CALIFORNIA

®TourBook

An annual catalog of selected travel information

American Automobile Association
1000 AAA Drive
Heathrow, FL 32746-5063

Valid through January 1994

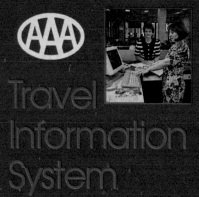

Travel Information System

AAA TRAVEL COUNSELORS are a unique and vital element of AAA's travel information system. They offer what no other auto club can: personalized, top-quality service. Our trained professionals are especially knowledgeable about geography and popular vacation destinations. They can tell you the fastest or most scenic way to get where you're going and update you on highway construction projects and local weather conditions.

TOURBOOKS are annually revised catalogs of selected travel information. Listings include AAA-approved attractions, lodgings and restaurants, plus details on sightseeing and valuable AAA discounts.

TRIPTIK MAPS show your driving route mile-by-mile. Conveniently spiral-bound, the maps indicate exit numbers and stops for food and gas as well as capsule summaries of places along the way.

SHEET MAPS are large-scale regional and state maps, completely researched, revised and reprinted regularly. Our network of AAA clubs and our Road Reporters make AAA maps the most detailed and accurate road maps available.

CAMPBOOKS contain comprehensive regional listings of AAA-approved public and private campgrounds across the continent.

CITIBOOKS provide complete information about major travel destinations like San Francisco and New York City. Not all clubs carry these booklets, which are extractions from the TourBooks.

CONTENTS

INTRODUCTION: USING YOUR TOURBOOK

TIPS FOR THE TOURBOOK TRAVELER

ATTRACTIONS

LODGINGS & RESTAURANTS

MAPS

FOR YOUR INFORMATION

INDEXES

Ⓥ SUPERNUMBER

Call 1-800-AAA-HELP for 24-hour road service when away from home and unable to find AAA or CAA in the phone book. 1-800-955-4TDD for hearing impaired. 21

COMMENTS   CAN YOU HELP US?

Write: AAA Member Comments
Box 61, 1000 AAA Dr.
Heathrow, FL 32746-5063

Please complete and return to us the brief questionnaire located at the back of this book. Also check the **Tell Us What You Think** survey, page A621.

ADVERTISING (407) 444-8280

published by **American Automobile Association**®   1000 AAA Drive, Heathrow, FL 32746-5063
Cover: *North slope of Lake Tahoe, NV* / David Muench ©

4605

USING YOUR TOURBOOK

This TourBook has one purpose: to make your trip as enjoyable as possible by providing reliable, detailed information about attractions, lodgings and restaurants in the area through which you are traveling.

No attraction, lodging or restaurant pays for a listing. Each is listed on the basis of merit alone after a AAA field inspector or a designated AAA representative has carefully evaluated it. AAA inspects each listed lodging property and restaurant every year. AAA's unique network of local club travel specialists checks information dealing with attractions and touring areas annually. Road reporters and cartographic researchers keep maps current.

Reading this introduction will help you understand the three components that comprise the book's information:

- Attractions
- Maps
- Lodgings & Restaurants

Knowing *about* these components—discussed here in the order in which you will discover them in the book—is your key to unlocking this Tour-Book, which AAA publishes to provide its members with the most accurate travel information available.

ABOUT ATTRACTIONS

The Attractions section of your TourBook serves as a guide to selected places rather than as a commercial, geographic or promotional encyclopedia. Communities or areas included offer something of particular or unusual interest—something for you to do or see that sets them apart from others in the area or nation. We call these "points of interest."

The text for each state begins by introducing you to historical, geographic, economic and other factors that contribute to the state's character. Factual data are highlighted in the Fast Facts and For Your Information boxes. The Recreation section outlines sports and recreational activities available in the state. The Recreation Areas chart lists facilities available in national and state parks and other areas; unusual or special features of a park are also mentioned.

READING THE LISTINGS

The Points of Interest listings are updated annually by local AAA clubs or other sources. Any attraction with a separate heading has been approved by a AAA field inspector or designated AAA representative. An attraction's quality is reflected in the length and scope of its general description. To assist you in selecting places to visit, we have placed a star (★) before attractions that are of exceptional interest and quality. An index to starred attractions appears with the orientation map. *(See ABOUT MAPS, page 7.)*

Attractions are listed alphabetically under the name of the nearest community; in most cases the distances given are computed from the center of town, unless otherwise specified, using the following highway designations: I (interstate highway), US (federal highway), SR (state route), CR (county road), FM (farm to market road) and FR (forest road).

Descriptive information about the attraction follows the location or directions. Next come the days, hours and seasons the attraction is *open.* These may be preceded by a suggested minimum visiting time. Following this are the admission prices, which are quoted *without* sales tax; children under the lowest age specified are admitted free when accompanied by an adult. Days, months and age groups written with a hyphen are *inclusive.*

Major credit cards accepted for admissions or fares may be indicated at the end of the listing as follows: AE, American Express; CB, Carte Blanche; DI, Diners Club; DS, Discover; ER, EnRoute; MC, MasterCard; VI, VISA. Minimum amounts that may be charged appear in parentheses after the last credit card designation when applicable.

ATTRACTION ADMISSION DISCOUNTS

Your AAA membership card is the key to reduced prices at certain attractions. Because they value your patronage and respect the AAA name, more than 1,500 attractions in the United States and Canada have agreed to offer members special discounts on their admission fees. If a TourBook listing shows a discount, present your valid AAA or CAA card when purchasing tickets. A full list of participating attractions appears in the Indexes section of your TourBook.

A participating attraction may offer one of two kinds of discount. The first, a simple reduction in price, is designated by "**Discount**" in the listing. The second, indicated by "**Two-for-one discount,**" means that for each regularly paid admission, one free admission of like kind is granted. Except where noted in the discount terms, discounts are offered for the validity period noted on the title page of this book.

The discount is given to both adults and children unless otherwise specified and applies to the member and his or her family traveling together, usually up to six persons. The discount may not apply if any other price reduction is offered or if tickets are purchased through an outlet other than the attraction's ticket office.

ATTRACTION SCHEDULES AND PRICES

All information in your TourBook was checked before the new edition was published and was accurate at press time. However, since the books are issued annually, changes often occur between editions. While we regret any inconvenience resulting from such instances, they are obviously beyond our control. If you're on a tight budget, you may want to use the phone numbers in the listings to check for possible increases in admission charges. **Increases in the admission fees charged by attractions are NOT covered under the rate guarantee,** which applies only to lodging accommodations whose listings contain the phrase "Rates Guaranteed" or "AAA Special Value Rates." *(See ABOUT LODGINGS & RESTAURANTS, page 9.)*

ABOUT MAPS

Maps created specifically for AAA travel books have very precise purposes and should be used in *conjunction* with the more complete sheet maps and Triptik maps provided by your AAA travel counselor. We recognize maps are crucial travel information. So to ensure your complete satisfaction, use book maps as *supplementary* guides only. Not every book will contain every map type listed below.

ORIENTATION MAPS

State, province and regional

State and province orientation maps appear before the Points of Interest listings in the Attractions section. Regional orientation maps appear with the description of the points of interest. Their purpose is to illustrate the relative positions of towns, recreation facilities and starred points of interest listed in the TourBooks. Only major road networks are portrayed on these larger-scale maps.

Coordinates (for example: A-3) following the place or city names in the Points of Interest listings refer to this map; stars next to town names on the maps indicate the presence of highly recommended attractions. An index to starred attractions appears with or adjacent to each orientation map.

Accommodations

Accommodations orientation maps are used for large geographical areas that are attractions in themselves (for example: the Finger Lakes region in New York and Michigan's Upper Peninsula). These maps are located in the Lodgings & Restaurants section of your book. Because the maps are on such a large scale, lodgings and restaurants are not shown, but the towns that have these types of facilities are printed in all capital letters and bold type so you can plan your trip accordingly.

SPOTTING MAPS

Spotting maps assist you in locating the facilities listed in the Lodgings & Restaurants section of your book. These maps locate, or "spot," lodgings with a dark-background numeral (**20**, for example); restaurants are spotted with a light-background numeral ((20), for example). Indexes found near the map match the number symbol to the property.

Downtown spotting maps

Downtown spotting maps are provided when spotted facilities are more concentrated. Every street in the area is shown.

City/Area spotting maps

City/Area spotting maps show the main roads required to find a dining or lodging facility, as well as the major landmarks that are near the lodgings and restaurants. Airports are also shown on city/area spotting maps.

POINTS OF INTEREST MAPS

Points of Interest maps assist you in locating establishments listed in the Attractions section of your book.

City maps

City maps show metropolitan areas where numerous attractions are concentrated. While reading an attraction description, refer to this map to see where it is located in relation to major roads, parks, airports, etc. Stars placed next to attractions on city maps indicate those that are highly recommended.

Walking-tour maps

Walking-tour maps provide an exceptional level of detail, showing specific routes corresponding to text in the TourBooks. Well-known buildings are often outlined for easier identification. Routes are well-marked with beginning and ending points as well as directional arrows.

NATIONAL PARK MAPS

National park maps familiarize drivers with the area in and around the park. The main features depicted are mountains, streams, hiking trails, canyons, ice fields, etc. Some of the campground sites and lodges spotted on the maps do not meet AAA criteria, but have been listed as a service to members who wish to stay at these facilities.

DRIVING DISTANCE MAPS

Located in the For Your Information section of the book, driving distance maps are to be used only for trip-distance and driving-time planning. Refer to more detailed AAA maps available from your club for actual route numbers. One set of numbers, printed in italics above the straight lines between cities, indicates how many miles are between the *center* of each city. The other set of numbers, printed below the lines in straight type, indicates the time needed to drive the speed limit between the *center* of each city. These times are for use in *approximating* how long a trip will take, based on AAA preferred routes.

ABOUT
LODGINGS & RESTAURANTS

AAA inspectors carefully evaluate every lodging establishment and restaurant listed in this publication at least once every year. Their rigorous inspection helps ensure that all properties meet AAA's exacting standards for quality.

AAA rating criteria are based on your needs and expectations and current standards in the lodging industry. Through your comments and surveys, AAA monitors member satisfaction. AAA rating criteria are continually updated to reflect members likes and dislikes.

Additionally, we monitor the pulse of the lodging industry to ensure that our criteria continue to reflect lodging industry standards. We maintain an open dialogue with individual establishment operators, the American Hotel and Motel Association and most major lodging chains. Annually, we invite a wide cross section of industry representatives to meet with us to discuss the AAA rating program. These discussions also provide AAA an opportunity to keep the lodging industry up-to-date on the needs and expectations of AAA members.

USING THE LODGING LISTINGS

Lodging and restaurant listings appear after the attraction listings and are introduced by a title page. Both types of properties are listed alphabetically under the nearest town or city, with lodgings listed first. To help you plan your trips, these towns and cities are printed in red on AAA regional, state, provincial and Triptik maps. The TourBook includes special accommodation "spotting" maps to help you find lodgings and restaurants. *(See ABOUT MAPS, page 7.)*

To use this book most effectively, read the sample lodging listing along with the explanation of the terms appearing on pages 14-15. General information includes the mailing address, phone number and directions. Directions are given from the center of town unless noted otherwise. Baths are not mentioned if all rooms have private baths. All showers are tub showers unless otherwise noted.

Parking facilities are mentioned only if the property is a hotel or if there is a parking charge. **Check-in** times are shown only if they are after 3 p.m.; **check-out** times are shown only if they are before 10 a.m. Service charges are not shown unless they are $1 or more, or at least 5 percent of the room rate.

READING THE LODGING DIAMONDS

Before a property may be listed in this book, it must satisfy a set of minimum requirements. These listing criteria reflect the basic lodging needs AAA members have identified. If a property meets those requirements, it is assigned a diamond rating reflecting the overall quality of the establishment. The rating ranges from one to five diamonds.

Ratings are assigned according to the property's classification, which appears just to the left of the diamond rating in the lodging listing. The classification represents the physical design and level of services provided by the property. For example, a motel offers limited services and recreational facilities. A resort hotel offers extensive guest services and recreational facilities. Comparing a motel to a resort hotel would be a lot like comparing an apple to an orange. By assigning ratings according to classification AAA compares apples to apples. A complete description of AAA lodging classifications is on page 16.

It should be noted that even though one diamond is AAA's lowest rating, it does not mean that the property is below standard. In fact, quite the opposite is true. Less than two-thirds of the lodging establishments open for business are listed in AAA TourBooks. While a few are not listed at the owner's request, the majority of unlisted properties do not meet AAA's exacting standards. This means that a one diamond AAA property is head and shoulders above many others. One diamond means clean, comfortable and well-maintained. Rates at one diamond properties are also generally very reasonable.

Criteria for Lodging Evaluation

Regardless of the rating, properties listed by AAA all provide:
- Staff in attendance 24 hours a day
- Clean and well-maintained facilities throughout
- Hospitable staff
- Adequate parking
- A well-kept appearance

Regardless of the rating, each guest room will have:
- Comfortable beds and good quality bedding
- Good locks on all doors and windows
- Comfortable furnishings and decor
- Smoke detectors
- Adequate towels and supplies
- At least one comfortable easy chair
- A desk or other writing surface
- Adequate illumination at each bed, the writing surface and easy chair

Here is a general description of what the lodging diamonds mean:

◆ provides good but unpretentious accommodations. Establishments are functional, emphasizing clean and comfortable rooms. They must meet the basic needs of comfort, privacy, cleanliness and safety.

◆◆ maintains the attributes offered at the ◆ level, while showing noticeable enhancements in decor and/or quality of furnishings. They may be recently constructed or older properties, both of which cater more to the needs of a budget-oriented traveler.

◆◆◆ rated establishments offer a degree of sophistication. Additional amenities, services and facilities may be offered. There is a marked upgrade in services and comfort.

◆◆◆◆ are excellent properties displaying a high level of service and hospitality. Properties offer a wide variety of amenities and upscale facilities, both inside the room, on the grounds and in the common areas.

◆◆◆◆◆ are renowned. They exhibit an exceptionally high degree of service; striking, luxurious facilities; and many extra amenities. Guest services are executed and presented in a flawless manner. The guest will be pampered by a very professional, attentive staff. The property's facilities and operation help set its standards in hospitality and service.

A few properties are listed in the TourBook without a rating. They are either under construction or are undergoing such a substantial renovation at press time that it is impossible to assign an accurate rating.

RATE OPTIONS AND DISCOUNTS

Annually, lodging operators are asked to update their rate line options for TourBook publication. Properties are not required to offer a discount to be listed in the book. But they have a choice of three rate options to offer AAA members: AAA Special Value Rates, Rates Guaranteed and Rates Subject to Change. Establishments that have a special interest in serving members offer **AAA Special Value Rates** or **Rates Guaranteed.**

AAA Special Value Rates — The establishment not only guarantees rates will not exceed the maximum rates printed in the TourBook, they also offer a minimum discount of 10 percent off printed rates. This is the only rate option that contains a discount. Since these rates are discounted only for AAA members, you *must* identify yourself as a AAA member and request the **AAA Special Value Rate** when making reservations. Also present your membership card at registration and verify the AAA Special Value Rate. *Note:* Exceptions may cause lodgings to temporarily increase their rates. See **Exceptions** below. *Note:* Members may take either the **AAA Special Value Rate** or the **Senior Discount**, but not both.

Rates Guaranteed — The establishment guarantees AAA members will not be charged more than the maximum rates printed in the TourBook. To receive these rates you *must* identify yourself as a AAA member and request the AAA guaranteed rate when making reservations. Also present your membership card at registration and verify the rate. *Note:* Exceptions may cause lodgings to temporarily increase their rates. See **Exceptions** below.

Rates Subject to Change — The printed rates are the establishment's estimated charges for the periods noted. The actual rates charged may be reasonably higher or lower than those printed in the TourBook.

Exceptions: Special events might cause lodgings to temporarily increase their room rates or modify their policies during the special event. Examples of such events range from Mardi Gras and the Kentucky Derby to college football homecoming games and state fairs. Other exceptions are holidays, when attending a convention, or when traveling as part of a group. During these times the **AAA Special Value Rate** option and the **Rates Guaranteed** option do not apply.

Lodging operators may offer a Senior Discount program:

Senior Discount — Some establishments offer the senior discount with either the **Rates Guaranteed** option or the **Rates Subject to Change** option. Where the words "Senior Discount" are included in a listing, a minimum discount of 10 percent off the prevailing or guaranteed rate is available to AAA members who are 60 years of age or older. This discount is in effect whenever the establishment is open. You *must* identify yourself as a AAA member *and* request the Senior Discount when making reservations. *Also* present your membership card at registration and verify the rate including the senior discount. Members may take this discount or the **AAA Special Value Rate**, but not both.

Rate lines: When the listing shows only one rate line, those rates are in effect either all year or during the main season. If only the dates for the main season are shown, then rates are lower at other times of the year. When off-season rates are significantly reduced, these dates also are shown. Rates are for typical rooms rather than special units.

Family rates: "F" at the end of a rate line stands for family rate, which means children stay free or at a reduced charge. Most lodgings limit children's eligibility and charge for rollaways and cribs.

Number of persons: Rates quoted are for one person (1P), for two persons and one bed (2P/1B) and for two persons and two beds (2P/2B). If a one-person rate is not shown, the minimum charge may be for two persons. Charges for extra persons (XP) include only standard room equipment; rollaways and other beds may cost more. Extra-person rates are shown, for example: XP 10 (each extra person $10) or XP 2-4 (each extra person $2-$4).

Taxes: State, city or other local taxes are not included in the listed rates.

USING THE RESTAURANT LISTINGS

We strive to approve consistently good dining establishments. In metropolitan areas, where many are above average, we select some of those known for the superiority of their food, service and atmosphere and also those offering a selection of quality food at moderate prices (including some cafeterias and family restaurants). In small communities the restaurants considered to be the best in the area may be listed. Dining rooms operated by a lodging and open to the public are designated in the lodging's listing by ● , which is followed by the operating hours. Other restaurants are listed separately.

Cuisine: Restaurants are classified by major cuisine type (Italian, French, etc.). Some listings indicate the availability of a senior discount for members 60 years or older; some also indicate the availability of "early-bird specials" if they are offered at least 5 days a week. Phone ahead for details on discounts and specially priced meals.

Dress codes: Listings including the words "dress code" indicate that certain attire is required. Phone the restaurant for details.

Price categories: $ meals are $10 or less.
$$ meals range from $11 to $20.
$$$ meals range from $21 to $30.
$$$$ meals start at $31 per person.

The range of prices is approximate and reflects dinner (salad or appetizer, a main course, a vegetable and a non-alcoholic beverage) for one person. Taxes and tips are not included.

READING THE RESTAURANT DIAMONDS

The restaurants listed are ◆ rated. Cafeterias, buffets and other self-service operations are rated, but only as compared to similar establishments. Listings in this category are very well suited to family dining.

◆ provides good but unpretentious dishes. Table settings are usually simple and may include paper placemats and napkins. If alcoholic beverages are offered, wine and beer selections may be limited. The restaurants are usually informal, with an atmosphere conducive to family dining.

◆◆ will usually have more extensive menus that represent more complex food preparation. A wider variety of alcoholic beverages will usually be available. The atmosphere is appealing and suitable for family or adult dining. Although service may be casual, host or hostess seating can be expected. Table settings may include tablecloths and cloth napkins.

◆◆◆ normally have extensive or specialized menus and a more complex cuisine preparation that requires a professional chef. Cloth table linens, above-average quality table settings, a skilled service staff and an inviting decor should all be provided. Generally, the wine list will include representatives of the best domestic and foreign wine-producing regions. Restaurants in this category can offer a formal dining experience or a special family occasion.

◆◆◆◆ will have an appealing ambience, frequently enhanced by fresh flowers and fine furnishings throughout. The overall sophistication and formal atmosphere visually creates a dining experience more for adults than for families. A wine steward presents an extensive list of the best wines. A smartly attired, highly skilled service staff will be capable of describing how any dish is prepared. Elegant silverware, china and correct glassware are typical. The menu will include creative dishes prepared from fresh ingredients by a chef who frequently has international training. Eye-appealing desserts will be offered at tableside.

◆◆◆◆◆ are world-class operations. They have the attributes of a four diamond restaurant with even more luxury and sophistication. A proportionally large staff, expert in preparing tableside delicacies, will provide flawless service, with impeccable linens, silver and crystal glassware.

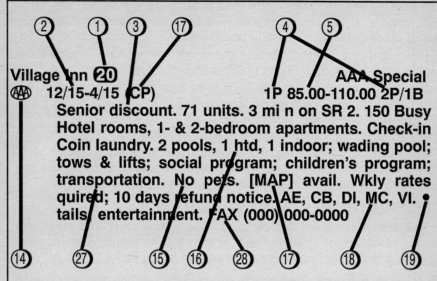

① Special maps help you select and locate lodgings and restaurants in or near large cities. Lodgings shown on these maps are assigned a 🄴 symbol; restaurants, a ㉔ symbol. See "About Maps" (page 7).

② The dates or days the rates listed to the right are available.

③ See "Senior Discount" (page 12).

④ Number of persons allowed and beds provided for rate listed.

⑤ When the listing shows only one set of rates, those rates are in effect all year or during the main season dates shown to the left. See "Rate Options and Discounts" (page 11).

⑥ Television: C/TV (color), CATV (cable) or C/CATV (color cable).

⑦ Movies are available on room TV.

⑧ Lodging classification (see page 16).

⑨ Phones are available in each room. There may be a charge for using the phone. If the charge is not listed in your room, ask the front desk.

⑩ Extra person charges (10=$10). Includes only standard room equipment; rollaways, cribs and other items may be extra.

⑪ "Kitchen" denotes full cooking equipment in an area separate from the sleeping area. "Efficiency" denotes cooking equipment within the sleeping area. The listing notes if utensils are included.

⑫ The overall quality of a lodging *within its classification* is reflected by the number of diamonds shown. See "Reading The Lodging Diamonds" (page 9).

⑬ A "family" plan enables children to stay free or at a discounted rate. Ask the establishment.

⑭ See "What The ⊕ Means" (page 17).

⑮ "Pets" or "No Pets" is shown as applicable. If the policy varies within the establishment, no mention of pets is made. By U.S. and Canada law, pet restrictions do not apply to guide dogs. There may be charges for pets.

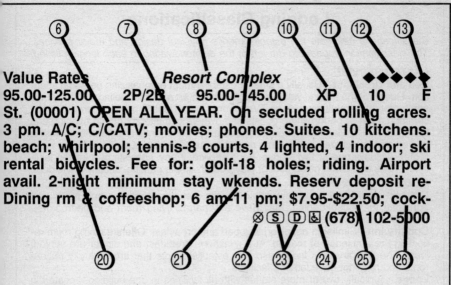

⑥ ⑦ ⑧ ⑨ ⑩ ⑪ ⑫ ⑬

Value Rates *Resort Complex* ◆◆◆◆◆
95.00-125.00 2P/2B 95.00-145.00 XP 10 F
St. (00001) OPEN ALL YEAR. On secluded rolling acres.
3 pm. A/C; C/CATV; movies; phones. Suites. 10 kitchens.
beach; whirlpool; tennis-8 courts, 4 lighted, 4 indoor; ski
rental bicycles. Fee for: golf-18 holes; riding. Airport
avail. 2-night minimum stay wkends. Reserv deposit re-
Dining rm & coffeeshop; 6 am-11 pm; $7.95-$22.50; cock-
⊗ⓈⒹ♿ (678) 102-5000

⑳ ㉑ ㉒ ㉓ ㉔ ㉕ ㉖

⑯ A heated pool is heated when it is reasonable to expect use of a pool. Outdoor pools may not open in winter.

⑰ Listed rates are for European Plan (no meals) unless marked AP for American Plan (three meals); MAP for Modified American Plan (two meals); BP for Breakfast Plan (full breakfast); or CP for Continental Plan (pastry, juice and another beverage).

⑱ Credit cards accepted are abbreviated AE (American Express), CB (Carte Blanche), DI (Diners Club), DS (Discover), ER (EnRoute), MC (MasterCard) and VI (VISA).

⑲ Dining rooms operated by lodgings and open to the public are noted by • .

⑳ Air conditioning is available in all rooms.

㉑ Friday and Saturday nights are considered weekends.

㉒ Nonsmokers' rooms available. Restaurants with this symbol offer nonsmoking sections.

㉓ "S" means that all rooms have sprinklers; "D" means that all rooms have smoke detectors. If all rooms have both, both symbols appear.

㉔ Lodgings including this symbol have at least one room accessible by wheelchair. Dining facilities at the lodging are also wheelchair accessible. Restaurants have an accessible dining area and restrooms.

㉕ Menu prices are for dinner meals.

㉖ Drinks served in lounge and dining room. If in lounge only, the listing will include "lounge."

㉗ Airport transportation is provided to and from the property by the lodging or by commercial limousine or bus. There may be a charge.

㉘ Appears when the establishment has a facsimile machine.

Lodging Classifications

Classifications delineate the establishment's physical design and major services. The classification appears to the left of the diamond rating in each lodging listing.

LIMITED SERVICE

Bed and Breakfast—Usually a smaller establishment emphasizing personal attention. Guest rooms are individually decorated with an *at home* feeling and may lack some modern amenities such as TVs, phones, etc. Usually owner-operated with a common room or parlor where guests and owners can interact during evening and breakfast hours. May have shared bathrooms. A Continental or full hot breakfast is served and is included in the room rate. Adequate parking is available.

Motel—Usually one or two stories. Food service, if any, consists of a limited facility or snack bar. Often has a pool or playground. Ample parking, usually at the door.

MODERATE SERVICE

Cottage—Individual bungalow, cabin or villa, usually containing one rental unit equipped for housekeeping. May have a separate living room and bedroom(s). Parking is usually at each unit.

Country Inn—Similar in definition to a bed and breakfast. Offers a dining room reflecting the ambience of the inn. At a minimum, breakfast and dinner are served. Note: The Country Inns Index also lists establishments that are primarily restaurants and may not have lodging facilities.

Lodge—Typically two or more stories with all facilities in one building. Located in vacation, ski, fishing areas, etc. Usually has food and beverage service. Adequate on-premises parking.

Motor Inn—Usually two or three stories, but may be a high-rise. Generally has recreation facilities and food service. May have limited banquet/meeting facilities. Ample parking.

FULL SERVICE

Complex—A combination of two or more kinds of lodgings.

Hotel—A multistory building usually including a coffee shop, dining room, lounge, room service, convenience shops, valet, laundry and full banquet/meeting facilities. Parking may be limited.

Ranch—May be any classification featuring outdoor, Western-type recreation.

The following are sub-classifications that may appear along with the classifications listed above to provide more description about the lodging:

Apartment—Usually four or more stories with at least half the units equipped for housekeeping. Often in a vacation destination area. Units typically provide a full kitchen, living room and one or more bedrooms, but may be studio-type rooms with kitchen equipment in an alcove. May require minimum stay and/or offer discounts for longer stays. This classification may also modify any of the other lodging types.

Condominium—A destination property located in a resort area; may apply to any classification. Guest units consist of a bedroom, living room and kitchen. Kitchens are separate from bedrooms and are equipped with a stove, oven or microwave, refrigerator, cooking utensils and table settings for the maximum number of people occupying the unit. Linens and maid service are provided at least twice weekly.

Historic—May apply to any type of lodging. Accommodations in restored, pre-1930 structures, reflecting the ambience of yesteryear and the surrounding region. Rooms may lack some modern amenities and have shared baths. Usually owner-operated and provides food service. Parking is usually available. Note: The Historical Lodgings and Restaurants Index also lists establishments that are primarily restaurants and may not have lodging facilities.

Resort—May apply to any other type of lodging. Has a vacation atmosphere offering extensive recreational facilities for such specific interests as golf, tennis, fishing, etc. Rates may include meals under American or Modified American plans.

Suite—One or more bedrooms and a living room, which may or may not be closed off from the bedrooms.

TIPS FOR THE TOURBOOK TRAVELER

OUR CUSTOMERS ALWAYS WRITE

We encourage your communication to tell us what we need to improve and what we have done well. We respond through our products and services, and we reply to thousands of letters from members every year.

Even at the most carefully managed establishments, problems will sometimes develop. This doesn't mean an attraction, hotel, motel or restaurant is uninterested in you as a guest or that AAA is not concerned with your travel welfare. Usually, it simply means that something has been misunderstood or has temporarily gone wrong.

We encourage you to report both pleasant and unpleasant experiences by visiting your local AAA club for assistance in completing a form prepared for this purpose. Or, if you prefer, write directly to AAA Member Comments, National Travel Dept., 1000 AAA Dr., Box 61, Heathrow, FL 32746-5063.

ADVERTISING

Attractions, lodgings and restaurants must be approved by a AAA inspector or other representative before they may purchase advertising in this book. Whether or not a business decides to advertise has no influence on that property's inspection, evaluation or rating. The information in this book is provided as a service to our members—so we review every ad carefully and impose rigorous standards. Some ads contain discount information; others have photos that can help you choose accommodations.

You also will find advertising for travel-related services and products, plus specific regions or promotional organizations. AAA does not endorse products, services, areas or organizations. However, many members indicate such information is useful.

WHAT THE ⦿ MEANS

Lodgings and restaurants approved by AAA are eligible for our Official Appointment Program, which permits the display and advertising of the ⦿ emblem. The ⦿ preceding a listing printed in bold type identifies that property as an Official Appointment establishment with a special interest in serving AAA members. The ⦿ sign helps traveling members—like you— find accommodations on which they can depend. These properties want AAA business.

WHEELCHAIR ACCESS

The international symbol of access, 🚹, appears only in listings of restaurants and lodging establishments that have met criteria adapted from *Making Buildings and Facilities Accessible To, and Usable By, the Physically Handicapped,* published by the American National Standards Institute

Inc. Lodgings must have at least one room and dining facilities, if offered, that are accessible to AAA members using wheelchairs. The presence of this symbol does not imply that a property conforms to guidelines outlined in the Americans with Disabilities Act of 1990.

Many attractions listed in the Attractions section of the TourBooks can be visited by AAA members who use wheelchairs. However, the wide range of attractions, the complexity of their sites and the diversity of their physical characteristics make it difficult to note those that are completely accessible. The attraction listings include a phone number so members can phone ahead to ask specific questions. **We strongly urge members with disabilities to call ahead.**

MAKING RESERVATIONS

Always make lodging reservations before leaving home. Your local club's Auto Travel Department can make reservations for you and will provide written confirmation if you request it. Remember that a room is most likely to be held if a deposit accompanies your request. Establishments don't always allow you to guarantee reservations with a credit card, although the card may be used for final payment. The establishment might require you to submit a check to guarantee your reservations absolutely. As a rule, a room reserved without a deposit will be released if it is not claimed by 6 p.m., unless the establishment agrees in advance to a late arrival time. Resorts invariably require a deposit.

Although it is not AAA's policy, some establishments accept reservations subject to certain age requirements. If applicable, you should explore this possibility with the property before placing a reservation.

When making reservations, you must identify yourself as a AAA member. Give all pertinent information about your planned stay. Request written confirmation to guarantee: type of room, rate, dates of stay, and cancellation and refund policies.

When making reservation deposits, be sure you understand the amount of notice required for cancellations and refunds. Most establishments give full deposit refunds if they have been notified at least 48 hours before the normal check-in time. Lodgings that require more time will so indicate in their listing. If you cancel too late, you have little recourse if a refund is denied. **AAA requires the full return of a deposit if the lodging received notice of your cancellation before the time specified in its cancellation policy.** When an establishment requires a full or partial payment in advance, and your trip is cut short, a refund may not be given.

When canceling reservations, call the lodging immediately. Make a note of the date and time you called, the cancellation number if there is one, and the name of the person who handled the cancellation. If your AAA club made your reservation, allow them to make the cancellation for you as well so you will have proof of cancellation.

When you are charged more than the rate listed in the TourBook, under the headings **Rates Guaranteed** or **AAA Special Value Rates**, or you qualify for the **Senior Discount** and did not receive it, question the additional charge. If management refuses to adhere to the published rate, pay for the room and submit your receipt and membership number to AAA *within 30 days (see address page 17)*. Include all pertinent information: dates of stay, rate paid, itemized paid receipts, number of persons in your party, the room number you occupied, and list any extra room equipment used. A refund of the amount paid in excess of the stated maximum will be made when our investigation indicates that unjustified charging has occurred.

When you find your room is not as specified, and you have written confirmation of reservations for a certain type of accommodation, you should be given the option of choosing a different room or finding one elsewhere. Should you choose to go elsewhere and a refund is refused or resisted, submit the matter to AAA *within 30 days* along with complete documentation, including your reasons for refusing the room and copies of your written confirmation and any receipts or canceled checks associated with this problem.

TIPPING

Tipping is an accepted practice and many service industry personnel depend upon tips for a large part of their incomes. At airports 50¢ to $1 per bag is appropriate for skycaps if the service is to the curb, more if the bag handling is farther. Taxi drivers expect 15 percent. In hotels it is appropriate to tip the bellperson or porter no less than $1, and often $1 per bag; the maid is left $2 per day in an envelope at the end of your stay; the doorman receives $1 to $5 depending upon the difficulty of the service he performs; the garage attendant is given $1 to $2; bathroom attendants receive 50¢ to $1. Barbers, hair stylists and similar personnel are tipped 15 to 20 percent of their bill.

Since the job of the concierge is to help guests, he or she usually should not be tipped unless an unusual or very difficult task is performed; then a minimum of $5 is appropriate. Desk clerks and elevator operators do not expect tips.

Tipping in restaurants depends upon the luxuriousness and sophistication of the establishment and, of course, upon the quality of the service. The standard for waiters and waitresses is 15 percent of the bill. If the captain, head waiter or some person other than your server takes your order or helps serve your meal, a 5 percent tip is appropriate; a tip of 10 to 15 percent of your wine bill is expected by the wine steward; in more luxurious restaurants the maitre d' expects $5 or $10. If you are paying by credit card it is acceptable and less awkward to put a 20 percent tip on the form and allow these personnel to sort out their portions.

GOLDEN PASSPORTS

Golden Age passports are free to permanent U.S. residents 62 and older. Golden Access passports are free to the medically blind and permanently disabled. Both cover entrance fees for the holder and accompanying private party to all national parks and historic sites, monuments and battlefields within the national park system, plus half off camping and other fees. Apply in person at most federally operated areas. For more information write: National Park Service, Public Inquiry, Dept. of the Interior, 18th & C Sts. NW, Washington, DC 20013.

The Golden Eagle Passport costs $25 annually and covers entrance fees for the holder and accompanying private party to all federally operated areas. Obtain the pass from the above address, or in person at any national park or regional office of the U.S. Park Service or Forest Service.

Hotel and Motel Fire Safety

The AAA inspection program is designed to provide you with the most useful information for selecting the lodgings best suited to your needs. Because of the highly specialized skills needed to conduct professional fire safety inspections, however, AAA inspectors cannot assess fire safety. Here are some important life-saving steps, as developed by the National Fire Protection Association and other sources, that you can take to protect yourself.

1. When you check in, ask at the front desk what type of fire alarm is used and how it sounds.

2. In your room, read the fire evacuation plan carefully. If one is not posted, call the front desk for assistance.

3. Find the two exits nearest your room and check to be sure they are unlocked and unblocked.

4. Count the doors between your room and the exits. This will help you find the exits if the corridor is unlighted or filled with smoke.

5. Take every alarm or unusual noise seriously. Should you hear an alarm, don't hesitate: **act.**

6. If the fire is in your room, get out immediately and close the door. Report the fire to the fire department and the front desk.

7. If the fire is not in your room, leave if possible. Touch the door to test it for heat. If it's cool, brace your shoulder against it and open slowly. Be ready to close it immediately if there are flames on the other side. Crawl low in the smoke to the exit; fresher air will be near the floor.

8. If your room door is hot, don't open it. Instead, seal the door with wet towels or sheets. Turn off any fans and air conditioners. Call the fire department, even if you can see firefighters outside, and give your exact location. Signal at your window. Leave your window closed if you can see smoke outside, since smoke and fire may enter through it. If there is smoke inside your room and it is clear outside, try opening the window. Be ready to close it if more smoke enters your room.

9. Fire exits and stairwells are your best escape routes. **Never use an elevator during a fire**—the elevator could stop at the fire floor.

Most listed establishments provide smoke detectors and/or automatic sprinkler systems in guest rooms. Lodgings that provide this added protection are identified with symbols (see the Sample Listing). At each establishment whose listing shows these symbols, a AAA inspector has evaluated a sampling of the rooms and verified that this equipment is in place.

When traveling away from home . . .

1-800-AAA-HELP
1-800-955-4TDD (Hearing Impaired)

a 24-hour toll-free Emergency Road Service information system.

It's easy to use Triple A's *SUPERNUMBER* ® when traveling outside your local club area.

1. Look in the white pages of the telephone book for a listing under "AAA" in the United States or "CAA" in Canada, since road service is dispatched by the local club in many communities.

2. If there is no listing, have your membership card handy and call *SUPERNUMBER* ® 1-800-AAA-HELP for the nearest road service facility. *Hearing impaired call 1-800-955-4TDD.*

SUPERNUMBER ® available 24 hours a day, is only for Emergency Road Service . . . and only when traveling outside the area served by your home club. Questions regarding other club services should be directed to the nearest club office.

You'll always find us in a great state.

Wherever you travel, there's a Hilton waiting to serve you. And many Hiltons* across the U.S. offer savings of 10%† off room rates when you present your AAA membership card upon arrival. For reservations, call the nearest AAA office or Hilton today at **1-800-HILTONS.**

CALIFORNIA
Anaheim area
*ANAHEIM HILTON AND TOWERS
*ANAHEIM HILTON SUITES (Orange)
Concord
*CONCORD HILTON
Dana Point (Orange County)
*DANA POINT HILTON-An All Suites Resort
Fresno
*FRESNO HILTON
Huntington Beach (Orange County)
*THE WATERFRONT HILTON BEACH RESORT
Lake Arrowhead
*LAKE ARROWHEAD HILTON RESORT
Long Beach
*LONG BEACH HILTON
Los Angeles area
*LOS ANGELES AIRPORT HILTON AND TOWERS
*LOS ANGELES HILTON AND TOWERS
*UNIVERSITY HILTON-LOS ANGELES
*SAN GABRIEL VALLEY HILTON
*THE BEVERLY HILTON (Beverly Hills)
*BURBANK AIRPORT HILTON AND CONVENTION CENTER (Burbank)

Los Angeles area (cont'd.)
*PASADENA HILTON (Pasadena)
*VALLEY HILTON (Sherman Oaks)
*UNIVERSAL CITY HILTON AND TOWERS (Universal City)
*WHITTIER HILTON (Whittier)
*WARNER CENTER HILTON AND TOWERS (Woodland Hills)
Oakland
*OAKLAND AIRPORT HILTON
Ontario
*ONTARIO AIRPORT HILTON
Oxnard
*FINANCIAL PLAZA HILTON
Palm Springs
*PALM SPRINGS HILTON RESORT
Pleasanton
*PLEASANTON HILTON AT THE CLUB
Sacramento
*SACRAMENTO HILTON INN
San Bernardino
*SAN BERNARDINO HILTON
San Diego area
*SAN DIEGO HILTON RESORT
*SAN DIEGO MISSION VALLEY HILTON

San Diego area (cont'd.)
*DEL MAR HILTON
San Francisco
*SAN FRANCISCO AIRPORT HILTON
*SAN FRANCISCO HILTON AND TOWERS
San Jose area
*SAN JOSE HILTON AND TOWERS
*NEWARK/FREMONT HILTON (Newark/Fremont)
*SUNNYVALE HILTON INN
Santa Maria
*SANTA MARIA AIRPORT HILTON
Stockton
*STOCKTON HILTON
Valencia
*VALENCIA HILTON GARDEN INN

NEVADA
Las Vegas
*FLAMINGO HILTON-LAS VEGAS
*LAS VEGAS HILTON
Laughlin
*FLAMINGO HILTON-LAUGHLIN
Reno
*FLAMINGO HILTON-RENO

Hilton

ATTRACTIONS

Whether your interests
are amusement parks
or historical monuments,
the attraction listings offer
a quick, concise overview
of descriptive information
on sightseeing destinations
throughout the United States
and Canada.

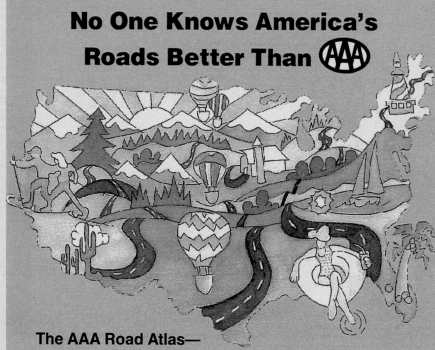

CALIFORNIA

An introduction to the state's history, geography, economy and recreation

MORE THAN A STATE, California is a state of mind. Surfer, cyclist, logger, vintner, migrant, magnate, starlet and politician—each has his or her own California. Yet these make up only a small part of the kaleidoscope that is the state itself. From its varied climate and topography, "land's end" geographical position and virtually boundless natural resources, California has developed a distinctive style that is evident in fashion, cuisine, architecture, art and business.

HISTORY

American Indians in California were characterized by diversity. Distinct language groups and regional dialects were represented in a population estimated to have exceeded 100,000 at its peak. Decimated by diseases introduced by Europeans and evicted from their lands by settlers and prospectors, these people were nearly obliterated within a century after the first European colonization.

In 1542 Juan Rodríguez Cabrillo, a Portuguese navigator, made the first European discovery of what is now California. In 1579 the English privateer Sir Francis Drake halted for repairs somewhere near Point Reyes and claimed the land for Elizabeth I. However, his chief interest was in preying on the Spanish treasure ships which plied the Pacific from the Philippines to Mexico.

In 1602 Sebastián Vizcaíno reaffirmed Spain's title to California; he explored extensively and named many coastal features. Spain allowed the region to languish until 1768 when King Charles, fearing possible encroachments by other countries, ordered the colonization of California. The next year Gaspar de Portolá's expedition marched from Mexico to San Diego, where Upper California's first permanent settlement was founded. One of Portolá's lieutenants later discovered San Francisco Bay.

Two important members of Portolá's expedition were Father Junípero Serra and Father

---

FAST FACTS

POPULATION: 29,760,000.

AREA: 158,693 square miles; ranks third.

CAPITAL: Sacramento.

HIGHEST POINT: Mount Whitney, 14,494 ft.

LOWEST POINT: Death Valley, 282 ft. below sea level.

TIME ZONE: Pacific. DST.

MINIMUM AGE FOR DRIVERS: 16 with drivers' training, 18 without.

SEAT BELT/CHILD RESTRAINT LAWS: Seat belts required for driver and front-seat passengers; child restraints for under age 4 or under 40 lbs.

HELMETS FOR MOTORCYCLISTS: Required.

RADAR DETECTORS: Permitted.

FIREARMS LAWS: Vary by state and/or county. Contact Department of Justice, Criminal Information and Inquiries, P.O. Box 903389, Sacramento, CA 94203-3870; phone (916) 739-2773.

HOLIDAYS: Jan. 1; Martin Luther King Jr.'s Birthday, Jan. (3rd Mon.); Lincoln's Birthday, Feb. 12; Washington's Birthday, Feb. (3rd Mon.); Memorial Day, May (last Mon.); July 4; Labor Day, Sept. (1st Mon.); Admission Day, Sept. 9; Columbus Day, Oct. (2nd Mon.); Veterans Day, Nov. 11; Thanksgiving; Dec. 25.

TAXES: California's statewide sales tax is 7.25 percent; an additional district tax of .25 to 1.25 percent may be imposed in various counties. There is a 0.02-percent Tourism Promotion Tax on meals and lodgings until July 1, 1993. Cities and counties may both impose Occupancy Taxes.

STATE INFORMATION CENTERS: are on US 199S at the Oregon border, I-55 near SR 96, I-80W near Truckee, I-15S near Halloran Springs, I-40W near Fenner, I-10W near Blythe and I-8W near Felicity.

Fermín Lasuén—leaders of a Franciscan movement that by 1823 had founded 21 missions and one *asistencia* along a 600-mile-long route from San Diego to Sonoma. The missions outlined *El Camino Real,* the King's Highway, that today is closely paralleled by US 101 *(see maps p. 30-31).*

Military fortresses called *presidios* were built at San Diego, Santa Barbara, Monterey and San Francisco, with the military government headquartered at Monterey. The first true town, or *pueblo,* to be established was San Jose in 1777. Four years later Los Angeles was founded. Growth was slow, however, and Spanish California was little more than a remote, ill-supplied outpost of European civilization.

FOR YOUR INFORMATION

SPECIAL REGULATIONS: At the borders the State Department of Food and Agriculture inspects all produce, plant materials and wild animals to see if they are admissible under current quarantine regulations. Dogs older than 4 months must be accompanied by a certificate stating that they have been vaccinated against rabies within 1 year prior to admission.

FURTHER INFORMATION FOR VISITORS:

California Office of Tourism
P.O. Box 9278, T98, Dept. 1003
Van Nuys, CA 91409
(800) 862-2543

RECREATION INFORMATION:

State Parks:

California State Park System
Dept. of Parks and Recreation
P.O. Box 942896
Sacramento, CA 94296-0001
(916) 653-6995

National Forests:

Pacific-Southwest Region,
U.S. Forest Service
630 Sansome St., Room 527
San Francisco, CA 94111
(415) 705-2874

National Parks:

National Park Service
Fort Mason, Bldg. 201
Bay and Franklin sts.
San Francisco, CA 94123
(415) 556-0560

FISHING AND HUNTING REGULATIONS:

Department of Fish and Game
1416 9th St.
Sacramento, CA 95814
(916) 653-7664

In 1822, when Mexico won its independence from Spain, California swore allegiance to Mexico but remained self-governing. The missions became secularized, and their vast land and cattle holdings were given away in huge land grants to several families. In 1842 there was a minor gold rush north of Los Angeles, but California's economy during the Mexican era was dominated by the *ranchos.* Foreigners, particularly Americans, began to arrive.

During the 1840s many Californians were suspicious of U.S. territorial intentions; others were discontented with Mexican rule and desired an American takeover. In 1846 a small group of American settlers organized the Bear Flag Revolt, which ended 23 days later when Commodore John Sloat, reacting to news that Mexico and the United States were at war, raised the U.S. flag at Monterey. The event left an important legacy: the Bear Flag standard carrying the words "California Republic" remains the official state flag.

The Mexican War brought little military action to California. One notable skirmish was the Battle of San Pasqual in 1846, which left 22 fatalities and numerous casualties. In 1847 hostilities ended and, with the signing of the Treaty of Guadalupe Hidalgo on Feb. 2, 1848, California became part of the United States.

Capt. John Sutter came to California in 1839, having received a large land grant along the Sacramento River; his outpost became known as Sutter's Fort. On Jan. 24, 1848, one of Sutter's foremen, James Marshall, was inspecting a millrace on the South Fork of the American River when he spotted a few shiny yellow flakes among the pebbles. News of the event leaked out and Marshall's discovery sparked one of history's largest, most frenzied migrations—the California gold rush.

Gold fever spread. Crews abandoned their ships and farmers left their land. New settlements sprang up, prices soared and speculations ballooned, fed by the thousands who poured across continent and sea to attain their El Dorado. Violence was common; often the only official "justice" was the hangman's rope. Conversely, some newcomers were well-educated, and often the new towns had opera and "society." The stories of Bret Harte and Mark Twain captured the flavor of this unique era.

Statehood came in 1850; Sacramento was designated capital in 1854. As the gold played out, national attention returned to politics, particularly the slavery question, and California was left to wallow in its own problems, including a series of boom and bust periods. Nevertheless California witnessed the completion of the transcontinental railroads, large-scale agricultural development, the growth of business and industry, and an influx of people looking for something more permanent than gold.

Two developments helped shape the character of today's California: a tremendous migration into the state and the introduction of the automobile. California's climate attracted the film industry. Farmers from the Midwest, blacks from the South, families from Asia and Latin America and Easterners escaping harsh winters—all came to California seeking a better life. The automobile fostered the growth of suburbia, dramatically transforming the pattern of the California's human settlement.

GEOGRAPHY

California is a state of remarkable geographic diversity. The highest point in the country outside Alaska, 14,494-foot Mount Whitney, is just 85 miles from the lowest, Death Valley, at 282 feet below sea level. One might swim in the ocean and ski on fresh snow in the same day. Ribbon Falls in California's Yosemite National Park is the continent's highest waterfall. Giant sequoias are the largest, coastal redwoods the tallest and bristlecone pines the oldest known living trees.

Mountains parallel the entire coastline. From the northwest corner the Coast Ranges extend almost to Los Angeles. Their moderate slopes wear evergreens in the north, stately oaks mid-state and brushy shrubs known as chaparral in the south. From the northeast the Sierra Nevada forms a continuous barrier that runs half the length of the state. It is a single block of granite that rises gradually from the west, then drops abruptly on the east, where its escarpment towers nearly 10,000 feet above the valleys.

Between Mount Whitney and Lake Tahoe is the true High Sierra—a land of granite, glacial ice and alpine lakes. At elevations of 6,000 to 9,000 feet along the western slope are forests of pine and fir, groves of giant sequoias, wildflower-covered meadows and steep, V-shaped river canyons.

Other major ranges include the White Mountains, east of the Sierra Nevada, and the volcanic Cascades, in the northern reaches of the state. Mount Shasta and Mount Lassen, both now quiescent, are California's biggest volcanoes. North of Los Angeles the Coast Ranges and the Sierra Nevada join to form the transverse ranges, which include the Tehachapi, San Gabriel and San Bernardino mountains. From Mount San Jacinto, a series of mountains called the peninsular range extends into Mexico.

Between the Coast Ranges and the Sierra Nevada is the great Central Valley, about 400 miles long and 40 to 50 miles wide. The northern half is called the Sacramento Valley; the southern part, San Joaquin. The Owens Valley lies between California's two highest mountain ranges, the Sierra Nevada and White Mountains. Elevations exceed 14,000 feet and 10,000-foot-high walls rise on either side. Death Valley is an independent basin shooting northward from the Mojave Desert between high, bare ranges.

Most of California's few large natural lakes are in the northern third of the state. The best known is Tahoe, which straddles the California-Nevada border. The largest natural lake entirely within California is Clear Lake, north of Napa Valley. Other natural lakes include Eagle Lake, near Susanville, and Mono Lake, in an ancient volcanic crater east of Yosemite National Park. Dams and reservoirs are numerous throughout the state.

THE COUNTRIES

California is a state of many "countries." The Mother Lode Country, the Wine Country, the Redwood Country, the Russian River Region, the Feather River Country, the Desert Country, the Big Sur Country, the Eastern Sierra Region—each is distinct in flavor and personality.

The wealth of the Mother Lode Country was instrumental in achieving statehood for California in 1850. The lode proper was the principal vein of gold-bearing quartz that lured the '49ers to the western foothills of the Sierra Nevada. Although the vein was only about a mile wide and 150 miles long, the Mother Lode Country extends approximately 245 miles from Mariposa to Sierra City. SR 49 runs its length, passing trails worn by the goldseekers. I-80 and US 50 are the major east-west routes.

The Wine Country is associated with the vineyards of Napa and Sonoma counties. Napa Valley, northeast of San Francisco, is the heartland of the Wine Country; SR 29 between Napa and St. Helena passes miles of vineyards. Other important wine-producing regions are in the San Joaquin Valley, the Sierra foothills, the Santa Cruz Mountains, the Salinas Valley, the central coast and Riverside County. Many wineries offer tours and/or tastings. For complete information visit any AAA office in California.

The domain of the giant coastal redwoods is the Redwood Country along the Redwood Highway, US 101. Redwood National Park between Crescent City and Orick includes the tallest specimens. Several state parks and reserves encompass significant stands between Alton and Leggett. The Avenue of the Giants, paralleling US 101 between Phillipsville and Pepperwood, winds through Humboldt Redwoods State Park. For more information write to The Redwood Empire Association, 1 Market Plaza, Spear Street Tower, San Francisco, CA 94105, or visit any AAA office in California.

The Russian River Region is a scenic recreational area. From its source near Ukiah, the Russian River flows southward for several miles, then turns west, passing redwood groves and vineyards before reaching the Pacific near Jenner. Resorts and the Armstrong Redwoods State Reserve lie along SR 116 between Guerneville and Duncans Mills. South of the river's mouth is Sonoma Coast State Beach.

The Feather River Country refers mainly to the segment of the North Fork of the Feather River that threads through Feather River Canyon. SR 70 between SR 89 and Lake Oroville follows the canyon through pine and fir forests. The highway and the tracks of the Western Pacific Railroad switch from one wall of the gorge to the other in a series of "leapfrog" bridges. Most of the area lies within Plumas National Forest.

The Desert Country encompasses thousands of square miles of arid and semiarid terrain in the southeastern part of the state. The landscape is dotted with cactuses, sagebrush, Joshua trees and palm oases. Wildflowers carpet the desert in late winter and early spring. Between November and May the region is visited by golfers in Palm Springs; anglers and boaters on the Colorado River; and campers and hikers in Death Valley and Joshua Tree national monuments and Anza-Borrego Desert State Park.

Big Sur is the section of ruggedly beautiful seacoast from about 10 miles south of Carmel to about 5 miles south of Lucia. The Santa Lucia Mountains rise abruptly from the ocean and steep-sided canyons contain groves of coastal redwoods. SR 1 twists along the headlands, offering breathtaking views. The best time to drive this route is in the afternoon; morning fog often obscures the view. During the summer months traffic can be heavy.

The Eastern Sierra Region extends along the eastern base of the Sierra Nevada from Olancha to Bridgeport. US 395 is the primary artery through this area, which makes a happy amalgam of magnificent views and year-round recreational opportunities. Bishop, Lone Pine and Mammoth lakes are the primary outfitting centers.

ECONOMY

California's economy is extremely diverse and not dominated by any single industry. Manufacturing accounts for about one-fifth of the state's total income and provides a wide variety of products. The San Jose area, more commonly known as Silicon Valley, is the leading center for the development and production of computers, electronic components, medical equipment and other electronic devices.

Southern California also is a major producer of electronic equipment. The Los Angeles and San Diego metropolitan areas are principal aerospace centers and employ more than 250,000 people. Aircraft and spacecraft manufacturing also is a major industry, as Los Angeles has nearly 20 percent of the nation's jobs in aircraft production.

California is the nation's center for film and television production, and the entertainment industry as a whole employs more than 200,000 people. The state's lodging and tourist attractions employ more than 725,000. Nearly a half-million more jobs are in some way related to tourism.

California is the nation's leading agricultural state because of the conducive climate. It provides about half of the fruits, nuts and vegetables grown in the country. California's vineyards produce a high percentage of the nation's wine and brandy. Napa Valley is the best known winegrowing area but many premium wines also

The Mother Lode

Mexican miners called it "La Veta Madre"—the Mother Lode—a rich vein of gold lacing the western slopes of the Sierra Nevada for 120 miles. The name eventually came to denote the entire band of territory extending roughly from Mariposa to Downieville, where the gleaming metal was mined during the frenetic years of the California gold rush.

The discovery of gold near Coloma in 1848 lured thousands of prospectors to the Mother Lode. Tales of nuggets littering the hillsides were not entirely unfounded during the early years of the gold rush, and the possibility of unearthing a mammoth find, like the 195-pound nugget found near Carson Hill, stoked the get-rich-quick dreams of many a '49er.

Nearly 550 mining towns proliferated in the Mother Lode; fewer than half remain today. Like the fortunes of many of the miners, the towns rose and fell precipitately, and often were simply abandoned when the miners moved on to more profitable stakes. A few, such as Sonora, Placerville, Auburn and Grass Valley, weathered the diminishing reserves to become prosperous small cities. Others survive as little more than intriguing names on a map.

Aptly numbered SR 49 traverses the length of the Mother Lode country. The facades of the surviving buildings, the historical parks along the route and the ghost towns and empty mines scattered throughout the hills still retain a sense of the atmosphere from this colorful period.

come from Sonoma, San Luis Obispo and Mendocino counties.

Although most of the trees found north of the tropics appear in California's woodlands, the active lumbering industry depends mostly on redwood and several varieties of pine and fir. Fishing also is an important industry; commercial fisheries net nearly 485 million pounds of seafood each year, including abalone, anchovies, cod, flounder, mackerel, sardines, salmon, shrimp and tuna.

RECREATION

From the surf of the Pacific to the snow of the High Sierra, from the desert sand dunes to the Klamath River rapids, there is something for everyone in California. Lake Tahoe is one of the country's foremost year-round resort centers. Clear Lake, north of San Francisco, and Lake Arrowhead and Big Bear Lake in the mountains east of Los Angeles are other popular resort areas. More than 100 reservoirs provide the setting for water sports where nature did not.

The recreational season in California's deserts is largely limited to late fall, winter and mid-spring. Those seeking winter sunshine frequent such resorts as Palm Springs, Borrego Springs and Death Valley for their luxurious accommodations, **golf, tennis, riding** and **swimming,** while others prefer **camping** at any of the dozens of well-equipped campgrounds.

California leads the nation in sales of **fishing** licenses; its lakes and rivers teem with a variety of species. Such northern streams as the Eel, Klamath, Sacramento, Pit, Trinity and Feather are especially good, as are Lake Almanor and Clear Lake. Saltwater sport fishing is available at commercial landings and public piers all along the coast. Much of California's wildlife is protected by law. Hunting is by license only.

Horse racing can be found at beautiful Santa Anita Park in Arcadia, at Del Mar, Los Alamitos, Hollywood Park in Inglewood, Golden Gate Fields in Albany and at Bay Meadows in San Mateo. Major **auto racing** events highlight a full calendar at Riverside International Raceway. California has collegiate and professional competition in all major sports; activity centers are in the Los Angeles, San Francisco and San Diego areas.

Approximately 25 million acres of public lands invite exploration and recreation: Kings Canyon, Lassen Volcanic, Redwood, Sequoia and Yosemite national parks, Point Reyes National Seashore, Golden Gate and Whiskeytown-Shasta-Trinity national recreation areas, eight national monuments, 18 national forests and numerous wilderness areas, as well as extensive tracts of desert country administered by the Bureau of Land Management.

Backpacking can be enjoyed in many of these areas. The John Muir Trail—extending from the summit of Mount Whitney to Yosemite National Park—is the state's best known back-country route. The Pacific Crest Trail extends from the Mexico border through California, Oregon and Washington to the Canadian border.

California's state park system encompasses a wide variety of sites—scenic, historic and scientific as well as recreational. Most parks are open all year. Campsite reservations are necessary in summer and on weekends and are available up to 8 weeks in advance at MISTIX outlets in California. Contact P.O. Box 85705, San Diego, CA 92138-5705; phone (619) 452-0150, or (800) 444-7275 in Calif.

Facilities at many national and state recreation areas are indicated on the Recreation Chart. For detailed listings of camping and trailering areas, both public and private, *see the AAA California and Nevada CampBook.*

RECREATION AREAS	MAP LOCATION	CAMPING	PICNICKING	HIKING TRAILS	BOATING	BOAT RAMP	BOAT RENTAL	FISHING	SWIMMING	PETS ON LEASH	BICYCLE TRAILS	NATURE PROGS.	VISITOR CENTER	LODGE/CABINS	FOOD SERVICE
NATIONAL PARKS *(See place listings)*															
Channel Islands 249,515 acres.															
Anacapa (J-4) Skin diving.		•	•	•				•	•				•		
San Miguel (J-3) Skin diving.		•	•	•				•	•				•		
Santa Barbara (K-4) Skin diving.		•	•	•				•	•				•	•	
Santa Cruz (J-4) Skin diving.		•	•	•				•	•				•		
Santa Rosa (J-3) Skin diving.		•	•	•				•	•				•		
Lassen Volcanic (B-3) 106,000 acres.		•	•	•				•	•	•		•	•	•	•
Redwood (A-1) 113,200 acres. Kayaking; horse rental.		•	•	•				•	•	•		•	•	•	•
Sequoia and Kings Canyon (H-5 & G-5) 1,351 square miles. Horse rental.		•	•	•				•		•		•	•	•	•
Yosemite (F-5) 1,189 square miles. Horse rental. Motorized vessels prohibited.		•	•	•				•	•	•		•	•	•	•
NATIONAL RECREATION AREAS *(See place listings)*															

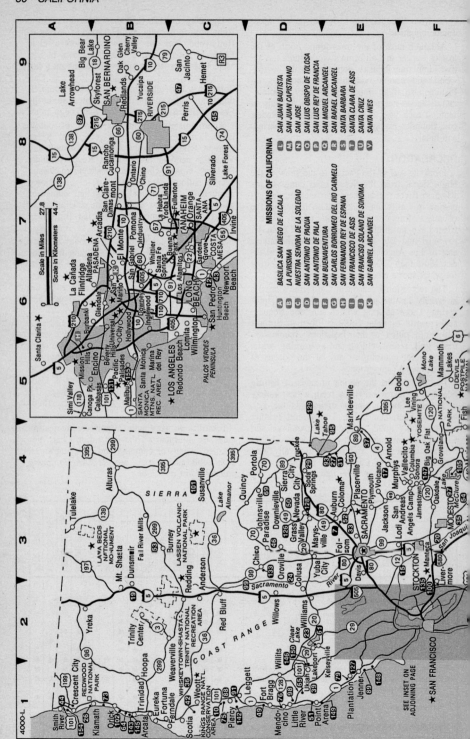

MISSIONS OF CALIFORNIA

- **A** BASILICA SAN DIEGO DE ALCALA
- **B** LA PURISIMA
- **C** NUESTRA SENORA DE LA SOLEDAD
- **D** SAN ANTONIO DE PADUA
- **E** SAN ANTONIO DE PALA
- **F** SAN BUENAVENTURA
- **G** SAN CARLOS BORROMEO DEL RIO CARMELO
- **H** SAN FERNANDO REY DE ESPANA
- **I** SAN FRANCISCO DE ASIS
- **J** SAN FRANCISCO SOLANO DE SONOMA
- **K** SAN GABRIEL ARCANGEL

- **L** SAN JUAN BAUTISTA
- **M** SAN JUAN CAPISTRANO
- **N** SAN JOSE
- **O** SAN LUIS OBISPO DE TOLOSA
- **P** SAN LUIS REY DE FRANCIA
- **Q** SAN MIGUEL ARCANGEL
- **R** SAN RAFAEL ARCANGEL
- **S** SANTA BARBARA
- **T** SANTA CLARA DE ASIS
- **U** SANTA CRUZ
- **V** SANTA INES

4000-L

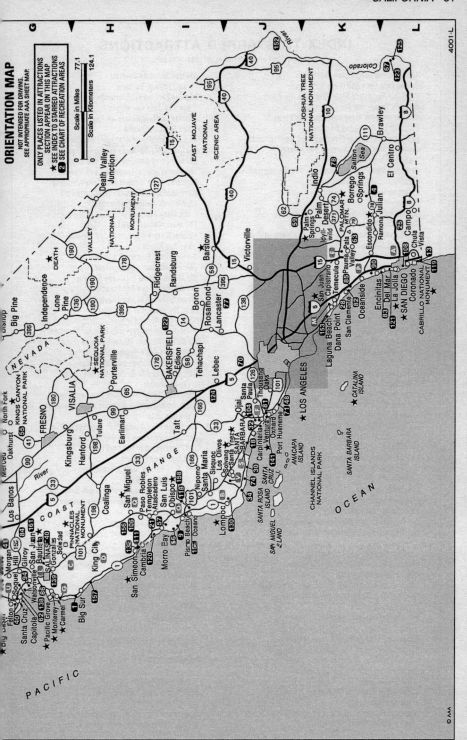

ORIENTATION MAP

NOT INTENDED FOR DRIVING,
SEE APPROPRIATE AAA SHEET MAP.

ONLY PLACES LISTED IN ATTRACTIONS
SECTION APPEAR ON THIS MAP
★ SEE INDEX TO STARRED ATTRACTIONS
❷ SEE CHART OF RECREATION AREAS

Scale in Miles   77.1

Scale in Kilometers   124.1

4001-L

© AAA

INDEX TO STARRED ATTRACTIONS
ATTRACTIONS OF EXCEPTIONAL INTEREST AND QUALITY

RECREATION AREAS	MAP LOCATION	CAMPING	PICNICKING	HIKING TRAILS	BOATING	BOAT RAMP	BOAT RENTAL	FISHING	SWIMMING	PETS ON LEASH	BICYCLE TRAILS	NATURE PROGS.	VISITOR CENTER	LODGE/CABINS	FOOD SERVICE
Golden Gate (O-1) 73,000 acres. Horse rental.		●	●	●				●	●	●	●		●		
Santa Monica Mountains (B-5) 150,000 acres. Horse rental.		●	●	●				●	●	●	●		●		
Whiskeytown-Shasta-Trinity (C-2) 243,000 acres. Horse rental.		●	●	●	●	●	●	●	●	●	●		●		●
NATIONAL FORESTS *(See place listings)*															
Angeles 651,874 acres. Southern California.		●	●	●	●	●		●	●	●	●	●	●		●
Cleveland 420,630 acres. Southwestern California.		●	●	●		●		●	●	●		●	●		●
Eldorado 676,780 acres. Central California. Horse rental.		●	●	●	●	●		●	●	●		●		●	●
Inyo 1,900,400 acres. Central California. Horse rental.		●	●	●	●	●		●	●	●	●	●	●	●	●
Klamath 1,726,000 acres. Northern California.		●	●	●	●	●		●	●	●		●	●	●	●
Lassen 1,200,000 acres. Northern California.		●	●	●	●	●	●	●	●	●		●	●		●
Los Padres 1,752,539 acres. Southern California. Horse rental.		●	●	●				●	●	●		●	●		●
Mendocino 894,339 acres. Northwestern California.		●	●	●				●	●	●			●		●
Modoc 1,654,392 acres. Northeastern California.		●	●	●				●		●			●		●
Plumas 1,162,863 acres. Northern California. Horse rental.		●	●	●	●	●		●	●	●			●		●
San Bernardino 657,360 acres. Southern California. Horse rental.		●	●	●	●	●		●	●	●	●	●	●		●
Sequoia 1,139,519 acres. South-central California. Horse rental.		●	●	●	●	●		●		●		●			●
Shasta-Trinity 2,129,524 acres. Northern California. Horse rental.		●	●	●	●	●		●	●	●		●	●		●
Sierra 1,304,476 acres. Central California. Horse rental.		●	●	●	●	●		●	●	●		●	●		●
Six Rivers 958,543 acres. Northwestern California. Horse rental.		●	●	●				●	●	●		●	●		●
Stanislaus 898,602 acres. Central California. Horse rental.		●	●	●	●	●	●	●	●	●		●	●		●
Tahoe 797,225 acres. North-central California. Horse rental.		●	●	●	●	●		●	●	●			●		●
NATIONAL CONSERVATION AREA															
King Range (C-1) 60,000 acres w. of Garberville.		●	●	●	●	●		●	●	●		●			
NATIONAL SCENIC AREA *(See place listing)*															
East Mojave (I-8) 1,500,000 acres.		●	●	●					●	●		●			
NATIONAL SEASHORE *(See place listing)*															
Point Reyes (O-1) 65,300 acres. Horse rental.		●	●	●				●		●		●	●		
ARMY CORPS OF ENGINEERS															
Lake Mendocino (D-2) 5,000 acres 5 mi. n.w. of Ukiah on SR 20.	150	●	●	●	●	●	●	●	●	●		●	●		●
Lake Sonoma (M-1) 17,600 acres 26 mi. n.w. of Santa Rosa on Dry Creek Rd. Fish hatchery.	144	●	●	●	●	●	●	●	●	●		●	●		●
STATE															
Anderson Marsh (D-2) 871 acres ¾ mi. n. of Lower Lake on SR 53. Nature trail.	61		●	●				●		●		●	●		
Andrew Molera (H-2) 4,800 acres 21 mi. s. of Carmel on SR 1. Horse rental.	1	●		●				●	●	●	●				
Angel Island (O-2) 758 acres in San Francisco Bay; ferry from San Francisco or Tiburon. Nature trails.	2	●	●	●	●			●			●	●	●		●
Annadel (M-2) 4,913 acres s.e. of Santa Rosa on Channel Dr. Horse rental.	3		●	●				●			●	●	●		
Anza-Borrego Desert (K-7) 600,000 acres. Horse rental, nature and off-road-vehicle trails. *(See Borrego Springs)*	4	●	●	●						●		●	●		
Armstrong Redwoods (M-1) 752 acres 2 mi. n. of Guerneville on Armstrong Woods Rd. Horse rental, nature trails.	5		●	●						●		●	●	●		
Auburn (E-3) 42,000 acres 1 mi. s. of Auburn on SR 49. Historic. Water skiing; horse rental.	7	●	●	●	●	●		●	●	●					

RECREATION AREAS

RECREATION AREAS	MAP LOCATION	CAMPING	PICNICKING	HIKING TRAILS	BOATING	BOAT RAMP	BOAT RENTAL	FISHING	SWIMMING	PETS ON LEASH	BICYCLE TRAILS	NATURE PROGS.	VISITOR CENTER	LODGE/CABINS	FOOD SERVICE
Austin Creek (M-1) 4,236 acres 2 mi. n. of Guerneville on Armstrong Woods Rd. Horse rental.	8	●	●	●						●	●	●			
Benbow Lake (C-1) 786 acres 3 mi. s. of Garberville on US 101. Horse rental. Motorboats not permitted.	10	●	●	●	●	●	●	●	●	●	●	●	●		
Bethany Reservoir (F-2) 300 acres n. of I-580 via Altamont Pass, Mountain House and Christensen rds. Windsurfing.	135		●		●	●		●	●						
Bidwell River (D-3) 180 acres 5 mi. w. of Chico on River Rd. Canoeing, tubing.	133		●	●	●	●	●		●	●					
Big Basin Redwoods (F-2) 16,000 acres. Horse rental, nature trails. *(See Big Basin)*	11	●	●	●						●		●	●	●	●
Bolsa Chica Beach (C-6) 164 acres 3 mi. w. of Huntington Beach on SR 1.	12		●					●	●	●		●			●
Border Field (L-7) 680 acres 15 mi. s. of San Diego on Monument Rd. Horse rental, nature trails.	13		●	●				●	●	●					
Bothe-Napa Valley (M-2) 1,916 acres 4 mi. n. of St. Helena on SR 29. Horse rental.	14	●	●	●					●	●		●	●	●	
Brannan Island (F-3) 336 acres 3¼ mi. s. of Rio Vista. Water skiing, windsurfing.	15	●	●	●	●	●		●	●	●		●	●		
Butano (Q-2) 3,200 acres 7 mi. s. of Pescadero on Cloverdale Rd.	16	●	●	●						●					
Calaveras Big Trees (E-4) 6,073 acres. Cross-country skiing; nature trails. *(See Arnold)*	17	●	●	●				●	●	●		●	●		
Candlestick Point (P-2) 37 acres e. of US 101 via Candlestick exit.	136		●	●				●		●					
Carpinteria Beach (J-4) 84 acres at Carpinteria.	18	●	●					●	●	●					
Castaic Lake (J-5) 8,000 acres ½ mi. e. of Castaic on Ridge Route Rd.	70	●	●		●	●	●	●	●	●			●		●
Castle Crags (B-2) 6,218 acres. Horse rental, nature trails. *(See Dunsmuir)*	19	●	●	●				●	●	●		●	●		
Castle Rock (Q-3) 3,600 acres 2 mi. s. of SR 9 and SR 35 on Skyline Blvd. Nature trails.	137	●	●	●						●		●			
Caswell Memorial (F-3) 258 acres 6 mi. s.w. of Ripon on Austin Rd.	20	●	●	●				●	●	●		●			
China Camp (O-2) 1,640 acres n. of San Rafael via US 101 and N. San Pedro Rd. Water skiing; horse rental.	22	●	●	●				●	●	●			●		
Clear Lake (D-2) 565 acres 3.5 mi. n. of Kelseyville on Soda Bay Rd. Water skiing; nature trails. *(See Kelseyville)*	23	●	●	●	●	●		●	●	●			●		
Colusa-Sacramento River (D-3) 67 acres at Colusa.	24	●	●	●	●	●		●	●				●		
Crystal Cove (K-6) 2,791 acres n. of Dana Point on SR 1.	153	●		●				●	●	●					
Cuyamaca Rancho (L-7) 24,677 acres 6 mi. n. of Descanso on SR 79. Horse rental, nature trails.	25	●	●	●				●	●	●		●	●		
Del Norte Coast Redwoods (A-1) 6,400 acres 7 mi. s. of Crescent City on US 101. Nature trails.	26	●	●	●					●	●		●			
D.L. Bliss (E-4) 1,237 acres 17 mi. s. of Tahoe on SR 89. Nature trails. *(See Lake Tahoe)*	27	●	●	●				●	●	●					
Doheny Beach (K-6) 62 acres 1 mi. s. of Dana Point.	28	●						●	●	●		●	●		●
Donner Memorial (D-4) 353 acres. Cross-country skiing; nature trails. *(See Truckee)*	29	●						●	●	●		●	●		
El Capitan Beach (J-4) 133 acres 20 mi. w. of Santa Barbara off US 101. Nature trails.	30	●	●	●				●	●		●	●	●		●
Emerald Bay (E-4) 593 acres on the s.w. shore of Lake Tahoe.	31	●	●	●	●			●	●	●					
Emma Wood Beach (J-4) 116 acres 4 mi. n. of Ventura on US 101.	32	●	●	●				●	●	●					
Empire Mine (D-3) 788 acres. Horse rental. *(See Grass Valley)*	128		●	●								●	●		
Folsom Lake (E-3) 17,718 acres 2 mi. n.w. of Folsom off US 50. Water skiing, windsurfing; horse rental, nature trails.	33	●	●	●	●	●	●	●	●	●		●	●	●	●
Forest of Nisene Marks (G-2) 9,960 acres 4 mi. n. of Aptos on Aptos Creek Rd.	138	●	●	●						●					
Fort Ross (E-1) 1,563 acres. *(See Jenner)*	127	●	●	●				●					●	●	
Fremont Peak (G-2) 244 acres 11 mi. s. of San Juan Bautista on San Juan Canyon Rd. Nature trails.	139	●	●	●						●		●			

WHEELCHAIR SIGHTSEERS

Many thousands of attractions listed in this book can be visited by AAA members who use wheelchairs. However, the wide range of attractions, the complexity of their sites and the diversity of their physical characteristics, some of which may pose partial limitations, make it difficult to note those that are completely accessible. The attraction listings include a phone number so members can call ahead to ask specific questions.

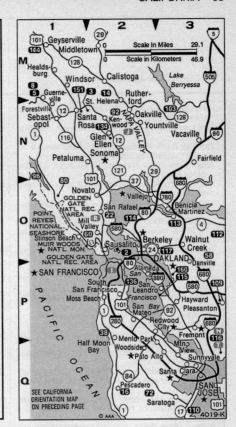

SEE CALIFORNIA ORIENTATION MAP ON PRECEDING PAGE

RECREATION AREAS	MAP LOCATION	CAMPING	PICNICKING	HIKING TRAILS	BOATING	BOAT RAMP	BOAT RENTAL	FISHING	SWIMMING	PETS ON LEASH	BICYCLE TRAILS	NATURE PROGS.	VISITOR CENTER	LODGE/CABINS	FOOD SERVICE
Gaviota (J-4) 2,776 acres at Gaviota, 30 mi. w. of Santa Barbara. Horse rental.	34	•	•	•	•	•		•	•			•			•
George J. Hatfield (F-3) 47 acres 28 mi. w. of Merced on Kelly Rd.	35	•	•					•	•						
Grizzly Creek Redwoods (C-1) 390 acres 15 mi. e. of Fortuna on SR 36. Nature trails.	36	•	•	•				•	•	•		•			
Grover Hot Springs (E-4) 539 acres 4 mi. w. of Markleeville on Hot Springs Rd. Nature trails.	37	•	•	•				•	•	•		•			
Half Moon Bay Beach (P-2) 170 acres ½ mi. w. of US 1 on Kelly Ave. Horse rental.	38	•	•					•		•		•			
Hendy Woods (D-1) 693 acres 3 mi. w. of Philo off SR 128. Horse rental, nature trails.	39	•	•	•				•	•	•		•			
Henry Cowell Redwoods (G-2) 4,082 acres 3 mi. e. of Felton on Graham Hill Rd. Horse rental, nature trails.	40	•	•	•				•	•	•	•	•	•		•
Henry W. Coe (G-3) 67,000 acres 14 mi. e. of Morgan Hill on E. Dunne Ave. Horse rental, nature trails.	41	•	•	•				•	•	•		•	•		
Hollister Hills (G-3) 3,322 acres 8 mi. s. of Hollister via Cienega Rd. Nature trails.	140	•	•							•		•			
Humboldt Lagoons (B-1) 1,036 acres 4 mi. s. of Orick on US 101. (See Orick)	102	•	•	•	•	•		•		•					
Humboldt Redwoods (C-1) 51,000 acres. Horse rental, nature trails. (See Weott)	42	•	•	•				•	•	•		•	•		

RECREATION AREAS	MAP LOCATION	CAMPING	PICNICKING	HIKING TRAILS	BOATING	BOAT RAMP	BOAT RENTAL	FISHING	SWIMMING	PETS ON LEASH	BICYCLE TRAILS	NATURE PROGS.	VISITOR CENTER	LODGE/CABINS	FOOD SERVICE
Huntington Beach (C-6) 78 acres at the s.e. edge of Huntington Beach.	43	•						•	•	•					•
Jack London (N-2) 800 acres. Horse rental. *(See Glen Ellen)*	134	•	•									•		•	
Jedediah Smith Redwoods (A-1) 9,560 acres 9 mi. n.e. of Crescent City. Nature trails.	44	•	•	•				•	•	•		•		•	
Julia Pfeiffer Burns (H-2) 3583 acres 37 mi. s. of Carmel on SR 1.	157	•	•	•											
Kings Beach (D-5) 8 acres 12 mi. n.e. of Tahoe City on SR 28.	129		•		•			•	•						
Lake Elsinore (C-8) 2,954 acres 1 mi. w. of Elsinore on SR 74. Water skiing, windsurfing.	45	•			•	•	•	•	•	•					
Lake Oroville (D-3) 31,600 acres 6 mi. n.e. of Oroville off SR 70. Water skiing, windsurfing; horse rental, nature trails.	46	•	•		•	•	•	•	•	•			•	•	
Lake Perris (C-9) 8,000 acres 4 mi. n.e. of Perris on the Ramona Expwy. Rock climbing, water skiing; horse rental.	47	•	•	•	•	•	•	•	•	•	•	•	•		
Lakes Earl and Talawa (A-1) 5,000 acres n. of Crescent City off US 101. Horse rental.	154	•	•	•	•	•		•				•	•		
La Purísima Mission (J-3) 967 acres. Horse rental. *(See Lompoc)*	130		•	•								•	•		
Leo Carrillo Beach (J-5) 2,000 acres 22 mi. n. of Santa Monica on SR 1. Windsurfing.	48	•	•	•				•	•				•		
Los Baños Creek Reservoir (G-3) 10 mi. s.w. of Los Baños via SR 165, Pioneer and Canyon rds.	161	•	•					•	•	•					
MacKerricher (D-1) 2,030 acres 3 mi. n. of Fort Bragg on SR 1. Horse rental.	49	•	•	•				•		•		•	•		
Malakoff Diggins (D-3) 3,000 acres n.e. of Nevada City on North Bloomfield Rd. Historic. Horse rental, nature trails.	50	•	•	•				•	•	•	•	•	•	•	
Malibu Creek (B-5) 6,600 acres 4 mi. s. of US 101 on Las Virgenes/Malibu Canyon Rd. in Calabasas. Horse rental.	131	•	•	•				•	•			•	•		
Malibu Lagoon Beach (B-5) 76 acres at US 101 and Malibu Creek. Nature trails.	155		•	•				•	•				•	•	
Manchester Beach (D-1) 1,419 acres 7 mi. n of Point Arena on SR 1.	51	•	•	•				•		•					
Manresa Beach (G-2) 5 mi. w. of Watsonville.	162	•	•					•	•	•					
Marshall Gold Discovery (E-3) 280 acres 8 mi. n. of Placerville on SR 49. Historic. Nature trails.	52		•	•				•		•			•		
McArthur-Burney Falls Memorial (B-3) 800 acres. Scenic. Water skiing; horse rental, nature trails. *(See Burney)*	53	•	•	•	•	•	•	•	•	•	•	•	•	•	•
McConnell (F-4) 74 acres 5 mi. e. of Delhi on Merced River.	54	•						•	•	•					
McGrath Beach (J-4) 295 acres s. of Ventura on Harbor Blvd. Nature trails.	141	•		•				•	•	•					
Millerton Lake (G-4) 6,553 acres 21 mi. n.e. of Fresno via SR 41. Historic. Water skiing, windsurfing; horse rental.	55	•	•	•				•	•	•			•	•	
Montana de Oro (I-3) 8,066 acres 6 mi. s. of Los Osos. Horse rental, nature trails.	56	•	•	•				•		•		•	•	•	
Morro Bay (I-3) 2,435 acres 3 mi. s. of Morro Bay. Birdwatching, golf.	57	•	•	•	•		•	•	•	•		•	•	•	•
Morro Strand Beach (I-3) 117 acres 1 mi. n. of Morro Bay on SR 1. Surfing.	120	•	•					•	•	•					
Mount Diablo (O-3) 18,000 acres. Horse rental. *(See Walnut Creek)*	58	•	•	•						•		•	•	•	
Mount San Jacinto Wilderness (J-7) 13,522 acres. Horse rental. *(See San Bernardino National Forest)*	59	•	•	•					•		•		•	•	•
Mount Tamalpais (O-1) 6,217 acres. Horse rental, nature trails. *(See Mill Valley)*	60	•	•							•	•	•	•	•	•
Navarro River Redwoods (D-1) 12 acres 6 mi. w. of Navarro on SR 128.	65	•	•					•	•						
New Brighton Beach (G-2) 94 acres 4 mi. s. of Santa Cruz.	62	•	•	•				•	•			•			

RECREATION AREAS	MAP LOCATION	CAMPING	PICNICKING	HIKING TRAILS	BOATING	BOAT RAMP	BOAT RENTAL	FISHING	SWIMMING	PETS ON LEASH	BICYCLE TRAILS	NATURE PROGS.	VISITOR CENTER	LODGE/CABINS	FOOD SERVICE
Palomar Mountain (K-7) 1,897 acres 4 mi. n. of jct. CR S6 and CR 57 via park road. Nature trails.	63	•	•	•				•		•					
Patrick's Point (B-1) 632 acres. Nature trails. (See Trinidad)	64	•	•	•				•		•		•	•		
Pfeiffer Big Sur (H-2) 821 acres. Nature trails. (See Big Sur)	66	•	•	•				•	•		•	•	•	•	•
Picacho (L-9) 4,880 acres 23 mi. n. of Winterhaven. Water skiing.	67	•	•	•	•	•	•	•	•						
Pismo Beach (I-4) 1,051 acres 3 mi. s. of city of Pismo Beach on SR 1. Surfing; nature trails.	68	•	•	•				•	•		•	•			•
Pismo Dunes (I-4) 2,500 acres 3 mi. s. of city of Pismo Beach on SR 1. Off-road vehicles permitted. Surfing; horse rental.	118	•	•	•				•	•						
Plumas-Eureka (D-4) 6,749 acres near Johnsville. Horse rental, nature trails.	69	•	•	•				•	•	•		•	•	•	
Point Mugu (J-5) 13,360 acres 15 mi. s. of Oxnard on SR 1. Horse rental.	71	•	•	•				•	•	•	•	•	•		
Portola (Q-2) 2,010 acres 20 mi. s.w. of Palo Alto. Nature trails.	72	•	•	•				•				•	•		
Prairie Creek Redwoods (B-1) 12,544 acres. (See Orick)	73	•	•	•				•				•	•		
Pyramid Lake (I-5) 1,297 acres 12 mi. n. of Frazier Park off I-5.	124	•	•		•	•	•	•	•	•					•
Red Rock Canyon (I-6) 4,000 acres 25 mi. n. of Mojave on SR 14. Scenic. Nature trails.	122	•	•	•				•				•			
Refugio Beach (J-4) 155 acres 22 mi. w. of Santa Barbara.	74	•	•	•				•	•		•				
Richardson Grove (C-1) 1,000 acres 8 mi. s. of Garberville on US 101. Nature trails.	75	•	•	•	•			•	•			•	•		•
Russian Gulch (D-1) 1,300 acres 2 mi. n. of Mendocino on US 101. Skin diving.	76	•	•	•				•	•		•	•	•		
Saddleback Butte (J-6) 2,875 acres 17 mi. e. of Lancaster. Nature trails.	77	•	•	•						•		•			
Salton Sea (K-8) 17,900 acres 11 mi. s.e. of Mecca. Water skiing; nature trails.	78	•	•	•				•	•			•	•		
Salt Point (E-1) 5,970 acres 24 mi. n. of Jenner on SR 1. Skin diving; horse rental.	79	•	•	•	•	•		•		•		•	•		
Samuel P. Taylor (O-1) 2,708 acres 18 mi. n.w. of San Rafael. Horse rental, nature trails.	80	•	•	•							•	•	•		
San Buenaventura Beach (J-5) 114 acres in Ventura.	81	•	•					•	•		•				•
San Clemente Beach (K-6) 110 acres at the s. edge of San Clemente.	82	•	•					•	•						
San Elijo Beach (L-6) 39 acres 1 mi. s. of Encinitas.	83	•						•	•			•			
San Luis Reservoir (G-3) 26,026 acres 12 mi. w. of Los Banos on SR 152. Water skiing, windsurfing; motorbike area.	84	•	•		•	•		•	•			•	•		
San Onofre Beach (K-6) 3,036 acres 1½ mi. s. of San Clemente.	85	•		•				•	•						
San Simeon Beach (H-3) 541 acres 5 mi. s. of San Simeon.	111	•	•		•			•	•			•			
Seacliff Beach (G-2) 85 acres 5½ mi. s. of Santa Cruz on SR 1.	86	•	•					•	•						•
Silver Strand Beach (L-6) 428 acres 4½ mi. s. of Coronado on SR 75.	119	•						•	•						
Silverwood Lake (A-8) 2,200 acres, e. of Cajon Junction on SR 138. Water skiing; nature trails.	87	•	•	•	•	•	•	•	•			•	•		
Sinkyone Wilderness (C-1) 7,000 acres 30 mi. w. of Redway on CR 435 (Briceland Rd.).	142	•		•				•				•	•		
Smithe Redwoods (C-1) 622 acres 4 mi. n. of Leggett on US 101.	88		•					•	•						
Sonoma Coast Beach (E-1) 5,000 acres n. of Bodega Bay on SR 1. Horse rental.	89	•	•	•	•	•		•				•	•	•	
South Carlsbad Beach (K-6) 135 acres 4 mi. n. of Encinitas.	90	•						•	•						
South Yuba River Project (D-3) 2,000 acres 8 mi. n.w. of Nevada City on SR 49. Nature trail.	126		•	•				•	•	•					

RECREATION AREAS	MAP LOCATION	CAMPING	PICNICKING	HIKING TRAILS	BOATING	BOAT RAMP	BOAT RENTAL	FISHING	SWIMMING	PETS ON LEASH	BICYCLE TRAILS	NATURE PROGS.	VISITOR CENTER	LODGE/CABINS	FOOD SERVICE
Standish-Hickey (C-1) 1,020 acres 1 mi. n. of Leggett on US 101.	91	•	•	•				•	•			•			
Sugarloaf Ridge (N-2) 2,700 acres 7 mi. e. of Santa Rosa on SR 12. Horse rental, nature trails.	92	•	•	•						•	•	•			
Sugar Pine Point (E-4) 2,011 acres 10 mi. s. of Tahoe City. Nature trails.	93	•	•	•	•			•	•			•	•		
Sunset Beach (G-3) 324 acres 4 mi. w. of Watsonville.	94	•	•	•				•		•					
Tahoe (E-4) 57 acres on Lake Tahoe ¼ mi. s. of Tahoe City.	95	•	•		•			•	•						
Tomales Bay (N-1) 1,857 acres 4 mi. n. of Inverness. Nature trails.	96	•	•	•				•	•			•	•		
Torrey Pines Beach (L-6) 41 acres 1 mi. s. of Del Mar on N. Torrey Pines Rd.	121		•					•	•						
Trinidad Beach (B-1) 159 acres 19 mi. n. of Eureka on US 101.	143		•	•				•				•	•		
Turlock Lake (F-4) 408 acres 23 mi. e. of Modesto off SR 132. Water skiing.	97	•	•	•	•	•		•	•						•
Van Damme (D-1) 2,163 acres 3 mi. s. of Mendocino on SR 1. Nature trails.	98	•	•	•				•				•	•		
William Randolph Hearst Memorial Beach (H-3) 8 acres in San Simeon on SR 1.	132		•		•			•	•						•
Woodson Bridge (D-2) 428 acres 6 mi. e. of Corning and I-5. Nature trails.	99	•	•	•	•			•	•						

OTHER

RECREATION AREAS	MAP LOCATION	CAMPING	PICNICKING	HIKING TRAILS	BOATING	BOAT RAMP	BOAT RENTAL	FISHING	SWIMMING	PETS ON LEASH	BICYCLE TRAILS	NATURE PROGS.	VISITOR CENTER	LODGE/CABINS	FOOD SERVICE
Anthony Chabot Regional Park and Lake Chabot Marina (P-3) 4,999 acres e. of Oakland. Horse rental, horse trails.	160	•	•	•	•		•	•		•	•				
Avila Beach (I-3) 10 acres in Avila. Surfing.	9		•		•	•		•	•						
Big Lagoon (B-1) 50 acres 7 mi. n. of Trinidad on US 101.	145	•	•		•	•		•	•	•					
Cayucos Beach (I-3) 16 acres s.w. of Cayucos on SR 1. Surfing.	21		•	•				•	•	•					
Contra Loma (O-3) 776 acres 1 mi. s. of Antioch. Windsurfing, sailboarding.	112		•	•				•	•	•	•				•
Cow Mountain (D-1) 50,000 acres e. of Ukiah on Talmage Rd.	146	•	•	•				•	•	•				•	
Del Valle (F-2) 4,000 acres 10 mi. s. of Livermore.	100	•	•	•	•	•		•	•	•		•			
Don Pedro Lake (F-4) 12,960 acres n.e. of La Grange on Bond's Flat Rd.	147	•	•	•	•	•	•	•	•	•		•		•	
Doran (E-1) 120 acres on Doran Park Rd., Bodega Bay.	148	•	•	•	•	•		•	•	•					
Eagle Lake (C-4) 22,000 acres 20 mi n.w. of Susanville.	101	•	•	•	•	•	•	•	•	•				•	•
Empire Landing (J-9) 10 acres 7 mi. s.w. of Parker Dam (Calif. side of Colorado River).	152	•	•	•				•	•						
Gualala Point (E-1) 300 acres off SR 1 s. of Gualala.	149	•	•	•				•	•	•	•		•		
Lake Berryessa (N-3) 13,000 acres 20 mi. n.w. of Napa on SR 121.	103	•	•	•	•	•	•	•	•	•	•		•	•	•
Lake Casitas (J-5) 6,000 acres 5 mi. s.w. of Ojai off SR 150.	104	•	•	•	•	•	•	•		•					•
Lake McClure (F-4) 7,100 acres 4 mi. w. of Coulterville on SR 132.	105	•	•	•	•	•	•	•	•	•					•
Lake Nacimiento (H-3) 5,370 acres 17 mi. w. of Paso Robles off US 101.	106	•	•	•	•	•	•	•	•	•		•		•	•
Lake San Antonio (H-3) 5,000 acres 40 mi. s. of King City off US 101. Birdwatching; horse rental.	156	•	•	•	•	•	•	•	•	•		•		•	•
Loch Lomond (F-2) 2,100 acres n. of Ben Lomond.	107		•	•	•	•	•	•		•		•			•
Lopez Lake (I-3) 4,376 acres 11 mi. n.e. of Arroyo Grande on Lopez Dr.	158	•	•	•	•	•	•	•	•	•				•	•
Martinez Shoreline (O-3) 343 acres in Martinez. Birdwatching; nature trails.	113		•	•				•		•	•	•	•		
Mission Bay (L-7) 4,600 acres. (See San Diego)	108	•	•		•	•	•	•	•	•			•	•	•
Oceano Memorial (I-3) 11.8 acres on Dewey Rd. in Oceano.	159	•	•					•	•	•					
Point Pinole Shoreline (O-2) 2,147 acres n.w. of San Pablo. Fishing pier.	114		•	•				•	•	•	•	•			

RECREATION AREAS	MAP LOCATION	CAMPING	PICNICKING	HIKING TRAILS	BOATING	BOAT RAMP	BOAT RENTAL	FISHING	SWIMMING	PETS ON LEASH	BICYCLE TRAILS	NATURE PROGS.	VISITOR CENTER	LODGE/CABINS	FOOD SERVICE
San Leandro Bay Shoreline (P-3) 1,220 acres in Oakland. Birdwatching; fishing pier.	115	•	•	•	•			•	•	•	•				•
Senator Wash Reservoir (L-9) 6 acres 20 mi. n. of Winterhaven on Senator Wash Rd. Skin diving.	123	•	•		•	•		•	•	•	•				
Shadow Cliffs (P-3) 249 acres at Pleasanton. Waterslide. *(See Pleasanton)*	109	•	•	•	•	•	•	•	•	•	•				•
Spring Lake (M-1) 320 acres e. of Santa Rosa at Newanga Ave.	151	•	•	•	•	•	•	•	•	•	•				•
Squaw Lake (L-9) 18 acres 20 mi. n. of Winterhaven at end of Senator Wash Rd.	125	•	•		•	•		•	•						
Sunol Wilderness (P-3) 5,924 acres 6 mi. s. of Sunol. Birdwatching; nature trails.	116	•	•							•			•	•	
Temescal (O-3) 48 acres in Oakland.	117	•						•	•	•					•
Vasona Park and Reservoir (Q-3) 151 acres near Los Gatos. Motorboats not permitted.	110	•	•	•	•			•	•	•			•		

Touring California

For descriptions of places in bold type, see individual listings.

California's Outback

Southern California's desert country is not just sand and occasional palm oases; it's a land of diversity and drama. Mountain peaks thousands of feet high look down on valleys that lie below sea level. A seemingly arid wilderness supports a variety of fascinating flora and fauna. The harsh terrain contains remnants of prosperous mines and boom towns.

To explore this backcountry, begin on I-10 in **Los Angeles** and head east. Seven miles past the Upland turnoff, go north on I-15 headed for **Victorville** and **Barstow**. In Barstow visit the California Desert Information Center for information on geology, desert plants and animals, recreation, and road and weather conditions.

Interstate 40 begins at Barstow; take it and go east. The highway stretches through an arid expanse where cactus and brush conceal small wildlife, dry lakes signify prehistoric seas and mountains shelter old mining sites.

Approximately 80 miles from Barstow, Kelbaker Road begins as 1½ miles of dirt road but is paved after that except for a 4-mile stretch of graded dirt. Mountains, lava beds and sand dunes are dramatic features of the landscape along this road. The only townsite is Kelso, once an important stop for the Union Pacific Railroad.

For a somewhat different perspective of the desert, stay on I-40 past Kelbaker Road and turn north on Essex Road to Providence Mountain State Recreation Area (*see listing under East Mojave National Scenic Area*). Red volcanic peaks punctuate this high desert area and within

its Mitchell Caverns are intricate limestone formations. Guided tours are available.

Because of the poor condition of the east-west roads between Essex and Kelbaker roads, it is advisable to return to I-40, then Kelbaker Road. Thirty-five miles north of Kelso, Kelbaker meets I-15 in the tiny town of Baker. North out of Baker, take SR 127 about 55 miles to SR 178.

Turn west and drive over the Greenwater mountain range and through Greenwater Valley into **Death Valley National Monument**. Here is a vast region of truly remarkable scenery: sand dunes and rocks sculpted by wind, and sub-sea-level valleys bordered by mountain walls of every hue. The lowest point in the United States (282 feet below sea level) lies within the monument, and not far away Telescope Peak rises to 11,049 feet.

As SR 178 curves north it becomes Badwater Road and, having offered some spectacular views along the way, reaches the visitor center at Furnace Creek. Another 55 miles north from Furnace Creek brings you to extravagant Scotty's Castle.

Leave Death Valley by driving south and west on SR 190, then south on Panamint Valley Road. Within 14 miles the highway becomes Trona-Wildrose Road as it goes through Panamint Valley, a smaller version of Death Valley. Mountains rise on either side of the highway and side roads lead to dry lakes or old mines.

At Trona pick up SR 178 leading southwest to **Ridgecrest**. From there China Lake Boulevard goes south to US 395. Continue down to the

Randsburg turnoff. Randsburg, along with the camps at Johannesburg and Red Mountain, was the site of frenzied gold and silver mining in the late 1800s.

Twenty-one miles west of Randsburg, Red Rock-Randsburg Road intersects SR 14. You can choose to make a side trip to **Red Rock Canyon State Park** by turning north on SR 14 and traveling 4 miles. The sight of the park's fantastically shaped cliffs and columns makes this a worthwhile detour.

Back on SR 14 head south through Mojave and **Rosamond**. Within about 1½ hours after leaving Red Rock Canyon you'll be in the Antelope Valley, with the San Gabriel Mountains just ahead. SR 14 takes you through the western portion of the **Angeles National Forest,** then ends at I-5, the highway leading south to Los Angeles.

Gold Country

For this tour along former stagecoach routes to the jewel of the Sierra—Lake Tahoe, haven for summer and winter sports and home of varied casinos and accommodations—it is strongly suggested you allow several days to enjoy the many scenic and historic attractions. During the tour you will ascend from an altitude of 30 feet in Sacramento to 7,382 feet at Echo Summit and then to 6,229 in Lake Tahoe.

Your vehicle should be in good condition with good brakes. Remember that down-shifting can sometimes be used to slow your vehicle instead of or in addition to using your brakes. Tire chains should be carried in all mountain areas from mid-October through April. For up-to-date travel advisory information, phone the California Highway Information Network at (415) 557-3755.

Perhaps one of the most exciting and scenic drives in northern California is that from the flat farmland of Sacramento to the resort area of Lake Tahoe. The area changes from rich, black soil with deciduous trees to red clay with its distinctive aroma and pines in the lower Sierras to craggy mountain peaks cloaked in snow.

Begin your trip in **Sacramento,** the state capital. The restored Old Sacramento area has restaurants, shops and museums, including the impressive California State Railroad Museum. Take US 50 east to **Placerville;** a *placer* is a deposit of sand or gravel containing valuable minerals. This once raucous mining town—infamous for its prosperity and consequent lawlessness—has reminders of its past in its museums, municipally owned gold mine and many buildings constructed 1850-70, including fine Victorian-style residences.

Continue east on US 50 through Camino, originally a station on the Placerville-Lake Tahoe stagecoach route. About 2 miles farther is a road to Apple Hill where some of the more than 40 apple farms are open to the public during the fall harvest from mid-September through December.

Taste locally made wines and purchase fruits, nuts, vegetables, apple products, arts and crafts or a Christmas tree from one of the nearly 20 Christmas tree farms. October offers the widest variety of events, but the Apple Blossom Festival from mid-April through May has many highlights, including hayrides and a trout derby.

About 10 miles from Camino you come to Pacific House, an 1859 inn which can boast of such guests as Horace Greeley and Mark Twain. On the 30 miles from Camino to Echo Summit you will pass several entrances to Desolation Wilderness, a hiking and backpacking area open by permit only. After passing through Strawberry, another stagecoach stop, you reach Echo Summit at an altitude of 7,382 feet and begin a 22-mile descent to **Lake Tahoe.**

Lake Tahoe is in a high valley between the Sierra Nevada and the Carson ranges and is one of the premier U.S. winter sports areas. Between 1860 and 1890 Tahoe's forests were nearly destroyed. Lumber was needed for fuel and to support the web of mines constructed beneath Virginia City. The decline of the Comstock Lode was likely the saving grace for Tahoe's forests.

The headquarters of the U.S. Forest Service-Lake Tahoe Basin Management Unit provides year-round information on forest activities, including camping, fishing and hiking in summer and cross-country skiing in winter. Phone (916) 573-2600.

Lake cruises are operated by several companies around the lake. These trips offer scenic views of the lakeshore as well as surrounding resorts and estates.

The State Line area of the South Shore is in Nevada and is the site of many gambling establishments, hotels and casinos. The larger casinos each have several restaurants and coffee shops in which the meals may be both above average in quality and below average in price—the casinos derive most of their income from gambling.

Follow US 50 north and east, a particularly scenic drive along the shore of the lake and through the **Toiyabe National Forest.** When US 50 merges with I-395 turn north and 3 miles later you are in **Carson City,** the capital of Nevada. The Carson City Chamber of Commerce, 1900 S. Carson St., has available a free self-guiding tour map which contains illustrations and descriptions of the town's historic sites.

In downtown Carson City, 2 blocks north of the State Museum and 1 block north of Washington Street at East William Street, US 50 diverges from US 395 and resumes its eastward course. Take US 50 east for about 7 miles to its intersection with scenic SR 341.

On SR 341 travel north for about 10 miles to **Virginia City.** This former haunt of such notables as Mark Twain and Bret Harte has been restored to its 1870 boomtown appearance. The town's restored buildings, its many large and small museums, its mine and its railroad can easily keep you busy for an entire day.

Continue northwest on SR 341 until it intersects US 395; take US 395 north into **Reno,** "The Biggest Little City in the World." While nationally known for easy and quick marriages and divorces as well as for gambling, it also has fine schools and museums. Not to be missed is the collection of more than 200 antique, classic and special interest automobiles.

Now it is time to leave the gambling fever of today and return to yesterday's gold fever. Leave Reno via I-80 heading west and after 32 miles you are in the small California town of **Truckee,** where restored 19th-century false-front buildings now house shops and restaurants. As with most of the lakes and rivers in the Sierras, the Truckee River is popular with trout fishermen.

Continuing west along I-80 you will find an exit to the 353-acre Donner Memorial State Park. Only 9 miles farther along I-80 you reach 7,239-foot Donner Pass.

Continuing west you pass exits to **Soda Springs,** which has a ski museum, and Cisco Grove. Near Emigrant Gap take SR 20 west; this road is lined with tall pines and offers views of old mining camps and sweeping views of the foothills, sometimes as far as 40 miles.

Nevada City was built on seven steep hills and the streets follow miners' trails. The chamber of commerce at 132 Main St. offers a brochure outlining a walking tour. Some of its many Victorian-era buildings are a hodgepodge of styles. The town has several museums, many restaurants and arts and crafts stores.

Continuing west on SR 49 for 5 miles you come to **Grass Valley,** once California's richest gold-mining town. The chamber of commerce at 248 Mill St. can provide you with walking-tour information. In addition to the 784-acre Empire Mine State Historic Park, with California's largest and richest gold mine, the Northstar Powerhouse Mining Museum has fine displays.

Head southwest on SR 49 to **Auburn** and its well-preserved 19th-century buildings. The chamber of commerce at 1101 High St. has walking tour brochures of Old Town. In addition to the museums, don't miss the 1891 firehouse and the 1849 post office.

Continuing southwest on SR 49 for about 25 miles you come to **Coloma,** the birthplace of the California gold rush. Most of the town is within the 300 acres of the Marshall Gold Discovery State Historic Park. The best way to see the park, with its many 1800s buildings and replica of Sutter's Mill, is to first visit the Gold Discovery Museum for a detailed brochure. If you are tired of looking and want to be doing, several local companies offer raft trips down the American River.

SR 49 intersects US 50 near Placerville; take US 50 south toward Sacramento. About 25 miles from Placerville is the exit for **Folsom.** Reminders of the past of this 1850s gold rush town remain in a restored four-block section of Sutter Street, which includes a theater offering melodramas on weekends. Folsom State Prison is 2 miles north of town. The nearly 18,000 acres of Folsom Lake State Recreation Area offer such a variety of recreational opportunities that it is one of the state's most popular multi-use parks.

Return to US 50 and after driving west about 22 miles you have returned to Sacramento.

The Northern California Coast and the Redwood Empire

Leave downtown **San Francisco** on US 101, north across the Golden Gate Bridge, to enjoy panoramic views of the city and the coastal mountains, passing suburban communities, San Pablo Bay and agricultural lands for about 50 miles to exit SR 116 west.

Your target is **Sebastopol,** a well-known Gravenstein apple orchard, berry and winery center. Small farms and antique and woodcarving shops are at the roadside; a weekend flea market is a popular mecca. In April the countryside blooms during the Sebastopol Apple Festival with music, food and fun for all as the downtown shops feature local wares.

The countryside is a carpet of orchards and pastures as you approach the redwood covered mountains where winding SR 116 enters the deep shade and passes occasional small rustic cabins. Crossing the Russian River on a narrow bridge you enter **Guerneville** where fine food, lodging and shops are an invitation to stop. Here you may swim, canoe and hike. Korbel Champagne Cellars offer wine tastings and guided tours.

Anglers driving along the Russian River to the coast through the tiny town of Monte Rio will bite at the sign "Monte Rio Angling Access," developed by the California Department of Fish and Game. Here too is a 7-mile byway drive to Occidental, a popular weekend dining spot.

Your ride will open out of the trees along riverbottom pasture lands to the junction with old SR 1. Turn right and another mile brings you to **Jenner** and an ocean view. Check your gas tank at Jenner, as there are few refueling facilities until **Fort Bragg.**

The 100-mile drive from Jenner to Fort Bragg and on to Rockport is one of the most scenic on the Pacific Coast, hugging the shoreline as it winds sharply around headlands high above the ocean and offering views of narrow coves and inlets. Occasionally it turns in for straight stretches, passing farms and cattle.

Visit Fort Ross, a trading post established by Russian fur traders in 1812. Most of the redwood buildings are faithfully reconstructed.

A few miles further is Salt Point State Park, extending 4 miles along the rugged coastline.

This is an excellent place for camping, picnicking, fishing and skindiving and has marked trails for hiking and horseback riding. The scenery varies dramatically from protected, sandy coves to sharp bluffs and sheer sandstone caves. The park has tidal pools rich in marine organisms.

Just down the road is Kruse Rhododendron State Reserve, a springtime mecca for flower lovers.

As you continue into Mendocino County the scenery is ever changing, always idyllic and peaceful, even when you pass through the few little towns along the way—Gualala, **Point Arena** and Elk. The light station at Point Arena, offering tours daily, is a great place for whale-watching during the annual migrations of the gray whales as they stop briefly in the cove near the lighthouse before voyaging down the coast to Baja California. The cove has a new concrete and steel 330-foot pier that is 15 feet above high-water level. Fishing from the pier requires no state license.

Little River, formerly a lumber port, is now a hostelry hub. Less than 3 miles north is Van Damme State Park, with an underwater skindiving park, a bike trail, fishing and excellent camping. Fern Canyon, via Ukiah Airport Road south of the park entrance on SR 1, or Pygmy Forest Self-Guiding Trail via Little River Road from SR 1, provide a view of freak dwarfed pines and cypress trees growing on the coastal shelf.

Continue your drive to **Mendocino,** a former lumber port that is now an artists'/vacation colony with quiet shops and an unhurried atmosphere. The Mendocino coastline, setting for many movies, is a spectacle of nature.

Five miles north of the town at Jughandle State Reserve is a remarkable "ecological staircase," a series of terraces formed beneath the ocean by the action of the waves. Five terraces support a distinctive association of plants, animals and soil that many scientists believe to be the finest record anywhere of the glacial movement during the great Pleistocene Ice Age.

Just 2 miles south of Fort Bragg is Mendocino Coast Botanical Gardens, a 17-acre seaside garden of native and ornamental plants in a woodland setting.

If you have not stayed overnight along the way, Fort Bragg offers traditional and bed and breakfast lodgings, restaurants, shops and entertainment. Stop for a map from the chamber of commerce, 332 N. Main St., and take the Historic Walking Tour. Enjoy sandy beaches, tidepools, year-round seal watching and December through April whale watching, riding and ocean fishing out of Noyo Harbor. Train buffs will enjoy riding the "Old 45" steam locomotive (The Skunk) through the redwoods from Fort Bragg to **Willits.**

State campsite reservations are available by phoning MISTIX, (800) 444-7275, for MacKer-

richer State Park just 3 miles north of Fort Bragg.

Continue north on SR 1, passing through the community of Westport, a picturesque remnant of a New England-like coastal mill town. Abalone and surf fishing are popular sports. Your route goes onward past Rockport for 28 miles on connector SR 208 to the junction of US 101 at **Leggett,** marking the official start of your journey north through vast preserves of towering coastal redwoods.

Richardson Grove State Park is the northbound traveler's first look at giant redwoods in the 1,000-acre park along US 101. Camping, swimming and fishing are permitted and there are trails for hiking, bicycling and scenic walks, including Lookout Trail and Toumey Trail.

After driving 5 miles north to Richardson Grove you will find Benbow Lake and State Recreation Area, with 786 forested acres and lake. The historic Benbow Inn holds a Shakespeare Festival in mid-summer.

There is a visitor center at the south exit of US 101 at Garberville. This also is a take-off point for Shelter Cove, King Range National Conservation Area, Sinkyone Wilderness and a section of Humboldt Redwoods State Park.

Ahead 6 miles on US 101 is the turn-off to scenic SR 254, a two-lane, 31-mile road parallel to US 101 from Sylvandale in the south to Jordan Creek in the north. The 52,222-acre Humboldt Redwood State Park winds along this beautiful section of highway sprinkled with memorial groves and picnic groves, an interpretive center, lodgings, restaurants, grocery, souvenir and art shops, and other services.

Continuing through **Scotia,** Rio Dell and **Fortuna,** you travel on to **Eureka** and **Arcata.** This has been a major lumber center, along with fishing and shipping, since the 1850s. The Carson Mansion, not open for tours, is a splendid example of classical Victorian architecture. An aviary delight is the National Wildlife Refuge at the south end of Humboldt Bay. As you continue on north, **Trinidad** and Patrick's Point State Park are fine beach and picnicking areas.

At **Orick,** a southern gateway to **Redwood National Park,** there is an information center at Freshwater Lagoon. You may purchase tickets there for the Tall Trees Shuttle. Visits to Lady Bird Johnson Grove and Elk Prairie are a must; however, watch out for the Roosevelt elk that roam the beaches and meadows.

Upon entering Del Norte County you will cross the Klamath Bridge into **Klamath.** This is part of the Yurok Indian Reservation and a magnet for steelhead and salmon fishermen. The Klamath Salmon Festival in early August is a very popular event. North of Klamath is The Trees of Mystery where Paul Bunyan stands guard over a variety of unusual redwoods. Indian artifacts fill a museum.

Within Del Norte Coast State Park, in the Redwood National Park, are more than 6,000 acres of redwoods, rhododendrons, azaleas and other spring and summer flowers.

Further north is **Crescent City**, with its beautiful crescent-shaped beach and harbor. At low tide, a walk to the Battery Point Lighthouse is a seasonal delight—just don't stay too long! There are many fine restaurants, museums, galleries and shops. Just ½ mile north are Earl and Talawa lakes, where dunes, marshes and ponds make for excellent bird-watching.

For a flower lover's treat, travel 1½ miles north to **Smith River**, the "Easter Lilly Capital of the World." The Easter-in-July Festival celebrates the harvest of the blooming plants.

To start the trip back to San Francisco, drive south on US 101 to Eureka. You may take a side trip and visit the beautiful Victorian village of **Ferndale**, now a State Historic Landmark; exit US 101 at Loleta and drive over the Fernbridge. A walking tour map is available at most shops. The wonderful gingerbread buildings are very well preserved. The services here are fine and varied.

You have a choice now of either returning to US 101 or, as an alternate route, experiencing the beautiful "Lost Coast of California" by continuing on the Mattole Road for 45 miles past Cape Mendocino and inland to Honeydew. If you wish to continue on to the King Range National Conservation Area and Shelter Cove via Wilder Range, be advised that this is an unpaved road.

Continue on Mattole Road from Honeydew through the Humboldt Redwoods State Park to US 101 and drive south to Redway. From Redway the 25-mile winding road to Shelter Cove and Sinkyone Wilderness State Park gives you breathtaking views of beaches and ocean. There are 4½ miles of tidal beach for avid beachcombers. South of Shelter Cove, Usal Road is an unpaved county road and very remote. Returning to Redway and US 101, continue back to Leggett.

The most direct route back to the Bay Area is south on US 101 and across the Golden Gate Bridge, but to continue on a scenic tour exit US 101 at Leggett to SR 208, which junctions with SR 1 at Rockport. Traveling south approximately 30 miles, leave SR 1, go inland on SR 128 and follow the Navarro River into Anderson Valley.

Northwest of Boonville 8 miles is Handy Woods State Park with its virgin redwoods, making a great camping spot. On through Philo, with vineyards close by to sample, then to Boonville. It helps to speak the native dialect, "Boontling," to get along with the locals! Continue to Yorkville and the junction with US 101 just above Cloverdale. The drive from Cloverdale to San Francisco is approximately 90 miles.

San Francisco to Monterey

Leave downtown **San Francisco** for a picturesque 1-day or weekend tour by driving south on US 101 to an immediate junction with I-280 to the junction of SR 1 in Daly City. Stay on SR 1 as the freeway turns toward the scenic community of Pacifica, nestled against the rolling Peninsula hills on the edge of the Pacific Ocean.

Soon you pass the rocky promontory Devil's Slide to gentle, fertile agricultural land where Brussels sprouts, artichokes and flowers grow in abundance and splendor.

Moss Beach has the James V. Fitzgerald Marine Reserve, just off SR 1 via California Avenue, one of the state's most diverse intertidal regions. Courageous surfers challenge the breaking waves along the beach at Pillar Point Harbor, while **Half Moon Bay's** beaches are popular for fishing and whale-watching cruises.

Another 10 miles south is San Gregorio State Beach, one of many tempting beaches along this tour. Ano Nuevo State Reserve, 13 miles south of **Pescadero,** is known for its large colony of northern elephant seals. Their population peaks during the December through March breeding season.

Davenport, about 10 miles north of **Santa Cruz,** was a whaling station in the 1850s. A nearby cement company is an oddity; it has churned concrete since 1915.

Still viewing the waving ocean shores you enter Santa Cruz, the site of one of Father Junípero Serra's historic California missions.

Santa Cruz and the other Monterey Bay communities of **Capitola, Soquel,** Aptos and Rio Del Mar are on your path. The 26 miles of the Santa Cruz County's coast is scalloped into a succession of state beaches that are the warmest and gentlest ocean waters in northern California.

In addition to Natural Bridges State Beach, where winter migrating Monarch butterflies stop, and Lighthouse Field, there's Twin Lakes, across from Schwan Lagoon where you can watch myriad waterfowl. New Brighton, Seacliff and Sunset offer camping among the evergreens. For camping reservations on all state beaches phone MISTIX at (800) 444-7275.

Capitola is an arts and crafts lover's haven, best known for its Begonia Wine and Art Festival in September. There are many fine galleries along the esplanade to stroll through and plenty of eateries.

Aptos, an Indian word for "meeting of the streams," adjoins SR 1 just past Capitola. The Forest of Nisene Marks State Park is the location of the epicenter of the 1989 earthquake. Except for a placard, there's no evidence above ground of the powerful quake.

As you continue on SR 1 toward Monterey the redwoods level to cultivated farmlands. Apples, strawberries and flowers are the basis of the **Watsonville** economy. Harvest time is celebrated in late September and early October with an apple festival.

Maps for walking and driving tours of Watsonville and the Pajaro Valley are available from the Greater Watsonville Chamber of Commerce and Agriculture at 444 Main St. The county's farm trail headquarters, Country Crossroads, 600 Main St., Suite 2, in Watsonville has information and a map of farms that you can visit and pick produce.

Crossing Elkhorn Slough at Moss Landing there is an 8-mile side drive inland to Elkhorn Slough National Estuarine Sanctuary. The slough is on a migratory flyway and is an important feeding and resting ground for many kinds of waterfowl and shorebirds.

Back on SR 1 it is a few miles to Castroville, "The Artichoke Capital of the World," and only 15 miles to your destination, **Monterey.**

The colorful blue Monterey Bay terminates in the vision of historic Monterey, rich with natural beauty and many attractions from Fisherman's Wharf to Cannery Row, the Monterey adobes to city parks and the Monterey Bay Aquarium.

Add the Seventeen-Mile Drive to your tour of the peninsula and end at the charming village of **Carmel** for delightful shopping, a stroll on the white sand beach and a visit to Mission San Carlos Borromeo del Rio Carmelo.

To enjoy some of the points you may have missed, return to San Francisco via SR 1 through Santa Cruz, where the boardwalk is fun with its arcade, rides, salt-water taffy, corndogs, cotton candy and "Neptune's Kingdom," an entertainment center.

The University of California, Santa Cruz offers many noteworthy attractions, including a Shakespeare Festival in July and August. You can visit the school's two art galleries, a world-class arboretum, a birds of prey project with wild falcons and a 25-acre farm and garden. Phone Public Information at (408) 459-2495. Campus tours, (408) 459-4008, cover the campus' fascinating architecture.

Leave Santa Cruz and SR 1 via a different scenic route immediately past the junction of SR 17. Exit SR 9 right, going north on the redwood-shaded highway.

In **Felton,** Henry Cowell Redwoods State Park has picnic areas and campgrounds. Consider taking the Roaring Camp & Big Trees Narrow Gauge Railroad from Felton to the Santa Cruz Beach Boardwalk and return.

The oldest state park in California is **Big Basin Redwoods State Park,** established in 1902. Access is via a 9-mile drive on SR 236 at Boulder Creek, a town with the nearest automotive and other service facilities.

The magnificent 18,000-acre park has about 100 miles of hiking trails, a museum/nature center, a large picnic area, family campsites, several group camping areas and backpacker trail camps. Reservations can be made through MISTIX, (800) 444-7275.

Leaving the park, SR 238 narrowly winds through the redwoods and rejoins SR 9 at Waterman Gap; therefore, campers and trailers must return on SR 238 to the Boulder Creek junction of SR 9. Whichever your exit route, proceed north on SR 9 for a gradual downhill ride to **Saratoga** and the junction of SR 58. Take SR 85 north to Cupertino and then continue north on the Junipero Serra Freeway, I-280.

To make a side tour to Sanford University in **Palo Alto,** exit at Page Mill Freeway to El Camino Real. Turn left to the campus entrance. Resuming your tour on I-280, a last stop can be enjoyed on a clear, sunny day from the top of 1,000-acre Sweeney Ridge, site of the Spanish explorer Gaspar de Portolá's discovery of San Francisco Bay in 1769. This part of the **Golden Gate National Recreation Area** has sweeping views of the Pacific coastline, San Francisco Bay and open space to the south.

To get there, exit I-280 on SR 35 (Skyline Boulevard) to Sneath Lane. Turn left. Major access is from the west end of Sneath Lane. It is a 1½-mile walk to the Discovery Site. In springtime the hills turn gold with California poppies and dozens of other wildflowers. The Ridge has a great diversity of wildlife.

Return on Sneath Lane to I-280 and enter, driving north to San Francisco and the junction of US 101 to downtown.

San Francisco to Yosemite

On this tour, leave **San Francisco** via I-80. Once across the Bay Bridge take I-580 through Alameda County and east into the Livermore Valley. Upon entering the Central Valley it's easy to understand why this is called the agricultural heartland of California. Nestled between the coastal foothills and the western slopes of the Sierra Nevada range, the valley is laced with waterways, orchards, fields and vineyards.

Continue on I-580 to SR 132 and turn east to **Modesto** where SR 99 intersects. Turning south on SR 99 and crossing the Tuolumne River, you travel approximately 8 miles then start winding north to **Mariposa.**

Renamed from Logtown, Mariposa is Spanish for "butterfly." It is one of the major towns along the Golden Chain. The mines around Mariposa yielded some of the richest finds in the Mother Lode. The California State Mining and Mineral Museum, 2 miles south of Mariposa at the county fairgrounds, has one of the world's largest gem and mineral collections. Climbing in altitude on SR 140, past Briceburg, the Merced River guides you through the **Stanislaus National Forest** to El Portal and the Arch Rock Entrance Station to **Yosemite National Park.**

When Abraham Lincoln signed the Yosemite Grant in 1864 he gave the state of California the deed to Yosemite Valley and the Mariposa Grove of Giant Sequoias. In 1890 Congress declared

Yosemite a national park, thanks to the tireless efforts of naturalist John Muir.

The center of activity in Yosemite is the Valley, which comprises only 7 of the almost 2,000 square miles of the park. One of the best ways to see Yosemite Valley is to leave your car at your hotel, campground or the Curry Village day-use lot (shuttle bus stop #1) and take a 2-hour Valley Floor Tour. An informed tour guide will be your narrator and take you to some of the most scenic sites in the park.

You won't want to miss beautiful Bridalveil Falls, which was named "Pohono, Spirit of the Puffing Wind" by the Ahwahneechee, the Yosemite Indians.

The highest waterfall in North America is Ribbon Falls, which drops 2,425 feet. Other equally beautiful falls are Vernal Fall, Nevada Fall and Horsetail Fall at El Capitan.

About midway through Yosemite Valley on the north side is El Capitan, the largest single granite monolith on Earth. Rock climbers come from all over the world to challenge the 4,000 foot summit.

The symbol of Yosemite National Park is Half Dome. At a height of 2,000 feet, the split rock is full of mystery. The Yosemite Indians tell a story of an Indian princess and her face stained on the side of the rock.

Most people find they can't limit their visit to the park to just a day. There are several different types of accommodations in Yosemite. You may camp in the high country along Tioga Pass, or there are house-keeping cabins in the valley. These facilities require reservations well in advance. You also may stay at several lodges throughout the park or, if you prefer an elegant hotel in a wooded setting, the Ahwahnee Hotel is open all year; the dining room has long been known for fine cuisine.

If you prefer accommodations away from the bustle of the valley, then the Wawona Hotel, south on SR 41, is the perfect choice. This National Historic Landmark with its Victorian architecture and beautiful, spacious grounds gives the weary traveler an excellent rest.

Leaving the valley floor from the northwest side, take the New Big Oak Flat Road entrance station past the Tuolumne and Merced groves of giant sequoias to the Big Oak Flat entrance station. Continue on SR 120 approximately 45 miles west down Priest Grade to Moccasin, where SR 49 junctions with SR 120. Heading north on SR 49 through the southern end of the Gold Country is **Jamestown,** one of the more commercially developed mining towns.

During the summer months, the Rail Town State Historic Park operates a 19th-century steam locomotive available for rides.

Continuing north to **Sonora,** the Tuolumne County Museum will have on display many gold rush-era artifacts.

The next stop is 2½ miles north in **Columbia,** the best preserved of all mining towns. Columbia is a State Historic Park which allows for leisurely walks through history.

From Columbia return on SR 49 to the junction of SR 49 and SR 108. Take SR 108 approximately 6 miles to the junction with SR 120 and proceed to Knights Ferry. This gold town boasts a covered bridge—a rare sight in California.

Starting back to San Francisco, stay on SR 120 through the Central Valley to I-205 for 12 miles, then take I-580. For the next 11 miles the windmill farms stand high on the hills. Continue to the Oakland Bay Bridge and back to "The City by the Bay."

The Sierras

A journey from the hectic pace of a big city to the quiet solitude of a mountain forest can be accomplished in less than a day in California. Begin by taking I-5 north from downtown **Los Angeles.** Make your first stop at **Lebec,** site of the long-ago U.S. Camel Corps, about 70 miles north of Los Angeles. Continue to Wheeler Ridge, where I-5 splits off to the west and SR 99 begins; travel north on SR 99 to **Bakersfield.**

The next 70 miles lead through farm and cattle country. Along the way you'll come to **Earlimart** and beyond that, **Tulare,** both with interesting histories to share.

Nine miles north of Tulare at Goshen, take SR 198 east. The highway goes through the attractive town of **Visalia,** then climbs through the foothills of the Sierra Nevada mountain range. Approximately 7 miles beyond Three Rivers, SR 198 becomes Generals Highway as it enters Sequoia National Park at Ash Mountain.

The highway connects **Sequoia and Kings Canyon National Parks** and provides an especially scenic 2-hour drive from the entrance station to Grant Grove. (Normally open year-round, the road may be closed for brief periods during heavy winter snowfalls.) On the mountainsides and in the meadows are giant sequoia trees, descendants of those that covered the Earth millions of years ago. Throughout the parks are wonderful places to picnic, hike or camp.

Just south of Grant Grove, SR 180 heads back down the mountains, across the Kings River and into **Fresno.** Then for a sampling of California's Mother Lode, take SR 41 north from Fresno to **Oakhurst** and turn northwest on SR 49 to **Mariposa.** Continue on the trail of the gold seekers as you drive to Coulterville.

Eleven miles north of Coulterville go east on SR 120 through **Big Oak Flat** and **Groveland.** Very soon you're back in the mountains as you travel through the **Stanislaus National Forest** and enter **Yosemite National Park** at the Big Oak Flat station. Here SR 120 becomes Tioga Road (closed in winter) and enables you to enjoy the grandeur of one of the world's most scenic spectacles. In addition to its magnificent cliffs and waterfalls, Yosemite offers a full range of recreational activities.

Exiting via the eastern side of the park on SR 120 takes you over breathtaking Tioga Pass and down through **Inyo National Forest.** At the highway's junction with US 395 is **Lee Vining,** gateway to Mono Lake. The lake and its surrounding landscape are worth exploring, for they contain unusual and dramatic geological formations. *(See Mono Basin National Forest Scenic Area.)*

Before starting back to Los Angeles, you might enjoy an interesting side trip of approximately 30 miles to **Bodie State Historic Park,** preserved site of a rip-roaring gold-rush town. Take US 395 north to Bodie Road (SR 270) and turn east to the park. (SR 270 is closed in the winter.)

From Lee Vining, a trip south on US 395 leads along the eastern base of the Sierra Nevada mountains, an area abounding in beautiful and varied landscapes. Among possible side trips, **Mammoth Lakes** and **Devil's Postpile National Monument,** west on SR 203, are well worth the day you'll want to spend there.

Thirty-eight miles south of Mammoth Lakes, US 395 reaches **Bishop** and from there goes through the Owens Valley to **Lone Pine.** The town is best known for its views of spectacular 14,494-foot Mount Whitney, the highest mountain in the contiguous United States. You can reach the 8,371-foot level of the mountain via Whitney Portal Road out of Lone Pine.

As you continue south on US 395, mountain scenery gives way to desert landscape. Sixty-three miles south of Lone Pine, pick up SR 14 where it intersects US 395 and turns southwest to Mojave. **Red Rock Canyon State Park** is just off SR 14 about 6 miles below that junction. Within the park there is ancient sedimentary rock that has eroded into fantastically shaped cliffs and columns.

Continue on SR 14 and approximately 25 miles south of the park you'll reach the high-desert town of Mojave. **Rosamond** is 5 miles farther south, and now you're in the Antelope Valley, with the San Gabriel Mountains on the southern horizon. SR 14 cuts through the **Angeles National Forest** on its way to I-5, the highway you'll take south to return to Los Angeles.

The Southern and Central Coast

Seasoned by salt air and sunshine, the southern and central California coast offers a variety of Pacific settings, from grassy bluffs above rocky shores to sandy beaches at quiet harbors. California history is reflected along the way in such places as bustling Santa Monica with its famous old pier, picturesque Santa Barbara that grew from a Hispanic settlement, and beautiful Monterey, the town that was once the capital of Spanish California. Inland detours lead to such diverse scenes as small towns, missions and farmland.

Interstate 10 west from downtown Los Angeles leads to **Santa Monica,** where the coastal highway turns north and west and, as SR 1, continues to **Malibu.** On your right are steep, eroded bluffs with plateaus on which houses perch precariously; here and there buildings cluster at the foot of the bluffs. On your left, wide beaches and oceanfront houses separate the highway from the ocean.

North of Malibu, SR 1 begins to climb through foothills covered with wild grasses. The coastline faces the Pacific on the south; to the north lies the **Santa Monica Mountains National Recreation Area.** At the line separating Los Angeles and Ventura counties is Leo Carrillo State Beach and farther west the highway cuts through Point Mugu State Park.

Now swinging northwest, SR 1 goes into **Oxnard.** Turn north on Oxnard Boulevard to pick up US 101 heading for **Ventura.** In Ventura watch for the Seward Avenue turn-off and follow signs to the **Channel Islands National Park** visitor center. Here you'll receive a good introduction to the five islands that make up a most unusual park. North of Ventura the ocean is lost to view for a few miles, then a seascape accompanies you until just before **Santa Barbara.**

At Santa Barbara either continue on US 101 along the coast or take an inland detour. US 101 goes west from Santa Barbara through Goleta, then along the coast past El Capitan and Refugio state beaches to Gaviota Pass. The pass cuts through the inland portion of Gaviota State Park and the western section of the Santa Ynez Mountains before meeting SR 154 about 5 miles past Buellton.

An alternate route begins at the western edge of Santa Barbara where San Marcos Pass Road (SR 154) goes north from US 101. This highway leads through the Santa Ynez Mountains past Lake Cachuma and through Santa Ynez Valley to rejoin US 101. On a clear day some of the Channel Islands are visible from the mountain road. Lake Cachuma is a pleasant place for a shoreline picnic. Within the valley are wineries to tour. And a side trip to **Solvang** provides a make-believe trip to Denmark.

Just beyond **Los Olivos** SR 154 rejoins US 101. As it heads toward San Luis Obispo County, the highway goes through oak-dotted ranchland backed by gently rolling hills.

About 12½ miles north of **Santa Maria** US 101 bisects the charming little town of Arroyo Grande, then heads out to the coast and through **Pismo Beach.** At Pismo State Beach it is possible to drive right onto the hard-packed sand.

Just out of Pismo Beach US 101 leads north to the university and mission city of **San Luis Obispo,** then meets SR 1. Turn north to **Morro Bay,** a small town with a big rock presiding over a bay where sea otters swim, seagulls soar and pelicans perch. The highway then makes its way along the coast to the pine groves and tempting shops of **Cambria**. Another 8 miles brings you to **San Simeon**, the home of the Hearst Castle, officially named Hearst San Simeon State Historical Monument.

North of San Simeon, SR 1 becomes a winding, cliff-top road that affords spectacular coastal views. A word of caution: Slides caused by storms may close the road periodically during the winter, and fog can sometimes make driving hazardous, particularly in the summer. **Big Sur**, 64 miles north of San Simeon, is the site of artists' secluded residences, as well as scenic Pfeiffer Big Sur State Park.

North of Big Sur, the Pacific is in sight almost continuously, and one of the best views is at Point Lobos State Preserve, with its Monterey cypress, tidepools, marine mammals and ocean birds. The lovely town of **Carmel** is less than 5 miles north, and **Monterey** is approximately 2 miles farther. Monterey, prominent in California history and the setting for John Steinbeck's "Cannery Row," is the terminus of this drive along California's coast.

For variety, the return trip to Los Angeles can be taken inland as far as San Luis Obispo. Southeast of Monterey, SR 68 leads to **Salinas,** self-proclaimed "Lettuce Capital of the World." Turning south on US 101 leads into an agricultural valley where, seasonally, fields of lettuce, beans, grain, beets, berries and other crops cover the landscape. Orchards and pastureland complete the bucolic scene. This is John Steinbeck country, with farms, small towns and distant hills seemingly from the pages of "The Red Pony," "Of Mice and Men" and "East of Eden."

Just south of **Soledad** there is an interesting side trip east on SR 146 to **Pinnacles National Monument,** with its volcanic spires and caves.

Return to US 101 and continue south along the Salinas River, over creek beds and through farming communities. To the east lies the Diablo mountain range; to the west, the Santa Lucias.

Sixty-three miles south of Soledad, tiny **San Miguel** and its well-preserved mission are just off US 101. About 12 miles farther south is **Paso Robles** where you will find rest and refreshment and a chance to visit nearby wineries. Not far south of Paso Robles are the small, quiet, attractive towns of **Templeton** and **Atascadero.** On US 101 San Luis Obispo lies 16½ miles south of Atascadero.

Southern California Sampler

Few places on Earth offer scenery as diverse as that in California, and nowhere is that diversity more concentrated than in the southern part of the state. This trip, whose farthest destination is no more than 165 miles from Los Angeles, will take you through cities and past farms, across deserts and along seashores, into mountains and around lakes.

Start your adventure on I-5 in **Los Angeles,** heading south to **San Diego.** In **San Juan Capistrano** look for the Ortega Highway turnoff and take it west into town. You'll want to spend at least 2 or 3 hours exploring the old Spanish mission and the charming town that grew up around it. Return to I-5, now a coastal highway, and continue south. In San Diego plan to spend at least 2 days exploring its many attractions.

To leave San Diego take I-8 east; within 25 miles you'll find yourself in **Cleveland National Forest.** You've gone from an altitude of about 10 feet in San Diego to over 2,000 feet near the forest boundary. Turn north on SR 79 and drive through Cuyamuca Rancho State Park, an area of meadows and mountain peaks.

About 8 miles beyond the park, at 4,220 feet, is the pleasant village of **Julian,** surrounded by apple orchards and horse ranches. From Julian go northeast on SR 78, out of the mountains and into **Anza-Borrego State Park,** a sandy landscape studded with a variety of cactus and, following sufficient rain, a profusion of wildflowers.

Watch for County Highway S3 and take it north into **Borrego Springs.** For an interesting introduction to the desert's flora, fauna and geology you'll want to spend a little time at the park's visitor center. It is located on Palm Canyon Drive just west of County Road S22.

Stay on County Road S22 and head east. Now you are driving through badlands where, over centuries, rugged canyons and gullies have been sculpted by erosion. Less than an hour after leaving Borrego Springs you'll reach SR 86. Turn north and drive up the west side of the Salton Sea.

You have reached one of the world's largest inland bodies of saltwater, with a surface that is 228 feet below sea level. If these facts prompt you to take a closer look, turn right off SR 86 on Brawley Avenue. You also might want to check the visitor center on the other side of the lake, 1½ miles south of North Shore off SR 111 at State Park Road.

Return to SR 86 and follow it north to SR 111. Follow the signs from SR 111 into the desert resort city of **Palm Springs.** This is a good place for some rest and relaxation (and shopping) before setting out on the next leg of the journey.

To leave Palm Springs return to SR 111 and take it northwest to I-10. From that junction travel 17 miles west to Calimesa on the north side of the highway. Go east on County Line Road to Bryant Street and turn north to SR 38. Turn right, and in less than 3 miles you are in the **San Bernardino National Forest;** at Angelus Oaks you've reached an elevation of 5,800 feet.

Continue on SR 38 as it winds along forest-clad mountainsides, reaching 8,443 feet at Onyx Summit. After about 40 miles you are in the town of **Big Bear Lake.** Make time here for a ski lift ride (winter or summer), a cruise on the lake or a walk through the woods.

At the west end of the lake, Rim of the World Highway (SR 18) is a well-maintained mountain-top thoroughfare that goes to the **Lake Arrowhead** area. About a mile west of **Skyforest** turn north on SR 173 to Lake Arrowhead and its pleasant lakeside village of alpine-style shops and restaurants.

To return to SR 18, go west on SR 189. This leads you through the mountain village of Blue Jay before taking you back to the highway. Continue west, and within 8 miles SR 18 turns south to **San Bernardino.** Watch for signs indicating SR 259, then I-215; they lead south to I-10. Travel west on I-10 to return to your starting point.

Wine Country

If Southern California is synonymous with motion pictures, then northern California is synonymous with wines. Just 40 miles north of San Francisco is one of the state's many wine-producing regions, Sonoma and Napa counties and their more than 150 wineries. The Wine Institute, a trade association, offers maps and information on wine-producing regions throughout California. For free copies, specify the area you are planning to visit and write to The Wine Institute, 425 Market St., Suite 1000, San Francisco, CA 94105.

Begin this tour by taking US 101 across the Golden Gate Bridge from **San Francisco** to **Sausalito.** Tourists flock to this small town to walk streets familiar to them from motion pictures and television shows and to frequent many quaint arts and crafts shops, eateries and bars.

Resume your northward journey on US 101 and continue until you reach the exit for SR 116 east at **Petaluma.** Don't be surprised if you experience déjà vu: Many scenes from the movies "American Graffiti" and "Peggy Sue Got Married" were filmed here. The nearby Petaluma Adobe State Historic Park is an unusual and popular attraction.

After sightseeing, continue east on Stage Gulch Road (SR 116) to **Sonoma,** with its reminders of California's multi-cultural heritage. Around Sonoma Plaza are many of the buildings of Sonoma State Historic Park. In the Plaza the Sonoma Valley Visitors Bureau is open daily 9-5 and offers a walking tour brochure and other information about the Sonoma area. To receive by mail a free copy of the 50-page Comprehensive Visitors Guide, write the Sonoma Valley Visitors Bureau, 453 First St. E., Sonoma, CA 95476 or phone (707) 996-1090.

The Sebastiani Vineyard is just a few blocks east of the Plaza; in addition to tours and tastings, it has a fine collection of Indian artifacts.

Within a 5-mile radius are more than 10 wineries. North of town near **Glen Ellen** is the 795-acre Jack London State Historic Park.

Continue east on SR 12/121 to find several wineries mostly open to the public by appointment only. At the junction with SR 29 turn north onto SR 29 heading to **Napa.**

Napa is an Indian word meaning "plenty" and is most appropriate for this fertile valley. The Napa Chamber of Commerce at 1556 First St. has local maps and information. The nearly 30-mile stretch of SR 29 between Napa and **Calistoga** runs past lush vineyards, farmhouses, wineries and small towns.

To the east and roughly parallel to SR 29 runs the Silverado Trail, never more than 3 miles from SR 29. Just off and between these roads lie more than 60 wineries, from small concerns to the very large, such as Beringer and Charles Krug. Most of the wineries are open daily 10-4. Some have picnic areas.

As you travel north on SR 29 the concentration of wineries really begins at **Yountville.** Here you can take a hot air balloon ride over the Napa Valley or eat and shop in the restaurants, boutiques and art galleries which now occupy Vintage 1870, a former winery.

Traveling north you come to **Oakville** and **Rutherford,** an area which produces some of the world's best Cabernet Sauvignons. **St. Helena,** with some 40 wineries, is considered by many to be the capital of this wine region.

St. Helena is a sophisticated town of stone buildings, parks, shops, restaurants and a resort. The Silverado Museum contains manuscripts and first editions of works by Robert Louis Stevenson. While learning about wine production and sampling its fruits, don't ignore the architecture, such as the Gothic style of the Rhine House at Beringer Vineyards.

Three miles north on SR 29 you come to Bale Grist Mill State Historical Park, with its 36-foot waterwheel. Continuing north toward **Calistoga** the number but not the quality of the wineries decreases. One interesting variation is 3 miles south of town at the Sterling Vineyards. An aerial tram takes visitors the 300 feet from the parking lot to the winery.

Calistoga, besides being a well-known spa and winery area, also offers visitors glimpses of Russian churches, as well as hot air balloon and glider flights. Three miles north of town is one of the world's three regularly erupting geysers. Five miles west of town is a petrified forest of giant redwoods.

Take SR 128 from Calistoga northwest to **Geyserville** to rejoin US 101 and head south to **Santa Rosa,** a large city with many lodgings and restaurants and several attractions, including the former home of horticulturist Luther Burbank. Either continue on US 101 to return to San Francisco or choose a more scenic route.

For a scenic return to San Francisco, head west on the Luther Burbank Memorial Highway/SR 12. **Sebastopol** is an apple-growing town with an ornate Buddhist temple on Gravenstein Highway. In Sebastopol Luther Burbank Memorial Highway/SR 12 becomes Bodega Highway and meanders west to intersect SR 1, the scenic Coast Highway.

Turn south onto SR 1, which travels between **Point Reyes National Seashore** on the west and the **Golden Gate National Recreation Area** on the east. South of Marshall, SR 1 intersects Sir Francis Drake Boulevard, which travels west to Point Reyes Light Station. Farther south on SR 1 near Olema, Bear Valley Road goes west to the park headquarters.

Point Reyes National Seashore is an area where blunt headlands jut into the sea, and grass-tufted dunes lie along miles of secluded beaches. Inland are rolling hills, freshwater lakes and Inverness Ridge, where the Douglas fir, typical of the northern California coastal ranges, and the Bishop pine of the southern forest areas merge.

Continue south on SR 1 to pass through **Stinson Beach** and then **Muir Woods National Monument,** one of the most beautiful and accessible of the redwood groves. Some of these coastal redwoods reach a height of 250 feet, with diameters of more than 12 feet.

Still continuing south on SR 1 you come to Mount Tamalpais State Park—6,233 acres of picturesque coastal hill country dominated by triple-peaked Mount Tamalpais. Hiking trails and a winding road lead to the summit, where spectacular vistas encompass much of Marin County, the San Francisco Bay area and beyond.

Just past Muir Beach SR 1 turns inland and merges with US 101 at Marin City. From here it is a short southward trip across the Golden Gate Bridge and back into "The City," San Francisco.

POINTS OF INTEREST

ALAMEDA (P-2) pop. 76,500, alt. 30′

Just west of Oakland in San Francisco Bay, Alameda was once a thriving resort community and is now home to the Alameda Naval Air Station. Fall and winter are the best times to observe such sea birds as loons, grebes and various ducks at Robert W. Crown Memorial Beach. The Crab Cove portion of the shoreline has been designated as an estuarine marine reserve, featuring exhibits on undersea creatures and Alameda's history.

ALAMEDA HISTORICAL MUSEUM, 2323 Alameda Ave., contains memorabilia of the city of Alameda. Displayed are vintage clothing, photographs, art, toys, household furnishings and a bicycle built for six. Allow 30 minutes minimum. Wed.-Fri. and Sun. noon-4, Sat. 11-4. Free. Phone (510) 521-1233.

ALTADENA (B-6) pop. 40,500, alt. 1,342′

Altadena, at the base of the San Gabriel Mountains, is famous for the towering Himalayan deodars that flank Santa Rosa Avenue, better known as "Christmas Tree Lane." The seeds of the deodar, an uncommon member of the cedar family, were brought from India and planted in 1885. Thousands of colored lights illuminate the trees from mid-December through New Year's Eve.

ALTURAS (B-4) pop. 3,300, alt. 4,366′

Until 1874, Alturas was called Dorris Bridge after the Dorris family, the town's first white settlers. The Dorrises built a simple wooden bridge across the Pit River at the south end of town and later erected a house that served as a stopover for

travelers. Alturas is now a county seat and marketing center for local ranchers, who primarily raise livestock, potatoes and alfalfa.

MODOC COUNTY MUSEUM, 600 S. Main St., documents the development of the area. Displays include Indian artifacts and an extensive collection of firearms, with pieces dating from the 15th century to World War II. A steam engine once used locally is displayed outside. Mon.-Sat. 10-4, Sun. 1-5, May-Oct. Donations. Phone (916) 233-2944.

ANAHEIM (C-7) pop. 266,400, alt. 160′

Its name taken from the Santa Ana River and the German word for home, Anaheim was settled by German immigrants in 1857. They brought cuttings from their Rhineland vineyards and developed Anaheim into California's wine capital. In the late 1800s a blight destroyed the vineyards, and the grape growers began growing oranges, thus beginning a new industry.

No longer a small town surrounded by orange groves, Anaheim is now a bustling suburb of Los Angeles. A variety of exhibitions, concerts and sports events take place at the Anaheim Convention Center on Harbor Boulevard. The NHRA Truck-Pull Championships in mid-January and the Disney Pigskin Classic in late August are held in Anaheim Stadium.

Shopping areas: Anaheim Plaza, I-5 at Euclid Street, has Mervyn's, Robinson's and 75 smaller stores.

ANAHEIM STADIUM, 2000 State College Blvd., seats 70,000. The California Angels baseball team plays mid-April to early October, and the Los Angeles Rams football team plays August through December. Guided tours covering the stadium from the press box to the dressing rooms depart from Gate 1 daily on the hour 11-2, except during stadium events; low-heeled shoes are recommended. Tour $3, senior citizens and children $2. Phone (714) 254-3120.

★**DISNEYLAND** is at 1313 Harbor Blvd. via I-5. Entering Disneyland through a 19th-century railroad station, you can board a train and circle the park, passing the 1890s Main Street, U.S.A. and six other theme areas: Tomorrowland, Frontierland, Fantasyland, Adventureland, Critter Country and New Orleans Square. Town Square faces the station; old-fashioned streetcars rumble past an ice cream parlor, bank and other enterprises—

all open for business. Walkways lead from the end of Main Street to the other six areas.

Entered through Sleeping Beauty's Castle, Fantasyland has rides based on such storybook characters as Snow White and Pinocchio. Other highlights include "It's a Small World" and a bobsled ride (on rails) through the Matterhorn. Frontierland re-creates the days of the Old West, featuring a stern-wheeler that plies the Rivers of America and Big Thunder Mountain, a high-speed "runaway" mining train ride. You can explore the jungle world of Adventureland by boat as well.

New Orleans Square reproduces the winding shop-lined streets and balconied facades of that city during the 1850s. Attractions include the "Pirates of the Caribbean" boat ride and the Haunted Mansion, where restless spirits cavort through dark, cobwebbed halls. The Country Bear Playhouse and the flume ride "Splash Mountain" highlight Critter Country, while Tomorrowland features the high-speed Space Mountain ride, the 3-D movie "Captain EO," starring superstar Michael Jackson, and "Star Tours," a simulated intergalactic shuttle adventure.

A monorail circles the park and travels to and from the Disneyland Hotel. In addition, you can ride the *Columbia,* a replica of a 1780s sailing ship; the stern-wheeler *Mark Twain;* antique cars; and keelboats, canoes, log rafts, canal boats and submarines.

Open Mon.-Fri. 10-6, Sat.-Sun. 9 a.m.-midnight. Extended hours during summer and on special holidays.

The Unlimited Passport covers admission to the park plus all rides and attractions, except the arcades: One-day Passport $28.75; ages 3-11, $23; over 60 (Sun.-Fri., Sept.-June), $23. Two-day Passport $52.50; ages 3-11, $42. Three-day Passport $71.25; ages 3-11, $57. Guided Tour One-day Passport $37; ages 3-11, $30. AE, MC, VI. Those holding A through E coupons from past visits may apply them toward the purchase of an Unlimited Passport.

Disneyland's parking lot (fee $5) can be entered from Harbor Boulevard or the Katella Avenue gate, which is open during peak traffic hours. Pets can be left in the kennel at the main gate for a fee. Phone (714) 999-4565 or (213) 626-8605, ext. 4565.

HOBBY CITY DOLL AND TOY MUSEUM, 1238 S. Beach Blvd., is in a half-scale model of the

White House. The museum contains more than 3,000 dolls and toys, including foreign dolls, composition dolls, antique French and German dolls, teddy bears and antique toy soldiers. Daily 10-6; closed major holidays. Admission $1; over 55 and under 12, 50c. Phone (714) 527-2323.

ANDERSON (C-2) pop. 8,300, alt. 430'

The railroad arrived in the area near Anderson in 1872. The town was named for Elias Anderson, the owner of the largest land grant in the area at that time.

COLEMAN NATIONAL FISH HATCHERY is 11 mi. s.e. via Balls Ferry Rd. and Jellys Ferry Rd. to Coleman Powerhouse Rd. The hatchery raises fingerlings in the rearing ponds year-round. From the first week in October to early February, salmon and steelhead migrate up the ladders to the hatchery. Picnicking is permitted. Self-guiding tours are available. Daily 8-4. Free. Phone (916) 365-8622.

ANGELES NATIONAL FOREST

John Muir described the San Gabriel Mountains as "one vast bee pasture, a rolling wilderness of honey-bloom." Covering more than 650,000 acres of these rugged mountains on the northern rim of the Los Angeles Basin, the Angeles National Forest encompasses terrain ranging from arid desert to heavily timbered high mountain ridges and meadows. Forest elevations range from a few hundred feet above sea level to 10,064 feet at the top of Mount San Antonio (Old Baldy).

Year-round recreation is available in the generally warm and dry climate. The forest, which includes the San Gabriel Wilderness and Sheep Mountain Wilderness, has more than 80 campgrounds as well as picnic areas and hiking trails for all levels of experience. During the summer three major areas— Chilao, Big Pines and Crystal Lake—offer campfire talks, lectures, films, nature walks and other interpretive programs. Visitor centers are available at all three areas.

A particularly scenic route is the 64-mile Angeles Crest Highway (SR 2), which runs from La Cañada Flintridge to Wrightwood. It continues along Hwy. 138 to connect with the Rim of the World Drive (see San Bernardino).

Six major areas offer skiing and other snow sports in winter. Although forest highways are generally open all year, heavy snows sometimes close the roads. Check with forest headquarters for information on weather conditions and wildland fire danger. For more information contact the Supervisor, Angeles National Forest, 701 N. Santa Anita Ave., Arcadia, CA 91006; phone (818) 574-5200. See Recreation Chart and the AAA California and Nevada CampBook.

ANGELS CAMP (F-3) pop. 2,400, alt. 1,379'

Angels Camp inspired Mark Twain to write his famous short story "The Celebrated Jumping Frog of Calaveras County"—his first published success. The third weekend in May the town perpetuates this institution with its annual Jumping Frog Jubilee in conjunction with the Calaveras County Fair. For more information contact the Calaveras County Visitor Center, P.O. Box 637, Angels Camp, CA 95222; phone (209) 763-0049 or (800) 225-3764.

ANGELS CAMP MUSEUM, 753 S. Main St., features early mining equipment, wagons, minerals and artifacts and a carriage house with horse-drawn vehicles from the gold rush days. The museum also contains the Calaveras Genealogical Society and its genealogical library. Allow 1 hour minimum. Daily 10-3, Apr. 1-day before Thanksgiving; Wed.-Sun. 10-3, rest of year. Closed major holidays. Admission $1; ages 6-12, 25c. Phone (209) 736-2963.

OUTDOOR ADVENTURE RIVER SPECIALISTS, 1¾ mi. s. on SR 49, offers 1- to 3-day whitewater raft trips on the American, Tuolumne, Merced, Carson, Stanislaus, Kern and California Salmon rivers. Meals are provided. Trips daily, Apr.-Oct. One-day trips $68-$115. AE, MC, VI. **Discount,** South Fork American River only. Under 7 not permitted; under 12 not permitted in high-water season, mid-May to mid-June.

Reservations are required; the cancellation fee varies. Write O.A.R.S., Box 67, Angels Camp, CA 95222. Phone (209) 736-4677. See ad p. 83.

ARCADIA (B-7) pop. 48,300, alt. 485'

Arcadia's largest shopping center is Santa Anita Fashion Park, Huntington Drive and Baldwin Avenue, where Broadway, JCPenney and Robinson's are the major stores.

★LOS ANGELES STATE AND COUNTY ARBORETUM, 301 N. Baldwin Ave., encompasses 127 acres of trees and shrubs arranged by continent of origin. The horticultural research center also has tropical and begonia greenhouses, a reference library and a bird sanctuary. Of special interest are the historic Queen Anne Cottage and coach barn, the Hugo Reid Adobe and the Santa Fe Railroad depot.

Guides conduct walking tours of the arboretum Wed. at 11. Arboretum open daily 9-5; closed Dec. 25. Begonia greenhouse open Mon.-Fri. 10-4:30. Tropical greenhouse open daily 9-4:30.

Admission $3; over 62, students with ID and ages 13-17, $1.50; ages 6-12, 75c; free to all third Tues. of the month. **Two-for-one discount,** except over 62, students with ID and ages 6-17. Under 18 must be accompanied by an adult. Tram tours Mon.-Fri. 12:15-3, Sat.-Sun. 10:30-4. Fare $1.50. Radios, televisions and athletic equipment are not permitted. Phone (818) 821-3222.

SANTA ANITA PARK, 285 W. Huntington Dr., is one of the most famous Thoroughbred horse racing tracks in the United States. Since its inception in 1934 Santa Anita has introduced and developed the magnetically-controlled starting gate, the photo finish, electrical timing and the totalisator.

Racing Wed.-Sun., early Oct.-early Nov. and late Dec.-late Apr.; post time 12:30 or 1, depending on time of year. Admission $3-$6.50, under 17 free when accompanied by an adult. Minimum betting age is 18. Morning workouts daily 7:30-9:30 during the racing seasons; free. Parking $3-$8. Phone (818) 574-7223.

ARCATA (B-1) pop. 15,200, alt. 33'

Founded in 1850 as a mining supply center, Arcata also was where author Bret Harte once worked as a journalist and miner; he used Arcata as the setting for some of his stories of mining camp life. Humboldt State University is based in Arcata.

Southwest of town on Humboldt Bay is the 175-acre Arcata Marsh and Wildlife Sanctuary, a recently transformed industrial area and county landfill that is now host to more than 200 species of birds. About 4½ miles of foot trails wind past seven different wetland habitats.

Self-guiding tours: Maps detailing a walking tour of Greek Revival structures and Victorian homes can be obtained at the chamber of commerce at 1062 G St., Arcata, CA 95521; phone (707) 822-3619.

AZALEA STATE RESERVE is 3 mi. n. on SR 200 via US 101; or use SR 200 exit from SR 299, 1 mi. e. of US 101. The reserve is loveliest when the flowers bloom from May through June. Parking is limited; the reserve is not recommended for trailers. Allow 30 minutes minimum. Daily dawn-dusk. Free. Phone (707) 445-6547.

HUMBOLDT STATE UNIVERSITY NATURAL HISTORY MUSEUM, 1315 G St., exhibits almost 2,000 animal and plant specimens from around the world. Displays date from 500 million years ago to the present. Highlights include dire wolves and manatees, the jaw of an ancient 70-foot great white shark, the intricate skeleton of a 50 million-year-old fish, saber-toothed cats, butterflies, insects, shore birds and Pacific seashells. Exhibits change periodically. Tues.-Sat. 10-4; closed Jan. 1, July 4, Thanksgiving and Dec. 25. Free. Phone (707) 826-4479.

ARNOLD (E-4) pop. 2,400, alt. 4,000'

CALAVERAS BIG TREES STATE PARK, 6,073 acres 4 mi. e. on SR 4, contains some of the finest specimens of Sierra sequoias. Interpretive programs are available in summer; snowshoeing and cross-country skiing are available in winter. Daily 24 hours. Day use fee $5 per vehicle, senior citizens $4. Phone (209) 795-2334. *See Recreation Chart and the AAA California and Nevada CampBook.*

ATASCADERO (I-3) pop. 23,100, alt. 834'

The Atascadero City Administration Building, Palma Avenue at West Mall, was built in the Italian Renaissance style. Completed in 1918, it houses the city hall, public library and the Atascadero Historical Society Museum, which has photographs and household items pertaining to Atascadero's early days.

About 1 mile southwest of the center of town off SR 41, Atascadero Park and Lake offer fishing, picnicking and the small Charles Paddock Zoo, open daily 10-4; closed Jan. 1, Thanksgiving and Dec. 25.

ATWATER (F-3) pop. 22,300, alt. 151'

CASTLE AIR MUSEUM, on Santa Fe Dr., is housed in a remodeled barracks. The museum is named for Brig. Gen. Frederick W. Castle, who earned a posthumous Medal of Honor for his role in a bombing mission over Europe in World War II. Historical photographs, weapons, uniforms and 41 vintage aircraft, including the SR-71 Blackbird, depict the development of the U.S. Air Force. Allow 1½ hours minimum. Daily 10-4; closed Jan. 1, Easter, Thanksgiving and Dec. 25. Donations. Phone (209) 723-2178.

AUBURN (E-3) pop. 10,600, alt. 1,255'

Historic Old Auburn, the central section of the city, has many restored buildings from the mid-1800s, including a firehouse and the oldest continuously used post office in California. The Gold Country Fair takes place in early September and Village Christmas in mid-December.

GOLD COUNTRY MUSEUM, 1273 High St. on the fairgrounds, depicts the early days of Placer County through old mining equipment and exhibits pertaining to early transportation and mining methods. Also featured are a stamp mill and period saloon. A small creek is available for visitors to try their hand at gold-panning. Bernhard Museum, a nearby adjunct to the Gold Country Museum, has a restored Victorian house and outbuildings with coopering, blacksmithing and winemaking displays.

Guided tours are available. Allow 1 hour, 30 minutes minimum. Gold Country Museum open Tues.-Sun. 10-4. Bernhard Museum open Tues.-Fri. 11 3, Sat. Sun. noon-4. Both closed holidays. Both museums $1; over 65 and ages 6-16, 50c. Phone (916) 889-6500.

BAKERSFIELD (I-5) pop. 174,800, alt. 408'

Bakersfield, near the southern end of the San Joaquin Valley, is an important shipping and marketing center for oil, natural gas and farm products. It also is known as California's country music capital. Mesa Marin Raceway hosts NASCAR stock car races and USAC midget car races in mid-May and mid-October. The Kern County Fair, with entertainment and a PRCA rodeo, is held late September to early October.

Shopping areas: The Valley Plaza Shopping Center, SR 99 at Ming Avenue, has a Broadway, Gottschalks, JCPenney, May Co. and Sears. East

Hills Mall, at Mall View Rd. and Oswell St. off SR 178, offer Gottschalks, Harris' and Mervyns.

CALIFORNIA LIVING MUSEUM, 3½ mi. n.w. of SR 178 at 14000 Old Alfred Harrell Hwy., contains a cross-section of California wildlife, some of which are rare or endangered. Included are the mountain lion, desert tortoise, kit fox and bald eagle. There also is a walk-in aviary as well as a farm-animal petting zoo. Picnic facilities are available. Tues.-Sun. and Mon. holidays 10-dusk; closed Thanksgiving and Dec. 25. Admission $3.50; over 60, $2.50; ages 4-17, $2. **Discount,** except over 60. Phone (805) 872-2256.

KERN COUNTY MUSEUM, 3801 Chester Ave., contains exhibits that represent the human and natural history of the area. The 14-acre, 56-building museum depicts life in the late 19th and early 20th centuries. Mon.-Fri. 8-5, Sat. and some holidays 10-5; closed Jan. 1, Thanksgiving and Dec. 24-25. Last admission 2 hours before closing. Admission $5; over 60, $4; ages 3-12, $3. **Discount.** Phone (805) 323-8368.

LORI BROCK CHILDREN'S MUSEUM, next to the Kern County Museum, has structures for climbing, hands-on displays, educational items and year-long special theme exhibits. Mon.-Fri. 10-5, Sat. 10-4, in summer; Mon.-Fri. 1-5, Sat. 10-4, rest of year. Closed major holidays. Admission $1.50, senior citizens $1, under 3 free. Phone (805) 395-1201.

BARSTOW (I-7) pop. 21,500, alt. 2,106'

A thriving mining center in the late 19th century, Barstow is at the juncture of three major highways—I-15, I-40 and SR 58—that provide access to the Mojave Desert. Several local military installations anchor the city's economy.

Shopping areas: Factory Merchants Outlet Plaza is 4 miles south of Barstow near the SR 15 Lenwood Road exit. There are nearly 50 factory outlet stores that include such manufacturers as Bass, Lenox, Levi's and London Fog.

CALICO EARLY MAN ARCHAEOLOGICAL SITE, 15 mi. n.e. via I-15 and Minneola Rd., is an excavation begun by Dr. Louis Leakey in 1964. More than 12,000 stone tools dating back about 200,000 years have been unearthed, making this the oldest prehistoric tool site yet discovered in the Western Hemisphere. Excavation site and visitor center open Thurs.-Sun. 8-4:30, Wed. noon-4:30; closed major holidays. Donations. Phone (619) 256-3591.

★CALICO GHOST TOWN is 11 mi. n.e. via I-15. Between 1881 and 1896, Calico (named after the varicolored surrounding mountains) was a booming silver-mining town of more than 2,500 people. Its mines produced more than $13 million in ore. In 1895 the price of silver dropped, the mines quit producing, and the town fell into ruin.

Calico's attractions include a mine tour, the Playhouse Theater, a museum, mystery shack, shooting gallery and train ride. Camping is permitted. A tram runs between the parking area and town; round-trip fare $1.

Daily 9-5; closed Dec. 25. Playhouse Theater $1.95; under 12, $1.25. Mine tour and train ride each $1.95; ages 6-15, $1.25. Mystery shack $1.95; ages 6-15, $1.25. Museum free. Shooting gallery $1 per round of ammunition. Parking $5; camping $9 per night with no hookups, $15 with hookups. Phone (619) 254-2122. *See ad.*

CALIFORNIA DESERT INFORMATION CENTER, 831 Barstow Rd., has exhibits depicting the natural history and environment of the Bureau of Land Management's California Desert District. The center also provides information on desert recreational opportunities and weather and road conditions. Daily 9-5; closed Jan. 1 and Dec. 25. Free. Phone (619) 256-8313.

RAINBOW BASIN NATIONAL NATURAL LANDMARK is 8 mi. n. via SR 58 to Irwin Rd., then n. to Fossil Bed Rd. (last 3 mi. unpaved). Here in the desert is a basin formed by millions of years of sediment that has taken dramatic shapes through the shifting and upheaval of Earth's crust. The rock walls, in shades of red, brown, green and white, hold many fossils and minerals.

Driving the 4-mile loop from Fossil Bed Road is a good way to view the colorful rock formations; hiking and horseback riding also are possible. Camping is available at Owl Canyon Campground for a fee; phone (619) 256-8313.

BENICIA (O-3) pop. 24,400, alt. 33'

Named after the wife of Mariano Guadalupe Vallejo, one of its founders, Benicia boasts California's oldest standing capitol building. The city supported an Army arsenal and barracks as well as the Pacific Mail Steamship Co. before becoming the state's third capital in 1853. Several well-preserved homes date back to those early years of statehood.

Benicia also boasts the oldest Masonic temple in the state and Saint Paul's Episcopal Church, the first Episcopal cathedral in northern California. Scandinavian shipwrights who worked on the church created a ceiling that resembles an inverted ship's hull, a design similar to those of Norwegian stave churches.

Self-guiding tours: The chamber of commerce distributes pamphlets for driving and walking tours of historic Benicia; pamphlets $1 each. The chamber is open Mon.-Fri. 8:30-5, Sat.-Sun. 11-3. For information contact 601 First St., Benicia, CA 94510; phone (707) 745-2120.

BENICIA CAPITOL STATE HISTORIC PARK, First and West G sts., preserves the Greek Revival building that served as the third state capitol from Feb. 4, 1853 to Feb. 25, 1854. The structure is restored and furnished in period. Allow 30 minutes minimum. Daily 10-5; closed Jan. 1, Thanksgiving and Dec. 25. Admission $2; ages 6-13, $1. Phone (707) 745-3385.

Fischer-Hanlon House, next to the park, is a renovated gold rush hotel furnished in period. Guided tours by appointment Sat.-Sun. noon-3:30. Phone (707) 745-3385.

BERKELEY (O-2) pop. 102,700, alt. 152′

Lively, inquiring and experimental, Berkeley exudes an atmosphere befitting its position as one of the country's leading educational centers. The University of California is often the vanguard of any campus movement, be it political, artistic or philosophic.

At the foot of University Avenue lies the center for one of the city's favorite activities—sport fishing. The Berkeley Marina, base for a large charter boat fleet, also has a free fishing pier. No license is required. Water sports and model yacht racing are popular on the mile-long saltwater lake in Aquatic Park at the foot of Bancroft Avenue. Golden Gate Fields offers horse racing; policies concerning the admittance of children to pari-mutuel facilities vary. For information phone (510) 559-7300.

BERKELEY MUNICIPAL ROSE GARDEN, Euclid Ave. and Bayview Pl., contains more than 4,000 varieties of roses and is especially lovely in late spring and early summer. A terraced amphitheater and arbor overlook the bay and Golden Gate Bridge. Daily dawn-dusk. Free. Phone (510) 644-6530.

CHARLES LEE TILDEN REGIONAL PARK, adjoining the city on the n.e. edge, is a 2,065-acre community playground with a botanic garden, golf course, picnic grounds, nature area, hiking and horse trails and tennis courts. The Environmental Education Center near Jewel Lake has a miniature farm with livestock, farm implements and an exhibit hall. Swimming in Lake Anza, a merry-go-round and pony and miniature train rides also are available; hours and prices vary

with the season. Daily 7 a.m.-10 p.m. Free. Phone (510) 635-0135.

GRIZZLY PEAK BOULEVARD winds along the crest of the hills behind the city at elevations up to 1,600 feet. It can be reached from the head of Spruce Street or from other points along the city's northeastern edge.

JUDAH L. MAGNES MUSEUM (Jewish Museum of the West), 2911 Russell St., displays ceremonial art and changing exhibits and houses two libraries. Tours Sun. and Wed. Allow 1 hour minimum. Open Sun.-Thurs. 10-4; closed Jewish and federal holidays. Donations. Phone (510) 549-6950.

PACIFIC FILM ARCHIVE, at the University Art Museum, 2625 Durant Ave., houses a large collection of films. Showings are held nightly. Admission $5.50; over 65, U.C. students and under 12, $3.50; second feature $1.50 extra. Phone (510) 642-1412.

PACIFIC SCHOOL OF RELIGION, LeConte and Scenic aves., is an interdenominational seminary. A museum displays Palestinian artifacts dating from 3200 B.C. and Bibles from the 15th through 18th centuries. Guided tours are offered by appointment. Allow 30 minutes minimum. Mon.-Fri. 9-4; closed holidays. Free. Phone (510) 848-0528.

TAKARA SAKE USA INC., 708 Addison St., presents on request a slide show pertaining to the Japanese rice wine. A tasting room also is available. Daily noon-6; closed Jan. 1, Easter, July 4, Thanksgiving and Dec. 25. Free. Phone (510) 540-8250.

★**UNIVERSITY OF CALIFORNIA** occupies a beautiful 1,232-acre campus e. of Oxford St., between Hearst St. and Bancroft Way. Tours of the Lawrence-Berkeley Laboratory are given by appointment, Mon.-Fri. 8-5, except on federal holidays; phone (510) 486-5122. Guided 1½-hour walking tours of the campus depart from the visitor center in the lobby of University Hall at Oxford St. and University Ave. Mon., Wed. and Fri. at 10 and 1 Phone 1 week in advance for Sat. tours. Phone (510) 642-5215.

Botanical Garden, 34 acres in Strawberry Canyon off Centennial Dr., contains 12,000 species of plants arranged according to their native regions. The complex includes a Chinese herb garden and a large collection of cactuses and other succulents. Greenhouse exhibits and a visitor center also are available. Allow 1 hour minimum. Daily 9-4:45; tours Sat.-Sun. at 1:30; closed Dec. 25. Free. Phone (510) 642-3343.

Campanile, at the center of the campus, is 307 feet tall and contains a 61-bell carillon. It chimes on the hour and plays music at 7:50 a.m., noon and 6 p.m. Open Mon.-Sat. 10-3:15, Sun. 10-1:15 and 2:45-4:15; closed university holidays. Admission 50c. Phone (510) 642-3666.

Lawrence Hall of Science, Centennial Dr. on the e. side of the campus, is a public science center with hands-on exhibits involving computers, telescopes, laboratory equipment and various animals.

Allow 2 hours minimum. The Holt Planetarium presents shows daily at 1, 2:15 and 3:30, in summer; Sat.-Sun. and holidays, rest of year. Science hall open Mon.-Fri. 10-4:30, Sat.-Sun. 10-5; closed Jan. 1, Labor Day, Thanksgiving and Dec. 24-25. Admission $5; senior citizens and students $4; ages 3-6, $2. Planetarium shows an additional $1.50. Phone (510) 642-5132.

Phoebe Apperson Hearst Museum of Anthropology, in Kroeber Hall on Bancroft Way, has exhibits on ethnology, archeology and anthropology. Tues.-Fri. 10-4:30, Sat.-Sun. noon-4:30; closed major holidays. Admission $1.50; over 60, 50c; under 16, 25c; free to all Thurs. Phone (510) 643-7648.

University Art Museum, on Bancroft Way between College Ave. and Bowditch St., features contemporary and Oriental art as well as 18th- and 19th-century works. Allow 1 hour, 30 minutes minimum. Wed.-Sun. 11-5. Admission $5; over 64 and ages 6-17, $4; free to all Thurs. 11-noon. Extra charge for special exhibits. Phone (510) 642-1207.

BEVERLY HILLS (B-5) pop. 32,000, alt. 225'

One of the most elegant residential communities in Southern California, Beverly Hills is completely surrounded by Los Angeles. Many well-known personalities of stage, screen and television live here. A great place for stargazing is Rodeo Drive, famous for its many art galleries and upscale clothing and jewelry shops.

Self-guiding tours: The "Guide to Beverly Hills" provides historical commentary as well as information on walking tours of the community. The free guide is available at the Beverly Hills Visitors Bureau, 239 S. Beverly Dr., Beverly Hills, CA 90212; phone (310) 271-8174 or (800) 345-2210.

GREYSTONE PARK, Doheny Rd. and Loma Vista Dr., embraces 18½ acres of formal gardens, woods, ponds and walkways. The 55-room mansion on the grounds is closed to the public. The park is open daily 10-6, May-Sept.; 10-5, rest of year. Closed Jan. 1, Thanksgiving and Dec. 25. Free. Phone (310) 550-4796.

BIG BASIN (G-2) pop. 100, alt. 1,000'

★**BIG BASIN REDWOODS STATE PARK** is on SR 236; the headquarters is 9 mi. n.w. of Boulder Creek. Covering more than 18,000 acres surrounding Big Basin, the park was established in 1902 as California's first state redwood park. Some trees have attained a diameter of 18 feet and a height of 330 feet. A natural history museum is open all year; supplies and naturalist services are available in summer.

Allow 2 hours minimum. Park and museum open daily 8-dusk, mid-Apr. through Sept. 30; 8-4:30, rest of year. Day use fee $5 per vehicle. Phone (408) 338-6132. *See Recreation Chart.*

BIG BEAR LAKE (A-9) pop. 5,400, alt. 6,754'

One of California's largest year-round recreation areas, Big Bear Lake and Valley lie about 30 miles northeast of San Bernardino in the eastern San Bernardino Mountains. Camping, picnicking and riding are popular in summer; skiing and sledding prevail in winter. Hunting and fishing are permitted in season. Swimming is permitted only in designated areas, including Meadow Park Swim Beach, which also has an indoor pool. Boat rentals and scenic boat tours also are available.

Self-guiding tours: The Gold Fever Trail Guide, a 3-hour auto tour map, covers several sites of the 1860-75 gold rush that occurred in Holcomb Valley just north of the lake. The guide is available at the Big Bear Ranger Station, 3 miles east of Fawnskin on SR 38. Guides 25c. Phone (909) 866-3437.

SIERRA BOAT TOUR, Pine Knot Landing at the foot of Pine Knot Ave., takes up to 38 passengers in a tri-hull excursion boat on a 1-hour narrated tour of Big Bear Lake, with views of China Island, Boulder Bay, the solar observatory and Mount San Gorgonio. Tours depart daily at 10, noon, 2, 4 and 6, in summer; otherwise varies, rest of year. Admission $8.50; over 52, $6.50; ages 4-12, $5. Phone (909) 866-2628.

BIG OAK FLAT (F-4) pop. 200, alt. 2,803'

Founded in 1850 by James Savage, who later discovered Yosemite Valley, Big Oak Flat was originally known as Savage Diggings. The name was later changed in deference to the large valley oak (11 feet in diameter) that stood in the center of town. Two pieces of this tree have been preserved in the monument that now stands in its place.

A few old stone and brick buildings are all that remain of the town's golden days. Scenic Big Oak Flat Highway (SR 120) leads to Yosemite Valley.

BIG PINE (G-6) pop. 1,500, alt. 3,985'

ANCIENT BRISTLECONE PINE FOREST, 28,000 acres in Inyo National Forest *(see place listing),* preserves these gnarled trees, some more than 4,000 years old—a millennium older than the redwoods. Two self-guiding trails and naturalist services are available at the Schulman Visitor Center in the White Mountain District.

The bristlecone area is reached from Big Pine by the Westgard Pass road (SR 168) and White

Mountain Road to Schulman Grove (alt. 10,000 ft.). Dress warmly, bring adequate water, and have a full tank of gas. Open early June-late Oct. Free. Phone (619) 873-4207.

BIG SUR (H-2) pop. 1,000, alt. 155'

PFEIFFER BIG SUR STATE PARK, 26 mi. s. of Carmel on SR 1, covers 821 acres of coastal redwood and chaparral on the Big Sur River. Rangers conduct naturalist and campfire programs in the summer. Daily 8-dusk; overnight camping permitted. Day use fee $6 per vehicle. Phone (408) 667-2315. *See Recreation Chart.*

BISHOP (G-6) pop. 3,700, alt. 4,147'

Near the northern end of the Owens River Valley, between the state's two highest mountain ranges, Bishop is the center of a vast recreation and resort area and an outfitting point for pack trips. Bishop Creek Canyon is west on Bishop Creek Highway (SR 168) within Inyo National Forest *(see place listing)*. Annual town events include the Blake Jones Early Opening Sierra Trout Derby in early March, the Memorial Day weekend Mule Days and the Labor Day weekend Tri-County Fair/Wild West Weekend.

LAWS RAILROAD MUSEUM AND HISTORICAL SITE, 5 mi. n.e. on US 6, is an 11-acre restoration and re-creation of the once-active railroad community of Laws and includes a narrow-gauge locomotive and cars. Daily 10-4, weather permitting. Closed Jan. 1, Thanksgiving and Dec. 25. Donations. Phone (619) 873-5950.

OWENS VALLEY PAIUTE-SHOSHONE INDIAN CULTURE CENTER, 2300 W. Line St. on the Bishop Paiute Reservation, features exhibits of historic American Indian food sources, clothing, shelter, tools and basketry. Mon.-Fri. 9-5, Sat.-Sun. 10-4; closed Jan. 1, Thanksgiving and Dec. 25. Donations. Phone (619) 873-4478.

BODIE (F-5) alt. 8,375'

BODIE STATE HISTORIC PARK, 495 acres embracing the ghost town of Bodie, is 20 mi. s.e. of Bridgeport via US 395 and SR 270 (last 3 mi. unpaved). It is often inaccessible in winter. The former community of 10,000 reportedly deserved and sustained its reputation as one of the toughest and most lawless gold-mining camps in the West. The local diggings yielded almost $100 million in ore. The 170 buildings that remain are preserved in a state of arrested decay; they will not be restored, but are prevented from decaying further.

Daily 9-7, Memorial Day weekend-Labor Day; 9-4, rest of year. Day use fee $5 per vehicle; $4 per vehicle for senior citizens. Fee for pets. Phone (619) 647-6445.

BORON (I-6) pop. 2,000, alt. 2,460'

TWENTY MULE TEAM MUSEUM, at Boron Ave. and Twenty Mule Team Rd., is a renovated

---

The Sea Otter

That pointy-nosed, long-whiskered creature floating on its back in northern California's waters isn't one of California's typical sunbathers—it's the sea otter.

The sea otter is a thickset, sturdy, fur-bearing marine mammal with small ears and short limbs. Its large hind feet are webbed and flipper-like; its front feet are comparatively small but agile enough to use rocks as tools to break open shellfish. The average adult weighs up to 80 pounds and can be 5 feet long including its tail, making it the largest otter.

The sea otter differs from most marine animals in that it doesn't have a layer of blubber under its skin to keep it warm. Instead, air trapped in its fur serves as a waterproof blanket, insulating the animal and helping it stay afloat.

Weaving through the water at speeds up to 10 miles per hour and diving as deep as 100 feet, sea otters swim with the ease of fish but they're not fast enough to escape their natural enemies, killer whales and sharks. Vast populations of sea otters once lived in kelp beds along the northern Pacific coast until man proved to be their worst enemy.

Like many species, the friendly sea otter learned to fear man when hunters virtually exterminated the species for its lustrous, brown-black fur. One pelt could bring as much as $2,500. By 1910 the U.S. government prohibited the hunting of sea otters in the Aleutian Islands; in 1911 Russia, Japan, Great Britain and the United States signed an international treaty protecting them.

The sea otter has reoccupied about one-fifth of its original range, re-establishing colonies in California, western Alaska and near the Commander and Kurile islands. Slowly, but in steadily increasing numbers, the bewhiskered sea otter is reclaiming its place in the Pacific ecosystem.

house that once stood near a borax mine campsite. The museum has exhibits on area history, Edwards Air Force Base and NASA, minerals, and local flora and fauna. Other highlights include a turn-of-the-20th-century railroad depot and mining equipment displays. Daily 10-4; closed Jan. 1, Thanksgiving and Dec. 25. Donations. Phone (619) 762-5810.

BORREGO SPRINGS (K-7) pop. 4,000, alt. 590'

ANZA-BORREGO DESERT STATE PARK, surrounding the town, encompasses 600,000 acres of the Colorado Desert, making it one of the largest state parks in the country. Points of interest are Font's Point, Borrego Palm Canyon, Split Mountain and Seventeen Palms Oasis. Canyons include Coyote, Palm, Fish Creek, Bow Willow and Carrizo Gorge.

A visitor center houses exhibits on weather, geology, history, desert plants and wildlife. A slide video presentation is shown every 20 minutes. Check with the visitor center or headquarters for road conditions before leaving the pavement.

Daily 9-5, Oct.-May; Sat.-Sun. 9-5, rest of year. Day use fee $5 per vehicle in developed campgrounds. Reservations for camping are recommended for weekends and holidays, Oct.-May; phone MISTIX at (800) 444-7275. For park information phone (619) 767-4684. *See Recreation Chart and the AAA California and Nevada CampBook.*

BRAWLEY (L-8) pop. 18,900, alt. -113'

While the Imperial Valley around Brawley produces cantaloupes, lettuce and alfalfa, the town is best known as a cattle-raising center. The annual Cattle Call and Rodeo during early November celebrates Brawley's premier industry.

IMPERIAL SAND DUNES can be reached via Gecko Rd., 19½ mi. e. off SR 78. Formed of sand from an ancient lake, the wind-sculpted crests and ripples extend more than 40 miles. The Imperial Sand Hills National Natural Landmark is a popular spot for primitive camping and off-highway vehicle recreation. Phone (619) 344-3919.

BUENA PARK (C-7) pop. 68,800, alt. 74'

The largest stores in Buena Park Mall, at La Palma and Stanton avenues, are JCPenney, May Co. and Sears. Knott's Berry Farm, Beach Boulevard and La Palma Avenue, has specialty shops in a Western-style setting.

★**KNOTT'S BERRY FARM,** 8039 Beach Blvd., re-creates the atmosphere of the Old West and encompasses five theme areas: Old West Ghost Town (including Indian trails), Fiesta Village,

Roaring '20s, Wild Water Wilderness and Camp Snoopy. In addition to rides there are 26 shops, a full-size reproduction of Independence Hall and the Good Time Theatre, where major entertainers perform.

Sun.-Thurs. 9 a.m.-11 p.m., Fri.-Sat. 9 a.m.-midnight, Memorial Day weekend-Labor Day; Mon.-Fri. 10-6, Sat. 10-10, Sun. 10-7, rest of year. Closed Dec. 25. Hours may vary; extended hours during most holiday periods. Unlimited-use ticket $22.95; over 60, $15.95; ages 3-11, $9.95. AE, DS, MC, VI. Discount, except over 60 and ages 3-11. Phone (714) 220-5200.

MEDIEVAL TIMES, 7662 Beach Blvd., offers 11th-century entertainment—tournament feats of skill and combat performed by costumed knights on horseback—in a castle setting, while guests feast on a four-course dinner. Self-guiding tours Mon.-Sat. 9-3. Performances nightly, matinees Sun.; phone for exact times. Reservations are required. Admission $27.95-$33.95; over 65, $23.95-$32.95; under 13, $18.95-$21.95. DS, MC, VI. Discount, except over 65 and on Sat. Phone (714) 521-4740 or (800) 899-6600.

★MOVIELAND WAX MUSEUM, 7711 Beach Blvd., displays more than 250 figures of movie and television stars in realistic settings. Daily 9-8, May-Sept.; 9-7, rest of year. Admission $12.95; over 55, $10.55; ages 4-11, $6.95. MC, VI. Discount, except over 55. Phone (714) 522-1155. See ad p. 57.

RIPLEY'S BELIEVE IT OR NOT MUSEUM, 7850 Beach Blvd., exhibits interesting, humorous and bizarre items collected from around the world. Daily 9-7, May-Sept.; 10-6, rest of year. Admission $8.95; over 55, $6.95; ages 4-11, $5.25. MC, VI. Discount, except over 55. Phone (714) 522-1152. See ad p. 57.

WILD BILL'S WILD WEST DINNER EXTRAVAGANZA, 7600 Beach Blvd., presents old-fashioned Western-style entertainment that includes hatchet throwing, lariat twirling, live music and cancan dancing; audience participation is encouraged. A family-style meal is served. Shows nightly, matinees Sat.-Sun.; phone for exact times. Reservations are required. Admission $26.50-$31.50; ages 3-11, $19.50. Discount, except Sat. evenings and Dec. 31. Phone (714) 522-6414.

BURBANK (A-6) pop. 93,600, alt. 598'

One of the largest cities in the San Fernando Valley, Burbank is best known for its film and television studios. A favorite shopping place is the Burbank Golden Mall on San Fernando Boulevard between Magnolia Boulevard and Angelino Street.

THE WARNER BROS. STUDIOS V.I.P. TOUR, 4000 Warner Blvd., showcases the many facets of a movie and television studio, including live filming when possible. Tours Mon.-Fri. at 10 and 2; additional tours at 9:30, 10:30 and 2:30, in summer. Closed major holidays. Reservations are required and should be made a week in advance in summer; tour entrance is through Gate 4. No cameras or tape recorders are permitted; comfortable walking shoes are recommended. Admission $25; under 10 not admitted. Phone (818) 954-1744.

BURNEY (C-3) pop. 3,200, alt. 3,173'

Named for an early English settler killed in an Indian raid in 1857, Burney is a marketing center for lumber, produce and livestock.

McARTHUR-BURNEY FALLS MEMORIAL STATE PARK, 6 mi. n. on SR 89, features a 129-foot waterfall that flows down several levels over moss-covered lava rock in a lush forest setting. Daily dawn-dusk. Admission $5 per vehicle; over 62, $4 per vehicle. Phone (916) 335-2777. See Recreation Chart.

★CABRILLO NATIONAL MONUMENT —
see San Diego, Point Loma section.

CALABASAS (B-5) pop. 200, alt. 928'
THE LEONIS ADOBE, 23537 Calabasas Rd., is a restored two-story ranch house built about 1844. Once the home of Miguel Leonis, a colorful figure prominent in early Los Angeles history, it is one of the best preserved Monterey-style adobes in the area. The Plummer House, the first house built in Hollywood, has been relocated here. Completely renovated, it serves as an entrance and visitor center and contains dioramas and period costumes. Wed.-Sun. 1-4; closed Thanksgiving and Dec. 25. Donations. Phone (818) 222-6511.

CALISTOGA (M-2) pop. 4,500, alt. 362'

At the head of Napa Valley, Calistoga is a health resort with natural hot-water geysers, mineral springs and mineralized mud baths. Some of California's finest vineyards cover the surrounding region. An extinct volcano lies north of town.

Calistoga is the southern terminus of a scenic 94 mile stretch of SR 128 that heads northeast to the coastal city of Albion. Scenic SR 29 runs 28 miles south to Napa through the valley.

OLD FAITHFUL GEYSER OF CALIFORNIA, 1 mi. n. on Tubbs Ln. between SRs 29 and 128, is one of the few regularly erupting geysers in the world. Fed by an underground river, the water heats to 350 F and erupts about every 40 minutes for 4 to 5 minutes, spewing 60 feet into the air. Earthquake activity might disrupt normal eruption patterns. Picnicking is permitted. Daily 9-6, in summer; 9-5, rest of year. Admission $3.50; ages 6-12, $2. Phone (707) 942-6463.

ONCE IN A LIFETIME HOT AIR BALLOON RIDES, 1458 Lincoln Ave., Depot Train car #12 off SR 29, offers 1-hour rides launched from

Hanns Kornell and Franciscan vineyards. Sunrise flights include gourmet brunch, photo and flight certificate. Transportation is provided from the depot to the launch site and back. Reservations are required. Fare $165; ages 7-12, $115; under 7 not permitted. AE, DS, MC, VI. **Discount.** Phone (707) 942-6541. *See ad p. 115.*

PETRIFIED FOREST, 5 mi. w. on Petrified Forest Rd., preserves the texture and fiber of giant petrified redwoods. The grounds also contain a museum and picnic facilities. Allow 30 minutes minimum. Daily 10-6, in summer; 10-5, rest of year. Admission $3; over 55, $2; ages 4-11, $1. Phone (707) 942-6667.

SHARPSTEEN MUSEUM, 1311 Washington St., displays artifacts, photographs and dioramas depicting 19th-century Calistoga; a scale model of the Calistoga Hot Springs Resort is included. Next to the museum is one of the resort's 1860s cottages. Special exhibits change every 3 months. Docents conduct tours on request. Daily 10-4, Apr.-Oct.; noon-4, rest of year. Closed Thanksgiving and Dec. 25. Free. Phone (707) 942-5916.

STERLING VINEYARDS, 3 mi. s. off SR 29 at 1111 Dunaweal Ln., occupies a hilltop overlooking Napa Valley. An aerial tram shuttles visitors between the parking lot and winery. Tours are self-guiding, and the tasting room offers a view of the valley. Daily 10:30-4:30; closed major holidays. Round-trip aerial tram ride $5, under 16 free. **Discount,** except Mon.-Fri. noon-4:30 and Sat.-Sun. Phone (707) 942-5151.

CAMBRIA (H-3) pop. 3,100, alt. 60'

Cambria, with its stately pines and panoramic ocean views, lies about 33 miles northwest of San Luis Obispo off SR 1. Originally developed in 1866, the town became a center for shipping, lumbering, whaling and mining. Today specialty shops, art galleries and restaurants line Main Street, which links the distinctly separate East and West villages.

Two coastal parks, Shamel County Park and Leffingwell Landing, a state day-use park, offer picnic areas, beachcombing, tidepools and vantage points for viewing sea otters, sea lions and the winter migration of California gray whales.

Cambria lies on a scenic stretch of SR 1 that extends from San Francisco to San Luis Obispo.

CAMPO (L-7) pop. 1,100, alt. 2,638'

SAN DIEGO RAILROAD MUSEUM, off SR 94 at the old Campo depot on Forest Gate Rd., has a large collection of vintage locomotives and freight and passenger cars. Train trips and tours of the equipment shops and restoration areas are offered. A 16-mile round trip is on a train pulled by either a restored diesel or steam locomotive. Picnic areas and food are available.

Sat.-Sun. and holidays 9-5; closed Jan. 1, Thanksgiving and Dec. 25. Tours depart at 11,

1:30 and 4; train rides depart at noon and 2:30. Museum free. Fare for train rides $10, over 62 and active military $8; ages 6-12, $3. Phone (619) 585-3030 Mon.-Fri. or 478-9937 Sat.-Sun.

CANOGA PARK (A-5) pop. 89,300, alt. 795'

Canoga Park's retail center is Topanga Plaza, Topanga Canyon Boulevard and Vanowen Street, where more than 180 specialty stores share space with three major department stores: Broadway, May Co. and Montgomery Ward.

ORCUTT RANCH HORTICULTURE CENTER, 23600 Roscoe Blvd., embraces a Spanish-style ranch house surrounded by huge oak trees, gardens and 16 acres of citrus trees. Grounds open daily 8-5; closed holidays. House tours conducted 2-5 on the last Sun. of the month, Sept.-June. Free. Phone (818) 883-6641.

CAPITOLA (G-2) pop. 10,200, alt. 50'

Capitola is a resort community on the north shore of Monterey Bay facing New Brighton Beach State Park *(see Recreation Chart)*. Capitola's begonia gardens bloom from July through September; the city celebrates its Begonia Festival each year in early September.

Capitola lies on a scenic stretch of SR 1 that extends from San Francisco to San Luis Obispo.

CARMEL (G-2) pop. 4,200, alt. 20'

Carmel was established in 1904 by a group of artists and writers as a bucolic retreat. As the settlement grew its founders fought the encroachment of paved streets, gas, electricity and other modern amenities, and stringent zoning ordinances have preserved Carmel's village flavor and individuality. Carmel is an architectural conglomerate of international styles, reflecting the whims of the residents.

The Bach Festival is held in mid-July. The holiday season begins a little bit early in Carmel with *Weihnachtsmarkt,* a celebration of the Feast Day of St. Nicholas in early December at the Barnyard.

Carmel lies on a scenic stretch of SR 1 that extends from San Francisco to San Luis Obispo. North of Carmel's white sand beach is an entrance to Seventeen-Mile Drive *(see Monterey).*

Shopping areas: The compact business center of Carmel contains many unusual shops and galleries that display the work of local artists. The Barnyard, a shopping and dining complex at the intersection of SR 1 and Carmel Valley Road with access from Carmel Rancho Boulevard, is as popular for its garden setting and country atmosphere as for its fine galleries and specialty shops.

★**MISSION SAN CARLOS BORROMEO DEL RIO CARMELO,** called Carmel Mission, is at 3080 Rio Rd. Established by Father Junípero Serra at Monterey in 1770 and moved to its present site the following year, the mission was Father Serra's residence and headquarters until his death in 1784. He is buried beneath the church floor in front of the altar. Relics of the mission's early days and some of Father Serra's books and documents are on display. The courtyard gardens and Moorish bell tower are of special interest.

A fiesta is usually held the last Sunday in September. Allow 1 hour minimum. Mon.-Sat. 9:30-4:30, Sun. and holidays 10:30-4:30; closed Thanksgiving and Dec. 25. Donations. Phone (408) 624-3600.

★POINT LOBOS STATE RESERVE, 4 mi. s., covers 1,325 acres of rugged seacoast. There are many well-marked trails along the cliffs. Plants specially adapted to the coastal climate abound in and among the rocks, particularly the Monterey cypress, Monterey pine, seaside daisy and bluff lettuce. The reserve also has a variety of wildlife, including deer, squirrel and rabbits.

About half of the reserve is designated as an underwater reserve. Harbor seals, gray whales and the California sea lion frequent the area, and the California sea otter also can be seen. Numerous sea birds, including cormorants and pelicans, nest along the coast. Diving is permitted by permit only; phone MISTIX at (800) 444-7275 for reservations. Nature walks are offered. Pets are not permitted. Allow 2 hours minimum. Daily 9-6:30, June-Sept.; 9-5, rest of year. Admission $6 per car. Phone (408) 624-4909.

CARPINTERIA (J-4) pop. 13,800, alt. 14'

Carpinteria is a popular resort community and a commercial flower-growing center 12 miles southeast of Santa Barbara. It is noted for its sandy beach and natural reef breakwater which prevents riptides. Nearby Carpinteria State Beach, which has one of California's largest public beach camping facilities, provides recreational opportunities (see Recreation Chart).

Carpinteria lies on a scenic stretch of US 101 that extends from San Luis Obispo south to Los Angeles.

★CATALINA ISLAND (K-5)

Twenty-two miles from the mainland, Catalina Island is 21 miles long and 8 miles wide with Avalon the principal town. The settlement of Two Harbors at Catalina's isthmus is about two-thirds of the way toward the island's northwest end. Discovered by Juan Rodríguez Cabrillo in 1542, the island was subsequently used as a base for smuggling and piracy.

The Santa Catalina Island Co., originally owned by the Banning family and later William Wrigley Jr., was responsible for all phases of the island's development as a resort and sport fisherman's paradise. In 1972, the Santa Catalina Island Conservancy was established as a non-profit organization dedicated to the preservation of the island's native flora and fauna and geographical features. Because the conservancy now owns 86 percent of the land, the island will be preserved in its present natural state and remain an open wilderness.

The island can be reached by sea and air. Channel crossing time by sea ranges from 75 minutes to 4 hours, depending upon the point of departure; service is provided by the following companies: Catalina Channel Express, (310) 519-1212, departing Long Beach and San Pedro (see ad and p. 89); Catalina Cruises, (213) 253-9800, departing Long Beach (see ad p. 61); Catalina Passenger Service, (714) 673-5245, departing Newport Bay; and SeaJet Cruise Lines, (619) 696-0088, departing Oceanside and San Diego.

Catalina-Vegas Airlines, (619) 292-7311, has a 40-minute flight from San Diego. Helicopter flight time averages 15 to 20 minutes via Island Express, (310) 491-5550; helicopters depart from Long Beach and San Pedro. It is necessary to make reservations well in advance, particularly during summer.

One of the leading resorts in the Los Angeles area, the island has fine beaches, tennis courts, horseback riding, hiking, camping, a golf course and deep-sea and pier fishing. It is, however, a fragile environment. Thus you may not bring

cars to the island; bicycles and small gasoline-powered carts can be rented for use around Avalon. Permits must be obtained from the Santa Catalina Island Conservancy, (310) 510-1421, for bicycling in the interior. Only pedestrians and tour buses are permitted outside the harbor area.

CATALINA ISLAND MUSEUM in the casino at the w. end of Avalon Bay, contains artifacts and mementos of the island's past. Daily 10:30-4. Admission $1, under 12 free. Phone (310) 510-2414.

TOURS of the island and surrounding waters are available from several companies; phone the Visitors Information Center at (310) 510-2500 or (800) 428-2566; or Catalina Adventure Tours, (310) 510-2888. For information on trips departing Two Harbors phone (310) 510-0303. Except where noted, regular fares usually begin at about $6.75; there are reduced rates for senior citizens and children.

Avalon Scenic Tour consists of a 50-minute jaunt along the ocean and into the hills above Avalon. Frequent departures daily.

Casino Tour is a guided tour of the Catalina Casino. Of particular interest are the ballroom, theater and circular balcony. Frequent departures daily.

Catalina Adventure Tours offers glass-bottom boat trips to the Marine Game Preserve; passengers can spot and feed a variety of colorful fish. Frequent departures daily for daylight and evening trips.

Coastal Cruise to Seal Rocks travels along Catalina's coastline to its eastern tip, where a large seal colony enter resides. Frequent departures daily, May-Sept.

Flying Fish Boat Trip provides views of nocturnal flying fish by the use of searchlights. One-hour night tours, mid-May to mid-Oct.

Glass-Bottom Boat Trip over Undersea Gardens offers 40-minute tours with views of marine life. Frequent departures daily for daylight trips. Evening tours offered May-Sept.

Inland Motor Tour is a 3¾-hour trip through the island's mountainous interior and along Skyline Drive overlooking the coast. Reservations are required. Departs daily at 9 a.m. with additional trips in summer. Fare $23; senior citizens $20; ages 2-11, $13. MC, VI.

Island Safari offers 2½- and 3½-hour guided motor tours departing from Two Harbors. The tours explore the island's natural history and include stops at various points of interest in the interior. Trips depart mornings May-Oct. The 3½-hour trip $22.50, 2½-hour trip $15.50, reduced rates for children. Phone (310) 510-0303 for schedule and reservations.

Skyline Drive Tour affords views of Avalon and the island's interior. The 1¾-hour tour includes a stop at Airport-in-the-Sky. Frequent daily tours in summer; daily at 1 p.m., rest of year. Reservations are required. Fare $12; senior citizens $10.75; ages 2-11, $8.

Sunset Buffet Cruise offers live entertainment, cocktails and a buffet dinner aboard a historic sidewheeler on a 2-hour coastal tour. Departures daily at 6 p.m., May-Sept. Fare $36.50; senior citizens $33; ages 2-11, $18.

Twilight Dining Cruise to Two Harbors is a cruise along 14 miles of scenic coastline to Two Harbors, where a buffet, complimentary beverage and a guided hike across the isthmus are provided. Flying fish are often seen on the return trip. Departures Tues. and Thurs., mid-June through Sept. 30. Fare $39.50; senior citizens $33; ages 2-11, $18.

Twilight Safari is a 2½-hour motor trip running through Catalina's interior from Two Harbors to Little Harbor. Late afternoon departures May-Oct. Phone (310) 510-2800 for fares and departure times.

WRIGLEY MEMORIAL AND BOTANICAL GARDEN is 2 mi. s. of Avalon via Avalon Canyon Rd. Daily 8-5. Admission $1, under 12 free. Phone (310) 510-2288.

CHANNEL ISLANDS NATIONAL PARK (K-4)

Of the eight islands in Southern California's Channel Islands chain, Anacapa, San Miguel, Santa Barbara, Santa Cruz and Santa Rosa constitute Channel Islands National Park. The water for 6 nautical miles around these five islands is protected as the Channel Islands National Marine Sanctuary. The closest island, Anacapa, is 11 miles from the mainland; access can be arranged at various locations in and around Ventura.

Visitors can observe the plants and animals that have evolved on these isolated havens; several species display traits uniquely suited to the island environment. Local wildlife includes colonies of cormorants, congregations of seals and

sea lions and major sea bird rookeries, most notably the endangered California brown pelican. The marine sanctuary contains giant kelp forests that shelter more than 1,000 species of ocean life.

Sections of the islands might be closed to protect the wildlife and their habitats. Fossils and evidence of volcanism and faulting can be found in the park.

General Information and Activities

The islands and their inhabitants represent a fragile balance of life that survives the constant wind and surging tides. Visitors are expected to remain on the trails; all objects, including plants, animals and archeological remains, should not be disturbed and may not be removed. Primitive camping is permitted on Anacapa, San Miguel, Santa Rosa and Santa Barbara; reservations are required.

Visitors must bring their own food and water; refreshments are not available on the islands. Clothing should be worn that accommodates both hot and cold weather.

Guided walks on San Miguel and Santa Rosa islands are conducted by rangers and must be arranged in advance through park headquarters; a landing permit also is required. Santa Cruz is privately owned, so permission to visit must be obtained from the landowners; contact park headquarters for more information.

Visitors must arrange their own transportation to the islands. The Island Packers Co. next to the park headquarters at 1867 Spinnaker Dr. offers trips to Santa Barbara, Santa Cruz, Santa Rosa and San Miguel, late Mar. to mid-Nov. Boats to Anacapa depart Ventura Harbor daily, phone for schedule. Round-trip fare to Anacapa Island $32-$37; under 13, $20.

Half-day, non-landing excursions also are available. Fares to Santa Barbara, San Miguel, Santa Rosa and Santa Cruz vary. A boat for campers departs daily in summer. Passengers must bring their own food and water on the boat. Reservations should be made 2 or more weeks in advance. For information contact 1867 Spinnaker Dr., Ventura, CA 93001; phone (805) 642 1393. *See Recreation Chart.*

VISITOR CENTER, 1901 Spinnaker Dr. in Ventura Harbor, contains the park headquarters and features exhibits, slide programs and a film about the islands. Special programs are offered during summer. Daily 8-5:30; closed Thanksgiving and Dec. 25. Free. Phone (805) 658-5730.

ADMISSION to the visitor center is free, but visitors must arrange their own transportation to the islands.

PETS are not permitted on the islands or at the visitor center.

ADDRESS inquiries to the Superintendent, Channel Islands National Park, 1901 Spinnaker Dr., Ventura, CA 93001.

CHERRY VALLEY(B-9) pop. 5,000, alt. 2,783'

EDWARD-DEAN MUSEUM OF DECORATIVE ARTS, 9401 Oak Glen Rd., exhibits priceless furniture and 17th-, 18th- and 19th-century European and Asian art. Changing displays present international art in various media. Tues.-Fri. 1-4:30, Sat.-Sun. 10-4:30, Sept.-July; closed holidays. Admission $1, under 12 free. Phone (909) 845-2626.

CHICO (D-3) pop. 40,100, alt. 200'

Bidwell Park, a 2,250-acre city park spanning an area from downtown to the foothills of the Sierra Nevada, offers hiking and bicycling trails, ball fields, a playground and facilities for swimming, golf and horseshoes.

BIDWELL MANSION STATE HISTORIC PARK, 525 The Esplanade, preserves a Victorian residence built 1865-68. Former home of city founder Gen. John Bidwell, it houses one of the largest collections of vintage clothing in northern California. Nearly 300 pieces of early 1900s men's and women's garments are on display. Guided tours are available. Allow 1 hour minimum. Daily 10-4; closed Jan. 1, Thanksgiving and Dec. 25. Admission $2; ages 6-12, $1. Phone (916) 895-6144.

CHICO MUSEUM, 2nd and Salem sts., contains galleries devoted to regional history and art, as well as a late-1800s Chinese temple that was shipped in pieces and reassembled. Tours available by reservation. Open Wed.-Sun. noon-4. Donations. Phone (916) 891-4336.

CHINO (B-7) pop. 59,700, alt. 735'

PLANES OF FAME AIR MUSEUM, 4½ mi. s. of SR 60 off Euclid Ave. at Chino Airport, displays restored American, British, German and Japanese military aircraft. A special collection of early aircraft includes an 1896 glider. The Jet Fighter Museum houses jet fighters that range from the early P-59 to the F-104, with most of the jets reflecting the Korean War era.

Daily 9-5, closed Thanksgiving and Dec. 25. Admission for either museum $4.95; ages 5-12, $1.95. Combination admission $7.95; ages 5-12, $1.95. **Discount,** except ages 5-12. Phone (909) 597-3722.

CHULA VISTA (L-7) pop. 135,200, alt. 75'

CHULA VISTA NATURE INTERPRETIVE CENTER is at 1000 Gunpowder Point Dr.; access is by shuttle bus, departing every 20 minutes from a parking lot 1 blk. w. of I-5 at E St. The center offers hands-on exhibits pertaining to the surrounding marshland habitat. Trails allow close-up views of indigenous flora and fauna and migratory birds. Tues.-Sun. and Mon. holidays 10-5; closed major holidays. Donations. Shuttle bus 50c, under 17 free. Phone (619) 422-2473.

CLAREMONT (B-7) pop. 32,500, alt. 1,165'

Claremont is best known as a college community, with Pomona College, Scripps College, Claremont McKenna College, The Claremont Graduate School, Harvey Mudd College and Pitzer College, as well as the School of Theology at Claremont.

Shopping areas: The Old Schoolhouse at Indian Hill and Foothill boulevards houses specialty shops and restaurants in a renovated high school building.

★RANCHO SANTA ANA BOTANIC GARDEN, 1500 N. College Ave., contains 85 acres of native California plants and flowers; it is most colorful February through June. Tours are given Sat.-Sun. at 2, Mar.-May. Open daily 8-5; closed Jan. 1, July 4, Thanksgiving and Dec. 25. Free. Phone (909) 625-8767.

CLEVELAND NATIONAL FOREST

Covering more than 420,000 acres in Southern California, Cleveland National Forest lies between the ocean and the desert. Within the forest are Palomar Observatory *(see Palomar Mountain)*, four wilderness areas, and Pine Creek, San Mateo, Palomar, Mount Laguna and Santa Ana Mountains recreation areas.

Information on forest naturalist programs, hiking and nature trails, camping and winter sports is available at ranger stations and information centers. The Laguna Mountain Visitor Information Office at Sunrise Highway and Shriner's Road is open Fri. 2-6, Sat. 9-5, Sun. 10-4, mid-May to mid-Sept.; phone (619) 473-8547. For information on Descanso District, Pine Creek and Hauser wilderness areas phone (619) 445-6235.

The 16,000-acre Agua Tibia Wilderness is at the northwest end of the Palomar District. A permit is required to enter the wilderness. Contact the U.S. Forest Service, Palomar Ranger District, 1634 Black Cyn Rd., Ramona, CA 92065; phone (619) 788-0250.

For information on the Santa Ana Mountains and the San Mateo Canyon Wilderness contact the El Cariso Visitor Information Center, (909) 678-3700, in the Trabuco District, 32-353 Ortega Hwy. in a fire station complex across from the campground, or the Trabuco District Office, (909) 736-1811, 1147 E. Sixth St. in Corona.

The forest supervisor's office is at 10845 Rancho Bernardo Rd., Rancho Bernardo, CA 92127; phone (619) 673-6180. It is open Mon.-Fri. 8-4:30. *See Recreation Chart and the AAA California and Nevada CampBook.*

COALINGA (H-3) pop. 8,200, alt. 671'

Coalinga began as a loading point for the Southern Pacific Railroad Co., which transported coal from area mines. Eventually "Coaling Station A" grew into a permanent oil-boomer settlement and its name was abbreviated. Nine miles north of town is a group of oil pumps decorated as animals, clowns and imaginary creatures.

The Annual Horned Toad Derby is held Memorial Day weekend in Olson Park. The 5-day event includes horned toad races, a carnival and a parade.

R.C. BAKER MEMORIAL MUSEUM, 297 W. Elm St., displays fossils, Indian artifacts, Western ranch hand equipment, a 1924 American La France fire engine and a large collection of oilfield equipment. Allow 1 hour minimum. Mon.-Fri. 10-noon and 1-5, Sat. 11-5, Sun. and holidays 1-5; closed Jan. 1, Easter, Thanksgiving and Dec. 24-25. Free. Phone (209) 935-1914.

COLOMA (E-4) pop. 1,100, alt. 750'

In January 1848 near Capt. John Sutter's sawmill on the American River, James Marshall discovered the first yellow flecks of metal that launched the great California gold rush. By the summer more than 2,000 miners were sifting for gold along the river near Sutter's mill, and Coloma, the first of the gold rush towns, was born. Finds grew scarce within a few years, and the thriving city of 10,000 dwindled to the quiet village it is today.

★MARSHALL GOLD DISCOVERY STATE HISTORIC PARK, 300 acres on SR 49, includes the 1860 cabin in which James Marshall lived. A statue of Marshall points toward the site of his discovery, a half-mile away. A replica of Sutter's mill stands nearby. Picnic facilities, a visitor center and a museum are available; fishing is permitted. Allow 1 hour minimum.

Park open daily 8-dusk. Museum open daily 10-5, Memorial Day weekend-Labor Day;

11-4:30, rest of year. Closed Jan. 1, Thanksgiving and Dec. 25. Day use fee $5 per private vehicle; $4 per private vehicle for senior citizens. Phone (916) 622-3470.

COLUMBIA (F-4) pop. 400, alt. 2,143'

In the foothills of the Sierra Nevada, Columbia was one of the largest and most important mining towns along the Mother Lode. Between 1850 and 1870, $87 million in gold was extracted from the local placer mines.

★COLUMBIA STATE HISTORIC PARK, covering 12 square blocks in the old business district, has been partially restored to its appearance in gold rush days. Among the buildings are a schoolhouse, bank, newspaper building, barbershop, saloons, the Wells Fargo Express Co. building and the City Hotel, which still houses guests. The Masonic Temple has been reconstructed on its original site. A museum presents slide shows on the history of Columbia. The annual Firemen's Muster is held in early May.

The restored Fallon House Theater presents plays Thurs.-Sat. at 8 p.m., Sun. at 2 during scheduled performances. Admission $12, senior citizens $10, students $7. Phone (209) 532-4644.

Park open daily 8-6, May-Oct.; 8-5, rest of year. Free. Tours on horseback are available; phone (209) 532-0663. Stagecoach and horseback rides daily, in summer; Sat.-Sun., rest of year, weather permitting. Fare $4-$5; under 13, $3.50-$4.50. Phone (209) 532-4301.

COLUSA (D-2) pop. 4,900, alt. 61'

More than 4,000 acres of seasonal marsh, permanent ponds, watergrass and uplands west of Colusa shelter large flocks of ducks and geese during fall and winter. The Colusa National Wildlife Refuge's 3-mile self-guiding auto tour route leads through part of the area; phone (916) 934-2801.

CORONA DEL MAR—see Newport Beach.

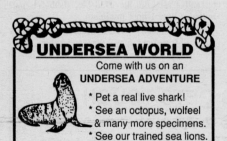

UNDERSEA WORLD

Come with us on an
UNDERSEA ADVENTURE

* Pet a real live shark!
* See an octopus, wolfeel
& many more specimens.
* See our trained sea lions.

*Open 7 days per week (707) 464-3522
SEE OUR LISTING IN CRESCENT CITY, CA
Mention AAA ad for a Free Souvenir

CORONADO (L-6) pop. 26,500, alt. 27'

On a peninsula between San Diego Bay and the Pacific Ocean, Coronado is a beach resort, convention center and attractive residential town. The San Diego-Coronado Bay Bridge connects Coronado to San Diego. The 1888 Hotel del Coronado is a well-known landmark and resort with Victorian turrets and cupolas. The hotel rents tapes for self-guiding tours.

Coronado Touring offers a narrated walking tour that highlights Coronado homes and the hotel's gardens. Tours leave from the Glorietta Bay Inn Tues., Thurs. and Sat. at 11. Fee $5; phone (619) 435-5993 or 435-5892.

Boat rentals and sightseeing charters are available at the dock next to the boathouse on Glorietta Bay. A ferry service runs from the Old Ferry Landing at B and 1st streets to San Diego (see San Diego, Boat Tours). Local businesses offer fishing charters and surfboard, bicycle and moped rentals. The Coronado Municipal Golf Course, bordering San Diego and Glorietta bays, and the nearby public Tennis Center cater to golf and tennis enthusiasts. Silver Strand State Beach, 7 miles south of town, allows picnicking and swimming (see Recreation Chart).

COSTA MESA (C-7) pop. 96,400, alt. 100'

A budding cultural center, Costa Mesa is the home of the South Coast Repertory Theater and the 8,542-seat Pacific Amphitheatre. Huntington State Beach is nearby. See Recreation Chart.

Shopping areas: One of Southern California's largest malls is South Coast Plaza at I-405 and Bristol Street. It has a Bullock's, I. Magnin, May Co., Nordstrom, Saks Fifth Avenue and Sears. Broadway and Robinson's are just across the street in Crystal Court at Bear Street and Sunflower Avenue.

LAGUNA ART MUSEUM SATELLITE AT SOUTH COAST PLAZA, 3333 Bristol St., Suite 1000, is an outreach of the Laguna Art Museum in Laguna Beach (see place listing). Its galleries offer changing exhibits of contemporary works. Mon.-Fri. 11-9, Sat. 10-6, Sun. 11-6. Free. Phone (714) 662-3366.

ORANGE COUNTY PERFORMING ARTS CENTER, 600 Town Center Dr. in South Coast Plaza Town Center, features the 3,000-seat Segerstrom Hall, where major symphony concerts, operas, ballets and Broadway musicals are presented. Free guided tours are offered Mon. and Wed. at 10 and 11 and the first Sat. of the month at 10 and 10:30. For ticket and tour information phone (714) 556-2787.

CRESCENT CITY (A-1) pop. 4,400, alt. 44'

Founded in 1853 as a gold mining supply center, Crescent City edges a harbor defined by a crescent-shaped beach. Point St. George, just above the harbor, protects the city from strong north winds; it was on Point St. George Reef that the sidewheeler *Brother Jonathan* wrecked on July 30, 1865. Brother Jonathan Cemetery, 9th Street and Pebble Beach Drive, contains the graves of many of the disaster victims.

The Lake Earl Wildlife Area, 5 miles north of Crescent City at the junction of Northcrest Drive and Old Mill Road, is 5,000 acres of wildlife habitat that is open for nature study, boating, hiking, waterfowl hunting and fishing. Year-round recreation is available at nearby Redwood National Park *(see place listing and Recreation Chart).*

The city celebrates the benefits of a coastal location with a series of events, including the World Championship Crab Races in February and a Seafood Festival in September. In early June is a Weekend in Bear Country.

Crescent City is the southern terminus of a scenic 42-mile stretch of US 199 that heads northeast to the Oregon border through Six Rivers National Forest.

DEL NORTE COAST REDWOODS STATE PARK, 6,375 acres 8 mi. s. on US 101, contains 15 memorial redwood groves. The growths extend down steep slopes almost to the ocean shore. Daily 24 hours, May-Oct. Day use fee $5 per vehicle; over 61, $4 per vehicle. Phone (707) 464-9533. *See Recreation Chart.*

OLD LIGHTHOUSE, on Battery Point Island at the end of A St., is a working 1856 lighthouse that houses a museum, nautical artifacts, antique clocks and photographs of shipwrecks and American and foreign lighthouses. Guided tours are available, tide permitting. Allow 30 minutes minimum. Wed.-Sun. 10-4, Apr.-Sept. Admission $2; under 12, 50c. To confirm hours phone (707) 464-3089.

RELLIM DEMONSTRATION FOREST, 4 mi s. off US 101 on Hamilton Rd., exhibits tools, photographs and a diorama of the early logging and lumber industry. Trails pass the remains of logging activities and evidence of forest regeneration. The trails are steep in some areas and take 15 to 30 minutes to complete. Allow 1 hour minimum. Tues.-Thurs. 8-6, Fri.-Mon. 8:30-4:30, early June-Labor Day. Free. Phone (707) 464-3144.

UNDERSEA WORLD, 304 US 101S, features a half-million-gallon tank with a sandy bottom and reef exhibit. Other highlights include a tidewater touch pool, shark petting tank and performances by trained sea lions. Guided tours are available. Daily 8-8, May-Sept.; 9-5, rest of year. Closed Thanksgiving and Dec. 25. Admission $5.95; over 55 and ages 13-18, $4.95; ages 6-12, $2.95. DS, MC, VI. Phone (707) 464-3522. *See ad p. 64.*

DANA POINT (K-6) pop. 31,900, alt. 10'

At the turn of the 19th century Dana Point was the only major port between Santa Barbara

and San Diego. Now the natural cove boasts a modern marina from which whale-watching cruises depart late December through March. In late February and early March the town celebrates its annual Harbor Whale Festival.

Shopping areas: Dana Point Harbor, Golden Lantern at Harbor Drive, consists of two dockside villages that offer shopping with a view.

ORANGE COUNTY MARINE INSTITUTE, 24200 Dana Point Harbor Dr., contains sea life exhibits. Next to the institute is a full-size replica of Richard Henry Dana's ship *Pilgrim,* which he described in "Two Years Before the Mast." Public area of institute open daily 10-3:30; closed major holidays. Ship tours Sun. 11-2:30. Institute and *Pilgrim* tours free. Phone (714) 496-2274.

DANVILLE (P-3) pop. 31,300, alt. 368'

Blackhawk Plaza is a mercantile and cultural center with museums, stores, restaurants, a waterway with fountains and reflecting gardens. Special events are held throughout the year.

THE BEHRING AUTO MUSEUM, 3750 Blackhawk Plaza Cir., at the intersection of Crow Canyon Rd. and Camino Tassajara, displays about 120 distinctive automobiles, many worth more than $1 million. The collection includes an 1897 Leon Bollee three-wheeler, Johnny Rutherford's Indy-winning McLaren, rare Bugattis and many more. The second floor has rotating exhibits as well as a video presentation.

Tues.-Sun. 10-5 (also Wed.-Fri. 5-9); closed major holidays. Admission $5, senior citizens and students $3; guided tours are available by reservation. **Two-for-one discount.** Phone (510) 736-2277.

DAVIS (E-3) pop. 46,200, alt. 50'

As a result of its foresight and commitment to conservation, Davis has received several energy conservation awards. Among them are The Energy Conservation Retrofit Program from the Sacramento Valley Section of the American Planning Association and Practical Uses of the Sun from the American Institute of Planners.

The University of California at Davis, 15 miles west of Sacramento, ranks among the top 20 research universities in the United States, with colleges of agriculture and environmental sciences, engineering, letters and sciences. There are more than 70 graduate programs offering work leading to advanced degrees. UC Davis offers professional studies at its school of law, management, medicine and veterinary medicine. Tours of the campus are available Sat.-Sun. 11:30-1:30. Phone (916) 752-0539.

SATIETY WINERY, 8 mi. n. of I-80 at SR 113 and CR 25-A, offers tours and tastings. Food is available. Daily 1-5. Free. Phone (916) 661-0680.

DEATH VALLEY JUNCTION (H-8) pop. 100, alt. 2,042'

MARTA BECKET'S AMARGOSA OPERA HOUSE, near jct. SRs 127 and 190, is the backdrop for dance-mime performances created and presented by Marta Becket. Performances Mon. and Fri.-Sat. at 8:15 p.m., Jan.-Apr.; Sat. only, in May, Oct. and Dec. Admission $8; ages 2-12, $5. **Discount.** Phone (619) 852-4316.

★DEATH VALLEY NATIONAL MONUMENT (H-7)

Death Valley's formation began about 3 million years ago when forces within the Earth broke the crust into blocks. Some of these blocks tilted and rotated, creating the alternating mountain and valley pattern. During the ice ages large lakes intermittently occupied the basin; their evaporation left alternating layers of mud and large salt deposits that are still visible today.

Several Indian cultures have occupied the area during the past 9,000 years, but the valley gained its forbidding name and reputation relatively recently. In the winter of 1849, a band of goldseekers started across the valley, believing that it was a shortcut to the goldfields. After runnning low on food and water, the band splintered into several frantic groups, each trying to escape the area on their own. Some of the pioneers died.

Although miners later found precious metal in the area, the discovery of another mineral—borax—initiated the exploitation of the valley. The first borax prospectors built the roads over which the famous 20-mule teams drew wagon loads weighing as much as 40 tons.

A place of unexpected contrasts, Death Valley ranges from less than 4 miles to about 16 miles in width and is about 120 miles long. Elevations range from 282 feet below sea level near Badwater (the lowest point in the Western Hemisphere) to 11,049 feet above sea level at Telescope Peak. One of the hottest regions in the world, the valley experiences daytime temperatures as high as 134 °F. Although summer thunderstorms often send flash floods tearing down narrow canyons, the average yearly rainfall on the valley floor is less than 2 inches.

Of the more than 900 species of plants and trees found, 21 are unique to the valley, including the Panamint daisy, the Death Valley sage and the Death Valley sandpaper plant.

The area also contains a wealth of geological phenomena. Large sand dune formations, sculpted rocks, isolated valleys and volcanic craters can be seen. The canyon and mountain walls change color with the shifting sunlight.

Mankind's marks on the desert are limited. The monument boundaries encompass the route of the Jayhawkers Trail followed from the Great Salt Lake in 1849; the route taken by the Darwin-French party in 1860; the first mine worked in the region; several beehive charcoal kilns; and the ghost town site of Skidoo.

Death Valley attracts many visitors between early November and late April. Washington's Birthday, Easter Week, Thanksgiving, Christmas and Death Valley Encampment in early November are particularly popular times. Artists Drive is a scenic 9-mile route among the foothills of the Black Mountains. Golden Canyon, about 5 miles north of the entrance to Artists Drive, is cut by an easy 2-mile trail that winds through carved rock formations; parking and trail guides are available at the trail entrance. East of Furnace Creek, SR 190 leads to Zabriskie Point.

The Furnace Creek Visitor Center has exhibits, literature and an 18-minute film on the monument. It is open daily 8-7, Nov. 1-Easter; 8-6, rest of year. Phone (619) 786-2331. Evening programs and naturalist walks are conducted Nov. 1-Easter; evening programs only are conducted Sat.-Sun., rest of year. Horses can be rented at Furnace Creek Ranch.

Leashed pets are allowed in the valley but not in public facilities or on the trails. Admission is by 7-day permit; fee $5 per private vehicle, $2 per person arriving by other means, free to U.S. residents over 62. *See the AAA California and Nevada CampBook.*

Note: Because of the intense heat, tours of the valley are not recommended during summer. If you must cross the valley, carry extra water or travel at night when temperatures are cooler. You also should boil or purify any water taken from valley springs before drinking it.

★**SCOTTY'S CASTLE,** at the valley's n. boundary, is an amazing sight in this isolated region. Built as a vacation retreat by a wealthy Chicagoan, it contains beautiful furnishings and art objects. Allow 1 hour minimum. Rangers in 1930s costumes conduct tours on the hour daily 9-5; grounds open daily 7-6. Admission $6; over 62 and ages 6-11, $3.

DEL MAR (L-6) pop. 4,900, alt. 122'

Del Mar's fairgrounds complex holds the Camel Grand Prix of Southern California in mid-October and is home to Thoroughbred racing from late July to mid-September.

TORREY PINES STATE RESERVE, 1,750 acres on N.Torrey Pines Rd., is the natural habitat of the Torrey pine, which Pacific winds often twist into unexpected shapes. Nature walks are conducted Sat.-Sun. at 11:30 and 1:30. Self-guiding tours are available; camping, pets and picnicking are not permitted. Reserve open daily 9-dusk; museum daily 11-5. Fee $4 per private vehicle; over 62, $3 per private vehicle. Pedestrians and bicyclists free. Phone (619) 755-2063.

★DEVILS POSTPILE NATIONAL MONUMENT (F-5)

Near Mammoth Lakes and surrounded by Inyo National Forest *(see place listing)*, Devils Postpile National Monument lies at an altitude of 7,600 feet in the eastern Sierra Nevada. The highlight of this 800-acre monument is a sheer wall of symmetrical basaltic columns more than 60 feet high. The formation is a remnant of a basalt flow worn smooth on top by glacial action. A trail leads to the top where the surface resembles a tile inlay.

The Middle Fork of the San Joaquin River drops about 100 feet at Rainbow Falls, 2 miles by trail from the Postpile. Fishing is permitted; anyone over 16 must have a California license. Hunting is prohibited.

The monument is reached via SR 203, which leads west from US 395 and the Mammoth Visitor Center to the Mammoth Mountain Ski Area parking lot, then by shuttle bus to the Postpile ranger station *(see Inyo National Forest for shuttle bus information)*. A ½-mile trail leads to the Postpile. Except for vehicles with camping permits, private vehicles are not allowed beyond Minaret Summit (just beyond the ski area parking lot) during the day, late June-Labor Day.

Rangers conduct interpretive walks and campfire programs early July-Labor Day. Leashed pets are permitted. Monument open mid-June through Oct. 31; ranger station open daily 8-5, July 1-Labor Day. Shuttle bus $6, children $5, round trip. Campsites are $8 per night. Phone (619) 934-2289.

★DISNEYLAND—*see Anaheim.*

DOWNEY (B-6) pop. 86,900, alt. 118′

DOWNEY MUSEUM OF ART, in Furman Park at 10419 Rives Ave., displays changing contemporary exhibits of professional art works that include paintings, sketches, ceramics, sculpture and other media. Wed.-Sun. noon-5; closed major holidays and periodically between exhibits. Donations. Phone (310) 861-0419.

DOWNIEVILLE (D-3) pop. 400, alt. 2,899′

Once the center of enormously rich diggings, Downieville retains much of its earlier atmosphere. Old brick and stone buildings with picturesque iron doors and shutters flank narrow, tree-lined Main Street. Some sections of sidewalk are still made of planks. Gold panning is available downtown in the Yuba River.

DOWNIEVILLE MUSEUM, Main St., was built in 1851 and features a miniature operating model of a stamp mill and a collection of horse snowshoes. Daily 10-5, Memorial Day weekend-Labor Day. Donations. Phone (916) 289-3261.

DUNSMUIR (B-3) pop. 2,100, alt. 2,289′

Dunsmuir is an old railroad town just south of Mount Shasta. The Sacramento River, which runs through town, offers fishing. Other recreational opportunities in the area include camping, hiking and skiing. The Dunsmuir Museum, 4101 Pine St., has displays on railroad history.

CASTLE CRAGS STATE PARK lies 6 mi. s. off I-5. The granite crags tower over the Sacramento River. Naturalist programs are available most Saturday evenings Memorial Day weekend-Labor Day. Park open daily 7:30 a.m.-10 p.m.; ranger on duty 7 a.m.-11 p.m. Day use fee $5 per vehicle; over 62, $4 per vehicle. Phone (916) 235-2684. *See Recreation Chart.*

EARLIMART (H-4) pop. 4,600, alt. 283′

COLONEL ALLENSWORTH STATE HISTORIC PARK, 8 mi. w. on SR 43, commemorates the only California town founded, financed and governed by black Americans. Several of the early 1900s buildings have been restored, including the school and Col. Allensworth's home. A 30-minute video presentation in the visitor center gives a history of the colonel and his town. Camping and picnicking are permitted.

Visitor center open daily 10-4; buildings open upon request. Closed Jan. 1, Thanksgiving and Dec. 25. Day use fee $3 per vehicle; additional fee for camping. Phone (805) 849-3433.

EAST MOJAVE NATIONAL SCENIC AREA (I-8)

Designated in 1980 as America's first national scenic area, the East Mojave comprises 1.5 million acres between I-15 and I-40 in southeastern California. It was established to preserve its prehistoric and historic features and to manage the natural resources found at this convergence of ecosystems.

The East Mojave desert ranges in elevation from less than 1,000 feet to almost 8,000 feet. The diverse landscape encompasses mountains, mesas, red volcanic spires, cinder cones and sand dunes. Since summer daytime temperatures typically exceed 100 F at lower elevations, the best months for visiting are October through May. Although yearly rainfall averages between 5 and 10 inches, summer storms sometimes cause flash floods, and occasional winter storms bring rain and even snow to the higher mountains.

Though not always visible, wildlife is abundant. Some of the nearly 300 different species of animals living in this area include bighorn sheep, mule deer, porcupines and mountain lions in the mountains; coyotes, kit fox, desert tortoises and antelope ground squirrels inhabit the lower elevations.

To survive the desert climate, many plants have small leaves to minimize moisture loss, while cactuses store large volumes of water and mesquite sends roots as deep as 100 feet. Common plants include yucca, sage, rabbitbrush and the spindly Joshua tree. Wildflower displays can be particularly colorful in April and May.

The East Mojave is rich in archeological and historical features that are protected by law. The many examples of Indian rock art include petroglyphs more than 10,000 years old. More recent are the abandoned mines and desert camps, evidence of the mining that once flourished and continues to a limited extent today. Cattle ranching, also important during the 1800s, is still practiced.

Semi-developed campgrounds are open all year at Mid Hills and Hole-in-the-Wall; primitive camping is permitted on most land adjacent to the roads. Hiking, backpacking and horseback riding are permitted, but horses are not allowed at developed campsites. Camping or parking within 600 feet of a watering spot is not allowed. Rockhounding, birdwatching, photography and star tracking also are popular.

Several paved roads and hundreds of miles of gravel and dirt roads lace the area. Vehicles must stay on existing routes; there are no off-road vehicle areas. Because gasoline availability is unpredictable, you should fill your tank at Needles, Goffs, Ludlow or Baker before entering the region, and check ahead for weather and road conditions. Contact the Needles Resource Area Office, Bureau of Land Management, 101 East Spikes Rd., P.O. Box 888, Needles, CA 92363; phone (619) 326-3896. *See Recreation Chart.*

CEDAR CANYON ROAD runs east and west between the Kelso-Cima and Lanfair roads, passing remnants of old ranches and homesteads—stark reminders of life in the East Mojave during the late 1800s. Part of this road follows the Mojave Road, or Old Government Road, one of the first routes developed through this region for wagon use in the 1850s and '60s.

Most of the Mojave Road is accessible only by four-wheel-drive vehicles. Guidebooks for the 130-mile route are available on loan from the Bureau of Land Management offices in Barstow, Needles and Riverside.

CIMA ROAD heads south from I-15 at Valley Wells; it passes east of the rounded and weathered granite of Cima Dome, which has one of the densest Joshua tree forests in California.

IVANPAH-LANFAIR ROAD begins 6½ mi. w. of Nipton near I-15 and extends s. to Goffs near I-40. The first stretch through Ivanpah Valley is one of the best places in California to spot the desert tortoise in spring. The road continues over the New York Mountains, where the presence of water accounts for the existence of 288 species of plants and a variety of wildlife. Both abandoned and working mines are scattered throughout the area.

KELBAKER ROAD provides north-south access between I-15 at Baker and I-40. Heading south

from Baker, the road passes the historic town of Kelso, the site of a classic Neo-Spanish railroad depot along the Union Pacific Railroad. Kelso Dunes southwest of town is one of the few dune fields in the continental United States where the sand cascading down the steep slopes emits a booming sound. Farther south the road passes between two of the area's highest ranges, the Providence Mountains on the east and the Granite Mountains on the west.

PROVIDENCE MOUNTAINS STATE RECREATION AREA is 17 mi. n. of I-40 on Essex-Black Canyon Rd. The nearby countryside consists of high desert framed by red volcanic peaks. A self-guiding nature trail begins near the visitor center. Guided tours of Mitchell Caverns are offered Mon.-Fri. at 1:30; Sat.-Sun. and holidays at 10, 1:30 and 3, mid-Sept. to mid-June, weather permitting. Tours $4; ages 6-17, $2. For information write P.O. Box 1, Essex, CA 92332; phone (619) 389-2281.

Essex-Black Canyon Road, which is narrow and rough in spots, continues north to the Hole-in-the-Wall country, the setting for the area's two developed campgrounds. Hills and mesas scattered with pinyon and juniper surround the broad sagebrush-covered valleys. Volcanic in origin, the mesas and buttes around Hole-in-the-Wall are pocked with holes that produce eerie sounds when the wind blows. Old mines dot the area, making it a favorite with rockhounds.

EDISON (I-5) pop. 1,000, alt. 567'

GIUMARRA VINEYARDS is off SR 58 on Edison Hwy. The vineyard produces varietal and generic wines. Storage and bottling facilities can be viewed, and tastings are offered. Tues.-Sat. 9-5. Free. Phone (805) 395-7088.

EL CENTRO (L-8) pop. 31,400, alt. -45'

El Centro is the market center for the Imperial Valley, one of the richest farming areas in the world. Irrigation has transformed a barren desert—much of it below sea level—into a verdant patchwork of productive fields and pastures. Tomatoes, cotton, sugar beets, melons and lettuce are raised. The Navy's Blue Angels flying team does its winter training at the nearby Naval Air Facility, and in mid-March the U.S. Navy Blue Angels Air Show zooms overhead.

ELDORADO NATIONAL FOREST

Bounded on the west by the Mother Lode Country and on the east by Lake Tahoe, Eldorado National Forest encompasses 676,780 acres in the rugged, lake-strewn Sierra Nevada. US 50 and SR 88 provide access to most of the forest's recreational facilities. The Carson Pass Highway (SR 88) is a 58-mile scenic route through the forest.

Although the forest is most popular in spring and summer, three downhill ski areas and trails for cross-country skiing and snowmobiling attract winter visitors as well. Segments of the Pacific Crest National Scenic Trail pass through the forest; snow renders some sections impassable until mid-June or July. Hikers wishing to camp on the trail should obtain campfire permits. Permits also are required for day use and overnight stays in the Desolation Wilderness and Mokelumne Wilderness.

Designated routes for off-road vehicles are outlined on a Vehicle Travel Plan Map. For information contact the Eldorado National Forest Visitor Center, 3070 Camino Heights Dr., Camino, CA 95709; phone (916) 644-6048. *See Recreation Chart and the AAA California and Nevada CampBook.*

EL MONTE (B-7) pop.106,200, alt. 283'

El Monte was known as the end of the Santa Fe Trail for westbound travelers. The water sources they found in the woodland in the 1850s now nourish the area's diminishing orange and walnut groves.

EL MONTE HISTORICAL SOCIETY MUSEUM, 3150 N. Tyler Ave., occupies the town's former library. Period furniture, clothing, household items and photographs are among the displays, many dating back to the late 19th century. An early 1900s schoolroom and Victorian-era parlor are replicated. Tues.-Fri. 10-4; closed holidays and the last 2 weeks of Dec. Donations. Phone (818) 580-2232.

ENCINITAS (K-6) pop. 55,400, alt. 92'

QUAIL BOTANICAL GARDENS, 230 Quail Gardens Dr., has rare plants, a waterfall and self-guiding trails. A chaparral area serves as a natural bird refuge. Guided tours are conducted Sat. at 10. Open daily 8-5. Free. Parking $1. Phone (619) 436-3036.

ENCINO (B-5) pop. 62,000, alt. 750'

LOS ENCINOS STATE HISTORIC PARK, 16756 Moorpark St., contains the restored 1849 de la Osa Adobe, a spring-fed lake, blacksmith shop and other American period buildings. The site is all that remains of Rancho El Encino, a 4,500-acre cattle and sheep ranch and stagecoach stop 1845-1915. Picnicking is permitted daily; reservations are required Sat.-Sun. House tours Wed.-Sun. 1-4. Grounds open Wed.-Sun. 10-5; closed Jan. 1, Thanksgiving and Dec. 25. Grounds free. Tours $2; ages 6-17, $1. Phone (818) 784-4849.

ESCONDIDO (K-7) pop. 108,600, alt. 654'

The Heritage Walk Museum, in Grape Day Park on Broadway near Woodward Avenue, features Escondido's first library (now the museum office), a furnished 1890 Victorian house and other 19th-century buildings, including a restored 1888 Santa Fe train depot. The museum is open Thurs.-Sat. 1-4.

Shopping areas: Escondido's favorite shopping destination is North County Fair, I-15 and Via Rancho Parkway, an enclosed mall that contains a Broadway, May Co., Robinson's and Sears.

BERNARDO WINERY, off Pomerado Rd. at 13330 Paseo del Verano Norte, offers self-guiding tours and tastings. Daily 9-5. Free. Phone (619) 487-1866.

DEER PARK, 29013 Champagne Blvd., combines a car museum and a winery. The museum occupies three buildings and displays about 70 automobiles, dating from 1903 to the 1970s. All are convertibles, including two 18-foot-long 1959 Cadillacs and a very small post-World War II Messerschmidt.

Deer Park Winery offers tours and tastings daily 10-6; picnicking is permitted. Park open daily noon-4. Admission $4; over 55, $2; under 12 free. Discount, except over 55 and during special events. Phone (619) 749-1666.

FERRARA WINERY, 1120 W. 15th Ave., produces varietal and generic wines, which can be sampled in the tasting room. The winery offers self-guiding tours. Mon.-Fri. 9-5:30, Sat.-Sun. 10-5:30. Free. Phone (619) 745-7632.

LAWRENCE WELK RESORT THEATRE, 7 mi. n. off I-15 at 8845 Lawrence Welk Dr. in the Lawrence Welk Resort, is a 330-seat dinner theater that offers musical and comedy productions. A museum contains memorabilia of Welk's life and musical career. Museum open daily at 10; closing time varies. Museum free. Phone (619) 749-3448. *See ad p. A136.*

★**SAN DIEGO WILD ANIMAL PARK** embraces 2,000 acres about 5 mi. e. of I-15, Rancho Pkwy. exit. More than 2,500 animals, including elephants, tigers, rhinos, zebras and giraffes roam over expanses of land that simulate Africa and Asia.

Visitors can view the preserve on a 50-minute monorail ride or from lookout points along a 1¾-mile walking trail. Animal and bird shows are presented daily in Nairobi Village, which also has small mammal exhibits and aviaries.

Park open daily 9-6, mid-June to Labor Day; 9-4, rest of year. Admission includes monorail, Nairobi Village, all animal shows and exhibits. Admission $16.50; over 55, $14.50; ages 3-15, $9.50. MC, VI. Parking $1. Pets are not allowed. Phone (619) 480-0100.

SAN PASQUAL BATTLEFIELD STATE HISTORIC PARK, 8 mi. e. on SR 78, covers 50 acres and commemorates an important battle in the conquest of California. In 1846, Gen. Stephen Watts Kearny and his American troops from Fort Leavenworth clashed with Californians under Gen. Andrés Pico. Thurs.-Mon. 10-5; closed Jan. 1, Thanksgiving and Dec. 25. Free. Phone (619) 238-3380 or 489-0076.

EUREKA (B-1) pop. 27,000, alt. 44'

The chief port between San Francisco Bay and the Columbia River, Eureka is a lumbering, industrial and commercial city on Humboldt Bay. Such ornate Victorian dwellings as the Carson Mansion at 2nd and M streets reflect the days of the lumber barons. Fort Humboldt, the 1853 headquarters of Gen. U.S. Grant, houses exhibits on past methods of logging. The renovated 19th-century Old Town consists of specialty shops, restaurants and art galleries and studios.

Humboldt Bay also is an important fishing port, boasting generous catches of crab, salmon, shrimp, albacore and bottom fish. Fishing fleets dock just across the Samoa bridge at the Woodley Island Marina, where a copper statue of a fisherman commemorates fishermen lost at sea. Eureka's seafaring history is chronicled at the Humboldt Bay Maritime Museum, 1410 2nd St., which displays marine artifacts and early photographs of the area.

BLUE OX MILLWORKS, at the foot of X St., 4 blks. n. of US 101, is a working mill that includes a sawmill building, moulding building, blacksmith shop and a re-creation of a logging "Skid Camp." Vintage equipment dating 1852-1940 is used in production. Visitors may watch the artisans at work via a self-guiding tour; casual dress and low-heeled shoes are advised. Allow 1 hour minimum. Mon.-Sat. 9-5, Sun. 11-4, Mar.-Sept.; Mon.-Sat. 9-5, rest of year. Admission $5; over 55, $4; ages 6-12, $2.50. Phone (707) 444-3437.

CLARKE MEMORIAL MUSEUM, 3rd and E sts., displays Indian artifacts, antique weapons and exhibits on regional and natural history. The museum also has a significant collection of northwestern California Indian basketry, including examples of Yurok, Karuk and Hupa ceremonial regalia. Allow 1 hour minimum. Tues.-Sat. noon-4; closed Jan. 1, Easter, Thanksgiving and Dec. 25. Donations. Phone (707) 443-1947.

HUMBOLDT BAY HARBOUR CRUISE leaves from the foot of C St. The M.V. *Madaket,* an original 1910 ferry, takes visitors on a cruise around Humboldt Bay. Departures require a minimum of six regular fares. Cruises depart daily 1-8, Apr.-Oct. Bring a sweater or jacket. Fare $8.50; over 60 and ages 12-17, $7.50; ages 6-11, $5.55. Cocktail cruise Tues.-Sat. at 5:30, mid-May through Sept. 30; fare $5.50. Tours of the ferry are conducted daily at 1, 2:30 and 4, June-Sept. Phone (707) 444-9440.

HUMBOLDT CULTURAL CENTER, 422 First St., sponsors exhibitions reflecting the cultural diversity of northwestern California through the visual arts, drama, music, sculpture and painting. The collections are housed in the 1875 E. Janssen and Co. building, which was once a ship's chandlery and features a narrow mezzanine with turned spindles and a spiral staircase, giving it the ap-

pearance of a ship's stern. Allow 30 minutes minimum. Tues.-Sat. 11-5, Sun. noon-5; closed major holidays. Donations. Phone (707) 442-2611.

SAMOA COOKHOUSE MUSEUM, off US 101 across the Samoa bridge, was established in the late 1800s as a large lumber camp chowhouse. The museum and dining rooms contain equipment, utensils and memorabilia from the lumber and logging industry. Daily 6-3:30 and 5-9; closed Thanksgiving and Dec. 24-25. Free. Phone (707) 442-1659.

SEQUOIA PARK, Glatt and W sts., contains a 52-acre grove of virgin redwoods, a formal flower garden, duck pond, zoo, bear grotto and deer and elk paddocks. A playground and picnic facilities are available. Park open daily 10-dusk. Zoo open Tues.-Sun. 10-7, May-Sept.; 10-5, rest of year. Petting zoo open Tues.-Sun. 11:30-3:30, mid-June through Labor Day. Free. Phone (707) 442-6552 or 443-8691.

FAIRFIELD (N-3) pop. 77,200, alt. 15'

ANHEUSER-BUSCH FAIRFIELD BREWERY TOUR, 3101 Busch Dr., is a 1½-hour guided tour of the brewery, during which the brewing process is demonstrated. A film of the brewing process also is shown. Open-toed shoes, tank tops and shorts are not permitted. Tours Mon.-Fri. at 10 and 2; reservations are required. Free. Phone (707) 429-7595.

SCANDIA FAMILY FUN CENTER, I-80 and Suisun Valley Rd., includes two 18-hole miniature golf courses, a large arcade, waterbug bumper boats, Little Indy race cars and a 10-minute train ride on the Copenhagen Express. Food is available. Allow 2 hours minimum. Indoor activities daily 10-10; outdoor activities Sun.-Thurs. 10-8:30, Fri.-Sat. 10-10. Super Saver admission, including golf, Indy cars, slick-track, boats and train, $13.75; individual prices for other rides $1.75-$5. Minigolf $5; over 65, $3; under 5 free. Phone (707) 864-8338 or 864-8558.

WESTERN RAILWAY MUSEUM, 12 mi. e. on SR 12, exhibits vintage streetcars, Key System trains, a Blackpool English open tram, a New York "L" train and other equipment. Streetcar rides from Rio Vista Junction to Dozier are available Mar.-Apr. and Sept.-Oct. Fare $10; ages 4-15, $6. Reservations are required; phone (415) 778-7245. Picnicking is permitted. Museum open Sat.-Sun. and holidays 11-5; closed Jan. 1, Thanksgiving and Dec. 25. Admission $4; ages 4-16, $2. AE, MC, VI. **Discount.** Phone (707) 374-2978.

FALL RIVER MILLS (B-3) pop. 300, alt. 3,291'

FORT CROOK MUSEUM, Fort Crook Ave., displays Indian artifacts, photographs and memorabilia from the 1800s, an authentic dug-out canoe and a 360-degree view of Fall River Mills. Next to the museum is an 1860 schoolhouse, a barn that houses a 1911 Wichita Flat-Bed Motorstage, log cabin, jailhouse and the James Showcase building. Genealogical records are available. Allow 30 minutes minimum. Daily noon-4, May-Oct. Donations. Phone (916) 336-5110.

FELTON (G-2) pop. 4,600, alt. 286′

One of the tallest covered bridges in the United States—and the only one made of redwood—can be found in Felton. Felton lies on a scenic stretch of SR 9 that extends from Los Gatos to Santa Cruz.

ROARING CAMP & BIG TREES NARROW GAUGE RAILROAD, 1 mi. s.e. on Graham Hill Rd., runs s. from the Roaring Camp Station through the redwoods of Santa Cruz County. An 1880 steam train makes a 6-mile, 75-minute round trip as the conductor recounts the history of the Santa Cruz Mountains. Picnicking is permitted at Roaring Camp; a barbecue lunch is offered Sat.-Sun., May-Oct. Departures several times daily; phone for schedule. Closed Dec. 25. Fare $11.15; ages 3-15, $8.15. AE, DS, MC, VI. Phone (408) 335-4400.

Santa Cruz Big Trees and Pacific Railway also departs the Roaring Camp station for a 2½-hour round-trip excursion to the beach boardwalk at Santa Cruz. The 1920s-style passenger coaches travel through Henry Cowell Redwoods State Park and along the San Lorenzo River Canyon. Conductors comment on the history of railroading on the central coast of California during the "golden age" of railroading, 1910-25. Departures several times daily, May-Oct.; otherwise varies, rest of year. Fare $9; ages 3-15, $3. AE, DS, MC, VI. Phone (408) 335-4400.

FERNDALE (C-1) pop. 1,300, alt. 30′

Ferndale was settled in 1852 by Vermonters Seth and Stephen Shaw, but it was Danish pioneers who established the town's dairying industry in the 1850s, producing the butter that Ferndale has been identified with ever since. The homes, known as "butterfat palaces," that the Danish and Portuguese dairymen built reflect the town's past and present. The village is a state historical landmark; it also plays host to a December Christmas gala.

The Ferndale Museum at Third and Shaw streets preserves local artifacts and memorabilia, including a blacksmith shop, seismograph, farm and logging equipment and microfilmed newspapers dating from 1878. Linden Hall, 1½ miles west of Ferndale Highway on Port Kenyon Road, is a 1901 Victorian farmhouse that features original period furnishings, gas lighting fixtures and the original parlor wallpaper.

Self-guiding tours: Brochures detailing a walking tour of the Victorian homes near the center of town can be obtained at various shops on Main Street.

FISH CAMP (F-5) pop. 100, alt. 4,990′

YOSEMITE MOUNTAIN-SUGAR PINE RAILROAD is 2 mi. s. on SR 41. The scenic narrow-gauge railroad offers 4-mile excursions aboard authentic steam-powered trains and gas-powered railcars. The scenic narrow-gauge runs daily Apr.-Oct. Departure times for the Logger steam train vary, May.-Oct.; phone ahead for schedule.

Jenny Rail cars operate daily every ½ hour from 9-4, Apr.-Oct., except when steam train is running; phone for limited winter schedule. A Moonlite Special with barbecue dinner and entertainment runs Sat. evenings, June 5-Sept. 5; reservations are recommended. Steam train $9.50; senior citizens $9; ages 3-12, $4.50. Rail cars $6.25; ages 3-12, $3. Moonlite Special $29; ages 3-12, $16. MC, VI. **Discount,** except senior citizens, rail cars and Moonlite Special. Phone (209) 683-7273.

FOLSOM (E-3) pop. 29,800, alt. 218′

A gold-mining town dating from the 1860s, Folsom retains much of its historic character. Many restored homes and buildings of that era line Sutter Street; they include the Wells Fargo Office—former terminus of the Pony Express.

At the intersection of Sutter and Wool streets is the old Southern Pacific Depot, which now houses the chamber of commerce. A Southern Pacific railcar, boxcar and caboose are on display. Alongside the cars is the 1868 Ashland Freight Depot, said to be the oldest standing station west of the Mississippi River. An old blacksmith shop and a miner's cabin are nearby.

Folsom City Park and Zoo, behind the city hall complex on Natoma Street, has picnic facilities, a children's play area and small zoo. Two miles north of town is the massive granite Folsom State Prison. An arts and gift shop at the main gate has items crafted by inmates; sales contribute to trust funds for the artists upon their release.

Shopping areas: The Natoma Station Factory Outlet, 13000 Folsom Blvd., has more than 45 factory-direct and specialty stores.

OLD POWERHOUSE, on the American River at the foot of Riley St., performed the first long-distance transmission of electric power to Sacramento in 1895. Now a state historic monument and national landmark, it is part of Folsom Lake State Recreation Area *(see Recreation Chart).* Powerhouse open Wed.-Sat. noon-4. Free tours of the powerhouse and dam are available with 2-weeks' notice. Phone (916) 988-0205 to arrange powerhouse tours and (916) 989-7275 for dam tours.

FORESTVILLE (N-1) pop. 500, alt. 63′

MARK WEST VINEYARDS & WINERY is 5½ mi. w. of US 101 via River Rd., then ½ mi. n. to 7000 Trenton-Healdsburg Rd. The family-owned winery offers tours and tastings by appointment. A picnic area is available. Daily 10:30-4. Free. Phone (707) 544-4813.

FORT BRAGG (D-1) pop. 6,100, alt. 80'

Fort Bragg was established in 1857 to oversee the Mendocino Indian Reservation. When the reservation was moved the fort was abandoned and subsequently became a lumber and port town. Noyo Harbor, at the south end of town, is a large commercial fishing port; fishing and whale-watching cruises are available. The harbor is the setting for the World's Largest Salmon BBQ, held in July.

Fort Bragg lies on a scenic stretch of SR 1 that extends from Leggett to Sausalito.

MENDOCINO COAST BOTANICAL GARDENS, 2 mi. s. on SR 1, encompasses 17 acres of lush woods, meadows and gardens. Paths lead from a nursery through the gardens, "Fern Canyon" and native forest to scenic ocean bluffs. The 1-mile loop trail to the Pacific is a leisurely 30-minute walk. Other paths pass rhododendrons and fuchsias. Free electric carts are available. Food is available.

Allow 1 hour minimum. Daily 9-5, Mar.-Oct.; 9-4, rest of year. Closed Jan. 1, Thanksgiving and Dec. 25. Admission $5; over 60, $4; students

and ages 13-17, $3. **Discount.** Phone (707) 964-4352.

SKUNK TRAIN travels from Fort Bragg, at an elevation of 80 feet, to Willits, at 1,365 feet. The scenic 40-mile trip passes through redwood groves and crosses and recrosses the Noyo River.

Full- and half-day trips daily from Fort Bragg or Willits, mid-June to mid-Sept.; full- and half-day trips daily from Fort Bragg only, rest of year. Closed Jan. 1, Thanksgiving and Dec. 25. Super Skunk, with open observation cars, also makes the run in summer. Round-trip fare $23; ages 5-11, $11.

Round trip to Northspur (3½ hours) $18.50; ages 5-11, $9. MC, VI. **Discount,** except when charged to credit card. For reservations write Skunk Train, P.O. Box 907, Fort Bragg, CA 95437; phone (707) 964-6371. *See ad.*

FORTUNA (B-1) pop. 8,800, alt. 51'

Established in 1875 as Springville, after the numerous springs in the surrounding hills, Fortuna was renamed Slide and finally, Fortuna by its "fortunate" citizens. The town is surrounded by the Redwood Empire.

CHAPMAN'S GEM AND MINERAL MUSEUM, 4 mi. s. off US 101, has displays of fossils, gems, minerals, petrified wood and Indian artifacts. Allow 30 minutes minimum. Mon.-Sat. 10-5, Sun. 1-5, May-Sept.; Wed.-Sat. 10-5, Sun.-Mon. 1-5, rest of year. Closed Easter, Thanksgiving and Dec. 25. Donations. Phone (707) 725-4732.

THE DEPOT MUSEUM, e. of US 101 in Rohner Park, presents local history exhibits in a restored Northwestern-Pacific depot. Allow 30 minutes minimum. Daily noon-5, June 1-Labor Day; Sat.-Wed. noon-5, rest of year. Free. Phone (707) 725-2495.

FREMONT (P-3) pop. 173,300, alt. 53'

Fremont was created in 1956 by the incorporation of five southeastern San Francisco Bay communities and their adjacent agricultural lands.

Spanish priests and native Uhiones founded a mission in this area in 1797. Reputedly, pioneer John Fremont, for whom the city is named, was so taken with the mission that he offered to buy the adjacent property for his home. The gold rush transformed the mission-based trade and agricultural center into a boisterous supply stop for miners. The use of salt in extracting silver from the Comstock Lode stimulated salt production along San Francisco Bay.

By the 1800s artesian springs had turned Fremont into a resort area. It was a motion picture location as well; in 1912 Essanay Studio began a 4-year production stint, and Charlie Chaplin filmed "The Tramp" in 1915.

Traces of the past remain, providing a backdrop for the futuristic city hall that overlooks

Lake Elizabeth and Central Park. Sailing on the lake is popular.

ARDENWOOD HISTORIC FARM on Ardenwood Blvd., ¼ mi. n. of SR 84, is a living-history project depicting farm life from the 1870s to the 1920s. The complex contains the Patterson house, a farmyard, gardens, period shops, picnic area and a collection of farm animals. Haywagon, carriage and horse-drawn rail car rides also are available. Thurs.-Sun. 10-4, early Apr. to mid-Nov. Admission $5; senior citizens $3; ages 4-17, $2.50. Phone (510) 796-0663.

COYOTE HILLS REGIONAL PARK is at 8000 Patterson Ranch Rd. The park is a 1,064-acre wildlife sanctuary containing 2,300-year-old Indian shell mounds and a reconstructed Indian village. The park also has more than 40 miles of hiking, bicycling and jogging trails; a boardwalk through a freshwater marsh; picnic facilities; and weekend nature programs.

Visitor center and museum open daily 9:30-5; closed Thanksgiving and Dec. 25. Park open daily 8-dusk. Fee $2.50 per private vehicle, Sat.-Sun. and holidays only, Easter-Labor Day. Leashed dogs are permitted; fee $1. Phone (510) 795-9385.

FREMONT CENTRAL PARK, 40000 Paseo Padre Pkwy., includes a waterfowl refuge, lake, library, bicycling and jogging trails and sailboat, canoe and paddleboat rentals. Picnicking is permitted. A golf driving range is located in Central Park East on Stevenson Place. Daily dawn-10 p.m. Free. Swimming fee $1.50, in summer. Phone (510) 791-4340.

★**MISSION SAN JOSE CHAPEL AND MUSEUM,** 43300 Mission Blvd., was founded in 1797. The reconstructed church has an unusually elegant interior, containing crystal chandeliers, murals, religious paintings and a goldleaf altar. The mission contains a small museum, which displays old paintings, photographs, pioneer artifacts and exhibits on the Ohlone Indians and the restoration of the mission. Slide shows are given hourly. Daily 10-5; closed Jan. 1, Easter, Thanksgiving and Dec. 25. Donations. Phone (415) 657-1797.

★**SAN FRANCISCO BAY NATIONAL WILDLIFE REFUGE**, on Marsh Land Rd., protects 20,000 acres for migratory birds using the Pacific flyway. An interpretive center overlooking the Dumbarton Bridge has dioramas depicting area wildlife as well as a changing film series and weekend interpretive walks. A fishing pier is located 2½ miles from the center. Wildlife viewing is best October through April. Open daily 10-5. Free. Phone (510) 792-0222.

WEIBEL CHAMPAGNE VINEYARDS, 1 mi. e. of I-680 at 1250 Stanford Ave., offers 15- to 20-minute guided tours Mon.-Fri. 10-3 and tastings daily 10-5; closed Dec. 25. Free. Phone (510) 656-2340.

FRESNO (G-4) pop. 354,200, alt. 294'

More than a million acres in the San Joaquin Valley are irrigated; on this land grow the grapes, figs and cotton that make Fresno County one of the nation's agricultural leaders. More turkeys are raised in this area than anywhere else in the country. The Blossom Trail is a scenic 85-mile self-guiding tour encompassing vineyards, orchards and historical points of interest.

FRESNO ART MUSEUM, 2233 N. First St. in Radio Park, offers changing exhibits of national and international artists in six galleries. The Bonner Auditorium features a Fresno Public Theater and concert series. Allow 1 hour minimum. Tues.-Sun. 10-5; closed major holidays and the last 2 weeks in Aug. Admission $2; over 60 and students over 16, $1; free to all on Tues. Phone (209) 485-4810.

FRESNO METROPOLITAN MUSEUM OF ART, HISTORY AND SCIENCE, 1555 Van Ness Ave., features an Asian art collection and the Salzer collection of European and American still life paintings displayed alternately with regional history, hands-on and temporary exhibits. Allow 1 hour minimum. Thurs.-Sun. 11-5, Wed. 11-7. Admission $3; senior citizens $2; ages 4-12, $1.50; free to all on Wed. Phone (209) 441-1444.

GOLDEN EAGLE AIR TOURS, 4885 E. Shields at the Fresno Airport, depart from the Fresno Air Terminal. The 90-minute flights tour Yosemite Valley, Tuolumne Meadows and the Cathedral and Ritter ranges. Allow 1 hour, 30 minutes minimum. Daily May-Oct.; winter reservations, weather permitting. Fare $109; ages 5-11, $69. DS, MC, VI. Reservations are required. Phone (209) 251-7501 or (800) 622-8687.

KEARNEY MANSION MUSEUM, 7 mi. w. at 7160 W. Kearney Blvd. in Kearney Park, was the home of one of the county's agricultural pioneers. The French Renaissance-style house contains many original furnishings and wallcoverings. Allow 1 hour minimum. Guided tours only Fri.-Sun. 1-4; closed holidays. Last tour departs 30 minutes before closing. Admission $3 ($4 in Dec.); students and ages 13-17, $2; ages 3-12, $1. **Discount**, except students and ages 3-17. Phone (209) 441-0862.

MEUX HOME MUSEUM, 1007 R St. at Tulare, was built in 1889 by Dr. Thomas R. Meux. The Victorian home contains some original furnishings and wall coverings and features Dr. Meux's office. Guided 45-minute tours are available. Thurs.-Sun. noon-3:30, June-Aug.; Fri.-Sun. noon-3:30, rest of year. Admission $3; ages 13-17, $2; ages 5-12, $1. Phone (209) 233-8007.

ROEDING PARK, US 99 via the Olive Ave. or Belmont Ave. exits, has a zoo, museum, recreational facilities, amusement rides and a variety of trees and other plants. Allow 1 hour, 30 minutes minimum. Chaffee Zoological Gardens open daily 10-6:30, Apr.-Sept.; 10-5, rest of year. Admission $4; over 61, $2.50; ages 4-14, $1.50. Fee $1 per private vehicle. Phone (209) 488-1111. Fort Miller Blockhouse Museum open Sat.-Sun. 1-4, May-Sept. Donations. Phone (209) 441-0862.

Storyland is a children's attraction with a fairytale theme featuring a castle and a giant beanstalk. Daily 10-5, May 1-Labor Day; Sat.-Sun., holidays and vacation periods 10-5, rest of year. Closed Dec. 1-Feb. 15. Admission $2.75; ages 3-14, $1.75. Phone (209) 264-2235.

WILD WATER ADVENTURES, 11413 E. Shaw Ave., 7 mi. e. of Clovis Ave., is a 50-acre water park offering water slides and flumes, a wave pool, large swimming pool, wading pool and a small fishing lake. Picnic facilities and food are available. Glass items and containers are not permitted. Daily 11-7, mid-June through Labor Day; Sat.-Sun. 10-7, mid-May to mid-June and day after Labor Day to mid-Sept. Admission $14.95, over age 62 and under 48 inches tall $8.95, under 2 free; reduced rates after 5 p.m. MC, VI. Phone (209) 438-9453.

FULLERTON (C-7) pop. 114,100, alt. 157'

MUCKENTHALER CULTURAL CENTER, 1201 W. Malvern Ave., was built in 1924 in the Italian Renaissance style. The first floor houses changing art exhibits. Dinner theater performances are held in the summer. Gallery open Tues.-Sat. 10-4, Sun. noon-5; closed major holidays. Donations. Phone (714) 738-6595.

GARDEN GROVE (C-7) pop. 143,000, alt. 85'

CRYSTAL CATHEDRAL OF THE REFORMED CHURCH IN AMERICA, Chapman Ave. and Lewis St., is an all-glass sanctuary enclosed by 10,000 mirrored windows; it was designed by Philip Johnson. The tower of the cathedral contains a 52-bell carillon. Tours Mon.-Sat. 9-3:30 (church functions affect tour times); closed major holidays. Donations. Phone (714) 971-4013.

GEYSERVILLE (M-1) pop. 1,000, alt. 209'

LAKE SONOMA VISITOR CENTER, 3333 Skaggs Springs Rd., displays local flora and fauna and provides information on recreational activities in the Lake Sonoma/Warm Springs Dam area. Catfish, small-mouthed bass and steelhead are raised at the Don Clausen Fish Hatchery. A developed swim area is available at Yorty Creek. Allow 2 hours minimum. Daily 10-6, in summer; Mon. and Thurs.-Fri. 9-4, Sat.-Sun. 10-5, rest of year. Free. Phone (707) 433-9483.

GILROY (G-3) pop. 31,500, alt. 194'

When Scotsman John Cameron jumped a British ship in Monterey Bay and traveled to the Ortega Ranch, he adopted his mother's maiden name, Gilroy, and married the ranch owner's daughter. A small town developed around his property; orchards were planted and cattle introduced, and the railroad found its way to the settlement. By 1870 Gilroy had lost the ranch to gambling debts but the town was incorporated and continued to thrive.

The Gilroy Historical Museum, in the Carnegie Library Building on the corner of Fifth and Church streets, displays historical photographs and artifacts of the area. The Garlic Festival in late July offers food, entertainment and arts and crafts.

Self-guiding tours: A booklet detailing a self-guiding walking tour of historic Fifth Street can be obtained from the Gilroy Historical Museum at 2nd and 4th sts.; phone (408) 848-0470.

GLENDALE (B-6) pop. 180,000, alt. 563'

At the east entrance to the San Fernando Valley, Glendale occupies the first land grant in California, given in 1784 by King Charles IV of Spain.

Shopping areas: The Glendale Galleria, a 250-store mall featuring Broadway, JCPenney, Mervyn's and Nordstrom, is bounded by Broadway, Central Avenue, Colorado Street and Columbus Avenue.

BRAND LIBRARY AND ART CENTER, 1601 W. Mountain St. in Brand Park, is a 1904 Moorish-style mansion with an art and music library and gallery, and studio and performance facilities. Wed. and Fri.-Sat. 12:30-6, Tues. and Thurs. 12:30-9; closed holidays. Free. Phone (818) 548-2051.

★FOREST LAWN MEMORIAL-PARK, 1712 S. Glendale Ave., comprises 300 landscaped acres and contains a collection of large Carrara marble statuary and stained-glass windows. The Memorial Terrace houses a stained-glass re-creation of Leonardo da Vinci's "Last Supper," shown daily on the half-hour 9:30-4. In the Hall of the Crucifixion-Resurrection is one of the world's largest religious oil paintings, Jan Styka's 45- by 195-foot "Crucifixion." Its companion, "Resurrection," is 51 by 70 feet. Both paintings are shown daily on the hour 10-4. Donations.

The Forest Lawn Museum displays all types of coins mentioned in the Bible, a famous gem collection, American bronze statuary, 11th- to 15th-century stained glass and a Michelangelo exhibit. Park open daily 9-6, in summer; 9-5, rest of year. Free. Phone (213) 254-3131.

GLEN ELLEN (N-2) pop. 1,000, alt. 230'

JACK LONDON STATE HISTORIC PARK, 800 acres 1 mi. w., encompasses the author's ranch, home and grave. The two-story house contains his papers, personal belongings and mementos of his travels, including South Pacific art objects. The burnt ruins of Wolf House, the 26-room mansion he built but never lived in, are nearby. No off-road vehicles are allowed. Allow 1 hour, 30 minutes minimum.

Museum open daily 10-5; closed Jan. 1, Thanksgiving and Dec. 25. Park open daily 10-7. Fee $5 per private vehicle, senior citizens $4 per private vehicle. Leashed dogs are permitted; fee $1. Phone (707) 938-5216. *See Recreation Chart.*

GOLDEN GATE NATIONAL RECREATION AREA (O-1)

Golden Gate National Recreation Area encompasses both the rolling coastal hill country north of the Golden Gate Bridge and the diverse urban parklands strung around San Francisco's northern and western edges. For a description of the parkland in the city see the Golden Gate National Recreation Area box under San Francisco.

The Marin Headlands across the Golden Gate Bridge contrast dramatically with the cityscape to the south. Smooth grassy ridges slope down through valleys to a craggy shoreline scalloped with sandy coves. Abandoned gun emplacements stud the hillsides above the Golden Gate and provide good vantage points for viewing the bridge and the city.

Northward from the Marin Headlands are Mount Tamalpais State Park *(see Mill Valley)* and Muir Woods National Monument *(see place listing).* Beyond the state park, the Olema Valley section of the recreation area abuts Point Reyes National Seashore *(see place listing).*

About 100 miles of hiking and riding trails traverse the pastoral countryside between Point Reyes and the Golden Gate. Hikers should stay on the trails, as the hillsides are often laced with poison oak. Because of the cool ocean winds and frequent fog, visitors should be prepared for changeable weather. Swimming is permitted only at Stinson Beach. Back-country campsites are available and require reservations. Fishing spots and picnic facilities are scattered throughout the parklands.

The Bay Area Discovery Museum in East Fort Baker is an interactive children's museum. The Building the City exhibit investigates the design and construction of homes, buildings and cities. The San Francisco Bay exhibit explores the impact and development of pollution on commerce, fishing, navigation, and animal and plant life.

The California Marine Mammal Center, 4 miles west of US 101 in Sausalito, is an animal hospital that rescues and rehabilitates sick, injured or distressed marine animals from the California coast. Self-guiding tours are available.

For further information write the General Superintendent, Golden Gate National Recreation Area, Building 201, Fort Mason, San Francisco, CA 94123; phone (415) 556-0560. *See Recreation Chart.*

GONZALES (G-3) pop. 4,700, alt. 131'

THE MONTEREY VINEYARD, 800 S. Alta St., offers tastings and guided tours of the aging cellars. An Ansel Adams collection of black and white photographs that demonstrate the making of wine from the bud on the vine to the final product is on permanent display. Guided tours Mon.-Wed. at noon, 2 and 3; Thurs.-Sun. on the hour. Allow 1 hour minimum. Open daily 10-5; closed major holidays. Free. Phone (408) 675-2316.

GRASS VALLEY (D-3) pop. 9,000, alt. 2,420'

In 1850, George Knight stubbed his toe on a piece of quartz laced with gold and put Grass Valley on the map. Aided by advanced mining techniques that were first developed and used in this region, Grass Valley ultimately became the richest gold-mining town in California. Unlike most gold rush towns, Grass Valley's prosperity outlasted its mining industry. Agriculture, high-tech manufacturing and tourism now anchor the local economy.

EMPIRE MINE STATE HISTORIC PARK, 1 mi. e. of SR 49 at 10791 E. Empire St., produced nearly 6 million ounces of gold during its operation. The park has 10 miles of hiking trails and a mine with 367 miles of passageways; restored buildings include the owner's cottage, clubhouse, a blacksmith shop, a hoist house and a machine shop. Films are shown daily at the visitor center. Tours and lectures are offered daily.

Allow 2 hours minimum. Grounds and gardens open daily 9-5, early May-early June; 9-6, early June-early Sept.; 10-5, rest of year. Visitor center closed Thanksgiving and Dec. 25. Admission $2; ages 6-17, $1; dogs $1. Phone (916) 273-8522. *See Recreation Chart.*

PELTON WHEEL MINING MUSEUM, on Allison Ranch Rd. at the s. end of Mill St., houses the Pelton Wheel and early mining equipment. The museum features one of the few operable Cornish pumps in the country. Daily 10-5, May-Oct. Donations. Phone (916) 273-4255.

GROVELAND (F-4) pop. 400, alt. 2,846'

ARTA RIVER TRIPS offers 1- to 3-day whitewater raft trips on the American, Merced, Tuolumne, Stanislaus and California Salmon rivers. Meals are provided. Some trips are not suitable for beginners. Trips daily, Apr.-Oct. One-day trips $80-$225. MC, VI. Reservations are recommended; refund policies vary. Write ARTA River Trips, Star Route 73, Groveland, CA 95321. Phone (209) 962-7873 or (800) 323-2782.

GUERNEVILLE (M-1) pop. 1,500, alt. 56'

KORBEL CHAMPAGNE CELLARS, 13250 River Rd., produces champagnes and brandy. Wine tastings and guided tours of the champagne cellars are available. Picnicking is permitted. Allow

30 minutes minimum. Tours Mon.-Fri. 10-3:45, Sat.-Sun. and holidays 10-noon and 12:45-3:45, May-Oct.; daily 10-3, rest of year. Tour times vary. Tastings 9-5, May-Sept.; 9-4:30, rest of year. Garden tours also are offered 10-3, May-Oct. Free. Phone (707) 887-2294.

HALF MOON BAY (Q-2) pop. 8,900, alt. 69'

Half Moon Bay has many sandy beaches for walking and exploring. The bay is a popular launching spot for sightseeing, fishing and whale-watching cruises; contact Huck Finn Sport Fishing. The Art and Pumpkin Festival is held in late October.

Half Moon Bay lies on a scenic stretch of SR 1 that extends from San Francisco to San Luis Obispo.

HANFORD (H-4) pop. 30,900, alt. 248'

Founded in 1882 in the San Joaquin Valley, Hanford was named for a Southern Pacific Railroad paymaster who became a power in the community. He paid millions of dollars of workers' wages in gold. Hanford once claimed one of the largest Chinese communities in California. In China Alley, a remnant of that community, are the Taoist Temple and a landmark restaurant operated by the descendants of the family who started the business in 1883.

Courthouse Square, the center of historic Hanford, includes the Kings County courthouse and the old brick jailhouse. Both have been renovated and now house shops, offices and a restaurant. Also on the square are an antique merry-go-round and ferris wheel and many specialty shops.

Self-guiding tours: Maps for self-guiding tours of historic Hanford are available at the chamber of commerce, 432 W. 7th St., Hanford, CA 93230; phone (209) 582-0483. Guided tours also can be arranged.

HANFORD CARNEGIE MUSEUM, 109 E. 8th St., contains exhibits depicting the history of Hanford and Kings County, including clothes, furniture, photographs and other items. Guided tours are available. Allow 30 minutes minimum. Tues.-Fri. noon-3. Free.

HAYWARD (P-3) pop. 111,500, alt. 111'

HAYWARD AREA HISTORICAL SOCIETY MUSEUM, 22701 Main St., is a former post office that houses memorabilia of early Hayward and southern Alameda County. Photographs, maps, tools and a vintage fire truck are on display. Changing exhibits also are presented. Allow 1 hour minimum. Mon.-Fri. 11-4, Sat. noon-4. Admission $1; ages 6-12, 50c. Phone (510) 581-0223.

JAPANESE GARDENS, 22372 N. Third St. off Crescent Ave., encompasses 3⅓ acres of Japanese and native California trees, rocks and plants arranged in the traditional Japanese style. The area includes a small pond containing koi and goldfish and a teahouse. Daily 10-4. Free. Phone (510) 881-6715.

THE McCONAGHY HOME & CARRIAGE HOUSE, 18701 Hesperian Blvd. next to Kennedy Park, is a spacious 1886 home, restored and furnished in period. A carriage house contains a jump-seat buggy and other vehicles of the era. Between the two buildings is a tank house that once pumped water for the estate. Allow 1 hour minimum. Guided tours Thurs.-Sun. 1-4, Feb.-Dec. Admission $2; senior citizens $1.50; ages 6-12, 50c. Special rates apply Dec. 25. Phone (510) 276-3010.

HEALDSBURG (M-1) pop. 9,500, alt. 106'

Healdsburg, founded in 1867, was once a part of the 48,800-acre Sotoyome Rancho owned by widow Josefa Fitch and her 11 children. While Fitch and her family sought refuge at Sutter's Fort during Indian uprisings and the Mexican War, Harmon Heald and many other failed gold miners illegally squatted on her land. Fitch won ownership of the original title to the rancho, but Heald donated some of the rancho he had bought for a park, school, cemetery and church and then named this new town after himself.

Self-guiding tours: Maps for self-guiding tours of Healdsburg are available at the chamber of commerce, 217 Healdsburg Ave., Healdsburg, CA 95448; phone (707) 433-6935, or (800) 648-9922 out of Calif.

JOHNSON'S ALEXANDER VALLEY WINES is 7 mi. s.e. at 8333 SR 128. Tastings and tours are offered. The winery also contains a 1925 theater pipe organ. Picnic facilities are available. Daily 10-5; closed Jan. 1, Thanksgiving and Dec. 25. Free. Phone (707) 433-2319.

SIMI WINERY, US 101 to Dry Creek Rd., e. to Healdsburg Ave., then 1 mi. n., offers tours and tastings. Allow 1 hour minimum. Tours daily at 11, 1 and 3; tastings 10-4:30. Closed major holidays. Tours and tastings free; fee charged for tastings of premium wines, by reservation. Picnicking is permitted. Phone (707) 433-6981.

★HEARST SAN SIMEON STATE HISTORICAL MONUMENT—see San Simeon.

HEMET (C-9) pop. 36,100, alt. 1,597'

RAMONA PAGEANT is a dramatization of Helen Hunt Jackson's 1884 novel, presented in the Ramona Bowl, 2 mi. s.e., Sat.-Sun. afternoons, late Apr.-early May. This historical revival has been presented every spring since 1923 and has a cast of more than 350. Send a request for a ticket application form with a stamped reply envelope to: Ramona Pageant Assoc., 27400 Ramona Bowl Rd., Hemet, CA 92544. Phone (909) 658-3111.

HOLLYWOOD (B-6) pop. 165,800, alt. 300'

Hollywood began as a religion-oriented agricultural community in 1903 and became part of

Los Angeles in 1910. A year later the first motion picture studio was established, and the fabulous legends of Hollywood began.

In keeping with the legends, the "Walk of Fame" extends for about a mile along Hollywood Boulevard between Gower Street and La Brea Avenue, and along a portion of Vine Street south of Hollywood Boulevard. Large metal stars embedded in the sidewalk honor past and present stars of the entertainment industry.

Today several major studios produce motion pictures, while some 60 independent studios are largely engaged in television productions. Entering the studios usually requires a personal contact, but some lots do have tours (see Burbank and Universal City).

ABC, CBS, FOX and NBC television studios offer a variety of audience participation shows (see Studio Tours, Los Angeles). The Playboy Jazz Festival in mid-June and the Hollywood Christmas Parade in late November are two of the town's events.

GUINNESS WORLD OF RECORDS MUSEUM, 6764 Hollywood Blvd., has video and hands-on displays illustrating historical and statistical information. Sun.-Thurs. 10 a.m.-midnight, Fri.-Sat. 10 a.m.-2 a.m.; closed major holidays. Admission $7.50; over 65, $6.50; ages 6-12, $5. Phone (213) 463-6433.

★**HOLLYWOOD BOWL** occupies a natural amphitheater in the foothills off Highland Ave. just w. of Cahuenga Blvd. Seating 18,000, the bowl plays host to concerts by the Los Angeles Philharmonic and the Hollywood Bowl Orchestra Tues.-Sat. at 8:30 p.m., Sunday Sunset Series at 7:30 p.m., early July to mid-Sept.

Ticket prices vary; student and senior citizen discounts are available the day before and the day of the performance, except Fri.-Sat. AE, MC, VI. Discount, except during special events. Easter sunrise services are held each year. Grounds open daily 9-5. Phone (213) 850-2000; for tickets phone (213) 480-3232.

Hollywood Bowl Museum near the pedestrian and vehicle entrance to the bowl grounds, has changing exhibits on the musical and visual arts of Southern California. Tues.-Sat. 9:30-8:30, July 1 to mid-Sept.; otherwise varies, rest of year. Free. Phone (213) 850-2058.

HOLLYWOOD STUDIO MUSEUM, e. side of Highland Ave. at the edge of the Hollywood Bowl parking area, is where Cecil B. DeMille made Hollywood's first Western, "The Squaw Man," in 1913. The museum houses filmmaking exhibits, early camera equipment, memorabilia of early film stars, a screening room and a replica of DeMille's office.

Thurs.-Fri. noon-4, Sat.-Sun. 10-4, in summer; Sat.-Sun. 10-4, rest of year. Closed holidays. Admission $3.50; over 55 and students with ID $2.50; ages 6-12, $1.50. Discount, except over

55, students with ID, ages 6-12 and during special screenings. Phone (213) 874-2276.

HOLLYWOOD WAX MUSEUM, 6767 Hollywood Blvd., presents life-size figures of people and sets, including displays on television, motion pictures, politics and religion. Low-heeled shoes are advised. Sun.-Thurs. 10 a.m.-midnight, Fri.-Sat. 10 a.m.-2 a.m.; closed major holidays. Admission $8; over 65, $6.50; ages 6-12, $5. Phone (213) 463-6433.

★**MANN'S CHINESE THEATRE** is at 6925 Hollywood Blvd. The handprints and footprints of many past and present stars are imprinted in the concrete of the courtyard in front of the theater.

SIGHTSEEING TOURS are a good way to see Hollywood's landmarks and celebrities' homes. Tour lengths and prices vary according to destination. Reservations should be made 24 hours in advance. Consult the telephone directory for other listings.

Hollywood Fantasy Tours, 6773 Hollywood Blvd., offers narrated tours of Beverly Hills and Hollywood daily, some in doubledecker, open-top buses. Fare $15-$25, depending on tour; $40 for combination tour. Phone (213) 469-8184 or (800) 782-7287.

HOOPA (B-2) pop. 1,000, alt. 300'

HOOPA TRIBAL MUSEUM, on SR 96 in the Hoopa Shopping Mall, displays baskets, jewelry, tools, a redwood canoe, hats and ceremonial clothing still used in Hupa tribal events. Tours may be arranged by appointment to the ceremonial grounds, Indian villages and the ruins of Fort Gaston, built in 1851, which includes a dwelling once occupied by Ulysses S. Grant. Allow 30 minutes minimum. Mon.-Fri. 8-5, Sat. 9-2, May-Sept.; Mon.-Fri. 8-5, rest of year. Donations. Phone (916) 625-4110.

HUNTINGTON BEACH (C-6) pop. 200,000, alt. 28'

Named after Henry E. Huntington, who brought the Pacific Electric Railway to what was then a small seaside village, Huntington Beach was incorporated in 1909. In 1920, an oil boom increased the population from 1,500 to 5,000 in less than a month, and in the following years agriculture and oil provided a base for continued growth. Huntington Beach is one of Orange County's larger cities; among its many amenities are beaches, parks and shopping centers.

Along the Pacific Coast Highway between Goldenwest Street and Brookhurst Street, Bolsa Chica, Huntington City and Huntington State beaches provide areas for swimming, picnicking and surfing. Parking fees are charged. The Huntington Beach International Surf Museum at 411 Olive Ave. has a collection of surfboards, photographs and other memorabilia commemorating this ocean sport.

Bolsa Chica Ecological Reserve, opposite the entrance to Bolsa Chica State Beach off the Pacific Coast Highway, is a wetland area that supports such rare waterfowl as avocets, egrets, plovers and terns. A walkway with explanatory signs leads through the reserve.

The largest of the city's many parks is Huntington Central Park, on Goldenwest Street between Slater and Ellis avenues. The park is home to hundreds of bird species, with walking and bicycling trails that wind past ponds, waterways and groves. Huntington Beach Central Library, 7111 Talbert Ave., has indoor fountains and one of the state's largest genealogy departments.

Shopping areas: Huntington Beach Mall, at Beach Boulevard and Center Avenue near I-405, has Broadway, JCPenney, Mervyn's and Montgomery Ward as well as specialty shops. Old World Village, across Center Avenue from the mall, maintains a Bavarian atmosphere with cobblestone streets winding among specialty shops and restaurants.

Seacliff Village, at Yorktown Avenue and Main Street, offers a few specialty shops and outdoor mosaics, murals, sculpture and showcase exhibits depicting Southern California waterfowl.

IDYLLWILD (K-7) pop. 3,000, alt. 5,303'

A mountain town within the southern unit of the San Bernardino National Forest *(see place listing)*, Idyllwild provides access to many recreational facilities and is the site of the 205-acre campus of the Idyllwild School of Music and the Arts.

INDEPENDENCE (G-6) pop. 1,000, alt. 3,925'

EASTERN CALIFORNIA MUSEUM, 3 blks. w. of the courthouse at 155 Grant St., illustrates the area's history, anthropology, botany and geology. Highlights include antique farm and mining equipment. Little Pine Village features restored and re-created structures from the 1880s, including a blacksmith shop and assay office. Wed.-Mon. 10-4; closed major holidays. Donations. Phone (619) 878-2411, ext. 2258.

INDIO (K-8) pop. 36,800, alt. -22'

Often called the date capital of the nation, Indio is a distribution point for the dates, grapefruit, grapes and melons produced in the Coachella Valley. The Riverside County Fair/National Date Festival is held in mid-February.

COACHELLA VALLEY MUSEUM AND CULTURAL CENTER, 82616 Miles Ave., is in a former home and medical office built in 1926. The museum displays Indian artifacts, old farm and household equipment and changing art exhibits. A large relief map shows the development of the desert's water system; dioramas explain the date-growing industry. Wed.-Sat. 10-4, Sun. 1-4, Oct.-May; Fri.-Sun. only, in June and Sept. Closed major holidays. Admission $1; senior citizens and under 12, 50c. Phone (619) 342-6651.

GENERAL PATTON MEMORIAL MUSEUM, 28 mi. e. off I-10 at Chiriaco Summit, is built on the site of the Gen. George S. Patton Desert Training Center. The museum contains World War II memorabilia, including displays of tanks and artillery. A 26-minute video highlights the general's life and career. The development of Southern California's water system and 11 desert training camp sites are indicated on a relief map. Daily 9-5. Admission $2.50; senior citizens, $2.25; under 12 free. Phone (619) 774-7388.

INDUSTRY (B-7) pop. 600, alt. 329'

HOMESTEAD MUSEUM, 15415 E. Don Julian Rd., consists of two main buildings. The Workman house is an 1842 adobe structure, later remodeled to incorporate mid-19th-century architectural elements; La Casa Nueva is a 1920s Spanish-Colonial Revival-style mansion noted for its craftmanship. A gallery contains exhibits on Southern California history. Tours are conducted on the hour Tues.-Fri. 1-4, Sat.-Sun. 10-4; closed holidays and the fourth weekend of each month. Free. Phone (818) 968-8492.

INGLEWOOD (B-6) pop. 109,600, alt. 118'

An annual Inglewood event in mid-February is the Times/Eagle Indoor Games.

THE GREAT WESTERN FORUM, 3900 W. Manchester Blvd. at Prairie Ave., is a Roman-inspired sports and entertainment arena, home of Los Angeles' professional basketball and ice hockey teams—the Lakers and the Kings—as well as the Strings tennis team. Parking $6. Phone (310) 673-1300.

HOLLYWOOD PARK, 1050 S. Prairie Ave. at Century Blvd., is one of the West Coast's largest racetracks. Open for racing Wed.-Sun., mid-Apr. to late July and mid-Nov. to late Dec.; post time 1 p.m. Admission $6-$25, under 17 free. Program and parking free. Phone (310) 419-1500.

INYO NATIONAL FOREST

Inyo National Forest parallels US 6 and US 395 for 165 miles between the eastern California towns of Inyokern and Lee Vining. Mount Whitney, at 14,494 feet, is the highest point in the contiguous United States. The forest also contains portions of the Pacific Crest Trail and the John Muir Trail. The eastern escarpment of the Sierra Nevada and the Ancient Bristlecone Pine Forest in the White Mountains rise to 14,246 feet between US 6 and the Nevada border. Almost all of the Sierra's highest peaks are within 10 to 15 miles of US 395.

Vehicle travel is restricted in the Devils Postpile National Monument (see place listing) and the Reds Meadow area of the forest: Only vehicles with camping permits are allowed beyond the Minaret Vista turnoff between 7:30 a.m. and 5:30 p.m., June 1-Labor Day.

All others are required to use a shuttle bus that operates during the restricted times. The 2-hour round trip makes 10 stops, including the Devils Postpile ranger station, where trails lead to recreation areas. Tickets and schedule and fare information are available at the Mammoth Mountain Inn. Parking is free.

Gondola rides to the top of Mammoth Mountain provide outstanding views and access to hiking trails. Gondola rides are available daily 9 3:30, mid-June to mid-Sept. Fare $8; ages 5-13, $4. Phone (619) 934-2571.

Minaret Vista, at 9,175 feet, offers a sweeping view of the Ritter Range. A store and cafe, as well as saddle and pack horses, are available at Reds Meadow. Permits are required for all overnight trips in wilderness areas. Contact the U.S. Forest Service at Mammoth Ranger District, (619) 924-5500, P.O. Box 148, Mammoth Lakes, CA 93546; Mono Lake Ranger District, (619) 647-6525, P.O. Box 429, Lee Vining, CA 93541; Mount Whitney Ranger District, (619) 876-5542, P.O. Box 8, Lone Pine, CA 93545; or White Mountain Ranger District, (619) 873-2500, 798 N. Main St., Bishop, CA 93514.

Roads throughout the remainder of the forest provide a variety of scenic drives. An interagency visitor center is south of Lone Pine at the junction of US 395 and SR 136; daily 8-4:30; hours are extended in summer. Closed Jan. 1, Thanksgiving and Dec. 24-25. Phone (619) 876-4252. See Recreation Chart and the AAA California and Nevada CampBook.

BISHOP CREEK CANYON is w. of Bishop on SR 168. Camping, hiking and fishing are permitted.

JUNE LAKE LOOP RECREATION AREA covers approximately 60,000 acres and contains portions of the Pacific Crest Trail, the John Muir Trail, Mono Basin National Forest Scenic Area (see place listing) and June Mountain Winter Sports Area. Mono Craters, Lee Vining Canyon, Tioga Pass and Lee Vining Ranger Station are nearby. Phone (619) 647-6595.

IRVINE (C-7) pop. 110,300, alt. 208'

Irvine is a planned community built on the Irvine Ranch, a former Spanish land grant. Old Town Irvine on Sand Canyon Rd. incorporates historic buildings that were once part of the Irvine Ranch. A lima bean warehouse built in 1895 now houses shops and a restaurant; former grain silos have become one wing of a major hotel; and among smaller buildings built in the early 1900s, one is now a post office. The Irvine campus of the University of California overlooks the upper end of Newport Bay.

IRVINE MEADOWS AMPHITHEATRE, 8808 Irvine Center Dr., presents outdoor concerts for audiences of up to 15,000 people. A large picnic area and parking lot are adjacent. Performances are offered at 8 p.m., Mar.-Oct. Amphitheater and lawn seating cost $18-$30. Phone (714) 855-2863.

WILD RIVERS WATERPARK, 8770 Irvine Center Dr., encompasses 20 acres devoted to more than 40 water rides and attractions. The park includes wave pools, wading pools, sunbathing areas, waterslides, curving flumes, picnic areas and a video game arcade.

Daily 10-8, mid-June through Labor Day; Sat.-Sun. and holidays 11-5, mid-May to mid-June and day after Labor Day Sept. 30. Admission $15.95; ages 3-9, $12.95; over 55, spectators and all after 4 p.m., $8.95. Admission includes all rides. MC, VI. Parking $3. Phone (714) 768-9453.

JACKSON (E-3) pop. 3,600, alt. 1,200'

Many buildings along Jackson's narrow streets were destroyed by fire in 1862 and subsequently rebuilt. North of town are several mine headframes; one shaft is approximately 6,000 feet deep.

AMADOR COUNTY MUSEUM is at 225 Church St. The museum features a working scale model of the Kennedy Mine. Allow 30 minutes minimum. Wed.-Sun. 10-4. Donations. Mine model tour (Sat.-Sun. or by appointment only) $1. Phone (209) 223-6386.

JAMESTOWN (F-3) pop. 2,200, alt. 1,405'

The first gold discovery in Tuolumne County was made near Jamestown in 1848. "Jimtown," as it was once called, has served as a backdrop for such movies as "High Noon" and "Butch Cassidy and the Sundance Kid." Several buildings in town date back to the 1870s.

RAILTOWN 1897 STATE HISTORIC PARK, on 5th Ave., comprises 26 acres which include a roundhouse, station, trains and yard facilities. Visitors can observe the maintenance and restoration of the railroad equipment. Guided tours include a slide presentation. Train rides are offered Sat.-Sun. and holidays. Tours offered daily 10-4, mid-May through Labor Day. Admission $2.50; ages 3-12, $1.50. Train fare $9; ages 3-12, $4.50. Phone (209) 984-3953.

JENNER (E-1) pop. 300, alt. 12'

FORT ROSS STATE HISTORIC PARK, 12 mi. n. on SR 1, was the site of a trading post and fort established by Russians in 1812. In 1841, Capt. John Sutter purchased and partially dismantled it. Further damage was done by the 1906 earthquake and by fire in 1970 and 1971. Restored or reconstructed buildings include the chapel, stockade, officers' barracks, commandant's house, blockhouses, a museum and a visitor center.

A special event is Living History Day on the last Saturday in July; admission $6. Russian Orthodox services are held on Memorial Day and July 4. Allow 1 hour minimum. Daily 10-4:30; closed Jan. 1, Thanksgiving and Dec. 25. Fee $5 per private vehicle; over 62, $4 per private vehicle. Phone (707) 847-3286. *See Recreation Chart.*

JOHNSVILLE (D-3)

PLUMAS-EUREKA STATE PARK AND MUSEUM, 4 mi. w. on CR A14 at 310 Johnsville Rd., has a collection of photographs, tools and memorabilia of mining days. A partially restored stamp mill is featured. Allow 30 minutes minimum. Museum open daily 8-4:30, June 15-Sept. 15. Park open year-round; camping available May Sept. Closed Jan. 1, Thanksgiving and Dec. 25. Admission $2, children $1. Phone (916) 836-2380. *See Recreation Chart.*

JOSHUA TREE NATIONAL MONUMENT (K-8)

Joshua Tree National Monument covers more than 870 square miles north of I-10 and east of Desert Hot Springs. This California desert country contains striking granite formations and mountain ranges rising from flat valleys about 1,000 feet above sea level to elevations of nearly 6,000 feet. The many spectacular desert plants include Joshua trees, cactuses, ocotillos, smoke trees, palo verdes, piñon pines, Mojave yuccas and a fine array of spring wildflowers.

The desert also supports a wide variety of wildlife, including many resident and migratory birds. The largest animal to be found is the desert bighorn.

Wood, gas and supplies must be carried into all of the monument's nine primitive campgrounds, and water must be carried into all but Cottonwood and Black Rock. There are entrance stations at Cottonwood Spring and Twentynine Palms. The Cottonwood station has variable hours. The Oasis Visitor Center at Twentynine Palms has displays providing an introduction to the flora, fauna and history of the desert monument. The center is open daily 8-4:30; closed Dec. 25. Park admission $5 per vehicle.

Direct inquiries to the Superintendent, Joshua Tree National Monument, 74485 National Monument Dr., Twentynine Palms, CA 92277-3597; phone (619) 367-7511. Phone MISTIX at (800) 444-7275 for reservations. *See the AAA California and Nevada CampBook.*

JULIAN (K-7) pop. 1,300, alt. 4,220'

Julian is a early 1900s mining town known for its spring wildflowers and autumn apple harvest. Orchards cover the surrounding land, and fall festivals celebrate the harvests. Such apple products as pies and cider are popular.

EAGLE MINING CO., n. end of C St., offers a guided tour through a gold mine. Dug into a hill, the mine brought gold seekers into the area more than 100 years ago. During the 1½-hour tour, visitors learn of the mine's history and the various methods for extracting the shiny mineral. Daily 10-3, weather permitting; closed major holidays. Admission $6; under 16, $3. Phone (619) 765-0036.

JULIAN PIONEER MUSEUM, 2811 Washington St., housed in a late 1800s structure, contains an assortment of 19th-century clothing, household furnishings, tools and photographs of early Julian. There also are Indian artifacts and stuffed and mounted animals indigenous to the area. Tues.-Sun. 10-4, Apr.-Nov.; Sat.-Sun. and some holidays 10-4, rest of year. Closed Jan. 1, Thanksgiving and Dec. 25. Donations. Phone (619) 765-0227.

KELSEYVILLE (E-2) pop. 1,600, alt. 1,386'

Called the "Bartlett Pear Capital of the World," Kelseyville is the agricultural center of Lake County. Pear and walnut orchards share the surrounding valley with vineyards.

CLEAR LAKE STATE PARK VISITORS CENTER, 4 mi. n.e. at 5300 Soda Bay Rd., has wildlife dioramas and exhibits depicting the lake environment both on land and in water. A theater presents videos, films and demonstrations. Allow 1 hour minimum. Daily 10-4, June 15-Sept. 30. Park admission $5 per private vehicle, senior citizens $4 per private vehicle. Phone (707) 279-4293. *See Recreation Chart.*

KENWOOD (N-2) pop. 1,000, alt. 415'

Wine Country Wagons offers horse-drawn tours of the vineyards and wineries of the Valley of the Moon (**discount**). A gourmet picnic is included. Reservations are required; phone (707) 833-2724.

CHATEAU ST. JEAN WINERY, 8555 Sonoma Hwy., produces white and red varietal and sparkling wines. Self-guiding tours are available. Tastings are held in the French Mediterranean mansion. Picnicking is permitted. Allow 30 minutes minimum. Daily 10-4:30; tours 10:30-4. Free. Limited production and reserve tastings $2. Phone (707) 833-4134.

KING CITY (H-3) pop. 7,600, alt. 330'

MISSION SAN ANTONIO DE PADUA is 20 mi. s.w. in Fort Hunter Liggett via Jolon Rd. Founded by Father Junípero Serra on July 14, 1771, it is one of the largest restored and rebuilt missions. Original remains include the well, gristmill, tannery and parts of the aqueduct system. A museum exhibits Indian artifacts. Mon.-Sat. 10-4:30, Sun. 11-5. Donations. Phone (408) 385-4478.

MONTEREY COUNTY AGRICULTURAL AND RURAL LIFE MUSEUM, in San Lorenzo Regional County Park at 1160 Broadway, features a restored barn with more than 20 exhibits tracing the evolution of agriculture in Monterey County. Other restored buildings include a farmhouse, blacksmith shop, a one-room schoolhouse of the late 1800s, a train depot and a caboose. Picnic facilities are available.

Allow 30 minutes minimum. Tours available by appointment. Museum open daily 10-5; school, farmhouse and blacksmith shop open daily 1-4. Closed Jan. 1, Thanksgiving and Dec. 25. Donations. Parking Mon.-Fri. $1.50, Sat.-Sun. $3. Phone (408) 385-5964.

KINGSBURG (G-4) pop. 7,200, alt. 297'

Kingsburg was established in 1875 by the Southern Pacific Railroad. Kingsburg's Swedish immigrants influenced the town's customs and architecture. Today Kingsburg is known as a Swedish village, with many restored buildings dating back to the early 1900s and featuring steep wood-shingled roofs, dormer windows and half-timbers. The annual Swedish Festival is held in late May.

★KINGS CANYON NATIONAL PARK—see
Sequoia and Kings Canyon National Parks.

KLAMATH (B-1) pop. 200, alt. 29'

TREES OF MYSTERY PARK, 4 mi. n. on US 101, is a forest of redwoods containing a number of oddly formed trees. Along the Trail of Tall Tales are chainsaw-carved redwood sculptures that depict the legend of Paul Bunyan and other log-gers' stories. The End of the Trail Indian Museum contains displays of artifacts and crafts from numerous Plains and Western Indian tribes.

Daily dawn-dusk; closed Thanksgiving and Dec. 25. Admission $5.50; over 60, $4.50; ages 6-12, $2.75; family rates available. MC, VI. **Discount.** Phone (800) 638-3389. *See ad p. A167.*

KLAMATH NATIONAL FOREST

Characterized by rugged forested ridges, rushing rivers and high mountain lakes and streams, Klamath National Forest covers about 1,726,000 acres. A small segment of the forest extends into Oregon. Much of this scenic area is included in the Marble Mountain Wilderness and Trinity Alps Wilderness, which are accessible only by trail. Vehicular traffic is prohibited in wilderness areas. Hunting, fishing and whitewater rafting opportunities are available.

The Klamath River Highway and forest roads and trails provide access to the region. Forest headquarters is in Yreka. *See Recreation Chart and the AAA California and Nevada CampBook.*

KLAMATH NATIONAL FOREST INTERPRETIVE MUSEUM, 1312 Fairlane Rd. in Yreka, has exhibits on national forests and how they are managed. Displays include dioramas on timber and wildlife preservation, geology, soils, mining and fire prevention. Another exhibit honors Hallie Daggett, the first woman forest-fire lookout in the country. Mon.-Fri. 8-5; closed holidays. Free. Phone (916) 842-6131.

LA CAÑADA FLINTRIDGE (A-6) pop. 19,400, alt. 1,318'

★DESCANSO GARDENS, s. of Foothill Blvd. at 1418 Descanso Dr., contains 100,000 camellias from throughout the world. Roses and assorted annuals bloom May through December. The camellias are in blossom October through March; lilacs and outdoor orchids peak in April. Shows throughout the year feature various flowers and plants.

Georgie Van de Kamp Hall accommodates horticultural events, lectures, classes and demonstrations. A teahouse in the Japanese Garden is open Tues.-Sun. 11-4. Pets, bicycles and radios are not permitted. Persons under 18 must be accompanied by an adult. Guided jeep tram tours Tues.-Fri. 1-3, Sat.-Sun. and holidays 11-4; fare $1.50.

Gardens open daily 9-4:30; closed Dec. 25. Admission $3; over 62, students with ID and ages 13-17, $1.50; ages 6-12, 75c. Free to all third Tues. of the month. **Two-for-one discount,** except students with ID, ages 6-17 and during Spring Festival of Flowers. Phone (818) 952-4400.

LAGUNA BEACH (K-6) pop. 23,200, alt. 25'

Laguna Beach, a picturesque resort community with steep hills rising from the coast, has long been a popular artists' colony. From early July to late August the Sawdust Festival is held to display the arts and crafts of local artisans.

FESTIVAL OF ARTS AND PAGEANT OF THE MASTERS takes place mid-July through Aug. 31 at Irvine Bowl Park, 650 Laguna Canyon Rd. The art festival highlights the work of local artisans. Admission $2; over 55, $1; under 13 free when accompanied by an adult. **Discount,** except over 55.

The pageant is a re-creation of great works of art posed as living tableaus by citizens from the community. Reservations for the pageant are recommended and can be made 8 months in advance; tickets cost $9 to $38. To obtain a ticket order form, send a self-addressed stamped envelope to Festival of Arts of Laguna Beach, P.O. Box 1659, Laguna Beach, CA 92652. Phone (714) 494-1145 for information or (800) 487-3378 for tickets.

LAGUNA ART MUSEUM, 307 Cliff Dr., has rotating exhibits that focus on the work of California artists. A satellite of the museum featuring contemporary works is in Costa Mesa *(see place listing).* Tues.-Sun. 11-5; closed holidays. Admission $3, senior citizens and students $1.50, under 12 free. Phone (714) 494-6531.

LA HABRA (B-7) pop. 51,300, alt. 298'

CHILDREN'S MUSEUM AT LA HABRA, 301 S. Euclid St., offers a creative hands-on environment for children; some exhibits are geared to toddlers. Highlights include a carrousel, a nature walk, science gallery, train caboose, theater and a bee observatory. There also are changing exhibits. Mon.-Sat. 10-4; closed major holidays. Admission $3; over 55 and ages 2-16, $2.50. Phone (310) 905-9793.

LA JOLLA (L-6) pop. 28,800, alt. 110'

Within the city limits of San Diego, La Jolla (Lah HOY-yah) is a popular resort graced with a rocky coast and fine beaches. La Jolla Cove affords excellent swimming, beachcombing and scuba and skindiving. The Shearson-Lehman Brothers Open PGA Golf Tournament is held in mid-February, and the National Senior Hardcourt Tennis Tournament takes place late November to early December.

CHILDREN'S MUSEUM OF SAN DIEGO, 8657 Villa La Jolla Dr. in La Jolla Village Sq., encourages children to learn by doing. Displays include a construction zone, art studio, health center, newsroom, theater backstage and the "Creative Journey" maze. Tues.-Fri. and Sun. noon-5, Sat. 10-5. Admission $3; over 65, $2; under 2 free. **Discount,** except over 65. Phone (619) 450-0767.

LA JOLLA CAVES, 1325 Coast Blvd., were formed by centuries of wave action on La Jolla's sandstone cliffs. Sunny Jim Cave is accessible by land via a staircase in a shell and souvenir shop. Mon.-Sat. 10-5, Sun. 11-5; closed Thanksgiving and Dec. 25. Admission $1; ages 3-11, 50c. Phone (619) 454-6080.

MUSEUM OF CONTEMPORARY ART, 700 Prospect St., displays paintings, sculpture, photography and architectural designs, emphasizing geometric abstraction, pop and contemporary international art from 1955 to the present. A satellite of the museum is in downtown San Diego at Kettner Blvd. and Broadway at American Plaza For information phone (619) 454-3541. The museum will close for renovations beginning spring 1993.

Tues.-Sun. 10-5 (also Wed. 5-9); closed Jan. 1, second week of Aug., Thanksgiving and Dec. 25. Admission $4; over 55 and students $2; ages 5-12, 50c. Free to all Wed. 5-9. **Two-for-one discount.** Phone (619) 454-3541.

THE SALK INSTITUTE, 10010 N. Torrey Pines Rd., is one of the world's largest independent centers for biological research, involving such issues as cancer, brain function, molecular medicine, AIDS research, plant biology and human genetics. Scientists from around the world collaborate with resident researchers using the institute's outstanding facilities. Tours on the hour

Mon.-Fri. 10-noon (phone for guide availability). Closed holidays. Free. Phone (619) 453-4100, ext. 200.

★STEPHEN BIRCH AQUARIUM-MUSEUM, 2300 Expedition Way, is on a hillside above the Scripps Institution of Oceanography at the University of California. The aquarium features marine animals from California and Mexico as well as the Indo-Pacific. Interactive exhibits and changing displays explore the latest developments in oceanography. Daily 9-5. Admission $6.50; senior citizens $5.50; active military and ages 13-18, $4.50; ages 4-12, $3.50. Phone (619) 534-6933.

LAKE ARROWHEAD (A-9) pop. 6,300, alt. 5,191'

Strict zoning laws have protected the appearance of Lake Arrowhead, a popular resort town and a highlight of the scenic Rim of the World Drive from San Bernardino (see place listing). Fishing is popular in this area, and nearby San Bernardino National Forest (see place listing) provides winter recreation facilities.

THE ARROWHEAD QUEEN offers a 50-minute narrated tour of Lake Arrowhead. The boat departs Lake Arrowhead Village waterfront on the hour daily 10-6, weather permitting. Closed Dec. 25. Tickets are available at LeRoy's Sports in Lake Arrowhead Village. Fare $9.50; over 60, $8.50; ages 2-12, $6.50. Discount. Phone (909) 336-6992.

LAKE FOREST (C-8) pop. 38,200, alt. 394'

HERITAGE HILL HISTORICAL PARK, near Lake Forest Dr. and Serrano Rd., has four preserved and restored structures that reflect part of Orange County's history. The Serrano Adobe dates from 1863, with furniture from the late 19th century. St. George's Episcopal Mission, built in 1891, has many of its original interior furnishings. The 1890 El Toro Grammar School recalls long-ago school days with period books, desks and other furnishings. The 1908 Bennet Ranch House reflects a citrus-ranching family's lifestyle in the early 20th century.

Wed.-Sun. 9-5; guided tours Wed.-Fri. at 2, Sat.-Sun. at 11 and 2; closed Dec. 25. Donations. Phone (714) 855-2028.

LAKE MENDOCINO—see Ukiah.

LAKEPORT (D-2) pop. 4,400, alt. 1,343'

On the western shore of Clear Lake (see Recreation Chart), one of California's largest, Lakeport is known for its excellent fishing (especially bass) and water recreation.

LAKE COUNTY HISTORICAL MUSEUM, 255 Main St., contains displays of arrowheads, Pomo Indian baskets, period rooms of the late 1800s and early 1900s and a gem and mineral collection that includes Lake County diamonds. A genealogical library has information on area pioneers. Allow 1 hour minimum. Wed.-Sat. 10-4, Sun. 11-4, May-Sept.; closed major holidays. Free. Phone (707) 263-4555.

★LAKE TAHOE (E-4) alt. 6,229'

Lake Tahoe, which holds enough water to cover the entire state of California to a depth of 14 inches, was named "big water" by the Washoe Indians. Their legend says Lake Tahoe was created when an Evil Spirit was in pursuit of an innocent Indian. Attempting to aid the Indian, the Great Spirit gave him a branch of leaves; each leaf dropped would produce a body of water that the Evil Spirit would have to circumvent. But during the chase, the Indian dropped the whole branch in fright—creating Lake Tahoe.

It is said that the water in Lake Tahoe is 99.7 percent pure, about the same as distilled water. Remarkably clear and deep blue, the lake is 22 miles long and 12 miles wide; about one-third lies in Nevada. Its average depth is 989 feet; the deepest point is 1,645 feet, making Tahoe the third deepest lake in North America. The first 12 feet below the surface can warm to 68 F in summer, while depths below 700 feet remain a constant 39 F.

The "lake in the sky" lies in a valley between the main Sierra Nevada and an eastern offshoot, the Carson Range. The mountains rise more than 4,000 feet above the resort-lined shore. Most of the surrounding area is within the Eldorado, Tahoe and Toiyabe national forests (see place listings).

Emigrants and miners were lured to the rugged Sierra by tales of fortunes made during the California gold rush. The discovery of the Comstock Lode increased traffic and depleted the Tahoe Basin's natural resources to a dangerously low level. Between 1860 and 1890 lumber was needed for fuel and to support the web of mines constructed beneath Virginia City. The decline of

the Comstock Lode was likely the saving grace for Tahoe's forests.

By the early 1900s the lake had become a retreat for the rich. Elaborate hotels began dotting the shores. Roads were paved during the 1920s and '30s, and Lake Tahoe was no longer available only to the wealthy. As development continued in the 1950s, roads were plowed during the winter, enabling year-round residence. In 1968, the Tahoe Regional Planning Agency was established, ensuring environmentally responsible development for years to come.

The headquarters of the U.S. Forest Service-Lake Tahoe Basin Management Unit provides year-round information on forest activities, including camping, fishing and hiking in summer and cross-country skiing in winter. For information contact Lake Tahoe Basin Management Unit, Box 731002, South Lake Tahoe, CA 95731; phone (916) 573-2600.

The U.S. Forest Visitor Center on SR 89 between Camp Richardson and Emerald Bay offers free orientation programs and guided walks daily 8-6, May-Sept. Phone (916) 573-2674.

D.L. BLISS STATE PARK, on the w. shore of Lake Tahoe between Meeks Bay and Emerald Bay, occupies 1,237 acres of forested mountain terrain. A sandy beach is at Rubicon Point near Emerald Bay. Naturalist programs are available in the summer. Allow 3 hours minimum. Daily 8 a.m.-10 p.m., mid-June to mid-Sept. Day use fee $5 per vehicle; over 62, $4 per vehicle. Phone (916) 525-7277. *See Recreation Chart.*

EHRMAN MANSION is 1 mi. s. of Tahoma on SR 89 in Sugar Pine Point State Park. The two-story Queen Anne style house was built in 1903 and is a fine example of a Tahoe summer home. Exhibits pertaining to area history as well as the Hellman-Ehrman family can be seen on the second floor. On the grounds are an 1870 cabin, a nature center and nature trails. Rangers conduct free guided tours of the mansion. Daily 10-4, June-Aug. Free. Parking $5 per private vehicle. Phone (916) 525-7232.

GATEKEEPER'S LOG CABIN MUSEUM is ¼ mi. s. on SR 89. The museum is a reconstruction of the original gatekeeper's cabin, which served as the residence for the dam attendant. Included are displays on area and natural history, Indian artifacts and photographs. Picnicking is permitted. Allow 30 minutes minimum. Daily 11-5, June 15-Labor Day; Wed.-Sun. 11-5, May 15-June 14 and day after Labor Day-Oct. 1. Donations. Phone (916) 583-1762.

HEAVENLY VALLEY TRAM, top of Ski Run Blvd., offers a 7-minute tram ride 2,000 feet above lake level. A panorama of the lake is possible from the summit. Hiking trails are available. Trips depart every 15 minutes on the quarter-hour daily 10-9, Memorial Day weekend-Labor Day; Mon.-Fri. 9-4, Sat.-Sun. 8:30-4, rest of year. Fare $10.50; over 65 and ages 3-12, $6.50. AE, MC, VI. Phone (916) 541-1330.

LAKE CRUISES are operated by several companies around the lake. These trips offer scenic views of the lakeshore as well as some of the surrounding resorts and estates.

The M.S. *Dixie* offers cruises from Zephyr Cove, Nev., to Emerald Bay daily at 11 and 2:15, mid-June to early Oct.; at noon, mid-Apr. to mid-June and early to late Oct. The South Shore Cruise departs Mon.-Sat. at 5:15, mid-June to early Sept. Breakfast, brunch and dinner dance cruises also are available. Reservations are strongly recommended.

Fare $12; senior citizens, $10; ages 3-11, $4. South Shore Cruise $9; under 12, $4. AE, MC, VI. Phone (702) 588-3508.

North Tahoe Cruises leave from Round House Mall and Marina in Tahoe City off SR 28 at 700 North Lake Blvd. The 2-hour historical trips along the northwest shore of the lake depart daily at 11, 1:30 and 3:30, mid-June to mid-Sept.; otherwise varies, May 1 to mid-June and mid-Sept. through Oct. 31, weather permitting.

The ship has a snack and cocktail bar. Sunset cocktail cruises depart at 6 p.m. Champagne continental breakfast cruises also are offered. Reservations are recommended. Fare $15; over 60, $13; ages 3-12, $5. **Discount,** except over 60. Phone (916) 583-0141.

The *Tahoe Queen,* South Lake Tahoe, offers a 2½-hour trip to Emerald Bay on a glass-bottom paddlewheeler. Departures from Ski Run Marina at the foot of Ski Run Blvd. are daily at 11, 1:30 and 3:55, early June-early Oct.; at noon only, rest of year. Fare $14; under 12, $5. Dinner cruise daily at 7, June-Oct.; at 6:30, rest of year. Boarding and fare $18; ages 2-11, $9. Dinner is extra.

Winter North Shore ski shuttle service to Squaw Valley and Alpine Meadows leaves Ski Run Marina Tues.-Fri. at 8 a.m. Round trip $18; ages 2-11, $8. AE, MC, VI accepted on ski shuttle and dinner cruises only. Phone (916) 541-3364 or (800) 23-TAHOE.

PONDEROSA RANCH, on SR 28 in Incline Village, Nev., is a Western theme park featuring the original Cartwright ranch house from the television show "Bonanza." Park highlights include a saloon, museum, kiddyland, playground, petting farm and mystery mine. Allow 2 hours minimum. Daily 9:30-5, May-Oct. Admission $7.50; ages 5-11, $5.50. Breakfast hay rides available 8-9:30, Memorial Day weekend-Labor Day. Admission $9.50; ages 5-11, $7.50; ages 2-4, $2. Ranch admission is included in the meal price. AE, DS, MC, VI. Phone (702) 831-0691.

SQUAW VALLEY CABLE CAR, 1960 Squaw Valley Rd., provides a full aerial view of Lake Tahoe and Squaw Valley, site of the 1960 Winter Olympics and a year-round recreation area. Passengers are taken to the trailhead of the Pacific

Crest Trail, where a variety of activities are offered, including ice skating, swimming and horseback riding. Daily 10-10, June-Aug.; 10-9, Dec.-Mar.; 10-4, rest of year, weather permitting. Fare $10; ages 3-12, $5; fee charged for activities. AE, CB, DS, MC, VI. Phone (916) 583-6955.

TALLAC HISTORIC SITE, on SR 89 n. of Camp Richardson, consists of three estates on the shore of Lake Tahoe. Some buildings are in the process of being restored. Highlights include a visitor center and an art gallery where visitors may watch the artists at work. Picnicking is permitted. Guided tours are available. Site open daily dawn-dusk, Memorial Day weekend-Labor Day. Artists at work program Mon.-Sat. 11-3, Memorial Day weekend-Labor Day. Visitor center open Mon.-Fri. 9-6, Memorial Day weekend-Labor Day. Free. Phone (916) 542-4166.

VIKINGSHOLM is at the s.w. end of Emerald Bay. Vikingsholm is a 38-room reproduction of a ninth-century Norse fortress. It is accessible by boat or by a steep 1-mile hiking trail. Guided tours are available. Allow 1 hour minimum. Daily 10-4, July 1-Labor Day; Sat.-Sun. 10-4, Memorial Day weekend-June 30. Admission $1; ages 5-17, 50c. Phone (916) 525-7277 or 541-3030.

LANCASTER (I-6) pop. 97,300, alt. 2,355'

NASA AMES-DRYDEN FLIGHT RESEARCH FACILITY, 25 mi. n.e. of SR 14 on Edwards Air Force Base, develops and tests new forms of aircraft design and flight operation techniques. Tours of the facility last 1½ hours, beginning with a film describing the history of the test programs, then continuing with a walk through a hangar and a look at experimental aircrafts. The facility also has a small aircraft and space museum. Tours Mon.-Fri. at 10:15 and 1:15; closed major holidays and space shuttle landing days. Free. Reservations are required. Phone (805) 258-3460.

LASSEN NATIONAL FOREST

Lassen National Forest covers approximately 1,200,000 acres surrounding Lassen Volcanic National Park (see place listing). Within the region are numerous lakes formed by ancient volcanic action.

Several highways, forest roads and trails afford access to the region. The Caribou, Thousand Lakes and Ishi wilderness areas allow backpacking. Campfire permits are required, except in campgrounds with developed facilities. Obtain permits in person at any Forest Service Bureau of Land Management or California Department of Forestry Office. Hunting and fishing are allowed, as well as cross-country skiing and snowmobiling.

Lake Almanor, one of the largest man-made bodies of water in California, offers fishing, sail-

ing, water skiing and swimming. Eagle Lake and Hat Creek offer trout fishing. Recreation sites are usually open mid-May to mid-October, weather permitting; the season is shorter at higher altitudes. For more information contact Lassen National Forest, 55 S. Sacramento St., Susanville, CA 96130; phone (916) 257-2151. See Recreation Chart and the AAA California and Nevada CampBook.

SUBWAY CAVE is off SR 89 about ½ mi. n. of SR 44. This lava tube winds 1,300 feet through a lava flow that covered the Hat Creek Valley nearly 2,000 years ago. Carry a jacket and a reliable lantern or flashlight.

★LASSEN VOLCANIC NATIONAL PARK (C-3)

Lassen Volcanic National Park covers 106,000 acres in northeastern California where the Cascades join the Sierra Nevada. The park is accessible via SR 36, 9 miles east of Mineral. In addition to Lassen Peak (10,457 ft.) and Cinder Cone (6,907 ft.), the park boasts Prospect Peak (8,338 ft.) and Mount Harkness (8,045 ft.), two shield volcanoes topped by cinder cones with trails leading to their summits. Other features include smaller volcanoes and lava flows, fumaroles, hot springs, boiling lakes and mudpots.

For a period of several thousand years Lassen Peak was quiescent; then in the spring of 1914 a series of relatively small eruptions began. After reaching its peak in 1915, the activity continued until about 1921.

A plug dome volcano, Lassen Peak once protruded from the north flank of ancestral Mount Tehama. This great stratovolcano was destroyed in glacial times. Mill Creek breached the south wall of Tehama's crater, draining any lake that might have formed there. Lassen Park Road winds around Lassen Peak, affording views of the volcano and evidence of its destructive might.

In the southern half of the park gurgling mudpots and roaring fumaroles contribute to the rather bizarre atmosphere. The eastern sector encompasses a splendid chain of lakes, extending from Juniper Lake at the northern base of Mount Harkness to Butte Lake near the eastern base of Prospect Peak.

General Information and Activities

Although the park is open all year, heavy snows render most sections inaccessible from late October to early June. Winter roads are maintained from the northern gate to the district ranger's office (about 1 mile) and from the southern gate to the ski area at Lassen Chalet, the hub of winter sports activity. Day lodge facilities, ski instruction, equipment rental, chairlift and rope tows are available from late November to mid-April. Cross-country skiing is usually possible from early December to late spring. Mountain bikes are not permitted in the park.

Some of the park's many lakes and streams contain trout. A state fishing license is required, and catch limits are posted. Wilderness permits issued by the park are required for back-country camping. Gates are open 24 hours daily, but the hours they are attended vary. Motorists entering the park in summer when the station is unattended must obtain a permit before leaving.

Park headquarters is 1 mile west of Mineral on SR 36. Maps, information and bulletins can be obtained at visitor centers at the northwest and southwest entrances. Interpretive and evening programs, guided nature walks and self-guiding trails are available. *See Recreation Chart.*

Note: Stay on established trails at all times in hot springs or steaming areas; small children should be kept under strict control. Ground crusts that appear safe can be dangerously thin.

ADMISSION to the park is $5 per passenger vehicle per day, $2 per person over age 16 per day by other means, or by annual permit. Entrance fees are good for 7 days with a receipt.

PETS are permitted in the park only if they are on a leash, crated or otherwise physically restrained at all times. Pets are not allowed on trails or in buildings.

ADDRESS inquiries to the Superintendent, Lassen Volcanic National Park, Box 100, Mineral, CA 96063-0100. Phone (916) 595-4444.

Points of Interest

BUMPASS HELL TRAIL, about ½ mi. beyond Emerald Lake, leads 1½ mi. off the Lassen Park Rd. to Bumpass Hell, a large area of spectacular hot springs, mudpots, boiling pools and other types of volcanic activity.

BUTTE LAKE is 6 mi. off SR 44 in the n.e. corner of the park. A marked nature trail leads to the Cinder Cone summit; interpretive leaflets are available at the campground.

CINDER CONE, accessible from a trail beginning at Butte Lake, has fantastic lava beds and multicolored volcanic ejecta. It is possible that some of the lava flows occurred as recently as 1850-51.

LASSEN PARK ROAD is a 30-mile drive between the s. entrance and Manzanita Lake in the n.w. region. A road guide ($1.65) to points of interest along the route is available at both of the park's entrance stations. Most of the road is impassable late Oct.-early June due to heavy snowfall.

Chaos Crags and Chaos Jumbles are 2 mi. s. from the n.w. boundary. The Chaos Crags are lava plugs believed to have been pushed up more than 1,000 years ago; subsequent rockfalls formed the Chaos Jumbles. The small coniferous trees in the Chaos Jumbles—some more than 300 years old—constitute the Dwarf Forest.

Devastated Area begins about 2½ mi. n. of Summit Lake. It was stripped of all vegetation by hot blasts and mudflows from the May 1915 eruptions of Lassen Peak. Natural reforestation is taking place. Another eruption remnant is Hot Rock, a large black lava rock near the north end of the area.

Diamond Peak is reached by Lassen Park Rd., which, from 2 mi. n. of the Sulphur Works, winds up the remains of old Mount Tehama. Rounding Diamond Peak, you can see steam vents across the canyon in Little Hot Springs Valley.

Kings Creek Meadows (7,400 ft.) are 4½ mi. n. from the summit. A trail leads 1⅓ miles to beautiful Kings Creek Falls. Both the cascades and falls are visible from the left side of the creek downstream.

Manzanita Lake, about 100 yards from the n.w. boundary, has a visitor contact station where park information and assistance are available.

Sulphur Works Thermal Area, about 1 mi. n. of the s.w. entrance station, has steam vents and mudpots. Stay on the trails in these areas at all times. Ground that appears safe might be dangerously thin.

Summit Lake, 5 mi. n.e. of Kings Creek Meadows, has two lakeside campgrounds with trailer spaces. They are convenient to hiking, fishing and points of interest. Nightly campfire programs are available in summer.

LASSEN PEAK TRAIL leaves Lassen Park Rd. less than 1 mi. beyond Lake Helen and travels 2½ miles to the top of the volcano. Round trip requires 4 to 5 hours.

WARNER VALLEY, in the s. part of the park, is reached by road from Chester or by trail from Summit Lake to Drakesbad. Marked trails lead to Boiling Springs Lake and Devil's Kitchen, a large area of boiling pools and other volcanic features.

BUDGETING YOUR TRAVEL TIME AND DISTANCE

Allow about 2½ hours' driving time for every 100 miles on the road. This includes stops for fuel, refreshments and rest.

★LAVA BEDS NATIONAL MONUMENT (B-3)

Centuries ago molten lava spewing from Medicine Lake Volcano cooled to form the rugged terrain of Lava Beds National Monument. The 46,500-acre area is characterized by cinder cones, deep chasms and nearly 200 lava tube caves of various sizes. Some of the caves contain permanent ice. The Modoc Indians used the volcanic formations as fortifications in 1872-73 during the only major Indian war fought in California.

Camping is allowed, but no lodgings, supplies, gas or oil are available. The monument is open all year, and although there are no specified visiting hours, those planning to camp should arrive before 5 p.m. The geology and history of the area is interpreted at a visitor center. Daily 9-6, June 15-Labor Day; 8-5, rest of year. Admission $3 per vehicle. Phone (916) 667-2282. *See the AAA California and Nevada CampBook.*

LEBEC (I-5) pop. 400, alt. 3,570'

FORT TEJON STATE HISTORIC PARK, 3½ mi. n. on I-5, is a restored U.S. Army Dragoon post in use 1854-64. Fort Tejon was the terminus for the U.S. Camel Corps, an experimental group of 25 camels that hauled supplies from San Antonio. A living-history program is held the first Sunday of each month. Civil War battle re-enactments are staged on the third Sunday of the month at 10, noon and 2, Apr.-Oct.; military demonstrations are given the day before every re-enactment.

Daily 10-4:30; closed Jan. 1, Thanksgiving and Dec. 25. Museum, living-history program and battle re-enactments $3; ages 6-12, $2. Phone (805) 248-6692.

LEE VINING (F-5) pop. 300, alt. 6,781'

Lee Vining is a center for recreational and scenic attractions around Mono Lake. Mono Lake County Park, 5 miles north off US 395, has a shady streamside picnic area and a boardwalk trail that winds through meadows to the lakeshore. The Mono Lake Visitor Center on US 395 provides information on the area and free naturalist tours daily, in summer. The center is open daily 9-9, in summer; 9-5, rest of year. Phone (619) 647-6595.

MONO LAKE TUFA STATE RESERVE, at S. Tufa Area off SR 120, 5 mi. e. of US 395, preserves tufa, a calcium-carbonate rock created by the interaction of freshwater springs under the lake with the alkaline lake waters. The lowering of the lake level due to stream diversion has exposed unusual tower formations. Tours daily, in summer; Sat.-Sun., rest of year. Reserve open daily 24 hours. Free. Phone (619) 647-6331.

LEGGETT (D-1) pop. 200

Leggett is at the crossroads of the Redwood Highway (US 101) and scenic SR 1. The town is located near the ocean, wine country and redwood forests. The area also contains several historic sites.

CHANDELIER TREE, in Drive-Thru Tree Park on US 101, towers 315 feet into the air and has a diameter of 21 feet. Visitors can drive a full-size automobile through the hand-hewn opening at the base of the tree. A picnic area is available. Daily 8-dusk. Admission $3 per vehicle. Phone (707) 925-6464.

LITTLE RIVER (D-1) alt. 90'

Founded as a lumber and shipbuilding town in the mid-19th century, Little River's architecture reflects its settlers' New England heritage. The town is a popular spot for divers. Little River lies on a scenic stretch of SR 1 on the north coast that runs from Leggett southward to Sausalito and the San Francisco Bay.

PYGMY FOREST, s. edge on SR 1 and 3 mi. e. on Little River-Comptche Rd., is thought to be the result of acidic soil. Even though they are decades old, some of the rare pygmy pine and pygmy cypress trees are only 2 feet high.

LIVERMORE (F-3) pop. 56,700, alt. 486'

Livermore is the principal community in Livermore Valley, a scenic area with vineyards and cattle lands. Sycamore trees—some more than 2 centuries old—grow along the banks of the Arroyo del Valle. The Livermore Rodeo is held the second weekend in June.

LAWRENCE LIVERMORE NATIONAL LABORATORY VISITORS CENTER, off Greenville Rd. about 2¼ mi. s. of I-580, highlights the laboratory's research on new energy sources through photographs, hands-on exhibits and a slide show. Allow 1 hour minimum. Mon.-Tues. and Thurs.-Fri. 9-4, Wed. 12:30-4, Sat. noon-5; closed Jan. 1, Thanksgiving, Dec. 25 and lab holidays. Free. Phone (510) 422-9797.

LIVERMORE VALLEY CELLARS, 1 mi. s. off SR 84 at 1508 Wetmore Rd., produces dry white varietal wines and offers tours and tastings. Picnic facilities and a park are nearby. Daily 11:30-5. Free. Phone (510) 447-1751.

WENTE BROTHERS, off I-580, 3 mi. s. on Vasco Rd., then w. to 5565 Tesla Rd., offers tours on the hour Mon.-Sat. at 10, 11 and 1-3; Sun. 1-3. Tasting room open Mon.-Sat. 10-4:30, Sun. 11-4:30; closed Jan. 1, Easter, Thanksgiving and Dec. 25. Free. Phone (510) 447-3603.

LODI (F-3) pop. 51,900, alt. 52'

With more than a dozen wineries nearby, Lodi is an important wine-producing center; a Grape Festival and Harvest Fair is held in April, and the National Wine Show takes place in September. Nearby Lake Lodi Park offers water skiing, boating, picnicking and swimming. The Hill House Museum is one of the few Victorian houses in Lodi; tours of the house are available by appointment.

MICKE GROVE REGIONAL PARK, 11793 Micke Grove Rd., has picnic facilities, a swimming pool, amusement rides, a Japanese garden, historical museum and zoo. Park open daily 8-dusk. Zoo open daily 10-5. Park admission Mon.-Fri. $2 per private vehicle, Sat.-Sun. and holidays $3 per private vehicle, senior citizens free. Zoo admission $1; senior citizens and ages 13-17, 50c; ages 6-12, 25c. Phone (209) 331-7400.

San Joaquin County Historical Museum contains permanent and changing exhibits on local history, agriculture, transportation and Indian culture. Of special interest is the Sunshine Trail, which re-creates a trip across California from west to east. An enclosed garden contains native California plants and a waterfall. The Weber Gallery contains personal belongings and a model of the first home site of Capt. Charles Weber, the founder of the city of Stockton.

The Jerald D. Kennedy Reference Library is available by appointment only. Allow 2 hours minimum. Museum open Wed.-Sun. 1-5. Admission $1; over 59 and ages 6-12, 50c. Phone (209) 368-9154 or 463-4119.

LOMITA (C-6) pop. 19,400, alt. 98′

LOMITA RAILROAD MUSEUM, 250th St. and Woodward Ave., is a Victorian-style passenger depot containing scale models, photographs and paintings of locomotives, and assorted railroading memorabilia. A 1902 Mogul locomotive and an all-wood 1910 Union Pacific caboose are outside. The museum annex has a 1913 box car and a 1923 oil tanker; picnicking is permitted. Wed.-Sun. 10-5; closed Thanksgiving and Dec. 25. Admission $1; under 13, 50c. Children must be accompanied by an adult. Phone (310) 326-6255.

LOMPOC (I-3) pop. 37,700, alt. 104′

Many of the nation's flower seeds are grown in Lompoc; local flower fields bloom May through September. The Civic Center Plaza between C and E streets has a display garden where new varieties of plants are identified. The Lompoc Valley Flower Festival is held in late June.

★LA PURÍSIMA MISSION STATE HISTORIC PARK is 4 mi. n.e. on SR 246. The original mission, founded in 1787, was demolished by an earthquake in 1812. Chumash Indians, directed by Franciscan priests, rebuilt it 1813-22 a few miles from the original site. One of the most complete mission restorations, the park includes nine buildings and a water system. The grounds comprise more than 900 acres and have 13 miles of hiking and riding trails. Rooms are furnished as they would have been in the 1820s; mission crafts are demonstrated periodically during the summer.

Daily 10-5; closed Jan. 1, Thanksgiving and Dec. 25. Admission $5 per vehicle; senior citizens $4 per vehicle. Phone (805) 733-3713. See Recreation Chart.

LOMPOC MUSEUM, 200 S. H St., contains a large collection of Indian artifacts representing the Chumash and other tribes. Exhibits trace Lompoc Valley history from the founding of La Purísima Mission to the present. Tues.-Fri. 1-5, Sat.-Sun. 1-4; closed major holidays. Donations. Phone (805) 736-3888.

LONE PINE (G-6) pop. 1,700, alt. 3,733′

Many Western movies have been filmed among the Alabama Hills, a mass of weatherbeaten rock bordering US 395 west and northwest of Lone Pine. The Early Opening Sierra Fishing Derby in early March and the Death Valley-Mount Whitney Bike Race in mid-May are popular events.

The Eastern Sierra Interagency Visitor Center, at US 395 and SR 136, has information and exhibits on Inyo National Forest, Sequoia and Kings Canyon National Parks, Yosemite National Park, Death Valley National Monument and Inyo and Mono counties recreation areas. The center is open daily 8-4:30; extended hours in summer. Closed Jan. 1, Thanksgiving and Dec. 24-25. Phone (619) 876-4252.

Vestiges of Manzanar are about 9 miles north off SR 395. This internment camp, the first of several established to hold Japanese Americans during World War II, ultimately had 10,000 inhabitants. Today little remains but stone entrance gates, some concrete foundations, a cemetery and roads in varying stages of disrepair.

MOUNT WHITNEY, the highest mountain in the contiguous United States, rises to a height of 14,494 feet west of Lone Pine. The summit is 10¾ miles by a strenuous trail from the end of Whitney Portal Road (8,367 ft.). Obtain the required wilderness permit from the Mount Whitney Ranger Station in Lone Pine. Station open daily 7-4:30, late May to mid-Sept.; daily 8-4:30, mid-Sept. to mid-Oct.; Mon.-Fri. 8-4:30, rest of year.

Wilderness permits can be reserved by written request postmarked Mar.-May. Quotas for overnight use are in effect late May to mid-Oct.; check with the Forest Service for details. For more information contact the U.S. Forest Service, P.O. Box 8, Lone Pine, CA 93545; phone (619) 876-5542.

LONG BEACH (C-6) pop. 429,400, alt. 32′

California's fifth largest city, Long Beach became popular in the late 19th century as a seaside resort. Long Beach Harbor, next to the Port of Los Angeles, is one of the busiest shipping centers on the Pacific Coast. The area is rich in petroleum resources, both on land and offshore.

The Long Beach Convention and Entertainment Center at Ocean and Long Beach boulevards includes the Long Beach Arena, Terrace Theater and Center Theater; concerts, plays, trade shows and sporting events are held here. Boat cruises to Catalina Island *(see place listing)* leave from the foot of Golden Shore Boulevard and from near the bow of the *Queen Mary.* The roar of Grand Prix race cars echoes through the city streets in late April during the Toyota Grand Prix of Long Beach.

A visitor information center is open Mon.-Sat. 9-5, Sun. 10-3. For more information contact the center at 3387 Long Beach Blvd., Long Beach, CA 90807; phone (213) 436-3645.

Shopping areas: Long Beach Plaza, with JCPenney and Montgomery Ward, occupies an area between Pine Avenue and Long Beach Boulevard between 3rd and 6th streets. The Broadway chain has a store at Los Altos Shopping Center, Bellflower Boulevard and Stearns Street.

Specialty shops abound along the waterfront. Londontowne, near Pier J, is an open-air mall designed to resemble an old English village. Shoreline Village, on Shoreline Village Drive at the foot of Pine Street, is a harborside shopping center with specialty stores, restaurants, a restored Looff carrousel and occasional live boardwalk entertainment.

EL DORADO NATURE CENTER, 7550 E. Spring St., is an 80-acre wildlife area with nature trails and a museum containing wildlife displays, hands-on exhibits for children, photographs and artwork. Museum open Tues.-Fri. 10-4, Sat.-Sun. 8:30-4. Trails open Tues.-Sun. 8-5. Admission free. Parking Mon.-Fri., $3; Sat.-Sun., $4; holidays $5. Phone (310) 421-9431, ext. 3415.

LONG BEACH CHILDREN'S MUSEUM, 445 Long Beach Blvd. at Long Beach Plaza, comprises areas devoted to interactive, imaginative play and creativity. Included are a make-believe supermarket, the front section of a full-sized bus, a doctor's and dentist's office, a race car, science exhibits and the "Art Cafe," where an array of materials is available for the art project of choice. Children must be accompanied by an adult at all times.

Thurs.-Sat. 11-4, Sun. noon-4. Admission $3.95, under 1 free. **Two-for-one discount.** Free parking in Long Beach Plaza lot off 3rd or 6th sts. Phone (310) 495-1163.

LONG BEACH MUSEUM OF ART, 2300 E. Ocean Blvd., houses contemporary paintings, sculpture, video art and photographs. Wed.-Sun. noon-5; closed holidays and occasionally to change exhibits. Admission $2, senior citizens and students $1. Phone (310) 439-2119.

RANCHO LOS ALAMITOS, 6400 E. Bixby Hill Rd., was once part of an 18th-century land grant. The 1806 ranch house contains late 19th- and early 20th-century furnishings. Also featured are six agricultural buildings, including a working barn, blacksmith shop and 4½ acres of gardens. Entrance is through a guarded gate. Tours are offered on the half-hour from 1-4; self-guiding garden tours also are available. Wed.-Sun. 1-5; closed holidays. Free. Phone (213) 431-3541.

RANCHO LOS CERRITOS, 4600 Virginia Rd., is one of the few two-story, Spanish Colonial-style adobes in Southern California and was once the headquarters for a 27,000-acre ranch. The 1844 house is furnished in 1870s decor. A reference library is surrounded by more than 4 acres of gardens; archives contain materials on California history. Picnicking is permitted. Open Wed.-Sun. 1-5; tours on the hour Sat.-Sun. 1-4; closed holidays. Free. Under 12 must be accompanied by an adult. Phone (310) 424-9423.

LOS ALAMITOS (C-6) pop. 11,700, alt. 25'

Los Alamitos Race Course, 4961 E. Katella Ave., conducts Thoroughbred, quarter horse and harness racing. For schedule information phone (310) 431-1361 or (714) 995-1234.

Los Angeles

Los Angeles is California's largest city, both in population and in territory (465 sq. mi.). The city ranks second in city and metropolitan area population in the United States.

Los Angeles is hardly a city in the traditional sense of a concentrated urban center with relatively distinct limits. Rather, it is a collection of intermingling communities, each with its own identity and character. For example, Hollywood lies entirely within the Los Angeles city limits. It is possible to travel 25 miles from city hall and still remain in the city; on the other hand, you can travel less than 3 miles in another direction and be in a separate town.

Early in this century towns that wanted to take advantage of water piped to Los Angeles from the Owens River had to become part of the city. Communities that refused to subscribe to the project under this stipulation remained separate from Los Angeles but in some cases found themselves entirely surrounded by it. Officially, the name Los Angeles applies to both city and county. The name is often used to designate the downtown nucleus, but it also can refer to the entire metropolitan area.

The area was first visited in 1769 by a Spanish expedition in search of the port of Monterey. In 1781 Governor Felipe de Neve and 11

THE INFORMED TRAVELER

POPULATION: 3,485,400; metro 14,531,500   **ALTITUDE:** 267 ft.

Whom to Call

Emergency: 911

Police (non-emergency): (213) 485-3294

Time and Temperature: 853-1212 (all area codes) or (213) 554-1212

Hospitals: Cedars-Sinai Medical Center, (310) 855-5000; Children's Hospital of Los Angeles, (213) 660-2450; Humana Hospital-West Hills, (818) 712-4100; San Pedro Peninsula Hospital, (310) 832-3311; University of California Los Angeles Medical Center, (310) 825-9111.

Where to Look

Newspapers

The major dailies in Los Angeles are the *Los Angeles Times* and the *Daily News*. Many surrounding communities publish daily newspapers as well; foreign-language and special interest papers also are plentiful.

Radio and TV

Los Angeles radio station KFWB (980 AM) is an all-news/weather station; KCRW (89.9 FM) is programmed by National Public Radio. Several stations in the Los Angeles area broadcast in Spanish and other languages as well as in English. The major TV channels include 2 (CBS), 4 (NBC), 7 (ABC), 11 (FOX) and 28

(PBS). For a complete list of radio and television programs, consult the daily newspapers.

Visitor Information

The following groups distribute visitor information: the Los Angeles Convention and Visitors Bureau, (213) 689-8822, 685 S. Figueroa St., Los Angeles, CA 90017 and 6541 Hollywood Blvd., (213) 461-4213, Hollywood, CA 90028; the chamber of commerce, (213) 629-0602, 404 S. Bixel St., Los Angeles, CA 90017; and the Los Angeles City Recreation and Parks Department, (213) 485-5555, City Hall East, 200 N. Main St., Los Angeles, CA 90012.

What to Wear

Los Angeles has a climate that many people might consider perfect if not for the smog. The average annual rainfall is just 14 inches, most of it occurring from November to March. Winters are mild, with days averaging 60 to 75 degrees and nights about 20 degrees cooler. However, temperature fluctuations can be quick and unpredictable; the Christmas season has been known to vary from 28 to 95 F.

Late spring is cool and frequently overcast. Summer days might dawn cloudy, but the skies usually clear before noon. Summer weather is comfortable, ranging from the low 80s in the daytime to the low 60s at night. The hottest months are August through November, when the hot, dry winds known as the Santa Anas periodically blow in from the desert, bringing the city some of its clearest days.

families founded El Pueblo de Nuestra Señora la Reina de Los Angeles (the Village of Our Lady the Queen of the Angels). Following Mexican independence from Spain in the early 19th century, Los Angeles sporadically served as capital of the Mexican province of Alta California. It was the last place to surrender to the United States in the Mexican War in 1847.

The original pueblo slowly branched into thriving cattle ranches and varied agricultural pursuits and trade. The climate, so conducive to the good life, undoubtedly contributed to an increasingly secular philosophy and the decline of the once-influential missions. By the 1800s many of the mission friars were complaining that the Angelenos were paying "more attention to gambling and playing the guitar than to tilling their lands and educating their children."

More recently the city's growth has been due to the development of a variety of industries. More than three-fourths of all motion pictures made in the United States are produced in the Los Angeles metropolitan area. This enormous amount of film production, combined with the major radio and television broadcasting companies, have made Los Angeles the entertainment center of the West.

The city also thrives on tourism, world trade and highly diversified industries—predominantly oil, electronics, finance, entertainment, real estate, aircraft and aerospace. But the city has not forgotten its past; it has preserved many of its early 19th-century homes.

The Museum Village at Heritage Square in the Highland Park district is a haven for the ornate Victorian structures that reflect the lifestyle of the city 1865-1914. A short distance from downtown, the Victorian-style suburb of Angelino Heights boasts stately 19th-century homes that have been restored to their original grandeur.

The city's educational institutions include the University of California at Los Angeles (UCLA), a campus of the state's oldest and most renowned university. Among the city's private institutions are the University of Southern California (USC), Loyola-Marymount University and Occidental College.

Behind these facts lies the most important element of all: the broad boulevards, palm-planted parks and gleaming new buildings that are the distillations of a thousand dreams. Here flock the aspiring star, the artist, the laborer, the imaginative businessperson and the student, each in search of his or her own El Dorado.

Some of them make it; most of them don't. But many stay, and their collective aspirations merge to produce the zest and variety that characterize their city. Smog and congestion, though undeniable, fail to smother the irrepressible enthusiasm that is Los Angeles.

Approaches
By Car

The major north-south route, I-5, is a heavily traveled freeway that bisects both Los Angeles proper and the entire metropolitan area. From the north this inland route approaches through the San Joaquin Valley, crosses the Tehachapi Mountains and enters the city as the Golden State Freeway; from the south at San Diego it follows the coast to Capistrano Beach, turns inland, then, as the Santa Ana Freeway, passes through Anaheim and sweeps into central Los Angeles.

I-405 (San Diego Freeway) joins I-5 at San Fernando and south of Irvine; a good alternate route, it avoids the busy downtown Los Angeles area, although it is typically as heavily traveled as the central route.

From the north, two other controlled-access routes, SR 99 and US 101, roughly parallel I-5 on the east and the west, respectively. SR 99 crosses the San Joaquin Valley and merges with I-5 a few miles south of Bakersfield. US 101 is a 204-mile scenic stretch from San Luis Obispo.

Almost continuously in sight of the Coast Ranges, US 101 follows the Salinas River Valley, runs along the coastline through Santa Barbara and terminates at I-5 in the center of Los Angeles. SR 1, which traverses the rugged coast, is slower and more dangerous when fog sets in or rain increases the possibility of slides. Outstanding coastal views make it the most scenic north-south route.

I-15 links Las Vegas and San Diego. Passing east of Los Angeles, it provides access to the area via freeway connections at San Bernardino and Riverside.

Direct access from the east is via I-10, which enters Los Angeles as the San Bernardino Freeway and ends at Santa Monica. Indirect access from points east is provided by I-40, a fast route across the desert that ends at I-15 in Barstow.

By Plane, Bus, Train and Boat

Los Angeles International Airport, at Century and Sepulveda boulevards near Inglewood, is one of the busiest airports in the world. Because of traffic congestion, bus transportation to and from the airport is advised. Contact the airport for information on airport bus service.

Airport Coach, (800) 772-5299, provides bus service to major hotels in Anaheim, Pasadena and Los Angeles International and John Wayne airports. Buses operated by the Southern California Rapid Transit District, (213) 626-4455, provide transportation between the airport and many communities.

FlyAway buses, (818) 994-5554, operate between Los Angeles International Airport and the Van Nuys Airport Bus Terminal in the San Fernando Valley at Woodley and Saticoy. Prime Time, (800) 262-7433, and Super Shuttle, (213) 777-8000 or (800) 258-3826, have door-to-door van service in Los Angeles and Orange counties.

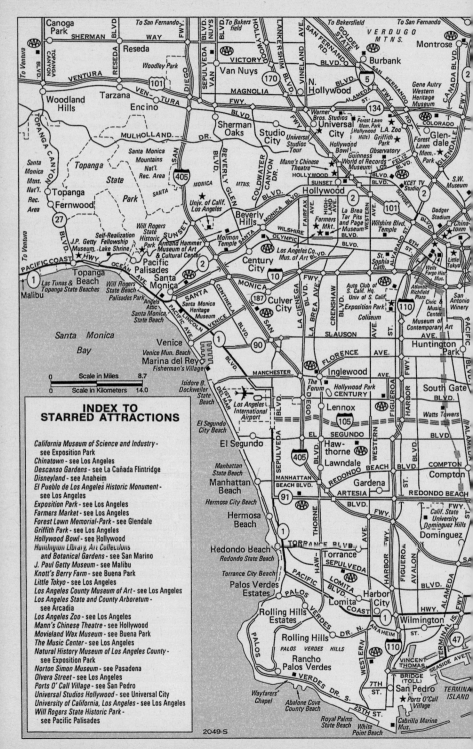

INDEX TO STARRED ATTRACTIONS

California Museum of Science and Industry - see Exposition Park
Chinatown - see Los Angeles
Descanso Gardens - see La Cañada Flintridge
Disneyland - see Anaheim
El Pueblo de Los Angeles Historic Monument - see Los Angeles
Exposition Park - see Los Angeles
Farmers Market - see Los Angeles
Forest Lawn Memorial-Park - see Glendale
Griffith Park - see Los Angeles
Hollywood Bowl - see Hollywood
Huntington Library, Art Collections and Botanical Gardens - see San Marino
J. Paul Getty Museum - see Malibu
Knott's Berry Farm - see Buena Park
Little Tokyo - see Los Angeles
Los Angeles County Museum of Art - see Los Angeles
Los Angeles State and County Arboretum - see Arcadia
Los Angeles Zoo - see Los Angeles
Mann's Chinese Theatre - see Hollywood
Movieland Wax Museum - see Buena Park
The Music Center - see Los Angeles
Natural History Museum of Los Angeles County - see Exposition Park
Norton Simon Museum - see Pasadena
Olvera Street - see Los Angeles
Ports O' Call Village - see San Pedro
Universal Studios Hollywood - see Universal City
University of California, Los Angeles - see Los Angeles
Will Rogers State Historic Park - see Pacific Palisades

2049-S

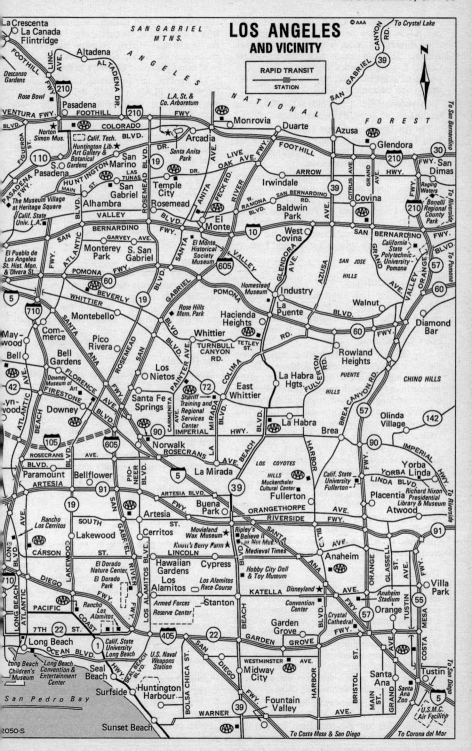

LOS ANGELES
AND VICINITY

Other metropolitan Los Angeles airports serving major airlines are Burbank-Glendale-Pasadena Airport, 14 miles northwest; Long Beach Airport, 22 miles south; John Wayne Orange County Airport, 30 miles southeast in Santa Ana; and Ontario International Airport, about 40 miles east in San Bernardino County.

Greyhound Lines Inc., (213) 620-1200, has a terminal at 6th and Los Angeles streets.

The Art Deco-style Union Passenger Terminal is at Los Angeles and Alameda streets near the Civic Center. Phone Amtrak at (800) 872-7245 for reservations and information.

Numerous steamship and cruise lines operate out of the city's man-made harbor, one of the largest deepwater ports in the United States. From San Pedro, part of the Port of Los Angeles along with Wilmington and Terminal Island, the best and fastest highway connection to the downtown Los Angeles area is the Harbor Freeway (I-110).

Getting Around

In sprawling Los Angeles the most popular way of getting around is by car. The result is a routine traffic volume seldom encountered elsewhere; in Los Angeles alone there is one car for every 1.8 residents.

City driving is usually least complicated on the major boulevards, such as Wilshire or Olympic. One big help is oversized street signs, easily legible from far enough away to permit decisions before reaching important intersections. In some outlying communities signs carry not only the name of the street but the name of the town as well.

The speed limit on most streets is 35 mph or as posted. Freeway speed is generally 55 mph. Motorists might be ticketed for driving at speeds considered dangerously slow as well as dangerously fast. Right turns on red are permitted, unless otherwise posted. U-turns at intersections also are permitted unless otherwise posted.

Pedestrians crossing the street in a marked crosswalk or at an intersection in an unmarked crosswalk **always** have the right-of-way.

The Freeways

Los Angeles has an extensive freeway system. Its involved interchanges, myriad access ramps and potentially confusing exit signs can bewilder a motorist unfamiliar with the territory. Without the freeways, getting around the metropolitan area would be nearly impossible. Although traffic flow on the city's surface streets is good, the freeways generally provide faster and safer transportation for the greater distances that area residents are accustomed to traveling daily.

The San Diego Freeway (I-405), the Foothill Freeway (I-210) and the Ventura Freeway (US 101, SR 134) are the completed freeway bypasses of downtown Los Angeles. Others, usually named for their ultimate destination, radiate from a loop around the central city. For example, the southbound Harbor Freeway leads to San Pedro and the harbor district; it is one of the most heavily traveled highways in the country.

The cardinal rule for driving the Los Angeles freeways is PLAN AHEAD. Before you start, study your map carefully and know the exact route that you intend to take. You might find it helpful to jot down highway numbers and directions, major interchanges and the names of a few main cross streets that precede the exit ramp you want to take.

It is especially important for a newcomer to avoid the rush hours, 6:30-9:30 a.m. and about 3:30-6:30 p.m. If you must drive during these times, have an alternate route in mind in case of exceptionally heavy congestion. Keep your radio on to catch Sigalert bulletins, which warn of freeway tie-ups.

Parking

Although downtown on-street parking is prohibited in most areas during the day, Los Angeles has hundreds of convenient lots and garages. Prices vary according to location. They are highest in the central city: about $2-$3.50 per half-hour and $12-$16 per day. Some hotels and stores provide free parking with validation.

Car Rentals

Automobile rental agencies maintain offices throughout the downtown Los Angeles area, in surrounding communities and at the airport. Hertz, (213) 629-1498, offers special rates to AAA members. For the names and phone numbers of other car rental agencies, consult the local telephone directory.

Rates vary with the size of the car. Standard insurance coverage is usually included, but companies may or may not include gas. Make reservations well in advance.

Taxis

Only taxicabs bearing the Los Angeles City franchise seal are authorized to solicit fares in the downtown area. Some of the largest companies include Checker, (213) 258-3231; Independent, (213) 385-8294; Taxi Systems, (213) 715-1968; and United Independent, (213) 653-5050. Some of these also serve the surrounding areas.

Fares are metered and are about $3.50 for the first mile and $1.80 for each additional mile. It is best to phone for a cab, since few taxis cruise outside areas of heavy tourist concentration, such as the airport and the major hotels.

Public Transportation

The public transportation system in Los Angeles is not as diversified as in many other large cities. Nevertheless, bus lines provide comprehensive coverage of the entire metropolitan region. Route maps of the largest public transportation agency, RTD (Southern California Rapid Transit District), are available Mon.-Fri. 7:30-3:30 at the RTD ticket counter on Level C of the ARCO Plaza, 515 S. Flower St.; phone (213) 626-4455. RTD will merge with the Metropolitan Transit Authority in February 1993.

A self-guiding brochure outlines RTD routes and scheduled stops for nearly 100 Southern California tourist attractions. Tickets, passes and brochures are available at the following RTD Customer Centers: Main Office, 419 S. Main St.; ARCO Plaza, 515 S. Flower St., Level C; California Mart, 1016 S. Main St.; East Los Angeles, 4501 "B" Whittier Blvd.; El Monte Station, 3501 N. Santa Anita Ave.; Hollywood, 6249 Hollywood Blvd.; South Bay, 281 Del Amo Fashion Center; South Central, 5425 S. Van Ness Ave.; San Fernando Valley, 14435 Sherman Way, Suite 107 (Van Nuys); and Wilshire Customer Service Center, 5301 Wilshire Blvd.

The first of three transit rail lines currently under construction, the Blue Line of the Los Angeles Metro System, opened in 1990. This light rail line runs 22 miles from Los Angeles to downtown Long Beach. The fare is $1.10; trains operate daily 5 a.m.-10 p.m. Phone (213) 639-6800 or 620-7245.

The Metro Red Line subway, running from Union Station to MacArthur Park, is scheduled to open in June 1993. Metrolink, a commuter rail service, operates three lines between Union Station (downtown at Macy and Alameda streets) and Santa Clarita, Pomona and Moorpark. For schedule and fare information phone (213) 620-7245.

DASH (Downtown Area Short Hop), a minibus shuttle system, operates at frequent intervals Mon.-Sat. The route of the silver and magenta minibuses passes close to most business centers, retail stores, points of interest and major hotels in the central city. The fare is 25c; exact change is required. Phone (800) 252-7433.

What To See

ARMAND HAMMER MUSEUM OF ART AND CULTURAL CENTER, 10899 Wilshire Blvd., has galleries set around an open courtyard. The museum's permanent collection includes more than 100 paintings by such artists as Rembrandt, Van Gogh, Monet and Wyeth. There is an extensive collection of works by Daumier and a manuscript with 360 drawings by Da Vinci.

Tues.-Sun. 10-6; closed Jan. 1, Thanksgiving and Dec. 25. Admission $4.50, senior citizens and students $3, under 16 free; free to all last Thurs. of the month. Phone (310) 443-7000.

ATLANTIC RICHFIELD PLAZA is bordered by 5th, Flower, 6th and Figueroa sts. ARCO Plaza, an underground shopping mall, is topped by the 52-floor ARCO/Bank of America twin towers, one of the largest office complexes in the West. Parking is available at 400 S. Flower St.

BRADBURY BUILDING, 304 S. Broadway, was built in 1893 by Louis Bradbury, who made his fortune in Mexican silver mining. Ornate iron railings line the five-story rectangular inner court, which rises to a large skylight. Marble stairs and Mexican tile complement the rich wood paneling and marble floors. Mon.-Fri. 9-5. Phone (213) 626-1893.

★CALIFORNIA MUSEUM OF SCIENCE AND INDUSTRY— see Exposition Park.

★CHINATOWN is bordered by Alpine, Spring and Yale sts. and Bamboo La. Chinese shops and restaurants line streets off Gin Ling Way, the "Street of the Golden Palace." Colorful Chinese festivals and processions are held in this area. A walking-tour map of the area is available for $1.50 from the visitor center in nearby El Pueblo de Los Angeles Historic Monument (see Sightseeing, Walking Tours).

CIVIC CENTER, roughly bounded by Sunset Blvd., Grand Ave., and First and San Pedro sts., houses city, county, state and federal offices. The Arthur Will Memorial Fountain is on Grand Avenue. The Department of Water and Power Building across from the Music Center is surrounded by reflecting pools.

City Hall, 200 N. Spring St., is 454 feet high. The tower and its observation deck are open daily 10-4; closed holidays. Free. Phone (213) 485-2891.

DODGER STADIUM, 1000 Elysian Park Ave., n. of the Civic Center, is visible from Academy Rd. The cantilevered structure, which seats 56,000, is open for baseball games and special events only. The Dodgers baseball season usually runs early Apr.-early Oct. For schedule and ticket information phone (213) 224-1400.

★EL PUEBLO DE LOS ANGELES HISTORIC MONUMENT consists of 44 acres bounded by Alameda, Arcadia, Spring and Macy sts. Historical landmarks have been restored. Free guided walking tours are given Tues.-Sat. at 10, 11, noon and 1, except Jan. 1, Thanksgiving and Dec. 25. For information contact the visitor center in the Sepulveda House, 622 N. Main St., Mon.-Fri. 10-3, Sat. 10-4:30; closed holidays. Phone (213) 628-1274.

Avila Adobe, 10 E. Olvera St., was built in 1818 by rancher Don Francisco Avila. Damaged by an earthquake in 1971, it has been restored to exemplify the California lifestyle of the 1840s. Tues.-Fri. 10-3, Sat.-Sun. 10-4:30; closed holidays. Free.

Masonic Hall, 416-418 N. Main St., was built in 1858. It has been restored with many furnishings and fixtures that were brought around Cape Horn by sailing ships. Tues.-Fri. 10-3; closed holidays. Free.

Old Plaza, N. Main St., was the center of activity in the old pueblo of Los Angeles. It contains an ornate kiosk, century-old Moreton Bay fig trees, a statue of Felipe de Neve, leader of the group that founded the city in 1781, and a statue of King Carlos III, ruler of Spain at that time.

Old Plaza Church (Nuestra Señora la Reina de Los Angeles), on N. Main St. at the Plaza, is the oldest church in the city. Completed by the Franciscans in 1822, it is still in service.

Old Plaza Firehouse, 134 Paseo de la Plaza, was built in 1884. It houses an original chemical wagon, antique firefighting equipment and historic photographs. Tues.-Fri. 10-3, Sat.-Sun. 10-4:30; closed holidays. Free.

★**Olvera Street** is n. of the Plaza between N. Main and Alameda sts. One of the oldest streets in the city, it was revitalized in 1930 as a Mexican marketplace. Sidewalk shops and stalls sell Mexican handicrafts; restaurants serve Mexican dishes. Las Posadas, the Mexican Christmas festival, is celebrated in December. Daily 10-8; some shops close later in summer.

Pico House, 424-436 N. Main St., was once an elegant hotel built in 1870 by Pio Pico, the last governor of California under the Mexican flag. The hotel is partially restored, but it is not open to the public.

Sepulveda House, 622 N. Main. St., is a two-story Eastlake Victorian building built in 1887. The original owner, Eloisa Martínez de Sepulveda, used the structure as a boarding house with shops and as her own residence. The house is partially restored and includes the historic monument's visitor center. An 18-minute film on the history of Los Angeles is shown Mon.-Sat. at 11 and 2. Visitor center open Mon.-Fri. 10-3, Sat. 10-4:30; closed holidays. Free. Phone (213) 628-1274.

★**EXPOSITION PARK,** bounded by Figueroa St., Exposition Blvd., Menlo Ave. and Martin Luther King Jr. Blvd., is a civic, cultural and recreational center. Within the park is a 7-acre sunken rose garden, where 16,000 specimens of 190 varieties are cultivated.

California Afro-American Museum is at 600 State Dr. The museum has a permanent fine arts and history collection relating to Afro-American life. There also are changing exhibits of paintings, photographs, films and artifacts. Daily 10-5; closed Jan. 1, Memorial Day, Thanksgiving and Dec. 25. Free. Phone (213) 744-7432.

★**California Museum of Science and Industry,** 700 State Dr., has hands-on exhibits related to mathematics, space, the environment, health, earthquakes and economics. The Aerospace Complex, dedicated to the history of air and space flight, contains the Aerospace Hall, the Air and Space Garden and the IMAX® Theater, which uses a large screen to re-create air, land, water and space travel.

Museum open daily 10-5; closed Jan. 1, Thanksgiving and Dec. 25. Theater schedule varies. Museum free. Theater admission $5.50; over 55 and ages 4-17, $4. MC, VI. **Discount,** except over 55. Parking $2. Phone (213) 744-2014 for theater, 744-7400 for museum.

Los Angeles Memorial Coliseum is at 3911 S. Figueroa St. The Coliseum is the home of the Los Angeles Raiders and the University of Southern California Trojans football teams. The Coliseum played host to both the 1932 Olympic Games and the 1984 Summer Olympics track and field events. It will undergo an extensive renovation in 1993. Phone (213) 748-6136.

Los Angeles Memorial Sports Arena, 3939 S. Figueroa St., is an indoor sports and entertainment facility. It is the home court for the Los Angeles Clippers and the University of Southern California basketball teams. Various events, including numerous concerts, a circus and an ice show take place here. Phone (213) 748-6136.

★**Natural History Museum of Los Angeles County** is at 900 Exposition Blvd. The museum contains detailed habitats of African, North American and exotic mammals. Exhibits include birds, insects and marine life; displays of dinosaurs and prehistoric fossils; a mineral collection; an outstanding cut gemstone collection; and Megamouth, said to be the world's rarest shark.

History galleries depict life in California and the Southwest 1540-1940, U.S. history from the Colonial period through 1914 and pre-Columbian archeology. The Discovery Center has hands-on exhibits for children and an insect zoo. Both areas are open Tues.-Sun. 11-3. Museum open Tues.-Sun. 10-5; closed Jan. 1, Thanksgiving and Dec. 25. Admission $5; over 65 and ages 12-17, $3.50; ages 5-11, $2; free to all first Tues. of the month. **Discount.** Phone (213) 744-3466.

★**FARMERS MARKET**— *see Where To Shop.*

FIRST BAPTIST CHURCH is at 760 S. Westmoreland Ave. The rose windows are patterned after those in the cathedral at Chartres, France, and the goldleaf embossed ceiling replicates that of an Italian palace. Mon.-Fri. 9-4:30, Sun. 8-1; closed holidays. Phone (213) 384-2151.

FOREST LAWN MEMORIAL-PARK—HOLLYWOOD HILLS, a 340-acre cemetery at 6300 Forest Lawn Dr., w. of Griffith Park, features Carrara marble and bronze statuary. In the 15-acre Court of Liberty are Thomas Ball's 60-foot bronze and marble Washington Memorial, a replica of the Liberty Bell and a 30- by 165-foot mosaic, "The Birth of Liberty." The Hall of Liberty presents the film "The Birth of Liberty" daily 11-4. Also in the hall is the Museum of Mexican History; an outdoor plaza contains reproductions of historic Mexican sculpture.

The park also contains a replica of Boston's Old North Church; it is closed during private services. Park open daily 9-6, in summer; 9-5, rest of year. Free. Phone (818) 241-4151.

GENE AUTRY WESTERN HERITAGE MUSEUM— see Griffith Park.

GEORGE C. PAGE MUSEUM OF LA BREA DISCOVERIES, 5801 Wilshire Blvd., exhibits reconstructed fossils of such ice-age animals as dire wolves, birds of prey and sabertooth cats. A 14-minute film, "The La Brea Story," provides an introduction to the museum and depicts prehistoric life in Southern California. Visitors can watch fossils being cleaned, identified and catalogued in the paleontological laboratory.
Tues.-Sun. 10-5; closed Jan. 1, Thanksgiving and Dec. 25. Admission $5; over 65 and students $2.50; ages 5-11, $1; free to all second Tues. of the month. **Discount.** Fee for parking in lot behind the museum. Phone (213) 936-2230 or 857-6311.

Rancho La Brea Tar Pits, Wilshire Blvd. and Curson Ave., are among the richest sources of ice-age fossils. These sticky asphalt beds trapped and preserved prehistoric plant and animal life. The viewing station and observation pit show how specimens appeared when they were discovered. Findings are displayed in the Page Museum. Guided tours of the grounds depart from the observation pit Wed.-Sun. at 1. Observation pit open Sat.-Sun. 10-5; no tours Jan. 1, Thanksgiving and Dec. 25. Free. Phone (213) 936-2230.

★**GRIFFITH PARK**, 4,107 acres at the e. end of the Santa Monica Mountains, contains recreational facilities, wilderness areas and many attractions. The visitor center and park ranger headquarters, 4730 Crystal Springs Dr., provides information on the park. The park is open and a ranger on duty daily 6 a.m.-10 p.m. Free. Phone (213) 665-5188.

Children's attractions near the Los Feliz Boulevard entrance include pony rides, a miniature stagecoach and a one-third scale model of an 1880s steam engine that runs a 1½-mile route through the park. Near the train station is the SR-2 Simulator, which uses film, sound effects and hydraulic motion to make participants feel as if they are experiencing roller-coaster rides and other thrills. For pony ride and stagecoach information, phone (213) 664-3266; train ride and simulator, (213) 664-6788.

Interpretive hikes conducted by the Sierra Club leave ranger headquarters at 9 a.m. on the first Saturday of the month. For more information on these and other hikes contact the ranger headquarters.

Gene Autry Western Heritage Museum, 4700 Western Heritage Way, uses paintings, artifacts and audiovisual materials to present the history of America's westward movement. Permanent and changing exhibits feature such displays as a firearms collection, a 19th-century fire engine, Frederic Remington paintings and "cowboy movie" excerpts. Food is available.
Tues.-Sun. 10-5. Last admission is at 4:15. Closed Thanksgiving and Dec. 25. Admission $6; over 60 and ages 13-18, $4.50; ages 2-12, $2.50. **Discount.** Phone (213) 667-2000.

Greek Theatre, in a natural amphitheater at 2700 N. Vermont Ave., is the scene of summer concerts and ballets. Tickets prices begin at about $20. Parking $5. AE, MC, VI. Phone (213) 665-1927.

Griffith Observatory and Planetarium, on the s. slopes of Mount Hollywood, is a popular spot for viewing both city lights and stars. The planetarium reproduces the night sky indoors, and special effects replicate celestial phenomena visible to the naked eye. Visitors may use the twin refracting telescope on clear evenings, nightly dusk-9:45 p.m., in summer; Tues.-Sun. 7-9:45 p.m., rest of year. Closed Thanksgiving and Dec. 24-25. Free. Phone (213) 664-1191.

The Hall of Science has exhibits on mankind's relationship with the universe. Daily 12:30-10, in summer; Tues.-Fri. 2-10, Sat.-Sun. 12:30-10, rest of year. Free.

A 24-hour recorded message describes astronomical phenomena visible in Southern California skies; phone (213) 663-8171.

Planetarium shows are presented Mon.-Fri. at 1:30, 3 and 7:30 p.m., Sat.-Sun. at 1:30, 3, 4:30 and 7:30 p.m., in summer; Tues.-Fri. at 3 and 7:30 p.m., Sat.-Sun. and holidays at 1:30, 3, 4:30 and 7:30 p.m., rest of year. Admission $3.50; senior citizens $2.50; ages 5-12, $2. Under 5 admitted only at 1:30 show when accompanied by a parent or guardian; free. Box office opens a half-hour before each show; there are no reserved seats.

Laserium shows are presented Tues.-Thurs. and Sun. at 6 and 8:45 p.m., Fri.-Sat. and various holidays at 6, 8:45 and 9:45 p.m. Admission $6.50; senior citizens and ages 5-12, $5.50. Under 5 not admitted. Phone (818) 997-3624.

★**Los Angeles Zoo**, near the jct. of the Golden State and Ventura frwys., covers 113 acres of landscaped hills. Five continental areas provide natural settings for more than 2,000 mammals, birds and reptiles. Adventure Island showcases animals native to the Southwest in their natural habitats. Wildlife shows are offered. Picnicking is permitted. Daily 10-6, in summer; 10-5, rest of year. Closed Dec. 25. Admission $6; over 65, $5; ages 2-12, $2.75. **Discount**, except over 65 and ages 2-12. Phone (213) 666-4090.

Travel Town, n. side of Griffith Park on N. Zoo Dr., is an outdoor transportation museum with steam locomotives and other early railroad equipment. An indoor area features wagons, period automobiles and Los Angeles firefighting equipment used 1869-1940. A miniature train circles the area. Mon.-Fri. 10-5, Sat.-Sun. and holidays 10-6, Apr.-Oct.; Mon.-Fri. 10-4, Sat.-Sun. and holidays 10-5, rest of year. Closed Dec. 25. Donations. Train rides are available; fare $1.75; ages 1½-13, $1.25; senior citizens $1. Phone (213) 662-5874.

HEBREW UNION COLLEGE SKIRBALL MUSEUM, 3077 University Ave. at Hoover and 32nd sts., contains Middle Eastern archeological artifacts, Judaic art and artifacts and folk art displays. Tues.-Fri. and some Sun. 11-4; closed public and Jewish holidays. Free. Phone (213) 749-3424.

HERITAGE SQUARE MUSEUM— *see The Museum Village at Heritage Square.*

HOLLYHOCK HOUSE, 4800 Hollywood Blvd. in Barnsdall Park, is considered one of Frank Lloyd Wright's finest works. Tours on the hour Tues.-Sun. noon-3. Admission $1.50, under 12 free with an adult. Phone (213) 662-7272.

LA BREA TAR PITS— *see George C. Page Museum of La Brea Discoveries.*

★**LITTLE TOKYO,** bounded by First, Alameda, 3rd and Los Angeles sts., is the social, cultural and economic center of Southern California's Japanese community. The 21-story New Otani Hotel and the Japanese American Cultural and Community Center attest to the area's vitality. Four shopping centers—Japanese Village Plaza, Weller Court, Yaohan Plaza and Honda Plaza—contain numerous restaurants and shops. For information on guided tours phone (213) 620-0570. Nisei Week is celebrated in August; phone (213) 687-7193.

Japanese American National Museum, 1st and Central sts., occupies a remodeled Buddhist temple with displays of photographs, personal objects, art works, agricultural implements and ceremonial clothing. Other highlights include an area where visitors may experiment with origami, examine Japanese family photo albums, learn about World War II internment camps and view the 15-minute film, "Through Our Own Eyes."

Tues.-Thurs. and Sat.-Sun. 10-5, Fri. 11-8; closed Jan. 1, Thanksgiving and Dec. 25. Admission $4, over 62, ages 6-17 and college students with ID $3. Phone (213) 625-0414.

LOS ANGELES CENTRAL LIBRARY, 630 W. 5th St. between Grand Ave. and Flower St., is a landmark structure designed by noted architect Bertram Goodhue. Damaged by fire in 1986, the building is closed and is being restored as part of a major redevelopment project. A temporary library location has opened in the Historic Title Insurance and Trust Building, 433 S. Spring St. Open Mon.-Tues. noon-8, Wed.-Sat. 10-5:30. Phone (213) 612-3200.

LOS ANGELES CHILDREN'S MUSEUM, 310 N. Main St. in the Los Angeles Mall, offers a hands-on environment designed to demystify everyday experiences for children. Interactive exhibits include a TV studio, recording studio, zoetrope (animation) and city streets. Mon.-Fri. 11:30-5, Sat.-Sun. 10-5, late June-Aug. 31; Wed.-Thurs. 2-4, Sat.-Sun. 10-5, rest of year; also open special hours on selected holidays. Closed major holidays. Admission $5. Phone (213) 687-8800.

★**LOS ANGELES COUNTY MUSEUM OF ART,** 5905 Wilshire Blvd., consists of several structures surrounding a central court. The Ahmanson Building houses a permanent collection of paintings, sculpture, graphic arts, costumes, textiles and decorative arts. The Hammer Building displays special loan exhibitions, while the Anderson Building features 20th-century paintings and sculpture.

The Pavilion for Japanese Art contains the renowned Shin'enkan paintings as well as a collection of other Japanese artworks. Lectures, films and other special events are presented in the Bing Center theater. There also are two sculpture gardens.

Guided tours are offered daily. Food is available. Tues.-Fri. 10-5 (also Fri. 5-9, except Pavilion for Japanese Art), Sat.-Sun. 11-6; closed Jan. 1, Thanksgiving and Dec. 25. Admission $5; over 62 and students $3.50; ages 6-17, $1; permanent exhibits free to all second Tues. of the month. A parking fee is charged. Phone (213) 857-6111.

LOS ANGELES MORMON TEMPLE, 10777 Santa Monica Blvd., is one of the largest temples of the Church of Jesus Christ of Latter-Day Saints. A 15-foot statue of Angel Moroni tops the temple's 257-foot tower. The temple is closed to non-Mormons. The visitor center showcases Mormon history and theology and is open daily 9-9. Free. Phone (310) 474-1549.

LOS ANGELES MUNICIPAL ART GALLERY, 4804 Hollywood Blvd. in Barnsdall Park, presents changing exhibits of contemporary art from Southern California. Tues.-Sun. 12:30-5; closed holidays and between exhibits. Admission $1, under 12 free with an adult. Phone (213) 485-4581.

LOS ANGELES TIMES, 202 W. First St., offers 45-minute tours of its editorial operations Mon.-Fri. at 11:15 and 3. Also offered are 1-hour tours of the Times' printing facilities, 2000 E. 8th St., on Tues. and Thurs. at 9:45 and 10 by reservation. Closed holidays. Under 10 are not permitted. Free. Phone (213) 237-5757.

★**LOS ANGELES ZOO**— *see Griffith Park.*

MUSEUM OF CONTEMPORARY ART, 250 S. Grand Ave. at California Plaza, houses a collection of international works from the 1940s to the present, including paintings, sculptures and environmental pieces. Mixed media and performing arts programs also are presented. The building, designed by Arata Isozaki, is itself considered a work of modern art.

Tues.-Sun. 11-5 (also Thurs. 5-8); closed Jan. 1, Thanksgiving and Dec. 25. Admission $4, over 65 and students with ID $2, under 12 free; free to all Thurs. 5-8. Phone (213) 626-6222.

THE MUSEUM VILLAGE AT HERITAGE SQUARE, 3800 Homer St., contains relocated and restored 19th-century buildings that reflect the lifestyle of the people of Los Angeles 1865-1914. Guided tours are available. Wed.-Sun. noon-4. Admission $5; over 65 and ages 12-17, $3; ages 7-11, $1. Phone (818) 449-0193.

★**THE MUSIC CENTER,** 1st St. and Grand Ave., is a three-theater complex at the crown of the Civic Center. One-hour guided tours include the Dorothy Chandler Pavilion (the center's largest building), the Ahmanson Theatre and the Mark Taper Forum. Tours Mon.-Tues. and Thurs.-Fri. 10-1:30, Sat. 10-noon, May-Oct.; Mon.-Thurs. 10-1:30, Sat. 10-noon, rest of year. Tours free; reservations are recommended. For tour reservations phone (213) 972-7483; for show information phone (213) 972-7211.

★**NATURAL HISTORY MUSEUM OF LOS ANGELES COUNTY**— *see Exposition Park.*

★**OLVERA STREET**— *see El Pueblo de Los Angeles Historic Monument.*

ST. JOHN'S CHURCH (Episcopal), W. Adams Blvd., just e. of Figueroa St., replicates an 11th-century church in Toscanella, Italy. The Martin Luther King Jr. window, dedicated in 1977, is on the west side of the clerestory. Mon. and Thurs. 9-5, Wed. 9-7, Fri. 9-3, Sat.-Sun. 9-noon; closed holidays. Phone (213) 747-6285.

ST. SOPHIA CATHEDRAL (Greek Orthodox) is at 1324 S. Normandie Ave. Stained-glass windows, large-scale murals, gilded woodwork and crystal chandeliers highlight the domed interior. Photography is not permitted. Fri.-Wed. 10-2; closed holidays. Phone (213) 737-2426.

ST. VINCENT DE PAUL CHURCH (Catholic), Adams Blvd. and Figueroa St., is an elaborate Spanish Colonial style church with mosaic tile from Mexico. Daily 9-5. Phone (213) 749-8950.

SAN ANTONIO WINERY, 737 Lamar St., produces varietals from jug wine to cognac. Food is available. Tours daily 10-3. Free. Phone (213) 223-1401.

SOUTHWEST MUSEUM, 234 Museum Dr., offers art exhibits and artifacts representing the diversity of American Indian cultures from prehistoric times to the present. Collections include basketry, pottery, paintings, textiles, religious icons and decorative arts. Changing exhibits explore various cultural aspects of different regions. Lectures, demonstrations and other special programs are scheduled periodically. Tues.-Sun. 11-5;

closed holidays. Admission $5; senior citizens and students $3; ages 7-18, $2. Phone (213) 221-2164.

★**UNIVERSITY OF CALIFORNIA, LOS ANGELES (UCLA),** 405 Hilgard Ave., occupies 419 acres in the foothills of the Santa Monica Mountains. Relocated here in 1929, the university encompasses several major complexes, including a large medical center, and enrolls more than 34,000 students each year. Phone (310) 825-4321.

Schoenberg Hall features free noon concerts October through May and houses the Erich Lachmann Collection of rare stringed instruments. UCLA Center for the Arts sponsors professional performances at Royce Hall throughout the year. Walking tours of the campus depart from the visitor center, 1417 Ueberroth Building, 10945 Le Conte Ave. Mon.-Fri. at 10:30 and 1:30. Fee for on-campus parking. Phone (310) 206-8147.

Edwin W. Pauley Pavilion, on the w. side of campus off Westwood Blvd., is a 13,000-seat arena that accommodates UCLA basketball, volleyball, wrestling, badminton and gymnastic events. For tickets phone (310) 825-2101.

Fowler Museum of Cultural History, on the n. side of campus w. of Royce Hall, is a three-story structure housing a collection of African, Oceanic and American Indian art and artifacts. Wed.-Sun. noon-5 (also Thurs. 5-8). Free. Phone (310) 825-4361.

Franklin D. Murphy Sculpture Gardens, on the n. portion of the campus in front of the Dickson Art Center, is an outdoor museum of 20th-century sculpture.

Mildred E. Mathias Botanical Gardens, Hilgard and Le Conte aves., consists of 8 acres of native, subtropical and exotic plants. Walking paths through the gardens are open Mon.-Fri. 8-5, Sat.-Sun. 8-4; closed university holidays. Phone (310) 825-3620.

Wight Art Gallery, on the n. part of campus in the Dickson Art Center, holds major art exhibits throughout the year. Open during exhibits Tues. 11-7, Wed.-Fri. 11-5, Sat.-Sun. 1-5; guided tours are offered Sat. and Sun. at 1:30 and by appointment. Phone (310) 825-9345.

UNIVERSITY OF SOUTHERN CALIFORNIA (USC), Exposition Blvd. and S. Figueroa St., was founded in 1880 and is one of the oldest private universities in the West. Widney Alumni House, USC's first building, is the second oldest school structure in California. Encompassing 180 acres, the university enrolls more than 30,000 students annually.

The McDonalds Swim Stadium, site of the 1984 Summer Olympics swimming and diving events, is on the northwest side of campus. One-hour walking tours of the campus are available by appointment Mon.-Fri. 10-2. Parking $5. Phone (213) 740-2300.

THE HOTTEST DOUBLE FEATURE EVER.

E.T.: THE RIDE OF A LIFETIME.

Soar beyond the stars – beyond your wildest dreams as Steven Spielberg's film classic becomes a breathtaking new ride for the whole family!

BACKDRAFT: 10,000 DEGREES OF LIVE EXCITEMENT.

We'll engulf you in a firestorm of special effects – blazing beams, exploding barrels, rocketing drums, even a raging river of fire – as Ron Howard's blockbuster movie roars to life! Then thrill to EARTHQUAKE,® KING KONG and much, much more!

Just show your AAA card at our ticket booth and save 10% on each admission for up to 6 people.

No one makes believe like we do.

UNIVERSAL STUDIOS
Hollywood

The university grounds contain several exhibits and statues. A life-size bronze figure of a Trojan warrior, the university's symbol, stands near the entrance to the Bovard Administration Building. Near the center of campus in Founders Park, a 400-pound boulder quarried before 1200 B.C. from the ancient city of Troy is displayed. Arnold Schoenberg Institute houses the complete archives and library of Schoenberg, a major 20th-century composer. Drama is presented throughout the year at Bing Theater; phone (213) 740-1247.

Fisher Gallery, 823 Exposition Blvd., displays rotating exhibits, including works of European old masters and contemporary artworks. Tues.-Fri. noon-5, Sat. noon-4, early Sept. to mid-May. Free. Phone (213) 740-4561.

Hancock Memorial Museum, in the Hancock Foundation Building, Trousdale Pkwy. and Childs Way, offers tours through four rooms of the 1890 Hancock Mansion. Furnishings include items from the palace of Emperor Maximilian of Mexico. Mon.-Fri. by appointment. Phone (213) 740-0433.

WATTS TOWERS OF SIMON RODIA STATE HISTORIC PARK (Towers of Simon Rodia), 1765 E. 107th St., are eight weblike towers of concrete-coated steel rods encrusted with shells, tile, pottery and glass. Tilesetter Simon Rodia spent 33 years creating these remarkable works of folk art. The Watts Towers Art Center, next to the towers, sponsors exhibits, classes and cultural events. The upper portions of the towers are readily visible from the center. Tours of the towers Sat.-Sun. noon-4. Admission $2, children $1.50. Phone (213) 569-8181.

WELLS FARGO HISTORY MUSEUM is in the Wells Fargo Center, 333 S. Grand Ave. Hundreds of items and a 17-minute multimedia show depict the history and development of the West and the Wells Fargo Bank since its founding in 1852.

Highlights include a 19th-century stagecoach, a 2-pound gold nugget, prospecting and assaying equipment, bank notes, maps, photographs and lithographs from the 1800s. Visitors can board a stagecoach and listen to a first-hand description of a 3-week journey from St. Louis to San Francisco taken in 1859. Mon.-Fri. 9-5; closed bank holidays. Free. Phone (213) 253-7166.

WILSHIRE BOULEVARD TEMPLE, Wilshire and Hobart blvds., is dominated by a 135-foot dome inlaid with mosaics. The interior walls have murals with Biblical and post-Biblical themes. A gallery contains exhibits explaining the history and customs of various Jewish celebrations. Mon.-Fri. 10-4; closed Jewish holidays. Phone (213) 388-2401.

Studio Tours
KCET-TV STUDIO TOUR, 4401 Sunset Blvd., is a 90-minute tour behind the scenes of one of the nation's leading public television stations. The technical aspects of television production are explained; visitors see sound stages and learn how the cameras operate. Reservations should be made 1 week in advance. Under 6th-grade level not allowed. Tours Tues. and Thurs. mornings by reservation. Free. Phone (213) 667-9242.

TELEVISION STUDIOS of the major broadcasting companies offer many studio audience shows. Ticket requests should be made well in advance; some shows have waiting lists several months long. For further information phone the following offices: ABC, (213) 557-4143; CBS Television City, (213) 852-2458; FOX, (213) 856-1520; NBC, (818) 840-4444, ext. 3537.

★**UNIVERSAL STUDIOS HOLLYWOOD**— *see Universal City.*

THE WARNER BROS. STUDIOS V.I.P. TOUR— *see Burbank.*

Suburban Areas
★**DESCANSO GARDENS**— *see La Cañada Flintridge.*

★**DISNEYLAND**— *see Anaheim.*

★**FOREST LAWN MEMORIAL-PARK**— *see Glendale.*

★**HOLLYWOOD BOWL**— *see Hollywood.*

★**HUNTINGTON LIBRARY, ART COLLECTIONS AND BOTANICAL GARDENS**— *see San Marino.*

★**J. PAUL GETTY MUSEUM**— *see Malibu.*

★**KNOTT'S BERRY FARM**— *see Buena Park.*

★**LOS ANGELES STATE AND COUNTY ARBORETUM**— *see Arcadia.*

★**MANN'S CHINESE THEATRE**— *see Hollywood.*

★**MOVIELAND WAX MUSEUM**— *see Buena Park.*

★**NORTON SIMON MUSEUM**— *see Pasadena.*

★**PORTS O' CALL VILLAGE**— *see San Pedro.*

★**RANCHO SANTA ANA BOTANIC GARDEN**— *see Claremont.*

★**UNIVERSAL STUDIOS HOLLYWOOD**— *see Universal City.*

★**WILL ROGERS STATE HISTORIC PARK**— *see Pacific Palisades.*

What To Do
Sightseeing
Bus, Limousine, Carriage and Train Tours
One way to get a comprehensive picture of Los Angeles is by taking an organized bus or limousine tour. Prices vary according to the itinerary and length of tour.

Bus tours of downtown Los Angeles depart on the first and third Wednesday mornings of the month from the Docent Center adjoining the Old Plaza Firehouse in El Pueblo de Los Angeles Historic Monument *(see attraction listing)*. Sponsored by Las Angelitas del Pueblo, the 2-hour tours visit St. Vibiana's Cathedral and Carroll Avenue. Reservations are required; phone (213) 628-1274.

Boat Tours

Boat tours of the Los Angeles harbor depart Ports O' Call Village *(see San Pedro)*. Ships also leave San Pedro for Catalina Island.

Walking Tours

The Los Angeles Conservancy offers 10 guided walking tours of historic downtown Los Angeles. Two-hour tours depart Saturday at 10 from the Biltmore Hotel's Olive Street entrance. Two-hour tours of Little Tokyo leave from the Japanese American Cultural Community Center Plaza on the first Saturday of the month at 10. One-hour tours of Union Station depart from the main entrance of the station on the third Saturday of the month at 10. The Conservancy also offers tours of the Art Deco-style I. Magnin/Bullocks Wilshire department store building. All tours cost $5; reservations are required. Phone (213) 623-2489.

RTD offers self-guiding tours to a number of Southern California tourist attractions on the bus route *(see Public Transportation)*. Other touring companies are listed in the telephone directory. Reservations should be made at least 24 hours in advance.

A walking-tour guide and map of Chinatown is available for $1.50 at El Pueblo de Los Angeles Historic Monument's visitor center, 622 N. Main St.

Self-guiding Tour

The best way to see downtown Los Angeles is on foot. The walking tour outlined here *(see map page 103)* is approximately 2½ miles long and will take at least 4 hours, allowing time for lunch and browsing. The tour is designed to return you to the starting point via the convenient DASH minibus. **Note:** DASH does not operate on Sunday, but other public transportation is available.

The tour starts on Bunker Hill atop the ARCO garage at Hope and Fourth sts. The location—next to the YMCA—can be reached by the garage elevator or from the bridge linking it with the futuristic Westin Bonaventure. The impressive buildings of the financial district are visible on all sides. Each building is distinctly different in color and shape, yet all blend harmoniously in accordance with the guiding agency's decree that all developments be architecturally compatible and spaced to allow plenty of sunlight to reach the plazas and streets below.

Extensive landscaping and artwork also play an important role in this district. The Bank of America water garden (1 block north), The Wells Fargo Court (diagonally across at Fourth and Hope) and the forecourt and tiered plazas of the 444 building are particularly attractive.

The First Interstate World Center, with its dramatic crown-like top, is America's tallest building west of Chicago. Next to the 1,017-foot tower is a beautiful Spanish-style stairway that leads in a series of cascades down to Fifth Street.

While still atop the ARCO garage, walk to the edge opposite the Westin Bonaventure. The landscaped parks covering the roofs of the buildings below also were a design requirement, as was the pedestrian skyway system that connects the complexes.

Leave the rooftop at Fourth and Hope and walk through The Wells Fargo Court to Grand Ave. (The Court is the glass-enclosed garden pavilion between the huge granite towers housing Wells Fargo Bank and IBM.) Across Grand is the California Plaza, which includes the Museum of Contemporary Art.

Although some construction remains to be done, the massive project includes three towering office buildings, nearly a thousand apartments, a major hotel, shops and restaurants, and the restored Angels Flight, a funicular railway that carried passengers up and down Bunker Hill 1901-69.

Continuing north on Grand you will notice that the roadway is elevated. Below is lower Grand Ave., which provides access to underground garages, thereby keeping the sidewalks on upper Grand free of automobile entranceways. Two blocks north is the Los Angeles Music Center, home of such famous companies as the Los Angeles Philharmonic Orchestra.

The huge building just west of the Music Center is the headquarters of the Los Angeles Department of Water and Power, the nation's largest public utility. The reflecting pool surrounding it is lined by a promenade from which you can see much of central Los Angeles.

Moving east from the Music Center, cross Grand Ave. to the plaza that leads toward the City Hall, the tall, pyramid-topped building straight ahead. You'll pass the impressive Arthur Will Memorial Fountain and see a great variety of subtropical foliage. The brilliant orange blooms of the bird-of-paradise plant—the city's official flower—can be found throughout the Civic Center.

Many of the Civic Center's major buildings surround the mall, including federal, state, county and city courthouses, record centers and administrative offices. Together they constitute one of the largest government complexes in the entire country outside of those in Washington, D.C.

Proceed east through the "Court of Flags" to Broadway, then turn south a half block to First St. and continue east past the mammoth headquarters of the *Los Angeles Times*. The *Times* lobby, with its giant globe of the world, is worth a look.

Two blocks farther east on First and next to the New Otani Hotel is Weller Court. An attractive development in the Little Tokyo district, the court contains many restaurants and shops. An excellent place to take a break is the Japanese Garden atop the south wing of the New Otani Hotel. The bustling city below and the skyscrapers on the horizon provide an intriguing contrast to the tumbling waterfalls, placid streams and serene landscaping of the garden.

An equally lovely garden is found at the Japanese American Cultural and Community Center, a half block south of 2nd St. on San Pedro St. It lies just beyond the spacious Noguchi Plaza, whose main focus is a striking work by the sculptor Isamu Noguchi. Fronting the plaza are the community center building and the Japan America Theatre, the scene of many performances from both Eastern and Western cultures.

Leading north from Noguchi Plaza, a pedestrian lane crosses Second St. and enters Japanese Village Plaza, a pleasant collection of small restaurants and stores. Cross the plaza to First St. At First and Central is the Japanese American National Museum, providing an insight into Japanese family life in the United States.

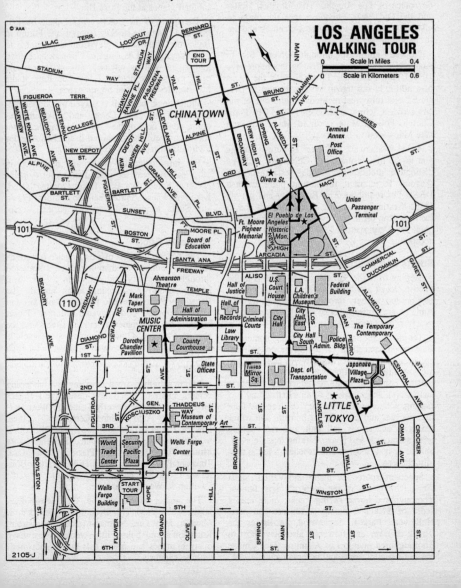

The rather drab area east and south of Little Tokyo is being redeveloped into artists' galleries and lofts. The "Art Scene" brochure pinpoints various galleries here and elsewhere in Los Angeles and is available from Los Angeles Contemporary Exhibitions (LACE); phone (213) 624-5650. Various galleries and museums throughout the city also distribute the brochure.

Turning back on First St. to Main St., you'll re-enter the Civic Center. Go north on Main past City Hall, Los Angeles Mall, a sunken shopping plaza containing the Triforium (a musical tower) and the Los Angeles Children's Museum to El Pueblo de Los Angeles Historic Monument, the birthplace of Los Angeles. Historic Pico House and the Old Plaza Firehouse face the plaza. A visitor information center has brochures and information on the park.

Proceed northeast through Olvera St. to Alameda St. Across the street is the impressive 1939 Union Passenger Terminal, now the focus of a 300-mile rail transit system. Return to Olvera St. and turn west to Main St. and one of the city's oldest religious structures—the Old Plaza Church. Follow Main north to Macy St., then take Macy west to Broadway.

A 3½-block walk north on Broadway brings you to the main entrance of Chinatown, with its distinctive architecture, shops, restaurants and dragons. To return to the starting point, catch a DASH bus southbound on Broadway and get off at the Westin Bonaventure. For a pleasant end to the tour, stop off at the revolving lounge atop the hotel for a panorama of the city; casual dress is acceptable.

Sports and Recreation

Sloping from the San Gabriel Mountains to the Pacific Ocean and blessed with a climate permitting outdoor activity throughout the year, the Los Angeles area offers recreational opportunities to satisfy every taste.

Tennis courts and golf courses are numerous. Beaches are excellent all along the coast; most are open to the public. Available at most beaches are swimming, surfing (sometimes restricted to the less congested hours to reduce the hazard to swimmers), scuba diving or snorkeling and surf fishing. Other areas offer pier or deep-sea fishing, marinas and facilities for boating and water skiing. Concessions sell bait and rent fishing gear, surfboards and boats. Parking lots are available at or near most public beaches; a fee is usually charged.

Spectator sports are many and varied. Santa Anita Park is one of the country's most famous Thoroughbred horse racing tracks; more than a score of $100,000 racing stakes are run here. Hollywood Park in Inglewood, known as the "track of lakes and flowers," also plays host to Thoroughbred racing; Los Alamitos Race Course has both quarter horse and harness racing.

Note: Policies concerning admittance of children to pari-mutuel betting facilities vary. Phone ahead for information.

Polo is frequently played at Will Rogers State Historic Park in Pacific Palisades, usually on Saturday and Sunday, weather permitting.

The college football event of the year is the Rose Bowl Game, played in Pasadena each New Year's Day. From August to mid-December the Los Angeles Rams generate football excitement at Anaheim Stadium. The home games of USC and the NFL Los Angeles Raiders football teams are played at the Los Angeles Memorial Coliseum in Exposition Park. UCLA plays its home football games at the Rose Bowl.

The home of the Los Angeles Lakers basketball and Kings ice hockey teams is the Forum in Inglewood. Both teams play from late October to mid-March. The Los Angeles Clippers basketball games, as well as circuses, athletic meets and other events, are held in Exposition Park at the Los Angeles Memorial Sports Arena.

Professional baseball is played in Dodger Stadium near the Civic Center and Anaheim Stadium, home field of the California Angels. Water sports competition is featured in the Los Angeles Swimming Stadium in Exposition Park.

For information on sports and recreation in other nearby areas see place listings for Angeles National Forest, Big Bear Lake, Catalina Island, Lake Arrowhead, San Bernardino National Forest and Santa Monica Mountains National Recreation Area.

Where To Shop

The decentralization of Los Angeles has given rise to a number of shopping centers scattered throughout the city and the metropolitan area. Major downtown shopping areas include Broadway Plaza, bounded by 7th, Hope, 8th and Flower streets, and Seventh Market Place, bounded by 7th, Figueroa, and 8th streets and the Harbor Freeway. Other shopping areas include Beverly Hills, Melrose Avenue between La Brea and Fairfax avenues, Century City and Westwood Village near UCLA.

Major suburban areas have regional shopping centers, many of which have distinctive architecture. These include Beverly Center in West Hollywood, Del Amo Fashion Center in Torrance, Fashion Island in Newport Beach, Fox Hills Mall in Culver City, the Glendale Galleria, Santa Monica Place, South Coast Plaza in Costa Mesa, Topanga Plaza in Woodland Hills, Ventura Boulevard in the San Fernando Valley and Westside Pavilion in West Los Angeles.

The major stores dotting the metropolitan landscape include The Broadway, Bullock's, I. Magnin, May Co., Neiman-Marcus, Nordstrom, Robinson's and Saks Fifth Avenue. Most have many branches and prices that range from moderate to expensive.

We Have A Hotel For Every Size Budget.

Wherever you're going and whatever size budget you have to get there, Choice Hotels has a room at a price that's right for you.

We also have many ways for AAA members to save, including a minimum 10% discount (even more at some of our hotels), and a family plan in which kids 18 and under stay free in their parent's room.

So to find the hotel you've been looking for, look no further than Choice Hotels. For reservations at more than 2,100 North American locations, call 1-800-228-1AAA or your local AAA club.

Only one discount per stay. All discounts subject to availability at participating hotels and do not apply to AAA Special Value Rates. Certain other restrictions apply.

CHOICE HOTELS
INTERNATIONAL

Call 1-800-228-1AAA

You can find gifts and unusual souvenirs from the Orient in the Chinatown and Little Tokyo districts of downtown Los Angeles. Mexican handicraft shops are abundant on Olvera Street. Many art galleries are along La Cienega Boulevard from Santa Monica to Beverly boulevards. Another concentration of galleries is near the Little Tokyo district downtown.

Also downtown are the garment district, where numerous wholesalers offer discount prices to the public, and the expanding jewelry district along Hill Street. At 7th and Wall streets is the Flower Mart, a huge wholesale flower center. Also popular is Grand Central Public Market, a bustling grocery and meat market at 3rd and Hill streets, which rivals Farmers Market for its color and variety.

The massive ARCO and Broadway plazas and the Westin Bonaventure combine modern shopping complexes and dramatic architecture. Fisherman's Village in Marina del Rey, Ports O' Call Village in San Pedro and Shoreline Village in Long Beach feature many art, craft and specialty shops.

★FARMERS MARKET, 3rd St. and Fairfax Ave., encompasses food, clothing and gift shops. The outdoor cafes also are popular. Mon.-Sat. 9-7, Sun. 10-6, in summer; Mon.-Sat. 9-6:30, Sun. 10-5, rest of year. Closed holidays. Phone (213) 933-9211.

Where To Dine

Los Angeles has restaurants specializing in the cuisine of almost every country. The city's heritage and proximity to the Mexican border account for the large number of establishments serving Mexican dishes; even the ubiquitous hot-dog-hamburger stands usually serve a third specialty—tacos. A number of Mexican restaurants along Olvera Street feature outdoor dining. North of Farmers Market along Fairfax Avenue are kosher delicatessens.

On the main steamship channel in San Pedro, Ports O' Call Village features mid-19th-century California and New England seaport architectural styles. Several restaurants serve a variety of cuisines, including Polynesian and Italian. Chinatown and Little Tokyo offer diners a wide variety of Oriental dishes.

Two areas noted for fine restaurants are the section of La Cienega Boulevard extending north from Wilshire Boulevard to Santa Monica Boulevard and along Ventura Boulevard in the San Fernando Valley. Other good restaurants and cafes are found throughout the metropolitan Los Angeles area, particularly in Beverly Hills and downtown.

Nightlife

Los Angeles' nightlife ranges from discotheques with light shows to theatrical and musical shows. Most nightspots are in Hollywood, the Sunset Strip area, Westwood and Marina del Rey.

Many hotels provide dinner, dancing and entertainment; notable are the Culver's Club at the Pacifica, Fantasia at the Westin Bonaventure, the Garden Pavilion in the Century Plaza, Moody's at the Sheraton Grande and Windows at the Holiday Inn-Hollywood.

The best sources of information concerning current offerings are the entertainment sections of the daily papers, especially the Calendar section of the Sunday Los Angeles Times. Key, Los Angeles and Where magazines, available in most hotel lobbies, provide similar details.

Note: The mention of any area or establishment in the preceding sections is for information only and does **not** imply endorsement by AAA.

Theater and Concerts

Thanks in part to the Music Center and the enormous talent pool created by the film and television industries, Los Angeles has become the nation's second major theatrical city.

Again, the best source of information is the Calendar section of the Sunday Times, which lists current and coming movie and stage features, as well as lectures, classical and pop music concerts, nightlife, museum exhibits and art shows. Numerous theaters present professional, amateur and college shows. Tickets for most can be obtained at the box office or through ticket agencies.

Presentations range from comedic theater in various media, such as that found at the Mayfair Music Hall in Santa Monica, to more serious works at such places as the Ahmanson and James Doolittle theaters.

The Music Center in downtown Los Angeles is host to opera, musical comedy, a celebrity series, symphony concerts and productions of the Center Theater Group, the Los Angeles Civic Light Opera, Los Angeles Master Chorale and the Los Angeles Philharmonic Orchestra. The Los Angeles Theatre Center, also downtown, presents varied dramatic productions. The Wiltern Theatre, noted for its elaborate Art Deco design, presents various stage events.

The Shubert Theatre in Century City stages an array of plays and musicals. The Universal Amphitheatre in Universal City is a fully enclosed year-round entertainment complex. The Pantages Theatre in Hollywood presents musical comedies and stage plays with top-name entertainers. The Henry Fonda Theatre in Hollywood and the Wilshire Theatre in Beverly Hills present dramatic fare with professional actors. Outdoor theaters include the Greek Theatre in Griffith Park and the Hollywood Bowl.

A special theater experience is provided by the Bob Baker Marionette Theater, 1345 W. First St. The beautifully crafted puppets and whimsical shows appeal to both children and adults. Tues.-Fri. at 10:30; Sat.-Sun. at 2:30. Admission (includes refreshments and a puppetry demonstration) $10; over 65, $8. Reservations are required; phone (213) 250-9995.

Especially for Children

The Calendar section of the Sunday *Los Angeles Times* lists theatrical productions geared especially to children. As a special help for parents, it also rates the regular stage and film productions according to their suitability for family audiences. Disneyland in Anaheim provides a day (or more) of rapt fascination for any child, as do Knott's Berry Farm in Buena Park and Six Flags Magic Mountain in Santa Clarita.

The Los Angeles Zoo in Griffith Park offers a chance to enjoy Adventure Island, designed especially for children, and to inspect an array of interesting animals. A day at the beach also can be a welcome respite after confining city touring. Any of the various boat tours offer a pleasant change of pace, while Wild Rivers Waterpark in Irvine and Raging Waters in San Dimas offer another way to have fun in the water.

The museums in Los Angeles can be interesting to children as well. Of particular note are the Los Angeles County Museum of Art, the Los Angeles Children's Museum in the Civic Center, the Rancho La Brea Tar Pits and the George C. Page Museum of La Brea Discoveries.

The California Museum of Science and Industry in Exposition Park and the Discovery Center in the Natural History Museum of Los Angeles present a wide variety of hands-on displays. Touchable exhibits also can be found at Kidspace in Pasadena, Long Beach Children's Museum and El Dorado Nature Center in Long Beach. For a combination of fun and history, visit El Pueblo de Los Angeles Historic Monument.

Special Events

Oshogatsui, the Japanese New Year, is celebrated in early January, while the Sunkist Invitational Indoor Track Meet is held mid-month. The Chinese New Year is celebrated in early February. The UCLA Gymnastics Invitational, held in Westwood, and the Nissan Los Angeles Open Golf Tournament occur later in the month. The Los Angeles Marathon is held in early March, and St. Patrick's Day brings a parade into Century City.

The Hispanic L.A. Fiesta fills the Broadway shopping district downtown with 500,000 people in late April. Cinco de Mayo celebrations in early May are scattered throughout the city at various locations. The Volvo Tennis Tournament at UCLA is held in early August as Japanese Americans celebrate Nisei Week. The Los Angeles Senior PGA Golf Tournament is held in late October.

For further information on these and other Los Angeles events contact the Automobile Club of Southern California.

LOS BAÑOS (G-3) pop. 14,500, alt. 1,120'

SAN LUIS DAM COMPLEX, 12 mi. w. on SR 152, is an important link in the Central Valley Project. Swimming, windsurfing, boating, camping and picnicking are permitted at San Luis Reservoir, San Luis Creek and O'Neill Forebay state recreation areas. Day use pass $5. Boat pass $5. Camping $14 in the developed area; $9 in the primitive area. Phone (209) 826-1196.

The Romero Visitors Center has movies, slide programs, a telescope and information about the project. Allow 30 minutes minimum. Daily 9-5; closed Jan. 1, Thanksgiving and Dec. 25. Free. Phone (209) 826-0718, ext. 253.

LOS GATOS (G-2) pop. 27,400, alt. 385'

South of San Francisco Bay, Los Gatos is guarded by two mountain ridges, El Sombroso (the shadowing one) and El Sereno (the night watchman). The town was founded about 1868 on a portion of an 1840 Spanish land grant. The original grant was known as *La Rinconada de los Gatos* (corner of the cats), a name derived from the many mountain lions and wildcats that inhabited the nearby hills.

By the early 1900s Los Gatos was a rural community mostly supporting orchards. Along with other bay area cities, the town was thrust into urbanization with the onset of World War II. The Forbes Mill Museum at 75 Church St. has exhibits on local and regional history.

Los Gatos is the northern terminus of a scenic 38-mile stretch of SR 9 to Santa Cruz.

LOS GATOS MUSEUM, Main and Tait sts., has art, science and nature displays. Tues.-Sun. 1-4; closed major holidays. Donations. Phone (408) 354-2646.

OAK MEADOW PARK, University Ave. and Blossom Hill Rd., is open daily 8 a.m.-dusk. Admission free. Parking fee of $3 charged daily, mid-June to mid-Sept.; Sat.-Sun., Mar. 1 to mid-June; free rest of year. Phone (408) 354-6809.

Billy Jones Wildcat Railroad, in the park, operates Mon.-Sat. 10:30-4:30, Sun. 11:30-5, June 13-Sept. 12; Sat. 10:30-4:30, Sun. 11:30-5, Sept. 13-early Nov.; weather permitting. Fare $1; physically impaired free. Phone (408) 395-7433.

OLD TOWN, 50 University Ave., with its many restored buildings of Spanish and Victorian architecture, topiary trees and gardens, encompasses specialty shops, restaurants and an outdoor amphitheater. Mon.-Sat. 10-6, Sun. 11-5; closed Jan. 1 and Dec. 25. Free. Phone (408) 354-6596.

LOS OLIVOS (I-4) pop. 250, alt. 825'

THE FIRESTONE VINEYARD, 2 mi. n. of jct. US 101 and SR 154 on Zaca Station Rd., offers guided tours of the winery and tastings. Picnic facilities are available. Daily 10-4. Free. Phone (805) 688-3940.

ZACA MESA WINERY, approximately 9 mi. n.w. on Foxen Canyon Rd., offers tours and tastings; picnicking is permitted. Daily 10-4. Free. Phone (805) 688-3310.

LOS PADRES NATIONAL FOREST

With more than 1,750,000 acres in Southern California, Los Padres National Forest covers terrain ranging from coastal areas through semidesert to pine-timbered elevations of almost 9,000 feet. Within this region are the Ventana, Machesna, San Rafael, Santa Lucia and Dick Smith wilderness areas and two condor sanctuaries. Phone (805) 683-6711. *See Recreation Chart and the AAA California and Nevada CampBook.*

MALIBU (B-5) pop. 11,700, alt. 5'

Stretching several miles along SR 1, Malibu is wedged between the Santa Monica Mountains and the Pacific Ocean. Many artists, writers and well-known entertainers are among its residents. Malibu Pier is a popular fishing spot.

★**J. PAUL GETTY MUSEUM,** 17985 Pacific Coast Hwy., houses collections of Greek and Roman antiquities; pre-20th-century European paintings, drawings, sculpture and decorative arts; illuminated manuscripts; and 19th- and 20th-century American and European photographs. The building was designed to re-create an ancient Roman villa.

Tues.-Sun. 10-5; gate closes at 4:30. Closed holidays. Free. Parking reservations must be made at least 1 week in advance; phone (310) 458-2003. No walk-in traffic. Visitors also can take RTD bus 434. For more information write P.O. Box 2112, Santa Monica, CA 90407; phone (310) 458-2003.

MALIBU LAGOON MUSEUM AND HISTORIC ADAMSON HOUSE, 23200 Pacific Coast Hwy., is a Moorish-Spanish Colonial-style residence built in the 1920s. Colorful tile, handcrafted woodwork and ironwork and other decorative features are found throughout the house. The adjoining museum depicts the history of the Malibu area. Guided tours offered Wed.-Sat. 11-3; closed major holidays. Tour admission $2, ages 7-17, $1. Parking $4. Phone (310) 456-8432.

MAMMOTH LAKES (F-5) pop. 4,800, alt. 7,860'

One of California's most popular four-season resorts, the Mammoth Lakes area provides access to the recreational facilities and points of interest in the Inyo National Forest *(see place listing).*

MAMMOTH LAKES RECREATION AREA, 200,000 acres, contains portions of the Pacific Crest Trail, the John Muir Trail, Devils Postpile National Monument *(see place listing),* Mammoth Mountain Ski Area, Rainbow Falls, Mammoth City Historical Site, Mammoth Lakes Basin and geothermal springs. Extensive self-guiding trails tour alpine lakes, mountain vistas, lodgepole and Jeffrey pine forests and unusual geologic formations.

The area has facilities for fishing, boating, snowmobiling, cross-country skiing and hiking. Naturalists conduct interpretive programs. The visitor center-ranger station is open daily 6-5, July 1 to mid-Sept.; Mon.-Fri. 8-4:30, rest of year. A gondola provides rides up and down Mammoth Mountain in the ski area daily 9-3:30, mid-June to mid-Sept. Fare $8; ages 5-13, $4. Phone (619) 934-2571 for gondola and ski information; phone (619) 934-6611 for weather information and road conditions.

MANTECA (F-3) pop. 40,800, alt. 38'

OAKWOOD LAKE WATER THEME PARK is between I-5 and SR 99 at 874 E. Woodward. The park features more than 20 waterslides and Castaway Bay. A 75-acre lake adjoins a campground and picnic sites. Daily 10-7, Memorial Day weekend-Labor Day; Sat.-Sun. 10-5, May 1-day before Memorial Day weekend and day after Labor Day-Sept. 30. All-day pass $15.95, general admission $7.95, under 48 inches tall free. Half-day pass available. DS, MC, VI. **Discount,** except general admission and half-day pass. Phone (209) 239-9566 or 239-2500.

MARINA DEL REY (B-5) pop. 8,100, alt. 5'

FISHERMAN'S VILLAGE, 13755 Fiji Way, overlooks the Marina del Rey harbor. The colorful Cape Cod-style buildings house specialty shops and restaurants, which are open daily 10-10, in summer; Sun.-Thurs. 10-9, Fri.-Sat. 10-10, rest of year. Phone (310) 823-5411.

Harbor cruises depart on the hour daily 11-5, mid-May through Sept. 30; Sat.-Sun. 11-5, rest of year. Fare $7; senior citizens and under 12, $4. For reservations phone (310) 301-6000.

MARIPOSA (F-4) pop. 1,200, alt. 1,953'

Originally called Logtown, Mariposa was renamed after the Spanish word for butterfly. Gold mining has been supplanted by the scenic riches of nearby Yosemite Valley, which draw thousands of visitors through the town each year.

CALIFORNIA STATE MINING AND MINERAL MUSEUM, 1.8 mi. s. on SR 49 at the county fairgrounds, has one of the world's largest gem and mineral collections. The mines surrounding Mariposa yielded some of the richest finds in the Mother Lode, and the museum's collection of more than 200,000 minerals, gold, diamonds and other gems reflects that wealth. Other exhibits are models of an assay office and stamp mill and a full-scale replica of a mine. Allow 1 hour minimum.

Wed.-Mon. 10-6, May-Sept.; Wed.-Sun. 10-4, rest of year. Closed Jan. 1 and Dec. 25. Admission $3.50; over 60, students and ages 14-18, $2.50; under 14 free. Phone (209) 742-7625.

COURTHOUSE, 5088 Bullion St., is the oldest in the state. It was built in 1854 and is still in use. Wooden pegs were used in the construction of the two-story white pine building; the second floor contains original furnishings. The old clock in the square clock tower was brought by way of Cape Horn. Tours Sat.-Sun. and holidays 10-5, late Mar. to mid-Oct. Open daily 8-5, Memorial Day weekend-Labor Day; Mon.-Fri. 8-5, rest of year. Donations. Phone (209) 966-3222.

MARIPOSA COUNTY HISTORY CENTER, SR 140 at 12th and Jessie sts., contains gold rush relics, including a five-stamp mill, horse-drawn vehicles and mining and printing equipment. Featured are replicas of a schoolroom, an Indian village, a miner's cabin, a print shop and an apothecary. Allow 1 hour minimum. Daily 10-4:30, Apr.-Oct.; Sat.-Sun. 10-4, Feb.-Mar. and Nov.-Dec. Donations. Phone (209) 966-2924.

MARKLEEVILLE (E-5) pop. 100, alt. 5,525'

ALPINE COUNTY HISTORICAL COMPLEX, ½ mi. w. of SR 89 at School and Montgomery sts., includes an 1882 schoolhouse and a jail that have been restored and furnished in period. A museum contains an exhibit on one of the earliest known settlements in North America. Wed.-Mon. noon-5, Memorial Day weekend-Oct. 31. Free. Phone (916) 694-2317.

MARTINEZ (O-3) pop. 31,300, alt. 23'

JOHN MUIR NATIONAL HISTORIC SITE, 4202 Alhambra Ave., was the residence of the naturalist, conservationist, author, explorer and co-founder (in 1892) of the Sierra Club. His crusade for the preservation of the nation's wilderness aided in the establishment of the national parks and forests. The 1882 house is furnished as it was in the early 19th century.

A self-guiding walking tour covers the 17 room mansion and the surrounding orchards where visitors can sample fruit picked by the gardener. A film on John Muir's life is shown at 10, 11, noon, 1:30, 2:30 and 3:30. The Martinez Adobe is a two-story adobe house built in 1849 and the former home of Muir's daughter. Allow 1 hour, 30 minutes minimum. Wed.-Sun. 10-4:30; closed Jan. 1, Thanksgiving and Dec. 25. Admission $1, over 62 and under 17 free. Phone (510) 228-8860.

MARYSVILLE (D-3) pop. 12,300, alt. 63'

Central to Marysville is Ellis Lake, named for W.T. Ellis, a prosperous town merchant in the early 1900s. Ellis was instrumental in obtaining funds necessary to expand and beautify the lake. The boulevard along the shore testifies to his ef-

forts; a jogging/exercise course also circles the lake. Paddleboats are available seasonally.

Riverfront Park is beneath the 5th and 10th street bridges, which link Marysville and Yuba City. Recreational facilities include a boat-launching dock, picnic area, playgrounds, soccer fields, baseball fields, and motorbike trails. The park also has a concert bowl with grassy slopes for seating.

MARY AARON MUSEUM, 704 D St., is a restored Victorian house built in 1855. Allow 30 minutes minimum. Open Tues.-Sat. 1:30-4:30; closed Dec. 24-Jan. 1. Donations. Phone (916) 743-1004.

MENDOCINO (D-1) pop. 1,000, alt. 90'

A picturesque community off scenic US 1 on the rugged northern California coast, Mendocino has many well-preserved 19th-century buildings and homes. The architecture reflects the New England roots of Mendocino's early settlers, who were drawn by the rich timber resources of the surrounding countryside. The stark beauty of the region has since attracted many artists to the town. The Mendocino Art Center, 45200 Little Lake Rd., offers exhibits and festivals throughout the year.

Mendocino lies on a scenic stretch of SR 1 that extends from Leggett to Sausalito.

KELLY HOUSE HISTORICAL MUSEUM, 45007 Albion St., includes a north coastal genealogy and research library and small museum. The museum contains a collection of photographs, watercolors and brief histories of many private buildings and homes in the area. The 1861 house has been restored. Library open Tues.-Fri. 9-4; museum open Fri.-Mon. 1-4. Admission $1. Phone (707) 937-5791.

MENDOCINO NATIONAL FOREST

Encompassing nearly 894,400 acres, Mendocino National Forest lies in the North Coast Mountain Range north of San Francisco. Roads and trails afford access to scenic points. Many roads within the forest are unsurfaced; driving can be hazardous, especially in the dusty, dry months. Hang gliding and motorcycling areas are available.

The Yolla Bolly-Middle Eel Wilderness at the north end of the forest and the Snow Mountain Wilderness in the south provide peaceful settings for horseback riding and hiking. Wilderness entry permits are not required, but users should sign the registry at trailheads.

Campfire permits are required in some areas; check with the Forest Supervisor, 420 E. Laurel St., Willows, CA 95988 or a district ranger. For recorded information phone (916) 934-2350. *See Recreation Chart and the AAA California and Nevada CampBook.*

MENLO PARK (Q-2) pop. 28,000, alt. 70'

ALLIED ARTS GUILD, off SR 82 at the end of Cambridge Ave. on Arbor Rd., stands on 3½ acres of land granted by the King of Spain to the Commandant of the Presidio de San Francisco in the early 19th century. Spanish-style buildings, courtyards, gardens, fountains, murals and frescoes create an Old World atmosphere where artisans practice their crafts. Food is available. Guild open Mon.-Sat. 10-5, Sun. noon-5, in Dec.; Mon.-Sat. 10-5, rest of year. Free. Phone (415) 325-3259.

LANE PUBLISHING CO., 80 Willow Rd. at Middlefield Rd., is the publisher of *Sunset* magazine. Guided tours of magazine offices, testing kitchens and gardens are available. An audiovisual presentation illustrates the magazine's history and the editorial process. Allow 1 hour minimum. Tours Mon.-Fri. at 10:30 and 2:30. Gardens open Mon.-Fri. 9-4. Closed major holidays. Free. Phone (415) 324-5479.

MERCED (G-4) pop. 56,200, alt. 167'

Merced, in the great agricultural San Joaquin Valley, is the principal western entrance to Yosemite National Park for travelers from the north.

The 1875 Old County Courthouse at 21st and N streets in Courthouse Park is built in the Italianate Renaissance style and closely resembles the state Capitol building. The Merced County Museum in the courthouse contains exhibits on local history. Merced National Wildlife Refuge is 16 miles southwest. Water sports are offered 7 miles northeast at Yosemite Lake. The Applegate Park and Zoo on 25th and R streets features wild animals, birds and kiddieland rides.

Self-guiding tours: The Merced Convention and Visitors Bureau at 690 West 16th St. distributes a guide to historic Merced; open Mon.-Fri. 8:30-5. For information contact the bureau at P.O. Box 3107, Merced, CA 95344; phone (209) 384-3333.

YOSEMITE WILDLIFE MUSEUM, 1 ml. e. of SR 99 at 2040 Yosemite Pkwy. (SR 140), features lifelike displays of America's wildlife in their natural habitats. Painted background murals, landscaped foregrounds and natural outdoor sounds create realistic settings. Allow 30 minutes minimum. Mon.-Sat. 10-5; closed major holidays. Admission $2.50; over 60 and ages 13-16, $1.75; ages 5-12, $1. MC, VI. Phone (209) 383-1052.

MIDDLETOWN (M-2) pop. 1,000, alt. 1,105'

GUENOC WINERY, 6 mi. n.e. off SR 29 at 21000 Butts Canyon Rd., offers tours and tastings. Picnicking is permitted. Allow 1 hour minimum. Thurs.-Sun. 10-4:30. Free. Phone (707) 987-2385.

MILL VALLEY (O-2) pop. 13,000, alt. 70'

Mill Valley is a residential community at the base of Mount Tamalpais. The heavy redwood frame of the sawmill for which the town was named still stands in Old Mill Park on Throckmorton Avenue. Hikers can follow a nearby trail up the mountain.

MOUNT TAMALPAIS STATE PARK, 6 mi. w., covers 6,233 acres of picturesque coastal hill country dominated by triple-peaked Mount Tamalpais, whose profile from the south is said to resemble a sleeping Indian girl. Though only slightly less than a ½-mile high, Mount Tamalpais rises from sea level and therefore appears much loftier than it is.

In 1884, a stagecoach road to the top was carved from the mountain slopes, followed 12 years later by the Mill Valley and Tamalpais Scenic Railway. Dubbed the "Crookedest Railroad in the World," it had 281 curves along its 8¼ miles, including the Double Bow Knot—a fivefold switchback.

In 1907, an additional line linked the summit with Muir Woods, and the railroad was renamed the Mount Tamalpais and Muir Woods Railway. But fires on the mountain, the Depression and the eventual completion of an auto route to the top spelled demise for the railroad; it was abandoned in the summer of 1930.

Hiking and bicycling trails and a winding road lead to the summit, where spectacular vistas encompass much of Marin County, the San Francisco Bay area and beyond. Both hawks and turkey vultures skim along the mountain's ridges. Plays and musical programs are presented in the Mountain Theater in spring. Daily dawn-dusk. Fee $5. Phone (415) 388-2070. *See Recreation Chart.*

MISSION HILLS (A-5) pop. 32,000, alt. 914'

★MISSION SAN FERNANDO REY DE ESPAÑA, midway between I-5 and I-405 at 15151 San Fernando Mission Rd., was founded Sept. 8, 1797. Restored structures include the church, monastery, majordomo's house, workrooms and living quarters around the quadrangle. The old gardens, now Brand Park, have flowers and shrubs from the other 20 missions. A 35-bell carillon rings hourly 9-5.

A museum theater offers three films illustrating the history of the mission, the Archdiocese of Los Angeles and the life of Father Junípero Serra. An Indian craft room is featured.

Mission and museum open daily 9-5. Last admission 45 minutes before closing. Archival Center open Mon. and Thurs.-Fri. 1-3; closed Thanksgiving and Dec. 25. Admission $3; ages 7-15, $1.50. Discount. Phone (818) 361-0186.

MODESTO (F-3) pop. 164,700, alt. 88'

In the northern San Joaquin Valley on the Tuolumne River, Modesto is near the geographic center of the state. When the Central Pacific Railroad founded the town in 1870, they wanted to name it after a San Francisco banker. When the banker rejected the idea, his modesty was commemorated in the town's chosen name. Modesto provides access to Sonora Pass in the Stanislaus National Forest, the Mother Lode Country and the Big Oak Flat route to Yosemite.

Graffiti U.S.A., held in mid-June, celebrates the "cruising" tradition made famous by the movie "American Graffiti." It features a street fair with '50s music, arts and crafts, a car show and the "Classic Car Cruz" on McHenry Avenue. Other annual events include the S & W Invitational Relays and Track Meet in early May and the Greek Food Festival the fourth weekend in September.

Miller's California Ranch, 10 miles east on SR 132 at 9425 Yosemite Blvd., has a small collection of motor vehicles and wagons and an old-fashioned store featuring antique and unusual bicycles. The Great Valley Museum of Natural History, 1100 Stoddard Ave., features exhibits on the Central Valley's ecosystems. St. Stan's Brewery at 9th and L streets offers tours and tastings.

CALIFORNIA ALMOND GROWERS EXCHANGE, 4800 Sisk Rd., is open Mon.-Fri. 10-5 (also Thurs. 5-6), Dec. 26-day before Thanksgiving; open daily with extended hours, rest of year. Closed major holidays. A movie is shown Mon.-Fri. A tasting room is available. Free. Phone (209) 545-3222.

McHENRY MANSION, 15th and I sts., is a restored 19th-century Victorian home furnished with period artwork and antiques. Tues.-Thurs. and Sun. 1-4. Free. Phone (209) 577-5344.

McHENRY MUSEUM, 1402 I St., includes a schoolroom, blacksmith shop, dentist's and doctor's offices, kitchen, country store, historical photographs and documents and changing exhibits. Tues.-Sun. noon-4; closed major holidays. Free. Phone (209) 577-5366.

MODOC NATIONAL FOREST

Modoc National Forest's 1,651,630 acres encompass much of the state's remote northeastern corner, which was covered millions of years ago by an immense lava flow. Although geologically the area is known as the Modoc Plateau, it doesn't look like a plateau: The region is distinguished by basins, mountains, lakes and meadows. And despite the relatively dry climate the plateau supports some of the country's most significant wetlands.

Three major national wildlife refuges—Tule Lake, Clear Lake and Modoc—are either within the forest's boundaries or nearby. Thousands of ducks, geese and other waterfowl frequent these sanctuaries as well as the forest's Big Sage, Medicine and Blue lakes.

Volcanism has left many marks on the forest's terrain, and some of the most dramatic examples are in the Medicine Lake highlands. There are such unusual features as Glass Mountain, a huge flow of obsidian, and the Burnt Lava Flow, which is a jumble of black lava interspersed with islands of timber. Medicine Lake itself fills an old volcanic crater and is popular for boating and swimming.

On the forest's eastern boundary, the Warner Mountains are a rolling upland that drops steeply on its eastern edge. Most of the range is above 5,000 feet and some of the peaks reach an altitude over 9,000 feet in the 70,385-acre South Warner Wilderness, which includes Modoc's highest mountain, Eagle Peak. The forest has 118 miles of trails, accessible by eight trailheads, suited for hikers and horseback riders. Carrying a topography map is advised.

Maps, brochures and information on a variety of recreational opportunities are available at the district ranger stations and the forest headquarters in Alturas. For more information write the Forest Supervisor, Modoc National Forest, 441 N. Main St. Alturas, CA 96101; phone (916) 233-5811. *See the Recreation Chart and AAA California and Nevada CampBook.*

MONO BASIN NATIONAL FOREST SCENIC AREA

Accessible via SRs 120 and 167, the scenic area is within Inyo National Forest *(see place listing)* near Lee Vining. The area covers 116,000 acres surrounding Mono Lake and includes volcanic hills on its borders. The Bodie Hills to the north and the Anchorite Hills to the east are about 11 million years old, while the Mono Craters to the south are the youngest mountain range in North America. One of the craters erupted about 600 years ago. The islands in Mono Lake also are volcanic, as evidenced by hot springs and steam vents.

The lake itself is more than 700,000 years old. Over time the salts and minerals in the water have become too concentrated for fish, but the brine shrimp and flies that thrive here attract millions of migratory birds and waterfowl. Most tourists come to see the tufa, spires and knobs formed of calcium carbonate that have been exposed as the lake's water level has dropped. Tufa, pumice and obsidian are protected by state and federal laws and may not be collected or damaged.

Many of the roads in the basin are unsuitable for conventional vehicles; off-road driving is not permitted. Self-guiding nature trails and interpretive exhibits are at the South Tufa and Panum Crater day-use areas. The scenic area is open daily 24 hours. A ranger station in Lee Vining is open daily 8. a.m.-9 p.m., Memorial Day weekend-Labor Day; Mon.-Fri. 9-5, rest of year. For more information contact Mono Lake Ranger District, P.O. Box 10, Lee Vining, CA 93541; phone (619) 647-6595.

MONTEREY (G-2) pop. 32,000, alt. 25'

The capital of Alta California under the Spanish, Mexican and American flags, Monterey lies on the Monterey Peninsula and ranges in altitude from sea level to 360 feet. The peninsula is a popular year-round playground boasting several golf courses. South of Monterey SR 1 winds through redwood forests and along the cliffs of the spectacular Big Sur coast.

On Cannery Row, the colorful locale of John Steinbeck's novels "Cannery Row" and "Sweet Thursday," galleries and restaurants have replaced the fish canneries. Along Fisherman's Wharf an art gallery, handicraft shops and the Wharf Theater have superseded the commercial fishing activities of the early 20th century.

The Monterey Presidio, 1 block from the theater on Pacific Street, was founded in 1770 by Capt. Gaspar de Portolá, assisted by fathers Junípero Serra and Juan Crespi. It is now the Defense Language Institute Presidio of Monterey.

Self-guiding tours: Walking-tour maps detailing local gardens, adobes and historic sites are available from the Monterey Peninsula Chamber of Commerce at 380 Alvarado St., Monterey, CA 93940; phone (408) 649-1770.

COLTON HALL, on Pacific St. facing Friendly Plaza and Colton Hall Park, is where the first Constitution of California was written in 1849. Adjoining Colton Hall, built in 1848, is the old jail, built in 1854. Allow 30 minutes minimum. Mon.-Fri. 10-5, Sat.-Sun. 10-noon and 1-5, Apr.-Oct.; Mon.-Fri. 10-4, Sat.-Sun. 10-noon and 1-4, rest of year. Closed Jan. 1, Thanksgiving and Dec. 25. Free. Phone (408) 375-9944.

DENNIS THE MENACE PLAYGROUND is in the park on El Estero. Hank Ketcham, creator of "Dennis the Menace," aided in its development. It contains climbing structures, slides, a balancing bridge, a maze, a railroad switch engine and a lion-shaped drinking fountain. Daily 10-dusk. Free. Phone (408) 646-3866.

★THE MONTEREY BAY AQUARIUM, 886 Cannery Row, is one of the largest aquariums in the world. Dramatic displays of nearly 600 species of marine life in 23 major habitat areas include a 90-foot-long re-creation of Monterey Bay, a two-story sea otter exhibit and a three-story kelp forest. The tanks are maintained by a flow of 2,000 gallons of fresh seawater per minute. The aquarium also has a hands-on tidepool, life-size models of marine animals, a shorebird aviary, a theater, historical displays and educational exhibits.

"Live from Monterey Canyon" is an innovative exhibit featuring transmissions from MBARI (Monterey Bay Aquarium Research Institute) scientists as they explore the ocean floor with a deep-diving robot research submersible. The broadcasts, from depths down to 3,000 feet, are shown Mon.-Tues. noon-3 in the auditorium and often showcase rare sealife. An accompanying video, "Exploring the Deep Canyon," is shown continuously in the aquarium theater.

Allow 3 hours minimum. Daily 10-6; closed Dec. 25. Admission $10.75; senior citizens, military and students $7.75; ages 3-12, $4.75. AE, MC, VI. Phone (408) 648-4888 for information or (800) 756-3737 in Calif. for advance tickets. *See ad p. A265.*

MONTEREY PENINSULA MUSEUM OF ART, 559 Pacific St., presents permanent and changing displays of regional, Oriental and folk art as well as photography. Allow 1 hour minimum. Tues.-Sat. 10-4, Sun. 1-4; closed Jan. 1, Thanksgiving and Dec. 25. Donations. Phone (408) 372-7591.

★MONTEREY STATE HISTORIC PARK, 20 Custom House Plaza, is a 7-acre site that preserves the historical and architectural heritage of old Monterey. Nearby is the original 1602 landing site of Sebastián Vizcaíno and—more than 150 years later— Father Junípero Serra. Park open daily 10-5, Memorial Day weekend-Labor Day; 10-4, rest of year. Closed Jan. 1, Thanksgiving and Dec. 25. Park admission (includes all buildings) $4; ages 6-17, $2. Phone (408) 649-2836.

The Boston Store, Scott and Olivier sts., has been a store, saloon, private residence and, reputedly, a gold depository. The restored building exhibits trade items of early Monterey. Wed.-Sun. noon-5; closed holidays.

Casa Soberanes, 336 Pacific St., was built in 1830 and occupied by members of the Soberanes family until 1922. The extremely well-preserved home contains period antiques. Sat.-Sun. 10-3; closed Jan. 1, Thanksgiving and Dec. 25.

Cooper-Molera Adobe, at Polk and Munras, is the restored Victorian home of the Yankee sea captain, rancher and adventurer who married the sister of Gen. Mariano Vallejo. The 2¼-acre grounds also have four other structures that are open to the public. Guided tours on the hour Thurs.-Tues. 10-1 and 2-4, June-Aug.; 2-3, rest of year.

Custom House, on Custom House Plaza at Fisherman's Wharf, is the oldest government building in California, its north section having been constructed about 1827. When Commodore John Drake Sloat raised the American flag over the building in 1846, approximately 600,000 square miles became part of the United States. The house displays trade goods from the 1840s. Wed.-Sun. 10-5, June-Aug.; 10-4, rest of year.

First Theater, Pacific and Scott sts., was once a lodging house for sailors as well as the first building in California to charge admission for a theatrical performance. The 1846 building contains relics of early California. Wed.-Sat. 1-8, Mar.-Oct.; 1-5, rest of year. Special evening performances held Wed.-Sat., July-Aug.; Fri.-Sat., rest of year. Check at the theater for times and fees. For reservations phone (408) 375-4916.

Larkin House is at Calle Principal and Jefferson St. Its combination of Spanish Colonial and New England architectural features has made it a prototype for other Monterey structures. The 1835 house served as the American consulate 1843-46. A 30-minute guided tour begins hourly Wed.-Mon. 10-4, June-Aug.; 10-3, rest of year. Closed holidays. Visitors should register for tours at the house.

Pacific House, Calle Principal and Scott St., was built in 1847 and now houses a museum of California history and Indian artifacts. Daily 10-5, June-Aug.; 10-4, rest of year.

Stevenson House, 530 Houston St., is the old "French Hotel" where Robert Louis Stevenson spent the fall of 1879. Here he wrote "Vendetta of the West" and an essay on Thoreau and blocked out the "Amateur Emigrant" and "Prince Otto." Restored and furnished in period, the house can be seen only during the 30-minute guided tours offered on the hour Thurs.-Tues. 10-4:30, June 1-Labor Day; 10-3:30, rest of year. Last tour departs 30 minutes before closing. Visitors must register for tours at the house.

SAN CARLOS CATHEDRAL, also known as the Royal Presidio Chapel, is on Church St. Founded in 1770 to be the mission church of the port, San Carlos Cathedral became the church for the Spanish colonists and soldiers instead, as the mission was moved to Carmel the following year. The present church has been in continuous use since 1795. Daily 8-6. Free. Phone (408) 373-2628.

SEVENTEEN-MILE DRIVE is the scenic route from Pacific Grove to Carmel and a highlight of any visit to this coastal region. Points of interest along the way include Seal Rock, Cypress Point and Lone Cypress. Also on the route are the Pebble Beach, Cypress Point, Spy Glass Hill and Monterey Peninsula golf courses, scene of the AT&T Pro-Am Golf Tournament each spring.

The toll for cars is $6; no motorcycles or motorbikes are permitted on the drive. Allow at least 1 hour to complete the drive. Bicycles are permitted during daylight hours when no major sporting event is scheduled. Bicyclists must enter through the Pacific Grove gate on weekends, holidays and when special events are scheduled, and must sign a release before using the drive. Phone (408) 625-8426.

THE SPIRIT OF MONTEREY WAX MUSEUM, 700 Cannery Row in the Monterey Cannery Building, displays wax replicas of local historical figures. Allow 30 minutes minimum. Daily 9 a.m.-10 p.m. Admission $5.95; senior citizens, military with ID and ages 7-13, $3.95. Phone (408) 375-3770.

TRIPS ON TAPE, for the Monterey Peninsula and Big Sur, is a self-guiding audio tape tour that describes the history, landmarks, events and attractions of Monterey, Pacific Grove, Carmel, Carmel Valley, Point Lobos and the Big Sur Coast. Maps are included. Tapes available for $11.95 by mail from The Rider's Guide, 484 Lake Park Ave., Suite 255, Oakland, CA 94610. Add $2 for postage. Phone (510) 653-2553.

MORGAN HILL (G-3) pop. 23,900, alt. 345'

Before the arrival of Spanish soldiers and priests in 1776, the area surrounding Morgan Hill was home to the peaceful Costanoan Indians. The first English-speaking community sprang up around a prosperous estate known as Morgan Hill's Ranch in 1845 and was incorporated in 1906. Morgan Hill is at the southern end of the agriculturally rich Santa Clara Valley, where the French prune was developed.

WAGONS TO WINGS MUSEUM, 15060 Foothill Rd., displays wagons, stagecoaches, surreys and related equipment along with airplanes, helicopters and many one-of-a-kind vehicles. Wed.-Sun. 10-5:30; closed Jan. 1 and Dec. 25. Free. Phone (408) 227-4607 or 779-4136.

MORRO BAY (I-3) pop. 9,700, alt. 80'

Both the town of Morro Bay and the bay that fronts it are named for Morro Rock, the great conical rock that juts 578 feet out of the Pacific Ocean. In the 1870s Morro Bay was a port for the region's cattle ranching and dairy industries. Later commercial fishing and oyster farming became prominent. Morro Bay still maintains a large commercial fishing fleet. A few miles south of SR 1 is Morro Bay State Park *(see Recreation Chart).*

MUSEUM OF NATURAL HISTORY, within Morro Bay State Park, has exhibits, programs and films. Daily 10-5; closed Jan. 1, Thanksgiving and Dec. 25. Admission $2; ages 6-12, $1. Phone (805) 772-2694.

TIGER'S FOLLY II **HARBOR CRUISES,** depart from 1205 Embarcadero. One-hour narrated trips on the stern-wheeler cruise past Morro Rock, the harbor entrance and the Embarcadero. Trips offered daily June-Sept.; Sat.-Sun. and holidays, rest of year. A brunch cruise is offered on Sun.; phone for schedule and reservations. Fare $7; under 12, $3.50. AE, MC, VI. Phone (805) 772-2257 or 772-2255.

MOSS BEACH (P-2) pop. 1,900, alt. 80'

JAMES V. FITZGERALD MARINE RESERVE, w. off SR 1 via California Ave., preserves marine life in one of the state's most diverse intertidal regions. Low tide is the best time to explore; consult a local tide chart or phone the reserve for information. Collecting shells, rocks and plants is strictly prohibited. Daily dawn-dusk. Donations. Phone (415) 728-3584.

MOUNTAIN VIEW (Q-3) pop. 67,500, alt. 97'

Mountain View is a busy industrial city in the Santa Clara Valley. To the east is Moffett Field, a U.S. naval air station.

AMES RESEARCH CENTER, off US 101, Moffett Field exit, is a NASA field laboratory that includes one of the world's largest wind tunnels and experimental research hangars. Tours of the lab must be arranged at least 2 weeks in advance; under 9 not permitted. The 2-hour tours involve a 2-mile walk. Visitor Center open Mon.-Fri. 8-4:30; closed holidays. Free. Phone (415) 604-6497.

MOUNT SHASTA (B-3) pop. 3,500, alt. 3,554'

A small city named for a tall mountain, Mount Shasta is the northern gateway via scenic SR 89 to the Whiskeytown-Shasta-Trinity National Recreation Area, Shasta-Trinity National Forest and nearby Lake Siskiyou.

MOUNT SHASTA STATE FISH HATCHERY AND SISSON HATCHERY MUSEUM, ½ mi. w. of I-5 via central Mount Shasta exit at Three, Old State Rd., produces 5 to 10 million trout annually to stock the streams and lakes of northern California. The museum has exhibits pertaining to the geological and human history of the region. Allow 1 hour minimum. Museum open daily 10-5, early May-Sept. 30; Mon.-Sat. noon-4, Sun. 1-4, rest of year. Hatchery open daily 7-dusk. Free. Phone (916) 926-2215 or 926-5508.

★MUIR WOODS NATIONAL MONUMENT (O-1)

The 550-acre Muir Woods National Monument, 17 miles northwest of San Francisco on the southwestern slope of Mount Tamalpais, is reached via the Golden Gate Bridge and SR 1. Muir Woods is one of the most beautiful and accessible of the famous redwood groves. The Sequoia sempervirens, tallest of all tree life—though not as large in girth as the Sequoia gigantea—is well represented. Some coastal redwoods in the monument reach a height of 250 feet with diameters of more than 12 feet.

Trails for hiking and exploring range from ½ mile to 2 miles long. Some trails combine with others in Mount Tamalpais State Park *(see Mill Valley and Recreation Chart)*.

Neither picnicking nor camping is permitted at the monument. Pets are not allowed. A visitor center is open daily 9-5. Food is available. Daily 8 a.m.-dusk. Free. Phone (415) 388-2595.

MURPHYS (E-4) pop. 1,200, alt. 2,171'

MERCER CAVERNS, 1½ mi. n. via Sheep Ranch Rd., has been open since 1885. Fifty-minute guided tours visit 10 rooms with various crystalline formations. Daily 9-5, Memorial Day weekend-Sept. 30; Sat.-Sun. and school holidays 11-4, rest of year. Closed Thanksgiving and Dec. 25. Admission $5; ages 5-11, $2.50. **Discount.** Phone (209) 728-2101.

STEVENOT WINERY, 3 mi. n. on Sheep Ranch Rd., then left ¼ mi. on San Domingo Rd., offers tours, tastings and picnic facilities. Daily 10-5. Free. Phone (209) 728-3436.

NAPA VALLEY (N-2)

Napa Valley, one of California's most famous wine-producing regions, began in the 1850s as a

gold rush center. The original grapevine cuttings were supplied by priests from the missions at Sonoma and San Rafael. Today Napa Valley is a leader in the American table wine industry. Popular tours of wineries and vineyards in Napa Valley are listed under Calistoga, Oakville, St. Helena, Rutherford and Yountville.

Napa is the southern terminus of a scenic 28-mile stretch of SR 29 that heads northwest through the valley to Calistoga.

Self-guiding tours: Maps for five different walking tours of Napa's architectural highlights are available for 20c each at the Napa City Hall, Second and School streets.

HOT AIR BALLOON RIDES over Napa Valley are available through several companies. Flights last about an hour, and they often include champagne afterwards. Prices range from $99 to $175 per person.

Contact: Above The West Ballooning, (707) 944-8638 or (800) 627-2759; Adventures Aloft, (707) 255-8688; American Balloon Adventures, (707) 944-8116 or (800) 333-4359; Balloon Aviation, (707) 252-7067, 944-4408 or (800) 367-6272; Balloons Above The Valley, (707) 253-2222; Bonaventura Balloon, (707) 944-2822 or (800) 243-6743 in Calif.; Napa's Great Balloon Escape, (707) 253-0860 or (800) 564-9399; Napa Valley Balloons, (707) 253-2224 or (800) 564-9399; or Once In A Lifetime Balloon Co. Inc., (707) 942-6541 *(see ad)*.

Note: The mention of the preceding hot air balloon rides is for information only and does **not** imply endorsement by AAA.

For information on plane rides contact the Napa Conference and Visitors Bureau, 1310 Napa Town Center, Napa, CA 94559; phone (707) 226-7459.

NAPA VALLEY WINE TRAIN, 1275 McKinstry St., is a 36-mile journey that winds through the heart of Napa Valley wine country. Brunch, lunch and dinner excursions are presented in the restored Pullman dining cars, while hors d'oeuvres and wine tasting are offered in the lounge cars.

Allow 3 hours minimum. Departures daily, times vary. Fare $29 per person on brunch or lunch train, $29 per couple on dinner train; meal and beverages not included. AE, DI, DS, MC, VI. Reservations and deposit are required; phone (707) 253-2111, (800) 427-4124 in Calif. or (800) 522-4142 out of Calif. *See ad p. 114.*

TRIPS ON TAPE is a self-guiding audio tape tour that describes the history, wineries and local attractions in the Napa Valley. Maps are included. Tapes available for $11.95 by mail from The Rider's Guide, 484 Lake Park Ave., Suite 255, Oakland, CA 94610. Add $2 for postage; Calif. residents add sales tax. Phone (510) 653-2553.

NEVADA CITY (D-3) pop. 2,900, alt. 2,525'

In the foothills of the High Sierras, Nevada City has been a gold-mining center for more than a century. It also is the seat of Nevada County, whose lode and placer mines have yielded more than one-half of California's total production of gold. Among the buildings dating from gold rush days is the Old Nevada Theater. Said to be the oldest theater in California, it opened in July 1865.

FIREHOUSE MUSEUM, at 214 Main St. in Firehouse No. 1, displays pioneer relics, Indian artifacts and antique guns. Allow 30 minutes minimum. Daily 11-4, Apr.-Oct., weather permitting; Tues. and Thurs.-Sun. 11-4, Mon. 11-2:30, rest of year. Closed Jan. 1, Thanksgiving and Dec. 25. Donations. Phone (916) 265-5468.

MALAKOF DIGGINS STATE HISTORIC PARK, 27 mi. n.e. of SR 49 off Tyler Foote Rd., was the world's largest hydraulic gold mine before it ceased operation in 1884. The park museum has exhibits and a 20-minute film explaining hydraulic mining methods and describing the miners' way of life. Highlights include a restored church, 1860s general store, drugstore, livery stable and house.

Camping and picnicking facilities are available; required reservations are available through MISTIX at (800) 444-7275. Allow 1 hour minimum. Daily 10-5, in summer; Sat.-Sun. 10-4, rest of year. Admission $5 per vehicle; over 62, $4 per vehicle. Phone (916) 265-2740.

MINERS FOUNDRY CULTURAL CENTER, 325 Spring St., has structures dating from 1856. Built for industrial metal working and metal casting, the complex is now a performing arts center. A free self-guiding tour of the historic site is available. Special programs are scheduled throughout the year. Historic site open Mon.-Fri. 9-5. Free. For information on special programs phone (916) 265-5040.

NEVADA CITY WINERY, 321 Spring St., produces varietal wines. Tastings and tours are

available. Daily noon-5. Free. Phone (916) 265-9463.

NEWHALL—*see Santa Clarita.*

NEWPORT BEACH (C-6) pop. 66,600, alt. 10'

The city of Newport Beach comprises Balboa, Balboa Island, Lido Isle, Corona del Mar, Newport Heights, Harbor Island, Bay Shores and Linda Isle. A 6-mile-long beach lies along the peninsula between the bay and the ocean. Newport Harbor is a leading Pacific Coast yacht rendezvous; it has one of the largest concentrations of pleasure craft in the nation with nearly 9,000 boats docked at the harbor.

Balboa Fun Zone, at the Newport Bay end of Main Street on the Balboa peninsula, has a carrousel, ferris wheel, shops and restaurants. In the same area is the Balboa Pavilion. Built in 1905 as an electric railway terminus, it now houses various businesses. Catalina Passenger Service has regularly scheduled trips to Catalina Island. Small ferry boats ply the channel between the peninisula and Balboa Island.

Shopping areas: Broadway, Bullock's Wilshire, Neiman-Marcus and Robinson's can all be found at Fashion Island, an open-air Mediterranean-style village on Newport Center Drive.

NEWPORT DUNES RV RESORT, Pacific Coast Hwy., at Jamboree Rd., on Upper Newport Bay, includes a 400-site RV park with full hook-ups, a swimming lagoon and beach, picnic and barbecue facilities, boat rentals and launching ramps and a marina. Daily 8 a.m.-10 p.m. Admission $5 per private vehicle; fee for RV camping. Phone (714) 729-3863.

NEWPORT HARBOR ART MUSEUM, 850 San Clemente Dr., offers changing exhibits of contemporary paintings, sculpture and photography. Tues.-Sun. 10-5; closed Jan. 1, July 4, Thanksgiving, Dec. 25 and periodically between exhibitions; phone ahead. Admission $4, over 62 and students $2; free to all on Tues. **Discount.** Phone (714) 759-1122.

NEWPORT HARBOR CRUISE, BALBOA PAVILION, 400 Main St., offers 45- and 90-minute cruises aboard the *Pavilion Queen* or *Pavilion Paddy,* departing from Balboa Pavilion. Departures daily 10-6, in summer; 11-3, rest of year. Closed Dec. 25. Fare for the 45-minute cruise $6; ages 5-12, $1. Fare for the 90-minute cruise $8; ages 5-12, $1. Phone (714) 673-5245.

NEWPORT HARBOR SHOWBOAT CRUISES leave from 700 E. Edgewater Ave. A 45-minute cruise departs daily on the hour 11-7, in summer; 11-3, rest of year. A 90-minute cruise leaves daily on the hour 11-6, in summer; 11-2, rest of year. Closed Dec. 24-25. Fare for the 45-minute cruise $6; ages 5-11, $1. Fare for the 90-minute cruise $8; ages 5-11, $1. Phone (714) 673-0240.

SHERMAN LIBRARY AND GARDENS, 2647 E. Coast Hwy., is a 2-acre cultural center with botanical gardens displaying tropical and subtropical flora, and a research library of Southwestern history. The complex also has a touch and smell garden and a tea garden. Gardens daily 10:30-4; library Mon.-Fri. 9-5; tea garden Sat.-Mon. 11-3. Closed Jan. 1, Thanksgiving and Dec. 25. Admission $2; ages 12-16, $1. Phone (714) 673-2261.

NIPOMO (I-3) pop. 10,000, alt. 330'

Originally a privately owned 38,000-acre ranch, Nipomo grew into a major stopover on El Camino Real between missions San Luis Obispo and Santa Barbara. Citrus orchards, vegetable farms and commercial nurseries thrive in the rich soil that washes down from the Nipomo Foothills. Thousands of blue gum eucalyptus trees, unsuccessfully planted to yield hardwood, clothe the mesa area of Nipomo. The Rancho Nipomo adobe house, built in 1839 with the help of mission Indians, still stands. Nipomo is on a scenic stretch of US 101.

ROSS-KELLER WINERY, 985 Orchard Ave., produces red and white varietal wines. Tours and tastings are offered. Picnicking is permitted. Daily noon-5, Apr.-Nov.; Wed.-Sun., rest of year. Free. Phone (805) 929-3627.

NORTH FORK (G-5) pop. 600, alt. 2,629'

SIERRA MONO INDIAN MUSEUM, jct. of CRs 225, 228 and 274, displays a variety of artifacts and items unique to the Mono Indians. Central to the museum's exhibits, as well as to the Mono culture, is an extensive collection of baskets. Other highlights include wildlife exhibits and tools, jewelry and baskets from other North American Indian tribes. During the first weekend in August the museum holds Indian Fair Days, which includes traditional dances, songs and demonstrations.

Mon.-Fri. 9-4, Sat. by appointment; closed Jan. 1, Thanksgiving and Dec. 25. Admission $1.50, high school students $1, elementary school students 75c. Phone (209) 877-2115.

NOVATO (O-2) pop. 47,600, alt. 18'

North of San Francisco on US 101, Novato was named for a chief of the Coast Miwok Indians and is now a community of homes while still retaining an outlying dairy region. The Renaissance Pleasure Faire, a re-created 16th-century harvest marketplace celebration, takes place on weekends from mid-August to early October.

The Novato History Museum, 815 DeLong Ave., is in one of the town's older houses. Exhibits include antique tools, photographs and relics relating to Novato's "Wild West" heritage.

MARIN MUSEUM OF THE AMERICAN INDIAN, 2200 Novato Blvd. in Miwok Park, displays Miwok Indian artifacts and exhibits of the prehistoric period in Marin County. Changing exhibits highlight various other American Indian cultures. The Trade Feast in early June features Indian dancing, food, arts and crafts displays and special children's activities. The museum also has a native plant garden. Free docent tour at 1:30. Allow 30 minutes minimum. Tues.-Sat. 10-4, Sun. noon-4. Donations. Phone (415) 897-4064.

OAKDALE (F-3) pop. 12,000, alt. 155′

HERSHEY CHOCOLATE U.S.A., a division of Hershey Foods, is at 120 S. Sierra Ave. The visitor center at S. Sierra Ave. and G St. is open Mon.-Fri. 8:30-5, Sat. 10-4:30. Thirty-minute tours are offered Mon.-Fri. 8:30-3; closed Good Friday and holidays. Free. Phone (209) 848-8126.

OAK GLEN (B-9) alt. 4,840′

Oak Glen is one of the largest apple-growing communities in Southern California. Most of the area's orchards are open September through December, including ranches where people may pick their own fruit. Several complexes in town offer specialty shops and restaurants; Oak Tree Village near the summit of Oak Glen Road also has a live-animal park, a small fishing pond and Mountaintown, where stuffed and mounted animals from around the world are displayed.

OAKHURST (G-4) pop. 2,000, alt. 2,289′

FRESNO FLATS HISTORICAL PARK, n.e. via SR 41 and CR 426 on School Rd., has a collection of historic buildings typical of those found in a local late 19th-century community. Highlights include the Taylor Log House, the Laramore House with its collection of antiques, a blacksmith shop, logging exhibit, late 1800s agricultural barn, schoolhouse and a collection of wagons and stagecoaches. Picnic tables are available. Wed.-Sat. 1-3, Sun. 1-4; closed Jan. 1, Easter and Dec. 25. Admission $2; ages 5-12, 75c. Phone (209) 683-6570.

OAKLAND (O-3) pop. 372,200, alt. 42′

Oakland stretches along the mainland side of San Francisco Bay and varies in altitude from sea level to 1,500 feet. The San Francisco-Oakland Bay Bridge links the city with San Francisco; a westbound toll of $1 is charged.

Oakland is a major West Coast port and manufacturing center. It also is home of the U.S. Naval Supply Depot and the U.S. Army Port of Embarkation and General Depot.

Nine regional parks adjoin Oakland: Anthony Chabot (*see Recreation Chart*), Charles Lee Tilden (*see Berkeley*), Claremont Canyon Regional

Preserve, Huckleberry Botanic Regional Preserve, Joaquin Miller, Lake Temescal *(see Recreation Chart)*, Redwood, Robert Sibley Volcanic Regional Preserve, and San Leandro Bay Regional Shoreline *(see Recreation Chart)*. Opportunities for hiking, picnicking, fishing and swimming are available. Facilities vary from park to park.

The Bret Harte Boardwalk on 5th Street between Jefferson and Clay streets adjoins the site of author Bret Harte's boyhood home. A block of renovated Victorian homes and barns have been converted to shops and restaurants.

GREEK ORTHODOX CHURCH OF THE ASCENSION, 4700 Lincoln Ave., overlooks Oakland and the bay. Designed in the Byzantine style, the copper-domed church houses colorful mosaics and icons of Christ and the disciples. It is crowned with a 12-foot cross set with light-catching Baccarat crystals. A Greek festival is held in mid-May. Allow 1 hour minimum. Mon.-Fri. 9-4; closed holidays. Free. Phone (510) 531-3400.

JACK LONDON WATERFRONT, bounded by Clay St., Alice St., the Embarcadero and the Oakland estuary, is a colorful waterfront area. Heinolds' First and Last Chance Saloon, a favorite haunt of the author, is at the foot of Webster Street. Jack London Village is an early 19th-century-style shopping and restaurant complex. Mon.-Sat. 10:30-6, Sun. noon-6. Phone (510) 893-7956.

KAISER CENTER ART GALLERY, 300 Lakeside Dr., is on the second floor of the international headquarters for Kaiser companies. Allow 30 minutes minimum. Gallery open Mon.-Fri. 8-6; roof garden open Mon.-Sat. 7-6:30. Closed holidays. Free. Phone (510) 271-2351.

LAKESIDE PARK embraces the n. shore of Lake Merritt, a saltwater tidal lake in the center of the city. The Oakland Municipal Band gives free concerts Sun. at 2:30, early July to mid-Sept. A tour boat plies the lake; fare $1; over 60 and under 12, 50c. Boat rentals, sailing lessons and bowling greens are available. Phone (510) 444-3807.

Children's Fairyland, Grand Ave., is a child-size attraction depicting fairy tales. Puppet shows are presented at 11, 2 and 4; animals are fed throughout the day. Children's rides are available. Allow 2 hours minimum. Daily 10-5:30, mid-June through Labor Day; Sat.-Sun. 10-4:30, rest of year. Closed Jan. 1, Thanksgiving and Dec. 25. Admission $2.25, children $1.75. Parking $2, Sat.-Sun. and holidays. Phone (510) 832-3609.

Lakeside Park Garden Center, 666 Bellevue Ave. between Bellevue Ave. and Perkins St., is surrounded by Japanese, Polynesian, cactus, dahlia, palm, fuchsia and chrysanthemum gardens, and also has an herb and fragrance garden. The center has a gardening library and presents flower shows in season. Allow 2 hours minimum. Mon.-Fri. 10-3, Sat.-Sun. and holidays 10-5, May-Nov.; 10-4, rest of year. Closed Jan. 1, Thanksgiving and Dec. 25. Parking $1.50, Sat.-Sun. and holidays. Phone (510) 238-2197.

Rotary Nature Center has seasonal displays of birds, mammals and reptiles. In winter hundreds of wild geese, herons, egrets and ducks take sanctuary at the state wildlife refuge outside the museum. Allow 1 hour minimum. Tues.-Sun. 10-5, Mon. noon-5. Free. Phone (510) 238-3739.

MILLS COLLEGE ART GALLERY AND ANTONIO PRIETO MEMORIAL GALLERY, on campus, offers changing exhibits. Allow 1 hour, 30 minutes minimum. Tues.-Sat. 11-4, Sun. noon-4, early Sept.-late May; closed holidays. Free. Phone (510) 430-2164.

MORCOM AMPHITHEATER OF ROSES, 1 blk. w. of Grand Ave. at 700 Jean St., has 8 acres of gardens, reflecting pools and trees. Various species are in bloom May through November; the peak season is May through September. Garden information is available. Additional street parking is on Olive Avenue. Daily dawn-dusk. Free. Phone (510) 658-0731.

MORMON TEMPLE, 4770 Lincoln Ave., is a magnificent example of religious architecture and offers a scenic vista of Oakland and San Francisco. Guided tours of the gardens and worship houses include a 12-minute slide show on the temple. The interior of the temple is closed to non-Mormons. A genealogical library is open to the public; phone for hours. Allow 1 hour minimum. Grounds open 9-9. Last tour departs 30 minutes before closing. Free. Phone (510) 531-1475.

OAKLAND-ALAMEDA COUNTY COLISEUM COMPLEX, Nimitz Frwy. (I-880) at the 66th Ave. exit, includes a stadium, indoor arena and exhibit hall. It is the home of Oakland's professional sports teams— the A's (baseball) and Warriors (basketball)—as well as concerts, wrestling and the circus. The complex is open only during scheduled events. Parking $5. Phone (510) 639-7700.

★**OAKLAND MUSEUM,** 10th and Oak sts., is a complex of gardens and galleries reflecting the ecology, history and art of California. Allow 1 hour minimum. Wed.-Sat. 10-5, Sun. noon-7; closed Jan. 1, July 4, Thanksgiving and Dec. 25. Free. A fee is charged for special exhibits. Phone (510) 834-2413.

OAKLAND ZOO AT KNOWLAND PARK, 98th Ave. at I-580 in southeastern Oakland, offers picnic facilities, playgrounds, amusement rides and a zoo. An aerial tram affords a bird's-eye view of the area. Allow 1 hour minimum. Zoo open daily 10-4; park open daily 9-5. Zoo admission $3.50;

over 55 and ages 2-14, $1.50. Closed Thanksgiving and Dec. 25. Park admission $2 per private vehicle; pedestrians free. Parking free first Mon. of each month, except holidays. Phone (510) 632-9523 or 632-9525.

Children's Zoo offers opportunities to feed and pet dozens of small and exotic animals. Children's Zoo included in zoo entrance fee.

SKYLINE BOULEVARD follows the rim of Oakland's low hills through a section of parks and private estates. On clear days the entire East Bay area is visible.

WOODMINSTER AMPHITHEATER is 1 mi. above the Mormon Temple on Joaquin Miller Rd. at the center of Joaquin Miller Park. Broadway plays and musicals and light opera are presented at 8 p.m., July 1 to early September. Tickets $7-$9; discounts are offered to senior citizens and under 13. MC, VI. Phone (510) 531-9597.

OAKVILLE (N-2) pop. 200, alt. 155′

ROBERT MONDAVI WINERY, ½ mi. n. on SR 29, offers tours of the facility; reservations are required. Daily 9-5, May-Oct.; 10-4:30, rest of year. Closed Jan. 1, Good Friday, Easter, Thanksgiving and Dec. 25. Free. Phone (707) 963-9611.

OCEANO (I-3) pop. 5,000, alt. 25′

THE GREAT AMERICAN MELODRAMA AND VAUDEVILLE, 1863 Pacific Ave. (SR 1), presents 19th-century melodramas and comedies Wed.-Thurs. at 7 p.m., Fri. at 8 p.m., Sat. at 5 and 9

p.m., Sun. at 6 p.m.; closed major holidays. Box office open Mon.-Sat. 10-6, Sun. 11-5. Tickets $10.50-$12.50; senior citizens and under 12, $9.50-$10.50. Reservations are recommended; phone (805) 489-2499.

OCEANSIDE (K-6) pop.128,400, alt. 47′

At the mouth of the San Luis Rey Valley, Oceanside's 3½ miles of beaches offer year-round opportunities for ocean recreation. There are several national surfing championships, including the World Body-Surfing Championships in mid-August. The harbor has facilities for boating, dining and sport fishing; whale-watching takes place during the winter.

CAMP PENDLETON, a Marine Corps base covering approximately 125,000 acres, is one of the world's leading amphibious training camps; it also serves as an ecological preserve. Self-guiding tours of the facility include the Amphibian Vehicle Museum, where amphibious vehicles used since World War II are displayed. Rancho Las Flores, the Bunkhouse Museum and a 19th-century adobe ranch house also are along the route.

Visitor passes and self-guiding tour brochures are available at the main gate. Visitors must present a driver's license, vehicle registration and verification of auto insurance to enter. Daily dawn-dusk. Phone (619) 725-5566.

MISSION SAN LUIS REY DE FRANCIA, 4 mi. e. on SR 76 at 4050 Mission Ave., was 18th in the chain of missions and one of the largest. Founded in 1798 by Father Fermín de Lasuén, it

---

Mission Architecture

The architecture of the 21 Spanish missions built along El Camino Real 1769-1823 reflects both the simple tastes of their Franciscan founders and the limited resources of material and skilled labor available in the California wilderness. The missions were constructed of stone and adobe, finished inside and out with whitewashed mud plaster and topped with pitched roofs of hewn timber covered with red tile. They were modestly adorned, compared to much of the Spanish architecture in the New World at that time.

The mission usually centered on a courtyard, which was enclosed by the church and a variety of other buildings. These minor structures included quarters for friars, Indian workers, servants and soldiers; guest rooms; workshops; a convent; a kitchen and a dining hall. Cloisters—arched covered passageways—fronted the courtyard and often the surrounding outer plaza as well.

The mission church followed one of three general designs. The first, typified by Mission San Miguel Arcangel in San Miguel, consisted of a simple nave, or central hall. A more elaborate design, such as Mission San Buenaventura's in Ventura, included a single bell tower. Two belfry towers adorned churches of the third design, exemplified by the graceful Mission Santa Barbara.

After the secularization of the missions in 1833, earthquakes and neglect took their toll; many of the missions were severely damaged or destroyed. Subsequent restoration and reconstruction have revitalized these historic structures, which remain the oldest and perhaps the most elegant architecture in California.

was named for Louis IX, King of France. The splendid interior has lofty beamed ceilings; the original decorations were done by American Indians. A museum includes artifacts from 18th- and 19th-century mission life. An annual fiesta takes place the third weekend in July.

Mon.-Sat. and holidays 10-4:30, Sun. noon-4:30; closed Jan. 1, Good Friday, Easter, Thanksgiving and Dec. 25. Admission $3; ages 5-12, $1. Phone (619) 757-3651.

OJAI (J-5) pop. 7,600, alt. 746'

In a valley surrounded by high mountains, Ojai (O-hi) is a popular artists' colony and retreat. The oldest tennis tournament in the country takes place in April. The Ojai Music Festival, the last weekend of May, features classical music. Local attractions include the Ojai Valley Museum in the old Ventura County Fire Station and nearby Lake Casitas and Los Padres National Forest *(see place listing)*. For further information contact the Ojai Chamber of Commerce and Visitors Bureau, 338 E. Ojai Ave., Ojai, CA 93023; phone (805) 646-8126.

ONTARIO (B-8) pop. 133,200, alt. 988'

Once an agricultural center, Ontario is now a largely residential community as well as the location of the Los Angeles area's second international airport.

Shopping areas: Plaza Continental Factory Stores, 3700 E. Inland Empire Blvd., has about 20 factory outlet stores, including Adolfo II, Converse, Corning/Revere and Gitano, as well as three restaurants.

GRABER OLIVE HOUSE, 315 E. Fourth St., was established in 1894. Free tours are conducted daily. During the harvest season visitors can watch the grading, curing and canning of olives. A picnic area is available. Open Mon.-Sat. 9-5:30, Sun. 9:30-6; closed major holidays. Free. Phone (909) 983-1761.

MUSEUM OF HISTORY AND ART, 225 S. Euclid Ave., is housed in the old city hall building. The history section contains private artifact collections and changing exhibits that reflect Ontario's role in such areas as agriculture, industry and aviation. Galleries display works of regional artists in various media. Wed.-Sun. noon-4; closed holidays. Free. Phone (909) 983-3198.

ORANGE (C-7) pop. 110,700, alt. 187'

In 1869, two lawyers planned the city of Orange from 1,300 acres they had received as payment from a client. The town was built around the circular central plaza at Chapman Avenue and Glassell Street. Chapman University is 2 blocks north of the plaza.

Self-guiding tours: Information on walking and driving tours of Orange's restored Victorian-style neighborhoods are available from the chamber of commerce at 80 Plaza Square, Orange, CA 92666; phone (714) 538-3581.

Shopping areas: Antique and specialty shops line Glassell Street just north of the plaza. Orange Circle Antique Mall, with 50 shops under one roof, is at 118 S. Glassell St. For everyday needs visit The City, Chapman Avenue and The City Drive, which has a JCPenney, May Co. and 100 other stores. Broadway, JCPenney and Sears have branches at the Mall of Orange, Tustin and Heim avenues.

ORICK (B-1) pop. 700, alt. 34'

HUMBOLDT LAGOONS STATE PARK, 1,886 acres 4 mi. s. on US 101, has a sandy beach, lagoon and rocky headlands. Wild azaleas and lilacs bloom in June. Daily 24 hours. Phone (707) 445-5435. *See Recreation Chart.*

PRAIRIE CREEK REDWOODS STATE PARK, 13,000 acres, is 6 mi. n. on US 101. A coastal redwood park, it protects one of the last herds of native Roosevelt elk. Beach access, guided nature hikes and campfire programs are available. Daily 24 hours. Day use fee $5 per vehicle, senior citizens $4 per vehicle. Phone (707) 488-2171. *See Recreation Chart.*

OROVILLE (D-3) pop. 12,000, alt. 174'

Cherokee Indians migrated to Oroville from Georgia in the 1850s to work in gold mines north of town. In 1870 alone, hydraulic mining operations at the site yielded $5 million in gold. Later diamonds were discovered; the Cherokee Diamond Mine opened in 1873 and produced some 300 diamonds of industrial quality.

The reserves were soon depleted, however, and Cherokee, like so many other mining towns in California, was forgotten. Shells of brick stores and foundations identified by markers are all that remain of this ghost town on Cherokee Road, 10 miles north of Oroville via SR 70/89.

CHINESE TEMPLE, is at Elma and Broderick sts. The 1863 temple contains furnishings donated by the Emperor of China. A self-guiding tour includes various temples, a courtyard garden and collections of puppets, costumes and tapestries. A 15-minute historical narration is available. Allow 30 minutes minimum. Thurs.-Mon. 11-4:30, Tues.-Wed. 1-4; closed mid-Dec. through Jan. 31. Admission $2, under 12 free. **Discount.** Phone (916) 538-2496.

FEATHER RIVER HATCHERY, 5 Table Mountain Blvd., releases more than 10 million salmon and steelhead yearlings into the Feather River each year. The best time to visit the hatchery is during the spawning season, October 1 to mid-November. Allow 30 minutes minimum. Daily 8-dusk. Free. Phone (916) 538-2222.

HISTORIC LOTT HOME IN SANK PARK is between 3rd and 4th aves. on Montgomery St. The

1856 home is furnished in period. Picnic facilities are available. Home open Fri.-Tues. 11-4:30, Wed.-Thurs. 1-4, Feb. 1-Dec. 14. Park open daily 9-9. Home $2, under 12 free. **Discount.** Phone (916) 538-2497.

LAKE OROVILLE VISITOR CENTER is 7 mi. n.e. of SR 162 to Kelly Ridge, then 1½ mi. n. The center, overlooking Lake Oroville and Oroville Dam, exhibits displays depicting the gold rush era, state water projects, wildlife and the Maidu Indians. Films are shown on request. Allow 1 hour minimum. Daily 9-5; closed Jan. 1, Thanksgiving and Dec. 25. Free. Phone (916) 538-2200.

OXNARD (J-5) pop. 142,200, alt. 52′

With a busy harbor and 7 miles of beaches, Oxnard offers opportunities for boating, sport fishing, swimming and bicycling. The city is the site of the California Strawberry Festival in May.

Shopping areas: The Esplanade, Vineyard Street and Esplanade Drive, has a May Co. and a Sears. Fisherman's Wharf is at the corner of Victoria Avenue and Channel Islands Boulevard. Styled after an early-American seacoast village, the complex houses numerous specialty shops and restaurants. Waterfront shops and restaurants are the attraction at Harbor Landing at Harbor and Channel Islands boulevards.

CARNEGIE ART MUSEUM, 424 S. C St., was built as a two-story library in 1906. The permanent collection focuses on 20th-century California painters. Changing exhibits include oil paintings, sketches, photographs and sculpture. Thurs.-Sat. 10-5, Sun. 1-5; closed Jan. 1, Thanksgiving, Dec. 25 and periodically between exhibits. Donations. Phone (805) 385-8157.

GULL WINGS CHILDREN'S MUSEUM, 418 W. 4th St., has a variety of hands-on exhibits and activities that include puppets and a stage, a make-believe campground with a tent and "fishing pond," a medical room with cutaway anatomical models and medical equipment, and a rock and mineral display that includes fossil remains. Wed.-Fri. and Sun. 1-5, Sat. 10-5. Admission $3, ages 2-12, $2. Phone (805) 483-3005.

VENTURA COUNTY MARITIME MUSEUM, 2731 S. Victoria Ave., just past Channel Islands Blvd., harbors a collection of ship models and artwork that reflects maritime history from ancient times to the present. Thurs.-Mon. 11-5; closed Jan. 1, Thanksgiving and Dec. 25. Admission $2; over 65, $1 (on Mon. only); ages 5-12, $1. Phone (805) 984-6260.

PACIFIC GROVE (G-2) pop. 16,100, alt. 55′

Adjoining Monterey, Pacific Grove is the starting point for the popular Seventeen-Mile Drive *(see Monterey).* Point Pinos Lighthouse, which has been in operation since 1855, is on Light-

house Avenue in Pacific Grove; tours are available. Phone (408) 648-3116.

Shopping areas: The American Tin Cannery, 125 Ocean View Blvd., has more than 45 factory-direct and specialty stores.

★**BUTTERFLY TREES,** on Ridge Rd. off Lighthouse Ave., are pine trees that are visited by monarch butterflies from late October through March. The colorful orange and black butterflies range from Canada to South America.

MUSEUM OF NATURAL HISTORY, 165 Forest Ave., emphasizes the natural history of Monterey County through an extensive collection of shore and aquatic birds, a marine life diorama and exhibit on monarch butterflies. Allow 1 hour minimum. Tues.-Sun. and holidays 10-5; closed Jan. 1, Thanksgiving and Dec. 24-25. Free. Phone (408) 648-3116.

PACIFIC PALISADES (B-5) pop. 23,100, alt. 260′

Many elaborate homes are precariously perched on Pacific Palisades' steep bluffs, overlooking the beaches below.

SELF-REALIZATION FELLOWSHIP LAKE SHRINE, 17190 Sunset Blvd., is a 10-acre site that includes a picturesque lake and a "wall-less temple" housing the Gandhi World Peace Memorial. A pathway encircling the lake affords views of a bird refuge, a sunken garden and various structures representing the five major religions of the world. Tues.-Sat. 9-4:45, Sun. 12:30-4:45; closed holidays and some Sat. Free. Phone (310) 454-4114.

★**WILL ROGERS STATE HISTORIC PARK,** 186 acres at 14253 Sunset Blvd., includes the humorist's home, as well as hiking trails and picnic facilities. Polo games are played Sat. at 2 and Sun. at 10, weather permitting. Home open daily 10-5, depending on availability of staff. Park open daily 8-7, in summer; 8-6, in winter. Both closed Jan. 1, Thanksgiving and Dec. 25. Admission $5 per private vehicle, senior citizens $4 per private vehicle. Phone (310) 454-8212.

PALA (K-7) pop. 500, alt. 410′

MISSION SAN ANTONIO DE PALA, n. of SR 76 on Pala Mission Rd., was originally a branch of Mission San Luis Rey de Francia. The first building, the granary, was built in 1810. Planned as part of a second chain of inland missions, it fell into disrepair after the project was rejected. It has since been restored and contains a museum and mineral room. Tues.-Sun. 10-3, weather permitting; closed Thanksgiving and Dec. 25. Mission free. Museum $1.50, students $1, children 50c. Phone (619) 742-3317.

PALM DESERT (K-7) pop. 23,300, alt. 243′

At the base of the Santa Rosa Mountains, Palm Desert is one of the satellite cities of Palm

Springs. The Bob Hope Cultural Center hosts live musical entertainment.

Shopping areas: The biggest mall in town is Palm Desert Town Center, SR 111 and Monterey Avenue, which has a Bullock's, JCPenney, May Co. and Robinson's.

HOT AIR BALLOON RIDES, over the Coachella Valley, offer an unusual perspective of the desert's landscape. Because of summer's heat, companies fly only from October through May. Flights are usually in the early morning or evening. Prices range from $100 to $150 per person for an approximately 1-hour flight. Reservations are required. Contact American Balloon Charters, (619) 327-8544 or (800) 359-6837; Desert Balloon Charters, (619) 346-8575; or Dream Flights Hot Air Balloon Adventures, (619) 321-5154 or (800) 933-5628.

Note: The mention of the preceding hot air balloon rides is for information only and does **not** imply endorsement by AAA.

THE LIVING DESERT, 1½ mi. s. off SR 111 at 47-900 Portola Ave., is a 1,200-acre wildlife and botanical park dedicated to interpreting the beauty of the world's desert lands. Among the animals are bighorn sheep, Arabian oryx, zebra and various reptiles. Gardens, American Indian culture exhibits, picnic areas and hiking trails are available.

Daily 9-4:30, Sept. 1-June 15. Admission $6; over 62, $5.25; ages 3-15, $3. **Discount,** except over 62. Phone (619) 346-5694. *See ad.*

PALM SPRINGS (K-7) pop. 40,200, alt. 466'

The fashionable resort of Palm Springs lies in the upper Colorado Desert at the foot of 10,804-foot San Jacinto Peak. The mineral springs have attracted visitors for years, and the idyllic setting has been the location of many Hollywood productions. Nationally known tournaments are held on Palm Springs' fine golf courses and on neighboring communities' courses. Information can be obtained from the Palm Springs Desert Resorts Convention and Visitors Bureau, 69-930 Hwy.

111, Suite 201, Rancho Mirage, CA 92270; phone (619) 770-9000. *See ad p. 123.*

VillageFest presents musical entertainment, food booths, arts and crafts displays and antiques each Thursday evening, September through July. The festivities take place on Palm Canyon Drive between Tahquitz Way and Baristo Road.

Shopping areas: Desert Fashion Plaza, at Palm Canyon Drive and Tahquitz Way, specializes in haute couture from the likes of Gucci, I. Magnin and Saks.

AGUA CALIENTE INDIAN RESERVATION, 5 mi. s., is a vast scenic area that includes hiking trails and picnic areas set aside for visitors by the Tribal Council. Daily 8-5, Sept.-June. Reservation entrance fee (includes Andreas, Murray and Palm canyons) $3.50; military and students $2.50; senior citizens $2; ages 6-12, $1. Phone (619) 325-5673.

Andreas Canyon offers many unusual rock formations, a hiking trail that follows a stream and picnic facilities. There also are Indian grinding stones, unusual rock formations and caves once used by the Agua Caliente.

Murray Canyon is smaller and less accessible than Andreas and Palm canyons, but contains spectacular rock formations, mortar holes and caves.

Palm Canyon is lined for 15 miles with 1,500- to 2,000-year-old Washingtonian palms that can be viewed by taking a steep walk down into the valley.

MOORTEN BOTANICAL GARDEN, 1701 S. Palm Canyon Dr., displays desert plants from around the world and also serves as a bird and wildlife sanctuary. Mon.-Sat. 9-4:30, Sun. 10-4. Admission $1.50; ages 5-16, 75c. Phone (619) 327-6555.

OASIS WATERPARK, 1500 Gene Autry Trail, has a wave pool, waterslides, river, spa and an outdoor pavilion. Daily 11-6, mid-Mar. to mid-June; daily 11-7, mid-June to early Sept.; Sat.-Sun. 11-6, early Sept.-Oct. 31. Admission $16.95;

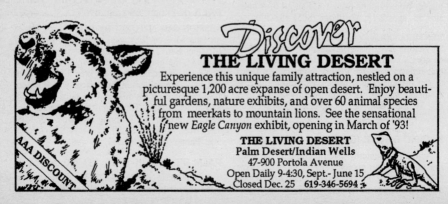

40-59 inches tall $11.95; over age 55, $10.95; reduced rates after 3:30. **Discount,** except 40-59 inches tall and over age 55. Foam surfboards and inner tubes can be rented for $5. Parking $2. Phone (619) 325-7873.

★**PALM SPRINGS AERIAL TRAMWAY,** on Tramway Rd., 3 mi. s.w. of SR 111, transports passengers 2½ mi. from Valley Station (2,643 ft.) in Chino Canyon to and from Mountain Station (8,516 ft.) at the e. edge of Long Valley. The tram affords spectacular views and access to the rugged San Jacinto Mountains. Both stations have observation decks and picnic areas; food is available.

Fifty miles of trails in the San Jacinto Wilderness Park make the area popular with hikers and cross-country skiers. Pets are not permitted on the tramway; there are no restrictions or extra fees for hiking or backpacking gear.

Tram rides are offered Mon.-Fri. beginning at 10 a.m., Sat.-Sun. and holidays beginning at 8 a.m. Last trip up departs at 9 p.m. and returns at 10:45 p.m. during DST; last trip up departs at 8 p.m. and returns at 9:45 p.m., rest of year. Closed up to 2 weeks beginning first Mon. in Aug. Fare $15.95; over 55, $13.25; ages 5-12, $10.95. AE, MC, VI. **Discount,** except over 55. Phone (619) 325-1391. *See ad.*

PALM SPRINGS DESERT MUSEUM, 101 Museum Dr., is dedicated to the visual and performing arts and the natural sciences. Exhibits focus on Western and contemporary art and the human and natural history of the Coachella Valley. Tues.-Fri. 10-4, Sat.-Sun. 10-5, Sept.-June; closed major holidays. Admission $4; over 62, $3; students and military with ID and ages 6-17, $2; free to all first Tues. of the month, except during special exhibits. Phone (619) 325-0189.

PALO ALTO (Q-2) pop. 55,900, alt. 23′

Palo Alto (tall tree) was named for a double-trunked redwood tree, a landmark used by travelers and explorers as early as 1769. A likeness of the tree appears on the seal of Stanford University. The opening of the university in 1891 provided the impetus for Palo Alto's development, and the livelihoods of the two remain closely intertwined.

Palo Alto is the southeastern teminus of a scenic 31-mile stretch of I-280 that heads northwest to San Francisco.

STANFORD UNIVERSITY, stands on what is known as the "Stanford Farm," an estate of 8,200 acres. The main buildings are about 1 mile from the city. Frederick Law Olmstead created the general concept for the grounds and the unifying architectural theme: Romanesque-style

As you ride the Palm Springs Aerial Tram, and the desert heat below gives way to the crisp mountain air above, you'll feel like you're in the Alps. So, go ahead and yodel all you want.

At the top of the Tram you can explore the tree-lined trails and perhaps even catch a glimpse of some wildlife (not the kind by the pool). Ride the Palm Springs Aerial Tram and prepare yourself for an Alpine experience. Leiderhosen optional.

Palm Springs Aerial Tram

Cars every ½ hour beginning 10am Mon-Fri; 8am Sat-Sun-Holidays. Last car up 8pm (9pm during Daylight Savings). For information call (619) 325-1391.

Vacation in "the village of Palm Springs" for unlimited sunshine and just as many options. Hike and picnic in the lush Indian Canyons, or shop on Palm Canyon Drive. Swim, play tennis, ride the Aerial Tramway, dine, dance, or simply relax by the pool under a palm tree. Call for a free 32-page vacation guide or to make hotel reservations.

Palm Springs
1(800) 34-Springs

sandstone buildings with arched arcades and red-tiled roofs. One-hour tours of the campus depart the information booth at the end of Palm Drive daily. Phone (415) 723-2560 or 723-2053.

Hoover Tower houses the Hoover Institution on War, Revolution and Peace, devoted to the study of world conflict. Tours depart daily at 11 and 3:15 from the Quad on Palm Drive; free. The building and observation platform are open daily 10-4:30; closed major holidays, exam weeks and during school breaks. Allow 30 minutes minimum. Admission $1; senior citizens and under 13, 50c; family rate $2.50. Phone (415) 723-2053 or 723-2560.

Stanford Art Gallery houses a variety of changing exhibits. Allow 30 minutes minimum. Tues.-Fri. 10-5, Sat.-Sun. 1-5; closed between exhibits. Free. Phone (415) 723-3469.

Stanford Linear Accelerator Center (SLAC), is a research facility with a 2-mile-long linear accelerator that generates high-energy electron beams. Stanford University operates the 426-acre basic research laboratory for the U.S. Department of Energy. An orientation precedes the guided bus tour. Allow 2 hours minimum. Free. For reservations and schedule information phone (415) 926-2204.

PALOMAR MOUNTAIN (K-7) pop. 200, alt. 5,202'

★**PALOMAR OBSERVATORY**, 4½ mi. n. on CR S6, consists of five domes; the largest houses the 200-inch Hale telescope, which is used to study distant celestial bodies. Also included are 48-inch Oschin and 18-inch Schmidt-type telescopes and a 60-inch reflecting telescope. The observatory primarily monitors the positions, distances, temperatures and physical properties of planets, stars and galaxies. The Greenway Museum contains a photographic display of some of the observatory's sightings.

Visitors' gallery at the 200-inch telescope open daily 9-4. Museum open daily 9-4:30; closed Dec. 24-25. Free. Phone (619) 742-2119.

PALOS VERDES PENINSULA (C-5) alt. 800'

Palos Verdes Peninsula is contoured by three coves that are accessible to the public. The widest and most easily reached is Malaga Cove, next to Torrance City Beach on Paseo de la Playa. Bluff Cove is reached by following Paseo del Mar west to a turnout for the cove. A trail winds down to the rocky inlet. Lunada Bay, a sand and pebble cove, can be reached by a short, very steep hike off the roadside turnoff on Paseo del Mar. Collecting plants or animals is prohibited in all of the coves. Just north of the peninsula are Redondo, Hermosa and Manhattan beaches.

POINT VICENTE INTERPRETIVE CENTER, next to the Point Vicente Lighthouse off Palos Verdes Dr. W., has exhibits on the Pacific gray whale and human and geologic history of the Palos Verdes Peninsula. An inside observation area on the second floor offers a panorama of the coast. The best season for whale-watching is from December through April. Daily 10-dusk; closed Jan. 1, Thanksgiving and Dec. 24-25. Admission $1.50; senior citizens and ages 4-14, 75c. Phone (310) 377-5370.

SOUTH COAST BOTANIC GARDEN, 26300 Crenshaw Blvd., has more than 2,000 plant species. Tram tours are available Sat.-Sun.; fare $1.50. Open daily 9-4:30; closed Dec. 25. Admission $3; over 62, students with ID and ages 13-17, $1.50; ages 6-12, 75c. **Two-for-one discount**, except over 62, students with ID and ages 6-17. Phone (310) 544-6815.

WAYFARERS CHAPEL, 5755 Palos Verdes Dr. S., was designed by Lloyd Wright, son of Frank Lloyd Wright. The "Glass Church" is surmounted by a 50-foot stone campanile, a landmark from both land and sea. The church has no members, although it is owned and operated by the Swedenborgian denomination. Daily 9-5. Free. Phone (310) 377-1650.

PARADISE (D-3) pop. 25,400, alt. 1,708'

GOLD NUGGET MUSEUM, 502 Pearson Rd., exhibits a miner's cabin, blacksmith shop, general store and a replica of a gold mine. Also displayed are exhibits depicting the history of Paradise and Magalia Ridge and a doll collection. Allow 1 hour minimum. Wed.-Sun. noon-4. Free. Phone (916) 872-8722.

PASADENA (B-6) pop. 131,600, alt. 865'

Pasadena, a residential community with many stately homes and the prestigious California Institute of Technology, is the site of the famed Tournament of Roses Parade, held annually on January 1, and the attendant Rose Bowl football game. Tickets for grandstand seats for the parade must be obtained months in advance. Football game tickets can be purchased from participating schools. To be outdone, participants in the farcical Doo Dah Parade take to the street in late November.

Ambassador Auditorium, on the campus of Ambassador College, and The Pasadena Center, a major auditorium and convention facility, play host to many of the city's cultural events. Several blocks west is the historic Old Town section of the city, featuring numerous shops and restaurants in an area bounded by Union Street, Raymond Avenue, Colorado Boulevard and Pasadena Avenue.

Shopping areas: Plaza Pasadena, bounded by Colorado Boulevard, Los Robles Avenue, and Green and Marengo streets, is an enclosed mall with a Broadway and JCPenney.

CALIFORNIA INSTITUTE OF TECHNOLOGY is at 1201 E. California Blvd. Caltech is a leading university where extensive research and instruction in science and engineering are conducted. Tours of the campus begin at the Public Relations office, 315 S. Hill Ave., Mon. and Thurs.-Fri. at 3 and Tues.-Wed. at 11; no tours on holidays or rainy days. Free. Phone (818) 356-6327.

The Jet Propulsion Lab (JPL), where the *Voyager* spacecraft was assembled and tracked in space, also is administered by the Institute. Two-hour tours are given occasionally by reservation only; under 10 not permitted. Phone (818) 354-9314.

THE GAMBLE HOUSE, 4 Westmoreland Pl., parallel to 300 blk. of N. Orange Grove Blvd., is part of the University of Southern California's School of Architecture. Designed by renowned architects Charles and Henry Greene in 1908, this bungalow-style home features sculptured woodwork, hand-shaped beams, projecting rafters and original furnishings. One-hour tours Thurs.-Sun. noon-3; closed holidays. Admission $4; over 65, $3; full-time students $2; under 12 free. Phone (818) 793-3334 or (213) 681-6427.

KIDSPACE, 390 S. El Molino Ave., is a participatory museum for ages 2-12. Children are encouraged to explore hands-on exhibits that include a TV studio, radio station, fire station and human habitrail. The museum also has special programs and workshops. Wed. 2-5, Sat.-Sun. 12:30-5, during school year; Tues.-Fri. 1-5, Sat.-Sun. 12:30-5, rest of year. Ages 3-12, $5; adults $4; over 65, $3.50; ages 1-2, $2.50. **Discount.** Phone (818) 449-9143.

★NORTON SIMON MUSEUM, 411 W. Colorado Blvd. at Orange Grove Blvd., exhibits art from the early Renaissance through the mid-20th century, including paintings by Monet, Renoir and Van Gogh; bronze models by Degas; and southeast Asian and Indian sculpture. Thurs.-Sun. noon-6; closed Jan. 1, Thanksgiving and Dec. 25. Admission $4, senior citizens and students with ID $2, under 12 free. Phone (818) 449-3730.

PACIFIC ASIA MUSEUM, 46 N. Los Robles Ave., houses historical, cultural and art exhibits of the Far East and the Pacific. The building, designed like a Chinese treasure house, surrounds a courtyard. Major exhibits change biannually. The museum also has a students' gallery and art shops. Wed.-Sun. noon-5; closed major holidays. Admission $3, over 55 and students with ID $1.50, under 12 free; free to all third Sat. of the month. **Discount.** Phone (818) 449-2742.

PASADENA PLAYHOUSE, 39 S. El Molino Ave., was founded in 1917 and has served as a training ground for numerous well-known actors and actresses. The 700-seat Mainstage Theatre presents stage productions throughout the year. Tickets $31.50. AE, MC, VI. Phone (818) 356-7529.

ROSE BOWL, in Brookside Park, is the site of the celebrated annual football game played on New Year's Day. UCLA home football games and other sporting events take place throughout the year. A huge swap meet is held on the grounds the second Sunday of each month; admission is charged. Mon.-Fri. 9-4; closed holidays and during events. Free. Phone (818) 577-3106.

TOURNAMENT HOUSE, 391 S. Orange Grove Blvd., is a mansion once owned by William Wrigley Jr. of chewing gum fame. As headquarters for the Pasadena Tournament of Roses Association's Rose Parade and Rose Bowl Game, it houses memorabilia commemorating notable parade and Rose Bowl events. A film and guided tour are offered Wed. 2-4, early Feb.-late Aug. Gardens open daily; closed Jan. 1 and Dec. 31. Free. Phone (818) 449-4100.

PASO ROBLES (H-3) pop. 15,500, alt. 721'

Paso Robles presents a variety of festivals and special events that draw visitors from around the state. The Mid-State Fair is held in August.

EBERLE WINERY, 4 mi. e. on SR 46, produces Chardonnay, Cabernet Sauvignon and Muscat Canelli. Large bay windows in the tasting room overlook the production facilities. Daily 10-6, May-Sept.; 10-5, rest of year. Free. Phone (805) 238-9607.

HELEN MOE'S ANTIQUE DOLL MUSEUM, US 101 at Wellsona Rd., houses about 700 antique and foreign dolls as well as various character and composition dolls. Included is a wooden stump doll that once belonged to Edward VI, son of England's King Henry VIII. Mon.-Sat. 10-5, Sun. 1-5; closed Easter, Mother's Day, Thanksgiving and Dec. 25. Admission $2; ages 5-12, $1. Phone (805) 238-2740.

PAUMA VALLEY (K-7) pop. 900, alt. 840'

SENGME OAKS WATER PARK, on the La Jolla Indian Reservation, 10½ mi. s.e. on SR 76, has a variety of waterslides and swimming pools in a 10-acre wooded setting. Picnic facilities, volleyball courts, showers and lockers are available. Wed.-Sun. 10-5:30, in summer, weather permitting. Admission $7.95; ages 4-11, $6.95. Phone (619) 742-1921.

PERRIS (C-8) pop. 21,500, alt. 1,457'

HOT AIR BALLOON RIDES over Perris Valley are available through several companies. Hot beverages, champagne and brunch are often included. Passengers may assist with lift-off and pack-up operations. Rides last from one-half hour to one hour, and prices range from $35 for children to $125 for adults; rides are not advisable for children under age 8. Reservations are required.

Contact Full of Hot Air Balloon Company, (714) 530-0110; Scorpion Balloons Inc., (909) 657-6930; or The Ultimate Ride Hot Air Balloon

Company, (310) 982-1570 or (800) 339-5139 in Southern Calif.

Note: The mention of the preceding hot air balloon rides is for information only and does **not** imply endorsement by AAA.

ORANGE EMPIRE RAILWAY MUSEUM, 2201 S. A St., displays trolleys and railway equipment. Daily 9-5; closed Thanksgiving and Dec. 25. Streetcar and train rides Sat.-Sun. and major holidays 9-5. Museum free; admission charged during special events. All-day ride pass $5; ages 6-11, $3. MC, VI. Phone (909) 657-2605.

PESCADERO (Q-2) pop. 500, alt. 30'

AÑO NUEVO STATE RESERVE is on SR 1, 13 mi. s. of Pescadero. The reserve harbors a variety of wildlife, but it is best known for its large colony of northern elephant seals. The seals spend most of their lives at sea, but come ashore to give birth, breed and molt. While seals can be seen all year, the greatest concentrations are found December through March during breeding season.

During this period the seals may be seen only on the scheduled guided walks that are conducted daily. Walks last 2½ hours and cover 3 miles. All walks leave on time and operate regardless of weather; no refunds are issued. Tickets cost $2 per person and must be purchased in advance by phone through MISTIX; phone (800) 444-7275. Entrance permits, required Apr.-Nov., can be obtained 8-3:30 at the entrance station. Donations. Parking $4. Phone (415) 879-0852.

PETALUMA (N-1) pop. 43,200, alt. 12'

Petaluma began as a hunter's camp on the Petaluma River and grew quickly as discouraged gold miners returned from the fields to take up hunting and farming. Today the poultry and dairy industries comprise much of the local economy. The Sonoma-Marin County Fair takes place at the fairgrounds in late June.

Tours on the Petaluma River are offered by Electric Nature Tours. The trips depart from the pedestrian bridge at the foot of Western and Water streets and highlights include an antique drawbridge, man-made island and opportunities for viewing native wildlife. For reservations phone (707) 874-1000.

Self-guiding tours: Brochures detailing a walking tour of 19th-century iron-front buildings and Victorian homes, survivors of the 1906 earthquake, can be obtained at the chamber of commerce at 215 Howard St. *See ad p. A331.*

CHEESE FACTORY is 9½ mi. s. via D St. Extension, Petaluma at 7500 Red Hill Rd. (Petaluma-Point Reyes Rd.). The factory offers tours of its cheesemaking operation. Allow 30 minutes minimum. Factory open daily 9-5, tours conducted

10-4; closed Jan. 1, Thanksgiving and Dec. 25. Free. Phone (707) 762-6001.

PETALUMA ADOBE STATE HISTORIC PARK, ¾ mi. e. on Adobe Rd., preserves a large adobe ranch headquarters built about 1836. Exhibits include candles, leather goods, clothing and tools made in this period. Allow 1 hour minimum. Daily 10-5; closed Jan. 1, Thanksgiving and Dec. 25. Admission, including house, $2; ages 6-12, $1. Phone (707) 762-4871.

PETALUMA HISTORICAL LIBRARY AND MUSEUM, 20 4th St., houses permanent and rotating exhibits reflecting life in early 19th-century Petaluma. Philanthropist Andrew Carnegie awarded the town $12,500 toward the building's construction in 1903. Exhibits include a collection of iron-front building facades popular in the last century. Allow 30 minutes minimum. Thurs.-Mon. 1-4. Free. Phone (707) 778-4398.

PIERCY (C-1) pop. 200, alt. 622'

CONFUSION HILL, on US 101, is an experience in contradictory optical and physical sensations in an apparently confused gravitational field. An optional 1¼-mile, 17-minute miniature train ride meanders through a redwood forest and a tree tunnel, weather permitting. Daily 8-7, late May-Labor Day; 10-4, rest of year. Allow 1 hour minimum. Admission $2.50; ages 6-12, $1.25. Train ride $2.50; ages 3-12, $1.25. Phone (707) 925-6456.

WORLD FAMOUS TREE HOUSE, 5 mi. s. on US 101, is in a 4,000-year-old living tree—250 feet high, 33 feet in diameter and 101½ feet in circumference. The room is built in a 50-foot-high cavity in the tree. Allow 30 minutes minimum. Daily 7 a.m.-8 p.m., June-Sept.; 8-5, rest of year. Closed Thanksgiving and Dec. 25. Free. Phone (707) 925-6406.

★PINNACLES NATIONAL MONUMENT (G-3)

The Pinnacles National Monument is entered from the east, 35 miles south of Hollister and 35 miles north of King City via SR 25 to SR 146, or from the west via SR 146, off US 101 near Soledad. It embraces about 16,000 acres of precipitous bluffs, spires and crags of colorful volcanic rock. A visitor center is accessible by car from the east entrance. The west entrance has a ranger station; the entrance road is narrow and not recommended for trailers or motorhomes. No roads connect the east and west districts.

Pinnacles is strictly a hiking park, although some of the major formations can be seen from the roadway into the monument. The best viewing by car is from the west side.

The monument is bisected from north to south by a 1,000-foot-high ridge. Most of the spirelike formations, some more than 600 feet high, are found on or alongside the ridge. This central backbone has been cut in two places by streams; huge fragments of rock have fallen into the resulting deep clefts, creating caves. Bear Gulch Caves and Balconies Caves require visitors to carry flashlights.

In addition to geological and scenic interest, the monument has an abundant bird population, as well as deer and wildflowers. An example of Coast Range chaparral thrives here. Picnic facilities are available. Pets must be kept under physical control and are not permitted on trails. Admission is $3 per private vehicle; parking areas fill up early during spring, which is the monument's busiest season. Phone (408) 389-4485. *See the AAA California and Nevada CampBook.*

PISMO BEACH (I-3) pop. 7,700, alt. 70'

Pismo Beach is perhaps best known for its namesake mollusk, the Pismo clam. At one time the clams were so plentiful that 45,000 could be commercially harvested in a single day. Decades of unrestricted clamming and the appetites of sea otters have depleted the supply, resulting in strict limits. Clamming for no more than 10 of the legal-size mollusks is permitted with California state license.

These days butterflies outrank clams as a local attraction. From late November through March thousands of migrating monarchs alight on Pismo Beach's Butterfly Trees, a grove of Monterey pine and eucalyptus. Some come from as far as Canada to pass the winter in this mild climate. The Mardi Gras Jazz Festival in late February and the Clam Festival in late October are other events.

The region offers numerous opportunities for fishing, scuba diving, bicycling and other active amusements. Pismo State Beach *(see Recreation Chart)* has camping and a dune area where off-highway vehicles are allowed. All vehicles are prohibited in Pismo Dunes Preserve, which contains some of the most extensive coastal dunes in California.

Pismo Beach lies on a scenic stretch of US 101 that extends from San Luis Obispo to Los Angeles.

PLACERVILLE (E-4) pop. 8,400, alt. 1,860'

Placerville, originally known as "Old Dry Diggin's," became so prosperous and lawless that lawbreakers were hanged first singly, then in pairs. As a result, the settlement was named Hangtown. By working as a wheelwright in a blacksmith shop, John Studebaker accumulated enough capital to establish the factory where the first Studebaker automobile was produced.

EL DORADO COUNTY HISTORICAL MUSEUM is 2 mi. w. at 100 Placerville Dr. in the El Dorado County Fairgrounds. The exhibits, which include ranching, logging, mining equipment,

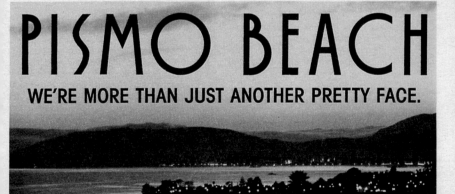

farming, housing, a country store, a stagecoach and a Shay locomotive, reflect local history and the gold rush days. Allow 1 hour minimum. Wed.-Sat. 10-4, Sun. noon-4, Mar.-Oct.; Wed.-Sat. 10-4, rest of year. Closed holidays. Donations. Phone (916) 621-5865.

PLANTATION (E-1) pop. 200, alt. 741'

KRUSE RHODODENDRON STATE RESERVE, 317 acres, is about 3 mi. w. on Kruse Ranch Rd. The rhododendrons, some to 14 feet tall, usually reach full bloom in April to early June. A variety of mosses, ferns, sorrel and other forest undergrowth bloom even earlier. Four miles of hiking trails wind through the reserve. The reserve is not suitable for vehicles larger than a van or pickup truck; trailers are not permitted. Allow 1 hour minimum. Daily dawn-dusk. Free. Phone (707) 865-2391.

PLEASANTON (P-3) pop. 50,600, alt. 352'

Many well-maintained old buildings and homes lend Pleasanton an early 19th-century atmosphere. The Amador-Livermore Valley Historical Society Museum at 603 Main St. depicts the history of the region.

The Alameda County Fairgrounds has one of the oldest racetracks in America; it was constructed in 1858 by the sons of a Spanish don, Augustin Bernal. The presence of limestone in the soil is credited with making this an exceptionally fine track. The Alameda County Fair is held from late June to early July.

The Shadow Cliffs Regional Recreation Area on the outskirts of town was developed from an abandoned gravel quarry. A lake in the park offers swimming, boating and fishing. *See Recreation Chart.*

RAPIDS WATERSLIDE AT SHADOW CLIFFS EAST BAY REGIONAL RECREATION AREA, 2 mi. e. on Stanley Blvd., 3 mi. s. of I-580 via Santa Rita Rd., has four flumes in a rustic corner of the site. Under 42 inches tall are not permitted on the slide. Daily 10:30-5:30, June-Aug.; Sat.-Sun. 10:30-5:30, Apr.-May and in Sept., weather permitting. All-day pass $12.50; half-day pass (Mon.-Fri. 10:30-2 or 2-5:30) $8; regular admission $5 per hour or $3 per half-hour. **Two-for-one discount,** except all-day and half-day passes. Parking $4. Phone (510) 829-6230.

PLUMAS NATIONAL FOREST

The 1,162,863 acres of Plumas National Forest straddle the transition zone between two of the West's great mountain ranges, the Sierra Nevada and the Cascades. Although the Sierra block disappears under the younger volcanic rock of the Cascades on the forest's northern boundary near Lake Almanor, it is difficult to tell where one range ends and the other begins.

The mountains of the northern Sierra Nevada, which make up most of the forest lands, are nei-

ther as high nor as spectacular as those south of Lake Tahoe. Yet within these mountains is a history of hidden treasure and a wealth of scenery.

The forest's principal gem is the Feather River watershed. The Feather River has carved numerous canyons and ravines full of cascades and white water. Portions of the Middle Fork of the river and three of its tributaries have been designated the Feather Falls Scenic Area. The centerpiece of this 15,000-acre scenic area is 640-foot Feather Falls, which is just above Lake Oroville and the highest of the numerous waterfalls on the 93-mile-long Middle Fork of the Feather River— a designated wild and scenic river.

Because of the rugged terrain and dangerous rapids, canoeing and tubing are recommended only in the recreation zone. Hiking trails and campgrounds are available along the river. Near the headwaters of the South Fork is Little Grass Valley Lake Recreation Area, which offers swimming, fishing and camping.

An extensive network of roads criss-crosses the national forest. Many of these routes, such as the designated scenic highway SR 70, which crosses the lowest pass in the Sierra Nevadas, are a legacy of the gold era when such towns as Rich Bar, Pulga and La Porte were flourishing mining camps. Anglers and hikers have replaced the miners and frequent such popular areas as Bucks Lake, Lake Davis and Antelope Lake. Sixty-seven miles of the Pacific Crest Trail runs through the national forest.

Information about campgrounds and recreational opportunities is available at the district ranger stations and the forest headquarters in Quincy. Maps and guides to the Pacific Crest Trail and the Feather Falls Scenic Area also are available at the headquarters. For more information contact Plumas National Forest, Box 11500, Quincy, CA 95971; phone (916) 283-2050. *See the Recreation Chart and AAA California and Nevada CampBook.*

PLYMOUTH (E-3) pop. 800, alt. 1,086'

SOBON ESTATE, 7½ mi. n.e. of SR 49 at 14430 Shenandoah Rd., was founded in 1856 by Adam Uhlinger when he dug the winery into a hill. It is among the oldest wineries in California and produces dry varietals and dessert wines. Wine tastings are offered. A museum displays agriculture and viticulture equipment. Allow 1 hour minimum. Daily 10-5; closed Easter, Thanksgiving and Dec. 25. Free. Phone (209) 245-6554.

POINT ARENA (D-1) pop. 400, alt. 220'

POINT ARENA LIGHTHOUSE AND MUSEUM are 1 mi. n.w. of SR 1 on Lighthouse Rd. The steel-reinforced concrete lighthouse was built in 1908 to replace an earlier structure that was destroyed by the 1906 earthquake; guided tours are available. The lighthouse also is a popular spot for whale-watching. Historical items are displayed in the adjacent maritime museum. Daily 11-2:30. Admission $2; under 12, 50c. Phone (707) 882-2777.

POINT REYES NATIONAL SEASHORE (O-1)

Blunt headlands jut into the sea, and grass-tufted dunes lie along miles of secluded beaches on Point Reyes, north of San Francisco. Inland are rolling hills, freshwater lakes and Inverness Ridge, where the Douglas fir, typical of the northern California coastal ranges, and the Bishop pine of the southern forest areas merge. More than 350 species of birds and 72 species of mammals inhabit Point Reyes National Seashore's 65,300 acres. In addition, fragile tidepool life can be observed at several locations.

Park headquarters is at Bear Valley, ¼ mile west of Olema. Nearby Bear Valley Visitor Center provides information on facilities, nature trails and exhibits; it is open daily. The Point Reyes Lighthouse and Visitor Center is open Thurs.-Mon. The Kenneth C. Patrick Visitor Center at Drakes Beach is open Sat.-Sun. and holidays. Admission, backpack camping and use of facilities are free.

The Point Reyes Morgan Horse Ranch; Kule Loklo, a replica of a Miwok Indian village; the Pierce Point Ranch, a working dairy ranch with self-guiding trail exhibits; and the Earthquake Trail are near park headquarters. At the end of Mesa Road is the Point Reyes Bird Observatory. Demonstrations are held Sat.-Sun. mornings.

The park has four hike-in campgrounds; the required free permits can be obtained at the Bear Valley Visitor Center. More than 140 miles of foot and horse trails fan out from the Bear Valley trailhead. Sixty miles of trails are open to bicyclists; obtain a map at the visitor center. Hikers and campers should carry a canteen, since the stream water is not potable. Pets are barred from all trails and campgrounds, but may be taken to North and South beaches and a portion of Limantour Beach if leashed.

A variety of educational programs are conducted; for additional information contact the Superintendent, Point Reyes National Seashore, Point Reyes, CA 94956; phone (415) 663-1092. *See Recreation Chart and the AAA California and Nevada CampBook.*

Point Reyes National Seashore lies on a scenic stretch of SR 1 that extends from Leggett south to Sausalito.

POMONA (B-7) pop. 131,700, alt. 850'

Pomona is the home of California State Polytechnic University, Pomona, whose beautifully landscaped campus reflects a full curriculum that includes agriculture and environmental design. Foals, piglets, lambs, calves and ducklings are seasonal residents.

Self-guiding tours of the campus during daylight hours are permitted daily; maps are avail-able at the information center at the campus entrance. Parking $1.50. Phone (909) 869-3210.

The Los Angeles County Fair, held in Pomona's Fairplex from mid-September to early October, is one of the largest county fairs in the nation. Throughout the rest of the year many events are held at the Fairplex, including the NHRA Winternationals in late January.

W.K. KELLOGG ARABIAN HORSE CENTER, off Kellogg Dr. on the campus of California State Polytechnic University, was part of the ranch that W.K. Kellogg donated to the university to perpetuate the breeding of Arabian horses. Horse shows are held the first Sun. of the month at 2, Oct.-June; admission $2; senior citizens $1.50; ages 6-17, $1. Center open daily 9-4. Free. Phone (909) 869-2224.

PORTERVILLE (H-5) pop. 29,600, alt. 455'

PORTERVILLE HISTORICAL MUSEUM is on D St. at Putnam Ave. This 1913 Mission Revival railroad depot houses exhibits on 19th- and early 20th-century life in the San Joaquin Valley, including a collection of American Indian baskets. Antique farming and firefighting equipment also are displayed. Open Thurs.-Sat. 10-4; closed major holidays and during Porterville Fair Week in May. Free. Phone (209) 784-2053.

ZALUD HOUSE, 393 Hockett St. at Morton Ave., was built about 1891 in the Mansard style for an established Porterville family. The house contains most of its original furnishings. Guided tours Wed.-Sat. 10-4, Sun. 2-4, Feb.-Dec.; closed major holidays. Admission $1; under 17, 50c. Phone (209) 782-7548.

PORT HUENEME (J-4) pop. 20,300, alt. 13'

CEC/SEABEE MUSEUM, U.S. Naval Construction Battalion at Ventura Rd. and Sunkist Ave., presents models of equipment and battle scenes, weapons, uniforms and arts and crafts by and about the Civil Engineer Corps and the Navy Seabees. Obtain a visitor pass at the Ventura Gate; under 16 must be accompanied by an adult. Mon.-Fri. 8-4:30, Sat. 9-4:30, Sun. 12:30-4:30; closed holidays. Phone to confirm hours. Free. Phone (805) 982-5163.

PORTOLA (D-4) pop. 2,200, alt. 4,850'

PORTOLA RAILROAD MUSEUM, 1 mi. s. of SR 70 on CR A15, contains more than 75 historical Western railroad locomotives and railcars, including a 1950 streamline diesel and a Union Pacific Centennial, which is billed as the world's largest diesel locomotive. Housed in a former Western Pacific diesel shop, the museum also displays railroad relics. Picnic facilities are available. Allow 1 hour minimum. Daily 10-5. Train rides every ½ hour 11-4, Memorial Day weekend-Labor Day. Museum admission free; train rides $2, family rate $5. Phone (916) 832-4131.

QUINCY (D-4) pop. 4,500, alt. 3,432'

PLUMAS COUNTY MUSEUM, 500 Jackson St., displays historical documents and photographs, period rooms of the late 1800s, mining and logging exhibits and woven baskets and artifacts from the native Maidu Indians. Allow 30 minutes minimum. Mon.-Fri. 8-5, Sat.-Sun. and holidays 10-4, May 1 to mid-Oct.; Mon.-Fri. 8-5, rest of year. Closed holidays mid-Oct. through Apr. 30. Donations. Phone (916) 283-6320.

RAMONA (K-7) pop. 8,200, alt. 1,442'

GUY B. WOODWARD MUSEUM, 645 Main St., was built as a private home in 1886 and has been restored and furnished in period. With its 2-foot-thick adobe walls and its raised veranda, the house is a good example of French provincial architecture. The old wine cellar and upstairs rooms have a variety of antique household items. Outside are historic buildings that include a bunkhouse, blacksmith shop and a dress and millinery shop with items dating to the 1700s. Thurs.-Sun. 1-4; closed holidays. Admission $2; under 12, 50c. Phone (619) 789-7644 or 789-1062.

RANCHO CUCAMONGA (B-8) pop. 101,400, alt. 1,200'

CASA DE RANCHO CUCAMONGA, at Vineyard Ave. and Hemlock St., also is known as the John Rains House. The oldest fired-brick house in San Bernardino County, it is restored and furnished in the style of the 1800s. Allow 30 minutes minimum. Wed.-Sun. noon-4; closed Jan. 1, last 2 weeks of Aug., Thanksgiving and Dec. 25. Free. Phone (909) 989-4970 or 798-8570.

RANDSBURG (I-6) pop. 200, alt. 3,523'

When gold was discovered in 1894, more than 3,000 prospectors and opportunists rushed to the camp and named it, with high expectations, after one of the richest mining districts in South Africa. Randsburg did so well that the Santa Fe Railway built a line to the camp in 1897.

While citizens were celebrating the arrival of the first locomotive, a dynamite explosion set off a fire that destroyed a number of buildings. The rest of the town went up in flames a few months later. However, in true gold rush spirit, the townsfolk persevered until the last traces of gold, silver and tungsten were mined in the 1920s.

This hillside town's character is kept alive in the restored 19th-century buildings along Butte Avenue, including antique shops and a general store.

DESERT MUSEUM, 161 Butte Ave., has Indian artifacts, minerals, mining photographs, a mine locomotive and a stone mill for pulverizing ore. Allow 30 minutes minimum. Sat.-Sun. and most holidays 10-5; closed Jan. 1, Thanksgiving and Dec. 25. Admission $1; ages 3-12, 50c. Phone (619) 374-2111.

RED BLUFF (C-2) pop. 12,400, alt. 304'

Named for the colored sand and gravel cliffs characteristic of the surrounding area, Red Bluff is a gateway to Lassen Volcanic National Park *(see place listing).*

SALMON VIEWING PLAZA, ⅛ mi. e. of I-5 on SR 36, then 2 mi. s. on Sale Ln., is at Diversion Dam on the Sacramento River. Underwater television cameras monitor the fish ladders. The best viewing time is September through October. There is no viewing November 1 through May 1. The plaza has exhibits on salmon, as well as camping, picnicking and boat-launching facilities. Daily 8-8. River ramp closed Aug. 1-Sept. 1. Free; camping $10 daily. Phone (916) 527-1408.

WILLIAM B. IDE ADOBE STATE HISTORIC PARK, 2 mi. n. on Adobe Rd., is an 1850 adobe that serves as a memorial to the founder and president of the short-lived California Republic. Ide, a Massachusetts carpenter, moved to northern California in 1845 when the area was still part of Mexico.

In 1846, rumors that Mexican authorities were planning to expel American settlers compelled Ide to join a band of 24 settlers in the "Bear Flag Revolt." Subsequently, California became an independent country with Ide as its president for 26 days until the outbreak of the Mexican-American War and the occupation of the area by U.S. troops. Picnic facilities are available. Daily 8-dusk. Parking $3. Phone (916) 527-5927.

REDDING (C-2) pop. 66,500, alt. 560'

Redding provides scenic access via I-5 to the surrounding Whiskeytown-Shasta-Trinity National Recreation Area and Shasta-Trinity National Forest *(see place listings).*

CARTER HOUSE NATURAL SCIENCE MUSEUM, 48 Quartz Hill Rd. in Caldwell Park, has displays on the natural history of northern California, featuring native animals. Changing exhibits also are presented. Open Tues.-Sun. 10-5. Admission $1; ages 2-18, 50c. Phone (916) 225-4125.

LAKE SHASTA CAVERNS is reached from Shasta Caverns Rd., 1½ mi. e. of I-5 at O'Brien. The 2-hour tour of more than 600 steps includes round-trip boat and bus transportation. Allow 3 hours minimum. Tours depart every hour daily 9-4, Apr.-Sept.; at 10, noon and 2, Oct.-Mar., weather permitting. Closed Thanksgiving and Dec. 25. Admission $12; ages 4-12, $6. Phone (916) 238-2341.

REDDING MUSEUM OF ART AND HISTORY, 56 Quartz Hill Rd., in Caldwell Park, has changing contemporary art exhibits, items depicting Shasta County history and displays of ethnic art, including American Indian exhibits. Also featured is the Shasta Historical Society Library which contains a variety of historical books and documents. American Indian Heritage Day and an arts and crafts fair are held in May. Tues.-Sun. 10-5, June-Aug.; Tues.-Fri. and Sun. noon-5, Sat. 10-5, rest of year. Closed holidays. Free. Phone (916) 225-4155.

SHASTA DAM is 6 mi. w. of I-5 from a point 8 mi. n. A 30-minute film depicting water usage in California is shown at the visitor center on request. Visitor center open daily 7:30-4, Memorial Day weekend-Labor Day; Mon.-Fri. 7:30-4, rest of year. Closed holidays. Free. Phone (916) 275-4463.

★SHASTA STATE HISTORIC PARK is 6 mi. w. on SR 299. Formerly a robust mining town with a population of 2,500, Shasta was the gateway to a large area of riches and a rendezvous for gamblers; it is now an interesting gold rush relic. The old courthouse has been converted to a museum; a restored barn and stagecoach also can be seen. Picnic facilities are available. Park open Thurs.-Mon. 10-5; closed Jan. 1, Thanksgiving and Dec. 25. Admission $2; ages 6-12, $1. Phone (916) 243-8194.

WATERWORKS PARK, ¼ mi. e. of SR 299 at 151 N. Boulder Dr., has three flumes, an inner tube ride, facilities for both water and beach volleyball and a children's pool with slides and a fountain. Lockers, dressing rooms, picnic tables and food are available. Daily 10-8, Memorial Day weekend-Labor Day. Admission $11.50; ages 4-11, $9.50; over 65 and under 4 free. Reduced prices after 5. DS, MC, VI. Phone (916) 246-9550.

REDLANDS (B-9) pop. 60,400, alt. 1,356'

Named for the color of the local soil, Redlands was once an important packing and distribution point for citrus fruit. Today the University of Redlands plays an important role in the life of the area; its campus occupies approximately 130 acres northeast of the city center.

Redlands is known for its carefully restored Victorian homes. A free map that can be used for a drive-by home tour is available at the chamber of commerce, 1 E. Redlands Blvd., Redlands, CA 93273; phone (909) 793-2546.

LINCOLN MEMORIAL SHRINE, behind A.K. Smiley Public Library in Smiley Park at Eureka and Vine sts., is a museum with art, photographs, manuscripts, artifacts and books on the life of Abraham Lincoln and the Civil War. Guided tours Tues.-Sat. and Lincoln's Birthday 1-5; closed other holidays. Free. Phone (909) 798-7632.

REDLANDS BOWL, in Smiley Park at Grant and Eureka sts., presents a variety of music and dance programs Tues. and Fri. at 8:15 p.m., late June-late Aug. Donations. Phone (909) 793-7316.

SAN BERNARDINO ASISTENCIA is 1½ mi. w. at 26930 Barton Rd. Built about 1830, it was a branch of the San Gabriel Mission. During the 1840s its buildings became part of a ranch. Restored, they consist of two museum rooms and a wedding chapel. Wed.-Sat. 10-5, Tues. and Sun. 1-5; closed holidays. Donations. Phone (909) 793-5402.

SAN BERNARDINO COUNTY MUSEUM, n. of I-10 at California St. and Orange Tree Ln., has regional anthropology, history and geology exhibits and an extensive collection of mammals, birds and bird eggs, fine arts and special exhibits. Tues.-Sat. 9-5, Sun. 11-5; closed Thanksgiving and Dec. 25. Donations; admission charged for special exhibits. Phone (909) 798-8570.

REDONDO BEACH (C-5) pop. 60,200, alt. 59'

A drive along SR 1 leads south from Redondo Beach to Palos Verdes Boulevard, affording views of the coastline and, on a clear day, Catalina Island. In early August Redondo Beach, along with neighboring communities, hosts the International Surf Festival.

Redondo Beach Pier, at the foot of Torrance Boulevard, offers fresh-fish stalls, souvenir shops and seafood restaurants. King Harbor, along Harbor Drive between Herondo and Beryl streets, has restaurants, hotels and facilities for such activities as boating, sport fishing, bicycling and racquetball. A wide pathway for bicyclists and pedestrians leads to the International Boardwalk, which has souvenir shops, an amusement center and fresh-fish markets.

Half-hour harbor cruises depart on summer weekends; whale-watching cruises are offered in winter.

Shopping areas: The Galleria at South Bay, at Hawthorne and Artesia boulevards, has a May Co., Mervyn's and Nordstrom. The Pier at Redondo, Horseshoe and Monstad piers at the foot of Torrance Boulevard, is a popular waterfront marketplace.

REDWOOD CITY (P-3) pop. 66,100, alt. 15'

LATHROP HOUSE is at 627 Hamilton Ave. off Marshall St. The restored 1863 house is an example of early Gothic Revival architecture and is furnished in period. The house was moved to its present site in 1905 and survived the earthquake of 1906. Tues.-Thurs. 11-3, Sept.-July; closed holidays. Donations. Phone (415) 365-5564.

REDWOOD NATIONAL PARK (A-1)

Encompassing 113,200 acres, Redwood National Park lies along the northern California coast between Crescent City and Orick, 330 miles north of San Francisco on US 101. Within its boundaries are the 28,504 combined acres of Del Norte Coast, Jedediah Smith and Prairie Creek Redwoods state parks *(see Recreation Chart)*. In addition to dense forests of coastal redwoods, the park embraces salt marshes, beaches, rugged coastline, rivers, streams and oak woodlands.

General Information and Activities

The beaches are open all year, but visitors should use caution when swimming or surfing. The coastline in northern California is a dangerous combination of steeply descending beaches, heavy undertows, very cold water and jagged rocky shoals. Visitors to the beach should be aware of the tides.

Coastal Drive, reached from the US 101 Klamath Beach Road exit, affords 8 miles of spectacular coastal scenery. Gold Bluffs Beach, off US 101 on Davison Road about 2 miles north of Orick, was the site of gold-mining operations in the 1850s. The Howland Hill Road east of Crescent City is a drive through old-growth redwoods along an unimproved stage route. Coastal Drive, Gold Bluffs and Howland Road are not suitable for RV travel.

Some public roads also serve adjoining private forest lands; logging truck traffic and other private activities take place along some of the routes.

Trails traverse the 40 miles of wild and untouched coastline along rock promontories that protrude into the sea, affording vistas of sea lion colonies and migrating whales. Birds inhabit bluffs, lagoons and offshore rocks; birdwatching is particularly rewarding during the waterfowl migrations. More than 150 miles of trails provide access to the magnificent redwood groves. The park staff provides free guided walks, evening programs and other activities from mid-June through Labor Day.

Several campgrounds are within the state parks and along US 101 nearby. There also are four primitive walk-in campsites in the park, although space is limited. A summer shuttle-bus service transports visitors from the Redwood Information Center, 1 mile south of Orick, to Tall Trees Grove; phone (707) 488-3461 for schedules and fares. Freshwater and surf fishing is permitted; a California fishing license is required. *See Recreation Chart.*

ADMISSION to the national park is free. The state parks within the national park's borders charge day use and overnight fees for developed picnicking and camping areas.

PETS must be kept under physical restraint while in the park and are prohibited on most trails. Campers are required to have proof of rabies shots for pets.

INFORMATION STATIONS are in Crescent City, Hiouchi and Orick. A beach interpretative center is just 4 miles south of Crescent City. Address inquiries to the Superintendent, Redwood National Park, 1111 2nd St., Crescent City, CA 95531; phone (707) 464-6101.

RIDGECREST (I-6) pop. 27,700, alt. 2,289'

MATURANGO MUSEUM, E. Las Flores Ave. at China Lake Blvd., has exhibits pertaining to the natural and cultural history of the upper Mojave Desert. Highlights include ancient American Indian petroglyphs and a gallery of changing artworks. A children's section offers hands-on displays. Tues.-Sun. 10-5; closed major holidays. Admission $1; ages 6-17, 50c. Phone (619) 375-6900.

RIVERSIDE (B-8) pop. 226,500, alt. 852'

Since rich soil and mild climate made it the ideal location for growing navel oranges, Riverside grew rapidly. By 1895, Riverside, then the metropolitan center of Southern California, was the wealthiest city per capita in the nation.

The citrus industry is a vital part of the local economy and is under constant scrutiny by the strong agricultural curriculum at the University of California at Riverside, which is on the east edge of town.

The Italian Renaissance-style old City Hall, a 1912 Classic Revival municipal museum, several elaborate Victorian homes and many fine examples of mission architecture and adobe houses reflect the city's early wealth and prestige. The Queen Anne-style Heritage House at 8193 Magnolia Ave. is open for tours.

Shopping areas: Riverside Plaza, Riverside Freeway (SR 91) at Central Avenue, has a Harris and Montgomery Ward. Also on Riverside Freeway is Tyler Mall, at the Tyler Street intersection, which contains a Broadway, JCPenney and May Co.

ALCOHOL AND NIGHT VISION

Studies show that a blood alcohol concentration of 0.12 percent reduces the distance from which a driver can see a pedestrian at night by about 20 percent. In many cases, this is enough to make the viewing distance much less than the stopping distance.

CALIFORNIA MUSEUM OF PHOTOGRAPHY, 3824 Main St., displays photographs, cameras and related equipment. Photographs range from early daguerreotypes to contemporary prints, while some of the many cameras on display date back to the invention of photography. The Interactive Gallery features hands-on exhibits.

In addition to the permanent collections there are changing exhibits from the museum's vast collection of photographic images and equipment. Wed.-Sat. 11-5, Sun. noon-5; closed Jan. 1, Thanksgiving and Dec. 25. Admission $2; senior citizens and ages 13-18, $1; free to all on Wed. Phone (909) 784-3686.

CASTLE AMUSEMENT PARK, 3500 Polk St., is a 25-acre park that includes four miniature golf courses, arcade games and a 1905 carrousel. Rides include a roller coaster, log flume and gentle rides for young children. The miniature golf courses and arcade open daily at 10, closing hours vary. Ride park open Tues.-Thurs. 6 p.m.-11 p.m., Fri.-6 p.m.-midnight, late June-Labor Day; Fri. 6 p.m.-11 p.m., Sat. noon-11, Sun. noon-8, rest of year. Admission to grounds free; prices for rides and games vary. Phone (909) 785-4141.

JURUPA MOUNTAINS CULTURAL CENTER, off SR 60 at 7621 Granite Hill Dr., has a museum of natural history with special emphasis on fossilized flora and fauna. Center open Tues.-Sat. 9-5; museum open Tues.-Fri. 1-4, Sat. 10:30-4. Dinosaur tour Sat. at 9. Closed Jan. 1, July 4 and Dec. 25. Museum admission $3, children $2.50. Dinosaur tour $3. **Discount.** Phone (714) 685-5818.

MARCH FIELD MUSEUM, s. on I-215/Van Buren Blvd. at March Air Force Base, is scheduled to open at this new location in February 1993. The museum emphasizes the evolution of air power. Displays feature military aviation relics, engines and trainers from 1918 to the present. Flight line aircraft include bombers, fighters, helicopters, the SR-71 and a U-2 spy plane. Shuttle trips to the flight line depart Tues.-Sun. at 1. Museum open Tues.-Fri. 10-4, Sat.-Sun. noon-4; closed Jan. 1, Easter, Thanksgiving and Dec. 25. Admission $4; over 55, $3; ages 6-17, $1.50. Phone (909) 655-3725.

MOUNT RUBIDOUX, at 1,337 feet, rises above the Santa Ana River at the city's w. edge. On the summit are the Father Serra Cross and the World Peace Tower. At the western foot of the mountain is the St. Francis Fountain. The summit road, which begins at 9th Street and Mount Rubidoux Drive, has many sharp turns and is open to vehicles Mon.-Wed. 9-3; Sun. 9-5, in winter; Sun.-Wed. 9-7, in summer.

RIVERSIDE MUNICIPAL MUSEUM, 3720 Orange St., houses exhibits depicting Riverside's human and natural history, including displays on American Indian cultures. Tues.-Fri. 9-5, Sat.-Sun. 1-5; closed holidays. Free. Phone (909) 782-5273.

UCR BOTANIC GARDENS, on the e. side of the University of California Riverside campus off N. Campus Circle Dr. near parking lot 13, occupies 39 hilly acres. Emphasis is on dry-climate plants; many of the 3,000 species bloom in the winter and spring, usually January through May. Under 16 must be accompanied by an adult. Allow 30 minutes minimum. Daily 8-5; closed Jan. 1, July 4, Thanksgiving and Dec. 25. Free. Phone (714) 787-4650.

ROSAMOND (I-6) pop. 7,400, alt. 2,330′

EXOTIC FELINE BREEDING COMPOUND, 3½ mi. w. of SR 14 at the w. end of Rhyolite Rd., is a breeding, research and educational facility with 35 to 40 rare and exotic cats in outdoor enclosures. Thirteen species are represented, including leopards, tigers, cougars and ocelots. Tour guides provide detailed information on these endangered felines. No pets are allowed. Thurs.-Tues. 10-4. Last tour departs 30 minutes before closing. Closed Dec. 25. Donations. Phone (805) 256-3332.

RUTHERFORD (M-2) pop. 400, alt. 170′

BEAULIEU VINEYARD, on SR 29, offers tours and tastings. Open daily 10-5; tastings daily 11-4:30. Closed Jan. 1, Easter, Thanksgiving and Dec. 25. Free. Phone (707) 963-2411.

INGLENOOK NAPA VALLEY, on SR 29, offers tours and tastings daily 10-4:30. Open daily 10-5; closed major holidays. Free. Phone (707) 963-3362.

RUTHERFORD HILL WINERY, e. off Silverado Trail at the end of Rutherford Hill Rd., offers free guided tours and tastings at 11:30, 12:30, 1:30 and 3:30. Open daily 10-4:30. Free; fee for tastings $3. Phone (707) 963-7194.

SACRAMENTO (E-3) pop. 369,400, alt. 30′

See map page 134.

Capt. John Sutter, a Swiss immigrant, settled at the confluence of the American and Sacramento rivers in 1839 on a 50,000-acre land grant from the Mexican government. The town of Sacramento was laid out on Sutter's property in 1848—the same year that James Marshall discovered gold near the South Fork of the American River, beginning the great California gold rush.

Sacramento quickly grew into a major supply center for the northern Mother Lode country. Between 1849 and 1853 it was devastated by two floods and two fires that leveled two-thirds of the town. Nonetheless, it was chosen as the state capital in 1854 and fought off subsequent challenges by Berkeley, San Jose and Monterey.

In 1856, the first railroad in California connected Sacramento with Folsom and became the western terminus of the Pony Express line from St. Joseph, Mo. The transcontinental railroad was completed in 1869. Agriculture took hold in the fertile Sacramento Valley, and the city's continued prosperity was assured.

Today Sacramento is an important highway, rail and river hub; the state capital; and the marketing center for a rich agricultural region. Nearby military installations and the space and aviation industries also contribute to Sacramento's economy. A deepwater channel to San Francisco Bay was completed in 1963, making the city a major inland port.

The Wells Fargo Bank History Museum, in the Wells Fargo Center at 400 Capitol Mall, has exhibits illustrating the commercial development of Sacramento, including historical items, photographs and lithographs.

Arco Arena at 1 Sports Pkwy., near the intersection of I-5 and I-80, is the home of the Sacramento Kings professional basketball team. The arena also is the scene of many other events and performances.

Sacramento celebrates its self-proclaimed status as "Camellia Capital of the World" in early March with the 10-day Camellia Festival. Memorial Day weekend festivities include the Sacramento Dixieland Jazz Jubilee. The California State Fair is held in late August.

Sacramento is the northern terminus of a scenic 33-mile stretch of SR 160 that heads south to Isleton along the Sacramento River.

Self-guiding tours: Maps and brochures for self-guiding walking tours of Old Sacramento are available daily 9-5 at the Old Sacramento Visitor Center, 1104 Front St., Sacramento, CA 95814; phone (916) 442-7644.

ACTION ADVENTURES WET N' WILD offers whitewater raft trips on several nearby rivers

DOWNTOWN SACRAMENTO

daily, May-Sept. Trips on the American, East Carson, Klamath, Sacramento, Salmon, Trinity and Tuolumne rivers last from half a day to 6 days and are appropriate for various ages and levels of experience. Prices for half-day and 1-day trips range from $50 to $125; meals are included. MC, VI. **Discount.** Reservations are required. Contact Box 828, Lotus, CA 95651; phone (916) 621-3510 or (800) 238-3688.

BLUE DIAMOND GROWERS, Blue Diamond Almond Plaza Visitor Center, 1701 C St., presents a film on almond growing and processing and offers free tours and tastings. Allow 1 hour minimum. Plant tours Mon.-Fri. at 10 and 1 by appointment only. Phone (916) 446-8409.

CALIFORNIA VIETNAM VETERANS MEMORIAL is at 15th and L sts., at the e. end of State Capitol Park. The 22 shiny black granite panels, built entirely with donations, are engraved with the 5,822 names of California's dead and missing. Full-relief bronze figures depict daily life during the war.

CROCKER ART MUSEUM is at 216 O St. The museum exhibits an extensive collection of paintings, drawings, sculpture and decorative arts, featuring both European and northern California artists. Guided tours are available on request. Wed.-Sun. 10-5 (also Thurs. 5-9); closed Jan. 1, July 4, Thanksgiving and Dec. 25. Admission $3; ages 7-17, $1.50. **Two-for-one discount,** except during special programs. Phone (916) 264-5423.

DELTA AND BAY CRUISES depart from the Port of Sacramento. They offer boat/bus excursions between Sacramento and San Francisco—one way by boat on the Sacramento Delta and San Francisco Bay and the other by bus. The 1-day trips depart Sat. and Sun., May-Oct. The 2-day riverboat cruise departs Sat. from San Francisco and returns by boat on Sun., May-Oct. Reservations are required. One-day fare $58. **Discount,** except 2-day trips. Phone (916) 372-3690.

GOVERNOR'S MANSION STATE HISTORIC PARK, 16th and H sts., features the 19th-century governor's mansion. Tours daily every hour 10-4; closed Jan. 1, Thanksgiving and Dec. 25. Admission $2; ages 6-12, $1. Phone (916) 445-9209.

THE HISTORIC PADDLEWHEELER *SPIRIT OF SACRAMENTO,* departing from the L Street Landing in Old Sacramento, is a 110-foot paddlewheel riverboat that conducts 1-hour sightseeing cruises on the Sacramento River. Dinner, lunch, happy hour and murder mystery excursions also are available.

Sightseeing cruises Wed.-Sun. at 1:30 and 3, June-Aug.; Fri.-Sun. at 1:30 and 3, Apr.-May and Sept.-Oct.; otherwise varies, rest of year. Fare $10; under 12, $5. AE, MC, VI. Reservations are recommended. Phone (916) 552-2933, or (800) 433-0263 in Calif.

OLD SACRAMENTO, a four-block section delineated by Capitol Mall, I St., 2nd St. and the Sacramento River, was the commercial district during the gold rush. The area has been redeveloped with museums, restaurants and shops that preserve its historical character.

B.F. Hastings Museum, 2nd and J sts., has exhibits on the Wells Fargo and Pony Express operations, both of which had offices here, and the California Supreme Court, which convened here 1855-69. Tues.-Sun. 10-5. Free. Phone (916) 445-4209.

★California State Railroad Museum, 2nd and I sts., is a three-story steel, brick and glass structure housing 21 restored locomotives and train cars. More than 40 interpretive exhibits, dioramas, pictures, murals and film presentations document the history of American railroading. A film is presented in the museum's theaters. The building's striking design and gleaming exhibits are impressive. Allow 2 hours minimum.

Daily 10-5; closed Jan. 1, Thanksgiving and Dec. 25. Admission $5; ages 6-12, $2. Tickets are good for a same-day visit to the Central Pacific Passenger Station. Phone (916) 448-4466, 445-4209 or 323-9280.

Central Pacific Passenger Station, Front and J sts. across from the railroad museum, was the first California terminal for the transcontinental railroad. The self-guiding tour of the reconstructed building recalls the 1870s. Allow 30 minutes minimum. Daily 10-5. Admission $5; ages 6-12, $2. Tickets are good for same-day visit to the California State Railroad Museum. Phone (916) 445-4209.

Eagle Theatre, 925 Front St., opened in October 1849 for a 3-month run and then was closed by the 1850 flood. The building was rebuilt in 1975. Performances Fri.-Sat. at 8 p.m. Admission $12, senior citizens and students $10. Phone (916) 445-4209; for other show times phone (916) 446-6761.

Sacramento History Museum, 101 I St., houses five galleries showcasing the role of gold in California's history. Exhibits include a million dollar Mother Lode gold collection, a 1928 family kitchen, ethnic photographs, a historic print shop and the California Gallery, which houses changing exhibits. Allow 1 hour minimum. Tues.-Sun. 10-5; closed holidays. Admission $3, under 18 free. **Two-for-one discount.** Phone (916) 264-7057.

PORT OF SACRAMENTO, s. of West Sacramento off I-80 along Harbor Blvd., is the terminus of the Sacramento River Deepwater Ship Channel. Self-guiding tours of the port begin at the main entrance; phone 1 day ahead for touring hours. Daily dawn-dusk. Free. Phone (916) 371-8000.

SACRAMENTO DELTA, reclaimed in the 19th-century with labor by Chinese coolies, is sometimes referred to as the Everglades of the West. Throughout this rich farmland winds a series of waterways punctuated by hundreds of islands and lined with historical towns and inns. Houseboating and rafting are favorite means of exploring the delta. Fishing and picnicking also are popular. Phone (916) 264-7777.

SACRAMENTO SCIENCE CENTER, 3615 Auburn Blvd., features hands-on science exhibitions and a self-guiding nature trail highlighting native California plants. Fifteen-minute planetarium shows are presented Wed.-Sun. Science of animal presentations are offered Sat.-Sun. Picnic facilities are available. Allow 1 hour minimum. Open Wed.-Fri. noon-5, Sat.-Sun. 10-5. Admission $2.50; ages 3-15, $1.50; a 45-minute planetarium show is extra. MC, VI. **Two-for-one discount,** except during special events. Phone (916) 277-6181.

★STATE CAPITOL, bounded by 10th, 15th, L and N sts., was built 1860-74 and is noted for its lofty dome, which rises 210 feet above the street. The main building contains historical and art exhibits, murals and statuary. Free guided tours cover the restored main building and chambers. A film on the capitol's history and construction is presented in the basement. The surrounding park has trees, shrubs and other plants from around the world.

A Capitol Tour is offered every hour daily 9-4; two additional tours are available, phone for schedule. Free tickets are available 30 minutes before the tour; phone for location. Allow 1 hour minimum. Daily 9-5; closed Jan. 1, Thanksgiving and Dec. 25. Free. Children must be accompanied by an adult. Phone (916) 324-0333.

STATE LIBRARY, 914 Capitol Mall, is a handsome granite structure. Murals in the general reading room depict California history. The files of early stage newspapers are especially interesting. The library also has a notable genealogical collection on California families. Mon.-Fri. 8-5, Free. Phone (916) 654-0261.

★SUTTER'S FORT, 27th and L sts., was the first European outpost in the California interior. The restored 1839 adobe fort has relics of pioneer and gold rush days; a diorama depicts life in the fort in the 1800s. Allow 1 hour minimum. Daily 10-5. Last tour departs 45 minutes before closing. Closed Jan. 1, Thanksgiving and Dec. 25. Admission $2; ages 6-12, $1; additional charge for Living History Days. Phone (916) 445-4209.

State Indian Museum, 2618 K St., on the grounds of Sutter's Fort, depicts aspects of California's Indian cultures with displays of feather baskets, jewelry, clothing and art. Daily 10-5; closed Jan. 1, Thanksgiving and Dec. 25. Admission $2; ages 6-12, $1. Phone (916) 445-4209.

TOWE FORD MUSEUM, Front St. at V St., displays more than 185 vintage automobiles. Virtually every year and every model Ford from 1903 to 1952 is represented, including Model A's, Model T's and early Ford V-8's. Allow 30 minutes minimum. Daily 10-6; closed Jan. 1, Thanksgiving and Dec. 25. Admission $5; over 65, $4.50; ages 14-18, $2.50; ages 5-13, $1. Phone (916) 442-6802.

WATERWORLD USA is at 1600 Exposition Blvd. This recreational water park has a pool, wading pool, wave pool, 10 speed slides, a river tube ride and a children's play area. Daily 10:30-6, Memorial Day weekend-Aug. 19; otherwise varies in May before Memorial Day weekend and in Sept. Admission, including all rides, $14.95; under 48 inches tall $9.95; under age 4 free. MC, VI. Phone (916) 924-0555 or 924-0556.

WILLIAM LAND PARK, bounded by Freeport Blvd., Riverside Blvd., 13th Ave. and Sutterville Rd., encompasses 600 acres. Within the park are the Sacramento Zoo and Fairytale Town. The park also has picnic facilities, a public golf course and a grove of cherry trees. Fairytale Town is a 2½-acre park with sets based on themes from popular children's nursery rhymes. Puppet shows and other activities take place regularly, weather permitting. Daily 10-5; closed Dec. 25. Admission Mon.-Fri. $2.25; ages 3-13, $1.75. Admission Sat.-Sun. $2.50; ages 3-13, $2. **Two-for-one discount.** Phone (916) 264-5233.

Sacramento Zoo, at Land Park Dr. park entrance, exhibits more than 400 animals, including Asian lions, Siberian tigers, Grevy zebras, African cheetahs and chimpanzees. Daily 10-4; closed Dec. 25. Admission Mon.-Fri. $3.50; ages 3-12, $2. Admission Sat.-Sun. $4; ages 3-12, $2.50. **Two-for-one discount.** Phone (916) 264-5885.

ST. HELENA (M-2) pop. 5,000, alt. 255'

St. Helena in Napa Valley has other industries besides its many wineries. The Hurd Beeswax Candle Factory, 2½ miles north on SR 29 in the Freemark Abbey Winery complex, produces handcrafted candles. St. Helena lies on a scenic stretch of SR 29 from Calistoga to Napa.

BERINGER WINES, 2000 Main St., offers tours daily 9:30-5. Tastings daily 10-6, in summer; 9:30-4, rest of year. Closed Jan. 1, Easter, Thanksgiving and Dec. 25. Fee for tastings of older vintages, $2-$3. Phone (707) 963-7115.

CHARLES KRUG WINERY, 2800 Main St., on SR 29, offers tours Thurs.-Tues. 10-4; tastings daily 10-5. Closed holidays. Fee for tastings $3. Fee for tours $1. Phone (707) 963-2761.

CHRISTIAN BROTHERS GREYSTONE CELLARS, 2555 Main St., offers self-guiding tours and tastings Sat.-Sun. 10-5; closed Jan. 1, Easter, Thanksgiving and Dec. 25. Fee for tastings $2. Phone (707) 963-0763.

GRIST MILL STATE HISTORIC PARK is 3 mi. n.w. on SR 29. The restored 1846 watermill has a 36-foot-diameter wheel that was once used to grind flour for local farmers. Hiking trails lead from the access road to the mill pond. Daily 10-5; closed Jan. 1, Thanksgiving and Dec. 25. Admission $5 per vehicle. Phone (707) 942-4575.

HANNS KORNELL CHAMPAGNE CELLARS, 3 mi. n. on SR 29 and ¼ mi. e. on Larkmead Ln., offers tours daily 10-4; tasting room open until 4:30. Closed Jan. 1, Easter, Thanksgiving and Dec. 25. Free. Phone (707) 963-2334.

LOUIS M. MARTINI, 254 St. Helena Hwy. S., offers winery tours daily 1:30-3:30 and tastings daily 10-5; closed Jan. 1, Easter, Thanksgiving and Dec. 24-25. Picnic facilities are available. Free. Phone (707) 963-2736.

NAPA'S GREAT BALLOON ESCAPE, offers 1-hour rides launched from the Franciscan, Charles Krug and Peju wineries. Sunrise flight includes a brunch, photograph and flight certificate. Transportation is provided from the Chateau Hotel in Napa to the launch site and back. Reservations are required. Fare $165; ages 7-12, $100, excluding brunch; under 7 not permitted. AE, DS, MC, VI. **Discount.** Phone (707) 253-0860.

SILVERADO MUSEUM, 1490 Library Ln., off E. Adams St., contains more than 8,000 items related to Robert Louis Stevenson. Tues.-Sun. noon-4; closed holidays. Free. Phone (707) 963-3757.

SALINAS (G-3) pop. 108,800, alt. 55'

Salinas is best known as the birthplace of John Steinbeck and the setting for many of his novels. Winner of the Nobel and Pulitzer prizes, Steinbeck continues to be a source of pride in Salinas. First editions, letters, photographs and memorabilia are displayed in a special room of the John Steinbeck Public Library, 110 W. San Luis St.

The California Rodeo, one of the largest in the nation, has been held in Salinas since 1911; the competition takes place on the third weekend in July. The California International Air Show is held in mid-October.

JOSE EUSIBIO BORONDA ADOBE, 333 Boronda Rd., was built 1844-48 and is the town's oldest structure. The wood shingles used on the restored adobe are a departure from the traditional red-clay tiles. The 1897 Old Lagunita School House also is at the site. Allow 30 minutes minimum. Office hours Mon.-Fri. 9-3. Tours Mon.-Fri. 10-2, Sun. 1-4. Donations. Phone (408) 757-8085.

SALINAS COMMUNITY CENTER, 940 N. Main St., displays a variety of artwork and stages many musical and theatrical performances throughout the year. Allow 30 minutes minimum. Mon.-Fri. 8-5. Free. Phone (408) 758-7351.

Hat In Three Stages of Landing, on the lawn of the Salinas Community Center, is a giant sculpture by Claes Oldenberg. The three hats, at various elevations, are painted a vivid yellow and weigh 3,500 pounds each. The sculpture is a tribute to farmers and ranchers and represents a Western hat tossed in the air from the nearby rodeo stands.

SALTON SEA (K-8)

The 35-mile-long, 15-mile-wide Salton Sea, 20 miles south of Indio, is one of the world's largest inland bodies of salt water. Created by flood waters from the Colorado River in 1905, the sea is shallow, having an average depth of less than 20 feet. The climate of the desert terrain surrounding the sea is typically hot and dry; summer temperatures regularly exceed 100 F. The area is most inviting to visitors between October and May, when temperatures fall to the 70s and 80s.

Camping, hiking, swimming, boating, fishing and water skiing are among the recreational opportunities in the area; parking fee $5. Limited supplies are sold in the surrounding small towns. For information contact the Salton Sea State Recreation Headquarters, P.O. Box 3166, North Shore, CA 92254; phone (619) 393-3052.

SAN ANDREAS (F-3) pop. 1,900, alt. 1,008'

Just 16 miles west of San Andreas via SR 12, Paloma Road, Watertown Road and Campo Seco-Chile Camp Road are the remains of Campo Seco, a once thriving gold and copper town. Dubbed Campo Seco (dry camp) by prospectors, the site produced some gold, but the real treasure was copper. In the early 1860s the Penn Copper Co. supplied the Union Army with the metal during the Civil War. Though considered a ghost town, Campo Seco has a post office and claims the largest cork oak tree in California.

For more information contact the Calaveras County Chamber of Commerce at 3 N. Main St., San Andreas, CA 95249; phone (209) 754-4009.

CALAVERAS COUNTY HISTORICAL MUSEUM AND ARCHIVES, 30 N. Main St., served as the county courthouse 1867-1962. Featured is a garden of native California plants and trees, mining relics and 1850-1900 period exhibits. Allow 30 minutes minimum. Museum open daily 10-4; closed major holidays. Archives open Thurs.-Fri. 8:30-4:30 or by appointment. Admission 50c, students 25c, under 6 free. Phone (209) 754-6513.

CALIFORNIA CAVERNS AT CAVE CITY is 8 mi. e. on Mountain Ranch Rd., then about 2½ mi. s.e. on Michel and Cave City Rd. Chambers and passageways contain glittering formations ranging from fragile soda straws on the ceiling to colossal stalagmites rising from the floor. The cavern was discovered in 1849, and many signatures dating back to the 1850s are visible on the walls. John Muir was reportedly among the signers, but his name has yet to be found.

A 3-hour wild downstream circuit tour and a 2-hour lakes rappel tour are available by reservation. An 80-minute guided tour leaves every hour daily 10-5, in summer; 10-4, in fall. Admission $5.75; senior citizens $5.25; ages 6-12, $2.75. DS, MC, VI. **Discount,** except senior citizens. Phone (209) 736-2708.

SAN BERNARDINO (B-9) pop. 164,200, alt. 1,040′

Settled by Mormons in the 1850s, San Bernardino lies in San Bernardino County, the largest county in the United States. The city is the gateway to the resort areas of the San Bernardino Mountains, including Lake Arrowhead and Big Bear Lake *(see place listings).*

In mid-April San Bernardino hosts the National Orange Show. Devore Renaissance Pleasure Faire is held in Devore late April to early June.

Shopping areas: Carousel Mall, bounded by 4th, E, 2nd and G streets, has a JCPenney and Montgomery Ward. Broadway, May Co. and Sears all have stores at Inland Center, I-215 and Inland Center Drive.

★RIM OF THE WORLD DRIVE, SR 18, leads to Lake Arrowhead, Big Bear Lake and other resort areas. This winding 40-mile road, at elevations of 5,000 to 7,200 feet, offers many panoramic views. One of the most spectacular vistas is from 7,203-foot Lakeview Point, which provides a glimpse of Big Bear Lake and a view of the road ahead twisting among the cliffs around the head of Bear Canyon.

Visitors can take either SR 38 or SR 18 around Big Bear Lake and continue past Baldwin Lake and over the Johnson and Cushenbury grades to Lucerne Valley, Apple Valley and then Victorville.

SANTA'S VILLAGE— *see Skyforest.*

SAN BERNARDINO NATIONAL FOREST

Wide variations in climate, vegetation, scenery, natural resources and outdoor recreation can be found within the nearly 660,000 acres of San Bernardino National Forest. The forest encompasses the highest mountains in Southern California, including 11,502-foot San Gorgonio Mountain. Some 114,000 acres are set aside as the Cucamonga, San Gorgonio, Santa Rosa and San Jacinto wilderness areas.

Walking and driving tours attract many visitors to the forest; maps cost $2. In addition to the resort centers of Lake Arrowhead and Big Bear Lake, there are campgrounds, picnic areas and six winter sports areas, as well as self-guiding tours of Barton Flats on SR 38 and the historic mining area in Holcomb Valley. For more information contact 1824 Commercenter Circle, San Bernardino, CA 92408-3430; phone (909) 383-5588. *See Recreation Chart and the AAA California and Nevada CampBook.*

MOUNT SAN JACINTO WILDERNESS STATE PARK embraces 13,522 acres at the e. edge of the forest, w. of Palm Springs and n. of Idyllwild. Crowned by 10,786-foot Mount San Jacinto, it is a popular area for backpacking *(see Recreation Chart).*

SAN CLEMENTE (K-6) pop. 41,100, alt. 208′

Built on hillsides overlooking the Pacific Ocean, San Clemente is known for its palm-fringed beach. The municipal pier is popular among fishermen and sightseers. The city beach offers swimming, surfing and picnic facilities. Camping is available at San Clemente State Beach *(see Recreation Chart).*

San Diego

Second largest city in California, San Diego is both a modern metropolis and a popular year-round resort. Spreading from the coast to the desert, encompassing cliffs, hills, mesas, canyons and valleys, San Diego possesses one of California's largest natural harbors; peninsulas shelter San Diego Bay from the ocean and provide miles of shoreline for both business and pleasure. This ideal location has been a dominant factor in determining the city's history, economy and future development.

Considered the birthplace of California, San Diego was first discovered in 1542 by Juan Rodríguez Cabrillo, who landed at Point Loma and claimed what is now California for the Spanish Crown. The first settlement came more than 2 centuries later in 1769, when Gaspar de Portolá and a group of Spanish settlers founded a military outpost on what is now Presidio Hill.

Accompanying Portolá was Franciscan friar Junípero Serra, who founded Mission Basilica San Diego de Alcalá, the first of a chain of 21 missions established along California's coast. In 1774, Serra moved the mission a few miles up the San Diego River to better soil and a more abundant water supply. The sites of the original mission and the fort can still be seen in Old Town San Diego.

After California achieved statehood in 1850, San Diego grew slowly, deferring to the northern coastal cities, Los Angeles and San Francisco. It maintained a fairly insular existence until the late

---

THE INFORMED TRAVELER

POPULATION: 1,110,500; metro 2,498,000   **ALTITUDE:** 13 ft.

Whom to Call

Emergency: 911

Police (non-emergency): (619) 531-2000

Time and Temperature: (619) 853-1212

Hospitals: Kaiser Foundation Hospital, (619) 528-5000; Mercy Hospital and Medical Center, (619) 294-8111; Naval Hospital, (619) 532-6407; Sharp Cabrillo Hospital, (619) 221-3400; Sharp Memorial Hospital, (619) 541-3400; V.A. Medical Center, (619) 552-8585.

Where to Look

Newspapers
Navy

The major daily in San Diego is the morning *San Diego Union*. The *Los Angeles Times* prints a daily San Diego edition. The host of other papers published locally includes the *San Diego Daily Transcript*. Several foreign-language and community newspapers also are available in San Diego.

Radio and TV

San Diego radio station XTRA (690 AM) is a news/weather station; KPBS (89.5 FM) is programmed by National Public Radio.

Major TV channels include 6 (FOX), 8 (CBS), 10 (ABC), 15 (PBS), 39 (NBC) and 51 and 69

(Independents). For a complete list of radio and television programs, consult one of the daily newspapers.

Visitor Information

The San Diego International Visitors Information Center, (619) 236-1212, is located at 11 Horton Plaza, San Diego, CA 92101. On the corner of First and F sts., the center offers brochures and maps of the city. Guides of Old Town San Diego can be purchased for $2 at the State Park Visitor Center, (619) 237-6770, in Old Town. Another visitor information center, (619) 276-8200, is at 2688 E. Mission Bay Dr., San Diego, CA 92109.

What to Wear

With an average daily temperature of 70 F, San Diego has an almost perfect climate. The average annual rainfall of 9½ inches falls mainly during December, January and February. Winters are mild, with daytime temperatures in the mid-60s and nights about 20 degrees cooler. Because San Diego lies so close to the ocean, some days are punctuated by early morning and late evening fog. Summers in the city are beautiful; temperatures reach about 76 F during the day and drop to about 64 F at night. August and September are the warmest months, but even mid-winter provides plenty of comfortable sunbathing days.

1800s when San Francisco merchant Alonzo E. Horton decided to move the nucleus of the town closer to its valuable harbor. Horton bought 960 acres of waterfront land and developed it into New Town, which is now part of downtown San Diego.

During the early 1900s San Diego made a concerted effort to attract people, industry and shipping and railroad commerce, but Los Angeles remained the leader. World War II had a major impact on the city: The United States, forced to move its Pacific naval headquarters from Pearl Harbor, chose San Diego as the new command center. This relocation produced an increase in industry and brought thousands of military personnel, many of whom stayed after the war.

San Diego is the home of the largest naval air station on the West Coast. San Diego Bay, headquarters for many Pacific Fleet operations of the U.S. Navy, also harbors a large tuna fleet. The federal government and the aerospace equipment industry rank high in economic importance, closely followed by tourism and agriculture.

San Diego has spread more than 20 miles north, south and east. It sprawls over the natural contours of the land, rather than following the traditional grid concept, and encompasses several distinct communities. Mission Bay, once a shallow wasteland, is a 4,600-acre aquatic park. Southeast of Mission Bay, Old Town preserves the town's rich Spanish-Mexican heritage, while downtown supports the business community, a convention center, theaters and naval and commercial shipping operations.

Balboa Park, an oasis in the midst of the city, provides numerous tourist attractions and recreational opportunities. Point Loma boasts a manmade resort, Shelter Island, and contains Cabrillo National Monument, where California began. A spectacular 2-mile bridge over San Diego Bay links the Coronado peninsula with downtown.

San Diego's institutions of higher education include San Diego State University and the University of California, San Diego. Within the city lies the community of La Jolla, home to Scripps Institute of Oceanography, a world-renowned marine studies center, and the Salk Institute, an outstanding biological research facility.

Business and pleasure coexist in unusual harmony. San Diego's climate, attractive setting and recreational facilities promote a casual lifestyle that has enticed many visitors to become permanent residents.

Approaches
By Car
Two major north-south routes, both originating at the Canadian border, converge on San Diego. I-5 comes down through Los Angeles, then heads for the coast; nearing San Diego it bisects the University of California San Diego campus at La Jolla, skirts Mission Bay Park and passes Old Town before entering the city center.

I-15 comes inland through Las Vegas and the Mojave Desert but changes to SR 15 as it avoids downtown San Diego and terminates at I-5 just south of the city proper. SR 163 (Cabrillo Freeway) leaves I-15 at the Miramar Naval Air Station, swings southwestward through Balboa Park, interchanges with I-5 and finally becomes Market Street in the heart of San Diego.

From the south the main route is I-5, which begins at the Mexican border, passes along the east side of San Diego Bay, then heads for the downtown area.

I-805 is the north-south bypass. It leaves I-5 north of La Jolla and rejoins I-5 just north of the Mexican border customs stations.

From points east, I-8 funnels traffic across the Colorado River at Yuma, Ariz., and roughly parallels the Mexican border to the town of Boulevard, from which it arcs northwestward through Alpine, interchanges with the major north-south routes just north of downtown San Diego and ends near the mouth of the San Diego River.

From I-8 at Boulevard, two-lane SR 94 continues to the border town of Tecate, then heads for San Diego via Spring Valley and La Mesa, where it becomes a multilane divided highway; this route terminates at the I-5 interchange in downtown San Diego.

By Plane, Bus and Train
San Diego International Airport (Lindbergh Field) off Harbor Drive is served by major domestic and foreign carriers. Taxi service to downtown costs $6 to $8. San Diego Transit Corporation's bus number 2 provides frequent service to downtown for $1.25; phone (619) 233-3004.

Greyhound Lines Inc., (619) 239-9171, has a depot at 1st Avenue and Broadway.

Amtrak, (800) 872-7245, has several daily round trips between San Diego and Los Angeles. The Amtrak depot is at Broadway and Kettner Boulevard.

Getting Around
Generally the most convenient way to get around San Diego is by car. Most major attractions and shopping areas are within easy freeway access. Traffic delays are infrequent except in the downtown areas during rush hours. The main thoroughfares, which include Pacific Highway, Harbor Drive, Nimitz Boulevard, El Cajon Boulevard, Mission Bay Drive, University Avenue, Friars Road and Market Street, also are easy travel routes.

Speed limits are usually 35 mph on streets and 55 mph on freeways. It is important to maintain freeway speed limits; drivers moving at dangerously slow speeds will be ticketed. Right turns on red and U-turns at intersections are both legal unless otherwise posted. Pedestrians crossing the street at intersections or in crosswalks **always** have the right-of-way.

Parking

San Diego has metered on-street parking downtown in addition to many lots and garages. Charges vary, but most average from $3 per half-hour to $10 per day. Some downtown hotels and stores provide free parking. Parking in other parts of the city is rarely a problem.

Car Rentals

There are many car rental agencies in San Diego. Among them is Hertz, (800) 654-3131, which offers discounts to AAA members. Consult the local telephone directory for the names and phone numbers of other agencies. All have offices in or near downtown San Diego and the airport. Rates vary depending on car size. Standard insurance coverage is usually included, but companies vary as to whether they include gas. Reservations are advised and should be made well in advance.

Taxis

The major taxi companies serving the San Diego metropolitan area are Coast, (619) 226-8294; Co-op Cab, (619) 280-5555; Red Cab, (619) 428-1107; USA, (619) 231-1144; and Yellow, (619) 234-6161. Other companies are listed in the telephone directory. Fares are metered and are about $2.20-$3.40 for the first mile, then $1.20-$1.90 for each additional mile. You should phone for a cab when in areas other than the airport and major hotels.

Public Transportation

San Diego Metropolitan Transit System (MTS) serves the area from Del Mar to the Mexican border, including several neighboring towns and unincorporated areas. One-way bus fare ranges from $1.25 to $2.75. Most transfers are free, but some require an extra charge.

The San Diego Trolley provides daily service on two lines. The South Line runs through downtown San Diego to the international border at San Ysidro, operating 5 a.m.-1 a.m. The last trolley leaves Columbia and C streets in downtown San Diego at 12:13 a.m. and from San Ysidro at 1:02 a.m.

The East Line runs from downtown San Diego to Marshall and Main streets in El Cajon 4:46 a.m.-1:16 a.m. The last trolley leaves downtown,

Imperial Ave. and 12th St., at 12:16 a.m. and El Cajon at 1:16 a.m. Fares are 50c to $2.50.

The Transit Store, downtown on Broadway at 5th Avenue, sells money-saving passes and multiride tickets for buses and trolleys, and provides maps, schedules and brochures. For information phone (619) 233-3004; hearing impaired (TTY/TDD) phone (619) 234-5005.

Greyhound Lines Inc., (619) 239-9171, and Mexicoach, (619) 232-5049, offer daily bus service between San Diego and downtown Tijuana, Mexico.

What To See
Balboa Park

★BALBOA PARK is a 1,158-acre recreation and cultural center at the n.e. edge of the business district. The park's most prominent feature, the 200-foot California Tower, contains a 100-bell carillon that chimes every 15 minutes. The park was the site of the Panama-California International Exposition in 1915-16, and many of the Moorish and Spanish Renaissance-style exhibit halls, such as the California Building and the ornate Casa del Prado, still remain along El Prado (The Promenade).

A $9 passport allows admission to up to four of Balboa Park's seven museums for a single price. Passports are available at participating museums and at the Balboa Park Information Center in the House of Hospitality. Phone (619) 239-0512.

Aerospace Historical Center, in the Ford Building, includes the Aerospace Museum and International Aerospace Hall of Fame. Museum highlights include a replica of Lindbergh's *Spirit of St. Louis* and a space capsule. The Hall of Fame honors heroes of aviation and space. Daily 10-4:30; closed Jan. 1, Thanksgiving and Dec. 25. Admission $4; ages 6-17, $1; free to all fourth Tues. of the month. **Discount.** Phone (619) 235-1100.

Botanical Building, at the n. end of the lilypond, is a reassembled Santa Fe Railroad station

in which tropical and subtropical plants are displayed. Tues.-Sun. 10-4; closed Jan. 1, Thanksgiving and Dec. 25. Free. Phone (619) 235-1100.

Hall of Champions Sports Museum contains photographs, memorabilia and video and audio tapes of San Diego sports history. Daily 10-4:30; closed Jan. 1, Thanksgiving and Dec. 25. Admission $3; over 65 and military $2; ages 6-17, $1. Free to all second Tues. of the month. **Discount.** Phone (619) 234-2544.

House of Pacific Relations comprises 15 cottages representing 31 nationality groups. Each cottage has exhibits pertaining to specific ethnic groups. Music and dance programs are held Sun. 2-3, mid-Mar. through Oct. 31. Cottages are open Sun. 12:30-4:30 and noon-3 the fourth Tues. of the month. Free. Phone (619) 234-0739.

Japanese Friendship Garden, just northeast of the Spreckels Organ Pavilion, includes a small entry garden, the Exhibit House, a traditional sand and stone garden and a picnic area overlooking a wooded canyon. Tues. and Fri.-Sun. 10-4. Admission $2; senior citizens, military and ages 7-18, $1; family rate $5; free to all Tues. Phone (619) 232-2780.

Museum of Photographic Arts, in the Casa de Balboa building, has changing exhibits of contemporary and historic photography. Guided tours are available Sat.-Sun. Open daily 10-5 (also Thurs. 5-9). Admission $3, under 12 free when accompanied by an adult; free to all second Tues. of the month. Phone (619) 239-5262.

Reuben H. Fleet Space Theater and Science Center, 1875 El Prado, houses the Space Theater where OMNIMAX® films create the illusion of motion. The Science Center is a hands-on museum with a variety of exhibits; free to all first Tues. of the month. Mon.-Fri. 9:30-9:30, Sat.-Sun. 9:30 a.m.-10-:30 p.m. Science Center $2.25; ages 5-15, $1. Space Theater and Science Center combination ticket $5.50; over 65, $4; ages 5-15, $3. Phone (619) 238-1233. *See ad.*

San Diego Automotive Museum near the Aerospace Historical Center, features more than 60 historic and special interest automobiles and motorcycles in its permanent and rotating collections. Daily 10-4:30; closed Jan. 1, Thanksgiving and Dec. 25. Admission $4; over 65, $3; ages 13-17, $2.50; ages 6-12, $1; free to all fourth Tues. of the month. **Two-for-one discount,** except over 65. Phone (619) 231-2886.

San Diego Model Railroad Museum in the Casa de Balboa building, has four scale-model railroad layouts that detail the geography and historical development of railroading in Southern California. Allow 30 minutes minimum. Wed.-Fri., first Tues. of the month and some holidays 11-4; Sat.-Sun. 11-5. Admission $2, under 15 free; free to all first Tues. of the month. Phone (619) 696-0199.

San Diego Museum of Art, in the center of the park, has a permanent collection of Italian Renaissance works; Spanish baroque old masters; American, Asian and Indian art and sculpture; contemporary California art; and special exhibitions. Tues.-Sun. 10-4:30; closed Jan. 1, Thanksgiving and Dec. 25. Admission $5, senior citizens $4, military $3, ages 6-18 and students $2; free to all third Tues. of the month. Phone (619) 232-7931.

San Diego Museum of Man comprises a group of buildings around the California Quadrangle. Exhibits depict the story of mankind with emphasis on the Indians of the three Americas. "Life Cycles and Ceremonies" details the human birth process and portrays rites of passage in various cultures. Daily 10-4:30; closed Jan. 1, Thanksgiving and Dec. 25. Admission $3; ages 13-18, $1; ages 6-12, 25c; free to military and to all on third Tues. of the month. **Discount.** Phone (619) 239-2001.

San Diego Natural History Museum, e. end of El Prado, houses exhibits of plants, animals and geology of the American Southwest. Daily 9:30-5:30, June-Aug.; 10-4:30, rest of year. Closed Jan. 1, Thanksgiving and Dec. 25. Admission $6; over 60, $5; ages 6-14, $2; free to all first Tues. of the month. Phone (619) 232-3821.

★**San Diego Zoo,** one of the largest in the world, exhibits some of the rarest specimens in captivity. More than 4,000 animals of 800 species are on display, separated from the public by moats. Highlights include free-flight, walk-through aviaries, koalas from Australia, an impressive assemblage of primates and a large reptile collection. Gorilla Tropics and Tiger River provide simulated rain forests similar to the animals' native habitats. Sun bears frolic on a hillside in Sun Bear Forest while lion-tailed macaques swing from the vines.

The zoo is beautifully landscaped with tropical and subtropical vegetation. Moving sidewalks stretch from the deep canyons to upper levels. An aerial tramway runs from the main entrance to the Horn and Hoof Mesa, ⅓-mile away. Narrated bus tours and picnic facilities also are available. Pets are not allowed in the zoo. Daily 9-5, July 1-Labor Day; 9-4, rest of year. General admission $12; ages 3-15, $4. Deluxe Tour (including admission, bus tour, aerial tram and children's zoo) $15; ages 3-15, $6.50. Phone (619) 234-3153.

The Children's Zoo, reached through the main zoo, covers 1⅓ acres and affords children the chance to pet the more gentle creatures. This area also contains two animal nurseries. Daily 9:30-5, July 1-Labor Day; 9:30-4, rest of year.

Simon Edison Centre for the Performing Arts includes the Old Globe Theatre, the Cassius Carter Centre Stage and the Lowell Davies Festival Theatre. A variety of productions are presented throughout the year; during the summer the focus is on works by Shakespeare. Tickets $17-$29.50. Under 5 not permitted. AE, DS, MC, VI. Phone (619) 239-2255.

Spanish Village Art Center contains studios where artisans create, display and sell their wares. Most studios open daily 11-4; closed Jan. 1, Thanksgiving and Dec. 25. Free. Phone (619) 233-9050.

Spreckels Organ Pavilion contains an outdoor organ said to be the largest in the world. Free concerts Sun. at 2. For program information phone (619) 235-1100.

Timken Art Gallery houses a collection of works by European masters from the 16th through 19th centuries as well as 18th- and 19th-century American paintings and Russian icons. Guided tours Tues.-Thurs. 10-noon. Gallery open Tues.-Sat. 10-4:30, Sun. 1:30-4:30, Oct.-Aug.; closed holidays. Free. Phone (619) 239-5548.

Mission Bay

Northwest of downtown, Mission Bay has two islands and many coves and inlets. Mission Bay Park has facilities for boating, boat rental, camping and fishing, as well as miles of shoreline for picnicking and swimming.

★**SEA WORLD,** on Mission Bay's south shore, is a 150-acre marine zoological park with shows, aquariums, marine-life exhibits, rides, a nautical theme playground, a marina and research and medical labs. Star performers include Shamu, a 2-ton orca ("killer whale"), Baby Shamu, a killer whale calf, and dolphins, sea lions, otters and walruses.

Other highlights include the Penguin Encounter, a 2½-acre exhibit containing nearly 400 penguins; a shark exhibit; and the dolphin pool. "Beach Blanket Ski Show" features a cast that shows off a variety of water ski maneuvers in Sea World's lagoon.

Through the use of underground viewing tunnels and shallow pools, the Forbidden Reef gives visitors an interactive experience with such sea creatures as moray eels and bat rays. Guided tours are offered. Pets are not permitted. Evening entertainment is offered in summer. Open daily 9 a.m.-11 p.m., mid-June to Labor Day; 9-dusk, rest of year; extended holiday hours. Admission $24.95; over 55, $21.20; ages 3-11, $18.95. DS, MC, VI. **Discount,** except over 55. Extra fee for some rides. Phone (619) 226-3901 or (714) 939-6212.

Old Town San Diego

JUNIPERO SERRA MUSEUM, 2727 Presidio Dr. in Presidio Park, interprets San Diego's historical Spanish and Mexican periods. Exhibits include artifacts from archeological excavations at the Presidio site. The museum marks the site of the 18th-century presidio and Father Junípero Serra's first mission in Alta California. Tues.-Sat.

10-4:30, Sun. noon-4:30; closed Jan. 1, Thanksgiving and Dec. 25. Admission $3, under 12 free. Phone (619) 297-3258.

OLD TOWN SAN DIEGO STATE HISTORIC PARK, a six-block area bounded by Wallace, Juan, Twiggs and Congress sts., commemorates the founding of the first permanent settlement in California. It contains many of San Diego's original buildings. Nearby Presidio Park is the site of California's first mission and military fortress, established in 1769.

Guided walking tours daily at 2. Brochures for self-guiding tours of Old Town are available at the visitor center *(see Robinson-Rose House)* for $2. All of the following buildings are closed Jan. 1, Thanksgiving and Dec. 25. Phone (619) 237-6770.

Alvarado House, next to the Johnson House, is a reconstruction of one of the town's oldest adobes. It was built 1824-30 and at one time was occupied by Tomasa Pico, sister of California's last Mexican governor. Daily 10-5. Free.

Black Hawk Smithy & Stable, Mason and Juan sts., was opened in the 1860s. Vintage blacksmithing techniques are demonstrated Wed. and Sat. 10-2.

Johnson House, Mason and Calhoun sts., is a reconstructed frame house built around 1869. Archeological displays from Old Town digs are featured. Daily 10-5. Free.

La Casa de Estudillo is at 4001 Mason St. The restored 1827 adobe features Spanish and early American relics, period furnishings and a garden. Daily 10-5; closed major holidays. Admission, including Seeley Stables, $2; ages 6-17, $1.

Mason Street School, Mason St. and San Diego Ave., is a one-room frame building erected in 1865. After being moved to another location and used for other purposes, the building was returned to its original site and restored. Daily 10-5. Free.

Old Town Plaza, bounded by San Diego Ave. and Wallace, Calhoun and Mason sts., was the center of community life after the formation of the pueblo of San Diego in 1835.

Robinson-Rose House, 4002 Wallace St., is a two-story adobe built in 1853. Today it houses the park's visitor center and has photo murals and carefully crafted scale models of Old Town as it appeared in the 1870s. Daily 10-5. Free.

San Diego Union Museum, 2626 San Diego Ave., is where the newspaper was founded in 1868. It is furnished to reflect the 1860s. Daily 10-5.

Seeley Stables, 2648 Calhoun St., is a reconstructed barn. The collection of horse-drawn vehicles includes several covered wagons and stagecoaches. Slide shows are presented. Daily 10-5; closed major holidays. Admission, including La Casa de Estudillo, $2; ages 6-17, $1.

Wells Fargo History Museum, near Mason Street School, occupies the 1851 Colorado House Hotel. The museum features a Concord stagecoach as well as historic documents and relics. Daily 10-5. Free.

WHALEY HOUSE, 2482 San Diego Ave., dates from 1856 and is thought to be the first two-story brick home built in Southern California. The building has served as a residence, store, courthouse and theater; it now showcases restored period furnishings. Wed.-Sun. 10-4:30; closed holidays. Admission $3; senior citizens $2.50; ages 12-16, $1.50; ages 5-11, $1. **Discount,** except senior citizens. Phone (619) 298-2482.

Point Loma

★**CABRILLO NATIONAL MONUMENT,** overlooking the city and harbor, is at the s. end of Cabrillo Memorial Dr. (SR 209); it is approached through the gates of the Naval Ocean Systems Center. The lighthouse, which beaconed ships to San Diego Harbor 1855-91, has been refurbished. An overlook provides a good vantage for observing the annual migration of California gray whales from December through February. Tidepools offer a chance to explore coastal marine life. Recorded information is provided at the lighthouse and whale overlook.

A coastal artillery system that defended San Diego Harbor during World Wars I and II is visible from the Bayside Trail. The visitor center presents films and has exhibits on Cabrillo's voyage and information on park activities. Daily 9-5:15; extended hours in summer. Admission $3 per vehicle or $1 per person arriving by other means; permanent U.S. residents over 62 and under 17 free. For more information contact Cabrillo National Monument, P.O. Box 6670, San Diego, CA 92166-0670; phone (619) 557-5450.

SUNSET CLIFFS along Sunset Cliffs Blvd. between Hill St. and Point Loma Ave., affords seascape views from rocky cliffs that have been carved into unusual shapes by the surf.

San Diego Bay

The U.S. Coast Guard Base, U.S. Naval and Marine Training Centers and the U.S. Naval Air Station flank the bay. Shipyards, docks and the repair base are next to the bay. Navy Open House is usually held aboard naval vessels at the Broadway Pier Sat.-Sun. 1-4; phone (619) 532-1430.

★MARITIME MUSEUM OF SAN DIEGO, on the Embarcadero at 1306 N. Harbor Dr., encompasses three historic vessels: the 1863 tall ship *Star of India,* the 289-foot 1898 ferry *Berkeley,* and the 1904 steam yacht *Medea.* Nautical and oceanographic exhibits are featured. Allow 1 hour minimum. Daily 9-8. Admission $5; over 62 and ages 13-16, $4; ages 5-12, $1.25; family rate $10. AE, MC, VI. **Two-for-one discount.** Phone (619) 234-9153.

SEAPORT VILLAGE, at Kettner Blvd. and West Harbor Dr., is a 14-acre landscaped dining, shopping and entertainment complex in a harborside setting. Within the village is a restored Looff carousel and an 8-acre park. Daily 10-10, June-Aug.; 10-9, rest of year. Free. Parking free for 2 hours with validation, 75c per half-hour thereafter. Phone (619) 235-4014.

Other Points of Interest

FIREHOUSE MUSEUM, 1572 Columbia St., contains antique fire equipment, a display of helmets and other items from around the world as well as an old steamer. Thurs.-Sun. 10-4. Donations. Phone (619) 232-3473.

★MISSION BASILICA SAN DIEGO DE ALCALA, 10818 San Diego Mission Rd. in Mission Valley, is reached via Mission Gorge Rd. (off I-8) and Twain Ave. The first of California's missions, it was founded by Father Junípero Serra on July 16, 1769, at Presidio Hill, moved to its present site in 1774, destroyed by earthquakes in 1803 and 1812 and subsequently rebuilt. Taped tours are available at the visitor center. Daily 9-5; closed Thanksgiving and Dec. 25. Admission $1, under 12 free. Phone (619) 281-8449.

★SAN DIEGO WILD ANIMAL PARK— *see Escondido.*

VILLA MONTEZUMA/JESSE SHEPARD HOUSE, 1925 K St., is a restored 1887 Victorian house. It contains exhibits pertaining to Victorian architecture and decorative arts as well as a fine example of residential stained glass. High-heeled shoes are not permitted. Fri.-Sun. noon-4; closed Jan. 1, Thanksgiving and Dec. 24-25. Admission $3, under 13 free. Phone (619) 239-2211.

Tijuana, Mexico—*see Baja California.*

What To Do
Sightseeing
Bus, Limousine, Carriage and Train Tours

A good way to become acquainted with the city is to take a bus or limousine tour. Bus tour destinations range from Los Angeles to San Felipe, Mexico. Gray Line Tours, (619) 491-0011, at 3855 Rosecrans St., offers more than 15 trips varying in price and itinerary. Tours pick up from most major hotels and depart from the terminal on Rosecrans Street.

San Diego Mini-Tours, (619) 477-8687, offers a variety of narrated trolley tours of San Diego, as well as trips to Tijuana, Ensenada and San Felipe. Other touring companies are listed in the local telephone directory. Reservations should be made a day in advance.

OLD TOWN TROLLEY TOURS offers 2-hour trolley bus excursions that visit Balboa Park, Horton Plaza, the Gaslamp Quarter, Seaport Village, the Embarcadero, Old Town and Coronado. Passengers have boarding and reboarding privileges at each stop. Tours begin daily at 9; closed Jan. 1, Thanksgiving and Dec. 25. Fare $15; ages 6-12, $7; senior citizens and military $12 on Mon. only. Phone (619) 298-8687. *See ad.*

Boat Tours

Since much of San Diego's activity centers on its harbor, a cruise provides an excellent perspective of the city.

BAHIA BELLE, a stern-wheeler, plies the waters of Mission Bay. Cruises depart from the Bahia Hotel and feature cocktails and dancing. Tues.-Sat. evenings, July-Aug.; Fri. and Sat. evenings only, Jan.-June and Sept.-Nov. Fare $5; minors are not permitted. Phone (619) 488-0551.

INVADER CRUISES, on the Embarcadero at 1066 N. Harbor Dr., offers narrated tours of San Diego Harbor. All trips are offered daily; phone for departure times. Dinner and Sun. brunch cruises are available. One-hour cruise $10; over 55 and military $8; ages 3-12, $5. Two-hour cruise $15; over 55 and military $13; ages 3-12, $7.50. Whale-watching cruise (Dec.-Feb.) $15; over 55 and military $13; ages 3-12, $7.50. AE, MC, VI. Discount, except over 55, military, 2-hour cruise and whale-watching cruise. Phone (619) 234-8687.

MARIPOSA, Sheraton Harbor Island East Hotel dock, is a 35-foot sailing craft that offers afternoon and evening cruises on San Diego Bay. Excursions are fully narrated, and passengers may take the wheel and participate in the sailing. There is a limit of six passengers per cruise. Daily 1-5 and 5:30-7:30, mid-Mar. to mid-Dec.;

8:30-12:30 and 1-5, rest of year. Fare $40. MC, VI. Reservations are required. Phone (619) 542-0646 or (800) 659-0141.

THE ORIGINAL SAN DIEGO HARBOR EXCURSION departs from 1050 N. Harbor Dr. near the foot of Broadway at Harbor Dr. Sights include the largest Navy fleet in the continental United States and the San Diego-Coronado Bay Bridge. Dinner cruises also are offered. The 1-hour trip departs Mon.-Fri. 10-4:15, Sat-Sun. and holidays 11:15-4:15. The 2-hour cruise departs Mon.-Fri. at 2, Sat.-Sun. and holidays 10-2.

One-hour fare $10; over 55 and military $8; ages 3-12, $5. Two-hour fare $15; over 55 and military $13; ages 3-12, $7.50. AE, MC, VI. Phone (619) 234-4111.

SAN DIEGO-CORONADO FERRY runs between the dock at Broadway and Harbor Dr. in San Diego and the Old Ferry Landing at B Ave. and 1st St. in Coronado. The ferry leaves San Diego on the hour and Coronado on the half-hour; crossings take approximately 15 minutes. Sun.-Thurs. 9 a.m.-10 p.m., Fri.-Sat. 9 a.m.-11 p.m. One-way fare $2; 55c additional for bicycles. Phone (619) 595-1490 or 234-4111.

Hot Air Balloon Tours

PACIFIC HORIZON BALLOON TOURS offers sunrise and sunset flights over the Temecula wine country or San Diego areas year-round, weather permitting. Champagne and hors d'oeuvres are included. Passengers may assist with lift-off and pack-up operations. Rides last approximately 1 hour; they are not advisable for under 4. Fares $125-$140; reservations are required. Phone (619) 756-1790 or (800) 244-1790.

Walking Tours

Pedestrians can take a self-guiding walking tour of Old Town San Diego State Historic Park, which is closed to vehicular traffic. Guide booklets giving a brief history of Old Town are available for $2 at the visitor center in the Robinson-Rose House, 4002 Wallace St.

Go south from the visitor center and turn east on San Diego Ave.; you'll pass a number of historic one-story buildings, including the 1832 Machado-Silvas Adobe. At the reconstructed first San Diego courthouse and the Wells Fargo History Museum, turn south on the walkway to the Machado-Stewart Adobe, once home of a shipmate of Richard Henry Dana. A visit to the adobe was described in Dana's classic "Two Years Before the Mast."

Diagonally north of the Machado-Stewart Adobe on Mason St. is the Mason Street School, a one-room frame building erected in 1865. This building served as the city's first publicly owned schoolhouse. Walk north on Mason St. to San Diego Ave. and continue east to Dodson's Corner, a group of small false-front shops where merchants sometimes dress in period costumes.

Across San Diego Ave. is the San Diego Union Museum, birthplace of Southern California's oldest continuously published newspaper.

Walk northward on Twiggs St.; around the corner at 2648 Calhoun St. are the Seeley Stables. Head north along the west side of the stables, then slightly east, to the Black Hawk Smithy & Stable. Adjacent stands the Casa de Bandini, an L-shaped structure built in 1849 for Juan Bandini. A second floor was added in 1869 and the building became a hotel; today it is a Mexican restaurant.

Walk west on Calhoun St. to the Johnson House and the neighboring Alvarado House. Retrace your steps and head south on Mason St., stopping for a visit at historic Casa de Estudillo. Directly across the street on Mason is Old Town Plaza, a good place to end the tour.

A stroll around downtown's Gaslamp Quarter, bounded by Broadway, 4th Ave., 6th Ave. and Harbor Dr., provides an excellent overview of the city's architectural and commercial history. Many buildings in this 16-block, 38-acre area have been restored to their original beauty.

The Nesmith-Greeley and Hubbell buildings, on the east side of 5th Ave. between E and F sts., are typical of Victorian-era commercial structures. The saltbox architectural style is exemplified by the William Heath Davis House at 4th and Island aves. Built in 1850, the house is now a museum that offers both guided walking tours of the Gaslamp Quarter and brochures for self-guiding tours.

Another historic building open to the public is the Horton Grand Hotel at 311 Island Ave., which has a small museum dedicated to the area's Oriental heritage. Guided walking tours of the Gaslamp Quarter are given Sat. at 11. Admission $5, senior citizens $3, under 12 free. For more information phone (619) 233-5227. Adjoining the district are arts and crafts shops and coffee houses well worth exploring, paticularly along the 600 and 800 blocks of G St. and 8th Ave.

Nature lovers will enjoy the bird-watching walks and trail walks at Point Loma. Led by knowledgeable volunteers, the tours leave from the Cabrillo National Monument visitor center. For information phone (619) 557-5450.

Driving Tours

A 59-mile scenic drive is marked at frequent intervals by blue and yellow signs with a white sea gull. The drive begins at Broadway Pier, although it can be joined at any point. It takes in the Embarcadero, Shelter and Harbor islands, Point Loma, Mission Bay, La Jolla, Old Town and Balboa Park. The loop can be driven in about 3 hours, but time should be allowed for sightseeing. Avoid driving during rush hours.

Sports and Recreation

Because of its mild climate, San Diego is a haven for year-round recreation. Outdoor sports draw nearly as many visitors to the city as the sightseeing attractions.

Miles of shoreline and two large, protected bays provide ideal settings for all types of water sports. **Swimming** opportunities include the ocean, Mission Bay and public pools. Ocean swimming is best June through November. Both ocean and bay beaches have lifeguards on duty daily during summer.

Surfing is an all-year activity, but wet suits are advised in winter. Among the popular surfing beaches are Windansea Beach and Tourmaline Surfing Park.

Water skiing conditions are excellent on the calm waters of the bays. San Diego Bay has restricted areas due to naval and commercial traffic, but water skiing is permitted within the secure waters around Shelter and Harbor islands and in Glorietta Bay. Skiing is permitted in certain sections of Mission Bay from dawn to dusk.

Boating is a favorite pastime; hundreds of pleasure boats dot the ocean and bays daily. The major boating centers are Shelter and Harbor islands, Glorietta Bay and Mission Bay marinas. Rental and launching facilities for paddle and fishing boats, sailboats and powerboats are available at these areas.

Fishing enthusiasts can enjoy many varieties of the sport: deep-sea, surf, pier, bay, shell and freshwater. Bottom-feeding fish are attracted by offshore kelp beds, and nearby Mexican waters contain barracuda, bass, bonito and yellowtail. Public piers are at Shelter Island, Ocean Beach and Imperial Beach. Fishing charters depart from Shelter and Harbor islands, Point Loma, Imperial Beach pier and Quivira Basin at Mission Bay Park.

Golf courses in San Diego County number more than 50, ranging from seaside to desert locations. The Mission Bay and River Valley golf courses are lighted for evening play.

Tennis courts for public play are scattered throughout the area. The best are at Point Loma, Mission Bay Youth Field, Robb Field and Cabrillo Playground. Most resort areas also have tennis facilities.

Bicycling is a good way to tour this sunshine city. There are several marked bike routes and numerous rental shops.

Horseback riding clubs offer horse rentals and riding facilities. Bonita and Bright Valley Ranch have hundreds of miles of riding trails.

Spectator sports are many and varied. San Diego Jack Murphy Stadium is the home of two major league teams: the Padres, **baseball,** and the Chargers, **football.** The San Diego Sports Arena plays host to special sports events. Local college and university teams provide additional entertainment.

Horse racing takes place at Del Mar Thoroughbred Club 15 miles north. Across the border in Tijuana, the Agua Caliente Race Track has both horse racing and **dog racing.** Two other prominent spectator sports in Mexico are **jai alai** and **bullfighting.**

Note: Policies concerning admittance of children to pari-mutuel betting facilities vary. Phone ahead for information.

For more information on sports and recreation contact the Automobile Club of Southern California, 815 Date St., San Diego, CA 92101; phone (619) 233-1000. Information on recreational opportunities can be obtained from the Community Park and Recreation Division, (619) 525-8285. The monthly *San Diego Sports Digest,* available at many newsstands, covers sports in the city.

Where To Shop

Mission Valley is the premier shopping area in the city. Its emergence can be attributed to its easy freeway access and its two large shopping centers—Fashion Valley and Mission Valley. The two centers are within a few minutes of each other and have a combined total of more than 175 stores and restaurants.

Other regional shopping centers in the area include the Grossmont Center in La Mesa and La Jolla Village Square and University Towne Centre in La Jolla. These contain a variety of major department stores, including Bullock's, JCPenney, May Co., Montgomery Ward, Robinson's, Saks Fifth Avenue and Walker Scott.

Seaport Village at Kettner Boulevard and Harbor Drive has an array of specialty shops (*see San Diego Bay*). The Olde Cracker Factory, 448 W. Market St., is an antique buff's delight. Within the three-story building more than 40 dealers display a wide variety of antiques and collectibles.

Among the historic sites in Old Town are numerous attractive shops, including those at Old San Diego Galleria. International items can be found at Bazaar del Mundo, and Old Town Mercado and Dodson's Corner re-create a 19th-century shopping atmosphere. At Rosecrans, Taylor and San Diego avenues is Pottery Village, where exhibits on 19th-century California life are interspersed with the departments of gift items.

Along the Embarcadero are many boutiques featuring such articles as clothing, jewelry and sea-related items. Downtown at 7th and L streets fresh fruits and vegetables, homemade foods and hand-crafted gifts attract shoppers to the Farmers Bazaar. Art, craft and specialty shops are featured in the downtown Gaslamp Quarter.

Shoppers in San Diego also will be lured to the Mexican border city of Tijuana. Because of its free port status, Tijuana offers tempting bargains on imported goods. Prices on Mexican products also are reasonable. Major shopping areas include a mall at the Agua Caliente Race Track, a center in the Río Tijuana area and

Avenida Revolución, the city's oldest tourist shopping area.

HORTON PLAZA CENTRE is bounded by Broadway, G St. and 1st and 4th aves. downtown. Distinguished by its fanciful and multicolored architecture, the three-level plaza houses four major department stores, more than 140 specialty shops, a seven-screen cinema, two theaters, a variety of restaurants and outdoor entertainment. Stores open Mon.-Sat. 10-9, Sun. 11-7, in summer; Mon.-Fri. 10-9, Sat. 10-6, Sun. 11-6, rest of year. Restaurants, theaters and some shops have extended hours. Parking is available in an adjacent garage. Phone (619) 238-1596.

Where To Dine

With the bounteous ocean in sight and a spicy influence just south of the border, it is not surprising that San Diego's most popular restaurants are known for their delicate seafood and substantial Mexican dishes.

Two locally popular seafood chains, Anthony's and the Chart House, provide family dining at affordable prices and the freshest catch of the day. Anthony's Fish Grotto downtown overlooks San Diego Harbor and serves fresh fish and shellfish. The Coronado Chart House offers steak and lobster in a cozy boathouse atmosphere with Tiffany lamps and a view of Glorietta Bay.

Sunday brunch is served in the Hotel del Coronado's Crown Room, which features wood-paneled ceilings and crown-shaped chandeliers. The Fontainebleau Room at Westgate is renowned for its white glove touch and Louis XIV furnishings. Mister A's at the top of the Financial Center specializes in scampi and Beef Wellington and provides a striking view of San Diego Harbor and Balboa Park. Other popular restaurants include Garcia's of Scottsdale, Lubach's and Anthony's Star of the Sea Room.

For the indecisive there are the Aztec Dining Room and Bit of Sweden. The Aztec Dining Room offers several combination plates and dinners with shredded beef and cheese tacos and chiles rellenos on the side. Bit of Sweden features a smorgasbord. Alfonso's prides itself on family recipes and its burrito or taco combination plates, while El Chalan introduces fine Peruvian cuisine.

Coats and ties are required at the most formal establishments. Reservations are advised on weekends and at the most popular places at all times; it is best to phone a day or two ahead.

Nightlife

Many San Diego hotels provide dinner, dancing and entertainment; notable are the Le Pavilion at the Town and Country Hotel and the Fontainebleau Room at Westgate. Lounges and dance clubs also have live entertainment. Croce's Restaurant & Jazz Bar, 802 5th Ave., is a local favorite. Top comedians perform at the Improv in Pacific Beach.

San Diego's proximity to Tijuana adds a number of possibilities for evening diversions; shops are open late for evening browsers, greyhounds race at Caliente, and jai alai is played at Frontón Palacio. Evening sightseeing tours of these Tijuana attractions, as well as San Diego Wild Animal Park in Escondido are offered by Gray Line.

Information sources for current show offerings are the entertainment sections of the daily newspapers and special-events publications available at most hotels and motels.

Note: The mention of any area or establishment in the preceding sections is for information only and does **not** imply endorsement by AAA.

Theater and Concerts

San Diego has become a major city in terms of its varied cultural offerings. The San Diego Concourse on 1st Avenue between A and C streets contains the City Administration Building, exhibit halls, the 3,000-seat Civic Theatre and the 4,000-seat Golden Hall. The theatre and hall host ballets, operas, plays, musicals and concerts. Copley Symphony Hall, a converted 1929 movie house at 7th and B streets, is the cornerstone of Symphony Towers, which also contains a hotel and shopping arcade.

The San Diego Convention Center, at 111 W. Harbor Dr., is done in a modern architectural style, with a portion of its roof line suggesting huge sails. The center has exhibit rooms, an open-air covered pavilion and an amphitheater.

Balboa Park's Simon Edison Centre for the Performing Arts encompasses the Lowell Davies Festival Theatre; the Old Globe Theatre; and Carter Centre Stage, where contemporary dramas are presented throughout the year. The Civic Theatre is home to the San Diego Opera Company and the bilingual theater company, Teatro Meta, which presents original and popular plays.

The Coronado Playhouse on the Silver Strand stages cabaret-style musicals, while the Lawrence Welk Resort Theatre in Escondido entertains guests with Broadway hits. The Theater in Old Town offers classic and experimental plays.

Mandell-Weiss Center on the University of California San Diego campus in La Jolla presents plays and musicals by both students and professional touring groups. The San Diego Sports Arena often books top-name shows.

TIMES ARTS TIX, a public service of the San Diego Theatre League, sells half-price performance-day tickets and full-price advance sale tickets for many local attractions. The box office is downtown at Broadway and Broadway Circle in Horton Plaza Park. Phone (619) 238-3810.

Especially for Children

San Diego's multitude of recreational activities makes the city a natural playground for children and adults. Water sports, bicycling and horseback riding offer an active day for all ages. Youngsters also can be enthusiastic spectators at athletic games; with two professional sports teams, San Diego never suffers from a lack of exciting sports competitions.

The three zoological attractions—the San Diego Zoo in Balboa Park, the San Diego Wild Animal Park in Escondido and Sea World—will capture hearts and imaginations. At the zoo, youngsters may pet and play with some of the gentler creatures; Sea World offers marine shows and exhibits and Cap'n Kid World, a 2-acre play area. Outer space fans are sure to enjoy the Reuben H. Fleet Space Theater and Science Center in Balboa Park. The park also offers carrousel rides and a puppet theater in the summer.

If you have nautical interests, a visit to the Embarcadero should include harbor tours for the seaworthy and the Maritime Museum of San Diego for landlubbers. A visit to Old Town provides a combination of fun and history.

Special Events

San Diego celebrates St. Patrick's Day with a parade in mid-March. April activities include the San Diego Crew Classic at Mission Bay, while May brings the Cinco de Mayo celebration early in the month and the San Diego American Indian Cultural Days Pow Wow in mid-month.

Miramar's Naval Air Show takes place in late July. In mid-September the Budweiser APA Thunderbolt Gold Cup Races are held in Mission Bay. The Dixieland Jazz Festival is a popular event held on Thanksgiving weekend, as is the Sea World Holiday Bowl football game in late December.

SAN DIMAS (B-7) pop. 27,100, alt. 940′

RAGING WATERS, 111 Raging Waters Dr., is a 44-acre aquatic recreation park featuring waterslides, speed slides, beaches for sunbathing and a children's pool. Daily at 10, mid-June to mid-Sept.; Sat.-Sun. at 9, May 1 to mid-June and mid-Sept. to mid-Oct. Closing times vary. Over 48 inches tall $18.50; over age 55, $10.50; 42-48 inches tall $9.95; under 42 inches tall free. **Discount.** Parking $3. Phone (909) 592-6453.

San Francisco

Civic devotion is the most noticeable characteristic of San Francisco residents; indeed, it is one of the few matters upon which they unanimously agree. The city is comparatively young, yet seldom is there found a greater passion for preservation of the past with all its colorful legends and architecture. This spirit is evident in the preservation of historic buildings as well as the famous cable cars.

Combined with this love of the city is the great determination and courage that rebuilt the city not once but seven times after devastating fires. Six of them came within a period of two boomtown years; the last one, which destroyed four-fifths of the town, blazed for days after the 1906 earthquake broke the water mains and rendered the firefighting equipment useless.

Possibly it is the beauty of San Francisco's setting that commands such loyalty. Varying in altitude from sea level to 929 feet, the city rests on 40 hills at the tip of a narrow peninsula, bounded on one side by the Pacific Ocean and on the other by San Francisco Bay, one of the largest land-locked harbors in the world.

It was the city's bayside location that attracted its earliest colonizers. A permanent European settlement was established in 1776, when the presidio, or Spanish military post, was begun at the end of the peninsula. During that same year the Franciscan fathers founded the Mission San Francisco de Asis.

A trail from the presidio to the mission was established, and about halfway between the two there sprang up a halting place known as El Paraje de Yerba Buena, the place of the good herb, around what is now Portsmouth Square. It was not until 1835 that the town of Yerba Buena—later to be called San Francisco—was founded.

THE INFORMED TRAVELER

POPULATION: 724,000; metro 6,253,300   **ALTITUDE:** 63 ft.

Whom to Call

Emergency: 911

Police (non-emergency): (415) 553-0123

Time and Temperature: (415) 767-1111

Hospitals: Davies Medical Center, (415) 565-6779; Pacific Presbyterian Medical Center, (415) 563-4321; St. Mary's Hospital and Medical Center, (415) 668-1000; University of California San Francisco Medical Center, (415) 476-1000; V.A. Medical Center, (415) 221-4810.

Where to Look

Newspapers

San Francisco has a number of papers in Chinese, Japanese and other foreign languages, but the major daily newspapers are the morning *Chronicle* and the evening *Examiner*. The two combine to produce a Sunday paper.

Radio and TV

San Francisco radio station KCBS (740 AM) is an all-news/weather station; KQED (88.5 FM) is programmed by National Public Radio.

Major TV channels are 2 (FOX), 4 (NBC), 5 (CBS), 7 (ABC) and 9 (PBS). Several stations have programs in Spanish and other languages.

For a complete list of radio and television programs, consult the daily newspapers.

Visitor Information

The San Francisco Visitor Information Center, (415) 391-2000, is at 900 Market St., San Francisco, CA 94102. In Hallidie Plaza the center is open Mon.-Fri. 9-5:30, Sat. 9-3, Sun. 10-2; closed Jan. 1, Thanksgiving and Dec. 25.

Information on northern California is available at the Redwood Empire Association Visitor Information Center, (415) 543-8334, 785 Market St., San Francisco, CA 94103.

What to Wear

San Francisco's weather is noted not for its extremes but for its consistency. Temperatures usually do not rise above 80 F or fall below 40 F. August and September are generally the warmest months; January is the coldest. Most of the average yearly rainfall of just over 20 inches falls in the winter, but the summer fog also dampens the air in mornings and evenings, making a raincoat a very useful item throughout the year.

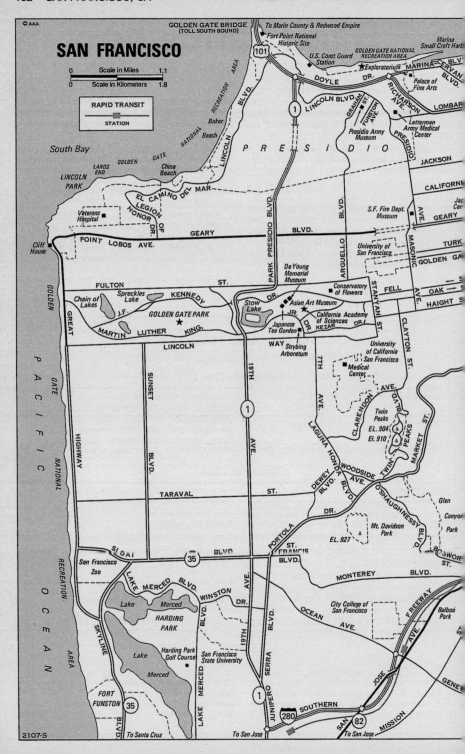

© AAA

SAN FRANCISCO

Scale in Miles	
0	1.1

Scale in Kilometers	
0	1.8

RAPID TRANSIT

■ STATION

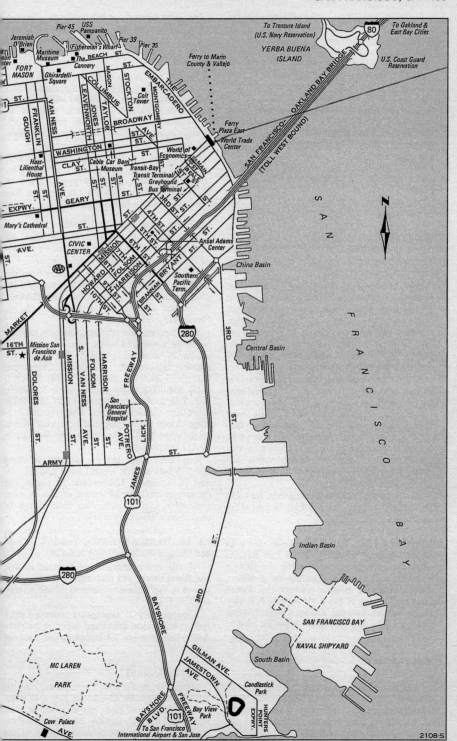

2108-S

For more than 13 years the village had fewer than 100 inhabitants, but with the discovery of gold in the American River in 1848 the population rapidly increased to well over 10,000. Through San Francisco poured thousands of hopefuls from all over the world, and back to it came most of the '49ers, both the successful and the disappointed, when it was all over.

San Francisco's population is composed of citizens of Chinese, Japanese, Hispanic, Italian, Russian and other ancestry. This diversity contributes to a spirit of broad-minded sophistication and tolerance. Cultural, cosmopolitan San Francisco has given birth to interesting offspring as well, from the United Nations to the topless dancer.

The best example of San Francisco's good-humored tolerance took place during the years jokingly called the Reign of Emperor Norton. A British businessman driven insane by financial failure, Joshua Norton in 1859 declared himself Emperor of these United States and Protector of Mexico.

For 21 years he "ruled" San Francisco, the residents of which gladly indulged his grandiose whims. Even some of his edicts were followed, as beneath his grand and flowery language flowed a strong, sane sense of humanitarian reform and practical public interest. When Emperor Norton I died in 1880, more than 30,000 San Franciscans attended his funeral.

Today's San Francisco, still fun loving, also is an important industrial, tourist and financial center. Its financial district at the lower end of Montgomery Street is often called "Wall Street West." Furthermore, the city port handles millions of tons of cargo annually. The George R. Moscone Convention Center occupies a city block between Third and Fourth streets and Howard and Folsom streets and is built almost entirely underground.

San Francisco provides scenic access via I-280 to San Jose and SR 1 to San Luis Obispo along the coast.

The crests of many of the city's hills, particularly Twin Peaks, afford matchless views of downtown San Francisco and the East Bay. At night when the bridges are lighted, the view is even more impressive. Standing on a hilltop, watching the fog swirl in through the Golden Gate and looking at the city's skyline, it is easy to understand Rudyard Kipling's lament: "San Francisco has only one drawback—'tis hard to leave."

Approaches
By Car
Scenic north-south routes passing directly through San Francisco are US 101 and SR 1. They enter the city separately from the south, merge on the San Francisco approach to the Golden Gate Bridge and continue as one through a few miles of southern Marin County. Because SR 1, the coastal route, is subject to dense fog and the likelihood of landslides, you should check weather and road conditions locally before driving it.

The fast north-south route, I-5, lies east of San Francisco; connections to the San Francisco-Oakland Bay Bridge are via I-580 and I-880 from the north and I-580 and I-880 (with a detour on I-980) from the south. Another route, SR 99, closely parallels I-5 and also has connections into the city.

Most traffic from the east approaches via I-80 across the Sierras. I-80 is closely paralleled by US 50 to Sacramento, from where the Interstate heads west, leading into the city over the San Francisco-Oakland Bay Bridge.

By Plane, Bus, Train and Boat
San Francisco International Airport, about 13 miles south near San Bruno, is served by all major domestic and foreign passenger carriers.

Airporter Coaches provides transfers from the airport to major downtown hotels every 20 minutes, 6 a.m.-11:10 p.m. Trips last approximately 20 minutes. One-way fare is $8; under 15, $4. Phone (415) 495-8404 or 673-2433.

Minivans provide door-to-door service between the airport and hotels, businesses and residences in most areas. Among the companies offering this service are Airport Connection, (415) 885-2666 or (800) 247-7678; Lorrie's, (415) 334-9000; Super Shuttle, (415) 558-8500; and Yellow Airport Shuttle, (415) 282-7433. There are frequent pickups from the red-and-white-striped zones marked at pedestrian islands on the upper level of the airport. One-way fare is $9-$12 per person.

Taxi fares vary, but the average is about $28-$30 between the Civic Center and the airport. A flat rate of $28 between the airport and the city is available for groups of two or more passengers with no more than three pickup or drop spots within a given area.

Greyhound buses depart from their depot at the San Francisco Trans-Bay Terminal at First and Mission sts. Phone (415) 558-6789.

All rail service terminates in Oakland at 16th and Wood streets, and passengers are transported by bus to the Trans-Bay Terminal. Phone Amtrak at (800) 872-7245.

Approximately 25 oceangoing steamship lines and 10 cruise lines arrive and depart at the piers that radiate from the Embarcadero and southern waterfront.

Getting Around
Market Street, the main thoroughfare, runs diagonally through the city. Major east-west arteries are Bush and Pine, one-way streets with synchronized traffic signals; Bush goes into the city, Pine out. The numbered streets are in the

eastern section; the numbered avenues are in the western section. The many one-way streets make a street map helpful.

San Francisco intersections are subject to strict enforcement of the Anti-Gridlock Act, which prohibits pulling into an intersection when traffic makes it questionable that you'll get through before the light turns red. Motorists convicted of violating the act are subject to a fine of $100.

"The Boot" (also known as "The Denver Boot") is a metal clamp which immobilizes a car when attached to the wheel. This device is applied when 10 or more parking tickets have accumulated; it is removed only when all outstanding fines and a $50 de-booting fee have been paid. If the fines are not paid, the car may be towed within 72 hours.

The downtown speed limit, unless otherwise posted, is 25 mph—15 mph at blind intersections. Right turns on red are legal unless otherwise posted. Pedestrians using designated crosswalks **always** have the right-of-way. Rush hours are generally 7-9 a.m. and 4-6 p.m.

Parking

Parking can present a problem, but the downtown area has some large garages and many conveniently located smaller garages and lots. On-street meter parking is permitted in some areas. Garage fees downtown range from $1.50 to $5.25 per hour and from $13 to $25 per day.

On-street parking in hilly San Francisco is strictly regulated. In addition to posted tow-away zones, the color of the curb also governs parking. Red means no stopping, standing or parking whatsoever; yellow curbs indicate limited stops for loading and unloading passengers or freight (7 a.m.-6 p.m.). Passenger cars left unattended in downtown yellow or special loading zones are subject to heavy fines and towing.

White curbs, usually found at entrances to public buildings, allow short stops to take on or discharge passengers during the hours that the building is in use. Green curbs indicate 10-minute parking 9 a.m.-6 p.m. Blue marks spaces for use by the disabled. In several areas of the city, local residents have priority parking rights; be sure to check all posted regulations wherever you park.

It is illegal to park a vehicle on any grade exceeding 3 percent without effectively setting the brakes and blocking the wheels by turning them against the curb or by other means. The minimum penalty for this violation is $20.

When parking uphill, the front wheels must be "heeled," or turned out, so that a tire is resting securely against the curb. They must be "toed," or turned in, when parking downhill. If there is no curb you must use a block. The emergency brake must always be firmly set, and it is strongly recommended that you have your brakes thoroughly checked before driving or parking in hilly San Francisco.

Car Rentals

One of the largest car rental agencies in San Francisco is Hertz, (415) 771-2200, which offers discounts to AAA members. Other car rental agencies are listed in the telephone directory. All agencies maintain offices in downtown San Francisco and at the airport. Basic charges range from $26 to $50 per day; most companies offer unlimited mileage and special weekend rates. Some include standard insurance. Reservations are recommended.

Taxis

Taxi companies are listed in the local telephone directory. The standard rate for most rides is $1.80 per mile.

Public Transportation

Public transportation, which consists of buses and streetcars, is provided by the San Francisco Municipal Railway. The fare is 85c; ages 5-17, 25c; senior citizens and the physically impaired 15c. Fare includes a free transfer good for use on any two other vehicles within a 90-minute period; be sure to ask for a transfer when paying your fare.

Service on some lines is available 24 hours a day. The SFMR Passport offers unlimited usage each day and is $6 for daily travel; $10 for three days. Drivers do not carry change. For schedules, details on routing and other information phone (415) 673-6864.

Preserved as national historic landmarks and purportedly the only such on wheels, San Francisco's famous cable cars are painted in their original 1873 colors—maroon with cream and blue trim. The cable cars operate 6 a.m.-1 a.m. and travel three routes: Powell and Market to Fisherman's Wharf, Powell and Market to Victorian Park at Beach and Hyde, and on California from Market to Van Ness. The fare is $2; ages 5-17, $1; senior citizens and the physically impaired 15c.

BART (Bay Area Rapid Transit) connects San Francisco with East Bay cities, terminating at Richmond (north), Concord (east) and Fremont (south). On the West Bay side the terminus is Daly City, approximately 10 minutes south of the Civic Center area. BART operates Mon.-Fri. 4 a.m.-midnight, Sat. 6 a.m.-midnight and Sun. 8 a.m.-midnight. Tickets must be purchased from dispensing machines. Information is posted near machines; phone (415) 788-BART.

In addition passenger ferries link San Francisco with the North Bay area. The Red and White Fleet, (415) 546-2896, operates daily commuter service to Tiburon, Sausalito and Vallejo.

The Golden Gate Bridge and Highway Transportation District, (415) 332-6600, operates ferries to Larkspur and Sausalito. Larkspur ferry rates Mon.-Fri. are $2.50; ages 6-12, $1.90; senior citizens and the physically impaired, $1.60. Sat.-Sun. and holidays $3.25; ages 6-12, $2.45;

senior citizens and the physically impaired, $1.60. Sausalito ferry rates daily are $3.75; ages 6-12, $2.80, senior citizens and the physically impaired, $1.85.

Golden Gate ferries depart from the Ferry Building at the foot of Market Street and north of the San Francisco-Oakland Bay Bridge. Red and White ferries depart Pier 41, Fisherman's Wharf. For schedules phone the respective companies at the above numbers.

What To See

ACRES OF ORCHIDS— *see South San Francisco.*

ALCATRAZ ISLAND, in San Francisco Bay, was formerly a maximum security federal penitentiary and is now part of Golden Gate National Recreation Area *(see box page 159).* Once interned here were such notorious criminals as Al Capone, Machine Gun Kelly and Robert Stroud, the "Birdman of Alcatraz." A self-guiding trail, cellblock tour, slide show and special ranger programs are available.

Round-trip admission $5.50; over 62, $4.60; ages 5-11, $3. Audio tapes for cellhouse tours $3; ages 5-11, $1. Wear comfortable walking shoes and warm clothing. Tickets can be purchased for the same day at the Red and White ticket booth, Pier 41 at Fisherman's Wharf where the tour departs; advance tickets can be obtained by phoning (415) 546-2700; tickets must be picked up at Pier 41. One-month advance ticket purchases are recommended May-Sept.; 2 days in advance, rest of year. AE, MC, VI for advance tickets only. Phone (415) 546-2628.

ANSEL ADAMS CENTER (The Friends of Photography), 250 4th St., features five galleries with ongoing displays of work by Ansel Adams and changing exhibits that cover the history of photography. Allow 1 hour minimum. Open Tues.-Sun. 11-6. Admission $4; students with ID $3; over 65 and ages 12-17, $2; free to all first Tues. of the month. Phone (415) 495-7000.

ASIAN ART MUSEUM, in Golden Gate Park, houses jades, bronzes, ceramics, paintings and other objects illustrating the major periods and stylistic development of Asian art. Wed.-Sun. 10-5. Admission $5; over 64, $3; ages 12-17, $2; free to all first Sat. of the month 10-noon, and first Wed. of the month. Combined admission with de Young Memorial Museum on same day. Phone (415) 668-8921.

CABLE CAR BARN MUSEUM, Washington and Mason sts., contains models, photographs and relics of San Francisco's early transit system, including the first cable car, built in 1873. A 16-minute film on the cable cars and how they work also is shown. An underground viewing room enables visitors to observe the huge sheaves that guide the cable cars from under the street. Allow 1 hour minimum. Daily 10-6, Apr.-Oct.; 10-5,

rest of year. Closed Jan. 1, Thanksgiving and Dec. 25. Free. Phone (415) 474-1887.

★CALIFORNIA ACADEMY OF SCIENCES, in Golden Gate Park, includes the Morrison Planetarium, the Natural History Museum and the Steinhart Aquarium. Daily 10-5; extended hours in summer. Admission $6; over 65 and ages 12-17, $3; ages 6-11, $1; free to all first Wed. of the month. **Discount,** except over 65 and ages 6-17. Admission includes the museum and aquarium; planetarium extra. Phone (415) 750-7145.

Morrison Planetarium houses a 5,000-pound star projector—a one-of-a-kind instrument specially built for the planetarium—under a 65-foot dome. Star shows are given daily on the hour noon-4, mid-June through Labor Day; daily at 2, rest of year. Additional shows are given Sat.-Sun., holidays and Easter and Christmas vacations; closed during program changeovers, Thanksgiving and Dec. 24-25. Admission, in addition to academy admission, $2.50; over 65 and under 17, $1.25.

Special Laserium shows are presented Thurs.-Sun. evenings; phone for times and program titles. Laserium admission $5.50-$6.50; over 65 and ages 6-12, $4. For planetarium show information phone (415) 750-7141. For Laserium information phone 750-7138.

Natural History Museum encompasses the Wild California Hall, Simson African Hall, Hall of Gems and Minerals, Wattis Hall of Human Cultures, The Far Side of Science Gallery and the Earth and Space Hall, where a shake table enables visitors to safely experience a simulated California earthquake. Another exhibit hall, Life Through Time—The Evidence For Evolution, demonstrates evolution based on scientific evidence. There also is a Discovery Room with hands-on exhibits especially for children; open Tues.-Fri. 1-4, Sat.-Sun. 11-3:30.

Steinhart Aquarium houses some 14,000 aquatic animals, including octopuses, alligators, turtles, reptiles, sharks, anemones and seahorses. Dolphins and seals are fed daily every 2 hours beginning at 10:30; penguins are fed at 11:30 and 4.

CHEVRON U.S.A. INC., "A World of Oil," 555 Market St., traces the history of the petroleum industry through a film, dioramas, electronic displays and other exhibits. Mon.-Fri. 8-4; closed major holidays. Free. Phone (415) 894-7700.

★CHINATOWN covers about 16 square blks. and is bounded by Broadway, Bush, Kearny and Stockton sts. More Chinese live in this "city within a city" than in any other place in the world outside of China or Hong Kong.

Grant Avenue, the main thoroughfare, is lined with tearooms, shops, temples, Christian missions, Chinese schools, theaters and grocery stores. The Bank of Canton, 743 Washington St., has an unusual exterior.

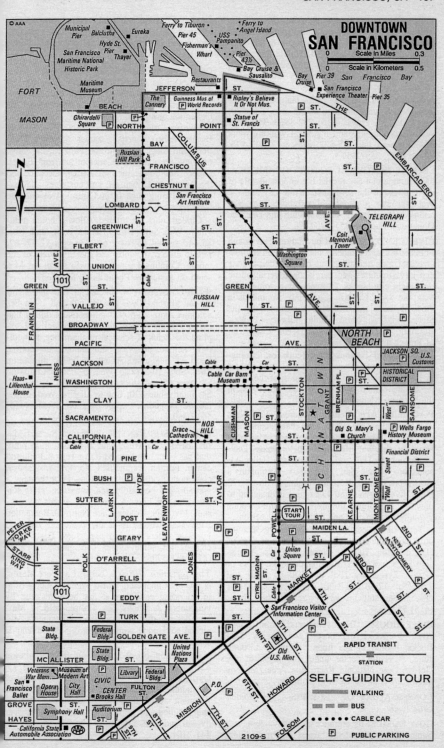

DOWNTOWN SAN FRANCISCO

The Chinese Culture Center, 3rd floor of the Holiday Inn at 750 Kearny St., displays Chinese art. Walking tours of Chinatown are by reservation only; phone (415) 986-1822. Heritage Tour $12; under 18, $2. Culinary Tour $25; under 12, $9. The center is open Tues.-Sat. 10-4; closed holidays. Free.

Chinatown Discovery Tours features the history, culture and traditions of the area. Fee $20; ages 5-11, $7. Phone (415) 982-8839. The Wok Wiz offers culinary and historical walking tours of Chinatown. Fee $15-$33; ages 6-12, $12-$25. Phone (415) 355-9657.

CHINESE HISTORICAL SOCIETY OF AMERICA, 650 Commercial St., recalls the important role of the Chinese in the settlement of the city and the West through a variety of exhibits. Tues.-Sat. noon-4; closed Jan. 1, Thanksgiving and Dec. 25. Donations. Phone (415) 391-1188.

CIVIC CENTER, bordered by Market, Hayes and Franklin sts. and Golden Gate Ave., is an impressive and monumental grouping of federal, state and city structures and parklands covering more than eight city blocks. Crowned by a dome taller than the U.S. Capitol, City Hall commands a view of the plaza, which is surrounded by the State Building, Main Public Library, Federal Building, Auditorium and the Health Center, all of French and Neo-Renaissance style.

The United Nations Conference on International Organization was held at the Civic Center in 1945; it culminated in the signing of the Charter of the United Nations on June 26, 1945, in the Veterans Memorial Building.

Performing Arts Center is across Van Ness Ave. opposite City Hall. The center comprises the Herbst Theater in the Veterans Memorial Building, the War Memorial Opera House, Davies Symphony Hall and San Francisco Ballet Association. The San Francisco Symphony's electro-pneumatic Ruffatti organ, with 7,373 pipes, five manuals and 132 ranks, is designed to play all the organ literature from pre-baroque through the romantic and contemporary periods.

Tours of the center are offered every 30 minutes from the Grove Street entrance of Davies Hall on Mon. 10-2:30; closed holidays. Admission $3, senior citizens and students $2. Tours of Davies Symphony Hall on Wed. at 1:30 and 2:30, Sat. 12:30 and 1:30. Admission $3, senior citizens and students $2. For reservations phone (415) 552-8338.

CLIFF HOUSE, Great Hwy. and Point Lobos Ave., overlooks the ocean and nearby Seal Rocks, habitat of sea lions September through June. A visitor center under the aegis of the Golden Gate National Recreation Area (see box page 159) is at the viewing platform.

CONSERVATORY OF FLOWERS— see Golden Gate Park.

COW PALACE, its entrance at Geneva Ave. and Santos St., is one of the largest indoor stadiums west of Chicago; it extends well across the city line into Daly City. Rodeos, trade and recreation shows and other programs are presented. Phone (415) 469-6000.

DE YOUNG MEMORIAL MUSEUM, on Teagarden Dr. in Golden Gate Park features American art from the Colonial period through the 20th century. Included are the John D. Rockefeller III Collection and paintings, sculpture, furniture and decorative arts by such artists as Winslow Homer, Albert Bierstadt, James McNeill Whistler, John Singer Sargent and Paul Revere. Also on view are exhibits of ancient art from Egypt, Greece and Rome; arts of Africa, Oceania and the Americas; British art; and costumes and textiles, including rugs from Central Asia and the Near East.

Guided tours are offered. Allow 2 hours minimum. Wed.-Sun. 10-5; Thanksgiving and Dec. 25. Admission $5; over 64, $3; ages 12-17, $2; free to all Sat. 10-noon and the first Wed. of the month. Combined admission with Asian Art Museum on same day. Phone (415) 563-7337.

★EXPLORATORIUM, entered at Bay and Lyon sts. or Marina Blvd. (eastbound) and Lyon St., contains more than 600 interactive exhibits that invite visitors to see, touch, hear, feel and explore the fields of science, mathematics, technology, animal behavior and human perception. Food is available. Allow 2 hours minimum. Tues.-Sun. 10-5 (also Wed. 5-9:30). Admission $8; over 65 and students with ID $6; ages 6-17, $4; family rate $20; free to all first Wed. of the month. Discount, except over 65. Phone (415) 561-0360.

FORT MASON CENTER, Buchanan St. and Marina Blvd., is a World War II embarkation point that has been transformed into a regional cultural center. Former warehouses are now workshops, classrooms, galleries and studios. Four theaters, a second-hand bookstore and numerous craft studios also are here. A variety of events are presented weekly. Golden Gate National Recreation Area headquarters is at the center at Bay and Franklin streets (see box page 159). Daily. Free; charges for some events and galleries. Phone (415) 441-5705.

The Jeremiah O'Brien, berthed at Fort Mason, is the only unaltered World War II Liberty Ship in operating condition; it has been restored by volunteers. A 5-hour Bay Cruise, held in May, includes a buffet luncheon and a Seamen's Memorial Ceremony commemorating World War II seamen.

Open Mon.-Fri. 9-3, Sat.-Sun. 9-4. Admission $2; over 59 and under 12, $1; family rate $5. During "Steaming" weekends (third weekend of the month, except May and Dec.) visitors can see the giant steam engine in operation and visit the ship's galley and slop chest. Admission $3; over 59 and under 12, $1; family rate $6. Phone (415) 441-3101.

Mexican Museum, Building D of the Fort Mason Center, has changing exhibits of works by Mexican and Mexican-American artists. Included are pre-conquest, colonial and folk pieces. Phone for information on specific exhibits. Wed.-Sun. noon-5; closed holidays. Admission $3, over 64 and students $2, under 10 free when accompanied by an adult; free to all first Wed. of the month. Phone (415) 441-0404.

Museo Italo-Americano, Building C of the Fort Mason Center, presents changing exhibits of Italian and Italo-American artwork. Wed.-Sun. noon-5. Admission $2, senior citizens and children $1. Phone (415) 673-2200.

FORT POINT NATIONAL HISTORIC SITE, reached by turning off Lincoln Blvd. at Long Ave. to the fort, is part of Golden Gate National Recreation Area *(see box page 159)*. Built by the U.S. Army and completed in 1861, Fort Point is similar in design to that of Fort Sumter, S.C. It was once the principal defense bastion on the West Coast. Tours and cannon-loading demonstrations are offered. Open daily 10-5; closed Jan. 1, Thanksgiving and Dec. 25. Donations. Phone (415) 556-1693.

GOLDEN GATE BRIDGE, over the bay, connects San Francisco with Marin County and the Redwood Hwy. (US 101). With an overall length of 8,981 feet and main span length of 4,200 feet, it is one of the longest single-span suspension bridges ever built. Its two massive towers are the world's highest bridge towers, at 746 feet above the water. A clearance of 220 feet allows passage of the largest oceangoing vessels. A crew of painters constantly maintains the bridge's distinctive coat of international orange. Toll is charged southbound; northbound free.

★GOLDEN GATE PARK is bordered by the Great Hwy. on the west, Lincoln Way on the south, Stanyan St. on the east and Fulton St. on the north. John McLaren, a Scottish landscape gardener and park superintendent 1887-1943, transformed a barren wasteland lapped by shifting dunes into this lush oasis with a dozen artificial lakes and a collection of trees and other plants of worldwide scope. Miles of roads, bridle paths and foot trails weave through the 1,017-acre park, which extends 3 miles from Fell and Stanyan streets to the ocean.

Among its many attractions are a buffalo paddock, a restored Dutch-style windmill, an equestrian center, trotting track, tennis courts, archery field, golf course, the polo field stadium and an outdoor music concourse, which offers concerts all year. Portals of the Past, a remnant of the 1906 earthquake, is on Kennedy Drive across from Speedway Meadows.

In the southeast corner of the park on Bowling Green is the Children's Playground with a restored 1912 Herschel Spillman carrousel. Boats can be rented at Stowe Lake, a moat ringing the steep slopes of Strawberry Hill, whose summit of over 400 feet is the highest point in the park. Certain roads are closed to automobile traffic on Sunday. Picnic facilities are available. Free guided tours of various parts of the park are offered Sat.-Sun., May-Oct. For times and locations phone (415) 221-1311.

Conservatory of Flowers on Kennedy Dr. was constructed in 1879. Seasonal displays include many rare plants and a wide variety of orchids. Two floral plaques that front the building are changed to depict current events and special themes. Daily 9-5. Admission $1.50; senior citizens and ages 6-12, 75c. Phone (415) 666-7017.

Japanese Tea Garden is beautifully landscaped with bridges, walks, ponds, miniature waterfalls, statuary and pagodas. The garden is spectacular in spring when the cherry trees bloom. Tea is served in the teahouse daily 10:30-5. Garden open daily 9:30-6. Admission $2; senior citizens and ages 6-12, $1. Free to all first Wed. of the month.

Strybing Arboretum, 9th Ave. and Lincoln Way, has more than 7,000 species of plants from

---

Golden Gate National Recreation Area

Golden Gate National Recreation Area encompasses both the rolling coastal hill country north of the Golden Gate Bridge and the diverse urban parklands strung around San Francisco's northern and western edges. For a description of the parkland north of the city see the separate place listing for *Golden Gate National Recreation Area.*

The southern extreme of the recreation area in San Francisco is Fort Funston, where hang gliders are commonly seen flying along the cliff. The long windswept strand of Ocean Beach links Fort Funston with the Cliff House, the Victorian gardens of Sutro Heights and Lands End at the northwestern shoulder of the city. The Coastal Trail threads through Lands End to China and Baker beaches and the abandoned coastal batteries just south of the Golden Gate Bridge.

The Golden Gate Promenade extends 3½ miles along San Francisco Bay and connects Fort Point below the Golden Gate Bridge with Crissy Field and Fort Mason. Alcatraz Island in the bay also is part of the recreation area.

An information center at the recreation area headquarters at Fort Mason is open Mon.-Fri. 9:30-4:30. For further information contact the General Superintendent, Golden Gate National Recreation Area, Building 201, Fort Mason, San Francisco, CA 94123; phone (415) 556-0560.

around the world. Within its 70 acres are demonstration gardens, a Mediterranean collection, a New World Cloud Forest collection, the Garden of Fragrance for the visually impaired and the Moonviewing Pavilion and adjacent waterfall. Guided tours are offered daily at 1:30, except major holidays. Gardens open Mon.-Fri. 8:30-4:30, Sat.-Sun. and holidays 10-5. A horticultural library is available; open daily 10-4, except major holidays. Free. Phone (415) 661-1316.

THE GUINNESS MUSEUM OF WORLD RECORDS, 235 Jefferson St., presents films, displays and participatory exhibits on superlative people and things. Daily 9 a.m.-midnight, July 4-Labor Day; Sun.-Thurs. 10-10, Fri.-Sat. 10 a.m.-midnight, rest of year. Admission $6.25; over 62, $5.25; ages 13-17, $5; ages 5-12, $3.25. AE, MC, VI. Discount, except over 62. Phone (415) 771-9890.

HAAS-LILIENTHAL HOUSE, 2007 Franklin St., is a furnished 1886 Queen Anne Victorian mansion. Tours Wed. noon-4, Sun. 11-5. Last tour departs 45 minutes before closing. Closed Jan. 1 and Dec. 25. Limited street parking is available. Admission $4; over 65 and under 12, $2. Phone (415) 441-3004.

JAPAN CENTER (Nihonmachi), bounded by Post, Geary, Laguna and Fillmore sts., is a multifaceted, 5-acre complex with many diverse cultural and commercial points of interest. The Miyako Hotel is within the center and adjoins the offices of the Japanese consulate. The Peace Pagoda, gift of the people of Japan, stands in the central plaza. Music, dance, tea ceremonies and martial arts presentations are given on many weekends in summer.

The area has several restaurants, art galleries, gardens, Japanese baths and shops offering the products of Japan (see Where To Shop). Underground parking is available.

JAPANESE TEA GARDEN— see Golden Gate Park.

LANDS END, overlooking the Pacific Ocean and the Golden Gate Bridge, is part of Golden Gate National Recreation Area (see box page 159). It has a memorial to the men who died on the USS San Francisco during the Battle of Guadalcanal, Nov. 12-13, 1942. The memorial is a part of the ship's bridge.

LINCOLN PARK, 193 acres at 34th Ave. and Clement St., contains San Francisco's memorial to the victims of the World War II Holocaust, created by American artist George Segal. The park also is noted for its encompassing views of the Golden Gate area and includes an 18-hole golf course.

LOMBARD STREET, between Hyde and Leavenworth sts., is often referred to as "the crookedest street in the world." In a series of S-curves, this one-block portion descends a 40-degree slope. Stairs are available. Campers and trailers are prohibited on this block of Lombard St.

★MISSION SAN FRANCISCO DE ASIS (Mission Dolores) is at 16th and Dolores sts. One of the oldest buildings in San Francisco, it was founded June 29 and opened Oct. 9, 1776, by Father Junípero Serra. The rough-hewn redwood roof timbers are still lashed together with rawhide. The altar was one of the most ornate among the missions; the original books and decorations were brought from Spain and Mexico. California's first book—Palou's "Life of Junípero Serra"—was written here. A small museum displays old manuscripts and mission relics.

The basilica next door, with its combination of Moorish, Mission and Corinthian styles, is a striking contrast to the mission's appearance. Daily 9-4; closed Thanksgiving and Dec. 25. Donations. Limited street parking is available. Phone (415) 621-8203.

MORRISON PLANETARIUM— see California Academy of Sciences.

NATURAL HISTORY MUSEUM— see California Academy of Sciences.

NOB HILL, in the vicinity of California, Sacramento, Jones and Taylor sts., was the center of luxurious living in the last half of the 19th century, when men who had made fortunes in railroading and gold mining built their homes in this territory. Today elegant apartment buildings and hotels occupy the hilltop.

Grace Cathedral (Episcopal), one of the nation's oldest, contains replicas of the bronze doors of the Baptistry in Florence by Lorenzo Ghiberti. Tours Mon.-Fri. 1-3, Sat. 11:30-1:30, Sun. 12:30-2. Donations. Phone (415) 776-6611.

NORTH BEACH, spread around Telegraph Hill and down to the waterfront, is noted for its art galleries, bookshops, international restaurants and informal approach to life.

OLD ST. MARY'S CHURCH is in Chinatown at Grant Ave. and California St. The 1854 church's interior was patterned after the Spanish church of California's first bishop, Joseph Sadoc Alemany. Sun.-Fri. 7:30-5:30, Sat. 7:30-6. Donations.

★OLD U.S. MINT, Fifth and Mission sts., was first opened in 1874 to serve the rich mineral districts of the West and the California gold rush. One of the few survivors of the 1906 earthquake, the mint is restored to its 1800s appearance.

A museum exhibits Western paintings and sculpture, gold bars and medals, coinage, assaying equipment, mining artifacts and a solid gold bear. One-hour tours, offered on the hour, include a film on the history of the building. Open Mon.-Fri. 10-4; closed holidays. Free. Phone (415) 744-6830.

PACIFIC HERITAGE MUSEUM, 608 Commercial St., displays changing exhibits chronicling the history and culture of immigrants from both sides of the Pacific Basin. Housed in the restored U.S. Subtreasury building, the museum also features an exhibit depicting the building's history. Allow 30 minutes minimum. Mon.-Fri. 10-4; closed major holidays. Free. Phone (415) 399-1124.

PALACE OF FINE ARTS, s.e. approach to the Golden Gate Bridge at Baker St. and Marina Blvd., is the last remaining structure of the 1915 Panama-Pacific Exposition. Preserved by the people of San Francisco, the temporary structure survived until 1962 when the Beaux Arts rotunda and colonnade were re-created in concrete from castings of the original ornamentation. The palace is now in a park with a lagoon where swans and ducks swim. Daily dawn-dusk. Free.

PRESIDIO, a 1,500-acre U.S. military reservation in northwest San Francisco, is headquarters of the Sixth Army. Established in 1776, it is one of the oldest military stations in America. All that remains of the original Spanish buildings is the Commandante's headquarters, now the Officers' Club. Miles of roads wind through the reservation. The higher hills offer spectacular bay and ocean vistas.

Presidio Army Museum, Lincoln Blvd. and Funston Ave., depicts more than 200 years of San Francisco area military history. Guided tours are available every Sat. by reservation; phone (415) 921-8193. Open Tues.-Sun. 10-4. Donations. Phone (415) 561-4115.

RANDALL MUSEUM, off Roosevelt Way on Museum Way, is a family museum with exhibits on science, arts and crafts, as well as live animals. Tues.-Sat. 10-5. Donations. Phone (415) 554-9600.

RIPLEY'S BELIEVE IT OR NOT MUSEUM, Fisherman's Wharf, displays the bizarre and unusual. Mon.-Thurs. 10-10, Fri.-Sun. 9 a.m.-midnight. Admission $7.25; over 62 and ages 13-17, $5.50; ages 5-12, $4. AE, MC, VI. Discount, except over 62. Phone (415) 771-6188.

ST. MARY'S CATHEDRAL, 1111 Gough St. on Cathedral Hill, is a modern structure of Italian marble. A baldachino of aluminum and gold, a large mosaic and a Ruffati organ highlight the interior of the cathedral. Mon.-Fri. 6:30-5, Sat. 6:30-6:30, Sun. 7:30-4:30, except during Masses. Donations. Phone (415) 567-2020.

SAN FRANCISCO ART INSTITUTE, 800 Chestnut St. at Jones St., presents artworks in two galleries, one of which contains a mural by Diego Rivera. The architecture of the institute effectively combines the traditional Spanish style of the original structure with the contemporary look of the new addition. Guided tours are available by appointment. Mon.-Fri. 9-5; closed holidays. Free. Phone (415) 771-7020.

"SAN FRANCISCO EXPERIENCE," 2 blks. e. of Fisherman's Wharf at Pier 39, Beach and Embarcadero, is a multimedia presentation on the history of San Francisco. Shows every 30 minutes daily 10-9:30. Admission $6; over 55 and active military, $5; ages 5-16, $3. Discount, except over 55 and active military. Phone (415) 982-7394.

SAN FRANCISCO FIRE DEPARTMENT MUSEUM (Pioneer Memorial Museum), 655 Presidio Ave., depicts more than 125 years of San Francisco Fire Department history through displays of equipment and relics. Guided tours Thurs.-Sun. 1-4. Free. Phone (415) 861-8000, ext. 0365.

SAN FRANCISCO MARITIME NATIONAL HISTORIC PARK, at the foot of Polk St. in Aquatic Park, includes a floating museum, the Hyde Street Pier and the Maritime Museum.

Hyde Street Pier, at the foot of Hyde St., displays ships dating from the late 19th century. The Balclutha is a three-masted square-rigged sailing vessel. It was launched in Scotland in 1886 carrying coal, wine and hardware from Europe for the Cape Horn trade and returned to Europe with California grain. Today it contains ship relics, marine paintings and photographs.

Anchored near the Balclutha are the Thayer, a coastal lumber schooner; the Eureka, the largest ferry operating on San Francisco Bay in her time; and the Eppleton Hall, a tugboat. The Balclutha, Thayer and Eureka can be boarded for self-guiding tours. Films and demonstrations on knot-tying and sea chanty singing are offered regularly. Open daily 10-5. Admission $3; ages 12-17, $1; over 62 free. Two-for-one discount. Phone (415) 556-3002.

Maritime Museum displays the history of water transportation from the 1800s to the present. Model ships and photographs are on display. Daily 10-5. Free. Phone (415) 556-3002.

San Francisco Maritime Library is located at Fort Mason, Building E. Open to the public Wed.-Fri. 1-5, Sat. 10-5, Tues. 5-8. Phone (415) 556-9870.

SAN FRANCISCO MUSEUM OF MODERN ART occupies the third and fourth floors of the War Memorial Veterans Building. Museum open Tues.-Fri. 10-5 (also Thurs. 5-9), Sat.-Sun. 11-5; closed holidays. Docent tours Tues. at 12:15 and 1:15; Wed. and Fri. at 1:15; Thurs. at 1:15, 7:15 and 7:45; Sat.-Sun. at 1:15 and 2:15. Admission $4; over 62 and under 16, $2; free to all first Tues. of the month. Reduced admission Thurs. 5-9, $2; over 62 and under 16, $1. Phone (415) 252-4000.

SAN FRANCISCO-OAKLAND BAY BRIDGE spans San Francisco Bay and links San Francisco with the East Bay cities. Including approaches, it is 8⅖ miles long, 4½ miles of it over navigable water. The east and west spans are connected by a double-deck tunnel through Yerba Buena Island. A toll is charged westbound only.

SAN FRANCISCO ZOO, in the s.w. corner of the city on Sloat Blvd. with entrance near 45th Ave., has more than 1,000 mammals and birds. Of special interest is the Primate Discovery Center, which features a nocturnal gallery and a discovery hall with participatory exhibits relating to primates. Koala Crossing is patterned after an Australian outback station and is the home of a growing collection of koalas.

Other attractions include Gorilla World, African Wild Dogs, Musk Ox Meadows and Penguin Island. Lions are fed Tues.-Sun. at 2. Open daily 10-5. Admission $6; over 65 and ages 12-15, $3; ages 5-11, $1; under 12 free when accompanied by an adult. Free to all first Wed. of the month. Phone (415) 753-7083.

Children's Zoo is within the zoo grounds. It includes nature trails, a barnyard, an insect zoo and live animals that may be petted and fed. Daily 10:30-4:30, in summer; Mon.-Fri. 11-4, Sat.-Sun. 10:30-4:30, rest of year. Admission $1, under 2 free.

STEINHART AQUARIUM— *see California Academy of Sciences.*

STRYBING ARBORETUM— *see Golden Gate Park.*

TELEGRAPH HILL, topped by a park, rises near the e. end of Lombard St. and affords a panorama. Coit Memorial Tower, built roughly in the shape of a firehose nozzle, memorializes the city's volunteer firefighters. The tower's observation deck is 542 feet above the bay. Daily 9-4, Mar.-Sept.; 10-5, rest of year. Closed Jan. 1, Thanksgiving and Dec. 25. Admission $3; over 64, $2; ages 6-12, $1. Phone (415) 274-0203.

TREASURE ISLAND MUSEUM, on Treasure Island, has displays depicting the history of the Navy, the Marine Corps and the Coast Guard in the Pacific. Included are exhibits on the 1939-40 Golden Gate International Exposition and the China Clipper Flying Boats. Allow 30 minutes minimum. Daily 10-3:30; closed Jan. 1, Easter, Thanksgiving and Dec. 25. Free. Phone (415) 395-5067.

USS *PAMPANITO,* at the end of Taylor St. at Pier 45, is a World War II submarine that saw action in the Pacific theater. Tours are self-guiding and require stooping through low passageways. Daily 9-9, mid-May to mid-Oct.; Sun.-Thurs. 9-6, Fri.-Sat. 9-9, rest of year. Admission $4; ages 12-18, $2; over 62 and ages 6-11, $1. **Two-for-one discount,** except over 62 and ages 6-11. Phone (415) 929-0202.

WAX MUSEUM, 145 Jefferson St. at Fisherman's Wharf, contains scenes of American presidents, world leaders and film stars, all in wax. Highlights include the Chamber of Horrors, Hall of Religion, King Tut's Tomb and the Haunted Gold Mine. Allow 1 hour minimum. Sun.-Thurs. 9 a.m.-10 p.m., Fri.-Sat. 9 a.m.-11 p.m. Museum $8.95; over 59 and ages 13-17, $6.95; ages 6-12, $4.95. Haunted Gold Mine $4.95; over 59 and ages 13-17, $3.95; ages 6-12, $2.95. MC, VI. **Discount,** except over 59 and ages 13-17. Phone (415) 885-4975.

WELLS FARGO HISTORY MUSEUM is in the Wells Fargo Bank Building at 420 Montgomery St. It contains a stagecoach, relics of the gold rush, nuggets, Western franks and stamps and other articles from 1848 to the present. Mon.-Fri. 9-5; closed bank holidays. Free. Phone (415) 396-2619.

WORLD OF ECONOMICS, at the Federal Reserve Bank, 101 Market St., has exhibits that explain economic principles, the U.S. economy and banking operations through cartoons, electronic interactive devices and computer games. A 20-minute movie is shown Mon.-Fri. at noon. Guided tours of the bank are available Mon.-Thurs. at 12:30 by reservation. Mon.-Fri. 9-4:30. Free. Phone (415) 974-3252.

What To Do
Sightseeing
Sightseeing tours are available by land, sea and air; particularly recommended if your time is

limited are the bus tours that touch briefly on the city's highlights. A list of events and sightseeing tips is recorded daily by the San Francisco Convention and Visitors Bureau; phone (415) 391-2001.

Bus, Limousine, Carriage and Train Tours

Many companies offer limousine tours of San Francisco, the Bay Area and Wine Country. See the telephone directory for information.

GRAY LINE offers a selection of full- and half-day excursions of San Francisco and the Bay Area. Day tours depart from Trans-Bay Terminal at First and Mission sts., and night tours depart from Union Square at Powell and Geary sts. The 3½-hour Deluxe City tour departs daily at 9, 10, 11, 1:30 and 2:30. There are additional departures May-Oct.

Daily tours include Muir Woods/Sausalito, Alcatraz and Bay Cruises, Wine Country, Monterey/Carmel, Yosemite and a variety of Night Life Tours. Reservations are required. Deluxe City fare $25, children $12.50. AE, MC, VI. **Discount.** Phone (415) 558-9400.

Boat Tours

Tours of the harbor operate from Fisherman's Wharf. The Red and White Fleet, (415) 546-2896, schedules 45-minute daytime cruises that depart from piers 41 or 43½ (see ad p. 162). The Alcatraz Tour, Tiburon and the Sausalito Ferry operate daily. Cruises to Marine World Africa USA in Vallejo depart from Pier 41. Tiburon ferry to Muir Woods departs from Pier 43½.

The Angel Island-Tiburon Ferry, (415) 546-2628, runs daily; times vary with the season. Angel Island State Park offers picnic facilities, beaches and hiking trails. The park includes the Angel Island Immigration Station, which received thousands of Chinese immigrants 1910-40.

The Blue and Gold Fleet, (415) 705-5555, has 1¼-hour trips leaving Pier 39 at frequent intervals daily all year. Fare $14; over 62 and ages 5-18, $7. **Discount.**

One-day Delta Riverboat Cruises between San Francisco and Sacramento (one-way cruise with return by bus) depart Pier 43½. Two-day riverboat cruises depart San Francisco on Saturday morning and return by boat on Sunday morning. Reservations are required for both cruises. Phone (916) 372-3690.

Hornblower Dining Yachts, (415) 394-8900, Pier 33 on the Embarcadero, offers dinner, lunch and brunch cruises aboard the motor yacht *City of San Francisco.* Live music is provided with dinner and brunch, and there are dance floors on two decks. Reservations are required. **Discount.**

Walking Tours

Perhaps the best way to get the feeling that instills such deep civic devotion in San Franciscans is to take a walking tour. The tour can be followed using this book's map of downtown San Francisco. Union Square is a good starting point. Stroll east on Post to Montgomery St. and make a sharp left. Here between Market and Sacramento sts. is "Wall Street West." Continue north on Montgomery to the Wells Fargo Bank Building, which has a collection of Western relics.

Return a quarter block to California St., turn right and continue up the hill on California to Grant Ave., passing Old St. Mary's Church. You are now entering Chinatown; turn right on Grant Ave., which is lined with many Chinese shops and restaurants.

At Columbus Ave. bear right to Union St., and, for the sake of your feet, take a number 39 bus (85c fare) to the top of Telegraph Hill and a breathtaking view from Coit Memorial Tower. Be sure to look west to view the section of Lombard St. known as "the crookedest street in the world." Descend via Lombard and return to Columbus Ave. for a block.

From Columbus make a right onto Taylor St.; 3 blocks farther is a fine statue of St. Francis by Bufano. At the end of Taylor St. is the Fisherman's Wharf area. Of interest here are the Ripley's Believe It Or Not Museum; the Guinness Museum of World Records; the Wax Museum; and the wharf itself, which boasts many fine seafood restaurants.

From the wharf walk a few blocks east to Pier 39 or a few blocks west to The Cannery; both have interesting shops, boutiques and restaurants. The Hyde Street Pier, a floating museum of ships including the *Balclutha,* an iron-hulled sailing ship, is at the foot of Hyde St.

Proceed south on Hyde St. and turn right onto Beach St. Continuing west on Beach, you will find the Maritime Museum on your right and Ghirardelli Square on your left. Do an about-face and return to the corner of Beach and Hyde sts., then take a cable car up one of the city's steepest hills and return to Union Square.

City guides provide free tours of historic Market Street, the Civic Center, North Beach, the Pacific Heights Victorians and other parts of the city; phone (415) 557-4266 for schedules and further information. Heritage Walks offers 2-hour tours of the Pacific Heights Victorians that cost $3. Tours of other areas also are available; phone (415) 441-3004.

Walking tours of the murals along Balmy Alley in the Mission District also are available. The tours depart Sat. at 1:30 from the Precita Eyes Mural Center at 348 Precita Ave. Fare $3; senior citizens and children, $1.

Driving Tours

Upon presentation of your AAA membership card, the California State Automobile Association can furnish a map with a suggested tour covering 49 miles of San Francisco.

Skyline Boulevard (SR 35) follows the scenic peninsula divide south of the city into the Santa

Cruz Mountains, affording simultaneous views of the bay and ocean.

NEAR ESCAPES offers two self-guiding audio tape tours. The first is a scenic driving tour of San Francisco. It includes Fort Point and Lombard Street—"the crookedest street in the world." The second is a walking tour of Chinatown that explores its alleys, temples and distinctive architecture. Maps are included. Both tapes available for $12 each by mail from Near Escapes Tapes, P.O. Box 19-3005J, San Francisco, CA 94119. Phone (415) 386-8687.

TRIPS ON TAPE is a self-guiding audio tape tour of San Francisco. It features nine excursions of major attractions by foot, ferry, car and cable car. Tapes available for $12.95 at the Cliff House Gift Shop, 1090 Point Lobos Ave., or by mail from The Rider's Guide, 484 Lake Park Ave., Suite 255, Oakland, CA 94610. Tapes for The Wine Country and Monterey available by mail only. Add $2 for postage, plus California sales tax. Phone (510) 653-2553.

Sports and Recreation

The recreational center of San Francisco is wooded Golden Gate Park, which offers facilities for all sorts of sports, including **hiking, bicycling,** boating, **horseback riding,** golf and tennis. The local telephone directory contains listings of bicycle rental agencies and riding academies.

The San Francisco Recreation and Park Department, (415) 666-7107, maintains 151 public **tennis** courts, eight indoor **swimming** pools and an outdoor pool open June through September.

Boating and **fishing** are popular on Lake Merced; rental boats with fishing gear are available, and supervised pier fishing is offered for children.

Municipal **golf** courses include the Golden Gate Park Golf Course (nine holes) in Golden Gate Park at 47th Avenue and John F. Kennedy Drive; Harding Park Golf Course on Lake Merced, Harding Road off Skyline Boulevard; Jack Fleming Golf Course (nine holes), Harding Road off Skyline Boulevard; and Lincoln Municipal Golf Course, between Lincoln Boulevard and Clement Street, overlooking the Golden Gate Bridge.

There also are private golf and country clubs that extend privileges to visitors who are members of recognized clubs in their hometowns; check with your own club.

Candlestick Park on Candlestick Point in southeastern San Francisco is home of the San Francisco Giants **baseball** team and the 49ers **football** team. The bay area's **basketball** team, the Golden State Warriors, plays in the Oakland-Alameda County Coliseum Complex in Oakland.

Where To Shop

Many of San Francisco's shopping areas would be attractions on their own without the shops and fashionable stores they offer. In general, the hours for downtown department stores are Mon.-Sat. 9:30-5:30; some stores are open evenings and Sun. noon-5. A few of the most popular areas are listed below.

At the foot of Stockton Street on the Embarcadero is Pier 39, a waterfront shopping and dining complex. Three stage areas present live entertainment, and the Palace of Fun Arts provides an amusement section for children. An information center is at the pier's entrance.

Embarcadero Center is bounded by Sacramento, California, Clay, Battery and Drumm streets. The four-tower complex houses the Hyatt Regency Hotel, shops, restaurants, offices and galleries; sculptures and tapestries are displayed throughout.

Chinatown, bounded by Broadway, Bush, Kearny and Stockton streets, has a variety of imports including fine ivory and jade items.

Japan Center is bordered by Post, Geary, Laguna and Fillmore streets. Three buildings (Kintetsu, East and Kinokuniya) contain malls that are lined with art galleries, antique stores, restaurants and many shops selling a wide variety of Japanese goods.

Union Square, with its flower stands, is the heart of the city's downtown shopping district; it is bounded by Powell, Geary, Post and Stockton streets. Around the square itself and extending a few blocks down each street are I. Magnin and Co., Lanz of California Inc., Neiman-Marcus and Saks Fifth Avenue, all elegant stores mainly devoted to apparel; Alfred Dunhill of London Inc., Brooks Brothers, Bullock and Jones, Gucci and Hermes; and The Emporium, Macy's and Nordstrom's department stores.

Also there is Gump's, famous for its selection of fine gifts, china and glass, as well as its jade collection; fine jewelers like Shreve and Co. and Tiffany and Co.; FAO Schwarz Fifth Avenue, the toy store for children of all ages; and bookstores and art galleries. At the corner of Post and Kearny streets, the Galleria at Crocker Center houses more than 50 specialty shops.

A section of Union Street between Van Ness Avenue and Steiner Street is an area of restored Victorian houses containing more than 50 restaurants and drinking establishments, as well as antique stores, gift shops, boutiques with men's and women's apparel from around the world, books and music and stereo equipment. This is the "main street" of historic Cow Hollow, serving residents of Marina and Pacific Heights as well as visitors.

THE CANNERY is on the e. side of the block bordered by Jefferson, Leavenworth, Beach and Hyde sts. Formerly a Del Monte fruit cannery, it houses specialty shops, art galleries and restaurants that are all linked by arcades, bridges and balconies.

FISHERMAN'S WHARF, with its picturesque sights and pungent smells, attracts millions of visitors annually. Along the waterfront are many excellent restaurants, markets, import houses and souvenir shops. Fresh seafood and sourdough bread are favorite buys. Parking is available in public lots along Beach, North Point, Bay and Francisco streets.

GHIRARDELLI SQUARE, between Beach, Polk, North Point and Larkin sts., is within walking distance of Fisherman's Wharf and the Cannery. The 2½-acre site comprises a complex of crenellated, white-trimmed brick buildings of the old Ghirardelli chocolate company, a woolen mill, apartments and other buildings that have been refurbished to house speciality shops, a theater, bakeries and international restaurants. Many "human statues" and mimes can be seen performing next to the square.

Where To Dine

San Francisco's skyview restaurants atop the tallest buildings offer enticing cuisines and captivating panoramas of this city by the bay. There are a multitude of atmospheres and locations from which to choose.

Places like the Carnelian Room, atop the Bank of America Headquarters Building; Cityscape, atop the San Francisco Hilton; the Crown at the Fairmont; the Equinox, revolving atop the Hyatt Regency; the Starlite Roof of the Sir Francis Drake; and Victor's, at the Westin St. Francis, provide rewarding panoramas of the city and bay. The Top of the Mark at Hotel Mark Hopkins serves cocktails and Sunday brunch with another sky-view panorama.

Among the city's most elegant restaurants are the Blue Fox, 659 Merchant St.; the Donatello, 501 Post St.; Ernie's, 847 Montgomery St.; and the French Room at Four Seasons Cliff Hotel, 495 Geary St. Chinatown offers fine Chinese dining in the Empress of China, Imperial Palace and Kan's, all on Grant Avenue. The Japan Center provides opportunities to sample Japanese cuisine. For formal or informal dining, Fisherman's Wharf is lined with many seafood restaurants and take-out stands selling seafood selections.

Reservations must always be made for San Francisco's better known restaurants; coats and ties are appropriate.

Nightlife

San Francisco's colorful nightlife has something for everyone. On any given night San Francisco vibrates with the sounds of jazz, pop and rock.

Popular music and dancing devotees will find both at the major hotels: the San Francisco Hilton or the Sir Francis Drake's Starlight Roof. The New Orleans Room of the Fairmont presents traditional and Dixieland jazz nightly. The Grand Hyatt San Francisco on Union Square has jazz piano nightly in Club 36. The Hyatt Regency of-

fers a jazz trio. Dancing is the main attraction nightly at Cityscape on the 46th floor of the San Francisco Hilton and at Oz at the Top in the Westin St. Francis.

Several clubs provide name entertainment. Some of them are the Great American Music Hall, Kimball's and Kimball's East (in Emeryville across the bay), Wolfgang's and Yoshi's in Oakland. Finocchio's, 506 Broadway, presents a lavish chorus line and colorful revues, all performed by female impersonators.

Comedy clubs provide an evening of laughter as well as an occasional opportunity to try your skill at making others chuckle. The Punch Line, 444A Battery St., is said to be the most elegant of the area's laugh spots. At Cobb's, 2801 Leavenworth Dr.; Holy City Zoo, 408 Clement St.; and the Improv, 401 Mason St., established comedy groups and new discoveries are spotlighted.

The colorful bars in San Francisco are numerous. North Beach and the downtown section are popular bar-hopping areas. The Buena Vista, 2765 Hyde St., where the cable cars turn around, is famed as the birthplace (in this country) of Irish coffee. To mix your nightcap or grog with a breathtaking view of San Francisco by night, it's hard to beat Cityscape at the top of the San Francisco Hilton, the Crown in the Fairmont Hotel atop Nob Hill or the Top of the Mark at Hotel Mark Hopkins.

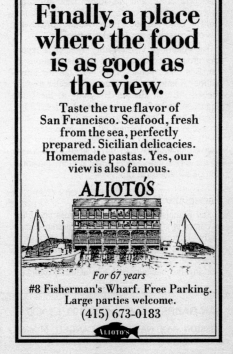

The *Date Book* supplement in the Sunday paper furnishes details of the week's stage, movie and music entertainment, as well as information on lectures and art exhibits. Also check the daily newspapers and the magazines available in most hotel lobbies.

Note: The mention of any area or establishment in the preceding sections is for information only and does **not** imply endorsement by AAA.

Theater and Concerts

The San Francisco Opera presents a full season of productions in the Opera House from mid-September into December. The San Francisco Symphony performs in the Louise M. Davies Symphony Hall from September through May; it also presents a Beethoven Festival in June and gives pops concerts in July.

Free Sunday orchestral and band concerts take place in Sigmund Stern Memorial Grove at Sloat Boulevard and 19th Avenue in summer and in Golden Gate Park all year. The San Francisco Conservatory of Music holds concerts by students and graduates at Hellman Hall; phone (415) 759-3477 for concert schedule and price information.

The San Francisco Ballet's repertory season is between late January and early May. The company also presents the Nutcracker Suite in December. All performances are at the War Memorial Opera House. Other principal theaters are the Curran, 445 Geary St.; the Orpheum, 1192 Market St.; and the Golden Gate at the intersection of Market and Taylor streets and Golden Gate Avenue. These feature Broadway hits or occasional pre-Broadway tryouts.

The American Conservatory Theater, a repertory group, presents plays at various locations in San Francisco; phone (415) 749-2228 for information. A uniquely San Francisco theater experience is "Beach Blanket Babylon" at the Club Fugazi, 678 Green St.; phone (415) 421-4222 for reservations. Community theater also flourishes in San Francisco. Various companies present revivals of stage classics, experimental plays and operas and musical reviews. The events sections of the city's newspapers carry current information on all theatrical offerings.

Especially for Children

San Francisco, with bridges to cross and hills to climb, is a fascinating city for children. Especially interesting activities include exploring Fisherman's Wharf, boarding the old vessels anchored at the Hyde Street Pier and Pier 43½, working the hands-on exhibits at the Explorato-

rium and visiting the San Francisco Fire Department Museum with its old firefighting relics. Aspiring cowboys will enjoy the Wells Fargo History Museum.

For children tired of sightseeing in the downtown confines, an active day in Golden Gate Park or at Ocean Beach is just the thing to restore spirits. Animal enthusiasts will enjoy Seal Rocks and the San Francisco Zoo and Children's Zoo. A harbor tour will thrill even travel-weary youngsters. And what young athlete wouldn't love to see a Giants' or 49ers' game in Candlestick Park?

Special Events

San Francisco's yearly calendar is packed with events ranging from gigantic exhibits of boats, cars, vacation equipment, furniture and antiques to small one-man sidewalk art shows.

The year begins with the East-West Shrine Game, held in January at Stanford University in Palo Alto. The Sports and Boat Show is a huge exhibition held in January at either Moscone Center or the Cow Palace. Following is one of the most colorful of all celebrations—Chinese New Year. Featuring a parade, complete with dragon, it is held in late February or early March in Chinatown. March's main event, the St. Patrick's Day Parade, is held on the Sunday nearest the 17th; it starts in the financial district.

In late March or early April the Junior Grand National Livestock Exposition and Rodeo is held at the Cow Palace. Mid-April brings the Japanese Cherry Blossom Festival to the city. The San Francisco International Film Festival has been held nearly every spring since 1956.

In May, Armed Forces Day is observed; the festivities include a parade, entertainment, arts and crafts and an open house at several nearby military installations. Also in May is the Bay to Breakers Footrace, involving as many as 100,000 runners. A parade from Market Street to the Civic Center is the highlight of the Lesbian-Gay Freedom Day Parade and Celebration in late June.

Medieval life is commemorated during the Renaissance Pleasure Faire, which is held in nearby Novato in September. The Festival of the Viewing of the Moon is observed in September as well. Mid-October presents the Columbus Day Parade and Fleet Week, and in late October the Cow Palace is the scene of the Grand National Rodeo, Horse and Stock Show. The Blessing of the Fishing Fleet is held the first Sunday in October.

SAN GABRIEL (B-6) pop. 37,100, alt. 430′

MISSION SAN GABRIEL ARCANGEL, Mission and Junipero Serra drs., was founded Sept. 8,

1771. The mission belltower, with its 200-year-old bell, was partially destroyed by an earthquake in 1812 and restored in 1815. The mission buildings are temporarily closed while undergoing restoration due to 1987 earthquake damage; they are expected to reopen in spring 1993. Grounds open daily 9:15-4:15. Admission $1. Phone (818) 282-5191.

SAN JACINTO (C-9) pop. 16,200, alt. 1,564'

SAN JACINTO MUNICIPAL MUSEUM, 181 E. Main St., contains items pertaining to the geologic and human history of Hemet and the San Jacinto Valley. Allow 30 minutes minimum. Daily noon-4; closed Jan. 1, Thanksgiving and Dec. 25. Free. Phone (909) 654-4952.

SAN JOSE (Q-3) pop. 782,200, alt. 94'

San Jose lies in the Santa Clara Valley between the Mount Hamilton Range on the east and the Santa Cruz Range on the west. Founded as Pueblo de San Jose de Guadalupe in November 1777, the settlement was established to raise crops and cattle for the nearby presidios of San Francisco and Monterey. In 1849, San Jose became the state's first capital—until 1851. The town claims as its oldest structure the Peralta Adobe at 184 W. St. John St.

The San Jose area, known for its table wines, has more than 50 wineries ranging from family-run establishments to large corporations. The primary harvest season is August through October. Festivals, concerts and other events celebrating viticulture are held April through October.

San Jose's Events Hotline is answered Mon.-Fri. 8:30-5 at (408) 295-2265, ext. 411, with a touchtone phone or (408) 295-9600 with a rotary or pulse phone. The Santa Clara County Transit System offers transportation to the various local wineries.

Self-guiding tours: Visitor packets and maps for driving tours of San Jose and vicinity are offered by the San Jose Convention/Visitors Bureau, 333 W. San Carlos St., Suite 1000, San Jose, CA 95110; phone (408) 295-9600. Open Mon.-Fri. 8-5.

Shopping Areas: The San Jose Flea Market, 12000 Berryessa Rd., is a 120-acre facility that features thousands of booths and 35 restaurants. An average of 80,000 people visit the market on a sunny weekend. Open Wed.-Sun. dawn-dusk; phone (408) 453-1110. *See ad.*

ALUM ROCK PARK, 776 acres in the foothills, is e. of US 101 on Alum Rock Ave. (SR 130). The park contains picnic facilities, mineral springs, marked trails and the Youth Science Institute. Dogs are not permitted. Allow 30 minutes minimum. Park open 8 a.m. until 30 minutes after dusk. Institute open Tues.-Fri. 9-4:30, Sat.-Sun. and holidays noon-4:30. Parking $2 per car Sat.-Sun. and holidays; free at other times. Museum admission 50c; under 16, 10c. Phone (408) 259-5477.

AMERICAN MUSEUM OF QUILTS AND TEXTILES is at 766 S. Second St. The museum houses a permanent collection of handwork; changing exhibits display fine examples of the art. Allow 30 minutes minimum. Tues.-Sat. 10-4; closed holidays. Free. Phone (408) 971-0323.

CHILDREN'S DISCOVERY MUSEUM OF SAN JOSE, intersection of Woz Way and Auzerais St., offers interactive exhibits and programs that lead children to discoveries about themselves and the world around them. Guadalupe Park surrounds the museum and has picnic facilities. Tues.-Sat. 10-5, Sun. noon-5. Admission $6, senior citizens and ages 4-18, $3; under 13 must be accompanied by an adult. Phone (408) 298-5437.

KELLEY PARK, Senter and Story rds., contains some of the city's most popular attractions. Entrance fee $3 per private vehicle in summer and Sat.-Sun. and holidays.

Happy Hollow, 1300 Senter Rd., is a family park with a playground, riverboat replica, treehouse, rides and a zoo. Allow 1 hour minimum. Mon.-Sat. 10-5, Sun. 11-6, May-Oct.; Mon.-Sat. 10-5, rest of year. Combination ticket for playground and zoo $2.50; ages 65-79 and ages 2-14, $2. Rides 50c each. Phone (408) 292-8188 or 295-8383.

Japanese Friendship Garden and Teahouse features landscaping and lanterns representing Japanese culture. Visitors may feed the koi fish with food purchased in the garden. Food also is available for visitors. Daily 10-dusk. Free. Parking fee $3, June 1-Labor Day. Phone (408) 292-8188 or 295-8383.

San Jose Historical Museum, Senter Rd. and Phelan Ave., has 21 original and fully restored Victorian buildings, including a printshop, candy store, bank, hotel, doctor's office, firehouse, livery and home. There also are exhibits on early Indian, Spanish and Mexican influences on the Santa Clara Valley. Allow 1 hour minimum. Mon.-Fri. 10-4:30, Sat.-Sun. and holidays noon-4:30; closed Jan. 1, Thanksgiving and Dec. 25. Admission $2; senior citizens $1.50; ages 6-17, $1. Phone (408) 287-2290.

★**LICK OBSERVATORY,** on the 4,209-foot summit of Mount Hamilton, is about 19 mi. e. via narrow, winding Mount Hamilton Rd. (not recommended in bad weather). The observatory is a division of the University of California, Santa Cruz. Guides are available for the main building daily 1-5. Allow 2 hours minimum. A visitor gallery at the 120-inch telescope is open daily 10-5; closed Thanksgiving, day after Thanksgiving and Dec. 24-26. Free. Phone (408) 274-5061. **Note:** Food and auto services are not available nearby.

MIRASSOU VINEYARDS, 3000 Aborn Rd., offers tours Mon.-Fri. and Sun. at noon and 2:30, Sat. at 11, 1 and 3, and a tasting room Mon.-Sat. 10-5, Sun. noon-4; closed major holidays. Free. Phone (408) 274-4000.

MUNICIPAL ROSE GARDENS is on Naglee Ave. between Dana Ave. and Garden Dr. The gardens contain more than 7,500 plants. The peak of color is in May and June. Allow 30 minutes minimum. Open daily 8 a.m.-30 minutes before dusk. Free. Phone (408) 287-0698.

OVERFELT GARDENS, Educational Park Dr. and McKee Rd., has a self-guiding arboreal trail, wildflower path, camellia garden, fragrance garden and three small lakes. The 5-acre Chinese Cultural Garden contains statues, memorials and displays devoted to ancient Chinese architecture and culture. Allow 1 hour, 30 minutes minimum. Daily 10-dusk; closed Jan. 1, Thanksgiving and Dec. 25. Free. Phone (408) 251-3323.

RAGING WATERS, off Capitol Expwy. at Tully Rd. in Lake Cunningham Regional Park, is a 14-acre water-theme park with more than 25 water-slides and other aquatic activities. Boating, fishing, windsurfing and bicycle paths are available at adjacent Lake Cunningham. Allow 4 hours minimum. Daily 10-7, mid-June through Labor Day; Sat.-Sun. 10-6, day after Labor Day to mid-Sept., weather permitting.

Admission $15.50; under 42 inches tall $11.50; over age 60, $9.95; under age 3 free; re-duced rates after 3. Parking fee $1. MC, VI. **Discount,** except under 42 inches tall and over age 60. Phone (408) 238-9900.

★**ROSICRUCIAN EGYPTIAN MUSEUM AND PLANETARIUM,** on Park Ave. between Naglee and Randolph, has a collection of Egyptian artifacts, including mummies, sculptures, jewelry, and objects from daily life; a replica of an Egyptian rock tomb; Babylonian and Assyrian artifacts; and a contemporary art gallery. Allow 2 hours minimum. Tues.-Sun. 9-5; closed Jan. 1, Thanksgiving and Dec. 25. Admission $4; over 65 and students with ID $3.50; ages 7-15, $2. AE, MC, VI. **Discount,** except over 65 and students with ID. Phone (408) 287-2807.

Planetarium and Science Center is open Tues.-Sun. 9-4:15; closed Jan. 1, Thanksgiving and Dec. 25. Phone for show subjects and times. Admission $3; over 65 and students with ID $2.50; ages 7-15, $1.50. Under 5 not admitted to planetarium show. AE, MC, VI. **Discount,** except over 65 and students with ID. Phone (408) 287-9172.

SAN JOSE MUSEUM OF ART, 110 S. Market St., was built in 1892 by local architect Willoughby Edbrooke. The museum and nearby annex contain changing exhibits of contemporary art. Text panels and tape tours are available in several languages. Guided tours are available. Allow 2 hours minimum. Open Wed.-Sun. 10-5 (also Thurs. 5-8); closed holidays. Admission $4; over 65 and ages 13-18, $2; under 13 free; free to all on Thurs. Phone (408) 294-2787.

★**WINCHESTER MYSTERY HOUSE,** 525 S. Winchester Blvd. between I-280 and Stevens Creek Blvd., was designed to baffle the evil spirits that haunted Sarah Winchester, eccentric heiress to the Winchester Arms fortune and mistress of the house. With 160 rooms, 2,000 doors, 13 bathrooms, 10,000 windows, 47 fireplaces, blind closets, secret passageways and 40 staircases, the house is so complex that even the owner and servants needed maps to find their way.

Guided tours of the mansion last about 65 minutes. Maps for self-guiding tours of the gardens and grounds, with tapes narrating the points of interest along the route, are available. Also on the estate are the Winchester Historic Firearms Museum and the Winchester Products Museum, which features sporting equipment, knives, tools and other items. Allow 2 hours minimum. Guided tours daily 9-5:30; closed Dec. 25. Grand Tour of the mansion and gardens $12.50; over 64, $9.50; ages 6-12, $6.50. AE, MC, VI. Phone (408) 247-2101.

SAN JUAN BAUTISTA (G-3) pop. 1,600, alt. 200'

★**MISSION SAN JUAN BAUTISTA,** founded June 24, 1797, was the largest of the mission churches. In recognition of its importance, a set of nine bells once graced the chapel area; only three remain. It is the only mission with a three-aisle entrance to the altar. The mission has period furnishings, and the convent wing contains relics. It is still an active Catholic church. Fiesta is held in late June. Daily 9:30-5, Mar.-Oct.; 9:30-4:30, rest of year. Closed Jan. 1, Thanksgiving and Dec. 25. Donations. Phone (408) 623-4528.

★SAN JUAN BAUTISTA STATE HISTORIC PARK, on the plaza, includes the old Plaza Hotel, built in 1858 on the site of the old Spanish soldiers' barracks, and the 1840 Castro House, headquarters of the Mexican government and later the home of the Patrick Breen family, survivors of the ill-fated Donner party. Other attractions include the 1868 Zanetta House, gardens, a Spanish orchard, a livery stable with old wagons and a slide show on the history of San Juan. Allow 30 minutes minimum. Daily 10-4:30. Admission $2; ages 6-12, $1. Phone (408) 623-4881.

SAN JUAN CAPISTRANO (K-6)
pop. 26,200, alt. 130'

San Juan Capistrano is set in rolling hills between the Santa Ana Mountains and the sea. It has many old adobe buildings, and its restored 1895 Santa Fe Railroad station is now an Amtrak terminal.

★MISSION SAN JUAN CAPISTRANO, 2 blks. w. of the SR 74/I-5 jct., was founded by Father Junípero Serra on Nov. 1, 1776. The mission had three churches: the Great Stone Church, of which only ruins remain; its likeness, the new seven-domed parish church containing a 104-foot bell-tower; and Padre Serra's Church, dedicated in 1778 and used daily. The cruciform stone church, built 1797-1806, was one of the most ambitious and elaborately adorned of the mission churches. The earthquake of 1812 razed the tower and heavy roof.

Today the mission is most famous for the swallows that arrive every March 19, St. Joseph's Day, and leave October 23. These remarkably constant birds fly approximately 6,000 miles from Goya, Argentina, to nest and rear their young in San Juan Capistrano. By 1777, when a record of their return was first noted in the mission archives, ceremonies welcoming the swallows were already a village tradition.

A self-guiding tour of mission buildings and grounds features artifacts, work buildings, the padres' living quarters, the soldiers' barracks, an Indian cemetery, a kitchen and smelter. Daily 8:30-5. Admission $3; ages 3-11, $2. Phone (714) 248-2048.

SAN LEANDRO (P-2) pop. 68,200, alt. 59'

San Leandro is across the bay from San Francisco, on land that was granted to Joaquin Estudillo in 1842. Visitor information, maps and recreation brochures are available at the chamber of commerce, 262 Davis St., San Leandro, CA 94577; phone (510) 351-1481. The chamber is open Mon.-Fri. 9-noon.

CASA PERALTA is at 384 W. Estudillo. The 1897 casa is being restored to its 1920s appearance. Spanish tiles inside the fence relate the story of Don Quixote. Allow 30 minutes minimum. Fri.-Sun. noon-4; closed holidays. Free. Phone (510) 577-3474.

SAN LUIS OBISPO (I-3) pop. 42,000, alt. 230'

Founded as a mission in 1772, San Luis Obispo grew into a full-fledged town only after completion of the Southern Pacific Railroad in 1894. Today the city is accessible via US 101 and is known as the home of California Polytechnic State University.

One of San Luis Obispo's most attractive sites is Mission Plaza, a developed wooded creek and urban oasis that offers special events all year. Town happenings include the Mozart Festival in late July and early August and the Central Coast Wine Festival in August.

San Luis Obispo is part of a scenic 252-mile stretch of SR 1 to San Francisco. Continuing southward, San Luis Obispo provides access to an interesting 204-mile drive on US 101 to Los Angeles.

APPLE FARM, 2015 Monterey St., features a working millhouse on San Luis Creek. Visitors can watch a 14-foot water wheel that, through a series of pulleys and gears, powers a gristmill, ice cream maker and cider press. Tours are available. Daily 10-4. Free. Phone (805) 544-2040.

FARMER'S MARKET takes place on the 600-900 blocks of Higuera St. Each Thurs. evening from

6:30 to 9 the area is closed to traffic and something like a street festival begins. There are stalls of fresh produce from local growers as well as barbecue stands serving cooked food. Many retail stores remain open, and street entertainment includes bands, jugglers and puppet shows.

★MISSION SAN LUIS OBISPO DE TOLOSA, Chorro and Monterey sts., is often called "The Prince of Missions." Named for a 13th-century French saint, the Bishop of Toulouse, the 1772 mission is now a parish church. A museum contains Chumash Indian artifacts and memorabilia from early settlers. There also are gardens. Daily 9-5, mid-June to mid-Sept.; 9-4, rest of year. Closed Jan. 1, Easter, Thanksgiving and Dec. 25. Donations. Phone (805) 543-6850.

SAN LUIS OBISPO COUNTY HISTORICAL MUSEUM, 696 Monterey St. in the historic Carnegie Library building, contains exhibits covering local history from the Chumash and Salinan Indian periods to the present. Wed.-Sun. 10-4; closed major holidays and Dec. 24. Free. Phone (805) 543-0638.

SAN MARINO (B-6) pop. 13,000, alt. 566′

EL MOLINO VIEJO (The Old Mill), 1120 Old Mill Rd. off Oak Knoll Ave., is a former gristmill built by Indians under supervision of the padres in 1816 for Mission San Gabriel. It is now Southern California headquarters for the California Historical Society. A working model of the mill, photographs and changing exhibits of Californiana are displayed. Tues.-Sun. 1-4; closed holidays. Free. Phone (818) 449-5450.

★HUNTINGTON LIBRARY, ART COLLECTIONS AND BOTANICAL GARDENS, 1151 Oxford Rd. (also at Orlando Rd. and Allen Ave.), houses one of the world's great collections of rare books and manuscripts, including a Gutenberg Bible, the Ellesmere Chaucer, and Benjamin Franklin's autobiography in his own handwriting. The Huntington Art Gallery contains 18th-century British and European paintings, rare tapestries, porcelains, miniatures, sculpture and period furniture.

The Virginia Steele Scott Gallery of American Art displays paintings from the 1730s to the 1930s, as well as period furnishings. The botanical gardens cover 150 acres of the 200-acre estate and embrace 14,000 varieties of plants, shrubs and trees. Garden tours depart Tues.-Sun. at 1; self-guiding tour brochures are available. Tues.-Fri. 1-4:30, Sat.-Sun. 10:30-4:30; closed major holidays. Donations. Phone (818) 405-2141.

SAN MATEO (P-2) pop. 85,600, alt. 29′

San Mateo is a residential suburb of San Francisco. Central Park contains a lovely Japanese garden. The San Mateo-Hayward Bridge, constructed with five steel spans, is one of the longest highway bridges in the country. Bay Meadows Race Track features horse racing.

Note: Policies concerning admittance of children to pari-mutuel betting facilities vary. Phone for information.

COYOTE POINT MUSEUM AND BIOPARK, on Coyote Point Dr. in Coyote Point Park, is a modern structure of natural woods designed to blend with the surrounding park. Exhibits on four descending levels lead visitors along a series of ramps symbolizing the eastward flow of water from the Santa Cruz Mountains to San Francisco Bay and its westward flow to the Pacific. Displays include dioramas of local environments, a working beehive and other insect colonies. Hands-on and electronic demonstration stations stress man's impact on nature.

The museum has picnic facilities and scenic views of San Francisco Bay. Wildlife habitats feature reptiles, birds and mammals. An environmental hall contains visual displays and hands-on exhibits relating to the development of the ecology and geography of the bay area. Both open Tues.-Sat. 10-5, Sun. 1-5; closed Jan. 1, Thanksgiving and Dec. 24-25. Admission $3; senior citizens $2; ages 6-17, $1; free to all first Wed. of the month. Park admission $4 per private vehicle. Phone (415) 342-7755.

SAN MATEO COUNTY HISTORICAL MUSEUM, 1700 W. Hillsdale Blvd. on the College of San Mateo campus, illustrates local history and cultures through exhibits on lumbering, architecture, transportation and agriculture. The museum also has a research library. Mon.-Thurs. 9:30-4:30, Sun. 12:30-4:30; closed holidays. Donations. Phone (415) 574-6441.

SAN MIGUEL (H-4) pop. 800, alt. 620′

★MISSION SAN MIGUEL ARCANGEL, 801 Mission St. on the s. edge of US 101, is still a parish church. In good repair, the 1797 mission has many original decorations, frescoes and paintings. The vaulted corridor is noted for its arches. The mission holds a fiesta the third Sunday in September. Daily 9:30-4:30; closed Jan. 1, Easter, Thanksgiving and Dec. 25. Donations. Phone (805) 467-3256.

RIOS-CALEDONIA ADOBE is at 700 Mission St. The adobe served as an inn and stage stop 1868-86; it is restored and furnished in period. Wed.-Sun. 10-4; closed Jan. 1 and Dec. 25. Free. Camping is available for a fee. Phone (805) 467-3357 for adobe, (805) 549-5219 for campground.

SAN PEDRO (C-6) pop. 70,900, alt. 100′

With Wilmington and Terminal Island, San Pedro forms the Port of Los Angeles, one of the largest deep-water ports in the nation. Fort MacArthur, once a formidable coastal defense, overlooks the harbor; Cabrillo Beach lies south. Cruises to Catalina Island (see place listing) leave the Catalina terminal near the Vincent Thomas Bridge. Harbor cruises are available as well.

CABRILLO MARINE MUSEUM, 3720 Stephen White Dr., specializes in the marine life of Southern California. Displays include 38 seawater aquariums with sealife native to Southern California and a multimedia show. Seasonal grunion programs and whale-watching tours also are offered. Tues.-Fri. noon-5, Sat.-Sun. 10-5; closed Thanksgiving and Dec. 25. Free. Parking $5.50. Phone (310) 548-7562.

LOS ANGELES MARITIME MUSEUM, berth 84 at the foot of 6th St., contains local nautical memorabilia, including historical photographs of Los Angeles Harbor, ship models and assorted maritime equipment from the USS *Los Angeles.* The museum also houses a 21-foot scale model of the *Queen Mary* and a 16-foot model of the *Titanic.* Allow 30 minutes minimum. Tues.-Sun. 10-5; closed Jan. 1, Thanksgiving and Dec. 25. Donations. Phone (310) 548-7618.

★**PORTS O' CALL VILLAGE,** on the main channel of Los Angeles Harbor at the s. end of Harbor Frwy., is a picturesque area featuring restaurants, shops and entertainment. Daily 11-9; closed Dec. 25. Free. Phone (310) 831-0287.

Buccaneer/Mardi Gras Cruises offers 1-hour harbor cruises aboard a square-rigged sailing ship. Lunch and sunset dinner cruises also are available; reservations are required. One-hour cruise $7; under 12, $3. For information and reservations phone (310) 548-1085.

Los Angeles Harbor Cruises offers 1-hour cruises of the inner and outer harbor past supertankers, cruise ships, a Coast Guard station, Terminal Island and Angels Gate Lighthouse. Trips depart from the Village Boat House Mon.-Fri. noon-4, Sat.-Sun. and holidays 11-6; closed Thanksgiving and Dec. 25. Fare $7; ages 2-12, $3. Phone (310) 831-0996.

Spirit Cruises offers trips aboard a 90-foot motor yacht, an 85-foot schooner or a 50-foot cruise boat. One and 1½ hour cruises offered daily, June-Oct.; Sat.-Sun., rest of year. Three-hour whale-watching cruises are offered Jan.-Mar. Dinner cruises are available on Sat. evenings. Reservations are suggested. One-hour cruise $7; ages 2-12, $4. One and one-half hour cruise $10; ages 2-12, $5. Whale-watching cruise $15; ages 2-12, $7.50. Dinner cruise $37.50; ages 2-12, $24.50. Phone (310) 831-1073.

SAN RAFAEL (O-2) pop. 48,400, alt. 34'

North of San Francisco, San Rafael began as a village that developed in the early 19th century around the Mission San Rafael. It is now a residential area and the seat of Marin County.

CALIFORNIA CENTER FOR WILDLIFE is at 76 Albert Park Ln. off B St. The center treats and shelters injured animals until they are able to return to their natural habitat in northern California. Reservations must be made for tours. Allow 30 minutes minimum. Tues.-Sun. 9-4:30. Donations. Phone (415) 456-7283.

MARIN COUNTY CIVIC CENTER, just n. off US 101, was the last major project of Frank Lloyd Wright. The 140 landscaped acres include fairgrounds, theaters, a lake and water conservation garden with drought-resistant plants. Tours can be arranged by appointment. Allow 1 hour minimum. Mon.-Fri. 8:30-4:30; closed holidays. Free. Phone (415) 499-7407.

MISSION SAN RAFAEL ARCANGEL, 1104 5th Ave. at A St., is a replica built in 1949 on the approximate site of the original mission. Relics and old pictures are displayed in the gift shop. Allow 30 minutes minimum. Mon.-Sat. 11-4, Sun. 10-4. Free. Phone (415) 454-8141.

SAN SIMEON (H-3) pop. 100, alt. 20'

San Simeon lies on a scenic stretch of SR 1 that extends from San Francisco to San Luis Obispo.

★**HEARST SAN SIMEON STATE HISTORICAL MONUMENT,** off SR 1, contains the castle, guesthouses and 127 acres of the estate of William Randolph Hearst. The grounds and dwellings occupy La Cuesta Encantada (The Enchanted Hill), a 1,600-foot mountain overlooking San Simeon and the Pacific Ocean.

The main residence is a huge Spanish-Moorish building called La Casa Grande, where millions of dollars' worth of Hearst's art collection and antiques are displayed. Pools, fountains and statuary grace the landscaped gardens. Construction was begun by William Randolph Hearst in 1919. Even though he continued to build for the next 32 years, he still had not completed La Cuesta Encantada at his death in 1951.

The estate is open by tour only, daily 8-5, in summer; 8:20-3:20, in winter. Closed Jan. 1, Thanksgiving and Dec. 25. Four 1¾-hour tours are available.

Tour I conducts visitors through the gardens, one guesthouse, pools and the ground floor of the main building, where a Hearst home movie is shown. Tour II visits the upper floors of the main building, including Mr. Hearst's private quarters, his study, library, guestrooms and kitchen.

Tour III includes the guest wing of the main building, one guesthouse, gardens, both pools and a video on the castle's construction. The Behind the Scenes Tour (Tour IV) covers mostly the gardens and includes the wine cellar, dressing rooms, two levels of a guesthouse and both pools. Tour IV is offered Apr.-Oct. only. Evening tours cover highlights of the estate and feature a living-history program. They are available Fri.-Sat., mid-Mar. through May 31 and mid-Sept. through Dec. 31. First-time visitors should take Tour I.

Comfortable walking shoes and a sweater or jacket are advised, since part of each tour is outdoors. Photography without the use of supports or flash attachments is permitted. Visitor parking is in a lot just off SR 1. Buses provide transportation to the castle.

A visitor center at the foot of the hill has exhibits highlighting the lives of Hearst and the estate's architect, Julia Morgan. Visitors also can watch conservators doing restoration work. Daily 7:30-30 minutes after last estate tour returns; closed holidays. Free.

Day tours $14; ages 6-12, $8. Evening tours $25; ages 6-12, $13. AE, DS, MC, VI. Reservations are recommended all year and can be obtained by phone; cancellation fee $4.75. Forms for reservations by mail can be obtained by writing MISTIX, P.O. Box 85705, San Diego, CA 92138-5705. To charge by telephone, phone (800) 444-7275.

JACK SMITH'S HEARST CASTLE SHOW, in San Simeon Lodge, 3½ mi. s. at 9520 Castillo Dr., offers a 1½-hour slide presentation that augments the sights and information furnished on tours of the estate. Among the topics covered are William Randolph Hearst's family background, corporations the family controlled and the castle's reflection of Hearst's interest in art and architecture. A half-hour film featuring Marion Davies is shown before the slide show.

Allow 2 hours minimum. Wed.-Mon. 8 p.m., Apr.-Nov. Admission $4; over 65 and under 12, $3. Phone (805) 927-4604.

SANTA ANA (C-7) pop. 293,700, alt. 110'

Shopping centers, restaurants and tourist attractions can be found all around Santa Ana or all in one place at South Coast Plaza Village, a European-style marketplace at Bear Street and Sunflower Avenue.

GOODWILL INDUSTRIES, 410 N. Fairview St., offers tours of the rehabilitation center and workshop. Reservations are suggested. Mon.-Fri. 9-3; closed holidays. Free. Phone (714) 547-6308, ext. 301.

SANTA ANA ZOO AT PRENTICE PARK, 1801 E. Chestnut Ave., houses small mammals, tropical birds and primates; the Children's Zoo houses a variety of barnyard animals, reptiles and amphibians. There also is a playground. Food is available. Daily 10-5, Memorial Day weekend-Labor Day; 10-4, rest of year. Closed Jan. 1 and Dec. 25. Admission $2; senior citizens and ages 3-12, 75c; handicapped persons free. Phone (714) 835-7484.

SANTA BARBARA (J-4) pop. 85,600, alt. 33'

Resting on a narrow shelf between the Santa Ynez Mountains and the Pacific coast, Santa Barbara is one of Southern California's foremost vacation areas. An especially scenic approach to the city is by way of US 101.

Santa Barbara traces its history back to the earliest days of Spanish settlement in Upper California. In 1602, Spanish conquistador Sebastián Vizcaíno sailed into Santa Barbara Bay and named it for the saint who held that birthdate. A military fortress was established in 1782; the mission was founded 4 years later by Father Fermín Francisco de Lasuén.

Santa Barbara's heritage is evident in its many whitewashed, tile-roofed buildings and Spanish street names. The Santa Barbara Historical Society administers the 1862 Fernald House, a traditional upper-class Victorian home with many original period furnishings, and the 1854 Trussell-Winchester Adobe, which represents the intermingling of New England and adobe architecture at 414 W. Montecito St. Phone (805) 966-1601.

The city's Old Spanish Days Fiesta takes place in early August. The Santa Barbara Arts and Crafts Show, in Chase Palm Park between Cabrillo Boulevard and the ocean near Stearns Wharf, features the works of more than 300 artists and craftspeople and is held Sundays and holidays year round.

Shopping areas: Two major department stores, Robinson's and Sears, have locations in La Cumbre Plaza at State Street and La Cumbre Road. Paseo Nuevo, anchored by a Broadway and Nordstrom's, is a large shopping mall on State Street between Canon Perdido and Ortega streets.

ALAMEDA PLAZA, bounded by Micheltorena, Sola, Anacapa and Garden sts., has picnic areas, playgrounds and more than 70 species of trees.

ALICE KECK PARK MEMORIAL GARDEN, bounded by Arrelaga, Garden, Santa Barbara and Micheltorena sts., contains a pond and a 4½-acre botanical garden landscaped with a variety of native ground covers, trees, shrubs and flowers. Daily 24 hours. Free.

BOTANIC GARDEN, 1212 Mission Canyon Rd., consists of 65 acres devoted to native California trees, flowers, shrubs and cactuses. Daily 8-dusk; guided tours daily at 2, also Thurs. and Sat.-Sun. at 10:30. Admission $3; senior citizens and ages 13-18, $2; ages 5-12, $1; family rate $8. Phone (805) 682-4726.

★COUNTY COURTHOUSE, 1100 Anacapa St., built in 1929, is a fine example of Spanish-Moorish-style architecture. Murals and Tunisian tile decorate the interior. Guided tours daily at 2 (also Wed. and Fri. at 10:30), in summer; Tues.-Sat. at 2 (also Wed. and Fri. at 10:30), rest of year. Open Mon.-Fri. 8-5, Sat.-Sun. 9-5; closed Dec. 25. Free. Phone (805) 962-6464.

EL PRESIDIO DE SANTA BARBARA STATE HISTORIC PARK, 122-129 E. Cañon Perdido, is the site of the 1782 Spanish outpost that first brought settlers to the area. Historic buildings within the park include the 1788 El Cuartel, the second-oldest surviving structure in California; the restored Canedo Adobe; the reconstructed Padre's Quarters; the chapel; and the Comandante's office, now under reconstruction.

Slide show and tours are available on request. Daily 10:30-4:30; closed Easter, Thanksgiving and Dec. 25. Free. Phone (805) 965-0093.

HISTORIC ADOBES are colorful reminders of the city's past. The 1828 Casa de la Guerra, 15 E. de la Guerra St., is part of El Paseo, a restoration. The 1817 Casa Covarrubias, 715 Santa Barbara St., is believed to have been used briefly as headquarters by the last Mexican governor of California, Pío Pico. The 1836 Historic Adobe, next to the Covarrubias, serves as the office of the Rancheros Visitadores. The 1826 Hill-Carrillo Adobe is at 11-15 E. Carrillo St.

HISTORICAL MUSEUM, 136 E. de la Guerra, is administered by the Santa Barbara Historical Society and has a library and local historical exhibits. Guided tours are conducted Wed. and Sat.-Sun. at 1:30. Allow 30 minutes minimum. Museum open Tues.-Sat. 10-5, Sun. noon-5; closed Jan. 1, Thanksgiving and Dec. 25. Library open Tues.-Fri. 10-4. Donations. Phone (805) 966-1601.

★**MISSION SANTA BARBARA** is at E. Los Olivos and Laguna sts. Called "Queen of the Missions," Mission Santa Barbara was founded on Dec. 4, 1786. Completed in 1820, it is one of the best preserved of the missions. The Little Fiesta is held in August. Daily 9-5; closed Easter, Thanksgiving and Dec. 25. Admission $2, under 16 free. Phone (805) 682-4149.

★**SANTA BARBARA MUSEUM OF ART,** 1130 State St., displays American, Asian and 19th-century French art; 20th-century works; Greek and Roman antiquities; and a major photographic collection. Tours Tues.-Sun. at 1. Museum open Tues.-Wed. and Fri.-Sat. 11-5, Thurs. 11-9, Sun. noon-5; closed Jan. 1, Thanksgiving and Dec. 25. Admission $3; over 65, $2.50; ages 6-16, $1.50; free to all Thurs. and first Sun. of the month. **Discount.** Phone (805) 963-4364.

SANTA BARBARA MUSEUM OF NATURAL HISTORY, 2559 Puesta del Sol Rd., houses exhibits on early American Indian tribes, as well as animals, birds, plants, minerals, gems and geology. For special exhibit and planetarium show information phone (805) 682-4334. Open Mon.-Sat. 9-5, Sun. and holidays 10-5; closed Jan. 1, Thanksgiving and Dec. 25. Admission $3; senior citizens and ages 13-17, $2; under 13, $1; free to all on Wed. Phone (805) 682-4711.

SANTA BARBARA ZOOLOGICAL GARDENS, a 40-acre park at 500 Ninos Dr., has more than 60 exhibits displaying exotic animals in natural habitats, as well as picnic areas, a playground and a

miniature train. Daily 9-6, mid-June through Labor Day; 10-5, rest of year. Closed Thanksgiving and Dec. 25. Admission $5; senior citizens and ages 2-12, $3. Train rides $1. Phone (805) 962-5339.

STEARNS WHARF, a landmark in Santa Barbara, was built in 1872 to serve cargo and passenger ships. In the 1930s it was the departure point for people trying to get aboard floating casinos. Today the wharf is the site of specialty shops, restaurants, a small museum and a fishing pier. It also affords excellent views of the harbor and the mountains behind Santa Barbara.

Sea Center, at the wharf, features a life-size model of a California gray whale and her calf. Through models, aquariums, photographs and a touch tank, this small museum gives a comprehensive introduction to the marine and bird life of the Santa Barbara Channel. Museum open daily 10-5; touch tank open Tues.-Sun. noon-4. Closed Jan. 1, Thanksgiving and Dec. 25. Admission $2; over 55, $1.50; under 17, $1. Phone (805) 962-0885.

UNIVERSITY OF CALIFORNIA AT SANTA BARBARA, 2 mi. s. off US 101, occupies 815 acres near the ocean. A major landmark is the 175-foot-high Storke Tower, which houses a 61-bell carillon heard twice each hour. In addition to traditional curricula, UCSB has an extensive Marine Sciences Institute. Admission Mon.-Fri. is by a $3 pass (includes campus map and parking fee), which can be purchased at the entrance gate. Free guided tours of the campus can be arranged; phone (805) 893-2485 or 893-8175.

★**SANTA CATALINA ISLAND—***see Catalina Island.*

SANTA CLARA (Q-3) pop. 93,600, alt. 88'

DE SAISSET MUSEUM, on the Santa Clara University campus, displays paintings, decorative arts, an early California history collection relating to Mission Santa Clara and changing exhibits. Allow 1 hour minimum. Tues.-Sun. 11-4; closed holidays. Free. Phone (408) 554-4528.

★**GREAT AMERICA,** on Great America Pkwy. between US 101 and SR 237, is a 100-acre family entertainment center. Through architecture and landscaping, boutiques, restaurants, craft shops and entertainment, it evokes North America's past in five major theme areas: Hometown Square, Yukon Territory, Yankee Harbor, County Fair and Orleans Place.

Among the amusement rides are the Columbia, a double-decker carrousel; a three-armed ferris wheel that stands 110 feet tall; a free-fall ride; a pendulum-like swinging ship; and five roller coasters—the Demon, Hot Ice, Skyhawk, Tidal Wave and the Grizzly wooden roller coaster. Another highlight is Rip Roaring Rapids, a 1,600-foot white-water raft ride. In addition, there are children's rides, an aerial gondola, a street trolley, narrow-gauge railway, water flume rides and an antique auto turnpike ride.

Restaurants offer international dining. Theaters present stage shows and films, and concerts are held in an outdoor amphitheater. Sidewalk entertainment, dolphin shows and game arcades also are featured. Sun.-Fri. 10-9, Sat. 10 a.m.-11 p.m., Easter season and late May-Labor Day; Sat.-Sun., in spring and fall. Hours and dates may vary; phone (408) 988-1776. Admission $23.95; over 54, $16.95; ages 3-6, $11.95. AE, MC, VI. Discount, except over 54 and ages 3-6. Phone (408) 988-1800.

★MISSION SANTA CLARA DE ASIS, on the Santa Clara University campus, was founded in 1777. The present building is a replica of the third mission, which was built in 1825. Relics include three bells given to the mission by the king of Spain. The original garden can still be seen; it is in full bloom April through May. Allow 30 minutes minimum. Mission open Mon.-Fri. 8-6; office open Mon.-Fri. 1-5. Free. Phone (408) 554-4023.

SANTA CLARITA (A-5) pop. 110,600, alt. 1,270'

★SIX FLAGS MAGIC MOUNTAIN, just w. of I-5 at 26101 Magic Mountain Pkwy., is a 260-acre entertainment complex with more than 100 rides, shows and attractions. Highlights include Tidal Wave, which plunges over a 50-foot waterfall; diving and dolphin shows; Ninja, a coaster suspended from an overhead track; Freefall, which gives the sensation of leaping from a 10-story building; Viper, a coaster with an initial drop of 188 feet, then vertical loops, a corkscrew and a boomerang turn; Psyclone, a classic wooden roller coaster; and the 384-foot Sky Tower.

An animal farm and Bugs Bunny World are especially for children. The Showcase Amphitheater offers name entertainment. The park also has restaurants.

Park opens daily at 10, mid-June to mid-Sept.; Sat.-Sun. and holidays, rest of year; closing hours vary. Closed Dec. 25. Unlimited-use ticket covering all shows and attractions $25; over age 55, $16; under 48 inches tall $14; under age 3 free. Discount, except over age 55 and under 48 inches tall. Parking $5. Free kennels are available in summer. Phone (805) 255-4111 or (818) 367-5965.

WILLIAM S. HART COUNTY PARK AND MUSEUM, 1¾ mi. n.w. of SR 14 via San Fernando Rd., embraces the home and 265-acre ranch of the Western movie star. The home, which sits on a hill at the end of a winding nature trail, contains original furnishings and Western art, American Indian artifacts and historical objects. American bison graze nearby. Picnic facilities are available.

Home open Wed.-Sun. 11-4, mid-June to mid-Sept.; Wed.-Fri. 10-1, Sat.-Sun. 11-4, rest of year. Tours are conducted about every half-hour. Park open daily 9-dusk; closed Jan. 1, Thanksgiving and Dec. 25. Free. Phone (805) 259-0855 or 254-4584.

SANTA CRUZ (G-2) pop. 49,000, alt. 20'

Santa Cruz, on the coast off scenic SR 1, is the site of one of Father Junípero Serra's 21 missions. A half-scale replica of the mission is on the grounds of Holy Cross Church facing the plaza. All that remains of the original mission,

---

California Missions

To secure its northern territorial claims in the New World, Spain ordered the creation of a series of Franciscan missions in California. Under the leadership of Father Junípero Serra, 21 missions and one *asistencia* were established 1769-1823, spaced about a day's journey apart along the northern extension of *El Camino Real*, the Royal Road.

Each mission had its own herd of cattle, fields and vegetable gardens, which were tended by Indian converts. For furniture, clothing, tools and other implements, the missions traded their surplus of meal, wine, oil, hemp, hides and tallow. Their attempts to "civilize" the indigenous population yielded mixed results: For the thousands of Indians brought under the wing of the church, thousands of others died at the hands of the Spanish or from their diseases. But the missions succeeded in other regards: Around them and their accompanying *presidios*, or military posts, grew the first permanent settlements in California.

After winning its independence from Spain, Mexico removed control of the missions from the Franciscans and subdivided much of their land among the Indians. During the ensuing years, neglect and earthquakes took their toll; many of the missions were severely damaged or destroyed. Subsequent restoration and reconstruction have revitalized these historic structures, and today US 101 roughly traces the route of the old El Camino Real.

built in 1791 and destroyed by the 1857 earthquake, are the ruins of the soldiers' barracks and part of the stone foundation. The chapel is open to visitors.

Also of interest are The McPherson Center for Art and History at the Santa Cruz County Art Museum, 705 Front St., which has family programs featuring exhibitions, films and lectures; the Santa Cruz County Historical Trust Museum at the McPherson Center, with exhibits and programs relating to local history; and the Surfing Museum on the ground level of the Mark Abbott Memorial Lighthouse on West Cliff Drive, displaying a collection of surfboards and surfing photographs from the 1930s to the present.

JOSEPH M. LONG MARINE LABORATORY, at the end of Delaware Ave., is a marine research and educational facility of the University of California. Examples of ongoing research, an aquarium, touch tank and 85-foot skeleton of a blue whale are on display. Allow 30 minutes minimum. Guided tours Tues.-Sun. 1-4; closed holidays. Donations. Phone (408) 459-4308.

MYSTERY SPOT, 2½ mi. n. on Market St., which becomes Branciforte Dr., is a section of redwood forest where the law of gravity seemingly does not apply. Allow 30 minutes minimum. Guided tours available daily 9:30-5. Admission $3; ages 5-11, $1.50. **Discount.** Phone (408) 423-8897.

NATURAL BRIDGES STATE BEACH, 65 acres on West Cliff Dr., has many tidepools for exploring. The migration of monarch butterflies can be observed from about mid-October through February. Allow 2 hours minimum. Open daily 8-dusk. Day use fee $6 per vehicle. Phone (408) 423-4609 or 688-3241. *See Recreation Chart.*

SANTA CRUZ ART LEAGUE GALLERIES, 526 Broadway, presents changing art exhibits in all forms of media, as well as performance space for theater, dance and music. Allow 30 minutes minimum. Galleries open Tues.-Sat. 11-5, Sun. noon-4; closed Jan. 1, Thanksgiving and Dec. 25. Donations. Phone (408) 426-5787.

SANTA CRUZ BEACH BOARDWALK, off SR 1, following signs to beach area, was established in 1868. A magnificent casino built in 1907 has been renovated to house an entertainment facility. The carrousel dates from 1911; the Giant Dipper roller coaster, built in 1924, ranks among the nation's most thrilling.

The boardwalk features Neptune's Kingdom Fun Complex, which includes an amusement park with miniature golf, games and historical displays. Allow 1 hour minimum. Open daily 11-10, Memorial Day weekend-Labor Day; Sat.-Sun. and holidays, rest of year. Closed Dec. 24-25. Boardwalk free; fees for rides range from $1.35 to $2.70 each or $16.95 for unlimited use.

MC, VI. **Discount.** Phone (408) 426-7433. *See ad p. A499.*

SANTA CRUZ CITY MUSEUM OF NATURAL HISTORY, 1305 E. Cliff Dr., contains displays of local Indian life, rocks, fossils, a touch tidepool exhibit and specimens of local flora and fauna. The museum sponsors a variety of programs, field trips and such special events as the annual winter Fungus Fair and spring Wild Flower Show. Allow 1 hour minimum. Tues.-Sat. 10-5, Sun. noon-5; closed holidays. Donations. Phone (408) 429-3773.

UNIVERSITY OF CALIFORNIA AT SANTA CRUZ (UCSC), corner of Bay and High sts., was founded in 1965 on a 2,000-acre hilltop of the Cowell Ranch overlooking Monterey Bay and Santa Cruz. Eight separate colleges surround a central academic core, connected by roads and walkways and situated among redwoods and meadows.

Obtain self-guiding tour maps at the main entrance information booth; student-led tours are available by reservation Mon.-Fri. at 10:30 and 1:30. Allow 3 hours minimum. Parking permits $3; limited metered spaces. Phone (408) 459-4008.

Agroecology Program Farm, reached by footpath from Coolidge Dr., is a 25-acre teaching and research facility. The farmorganic farm supports a variety of vegetable crops, flowers, herbs and fruit trees. Self-guiding tours are available daily dawn-dusk. Docents are available Thurs. at noon and Sun. at 2. Free. Phone (408) 459-4140.

Arboretum, on High St., ¼ mi. w. of the main entrance, maintains rare plant collections. Many of the specimens are not otherwise available for study in American botanical gardens. Hummingbirds and butterflies can frequently be seen. Open daily 9-5. Docents are available Wed. and Sat.-Sun 2-4. Phone (408) 427-2998.

Barn Theater, w. of the main entrance, is a converted horse barn that now functions as a 150-seat theater used by both campus and community groups.

Cook House, now the admissions office, is a former Cowell Ranch cookhouse. The well-preserved building also has served as the chancellor's office and headquarters for the campus police.

Performing Arts Center, Meyer Dr., contains a 537-seat stage theater as well as dance, drama and sound recording studios; a 231-seat concert hall; and specialized visual arts facilities. Shakespeare Santa Cruz, a month-long performing arts festival held in late July through August, features professional actors from throughout the United States and members of England's Royal Shakespeare Company. Phone (408) 459-2121.

SANTA FE SPRINGS (B-6) pop. 15,500, alt. 158'

HERITAGE PARK, 12100 Mora Dr., was developed on the site of an 1880s citrus ranch. Highlights of the area include the reconstructed carriage barn, now used to exhibit items reflecting a turn-of-the-20th-century lifestyle, a windmill, remains of the ranch house, a Victorian-style formal garden, an aviary and a plant conservatory. Picnicking is permitted. Food is available. Daily 7 a.m.-10 p.m.; carriage barn Tues. and Fri.-Sun. noon-4, Wed.-Thurs. 9-4. Free. Phone (310) 946-6476.

SANTA MARIA (I-4) pop. 61,300, alt. 217'

Santa Maria's scenic location can best be viewed by a drive along US 101. The city's largest mall is Santa Maria Town Center, at Broadway and Main Street; it has a Gottschalks and Sears.

BYRON VINEYARD & WINERY, 12 mi. s.e. at 5230 Tepusquet Rd., offers wines from estate-grown grapes or those purchased from vineyards in the Santa Ynez and Santa Maria valleys. Picnicking is permitted. Tours and tastings daily 10-4; closed major holidays. Free. Phone (805) 937-7288.

SANTA MARIA VALLEY HISTORICAL MUSEUM, 616 S. Broadway, depicts the early history of the area. Changing displays include artifacts from the Chumash Indian, Spanish rancho and American pioneer eras. The museum also has a children's corner. Tues.-Sat. noon-5; closed major holidays. Free. Phone (805) 922-3130.

SANTA MONICA (B-5) pop. 86,900, alt. 101'

Bounded by Los Angeles on three sides and by the Pacific on the fourth, Santa Monica is a popular ocean resort. Shops, restaurants and boutiques line sections of Main Street, Montana Avenue and Third Street. The Santa Monica Municipal Pier at the foot of Colorado Avenue also has shops and restaurants, as well as a fishing pier, carnival games and a restored antique carrousel with hand-carved wooden horses. The pier is a favorite filming location with Hollywood moviemakers.

Palisades Park lies along the clifftops overlooking Santa Monica's broad beachfront and affords scenic spots for picnicking. The visitor information center, 1400 Ocean Ave., is open daily 10-5, in summer; 10-4, rest of year. Phone (310) 393-7593.

Shopping areas: Santa Monica Place, bounded by Broadway and 4th, Colorado and 2nd streets, contains a Broadway, Robinson's and 163 smaller stores.

ANGELS ATTIC, 516 Colorado Ave., is a restored Victorian house containing antique dollhouses, miniatures, dolls and toys. Thurs.-Sun.

12:30-4:30; closed major holidays and the first week in Sept. Admission $4; over 65, $3; under 12, $2. Phone (310) 394-8331.

MUSEUM OF FLYING, 2772 Donald Douglas Loop N. near the s. end of 28th St., displays historic aircraft. Included are a World War I "Jenny" and the *New Orleans,* a plane that flew around the world in 1924. Open Wed.-Sun. 10-5; closed Jan. 1 and Dec. 25. Admission $5; over 65, $3; ages 3-17, $2. MC, VI. Phone (310) 392-8822.

SANTA MONICA HERITAGE MUSEUM, 2612 Main St., contains a series of restored period rooms dating from the 1890s through the 1930s. The house also has changing contemporary art exhibits and displays depicting the history and culture of Southern California. Thurs.-Sat. 11-4, Sun. noon-4; closed holidays. Donations. Phone (310) 392-8537.

SANTA MONICA MOUNTAINS NATIONAL RECREATION AREA (B-5)

The Santa Monica Mountains National Recreation Area, stretching west from Griffith Park in Los Angeles to the Ventura County line, embraces 150,000 acres of rugged mountains, steep canyons, rolling woodlands and 50 miles of beach. Within its boundaries are 70,000 acres of city, county, state and federal parklands. Major state parks include Leo Carrillo, Malibu Creek, Point Mugu, Topanga Canyon and Will Rogers; in addition there are state and county beaches and parks from Point Mugu to Santa Monica.

Among the many scenic crestline and canyon roads within the recreation area are Decker, Encinal Canyon, Potrero and Yerba Buena roads. Tuna Canyon and Saddle Peak roads provide coastal views, while Corral Canyon Road offers a view of the interior canyons and rugged crests.

Paralleling the Pacific Coast Highway (SR 1) and the Ventura Freeway (US 101), the Mulholland Highway traverses the Santa Monica Mountains from the Hollywood Freeway (US 101) on the east to the Pacific Ocean at Leo Carrillo State Beach on the west.

Note: A 10-mile section of Mulholland Highway from the San Diego Freeway (I-405) west to Topanga Canyon Boulevard is a graded dirt road that can be hazardous in rainy weather.

Recreation in the area includes hiking, picnicking, birdwatching, camping, swimming, snorkeling, fishing, surfing, bicycling and horseback riding. Rangers conduct nature hikes and educational programs; check with the park service for schedules. Reservations are required on some hikes. For information contact the Santa Monica Mountains National Recreation Area, 30401 Agoura Rd., Suite 100, Agoura Hills, CA 91301; phone (818) 597-9192, or (800) 533-7275 in Calif. *See Recreation Chart and the AAA California and Nevada CampBook.*

CHEESEBORO CANYON, off Cheeseboro Rd. in Agoura, has more than 2,000 acres of rolling oak woodland that is suitable for hiking, horseback riding and picnicking. Daily dawn-dusk.

CIRCLE X RANCH, 5 mi. off Pacific Coast Hwy. on Yerba Buena Rd., has 1,665 acres of trails. Camping, picnicking, hiking and horseback riding are available. Daily dawn-dusk. Fee for camping.

FRANKLIN CANYON RANCH, on Lake Dr. off Franklin Canyon Dr. n. of Beverly Hills, is a wilderness area amid a highly developed suburban neighborhood. Mountaintop trails provide both mountain and city vistas; streamside walks and grassy picnic areas also are available. Nature walks and educational programs are offered periodically. Food and water are not available. Daily dawn-dusk.

Note: Part of Franklin Canyon Drive is unpaved and can be hazardous in rainy weather.

PARAMOUNT RANCH, on Cornell Rd. off Kanan Rd. in Agoura, was owned by Paramount Studios and used as a Western movie set. Tour guides describe the history of the area and the set. Picnicking, hiking and equestrian trails are available; rangers lead hikes and conduct naturalist programs. Daily dawn-dusk.

PETER STRAUSS RANCH (Lake Enchanto), 30000 Mulholland Hwy., has a 250-seat outdoor amphitheater, cactus garden, information center, loop nature trails, ranger-conducted hikes and picnic tables. Concerts are held periodically at 2 on Sundays. Daily 8-5. Free.

RANCHO SIERRA VISTA/SATWIWA, on Potrero Rd. off Wendy Dr. s. of Newbury Park, is an area of chaparral-covered hillsides and large grassy fields ideal for picnicking, hiking and horseback riding. Rancho Sierra Vista also provides access to the extensive trail system of Point Mugu State Park. Rangers periodically conduct hikes, nature tours and naturalist programs. The Satwiwa Native American Culture Center presents exhibits and craft demonstrations every Sunday. Center open Sun. 9-5; ranch open daily dawn-dusk.

ROCKY OAKS, Kanan Rd. and Mulholland Hwy. in Agoura, consists of shady oak groves and a small pond. Popular pursuits include picnicking, hiking, birdwatching and horseback riding. Rangers conduct hikes and naturalist programs periodically. Daily dawn-dusk.

SANTA PAULA (J-5) pop. 25,100, alt. 274'
UNOCAL OIL MUSEUM, 1001 E. Main St., depicts the history of oil exploration in California through relics, photographs, computer games, videos and a working model of a drilling rig. Wed.-Sun. 10-4; closed major holidays. Free. Phone (805) 933-0076.

SANTA ROSA (N-1) pop. 113,300, alt. 164'
CHURCH OF ONE TREE/ROBERT L. RIPLEY MUSEUM, in Juilliard Park at 492 Sonoma Ave., was built from a single redwood tree. Once fea-

tured in Robert Ripley's renowned syndication, the museum has displays on the cartoonist's life and historical exhibits of Santa Rosa. Allow 30 minutes minimum. Wed.-Sun. 11-4; Mar.-Oct. Admission $1.50; senior citizens and ages 7-18, 75c. Phone (707) 524-5233.

DeLOACH VINEYARDS, 1791 Olivet Rd., offers tours daily by appointment. Picnicking is permitted. Allow 30 minutes minimum. Tastings daily 10-4; closed major holidays. Free. Phone (707) 526-9111.

LUTHER BURBANK HOME AND GARDENS is at the corner of Santa Rosa and Sonoma aves. The 30-minute tours describe the life and work of the horticulturist who introduced 800 varieties of plants and more than 200 varieties of fruits, vegetables, nuts, grains and ornamental flowers. The house contains original furnishings, memorabilia and a Burbank-designed greenhouse. Gardens open daily dawn-dusk. Home tours Wed.-Sun. 10-3:30, Apr.-Oct. Gardens free; home tours $1, under 12 free when accompanied by an adult. Phone (707) 524-5445.

SONOMA COUNTY MUSEUM, in the restored post office building at 425 7th St., exhibits photographs, paintings and other items pertaining to regional history and culture. Special programs and lectures are scheduled periodically. Allow 30 minutes minimum. Wed.-Sun. 11-4. Admission $1; ages 12-18, 50c. Phone (707) 579-1500.

SANTA YNEZ (J-4) pop. 3,300, alt. 600'
THE GAINEY VINEYARD, 1 mi. e. on SR 246, offers tastings and comprehensive tours of the winemaking process; picnic facilities are available. Daily 10-5. Free; fee for tastings. Phone (805) 688-0558.

SANTA YNEZ VALLEY HISTORICAL SOCIETY MUSEUM AND PARKS-JANEWAY CARRIAGE HOUSE is at 3596 Sagunto St. The museum has exhibits on the Chumash Indian culture and 19th-century life in the Santa Ynez Valley; the carriage house displays such antique vehicles as stagecoaches and carriages. Museum open Fri.-Sun. 1-4; carriage house open Tues.-Thurs. 10-4, Fri.-Sun. 1-4. Closed major holidays. Donations. Phone (805) 688-7889.

SANTA YNEZ WINERY, s. of SR 246 at 343 N. Refugio Rd., offers self-guiding tours, tastings and a picnic area. Daily 10-4. Free. Phone (805) 688-8381.

SARATOGA (Q-3) pop. 28,000, alt. 480'
Saratoga is the northern terminus of a scenic 38-mile stretch of SR 9.

HAKONE GARDENS, 21000 Big Basin Way, is a 15-acre park containing formal Japanese gardens and a bamboo park, specializing in Japanese bamboos. Allow 1 hour minimum. Open Mon.-Fri. 10-5, Sat.-Sun. 11-5; closed holidays. Donations. Phone (408) 741-4994.

VILLA MONTALVO CENTER FOR THE ARTS AND ARBORETUM is ½ mi. s.e. on SR 9, then 1 mi. s.w. on Montalvo Rd.; from SR 17 at Los Gatos take SR 9 n.w. 3½ mi. The estate was the summer home of U.S. senator and San Francisco mayor James D. Phelan. It now serves as a center for fine arts. The 1912 Mediterranean-style structure is set on landscaped grounds with a formal garden and trails to lookout points on the surrounding hills.

The villa regularly sponsors art exhibits as well as theater and concerts. The arboretum has approximately 400 species of plants and 85 species of birds. Allow 1 hour minimum. Arboretum open Mon.-Fri. 8-5, Sat.-Sun. 9-5; gallery open Fri. 1-4, Sat.-Sun. 11-4. Free. The garden sometimes closes for special events. Phone (408) 741-3421.

SAUSALITO (O-2) pop. 7,200, alt. 14'

A focal point for artists, Sausalito (originally *Saucelito*, meaning "little willow") is a pleasant blending of bohemian and marine influences. Its setting of hilly terrain plunging into the bay contributes to its popularity. Some of the town's narrow streets become broad stairs between buildings, and houses cling precariously to or are cantilevered from the hillsides. Locally made handicrafts are displayed and sold at the Village Fair.

Ferry service links Sausalito with San Francisco; the entire bay area is visible from Sausalito and from Vista Point at the north end of the Golden Gate Bridge. Sausalito is the southern terminus of a scenic 212-mile stretch of SR 1 that heads north along the ocean to Leggett.

BAY MODEL VISITOR CENTER, 2100 Bridgeway at the foot of Spring St., reproduces the tidal action, flow and current as well as the mixing of salt and fresh water in a 2-acre scale model of the San Francisco Bay and Delta region. The model operates only when an experiment is in progress. Audio tours, videos and interactive exhibits are available. For guided tour information, phone (415) 332-3871. Open Tues.-Fri. 9-4, Sat.-Sun. and holidays 10-6, in summer; Tues.-Sat. 9-4, rest of year. Free. Phone (415) 332-3870.

SCOTIA (C-1) pop. 1,000, alt. 164'

PACIFIC LUMBER CO., Main St., offers self-guiding tours of their redwood-processing plant. A logging museum features samples of former and current products, logging equipment, Scotia coins (produced for and used by employees), and photographs. Allow 1 hour minimum. Mon.-Fri. 7:30-10:30 and 12:30-2:30; closed holidays and weeks of July 4 and Dec. 25. Free. Phone (707) 764-2222.

SEBASTOPOL (N-1) pop. 7,000, alt. 78'

When apple blossoms reach their peak in late March and early April, signs marking a self-guiding tour are posted through a 35-mile section

---

High-Altitude Health

Temples throbbing, gasping for breath and nauseated, you barely notice the sparkling snow, the scudding clouds or the spectacular view below.

You might be suffering from Acute Mountain Sickness (AMS). Usually striking at around 8,000 feet (2,500 m) in altitude, AMS is your body's way of coping with the reduced oxygen and humidity of high altitudes. Among the symptoms are headaches, shortness of breath, loss of appetite, insomnia and lethargy. Some people complain of temporary weight gain or swelling in the face, hands and feet.

If your AMS is severe, you should stop ascending; you will recover in a few days. On the other hand, a quick descent will end the suffering immediately.

You can reduce the impact of high altitude by being in top condition. If you smoke or suffer from heart or lung ailments, consult your physician. Alcohol and certain drugs will intensify the symptoms.

A gradual ascent with a couple days of acclimatization is the best bet if you have time. On the way up, eat light, nutritious meals and drink water copiously. A spicy, high-carbohydrate diet might mitigate the effects of low oxygen and encourage you to drink more. But beware of those crystal-clear mountain streams where parasites might lurk. Boil such water at least 10 minutes.

Other high-altitude health problems include sunburn and hypothermia. Dress in layers to protect yourself from the intense sun and wide fluctuations in temperature.

Finally, after you unwind in the sauna or whirlpool bath at your lodgings, remember to stand up carefully, for the heat has relaxed your blood vessels and lowered your blood pressure. Then enjoy the view.

of Sebastopol. The Apple Blossom Festival in early April features a parade, crafts displays and entertainment. In mid-August residents celebrate apple-picking time with the Sebastopol Gravenstein Apple Fair, which includes arts and crafts, country music, locally produced food and wine and roving entertainers.

★SEQUOIA AND KINGS CANYON NATIONAL PARKS (H-5 & G-5)

One way to turn back the pages of time 3,000 years is to take a trip through Sequoia and Kings Canyon National Parks. The landscape is studded with the largest of living things, the giant sequoia trees (Sequoiadendron giganteum). Many of the trees are more than 200 feet high and some have trunks more than 30 feet in diameter. The parks, which abut, extend from the foothills of the San Joaquin Valley to the crest of the High Sierra. Mount Whitney, at 14,494 feet the highest point in the contiguous United States, is within Sequoia National Park.

Although the sequoias sparked the formation of these parks, magnificent forests of sugar and ponderosa pine, white and red fir and incense cedar also exist here. Sugar pines have been known to grow to a base diameter of 11 feet.

Its variable climate has endowed this region with a significant variety of plants. About 1,200 different trees, shrubs, plants and flowers have been identified.

Mule deer, black bears, marmots, chipmunks and squirrels are common. Raccoons, gray foxes and bobcats can be seen occasionally at night. Rarely seen, however, are the Sierra bighorn, mountain lion, pine marten, wolverine and fisher. About 150 species of birds, including the golden eagle, have been spotted in the parks. The lakes and streams support rainbow, brook, brown and golden trout.

Only trails penetrate the alpine wilderness of both parks; therefore, the beauties of the High Sierra or back country are available only to hikers and horseback riders. *See Recreation Chart and the AAA California and Nevada CampBook.*

General Information and Activities

Sequoia and Kings Canyon National Parks are open all year, although the more remote areas are inaccessible in winter. High mountain passes are seldom open to travel before July 1. The roads to Giant Forest, Lodgepole and the Big Stump entrance are open all year; however, the Generals Highway between Lodgepole in Sequoia National Park and Grant Grove in Kings Canyon is closed by heavy snow for brief periods during winter.

Bus tours are available daily, in summer. Accommodations and campgrounds in the higher elevations usually operate from late May to late October. Some facilities are open throughout the year.

Lodgepole and Grant Grove visitor centers, in Sequoia and Kings Canyon National Parks, respectively, are headquarters for special activities. Naturalists give illustrated talks or campfire programs several nights a week in summer at the Lodgepole, Giant Forest, Grant Grove, Cedar Grove and Mineral King amphitheaters. Schedules of programs and daily guided walks are posted on bulletin boards and in prominent public places. The parks' free newspaper, the *Sequoia Bark,* is available at park entrance stations and visitor centers.

A state fishing license is required for all persons 16 years and over; fee for residents $22.60, non-residents $57.75. A 1-day resident or non-resident license costs $8.15. Hunting is strictly prohibited.

Horseback trips over the hundreds of miles of backpacking trails are popular. Current information is available at the park visitor centers. Guided trail rides and pack trips or rental saddle stock are available from Grant Grove, Cedar Grove, Giant Forest at Wolverton, and Mineral King at the southern section of Sequoia. Pack trips also can be arranged from the Owens Valley area on the east side of the Sierra. Cross-country ski rentals and tours are available at Grant Grove and Wolverton.

HEADQUARTERS for both parks, which are administered jointly, is at Ash Mountain, on the Generals Hwy. 7 mi. above Three Rivers via SR 198. Phone (209) 565-3341.

ADMISSION to the park is $5 per vehicle, good for 7 days, or $2 per person by other means. An annual pass costs $15. Chains might be required at any time.

PETS are permitted only if they are on a leash, crated or otherwise restricted at all times. They are prohibited on trails and in buildings.

ADDRESS inquiries to the Superintendent, Sequoia and Kings Canyon National Parks, Three Rivers, CA 93271.

Points of Interest

Connecting the two national parks is the Generals Highway, a 46-mile-long scenic road that extends from SR 198 at Ash Mountain through Giant Forest to SR 180 at Grant Grove in Kings Canyon National Park. The highway reaches 7,643 feet at Big Baldy Saddle. From Ash Mountain to Giant Forest, the road is particularly difficult for motorhomes and large trailers. Vehicles over 20 feet are not recommended. Vehicle combinations over 50 feet are prohibited between Hospital Rock and Giant Forest.

ALTA PEAK (Sequoia), 11,204 feet high, is about 7 mi. from the Wolverton parking area; it can be reached on foot or on horseback.

CEDAR GROVE (Kings Canyon) is within the canyon of the South Fork of the Kings River.

Peaks rise nearly a mile above the stream, and spectacular views are available from road and trail. The level valley floor is especially well suited to leisurely bicycling. Cedar Grove also is a popular base point for trail trips into the high country. The area is inaccessible during winter.

GENERAL GRANT AND REDWOOD MOUNTAIN GROVES are in Kings Canyon. In Grant Grove is the General Grant Tree, third largest of known sequoias. It is 267 feet high with a circumference of 107.6 feet. The General Lee is the second largest sequoia in Grant Grove. Centennial Stump was cut in 1875 as an exhibit for the Philadelphia World's Fair, and Big Stump Basin, the result of early lumbering pursuits, is nearby. The Hart Tree, another very large sequoia, is in Redwood Mountain Grove.

Grant Grove Visitor Center is 3 mi. e. of Big Stump entrance station on SR 180. The center contains exhibits on the logging history of the sequoias and the wildlife and early Indian inhabitants of the region. Daily 8-5.

GIANT FOREST (Sequoia) is one of the largest sequoia groves. The General Sherman Tree is approximately 275 feet high and 103 feet in circumference, with a maximum diameter of 36½ feet at the base. The volume of its trunk alone is 52,500 cubic feet; it is the world's largest known sequoia.

Giant Forest has within its boundaries a lodge, cabins, stores and other facilities. Numerous trails lead from this location.

HEATHER LAKE (Sequoia), 4 mi. by trail from Wolverton, is the most easily accessible of the parks' alpine lakes. Two miles beyond is Pear Lake, in a barren granite basin.

THE HIGH COUNTRY extends from Coyote Peaks at the s. border of Sequoia to the n. boundary of Kings Canyon at Pavilion Dome. Trail trips are the only way to become acquainted with this rugged country. Mount Whitney is 70 miles from Giant Forest along the High Sierra Trail.

HOSPITAL ROCK (Sequoia) is 5 mi. beyond Ash Mountain on the road that leads to Giant Forest. Indian pictographs on the boulder mark the old headquarters of the Potwisha tribe of the Western Mono Indians. Exhibits are on the site of an ancient village.

LODGEPOLE VISITOR CENTER (Sequoia) is 4 mi. e. of Giant Forest on the Generals Hwy. The center has displays about the sequoias, geologic history and plant life. Daily 8-5, in summer; 9-5, in winter. For camping reservations phone MISTIX at (800) 365-2267.

MINERAL KING is 29 mi. e. of Three Rivers via SR 198 and a narrow, winding and partially paved road. Once a silver-mining area, it is now a peaceful valley retreat lying at an altitude of

7,500 feet beneath the towering peaks of the Great Western Divide. Rangers lead walks and campfire programs in summer. The area is unsuitable for RVs (trailers are not permitted) and is inaccessible in winter.

MORO ROCK (Sequoia), 2 mi. by road or trail from Giant Forest, is 6,725 feet above sea level and more than 6,000 feet above the San Joaquin Valley floor. A stairway leads to the summit.

PANORAMIC POINT (Kings Canyon), at the e. boundary of General Grant Grove, offers views of the High Sierra to the east and the San Joaquin Valley and Coast Range to the west. Other observation points—Park Ridge, Rocking and Balcony rocks, Point of View and Lookout Point—are within walking distance of Panoramic Point. The roads are narrow and winding; motorhomes are prohibited.

THARPS LOG (Sequoia) is at the end of Log Meadow, a mile by trail from Crescent Meadow; or by Circle Meadow and Congress trails. It is a cabin within a hollow sequoia log.

SEQUOIA NATIONAL FOREST

Sequoia National Forest, in central California at the southern end of the Sierra Nevada, extends from Kings River southward to the Kern River and Piute Mountains and westward from the Sierra Nevada summit to the brush-covered foothills of the San Joaquin Valley.

Giant sequoias, the Kern Plateau and the Golden Trout, Monarch, Jennie Lakes, South Sierra and Dome Land wildernesses are among the most popular attractions of this approximately 1,139,500-acre forest. South Fork Kings Wild and Scenic River, Kings River Special Management Area, North Fork Kern Wild and Scenic River, and South Fork Kern Wild and Scenic River also are among the attractions.

More than 50 campgrounds and picnic areas provide bases for fishing, swimming, boating, hiking, horseback riding, rock climbing and hunting. Whitewater rafting is popular on the Kern and Kings rivers. Swimming along the shoreline and limited boating are permitted on 87-acre Hume Lake. Fall color is particularly spectacular at Quaking Aspen, Indian Basin and Kern Plateau. Winter activities include cross-country and downhill skiing and snowmobiling.

For information contact the Recreation Officer, Sequoia National Forest, 900 W. Grand Ave., Porterville, CA 93257-2035; phone (209) 784-1500. *See Recreation Chart and the AAA California and Nevada CampBook.*

BALCH PARK is a 160-acre county park within Mountain Home State Forest and the general boundary of the Sequoia National Forest, 32 mi. n.e. of Porterville. At an elevation of 6,325 feet stands a beautiful sequoia grove. Two small stocked ponds are in the park.

BOYDEN CAVERNS is 22 mi. n.e. of Grant Grove on SR 180 within Sequoia National Forest. Guided tours, offered every hour on the hour, wind through a variety of underground formations. The temperature inside is a cool 55 F. Allow 1 hour minimum. Daily 9-6, June-Sept.; 10-5, in May and Oct. Admission $5; senior citizens $4.50; ages 6-12, $2.50. MC, VI. **Discount,** except senior citizens. Phone (209) 736-2708.

LAKE ISABELLA is one of Southern California's largest reservoirs, with more than 11,000 surface acres. With fishing, boating, camping and picnicking, the lake offers freshwater recreation well within a day's drive of either Los Angeles or Bakersfield.

SHASTA-TRINITY NATIONAL FOREST

Shasta-Trinity National Forest in northern California covers more than 2,100,000 acres, including portions of the Yolla Bolly-Middle Eel Wilderness Area and the Trinity Alps Wilderness. Mount Shasta, a dormant volcano with five living glaciers, towers to 14,162 feet.

Three impounded lakes—Whiskeytown, Shasta and Clair Engle—are within Whiskeytown-Shasta-Trinity National Recreation Area *(see place listing)*. Some 1,269 miles of trails lace the area, including 154 miles of the Pacific Crest Trail. The forest offers opportunities for lake and stream fishing, as well as hunting for waterfowl, upland birds, deer, bear and small game. For park reservations phone MISTIX at (800) 283-2267. *See Recreation Chart and the AAA California and Nevada CampBook.*

SIERRA CITY (D-4) pop. 100, alt. 4,187′

KENTUCKY MINE PARK AND MUSEUM, 1 mi. n.e. via SR 49 in Sierra County Historical Park, is on the site of a hard-rock gold mine. Guided walking tours go from the mine portal through an operable tin stampmill. Tools, photographs, documents and mineral samples displayed in the museum depict mining-camp life during California's gold rush era. Picnic facilities are available. Concerts take place Friday evenings July through August in the outdoor amphitheater. Phone for concert information.

Wed.-Sun. 10-5, Memorial Day weekend-late Sept.; Sat.-Sun. 10-5, in Oct., weather permitting. Tours $4; ages 13-16, $2. Museum only, $1. Phone (916) 862-1310.

SIERRA NATIONAL FOREST

Sierra National Forest is a gem set between two of California's crown jewels, Yosemite and Kings Canyon national parks *(see place listings).* The forest's 1,300,000 acres embrace almost all the land between these national parks—from the gently rolling foothills bordering the San Joaquin Valley to the jagged Sierra crest. Within the forest's boundaries is much of John Muir's famed "Range of Light." More commonly called the High Sierra, this is a landscape of craggy peaks, giant glacial stairways, and mountainside amphitheaters filled with lakes and open meadows.

How this rugged landscape came to be was a major issue among many 19th-century scientists. Yet it was Muir's remark that "tender snowflowers noiselessly falling through unnumbered centuries" came closest to the truth. Glacial ice gave these peaks their distinctive shape, a profile further refined by the swift streams and rivers fed by the yearly snowpack. Such major rivers as the San Joaquin, the Kings and their tributaries carved deep canyons and gorges into the forest floor.

Hidden deep within these watersheds are clusters of sequoias. One stand of these majestic trees is the Nelder Grove south of Yosemite National Park near Bass Lake; another is farther south near Dinkey Creek in the McKinley Grove.

Two major highways that penetrate the forest are SRs 41 and 168; the most accessible recreation areas lie along or just off these routes. Huntington and Bass lakes are two of the most popular destinations, offering camping and a variety of water sports. Other recreation areas, such as Florence Lake, Edison Lake, Redinger Lake and Pine Flat Reservoir are accessible from forest roads branching off SR 168.

The John Muir and Ansel Adams wilderness areas straddle the forest's eastern border and the Sierra crest. The former, with its snowcapped peaks, dense forests and numerous lakes, is one of California's largest wilderness areas. Highlights of this wild area include the John Muir Trail—a segment of the Pacific Crest Trail—and Humphreys Basin, with its countless lakes and views of Mount Humphreys, a favorite for world-class climbers.

Within the Ansel Adams Wilderness Area are the jagged peaks of the Ritter Range, one of the most dramatic mountain ranges in the national forest. Smaller areas include the Monarch, Dinkey Lakes and Kaiser wilderness areas. The John Muir, Kaiser and portions of the Ansel Adams wilderness areas are so popular that a quota system for visitors is in effect. Other recreation highlights include 1,100 miles of hiking trails, 411 lakes and five wilderness areas.

Although the forest has no visitor center, information about campgrounds and recreational opportunities is available at the district ranger stations and the forest headquarters in Clovis. Campground reservations, usually required for June, July and August at Huntington, Dinkey Creek and Bass Lake, can be made through MISTIX, (800) 283-2267. Downhill skiing is available at Sierra Summit Ski Area.

For more information contact the Forest Supervisor, Sierra National Forest, 1600 Tollhouse Rd., Fresno, CA 93612; phone (209) 487-5155 or

487-5456. *See the Recreation Chart and AAA California and Nevada CampBook.*

SILVERADO (C-8) pop. 800, alt. 1,800'

TUCKER WILDLIFE SANCTUARY, 7 mi. s. off Santiago Canyon Rd. at 29322 Modjeska Canyon Rd., is notable for its hummingbirds and native plants. An observation porch affords views of the area, and an attendant aids in identification. A nature center displays several small animals, live as well as stuffed and mounted, most of which are native to California. Nature trails wind through the 12-acre site. Daily 9-4; closed Dec. 25. Tours $3. Phone (714) 649-2760.

SIMI VALLEY (A-5) pop. 101,600, alt. 820'

RONALD REAGAN PRESIDENTIAL LIBRARY, 40 Presidential Dr., is a Spanish Mission-style structure built around a courtyard and set on a hilltop that affords a view of the surrounding countryside. Within the library's museum are photographs and memorabilia of President Reagan's life, gifts of state received during his administration, a replica of the Oval Office and a large section of the Berlin Wall. Open Mon.-Sat. 10-6, Sun. noon-6, in summer; Mon.-Sat. 10-5, Sun. noon-5, rest of year. Closed Jan. 1, Thanksgiving and Dec. 25. Admission $2; over 65, $1; under 16 free. Phone (805) 522-8444.

SISQUOC (I-4) pop. 200, alt. 440'

RANCHO SISQUOC WINERY, on Foxen Canyon Rd., offers tastings; picnicking is permitted. Daily 10-4. Free. Phone (805) 934-4332.

SIX RIVERS NATIONAL FOREST

Covering almost 990,000 acres, Six Rivers National Forest extends 135 miles south from the Oregon border along the west slope of the Coast Range; it is named for the Smith, Klamath, Trinity, Mad, Van Duzen and Eel rivers.

Many routes, including SR 96 along the Trinity and Klamath rivers northward from Willow Creek through the Hoopa Valley Indian Reservation, penetrate the forest. Much of the region is accessible only on foot or by horseback.

Trout, steelhead and salmon fishing and deer hunting are popular. For information contact the Office of Information, Six Rivers National Forest; phone (707) 442-1721, ext. 3523. *See Recreation Chart and the AAA California and Nevada CampBook.*

SKYFOREST (B-9) pop. 300, alt. 5,800'

SANTA'S VILLAGE is 1 mi. e. on SR 18. Highlights of the village include the Gingerbread House, Puppet Theater and bobsled, monorail and burro rides. Daily 10-5, mid-June to mid-Sept. and mid-Nov. through Jan. 2; Sat.-Sun. only, rest of year. Phone to confirm dates. Closed Dec. 25. Admission $9; over 65, $4.50; under 3 free. AE, DS, MC, VI. **Discount,** except over 65. Phone (909) 337-2481.

SMITH RIVER (A-1) pop. 2,000, alt. 69'

Although its namesake flows nearby, the town of Smith River is on the banks of Rowdy Creek. The river was named for Jedediah Strong Smith, an adventurer and trapper who explored the northwestern corner of California in 1828. Smith River serves the surrounding dairy country and supports a seasonal influx of hunters and fishermen. The Easter in July Lily Festival is held in mid-July.

SODA SPRINGS (D-4) pop. 300, alt. 6,768'

WESTERN SKISPORT MUSEUM, s. of I-80 at the Boreal Ski Area, has displays depicting the development of snow skiing as a sport. Exhibits date from 1850 to the present. Films are shown on request. Allow 30 minutes minimum. Tues.-Sun. 11-5, during ski season; Wed.-Sun. 11-5, rest of year. Free. Phone (916) 426-3313.

SOLEDAD (G-3) pop. 7,100, alt. 190'

MISSION NUESTRA SEÑORA DE LA SOLEDAD, 3 mi. s. on Fort Romie Rd., was founded in 1791. It consists of adobe ruins, a museum and a restored chapel. Allow 30 minutes minimum. Wed.-Mon. 10-4; closed Thanksgiving and Dec. 25. Donations. Phone (408) 678-2586.

★SOLVANG (I-4) pop. 4,700, alt. 480'

Danish in heritage, customs and atmosphere, Solvang is about 45 miles northwest of Santa Barbara in the Santa Ynez Valley. The town was established in 1911 by a group of Danish educators from the Midwest who were looking for a site on which to build a Danish folk school. Visitors delight in the traditional Danish architecture, windmills, gaslights and cobblestone walks. A Danish streetcar tours the town, drawn by two muscular blonde Belgian horses. Perched on many roofs are artificial nesting storks, considered good luck charms by the Danes.

Outstanding among the events in Solvang are Danish Days the third weekend in September and the Solvang Theater Festival, held in the outdoor Solvang Festival Theater from early June to mid-September.

Shopping areas: Solvang's distinctly Danish flavor pervades its roughly 300 stores, which sell

---

Long trips can tire you out! Be sure to stop every 2 hours for at least 10 minutes and get out of the car and stretch.

everything from hand-crafted furniture to freshly baked bread.

BALLARD CANYON WINERY, 1825 Ballard Canyon Rd., produces chardonnay, riesling and cabernet sauvignon. Self-guiding tours and tastings are offered; picnicking is permitted. Daily 11-4. Free. Phone (805) 688-7585.

CAREY CELLARS, off SR 246 at 1711 Alamo Pintado Rd., offers tours and tastings; picnicking is permitted. Daily 10-4. Free. Phone (805) 688-8554.

NOJOQUI FALLS COUNTY PARK, 6½ mi. s.w. on Alisal Rd., was named for a 164-foot-high falls that, after a sufficient rainy season, cascades over a mossy cliff. The park offers picnic facilities, a ballfield, volleyball courts, playgrounds and a trail to the falls.

★**OLD MISSION SANTA INES**, 1760 Mission Dr., contrasts with the town's Scandinavian motif. The mission was founded in 1804; at the peak of its prosperity in 1820, it owned 12,000 head of stock. The mission now contains a museum. Mon.-Fri. 9-5, Sat. 9-4:30, Sun. noon-5, May-Oct.; Mon.-Sat. 9:30-4:30, Sun. noon-4:30, rest of year. Closed Jan. 1, Easter, Thanksgiving and Dec. 25. Admission $2, under 16 free when accompanied by an adult. Phone (805) 688-4815.

SONOMA (N-2) pop. 8,100, alt. 84'

To proclaim California a republic, the Bear Flag was raised on June 14, 1846, in Sonoma Plaza; on July 9 it was replaced by the Stars and Stripes. The Depot Park Museum in the original town depot preserves the history of the California Republic through displays of 19th-century clothing and furniture.

BUENA VISTA WINERY is 2 mi. n.e. at the end of Old Winery Rd. Hungarian nobleman Count Agoston Haraszthy planted the experimental vineyards here, from which California's vast grape industry developed. A historical landmark, the winery has the oldest stone wine cellars in the state. Some huge eucalyptus trees can be seen.

The winery offers self-guiding tours, a tasting room, an art gallery and a historical presentation daily at 2. Picnicking is permitted. Allow 1 hour minimum. Daily 10-5; closed Jan. 1, Thanksgiving and Dec. 25. Free. Phone (800) 926-1266.

SEBASTIANI VINEYARDS, 389 4th St. E., has one of the world's largest collections of carved wood wine casks. Allow 1 hour minimum. Tours daily 10:30-4. Tasting room daily 10-5; closed major holidays. Free. Phone (707) 938-5532.

★**SONOMA STATE HISTORIC PARK** includes the Toscano Hotel and Sonoma Barracks on the Plaza, the Mission San Francisco Solano and the home of Sonoma's founder, Gen. Mariano Guadalupe Vallejo. The mission houses the Jorgensen watercolors of Missions of California. The Vallejo home has gardens and furnishings from the family estate.

Guided tours of the mission and Vallejo home are available Mon.-Fri. with at least a 15-day advance reservation. Allow 1 hour minimum. Open daily 10-5; closed Jan. 1, Thanksgiving and Dec. 25. Home $2; ages 6-12, $1. Phone (707) 938-1519.

TRAIN TOWN, 1 mi. s. on SR 12, offers a 20-minute miniature steam train ride through a forested railroad park past scaled-down reproductions of buildings and waterfalls. A petting zoo is on the grounds. Allow 30 minutes minimum. Weather permitting, trips daily 10:30-5:30, mid-June through Labor Day; Sat.-Sun. and holidays only, rest of year. Closed Dec. 25. Admission $2.50; ages 16 months-16, $1.80. Phone (707) 938-3912.

TRIPS ON TAPE, for the Sonoma Valley, is a self-guiding audio tape tour featuring the valley's wineries, historic Sonoma Plaza, Jack London State Historic Park, community events and Sonoma Valley landmarks. Maps are included. Tapes available for $11.95 at the Sonoma Valley Visitors Bureau, 453 First St. East, or by mail from The Rider's Guide, 484 Lake Park Ave., Suite 255, Oakland, CA 94610. Add $2 for postage. Phone (510) 653-2553.

SONORA (F-4) pop. 4,200, alt. 1,796'

Sonora was first settled by miners from Sonora, Mexico, and became one of the largest and wealthiest towns in the Mother Lode country. Still a bustling community, Sonora now relies on tourism, lumbering and agriculture. It also is the seat of Tuolumne County and a market center for the surrounding region. Sonora's past is proudly reflected in its fine collection of Victorian homes.

BRADFORD STREET PARK, Bradford St. at SR 49, has exhibits of mining equipment used in Sonora during the gold rush era. An arrastra, stamp mill and pelton wheel are included. Picnic areas are available.

TUOLUMNE COUNTY MUSEUM, 158 W. Bradford Ave., is housed in the 1857 county jail. Displays depicting the gold rush era include photographs, guns, antiques, artifacts and gold exhibits. The Tuolumne County Genealogy Society also is available. Picnicking is permitted. Mon., Wed. and Fri. 9-4:30, Tues., Thurs. and Sat. 10-3:30. Free. Phone (209) 532-1317.

SOQUEL (G-2) pop. 6,200, alt. 40'

BARGETTO'S SANTA CRUZ WINERY, 3535 N. Main St., offers 20-minute tours Mon.-Fri. at 11 and 2. Tasting room open Mon.-Sat. 10-5:30, Sun. noon-5:30; closed Jan. 1, Easter, Thanksgiving and Dec. 25. Free. Phone (408) 475-2258.

SOUTH SAN FRANCISCO (P-2)
pop. 54,300, alt. 19'

ACRES OF ORCHIDS (Rod McLellan Co.) is reached by taking Hickey Blvd. exit e. from I-280 to El Camino (SR 82), then right 1 blk. It displays a large variety of orchids and floral crops. Cloning can be observed in laboratories on 1-hour tours at 10:30 and 1:30. Open daily 8-5; closed holidays. Free. Phone (415) 871-5655.

STANISLAUS NATIONAL FOREST

Ranging in altitude from 1,100 to 11,570 feet and covering nearly 900,000 acres on the western slope of the Sierra Nevada Range, Stanislaus National Forest outlines the northwestern boundary of Yosemite National Park (see place listing). The Merced, Mokelumne, Clavey, Stanislaus and Tuolumne rivers cut deep canyons through this region.

Popular summer activities include swimming, camping, picnicking, hiking, boating, fishing and hunting. Snow skiing is available at Dodge Ridge off SR 108 and at Mount Reba off SR 4. Snowmobiling and cross-country skiing also are popular during the winter. Reservations for Pinecrest campground can be made through MISTIX, (800) 283-2267, during the summer months. For detailed campground information phone (209) 532-3671.

Visitor tours and programs are offered in July and August in Pinecrest. The Emigrant and Carson-Iceberg wildernesses are on the eastern side of the forest. Contact the Summit Ranger Station for permit information; phone (209) 965-3434. For general forest information contact the Supervisor's Office, Stanislaus National Forest, 19777 Greenley Rd., Sonora, CA 95370; phone (209) 532-3671. See Recreation Chart and the AAA California and Nevada CampBook.

STINSON BEACH (O-1) pop. 800, alt. 18'

AUDUBON CANYON RANCH, 3½ mi. n. on SR 1, is a former dairy ranch that is now a wildlife sanctuary and educational center. The ranch contains a major heronry frequented by great blue herons and great egrets. Allow 2 hours minimum. Sat.-Sun. and holidays 10-4, during the mid-Mar. to mid-July nesting period. Donations. Phone (415) 868-9244.

STOCKTON (F-3) pop. 210,900, alt. 14'

The first of California's two inland seaports, Stockton is connected with San Francisco Bay by a channel 60 miles long and 37 feet deep. The San Joaquin waterways, 1,000 miles of navigable inland waters, offer boating and fishing. The city also is the home of the University of the Pacific, the first chartered university in California.

Stockton honors its favorite vegetable with the annual spring Asparagus Festival, which includes an auto show, craft booths, live entertainment and, naturally, an asparagus recipe contest.

THE HAGGIN MUSEUM, Rose St. and Pershing Ave. in Victory Park, houses European and American paintings and local relics. Tues.-Sun. 1:30-5. Donations. Phone (209) 462-4116.

PIXIE WOODS WONDERLAND, in Louis Park, is a children's playland featuring sets from popular children's stories and legends. Theater programs are held during the afternoon. The park also offers amusement rides. Wed.-Fri. and holidays 11-5, Sat.-Sun. 11-6, mid-June to early Sept.; Sat.-Sun. and holidays noon-5, late Feb.-early June and mid-Sept. to late Oct. Admission $1.25; under 13, $1; rides 50c each. Phone (209) 944-8220 or 466-9890.

SUNNYVALE (Q-3) pop. 117,200, alt. 105'

Although Silicon Valley doesn't appear on any map, people the world over know that the nickname refers to the area around Sunnyvale. The city is the headquarters of more than 650 computer-related manufacturers whose products, whether software or hardware, are based on silicon chip technology.

Local manufacturers make good use of the Patent Information Clearinghouse at 1500 Partridge Ave., Building 7. The clearinghouse has facilities for patent and trademark research. Phone (408) 730-7290.

SUSANVILLE (C-4) pop. 7,300, alt. 4,258'

EAGLE LAKE, 16 mi. n.w. on Eagle Lake Rd., is the second largest natural lake in California. In summer campfire programs are held on Wednesday evenings, slide presentations are shown on Saturday evenings and trail walks are given Tues.-Fri. Facilities open daily dawn-dusk, Memorial Day weekend to mid-Oct. Free. Phone (916) 257-2151. See Recreation Chart.

TAFT (I-4) pop. 5,900, alt. 984'

TULE ELK STATE RESERVE, 964 acres 20 mi. n.e. via SR 119 and Tupman Rd., protects a herd of Tule elk, sometimes called dwarf elk. The elk can be observed best in the viewing area near park headquarters. A visitor center with natural history displays and information about the Tule elk is open Sat.-Sun. 1-5, Mar.-June and Sept. 1 to mid-Nov. Picnicking is permitted. Daily 8-dusk. Day use fee $3 per vehicle. Phone (805) 765-5004.

WEST KERN OIL MUSEUM, w. of SR 33 on Wood St., preserves relics from the early oilfields. Displays include Indian artifacts, gas engines, handwrought cable tools, photographs and a wooden derrick constructed in 1917. Tues.-Sat. 10-4, Sun. 1-4; closed Jan. 1, Thanksgiving and Dec. 25. Donations. Phone (805) 765-6664.

TAHOE NATIONAL FOREST

Despite its name, Tahoe National Forest has little to do with the lake. All of its 829,362 acres are north and west of Lake Tahoe, while the lake and its immediate environs are part of the Lake Tahoe Basin Management Unit. Much of the national forest lies in the Yuba River drainage, a region renowned in the 19th century as the northern mines. Here miners used the placer pan, pick and hydraulic cannon, which used tons of pressurized water to tear away the hillsides, in their frantic pursuit of gold.

Today, where pack trains and stagecoaches once traveled, automobiles now follow SR 49 past the remnants of mining camps since reclaimed by forest. Along the twisting course of the North Yuba River are steep-walled canyons and the dramatic Sierra Buttes, which are riddled with old quartz mines.

Miners weren't the only ones to leave their mark on the landscape. Touring the region as an entertainer in 1853, famed *femme-fatale* Lola Montez christened Independence Lake during a Fourth of July picnic. Just north of the site of her picnic, Mount Lola honors the adventuress.

Independence Lake is but one of many lakes within the forest boundaries. Some of the most popular areas are the French Meadows Reservoir, cradled in the upper reaches of the American River watershed; a cluster of glacial lakes north of Sierra City; and Bullards Bar Reservoir, on the edge of the Sacramento Valley.

A variety of publications on recreational opportunities and maps are available at most forest service stations and the forest headquarters in Nevada City. For more information contact the Forest Supervisor, Tahoe National Forest, 631 Coyote St., P.O. Box 6003, Nevada City, CA 95959; phone (916) 265-4531. *See the Recreation Chart and AAA California and Nevada CampBook.*

TEHACHAPI (I-5) pop. 5,800, alt. 3,973'

TEHACHAPI LOOP, 8½ mi. n.w. on the railroad, was conceived by a railroad engineer in 1876 to surmount a steep grade. The loop enables the caboose of an 85-car train to pass over the engine in the tunnel below.

TEMECULA (K-6) pop. 27,000, alt. 1,006'

CALLAWAY VINEYARD AND WINERY, 32720 Rancho California Rd., offers tours and picnic facilities. Daily 10-5; tours Mon.-Fri at 11, 1 and 3; Sat.-Sun. 11-4. Fee for tastings. Allow 30 minutes minimum. Phone (909) 676-4001.

CILURZO VINEYARD AND WINERY, 5½ mi. e. off Rancho California Rd. at 41220 Calle Contento, is a small family owned and operated winery offering tours and tastings. Picnicking is permitted. Daily 9:30-4:45. Free; fee for tastings. Phone (909) 676-5250.

CULBERTSON WINERY, 32575 Rancho California Rd., produces méthode champenoise spar-

kling wine. Daily 10-6. Fee for tastings. Phone (909) 699-0099.

MOUNT PALOMAR WINERY, 33820 Rancho California Rd., offers tours, tastings and picnic facilities. Daily 9-5; tours daily at 1:30 and 3:30 (also Sat.-Sun. at 11:30). Free; fee for tastings. Phone (909) 676-5047.

TEMPLETON (H-3) pop. 800, alt. 770'

Templeton was established in 1886 when the Southern Pacific Railroad ran track to this area. The town thrived until 1897 when a fire destroyed most of its downtown. Rebuilt, Templeton offers numerous antique shops, wineries and 19th-century structures.

PESENTI WINERY, 3 mi. w. at 2900 Vineyard Dr., offers tastings Mon.-Sat. 8-6, Sun. 9-6. Free. Phone (805) 434-1030.

THOUSAND OAKS (J-5) pop. 104,400, alt. 800'

STAGECOACH INN MUSEUM, 51 S. Ventu Park Rd., first opened in 1876 as a stopping place for travelers journeying between Los Angeles and Santa Barbara. The reconstructed Monterey-style building houses Victorian furnishings and changing exhibits. A restored carriage house, pioneer house and adobe with displays of Chumash artifacts are open Sun. only. Museum open Wed.-Fri.

and Sun. 1-4; closed holidays. Donations. Phone (805) 498-9441.

TOIYABE NATIONAL FOREST—*see Nevada.*

TRINIDAD (B-1) pop. 400, alt. 175'

PATRICK'S POINT STATE PARK, 632 acres 5 mi. n., is noted for its agate beach, numerous tide-pools and variety of spring wildflowers. A natu-ralist service is available in summer. Dogs are restricted from the beach and trails. Daily dawn-dusk. Day use fee $5 per vehicle; over 62, $4; dogs $1. Phone (707) 677-3570. *See Recreation Chart.*

TRINITY CENTER (B-2) pop. 200, alt. 2,311'

SCOTT MUSEUM OF TRINITY CENTER is ¼ mi. e. off SR 3 on Airport Rd. Among the exhib-its are a stagecoach and other early vehicles, a barbed wire collection, Indian artifacts and old utensils. Free guide service is available. Tues.-Sun. 1-4, May 15-Sept. 15. Donations. Phone (916) 266-3378.

TRINITY NATIONAL FOREST—*see Shasta-Trinity National Forest.*

TRUCKEE (D-4) pop. 2,400, alt. 5,820'

Truckee was once a lawless lumber and rail-road town, and much of its Old West charm re-mains; 19th-century false-front buildings and a train running through the middle of town can be seen.

DONNER MEMORIAL STATE PARK, 1 mi. w. on Donner Pass Rd., covers 353 acres near the site where the Donner party was stranded without food during the winter of 1846-47. As members of the 89-person party died, those remaining re-sorted to cannibalism. Only 47 were rescued. A 25-minute slide show of the Donner party experi-ences is presented at 10:15, 11, noon, 1, 2 and 3.

The Emigrant Trail Museum displays exhibits of the area's railroad history, logging, natural his-tory and immigrants. Park open daily 8-dusk, June 1-Oct. 1. Day use fee $5 per vehicle. Mu-seum open daily 10-4, mid-May through Sept. 30; 10-noon and 1-4, rest of year. Both closed Jan. 1, Thanksgiving and Dec. 25. Admission $2; ages 6-12, $1. Phone (916) 587-3841. *See Recre-ation Chart.*

TULARE (H-4) pop. 33,200, alt. 288'

TULARE HISTORICAL MUSEUM, 444 W. Tulare Ave., displays dioramas, relics, photographs and replicas of rooms and small businesses which re-veal the colorful history of the town, from Yokut Indian villages to the arrival of the railroad in 1872 to modern-day Tulare. Thurs.-Sat. 10-4, Sun. 12:30-4; closed major holidays. Admission $1.50; ages 13-17, 75c; ages 1-12, 50c. Phone (209) 686-2074.

TULELAKE (A-3) pop. 1,000, alt. 4,035'

KLAMATH BASIN NATIONAL WILDLIFE REF-UGES, near Tulelake, include the Lower Klamath and Tule Lake refuges. They offer some 30 miles of self-guiding auto tour routes for observing wildlife. An estimated 60 to 70 percent of Pacific flyway waterfowl stop here in the fall; the peak migration period is from late October to mid-No-vember. Hunting is allowed during state seasons.

The Klamath Basin regularly attracts as many as 500 bald eagles during January and February; many can be seen from the auto tour routes. A self-guiding canoe trail at Tule Lake Refuge is open July-Sept. The visitor center is open Mon.-Fri. 8-4:30, Sat.-Sun. and holidays 8-4. Entrance fee $3 per private vehicle. For more information contact the Refuge Manager, Klamath Basin Ref-uges, Rte. 1, Box 74, Tulelake, CA 96134; phone (916) 667-2231.

UKIAH (D-1) pop. 14,600, alt. 635'

Ukiah, center of a flourishing wine region, gets its name from a Pomo Indian word meaning "deep valley." It is home to the Redwood Em-pire Fairgrounds.

GRACE HUDSON MUSEUM AND SUN HOUSE, 431 S. Main St., is a 4½-acre complex that in-cludes a museum of art, history and anthropol-ogy, a historic house and a park. The museum displays works by noted Indian painter Grace Carpenter Hudson, an extensive collection of Pomo Indian basketry and historical photographs. Also featured are manuscripts collected by the artist and her husband, ethnologist John W. Hud-son, whose original manuscripts and collection of Pomo Indian materials also are on display. Allow 1 hour minimum.

Guided tours of the Sun House are available on the hour Wed.-Sun. noon-3. Museum and Sun House open Wed.-Sat. 10-4:30, Sun. noon-4:30; closed major holidays. Donations. Phone (707) 462-3370.

LAKE MENDOCINO VISITOR CENTER is ¼ mi. s. of SR 20 at 1160 Lake Mendocino Dr. The center offers a variety of programs and visitor in-formation that feature the lake, Pomo Indian cul-ture and the Coyote Valley. Highlights include the Interpretive Cultural Center, with exhibits of Pomo Indian crafts, pottery, jewelry and decora-tive arts. Picnicking is permitted. Open Wed.-Sun. 9-5. Donations. Phone (707) 462-7582.

PARDUCCI WINE CELLARS, 501 Parducci Rd., offers a tasting room and tours. A 45-minute video of the winery's operation from harvest to final product is shown. Picnicking is permitted. Allow 1 hour minimum. Tours on the hour daily 10-3, weather permitting. Tasting room open daily 9-5. Closed major holidays. Free. Phone (707) 462-9463.

UNIVERSAL CITY (B-6) alt. 609'

★UNIVERSAL STUDIOS HOLLYWOOD, Hollywood Frwy. (US 101) at Lankershim Blvd., consists of two parts. The first part is a narrated tram and walking tour showing where and how Universal movies are made. Visitors see costumes and props, sound stages and sets and demonstrations of special effects, including a simulated 8.3 earthquake in a subway setting, an "attack" by King Kong and a bike ride with E.T. the extraterrestrial.

The second part is a self-guiding tour of the Entertainment Center where live shows are performed: "Wild, Wild, Wild West," a stunt show; Animal Actors; the Adventures of Conan; "Star Trek Adventure," which allows visitor participation; and the Miami Vice Action Spectacular. Tours are offered continuously.

Open daily at 8, in summer; at 9, rest of year; closing times vary. Tours in Spanish are available Sat.-Sun. Closed Thanksgiving and Dec. 25. Admission $26; over 60 and ages 3-11, $20. AE, CB, DI, MC, VI. **Discount,** except over 60 and ages 3-11. Phone (818) 777-3801. *See ad p. 100.*

VACAVILLE (N-3) pop. 71,500, alt. 179'

VACAVILLE MUSEUM, 213 Buck Ave., displays photographs, documents and memorabilia pertaining to the history of Solano County. The museum also contains changing exhibits and an interpretive garden of native plants. Walking tours of the old downtown area of Vacaville are offered periodically; phone for schedule. Allow 30 minutes minimum. Wed.-Sun. 1-4:30. Donations. Phone (707) 447-4513.

VALLECITO (F-4) pop. 300, alt. 1,745'

MOANING CAVERN, 2 mi. s.w. on Parrots Ferry Rd., was explored in 1851 by miners, who discovered not the precious metal they were seeking, but prehistoric human remains. Guided 45-minute tours descend 165 feet, 100 feet of which descend a steel spiral staircase into a room big enough to hold the Statue of Liberty.

Visitors also can descend into the cavern on a 180-foot rappel (no experience necessary) or take the 3-hour Adventure Tour to the farthest depths of the cavern; reservations are required. Daily 9-6, in summer; 10-5, rest of year. Admission $5.75; senior citizens $5.25; ages 6-12, $2.75. DS, MC, VI. **Discount,** except senior citizens. Phone (209) 736-2708.

VALLEJO (O-2) pop. 109,200, alt. 40'

In 1851, Gen. Mariano Guadalupe Vallejo (val-LEH-hoh) founded the town that bears his name at the junction of the Carquinez Straits and the Napa River. The general was a citizen of California under both Mexican and U.S. rule. His namesake served as state capital twice between 1851 and 1853.

The Mare Island Naval Shipyard, on a peninsula across the Napa River from Vallejo, was established in 1854 by Adm. David Glasgow Farragut. Among the more than 520 ships built at the shipyard were the 1858 USS *Saginaw,* the first U.S. warship in the Pacific, and the 1920 battleship *California,* the largest naval craft built on the West Coast.

Today Vallejo is the home of the California Maritime Academy and the Sperry Division of General Mills.

Red and White Fleet ferry service is offered from Fisherman's Wharf in San Francisco to Vallejo, where shuttle buses can transport visitors to Marine World Africa USA.

★MARINE WORLD AFRICA USA, Marine World Pkwy. (SR 37) exit off I-80, is a 160-acre park with more than 1,000 animals in themed shows and naturalistic settings. Killer whales, dolphins, sea lions, tigers, elephants and chimpanzees perform in various shows. There also is a boat and water-skiing show, a wildlife theater, butterfly world, elephant encounter, an extensive bird habitat and a shark exhibit.

Children will especially enjoy the playground, petting zoo, life-size blue whale play area and elephant rides. Food is available. Allow full day. Daily 9:30-6:30, Memorial Day weekend-Labor Day; Wed.-Sun. 9:30-5, rest of year. Closed Thanksgiving and Dec. 25. Admission $21.95; over 60, $18.95; ages 4-12, $16.95. Parking $3. AE, CB, DI, MC, VI. **Discount,** except over 60. Phone (707) 643-6722.

VALLEJO NAVAL AND HISTORICAL MUSEUM, in the old Vallejo City Hall building at 734 Marin St., offers exhibits on naval history, including relics and papers from the Mare Island Naval Shipyard. Ship models, murals and an operating periscope are on display. The museum also offers changing exhibits, a maritime research library and exhibits of local and regional history. Guided tours are available by reservation. Tues.-Sat. 10-4:30; closed holidays. Admission $1.50; senior citizens and ages 12-17, 75c. Phone (707) 643-0077.

VAN NUYS (A-6) alt. 708'

DONALD C. TILLMAN WATER RECLAMATION PLANT AND JAPANESE GARDEN, 6100 Woodley Ave., is a water treatment facility highlighted by a 6½-acre Japanese garden. Paths wind by small lakes and among lawns, bonsai trees and decorative rocks. The gardens feature a tea house, zigzag bridges and stone lanterns. Tours of the garden and treatment plant depart Tues., Thurs. and Sat. at 9, 9:45 and 10:30. Evening tours are conducted in summer; phone for schedule. Reservations are required; under 12 not admitted. Free. Phone (818) 989-8166.

VENTURA (J-4) pop. 88,700, alt. 35'

Originally the site of a Chumash Indian settlement, Ventura is one of the oldest towns in the state. The town has beaches, a public pier and a large marina.

Ventura lies on a scenic stretch of US 101 that extends from San Luis Obispo to Los Angeles.

Shopping areas: Buenaventura Plaza, a fabric-enclosed mall at Mills Road and Main Street, contains a Broadway, JCPenney and numerous smaller stores.

ALBINGER ARCHAEOLOGICAL MUSEUM, 113 E. Main St., displays artifacts spanning 3,500 years; all were excavated from a single site next to Mission San Buenaventura. Evidence of an early Indian culture dating from 1600 B.C. and the later Chumash Indians dating from A.D. 1500 is exhibited, along with objects dating from the mission's founding to the early 1900s. The original mission foundation and an earth oven lie outside in the dig area. Two audiovisual programs are presented to visitors on request. Allow 30 minutes minimum.

Tues.-Sun. 10-4, Memorial Day weekend-Labor Day; Tues.-Fri. 10-2, Sat.-Sun. 10-4, rest of year. Closed Jan. 1, Easter, Thanksgiving and Dec. 25. Free. Phone (805) 648-5823.

★**MISSION SAN BUENAVENTURA** is at 225 E. Main St.; entrance is through a gift shop just east of the mission. Founded in 1782 and completed in 1809, the present mission includes a restored church, the Holy Cross School and a small museum. Mon.-Sat. 10-5, Sun. 10-4; closed major holidays. Admission 50c; under 16, 25c. Phone (805) 648-4496.

OLIVAS ADOBE HISTORICAL PARK, 4200 Olivas Park Dr., was built in 1847 in the Monterey style by Raymundo Olivas and has displays of period furnishings and handicrafts. An adjacent building contains artifacts from the adobe and rancho eras in Ventura County; an audiovisual program is presented upon request. The grounds include a small adobe, an adobe pit and rose gardens. Grounds open Mon.-Fri. 10-4; house open Sat.-Sun. 10-4; guided tours Sat.-Sun. at 11, 1 and 2. Closed major holidays. Free. Phone (805) 644-4346.

PADRE SERRA CROSS is on Mission Hill in Grant Park, which offers an impressive view. The first cross was erected on this spot by Father Junípero Serra on March 31, 1782. Easter sunrise services are offered.

VENTURA COUNTY MUSEUM OF HISTORY & ART, 100 E. Main St., reflects American Indian, Spanish and pioneer influences in the area. The museum includes displays of agricultural equipment, the George Stuart Historical Figures, changing exhibits and a research library. Tues.-Sun. 10-5; closed Jan. 1, Thanksgiving and Dec. 25. Admission $2; ages 6-12 free when accompanied by an adult; free to all second Tues. of the month. Phone (805) 653-0323.

VICTORVILLE (J-7) pop. 40,700, alt. 2,714'

The widest shopping selection in Victorville can be found at The Mall of Victor Valley, I-15 and Bear Valley Road, where Harris, JCPenney and Mervyn's are the biggest stores.

ROY ROGERS-DALE EVANS MUSEUM is at 15650 Seneca Rd. off I-15 via the Palmdale Rd. exit. The museum exhibits personal and professional memorabilia of the famous Western stars. Daily 9-5; closed Thanksgiving and Dec. 25. Admission $3; over 65 and ages 13-16, $2; ages 6-12, $1. **Discount,** except over 65 and ages 6-16. Phone (619) 243-4547.

VISALIA (H-5) pop. 65,200, alt. 331'

Founded in 1852, Visalia is the oldest city between Stockton and Los Angeles. By the early 19th century its countryside was rich with ranches and farms, and the city's prosperity was reflected in its many lavish homes.

Self-guiding tours: Free brochures outlining self-guiding walking tours of the city's historic district are available through the Visalia Chamber of Commerce and Convention and Visitors Bureau, 720 W. Mineral King Ave., Visalia, CA 93291; phone (209) 734-5876.

MOONEY GROVE PARK, 5 mi. s., embraces 155 grassy acres covered with valley oaks and date palms, picnic areas, a lake and recreational facilities. Mon.-Fri. 8-dusk, Sat.-Sun. 8 a.m.-9 p.m., in summer; Thurs.-Mon. 8-dusk, rest of year. Admission $2 per private vehicle, senior citizens free.

Tulare County Museum, in the park, displays American Indian artifacts and Tulare County pioneer memorabilia of the early 1800s. Allow 30 minutes minimum. Mon. and Wed.-Fri. 10-4, Sat.-Sun. noon-6, in summer; Wed.-Mon. 10-4, rest of year. Closed holidays. Admission $1, children 50c; under 12 must be accompanied by an adult. Phone (209) 733-6616.

VOLCANO (E-4) pop. 100, alt. 2,053'

Volcano, in a deep depression resembling a crater, was aptly named. During the gold rush the city was famous for its dancehalls and saloons. Daffodil Hill, 3 miles north of town, is covered with daffodils originally planted during the 1850s. Blooming season is late March to mid-April.

INDIAN GRINDING ROCK STATE HISTORIC PARK, ½ mi. off SR 88 at 14881 Pine Grove-Volcano Rd., is a 135-acre park where Miwok Indians chiseled in the main bedrock more than a thousand mortar cups in which they pulverized acorns and other seeds for food. A ceremonial roundhouse and re-created village are featured. The Chaw Se' Regional Indian Museum includes artifacts, presentations, exhibits and audiovisual programs representing 10 Sierra Nevada Indian tribes. Camping and picnicking are permitted.

Museum open daily 10-4, Memorial Day weekend-Labor Day; Mon.-Fri. 11-3, Sat.-Sun.

10-4, rest of year. Park open daily 8-5. The museum is closed Jan. 1, Thanksgiving and Dec. 25. Admission $5 per vehicle; over 62, $4 per vehicle. Phone (209) 296-7488.

WALNUT CREEK (O-3) pop. 60,600, alt. 135'

Whitewater enthusiasts may enjoy a trip down the American, Stanislaus, Merced, Tuolumne, Klamath, California or Salmon river with All-Outdoors Whitewater Trips. Half- to 3-day trips are offered; meals and transportation are provided. Trips depart from Walnut Creek daily, April through October. For information phone (800) 24-RAFTS. **Discount.**

LINDSAY MUSEUM, 1901 First Ave., has a collection of live animals, some of which children may pet. Wed.-Sun. 1-5; phone for holiday schedule. Free. Phone (510) 935-1978.

MOUNT DIABLO STATE PARK is 17 mi. s.e. on Diablo Rd. A paved road leads to the 3,849-foot summit, from which as much as 600 miles of the Sierra Nevada Range and portions of 35 counties are visible on clear days. The Interpretive Center on the summit is open Sat.-Sun. 11-4. Park open daily 8-dusk. Day use fee $5 per vehicle; over 62, $4 per vehicle. Phone (510) 837-2525. *See Recreation Chart.*

WATSONVILLE (G-2) pop. 31,100, alt. 23'

Watsonville's economy relies heavily on the growing of apples, strawberries and flowers. The main harvest time is celebrated in late September and early October. The Fats Waller Memorial Jazz Festival takes place in late June, and the Watsonville Antique Fly-In is held over Memorial Day weekend.

Self-guiding tours: Maps for walking and driving tours of Watsonville and the Pajaro Valley are available from the Pajaro Valley Chamber of Commerce at 444 Main St., Watsonville, CA 95076; phone (408) 724-3900.

ELKHORN SLOUGH NATIONAL ESTUARINE RESEARCH RESERVE is e. of US 1 off Dolan Rd. exit. This 1,340-acre coastal area protects the habitat of hundreds of species of birds, fish and invertebrates. Elkhorn Slough is one of the few relatively undisturbed coastal wetlands remaining in California. It also is an important feeding and resting ground for many kinds of waterfowl and migratory shorebirds. Walking trails wend through live oak and eucalyptus groves.

Picnicking is permitted in designated areas; smoking is prohibited on the trails. Guided nature walks originate at the visitor center near the Elkhorn Road entrance and are offered Sat.-Sun. 10-1. Open Wed.-Sun. 9-5. Admission $2.50, under 16 free. Phone (408) 728-2822.

WEAVERVILLE (C-2) pop. 2,800, alt. 2,045'

A mining town in the days of '49, Weaverville retains much of the flavor and colorful atmosphere depicted by author Bret Harte. The town is a starting point for trips into the Shasta-Trinity National Forest and the Whiskeytown-Shasta-Trinity National Recreation Area *(see place listings).*

J.J. "JAKE" JACKSON MEMORIAL MUSEUM, in town, displays Indian relics, Chinese weapons, fossils, a bottle collection and old jail cells with an emphasis on the early pioneer era. Picnic facilities are available. Daily 10-5, May-Oct.; noon-4, in Apr. and Nov.; Tues. noon-4, rest of year. Donations. Phone (916) 623-5211.

JOSS HOUSE STATE HISTORIC PARK, Oregon and Main sts., contains the oldest Chinese temple still in use in California. Exhibits depict Chinese life, early history and contributions to the state's development. Tours are given every hour from 10-4, with additional tours July-Aug. Open Thurs.-Mon. 10-5; closed Jan. 1, Thanksgiving and Dec. 25. Admission $2; ages 6-13, $1. Phone (916) 623-5284.

WEOTT (C-1) pop. 400, alt. 338'

HUMBOLDT REDWOODS STATE PARK covers more than 50,000 acres along the Redwood Hwy. between Miranda and Redcrest. The park is famous for the 362-foot Dyerville Giant Tree, considered the world's tallest until it was felled by a lightning strike in 1991; the 356-foot Rockefeller Tree; and more than 100 memorial redwood groves. Naturalist service is offered during the summer.

A visitor center contains redwood and wildlife exhibits. Park open daily 24 hours. Day use fee $5 per vehicle; over 62, $4. Visitor center open daily 9-5, Mar. 1 to mid-Sept.; otherwise varies, rest of year. Free. Phone (707) 946-2311 for the park, or (707) 946-2263 for the visitor center. *See Recreation Chart.*

★**Avenue of the Giants,** a 33-mile section of highway paralleling US 101 between Phillipsville and Pepperwood, winds along the course of the Eel River. While the surrounding hills also support oak, maple, madrone and pepperwood trees, the magnificent redwoods along this route overshadow all. The two-lane road has numerous parking areas, picnic sites and nature trails that afford a closer look at some of California's most beautiful redwood groves.

WHISKEYTOWN-SHASTA-TRINITY NATIONAL RECREATION AREA (C-2)

The 243,000-acre Whiskeytown-Shasta-Trinity National Recreation Area is at the head of the Sacramento Valley and Upper Trinity River country, north and west of Redding. Its three components embrace four major dam-created lakes: Whiskeytown, about 8 miles west of Redding via SR 299; Clair Engle and Lewiston, northeast of Weaverville; and Shasta, north of Redding.

Recreational gold panning using a metal or plastic gold pan is permitted in the Whiskeytown unit only. For park reservations phone MISTIX at (800) 283-2267. *See Recreation Chart and the AAA California and Nevada CampBook.*

WHITTIER (B-6) pop. 77,700, alt. 365'

The primary shopping area in Whittier is Whittwood Mall, Whittier and Santa Gertrudes boulevards. The largest stores are Broadway, JCPenney and Mervyn's.

ROSE HILLS MEMORIAL PARK, 3900 S. Workman Mill Rd., is one of the world's largest memorial parks. The east park features the 3½-acre Pageant of Roses Garden with more than 7,000 bushes and 750 varieties. The west park has a Japanese garden with a meditation house; lakes and arched bridges further enhance the park. Daily 8-5. Free. Phone (310) 699-0921.

SHERIFFS TRAINING AND REGIONAL SERVICES (STARS) CENTER, 11515 S. Colima Rd., near the n.w. corner of S. Colima and Telegraph rds., includes a museum depicting the history and current activities of the Los Angeles County Sheriffs Department. Highlights are a Hughes 300 helicopter, a replica of a 19th-century sheriff's office and jail and videos of famous cases that involved the department. Tues.-Fri. 10-3. Free. Guided tours of the museum and a portion of the campus are available by reservation; phone Wed.-Fri. at (310) 946-7081.

WILLIAMS (D-2) pop. 1,800, alt. 80'

SACRAMENTO VALLEY MUSEUM is 1 mi. w. of I-5 at 1491 E St., in the 1911 Williams High School building. The museum includes room displays depicting life in the Colusa County area from the mid-1800s to 1930. Wed.-Sat. 10-4, Sun. 1-4, Apr.-Nov.; Fri.-Sat. 10-4 or by appointment, rest of year. Closed major holidays. Admission $1. Phone (916) 473-2978.

WILLITS (D-1) pop. 5,000, alt. 1,364'

Willits is the terminus for the California Western Railroad trip aboard "The Skunk" from Fort Bragg *(see place listing). See ad p. 72.*

MENDOCINO COUNTY MUSEUM, 400 E. Commercial St., displays collections of Pomo and Yuki Indian baskets, local relics of Mendocino County and contemporary and traditional art. Allow 30 minutes minimum. Wed.-Sat. 10-4:30; closed holidays. Donations. Phone (707) 459-2736.

WILLOWS (D-2) pop. 5,300, alt. 135'

SACRAMENTO NATIONAL WILDLIFE REFUGE, 7 mi. s. of Willows on SR 99W, affords a 10,783-acre wintering area for migratory birds, especially ducks and geese. The best season to view waterfowl is September through March. Among the more than 175 bird species frequent-ing the area are hawks, egrets and herons. A variety of birds and mammals can be seen year round.

A 6-mile auto route and a 2-mile hiking trail lead through part of the refuge. Visitors should contact headquarters for information on current regulations and on refuge access for controlled hunting. Daily dawn-dusk; office open daily 8-4:30, Oct.-Mar.; Mon.-Fri. 8-4:30, rest of year. Free. Phone (916) 934-7774 or 934-2801.

The other three refuges that constitute the Sacramento Valley national wildlife refuges are Colusa *(see place listing),* Delevan and Sutter.

WILMINGTON (C-6) pop. 40,000, alt. 22'

BANNING RESIDENCE MUSEUM, 401 E. M St., is the restored 18-room 1864 Greek Revival home of Gen. Phineas Banning, who founded Wilmington in 1858. The museum is a major center for the interpretation of 19th-century Los Angeles history. Guided tours given Tues.-Thurs. at 12:30, 1:30 and 2:30, Sat.-Sun. at 12:30, 1:30, 2:30 and 3:30; closed holidays. Donations. Phone (310) 548-7777.

DRUM BARRACKS CIVIL WAR MUSEUM, 1052 Banning Blvd., was once the "Accompanied Officers Quarters" and is the only remaining structure of the more than 20 that composed Camp Drum 1862-73. The camp, quartering up to 7,000 men, was established as a Civil War garrison and depot and also was a base of operations in the Indian wars.

The rooms now display items from that period, including a rare Gatling gun, furniture, photographs, documents and a scale model of the original 60-acre camp. Tours depart Tues.-Thurs. at 10, 11 and noon; Sat. at 12:30, 1:30 and 2:30. Donations. Phone (310) 548-7509.

WINDSOR (M-1) pop. 2,400, alt. 118'

RODNEY STRONG VINEYARDS, 11455 Old Redwood Hwy., offers tours, tastings and a picnic area. Allow 30 minutes minimum. Tours offered daily on the hour 11-4; tasting room open daily 10-5; closed Jan. 1, Thanksgiving and Dec. 25. Free; fee charged for special wines on weekends. Phone (707) 433-6511.

WINDSOR WATERWORKS AND SLIDES, 8225 Conde Ln., has two winding water flumes, an aqua tube, a splash fountain and a heated pool. Under 48 inches tall not permitted on slides. Picnic facilities and food are available. Allow 4 hours minimum. Mon.-Fri. 11-7, Sat.-Sun. 10-8, mid-June to early Sept.; Sat.-Sun. 10-7, May 1 to mid-June. All-day pass Sat.-Sun. $11.95; ages 2-12, $10.95. All-day pass Mon.-Fri. $10.95; ages 2-12, $9.95. Pool and picnic area only, $4.95; under 13, $3.95. MC, VI. **Discount.** Phone (707) 838-7760.

WOODSIDE (Q-2) pop. 5,000, alt. 382'

FILOLI, off I-280 via Edgewood Rd. to Cañada Rd., was built 1916-19. The 654-acre estate includes a mansion and 16 acres of themed formal enclosed gardens. Self-guiding tours are available Fri. and the first Sat. and second Sun. of each month, mid-Feb. to mid-Nov.; fee $8. Guided hikes are offered by reservation; fee $4, children $1. Mansion and gardens tours Tues.-Sat. at 10 and 1; reservations are required. Admission $8; under 12 not permitted. Phone (415) 364-2880.

YORBA LINDA (B-7) pop. 52,400, alt. 397'

RICHARD NIXON PRESIDENTIAL LIBRARY AND BIRTHPLACE, 18001 Yorba Linda Blvd., includes a museum, gardens and the small house in which Nixon was born. Within the museum are films, interactive video displays, exhibits and personal memorabilia that reflect the former president's public and private life. The house is furnished with items reflective of early 20th-century, middle-class Americans. Mon.-Sat. 10-5, Sun. 11-5; closed Jan. 1, Thanksgiving and Dec. 25. Admission $4.95; over 62, $2.95; ages 8-11, $1. **Discount.** Phone (714) 993-3393.

★YOSEMITE NATIONAL PARK (F-5)

See map page 192.

Glaciers transformed the rolling hills and meandering streams of pre-Pleistocene Yosemite into the colossal landscape of the present. To preserve it for posterity, Abraham Lincoln set aside the valley as the nation's first state park on June 30, 1864. Twenty-six years later Yosemite became a national park.

A region of unusual beauty, Yosemite National Park lies in central California on the western slope of the Sierra Nevada. The park is much greater both in area and beauty than most people generally realize; Yosemite Valley actually comprises only 7 of the 1,189 square miles of park land. The territory above the rim of the valley is less celebrated principally because it is less well known. However, 360 miles of primary roads and 800 miles of trails now make much of this mountain region easily accessible to both motorist and hiker.

The crest of the Sierra Nevada is the park's eastern boundary, and the two rivers that flow through the park—the Merced and Tuolumne—originate among the snowy peaks. The Merced River flows through Yosemite Valley, and the Tuolumne River carves a magnificent gorge through the northern half of the park. Though spectacular through most of the year, many of the park's famous waterfalls are often dry during the late summer months.

The main paved route to Yosemite is SR 140 from Merced. SR 41 (Wawona Rd.) from Fresno passes the Mariposa Grove of Big Trees near the park's south entrance, 36 miles from the Yosemite Valley. Both of these routes are open all year. The park also can be reached by Big Oak Flat Road (SR 120), also open all year, and by Tioga Pass Road (SR 120E), open only in summer.

The road to Mirror Lake and Happy Isles, at the eastern end of Yosemite Valley, is closed to cars but is served by a free shuttle bus. Southside Drive is one-way eastbound from Bridalveil Falls to Camp Curry; Northside Drive is one-way westbound from Yosemite Lodge; and the road between Camp Curry and Yosemite Village also is one-way westbound.

TIOGA PASS ROAD (SR 120) traverses the park and provides the only entrance from the east; it begins at the junction with US 395 just south of Lee Vining.

The first 12 miles of the two-lane paved road ascend nearly a mile and overlook a vast canyon. The road traverses Tuolumne Meadows and descends to Tenaya Lake. From the rocky area surrounding the lake, it continues west to a junction with Big Oak Flat Road. This route offers a very pleasant and scenic trip with frequent overlooks.

Although portions of the drive are more demanding than relaxing, the magnificent scenery attracts many motorists. The road is usually open Memorial Day weekend-November 1, weather permitting. Motorists should carry tire chains, since weather and road conditions can change quickly. For road conditions phone (619) 873-6366 or (209) 372-0200.

General Information and Activities

Yosemite National Park is open daily all year. Maps and information are available at the Yosemite Valley visitor center, and schedules of events are provided at park entrances and posted throughout the valley. A free shuttle bus operates in the east end of the valley, passing any given point, including some valley trailheads, regularly 9 a.m.-10 p.m., early Apr.-late Oct.; 10-9, rest of year.

Wilderness permits, required of all overnight backpackers, can be obtained free at visitor centers and ranger stations. A California fishing license is required for all park waters; an annual permit costs $23.65 for residents and $63.55 for non-residents. A 1-day non-resident license costs $8.40. Information on bicycle rentals is available at Camp Curry and Yosemite Lodge; tour bus information also is given at these spots and at the Ahwahnee Hotel.

Naturalists conduct year-round nature walks that last from a half-hour to all day. Evening programs are presented all year at the Valley Visitor Center and Yosemite Lodge, and in summer at Lower River, Camp Curry, Lower Pines, Glacier Point, Tuolumne Meadows, Crane Flat, Wawona, White Wolf and Bridalveil Creek campgrounds. Happy Isles offers exhibits and a slide program daily 10-4, in summer; several day-hike trails also are available.

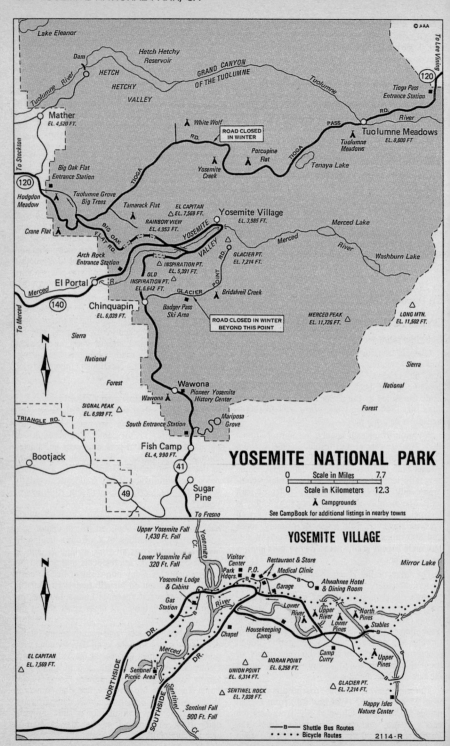

S uper 8 Lodges

We're Everywhere You Want to Go!

For reservations, phone toll-free 1-800-800-8000

Modesto
2025 W. Orangeburg Ave.
209/577-8008
Hwy. 99, Briggsmore Exit
$42*

Pleasanton
5375 Owens Ct.
510/463-1300
I-580, Hopyard Rd. Exit
$50*

Sacramento
4317 Madison Ave.
916/334-7430
I-80, Madison Ave. Exit
$42*

San Bernardino
294 E. Hospitality Ln.
714/381-1681
I-10, Waterman Exit
$41*

Santa Rosa
2632 Cleveland Ave.
707/542-5544
Hwy. 101, Steele Ln. Exit
$38*

San Francisco
International Airport
(Southern Region)
111 Mitchell Ave.
415/877-0770
Hwy. 101,
S. Airport Blvd. Exit
$53*

H oliday Inn

For reservations,
phone toll-free 1-800-HOLIDAY

Barstow
1511 East Main Street
619/256-5673
I-15 at East Main
$54*

...and while you're here, enjoy a meal at our Garden Court Cafe. Choose our **ALL YOU CAN EAT BUFFET** or our delicious menu items.
• Cocktail lounge with big screen T.V.
• Open 6 am–10 pm
• Serving breakfast, lunch and dinner

* Must mention this ad to receive the discounted rates listed
  above, single or double occupancy. Discounted rate cannot
  be used in conjunction with any other discount or promotion.
  Offer expires 1/31/94

An open tram offers frequent 2-hour tours of the valley during summer and occasional trips after Labor Day; reservations can be made at the Ahwahnee Hotel, Camp Curry and Yosemite Lodge. Other tours depart daily in summer to Glacier Point and Mariposa Grove. Guided horseback tours of Yosemite Valley, Wawona, White Wolf and Tuolumne Meadows also are available.

Narrated 1½-hour air tours over the valley, Tuolumne Meadows and the Cathedral and Ritter mountains are conducted by Golden Eagle Air Tours (*see Fresno*). Four- and 6-day saddle trips and a 7-day guided hiking trip are available as well; contact Yosemite Park and Curry Co., Yosemite National Park, CA 95389.

Skiing and skating can be enjoyed in winter. Camp Curry has an outdoor skating rink; Badger Pass Ski Area has downhill and cross-country skiing. Ski touring trails lead from Badger Pass and Crane Flat areas. One-hour snowcat tours around the Badger Pass area are given, weather permitting. Snowshoe tours also are offered.

Child care is available in winter for a fee at Ski Tots Playhouse at Badger Pass. During the summer the Junior Ranger Program of nature walks and classes welcomes students in grades 3 through 6; for grades 7 and up, a special program of hiking activities is provided; phone (209) 372-0200.

For recorded information on camping, roads, weather conditions and recreation phone (209) 372-0200. Campground reservations are available through MISTIX, (800) 365-2267, P.O. Box 85705, San Diego, CA 92138-5705. *See Recreation Chart and the AAA California and Nevada CampBook.*

VISITOR CENTER in Yosemite Valley is open all year. The center has exhibits and audiovisual programs, and the adjacent Indian Cultural Museum depicts the history of the Miwok and Paiute. Visitor centers at Big Oak Flat and Tuolumne Meadows are staffed by park naturalists during summer.

ADMISSION to the park is by $5 entry fee. Chains might be required at any time.

PETS are not allowed on the trails or in public buildings and must be leashed at all times. Cats and dogs are permitted in Upper Pines in Yosemite Valley, the west end of the campground at Tuolumne Meadows, and at White Wolf (Section C), Bridalveil (Section A), Crane Flat (Section A), Wawona, Hodgdon Meadows and Yosemite Creek campgrounds. Dogs can be boarded in Yosemite Valley from late May to mid-October.

ADDRESS inquiries concerning the park to the Superintendent, P.O. Box 577, Yosemite National Park, CA 95389.

Points of Interest

GLACIER POINT, 30 mi. from Yosemite Valley via Wawona Rd. to Chinquapin, then Glacier Point Rd., offers a panorama of the area's domes, pinnacles, waterfalls and—dominating all—Half Dome. On the valley floor 3,214 feet below, automobiles appear as moving specks, and the Merced River resembles a silver thread. From the stone lookout you can study the detail of the High Sierra and its flanking ranges, miles away.

The paved road to the point winds through forests of pine and fir. During summer, bus tours to Glacier Point are available and ranger-naturalists are on duty. A 1-mile walk from the parking area leads to Sentinel Dome at 8,122 feet. The road to Glacier Point is open from June through October.

THE GRAND CANYON of the Tuolumne can be traversed on foot. Waterwheel Falls is accessible by a good trail 6 miles from Tioga Road down the Tuolumne River Gorge to Glen Aulin High Sierra Camp, then 3 miles down the river. At the falls, the river rushing down the canyon hits shelves of projecting rock with terrific force, throwing enormous arcs of water into the air. This spectacle is best viewed from mid-June to mid-July.

Below the waterfalls the river descends abruptly, plunging through a mile-deep gorge. Trails penetrate to the heart of the region and lead to Pate Valley, where only ancient mortar holes remain of the Indians who once lived in this region.

North of the Tuolumne River is a vast area of lakes and valleys. Though it is threaded with numerous trails, it remains lightly visited and offers a true wilderness experience.

HETCH HETCHY RESERVOIR is reached from Yosemite Valley via Big Oak Flat Rd. (You should carry tire chains in the fall, winter and spring.) The 38-mile drive from the valley through fine stands of sugar pine and white fir can be covered easily in 2 hours. A paved road leads 9 miles from Mather to the 312-foot dam, which impounds San Francisco's water supply. Before the dam was built in 1913, the Hetch Hetchy Valley rivaled Yosemite Valley in beauty. The valley floor is now under 300 feet of water.

MARIPOSA GROVE, in the extreme southern end of the park, is reached via Wawona Road (SR 41), an easy 36-mile paved drive from Yosemite Valley. The giant sequoia grove is one of the finest in the Sierra.

Grizzly Giant, the oldest tree in Mariposa Grove, has a maximum base diameter of 30.7 feet, a girth of 96.5 feet and a height of 210 feet. Two tunnel trees are in the park: the 232-foot California Tree in Mariposa Grove and the 40-foot stump Dead Giant in Tuolumne Grove. The Wawona Tunnel Tree fell during the 1968-69 winter storms.

Guided bus tours run from the valley to the grove, with a stop in Wawona. Along the way an overlook at the east portal of the 4,233-foot Wawona tunnel offers a view of the entire valley; farther south is the Merced South Fork Basin. Cars are not permitted in the grove. Daily 9-6 from about May to October, 1-hour tram tours leave from the parking area every 10-15 minutes. Admission $5.25; over 64, $4.50; ages 4-12, $2.50. For those who want to explore on foot, a 2½-mile trail leads to the upper grove.

The Mariposa Grove Museum contains exhibits on the giant sequoias and is open on the same schedule as the trams. During the summer a naturalist gives talks on the park. Nearby is the fallen Massachusetts Tree, 280 feet long and 28 feet in diameter; several broken sections provide opportunities to study the wood.

TUOLUMNE GROVE, on Big Oak Flat Rd., 17 mi. from Yosemite Valley, contains 20 giant sequoia trees, including the Dead Giant. The grove is traversed by a one-way road that begins south at Crane Flat. No trailers or motorhomes are allowed.

TUOLUMNE MEADOWS is in the High Sierra, 8,600 feet in elevation, surrounded by lofty peaks. This area, about 56 miles from Yosemite Valley over the Big Oak Flat and Tioga roads, is an ideal camping place and an excellent starting point for fishing, hiking and mountain-climbing trips. It is accessible by car from about late May through October.

Trips can be taken on foot or horseback to Waterwheel Falls, Mount Lyell and Lyell Glacier, Lembert Dome, Glen Aulin, Muir Gorge, Soda Springs, Tenaya Lake and other points. Daily bus service is available in summer to Tuolumne Meadows, Tioga Pass and Mono Lake. Nature walks, hikes and evening campfire programs are conducted in summer; saddle horses and gas station, store and post office services also are available, along with a mountaineering school and guide service.

WASHBURN AND MERCED LAKES are typical of the many lakes bordering the western slopes of the Sierras. One of six High Sierra camps is at the head of Merced Lake and can be reached by trail from Yosemite Valley, Tenaya Lake or Tuolumne Meadows.

WAWONA BASIN provides a recreation area of several square miles that includes camping, riding, golf, swimming and tennis facilities. Wawona, in a beautiful meadow on Wawona Road, is 27 miles south of the Yosemite Valley near Mariposa Grove. Saddle and pack animals are available in summer.

YOSEMITE PIONEER HISTORY CENTER, at Wawona, has historic cabins and exhibits on stagecoach days in Yosemite. Rides are offered in summer: fare $3, children $2. Living-history

demonstrations are given Wed.-Sun. 9-5, July-Aug.

YOSEMITE VALLEY is open all year. The valley extends for 7 miles and averages ¾ miles in width; its walls rise to 3,200 feet. The sheer immensity of the precipices on either side of the valley and the loftiness of the many waterfalls never fail to impress even the most jaded eyes.

Upper Yosemite Falls drops 1,430 feet in one staggering fall, a height equal to nine Niagaras. Lower Yosemite Falls, immediately below, has a comparatively modest drop of 320 feet. Counting the cascades in between, the total drop from the crest of Yosemite Falls to the valley floor is 2,425 feet—nearly half a mile. Vernal Falls drops 317 feet; Illilouette Falls, 370 feet; Nevada Falls, 594 feet; Bridalveil Falls, 620 feet; and Ribbon Falls, 1,612 feet.

The falls are at their fullest in May and June, while winter snows are melting. Fairly abundant up to mid-July, many of the falls practically disappear for the balance of the summer, then reappear with the first storm of autumn and run lightly during winter.

The great domes and pinnacles of Yosemite Valley—Three Brothers, El Capitan, Cathedral Spires, North Dome and Half Dome—are as celebrated as the falls.

YOUNTVILLE (N-2) pop. 3,300, alt. 100'

A "Wine Country" community, Yountville is the base for Napa Valley Balloons, a company offering balloon rides over Napa Valley's colorful vineyards. Rides depart from Yountville Park north of town. The Vintage 1870 is an interesting shopping and dining complex in a restored 19th-century winery.

Yountville lies on a scenic stretch of SR 29 that extends from Calistoga to Napa.

ADVENTURES ALOFT offers 1-hour balloon rides launched from the Vintage 1870 in Yountville. Flights include a continental breakfast, champagne brunch and flight certificate. Transportation is provided from Napa-area accommodations to the launch site and back. Reservations are required. Fare $165; ages 8-12, $82.50. AE, MC, VI. **Discount.** Phone (707) 255-8688.

BALLOON AVIATION offers 1-hour balloon excursions departing from the Vintage 1870. Flights include a continental breakfast, champagne brunch and flight certificate. Transportation is provided from Napa-area hotels to the launch site and back. Reservations are required. Fare $165; ages 8-12, $82.50. AE, MC, VI. **Discount.** Phone (707) 252-7067.

Note: The mention of the preceding hot air balloon rides is for information only and does **not** imply endorsement by AAA.

DOMAINE CHANDON, W. California Dr., produces sparkling wines. A 19th-century champagne press and other items from artisans, glassblowers, and corkmakers are on display in the gallery. Tours daily 11-5, May-Oct.; Wed.-Sun. 11-5, rest of year. Tasting room open until 6. Closed Jan. 1, Easter, Thanksgiving and Dec. 25. Cabarets and concerts on some Sun. and Mon.; fee charged. Tours free; tastings $3-$4 per glass with complimentary hor d'oeuvres. Phone (707) 944-2280.

YREKA (A-2) pop. 7,000, alt. 2,625'

Yreka was incorporated in 1857, 6 years after Abraham Thompson's mules pulled gold flecks up on the roots of the grass they were eating. Miners soon swarmed into this lush valley, which had long been a home to the Modoc and Shasta Indians.

I-5 provides a scenic route to Yreka. An even closer look at the countryside is offered by Orange Torpedo Trips, which conducts 1-, 2- and 3-day whitewater trips in inflatable kayaks and rafts on the Klamath River; phone (503) 479-5061 (Grants Pass, Oreg.).

BLUE-GOOSE SHORT LINE RAILROAD departs the depot at the Center exit in Yreka. The 3-hour tour provides views of Mount Shasta, Shasta Valley and cattle ranch country as well as a visit to the old railroad town of Montague. Steam train departs Wed.-Sun. at 10 a.m., mid-June through Labor Day; Sat.-Sun. at 10 a.m., late May to mid-June and mid-Sept. to mid-Oct.; phone for schedule in spring and fall. Fare $9, children $4.50. Phone (916) 842-4146.

GREENHORN PARK, s. off Greenhorn Rd. at Greenhorn Reservoir, features a restored miner's cabin and mining equipment. A nature trail, playground and picnic facilities are available. Daily 7 a.m.-10 p.m., May 1-Oct. 1; 7-6, rest of year. Free. Phone (916) 842-4386.

SISKIYOU COUNTY COURTHOUSE, 311 Fourth St., exhibits various forms of gold. Mon.-Fri. 8-5, Sat. 10-3, Memorial Day weekend-Labor Day; Mon.-Fri. 8-5, rest of year. Closed holidays. Free. Phone (916) 842-8005.

SISKIYOU COUNTY MUSEUM, 910 S. Main St., contains exhibits on Indians, agriculture, geology and mining. Period rooms include a blacksmith shop, general store, music store, milliner's shop, parlor, children's room and office. The outdoor museum displays equipment and restored buildings in an 1800s village setting. A special candlelight tour takes place in December. Allow 2 hours minimum. Mon.-Sat. 9-5, Memorial Day weekend-Labor Day; Tues.-Sat. 9-5, rest of year. Closed major holidays. Free. Phone (916) 842-3836.

YUBA CITY (E-3) pop. 27,400, alt. 60'

Yuba City was founded in 1849 as a gold rush development; it is now a marketing center for the surrounding agricultural area.

COMMUNITY MEMORIAL MUSEUM, 1333 Buttehouse Rd., contains Indian and pioneer artifacts, furniture, clothing, agricultural equipment, photographs and historical documents from Sutter County. Tues.-Fri. 9-5, Sat.-Sun. noon-4. Donations. Phone (916) 741-7141.

GRAY LODGE REFUGE, 15 mi. n.w. off SR 99, comprises 8,400 acres. The refuge is an important Pacific flyway stopover for waterfowl, in addition to being a nesting ground for dove, pheasant, coot and hawk. In all, more than 200 species of bird use the refuge. An auto route traverses the area; fishing and hunting are permitted in season.

Daily dawn-dusk, except during waterfowl season, when hours coincide with the operational hunting regulations. Admission $2.50; free to holders of current California fishing and hunting licenses or California Wildlife Pass. For more information contact the area headquarters office at P.O. Box 37, Gridley, CA 95948; phone (916) 846-3315 (Mon.-Fri. 8-4:30). For information on interpretive programs phone (916) 846-5176.

SUTTER BUTTES is sometimes referred to as the world's smallest mountain range. This brooding cluster of dark rocks rises some 2,000 feet above the surrounding plain and covers about 75 square miles. The buttes are a volcanic upthrust formation—something of a geologic anomaly for this area—and are popular with nature lovers, who enjoy the abundant birdlife and wildflowers.

Although much of the region is private property, visitors can join nature study groups and guided hikes. For more information contact Yuba College Community Education, 2088 N. Beale Rd., Marysville, CA 95901; phone (916) 741-6825.

YUCAIPA (B-9) pop. 32,800, alt. 2,622'

MOUSLEY MUSEUM OF NATURAL HISTORY, 35308 Panorama Dr., is a branch of the San Bernardino County Museum that houses extensive collections of seashells and minerals, exhibits of small plant and animal fossils and a number of artifacts that reflect various world cultures. Allow 30 minutes minimum. Thurs.-Sat. 1-5; closed Jan. 1, Thanksgiving and Dec. 25. Free. Phone (714) 790-3163 or 798-8570.

Roads are the most slippery for the first 10 to 15 minutes after it begins to rain.

NEVADA

An introduction to the state's history, geography, economy and recreation

WHATEVER THE COIN, Nevada displays both sides. It is the seventh largest state yet has one of the smallest populations. Half an hour from the clatter of Las Vegas the only sound is wind brushing across miles of sage. While the skeletal buildings of old mining towns stare back at their boom-and-bust yesterdays, students and ideas at the University of Nevada keep a steady eye on tomorrow. These contrasts help contribute to the state's intriguing image.

HISTORY

Historians believe the first European to enter Nevada was the Spanish priest Father Francisco Garces. His expedition may have crossed the southern edge of the state in 1776 while seeking a new route to California. Further incursions were made into the arid, forbidding region in the 1820s, but the first official expeditions were those of Capt. John C. Fremont in 1843-45.

The first permanent settlement was Mormon Station, now called Genoa, which grew up around a trading post established in 1850 by Mormons from Salt Lake City. In 1855 the Mormons settled another mission fort that was destined to become glittery Las Vegas after the railroad's arrival in 1905.

Nevada, with its formidable deserts, was an obstacle that had to be crossed on the way to California. It gained allure of its own with the discovery of gold at the mouth of Gold Canyon in 1850. Nearly 10 years later miners realized that the pesky blue clay they had been scraping out of their gold claims was silver ore. The Comstock Lode, one of the richest silver and gold ore bodies ever discovered, suddenly turned Nevada into the place to go.

Its new mineral wealth made the region a desirable addition to the United States. Originally part of Utah Territory, Nevada became a territory in its own right in 1861. Statehood followed in 1864, mainly because two more votes were

---

FAST FACTS

POPULATION: 1,201,800.

AREA: 110,540 square miles; ranks seventh.

CAPITAL: Carson City.

HIGHEST POINT: 13,143 ft., Boundary Peak, White Mountains.

LOWEST POINT: 470 ft., on the Colorado River.

TIME ZONE: Pacific. DST.

MINIMUM AGE FOR DRIVERS: 16.

SEAT BELT/CHILD RESTRAINT LAWS: Seat belts required for driver and all passengers; child restraints required for under 5 and under 40 pounds.

HELMETS FOR MOTORCYCLISTS: Required.

RADAR DETECTORS: Permitted.

FIREARMS LAWS: Vary by state and/or county. Contact the Legislative Council Bureau, Capitol Complex, Carson City, NV 89710; phone (702) 687-6800.

HOLIDAYS: Jan. 1; Washington's Birthday, Feb. (3rd Mon.); Memorial Day, May (last Mon.); July 4; Labor Day; Nevada Day, Oct. 31; Veterans Day, Nov. 11; Thanksgiving; Dec. 25.

TAXES: Nevada's statewide sales tax is 6.75 percent (7 percent in Clark County), with local options for an additional 0.25 - 0.50 percent. Cities and counties impose a 1 percent lodgings tax.

If only trees could talk.

Discover
Both Sides Of
NEVADA ©

These would sure have some tales to tell. After all, they're the oldest living things on earth! They're Bristlecone Pines, just one of the wild wonders of Eastern Nevada's Great Basin National Park. And it's just 70 miles east of Ely.

Come discover it for yourself. But keep your ears open, you never know what you might hear!

Call 1-800-NEVADA-8.

Nevada Commission On Tourism, P.O. Box 30032, Reno, NV 89520.   AA

needed to propose the 13th amendment, which abolished slavery.

Statehood furthered other causes as well. President Abraham Lincoln wanted more support for his war programs and for the Republican Party, while Nevadans sought to protect their mining claims. Above all, the Comstock Lode financed the Union's efforts in the Civil War.

During this period of frantic boom, the wry countenance of Samuel Clemens began to appear at the diggings. Following a brief flirtation with mining, he turned to journalism via the Virginia City *Territorial Enterprise*. By the time Clemens left in 1864, his writings had already made the immortal pen name of Mark Twain and life in the Nevada gold camps famous.

As the mines went, so did the state. The "Big Bonanza" of 1873-78 created millionaires, some of whom built sumptuous mansions that are still the pride of Virginia City's residential district. But when the best of the Comstock mines flooded and the remainder began to fail Nevada slumped into a 20-year depression.

Revival came in 1900 with a gold and silver discovery in the south; Tonopah, on a mountainside above the sage flats, leaped to life. Prospectors hit another big strike in 1902 at Goldfield. About that time, copper was found at Ely. As lucrative as the mines were, however, Nevadans determined they needed to develop a more stable economy than one based on the volatile silver and gold markets.

Irrigation made the largest valleys productive. Basque shepherds arrived to raise sheep on the grassy mountain meadows. But the greatest boost to revenue was the legalization of gambling in 1931. Along with the liberalization of marriage and divorce laws, this legislation paved the way for the state to become one of the busiest year-round resorts in the country, a distinction it still claims.

GEOGRAPHY

Nevada lies almost entirely within the Great Basin. Most of its rivers, except for the Colorado, flow inward and are impounded by dams that now hold water once lost to evaporation. The most important river is the Humboldt, which loops southwestward across the northern part of the state. In the southeast region the Colorado River marks 150 miles of the Nevada-Arizona border. Several streams in the northeast feed into the Snake River-Columbia River watershed.

North-south mountain ranges crease the level floor of the Great Basin. Several have peaks more than 10,000 feet high; Boundary Peak in the White Mountains and Wheeler Peak in the Snake Range exceed 13,000 feet. The Toiyabe and Humboldt national forests embrace most of the wooded areas.

Of the more than 300 mountain ranges in Nevada, 14 of the highest peaks, covering approximately 750,000 acres, are designated protected areas by the Wilderness Protection Act, signed into law by President George Bush on Dec. 5, 1989. Administered by the U.S. Forest Service, these areas are protected from encroachment via roads, automobiles, mechanical equipment or man-made structures; access is allowed only on foot or horseback.

Several natural lakes, remnants of prehistoric Lake Lahontan that once covered most of northwestern Nevada, are set like blue jewels in the dry desert. The largest lake totally within the state is Pyramid Lake, 32 miles long and about 12 miles wide, northeast of Reno within the Pyramid Lake Indian Reservation. Captain Fremont named it for the sharp island that juts 475 feet above the water.

Anaho Island, a federal bird sanctuary, provides a breeding ground for more than 10,000 white pelicans. Walker Lake, in the bleak desert near Hawthorne, contrasts with Lake Tahoe, the year-round resort center that Nevada shares with California. Such artificial lakes as Rye Patch Reservoir, on the Humboldt, hold irrigation water for a large section of northwestern Nevada.

Modern Lake Lahontan, a reservoir formed by the damming of the Carson River in 1915 for reclamation purposes, is one of Nevada's most popular recreation areas. Mighty Lake Mead, impounded behind Hoover Dam, provides plenty of

---

recreation for southern Nevada, but most of its irrigation water goes to Arizona and California.

ECONOMY

One in every three jobs in Nevada is related to tourism, making the serving of visitors the state's leading business. Many are drawn by one of the state's other leading businesses: gambling.

To the visitor gambling is sport, but to Nevada it is a major industry. Luring millions with plush casinos and top-name shows, Reno and Las Vegas draw enough hotel patrons to make "no vacancy" signs as common as slot machines. Due to liberal tax laws, warehousing is another big business.

Mineral production, a multimillion-dollar source of income, is increasing after a slight decline. Gold is the leading mineral commodity, followed by sand/gravel and barite. New mining facilities are operating throughout the state. The Carlin County Mine, opened in 1965, represented the first new gold mine venture in the United States since the 1930s.

Silver, responsible for the state's nickname, is still being mined, as are mercury, gypsum and nickel. Turquoise is mined in Lander County near Battle Mountain. Already discovered sources of geothermal energy may become important in the production of electricity. Mining and related industries are estimated to have yielded $2.6 billion in 1990.

In the arid shadow of the Sierra Nevada, Nevada depends almost entirely on irrigation for its agricultural output. Once watered, the valley soils prove rich, producing bountiful crops of alfalfa, hay, wheat and barley. Potatoes, sugar beets, orchard fruits and the well-known "Hearts o' Gold" cantaloupes grow in quantity around Lovelock and Fallon.

In the south, cotton, tomatoes, almonds, figs, grapes and pomegranates are cultivated. Livestock, however, is more important. Cattle and sheep graze on more than 50 million acres of rangeland, augmented by an additional 5 million acres of national forest pasturage. Fallon bronze turkeys are prized by epicures.

RECREATION

Las Vegas and Reno are Nevada's largest centers of recreational activity. Besides gambling and nightclub entertainment, **swimming, boating, horseback riding, tennis, golf** and **winter sports** are available near both cities. The recreational satellite of Reno is Lake Tahoe; Lake Mead National Recreational Area and Mount Charleston serve Las Vegas.

Stocked with bass, crappie, mackinaw and other trout, channel catfish and walleye, Nevada's lakes and reservoirs provide **fishing** as well as boating, **water skiing** and other water sports. Two popular small lakes are Lake Topaz, off US 395 south of Gardnerville, and Wild Horse Reservoir, off SR 225 between Mountain City and North Fork. One of the finest fishing spots for brown trout is Cave Lake State Park near Ely.

Hunting is available, and rabbits are the most common small quarry. Quail, pheasant, sage grouse, chukar (partridge), doves, duck and geese also are hunted. The national wildlife refuges of Pahranagat, south of Alamo, Ruby Lake, in the Ruby Valley, and Stillwater, in the Fallon area, are good for duck hunting. Northwest of Las Vegas is the Desert National Wildlife Range, where hunting for deer, elk and pronghorn is carefully controlled.

Most of Nevada's winter sports areas cluster around Lake Tahoe. The 16 developments of the Ski Reno complex offer equipment rentals, accommodations and instruction in skiing and skating. Southern Nevada's snow center is Lee Canyon, northwest of Las Vegas in the Toiyabe National Forest.

A favorite pastime in this stony desert country is **rockhounding.** Turquoise, fire opal, agate, jasper and various crystals are abundant. The state's numerous trails make it popular for **hiking.** A map describing the trails' levels of difficulty and offering safety hints is available from the Nevada Division of State Parks, Capitol Complex, Carson City, NV 89710.

Indoor diversions also are plentiful in this doer's state. The casinos and nightclubs of Reno and Las Vegas offer participant activity as well as top entertainment and cuisine.

The state park system includes a well-rounded selection of scenic, historical and recreational parks. Though most state parks are open all year, severe winter weather may limit their accessibility. Most charge user fees for camping, day use, boat launching and group use; annual permits can be purchased to cover all user fees.

Tribal permits are required for boating and fishing on Indian reservations along Pyramid Lake, Walker River, Colorado River and Lake Mead; permits can be obtained from the tribal council at the reservation site or at sporting goods stores. For detailed listings of camping and trailering areas *see the AAA California/ Nevada CampBook.*

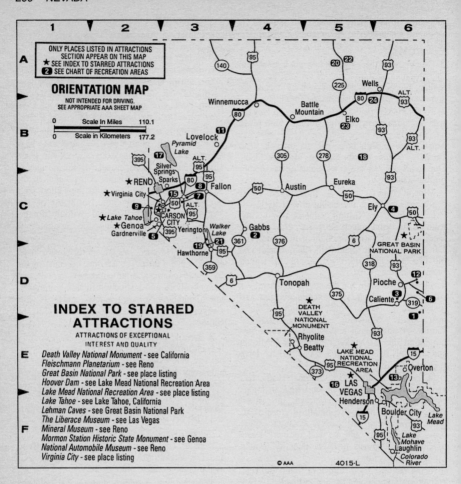

ONLY PLACES LISTED IN ATTRACTIONS SECTION APPEAR ON THIS MAP
★ SEE INDEX TO STARRED ATTRACTIONS
❷ SEE CHART OF RECREATION AREAS

ORIENTATION MAP

NOT INTENDED FOR DRIVING.
SEE APPROPRIATE AAA SHEET MAP

Scale In Miles   110.1
Scale in Kilometers   177.2

INDEX TO STARRED ATTRACTIONS

ATTRACTIONS OF EXCEPTIONAL INTEREST AND QUALITY

Death Valley National Monument - see California
Fleischmann Planetarium - see Reno
Great Basin National Park - see place listing
Hoover Dam - see Lake Mead National Recreation Area
Lake Mead National Recreation Area - see place listing
Lake Tahoe - see Lake Tahoe, California
Lehman Caves - see Great Basin National Park
The Liberace Museum - see Las Vegas
Mineral Museum - see Reno
Mormon Station Historic State Monument - see Genoa
National Automobile Museum - see Reno
Virginia City - see place listing

© AAA   4015-L

RECREATION AREAS	MAP LOCATION	CAMPING	PICNICKING	HIKING TRAILS	BOATING	BOAT RAMP	BOAT RENTAL	FISHING	SWIMMING	PETS ON LEASH	BICYCLE TRAILS	WINTER SPORTS	VISITOR CENTER	LODGE/CABINS	FOOD SERVICE
NATIONAL PARK *(See place listing)*															
Great Basin 77,109 acres 5 mi. w. of Baker near the Nevada-Utah border.		•	•	•				•		•		•	•		•
NATIONAL FORESTS *(See place listings)*															
Humboldt 2,474,985 acres. Central and northern Nevada. Horse rental.		•	•	•				•	•	•		•			
Toiyabe 3,861,166 acres. Central, western and southern Nevada and eastern California. Horse rental.		•	•	•				•		•		•			
NATIONAL RECREATION AREA *(See place listing)*															
Lake Mead (E-5)		•	•	•	•	•	•	•	•	•			•	•	•

RECREATION AREAS

RECREATION AREAS	MAP LOCATION	CAMPING	PICNICKING	HIKING TRAILS	BOATING	BOAT RAMP	BOAT RENTAL	FISHING	SWIMMING	PETS ON LEASH	BICYCLE TRAILS	WINTER SPORTS	VISITOR CENTER	LODGE/CABINS	FOOD SERVICE
STATE															
Beaver Dam (D-6) 2,218 acres 35 mi. n.e. of Caliente. Interpretive trails.	1	•	•	•				•	•	•					
Berlin-Ichthyosaur (C-4) 1,127 acres. Historic. *(See Gabbs)*	2	•	•	•						•			•		
Cathedral Gorge (D-6) 1,633 acres 2 mi. n. of Panaca off US 93. Scenic. Interpretive trails.	3	•	•	•						•					
Cave Lake (C-6) 1,208 acres 8 mi. s. of Ely off US 93, then 7 mi. e. on Success Summit Rd. Cross-country skiing, snowmobiling.	4	•	•	•	•	•		•	•	•		•			
Dayton (C-3) 152 acres 12 mi. e. of Carson City on US 50. Nature trail.	5	•	•	•						•					
Echo Canyon (D-6) 920 acres 4 mi. e. of Pioche, then 8 mi. s.e.	6	•	•	•	•	•		•		•					
Fort Churchill (C-3) 1,232 acres. Historic. *(See Silver Springs)*	7	•	•	•						•					
Lahontan (C-3) 30,362 acres 18 mi. w. of Fallon off US 50.	8	•	•		•	•		•	•	•					
Lake Tahoe-Nevada (C-2) 14,242 acres 4 mi. s. of Incline Village on SR 28. Cross-country skiing.	9		•	•	•	•		•	•	•		•	•	•	
Rye Patch (B-3) 20,241 acres 22 mi. n. of Lovelock off I-80.	11	•	•	•	•	•		•	•	•					
South Fork (B-5) 3,924 acres s.w. of Elko via SR 228 to Lower South Fork Rd. Water skiing.	23				•	•		•	•	•					
Spring Valley (D-6) 1,230 acres 20 mi. e. of Pioche. Horse rental.	12	•	•	•	•	•		•		•					
Valley of Fire (E-6) 38,480 acres. *(See Overton)*	13	•	•	•						•			•		
Walker Lake (D-3) 280 acres 11 mi. n.w. of Hawthorne on US 95. Water skiing.	21	•	•		•	•		•	•	•					
Washoe Lake (C-3) 7,778 acres between Reno and Carson City e. of US 395.	15	•	•	•	•	•		•	•	•					
Wild Horse (A-5) 120 acres 65 mi. n. of Elko via SR 225. Cross-country skiing, snowmobiling.	20	•	•		•	•		•	•	•		•			
OTHER															
Angel Lake (B-5) 13 mi. s.w. of Wells via SR 582.	24	•	•	•				•		•					
Mount Charleston (E-5) 30 mi. n.w. of Las Vegas via US 95 and SR 157.	16	•	•	•						•	•	•	•	•	•
Pyramid Lake (B-3) *(See Reno)*	17	•	•		•	•		•	•	•					
Ruby Lake (B-5) 60 mi. s.e. of Elko.	18	•	•		•	•		•	•	•			•		•
Walker Lake (D-3) 4 mi. n. of Hawthorne.	19	•	•		•	•		•	•	•					•
Wild Horse Reservoir (A-5) 65 mi. n. of Elko on SR 225.	22	•	•	•	•	•		•	•	•			•	•	•

POINTS OF INTEREST

AUSTIN (C-4) pop. 400

Popular legend says that Austin sprang up in 1862 after a Pony Express horse kicked over a rock that capped the mouth of a silver-laden cavern just west of the present townsite. Within 2 years Austin boasted a population of 10,000 as bullion poured from its 11 ore-reduction mills. By 1867, some 6,000 mining claims had been filed.

Despite appearances, Austin is not a ghost town. Gold and barite mining operations have been reactivated, and Austin remains a base for mining exploration crews in central Nevada. The search for silver has been replaced by an interest in the turquoise deposits that dot the region.

Austin lies along US 50. Once part of the Pony Express Trail across central Nevada, the route has long stretches without roadside services and passes through such other historic mining towns as Eureka and Ely *(see place listings)*. Austin also is at the southern end of scenic SR 305, which follows the Reese River and Shoshone Ridge to Battle Mountain.

A reminder of Austin's former affluence is Stoke's Castle, built in 1897 for Anson Phelps Stokes, an eastern financier who had considerable mining interests in the area. Built of hand-hewn granite slabs, the deserted three-story replica of a Roman tower can be seen for miles in the desert.

Near Austin are a number of historical sites. The Hickson Petroglyph Recreation Site, 24 miles east on US 50 near the old Pony Express Trail, features stones etched with Indian drawings dating from 1000 B.C. to A.D. 1500. Toiyabe National Forest *(see place listing)* offers trout fishing and fowl hunting.

About 65 miles west of Austin off SR 50 are the remains of the Cold Springs Pony Express Station. A sign near the highway explains the history of the site and marks the beginning of an interpretive self-guiding 1½-mile trail that leads to the station.

BATTLE MOUNTAIN (B-4) alt. 4,507'

Battle Mountain took its name from a nearby range of mountains whose name originated with an Indian raid against pioneers in 1857. The discovery of minerals in Copper Canyon in 1870 brought permanent settlers, and Battle Mountain became the point where mining supplies were transferred between stage lines and railroads.

Ranching and transportation have largely replaced mining. There are two barite mines in the vicinity of Battle Mountain and a gold and silver mine at Copper Canyon. Battle Mountain straddles I-80, which follows the old Bidwell, Donner and Fremont pioneer trails. To the south along SR 305 is the scenic Reese River Valley.

BEATTY (E-5) pop. 3,500

A picturesque desert town in the Amargosa River Valley, Beatty is the Nevada approach to Death Valley National Monument *(see place listing in California)*. Chloride Cliff, reached via a rough 5-mile dirt road off SR 374, offers an excellent view of Death Valley. Also en route to the national monument are the ghost towns of Rhyolite *(see place listing)* and Bullfrog. Six miles north of Beatty on US 95 are Bailey's Hot Springs. With a water temperature of about 104 degrees Fahrenheit, the springs are open throughout the year.

BOULDER CITY (F-6) pop. 12,600

An access point to the Lake Mead National Recreation Area *(see place listing)*, Boulder City was built by the federal government as a residential community for employees of the Bureau of Reclamation, Park Service and Bureau of Mines branches in the area.

Because gambling was prohibited in Boulder City under the original land agreement, the town is still the only community in Nevada without legalized gambling. Boulder City celebrates the Spring Jamboree and Artisans Fair in March and displays local talent in the open-air Art in the Park festival in early October.

★HOOVER DAM—*see Lake Mead National Recreation Area.*

CALIENTE (D-6) pop. 1,100, alt. 4,403'

Caliente is near several state parks, including Beaver Dam, Cathedral Gorge, Echo Canyon and Spring Valley *(see Recreation Chart)*. Also nearby is the ghost town Delamar, marked by a few rock buildings, mill ruins and a cemetery. Check locally on road conditions. On Memorial Day weekend, the town holds its Lincoln County Homecoming, which consists of a rodeo, arts show and various sporting events.

A mural displaying points of interest in Lincoln and Clark counties is in the lobby of the Amtrak station, a Spanish-style railroad depot built in 1923. Guided tours of the Lincoln County Art Room, also in the lobby of the station, and other area attractions can be arranged through the chamber of commerce; write P.O. Box 553, Caliente, NV 89008, or phone (702) 726-3129.

CARSON CITY (C-3) pop. 40,400, alt. 4,660'

Carson City, named for Kit Carson when it was founded in 1858, was designated as the state capital in 1864. The original silver-domed Capitol, with later additions and restorations, is still in use. The old Assembly and Senate chambers, including a museum display about the Capitol, can be visited. Self-guiding tours are available Mon.-Fri. 8-5; phone (702) 687-4810. The Legislative Building south of the Capitol is open Mon.-Fri. 9-4.

As the social center for nearby mining settlements in the mid-1800s, Carson City prospered. The federal government established a mint for coining the copious silver output of the Comstock Lode, 15 miles northeast near Virginia City. Gold found its way here also, as evidenced by the rare gold display at the Carson City Nugget, across from the Capitol.

Antique firefighting equipment, old photographs and a series of Currier & Ives prints dealing with firefighters are on display at the Warren Engine Company No. 1 Fire Museum at 111 N. Curry St. (second floor); phone (702) 883-4855.

The Sierra Seminary, one of the first coeducational schools in the West, was established in Carson City in 1860 by Hannah Clapp. An outspoken advocate of women's rights, Clapp operated the school for about 25 years before moving to Reno. There she and the university president temporarily served as the entire staff of the infant University of Nevada.

Carson City lies along US 50, which has been called "the loneliest road in America." Once part of the Pony Express Trail across central Nevada, the route consists of long stretches without roadside services and passes through such historic mining towns as Austin, Eureka and Ely *(see place listings).*

The portion of US 50 heading west to Lake Tahoe and the California border is especially scenic. From its junction with US 395 downtown, US 50 cuts through the Toiyabe National Forest *(see place listing)* and then follows the lake's southeastern shoreline. Beginning at its junction with US 50 at Spooner Summit, SR 28, another scenic route, follows the lake's northeastern shoreline into California.

Carson City's Spring Fun Fair takes place at the end of April, while Kit Carson Rendezvous and Wagon Train Ride are held in mid-June. The Nevada Day Celebration and Parade occurs in late October.

Self-guiding tours: The Carson City Chamber of Commerce, 1900 S. Carson St., has a free self-guiding tour map which contains illustrations and descriptions of the town's historic sites; phone (702) 882-1565.

BOWERS MANSION PARK, 10 mi. n. on old US 395, overlooks Washoe Lake. The restored mansion, built by a Comstock Lode millionaire at a cost of $200,000 in 1864, contains some of the original furnishings. The surrounding park has picnic facilities, a playground and a swimming pool.

Guided tours of the mansion are available every half-hour. Park open daily 8-8, mid-May through Oct. 31; 8-5:30, rest of year. Mansion tours daily 11-1 and 1:30-4:30, mid-May through Oct. 31. Park free. Tours $2; under 13, $1. Pool $2; ages 13-17, $1.50; under 13, $1. Phone (702) 849-0644.

NEVADA STATE RAILROAD MUSEUM, 2180 S. Carson St. (US 395), consists of more than 26 pieces of the Virginia and Truckee Railroad line, including three restored steam engines. Established in 1869, the celebrated line carried ore from the Comstock Lode to the Carson River for 69 of its 81 years. In retirement, the line was discovered by Hollywood, which used V & T passenger and freight cars and vintage engines in movies during the late 1930s.

Allow 30 minutes minimum for museum, 1 hour for museum and train ride. Museum open Wed.-Sun. 8:30-4:30; closed Jan. 1, Thanksgiving and Dec. 25. Rides on historic railroad equipment are offered weekends, Memorial Day-Labor Day; phone for schedule. Train $2.50; under 12, $1 Museum $1, under 18 free. Phone (702) 687-6953.

STATE MUSEUM, 600 N. Carson St., is in the Mint Building where the Carson City silver dollars were stamped. Exhibits include historical relics, a ghost town replica, a mint mark coin collection, minerals and ores. In addition, an Indian room displays baskets woven by Dot-So-La-Lee of the Washoe tribe. Allow 1 hour, 30 minutes minimum. Daily 8:30-4:30; closed Jan. 1, Thanksgiving and Dec. 25. Admission $5, under 18 free. Phone (702) 687-4810.

STEWART INDIAN MUSEUM, 5366 Snyder Ave., has displays of Indian artifacts, basketry, pottery and E.S. Curtis photogravures. Changing exhibits highlight American Indian history and culture. The museum trading post offers rugs, silver and turquoise jewelry, beadwork and original art. Allow 1 hour minimum. Daily 9-4. Free. Phone (702) 882-1808.

★DEATH VALLEY NATIONAL MONUMENT—*see California.*

ELKO (B-5) pop. 14,700, alt. 5,060'

The center for Nevada's cattle country, Elko served as a way station for wagon trains during the western migration. Tourism accounts for a good portion of the town's revenue. Elko holds several events—the Cowboy Poetry Gathering from late January to early February; Mardi Gras in mid-February; the Western Festival and the Elko Mining Expo and Open Golf Tournament in early June; and the Basque Festival on the first weekend in July.

South of Elko lie the Ruby Mountains, where miles of trails lead to back-country lakes and marshes offering hunting, fishing and boating. Lamoille Canyon *(see Humboldt National Forest)* in the Ruby Mountains is known for its 12-mile-long steep glacial walls, free-flowing streams and scenic vistas.

NORTHEASTERN NEVADA MUSEUM, 11 blks. e. on I-80 business route at 1515 Idaho St., chronicles natural history through exhibits pertaining to the area's Indian heritage and mining tradition. Frontier displays depict a pioneer kitchen, schoolroom and printing plant. Changing art exhibitions also are featured.

An 1860 Pony Express cabin, a "mudwagon" stagecoach and other pioneer vehicles are on the grounds, as well as a 1918 Dodge touring car and a 1925 Seagraves fire engine. Allow 1 hour minimum. Mon.-Sat. 9-5, Sun. 1-5; closed Jan. 1, Thanksgiving and Dec. 25. Free. Phone (702) 738-3418.

ELY (C-6) pop. 4,800, alt. 6,421'

Founded in 1868 as a silver-mining camp, Ely bloomed with the arrival of the Nevada Northern Railway, which chugged into town in 1906 bedecked with flags, bunting and sagebrush wreaths. When it converted to large-scale copper mining, Ely grew from 500 to 3,000 residents in 1 year.

Kennecott Copper Corp.'s renowned Liberty Pit produced more than $550 million in copper, gold and silver deposits. Kennecott also operated the giant Ruth pit, which produced from about 1905 to the late 1970s. The seat of White Pine County, Ely continues to be a center for mining as well as ranching and recreation.

The surrounding mountain ranges provide fine hunting and trout fishing. High-country hikers are fond of nearby Wheeler Peak Scenic Area, which includes 13,063-foot Wheeler Peak, Baker and Snake creeks, Big Wash Canyon and the upper parts of Lehman Creek. The garnet-studded rhyolite outcropping at the peak of Garnet Hill, 5 miles west off US 50, is popular with rockhounds. Swimming and fishing are available at Cave Lake State Recreation Area *(see Recreation Chart)*.

The Bristlecone Chariot and Futurity Races, held in early March, draw horse racing fans. In late August, the town pays tribute to the Old West with the celebration of Pony Express Days and Horse Race.

Several old mining camps and ghost towns can still be found in the Ely vicinity; these include Hamilton, Cherry Creek, Fort Schellbourne, Lane City, Osceola, Taylor and Ward. Ely also is the western terminus of a scenic route consisting of US 93, US 50/6 and SR 487. Crossing the Schell Creek and Snake ranges, the route leads to the Utah border.

NEVADA NORTHERN RAILWAY MUSEUM, in a train depot at 1100 Ave. A in East Ely, contains a restored dispatcher's office, roundhouse, machine shop, locomotives and cars from various eras. Guided tours are conducted hourly. Museum open Wed.-Sun. 9-5, mid-May through Sept. 30. Admission $2.50; over 64 and ages 12-18, $1; ages 5-11, 50c. Phone (702) 289-2085.

On weekends the Ghost Train of Old Ely makes a 1½-hour trip from the museum through downtown Ely, the Lane City ghost town, Robinson Canyon and the Keystone mining district. The train consists of preserved Nevada Northern Railway cars, which include a Pullman coach, baggage car, flat car and a 1910, 10-wheel Baldwin steam engine. On alternate weekends a diesel engine is used.

Since the steam engine may emit coal cinders, riders should wear protective eye and headgear. Train departures and prices vary; write to P.O. Box 150040, East Ely, NV 89315; phone (702) 289-2085.

WARD CHARCOAL OVENS HISTORIC STATE MONUMENT is 5 mi. s.e. on US 6/50/93, then 11 mi. w. on a gravel road. The six 30-foot-high stone "beehive" ovens were constructed during the 1870s mining boom. The monument is open all year but may not be accessible during winter months.

WHITE PINE PUBLIC MUSEUM, 2000 Aultman St., displays gems and minerals, mining equipment, Pony Express memorabilia, Indian relics, furniture, clothes and guns. In addition, the museum has a collection of 700 dolls, 200 of which are displayed at a time on a rotating basis. An outdoor train exhibit includes a 1905 coach and 1909 and 1917 steam locomotives. Mon.-Fri. 9-5, Sat.-Sun. 10-4. Free. Phone (702) 289-4710.

EUREKA (C-5) pop. 800, alt. 6,837'

Eureka lies along US 50, at the southern end of scenic SR 278. During the town's heyday in the 1870s, its lead-based economy and the atten-

dant smelters led the town to be called the "Pittsburgh of the West." The population, which at one point reached nearly 11,000, supported 100 saloons, several newspapers, hotels, an opera house, five fire companies and a brass band.

The opera house presents historical theater productions and is used by the chamber of commerce for special events and exhibits. The Eureka Sentinel Museum, at Bateman and Monroe roads, houses the original printing equipment of the newspaper, which began operations in 1870, and displays reprints, posters and placards printed by the *Sentinel* in the 1870s and '80s. The Eureka County Chamber of Commerce also is located within the building. For information on the area contact the chamber of commerce; phone (702) 237-5484.

FALLON (C-3) pop. 6,400

Completion of Lahontan Dam in 1914 and subsequent reclamation and irrigation changed the area from barren desert to one of the state's largest farming districts. The major farm products include livestock, alfalfa and "Hearts o' Gold" cantaloupes. Besides supplying water for irrigation, the impounded lake is popular for recreation as part of the Lahontan State Recreation Area *(see Recreation Chart)*.

East of Fallon SR 50 parallels the old route of the Pony Express for a number of miles. About 20 miles east of town an unimproved road (often impassable after storms) leads to Sand Mountain and the Sand Springs Pony Express Station, a short hike away. One of the few "singing mountains" in the country, Sand Mountain is composed of grains of sand that sometimes create a low moan as they shift.

Fallon's International Invitational High School Rodeo is held in early July; mid-July features the All-Indian Stampede and Pioneer Days. Other events include the Hearts o' Gold Cantaloupe Festival and the Lions Club Jr. Rodeo on Labor Day weekend.

CHURCHILL COUNTY MUSEUM AND ARCHIVES, 1050 S. Maine St., features an extensive collection of Western Americana focusing on the history of Churchill County and the Lahontan Valley. Displays of memorabilia pertain to the Emigrant Trail, Pony Express and Transcontinental Telegraph, while notable collections include rocks, minerals and gemstones, and artifacts of Nevada Indian tribes.

Allow 1 hour minimum. Museum open Mon.-Sat. 10-5, Sun. noon-5, June-Sept.; Mon.-Wed. and Fri.-Sat. 10-4, Sun. noon-4, rest of year. Free. Phone (702) 423-3677.

The museum offers expeditions on the second and fourth Saturday of each month to Grimes Point, an archeological zone 12 miles east on US 50; visitors can explore Hidden Cave with a guide or take a self-guiding hike along a petroglyph trail. Allow 2 hours minimum for the guided tour, 1½ hours for the hike. Tours are free; phone for schedule.

GABBS (C-4) pop. 700

Gabbs has one of the few golf courses in the area. The nine-hole set of links at Sandy Bottom Golf Course, 3 miles north of town, is unusual in that all its greens are made of desert sand. For directions, phone the Town Hall at (702) 285-2671.

BERLIN-ICHTHYOSAUR STATE PARK is 23 mi. e. via SR 844. This 1,127-acre park has fossils of reptiles that once swam the ancient ocean covering Nevada 225 million years ago, as well as the late 19th-century ghost town of Berlin. Interpretive signs outline self-guiding tours among the town's 13 preserved buildings.

Guided tours of the townsite are offered Sat.-Sun. at 11 a.m., May-Sept. The park is open daily, weather permitting; it may be inaccessible in winter. Guided tours of the Ichthyosaur Fossil Shelter are given Fri.-Mon. at 10, 2 and 4, May 21-Sept. 6; Fri.-Mon. at 10 and 2, Mar. 12-May 20 and Sept. 7-Nov. 15. Park free. Guided tours $1; ages 6-12, 50c. Phone (702) 964-2440. *See Recreation Chart.*

GARDNERVILLE (C-2) pop. 2,200

The Lahontan National Fish Hatchery is located 4 miles south on US 395. The hatchery rears the threatened cutthroat trout for stocking in western Nevada waters. Picnicking is permitted. The hatchery is open daily 8-3; phone (702) 265-2425.

GENOA (C-2) alt. 4,800′

Founded by one of the traders sent out by Brigham Young in 1849, Genoa became the first permanent settlement in Nevada. In 1859 Nevada's first territorial legislature met in Genoa for a 9-day session that drafted a declaration of cause for separation from Utah Territory. Recognizing the value of the famed Comstock Lode in financing the Union's efforts in the Civil War, Congress established the Territory of Nevada in 1861.

GENOA COURTHOUSE MUSEUM, Main St., contains a Virginia and Truckee Railroad display and replicas of an old schoolroom, courtroom, jail and kitchen, as well as Indian basketry, needlework and artifacts. Allow 1 hour minimum. Daily 10-4:30, May 15 to mid-Oct. Donations. Phone (702) 782-4325.

★**MORMON STATION HISTORIC STATE MONUMENT**, off I-395 then w. on Genoa Ln. to jct. with SR 206, is a restored log stockade and trading post built in 1851 in the Carson Valley, where emigrants often rested before continuing over the Sierra Nevada to California. There also is a museum on the grounds. Daily 9-5, May 1-Oct. 15. Donations. Phone (702) 782-2590.

★GREAT BASIN NATIONAL PARK (C-6)

Great Basin National Park is 68 miles east of Ely off US 50; from US 50 go 5 miles south on SR 487 to Baker, then 5 miles west on SR 488 to the park headquarters. Established in 1986, the 77,109-acre park contains many of the features common to the Great Basin, including impressive mountain peaks, lush meadows, sparkling streams and alpine lakes, in addition to a small icefield.

Rising abruptly 5,300 feet from the desert floor, the park exhibits a wide variety of plant and animal habitats that range from the Upper Sonoran life zone with its jack rabbits, sagebrush and cacti to the frigid Arctic-Alpine Tundra life zone at the highest elevations.

In spring and summer many kinds of wildflowers bloom on the mountain slopes. Pine, spruce, fir and mountain mahogany make up the forests, and wildlife includes mule deer, mountain lion, coyote, porcupine and golden eagles. Rocky Mountain bighorn sheep, once locally extinct, were reintroduced to this area in 1971.

General Information and Activities

A highlight of the park is Lehman Caves, a limestone solution cave. The visitor center is open daily 8-5 and offers 90-minute cave tours, exhibits, films, maps and park information. A cafe is open April through October.

Wheeler Peak Scenic Drive extends 12 miles to the 10,000-foot elevation on the flank of Wheeler Peak. Hiking trails lead past several alpine lakes to the 13,063-foot summit or to a rare ancient bristlecone pine forest. Park interpreters conduct various campfire programs throughout the summer.

Camping is permitted at three campgrounds along Wheeler Peak Scenic Drive. Fishing for rainbow trout is popular in the park's many clear creeks. Anglers over 11 need a Nevada fishing license and a trout stamp; both are available in Ely and Baker. There are no developed cross-country ski trails, but winter brings ample opportunity for back-country skiing.

A few warnings should be kept in mind when visiting the park. The area is quite dry, so carry plenty of drinking water when hiking and treat any surface water before use. Rattlesnakes are found at the lower elevations during warm weather, and extreme weather conditions are likely in winter. *See Recreation Chart and the AAA California/Nevada CampBook.*

ADMISSION to the park is free. There is a fee for cave tours.

PETS must be on a leash at all times. They are not allowed in buildings, in the cave or on trails.

ADDRESS inquiries to the Superintendent, Great Basin National Park, Baker, NV 89311.

Points of Interest

BRISTLECONE PINE FOREST consists of 150 acres of trees considered to be among the oldest living things on Earth. One stand includes pines approaching 4,000 years old. An interpretive trail through the forest branches off the scenic area's main loop trail. Another spur off the main loop climbs to the summit of Wheeler Peak, the second highest peak in Nevada. Park interpreters lead walks through the bristlecone pine forest daily, June 15-Sept. 8.

★**LEHMAN CAVES**, at the foot of Wheeler Peak and 5 mi. w. of Baker, consist of illuminated marble and limestone passages that have many colorful formations and curious shieldlike or palettelike shapes.

Although the first written mention of the cave was found in an 1885 newspaper, it is possible that it was discovered earlier by homesteaders or miners. Absolom S. Lehman was probably the first to realize the significance of the underground galleries. After conducting his own exploration, he guided parties through the cave that bears his name until his death in 1891.

Guided 1½-hour cave tours are offered daily on the hour 8-5, Memorial Day-Labor Day; at 9, 11, 2 and 4, rest of year. Admission $3; over 62 (Golden Age Passport holders) $1.50; ages 6-15 (with an adult) $2. The tour covers about a half mile and includes 10 stairways. Flash cameras are allowed, but tripods and backpacks are not. The cave temperature is a cool 50 degrees Fahrenheit, so a sweater or light jacket is highly recommended.

A 45-minute historic candlelight tour, which uses candle lanterns carried by visitors to illuminate the cave, is offered daily at 6 p.m., Memorial Day-Labor Day. Admission is the same as for the regular tours. Children unable to carry a candle are not permitted.

A 3-hour spelunking tour of another of the park's caves, Little Muddy Cave, is offered Sat.-Sun. at 1:30, Memorial Day-Labor Day. Tours are limited to six people over 14, and participants must be able to fit through a 10-by-20-inch space. Admission $6; reservations are required. Phone (702) 234-7331.

HAWTHORNE (D-3) alt. 4,375'

MINERAL COUNTY MUSEUM, 10th and D sts., features American Indian artifacts, clothing, housewares and archeological specimens from the area's early days. Mon.-Fri. 11-5, Apr.-Oct.; noon-4, rest of year. Donations. Phone (702) 945-5142.

HENDERSON (F-5) pop. 64,900

Henderson was settled during World War II as a housing area for employees of a magnesium plant, but has since expanded into Nevada's main industrial center, with many plants concerned principally with chemical and metal production.

The town is the southwest terminus of scenic SR 147, which follows the spectacular Lake Mead shoreline from Hoover Dam to Overton Beach.

CLARK COUNTY HERITAGE MUSEUM, 1830 S. Boulder Hwy., offers three exhibit areas, including a chronological history of southern Nevada from dinosaur fossils to the first white settlements, a group of historic residential and commercial structures called Heritage Street, and a re-created ghost town with a number of original structures and old railroad cars.

Allow 1 hour minimum. Daily 9-4:30; closed Jan. 1 and Dec. 25. Admission $1; over 54 and ages 3-16, 50c. Phone (702) 455-7955.

ETHEL M. CHOCOLATE FACTORY AND CACTUS GARDEN are in the Green Valley Business Park, 2 Cactus Garden Dr. The factory makes gourmet chocolates; a self-guiding tour is available. Adjacent is the Cactus Garden, a 2½-acre collection of more than 350 species of desert plants from the Southwest and other arid areas of the world.

Guided tours are offered by advance arrangement. Factory open daily 9-5:30; garden 8:30-6. Closed Thanksgiving and Dec. 25. Free. Phone (702) 458-8864.

HUMBOLDT NATIONAL FOREST

The 2,474,985 acres of Humboldt National Forest are scattered along the Independence, Santa Rosa, Ruby, White Pine, Jarbidge, Schell Creek and Quinn Canyon ranges in north-central Nevada. Jarbidge Wilderness is north of Elko; no motorized vehicles are allowed, but six trails suitable for hiking and horseback riding traverse the area.

The Ruby Mountains Wilderness, southeast of Elko, offers backpacking and other recreational opportunities within 90,000 acres of alpine lakes, glaciated canyons and rugged mountains. Other wilderness areas include East Humboldt, Mount Moriah, Currant Mountain, Quinn Canyon, Grant Range and Santa Rosa-Paradise Peak.

The forest headquarters are at 976 Mountain City Hwy., Elko, NV 89801; phone (702) 738-5171. See Recreation Chart and the AAA California/Nevada CampBook.

LAMOILLE CANYON is in Humboldt National Forest, 18 mi. s.e. of Elko via SR 227. A paved, two-lane scenic drive, overshadowed by towering cliffs, winds 12 miles along the canyon. Several overlooks with posted information enable visitors to observe the effects of glacial activity. Picnicking, rest areas and limited campgrounds are available.

INCLINE VILLAGE

PONDEROSA RANCH—*see Lake Tahoe, Calif.*

★**LAKE MEAD NATIONAL RECREATION AREA (E-5)**

Extending about 140 miles along the Colorado River from Grand Canyon National Park, Ariz., to a point 67 miles below Hoover Dam, Lake Mead National Recreation Area embraces Lake Mohave, Lake Mead and an isolated pocket of land north of Grand Canyon National Park. Fishing is popular in both lakes all year; licenses are required. Bass and catfish are the chief catches in Lake Mead, while rainbow trout and bass are plentiful in Lake Mohave.

★HOOVER DAM, 726 feet tall, is one of the highest dams ever constructed. Begun in 1931 and completed in 1935, it is considered one of the engineering wonders of the United States. The dam impounds Lake Mead, one of the largest man-made lakes in the Western Hemisphere. A free movie illustrating the construction of Hoover Dam is shown continuously in a portable movie theater near the Nevada Spillway.

Until the spring of 1993 construction of new visitor facilities may cause traffic delays. Free shuttle service is provided from several well-marked lots along US 93 in the vicinity of the dam during most tour hours.

Elevators carry passengers down to the power plant for a 40-minute guided tour daily 8-6:45, Memorial Day weekend-Labor Day; 9-4:15, rest of year. Last tour 1 hour before closing. Closed Dec. 25. Admission $1, bearers of Golden Age or Golden Access Passports 50c, under 15 free.

The Exhibit Building at the west end of the dam houses a model of the river basin; a recorded lecture is available. Open daily 8-6; Memorial Day weekend-Labor Day; 9-4:30, rest of year. Closed Dec. 25. Free. Phone (702) 293-8367.

LAKE MEAD, one of the world's largest artificial lakes in volume, is 115 miles long and averages 200 feet in depth. The 550-mile shoreline encircles 157,900 acres of water in Nevada and Arizona. A drive along SR 147 reveals the beauty of Nevada's northwestern and western portions of the shoreline. In December, the boats at Lake Mead sport holiday decorations during the Lake Mead Parade of Lights.

There are six major recreational centers on the lake. In Arizona, Temple Bar is about 80 miles north of Kingman. In Nevada are Boulder Beach, 6 miles northeast of Boulder City; Las Vegas Wash, 13 miles northeast of Boulder City; Callville Bay, 22 miles east of North Las Vegas; and the Overton Beach and Echo Bay areas, both south of Overton.

An orientation film, slides, information services and natural history exhibits are offered at the Alan Bible Visitor Center, 4 miles east of Boulder City at the junction of US 93 and Lakeshore Road. A botanical garden surrounding the visitor center contains varieties of desert flora. Center open daily 8:30-4:30; closed Jan. 1, Thanksgiving and Dec. 25. Free. Phone (702) 293-8906. *See Recreation Chart and the AAA California/Nevada CampBook.*

Boat Excursion to Hoover Dam leaves Lake Mead Resort Marina for a 1½-hour trip daily at 11:30, 1:30 and 3:30, Mar. 15-Nov. 15; 11:30 and 1:30, rest of year. Fare $12; ages 3-12, $5. AE, MC, VI. Breakfast and dinner cruises also are available. For information phone (702) 293-6180.

LAKE MOHAVE extends 67 mi. s. from Hoover Dam to Davis Dam; the latter is open daily 7:30-3:30 for self-guiding tours. Concessionaires offer trailer sites, food, overnight lodgings and boat rentals at Katherine's Landing, just north of Davis Dam in Arizona; Cottonwood Cove, 14 miles east of Searchlight in Nevada; and Willow Beach, 28 miles east of Boulder City on US 93 in Arizona. Information/ranger stations, launch ramps and picnic facilities are available at all three sites.

Swimming is permitted anywhere along the lakeshore except in harbors. Camping is available at Cottonwood Cove *(see the AAA California/Nevada CampBook)* and at Katherine's Landing *(see the AAA Southwestern CampBook).*

★LAKE TAHOE—*see place listing in California.*

Las Vegas

The neon memorial to tinseled affluence, Las Vegas booms 24 hours a day with a heady atmosphere of "get rich quick." The lure of easy money, the whirling wheels and gaming tables, and numerous plush hotels provide ready entertainment for visitors.

Las Vegas, once an oasis on the route to California, began as a Mormon settlement and boomed fleetingly during the silver rush. But unlike towns that went bust and stayed bust, the townsite revived with ranching in the late 1800s and the coming of the railroad in 1905. The Union Pacific successfully auctioned off 1,200 lots in one day—lots which were to become the breeding ground for saloons, businesses and gambling houses.

During the Great Depression, a stampede of unemployed men streamed into the Las Vegas-Boulder City area to find work constructing Hoover Dam on the Colorado River. The hydroelectric wonder they created helped to light the neon signs synonymous with the city.

In 1931, the same year construction began on Hoover Dam, the desert town received its greatest windfall: legalized gambling. The ever-practical state legislators, cognizant of widespread gambling, decided to capitalize on it and eliminate the attendant bribery and corruption. Almost overnight casinos sprang up downtown, gamblers flooded the city and Las Vegas was on its way.

After World War II came the big resort hotels, and with them big entertainment. The purpose was simply to lure people in so they would sample the thrill of slot machines and blackjack. As more hotels moved onto the Strip, each vied with the others for the plushest casino, most opulent showroom and most glamorous stars.

The siren song was simple: Visit Las Vegas and see the world's largest and best collection of singers, comedians, dancers and musicians. People heeded the call in increasing numbers. Hotels and casinos, enriched by the increased revenue, offered more and more—shows grew bigger, the Strip flashier, the casinos slicker. Las Vegas became a city that thrived on illusion and fantasy.

Glitz and escapist fun are supplied in quantity by colossal hotel/casino complexes. The Mirage, located on the Strip, offers gardens, waterfalls

---

THE INFORMED TRAVELER

POPULATION: 258,300, metro 741,500   **ALTITUDE:** 2,174 ft.

Whom to Call

Emergency: 911
Police (non-emergency): (702) 795-3111
Fire: (702) 383-2888
Weather: (702) 734-2010

Time: 118

Hospitals: Humana-Sunrise, (702) 731-8000; University Medical Center, (702) 383-2000.

Where to Look

Newspapers

Las Vegas has two daily newspapers, the morning *Review-Journal* and the evening *Sun.* Check the daily events section for current entertainment offerings.

Radio and TV

Las Vegas radio station KNEWS (970 AM) is an all-news/weather station; KNPR (89.5 FM) is programmed by National Public Radio. The major TV channels are 3 (NBC), 5 (FOX), 8 (CBS), 10 (PBS) and 13 (ABC).

Visitor Information

The Las Vegas Convention and Visitors Authority, 3150 S. Paradise Rd., Las Vegas, NV 89109, provides entertainment, transportation, recreation, city tour and visitor information. The authority is open Mon.-Fri. 8-5; phone (702) 892-0711.

What to Wear

Las Vegas receives only 4 inches of rain and an estimated 320 days of sunshine annually. Though days can be furnace-hot from May to October, low humidity and air conditioning dispel discomfort.

Temperatures range between 25 and 70 degrees Fahrenheit from November through February, climb to warmer levels in March and reach well over 100 degrees Fahrenheit from June through August.

and a man-made volcano which erupts 100 feet above the water every 15 minutes from dusk to 1 a.m. Inside, Siegfried and Roy perform illusions with disappearing animals and rare royal white tigers in a $25-million theater designed especially for their show. An elaborate habitat for the royal white tigers has been constructed within the hotel.

The Excalibur, the world's largest hotel, boasts 4,032 rooms in a castlelike structure featuring 14 spires of red, blue and gold and four stone turrets. Visitors must cross a moat complete with drawbridge to gain access, and once inside, they can witness a jousting tournament or watch the Lipizzan stallions perform.

Approaches
By Car

The major route into Las Vegas is I-15, which passes through the city from southern California to Arizona and Utah. Other routes are US 95 from the northwest, which becomes the Las Vegas Expressway in the downtown area, and US 93/95 from the southeast.

Travelers from California should be prepared for desert driving, regardless of their departure point. Basic precautions include making certain that the car's engine and cooling system are in good working order and that tires are properly inflated, as well as keeping a constant watch on the gas gauge. It is always prudent to carry extra coolant or water in case of overheating.

By Plane, Train and Bus

McCarran International Airport is 5 miles south of the business district via Paradise Road and the Strip. Limousine, taxi and bus service are available.

Daily train service is provided by Amtrak, (800) 872-7245; the station is at the Union Plaza Hotel, 1 Main St. Greyhound Lines Inc., 200 S. Main St., is the major bus carrier serving Las Vegas; phone (702) 382-2640.

Getting Around
Street System

Las Vegas Boulevard, known as the Strip, and Main Street are the primary north-south thoroughfares. The primary east-west thoroughfares are Charleston Boulevard and Sahara Avenue. Four east-west streets that intersect both the Strip and I-15 are Sahara Avenue, Spring Mountain Road, Dunes-Flamingo Road and Tropicana Avenue. There also is an interchange for the Strip on I-15.

Downtown is roughly bordered by Charleston Boulevard on the south, Bonanza Road on the north, Maryland Parkway on the east and Main Street on the west. Since Las Vegas is laid out in the traditional grid system, most streets in the city travel north to south or east to west.

Parking

Parking is seldom a problem, since most hotels, casinos and businesses provide guest, valet and customer parking. Should neither free nor on-street parking be available, rates at lots and garages average from 50c to $1 per hour. If you leave your car in a commercial lot, check the hours of the lot's operation, since many commercial lots close at 6 p.m. However, several downtown hotels and the city of Las Vegas operate 24-hour garages.

Rental Cars

Several rental car agencies serve the Las Vegas area; check the telephone directory. Hertz, (702) 736-4900/airport and (702) 735-4597/Strip, offers discounts to AAA members.

Taxis

Cabs are available at the airport, hotels and taxi stands. The fare is determined by both the number of passengers and the mileage; the basic rate is $3.50 for the first mile and $1.70 for each additional mile. Usually the tip is 15 to 20 percent of the meter reading. The largest taxi companies are ABC Union, (702) 736-8444; Ace, (702) 736-8383; Checker, (702) 873-2227; Desert, (702) 736-1702; Nellis Cab, (702) 798-1149; N. Las Vegas Cab, (702) 643-1041; Vegas Western Cab, (702) 736-6121; Western, (702) 736-8000; Whittlesea Blue Cab, (702) 384-6111; and Yellow, (702) 873-2227.

Public Transportation

The Las Vegas Transit System provides bus service to most parts of the city. The bus serving the Strip, or Las Vegas Boulevard, runs every 15-20 minutes until 1 a.m., after which it runs every 30 minutes until 4:15 a.m., then every hour until 7 a.m. The fare is $1.25 and a transfer costs 20c. Exact fare is required. A 10-ride ticket costs $8 (senior citizens $4.60).

The Mall Hopper, a shuttle bus service circulating among the city's three shopping malls every half-hour from 6:15 a.m. to 6:30 p.m., costs $1.15. Bus service also is available to Henderson Mon.-Sat. 6:10 a.m.-5:40 p.m. For schedule and route information phone (702) 384-3540.

What To See

BINION'S HORSESHOE, a casino at 128 Fremont St., features 100 U.S. banknotes bound between sheets of bulletproof glass and suspended from a giant golden horseshoe. Worth $10,000 each, the bills display the visage of Salmon P. Chase, chief justice of the U.S. Supreme Court from 1864-73. Open daily 24 hours. Phone (702) 382-1600.

CIRCUS CIRCUS, a tent-shaped hotel casino on the Strip, features trapeze stars, high-wire artists, clowns, unicyclists and aerial dancers, all performing high above the floor to a brass band.

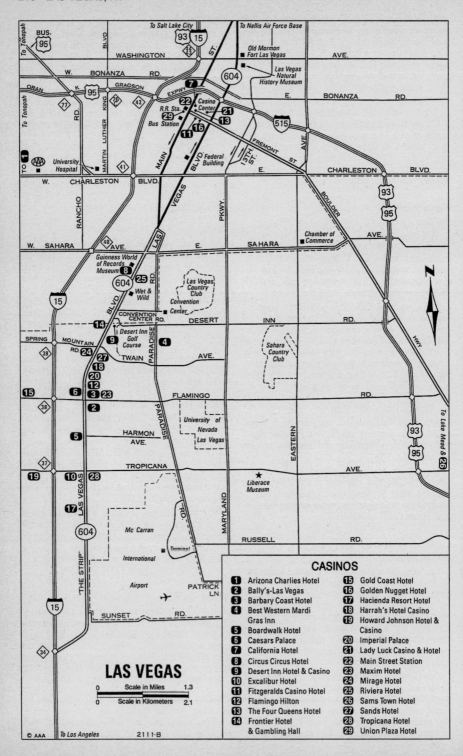

CASINOS

1. Arizona Charlies Hotel
2. Bally's-Las Vegas
3. Barbary Coast Hotel
4. Best Western Mardi Gras Inn
5. Boardwalk Hotel
6. Caesars Palace
7. California Hotel
8. Circus Circus Hotel
9. Desert Inn Hotel & Casino
10. Excalibur Hotel
11. Fitzgeralds Casino Hotel
12. Flamingo Hilton
13. The Four Queens Hotel
14. Frontier Hotel & Gambling Hall
15. Gold Coast Hotel
16. Golden Nugget Hotel
17. Hacienda Resort Hotel
18. Harrah's Hotel Casino
19. Howard Johnson Hotel & Casino
20. Imperial Palace
21. Lady Luck Casino & Hotel
22. Main Street Station
23. Maxim Hotel
24. Mirage Hotel
25. Riviera Hotel
26. Sams Town Hotel
27. Sands Hotel
28. Tropicana Hotel
29. Union Plaza Hotel

LAS VEGAS

Scale in Miles   0 — 1.3
Scale in Kilometers   0 — 2.1

© AAA   To Los Angeles   2111-B

Bordering the floor at performer level is an observation gallery lined with food, game and carnival concessions. Children are permitted on the observation levels only.

Allow 1 hour minimum. The casino is open daily 24 hours, the circus arena daily 11-11. The Midway, with games of skill and chance, is open daily 9 a.m.-1 a.m., Memorial Day-Labor Day; Mon.-Fri. 10 a.m.-midnight, Sat.-Sun. 10 a.m.-1 a.m., rest of year. Free. Phone (702) 734-0410.

GUINNESS WORLD OF RECORDS MUSEUM, 2780 Las Vegas Blvd. S., features exhibits, videotape presentations, computerized data banks and interactive computers of world records, feats and facts from the "Guinness Book of Records." A special display highlights the history of Las Vegas. Daily 9 a.m.-10 p.m. Admission $4.95; over 62 and ages 13-18, $3.95; ages 5-12, $2.95. AE, DS, MC, VI. Phone (702) 792-0640.

IMPERIAL PALACE AUTO COLLECTION, on the parking terrace of the Imperial Palace Hotel, includes more than 200 antique, classic and special-interest automobiles dating back to an 1897 Haynes-Apperson, displayed in a gallerylike setting. The King of Siam's 1928 Delage limousine, President Eisenhower's parade car, a 1947 Tucker and Model J Duesenbergs owned by James Cagney and Max Baer are among the hotel's collection.

Allow 1 hour minimum. Daily 9:30 a.m.-11:30 p.m. Admission $6.95; senior citizens, military with ID and ages 5-11, $3. **Free admission** for AAA/CAA members with card. Phone (702) 731-3311.

LAS VEGAS NATURAL HISTORY MUSEUM, 900 Las Vegas Blvd. N., features walk-through dioramas of animals in re-created natural habitats, including birds, bugs, bats, butterflies and prehistory animals. Also highlighted are 28 mounted sharks, a shark videotape presentation and hands-on exhibits. Allow 30 minutes minimum. Daily 9-4; closed Thanksgiving and Dec. 25. Admission $5; senior citizens, military and students $4; ages 4-11, $2.50. Phone (702) 384-3466.

★THE LIBERACE MUSEUM, 1775 E. Tropicana Ave., houses a rare piano collection, priceless and customized automobiles, and costumes from the entertainer's million-dollar wardrobe. Of particular interest is an authentic Czar Nicholas uniform, a piano played by Frédéric François Chopin and a concert grand owned by George Gershwin. Mon.-Sat. 10-5, Sun. 1-5; closed Jan. 1, Thanksgiving and Dec. 25. Admission $6.50; over 60, $4.50; ages 6-12, $3.50. Phone (702) 798-5595.

LIED DISCOVERY CHILDREN'S MUSEUM, 833 Las Vegas Blvd. N., consists of 100 hands-on exhibits that teach as well as entertain. An everyday living section, where children pick a job, earn a paycheck, deposit savings in a bank and buy groceries, offers an opportunity to experience a bit of grown-up reality. Another section allows children to experience the use of a wheelchair and/or crutches and to feel what it is like to be blind or deaf.

Allow 2 hours minimum. Tues.-Sat. 10-5 (also Wed. 5-7), Sun. noon-5. Admission $5; over 55 and ages 12-18, $4; ages 4-11, $3. Phone (702) 382-5437.

NEVADA STATE MUSEUM AND HISTORICAL SOCIETY, 700 Twin Lakes Dr. in Lorenzi Park, portrays the history, cultures, geography and wildlife of southern Nevada. The rambling Spanish Colonial-style museum also houses the Nevada Historical Society's research library. Daily 8:30-4:30. Admission $1, under 18 free. Phone (702) 486-5205.

OLD MORMON FORT, at Washington Ave. and Las Vegas Blvd., was built by Mormons in 1855 to give refuge to travelers bound for the California goldfields along the Salt Lake-Los Angeles Trail. The fort prospered enough to become a Union Pacific Railroad stop, prompting land speculation that transformed the town into what would become Las Vegas. The restored fort contains more than half its original brick. Antiques and relics help re-create a late 19th-century Mormon living room.

Guided tours are available; there also is a self-guiding exhibit. Allow 30 minutes minimum. Fri.-Mon. 8-4, Memorial Day-Labor Day; Mon. and Sat. 10-4, Sun. 1-4, rest of year. Free. Phone (702) 486-3511.

RED ROCK CANYON RECREATION LANDS, 20 mi. w. off Charleston Blvd. (SR 159), contain such outstanding geological formations as the Keystone Thrust Fault, which reveals the contrast between layers of gray limestone and red sandstone. A 13-mile scenic loop road passes a visitor center, then winds through unusual high-desert terrain that includes the 3,000-foot-high Red Rock Escarpment. Bighorn sheep and wild burros inhabit the sandstone cliffs of the canyon.

Self-guiding hiking tours lead to a spring, a waterfall, water catchment areas, small canyons and the ruins of an old homestead. Because of the danger of flash floods, avoid low-lying areas. Picnicking at Willow Spring on the scenic loop road and primitive camping at Oak Creek Canyon are permitted. The visitor center is open daily 9-4. Free. Phone (702) 363-1921.

RIPLEY'S BELIEVE IT OR NOT, Four Queens Hotel at 202 E. Fremont St., contains more than 4,000 exotic artifacts in 10 theme rooms. The displays concern mankind, nature and the supernatural. Allow 1 hour minimum. Sun.-Thurs. 9 a.m.-midnight, Fri.-Sat. 9 a.m.-1 a.m. Admission $4.95; over 50, $3.95; ages 6-12, $2.50. Phone (702) 385-4011.

SOUTHERN NEVADA ZOOLOGICAL PARK, 1½ mi. n. of US 95N at 1775 N. Rancho Dr., is a

2¼-acre zoo featuring African, Asian and Western American animals. Of special interest is the children's petting zoo. Allow 30 minutes minimum. Daily 9-5; closed Jan. 1, Thanksgiving and Dec. 25. Admission $5; over 60 and ages 2-12, $3. AE, MC, VI. Phone (702) 648-5955.

UNIVERSITY OF NEVADA, LAS VEGAS, 1½ mi. e. of the Strip at 4505 Maryland Pkwy., offers campus tours; phone (702) 739-3443. *Also see What To Do, Theater and Concerts.*

The Donna Beam Fine Arts Gallery displays works of modern art by professional touring artists, faculty and students. Allow 30 minutes minimum. Mon.-Fri. 8-5 (also Wed. 5-8), Sun. 1-5. Free. For guided tour information phone (702) 739-3751.

The Marjorie Barrick Museum of Natural History focuses on the natural history of southern Nevada and the Mojave Desert. Allow 1 hour minimum. Mon.-Fri. 9-4:45, Sat. 10-2. Free. Phone (702) 739-3893.

Flashlight is in the small plaza next to the Judy Bayley Theatre on Maryland Ave. on the campus. The university commissioned Claes Oldenburg to create a work symbolizing the school. Oldenburg delivered a 38-foot black steel flashlight, which is mounted lens down.

VALLEY OF FIRE STATE PARK—*see Overton.*

WET 'N WILD, 2600 Las Vegas Blvd., is a 26-acre water park. Attractions include a 500,000-gallon wave pool, three water flumes, a water roller coaster and a hydra-hurricane ride, which carries 50 to 100 riders on inner tubes clockwise around a 90-foot diameter pool at a rate of 15 miles per hour. Allow 3 hours minimum. Daily 10-5, Apr. 17-Sept. 19; Sat.-Sun. 10-5, Sept. 25-26 and Oct. 2-3; extended hours available June-Aug. Admission $17.95; ages 3-9, $14.95;

over 54, $8.50. **Discount,** except over 54. Phone (702) 737-3819.

What To Do
Gambling

The rattle of the "bones," then a sigh of disappointment or a cry of exultation—such are the sounds of Las Vegas, where gambling is by no means limited to the craps table. Slot machines, "21" or blackjack, keno, bingo, poker, baccarat and roulette all await the hopeful.

Gambling is easier than buying toothpaste, since casinos never close and most drugstores do. Many hotels strategically place their casinos near the registration desk, so you can practically yank the one-armed bandit with one hand while you fill in the guest card with the other. Rows of slot machines stand like sentries in most establishments—restaurants, drugstores, supermarkets, even laundermats.

Visitors who resist the temptation to gamble are rare. If you decide to take a chance, obtain a book on gambling and bone up. Generally speaking, beginners should never approach any gaming table without some knowledge of the game to be played. Many casinos provide literature and some even give classes for novice patrons. Although the state regulates casinos and gambling, the odds ultimately favor the house.

In terms of betting and playing strategies, poker in all its varieties can be termed the most complex. Baccarat requires a high stake to be successful, though "mini-baccarat," in which the dealer keeps the bank, provides cheaper play.

The many ways of playing number combinations, the difficulty in understanding the payoffs and general unfamiliarity with the game have made craps the toughest game of all. It also is the most difficult game for dealers to learn.

While not a game for the novice, craps is mesmerizing to watch.

Casinos and separate betting parlors also have sports books that allow patrons to wager on almost any horse race, boxing match or professional or collegiate game.

Remember that if you are a first-time visitor to Las Vegas, credit at the gaming tables will be tight or nonexistent. With further visits, once credit has been established, you will be able to get $1,000 as easily as you can obtain $1.

Sightseeing

There are other ways to spend one's time and money in Las Vegas than at the tables. A day-long sightseeing tour of the city and nearby attractions can be a relaxing intermission from the evening's hectic agenda of casino hopping and shows.

Bus, Limousine, Carriage or Train Tours

Guided bus tours of downtown and surrounding points of interest, including the Grand Canyon, Lake Mead and Valley of Fire State Park, are offered by Gray Line; phone (702) 384-1234.

Plane or Helicopter Tours

Air tours of the Grand Canyon or Lake Mead area are available from Las Vegas or Boulder City; companies include Lake Mead Air, (702) 293-1848 or 293-9906, and Scenic Airlines, (702) 739-1900 or (800) 634-6801. A combination tour of Hoover Dam and a cruise on Lake Mead is offered by Lake Mead Cruises; phone (702) 293-6180.

AIR NEVADA AIRLINES-GRAND CANYON/ BRYCE CANYON TOURS, based at McCarran International Airport, schedules several flights daily—from air tours over Hoover Dam, Lake Mead and the west entrance to the Grand Canyon to an all-day deluxe tour including a motorcoach excursion through portions of the national park, lunch, stops at lookout points and opportunities to shop for arts and crafts. Another deluxe package to Bryce Canyon in Utah is available April through November.

All flights include hotel pick-up, in-flight multilingual narration and spectacular scenery. Reservations are suggested. Air tour of the west rim of the Grand Canyon $79, under 2 free. Deluxe package $179; ages 2-11, $139. Combined 1-day Grand Canyon/Bryce Canyon deluxe tour $299. **Discount.** Phone (702) 736-8900 or (800) 634-6377.

Driving Tours

For do-it-yourselfers, a 13-mile scenic road in nearby Red Rock Canyon winds through unusual high-desert terrain and also is the site of Spring Mountain Ranch, a working ranch and luxurious retreat for such past owners as billionaire Howard Hughes and Vera Krupp, wife of a wealthy German munitions industrialist.

The ranch, now a state park, has a visitor center that is open Mon.-Fri. noon-4, Sat.-Sun. and holidays 10-4. Guided tours of the park leave from the center on weekends and Nevada state holidays; self-guiding tours of the grounds are permitted daily. The park is open daily 8 a.m.-dusk. An entrance fee is charged; phone (702) 875-4141.

Sports and Recreation

Las Vegas has a royal flush of recreational pursuits that include **golf, tennis, racquetball** and **swimming**. Lake Mead *(see place listing)*, 24 miles south, is ideal for water sports. Less than an hour's drive northwest is Toiyabe National Forest *(see place listing)*. Mount Charleston, within the forest, offers **hunting, mountain climbing** and **winter sports** and includes the Lee Canyon Ski Area.

Golf enthusiasts enjoy the excellent playing conditions of Las Vegas' desert climate. Numerous championship and less demanding golf courses are open to the public.

Area courses include Craig Ranch (18 holes), 2½ miles north off I-15 at 628 W. Craig Rd. (North Las Vegas); Desert Inn and Country Club (18), three-fourths of a mile east of I-15 off Flamingo Road at 3145 Las Vegas Blvd.; Desert Rose Golf Course (18), 6 miles east of I-15 off Sahara Avenue at 5483 Clubhouse Dr.; Dunes "Emerald Green" Country Club (18), east of I-15 off Dunes Road at 3650 Las Vegas Blvd.; and Las Vegas Golf Club (18), 1 mile west of US 95 on Washington Avenue.

Others include Los Prados Golf Course (18), 8 miles northwest of US 95 via Lone Mountain Road and Los Prados Boulevard at 5150 Los Prados Cir.; North Las Vegas Community Golf Course (nine), a half mile west of I-15 off Cheyenne Avenue at 324 W. Brooks Ave.; Painted Desert Country Club (18), 8½ miles northwest off US 95 and Ann Road at 5555 Painted Mirage Rd.; Showboat Country Club (18), 8 miles east of Las Vegas at 1 Green Valley Pkwy.; and Sun City Summerlin Golf Club (18), 10 miles northwest of US 95 and Smoke Ranch Road at 9101 Del Webb Blvd.

All courses include a clubhouse, golf shop, equipment rental and some food service. None are lighted for night play. Early starts are recommended during the summer months.

Tennis players seldom have difficulty finding an empty court, since there are many public courts scattered throughout the city. Those that follow have at least two lighted courts: East Las Vegas Park and Recreation Center, Missouri Avenue and Boulder Highway; Paradise Park Recreation Center, 4770 S. Harrison Dr.; Sunrise Recreation Center, 2240 Linn Ln.; Sunset Park, Sunset Drive and Eastern Avenue; Winchester Recreation Center, 3130 S. McLeod; and Winterwood Park, Sahara Avenue and Winterwood Boulevard.

Many resort hotels and private clubs have tennis courts that visitors are allowed to use, but it is always a good idea to confirm the hotel's current visitor policy by phone.

Many swimming pools are open daily Memorial Day-Labor Day. Admission $1.50; under 17, 75c. Contact the Las Vegas Parks and Recreation Department for information on pools open other times of the year; phone (702) 229-6309.

Bowling is available at several locations. The Showboat Hotel, 2800 E. Fremont St., has 106 lanes and an attended room where children can be left free of charge; phone (702) 385-9153. Other bowling centers can be found at Arizona Charlie's Hotel, 740 S. Decatur Blvd.; El Rancho Hotel, 2755 Las Vegas Blvd.; Gold Coast Hotel, 3111 S. Valley View Blvd.; Sam's Town Hotel, 5111 Boulder Hwy.; and West Hill Lanes, 4747 W. Charleston Blvd. The Santa Fe Hotel, 4949 N. Rancho Dr., has bowling facilities in addition to an ice skating rink.

Fans of **baseball** will find the Las Vegas Stars, the AAA farm club of the San Diego Padres, playing at Cashman Field, 850 N. Las Vegas Blvd., April through October. Phone (702) 386-7200 for ticket and schedule information.

The Scandia Family Fun Center, 2900 Sirius Rd., offers a variety of amusements including miniature golf, go-cart racing, bumper boats, a video arcade and batting cages.

Where To Shop

Las Vegas offers a wide variety of boutiques, haberdasheries and specialty stores. Shops in the Boulevard, Fashion Show and Meadows malls generally are open Mon.-Fri. 10-9, Sat. 10-6 and Sun. noon-5.

The Fashion Show, at Las Vegas Boulevard and Spring Mountain Road, contains such major department stores as Bullock's, Dillards, The May Co., Neiman-Marcus and Saks Fifth Avenue, which generally have additional hours Sunday noon-5. The Forum Shops, in Caesars Palace on the Strip, is an upscale complex with 70 specialty shops and restaurants.

Where To Dine

Many restaurants in Las Vegas' major hotels stay open 24 hours a day, as do most coffee shops. Hotel restaurants usually offer lavish buffets ranging in cost from $2.95 to $15.

The Alpine Village Inn, opposite the Las Vegas Hilton, 3003 Paradise Rd., presents German, Swiss and American dishes. For dining in a hedonistic fashion, the Bacchanal in Caesars Palace serves expensive fare in an opulent garden reminiscent of a Roman villa.

For steak lovers there are Barrymores Steak House in the Bally's Casino Resort, Golden Steer, 308 W. Sahara Ave., and Ruth Cris Steak House, 3900 Paradise Rd. The Philips Supper House, 4545 W. Sahara Ave., offers lobster, beef, clambakes and Italian dishes, while the Starboard Tack, 2601 Atlantic Ave., offers a mix of steak and seafood. Tony Roma's, 620 E. Sahara Ave., specializes in ribs.

The downtown area offers several hotel restaurants including Hugos Cellar in the Four Queens Hotel, Elaines Gourmet and Stefanos in the Golden Nugget and Center Stage in the Union Plaza Hotel.

The area also offers many ethnic restaurants. Andre's, 401 S. 6th St., offers French delicacies. Surrounded by Japanese gardens and flowing streams, Benihana Village, in the Las Vegas Hilton, features a choice of five restaurants. Italian food can be found at Amore, 3310 S. Sandhill Rd., Battista's Hole in the Wall, 4041 Audrie, and the Olive Garden, 1545 E. Flamingo Rd. and 1361 S. Decatur Blvd.

A Continental menu is offered at Anthony's, 3620 E. Flamingo Rd., and Cafe Michelle, 1350 E. Flamingo Rd. Country Inn, 2425 E. Desert Inn Rd. and 1401 S. Rainbow Blvd., features traditional American food. For a variety The Mirage, 3400 Las Vegas Blvd., offers seafood, Japanese, Italian, Chinese, French and a buffet.

Nightlife

Lured to Las Vegas by the wealth—headline stars command fees of up to six figures per week—entertainers play to happy, receptive audiences in Las Vegas. The city also is a proving ground for younger entertainers, and often the big names are backed up by these talented newcomers, as well as by revues, shortened versions of Broadway hits, burlesque and magic shows.

Entertainment loses money, but the owners and managers of the hotels and casinos agree that nothing is too good for the visiting gambler. Guests might catch the Folies Bergere for an hour of exotic burlesque before discovering they would have spent much less for comparable entertainment elsewhere. Cab fares for casino hopping, however, can be expensive.

Las Vegas entertainment falls into two categories: big room and lounge. The big rooms, seating 600 to 1,500, offer three types of shows, the best known of which is the star performer, backed up by an orchestra and supported by a lesser known singer or comic.

The second most common is the "Continental" production show featuring European-style revues: Folies Bergere dancers at the Tropicana and Jubilee at Bally's. The third type of big room show is a Broadway play, usually a musical or comedy.

Big room shows (except plays) generally run about 90 minutes. Check in advance with the hotel or casino regarding showtimes, minimums and reservation policies. Guests for cocktail shows should arrive about 45 minutes early; for dinner shows arriving 2 hours in advance is recommended. Children are not admitted to shows with nude performers.

There is never a cover charge for the shows in the big rooms, but depending on the entertainer being featured, minimums can range from $25 to $75 per person. Production show minimums vary from $9.95 to $25 per person. Big rooms usually require reservations; for the more popular performances, be sure to make your reservations at least 24 to 48 hours in advance and give the name of your hotel.

Chances of getting into a show are always better when staying at a hotel where a popular entertainer is performing. Ticket agencies specializing in booking entertainment often have permanent reservations for tables at some showrooms; refer to the phone directory. A reservation, however, usually only admits a guest to the room—tipping the maitre d' $5 to $10 for a couple and double that for a larger party helps get a good seat close to the stage.

Waiters at a dinner show also expect a tip, and the same rules for tipping in restaurants apply here as well. But remember that the bill includes the entertainment costs as well as the food. Check in advance with the hotel or casino regarding showtimes, minimums and reservation policies.

Lounges seat 200 to 400 in more intimate surroundings, frequently providing visitors on a budget moderate-to-big name performers with supporting acts. Lounge shows vary from those that offer 24-hour entertainment to those that feature two or three acts a night, usually from 7 p.m. to 4 a.m.

The prevailing minimum is usually two drinks per person. Here, too, a folding favor for the captain will spur him to seat you quickly and at a good table on crowded nights. To ensure the act you want to see is performing on a given night (Monday and Tuesday are commonly dark nights), and to find out exact times, check with the hotel or casino in advance.

Note: The mention of any area or establishment in the preceding sections is for information only and does **not** imply endorsement by AAA.

Theater and Concerts

Concerts and plays are presented periodically at the Reed Whipple Cultural Center on Las Vegas Boulevard and at the Charleston Heights Arts Center, on Brust Street west of Decatur Boulevard north of Charleston Boulevard. Free concerts are regularly performed by the Nevada String Quartet in the Flamingo Library auditorium at 1401 E. Flamingo; phone (702) 733-3613 for schedule information.

The award-winning Theatre Arts Department of the University of Nevada stages both contemporary plays and the classics throughout the year in the 600-seat Judy Bayley Theater on Maryland Parkway. The popular Nevada Dance Theater also performs on a regular basis; phone (702) 739-3801.

The Artemus W. Ham Concert Hall, also on the University of Nevada campus and a few miles from the Strip, presents symphony, ballet, opera, jazz and popular music performances, often under the direction of prominent musicians. For schedule information phone (702) 739-3801.

For a different form of theater, Caesars Palace's futuristic Omnimax® Theater offers a different film each year on a huge screen with a "sensaround" sound system designed to allow the audience to experience the action. Housed in a geodesic dome, the theater is accessible via a moving sidewalk or the Olympic Tower escalator. Shows are presented daily; phone (702) 731-7900.

The Red Rock Theaters, 5201 W. Charleston Blvd., consists of 11 movie theaters in an enclosed mall decorated with antiques; phone (702) 870-1423.

Information on performances and exhibits is available from the newspapers or from the Allied Arts Council, 3750 S. Maryland Pkwy., Mon.-Fri. 9-5; phone (702) 731-5419.

Especially for Children

Although the neon excitement of Las Vegas caters mainly to adults, there are diversions for children. They will love the highwire gymnastics at Circus Circus, marvel at the size of Hoover Dam, frolic in the waters at Wet 'n Wild and enjoy the swimming, fishing and boat tours at Lake Mead. Children will love to visit the grounds of the Mirage where dolphins have taken up residence in a marine facility with more than 1 million gallons of man-made sea water and coral reefs. In addition, some hotels provide entertainment centers for use by guests.

Special Events

Events in Las Vegas are as varied as entertainment on the Strip. The Desert Inn LPGA Golf Tournament tees off in March. The All Indian Pow Wow is held in April; in May the Old West is relived during Helldorado Days, which features Western costumes, parades and a championship rodeo. The Jerry Lewis Telethon takes place in September. The Jaycee State Fair is presented in late September or early October.

The Fairshow, held in North Las Vegas in late October, includes national championship hot air balloon races, a chili cookoff, a huge bicycle relay and softball tournaments, as well as other activities and entertainment.

Las Vegas' sports events are of both the indoor and outdoor variety. They include the Showboat Invitational Bowling Tournament in January; the Nissan/400 Off-Road Race, the Las Vegas Invitational Golf Tournament and the World Series of Poker, all held in the spring; and the National Rodeo Finals in December.

LAUGHLIN (F-6) pop. 3,000

Laughlin, located near the California border and across the Colorado River from Arizona, was little more than a nameless bait shack on the Colorado River in 1970. It is now a gambling mecca in the middle of the desert, attracting 2.5 million visitors in 1989. Buses and ferries provide transportation between the glittery casinos in Laughlin and parking areas in nearby Bullhead, Ariz. In May, the town celebrates Laughlin River Days.

LOVELOCK (B-3) pop. 2,100, alt. 3,900'

Lovelock, with the only round courthouse said to be in use in the country, offers such recreational diversions as gaming casinos, stock car racing and rodeos. Hunting and fishing are abundant in the surrounding area. The Giant Tufa Park, 7 miles west of town, features geological deposits created by ancient Lake Lahontan, which covered the area thousands of years ago.

About 22 miles northeast is Rye Patch State Recreation Area, with facilities for camping, fishing, swimming, boating and picnicking. *See Recreation Chart and the AAA California/ Nevada CampBook.*

MARZEN HOUSE, n. of I-80 exit 105 at the w. end of Cornell Ave., houses the Pershing County Museum. Displays of antiques, mineral ores, Piute Indian artifacts and pioneer memorabilia are exhibited in the 1876 two-story frame house. Mon.-Sat. 9-4, Sun. and holidays 1:30-4, Apr. 1-Nov. 25; Mon.-Fri. 9-1:30, rest of year. Closed Jan. 1, Thanksgiving and Dec. 25. Donations. Phone (702) 273-7213.

OVERTON (E-6) pop. 1,800, alt. 1,250'

Founded by Mormon pioneers, Overton lies just north of a 2,000-year-old settlement known as the Lost City, which extended 30 miles on both sides of the Muddy River. The Puebloans who lived in Lost City were farmers who built above-ground dwellings with several rooms that were used to store crops.

Overton also lies at the northern end of a scenic route which follows the northwestern shore of Lake Mead. The route is made up of SR 169 to Overton Beach and SR 147 from Overton Beach to US 95/93 and Hoover Dam.

LOST CITY MUSEUM OF ARCHEOLOGY, on a restored part of Pueblo Grande de Nevada, contains such Indian relics as baskets, pottery and tools excavated from the Lost City pueblos and other sites that date as far back as 10,000 years. On the museum grounds are several Pueblo-type houses of wattle and daub reconstructed on original foundations.

Allow 30 minutes minimum. Daily 8:30-4:30; closed Jan. 1, Thanksgiving and Dec. 25. Admission $1, under 18 free. Phone (702) 397-2193.

VALLEY OF FIRE STATE PARK, 14 mi. s.w. on SR 169, occupies a basin about 6 miles long and 3 to 4 miles wide. The rough floor and jagged walls contain formations of eroded red sandstone that often appear to be on fire when reflecting the sun's rays. Some cliffs and rocks, mainly in the area of Atlatl Rock, are covered with prehistoric petroglyphs probably sketched from 300 B.C. to A.D. 1150 by the Basketmaker people and later the Anasazi Pueblo farmers.

Mouse Tank, a natural basin that collects scarce rainwater, was named for a reclusive Paiute Indian who lived in this area in the early 1900s. A ¼-mile trail to the tank offers views of prehistoric petroglyphs.

Exhibits on the park's history, geology and ecology are housed in the visitor center on SR 169, about 4 miles east of the park boundary. Park open daily dawn-dusk. Center open daily 8:30-4:30. Closed Jan. 1 and Dec. 25. Free. Phone (702) 397-2088. *See Recreation Chart.*

PIOCHE (D-6) pop. 800, alt. 6,018'

Pioche was one of the roughest mining camps in the West during the 1870s. The town's Boot Hill boasted 75 graves before its first interment due to natural causes. Residents balanced their lack of creativity in solving disagreements with such epitaphs as "Fanny Peterson, July 12, 1872. They loved til death did them part. He killed her." The past is re-created during Heritage Days festivities at the end of July.

Pioche is known for its Million Dollar Courthouse, a $30,000 building that cost the county almost $1 million by the time it was completed in the late 1800s. Condemned in 1933, the building and the four lots on which it stands were sold 25 years later for $150. The courthouse has been restored and is open for guided tours, but may be closed during bad weather.

LINCOLN COUNTY HISTORICAL MUSEUM, on Main St. adjacent to the library, houses local historical articles that include tools, furniture, photo graphs, documents and early 20th-century clothing. Mon.-Sat. 9-12:30 and 1:30-5, Sun. and holidays 10-12:30 and 1:30-5; closed Thanksgiving and Dec. 25. Free. Phone (702) 962-5207.

RENO (C-2) pop. 133,900, alt. 4,490'

Full of stage shows and gambling establishments that operate 24 hours a day, Reno is a city of diverse extremes, calling itself "the biggest little city in the world." Its neon lights supply the same excitement as Las Vegas, but Reno also is the home of the University of Nevada-Reno. The city is an important distribution and merchandising center that also has extensive residential areas. More couples are married in its courthouse than divorced.

Reno's sunny, dry climate attracts summer and winter sports enthusiasts. Skiers flock to the Sierras for downhill and cross-country skiing; golfers can tee off at several area courses. Facilities for boating, swimming, snowmobiling, tennis, hiking and white-water rafting are available in the Reno area.

A more sedate side of Reno can be found in the rose garden of Idlewild Park, along the Truckee River on the city's west side, and during the noontime band concerts on Monday, Wednesday and Friday in Wingfield Park, along the river in the downtown area. A tree-shaded paved path along the river connects the two parks.

Several businesses contain exhibits and provide entertainment. Harolds Club, 250 N. Virginia St., features a display of antique firearms, music boxes, slot machines and exhibits of Western Americana, including carriages, illustrations and curios recalling pioneer days.

Antique slot machines and player pianos are on display in the back room of the Liberty Belle, 4250 S. Virginia St., while free circus acts are offered at the Circus Circus Hotel, 500 N. Sierra St. Exhibitions of works by international, regional and local artists are held by the Sierra Nevada Museum of Art in the Hawkins House at 549 Court St.

Reno is at the southwestern end of a scenic route consisting of SRs 445, 446 and 447. These highways run through Pyramid Lake Indian Reservation and follow the southern shoreline of Pyramid Lake.

Reno's annual events range from offbeat to crowd pleasing and offer something for everyone. The International Jazz Festival occurs the last week in March; the Reno Rodeo takes place the last week in June; the Basque Festival is celebrated in August; the Nevada State Fair is held in mid-August; the Great Balloon Race is held the weekend after Labor Day; the National Air Races follow the second weekend after Labor Day; and the Snafflebit Futurity happens the last week in September.

CHURCH FINE ARTS BUILDING, University of Nevada, presents changing exhibits, principally of contemporary art, in the Sheppard Fine Arts Gallery. Allow 30 minutes minimum. Mon.-Fri. 9-4. Free. Theatrical productions are staged by the university in the Church Fine Arts Theatre; call for schedule and prices. Phone (702) 784-6682 (gallery) or 784-6839 (theater).

★**FLEISCHMANN PLANETARIUM,** at the n. edge of the University of Nevada campus on N. Virginia St., presents programs on the night sky. Periodically changing Star Shows depict astronomical events of the past, present and future. Astronomy and earth science exhibits also are featured. Hours and programs vary. Under 6 are admitted to daytime shows only.

Allow 1 hour, 30 minutes minimum. Open Mon.-Thurs. 8-5 and 7-10, Fri. 8 a.m.-10 p.m., Sat.-Sun. 10:30-10; closed Jan. 1, Easter, Thanksgiving, Dec. 24 after 5 p.m., Dec. 25 and Dec. 31 after 5 p.m. Planetarium building free. Star Show $5; over 59 and under 13, $3.50. MC, VI. **Discount.** Phone (702) 784-4811.

★**MINERAL MUSEUM,** at the university's Mackay School of Mines on N. Center St., contains mining, metallurgical, geological and mineralogical collections. Exhibits illustrate procedures and depict significant events in the mining history of the surrounding area. Mon.-Fri. 8-5; closed holidays. Free. Phone (702) 784-6988.

★**NATIONAL AUTOMOBILE MUSEUM,** 10 Lake St. S., displays 200 antique, vintage, classic and special interest automobiles. The facility offers interactive exhibits, period street scenes and a multimedia theater presentation. Also featured are antique clothing and an automotive research library. Food is available. Allow 1 hour, 30 minutes minimum. Daily 9:30-5; closed Dec. 25. Admission $7.50; over 62, $6.50; ages 6-18, $2.50. **Discount.** Phone (702) 333-9300. *See ad p. 218.*

NEVADA HISTORICAL SOCIETY MUSEUM, 1650 N. Virginia St., displays Indian artifacts, pioneer relics, antique furniture, guns and rocks. A research library contains records dating from 1859. Library open Tues.-Sat. 10-5. Museum open Mon.-Sat. 10-5. Closed Jan. 1, Easter, July 4, Oct. 31, Thanksgiving and Dec. 25. Free. Phone (702) 789-0190.

PYRAMID LAKE is 36 mi. n. of the city on SR 445. Though smaller in size than prehistoric Lake Lahontan, which once covered 8,400 square miles of western Nevada and northeastern California, it is still Nevada's largest natural lake. About 30 miles long and 7 to 9 miles wide, Pyramid Lake is surrounded by red and brown sandstone mountains and punctuated by porous rock islands.

Long before it became a 475,000-acre Paiute Indian reservation in 1874, the lake area served as the tribe's homeland. The lake's north end, surrounded by huge rock monoliths, is sacred to the Paiutes and off limits to visitors. Fragmentary remains of an elephant, bison and camel found at the nearby Astor Pass railroad excavations offer clues to the lake's inhabitants during prehistoric times.

Pyramid Lake is considered one of the state's best recreation areas. Unique to the lake is the cui-cui fish—an endangered lake sucker fish—and trout weighing up to 40 pounds. Warrior Point, a park 9 miles north of Sutcliffe, offers various shoreline facilities. Applications for fishing and boating permits can be obtained at Pyramid Lake Indian Tribal Enterprises, Star Rte., Sutcliffe, NV 89510. *See Recreation Chart.*

WILBUR D. MAY MUSEUM AND ARBORETUM is in Rancho San Rafael Park at 1502 Washington St. Containing objects collected by adventurer Wilbur D. May during his world travels, the museum is a replica of his Double Diamond Ranch. Highlights of the collection include May memorabilia, souvenirs of his African safaris, rare Tang Dynasty horse sculptures and 18th-century sterling silver.

The adjacent arboretum consists of 12 gardens representing plant habitats at different elevations in the eastern Sierra Nevada Mountains. Picnicking is permitted.

Allow 1 hour minimum for both attractions. Museum and arboretum open Tues.-Sun. 10-5, May 30-Sept. 5; Wed.-Sun. 10-5, rest of year. Museum $2; over 62 and under 12, $1. Arboretum $3; over 62 and under 12, $1. Phone (702) 785-5961 (museum) or 785-4153 (arboretum).

RHYOLITE (E-5)

On a dirt road 2½ miles west of Beatty, Rhyolite was a city of 12,000 inhabitants in 1907. Mine failure caused its desertion, and only stone foundations and brick fronts remain of the town that once boasted telephone service, water companies, saloons, hundreds of homes, an opera house, electric street lights and even a red-light district.

An elaborate railroad depot and a house constructed almost entirely of bottles are two of the few surviving structures in Rhyolite; neither is open to the public. Visitors are cautioned to be careful if climbing the old remains; trembling caused by mining in nearby areas could make it a treacherous climb.

SILVER SPRINGS (C-3)

FORT CHURCHILL STATE HISTORIC PARK is 7 mi. s. on US 95, then 1 mi. w. on Old Fort Churchill Rd. Built in 1860 as protection against Indian attacks, this U.S. Army outpost also guarded the Pony Express and other mail routes. Although the fort is now in ruins, a visitor center reconstructs its colorful history with interpretive exhibits. Park open all year. Visitor center open daily 8:30-4:30, Memorial Day-Labor Day; otherwise varies, rest of year. Free. Day use of picnic facilities $2, camping $4. Phone (702) 577-2345. *See Recreation Chart.*

SPARKS (C-3) pop. 53,400, alt. 4,407'

Sparks was established in 1904 when railroad buildings were moved by the Southern Pacific Railroad to Reno's eastern border. It was named after the state's governor, John Sparks.

An outdoor railroad exhibit, the chamber of commerce and a number of casinos are on B Street. Victorian Square, a pedestrian mall off I-80 via Rock Boulevard or Pyramid Way, holds special events year-round on the mall and in the 400-seat Victorian Amphitheater. Situated on the mall are restaurants, casinos, hotels and the free Sparks Heritage Museum, which is open Wed.-Sun. 1-5.

The Wildcreek Golf Course, offering both nine- and 18-hole courses, is approximately 1 mile east of US 395 via McCarran Boulevard at 3500 Sullivan Ln.

WILD ISLAND, I-80 E. and Sparks Blvd., has eight outdoor water rides, a wave pool, volleyball court, children's play area, game arcade, miniature golf and picnic facilities. Food is available. Daily 11-5, Memorial Day-Labor Day. Admission $13.50; ages 4-9, $9.95; over 63, $6.95. MC, VI. Phone (702) 331-9453.

TOIYABE NATIONAL FOREST

Toiyabe National Forest covers 3,861,166 acres in central, western and southern Nevada and eastern California. It lies along the rugged Monitor, Toquima, Toiyabe, Shoshone and Paradise ranges of central Nevada and along the eastern slopes of the Sierras and the Spring Mountains near Las Vegas. Fishing, hunting and camping are popular. Winter sports areas can be found at Lee Canyon, Heavenly Valley and Slide Mountain.

Within the forest are eight wilderness areas and three national hiking trails. The Pacific Crest National Scenic Trail traverses 74 miles of forest land; the Toiyabe Crest National Recreation Trail runs 67 miles along the Toiyabe Range; and the Mount Charleston National Recreation Trail ascends the 11,918-foot summit of Charleston Peak, the fourth highest peak in Nevada.

Because of unpredictable weather conditions, hiking on these trails should be limited to June through October; high elevations can receive snow during any month of the year.

Other areas noted for visual and recreational appeal are Lake Tahoe, the Sierras near Bridgeport, Calif., and Mount Rose. Phone (702) 331-6444. *See Recreation Chart and the AAA California/Nevada CampBook.*

TONOPAH (D-4) pop. 2,700

Tonopah had its beginning in 1900 when a prospector, Jim Butler, idly chipped away at a ledge that sheltered him during a thunderstorm and noticed that the rock looked like silver ore. By the time the boom he started reached its peak 13 years later, production in the area had netted $9,500,000. The town shared the area's mineral wealth with nearby Goldfield.

Residents and visitors celebrate Jim Butler Days each Memorial Day weekend. The festivities include parades, mining contests, camel and burro races and barbecues.

CENTRAL NEVADA MUSEUM, on Logan Field Rd. s. of Nye General Hospital, depicts the history of the area through displays dealing with American Indians, settlements, boomtowns, railroads and mining. The grounds contain heavy industrial and mining equipment. Allow 30 minutes minimum. Daily 10-5, May-Sept.; Tues.-Sat. noon-5, rest of year. Closed Jan. 1, Thanksgiving and Dec. 25. Donations. Phone (702) 482-9676.

★VIRGINIA CITY (C-2) pop. 1,500

With 30,000 residents, banks, churches, theaters, 110 saloons and the only elevator between Chicago and San Francisco, the Virginia City of the 1870s was the West's mining metropolis. The Comstock Lode had given the town unequaled prosperity. The ore extracted from the Consolidated Virginia Mine has been estimated to have a gross value of at least $234 million, some of which was used to build San Francisco and finance the Union Army during the Civil War.

Notable residents included Mark Twain and Bret Harte, who worked as reporters on the *Territorial Enterprise,* Nevada's first newspaper and one known for occasionally making up the news. The National Championship Camel Races, held on Labor Day weekend, began as a fictitious story in 1959 and has since become one of the state's major events.

Much has been done to restore Virginia City to its 1870 boomtown appearance. Many small museums along C Street preserve the town's illustrious past. They include The Way It Was Museum, Delta Saloon, The Wild West Museum, Museum of Memories, Bucket of Blood Saloon and Ponderosa Saloon, which offers underground mine tours every 20 minutes.

Saint Mary's in the Mountains is a brick church built on the site of an earlier church destroyed by fire in 1875. The building has been restored and can be visited daily in summer and on weekends all year.

The Virginia City Visitors Bureau, on C Street between Taylor and Union streets, shows a slide presentation on the history of the town; phone (702) 847-0177 for the schedule. The chamber of commerce, in the Virginia and Truckee Railroad car across from the post office, has brochures and further information on the area; phone (702) 847-0311.

Virginia City lies along a scenic route consisting of SR 341 northwest to the junction of US 395. From that point the route follows SR 431 through the Toiyabe National Forest to the northern shore of Lake Tahoe.

THE CASTLE is at 70 S. B St. The 1868 structure, which reflects the prosperity of mining towns through antique furnishings, includes 200-year-old Czechoslovakian crystal chandeliers, Italian marble fireplaces and silver doorknobs. Allow 30 minutes minimum. Guided tours are offered daily 10-5, July 1-Labor Day; 11-5, Memorial Day-June 30 and day after Labor Day-Oct. 31. Admission $2.75; ages 6-12, 25c. Phone (702) 847-0275.

CHOLLAR MINE, S. F St., is an 1861 Comstock gold and silver mine with original square-set timbering. Allow 30 minutes minimum. Daily noon-5, June-Sept.; also open May and Oct., weather permitting. Admission $4; ages 4-14, $1. Phone (702) 847-0155.

MACKAY MANSION, 129 D St., is a 10-room, 1861 home that served as the original headquarters of the Gould and Curry Mine Co. Later it was the residence of John Mackay, an early leader of Virginia City who donated millions to Nevada education.

The original furnishings, old Chinese laundry and a woodshed with original implements have been retained. Daily 10-5, Apr.-Nov.; 11-5, rest of year, weather permitting. Admission $3; ages 8-11, $1; over 80 and under 8 free. Phone (702) 847-0173.

MARK TWAIN MUSEUM OF MEMORIES, C and Taylor sts., contains a collection of rare nickelodeons, telephones and radios, Indian artifacts, railroad memorabilia, a 1,000-year-old human skeleton and late 19th-century ladies' fashions. An animated mannequin of Mark Twain recites the author's works. Allow 1 hour minimum. Daily 10-5, May-Oct.; 10-4, rest of year. Donations. Phone (702) 847-0454.

NEVADA STATE FIRE MUSEUM AND COMSTOCK FIREMEN'S MUSEUM, 51 S. C St., displays antique fire wagons dating from 1839 as well as firefighters' uniforms, leather helmets, photographs and firefighting accessories. The collection spans the early volunteer fire department period in the Virginia City-Gold Hill area from 1861-77; relics from later periods also are displayed. Daily 10-5, May-Oct. Donations. Phone (702) 847-0717.

PIPER'S OPERA HOUSE, B and Union sts., has witnessed the coming of age of two generations of traveling players since it was built in the 1880s. Such greats as Edwin Booth, Wilson Barrett, Lotta Crabtree, Adah Isaacs Menken, Maude Adams and David Belasco have performed for the bonanza kings of Comstock silver wealth.

Interesting features include original 19th-century scenery, an auditorium floor built on ore car springs, a raked stage and a beautiful suspended balcony, as well as a museum of playbills, posters, photographs and other theater memorabilia. Guided tours are available. Daily 11-5, mid-May to late Oct.; by appointment, rest of year. Admission $3. Phone (702) 847-0433.

VIRGINIA AND TRUCKEE RAILROAD, a partially restored standard gauge railroad, operates a 35-minute run between Virginia City and Gold Hill. Daily 10:30-5:45, Memorial Day-Sept. 30; Sat.-Sun., in Oct., weather permitting. Round-trip fare $4; ages 5-12, $2. **Discount.** Phone (702) 847-0380.

WELLS (B-5) pop. 1,300, alt. 5,625′

Wells took its name from a number of calm springs. This area, where I-80 and US 93 intersect, was an important stop for late 19th-century pioneers following the Humboldt Trail. The ruts left by the iron-rimmed wheels of their wagons can still be seen in nearby rocks.

Wells holds its Chariot Races in February, and five-man teams compete on a 20-mile course during the Pony Express Races in mid-May. The local high school holds a Buckaroo Rodeo the second week in May; a junior rodeo is held in August.

For a panorama of the area, summer visitors can hike on trails leading from nearby Angel Lake (see Recreation Chart) to the 11,000-foot "Hole-in-the-Mountain Peak." Angel Lake is accessible from Wells from mid-June through September via SR 582, a precipitous two-lane road. Information on the vicinity may be obtained through the chamber of commerce; phone (702) 752-3540.

WINNEMUCCA (B-4) pop. 6,100, alt. 4,324′

Thousands of pioneers passed through Winnemucca on their way to California and Oregon. In 1845 children in a wagon train bound for California played a game of tossing pebbles into blue buckets hanging from the wagons. The "pebbles" were later identified as gold nuggets, and although many have searched, the "Blue Bucket Mine" has never been found.

The infamous duo of Butch Cassidy and the Sundance Kid were said to have left their mark on Winnemucca. In 1900 they purportedly celebrated their robbery of the First National Bank by sending the bank president a studio portrait of themselves.

The Humboldt County Museum at Maple Avenue and Jungo Road chronicles the region's history with antiques and memorabilia. Minerals found in the area include gold, silver, tungsten, barite and mercury; opals and turquoise appeal to rockhounds.

Winnemucca is the site of a number of events. The first weekend in June the Winnemucca Draft Horse and Mule Show and Races are held. Residents of Basque ancestry remember their heritage by celebrating the Basque Festival during the second weekend in June. Festivities include a parade, games of strength and colorful dancing exhibitions, as well as hearty servings of traditional Basque food.

Labor Day weekend is enlivened by Nevada's Oldest Rodeo, a Tri-County Fair and the Western Art Round-up, which features buckaroo poetry, handmade horse gear and artists from throughout the West. In mid-September, the town participates in pari-mutuel Thoroughbred, quarter horse and mule racing events.

Information on activities in the area is available Mon.-Fri. 8-5 from the convention and visitors bureau, 50 Winnemucca Blvd. W., (702) 623-5071, or from the chamber of commerce, 30 W. Winnemucca Blvd. The chamber is open daily 8-4 and most holidays; phone (702) 623-2225.

YERINGTON (C-3) pop. 2,400

One of the state's most prosperous agricultural and livestock centers, Yerington was founded in the 1860s along the fertile banks of the Walker River in the Mason Valley. Named after H.M. Yerington, an official of the Virginia and Truckee Railroad, the town lies at the northwestern end of scenic SR 208, which leads to the Sierra Nevada Mountains and the California border.

Further Reading

The following sampling of books has been selected for the pleasure and enrichment of our members who wish to discover more about the region they are visiting. This list is not intended to be a complete survey of works available, nor does it imply AAA endorsement of a particular author, work or publisher.

California:

Bean, Walton. "California, an Interpretive History." A historical reference about California.

Berg, Scott. "Goldwyn." An autobiography of the man who helped to build Hollywood and the film industry.

Birmingham, Stephen. "California Rich." Insights into the lives of those who made and reinvested their fortunes in California.

Jakes, John. "California Gold." A novel about California from railroad barons of the late 1880s to the 1920s birth of the movie industry.

L'Amour, Louis. "The Californios." The popular storyteller of the Old West brings life to the California gold rush.

Michaels, Leonard. "West of the West: Imagining California." A diverse collection of both literary and documentary writings on the people, geography and weather of California.

Rorabaugh, W.J. "Berkeley at War: The 1960s." An informative account of the impetus of the political, social and cultural upheaval of the 1960s.

Wilhelm, Kate. "Fault Lines." An old woman relives her life when she is trapped by an earthquake.

Nevada:

Clark, Walter Van Tillburg. "The Track of the Cat." A symbolic struggle of good versus evil on a small-town Nevada ranch.

Graham, Jefferson. "Vegas Live and in Person." An illustrated history of Nevada's most colorful city.

Puzo, Mario. "Fools Die." A story about the glamour, power and brutality of Las Vegas in the '50s and '60s.

Ross, Dana Fuller. "Nevada." A saga of men and women carving a new life on the Nevada frontier.

PLAN AHEAD FOR ECONOMY

- Select the optimum route in terms of distance and type of highway. A AAA Travel Counselor can assist you.
- Travel light and avoid using a car-top rack. The less weight and wind resistance, the better the mileage.
- Combine short trips, such as visits, errands and shopping.

Baja California
Mexico

In 1535, an officer under the command of Hernán Cortés became the first European to land in Baja (Lower) California. The reports he brought back, particularly with respect to the existence of pearls in the Gulf of California, were so encouraging that a year later Cortés himself led settlers to the present site of La Paz (see place listing).

However, the many hardships far exceeded the Spaniards' expectations, and they abandoned their colony. Not until 1697 was a permanent settlement established—a Jesuit mission and presidio at Loreto (see place listing), about 220 miles (360 km) north of La Paz.

During the next 137 years the Jesuits, followed by the Franciscans and Dominicans, founded 29 more missions throughout the peninsula. In 1769 Loreto served as the advance base for the colonization of Alta (Upper) California, the present state of California.

Baja California extends almost 800 miles southward from the international boundary, parallel to the Mexican mainland. Varying from 30 to 145 miles in width, this long, narrow strip of land is bounded by the Gulf of California (also known as the Sea of Cortés) on the east and the Pacific Ocean on the west. Both coastlines are indented by an endless string of bays and coves, with many islands scattered offshore. Numerous fishing villages and many fine resort lodges cater to fishing and swimming in addition to water sports along Baja California's more than 2,000 miles of coastline.

Although generally arid in character, the terrain is more varied than is commonly believed. The backbone of the peninsula comprises several westward-sloping mountain ranges. Sierra de San Pedro Mártir dominates the north; Sierra de la Giganta, the south. In the former, Picacho del Diablo attains an elevation of 10,073 feet, the highest point on the peninsula. Near the center is the parched Desierto Vizcaíno, which Mex. 1 passes through from a point just south of San Agustin, B.C., to just north of Punta Prieta, B.C. Other areas support more vegetation, particularly the agricultural north and the tropical south.

Baja California's climate varies with the peninsula's disparate physical geography. The northern section along the Pacific coast is similar to coastal southern California: warm and dry in summer, cool and rather wet in winter. The eastern side of the peninsula along the Gulf of California is a desert climate that is very hot and dry from May through October and mild to warm with small amounts of rainfall during the rest of the year.

The central section of Baja California from about San Quintín to La Paz is true desert. This area receives occasional rainfall from southward-moving winter storms and from late-summer tropical storms (chubascos) that come from the south. The portion of the peninsula from La Paz south is semiarid but receives some heavy rainfall from late-summer tropical storms. Winters are warm and sunny, summers hot and dry, with occasional humid spells. The nicest weather in this region occurs from November through April.

The peninsula is politically divided by the 28th parallel, about 440 miles south of the border. The area north of this line, which has experienced considerable economic growth, is the state of Baja California; its capital is Mexicali. The rapidly developing southern section is the state of Baja California Sur, with its seat of government at picturesque La Paz.

While Baja California is experiencing an increase in tourism, it remains a last frontier in many ways— isolated from the rest of Mexico, thinly populated and ruggedly scenic. Almost two-thirds of the population resides in or near the U.S. border cities of Tijuana and Mexicali. Much of the land is harsh. Outdoor recreation is the lure for visitors, who come to frolic on the white sand beaches, surf the Pacific breakers and fish the rich waters of the Gulf of California.

Points of interest on the peninsula include the prehistoric rock paintings near Cataviña, B.C., and San Ignacio, B.C.S., and the striking seascapes of Puerto Escondido, B.C.S. The following are well-known sports fishing sites: Bahía de Los Angeles, B.C.; Cabo San Lucas, B.C.S.; La Paz, B.C.S.; Loreto, B.C.S.; Los Barriles, B.C.S; and San Quintín, B.C.

An easily reached resort town is Rosarito Beach, 13 miles (21 km) south of Tijuana on Mex. 1. An alternative route from Tijuana is Mex. 1-D (toll). This coastal playground, a major tourist destination, offers swimming, surfing, windsurfing, hang gliding and camping.

From January through April, whale watching along the Pacific coast is popular in such sanctuaries as Scammon's (see Guerrero Negro) and San Ignacio lagoons.

The cave paintings that cover huge expanses of canyon walls in the Sierra de San Francisco Mountains of central Baja, long revered by local inhabitants, have mystified researchers. The age of these rock murals—some 10 feet tall—is unknown. Scenes depict running deer and mountain goats, warriors with elaborate headdresses and even a whale. According to one 18th-century Jesuit legend, the cave artists were a race of giants invading from the north. Rediscovered in the early 1960s, the deterioration of some paintings due to damage from wind erosion and water seepage is causing concern among scientists and conservationists.

Although difficult to reach, the Sierra de San Francisco, north of Santa Rosalía *(see place description)*, harbor the most important petroglyphs yet discovered in Mexico. They are contained inside the Cueva de la Flecha (Arrow Cave), Cueva de San Julio (Cave of San Julio), Cueva del Raton (Cave of the Mouse) and Cueva Pintada (Painted Cave), and also decorate the Piedras Pintadas (Painted Rocks). Access to these areas is by horse; guides can be hired in Santa Rosalía.

The peninsula is the site of several road races, including the Las Mil Millas de Baja California (also known as Baja Mil—the Baja Thousand), an event lasting several days and run between Cabo San Lucas and Tijuana; phone (905) 705-0258 or 705-0251 for information.

Driving in Baja California

Motoring off the paved roads in Baja California becomes a test of skill and patience, for much of the peninsula is truly an undeveloped wilderness. There are several good highways, including those that radiate from the cities of Tijuana, Mexicali, Tecate and Ensenada. Mex. 1 extends the length of the peninsula from Tijuana to Cabo San Lucas. Drivers should note that sharp curves, steep shoulders and infrequently marked narrow stretches make it crucial that they not exceed the speed limit. Driving is dangerous at night, when cattle often sleep on or wander onto unlit roads. If driving after dark is unavoidable, greatly reduce your speed.

All gasoline facilities in Baja are concessions granted by the federally run oil company, Pemex. Fuel prices are fixed by the Mexican government. Be sure you are charged the right amount; make sure the pump is at zero before having your tank filled; know just how many gallons your tank holds; and keep smaller denominations of pesos in case attendants run out of change. Stations on major routes are spaced at adequate intervals but occasionally run out of supplies. Therefore you should always keep your gas tank at least half full.

The Mexican gasoline octane rating method differs from the method used in the United States. Octane ratings on Mexican gas pumps can thus be misleading. Mexican gasoline comes in two grades. Magna Sin is similar to regular unleaded gasoline. It has a U.S. octane rating of 87 and a Mexican rating of 92. (Regular unleaded in the United States has an octane rating

of 87; midgrade, 89; and premium, 93.) Pemex Nova (leaded fuel subregular to that in the United States) has a U.S. octane rating of 80 and a Mexican rating of 82. Magna Sin is found in green pumps; Pemex Nova, in blue pumps.

Nova is sold at all gasoline stations. Magna Sin is available in all cities and in larger towns; some villages on the paved highways also carry it. Diesel fuel is available at most stations that carry Magna Sin.

Cars requiring leaded gas but higher octane can use a mixture of Magna Sin and Nova to get a medium-octane, slightly leaded gas. Also, a gas additive can be helpful in adapting Nova for use in cars requiring high-octane leaded gas. Since unleaded pump nozzles in Mexico are sometimes larger than those in the United States, it's a good idea to keep a funnel in the car.

A tourist card is necessary if you plan to stay in Baja California longer than 72 hours or if you wish to proceed south of either Mexicali on Mex. 5 or Maneadero on the Pacific coast. A car permit also is required for motorists traveling in mainland Mexico or planning to ferry their vehicle to the mainland. To obtain a car permit, the vehicle owner must pay a $10 fee using a major credit card (American Express, VISA or MasterCard). The word bank must appear on the card. Cash, checks, money orders or a credit card issued on a Mexican bank will not be accepted.

If the owner does not have an acceptable credit card or prefers not to pay the $10 fee, he or she may post a bond with a Mexican bonding firm (Afianzadora) for the total value of the vehicle; a notarized letter from the owner, lienholder, car rental company or business company owning the vehicle must be presented, authorizing the driver to take the vehicle out of the United States or Canada and into Mexico.

The car permit may be obtained from a Mexican customs office (Aduana) at any Baja California ferry port. Complete border crossing information is presented in AAA's *Mexico TravelGuide* or the Automobile Club of Southern California publication *Baja California*.

Because U.S. automobile insurance is **not valid** in Mexico, an insurance policy that is issued through a licensed Mexican company is a necessity for anyone driving in the country. If you are involved in an accident and cannot produce an acceptable insurance policy, you may be held by the authorities pending investigation, determination of liability and payment of fines and damages. A policy written by the day, month or year can be purchased at offices of the Automobile Club of Southern California or the California State Automobile Association. Policies are written in both English and Spanish.

When driving within the peninsula, carry proof of citizenship, a tourist card, a valid driver's license, and the original as well as a copy of the vehicle title or registration. Rental vehicles require a rental agreement and a notarized affidavit from the rental car company stating the company's permission to bring the car into Mexico. Owners of vehicles who carry only temporary registration papers must have the notarized bill of sale. If the car is not fully paid for or if it is registered in a business firm's name, a notarized letter from the lienholder or owner authorizing use of the vehicle in Mexico for a specified period must be presented at the border. The above proof of ownership **must** be carried in the car at all times while in Mexico.

Calling In and Out of Baja California

When calling Mexican phone numbers from outside the country, it is necessary to dial 011 (the international code) and 52 (the country code) before dialing the phone number. When placing long distance calls within Mexico, dial 91, then the long distance code and the phone number.

Travel by Air

Aero California offers daily flights from Los Angeles to Loreto, La Paz and Los Cabos Airport (San José del Cabo), from San Diego to Los Cabos and from Phoenix to Los Cabos. There also are daily flights from Tijuana to La Paz. Phone (310) 322-2644 or (800) 237-6225 in the United States, (66) 84-2100 (Tijuana) in Mexico.

Aeroméxico offers flights from Los Angeles to La Paz; it also flies from Tucson and Tijuana to La Paz. Phone (800) 237-6639. Alaska Airlines flies daily from Los Angeles and San Diego to Los Cabos. Phone (800) 426-0333. Mexicana Airlines offers flights daily from Los Angeles and San Francisco to Los Cabos Airport. Phone (310) 646-9500 or (800) 531-7921.

Charter service from any southern California airport to destinations throughout Baja California is offered by Gunnell Aviation Inc.; phone (310) 870-3778.

Travel by Bus

Frequently scheduled bus service is furnished by Greyhound Lines Inc. from Los Angeles and San Diego to Tijuana. Phone (310) 620-1200 in Los Angeles or (619) 239-9171 in San Diego for information on prices and schedules. Mexicoach also provides bus service from San Diego and San Ysidro to Tijuana; for information on schedules and fares phone (619) 232-5049 in San Diego.

Regular passenger bus service between Tijuana, Ensenada, Tecate and Mexicali is offered by Autotransportes de Baja California, Transportes Aguila, Transportes Norte de Sonora and Tres Estrellas de Oro. These companies operate from the Central Bus Terminal (Central de Autobuses) on Bulevar Lázaro Cárdenas at Calle Alamar near Tijuana International Airport in La Mesa. Phone (66) 86-9060 for reservations.

Tres Estrellas de Oro and Autotransportes de Baja California buses provide service between Tijuana and La Paz. The trip takes about 24 hours and costs about $29 (U.S.) one way. Phone (66) 86-9515 for information.

Travel by Ferry

A private company, Grupo Sematur, operates regularly scheduled ferry service between the Baja California peninsula and the Mexican mainland; for information phone (5) 553-7957. Round trips connect the ports of La Paz (see place listing) and Mazatlán, La Paz and Topolobampo (Los Mochis), and Santa Rosalía (see place listing) and Guaymas.

Reservations, necessary at all times, must be made at the ferry office several days in advance and at least 1 month before the departure date for holiday periods: La Paz, on Guillermo Prieto at 5 de Mayo, phone (682) 5-3833 or 5-4666; Santa Rosalía, at the ferry terminal, phone (685) 2-0013 or 2-0014; Topolobampo, at the ferry terminal, phone (686) 2-0035 or 2-0141; Guaymas, at the ferry terminal, phone (622) 2-3390 or 2-3393; and Mazatlán, at the ferry terminal, phone (69) 81-7020 or 81-7021. Rates and space availability should be reconfirmed. Even so, passage cannot be guaranteed, since trucks bearing food and provisions between the mainland and the peninsula have priority.

Visitors to Mexico should remember that schedules are subject to periodic change without notice. Schedule and fee information is available from Grupo Sematur, Paseo de la Reforma, 509-4 Piso, Col. Juárez, Mexico City, D.F., Mexico; phone (5) 553-7935 or 553-7957. Information also is available through the Automobile Club of Southern California and the club publication Baja California.

In Case of Emergency

The Mexican Government Tourist Secretariat, Presidente Masaryk 172, Mexico City, D.F., governs all tourism policies and activities in the country. Bilingual operators and receptionists provide valuable information and advice, including how to get around, what to do and see, what laws there are for the protection of tourists, and where to turn for assistance. The secretariat is open Mon.-Fri. 8-8; a 24-hour hotline can be reached by phoning (5) 250-0123. The hotline also can be used to summon the "Green Angels."

Branch offices are in all Mexican state capitals; delegates serve other major cities. Offices can usually be found in the local city hall (palacio municipal). If not, ask your hotel for directions to the Delegación or Subdelegación Federal de Turismo.

Contact a state tourism office in cases of immediate emergency. If these offices cannot be reached, then contact the local police. In rural areas the authority to contact is the delegado, who can be found at the delegación municipal or sub-delegación. In very isolated areas ask for assistance from the appointed citizen who reports to the nearest *delegado*.

For emergency road service on Mexico's major highways contact the "Green Angels." These are patrols, usually bilingual, employed by the Tourist Secretariat to help stranded motorists. Their services include mechanical aid, towing, tire changing, tourist information, basic supplies and medical first aid. The patrols cruise the main tourist routes in green-and-white pickup trucks daily 8-8.

To summon a "Green Angel," pull completely off the highway and lift the hood of your car. It is a good idea to hail a passing motorist, especially a truck or bus driver, and ask the driver to call the patrol for you. Motorists are charged for the cost of parts, gasoline and oil, but the labor is free. The "Angels" are carefully picked for their knowledge of first aid, history and geography, and should be well-acquainted with the facilities available along their routes.

Travelers experiencing an emergency anywhere in Baja California can contact the Binational Emergency Medical Commission, located in Chula Vista, Calif.; phone (619) 425-5080. This voluntary organization will help those stranded due to accident, illness, legal difficulty or lack of money. The commission works with both Mexican and American authorities.

For medical assistance ask at your hotel desk for information on the nearest hospital and English-speaking doctor. A 24-hour emergency medical evacuation service is provided by Air-Evac International Inc. in Chula Vista, Calif., phone (619) 278-3822, and in Houston, Tex., phone (713) 880-9767; or by Critical Air Medicine Inc. of San Diego, phone (619) 571-0482.

Assistance to visitors experiencing legal difficulties with local businesses or public officials in Mexico is provided by the Mexican Tourism Protection Agency. Tourist protection offices are in Ensenada, Mexicali, San Felipe and Tijuana. Federal consumer protection agency offices (Procuraduría Federal del Consumidor) also are in most major cities.

The United States Embassy in Mexico City and consulates in other large Mexican cities also give advice and render assistance to American tourists in the event of accident, serious illness or death. In Baja California, the consulate is located in Tijuana; phone (66) 81-7700 or 81-7400. In addition, there is a consular agent in Mulegé to assist with matters such as lost passports or other unforeseen snags; phone (685) 3-0111.

Canadians can receive assistance from the Canadian consulate in Tijuana; phone (66) 84-0461.

Note: Regulations prohibit tourists from sending *collect* wires outside Mexico without full deposit, which *may* become refundable. Collect telephone calls can be made from any Mexican city to U.S. and Canadian points and to several other countries.

POINTS OF INTEREST

CABO SAN LUCAS pop. 16,000

Cabo San Lucas (KAH-boh sahn LOO-kahs) marks the convergence of the Gulf of California and the Pacific Ocean. Fronting a small harbor on the gulf side, this former cannery village has emerged as an international resort renowned for its sport fishing.

Impressive condominiums, boutiques and restaurants line the hillsides and waterfront of Cabo San Lucas. The town's bay, a pirate hideout in the 16th and 17th centuries, now accommodates fishing boats and private yachts. At the tip of the peninsula is Cabo Falso, where an old lighthouse once guided ships between the U.S. west coast and Panama. Playa del Amor, also at the tip of the peninsula, is overlooked by rocky pinnacles.

Fishing for marlin and sailfish, as well as for smaller game fish, is excellent all year, and charters are available; arrangements can be made at many local hotels or on the docks by the harbor. A 1-hour excursion by skiff around the tip of the peninsula and its natural arch also is available.

Tourism and industry have combined to create intriguing contradictions with long-established ways. New yachts crowd the harbor, while rocks sculpted by untold crashing waves form Land's End, the southern tip of the Baja peninsula. Chickens scratch in dusty yards near hotels where satellite dishes pull in the latest football game.

Craft shops in the center of town feature artisans making distinctive black coral jewelry. For those who crave a little more excitement, there's the Cabo Wabo Cantina, a rock 'n' roll watering hole owned by members of the rock group Van Halen.

Aero California offers direct flights to Los Cabos Airport from Los Angeles, Phoenix and San Diego. Alaska Airlines has flights from Los Angeles and San Diego. Mexicana Airlines flies direct from Los Angeles and San Francisco.

ENSENADA pop. 169,400

One of Baja California's foremost resorts, Ensenada (ehn-seh-NAH-dah) was relatively isolated before the completion of the highway from Tijuana and the development of a seaport in the mid-1930s. For centuries a lack of fresh water prevented any permanent settlement from taking hold, though the bay often sheltered whaling ships, treasure-laden galleons and privateers. Ensenada temporarily boomed in 1870 with the discovery of gold at nearby Real de Castillo. The town became the capital of the Baja California Territory 12 years later, only to lapse into obscurity when the mines gave out.

Ensenada's seaport became revitalized with agricultural reform and development in the Mexicali Valley. Connected to Tijuana by the Mex. 1-D tollway, Ensenada attracts many Americans with its warm weather and broad, sandy beaches.

On the protected harbor of Todos Santos, this Pacific port is a well-known sport and commercial fishing center. Barracuda, bonito, mackerel, marlin, tuna and yellowtail abound in nearby waters. Sport fishing trips can be arranged at various shops along Bulevar Lázaro Cárdenas and Avenida López Mateos. Surf fishing is equally rewarding along the sandy beaches and rocky shorelines surrounding the city.

Swimming beaches are just south of town and at Estero Beach. The rocky beach near the village of San Miguel north of town is a favorite destination for surfers. Punta Banda, on the southern shore of Bahía de Todos Santos, is popular with scuba divers and skin divers. A fascinating spectacle near Punta Banda is La Bufadora (the Snort), a hollow, cavelike rock through which surf explodes like a geyser during high tide.

Muelle de Pesca Deportiva (Gordo's Sport Fishing) offers 4-hour weekend tours to observe migrating gray whales during the winter and early spring and also to view La Bufadora from the ocean. Departures are at 10 a.m. from Gordo's pier. Admission is charged.

In Ensenada is Bodegas de Santo Tomás, Mexico's largest winery. Tours are offered daily at 11, 1 and 3; phone (667) 8-2509. The popular Hobie Cat Regatta from Newport Beach, Calif., to Ensenada is held each year in late April. For local visitor information contact the Delegación de Turismo del Estado, avenidas López Mateos and Espinoza, Mon.-Fri. 9-7, Sat.-Sun. 10-2; phone (667) 6-2222 or 6-3718 (English spoken). The Comité de Turismo y Convenciones de Ensenada (Ensenada Tourist and Convention Bureau), phone (667) 8-2411 (English spoken), and the Conaco Servitur (Chamber of Commerce), phone (667) 8-2322 or 8-3770, also offer visitor information.

Mex. 1 provides access to the ruins of two missions built in the 18th century by Dominican friars. The ruins are in La Misión, 26 miles (42 km) north, and Santo Tomás, in a picturesque valley of olive trees and vineyards 28 miles (45 km) south.

Constitution of 1857 National Park (Parque Nacional Constitución de 1857), in the high plateau country of the Sierra de Juárez, offers a contrast to Ensenada's seaside milieu. The park's rugged terrain, blanketed by thick forests of ponderosa pine and unusual rock formations, is highlighted by Laguna Hanson, a small lake surrounded by primitive campsites. The park is accessible via a paved spur and dirt roads off Mex. 3 at Ojos Negros, 16 miles (26 km) east of Ensenada.

Ensenada also is the closest city in Baja from which to approach Sierra San Pedro Mártir National Park, an alpine preserve characterized by rocky peaks, pine and fir forests, freshwater streams, mountain meadows and hot springs. In

1947 the Mexican government built the National Observatory within the park. Although the observatory is closed to the public, a viewpoint offers a striking panorama that includes 10,073-foot Picacho del Diablo, the desert below and the Gulf of California.

Fishing, hiking, camping and backpacking are possible in the undeveloped park, which is reached by a graded dirt road that begins at a signed junction 9.5 miles (15 km) south of Colonet on Mex. 1. An entrance fee is charged.

SCIENCE MUSEUM OF ENSENADA (Museo de Ciencias de Ensenada), calles Obregón and 14th, contains oceanography and marine life exhibits pertaining to the area. Daily 9-5. Free. Phone (667) 8-7192.

GUERRERO NEGRO pop. 7,200

In the barren Vizcaíno Desert, Guerrero Negro (geh-REH-roh NEH-groh) is one of the world's largest producers of salt, which is shipped to mainland Mexico, Canada, Japan and the United States.

The town has become a popular observation point for viewing gray whales, which end their 6,000-mile migration from the Bering Sea at nearby Scammon's Lagoon (Laguna Ojo de Liebre), where they bear their young during January, February and early March. Their cavorting can be observed from the beach of the lagoon or from the old salt wharf 7 miles (11 km) northwest of town via a paved, bumpy road. From Mex. 1 the junction to the dirt road to Scammon's Lagoon is about 5 miles (8 km) south of the turnoff to Guerrero Negro and is signed Gray Whale Natural Park (Parque Natural Ballena Gris).

LA PAZ pop. 137,600

La Paz (lah PAHS) lies on Bahía de La Paz, 99 miles (160 km) north from the tip of the peninsula via Mex. 19. Its fine port facilities make it the commercial as well as governmental capital of the state of Baja California Sur.

For nearly 3 centuries isolation and hardship prevented permanent settlement. Two years after the bay was discovered by a Spanish expedition in 1533, supply problems doomed a colonization attempt by Hernán Cortés. The most persistent inhabitants were the privateers who sought haven in the bay. The name of one—Cromwell—lives on (hispanicized) in the *coromueles,* or offshore breezes, and in such local place names as Playa Coromuel.

The Jesuits founded a mission at La Paz in 1720, but abandoned it nearly 3 decades later after disease virtually wiped out the area's Indian population. A group of determined Spaniards finally established a settlement in 1811.

Pearl diving and some mining provided impetus for growth, and the city soon replaced Loreto as territorial capital. Beautiful black and pink pearls discovered in the rich oyster beds in nearby gulf waters filled the coffers of the Spanish royal treasury. Both industries gave out around 1930, and La Paz languished until sportsmen and tourists rediscovered its balmy climate and fine fishing. La Paz now integrates vestiges of its colonial past within a progressive city structure.

The city, with its shady plazas and palm-fringed *malecón,* has a growing number of resorts and fleets of pleasure craft. On the southeastern end of Bahía de La Paz, the city faces northwest, an ideal location to view the spectacular sunsets that make the waters of the Gulf of California (Sea of Cortés) appear red. Much activity centers around the kiosk on the esplanade extending off the *malecón,* where pop music concerts are performed on Sunday nights.

A free port, La Paz has shops stocked with goods from around the world at duty-free prices. Shops geared to tourists are found along Paseo Alvaro Obregón, opposite the *malecón.* Small stores offering bargains also are scattered throughout the downtown area. The Regional Art Center (Centro de Arte Regional) at calles Chiapas and Encinas is a pottery workshop with reasonably priced merchandise.

Such local handicrafts as black coral jewelry, seashell knickknacks, leather products and woven baskets are displayed at Casa de las Artesanias de Baja California Sur, on Paseo Obregón just east of Hotel Los Arcos. La Perla de la Paz, on Mutualismo, is a giant downtown department store offering everything from auto parts to sporting goods.

Marlin weighing up to 1,000 pounds are found in the waters off La Paz from mid-March through October; sailfish are caught from the end of May through October. Yellowtail, roosterfish and bonito are available all year. The best months for catching big fish are March through September. Boats for deep-sea fishing can be hired along the *malecón* and at Hotel Los Arcos. Rental rates usually include tackle, bait and crew. Reservations are advised from April to early July.

Other popular water sports are scuba diving, skin diving, water skiing and swimming. The area around El Mogote, a long sandbar that protects the city from the open waters of the Gulf of California, is particularly suited to scuba diving.

Playa Coromuel, about 1.9 miles (3 km) from Avenida 5 de Mayo, is the most popular beach. The easy drive on Mex. 11 to Pichilingue, 8 miles (13 km) north, follows the scenic shore of Bahía de La Paz. At the Pichilingue Ferry Terminal a graded road continues to Playa Pichilingue, Puerto Balandra, Playa Tecolote and Punta San Lorenzo. Baja Diving, Independencia 107-B, offers trips to Playa Encantada and Isla de las Focas (home to a colony of sea lions) as well as snorkeling and scuba diving at Isla Espiritu

Santo; phone (682) 2-1826 or 5-2575 daily 8-3:30.

Two-hour sightseeing cruises of Bahía de La Paz and to such nearby beaches as Puerto Balandra depart daily from the *malecón*. The state tourism office is at Paseo Alvaro Obregón and 16 de Septiembre; phone (682) 2-5939 (English spoken).

Flights to and from several Mexican mainland cities and major southwestern U.S. cities regularly operate out of the jet-capacity airport. Aero California offers direct flights from Los Angeles and Tijuana; Aeroméxico has direct flights from Los Angeles and Tucson. Several buslines depart from the station at Paseo Alvaro Obregón 125.

Air-conditioned, automobile-passenger ferries link La Paz with the mainland cities of Mazatlán and Topolobampo, near Los Mochis. The ferry office in La Paz is on Guillermo Prieto at 5 de Mayo; phone (682) 5-3833 or 5-4666. Try to make reservations well in advance. A 315-passenger boat makes the trip to Topolobampo in 3½ hours. Departures are at 4:30 from the *malecón*, Av. Alvaro Obregón; phone (682) 5-6311.

ANTHROPOLOGICAL MUSEUM OF BAJA CALIFORNIA (Museo Antropologico Baja California), at Ignacio Altamirano and 5 de Mayo, has prehistoric paintings and pictures, fossils and exhibits devoted to anthropology, geology and the history of Baja California Sur. Tues.-Sat. 9-6.

LORETO pop. 7,200

Dating from 1697 with the founding of a mission by a Jesuit padre, Loreto (loh-REH-toh) became the first capital of both Alta and Baja California. The base from which exploration and colonization efforts began in what is now California, Loreto was also the departure point from which Junípero Serra launched his northward quest in 1769 to establish a chain of missions in Alta California. The town's natural beauty began attracting visitors and fishermen after a period of near oblivion, the result of a devastating hurricane that caused the capital to be moved to La Paz in 1829.

Loreto lies on the Gulf of California in a scenic palm grove overshadowed by the jagged peaks of the Sierra de la Giganta to the west. The economy is based on farming, fishing and tourism. A favorite destination with fly-in anglers for many years, Loreto is easily reached via the transpeninsular highway (Mex. 1) and continues to attract those in search of roosterfish, marlin, sailfish and just about every other major game species.

Near the central plaza is the restored mission of Nuestra Señora de Loreto. Severely damaged by earthquakes, the 1752 mission—including the tower with its modern clock—has been rebuilt.

Interesting side trips include a boat excursion to Isla Coronado, the home of a large colony of sea lions, and to Mission San Javier, an impressively restored 1699 mission constructed of dark volcanic rock in the *mudéjar* (Moorish) style. The road to San Javier south of the Loreto junction is one of Baja California's most rewarding jaunts; it runs 20 miles (33 km) through stunning mountain and canyon scenery. The trip should be attempted by high-clearance vehicles only. The mission, still active as a parish church, displays exemplary stonework and a gilded altar from Mexico City.

A large government-managed resort project is located at Nopoló, approximately 3 miles (5 km) south of Loreto. About 6 miles (10 km) farther a short paved road off Mex. 1 leads to Puerto Escondido, a deepwater port that also has resort facilities. Its partially landlocked bay just north of the dock offers fine fishing and diving, a well-developed campground and a protected marina for small boats. Loreto's airport receives regular flights from southern California; direct flights are offered from Los Angeles by Aero California.

MUSEUM OF BAJA CALIFORNIA MISSIONS (Museo de Las Misiones de Baja California) is beside the Nuestra Señora de Loreto Mission. The artifacts and manuscripts on display relate to Baja California's historic missions. Other exhibits include saddles used in colonial times and a wooden carving of Christ. Admission is charged.

MEXICALI pop. 438,400

Capital of the state of Baja California, Mexicali (meh-hee-CAH-lih) is a border city and duty-free port opposite Calexico, Calif. Customs offices are open 24 hours daily. Tourists in need of assistance can contact the Secretaría de Turismo del Estado; phone (65) 52-5877 Mon.-Fri. 9-4 and 5-7, Sat. 9-1 (English spoken).

Mexicali developed as a market center for surrounding farms in the early 20th century. It became the capital of the territory of Baja California Norte in 1915. Visitors from across the border were attracted by legalized alcohol and gambling as well as by land speculation. In the late 1930s, however, the fertile land of the Mexicali Valley was distributed, under the leadership of President Lazaro Cárdenas, among Mexican farmers and *ejidos* (collective agricultural colonies).

Water has been integral to the city's subsequent growth. The aridity of the valley—it receives on average only 2 inches of rain yearly—prevented the silt-laden soil from being exploited. When the flow of irrigation water from the Colorado River was guaranteed by international treaty, Mexicali bloomed both agriculturally and industrially.

This extension of the Imperial Valley of California is now invaluable to the economy of the republic. Wheat, cotton, cantaloupes and many other truck crops are grown in abundance. A brewery, large cotton gins and its status as the terminus of a major Mexican railroad contribute to the city's livelihood. Tourism and the electronics industry have further bolstered the economy.

Indicative of Mexicali's prosperity is the Civic-Commercial Center (Centro Cívico y Comercial) along Calzada Independencia on the southern edge of the city. The extensive urban project includes state and federal government offices, hospitals, a bullring and restaurants. Zona Rosa, next to the center, is an attractive shopping area.

Most of Mexicali's shops, restaurants and nightclubs are near the international border in an irregular rectangle bounded by avenidas Cristóbal Colón and Alvaro Obregón, the Río Nuevo and Calle C. In the former state governor's residence at Av. Alvaro Obregón 1209, between calles D and E, is Galería de la Ciudad, an art gallery displaying works by Mexican artists.

Bullfights are held in September and October at Plaza de Toros Calafia in the Civic-Commercial Center on Calle Calafia. *Charreadas,* the Mexican forerunner of Western-style rodeos, are usually held one Sunday each month during the winter and on Mexican holidays. These equestrian events occur at two sites, one west of Mexicali on Mex. 2 and another approximately 3 miles (5 km) east of Calzada Justo Sierra on Calle Compuertas.

About 20 miles (32 km) west of Mexicali on Mex. 2 is the junction with a dirt road to Cañon de Guadalupe, a scenic palm canyon with hot springs and campground facilities. Between the turnoff to Cantú Palms and La Rumorosa, Mex. 2 climbs 4,260 feet and offers views of Laguna Salada, site of Mexico's most important geothermal power plant, and the moonlike desertscape below.

Also in this area is Macahui (mah-KAH-wee), a point of departure from which to observe part of a huge archeological zone that extends north to Blythe, Calif. The landscape is almost totally covered with strange designs formed by piling desert rocks on top of one another. No one has been able to explain how the mostly vertical and spiral formations were created, or by whom. These rock sculptures are seen to even better advantage from the air.

"Deluxe" bus service is provided by Tres Estrellas; phone (65) 57-2420.

REGIONAL MUSEUM, UNIVERSITY OF BAJA CALIFORNIA (Museo Regional, Universidad de Baja California), Av. Reforma and Calle L, offers a cultural perspective of the city. Its exhibits focus on paleontology, archeology, ethnography, landscape photography and the missions of Baja California. Allow 30 minutes minimum.

MULEGE pop. 3,100

Mulegé (moo-leh-HEH) is an attractive oasis on the Santa Rosalía River midway down the Baja California peninsula. Fishing and boating opportunities make this a popular gulf resort.

Cabin cruisers and outboards can be rented by the day. Placid Bahía Concepción south of Mulegé is a good spot for seaside camping. Playa Coyote fronts a sparkling cove and has several trees, rare on Baja's desert beaches.

The 1766 Mission Santa Rosalía de Mulegé, just upstream from the Mex. 1 bridge over the Santa Rosalía River, has been restored. Another nearby attraction is El Sombrerito, a hat-shaped monolith at the mouth of the Mulegé River. Stone steps to the summit begin at the beach, which is reached via an eastward extension of the town's main street.

NUEVO ROSARITO pop. 100

The village of Nuevo Rosarito (roh-sah-REE-toh) is off Mex. 1, 70 miles (113 km) north of Guerrero Negro. The Mission San Borja, 22 miles (35 km) east over a very rough open-desert dirt road, is one of Baja's most interesting missions, partly because of its remoteness. Founded in 1759 by the Jesuits shortly before they were expelled from the New World, the mission once served more than 3,000 Indians and remains largely intact.

SAN FELIPE pop. 9,300

San Felipe (sahn feh-LEE-peh), one of the towns on the Gulf of California chosen by the Mexican government for development as a future resort, was settled as a fishing community in the 1920s. Since the completion of Mex. 5 from Mexicali in 1951, a steady stream of American sportsmen has helped transform San Felipe into a major winter vacation destination. Attractive beaches line the coastline southeastward from the town's crescent-shaped bayfront to Punta Estrella, about 12 miles (19 km) distant.

The high Sierra de San Pedro Mártir, crowned by 10,073-foot Picacho del Diablo, is visible to the west as the highway nears town. Equally spectacular is Bahía San Felipe's extreme tidal range, often reaching more than 20 feet. A splendid view of the town and coastline is available at the Virgin of Guadalupe Shrine, atop a hill just north of San Felipe. Southbound, Mex. 5 passes the airport and continues, paved but rough, 51 miles (83 km) to Puertecitos.

At this major fishing center shrimp are caught commercially. Surf fishing and package or chartered fishing trips appeal to visitors. White sea bass, cabrilla, corbina, sierra and many other species are found in the gulf waters. Boat rentals can be arranged locally. Air service to San Felipe is available through Air Resorts Airline; phone (619) 438-4926 from San Diego.

SAN IGNACIO pop. 800

Verdant San Ignacio (sahn eeg-NAH-syoh) appears as a mirage in Baja California's inhospitable desert. In a wide valley among numerous date palms, San Ignacio has thatched-roof dwellings and pastel-colored buildings clustered around an imposing 18th-century stone mission and a tree-shaded plaza. Built by the Dominicans in 1786, the well-preserved church still serves an active local parish.

The town's agricultural foundation was laid by the Jesuits, who founded a mission in 1728 and planted date palms around the former Indian settlement. While dates remain the chief crop, figs, oranges and grapes also are grown. San Ignacio serves as the commercial center for isolated ranching operations to the north and south.

Many mysterious cave paintings done by prehistoric Indian artists are hidden in the remote Sierra de San Francisco Mountains; the most significant are Arrow Cave, Cave of the Mouse, Painted Cave, Painted Rocks and San Julio Cave. Mule trips to the cave sites can be arranged in town.

Bahía de Ballenas and Laguna San Ignacio, 43.5 miles (70 km) southwest via the passable dirt road to La Fridera fishing camp, are wintering grounds for gray whales; boat rides to observe them are available.

SAN JOSE DEL CABO pop. 14,900

Tropical San José del Cabo (sahn hoh-SEH dehl KAH-boh) has emerged as a resort and commercial center at the southern tip of the Baja peninsula. It also serves as the market for the surrounding agricultural and cattle-raising areas. An abundance of mangoes, avocados and oranges are produced in the region.

Most resort development lies just south of town. There are several swimming beaches, and surf fishing is good in the surrounding area. Playa Barco Varado (Shipwreck Beach), between San Jose del Cabo and Cabo San Lucas (see place listing), curves around the remains of a Japanese freighter jutting from a rocky shelf. For boaters, skiffs and cruisers are available. Campo de Golf Los Cabos, a nine-hole public course, is situated among condominiums and hotels in the resort area. The Paseo Mijares, lined by stone arches, is suitable for leisurely hikes. There is air service to San José del Cabo from Los Angeles via Mexicana Airlines, Aero California and Alaska Airlines.

SANTA ROSALIA pop. 10,200

A mining town that has been designated a national historic monument, Santa Rosalía (SAHN-tah roh-sah-LEE-ah) was established by the French-owned El Boleo Copper Co. during the 1880s. Prosperity reigned until the mines gave out in 1953. Mining operations were later reactivated with the discovery of new copper and manganese deposits, but these too failed. Boat-building is a major factor in today's economy.

In keeping with its mineral assets, the town's most interesting feature is a prefabricated galvanized-iron church. Designed by A.G. Eiffel for the 1898 Paris World's Fair, the metal church was shipped in pieces to Santa Rosalía from France.

Also of interest are the nearby caves of San Borjita, which contain the oldest cave paintings yet discovered in Baja California. Reached by an inferior side road off the highway south of town, the best time to visit the caves is in the afternoon when the sun illuminates the vibrantly executed paintings.

A worthwhile side trip for high-clearance vehicles only is the picturesque old village of San José de Magdalena, reached by a graded dirt road that branches west off Mex. 1, about 17 miles (27 km) south of Santa Rosalía. Graced by palm groves and colorful flower gardens, this oasis village dates from Baja California's Spanish colonial period, when it served as a visiting station of the Mulegé mission. Ruins of a chapel built by the Dominicans in 1774 testify to the village's antiquity.

Ferry service is available between Santa Rosalía and Guaymas; make reservations well in advance. The ferry office is in the terminal building; for information phone (685) 2-0013 or 2-0014.

TECATE pop. 40,200

A port of entry about 32 miles (51 km) southeast of San Diego, Calif., Tecate (teh-KAH-teh) has managed to maintain a Mexican small-town atmosphere. Life centers on a tranquil, tree-shaded plaza. Tecate lies in a bowl-shaped valley below 5,884-foot Tecate Peak. The border is open 6 a.m.-midnight.

Tecate was first settled in the 19th century by farmers and ranchers attracted by its abundant water and fertile soil. Although industry—beer and instant coffee production—and tourism continue to grow in importance, the town remains a commercial center for the surrounding grape-, olive- and grain-growing area.

The Tecate Brewery on the outskirts of town offers tours; phone (665) 4-1709 for a schedule. Visitor information also can be obtained at SECTURE (State Tourism Bureau), at 1305 Callejón Libertad on the south side of the plaza. The office is open Mon.-Fri. 8-7, Sat. 9-3, Sun. 10-2; phone (665) 4-1095.

TIJUANA pop. 698,800

Tijuana (tee-HWAH-nah), south of San Diego, is a main port of entry to the Baja California peninsula. A booming tourism industry has helped transform this former tawdry border town into a bustling metropolis of high-rise buildings, huge shopping centers and broad boulevards.

A growing commercial center, Tijuana offers shopping bargains, horse and dog racing, jai alai, golf and a temperate climate. A seven-block stretch of Avenida Revolución, the traditional tourist zone, is lined with everything from cafes and curio shops to nightclubs and strip joints. At the corner of Paseo de los Héroes and Avenida Independencia, the Plaza Río Tijuana complex contains major department stores.

Gastronomic lore names Tijuana as the birthplace of the Caesar salad, invented to serve a crowd of late diners from a restaurant's depleted food supply.

Bullfights are held every Sunday afternoon from mid-May to mid-September. During the season sites alternate between El Toreo, 1.9 miles (3 km) east on Bulevar Agua Caliente, and Plaza de Toros Monumental (Bullring-by-the-Sea), 6 miles (10 km) west via Mex. 1-D. Reserved and general admission seating is available.

Jai alai games are played at the Frontón Palacio, Avenida Revolución at Calle 7. The Agua Caliente Track, Bulevar Agua Caliente, presents dog racing in the evening and on some afternoons; the track also offers horse racing on weekends at noon. The Country Club (Club Campestre), also on Bulevar Agua Caliente, has golf and tennis facilities.

Las Playas de Tijuana, 6 miles (10 km) from the city, is a popular seaside community. Rosarito Beach, about 13 miles (21 km) south via Mex. 1, is a rapidly growing resort town with facilities catering mainly to tourists. Diversions include swimming in the Pacific Ocean and horseback riding along the wide, sandy beach.

Information can be obtained at SECTURE, the state tourism bureau, in the Plaza Patria on Bulevar Agua Caliente. The bureau is open Mon.-Fri. 9-3 and 5-7; phone (66) 81-9492, 81-9493 or 81-9494 (English spoken). The Procuraduría de Protección al Turismo (Tourist Protection Agency), Av. Revolución and 1st Street, is open Mon.-Fri. 9-7; phone (66) 88-0555. Information booths also are at the border and at the Tijuana Chamber of Commerce on Avenida Revolución.

Mexican and U.S. customs offices are open 24 hours daily. There are two border crossings—at Tijuana-San Ysidro and at Otay Mesa, just east of the Tijuana International Airport and south of SR 117 (Otay Mesa Road). Open daily 6 a.m.-10 p.m., the Otay Mesa crossing is particularly useful for travelers who are returning from Baja on weekends.

Aero California and Mexicana Airlines provide regular flights from Tijuana to La Paz and several cities on the Mexican mainland. "Deluxe" bus service is provided by Tres Estrellas; phone (66) 26-1146.

THEME PARK (Mexitlan Parque Tematico), Calle 2 and Av. Ocampo, features an outdoor display of 150 scale models. Covering a city block, the representations include some of the nation's outstanding monuments, churches, buildings, plazas, stadiums and architectural treasures. The display spans 4 centuries of history and focuses on Mexico's south-central plateau region. Music characteristic of each area plays at the different exhibits.

Mexitlan also includes a beach resort map, restaurants and souvenir and handicraft shops. Live folk music and dancing are featured; a sound-and-light show is presented at dusk. Daily 10-10, May-Sept.; Wed.-Fri. noon-8, Sat.-Sun. noon-10, rest of year. Admission $9.50; over 60, $7.50; ages 5-12, $4.75. Phone (66) 38-4101.

TIJUANA CULTURAL CENTER is at Paseo de los Héroes and Av. Independencia. The complex has a museum with archeological and handicraft displays; a spherical Omnitheater, which features a film on the history and culture of Mexico; craft shops; and a 1,000-seat performing arts center. The Omnitheater film is shown in English at 2 p.m. Allow 1 hour, 30 minutes minimum. Admission is charged to the museum and the film. Phone (66) 84-1111 or 84-1132.

Discounts to go

For sightseeing, staying overnight or going from here to there **there's more than one way to save money** when you travel with AAA.

 AT ATTRACTIONS

Over 2,000 attractions discount their admission fees to AAA members. Look for the word **"discount"** in the TourBook listings.

 AT ACCOMMODATIONS*

Special Value—Lodgings whose listings contain **"Special Value Rates"** give you at least 10 percent off.

Senior Discount—If you're 60 or older, you can save at least 10 percent where **"Senior Discount"** appears in a listing.

Special Discounts—By separate arrangement with AAA, several large hotel chains offer special discounts or rates to AAA members. Call your AAA office for details.

✓ **ON THE ROAD**

AAA has approved a very special and exclusive package with **Hertz Rent-A-Car.** You don't have to worry about hidden charges; you know you'll get a high-quality, dependable vehicle and first-class service. As a AAA member you're entitled to special rates and discounts and a whole package of benefits. Call your AAA office for details and a discount card.

*Only one of the lodging discounts may be used at a time. The discounts cannot be combined.

 MEMBER DISCOUNT PROGRAM

LODGINGS & RESTAURANTS

AAA knows how important
accommodations and dining
experiences are for the traveler.
Lodgings and Restaurants
are annually inspected
and approved by AAA.
Diamond quality ratings, directions,
price ranges and other helpful
information are noted.

With Ramada's Four-For-One Program*, Up to Four People Can Stay For The Price Of One.

Ramada offers a great value with our Four-For-One Program. For one low rate, up to four people can share a room for the price of one.

This program is great when visiting family and friends, or traveling together to gatherings and reunions, for extended business trips and vacation stays.

What's more, you'll enjoy all the features Ramada is known for...like big, comfortable rooms, a sparkling pool and spa, great restaurants and a cozy lounge.

So next time you're traveling, don't feel you have to go alone just to save a few dollars.

Call Ramada and ask for the Four-For-One rate.

RAMADA®

INNS, HOTELS, SUITES AND RESORTS.

FOR RESERVATIONS CALL

1-800-2-RAMADA

(1-800-272-6232)

OR YOUR LOCAL TRAVEL PROFESSIONAL

CALIFORNIA

ADELANTO
Days Inn
All year [CP]
| | AAA Special Value Rates | | | | | Motel | ◆◆ |
| 1P 35.00- | 40.00 | 2P/1B | 40.00- 45.00 | 2P/2B | 50.00- 55.00 | XP 6 | F |

36 units. On US 395. 11628 Bartlett Ave. (92301) Refrigerators; A/C; C/CATV; movies; phones; comb or shower baths. Htd pool. Small pets only. 4 rooms with whirlpool tub & VCP, $80 for 1 to 2 persons. Wkly rates avail. Reserv deposit required. AE, DI, DS, MC, VI. Coffeeshop opposite. FAX (619) 246-4350 ⊗ Ⓓ 🅖 (619) 246-8777

AGOURA HILLS — 20,400
Ramada Hotel
All year
| | Rates Guaranteed | | | | | Hotel | ◆◆◆ |
| 1P .... | 59.00 | 2P/1B | .... 59.00 | 2P/2B | .... 59.00 | XP 10 | F |

Senior discount. 281 units. 1/4 mi s of US 101, exit Reyes Abode Rd. 30100 Agoura Rd. (91301) Check-in 3 pm. A/C; C/CATV; pay movies; radios; phones. Rental refrigerators. Htd pool; whirlpool; exercise rm. Parking lot. Pets, $10 extra charge. Wkly & monthly rates avail. AE, DI, DS, MC, VI. ● Restaurant; 6:30 am-10 pm; $9-$19; cocktails; entertainment. FAX (818) 707-6298 (See ad p A4) ⊗ Ⓢ Ⓓ 🅖 (818) 707-1220

ALBION — 400

Albion River Inn

@ All year [BP]   Rates Subject to Change   *Cottages* ◆◆◆
1P 85.00- 225.00 2P/1B 85.00- 225.00 .... XP 20
20 units. On SR 1, 6 mi s of Mendocino; nw end of bridge. (PO Box 100, 95410) On a bluff; most rooms with fireplace & ocean view; few motel units. Check-in 3 pm. 3 refrigerators; radios; phones; comb or shower baths. 2 rooms with whirlpool bath. No pets. Reserv deposit required; 7 days refund notice. MC, VI. ● see separate listing. ⊗ Ⓓ Ⓖ (707) 937-1919

RESTAURANT

Albion River Inn Restaurant   American $$ ◆◆◆
In Albion River Inn. 3790 N Hwy.1. Fresh seafood. On cliff overlooking river & ocean. Smoke free premises. Open 5:30 pm-9:30 pm; Sat & Sun from 5 pm. Cocktails. Minimum $10. Reserv advised. MC, VI. ⊗ (707) 937-4044

ALHAMBRA — 82,100

Best Western Alhambra Inn

@ All year [CP]   AAA Special Value Rates   *Motel* ◆◆◆
1P .... 49.00 2P/1B .... 55.00 2P/2B .... 59.00 XP 5
58 units. 2 mi ne of I-10; exit Fremont Ave. 2451 W Main St. (91801) Refrigerators; A/C; C/TV; movies; radios; phones. Coin laundry. Small htd pool; whirlpool. No pets. AE, DI, DS, MC, VI. FAX (818) 576-5937 ⊗ Ⓢ Ⓓ Ⓖ (818) 284-5522

Quality Inn

@ All year [CP]   Rates Subject to Change   *Motel* ◆◆◆
1P .... 60.00 2P/1B .... 68.00 2P/2B .... 72.00 XP 10 F
Senior discount. 73 units. 1 1/2 mi ne of I-10; exit Fremont Ave. 2221 W Commonwealth Ave. (91801) Rooms & 1-bedroom suites with living room. 41 refrigerators; A/C; C/CATV; movies; radios; phones. Htd pool. No pets. AE, DI, DS, MC, VI. Restaurant adjacent. FAX (818) 281-8297 ⊗ Ⓢ Ⓓ Ⓖ (818) 300-0003

RESTAURANT

Bangkok Siam Cafe   Ethnic $ ◆
1 3/4 mi n of I-10; exit Garfield Ave. 29 S Garfield Ave. Extensive selection of authentic Thai dishes, served in a casual, high tech dining room. Open 11 am-10 pm; Fri & Sat-11 pm; Sun 11 am-10 pm. Beer & wine. MC, VI. (818) 281-6255

ALPINE — 5,400

Country Side Inn

@ All year [CP]   Rates Guaranteed   *Motel* ◆◆◆
1P .... 40.00 2P/1B .... 45.00 2P/2B .... 50.00 XP 5 F
59 units. Adjacent to I-8, exit Tavern Rd. 1251 Tavern Rd. (92001) Refrigerators; A/C; C/CATV; movies; phones. Htd pool; whirlpool. No pets. Wkly rates avail. AE, DI, MC, VI. Restaurant opposite. FAX (619) 445-6730 *(See ad p A295)* ⊗ Ⓢ Ⓓ Ⓖ (619) 445-5800

RESTAURANT

Donato's   Italian $ ◆◆
1/2 mi e. 2654 Alpine Blvd. Nicely prepared entrees & variety of pizzas. A/C. Children's menu. Open 3 pm-10 pm; Fri-Sun from 11 am; closed Major holidays & 4/11. Cocktails & lounge. Reserv advised Fri & Sat. MC, VI. ⊗ (619) 445-4006

ALTURAS — 3,200

Best Western Trailside Inn

@ 5/1-11/1   Rates Subject to Change   *Motel* ◆◆
1P 40.00- 46.00 2P/1B 44.00- 46.00 2P/2B .... 46.00 XP 4
11/2-4/30 1P 36.00- 44.00 2P/1B 38.00- 44.00 2P/2B .... 40.00 XP 4
39 units. On US 395. 343 N Main St. (96101) A/C; C/CATV; movies; phones. Small pool open 6/1-9/30. Pets, $5 extra charge. 4 units with microwave & refrigerator, $5 extra. AE, DI, DS, MC, VI. ⊗ Ⓓ (916) 233-4111

Dunes Motel

@ 4/1-10/31   Rates Guaranteed   *Motel* ◆◆
1P 38.00- 50.00 2P/1B 40.00- 50.00 2P/2B 45.00- 54.00 XP 4
11/1-3/31 1P 34.00- 42.00 2P/1B 36.00- 44.00 2P/2B 38.00- 48.00 XP 4
Senior discount. 49 units. On US 395. 511 N Main St. (96101) Few small rooms. A/C; C/CATV; movies; phones. AE, CB, DI, MC, VI. Coffeeshop adjacent. ⊗ Ⓓ (916) 233-3545

ANAHEIM — 266,400 (See ANAHEIM-BUENA PARK spotting map pages A6 & A7; see index starting below) See also BUENA PARK, CYPRESS, FULLERTON, GARDEN GROVE, ORANGE & SANTA ANA

Index of Establishments on the ANAHEIM-BUENA PARK AREA Spotting Map

(See ANAHEIM-BUENA PARK spotting map pages A6 & A7)

Travelodge Westgate Inn.....................	⑱
Anaheim Carriage Inn........................	⑲
Quality Hotel & Conference Center.................................	⑳
Anaheim Marriott Hotel	㉑
Anaheim Hilton and Towers.................	㉒
Convention Center Inn.......................	㉓
Inn At The Park..............................	㉔
Jolly Roger Inn Hotel	㉕
Magic Carpet Motel.........................	㉖
Magic Lamp Motel	㉗
Alpine Motel................................	㉘
Anaheim Angel Inn	㉙
Travelodge Maingate........................	㉚
Anaheim Plaza Hotel........................	㉛
Grand Hotel	㉜
Saga Inn	㉝
Best Western Anaheim Inn	㉞
Marco Polo Inn..............................	㉟
Anaheim Desert Inn & Suites................	㊱
Best Western Park Place Inn	㊲
Anaheim Penny Sleeper Inn.................	㊳
Howard Johnson Lodge......................	㊴
Holiday Inn Anaheim Center	㊵
Anaheim Courtesy Lodge	㊶
Ramada Maingate Anaheim	㊷
Residence Inn By Marriott	㊸
Econo Lodge-East...........................	㊹
Travelodge Anaheim/Beach Blvd	㊺
Sheraton-Anaheim Hotel	㊻
Best Western Anaheim Stardust..............	㊼
Super 8 Motel-Anaheim Park	㊽
Park Vue Inn	㊾
Days Inn Suites	㊿
Best Western Courtesy Inn..................	51
Anaheim Maingate Inn	52
Candy Cane Inn	53
Conestoga Hotel............................	54
Best Western Abby's Anaheimer Inn.........	55
The Pan Pacific Hotel.......................	56
TraveLodge Apollo Inn......................	57
Best Western Stovall's Inn	58
Best Western Pavilions	59
Disneyland Hotel	60
Crystal Inn.................................	61
Granada Inn................................	62
Anaheim Regency Inn	63
Quality Inn-Brookhurst......................	64
Best Western Station Inn....................	65
Carousel Inn & Suites.......................	66
Tropicana Inn	67

Econo Lodge-West	68
Quality Inn Anaheim-West	69
Anaheim La Palma Inn.......................	72
Anaheim/Buena Park Travelodge	73
Polynesian Motel	74
Hampton Inn................................	75
Cavalier Inn & Suites	76
Comfort Suites Anaheim Hills	77
Parkside Inn & Suites........................	78
Holiday Inn Express	79
Econo Lodge-Anaheim Stadium.................................	80
Akua Motor Inn..............................	81
Travelodge Cornerstone Inn..................	82

RESTAURANTS

Foxfire Restaurant...........................	①
Thee White House Restaurant................	②
Mr Stox Restaurant	③
Charley Brown's.............................	⑤
The Catch	⑥
Hansa House Smorgasbord	⑦
JW's	⑧
El Torito Restaurant.........................	⑩
Spaghetti Station	⑪
California Bistro	⑫
Cattleman's Wharf	⑬
The Overland Stage	⑭
Mimi's Cafe	⑮
Plantation Restaurant	⑯
Pavia.......................................	⑰

BUENA PARK

Fairfield Inn by Marriott......................	92
Hampton Inn	93
Travelers Inn	94
Siesta Inn..................................	95
Plaza Inn...................................	96
Days Inn-La Palma..........................	97
Best Western Buena Park Inn	98
Embassy Suites Hotel-Buena Park...........	99
Courtyard by Marriott........................	100
Holiday Inn Buena Park......................	102

RESTAURANTS

Marie Callenders............................	㉒
Knott's Berry Farm Chicken Dinner Restaurant..................................	㉓
El Torito	㉔
Velvet Turtle Restaurant	㉕

Akua Motor Inn 81
All year   **Rates Guaranteed**   *Motel* ◆
1P 30.00- 34.00   2P/1B   36.00- 40.00   2P/2B   40.00- 44.00 XP 2
Senior discount. 62 units. 3 blks e of Harbor Blvd; 1/4 mi n of SR 91, exit Raymond Ave. 1018 E Orangethorpe Ave (92001) A/C; C/CATV; movies; phones; shower baths. 2 3-bedrm units, 7 efficiencies, no utensils. Coin laundry. Pool. No pets. Wkly rates avail. Reserv deposit required; 3 days refund notice. AE, CB, MC, VI. *(See ad below)*   Ⓓ (714) 871-2830

Alpine Motel 28
6/8-9/3   **Rates Subject to Change**   *Motel* ◆◆
6/8-9/3   1P 48.00- 52.00   2P/1B   48.00- 52.00   2P/2B   50.00- 58.00 XP 4
9/4-6/7   1P 32.00- 44.00   2P/1B   32.00- 44.00   2P/2B   40.00- 50.00 XP 4
41 units. 715 W Katella Ave. (92802) A/C; C/CATV; movies; phones; comb or shower baths. Rental refrigerators. 7 2-bedrm units. Pool. No pets. Reserv deposit required. AE, DI, DS, MC, VI. Restaurant adjacent. FAX (714) 535-3714   Ⓓ (714) 535-2186

(See ANAHEIM-BUENA PARK spotting map pages below & A7)

Anaheim Angel Inn 29
			AAA Special Value Rates					*Motel*		◆
6/12-9/4	1P	39.00-	45.00	2P/1B	39.00-	49.00	2P/2B	45.00-	59.00	XP 5
9/5-6/11	1P	32.00-	39.00	2P/1B	34.00-	45.00	2P/2B	34.00-	49.00	XP 5

61 units. 1 mi e of I-5, exit Katella Ave. 1800 E Katella at State College Blvd. (92805) A/C; C/CATV; movies; phones. Coin laundry. Pool. No pets. AE, DS, MC, VI. Restaurant adjacent. FAX (714) 978-1608 Ⓓ (714) 634-9121

Anaheim Ascot Inn 6
			AAA Special Value Rates					*Motel*		◆
6/15-9/5 [CP]	1P	48.00-	52.00	2P/1B	52.00-	58.00	2P/2B	54.00-	62.00	XP 4 F
9/6-6/14 [CP]	1P	36.00-	36.00	2P/1B	36.00-	45.00	2P/2B	36.00-	42.00	XP 4 F

53 units. 1/2 blk s of Orangewood. 2145 S Harbor Blvd. (92802) Refrigerators; A/C; C/CATV; movies; rental VCPs. Radios; phones. 5 2-bedrm units. Coin laundry. Pool; whirlpool. No pets. AE, DI, DS, MC, VI. FAX (714) 748-4183 *(See ad p A12)* ⊗ Ⓓ (714) 971-5556

Anaheim/Buena Park Travelodge 73
			Rates Subject to Change					*Motel*		◆◆
6/5-9/4	1P	39.00-	45.00	2P/1B	45.00-	49.00	2P/2B	49.00-	59.00	XP 6 F
9/5-6/4	1P	32.00-	45.00	2P/1B	36.00-	45.00	2P/2B	45.00-	49.00	XP 6 F

Senior discount. 42 units. On SR 39, 1/2 mi n of Ball Rd. 735 S Beach Blvd. (92804) A/C; C/CATV; pay movies; radios; phones. Small pool; whirlpool. No pets. Wkly & monthly rates avail. AE, DI, DS, MC, VI. FAX (714) 821-0171 *(See ad below)* ⊗ Ⓓ 🅖 (714) 761-4255

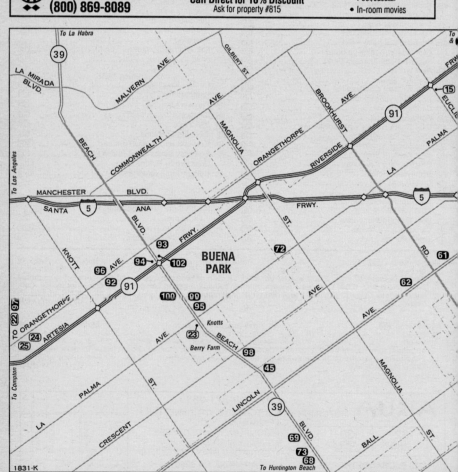

1831-K

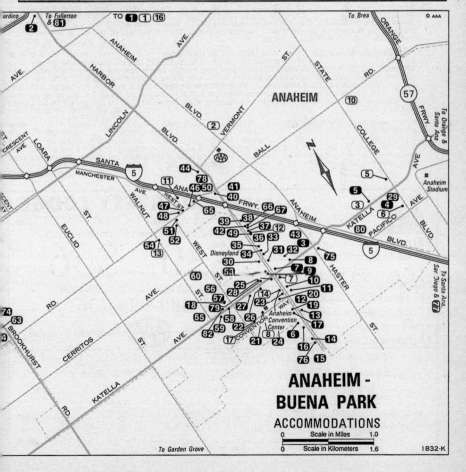

ANAHEIM - BUENA PARK
ACCOMMODATIONS

(See ANAHEIM-BUENA PARK spotting map pages A6 & A7)

Anaheim Carriage Inn ⑲   AAA Special Value Rates   *Motel* ◆◆◆

⊕ 6/10-9/4	1P	49.00- 65.00	2P/1B	49.00- 65.00	2P/2B	59.00- 79.00	XP 4	F
9/5-6/9	1P	35.00- 49.00	2P/1B	35.00- 49.00	2P/2B	39.00- 59.00	XP 4	F

51 units. 1 blk s of Orangewood Ave. 2125 S Harbor Blvd. (92802) Refrigerators; A/C; C/CATV; movies; radios; phones. 5 kitchens. Coin laundry. Htd pool; whirlpool; 3 rooms with whirlpool tub. Limited parking lot. No pets. 17 2-bedroom units, $69-$139 for 2-8 persons. Reserv deposit required; 3 days refund notice. AE, DI, DS, MC, VI. Coffeeshop opposite. FAX (714) 971-5330 *(See ad p A16)*   ⊗ Ⓓ ⑤ (714) 740-1440

Anaheim Courtesy Lodge ㊶   Rates Subject to Change   *Motel* ◆

⊕ 6/10-9/4 [CP]	1P	36.00- 42.00	2P/1B	36.00- 42.00	2P/2B	42.00- 48.00	XP 4	F
9/4-6/9 [CP]	1P	32.00- 36.00	2P/1B	32.00- 36.00	2P/2B	36.00- 40.00	XP 4	F

Senior discount. 26 units. 1/4 mi e of I-5; 1 blk e of Harbor Blvd. 414 W Ball Rd. (92805) A/C; C/TV; movies; radios; phones. Small pool. No pets. 3 kitchens, $5-$7 extra; no utensils. Wkly rates avail. Reserv deposit required; 3 days refund notice. AE, DI, DS, MC, VI. *(See ad below)*   Ⓓ (714) 533-2570

Anaheim Desert Inn & Suites ㊱   Rates Guaranteed   *Motel* ◆◆◆

⊕ 6/12-9/1 [CP]	1P	49.00- 69.00	2P/1B	49.00- 69.00	2P/2B	59.00- 79.00	XP 4	
9/2-6/11 [CP]	1P	42.00- 59.00	2P/1B	49.00- 59.00	2P/2B	49.00- 69.00	XP 4	

Senior discount. 143 units. 1600 S Harbor Blvd. (92802) Refrigerators; A/C; C/CATV; movies; VCPs. Radios; phones. 15 2-bedrm units. Coin laundry. Htd indoor pool; whirlpool. Garage. No pets. 2 & 3-room suites for 5-10 persons, $59-$169. Microwaves. Reserv deposit required; 3 days refund notice. AE, DI, DS, MC, VI. Coffeeshop adjacent. FAX (714) 778-2754 *(See ad starting on p A18)*   ⊗ ⑤ Ⓓ (714) 772-5050

Anaheim Desert Palm Inn & Suites ⑨   Rates Subject to Change   *Motel* ◆◆◆

⊕ 6/7-9/2	1P	59.00- 69.00	2P/1B	59.00- 69.00	2P/2B	69.00- 89.00	XP	F
9/3-6/6	1P	49.00- 59.00	2P/1B	49.00- 59.00	2P/2B	59.00- 79.00	XP	F

Senior discount. 100 units. 631 W Katella Ave. (92802) Refrigerators; A/C; C/CATV; movies; VCPs. Radios; phones. Coin laundry. Htd pool; sauna; whirlpool; exercise rm. No pets. 12 rooms with whirlpool tub, $79-$109. 52 2-bedroom units for up to 8 persons, $89-$169. 6-efficiencies, $15 extra. Reserv deposit required; 3 days refund notice. AE, DI, DS, MC, VI. Restaurant opposite. FAX (714) 491-7409 *(See ad starting on p A20)*   ⊗ ⑤ Ⓓ (714) 535-1133

Anaheim Harbor Inn ⑯   Rates Subject to Change   *Motel* ◆◆◆

⊕ 6/1-8/31	1P	59.00- 79.00	2P/1B	59.00- 79.00	2P/2B	59.00- 79.00	XP 5	F
9/1-5/31	1P	49.00- 69.00	2P/1B	49.00- 69.00	2P/2B	49.00- 69.00	XP 5	F

Senior discount. 128 units. 1 blk s of Orangewood Ave. 2171 S Harbor Blvd. (92802) Check-in 3 pm. A/C; C/TV; phones. Coin laundry. Htd pool; whirlpool. No pets. Reserv deposit required. AE, DI, DS, MC, VI. Coffeeshop adjacent. FAX (714) 748-9809 *(See ad p A22)*   ⊗ Ⓓ ⑤ (714) 750-3100

Anaheim Hilton and Towers ㉒   AAA Special Value Rates   *Hotel* ◆◆◆

⊕ All year	1P	150.00- 210.00	2P/1B	170.00- 230.00	2P/2B	170.00- 230.00	XP 20	F

1576 units. 1/2 blk s of Katella Ave. 777 Convention Way. (92802) Next to Anaheim Convention Center. Large convention hotel with many recreational facilities & specialty shops. Check-in 3 pm. A/C; C/CATV; free & pay movies; radios; phones. 2 htd pools; saunas; whirlpools. Fee for: health club & massage. Pay garage. Small pets only. Luxury level rooms avail. Reserv deposit required; 3 days refund notice. AE, DI, DS, MC, VI. ● 4 restaurants; 6 am-midnight; $8.50-$35; cocktails; entertainment. Also, Pavia, see separate listing. FAX (714) 740-4252 *(See ad p 22)*   ⊗ ⑤ Ⓓ (714) 750-4321

Anaheim International Inn & Suites ⑫   Rates Subject to Change   *Motel* ◆◆

⊕ 6/1-8/31 [CP]	1P	.... 59.00	2P/1B	.... 59.00	2P/2B	.... 59.00	XP 7	F
9/1-5/31 [CP]	1P	.... 49.00	2P/1B	.... 49.00	2P/2B	.... 49.00	XP 7	F

Senior discount. 119 units. 1/2 mi s of Katella Ave. 2060 S Harbor Blvd. (92802) Check-in 3 pm. A/C; C/CATV; movies; radios; phones; comb or shower baths. 3 2-bedrm units, 6 efficiencies, no utensils. Coin laundry. Htd pool; whirlpool. Limited parking lot. No pets. AE, DI, DS, MC, VI. FAX (714) 971-2706 *(See ad p A9)*   ⊗ Ⓓ ⑤ (714) 971-9393

(See ANAHEIM-BUENA PARK spotting map pages A6 & A7)

Anaheim La Palma Inn **72**

	Rates Subject to Change					Motel		◆
6/11-9/3	1P	....	35.00	2P/1B	....	40.00	2P/2B	....	40.00	XP	3
9/4-6/10	1P	....	30.00	2P/1B	....	33.00	2P/2B	....	33.00	XP	3

68 units. 1 mi e of SR 39, Beach Blvd. 2691 W La Palma Ave. (92801) A/C; C/CATV; movies; radios; phones. 3 2-bedrm units, 2 3-bedrm units. Coin laundry. Htd pool; 2 rooms with whirlpool tub. No pets. 6 efficiencies, $5 extra; no utensils. AE, DI, DS, MC, VI. ⊗ Ⓓ 🅖 (714) 826-8100

Anaheim Maingate Inn **52**

	AAA Special Value Rates					Motel		◆◆
♿ 6/1-8/31 [CP]	1P	....	58.00	2P/1B	....	58.00	2P/2B	....	58.00	XP	5	F
9/1-5/31 [CP]	1P	....	48.00	2P/1B	....	48.00	2P/2B	....	48.00	XP	5	F

29 units. 2 blks w of I-5. 1211 S West St at Ball Rd. (92802) Formerly Excalibur Inn & Suites. Refrigerators; A/C; C/CATV; movies; radios; phones. Coin laundry. Whirlpool. No pets. 7 units with whirlpool tub & microwave, $48-$98. Wkly rates avail. Reserv deposit required. AE, DI, DS, MC, VI. FAX (714) 520-0578 *(See ad p A23)* ⊗ Ⓓ (714) 533-2500

DIAMONDS tell the story—read Using Your TourBook.

ALL NEW. ALL SUITES. ALL RADISSON.

Centrally Located ... Within 15 Minutes from all the Magic of Disneyland Park (free shuttle), Newport Beach, Orange County Airport, Exclusive Shopping Malls and Miles of Sandy Beaches

In the tradition of Radisson elegance, and luxury you will find all comforts & services possible to make your stay pure pleasure. ... elegantly furnished two room suites with a spacious living room and private bedroom.

There is an outdoor pool, sundeck & whirlpool hot spa, sundries store, guest coin laundry, exercise room free shuttle to Orange County Airport & Disneyland Park... and much more.

THREE DIAMOND AWARD

KNOTT'S BERRY FARM
DISNEYLAND PARK
ANAHEIM STADIUM
55
HOTEL TERRACE DR.
HOTEL
5
405
MALL
SOUTH COAST PLAZA
DYER RD (EAST) EXIT
ORANGE COUNTY AIRPORT
NEWPORT BEACH
FASHION ISLAND

Radisson SUITE HOTEL SANTA ANA ®

(See ANAHEIM-BUENA PARK spotting map pages A6 & A7)

Anaheim Marriott Hotel **21**   Rates Guaranteed   *Hotel* ◆◆◆
All year   1P 160.00- 169.00   2P/1B 180.00- 189.00   2P/2B 180.00- 189.00 XP 10   F
1039 units. 1 blk w of Harbor Blvd. 700 W Convention Way. (92802) Adjacent to Anaheim Convention Center.
Check-in 4 pm. A/C; C/CATV; free & pay movies; radios; phones. Coin laundry. 2 htd pools, 1 indoor/outdoor;
saunas; whirlpools; exercise rm. Pay valet parking ramp. Pets. Reserv deposit required; 3 days refund notice.
AE, DI, DS, MC, VI. ● 2 dining rms; 6:30 am-11 pm; $7.50-$35; cocktails. Also, JW's, see separate listing.
FAX (714) 750-9100 *(See ad p A9)*   ⊗ Ⓢ Ⓓ Ⓛ (714) 750-8000

(See ANAHEIM-BUENA PARK spotting map pages A6 & A7)

Anaheim Penny Sleeper Inn 38	Rates Guaranteed					*Motel*	◆
6/10-8/31, 12/25-1/1 [CP]	1P	....	42.00	2P/1B	.... 42.00	2P/2B	.... 52.00 XP
1/2-6/9, 9/1-12/24 [CP]	1P	....	33.00	2P/1B	.... 33.00	2P/2B	.... 36.00 XP

205 units. Adjacent to I-5; northbound Harbor Blvd exit, southbound Freedman Way exit; 1 blk e of Harbor Blvd. 1441 S Manchester Ave. (92802) A/C; C/CATV; movies; VCPs. Phones. Coin laundry. Htd pool. No pets. Reserv deposit required. AE, DS, MC, VI. FAX (714) 533-6430 *(See ad below)*   ⊗ Ⓓ ⑤ (714) 991-8100

Anaheim Plaza Hotel 31	Rates Subject to Change				*Motor Inn*	◆◆◆
6/1-9/1	1P 92.00- 107.00	2P/1B	107.00- 117.00	2P/2B 107.00- 117.00	XP 10	F

Senior discount. 297 units. 1700 S Harbor Blvd. (92802) OPEN ALL YEAR. Check-in 3 pm. A/C; C/CATV; movies; radios; phones. Htd pool; whirlpool. Pay parking lot. No pets. AE, DI, MC, VI. ● Dining rm; 6:30 am-10 pm; $7.50-$15; cocktails. FAX (714) 772-8386 *(See ad p A24)*   ⊗ Ⓓ ⑤ (714) 772-5900

Anaheim Regency Inn 63	Rates Subject to Change					*Motel*	◆
6/15-8/31	1P	....	35.00	2P/1B	.... 38.00	2P/2B	.... 42.00 XP 2- 3
9/1-6/14	1P	....	30.00	2P/1B	.... 32.00	2P/2B	.... 34.00 XP 2

32 units. 1 1/4 mi s of I-5, Brookhurst St exit. 701 S Brookhurst St. (92804) A/C; C/TV; phones. Pool. No pets. 4 kitchens, $7 extra. Reserv deposit required. AE, CB, DI, MC, VI. *(See ad p A12)*   Ⓓ (714) 776-2600

The Anaheim **Penny Sleeper INN**

Take Advantage of Penny Sleeper Inn's Many Tour Packages Designed to Take the Hassle out of a Southern California Vacation.

PENNY SLEEPER HOLIDAY PACKAGES FEATURE:
A Disneyland® Park passport with unlimited rides and attractions • Universal Studios • Knott's Berry Farm • Hard Rock Cafe & Venice Beach • Magic Mountain • Sea World • San Diego Zoo • L.A & Hollywood - Tour by day or night • Tijuana, Mexico • Las Vegas & The Grand Canyon - CALL US FOR A FREE BROCHURE.

Each of our 202 spacious guest rooms feature:
- FREE HBO (Premium Movies), CNN & ESPN
- In-room VCR & Nintendo rentals
- FREE in-room coffee & tea
- Direct dial phones
- AM/FM- alarm clock radio

We offer our guests:
- Year round heated pool
- Game room/Video arcade
- FREE Safe deposit boxes
- FREE Continental breakfast
- Laundromat & valet service
- Car rental available
- One day photo service
- Fax, copying and postal services
- FREE shuttle to Disneyland® Park, Anaheim Convention Center, Anaheim Greyhound & Anaheim Amtrak
- Shuttles to three major shopping centers (nominal charge)
- One block from Disneyland® Park and two blocks from Anaheim Convention Center
- All sightseeing tours arranged.
- Direct pick up & drop off by airport shuttles
- Easy walking distance to a variety of restaurants
- Gift Shop

AAA Special Rates

One Queen	Two Doubles
Low season **$33.00**	Low season **$36.00**
High season **$42.00**	High season **$52.00**

BALL RD.
SANTA ANA FWY.
Disneyland Park®
MANCHESTER AVE.
HARBOR BLVD.
PENNY SLEEPER
KATELLA AVE.
CONVENTION CENTER
ANAHEIM STADIUM →

(800) 854-6118
TOLL FREE

1441 S. Manchester Ave., Anaheim, California 92802-2995
Reservations (714) 991-8100 • (800) 854-6118 • (800) 44 UTELL • FAX (714) 533-6430
Apollo UI-17005, Sabre UI-5429, Pars UI-2786

■ ALL SUITES INCLUDE: ■
Entertainment Center with Microwave, Refrigerator, Coffee Maker
Two Remote TV's • Individual Climate Control • Game Table
In-Suite Safe • Three Phones (1 in the Bath) • Fine Personal Amenities

■ COMPLIMENTARY ■
Daily Continental Breakfast served in our Crystal Cafe
Shuttle Service to Disneyland Park and the Convention Center
In-Suite Movies (HBO, CNN, ESPN) • Fresh Brewed Coffee in Suites

TYPICAL BEDROOM

TWO ROOM SUITE

$69

1-4 Persons Per Suite

SPACIOUS LIVING ROOM

■ TWO ROOM SUITES ■

A
UP TO 4 PERSONS

Bedroom with King Bed
Spacious Living Room
with Full Size Sofabed.
Sept. 1 - June 16: $69

B
UP TO 6 PERSONS

Bedroom with 2 Beds
Spacious Living Room
with Full Size Sofabed.
Sept. 1 - June 16: $79

C
UP TO 8 PERSONS

Bedroom with 3 Beds
Spacious Living Room
with Full Size Sofabed.
Sept. 1 - June 16: $89

June 17 - August 31, Holidays & Special Events Add $15

■ THREE ROOM SUITE ■
Two Private Bedrooms (Up to 8 Persons) • One with a King Bed
& Full Bath • One with Two Beds & Full Bath
Three TV's • Spacious Living Room with Full Sofabed
Sept. 1 - June 16: $129 • June 17 - Aug. 31 & Holidays: $159

■ HONEYMOON SPA SUITE ■
Uniquely contoured Bedroom
Luxurious Living Room • Private Jacuzzi & Separate Shower
Sept. 1 - June 16: $99 • June 17 - Aug. 31 & Holidays: $129

**24 HOUR
RESERVATIONS: 800-992-4884**

Three day refund cancellation notice required. Subject to limited availability.

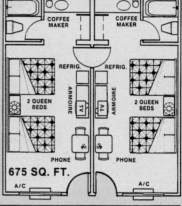
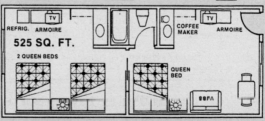

WE'RE RIGHT IN THE MIDDLE OF ALL THE FUN

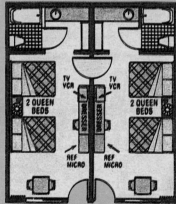

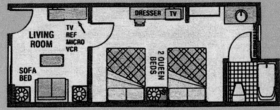
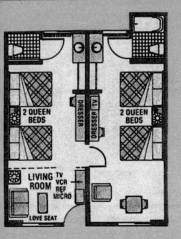
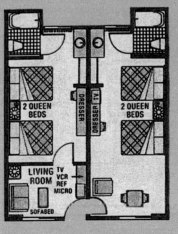

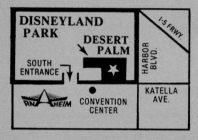

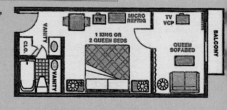

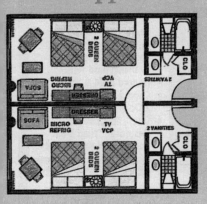

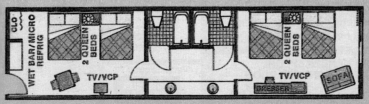

(See ANAHEIM-BUENA PARK spotting map pages A6 & A7)

Anaheim Stadium Travelodge **4**		Rates Subject to Change						*Motel*			◆◆
6/16-8/22 [CP]	1P	....	54.00	2P/1B	....	58.00	2P/2B	....	63.00	XP 6	F
8/23-6/15 [CP]	1P	....	50.00	2P/1B	....	50.00	2P/2B	....	56.00	XP 6	F

Senior discount. 72 units. 1 mi e of I-5. 1700 E Katella Ave. (92805) 57 refrigerators; A/C; C/CATV; movies; radios; phones. Htd pool; whirlpool. No pets. Reserv deposit required. AE, DI, DS, MC, VI. Restaurant adjacent. FAX (714) 634-0366 *(See ad p A24)* ⊗ Ⓓ 🅖 (714) 634-1920

Anaheim Westward Ho **8**		Rates Subject to Change						*Motel*		◆◆
6/1-9/3	1P 42.00-	46.00	2P/1B	42.00-	46.00	2P/2B	54.00-	62.00	XP 6	
9/4-5/31	1P 39.00-	42.00	2P/1B	39.00-	46.00	2P/2B	44.00-	58.00	XP 6	

175 units. 1/2 blk e of Harbor Blvd. 415 W Katella Ave. (92802) Check-in 3 pm. A/C; C/TV; rental VCPs; phones. Htd pool; whirlpool. No pets. Reserv deposit required. AE, DS, MC, VI. FAX (714) 535-5659 *(See ad p A30)* ⊗ Ⓓ (714) 778-6900

Best Western Abby's Anaheimer Inn **55**		Rates Subject to Change						*Motel*		◆◆
6/1-8/31 [CP]	1P	....	50.00	2P/1B	....	55.00	2P/2B	....	65.00	XP 6	F
9/1-5/31 [CP]	1P	....	39.00	2P/1B	....	42.00	2P/2B	....	44.00	XP 6	F

28 units. 1201 W Katella Ave at Walnut. (92802) A/C; C/TV; radios; phones. Coin laundry. Htd pool; whirlpool. No pets. AE, DI, DS, MC, VI. *(See ad p A7)* ⊗ Ⓓ (714) 774-0211

(See ANAHEIM-BUENA PARK spotting map pages A6 & A7)

Best Western Anaheim Inn 34   **AAA Special Value Rates**   **Motel** ◆◆◆
3/9-4/14, 5/27-9/6 & 12/24-1/3 1P 75.00- 85.00 2P/1B 75.00- 85.00 2P/2B 75.00- 85.00 XP F
1/4-3/18, 4/15-5/26 & 9/7-12/23 1P 55.00- 65.00 2P/1B 55.00- 65.00 2P/2B 55.00- 65.00 XP F
88 units. 1630 S Harbor Blvd. (92802) Refrigerators; A/C; C/TV; rental VCPs; radios; phones. 5 2-bedrm units, 1
kitchen. Coin laundry. Htd pool; saunas; whirlpool. Limited parking lot. No pets. Reserv deposit required. AE,
DI, DS, MC, VI. Restaurant adjacent. FAX (714) 776-6305 *(See ad p A31)*   ⊗ Ⓓ (714) 774-1050

Best Western Anaheim Stardust 47   **Rates Guaranteed**   **Motel** ◆◆◆
All year   1P 38.00- 60.00 2P/1B 42.00- 64.00 2P/2B 46.00- 68.00 XP 8
103 units. 1 blk w of I-5. 1057 W Ball Rd. (92802) Check-in 3 pm. A/C; C/TV; radios; phones. Rental refrigerators.
Coin laundry. Htd pool; whirlpool. No pets. Reserv deposit required. AE, DI, DS, MC, VI. Restaurant adjacent.
FAX (714) 535-6953 *(See ad p A32)*   Ⓓ Ⓚ (714) 774-7600

Best Western Angels Inn 14   **Rates Subject to Change**   **Motel** ◆◆
4/2-4/17, 6/1-8/28 & 12/25-1/31 1P .... 48.00 2P/1B .... 52.00 2P/2B .... 58.00 XP 4 F
2/1-4/1, 4/18-5/31 & 8/29-12/24 1P .... 38.00 2P/1B .... 42.00 2P/2B .... 44.00 XP 4 F
Senior discount. 55 units. 3/4 mi s of Katella Ave. 11851 S Harbor Blvd. (92802) A/C; C/CATV; movies; radios;
phones. Htd pool; whirlpool. No pets. Reserv deposit required. AE, DI, DS, MC, VI. Restaurant adjacent. *(See ad
p A24)*   ⊗ Ⓓ (714) 971-0255

(See ANAHEIM-BUENA PARK spotting map pages A6 & A7)

Best Western Courtesy Inn 51   Rates Subject to Change   *Motor* ◆◆
6/12-9/12 & 12/17-1/4 [CP]   1P 59.00- 72.00 2P/1B 62.00- 72.00 2P/2B 62.00- 72.00 XP 4   F
4/1-6/11 [CP]   1P 42.00- 62.00 2P/1B 45.00- 62.00 2P/2B 45.00- 62.00 XP 4   F
1/5-3/31 & 9/13-12/16 [CP]   1P 39.00- 59.00 2P/1B 42.00- 59.00 2P/2B 42.00- 59.00 XP 4   F
Senior discount. 35 units. 1 blk w of I-5. 1200 S West St at Ball Rd. (92802) 10 refrigerators; A/C; C/TV; movies; radios; phones. 2 2-bedrm units. Pool; whirlpool. No pets. Reserv deposit required; 7 days refund notice. AE, DI, DS, MC, VI. FAX (714) 774-3425 *(See ad p A32)*   ⊗ Ⓓ (714) 772-2470

Best Western Park Place Inn 37   AAA Special Value Rates   *Motor Inn* ◆◆◆
3/7-4/6, 5/24-9/2 & 12/20-1/5
[CP]   1P 80.00- 85.00 2P/1B 80.00- 85.00 2P/2B 85.00- 95.00 XP
1/6-3/6, 4/7-5/23 & 9/3-12/19
[CP]   1P 55.00- 65.00 2P/1B 55.00- 65.00 2P/2B 65.00- 75.00 XP
199 units. 1544 S Harbor Blvd. (92802) A/C; C/TV; rental VCPs; radios; phones. Coin laundry. Htd pool; sauna; whirlpool. Limited parking lot. No pets. Reserv deposit required. AE, DI, DS, MC, VI. ● Restaurant; 6:30 am-10 pm; $6-$12; cocktails. FAX (714) 758-1396 *(See ad p A31)*   ⊗ Ⓓ (714) 776-4800

San Diego

Vacation Values For AAA Members

See other side for additional hotels

San Diego

Vacation Values For AAA Members

Suite Type A
Two Room Suite up to 8 persons
$85 including Hot Breakfast
$75 without Breakfast.

June-Aug, & Special Events
$115 Including Hot Breakfast
$105 without Breakfast

Two Separate rooms each with full bath, TV,
refrigerator, safe, coffee maker and hair dryer.
Bedroom has 2 Queen beds and Living room
has 1 Sofa bed and 1 Queen Bed.

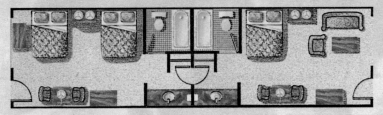

"Suite Dreams"

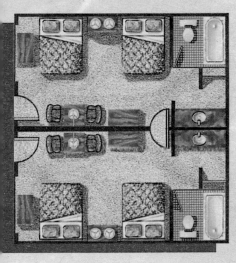

Suite Type B
Two Room Suite up to 10 persons
$95 Including Hot Breakfast
$75 Without Breakfast.

June-Aug, & Special Events
$115 Including Hot Breakfast
$105 Without Breakfast

Two adjoining rooms each with 2 Queen
beds, full bathroom, T.V., refrigerator,
safe, coffee maker and hair dryer.

Local # (714) 999-0684 • Fax (714) 635-0964
921 S. Harbor Blvd., Anaheim, CA 92805

Stay Directly Across From The Main Entrance To Disneyland Park!

Luxurious Suites

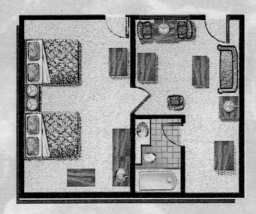

SUITE TYPE A
6 Person • Two Room Suite

$55.00

Off Season

Private room with 2-Queen beds
Living Room with sofabed.
2 TV's, Microwave, Refrigerator, Hair
Dryer & Coffee Maker.
June-August & Special Events $75

SUITE TYPE B
8 Person • Two Room Suite

$75.00

Off Season

Bedroom with 2-Queen beds and full
bath. Living room with sofa bed,
Queen bed and full bath. TV and
phone in both rooms
June-August & Special Events
$110.00

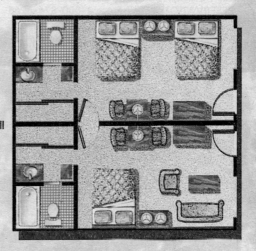

SUITE TYPE C
Same as Suite Type B except,
2-Queen beds in each room.

Toll Free Reservations (800) 854-0199

**1570 S. Harbor Blvd.
Anaheim, CA 92802
Telephone: (714) 772-5721
Fax: (714) 635-0964**

(See ANAHEIM-BUENA PARK spotting map pages A6 & A7)

Best Western Pavilions ⑤⑨   Rates Guaranteed   *Motel*   ◆◆◆
🆎 3/21-4/8, 5/28-9/6 & 12/24-1/2 1P 60.00- 75.00 2P/1B   60.00- 75.00 2P/2B   65.00- 80.00 XP   F
1/3-3/20, 4/9-5/27 & 9/7-12/23 1P 50.00- 65.00 2P/1B   50.00- 65.00 2P/2B   55.00- 70.00 XP 6   F
Senior discount. 100 units. 1 mi w of I-5. 1176 W Katella Ave. (92802) 58 refrigerators; A/C; C/CATV; radios;
phones. 1 2-bedrm unit. Htd pool; sauna; whirlpool. No pets. Reserv deposit required. AE, CB, DI, MC, VI. Restaurant adjacent. FAX (714) 776-5801 *(See ad p A31)*   ⊗ Ⓓ (714) 776-0140

Best Western Station Inn ⑥⑤   Rates Guaranteed   *Motel*   ◆◆
🆎 5/25-9/7 [CP]   1P .... 55.00 2P/1B   .... 68.00 2P/2B   .... 68.00 XP 10   F
9/8-5/24 [CP]   1P .... 42.00 2P/1B   .... 52.00 2P/2B   .... 52.00 XP 10   F
Senior discount. 55 units. Adjacent to I-5, exit Ball Rd. 989 W Ball Rd. (92802) Check-in 3 pm. A/C; C/TV; radios;
phones. 3 2-bedrm units. Coin laundry. Htd pool; whirlpool. No pets. 6 rooms with whirlpool tub, $130-$165. Reserv deposit required. AE, CB, DI, MC, VI. *(See ad below)*   ⊗ Ⓢ Ⓓ (714) 991-5500

Check out our **bold** listings!

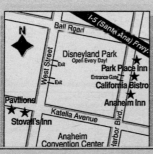

(See ANAHEIM-BUENA PARK spotting map pages A6 & A7)

Best Western Stovall's Inn 58   AAA Special Value Rates   *Motel*   ◆◆◆
(AAA) 3/19-4/8, 5/28-9/6 &
12/24-12/31   1P 70.00- 75.00 2P/1B   70.00- 75.00 2P/2B 75.00- 85.00 XP
1/1-3/18, 4/9-5/27 & 9/7-12/23   1P 50.00- 60.00 2P/1B   50.00- 60.00 2P/2B 55.00- 70.00 XP
290 units. Katella Ave at S West St. 1110 W Katella Ave. (92802) Check-in 3 pm. A/C; C/TV; rental VCPs; radios;
phones. Rental refrigerators. Coin laundry. 2 htd pools; wading pool; whirlpools. No pets. Reserv deposit required. AE, DI, DS, MC, VI. Cocktail lounge; coffeeshop adjacent. FAX (714) 778-3805 *(See ad p A31)*
                                                                                  ⊗ Ⓓ (714) 778-1880

Candy Cane Inn 53   Rates Subject to Change   *Motel*   ◆◆◆
(AAA) All year [CP]   1P 59.00- 69.00 2P/1B   59.00- 69.00 2P/2B 59.00- 95.00 XP
173 units. 1/2 blk n of Katella Ave. 1747 S Harbor Blvd. (92802) Nicely landscaped. 20 refrigerators; A/C; C/CATV;
movies; phones. Coin laundry. Htd pool; wading pool; whirlpool. No pets. Reserv deposit required. AE, DS, MC,
VI. FAX (714) 772-5462 *(See ad p A34)*   Ⓓ Ⓑ (714) 774-5284

(See ANAHEIM-BUENA PARK spotting map pages A6 & A7)

Carousel Inn & Suites 66   AAA Special Value Rates   Motel   ◆◆
♿ 6/15-9/15 [CP]   1P .... 48.00 2P/1B .... 48.00 2P/2B .... 48.00 XP 8   F
9/16-6/14 [CP]   1P .... 45.00 2P/1B .... 45.00 2P/2B .... 45.00 XP 8   F
131 units. 1530 S Harbor Blvd. (92802) A/C; C/CATV; free & pay movies; radios; phones. Coin laundry. Htd pool.
No pets. 65 rooms with small refrigerators & microwaves. AE, DS, MC, VI. Restaurant adjacent.
FAX (714) 772-9965   ⊗ Ⓓ (714) 758-0444

Castle Inn & Suites 7   Rates Guaranteed   Motel   ◆◆◆
♿ All year   1P 52.00- 82.00 2P/1B 62.00- 92.00 2P/2B 62.00- 92.00 XP 4
200 units. 1/2 blk n of Katella Ave. 1734 S Harbor Blvd. (92802) Refrigerators; A/C; C/TV; movies; VCPs. Radios;
phones. Coin laundry. Htd pool; wading pool; whirlpool; 6 rooms with whirlpool tub. No pets. Suites, $82-$112.
Reserv deposit required. AE, DI, DS, MC, VI. Restaurant adjacent. FAX (714) 956-4736 *(See ad
starting on p A36)*   ⊗ Ⓢ Ⓓ 🅖 (714) 774-8111

Check out our **bold** listings!

AAA Trip Interruption Protection is designed
to assist you in reaching your destination if your vehicle
becomes disabled as a result of a traffic collision.

(See ANAHEIM-BUENA PARK spotting map pages A6 & A7)

Cavalier Inn & Suites [76]

				Rates Subject to Change				Motel		◆◆
6/1-8/31 [CP]	1P	49.00- 65.00	2P/1B	49.00- 65.00	2P/2B	49.00- 65.00	XP			F
3/1-5/31 [CP]	1P	39.00- 55.00	2P/1B	39.00- 55.00	2P/2B	39.00- 55.00	XP			F
9/1-2/28 [CP]	1P	36.00- 52.00	2P/1B	36.00- 52.00	2P/2B	36.00- 52.00	XP			F

Senior discount. 93 units. 3/4 mi s of Katella Ave. 11811 S Harbor Blvd. (92802) Check-in 3 pm. A/C; C/TV; movies; phones; comb or shower baths. Coin laundry. Htd pool; whirlpool. No pets. 27 rooms with small refrigerator & microwave. Reserv deposit required. AE, DI, DS, MC, VI. FAX (714) 971-3539 *(See ad p A35)*
⊗ Ⓓ (714) 750-1000

Comfort Inn-North [2]

				Rates Subject to Change				Motel		◆◆
6/1-8/31 [CP]	1P	.... 50.00	2P/1B	.... 50.00	2P/2B	.... 55.00	XP	5		F
9/1-5/31 [CP]	1P	.... 40.00	2P/1B	.... 40.00	2P/2B	.... 45.00	XP	5		F

118 units. 1/4 blk s of SR 91, Harbor Blvd exit. 1251 N Harbor Blvd. (92801) A/C; C/TV; radios; phones. Rental refrigerators. Coin laundry. Htd pool; whirlpool. No pets. Reserv deposit required. AE, DI, DS, MC, VI. *(See ad p A33)*
⊗ Ⓓ (714) 635-6461

(See ANAHEIM-BUENA PARK spotting map pages A6 & A7)

Comfort Inn-South 13		Rates Subject to Change					Motel			◆◆
⊕ 5/24-8/31 [CP]	1P 51.00- 59.00	2P/1B	56.00- 64.00	2P/2B	56.00- 64.00	XP 5				F
9/1-5/23 [EP]	1P 39.00- 48.00	2P/1B	44.00- 53.00	2P/2B	44.00- 53.00	XP 5				F

Senior discount. 66 units. 3/4 mi s of Katella Ave. 2200 S Harbor Blvd. (92802) A/C; C/TV; movies; phones. Coin laundry. Htd pool; whirlpool. No pets. AE, DI, DS, MC, VI. *(See ad p A35)* ⊗ Ⓓ ⓐ (714) 750-5211

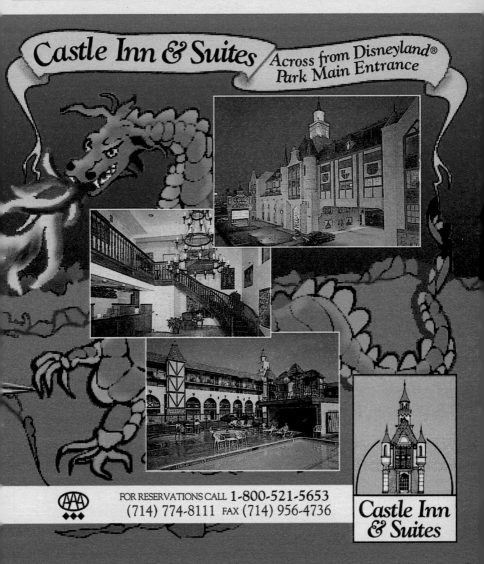

(See ANAHEIM-BUENA PARK spotting map pages A6 & A7)

Comfort Suites Anaheim Hills 🛇 Rates Subject to Change Motel ◆◆◆
ⓐⓐⓐ All year [CP] 1P .... 64.00 2P/1B .... 74.00 2P/2B .... 84.00 XP 10
160 units. Adjacent to SR 91; exit Imperial Ave, 1 blk s to Santa Ana Canyon Rd, then 1 blk e to Via Cortez. 201 N Via Cortez St. (92807) Check-in 3 pm. Refrigerators; A/C; C/CATV; movies; radios; phones. Coin laundry. Htd pool; saunas; whirlpool; exercise rm. No pets. Wkly & monthly rates avail. AE, DI, DS, MC, VI. Restaurant adjacent. FAX (714) 637-8790 ⊗ Ⓢ Ⓓ (714) 921-1100

Comfort Suites at The Park 🛇 AAA Special Value Rates Motel ◆◆◆
ⓐⓐⓐ 6/18-9/10 [CP] 1P 78.00- 88.00 2P/1B 83.00- 93.00 2P/2B 93.00- 108.00 XP
4/1-6/17 & 9/11-1/31 [CP] 1P 68.00- 78.00 2P/1B 73.00- 83.00 2P/2B 83.00- 98.00 XP
2/1-3/31 [CP] 1P 63.00- 73.00 2P/1B 67.00- 78.00 2P/2B 78.00- 93.00 XP
79 units. 2141 S Harbor Blvd. (92802) Formerly Anaheim Travelodge Suites. Refrigerators; A/C; C/TV; free & pay movies; radios; phones. Coin laundry. Small htd pool; whirlpool. Limited parking lot. No pets. 13 suites with whirlpool tub, $69-$99. Microwaves. Reserv deposit required. AE, DI, DS, MC, VI. FAX (714) 971-4609 *(See ad below and starting on p A40)* ⊗ Ⓢ Ⓓ ⓘ (714) 971-3553

Conestoga Hotel 🛇 Rates Guaranteed Hotel ◆◆◆
ⓐⓐⓐ 6/1-8/31 1P .... 79.00 2P/1B .... 79.00 2P/2B .... 79.00 XP 10 F
9/1-5/31 1P .... 65.00 2P/1B .... 65.00 2P/2B .... 65.00 XP 10 F
Senior discount. 252 units. 1/2 mi w of I-5; 1/2 blk s of Ball Rd. 1240 S Walnut St. (92802) Check-in 3 pm. A/C; C/TV; pay movies; radios; phones. Htd pool; whirlpool. Parking lot. No pets. Reserv deposit required. AE, DI, DS, MC, VI. ● Coffeeshop; 6:30 am-10 pm; $6.50-$15; cocktails; entertainment. Also, Cattleman's Wharf, see separate listing. FAX (714) 491-8953 *(See ad p A42)* ⊗ Ⓓ (714) 535-0300

Convention Center Inn 🛇 Rates Subject to Change Motel ◆◆◆
ⓐⓐⓐ All year [CP] 1P 48.00- 88.00 2P/1B 48.00- 88.00 2P/2B 48.00- 88.00 XP
122 units. 2017 S Harbor Blvd. (92802) A/C; C/TV; pay movies; radios; phones. Coin laundry. Htd pool; whirlpool; 3 rooms with whirlpool tub. No pets. 34 1-bedroom suites with refrigerator. Reserv deposit required. AE, DI, DS, MC, VI. Restaurant adjacent. FAX (714) 750-5676 *(See ad p A39)* ⊗ Ⓓ ⓘ (714) 740-2500

(See ANAHEIM-BUENA PARK spotting map pages A6 & A7)

Crown Sterling Suites **1** ◆◆◆
⊛ All year [BP]   AAA Special Value Rates   *Suites Motor Inn*   F
1P 129.00- 139.00   2P/1B 139.00- 149.00   2P/2B 139.00- 149.00   XP 10
224 units. Adjacent to SR 91, Glassell St exit. 3100 E Frontera St. (92806) Attractively decorated & landscaped atrium area. Check-in 3 pm. Refrigerators; A/C; C/CATV; free & pay movies; radios; phones. Coin laundry. Htd indoor pool; sauna; whirlpool; steamroom. No pets. Monthly rates avail. Complimentary beverages each evening. AE, DI, DS, MC, VI. ● Dining rm & restaurant; 11 am-11 pm; $12-$18; cocktails. FAX (714) 632-9963 *(See ad below)*   ⊗ Ⓢ Ⓓ (714) 632-1221

Crystal Inn **61** ◆
⊛ 6/9-9/5   Rates Subject to Change   *Motel*   F
1P 36.00- 40.00   2P/1B   36.00- 40.00   2P/2B   38.00- 42.00   XP 3
  9/6-6/8   1P 32.00- 36.00   2P/1B   32.00- 36.00   2P/2B   34.00- 38.00   XP 3   F
Senior discount. 23 units. 1 1/2 mi w of I-5. 2123 W Lincoln Ave. (92801) Formerly Ana-Lin Motel. A/C; C/CATV; movies; radios; phones; shower or comb baths. Pool; whirlpool. No pets. 3 efficiencies, $5-$7 extra; no utensils. Wkly rates avail. Reserv deposit required; 3 days refund notice. AE, DI, DS, MC, VI. *(See ad p A38)*
                                                                      Ⓓ (714) 535-8446

CHECK-IN TIME? If after 3 p.m., it is noted in the listing.

❖

SERVICES

Complimentary continental breakfast, courtesy shuttle to Disneyland® Park, non-smoking suites, in suite safe & VCR's available, fax/copy service, guest laundry, free limited parking, indoor petite heated pool & spa and restaurants nearby.

Closest to Disneyland® Park and Convention Center

❖

AMENITIES

All one and two room suites have refrigerator, microwave, wet bar, sofa sleepers and two remote control T.V.'s with in-suite movies. Children under 18 stay free in parent's suite.

Group Rates Available

❖

LOCATION

Two blocks from Disneyland® Park and the Anaheim Convention Center. Ideally located for visiting all the sights & entertainment of Southern California. Front door pick-up for tours, Airport shuttles available.

Packages For Disneyland® Park Available!

Ask For AAA Special

1 800 526-9444

2141 S. Harbor Blvd. Anaheim CA. 92802
(714) 971-3553 • Fax (714) 971-4609

(See ANAHEIM-BUENA PARK spotting map pages A6 & A7)

Crystal Suites ③   Rates Subject to Change   *Suites Motel* ◆◆◆
🏩 6/17-8/31 [CP]   ....   2P/1B   89.00- 99.00   2P/2B   99.00-109.00   XP 10
    9/1-6/16 [CP]   ....   2P/1B   79.00- 89.00   2P/2B   89.00- 99.00   XP 10
130 units. 1/2 blk n of Katella Ave. 1752 Clementine St. (92802) Refrigerators; A/C; C/CATV; movies; radios; phones. Htd pool; whirlpool; exercise rm. No pets. 12 2-bedroom suites with microwave, $129-$169. Reserv deposit required; 3 days refund notice. AE, DI, DS, MC, VI. FAX (714) 776-9071 *(See ad starting on p A14)*
                                           ⊗ Ⓢ Ⓓ (714) 535-7773

Days Inn Suites ㊿   AAA Special Value Rates   *Motel* ◆◆
🏩 6/10-9/5 [CP]   1P   49.00- 69.00   2P/1B   49.00- 69.00   2P/2B   49.00- 59.00   XP   F
    9/6-6/9 [CP]   1P   39.00- 59.00   2P/1B   39.00- 59.00   2P/2B   39.00- 49.00   XP   F
80 units. 1/2 blk n of Ball Rd. 1111 S Harbor Blvd. (92805) Check-in 3 pm. A/C; C/CATV; movies; phones. Coin laundry. Htd pool; whirlpool. No pets. AE, CB, DS, MC, VI. FAX (714) 758-0573 *(See ad p A43)*
                                           ⊗ Ⓓ (714) 533-8830

Disneyland Hotel ㊿   Rates Subject to Change   *Resort Complex* ◆◆◆
🏩 All year   1P 140.00- 245.00   2P/1B   140.00- 245.00   2P/2B   140.00- 245.00   XP 15   F
1131 units. 1150 W Cerritos Ave. (92802) Rooms in towers & 2-story garden buildings on several acres of nicely landscaped grounds. Many recreational & shopping facilities. Check-in 3 pm. A/C; radios; phones. 3 htd pools; whirlpool; Disneyland Monorail Station. Fee for: pedal boats; tennis-10 courts, 9 lighted. Pay valet parking lot. Airport transp. No pets. Reserv deposit required. AE, CB, DI, MC, VI. ● 5 restaurants & coffeeshop; 6 am-1 am; $6-$30; cocktails; entertainment. Dancing. FAX (714) 956-6597 *(See ad p A44)* ⊗ Ⓢ Ⓓ 🔔 (714) 778-6600

Econo Lodge-Anaheim Stadium ⑧⓪   Rates Subject to Change   *Motel* ◆◆
🏩 All year [CP]   1P ....   42.00   2P/1B ....   46.00   2P/2B ....   52.00   XP   5
63 units. East side of I-5, exit Katella Ave, then 1/2 mi s on frontage Rd. 1914 S Anaheim Blvd. (92805) Refrigerators; A/C; C/CATV; movies; phones. No utensils. Coin laundry. Htd pool; whirlpool. No pets. Rooms with efficiencies or whirlpool tubs, $75. AE, CB, DI, MC, VI. FAX (714) 635-4953
                                           ⊗ Ⓓ (714) 533-2666

DAYS INN
SUITES
AAA

AFFORDABLE ELEGANCE AT DISNEYLAND

Walk to Disneyland or
Ride the Courtesy Shuttle.
Enjoy the Free Continental
Breakfast and Free Ice.
Coupons to Attractions
(Only Minutes Away).
Tour Arrangements in the Lobby.
Car Rental Service.
In-Room Movies/Cable TV.
Heated Pool/Jacuzzi.
Adjacent Restaurant, Gas, Gift Shop.
Meeting Room, FAX, Copier.
Valet Service, Laundry Facilties.

For Reservations, Call Toll Free,
and *Mention Your Membership*:

1-800-654-7503

1111 So. Harbor Blvd., Anaheim, CA 92805
(714) 533-8830   FAX (714) 758-0573

Standard Rooms   **Suites**

$39 - $62 $49 - $125

Rates Are Per Night
For Up to 4 Persons
Subject to Availability Only
No Other Discounts Apply

The
Disneyland Hotel.
Everything You
Would Expect
A Disney Hotel
To Be. There's a fresh new look.
With 1,131 guest rooms refurbished to the
finest detail. It's quality you've come to
expect. And exclusive Monorail service to
Disneyland Park. Call (714) 956-MICKEY
or see your travel planner. Special
discount for AAA members. We'll be
expecting you. **Disneyland
Hotel**

(See ANAHEIM-BUENA PARK spotting map pages A6 & A7)

Econo Lodge-East 44 ◆
🉐 6/1-9/1   AAA Special Value Rates   *Motel*

6/1-9/1	1P	....	48.00	2P/1B	....	54.00	2P/2B	....	62.00	XP 6	F
9/2-5/31	1P	....	42.00	2P/1B	....	48.00	2P/2B	....	52.00	XP 6	F

52 units. 2 blks n of Ball Rd. 871 S Harbor Blvd. (92805) A/C; C/CATV; movies; radios; phones. 13 efficiencies, no utensils. Coin laundry. Small pool; whirlpool. Pets. 12 rooms with whirlpool bath, $15 extra. Wkly & monthly rates avail 9/1-5/14. Reserv deposit required. AE, DS, MC, VI. FAX (714) 567-5870 *(See ad p A42)*
⊗ Ⓓ 🄳 (714) 535-7878

Econo Lodge-West 68 ◆
🉐 All year   AAA Special Value Rates   *Motel*

All year	1P	....	35.00	2P/1B	....	38.00	2P/2B	....	40.00	XP 5

45 units. On SR 39, 1/4 mi n of Ball Rd. 837 S Beach Blvd. (92804) A/C; C/CATV; movies; phones. Small pool. No pets. AE, DI, DS, MC, VI.
⊗ Ⓓ (714) 952-0898

Granada Inn 62 ◆◆
🉐 All year [CP]   AAA Special Value Rates   *Motor Inn*

All year [CP]	1P	....	45.00	2P/1B	....	50.00	2P/2B	....	55.00	XP 5

80 units. 1/2 mi w of Brookhurst St. 2375 W Lincoln Ave. (92801) A/C; C/CATV; movies; radios; phones. Htd pool. Pets. Kitchens, $5 extra. Wkly rates avail. Reserv deposit required. AE, DI, DS, MC, VI. ● Restaurant; 6:30 am-10 pm; Sun-3:30 pm; $5-$8; beer & wine. FAX (714) 774-8068 *(See ad below)*
⊗ Ⓓ (714) 774-7370

Grand Hotel 32 ◆◆◆
🉐 All year   AAA Special Value Rates   *Hotel*

All year	1P	85.00- 135.00	2P/1B	95.00- 155.00	2P/2B	95.00- 155.00	XP 10	F

242 units. 1 blk e of Harbor Blvd. No. 1 Hotel Way. (92802) Check-in 3 pm. 75 refrigerators; A/C; C/TV; pay movies; radios; phones. Htd pool; whirlpools; exercise rm. Parking lot. No pets. AE, CB, DI, MC, VI. ● Dining rm & coffeeshop; 6 am-11 pm; $7.50-$18; dinner theater; cocktails; entertainment. FAX (714) 774-7281
⊗ Ⓓ (714) 772-7777

Hampton Inn 75 ◆◆◆
5/25-9/5 [CP]   Rates Subject to Change   *Motel*

5/25-9/5 [CP]	1P	63.00- 72.00	2P/1B	73.00- 82.00	2P/2B	73.00- 82.00	XP	
9/6-5/24 [CP]	1P	55.00- 64.00	2P/1B	65.00- 74.00	2P/2B	65.00- 74.00	XP	

Senior discount. 136 units. 1 blk w of I-5, Katella Ave exit. 300 E Katella Way. (92802) A/C; C/CATV; free & pay movies; radios; phones. Htd pool. Pets. AE, DI, DS, MC, VI. FAX (714) 778-1235
⊗ Ⓢ Ⓓ 🄳 (714) 772-8713

(See ANAHEIM-BUENA PARK spotting map pages A6 & A7)

Holiday Inn Anaheim Center **40**   Rates Guaranteed   *Motor Inn*   ◆◆◆
5/1-9/15   1P .... 89.00 2P/1B .... 89.00 2P/2B .... 89.00 XP 10   F
9/16-4/30   1P .... 75.00 2P/1B .... 75.00 2P/2B .... 79.00 XP 10   F
256 units. Adjacent to I-5, southbound exit Ball Rd, northbound Harbor Blvd. 1221 S Harbor Blvd at Ball Rd. (92805) Attractively landscaped pool area. Check-in 3 pm. A/C; C/CATV; movies; radios; phones. Coin laundry. Htd pool; whirlpool.
AE, DI, DS, MC, VI. ● Restaurant; 6 am-10 pm; Fri & Sat-11 pm; $10-$15; cocktails. FAX (714) 533-1804 *(See ad
below)*   ⊗ Ⓢ Ⓓ ⓘ (714) 758-0900

Holiday Inn Express **79**   Rates Subject to Change   *Motel*   ◆◆◆
🅰🅱 6/8-9/2 [CP]   1P 70.00- 80.00 2P/1B 70.00- 80.00 2P/2B 75.00- 85.00 XP 5   F
9/3-6/7 [CP]   1P 55.00- 60.00 2P/1B 55.00- 60.00 2P/2B 60.00- 70.00 XP 5   F
Senior discount. 104 units. 435 W Katella Ave. (92802) Formerly Lucky Star Inn. Refrigerators; A/C; C/CATV;
movies; VCPs. Radios; phones. Coin laundry. Htd pool; whirlpool. Limited garage & parking lot. No pets. 5
rooms with whirlpool tub, $105-$125. Reserv deposit required. AE, DI, DS, MC, VI. FAX (714) 772-2727 *(See ad
p A47)*   ⊗ Ⓢ Ⓓ (714) 772-7755

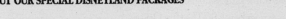

Holiday Inn
EXPRESS®
ANAHEIM

☆ **GRAND OPENING**
FIRST IN ANAHEIM

AAA ▽▽▽

ACCOMMODATIONS

Spacious Rooms w/2 Queen beds. King Leisure Mini-suite w/sitting area and sofabed. Family Mini-suite w/2 queen beds, sitting area and sofabed. Two Room Suite w/separate living room w/sofabed and bedroom w/2 queen beds. Special Jacuzzi King Suite with wet bar. ALL accommodations have a refrigerator, remote TV with VCP, and the best cable channels, Hair Dryer, Bath Amenities, AM/FM Alarm Clock. ALL suites also have a microwave. Some fireworks views available. Non-smoking and Handicap equipped rooms.

SPECIAL FEATURES

- Gated Underground Parking • Outdoor Pool & Spa • Sauna • Exercise Room • Guest Laundry • Movie Rental • FAX Service • Meeting Room • Disneyland Park® Tickets at Front Desk • Arrangements made for Tours, Shopping Mall Trips and Airport Service. Buses pick up at front door

COMPLIMENTARY

- Breakfast Bar Every Day in the Great Room • Disneyland Park® Shuttle Service • Selection of Local Telephone Calls

PRIME LOCATION

ONE BLOCK FROM DISNEYLAND PARK® AND THE ANAHEIM CONVENTION CENTER

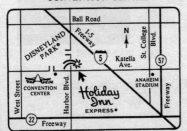

RESERVATIONS

DIRECT 800- 833-7888
-OR- CALL 800-HOLIDAY

HOLIDAY INN EXPRESS® -ANAHEIM
435 W. KATELLA AVENUE
ANAHEIM, CALIFORNIA 92802
LOCAL 714/772-7755 • FAX 714/772-2727

(See ANAHEIM-BUENA PARK spotting map pages A6 & A7)

Holiday Inn-Maingate Anaheim **10**   Rates Subject to Change   *Motor Inn*   ◆◆◆
   All year   1P 85.00- 95.00   2P/1B   .... 95.00   2P/2B   .... 85.00 XP 10   F
Senior discount. 312 units. 1850 S Harbor Blvd. (92802) A/C; C/CATV; movies; phones. Coin laundry. Htd pool; wading
pool. Fee for: airport transp. No pets. Reserv deposit required. AE, DI, DS, MC, VI. ● Dining rm; 6 am-2 & 5-10 pm;
$6-$13; cocktails; entertainment. FAX (714) 971-4754 *(See ad p A46)*   ⊗ Ⓓ 🅰 (714) 750-2801

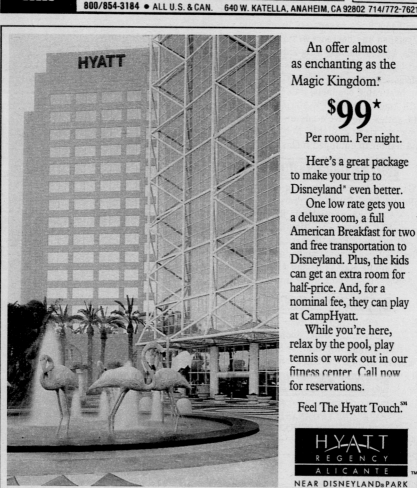

(See ANAHEIM-BUENA PARK spotting map pages A6 & A7)

Howard Johnson Lodge 39 · · · · · · · · · · Rates Subject to Change · · · · · · · · · · *Motor Inn* ◆◆◆
All year · 1P .... 78.00 2P/1B .... 78.00 2P/2B .... 78.00 XP 7 · · · F
Senior discount. 318 units. 1380 S Harbor Blvd. (92802) Attractively landscaped grounds. A/C; C/CATV; pay movies; radios; phones. Coin laundry. 2 htd pools; wading pool; whirlpool. No pets. Reserv deposit required. AE, DI, MC, VI. ● Restaurant; 6 am-midnight; $5.50-$12; beer & wine. FAX (714) 533-3578 ⊗ Ⓓ (714) 776-6120

Hyatt Regency Alicante 15 · · · · · · · · · · Rates Subject to Change · · · · · · · · · · *Hotel* ◆◆◆
Mon-Thurs · 1P .... 119.00 2P/1B .... 139.00 2P/2B .... 139.00 XP 20 · · · F
Fri-Sun · 1P .... 79.00 2P/1B .... 79.00 2P/2B .... 79.00 XP
Senior discount. 400 units. Chapman Ave at Harbor Blvd. 100 Plaza Alicante. (PO Box 4669, 92803) Contemporary decor. 17-story atrium area. Check-in 3 pm. A/C; C/CATV; free & pay movies; radios; phones. Htd pool; whirlpool; lighted tennis-2 courts; exercise rm. Pay valet parking lot. Airport transp. No pets. AE, DI, DS, MC, VI. ● Dining rm & restaurant; 6:30 am-midnight; $7-$22; cocktails. FAX (714) 740-0465 *(See ad p A48)* ⊗ Ⓢ Ⓓ ⬧ (714) 950-1234

Inn At The Park 24 · · · · · · · · · · · · · · Rates Guaranteed · · · · · · · · · · · · · · *Hotel* ◆◆◆
All year · 1P .... 85.00 2P/1B .... 95.00 2P/2B .... 95.00 XP · · · F
500 units. 1/2 blk s of Katella Ave. 1855 S Harbor Blvd. (92802) Check-in 3 pm. A/C; C/CATV; free & pay movies; radios; phones. Htd pool; whirlpool; exercise rm. Pay parking lot. No pets. AE, DI, DS, MC, VI. ● Restaurant & coffeeshop; 6 am-11 pm; $7-$18; cocktails; entertainment. Also, The Overland Stage, see separate listing. FAX (714) 971-3626 ⊗ Ⓓ (714) 750-1811

Jolly Roger Inn Hotel 25 · · · · · · · · · · Rates Guaranteed · · · · · · · · · · *Motor Inn* ◆◆◆
All year · · · · · · · · · 1P 65.00- 85.00 2P/1B 70.00- 90.00 2P/2B 70.00- 90.00 XP 10
235 units. 640 W Katella Ave at Harbor Blvd. (92802) 30 refrigerators; A/C; C/CATV; movies; radios; phones; comb or shower baths. 10 2-bedrm units. 2 pools, 1 htd; wading pool; whirlpool. 1 unit with private pool, $200. Reserv deposit required. AE, CB, DI, MC, VI. ● Dining rm & coffeeshop; 6:30 am-12:30 am; $5-$11; cocktails. FAX (714) 772-2308 *(See ad p A48)* ⊗ Ⓓ ⬧ (714) 772-7621

Magic Carpet Motel 26 · · · · · · · · · · AAA Special Value Rates · · · · · · · · · · *Motel* ◆◆
6/21-8/31 · 1P .... 50.00 2P/1B .... 54.00 2P/2B .... 54.00 XP 4
9/1-6/20 · 1P .... 35.00 2P/1B .... 37.00 2P/2B .... 39.00 XP 4
136 units. 1 mi w of I-5. 1016 W Katella Ave. (92802) A/C; C/TV; phones; comb or shower baths. 35 2-bedrm units. Coin laundry. Htd pool. Limited parking lot. No pets. 75 kitchens, $5 extra. Reserv deposit required. AE, DI, DS, MC, VI. FAX (714) 772-5461 *(See ad p A50)* Ⓓ (714) 772-9450

Magic Lamp Motel 27 · · · · · · · · · · AAA Special Value Rates · · · · · · · · · · *Motel* ◆◆
6/21-8/31 · 1P .... 50.00 2P/1B .... 54.00 2P/2B .... 54.00 XP 4
9/1-6/20 · 1P .... 35.00 2P/1B .... 39.00 2P/2B .... 39.00 XP 4
79 units. 1 mi w of I-5. 1030 W Katella Ave. (92802) A/C; C/TV; phones; comb or shower baths. 2 2-bedrm units. Coin laundry. Htd pool. Limited parking lot. No pets. 20 efficiencies, $5 extra. Reserv deposit required. AE, DI, DS, MC, VI. Restaurant adjacent. FAX (714) 772-5461 *(See ad p A51)* Ⓓ ⬧ (714) 772-7242

(See ANAHEIM-BUENA PARK spotting map pages A6 & A7)

Marco Polo Inn 35 ◆◆◆
 AAA Special Value Rates *Motel*
6/10-9/4 [CP] 1P 52.00- 60.00 2P/1B 52.00- 60.00 2P/2B 54.00- 84.00 XP 5
9/5-6/9 [CP] 1P 36.00- 44.00 2P/1B 36.00- 44.00 2P/2B 44.00- 55.00 XP 4
58 units. 1604 S Harbor Blvd. (92802) Refrigerators; A/C; C/CATV; rental VCPs; radios; phones. 1 2-bedrm unit. Coin laundry. Htd pool; whirlpool. Limited parking lot. No pets. Microwaves. Reserv deposit required; 3 days refund notice. AE, DI, DS, MC, VI. Coffeeshop adjacent. *(See ad p A25)* ⊗ Ⓓ (714) 635-3630

The Pan Pacific Hotel 56 ◆◆◆
 AAA Special Value Rates *Hotel*
All year 1P 99.00- 155.00 2P/1B 99.00- 155.00 2P/2B 99.00- 155.00 XP 10
502 units. 1 blk n of Katella Ave. 1717 S West St. (92802) Check-in 3 pm. 70 refrigerators; A/C; C/CATV; free & pay movies; radios; phones. Htd pool; whirlpool. Pay parking ramp. No pets. AE, DI, DS, MC, VI. ● Dining rm & restaurant; 6:30 am-11 pm; $7-$24; cocktails. FAX (714) 776-5763 *(See ad p A51)* ⊗ Ⓢ Ⓓ ⅌ (714) 999-0990

Look for the 🆎 in our listings!

(See ANAHEIM-BUENA PARK spotting map pages A6 & A7)

Parkside Inn & Suites 78   Rates Subject to Change   *Motel* ◆◆◆
♨ 6/10-9/4 [BP]   1P   46.00-   60.00   2P/1B   46.00-   60.00   2P/2B   54.00-   68.00   XP   4
9/5-6/9 [BP]   1P   34.00-   44.00   2P/1B   38.00-   48.00   2P/2B   40.00-   54.00   XP   4
93 units. 1 blk n of Ball Rd. 921 S Harbor Blvd. (92802) Formerly Anaheim Sandman Inn. Check-in 3 pm. Refrigerators; A/C; C/CATV; movies; phones. 1 2-bedrm unit. Coin laundry. Htd pool; exercise rm. No pets. Reserv deposit required; 3 days refund notice. AE, CB, DI, MC, VI. Restaurant adjacent. FAX (714) 635-0964 *(See ad starting on p A26)*   ⊗ Ⓓ 🅛 (714) 999-0684

The real magic happens across the street from Disneyland Park

World-class facilities. Uncompromising personal service. Two first-class restaurants. All just a monorail ride away from Disneyland Park and two blocks from the Anaheim Convention Center. The

next time you're planning a trip to Anaheim, for business or for pleasure, just say the magic words: The Pan Pacific Hotel.

> ### 20% AAA discount
> ### off rack rates.

THE PAN PACIFIC HOTEL *Anaheim*

1717 South West Street, Anaheim, California 92802. 714/999-0990.

Magic Lamp Motel

Across the street from Disneyland Park and next to the Convention Center

1030 W. KATELLA, ANAHEIM, CALIFORNIA 92802
(714) 772-7242

Air-Conditioned
79 Rooms   20 Full Kitchen Units   No Pets
Color TV   Heated Pool   Direct Dial Phones
Laundromat   Major Credit Cards
Kitchens $5

1 Person	$35.00
2 Persons	$39.00
3 Persons	$43.00
4 Persons	$45.00
5 & 6 Persons	$49.00

Low Season Rates in Effect
2/01-6/21, 9/01-12/25, 1/01/93-1/31/93

(See ANAHEIM-BUENA PARK spotting map pages A6 & A7)

Park Vue Inn **49**   Rates Subject to Change   Motel   ◆◆
🏨 6/10-9/7 [CP]   1P 47.00- 54.00 2P/1B   48.00- 54.00 2P/2B 50.00- 68.00 XP 4
   9/8-6/9 [CP]   1P 36.00- 44.00 2P/1B   37.00- 44.00 2P/2B 44.00- 56.00 XP 4
Senior discount. 90 units. 1570 S Harbor Blvd. (92802) 47 refrigerators; A/C; C/TV; movies; rental VCPs. Phones.
7 2-bedrm units, 4 efficiencies. Coin laundry. Htd pool; wading pool. No pets. Reserv deposit required; 3 days
refund notice. AE, DI, DS, MC, VI. Restaurant adjacent. FAX (714) 635-0964 *(See ad starting on p A28)*
                                                                            ⊗ ⒟ (714) 772-5721

Polynesian Motel **74**   Rates Guaranteed   Motel   ◆
🏨 6/12-9/2   1P .... 32.00 2P/1B   .... 32.00 2P/2B .... 34.00 XP 2
   9/3-6/11   1P .... 28.00 2P/1B   .... 28.00 2P/2B .... 30.00 XP 2
Senior discount. 28 units. 1 1/4 mi s of I-5. 641 S Brookhurst St. (92804) A/C; C/TV; radios; phones; shower or
comb baths. 4 2-bedrm units. Pool. No pets. 4 efficiencies, $5 extra, no utensils. Wkly rates avail. Reserv deposit
required. AE, MC, VI. *(See ad below)*   ⒟ (714) 778-6892

Quality Hotel & Conference Center **20**   Rates Subject to Change   Motor Inn   ◆◆◆
🏨 All year   1P 62.00- 80.00 2P/1B   67.00- 85.00 2P/2B 67.00- 85.00 XP ... F
284 units. 1 blk s of Katella Ave. 616 Convention Way at Harbor Blvd. (92802) Check-in 4 pm. A/C; C/TV; pay
movies; 200 radios; phones. Htd pool. Pay parking lot. Pets. Reserv deposit required. AE, DI, DS, MC,
VI. ● Dining rm & coffeeshop; 6 am-10 pm; $7-$18; cocktails. FAX (714) 750-9027   ⊗ ⒟ (714) 750-3131

Quality Inn Anaheim-West **69**   Rates Guaranteed   Motor Inn   ◆◆
🏨 6/1-8/31   1P 42.00- 52.00 2P/1B   48.00- 56.00 2P/2B 48.00- 56.00 XP 6 F
   9/1-5/31   1P 40.00- 44.00 2P/1B   42.00- 48.00 2P/2B 45.00- 52.00 XP 6 F
Senior discount. 99 units. On SR 39; 1/2 mi n of Ball Rd. 727 S Beach Blvd. (92804) Refrigerators; A/C; C/CATV; movies;
radios; phones. 6 2-bedrm units. Coin laundry. Htd pool; sauna; whirlpool; 4 rooms with whirlpool tub; 1 steambath. No
pets. 6 efficiencies, $5 extra. No utensils. Reserv deposit required. AE, DI, DS, MC, VI. ● Restaurant; 7 am-10 pm;
closed Sun; $10-$14; cocktails.   ⊗ ⒟ (714) 220-0100

Quality Inn-Brookhurst **64**   Rates Subject to Change   Motel   ◆◆
All year   1P 52.00- 56.00 2P/1B   56.00- 62.00 2P/2B 62.00- 68.00 XP 10
91 units. 1 1/4 mi s of I-5, Brookhurst St exit. 711 S Beach Blvd. (92804) Refrigerators; A/C; C/CATV; movies; rental
VCPs. Radios; phones. Coin laundry. Htd pool; sauna; whirlpool. No pets. 6 efficiencies, $5 extra; no utensils. 6 rooms
with whirlpool tub, $15 extra. Reserv deposit required. AE, CB, DI, MC, VI.   ⊗ ⒟ (714) 999-1220

Raffles Inn & Suites **11**   AAA Special Value Rates   Motel   ◆◆◆
🏨 6/1-9/7   1P 77.00- 97.00 2P/1B   77.00- 97.00 2P/2B 77.00- 97.00 XP 5 F
   9/8-5/31   1P 54.00- 74.00 2P/1B   54.00- 74.00 2P/2B 54.00- 74.00 XP 5 F
122 units. 1/2 mi s of Katella Ave. 2040 S Harbor Blvd. (92802) Check-in 3 pm. 27 refrigerators; A/C; C/TV; pay
movies; radios; phones. 8 2-bedrm units. Coin laundry. Htd pool; whirlpool. Limited parking lot. Pets, $10 extra
charge. Reserv deposit required. AE, DI, DS, MC, VI. FAX (714) 740-0639 *(See ad p A53)*
                                                                         ⊗ ⒟ ♿ (714) 750-6100

Ramada Inn-Anaheim **5**   Rates Subject to Change   Motor Inn   ◆◆
🏨 6/1-9/8   1P .... 64.00 2P/1B   .... 64.00 2P/2B .... 74.00 XP
   9/9-5/31   1P .... 47.00 2P/1B   .... 47.00 2P/2B .... 47.00 XP
240 units. 3/4 mi e of I-5, Katella Ave exit. 1331 E Katella Ave. (92805) Check-in 3 pm. A/C; C/CATV; free & pay
movies; radios; phones. Coin laundry. Htd pool; sauna; whirlpool. No pets. Reserv deposit required; 3 days refund notice. AE, DI, DS, MC, VI. ● Restaurant; 6 am-11 pm; $5-$10; cocktails. FAX (714) 937-5622
                                                                            ⊗ ⒟ (714) 978-8088

Ramada Maingate Anaheim **42**   AAA Special Value Rates   Motor Inn   ◆◆◆
🏨 5/25-8/31   1P 89.00- 99.00 2P/1B   99.00- 109.00 2P/2B 99.00- 109.00 XP 10 F
   9/1-5/24   1P 79.00- 89.00 2P/1B   89.00- 99.00 2P/2B 89.00- 99.00 XP 10 F
465 units. 1460 S Harbor Blvd. (92802) Check-in 3 pm. 70 refrigerators; A/C; C/CATV; pay movies; radios;
phones. Coin laundry. Htd pool; whirlpool. No pets. Reserv deposit required. AE, DI, DS, MC, VI. ● Restaurant;
6 am-midnight; $6-$9; beer & wine. FAX (714) 999-1727 *(See ad p A54)*   ⊗ Ⓢ ⒟ ♿ (714) 772-6777

Residence Inn By Marriott **43**   AAA Special Value Rates   Apartment Motel ◆◆◆
All year [CP]   1P 159.00- 189.00 2P/1B 159.00- 189.00 2P/2B 169.00- 189.00 XP 10 F
200 units. 1/8 mi sw of I-5, exit Katella Ave. 1700 S Clementine St at Freedman Way. (92802) Nicely landscaped
grounds. Many rooms with fireplace. Check-in 4 pm. A/C; C/CATV; movies; radios; phones. 7 2-bedrm units, kitchens.
Coin laundry. Htd pool; wading pool; whirlpools. Some units with private patio & whirlpool, $259. Pets, $200 deposit, $75
per stay, $6 extra per day. Wkly & monthly rates avail. Reserv deposit required. AE, DI, MC, VI. FAX (714) 535-7626
                                                                             ⒳ (714) 533-3555

(See ANAHEIM-BUENA PARK spotting map pages A6 & A7)

Saga Inn 33		AAA Special Value Rates			Motel	◆◆◆		
5/28-9/6	1P 60.00	2P/1B 68.00- 74.00	2P/2B 73.00	XP 5	F
9/7-5/27	1P 50.00	2P/1B 56.00- 66.00	2P/2B 60.00- 70.00	XP 4	F

185 units. 1650 S Harbor Blvd. (92802) A/C; C/TV; phones. Coin laundry. Htd pool; whirlpool. No pets. 7 rooms with whirlpool tub, $76-$95. 2 room suites, $90-$120. Reserv deposit required; 3 days refund notice. AE, DI, DS, MC, VI. Restaurant adjacent. FAX (714) 991-8219 *(See ad p A55)*   ⊗ Ⓓ 🅢 (714) 772-0440

Sheraton-Anaheim Hotel 46		Rates Subject to Change			Hotel	◆◆◆		
6/1-9/3	1P 100.00- 130.00	2P/1B 120.00- 145.00	2P/2B 120.00- 145.00	XP 15	F
2/1-5/31	1P 95.00- 115.00	2P/1B 110.00- 130.00	2P/2B 110.00- 130.00	XP 15	F
9/4-1/31	1P 85.00- 115.00	2P/1B 100.00- 130.00	2P/2B 100.00- 130.00	XP 15	F

491 units. Adjacent to I-5. 1015 W Ball Rd. (92802) Check-in 3 pm. A/C; C/CATV; free & pay movies; radios; phones. Coin laundry. Htd pool. Parking lot. No pets. Reserv deposit required. AE, DI, DS, MC, VI. ● Restaurant; 6 am-11 pm; $8-$16; cocktails. FAX (714) 535-3889   🆂 Ⓓ (714) 778-1700

The best reservation is a *confirmed* reservation.

(See ANAHEIM-BUENA PARK spotting map pages A6 & A7)

Super 8 Motel-Anaheim Park 48		Rates Subject to Change				*Motel*		◆◆
6/1-8/31 [CP]	1P 48.00	2P/1B 48.00	2P/2B 50.00	XP 6				
9/1-5/31 [CP]	1P 38.00	2P/1B 38.00	2P/2B 40.00	XP 6				

113 units. 2 blks w of I-5; 1/2 blk n of Ball Rd. 915 S West St. (92802) A/C; C/TV; movies; phones; comb or shower baths. Coin laundry. Htd pool; whirlpool. Limited parking lot. No pets. Reserv deposit required; 7 days refund notice. AE, DI, DS, MC, VI. FAX (714) 778-3878 *(See ad p A7)*   ⊗ Ⓓ Ⓢ (714) 778-0350

Travelodge Anaheim/Beach Blvd 45		Rates Subject to Change			*Motel*		◆◆
6/15-9/15 & 12/15-12/31	1P 35.00- 45.00	2P/1B 39.00- 55.00	2P/2B 45.00- 75.00	XP 5	F		
9/16-12/14 & 1/1-6/14	1P 32.00- 39.00	2P/1B 35.00- 45.00	2P/2B 39.00- 55.00	XP 5	F		

Senior discount. 60 units. 1/2 blk e of Beach Blvd. 328 N Stanton Ave. (92801) 1/2 mi s of Knott's Berry Farm. A/C; C/CATV; movies; radios; phones. Coin laundry. Htd pool. No pets. 6 rooms with whirlpool tub, $79-$95. Wkly rates avail. Reserv deposit required. AE, CB, DI, MC, VI. FAX (714) 236-0261   ⊗ Ⓢ Ⓓ (714) 229-0101

Look for the ⊛ in our listings!

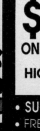

(See ANAHEIM-BUENA PARK spotting map pages A6 & A7)

TraveLodge Apollo Inn 🏨 57   Rates Subject to Change   *Motor Inn* ◆◆

3/7-4/6, 5/24-9/2 & 12/20-1/5	1P 65.00-	70.00	2P/1B	65.00- 70.00	2P/2B	70.00- 80.00	XP	F
1/6-3/6, 4/7-5/23 & 9/3-12/19	1P 55.00-	65.00	2P/1B	55.00- 65.00	2P/2B	60.00- 65.00	XP	F

136 units. 1/2 blk n of Katella Ave. 1741 S West St. (92802) Formerly Anaheim Parkside TraveLodge. Refrigerators; A/C; C/TV; pay movies; rental VCPs. Radios; phones. Coin laundry. Htd pool; wading pool; saunas; whirlpool. No pets. Reserv deposit required. AE, CB, DI, MC, VI. ● Coffeeshop; 6:30 am-noon & 5:30-10 pm; $5.50-$8. FAX (714) 772-5842 *(See ad below)*   ⊗ (714) 772-9750

Travelodge Cornerstone Inn 🏨 82   Rates Subject to Change   *Motel* ◆◆

6/10-8/31 & 12/20-12/31	....	2P/1B	.... 53.00	2P/2B	.... 58.00	XP
1/1-6/9 & 9/1-12/19	....	2P/1B	.... 38.00	2P/2B	.... 43.00	XP

Senior discount. 44 units. 1/4 blk n of Katella Ave. 1765 S West St. (92802) A/C; C/CATV; movies; phones; comb or shower baths. Htd pool; whirlpool. Limited parking lot. No pets. Reserv deposit required. AE, DI, DS, MC, VI. FAX (714) 774-2709 *(See ad below)*   ⊗ Ⓓ (714) 774-6427

Travelodge Maingate 🏨 30   Rates Subject to Change   *Motel* ◆◆

6/10-8/31 & 12/20-12/31	....	2P/1B	.... 78.00	2P/2B	.... 83.00	XP
1/1-6/9 & 9/1-12/19	....	2P/1B	.... 58.00	2P/2B	.... 63.00	XP

Senior discount. 254 units. 1717 S Harbor Blvd. (92802) Check-in 3 pm. A/C; C/CATV; radios; phones; comb or shower baths. 25 2-bedrm units. Coin laundry. 2 htd pools; wading pool; saunas; whirlpool. No pets. Reserv deposit required. AE, DI, DS, MC, VI. Restaurant adjacent. FAX (714) 635-1502 *(See ad below)*   ⊗ Ⓓ (714) 635-6550

Travelodge Westgate Inn 🏨 18   Rates Subject to Change   *Motel* ◆◆

6/11-8/31 & 12/21-12/31	....	2P/1B	.... 55.00	2P/2B	.... 60.00	XP
1/1-6/10 & 9/1-12/20	....	2P/1B	.... 45.00	2P/2B	.... 50.00	XP

Senior discount. 56 units. 1/2 blk n of Katella Ave. 1759 S West St. (92802) A/C; C/CATV; movies; radios; phones; comb or shower baths. 10 2-bedrm units. Htd pool. Limited parking lot. No pets. Reserv deposit required. AE, DI, DS, MC, VI. FAX (714) 778-3918 *(See ad below)*   ⊗ Ⓓ (714) 774-2136

Tropicana Inn 🏨 67   Rates Guaranteed   *Motel* ◆◆

5/24-9/6	1P 68.00-	80.00	2P/1B	68.00- 80.00	2P/2B	68.00- 80.00	XP	10
9/7-5/23	1P 48.00-	68.00	2P/1B	48.00- 68.00	2P/2B	48.00- 68.00	XP	10

195 units. 1540 S Harbor Blvd. (92802) A/C; C/TV; pay movies; phones; comb or shower baths. Coin laundry. Htd pool; whirlpool. Limited parking lot. No pets. 14 efficiencies, $12 extra charge. Reserv deposit required. AE, DI, DS, MC, VI. Restaurant adjacent. FAX (714) 635-1535 *(See ad p A57)*   ⊗ Ⓓ (714) 635-4082

RESTAURANTS

California Bistro 🍴 12   American $$ ◆◆
    Adjacent to Best Western Park Place Inn. Casual dining. Nice selection of sandwiches, salads & entrees. A/C. Early bird specials; children's menu. Open 6:30 am-10 pm. Cocktails & lounge. Reserv advised. AE, MC, VI. ⊗ (714) 776-5300

(See ANAHEIM-BUENA PARK spotting map pages A6 & A7)

The Catch ⑥ — Steak & Seafood — $$ ◆◆
Opposite Anaheim Stadium. 1929 S State College Blvd. Attractively decorated with decor of the 1920's. A/C. Children's menu. Open 11 am-2:30 & 5-9:30 pm; Fri-10:30 pm; Sat 5 pm-10:30 pm; Sun 5 pm-9 pm; closed 11/25 & 12/25. Cocktails & lounge. Reserv advised. AE, CB, DI, MC, VI. — ⊗ (714) 634-1829

Cattleman's Wharf ⑬ — American — $$ ◆◆
Adjacent to Conestoga Hotel. 1160 W Ball Rd. Attractive restaurant with 5 theme dining rooms. Nice selection of beef, steaks, prime rib, seafood & poultry. Desserts made on premises. A/C. Children's menu. Open 5 pm-10 pm; Fri-11 pm; Sat 5 pm-11 pm; Sun 10 am-2 & 5-10 pm. Cocktails & lounge. Entertainment & dancing. Valet parking. Reserv advised. AE, DI, DS, MC, VI. *(See ad p A42)* — ⊗ (714) 535-1622

Charley Brown's ⑤ — American — $$ ◆◆
1/4 blk n of Katella Ave. 1751 S State College Blvd. Nice selection of steaks, prime rib & seafood. A/C. Children's menu. Open 11:30 am-2:30 & 5-10 pm; Sat 4:30 pm-10:30 pm; Sun 10 am-2 & 4-9 pm. Cocktails & lounge. AE, DI, DS, MC, VI. — ⊗ (714) 634-2211

El Torito Restaurant ⑩ — Mexican — $
1/2 blk e of State College Blvd. 2020 E Ball Rd. Popular, Colorfully decorated restaurant. A/C. Children's menu. Open 11 am-10 pm; Fri & Sat-11 pm; Sun 9:30 am-10 pm; closed 11/25 & 12/25. Cocktails & lounge. AE, MC, VI. — ⊗ (714) 956-4880

Foxfire Restaurant ① — American — $$ ◆◆◆
In Anaheim Hills; adjacent to SR 91, Imperial Hwy exit; in Canyon Plaza. 5717 E Santa Ana Canyon Rd. Dining in casual elegance. Sun buffet brunch. A/C. Children's menu. Open 11 am-3 & 5-10 pm; Sat from 5 pm; Sun 10 am-2:30 & 5-10 pm; closed major holidays. Cocktails & lounge. Entertainment & dancing. Reserv advised. AE, CB, DI, MC, VI. — ⊗ (714) 974-5400

Hansa House Smorgasbord ⑦ — Ethnic — $
🏵 1/4 blk s of Katella Ave. 1840 S Harbor Blvd. Scandinavian decor. Large selection of salads & entrees served buffet style. Sun brunch 11:30 am-3 pm. A/C. Children's menu. Open 7-10:30 am, 11:30-3 & 4:30-9 pm. Cocktails & lounge. AE, DS, MC, VI. — ⊗ (714) 750-2411

JW's ⑧ — Continental — $$$$ ◆◆◆
In Anaheim Marriott Hotel. Elegant dining in refined atmosphere. A/C. Open 6 pm-10 pm; closed Sun. Cocktails & lounge. Reserv advised. AE, CB, DI, MC, VI. *(See ad p A9)* — ⊗ (714) 750-0900

Mimi's Cafe ⑮ — American — $
1 blk s of SR 91. 1240 N Euclid Ave. Delightful family restaurant with decor of a French cafe. A/C. Children's menu. Open 7 am-11 pm; closed 11/25 & 12/25. Beer & wine. AE, MC, VI. — ⊗ (714) 535-1552

Mr Stox Restaurant ③ — American — $$$ ◆◆◆
🏵 1/4 mi e of I-5. 1105 E Katella Ave. Pleasant dining featuring California contemporary cuisine. A/C. Children's menu. Open 11:30 am-3 & 5:30-10 pm; Sat 5:30 pm-10 pm; Sun 5 pm-9 pm; closed major holidays. Cocktails & lounge. Entertainment. Valet parking. Reserv advised. AE, CB, DI, MC, VI. — ⊗ (714) 634-2994

(See ANAHEIM-BUENA PARK spotting map pages A6 & A7)

The Overland Stage ⑭   American $$ ◆◆
In Inn At The Park. Attractive Western decor. Features beef, poultry, seafood & daily selection of wild game. A/C. Open 11:30 am-2:30 & 5-11 pm; Sat & Sun from 5 pm. Cocktails & lounge. Reserv advised. AE, DI, DS, MC, VI.   ⊗ (714) 971-4570

Pavia ⑰   Italian $$$ ◆◆◆
In Anaheim Hilton and Towers. Elegant decor. Formal service. Nice selection of homemade pasta & fresh seafood. A/C. Open 6 pm-11 pm; closed Mon. Cocktails. Entertainment. Valet parking. Reserv advised. AE, CB, DI, MC, VI.   ⊗ (714) 750-4321

Plantation Restaurant ⑯   American $ ◆
1/4 mi e of Raymond Ave. 601 E Orangethorpe Ave. Attractive cafeteria serving a la carte or limited buffet style. A/C. Children's menu. Open 11 am-8 pm; closed Mon & 12/25. DS, MC, VI.   ⊗ (714) 870-1020

Spaghetti Station ⑪   Italian $ ◆
Adjacent to I-5. 999 W Ball Rd. Specializing in spaghetti with varied sauces. Antique rifle, pistol, western memorabilia collection on display. A/C. Children's menu. Open 11 am-2 & 4:30-10 pm; Sat & Sun 4:30 pm-10:30 pm; closed 11/25 & 12/25. Cocktails & lounge. AE, MC, VI.   ⊗ (714) 956-3250

Thee White House Restaurant ②   Northern Italian $$$ ◆◆
🕮 3 blks n of Ball Rd. 887 S Anaheim Blvd. Fine dining in a restored home with colonial theme. A/C. Open 11:30 am-2 & 5:30-10 pm; Sat & Sun from 5:30 pm; closed major holidays. Cocktails. Reserv advised. AE, CB, DI, MC, VI.   ⊗ (714) 772-1381

ANDERSON ⊢ 8,300

Anderson Valley Inn   Rates Subject to Change   *Motel*   ◆◆◆
🕮 All year [CP]   1P 40.00- 55.00   2P/1B 48.00- 55.00   2P/2B 48.00- 60.00   XP 4
Senior discount. 62 units. E of & Adjacent to I-5, exit Central Anderson. 2861 Mc Murry Dr. (96007) A/C; C/CATV; phones. Small pool. No pets. Reserv deposit required. AE, DI, DS, MC, VI. Restaurant adjacent.   ⊗ Ⓓ 🅱 (916) 365-2566

Best Western Knights Inn   Rates Subject to Change   *Motel*   ◆◆
🕮 All year   1P 40.00- 46.00   2P/1B 44.00- 50.00   2P/2B 48.00- 54.00   XP 4
Senior discount. 40 units. Exit I-5 at the Central Anderson, Lassen Park exit. 2688 Gateway Dr. (96007) A/C; C/CATV; movies; radios; phones. Pool. Small pets only. Reserv deposit required. AE, DI, DS, MC, VI. Restaurant adjacent.   ⊗ Ⓓ 🅱 (916) 365-2753

ANGELS CAMP — 2,400

Gold Country Inn   Rates Subject to Change   *Motel*   ◆
🕮 All year   1P .... 50.00   2P/1B .... 55.00   2P/2B .... 60.00   XP 5
40 units. 1 mi n on SR 49. (PO Box 188, 95222) A/C; C/CATV; radios; phones. No pets. Reserv deposit required. AE, DS, MC, VI. Coffeeshop adjacent.   ⊗ Ⓓ (209) 736-4611

RESTAURANT

Utica Mansion Inn Restaurant   Continental $$$ ◆◆
SR 49, 1 blk w; opposite Utica Park. 1090 Utica Ln. In a Victorian house built in 1882. Smoking not permitted. A/C. Children's menu. Open 5:30 pm-9:30 pm; closed Tues, Wed, 1st week in Jan & 1st 2 weeks in July. Beer & wine. Reserv advised. MC, VI.   ⊗ (209) 736-4209

ANTIOCH — 62,200

Best Western Heritage Inn   Rates Guaranteed   *Motel*   ◆◆◆
🕮 All year [CP]   1P 52.00- 60.00   2P/1B 52.00- 74.00   2P/2B 62.00- 66.00   XP 5   F
Senior discount. 75 units. Exit SR 4 at Somersville Rd. 3210 Delta Fair Blvd. (94509) 26 refrigerators; A/C; C/CATV; movies; phones. 2 2-bedrm units. Pool; whirlpool. No pets. Some rooms with whirlpool tub & wet bar. Reserv deposit required. AE, CB, DI, MC, VI. Coffeeshop adjacent. *(See ad p A364)*   ⊗ Ⓢ Ⓓ 🅱 (510) 778-2000

Ramada Inn   Rates Subject to Change   *Motel*   ◆◆
All year [CP]   1P 50.00- 70.00   2P/1B 60.00- 81.00   2P/2B 67.00- 85.00   XP 8
116 units. At Hwy 4 & Somersville Rd. 2436 Mahogany Way. (94509) Refrigerators; A/C; C/CATV; movies; radios; phones; comb or shower baths. Coin laundry. Pool; whirlpool. No pets. Parlor suites with microwave. Reserv deposit required. AE, DI, DS, MC, VI. Coffeeshop opposite. FAX (510) 754-6828   ⊗ Ⓓ (510) 754-6600

RESTAURANT

Riverview Lodge Restaurant   Seafood $ ◆
🕮 1/2 mi n off SR 4 on river, at foot of I St. Rustic decor. Boat docking. Varied menu; steak specialties. A/C. Children's menu. Open 11 am-midnight; closed 12/25. Cocktails & lounge. Reserv advised. AE, DI, MC, VI.   ⊗ (510) 757-2272

APTOS — 7,000

Best Western Seacliff Inn   Rates Subject to Change   *Motor Inn*   ◆◆◆

🕮 Fri & Sat	1P	....	69.00	2P/1B	....	89.00	2P/2B	.... 89.00 XP 10 F
Sun-Thurs 3/31-10/31	1P	....	59.00	2P/1B	....	79.00	2P/2B	.... 89.00 XP 10 F
Sun-Thurs 11/1-3/30	1P	....	49.00	2P/1B	....	69.00	2P/2B	.... 79.00 XP 10 F

Senior discount. 140 units. N of & adjacent to SR 1, exit Seacliff; 5 1/2 mi se of Santa Cruz. 7500 Old Dominion Ct. (95003) Attractively landscaped. Check-in 3 pm. A/C; C/CATV; pay movies; radios; phones. Pool; whirlpool. No pets. 10 suites with whirlpool bath & wet bar, $110-$195 for 2 persons. 2-night minimum stay weekends 5/25-10/31. AE, DI, DS, MC, VI. ● Dining rm; 7 am-2 & 5-10 pm; $10-$19; cocktails; entertainment. FAX (408) 685-3603   ⊗ Ⓢ Ⓓ 🅱 (408) 688-7300

Rio Sands Motel　　　　　　　　　　　　　　AAA Special Value Rates　　　　*Apartment Motel*　　◆◆

◐ Fri & Sat 6/1-9/6 [CP]	....	2P/1B	....	89.50	2P/2B	....	89.50	XP	5
Fri & Sat 9/7-5/31 [CP]	.... -	2P/1B	....	79.50	2P/2B	....	79.50	XP	5
Sun-Thurs 6/1-9/6 [CP]	....	2P/1B	....	69.50	2P/2B	....	69.50	XP	5
Sun-Thurs 9/7-5/31 [CP]	....	2P/1B	....	49.50	2P/2B	....	49.50	XP	5

50 units. Exit SR 1 via Rio Del Mar Blvd; 7 mi se of Santa Cruz. 116 Aptos Beach Dr. (95003) Attractively landscaped. Patios or balconies; garden spa. C/CATV; 25 radios; phones; comb or shower baths. Htd pool; whirlpool. No pets. 25 kitchens, $60-$109 for 2 persons. 2-night minimum stay weekends. Wkly rates avail. Reserv deposit required. AE, MC, VI. *(See ad p A501)*　　　　　　　　　　⊗ Ⓓ (408) 688-3207

Seascape Resort & Conference Center　　AAA Special Value Rates　　　　*Apartment Motel*
　　All year　　　　　　　　1P 165.00- 215.00　2P/1B　165.00- 215.00　　　　　　　　XP

84 units. 1 mi w of SR 1; Larkin Valley Rd exit; w via San Andreas Rd, right on Seascape Blvd. Seascape Blvd at Sumner Ave. (95003) On coastal bluff; fireplaces; patios or decks. Rating withheld pending completion of construction. Scheduled to open summer, 1993. Check-in 4 pm. C/TV; pay movies; radios; phones. Efficiencies. Coin laundry. Pool; whirlpool; rental bicycles. Fee for: airport transp. No pets. Maximum rate for up to 4 persons. Advanced payment required for stay. Reserv deposit required; 14 days refund notice. AE, MC, VI. ● Restaurant; 7 am-10 & 6-10 pm; a la carte entrees about $14-$20; cocktails. *(See ad below)*　　　　　　　　　　　⊗ (408) 688-6800

RESTAURANTS

Cafe Rio　　　　　　　　　　　Steak & Seafood　　　　　　　$$　　　　　◆◆
　7 mi se of Santa Cruz; exit SR 1 via Rio Del Mar Blvd. 131 Explanade. Casual atmosphere; at the beach. Children's menu. Open 5 pm-9:30 pm; Sat 5 pm-10:30 pm; Sun 4 pm-9:30 pm; closed 11/25. Cocktails & lounge. Entertainment. Reserv advised. AE, MC, VI.　　　　　　　　　　　　　　　　⊗ (408) 688-8917

Deer Park Tavern　　　　　　　　　American　　　　　　　　$$　　　　　◆◆
　7 mi se of Santa Cruz; exit w SR 1 via Rio Del Mar Blvd. 783 Rio Del Mar Blvd. Casual atmosphere. A/C. Early bird specials; children's menu. Open 11:30 am-2:30 & 4:30-9 pm; Fri & Sat-10 pm; closed 12/25. Cocktails & lounge. Reserv advised. AE, DI, MC, VI.　　　　　　　　　　　　　　⊗ (408) 688-5800

Palapas　　　　　　　　　　　　Mexican　　　　　　　　　$$　　　　　◆◆◆
　1 mi w of SR 1; Larken Valley Rd exit; w via San Andreas Rd, right on Seascape Blvd. 21 Seascape Village. Mexican cuisine & seafoods; emphasis on fresh ingredients & own sauces. A/C. Children's menu. Open 11:30 am-2:30 & 5-10 pm; Sun 11:30 am-2:30 & 4:30-9:30 pm. Cocktails & lounge. Reserv advised. AE, DI, MC, VI. ⊗ Ⓖ (408) 662-9000

In the listings, the meal plan included in the rates follows the open dates.

ARCADIA — 48,300   (See PASADENA & VICINITY AREA spotting map page A327; see index starting on page A326)

Best Western Westerner Inn ❸   AAA Special Value Rates   *Motel*   ◆◆
All year [CP]   1P 40.00- 56.00   2P/1B   40.00- 56.00   2P/2B   40.00- 56.00   XP 10
70 units. 1 mi s of I-210, Santa Anita Ave exit; w on Huntington Dr, across from Santa Anita Race Track. 161 Colorado Pl. (91006) Nicely landscaped grounds. 30 refrigerators; A/C; C/CATV; movies; radios; phones; comb or shower baths. 15 efficiencies. Htd pool; whirlpool. No pets. 1-bedroom apartments, 11 suites $66-$85. Kitchen units $50-$65. AE, DI, DS, MC, VI. Restaurant adjacent. FAX (818) 447-4739 *(See ad p A329)*
   ⊗ Ⓓ Ⓛ (818) 447-3501

Embassy Suites ❶   Rates Subject to Change   *Suites Motor Inn*   ◆◆◆
All year [BP]   1P .... 107.00   2P/1B .... 117.00   2P/2B .... 117.00   XP 10   F
194 units. 1/4 mi w of I-210; exit Huntington Dr (Monrovia). 211 E Huntington Dr. (91006) Beautifully landscaped atrium area. A/C; C/CATV; free & pay movies; radios; phones. Coin laundry. Htd indoor pool; sauna; whirlpool; steamroom. Pets, $5 extra charge. Refrigerators & microwaves. Monthly rates avail. Reserv deposit required; 3 days refund notice. Complimentary beverages each evening. AE, DI, DS, MC, VI. ● Restaurant; 11 am-3 & 5-10 pm; $13.50-$18; cocktails. FAX (818) 445-8548
   ⊗ Ⓢ Ⓓ (818) 445-8525

Hampton Inn ❷   Rates Subject to Change   *Motel*   ◆◆◆
All year [CP]   1P 60.00- 70.00   2P/1B 65.00- 75.00   2P/2B .... 75.00   XP 10
Senior discount. 132 units. 1/2 mi w of I-210, exit Huntington Dr. 311 E Huntington Dr. (91006) A/C; C/CATV; free & pay movies; radios; phones. Htd pool. Pets. AE, DI, DS, MC, VI. Restaurant adjacent. FAX (818) 446-2748
   ⊗ Ⓢ Ⓓ (818) 574-5600

Residence Inn by Marriott ❹   AAA Special Value Rates   *Apartment Motel*   ◆◆◆
All year [CP]   1P 109.00- 129.00   2P/1B 109.00- 129.00   2P/2B 139.00- 159.00   XP 10
120 units. 1/2 mi w of I-210, exit Huntington Dr. 321 E Huntington Dr. (91006) Studios & split level 2-bedroom units. 60 fireplaces. Check-in 3 pm. A/C; C/CATV; movies; radios; phones. 22 2-bedrm units, kitchens. Coin laundry. Htd pool; whirlpool. Pets, $250 deposit, $50-$75 non-refundable & $6 per night. Reserv deposit required. AE, DI, DS, MC, VI. Restaurant adjacent. FAX (818) 446-5824
   ⊗ Ⓢ Ⓓ Ⓛ (818) 446-6500

RESTAURANTS

Chez Sateau ②   French $$$ ◆◆
1/2 blk s of Huntington Dr. 850 S Baldwin Ave. Fine dining in very attractively decorated dining room. A/C. Open 11:30 am-2:30 & 5:30-9 pm; Sat 5:30 pm-10 pm; Sun 10:30 am-2:30 & 5:30-9 pm; closed Mon & 12/25. Cocktails & lounge. Valet parking. Reserv advised. AE, CB, DI, MC, VI.
   ⊗ (818) 446-8806

Reubens ①   American $$ ◆◆
Adjacent to I-210. 1150 W Colorado Blvd at Michillinda. Nice selection of steaks & seafood. A/C. Early bird specials; children's menu. Open 11:30 am-3 & 5-10 pm; Fri-11 pm; Sat 5 pm-11 pm; Sun 10 am-3 & 4-10 pm. Cocktails & lounge. Reserv advised. AE, DI, DS, MC, VI.
   ⊗ (818) 446-5551

ARCADA — 15,200

Arcata Super 8   AAA Special Value Rates   *Motel*   ◆◆
6/1-9/30   1P .... 49.88   2P/1B .... 54.88   2P/2B .... 57.88   XP 5   F
4/1-5/31   1P .... 39.88   2P/1B .... 44.88   2P/2B .... 47.88   XP 5   F
10/1-3/31   1P .... 32.88   2P/1B .... 37.88   2P/2B .... 39.88   XP 5   F
Senior discount. 62 units. 2 mi n, exit US 101 Guintoli Ln E. 4887 Valley West Blvd. (95521) A/C; C/CATV; rental VCPs; radios; phones. Pets, $50 deposit required. AE, DI, DS, MC, VI. FAX (707) 822-2513
   ⊗ Ⓓ Ⓛ (707) 822-8888

Best Western Arcata Inn   AAA Special Value Rates   *Motel*   ◆◆
5/15-9/15 [CP]   1P .... 74.00   2P/1B .... 78.00   2P/2B .... 78.00   XP 5
9/16-5/14 [CP]   1P .... 52.00   2P/1B .... 56.00   2P/2B .... 56.00   XP 5
Senior discount. 37 units. E of US 101, exit Guintoli Rd. 4827 Valley West Blvd. (95521) A/C; C/CATV; movies; radios; phones; comb or shower baths. Htd indoor/outdoor pool; enclosed whirlpool. Pets, $5 extra charge. AE, DI, DS, MC, VI.
   ⊗ Ⓢ Ⓓ Ⓛ (707) 826-0313

Comfort Inn   Rates Subject to Change   *Motel*
6/1-9/30   1P .... 48.00   2P/1B .... 55.00   2P/2B .... 60.00   XP 5
4/1-5/31   1P .... 35.00   2P/1B .... 45.00   2P/2B .... 50.00   XP 5
10/1-3/31   1P .... 32.00   2P/1B .... 35.00   2P/2B .... 40.00   XP 5
46 units. Exit US 101, Guintoli Ln. 4701 Valley Nest Blvd. (95521) Rating withheld pending completion of construction. A/C; C/TV; phones. Whirlpool. No pets. AE, CB, DI, MC.
   ⊗ (707) 826-2827

Fairwinds Motel   Rates Guaranteed   *Motel*   ◆◆
5/1 0/1   1P .... 45.00   2P/1B .... 48.00   2P/2B .... 54.00   XP 6
9/2-4/30   1P .... 34.00   2P/1B .... 44.00   2P/2B .... 46.00   XP 6
27 units. Exit US 101 14th St, w to G St, 1/4 mi n. 1674 G St. (95521) C/CATV; movies; radios; phones; shower baths. 1 2-bedrm unit. Limited parking lot. No pets. Reserv deposit required. AE, DS, MC, VI.
   ⊗ Ⓓ (707) 822-4824

Hotel Arcata   Rates Subject to Change   *Historic Hotel*   ◆
6/1-9/7 [CP]   1P .... 70.00   2P/1B .... 120.00   2P/2B .... 120.00   XP
9/8-5/31 [CP]   1P .... 45.00   2P/1B .... 70.00   2P/2B .... 70.00   XP
Senior discount. 32 units. At Central Plaza. 708 9th St. (95521) Refurbished 1915 hotel. Smoke free premises. Check-in 3 pm. C/CATV; phones. Parking lot. Pets, $100 deposit required. Reserv deposit required; 7 days refund notice. CB, DI, MC, VI. ● Dining rm; 11:30 am-2 & 5-10 pm; $12-$20; cocktail lounge. FAX (707) 826-1737
(See ad below)   ⊗ Ⓢ Ⓓ (707) 826-0217

Quality Inn-Mad River Rates Subject to Change *Motor Inn* ◆◆◆
6/1-9/30 [CP] 1P .... 69.00 2P/1B .... 76.00 2P/2B .... 76.00 XP 7 F
10/1-10/31 & 3/1-5/31 [CP] 1P .... 45.00 2P/1B .... 52.00 2P/2B .... 52.00 XP 7 F
11/1-2/28 [CP] 1P .... 38.00 2P/1B .... 45.00 2P/2B .... 45.00 XP 7 F
Senior discount. 64 units. Exit US 101 Guintoli Rd, w 1/4 mi. 3535 Janes Rd. (95521) Attractive decor. Check-in 3 pm. A/C; C/CATV; movies; radios; phones. Coin laundry. Pool; whirlpool; tennis-1 court; exercise rm. Pets. AE, DI, DS, MC, VI. Restaurant adjacent. FAX (907) 822-1074 ⊗ Ⓓ ⬛ (707) 822-0409

ARROYO GRANDE — 14,400
Arroyo Village Inn Bed & Breakfast Rates Subject to Change *Bed & Breakfast* ◆◆◆
All year [BP] 1P 80.00- 105.00 2P/1B 95.00- 165.00 2P/2B 105.00- 135.00 XP 20
7 units. Adjacent to US 101; exit Grand Ave, w side via Barnett St. 407 El Camino Real. (93420) Victorian house built in 1988. Designated smoking areas. Check-in 3 pm. A/C; 5 radios. No pets. Wkly rates avail. Reserv deposit required; 14 days refund notice. AE, DI, DS, MC, VI. *(See ad p A466)* ⊗ Ⓓ (805) 489-5926

Best Western Casa Grande Inn Rates Subject to Change *Motor Inn* ◆◆◆
4/1-10/31 [CP] 1P 58.00- 76.00 2P/1B 63.00- 82.00 2P/2B 75.00- 88.00 XP 7
114 units. 1 blk e of US 101, exit Oak Park Rd. 850 Oak Park Rd. (93420) OPEN ALL YEAR. 41 refrigerators; A/C; C/CATV; phones; movies; comb or shower baths. 6 2-bedrm units. Coin laundry. Htd pool; saunas; whirlpools; exercise rm. Pets, $10 extra charge. 7 suites with efficiency; utensils avail, $70-$125. Wkly & monthly rates avail. Complimentary beverages each evening. AE, DI, DS, MC, VI. ● Coffeeshop; 7 am-10 pm; $5.95-$10.95. *(See ad p A335)* ⊗ Ⓓ ⬛ (805) 481-7398

ARTESIA — 15,500
Best Western Pioneer Inn Rates Subject to Change *Motel* ◆◆
All year [CP] 1P .... 54.00 2P/1B .... 59.00 2P/2B .... 59.00 XP 5
Senior discount. 163 units. Adjacent to SR 91, Artesia Frwy, exit Pioneer Blvd. 16905 S Pioneer Blvd. (90701) Refrigerators; A/C; C/CATV; movies; radios; phones. Htd pool; whirlpool. No pets. 10 rooms with whirlpool, $95. AE, DI, DS, MC, VI. ● Coffeeshop; 24 hrs; $5-$7.95; beer & wine. FAX (310) 928-3623 *(See ad below)* ⊗ Ⓓ ⬛ (310) 402-2202

RESTAURANT
Peppers Mexican $$ ◆◆
Adjacent to s side of SR 91, Artesia Frwy, exit Pioneer Blvd. 17104 Pioneer Blvd. Colorful; uniquely furnished & decorated. Few American food items & fresh fish. Sun brunch 9:30 am-2:30 pm. A/C. Children's menu. Open 11:30 am-10 pm; Fri & Sat-11 pm; Sun 9:30 am-10 pm. Cocktails & lounge. Entertainment & dancing. AE, MC, VI. ⊗ (310) 809-8400

ATASCADERO — 23,100
Best Western Colony Inn Rates Subject to Change *Motor Inn* ◆◆◆
4/15-9/8 1P 55.00- 68.00 2P/1B 60.00- 75.00 2P/2B 66.00- 75.00 XP 8
9/9-4/14 1P 46.00- 63.00 2P/1B 50.00- 70.00 2P/2B 56.00- 72.00 XP 8
Senior discount. 75 units. Adjacent to US 101; exit San Anselmo Rd, 1/2 mi ne. 3600 El Camino Real. (93422) Refrigerators; A/C; C/CATV; movies; phones. Htd pool; saunas; whirlpool; 11 rooms with whirlpool tub. No pets. AE, DI, DS, MC, VI. ● Restaurant; 6 am-10 pm; $5-$9. FAX (805) 466-2119 *(See ad p A466)* ⊗ Ⓓ ⬛ (805) 466-4449

Super 8 Motel Rates Guaranteed *Motel* ◆◆
All year 1P .... 48.00 2P/1B .... 53.00 2P/2B .... 56.00 XP 5 F
Senior discount. 30 units. On SR 41, 1/2 blk w of jct US 101. 6505 Morro Rd. (93422) Formerly Atascadero Inn Motel. A/C; C/CATV; movies; radios; phones. Whirlpool. No pets. Reserv deposit required. AE, MC, VI. ⊗ Ⓓ ⬛ (805) 466-6835

ATWATER — 22,300
Applegate Inn Rates Guaranteed *Motel* ◆◆◆
All year 1P 39.95- 47.95 2P/1B 44.95- 52.95 2P/2B .... 44.95 XP 5 F
Senior discount. 80 units. 1 blk ne of SR 99, Applegate Rd exit. 1501 Sycamore Ave. (95301) Refrigerators; A/C; C/CATV; phones. Pool. No pets. AE, DI, MC, VI. Coffeeshop opposite. FAX (209) 357-0798 *(See ad below)* ⊗ Ⓢ Ⓓ ⬛ (209) 357-0202

AUBURN — 10,600
Auburn Inn Rates Subject to Change *Motel* ◆◆◆
All year 1P 52.00- 60.00 2P/1B 58.00- 66.00 2P/2B 62.00- 66.00 XP 6 F
Senior discount. 81 units. 1 1/4 mi e; exit I-80N via Foresthill & Auburn Ravine rds. 1875 Auburn Ravine Rd. (95603) Check-in 4 pm. A/C; C/CATV; radios; phones; comb or shower baths. Coin laundry. Pool; whirlpool. No pets. AE, DD, DI, MC, VI. Coffeeshop opposite. FAX (916) 888-6424 *(See ad p A62)* ⊗ Ⓓ ⬛ (916) 885-1800

Best Western Golden Key Motel Rates Subject to Change *Motel* ◆◆◆
(ⓐ) All year 1P 46.00- 50.00 2P/1B 46.00- 56.00 2P/2B 50.00- 60.00 XP 2- 4
Senior discount. 68 units. Off & adjacent to I-80; via Foresthill Rd. 13450 Lincoln Way. (95603) Spacious lawn
area with many seasonal flowers. A/C; C/TV; movies; 50 radios; phones; comb or shower baths. Coin laundry.
Htd pool, enclosed in winter. Pets, $20 deposit required. AE, DI, DS, MC, VI. Restaurant adjacent.
⊗ ⓓ ⓛ (916) 885-8611

Country Squire Inn Rates Subject to Change *Motor Inn* ◆
(ⓐ) All year 1P 37.00- 47.00 2P/1B 41.00- 45.00 2P/2B 46.00- 52.00 XP 5
Senior discount. 80 units. 1 1/4 mi e off I-80; via Foresthill Rd exit. 13480 Lincoln Way. (95603) A/C; C/CATV; 36
radios; phones; shower or comb baths. Pool; whirlpool. AE, DI, DS, MC, VI. ● Restaurant; 11 am-10 pm; Fri &
Sat 7 am-11 pm; Sun 7 am-10 pm; a la carte entrees about $7-$11. ⊗ ⓓ ⓛ (916) 885-7025

Super 8 Motel Rates Subject to Change *Motel* ◆◆
(ⓐ) All year 1P .... 59.88 2P/1B 62.88- 64.88 2P/2B .... 64.88 XP 5
Senior discount. 52 units. 1 1/4 mi e; exit I-80 n via Foresthill & Auburn Ravine rds. 150 Hillcrest Dr. (95603)
Check-in 3 pm. 15 refrigerators; A/C; C/CATV; radios; phones. Pool; whirlpool. 6 rooms with whirlpool bath,
$74.88 for 2 persons. AE, CB, VI. ⊗ ⓓ ⓛ (916) 888-8808

RESTAURANTS

Dingus McGees American $$ ◆
(ⓐ) 16 mi n in Colfax; n side of I-80; westbound exit via Placer Hills Rd; eastbound exit Canyon Way. 2121 S Auburn
St. Beef, seafood & pasta. A/C. Children's menu. Open 11:30 am-9:30 pm; Fri & Sat-10:30 pm; Sun 4 pm-9:30 pm;
closed 11/25 & 12/25. Cocktails. Reserv advised. AE, MC, VI. ⊗ (916) 346-2235

The Headquarter House American $$ ◆◆
(ⓐ) 1 1/2 mi e; s off I-80 via Bell Rd. 14500 Musso Rd. On the Dunipace Angus Ranch, in the pines. Beef, seafood &
chicken. Smoke free premises. A/C. Open 11:30 am-3 & 5-9:30 pm; Fri & Sat-11 pm; Sun 10:30 am-2 & 4:30-9:30
pm; closed 1/1, 7/4, 12/24 & 12/25. Minimum $5. Reserv advised. AE, DI, DS, MC, VI. ⊗ (916) 878-1906

AVALON (Catalina Island) — 2,900

Casa Mariquita Rates Subject to Change *Motel* ◆◆
(ⓐ) 6/15-9/30 1P 110.00- 275.00 2P/1B 110.00- 275.00 2P/2B 110.00- 275.00 XP 15
4/1-6/16 1P 90.00- 225.00 2P/1B 90.00- 225.00 2P/2B 90.00- 225.00 XP 15
10/1-3/31 1P 80.00- 200.00 2P/1B 80.00- 200.00 2P/2B 80.00- 200.00 XP 15
19 units. 1 blk from harbor. 229 Metropole Ave. (PO Box 2487, 90704) Refrigerators; A/C; C/CATV. No pets.
2-night minimum stay weekends. Reserv deposit required; 14 days refund notice. AE, DI, MC, VI.
ⓢ ⓓ (310) 510-1192

Catalina Canyon Island Rates Subject to Change *Motor Inn* ◆◆
(ⓐ) 5/1-10/31 1P 120.00- 135.00 2P/1B 120.00- 135.00 2P/2B 120.00- 135.00 XP 20 F
11/1-4/30 1P 75.00- 100.00 2P/1B 75.00- 100.00 2P/2B 75.00- 100.00 XP 20 F
Senior discount. 61 units. 1/2 mi from Harbor. 888 Country Club Dr. (90704) A/C; C/CATV; radios; phones. Coin
laundry. Htd pool; sauna; whirlpool; exercise rm. Reserv deposit required; 3 days refund notice. AE, CB, DS, MC,
VI. ● Restaurant; 7:30 am-11 & 5:30-10 pm; closed Mon-Thurs off season; $9-$18; cocktails. FAX (310) 510-0900
⊗ ⓓ (310) 510-0325

El Terado Terrace Rates Subject to Change *Motel* ◆◆
(ⓐ) 5/23-10/31 .... 2P/1B 100.00- 130.00 .... XP 10
11/1-5/22 .... 2P/1B 55.00- 85.00 .... XP 10
18 units. 230 Marilla Ave. (PO Box 1295, 90704) On hill, 1 1/2 blocks from harbor. Some rooms with ocean view.
C/CATV; rental VCPs; shower or comb baths. 2 kitchens, 10 efficiencies. Whirlpool. No pets. 2-night minimum
stay weekends. Reserv deposit required; 5 days refund notice. AE, DS, MC, VI. FAX (310) 510-1495
ⓓ (310) 510-0831

Garden House Inn Rates Guaranteed *Bed & Breakfast* ◆◆◆
(ⓐ) 4/2-10/31 [CP] 1P 125.00- 250.00 2P/1B 125.00- 250.00 2P/2B 125.00- 250.00 XP 25
11/1-4/1 [CP] 1P 95.00- 200.00 2P/1B 95.00- 200.00 2P/2B 95.00- 200.00 XP 25
Senior discount. 9 units. 1 blk from beach. 125 Claressa. (90704) Restored home built in 1923. Nicely furnished rooms.
Smoke free premises. C/CATV; movies; VCPs. Phones; comb or shower baths. No pets. 2-night minimum stay weekends, 4/2-10/31. Reserv deposit required; 10 days refund notice. AE, MC, VI. ⊗ ⓢ ⓓ (310) 510-0356

Gull House-Bed & Breakfast   Rates Subject to Change   *Motel*   ◆◆
🚭 Fri-Sun [CP]   ·······   2P/1B   100.00- 145.00   ·······   XP
Mon-Thurs [CP]   ·······   2P/1B   90.00- 140.00   ·······   XP
4 units. 344 Whittley Ave. (PO Box 1381, 90704) OPEN 4/1-10/31. On hill in quiet residential area. 1/4 mi from harbor. 2 1-bedroom suites & 2 guest rooms. Check-out 10 am. 2 refrigerators; C/CATV; comb or shower baths. Small pool; whirlpool. No pets. 2-night minimum stay. Reserv deposit required; 10 days refund notice.
Ⓢ Ⓓ (310) 510-2547

Hotel MacRae   Rates Subject to Change   *Motel*   ◆
🚭 Fri & Sat 6/1-10/31 [CP]   1P 105.00- 170.00   2P/1B   105.00- 170.00   2P/2B   .... 125.00 XP
Sun-Thurs 6/1-10/31 [CP]   1P 90.00- 150.00   2P/1B   90.00- 150.00   2P/2B   .... 110.00 XP
11/1-5/31 [CP]   1P 60.00- 110.00   2P/1B   60.00- 110.00   2P/2B   .... 80.00 XP
Senior discount. 24 units. 409 Crescent Ave. (90704) Across from beach. Nicely decorated, cozy rooms. C/CATV; VCPs; shower baths. No pets. Reserv deposit required; 3 days refund notice. MC, VI. FAX (310) 510-9632
Ⓓ (310) 510-0246

Hotel Metropole   Rates Subject to Change   *Motel*   ◆◆◆
🚭 5/1-10/31 [CP]   1P 125.00- 175.00   2P/1B   125.00- 179.00   ·······   XP
Fri & Sat 11/1-4/30 [CP]   1P 100.00- 150.00   2P/1B   100.00- 150.00   ·······   XP 15
Sun-Thurs [CP]   1P 85.00- 125.00   2P/1B   85.00- 125.00   ·······   XP
47 units. Crescent Ave at Whittley. (PO Box 1900, 90704) Across from harbor at Metropole Market Place. Many ocean view rooms, some with balconies & gas fireplaces. Designated smoking areas. A/C; C/CATV; movies; radios; phones. Whirlpool; 11 rooms with whirlpool tub. No pets. 4 large ocean view rooms, $275 5/1-10/31; $190 11/1-4/30. Reserv deposit required; 3 days refund notice. AE, MC, VI. 2 restaurants adjacent. FAX (310) 510-2534
⊗ Ⓢ Ⓓ Ⓛ (310) 510-1884

Hotel St. Lauren   Rates Subject to Change   *Motel*   ◆◆◆
🚭 5/20-10/15 [CP]   1P 85.00- 200.00   2P/1B   85.00- 200.00   ·······   XP 20
10/16-5/19 [CP]   1P 60.00- 160.00   2P/1B   60.00- 160.00   ·······   XP 20
Senior discount. 42 units. 231 Beacon St at Metropole. (PO Box 497, 90704) Victorian style hotel. 1 block from harbor. Many ocean view rooms. 14 A/C; C/CATV; rental VCPs; phones. 6 rooms with whirlpool tub. No pets. 2-night minimum stay weekends 3/1-11/30. Reserv deposit required; 7 days refund notice. MC, VI. FAX (310) 510-1369
Ⓢ Ⓓ (310) 510-2299

Hotel Villa Portofino   Rates Subject to Change   *Motor Inn*   ◆◆
🚭 5/15-10/31, Fri & Sat 11/1-5/14
[CP]   1P 86.00- 140.00   2P/1B   86.00- 250.00   2P/2B   100.00- 250.00 XP 10
Sun-Thurs 11/1-5/14 [EP]   1P 48.00- 115.00   2P/1B   48.00- 150.00   2P/2B   48.00- 175.00 XP 10
34 units. 111 Crescent Ave. (PO Box 127, 90704) Across from harbor. Some ocean view rooms. 6 refrigerators; C/CATV; shower or comb baths. 6 2-bedrm units. No pets. 2-night minimum stay weekends, 4/1-10/31. Reserv deposit required; 3 days refund notice. AE, DI, DS, MC, VI. ● Restaurant, see separate listing. FAX (310) 510-0839 *(See ad below)*
Ⓓ (310) 510-0555

Hotel Vincentes   Rates Subject to Change   *Motel*   ◆◆
🚭 5/15-10/31   1P 75.00- 110.00   2P/1B   85.00- 135.00   2P/2B   95.00- 150.00 XP 15-25
11/1-5/14   1P 65.00- 85.00   2P/1B   75.00- 110.00   2P/2B   95.00- 140.00 XP 15-25
12 units. 1/4 blk from harbor. 108 Marilla Ave. (PO Box 187, 90704) Refrigerators; 4 A/C; C/CATV; VCPs; radios; shower or comb baths. No pets. 2 ocean view suites, $250-$295 for up to 2 persons in season; $100-$175 off season. Reserv deposit required; 7 days refund notice. AE, DS, MC, VI.
Ⓓ (310) 510-1115

Hotel Vista Del Mar   Rates Subject to Change   *Motel*   ◆◆◆
🚭 5/1-10/31 [CP]   1P 95.00- 165.00   2P/1B   95.00- 165.00   ·······   XP 15
11/1-4/31 [CP]   1P 65.00- 135.00   2P/1B   65.00- 135.00   ·······   XP 15
15 units. 417 Crescent Ave. (PO Box 1979, 90704) Across from beach. Most rooms with gas fireplace. Smoke free premises. Refrigerators; A/C; C/CATV; movies; radios; phones. No pets. 2-night minimum stay weekends. 2 large rooms with balcony, whirlpool & ocean view, $195-$275. Reserv deposit required; 5 days refund notice. AE, DS, MC, VI. Restaurant adjacent. FAX (310) 510-2917 *(See ad below)*
⊗ Ⓢ Ⓓ (310) 510-1452

Pavilion Lodge   Rates Guaranteed   *Motel*   ◆◆◆
🚭 6/18-9/11   1P 129.00- 158.00   2P/1B   129.00- 158.00   2P/2B   129.00- 158.00 XP 12   F
9/12-10/30   1P 84.00- 104.00   2P/1B   84.00- 104.00   2P/2B   84.00- 104.00 XP 8   F
3/26-6/17   1P 79.00- 99.00   2P/1B   79.00- 99.00   2P/2B   79.00- 99.00 XP 8   F
10/31-3/25   1P 49.00- 79.00   2P/1B   49.00- 79.00   2P/2B   49.00- 79.00 XP 8   F
Senior discount. 72 units. 513 Crescent Ave. (PO Box 737, 90704) Across from beach. Nicely landscaped grounds. Check-out 10:30 am. Refrigerators; A/C; C/CATV; movies; radios; comb or shower baths. No pets. For reservations: (310) 510-2500. Reserv deposit required; 3 days refund notice. AE, CB, DS, MC, VI. *(See ad p A64)*
Ⓓ (310) 510-1788

Seacrest Inn
◉ 5/1-10/31 [CP]   Rates Subject to Change   *Motel*   ◆◆
 1P 135.00- 185.00   2P/1B   135.00- 185.00   ....   XP
 11/1-4/30 [CP]   1P 95.00- 145.00   2P/1B   95.00- 145.00   ....   XP
 Senior discount. 6 units. 1 blk from beach. 201 Claressa. (PO Box 128, 90704) Small well-appointed rooms in a
 restored 2-story home. Smoke free premises. Refrigerators; A/C; C/CATV; movies; VCPs. Radios; comb or
 shower baths. 3 rooms with whirlpool tub. No pets. Reserv deposit required; 7 days refund notice. AE, DS, MC,
 VI.
 ⊗ Ⓓ (310) 510-0196

RESTAURANTS

El Galleon   American $$ ◆
◉ Across from harbor & beach. 411 Crescent Ave. Attractive Mediterranean/nautical decor. Selection of seafood &
 steaks. Children's menu. Open 11 am-2:30 & 5-10 pm. Cocktails & lounge. Entertainment. AE, MC, VI.
 (310) 510-1188

Pirrone's   American $$ ◆◆
◉ 417 Crescent Ave. On 2nd floor overlooking the harbor. Selection of seafood, pasta, beef & chicken specialties.
 Sun brunch. Early bird specials. Open 5 pm-9 pm; also 11 am-2 pm in summer; Sun 10 am-2 & 5-9 pm. Cocktails
 & lounge. AE, DI, DS, MC, VI.
 (310) 510-0333

Ristorante Villa Portofino   Italian $$$ ◆◆◆
 At the Hotel Villa Portofino. Attractive dining room with a nice selection of seafood, pasta & veal. Children's menu. Open
 5 pm-10 pm; closed 1/1. Cocktails. Reserv advised. AE, MC, VI. *(See ad p A63)*   (310) 510-0508

Solomon's Landing   American $$ ◆
◉ 101 Marilla at Crescent Ave. Indoor & outdoor patio dining overlooking harbor. Nice selection of seafood, steaks
 & Mexican cuisine. Children's menu. Open 11 am-2 & 5-9 pm; 11 am-9 pm in summer; closed 12/1-2/1 & Mon-
 Tues 10/1-11/30 & 2/1-6/1. Cocktails & lounge. Entertainment & dancing. AE, DI, DS, MC, VI.   (310) 510-1474

AVENUE OF THE GIANTS — See GARBERVILLE & MIRANDA

AZUSA — 41,300
Corporate Inn   Rates Guaranteed   *Motel*   ◆◆
◉ All year   1P 36.00- 40.00   2P/1B   36.00- 40.00   2P/2B   38.00- 50.00 XP 5
 44 units. On SR 39; 1 blk n of I-210; exit Azusa Ave. 117 N Azusa Ave. (91702) A/C; C/CATV; movies; radios;
 phones. Coin laundry. Whirlpool. No pets. 14 efficiencies, $5 extra; no utensils. Wkly rates avail. AE, CB, DI, MC,
 VI.
 Ⓓ 🚲 (818) 969-8871

RESTAURANT

El Encanto Inn   American $$ ◆◆
◉ 3 mi n on SR 39, in San Gabriel Canyon. 100 N San Gabriel Canyon Rd. Country setting. Selections of chicken,
 lamb, pork, steaks, seafood & prime rib. A/C. Children's menu. Open 5 pm-10 pm; Fri & Sat-11 pm; Sun 4 pm-9
 pm; closed 1/1 & 12/25. Cocktails & lounge. Entertainment. AE, DI, DS, MC, VI.   ⊗ (818) 969-8877

BAKER — 600
Bun Boy Motel   Rates Subject to Change   *Motor Inn*   ◆
◉ All year   1P .... 29.00   2P/1B   .... 40.00   2P/2B   .... 44.00 XP 8
 20 units. At jct I-15 & SR 127. (PO Box 130, 92309) A/C; C/CATV; movies; radios; phones; shower baths. Pets.
 AE, DI, DS, MC, VI. ● Restaurant; 24 hours; $6.95-$11.95; 24 hour room service.   ⊗ Ⓓ (619) 733-4363

BAKERSFIELD — 174,800   See also BUTTONWILLOW

Bakersfield Plaza Inn Travelodge   AAA Special Value Rates   *Motel* ◆◆
⊕ All year [CP]   1P 36.00- 38.00 2P/1B 38.00- 40.00 2P/2B 40.00- 42.00 XP 4
61 units. Adjacent to SR 99, 1/2 mi ne, exit Ming Ave. 1030 Wible Rd. (93304) Refrigerators; A/C; C/CATV; movies; radios; phones. Coin laundry. Pool; saunas; whirlpool. No pets. Microwaves. Reserv deposit required. AE, DI, MC, VI. FAX (805) 834-4439   ⊗ ⒟ Ⓖ (805) 834-3377

Bakersfield South-Travelodge   AAA Special Value Rates   *Motel* ◆◆
⊕ All year   1P 36.00- 40.00 2P/1B 40.00- 44.00 2P/2B 42.00- 45.00 XP 4   F
60 units. Adjacent to SR 99, 1/2 mi nw, exit White Ln. 3620 Wible Rd. (93309) Refrigerators; A/C; C/TV; movies; VCPs. Radios; phones. Coin laundry. Small pool; whirlpool. No pets. 14 efficiencies, $3 extra. 4 rooms with whirlpool bathtub, $60-$65. AE, DI, DS, MC, VI. Coffeeshop adjacent. FAX (805) 832-3212 *(See ad below)*
     ⊗ Ⓢ ⒟ Ⓖ (805) 833-1000

Best Western Hill House   Rates Subject to Change   *Motor Inn* ◆◆◆
All year [BP]   .... 2P/1B .... 46.00 2P/2B .... 50.00 XP 5
99 units. 2 mi e of SR 99, California Ave exit. 700 Truxtun Ave at S St. (93301) Refrigerators; A/C; C/CATV; movies; 40 radios; phones. Pool. Pets, $3 extra charge. AE, DI, DS, MC, VI. ● Dining rm & coffeeshop; 6 am-2:30 pm; Sat 7 am-noon; Sun 7 am-2 pm; $4-$8.25; cocktails. FAX (805) 327-1247   ⊗ ⒟ (805) 327-4064

Best Western Inn   AAA Special Value Rates   *Motor Inn* ◆◆
⊕ All year   1P 47.00- 62.00 2P/1B 60.00- 72.00 2P/2B 60.00- 72.00 XP 6   F
196 units. Adjacent east side SR 99 northbound exit Pierce Rd, southbound exit Rosedale Hwy. 2620 Pierce Rd. (93308) A/C; C/CATV; free & pay movies; radios; phones. Coin laundry. Pool; whirlpool. Small pets only. AE, DI, DS, MC, VI. ● Dining rm & coffeeshop; 6 am-10 pm; $6.50-$12.95; cocktails; entertainment. FAX (805) 334-1820 *(See ad below)*   ⊗ ⒟ (805) 327-9651

Best Western Oak Inn   AAA Special Value Rates   *Motel* ◆◆
⊕ All year [CP]   1P 48.00- 52.00 2P/1B 52.00- 56.00 2P/2B 52.00- 56.00 XP 5   F
42 units. Adjacent to SR 99, 1/2 mi se, California Ave exit. 889 Oak St. (93304) A/C; C/CATV; pay movies; radios; phones; comb or shower baths. Pool. Pets. Some rooms with microwave & refrigerator. Reserv deposit required. AE, DI, DS, MC, VI. *(See ad below)*   ⊗ ⒟ (805) 324-9686

California Inn   Rates Guaranteed   *Motel* ◆◆
⊕ All year   1P .... 41.00 2P/1B .... 43.00 2P/2B .... 45.00 XP 4
Senior discount. 74 units. 1/4 mi sw of SR 99; exit California Ave, at Real Rd. 3400 Chester Ln. (93309) Refrigerators; A/C; C/CATV; movies; radios; phones. 10 efficiencies. Coin laundry. Small pool; sauna; whirlpool; 10 rooms with whirlpool tub; 3 rooms with spa. No pets. Microwaves. Wkly rates avail. Reserv deposit required. AE, DI, MC, VI. FAX (805) 328-0433 *(See ad p A66)*   ⊗ Ⓢ ⒟ Ⓖ (805) 328-1100

Comfort Inn-Central   Rates Subject to Change   *Motel* ◆◆
⊕ All year [CP]   1P 35.00- 38.00 2P/1B 38.00- 40.00 2P/2B 40.00- 44.00 XP 4   F
Senior discount. 52 units. Adjacent to SR 99, 3/4 mi ne of Ming Ave exit. 830 Wible Rd. (93304) Refrigerators; A/C; C/CATV; free & pay movies; radios; phones. 10 efficiencies, no utensils. Coin laundry. Small pool; whirlpool; 4 rooms with whirlpool bathtub. No pets. AE, DI, DS, MC, VI. FAX (805) 831-1879 ⊗ ⒟ Ⓖ (805) 831-1922

Courtyard by Marriott .... Rates Subject to Change .... *Motor Inn* ◆◆◆
Sun-Thurs .... 1P .... 69.00 2P/1B .... 79.00 2P/2B .... 79.00 XP
Fri & Sat .... 1P .... 55.00 2P/1B .... 55.00 2P/2B .... 55.00 XP
Senior discount. 146 units. Adjacent west side of SR 99 & SR 58W, Rosedale Hwy exit. 3601 Marriott Dr. (93308) Many rooms with patio or balcony, facing courtyard area. Check-in 3 pm. A/C; C/CATV; free & pay movies; radios; phones. Coin laundry. Htd pool; indoor whirlpool; exercise rm. No pets. Reserv deposit required. AE, DI, MC, VI. ● Dining rm; 6:30 am-2 & 5-10 pm; Sat & Sun from 7 am; $8.75-$12.50; cocktails. FAX (805) 324-1185 *(See ad below)*
⊗ Ⓢ Ⓓ Ⓚ (805) 324-6660

Days Inn .... Rates Guaranteed .... *Motor Inn* ◆◆
⊛ Mon-Thurs .... 1P 55.00- 65.00 2P/1B 60.00- 75.00 2P/2B 60.00- 75.00 XP 10   F
Fri-Sun .... 1P 48.00- 58.00 2P/1B 48.00- 58.00 2P/2B 48.00- 58.00 XP 10   F
Senior discount. 122 units. Adjacent west side of SR 99 & SR 58W, Rosedale Hwy exit. 3540 Rosedale Hwy. (93308) A/C; C/CATV; free & pay movies; radios; phones. Htd pool; whirlpool. No pets. Wkly & monthly rates avail. Reserv deposit required. Complimentary beverages each evening. AE, DI, DS, MC, VI. ● Coffeeshop; 6 am-1:30 & 5-11 pm; $7.95-$11.95; cocktails. FAX (805) 326-1513
Ⓢ Ⓓ Ⓚ (805) 326-1111

Downtowner Inn .... AAA Special Value Rates .... *Motel* ◆◆
⊛ All year .... 1P 33.00- 49.00 2P/1B 38.00- 49.00 2P/2B 43.00- 48.00 XP 5   F
50 units. 1 1/4 mi e of SR 99; California Ave exit; at 13th St. 1301 Chester Ave. (93301) A/C; C/CATV; movies; rental VCPs. Phones; comb or shower baths. Rental refrigerators. Pool. Garage. No pets. Wkly & monthly rates avail. Reserv deposit required. AE, DI, DS, MC, VI.
⊗ Ⓢ Ⓓ (805) 327-7122

Garden Suites Inn .... Rates Guaranteed .... *Suites Motor Inn* ◆◆◆
⊛ All year [BP] .... 1P 48.00- 54.00 2P/1B 54.00- 60.00 2P/2B 58.00- 64.00 XP 6
67 units. Adjacent to SR 99; 3/4 mi se of Ming Ave exit. 2310 Wible Rd. (93304) All rooms with microwave & refrigerator. Check-in 3 pm. A/C; C/CATV; movies; radios; phones. Small pool; whirlpool. No pets. 8 rooms with whirlpool, $68-$78. Reserv deposit required; 3 days refund notice. AE, DI, DS, MC, VI. ● Coffeeshop; 6 am-9 pm; $4.25-$8.95. FAX (805) 397-5464
⊗ Ⓢ Ⓓ Ⓚ (805) 833-6066

La Quinta Motor Inn   Rates Subject to Change   *Motel* ◆◆◆
◉ All year   1P 50.00- 57.00   2P/1B   55.00- 62.00   2P/2B .... 55.00 XP 6   F
129 units. Adjacent east side SR 99, southbound exit Rosedale Hwy, northbound exit Pierce Rd. 3232 Riverside
Dr. (93308) A/C; C/TV; free & pay movies; radios; phones. Htd pool. Pets. AE, DI, DS, MC, VI. Restaurant adjacent.   ⊗ Ⓢ Ⓓ Ⓛ (805) 325-7400

Lone Oak Inn   Rates Guaranteed   *Apartment Motel* ◆◆
◉ All year   1P .... 39.00   2P/1B   .... 43.00   2P/2B .... 49.00 XP 5
Senior discount. 19 units. 4 1/2 mi w of SR 99 via Rosedale Hwy exit. 10614 Rosedale Hwy. (93312) A/C; C/CATV;
movies; phones. No pets. 19 kitchens, $6 extra. Reserv deposit required. AE, MC, VI. *(See ad p A66)*
                                                                         Ⓓ (805) 589-6600

Quality Inn   Rates Subject to Change   *Motel* ◆◆◆
◉ All year   1P 42.00- 52.00   2P/1B   46.00- 61.00   2P/2B 51.00- 61.00 XP 5   F
Senior discount. 89 units. Adjacent to SR 99, exit California Ave. 1011 Oak St. (93304) 14 refrigerators; A/C;
C/CATV; movies; phones. Coin laundry. Htd pool; sauna; indoor whirlpool; exercise rm. Pets. AE, DI, DS, MC, VI.
Coffeeshop adjacent. *(See ad below)*   ⊗ Ⓓ (805) 325-0772

Ramada Inn   Rates Guaranteed   *Motor Inn* ◆◆
◉ All year   1P 53.00- 57.00   2P/1B   59.00- 65.00   2P/2B 59.00- 65.00 XP 6
197 units. Adjacent west side of SR 99, via SR 58W, Rosedale Hwy exit. 3535 Rosedale Hwy. (93308) Check-in 4
pm. 10 refrigerators; A/C; C/CATV; movies; VCPs. 100 radios; phones. Coin laundry. Pool; whirlpool. Pets.
Wkly & monthly rates avail. AE, DI, DS, MC, VI. ● Dining rm & coffeeshop; 6:30 am-10 pm; Fri & Sat-11 pm; $10-
$14; cocktails. FAX (805) 327-0681 *(See ad below)*   ⊗ Ⓓ Ⓛ (805) 327-0681

Red Lion Hotel   Rates Subject to Change   *Motor Inn* ◆◆◆
All year   1P 103.00- 128.00   2P/1B 112.00- 138.00   2P/2B 112.00- 138.00 XP 10   F
262 units. Adjacent west side SR 99 & SR 58W, Rosedale Hwy exit. 3100 Camino Del Rio Ct. (93308) Spacious rooms.
Check-in 3 pm. A/C; C/CATV; pay movies; radios; phones. Rental refrigerators. 7 2-bedrm units. Htd pool; whirlpool. Air-
port transp. Pets. AE, DI, DS, MC, VI. ● Coffeeshop; 6 am-11 pm; Fri & Sat-midnight; $7-$17; cocktails; entertainment.
Also, Misty's, see separate listing. FAX (805) 323-0331 *(See ad p A3)*   ⊗ Ⓓ Ⓛ (805) 323-7111

Residence In by Marriott   Rates Subject to Change   *Suites Motel* ◆◆◆
Sun-Thurs [CP]   1P 89.00- 114.00   2P/1B   89.00- 114.00   2P/2B .... 114.00 XP
Fri & Sat [CP]   1P .... 65.00   2P/1B   .... 65.00   2P/2B .... 65.00 XP
114 units. 2 blks w of SR 99, then 1/2 blk n, exit California Ave. 4241 Chester Ln. (93309) 1- & 2-bedroom suites with
living room. 52 fireplaces. Check-in 3 pm. A/C; C/CATV; movies; rental VCPs. Radios; phones. Kitchens. Coin laundry.
Htd pool; whirlpool; putting green; sports court; exercise rm. Parking lot. Pets, under 40lbs. $250 deposit required,
$40-$60 non-refundable; $6 extra charge. Wkly & monthly rates avail. AE, DI, DS, MC, VI. FAX (805) 321-0720
                                                                 ⊗ Ⓢ Ⓓ (805) 321-9800

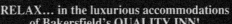

Rio Mirada Motor Inn
Rates Subject to Change — *Motel* ◆◆
All year [CP]   1P .... 48.00   2P/1B .... 48.00   2P/2B .... 53.00   XP 5   F
203 units. Adjacent east side SR 99, 1 mi n of Rosedale Hwy southbound exit Rosedale Hwy, northbound exit Pierce Rd. 4500 Pierce Rd. (93308) A/C; C/CATV; movies; rental VCPs. Phones. Rental refrigerators. Coin laundry. Htd pool; sauna; whirlpool; exercise rm. Pets, $10 non-refundable deposit required. Efficiencies, $59-$64. Complimentary beverages each evening. AE, DI, DS, MC, VI. FAX (805) 324-5555   ⊗ Ⓢ Ⓓ ⓛ (805) 324-5555

Sheraton Inn Bakersfield
Rates Subject to Change — *Motor Inn* ◆◆◆
⊛ All year   1P 65.00- 110.00   2P/1B 65.00- 110.00   2P/2B 65.00- 110.00   XP 10   F
Senior discount. 198 units. 1 1/4 mi w of SR 99, exit California Ave. 5101 California Ave. (93309) Spacious landscaped grounds. Check-in 3 pm. 15 refrigerators; A/C; C/CATV; free & pay movies; radios; phones. Htd pool; whirlpool; exercise rm. Pets. AE, CB, DI, MC, VI. ● Restaurant; 6:30 am-10 pm; $11.95-$20; cocktails. Also, The Bistro, see separate listing. FAX (805) 323-3508 *(See ad p A67)*   ⊗ Ⓢ Ⓓ ⓛ (805) 325-9700

RESTAURANTS

The Bistro   Continental $$$ ◆◆◆
At the Sheraton Inn Bakersfield. Selections of prime rib, fresh seafood, pastas, steaks, lamb, pork & duck. A/C. Early bird specials; children's menu. Open 6:30-10 am, 11-2 & 6-10 pm; Sat 7:30-10 am, 11-2 & 6-10 pm; Sun 9 am-2 & 6-10 pm. Cocktails & lounge. Entertainment & dancing. Reserv advised. AE, DI, DS, MC, VI.   (805) 323-3905

Blu Note Restaurant   Continental $$ ◆◆
Ne corner of Planz Rd & Stine, in the Stockdale Town Center. 4705 Planz Rd. Chicken, veal, pork, New York strip, lamb chops, fresh fish & pastas. Live jazz music Wed-Sun evenings. A/C. Early bird specials. Open 11:30 am-2 & 5:30-10:30 pm; Fri-11 pm; Sat 5:30 pm-10:30 pm; Sun 5:30 pm-9 pm; closed 1/1, 7/4, 11/25, 12/24 & 12/25. Cocktails & lounge. Reserv advised. AE, MC, VI.   ⊗ (805) 835-0463

Mama Tosca's Ristorante Italiano   Italian $$ ◆◆
2 mi w of SR 99, in Laurelglen Plaza, sw corner of Ashe & Ming Ave; exit Ming Ave. 6631 Ming Ave. Fine dining featuring home cooking in an attractive setting. Some pasta & all desserts made on premises; also selections of chicken, veal, fish, steaks & lamb. A/C. Children's menu. Open 11:30 am-2 & 5:30-10 pm; Sat from 5:30 pm; closed Sun & major holidays. Cocktails & lounge. Reserv advised. AE, DI, MC, VI.   ⊗ (805) 831-1242

Misty's   Continental $$ ◆◆
In Red Lion Hotel. Nice selection of American entrees. A/C. Open 11:30 am-1:30 & 5:30-10 pm; Fri-11 pm; Sat 5:30 pm-11 pm; Sun 9 am-2 & 5:30-10 pm. Cocktails & lounge. Entertainment & dancing. Reserv advised. AE, DI, DS, MC, VI.   ⊗ (805) 323-7111

The Olive Garden   Italian $ ◆◆
1 1/4 mi w of SR 99, via Ming Ave, just n of Ming Ave. 1701 New Stine Rd. Casual dining; friendly service. Selection of pastas, chicken, pizza, steak & fresh fish. A/C. Children's menu. Open 11 am-10 pm; Fri & Sat-11 pm; Sun-10:30 pm; closed 11/25 & 12/25. Cocktails & lounge. AE, DI, DS, MC, VI.   ⊗ (805) 832-1278

Piccadilly Cafeteria   American $ ◆◆
1 blk e of SR 99 inside The Valley Plaza Mall; exit Ming Ave. 2701 Ming Ave, Suite 109. Casual atmosphere. Varied selection of salads, entrees & desserts. A/C. Open 11 am-8:30 pm; Sat-7:30 pm; Sun-6:30 pm. AE, DS, MC, VI.   ⊗ (805) 837-8233

Piccadilly Cafeteria   American $ ◆◆
1/4 mi w of Union St. 501 34th St. Casual atmosphere. Varied selection of salads, entrees & desserts. A/C. Open 11 am-8:30 pm; closed 12/24 at 7 pm & 12/25. AE, DS, MC, VI.   ⊗ ⓛ (805) 327-9934

BALDWIN PARK — 69,300

Howard Johnson Lodge
AAA Special Value Rates — *Motel* ◆◆
All year [CP]   1P 35.00- 58.00   2P/1B 45.00- 67.00   2P/2B 45.00- 71.00   XP 8   F
69 units. S side of I-10, exit Puente Ave. 14624 Dalewood St. (91706) A/C; C/TV; pay movies; phones. Pool. No pets. AE, DI, DS, MC, VI. Restaurant adjacent. FAX (818) 338-7989   ⊗ Ⓓ (818) 962-8761

San Gabriel Valley Hilton
Rates Subject to Change — *Hotel* ◆◆◆
All year   1P 99.00- 109.00   2P/1B 109.00- 119.00   2P/2B 109.00- 119.00   XP 10   F
Senior discount. 196 units. N side of I-10, exit Puente Ave. 14635 Baldwin Park Towne Center. (91706) Formerly Baldwin Park Hilton. 120 refrigerators; A/C; C/CATV; movies; radios; phones. Htd pool; whirlpool; exercise rm. Parking lot. Airport transp. No pets. Monthly rates avail. AE, DI, DS, MC, VI. ● Restaurant; 6 am-10 pm; $8-$17; cocktails. FAX (818) 962-6000   ⊗ Ⓢ Ⓓ (818) 962-6000

Travelodge Baldwin Park
Rates Subject to Change — *Motel* ◆◆◆
⊛ All year   1P 42.00- 40.00   2P/1B 42.00- 48.00   2P/2B 48.00- 60.00   XP 5   F
Senior discount. 107 units. Adjacent south side I-10; Francisquito Ave. 13921 Francisquito Ave. (91706) 30 refrigerators; A/C; C/CATV; movies; radios; phones. Coin laundry. Pool; whirlpool. No pets. 6 rooms with whirlpool, 6 suites $65-$85. Wkly rates avail. Reserv deposit required; 3 days refund notice. AE, DI, DS, MC, VI. Restaurant opposite. FAX (818) 337-1190   ⊗ Ⓢ Ⓓ (818) 814-0808

RESTAURANT

Rosa Ristorante Italiano   Italian $$$ ◆◆◆
⊛ Adjacent to I-10, exit Baldwin Park Blvd. 3077 Baldwin Park Blvd. Very attractive dining room. Features a large selection of cuisine. A/C. Open 11:30 am-2 & 5-9 pm; Sat from 5 pm; closed Sun & major holidays. Cocktails. Reserv advised. AE, DI, DS, MC, VI.   (818) 960-2788

BALLARD

The Ballard Inn Rates Subject to Change *Bed & Breakfast* ◆◆◆
All year [BP] 1P 155.00- 185.00 2P/1B 155.00- 185.00 .... XP
15 units. 3 1/2 mi ne of Solvang, via Alamo Pintado Rd. 2436 Baseline. (93463) A charming inn with individually decorated rooms, 7 with fireplace. Afternoon tea & beverages. Smoke free premises. Check-in 3 pm. A/C; comb or shower baths. Rental bicycles. No pets. Reserv deposit required; 7 days refund notice. AE, MC, VI. ⊗ Ⓓ Ⓛ (805) 688-7770

RESTAURANT

The Ballard Store Restaurant Continental $$ ◆◆◆
3 1/2 mi ne of Solvang, via Alamo Pintado Rd. 2449 Baseline Ave. Fine dining in a French country atmosphere. International cuisine. Extensive selection of California wines. A/C. Open noon-2:30 & 6-9:30 pm; Sun 10:30 am-2 & 5-8:30 pm; closed Mon, Tues, 12/24 & 12/25. Wine. Reserv advised. MC, VI. (805) 688-5319

BANNING — 20,600

Banning Travelodge AAA Special Value Rates *Motel* ◆◆◆
⑯ All year [CP] 1P .... 36.00 2P/1B .... 40.00 2P/2B .... 45.00 XP 3 F
40 units. Adjacent to I-10, exit 22nd St, then 1/2 mi e. 1700 W Ramsey St. (92220) A/C; C/CATV; movies; rental VCPs. Phones; comb or shower baths. Rental refrigerators. Small htd pool. No pets. Wkly & monthly rates avail. AE, CB, DI, MC, VI. FAX (909) 849-4071 ⊗ Ⓢ Ⓓ Ⓛ (909) 849-1000

Days Inn Rates Subject to Change *Motel* ◆◆
⑯ All year 1P .... 44.00 2P/1B .... 46.00 2P/2B .... 48.00 XP 2
43 units. Adjacent to I-10; exit 22nd St. 2320 W Ramsey St. (92220) Spacious rooms. A/C; C/CATV; movies; radios; phones; comb or shower baths. Htd pool. Pets, $5 extra charge. 3 rooms with whirlpool tub, $56. AE, CB, DS, MC, VI. FAX (909) 849-0509 ⊗ Ⓢ Ⓓ Ⓛ (909) 849-0092

Super 8 Motel Rates Subject to Change *Motel* ◆◆
⑯ All year 1P .... 31.88 2P/1B .... 35.88 2P/2B .... 39.88 XP 4 F
Senior discount. 51 units. Adjacent to I-10, 22nd St exit. 1690 W Ramsey St. (92220) A/C; C/CATV; movies; rental VCPs. Radios; phones. Pool. Pets. Wkly rates avail. AE, DI, DS, MC, VI. ⊗ Ⓓ Ⓛ (909) 849-6887

BARSTOW — 21,500

Astro Budget Motel Rates Subject to Change *Motel* ◆
⑯ All year 1P 22.00- 28.00 2P/1B 25.00- 32.00 2P/2B 28.00- 38.00 XP 3
30 units. 1/2 mi w of I-15; from I-15 & westbound I-40, E Main St exit. 1271 E Main St. (92311) A/C; C/CATV; movies; radios; phones. Pool. Pets. Wkly rates avail. Reserv deposit required. AE, DI, DS, MC, VI. FAX (619) 256-6471 ⊗ Ⓓ (619) 256-2204

Barstow Holiday Inn Rates Guaranteed *Motor Inn* ◆◆◆
All year 1P .... 58.00 2P/1B .... 61.00 2P/2B .... 64.00 XP 4
Senior discount. 148 units. 1/4 mi w of I-15; from I-15 & westbound I-40, E Main St exits. 1511 E Main St. (92311) A/C; C/CATV; radios; phones. Rental refrigerators. Htd pool; whirlpool; exercise rm. No pets. AE, DI, DS, MC, VI. Restaurant adjacent. FAX (619) 256-5917 ⊗ Ⓢ Ⓓ Ⓛ (619) 256-5673

Barstow Inn Rates Subject to Change *Motel* ◆
⑯ All year 1P 22.00- 30.00 2P/1B 27.00- 30.00 2P/2B 33.00- 40.00 XP 3
Senior discount. 32 units. 3/4 mi w of I-15; from I-15 & westbound I-40, E Main St exits. 1261 E Main St. (92311) Refrigerators; A/C; C/CATV; movies; radios; phones. Pool. Pets. 10 kitchens, $5 extra, no utensils. Wkly rates avail. AE, CB, DI, MC, VI. ⊗ Ⓓ (619) 256-7581

Best Motel Rates Guaranteed *Motel* ◆
⑯ All year 1P .... 24.00 2P/1B .... 28.00 2P/2B .... 32.00 XP 4
28 units. 1/2 mi w of I-15; from I-15 & westbound I-40, E Main St exit. 1281 E Main St. (92311) A/C; C/CATV; phones. Pool. Wkly & monthly rates avail. AE, DS, MC, VI. *(See ad below)* ⊗ Ⓓ (619) 256-6836

Best Western Desert Villa Motel Rates Subject to Change *Motel* ◆◆◆
⑯ All year [CP] 1P 48.00- 58.00 2P/1B 50.00- 60.00 2P/2B 52.00- 62.00 XP 4
Senior discount. 97 units. Adjacent to I-40, exit Montara; 1/2 mi e of I-15 & Main St exits. 1984 E Main St. (92311) A/C; C/CATV; movies; phones. Coin laundry. Pool; whirlpool. No pets. 9 efficiencies, $5 extra; no utensils. 18 deluxe suites. AE, CB, DI, MC, VI. Coffeeshop; 4:30 pm-9 pm; $6.95-$8.25; cocktails. FAX (619) 256-9265 Ⓓ Ⓛ (619) 256-1781

Desert Inn Motel Rates Subject to Change *Motel* ◆
⑯ All year 1P .... 28.00 2P/1B .... 38.00 2P/2B .... 38.00 XP 6
95 units. 3/4 mi w of I-15; from I-15 & westbound I-40, E Main St exits. 1100 E Main St. (92311) 32 refrigerators; A/C; C/CATV; movies; 54 radios; phones; shower baths. 12 2-bedrm units. Htd pool. Pets. Reserv deposit required. AE, CB, DI, MC, VI. Restaurant adjacent. Ⓓ (619) 256-2146

Econo Lodge Rates Subject to Change *Motel* ◆◆
⑯ 6/15-9/15 1P 27.95- 39.95 2P/1B 32.95- 52.95 2P/2B 32.95- 52.95 XP 5
9/16-6/14 1P 24.95- 34.95 2P/1B 28.95- 48.95 2P/2B 28.95- 48.95 XP 5
50 units. 3/4 mi w of I-15; from I-15 & westbound I-40, E Main St exits. 1230 E Main St. (92311) 49 refrigerators; A/C; C/CATV; movies; phones; shower or comb baths. 2 kitchens. Htd pool. Pets, $10 deposit required. Wkly & monthly rates avail. Reserv deposit required; 3 days refund notice. AE, DI, DS, MC, VI. *(See ad p A68)* ⊗ Ⓓ (619) 256-2133

Gateway Motel Rates Subject to Change *Motel* ◆
⑯ All year 1P 22.00- 28.00 2P/1B 25.00- 32.00 2P/2B 32.00- 40.00 XP 3
Senior discount. 33 units. 1/4 mi w of I-15; from I-15 & westbound I-40, E Main St exits. 1630 E Main St. (92311) A/C; C/CATV; radios; phones. Pool. Pets. Wkly rates avail. AE, DI, DS, MC, VI. Coffeeshop adjacent. Ⓓ (619) 256-8931

Howard Johnson Lodge — Rates Subject to Change — *Motel* ◆◆
All year   1P 55.00- 65.00   2P/1B   60.00- 70.00   2P/2B   65.00- 75.00   XP 10
64 units. 1/2 mi w of I-15; from I-15 & westbound I-40, E Main St exits. 1431 E Main St. (92311) A/C; C/CATV; movies; phones. Coin laundry. Htd pool; wading pool. No pets. AE, DI, DS, MC, VI. Restaurant adjacent. FAX (619) 256-8392
⊗ Ⓓ (619) 256-0661

Quality Inn ⑭ — Rates Subject to Change — *Motor Inn* ◆◆
All year   1P 46.00- 64.00   2P/1B   49.00- 64.00   2P/2B   .... 55.00 XP 5
Senior discount. 100 units. 1/4 mi w of I-15; from I-15 & westbound I-40, E Main St exits. 1520 E Main St. (92311) A/C; C/CATV; free & pay movies; 30 radios; phones. Coin laundry. Htd pool. Pets. Refrigerator, $5 extra. Reserv deposit required; 7 days refund notice. AE, DI, DS, MC, VI. ● Dining rm; 6 am-10 pm; $7.95-$18.95; cocktails. FAX (619) 256-3850
⊗ Ⓓ Ⓢ (619) 256-6891

Sleep Inn ⑭ — AAA Special Value Rates — *Motel* ◆◆
All year   1P .... 32.95   2P/1B   .... 38.95   2P/2B   .... 49.95 XP 6   F
65 units. 1 1/2 mi w on Business Rt 15. 1841 W Main St. (92311) A/C; C/CATV; movies; VCPs. Phones; shower or comb baths. Small pool. No pets. Reserv deposit required. AE, DI, DS, MC, VI. Coffeeshop opposite. FAX (619) 256-6825
⊗ Ⓢ Ⓓ (619) 256-1300

Stardust Inn ⑭ — Rates Subject to Change — *Motel* ◆
All year   1P 24.00- 30.00   2P/1B   28.00- 35.00   2P/2B   35.00- 45.00 XP 3
24 units. 1 1/4 mi w of I-15; from I-15 & westbound I-40, E Main St exits. 901 E Main St. (92311) 18 refrigerators; A/C; C/CATV; movies; radios; phones. Pool. No pets. 4-night minimum stay in 6 kitchens, $5 extra; no utensils. Wkly rates avail. Reserv deposit required. AE, DI, DS, MC, VI.
Ⓓ Ⓢ (619) 256-7116

Vagabond Inn ⑭ — Rates Subject to Change — *Motel* ◆
All year [CP]   1P 38.00- 51.00   2P/1B   43.00- 58.00   2P/2B   48.00- 63.00 XP 5   F
67 units. 3/4 mi w of I-15; from I-15 & westbound I-40, E Main St exits. 1243 E Main St. (92311) A/C; C/CATV; movies; rental VCPs. Radios; phones. Rental refrigerators. 2 2-bedrm units. Htd pool. Pets, $5 extra charge. AE, DI, DS, MC, VI. Coffeeshop opposite. FAX (619) 256-1451 *(See ad below)*
⊗ Ⓓ (619) 256-5601

RESTAURANTS

Garden Court Cafe — American — $ ◆◆
1/4 mi w of I-15: from I-15 & westbound I-40, e Main St exits. 1505 E Main St. A/C. Open 6 am-10 pm. Cocktails & lounge. MC, VI.
⊗ (619) 256-8806

Idle Spurs Steak House ⑭ — Steakhouse — $$ ◆◆◆
On SR 58W; 3 mi w of I-15. 29557 Hwy 58W. Attractive western decor with enclosed patio dining area. Also features prime rib & seafood. A/C. Open 11 am-2:30 & 5-9:30 pm; Fri-10:30 pm; Sat 5 pm-10:30 pm; Sun 5 pm-9 pm; closed 1/1, 11/25 & 12/25. Cocktails & lounge. MC, VI.
(619) 256-8888

BASS LAKE — 200

Ducey's on the Lake ⑭ — Rates Subject to Change — *Resort Motor Inn* ◆◆◆
4/1-10/31   1P 160.00- 195.00   2P/1B   160.00- 195.00   ....   XP 10
11/1-3/31   1P 105.00- 160.00   2P/1B   105.00- 160.00   ....   XP 10
20 units. 6 mi e of SR 41 via Rd 222 & 274, then s on Rd 434; in Pines Village. (PO Box 329, 93604) Fireplaces, wet bars, decks & lake view. Check-in 3 pm. Refrigerators; A/C; C/CATV; pay movies; radios; phones. Coin laundry. Pool; whirlpool; fishing; tennis-2 courts; exercise rm. Fee for: marina & ramp, water skiing. No pets. 2 units with 2 fireplace & whirlpool bath, $175 off season; $300 in season for up to 2 persons. 2 night minimum stay weekends. Wkly rates avail. Reserv deposit required. CB, DI, MC, VI. ● Dining rm & coffeeshop; 11 am-10 pm; $13-$22; cocktail lounge; entertainment. FAX (209) 642-3902
⊗ Ⓢ Ⓓ (209) 642-3131

The Pines Resort ⑭ — Rates Subject to Change — *Cottages* ◆◆◆
4/1-10/31   1P 125.00- 160.00   2P/1B   125.00- 160.00   2P/2B   125.00- 160.00 XP 6   F
11/1-3/31   1P 88.00- 120.00   2P/1B   88.00- 120.00   2P/2B   88.00- 120.00 XP 6   F
84 units. Exit e off SR 41, 6 mi e on Rd 222 & 274, then s on Rd 434; in Pines Village. (PO Box 329, 93604) 1-bedroom duplexes with kitchen, some with view of lake; most with fireplace. Check-in 3 pm. C/CATV; radios; phones. Coin laundry. Swimming; sauna; whirlpool; fishing; water skiing; tennis-2 courts. No pets. 2-night minimum stay weekends. Wkly rates avail. Reserv deposit required. CB, DI, MC, VI. ● Restaurant; 7 am-9 pm; Fri & Sat-10 pm; $6-$16. FAX (209) 642-3902 *(See ad p A552)*
Ⓓ (209) 642-3121

BEAUMONT — 9,700

Best Western El Rancho Motel ⑭ — Rates Subject to Change — *Motor Inn* ◆◆
All year   1P 40.00- 43.00   2P/1B   43.00- 46.00   2P/2B   46.00- 52.00 XP 2
Senior discount. 52 units. Adjacent to I-10, exit Beaumont Ave. 550 Beaumont Ave. (92223) A/C; C/CATV; movies; phones; shower or comb baths. 4 2-bedrm units. Htd pool. No pets. AE, DI, DS, MC, VI. ● Restaurant; 6 am-9:30 pm; $5.95-$9.25; cocktails. FAX (909) 845-7559
⊗ Ⓓ (909) 845-2176

Golden West Motel ⑭ — AAA Special Value Rates — *Motel* ◆◆
All year   1P .... 32.00   2P/1B   .... 36.00   2P/2B   .... 40.00 XP 3
Senior discount. 24 units. Adjacent to I-10 exit Beaumont Ave, then 2 blks e. 625 E 5th St. (92223) A/C; C/TV; movies; radios; phones; shower baths. 2 2-bedrm units. Small pool; whirlpool. Pets, $2 extra charge. Wkly rates avail. Reserv deposit required. AE, DI, DS, MC, VI.
Ⓓ (909) 845-2185

Highland Springs Resort Rates Subject to Change *Resort Complex* ◆◆
All year [MAP] 1P 120.00- 235.00 .... 2P/2B 140.00- 255.00 XP 45-55
94 units. 3 mi n of I-10, Highland Springs Ave exit. (PO Box 218, Cherry Valley, 92223) Long-established resort on several acres of tree-shaded grounds. Small, modestly furnished to large nicely furnished rooms. Check-in 3 pm. Refrigerators; A/C; C/TV; radios; phones; comb & shower baths. Htd pool; saunas; whirlpool; tennis-3 courts, 2 lighted; children's program in summer; rental bicycles; exercise rm. No pets. Reserv deposit required; 3 days refund notice. MC, VI. Dining rm; open to public by reservation only; cocktails. FAX (909) 845-8090 (D) (909) 845-1151

Windsor Motel Rates Guaranteed *Motel* ◆
🐾 All year 1P .... 26.00 2P/1B .... 28.00 2P/2B .... 30.00 XP 2
Senior discount. 16 units. From I-10, westbound exit Pennsylvania Ave, eastbound exit Beaumont Ave; 1 mi e of Beaumont Ave. 1265 E 6th St. (92223) Refrigerators; A/C; C/CATV; movies; VCPs. 4 radios; phones; shower or comb baths. Pool; whirlpool. Small pets only, $2 extra. 1 room with whirlpool spa, $55-$60. Wkly rates avail. Reserv deposit required. AE, MC, VI. FAX (909) 845-1436 ⊗ (D) (909) 845-1436

BELLFLOWER — 61,800

RESTAURANT

Furr's Family Dining American $ ◆◆
1/4 mi w of I-605. 10460 Rosecrans Ave. Formerly Furr's Cafeteria. Large selection of salads, entrees & desserts. A/C. Open 11 am-8 pm; Fri & Sat-8:30 pm; Sun 11 am-8 pm. AE, MC, VI. ⊗ (310) 804-4611

BELL GARDENS — 42,400

Fiesta Inn Rates Subject to Change *Motel* ◆◆
🐾 All year 1P 40.00- 50.00 2P/1B 40.00- 50.00 2P/2B 51.00- 61.00 XP 5
50 units. 1 1/2 mi e of I-710, exit Florence Ave. 6442 Florence Ave. (90201) 25 refrigerators; A/C; C/TV; movies; phones. Coin laundry. Htd pool. No pets. 2 rooms with whirlpool tub, $70-$90. 1 suite with whirlpool tub, $120. Wkly rates avail. AE, DI, DS, MC, VI. FAX (310) 928-5159 ⊗ (D) (玉) (310) 928-6252

Quality Inn Rates Subject to Change *Motel* ◆◆
All year 1P 65.00- 98.00 2P/1B 71.00- 104.00 2P/2B 71.00- 104.00 XP 6
118 units. 3 blks se of I-710; use Florence Ave exit. 7330 Eastern Ave. (90201) Rooms & 1-bedroom suites with living room. Refrigerators; A/C; C/CATV; movies; radios; phones. Coin laundry. Htd pool; whirlpool; 5 rooms with whirlpool tub. No pets. AE, DI, DS, MC, VI. FAX (310) 928-9851 ⊗ (D) (玉) (310) 928-3452

**BELMONT — 24,100   (See SAN FRANCISCO (Southern Region) AREA spotting map page A444;
see index starting on page A443)**

Holiday Inn-Belmont 〔107〕 AAA Special Value Rates *Motor Inn* ◆◆
🐾 All year 1P 65.00- 90.00 2P/1B 65.00- 90.00 2P/2B 65.00- 90.00 XP 10 F
Senior discount. 191 units. E of US 101, exit Ralston/Marine World Pkwy, s on Shoreway Rd. 1101 Shoreway Rd. (94002) 51 refrigerators; A/C; C/CATV; free & pay movies; radios; phones. 1 2-bedrm unit, 1 kitchen. Coin laundry. Pool; whirlpool. Airport transp. No pets. 1-bedroom unit with living room & kitchen, $125 for 2 persons. AE, DI, DS, MC, VI. ● Restaurant; 6 am-10 & 11:30-10 pm; $8-$16; cocktails; entertainment. FAX (415) 593-6415 ⊗ (D) (玉) (415) 591-1471

RESTAURANTS

Lemon Tree 〔48〕 American $$ ◆◆
W of El Camino Real. 968 Ralston Ave. Casual family atmosphere, emphasis on fresh ingredients. Smoke free premises. A/C. Children's menu. Open 6:30 am-9:30 pm; Sat 7 am-9:30 pm; Sun 8 am-9 pm; closed 11/25 & 12/25. Beer & wine. Reserv advised. MC, VI. ⊗ (415) 592-7273

Pine Brook Inn 〔47〕 Continental $$ ◆◆
At Ralston Ave; in Carlmont Village Shopping Center. 1015 Alameda de las Pulgas. Popular, long established, family owned; fresh seafood & German specialties, some tables have brookside view. A/C. Early bird specials; children's menu. Open 11:30 am-2:30 & 5:30-9:30 pm; Fri-10 pm; Sat 11:30 am-10 pm; Sun 10:30 am-2 & 5-9 pm; closed major holidays, 1/1-1/7 & 7/1-7/7. Cocktails & lounge. Reserv advised. AE, MC, VI. ⊗ (415) 591-1735

BENICIA — 24,400

Best Western Heritage Inn Rates Guaranteed *Motel* ◆◆◆
🐾 All year [OP] 1P 60.00- 65.00 2P/1B .... 65.00 2P/2B .... 60.00 XP 5 F
101 units. E off I-780, exit Central Benicia/E 2nd St. 1955 E 2nd St. (94510) 40 refrigerators; A/C; C/CATV; movies; phones. 7 efficiencies. Small pool; whirlpool. Pets, $50 deposit required. 2 units with kitchen, $90 for 2 persons. 30 rooms with whirlpool tubs, $67. AE, DI, DS, MC, VI. FAX (707) 745-0842 *(See ad p A364)* ⊗ (S) (D) (玉) (707) 746-0401

Union Hotel AAA Special Value Rates *Historic Hotel* ◆◆
🐾 Fri & Sat [CP] 1P 95.00- 135.00 2P/1B 95.00- 135.00 .... XP 15
Sun-Thurs [CP] 1P 80.00- 115.00 2P/1B 80.00- 115.00 .... XP 15
12 units. 2 mi sw of I-780 via 2nd St exit; Central Benicia. 401 1st St. (94510) Restored 1882 hotel, furnished in antiques. Few units with view of waterfront. Check-in 3 pm. A/C; C/CATV; phones. All rooms with whirlpool tub. Parking lot. No pets. Reserv deposit required. AE, DI, DS, MC, VI. ● Restaurant, see separate listing. (D) (707) 746-0100

RESTAURANTS

Stevenson's Mallard House Continental $$ ◆
🐾 Exit I-780 at e 2nd St. 1654 E 2nd St. Varied menu; comfortable atmosphere, seafood & pasta specialties. A/C. Children's menu. Open 11:30 am-3 & 5-10 pm; Fri-11 pm; Sat 5 pm-11 pm; Sun 4 pm-9 pm; closed major holidays & week of July 4th. Lounge. AE, CB, DI, MC, VI. ⊗ (707) 746-1747

Union Hotel Restaurant American $$$ ◆◆
In Union Hotel. Historic 1882 hotel, emphasis on fresh local ingredients & creative preparation. Smoke free premises. A/C. Open 11:30 am-2:30 & 6-10 pm; Sun 9:30 am-2:30 & 6-9:30 pm. Cocktails & lounge. Reserv advised. MC, VI. ⊗ (707) 746-0100

BEN LOMOND — 7,200

Ben Lomond Hylton Motel		Rates Subject to Change			Motel	◆
㊹ Fri & Sat 7/1-9/30	1P 60.00	2P/1B 66.00	2P/2B 70.00	XP 6		
Fri & Sat 5/1-6/30	1P 50.00	2P/1B 54.00	2P/2B 58.00	XP 6		
Sun-Thurs 5/1-9/30	1P 42.00	2P/1B 48.00	2P/2B 54.00	XP 6		
10/1-4/30	1P 38.00	2P/1B 44.00	2P/2B 48.00	XP 6		

21 units. 1/4 mi n on SR 9; on San Lorenzo River. 9733 Hwy 9. (95005) In the redwoods. C/CATV; phones; comb or shower baths. Pool; fishing. No pets. 1 apartment & 1 housekeeping cottage, $12 extra. Wkly rates avail. Reserv deposit required. AE, MC, VI.   Ⓧ Ⓓ (408) 336-2292

BERKELEY — 102,700   (See OAKLAND/BERKELEY AREA spotting map pages A300 & A301; see index starting on page A298)

Berkeley Marina Marriott ㉚		Rates Subject to Change		Motor Inn	◆◆◆
All year	1P 99.00- 155.00	2P/1B 99.00- 155.00	2P/2B 99.00- 155.00	XP 12	

373 units. On Berkeley Marina, exit I-80 University Ave w 1/2 mi. 200 Marina Blvd. (94710) Some rooms with view of Marina & San Francisco Bay. Check-in 3 pm. A/C; C/CATV; movies; radios; phones. Coin laundry. 2 htd indoor pools, 1 small; sauna; whirlpools; dock; pier; health club. No pets. AE, DI, DS, MC, VI. ● Restaurant; 6:30 am-10 pm; Sat 7 am-11 pm; $11-$20; cocktails; entertainment. FAX (510) 548-7944   Ⓧ Ⓢ Ⓓ (510) 548-7920

Golden Bear Motel ㉙		Rates Subject to Change		Motel	◆
㊹ All year	1P 45.00	2P/1B 45.00	2P/2B 49.00	XP 4	

42 units. Exit I-80 Gilman St e, 3/4 mi s on SR 123. 1620 San Pablo Ave. (94702) C/TV; radios; phones; shower or comb baths. 4 2-bedrm units. AE, CB, DI, MC, VI. Coffeeshop adjacent.   Ⓓ (510) 525-6770

Hotel Durant ㉛		Rates Subject to Change		Hotel	◆◆
㊹ All year [CP]	1P 73.00- 78.00	2P/1B 83.00- 88.00	2P/2B 83.00- 88.00	XP 10	

Senior discount. 140 units. E off I-80 on Ashby to Telegraph then n to Durant; westbound from SR 13 & 24 exit Berkeley, w on Ashby to Telegraph, then n to Durant. 2600 Durant Ave. (94704) 1 block from university. C/CATV; movies; radios; phones; comb or shower baths. Pay parking lot & garage. Airport transp. No pets. Reserv deposit required. AE, DI, DS, MC, VI. ● Dining rm; 11:30 am-10 pm; $7.50-$16; cocktails. FAX (510) 486-8336   Ⓧ Ⓓ (510) 845-8981

RESTAURANTS

Skates on the Bay ㉙	American	$$	◆◆

On Berkeley Marina, exit I-80 University Ave, w 1/4 mi. 100 Seawall Dr. Varied menu, mesquite grilled fish, duck & pasta. Casual atmosphere with view of bay. A/C. Children's menu. Open 11:15 am-3 pm & 5-10 pm; Fri & Sat-10:30 pm; Sun 10:15 am-3 & 4-10:30 pm; closed 7/4 & 12/25. Cocktails & lounge. Reserv advised. AE, MC, VI.   Ⓧ (510) 549-1900

Spenger's Fish Grotto ㉚	Seafood	$$	◆

3 blks e off I-80, University Ave exit. 1919 4th St. Very popular & lively; rustic-nautical atmosphere. Oyster bar 11:30 am-8:30 pm. A/C. Children's menu. Open 6 am-11 pm; Thurs-Sun to midnight; closed 11/26 & 12/25. Cocktails & lounge. Reserv advised. AE, DI, DS, MC, VI.   Ⓧ (510) 845-7771

BERMUDA DUNES   (92201) — 103,700

The New Inn at Bermuda Dunes Country Club	Rates Subject to Change			Motel	◆◆◆
11/1-6/30	1P 105.00	2P/1B 105.00	2P/2B 125.00	XP	
7/1-10/31	1P 75.00	2P/1B 75.00	2P/2B 90.00	XP	

41 units. From I-10, exit Washington St; 1 1/2 mi se via 42nd Ave. 42-325 Adams St. Some units overlook 17th fairway of Bermuda Dunes golf course. A/C; C/CATV; radios; phones; shower or comb baths. Htd pool; whirlpool. No pets. 9 2-bedroom villas with private outdoor spa, $175-$250 for 2 persons. Monthly rates avail. Reserv deposit required. AE, DS, MC, VI. FAX (619) 322-5428   Ⓓ (619) 345-2577

BEVERLY HILLS — 32,000   (See LOS ANGELES (Central & Western Areas) spotting map pages A212 & A213; see index starting on page A210)   See also LOS ANGELES (Central & Western Areas)

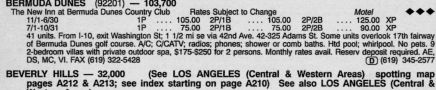

Beverly Hilton ⑲⓪	Rates Subject to Change			Hotel	◆◆◆
㊹ All year	1P 190.00- 230.00	2P/1B 210.00- 250.00	....	XP 20	F

Senior discount. 592 units. 9876 Wilshire Blvd at Santa Monica Blvd. (90210) Very popular, elegant hotel. Refrigerators; A/C; C/CATV; movies; radios; phones. Htd pool; wading pool; exercise rm. Pay valet garage & parking ramp. Pets. Wkly & monthly rates avail. AE, DI, DS, MC, VI. ● Dining rm, restaurant & 2 coffeeshops; 6:30 am-11 pm; $6-$20. Also, L'Escoffier & Trader Vic's, see separate listing. FAX (310) 285-1313 *(See ad p 22)*   Ⓧ Ⓢ Ⓓ (310) 274-7777

The Peninsula Beverly Hills ⑱⑧	Rates Subject to Change			Hotel	◆◆◆◆
All year	1P 265.00- 320.00	2P/1B 265.00- 320.00	2P/2B 265.00- 320.00	XP	

200 units. 9882 Santa Monica Blvd at Wilshire Blvd. (90212) An elegant hotel with luxurious public areas. Afternoon tea served from 3 pm-6 pm. A/C; C/CATV; VCPs; radios; phones. 3 pools; sauna; heated rooftop pool & whirlpool; steamroom; health club. Fee for: massage. Pay valet garage. No pets. 32 suites in main building & 16 suites in 5 2-story villas; some with private terrace & fireplace, $340-$625. Reserv deposit required. AE, CB, DI, MC, VI. ● 2 dining rms; 6:30 am-11 pm; a la carte entrees about $12-$40; 24 hour room service; cocktails; entertainment. Also, The Georgian Room, see separate listing. A *Preferred Hotel.* FAX (310) 858-6663   Ⓧ Ⓢ Ⓓ Ⓚ (310) 273-4888

Regent Beverly Wilshire ⑱⑨	Rates Subject to Change			Hotel	◆◆◆
All year	1P 255.00- 600.00	2P/1B 255.00- 600.00	2P/2B 255.00- 600.00	XP 30	

383 units. 9500 Wilshire Blvd at Rodeo Dr. (90212) Refrigerators; A/C; C/CATV; radios; phones. Htd pool; saunas. Fee for: health club & massage. Pay valet garage. No pets. Monthly rates avail. AE, CB, DI, MC, VI. ● Dining rm & coffeeshop; 7 am-11 pm; $10-$30; cocktails; entertainment. FAX (310) 274-2851   Ⓓ (310) 275-5200

RESTAURANTS

El Torito Grill ⑨③	Mexican	$$	◆◆◆

At Camden Dr. 9595 Wilshire Blvd. Contemporary Southwestern cuisine. A/C. Open 11 am-10 pm; Fri & Sat-11 pm; Sun 10 am-10 pm; closed 11/25 & 12/25. Cocktails & lounge. Reserv advised. AE, CB, DI, MC, VI.   Ⓧ (310) 550-1599

La Scala Boutique ⑧⑨	Italian	$$$	◆◆◆

410 N Canon Dr. Italian-oriented continental menu. A/C. Open 11:30 am-2:30 & 5:30-11 pm; Sat 11:30 am-11 pm; closed Sun & major holidays. Cocktails. Valet parking. Reserv required. AE, CB, DI, MC, VI.   Ⓧ (310) 275-0579

La Veranda ⑨⑥	Ethnic	$$$	◆◆◆

2 blks s of Wilshire Blvd. 225 S Beverly Dr. California-Italian cuisine. A/C. Open 11:30 am-2 & 5-10:30 pm; Fri-11:30 pm; Sat 5 pm-11:30 pm; closed Sun. Cocktails & lounge. Valet parking. Reserv advised. AE, DI, MC, VI. Ⓧ (310) 274-7246

You'll love the look, the touch, the feeling... *the total value experience.*

• Large, quiet, stylish rooms • Free cable tv • Free local calls • Free Continental breakfasts at many locations • Non-smoker and smoker rooms • Children stay free • Free coffee in the lobby • Adjacent restaurants • **AAA** approved at over 200 locations coast-to-coast

LA QUINTA INNS®
America's Hotel Value℠

RESERVATIONS **1-800-531-5900**   © 1992, La Quinta Motor Inns, Inc.

LA QUINTA INNS®
America's Hotel Value℠

NEW MEXICO
Albuquerque (3)
Farmington
Las Cruces
Santa Fe

NORTH CAROLINA
Charlotte (2)

OHIO
Cincinnati-Sharonville
Columbus

OKLAHOMA
Oklahoma City (2)
Tulsa (3)

PENNSYLVANIA
Pittsburgh

SOUTH CAROLINA
Charleston
Columbia
Greenville

TENNESSEE
Knoxville
Memphis (3)
Nashville (2)

TEXAS
Abilene
Amarillo (2)
Arlington
Austin (5)
Baytown
Beaumont
Brownsville
Clute
College Station
Corpus Christi (2)
Dallas (14)
Denton
Eagle Pass
El Paso (3)
Fort Worth (2)
Galveston
Harlingen

Houston (16)
Killeen
La Porte
Laredo
Longview
Lubbock
Lufkin
McAllen
Midland
Nacogdoches
Odessa
Round Rock
San Angelo
San Antonio (11)
Temple
Texarkana
Texas City
Tyler
Victoria
Waco
Wichita Falls

UTAH
Layton
Salt Lake City-
  Midvale

VIRGINIA
Hampton/Newport
  News
Richmond
Virginia Beach

WASHINGTON
Seattle (2)
Tacoma

WYOMING
Casper
Cheyenne
Rock Springs

MEXICO
Saltillo
  Opening Soon

ALABAMA
Birmingham
Huntsville (2)
Mobile
Montgomery
Tuscaloosa

ARIZONA
Phoenix
Tempe
Tucson (2)

ARKANSAS
Little Rock (4)

CALIFORNIA
Bakersfield
Costa Mesa
Fresno
Irvine
Sacramento
San Bernardino
San Diego (2)
San Francisco
Stockton
Ventura
Vista

COLORADO
Colorado Springs
Denver (7)

FLORIDA
Altamonte Springs
Clearwater
Daytona Beach
Deerfield Beach
Fort Myers
Gainesville
Jacksonville (3)
Miami
Orlando
Pensacola
Pinellas Park
St. Petersburg
Tallahassee (2)
Tampa (2)

GEORGIA
Atlanta (7)
Augusta
Columbus
Savannah

ILLINOIS
Champaign
Chicago (5)
Moline

INDIANA
Indianapolis (2)
Merrillville

KANSAS
Kansas City-Lenexa
Wichita

KENTUCKY
Lexington

LOUISIANA
Baton Rouge
Bossier City
Lafayette
Monroe
New Orleans (5)
Sulphur/Lake Charles

MICHIGAN
Kalamazoo

MISSISSIPPI
Jackson

MISSOURI
St. Louis

NEBRASKA
Omaha

NEVADA
Las Vegas
Reno

RESERVATIONS
1-800-531-5900

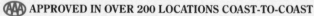

(See LOS ANGELES (Central & Western Areas) spotting map pages A212 & A213)

Lawry's The Prime Rib 88 American $$$ ◆◆◆
1/2 blk n of Wilshire Blvd. 55 N La Cienega Blvd. Famous for its 1 entree of prime rib. A/C. Children's menu. Open 5 pm-11 pm; Fri & Sat-midnight; Sun 3 pm-10 pm; closed 7/4 & 12/25. Cocktails & lounge. Pay valet parking. AE, CB, DI, MC, VI. ⊗ (310) 652-2827

L'Escoffier 90 French $$$$
On top floor of The Beverly Hilton. Elegant decor. A/C. Dress code. Open 6:30 pm-10:30 pm; Fri & Sat-11:30 pm; closed Sun, 11/25 & 12/25. Cocktails. Entertainment & dancing. Valet parking. Reserv required. AE, DI, DS, MC, VI. *(See ad p 22)* ⊗ (310) 285-1333

Matsuhisa 95 Ethnic $$$$ ◆◆◆
129 N La Cienega Blvd. Extensive Japanese entrees featuring sushi & seafood. A/C. Open 11:45 am-2:15 & 5:45-10:15 pm. Beer & wine. Valet parking. Reserv required. AE, MC, VI. (310) 659-9639

Prego 94 Italian $$$ ◆◆◆
1 blk n of Wilshire Blvd. 362 N Camden Dr. Northern Italian cuisine featuring homemade pasta & grilled seafood entrees. A/C. Open 11:30 am-midnight; Sun 5:30 pm-midnight. Cocktails & lounge. Valet parking. Reserv advised. AE, DI, MC, VI. ⊗ (310) 277-7346

Ruth's Chris Steak House 92 American $$$ ◆◆◆
2 blks s of Wilshire Blvd. 224 S Beverly Dr. Nicely decorated; casual atmosphere. A/C. Open 11:30 am-3 & 5-10 pm; Fri-11 pm; Sat 5 pm-11 pm; Sun 5 pm-10 pm; closed major holidays. Cocktails & lounge. Valet parking. Reserv advised. AE, DI, MC, VI. ⊗ (310) 859-8744

Trader Vic's 91 Ethnic $$$ ◆◆◆
In the Beverly Hilton. Large selection of Cantonese & Polynesian cuisine. A/C. Open 5 pm-11:30 pm; closed 11/25 & 12/25. Cocktails & lounge. Valet parking. Reserv advised. AE, DI, DS, MC, VI. *(See ad p 22)* ⊗ (310) 276-6345

BIG BEAR CITY — 11,200 See also BIG BEAR LAKE

Cathy's Country Cottages AAA Special Value Rates *Motel* ◆◆◆
Ⓐ Fri-Sun [CP] .... 2P/1B 89.00- 199.00 .... XP 10
 Mon-Thurs [CP] 1P .... 49.00 2P/1B 69.00- 169.00 .... XP
6 units. On SR 18; 3/4 mi e of Division St across from airport. 600 W Big Bear Blvd. (PO Box 3706, Big Bear Lake, 92315) All rooms with whirlpool tub, fireplace & microwave. 1 small unit. Designated smoking areas. Refrigerators; C/CATV; 5 radios; phones; comb or shower baths. No pets. 2-night minimum stay weekends. Wkly rates avail. Reserv deposit required; 15 days refund notice. CB, DI, DS, MC, VI. ⊗ Ⓓ (909) 866-7567

Gold Mountain Manor Bed & Breakfast Inn Rates Subject to Change *Bed & Breakfast* ◆◆
All year [BP] 1P 75.00- 180.00 2P/1B 75.00- 180.00 .... XP 20
7 units. 2 mi ne, 1 mi e of Division, 1/2 blk n of Northshore Dr. 1117 Anita. (PO Box 2027, 92314) 1931 mountain mansion. Located on 1 acre of pine trees & grassy areas. Most rooms with woodburning fireplace. 3 shower or comb baths. No pets. 1 2-room suite with whirlpool, private bath & entrance, $180; 2-night minimum stay weekends. Monthly rates avail. Reserv deposit required; 7 days refund notice. MC, VI. ⊗ Ⓓ (909) 585-6997

Krausmeier Haus Bavarian Village Rates Subject to Change *Motel* ◆◆
Ⓐ Fri-Sat [CP] 1P 75.00- 110.00 2P/1B 75.00- 110.00 2P/2B 85.00- 110.00 XP 10
 Sun-Thurs [CP] 1P 65.00- 100.00 2P/1B 65.00- 100.00 2P/2B 65.00- 100.00 XP 10
14 units. 1 1/4 mi e on SR 38, 1/4 mi ne on Shay Rd to Midway Blvd. 1351 Midway Blvd. (PO Box 495, 92314) Rooms in lodge & Bavarian style duplex cottages. Spacious grounds in a quiet picturesque setting. Many fireplaces. Comb or shower baths. 2 2-bedrm units, 6 kitchens. Whirlpool. No pets. 2-night minimum stay weekends. Wkly rates avail. Reserv deposit required; 7 days refund notice. MC, VI. *(See ad below)* Ⓓ (909) 585-2886

BIG BEAR LAKE — 5,400 See also BIG BEAR CITY

Bear Manor Rates Subject to Change *Cottages* ◆◆
Ⓐ All year 1P .... 89.00 2P/1B .... 149.00 2P/2B .... 99.00 XP 10
Senior discount. 14 units. 3/4 mi w on SR 18. 40393 Big Bear Blvd. (PO Box 3874, 92315) Tree-shaded grounds. Fireplaces. Check-in 3 pm. C/CATV; phones. 5 efficiencies. No pets. 10 units with whirlpool tub, $159. Wkly rates avail. Reserv deposit required; 30 days refund notice. AE, DS, MC, VI. FAX (909) 866-6530 Ⓓ (909) 866-6817

Bear Manor Too Rates Subject to Change *Motel* ◆◆
Fri & Sat 1P .... 189.00 2P/1B .... 189.00 2P/2B .... 189.00 XP
Sun-Thurs 1P .... 149.00 2P/1B .... 149.00 2P/2B .... 149.00 XP
Senior discount. 7 units. 1/8 mi w on SR 18. 706 Paine Rd. (PO Box 3874, 92315) Each unit with fireplace, washer & dryer. C/CATV; phones. 1 2-bedrm unit, kitchens. Coin laundry. 6 rooms with whirlpool tub. No pets. Wkly rates avail. Reserv deposit required; 30 days refund notice. AE, DS, MC, VI. FAX (909) 866-6530 Ⓓ (909) 866-6800

Big Bear Cabins

		Rates Subject to Change			*Cottages*			
Fri & Sat 11/16-3/14	....	2P/1B	59.00- 99.00	2P/2B	69.00- 99.00	XP 10		
Sun-Thurs 11/16-3/14	....	2P/1B	49.00- 89.00	2P/2B	49.00- 89.00	XP 10		
Fri & Sat 3/15-11/15	....	2P/1B	49.00- 79.00	2P/2B	49.00- 89.00	XP 10		
Sun-Thurs 3/15-11/15	....	2P/1B	49.00- 69.00	2P/2B	49.00- 79.00	XP 10		

Senior discount. 14 units. 1 1/4 mi w on SR 18. 39774 Big Bear Blvd. (PO Box 1533, 92315) Cabins with fireplace; 11 with kitchen. Check-out 10 am. Refrigerators; C/CATV; comb or shower baths. 2 2-bedrm units. Htd pool. Pets, $10 deposit required. Wkly rates avail. Reserv deposit required; 3 days refund notice. MC, VI. *(See ad below)*
Ⓓ (909) 866-2723

Big Bear Lake Inn-Cienega [CP]

		Rates Subject to Change			*Motel*			
Fri & Sat [CP]	....	2P/1B	69.50- 74.50	2P/2B	75.00- 84.50	XP 5	F
Sun-Thurs [CP]	....	2P/1B	46.00- 57.00	2P/2B	56.00- 66.00	XP 5	F

52 units. 2 1/4 mi w on SR 18. 39471 Big Bear Blvd. (PO Box 1665, 92315) Refrigerators; A/C; C/CATV; phones. 9 efficiencies, no utensils. Htd pool; whirlpool. No pets. Reserv deposit required; 3 days refund notice. AE, MC, VI. *(See ad below)*
⊗ Ⓓ (909) 866-3477

Cape Cod Mountain Cottages

		Rates Subject to Change			*Cottages*		
Fri & Sat 11/1-3/31	....	2P/1B	84.00- 145.00	2P/2B	84.00- 145.00	XP
Sun-Thurs 11/1-3/31	....	2P/1B	63.00- 109.00	2P/2B	63.00- 109.00	XP
Fri & Sat 4/1-10/31	....	2P/1B	67.00- 105.00	2P/2B	67.00- 105.00	XP
Sun-Thurs 4/1-10/31	....	2P/1B	51.00- 80.00	2P/2B	51.00- 80.00	XP

12 units. 1/2 mi e on SR 18, 1 blk s. 652 Jeffries. (PO Box 3329, 92315) 6 2-bedroom & 1 1-bedroom 2-story housekeeping units with fireplace; also, 1 2-bedroom & 5 1-bedroom rustic housekeeping cottages. C/CATV; comb or shower baths. Playground. No pets. Rates for up to 6 persons. Wkly rates avail. Reserv deposit required; 15 days refund notice. AE, DS, MC, VI. *(See ad below)*
Ⓓ (909) 866-8296

Club View Chalets ◆◆
⊕ All year .... Rates Subject to Change — Apartment Motel — 2P/1B 55.00- 165.00   2P/2B 95.00- 250.00   XP 30   F
Senior discount. 7 units. 1 1/2 mi e on SR 18, 1 3/4 mi s via Moonridge Rd & Club View Dr at base of Bear Mountain Ski area & Goldmine Golf Course. 1302 Club View Dr. (PO Box 2817, 92315) Pine shaded grounds, many units with fireplace. Additional houses off premises, not AAA approved. C/CATV. No pets. 2 2-bedroom housekeeping units; utensils, deposit required. Wkly rates avail. Reserv deposit required; 30 days refund notice. AE, DS, MC, VI.   (D) (909) 866-5753

Cozy Hollow Lodge ◆◆
⊕ Fri & Sat — Rates Guaranteed — Cottages — 1P 69.00- 79.00   2P/1B 69.00- 79.00   2P/2B 79.00- 129.00   XP 10   F
Sun-Thurs   1P 49.00- 69.00   2P/1B 49.00- 69.00   2P/2B 79.00- 129.00   XP 10   F
10 units. 3/4 mi w on SR 18. 40409 Big Bear Blvd. (PO Box 1288, 92315) Tree-shaded grounds. Fireplaces. Refrigerators; C/CATV; phones. 1 2-bedrm unit, 1 kitchen, 6 efficiencies. Whirlpool; playground. Units with whirlpool, $99-$135. 2-night minimum stay weekends. Pets, $50 cash deposit, $5 extra per pet. Wkly rates avail. Reserv deposit required; 10 days refund notice. AE, DS, MC, VI.   (D) (909) 866-8886

Eagle's Nest Bed & Breakfast ◆◆
⊕ Fri & Sat [CP] .... Rates Guaranteed — Bed & Breakfast — 2P/1B 90.00- 140.00   ....   XP
Sun-Thurs [CP] ....   2P/1B 75.00- 90.00   ....   XP
8 units. 1 mi e on SR 18. 41675 Big Bear Blvd. (PO Box 1003, 92315) Charming bed & breakfast inn with country antiques. 3 additional cottage units with fireplace; breakfast excluded. 3 refrigerators; 3 C/CATV; comb or shower baths. 1 kitchen. Bicycles. Pets, $50 deposit required. 2 units with whirlpool. Wkly rates avail. Reserv deposit required; 14 days refund notice.   ⊗ (D) (909) 866-6465

Forest Shores Estates ◆◆
⊕ Fri & Sat — Rates Subject to Change — Apartment Motel — 1P 95.00- 195.00   2P/1B 95.00- 195.00   2P/2B 95.00- 195.00   XP 5   F
Sun-Thurs   1P 76.00- 156.00   2P/1B 76.00- 156.00   2P/2B 76.00- 156.00   XP 5   F
23 units. 1 blk w of SR 18 on Lakeview Dr. 40670 Lakeview Dr. (PO Box 946, 92315) Lakefront; all units with view of lake. 11 studio units with efficiency & nicely furnished 1-to 3-bedroom apartments. Refrigerators; C/CATV; rental VCPs; radios; phones. Sauna; whirlpool; dock; fishing; water skiing. Garage. No pets. 12 2-bedroom units with kitchen. 2-night minimum stay weekends. Wkly rates avail. Reserv deposit required; 3 days refund notice. AE, CB, DI, MC, VI. *Independant Motels of America. (See ad below)*   (D) (909) 866-6551

Frontier Lodge & Motel ◆
⊕ All year [CP] — Rates Subject to Change — Cottages — 1P 50.00- 85.00   2P/1B 50.00- 85.00   2P/2B 77.00- 132.00   XP 10
Senior discount. 47 units. 1/2 mi w on SR 18. 40472 Big Bear Blvd. (PO Box 687, 92315) Studio units & 1-to 3-bedroom housekeeping cabins with fireplace. Lakefront motel units; also 17 rental cabins off premises, not AAA approved. C/CATV; rental VCPs; 18 radios; phones; comb, shower, or tub baths. 16 kitchens, 12 efficiencies. Pool; saunas; dock; playground. 2-night minimum stay wkends. 3 rms with whirlpool tub, $105; cabins with whirlpool, $150-$250. Pets, $75 deposit, also $15 extra. Permitted in Frontier 2 only. Reserv deposit required; 14 days refund notice. AE, DS, MC, VI. FAX (909) 866-4372   (D) (909) 866-5888

Goldmine Lodge ◆◆
⊕ 11/1-3/31 [CP] — AAA Special Value Rates — Motel — 2P/1B 59.00- 99.00   ....   XP 10   F
4/1-10/31 [CP] ....   2P/1B 49.00- 89.00   ....   XP 10   F
11 units. 1 1/2 mi e on SR 18; 1/4 mi s on Moonridge Rd. 42268 Moonridge Rd. (PO Box 198, 92315) Amid tall pines. C/CATV; movies; radios; phones; shower or comb baths. Whirlpool. No pets. 5 suites with living room, bedroom, kitchen & woodburning fireplace, $79-$129. Wkly rates avail. Reserv deposit required; 3 days refund notice. AE, DS, MC, VI. FAX (909) 866-1592   (D) (909) 866-8786

Grey Squirrel Resort ◆◆◆
⊕ All year — Rates Subject to Change — Cottages — 1P 62.00- 72.00   2P/1B 62.00- 72.00   2P/2B 72.00- 88.00   XP 10
16 units. 2 mi w on SR 18. (PO Box 5404, 92315) Spacious, attractive grounds. 1-to 3-bedroom cottages & 2 motel units. 1 room with whirlpool tub, $110-$125. Pets, $100 deposit; also $5 daily extra charge. Refrigerators; C/CATV; pay movies; rental VCPs. 4 radios; phones; comb or shower baths. 14 kitchens. Coin laundry. Htd pool, enclosed in winter; whirlpool. 2-day minimum stay wkends. 7 2-bedrm cottages with fireplace for up to 6 persons, $72-$115. 3 bedrm cottage for up to 8 persons, $145. Wkly rates avail. Reserv deposit required; 14 days refund notice. AE, DS, MC, VI. FAX (909) 866-6271 *(See ad below)*   (D) (909) 866-4335

Happy Bear Village ◆◆
⊕ All year [CP] — Rates Subject to Change — Cottages — 1P 70.00- 80.00   2P/1B 70.00- 80.00   2P/2B 80.00- 100.00   XP 10
Senior discount. 10 units. 1 mi w on SR 18. 40154 Big Bear Blvd. (PO Box 3939, 92315) All units with fireplace. Large grassy area with barbecue & picnic tables. C/CATV; rental VCPs; 2 radios; phones; shower baths. 5 2-bedrm units, kitchens. Pool; whirlpool; playground. 2-night minimum stay weekends. Pets, $75 deposit required, also $15 daily. Wkly & monthly rates avail. Reserv deposit required; 14 days refund notice. MC, VI. FAX (909) 000-4372   (D) (000) 866-2360

Hillcrest Lodge ◆◆
Rates Subject to Change — *Motel*

⊕ Fri-Sat & 12/16-4/14   1P   59.00- 102.00   2P/1B   59.00- 102.00   2P/2B   69.00- 118.00   XP
Sun-Thurs & 4/15-12/15   1P   35.00- 64.00   2P/1B   35.00- 64.00   2P/2B   .... 64.00   XP
Senior discount. 12 units. 3/4 mi w on SR 18. 40241 Big Bear Blvd. (PO Box 3945, 92315) Many rooms with fireplace. C/CATV; 3 radios; phones; comb or shower baths. 10 kitchens. Whirlpool. No pets. 2 units with whirlpool
tub, $95-$139; 1 2-bedroom unit, $79-$118. Reserv deposit required; 3 days refund notice. AE, DI, DS, MC, VI.
Ⓓ (909) 866-7330

The Inn at Fawnskin Bed & Breakfast   Rates Subject to Change   *Bed & Breakfast* ◆◆
All year [CP]   1P   75.00- 155.00   2P/1B   75.00- 155.00   ....   XP 20
4 units. In Fawnskin; at jct SR 38 & Canyon Rd. 880 Canyon Rd. (PO Box 378, Fawnskin, 92333) Contemporary 2-story
log lodge surrounded by pine trees. Knotty pine interior. Living room equipped with baby grand piano. Designated
smoking areas. Check-in 3 pm. 2 comb baths. 2-night minimum stay weekends. Reserv deposit required; 10 days refund
notice. MC, VI.   ⊗ Ⓓ (909) 866-3200

Janet Kay's   Rates Subject to Change   *Bed & Breakfast* ◆◆◆
Fri & Sat [BP]   1P   69.00- 149.00   2P/1B   89.00- 149.00   2P/2B   89.00- 189.00   XP
Sun-Thurs [BP]   1P   59.00- 129.00   2P/1B   79.00- 129.00   2P/2B   79.00- 149.00   XP
5 units. 1/8 mi w on SR 18. 695 Paine Rd. (PO Box 3874, 92315) Traditional southern colonial house, each room decorated in a different theme. Many rooms with gas fireplace. C/CATV; phones; 4 comb baths. No pets. Suites with whirlpool tub, $149-$199. Wkly & monthly rates avail. Reserv deposit required; 30 days refund notice. AE, DS, MC, VI.
FAX (909) 866-6530   ⊗ Ⓓ (909) 866-6800

The Knickerbocker Mansion Bed & Breakfast   Rates Subject to Change   *Bed & Breakfast* ◆◆
All year [CP]   1P   85.00- 95.00   2P/1B   95.00- 165.00   2P/2B   .... 95.00   XP 10
9 units. 1/4 mi e on SR 18, 1/2 mi s. 869 S Knickerbocker Rd. (92315) Turn-of-the-century 4-story log mansion with
country-motif furnishings. Grounds surrounded by heavily wooded forest. Smoke free premises. C/CATV; 7 comb baths.
Whirlpool. No pets. Suite with whirlpool, $165. 2-night minimum stay weekends. Wkly rates avail. Reserv deposit re-
quired; 7 days refund notice. MC, VI.   ⊗ Ⓢ Ⓓ (909) 866-8221

Marina Riviera Resort   Rates Subject to Change   *Motel* ◆◆◆
⊕ Fri & Sat   ....   2P/1B   89.00- 99.00   2P/2B   89.00- 99.00   XP 8
Sun-Thurs   ....   2P/1B   75.00- 85.00   2P/2B   75.00- 85.00   XP 8
41 units. 1 blk w of SR 18, Pine Knot Blvd. 40770 Lakeview Dr. (Box 979, 92315) Lakefront. All rooms with lake
view. Nicely furnished rooms; many with private patio. Check-in 3 pm. 7 refrigerators; C/CATV; radios; phones.
Htd pool; beach; whirlpool. Fee for: dock. No pets. 3 efficiencies, $105-$150; 13 rooms with whirlpool tub, $85-
$115. Reserv deposit required; 7 days refund notice. MC, VI. Restaurant opposite. FAX (909) 866-6705 *(See ad
below)*   ⊗ Ⓓ (909) 866-7545

Pine Knot Guest Ranch   Rates Guaranteed   *Cottages*
⊕ 11/22-4/15   ....   2P/1B   .... 149.00   2P/2B   .... 149.00   XP 10   F
4/16-11/21   ....   2P/1B   .... 129.00   2P/2B   .... 129.00   XP 10   F
Senior discount. 5 units. 1/4 mi s of SR 18. 888 Pine Knot Blvd. (92315) Rating withheld pending completion of
construction. Scheduled to open Aug 1992. 5 individual cabins with fireplace, in-room jaccuzzi, microwave & refrigerator. C/CATV; VCPs; radios; phones; shower baths. Bicycles. No pets. Reserv deposit required. AE, DS,
MC, VI.   ⊗ Ⓓ (909) 866-6500

Robinhood Inn & Lodge · · · · · AAA Special Value Rates · · · · · *Motel* ◆

Fri-Sun [CP]		·······	2P/1B	89.00- 109.00		·······	XP 10	F
Mon-Thurs [CP]	1P	.... 69.00	2P/1B	69.00- 89.00		·······	XP 10	F

21 units. On SR 18; Lakeview Dr at Pine Knot Blvd. (PO Box 3706, 92315) Some rooms with fireplace. 3 refrigerators; C/CATV; phones. 4 2-bedrm units, 1 kitchen. Whirlpool. No pets. 2-night minimum stay weekends. 4 rooms with whirlpool tub, $139-$199. Wkly rates avail. Reserv deposit required; 15 days refund notice. DI, DS, MC, VI. (D) (909) 866-4643

Sleepy Forest Cottages · · · · · AAA Special Value Rates · · · · · *Cottages* ◆◆◆

Fri-Sun [CP]		·······	2P/1B	99.00- 179.00		·······	XP 10	F
Mon-Thurs [CP]	1P	.... 59.00	2P/1B	79.00- 159.00		·······	XP 10	F

17 units. 1 mi e on SR 18, 1 blk n. 426 Eureka Dr. (PO Box 3706, 92315) Pine shaded grounds. Refrigerators; C/CATV; pay movies; phones; comb or shower baths. 1 2-bedrm unit, 1 kitchen, 7 efficiencies. Coin laundry. 4 rooms with whirlpool tub. No pets. Fireplaces. 2-night minumum stay weekends. 1 2-story unit with loft bedroom. 1 deluxe unit $189-$229. Wkly rates avail. Reserv deposit required; 15 days refund notice. CB, DI, DS, MC, VI. ⊗ (D) (909) 866-7567

Thundercloud Resort · · · · · Rates Subject to Change · · · · · *Motel* ◆

Fri & Sat 11/1-3/31	1P	.... 85.00	2P/1B	.... 85.00	2P/2B	.... 85.00	XP 10			F
Fri & Sat 4/1-10/31	1P	.... 75.00	2P/1B	.... 75.00	2P/2B	.... 75.00	XP 10			F
Sun-Thurs 11/1-3/31	1P	.... 65.00	2P/1B	.... 65.00	2P/2B	.... 65.00	XP 10			F
Sun-Thurs 4/1-10/31	1P	.... 55.00	2P/1B	.... 55.00	2P/2B	.... 55.00	XP 10			F

Senior discount. 64 units. 2 blks w on Lakeview Dr. 40598 Lakeview Dr. (PO Box 1773, 92315) Check-in 3 pm. 31 refrigerators; C/CATV; phones; shower or comb baths. 1 2-bedrm unit. Coin laundry. 2 pools, 1 htd, 1 indoor; saunas. No pets. 15 kitchens, $75-$100. Reserv deposit required; 7 days refund notice. AE, CB, DI, MC, VI. FAX (909) 866-4543 *(See ad p A76)* ⊗ (D) (909) 866-7594

Timber Haven Lodge · · · · · AAA Special Value Rates · · · · · *Cottages* ◆◆

Fri-Sun [CP]		·······	2P/1B	109.00- 169.00		·······	XP 10	F
Mon-Thurs [CP]	1P	.... 59.00	2P/1B	79.00- 139.00		·······	XP 10	F

8 units. 1 3/4 mi w on SR 18, 1/4 blk s. 877 Tulip Ln. (PO Box 430, 92315) Pine shaded grounds. All units with fireplace. C/CATV; phones; shower or comb baths. 7 kitchens. Whirlpool. No pets. 1 larger unit, $119-$169 for up to 5 persons. 2-night minimum stay weekends. 1 unit with whirlpool tub. Microwaves. Wkly rates avail. Reserv deposit required; 15 days refund notice. AE, DI, DS, MC, VI. *(See ad below)* (D) (909) 866-3568

Wainwright Inn Bed & Breakfast · · · · · Rates Guaranteed · · · · · *Bed & Breakfast* ◆◆

11/25-4/12 & 7/1-9/7 [BP]		·······	2P/1B	85.00- 145.00		·······	XP	
4/13-6/30 & 9/8-11/24 [BP]		·······	2P/1B	75.00- 120.00		·······	XP	

4 units. 1 1/2 mi e on SR 18; 1 1/2 mi s on Moonridge Rd; 3/4 mi n of Bear Mountain Ski area. 43113 Moonridge Rd. (PO Box M4-6, 92315) Contemporary, 3-story Tudor-style house. Rooms furnished with English & Victorian antiques. Designated smoking areas. Radios; 2 comb baths. Airport transp. No pets. 1 room with whirlpool tub & gas fireplace. 2-night minimum stay weekends. Wkly rates avail. Reserv deposit required; 10 days refund notice. AE, CB, DI, MC, VI. ⊗ (D) (909) 585-6914

Wishing Well Motel · · · · · AAA Special Value Rates · · · · · *Motel* ◆◆

Fri & Sat [CP]		·······	2P/1B	.... 79.00	2P/2B	.... 89.00	XP 10			F
Sun-Thurs [CP]	1P	.... 49.00	2P/1B	.... 59.00	2P/2B	.... 69.00	XP 10			F

15 units. On SR 18, Pine Knot Blvd. 540 Pine Knot Blvd. (PO Box 577, 92315) Pine-shaded grounds in downtown area. C/CATV; radios; phones; shower baths. No pets. Wkly rates avail. Reserv deposit required; 3 days refund notice. AE, CB, DI, MC, VI. Restaurant adjacent. FAX (909) 866-6821 (D) (909) 866-3505

RESTAURANTS

Bear Valley Winery/Vines Restaurant · · · · · Italian · · · · · $$ ◆◆
1/4 mi ne on SR 18. 625 Pine Knot Blvd. A pleasant restaurant with wine tasting room & gift shop. Sun brunch 10 am-2 pm. Early bird specials & senior discount. Open 11:30 am-2:30 & 5:30-9 pm; Fri & Sat-10 pm. Beer & wine. Reserv advised. DS, MC, VI. ⊗ (909) 866-3033

The Iron Squirrel Restaurant · · · · · French · · · · · $$ ◆◆
Downtown; on SR 18. 646 Pine Knot Blvd. A charming restaurant. Sun brunch 10 am-2 pm. Smoke free premises. A/C. Open 5:30 pm-9 pm; Sat from 5 pm; Sun 10 am-2 & 5-9 pm; closed 12/24 & 12/25. Cocktails. Reserv advised. AE, MC, VI. ⊗ (909) 866-9121

BIG PINE — 1,500   See (Do not confuse with BIG PINES & WRIGHTWOOD Recreational Area)

Big Pine Motel · · · · · Rates Subject to Change · · · · · *Motel* ◆◆

4/1-11/31	1P	.... 35.00	2P/1B	.... 38.00	2P/2B	.... 42.00	XP	4
12/1-3/31	1P	.... 30.00	2P/1B	.... 35.00	2P/2B	.... 36.00	XP	4

14 units. On US 395. 370 S Main. (93513) 4 refrigerators; A/C; C/CATV; phones; shower or comb baths. Pets. 2 units with kitchen, $5 extra. Reserv deposit required. AE, MC, VI. (D) (619) 938-2282

Starlight Motel						Motel	◆◆
⊕ 4/1-12/1	1P 32.00	2P/1B 36.00	2P/2B 40.00	XP 5
12/2-3/31	1P 28.00	2P/1B 32.00	2P/2B 36.00	XP 5

8 units. On US 395. 511 S Main St. (PO Box 575, 93513) Refrigerators; A/C; C/CATV; movies; radios; phones; shower baths. Fish cleaning & freezing facilities. No pets. Reserv deposit required; 3 days refund notice. AE, DS, MC, VI.
Ⓓ (619) 938-2011

RESTAURANT

Rossi's Steak & Spaghetti	American	$$	◆◆

On US 395. 100 N Main St. Casual dining in pleasant surroundings. Interesting selection of family & regional memorabilia. A/C. Early bird specials; children's menu. Open 5:30 pm-10 pm; closed major holidays. Beer & wine. Reserv advised weekends. MC, VI.
⊗ (619) 938-2254

BIG SUR — 1,000

Big Sur Lodge		Rates Subject to Change		Cottages	◆◆
⊕ 5/28-9/18 [CP]	1P 110.00	2P/1B 115.00- 125.00	2P/2B 125.00- 145.00 XP 20
3/2-5/27 & 9/19-10/31 [CP]	1P 110.00	2P/1B 115.00	2P/2B .... 125.00 XP 20
11/1-3/1 [CP]	1P 90.00	2P/1B 90.00	2P/2B 90.00- 100.00 XP 20

61 units. 26 mi s of Carmel on SR 1; in Pfeiffer Big Sur State Park. (PO Box 190, 93920) Spacious wooded surroundings. Check-in 4 pm. Shower or comb baths. 40 2-bedrm units, no utensils. Pool; hiking trails. No pets. Units with fireplace $15; kitchen $20 extra. 2-night minimum stay weekends. Reserv deposit required; 3 days refund notice. MC, VI. ● Coffeeshop; 8 am-11:30 & 5-9 pm; in summer; $9-$16; beer & wine. FAX (408) 667-3110 *(See ad p A77 and p A472)*
Ⓓ (408) 667-2171

Ventana Inn		Rates Subject to Change		Motor Inn	◆◆
All year [CP]	1P 170.00- 785.00	2P/1B 170.00- 785.00	2P/2B 170.00- 785.00 XP 50

63 units. 28 mi s of Carmel; 1/2 mi e of SR 1. SR 1. (93920) Wooded hilltop location; some ocean views; unfinished-cedar interior. Many with woodburning fireplace. Townhouses; some with whirlpool. Check-in 4:30 pm. Refrigerators; A/C; C/CATV; pay movies; VCPs. Radios; phones; comb or shower baths. 1 2-bedrm unit. 2 pools; sauna; whirlpools; nature trails. No pets. 2-night minimum stay weekends. Reserv deposit required; 3 days refund notice. Complimentary beverages each evening. AE, DI, DS, MC, VI. ● Restaurant, see separate listing. FAX (408) 667-2419 Ⓓ (408) 667-2331

RESTAURANTS

Glen Oaks	Regional American	$$$	◆◆

On SR 1, 1 1/4 mi n of Pfeiffer Big Sur State Park. Hwy 1. California cuisine. Mesquite broiler. Smoking not permitted. Children's menu. Open 6 pm-10 pm. Beer & wine. Minimum $4. Reserv advised. MC, VI.
⊗ (408) 667-2623

Ventana	American	$$$	◆◆◆

1/4 mi e of SR 1. Hwy 1. California cuisine, oakwood broiler. Casual atmosphere on wooded hilltop. A/C. Open noon-3 & 6-9:30 pm; Sat & Sun from 11 am; closed 12/2-12/18. Cocktails & lounge. Minimum $10. Reserv required. AE, CB, DI, MC, VI.
⊗ (408) 667-2331

BISHOP — 3,500

Best Western Holiday Spa Lodge		Rates Subject to Change		Motel	◆◆◆
⊕ All year	1P 50.00- 55.00	2P/1B 60.00- 67.00	2P/2B 64.00- 68.00 XP 5

Senior discount. 89 units. 3/4 mi n on US 395. 1025 N Main St. (93514) 60 refrigerators; A/C; C/CATV; movies; radios; phones; comb or shower baths. Coin laundry. Pool; indoor whirlpool; fish cleaning & freezing facilities. Some rooms with microwave. Reserv deposit required. AE, DI, MC, VI. Restaurant opposite. FAX (619) 872-4777
Ⓒ Ⓓ Ⓛ (619) 873-3543

Best Western Westerner Motel		AAA Special Value Rates		Motel	◆◆
⊕ 5/13-10/1	1P 55.00	2P/1B 55.00- 60.00	2P/2B 60.00- 65.00 XP 5
10/2-5/12	1P 45.00- 50.00	2P/1B 50.00- 55.00	2P/2B 55.00- 60.00 XP 5

55 units. 1/2 blk e of US 395. 150 E Elm St. (93514) 10 refrigerators; A/C; C/CATV; movies; radios; phones; comb or shower baths. 1 2-bedrm unit. Htd pool; fish cleaning & freezing facilities. Small pets only. Reserv deposit required. AE, DI, DS, MC, VI. FAX (619) 873-6936 *(See ad below)*
⊗ Ⓓ (619) 873-3564

Bishop Days Inn		Rates Subject to Change		Motel	
⊕ All year	1P 49.00- 70.00	2P/1B 55.00- 85.00	2P/2B 55.00- 90.00 XP 6

34 units. 3 blks w of US 395 at the corner of Home Ave. 724 Westline St. (93514) Rating withheld pending completion of construction. Scheduled to open August, 1992. A/C; C/CATV; movies; phones. Whirlpool. AE, DI, DS, MO, VI.
⊗ (619) 872-1099

Bishop Elms Motel — Rates Subject to Change — *Motel* ◆
⊕ All year .... 2P/1B 33.00- 42.00 2P/2B 38.00- 46.00 XP 4
19 units. 1 blk e of US 395. 233 E Elm St. (93514) Shaded grounds. Quiet location adjacent to public park. A/C; C/CATV; shower baths. Fish cleaning & freezing facilities; barbecues. No pets. MC, VI.   ⒹD (619) 873-8118

Bishop Inn — Rates Subject to Change — *Motel* ◆◆◆
⊕ All year 1P 47.00- 62.00 2P/1B 56.00- 62.00 2P/2B 59.00- 62.00 XP 5
Senior discount. 52 units. 1/2 mi n on US 395. 805 N Main St. (93514) Refrigerators; A/C; C/CATV; movies; 5 radios; phones. 1 2-bedrm unit. Coin laundry. Htd pool; whirlpool; fish cleaning & freezing facilities. Pets. Some rooms with microwave. AE, CB, DI, MC, VI. Restaurant adjacent. FAX (619) 873-8563   Ⓓ Ⓑ (619) 873-4284

Chalfant House Bed & Breakfast — Rates Subject to Change — *Bed & Breakfast* ◆◆◆
All year [BP] 1P 50.00- 65.00 2P/1B 60.00- 75.00 2P/2B 60.00- 75.00 XP 15
6 units. 1 blk n of US 395. 213 Academy St. (93514) Smoke free premises. Check-in 3 pm. A/C; 1 radio; shower or comb baths. No pets. Reserv deposit required; 7 days refund notice. AE.   ⊗ Ⓓ (619) 872-1790

El Rancho Motel — Rates Subject to Change — *Motel* ◆◆
⊕ All year 1P 30.00- 38.00 2P/1B 30.00- 38.00 2P/2B 34.00- 42.00 XP 4   F
Senior discount. 16 units. 1 1/2 blks w of US 395. 274 Lagoon St. (93514) 11 refrigerators; A/C; C/CATV; shower or comb baths. Fish cleaning & freezing facilities. No pets. 3 kitchens, $8 extra. Reserv deposit required; 3 days refund notice. MC, VI. *(See ad p A78)*   Ⓓ (619) 872-9251

Mountain View Motel — AAA Special Value Rates — *Motel* ◆◆
⊕ All year 1P 36.00- 40.00 2P/1B 45.00- 50.00 2P/2B 48.00- 55.00 XP 5   F
35 units. 1/2 mi w of US 395. 730 W Line St. (93514) Refrigerators; A/C; C/CATV; phones; shower or comb baths. Htd pool; fish cleaning & freezing facilities. No pets. 3 efficiency units, $60-$70; 2 kitchen suites, $85-$90. Reserv deposit required. AE, DI, DS, MC, VI. FAX (619) 873-3409   ⊗ Ⓓ (619) 873-4242

National 9 Inn-High Sierra Lodge — Rates Subject to Change — *Motel* ◆◆
⊕ 5/1-10/31 1P 42.00- 48.00 2P/1B 46.00- 58.00 2P/2B 56.00- 60.00 XP 5
11/1-4/30 1P 36.00- 42.00 2P/1B 40.00- 48.00 2P/2B 48.00- 50.00 XP 5
51 units. 3/4 mi n on US 395. 1005 N Main St. (93514) 49 refrigerators; A/C; C/CATV; movies; phones. 2 efficiencies. Small htd pool; indoor whirlpool; fish cleaning & freezing facilities. No pets. AE, DI, DS, MC, VI. Restaurant opposite. FAX (619) 873-8060   ⊗ Ⓓ Ⓑ (619) 873-8426

Sierra Foothills Motel — Rates Subject to Change — *Motel* ◆◆
⊕ All year 1P 33.00- 38.00 2P/1B 40.00- 43.00 2P/2B .... 46.00 XP 5- 6
43 units. 1/4 mi s on US 395. 535 S Main St. (93514) A/C; C/CATV; movies; radios; phones. Htd pool; sauna; indoor whirlpool; fish cleaning & freezing facilities. Pets, $10 deposit required. AE, DI, DS, MC, VI.
  ⊗ Ⓓ Ⓑ (619) 872-1386

Thunderbird Motel — Rates Subject to Change — *Motel* ◆◆
⊕ 5/15-10/31 1P 34.00- 40.00 2P/1B 38.00- 44.00 2P/2B 44.00- 50.00 XP 4
11/1-5/14 1P 30.00- 36.00 2P/1B 34.00- 40.00 2P/2B 40.00- 46.00 XP 4
23 units. 1/2 blk w of US 395. 190 W Pine St. (93514) 1 small unit. 6 refrigerators; A/C; C/CATV; movies; phones. Fish freezing facilities. Pets. Reserv deposit required; 3 days refund notice. AE, MC, VI. *(See ad below)*   ⊗ Ⓓ (619) 873-4215

Vagabond Inn — Rates Subject to Change — *Motel* ◆◆
⊕ All year [CP] 1P 44.00- 56.00 2P/1B 49.00- 61.00 2P/2B 54.00- 66.00 XP 5   F
80 units. 3/4 mi n on US 395. 1030 N Main St. (93514) 4 family units each with king bed & 4 bunk beds. A/C; C/CATV; movies; radios; phones. Coin laundry. Pool; fish cleaning & freezing facilities; playground. Pets, $5 extra charge. AE, DI, DS, MC, VI. Coffeeshop adjacent. FAX (619) 873-3067 *(See ad below)* ⊗ Ⓓ (619) 873-6351

RESTAURANTS

Firehouse Grill — American — $$ ◆◆
1 3/4 mi n on US 395. 2206 N Sierra Hwy. Country decor. Nice selection of steaks, seafood, chicken & pasta. A/C. Early bird specials; children's menu. Open 4:30 pm-10 pm. Cocktails. AE, DS, MC, VI.   ⊗ (619) 873-4888

Whiskey Creek Homestyle Fare — American — $$ ◆◆
1/4 mi n on US 395. 524 N Main St. Country Inn decor. Beef, chicken & fish entrees. Also nice selection of soups, salads & sandwiches. Patio dining weather permitting. Bakery & gift shop. A/C. Senior discount; children's menu. Open 7 am-9 pm; 5/31-10/1 to 10 pm; closed 12/25. Cocktails & lounge. Reserv advised. AE, CB, DI, MC, VI.   ⊗ (619) 873-7174

BLYTHE — 8,400

Best Western Sahara Motel — Rates Subject to Change — *Motel* ◆◆
⊕ All year [CP] 1P 49.00- 64.00 2P/1B 54.00- 64.00 2P/2B 54.00- 64.00 XP 5   F
Senior discount. 47 units. 2 blks n of I-10, Lovekin Blvd exit. 825 W Hobsonway. (92225) A/C; C/CATV; movies; VCPs. Radios; phones. Htd pool; whirlpool. Pets. Microwaves & refrigerators. AE, DI, DS, MC, VI. Coffeeshop opposite. FAX (619) 922-5836 *(See ad p A80)*   ⊗ Ⓓ (619) 922-7105

Blythe Travelodge

		Rates Guaranteed							Motel			◆◆
8/31-9/1	1P	70.00-	75.00	2P/1B	70.00-	75.00	2P/2B	80.00-	85.00	XP	5	F
1/15-2/6	1P	56.00-	58.00	2P/1B	56.00-	58.00	2P/2B	58.00-	60.00	XP	3	F
2/7-8/30 & 9/2-1/14	1P	42.00-	44.00	2P/1B	42.00-	44.00	2P/2B	46.00-	48.00	XP	3	F

50 units. 2 blks nw of I-10, exit Lovekin Blvd. 850 W Hobsonway. (92225) Refrigerators; A/C; C/CATV; movies; phones; shower or comb baths. Pool. No pets. AE, DI, DS, MC, VI. Restaurant adjacent. *(See ad below)*
⊗ Ⓓ (619) 922-5145

Comfort Inn

		AAA Special Value Rates							Motel			◆◆
All year	1P	38.00-	54.00	2P/1B	45.00-	59.00	2P/2B	52.00-	62.00	XP	5	F

48 units. 1 1/2 blks nw of I-10, exit Lovekin Blvd. 903 W Hobsonway. (92225) Refrigerators; A/C; C/CATV; movies; rental VCPs. Phones. Pool. Small pets only. AE, DI, DS, MC, VI.
⊗ Ⓓ (619) 922-4146

Comfort Suites

		Rates Subject to Change							Suites Motel			◆◆◆
All year [CP]	1P	59.00-	69.00	2P/1B	69.00-	79.00	2P/2B	79.00-	89.00	XP	8	F

Senior discount. 67 units. 1/2 mi nw of I-10; exit 7th St. 545 E Hobsonway. (92225) A/C; C/CATV; movies; VCPs. Radios; phones. Coin laundry. Htd pool; whirlpool; exercise rm. No pets. Microwaves & refrigerators. Reserv deposit required. AE, DI, DS, MC, VI. FAX (619) 922-9209
⊗ Ⓢ Ⓓ Ⓛ (619) 922-9209

BODEGA BAY — 300

Bodega Bay Lodge Best Western   Rates Subject to Change   *Motel*   ◆◆◆◆
⊕ All year [CP]   1P 118.00- 198.00   2P/1B   118.00- 198.00   2P/2B   118.00- 198.00   XP 10
Senior discount. 78 units. 1/2 mi s off SR 1 via Doran Beach Rd. (94923) Balconies or patios with view of bay & ocean. Many fireplaces. Check-in 3 pm. Refrigerators; C/CATV; free & pay movies; radios; phones. 2 2-bedrm units. Pool; sauna; whirlpool; rental bicycles; exercise rm. No pets. Reserv deposit required. AE, DI, DS, MC, VI. ● Restaurant; 6 am-9 pm; Fri & Sat set menu $34; a la carte entrees about $11-$25. FAX (707) 875-2428 *(See ads inside back cover and p A80)*   ⊗ Ⓓ (707) 875-3525

Bodega Coast Inn   Rates Subject to Change   *Motel*   ◆◆◆
⊕ Sat 4/1-11/30   1P 130.00- 180.00   2P/1B   130.00- 180.00   2P/2B   130.00- 180.00   XP 10   F
Sat 12/1-3/31   1P 98.00- 140.00   2P/1B   98.00- 175.00   2P/2B   98.00- 175.00   XP 10   F
Sun-Fri 4/1-11/30   1P 82.00- 125.00   2P/1B   84.00- 125.00   2P/2B   95.00- 125.00   XP 10   F
Sun-Fri 12/1-3/31   1P 60.00- 95.00   2P/1B   70.00- 115.00   2P/2B   70.00- 115.00   XP 10   F
45 units. 2 blks s on SR 1. 521 SR 1 N. (PO Box 55, 94923) Many rooms with view of bay; some with patio or balcony. Few rooms with woodburning fireplace and/or whirlpool. Refrigerators; C/CATV; free & pay movies; VCPs. Radios; phones. Whirlpool. Pets, $10 extra charge. 1 apartment, $175-$275 for up to 6 persons. Reserv deposit required. AE, DI, DS, MC, VI. ● Restaurant; 8 am-10 pm; $10-$18. FAX (707) 875-2964 *(See ad p A80)*   ⊗ Ⓢ Ⓓ (707) 875-2217

Inn at the Tides   AAA Special Value Rates   *Motel*   ◆◆◆
⊕ Sat [CP]   1P 130.00- 210.00   2P/1B   130.00- 210.00   2P/2B   130.00- 150.00   XP 20   F
Sun-Fri [CP]   1P 105.00- 185.00   2P/1B   105.00- 185.00   2P/2B   105.00- 130.00   XP 20
86 units. Center; on SR 1. 800 SR 1. (PO Box 640, 94923) Many with woodburning fireplaces & view of bay. Check-in 3 pm. Refrigerators; C/CATV; movies; radios; phones. Coin laundry. Pool; sauna; whirlpool. No pets. Reserv deposit required. AE, MC, VI. Dining rm; Wed-Sun 6 pm-10 pm; Sun brunch 11 am-2 pm, $16; a la carte entrees about $20; cocktails. FAX (707) 875-3023 *(See ad below)*   Ⓓ Ⓢ (707) 875-2751

RESTAURANT

Lucas Wharf Restaurant   Seafood $$ ◆◆
⊕ Center. 595 SR 1. Also, steak & pasta. On the bay. Early bird specials; children's menu. Open 11 am-9:30 pm; Fri-Sun to 10 pm; closed 11/26, 12/24 & 12/25. Lounge. Minimum, $4. MC, VI.   ⊗ (707) 875-3522

BONSALL — 500

RESTAURANT

Rio Rico Restaurant   Mexican $ ◆◆
1 mi e on SR 76, in River Village Shopping Center. 5256 S Mission Rd. Colorfully decorated dining room & outdoor patio. A/C. Open 11:30 am-9 pm; Fri & Sat-10 pm; Sun 9:30 am-9 pm; closed 11/25 & 12/25. Cocktails & lounge. MC, VI.   ⊗ (619) 945-1250

Look for the ⊕ in our listings!

BORREGO SPRINGS — 1,400

La Casa Del Zorro Resort Hotel Rates Subject to Change *Resort Complex* ◆◆◆
⊛ 11/16-4/30 1P 98.00- 200.00 2P/1B 98.00- 200.00 2P/2B 98.00- 200.00 XP 10
5/1-6/15 & 10/1-11/15 1P 55.00- 150.00 2P/1B 55.00- 150.00 2P/2B 55.00- 150.00 XP 10
6/16-9/30 1P 47.50- 100.00 2P/1B 47.50- 100.00 2P/2B 47.50- 100.00 XP 10
77 units. 5 1/2 mi se on CR S-3 at jct Yaqui Pass Rd & Borrego Springs Rd. (PO Box 127, 92004) Long-established resort on spacious, attractive, tree-shaded & open grounds. Beautifully appointed suites & villas. Check-in 3 pm. 65 refrigerators; A/C; C/CATV; movies; rental VCPs. Phones. Coin laundry. 3 htd pools; whirlpools; putting green; lighted tennis-6 courts; rental bicycles; exercise rm. No pets. 2 to 3-bedroom villas, $250-$500 in season; private villas with pool. Wkly rates avail. Reserv deposit required. AE, DI, DS, MC, VI. ● Dining rm; 7 am-3 & 4-11 pm; $14-$26; cocktails; entertainment. FAX (619) 767-5963 *(See ad p A81)*
⊗ Ⓓ Ⓛ (619) 767-5323

Oasis Motel Rates Subject to Change *Motel* ◆
1/1-5/31 & Fri-Sat 6/1-12/31 1P 55.00- 65.00 2P/1B 55.00- 65.00 2P/2B 55.00- 65.00 XP 5
Sun-Thurs 6/1-12/31 1P 30.00- 40.00 2P/1B 30.00- 40.00 2P/2B 30.00- 40.00 XP 5
7 units. 1 mi w on CR S-22. 366 Palm Canyon Dr. (PO Box 221, 92004) A/C; C/CATV; shower baths. 2 kitchens. Pool; whirlpool. No pets. Wkly rates avail. Reserv deposit required; 3 days refund notice. MC, VI.
Ⓓ (619) 767-5409

Palm Canyon Resort Rates Subject to Change *Motor Inn* ◆◆◆
⊛ 10/1-5/31 1P 85.00- 99.00 2P/1B 85.00- 99.00 2P/2B 85.00- 99.00 XP 8
6/1-9/30 1P 56.00- 66.00 2P/1B 56.00- 66.00 2P/2B 56.00- 66.00 XP 8
44 units. 1 1/2 mi w on CR S-22. 221 Palm Canyon Dr. (PO Box 956, 92004) A/C; C/CATV; rental VCPs; phones. Coin laundry. Htd pool; whirlpool; rental bicycles; suite with whirlpool. Pets, $25 deposit required. Reserv deposit required. AE, DI, DS, MC, VI. ● Restaurant; 11 am-10 pm; Sat & Sun from 7 am; $6.95-$16.95; cocktails. FAX (619) 767-4073 *(See ad below)*
⊗ Ⓓ Ⓛ (619) 767-5341

BOULDER CREEK — 5,700

Merrybrook Lodge Rates Guaranteed *Cottages* ◆◆
⊛ 5 1P .... 64.00 2P/1B 64.00- 80.00 .... XP 8
8 units. 3 blks n on Big Basin Hwy, SR 236. 13420 Big Basin Way. (PO Box 845, 95006) OPEN ALL YEAR. Rustic setting; few units overlook creek; in the redwoods. Check-out 10:30 am. Refrigerators; C/CATV; shower baths. No pets. 6 housekeeping cottages, 3 with fireplace & 3 with woodstove. 2 motel units, $50-$66 for up to 2 persons; 2-night minimum stay weekends. Wkly rates avail. Reserv deposit required; 7 days refund notice. MC, VI.
Ⓓ (408) 338-6813

BRAWLEY — 18,900

Town House Lodge AAA Special Value Rates *Motel* ◆◆
⊛ All year 1P .... 43.00 2P/1B .... 46.00 2P/2B .... 47.00 XP 3
39 units. At jct SR 78 & 86. 135 Main St. (92227) A/C; C/CATV; movies; phones. Small pool. Pets. All rooms with microwave & refrigerator. Wkly rates avail. AE, CB, DI, MC, VI.
⊗ Ⓓ (619) 344-5120

BREA — 32,900

Embassy Suites Hotel Rates Subject to Change *Suites Motor Inn* ◆◆◆
⊛ Sun-Thurs [BP] .... 2P/1B 104.00- 129.00 2P/2B 104.00- 129.00 XP 15
Fri & Sat [BP] 1P .... 89.00 2P/1B .... 89.00 2P/2B .... 89.00 XP 15
Senior discount. 229 units. 1/2 mi w of SR 57, exit Imperial Hwy, adjacent to Brea Mall. 900 E Birch St. (92621) Check-in 3 pm. A/C; C/CATV; free & pay movies; radios; phones. Coin laundry. Htd pool; sauna; whirlpool; exercise rm. No pets. 2-room suites with living room, refrigerator & microwave. Complimentary beverages each evening. AE, DI, DS, MC, VI. ● Restaurant; 11 am-2:30 & 5-10 pm; Fri & Sat 11-pm; $10-$18; cocktail lounge. FAX (714) 990-1653
⊗ Ⓢ Ⓓ Ⓛ (714) 990-6000

Hyland Motel Rates Subject to Change *Motel* ◆
⊛ All year 1P .... 36.00 2P/1B .... 38.00 2P/2B .... 40.00 XP 2
Senior discount. 26 units. 3/4 mi ne of Bastanchury Rd. 727 S Brea Blvd. (92621) A/C; C/CATV; movies; radios; phones. Small pets only. Wkly rates avail. Reserv deposit required. AE, DS, MC, VI. ⊗ Ⓓ (714) 990-6867

RESTAURANTS

Bobby McGee's Conglomeration Steak & Seafood $$ ◆◆
200 S State College Blvd at Birch St. Casual, informal service by costumed waiters & waitresses. A/C. Early bird specials; children's menu. Open 5 pm-10 pm; Fri & Sat-11 pm; closed 12/25. Cocktails & lounge. Reserv advised. AE, CB, DI, MC, VI.
⊗ (714) 529-1998

La Vie en Rose French $$$ ◆◆◆
Adjacent to SR 57, Imperial Hwy exit. 240 S State College Blvd. Elegant atmosphere. A/C. Open 11:30 am-2:30 & 5:30-9:30 pm; Sat from 5:30 pm; closed Sun & major holidays. Cocktails & lounge. Reserv advised. AE, CB, DI, MC, VI.
Ⓜ Ⓛ (714) 000 0000

Reuben's Steak & Seafood $$ ◆◆◆
1/4 mi sw of SR 57; exit Imperial Hwy. 390 S State College Blvd. A/C. Early bird specials; children's menu. Open 11 am-4 & 5-9 pm; Wed-Fri 10 pm; Sat 5 pm-10 pm; Sun 5 pm-9 pm. Cocktails & lounge. Entertainment & dancing. Reserv advised Weekends. AE, DI, DS, MC, VI.
⊗ (714) 529-4804

Rusty Pelican Restaurant Seafood $$ ◆◆◆
3/4 mi n of Imperial Hwy. 190 S State College Blvd at Birch St. Popular, attractive restaurant serving large selection of fresh seafood. A/C. Early bird specials; children's menu. Open 11 am-2:30 & 5-10 pm; Fri-11 pm; Sat 4:30 pm-11 pm; Sun 4:30 pm-10 pm; closed 11/25 & 12/25. Cocktails & lounge. Entertainment & dancing. Reserv advised. AE, DI, DS, MC, VI.
⊗ (714) 671-3020

BRIDGEPORT — 500

Best Western Ruby Inn ● ● ●
| | | | Rates Guaranteed | | | *Motel* |
4/15-9/15 — 1P 60.00- 90.00 2P/1B 65.00- 90.00 2P/2B 72.00- 90.00 XP 5 F
9/16-4/14 — 1P 55.00- 75.00 2P/1B 60.00- 75.00 2P/2B 65.00- 80.00 XP 5 F
Senior discount. 30 units. Center on US 395. (PO Box 475, 93517) A/C; C/CATV; movies; radios; phones. 1 2-bedrm unit. Whirlpool; fish freezing facilities. Pets. AE, DI, DS, MC, VI. ⊗ Ⓓ Ⓛ (619) 932-7241

Historic Bed & Breakfast
The Cain House [BP] ● ● ●
1P 79.00- 80.00 2P/1B 80.00-130.00 2P/2B .... 135.00 XP 20
6 units. Center; on US 395. 11 Main St. (PO Box 454, 93517) Western historical home restored with a comfortable elegance. Designated smoking areas. Phones avail upon request. Check-in 3 pm. C/CATV; movies. Parking lot. No pets. Reserv deposit required. Complimentary beverages each evening. AE, DI, DS, MC, VI. Restaurant opposite. FAX (619) 932-7419 ⊗ Ⓓ (619) 932-7040

Silver Maple Inn ●
| | | | Rates Guaranteed | | | *Motel* |
4/25-11/1 — 1P 45.00- 55.00 2P/1B 50.00- 70.00 2P/2B 65.00- 80.00 XP 10
20 units. Center; on US 395. 9 Main St. (PO Box 327, 93517) OPEN 4/25-11/1. C/CATV; movies; shower or comb baths. Pets. Reserv deposit required. AE, DI, DS, MC, VI. Restaurant opposite. Ⓓ Ⓛ (619) 932-7383

Walker River Lodge ● ● ●
| | | | Rates Subject to Change | | | *Motel* |
4/1-10/31 — 1P 65.00- 85.00 2P/1B 75.00- 95.00 2P/2B 85.00-110.00 XP 10
11/1-3/31 — 1P 45.00- 60.00 2P/1B 55.00- 65.00 2P/2B 60.00- 80.00 XP 10
Senior discount. 36 units. 2 blks s on US 395. 1 Main St. (PO Box 695, 93517) On east fork of Walker River. 17 refrigerators; 34 A/C; C/CATV; movies; phones. 4 2-bedrm units. Small htd pool; whirlpool; fishing; fish cleaning & freezing facilities. Pets. 2 1-bedroom apartments, $95-$120 for 2 persons. Reserv deposit required in season. AE, DI, DS, MC, VI. *(See also below)* ⊗ Ⓓ (619) 932-7021

BUELLTON — 2,400

Best Western Pea Soup Andersen's Inn ● ● ●
| | | | Rates Subject to Change | | | *Motel* |
5/1-9/30 [CP] — 1P 47.00- 57.00 2P/1B 53.00- 63.00 2P/2B 57.00- 67.00 XP 6
97 units. On SR 246; 1 blk w of jct US 101. 51 E Hwy 246. (PO Box Y, 93427) OPEN ALL YEAR. 6 refrigerators; A/C; C/CATV; rental VCPs; phones. Htd pool; whirlpool; putting green. No pets. Microwaves. AE, DI, DS, MC, VI. Restaurant adjacent. FAX (805) 688-9767 *(See also below)* ⊗ Ⓢ (805) 688-3216

Econo Lodge ● ●
| | | | Rates Subject to Change | | | *Motel* |
All year — 1P .... 35.95 2P/1B .... 49.95 2P/2B .... 49.95 XP 10
60 units. Adjacent to US 101; southbound first Buellton exit; northbound Frontage Rd exit, then 1 blk w over the frwy. 630 Ave of Flags. (93427) A/C; C/CATV; phones. Coin laundry. 16 efficiencies, $59.95-$68.95 for 2 persons. Wkly & monthly rates avail. Reserv deposit required in summer. AE, DS, MC, VI. FAX (805) 688-7448 ⊗ Ⓢ Ⓓ (805) 688-0022

Holiday Inn-Solvang/Buellton ● ● ●
| | | | Rates Subject to Change | | | *Motor Inn* |
All year — 1P 69.00- 85.00 2P/1B 69.00- 95.00 2P/2B 69.00- 95.00 XP 10 F
Senior discount. 149 units. Adjacent to US 101, exit SR 246. 1/4 mi n. 555 McMurray Rd. (93427) A/C; C/CATV; free & pay movies; radios; phones. Coin laundry. Htd pool; whirlpool; tennis-1 court; racquetball-2 courts; exercise rm. No pets. 7 suites with whirlpool tub. AE, CB, DI, MC, VI. ● Restaurant & coffeeshop; 7 am-10 pm; $7.95-$12.95. Also, Federico's, see separate listing. FAX (805) 688-0380 ⊗ Ⓢ Ⓓ (805) 688-1000

Ramada Inn At the Windmill ● ● ●
| | | | Rates Subject to Change | | | *Motel* |
Fri & Sat 5/24-9/21 — 1P .... 88.00 2P/1B .... 94.00 2P/2B .... 94.00 XP 6 F
Fri & Sat 9/22-5/23 — 1P .... 86.00 2P/1B .... 92.00 2P/2B .... 92.00 XP 6 F
Sun-Thurs 5/24-9/21 — 1P 56.00- 62.00 2P/1B 66.00- 72.00 2P/2B 66.00- 72.00 XP 6 F
Sun-Thurs 9/22-5/23 — 1P 44.00- 54.00 2P/1B 50.00- 60.00 2P/2B 50.00- 60.00 XP 6 F
Senior discount. 110 units. Adjacent to US 101, at jct SR 246. 114 E Hwy 246. (93427) Check-in 3 pm. 13 refrigerators; A/C; C/CATV; movies; radios; phones. Htd pool; whirlpool. No pets. Wkly & monthly rates avail. AE, DI, DS, MC, VI. Cocktail lounge. FAX (805) 686-1338 ⊗ Ⓓ Ⓛ (805) 688-8448

RESTAURANTS

A J Spurs *American* $$ ● ●
On SR 246, 1/4 mi e of US 101. 350 E Hwy 246. Casual, western-style family dining featuring steaks, ribs, barbecue chicken & seafood. A/C. Early bird specials; children's menu. Open 3:30 pm-9:30 pm; Fri-10 pm; Sat 2 pm-10 pm; Sun 2 pm-9:30 pm; closed 1/1, 11/25, 12/24 & 12/25. Cocktails & lounge. Reserv advised. MC, VI. (805) 686-1655

Federico's *Mexican* $$ ● ●
At Holiday Inn Solvang/Buellton. Large, attractively decorated. A/C. Children's menu. Open 11:30 am-10 pm; Sun 10:30 am-9 pm. Cocktails & lounge. AE, CB, DI, MC, VI. ⊗ (805) 688-0606

The Hitching Post II   Steakhouse $$ ◆◆
On SR 246, 1/2 mi e of jct US 101. 406 E Hwy 246. Well-known for steak & barbecue specialties. A/C. Open 5 pm-10 pm; Sun 4 pm-9 pm; closed Mon & major holidays. Cocktails & lounge. Reserv advised. AE, MC, VI. ⊗ (805) 688-0676

Zaca Creek Restaurant   American $$ ◆◆
1 1/2 mi n via Ave of Flags & Jonata Park Rd. 1297 N Hwy 101. Western decor. Nice selection of steaks, prime rib & seafood. A/C. Children's menu. Open 5:30 pm-10 pm; Sat & Sun from 5 pm; closed 11/25, 12/24 & 12/25. Cocktails & lounge. AE, DI, MC, VI. ⊗ (805) 688-2412

BUENA PARK — 68,800   (See ANAHEIM-BUENA PARK spotting map pages A6 & A7; see index starting on page A4)   See also CYPRESS, FULLERTON & LA MIRADA

Best Western Buena Park Inn **98**   AAA Special Value Rates   *Motel*   ◆◆
ⓐ	5/25-9/15	1P	....	42.00	2P/1B	....	48.00	2P/2B	....	52.00 XP 5 F
	9/16-5/24	1P	....	36.00	2P/1B	....	42.00	2P/2B	....	46.00 XP 5 F

63 units. 1 blk e of SR 39, 1 blk s of Crescent Ave. 8580 Stanton Ave. (90620) A/C; C/CATV; movies; phones. 2 2-bedrm units. Coin laundry. Htd pool. Small pets, $50 deposit; also $6 daily. Refrigerators & microwaves avail. Reserv deposit required. AE, DI, DS, MC, VI. Restaurant opposite. FAX (714) 826-3716 *(See ad below)*
⊗ Ⓓ ⓵ (714) 828-5211

Courtyard by Marriott **100**   Rates Subject to Change   *Motor Inn*   ◆◆◆
Sun-Thurs	1P	....	80.00	2P/1B	....	90.00	2P/2B	....	90.00 XP 10
Fri & Sat	1P	....	64.00	2P/1B	....	74.00	2P/2B	....	74.00 XP 10

Senior discount. 145 units. On SR 39; 1/4 mi s of jct SR 91. 7621 Beach Blvd. (90620) Patios or balconies. Check-in 3 pm. 10 refrigerators; A/C; C/CATV; free & pay movies; radios; phones. Coin laundry. Htd pool; whirlpool; exercise rm. No pets. Wkly rates avail. AE, DI, DS, MC, VI. ● Restaurant; 6:30 am-2 & 5-10 pm; Sat & Sun 7:30 am-2 & 5-10 pm; $8-$12; cocktails. FAX (714) 670-0360 *(See ad p A33)*
⊗ Ⓢ Ⓓ ⓵ (714) 670-6600

Days Inn-La Palma **97**   AAA Special Value Rates   *Motor Inn*   ◆◆◆
ⓐ	All year	1P 49.00- 58.00	2P/1B	49.00- 64.00	2P/2B	49.00- 64.00 XP 6		F

161 units. 1/4 mi nw of SR 91; exit Orangethorpe Ave. 3 Center Pointe Dr. (La Palma, 90623) Many balconies. Check-in 3 pm. A/C; C/CATV; free & pay movies; radios; phones. Htd pool; whirlpool. No pets. Wkly & monthly rates avail. AE, DI, MC, VI. ● Coffeeshop; 6 am-1 & 5:30-10 pm; $6-$12.50; cocktails. FAX (714) 522-4698 *(See ad below)*
⊗ Ⓢ Ⓓ (714) 670-1400

Embassy Suites Hotel-Buena Park **99**   Rates Subject to Change   *Suites Motor Inn*   ◆◆◆
ⓐ	Sun-Thurs [BP]	1P 99.00-109.00	2P/1B	.... 119.00	2P/2B	.... 109.00 XP 15		
	Fri & Sat [BP]	1P 94.00	2P/1B	.... 94.00	2P/2B	.... 94.00 XP		

203 units. 7762 Beach Blvd. (90620) Check-in 3 pm. A/C; C/CATV; free & pay movies; radios; phones. Coin laundry. Htd pool; whirlpool. No pets. 1-bedroom suites with refrigerator & microwave. Complimentary beverages each evening. AE, DI, DS, MC, VI. ● Restaurant; 11:30 am-2:30 & 5-10 pm; $9-$18.50; cocktails. FAX (714) 521-9650
⊗ Ⓢ Ⓓ (714) 739-5600

Fairfield Inn by Marriott **92**   Rates Subject to Change   *Motel*   ◆◆
All year	1P 38.95- 42.95	2P/1B	43.95- 48.95	2P/2B	47.95- 52.95 XP 3 F

135 units. 1 blk n of SR 91, exit Knott Ave. 7032 Orangethorpe Ave. (90621) A/C; C/CATV; movies; radios; phones. Htd pool. No pets. AE, DI, DS, MC, VI. FAX (714) 523-1488 *(See ad p A33)*
⊗ Ⓓ ⓵ (714) 523-1488

Hampton Inn **93**   Rates Subject to Change   *Motel*   ◆◆
ⓐ	All year [CP]	1P 51.00- 61.00	2P/1B	56.00- 66.00	2P/2B .... 61.00 XP 5

184 units. 1 blk n of SR 91, exit Beach Blvd. 7828 Orangethorpe Ave. (90620) A/C; C/CATV; free & pay movies; phones. Rental refrigerators. Coin laundry. Htd pool; whirlpool. No pets. AE, DI, DS, MC, VI. Restaurant adjacent. FAX (714) 522-3319
⊗ Ⓢ Ⓓ ⓵ (714) 670-7200

PLAZA INN

MINUTES AWAY FROM DISNEYLAND AND KNOTTS BERRY FARM

♦♦♦ RATED LUXURY

ALL RATES GUARANTEED ♦ SPECIAL WEEKLY RATES AVAILABLE

Deluxe Room	King Bed 1-2 People	2 Double Beds 2 People
February 1, 1993 to June 1, 1993		
June 2, 1993 to September 1,1993	$42-46	$50-$54
September 2,1993 to January 31,1994	$38-$42	$42-$46

❖ Complimentary Deluxe Continental Breakfast ❖ Spa & Sauna ❖ Heated Pool ❖ Color T.V. with Clock Radio ❖ In-Room Coffee/Tea Service ❖ Free Parking ❖ Refrigerators in Every Room ❖ Laundry Facilities ❖ Complimentary Coffee and Cookies Every Evening ❖ Tours from Lobby to Local Attractions ❖ All Rooms Redecorated 1988 ❖ Free 24 HR Movies & Sports ❖ King Size Beds ❖ Direct Dial Phones ❖ BBQ Picnic Area ❖ Tub/Shower-Massage ❖ Kitchens Available ❖ Deluxe Mini Suites ❖ Free Ice ❖ Discount Coupons for Local Attractions ❖ Game Room ❖ Air Conditioning

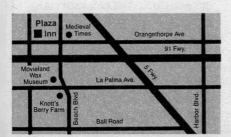

For Reservations CALL:

(714) 521-9220

In the Continental U.S. 1-800-854-8299
In California 1-800-854-7725
In Canada 1-800-225-5251

7039 Orangethorpe Avenue
Buena Park, CA 90621

Member of Sunset Affiliated Hotels

(See ANAHEIM-BUENA PARK spotting map pages A6 & A7)

Holiday Inn Buena Park 102   **Rates Guaranteed**   *Motor Inn* ◆◆◆

6/15-9/7	1P	....	85.00	2P/1B	85.00-	95.00	2P/2B	85.00-	95.00	XP 10	F
9/8-6/14	1P	....	75.00	2P/1B	75.00-	85.00	2P/2B	75.00-	85.00	XP 10	F

Senior discount. 246 units. On SR 39, at jct SR 91. 7000 Beach Blvd. (90620) Check-in 3 pm. A/C; C/CATV; pay movies; radios; phones. Coin laundry. Htd pool; wading pool; whirlpool. Airport transp. No pets. Reserv deposit required. AE, DI, DS, MC, VI. ● Dining rm; 6:30 am-2 & 5-10 pm; $9-$15; cocktails. FAX (714) 522-3230 *(See ad below)*   ⊗ Ⓓ Ⓑ (714) 522-7000

Plaza Inn 96   **Rates Subject to Change**   *Motel* ◆◆◆

6/1-8/31 [CP]	1P	42.00-	46.00	2P/1B	44.00-	46.00	2P/2B	50.00-	54.00	XP 4
9/1-5/31 [CP]	1P	38.00-	40.00	2P/1B	38.00-	42.00	2P/2B	42.00-	46.00	XP 4

Senior discount. 101 units. 1 blk e of Knott Ave. 7039 Orangethorpe Ave. (90621) A/C; C/CATV; movies; VCPs. Radios; phones. 35 efficiencies. Coin laundry. Htd pool; saunas; whirlpool. No pets. Some rooms with microwave & refrigerator. Wkly rates avail. Reserv deposit required. AE, DI, DS, MC, VI. FAX (714) 521-6706 *(See ad p A85)*   ⊗ Ⓓ (714) 521-9220

Siesta Inn 95   **Rates Subject to Change**   *Motel* ◆◆

6/1-8/31 [CP]	1P	42.00-	46.00	2P/1B	44.00-	46.00	2P/2B	50.00-	54.00	XP 4
9/1-5/31 [CP]	1P	38.00-	40.00	2P/1B	38.00-	42.00	2P/2B	42.00-	46.00	XP 4

Senior discount. 78 units. On SR 39, 1/2 mi s of jct SR 91. 7930 Beach Blvd. (90620) Many balconies. Refrigerators; A/C; C/CATV; movies; radios; phones. 4 2-bedrm units, 40 efficiencies, no utensils. Coin laundry. Htd pool; whirlpool. No pets. Wkly rates avail. Reserv deposit required. AE, DI, DS, MC, VI. Coffeeshop adjacent. FAX (714) 994-3874 *(See ad p A87)*   ⊗ Ⓓ (714) 522-2422

Travelers Inn 94   **AAA Special Value Rates**   *Motel* ◆◆

5/1-8/31 [CP]	1P	....	42.00	2P/1B	....	48.00	2P/2B	....	48.00	XP 5

Senior discount. 132 units. Adjacent to SR 91 at jct SR 39. 7121 Beach Blvd. (90620) OPEN ALL YEAR. A/C; C/CATV; movies; radios; phones. Htd pool; whirlpool. No pets. AE, CB, DI, MC, VI. Restaurant adjacent. FAX (714) 522-7280 *(See ad below)*   ⊗ Ⓢ Ⓓ Ⓑ (714) 670-9000

RESTAURANTS

El Torito 24   Mexican $ ◆◆
1/2 blk w of Valley View. 5980 Orangethorpe Ave. Buffet lunch Mon-Fri 11 am-2 pm, $5.45. Sat buffet 9 am-noon, $4.95; Sun brunch 9 am-2 pm, $8.95. A/C. Children's menu. Open 11 am-11 pm; Fri-midnight; Sat 9 am-midnight; Sun 9 am-10 pm; closed 11/25 & 12/25. Cocktails & lounge. AE, DI, DS, MC, VI.   ⊗ Ⓑ (714) 521-8331

Knott's Berry Farm Chicken Dinner
Restaurant 23   American $ ◆
Beach Blvd at La Palma Ave. Very popular, well-known restaurant specializing in complete chicken dinners. Also sandwiches & salads at lunch. A/C. Children's menu. Open 7 am-8:30 pm; Fri & Sun-9 pm; Sat-10 pm; closed 12/25. AE, DI, DS, MC, VI.   ⊗ Ⓑ (714) 220-5080

Marie Callenders 22   American $ ◆◆
1/2 blk w of Valley View. 5960 Orangethorpe Ave. Casual atmosphere. Sun brunch 9 am-2 pm, $8.95. Large selection of pies. A/C. Children's menu. Open 11 am-10 pm; Fri & Sat-11 pm; Sun 9 am-10 pm. Cocktails & lounge. AE, DS, MC, VI.   ⊗ Ⓑ (714) 522-0170

Velvet Turtle Restaurant 25   Continental $$ ◆◆
1/2 blk w of Valley View. 5970 Orangethorpe Ave. Casual atmosphere. Featuring seafood, steaks, pasta & prime rib. Sun brunch 10 am-2:30 pm, $10.95. A/C. Children's menu. Open 11 am-2:30 & 5-10 pm; Fri 11:30 am-2:30 & 5-11 pm; Sat 5 pm-11 pm; Sun 10 am-2:30 & 5-10 pm. Cocktails & lounge. AE, DI, DS, MC, VI.   ⊗ Ⓑ (714) 523-5262

SIESTA INN

Walk to Knotts Berry Farm,
Movieland Wax Museum, and Medieval Times.
Only minutes from Disneyland.

AAA ♦♦♦ RATED LUXURY

ALL RATES GUARANTEED ♦ SPECIAL WEEKLY RATES AVAILABLE

Deluxe Room	King Bed 1-2 People	2 Double Beds 2 People
February 1, 1989 to June 1, 1989 September 1, 1989 to January 31, 1990	$36-$40	$40-$44
June 1, 1989 to September 1, 1989	$40-$44	$48-$52

♦ Complimentary Deluxe Continental Breakfast ♦ Free 24 Hour Movies & Sports ♦ In-room Coffee/Tea Service ♦ Color T.V. with Clock Radio ♦ All Rooms Redecorated 1986 ♦ Restaurant/Coffee Shop Adjacent to Hotel ♦ 2 Bedroom Suites Available ♦ Complimentary Coffee and Cookies Every Evening ♦ Refrigerators in Every Room ♦ Tours from Lobby to Local Attractions ♦ Deluxe Mini Suites ♦ King Size Beds ♦ Direct Dial Phones ♦ Air Conditioning ♦ Free Parking ♦ Kitchens Available ♦ Laundry Facilities ♦ Heated Pool and Spa ♦ Free Ice ♦ Tub/Shower-Massage ♦ BBQ Picnic Area ♦ Discount Coupons for Local Attractions ♦ Game Room

For Reservations CALL:

(714) 994-6480

In the Continental U.S. 1-800-854-6031
In California 1-800-854-7750
In Canada 1-800-225-5251

7930 Beach Boulevard
Buena Park, CA 90620

Member of Sunset Affiliated Hotels

BURBANK — 93,600 (See LOS ANGELES (San Fernando Valley) AREA spotting map page A236 ; see index starting on page A235) See also LOS ANGELES (San Fernando Valley)

Airport Accommodations-See listing for:

ⓑ Burbank Airport Hilton & Convention Center, at airport entrance

Burbank Airport Hilton & Convention
Center 60   Rates Subject to Change   Hotel   ◆◆◆
ⓑ All year   1P 106.00- 156.00 2P/1B 121.00- 171.00 2P/2B 121.00- 171.00 XP 15
487 units. 1 mi s of I-5, exit Hollywood Way; at airport entrance. 2500 Hollywood Way. (91505) 100 refrigerators; A/C; C/CATV; movies; VCPs. Radios; phones. Coin laundry. 2 htd pools; saunas; whirlpool; exercise rm. Pay parking lot. Airport transp. Pets. Monthly rates avail. AE, CB, DI, MC, VI. ● Dining rm & coffeeshop; 6 am-11 pm; $8-$14; cocktails; entertainment. FAX (818) 842-9720 *(See ad p 22)*   ⊗ Ⓢ Ⓓ Ⓛ (818) 843-6000

Holiday Inn-Burbank 61   Rates Subject to Change   Hotel   ◆◆
All year   1P 96.00- 135.00 2P/1B 106.00- 135.00 2P/2B 106.00- 135.00 XP 10   F
Senior discount. 500 units. 1 blk e of I-5; northbound exit Olive Ave, southbound exit Verdugo Ave. 150 E Angeleno. (91510) A/C; C/CATV; free & pay movies; phones. Coin laundry. Htd pool; saunas. Parking lot. Airport transp. Pets. Suites, $135-$155. Reserv deposit required. AE, DI, DS, MC, VI. ● Dining rm; 6:30 am-10 pm; $8-$16; cocktails.
⊗ Ⓢ Ⓓ Ⓛ (818) 841-4770

Ramada Inn-Burbank 62   Rates Subject to Change   Motor Inn ◆◆
ⓑ All year   1P 75.00- 85.00 2P/1B   85.00- 95.00 2P/2B   85.00- 95.00 XP 10
Senior discount. 144 units. Adjacent to I-5, exit Buena Vista St. 2900 N San Fernando Rd. (91504) A/C; C/CATV; movies; radios; phones. Pool; 9 rooms with whirlpool. Airport transp. Pets, $50 extra charge. Wkly & monthly rates avail. AE, DI, DS, MC, VI. ● Restaurant; 6 am-2 & 5-10 pm; $9-$16; cocktails. FAX (818) 845-9030
⊗ Ⓢ Ⓓ (818) 843-5955

Safari Inn 63   Rates Subject to Change   Motor Inn ◆◆
ⓑ All year   1P 55.00- 65.00 2P/1B   65.00- 75.00 2P/2B   70.00- 80.00 XP 10
104 units. 1 1/4 mi sw of I-5; Olive Ave exit. 1911 W Olive Ave. (91506) Good rooms in original motel section, very good rooms in adjacent 3-story motor inn section. Refrigerators; A/C; C/TV; VCPs; phones; comb or shower baths. 2 2-bedrm units, 18 kitchens, 2 efficiencies. Htd pool; whirlpool. No pets. Wkly rates avail for kitchens. Reserv deposit required. AE, CB, DI, MC, VI. ● Restaurant; 6:30-10:30 am, 11:30-2:30 & 5-10 pm; a la carte entrees about $10-$17; cocktails. FAX (818) 845-0054   ⊗ Ⓢ Ⓓ (818) 845-8586

RESTAURANT

Bobby McGee's Comglomeration 40   American $$ ◆◆
Adjacent to n side of I-5; northbound exit Olive Ave, southbound exit Verdago Ave. 107 S 1st St. Uniquely decorated restaurant. Informal, casual service by costumed staff. Features steaks, prime rib & seafood. A/C. Early bird specials; children's menu. Open 11 am-10 pm; Fri-11 pm; Sat 5 pm-11 pm; Sun 5 pm-10 pm; closed 12/25. Cocktails & lounge. Entertainment & dancing. Pay valet parking. Reserv advised. AE, DI, MC, VI.   ⊗ (818) 841-1935

BURLINGAME — 26,800   See SAN FRANCISCO (Southern Region)

BURNEY — 3,200
Charm Motel   Rates Subject to Change   Motel   ◆
ⓑ All year   1P 46.00- 69.00 2P/1B   51.00- 74.00 2P/2B   51.00- 74.00 XP 9
42 units. 3/4 mi e on SR 299. (PO Box 50, 96013) Tree-shaded grounds. Some small units. Refrigerators; A/C; C/CATV; movies; phones; shower or comb baths. 1 2-bedrm unit. Pets, $4 extra charge. 2 efficiencies & 3 kitchens, $6 extra. Reserv deposit required. AE, DI, MC, VI. FAX (916) 335-4147   Ⓓ Ⓛ (916) 335-2254

BUTTONWILLOW — 1,400   See also BAKERSFIELD
Econo Lodge   Rates Subject to Change   Motel   ◆
ⓑ All year   1P 34.95- 36.95 2P/1B   38.95- 40.95 2P/2B   43.95- 46.95 XP 5
Senior discount. 53 units. Eastside of I-5 Frwy at Stockdale Hwy. 200 Trask St. (Bakersfield, 93312, 93206) A/C; C/CATV; free & pay movies; rental VCPs. Phones. Small pool. No pets. Reserv deposit required. AE, MC, VI. Restaurant adjacent.   ⊗ Ⓓ Ⓛ (805) 764-5221

Nice Inn   Rates Subject to Change   Motel   ◆
ⓑ All year   1P ....   26.95 2P/1B   ....   32.95 2P/2B   ....   36.95 XP 4
Senior discount. 90 units. At Hwy 58 off ramp of I-5 Frwy. 20681 Tracy Ave. (93206) A/C; C/TV; movies; phones; comb or shower baths. Pool; whirlpool. Pets. Wkly rates avail. Reserv deposit required; 3 days refund notice. AE, DS, MC, VI. Coffeeshop adjacent.   ⊗ Ⓓ Ⓛ (805) 764-5117

CALABASAS — 200
Country Inn at Calabasas   Rates Guaranteed   Motel   ◆◆◆
ⓑ Sun-Thurs [BP]   1P ....   85.00 2P/1B   ....   85.00 2P/2B   ....   85.00 XP 10   F
Fri & Sat [BP]   1P ....   77.00 2P/1B   ....   77.00 2P/2B   ....   77.00 XP 10   F
Senior discount. 120 units. Adjacent to US 101, 1/2 mi sw; exit Mulholland Dr. 23627 Calabasas Rd. (91302) Refrigerators & microwaves. 12 units with gas fireplace. Check-in 3 pm. Refrigerators; A/C; C/TV; pay movies; VCPs. Radios; phones. 2 2-bedrm units. Coin laundry. Htd pool; whirlpool. Garage & parking lot. No pets. Complimentary beverages each evening. AE, DI, MC, VI. *(See ad p A89)*   ⊗ Ⓢ Ⓓ Ⓛ (818) 222-5300

CALIMESA — 1,000

Calimesa Inn Motel

		Rates Subject to Change			*Motel*	◆◆
⊛ 6/1-9/1	1P 39.00	2P/1B 42.00	2P/2B 47.00	XP 3	
9/2-5/31	1P 35.00	2P/1B 38.00	2P/2B 42.00	XP 3- 5	

36 units. 1 blk n of I-10, exit Calimesa Blvd. 1205 Calimesa Blvd. (92320) 10 refrigerators; A/C; C/TV; radios; phones. Whirlpool. Pets, $5 extra charge. Reserv deposit required. AE, DS, MC, VI.

⊗ Ⓢ Ⓓ Ⓛ (909) 795-2536

CALISTOGA — 4,500

Calistoga Village Inn and Spa

		AAA Special Value Rates			*Motel*	◆
⊛ Fri & Sat [CP]	1P 80.00	2P/1B 80.00	2P/2B 105.00	XP 6	F
Sun-Thurs 5/1-10/31 [CP]	1P 70.00	2P/1B 70.00	2P/2B 90.00	XP 6	F
Sun-Thurs 11/1-4/30 [CP]	1P 65.00	2P/1B 65.00	2P/2B 75.00	XP 6	

32 units. 3/4 mi n on SR 29. 1880 Lincoln Ave. (94515) 11 refrigerators; A/C; C/CATV; movies; radios; phones; comb or shower baths. 6 2-bedrm units. Wading pool; whirlpool; geothermal mineral water pool & tubs. Fee for: mudbaths; massage. 7 rooms with whirlpool bath, vcp & microwave, $125-$175 for up to 2 persons. AE, DI, DS, MC, VI. Restaurant adjacent. FAX (707) 942-5306 *(See ad p A88)*

⊗ Ⓓ (707) 942-0991

Comfort Inn Napa Valley North

		AAA Special Value Rates			*Motel*	◆◆
⊛ Fri & Sat [CP]	1P 95.00	2P/1B 99.00	2P/2B 105.00	XP 7	F
Sun-Thurs 4/1-10/31 [CP]	1P 80.00	2P/1B 85.00	2P/2B 95.00	XP 7	F
Sun-Thurs 11/1-3/31 [CP]	1P 62.00	2P/1B 68.00	2P/2B 75.00	XP 7	F

54 units. 1/2 mi n on SR 29. 1865 Lincoln Ave. (94515) Many units with view of gardens or hills. Check-in 3 pm. A/C; C/CATV; radios; phones. Small pool; sauna; whirlpool; steamroom. No pets. Reserv deposit required. AE, CB, DI, MC, VI. FAX (707) 942-5306

⊗ Ⓓ (707) 942-9400

Choose an establishment with the ⊛ next to its listing!

Roman Spa

| | | | | | | | Rates Subject to Change | | | | *Motel* | | ◆◆ |

⊕ 6/25-9/5 & Fri-Sat .... 2P/1B 70.00- 110.00 2P/2B 80.00- 94.00 XP 8
Sun-Thurs 3/11-6/24 &
9/6-10/30 .... 2P/1B 64.00- 100.00 2P/2B 72.00- 84.00 XP 8
Sun-Thurs 10/31-3/10 .... 2P/1B 55.00- 88.00 2P/2B 65.00- 75.00 XP 8
61 units. Center; 1 blk n of Lincoln Ave, SR 29. 1300 Washington St. (94515) Garden setting. Refrigerators; A/C; C/CATV; phones; comb or shower baths. 2 2-bedrm units, 28 kitchens. Coin laundry. Saunas; 2 hot mineral pools, 1 indoor. Fee for: geothermol tubs, mudbaths; massage. No pets. 2 night minimum stay weekends. 2-bedroom units, $90-$120 for 2 persons. Wkly rates avail. Reserv deposit required; 3 days refund notice. AE, MC, VI. *(See ad p A89 and p A289)* ⊗ Ⓓ (707) 942-4441

CAMARILLO — 47,000

Best Western Camarillo Inn — AAA Special Value Rates — *Motel* ◆◆◆
⊕ All year [CP] 1P .... 50.00 2P/1B .... 55.00 2P/2B .... 60.00 XP 5 F
58 units. Adjacent to US 101; 1/4 mi ne, exit Los Posas Rd. 295 E Daily Dr. (93010) 5 refrigerators; A/C; C/TV; movies; rental VCPs. Radios; phones. Small htd pool; whirlpool; 5 rooms with whirlpool tub. No pets. AE, DI, DS, MC, VI. Restaurant adjacent. FAX (805) 388-3679 ⊗ Ⓓ (805) 987-4991

Comfort Inn — AAA Special Value Rates — *Motel* ◆◆◆
⊕ 5/1-9/15 1P .... 47.00 2P/1B .... 53.00 2P/2B .... 59.00 XP 6 F
9/16-4/30 1P .... 45.00 2P/1B .... 49.00 2P/2B .... 53.00 XP 6 F
70 units. Adjacent to US 101, 1/2 mi se; exit Central Ave. 984 Ventura Blvd. (93010) 12 refrigerators; A/C; C/CATV; radios; phones. Small htd pool; whirlpool. No pets. 11 suites, $65-$69. In-house movies. Wkly & monthly rates avail. AE, DI, DS, MC, VI. FAX (805) 987-3450 *(See ad below)* ⊗ ⓈⒹ🄻 (805) 987-4188

Country Inn at Camarillo — Rates Guaranteed — *Motel* ◆◆◆
⊕ All year [BP] 1P .... 66.00 2P/1B .... 66.00 2P/2B .... 66.00 XP 10
Senior discount. 100 units. Adjacent to US 101, n side, 1/2 mi w; exit Central Ave. 1405 Del Norte Rd. (93010) Check-in 3 pm. Refrigerators; A/C; C/CATV; VCPs; radios; phones. Coin laundry. Small htd pool; whirlpool; 10 rooms with whirlpool tub. No pets. Microwaves. Complimentary beverages each evening. AE, DI, DS, MC, VI. FAX (805) 983-1838 *(See ad below)* ⊗ ⓈⒹ🄻 (805) 983-7171

Courtyard by Marriott — Rates Subject to Change — *Motel* ◆◆◆
Sun-Thurs 1P .... 64.00 2P/1B .... 74.00 2P/2B .... 74.00 XP 10
Fri & Sat .... 2P/1B .... 56.00 2P/2B .... 56.00 XP
Senior discount. 130 units. Adjacent n side of US 101; exit Pleasant Valley Rd/Santa Rosa Rd. 4994 Verdugo Way. (93012) A/C; C/CATV; free & pay movies; radios; phones. Htd pool; whirlpool; exercise rm. No pets. Wkly & monthly rates avail. AE, DS, MC, VI. Restaurant; 6:30 am-2 & 5-10 pm; $7.95-$12.25; cocktails. FAX (805) 987-6274 *(See ad below)* ⊗ ⓈⒹ🄻 (805) 388-1020

Days Inn — AAA Special Value Rates — *Motel* ◆◆
⊕ All year [CP] 1P .... 45.00 2P/1B .... 50.00 2P/2B .... 55.00 XP 5 F
82 units. Adjacent to US 101; exit Los Posas Rd. 165 Daily Dr. (93010) A/C; C/TV; movies; rental VCPs. Radios; phones; comb or shower baths. Htd pool; 2 rooms with whirlpool. No pets. Monthly rates avail. AE, DI, DS, MC, VI. Restaurant adjacent. ⊗ Ⓓ (805) 482-0761

Del Norte Inn — Rates Guaranteed — *Motel* ◆◆◆

All year [CP] 1P .... 49.00 2P/1B .... 49.00 2P/2B .... 49.00 XP 10 F
Senior discount. 111 units. Adjacent to US 101, n side; exit Central Ave. 4444 E Central Ave. (93010) Patio or balcony. Check-in 3 pm. Refrigerators; A/C; C/CATV; VCPs; radios; phones. 24 efficiencies. Coin laundry. Small htd pool; whirlpool. No pets. AE, DI, MC, VI. Restaurant adjacent. FAX (805) 485-1820 *(See ad below)*
Ⓧ Ⓢ Ⓓ Ⓛ (805) 485-3999

RESTAURANTS

Giovanni's — Northern Italian — $$$ — ◆◆
2 1/2 mi ne of US 101, via Dawson Rd & Mission Oaks Blvd, exit Dawson Rd (Mission Oaks Plaza). 5227 Mission Oaks Blvd. Semi-formal atmosphere. Homemade pastas, fresh fish & eastern veal. A/C. Open 11 am-2:30 & 5-10 pm; Sat & Sun from 5 pm; closed Mon. Cocktails & lounge. AE, MC, VI. Ⓧ (805) 484-4376

Ottavio's — Italian — $$ — ◆◆
1/2 blk se of US 101; exit Carmen Dr. 1620 Ventura Blvd. Informal atmosphere. Selection of seafood, steaks & pastas. Buffet lunch Mon-Fri 11:30 am-1:30 pm. A/C. Open 11 am-10 pm; Sun-9 pm; closed 12/25. Cocktails & lounge. Minimum $5.50 weekends. Reserv advised weekends. AE, CB, DI, MC, VI. Ⓧ (805) 482-3810

CAMBRIA — 3,100 See also SAN SIMEON

Best Western Fireside Inn — Rates Subject to Change — *Motel* ◆◆◆

4/1-10/31 [CP]	1P	95.00-140.00	2P/1B	95.00-140.00	2P/2B	95.00-105.00	XP 10
11/1-3/31 [CP]	1P	85.00-125.00	2P/1B	85.00-125.00	2P/2B	85.00- 95.00	XP 10

Senior discount. 46 units. 2 1/4 mi n, adjacent to SR 1. 6700 Moonstone Beach Dr. (93428) Across from beach. Spacious rooms, many with gas fireplace. Refrigerators; C/CATV; movies; radios; phones. Htd pool; whirlpool; 9 rooms with whirlpool tub. No pets. Reserv deposit required. AE, DI, DS, MC, VI. FAX (805) 927-8584
Ⓧ Ⓓ Ⓛ (805) 927-8661

Best Western Mariners Inn — Rates Subject to Change — *Motel* ◆◆

Fri & Sat 7/1-8/31 [CP]	1P	60.00- 70.00	2P/1B	65.00- 75.00	2P/2B	70.00- 80.00	XP 5
Sun-Thurs 5/15-9/30 [CP]	1P	45.00- 55.00	2P/1B	55.00- 65.00	2P/2B	60.00- 70.00	XP 5
Sun-Thurs 10/1-5/14 [CP]	1P	40.00- 50.00	2P/1B	45.00- 55.00	2P/2B	50.00- 60.00	XP

26 units. 1 3/4 mi n; adjacent to SR 1. 6180 Moonstone Beach Dr. (93428) Across from beach. Nicely decorated rooms, many with gas fireplace. 5 refrigerators; C/CATV; movies; VCPs. Radios; phones; comb or shower baths. Whirlpool; 2 whirlpool tubs. Reserv deposit required. AE, DI, DS, MC, VI. FAX (805) 927-3425
Ⓧ Ⓓ (805) 927-4624

Blue Bird Motel — Rates Subject to Change — *Motel* ◆◆

3/15-10/31 & Fri-Sat 11/1-3/14	1P	42.00- 78.00	2P/1B	44.00- 78.00	2P/2B	48.00- 78.00	XP 6
Sun-Thurs 11/1-3/14	1P	38.00- 58.00	2P/1B	42.00- 68.00	2P/2B	46.00- 68.00	XP 6

31 units. 1/4 mi w; 1/2 mi e of SR 1. 1880 Main St. (93428) C/CATV; radios; shower or comb baths. 1 2-bedrm unit. No pets. Wkly rates avail. Reserv deposit required. AE, DI, DS, MC, VI. *(See ad below and p A473)*
Ⓓ (805) 927-4634

Blue Dolphin Inn — Rates Subject to Change — *Motel* ◆◆◆◆

4/1-10/30 Fri & Sat [CP]	....		2P/1B	85.00-155.00	2P/2B	85.00-155.00	XP 5
11/1-3/31 [CP]	....		2P/1B	75.00-125.00	2P/2B	75.00-125.00	XP 5

18 units. 2 1/2 mi n; adjacent to SR 1. 6470 Moonstone Beach Dr. (93428) All rooms with gas fireplace, most with ocean view. French country decor. Check-in 3 pm. Refrigerators; C/CATV; movies; VCPs. Radios; phones. No pets. 5 rooms with whirlpool tub, $125-$185. Reserv deposit required; 3 days refund notice. AE, DI, MC, VI. *(See ad p A92 and p A477)* Ⓧ Ⓢ Ⓓ Ⓛ (805) 927-3300

Blue Whale Inn Bed & Breakfast   Rates Subject to Change   *Bed & Breakfast*   ◆◆◆◆
ⓐⓐ All year [BP]   ....   2P/1B   135.00- 165.00   ....   XP
6 units. 2 1/4 mi n, adjacent to SR 1. 6736 Moonstone Beach Dr. (93428) Individually decorated rooms in European country decor with canopy beds & gas fireplaces. Refrigerators; C/CATV; radios; phones. No pets. Complimentary afternoon refreshments. Reserv deposit required; 10 days refund notice. MC, VI. *(See ad below)*
       ⊗ Ⓓ (805) 927-4647

Check out our **bold** listings!

Cambria Landing on Moonstone Beach   Rates Subject to Change   *Motel*   ◆◆◆
⊛ All year [CP]   1P 85.00- 180.00   2P/1B 85.00- 180.00   2P/2B 85.00- 180.00 XP
20 units. 2 1/4 mi n, adjacent to SR 1, on Moonstone Beach Dr. 6530 Moonstone Beach Dr. (93428) All rooms with
fireplace, some balconies & ocean view. Check-in 3 pm. Refrigerators; C/CATV; VCPs; phones. 2 indoor whirlpools. No pets. Reserv deposit required; 7 days refund notice. MC, VI. Restaurant adjacent. *(See ad p A472)*
                                                                    Ⓢ Ⓓ (805) 927-1619

Cambria Pines Lodge   Rates Subject to Change   *Lodge*   ◆◆
⊛ 5/24-9/6 & Fri-Sat   1P 60.00- 100.00   2P/1B 60.00- 100.00   2P/2B 60.00- 100.00 XP 5
Sun-Thurs 9/7-5/23   1P 55.00- 95.00   2P/1B 55.00- 95.00   2P/2B 55.00- 95.00 XP 5
124 units. 1/2 mi e via Burton Dr from SR 1. 2905 Burton Dr. (93428) 100 units with woodburning fireplace. Cabins
& motel units on spacious natural & landscaped grounds. Check-in 3 pm. C/CATV; rental VCPs; phones; 64
phones. Htd indoor pool; whirlpool; exercise rm. No pets. 54 suites with microwave & refrigerator. AE, DS, MC,
VI. ● Restaurant; 7 am-10 pm; $10-$16.20; cocktails. FAX (805) 927-4016 *(See ad p A476)* ⊗ Ⓓ (805) 927-4200

Cambria Shores Inn   Rates Subject to Change   *Motel*   ◆◆
⊛ 6/1-9/30 & Fri-Sat 10/1-5/31
[CP]   1P 55.00- 85.00   2P/1B 55.00- 85.00   2P/2B 65.00- 95.00 XP 5
Sun-Thurs 10/1-5/31 [CP]   1P 45.00- 65.00   2P/1B 45.00- 65.00   2P/2B 55.00- 75.00 XP 5
24 units. 2 mi n, adjacent to SR 1, on Moonstone Beach Dr. 6276 Moonstone Beach Dr. (93428) Across from
beach. Most rooms with ocean view. Refrigerators; C/CATV; phones; shower or comb baths. No pets. Wkly rates
avail. Reserv deposit required; 3 days refund notice. AE, MC, VI. *(See ad below)*   Ⓓ (805) 927-8644

Castle Inn By The Sea   Rates Subject to Change   *Motel*   ◆◆
⊛ 5/1-10/31   1P 55.00- 95.00   2P/1B 55.00- 95.00   2P/2B 65.00- 95.00 XP 5
11/1-4/31   1P 45.00- 80.00   2P/1B 45.00- 80.00   2P/2B 50.00- 85.00 XP 5
31 units. 2 1/4 mi n, adjacent to SR 1, on Moonstone Beach Dr. 6620 Moonstone Beach Dr. (93428) Across from
beach. Many ocean view rooms. 20 refrigerators; C/CATV; movies; phones; shower or comb baths. Htd pool;
whirlpool. No pets. Reserv deposit required. AE, DS, MC, VI. Restaurant adjacent. FAX (805) 927-3179 *(See ad
below)*   Ⓓ (805) 927-8605

Creekside Inn   Rates Subject to Change   *Motel*   ◆◆
⊛ 4/2-11/30   1P 35.00- 80.00   2P/1B 35.00- 80.00   2P/2B 35.00- 80.00 XP 5
12/1-4/1   1P 35.00- 70.00   2P/1B 35.00- 70.00   2P/2B 35.00- 70.00 XP 5
21 units. 1/4 mi e. 2618 Main St. (93428) Check-in 3 pm. C/CATV; movies; VCPs. Phones; comb or shower baths.
No pets. MC, VI. *(See ad p A472)*   Ⓓ (805) 927-4021

Fog Catcher Inn   Rates Subject to Change   *Motel*   ◆◆◆
All year [BP]   1P 75.00- 135.00   2P/1B 75.00- 135.00   2P/2B 75.00- 135.00 XP 10
58 units. 2 1/2 mi n; adjacent to SR 1. 6400 Moonstone Beach Dr. (93428) Across from beach. All units with microwave
& fireplace. Many with ocean view. 6 suites with bedroom & living room. Check-in 3 pm. Refrigerators; C/CATV; VCPs;
radios; phones. Htd pool; whirlpool. No pets. 1 larger unit with private balcony, gas fireplace & ocean view,
$150. Reserv deposit required. AE, MC, VI. *(See ad p A476)*   ⊗ Ⓓ (805) 927-1400

The J Patrick House Bed and Breakfast Inn   Rates Subject to Change   *Bed & Breakfast*   ◆◆◆
All year [CP]   1P 100.00- 120.00   2P/1B 100.00- 120.00   ....   XP 30
8 units. 1/2 mi s. 2990 Burton Dr. (93428) Smoke free premises. 7 woodburning fireplaces & 1 woodburning stove. Comb
or shower baths. No pets. Reserv deposit required; 3 days refund notice. MC, VI.   ⊗ Ⓓ (805) 927-3812

Moonstone Inn Motel   Rates Subject to Change   *Motel*   ◆◆◆
⊛ All year [CP]   1P 90.50- 130.50   2P/1B 90.50- 130.50   ....   XP 10
7 units. 1 3/4 mi n; adjacent to SR 1. 5860 Moonstone Beach Dr. (93428) A small, charming motel with the atmosphere of a country inn. Across from beach. Ocean view. Six units with gas fireplace & refrigerator. Check-in 3
pm. C/CATV; movies; VCPs. Radios; phones; shower baths. Whirlpool; 2 rooms with whirlpool tub. No pets.
Complimentary afternoon refreshments. Reserv deposit required; 7 days refund notice. AE, MC, VI. *(See ad
p A477)*   Ⓓ (805) 927-4815

Olallieberry Inn
All year [BP]

Rates Subject to Change

Historic Bed & Breakfast ◆◆

1P 85.00- 115.00 2P/1B 85.00- 115.00 .... XP

Senior discount. 6 units. 2 blks s of Burton Dr. 2476 Main St. (93428) Restored 1870 2-story wood home furnished with turn-of-the-century antiques. Smoke free premises. 3 gas fireplaces. Check-in 3 pm. Comb, shower, or tub baths. No pets. Reserv deposit required; 5 days refund notice. MC, VI. ⊗ Ⓓ (805) 927-3222

Pickford House Bed & Breakfast
🚗 All year [BP]

Rates Subject to Change

Bed & Breakfast ◆◆

.... 2P/1B 85.00- 120.00 2P/2B .... 125.00 XP 20

8 units. 1 mi s; adjacent to SR 1, via Main St, Eton & Wood rds. 2555 MacLeod Ave. (93428) Designated smoking areas. C/CATV. No pets. 3 rooms with fireplace. Complimentary evening refreshments. Reserv deposit required; 7 days refund notice. MC, VI. ⊗ Ⓓ (805) 927-8619

Sand Pebbles Inn
🚗 4/1-10/31 & Fri-Sat [CP]
11/1-3/31 [CP]

Rates Subject to Change

Motel ◆◆◆◆

.... 2P/1B 85.00- 155.00 2P/2B 85.00- 155.00 XP 5
.... 2P/1B 75.00- 125.00 2P/2B 75.00- 125.00 XP 5

23 units. 2 mi n; adjacent to SR 1. 6252 Moonstone Beach Dr. (93428) All rooms with gas fireplace; most with ocean view, French country decor. Check-in 3 pm. Refrigerators; C/CATV; movies; VCPs. Radios; phones. No pets. 6 rooms with whirlpool tub, $125-$185. Reserv deposit required; 3 days refund notice. AE, DI, MC, VI. *(See ad below and p A477)* ⊗ Ⓢ Ⓓ 🛗 (805) 927-5600

San Simeon Pines Seaside Resort — Rates Subject to Change — *Motel* ◆◆
All year .... 2P/1B 70.00- 98.00 2P/2B 70.00- 84.00 XP
60 units. 3 mi n, adjacent to SR 1, on Moonstone Beach Dr. (PO Box 117, San Simeon, 93452) Spacious & nicely landscaped grounds. Private access to beach. 22 rooms with woodburning fireplace. Check-in 3 pm. C/CATV; phones; shower or comb baths. Htd pool; par-3 golf; playground. No pets. Reserv deposit required. AE, MC, VI. *(See ad below and p A474)* ⊗ Ⓓ 🖭 (805) 927-4648

Sea Otter Inn — Rates Guaranteed — *Motel* ◆◆◆
4/1-10/31 & Fri-Sat 11/1-3/31 1P 65.00- 90.00 2P/1B 70.00- 100.00 2P/2B 70.00- 110.00 XP 5
Sun-Thurs 11/1-3/31 1P 55.00- 75.00 2P/1B 60.00- 80.00 2P/2B 60.00- 80.00 XP 5
25 units. 2 1/4 mi n; adjacent to SR 1. 6656 Moonstone Beach Dr. (93428) All rooms with gas fireplace. Check-in 3 pm. Refrigerators; C/CATV; VCPs; radios; phones. Htd pool; whirlpool; 5 rooms with whirlpool tub. No pets. Reserv deposit required. DS, MC, VI. Ⓓ 🖭 (805) 927-5888

Sylvia's Rigdon Hall Inn — Rates Subject to Change — *Suites Motor Inn*
All year [CP] .... 2P/1B 100.00- 150.00 .... XP
8 units. 2 blks s of Main St. 4036 Burton Dr. (93428) Rating withheld pending completion of renovation, scheduled to open September, 1992. 1 bedroom suites with living room. C/CATV; movies; radios; phones. No pets. Microwave & refrigerator. Reserv deposit required. MC, VI. ● Dining rm, see separate listing.
⊗ Ⓓ (805) 927-5125

White Water Inn — Rates Subject to Change — *Motel* ◆◆◆
All year [CP] 1P 85.00- 100.00 2P/1B 85.00- 100.00 2P/2B 85.00- 100.00 XP 10
17 units. 2 1/2 mi n, adjacent to SR 1, on Moonstone Beach Dr. 6790 Moonstone Beach Dr. (93428) All rooms with gas fireplace. Refrigerators; C/CATV; movies; radios; phones. No pets. 2 rooms with private patio & whirlpool tub, $160; 6 rooms with whirlpool tub $110. Reserv deposit required; 3 days refund notice 9/1-5/31. AE, DI, DS, MC, VI. *(See ad p A474)* ⊗ ⑤Ⓓ🖭 (805) 927-1066

RESTAURANTS

The Hamlet Restaurant at Moonstone Gardens — American — $$ ◆◆
3 mi n on SR 1, across from jct Moonstone Beach Dr. Ocean view dining. Outdoor patio dining in garden. Lunches & light suppers served in upstairs lounge. Open 11:30 am-9 pm; closed 11/29-12/25. Cocktails & lounge. MC, VI.
(805) 927-3535

Moonraker — Seafood — $$ ◆◆
2 1/4 mi n; adjacent to SR 1. 6550 Moonstone Beach Dr. Attractive setting with ocean view. Nice selection of seafood, steaks, chicken, frog legs & Cajun cuisine. Sun brunch 9 am-1 pm. Children's menu. Open 11:30 am-2:30 & 4:30-9 pm; Sat, Sun & 6/1-8/31 8 am-9 pm; closed Wed, 9/1-5/30, 11/25 & 1/4-1/17. Cocktails. Reserv advised. AE, MC, VI. ⊗ (805) 927-3859

Mustache Pete's Italian Eatery — Italian — $$ ◆◆
Center. 4090 Burton Dr. Casual family dining. Enclosed patio dining. Selection of seafood, chicken & beef, pasta & pizza entrees. Sun brunch 10 am-1 pm. Early bird specials; children's menu. Open 11 am-9 pm; Fri & Sat-10 pm; Sun 10 am-9 pm; closed 12/25. Cocktails. Entertainment. AE, DS, MC, VI. ⊗ (805) 927-8589

Robin's — Ethnic — $$ ◆◆
1 blk s of Main St. 4095 Burton Dr. India, Mexican, Thai & Chinese cuisines. Also pasta, seafood, beef & chicken. Smoke free premises. Open 5 pm-9 pm; closed 12/25. Beer & wine. Reserv advised weekends. MC, VI.
(805) 927-5007

Sow's Ear — American — $$ ◆◆
Center. 2248 Main St. Small, casual restaurant with nice selection of fresh seafood. Pastries & bread made on premises. Children's menu. Open 5:30 pm-9 pm; Sat-10 pm; closed 11/25, 12/24 & 12/25. Beer & wine. Reserv advised. MC, VI.
⊗ (805) 927-4865

Sylvia's Rigdon Hall Restaurant American $$ ◆◆
ⓐ 2 blks s of Main St. 4022 Burton Dr. Fine dining in a refined atmosphere. A/C. Early bird specials; children's menu. Open 5 pm-10 pm; closed 12/25. Beer & wine. Reserv advised weekends. MC, VI. *(See ad p A476)*
⊗ (805) 927-5125

CAMERON PARK — 5,600

Best Western Cameron Park Inn AAA Special Value Rates Motel ◆◆◆
ⓐ All year [CP] 1P 54.00- 64.00 2P/1B 59.00- 69.00 2P/2B 66.00- 76.00 XP 6
63 units. 12 mi w of Placerville on US 50, exit Cameron Park Dr. 3361 Coach Ln. (95682) Check-in 3 pm. A/C; C/CATV; movies; radios; phones. Coin laundry. Pool. Pets. 10 kitchens, $15 extra. Wkly & monthly rates avail. Reserv deposit required. AE, DI, DS, MC, VI. Coffeeshop adjacent. FAX (916) 676-1422 ⊗ Ⓓ (916) 677-2203

Super 8 Motel Rates Guaranteed Motel ◆◆
All year 1P .... 41.50 2P/1B .... 46.50 2P/2B .... 49.50 XP 5
Senior discount. 60 units. 12 mi w of Placerville on US 50, exit Cameron Park Dr. 3444 Coach Ln. (95682) Check-in 3 pm. A/C; C/TV; phones. Coin laundry. Small pool; whirlpool. Pets, $100 deposit required. 3 extra large rooms, $48.50-$58.50 for up to 2 persons. Wkly rates avail. AE, DS, MC, VI. Coffeeshop adjacent. FAX (916) 677-2235
⊗ Ⓢ Ⓓ (916) 677-7177

CAMPBELL — 36,000 See also SAN JOSE

Campbell Inn Rates Subject to Change Motel ◆◆◆
ⓐ Sun-Thurs [CP] 1P 109.00- 175.00 2P/1B 119.00- 175.00 2P/2B 119.00- 175.00 XP 10 F
Fri & Sat [CP] 1P 89.00- 175.00 2P/1B 99.00- 175.00 2P/2B 99.00- 175.00 XP 10 F
99 units. Exit SR 17 Hamilton Ave E; 1/4 mi to Bascom Ave, 1/4 mi s; 1/4 mi w on Campbell Ave. 675 E Campbell Ave. (95008) Tastefully appointed. Refrigerators; A/C; C/CATV; VCPs; radios; phones. Small pool; whirlpool; lighted tennis-1 court; bicycles; 25 units with whirlpool bath; 5 steambaths; jogging track. Airport transp. Pets, $10 extra charge. 4 suites with fireplace & whirlpool tub. Complimentary beverages each evening. AE, CB, DI, MC, VI. Restaurant opposite. FAX (408) 379-0695 ⊗ Ⓢ Ⓓ (408) 374-4300

Executive Inn Suites Rates Subject to Change Motel ◆◆◆
ⓐ All year [CP] 1P .... 80.00 2P/1B .... 85.00 2P/2B .... 85.00 XP 10 F
Senior discount. 38 units. Exit SR 17 at Camden Ave E. 1300 Camden Ave. (95008) Attractively appointed rooms. A/C; C/CATV; movies; radios; phones; comb or shower baths. 35 efficiencies, no utensils. Coin laundry. Garage. No pets. Some rooms with whirlpool tub. Wkly rates avail. AE, DI, DS, MC, VI. Coffeeshop opposite. FAX (408) 371-5721 *(See ad p A95)* ⊗ Ⓢ Ⓓ (408) 559-3600

The Pruneyard Inn Rates Subject to Change Motel ◆◆◆◆
ⓐ Sun-Thurs [CP] 1P 109.00- 245.00 2P/1B 119.00- 245.00 2P/2B 119.00- 245.00 XP 10 F
Fri & Sat [CP] 1P 89.00- 220.00 2P/1B 85.00- 220.00 2P/2B 85.00- 220.00 XP 10 F
Senior discount. 118 units. Exit SR 17 Hamilton Ave, 1/4 mi e, s on Bascom Ave, at nw corner of Pruneyard Shopping Center. 1995 S Bascom Ave. (95008) Attractive decor. Refrigerators; A/C; C/CATV; movies; VCPs. Radios; phones; comb or shower baths. 11 efficiencies. Small pool; whirlpool; bicycles; jogging track. Airport transp. No pets. Some rooms with whirlpool tub & fireplace. Reserv deposit required. Complimentary beverages each evening. AE, CB, DI, MC, VI. FAX (408) 559-9919 ⊗ Ⓢ Ⓓ (408) 559-4300

Residence Inn By Marriott-San Jose Rates Subject to Change Suites Motel ◆◆◆
Sun-Thurs [CP] 1P .... 124.00 2P/1B .... 124.00 2P/2B .... 149.00 XP
Fri & Sat [CP] 1P .... 89.00 2P/1B .... 89.00 2P/2B .... 119.00 XP
Senior discount. 80 units. Exit SR 17 via Camden Ave E; n on Bascom Ave. 2761 S Bascom Ave. (95008) 1- & 2-bedroom suites with living room, dining area & kitchen; some fireplaces. A/C; C/CATV; movies; radios; phones. Coin laundry. Small pool; whirlpool; bicycles. Parking lot. Airport transp. Pets, $50 extra charge; also $6 daily. AE, DI, DS, MC, VI. FAX (408) 371-9808 ⊗ Ⓓ Ⓖ (408) 559-1551

CANOGA PARK — 89,300 See LOS ANGELES (San Fernando Valley)

CAPISTRANO BEACH — 6,200

Capistrano Edgewater Inn Rates Subject to Change Motel ◆◆◆
ⓐ Fri & Sat [CP] 1P 85.00- 120.00 2P/1B 85.00- 120.00 2P/2B 85.00- 120.00 XP 10 F
Sun-Thurs [CP] 1P 75.00- 110.00 2P/1B 75.00- 110.00 2P/2B 75.00- 110.00 XP 10 F
Senior discount. 30 units. 3/4 mi se. 34744 Pacific Coast Hwy. (92624) Across from beach. Most rooms with ocean view. A/C; C/CATV; movies; radios; phones. Efficiencies. Sauna; indoor whirlpool. Garage. No pets. Wkly & monthly rates avail. Reserv deposit required. AE, DI, MC, VI. FAX (714) 493-3692 *(See ad p A125)*
Ⓢ Ⓓ (714) 240-0150

Capistrano Seaside Inn Rates Subject to Change Motel ◆◆
ⓐ Fri & Sat 5/1-9/7 [CP] .... 2P/1B 60.00- 75.00 2P/2B 60.00- 75.00 XP F
Sun-Thurs 5/1-9/7 [CP] .... 2P/1B 48.00- 60.00 2P/2B 48.00- 60.00 XP F
Fri & Sat 9/8-4/30 [CP] .... 2P/1B 48.00- 60.00 2P/2B 48.00- 60.00 XP F
Sun-Thurs 9/8-4/30 [CP] .... 2P/1B 40.00- 52.00 2P/2B 40.00- 52.00 XP F
28 units. 34862 Pacific Coast Hwy. (92624) Across highway from beach. Rooms decorated in a country inn style with fireplace & patio. 23 refrigerators; C/CATV; radios; phones; shower baths. 1 2-bedroom suite, $95-$105. AE, DI, DS, MC, VI. FAX (714) 240-8977 ⊗ Ⓓ (714) 496-1399

Capistrano Surfside Inn AAA Special Value Rates Suites Motel ◆◆◆
ⓐ 6/15-9/15 1P 145.00- 185.00 2P/1B 145.00- 185.00 2P/2B 145.00- 185.00 XP
9/16-10/31 & 4/1-6/14 1P 120.00- 150.00 2P/1B 120.00- 150.00 2P/2B 120.00- 150.00 XP
11/1-3/31 1P 100.00- 125.00 2P/1B 100.00- 125.00 2P/2B 100.00- 125.00 XP
15 units. 34680 Pacific Coast Hwy. (92624) All rooms with whirlpool bath. Balconies with gas barbecue. Some ocean views. Check-in 4 pm. Check-out 10 am. A/C; C/CATV; movies; radios; phones. 4 2-bedrm units, kitchens. Coin laundry. Htd pool; sauna; whirlpool; recreational program; bicycles; exercise rm. Garage. No pets. Wkly rates avail. Reserv deposit required; 3 days refund notice. MC, VI. Ⓢ Ⓓ (714) 240-7681

CAPITOLA — 10,200

Capitola Inn Rates Subject to Change Motel ◆◆◆
ⓐ 5/1-9/30 1P 65.00- 95.00 2P/1B 70.00- 120.00 2P/2B 85.00- 125.00 XP 5
10/1-4/30 1P 55.00- 75.00 2P/1B 55.00- 85.00 2P/2B 65.00- 90.00 XP 5
56 units. 3 mi se of Santa Cruz, off SR 1; 1 blk w via Capitola-Soquel exit. 822 Bay Ave. (95010) 14 refrigerators; A/C; C/CATV; pay movies; 20 radios; phones. Pool. No pets. 6 efficiencies, $15 extra; 3 units with gas fireplace & whirlpool bath. $175 for up to 4 persons. Reserv deposit required. AE, DI, MC, VI. Coffeeshop adjacent.
⊗ Ⓓ Ⓖ (408) 462-3004

The Inn at Depot Hill   Rates Subject to Change   *Bed & Breakfast*   ◆◆◆
  All year [BP]   1P 165.00- 265.00   2P/1B 165.00- 265.00   ....   XP 25
  8 units. 1 mi w of SR 1 via Bay Ave; Capitola/Soquel exit. 250 Monterey Ave. (95010) Individually decorated rooms &
  common areas in converted former railroad station. Smoke free premises. Check-in 3 pm. C/CATV; radios; phones; comb
  or shower baths. No pets. 4 units with hot tub. VCP's avail. Reserv deposit required; 10 days refund notice. AE, MC, VI.
  FAX (408) 458-0989   ⊗ Ⓓ (408) 462-3376

RESTAURANT

Shadowbrook   Steak & Seafood $$ ◆◆◆
  4 mi se of Santa Cruz; 41st Ave, exit off SR 1, 1/2 mi s, then 1/2 mi e on Capitoa Rd. 1750 Wharf Rd. In unique rustic
  setting overlooking creek. Lush landscaping. Funicular railway down to dining room. Specialty, prime rib. Variety of fresh
  seafood. Children's menu. Open 5:30 pm-9:30 pm; Sat 11 am-2:30 & 4-10:30 pm; Sun 10 am-2:30 & 4-9 pm. Cocktails
  & lounge. Entertainment. Reserv advised. AE, DI, DS, MC, VI.   ⊗ (408) 475-1511

CARDIFF-BY-THE-SEA — 10,100

Cardiff-By-The-Sea Lodge   Rates Subject to Change   *Motel*   ◆◆◆
  ㊈ All year [CP]   ....   2P/1B 85.00- 160.00   2P/2B 85.00- 160.00 XP
  Senior discount. 17 units. 1/4 mi w of I-5, exit Birmingham Dr. 142 Chesterfield Ave. (92007) Beautifully decorated
  & furnished rooms. Rooftop garden with ocean view, whirlpool & fire pit. Smoke free premises. Check-in 3 pm.
  6 refrigerators; A/C; C/CATV; phones; comb or shower baths. No pets. 5 rooms with fireplace & whirlpool tub.
  Wkly rates avail. Reserv deposit required; 7 days refund notice. AE, MC, VI. FAX (619) 944-6841
                                                              ⊗ Ⓢ Ⓓ (619) 944-6474

Country Side Inn   Rates Guaranteed   *Motel*   ◆◆◆
  ㊅ 5/1-9/15 [BP]   1P 65.00- 75.00   2P/1B 70.00- 80.00   2P/2B 72.00- 82.00 XP   8   F
  9/16-4/30 [BP]   1P 59.00- 69.00   2P/1B 64.00- 74.00   2P/2B 66.00- 76.00 XP   8   F
  Senior discount. 102 units. Adjacent to I-5, exit Birmingham Dr. 1661 Villa Cardiff Dr. (92007) Attractive, colonial
  decor. Refrigerators; A/C; C/CATV; movies; radios; phones. Small htd pool; whirlpool. No pets. Wkly rates avail.
  Complimentary beverages each evening. AE, DI, DS, MC, VI. FAX (619) 844-7708 *(See ad p A295)*
                                                              ⊗ Ⓢ Ⓓ Ⓛ (619) 944-0427

RESTAURANT

Chart House — Steak & Seafood — $$ — ◆◆
1/2 mi s of Chesterfield. 2588 S Hwy 101. Nautical decor overlooking ocean. Sun brunch 10 am-2 pm. A/C. Early bird specials; children's menu. Open 5 pm-10 pm; Fri & Sat-11 pm; Sun 4:30 pm-10 pm; closed 11/25. Cocktails & lounge. Valet parking. AE, DI, DS, MC, VI.   ⊗ (619) 436-4044

CARLSBAD — 63,100   See also LA COSTA

Best Western Andersen's Inn — Rates Subject to Change — *Motor Inn* — ◆◆◆
⊛
5/24-9/14	1P 75.00- 85.00	2P/1B	85.00- 95.00	2P/2B	85.00- 95.00	XP 10	F
9/15-5/23	1P 65.00- 75.00	2P/1B	75.00- 85.00	2P/2B	75.00- 85.00	XP 10	F

Senior discount. 143 units. Adjacent to I-5; exit Palomar Airport Rd. 850 Palomar Airport Rd. (92008) Spacious, nicely landscaped grounds. A/C; C/CATV; radios; phones. Coin laundry. Htd pool; whirlpool. No pets. Reserv deposit required; 3 days refund notice. AE, CB, DI, MC, VI. ● Pea Soup Andersen's Restaurant, see separate listing. FAX (619) 438-1015   ⊗ (D) (&) (619) 438-7880

Best Western Beach Terrace Inn — Rates Subject to Change — *Motel* — ◆◆◆
⊛
6/15-9/15 [CP]	1P 95.00- 170.00	2P/1B	95.00- 170.00	2P/2B	105.00- 180.00	XP 10	
9/16-6/14 [CP]	1P 80.00- 130.00	2P/1B	80.00- 130.00	2P/2B	90.00- 140.00	XP 10	

49 units. 1 mi w of I-5, exit Carlsbad Village Dr. 2775 Ocean St. (92008) Directly on beach. Many rooms with ocean view. Gas fireplace & microwave, many balconies. Refrigerators; A/C; C/CATV; movies; radios; phones. 6 efficiencies. Coin laundry. Htd pool; sauna; whirlpool. No pets. 28 1-bedroom suites with kitchen. Monthly rates avail 10/1-4/30. Reserv deposit required. AE, DI, DS, MC, VI. FAX (619) 729-1078 *(See ad p A97)*   (D) (619) 729-5951

Best Western Beach View Lodge — Rates Subject to Change — *Motel* — ◆◆◆
⊛
6/15-9/15 [CP]	1P 85.00- 95.00	2P/1B	95.00- 100.00	2P/2B	95.00- 100.00	XP 8	
9/16-6/14 [CP]	1P 68.00- 78.00	2P/1B	78.00- 86.00	2P/2B	78.00- 86.00	XP 8	

41 units. From I-5, exit Carlsbad Village Dr, 3/4 mi w then 2 blks s. 3180 Carlsbad Blvd. (92008) Across from Carlsbad State Beach. Few ocean view rooms. Some gas fireplaces & balconies. Refrigerators; A/C; C/CATV; movies; radios; phones. Coin laundry. Htd pool; sauna; whirlpool. No pets. 16 kitchens & 12 efficiencies, $10 extra. 6 1-bedroom apartments, $110-$135 for 2 persons. Monthly rates avail 10/1-4/30. Reserv deposit required. AE, DI, DS, MC, VI. FAX (619) 434-5405 *(See ad p A97)*   (D) (619) 729-1151

Carlsbad Inn Beach Resort — AAA Special Value Rates — *Motor Inn* — ◆◆◆
⊛
All year	1P 105.00- 125.00	2P/1B	115.00- 135.00	2P/2B	115.00- 135.00	XP 10	F

62 units. 3/4 mi w of I-5, exit Carlsbad Village Dr. 3075 Carlsbad Blvd. (92008), Across the street from stairway to beach Old World decor. Check-in 4 pm. C/CATV; VCPs; radios; phones; comb or shower baths. 29 efficiencies. Coin laundry. Htd pool; sauna; whirlpool; exercise rm. Garage & parking lot. No pets. Wkly & monthly rates avail. Reserv deposit required. AE, CB, DI, MC, VI. ● Restaurant & coffeeshop; 6 am-11 pm; $6-$12; cocktails. FAX (619) 729-4853   (S) (D) (619) 434-7020

Carlsbad/La Costa Travelodge   Rates Subject to Change   *Motel* ◆◆

5/3-9/15	1P	....	49.00	2P/1B	....	54.00	2P/2B	....	63.00	XP 5	F
9/16-5/2	1P	....	39.00	2P/1B	....	42.00	2P/2B	....	42.00	XP 5	F

Senior discount. 126 units. Adjacent to I-5, exit Poinsettia Ln, 1 blk w to Ave Encinas, then 2 blks n. 760 Macadamia Dr. (92009) Check-in 3 pm. 8 refrigerators; A/C; C/TV; phones. Coin laundry. Small htd pool; whirlpool. No pets. Wkly rates avail. AE, DS, MC, VI. FAX (619) 438-8181 *(See ad p A97)*   ⊗ ⒟ Ⓛ (619) 438-2828

Inns of America   AAA Special Value Rates   *Motor Inn* ◆◆

6/15-9/8 [CP]	1P	....	39.90	2P/1B	....	49.90	2P/2B	....	49.90	XP 7
9/9-6/14 [CP]	1P	....	39.90	2P/1B	....	39.90	2P/2B	....	39.90	XP 7

126 units. Adjacent to I-5, exit Poinsettia Ln. 751 Raintree Dr. (92009) A/C; C/CATV; movies; radios; phones. Htd pool. Pets. AE, MC, VI. ● Restaurant; 11 am-11 pm, Sat 7 am-midnight, Sun 8 am-10 pm; $10-$17; cocktails.   ⊗ Ⓢ ⒟ (619) 931-1185

Ocean Manor Motel   Rates Subject to Change   *Apartment Motel* ◆◆

6/15-9/14	1P	69.00- 120.00	2P/1B	69.00- 120.00	2P/2B	119.00- 127.00 XP
9/15-6/14	1P	49.00- 77.00	2P/1B	49.00- 77.00	2P/2B	75.00- 83.00 XP

Senior discount. 47 units. 1 mi w of I-5, exit Carlsbad Village Rd. 2950 Ocean St. (92008) Across from stairway to beach. Studio, 1- & 2-bedroom apartments. C/CATV; radios; phones; shower or comb baths. 12 2-bedrm units, 46 kitchens, 21 efficiencies. Coin laundry. Htd pool; whirlpool. No pets. Wkly rates avail. Reserv deposit required; 3 days refund notice; 30 days for stay over 7 days. AE, CB, DI, MC, VI. FAX (619) 729-0579   ⒟ (619) 729-2493

Pelican Cove Inn   AAA Special Value Rates   *Bed & Breakfast* ◆◆◆

All year [CP]	1P	75.00- 140.00	2P/1B	85.00- 150.00	....	XP 10

8 units. 2 blks e of Carlsbad Blvd. 320 Walnut Ave. (92008) Beautifully decorated rooms. Gas fireplaces. Feather beds. Check-in 3 pm. C/CATV; radios; comb or shower baths. 2 rooms with whirlpool tub. No pets. Wkly rates avail. Reserv deposit required; 7 days refund notice. AE, MC, VI.   ⒟ (619) 434-5995

Sun Coast Inn   Rates Subject to Change   *Motel* ◆◆

5/28-9/14	1P	43.00- 48.00	2P/1B	46.00- 51.00	2P/2B	....	55.00	XP 15
9/15-5/27	1P	37.00- 48.00	2P/1B	41.00- 44.00	2P/2B	....	48.00	XP 15

47 units. E side of I-5, exit Tamarack Ave; then 1/4 mi n. 3700 Pio Pico Dr. (92008) All units with small microwave & refrigerator. A/C; C/CATV; movies; radios; phones. 3 2-bedrm units. Coin laundry. Small htd pool. No pets. Wkly rates avail. Reserv deposit required. AE, DI, DS, MC, VI.   ⊗ Ⓢ ⒟ (619) 720-0808

Surf Motel   Rates Subject to Change   *Motel* ◆◆

6/1-8/31	1P	50.00- 65.00	2P/1B	50.00- 65.00	2P/2B	65.00- 75.00 XP 5	F
9/1-5/31	1P	34.00- 50.00	2P/1B	34.00- 50.00	2P/2B	40.00- 60.00 XP 5	F

26 units. From I-5, exit Carlsbad Village Dr, 3/4 mi/w, then 1 1/2 blks s. 3136 Carlsbad Blvd. (92008) 14 refrigerators; A/C; C/CATV; phones; comb or shower baths. Coin laundry. Htd pool. No pets. 5 kitchens, $25 utensil deposit required; 5 rooms with whirlpool tub, $5-$10 extra. Reserv deposit required; 3 days refund notice. AE, DS, MC, VI. *(See ad p A98 & A378)*   ⊗ ⒟ (619) 729-7961

RESTAURANTS

The Cove   American $$
1/2 blk w of I-5. 1025 Carlsbad Village Dr. Attractive, informal restaurant featuring a nice selection of salads, sandwiches & entrees. A/C. Open 11 am-9 pm; Fri-10 pm; Sat 9 am-10 pm; closed Sun & major holidays. Beer & wine. MC, VI.   ⊗ (619) 434-2683

Fidel's Norte   Mexican $
1 mi w of I-5, exit Carlsbad Village Dr. 3003 Carlsbad Blvd. Colorful, informal restaurant featuring nice selection of Mexican cuisine. A/C. Open 11:30 am-9 pm; Fri & Sat-10 pm; closed 11/25 & 12/25. Cocktails & lounge. MC, VI.   ⊗ (619) 729-0903

Henry's   American $$ ◆◆
1 mi w of I-5. 264 Carlsbad Village Dr. Nice selection of beef, veal, chicken & pasta. A/C. Open 11 am-2:30 & 4:30-9:30 pm; Fri-10:30 pm; Sat 5:30 pm-10:30 pm; Sun 5:30 pm-9:30 pm; closed 4/11, 9/6, 11/25 & 12/25. Cocktails & lounge. Entertainment. AE, CB, DI, MC, VI.   Ⓛ (619) 729-9244

Neiman's   American $$ ◆◆◆
3/4 mi w of I-5, exit Carlsbad Village Dr. 2978 Carlsbad Blvd. In restored Victorian building. Very attractive restaurant featuring seafood, chicken & prime rib. Sun buffet brunch. A/C. Open 11:30 am-11:30 pm; Sun 9:30 am-2 & 5-10 pm. Cocktails & lounge. AE, MC, VI.   ⊗ (619) 729-4131

Pea Soup Andersen's Restaurant   American $$ ◆
At Best Western Andersen's Inn. Coffeeshop & dining room featuring a nice selection of salads, sandwiches & entrees. A/C. Open 6:30 am-10 pm. Cocktails & lounge. AL, CB, MC, VI.   ⊗ Ⓛ (619) 438-7880

CARMEL — 4,200   (See MONTEREY PENINSULA spotting map pages A262 & A263; see index starting on page A260)

Adobe Inn-Carmel 🅼   Rates Subject to Change   *Motel* ◆◆◆◆

6/1-10/31 [CP]	1P 140.00- 185.00	2P/1B	140.00- 190.00	2P/2B	155.00- 270.00 XP 20
11/1-5/31 [CP]	1P 110.00- 150.00	2P/1B	120.00- 170.00	2P/2B	145.00- 240.00 XP 20

20 units. 2 blks s off Ocean Ave at Dolores St & 8th Ave. (PO Box 4115, 93921) Woodburning fireplaces; many balconies & wet bar. Check-in 3 pm. Refrigerators; C/CATV; VCPs; radios; phones. 3 2-bedrm units. Small pool; sauna. Garage. No pets. 3-night minimum stay weekends. Reserv deposit required; 3 days refund notice. AE, MC, VI. Restaurant adjacent. *(See ad p A100)*   ⊗ ⒟ (408) 624-3933

(See MONTEREY PENINSULA spotting map pages A262 & A263)

Best Western Bay View Inn 79   Rates Subject to Change   *Motel*   ◆◆◆
4/15-10/31 [CP]   1P 110.00- 150.00   2P/1B   110.00- 150.00   2P/2B   110.00- 160.00   XP
56 units. 1 blk n; Junipero St between 5th & 6th aves. (PO Box 3715, 93921) OPEN ALL YEAR. Hilltop units with
ocean view. Some balconies & all gas burning fireplaces. Few small units. 12 refrigerators; C/CATV; phones;
comb or shower baths. Pool. No pets. 4 suites, $149-$210 for up to 4 persons. Reserv deposit required; 3 days
refund notice. AE, DI, DS, MC, VI. Restaurant opposite. *(See ad p A101)*   ⒟ (408) 624-1831

Best Western Carmel's Town House
Lodge 77   Rates Subject to Change   *Motel*   ◆◆
4/1-10/31 [CP]   1P 84.00- 96.00   2P/1B   84.00- 96.00   2P/2B   94.00- 145.00   XP   6
11/1-3/31   1P 64.00- 76.00   2P/1B   64.00- 76.00   2P/2B   74.00- 125.00   XP   6
28 units. 2 blks n, at 5th Ave & San Carlos St. (PO Box 3574, 93921) 6 refrigerators; C/CATV; phones; shower or
comb baths. 1 2-bedrm unit. Small pool. Limited parking lot. No pets. 2-night minimum stay weekends 4/1-10/31;
3 night minimum for major holidays & special events. Reserv deposit required; 3 days refund notice. AE, DI, DS,
MC, VI. *(See ad p A99)*   ⒟ (408) 624-1261

(See MONTEREY PENINSULA spotting map pages A262 & A263)

Candle Light Inn 109 ◆◆◆
5/28-10/31 & Fri-Sat [CP]   1P 115.00- 135.00   2P/1B 115.00- 135.00   2P/2B 115.00- 135.00   XP 15   F
11/1-5/27 [CP]   1P 89.00- 105.00   2P/1B   89.00- 105.00   2P/2B   89.00- 105.00   XP 15   F
Senior discount. 19 units. 2 blks n on San Carlos St, between 4th & 5th aves. (PO Box 1900, 93921) Some rooms
with fireplace. Check-in 3 pm. Refrigerators; C/CATV; phones; shower or comb baths. 1 2-bedrm unit, 7 kitchens.
Small pool. No pets. 2-night minimum stay weekends. 1 unit with whirlpool bath. Reserv deposit required; 3 days
refund notice. AE, DI, DS, MC, VI. FAX (408) 624-2967 *(See ad p A102)*   Ⓓ (408) 624-6451

Carmel Fireplace Inn 104 ◆
6/1-10/31 & Fri-Sat [CP]   1P 65.00- 140.00   2P/1B   65.00- 140.00   2P/2B   65.00- 150.00   XP 15
11/1-5/31 & Sun-Thurs [CP]   1P 60.00- 100.00   2P/1B   60.00- 100.00   2P/2B   60.00- 100.00   XP 15
Senior discount. 18 units. 3 blks n at San Carlos St & 4th Ave. (PO Box 5245, 93921) Few small rooms; few large
units. Many woodburning fireplaces. Refrigerators; C/CATV; radios; phones; comb or shower baths. 1 2-bedrm
unit. Limited parking lot. 2-night minimum stay weekends. Reserv deposit required; 3 days refund notice. MC,
VI. *(See ad p A100)*   Ⓓ (408) 624-4862

Carmel Garden Court 108 *Motel*
All year [CP]   1P 75.00- 165.00   2P/1B   75.00- 165.00   2P/2B   75.00- 165.00   XP 15
10 units. 3 blks n at 4th Ave & Torres St. (PO Box 2077, 93921) Formerly Rosita Lodge. Picturesque garden area.
Rating withheld pending completion of renovation. Refrigerators; C/CATV; radios; comb or shower baths. 1
kitchen. Limited parking lot. No pets. 2-night minimum stay weekends. Reserv deposit required; 3 days refund
notice. AE, MC, VI. *(See ad p A103 and p A270)*   Ⓓ (408) 624-6942

Carmel Mission Inn-Best Western 92 *Motor Inn* ◆◆◆
5/20-10/31   1P 89.00- 139.00   2P/1B   89.00- 149.00   2P/2B   99.00- 149.00   XP 10   F
11/1-5/19   1P 79.00- 119.00   2P/1B   79.00- 119.00   2P/2B   89.00- 129.00   XP 10   F
Senior discount. 165 units. 1 mi s on SR 1, at Rio Rd. 3665 Rio Rd. (93922) Some balconies. Check-in 4 pm. Refrigerators; A/C; C/CATV; radios; phones. Pool; whirlpools. Reserv deposit required; 3 days refund notice. AE,
DI, DS, MC, VI. ● Dining rm; 6:30 am-2 & 5-10 pm; $10-$22; cocktails; entertainment. FAX (408) 624-8684
                                                                          ⊗ Ⓓ (408) 624-1841

A102   CARMEL, CA

(See MONTEREY PENINSULA spotting map pages A262 & A263)

Carmel Normandy Inn [83]　　　　Rates Subject to Change　　　　Motel ◆◆◆
ⓐ All year [CP]　　1P 89.00- 135.00　2P/1B　89.00- 135.00　2P/2B　.... 125.00　XP 10　F
48 units. On Ocean Ave between Monte Verde & Casanova. (PO Box 1706, 93921) Some rooms with wood-burning fireplace. 24 refrigerators; C/CATV; radios; phones; comb or shower baths. Small pool. Limited parking lot. No pets. 2-night minimum stay weekends. 3 kitchen cottage units with woodburning fireplace, $250-$300. Reserv deposit required; 3 days refund notice. AE, MC, VI. *(See ad p A104)*　　⊗ Ⓓ (408) 624-3825

Carmel Oaks Inn [96]　　　　Rates Subject to Change　　　　Motel ◆◆◆
ⓐ 6/1-10/31 & weekends [CP]　1P 89.00- 121.00　2P/1B　89.00- 121.00　2P/2B　.... 121.00　XP 15
17 units. 2 blks n at 5th & Mission. (PO Box 3696, 93921) OPEN ALL YEAR. Check-in 4 pm. Refrigerators; C/CATV; VCPs; radios; phones; shower or comb baths. No pets. 2-night minimum stay weekends. 1 efficiency, $15-$25 extra. Reserv deposit required; 3 days refund notice. AE, MC, VI. *(See ad p A105)*　Ⓓ (408) 624-5547

Carmel River Inn [93]　　　　Rates Subject to Change　　　　Motel ◆◆
ⓐ 6/1-10/31　　1P 60.00- 85.00　2P/1B　70.00- 85.00　2P/2B　.... 90.00　XP 5
　11/1-5/31　　1P 50.00- 70.00　2P/1B　50.00- 70.00　2P/2B　.... 75.00　XP 5
43 units. 1 mi s on SR 1; at Carmel River Bridge. (PO Box 221609, 93922) Many balconies & patios overlooking river-bed. 33 refrigerators; C/CATV; phones; shower or comb baths. 6 2-bedrm units, 13 kitchens. Htd pool. No pets. 24 cottages $65-$120 for up to 4 persons. 3-night minimum stay weekends. Reserv deposit required; 3 days refund notice. MC, VI. FAX (408) 624-0290 *(See ad p A105)*　Ⓓ (408) 624-1575

Carmel Sands Lodge [98]　　　　Rates Guaranteed　　　　Motel ◆◆
ⓐ 5/1-10/31 [CP]　1P 75.00- 145.00　2P/1B　75.00- 145.00　2P/2B　75.00- 145.00　XP 10
　11/1-4/30 [CP]　1P 69.00- 125.00　2P/1B　69.00- 125.00　2P/2B　69.00- 125.00　XP 10
39 units. 2 blks n on ne San Carlos St & 5th ave. (PO Box 951, 93921) Few small rooms; few fireplaces & balconies. Check-in 3 pm. 12 refrigerators; C/CATV; phones; comb or shower baths. Pool. No pets. Reserv deposit required; 3 days refund notice. AE, CB, DI, MC, VI. FAX (408) 624-2576 *(See ad p A101)*　⊗ Ⓓ (408) 624-1255

CARMEL VALLEY INN $49 PER ROOM
A TENNIS RESORT IN THE COUNTRY
10 Minutes From the Barnyard in Carmel (Hwy 1).
See listing and ad under Carmel Valley. Special AAA rate.
* Not available July or August and Weekends.
Calif. (800) 541-3113 or (408) 659-3131

Experience the best values on the Monterey Peninsula

7 Exceptional Inns, 7 Terrific Locations, 1 Phone Call!

Monterey
• El Adobe Inn • Cypress Gardens Inn

Carmel
• Wayside Inn • Candlelight Inn
• The Dolphin Inn • Svendsgaard's Inn
• Carriage House Inn

Ask about our 10% discount for AAA Members!

Inns by the Sea
Call Toll Free for Reservations
(800) 433-4732

(See MONTEREY PENINSULA spotting map pages A262 & A263)

Carmel Studio Lodge 78
AAA Special Value Rates — Motel ◆◆◆
- 5/15-10/31 & Fri-Sat [CP] 1P 70.00- 144.00 2P/1B 75.00- 150.00 2P/2B 80.00- 150.00 XP 10 F
- Sun-Thurs 11/1-5/14 [CP] 1P 45.00- 120.00 2P/1B 50.00- 130.00 2P/2B 60.00- 130.00 XP 10 F
19 units. 2 blks n of Ocean Ave at Junipero St & 5th aves. (PO Box 2388, 93921) 12 refrigerators; C/CATV; phones; comb or shower baths. 6 efficiencies. Small pool. Limited parking lot. No pets. Reserv deposit required; 3 days refund notice. AE, DI, DS, MC, VI. Restaurant opposite. *(See ad p A104)*   ⊗ Ⓓ (408) 624-8515

Carmel Tradewinds Inn 101
Rates Subject to Change — Motel ◆◆◆
- All year [CP] 1P 69.00- 150.00 2P/1B 69.00- 150.00 2P/2B 69.00- 150.00 XP 10
27 units. 4 blks n off Ocean Ave at Mission St & 3rd Ave. (PO Box 3403, 93921) Large units; many gas fireplaces; view of ocean or mountains. Balconies. 3-story, no elevator. C/CATV; radios; phones; shower or comb baths. Pool. No pets. Luxury level rooms avail. Wkly & monthly rates avail. Reserv deposit required; 3 days refund notice. AE, MC, VI. FAX (408) 624-0634   Ⓓ (408) 624-2776

Carmel Village Inn 81
Rates Subject to Change — Motel ◆◆◆
- 3/1-10/31 & weekends [CP] 1P 79.00- 125.00 2P/1B 79.00- 125.00 2P/2B 79.00- 125.00 XP 10
- 11/1-2/28 [CP] 1P 69.00- 98.00 2P/1B 69.00- 98.00 2P/2B 69.00- 98.00 XP 10
34 units. At Ocean Ave & Junipero St. (PO Box 5275, 93921) Refrigerators; C/CATV; radios; phones. No pets. 2 studio apartments with kitchen or efficiency & gas burning fireplace, $89-$179 for up to 5 persons. Reserv deposit required; 3 days refund notice. AE, MC, VI. *(See ad p A106)*   ⊗ Ⓓ (408) 624-3864

(See MONTEREY PENINSULA spotting map pages A262 & A263)

Carmel Wayfarer Inn [107]   **AAA Special Value Rates**   *Motel*   ◆◆
   7/1-10/31 Fri & Sat [BP]   1P 67.50- 87.50 2P/1B 77.50- 97.50 2P/2B 87.50- 107.50 XP 16
   3/1-6/30 Sun-Thurs [BP] 1P 57.50- 77.50 2P/1B 67.50- 87.50 2P/2B 77.50- 97.50 XP 13
   11/1-2/29 Sun-Thurs [BP] 1P 47.50- 67.50 2P/1B 57.50- 77.50 2P/2B 67.50- 87.50 XP 11
15 units. 3 blks n, at 4th Ave & Mission St. (PO Box 1896, 93921) Most units with gas burning fireplace; few with ocean view. Designated smoking areas. Check-in 3 pm. Refrigerators; C/CATV; movies; radios; phones; shower or comb baths. 2 2-bedrm units, 3 kitchens. Limited parking lot. No pets. 2-bedroom units, $87.50-$147.50. Reserv deposit required; 3 days refund notice. AE, DI, DS, MC, VI. *(See ad p A106)*   ⊗ Ⓓ (408) 624-2711

Carriage House Inn [88]   **Rates Subject to Change**   *Bed & Breakfast* ◆◆◆◆
   5/28-10/31 & Fri-Sat [CP] 1P 165.00- 225.00 2P/1B 165.00- 225.00 .... XP
   11/1-5/27 & Sun-Thurs [CP] 1P 130.00- 195.00 2P/1B 130.00- 195.00 .... XP
Senior discount. 13 units. 2 blks s off Ocean Ave, on Junipero St between 7th & 8th aves. (PO Box 1900, 93921) All units with fireplace; most with bay windows. Check-in 3 pm. Refrigerators; C/CATV; movies; radios; phones. No pets. 1 suite with 2 fireplaces; 1 unit with whirlpool bath. Reserv deposit required; 3 days refund notice. Complimentary beverages each evening. AE, DI, DS, MC, VI. FAX (408) 624-2967 *(See ad p A102)*
   ⊗ Ⓢ Ⓓ (408) 625-2585

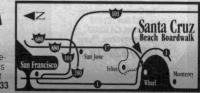

(See MONTEREY PENINSULA spotting map pages A262 & A263)

Coachman's Inn **86**
  All year [CP]   Rates Subject to Change   *Motel*   ◆◆
1P 65.00- 135.00   2P/1B   85.00- 150.00   2P/2B   95.00- 150.00   XP 10
Senior discount. 30 units. 1 blk s; San Carlos St between 7th & 8th aves. (PO Box C-1, 93921) Refrigerators; C/CATV; radios; phones. Pets. Reserv deposit required; 3 days refund notice. AE, MC, VI. *(See ad p A107)*
  ⊗ ⒟ (408) 624-6421

Cobblestone Inn **89**
  All year [BP]   Rates Subject to Change   *Motel*   ◆◆
1P 95.00- 160.00   2P/1B   95.00- 160.00   ....   XP 15
24 units. On Junipero St between 7th & 8th aves. (PO Box 3185, 93921) Quaint appointments. All rooms with gas fireplace. Refrigerators; C/CATV; radios; phones; shower or comb baths. 2 2-bedrm units. Limited parking lot. No pets. Reserv deposit required. Complimentary beverages each evening. AE, DI, MC, VI. Wine. FAX (408) 625-0478
  ⒟ (408) 625-5222

Colonial Terrace Inn **91**
  6/1-10/31 [CP]   Rates Subject to Change   *Motel*   ◆◆
1P 65.00- 175.00   2P/1B   65.00- 175.00   2P/2B   95.00- 185.00   XP 15
  11/1-5/31 [CP]   1P 55.00- 165.00   2P/1B   55.00- 165.00   2P/2B   85.00- 165.00   XP 15
25 units. On San Antonio between 12th & 13th aves. (PO Box 1375, 93921) Attractive gardens; gas burning fireplaces. Refrigerators; C/CATV; radios; phones; comb or shower baths. 6 kitchens, 2 efficiencies. 2 rooms with whirlpool bath. Limited parking lot. No pets. 3-night minimum stay weekends. Reserv deposit required; 3 days refund notice. AE, MC, VI. *(See ad p A107)*
  ⊗ ⒟ (408) 624-2741

(See MONTEREY PENINSULA spotting map pages A262 & A263)

Cypress Inn 85   Rates Subject to Change   *Historic Hotel* ◆◆◆
All year [CP]   1P 78.00- 185.00   2P/1B   78.00- 185.00   2P/2B   .... 106.00 XP 15
33 units. 1 blk s off Ocean Ave; at Lincoln St & 7th Ave. (PO Box Y, 93921) Mediterranean setting with garden courtyard. Check-in 3 pm. C/CATV; phones; comb or shower baths. Limited parking lot. Pets, $15 extra charge. Reserv deposit required; 3 days refund notice. AE, MC, VI. Cocktail lounge.   D Ⓖ (408) 624-3871

Dolores Lodge 103   Rates Subject to Change   *Motel* ◆◆
All year [CP]   1P 75.00- 110.00   2P/1B   75.00- 110.00   2P/2B 110.00- 125.00 XP 15
12 units. 4 blks n of Ocean Ave; at Dolores & 3rd Ave. (PO Box 3756, 93921) Many large rooms with wet bar; few gas burning fireplaces. Refrigerators; C/CATV; radios; phones; comb or shower baths. 5 2-bedrm units. No pets. Wkly rates avail. Reserv deposit required; 3 days refund notice. MC, VI.   ⊗ D (408) 625-3263

Dolphin Inn 105   Rates Subject to Change   *Motel* ◆◆◆
5/28-10/31 & Fri-Sat [CP]   1P 95.00- 130.00   2P/1B   95.00- 130.00   2P/2B   95.00- 130.00 XP 15   F
11/1-5/27 [CP]   1P 75.00- 105.00   2P/1B   75.00- 105.00   2P/2B   75.00- 105.00 XP 15   F
Senior discount. 26 units. 3 blks n at San Carlos St & 4th Ave. (PO Box 1900, 93921) Many fireplaces, some balconies & patios. Check-in 3 pm. Refrigerators; C/CATV; radios; phones. 1 efficiency. Small pool. No pets. 2-night minimum stay weekends. 3 suites, $180-$195 for up to 2 persons. 1 with whirlpool bath. Reserv deposit required; 3 days´ refund notice. Complimentary beverages each evening. AE, DI, DS, MC, VI. Restaurant adjacent. FAX (408) 624-2967 (See ad p A102)   ⊗ D (408) 624-5356

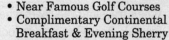

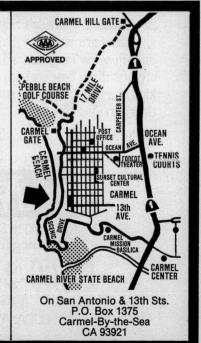

Make The Intelligent Choice. Choose Ramada.

When traveling the road, whether it's for business or leisure, Ramada has what you're looking for. Ramada's economical rates offer the best lodging value available, while our long list of outstanding features...spacious, well-appointed rooms, pools and spas, delightful restaurants and cozy lounges, assure you of comfort and convenience. And, our "You're Somebody Special" service will make you feel at home when you're on the road.

In addition to Ramada's regular low rates, a variety of package plans are available. Super Saver Weekends, Ramada's Four-For-One Program and the Best Years Senior Program are just three cost saving plans available. And don't forget, kids 18 and under always stay free when sharing a room with their parents.

So the next time you're on the road, choose Ramada.

RAMADA®

INNS, HOTELS, SUITES AND RESORTS.
FOR RESERVATIONS CALL

1-800-2-RAMADA

(1-800-272-6232)
OR YOUR LOCAL TRAVEL PROFESSIONAL

©1993 Ramada Franchise Systems, Inc.

(See MONTEREY PENINSULA spotting map pages A262 & A263)

Highlights Inn 🄼   Rates Guaranteed   *Motor Inn*   ◆◆◆◆
🏶 All year   1P 225.00- 650.00   2P/1B 225.00- 650.00   ....   XP 25   F
142 units. 4 mi s on SR 1, in Carmel Highlands. (PO Box 1700, 93921) Outstanding ocean view. Units with wood-burning fireplace. All suites with whirlpool bath. Check-in 4 pm. Refrigerators; C/CATV; pay movies; VCPs. Radios; phones; comb or shower baths. 103 kitchens. Pool; whirlpools; bicycles. Airport transp. Pets, $50 non-refundable deposit required. Reserv deposit required; 7 days refund notice. AE, CB, DI, MC, VI. ● Dining rm & restaurant; 7:30 am-10 pm; a la carte entrees about $20-$30; cocktail lounge; entertainment. Pacific's Edge. FAX (408) 626-1574   ⊗ Ⓓ 🄻 (408) 624-3801

Hofsas House 🄻🄾🄻   Rates Subject to Change   *Motel*
🏶 All year [CP]   1P 75.00- 120.00   2P/1B   75.00- 120.00   ....   XP
38 units. 3 blks n off Ocean Ave, between 3rd & 4th aves, on San Carlos St. (PO Box 1195, 93921) Few very small rooms. Check-in 3 pm. C/CATV; phones; shower or comb baths. 5 2-bedrm units, 5 kitchens, 15 efficiencies. Pool; sauna. Limited parking lot. No pets. 12 units with fireplace. 2-bedroom units, $140-$155 for 2 persons. Reserv deposit required; 3 days refund notice. AE, MC, VI. *(See ad below)*   ⊗ Ⓓ (408) 624-2745

Horizon Inn 🄻🄾🄾   Rates Subject to Change   *Motel*   ◆◆◆
🏶 5/15-10/31 & weekends [CP] 1P 95.00- 155.00 2P/1B   95.00- 155.00 2P/2B 95.00- 155.00 XP 15
20 units. 4 blks n; at Junipero St & 3rd Ave. (PO Box 1693, 93921) OPEN ALL YEAR. Some rooms with view of ocean or mountains. Some balconies, patios & gas-burning fireplaces. Check-in 4 pm. Refrigerators; C/CATV; radios; phones; comb or shower baths. Small pool. No pets. 3 efficiencies & 1 kitchen, $15-$25 extra. 2-night minimum stay weekends. Wkly rates avail. Reserv deposit required; 3 days refund notice. AE, MC, VI. FAX (408) 626-8253 *(See ad p A105)*   Ⓓ (408) 624-5327

La Playa Hotel 🄯⁷   Rates Subject to Change   *Hotel*   ◆◆◆
All year   1P 110.00- 200.00   2P/1B 110.00- 200.00   2P/2B 110.00- 200.00 XP 15
80 units. 2 blks s of Ocean Ave. Camino Real at 8th Ave. (PO Box 900, 93921) Mediterranean-style architecture, landscaped grounds; few small rooms; 3-story, no elevator. Check-in 3 pm. Refrigerators; C/CATV; radios; phones; comb or shower baths. Pool. Limited pay valet parking lot. No pets. 5 cottages, 1-to 4-bedrooms with fireplace & kitchen, $200-$475 for up to 8 persons. Reserv deposit required. AE, CB, MC, VI. ● Dining rm; 7 am-10 pm; a la carte entrees about $16-$24; cocktails.   Ⓢ Ⓓ (408) 624-6476

Lobos Lodge 🄤   Rates Subject to Change   *Motel*   ◆◆◆
🏶 All year [CP]   1P 87.00- 160.00 2P/1B   87.00- 160.00 2P/2B   87.00- 160.00 XP 20
30 units. Ocean Ave & Monte Verde. (PO Box L-1, 93921) Some rooms with ocean view; all with gas fireplace. Refrigerators; C/CATV; phones. No pets. Reserv deposit required; 3 days refund notice. AE, MC, VI.
                                                                       Ⓓ (408) 624-3874

Ocean View Lodge 🄴🄴   Rates Subject to Change   *Motel*   ◆◆◆
🏶 5/15-10/31 & weekends [CP] 1P 79.00- 175.00 2P/1B   79.00- 175.00 2P/2B 140.00- 175.00 XP 15
6 units. 4 blks n. Junipero St & 3rd Ave. (PO Box 3696, 93921) OPEN ALL YEAR. Landscaped courtyard. Check-in 4 pm. Refrigerators; C/CATV; phones. No pets. 2-night minimum stay weekends. 1 unit with whirlpool bath. 5 suites with kitchen & fireplace. Wkly rates avail. Reserv deposit required; 3 days refund notice. AE, MC, VI. FAX (408) 626-8253 *(See ad p A105)*   Ⓓ (408) 624-7723

(See MONTEREY PENINSULA spotting map pages A262 & A263)

Pine Inn 82   Rates Subject to Change   *Hotel*   ◆◆◆
All year   1P 85.00- 205.00   2P/1B   85.00- 205.00   2P/2B   85.00- 100.00   XP 10
Senior discount. 49 units. Ocean Ave; between Lincoln & Monte Verde. (PO Box 250, 93921) Turn-of-the-century
& oriental decor. Some units with ocean view. Few small units. 3-story, no elevator. Check-in 4 pm. 9 refrigerators; C/CATV; phones. Limited parking lot. No pets. Reserv deposit required. AE, CB, DI, MC, VI. ● Dining rm;
7 am-10 pm; $10-$20; cocktails; cocktail lounge. *(See ad p A109)*   Ⓓ (408) 624-3851

Svendsgaard's 106   Rates Subject to Change   *Motel*   ◆◆◆
5/28-10/31 & Fri & Sat [CP]   1P   95.00- 130.00   2P/1B   95.00- 130.00   2P/2B   110.00- 130.00   XP 15   F
11/1-5/27 [CP]   1P   75.00- 105.00   2P/1B   75.00- 105.00   2P/2B   89.00- 105.00   XP 15   F
Senior discount. 34 units. 3 blks n at San Carlos St & 4th Ave. (PO Box 1900, 93921) Landscaped grounds. Large
& studio rooms, some gas burning fireplaces. Check-in 3 pm. Refrigerators; C/CATV; radios; shower or
comb baths. 3 2-bedrm units, 16 efficiencies. Pool. No pets. 2-night minimum stay weekends. 2 suites, $175 for
up to 2 persons. 1 family unit, $195 for up to 4 persons. Reserv deposit required; 3 days refund notice. AE, DI,
DS, MC, VI. FAX (408) 624-2967 *(See ad p A102)*   ⊗ Ⓓ (408) 624-2967

Tickle Pink Inn 95   Rates Subject to Change   *Motel*   ◆◆◆
All year [CP]   1P 149.00- 259.00   2P/1B   149.00- 259.00   2P/2B   149.00- 259.00   XP 25   F
35 units. 4 mi s on SR 1 in Carmel Highlands. 155 Highland Dr. (93923) Spectacular view. Large units with balcony & some fireplaces. Check-in 3 pm. Refrigerators; C/CATV; VCPs; radios; phones; shower or comb baths.
No pets. 2-night minimum stay weekends. 1 suite with fireplace & whirlpool bath. Wkly rates avail. Reserv deposit required; 3 days refund notice. AE, MC, VI. Restaurant adjacent. FAX (408) 626-9516 *(See ad p A111)*
                                                    Ⓓ (408) 624-1244

Wayside Inn 87   Rates Subject to Change   *Motel*   ◆◆
5/28-10/31 & Fri-Sat [CP]   1P   95.00- 135.00   2P/1B   95.00- 135.00   2P/2B   95.00- 135.00   XP 15   F
11/1-5/27 [CP]   1P   75.00- 105.00   2P/1B   75.00- 105.00   2P/2B   75.00- 105.00   XP 15   F
Senior discount. 22 units. 1 blk s off Ocean Ave, corner Mission St & 7th Ave. (PO Box 1900, 93921) Most units
with fireplace. Few small units. Check-in 3 pm. Refrigerators; C/CATV; radios; phones; comb or shower baths.
1 2-bedrm unit, 10 kitchens. Limited parking lot. Pets. 10 small suites. 2-night minimum stay weekends. 1 unit,
$225 for up to 6 persons. Reserv deposit required; 3 days refund notice. AE, DI, DS, MC, VI. FAX (408) 624-2967
(See ad p A102)   ⊗ Ⓓ (408) 624-5336

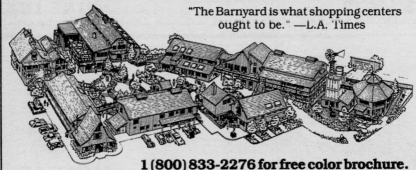

(See MONTEREY PENINSULA spotting map pages A262 & A263)

RESTAURANTS

Adobe Inn Bully III (25)   Steak & Seafood $$ ◆◆
Dolores St & 8th Ave. Prime rib cut to order & fresh seafood. Short order items in the Pub 11:30 am-10 pm. Early bird specials. Open 5 pm-9:30 pm; Fri & Sat-10 pm; closed 11/25 & 12/25. Cocktails & lounge. Reserv advised. MC, VI. *(See ad p A100)*   ⊗ (408) 625-1750

Anton & Michel (24)   Continental $$$
🅰 Mission St between Ocean & 7th St. Attractive courtyard view. Lamb & seafood specialties. Children's menu. Open 11:30 am-3 & 5:30-9:30 pm; Sat-10 pm. Cocktails & lounge. Reserv advised. AE, CB, DI, MC, VI.
     (408) 624-2406

Casanova (21)   Northern Italian $$$ ◆◆
On 5th Ave between San Carlos & Mission sts; 2 blks n off Ocean Ave. Rustic atmosphere. Also French cuisine. Open 8 am-10:30 pm; Sun 9 am-3 & 5:30-10:30 pm; closed 12/9-12/26. Beer & wine. MC, VI.   ⊗ (408) 625-0501

Clam Box (22)   American $$ ◆◆
On Mission St, between 5th & 6th aves. Seafood & chicken; casual atmosphere. Popular with local families. Children's menu. Open 4:30 pm-9 pm; closed Mon, 11/25 & 12/14-12/26. Cocktails. Minimum $5.   ⊗ (408) 624-8597

From Scratch (27)   American $$ ◆
1 mi s exit SR 1 at Carmel Valley Rd, in the Barnyard Shopping Center; Lobos Barn level 1. 3626 The Barnyard. Homemade soups & quiches. Smoke free premises. Open 8 am-9:30 pm; Sun-2:30 pm. Beer & wine. MC, VI.   ⊗ (408) 625-2448

Rio Grill (23)   American $$ ◆◆
1 blk e of SR 1; in the Crossroads Shopping Center. 101 Crossroads Blvd. Creative regional cuisine; contemporary southwestern decor. A/C. Children's menu. Open 11:30 am-11 pm; Sun from 11 am; closed 7/4, 11/25 & 12/25. Cocktails & lounge. Reserv advised. AE, MC, VI.   ⊗ (408) 625-5436

Sans Souci (26)   French $$$ ◆◆◆
🅰 1 12/ blks n of Ocean Ave, between 5th & 6th aves. Lincoln St. Fresh seafood specialties. Cozy, warm & quiet. Dress code. Children's menu. Open 6 pm-12 pm; closed Wed & 12/8-12/20 & 12/24. Cocktails. Reserv advised. AE, MC, VI.   ⊗ (408) 624-6220

Silver Jones (28)   American $$
1 mi s on SR 1; in The Barnyard Shopping Center. 3690 The Barnyard. Santa Fe decor. Casual atmosphere. Open 11:30 am-9:30 pm; closed 11/25 & 12/25. Beer & wine. AE, DI, MC, VI.   ⊗ (408) 624-5200

CARMEL VALLEY — 4,000

Acacia Lodge   Rates Subject to Change   *Motel*   ◆◆
🅰 All year   1P 58.00- 85.00   2P/1B   58.00- 95.00   2P/2B   60.00-100.00   XP 10
Senior discount. 18 units. 12 3/4 mi e of SR 1; on Via Contenta; 1 blk n of Carmel Valley Rd in Carmel Valley Village. 20 Via Contenta. (PO Box 87, 93924) Quiet secluded area. Nicely landscaped grounds with view of mountains. Patios. Refrigerators; C/CATV; radios; phones; comb or shower baths. Pool; whirlpool. No pets. 8 kitchens, $15 extra. 2-night minimum stay weekends. Reserv deposit required; 4 days refund notice. MC, VI.
     Ⓓ (408) 659-2297

Carmel Valley Inn — AAA Special Value Rates — *Motor Inn* ◆◆

5/1-10/31	1P	69.00- 99.00	2P/1B	79.00- 119.00	2P/2B	79.00- 119.00	XP 10		F
3/1-4/30	1P	59.00- 89.00	2P/1B	69.00- 99.00	2P/2B	69.00- 99.00	XP 10		F
11/1-2/28	1P	49.00- 69.00	2P/1B	59.00- 79.00	2P/2B	59.00- 79.00	XP 10		F

46 units. 10 mi e of SR 1 via Carmel Valley Rd. (PO Box 115, 93924) Country atmosphere on spacious landscaped grounds. Some small units. A/C; C/CATV; phones; comb or shower baths. Pool; whirlpool; tennis-7 courts. Pets, $10 extra charge. Reserv deposit required; 3 days refund notice. AE, CB, DI, MC, VI. ● Restaurant; 8 am-10 pm; a la carte entrees about $8-$16; cocktails. FAX (408) 659-0137 *(See ad p A102 and p A111)*
⊗ Ⓓ (408) 659-3131

Carmel Valley Ranch Resort — Rates Subject to Change — *Resort* ◆◆◆◆

All year	1P	235.00- 305.00	2P/1B	235.00- 305.00	2P/2B	235.00- 305.00	

100 units. 6 1/4 mi e of SR 1 via Carmel Valley Rd, exit at Robinson Canyon Rd & follow signs. 1 Old Ranch Rd. (93923) Hillside location overlooking valley & golf course. Woodburning fireplaces. Check-in 4 pm. Refrigerators; A/C; C/CATV; pay movies; VCPs. Radios; phones. 2 2-bedrm units. 2 pools; saunas; whirlpools; tennis-12 courts. Fee for: golf-18 holes. Airport transp. No pets. 4 suites with outdoor whirlpool, $650-$700 for 2 to 4 persons. Reserv deposit required; 7 days refund notice. AE, CB, DI, MC, VI. ● Dining rm, coffeeshop & cafeteria; 7 am-2 & 6-10:30 pm; guest only; a la carte entrees about $22-$35; cocktails. FAX (408) 624-2858
Ⓢ Ⓓ ♿ (408) 625-9500

Hidden Valley Inn — Rates Subject to Change — *Motel* ◆◆

4/1-11/30 [CP]	....		2P/1B	89.00- 169.00	2P/2B	99.00- 129.00	XP 20
12/1-3/31 [CP]	....		2P/1B	79.00- 129.00	2P/2B	89.00- 99.00	XP 20

24 units. 10 mi e of SR 1, Carmel Valley Rd. (PO Box 504, 93924) Quiet scenic location. Rooms with patio or deck. 7 refrigerators; C/CATV; phones; comb or shower baths. 2 efficiencies, no utensils. Small pool. No pets. 2-night minimum stay weekends. Wkly & monthly rates avail. Reserv deposit required. Complimentary beverages each evening. AE, MC, VI.
⊗ Ⓓ (408) 659-5361

Los Laureles — Rates Guaranteed — *Motor Inn* ◆◆

4/1-10/31	1P	98.00- 135.00	2P/1B	98.00- 135.00	2P/2B	98.00- 135.00	XP 20		F
11/1-1/31	1P	85.00- 120.00	2P/1B	85.00- 120.00	2P/2B	85.00- 120.00	XP 20		F
2/1-3/31	1P	78.00- 110.00	2P/1B	78.00- 110.00	2P/2B	78.00- 110.00	XP 20		F

30 units. 10 mi e of SR 1. 150 E Carmel Valley Rd. (93924) Restored historic California ranch; few small rooms; few fireplaces. Check-in 3 pm. 9 refrigerators; C/CATV; radios; phones; shower or comb baths. 1 3-bedrm unit, 1 kitchen. Pool; whirlpool; playground. Fee for: riding. No pets. 3-bedroom house, $400 for up to 5 persons. Reserv deposit required; 3 days refund notice. AE, MC, VI. ● Restaurant; 7 am-9:30 pm; $15-$22; cocktails; cocktail lounge. FAX (408) 659-0481
⊗ Ⓓ (408) 659-2233

Quail Lodge Resort & Golf Club — Rates Guaranteed — *Resort Complex* ◆◆◆

3/1-11/30	1P	195.00- 295.00	2P/1B	195.00- 295.00	2P/2B	195.00- 295.00	XP 25
12/1-2/28	1P	155.00- 230.00	2P/1B	155.00- 230.00	2P/2B	155.00- 230.00	XP 25

100 units. 3 1/2 mi e of SR 1, via Carmel Valley Rd. 8205 Valley Greens Dr. (Carmel, 93923) On manicured grounds of country club. Some fireplaces; patios & balconies. Check-in 4 pm. Refrigerators; C/CATV; pay movies; VCPs. Radios; phones; comb or shower baths. 2 pools; whirlpool; putting green. Fee for: golf-18 holes, tennis-4 courts. Pets. Reserv deposit required; 3 days refund notice. AE, CB, DI, MC, VI. ● Restaurant; at clubhouse, 1/4 mi; 7 am-3 pm; 15% service charge; cocktails. Also, The Covey, see separate listing. A *Preferred Hotel.* FAX (408) 624-3726 *(See ad p A279)*
⊗ Ⓓ (408) 624-1581

Valley Lodge — Rates Guaranteed — *Complex* ◆◆◆

All year [CP]	1P	95.00- 135.00	2P/1B	95.00- 135.00	2P/2B	.... 115.00	XP 10

Senior discount. 31 units. 11 1/2 mi e of SR 1; Carmel Valley Rd, at Ford Rd. (PO Box 93, 93924) Quiet location; landscaped grounds with garden patios. Some antiques & reproductions. C/CATV; radios; phones. Pool; sauna; whirlpool; exercise rm. Pets, $10 extra charge. 8 1-bedroom cottages, $155 for 2 persons; 4 2-bedroom cottages, $235 for 4 persons with kitchen & fireplace. 2-night minimum weekends. Microwaves avail. Reserv deposit required; 3 days refund notice. AE, MC, VI. FAX (408) 659-4558 *(See ad below)*
Ⓓ (408) 659-2261

RESTAURANTS

The Covey   Continental $$$ ◆◆◆
In Quail Lodge. Overlooking duck pond. Dress code. Open 6:30 pm-10 pm; Sat 6 pm-11 pm. Cocktails & lounge. Reserv advised. AE, CB, DI, MC, VI.   ⊗ (408) 624-1581

Will's Fargo Restaurant   Steakhouse $$$
In the Village. 1880's decor; garden setting. Varied menu. Steaks cut to order. A/C. Early bird specials; children's menu. Open 5:30 pm-9:30 pm; Sun from 5 pm; closed Mon, 1/1, 11/25 & 12/25. Cocktails & lounge. Reserv advised. AE, CB, DI, MC, VI.   ⊗ (408) 659-2774

CARMICHAEL — 43,100   See SACRAMENTO

CARPINTERIA — 13,700

Best Western Carpinteria Inn   Rates Subject to Change   *Motor Inn*   ◆◆
🏧 5/15-9/7   1P 95.00- 115.00   2P/1B 109.00- 119.00   2P/2B 105.00- 115.00 XP 10
9/8-5/14   1P 85.00- 105.00   2P/1B 99.00- 109.00   2P/2B 89.00- 99.00 XP 10
144 units. Adjacent to US 101; northbound exit Santa Monica Rd, southbound exit Reynolds Ave. 4558 Carpinteria Ave. (93013) A/C; C/CATV; phones. Small htd pool; whirlpool. Reserv deposit required in summer. AE, CB, DI, MC, VI. ● Dining rm; 5 pm-10 pm; $8.50-$17.50; cocktails. FAX (805) 684-4015 ⊗ Ⓢ Ⓓ ⓑ (805) 684-0473

CARSON — 84,000

Comfort Inn   Rates Subject to Change   *Motel*   ◆◆
🏧 All year [CP]   1P 43.00- 53.00   2P/1B 49.00- 59.00   2P/2B 54.00- 64.00 XP 6   F
Senior discount. 31 units. 1/4 mi e of I-405, exit Carson St. 1325 E Carson St. (90745) 25 refrigerators; A/C; C/TV; movies; radios; phones. Small pool. No pets. 7 rooms with whirlpool tub, $65-$95. Wkly rates avail. AE, DI, DS, MC, VI. FAX (310) 518-5575   ⊗ Ⓓ (310) 830-8044

Days Inn   Rates Subject to Change   *Motel*   ◆◆
🏧 All year   1P .... 49.00   2P/1B .... 49.00   2P/2B .... 54.00 XP 5
35 units. 1/4 mi e of I-110; exit Carson St. 415 W Carson St. (90745) Check-in 3 pm. A/C; C/CATV; movies; radios; phones; tub or shower baths. AE, DI, DS, MC, VI.   ⊗ Ⓓ ⓑ (310) 328-2622

Hampton Inn   Rates Subject to Change   *Motel*   ◆◆◆
All year   1P 48.00- 58.00   2P/1B 52.00- 62.00   2P/2B 52.00- 58.00 XP 6
134 units. Adjacent to s side of SR 91 (Artesia Frwy); exit Avalon Blvd. 767 Albertoni St. (90746) A/C; C/CATV; movies; radios; phones. Pool; whirlpool. No pets. Wkly rates avail. AE, DI, DS, MC, VI. FAX (310) 768-2022 (See ad p A112)   ⊗ Ⓢ Ⓓ ⓑ (310) 768-8833

Ramada Inn   Rates Subject to Change   *Motor Inn*   ◆◆
🏧 All year [BP]   1P 52.00- 60.00   2P/1B 52.00- 60.00   2P/2B 56.00- 68.00 XP 5   F
Senior discount. 167 units. 1/4 mi ne of I-405, exit Avalon Blvd. 850 E Dominguez St. (90746) Check-in 3 pm. 6 refrigerators; A/C; C/CATV; movies; rental VCPs. Radios; phones. Pool; exercise rm. No pets. Wkly & monthly rates avail. Reserv deposit required; 7 days refund notice. AE, DI, DS, MC, VI. ● Restaurant; 6:30 am-10 pm; Sat & Sun 6:30 am-10 am; $8-$15; cocktails; entertainment. FAX (310) 715-2956   ⊗ Ⓓ ⓑ (310) 538-5500

CASTAIC — 600

Castaic Inn   Rates Subject to Change   *Motel*   ◆◆
🏧 All year   1P 35.00- 59.00   2P/1B 45.00- 59.00   2P/2B 45.00- 69.00 XP 5
Senior discount. 50 units. Adjacent to I-5; northbound exit Parker Rd, southbound exit Lake Hughes Rd, 3/4 mi se. 31411 Ridge Rt. (91384) 23 refrigerators; A/C; C/CATV; movies; radios; phones. Coin laundry. Small pool; whirlpool. No pets. 6 rooms with whirlpool, $50-$75. Reserv deposit required. AE, DI, DS, MC, VI. FAX (805) 257-0980 (See ad below and p A498)   ⊗ Ⓢ Ⓓ ⓑ (805) 257-0229

Comfort Inn   Rates Subject to Change   *Motel*   ◆◆
🏧 All year [CP]   1P 40.00- 65.00   2P/1B 43.00- 70.00   2P/2B 45.00- 70.00 XP 5
Senior discount. 120 units. From I-5, northbound exit Parker Rd, 1/4 mi ne, southbound exit Lake Hughes Rd, 1/2 mi se. 31558 Castaic Rd. (91384) A/C; C/CATV; movies; phones. Coin laundry. Small htd pool. Pets. AE, DI, DS, MC, VI. FAX (805) 295-0379 (See ad below)   ⊗ Ⓓ ⓑ (805) 295-1100

Econolodge   Rates Subject to Change   *Motel*   ◆◆
🏧 All year   1P 40.00- 54.00   2P/1B 45.00- 60.00   2P/2B 45.00- 60.00 XP 5
54 units. Northbound exit Parker Rd, 1/4 mi se of I-5, southbound exit Lake Hughes Rd, 3/4 mi se of I-5. 31410 Castaic Rd. (91384) Formerly South Lake Inn. A/C; C/CATV; movies; radios; phones. Small htd pool; whirlpool. No pets. AE, MC, VI.   ⊗ Ⓓ ⓑ (805) 295-1070

CASTRO VALLEY — 44,000   (See OAKLAND/BERKELEY AREA spotting map pages A300 & A301; see index starting on page A298)

Castro Valley Travelodge ⑦		Rates Subject to Change				Motel	◆◆
All year [CP]	1P 48.00- 53.00	2P/1B	48.00- 53.00	2P/2B	.... 58.00	XP 6	

59 units. Exit I-580 Castro Valley Blvd, 1/4 mi n. 2532 Castro Valley Blvd. (94546) Spacious rooms. 20 refrigerators; A/C; C/CATV; movies; phones. Small pool. Garage & parking lot. No pets. 9 rooms with whirlpool, $20 extra. AE, CB, DI, MC, VI.   ⊗ ⑤ Ⓓ 🅛 (510) 538-9501

Econo Lodge ⑥		Rates Subject to Change				Motel	◆◆
All year	1P 45.00	2P/1B	.... 50.00	2P/2B	.... 55.00	XP 10	

Senior discount. 33 units. I-580 exit Crow Canyon Rd N, 1/4 mi e. 3954 E Castro Valley Blvd. (94546) Most rooms with view of valley & bay. A/C; C/CATV; movies; VCPs. Radios; phones. Pool; whirlpool. No pets. 14 rooms with whirlpool tub, $75 for 2 persons. Reserv deposit required; 3 days refund notice. AE, DI, DS, MC, VI.
⊗ ⑤ Ⓓ 🅛 (510) 537-8833

CATALINA ISLAND — See AVALON (Catalina Island)

CAYUCOS — 2,300

Estero Bay Motel							◆◆
5/1-10/15	1P 50.00- 82.00	2P/1B	50.00- 82.00	2P/2B	55.00- 85.00	XP 5	
10/16-4/30	1P 30.00- 68.00	2P/1B	30.00- 68.00	2P/2B	42.00- 75.00	XP 5	

Senior discount. 12 units. 25 S Ocean Ave. (93430) 1/2 block to beach. C/CATV; movies; VCPs. Phones; comb or shower baths. No pets. 4 kitchens & 1 efficiency, $10 extra. Wkly & monthly rates avail in winter. Reserv deposit required; 3 days refund notice. AE, MC, VI.   Ⓓ 🅛 (805) 995-3614

CENTURY CITY — See LOS ANGELES (Central & Western Areas)

CERRITOS — 53,200

Sheraton Cerritos Hotel at Towne Center		Rates Guaranteed				Hotel	◆◆◆
Sun-Thurs	1P 99.00- 139.00	2P/1B	109.00- 149.00	2P/2B	109.00- 149.00	XP 15	F
Fri & Sat	1P 82.00	2P/1B	.... 82.00	2P/2B	.... 82.00	XP 15	F

Senior discount. 203 units. 1/4 mi s of SR 91 Artesia Frwy; westbound exit, Artesia/Bloomfield, eastbound exit Shoemaker Rd. 12725 Center Court Dr. (90701) A/C; C/CATV; free & pay movies; radios; phones. Htd pool; whirlpool; Airport transportation to Long Beach Airport; exercise rm. Parking lot. Monthly rates avail. AE, CB, DI, MC, VI. ● Dining rm; 6:30 am-10:30 pm; $8.50-$16; cocktails. FAX (310) 403-2080 *(See ad p A50)*
⊗ ⑤ Ⓓ 🅛 (310) 809-1500

CHATSWORTH — 47,100   See LOS ANGELES (San Fernando Valley)

CHICO — 40,100

Best Western Heritage Inn		Rates Subject to Change				Motel	◆◆
All year	1P 56.00- 62.00	2P/1B	60.00- 70.00	2P/2B	.... 60.00	XP 7	F

Senior discount. 103 units. 1 1/2 mi nw; e off SR 99 bypass, via Cohasset Rd. 25 Heritage Ln. (95926) Check-in 3 pm. A/C; C/CATV; movies; radios; phones. Pool; whirlpool; exercise rm. No pets. Reserv deposit required. AE, DI, DS, MC, VI. FAX (916) 894-8600 *(See ad p A364)*   ⊗ ⑤ Ⓓ (916) 894-8600

Holiday Inn of Chico		AAA Special Value Rates				Motor Inn	◆◆◆
All year	1P 69.00- 77.00	2P/1B	75.00- 85.00	2P/2B	75.00- 80.00	XP 6	F

174 units. W off SR 99 bypass, via Cohasset Rd; across from North Valley Mall Shopping Center. 685 Manzanita Ct. (95926) A/C; C/CATV; free & pay movies; phones. Coin laundry. Pool; whirlpool. Airport transp. Pets. Wkly & monthly rates avail. AE, DI, DS, MC, VI. ● Restaurant; 6 am-2 & 5-10 pm; $8-$18; cocktails; entertainment. FAX (916) 893-3040
⊗ Ⓓ 🅛 (916) 345-2491

Motel Orleans		Rates Subject to Change				Motel	◆
All year	1P 32.00	2P/1B	.... 37.00	2P/2B	.... 39.00	XP 5	

Senior discount. 53 units. Exit SR 99 at Cohasset Rd, 1/4 mi w. 655 Manzanita Ct. (95926) 3-story, no elevator. A/C; C/CATV; phones; comb or shower baths. Pool. No pets, $25. Reserv deposit required; 3 days refund notice. AE, DI, DS, MC, VI. Coffeeshop adjacent.   ⊗ Ⓓ (916) 345-2533

Safari Garden Motel		Rates Subject to Change				Motel	◆
All year	1P 32.00- 37.00	2P/1B	40.00- 42.00	2P/2B	42.00- 44.00	XP 4	

Senior discount. 50 units. 2 mi n on SR 99 business rt. 2352 Esplanade. (95926) Tree-shaded grounds. A/C; C/CATV; movies; 19 radios; phones; shower or comb baths. Pool. Pets, $25 deposit required. 4 kitchens & 1 efficiency, $8 extra. Reserv deposit required. AE, DI, DS, MC, VI. FAX (916) 343-2364   ⊗ Ⓓ (916) 343-3201

Town House Motel		Rates Subject to Change				Motel	◆
All year	1P 28.00- 32.00	2P/1B	34.00- 40.00	2P/2B	35.00- 42.00	XP 5	

Senior discount. 30 units. 1 3/4 mi n on SR 99 business rt. 2231 Esplanade. (95926) A/C; C/CATV; movies; radios; phones; shower baths. 2 efficiencies, no utensils. Pool. Pets, $25 deposit, small pets only. Wkly rates avail. Reserv deposit required. AE, CB, DI, MC, VI. Coffeeshop opposite.   ⊗ Ⓓ (916) 343-1621

RESTAURANTS

Hatch Cover	Seafood	$$	◆◆

1 1/2 mi n on SR 99 business rt. 1720 Esplanade. Varied menu. A/C. Children's menu. Open 5 pm-9:30 pm; Fri & Sat-10:30 pm; closed 1/1, 7/4, 11/26 & 12/25. Cocktails & lounge. Reserv advised. AE, MC, VI.   ⊗ (916) 345-5862

Marie Callender's	American	$$	◆

US 99 exit e; adjacent to US 99 in Chico Mall. 1910 E 20th St. Homestyle cooking. Noted for homemade pies. A/C. Children's menu. Open 7 am-10 pm; Fri & Sat-11 pm; closed 11/25 & 12/25. Cocktails. AE, MC, VI.   ⊗ (916) 345-8800

CHINO — 59,700

Best Western Pine Tree Motel		AAA Special Value Rates				Motel	◆◆
All year	1P 39.00- 46.00	2P/1B	45.00- 53.00	2P/2B	47.00- 59.00	XP 4- 5	

44 units. 2 blks n of SR 60, Central Ave exit. 12018 Central Ave. (91710) A/C; C/CATV; movies; radios; phones; comb or shower baths. Pool. No pets. Reserv deposit required. AE, CB, DI, MC, VI. FAX (909) 465-0748
⊗ Ⓓ (909) 628-6021

Chino Motel		Rates Subject to Change				Motel	◆◆
All year	1P 39.00- 43.00	2P/1B	43.00- 48.00	2P/2B	.... 43.00	XP 4	

52 units. 2 1/2 blks n of SR 60, Central Ave exit. 11885 Central Ave. (91710) A/C; C/TV; radios; phones. Small pool. No pets. AE, DI, DS, MC, VI.   Ⓓ 🅛 (909) 591-9505

RESTAURANT

Cask'n Cleaver American $$ ◆
1 blk n of SR 60. 12206 Central Ave. Casual dining. Nice selection of steaks, seafood & chicken. A/C. Early bird specials. Open 11:30 am-2 & 5-10 pm; Fri-11 pm; Sat 5 pm-11 pm; Sun 4:30 pm-9:30 pm; closed 11/25 & 12/25. Cocktails & lounge. AE, MC, VI. ⊗ (909) 627-6011

CHULA VISTA — 135,200 (See SAN DIEGO spotting map pages A376 & A377; see index starting on page A374)

All Seasons Inns 139 Rates Guaranteed *Motel* ◆◆◆
All year [CP] 1P 45.00- 60.00 2P/1B 50.00- 59.00 2P/2B 50.00- 65.00 XP 5 F
Senior discount. 108 units. 1 blk e of I-5, exit E St. 699 E St. (91910) Refrigerators; A/C; C/CATV; movies; VCPs. Radios; phones. Coin laundry. Htd pool; whirlpool. Airport transp. No pets. Reserv deposit required. AE, DI, DS, MC, VI. Restaurant opposite. FAX (619) 427-3748 ⊗ Ⓓ (619) 585-1999

Best Western Cavalier Motor Hotel 137 Rates Subject to Change *Motel* ◆◆
All year 1P 42.00- 52.00 2P/1B 48.00- 58.00 2P/2B 51.00- 61.00 XP 5- 6 F
Senior discount. 76 units. 1 blk e of I-5, E St exit. 710 E St. (91910) A/C; phones. 3 2-bedrm units. Htd pool. No pets. Reserv deposit required; 7 days refund notice. AE, DI, DS, MC, VI. Coffeeshop adjacent. ⊗ Ⓓ (619) 420-5183

Chula Vista Travelodge 145 Rates Subject to Change *Motel* ◆◆◆
All year 1P 43.00- 52.00 2P/1B 49.00- 56.00 2P/2B 54.00- 60.00 XP 6 F
Senior discount. 62 units. 3/4 mi e of I-5; exit E St. 394 Broadway. (91910) A/C; C/CATV; movies; rental VCPs. Radios; phones. 20 2-bedrm units, 5 efficiencies, no utensils. Coin laundry. Pool; whirlpool; 3 rooms with whirlpool tub. No pets. Microwave or refrigerator avail, extra charge. Wkly rates avail. AE, DI, DS, MC, VI. FAX (619) 420-5556 *(See ad p A378)* ⊗ Ⓢ Ⓓ Ⓚ (619) 420-6600

La Quinta Inn 141 Rates Subject to Change *Motel* ◆◆◆
All year 1P 61.00- 68.00 2P/1B 69.00- 76.00 2P/2B .... 69.00 XP 5 F
142 units. Adjacent to I-805, E St & Bonita Rd exit. 150 Bonita Rd. (91910) Check-in 3 pm. A/C; C/CATV; movies; radios; phones. Htd pool. Pets. AE, DI, DS, MC, VI. Restaurant adjacent. FAX (619) 427-0135 ⊗ Ⓓ Ⓚ (619) 691-1211

Otay Valley Inn 144 Rates Subject to Change *Motel* ◆◆◆
All year [CP] 1P .... 48.00 2P/1B .... 48.00 2P/2B .... 58.00 XP 10 F
Senior discount. 121 units. Adjacent to I-805; exit Otay Valley Rd. 4450 Otay Valley Rd. (91911) A/C; C/CATV; movies; radios; phones. Rental refrigerators. Coin laundry. Htd pool; whirlpool. No pets. Wkly & monthly rates avail. AE, DI, DS, MC, VI. FAX (619) 422-2600 ⊗ Ⓢ Ⓓ Ⓚ (619) 422-2600

Palomar Inn 143 Rates Subject to Change *Motel* ◆◆◆
Fri-Sun 1P 37.00- 45.00 2P/1B 42.00- 49.00 2P/2B 42.00- 49.00 XP 5
Mon-Thurs 1P 35.00- 39.00 2P/1B 39.00- 45.00 2P/2B 39.00- 45.00 XP 5
Senior discount. 37 units. Adjacent to I-5, exit Palomar St. 801 Palomar St. (91911) A/C; C/CATV; movies; radios; phones. 2 2-bedrm units. No pets. 16 rooms with refrigerator & microwave. Wkly rates avail. AE, MC, VI. Ⓢ Ⓓ (619) 423-8889

Ramada Inn-San Diego South 140 Rates Guaranteed *Motel* ◆◆◆
6/15-9/30 1P 55.00- 67.00 2P/1B 67.00- 73.00 2P/2B .... 63.00 XP 8 F
Senior discount. 97 units. Adjacent to I-805, exit Bonita Rd & E St. 91 Bonita Rd. (91910) OPEN ALL YEAR. Check-in 4 pm. A/C; C/CATV; movies; radios; phones. Htd pool; whirlpool. No pets. AE, CB, DI, MC, VI. Restaurant adjacent. FAX (619) 425-8934 ⊗ Ⓓ Ⓚ (619) 425-9999

Rodeway Inn 142 Rates Guaranteed *Motel* ◆
5/15-9/15 1P 39.00- 45.00 2P/1B 43.00- 49.00 2P/2B 45.00- 54.00 XP
9/16-5/14 1P 33.00- 39.00 2P/1B 37.00- 43.00 2P/2B 40.00- 50.00 XP
Senior discount. 50 units. 1/4 blk n of K St. 778 Broadway. (91910) A/C; C/CATV; movies; radios; phones. Htd pool; whirlpool. No pets. Microwave & refrigerator avail. Wkly & monthly rates avail. AE, DI, DS, MC, VI. ⊗ Ⓓ (619) 476-9555

Vagabond Inn 138 Rates Subject to Change *Motel* ◆
All year [CP] 1P 36.00- 47.00 2P/1B 39.00- 51.00 2P/2B 42.00- 55.00 XP 5 F
91 units. 1/2 mi e of I-5, exit E St. 230 Broadway. (91910) Check-in 3 pm. 46 refrigerators; A/C; C/CATV; movies; VCPs. Radios; phones. 6 2-bedrm units, 1 kitchen, 2 efficiencies. 2 pools, 1 htd; playground. Pets, $5 extra charge. AE, DI, DS, MC, VI. Restaurant adjacent. FAX (619) 425-0645 *(See ad p A412)* ⊗ Ⓓ (619) 422-8305

RESTAURANTS

Anthony's Fish Grotto 55 Seafood $$ ◆
Adjacent to I-5, E St exit. 215 W Bay Blvd. Popular family dining. A/C. Children's menu. Open 11:30 am-8:30 pm; closed Mon, 1/1, 4/11, 11/25 & 12/25. Cocktails & lounge. AE, MC, VI. ⊗ Ⓚ (619) 425-4200

Furr's Family Dining 58 American $ ◆◆
1 1/2 mi s. 1032 3rd Ave. Nice selection of salads, entrees & desserts. A/C. Open 11 am-9 pm; Sun-8 pm; closed 12/25. MC, VI. ⊗ (619) 427-3840

La Fonda Roberto's 56 Mexican $
300 Third Ave at F St. A small, unpretentious restaurant serving an interesting selection of Mexican cuisine. A/C. Open 11 am-9 pm; Sat 11 am-10 pm; Sun 11 am-8 pm; closed 1/1 & 12/25. Beer & wine. MC, VI. (619) 585-3017

CLAREMONT — 32,500
Griswold's Inn AAA Special Value Rates *Motor Inn* ◆◆
All year 1P .... 75.00 2P/1B .... 85.00 2P/2B .... 85.00 XP 10 F
276 units. On SR 66, 1 blk w of Indian Hill Blvd, 1 3/4 mi n of jct I-10. 555 W Foothill Blvd. (91711) Attractive grounds. 15 refrigerators; A/C; C/CATV; movies; radios; phones. Coin laundry. Htd pool; whirlpool. Airport transp. Small pets only, $25 deposit. Monthly rates avail. AE, DI, DS, MC, VI. ● 2 restaurants; 6:30 am-10 pm; $6-$18; dinner theatre; cocktails; entertainment. Also, Indian Hills Restaurant, see separate listing. FAX (909) 624-0756 Ⓓ (909) 626-2411

Ramada Inn   Rates Subject to Change   *Motel* ◆◆
ⓐ All year   1P 54.00- 65.00 2P/1B   58.00- 65.00 2P/2B   .... 64.00 XP 8
124 units. Adjacent to I-10. 840 S Indian Hill Blvd. (91711) Refrigerators; A/C; C/CATV; movies; radios; phones.
10 efficiencies, no utensils. Coin laundry. Htd pool; wading pool; whirlpool; lighted tennis-8 courts. Airport
transp. No pets. Reserv deposit required. AE, DI, DS, MC, VI. Restaurant adjacent. FAX (909) 626-8452
    ⊗ Ⓓ 🛆 (909) 621-4831

RESTAURANTS

Furr's Family Dining   American $ ◆◆
Adjacent to I-10, exit Indian Hill Blvd, 1/4 blk s, then 1 blk w. 507 Claremont Center Dr. Nice selection of salads, entrees
& desserts. A/C. Open 11 am-8 pm; closed 12/25. MC, VI.   ⊗ (909) 624-7759

Indian Hills Restaurant   Continental $$ ◆◆
In Griswold's Inn. Attractive dining room. Sun brunch. A/C. Early bird specials. Open 6:30 am-9:30, 11:30-2 & 6-10 pm;
Sat from 11:30 am; Sun 10 am-2 & 6-9 pm. Cocktails & lounge. Entertainment. Reserv advised. AE, CB, DI, MC, VI.
    🛆 (909) 621-3200

CLEARLAKE — 11,800 See also KELSEYVILLE & LAKEPORT

Best Western El Grande Inn   Rates Subject to Change   *Motor Inn* ◆◆◆
ⓐ 4/1-12/31   1P .... 67.00 2P/1B   .... 73.00 2P/2B   .... 73.00 XP 6
68 units. 3 mi n on SR 53 from jct SR 29, 1 blk w on Lakeshore Dr, via 40th Ave. 15135 Lakeshore Dr. (PO Box
4598, 95422) OPEN ALL YEAR. 24 refrigerators; A/C; C/CATV; pay movies; radios; phones; comb or shower
baths. Whirlpool; indoor sitting pool. No pets. Luxury level rooms avail. AE, DI, DS, MC, VI. ● Dining rm; 6
am-10 pm; $8-$15; cocktails. FAX (707) 994-2042   ⊗ Ⓢ Ⓓ (707) 994-2000

Highlands Inn   Rates Subject to Change   *Motel* ◆◆
ⓐ 5/26-9/30   1P 45.00- 55.00 2P/1B   50.00- 55.00 2P/2B   .... 65.00 XP 5
10/1-5/25   1P 40.00- 45.00 2P/1B   45.00- 50.00 2P/2B   .... 55.00 XP 5
Senior discount. 20 units. 4 mi nw of jct SR 29 & SR 53 via 40th Ave. 13865 Lakeshore Dr. (PO Box 515, 95422)
On the lake; view rooms. 5 refrigerators; A/C; C/CATV; radios; phones. Coin laundry. Small pool; dock; fishing;
water skiing. No pets. 1 suite, $75; 10/1-5/26 $65, for up to 2 persons. Wkly rates avail. Reserv deposit required;
3 days refund notice. AE, DI, DS, MC, VI. FAX (707) 994-0613   ⊗ Ⓢ Ⓓ (707) 994-8982

Lakeside Inn   Rates Subject to Change   *Motel* ◆
ⓐ 5/1-10/15   1P .... 46.00 2P/1B   .... 52.00 2P/2B   .... 55.00 XP 6
10/16-4/30   1P .... 38.00 2P/1B   .... 42.00 2P/2B   .... 48.00 XP 6
Senior discount. 31 units. 2 1/2 mi n on SR 53 from jct SR 29; left on Old Hwy 53. 4775 Old Hwy 53. (PO Box
5166, 95422) A/C; C/CATV; radios; phones. Coin laundry. No pets. AE, DI, DS, MC, VI. ⊗ Ⓓ 🛆 (707) 994-1499

COALINGA — 8,200

Big Country Inn   Rates Subject to Change   *Motel* ◆◆
ⓐ All year   1P 44.00- 46.00 2P/1B   52.00- 54.00 2P/2B   .... 56.00 XP 6
Senior discount. 48 units. W of & adjacent to I-5, at SR 198, Hanford-Lemoore off-ramp. 25020 W Dorris Ave.
(93210) A/C; C/TV; movies; phones. Pool. MC, VI. Coffeeshop adjacent.   Ⓓ (209) 935-0866

The Inn at Harris Ranch   Rates Subject to Change   *Motor Inn* ◆◆ F
ⓐ 2/1-9/30   1P 83.00- 104.00 2P/1B   91.00- 107.00 2P/2B   86.00- 95.00 XP 8
Senior discount. 123 units. E side & adjacent to I-5; at SR 198, Hanford-Lemoore off-ramp. (Rt 1, Box 777, 93210)
OPEN ALL YEAR. Spacious landscaped grounds. Spanish architecture. Check-in 3 pm. A/C; C/CATV; pay
movies; phones; shower or comb baths. Htd pool; whirlpool; lighted tennis-2 courts; private airstrip; exercise
rm. Pets, $10 cleaning fee. 1-bedroom suite, $150-$215 for up to 2 persons. Wkly rates avail. Reserv deposit re-
quired. AE, CB, DI, MC, VI. ● Coffeeshop; 6 am-11 pm; $8-$20. Also restaurant, see separate listing.
FAX (209) 935-5061   ⊗ Ⓢ Ⓓ 🛆 (209) 935-0717

RESTAURANT

Harris Ranch Restaurant   Steakhouse $$ ◆◆◆
In The Inn at Harris Ranch. Coffeeshop & dining room. Specializing in Harris-raised beef & Harris-grown fruit & vegeta-
bles. Early California elegance. A/C. Children's menu. Open 6 am-11 pm. Cocktails & lounge. Minimum, $5. Reserv ad-
vised. AE, DI, MC, VI.   ⊗ 🛆 (209) 935-0717

COLTON — 40,200

Patriot Inn & Suites   Rates Subject to Change   *Motel* ◆◆
ⓐ All year [CP]   1P .... 44.00 2P/1B   .... 48.00 2P/2B   .... 48.00 XP 4 F
Senior discount. 149 units. Adjacent to I-215, northbound exit La Cadena Dr, southbound exit Iowa St. 2830 Iowa
St (92324) Formerly Comfort Inn. A/C; C/CATV; movies; rental VCPs. Radios; phones. Coin laundry. Pool; whirl-
pool. Small pets only, $20 deposit. 4 suites with microwave & refrigerator, $75 for up to 2 persons. Wkly &
monthly rates avail. AE, DI, DS, MC, VI. Restaurant adjacent. FAX (909) 788-7096 ⊗ Ⓢ Ⓓ 🛆 (909) 788-9900

COLUMBIA — 400

Columbia Gem Motel   Rates Subject to Change   *Cottages* ◆
ⓐ 4/1-12/31   1P 30.00- 40.00 2P/1B   35.00- 45.00 2P/2B   50.00- 65.00 XP 3
1/1-3/31   1P .... 25.00 2P/1B   35.00- 40.00 2P/2B   45.00- 50.00 XP 3
12 units. 3 mi n of Sonora, on Parrotts Ferry Rd; 1 mi from Columbia State Historic Park. (PO Box 874, 95310)
Among pines. Rustic individual & duplex cottages, some small; 4 motel rooms. A/C; C/CATV; comb or shower
baths. Wkly rates avail. Reserv deposit required. MC, VI.   Ⓓ (209) 532-4508

RESTAURANT

City Hotel Dining Room   French $$$ ◆◆
In Columbia State Historic Park. Authentically furnished saloon of the Gold Rush Days; fine California wine selection in
restored landmark circa 1870's. Smoking not permitted on premises. A/C. Children's menu. Open 11:30 am-2 & 5:30-
8:30 pm; Mon-Wed from 5:30 pm; Sat-9 pm; Sun 11 am-2 & 5-9 pm; closed Mon 9/1-6/30 & for lunch 1/1-3/31. Cock-
tails. Reserv advised. AE, MC, VI.   ⊗ (209) 532-1479

COMMERCE — 12,100

Radisson City of Commerce Hotel   Rates Subject to Change   *Hotel* ◆◆◆
All year [BP]   1P .... 79.00 2P/1B   .... 94.00 2P/2B   .... 94.00 XP 15
283 units. Adjacent to I-5, Washington Blvd exit. 6300 E Telegraph Rd. (90040) Check-in 3 pm. A/C; C/CATV; free & pay
movies; radios; phones; shower or comb baths. Rental refrigerators. Htd pool; sauna; whirlpool; exercise rm. Garage &
parking lot. Wkly rates avail. AE, DI, DS, MC, VI. ● Dining rm & coffeeshop; 6 am-11 pm; $8.50-$16.50; cocktails; en-
tertainment. FAX (310) 888-9629   ⊗ Ⓓ (310) 722-7200

Ramada Inn Rates Guaranteed *Motel* ◆◆◆
All year 1P 61.00- 68.00 2P/1B 67.00- 74.00 2P/2B 67.00- 74.00 XP 7
Senior discount. 158 units. 1/4 mi w of I-5, exit Slauson Ave. 7272 Gage Ave. (90040) A/C; C/CATV; free & pay movies; VCPs. Radios; phones. Htd pool; exercise rm. No pets. Reserv deposit required. AE, DI, DS, MC, VI. Cocktail lounge; restaurant adjacent. FAX (310) 806-4777 ⊗ Ⓢ Ⓓ 🔊 (310) 806-4777

Westland Inn AAA Special Value Rates *Motel* ◆◆
All year [CP] 1P .... 44.00 2P/1B .... 50.00 2P/2B .... 50.00 XP 6 F
120 units. Adjacent to I-5; exit Slauson Ave. 7810 E Telegraph Rd. (90040) A/C; C/CATV; free & pay movies; radios; phones. Coin laundry. Htd pool; sauna; whirlpool. No pets. Wkly rates avail. AE, DI, DS, MC, VI. Ⓓ 🔊 (310) 806-3791

Wyndham Garden Hotel Rates Subject to Change *Hotel* ◆◆◆
All year 1P .... 119.00 2P/1B .... 129.00 2P/2B .... 129.00 XP 10 F
201 units. Adjacent e side of I-5, between Washington Blvd & Atlantic Ave off ramps. 5757 Telegraph Rd. (90040) South end of the Citadel. Check-in 3 pm. A/C; C/CATV; pay movies; radios; phones. Rental refrigerators. Htd pool; saunas; whirlpool; exercise rm. Pets. 14 suites with living room & bedroom, $129-$139. Wkly & monthly rates avail. AE, DI, DS, MC, VI. ● Restaurant; 6:30 am-10 pm; $10.95-$16.95. FAX (213) 887-4343 *(See ad below)* ⊗ Ⓢ Ⓓ (213) 887-8100

RESTAURANT

Tamayo Mexican $$ ◆◆
From I-5 Santa Ana Frwy, exit Atlantic Ave, 1/2 mi n. 5300 E Olympic Blvd. Very attractive restaurant in a historical building. A/C. Open 11 am-10 pm; Fri-11 pm; Sat 5 pm-11 pm; closed Sun, 11/25 & 12/25. Cocktails & lounge. Valet parking. Reserv advised. AE, CB, DI, MC, VI. ⊗ (310) 260-4700

COMPTON — 90,500

Best Western Willow Tree Inn Rates Subject to Change *Motor Inn* ◆◆◆
All year 1P 48.00- 56.00 2P/1B 52.00- 60.00 2P/2B 53.00- 65.00 XP 4 F
Senior discount. 96 units. Adjacent to SR 91, Central Ave exit. 1919 W Artesia Blvd. (90220) A/C; C/CATV; movies; rental VCPs. Radios; phones. Rental refrigerators. Coin laundry. Pool. No pets. AE, DI, DS, MC, VI. ● Restaurant; 24 hours; $7-$12; cocktails. ⊗ Ⓓ 🔊 (310) 537-6700

CONCORD — 111,300   See also MARTINEZ

Best Western Heritage Inn — Rates Guaranteed — *Motel* ◆◆◆
All year   1P 60.00- 65.00 2P/1B 60.00- 65.00 2P/2B 55.00- 60.00 XP 5   F
Senior discount. 132 units. 3 mi e at Wharton Way. 4600 Clayton Rd. (94521) Refrigerators; A/C; C/CATV; movies; radios; phones. 7 efficiencies. Pool; sauna; whirlpool. Pets, $50 deposit required. Wkly rates avail. AE, DI, DS, MC, VI. Restaurant adjacent. FAX (510) 825-0581 *(See ad p A364)*   ⊗ Ⓢ Ⓓ Ⓔ (510) 686-4466

Concord Hilton — Rates Guaranteed — *Hotel* ◆◆◆◆
All year   1P .... 72.00 2P/1B .... 72.00 2P/2B .... 72.00 XP 10   F
330 units. E of I-680 via Willow Pass Rd. 1970 Diamond Blvd. (94520) Check-in 3 pm. A/C; C/CATV; movies; radios; phones. Pool; whirlpool; exercise rm. Parking lot. No pets. Wkly & monthly rates avail. AE, DI, DS, MC, VI. ● Restaurant; 6:30 am-10 pm; $10-$30; cocktails. FAX (510) 671-0984 *(See ads p 22 and p A117)*   ⊗ Ⓢ Ⓓ Ⓔ (510) 827-2000

Days Inn — Rates Subject to Change — *Motel* ◆◆
5/1-9/30 [CP]   1P 45.00- 60.00 2P/1B 45.00- 60.00 2P/2B 50.00- 65.00 XP 6   F
10/1-4/30 [CP] 1P 40.00- 55.00 2P/1B 40.00- 55.00 2P/2B 45.00- 58.00 XP 6   F
Senior discount. 63 units. 1 mi e at Babel Rd. 3606 Clayton Rd. (94521) Attractively decorated rooms. A/C; C/CATV; movies; radios; phones. Pool. No pets. Luxury level rooms avail. Most rooms with VCP, microwave & refrigerator. Some suites with wet bar & large whirlpool tub, $85-$105 for 2 persons. Reserv deposit required. AE, DI, DS, MC, VI. Restaurant adjacent. FAX (510) 676-7547   ⊗ Ⓓ Ⓔ (510) 682-7850

El Monte Motor Inn — Rates Guaranteed — *Motel* ◆◆
All year [CP]   1P 43.00- 45.00 2P/1B 43.00- 45.00 2P/2B .... 55.00 XP
42 units. 2 mi e of jct I-680 & SR 24, exit SR 24 at Clayton Rd. 3555 Clayton Rd. (94519) Refrigerators; A/C; C/CATV; movies; 20 radios; phones; shower or comb baths. 24 kitchens. Coin laundry. Pool; whirlpool. No pets. Wkly rates avail. AE, DI, DS, MC, VI.   ⊗ Ⓓ (510) 682-1601

Holiday Inn Concord — Rates Subject to Change — *Motor Inn* ◆◆
All year [BP]   1P 59.00- 95.00 2P/1B 59.00- 95.00 2P/2B 69.00- 95.00 XP 10
Senior discount. 195 units. Exit I-680 E Concord Ave; Diamond Ave S; Burnett Ave W. 1050 Burnett Ave. (94520) A/C; C/CATV; movies; radios; phones. Pool; whirlpool; exercise rm. Complimentary beverages each evening. AE, DI, DS, MC, VI. ● Restaurant; 6:30 am-2 & 5:30-10 pm; $8-$18; cocktails. FAX (510) 687-5500   ⊗ Ⓓ (510) 687-5500

Sheraton Hotel & Conference Center — AAA Special Value Rates — *Motor Inn* ◆◆◆
All year   1P 80.00- 95.00 2P/1B 90.00- 100.00 2P/2B 90.00- 100.00 XP 15   F
325 units. E off I-680 exit Concord Ave. 45 John Glenn Dr. (94520) A/C; C/CATV; movies; radios; phones. Small indoor pool; whirlpool; putting green; exercise rm. Pets. AE, DI, DS, MC, VI. ● Restaurant; 6 am-10:30 pm; $10-$16; cocktails; entertainment. FAX (510) 674-9567 *(See ad below)*   ⊗ Ⓢ Ⓓ (510) 825-7700

The Trees Inn — Rates Subject to Change — *Apartment Motel* ◆◆◆
All year [CP]   1P 54.00- 80.00 2P/1B 54.00- 80.00 2P/2B 54.00- 80.00 XP 5   F
Senior discount. 42 units. 1/2 mi e of I-680, northbound exit Monument Blvd; southbound exit Gregory Ln. 1370 Monument Blvd. (94520) Check-in 3 pm. A/C; C/CATV; movies; radios; phones. 11 2-bedrm units, efficiencies. Coin laundry. Pool. Wkly & monthly rates avail. Reserv deposit required. AE, CB, DI, MC, VI.   Ⓢ Ⓓ Ⓔ (510) 827-8998

CORCORAN — 13,400

Budget Inn — Rates Subject to Change — *Motel* ◆
All year [CP]   1P 47.00- 55.00 2P/1B 47.00- 55.00 2P/2B .... 60.00 XP 6   F
45 units. 1 mi w of SR 43; Whitley Ave exit. 1224 Whitley Ave. (93212) Formerly Shilo Inn. Few small rooms. 3-story, no elevator. A/C; C/CATV; radios; phones. Coin laundry. Pets, $6 extra charge. Reserv deposit required. AE, DI, DS, MC, VI. Coffeeshop adjacent. FAX (209) 992-5681   ⊗ Ⓢ Ⓓ (209) 992-3171

CORNING — 5,900

Corning Olive Inn Motel — Rates Guaranteed — *Motel* ◆◆
5/16-9/30   1P .... 36.00 2P/1B .... 46.00 2P/2B .... 48.00 XP 5   F
10/1-5/15   1P .... 34.00 2P/1B .... 42.00 2P/2B .... 44.00 XP 5   F
41 units. Exit I-5 e via Corning exit, 1 blk e. 2165 Solano St. (96021) A/C; C/CATV; movies; phones. Pool. Reserv deposit required. AE, DI, DS, MC, VI. Coffeeshop opposite.   ⊗ Ⓓ Ⓔ (916) 824-2468

Days Inn — Rates Subject to Change — *Motel* ◆◆
All year [CP]   1P 28.00- 40.00 2P/1B 32.00- 50.00 2P/2B 35.00- 60.00 XP 5   F
Senior discount. 62 units. Exit I-5 at South Ave, 1/4 mi s. 3475 Hwy 99W. (96021) A/C; C/CATV; VCPs; phones; comb or shower baths. Coin laundry. Pool. Pets, $25 deposit required. AE, DI, DS, MC, VI. FAX (916) 824-2736   ⊗ Ⓓ Ⓔ (916) 824-2000

Shilo Inn Rates Subject to Change *Motel* ◆◆◆
All year [CP] .... 2P/1B 60.00- 67.00 2P/2B 54.00- 61.00 XP 8 F
Senior discount. 78 units. 1 mi s; e & adjacent to I-5, exit South Ave. 3350 Sunrise Way. (96021) A/C; C/CATV; movies; radios; phones. Coin laundry. Small pool; sauna; whirlpool; steamroom; exercise rm. Pets, $6 extra charge. Some rooms with wet bar, microwave & refrigerator $59-$65. Wkly rates avail. AE, DI, DS, MC, VI. Restaurant opposite.
FAX (916) 824-2983 ⊗ Ⓢ Ⓓ Ⓛ (916) 824 2940

RESTAURANT

D2 (Squared) Italian $$ ◆◆
Exit Central Corning, 1 mi e. 410 Solano St. Comfortable atmosphere, emphasis on fresh ingredients. Creative preparation. A/C. Children's menu. Open 11 am-2 & 5-9 pm; 6/1-9/31 to 10 pm; Sat from 5 pm; Sun 1 pm-9 pm; closed Mon, 1.1 & 12/25. Beer & wine. CB, DI, MC, VI. ⊗ (916) 824-4170

CORONA — 76,100

Best Motel Rates Subject to Change *Motel* ◆◆
⊕ All year 1P 36.00- 38.00 2P/1B 38.00- 40.00 2P/2B .... 45.00 XP 4
57 units. 3/4 mi s of SR 71 & 91, 6th St or Lincoln Ave exit. (91720) 37 refrigerators; A/C; C/CATV; movies; rental VCPs. Phones. Coin laundry. Small pool; whirlpool. No pets. 27 efficiencies, $5 extra; Suites with refrigerator $49-$55. 2 units with whirlpool tub, $65. Wkly & monthly rates avail. Reserv deposit required. AE, DI, DS, MC, VI. Restaurant adjacent. FAX (909) 737-8003 Ⓓ (909) 272-4900

Best Western Kings Inn Rates Subject to Change *Motel* ◆◆◆
⊕ All year [CP] 1P 49.00- 57.00 2P/1B 49.00- 57.00 2P/2B 49.00- 54.00 XP 5
87 units. Adjacent to SR 91, Lincoln Ave exit. 1084 Pomona Rd. (91720) 31 refrigerators; A/C; C/CATV; movies; rental VCPs. Radios; phones; comb & shower baths. Htd pool; whirlpool. No pets. Microwaves. AE, DI, DS, MC, VI. Restaurant adjacent. FAX (909) 279-5371 ⊗ Ⓓ Ⓛ (909) 734-4241

Corona Travelodge Rates Subject to Change *Motel* ◆◆
⊕ All year 1P .... 33.00 2P/1B .... 38.00 2P/2B .... 41.00 XP 5 F
Senior discount. 46 units. 1701 W 6th St. (91720) 9 refrigerators; A/C; C/TV; radios; phones. Pool. Reserv deposit required. AE, DI, DS, MC, VI. Restaurant adjacent. ⊗ (909) 735-5505

Country Side Inn Rates Guaranteed *Motel* ◆◆◆
⊕ All year [BP] 1P .... 59.00 2P/1B .... 69.00 XP 10 F
Senior discount. 102 units. Adjacent to SR 91, exit McKinley. 2260 Griffin Way. (91719) Check-in 3 pm. Refrigerators; A/C; C/CATV; movies; radios; phones. Small htd pool; whirlpool. No pets. Wkly rates avail. Complimentary beverages each evening. AE, DI, DS, MC, VI. Restaurant opposite. FAX (909) 734-4056 *(See ad p A295)*
⊗ Ⓢ Ⓓ Ⓛ (909) 734-2140

Flaming Arrow Motel Rates Subject to Change *Motel* ◆
⊕ All year 1P 25.00- 28.00 2P/1B 28.00- 32.00 2P/2B 30.00- 35.00 XP 4 F
Senior discount. 18 units. 1/2 mi s of SR 71 & 91, Lincoln Ave exit. 1030 W 6th St. (91720) A/C; C/CATV; movies; phones; shower baths. 1 2-bedrm unit. Pool. No pets. Wkly rates avail. Reserv deposit required. AE, CB, DI, MC, VI. Ⓓ (909) 737-0491

RESTAURANTS

Furr's Family Dining American $ ◆◆
1/4 mi n of SR 91. 705 N Main St. Large selection of salads, entrees & desserts. A/C. Open 11 am-8 pm; closed 12/25. MC, VI. ⊗ (909) 735-6680

Reubens American $$ ◆◆
Adjacent to SR 91, Lincoln Ave exit. 103 N Lincoln Ave. A/C. Children's menu. Open 11:30 am-2:30 & 5-10 pm; Fri-11 pm; Sat 5 pm-11 pm; Sun 4 pm-9 pm; closed 12/25. Cocktails & lounge. Entertainment. AE, CB, DI, MC, VI.
⊗ Ⓛ (909) 735-1100

CORONADO — 26,500 See SAN DIEGO

CORTE MADERA — 8,300

Best Western Corte Madera Inn Rates Subject to Change *Motor Inn* ◆◆◆
⊕ All year [CP] 1P 77.00- 92.00 2P/1B 87.00-105.00 2P/2B 87.00-105.00 XP 8 F
110 units. W off & adjacent to US 101; southbound exit Madera Blvd; northbound 1 blk w via Tamalpias Rd-Paradise Dr exit, then 3 blks n via Madera Blvd. 1815 Redwood Hwy. (94925) Attractively landscaped garden area. Many rooms with patio. Check-in 3 pm. Refrigerators; A/C; C/CATV; movies; radios; phones; comb & shower baths. 7 2-bedrm units. Coin laundry. Pool; wading pool; whirlpools; playground; 2 units with whirlpool tub; exercise rm. No pets. Reserv deposit required. AE, DI, DS, MC, VI. ● Coffeeshop; 6:30 am-midnight; Fri & Sat-2 am; $9-$16; cocktails. FAX (415) 924-5419 *(See ad p A422)* ⊗ Ⓓ (415) 924-1502

COSTA MESA — 96,400

Ana Mesa Suites AAA Special Value Rates *Suites Motel* ◆◆
⊕ All year [CP] .... 2P/1B 51.00- 77.00 2P/2B 51.00- 77.00 XP 5 F
51 units. 3/4 mi n of I-405, Harbor Blvd exit. 3597 Harbor Blvd. (92626) Rooms & 1-bedroom suites with kitchen or efficiency. Whirlpool tubs. Refrigerators; A/C; C/CATV; movies; radios; phones. 15 kitchens, 11 efficiencies. Coin laundry. Small pool. Pets, $50 deposit required; also, $20 extra charge. Wkly rates avail. AE, DI, DS, MC, VI. FAX (714) 549-7126 Ⓓ (714) 662-3500

Best Western Newport Mesa Inn AAA Special Value Rates *Motor Inn* ◆◆◆
⊕ All year 1P 52.00- 59.00 2P/1B 54.00- 64.00 2P/2B 59.00- 68.00 XP 6-10 F
97 units. 2 mi n, adjacent to SR 55. 2642 Newport Blvd. (92627) Spacious, nicely furnished rooms. 63 refrigerators; A/C; C/CATV; movies; radios; phones. Coin laundry. Htd pool; sauna; indoor whirlpool; exercise rm. Garage. Airport transp. No pets. 3 rooms with whirlpool tub, $99. Wkly & monthly rates avail. AE, DI, MC, VI. ● Restaurant; 11:30 am-2:30 & 5-9:30 pm; $5-$8.50; beer & wine. FAX (714) 642-1220 *(See ad p A163)*
⊗ Ⓢ Ⓓ (714) 650-3020

Beverly Heritage Hotel Rates Subject to Change *Hotel* ◆◆◆
All year [CP] 1P 95.00-120.00 2P/1B 95.00-120.00 2P/2B 95.00-120.00 XP 10
238 units. From I-405, exit Bristol St, 1 blk n, then 2 blks e. 3350 Ave of the Arts. (92626) 1 block to Orange County Performing Arts center. Check-in 3 pm. A/C; C/CATV; movies; radios; phones. Htd pool; whirlpool; bicycles; exercise rm. Garage. Airport transp. No pets. AE, CB, DI, MC, VI. ● Restaurant; 7 am-10 pm; Sun from 7:30 am; a la carte entrees about $12-$20; 24 hour room service; cocktails; entertainment. FAX (714) 751-0129 ⊗ Ⓢ Ⓓ Ⓛ (714) 751-5100

Comfort Inn AAA Special Value Rates *Motel* ◆◆
⊕ All year [CP] 1P 48.00- 58.00 2P/1B 51.00- 55.00 2P/2B .... 58.00 XP 3 F
Senior discount. 58 units. Adjacent to SR 55, 1 1/2 mi n of jct Harbor Blvd. 2430 Newport Blvd. (92627) 25 refrigerators; A/C; C/CATV; movies; phones. Pool; whirlpool. No pets. Wkly rates avail. Reserv deposit required. AE, DI, DS, MC, VI. FAX (714) 548-3720 *(See ad p A120)* ⊗ Ⓓ (714) 631-7840

Costa Mesa Marriott Suites — Rates Subject to Change — *Suites Hotel* ◆◆◆
All year   1P .... 139.00   2P/1B .... 159.00   2P/2B .... 159.00   XP 15
253 units. From I-405, use Bristol St exit, 1 blk n, then 3 blks e. 500 Anton Blvd. (92626) Check-in 3 pm. Refrigerators; A/C; C/CATV; movies; radios; phones. Coin laundry. Htd pool; whirlpool; exercise rm. Parking ramp. Airport transp. No pets. Wkly & monthly rates avail. AE, DI, DS, MC, VI. ● Dining rm; 6:30 am-10 pm; $12-$18; cocktails. FAX (714) 966-8495   ⊗ ⑤ Ⓓ 🕭 (714) 957-1100

Country Side Inn & Suites — Rates Guaranteed — *Motor Inn* ◆◆◆
🏧 All year [BP]   1P 70.00- 90.00   2P/1B 80.00- 100.00   2P/2B 80.00- 100.00   XP 10   F
Senior discount. 290 units. Adjacent to SR 73; 1/4 blk e of Red Hill Ave. 325 Bristol St. (92626) Attractive country French atmosphere, 27 1-bedroom suites. Refrigerators; A/C; C/CATV; VCPs; radios; phones; comb or shower baths. Coin laundry. 2 htd pools; whirlpools; 120 rooms with whirlpool tub; exercise rm. Airport transp. No pets. Many rooms with small microwave. Complimentary beverages each evening. AE, CB, DI, MC, VI. ● Dining rm; 7 am-9 pm; Fri & Sat-10 pm; a la carte entrees about $10-$20; cocktails. FAX (714) 662-0828 *(See ad p A295)*   ⊗ ⑤ Ⓓ 🕭 (714) 549-0300

Cozy Inn — Rates Guaranteed — *Motel* ◆◆
🏧 6/1-9/15   1P 38.00- 40.00   2P/1B 42.00- 46.00   2P/2B .... 48.00   XP 4
9/16-5/31   1P 34.00- 36.00   2P/1B 38.00- 40.00   2P/2B .... 42.00   XP 4
Senior discount. 30 units. 1/4 blk w of SR 55, Newport Blvd. 325 W Bay St. (92627) Spacious rooms. A/C; C/TV; radios; phones. Small htd pool. No pets. 11 efficiencies, $8 extra. Wkly rates avail. Reserv deposit required. AE, DI, DS, MC, VI.   Ⓓ (714) 650-2055

Days Inn — Rates Subject to Change — *Motel* ◆◆◆
🏧 5/15-9/15   1P 42.00- 48.00   2P/1B 46.00- 50.00   2P/2B 48.00- 52.00   XP 4
9/16-5/14   1P 38.00- 44.00   2P/1B 44.00- 48.00   2P/2B .... 48.00   XP 4
31 units. Adjacent to SR 55; 3/4 mi n of jct Harbor Blvd. 2100 Newport Blvd. (92627) Formerly Don Quixote Motel. Refrigerators; A/C; C/CATV; movies; 18 radios; phones. 3 2-bedrm units. Pool. No pets. 3-night minimum stay in 4 efficiencies, $5 extra. Wkly rates avail. AE, DI, DS, MC, VI.   Ⓓ (714) 642-2670

Holiday Inn Bristol Plaza Hotel — Rates Subject to Change — *Motor Inn* ◆◆◆
All year   1P 80.00- 88.00   2P/1B 88.00- 96.00   2P/2B 88.00- 96.00   XP 8   F
Senior discount. 230 units. Adjacent to I-405, Bristol St exit. 3131 Bristol St. (92626) 60 refrigerators; A/C; C/CATV; movies; radios; phones. Coin laundry. Htd pool; wading pool; sauna; exercise rm. Airport transp. No pets. AE, CB, DI, MC, VI. ● Dining rm; 6 am-2 & 5-10 pm; $7-$14; cocktails. FAX (714) 957-8185   ⊗ ⑤ Ⓓ 🕭 (714) 557-3000

Inn at Costa Mesa — Rates Subject to Change — *Motel* ◆◆
🏧 All year   1P 41.00- 51.00   2P/1B 47.00- 57.00   2P/2B 50.00- 60.00   XP 5
Senior discount. 50 units. 1 1/2 blks s of I-405. 3151 Harbor Blvd. (92626) A/C; C/TV; movies; radios; phones. 1 2-bedrm unit. Pool. No pets. AE, DI, DS, MC, VI. FAX (714) 979-9647   ⊗ Ⓓ (714) 540-8571

La Quinta Motor Inn — Rates Subject to Change — *Motel* ◆◆◆
🏧 All year   1P 45.00- 52.00   2P/1B 48.00- 55.00   2P/2B .... 48.00   XP 3   F
162 units. Adjacent to I-405, 2 blks nw of Harbor Blvd exit. 1515 S Coast Dr. (92626) A/C; C/CATV; movies; radios; phones. Htd pool. Airport transp. Pets. AE, DI, DS, MC, VI. Restaurant adjacent. FAX (714) 432-7159   ⊗ Ⓓ 🕭 (714) 957-5841

New Harbor Inn — Rates Guaranteed — *Motel* ◆◆
🏧 6/1-9/15   1P 38.00- 40.00   2P/1B 42.00- 46.00   2P/2B .... 48.00   XP 4
9/16-5/31   1P .... 35.00   2P/1B .... 38.00   2P/2B .... 40.00   XP 4
Senior discount. 35 units. 1 mi n of jct SR 55, Newport Blvd. 2205 Harbor Blvd. (92627) Rating withheld pending completion of construction. Scheduled to open August, 1992. A/C; C/CATV; movies; phones. Pool. No pets. MC, VI.   Ⓓ (714) 646-3277

Newport Bay Inn [CP] — AAA Special Value Rates — *Motel* ◆◆◆
🏧 All year [CP]   1P 48.00- 60.00   2P/1B 48.00- 60.00   2P/2B 56.00- 65.00   XP 5   F
60 units. Adjacent to SR 55; 3/4 mi n of jct Harbor Blvd. 2070 Newport Blvd. (92627) Spacious rooms. 50 refrigerators; A/C; C/CATV; rental VCPs; 30 radios; phones; comb or shower baths. Coin laundry. Garage. No pets. Wkly rates avail. Reserv deposit required. AE, DI, DS, MC, VI. FAX (714) 631-4952   ⊗ ⑤ Ⓓ 🕭 (714) 631-6000

Park Place Inn — Rates Subject to Change — *Motel* ◆
🏧 All year   1P .... 44.50   2P/1B .... 44.50   2P/2B .... 48.00   XP 4
Senior discount. 59 units. On SR 55 1/2 mi s of jct Harbor Blvd. 1662 Newport Blvd. (92627) A/C; C/CATV; movies; phones. 3 2-bedrm units. Pool. No pets. Wkly & monthly rates avail. MC, VI.   Ⓓ (714) 642-0977

Ramada Limited [CP] — Rates Subject to Change — *Motel* ◆◆
🏧 All year [CP]   1P 42.00- 50.00   2P/1B 50.00- 60.00   2P/2B 42.00- 50.00   XP 5
141 units. 1 blk w of SR 55, Newport Blvd. 1680 Superior Ave at 17th St. (92627) Formerly Marina Gateway Westway Inn. A/C; C/TV; phones; comb baths. 2 2-bedrm units. Coin laundry. Htd pool; whirlpool. No pets. Wkly & monthly rates avail. AE, DB, DI, MO, VI. *(See ads p A121)*   Ⓓ 🕭 (714) 645-2221

Red Lion Hotel/Orange County Airport   Rates Subject to Change   *Hotel* ◆◆◆
All year   1P 123.00- 152.00   2P/1B 132.00- 172.00   2P/2B 132.00- 172.00 XP 15   F
484 units. 1 blk s of I-405, exit Bristol St. 3050 Bristol St. (92626) Check-in 3 pm. A/C; C/CATV; free & pay movies; radios; phones. Htd pool; sauna; whirlpool; steamroom; exercise rm. Fee for: massage. Pay valet garage. Airport transp. Small pets only. AE, DI, DS, MC, VI. ● Dining rm & restaurant; 6 am-midnight; $7-$25; cocktails; entertainment. FAX (714) 540-9176 *(See ad p A3)*   ⊗ Ⓢ Ⓓ Ⓔ (714) 540-7000

Residence Inn by Marriott   Rates Subject to Change   *Apartment Motel* ◆◆◆
All year [CP]   1P 97.00- 132.00   2P/1B 97.00- 132.00   2P/2B 97.00- 132.00 XP 10
144 units. Adjacent to SR 73, use Bear St exit; from SR 55 Baker St exit. 881 W Baker St. (92626) 1-bedroom studios & 36-split level, 2-bedroom suites with living room & kitchen. Many fireplaces. A/C; C/CATV; movies; VCPs. Radios; phones. Coin laundry. Htd pool; whirlpool; exercise rm. Pets, $200 deposit, $60 non-refundable, & $7 daily extra charge. Wkly rates avail. Reserv deposit required. AE, CB, DI, MC, VI. FAX (714) 546-4308   ⊗ Ⓓ Ⓔ (714) 241-8800

Super 8 Motel, Costa Mesa   AAA Special Value Rates   *Motel* ◆◆◆
Ⓐ All year [CP]   1P 42.00- 52.00 2P/1B 45.00- 58.00 2P/2B 47.00- 57.00 XP 5   F
49 units. 1 mi s of I-405. 2645 Harbor Blvd. (92626) Refrigerators; A/C; C/CATV; movies; radios; phones; shower or comb baths. Htd pool; sauna; whirlpool. No pets. 7-night minimum stay in kitchen units; $7 extra. Wkly rates avail. Reserv deposit required. Complimentary beverages each evening. AE, DI, DS, MC, VI. FAX (714) 432-8129 *(See ad below)*   ⊗ Ⓓ (714) 545-9471

Travelodge-Orange County Airport   Rates Subject to Change   *Motel*   ◆◆
All year [CP]   1P .... 43.00   2P/1B .... 47.00   2P/2B .... 47.00   XP 5
122 units. 1/2 mi e of SR 55. 1400 SE Bristol St. (Santa Ana, 92707) 70 refrigerators; A/C; C/CATV; free & pay movies; radios; phones. Pool; whirlpool; 12 steambaths; exercise rm. Airport transp. AE, DI, DS, MC, VI. Restaurant adjacent. FAX (714) 557-9164   ⊗ (D) (714) 557-8700

Vagabond Inn   Rates Subject to Change   *Motel*   ◆◆
All year [CP]   1P 40.00- 50.00   2P/1B 45.00- 55.00   2P/2B 50.00- 60.00   XP 5   F
127 units. 1/4 blk s of I-405, Harbor Blvd exit. 3205 Harbor Blvd. (92626) A/C; C/CATV; movies; VCPs. Radios; phones. Rental refrigerators. 3 2-bedrm units. Htd pool; whirlpool; exercise rm. Pets, $5 extra charge. Reserv deposit required. AE, DI, DS, MC, VI. Restaurant adjacent. FAX (714) 662-7596 *(See ad p A121)*
    ⊗ (D) (714) 557-8360

The Westin South Coast Plaza Hotel   Rates Subject to Change   *Hotel* ◆◆◆◆
All year   1P 139.00- 164.00   2P/1B 139.00- 164.00   2P/2B 139.00- 164.00   XP 20   F
392 units. 1 blk n of I-405, Bristol St exit. 686 Anton Blvd. (92626) A/C; C/CATV; free & pay movies; radios; phones. Htd pool; lighted tennis-2 courts. Pay valet parking ramp. Airport transp. Pets. AE, CB, DI, MC, VI. ● Restaurant; 6:30 am-11 pm; Sat & Sun from 7 am; $9-$18; 24 hour room service; cocktails. FAX (714) 754-7996   ⊗ (S) (D) (714) 540-2500

Birraporetti's   Italian $$ ◆◆
1/4 mi n of I-405, in South Coast Plaza, adjacent to Sears. 333 Bristol St. A large, popular restaurant featuring a nice selection of pasta, chicken, veal, seafood & pizza. A/C. Open 11 am-2 am; closed 11/25 & 12/25. Cocktails & lounge. AE, CB, DI, MC, VI.   ⊗ (714) 850-9090

Mimi's Cafe   American $ ◆◆
On SR 55. 1835 Newport Blvd at jct Harbor Blvd. Attractive family restaurant in a French cafe atmosphere. Nice selection of salads, sandwiches & entrees. A/C. Children's menu. Open 7 am-11 pm; Fri & Sat-midnight; closed 11/25 & 12/25. Beer & wine. AE, MC, VI.   ⊗ (714) 722-6722

Riviera Restaurant   Continental $$$ ◆◆◆
1 blk n of I-405, in South Coast Plaza Shopping Center; adjacent to May Co. 3333 Bristol St. Small charming restaurant. A/C. Open 11:30 am-3 & 5-11 pm; closed Sun & major holidays. Cocktails & lounge. Reserv advised. AE, CB, DI, MC, VI.   (714) 540-3840

Scott's Seafood Grill   Seafood $$$ ◆◆◆
1 blk n of I-405, exit Bristol St. 3300 Bristol St. A popular attractive restaurant featuring fresh seafood. Also pasta & gourmet pizza. A/C. Open 11:30 am-3 & 5-11 pm; closed 1/1, 11/25 & 12/25. Cocktails & lounge. Valet parking. Reserv advised. AE, CB, DI, MC, VI.   ⊗ (714) 979-2400

COULTERVILLE — 100

Hotel Jeffery   Rates Subject to Change   *Historic Hotel*   ◆
All year [CP]   ....   2P/1B 59.00- 74.00   2P/2B 59.00- 74.00   XP 10   F
Senior discount. 21 units. At jct SR 49 & SR 132. 1 Main St. (PO Box 440, 95311) Built in 1851. 5 shower or comb baths. Parking lot. No pets. 2-bedroom units, $99-$133 for 4-6 persons. Reserv deposit required. MC, VI. Restaurant adjacent. *(See ad p A548)*   (S) (D) (209) 878-3471

Yosemite Americana Inn   Rates Subject to Change   *Motel*
5/15-9/10   1P 42.50- 49.50   2P/1B 42.50- 49.50   2P/2B .... 49.50   XP 6
9/11-5/14   1P 38.00- 45.00   2P/1B 38.00- 45.00   2P/2B .... 45.00   XP 6
Senior discount. 9 units. 1/2 mi n on SR 49. 10407 Hwy 49. (PO Box 265, 95311) A/C; C/TV; phones; comb or shower baths. No pets. Reserv deposit required; 3 days refund notice. MC, VI.   ⊗ (D) (209) 878-3407

CRESCENT CITY — 4,400

American Best Motel   Rates Subject to Change   *Motel*   ◆◆
6/13-9/30   1P 50.00- 62.50   2P/1B 50.00- 62.50   2P/2B 55.00- 72.50   XP
10/1-6/12   1P 39.50- 50.00   2P/1B 39.50- 50.00   2P/2B 45.00- 57.50   XP
49 units. 1/4 mi s on US 101. 685 Hwy 101S. (95531) Large rooms. Attractive decor. C/CATV; movies; phones; shower or comb baths. No pets. Reserv deposit required. AE, DS, MC, VI.   ⊗ (D) (§) (707) 464-4111

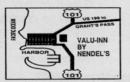

Best Western Northwoods Inn
		Rates Subject to Change					Motel		◆◆
6/15-8/31	1P 65.00- 75.00	2P/1B	65.00- 75.00	2P/2B	75.00- 85.00	XP	6		
5/15-6/14 & 9/1-9/30	1P 50.00- 55.00	2P/1B	50.00- 55.00	2P/2B	59.00- 65.00	XP	6		
10/1-5/14	1P 42.00- 52.00	2P/1B	42.00- 52.00	2P/2B	47.00- 57.00	XP	6		

Senior discount. 52 units. 1/4 mi s on US 101. 655 Hwy 101S. (95531) Comfortable modern rooms. C/CATV; movies; radios; phones. Coin laundry. Whirlpool. No pets. AE, DS, DI, MC, VI. ● Restaurant, see separate listing. FAX (707) 464-9461 *(See ad below)*   ⊗ Ⓓ (707) 464-9771

Curly Redwood Lodge
		Rates Subject to Change					Motel		◆◆
6/1-9/30	1P 50.00- 57.00	2P/1B	50.00- 57.00	2P/2B	54.00- 62.00	XP	5		
10/1-5/31	1P 35.00	2P/1B	.... 35.00	2P/2B	.... 37.00	XP	5		

36 units. 1/2 mi s on US 101. 701 Redwood Hwy S. (95531) Many large rooms. C/CATV; phones; shower or comb baths. No pets. 3 2-bedroom units, $75. Reserv deposit required; 3 days refund notice. AE, CB, DI, MC, VI. *(See ad p A122)*   ⊗ Ⓓ (707) 464-2137

Econo Lodge
		Rates Subject to Change					Motel		◆
7/1-8/31	1P 50.00- 55.00	2P/1B	50.00- 55.00	2P/2B	55.00- 70.00	XP	5		
5/1-6/30 & 9/1-10/31	1P 35.00- 45.00	2P/1B	35.00- 45.00	2P/2B	40.00- 50.00	XP	5		
11/1-4/30	1P 30.00- 40.00	2P/1B	30.00- 40.00	2P/2B	35.00- 45.00	XP	5		

Senior discount. 48 units. On US 101 southbound at Front St. 119 L St. (95531) C/CATV; movies; phones; shower baths. No pets. Reserv deposit required. MC, VI. *(See ad below)*   ⊗ Ⓓ (707) 464-2181

Nendels Valu-Inn
		Rates Subject to Change					Motel		◆◆
7/1-8/31	1P 62.00- 69.00	2P/1B	65.00- 72.00	2P/2B	69.00- 74.00	XP	6		
5/1-6/30 & 9/1-9/30	1P 35.00- 42.00	2P/1B	37.00- 45.00	2P/2B	42.00- 49.00	XP	6		
10/1-4/30	1P 32.00- 38.00	2P/1B	32.00- 38.00	2P/2B	35.00- 42.00	XP	6		

27 units. Between US 101 northbound & southbound. 353 L St. (95531) C/CATV; movies; radios; phones; comb or shower baths. Sauna. No pets. Reserv deposit required; 3 days refund notice. AE, DI, DS, MC, VI. *(See ad p A122)*   ⊗ Ⓓ (707) 464-6124

Pacific Motor Hotel
		Rates Subject to Change					Motel		◆◆
5/1-10/15	1P 47.00	2P/1B	.... 59.00	2P/2B	.... 62.00	XP	5		
10/16-4/30	1P 39.00	2P/1B	.... 52.00	2P/2B	.... 57.00	XP	5		

Senior discount. 62 units. 1 mi n; on US 101. 440 Hwy 101N. (PO Box 595, 95531) C/CATV; movies; radios; phones; shower or comb baths. 3 2-bedrm units. Sauna; indoor whirlpool. Small pets only. AE, DI, DS, MC, VI. Restaurant adjacent.-. *(See ad below)*   Ⓓ (707) 464-4141

Travelodge
		Rates Subject to Change					Motel		◆◆
6/1-9/15	1P 57.00	2P/1B	.... 57.00	2P/2B	.... 67.00	XP	5	F
9/16-5/31	1P 37.00	2P/1B	.... 37.00	2P/2B	.... 47.00	XP	5	F

Senior discount. 52 units. 1 1/4 mi n on US 101. 725 Hwy 101N. (95531) C/CATV; movies; radios; phones. Coin laundry. Sauna; whirlpool. No pets. AE, MC, VI.   ⊗ Ⓓ Ⓖ (707) 464-6106

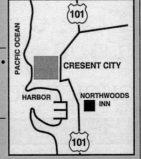

RESTAURANTS

Harbor View Grotto   Steak & Seafood $$ ◆
1/2 mi s, 1 blk w of US 101. 155 Citizen's Dock Rd. Informal dining upstairs, overlooking boat basin. A/C. Children's menu. Open 11:30 am-10 pm; closed 1/1, 11/25, 12/24 & 12/25. Cocktails & lounge.   ⊗ (707) 464-3815

House of Rowland's Restaurant   Continental $$ ◆
1 mi n on US 101. 400 Hwy 101N. Casual atmosphere, seafood specialties. Children's menu. Open 6 am-10 pm; closed 12/25. Cocktails & lounge. AE, DS, MC, VI.   (707) 464-4727

Jim's Bistro   Steak & Seafood $$ ◆◆
On US 101; opposite fairgrounds. 200 Hwy 101 N. Mesquite grilled, fresh seafood specialties, emphasis on light cooking. Children's menu. Open 5 pm-9 pm; closed major holidays. Beer & wine.   ⊗ (707) 464-4878

Northwood's Restaurant   American $$ ◆
At BW Northwoods Inn. 675 Hwy 101S. Fresh seafood specials in casual atmosphere. Children's menu. Open 7 am-10 pm; closed 11/25 & 12/25. Cocktails & lounge. AE, DI, DS, MC, VI.   ⊗ (707) 465-5656

CULVER CITY — 38,800   See LOS ANGELES (Central & Western Areas)

CUPERTINO — 40,300   See also SAN JOSE

Courtyard by Marriott   Rates Subject to Change   *Motor Inn*   ◆◆◆

Sun-Thurs	1P	.... 94.00	2P/1B	.... 104.00	2P/2B	.... 104.00	XP 10
Fri & Sat	1P	.... 68.00	2P/1B	.... 68.00	2P/2B	.... 68.00	XP	F

149 units. N of & adjacent to I-280; exit Wolfe Rd N, w on Pruneridge Rd. 10605 N Wolfe Rd. (95014) Check-in 3 pm. A/C; C/CATV; movies; radios; phones. Coin laundry. Pool; indoor whirlpool; exercise rm. No pets. Wkly rates avail. Reserv deposit required. AE, DI, DS, MC, VI. ● Restaurant; 6:30 am-2 & 5-10 pm; Sat & Sun from 7 am; $10-$15; cocktail lounge. FAX (408) 252-0632 *(See ad p A447)*   ⊗ Ⓢ Ⓓ Ⓚ (408) 252-9100

Cupertino Inn   Rates Subject to Change   *Motel*   ◆◆◆

Sun-Thurs [BP]	1P 104.00- 121.00	2P/1B	119.00- 136.00	2P/2B	119.00- 136.00	XP 15	F
Fri & Sat [BP]	1P	.... 79.00	2P/1B	.... 79.00	2P/2B	.... 79.00	XP 20	F

125 units. N of & adjacent to I-280; exit Sunnyvale-Saratoga Rd. 10889 N De Anza Blvd. (95014) Some fireplaces & whirlpool baths. Nicely appointed rooms. A/C; C/TV; movies; VCPs. Radios; phones. Small pool; whirlpool. Airport transp. No pets. Luxury level rooms avail. Monthly rates avail. Reserv deposit required. Complimentary beverages each evening. AE, CB, DI, MC, VI. FAX (408) 257-0578   ⊗ Ⓢ Ⓓ Ⓚ (408) 996-7700

CYPRESS — 42,700

Country Club Inn   Rates Subject to Change   *Motel*   ◆

All year	1P	.... 32.00	2P/1B	.... 40.00	2P/2B	.... 45.00	XP 5

45 units. 2 1/2 mi s of SR 91; 3/4 mi w of Valley View. 5311 Lincoln Ave. (90630) Refrigerators; A/C; C/CATV; movies; radios; phones. Indoor whirlpool. No pets. 8 rooms with whirlpool tub, $47. Wkly & monthly rates avail. MC, VI. FAX (714) 952-4265   ⊗ Ⓢ Ⓓ (714) 952-9388

Ramada Inn   AAA Special Value Rates   *Hotel*   ◆◆◆

All year	1P	.... 81.00	2P/1B	.... 91.00	2P/2B	.... 91.00	XP 10	F

180 units. 1/2 blk w of Valley View. 5865 Katella Ave. (90630) A/C; C/CATV; pay movies; radios; phones. Coin laundry. Htd pool; whirlpool; transporation to Long Beach Airport; exercise rm. Parking lot. AE, CB, DI, MC, VI. ● Dining rm; 6:30 am-2 & 5-10:30 pm; $8-$15; cocktails. FAX (714) 220-0543 ⊗ Ⓢ Ⓓ Ⓚ (714) 827-1010

RESTAURANT

El Torito Restaurant   Mexican $ ◆◆
5995 Katella Ave at Valley View. A popular, colorfully decorated restaurant. A/C. Open 11 am-11 pm; Fri & Sat-midnight; Sun 9 am-11 pm; closed 11/25 & 12/25. Cocktails & lounge. AE, CB, DI, MC, VI.   ⊗ (714) 761-8155

DANA POINT — 31,900   See also LAGUNA BEACH & LAGUNA NIGUEL

Best Western Marina Inn   Rates Subject to Change   *Motel* ◆◆◆
@ 5/16-9/15   1P 60.00- 83.00 2P/1B 65.00- 83.00 2P/2B 79.00- 89.00 XP 6
 9/16-5/15   1P 60.00- 76.00 2P/1B 60.00- 76.00 2P/2B 72.00- 82.00 XP 6
Senior discount. 138 units. 1/2 mi w of SR 1, Pacific Coast Hwy, At Dana Point Harbor Dr. 24800 Dana Point
Harbor Dr. (92629) Check-in 3 pm. Refrigerators; A/C; C/CATV; free & pay movies; phones. 48 efficiencies, no
utensils. Coin laundry. Htd pool; exercise rm. No pets. Suites, $120-$150; harbor view $92-$102. Wkly rates avail.
AE, DI, DS, MC, VI. Restaurant adjacent. FAX (714) 248-0360 *(See ad p A124)*   Ⓓ Ⓛ (714) 496-1203

Blue Lantern Inn   Rates Subject to Change   *Bed & Breakfast* ◆◆◆◆
All year [BP]   1P 135.00- 350.00 2P/1B 135.00- 350.00 2P/2B 135.00- 350.00 XP 15
Senior discount. 29 units. 1 blk w Pacific Coast Hwy. 34343 Street of the Blue Lantern. (92629) Beautifully decorated
rooms & public areas. On bluff overlooking Dana Point Harbor. Many rooms with ocean view. Refrigerators; A/C; C/CATV;
radios; phones. Bicycles; exercise rm. No pets. All rooms with fireplace & whirlpool bathtub. Reserv deposit required. AE,
MC, VI. Restaurant adjacent. FAX (714) 496-1483   ⊗ Ⓢ Ⓓ (714) 661-1304

Dana Point Hilton an All Suite Resort   Rates Subject to Change   *Suites Hotel* ◆◆◆
All year [CP]   . . . . 2P/1B 99.00- 165.00 2P/2B 99.00- 165.00 XP 15   F
200 units. Exit I-5 northbound Beach Cities Dr, southbound Hwy 1, Camino Las Ramblas; across from Doheny State
Beach. 34402 Pacific Coast Hwy. (92629) Check-in 4 pm. Refrigerators; A/C; C/CATV; movies; VCPs. Radios; phones.
Htd pool; sauna; whirlpool; rental bicycles; exercise rm. Fee for: massage. Pay valet garage. Microwaves. Complimen-
tary beverages each evening. AE, DI, DS, MC, VI. ● Restaurant & coffeeshop; 6:30 am-2 & 5-10 pm; $6.95-$10.95.
FAX (714) 489-0628   ⊗ Ⓢ Ⓓ Ⓛ (714) 661-1100

Dana Point Resort   AAA Special Value Rates   *Hotel* ◆◆◆
@ All year [CP]   1P 180.00- 280.00 2P/1B 180.00- 280.00 2P/2B 180.00- 280.00 XP 20
341 units. 1 blk w of SR 1, Pacific Coast Hwy. 25135 Park Lantern. (92629) Rooms overlook yacht harbor.
Check-in 3 pm. Refrigerators; A/C; C/CATV; free & pay movies; radios; phones. 2 htd pools; sauna; whirlpools;
exercise rm. Fee for: lighted tennis-3 courts; massage. Parking lot. No pets. Wkly & monthly rates avail. Reserv
deposit required; 3 days refund notice. AE, MC, VI. ● Restaurant; 6:30 am-11 pm; $9.95-$30; cocktails; entertainment. FAX (714) 661-3688   ⊗ Ⓢ Ⓓ Ⓛ (714) 661-5000

Don Carlos Motel   Rates Subject to Change   *Motel* ◆◆
@ Fri & Sat   1P 69.00- 89.00 2P/1B 69.00- 89.00 2P/2B 69.00- 89.00 XP 5   F
 Sun-Thurs   1P 55.00- 60.00 2P/1B .... 60.00 2P/2B .... 60.00 XP 5   F
46 units. 1/4 blk w of SR 1, Pacific Coast Hwy. 25325 Dana Point Harbor Dr. (92629) Across from entrance to
Doheny State Beach. 10 refrigerators; A/C; C/CATV; movies; rental VCPs. Phones. Htd pool. No pets. Wkly &
monthly rates avail. Reserv deposit required. AE, DS, MC, VI. FAX (714) 830-9650   ⊗ Ⓓ (714) 493-5001

RESTAURANTS

Casa Maria   Mexican $ ◆◆
1/2 mi w of SR 1, at Dana Point Harbor Dr. 34521 Golden Lantern. Casual, informal, colorfully decorated restaurant
overlooking marina. Sun brunch 9 am-3 pm. A/C. Children's menu. Open 11 am-10 pm; Fri & Sat-11 pm; Sun 9 am-10
pm; closed 11/25 & 12/25. Cocktails & lounge. AE, CB, DI, MC, VI.   ⊗ (714) 496-6311

Delaney's   Seafood $$ ◆◆
At Dana Point Harbor Dr. 25001 Dana Point Harbor Dr. Overlooking marina. Sun brunch, 10 am-3 pm. A/C. Children's
menu. Open 11:30 am-10 pm; closed 11/25 & 12/25. Cocktails & lounge. AE, MC, VI.   ⊗ Ⓛ (714) 496-6195

DANVILLE — 31,300   (See OAKLAND/BERKELEY AREA spotting map pages A300 & A301; see index starting on page A298)

Econo Lodge 🔵   Rates Subject to Change   *Motel* ◆◆
@ All year   1P 55.00- 65.00 2P/1B 60.00- 70.00 2P/2B 70.00- 75.00 XP 5   F
Senior discount. 59 units. E of & adjacent to I-680; exit via Sycamore Valley Rd. 803 Camino Ramon. (94526) A/C;
C/CATV; movies; radios; phones. Small pool. No pets. Monthly rates avail. AE, CB, DI, MC, VI. Coffeeshop adja-
cent.   ⊗ Ⓓ Ⓛ (510) 838-8080

DAVIS — 46,200

Aggie Inn   AAA Special Value Rates   *Motel* ◆◆
@ All year [CP]   1P 62.00- 70.00 2P/1B 62.00- 70.00 2P/2B .... 66.00 XP 5
20 units. 1/2 mi n of I-80; Davis exit, w on First St, then 2 blks. 245 First St. (95616) Refrigerators; A/C; C/CATV;
radios; phones. Sauna; whirlpool. No pets. Some microwaves. Wkly rates avail. Reserv deposit required. AE, DI,
DS, MC, VI.   ⊗ Ⓢ Ⓓ (916) 756-0352

Best Western Executive Suites   Motel   Under Construction
26 units. Exit I-80 at Contra/Davis exit 234 D St. (95616) Scheduled to open February, 1990. Refrigerators, A/C,
C/CATV; movies; VCPs. Radios; phones. No pets. All rooms with microwave. AE, CB, DI, MC, VI. ⊗ (916) 753-7100

Best Western University Lodge   Rates Subject to Change   *Motel*   ◆◆
🚲 All year   1P 50.00- 55.00   2P/1B   55.00- 60.00   2P/2B   55.00- 70.00   XP 5
Senior discount. 53 units. 1 blk e of U of C campus. 123 B St. (95616) Some large rooms. Refrigerators; A/C;
C/CATV; movies; radios; phones; comb or shower baths. 2 kitchens, 1 efficiency, no utensils. Whirlpool; bicy-
cles; exercise rm. Pets, $10 extra charge. Microwaves. Wkly & monthly rates avail. Reserv deposit required. AE,
DI, DS, MC, VI. Coffeeshop opposite. *(See ad p A124)*   Ⓓ (916) 756-7890

Econo Lodge   Rates Subject to Change   *Motel*   ◆◆
🚲 All year [CP]   1P .... 45.00   2P/1B .... 47.00   2P/2B .... 50.00   XP 5
Senior discount. 26 units. Downtown; I-80 2nd exit. 221 D St. (95616) Formerly Campus Welcome Inn. Refriger-
ators; A/C; C/TV; radios; phones. Pets, $10 extra charge. Microwaves. Wkly & monthly rates avail. AE, CB, DI,
MC, VI. FAX (916) 756-2842 *(See ad p A124)*   ⊗ Ⓓ 🔥 (916) 756-1040

Ramada Inn-Davis   Rates Subject to Change   *Motor Inn*   ◆◆
🚲 All year   1P .... 68.00   2P/1B .... 68.00   2P/2B .... 58.00   XP 10
135 units. I-80 westbound exit Davis, eastbound exit Central Davis. 110 F St. (95616) Check-in 3 pm. A/C; C/TV;
pay movies; radios; phones. Pool. No pets. A few units with microwave & refrigerator, $5 extra. Wkly & monthly
rates avail. Reserv deposit required. AE, DI, DS, MC, VI. Coffeeshop adjacent. FAX (916) 758-8623
    ⊗ Ⓢ Ⓓ (916) 753-3600

DEATH VALLEY NATIONAL MONUMENT

Furnace Creek Inn   Rates Subject to Change   *Resort Hotel*   ◆◆◆
🚲 10/15-5/10 [MAP]   1P 210.00- 285.00   2P/1B 243.00- 325.00   2P/2B 243.00- 325.00   XP 50
67 units. On SR 190; 1 mi s of visitor center. (PO Box 1, 92328) OPEN 10/17-5/10. Long-established. Picturesque
location overlooking Death Valley. Palm-shaded terrace gardens. Check-in 4 pm. Refrigerators; A/C; C/CATV; radios; phones; comb or shower baths. Htd pool; saunas; whirlpool; lighted tennis-4 courts; archery range; exercise rm. Fee for: golf-18 holes, riding, massage. Parking lot. No pets. Reserv deposit required. AE, CB, DS, MC,
VI. ● 2 dining rms; 7-10 am, 11-4 & 6-9 pm; Sun brunch 11 am-2 pm; $12-$28; dress code; cocktails; entertainment. FAX (619) 786-2307 *(See ad p A127)*   Ⓢ Ⓓ (619) 786-2345

Furnace Creek Ranch   Rates Subject to Change   *Resort Complex*   ◆◆
All year   1P 65.00- 94.00   ....   2P/2B 65.00- 94.00   XP 14
224 units. On SR 190, adjacent to visitor center. (PO Box 1, 92328) On spacious grounds. Check-in 4 pm. 200 refrigerators; A/C; 200 C/CATV; 200 phones; comb or shower baths. Coin laundry. Htd pool; lighted tennis-2 courts; playground; Borax Museum, general store, gas station, landing strip for light aircraft; unicom 122.8. Fee for: golf-18 holes,
riding, hayrides & carriage rides. Parking lot. Reserv deposit required. AE, DS, MC, VI. ● 2 restaurants, coffeeshop &
cafeteria; 6 am-10 pm; cafeteria 5:30 pm-11:30 pm; $4.95-$16; cocktails. FAX (619) 786-2514 *(See ad p A127)*
    ⊗ Ⓢ Ⓓ (619) 786-2345

Stove Pipe Wells Village   Rates Subject to Change   *Motor Inn*   ◆
All year   ....   2P/2B 50.00- 69.00   XP 9
82 units. On SR 190, 24 mi nw of visitor center. (92328) Some very good rooms. Water in some rooms unsuitable for
drinking. Check-in 3 pm. 26 refrigerators; A/C; comb or shower baths. Htd pool; heated mineral water pool; service station, grocery store, landing strip for light aircraft. Small pets only. Reserv deposit required. AE, MC, VI. ● Restaurant;
7 am-2 & 5:30-9 pm; $7.95-$13.50; cocktails. FAX (619) 786-2389   ⊗ Ⓓ (619) 786-2387

DELANO — 22,800

Comfort Inn   Rates Subject to Change   *Motel*   ◆◆
🚲 5/2-9/31 [CP]   1P .... 49.95   2P/1B .... 54.95   2P/2B .... 58.95   XP 5   F
10/1-5/1 [CP]   1P .... 42.95   2P/1B .... 47.95   2P/2B .... 52.95   XP 5   F
Senior discount. 45 units. E side of SR 99; exit County Line. 2211 Girard St. (93215) A/C; C/CATV; movies;
phones. Small pool. 2 rooms with whirlpool tub 10/1-5/1, $65; 5/2-9/31, $75. AE, DI, DS, MC, VI. Restaurant opposite.   ⊗ Ⓢ Ⓓ 🔥 (805) 725-1022

Shilo Inn   Rates Subject to Change   *Motel*   ◆◆
All year [CP]   1P 49.00- 58.00   2P/1B 49.00- 58.00   2P/2B 54.00- 60.00   XP 8   F
Senior discount. 48 units. Adjacent to SR 99; on e side of hwy, County Line exit. 2231 Girard St. (93215) A/C; C/CATV;
movies; radios; phones. Coin laundry. Small htd pool; whirlpool. Small pets only, $6 extra. Monthly rates avail. Reserv
deposit required. AE, DI, DS, MC, VI. Restaurant opposite. FAX (805) 725-7524   ⊗ Ⓢ Ⓓ 🔥 (805) 725-7551

DEL MAR — 4,900

Clarion Carriage House Del Mar Inn   Rates Guaranteed   *Motel*   ◆◆◆
🚲 6/15-9/14 [CP]   1P 85.00- 105.00   2P/1B 90.00- 105.00   2P/2B 105.00- 115.00   XP 10   F
9/15-6/14 [CP]   1P 80.00- 99.00   2P/1B 85.00- 105.00   2P/2B 99.00- 105.00   XP 10   F
Senior discount. 80 units. From I-5, Del Mar Heights Rd exit 1 mi w, then 1/4 mi n. 720 Camino Del Mar. (92014)
English Tudor design. Beautifully landscaped pool area. Many rooms with ocean view & balcony. 55 refrigerators; C/CATV; movies; phones; comb or shower baths. 20 efficiencies. Coin laundry. Htd pool; whirlpool. No
pets. Monthly rates avail. Reserv deposit required. AE, DI, DS, MC, VI. Afternoon tea 3 pm-4:30 pm.
FAX (619) 752-8130 *(See ad below)*   ⊗ Ⓣ (619) 755-9765

Furnace Creek Inn
& Ranch Resort
Including Stovepipe Wells Village

A Magnificent Spring-Fed Oasis Open All Year
In The Heart Of Death Valley National Monument.

- 374 rooms at Furnace Creek Inn, Furnace Creek Ranch, and Stovepipe Wells Village from $45 to $325
- RV spaces – both full and dry available
- 14 dining options
- 6 bars, some featuring dancing and entertainment
- 18-hole championship golf course – 214 feet below sea level with driving range, putting greens and Pro Shop
- 3 spring-fed swimming pools
- 6 lighted tennis courts
- Horseback riding, carriage and hay rides
- Jogging, bicycle and hiking trails
- Volleyball, basketball, shuffleboard and playground
- Borax Museum

- Escorted Fred Harvey Motorcoach Tours
- 3 gift shops and 2 general stores
- 2 gas stations with AAA towing and garage services
- A lighted airfield and landing strip
- Meeting facilities for 10 to 400

    All within a 23 mile radius, including some of nature's most spectacular scenery. **Open year round.**

FURNACE CREEK
INN & RANCH RESORT
INCLUDING STOVEPIPE WELLS VILLAGE

A Magnificent Spring-Fed Oasis
DEATH VALLEY, CALIFORNIA

For reservations call:
Inn: 619-786-2361 • Ranch: 800-528-6367, 619-786-2345 • Stovepipe Wells: 619-786-2387
Traditional Hospitality since 1876 by *Fred Harvey*.

Del Mar Hilton North San Diego
7/1-9/30 — 1P 90.00-135.00 2P/1B 120.00-165.00 2P/2B 120.00-165.00 XP 15 F
1/1-6/30 & 10/1-12/31 — 1P 75.00-120.00 2P/1B 90.00-135.00 2P/2B 75.00-135.00 XP 15 F
Rates Subject to Change *Motor Inn* ◆◆◆
Senior discount. 245 units. Adjacent to I-5; exit Via de la Valle. 15575 Jimmy Durante Blvd. (92014) Some balconies or patios. Check-in 4 pm. 3 refrigerators; A/C; C/CATV; free & pay movies; radios; phones. Htd pool; whirlpools. Parking lot. No pets. Monthly rates avail. Reserv deposit required. AE, DI, DS, MC, VI. ● Dining rm & restaurant; 6 am-11 pm; $10-$16; cocktails; entertainment. FAX (619) 792-0353 *(See ad p 22)*
Ⓧ Ⓢ Ⓓ ⑤ (619) 792-5200

Doubletree Club Hotel Del Mar
6/19-8/30 [BP] — 1P .... 79.00 2P/1B .... 79.00 2P/2B .... 79.00 XP 10
1/1-6/18 & 9/1-12/31 [BP] — 1P ..//. 69.00 2P/1B .... 69.00 2P/2B .... 69.00 XP 10
Rates Subject to Change *Hotel* ◆◆◆
Senior discount. 226 units. 1/4 mi e of I-5, exit Carmel Valley Rd. 11915 El Camino Real. (San Diego, 92130) Check-in 3 pm. A/C; C/CATV; pay movies; radios; phones. Htd pool; wading pool; whirlpool; exercise rm. Parking lot. No pets. 6 suites, $89-$198. Wkly & monthly rates avail. Complimentary beverages each evening. AE, DI, DS, MC, VI. ● Restaurant; 6-9 am, 11:30-2 & 5-10 pm; $7.95-$16.95; cocktail lounge. FAX (619) 481-0990 *(See ad below)*
Ⓧ Ⓢ Ⓓ ⑤ (619) 481-5900

L'Auberge Del Mar
All year — 2P/1B 165.00-225.00 2P/2B 165.00-225.00 XP 20
Rates Subject to Change *Motor Inn* ◆◆◆
Senior discount. 123 units. From I-5, Del Mar Heights Rd exit 1 mi w, then 1 mi n. 1540 Camino Del Mar. (92014) Many rooms with ocean view, balcony & gas fireplace. Check-in 4 pm. Refrigerators; A/C; C/CATV; radios; phones. 2 htd pools; sauna; whirlpool; health club. Fee for: lighted tennis-2 courts. Pay valet garage. No pets. Reserv deposit required; 3 days refund notice. AE, DI, DS, MC, VI. ● Dining rm; 6:30 am-10 pm; $12-$28; cocktails; entertainment. Also restaurant, see separate listing. FAX (619) 755-4940 Ⓧ Ⓢ Ⓓ ⑤ (619) 259-1515

Ramada Inn
6/15-9/14 [CP] — 1P 85.00-99.00 2P/1B 93.00-107.00 2P/2B 93.00-107.00 XP 10
9/15-6/14 [CP] — 1P 75.00-89.00 2P/1B 75.00-89.00 2P/2B 75.00-89.00 XP 5
Rates Subject to Change *Motel* ◆◆◆
115 units. 1 mi w of I-5; exit Via del La Valle. 717 Hwy 101S. (Solana Beach, 92075, 92014) 1/2 blk from beach. Patio or balcony. Check-in 3 pm. A/C; C/CATV; movies; radios; phones. 42 efficiencies. Coin laundry. Htd pool; whirlpools; rental bicycles; 29 rooms with oversized whirlpool tub; exercise rm. Garage. No pets. Reserv deposit required in season. AE, DI, DS, MC, VI. Restaurant adjacent. FAX (619) 792-2370 *(See ad below)* Ⓧ Ⓢ Ⓓ ⑤ (619) 792-8200

Stratford Inn
6/15-9/15 [CP] — 1P 60.00-135.00 2P/1B 60.00-135.00 2P/2B 70.00-130.00 XP 10 F
9/16-6/14 [CP] — 1P 55.00-90.00 2P/1B 55.00-110.00 2P/2B 65.00-100.00 XP 10 F
AAA Special Value Rates *Motel* ◆◆◆
100 units. From I-5, Del Mar Heights Rd exit 1 mi w, then 1/4 mi n. 710 Camino Del Mar. (92014) Some rooms with ocean view, balcony or patio. 67 A/C; C/CATV; pay movies; radios; phones; comb or shower baths. 32 2-bedrm units, 6 kitchens, 39 efficiencies. Coin laundry. 2 htd pools; whirlpool. No pets. Wkly & monthly rates avail. Reserv deposit required; 3 days refund notice. AE, DI, DS, MC, VI. Restaurant adjacent. FAX (619) 755-4704 *(See ad p A129 and p A379)* Ⓓ ⑤ (619) 755-1501

RESTAURANTS

Del Mar Bistro Gardens   Continental $$$ ◆◆◆
In L'Auberge Del Mar. Semi-formal atmosphere. Features steak, pasta & fresh seafood. A/C. Open 6:30 am-10 pm; Fri & Sat-11 pm. Cocktails & lounge. Entertainment. Valet parking. AE, DI, DS, MC, VI.   ⊗ (619) 259-1515

Il Fornaio   Italian $$
From I-5, Del Mar Heights Rd exit 1 mi w, then 1 mi n. 1555 Camino Del Mar. Continental breakfast 8 am-11:30 am, Sat & Sun brunch 8 am-3 pm. Patio dining, weather permitting. Pastries, bread & cookies baked on premises. Open 11:30 am-11 pm; Fri-midnight; Sat 9 am-midnight; Sun 9 am-11 pm; closed 11/25 & 12/25. Cocktails & lounge. Reserv advised. AE, MC, VI.   ⊗ (619) 755-8876

DESERT HOT SPRINGS — 11,700   (See map page A315)

Cactus Springs Lodge   Rates Subject to Change   Motel   ◆◆
11/16-4/30	....	2P/1B	....	50.00	2P/2B	....	60.00 XP 10
5/1-6/15 & 10/1-11/15	....	2P/1B	....	40.00	2P/2B	....	50.00 XP 10
6/16-9/30	....	2P/1B	....	29.00	2P/2B	....	39.00 XP 10

11 units. 2 mi e, 1 blk n of Hacienda Dr. 68075 Club Circle Dr. (92240) Refrigerators; A/C; C/CATV; shower baths. Hot mineral swimming pool, 1 indoor & 1 outdoor hot mineral water whirlpool. No pets. 5 kitchens, $10-$15 extra. Wkly & monthly rates avail. Reserv deposit required; 5 days refund notice. MC, VI.   Ⓓ (619) 329-5776

Desert Hot Springs Spa Hotel   Rates Subject to Change   Motor Inn   ◆◆◆
12/25-5/31	1P 59.00- 89.00	2P/1B	59.00- 89.00	2P/2B	66.00- 99.00 XP 6
10/1-12/24	1P 49.00- 59.00	2P/1B	49.00- 59.00	2P/2B	55.00- 65.00 XP 6
6/1-9/30	1P 39.00- 49.00	2P/1B	39.00- 49.00	2P/2B	45.00- 54.00 XP 6

Senior discount. 50 units. 1 mi n. 10805 Palm Dr. (92240) Popular spa facility open to the public. Check-in 3 pm. A/C; C/CATV; 25 radios; phones. Rental refrigerators. Wading pool; saunas; 3 hot natural mineral water pools, 4 mineral water whirlpools. Fee for: massage. Airport transp. Pets, $50 deposit required. Wkly & monthly rates avail. Reserv deposit required; 3 days refund notice. AE, CB, DI, MC, VI. ● Dining rm & coffeeshop; 7 am-9 pm; Fri & Sat-10 pm; $8.95-$14.95; cocktails. FAX (619) 329-6915 *(See ads inside front cover, below and p A323)*   Ⓓ (619) 329-6495

Desert Palms Spa Motel   Rates Subject to Change   Motel   ◆◆◆
12/21-5/31	....	2P/1B	49.00- 59.00	2P/2B	59.00- 69.00 XP 10
10/1-12/20	....	2P/1B	45.00- 55.00	2P/2B	49.00- 59.00 XP 10
6/1-9/30	....	2P/1B	39.00- 49.00	2P/2B	45.00- 55.00 XP 10

40 units. 1 mi e of Palm Dr. 67-485 Hacienda Dr. (92240) A/C; C/CATV; movies; phones. 15 efficiencies. Coin laundry. Sauna; natural hot mineral water pool, 5 natural mineral water whirlpools. Fee for: massage. No pets. Wkly & monthly rates avail. Reserv deposit required; 3 days refund notice. MC, VI.   ⊗ Ⓢ Ⓓ (619) 329-4443

Lido Palms Spa   Rates Subject to Change   Motel   ◆◆
10/1-5/31	1P 65.00- 75.00	....		2P/2B	65.00- 75.00 XP 10	F
6/1-9/30	1P 45.00- 55.00	....		2P/2B	55.00 XP 10	

11 units. 3/4 mi e on Hacienda Dr, 1/2 blk n. 12801 Tamar Dr. (92240) Spacious rooms. A/C; C/CATV; movies; radios; comb or shower baths. 10 kitchens. 1 hot natural mineral water pool, 1 outdoor & 1 indoor natural mineral water whirlpool. Fee for: massage. No pets. 5 rooms with microwave. Wkly & monthly rates avail. Reserv deposit required; 10 days refund notice. MC, VI.   Ⓓ (619) 329-6033

Linda Vista Lodge   Rates Subject to Change   Motel   ◆
12/1-3/31	1P 36.00- 55.00	2P/1B	36.00- 55.00	2P/2B	36.00- 55.00 XP 7
4/1-5/31 & 10/1-11/30	1P 34.00- 48.00	2P/1B	34.00- 48.00	2P/2B	34.00- 48.00 XP 7
6/1-9/30	1P 32.00- 45.00	2P/1B	32.00- 45.00	2P/2B	32.00- 45.00 XP 7

42 units. 3/4 mi e. 67-200 Hacienda Dr. (92240) A/C; C/CATV; phones; comb or shower baths. 1 2-bedrm unit, 28 efficiencies. Sauna; hot mineral water pool, 2 indoor & 1 outdoor mineral water whirlpools. No pets. Wkly & monthly rates avail. Reserv deposit required; 3 days refund notice. AE, MC, VI.   Ⓓ (619) 329-6401

(See map page A315)

Royal Fox Inn — *Motor Inn* ◆◆◆

		Rates Subject to Change					
11/1-5/31	1P 51.00- 62.00	2P/1B 61.00- 65.00	2P/2B 70.00	XP 6
6/1-10/30	1P 31.00- 46.00	2P/1B 41.00- 46.00	2P/2B 50.00	XP 6

Senior discount. 115 units. 1 1/2 mi s. 14500 Palm Dr. (92240) A/C; C/CATV; rental VCPs; phones. Rental refrigerators. 1 2-bedrm unit, 6 kitchens. Htd pool; sauna; whirlpool; 10 rooms with small pool; exercise facilities. Fee for: massage. No pets. Wkly & monthly rates avail. Reserv deposit required. AE, DS, MC, VI. ● Coffeeshop; 6:30 am-9 pm; $6-$10. FAX (619) 329-1409 *(See ad below)* ⊗ Ⓢ Ⓓ (619) 329-4481

Sam's Family Spa Motel — *Motel* ◆

		Rates Subject to Change			
All year	....	2P/1B 55.00- 70.00	2P/2B 66.00- 90.00	XP 7

13 units. 7 mi se. 70-875 Dillon Rd. (92240) Check-in 3 pm. 9 refrigerators; A/C; C/CATV; comb or shower baths. 1 2-bedrm unit. Coin laundry. Htd pool; wading pool; sauna; whirlpool; 2 natural hot mineral water whirlpools & 2 natural hot mineral pools; playground; exercise rm. No pets. 5 kitchens, $10 extra. 2-night minimum stay weekends. Wkly & monthly rates avail. Reserv deposit required. Restaurant adjacent. FAX (619) 329-8267 Ⓓ (619) 329-6457

Sandpiper Inn — *Motel* ◆

		Rates Subject to Change			
12/1-3/31	....	2P/1B 55.00	2P/2B 55.00	XP 10
4/1-5/31 & 10/1-11/30	....	2P/1B 50.00	2P/2B 50.00	XP 10
6/1-9/30	....	2P/1B 42.00- 47.00	2P/2B 42.00- 47.00	XP 10

26 units. 3/4 mi e on Hacienda Dr, 1 blk n. 12-800 Foxdale Dr. (92240) A/C; C/CATV; phones. 22 efficiencies. Sauna; hot mineral water pool, 1 indoor & 1 outdoor hot mineral water whirlpool. No pets. Reserv deposit required; 7 days refund notice. MC, VI. Ⓓ (619) 329-6455

Stardust Motel — *Motel* ◆

		Rates Subject to Change					
12/1-5/15	1P 43.00	2P/1B 43.00	2P/2B 47.00	XP 7
5/16-6/30 & 10/1-11/30	1P 40.00	2P/1B 40.00	2P/2B 45.00	XP 7
7/1-9/30	1P 37.00	2P/1B 37.00	2P/2B 40.00	XP 7

17 units. 1/2 mi n, 1 blk e of Palm Dr. 66634 5th St. (92240) A/C; C/CATV; shower or comb baths. Htd pool; hot mineral water whirlpool. Pets. 12 kitchens, $9-$15 extra. Wkly & monthly rates avail. Reserv deposit required. MC, VI. Ⓓ (619) 329-5443

Sunset Inn — *Motor Inn* ◆◆◆

		Rates Subject to Change			
12/24-5/30	....	2P/1B 65.00- 75.00	2P/2B 70.00- 80.00	XP 10
10/1-12/23	....	2P/1B 48.00- 58.00	2P/2B 53.00- 63.00	XP 10
5/31-9/30	....	2P/1B 40.00- 50.00	2P/2B 45.00- 55.00	XP 10

20 units. 1 mi e of Palm Dr. 67-585 Hacienda Dr. (92240) Refrigerators; A/C; C/CATV; phones; comb or shower baths. 2 kitchens. Sauna; hot mineral water pool, 2 mineral water whirlpools; steamroom. Fee for: massage. Airport transp. No pets. 2 efficiencies, $10-$15 extra. 2-night minimum stay in season. Wkly rates avail. Reserv deposit required. MC, VI. ● Dining rm & coffeeshop; 7 am-9 pm; $7.95-$14.95; cocktails. FAX (619) 329-0283 Ⓢ Ⓓ (619) 329-4488

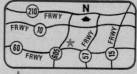

(See map page A315)

RESTAURANT

Hayden's Wharf　　　　　　　　　　American　　　　　　　$$　　　　　◆
1/4 mi w. 66230 Pierson Blvd. A selection of steaks, chicken & pasta with emphasis on seafood. A/C. Children's menu. Open 5 pm-9 pm; closed Wed, 12/24 & 12/25. Cocktails. Reserv advised. AE, MC, VI.　　　Ⓧ (619) 329-5622

DIAMOND BAR — 53,700

Best Western Hotel Diamond Bar　　　　Rates Subject to Change　　　　　*Motel*　　◆◆◆
🏵 All year [BP]　　　　1P 59.00- 79.00　2P/1B　69.00- 89.00　2P/2B　69.00- 89.00　XP 10
100 units. At jct SR 60 & 57 frwy; 1 blk w of Diamond Bar Blvd. 259 Gentle Springs Ln. (91765) Spacious rooms. Check-in 3 pm. 40 refrigerators; A/C; C/CATV; movies; radios; phones. Htd pool; whirlpool; airport transportation to Ontario Airport. No pets. AE, CB, DI, MC, VI. FAX (909) 860-2110　　Ⓧ Ⓓ ♿ (909) 860-3700

Radisson Inn Diamond Bar　　　　　　Rates Subject to Change　　　　*Motor Inn*　◆◆◆
🏵 Sun-Thurs　　　　　1P 65.00- 75.00　2P/1B　75.00- 85.00　2P/2B　75.00- 85.00　XP 10
　　Fri & Sat　　　　　1P 59.00- 69.00　2P/1B　59.00- 69.00　2P/2B　69.00- 72.00　XP 10
Senior discount. 184 units. At Golden Springs Dr; adjacent to SR 60, exit Grand Ave E. 21725 E Gateway Dr. (91765) Formerly Days Hotel. A/C; C/CATV; movies; phones. Htd pool; whirlpool; airport transportation to Ontario Airport. No pets. AE, DI, DS, MC, VI. ● Restaurant; 6 am-11 pm; $7.95-$13.95; cocktails. FAX (909) 860-8224
(See ad p A130 and p A341)　　　　　　　　　　　　　　　Ⓧ Ⓢ Ⓓ ♿ (909) 860-5440

DISNEYLAND — See ANAHEIM, BUENA PARK, FULLERTON, GARDEN GROVE, ORANGE & SANTA ANA

DIXON

Best Western Inn　　　　　　　　　Rates Subject to Change　　　　　*Motel*
　　All year [CP]　　　　1P 45.00- 55.00　2P/1B　45.00- 55.00　2P/2B　55.00- 65.00　XP 4
55 units. Adjacent to I-80. 1345 Commercial Way. (95620) All rooms with microwave. Rating withheld pending completion of construction. Refrigerators; A/C; C/CATV; VCPs; radios; phones. Pool; sauna; whirlpool. No pets. 4 rooms with whirlpool, $10 extra. AE, CB, DI, MC, VI.　　　　　　　　　　　Ⓧ Ⓓ (916) 678-1400

DOWNEY — 91,400

Comfort Inn　　　　　　　　　　　Rates Subject to Change　　　　　*Motel*　　◆◆
🏵 All year [CP]　　　　1P .... 49.00　2P/1B　.... 49.00　2P/2B　.... 54.00　XP
Senior discount. 33 units. 3/4 mi w of I-605, Firestone Blvd exit. 9438 Firestone Blvd. (90241) A/C; C/CATV; movies; radios; phones. Whirlpool. No pets. 6 rooms with whirlpool bath, $5 extra. Wkly rates avail. AE, DI, DS, MC, VI. FAX (310) 830-0551 *(See ad below)*　　　　　　Ⓧ Ⓢ Ⓓ ♿ (310) 803-3555

Downey Inn Luxury Suites　　　　　　Rates Guaranteed　　　　　　*Motel*　　◆◆
🏵 All year [CP]　　　　1P .... 49.00　2P/1B　.... 49.00　2P/2B　.... 54.00　XP 6
Senior discount. 34 units. 2 blks s of Firestone Blvd. 11510 Lakewood Blvd. (90241) 1/2 mi n of Rockwell International Space Center. 2 room suites & motel units. Refrigerators; A/C; C/CATV; movies; radios; phones. Coin laundry. Small htd pool; sauna. No pets. Suites with whirlpool tub, $69-$89. Wkly rates avail. AE, DS, MC, VI. FAX (310) 923-4240 *(See ad below)*　　　　　　　Ⓧ Ⓓ ♿ (310) 862-5050

Embassy Suites Hotel　　　　　　　Rates Guaranteed　　　　*Suites Hotel*　◆◆◆
🏵 All year [BP]　　　　1P .... 89.00　2P/1B　.... 99.00　2P/2B　.... 99.00　XP 15　F
Senior discount. 220 units. 2 mi w of I-605, exit Firestone Blvd. 8425 Firestone Blvd. (90241) 1-bedroom suites with living room. Refrigerators; A/C; C/CATV; free & pay movies; radios; phones. Htd indoor pool; sauna; whirlpool; steamroom; exercise rm. Parking lot. Pets. Monthly rates avail. Complimentary beverages each evening. AE, DI, DS, MC, VI. ● Restaurant; 11 am-3 & 5-10 pm; $8.95-$16.95; cocktails. FAX (310) 923-5847
　　　　　　　　　　　　　　　　　　　Ⓧ Ⓢ Ⓓ ♿ (310) 861-1900

DOWNIEVILLE — 400 See SIERRA CITY

DUARTE — 20,700
Rodeway Inn, Duarte/Arcadia   AAA Special Value Rates   *Motel*   ◆◆
⊛ All year [CP]   1P 40.00- 42.00 2P/1B 45.00- 55.00 2P/2B .... 46.00 XP 6   F
50 units. 1/2 mi ne of I-210, use Buena Vista St exit. 1533 E Huntington Dr. (91010) A/C; C/CATV; movies; radios; phones. Coin laundry. No pets. 1 suite, $75 for 2 persons. Wkly rates avail. Reserv deposit required. AE, CB, DI, MC, VI.   ⊗ Ⓢ Ⓓ 🅖 (818) 303-4544

Travelodge Duarte   Rates Subject to Change   *Motel*   ◆
⊛ All year [CP]   1P .... 35.00 2P/1B .... 39.00 2P/2B .... 45.00 XP 5   F
68 units. 1/2 mi nw of I-210; exit Buena Vista St. 1200 E Huntington Dr. (91010) A/C; C/CATV; movies; rental VCPs. Radios; phones. Small pool; whirlpool; 7 rooms with whirlpool tub. No pets. Wkly & monthly rates avail. AE, DI, DS, MC, VI.   ⊗ Ⓢ Ⓓ 🅖 (818) 357-0907

RESTAURANT

Fanara's Italian Restaurant   Italian $ ◆
1/2 mi ne of I-10; Buena Vista exit. 1845 E Huntington Dr. A nice selection of pasta, chicken & seafood. A/C. Open 11:30 am-10:30 pm; Sat & Sun 4:30 pm-9:30 pm. Cocktails. MC, VI.   ⊗ (818) 358-0128

DUNNIGAN — 300
Best Western Country   AAA Special Value Rates   *Motel*   ◆◆◆
⊛ 5/16-9/30   ....   2P/1B 60.00- 64.00 2P/2B 62.00- 68.00 XP 4
    10/1-5/15   ....   2P/1B 56.00- 62.00 2P/2B 58.00- 64.00 XP 4
55 units. I-5 at Dunnigan exit. (PO Box 740, 95937) Refrigerators; A/C; C/CATV; movies; phones. Coin laundry. Pool; whirlpool. Pets. 6 kitchens, $60-$80; no utensils. 10 units with microwave, extra charge. Reserv deposit required; 3 days refund notice. AE, DI, DS, MC, VI. Coffeeshop opposite. FAX (916) 724-4423 *(See ad below)*   ⊗ Ⓓ 🅖 (916) 724-3471

Value Lodge   AAA Special Value Rates   *Motel*   ◆◆
⊛ 5/16-9/30   1P .... 42.00 2P/1B .... 52.00 2P/2B .... 56.00 XP
    10/1-5/15   1P .... 39.00 2P/1B .... 50.00 2P/2B .... 50.00 XP 4   F
40 units. I-5 at Dunnigan exit. (PO Box 740, 95937) Refrigerators; A/C; C/CATV; movies; phones. Coin laundry. Pool. Pets. Reserv deposit required; 3 days refund notice. AE, DI, DS, MC, VI. Coffeeshop opposite. FAX (916) 724-4423   ⊗ Ⓢ Ⓓ 🅖 (916) 724-3333

DUNSMUIR — 2,100
Caboose Motel   Rates Subject to Change   *Motel*   ◆◆◆
⊛ 5/16-10/14   1P 50.00- 60.00 2P/1B 67.50- 80.00 2P/2B 67.50- 80.00 XP 5
    10/15-5/15   1P 45.00- 55.00 2P/1B 62.50- 75.00 2P/2B 62.50- 75.00 XP 5
27 units. 1 mi s exit I-5, Railroad Park Rd. 100 Railroad Park Rd. (96025) Restored & nicely furnished caboose cars; 4 motel rooms. Attractively landscaped with views of Castle Crags Peaks. 9 refrigerators; A/C; C/CATV; movies; phones; comb or shower baths. 1 2-bedrm unit, 3 kitchens. Pool; whirlpool. Pets, $2.50 extra charge. Reserv deposit required. AE, DS, MC, VI. ● Railroad Park Resort Restaurant, see separate listing. FAX (916) 235-4470 *(See ad p A133)*   ⊗ Ⓓ (916) 235-4440

Cedar Lodge Motel   Rates Subject to Change   *Motel*   ◆◆
⊛ All year   1P 28.00- 32.00 2P/1B 36.00- 40.00 2P/2B 46.00- 50.00 XP 4
Senior discount. 13 units. Exit I-5 at Dunsmuir/Siskiyou; w 1/2 mi. 4201 Dunsmuir Ave. (96025) Quiet tree-shaded grounds, large exotic bird aviaries. A/C; C/CATV; movies; phones; comb or shower baths. 2 kitchens, $10 extra. Family unit for up to 6 persons, $68-$76. Reserv deposit required. AE, CB, DI, MC, VI.   Ⓓ (916) 235-4331

Dunsmuir Travelodge ◆◆
♿ AAA Special Value Rates · Motel

5/25-9/4	1P	....	45.00	2P/1B	....	55.00	2P/2B	....	60.00 XP 5	F
9/5-5/24	1P	....	40.00	2P/1B	....	50.00	2P/2B	....	5.00 XP 5	F

18 units. Exit I-5 Central Dunsmuir. 5400 Dunsmuir Ave. (96025) Attractive comfortable modern rooms. A/C; C/CATV; movies; phones. 3 2-bedrm units. Pets, $5 extra charge. 3 2-bedroom units, $75-$85 for 4-6 persons. AE, DI, DS, MC, VI.   ⊗ Ⓓ (916) 235-4395

RESTAURANT

Railroad Park Resort Restaurant   American $$ ◆◆
♿ At Caboose Motel. 100 Railroad Park Rd. Attractively restored 100 year old railroad cars; varied menu. A/C. Children's menu. Open 5 pm-9 pm; closed Tues, 11/25 & 12/25 from 10/15-5/15 closed Mon. Cocktails & lounge. Dancing. Reserv advised. AE, DS, MC, VI. *(See ad below)*   ⊗ (916) 235-4611

EL CAJON — 88,700

Best Western Continental Inn ◆◆◆
♿ Motel

6/14-9/8 [CP]	1P 45.00- 75.00	2P/1B	50.00- 75.00	2P/2B	55.00- 75.00	XP 5
9/9-6/13 [CP]	1P 38.00- 70.00	2P/1B	42.00- 70.00	2P/2B	46.00- 70.00	XP 5

97 units. Adjacent to I-8, exit Mollison Ave. 650 N Mollison Ave. (92021) Rooms & 1-bedroom suites with living room. Many balconies. 66 refrigerators; A/C; C/CATV; movies; 18 radios; phones. Coin laundry. Htd pool; whirlpool; 11 rooms with whirlpool tub. No pets. 20 efficiencies, $55-$85 for 2 persons. Wkly & monthly rates avail. Reserv deposit required; 14 days refund notice. AE, DI, DS, MC, VI. Coffeeshop opposite. FAX (619) 442-0152
⊗ Ⓓ Ⓛ (619) 442-0601

Best Western Courtesy Inn ◆◆
♿ Rates Subject to Change · Motel

All year	1P 38.00- 48.00	2P/1B	44.00- 58.00	2P/2B	44.00- 58.00 XP 5

Senior discount. 47 units. On Business Loop I-8; 1/2 mi s of I-8; westbound exit E Main St, eastbound exit 2nd Ave, s to Main St, then e. 1355 E Main St. (92021) 30 refrigerators; A/C; C/CATV; movies; rental VCPs. Radios; phones. 10 2-bedrm units. Coin laundry. Pool; whirlpool; 2 rooms with whirlpool. No pets. Wkly rates avail. Reserv deposit required. AE, DI, DS, MC, VI. FAX (619) 588-0582   Ⓢ Ⓓ Ⓛ (619) 440-7378

Budget Host Hacienda ◆◆
♿ Rates Guaranteed · Motel

All year	1P 31.00	2P/1B	.... 36.00	2P/2B	.... 36.00 XP 4

Senior discount. 73 units. Adjacent to I-8, exit Mollison Ave. 588 N Mollison Ave. (92021) Spacious rooms. Refrigerators; A/C; C/CATV; phones. 16 efficiencies. Pool; whirlpool. Small pets only. Wkly rates avail. Reserv deposit required. AE, DI, MC, VI. Restaurant adjacent.   ⊗ Ⓓ (619) 579-1144

Days Inn-La Mesa ◆
♿ Rates Subject to Change · Motel

6/1-9/4 [CP]	1P 39.00	2P/1B	.... 45.00	2P/2B	.... 49.00 XP 6
9/5-5/31 [CP]	1P 35.00	2P/1B	.... 42.00	2P/2B	.... 47.00 XP 6

Senior discount. 110 units. Adjacent to I-8, westbound exit Murray Dr; eastbound exit El Cajon Blvd. 1250 El Cajon Blvd. (92020) 10 refrigerators; A/C; C/CATV; phones. Coin laundry. Htd pool; whirlpool. Pets, $6 extra charge. Wkly & monthly rates avail. Reserv deposit required. AE, DI, DS, MC, VI. FAX (619) 441-2853 *(See ad below)*   ⊗ Ⓢ Ⓓ (619) 588-8808

Plaza International Inn ◆◆
♿ Rates Guaranteed · Motel

All year	1P 29.00	2P/1B	.... 35.00	2P/2B	.... 38.00 XP	F

60 units. Adjacent to I-8, exit Mollison Ave. 683 N Mollison Ave. (92021) Refrigerators; A/C; C/CATV; movies; phones. Pool; saunas; indoor whirlpool. No pets. 4 efficiencies, weekly rental only. Wkly rates avail. AE, DI, DS, MC, VI. Coffeeshop adjacent.   ⊗ Ⓓ (619) 442-0973

Singing Hills Lodge ◆◆◆
♿ Rates Subject to Change · Resort Motor Inn

Fri & Sat	1P 85.00- 135.00	....	2P/2B	85.00- 135.00 XP 12	F
Sun-Thurs	1P 74.00- 120.00	....	2P/2B	78.00- 120.00 XP 12	F

102 units. From I-8 exit 2nd Ave & Jamacha Rd, 1 mi s; 3 mi e on Washington St & Dehesa Rd. 3007 Dehesa Rd. (92021) Golf resort on attractive, tree-shaded grounds. Check-in 4 pm. A/C; C/TV; phones; shower baths. 2 2-bedrm units. Coin laundry. 2 htd pools; whirlpools. Fee for: golf-54 holes, tennis-11 courts, 12 lighted. No pets. 2 room suites for up to 6 persons, $172-$208. Reserv deposit required; 14 days refund notice. AE, DS, MC, VI. ● Dining rm & coffeeshop; 6 am-10 pm; Sun & Mon-9 pm; $8.50-$15; cocktails. FAX (619) 442-9574   Ⓓ Ⓛ (619) 442-3425

Travelodge El Cajon/Magnolia ◆◆
♿ Rates Guaranteed · Motel

6/1-9/30	1P 32.00	2P/1B	.... 35.00	2P/2B	.... 38.00 XP 5
10/1-5/31	1P 30.00	....	2P/2B	.... 35.00 XP 5

47 units. 2 blks s of I-8. 471 N Magnolia Ave. (92020) A/C; C/CATV; movies; phones. 2 2-bedrm units. Coin laundry. Small pool. No pets. Wkly rates avail. Reserv deposit required; 3 days refund notice. AE, DI, MC, VI. Restaurant adjacent. FAX (619) 447-0400   ⊗ Ⓢ Ⓓ (619) 447-3999

Villa Embasadora   Rates Subject to Change   *Motel*   ◆
⊕ All year [CP]   1P 25.00- 35.00   2P/1B   29.00- 40.00   2P/2B   32.00- 42.00   XP 3- 6
85 units. Adjacent to I-8; exit Greenfield Dr, then 3/4 mi w, westbound exit E Main St. 1556 E Main St. (92021)
Formerly Penny Lodge. Check-in 4 pm. A/C; C/CATV; movies; 22 radios; phones. Coin laundry. Htd pool; sauna;
whirlpool. Pets, $5 extra charge. 12 deluxe rooms with refrigerator & microwave, $35-$65 for up to 4 persons.
Wkly rates avail. MC, VI. *(See ad p A132)*   ⊗ ⒟ (619) 442-9617

RESTAURANT

Hungry Hunter   Steak & Seafood $$ ◆◆◆
1 1/2 blks w of Magnolia Ave. 402 Fletcher Pkwy. Attractive hunting lodge decor. A/C. Open 11:30 am-2 & 5-10 pm; Fri-11
pm; Sat 4:30 pm-11 pm; Sun 4 pm-10 pm; closed 12/25. Cocktails & lounge. AE, MC, VI.   ⊗ (619) 442-0517

EL CENTRO — 31,400

Barbara Worth Country Club & Hotel   Rates Guaranteed   *Motor Inn*   ◆◆◆
⊕ All year   1P .... 48.00   2P/1B .... 54.00   2P/2B .... 54.00   XP 6   F
103 units. 9 mi e from I-8, Bowker exit, 2 mi n then 3 mi e on SR 80. 2050 Country Club Dr. (Holtville, 92250)
Quiet, restful setting. Check-in 3 pm. A/C; C/CATV; movies; radios; phones. Coin laundry. 2 htd pools; putting
green. Fee for: golf-18 holes. Pets. Wkly & monthly rates avail. Reserv deposit required. AE, DI, DS, MC,
VI. ● Dining rm; 6 am-10 pm; $9-$20; cocktails. Also restaurant, see separate listing. FAX (619) 356-4653
      ⊗ ⒟ (619) 356-2806

Brunner's   AAA Special Value Rates   *Motor Inn*   ◆◆◆
⊕ All year   1P 46.00- 53.00   2P/1B   49.00- 55.00   2P/2B   49.00- 52.00   XP 3
88 units. 1 mi n of I-8, exit Imperial Ave. 215 N Imperial Ave. (92243) A/C; C/CATV; movies; phones. 12 efficien-
cies. Coin laundry. Pool; whirlpool. Pets. 20 1-bedroom housekeeping units, $65-$75 for 2 persons. All units with
microwave & refrigerator. Some rooms with VCR. Wkly rates avail. AE, CB, DI, MC, VI. ● Dining rm & coffee-
shop; 5 am-10 pm; $5-$23; cocktails. FAX (619) 352-6431   ⊗ ⒟ (619) 352-6431

Executive Inn of El Centro   Rates Subject to Change   *Motel*   ◆
⊕ All year   1P .... 27.00   2P/1B .... 35.00   2P/2B .... 40.00   XP 5
42 units. Downtown. 725 State St. (92243) 19 refrigerators; A/C; C/CATV; phones. 5 efficiencies. Coin laundry. Htd
pool. No pets. 2 suites with kitchen. Wkly & monthly rates avail. Reserv deposit required. MC, VI.
      ⒟ (619) 352-8500

Sands Motel   AAA Special Value Rates   *Motel*   ◆
⊕ All year   1P 30.00- 33.00   2P/1B   35.00- 38.00   2P/2B   40.00- 44.00   XP 5
50 units. 1 1/4 mi n of I-8, exit Imperial Ave. 611 N Imperial Ave. (92243) Check-in 3 pm. Refrigerators; A/C;
C/CATV; movies; phones. Coin laundry. Pool. Small pets only. Wkly rates avail. Reserv deposit required; 3 days
refund notice. AE, DI, DS, MC, VI. Coffeeshop adjacent. FAX (619) 353-9636   ⊗ ⒟ (619) 352-0715

Vacation Inn   Rates Subject to Change   *Motor Inn*   ◆
All year   1P .... 43.00   2P/1B .... 45.00   2P/2B .... 48.00   XP 5   F
189 units. Adjacent to I-8, exit Imperial Ave. 2000 Cottonwood Cir. (92243) 44 refrigerators; A/C; C/CATV; movies; ra-
dios; phones. 20 efficiencies. Coin laundry. 2 htd pools; whirlpools. AE, DI, DS, MC, VI. ● Dining rm; 6 am-2 & 5-10
pm; $10-$17; cocktails. FAX (619) 352-9523 *(See ad below)*   ⊗ ⒧ (619) 352-9523

RESTAURANTS

Barbara Worth Country Club Restaurant   American $$ ◆◆◆
At Barbara Worth Country Club & Hotel. Attractive restaurant with view of golf course. Sun brunch 10:30 am-2:30 pm,
$11.95; Fri night seafood buffet, $15.95. A/C. Open 6 am-10 pm; closed 12/25. Cocktails & lounge. AE, DI, DS, MC, VI.
      (619) 356-2806

Caston's   American $$ ◆◆◆
1/2 mi e of Imperial Ave, 1 blk n of Main. 548A Broadway. Casual dining in tastefully decorated room. A/C. Children's
menu. Open 5 pm-10 pm; closed Sun, Mon & 12/25. Cocktails & lounge. Reserv advised. MC, VI.   (619) 352-8671

Grasso's Italian Restaurant   Italian $$ ◆◆◆
1/4 mi w of Imperial Ave. 1902 W Main. Unpretentious, casual; also serves steak & chicken. Smaller portions avail. A/C.
Children's menu. Open 5:30 pm-10 pm; closed Mon, Tues & major holidays. Beer & wine. DS, MC, VI. (619) 352-4635

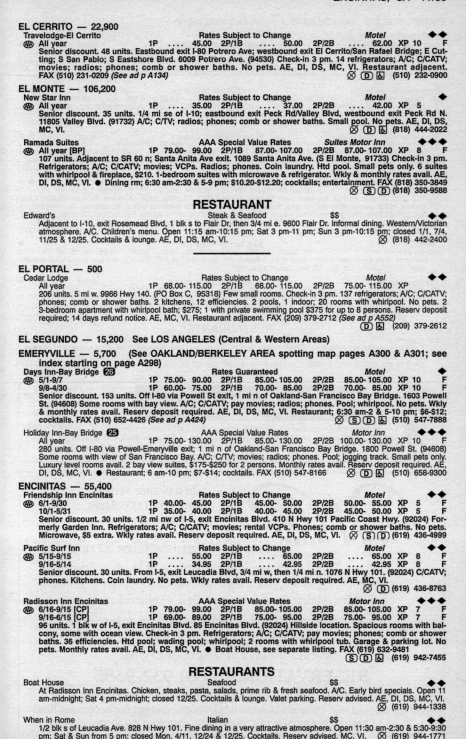

EL CERRITO — 22,900

Travelodge-El Cerrito   **Rates Subject to Change**   *Motel*   ◆◆
⊛ All year   1P .... 45.00 2P/1B .... 50.00 2P/2B .... 62.00 XP 10   F
Senior discount. 48 units. Eastbound exit I-80 Potrero Ave; westbound exit El Cerrito/San Rafael Bridge; E Cutting; S San Pablo; S Eastshore Blvd. 6009 Potrero Ave. (94530) Check-in 3 pm. 14 refrigerators; A/C; C/CATV; movies; radios; phones; comb or shower baths. No pets. AE, DI, DS, MC, VI. Restaurant adjacent. FAX (510) 231-0209 *(See ad p A134)*   ⊗ Ⓓ 🔥   (510) 232-0900

EL MONTE — 106,200

New Star Inn   **Rates Subject to Change**   *Motel*   ◆
⊛ All year   1P .... 35.00 2P/1B .... 37.00 2P/2B .... 42.00 XP 5
Senior discount. 35 units. 1/4 mi se of I-10; eastbound exit Peck Rd/Valley Blvd, westbound exit Peck Rd N. 11805 Valley Blvd. (91732) A/C; C/TV; radios; phones; comb or shower baths. Small pool. No pets. AE, DI, DS, MC, VI.   ⊗ Ⓓ 🔥   (818) 444-2022

Ramada Suites   **AAA Special Value Rates**   *Suites Motor Inn*   ◆◆
⊛ All year [BP]   1P 79.00- 99.00 2P/1B 87.00- 107.00 2P/2B 87.00- 107.00 XP 8   F
107 units. Adjacent to SR 60 n; Santa Anita Ave exit. 1089 Santa Anita Ave. (S El Monte, 91733) Check-in 3 pm. Refrigerators; A/C; C/CATV; movies; VCPs. Radios; phones. Coin laundry. Htd pool. Small pets only. 6 suites with whirlpool & fireplace, $210. 1-bedroom suites with microwave & refrigerator. Wkly & monthly rates avail. AE, DI, DS, MC, VI. ● Dining rm; 6:30 am-2:30 & 5-9 pm; $10.20-$12.20; cocktails; entertainment. FAX (818) 350-3849   ⊗ Ⓢ Ⓓ   (818) 350-9588

RESTAURANT

Edward's   Steak & Seafood $$ ◆◆
Adjacent to I-10, exit Rosemead Blvd, 1 blk s to Flair Dr, then 3/4 mi e. 9600 Flair Dr. Informal dining. Western/Victorian atmosphere. A/C. Children's menu. Open 11:15 am-10:15 pm; Sat 3 pm-11 pm; Sun 3 pm-10:15 pm; closed 1/1, 7/4, 11/25 & 12/25. Cocktails & lounge. AE, DI, DS, MC, VI.   ⊗   (818) 442-2400

EL PORTAL — 500

Cedar Lodge   **Rates Subject to Change**   *Motel*   ◆◆
All year   1P 68.00- 115.00 2P/1B 68.00- 115.00 2P/2B 75.00- 115.00 XP
206 units. 5 mi w. 9966 Hwy 140. (PO Box C, 95318) Few small rooms. Check-in 3 pm. 137 refrigerators; A/C; C/CATV; phones; comb or shower baths. 2 kitchens, 12 efficiencies. 2 pools, 1 indoor; 20 rooms with whirlpool. No pets. 2 3-bedroom apartment with whirlpool bath; $275; 1 with private swimming pool $375 for up to 8 persons. Reserv deposit required; 14 days refund notice. AE, MC, VI. Restaurant adjacent. FAX (209) 379-2712 *(See ad p A552)*   Ⓓ 🔥   (209) 379-2612

EL SEGUNDO — 15,200   See LOS ANGELES (Central & Western Areas)

EMERYVILLE — 5,700   (See OAKLAND/BERKELEY AREA spotting map pages A300 & A301; see index starting on page A298)

Days Inn-Bay Bridge ㉖   **Rates Guaranteed**   *Motel*   ◆
⊛ 5/1-9/7   1P 75.00- 90.00 2P/1B 85.00- 105.00 2P/2B 85.00- 105.00 XP 10   F
9/8-4/30   1P 60.00- 75.00 2P/1B 70.00- 85.00 2P/2B 70.00- 85.00 XP 10   F
Senior discount. 153 units. Off I-80 via Powell St exit, 1 mi n of Oakland-San Francisco Bay Bridge. 1603 Powell St. (94608) Some rooms with bay view. A/C; C/CATV; pay movies; radios; phones. Pool; whirlpool. No pets. Wkly & monthly rates avail. Reserv deposit required. AE, DI, DS, MC, VI. Restaurant; 6:30 am-2 & 5-10 pm; $6-$12; cocktails. FAX (510) 652-4426 *(See ad p A424)*   ⊗ Ⓢ Ⓓ   (510) 547-7888

Holiday Inn-Bay Bridge ㉕   **AAA Special Value Rates**   *Motor Inn*   ◆◆◆
All year   1P 75.00- 130.00 2P/1B 85.00- 130.00 2P/2B 100.00- 130.00 XP 10   F
280 units. Off I-80 via Powell-Emeryville exit; 1 mi n of Oakland-San Francisco Bay Bridge. 1800 Powell St. (94608) Some rooms with view of San Francisco Bay. A/C; C/TV; movies; radios; phones. Pool; jogging track. Small pets only. Luxury level rooms avail. 2 bay view suites, $175-$250 for 2 persons. Monthly rates avail. Reserv deposit required. AE, DI, DS, MC, VI. ● Restaurant; 6 am-10 pm; $7-$14; cocktails. FAX (510) 547-8166   ⊗ Ⓓ 🔥   (510) 658-9300

ENCINITAS — 55,400

Friendship Inn Encinitas   **Rates Subject to Change**   *Motel*   ◆◆
⊛ 6/1-9/30   1P 40.00- 45.00 2P/1B 45.00- 50.00 2P/2B 50.00- 55.00 XP 5   F
10/1-5/31   1P 35.00- 40.00 2P/1B 40.00- 45.00 2P/2B 45.00- 50.00 XP 5   F
Senior discount. 30 units. 1/2 mi nw of I-5, exit Encinitas Blvd. 410 N Hwy 101 Pacific Coast Hwy. (92024) Formerly Garden Inn. Refrigerators; A/C; C/CATV; movies; rental VCPs. Phones; comb or shower baths. No pets. Microwave, $5 extra. Wkly rates avail. Reserv deposit required. AE, DI, DS, MC, VI.   ⊗ Ⓢ Ⓓ   (619) 436-4999

Pacific Surf Inn   **Rates Subject to Change**   *Motel*   ◆◆
⊛ 5/15-9/15   1P .... 55.00 2P/1B .... 65.00 2P/2B .... 65.00 XP 8   F
9/16-5/14   1P .... 34.95 2P/1B .... 42.95 2P/2B .... 42.95 XP 8   F
Senior discount. 30 units. From I-5, exit Leucadia Blvd, 3/4 mi w, then 1/4 mi n. 1076 N Hwy 101. (92024) C/CATV; phones. Kitchens. Coin laundry. No pets. Wkly rates avail. Reserv deposit required. AE, MC, VI.   ⊗ Ⓓ   (619) 436-8763

Radisson Inn Encinitas   **AAA Special Value Rates**   *Motor Inn*   ◆◆◆
⊛ 6/16-9/15 [CP]   1P 79.00- 99.00 2P/1B 85.00- 105.00 2P/2B 85.00- 105.00 XP 7   F
9/16-6/15 [CP]   1P 69.00- 89.00 2P/1B 75.00- 95.00 2P/2B 75.00- 95.00 XP 7   F
96 units. 1 blk w of I-5, exit Encinitas Blvd. 85 Encinitas Blvd. (92024) Hillside location. Spacious rooms with balcony, some with ocean view. Check-in 3 pm. Refrigerators; A/C; C/CATV; pay movies; phones; comb or shower baths. 36 efficiencies. Htd pool; wading pool; whirlpool; 2 rooms with whirlpool tub. Garage & parking lot. No pets. Monthly rates avail. AE, DI, DS, MC, VI. ● Boat House, see separate listing. FAX (619) 632-9481   Ⓢ Ⓓ 🔥   (619) 942-7455

RESTAURANTS

Boat House   Seafood $$ ◆◆
At Radisson Inn Encinitas. Chicken, steaks, pasta, salads, prime rib & fresh seafood. A/C. Early bird specials. Open 11 am-midnight; Sat 4 pm-midnight; closed 12/25. Cocktails & lounge. Valet parking. Reserv advised. AE, DI, DS, MC, VI.   ⊗   (619) 944-1338

When in Rome   Italian $$ ◆◆
1/2 blk s of Leucadia Ave. 828 N Hwy 101. Fine dining in a very attractive atmosphere. Open 11:30 am-2:30 & 5:30-9:30 pm; Sat & Sun from 5 pm; closed Mon, 4/11, 12/24 & 12/25. Cocktails. Reserv advised. MC, VI.   ⊗   (619) 944-1771

ENCINO — 62,000   See LOS ANGELES (San Fernando Valley)

ESCONDIDO — 108,600

Best Western Escondido   Rates Subject to Change   *Motel*   ◆◆◆
Ⓐ All year [CP]   1P 55.00- 61.00   2P/1B   61.00- 70.00   2P/2B .... 61.00 XP 6
Senior discount. 100 units. 1 blk e of I-15; exit El Norte Pkwy. 1700 Nutmeg St. (92026) Refrigerators; A/C;
C/CATV; movies; phones. Coin laundry. Htd pool; whirlpool. No pets. 20 1-bedroom suites $87. Microwaves. AE,
CB, DI, MC, VI. FAX (619) 740-9832   ⊗ Ⓢ Ⓓ Ⓛ (619) 740-1700

Escondido Econo Lodge   Rates Subject to Change   *Motel*   ◆◆
Ⓐ All year [BP]   1P .... 44.00   2P/1B   .... 49.00   2P/2B .... 49.00 XP 5
Senior discount. 110 units. Adjacent to I-15, exit Valley Pkwy. 1250 W Valley Pkwy. (92029) A/C; 104 C/CATV; radios; phones. Coin laundry. Htd pool; whirlpool. Small pets, $50 deposit. also $10 daily extra charge. Wkly rates
avail. AE, DI, DS, MC, VI. Restaurant adjacent. FAX (619) 741-5058   ⊗ Ⓓ (619) 741-7117

Escondido West Travelodge   Rates Subject to Change   *Motel*   ◆◆
Ⓐ All year [BP]   1P .... 52.00   2P/1B   .... 56.00   2P/2B .... 60.00 XP 5   F
Senior discount. 94 units. 1 blk w of I-15, exit Valley Pkwy. 1290 W Valley Pkwy. (92029) A/C; C/CATV; rental
VCPs; radios; phones. Pool; whirlpool. No pets. AE, CB, DS, MC, VI. Restaurant adjacent. FAX (619) 489-7847
                                                                      ⊗ Ⓓ (619) 489-1010

Lawrence Welk Resort   AAA Special Value Rates   *Resort Motor Inn*   ◆◆◆
Ⓐ All year   1P 100.00- 110.00   2P/1B 100.00- 110.00   2P/2B 100.00- 110.00 XP 10   F
132 units. 9 mi n on I-15, between Deer Springs & Old Castle Rd exits. 8860 Lawrence Welk Dr. (92026) Large
rooms, most overlooking golf course. Balconies or patios. Rural location, nicely landscaped. 25 refrigerators;
A/C; C/CATV; radios; phones. 2 htd pools; whirlpools; lighted tennis-3 courts. Fee for: golf-18 holes, par-3 golf.
Pets. Wkly & monthly rates avail. AE, CB, DI, MC, VI. ● Restaurant; 7 am-9 pm; $10-$17; cocktails.
FAX (619) 749-6182 *(See ad below)*   ⊗ Ⓓ Ⓛ (619) 749-3000

Palms Inn   AAA Special Value Rates   *Motel*   ◆
Ⓐ All year   1P 29.00- 45.00   2P/1B   45.00- 65.00   2P/2B   45.00- 65.00 XP 6   F
44 units. 2 mi s on Centre City Pkwy. 2650 S Escondido Blvd. (92025) A/C; C/CATV; movies; phones. 13 efficiencies. Coin laundry. DS, MC, VI. Restaurant adjacent.   ⊗ Ⓓ (619) 743-9733

The Sheridan Inn   AAA Special Value Rates   *Motel*   ◆◆◆
Ⓐ All year [CP]   1P 51.00- 57.00   2P/1B   51.00- 57.00   2P/2B .... 51.00 XP   F
59 units. 1 mi e of I-15; 1 blk e of Centre City Pkwy; from I-15, exit El Norte. 1341 N Escondido Blvd. (92026) 11
refrigerators; A/C; C/CATV; movies; phones. Htd pool; whirlpool. No pets. Wkly & monthly rates avail. AE, DI, DS,
MC, VI. FAX (619) 743-0840 *(See ad below)*   ⊗ Ⓓ Ⓛ (619) 743-8338

RESTAURANTS

The Brigantine   Seafood $$ ◆◆
1 1/2 mi s on I-15 business loop. 421 W Felicita Ave at Centre City Pkwy. Nautical decor. Nice selection of seafood &
steaks. Sun brunch 11 am-2:30 pm. A/C. Open 11:30 am-2:30 & 5-9:30 pm; Fri-10:30 pm; Sat 5 pm-11 pm; Sun 4:30
pm-9:30 pm; closed 11/25 & 12/25. Cocktails & lounge. AE, CB, DI, MC, VI.   ⊗ (619) 743-4718

Fireside Restaurant   Steak & Seafood $$ ◆◆
On I-15 business loop. 439 W Washington Ave at Centre City Pkwy. Nice selection of steaks, prime rib & seafood. A/C.
Open 11 am-9 pm; Sat & Sun from 4 pm. Cocktails & lounge. Entertainment. AE, DS, MC, VI.   ⊗ (619) 745-1931

Marie Callender's   American $ ◆◆
1 mi s on I-15 business loop; Centre City Pkwy. 515 W 13th St. Family type restaurant with nice selection of sandwiches,
salads & entrees. Pies are a specialty. A/C. Open 11 am-10 pm; Fri & Sat-11 pm; Sun 10 am-10 pm; closed 12/25.
Cocktails & lounge. AE, DS, MC, VI.   ⊗ (619) 741-3636

EUREKA — 27,000   See also ARCATA, FORTUNA & TRINIDAD

An Elegant Victorian Mansion		Rates Subject to Change		*Historic Bed & Breakfast*		◆◆
6/1-9/30 & 12/1-1/2 [BP]	1P 70.00- 100.00	2P/1B 75.00- 115.00	2P/2B 125.00- 150.00	XP		
10/1-11/30 & 1/3-5/31 [BP]	1P 60.00- 90.00	2P/1B 65.00- 105.00	2P/2B 115.00- 140.00	XP		

4 units. Exit US 101 at C St, 1/2 mi e. 1406 C St. (95501) 1888 historic Victorian mansion. Ice cream sodas served in
evening. Check-in 3 pm. 1 comb or shower baths. 1 2-bedrm unit. Sauna; bicycles; croquet field. Fee for: massage. Lim-
ited parking lot. No pets. MC, VI.   ⊗ Ⓓ (707) 444-3144

Best Western Thunderbird Lodge   Rates Subject to Change   *Motel*   ◆◆◆
Ⓐ 5/15-9/30   1P 70.00- 80.00   2P/1B 74.00- 84.00   2P/2B 74.00- 84.00 XP 5
    10/1-5/14   1P 54.00- 64.00   2P/1B 56.00- 66.00   2P/2B 56.00- 66.00 XP 5
115 units. On US 101, at Broadway. 232 W 5th St. (95501) Many large rooms. 25 refrigerators; 23 A/C; C/CATV;
movies; radios; phones; shower or comb baths. 3 2-bedrm units. Coin laundry. Pool; whirlpool. No pets.
2-bedroom units, $80-$140 for 6-8 persons. Some executive rooms with refrigerator & air conditioning. Monthly
rates avail. AE, DI, DS, MC, VI. Coffeeshop adjacent. FAX (707) 443-3489 *(See ad below)*
                                                                              ⊗ Ⓓ Ⓛ (707) 443-2234

Budget Host Townhouse Motel   Rates Subject to Change   *Motel*   ◆
Ⓐ 7/1-9/6   ....   2P/1B .... 48.00   2P/2B .... 52.00 XP 7
    9/7-9/30 & 5/28-6/30   1P .... 38.00 2P/1B .... 42.00   2P/2B .... 48.00 XP 6
    10/1-10/31 & 5/1-5/27 1P .... 34.00 2P/1B .... 38.00   2P/2B .... 42.00 XP 6
    11/1-4/30   1P .... 30.00   2P/1B .... 34.00   2P/2B .... 38.00 XP 6
20 units. On US 101 southbound, corner 4th & K sts. 933 4th St. (95501) C/CATV; movies; phones; shower or
comb baths. 4 2-bedrm units. Parking ramp. 6 rooms with whirlpool, extra charge. 2 bedroom units, $60-$85 for
4 persons. Reserv deposit required. AE, DI, DS, MC, VI. *(See ad below)*   ⊗ (707) 443-4536

Carson House Inn   Rates Subject to Change   *Motel*   ◆◆
Ⓐ 6/1-10/15   1P 60.00- 85.00   2P/1B 75.00- 95.00   2P/2B 85.00- 110.00 XP 10
Senior discount. 60 units. On US 101 southbound, between M & N sts; 1 blk from the Carson Mansion. 1209 4th
St. (95501) OPEN ALL YEAR. Spacious rooms. C/CATV; movies; phones; comb or shower baths. 4
2-bedrm units. Pool; sauna; whirlpool. No pets. 15 units with whirlpool tub, extra charge. Reserv deposit re-
quired. AE, DI, DS, MC, VI. Coffeeshop opposite. FAX (707) 444-8365   ⊗ Ⓓ (707) 443-1601

Hotel Carter   Rates Subject to Change   *Bed & Breakfast* ◆◆◆
  5/1-9/30 [BP]   1P 89.00- 99.00   2P/1B 99.00- 109.00   2P/2B 99.00- 109.00 XP 15
    10/1-4/30 [BP]   1P 69.00- 79.00   2P/1B 79.00- 89.00   2P/2B 79.00- 89.00 XP 15
20 units. 1 blk w of US 101S. 301 L St. (95501) Victorian replica in Old Town. Smoke free premises. C/CATV; radios;
phones. 8 units with whirlpool tub. Limited parking lot. No pets. 3 rooms with fireplace, 2 with whirlpool baths, $159-$169
for 2 persons. Reserv deposit required; 3 days refund notice. AE, DS, MC, VI. ● Dining rm; 6 pm-9 pm Thurs-Sun; a
la carte entrees about $11.95-$17.95; beer & wine.   ⊗ Ⓢ Ⓓ (707) 444-8062

Comfort Inn — Rates Subject to Change — *Motel* ◆◆
5/1-10/31   1P 45.00- 60.00   2P/1B 49.00- 70.00   2P/2B 60.00- 85.00   XP 6
11/1-4/30   1P 38.00- 42.00   2P/1B 42.00- 46.00   2P/2B 48.00- 55.00   XP 6
27 units. On US 101; southbound, corner 4th & V sts. 2014 4th St. (95501) Formerly Tradewind Inn. C/CATV; movies; phones; comb or shower baths. 4 2-bedrm units. No pets. 4 2-bedroom units, $90-$160 for 4-6 persons. Reserv deposit required. AE, DI, DS, MC, VI. FAX (707) 442-8145 *(See ad below)* ⊗ Ⓓ 🅶 (707) 444-0401

Eureka Inn — Rates Subject to Change — *Historic Hotel* ◆◆◆
All year   1P 70.00- 110.00   2P/1B 85.00- 135.00   2P/2B 95.00- 135.00   XP 10   F
105 units. 7th & F sts. (95501) Charming English Tudor design. Excellent facilities. C/CATV; phones; comb or shower baths. 2 2-bedrm units. Pool; sauna; whirlpool. Limited parking lot. Airport transp. AE, DI, DS, MC, VI. ● Dining rm & restaurant; 6:30 am-11 pm; Sat & Sun from 7 am; $5-$17; cocktails. Also, The Rib Room, see separate listing. FAX (707) 442-0637 ⊗ Ⓢ Ⓓ 🅶 (707) 442-6441

Eureka Super 8 Motel — Rates Subject to Change — *Motel* ◆◆
5/8-9/30   ....   2P/1B 59.00- 75.00   2P/2B 64.00- 79.00   XP 6
10/1-4/30   ....   2P/1B 38.00- 48.00   2P/2B 42.00- 52.00   XP 6
50 units. 8 blks n on US 101, at N St. 1304 4th St. (95501) C/CATV; movies; radios; phones; comb or shower baths. 1 2-bedrm unit, 2 efficiencies. Small htd indoor pool; sauna; indoor whirlpool; steamroom. No pets. 2 room apartment, $110-$185 for up to 6 persons. Reserv deposit required. AE, DI, DS, MC, VI. Cocktail lounge; coffeeshop opposite. *(See ad below)* ⊗ Ⓓ (707) 443-3193

Nendels Valu Inn — Rates Subject to Change — *Motel* ◆◆
5/20-9/10 [CP]   1P .... 55.00   2P/1B .... 65.00   2P/2B .... 65.00   XP 5   F
9/11-5/19 [CP]   1P .... 40.00   2P/1B .... 45.00   2P/2B .... 55.00   XP 5   F
Senior discount. 25 units. Northbound exit US 101 w on V St, n on 3rd, southbound exit US 101 at X St. 2223 4th St. (95501) C/CATV; movies; VCPs. Phones; comb or shower baths. 5 kitchens. Coin laundry. Pets, $10 small dogs deposit required. Reserv deposit required. AE, DI, DS, MC, VI. ⊗ Ⓢ Ⓓ 🅶 (707) 442-3261

Red Lion Inn — Rates Subject to Change — *Motor Inn* ◆◆◆
All year   1P 75.00- 135.00   2P/1B 90.00- 135.00   2P/2B 100.00- 135.00   XP 15   F
179 units. 14 blks n on US 101 southbound; between T & V sts. 1929 4th St. (95501) Attractively decorated rooms. A/C; C/CATV; pay movies; radios; phones. 8 2-bedrm units. Small pool; whirlpool. Pets. AE, DI, DS, MC, VI. ● Dining rm & coffeeshop; 6 am-11 pm; $10-$22; cocktails. FAX (707) 445-2752 *(See ad p A3)* ⊗ Ⓓ 🅶 (707) 445-0844

Seafarer Motor Inn — Rates Subject to Change — *Motel* ◆◆
5/1-9/30   1P 51.00- 69.00   2P/1B 57.00- 75.00   2P/2B 63.00- 83.00   XP 6
10/1-4/30   1P 41.00- 53.00   2P/1B 45.00- 57.00   2P/2B 47.00- 65.00   XP 5
Senior discount. 40 units. On US 101 northbound. 270 5th St. (95501) C/CATV; movies; 6 radios; phones. Sauna; indoor whirlpool. No pets. 1 efficiency, $6 extra. 1 kitchen apartment, $92 for 2 persons. Reserv deposit required. AE, DI, DS, MC, VI. FAX (707) 443-2029 *(See ad p A139)* ⊗ Ⓓ 🅶 (707) 443-2206

RESTAURANTS

Cafe Marina — American — $ — ◆◆
Exit US 101 at SR 255W, exit to Marina on Woodley Island. Startare Dr. Specializing in fresh local seafood; casual atmosphere overlooking marina. Outside dining, weather permitting. A/C. Early bird specials; children's menu. Open 7 am-9 pm, 6 am-10 pm 6/1-8/31; Fri & Sat-10 pm; closed 11/25 & 12/25. Cocktails & lounge. AE, DI, DS, MC, VI. ⊗ (707) 443-2233

The Rib Room — Continental — $$ — ◆◆◆
In Eureka Inn. English Tudor decor. Prime rib & fresh seafood in season. A/C. Children's menu. Open 5 pm-11 pm. Cocktails & lounge. Entertainment. Reserv advised. AE, CB, DI, MC, VI. ⊗ (707) 442-6441

FAIRFIELD — 77,200

Best Western Cordelia Inn
All year [CP]   Rates Subject to Change   *Motel* ◆◆ F
1P .... 42.00   2P/1B .... 48.00   2P/2B .... 54.00   XP 6
Senior discount. 60 units. 3 1/2 mi w; exit I-80 Suisun Valley Rd, 1 blk s to Central Pl. 4373 Central Pl, Cordelia Village. (94585) A/C; C/CATV; movies; radios; phones. Coin laundry. Pool; whirlpool. Pets. AE, DI, DS, MC, VI.
(See ad below)   ⊗ Ⓢ Ⓓ ⓑ (707) 864-2029

Hampton Inn
Fri & Sat 6/28-8/1 [CP]   Rates Subject to Change   *Motel* ◆◆
1P .... 54.00   2P/1B .... 54.00   2P/2B .... 64.00   XP
Fri & Sat 5/31-6/27 [CP]   1P .... 52.00   2P/1B .... 52.00   2P/2B .... 62.00   XP
Sun-Thurs & Fri-Sat 8/2-5/30
[CP]   1P .... 49.00   2P/1B .... 49.00   2P/2B .... 59.00   XP
57 units. Exit I-80 at Suisun Valley Rd. 4441 Central Pl. (94585) A/C; C/CATV; movies; radios; phones. Coin laundry. Pool; exercise rm. No pets. Luxury level rooms avail. 3 rooms with whirlpool tub, refrigerator & microwave, $105 for 2 persons. AE, DI, DS, MC, VI. FAX (707) 864-4288   ⊗ Ⓢ Ⓓ ⓑ (707) 864-1446

Holiday Inn of Fairfield
All year   AAA Special Value Rates   *Motor Inn* ◆◆◆
1P 59.00- 79.00   2P/1B 59.00- 86.00   2P/2B 59.00- 86.00   XP 7   F
140 units. Exit I-80 Travis Blvd W, 1/4 mi s. 1350 Holiday Ln. (94533) A/C; C/CATV; movies; radios; phones. Coin laundry. Pool; wading pool. Small pets only. Monthly rates avail. AE, DI, DS, MC, VI. ● Restaurant; 6 am-2 & 5-10 pm; $8-$16; cocktails. FAX (707) 428-3452   ⊗ Ⓓ ⓑ (707) 422-4111

RESTAURANTS

Fairfield Landing   Steak & Seafood $$ ◆◆
N of & adjacent to I-80; exit Waterman Travis. 2440 Martin Rd. Casual atmosphere, popular with locals. A/C. Early bird specials; children's menu. Open 11:30 am-2:30 & 5:30-9 pm; Fri-10 pm; Sat 11:30 am-2:30 & 5-10 pm; Sun 10 am-2:30 & 5-9 pm; closed 7/4, 11/25 & 12/25. Cocktails & lounge. Dancing. Minimum, $5. Reserv advised. AE, MC, VI.   ⊗ ⓑ (707) 429-2370

Marie Callender   American $$
Exit I-80 Travis Blvd E. 1750 Travis Blvd. Varied menu, specializing in homemade pies, on site bakery, pasta & fresh specials. A/C. Children's menu. Open 8 am-10 pm; Fri & Sat-11 pm; closed 11/25 & 12/25. Cocktails & lounge. AE, DS, MC, VI.   ⊗ (707) 428-4745

FALLBROOK (92028) — **14,000**

Best Western Franciscan Inn
All year   Rates Guaranteed   *Motel* ◆◆
1P 45.00- 55.00   2P/1B 50.00- 65.00   2P/2B 55.00- 65.00   XP 5   F
Senior discount. 51 units. 1 mi s on CR S-13. 1635 S Mission Rd. 14 refrigerators; A/C; C/CATV; movies; phones. No utensils. Htd pool; whirlpool. Small pets only. 9 efficiencies $5 extra, no utensils. Wkly & monthly rates avail. Reserv deposit required. AE, DI, DS, MC, VI. FAX (619) 731-6404   ⊗ Ⓓ ⓑ (619) 728-6174

Fallbrook Travelodge   AAA Special Value Rates   *Motel*   ◆◆
🅖 All year   1P 45.00- 50.00   2P/1B   50.00- 55.00   2P/2B   55.00- 60.00 XP 5
36 units. 1 mi s on CR S-13. 1608 Mission Rd. A/C; C/CATV; movies; radios; phones. 8 efficiencies, no utensils. Whirlpool. No pets. Wkly & monthly rates avail. AE, DI, DS, MC, VI. FAX (619) 723-2917 *(See ad below)*
Ⓧ Ⓢ Ⓓ (619) 723-1127

La Estancia Inn   Rates Subject to Change   *Motor Inn*   ◆◆◆
🅖 All year   1P 68.00- 78.00   2P/1B   68.00- 78.00   2P/2B   68.00- 78.00 XP 10   F
Senior discount. 41 units. Adjacent to I-15, exit Pala Rd & SR 76, then 1/2 mi n. 3135 S Old Hwy 395. 12 refrigerators; A/C; C/CATV; radios; phones. 6 efficiencies. Htd pool; whirlpool; 10 rooms with whirlpool tub. No pets. Wkly & monthly rates avail. AE, DI, MC, VI. ● Dining rm; 11:30 am-10 pm; closed Mon; $15-$20; cocktails.
Ⓓ (619) 723-2888

Pala Mesa Resort   —   AAA Special Value Rates   *Resort Complex*   ◆◆◆
Fri & Sat   1P .... 130.00   2P/1B .... 130.00   2P/2B .... 130.00 XP   F
Sun-Thurs   1P .... 110.00   2P/1B .... 110.00   2P/2B .... 110.00 XP   F
131 units. Adjacent to I-15; 1 1/4 mi n of jct SR 76. 2001 Old Hwy 395. Attractively landscaped grounds. Country club atmosphere. Spacious rooms. Some patios & balconies. Check-in 4 pm. A/C; C/CATV; movies; radios; phones; comb or shower baths. Htd pool; whirlpool; exercise rm. Fee for: golf-18 holes, lighted tennis-4 courts; airport transp. No pets. Golf package plans. Reserv deposit required weekends. AE, DI, MC, VI. ● Dining rm; 6:30 am-10 pm; $7.50-$22; cocktails; entertainment. FAX (619) 723-8292
Ⓧ Ⓓ (619) 728-5881

RESTAURANT

Square One   American $ ◆
🅖 Downtown. 119 N Main. Dining in a charming outdoor patio area & indoor dining rooms. Interesting selection of salads, sandwiches, entrees & desserts. Open 11 am-4 pm; closed Sun & major holidays. Beer & wine. MC, VI.
Ⓧ (619) 728-5154

FEATHER RIVER AREA — See GRAEAGLE, MARYSVILLE, OROVILLE & YUBA CITY

FELTON — 4,600

Fern River Resort   Rates Subject to Change   *Cottages*   ◆◆
🅖 4/1-12/15   1P 49.00- 69.00   2P/1B   49.00- 69.00   2P/2B   59.00- 69.00 XP 8
12/16-3/31   1P 42.00- 59.00   2P/1B   42.00- 59.00   2P/2B   53.00- 59.00 XP 8
13 units. 1 mi s on SR 9; across river from Henry Cowell State Park. 5250 Hwy 9. (95018) Rustic setting along San Lorenzo River. Single & duplex housekeeping cottages. Few fireplaces. CATV, 11 color; shower baths. 4 2-bedrm units, 10 kitchens, 2 efficiencies, no utensils. Swimming; playground. No pets. 2 studios, $56 for up to 2 persons. Wkly & monthly rates avail. Reserv deposit required; 30 days refund notice. MC, VI.
Ⓓ (408) 335-4412

FERNDALE — 1,300

Gingerbread Mansion   Rates Subject to Change   *Bed & Breakfast*   ◆◆◆
Fri-Sat & 5/1-10/31 [CP]   1P 90.00- 160.00   2P/1B   105.00- 175.00   2P/2B   105.00- 175.00 XP 20
Sun-Thurs 11/1-4/30 [CP]   1P 75.00- 145.00   2P/1B   90.00- 160.00   2P/2B   90.00- 160.00 XP 20
9 units. 1 blk e of Main St. 400 Berding St. (95536) 90 year old mansion, very attractive building & garden, afternoon tea. Smoke free premises. Check-in 3 pm. Comb or shower baths. Bicycles. No pets. Reserv deposit required; 14 days refund notice. MC, VI.
Ⓧ Ⓓ (707) 786-4000

FILLMORE — 12,000

Best Western La Posada Motel   Rates Guaranteed   *Motel*   ◆◆
🅖 All year   1P 40.00- 50.00   2P/1B   45.00- 55.00   2P/2B   45.00- 65.00 XP 5
Senior discount. 49 units. 1/2 mi w on SR 126. 827 Ventura St. (93015) A/C; C/CATV; movies; 10 radios; phones; comb or shower baths. Pool; sauna; whirlpool. No pets. AE, DI, DS, MC, VI. Restaurant adjacent. FAX (805) 524-1463
Ⓓ (805) 524-0440

FISH CAMP

Marriott's Tenaya Lodge   Rates Subject to Change   *Resort Hotel*   ◆◆◆◆
🅖 5/24-9/5   1P .... 225.00   2P/1B .... 225.00   2P/2B .... 225.00 XP 15   F
Fri & Sat 9/6-11/28 & 3/28-5/23   1P .... 179.00   2P/1B .... 179.00   2P/2B .... 179.00 XP 15   F
Fri & Sat 11/29-3/27   1P .... 139.00   2P/1B .... 139.00   2P/2B .... 139.00 XP 15   F
Sun-Thurs 11/29-3/27   1P .... 109.00   2P/1B .... 109.00   2P/2B .... 109.00 XP 15   F
242 units. 2 mi s of Yosemite National Park entrance, on SR 41. 1122 Hwy 41. (PO Box 159, 93623) Landscaped grounds, surrounded by national forest. Check-in 3 pm. A/C; C/CATV; pay movies; radios; phones. Coin laundry. 2 htd pools, 1 indoor; saunas; whirlpools; nature program; rental bicycles; exercise rm. Fee for: skiing, riding, massage. Valet parking lot. No pets. 9 units with Japanese sunken-tub & wet bar, $295 for 2 persons. Reserv deposit required; 10 days refund notice. AE, DI, DS, MC, VI. ● Dining rm & coffeeshop; 7 am-11 pm; $13-$29. FAX (209) 683-8684 *(See ad p A551)*
Ⓧ Ⓢ Ⓓ Ⓛ (209) 683-6555

The Narrow Gauge Inn — Rates Subject to Change — *Motor Inn* ◆◆
4/1-10/25   1P 80.00-125.00   2P/1B 80.00-125.00   2P/2B 100.00-125.00   XP 5-10
26 units. 4 mi s of Yosemite National Park entrance, on SR 41. 48571 Hwy 41. (93623) OPEN 4/1-10/25. Picturesque mountain setting. Most balconies with view. Check-in 3 pm. C/TV; shower baths. Small pool; whirlpool. No pets. Reserv deposit required; 4 days refund notice. AE, DI, MC, VI. ● Dining rm; 7:30 am-10:30 & 5:30-9 pm; smoking not permitted in dining room; $14-$25; cocktails. FAX (209) 683-2139 *(See ad p A550)*
(D) (209) 683-7720

FONTANA — 87,500

Comfort Inn — Rates Subject to Change — *Motel* ◆◆
All year   1P 40.00- 45.00   2P/1B 40.00- 45.00   2P/2B 45.00- 48.00   XP 4
Senior discount. 50 units. 2 blks nw of I-10; exit Sierra Ave. 16780 Valley Blvd. (92335) A/C; C/TV; radios; phones. Coin laundry. Pool. No pets. AE, DI, DS, MC, VI. FAX (909) 822-0337
⊗ (D) 🅖 (909) 822-3350

Valley Motel — Rates Subject to Change — *Motel* ◆
All year   1P .... 35.00   2P/1B .... 40.00   2P/2B .... 45.00   XP 5
24 units. 2 blks nw of I-10, exit Sierra Ave. 16762 Valley Blvd. (92335) A/C; C/CATV; movies; radios; phones. No pets. 2 rooms with whirlpool tub, $80. Reserv deposit required. AE, DS, MC, VI. FAX (909) 829-8874
⊗ (S) (D) (909) 829-8874

FORT BRAGG — 6,100   See also LITTLE RIVER

Best Western Vista Manor Lodge — Rates Subject to Change — *Motel* ◆◆
5/1-10/31   1P 67.00- 95.00   2P/1B 79.00-105.00   2P/2B 79.00-105.00   XP 7
11/1-4/30   1P 46.00- 80.00   2P/1B 53.00- 85.00   2P/2B 53.00- 85.00   XP 5
Senior discount. 56 units. 1 mi n on SR 1. 1100 N Main St. (95437) Many rooms with ocean view. Check-in 3 pm. C/CATV; phones; comb or shower baths. 2 kitchens. Htd indoor pool. No pets. 2 2-bedroom cottages, $110-$200 for up to 6 persons. Reserv deposit required; 3 days refund notice. AE, DI, DS, MC, VI. ⊗ (D) (707) 964-4776

Harbor Lite Lodge — Rates Subject to Change — *Motel* ◆◆
5/1-10/31 & Fri-Sat   1P 53.00- 72.00   2P/1B 57.00- 72.00   2P/2B 61.00- 68.00   XP 6
Sun-Thurs 11/1-4/30   1P 45.00- 62.00   2P/1B 45.00- 62.00   2P/2B 45.00- 55.00   XP 6
79 units. 1/2 mi s at n end of Noyo Bridge, off SR 1. 120 N Harbor Dr. (95437) Many balconies with view of river & fishing fleet. 15 refrigerators; C/CATV; movies; phones. 1 2-bedrm unit. Sauna. No pets. 6 units with wood-burning fireplace, $94 for up to 2 persons. Reserv deposit required. AE, DI, DS, MC, VI. *(See ad below)*
⊗ (D) 🅖 (707) 964-0221

Noyo River Lodge — Rates Subject to Change — *Bed & Breakfast* ◆◆
All year [CP]   1P 75.00-125.00   2P/1B 80.00-150.00   2P/2B .... 90.00   XP 15
Senior discount. 13 units. 3 blks e of SR 1 via Harbor Dr. 500 Casa del Noyo Dr. (95437) Some units overlooking river & fishing fleet. Some fireplaces & balconies. Smoke free premises. 7 C/CATV; radios; comb or shower baths. No pets. 2-night minimum stay weekends. Wkly rates avail. Reserv deposit required; 3 days refund notice. DS, MC, VI. FAX (707) 964-5368 *(See ad p A140)*
⊗ (D) (707) 964-8045

Pine Beach Inn — Rates Subject to Change — *Motor Inn* ◆◆
4/1-10/30   1P 70.00- 90.00   2P/1B 70.00- 90.00   2P/2B 70.00- 90.00   XP 10
11/1-3/31   1P 55.00- 65.00   2P/1B 55.00- 70.00   2P/2B 55.00- 70.00   XP 10
51 units. 4 mi s on SR 1. (PO Box 1173, 95437) Spacious grounds. Few units overlooking ocean. C/CATV; phones; comb or shower baths. 5 2-bedrm units. Beach; fishing; tennis-2 courts. No pets. Reserv deposit required; 3 days refund notice. AE, MC, VI. ● Restaurant; 7 am-11 & 5:30-9:30 pm, 4/1-10/15; $11-$18; cocktails.
(D) (707) 964-5603

Seabird Lodge   Rates Guaranteed   *Motel*   ◆◆
⊕ 5/1-9/30   ....   2P/1B   65.00- 80.00   2P/2B   70.00- 80.00 XP 5   F
   10/1-4/30   ....   2P/1B   55.00- 65.00   2P/2B   60.00- 70.00 XP 5   F
Senior discount. 65 units. 3/4 mi n of Noyo Bridge; 1 blk e off SR 1. 191 South St. (95437) Refrigerators; C/CATV; movies; radios; phones. Coin laundry. Htd indoor pool; whirlpool. No pets. 3 kitchens, $15 extra. Wkly rates avail. Reserv deposit required; 3 days refund notice. AE, DI, DS, MC, VI. Restaurant adjacent. FAX (707) 961-1779 *(See ad p A141)*   ⊗ Ⓢ Ⓓ (707) 964-4731

Surf Motel   Rates Subject to Change   *Motel*   ◆◆
⊕ 5/21-9/25   1P 57.00- 82.00   2P/1B   59.00- 84.00   2P/2B   63.00- 90.00 XP 6
   4/2-5/20 & 9/26-10/30 1P 44.00- 66.00 2P/1B 50.00- 70.00 2P/2B 54.00- 74.00 XP 6
   10/31-4/1   1P 40.00- 60.00   2P/1B   45.00- 60.00   2P/2B   49.00- 65.00 XP 6
54 units. 1 mi s on SR 1; s of Noyo River Bridge; 1/4 mi n of jct SR 20. (PO Box 488, 95437) Spacious landscaped grounds. 7 refrigerators; C/CATV; radios; phones; comb or shower baths. Airport transp. No pets. 2 2-bedroom studio efficiencies. Reserv deposit required; 3 days refund notice. AE, CB, DI, MC, VI. FAX (707) 964-5361 *(See ad below)*   Ⓓ (707) 964-5361

Surrey Inn   Rates Subject to Change   *Motel*   ◆
⊕ 4/16-10/15   1P   ....   46.00   2P/1B   ....   53.00   2P/2B   ....   58.00 XP 5
   10/16-4/15   1P   ....   34.00   2P/1B   ....   37.00   2P/2B   ....   42.00 XP 5
53 units. 1/2 mi s; n end of Noyo Bridge on SR 1. 888 S Main St. (95437) Some rooms with ocean view. C/CATV; phones. No pets. Reserv deposit required. AE, MC, VI. Coffeeshop adjacent.   ⊗ Ⓓ (707) 964-4003

Tradewinds Lodge   Rates Guaranteed   *Motor Inn*   ◆◆
⊕ 5/1-9/30   1P   ....   60.00   2P/1B   64.00- 74.00   2P/2B   ....   74.00 XP 8
   10/1-4/30   1P   ....   49.00   2P/1B   ....   54.00   2P/2B   ....   64.00 XP 8
92 units. 6 blks s on SR 1. 400 S Main St. (95437) Many large rooms. Check-in 3 pm. Refrigerators; C/CATV; pay movies; phones; comb or shower baths. 2 2-bedrm units. Coin laundry. Indoor pool; whirlpool. No pets. 7 units, $85-$105 for up to 6 persons. Reserv deposit required. AE, DI, DS, MC, VI. ● Restaurant; 4:30 am-midnight; $9-$15; cocktails. FAX (707) 964-0372 *(See ad below)*   ⊗ Ⓓ (707) 964-4761

RESTAURANTS

Cliff House   Steak & Seafood $$ ◆◆◆
⊕ 8 blks s on SR 1; at s end of Noyo Bridge. 1011 S Main St. Overlooking ocean & Noyo River entrance from four dining levels. Open 4 pm-9:30 pm; closed 12/24 & 12/25. Cocktails & lounge. Reserv advised. AE, DI, DS, MC, VI.
                                                                                        ⊗ (707) 961-0255

The Restaurant   American $$
2 blks n on SR 1. 418 N Main St. California cuisine. Family owned & operated since 1973. Children's menu. Open 5 pm-9 pm; Thurs & Fri 11:30 am-2 & 5-9 pm; Sun 9 am-1 & 5-9 pm; closed Wed, 11/25, 12/25 & 2/22-3/15. Beer & wine. Reserv advised. MC, VI.   ⊗ (707) 964-9800

FORTUNA — 8,800
Econo Lodge   Rates Subject to Change   *Motel*   ◆◆
⊕ All year [CP]   1P 48.00- 52.00   2P/1B   52.00- 58.00   2P/2B   58.00- 68.00 XP 6
25 units. 2 blks e of US 101, 12th St exit. 275 12th St. (95540) Formerly Fortuna Motor Lodge. C/CATV; movies; radios; phones; comb or shower baths. No pets. Reserv deposit required. AE, DI, DS, MC, VI.
                                                                            ⊗ Ⓓ Ⓖ (707) 725-6993

Fortuna Super 8   Motel   Under Construction
47 units. Exit US 101 at Kenmar exit. Alamar Way. (95540) Scheduled to open February, 1993. 10 refrigerators; A/C; C/CATV; phones. Coin laundry. AE, CB, DI, MC, VI.   ⊗ (707) 725-2888

FOSTER CITY — 28,200   (See SAN FRANCISCO (Southern Region) AREA spotting map page A444 ; see index starting on page A443)

Courtyard by Marriott 151		Rates Subject to Change					Motor Inn		◆◆◆
Sun-Thurs	1P	.... 91.00	2P/1B	.... 101.00	2P/2B	.... 101.00	XP 10		
Fri & Sat	1P	.... 69.00	2P/1B	.... 69.00	2P/2B	.... 69.00	XP		

147 units. SE of jct US 101 & SR 92, exit SR 92 at Foster City Blvd S. 550 Shell Blvd. (94404) Check-in 3 pm. A/C; C/CATV; free & pay movies; radios; phones. Coin laundry. Indoor pool; indoor whirlpool; exercise rm. Airport transp. No pets. Wkly rates avail. AE, CB, DI, MC, VI. ● Restaurant; 6:30 am-2 & 5-10 pm; $9-$13; cocktails. FAX (415) 377-1983 *(See ad p A447)*   ⊗ Ⓢ Ⓓ 🅫 (415) 377-0600

Holiday Inn-Foster City 150		Rates Subject to Change					Hotel		◆◆◆
⊛ Sun-Thurs	1P	85.00- 145.00	2P/1B	85.00- 145.00	2P/2B	95.00- 145.00	XP 10		
Fri & Sat	1P	65.00- 95.00	2P/1B	65.00- 95.00	2P/2B	65.00- 105.00	XP 10		

Senior discount. 248 units. 1 mi e of jct US 101 & SR 92; exit SR 92 at Foster City Blvd, 1/4 mi n. 1221 Chess Dr. (94404) A/C; C/CATV; movies; radios; phones. Htd pool; sauna; whirlpool. Parking ramp. Airport transp. Pets $100 deposit, $20 retained for cleaning. Reserv deposit required. AE, DS, DI, MC, VI. ● Dining rm & restaurant; 6 am-10 pm; $7-$16; cocktails. FAX (415) 570-0540   ⊗ Ⓢ Ⓓ 🅫 (415) 570-5700

RESTAURANT

Seven Ports Restaurant 73	Greek	$$	◆◆

1 mi e of San Mateo via Hillsdale Blvd; se of jct US 101 & SR 92, in Charter Square Shopping Center. 1088 C-D Shell Blvd. Charming, Mediterranean cuisine & ambiance. A/C. Children's menu. Open 5:30 pm-10 pm; closed Mon, 1/1, 11/26 & 12/25. Cocktails & lounge. Reserv advised. AE, CB, MC, VI.   ⊗ (415) 345-3010

FOUNTAIN VALLEY — 53,700

Courtyard by Marriott		Rates Subject to Change					Motor Inn		◆◆◆
All year	1P	.... 69.00	2P/1B	.... 69.00	2P/2B	.... 69.00	XP 10		F

Senior discount. 150 units. 1 blk n of I-405, exit Brookhurst St. 9950 Slater Ave. (92708) A/C; C/CATV; free & pay movies; phones. Htd pool; whirlpool; exercise rm. No pets. AE, DI, DS, MC, VI. ● Restaurant; 6:30 am-2 & 5-11 pm; $8-$13; cocktails. FAX (714) 968-0112   ⊗ Ⓢ Ⓓ (714) 968-5775

Residence Inn by Marriott		AAA Special Value Rates					Apartment Motel		◆◆◆
All year	1P	99.00- 127.00	2P/1B	99.00- 109.00	2P/2B	99.00- 127.00	XP 10		F

122 units. 1 blk n of I-405, exit Brookhurst St. 9930 Slater Ave. (92708) Studio, 1- & 2-bedroom apartments. Some with fireplace. A/C; C/CATV; movies; radios; phones. 28 2-bedrm units. Coin laundry. Htd pool; whirlpool; exercise rm. Pets, $200 deposit, minimum $50 non-refundable, also $6 daily extra charge. Wkly & monthly rates avail. Reserv deposit required. Complimentary beverages each evening. AE, DI, DS, MC, VI. Restaurant adjacent. FAX (714) 962-3439   ⊗ Ⓢ Ⓓ (714) 965-8000

FREMONT — 173,300   See also NEWARK

Best Western Thunderbird Inn		Rates Guaranteed					Motel		◆◆◆
⊛ Mon-Thurs [CP]	1P	60.00- 70.00	2P/1B	65.00- 75.00	2P/2B	65.00- 75.00	XP 10		
Fri-Sun [CP]	1P	50.00- 60.00	2P/1B	55.00- 65.00	2P/2B	55.00- 65.00	XP 5		

Senior discount. 122 units. Exit I-880 Mowry Ave E. 5400 Mowry Ave. (94538) Spacious, landscaped grounds. A/C; C/CATV; movies; radios; phones. Pool; saunas; whirlpool. No pets. Wkly & monthly rates avail. AE, DI, DS, MC, VI. Restaurant 11 am-11 pm, Sat & Sun 8 am-11 pm adjacent. $10-$20. FAX (510) 792-2643   ⊗ Ⓓ (510) 792-4300

Courtyard by Marriott		Rates Subject to Change					Motor Inn		◆◆◆
Mon-Thurs	1P	82.00- 97.00	2P/1B	92.00- 107.00	2P/2B	92.00- 107.00	XP		
Fri-Sun	1P	.... 60.00	2P/1B	.... 60.00	2P/2B	.... 60.00	XP		

Senior discount. 146 units. W of & adjacent to I-880; northbound exit Gateway Blvd, southbound exit Warren Ave. 47000 Lakeview Blvd. (94538) Attractive courtyard setting. Check-in 3 pm. A/C; C/CATV; movies; radios; phones. Coin laundry. Indoor pool; indoor whirlpool; exercise rm. No pets. Wkly rates avail. AE, DI, DS, MC, VI. ● Restaurant; 6:30 am-2 & 4-10 pm; Sat & Sun from 7 am; $7-$12; cocktails. FAX (510) 656-2441 *(See ad below)* ⊗ Ⓢ Ⓓ 🅫 (510) 656-1800

Residence Inn By Marriott		Rates Subject to Change					Suites Motel		◆◆◆
All year [CP]	1P	.... 104.00	2P/1B	.... 104.00	2P/2B	.... 134.00	XP		

Senior discount. 80 units. E of I-880, exit Mowry Ave. 5400 Farwell Pl. (94536) A/C; C/CATV; movies; radios; phones. 20 2-bedrm units, kitchens. Coin laundry. Pool; whirlpool; sports court. Airport transp. Pets, $75 extra charge. 1- & 2-bedroom units, some with fireplace. Wkly & monthly rates avail. Reserv deposit required. Complimentary beverages each evening. AE, DI, DS, MC, VI. Restaurant adjacent. FAX (510) 793-6687   ⊗ Ⓓ (510) 794-5900

FRESNO — 354,200

Best Western Parkside Inn Motel Rates Subject to Change *Motel* ◆◆
5/1-9/30   1P 46.00- 52.00 2P/1B 50.00- 56.00 2P/2B 52.00- 60.00 XP 4   F
10/1-4/30 1P 44.00- 48.00 2P/1B 48.00- 52.00 2P/2B 50.00- 54.00 XP 4   F
Senior discount. 48 units. 2 1/2 mi nw; exit SR 99 Frwy via Olive Ave. 1415 W Olive Ave. (93728) 25 refrigerators; A/C; C/CATV; radios; phones. Coin laundry. Pool; wading pool; whirlpool. No pets. Reserv deposit required. AE, DI, DS, MC, VI. Restaurant adjacent. FAX (209) 264-9304 *(See ad p A143)*   ⊗ Ⓓ (209) 237-2086

Best Western Tradewinds Motor Inn Rates Subject to Change *Motel* ◆◆◆
6/1-10/31 1P 45.00- 56.00 2P/1B 49.00- 59.00 2P/2B 49.00- 59.00 XP 5   F
11/1-5/31 1P 42.00- 50.00 2P/1B 45.00- 55.00 2P/2B 45.00- 55.00 XP 5   F
110 units. 3 1/2 mi nw; w of SR 99, Clinton Ave exit. 2141 N Parkway Dr. (93705) Spacious landscaped courtyard. A/C; C/CATV; radios; phones; comb or shower baths. Pool; whirlpool. AE, DI, DS, MC, VI. Restaurant adjacent. Cocktails. FAX (209) 237-9719   ⊗ Ⓓ (209) 237-1881

Best Western Village Inn Rates Subject to Change *Motel* ◆◆◆
All year [CP] 1P 50.00- 56.00 2P/1B 54.00- 60.00 2P/2B 56.00- 62.00 XP 3   F
Senior discount. 153 units. Northbound SR 99 exit SR 41, 2 3/4 mi n exit Shields Ave; southbound exit Clinton Ave. 3110 N Blackstone Ave. (93703) Some small rooms. A/C; C/CATV; pay movies; 50 radios; phones. Pool; whirlpool. No pets. AE, CB, DS, MC, VI. Coffeeshop adjacent. FAX (209) 226-0539 *(See ad below)*   ⊗ Ⓓ (209) 226-2110

Best Western Water Tree Inn Rates Subject to Change *Motel* ◆◆◆
All year 1P 52.00- 60.00 2P/1B 58.00- 64.00 2P/2B 58.00- 64.00 XP 4   F
Senior discount. 136 units. 3 3/4 mi n on SR 41; SR 99 Frwy, Ashlan Ave exit. 4141 N Blackstone Ave. (93726) Refrigerators; A/C; C/CATV; pay movies; VCPs. Radios; phones; comb or shower baths. Pool. No pets. Reserv deposit required. AE, DI, DS, MC, VI. Coffeeshop adjacent. FAX (209) 226-4589 *(See ad below)*   ⊗ Ⓓ (209) 222-4445

Brooks Ranch Inn Rates Subject to Change *Motel* ◆
All year 1P 28.95- 34.95 2P/1B 32.95- 38.95 2P/2B 34.95- 42.95 XP 5
120 units. 6 mi nw; 1/2 blk w off SR 99 Frwy. 4278 W Ashlan Ave. (93722) A/C; C/CATV; phones. Coin laundry. Pool. Pets, $5 extra charge. AE, MC, VI. Restaurant adjacent.   ⊗ Ⓓ (209) 275-2727

Chateau by Piccadilly Inn Rates Subject to Change *Motel* ◆◆
All year 1P 45.00- 55.00 2P/1B 52.00- 62.00 2P/2B 58.00- 68.00 XP 10   F
78 units. 5 mi ne; exit SR 99 via McKinley, 6 mi e. 5113 E McKinley. (93727) Check-in 3 pm. 20 refrigerators; A/C; C/TV; pay movies; radios; phones; shower or comb baths. Small pool. Airport transp. No pets. Monthly rates avail. Reserv deposit required. AE, DI, DS, MC, VI. Coffeeshop adjacent. FAX (209) 456-1418   ⊗ ⓈⒹⒼ (209) 456-1418

Courtyard by Marriott Rates Subject to Change *Motor Inn* ◆◆◆
Sun-Thurs 1P .... 75.00 2P/1B .... 85.00 2P/2B .... 85.00 XP
Fri & Sat   1P .... 68.00 2P/1B .... 68.00 2P/2B .... 68.00 XP
146 units. 4 1/2 mi n on SR 168; SR 99 Frwy exit Shaw Ave E. 140 E Shaw Ave. (93710) Check-in 4 pm. A/C; C/CATV; pay movies; radios; phones. Coin laundry. Pool; whirlpool; exercise rm. No pets. Maximum rates for up to 4 persons. AE, DI, DS, MC, VI. ● Dining rm; 6:30 am-2 & 5-10 pm; $8-$13; cocktails. FAX (209) 221-0368 *(See ad below)*   ⊗ ⓈⒹⒼ (209) 221-6000

Econo Lodge Rates Subject to Change *Motel* ◆
All year 1P .... 40.00 2P/1B .... 45.00 2P/2B .... 50.00 XP 6
56 units. 1 blk w of SR 99, Olive Ave exit. 1804 W Olive Ave. (93728) Many large rooms. Check-in 3 pm. A/C; C/CATV; phones. No pets. Reserv deposit required; 7 days refund notice. AE, DS, MC, VI.   ⊗ ⓈⒹ (209) 442-1082

Fresno Hilton — Rates Subject to Change — *Hotel* ◆◆◆
All year — 1P 65.00-119.00 — 2P/1B 72.00-119.00 — 2P/2B 74.00-119.00 XP 10 F
Senior discount. 192 units. Southbound exit SR 99, Ventura St, 3/4 mi s to Van Ness Ave, then 4 blks n; northbound exit SR 41, then Van Ness Ave. 1055 Van Ness Ave. (93721) Check-in 3 pm. 10 refrigerators; A/C; C/CATV; movies; radios; phones. Pool; whirlpool. Garage. Airport transp. Pets, $15 extra charge. AE, CB, DI, MC, VI. ● Dining rm & coffeeshop; 6:30 am-10 pm; $10-$18; cocktails. FAX (209) 485-7666 *(See ad p 22)* ⊗ Ⓢ Ⓓ Ⓛ (209) 485-9000

Hampton Inn — Rates Guaranteed — *Motel* ◆◆
All year [CP] — 1P 59.00-67.00 — 2P/1B 67.00-75.00 — 2P/2B 67.00-75.00 XP F
Senior discount. 118 units. 5 mi ne; exit SR 99 via McKinley, 6 mi e. 1551 N Peach Ave. (93727) A/C; C/CATV; free & pay movies; radios; phones. Coin laundry. Pool; exercise rm. Airport transp. No pets. Maximum rates for up to 5 persons. Wkly rates avail. Reserv deposit required. AE, DI, DS, MC, VI. FAX (209) 454-0552 ⊗ Ⓢ Ⓓ Ⓛ (209) 251-5200

Holiday Inn-Airport — AAA Special Value Rates — *Motor Inn* ◆◆◆
All year — 1P 76.00-105.00 — 2P/1B 76.00-105.00 — 2P/2B 76.00-92.00 XP 8 F
Senior discount. 210 units. 5 mi ne; exit SR 99 Frwy via Clinton Ave, then 6 mi e. 5090 E Clinton Ave. (93727) Check-in 3 pm. A/C; C/CATV; pay movies; radios; phones. Coin laundry. 2 htd pools; 1 indoor; sauna; indoor whirlpool; putting green. Airport transp. Pets. Wkly & monthly rates avail. AE, DI, DS, MC, VI. ● Restaurant; 6 am-10:30 pm; $8-$18; cocktails. FAX (209) 456-8243 ⊗ Ⓓ (209) 252-3611

Holiday Inn Centre Plaza — Rates Subject to Change — *Hotel* ◆◆◆
All year — 1P 72.00-78.00 — 2P/1B .... 86.00 — 2P/2B .... 80.00 XP 8
Senior discount. 320 units. E of SR 99, by Convention Center; northbound exit via SR 41 & Van Ness Ave, southbound via Ventura St. 2233 Ventura St. (93709) Check-in 3 pm. 37 refrigerators; A/C; C/CATV; pay movies; radios; phones. Indoor pool; saunas; whirlpool; fitness center. Parking ramp & parking lot. Airport transp. Pets. Monthly rates avail. Reserv deposit required. AE, DI, DS, MC, VI. ● Restaurant & coffeeshop; 6 am-10 pm; $8-$19; cocktails. FAX (209) 486-6625 ⊗ Ⓢ Ⓓ Ⓛ (209) 268-1000

Howard Johnson Hotel — Rates Subject to Change — *Motel* ◆◆
4/1-10/31 — 1P .... 42.00 — 2P/1B .... 48.00 — 2P/2B .... 48.00 XP 6 F
1/1-3/31 — 1P .... 36.00 — 2P/1B .... 42.00 — 2P/2B .... 42.00 XP 6 F
11/1-12/31 — 1P .... 36.00 — 2P/1B .... 40.00 — 2P/2B .... 40.00 XP 6 F
Senior discount. 115 units. 3 1/2 mi n on SR 41; exit SR 99 via Ashlan Ave. 4061 N Blackstone. (93726) A/C; C/CATV; movies; radios; phones. Pool. Pets, $25 deposit required. AE, MC, VI. Coffeeshop adjacent. Cocktails. FAX (209) 225-0144 ⊗ Ⓓ (209) 222-5641

La Quinta Motor Inn — Rates Subject to Change — *Motel* ◆◆◆
⊛ All year — 1P 50.00-57.00 — 2P/1B 58.00-65.00 — 2P/2B .... 58.00 XP 5 F
130 units. E of SR 99; southbound exit Fresno St, northbound exit SR 41, n to Tulare St exit. 2926 Tulare St. (93721) Check-in 3 pm. A/C; C/CATV; free & pay movies; radios; phones. Pool. Airport transp. Reserv deposit required. AE, DI, DS, MC, VI. Restaurant adjacent. FAX (209) 237-0415 ⊗ Ⓢ Ⓓ Ⓛ (209) 442-1110

Phoenix Lodge — Rates Subject to Change — *Motel* ◆
⊛ All year — 1P .... 25.00 — 2P/1B .... 29.00 — 2P/2B .... 33.00 XP 4
116 units. 3 1/2 mi nw; exit SR 99, at Clinton Ave. 2345 N Parkway Dr. (93705) A/C; C/CATV; 25 radios; phones; comb or shower baths. Coin laundry. Pool. Pets, $4 extra charge. Wkly rates avail. AE, MC, VI. Coffeeshop adjacent. FAX (209) 485-3268 *(See ad below)* Ⓓ (209) 268-0711

Piccadilly Inn Airport — Rates Subject to Change — *Motor Inn* ◆◆◆
⊛ Mon-Thurs — 1P .... 82.00 — 2P/1B .... 89.00 — 2P/2B .... 89.00 XP 10 F
Fri-Sun — 1P .... 65.00 — 2P/1B .... 70.00 — 2P/2B .... 70.00 XP 10 F
Senior discount. 185 units. 5 mi ne; exit SR 99 via McKinley, 6 mi e. 5115 E McKinley. (93727) Check-in 3 pm. 44 refrigerators; A/C; C/CATV; pay movies; radios; phones. Coin laundry. Pool; whirlpool; exercise rm. Airport transp. No pets. Wkly & monthly rates avail. AE, DI, DS, MC, VI. ● Restaurant & coffeeshop; 6 am-10 pm; $7-$15. FAX (209) 251-6956 ⊗ Ⓓ (209) 251-6000

Piccadilly Inn-Shaw   Rates Subject to Change   *Motor Inn* ◆◆◆◆
| ⑳ | Mon-Thurs | 1P | .... | 82.00 | 2P/1B | .... | 89.00 | 2P/2B | .... | 89.00 | XP 10 | F |
| | Fri-Sun | 1P | .... | 65.00 | 2P/1B | .... | 70.00 | 2P/2B | .... | 70.00 | XP 10 | F |

Senior discount. 196 units. 5 1/2 mi nw; 3 mi e off SR 99 Frwy exit Shaw Ave. 2305 W Shaw Ave. (93711) Quiet location. Spacious grounds. Check-in 3 pm. 145 refrigerators; A/C; C/CATV; pay movies; radios; phones. Coin laundry. Pool; whirlpool; exercise rm. Airport transp. No pets. [MAP] avail. Wkly & monthly rates avail. AE, DI, DS, MC, VI. ● Restaurant; 6 am-2 & 5-10 pm; $10-$20; cocktails. FAX (209) 226-2448 ⊗ Ⓓ Ⓢ (209) 226-3850

Piccadilly Inn-University   Rates Subject to Change   *Motel* ◆◆◆◆
| ⑳ | Mon-Thurs | 1P | .... | 82.00 | 2P/1B | .... | 89.00 | 2P/2B | .... | 89.00 | XP 10 | F |
| | Fri-Sun | 1P | .... | 65.00 | 2P/1B | .... | 70.00 | 2P/2B | .... | 70.00 | XP 10 | F |

Senior discount. 190 units. 7 1/2 mi N; 3 mi e of SR 99, Shaw Ave exit. 4961 N Cedar Ave. (93726) Large rooms. Check-in 3 pm. 60 refrigerators; A/C; C/CATV; pay movies; radios; phones. Coin laundry. Pool; whirlpool; exercise rm. Valet parking lot. Airport transp. No pets. Wkly & monthly rates avail. Reserv deposit required. AE, DI, DS, MC, VI. Breakfast 6:30-11 am; restaurant adjacent; cocktail lounge. FAX (209) 227-2382 ⊗ Ⓢ Ⓓ Ⓢ (209) 224-4200

Ramada Inn   Rates Guaranteed   *Motor Inn* ◆◆◆
| ⑳ | All year | 1P | .... | 55.00 | 2P/1B | .... | 60.00 | 2P/2B | .... | 60.00 | XP 6 | F |

Senior discount. 167 units. 4 3/4 mi n on SR 168; SR 99 Frwy exit Shaw Ave. 324 E Shaw Ave. (93710) Check-in 3 pm. A/C; C/CATV; movies; radios; phones. Pool; whirlpool. Airport transp. No pets. AE, DI, DS, MC, VI. ● Dining rm & coffeeshop; 6:30 am-1:30 & 5-10 pm; Sun-9 pm; $11-$15; cocktails. FAX (209) 222-4017 *(See ad p A145)* ⊗ Ⓓ (209) 224-4040

The San Joaquin   Rates Subject to Change   *Suites Motel* ◆◆◆◆
| ⑳ | All year [CP] | 1P 70.00- 115.00 | 2P/1B | 70.00- 115.00 | 2P/2B | 85.00- 140.00 | XP 10 |

68 units. 5 1/4 mi nw; 3 1/2 mi e of SR 99, Shaw Ave exit. 1309 W Shaw Ave. (93711) Attractive landscaped grounds. Refrigerators; A/C; C/CATV; pay movies; radios; phones; comb or shower baths. 8 2-bedrm units, 18 kitchens. Pool; whirlpool. Airport transp. No pets. 40 units with microwaves. Wkly & monthly rates avail. AE, DS, MC, VI. FAX (209) 225-6021 ⊗ Ⓢ Ⓓ (209) 225-1309

Sheraton Smugglers Inn   Rates Subject to Change   *Motel* ◆◆◆◆
| ⑳ | All year | 1P 75.00- 90.00 | 2P/1B | 80.00- 100.00 | 2P/2B | 80.00- 100.00 | XP 5 | F |

Senior discount. 205 units. 3 1/4 mi on SR 41; southbound SR 99 Frwy exit Shaw Ave, northbound exit Clinton Ave. 3737 N Blackstone Ave. (93726) Very nicely landscaped grounds. Some patios. Check-in 3 pm. 185 refrigerators; A/C; C/CATV; pay movies; radios; phones. Coin laundry. Pool; whirlpool; exercise rm. Airport transp. No pets. AE, DI, DS, MC, VI. Restaurant adjacent. FAX (209) 222-7147 *(See ad p A145)* ⊗ Ⓢ Ⓓ (209) 226-2200

RESTAURANTS

Nicola's   Italian $$ ◆◆◆
4 blks w of SR 41 Frwy; Shields Ave exit. 3075 N Maroa Ave. Also seafood entrees; stuffed steak & pasta house specialty. A/C. Open 11:30 am-4 & 5:30-10 pm; Fri-11:30 pm; Sat 5 pm-11 pm; Sun 4 pm-9:30 pm; closed major holidays. Cocktails & lounge. Minimum, $6. Reserv advised. AE, CB, DI, MC, VI. ⊗ Ⓢ (209) 224-1660

Piccadilly Cafeteria   American $
At West St. 2066 W Shaw Ave. A/C. Open 11 am-8:30 pm; closed 12/25. AE, DS, MC, VI. ⊗ (209) 438-6462

Reuben's   Steak & Seafood $$$ ◆◆
On SR 168; at Fashion Fair Mall. 575 E Shaw Ave. Casual atmosphere. A/C. Early bird specials; children's menu. Open 11:30 am-3 & 5-9:30 pm; Fri & Sat-10:30 pm; Sun 10 am-2 & 4:30-9 pm. Cocktails & lounge. Entertainment. Reserv advised. AE, CB, DI, MC, VI. ⊗ Ⓢ (209) 222-6911

FULLERTON — 114,100

Fullerton Inn   Rates Guaranteed   *Motel* ◆◆
| ⑳ | All year | 1P 35.00- 40.00 | 2P/1B | 35.00- 40.00 | 2P/2B | 40.00- 45.00 | XP 4 |

43 units. 1/4 mi ne of SR 91, Riverside Frwy, exit Magnolia Ave. 2601 W Orangethorpe Ave. (92633) A/C; C/CATV; movies; phones. Coin laundry. Small htd pool; whirlpool. No pets. Refrigerators & microwaves avail. Wkly rates avail. Reserv deposit required. AE, DS, MC, VI. Ⓓ Ⓢ (714) 773-4900

Fullerton Marriott Hotel at California State University   Rates Subject to Change   *Motor Inn* ◆◆◆
| ⑳ | All year | 1P | .... | 79.00 | 2P/1B | .... | 79.00 | 2P/2B | .... | 89.00 | XP |

Senior discount. 225 units. Adjacent w side of SR 57; exit Nutwood Ave. 2701 E Nutwood Ave. (92631) Check-in 4 pm. 15 refrigerators; A/C; C/CATV; free & pay movies; radios; phones. Htd pool; saunas; whirlpool; exercise rm. Garage & parking lot. Small pets only. AE, DI, DS, MC, VI. ● Restaurant; 6:30 am-10 pm; $7-$12; cocktails. FAX (714) 738-0288 ⊗ Ⓢ Ⓓ Ⓢ (714) 738-7800

Heritage Inn   Rates Subject to Change   *Motel* ◆◆◆
| ⑳ | All year [CP] | 1P | .... | 56.00 | 2P/1B | .... | 60.00 | 2P/2B | .... | 63.00 | XP 6 | F |

Senior discount. 124 units. On SR 90, 1 blk e of Harbor Blvd. 333 E Imperial Hwy. (92635) Check-in 3 pm. Refrigerators; A/C; C/CATV; free & pay movies; radios; phones. Coin laundry. Htd pool; whirlpool; exercise rm. No pets. 4 suites & 10 large rooms with refrigerator & microwave, $80-$95 for up to 2 persons. Reserv deposit required. AE, DI, DS, MC, VI. FAX (714) 773-0685 ⊗ Ⓢ Ⓓ Ⓢ (714) 447-9200

Holiday Inn-Fullerton   AAA Special Value Rates   *Motor Inn* ◆◆◆
| ⑳ | All year | 1P 80.00- 90.00 | 2P/1B | 90.00- 100.00 | 2P/2B | 90.00- 100.00 | XP 10 | F |

289 units. Adjacent to SR 91, exit Harbor Blvd, Fullerton. 222 W Houston Ave. (92632) Check-in 3 pm. A/C; C/CATV; free & pay movies; radios; phones. Coin laundry. Htd pool; wading pool; exercise rm. Pets. Wkly rates avail. Reserv deposit required; 3 days refund notice. AE, DI, DS, MC, VI. ● Dining rm; 6 am-10 pm; $6.50-$15; cocktails. FAX (714) 992-4843 ⊗ Ⓓ Ⓢ (714) 992-1700

Radisson Suite Hotel Fullerton   Rates Subject to Change   *Motel* ◆◆◆
| ⑳ | All year [CP] | 1P 89.00- 149.00 | 2P/1B | 99.00- 149.00 | 2P/2B | 99.00- 149.00 | XP 10 |

Senior discount. 96 units. Adjacent to e side of SR 57; exit Nutwood Ave. 2932 E Nutwood Ave. (92631) Check-in 3 pm. Refrigerators; A/C; C/CATV; free & pay movies; radios; phones. Coin laundry. Small htd pool; all rooms with whirlpool; exercise rm. Garage, ramp & parking lot. No pets. Wkly & monthly rates avail. Complimentary beverages each evening. AE, DI, DS, MC, VI. Restaurant adjacent. FAX (714) 528-7945 ⊗ Ⓢ Ⓓ (714) 579-7400

RESTAURANTS

The Cellar   French $$$ ◆◆◆◆
1 1/4 mi n of SR 91, exit Harbor Blvd; in Villa Del Sol Shopping Plaza. 305 N Harbor Blvd. Refined atmosphere. Expertly prepared cuisine. A/C. Open 6 pm-11 pm; Fri & Sat-midnight; closed Sun, Mon & major holidays. Cocktails & lounge. Reserv advised. AE, DI, DS, MC, VI. ⊗ (714) 525-5682

The Old Spaghetti Factory   Italian $ ◆
   Adjacent to Amtrak station. 110 E Santa Fe. Uniquely decorated informal restaurant serving spaghetti with a variety of
   sauces. A/C. Children's menu. Open 11:30 am-2 & 5-10 pm; Fri-10:30 pm; Sat 5 pm-10:30 pm; Sun 4 pm-10 pm; closed
   11/25, 12/24 & 12/25. Cocktails & lounge. MC, VI.   ⊗ (714) 526-6801

GARBERVILLE — 1,000   See also MIRANDA
Benbow Inn   **Rates Subject to Change**   *Historic Country Inn*   ◆◆◆◆
🐘 4/15-11/26 & 12/20-1/2   1P 88.00- 145.00   2P/1B   88.00- 145.00   2P/2B   88.00- 145.00 XP 15
   Senior discount. 55 units. 2 mi s on US 101, opposite Benbow Lake State Recreation Area, on Eel River. 445 Lake
   Benbow Dr. (95542) OPEN 4/15-11/26 & 12/20-1/2. Tudor English Inn design. 3-story, no elevator. Afternoon tea &
   scones. Designated as a national historic landmark. 22 refrigerators; A/C; 18 C/CATV; comb or shower baths.
   Pool; whirlpool. Pets. 3 units with fireplace, $190-$260. Large garden unit with fireplace, whirlpool tub & VCP for
   2 persons $260. Reserv deposit required; 5 days refund notice. MC, VI. ● Dining rm, see separate listing. *(See
   ad below)*   Ⓢ Ⓓ (707) 923-2124

BENBOW INN

Set in the midst of the giant redwoods just 200 miles
north of San Francisco, the fabled Benbow Inn is one
of the last of the true English carriage house inns in
North America. The aura and comfort of old English
tradition seeps throughout this historical establishment
from its exquisitely decorated rooms with fine antiques,
some having fireplaces, to the many lush gardens that
surround the inn. It also has a world class dining
room serving 3 meals daily offering fine American/
Continental cuisine and a cocktail lounge. Golf and
horseback riding are nearby with swimming and
boating on the lake and river right on the grounds.

🦃🦃🦃🦃

for reservations: (707) 923-2124
445 Lake Benbow Drive, Garberville, CA 95440
(on Hwy. 101, 2 mi. South of Garberville)

A National
Historical Landmark

IN AAA LISTINGS, "WEEKENDS" MEANS FRIDAY AND SATURDAY NIGHTS.

Best Western Humboldt House Inn   Rates Subject to Change   *Motel* ◆◆◆

5/10-10/31 [CP]	1P	66.00-	79.00	2P/1B	66.00-	79.00	2P/2B	69.00- 77.00 XP 5
11/1-5/9 [CP]	1P	52.00-	59.00	2P/1B	57.00-	65.00	2P/2B	60.00- 68.00 XP 5

75 units. US 101 1st exit. 701 Redwood Dr. (95542) Many rooms with balcony or patio. Check-in 3 pm. 38 refrigerators; A/C; C/CATV; movies; phones. 6 2-bedrm units, 2 kitchens. Coin laundry. Pool; whirlpool. 37 deluxe rooms with refrigerator, $5 extra. Reserv deposit required. AE, DI, DS, MC, VI. Restaurant opposite. FAX (707) 923-4259 *(See ad p A147)*   ⊗ Ⓓ 🛇 (707) 923-2771

Dean Creek Resort   Rates Subject to Change   *Motel* ◆◆

7/1-9/30	1P	....	48.00	2P/1B	....	55.50	2P/2B	.... 57.50 XP 15

Senior discount. 11 units. 3 mi n, exit US 101 Redway. 4112 Redwood Dr. (PO Box 157, Redway, 95560) OPEN ALL YEAR. A/C; C/CATV; 10 radios; phones; shower or comb baths. Coin laundry. Pool; sauna; whirlpool. No pets. 5 efficiencies, $60-$72.50 for up to 2 persons. Wkly rates avail. Reserv deposit required. MC, VI.   ⊗ Ⓓ 🛇 (707) 923-2555

Motel Garberville   Rates Subject to Change   *Motel* ◆◆

5/1-10/31	1P	40.00-	44.00	2P/1B	44.00-	48.00	2P/2B	48.00- 54.00 XP 6
10/15-4/30	1P	36.00-	40.00	2P/1B	38.00-	44.00	2P/2B	40.00- 48.00 XP 6

30 units. On US 101 business rt. 948 Redwood Dr. (95542) A/C; C/CATV; movies; phones; comb or shower baths. 1 2-bedrm unit, 1 kitchen. Reserv deposit required. AE, DI, DS, MC, VI. Restaurant adjacent. *(See ad below)*   ⊗ Ⓓ 🛇 (707) 923-2422

Rancho Motel   Rates Subject to Change   *Motel* ◆

5/22-9/30	1P	36.00-	58.00	2P/1B	40.00-	58.00	2P/2B	42.00- 62.00 XP 6
10/1-5/21	1P	30.00-	34.00	2P/1B	34.00-	38.00	2P/2B	36.00- 40.00 XP 4

22 units. On US 101 business rt. 987 Redwood Dr. (95542) A/C; C/CATV; movies; 12 radios; phones; shower or comb baths. 2 2-bedrm units. Pool. No pets. Reserv deposit required. AE, CB, DI, MC, VI. ⊗ Ⓓ (707) 923-2451

Sherwood Forest Motel   Rates Subject to Change   *Motel* ◆◆

5/1-10/31	1P	....	50.00	2P/1B	....	50.00	2P/2B	.... 54.00 XP 6
11/1-4/30	1P	....	46.00	2P/1B	....	46.00	2P/2B	.... 50.00 XP 6

33 units. North & southbound US 101 1st exit. 814 Redwood Dr. (95542) A/C; C/CATV; movies; radios; phones; comb or shower baths. 2 2-bedrm units. Coin laundry. Pool; whirlpool. 2 kitchens, $15 extra. 18 rooms with microwave & refrigerator. Reserv deposit required. AE, MC, VI. Coffeeshop opposite. FAX (707) 923-3677   ⊗ Ⓓ (707) 923-2721

RESTAURANT

Benbow Inn Dining Room   American $$$ ◆◆◆

In Benbow Inn. Pleasant dining. Patio service in summer. Smoke free premises in dining room. Varied menu, fresh local ingredients. Listed as a National Historic landmark. Open 8 am-11, noon-1 & 6-9 pm; Sun 10 am-1 & 6-9 pm; closed 1/2-4/15, 12/1-12/20 & for lunch 9/16-6/14. Cocktails & lounge. Reserv required. MC, VI. *(See ad p A147)*   ⊗ (707) 923-2125

GARDENA — 49,800

Days Inn   AAA Special Value Rates   *Motel* ◆◆

All year	1P	45.00-	50.00	2P/1B	50.00-	55.00	2P/2B	.... 50.00 XP 5 F

40 units. 1/4 mi s of Redondo Beach Blvd. 16427 Western Ave. (90247) 7 refrigerators; A/C; C/CATV; movies; radios; phones. 15 rooms with whirlpool bath. Garage. No pets. Wkly rates avail. Reserv deposit required. AE, DI, DS, MC, VI. FAX (310) 532-3285   ⊗ Ⓢ Ⓓ (310) 329-1188

Premier Residential Suites   Rates Guaranteed   *Motel* ◆◆

All year [CP]	1P	39.00-	55.00	2P/1B	39.00-	55.00	2P/2B	.... 79.00 XP 10

40 units. 1 blk n of I-405: exit Normandie Ave. 18600 S Normandie Ave. (90248) 24 units with gas fireplace. Refrigerators; A/C; C/CATV; movies; radios; phones. 10 2-bedrm units, 26 kitchens, 10 efficiencies. Coin laundry. Garage. No pets. 10 loft units. Monthly rates avail. AE, MC, VI. FAX (310) 532-6704   Ⓓ (310) 532-8200

RESTAURANT

Paradise Restaurant   American $$ ◆◆

At Vermont Ave. 889 W 190th St. Popular; decorated in oasis theme. Sun brunch, 10 am-2 pm. A/C. Open 11 am-2:30 & 5-10 pm; Sat 5 pm-11 pm; Sun 10 am-2 & 5-9 pm. Cocktails & lounge. AE, DI, MO, VI.   ⓂⒸ (310) 324-1900

GARDEN GROVE — 143,100

Best Western Plaza International Inn — Rates Subject to Change — Motel ◆◆
5/28-9/30	1P	....	46.00	2P/1B	48.00-	50.00	2P/2B	....	48.00	XP 5	F
10/1-5/27	1P	....	40.00	2P/1B	44.00-	50.00	2P/2B	....	44.00	XP 5	F

101 units. Adjacent to SR 22, n of jct SR 39 Beach Blvd. 7912 Garden Grove Blvd. (92641) Formerly Royal Plaza International Inn. 50 refrigerators; A/C; C/CATV; movies; radios; phones. Htd pool; saunas. No pets. AE, DI, MC, VI. Restaurant adjacent. ⊗ ⓓ (714) 894-7568

Ramada Inn — Rates Subject to Change — Hotel ◆◆◆
All year	1P	....	59.00	2P/1B	....	69.00	2P/2B	....	69.00	XP

116 units. From SR 22 Freeway exit Brookhurst St, 1/2 mi n, then 1 blk w. 10022 Garden Grove Blvd. (92644) A/C; C/CATV; movies; radios; phones. Small htd pool; whirlpool. Garage & parking lot. No pets. Reserv deposit required. AE, MC, VI. ● Dining rm; 7 am-midnight; Sun-10 pm; $8-$15; cocktails. FAX (714) 539-9930 ⊗ ⓢⓓ⧉ (714) 534-1818

RESTAURANT

Mimi's Cafe — American — $ — ◆◆
On SR 39; 1 blk n of SR 22. 7955 Garden Grove Blvd at Beach Blvd. Delightful restaurant with decor of a French cafe. Nice selection of salads, sandwiches & entrees. A/C. Children's menu. Open 7 am-11 pm; closed 11/25 & 12/25. Beer & wine. AE, MC, VI. ⊗ (714) 898-5042

GILROY — 31,500

Best Western Inn — Rates Subject to Change — Motel ◆◆◆
5/1-9/30	1P 48.50-	58.50	2P/1B	52.50-	62.50	2P/2B	....	64.50	XP 8
10/1-4/30	1P 42.50-	52.50	2P/1B	48.50-	58.50	2P/2B	....	58.50	XP 8

Senior discount. 42 units. Exit 101 Leavesley Rd, 1/4 mi w. 360 Leavesley Rd. (95020) Refrigerators; A/C; C/CATV; pay movies; phones; comb or shower baths. 2 2-bedrm units. Coin laundry. Small pool; whirlpool. Pets. Reserv deposit required; 3 days refund notice. AE, DI, DS, MC, VI. Coffeeshop opposite. FAX (408) 848-1424 ⊗ ⓢⓓ⧉ (408) 848-1467

Forest Park Inn — Rates Subject to Change — Motel ◆◆◆
All year	1P	....	38.00	2P/1B	....	50.00	2P/2B	....	50.00	XP

Senior discount. 77 units. Northwest corner of US 101, exit Leavesley Rd. 375 Leavesley Rd. (95020) 21 refrigerators; A/C; C/CATV; pay movies; radios; phones. 3 2-bedrm units. Coin laundry. Small htd pool; sauna; whirlpool. No pets. 3 rooms with whirlpool bath & 10 rooms with gas fireplace, $10-$20 extra. Wkly & monthly rates avail. Reserv deposit required; 7 days refund notice. AE, CB, DI, MC, VI. Coffeeshop adjacent. FAX (408) 848-1138 ⊗ ⓢⓓ⧉ (408) 848-5144

Leavesley Inn — Rates Subject to Change — Motel ◆◆
All year [CP]	1P	....	38.00	2P/1B	....	45.00	2P/2B	....	50.00	XP 5

Senior discount. 48 units. W of US 101; Leavesley Rd exit. 8430 Murray Ave. (95020) Refrigerators; A/C; C/CATV; radios; phones. Coin laundry. Small pool; whirlpool. Pets, $10 deposit required. Reserv deposit required. AE, CB, DI, MC, VI. Restaurant adjacent. FAX (408) 847-2241 *(See ad below)* ⊗ ⓢⓓ⧉ (408) 847-5500

SunRest Inn — Rates Subject to Change — Motel ◆◆◆
All year [CP]	....	2P/1B	42.50-	62.50	2P/2B	48.50-	68.50	XP 8

65 units. W of US 101, exit SR 152. 8292 Murray Ave. (95020) Refrigerators; A/C; C/CATV; pay movies; radios; phones. Coin laundry. Pool; sauna; whirlpool; exercise rm. 2 units with whirlpool bath, $65-$125 for 2 persons. Reserv deposit required; 3 days refund notice. AE, DI, DS, MC, VI. FAX (408) 848-1569 ⊗ ⓢⓓ⧉ (408) 848-3500

AAA restaurant expertise
saves you time and costly explorations.

Super 8 Motel
Rates Subject to Change   *Motel*   ◆
🏵 All year   1P .... 39.88 2P/1B .... 43.88 2P/2B .... 47.88 XP 4
Senior discount. 53 units. E of & adjacent to US 101, Leavesley Rd exit. 8435 San Ysidro. (95020) A/C; C/CATV;
pay movies; radios; phones. Pool. Pets, $30 deposit required. Wkly & monthly rates avail. Reserv deposit re-
quired. AE, DI, DS, MC, VI. Coffeeshop opposite. FAX (408) 848-2651   ⊗ Ⓢ Ⓓ Ⓑ (408) 848-4108

**GLENDALE — 180,000   (See PASADENA & VICINITY AREA spotting map page A327; see index
starting on page A326)**

Best Western Eagle Rock Inn 32
Rates Subject to Change   *Motel*   ◆◆
🏵 All year [CP]   1P 55.00- 60.00 2P/1B   55.00- 60.00 2P/2B 65.00- 70.00 XP 10
50 units. 3 blks e of Verdugo Rd. 2911 Colorado St. (Los Angeles, 90041) Refrigerators; A/C; C/CATV; movies;
VCPs. Phones. Whirlpool; small heated pool 4/16-10/31; 4 rooms with whirlpool tub. No pets. AE, DI, DS, MC, VI.
FAX (213) 255-6750 *(See ad p A151)*   ⊗ Ⓓ Ⓑ (213) 256-7711

Best Western Golden Key Motor Hotel 35
AAA Special Value Rates   *Motel*   ◆◆◆
🏵 All year [CP]   1P 79.00- 105.00 2P/1B   84.00- 110.00 2P/2B 89.00- 120.00 XP 5
55 units. 1 mi s of SR 134, Brand Blvd exit. 123 W Colorado St. (91204) A/C; C/CATV; movies; VCPs. Radios;
phones. Htd pool; whirlpool. No pets. Microwave & refrigerator. AE, DI, DS, MC, VI. Coffeeshop opposite.
FAX (818) 545-9393 *(See ad p A237)*   ⊗ Ⓓ Ⓑ (818) 247-0111

Chariot Inn Motel 33
Rates Subject to Change   *Motel*   ◆
🏵 All year [CP]   1P 45.00- 50.00 2P/1B   45.00- 50.00 2P/2B 55.00- 60.00 XP 4
Senior discount. 31 units. 1 1/2 mi se of SR 134, exit Glendale Ave. 1118 E Colorado Blvd. (91205) Refrigerators;
A/C; C/CATV; movies; radios; phones. Whirlpool; 4 rooms with whirlpool. No pets. Reserv deposit required. AE,
DI, DS, MC, VI. *(See ad below)*   ⊗ Ⓓ Ⓑ (818) 507-9600

Econo Lodge 30
Rates Guaranteed   *Motel*   ◆
🏵 All year [CP]   1P 45.00- 50.00 2P/1B   45.00- 50.00 2P/2B 50.00- 60.00 XP 5
Senior discount. 30 units. 3/4 blk e of Verdugo Rd. 1437 E Colorado St. (91205) Refrigerators; A/C; C/CATV;
movies; radios; phones. Small pool; whirlpool. No pets. 4 efficiencies, $5 extra. Wkly rates avail. Reserv deposit
required. AE, DI, DS, MC, VI. FAX (818) 246-8374 *(See ad below)*   ⊗ Ⓓ Ⓑ (818) 246-8367

(See PASADENA & VICINITY spotting map page A327)

Holiday Inn 29   Rates Subject to Change   *Motor Inn* ◆◆
All year   1P .... 47.00   2P/1B .... 57.00   2P/2B .... 57.00 XP 10
600 units. 1 blk s of SR 134, exit Pacific Ave. 600 N Pacific Ave. (91203) A/C; C/CATV; movies; phones. Coin laundry. Htd pool; whirlpool. Parking lot. Airport transp. Pets. 10 efficiencies, $10 extra; no utensils. AE, DI, DS, MC, VI. ● Dining rm; 6:30 am-9 pm; $6-$12.50; cocktails; entertainment. FAX (818) 502-0843   ⊗ Ⓢ Ⓓ Ⓛ (818) 956-0202

Motel Sakura 31   Rates Subject to Change   *Motel* ◆
Ⓐ All year   1P 38.00- 46.00   2P/1B 42.00- 54.00   2P/2B 46.00- 58.00 XP 2
27 units. 2 blks e of Verdugo Rd. 1500 E Colorado St. (91205) Refrigerators; A/C; C/CATV; movies; radios; phones. Coin laundry. No pets. Reserv deposit required. AE, DI, DS, MC, VI. FAX (818) 246-6800 *(See ad below)*
                                                    ⊗ Ⓓ (818) 243-8999

Red Lion Hotel/Glendale 36   Rates Subject to Change   *Hotel*
Ⓐ All year   1P 125.00- 150.00   2P/1B 125.00- 150.00   2P/2B 125.00- 150.00 XP 20   F
348 units. 1/4 mi n of SR 134; between Central Ave & Brand Blvd. 100 W Glenoaks Blvd. (91203) Rating withheld pending completion of construction. Scheduled to open November, 1992. Check-in 3 pm. A/C; C/CATV; free & pay movies; radios; phones. Htd pool; sauna; whirlpool; exercise rm. Garage & parking ramp. Pets. AE, DI, DS, MC, VI. ● Dining rm & restaurant; 6 am-11 pm; $12-$20; cocktails; cocktail lounge.   ⊗ Ⓢ Ⓓ (818) 956-5466

Vagabond Inn 34   Rates Subject to Change   *Motel* ◆◆
Ⓐ All year [CP]   1P 61.00- 71.00   2P/1B 66.00- 76.00   2P/2B 71.00- 81.00 XP 5   F
52 units. 1 mi s of SR 134, Brand Blvd exit. 120 W Colorado St. (91204) A/C; C/TV; radios; phones. Pool. Pets, $5. AE, DI, DS, MC, VI. Coffeeshop adjacent. FAX (818) 548-8428 *(See ad p A150)*   ⊗ Ⓓ (818) 240-1700

RESTAURANTS

Fresco Ristorante 19   Italian $$$ ◆◆
2 1/2 blks s of Colorado St. 514 S Brand Blvd. Selections of salads, pasta, seafood, chicken, beef & veal. A/C. Open 11:30 am-2:30 & 5:30-10:30 pm; Fri & Sat-11 pm; closed Sun. Cocktails & lounge. Entertainment. Pay valet parking. Reserv advised. AE, MC, VI.   (818) 247-5541

Rusty Pelican 20   Seafood $$ ◆
At SR 134 & Glendale Frwy. 300 Harvey Dr. Informal atmosphere. Chicken, lamb, salads, prime rib & seafood. Sun brunch 10 am-2:30 pm. A/C. Children's menu. Open 11:30 am-3 & 4:30-10 pm; Fri & Sat-11:30 pm; Sun 10 am-2:30 & 3-10 pm; closed 12/25. Cocktails & lounge. Entertainment. Valet parking. AE, DI, DS, MC, VI.   ⊗ Ⓛ (818) 242-9191

Tam O'Shanter Inn 18   American $$
1/2 mi e of I-5. 2980 Los Feliz Blvd. A popular, long-established restaurant. Attractive, early Scottish decor. Ale & sandwich bar Mon-Sat 11 am-11 pm & Sun 1-9 pm. A/C. Children's menu. Open 11 am-3 & 5-10 pm; Fri & Sat-11 pm; Sun 10:30 am-2:30 & 4-10 pm; closed 7/4 & 12/25. Cocktails & lounge. Entertainment. Valet parking. Reserv advised for brunch & dinner. AE, DI, DS, MC, VI.   ⊗ (213) 664-0228

GLENDORA — 47,800

Comfort Inn   Rates Subject to Change   *Motel* ◆◆
Ⓐ All year [CP]   1P 49.00- 55.00   2P/1B 55.00- 65.00   2P/2B 59.00- 69.00 XP 6   F
Senior discount. 38 units. 1 blk w of Grand Ave; 3/4 mi nw of I-210. 606 W Alosta. (91740) Refrigerators; A/C; C/TV; pay movies; radios; phones. 28 efficiencies. Coin laundry. Indoor whirlpool. No pets. Reserv deposit required. AE, DI, DS, MC, VI.   ⊗ Ⓓ (818) 963-9361

RESTAURANT

Cafe Chantrell's   American $ ◆◆
870 Arrow Hwy at Grand Ave. Casual dining. Attractive country French atmosphere. A/C. Children's menu. Open 6 am-11 pm; Fri & Sat-midnight; closed 11/25 & 12/25. Cocktails. AE, MC, VI.   ⊗ (818) 339-8337

GRAEAGLE — 300

Graeagle Meadows   Rates Subject to Change   *Apartment Motel* ◆◆◆
All year Wkly   ....   2P/2B 560.00- 770.00 XP 20
56 units. 1/4 mi s on SR 89; 1 1/2 mi s of jct SR 70, Feather River Hwy. (PO Box 20344, 96103) 2 & 3-bedroom, 2-bath, 1 or 2-story duplexes; fireplace, patio & laundry facilities. Check-in 3 pm. Check-out 10:30 am. C/CATV; 35 radios; phones. Fee for: golf-18 holes. No pets. Damage deposit $200; 3-night minimum stay 7/1-9/30. Some units with micro wave & VCP. [MAP] avail. Reserv deposit required; 14 days refund notice.   Ⓓ (916) 836-2221

GRASS VALLEY — 9,000   See also NEVADA CITY

Alta Sierra Resort Motel — Rates Subject to Change — *Motel* ◆◆
Ⓐ **All year** — 1P 45.00- 57.50 — 2P/1B 64.00- 67.50 — 2P/2B 64.00- 85.00 — XP 5
14 units. 6 mi s; 2 1/2 mi e off SR 49, in the Alta Sierra Country Club. 135 Tammy Way. (95949) Decks overlooking small lake. Rustic decor. A/C; C/TV; 13 radios; comb or shower baths. 1 kitchen. Pool, golf & tennis privileges. Pets, $8 extra charge. 2-bedroom unit, $145. MC, VI. Restaurant opposite. Ⓓ (916) 273-9102

Best Western Gold Country Inn — Rates Subject to Change — *Motel* ◆◆
Ⓐ **3/16-12/31** — 1P 49.00- 62.00 — 2P/1B 58.00- 66.00 — 2P/2B 66.00- 70.00 — XP 6 — F
1/1-3/15 — 1P 48.00- 56.00 — 2P/1B 58.00- 60.00 — 2P/2B 58.00- 62.00 — XP 6 — F
Senior discount. 84 units. 1 mi e; off & adjacent to SR 20 & 49; midway between Grass Valley & Nevada City; exit Brunswick Rd. 11972 Sutton Way. (95945) Check-in 4 pm. 39 refrigerators; A/C; C/CATV; 42 radios; phones. 3 2-bedrm units, no utensils. Small pool; whirlpool. No pets. 10 kitchens & 6 efficiencies, $6-$10 extra. Reserv deposit required. AE, DI, DS, MC, VI. *(See ad p A364)* ⊗ Ⓓ (916) 273-1393

Golden Chain Resort Motel — Rates Subject to Change — *Motel* ◆◆
Ⓐ **Fri & Sat 5/1-10/15** — 1P 48.00- 56.00 — 2P/1B 56.00- 66.00 — 2P/2B 58.00- 70.00 — XP 5
Sun-Thurs 5/1-10/15 — 1P 38.00- 48.00 — 2P/1B 44.00- 54.00 — 2P/2B 44.00- 58.00 — XP 5
10/16-4/30 — 1P 34.00- 44.00 — 2P/1B 38.00- 48.00 — 2P/2B 42.00- 52.00 — XP 4
21 units. 2 1/2 mi s on SR 49. 13363 SR 49. (95949) Spacious tree-shaded grounds. A/C; C/TV; shower or comb baths. Pool; putting green. Pets, $4 extra charge. Reserv deposit required; 3 days refund notice. AE, MC, VI. ⊗ Ⓓ (916) 273-7279

Holbrooke Hotel — Rates Subject to Change — *Historical* ◆◆
Ⓐ **Fri & Sat [CP]** — 1P 76.00- 106.00 — 2P/1B 76.00- 106.00 — 2P/2B .... 76.00 — XP 15
Sun-Thurs [CP] — 1P 66.00- 86.00 — 2P/1B 66.00- 86.00 — 2P/2B .... 66.00 — XP 15
28 units. SR 49 exit Central Grass Valley. 212 W Main St. (95945) 1851 restored hotel. 10 rooms located in restored 1870 Victorian annex. A California historical landmark. Check-in 3 pm. A/C; C/CATV; phones; comb or shower baths. Limited parking lot. No pets. Wkly & monthly rates avail. Reserv deposit required; 7 days refund notice. AE, MC, VI. ● Dining rm; 11:30 am-3 & 5-9 pm; Fri & Sat-10 pm; Sun brunch 10 am-3 pm; $7.95-$21.95; cocktails. ⊗ Ⓓ (916) 273-1353

Holiday Lodge — Rates Subject to Change — *Motel* ◆
Ⓐ **All year** — 1P 38.00- 42.00 — 2P/1B 44.00- 48.00 — 2P/2B 46.00- 50.00 — XP 6 — F
Senior discount. 36 units. 1 1/4 mi e; 3/4 mi e on Old Hwy 20 & 49; exit SR 49 Frwy via Idaho-Maryland Rd exits. 1221 E Main St. (95945) A/C; C/CATV; movies; radios; phones; shower or comb baths. Pool; sauna; whirlpool. Pets, $25 deposit required. Some gold rush theme rooms, $60 for 2 persons. Reserv deposit required. AE, CB, DI, MC, VI. ⊗ Ⓓ (916) 273-4406

RESTAURANT

Scheidel's Old European Restaurant — German — $$ ◆◆
6 mi s on SR 49, at entrance to Alta Sierra Dr. 10140 Alta Sierra Dr. Charming Bavarian atmosphere. European & continental specialties. A/C. Children's menu. Open 5:30 pm-9 pm; Fri-10 pm; Sat 4 pm-10 pm; Sun 4 pm-9 pm; closed Mon, Tues & 12/24. Cocktails & lounge. Minimum $8. Reserv advised. MC, VI. ⊗ 🅱 (916) 273-5553

GROVER CITY — 11,700

Oak Park Inn — Rates Subject to Change — *Motel* ◆◆◆
Ⓐ **5/15-10/1 [CP]** — 1P 49.00- 67.00 — 2P/1B 59.00- 75.00 — 2P/2B 59.00- 83.00 — XP 5 — F
Senior discount. 35 units. 1 blk w of US 101, exit Oak Park Blvd. 775 Oak Park Blvd. (93433) OPEN ALL YEAR. 5 refrigerators; A/C; C/CATV; movies; radios; phones. Htd pool; whirlpool; exercise rm. No pets. 4 rooms with whirlpool tub & fireplace, $85. Wkly rates avail. Reserv deposit required; 3 days refund notice. AE, DS, MC, VI. Restaurant adjacent. FAX (805) 473-3609 *(See ad p A337)* ⊗ Ⓢ Ⓓ (805) 481-4448

GUALALA — 600

RESTAURANT

St Orres Dining Room — American — $$$$ ◆◆◆
2 mi n on SR 1. 36601 S Hwy 1. Unique Russian architecture. 3-story domed dining room. Prix fixe with several choices of entree. Designated smoking areas. Open 6 pm-9 pm; Sat from 5 pm; closed Wed 10/6-5/27 & 11/29-12/16. Beer & wine. Reserv required. ⊗ (707) 884-3303

HACIENDA HEIGHTS — See INDUSTRY

HALF MOON BAY — 8,900   (See SAN FRANCISCO (Southern Region) AREA spotting map page A444 ; see index starting on page A443)

Cypress Inn on Miramar Beach 🅸🅶🅸 — Rates Subject to Change — *Bed & Breakfast* ◆◆◆
Ⓐ **Fri-Sun [BP]** — 1P 135.00- 175.00 — 2P/1B 135.00- 175.00 — 2P/2B .... 250.00 — XP 20
8 units. 3 mi n of SR 92, off SR 1; exit Medio Ave w. 407 Mirada Rd. (94019) OPEN 12/26-12/24. Beach opposite. Modern decor. All rooms have fireplace & balcony overlooking ocean. 3-story, no elevator. Smoke free premises. Check-in 4 pm. 3 C/TV; radios; phones; comb or shower baths. Fee for: massage. Parking lot. No pets. Reserv deposit required; 3 days refund notice. Complimentary beverages each evening. AE, DS, MC, VI. ⊗ Ⓢ Ⓓ (415) 726-6002

(See SAN FRANCISCO (Southern Region) spotting map page A444)

Half Moon Bay Lodge Best Western 🈴   Rates Subject to Change   *Motel*   ◆◆◆
🈴 All year   1P 96.00-120.00   2P/1B   99.00-150.00   2P/2B   99.00-150.00   XP 12   F
Senior discount. 81 units. 2 1/2 mi s of jct SR 92 on w side of SR 1. 2400 S Cabrillo Hwy. (94019) Rooms with
view of golf course; balcony or patio; 25 fireplaces. Check-in 3 pm. Refrigerators; C/CATV; movies; radios;
phones. 4 2-bedrm units. Pool; sauna; exercise rm. No pets. AE, DI, DS, MC, VI. Restaurant adjacent.
FAX (415) 726-7951 *(See ads inside back cover and below)*   ⊗ Ⓓ (415) 726-9000

Harbor View Inn 🈲   Rates Subject to Change   *Motel*   ◆◆
🈴 4/15-1/2 & Fri-Sat   1P ....   64.00   2P/1B   ....   64.00   2P/2B   69.00- 74.00   XP
1/3-4/14 Sun-Thurs   1P ....   58.00   2P/1B   ....   58.00   2P/2B   62.00- 67.00   XP
17 units. 4 mi n in El Granada; 1/2 blk e of SR 1. 11 Ave Alhambra. (PO Box 127, El Granada, 94018) Across the
highway from Pillar Point Harbor. Ocean view. C/CATV; radios; phones; shower baths. No pets. Wkly & monthly
rates avail. Reserv deposit required. AE, MC, VI. Restaurant opposite. *(See ad p A152)*
      ⊗ Ⓢ Ⓓ (415) 726-2329

Mill Rose Inn, Spa & Garden Suites 🈴   Rates Subject to Change   *Bed & Breakfast*   ◆◆◆◆
🈴 All year [BP]   1P 155.00- 250.00   2P/1B   155.00- 250.00   2P/2B   155.00- 250.00   XP 20
6 units. 1 blk w. 615 Mill St. (94019) Elegant & charming decor; most fireplaces. Lavish flower gardens. Smoke
free premises. Check-in 3 pm. Refrigerators; C/CATV; movies; VCPs. Radios; phones; comb or shower baths.
Enclosed whirlpool. Fee for: massage. No pets. 2 2-room suites with fireplace & 1 with large whirlpool tub, $225-
$250 for 2 persons. Reserv deposit required; 14 days refund notice. Complimentary beverages each evening.
AE, MC, VI. FAX (415) 726-3031   ⊗ Ⓓ (415) 726-9794

Pillar Point Inn 🈲   AAA Special Value Rates   *Bed & Breakfast*   ◆◆◆
🈴 Fri & Sat [BP]   1P 150.00- 165.00   2P/1B   150.00- 165.00   ....   XP 20
Sun-Thurs [BP]   1P 130.00- 140.00   2P/1B   130.00- 140.00   ....   XP 20
11 units. 4 mi n of jct SR 92 & SR 1; in Princeton-by-the-Sea. 380 Capistrano Rd. (PO Box 388, El Granada, 94018) Overlooking harbor. All rooms with fireplace. Smoke free premises. Refrigerators; C/CATV; radios;
phones; comb or shower baths. 5 steambaths. No pets. Reserv deposit required. Complimentary beverages
each evening. AE, MC, VI. Restaurant adjacent. FAX (415) 728-8345   ⊗ Ⓢ Ⓓ Ⓛ (415) 728-7377

Ramada Limited 🈲   Rates Subject to Change   *Motel*   ◆◆
🈴 All year [CP]   1P 55.00- 75.00   2P/1B   55.00- 85.00   2P/2B   55.00-105.00   XP
Senior discount. 20 units. 2 mi n of SR 92 on SR 1. 3020 Hwy 1. (94019) 6 refrigerators; A/C; C/CATV; phones.
No pets. Reserv deposit required. AE, DI, DS, MC, VI.   ⊗ Ⓢ Ⓓ (415) 726-9700

RESTAURANT

The Shore Bird 🈸   Seafood $$ ◆◆
🈴 4 mi n of jct SR 92 & SR 1 in Princeton-by-the-Sea. 390 Capistrano Rd. New England fishing village atmosphere
overlooking Pillar Point Harbor. Steaks & chicken served also. Open 11:30 am-3 & 5:30-9 pm; Sat 11:30 am-3 &
5-10 pm; Sun 10:30 am-3 & 4-9 pm; closed 11/25, 12/24 & 12/25. Cocktails & lounge. AE, DI, DS, MC, VI.
      ⊗ (415) 728-5541

HANFORD — 30,900
Best Western Hanford Inn 🈲   Rates Subject to Change   *Motel*   ◆◆
🈴 All year   1P 40.00- 45.00   2P/1B   46.00- 47.00   2P/2B   ....   48.00   XP 6   F
Senior discount. 40 units. S of & adjacent to SR 198; eastbound exit 11th Ave; westbound exit Reddington St.
755 Cadillac Ln. (93230) A/C; C/CATV; radios; phones. Coin laundry. Small pool. No pets. AE, DI, DS, MC, VI. Cof-
feeshop opposite.   ⊗ Ⓢ Ⓓ Ⓛ (209) 583-7300

HAPPY CAMP — 1,100

Forest Lodge Motel		Rates Guaranteed				Motel	◆
⑱ 3/2-11/30	1P 40.00	2P/1B	.... 50.00	2P/2B	.... 55.00	XP 10	
12/1-3/1	1P 35.00	2P/1B	.... 45.00	2P/2B	.... 50.00	XP 10	

15 units. 63712 Hwy 96. (PO Box 1535, 96039) 6 refrigerators; A/C; C/CATV; phones; shower baths. 3-night minimum stay in 2 kitchen units; $15 extra. Seasonal rates avail. Reserv deposit required. MC, VI.

Ⓓ (916) 493-5424

RESTAURANT

Indian Creek Cafe   American $$ ◆

⑱ S off SR 96, 1/4 mi e. 106 Indian Creek Rd. Homemade bread, soups & desserts. Steaks, chops & seafood, Mexican, & vegetarian specialities. A/C. Children's menu. Open 6:30 am-9 pm; closed 4/11, 11/25 & 12/25. Beer & wine. AE, DI, MC, VI.

(916) 493-5180

HARBOR ISLAND — See SAN DIEGO

HARMONY — See CAMBRIA

HAWTHORNE — See LOS ANGELES (Central & Western Areas)

HAYWARD — 111,500

Best Western Inn		Rates Guaranteed				Motel	◆◆◆
⑱ All year [CP]	1P 49.00- 59.00	2P/1B	59.00- 69.00	2P/2B	.... 62.00	XP 6	

Senior discount. 91 units. E of I-880. 360 West A St. (94541) 37 refrigerators; A/C; C/CATV; movies; radios; phones; comb or shower baths. Pool; sauna; whirlpool; 16 rooms with whirlpool tub; exercise rm. No pets. 4 kitchens, $8 extra. 2 units with hot tub $140. Reserv deposit required. AE, DS, DI, MC, VI. FAX (510) 782-0850

⊗ Ⓓ (510) 785-8700

Comfort Inn		Rates Guaranteed				Motel	◆◆
⑱ All year [CP]	1P 46.00- 56.00	2P/1B	48.00- 58.00	2P/2B	52.00- 62.00	XP 5	F

Senior discount. 62 units. 1 3/4 mi e of I-880; exit Jackson Blvd/SR92, s 1/2 mi on SR 238 (Mission Blvd). 24997 Mission Blvd. (94544) Refrigerators; A/C; C/CATV; movies; radios; phones. 18 efficiencies, no utensils. Coin laundry. Sauna. No pets. 5 units with whirlpool bath & VCP'S. Wkly rates avail. Reserv deposit required. AE, DI, DS, MC, VI. FAX (510) 581-8029 *(See ad p A153)*

⊗ Ⓓ (510) 538-4466

Executive Inn-Hayward Airport		AAA Special Value Rates				Motel	◆◆◆
⑱ All year [CP]	1P 68.00- 81.00	2P/1B	72.00- 85.00	2P/2B	.... 72.00	XP 4	F

145 units. Exit I-880; A St, 1/2 mi w. 20777 Hesperian Blvd. (94541) Modern attractive decor, spacious rooms. Check-in 3 pm. 23 refrigerators; A/C; C/CATV; movies; radios; phones; comb or shower baths. Coin laundry. Htd pool; whirlpool. No pets. AE, DI, DS, MC, VI. Restaurant opposite. FAX (510) 783-2265 *(See ad p A299)*

⊗ Ⓢ Ⓓ (510) 732-6300

Phoenix Lodge		Rates Subject to Change				Motel	◆
⑱ All year	1P 36.00	2P/1B	.... 40.00	2P/2B	.... 42.00	XP 2	

70 units. W of I-880, A St exit. 500 West A St. (94541) 3-story, no elevator. 20 refrigerators; A/C; C/CATV; movies; phones; comb or shower baths. No pets. Reserv deposit required. AE, MC, VI.

Ⓓ Ⓖ (510) 786-0417

Phoenix Lodge		Rates Subject to Change				Motel	◆
⑱ All year	1P 36.00	2P/1B	.... 40.00	2P/2B	.... 42.00	XP 4	

70 units. W of I-880, exit southbound Industrial Pkwy, northbound Whipple/Industrial Pkwy. 2286 Industrial Pkwy West. (94544) 3-story, no elevator. A/C; C/TV; movies; phones; comb or shower baths. Coin laundry. No pets. Reserv deposit required. AE, MC, VI. ● Coffeeshop; 6 am-9 pm; $8-$11.

Ⓓ Ⓖ (510) 786-2844

Vagabond Inn		Rates Subject to Change				Motel	◆◆
⑱ All year [CP]	1P 50.00- 60.00	2P/1B	55.00- 65.00	2P/2B	60.00- 70.00	XP 5	F

Senior discount. 99 units. 1/2 mi w off I-880 via West A St. 20455 Hesperian Blvd. (94541) Spanish exterior design. A/C; C/TV; movies; radios; phones. Htd pool; whirlpool. Pets, $3 extra charge. Reserv deposit required. AE, DI, DS, MC, VI. Restaurant adjacent. FAX (510) 785-9142 *(See ad below)*

⊗ Ⓓ (510) 785-5480

RESTAURANT

Rue de Main   French $$ ◆◆◆

Exit 880 at A St, e 1 1/2 mi; s on Main St between B & C sts. 22622 Main St. Creative preparation & presentation; unique Paris street-cafe decor. Pleasant, quiet atmosphere. A/C. Open 11:30 am-2:15 & 5:30-9:30 pm; Sat 5:30 pm-10:30 pm; closed Sun, Mon & major holidays. Beer & wine. Reserv advised. CB, DI, MC, VI.

⊗ (510) 537-0812

HEALDSBURG — 9,500

Best Western Dry Creek Inn   Rates Subject to Change   *Motel* ◆◆

Fri & Sat 4/1-10/31	1P	65.00-	79.00	2P/1B	65.00-	79.00	2P/2B	65.00-	79.00	XP	10		F
Fri & Sat 11/1-3/31	1P	59.00-	69.00	2P/1B	59.00-	69.00	2P/2B	59.00-	69.00	XP	10		
Sun-Thurs 4/1-10/31	1P	....	59.00	2P/1B	....	59.00	2P/2B	....	59.00	XP	10		
Sun-Thurs 11/1-3/31	1P	....	49.00	2P/1B	....	49.00	2P/2B	....	49.00	XP	10		

102 units. E of US 101, Dry Creek Rd exit. 198 Dry Creek Rd. (95448) Spanish-style building. 8 refrigerators; A/C; C/CATV; pay movies; radios; phones. Coin laundry. Small pool; indoor whirlpool. Reserv deposit required; 3 days refund notice. AE, DI, DS, MC, VI. Coffeeshop adjacent. FAX (707) 433-1129 *(See ad below)*   ⊗ Ⓢ Ⓓ 🅖 (707) 433-0300

Fairview Motel   Rates Subject to Change   *Motel* ◆◆
All year [CP]   1P .... 38.00   2P/1B .... 46.00   2P/2B .... 50.00 XP 5
18 units. 1/2 mi s off US 101; northbound 2nd exit, southbound exit Healdsburg. 74 Healdsburg Ave. (95448) Refrigerators; A/C; C/CATV; movies; radios; phones; shower or comb baths. Pool; whirlpool; playground. No pets. Reserv deposit required. AE, DI, DS, MC, VI.   ⊗ Ⓓ (707) 433-5548

Madrona Manor   Rates Subject to Change   *Country Inn* ◆◆
4/1-10/31 [BP]   ....   2P/1B 125.00- 200.00   2P/2B 125.00- 200.00 XP 29
11/1-3/31 [BP]   ....   2P/1B 115.00- 185.00   2P/2B 115.00- 185.00 XP 29
21 units. 1/2 mi w of US 101; northbound 2nd exit, southbound Westside Rd. 1001 Westside Rd. (PO Box 818, 95448) Renovated 1881 mansion & buildings; some units furnished in original antiques, many with fireplace. Check-in 3 pm. A/C; radios; phones. Pool. Suite with whirlpool bath, $200 for 2 persons. Reserv deposit required; 5 days refund notice. AE, CB, DI, MC, VI. ● Dining rm; 8:30 am-9:30 & 6-9 pm; Sun 11 am-2 & 6-9 pm; $25-$50; beer & wine. FAX (707) 433-0703   Ⓓ (707) 433-4231

Vineyard Valley Inn   Rates Subject to Change   *Motel* ◆◆
Fri & Sat 4/1-10/31   1P .... 65.00   2P/1B .... 65.00   2P/2B .... 75.00 XP 10
Fri & Sat 11/1-3/31   1P .... 55.00   2P/1B .... 55.00   2P/2B .... 60.00 XP 10
Sun-Thurs   1P .... 45.00   2P/1B .... 45.00   2P/2B .... 50.00 XP 10
24 units. 1 blk e of US 101; Dry Creek Rd exit. 178 Dry Creek Rd. (95448) 3-story building, no elevator. A/C; C/CATV; phones. Sauna; whirlpool; exercise rm. No pets. 2 units with refrigerator, microwave & whirlpool bath, $90-$115 for up to 2 persons. Reserv deposit required; 3 days refund notice. AE, DS, MC, VI. Coffeeshop opposite. FAX (707) 433-1466 *(See ad p A154)*   ⊗ Ⓢ Ⓓ (707) 433-0101

RESTAURANTS

Chateau Souverain   American $$$ ◆◆◆
8 1/2 mi n; w of US 101 via Independenc e La & Souverain Rd. 400 Souverain Rd. California cuisine, seasonal menu changes. View of vineyards. Smoking in lounge only. Dining room. A/C. Dress code. Open 11:30 am-3 & 5:30-9 pm; Sun 10:30 am-2:30 & 5:30-9 pm; closed Mon, Tues, 12/24, 12/25 & 12/31-1/16. Wine. Reserv advised. AE, CB, DI, MC, VI.   ⊗ 🅖 (707) 433-3141

Jacob Horner   American $$ ◆◆◆
On The Plaza. 106 Matheson St. California cuisine. Smoking in lounge only. A/C. Open 11:30 am-2 & 5:30-9 pm; closed Sun, 1/1, 12/25 & dinner Mon. Cocktails & lounge. Reserv advised. AE, MC, VI.   ⊗ (707) 433-3939

HEARST-SAN SIMEON STATE HISTORICAL MONUMENT — See CAMBRIA & SAN SIMEON

HEMET — 36,100

Best Western Hemet   Rates Guaranteed   *Motel* ◆◆
All year   1P 40.00- 44.00   2P/1B 46.00- 50.00   2P/2B .... 50.00 XP 6
Senior discount. 72 units. 1 1/4 mi w on SR 74 & 79. 2625 W Florida Ave. (92545) Refrigerators; A/C; C/TV; movies; radios; phones. 2 2-bedrm units. Coin laundry. Htd pool; whirlpool. No pets. 29 efficiencies, $6 extra. Wkly & monthly rates avail. Reserv deposit required. AE, DI, DS, MC, VI. Coffeeshop adjacent. *(See ad p A154)*   ⊗ Ⓓ (909) 925-6605

Coach Light Motel   Rates Guaranteed   *Motel* ◆
⊛ All year   1P 28.00- 32.00   2P/1B   34.00- 36.00   2P/2B   34.00- 40.00   XP 3
Senior discount. 32 units. 1 mi w on SR 74 & SR 79. 1640 W Florida Ave. (92545) 7 refrigerators; A/C; C/TV; radios; phones; shower or comb baths. Pool. Pets, $5 extra charge. Wkly rates avail. Reserv deposit required. AE, DI, DS, MC, VI. *(See ad below)*   ⊗ Ⓓ (909) 658-3237

Hemet TraveLodge   Rates Subject to Change   *Motel* ◆◆
⊛ All year   1P .... 48.00   2P/1B   .... 50.00   2P/2B   .... 55.00   XP 5
Senior discount. 46 units. 3/4 mi w on SR 74 & 79. 1201 W Florida Ave. (92543) A/C; C/CATV; movies; radios; phones. Pool; whirlpool. No pets. 4 rooms with whirlpool, $80. 26 rooms with microwave & refrigerator. Wkly rates avail. AE, CB, DI, MC, VI. FAX (909) 766-7739 *(See ad below)*   ⊗ Ⓢ Ⓓ (909) 766-1902

Quality Inn   Rates Subject to Change   *Motel* ◆◆◆
⊛ All year [CP]   1P .... 45.00   2P/1B   .... 52.00   2P/2B   .... 55.00   XP 6   F
Senior discount. 65 units. 3/4 mi w on SR 74 & 79. 800 W Florida Ave. (92543) A/C; C/CATV; movies; radios; phones; comb or shower baths. Coin laundry. Htd pool; whirlpool; exercise rm. Pets, $5 extra charge. 30 efficiencies, $6 extra; utensils, deposit required. Wkly & monthly rates avail. AE, DI, DS, MC, VI. Restaurant adjacent. FAX (909) 925-3016   ⊗ Ⓓ Ⓗ (909) 929-6366

Ramada Inn   Rates Guaranteed   *Motel* ◆◆
⊛ 1/1-5/15   1P .... 56.00   2P/1B   .... 59.00   2P/2B   .... 59.00   XP 5   F
5/16-12/31   1P .... 51.00   2P/1B   .... 54.00   2P/2B   .... 54.00   XP 5   F
Senior discount. 99 units. 2 1/4 mi w on SR 74 & 79. 3885 W Florida Ave. (92545) 60 refrigerators; A/C; C/CATV; movies; phones. Coin laundry. Htd pool; whirlpool. No pets. Wkly & monthly rates avail. AE, CB, DI, DS, MC, VI. Restaurant adjacent. FAX (909) 929-3716   ⊗ Ⓓ Ⓗ (909) 929-8900

Super 8 Motel   Rates Guaranteed   *Motel* ◆
⊛ All year   1P .... 38.88   2P/1B   .... 42.88   2P/2B   .... 46.88   XP 4   F
Senior discount. 69 units. 2 mi w on SR 74 & 79. 3510 W Florida Ave. (92545) Refrigerators; A/C; C/CATV; movies; radios; phones. Small htd pool; whirlpool. Pets. 29 rooms with small microwave. Wkly rates avail. AE, DI, DS, MC, VI.   ⊗ Ⓢ Ⓓ Ⓗ (909) 658-2281

RESTAURANTS

Alejandro's   Mexican $$ ◆◆
2 1/4 mi w on SR 74 & 79. 3909 W Florida Ave. An attractive, colorfully decorated restaurant. A/C. Open 11 am-10 pm; Fri & Sat-11 pm; Sun 9 am-9 pm; closed 1/1, 11/25 & 12/25. Cocktails & lounge. MC, VI.   ⊗ (909) 766-1192

Furr's Family Dining   American $ ◆
1 1/2 mi w on SR 74 & 79. 3000 W Florida Ave. Popular cafeteria serving a large selection of salads, entrees & desserts. A/C. Open 11 am-8 pm; closed 12/25. AE, MC, VI.   ⊗ (909) 652-4485

Marie Callender's   American $
2 1/4 mi w on SR 74 & 79. 3969 W Florida Ave. Attractively decorated. Nice selection of salads, sandwiches, entrees & pies. A/C. Senior discount; children's menu. Open 7 am-9:30 pm; Fri & Sat-10:30 pm; closed 12/25. Cocktails & lounge. AE, MC, VI.   ⊗ Ⓗ (909) 925-7727

HERMOSA BEACH — 18,200
Hotel Hermosa   Rates Subject to Change   *Motel* ◆◆◆
⊛ All year [CP]   1P 72.00- 102.00   2P/1B   82.00- 115.00   2P/2B   82.00- 115.00   XP 10
80 units. Corner of Artesia Blvd & Pacific Coast Hwy. 2515 Pacific Coast Hwy. (90254) Many rooms with ocean view & balconies. Refrigerators; A/C; C/TV; movies; radios; phones. 14 efficiencies, no utensils. Coin laundry. Small htd pool; whirlpool. Garage & parking ramp. No pets. 8 loft units, $115-$150. Rooms with whirlpool, $109-$119. AE, DI, DS, MC, VI. FAX (310) 318-6936   ⊗ Ⓢ Ⓓ Ⓗ (310) 318-6000

Travelodge Hermosa Beach   AAA Special Value Rates   *Motel* ◆◆
⊛ All year   1P .... 59.00   2P/1B   .... 64.00   2P/2B   .... 69.00   XP 5   F
67 units. 1 blk e of SR 1, Pacific Coast Hwy. 901 Aviation Blvd. (90254) Refrigerators; A/C; C/CATV; movies; VCPs. Radios; phones. 7 efficiencies, no utensils. Coin laundry. Whirlpool. Garage & parking lot. No pets. 8 rooms with whirlpool tub, $85. AE, DI, DS, MC, VI. FAX (310) 379-3797 *(See ad p A157)*   ⊗ Ⓢ Ⓓ Ⓗ (310) 374-2666

HESPERIA — 50,400
Days Inn Suites   Rates Subject to Change   *Motel* ◆◆
⊛ All year [CP]   1P 39.00- 69.00   2P/1B   39.00- 69.00   2P/2B   45.00- 69.00   XP   F
Senior discount. 24 units. 2 blks e of I-15, exit Bear Valley Rd. 14865 Bear Valley Rd. (92345) 19 refrigerators; A/C; C/CATV; movies; 9 radios; phones; comb, shower, or tub baths. Coin laundry. Indoor whirlpool; 9 rooms with whirlpool tub; exercise rm. Pets. Reserv deposit required. AE, DI, DS, MC, VI. Restaurant opposite. FAX (619) 956-8645   ⊗ Ⓢ Ⓓ Ⓗ (619) 948-0600

TAXES—state, city and local—are extra. Allow for them; our listed rates do not.

HIGHLAND — 34,400

Super 8 Motel   Rates Subject to Change   *Motel*   ◆◆
(AAA) All year   1P .... 36.00 2P/1B .... 39.00 2P/2B .... 41.00 XP 3   F
Senior discount. 40 units. On SR 30, 5 mi e of I-215, across from Patton State Hospital. 26667 E Highland Ave.
(92346) Refrigerators; A/C; C/CATV; movies; phones. Pool. Pets, $5 extra charge. Wkly & monthly rates avail. AE,
DI, DS, MC, VI. Restaurant adjacent. FAX (909) 425-0612   ⊗ Ⓢ Ⓓ Ⓛ (909) 864-0100

HOLLISTER — 19,200

Best Western San Benito Inn   Rates Subject to Change   *Motel*   ◆◆
(AAA) 5/1-9/30 [CP]   1P .... 45.00 2P/1B .... 50.00 2P/2B .... 55.00 XP 5   F
10/1-4/30 [CP]   1P .... 40.00 2P/1B .... 45.00 2P/2B .... 50.00 XP 5   F
Senior discount. 42 units. 1 1/2 mi n on SR 25 & 156. 660 San Felipe Rd. (95023) A/C; C/TV; movies; 10 radios;
phones. Small pool. Pets, $2 extra charge. Reserv deposit required; 3 days refund notice. AE, DI, DS, MC, VI.
FAX (408) 637-4584   ⊗ Ⓓ Ⓛ (408) 637-9248

Hollister Inn   Rates Subject to Change   *Motel*   ◆◆
(AAA) 5/15-10/14   1P 40.00- 48.00 2P/1B 46.00- 58.00 2P/2B 46.00- 64.00 XP 4
10/15-5/14   1P 36.00- 40.00 2P/1B 38.00- 46.00 2P/2B 44.00- 52.00 XP 4
Senior discount. 31 units. 3 blks n on SR 25 & 156. 152 San Felipe Rd. (95023) 20 refrigerators; A/C; C/CATV;
radios; phones. Whirlpool. No pets. 15 units with microwave. Reserv deposit required; 7 days refund notice. AE,
CB, DI, MC, VI. Coffeeshop opposite. FAX (408) 637-1641 *(See ad p A157)*   ⊗ Ⓓ (408) 637-1641

Ridgemark Guest Cottages   Rates Subject to Change   *Motor Inn* ◆◆◆
(AAA) Fri & Sat   1P .... 75.00 2P/1B .... 80.00 2P/2B .... 100.00 XP 10
32 units. 2 1/2 mi se off SR 25; at Ridgemark Golf & Country Club. 3800 Airline Hwy. (95023) OPEN ALL YEAR.
Many rooms overlooking golf course. A/C; C/CATV; movies; radios; phones. Fee for: golf-36 holes, lighted
tennis-4 courts. No pets. 22 rooms with whirlpool bath, $5 extra. Reserv deposit required; 30 days refund no-
tice. AE, DI, MC, VI. ● Restaurant & coffeeshop; 7 am-9 pm; $10-$19; cocktail lounge. FAX (408) 636-3168
                                                                              Ⓓ (408) 637-8151

RESTAURANT

Sugar Plum Farm   American $ ◆
7 3/4 mi n on SR 156; 1/4 mi s of jct SR 152. 7511 Pacheco Pass Hwy. Family restaurant. Also fountain service. A/C.
Children's menu. Open 8 am-8 pm; closed 1/1, 11/25 & 12/25. MC, VI.   ⊗ (408) 637-3788

HOLLYWOOD — 165,800 See LOS ANGELES (Central & Western Areas)

HOOPA — 1,000

Best Western Tsewenaldin Inn   AAA Special Value Rates   *Motel*   ◆◆◆
(AAA) 5/1-9/30   1P .... 50.00 2P/1B .... 65.00 2P/2B .... 70.00 XP 10   F
10/1-4/30   1P .... 45.00 2P/1B .... 55.00 2P/2B .... 60.00 XP 10   F
22 units. At Hoopa Shopping Center. Hwy 96. (PO Box 219, 95546) Very attractive decor. All rooms have view of
Trinity River. A/C; C/TV; movies; radios; phones. Htd pool; whirlpool. Small pets only. Reserv deposit required;
14 days refund notice. AE, DI, DS, MC, VI. Beer & wine; restaurant adjacent. *(See ad p A138)*
                                                                          ⊗ Ⓓ Ⓛ (916) 625-4294

HOPLAND

Thatcher Inn   Rates Subject to Change   *Country Inn* ◆◆
(AAA) All year [BP]   1P 75.00- 130.00 2P/1B 85.00- 140.00 2P/2B .... 90.00 XP 25   F
Senior discount. 20 units. Center. 13401 S Hwy 101. (PO Box 660, 95449) Restored 1890's Victorian hotel.
3-story, no elevator. Designated smoking areas. Check-in 3 pm. 2 A/C; radios; phones; comb, shower, or tub
baths. Small pool open 5/1-10/31. No pets. Reserv deposit required; 5 days refund notice. AE, MC, VI. ● Dining
rm; 8-10:30 am, 11:30-2 & 5:30-9:30 pm; $10-$20; cocktails. FAX (707) 744-1219   ⊗ Ⓢ Ⓓ (707) 744-1890

HUNTINGTON BEACH — 181,500 See also SUNSET BEACH

Best Western Regency Inn   Rates Subject to Change   *Motel*   ◆◆
(AAA) 5/14-9/14   1P .... 69.00 2P/1B .... 69.00 2P/2B .... 79.00 XP 6
9/15-5/13   1P .... 59.00 2P/1B .... 59.00 2P/2B .... 69.00 XP 6
Senior discount. 66 units. 2 mi n on SR 39, 4 mi s of I-405. 19360 Beach Blvd. (92648) A/C; C/CATV; movies; radios; phones. Coin laundry. Pool; whirlpool. No pets. 11 efficiencies, $5 extra; no utensils. 15 rooms with whirl-
pool tub, $95-$120. Reserv deposit required. AE, DI, DS, MC, VI. FAX (714) 963-4724 Ⓢ Ⓓ (714) 962-4244

Comfort Suites   AAA Special Value Rates   *Motel*   ◆◆
(AAA) 2/1-9/15 [CP]   1P 54.00- 59.00 2P/1B 59.00- 64.00 2P/2B .... 69.00 XP 5   F
9/16 1/01 [CP]   1P 49.00- 54.00 2P/1B 54.00- 59.00 2P/2B .... 64.00 XP 5   F
102 units. On SR 39, 1/3 mi s of I-405. 16301 Beach Blvd. (92647) Refrigerators; A/C; C/CATV; movies; radios,
phones. Coin laundry. Htd pool; whirlpool; exercise rm. No pets. 3 rooms with whirlpool tub, $74. Wkly &
monthly rates avail. AE, DI, DS, MC, VI. Restaurant opposite. FAX (714) 841-0214 *(See ad below)*
                                                                          ⊗ Ⓢ Ⓓ Ⓛ (714) 841-1812

Friendship Beach Inn Motel   Rates Subject to Change   *Motel*   ◆
(AAA) 6/1-9/15 [CP]   1P 44.00- 54.00 2P/1B 48.00- 58.00 2P/2B 52.00- 63.00 XP 5-10
1/1-5/31 [EP]   1P 40.00- 50.00 2P/1B 44.00- 54.00 2P/2B 48.00- 58.00 XP 5-10
9/16-12/31 [EP]   1P 39.00- 49.00 2P/1B 43.00- 53.00 2P/2B 46.00- 57.00 XP 5-10
Senior discount. 38 units. 3 1/2 mi n on SR 39, 2 3/4 mi s of I-405. 18112 Beach Blvd. (92648) Refrigerators; A/C;
C/CATV; movies; phones. Small htd pool; whirlpool. No pets. 8 efficiencies, $7-$10 extra; no utensils. AE, DS,
MC, VI.   Ⓢ Ⓓ (714) 841-6606

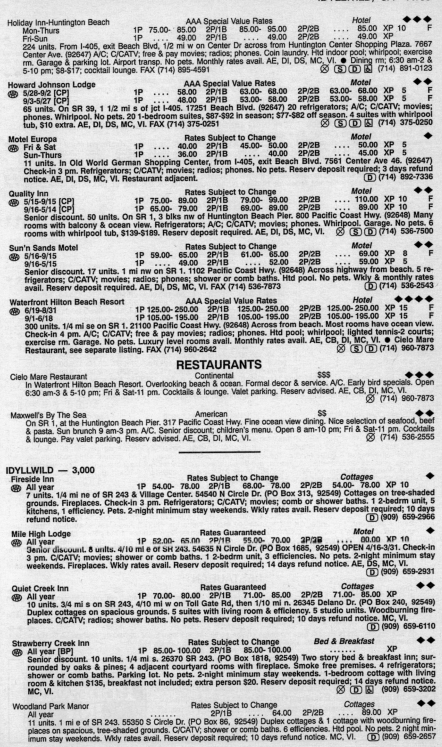

Holiday Inn-Huntington Beach　　　　AAA Special Value Rates　　　　*Hotel*　◆◆◆
　Mon-Thurs　　1P 75.00- 85.00　2P/1B　85.00- 95.00　2P/2B　.... 85.00　XP 10　　F
　Fri-Sun　　　1P　.... 49.00　2P/1B　.... 49.00　2P/2B　.... 49.00　XP
　224 units. From I-405, exit Beach Blvd, 1/2 mi w on Center Dr across from Huntington Center Shopping Plaza. 7667 Center Ave. (92647) A/C; C/CATV; free & pay movies; radios; phones. Coin laundry. Htd indoor pool; whirlpool; exercise rm. Garage & parking lot. Airport transp. No pets. Monthly rates avail. AE, DI, DS, MC, VI. ● Dining rm; 6:30 am-2 & 5-10 pm; $8-$17; cocktail lounge. FAX (714) 895-4591　⊗ Ⓢ Ⓓ ⓖ (714) 891-0123

Howard Johnson Lodge　　　　　　AAA Special Value Rates　　　　*Motel*　◆◆
⊕ 5/28-9/2 [CP]　1P　.... 58.00　2P/1B　63.00- 68.00　2P/2B　63.00- 68.00　XP 5　　F
　9/3-5/27 [CP]　1P　.... 48.00　2P/1B　53.00- 58.00　2P/2B　53.00- 58.00　XP 5　　F
　65 units. On SR 39, 1 1/2 mi s of jct I-405. 17251 Beach Blvd. (92647) 20 refrigerators; A/C; C/CATV; movies; phones. Whirlpool. No pets. 20 1-bedroom suites, $87-$92 in season; $77-$82 off season. 4 suites with whirlpool tub, $10 extra. AE, DI, DS, MC, VI. FAX (714) 375-0251　⊗ Ⓢ Ⓓ ⓖ (714) 375-0250

Motel Europa　　　　　　　Rates Subject to Change　　　　　*Motel*　◆
⊕ Fri & Sat　　1P　.... 40.00　2P/1B　45.00- 50.00　2P/2B　.... 50.00　XP 5
　Sun-Thurs　　1P　.... 36.00　2P/1B　.... 40.00　2P/2B　.... 45.00　XP 5
　11 units. In Old World German Shopping Center, from I-405, exit Beach Blvd. 7561 Center Ave 46. (92647) Check-in 3 pm. Refrigerators; C/CATV; movies; radios; phones. No pets. Reserv deposit required; 3 days refund notice. AE, DI, DS, MC, VI. Restaurant adjacent.　Ⓓ (714) 892-7336

Quality Inn　　　　　　　Rates Subject to Change　　　　　*Motel*　◆◆
⊕ 5/15-9/15 [CP]　1P 75.00- 89.00　2P/1B　79.00- 99.00　2P/2B　.... 110.00　XP 10　F
　9/16-5/14 [CP]　1P 65.00- 79.00　2P/1B　69.00- 89.00　2P/2B　.... 89.00　XP 10　F
　Senior discount. 50 units. On SR 1, 3 blks nw of Huntington Beach Pier. 800 Pacific Coast Hwy. (92648) Many rooms with balcony & ocean view. Refrigerators; A/C; C/CATV; movies; phones. Whirlpool. Garage. No pets. 6 rooms with whirlpool tub, $139-$189. Reserv deposit required. AE, DI, DS, MC, VI.　⊗ Ⓢ Ⓓ (714) 536-7500

Sun'n Sands Motel　　　　　Rates Subject to Change　　　　　*Motel*　◆◆
⊕ 5/16-9/15　　1P 59.00- 65.00　2P/1B　61.00- 65.00　2P/2B　.... 69.00　XP 8　　F
　9/16-5/15　　1P　.... 49.00　2P/1B　.... 52.00　2P/2B　.... 59.00　XP 5
　Senior discount. 17 units. 1 mi nw on SR 1. 1102 Pacific Coast Hwy. (92648) Across highway from beach. 5 refrigerators; C/CATV; movies; radios; phones; shower or comb baths. Htd pool. No pets. Wkly & monthly rates avail. Reserv deposit required. AE, DI, DS, MC, VI. FAX (714) 536-7873　⊗ Ⓢ Ⓓ (714) 536-2543

Waterfront Hilton Beach Resort　　　AAA Special Value Rates　　　　*Hotel*　◆◆◆
⊕ 6/19-8/31　　1P 125.00- 250.00　2P/1B　125.00- 250.00　2P/2B　125.00- 250.00　XP 15　F
　9/1-6/18　　1P 105.00- 195.00　2P/1B　105.00- 195.00　2P/2B　105.00- 195.00　XP 15　F
　300 units. 1/4 mi se on SR 1. 21100 Pacific Coast Hwy. (92648) Across from beach. Most rooms have ocean view. Check-in 4 pm. A/C; C/CATV; free & pay movies; radios; phones. Htd pool; whirlpool; lighted tennis-2 courts; exercise rm. Garage. No pets. Luxury level rooms avail. AE, CB, DI, MC, VI. ● Cielo Mare Restaurant, see separate listing. FAX (714) 960-2642　⊗ Ⓢ Ⓓ (714) 960-7873

RESTAURANTS

Cielo Mare Restaurant　　　　　Continental　　　　　$$$　◆◆
　In Waterfront Hilton Beach Resort. Overlooking beach & ocean. Formal decor & service. A/C. Early bird specials. Open 6:30 am-3 & 5-10 pm; Fri & Sat-11 pm. Cocktails & lounge. Valet parking. Reserv advised. AE, CB, DI, MC, VI.　⊗ (714) 960-7873

Maxwell's By The Sea　　　　　American　　　　　$$　◆
　On SR 1, at the Huntington Beach Pier. 317 Pacific Coast Hwy. Fine ocean view dining. Nice selection of seafood, beef & pasta. Sun brunch 9 am-3 pm. A/C. Senior discount; children's menu. Open 8 am-10 pm; Fri & Sat-11 pm. Cocktails & lounge. Pay valet parking. Reserv advised. AE, CB, DI, MC, VI.　⊗ (714) 536-2555

IDYLLWILD — 3,000
Fireside Inn　　　　　　　Rates Subject to Change　　　　　*Cottages*　◆
⊕ All year　　　1P 54.00- 60.00　2P/1B　68.00- 78.00　2P/2B　54.00- 78.00　XP 10
　7 units. 1/4 mi ne of SR 243 & Village Center. 54540 N Circle Dr. (PO Box 313, 92549) Cottages on tree-shaded grounds. Fireplaces. Check-in 3 pm. Refrigerators; C/CATV; movies; comb or shower baths. 1 2-bedrm unit, 5 kitchens, 1 efficiency. Pets. 2-night minimum stay weekends. Wkly rates avail. Reserv deposit required; 10 days refund notice.　Ⓓ (909) 659-2966

Mile High Lodge　　　　　　Rates Guaranteed　　　　　*Motel*　◆
⊕ All year　　　1P 52.00- 65.00　2P/1B　55.00- 70.00　2P/2B　.... 80.00　XP 10
　Senior discount. 8 units. 4/10 mi e of SR 243. 54635 N Circle Dr. (PO Box 1685, 92549) OPEN 4/16-3/31. Check-in 3 pm. C/CATV; movies; shower or comb baths. 1 2-bedrm unit, 3 efficiencies. No pets. 2-night minimum stay weekends. Fireplaces. Wkly rates avail. Reserv deposit required; 14 days refund notice. AE, DS, MC, VI.　Ⓓ (909) 659-2931

Quiet Creek Inn　　　　　　Rates Guaranteed　　　　　*Cottages*　◆◆
⊕ All year　　　1P 70.00- 80.00　2P/1B　71.00- 85.00　2P/2B　71.00- 85.00　XP
　10 units. 3/4 mi s on SR 243, 4/10 mi w on Toll Gate Rd, then 1/10 mi n. 26345 Delano Dr. (PO Box 240, 92549) Duplex cottages on spacious grounds. 5 suites with living room & efficiency. 5 studio units. Woodburning fireplaces. C/CATV; radios; shower baths. No pets. Reserv deposit required; 10 days refund notice. MC, VI.　Ⓓ (909) 659-6110

Strawberry Creek Inn　　　　Rates Subject to Change　　　*Bed & Breakfast*　◆◆
⊕ All year [BP]　1P 85.00- 100.00　2P/1B　85.00- 100.00　　　　　　　　　XP
　Senior discount. 10 units. 1/4 mi s. 26370 SR 243. (PO Box 1818, 92549) Two story bed & breakfast inn; surrounded by oaks & pines; 4 adjacent courtyard rooms with fireplace. Smoke free premises. 4 refrigerators; shower or comb baths. Parking lot. No pets. 2-night minimum stay weekends. 1-bedroom cottage with living room & kitchen $135, breakfast not included; extra person $20. Reserv deposit required; 14 days refund notice. MC, VI.　⊗ Ⓓ (909) 659-3202

Woodland Park Manor　　　　Rates Subject to Change　　　　*Cottages*　◆◆
　All year　　　........　2P/1B　.... 64.00　2P/2B　.... 89.00　XP
　11 units. 1 mi e of SR 243. 55350 S Circle Dr. (PO Box 86, 92549) Duplex cottages & 1 cottage with woodburning fireplaces on spacious, tree-shaded grounds. C/CATV; shower or comb baths. 6 efficiencies. Htd pool. No pets. 2 night minimum stay weekends. Wkly rates avail. Reserv deposit required; 10 days refund notice. MC, VI.　Ⓓ (909) 659-2657

RESTAURANTS

The Chart House   Steak & Seafood $$ ◆
1/2 mi ne at Fern Valley Corner. 54905 N Circle Dr. Attractive dining area with view of forest. Sun brunch. Early bird specials; children's menu. Open 5 pm-9 pm; Fri-10 pm; Sat 11:30 am-2:30 & 4:30-10 pm; Sun 10 am-2 & 4:30-9 pm; closed Mon-Wed 10/1-6/1. Cocktails & lounge. AE, DI, DS, MC, VI.   ⊗ (909) 659-4645

Gastrognome Restaurant   American $$ ◆◆
1 blk e of SR 243, in village center. 54381 Ridgeview Dr. Attractive restaurant featuring steaks, seafood & continental entrees. Sun brunch. Children's menu. Open 5 pm-9 pm; Fri & Sat-10 pm; Sun 10 am-9 pm. Cocktails. Reserv advised weekends. CB, MC, VI.   ⊗ (909) 659-5055

IMPERIAL BEACH — 26,500   (See SAN DIEGO spotting map pages A376 & A377; see index starting on page A374)   See also SAN YSIDRO

Hawaiian Gardens Suite-Hotel 150		AAA Special Value Rates		Apartment Motel			◆◆◆
🏵	6/15-9/14 & 12/15-4/14 [CP]	1P	65.00- 90.00	2P/1B	70.00- 100.00	2P/2B	80.00- 125.00	XP	5-10	F
	9/15-12/14 & 4/15-6/14 [CP]	1P	60.00- 79.00	2P/1B	65.00- 85.00	2P/2B	75.00- 115.00	XP	5-10	F

32 units. 2 mi w of I-5, Coronado Ave exit. 1031 Imperial Beach Blvd. (91932) Studio, 1- & 2-bedroom apartments. Check-in 3 pm. C/CATV; movies; VCPs. Phones. Kitchens. Coin laundry. Htd pool; sauna. Pets. Wkly & monthly rates avail. Reserv deposit required; 14 days refund notice. AE, DI, DS, MC, VI. FAX (619) 429-5304 *(See ad p A390)*   Ⓓ (619) 429-5303

RESTAURANT

Hungry Hunter Restaurant 62   Steak & Seafood $$ ◆◆
On SR 75, 3/4 mi w of I-5. 1344 Palm Ave. Attractive Early American country atmosphere. A/C. Open 11 am-2:30 & 5-10 pm; Fri-11 pm; Sat 11:30 am-2:30 & 4-11 pm; Sun 4 pm-10 pm; closed 12/25. Cocktails & lounge. AE, MC, VI.   ⊗ (619) 423-0953

INDIAN WELLS — 2,600   (See map page A315)

Erawan Garden Hotel		Rates Subject to Change		Motor Inn			◆◆◆
🏵	12/21-5/31	1P	90.00- 140.00	2P/1B	90.00- 140.00	2P/2B	90.00- 140.00	XP
	9/30-12/20	1P	65.00- 130.00	2P/1B	65.00- 130.00	2P/2B	65.00- 130.00	XP
	6/1-6/14 & 9/9-9/29	1P	55.00- 85.00	2P/1B	55.00- 85.00	2P/2B	55.00- 85.00	XP

Senior discount. 223 units. On SR 111. 76-477 Hwy 111. (92210) OPEN 9/9-6/14. Attractively landscaped grounds. Check-in 3 pm. Refrigerators; A/C; C/CATV; 50 radios; phones. 2 htd pools; saunas; whirlpool; putting green. No pets. Monthly rates avail. Reserv deposit required. AE, DI, DS, MC, VI. ● Dining rm & restaurant; 6:30 am-10 pm; $9-$22; cocktails; entertainment. FAX (619) 568-0541   Ⓓ (619) 346-8021

Hotel Indian Wells		Rates Subject to Change		Hotel			◆◆◆
🏵	2/1-5/27	1P	95.00- 135.00	2P/1B	95.00- 135.00	2P/2B	95.00- 135.00	XP	F
	9/3-1/31	1P	85.00- 125.00	2P/1B	85.00- 125.00	2P/2B	85.00- 125.00	XP	F
	5/28-9/2	1P	69.00- 119.00	2P/1B	69.00- 119.00	2P/2B	69.00- 119.00	XP	F

151 units. On SR 111. 76-661 Hwy 111. (92210) Check-in 3 pm. A/C; C/CATV; pay movies; radios; phones. 10 2-bedrm units. Htd pool; whirlpool. Valet parking lot. No pets. Reserv deposit required. AE, DI, DS, MC, VI. ● Dining rm; 7 am-9 pm; Fri & Sat-10 pm; $14-$25; cocktails. FAX (619) 772-5083   ⊗ Ⓢ Ⓓ ⅙ (619) 345-6466

Hyatt Grand Champions Resort		Rates Subject to Change		Resort Hotel			◆◆◆
🏵	1/1-5/31	1P	215.00- 325.00	2P/1B	215.00- 325.00	2P/2B	215.00- 325.00	XP 25	F
	9/30-12/31	1P	190.00- 255.00	2P/1B	190.00- 255.00	2P/2B	190.00- 255.00	XP 25	F
	6/1-9/29	1P	105.00- 180.00	2P/1B	105.00- 180.00	2P/2B	105.00- 180.00	XP 25	F

335 units. On SR 111. 44-600 Indian Wells Ln. (92210) Spacious, beautifully landscaped grounds. 20 1 & 2-bedroom villas with whirlpool & butler service. Check-in 4 pm. A/C; C/CATV; movies; radios; phones. 4 htd pools; saunas; whirlpools; exercise room; steamroom. Fee for: golf-36 holes, tennis-14 courts, 8 lighted; health club. Pay valet garage. No pets. Reserv deposit required. AE, DI, DS, MC, VI. ● 2 dining rms & restaurant; 6:30 am-10 pm; a la carte entrees about $9.75-$25; cocktails; entertainment. FAX (619) 569-2236   Ⓢ Ⓓ ⅙ (619) 341-1000

Stouffer Esmeralda Resort		Rates Guaranteed		Resort Hotel			◆◆◆
🏵	2/1-5/31	1P	229.00- 380.00	2P/1B	229.00- 380.00	2P/2B	229.00- 380.00	XP 25	F
	9/28-1/31	1P	179.00- 275.00	2P/1B	179.00- 275.00	2P/2B	179.00- 275.00	XP 25	F
	6/1-9/27	1P	119.00- 170.00	2P/1B	119.00- 170.00	2P/2B	119.00- 170.00	XP 25	F

Senior discount. 560 units. On SR 111. 44-400 Indian Wells Ln. (92210) Spacious, beautifully landscaped grounds. Check-in 3 pm. A/C; C/CATV; movies; radios; phones. Coin laundry. 3 htd pools; saunas; whirlpools; rental bicycles. Fee for: golf-36 holes, lighted tennis-7 courts; steamroom; health club & massage. Garage & parking lot. Airport transp. Pets. Reserv deposit required; 3 days refund notice. AE, DI, DS, MC, VI. ● Dining rm & restaurant; 6 am-11 pm; $10-$30; cocktails; entertainment. Also, Sirocco, see separate listing. FAX (619) 773-9250   ⊗ Ⓢ Ⓓ ⅙ (619) 773-4444

RESTAURANTS

Don Diego's   Mexican $$ ◆◆
At Cook St. 74-969 Hwy 111. Colorfully decorated restaurant. Sun brunch 10:30 am-3 pm. A/C. Children's menu. Open 11 am-9 pm; Fri & Sat-10 pm; Sun 10:30 am-9 pm; closed 11/25. Cocktails. Reserv advised. AE, MC, VI.   ⊗ (619) 340-5588

Sirocco   Ethnic $$$$ ◆◆◆
In Stouffer Esmeralda Resort. Mediterranean cuisine served in an elegant, but relaxed atmosphere. A/C. Dress code. Open 6 pm-10:30 pm. Cocktails. Valet parking. Reserv advised. AE, CB, DI, MC, VI.   ⊗ (619) 773-4444

INDIO — 36,800   (See map page A315)

Best Western Date Tree Motor Hotel   Rates Subject to Change   Motel ◆◆

1/1-5/31 [CP]	1P	48.00-	64.00	2P/1B	58.00-	72.00	2P/2B	64.00-	78.00	XP 6	F
10/1-12/31 [CP]	1P	46.00-	54.00	2P/1B	54.00-	68.00	2P/2B	62.00-	74.00	XP 6	F
6/1-9/30 [CP]	1P	42.00-	54.00	2P/1B	54.00-	64.00	2P/2B	58.00-	68.00	XP 6	F

Senior discount. 120 units. 1/2 mi s of I-10, exit Monroe St. 81-909 Indio Blvd. (92201) Refrigerators; A/C; C/CATV; pay movies; 50 radios; phones; shower or comb baths. 3 2-bedrm units, 3 efficiencies. Coin laundry. Htd pool; whirlpool; 1 room with whirlpool tub. Small pets only, $25 deposit. Wkly & monthly rates avail. AE, CB, DI, MC, VI. Restaurant adjacent. FAX (619) 347-3421   ⊗ Ⓓ (619) 347-3421

Comfort Inn   Rates Subject to Change   Motel ◆◆

11/1-5/31	1P	54.00-	64.00	2P/1B	64.00-	74.00	2P/2B	69.00-	79.00	XP 6	F
6/1-10/31	1P	44.00-	49.00	2P/1B	49.00-	59.00	2P/2B	54.00-	64.00	XP 6	F

Senior discount. 63 units. 1/2 mi s of I-10; exit Monroe St. 43-505 Monroe St. (92201) 15 refrigerators; A/C; C/CATV; movies; phones. Htd pool; whirlpool. AE, DI, DS, MC, VI. Coffeeshop adjacent. FAX (619) 347-4044   ⊗ Ⓓ (619) 347-4044

Indio Travelodge   Rates Subject to Change   Motel ◆

12/1-4/30	1P	....	55.00	2P/1B	....	60.00	2P/2B	....	69.00	XP 6	F
5/1-11/30	1P	....	40.00	2P/1B	....	45.00	2P/2B	....	49.00	XP 5- 6	F

Senior discount. 50 units. 2 mi w on SR 111. 80-651 Hwy 111. (92201) A/C; C/CATV; radios; phones. 2 2-bedrm units. Coin laundry. Htd pool; whirlpool; lighted tennis-1 court. No pets. 25 efficiencies, $5 extra. Wkly rates avail. Reserv deposit required. AE, DI, DS, MC, VI.   ⊗ Ⓓ (619) 342-0882

Rodeway Inn at Big America   Rates Subject to Change   Motor Inn ◆◆◆

1/1-4/30 & 9/6-12/31	1P	39.95-	76.95	2P/1B	45.95-	76.95	2P/2B	45.95-	76.95	XP 6
5/1-9/5	1P	39.95-	60.95	2P/1B	45.95-	66.95	2P/2B	45.95-	66.95	XP 6

Senior discount. 125 units. Adjacent to I-10, exit Auto Center Dr, then 1/4 mi ne. 84-096 Indio Springs Dr. (92201) Refrigerators; A/C; C/CATV; pay movies; phones. Pool; whirlpool. Pets. Wkly & monthly rates avail. Reserv deposit required. AE, CB, MC, VI. ● Dining rm; 6 am-9 pm; $6.25-$9.95; beer & wine. (See ad p A160)   ⊗ Ⓓ ♿ (619) 342-6344

Royal Plaza Inn   AAA Special Value Rates   Motor Inn ◆◆

10/31-4/30	1P	44.00-	55.00	2P/1B	48.00-	55.00	2P/2B	50.00-	60.00	XP 6
5/1-10/30	1P	36.00-	45.00	2P/1B	42.00-	45.00	2P/2B	44.00-	50.00	XP 6

99 units. On SR 111, 1 blk e of Monroe St. 82-347 Hwy 111. (92201) 11 refrigerators; A/C; C/CATV; movies; phones. Coin laundry. Htd pool; whirlpool. Pets, $50 deposit required. AE, DI, DS, MC, VI. ● Restaurant; 5 am-11 pm; $8-$23; cocktails. FAX (619) 347-8644   ⊗ Ⓓ (619) 347-0911

INDUSTRY — 600   See also ROWLAND HEIGHTS

Courtyard by Marriott   Rates Subject to Change   Motor Inn ◆◆◆

Sun-Thurs	1P	....	59.00	2P/1B	....	69.00	2P/2B	....	69.00	XP 10
Fri & Sat	1P	....	59.00	2P/1B	....	59.00	2P/2B	....	59.00	XP 10

150 units. 1/2 mi s of SR 60, exit Azusa Ave. 1905 S Azusa Ave. (Hacienda Heights, 91745) A/C; C/CATV; free & pay movies; radios; phones. Coin laundry. Htd pool; indoor whirlpool; exercise rm. No pets. Wkly rates avail. AE, CB, DI, MC, VI. ● Dining rm; 6:30 am-2 & 5-10 pm; Sat & Sun from 7 am; $8-$12; cocktails. FAX (909) 965-1367 (See ad p A221)   ⊗ Ⓢ Ⓓ (909) 965-1700

Holiday Inn Express   AAA Special Value Rates   Motel ◆◆◆

All year [CP]	1P	....	59.00	2P/1B	....	64.00	2P/2B	....	69.00	XP 5	F

95 units. 1/4 mi s of SR 60. 1170 Fairway Dr. (Walnut, 91789) Formerly Comfort Suites. Refrigerators; A/C; C/CATV; radios; phones. Coin laundry. Htd pool; sauna; whirlpool; exercise rm. No pets. Wkly & monthly rates avail. AE, CB, DI, MC, VI. FAX (909) 594-9343 (See ad below)   ⊗ Ⓢ Ⓓ (909) 594-9999

Industry Hills & Sheraton Resort   Rates Subject to Change   Resort Hotel ◆◆◆

All year	1P 110.00-	130.00	2P/1B	115.00-	145.00	2P/2B	115.00-	145.00	XP 15

296 units. 1 3/4 mi n of SR 60, Azusa Ave exit. One Industry Hills Pkwy. (91744) Hilltop location on spacious grounds. Check-in 3 pm. 45 refrigerators; A/C; C/CATV; pay movies; radios; phones; comb or shower baths. 2 htd pools; saunas; whirlpools. Fee for: golf-36 holes, lighted tennis-17 courts; health club. Pay valet parking lot & ramp. No pets. Reserv deposit required. AE, CB, DI, MC, VI. ● Dining rm & coffeeshop; 6 am-11:30 pm; $8-$25; dancing; cocktails; entertainment. FAX (909) 064-9505   ⊗ Ⓢ Ⓓ (909) 905-0861

RESTAURANTS

Frere Jacques Restaurant   French $$ ◆◆
1/2 mi w of Hacienda Blvd. 15200 E Valley Blvd. A small, charming French restaurant. A/C. Open 11 am-2:30 & 5:30-10 pm; Sat 5:30 pm-10 pm; closed Sun, 1/1, 4/11 & 12/25. Cocktails & lounge. AE, CB, DI, MC, VI.   ⊗ (909) 330-8119

Mimi's Cafe   American $ ◆◆
Southside of SR 60, between Azusa Ave & Fullerton Ave exits. 17919 E Gale. Casual dining in a French cafe atmosphere. Nice selection of salads, sandwiches & entrees. A/C. Children's menu. Open 7 am-11 pm; closed 11/25 & 12/25. Beer & wine. AE, MC, VI.   ⊗ (909) 912-3350

INGLEWOOD — 109,600   See LOS ANGELES (Central & Western Areas)

IRVINE — 110,300

Airporter Hotel
| | Rates Subject to Change | | | | | Motor Inn |
All year   1P .... 80.00   2P/1B   .... 85.00   2P/2B   .... 90.00 XP

215 units. 1/2 mi s of I-405, opposite John Wayne Orange County Airport. 18700 MacArthur Blvd. (92715) Rating withheld pending completion of renovation. 16 refrigerators; A/C; C/CATV; free & pay movies; radios; phones; comb or shower baths. Htd pool; 1 room with private pool; steamroom; exercise rm. Airport transp. No pets. Wkly & monthly rates avail. AE, DI, DS, MC, VI. ● Dining rm & coffeeshop; 6 am-10 pm; $5.95-$18.95; cocktails; entertainment. FAX (714) 757-1228   (714) 833-2770

Courtyard By Marriott Irvine/Orange County
Airport   Rates Subject to Change   Motor Inn   ◆◆◆
Sun-Thurs   1P 79.00- 82.00   2P/1B   89.00- 92.00   2P/2B   89.00- 92.00 XP 10   F
Fri & Sat   1P 60.00- 62.00   2P/1B   70.00- 72.00   2P/2B   70.00- 72.00 XP 10   F

153 units. Corner Jamboree Blvd. 2701 Main St. (92714) Check-in 3 pm. A/C; C/CATV; free & pay movies; radios; phones. Coin laundry. Htd pool; whirlpool; exercise rm. No pets. Wkly rates avail. AE, DI, DS, MC, VI. ● Restaurant; 6:30 am-10 pm; $6.95-$12.50; cocktails. FAX (714) 757-1596 *(See ad p A33)*   ⊗ Ⓢ Ⓓ 🖥 (714) 757-1200

Minutes to Newport Beach & John Wayne Airport • Deluxe rooms/ suites • In-room Coffeemakers • Microwaves & Refrigerators • Cable/Satellite T.V. • Videocassette Players • Complimentary Continental Breakfast • Restaurant & Lounge • Heated pool, spa & sauna • Airport Shuttle • Coin Laundry

SEE LISTING, SANTA ANA
Make reservations at any Best Western or call toll-free 1-800-528-1234

Best Western
IRVINE HOST
Independently owned and operated

For Reservations
Call 714-261-1515 or toll-free 800-433-4374
FAX (714) 261-1265

Best Western

1717 East Dyer Rd. • At the Newport Freeway • Irvine, CA 92705

Embassy Suites-Irvine-Orange County Airport   Rates Subject to Change   *Suites Motor Inn*   ◆◆◆
Sun-Thurs [BP]   1P .... 139.00   2P/1B .... 149.00   2P/2B .... 149.00   XP 10   F
Fri & Sat [BP]   1P .... 99.00   2P/1B .... 99.00   2P/2B .... 99.00   XP
Senior discount. 293 units. From I-405 exit MacArthur Blvd, n to Main St, then 1/2 mi e. 2120 Main St. (92714)
1-bedroom suites with living room & microwave. Few smaller rooms. Check-in 3 pm. Refrigerators; A/C; C/CATV;
free & pay movies; radios; phones. Htd indoor pool; sauna; indoor whirlpool. Parking ramp. Airport transp. No
pets. Reserv deposit required. Complimentary beverages each evening. AE, DI, DS, MC, VI. ● Dining rm; 11:30
am-3 & 5-10 pm; $8.25-$21; cocktails. FAX (714) 261-5301   ⊗ Ⓢ Ⓓ (714) 553-8332

Holiday Inn-Irvine/Orange County Airport   Rates Subject to Change   *Motor Inn*   ◆◆◆
All year   1P 85.00- 125.00   2P/1B 98.00- 139.00   2P/2B 98.00- 139.00   XP 15   F
Senior discount. 340 units. Adjacent to I-405, exit Jamboree Rd, n to Main, then w to Von Karman Ave. 17941 Von
Karman Ave. (92714) A/C; C/CATV; free & pay movies; radios; phones. Coin laundry. Htd indoor pool; wading pool;
saunas; whirlpool; rental bicycles; exercise rm. Airport transp. Pets. AE, DI, DS, MC, VI. ● Dining rm; 6 am-11 pm;
$8.50-$17.50; cocktails. FAX (714) 474-7236   ⊗ Ⓢ Ⓓ (714) 863-1999

Hyatt Regency Irvine   Rates Subject to Change   *Hotel*   ◆◆◆
All year   1P 89.00- 149.00   2P/1B 99.00- 159.00   2P/2B 109.00- 169.00   XP 20   F
Senior discount. 536 units. Adjacent to I-405, exit Jamboree Blvd. 17900 Jamboree Blvd. (92714) Check-in 3 pm. A/C;
C/CATV; free & pay movies; radios; phones. Htd pool; saunas; whirlpool; lighted tennis-4 courts; rental bicycles; exer-
cise rm. Pay valet parking lot. Airport transp. No pets. Wkly & monthly rates avail. AE, DI, DS, MC, VI. ● Dining rm &
coffeeshop; 6 am-midnight; $9.50-$25; cocktails; entertainment. FAX (714) 863-0531   ⊗ Ⓢ Ⓓ (714) 975-1234

Irvine Marriott Hotel   Rates Subject to Change   *Hotel*   ◆◆◆◆
Sun-Thurs   1P .... 139.00   2P/1B .... 139.00   2P/2B .... 139.00   XP
Fri & Sat   1P .... 89.00   2P/1B .... 89.00   2P/2B .... 89.00   XP
484 units. Adjacent to I-405, exit Jamboree Blvd; s to Michelson Dr, w to Von Karman Ave. 18000 Von Karman Ave.
(92715) Check-in 4 pm. A/C; C/CATV; free & pay movies; radios; phones. Coin laundry. Htd pool; sauna; whirlpool; rental
bicycles; exercise rm. Fee for: lighted tennis-4 courts; massage. Pay valet parking lot. Airport transp. Pets. AE, DI, DS,
MC, VI. ● Restaurant & coffeeshop; 6 am-10 pm; Sat & Sun from 7 am; $7-$18; cocktails. FAX (714) 261-7059
                                                                              ⊗ Ⓢ Ⓓ Ⓑ (714) 553-0100

La Quinta Inn   Rates Subject to Change   *Motel*   ◆◆◆
All year   1P 56.00- 63.00   2P/1B 64.00- 74.00   2P/2B .... 64.00   XP 5   F
148 units. 1/2 blk w of I-5, exit Sand Canyon Ave. 14972 Sand Canyon Ave. (92718) Units vary from modern day
to 98 rooms situated in 32 historic hexagonal grain silos; each decorated in turn-of-century replica furnishings.
8 refrigerators; A/C; C/CATV; free & pay movies; radios; phones. Coin laundry. Htd pool; whirlpool; transportation to John Wayne Orange County Airport; exercise rm. Pets. AE, DI, DS, MC, VI. Restaurant & 2 coffeeshops
adjacent. FAX (714) 551-2945   ⊗ Ⓓ Ⓑ (714) 551-0909

Radisson Plaza Hotel-Orange County Airport   Rates Subject to Change   *Hotel*   ◆◆◆
Sun-Thurs   1P 89.00- 125.00   2P/1B 89.00- 125.00   2P/2B 89.00- 125.00   XP 20
Fri & Sat   1P 69.00- 79.00   2P/1B 69.00- 79.00   2P/2B 69.00- 79.00   XP 20
Senior discount. 289 units. Opposite John Wayne Orange County Airport. 18800 MacArthur Blvd. (92715)
Check-in 3 pm. A/C; C/CATV; pay movies; radios; phones. Htd pool; whirlpool; lighted tennis-1 court; exercise
rm. Pay valet parking lot. Airport transp. No pets. Wkly & monthly rates avail. Reserv deposit required. AE, DI,
DS, MC, VI. ● Restaurant & coffeeshop; 6 am-midnight; $9.95-$22; cocktails. FAX (714) 833-3317
                                                                              ⊗ Ⓢ Ⓓ Ⓑ (714) 833-9999

Residence Inn by Marriott-Irvine   Rates Guaranteed   *Apartment Motel*   ◆◆◆
All year [CP]   1P 102.00- 134.00   2P/1B 102.00- 134.00   2P/2B 134.00- 160.00   XP 10
Senior discount. 112 units. 2 mi e of I-5, exit Alton Pkwy. 10 Morgan. (92718) A/C; C/CATV; movies; radios; phones.
Kitchens. Coin laundry. Htd pool; whirlpool; sports court. Small pets only; $200 deposit, plus $6 daily extra charge. Some
VCP's. Wkly & monthly rates avail. AE, DI, DS, MC, VI. FAX (714) 588-7743   ⊗ Ⓢ Ⓓ Ⓑ (714) 380-3000

RESTAURANTS

Chanteclair   French $$$ ◆◆◆◆
3/4 mi s of I-405. 18912 MacArthur Blvd. An elegant restaurant with the atmosphere of a French country inn. Sun brunch
10:30 am-2 pm, $16-$22.95. A/C. Dress code. Open 11:30 am-2:30 & 5-10 pm; Sat 5:30 pm-11 pm; Sun 10:30 am-2 &
5-10 pm; closed major holidays. Cocktails & lounge. Valet parking. Reserv advised. AE, DI, DS, MC, VI.
                                                                              ⊗ Ⓑ (714) 752-8001

Reuben's   Steak & Seafood $$ ◆◆
2 blks s of I-405. 18542 MacArthur Blvd. Nice selection of steaks, prime rib & seafood. A/C. Early bird specials; children's
menu. Open 11 am-10 pm; Fri-11 pm; Sat 5 pm-11 pm; Sun 5 pm-10 pm; closed 12/25. Cocktails & lounge. Entertainment. AE, DI, DS, MC, VI.   ⊗ Ⓑ (714) 833-9111

ISLETON — 900

Delta Daze Inn
🏵 All year [CP]   *Bed & Breakfast*   ◆◆
Rates Subject to Change
1P 90.00- 125.00 2P/1B 90.00- 125.00 2P/2B 90.00- 125.00 XP 20
12 units. 20 Main St. (PO Box 607, 95641) A/C; C/CATV; movies; radios; phones; shower baths. Bicycles. No pets. Reserv deposit required; 7 days refund notice. Complimentary beverages each evening. AE, MC, VI.
⊗ Ⓓ (916) 777-7777

JACKSON — 3,500

Amador Motel
🏵 All year   *Motel*   ◆
Rates Subject to Change
1P .... 37.00 2P/1B .... 37.00 2P/2B 40.00- 42.00 XP 5
10 units. 1 1/2 mi w in Martell at jct SR 49 & 88 on Frontage Rd. 12408 Kennedy Flat Rd. (95642) Some small rooms. A/C; C/TV; shower baths. Pool. Pets. Reserv deposit required. DS, MC, VI.
Ⓓ (209) 223-0970

Best Western Amador Inn
🏵 Fri & Sat   *Motor Inn*   ◆◆
Rates Subject to Change
1P .... 50.00 2P/1B .... 64.00 2P/2B .... 64.00 XP 8
Sun-Thurs   1P .... 46.00 2P/1B .... 60.00 2P/2B .... 60.00 XP 8
Senior discount. 118 units. On SR 49. 200 s Hwy 49. (PO Box 758, 95642) Check-in 3 pm. A/C; C/CATV; movies; 55 radios; phones. Pool. Pets, $6 extra charge. 4 kitchens, $10 extra. Some gas burning fireplaces, $10 extra. Reserv deposit required. AE, DI, DS, MC, VI. Coffeeshop adjacent. FAX (209) 223-4836 ⊗ Ⓓ 🔊 (209) 223-0211

El Campo Casa Resort Motel
🏵 2/5-10/17   *Motel*   ◆◆
Rates Subject to Change
1P 37.00- 56.00 2P/1B 44.00- 66.00 2P/2B 47.00- 70.00 XP 5
10/18-2/4   1P 33.00- 39.00 2P/1B 37.00- 47.00 2P/2B 39.00- 49.00 XP 3
15 units. 1 1/2 mi w in Martell, at jct SR 49 & 88 on Frontage Rd; approach off SR 88. 12548 Kennedy Flat Rd. (95642) Well-landscaped grounds. A/C; C/TV; radios; shower baths. Pool; playground. Reserv deposit required; 5 days refund notice. AE, CB, DI, MC, VI.
⊗ Ⓓ (209) 223-0100

Jackson Holiday Lodge
🏵 All year   *Motel*   ◆◆
Rates Subject to Change
1P 37.00- 55.00 2P/1B 42.00- 60.00 2P/2B 42.00- 60.00 XP 5
36 units. 1/2 mi w on SR 49 & 88. (PO Box 1147, 95642) A/C; C/CATV; movies; phones; comb or shower baths. Pool. Pets, $10 deposit required. 8 duplex housekeeping cottages, $58-$68 for up to 2 persons. AE, MC, VI.
⊗ Ⓓ (209) 223-0486

JULIAN — 1,300

Julian Lodge
🏵 All year [CP]   *Lodge*   ◆◆
Rates Subject to Change
1P .... 74.00 2P/1B 74.00- 84.00 2P/2B .... 84.00 XP 10
23 units. 1/2 blk s of Main St, SR 78. 2720 C St. (PO Box 1930, 92036) Attractive country atmosphere. Check-in 3 pm. 11 refrigerators; A/C; C/CATV. No pets. Reserv deposit required. AE, MC, VI.
⊗ Ⓓ (619) 765-1420

JUNE LAKE — 600

Boulder Lodge
🏵 11/20-10/1   *Motel*   ◆◆
Rates Subject to Change
2P/1B 52.00- 95.00 2P/2B 60.00- 120.00 XP 8
10/2-11/19   .... 2P/1B 40.00- 80.00 2P/2B 45.00- 100.00 XP 8
Senior discount. 60 units. 2 1/4 mi w of US 395 on SR 158 via s jct June Lake Loop turnoff. (PO Box 68, 93529) On 5 acres of wooded, lakefront grounds. Varied accommodations in rooms, housekeeping cabins & 1-to 3-bedroom apartments with kitchen; 1 5-bedroom cottage. Check-in 4 pm. C/CATV; 30 radios; comb or shower baths. 23 2-bedrm units. Htd indoor pool; sauna; whirlpool; fishing; fish cleaning & freezing facilities avail; tennis-1 court; playground. No pets. 3-night minimum stay for kitchen units, 4 days in Aug; cleaning deposit required 2 cabins with private whirlpool & fireplace. Wkly rates avail. Reserv deposit required; 30 days refund notice. AE, DS, MC, VI. FAX (619) 648-7330 *(See ad p A165)*
⊗ (619) 648-7533

Gull Lake Lodge
🏵 Fri & Sat 11/15-4/15   *Apartment Motel*   ◆◆
AAA Special Value Rates
2P/1B .... 75.00 2P/2B .... 75.00 XP 9
4/16-11/14   .... 2P/1B .... 65.00 2P/2B .... 65.00 XP 9
Sun-Thurs 11/15-4/15   .... 2P/1B .... 59.00 2P/2B .... 59.00 XP 9
15 units. 3 mi w of US 395 via s jct June Lake Loop turnoff, then 3 blks n via Knoll & Bruce sts, between June & Gull Lakes. (PO Box 25, 93529) 1-bedroom housekeeping apartments. Check-out 10 am. C/CATV; movies; radios; shower or comb baths. Coin laundry. Fish cleaning & freezing facilities. Pets, $6 extra charge. 1 2-bedroom cottage with fireplace & kitchen, $105-$165. Wkly rates avail 4/1-8/1 & 9/1-11/1. Reserv deposit required; 21 days refund notice. AE, DS, MC, VI.
Ⓓ (619) 648-7516

June Lake Motel & Cabins   Rates Subject to Change   *Motel*   ◆◆

5/1-11/15	....	2P/1B	....	48.00	2P/2B	50.00- 75.00	XP	8
Sun-Thurs 11/16-4/30	....	2P/1B	....	42.00	2P/2B	44.00- 66.00	XP	8
Fri & Sat 11/16-4/30	....	2P/1B	....	52.00	2P/2B	.... 54.00	XP	8

Senior discount. 26 units. 3 mi w of US 395 on SR 158 via s jct June Lake Loop turnoff. (PO Box 98, 93529) Check-out 10 am. C/CATV; movies; phones; shower or comb baths. Sauna; indoor whirlpool; fish cleaning & freezing facilities avail. Pets, $3 extra charge. 22 kitchens, $4 extra. 2 1-bedroom & 1 2-bedroom apartments. 4 2-bedroom housekeeping cabins with fireplace. Wkly rates avail in summer. Reserv deposit required; 14 days refund notice. DS, MC, VI. *(See ad p A164)*   Ⓓ (619) 648-7547

Whispering Pines Chalets & Motel   Rates Subject to Change   *Motel*   ◆◆

Fri & Sat 11/1-4/25	....	2P/1B	55.00- 65.00	2P/2B	55.00- 145.00	XP	7
Sun-Thurs 11/1-4/25	....	2P/1B	45.00- 65.00	2P/2B	45.00- 145.00	XP	7
8/1-9/6	....	2P/1B	.... 55.00	2P/2B	55.00- 105.00	XP	7
Sun-Thurs 4/26-7/31 & 9/7-10/31	....	2P/1B	44.00- 55.00	2P/2B	44.00- 105.00	XP	7

24 units. 5 1/2 mi w of US 395 on SR 158 via s jct June Lake Loop turnoff. (Star Rt 3, Box 14B, 93529) Motel units with kitchens, housekeeping cabins & A-frame chalets; view of Carson Peak. Some units with microwave. Check-out 10 am. C/CATV; movies; radios; phones; shower or comb baths. 6 2-bedrm units, kitchens. Fish cleaning & freezing facilities. No pets. 6 units with VCP. Reserv deposit required; 30 days refund notice. MC, VI. *(See ad p A164)*   Ⓓ (619) 648-7762

RESTAURANTS

Carson Peak Inn   American $$ ◆◆
5 mi w of US 395 on SR 158 via s jct June Lake Loop turnoff. Beautiful country setting at foot of Carson Peak. Children's menu. Open 5 pm-10 pm. Beer & wine. Reserv advised. MC, VI.   (619) 648-7575

Sierra Inn   American $$ ◆
2 1/2 mi w of US 395 on SR 158 via s jct June Lake Loop turnoff. Attractive dining room overlooking June Lake. Selection of seafood, chicken, steaks, pasta & pizza. Buffet dinner Sat $13.95. A/C. Senior discount; children's menu. Open 5 pm-10 pm; coffeeshop 7 am-2 pm; closed 11/1-11/19. Cocktails & lounge. Reserv advised weekends. AE, DS, MC, VI. *(See ad below)*   (619) 648-7774

KELSEYVILLE — 1,600

Bell Haven Resort   Rates Subject to Change   *Apartment Cottages*   ◆

2/1-11/30	....	....	2P/2B	.... 62.00	XP	8

8 units. On Soda Bay; 6 mi se off Soda Bay Rd. 3415 White Oak Way. (95451) OPEN 2/1-11/30. Nice wooded area on southwest shore of Clear Lake. Shower baths. 6 2-bedrm units, 7 kitchens. Beach; swimming; boating; dock; fishing. No pets. Wkly rates avail. Reserv deposit required; 30 days refund notice. MC, VI.   Ⓓ (707) 279-4329

Konocti Harbor Resort & Spa   Rates Subject to Change   *Resort Complex*   ◆◆

4/15-11/15	1P	59.00- 80.00	2P/1B	59.00- 80.00	2P/2B	59.00- 80.00	XP 10
11/16-4/14	1P	45.00- 70.00	2P/1B	45.00- 70.00	2P/2B	45.00- 70.00	XP 10

250 units. 5 mi ne of SR 29 via SR 281. 8727 Soda Bay Rd. (95451) Beautifully landscaped, terraced hillside location. Excellent recreational facilities. Few modest rooms. Check-in 4 pm. A/C; C/CATV; VCPs; phones; shower or comb baths. Coin laundry. 2 pools; 2 wading pools; rental boats; fishing; water skiing; social program in summer; recreational program; playground. Fee for: marina & ramp, miniature golf, lighted tennis-8 courts; herbal wraps; health club & massage. No pets. 100 kitchen apartments $130-$175; 11/16-4/14 $100-$175, for up to 2 persons. Reserv deposit required. AE, DI, DS, MC, VI. ● Dining rm & coffeeshop; 7 am-10 pm; $10-$20; cocktails. FAX (707) 279-9205   ⊗ Ⓓ (707) 279-4281

KERNVILLE — 1,700

Hi-Ho Resort Lodge   Rates Guaranteed   *Apartment Motel*   ◆

5/2-1/31	....	2P/1B	.... 60.00	2P/2B	.... 80.00	XP 10	F

Senior discount. 7 units. 1 1/4 mi s on Sierra Way. 11901 Sierra Way. (Rt 1, Box 21, 93238) OPEN ALL YEAR. Spacious grounds. 2-bedroom housekeeping units for up to 6 persons. A/C; C/CATV. Coin laundry. Pool; whirlpool; fish cleaning facilities; recreational program; playground. Small pets only. 5 rooms with fireplace, $5 extra. 7 kitchens, $10 extra. Wkly & monthly rates avail. Reserv deposit required; 5 days refund notice. MC, VI.   Ⓓ (619) 376-2671

Kern Lodge Motel   Rates Guaranteed   *Motel*   ◆

All year	....	2P/1B	.... 47.00	2P/2B	.... 53.00	XP 7

15 units. 67 Valley View Corner of Sierra Way. (PO Box 66, 93238) 3 blocks from the Kern River. Refrigerators; C/CATV; phones; shower baths. Pool; recreational program. Pets, $7 extra charge. 2 2-bedroom units, $85 for up to 5 persons. 6 kitchen units, $55-$75. 2-night minimum stay Fri & Sat, 3/31-10/1. Reserv deposit required; 7 days refund notice 3/1-10/1. AE, CB, DS, MC, VI. Restaurant adjacent.   Ⓓ (619) 376-2223

Kern River Inn Bed & Breakfast   Rates Guaranteed   *Bed & Breakfast*   ◆◆◆

4/1-10/31 [BP]	1P	69.00- 79.00	2P/1B	79.00- 89.00	....	XP 15
11/1-3/31 [BP]	1P	59.00- 69.00	2P/1B	69.00- 79.00	....	XP 15

6 units. In town off of Kernville Rd. 119 Kern River Dr. (PO Box 1725, 93238) Across from Riverside Park & Kern River. Designated smoking areas. Afternoon refreshments. Check-in 3 pm. A/C; radios. No pets. 3 rooms with fireplace & 2 rooms with whirlpool tub. Wkly rates avail. Reserv deposit required; 7 days refund notice. MC, VI.   ⊗ Ⓓ (619) 376-6750

Whispering Pines Lodge Bed & Breakfast   Rates Guaranteed   *Lodge* ◆◆
All year [BP]   1P 69.00- 119.00   2P/1B   79.00- 129.00   ....   XP 10
Senior discount. 11 units. 1/4 mi n. 13745 Sierra Way. (Rt 1, Box 41, 93238) 7 woodburning fireplaces; 10 rooms with balcony. Smoke free premises. Check-in 3 pm. Refrigerators; A/C; C/CATV; movies; VCPs. Radios; phones. 4 efficiencies. Pool; 2 room with whirlpool tub. No pets. Wkly rates avail. Reserv deposit required; 7 days refund notice. AE, DI, MC, VI. FAX (619) 376-3735   ⊗ Ⓢ Ⓓ (619) 376-3733

RESTAURANTS

Johnny McNally's Fairview Lodge   Steakhouse $$ ◆
15 mi ne on Sierra Way. Old west decor featuring oversize steaks including 40 oz Porterhouse, also fish & poultry. Located on Kern River. Snack bar open 10 am-5 pm featuring sandwiches. Children's menu. Open 5 pm-10 pm; Sat from 5 pm; Sun from 4 pm; closed Mon-Thurs, Nov-March except 11/25, 1 pm-7 pm. Cocktails & lounge. Reserv advised. MC, VI.
(619) 376-2430

Peacock Inn   Chinese $
Center of town. 21 Sierra Dr. Casual atmosphere. Open 11 am-9 pm; closed Tues, 11/25, 12/24 & 12/25. Beer & wine. Reserv advised. MC, VI.
(619) 376-3937

KETTLEMAN CITY — 600

Best Western Olive Tree Inn   Rates Subject to Change   *Motel* ◆◆
6/1-9/30   1P .... 56.00 2P/1B .... 58.00 2P/2B .... 62.00 XP 6
Senior discount. 60 units. 2 mi sw; 1/2 blk e off I-5, jct SR 41; exit Kettleman City-Paso Robles. (PO Box 540, 93239) OPEN ALL YEAR. A/C; C/CATV; pay movies; phones. Pool. AE, CB, DI, MC, VI. Coffeeshop opposite.
⊗ Ⓓ (209) 386-9530

KING CITY — 7,600

Best Western King City Inn   Rates Subject to Change   *Motel* ◆◆
All year   1P 42.00- 50.00 2P/1B 44.00- 55.00 2P/2B .... 47.00 XP 8
47 units. Exit US 101 at Broadway. 1190 Broadway. (93930) 40 refrigerators; A/C; C/CATV; phones. Small pool; whirlpool. Pets. 6 rooms with whirlpool, $10 extra. Some microwaves. Reserv deposit required; 3 days refund notice. AE, DI, DS, MC, VI. FAX (408) 385-0714 *(See ad below)*   ⊗ Ⓓ Ⓛ (408) 385-6733

Courtesy Inn   Rates Subject to Change   *Motel* ◆◆◆
All year [CP]   1P 42.00- 94.00 2P/1B 44.00- 94.00 2P/2B .... 94.00 XP 5   F
Senior discount. 63 units. W of US 101; exit Broadway 1/4 mi s. 4 Broadway Cir. (93930) Refrigerators; A/C; C/CATV; phones. Coin laundry. Small htd pool; whirlpool. Pets, $10 extra charge. Microwaves. AE, DI, DS, MC, VI. Coffeeshop adjacent. FAX (408) 385-6024 *(See ad below)*   ⊗ Ⓢ Ⓓ Ⓛ (408) 385-4646

Fireside Inn   Rates Subject to Change   *Motel* ◆
1/1-9/30   1P .... 24.95 2P/1B .... 29.95 2P/2B .... 34.95 XP 5
10/1-12/31   1P .... 19.95 2P/1B .... 23.95 2P/2B .... 28.95 XP 5
Senior discount. 18 units. 4 blks n on US 101 business rt; exit via Canal St or Broadway Cir. 640 Broadway Cir. (93930) Few microwaves. Refrigerators; C/CATV; phones; shower baths. No pets. Wkly rates avail. Reserv deposit required. AE, CB, DI, MC, VI.
Ⓓ (408) 385-3248

Keefer's Inn   Rates Subject to Change   *Motor Inn* ◆◆
All year [CP]   1P 45.00- 48.00 2P/1B 48.00- 53.00 2P/2B .... 51.00 XP 5   F
48 units. W off & adjacent to US 101; exit via Canal St. 615 Canal St. (93930) Refrigerators; A/C; C/CATV; movies; radios; phones. Coin laundry. Small pool; whirlpool. No pets. AE, MC, VI. ● Restaurant, see separate listing.
⊗ Ⓓ (408) 385-4843

RESTAURANT

Keefer's Restaurant   American $$ ◆◆
W of & adjacent to US 101. 611 Canal St. Family restaurant. A/C. Children's menu. Open 7 am-9:45 pm; closed 12/25. Cocktails. MC, VI.   ⊗ Ⓛ (408) 385-3543

KINGSBURG — 5,700

Swedish Inn   Rates Subject to Change   *Motel* ◆◆
All year   1P 40.00- 44.00 2P/1B 42.00- 46.00 2P/2B 44.00- 48.00 XP 5
47 units. 1 blk w of SR 99; Conejo exit. 401 Conejo St. (93631) A/C; C/CATV; phones. 1 kitchen. Pool; whirlpool. No pets. 3 units with sitting area, $52-$89 for up to 2 persons. [MAP] avail. Reserv deposit required; 3 days refund notice. AE, DI, DS, MC, VI. Restaurant adjacent.   Ⓓ (209) 897-1022

KINGS CANYON NATIONAL PARK — See SEQUOIA and KINGS CANYON NATIONAL PARKS & THREE RIVERS

KIRKWOOD

Kirkwood Resort — AAA Special Value Rates — Resort Complex ◆◆
11/1-5/10   1P 65.00- 125.00 2P/1B 85.00- 190.00 2P/2B 115.00- 245.00 XP
5/11-10/31   1P 55.00- 60.00 2P/1B 80.00- 90.00 2P/2B 110.00- 120.00 XP
120 units. 30 mi s of Lake Tahoe; 14 mi w of jct SR 89 & SR 88; on SR 88. (PO Box 1, 95646) 1-to 3-bedroom condominiums, all with woodburning fireplaces. Check-in 4 pm. Check-out 10 am. Refrigerators; C/CATV; radios; phones. 33 2-bedrm units, 89 kitchens, 31 efficiencies. Coin laundry. Tennis-4 courts; cross country skiing. Fee for: ski tows & lifts, riding. No pets. Reserv deposit required; 14 days refund notice. AE, CB, DI, MC, VI. ● Restaurant; 6 am-10 pm; $5.50-$15; cocktails. FAX (209) 258-7400   (D) (209) 258-6000

KIT CARSON — 300

Kit Carson Lodge — Rates Subject to Change — Cottages ◆◆
5/28-10/11   1P 95.00- 160.00 2P/1B 95.00- 160.00 2P/2B 95.00- 160.00 XP
27 units. 1/4 mi off SR 88, on Silver Lake. On Hwy 88 at Silver Lake. (95644) OPEN 5/28-10/11. Wooded mountainside location at 7200 ft elevation. Rooms with scenic views. Many units with decks & fireplaces. Check-in 4 pm. Shower baths. 8 2-bedrm units. Coin laundry. Beach; swimming; boats, rental motors & canoes; dock; fishing; nature trails. No pets. 8 motel units for up to 3 persons; 19 efficiency cottages for up to 6 persons. Wkly rates avail in cottages 6/13-9/8, $380-$695. Reserv deposit required; 30 days refund notice. MC, VI. ● Restaurant; 6 pm-9 pm; closed Sun & Mon evenings; $11-$18; Continental breakfast, 8 am-10 am; beer & wine.   (D) (209) 258-8500

KLAMATH — 200

Motel Trees — Rates Subject to Change — Motel ◆◆
3/1-11/1   1P .... 40.00 2P/1B .... 44.00 2P/2B .... 48.00 XP 4
23 units. 4 mi n on US 101. (PO Box 309, 95548) OPEN ALL YEAR. Opposite Trees of Mystery. Check-in 3 pm. C/CATV; movies; 5 radios; phones; shower or comb baths. 4 2-bedrm units. Tennis-1 court. No pets. Wkly & monthly rates avail. Reserv deposit required. MC, VI. Coffeeshop adjacent. *(See ad below)* (D) (707) 482-3152

LA COSTA

La Costa Resort and Spa — Rates Guaranteed — Resort Complex ◆◆◆◆
All year   1P 215.00- 400.00 2P/1B 215.00- 400.00 2P/2B 215.00- 400.00 XP 35
480 units. 2 mi e of I-5, exit La Costa Ave to El Camino Real. Costa Del Mar Rd. (Carlsbad, 92009) Acres of nicely landscaped grounds. Check-in 4 pm. Refrigerators; A/C; C/CATV; pay movies; radios; phones. 2 htd pools; rental bicycles; playground; jogging track. Fee for: golf-36 holes, tennis-23 courts, 8 lighted; theatre; health club; airport transp. No pets. [MAP] avail. Monthly rates avail. Reserv deposit required; 7 days refund notice. AE, CB, DI, MC, VI. ● 3 dining rms & 2 restaurants; 6 am-1 am; $15-$45; cocktails; entertainment. FAX (619) 438-3758   (X) (S)(D) (619) 438-9111

LAFAYETTE — 23,500   (See OAKLAND/BERKELEY AREA spotting map pages A300 & A301; see index starting on page A298)

Lafayette Park Hotel/Best Western [36] — Rates Subject to Change — Hotel ◆◆◆
All year   1P 115.00- 145.00 2P/1B 115.00- 155.00 2P/2B 115.00- 155.00 XP 10
Senior discount. 139 units. Exit SR 24 at Pleasant Hill Rd, 1 blk s. 3287 Mt Diablo Blvd. (94549) Norman French architecture. Spacious elegant rooms. Check-in 3 pm. Refrigerators; A/C; C/CATV; pay movies; radios; phones. Pool; sauna; whirlpool; exercise rm. Garage & parking lot. No pets. Some rooms & suites with fireplace. Monthly rates avail. Reserv deposit required. AE, DI, DS, MC, VI. ● Restaurant; 6:30 am-10 pm; $10-$22; cocktails. FAX (510) 284-1621 *(See ad inside back cover)*   (X) (S)(D)(L) (510) 283-3700

RESTAURANT

Cape Cod House [36] — Seafood — $$ ◆◆
Exit SR 24 Central, 1 mi e. 3666 Mt Diablo Blvd. Quiet comfortable atmosphere, nice selection of meats & poultry. A/C. Children's menu. Open 11:30 am-10 pm; Fri & Sat-10:30 pm; Sun-9 pm. Cocktails & lounge. Reserv advised. AE, DI, VI.   (X) (510) 283-8288

LAGUNA BEACH — 23,200   See also DANA POINT & LAGUNA NIGUEL

Aliso Creek Inn AAA Special Value Rates *Apartment Motor Inn* ◆◆◆
5/20-9/30	1P 112.00- 140.00	2P/1B	112.00- 140.00	2P/2B	130.00- 188.00	XP 10			
10/1-5/19	1P 88.00- 114.00	2P/1B	88.00- 162.00	2P/2B	104.00- 162.00	XP 10			

62 units. 2 mi se on SR 1; 1/4 mi e of Aliso Beach Park. 31106 S Coast Hwy. (South Laguna, 92677) Picturesque canyon setting adjoining golf course. Studio & 1 to 2-bedroom housekeeping units. Patios. Check-in 3 pm. C/CATV; movies; phones. Coin laundry. Htd pool; wading pool; whirlpool. Fee for: golf-9 holes. No pets. Reserv deposit required. AE, MC, VI. ● Restaurant; 8 am-10 pm; Fri & Sat-11 pm; Sun 8 am-3 & 5-9 pm; $10.50-$18; cocktails; entertainment. FAX (714) 499-4601 ⊗ Ⓓ (714) 499-2271

Best Western Laguna Reef Inn Rates Subject to Change *Motel* ◆◆◆
7/1-9/8 [CP]	1P 84.00	2P/1B	.... 84.00	2P/2B	.... 84.00	XP 10	
Fri & Sat 9/9-6/30 [CP]	1P 72.00	2P/1B	.... 72.00	2P/2B	.... 72.00	XP 10	
Sun-Thurs [CP]	1P 62.00	2P/1B	.... 62.00	2P/2B	.... 62.00	XP 10	

43 units. 1 3/4 mi se on SR 1. 30806 S Coast Hwy. (92651) Nicely landscaped. A/C; C/CATV; pay movies; VCPs. Phones; shower or comb baths. Htd pool; sauna; whirlpool. No pets. 14 efficiencies with refrigerator & small microwave. 6 kitchens, $15 extra. Wkly rates avail. AE, DI, DS, MC, VI. FAX (714) 495-5575 *(See ad p A167)*
⊗ (714) 499-2227

By-The-Sea Motel AAA Special Value Rates *Motel* ◆◆
Fri & Sat 6/15-9/15	1P 99.00- 169.00	2P/1B	99.00- 169.00	2P/2B	99.00- 159.00	XP 10	
Sun-Thurs 6/15-9/15	1P 89.00- 149.00	2P/1B	89.00- 149.00	2P/2B	89.00- 149.00	XP 10	
Fri & Sat 9/16-6/14	1P 79.00- 139.00	2P/1B	79.00- 139.00	2P/2B	79.00- 139.00	XP 10	
Sun-Thurs 9/16-6/14	1P 69.00- 129.00	2P/1B	69.00- 129.00	2P/2B	69.00- 129.00	XP 10	

36 units. 1/2 mi n on SR 1. 475 N Coast Hwy. (92651) 1 block to oceanfront. A/C; C/CATV; pay movies; VCPs. Radios; phones. Coin laundry. Small htd pool; sauna; whirlpool; 3 rooms with whirlpool bath. Garage. No pets. 4 efficiencies with refrigerator & microwave. Wkly & monthly rates avail. Reserv deposit required; 3 days refund notice. AE, DI, DS, MC, VI. FAX (714) 497-7499 *(See ad p A167)*
⊗ Ⓓ Ⓛ (714) 497-6645

Capri Laguna Rates Subject to Change *Motel* ◆◆
6/14-9/13 [CP]	....	2P/1B	90.00- 250.00	2P/2B	90.00- 250.00	XP 15
3/28-6/13 [CP]	....	2P/1B	75.00- 175.00	2P/2B	75.00- 175.00	XP 10
9/14-3/27 [CP]	....	2P/1B	70.00- 150.00	2P/2B	70.00- 150.00	XP 10

Senior discount. 35 units. 1441 S Coast Hwy. (92651) Refrigerators; C/CATV; movies; radios; phones. 3 kitchens, 28 efficiencies, no utensils. Coin laundry. Htd pool; beach; sauna; exercise rm. No pets. AE, CB, DI, MC, VI. FAX (714) 497-6962 *(See ad below)* ⊗ Ⓓ (714) 494-6533

The Carriage House-Bed & Breakfast Rates Guaranteed *Historical*
All year [CP]	....	2P/1B	95.00- 150.00	2P/2B	95.00- 150.00	XP 10-20

Senior discount. 6 units. 1 mi s; 2 blks e of SR 1, via Cress St. 1322 Catalina St. (92651) A charming bed & breakfast inn with 1- & 2-bedroom suites. Refrigerators; C/CATV; radios; comb or tub baths. 5 kitchens. No pets. Reserv deposit required; 7 days refund notice. Ⓓ (714) 494-8945

Casa Laguna Inn Rates Subject to Change *Historic Bed & Breakfast* ◆
5/20-9/30 [CP]	1P 90.00- 150.00	2P/1B	90.00- 150.00	2P/2B	90.00- 150.00	XP 20
10/1-5/19 [CP]	1P 79.00- 109.00	2P/1B	79.00- 109.00	2P/2B	79.00- 109.00	XP 10

Senior discount. 20 units. 1 1/4 mi se on SR 1. 2510 S Coast Hwy. (92651) Landscaped, terraced grounds overlooking the ocean. Smaller, nicely furnished rooms to spacious sites. Check-in 3 pm. 10 refrigerators; C/CATV; movies; phones; shower baths. 1 2-bedrm unit, 5 kitchens. Htd pool. No pets. 2-night minimum stay weekends, 7/1-8/31. 1 cottage, $169-$205. Monthly rates avail. Reserv deposit required; 3 days refund notice. AE, DI, DS, MC, VI. FAX (714) 494-5009 *(See ad below)* Ⓓ (714) 494-2996

Inn at Laguna Beach AAA Special Value Rates *Motel* ◆◆◆
5/22-9/7 [CP]	1P 149.00- 299.00	2P/1B	149.00- 299.00	2P/2B	149.00- 299.00	XP 20	F
9/8-1/31 & 2/1-5/21 [CP]	1P 99.00- 279.00	2P/1B	99.00- 279.00	2P/2B	99.00- 279.00	XP 20	F

70 units. 211 N Coast Hwy. (92651) Located on bluff above the ocean. Many rooms with ocean view. Check-in 4 pm. Refrigerators; A/C; C/CATV; pay movies; VCPs. Radios; phones; shower or comb baths. Htd pool. No pets. Reserv deposit required. AE, CB, DI, MC, VI. FAX (714) 497-9972 ⊗ Ⓢ Ⓓ (714) 497-9722

Laguna Riviera Beach Resort & Spa Rates Guaranteed *Motel* ◆◆
6/15-9/15 [CP]	1P 75.00- 170.00	2P/1B	75.00- 170.00	2P/2B	75.00- 170.00	XP 10
9/16-6/14 [CP]	1P 63.00- 155.00	2P/1B	63.00- 155.00	2P/2B	63.00- 155.00	XP 10

41 units. 1/2 mi se on SR 1. 825 S Coast Hwy. (92651) 5 terrace levels on oceanfront. Large variety of rooms, some with ocean view & enclosed lanai. Check-in 3 pm. Refrigerators; C/CATV; movies; 15 radios; phones; shower or comb baths. 5 2-bedrm units, 10 kitchens, 16 efficiencies. Htd indoor pool; beach; sauna; whirlpool; 2 rooms with whirlpool. No pets. 8 rooms with microwave. 2 night minimum stay weekends 6/15-9/15. Wkly & monthly rates avail 9/16-6/14. Reserv deposit required. AE, DI, DS, MC, VI. FAX (714) 494-8421 Ⓓ (714) 494-1196

Surf & Sand Hotel   Rates Subject to Change   Hotel   ◆◆◆◆
🏵 5/25-10/31   1P 160.00- 275.00   2P/1B 160.00- 275.00   2P/2B 215.00- 275.00 XP 10
   11/1-5/24   1P 150.00- 225.00   2P/1B 150.00- 225.00   2P/2B 150.00- 225.00 XP 10
   157 units. 1 mi se on SR 1. 1555 S Coast Hwy. (92651) Oceanfront. Most rooms with ocean view & balcony.
   Check-in 3 pm. Refrigerators; 6 A/C; C/CATV; pay movies; VCPs. Radios; phones; comb or shower baths. 12
   2-bedrm units. Htd pool; beach. Valet parking ramp. No pets. 2-night minimum stay 7/1-7/31; also weekends
   6/1-6/30 & 9/1-9/30; 3-day minimum stay 8/1-8/31. Reserv deposit required. AE, CB, DI, MC, VI. ● 2 dining rms;
   6:30 am-10:30 pm; $11-$25; cocktails; entertainment. Also, Towers Restaurant, see separate listing.
   FAX (714) 494-7653 (See ad p 82)   ⊗ Ⓓ ⓹ (714) 497-4477

RESTAURANTS

The Beach House   Seafood $$ ◆◆
🏵 1/2 mi se on SR 1; 1 blk w. 619 Sleepy Hollow Ln. Charming restaurant located on the beach. Early bird spe-
   cials; children's menu. Open 8-11:15 am, 11:30-3:30 & 4:30-10 pm; Sat 8 am-11:45, noon-3:30 & 4:30-11 pm; Sun
   8 am-3:30 & 4:30-10 pm; closed 11/25 & 12/25. Cocktails & lounge. Valet parking. Reserv advised. AE, MC, VI.
                                                                                      ⊗ (714) 494-9707

Cedar Creek Inn   American $$ ◆◆◆
   Downtown, 2 blks e of SR 1. 384 Forest Ave. Very attractive restaurant featuring a large selection of homemade des-
   serts, fresh fish, beef, chicken, veal & sandwiches. Oyster bar 4 pm-midnight. Casual. A/C. Open 11 am-10 pm; closed
   major holidays. Cocktails & lounge. Entertainment. Minimum, $5. AE, MC, VI.   ⊗ (714) 497-8696

Las Brisas   Mexican $$ ◆◆◆
   1/4 mi nw on SR 1. 361 Cliff Dr. Beautiful ocean view. Features cuisine of the west coast of Mexico. Sun brunch 9 am-
   2:30 pm $16.75 All you can eat buffet Mon-Sat 8 am-11 am $6.95. Open 8 am-3:30 & 5-10 pm; Fri & Sat-11 pm; Sun 9
   am-3 & 4-10 pm; closed 11/25 & 12/25. Cocktails & lounge. Pay valet parking. Reserv advised. AE, DI, DS, MC, VI.
                                                                                      ⊗ (714) 497-5434

Towers Restaurant   Continental $$$ ◆◆◆
   In Surf & Sand Hotel. On top floor overlooking beach & ocean. Beautiful, contemporary decor. Formal service. A/C. Dress
   code. Open 5:30 pm-10 pm; Fri & Sat-11 pm. Cocktails & lounge. Entertainment. Valet parking. Reserv advised. AE, CB,
   DI, MC, VI. (See ad p 82)   ⊗ (714) 497-4477

LAGUNA HILLS — 33,600   See also LAKE FOREST & MISSION VIEJO

Comfort Inn   Rates Subject to Change   Motel   ◆◆
   All year   1P .... 40.00   2P/1B   .... 40.00   2P/2B   .... 50.00 XP   F
   76 units. 1 blk w of I-5, exit Lake Forest Dr. 23061 Avenida de la Carlota. (92653) 10 refrigerators; A/C; C/CATV; movies;
   rental VCPs. Radios; phones. Htd pool; whirlpool. No pets. Wkly rates avail. AE, DI, DS, MC, VI. FAX (714) 859-2468
                                                                                      Ⓓ ⓹ (714) 859-0166

Courtyard By Marriott   Rates Subject to Change   Motor Inn   ◆◆◆
   Sun-Thurs   1P .... 72.00   2P/1B   .... 82.00   2P/2B   .... 82.00 XP
   Fri & Sat   1P .... 62.00   2P/1B   .... 62.00   2P/2B   .... 62.00 XP
   137 units. W side of I-5; exit Lake Forest Rd. 23175 Avenida De La Carlota. (92653) Check-in 3 pm. 30 refrigerators;
   A/C; C/CATV; free & pay movies; radios; phones. Coin laundry. Htd pool; whirlpool; exercise rm. No pets. Wkly rates
   avail. AE, DI, DS, MC, VI. ● Restaurant; 6 am-11 pm; Sat & Sun from 7 am; $6.95-$12.95; cocktails.
   FAX (714) 454-2158 (See ad p A33)   ⊗ Ⓢ Ⓓ ⓹ (714) 859-5500

Holiday Inn   AAA Special Value Rates   Motor Inn   ◆◆◆
🏵 All year [CP]   1P 69.00- 89.00   2P/1B 79.00- 99.00   2P/2B 79.00- 99.00 XP 10   F
   150 units. 1 blk w of I-5, La Paz Rd exit. 25205 La Paz Rd. (92653) A/C; C/CATV; pay movies; radios; phones.
   Rental refrigerators. Pool; transportation to John Wayne/Orange County Airport. No pets. AE, DI, DS, MC,
   VI. ● Coffeeshop; 6 am-3 & 4:30-10 pm; $9.95-$16.95; cocktails; entertainment. FAX (714) 581-7410
                                                                                      ⊗ Ⓓ ⓹ (714) 586-5000

RESTAURANTS

Delaney's   Seafood $$ ◆◆
   1/2 mi w of I-5. 24035 El Toro Rd. Attractive, informal dining. Sun brunch 10 am-2 pm. A/C. Early bird specials; children's
   menu. Open 11:30 am-9 pm; Fri & Sat-10 pm; Sun 10 am-10 pm; closed 11/25 & 12/25. Cocktails & lounge. Reserv ad-
   vised weekends. AE, DS, MC, VI.   ⊗ (714) 830-6670

Mon Chateau   French $$ ◆◆
   In El Toro, 1/2 mi e of I-5; in se corner of Saddleback Valley Plaza. 23642 El Toro Rd. A small, charming restaurant, also
   specializing in Belgian cuisine. A/C. Open 11:30 am-2 & 5:30-9:30 pm; Fri-10 pm; Sat 5:30 pm-9:30 pm; closed Sun,
   Mon, 1/1, 11/25 & 12/25. Beer & wine. Reserv advised. AE, CB, DI, MC, VI.   ⊗ (714) 830-3810

Reuben's   Steak & Seafood $$ ◆◆
   1 blk w of I-5, exit El Toro Rd; adjacent to Laguna Hills Mall. 24001 Avenida de la Carlota. Attractive, contemporary decor.
   Sun brunch 10 am-2 pm, $12.99. A/C. Early bird specials; children's menu. Open 11:30 am-10 pm; Fri & Sat-10 pm; Sun
   10 am-2 & 4-10 pm. Cocktails & lounge. Entertainment. AE, DI, DS, MC, VI.   ⊗ (714) 830-9010

Velvet Turtle   American $$ ◆◆
   In El Toro. 23732 El Toro Rd. Attractive dining room. Sun brunch 10 am-3 pm, $12.95. A/C. Early bird specials; children's
   menu. Open 11:30 am-3 & 5-9 pm; Fri-10:30 pm; Sat 5 pm-10 pm; Sun 10 am-2:30 & 4-9 pm. Cocktails & lounge. Reserv advised. AE, DI, DS, MC, VI.   ⊗ ⓹ (714) 859-7885

LAGUNA NIGUEL — 44,400

The Ritz-Carlton, Laguna Niguel   Rates Subject to Change   Resort Hotel ◆◆◆◆◆
🏵 All year   1P 195.00- 390.00   2P/1B 195.00- 390.00   2P/2B 195.00- 390.00 XP 50
   393 units. 1 blk w of SR 1. 33533 Ritz-Carlton Dr. (92677) An elegant hotel on a bluff overlooking the ocean.
   Beautiful public facilities, pool area & guest rooms. Check-in 3 pm. A/C; C/CATV; movies; rental VCPs. Radios;
   phones. 2 htd pools; beach; saunas; whirlpools; fitness center. Fee for: golf-18 holes, tennis-4 courts. Pay valet
   garage. No pets. AE, CB, DI, MC, VI. ● 2 dining rms & restaurant; 6:30 am-10:30 pm; a la carte entrees about
   $12-$40; dress code; 24 hour room service; cocktails; entertainment. Also, The Dining Room, see separate
   listing. FAX (714) 240-1061 (See ad p A170)   Ⓢ Ⓓ ⓹ (714) 240-2000

RESTAURANTS

Crown House   Continental $$ ◆◆
   On SR 1; (Pacific Coast Hwy). 32802 Pacific Coast Hwy. Sun brunch 9:30 am-3:30 pm. A/C. Early bird specials. Open
   11 am-11 pm; Sun from 9:30 am. Cocktails & lounge. Entertainment & dancing. Reserv advised. AE, DI, DS, MC, VI.
                                                                                      ⊗ (714) 499-2626

The Dining Room   Continental $$$$ ◆◆◆
At the Ritz Carlton, Laguna Niguel. Formal, beautifully decorated dining room. A/C. Dress code. Open 6 pm-10 pm; Fri
& Sat-10:30 pm; closed Sun & Mon. Cocktails. Pay valet parking. AE, DI, DS, MC, VI. *(See ad below)*
⊗ (714) 240-2000

LA HABRA — 51,300

RESTAURANTS

Cafe El Cholo & The Burro Alley Tortilla Factory   Mexican $ ◆◆
1 1/2 mi e of Hwy 39 (Beach Blvd). 840 E Whittier Blvd. Both restaurants located under the same roof. Burro Alley Tortilla Factory specializes in foods from Baja CA. Sun brunch. A/C. Children's menu. Open 11:30 am-10 pm; Sun 10 am-9
pm; closed 7/4, 11/25 & 12/25. Cocktails & lounge. AE, MC, VI.   ⊗ (310) 691-4618

The Cat & The Custard Cup   American $$ ◆◆◆
⊕ 1 1/2 mi e of Hwy 39 (Beach Blvd). 800 E Whittier Blvd. English inn & pub atmosphere. Pastries made on pre-
mises. A/C. Open 11:30 am-2:30 & 5:30-9 pm; Tues-Fri 10 pm; Sat 5:30 pm-10 pm; Sun 5 pm-9 pm; closed 7/4,
11/25 & 12/25. Cocktails & lounge. Entertainment. Reserv advised. AE, MC, VI.   ⊗ (310) 694-3812

LA JOLLA — 28,800   (See SAN DIEGO spotting map pages A376 & A377; see index starting on page A374)

Andrea Villa Inn **5**   AAA Special Value Rates   *Motel*   ◆◆◆
⊕ 6/15-9/14 [CP]   1P 75.00- 95.00 2P/1B   75.00- 95.00   2P/2B   80.00- 100.00 XP 10   F
   9/15-6/14 [CP]   1P 70.00- 90.00 2P/1B   70.00- 90.00   2P/2B   75.00- 95.00 XP 5   F
49 units. 1 1/2 mi n. 2402 Torrey Pines Rd. (92037) Nicely landscaped pool area. A/C; C/CATV; free & pay movies;
radios; phones. Coin laundry. Htd pool; whirlpool. No pets. 20 efficiencies, $5 extra. Wkly & monthly rates avail.
Reserv deposit required; 3 days refund notice. AE, DI, DS, MC, VI. FAX (619) 459-1320 *(See ad p A171 and
p A379)*   Ⓓ (619) 459-3311

Best Western Inn By The Sea **10**   AAA Special Value Rates   *Motor Inn*   ◆◆◆
⊕ All year   1P 85.00- 115.00 2P/1B   95.00- 125.00   2P/2B   95.00- 125.00 XP 10   F
132 units. 7830 Fay Ave & Prospect St. (92037) Spacious rooms, some with ocean view, balconies. 10 refrigera-
tors; A/C; C/CATV; movies; phones. Htd pool; enclosed whirlpool; exercise rm. Garage & parking lot. No pets.
Wkly & monthly rates avail. Reserv deposit required. AE, DI, DS, MC, VI. ● Coffeeshop; 24 hours; $7.25-$10.
FAX (619) 456-2578 *(See ad p A378)*   ⊗ Ⓓ Ⓛ (619) 459-4461

Colonial Inn **9**   Rates Subject to Change   *Hotel*   ◆◆◆
⊕ All year [CP]   1P 120.00- 220.00 2P/1B   120.00- 220.00   2P/2B   120.00- 220.00 XP 10
75 units. 910 Prospect St. (92037) Some ocean view rooms. Afternoon tea 3:30 pm-5:30 pm, Wed-Sun. Check-in
3 pm. Refrigerators; C/CATV; movies; radios; phones. Htd pool. Valet parking lot. No pets. Monthly rates avail.
Reserv deposit required; 3 days refund notice. AE, DI, MC, VI. ● Dining rm; 7 am-2:30 & 5-10 pm; $12-$25; cock-
tails. FAX (619) 454-5679   ⊗ Ⓓ (619) 454-2181

(See SAN DIEGO spotting map pages A376 & A377)

Embassy Suites ❸   Rates Guaranteed   Suites Hotel ◆◆◆
Mon-Thurs 5/15-10/15 [BP]   1P .... 154.00   2P/1B .... 164.00 ....   XP 10   F
Fri-Sun 5/15-10/15 [BP]   1P .... 119.00   2P/1B .... 119.00 ....   XP 10   F
Senior discount. 335 units. 3/4 mi e of I-5. 4550 La Jolla Village Dr. (San Diego, 92122) 1- & 2-bedroom suites with living room, refrigerator & microwave. Check-in 4 pm. A/C; C/CATV; free & pay movies; radios; phones. Coin laundry. Htd indoor pool; sauna; whirlpool; exercise rm. Garage & parking lot. No pets. Reserv deposit required. Complimentary beverages each evening. AE, DI, DS, MC, VI. ● Restaurant; & deli; 11 am-11 pm; $8.95-$19.95; cocktails. FAX (619) 453-4226   ⊗ Ⓢ Ⓓ 🄴 (619) 453-0400

The Empress Hotel of La Jolla ⓫   AAA Special Value Rates   Hotel ◆◆◆
6/16-9/14 [CP] ....   2P/1B   90.00- 130.00   2P/2B   90.00- 130.00   XP 10
9/15-6/17 [CP] ....   2P/1B   85.00- 130.00   2P/2B   85.00- 130.00   XP 10
72 units. 7766 Fay Ave at Silverado St. (92037) Refrigerators; A/C; C/TV; free & pay movies; radios; phones. Sauna; whirlpool; exercise rm. Limited pay garage. Airport transp. No pets. Wkly & monthly rates avail. Reserv deposit required. AE, DI, DS, MC, VI. ● Dining rm; 11:30 am-2 & 5:30-10 pm; $17-$25; cocktails. FAX (619) 454-6387 (See ads below)   ⊗ Ⓓ 🄴 (619) 454-3001

Hyatt Regency La Jolla ⓳   Rates Subject to Change   Hotel ◆◆◆◆
All year   1P 109.00- 160.00   2P/1B   109.00- 185.00   2P/2B   109.00- 185.00   XP 10
Senior discount. 400 units. 1 blk e of I-5; exit La Jolla Village Dr. 3777 La Jolla Village Dr. (San Diego, 92122) Check-in 3 pm. 15 refrigerators; A/C; C/CATV; free & pay movies; radios; phones. Htd pool; sauna; whirlpool. Fee for: lighted tennis-2 courts; health club. Pay valet garage. No pets. Wkly & monthly rates avail. Reserv deposit required. AE, DI, DS, MC, VI. ● Restaurant; 6 am-10:30 pm; $9-$16; cocktails; entertainment. FAX (619) 552-6066
⊗ Ⓢ Ⓓ 🄴 (619) 552-1234

The Inn at La Jolla ⓮   AAA Special Value Rates   Motel ◆◆
6/15-9/15 [CP] ....   2P/1B   75.00- 95.00   2P/2B   75.00- 95.00   XP 10   F
9/16-6/14 [CP] ....   2P/1B   59.00- 79.00   2P/2B   69.00- 89.00   XP 5   F
45 units. 3 mi s. 5440 La Jolla Blvd. (92037) 26 refrigerators; C/CATV; movies; radios; phones; comb or shower baths. 1 2-bedrm unit, 19 kitchens, 2 efficiencies. Htd pool; whirlpool; putting green. No pets. Wkly & monthly rates avail. Reserv deposit required; 3 days refund notice. AE, DI, DS, MC, VI. FAX (619) 459-1377 (See ad below and p A379)   ⊗ Ⓓ (619) 454-6121

(See SAN DIEGO spotting map pages A376 & A377)

La Jolla Beach Travelodge 🔢 12   Rates Subject to Change   *Motel*   ◆◆
🏍 7/1-9/15   1P .... 67.00   2P/1B   .... 73.00   2P/2B   .... 79.00   XP   6
   1/1-6/30   1P .... 49.00   2P/1B   .... 54.00   2P/2B   .... 62.00   XP   5
   9/16-12/31   1P .... 45.00   2P/1B   .... 48.00   2P/2B   .... 56.00   XP   5
Senior discount. 44 units. 1 1/2 mi s. 6750 La Jolla Blvd. (92037) 16 refrigerators; A/C; C/TV; radios; phones; shower or comb baths. Htd pool. Limited parking lot. No pets. 10 efficiencies, $10 extra. Wkly & monthly rates avail. AE, DI, DS, MC, VI. Restaurant opposite. FAX (619) 454-1075   Ⓓ (619) 454-0716

La Jolla Cove Travelodge 🔢 21   Rates Subject to Change   *Motel*   ◆◆
🏍 7/11-8/29 [CP]   1P 54.00- 69.00   2P/1B   59.00- 74.00   2P/2B   64.00- 79.00   XP   5   F
   8/30-7/10 [CP]   1P 39.00- 54.00   2P/1B   44.00- 59.00   2P/2B   44.00- 59.00   XP   5   F
Senior discount. 30 units. 2 blks s of Prospect St, via Herschel Ave. 1141 Silverado St. (92037) 4 refrigerators; A/C; C/CATV; movies; radios; phones; shower or comb baths. No pets. Wkly & monthly rates avail. AE, DI, DS, MC, VI. Restaurant opposite. FAX (619) 459-8534   ⊗ Ⓓ (619) 454-0791

La Jolla Marriott 🔢 1   Rates Subject to Change   *Hotel*   ◆◆◆◆
🏍 All year   1P 139.00- 149.00   2P/1B   159.00- 169.00   2P/2B   159.00- 169.00   XP
360 units. 1/2 mi e of I-5. 4240 La Jolla Village Dr. (92037) Check-in 4 pm. 10 refrigerators; A/C; C/CATV; free & pay movies; radios; phones. Coin laundry. 2 htd pools, 1 indoor; saunas; whirlpool; exercise rm. Pay valet garage. No pets. Monthly rates avail. Reserv deposit required. AE, CB, DS, MC, VI. ● 2 dining rms; 6:30 am-10 pm; $8.95-$25; cocktails; entertainment. FAX (619) 546-8518   ⊗ Ⓢ Ⓓ 🄴 (619) 587-1414

La Jolla Palms Inn 🔢 18   AAA Special Value Rates   *Motel*   ◆◆
🏍 6/15-9/15 [CP]   1P 65.00- 99.00   2P/1B   65.00- 99.00   2P/2B   71.00- 99.00   XP   F
   9/16-6/14 [CP]   1P 49.00- 83.00   2P/1B   49.00- 83.00   2P/2B   61.00- 83.00   XP   F
59 units. 1 1/2 mi s. 6705 La Jolla Blvd. (92037) Refrigerators; 45 A/C; C/CATV; movies; 29 radios; phones; comb or shower baths. 12 kitchens, 4 efficiencies. Coin laundry. Htd pool; whirlpool. Small pets only, $5. Wkly & monthly rates avail. Reserv deposit required. AE, DI, DS, MC, VI. Restaurant adjacent. FAX (619) 454-6957 *(See ad below)*   Ⓓ (619) 454-7101

La Valencia Hotel 🔢 8   Rates Subject to Change   *Hotel*   ◆◆◆◆
🏍 All year   1P 140.00- 285.00   2P/1B   140.00- 285.00   2P/2B   140.00- 285.00   XP 10
100 units. 1132 Prospect St. (92037) Charming, long-established hotel. Many rooms with ocean view. Check-in 3 pm. 97 refrigerators; A/C; C/CATV; movies; radios; phones; comb or shower baths. 12 efficiencies. Htd pool; sauna; whirlpool; 16 rooms with whirlpool tub; exercise rm. Pay valet garage. No pets. Reserv deposit required. AE, CB, DI, MC, VI. ● 3 dining rms; 6:30 am-11 pm; $14.25-$27; cocktails. Also, Sky Room, see separate listing. A *Preferred Hotel*. FAX (619) 456-3921   Ⓢ Ⓓ (619) 454-0771

Prospect Park Inn 🔢 20   Rates Subject to Change   *Motel*   ◆◆
🏍 All year [CP]   1P .... 79.00   2P/1B   .... 89.00   2P/2B   99.00- 109.00   XP
Senior discount. 23 units. 1110 Prospect St. (92037) Smoke free premises. Ocean view from roof patio. Some balconies & ocean views. Check-in 3 pm. A/C; C/CATV; movies; radios; phones. 3 kitchens, 4 efficiencies. No pets. 2 1-bedroom suites with kitchen, $199-$259. 4 1-bedroom units with efficiencies, $119. Monthly rates avail. Reserv deposit required. AE, MC, VI. *(See ad below)*   ⊗ Ⓓ (619) 454-0133

Radisson Hotel La Jolla 🔢 2   Rates Guaranteed   *Motor Inn*   ◆◆◆
🏍 All year   1P 75.00- 149.00   2P/1B   85.00- 159.00   2P/2B   85.00- 159.00   XP 10   F
Senior discount. 200 units. Adjacent to I-5, La Jolla Village Dr exit. 3299 Holiday Ct. (92037) Formerly La Jolla Village Inn. Check-in 4 pm. 25 refrigerators; A/C; C/CATV; VCPs; radios; phones. Htd pool; whirlpool; tennis-2 courts; exercise rm. Airport transp. No pets. Reserv deposit required. AE, DI, DS, MC, VI. ● Dining rm & restaurant; 7 am-10 pm; $8-$15; cocktails; entertainment. FAX (619) 453-5550 *(See ad p A172)*   ⊗ Ⓓ 🄴 (619) 453-5500

Residence Inn by Marriott 🔢 16   Rates Subject to Change   *Suites Motel*   ◆◆◆
🏍 All year [CP]   1P .... 85.00   2P/1B   .... 85.00   2P/2B   .... 139.00   XP 10   F
287 units. 1 blk s of La Jolla Village Dr on Gilman Dr. 8901 Gilman Dr. (92037) 1- & 2-bedroom suites with living room. Some with fireplace. Check-in 4 pm. A/C; C/CATV; movies; VCPs. Radios; phones. 72 2-bedrm units, kitchens, 48 efficiencies. Coin laundry. 2 htd pools; whirlpools. Airport transp. Pets $150 deposit, also $6 daily extra charge & $50 cleaning fee. Wkly & monthly rates avail. Complimentary beverages each evening. AE, DI, DS, MC, VI. Restaurant opposite. FAX (619) 552-0387   ⊗ Ⓓ (619) 587-1770

Sands of La Jolla 🔢 13   Rates Subject to Change   *Motel*   ◆◆
🏍 6/14-9/14 [CP]   1P 69.00- 89.00   2P/1B   69.00- 89.00   2P/2B   79.00- 89.00   XP 10   F
   9/15-6/13 [CP]   1P 49.00- 69.00   2P/1B   59.00- 79.00   2P/2B   59.00- 79.00   XP 10
Senior discount. 38 units. 3 mi s. 5417 La Jolla Blvd. (92037) Many balconies. Some rooms with ocean view. Refrigerators; C/CATV; movies; radios; phones; shower or comb baths. 2 kitchens. Htd pool. No pets. Wkly & monthly rates avail. Reserv deposit required; 3 days refund notice. AE, DI, DS, MC, VI. *(See ad p A174)*   Ⓓ (619) 459-3336

(See SAN DIEGO spotting map pages A376 & A377)

Scripps Inn **7**

		Rates Subject to Change			*Motel*		◆◆
6/1-9/15 [CP]	1P 110.00- 165.00	2P/1B 110.00- 165.00	2P/2B 110.00- 165.00	XP 10			
9/16-5/31 [CP]	1P 90.00- 130.00	2P/1B 90.00- 130.00	2P/2B 90.00- 130.00	XP 10			

13 units. 1 blk w of Prospect St via Cuvier St. 555 Coast Blvd S. (92037) Across from bluff overlooking ocean. Check-in 3 pm. Refrigerators; C/CATV; phones; comb or shower baths. Pets. 5 1-bedroom efficiency suites. Wkly & monthly rates avail. Reserv deposit required. AE, MC, VI. Ⓓ (619) 454-3391

Sea Lodge at La Jolla Shores **4**

		Rates Subject to Change			*Motor Inn*		◆◆◆
6/16-9/15	1P 145.00- 215.00	2P/1B 160.00- 230.00	2P/2B 160.00- 305.00	XP 15			
9/16-6/15	1P 105.00- 160.00	2P/1B 120.00- 175.00	2P/2B 120.00- 235.00	XP 15			

128 units. 1 1/2 mi n, on the beach; via La Jolla Shores Dr & Avenida de la Playa. 8110 Camino Del Oro. (92037) Attractive, early California decor. Balconies or patios, many with ocean view. Check-in 3 pm. Refrigerators; A/C; C/CATV; movies; VCPs. Radios; phones. 18 efficiencies. Coin laundry. Htd pool; wading pool; sauna; whirlpool; tennis-2 courts. Garage. No pets. Wkly & monthly rates avail. Reserv deposit required. AE, DI, DS, MC, VI. ● Dining rm; 7 am-11, noon-2:30 & 6-10 pm; $13.95-$21.95; cocktails. FAX (619) 456-9346 Ⓓ (619) 459-8271

Sheraton Grande Torrey Pines **17**

	Rates Guaranteed			*Hotel*		◆◆◆◆
All year	....	2P/1B 165.00- 250.00	2P/2B 165.00- 250.00	XP 20		F

Senior discount. 400 units. 10950 N Torrey Pines Rd. (92037) Balconies or patios. Many ocean views. Check-in 3 pm. Refrigerators; A/C; C/CATV; free & pay movies; radios; phones. Htd pool; saunas; whirlpool; putting green; lighted tennis-3 courts; rental bicycles. Fee for: health club. Pay valet garage. No pets. Wkly & monthly rates avail. AE, DI, DS, MC, VI. ● Restaurant; 6:30 am-11 pm; $12-$19; cocktails; entertainment. FAX (619) 450-4584 ⊗ Ⓢ Ⓓ (619) 558-1500

Summer House Inn **6**

		AAA Special Value Rates			*Hotel*		◆◆◆
7/24-9/14	1P 89.00- 105.00	2P/1B 99.00- 125.00	2P/2B 99.00- 125.00	XP			F
9/15-7/23	1P 79.00- 96.00	2P/1B 89.00- 116.00	2P/2B 89.00- 116.00	XP			F

90 units. 1 1/2 mi n. 7955 La Jolla Shores Dr. (92037) Many ocean view rooms. Balconies. Check-in 3 pm. Refrigerators; A/C; C/CATV; movies; radios; phones. Coin laundry. Htd pool; saunas; whirlpool. Parking lot. Airport transp. 36 efficiencies, $6 extra. 10 corner suites with whirlpool. Wkly & monthly rates avail. AE, DI, DS, MC, VI. ● Dining rm; 7 am-10 pm; Fri & Sat-11 pm; $16.75-$25; cocktails; entertainment. Also, Elario's, see separate listing. FAX (619) 459-7649 Ⓢ Ⓓ (619) 459-0261

Torrey Pines Inn **15**

	Rates Guaranteed			*Motor Inn*		◆◆
All year	1P 70.00- 90.00	2P/1B 75.00- 95.00	2P/2B 75.00- 95.00	XP 10		F

Senior discount. 71 units. 11480 N Torrey Pines Rd. (92037) C/TV; rental VCPs; radios; phones. Rental refrigerators. Coin laundry. Htd pool; putting green. Fee for: golf-36 holes, airport transp. No pets. 5 microwaves. Wkly rates avail. AE, DI, DS, MC, VI. ● Dining rm & coffeeshop; 4:30 am-10 pm; a la carte entrees about $8.90-$15.95; cocktails. FAX (619) 453-0691 ⊗ Ⓓ (619) 453-4420

RESTAURANTS

Anthony's Fish Grotto ① Seafood $$ ◆◆
1/2 mi e of I-5, La Jolla Village Dr exit, corner Regents Rd & La Jolla Village Dr. 4120 La Jolla Village Dr. Fresh fish, chicken & beef served in intimate setting with contemporary decor. Economy dining in adjoining Fishette; also, oyster bar & lounge. A/C. Children's menu. Open 11:30 am-10 pm; closed major holidays. Cocktails & lounge. Reserv advised. AE, DI, DS, MC, VI. ⊗ Ⓖ (619) 457-5008

Cafe Japengo ② Ethnic $$ ◆◆
1 blk e of I-5; exit La Jolla Village Dr. 8960 University Center Ln. Casual atmosphere. Features contemporary Japanese dishes. Sushi bar. A/C. Children's menu. Open 11 am-2:30 & 6-midnight; Sat & Sun 6 pm-midnight. Cocktails & lounge. Pay valet parking. Reserv advised. AE, DI, DS, MC, VI. ⊗ (619) 450-3355

Chart House ⑥ Steak & Seafood $$$ ◆◆◆
1270 Prospect St. Seafood, prime rib, lamb, steak & chicken. Ocean view. A/C. Children's menu. Open 5 pm-10 pm; Fri & Sat-11 pm; Sun 4:30 pm-10 pm. Cocktails & lounge. Reserv advised. AE, DI, DS, MC, VI. ⊗ (619) 459-8201

Coast Cafe ⑧ American $$ ◆◆
At Embassy Suites. Casual decor & atmosphere. Features prime rib & fresh seafood. A/C. Open 11 am-3 & 5-11 pm. Cocktails & lounge. AE, DI, DS, MC, VI. ⊗ Ⓖ (619) 453-1418

Elario's ⑤ Continental $$$ ◆◆◆
In Summer House Inn on the 11th floor. Fresh seafood, rack of lamb, chicken, veal, duckling, steak, prime rib & pasta. On the 11th floor; view of La Jolla Shores & ocean. Sun brunch, 10 am-2 pm. A/C. Open 7 am-10 pm; Fri-Sun til 11 pm. Cocktails & lounge. AE, DI, DS, MC, VI. (619) 459-0541

(See SAN DIEGO spotting map pages A376 & A377)

Marine Room Restaurant ③   American $$ ◆◆
1 mi n; adjacent to La Jolla Beach & Tennis Club. 2000 Spindrift Dr. Located on the beach with a beautiful view of surf & coastline. Fresh seafood, beef & veal specialties. Semi-formal atmosphere. A/C. Open 11:30 am-2:30 & 6-10 pm; Sun from 10:30 am. Cocktails & lounge. Entertainment & dancing. Parking avail. Reserv advised. AE, CB, DI, MC, VI.
     ⊗ Ⓛ (619) 459-7222

Sky Room ⑦   French $$$$ ◆◆◆◆
10th floor of La Valencia Hotel. 1132 Prospect St. Features fresh seafood, chicken, duck, lamb & steak. Desserts prepared daily. Ocean view. Prix fixe dinner menu. A/C. Open 11:30 am-2:30 & 6-10 pm; Sat from 6 pm; closed Sun. Cocktails. Valet parking. Reserv advised Fri & Sat. AE, DI, MC, VI.   (619) 454-0771

Top O' The Cove Restaurant ④   Continental $$$$ ◆◆◆◆
1216 Prospect St. Charming restaurant, ocean view from some tables. Sun brunch 10:30 am-3 pm. Open 11:30 am-3 & 5:30-10:30 pm. Cocktails & lounge. Reserv advised. AE, DI, MC, VI.   ⊗ (619) 454-7779

LAKE ARROWHEAD — 6,300

Arrowhead Tree Top Lodge   Rates Subject to Change   *Motel*   ◆◆

6/7-1/2	....	2P/1B	68.00- 92.00	2P/2B	79.00- 125.00	XP
1/3-6/5	....	2P/1B	55.00- 84.00	2P/2B	70.00- 125.00	XP

19 units. On SR 173, 1/2 mi s of Lake Arrowhead Village. (PO Box 186, 92352) Picturesque forest setting. Some fireplaces. Refrigerators; C/CATV; shower baths. Htd pool. 2-night minimum stay weekends 6/7-1/2. 6 efficiency apartments, $80-$145 for up to 6 persons. Reserv deposit required; 7 days refund notice. AE, CB, DI, MC, VI. Ⓓ (909) 337-2311

Bluebelle House Bed & Breakfast   Rates Subject to Change   *Bed & Breakfast*   ◆◆◆

All year [BP]	1P	75.00- 110.00	2P/1B	75.00- 95.00	2P/2B	.... 110.00 XP 10

5 units. On SR 173, 1/4 mi ne of Lake Arrowhead Village. 263 S SR 173. (PO Box 2177, 92352) European-style house with country English decor. Large second story deck surrounded by pine trees. Closed 12/24-12/27. Designated smoking areas. Check-in 3 pm. 3 shower or comb baths. No pets. 2-night minimum stay weekends. Reserv deposit required; 7 days refund notice. MC, VI.   ⊗ Ⓓ (909) 336-3292

Lake Arrowhead Hilton Resort   AAA Special Value Rates   *Resort Complex*   ◆◆◆

5/24-9/12 & 12/20-1/2	1P 159.00- 239.00	2P/1B	159.00- 239.00	2P/2B	159.00- 239.00	XP 15
9/13-12/19	1P 149.00- 229.00	2P/1B	149.00- 229.00	2P/2B	149.00- 229.00	XP 15
1/3-3/14	1P 139.00- 219.00	2P/1B	139.00- 219.00	2P/2B	139.00- 219.00	XP 15
3/15-5/23	1P 99.00- 179.00	2P/1B	99.00- 179.00	2P/2B	99.00- 179.00	XP 15

261 units. In Lake Arrowhead Village. (PO Box 1699, 92352) Many rooms with view of lake. Check-in 4 pm. 133 refrigerators; A/C; C/CATV; pay movies; radios; phones. Htd pool; beach; whirlpools; dock; children's program in summer. Fee for: fishing, lighted tennis-2 courts; racquetball-2 courts; health club & massage. Pets. 1- & 2-bedroom suites, $259-$399. Monthly rates avail. Reserv deposit required weekends. AE, CB, DS, MC, VI. ● Dining rm & restaurant; 7 am-10 pm; Sat from 6:30 am, Sun brunch 10 am-2 pm; $10.95-$21.95; cocktails. FAX (909) 336-1378 *(See ad p 22)*
     ⊗ Ⓓ Ⓛ (909) 336-1511

Romantique Lakeview Lodge Bed & Breakfast   Rates Guaranteed   *Lodge*   ◆◆◆

Fri & Sat 6/15-9/15 [CP]	1P 95.00- 210.00	2P/1B	95.00- 210.00	2P/2B	95.00- 210.00	XP
Fri & Sat 9/16-6/14 [CP]	1P 75.00- 175.00	2P/1B	75.00- 175.00	2P/2B	75.00- 175.00	XP
Sun-Thurs 6/15-9/15 [CP]	1P 65.00- 125.00	2P/1B	75.00- 125.00	2P/2B	65.00- 125.00	XP
Sun-Thurs 9/16-6/14 [CP]	1P 65.00- 120.00	2P/1B	65.00- 120.00	2P/2B	65.00- 120.00	XP

Senior discount. 9 units. Across from Lake Arrowhead Village. 28051 Hwy 189. (PO Box 128, 92352) Some lakeview rooms. Charming rooms with Victorian decor; many with fireplace. Check-in 3 pm. C/CATV; movies; VCPs. Radios; comb or shower baths. No pets. Reserv deposit required; 7 days refund notice. AE, MC, VI. Restaurant opposite.
     ⊗ Ⓓ (909) 337-6633

Saddleback Inn-Arrowhead   Rates Guaranteed   *Country Inn*   ◆◆

Fri & Sat 7/4-1/2 [BP]	....	2P/1B	100.00- 165.00	2P/2B	200.00- 340.00	XP
Fri & Sat 1/3-7/3 [BP]	....	2P/1B	100.00- 150.00	2P/2B	175.00- 275.00	XP
Sun-Thurs [BP]	1P 85.00	2P/1B	.... 100.00	2P/2B	.... 140.00	XP

34 units. On SR 173; across from entrance to Lake Arrowhead Village. (PO Box 1890, 92352) Very attractive country motif. Rooms & 1-to 3-bedroom suites in main lodge & individual chalets. Many fireplaces. Check-in 3 pm. 32 refrigerators; 10 A/C; C/CATV; VCPs; radios; phones; comb or shower baths. 32 rooms with whirlpool tub. No pets. 2-night minimum stay weekends. Reserv deposit required. AE, DI, DS, MC, VI. ● Dining rm; 8 am-3 & 5-9 pm; Fri & Sat-10 pm; $14.95-$20.95; cocktails. FAX (909) 337-4277   Ⓓ (909) 336-3571

RESTAURANT

The Royal Oak Restaurant   American $$ ◆◆
In Blue Jay; 1 1/2 mi ow of Lake Arrowhead Village. 27187 Hwy 189. Large selection of seafood, beef, pasta & continental entrees. Olde English Tudor atmosphere. A/C. Early bird specials; children's menu. Open 5 pm-9:30 pm; Fri & Sat-11 pm; Sun 11 am-3 & 5-9:30 pm; closed Mon, 4/11, 11/25 & 12/25. Cocktails & lounge. Reserv advised. MC, VI.
     ⊗ (909) 337-6018

LAKE ELSINORE — 18,300

Lakeview Inn   AAA Special Value Rates   *Motel*   ◆◆

⏆ All year	1P 38.00	2P/1B	.... 42.00	2P/2B	.... 42.00	XP 5 F

55 units. Adjacent to I-15, exit Railroad Canyon Rd, 1 blk w, then 1/2 mi s. 31808 Casino Dr. (92530) A/C; C/CATV; phones. Coin laundry. Small htd pool; whirlpool. No pets. 4 rooms with whirlpool tub, $60. Reserv deposit required. AE, DI, DS, MC, VI. FAX (909) 245-9249 *(See ad below)*   ⊗ Ⓓ (909) 674-9694

LAKE FOREST — 300

Best Western Laguna/El Toro Inn
Rates Subject to Change   *Motor Inn*   ◆◆◆
All year [CP]   1P 55.00- 65.00 2P/1B 61.00- 71.00 2P/2B 61.00- 71.00 XP 6
113 units. 1 blk e of I-5, exit Lake Forest Dr. 23702 Rockfield Blvd. (92630) Refrigerators; A/C; C/CATV; movies; radios; phones. Coin laundry. Pool; sauna; whirlpool; 2 rooms with whirlpool; exercise rm. No pets. Reserv deposit required. AE, DI, DS, MC, VI. ● Restaurant; 11:30 am-2:30 & 4:30-9:30 pm; $5.95-$10.95; cocktails. FAX (714) 830-3325 *(See ad p A54)*   Ⓧ Ⓢ Ⓓ Ⓛ (714) 458-1900

Quality Suites
AAA Special Value Rates   *Suites Motel*   ◆◆◆
All year [BP]   1P 79.00- 99.00 2P/1B 89.00- 109.00 2P/2B 89.00- 109.00 XP 10
90 units. 1 1/2 blks e of I-5, Lake Forest Dr exit. 23192 Lake Center Dr. (92630) 1-bedroom suites with living room. Some suites with whirlpool. Refrigerators; A/C; C/CATV; movies; VCPs. Radios; phones. Htd pool; whirlpool; exercise rm. No pets. Monthly rates avail. Reserv deposit required. Complimentary beverages each evening. AE, DI, DS, MC, VI. FAX (714) 380-8307   Ⓧ Ⓢ Ⓓ Ⓛ (714) 380-9888

LAKEPORT — 4,400

Anchorage Inn
Rates Subject to Change   *Motel*   ◆
All year   1P .... 35.00 2P/1B .... 47.00 2P/2B .... 50.00 XP 5
34 units. SR 29 Frwy exit via 11th St/Scotts Valley Rd. 950 N Main St. (95453) 20 refrigerators; A/C; C/CATV; 17 radios; phones; shower or comb baths. 8 2-bedrm units. Coin laundry. Small pool; sauna; whirlpool; boating; dock; fishing; water skiing. No pets. 12 kitchen apartments no utensils; $55-$70 for 2 persons. Wkly rates avail in winter. Reserv deposit required; 7 days refund notice. AE, DI, MC, VI.   Ⓓ (707) 263-5417

Clear Lake Inn
Rates Subject to Change   *Motel*   ◆
3/1-11/30   1P .... 39.00 2P/1B .... 49.00 .... XP 6
12/1-2/28   1P .... 32.00 2P/1B .... 42.00 .... XP 6
40 units. SR 29 Frwy exit 11th St/Scotts Valley Rd. 1010 N Main St. (95453) A/C; C/CATV; fishing. Small pool; boating; fishing; water skiing. No pets. Reserv deposit required; 3 days refund notice. AE, DI, DS, MC, VI.   Ⓓ (707) 263-3551

Skylark Shores Resort Motel
Rates Subject to Change   *Motel*   ◆◆
5/21-9/25   .... 2P/1B 52.00- 97.00 2P/2B 60.00- 97.00 XP 6
4/2-5/20 & 9/26-10/30   .... 2P/1B 47.00- 85.00 2P/2B 52.00- 85.00 XP 6
10/31-4/1   .... 2P/1B 37.00- 75.00 2P/2B 43.00- 75.00 XP 6
45 units. SR 29 Frwy exit 11th St/Scotts Valley Rd. 1120 N Main St. (95453) On spacious grounds. 16 lakefront units with patio or balcony. Check-in 3 pm. A/C; C/CATV; radios; phones; shower or comb baths. Small pool; boating; dock; fishing; playground. No pets. 9 efficiencies & 9 kitchens, $15 extra. 5 1- & 2-bedroom cottages, with kitchen, $450-$575 weekly for 2-8 persons. Reserv deposit required; 3 days refund notice. AE, CB, DI, MC, VI. FAX (707) 263-7733 *(See ad below)*   Ⓧ Ⓓ (707) 263-6151

RESTAURANT

Anthony's
Italian $$ ◆
3/4 mi n on SR 29 business rt. 2509 Lakeshore Blvd. Also, American cuisine. A/C. Children's menu. Open 5 pm-10 pm; closed 4/11, 11/25 & 12/25. Cocktails & lounge. Minimum $3. Reserv advised. AE, DI, DS, MC, VI.
(707) 263-4905

LAKE TAHOE

> Establishments in Lake Tahoe are divided into Northern Region and Southern Region. Some establishments in the Lake Tahoe area may require payment in full upon arrival.

LAKE TAHOE (Northern Region) (See LAKE TAHOE AREA spotting map page A177; see index starting below)

Index of Establishments on the LAKE TAHOE AREA Spotting Map

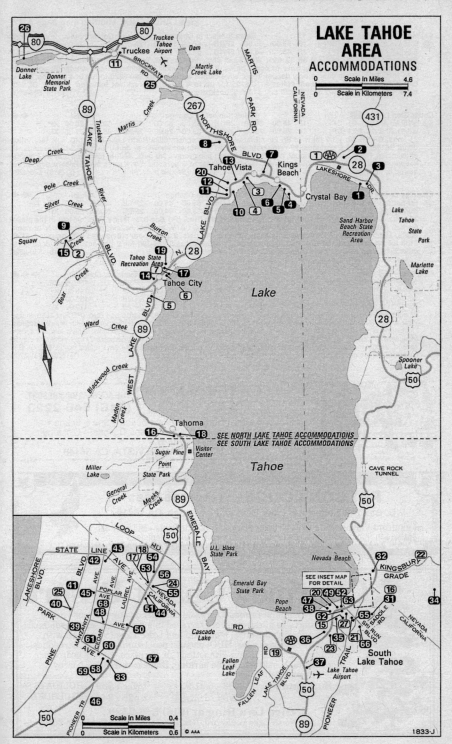

LAKE TAHOE AREA ACCOMMODATIONS

Scale in Miles 0 — 4.6
Scale in Kilometers 0 — 7.4

SEE NORTH LAKE TAHOE ACCOMMODATIONS
SEE SOUTH LAKE TAHOE ACCOMMODATIONS

Scale in Miles 0 — 0.4
Scale in Kilometers 0 — 0.6

© AAA

1833-J

(See LAKE TAHOE spotting map page A177)

Captain's Alpenhaus 🔟   Rates Subject to Change   *Country Inn*   ◆◆
🏅 6/15-9/8 & 12/15-3/31 [BP]   1P 55.00- 95.00   2P/1B   60.00-100.00   2P/2B   ....   75.00   XP 12   F
9/9-12/14 & 4/1-6/14 [BP]   1P 45.00- 85.00   2P/1B   55.00- 95.00   2P/2B   ....   65.00   XP 12   F
Senior discount. 13 units. On SR 89. 6941 West Lake Blvd. (PO Box 262, Tahoma, 96142) Smoke free premises.
C/CATV; radios; phones; 12 shower or comb baths. 6 2-bedrm units, 5 kitchens. Pool; whirlpool; pool open
5/24-10/1. Pets, $50 in cabins only deposit required. 4 cabins with kitchen, $90-$120 for up to 4 persons, break-
fast not included. 2 2-bedroom suites $110-$135 for up to 4 persons, breakfast included. AE, CB, DI, MC,
VI. ● Restaurant; 8 am-2 & 5:30-9:30 pm; $14-$25; cocktails.   ⊗ Ⓓ (916) 525-5000

Cedar Glen Lodge 🔟   Rates Subject to Change   *Motel*   ◆◆
🏅 6/15-9/5 & 11/21-4/1 [CP]   1P 45.00- 80.00   2P/1B   45.00- 80.00   2P/2B   55.00- 80.00   XP 5
9/6-11/20 & 4/2-6/14 [CP]   1P 39.00- 75.00   2P/1B   39.00- 75.00   2P/2B   45.00- 75.00   XP 5
31 units. On SR 28, 1 1/2 mi w of SR 267; 3 mi w of casino center. 6589 North Lake Blvd. (PO Box 188, Tahoe
Vista, 96148) Motel & cottages. 27 refrigerators; C/CATV; phones; shower or comb baths. 2 2-bedrm units, 10
efficiencies. Pool; sauna; whirlpool, enclosed in winter; playground. No pets. 3-night minimum stay in 7 housekeeping units. 2 2-bedroom kitchen units, $90-$105 for up to 6 persons. Wkly rates avail. Reserv deposit required in high season; 14 days refund notice. AE, DS, MC, VI. *(See ad p A179)*   Ⓓ (916) 546-4281

Charmey Chalet Resort 🔟   Rates Subject to Change   *Motel*   ◆◆
🏅 Fri-Sat & 6/16-9/15 [CP]   1P 55.00- 65.00   2P/1B   55.00- 65.00   2P/2B   60.00- 75.00   XP 7
Sun-Thurs 9/16-6/15 [CP]   1P 39.00- 54.00   2P/1B   39.00- 54.00   2P/2B   44.00- 59.00   XP 7
29 units. On SR 28, 1 1/2 mi w of SR 267. 6549 North Lake Blvd. (PO Box 316, Tahoe Vista, 96148) In the pines.
Garden patios & few rooms with lake view. Refrigerators; C/CATV; movies; radios; phones; shower or comb
baths. 10 efficiencies. Pool; whirlpool; beach opposite. No pets. 2 2-bedroom efficiencies with fireplace, $130-
$150 for up to 6 persons; $74-$100 for 2 persons. 1 whirlpool unit $64-$90 for 2 persons. Reserv deposit re-
quired; 14 days refund notice. AE, DS, MC, VI. *(See ad below)*   Ⓓ (916) 546-2529

Club Tahoe 2   Rates Subject to Change   *Apartment Complex*   ◆◆◆
12/12-1/4 [CP]   1P .... 155.00   2P/1B   .... 155.00   2P/2B   .... 155.00   XP
6/16-9/7 [CP]   1P .... 145.00   2P/1B   .... 145.00   2P/2B   .... 145.00   XP
1/5-3/30 [CP]   1P .... 130.00   2P/1B   .... 130.00   2P/2B   .... 130.00   XP
9/8-12/11 & 3/31-6/15 [CP]   1P .... 110.00   2P/1B   .... 110.00   2P/2B   .... 110.00   XP
92 units. Exit SR 28 at Village Blvd, 1 blk n then 1 blk e on Northwood Blvd. 914 Northwood Blvd. (PO Box 4650, Incline
Village, NV, 89450) Attractive landscaped grounds with creek & tall pine trees. 2-bedroom units, with laundry facilities.
Check-in 4 pm. Check-out 10 am. C/CATV; radios; phones. Kitchens. Pool; sauna; whirlpools; lighted tennis-2 courts;
racquetball-2 courts; recreational program; exercise rm. No pets. Rates for up to 6 persons. 7-night minimum stay in
season. 2-night minimum stay off season. Wkly rates avail. Reserv deposit required; 14 days refund notice. MC, VI. Deli
& cocktail lounge guests only.   Ⓓ (702) 831-5750

(See LAKE TAHOE spotting map page A177)

Cottonwood Lodge ⑩ ♦
♠ 6/1-9/15
Rates Subject to Change   *Cottages*
1P 74.00-100.00   2P/1B   74.00-100.00   2P/2B   74.00-100.00   XP   5
18 units. On SR 28, 1 1/2 mi w of SR 267. 6542 N Lake Blvd. (PO Box 86, Tahoe Vista, 96148) OPEN ALL YEAR.
Duplex log cabins & lakeside cottages. 17 refrigerators; C/CATV; movies; radios; shower baths. Beach; swimming; sauna; whirlpool; pool open 5/30-9/15. No pets. 3-night minimum stay 6/1-9/15. 9 kitchens & 4 efficiencies,
$8-$10 extra. Wkly rates avail. Reserv deposit required; 30 days refund notice. AE, DI, DS, MC, VI. *(See ad
p A178)*   Ⓓ (916) 546-2220

Crown Motel ④ ♦
♠ All year
Rates Subject to Change   *Motel*
1P 35.00-100.00   2P/1B   45.00-100.00   2P/2B   45.00-100.00   XP   5
Senior discount. 37 units. On SR 28, 1/4 mi e of SR 267. 8200 N Lake Blvd. (PO Box 845, Kings Beach, 96143)
15 attractively decorated lakefront units with electric fireplace. Some small rooms. 16 A/C; C/CATV; phones;
comb or shower baths. 8 2-bedrm units. Pool; beach; indoor whirlpool. No pets. 10 units on lake with microwave
& refrigerator, $100 for 2 persons. Reserv deposit required; 7 days refund notice. AE, MC, VI. Ⓓ (916) 546-3388

Are you a Wheelchair traveler? Eat and sleep at the Ⓗ listings.

(See LAKE TAHOE spotting map page A177)

Falcon Motor Lodge 🔷5️⃣   **Rates Subject to Change**   *Motel*   ◆
🏵️ 6/15-9/15   1P 38.00- 78.00 2P/1B   38.00- 78.00 2P/2B 53.00- 88.00 XP 10
     9/16-6/14   1P 30.00- 78.00 2P/1B   30.00- 78.00 2P/2B 43.00- 88.00 XP 10
31 units. 2 blks e of SR 267, on SR 28. 8258 N Lake Blvd. (PO Box 249, Kings Beach, 96143) Some rooms with lake view; few small rooms. Refrigerators; C/CATV; movies; phones; shower or comb baths. 4 2-bedrm units, 1 3-bedrm unit, 2 kitchens. Coin laundry. Pool; beach; whirlpool. No pets. Some rooms with microwave. Reserv deposit required. AE, MC, VI. *(See ad p A178)*   Ⓓ (916) 546-2583

Franciscan Lakeside Lodge 🔷1️⃣3️⃣   **Rates Subject to Change**   *Cottages*   ◆◆
🏵️ All year   1P 50.00-110.00 2P/1B 50.00- 110.00 2P/2B 85.00-155.00 XP 10
63 units. On SR 28; 1 mi w of SR 267. 6944 N Lake Blvd. (PO Box 280, Tahoe Vista, 96148) Some motel rooms in pines, few cottages on lake. Check-in 3 pm. C/CATV; movies; shower or comb baths. Kitchens. Pool; beach; fishing; playground. No pets. 6 2-bedroom units, $130-$155 for up to 7 persons. Reserv deposit required in high season; 14 days refund notice. AE, DS, MC, VI. *(See ad p A179)*   Ⓓ (916) 546-7234

Goldcrest Resort Motel 🔷6️⃣   **Rates Subject to Change**   *Motel*   ◆
🏵️ 6/16-9/20 & Fri-Sat [CP]   1P 43.00- 90.00 2P/1B 48.00- 90.00 2P/2B 60.00- 95.00 XP 5
     9/21-6/15 [CP]   1P 38.00- 75.00 2P/1B 43.00- 75.00 2P/2B 50.00- 75.00 XP 5
Senior discount. 25 units. On SR 28; 1/4 mi e of SR 267. 8194 North Lake Blvd. (PO Box 579, Kings Beach, 96143) 8 refrigerators; C/CATV; movies; phones; shower or comb baths. 4 2-bedrm units. Pool; beach; whirlpool. Fee for: water skiing. No pets. 4 kitchens, $15 extra. Wkly rates avail. Reserv deposit required; 7 days refund notice. AE, DI, DS, MC, VI. Coffeeshop opposite. FAX (916) 546-4395 *(See ad below)* Ⓓ (916) 546-3301

Hyatt Regency Lake Tahoe Resort &
Casino 🔷1️⃣   **Rates Subject to Change**   *Resort Hotel*   ◆◆◆
🏵️ 6/15-9/30 & 12/21-12/31   1P 229.00- 895.00 2P/1B 229.00- 895.00 2P/2B 229.00- 895.00 XP 10
     1/1-6/14 & 10/1-12/20   1P 179.00- 685.00 2P/1B 179.00- 685.00 2P/2B 179.00- 695.00 XP 10
458 units. 1/2 mi w of SR 28, toward lake via Country Club Dr; 2 mi s of Mt Rose Hwy. Lakeshore at Country Club Dr. (PO Box 3239, Incline Village, NV, 89450) Exceptional facilities; nestled in the pines on beautifully landscaped grounds. Check-in 3 pm. A/C; C/CATV; free & pay movies; radios; phones. Rental refrigerators. Htd pool; beach; saunas; whirlpool; tennis-2 courts; children's program; rental bicycles; health club. Fee for: jet ski, sailboats, kayak; massage. Valet parking lot. Airport transp. No pets. 24 1-to 2-bedroom lakeside cottages, $475-$895 for 2-4 persons. Reserv deposit required; 7 days refund notice. AE, CB, DI, MC, VI. ● 2 dining rms & coffeeshop; 24 hours; $8-$25; cocktails. Casino. FAX (702) 831-7508 *(See ad below)* ⊗ Ⓢ Ⓓ (702) 831-1111

The Inn at Incline 🔷3️⃣   **Rates Subject to Change**   *Motel*   ◆◆
🏵️ 6/11-9/30 [CP]   1P 75.00- 95.00 2P/1B 79.00- 99.00 2P/2B 89.00- 99.00 XP 10   F
     12/24-3/15 [CP]   1P 65.00- 85.00 2P/1B 69.00- 89.00 2P/2B 79.00- 89.00 XP 10   F
     3/16-6/10 & 10/1-12/23 [CP]   1P 55.00- 75.00 2P/1B 59.00- 79.00 2P/2B 69.00- 79.00 XP 10   F
38 units. 2 mi s of Mt. Rose Hwy on SR 28. 1003 Tahoe Blvd. (PO Box 4545, Incline Village, NV, 89450) Refrigerators; C/CATV; movies; radios; phones. Htd indoor pool; sauna; whirlpool. Parking ramp & parking lot. No pets. Wkly rates avail. Reserv deposit required; 14 days refund notice. AE, DS, MC, VI. *(See ad below)*   Ⓓ (702) 831-1052

(See LAKE TAHOE spotting map page A177)

Lake of the Sky Motor Inn ⑲   Rates Subject to Change   *Motel*   ◆◆
⊕ 11/14-1/1, 6/13-9/21 &

2/14-2/16	1P 56.00- 90.00	2P/1B	66.00- 90.00	2P/2B	71.00- 95.00	XP 5	F
1/2-2/13 & 2/17-4/12	1P 56.00- 76.00	2P/1B	66.00- 76.00	2P/2B	71.00- 81.00	XP 5	F
9/22-11/13 & 4/13-6/12	1P 49.00- 54.00	2P/1B	54.00- 59.00	2P/2B	59.00- 64.00	XP 5	F

23 units. 1 mi e of jct SR 89. 955 North Lake Blvd. (PO Box 227, Tahoe City, 95730) View of Lake Tahoe from some rooms. Check-in 3 pm. C/CATV; phones; shower baths. Pool. No pets. Reserv deposit required; 7 days refund notice. AE, CB, MC, VI. *(See ad below)*   Ⓓ (916) 583-3305

Northstar at Tahoe ⑧   Rates Subject to Change   *Complex*   ◆◆◆
⊕ 11/16-4/30   ....   2P/2B 111.00- 270.00 XP
6/26-9/13   ....   2P/2B 89.00- 196.00 XP
5/1-6/25 & 9/14-11/15   ....   2P/2B 77.00- 159.00 XP
230 units. Exit I-80 at SR 267, 7 mi se; exit SR 28 at Kings Beach SR 267 n 6 mi. SR 267 & Northstar Dr. (PO Box 2499, Truckee, 96160) Spacious grounds, mountain setting. Varied accommodations in 1-to 4-bedroom housekeeping units, most with fireplace. Some 3-story, no elevator. Check-in 3 pm. C/CATV; VCPs; radios; phones. Coin laundry. Pool; saunas; whirlpools; tennis-10 courts; children's program; rental bicycles; exercise rm. Fee for: golf-18 holes, ski tows & lifts, cross country ski trails; ski equipment; riding. No pets. 2-night minimum stay 6/26-9/13; 2 night minimum stay 11/16-4/30. Wkly rates avail. Reserv deposit required; 14 days written refund notice. AE, DS, MC, VI. ● Restaurant & coffeeshop; 8 am-9 pm; $11-$18; cocktails. FAX (916) 587-0215
Ⓓ (916) 562-1113

Resort at Squaw Creek ⑨   Rates Guaranteed   *Resort Complex*   ◆◆◆◆
⊕ 12/19-4/11   ....   2P/2B 195.00- 350.00 XP 35   F
6/18-9/7   ....   2P/2B 165.00- 290.00 XP 35   F
9/8-12/18 & 4/12-6/17   ....   2P/2B 145.00- 250.00 XP 35   F
Senior discount. 405 units. 1/4 mi from entrance to Squaw Valley. 400 Squaw Creek Rd. (P O Box 3333, Olympic Valley, 96146) All season resort, exceptional facilities. Many rooms have extraordinary views. Check-in 3 pm. Refrigerators; A/C; C/CATV; free & pay movies; radios; phones. 18 2-bedrm units, 14 kitchens. 3 pools, 1 htd; wading pool; saunas; whirlpools; waterslide pool open 7/1-9/7; indoor whirlpool; ice skating; children's program in summer; rental bicycles; health club. Fee for: golf-18 holes, tennis-8 courts, 6 lighted; skiing, riding, massage. Pay valet parking lot. No pets. Luxury level rooms avail. 18 bi-level suites from $475-$845. Reserv deposit required ski season only; 14 days refund notice. AE, DI, DS, MC, VI. ● Dining rm & 2 restaurants; 6:30 am-10 pm; $15-$55; cocktails. Also, Glissandi, see separate listing. FAX (916) 581-5407   Ⓢ Ⓓ (916) 583-6300

Rodeway Inn ⑰   Rates Subject to Change   *Motel*   ◆◆
⊕ All year   1P 54.00- 79.00 2P/1B 59.00- 89.00 2P/2B 64.00- 99.00 XP 5
51 units. On SR 28, 1/2 mi n of SR 89. 645 N Lake Blvd. (PO Box 29, Tahoe City, 96145) Formerly Pepper Tree Inn. Check-in 3 pm. C/CATV; phones; shower baths. Coin laundry. Pool; indoor whirlpool. Garage & parking lot. No pets. Reserv deposit required. AE, DI, DS, MC, VI. Restaurant opposite. *(See ad below)*   Ⓓ (916) 583-3711

Squaw Valley Lodge ⑮   Rates Subject to Change   *Apartment Lodge*   ◆◆◆◆
⊕ Fri & Sat 11/15-4/30   ....   2P/2B 150.00- 295.00 XP
Sun-Thurs 11/15-4/30   ....   2P/2B 120.00- 295.00 XP
5/1-11/14   ....   2P/2B 100.00- 150.00 XP
Senior discount. 154 units. In Olympic Valley at Squaw Valley Ski area. 201 Squaw Peak Rd. (PO Box 3730, Olympic Valley, 96146) Located at foot of slopes, 150 feet from Cable car. Most rooms with view of slopes or valley. Check-in 4 pm. Check-out 10 am. C/CATV; pay movies; VCPs. Radios; phones. Kitchens. Coin laundry. Pool; sauna; whirlpool; 3 indoor whirlpool; tennis-2 courts; nature trails; steamroom; exercise rm. Fee for: ski lifts, massage. Valet parking ramp. No pets. Wkly rates avail. Reserv deposit required ski season only; 30 days refund notice. AE, MC, VI. FAX (916) 583-0326 *(See ad below)*   Ⓓ Ⓛ (916) 583-5500

(See LAKE TAHOE spotting map page A177)

Tahoe Cedars Lodge **18**   Rates Guaranteed   *Cottages*   ◆
5/4-10/1   1P .... 45.00 2P/1B .... 45.00 2P/2B .... 48.00 XP 6
19 units. 9 mi s of Tahoe City, on SR 89. 6980 W Lake Blvd. (PO Box 269, Tahoma, 96142) OPEN 5/14-10/1. Spacious lakefront grounds. Rustic cottages, some with view. Credit cards not accepted. Shower baths. 2 2-bedrm units. Beach; swimming; dock. No pets. 9 kitchens, $51-$54 for 2 persons. 4 duplex units for up to 5 persons, $105 also 2 2-story units, $100-$115 for up to 6 persons. Wkly rates avail. Reserv deposit required; 7 days refund notice. Restaurant opposite.
Ⓓ (916) 525-7515

Tahoe City Travelodge **14**   AAA Special Value Rates   *Motel*   ◆◆
⊛ 12/24-1/3   1P 99.00- 104.00 2P/1B   99.00- 104.00 2P/2B 109.00- 126.00 XP 5 F
1/4-4/24 & 7/2-9/6   1P 60.00- 86.00 2P/1B   66.00- 91.00 2P/2B   71.00- 97.00 XP 5 F
5/29-7/1 & 9/7-12/23   1P 54.00- 76.00 2P/1B   59.00- 81.00 2P/2B   63.00- 86.00 XP 5 F
4/25-5/28   1P 42.00- 55.00 2P/1B   44.00- 58.00 2P/2B   49.00- 63.00 XP 5 F
47 units. On SR 28, 1/4 mi e of jct SR 89. 455 North Lake Blvd. (PO Box 84, Tahoe City, 96145) Lake opposite & golfing adjacent; attractive comfortable rooms. C/CATV; movies; radios; phones; shower or comb baths. Pool; sauna; whirlpool. No pets. Reserv deposit required. AE, DI, DS, MC, VI. Restaurant adjacent. FAX (916) 583-8045
(See ad below)   ⊗ Ⓓ (916) 583-3766

Vista Shores Resort **20**   Rates Subject to Change   *Cottages*   ◆◆
⊛ 6/15-9/15   1P 60.00- 85.00 2P/1B   60.00- 85.00 2P/2B   75.00- 95.00 XP 10
Fri & Sat 9/16-6/14   1P 55.00- 75.00 2P/1B   55.00- 95.00 2P/2B   65.00- 85.00 XP 10
Sun-Thurs 9/16-6/14   1P 45.00- 60.00 2P/1B   45.00- 60.00 2P/2B   55.00- 75.00 XP 10
Senior discount. 27 units. On SR 28 1 mi w of SR 267. 6731 North Lake Blvd. (PO Box 487, Tahoe Vista, 96148) Some cottages on the beach. Refrigerators; C/CATV; shower or comb baths. 4 2-bedrm units, 1 3-bedrm unit, 14 kitchens, 2 efficiencies. Pool; beach; sauna; whirlpool. No pets. 1-3 bedroom cottages, $75-$180 for 2-4 persons. Reserv deposit required; 14 days refund notice. MC, VI. Restaurant adjacent. FAX (916) 546-7145 *(See ad below)*
Ⓓ (916) 546-3635

Woodvista Lodge **7**   Rates Subject to Change   *Motel*   ◆
⊛ 6/15-9/30, 11/25-4/15 & week-
ends   1P 40.00- 85.00 ....   2P/2B 45.00- 90.00 XP 5 F
10/1-11/24 & 4/16-6/14 1P 35.00- 75.00 ....   2P/2B 40.00- 80.00 XP 5 F
16 units. On SR 28, 1/4 mi w of SR 267. 7699 N Lake Blvd. (PO Box 439, Tahoe Vista, 96148) Tree-shaded grounds. Spacious lawn. Refrigerators; C/CATV; phones; shower baths. Pool; whirlpool; playground. No pets. Reserv deposit required; 10 days refund notice. AE, DS, MC, VI.
Ⓓ (916) 546-3839

RESTAURANTS

Azzara's Italian Restaurant ①   Italian $$ ◆◆
930 Tahoe Blvd. Charming European decor, varied menu with seafood specialties, very popular. A/C. Open 5 pm-9:30 pm; closed Mon, 4/11, 11/25, 12/24 & 12/25. Cocktails. Minimum $3. AE, MC, VI.   (702) 831-0346

(See LAKE TAHOE spotting map page A177)

Christy Hill Restaurant ⑥   American $$$ ◆◆
E off SR 28 toward lake. 115 Grove St, Tahoe City. Varied menu with emphasis on California & French style; fresh local ingredients & pacific seafood. Attractive decor, view of lake. Smoke free premises. Open 5:30 pm-9:30 pm; closed Mon, 11/25 & 12/25. Beer & wine. Reserv advised. MC, VI.   ⊗ (916) 583-8551

Glissandi ②   French $$$$ ◆◆◆◆
In Olympic Valley at Resort, Squaw Creek. 1000 Squaw Creek Rd. Dress code. Open 6 pm-10 pm; closed Sun. Cocktails & lounge. Valet parking. Reserv required. AE, CB, DI, MC, VI.   ⊗ (916) 581-6621

La Playa ③   Seafood $$$ ◆◆
On SR 28, 1 mi w of SR 267 in Tahoe Vista; 7 mi e of Tahoe City, on lake. 7042 N Lake Blvd. Patio dining in summer; comfortable seating. Open 11 am-3 & 5-10 pm; closed for lunch 9/1-5/31. Cocktails & lounge. Minimum, $8. Reserv advised. AE, DI, MC, VI.   (916) 546-5903

Le Petit Pier ④   French $$$$ ◆◆◆
On SR 28; 1/2 mi w of SR 267. 7238 N Lake Blvd. View of lake & mountains; quiet atmosphere. A/C. Open 6 pm-10 pm; closed Tues. Cocktails & lounge. Reserv advised. AE, DI, MC, VI.   ⊗ (916) 546-4464

Mackinaw Inn ⑦   Continental $$ ◆◆
On SR 28 1/2 mi e of SR 89 in Round House Mall. 700 N Lake Blvd. Overlooking Lake Tahoe & mountains. Sun brunch 10 am-2 pm. Children's menu. Open 11:30 am-10 pm; Fri & Sat-11 pm; Sun 10 am-10 pm. Cocktails & lounge. Reserv advised. MC, VI.   ⊗ (916) 583-0233

Tahoe House ⑤   Ethnic $$
3/4 mi s of Tahoe City on SR 89. 625 W. Lake Blvd. Swiss, also California cuisine. Fresh baked breads. Homemade desserts; European atmosphere. A/C. Children's menu. Open 5 pm-10 pm. Cocktails & lounge. Minimum $5. Reserv advised. AE, MC, VI.   ⊗ (916) 583-1377

LAKE TAHOE (Southern Region) (See LAKE TAHOE AREA spotting map page A177; see index below)

Alder Inn & Cottages ⑥⑤   Rates Subject to Change   *Motel*   ◆

All year	1P	38.50- 75.50	2P/1B	42.50- 85.50	2P/2B	48.50- 95.50	XP 10	

Senior discount. 28 units. 2 1/2 blks s off US 50 on Ski Run Blvd; 3/4 mi below Heavenly Valley ski lift terminal. 1072 Ski Run Blvd. (PO Box 5414, South Lake Tahoe, 96157) Refrigerators; C/CATV; phones. 4 kitchens. Coin laundry. Pool; enclosed whirlpool. Pets, $10 daily extra charge. 2-night minimum stay weekends 7/1-8/31. Reserv deposit required; 30 days refund notice. MC, VI. FAX (916) 544-8119   ⊗ ⒟ (916) 544-4485

Best Tahoe West Inn ④①   Rates Subject to Change   *Motel*   ◆◆

Fri-Sat 6/15-9/7 & Sun-Thurs 7/30-8/31	1P	42.00- 64.00	2P/1B	42.00- 64.00	2P/2B	48.00- 68.00	XP 6		F
Fri & Sat 9/8-6/14	1P	38.00- 46.00	2P/1B	38.00- 46.00	2P/2B	42.00- 52.00	XP 6		F
Sun-Thurs 6/15-7/29 & 9/1-9/14	1P	34.00- 48.00	2P/1B	34.00- 48.00	2P/2B	40.00- 52.00	XP 6		F
Sun-Thurs 9/15-6/14	1P	29.95- 38.00	2P/1B	29.95- 38.00	2P/2B	34.00- 44.00	XP 6		F

Senior discount. 61 units. N off US 50, via Park Ave; on Pine Blvd, between Stateline & Park aves. 4107 Pine Blvd. (PO Box CCC, South Lake Tahoe, 96157) On both sides of Pine Blvd. 3-story, no elevator. C/CATV; phones; comb or shower baths. Small pool; sauna; whirlpool. No pets. 11 efficiencies, $7 extra. Reserv deposit required. 2 night minimum stay, weekends in ski season. AE, CB, DI, MC, VI. FAX (916) 544-0588 *(See ads inside front cover and p A184)*   ⒟ (916) 544-6455

Checkout time is noted in the listing if the required time is before 10 a.m.

(See LAKE TAHOE spotting map page A177)

Best Western Lake Tahoe Inn �51		AAA Special Value Rates				Motor Inn		◆◆
ⓐ Fri & Sat 6/25-9/6	1P 82.00-102.00	2P/1B	82.00-102.00	2P/2B	92.00-112.00	XP 10	F
Fri & Sat 9/7-6/24	1P 72.00- 92.00	2P/1B	72.00- 92.00	2P/2B	82.00-102.00	XP 10	F
Sun-Thurs 6/25-9/6	1P 67.00- 87.00	2P/1B	67.00- 87.00	2P/2B	77.00- 97.00	XP 10	F
Sun-Thurs 9/7-6/24	1P 57.00- 77.00	2P/1B	57.00- 77.00	2P/2B	67.00- 87.00	XP 10	F

400 units. On US 50, adjacent to casinos. 4110 Lake Tahoe Blvd. (South Lake Tahoe, 96150) Spacious grounds. A/C; C/CATV; pay movies; 200 radios; phones; shower or comb baths. 8 2-bedrm units. 2 pools, 1 small; hot tub. No pets. Reserv deposit required; 3 days refund notice. AE, DI, DS, MC, VI. ● Restaurant; 7 am-10 pm; 9/1-6/1, 7 am-1:30 & 5:30-9:30 pm; a la carte entrees about $7-$10; cocktails. FAX (916) 542-1428 *(See ad p A185)*
⊗ Ⓓ (916) 541-2010

Best Western Station House Inn 🆗40		AAA Special Value Rates				Motor Inn	◆◆◆
ⓐ Fri & Sat 6/1-10/31 [EP]	1P 98.00	2P/1B	.... 98.00	2P/2B	.... 108.00	XP 10	
Fri & Sat 11/1-5/31 & Sun-							
Thurs 6/1-10/31 [BP]	1P 88.00	2P/1B	.... 88.00	2P/2B	.... 98.00	XP 10	
Sun-Thurs 11/1-5/31 [BP]	1P 78.00	2P/1B	.... 78.00	2P/2B	.... 88.00	XP 10	

102 units. 3 1/2 blks from casino center; 2 blks n off US 50 via Park-Loop Rd. 901 Park Ave. (PO Box 4009, South Lake Tahoe, 96157) Attractive rooms. Check-in 3 pm. 100 A/C; C/CATV; movies; radios; phones; comb or shower baths. 1 3-bedrm unit. Pool; whirlpool. No pets. 1 2-bedroom cabin with kitchen for up to 6 persons, $150-$200. 1 3-bedroom cabin with kitchen for up to 6 persons, $175-$235. AE, DI, DS, MC, VI. ● Lew Mar Nels, see separate listing. FAX (916) 542-1714
Ⓓ (916) 542-1101

Best Western Timber Cove Lodge �52		AAA Special Value Rates				Motor Inn		◆◆◆
ⓐ Fri & Sat 6/25-9/6	1P 92.00-112.00	2P/1B	92.00-112.00	2P/2B	102.00-112.00	XP 10	F
Sun-Thurs 6/25-9/6	1P 82.00-102.00	2P/1B	82.00-102.00	2P/2B	92.00-112.00	XP 10	F
Fri & Sat 9/7-6/24	1P 72.00- 92.00	2P/1B	72.00- 92.00	2P/2B	82.00-102.00	XP 10	F
Sun-Thurs 9/7-6/24	1P 57.00- 77.00	2P/1B	57.00- 77.00	2P/2B	67.00- 87.00	XP 10	F

262 units. On lake 1 1/2 mi w of casino center, 1/2 mi w of Ski Run Blvd. 3411 Lake Tahoe Blvd. (South Lake Tahoe, 96150) Spacious grounds; some rooms with lake view. Check-in 3 pm. A/C; C/CATV; pay movies; radios; phones; shower or comb baths. Htd pool; beach; whirlpool; rental boats & motors; marina; fishing; water skiing; pier. No pets. Reserv deposit required. AE, DI, DS, MC, VI. ● Restaurant; 7 am-10 pm; in winter-9 pm; $9-$20; cocktails. FAX (916) 541-7959 *(See ad p A185)*
⊗ Ⓓ (916) 541-6722

Caesars Tahoe 🆖56		Rates Subject to Change				Hotel		◆◆◆◆
7/1-8/31	1P 115.00-175.00	2P/1B	115.00-175.00	2P/2B	115.00-175.00	XP 10	
9/1-6/30	1P 105.00-165.00	2P/1B	105.00-165.00	2P/2B	105.00-165.00	XP 10	

440 units. At casino Center. (PO Box 5800, Stateline, NV, 89449) Many rooms with view of Lake Tahoe. Check-in 3 pm. A/C; C/CATV; free & pay movies; radios; phones; comb or shower bath. Htd indoor pool; saunas; whirlpool. Fee for: lighted tennis-4 courts; health club. Valet garage & parking lot. No pets. Reserv deposit required. AE, CB, DI, MC, VI. ● 4 restaurants & coffeeshop; 24 hours; $7-$25; cocktails; name entertainment; nightclub. FAX (702) 586-2056
Ⓢ Ⓓ Ⓖ (702) 588-3515

Casino Area Travelodge 🆕50		AAA Special Value Rates				Motel		◆◆
ⓐ 7/1-8/31 & 12/21-12/31	1P 75.00- 90.00	2P/1B	80.00- 95.00	2P/2B	86.00-101.00	XP 5	F
5/1-6/30 & 9/1-10/31	1P 65.00- 80.00	2P/1B	70.00- 85.00	2P/2B	76.00- 91.00	XP 5	F
1/1-1/31	1P 56.00- 71.00	2P/1B	61.00- 76.00	2P/2B	67.00- 82.00	XP 5	F
2/1-4/30 & 11/1-11/12/20	1P 53.00- 68.00	2P/1B	58.00- 73.00	2P/2B	64.00- 79.00	XP 5	F

66 units. 2 blks w of casino center, on US 50. (PO Box 6500, South Lake Tahoe, 96157) A/C; C/CATV; movies; radios; phones; shower baths. Pool. No pets. Reserv deposit required. AE, DI, DS, MC, VI. FAX (916) 544-6910 *(See ad p A187)* ⊗ Ⓓ (916) 541-5000

Cedar Lodge 🆘48		Rates Subject to Change				Motel		◆◆
ⓐ Fri & Sat 12/26-12/31	....	2P/1B	48.00- 88.00	2P/2B	42.00- 94.00	XP 14	
Sun-Thurs 6/12-9/30	....	2P/1B	.... 52.00	2P/2B	.... 58.00	XP 14	
Sun-Thurs 10/1-12/25 &							
1/1-6/11	....	2P/1B	.... 42.00	2P/2B	.... 48.00	XP 10	

32 units. N off US 50, toward the lake; at Cedar & Friday aves; 3 blks from the casino center. 4069 Cedar Ave. (PO Box 4547, South Lake Tahoe, 96157) C/CATV; movies; radios; phones; shower or comb baths. 2 2-bedrm units. Pool; whirlpool open 10/1-5/15. No pets. Package plans avail. Reserv deposit required during holidays; 14 days refund notice. MC, VI.
Ⓓ (916) 544-6453

(See LAKE TAHOE spotting map page A177)

Days Inn-Stateline/South Lake Tahoe 60   Rates Subject to Change   *Motel* ◆

6/15-9/15 & weekends [CP]	1P	66.00- 70.00	2P/1B	70.00- 74.00	2P/2B	78.00- 92.00	XP 6
9/16-6/14 [CP]	1P	56.00- 60.00	2P/1B	60.00- 64.00	2P/2B	68.00- 82.00	XP 6

Senior discount. 59 units. 5 blks w of casino center; 1 blk n off US 50 toward lake at Park & Cedar aves. (PO Box 6499, South Lake Tahoe, 96157) A/C; C/CATV; radios; phones. Small pool; sauna; indoor whirlpool. 3 2-bedroom units for up to 4 persons, $100. Pets, $25 deposit, plus $5 daily extra charge. Reserv deposit required; 3 days refund notice. AE, DI, DS, MC, VI. FAX (916) 544-4643   ⊗ Ⓓ (916) 541-4800

Embassy Suites Resort 44   Rates Subject to Change   *Suites Hotel* ◆◆◆◆

12/20-1/1 [BP]	1P	.... 200.00		.... 200.00	2P/2B	.... 200.00	XP 20	F
1/2-2/16 & 7/1-9/7 [BP]	1P	159.00- 179.00	2P/1B	159.00- 179.00	2P/2B	159.00- 179.00	XP 20	F
2/17-6/30 & 9/8-12/19 [BP]	1P	119.00- 159.00	2P/1B	119.00- 159.00	2P/2B	119.00- 159.00	XP 20	F

400 units. At Casino Center. 4130 Lake Tahoe Blvd. (South Lake Tahoe, 96150) Check-in 3 pm. A/C; C/CATV; free & pay movies; radios; phones. Efficiencies, no utensils. Coin laundry. Htd pool; sauna; whirlpool. Valet parking lot. Airport transp. No pets. Reserv deposit required. Complimentary beverages each evening. AE, CB, DI, MC, VI. ● Restaurant; cocktails. Also, Zachary's, see separate listing. FAX (916) 544-4900 *(See ad p A187)*   ⊗ Ⓢ Ⓓ (916) 544-5400

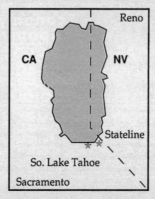

The South Lake Tahoe Flamingo Lodge

3 ◆◆◆ 3 Diamond Rating
10% Discount to AAA Members

Room Rates for Two People/One Bed

LOW SEASON *Sunday thru Thursday January 3 thru June 24 and September 12 thru December 23.*

	Economy Room	Standard Room
Room Rate	49.00	64.00
AAA Discount	-4.90	-6.40
Net Rate for AAA Members	44.10	57.60

HIGH SEASON *Every Friday, Saturday and Holiday Year-round. Plus every weekday from June 25 thru September 11 and December 24 thru January 2. Two-night minimum on some Saturdays and Holidays.*

	Economy Room	Standard Room
Room Rate	74.00	89.00
AAA Discount	-7.40	-8.90
Net Rate for AAA Members	66.60	80.10

All rooms are newly refurbished and equipped with Air Conditioning, Refrigerators, Ice and Coffee • Non-Smoking Rooms, Wet Bars, Kitchens and Fireplaces are available • Superb Honeymoon Accommodations • Luxurious Indoor Spa with Whirlpool, Sauna and Steam • Plus an outdoor Spa and Heated Pool • Free Casino Shuttle Service and Casino Coupons • Adjacent to Restaurant

Three Blocks from Harrah's and Harvey's Casinos

For Reservations call (800) 544-5288
3961 Lake Tahoe Blvd (Highway 50)
South Lake Tahoe, CA 96150

(See LAKE TAHOE spotting map page A177)

Flamingo Lodge 59
6/25-9/11, 12/24-1/2 & Fri-Sat 1P 69.00- 89.00 2P/1B 74.00- 89.00 2P/2B 79.00- 94.00 XP 10 F
Sun-Thurs 1/3-6/24 &
9/12-12/23   1P 44.00- 64.00 2P/1B 49.00- 64.00 2P/2B 54.00- 69.00 XP 10 F
AAA Special Value Rates — *Motel* ◆◆◆
90 units. 1/4 mi w of casino center, on US 50; at Pioneer Tr. 3961 Lake Tahoe Blvd. (South Lake Tahoe, 96150)
Refrigerators; A/C; C/CATV; phones; comb or shower baths. Coin laundry. Pool; sauna; indoor whirlpool, outdoor hot tub; steamroom. No pets. 1- & 2-bedroom suites, some with kitchen, $99-$159 for 4 persons. 1 large
unit with fireplace, whirlpool & VCP, $129-$159 for 2 persons. Reserv deposit required. AE, DI, DS, MC, VI. Coffeeshop adjacent. *(See ad p A186)*   ⊗ Ⓓ (916) 544-5288

Forest Inn 57
5/21-9/15   1P 86.00- 99.00 2P/1B 86.00- 99.00 2P/2B 99.00- 125.00 XP 10
9/16-5/20   1P 76.00- 94.00 2P/1B 76.00- 94.00 2P/2B 94.00- 115.00 XP 10
Rates Subject to Change — *Apartment Motel* ◆◆◆
123 units. 1 blk se off US 50, adjacent to casinos on Park Ave. 1101 Park Ave. (PO Box 4300, South Lake
Tahoe, 96157) Shaded, landscaped grounds. 17 A/C; C/CATV; VCPs; radios; phones. Coin laundry. Saunas;
whirlpools; 2 pools enclosed in winter. No pets. 2-night minimum stay. 1-bedroom suites for up to 2 persons,
$94-$99; 2-bedroom suites for up to 4 persons, $115-$185; 108 kitchens, $6 extra. Reserv deposit required; 4
days refund notice. AE, MC, VI. *(See ad starting on p A188)*   Ⓓ (916) 541-6655

Standard Rates – February 1, 1993

Accommodations	# in party	May 21 Sept. 15	Sept16 May 20
Hotel Room	1-2	$86	$76
1 Bed/1 Bath Suite	1-2	$99	$94
2 Bed/2 Bath Suite	1-4	$125	$115
Additional Guests	1	$10	$10

SPECIAL DISCOUNTS

AAA Members
Senior Citizens
$5.00 OFF Standard
Rates per night
Minimum 2 night stay

**CHECK-IN 3:00 PM
CHECK-OUT 11:00 AM**

Valid:
**September 1
thru May 20**
Sunday thru Thursday
Holidays Excluded

Due to high occupancy,
please make
your reservations
well in advance

SPECIAL PACKAGE RATES

Accommodations	# in party	3 Day Pkg.	4 Day Pkg.	5 Day Pkg.
1 Bed/1 Bath Suite	1-2	$246	$316	$375
2 Bed/2 Bath Suite	1-4	$336	$424	$490
Additional Guests	1	$30	$40	$50

FOREST INN SUITES

1101 Park Ave.
P.O. Box 4300
So. Lake Tahoe
CA 96157

800 822-5950
(U.S. & Canada)
916 541-6655
FAX 916 544-3135

*Follow arrows
on map to
avoid traffic*

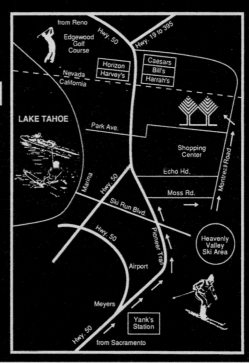

(See LAKE TAHOE spotting map page A177)

Green Lantern Motel 45 ◆
7/1-9/7 & Fri-Sat

1P	42.00- 60.00	2P/1B	42.00- 60.00	2P/2B	46.00- 66.00	XP	5

Sun-Thurs 5/22-6/30 &
9/8-10/17

1P	32.00- 42.00	2P/1B	32.00- 42.00	2P/2B	36.00- 50.00	XP	5

Sun-Thurs 10/18-5/21

1P	28.00- 38.00	2P/1B	28.00- 38.00	2P/2B	32.00- 42.00	XP	5

40 units. 3 blks toward the lake from casino area, on Manzanita Ave at Poplar St. 4097 Manzanita. (PO Box SV, South Lake Tahoe, 96157) C/CATV; 24 radios; phones; shower baths. Small pool; whirlpools. No pets. 1 2-bedroom kitchen unit with fireplace, $102-$160. Reserv deposit required; 5 days refund notice. AE, DI, DS, MC, VI. *(See ad below)* D (916) 544-6336

Harrah's Hotel & Casino 55 ◆◆◆◆
6/12-9/19

Rates Subject to Change   *Hotel*

1P	135.00- 175.00	2P/1B	135.00- 175.00	2P/2B	135.00- 175.00	XP	20

9/20-11/12 & 12/18-6/11

1P	115.00- 145.00	2P/1B	115.00- 145.00	2P/2B	115.00- 145.00	XP	20

11/13-12/17

1P	105.00- 125.00	2P/1B	105.00- 125.00	2P/2B	105.00- 125.00	XP	20

Senior discount. 534 units. In casino area. (PO Box 8, Stateline, NV, 89449) Many with views of mountains or lake. Check-in 3 pm. A/C; C/CATV; radios; phones. Htd indoor pool; 2 indoor whirlpools; health club. Fee for: massage. Valet garage & parking lot. Airport transp. Pets. Reserv deposit required. AE, DI, DS, MC, VI. ● 4 restaurants & coffeeshop; 24 hours; $8-$60; buffet $9-$15; casino; cocktails; entertainment. Also, The Summit Room, see separate listing. FAX (702) 586-6607 ⊗ Ⓢ Ⓓ (702) 588-6611

Harvey's Resort Hotel 53 ◆◆◆
7/1-9/30 [BP]

Rates Subject to Change   *Hotel*

1P	135.00- 180.00	2P/1B	135.00- 180.00	2P/2B	135.00- 180.00	XP	20	F

10/1-6/30 [BP]

1P	90.00- 165.00	2P/1B	90.00- 165.00	2P/2B	90.00- 165.00	XP	20	F

Senior discount. 740 units. On US 50, casino center. (PO Box 128, Stateline, NV, 89449) Check-in 3:30 pm. 544 refrigerators; A/C; C/CATV; pay movies; radios; phones; comb or shower baths. Htd pool; whirlpool; tennis-3 courts, 1 lighted; steamroom; health club. Fee for: massage. Valet ramp & parking lot. Airport transp. No pets. Suites with whirlpool tub, Most with balcony, $175-$500. AE, DI, DS, MC, VI. ● 4 restaurants & coffeeshop; 24 hours; $10-$31; buffet about $4-$13; casino; cocktails; entertainment. Also, Sage Room Steakhouse & Lewel-lyn's, see separate listing. FAX (702) 588-6643 *(See ad p A191)* ⊗ Ⓢ Ⓓ Ⓛ (702) 588-2411

High Country Lodge 37 ◆
Fri & Sat 6/30-9/30

Rates Subject to Change   *Motel*

1P	.... 60.00	2P/1B	.... 60.00	2P/2B	.... 70.00	XP	10

Fri & Sat 10/1-6/29

1P	.... 50.00	2P/1B	.... 55.00	2P/2B	.... 60.00	XP	10

Sun-Thurs

1P	.... 30.00	2P/1B	.... 40.00	2P/2B	.... 40.00	XP	10

Senior discount. 15 units. 1/2 mi n of airport; on US 50. 1227 Emerald Bay Rd. (South Lake Tahoe, 96150) Tree shaded grounds. 5 refrigerators; C/CATV; movies; VCPs. Radios; phones; shower or comb baths. Whirlpool. Pets, $5 extra charge. Reserv deposit required; 7 days refund notice. AE, MC, VI. FAX (916) 542-4385 *(See ad below)* D (916) 541-0508

Horizon Casino Resort 54 ◆◆
Fri & Sat 6/18-9/18

AAA Special Value Rates   *Hotel*

1P	.... 129.00	2P/1B	.... 129.00	2P/2B	.... 129.00	XP	10

Sun-Thurs 6/18-9/18 & Fri-Sat
9/19-6/17

1P	.... 110.00	2P/1B	.... 110.00	2P/2B	.... 110.00	XP	10

Sun-Thurs 9/19-10/30,
2/28-6/17

1P	.... 95.00	2P/1B	.... 95.00	2P/2B	.... 95.00	XP	10

Sun-Thurs 10/31-2/27

1P	.... 85.00	2P/1B	.... 85.00	2P/2B	.... 85.00	XP	10

539 units. On US 50 in the casino area. (PO Box C, Stateline, NV, 89449) Check-in 3 pm. A/C; C/CATV; pay movies; radios; phones. Wading pool; pool open 5/30-9/30; hot tubs. Parking ramp & parking lot. No pets. Lake view rooms, $10 extra. AE, DI, DS, MC, VI. ● Dining rm, 2 restaurants & coffeeshop; 24 hours; $6-$18; buffet about $8; cocktails; entertainment. Casino. FAX (702) 588-1344 ⊗ Ⓢ Ⓓ (702) 588-6211

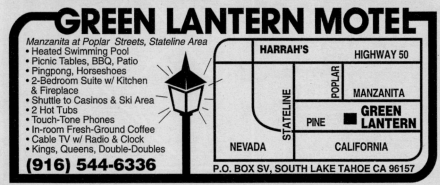

Just think, all this and you don't have to go camping.

Natural splendor. Spectacular mountain and lake views. You're familiar with the great outdoors of Lake Tahoe. Now let us introduce you to our great indoors. Imagine a luxurious room. A complimentary buffet breakfast each morning of your stay. Eight great restaurants. A state-of-the-art health club, year-round pool and spa. And of course, 24-hour casino action. Plus, when you show your AAA card upon check-in, you'll receive 10% off your posted room rate. So leave your tent at home. Just call 1-800-648-3361 for reservations.

The Party's At Harveys!
RESORT HOTEL / CASINO · LAKE TAHOE

Call 1-800-648-3361.

(See LAKE TAHOE spotting map page A177)

Inn By The Lake 35	Rates Subject to Change					Motel	◆◆◆

Inn By The Lake 35   **Rates Subject to Change**   *Motel* ◆◆◆

⊛ 6/26-9/7 & 12/18-1/4 [CP]   1P   98.00- 148.00   2P/1B   98.00- 148.00   2P/2B   138.00- 148.00   XP
1/5-4/19 & 9/8-9/30 [CP]   1P   98.00- 138.00   2P/1B   98.00- 138.00   2P/2B   128.00- 138.00   XP
4/20-6/25, 10/1-12/17 [CP]   1P   84.00- 138.00   2P/1B   84.00- 138.00   2P/2B   108.00- 128.00   XP

Senior discount. 99 units. 2 mi s of casino center on US 50. 3300 Lake Tahoe Blvd. (South Lake Tahoe, 96150) Some rooms with lake view. Check-in 3 pm. 36 refrigerators; A/C; C/CATV; movies; radios; phones; comb or shower baths. 2 2-bedrm units, 6 kitchens. Coin laundry. Htd pool; sauna; whirlpool. No pets. Rates for up to 4 persons. 2-night minimum stay weekends. Reserv deposit required. AE, DI, DS, MC, VI. Coffeeshop adjacent. FAX (916) 541-6596 *(See ad below)*   ⊗ Ⓢ Ⓓ ▣ (916) 542-0330

AAA'S REDUCING PLAN.
AAA Special Value Rates means a 10-percent minimum reduction
from the rates printed in the TourBook.

(See LAKE TAHOE spotting map page A177)

Lakeland Village 🆔 49 ◆◆
🏅 12/18-1/3   1P 100.00- 235.00 2P/1B 100.00- 235.00 2P/2B 100.00- 235.00 XP
1/4-3/28 & 7/1-9/7   1P 95.00- 225.00 2P/1B   95.00- 225.00 2P/2B   95.00- 225.00 XP
3/29-6/30 & 9/8-12/17 1P 85.00- 175.00 2P/1B   85.00- 175.00 2P/2B   85.00- 175.00 XP
Senior discount. 260 units. 1 1/4 mi w of casino center, on US 50. 3535 Lake Tahoe Blvd. (PO Box 1356, South Lake Tahoe, 96156) Spacious grounds. Some units on lakefront. Check-in 3 pm. 87 A/C; C/CATV; movies; phones. Coin laundry. 2 pools; wading pool; beach; saunas; whirlpool; rental boats; fishing; pier. Fee for: tennis-2 courts. Parking ramp & parking lot. No pets. 1-to 4-bedroom housekeeping townhouse units with fireplace, $140-$400 for up to 10 persons. Reserv deposit required; 14 days refund notice. AE, MC, VI. Restaurant adjacent. FAX (916) 541-6278 *(See ad p A192)*   Ⓓ (916) 541-7711

Lakeside Inn 🆔 32 ◆◆◆
🏅 5/16-9/30   AAA Special Value Rates   *Motor Inn*
5/16-9/30   1P 79.00- 110.00 2P/1B   79.00- 110.00 2P/2B   79.00- 110.00 XP 10
10/1-5/15   1P 59.00- 99.00   2P/1B   59.00- 99.00   2P/2B   59.00- 99.00   XP 10
123 units. On US 50; 1 mi e of state line at Kingsbury Grade. (PO Box 5640, Stateline, NV, 89449) Check-in 3:30 pm. A/C; C/CATV; movies; 50 radios; phones. 1 2-bedrm unit. Pool; Pool open 6/1-9/30. No pets. 1 & 2-bedroom suites with wet bar & whirlpool tub, $210 for up to 4 persons. Reserv deposit required. AE, DI, DS, MC, VI. ● Restaurant; 24 hrs; $8-$18; cocktails; entertainment. Casino. FAX (702) 588-4092 ⊗ Ⓓ (702) 588-7777

Pacifica Lodge 🆔 39 ◆◆
🏅 6/15-9/30   Rates Subject to Change   *Motel*
6/15-9/30   1P 65.00- 70.00 2P/1B   65.00- 70.00 2P/2B   65.00- 70.00 XP 6
10/1-6/14   1P 50.00- 60.00 2P/1B   50.00- 60.00 2P/2B   50.00- 60.00 XP 6
Senior discount. 67 units. 6 blks w of casino center; 2 blks n off US 50 toward lake at Park & Manzanita Ave. 931 Park Ave. (PO Box 4298, South Lake Tahoe, 96157) Some woodburning fireplace units. 35 refrigerators; C/CATV; phones. 12 2-bedrm units, 6 kitchens. Pool; whirlpool. No pets. AE, DI, DS, MC, VI. *(See ad below)*   Ⓓ (916) 544-4131

Parkwood Lodge 🆔 58 ◆◆
🏅 Fri-Sat 7/1-9/18   Rates Subject to Change   *Motel*
Fri-Sat 7/1-9/18   1P 48.00- 68.00 2P/1B   48.00- 68.00 2P/2B   68.00- 78.00 XP 8
Sun-Thurs 7/1-9/18 & Fri-Sat
9/19-6/30   1P 38.00- 54.00 2P/1B   38.00- 54.00 2P/2B   48.00- 68.00 XP 8
Sun-Thurs 9/19-6/30 1P 32.00- 38.00 2P/1B   32.00- 38.00 2P/2B   42.00- 58.00 XP 8
16 units. 1 blk n off US 50 toward lake, at Park & Cedar aves; 3 blks w of casino center. 954 Park Ave. (96150) Covered parking. C/CATV; movies; phones. Enclosed whirlpool. No pets. Covered parking. Reserv deposit required; 3 days refund notice. AE, MC, VI. FAX (916) 541-7519 *(See ad below)*   ⊗ Ⓓ (916) 544-4114

See the Sample Listing.

(See LAKE TAHOE spotting map page A177)

The Ridge Tahoe 🟥34 ◆◆◆◆
12/11-4/16	1P	155.00- 225.00	2P/1B	155.00- 225.00	2P/2B	225.00- 330.00	XP
6/19-9/10	1P	125.00- 195.00	2P/1B	125.00- 195.00	2P/2B	195.00- 285.00	XP
9/11-12/10 & 4/17-6/18	1P	105.00- 175.00	2P/1B	105.00- 175.00	2P/2B	175.00- 265.00	XP

Resort Complex

343 units. 3 mi e of US 50 via Kingsbury Rd, 3/4 mi s via Tramway Dr, then 1 1/4 mi e on Quaking Aspen Ln. 400 Ridge Club Dr. (PO Box 5790, Stateline, NV, 89449) At 7300 ft elevation, gondola to ski lift. 1- & 2-bedroom units with fully equipped kitchen & gas fireplace; some motel units, some with view of Carson Valley. Check-in 4 pm. Check-out 10 am. Refrigerators; C/CATV; pay movies; VCPs. Radios; phones. Coin laundry. 2 htd pools, 1 indoor/outdoor; saunas; indoor & outdoor whirlpools; putting green; tennis-4 courts, 2 lighted, 1 indoor; racquetball-2 courts; social program; recreational program; children's program; playground; transportation to casinos; game room; health club. Fee for: ski lifts, massage. Garage & parking lot. No pets. Maximum rates for up to 6 persons. Wkly rates avail. Reserv deposit required; 15 days refund notice in high season. AE, CB, DI, MC, VI. ● Dining rm & coffeeshop; 9 am-10 pm, dining room closed Mon & Tues; Sun brunch 10 am-1:30 pm, for Resort guests only; a la carte entrees about $10-$30; cocktails. FAX (702) 588-7099 *(See ad p A193)* ⊗ Ⓢ Ⓓ (702) 588-3553

Royal Valhalla Motor Lodge 🟥42   Rates Subject to Change   *Motel* ◆◆◆
5/15-9/30 [CP]	....		2P/1B	74.00- 94.00	2P/2B	79.00- 99.00	XP 5
10/1-5/14 [CP]	....		2P/1B	54.00- 74.00	2P/2B	59.00- 79.00	XP 5

80 units. N off Hwy 50; at Lakeshore & Stateline Ave. 4104 Lakeshore. (96150) Beach opposite. Some balconies, with lake view. 2- & 3-bedroom bi-level suites; some with covered parking. C/CATV; phones; comb or shower baths. 26 2-bedrm units. Coin laundry. Pool. No pets. 29 kitchens, $5 extra. Reserv deposit required. AE, CB, DI, MC, VI. FAX (916) 544-1436   Ⓓ (916) 544-2233

---

7 Seas Motel 🟥43   Rates Subject to Change   *Motel* ◆
Fri-Sat 6/28-9/11	1P	.... 53.00	2P/1B	.... 58.00	2P/2B	.... 63.00	XP 5
Fri-Sat 5/21-6/25 & 9/12-10/3	1P	.... 49.00	2P/1B	.... 49.00	2P/2B	.... 54.00	XP 5
Fri-Sat 10/4-5/20 & Sun-Thurs 6/23-9/11	1P	.... 41.00	2P/1B	.... 41.00	2P/2B	.... 46.00	XP 5
Sun-Thurs 9/12-6/22	1P	.... 30.00	2P/1B	.... 30.00	2P/2B	.... 35.00	XP 5

17 units. 2 1/2 blks from casino center; 2 blks n off US 50 towards lake on Manzanita Ave, between Stateline & Poplar aves. 4145 Manzanita Ave. (PO Box 4362, South Lake Tahoe, 96157) Refrigerators; C/CATV; pay movies; radios; phones; shower or comb baths. Whirlpool. No pets. Reserv deposit required; 3 days refund notice. MC, VI. FAX (916) 544-1208 *(See ad below)*   ⊗ Ⓓ (916) 544-7031

Slalom Inn 🟥66   Rates Subject to Change   *Motel* ◆
7/1-9/30, 12/1-4/19 & Fri-Sat Sun-Thurs 10/1-11/30 &	1P	.... 47.00	2P/1B	.... 54.00	2P/2B	.... 59.00	XP 6
4/20-6/30	1P	.... 34.00	2P/1B	.... 38.00	2P/2B	.... 42.00	XP 6

28 units. 8 blks s off US 50, via Ski Run Blvd. 1195 Ski Run Blvd. (PO Box 13534, South Lake Tahoe, 96151) Tree-shaded grounds. C/CATV; movies; phones. Coin laundry. Small pool. No pets. 8 efficiencies, $8 extra. Wkly & monthly rates avail. Reserv deposit required; 3 days refund notice. AE, MC, VI.   Ⓓ (916) 544-5765

South Shore Inn 🟥46   Rates Subject to Change   *Motel* ◆◆
6/15-9/30 & 12/15-1/2	1P	46.00- 88.00	2P/1B	50.00- 88.00	2P/2B	58.00- 98.00	XP 6
Fri-Sat 1/3-6/14 & 10/1-12/14	1P	44.00- 68.00	2P/1B	48.00- 68.00	2P/2B	58.00- 78.00	XP 6
Sun-Thurs 1/3-6/14 & 10/1-12/14	1P	.... 32.00	2P/1B	.... 36.00	2P/2B	.... 42.00	XP 4

Senior discount. 22 units. 4 blks w of casino area. 3900 Pioneer Tr. (PO Box 6470, South Lake Tahoe, 96150) C/CATV; movies; phones. 2 2-bedrm units. No pets. Some covered parking. Reserv deposit required; 3 days refund notice. MC, VI.   ⊗ Ⓓ (916) 544-1000

South Tahoe Travelodge 🟥38   AAA Special Value Rates   *Motel* ◆◆◆
7/1-8/31 & 12/21-12/31	1P	75.00- 90.00	2P/1B	80.00- 95.00	2P/2B	86.00- 101.00	XP 5	F
5/1-6/30 & 9/1-10/31	1P	65.00- 80.00	2P/1B	70.00- 85.00	2P/2B	76.00- 91.00	XP 5	F
1/1-1/31	1P	56.00- 71.00	2P/1B	61.00- 76.00	2P/2B	67.00- 82.00	XP 5	F
2/1-4/30 & 11/1-12/20	1P	53.00- 68.00	2P/1B	58.00- 73.00	2P/2B	64.00- 79.00	XP 5	F

59 units. 1 1/2 mi w of casino center on US 50. 3489 Hwy 50. (PO Box 70512, South Lake Tahoe, 96156) A/C; C/CATV; movies; radios; phones; shower or comb baths. Pool. No pets. Reserv deposit required. AE, DI, DS, MC, VI. Restaurant adjacent. FAX (916) 544-6985 *(See ad p A187)*   ⊗ Ⓓ (916) 544-5266

(See LAKE TAHOE spotting map page A177)

Stateline Travelodge 〔33〕   Rates Subject to Change   *Motel*   ◆◆
〔AAA〕 7/1-8/31 & 12/21-12/31   1P 75.00- 90.00   2P/1B   80.00- 95.00   2P/2B   86.00-101.00 XP 5   F
     5/1-6/30 & 9/1-10/31   1P 65.00- 80.00   2P/1B   70.00- 85.00   2P/2B   76.00- 91.00 XP 5   F
     1/1-1/31   1P 56.00- 71.00   2P/1B   61.00- 76.00   2P/2B   67.00- 82.00 XP 5   F
     2/1-4/30 & 11/1-12/20   1P 53.00- 68.00   2P/1B   58.00- 73.00   2P/2B   64.00- 79.00 XP 5   F
50 units. 4011 Lake Tahoe Blvd. 4011 Lake Tahoe Blvd. (PO Box 6600, South Lake Tahoe, 96157) A/C; C/CATV; radios; phones; shower baths. No pets. Reserv deposit required. AE, DI, DS, MC, VI. FAX (916) 544-6869
⊗ Ⓓ (916) 544-6000

Tahoe Beach & Ski Club 〔63〕   AAA Special Value Rates   *Apartment Motel*   ◆◆
〔AAA〕 12/25-1/2   1P 85.00- 290.00   2P/1B   85.00- 290.00   2P/2B   85.00- 290.00 XP 15
     2/6-4/2 & 6/23-9/18   1P 80.00- 255.00   2P/1B   80.00- 255.00   2P/2B   80.00- 255.00 XP 15
     1/3-2/5 & 9/19-10/15   1P 60.00- 220.00   2P/1B   60.00- 220.00   2P/2B   60.00- 220.00 XP 15
     4/3-6/22 & 10/16-12/24   1P 50.00- 190.00   2P/1B   50.00- 190.00   2P/2B   50.00- 190.00 XP 15
135 units. On US 50; 1 blk w of Ski Run Blvd. 3601 Lake Tahoe Blvd. (South Lake Tahoe, 96150) Spacious grounds. Some units with lake view; many with whirlpool bath. Check-in 3 pm. C/CATV; rental VCPs; radios; phones; comb or shower baths. 4 2-bedrm units, 7 kitchens, 75 efficiencies. Coin laundry. Beach; swimming; sauna; whirlpool; pool open 5/25-10/1; putting green. No pets. 5-night minimum stay 12/25-1/2. Reserv deposit required. AE, CB, DI, MC, VI. Restaurant adjacent.
Ⓓ (916) 541-6220

Tahoe Marina Inn 〔47〕   Rates Subject to Change   *Apartment Motel*   ◆◆
〔AAA〕 6/1-9/30   ······· 2P/1B   89.00- 140.00   2P/2B   89.00- 140.00 XP 5
     Fri & Sat 10/1-5/31   ······· 2P/1B   79.00- 99.00   2P/2B   79.00- 99.00 XP 5
     Sun-Thurs 10/1-5/31   ······· 2P/1B   56.00- 99.00   2P/2B   56.00- 99.00 XP 5
77 units. On lake, 1 1/2 mi w of casino center; off US 50. 930 Bal BiJou Rd. (South Lake Tahoe, 96150) Many rooms with lake view. Check-in 3 pm. C/CATV; movies; phones; comb or shower baths. 43 kitchens. Pool; beach; sauna. No pets. 29 condominiums with kitchen & fireplace, $125-$180; $79-$145 in winter for 2 persons. Reserv deposit required; 7 days refund notice. AE, MC, VI. Restaurant adjacent.
Ⓓ (916) 541-2180

Tahoe Sands Inn 〔62〕   Rates Subject to Change   *Motel*   ◆◆
〔AAA〕 1/1-4/1, 6/1-9/1 & Fri-Sat   1P ···· 73.00   2P/1B ···· 78.00   2P/2B ···· 78.00 XP 6   F
     Sun-Thurs 4/2-5/31 &
     9/2-12/31   1P ···· 53.00   2P/1B ···· 58.00   2P/2B ···· 58.00 XP 6   F
Senior discount. 110 units. On US 50; 1 blk w of Ski Run Blvd. 3600 Lake Tahoe Blvd. (PO Box 18692, South Lake Tahoe, 96151) Attractively landscaped grounds. C/CATV; rental VCPs; radios; phones; or comb baths. 1 2-bedrm unit, 1 kitchen, 1 efficiency. Pool; whirlpool; playground. Pets, $6 extra charge. 1 large suite with fireplace, $85-$110 for 2 persons. Reserv deposit required. AE, DI, DS, MC, VI. Coffeeshop; 6 am-2 pm; cocktail lounge. FAX (916) 542-4011
Ⓓ (916) 544-3476

The Tahoe Seasons Resort 〔31〕   AAA Special Value Rates   *Hotel*   ◆◆◆
     12/16-3/31 & 7/1-9/15   1P 128.00- 195.00   2P/1B   128.00- 195.00   ······· XP
     4/1-6/30 & 9/16-12/15   1P 95.00- 160.00   2P/1B   95.00- 160.00   ······· XP
160 units. 1 1/4 mi se off US 50; 1/2 mi ne on Saddle Rd; across from Heavenly Valley ski area. Saddle Rd at Keller Rd. (PO Box 5656, South Lake Tahoe, 96157) In the pines. Check-in 4 pm. C/CATV; rental VCPs; radios; phones; comb or shower baths. 12 2-bedrm units. Pool; whirlpool; whirlpool baths; tennis-2 courts; paddleball-1 court; recreational program. Valet garage. Airport transp. No pets. Maximum rates for up to 4 persons. All rooms with microwave. Reserv deposit required. AE, MC, VI. ● Restaurant; 7 am-noon; open for lunch in dinner in ski season; a la carte entrees about $8-$15; cocktails. FAX (916) 541-0653
Ⓢ Ⓓ (916) 541-6700

(See LAKE TAHOE spotting map page A177)

Tahoe Valley Motel 36   AAA Special Value Rates   *Motel* ◆◆

12/25-1/2, 2/14-2/16 & 9/4-9/16 1P	....	125.00	2P/1B	....	125.00	2P/2B	.... 150.00 XP 25
1/3-2/13, 2/17-9/3 & 9/17-12/24 1P	....	85.00	2P/1B	....	85.00	2P/2B	.... 95.00 XP 15

21 units. 1/2 mi e of jct US 50 & SR 89, at Tahoe Keys Blvd. 2241 Lake Tahoe Blvd. (South Lake Tahoe, 96150) 3 refrigerators; 17 A/C; C/CATV; movies; radios; phones; shower or comb baths. Pool. Fee for: hot tub. Pets, $10 extra charge. Few combination baths with private whirlpool. 2-night minimum stay weekends. Wkly rates avail. Reserv deposit required; 7 days refund notice. AE, DI, DS, MC, VI. *(See ad p A195)*   ⊗ Ⓓ (916) 541-0353

Torchlite Inn 61   Rates Subject to Change   *Motel* ◆

Fri & Sat 6/15-9/15	1P	....	58.00	2P/1B	.... 68.00	2P/2B	.... 68.00 XP 5
Fri & Sat 9/16-6/14	1P	....	52.00	2P/1B	.... 62.00	2P/2B	.... 68.00 XP 5
Sun-Thurs 6/15-9/15	1P	....	42.00	2P/1B	.... 52.00	2P/2B	.... 58.00 XP 5
Sun-Thurs 9/16-6/14	1P	....	38.00	2P/1B	.... 48.00	2P/2B	.... 52.00 XP 5

Senior discount. 33 units. 1 1/2 blks from casino center; 1 blk n off US 50 via Park-Loop Rd. 965 Park Ave. (PO Box 4335, South Lake Tahoe, 96157) C/CATV; phones; shower or comb baths. Enclosed whirlpool. No pets. Reserv deposit required; 3 days refund notice. AE, DI, DS, MC, VI. *(See ad p A195)*   Ⓓ (916) 541-2363

Viking Motor Lodge 68   Rates Subject to Change   *Motel* ◆◆

5/15-10/31 [CP]	1P	....	55.00	2P/1B	.... 55.00	2P/2B 60.00-	70.00 XP 5
11/1-5/14 [CP]	1P	....	45.00	2P/1B	.... 45.00	2P/2B 50.00-	60.00 XP 5

58 units. 2 blks off Hwy 50, via Friday Ave, toward lake on Cedar Ave; 1 1/2 blks from casino Center. 4083 Cedar Ave. (96150) C/CATV; phones; comb or shower baths. Utensils, extra charge. Pool; whirlpool. No pets. 14 efficiencies, $5 extra. Reserv deposit required. AE, DI, DS, MC, VI.   Ⓓ (916) 541-5155

RESTAURANTS

Carlos Murphy's 27   Mexican $$ ◆◆
1 mi w of casino center, on Hwy 50. 3678 Lake Tahoe Blvd. Casual dining. Open 11 am-10 pm; Sat-11 pm; Sun from 10 am. Cocktails & lounge. AE, CB, DI, MC, VI.   ⊗ (916) 542-1741

The Chart House 22   Steak & Seafood $$ ◆◆
E of Stateline on Kingsbury Grade, 1 1/2 mi off US 50. Panoramic view of lake. Varied menu, casual atmosphere. Children's menu. Open 5:30 pm-10 pm; Sat from 5 pm. Cocktails & lounge. AE, CB, DI, MC, VI.   ⊗ (702) 588-6276

Evans American Gourmet Cafe 19   American $$$ ◆◆◆
On SR 89; 1 mi n of US 50. 536 Emerald Bay Rd. Quiet cozy atmosphere; creative California cuisine with emphasis on fresh ingredients. Smoke free premises. A/C. Dress code. Open 6 pm-10 pm; closed Sun, 4/11, 11/25 & 12/25. Beer & wine. Minimum $8. Reserv advised. CB, DI, MC, VI.   ⊗ (916) 542-1990

Heidi's Restaurant 20   American $$ ◆◆
1 1/2 mi w of Stateline on US 50. 3485 Hwy 50. Family dining. German & European dishes. A/C. Open 7 am-9 pm; Tues-Wed 5/1-5/31 & 10/1-11/30 to 3 pm. Beer & wine. MC, VI. *(See ad p A195)*   ⊗ (916) 544-8113

LewMarNel's 25   Continental $$ ◆◆◆
At Best Western Station House Inn. Formerly Maison Marguite. Rustic, Western atmosphere, varied menu featuring steak & seafood. A/C. Open 5:30 pm-10 pm; Fri & Sat-10:30 pm; closed Wed. Cocktails & lounge. Reserv advised. AE, CB, DI, MC, VI.   (916) 542-1072

Llewellyn's 18   Continental $$$$ ◆◆◆◆
Atop Harvey's Resort Hotel. Elegant surroundings, spectacular view of Lake Tahoe & mountains. Inovative preparation. A/C. Open 11:30 am-2:30 & 6-10 pm; Fri & Sat-11 pm; Sun 10 am-2:30 & 6-10 pm. Cocktails & lounge. Valet parking. Reserv required in season. AE, CB, DI, MC, VI.   ⊗ (702) 588-2411

Marie Callender South Lake Tahoe 21   American $ ◆
Hwy 50. 3601 Lake Tahoe Blvd. Casual atmosphere. Home baked pies. A/C. Children's menu. Open 8 am-10 pm. Cocktails & lounge. MC, VI.   ⊗ (916) 544-5535

Sage Room Steak House 17   Steakhouse $$$ ◆◆◆
In Harvey's Hotel. Rustic quiet atmosphere, extensive selection of beef. A/C. Open 6 pm-11 pm. Cocktails & lounge. Reserv advised. AE, CB, DI, MC, VI. *(See ad p A191)*   ⊗ (702) 588-2411

The Summit Room 24   Continental $$$$ ◆◆◆◆
On 18th floor of Harrah's Tahoe Hotel. Panoramic view of lake & mountains. Excellently prepared dishes, varied menu. Intimate, elegant environment. A/C. Dress code. Open 6 pm-10 pm; Fri & Sat-11 pm; closed 12/1-12/22. Cocktails & lounge. Parking avail. Reserv required. AE, CB, DI, MC, VI.   ⊗ (702) 588-6611

The Swiss Chalet 23   Continental $$ ◆◆
4 mi w of Stateline; on US 50 at Sierra Blvd. 2540 Tahoe Blvd. Chalet decor & atmosphere, casual dining. European, German & Swiss cuisine. A/C. Children's menu. Open 5 pm-10 pm; closed Mon, 11/26, 12/25 & Easter. Cocktails & lounge. Reserv required. AE, MC, VI.   (916) 544-3304

Tep's Villa Roma 15   Italian $$ ◆
2 mi w of Stateline. 3450 Lake Tahoe Blvd. Casual atmosphere, large varied salad bar & fresh seafood specialties. Smoke free premises after 5 pm. A/C. Children's menu. Open 11:30 am-3:30 & 5-10:30 pm; closed Mon & 12/25. Cocktails & lounge. Minimum, $7. AE, MC, VI.   ⊗ (916) 541-8227

Zachary's 16   Continental $$ ◆◆◆
In Embassy Suites at Casino Center. 4130 Lake Tahoe Blvd. Casual atmosphere, varied menu featuring fresh local ingredients & fresh seafood specialties. Lunch on Deck Weather permitting. A/C. Children's menu. Open 11 am-2 & 5-11 pm. Cocktails & lounge. Reserv advised. AE, DI, DS, MC, VI.   ⊗ (916) 544-5400

LAKEWOOD — 73,600

Crazy 8 Motel   AAA Special Value Rates   *Motel* ◆

All year	1P 36.00-	45.00	2P/1B	39.00-	48.00	2P/2B	42.00- 48.00 XP 3 F

31 units. 1 blk w of I-605. 11535 E Carson St. (90715) Refrigerators; A/C; C/CATV; movies; radios; phones; shower or comb baths. 1 efficiency. Coin laundry. Wkly rates avail. AE, DS, MC, VI. Restaurant adjacent. FAX (310) 402-3572   Ⓓ (310) 860-0546

LA MESA — 52,900   See SAN DIEGO

LA MIRADA — 40,500

Holiday Inn/Gateway Plaza   AAA Special Value Rates   *Hotel* ◆◆◆
🏨 All year   1P 65.00- 85.00   2P/1B   65.00- 85.00   2P/2B 65.00- 85.00 XP 10   F
300 units. 1 blk ne of I-5, exit Valley View. 14299 Firestone Blvd. (90638) Check-in 3 pm. 14 refrigerators; A/C;
C/CATV; movies; radios; phones. Coin laundry. Htd pool; saunas; whirlpool; exercise rm. Parking lot. No pets.
Wkly & monthly rates avail. AE, DI, DS, MC, VI. ● Dining rm; 6 am-10:30 pm; $6.50-$15.95; cocktails.
FAX (714) 739-8500 *(See ad p A49)*   ⊗ Ⓢ Ⓓ 🅰 (714) 739-8500

Residence Inn by Marriott   Rates Subject to Change   *Suites Motel* ◆◆◆
All year [CP]   1P 115.00- 140.00 2P/1B 115.00- 140.00 2P/2B 115.00- 140.00 XP 10   F
141 units. 2 blks ne of I-5, exit Valley View. 14419 Firestone Blvd. (90638) 1- & 2-bedroom suites with living room &
kitchen; many with fireplace. Check-in 3 pm. A/C; C/CATV; free & pay movies; VCPs. Radios; phones. 36 2-bedrm units.
Coin laundry. Pool; whirlpool; sports court; exercise rm. Pets, $50 deposit required; also $8 extra charge. Wkly & monthly
rates avail. Reserv deposit required. Complimentary beverages each evening. AE, DI, DS, MC, VI. Restaurant adjacent.
FAX (714) 522-5884   ⊗ Ⓢ Ⓓ 🅰 (714) 523-2800

LANCASTER — 97,300

Best Western Antelope Valley Inn   Rates Guaranteed   *Motor Inn* ◆◆◆
🏨 All year   1P 50.00- 65.00   2P/1B   55.00- 70.00   2P/2B 55.00- 70.00 XP 6
Senior discount. 148 units. 2 1/4 mi e of SR 14 & 138; exit Ave J. 44055 N Sierra Hwy. (93534) 100 refrigerators;
A/C; C/CATV; free & pay movies; phones; comb or shower baths. Htd pool; whirlpool. No pets. Wkly & monthly
rates avail. Reserv deposit required; 7 days refund notice. AE, DI, DS, MC, VI. ● Coffeeshop; 6 am-midnight;
$10-$20. Also, Desert Rose, see separate listing. FAX (805) 948-4651   ⊗ Ⓓ 🅰 (805) 948-4651

Desert Inn Motor Hotel   Rates Subject to Change   *Motor Inn* ◆◆◆
🏨 All year   1P 62.00- 75.00   2P/1B   67.00- 80.00   2P/2B 68.00- 80.00 XP 2
144 units. 2 mi e of SR 14 & 138; exit Ave J. 44219 N Sierra Hwy. (93534) Refrigerators; A/C; C/CATV; movies;
radios; phones; comb or shower baths. 6 2-bedrm units. Coin laundry. 2 htd pools; wading pool; saunas; whirlpools; racquetball-2 courts; exercise rm. No pets. Wkly rates avail. AE, CB, DI, MC, VI. ● Coffeeshop; 5:30
am-10 pm; Fri & Sat 11 pm; $7-$15; cocktails; entertainment. Also, Granada Room, see separate listing.
FAX (805) 942-8950   ⊗ Ⓓ (805) 942-8401

Inn of Lancaster   Rates Guaranteed   *Motel* ◆◆◆
All year [CP]   1P 54.00- 62.00   2P/1B   54.00- 62.00   2P/2B 60.00- 68.00 XP 4   F
103 units. 2 mi e of SR 14 & 138, exit Ave J. 44131 Sierra Hwy. (93534) Refrigerators; A/C; C/CATV; free & pay movies;
phones. Coin laundry. Htd pool; whirlpool; exercise rm. No pets. Microwaves. AE, DI, DS, MC, VI. FAX (805) 948-3355
                                                                          ⊗ Ⓓ 🅰 (805) 945-8771

Quality Inn   AAA Special Value Rates   *Motor Inn* ◆◆◆
🏨 All year   1P 40.00- 60.00   2P/1B   45.00- 65.00   2P/2B 60.00- 70.00 XP 7   F
87 units. 1 3/4 mi e of SR 14 & 138, exit Ave K. 43321 N Sierra Hwy. (93534) Check-in 3 pm. 27 refrigerators; A/C;
C/TV; movies; phones. Htd pool; wading pool; whirlpool. No pets. 7 1-bedroom housekeeping apartments, $357-
$487 weekly for up to 4 persons. Wkly rates avail. AE, DI, DS, MC, VI. ● Dining rm & coffeeshop; 6 am-9 pm; Fri
& Sat 24 hours; $10-$22; cocktails; entertainment. FAX (805) 945-2363   ⊗ Ⓓ (805) 948-2691

RESTAURANTS

Casa de Miguel   Mexican $ ◆◆
2 mi e of SR 14 & 138; exit Ave J. 44245 N Sierra Hwy. Attractive Mexican decor. Nice selection of Mexican entrees.
Champagne brunch Sun 10 am-1 pm. A/C. Children's menu. Open 11 am-10 pm; Fri & Sat-11 pm; Sun 10 am-10 pm;
closed 11/25 & 12/25. Cocktails & lounge. AE, DI, MC, VI.   ⊗ 🅰 (805) 948-0793

Desert Rose   American $$ ◆◆
At Best Western Antelope Valley Inn. Chicken, lamb, salads, seafood & prime rib. Buffet lunch or order from menu. A/C.
Early bird specials; children's menu. Open 11 am-2 & 5-10 pm; Sat from 5 pm; Sun 9:30 am-2 pm. Cocktails & lounge.
Entertainment & dancing. AE, DI, DS, MC, VI.   ⊗ (805) 948-4651

Granada Room   American $$ ◆◆
At Desert Inn Motor Hotel. Attractive dining room with a nice selection of entrees. Semi-formal atmosphere. A/C. Open
11:30 am-2 & 5-9:30 pm; Fri & Sat-10 pm; Sun from 10 am. Cocktails & lounge. Entertainment & dancing. AE, CB, DI,
MC, VI.   ⊗ 🅰 (805) 942-8401

LA PUENTE — 37,000

Travelodge La Puente   Rates Subject to Change   *Motel* ◆◆
🏨 All year   1P .... 34.00   2P/1B   .... 37.00   2P/2B   .... 49.00 XP 5
46 units. From I-10, exit Glendora Ave; 1 1/2 mi s. 15412 Francisquito Ave. (91744) Refrigerators; A/C; C/CATV;
movies; radios; phones; comb or shower baths. Coin laundry. No pets. 5 rooms with whirlpool spa, $62 for 2
persons. AE, DI, DS, MC, VI. FAX (818) 917-5608   Ⓢ Ⓓ 🅰 (818) 918-2315

LA QUINTA — 11,200   (See map page A315)

RESTAURANT

La Quinta Garden Cafe   Italian $$$ ◆◆◆
4 mi s of SR 111, via Washington St. 78-073 Calle Barcelona. Light opera & broadway music by strolling singers. A/C.
Early bird specials. Open 9/15-6/15 from 4:30 pm-9:30 pm; closed Mon & 12/25. Cocktails & lounge. Valet parking. Re-
serv advised. AE, CB, DI, MC, VI.   ⊗ (619) 564-0169

LARKSPUR — 11,100

Courtyard by Marriott   Rates Subject to Change   *Motor Inn* ◆◆◆
All year   1P .... 89.00   2P/1B   .... 99.00   2P/2B   .... 99.00 XP
Senior discount. 146 units. 1/4 mi e of US 101; exit E Sir Francis Drake Blvd. 2500 Larkspur Landing Cir. (94939)
Check-in 4 pm. A/C; C/CATV; free & pay movies; radios; phones. Coin laundry. Pool; whirlpool; exercise rm. No pets.
Reserv deposit required. AE, DI, DS, MC, VI. ● Restaurant; 6:30 am-2 & 5-10 pm; $7-$12; cocktails.
FAX (415) 925-1107 *(See ad p A447)*   ⊗ Ⓢ Ⓓ 🅰 (415) 925-1800

RESTAURANT

Lark Creek Inn   Regional American $$$$ ◆◆◆
1 1/4 mi w of US 101, exit Tamalpais Dr. 234 Magnolia Ave. A restored Victorian home built in 1888. Pleasant garden setting. Smoking not permitted. Open 11:30 am-2:30 & 5:30-10 pm; Fri-10:30 pm; Sat 5 pm-10:30 pm; Sun 10 am-1:30 & 5-10 pm; closed 7/4, 11/26, 12/24 & 12/25. Cocktails & lounge. Reserv advised. AE, MC, VI.   ⊗ (415) 924-7766

LASSEN VOLCANIC NATIONAL PARK

The establishment below does not meet AAA standards but is listed as a service to members who may wish to stay in the park.

Drakesbad Guest Ranch   Rates Subject to Change   *Resort Complex*
6/4-10/3 [AP]   1P   .... 116.00   ....   2P/2B   .... 170.00 XP 66
20 units. 47 mi se of Park Hdqtrs; 17 mi nw of Chester on CR Chester-Warner Valley; last 3 mi rocky-gravel/dirt road. (Chester, 96020) OPEN 6/4-10/3. Beautiful setting overlooking meadows primitive area. Check-out 10:30 am. 10 shower baths. 1 2-bedrm unit. Htd pool; fishing. Fee for: riding. No pets. 4 cabins & 6 lodge rooms with half-bath for up to 6 persons, $75-$250. No electricity. Wkly rates avail. Reserv deposit required; 30 days refund notice. MC, VI. ● Dining rm; 7:30 am-8:30, noon-1 & 6-7 pm; $13; beer & wine.
            Ⓓ Phone Susanville operator, Drakesbad No. 2, thru your long-distance operator; in winter (916) 529-1512.

LAWNDALE — 27,300
Best Western South Bay Hotel   **AAA Special Value Rates**   *Motor Inn*   ◆◆◆
㊌ All year [CP]   1P   .... 45.00 2P/1B   .... 48.00 2P/2B   .... 53.00 XP 5   F
101 units. On SR 107; 3/4 mi n of jct I-405, San Diego Frwy. 15000 Hawthorne Blvd. (90260) Refrigerators; A/C; C/CATV; movies; radios; phones. Coin laundry. Htd pool; sauna; whirlpool. Airport transp. No pets. 2 rooms with whirlpool, $95. Wkly rates avail. AE, DI, DS, MC, VI. ● Dining rm; 11 am-2:30 & 5-9:30 pm; buffet about $5.55-$9.95; cocktails. FAX (310) 978-0022 *(See ad p A232)*   Ⓢ Ⓓ Ⓖ (310) 973-0998

Days Inn Airport South   **AAA Special Value Rates**   *Motel*   ◆◆
㊌ 6/1-8/31 [CP]   1P 49.00- 59.00 2P/1B   54.00- 64.00 2P/2B   56.00- 66.00 XP 5   F
43 units. On SR 107; 1/2 mi n of jct I-405, San Diego Frwy. 15636 Hawthorne Blvd. (90260) OPEN ALL YEAR. Refrigerators; A/C; C/CATV; movies; radios; phones. Coin laundry. Whirlpool. Airport transp. No pets. 2 rooms with whirlpool, $85-$100. Wkly rates avail. Reserv deposit required; 7 days refund notice. AE, DI, DS, MC, VI. Restaurant adjacent. FAX (310) 676-3138 *(See ad p A222)*   ⊗ Ⓢ Ⓓ Ⓖ (310) 676-7378

LEE VINING — 300
Best Western Lake View Lodge   Rates Subject to Change   *Motel*   ◆◆◆
㊌ 4/20-10/31   1P 68.00- 78.00 2P/1B   68.00- 78.00 2P/2B   68.00- 78.00 XP 3
   11/1-1/4   1P 50.00- 68.00 2P/1B   50.00- 68.00 2P/2B   50.00- 78.00 XP 3
   1/5-4/19   1P 48.00- 58.00 2P/1B   48.00- 58.00 2P/2B   48.00- 58.00 XP 3
47 units. On US 395. (PO Box 345, 93541) Attractively landscaped. Check-in 4 pm. 34 A/C; C/CATV; movies; phones; comb or shower baths. 3 2-bedrm units. Coin laundry. No pets. 3-night minimum stay in 3 kitchens, $8 extra. Reserv deposit required. AE, DI, DS, MC, VI. FAX (619) 647-6325   ⊗ Ⓓ Ⓖ (619) 647-6543

Gateway Motel   Rates Subject to Change   *Motel*   ◆◆
㊌ 4/26-11/2   1P 65.00- 70.00 2P/1B   55.00- 70.00 2P/2B   57.00- 70.00 XP 4
   11/3-12/31   1P 40.00- 45.00 2P/1B   40.00- 45.00 2P/2B   42.00- 54.00 XP 4
   1/1-4/25   1P 30.00- 35.00 2P/1B   30.00- 35.00 2P/2B   32.00- 48.00 XP 4
12 units. On US 395. (PO Box 250, 93541) Overlooks Mono Lake. Check-out 10 am. C/CATV; phones; shower or comb baths. Rental refrigerators. Fish freezing facilities. No pets. 1 2-bedroom unit with refrigerator, $57-$85 for up to 4 persons. Reserv deposit required. AE, MC, VI. Restaurant opposite.   ⊗ Ⓓ (619) 647-6467

Murphey's Motel   Rates Subject to Change   *Motel*   ◆◆
㊌ 4/23-11/1   1P 48.00- 68.00 2P/1B   58.00- 68.00 2P/2B   58.00- 68.00 XP 5
   11/2-4/22   1P 32.00- 48.00 2P/1B   32.00- 48.00 2P/2B   32.00- 52.00 XP 5
43 units. On US 395. (PO Box 57, 93541) Check-out 10 am. C/CATV; phones; comb or shower baths. 2 kitchens. Sauna; whirlpool open 5/1-11/1; fish cleaning & freezing facilities; recreation room. Pets. Reserv deposit required. AE, DI, DS, MC, VI. Restaurant opposite. *(See ad below)*   Ⓓ Ⓖ (619) 647-6316

LEMON GROVE — 24,000   See SAN DIEGO

LEMOORE — 13,600
Best Western Vineyard Motel   Rates Subject to Change   *Motor Inn*   ◆◆
㊌ All year   1P   .... 44.00 2P/1B   .... 46.00 2P/2B   .... 46.00 XP 3
Senior discount. 67 units. 3/4 mi nw of SR 198; Houston St exit eastbound; D St exit westbound. 877 East D St. (93245) A/C; C/CATV; pay movies; phones. Coin laundry. Small pool. Reserv deposit required; 3 days refund notice. AE, DI, DS, MC, VI. ● Coffeeshop; 24 hours; $6-$12. FAX (209) 924-4270   ⊗ Ⓓ (209) 924-1261

RESTAURANT

The Cotton Mill   Steakhouse $$ ◆◆
3/4 mi nw of SR 198; Houston St exit eastbound, D St exit westbound. 850 East D St. California cuisine; local beef & fish; oakwood pit. A/C. Open 5 pm-10 pm; Sun 9 am-2 & 5-10 pm; closed Mon, Tues & major holidays. Cocktails & lounge. Reserv advised. AE, MC, VI.   ⊗ (209) 924-1256

LINDSAY — 8,300

Olive Tree Inn
| | | Rates Subject to Change | | | *Motor Inn* ◆◆ |
5/1-10/31 [CP] — 1P .... 48.00 2P/1B .... 54.00 2P/2B .... 56.00 XP 6 F
11/1-4/30 [CP] — 1P .... 45.00 2P/1B .... 51.00 2P/2B .... 53.00 XP 6 F
Senior discount. 51 units. 390 N Hwy 65. (93247) Refrigerators; A/C; C/CATV; movies; radios; phones. Coin laundry. Pool; whirlpool. No pets. 6 efficiencies, $5 extra. 8 units with refrigerator & microwave. AE, DI, DS, MC, VI. ● Coffeeshop; 5:30 am-10 pm; $5-$10. FAX (209) 562-2113   ⊗ Ⓓ ⓛ (209) 562-5188

LITTLE RIVER

The Inn at Schoolhouse Creek — Rates Subject to Change — *Cottages* ◆
All year — 1P 65.00- 105.00 2P/1B 65.00- 105.00 2P/2B 65.00- 115.00 XP 10
12 units. 3 mi s of Mendocino; e of Coast Hwy. 7051 N Hwy 1. (95456) Landscaped grounds; few motel rooms; small single & duplex units. Unpretentious. Office & guest lounge in former home, circa 1862. Few fireplaces. Shower, comb, or tub baths. 4 kitchens. No pets. [BP] avail. Reserv deposit required; 3 days refund notice. MC, VI. *(See ad p A254)*   ⊗ Ⓓ (707) 937-5525

Stevenswood Lodge — Rates Subject to Change — *Bed & Breakfast* ◆◆◆◆
3/1-11/30 [BP] — 1P 90.00- 195.00 2P/1B 90.00- 195.00 .... XP 25
12/1-2/29 [BP] — 1P 85.00- 145.00 2P/1B 85.00- 145.00 .... XP 25
10 units. 2 mi s of Mendocino; e of SR 1. 8211 N Hwy 1. (PO Box 170, Mendocino, 95460) Quiet forest setting. Fireplaces, many ocean view. Smoke free premises. Check-in 3 pm. Refrigerators; C/CATV; phones; comb or shower baths. Hiking. No pets. Reserv deposit required; 3 days refund notice. Complimentary beverages each evening. DS, MC, VI. FAX (707) 937-2405 *(See ad p A254)*   ⊗ Ⓓ ⓛ (707) 937-2810

RESTAURANT

Little River Inn Restaurant — American — $$ ◆◆
E side of SR 1, on a knoll. Prime rib Sat & Sun. Smoking in designated areas. Charming Victorian circa 1853. A/C. Open 7:30 am-11 & 6-9 pm; Fri & Sat-10 pm; Sun 7:30 am-1 & 6-9 pm; closed 12/24 & 1/2-1/31. Cocktails & lounge. Reserv advised.   ⊗ (707) 937-5942

LIVERMORE — 56,700   See also PLEASANTON & SAN RAMON

Holiday Inn-Livermore — Rates Subject to Change — *Motor Inn* ◆◆
All year — 1P 53.00- 65.00 2P/1B 59.00- 65.00 2P/2B 59.00- 65.00 XP 7 F
Senior discount. 125 units. N of & adjacent to I-580, exit Springtown Blvd. 720 Las Flores Rd. (94550) A/C; C/CATV; phones. Rental refrigerators. Coin laundry. Pool; exercise rm. Pets. AE, CB, DI, MC, VI. ● Restaurant; 6:30 am-10 pm; $6.50-$13; cocktails. FAX (510) 449-9059   ⊗ Ⓓ ⓛ (510) 443-4950

Residence Inn By Marriott — AAA Special Value Rates — *Suites Motel* ◆◆◆
Sun-Thurs [CP] — 1P 89.00- 113.00 2P/1B 89.00- 113.00 2P/2B .... 113.00 XP
Fri & Sat [CP] — 1P 75.00- 106.00 2P/1B 75.00- 106.00 2P/2B .... 106.00 XP
96 units. Exit I-580 Airway/Collier Canyon Rd N. 1000 Airway Blvd. (94550) Some rooms with 2 double beds, some units have loft bedrooms. A/C; C/CATV; movies; radios; phones. 20 2-bedrm units, kitchens. Coin laundry. Pool; sauna; whirlpool; sports court; exercise rm. Pets, $150 deposit, $50 non-refundable; $6 extra per day. AE, DI, DS, MC, VI. FAX (510) 373-7252   ⊗ Ⓢ Ⓓ ⓛ (510) 373-1800

RESTAURANT

The Restaurant at Wente Bros — American — $$$$ ◆◆◆
5 mi s, exit I-580 Portola Ave or Livermore Ave, s to L St; at Wente Brothers Winery. 5050 Arroyo Rd. Serving New American fare; attractive vineyard surroundings. Smoke free premises. A/C. Open 11:30 am-2:30 & 5:30-9:30 pm; Sun 10:30 am-2:30 & 5-9 pm; closed 1/1, 11/25, 12/24 & 12/25. Wine. Reserv advised. AE, DI, MC, VI. ⊗ (510) 447-3696

LODI — 51,900

Best Western Royal Host Inn — AAA Special Value Rates — *Motel* ◆◆
All year — 1P 45.00- 50.00 2P/1B 49.00- 53.00 2P/2B 51.00- 56.00 XP 6 F
48 units. 3/4 mi s on SR 99 business rt. 710 S Cherokee Ln. (95240) Large rooms. 15 refrigerators; A/C; C/CATV; movies; radios; phones; comb or shower baths. 4 2-bedrm units. Small pool. Pets, $20 deposit required. Monthly rates avail. AE, DI, DS, MC, VI. Restaurant adjacent. FAX (209) 369-0654   Ⓓ (209) 369-8484

Lodi Motor Inn — Rates Subject to Change — *Motel* ◆◆
All year [CP] — 1P 53.00- 60.00 2P/1B 53.00- 60.00 2P/2B .... 60.00 XP 6 F
Senior discount. 95 units. 1 blk e of jct SR 99 & 12; exit SR 99, Kettlemen Ln. 1140 S Cherokee Ln. (95240) A/C; C/CATV; radios; phones. Coin laundry. Small pool; sauna; whirlpool; exercise rm. No pets. AE, DI, DS, MC, VI. FAX (209) 368-7967   ⊗ Ⓓ (209) 334-6422

Wine and Roses Country Inn — Rates Guaranteed — *Bed & Breakfast* ◆◆◆
Fri & Sat [BP] — 1P .... 99.00 2P/1B .... 99.00 2P/2B .... 99.00 XP 15
Sun-Thurs [BP] — 1P .... 79.00 2P/1B .... 79.00 2P/2B .... 79.00 XP 15
10 units. I-5 exit Turner Rd, e 5 mi; SR 99 exit Turner Rd, w 2 mi. 2505 W Turner Rd. (95242) 1902 historical estate located on 5 acres of landscaped grounds. A/C; C/TV; radios; phones; comb or shower baths. No pets. Reserv deposit required; 3 days refund notice. AE, MC, VI. Dining rm; Tues 11:30 am-1:30 pm; Wed-Fri 11:30 am-1:30 & 6-9:30 pm; Sat 6 pm-9:30 pm; Sun 10:30 am-1:30 pm; $12-$20; beer & wine.   ⊗ Ⓓ (209) 334-6988

LOMITA — 19,400

Best Western Eldorado Inn — Rates Subject to Change — *Motel* ◆◆◆
6/1-9/15 [CP] — 1P .... 54.00 2P/1B .... 61.00 2P/2B .... 61.00 XP 7
Senior discount. 60 units. On SR 1, 2 mi w of I-110. 2037 Pacific Coast Hwy. (90717) OPEN ALL YEAR. Refrigerators; A/C; C/CATV; movies; radios; phones. Small htd pool; sauna; whirlpool. Small pets only, $50 deposit. 5 efficiencies, $3 extra. 2 rooms with whirlpool tub, $65. Wkly rates avail. Reserv deposit required; 3 days refund notice. AE, DI, DS, MC, VI. FAX (310) 539-5223   ⊗ Ⓓ ⓛ (310) 534-0700

LOMPOC — 37,600

Best Western Flagwaver Motor Hotel — Rates Guaranteed — *Motel* ◆◆
All year [CP] — 1P 38.00- 55.00 2P/1B 40.00- 55.00 2P/2B 45.00- 55.00 XP 6
Senior discount. 22 units. 1 mi n on SR 1. 937 North H St. (93436) Refrigerators; A/C; C/CATV; movies; radios; phones. Pool; whirlpool. No pets. 6 1-bedroom suites with efficiency, $60-$80 for 2 persons. Wkly rates avail. Reserv deposit required; 3 days refund notice. AE, DI, DS, MC, VI. Coffeeshop opposite. FAX (805) 736-6423   Ⓓ (805) 736-5605

Embassy Suites Hotel   Rates Subject to Change   *Suites Motor Inn*   ◆◆◆
Mon-Thurs [BP]   1P .... 69.00   2P/1B .... 79.00   ....   XP 10
Fri-Sun [BP]   1P .... 69.00   2P/1B .... 69.00   ....   XP 10
155 units. 1 1/4 mi n on SR 1. 1117 North H St. (93436) A/C; C/CATV; free & pay movies; radios; phones. Coin laundry. Htd pool; whirlpool; exercise rm. No pets. 1 2-bedroom apartment, $125. Refrigerators & microwaves. Complimentary beverages each evening. AE, DI, DS, MC, VI. Restaurant adjacent. FAX (805) 735-8459
     ⊗ Ⓢ Ⓓ 🅴 (805) 735-8311

Inn of Lompoc   Rates Subject to Change   *Motel*   ◆◆◆
🆔 All year [CP]   1P .... 51.00   2P/1B .... 57.00   2P/2B .... 57.00 XP 6   F
Senior discount. 90 units. 1 1/4 mi n on SR 1. 1122 North H St. (93436) Formerly Days Inn. Spacious, nicely furnished rooms. Refrigerators; A/C; C/CATV; movies; rental VCPs. Radios; phones; shower or comb baths. Coin laundry. Htd indoor pool; indoor whirlpool; exercise rm. No pets. Microwaves, $6 extra. Wkly & monthly rates avail. AE, DI, DS, MC, VI. Restaurant adjacent. FAX (805) 736-0421
     ⊗ Ⓓ 🅴 (805) 735-7744

Porto Finale Inn   AAA Special Value Rates   *Motel*   ◆◆◆
🆔 3/15-9/30 [CP]   1P 35.00- 42.00   2P/1B   35.00- 40.00   2P/2B   40.00- 50.00 XP 5
10/1-3/14 [CP]   1P .... 30.00   2P/1B .... 35.00   2P/2B   38.00- 44.00 XP 5
83 units. 1 mi e on SR 1 & 246. 940 E Ocean Ave. (93436) Refrigerators; A/C; C/CATV; radios; phones. Coin laundry. Htd pool; whirlpool. Pets, $10 extra charge. Wkly rates avail. Reserv deposit required. AE, DI, DS, MC, VI.
     ⊗ Ⓓ 🅴 (805) 735-7731

Quality Inn & Executive Suites   Rates Guaranteed   *Motel*   ◆◆◆
🆔 All year [CP]   1P 46.00- 59.00   2P/1B   54.00- 69.00   2P/2B   54.00- 69.00 XP 5   F
Senior discount. 220 units. 1 3/4 mi n on SR 1. 1621 North H St. (93436) A/C; C/CATV; movies; radios; phones. 4 2-bedrm units, 93 efficiencies. Coin laundry. Htd pool; whirlpool. Pets, $10. Wkly & monthly rates avail. Complimentary beverages each evening. AE, CB, DI, MC, VI. Restaurant adjacent. FAX (805) 735-8566 *(See ad below)*
     ⊗ Ⓢ Ⓓ 🅴 (805) 735-8555

Redwood Motor Lodge   Rates Subject to Change   *Motel*   ◆
🆔 All year   1P 40.00- 45.00   2P/1B   40.00- 45.00   2P/2B   40.00- 45.00 XP 2
Senior discount. 60 units. 1 1/4 mi n on SR 1. 1200 North H St. (93436) Refrigerators; C/CATV; movies; rental VCPs. Phones; shower or comb baths. Coin laundry. Sauna. Pets, $10. Microwave rentals. Wkly & monthly rates avail. AE, DI, DS, MC, VI. Restaurant adjacent. FAX (805) 735-3510
     ⊗ Ⓓ 🅴 (805) 735-3737

Tally Ho Motor Inn   AAA Special Value Rates   *Motel*   ◆◆
🆔 All year   1P .... 40.00   2P/1B .... 40.00   2P/2B .... 45.00 XP
Senior discount. 53 units. 1 mi e on SR 1 & 246. 1020 E Ocean Ave. (93436) Refrigerators; A/C; C/CATV; radios; phones. 2 efficiencies. Coin laundry. Sauna; indoor whirlpool. Pets, $10 extra charge. Microwaves. Monthly rates avail. Reserv deposit required. AE, CB, DS, MC, VI.
     Ⓓ (805) 735-6444

LONE PINE — 1,700

Best Western Frontier Motel
4/1-10/31 [CP]   Rates Subject to Change   *Motel*   ◆◆◆
1P 42.00- 75.00 2P/1B 46.00- 75.00 2P/2B 46.00- 75.00 XP 3
Senior discount. 73 units. 1/2 mi s on US 395. 1008 S Main St. (93545) OPEN ALL YEAR. 39 refrigerators; A/C;
C/CATV; movies; phones; comb or shower baths. Coin laundry. Htd pool. Reserv deposit required. AE, DI, DS,
MC, VI. FAX (619) 876-5357 *(See ad p A200)*   ⊗ ⅅ Ⓛ (619) 876-5571

Dow Villa Motel
All year   Rates Subject to Change   *Motel*   ◆◆◆
1P 52.00- 60.00 2P/1B 54.00- 60.00 2P/2B 54.00- 60.00 XP 4
39 units. On US 395. 310 S Main St. (93545) Refrigerators; A/C; C/CATV; movies; 10 radios; phones.
Htd pool; whirlpool. Pets. 2 rooms with microwave, $60. Reserv deposit required. AE, CB, DI, MC, VI. Coffeeshop
adjacent. *Independant Motels of America.* FAX (619) 876-5643 *(See ad p A200)*   ⊗ ⅅ (619) 876-5521

National 9 Trails Motel
All year   Rates Subject to Change   *Motel*   ◆
1P 32.00- 49.00 2P/1B 34.00- 49.00 2P/2B 36.00- 49.00 XP 4
17 units. 1/4 mi s on US 395. 633 S Main St. (93545) 15 refrigerators; A/C; C/CATV; movies; phones; shower or
comb baths. Pool; fish freezing facilities. Small pets only, $4. Some microwaves. AE, DS, MC, VI.
⊗ ⅅ (619) 876-5555

The Portal Motel
All year   Rates Subject to Change   *Motel*   ◆
1P 36.00- 54.00 2P/1B 36.00- 54.00 2P/2B 36.00- 54.00 XP 4
17 units. On US 395. 425 S Main St. (PO Box 97, 93545) A/C; C/CATV; movies; 6 radios; shower or comb baths.
No pets. Some units with microwave & refrigerator. AE, DS, MC, VI. Coffeeshop opposite.   ⅅ (619) 876-5930

RESTAURANT

Margie's Merry Go-Round   American $$ ◆
On US 395. 212 S Main St. Small restaurant specializing in charcoal-broiled steaks, pork chops & barbecue spe-
cialties. Limited menu. A/C. Children's menu. Open 5:30 pm-9 pm; closed Mon 11/1-3/31, 4/11 & major holidays.
Beer & wine. Reserv advised. MC, VI.   (619) 876-4115

LONG BEACH — 429,400   See also SEAL BEACH

Airport Accommodations-See listings for:

- Holiday Inn-Long Beach Airport, 1 mi s of airport.
- Long Beach Airport Marriott, 1/2 mi e of airport.

Best Western Golden Sails Hotel   Rates Guaranteed   *Motor Inn*   ◆◆
All year   1P 59.00- 89.00 2P/1B 59.00- 89.00 2P/2B 59.00- 89.00 XP 10
175 units. 7 1/2 mi e on SR 1. 6285 E Pacific Coast Hwy. (90803) Refrigerators; A/C; C/CATV; movies; 155 radios;
phones; comb or shower baths. Coin laundry. Htd pool; whirlpool; 5 rooms with whirlpool. Airport transp. No
pets. Reserv deposit required. AE, CB, MC, VI. ● Restaurant; 6:30 am-10 pm; $9-$16; cocktails; entertainment.
FAX (310) 594-0623 *(See ad p A200)*   ⊗ ⅅ (310) 596-1631

Best Western of Long Beach   Rates Subject to Change   ◆◆◆
All year [CP]   1P .... 48.00 2P/1B .... 54.00 2P/2B .... 54.00 XP 6   F
Senior discount. 99 units. 1/4 blk s of Pacific Coast Hwy. 1725 Long Beach Blvd. (90813) Refrigerators; A/C; C/CATV;
movies; radios; phones. Htd pool. Garage & parking lot. Airport transp. No pets. 6 suites with living room, bedroom, mi-
crowave & refrigerator, $74-$80. AE, DI, DS, MC, VI. FAX (310) 599-1212   ⊗ Ⓢ ⅅ (310) 599-5555

Best Western Queen City Motel   Rates Subject to Change   *Motel*   ◆◆
All year [CP]   1P .... 52.00 2P/1B .... 54.00 2P/2B .... 56.00 XP 4
Senior discount. 44 units. On SR 1; 1/4 mi w of Lakewood Blvd. 3555 E Pacific Coast Hwy. (90804) A/C; C/CATV;
movies; radios; phones. Coin laundry. Small htd pool. No pets. Wkly rates avail. Reserv deposit required. AE,
DI, DS, MC, VI. FAX (310) 494-3186 *(See ad below)*   ⊗ ⅅ (310) 597-4455

Clarion Hotel Edgewater — Rates Guaranteed — *Motor Inn* ◆◆
All year 1P .... 63.00 2P/1B .... 63.00 2P/2B .... 63.00 XP 10 F
Senior discount. 249 units. 8 mi se on SR 1. 6400 E Pacific Coast Hwy. (90803) Check-in 3 pm. A/C; C/CATV; pay movies; radios; phones; shower or comb baths. Htd pool; whirlpool. Pets, $30. Wkly & monthly rates avail. AE, DI, DS, MC, VI. ● Dining rm & coffeeshop; 6 am-10 pm; $7-$25; cocktails; entertainment. FAX (310) 598-6028
⊗ (D) (310) 434-8451

Comfort Inn — Rates Subject to Change — *Motel* ◆◆
⊕ 5/1-9/15 [CP] 1P 55.00- 65.00 2P/1B 60.00- 65.00 .... XP 6 F
Senior discount. 65 units. On SR 1, 3/4 mi w of Lakewood Blvd. 3201 E Pacific Coast Hwy. (90804) OPEN ALL YEAR. Check-in 3 pm. A/C; C/CATV; radios; phones. Rental refrigerators. 1 2-bedrm unit. Coin laundry. Htd pool; whirlpool. No pets. AE, DI, DS, MC, VI. FAX (310) 985-3142 *(See ad p A201)* ⊗ (D) (310) 597-3374

Holiday Inn-Long Beach Airport — AAA Special Value Rates — *Motor Inn* ◆◆
All year 1P .... 104.00 2P/1B .... 114.00 2P/2B .... 114.00 XP 10 F
233 units. On SR 19 at jct I-405; from I-405, southbound exit Lakewood Blvd N; northbound exit Lakewood Blvd, 1 mi s of Long Beach Airport. 2640 Lakewood Blvd. (90815) A/C; C/CATV; free & pay movies; radios; phones. Coin laundry. Htd pool; exercise rm. Airport transp. Pets. Wkly & monthly rates avail. AE, DI, DS, MC, VI. ● Dining rm; 6 am-2 & 5:30-10:30 pm; $9.50-$15; cocktails; entertainment. FAX (310) 597-0601 ⊗ (D) (310) 597-4401

Howard Johnson Hotel — Rates Subject to Change — *Motor Inn* ◆◆◆
⊕ All year 1P 71.00- 79.00 2P/1B 71.00- 79.00 2P/2B 79.00- 87.00 XP 8 F
Senior discount. 135 units. 1 mi n of Ocean Blvd. 1133 Atlantic Ave. (90813) Check-in 3 pm. Refrigerators; A/C; C/CATV; movies; rental VCPs. Radios; phones. Coin laundry. Htd pool; whirlpool. No pets. Wkly & monthly rates avail. Reserv deposit required; 3 days refund notice. AE, DI, DS, MC, VI. ● Dining rm; 7 am-10 pm; $7.75-$10.75; cocktails. ⊗ (S) (D) (310) 590-8858

Hyatt Regency Long Beach — Rates Subject to Change — *Hotel* ◆◆◆◆
Sun-Thurs 1P 119.00- 139.00 2P/1B 139.00- 169.00 2P/2B 139.00- 169.00 XP 15
Fri & Sat 1P 79.00- 99.00 2P/1B 79.00- 99.00 2P/2B 79.00- 99.00 XP 15
Senior discount. 521 units. Adjacent to Convention Center. 200 S Pine Ave at Shoreline Dr. (90802) Many rooms with ocean view. Check-in 3 pm. A/C; C/CATV; free & pay movies; radios; phones. Htd pool; whirlpool; exercise rm. Pay valet parking ramp. Airport transp. No pets. Wkly rates avail. AE, DI, DS, MC, VI. ● Dining rm & restaurant; 6 am-midnight; $7-$15; cocktail lounge; entertainment. Also, The Beacon, see separate listing. FAX (310) 432-1972
⊗ (S) (D) (310) 491-1234

Long Beach Airport Marriott — Rates Subject to Change — *Hotel* ◆◆◆
⊕ Mon-Thurs [EP] 1P .... 154.00 2P/1B .... 169.00 2P/2B .... 169.00 XP 15
Fri-Sun [BP] 1P .... 59.00 2P/1B .... 59.00 2P/2B .... 59.00 XP 15
311 units. 1 mi n of I-405, exit Lakewood Blvd; 1/2 mi s of Long Beach Airport. 4700 Airport Plaza Dr at Spring St. (90815) Nicely landscaped pool area. Check-in 3 pm. A/C; C/CATV; free & pay movies; radios; phones. 2 htd pools, 1 indoor; sauna; whirlpool; exercise rm. Parking lot. Airport transp. No pets. Monthly rates avail. AE, DI, DS, MC, VI. ● Dining rm & restaurant; 6:30 am-11 pm; $8-$22; cocktails. FAX (310) 421-1075
⊗ (S) (D) (310) 425-5210

Long Beach Hilton at World Trade Center — Rates Subject to Change — *Hotel* ◆◆◆◆
All year 1P 99.00- 130.00 2P/1B 119.00- 150.00 2P/2B 119.00- 150.00 XP 10 F
Senior discount. 398 units. From I-710 exit Broadway, Ocean Ave & Golden Shore St. Two World Trade Center. (90831) Some balconies. At The World Trade Center. Check-in 3 pm. A/C; C/CATV; free & pay movies; radios; phones. 2 2-bedrm units, 1 3-bedrm unit. Htd pool; whirlpool; rental bicycles; steamroom; health club. Valet garage & parking lot. Airport transp. Small pets only. Monthly rates avail. AE, DI, DS, MC, VI. Restaurant; 6 am-midnight; $7.95-$16.95; cocktails; entertainment. FAX (310) 983-1200 ⊗ (S) (D) (310) 983-3400

Lord Mayor's Inn — Rates Subject to Change — *Bed & Breakfast* ◆◆
All year [BP] 1P .... 70.00 2P/1B 85.00- 95.00 2P/2B 85.00- 95.00 XP
5 units. 4 1/2 blks n of Ocean Blvd. 435 Cedar Ave. (90802) 1904 Edwardian-style house, home of the first mayor of Long Beach. Smoking in designated areas. Check-in 4 pm. Radios; tub or shower baths. No pets. Complimentary evening refreshments. Reserv deposit required; 7 days refund notice. AE, MC, VI. ⊗ (D) (310) 436-0324

Ramada Inn — AAA Special Value Rates — *Motor Inn* ◆◆
⊕ All year 1P 65.00- 90.00 2P/1B 70.00- 95.00 2P/2B 90.00- 95.00 XP 5 F
144 units. 5 mi se on SR 1. 5325 E Pacific Coast Hwy. (90804) Check-in 3 pm. 19 refrigerators; A/C; C/CATV; free & pay movies; radios; phones. 4 2-bedrm units. Htd pool; 11 rooms with whirlpool bathtub; 5 rooms with whirlpool. Airport transp. Pets, $150 deposit required. Wkly & monthly rates avail. AE, DI, DS, MC, VI. ● Restaurant; 6:30 am-10 pm; Fri & Sat-midnight; $9-$15; cocktails. FAX (310) 597-1664 *(See ad below)* (D) (310) 597-1341

Ramada Renaissance Hotel — Rates Subject to Change — *Hotel* ◆◆◆◆
All year 1P 126.00- 166.00 2P/1B 140.00- 170.00 2P/2B 140.00- 170.00 XP 15 F
Senior discount. 374 units. Downtown. 111 E Ocean Blvd at Pine Ave. (90802) Many rooms with ocean view. 23 rooms with a balcony. Check-in 3 pm. A/C; C/CATV; free & pay movies; radios; phones. Rental refrigerators. Htd pool; saunas; whirlpool; health club. Pay valet parking ramp. Airport transp. No pets. AE, DI, DS, MC, VI. ● Dining rm & restaurant; 6 am-midnight; $12-$25; cocktails. FAX (310) 499-2509 ⊗ (S) (D) (310) 437-5900

Sheraton Long Beach at Shoreline Square — Rates Subject to Change — *Hotel* ◆◆◆◆
⊕ All year 1P 135.00- 145.00 2P/1B 155.00- 165.00 2P/2B 125.00- 160.00 XP 20 F
Senior discount. 460 units. Downtown, across from Convention Center. 333 E Ocean Blvd. (90802) A/C; C/CATV; free & pay movies; radios; phones. Htd pool; sauna; whirlpool; exercise rm. Pay valet parking ramp. Airport transp. Pets. Reserv deposit required. AE, DI, DS, MC, VI. ● Dining rm; 6:30 am-midnight; a la carte entrees about $10.50-$16; cocktails; entertainment. FAX (310) 436-9176 ⊗ (S) (D) (310) 436-3000

Super 8 Motel-Long Beach Traffic Circle AAA Special Value Rates *Motel* ◆◆
All year [CP] 1P 49.00- 59.00 2P/1B 53.00- 63.00 2P/2B 56.00- 66.00 XP 5 F
49 units. On SR 1; 1 mi s of I-405, exit Lakewood Blvd. 4201 E Pacific Coast Hwy. (90804) Formerly Oak Creek Inns-Beachtown Motel. Refrigerators; A/C; C/CATV; movies; radios; phones. Htd pool; sauna; whirlpool. No pets. 7-night minimum stay in 11 kitchen units, $7 extra. Reserv deposit required. Complimentary beverages each evening. AE, DI, DS, MC, VI. FAX (310) 494-7373 *(See ad below)* (D) (310) 597-7701

Travelodge/Downtown AAA Special Value Rates *Motor Inn* ◆◆
All year 1P .... 49.00 2P/1B .... 54.00 2P/2B .... 59.00 XP 5 F
63 units. 1 blk n of Ocean Blvd. 80 Atlantic Ave. (90802) Many balconies. Refrigerators; A/C; C/CATV; movies; 22 radios; phones; shower or comb baths. Pool. Pets. Wkly & monthly rates avail. AE, DI, DS, MC, VI. ● Coffeeshop; 5 am-10 pm; Sat & Sun from 6 am; $4-$6.50; beer & wine. FAX (310) 437-1995 (X) (D) (310) 435-2471

Travelodge Hotel Resort & Marina Rates Guaranteed *Motor Inn* ◆◆◆
All year 1P .... 75.00 2P/1B .... 85.00 2P/2B .... 85.00 XP 10
Senior discount. 194 units. 1/2 mi nw of Queensway Dr exit. 700 Queensway Dr. (90802) Many ocean view rooms & balconies. Check-in 3 pm. A/C; C/CATV; free & pay movies; radios; phones. Htd pool; dock; lighted tennis-2 courts; bicycles. Airport transp. No pets. Wkly & monthly rates avail. AE, DI, DS, MC, VI. ● Dining rm; 6:30 am-2 & 5:30-10 pm; $12-$18; cocktails; entertainment. FAX (310) 437-0866 (X) (D) (L) (310) 435-7676

RESTAURANT

The Beacon American $$$ ◆◆
In Hyatt Regency Long Beach. Fine dining with a view of the downtown marina. Sun brunch. A/C. Open 11:30 am-2:30 & 6-10:30 pm; Sat from 6 pm; Sun 10:30 am-2 & 6-10:30 pm. Cocktails & lounge. Entertainment. Pay valet parking. Reserv advised. AE, DI, DS, MC, VI. (X) (310) 491-1234

Bobby McGee's Conglomeration American $$ ◆◆
8 mi e on SR 1; in The Market Place Shopping Center. 6501 E Pacific Coast Hwy. Uniquely decorated restaurant. Informal, casual service by costumed waiters & waitresses. Features steaks, prime rib & seafood. A/C. Early bird specials; children's menu. Open 5 pm-10 pm; Fri-11 pm; Sat 5 pm-11 pm; Sun 4 pm-10 pm; closed 12/25. Cocktails & lounge. Reserv advised. AE, CB, DI, MC, VI. (X) (310) 594-8627

Caffe' Gazelle Italian $ ◆◆
In Belmont Shore area. 5325 E 2nd St, at Pomona. Small restaurant featuring nice selection of regional specialties. A/C. Open 5 pm-10 pm; Fri & Sat-11 pm; closed 11/25. Cocktails. Reserv advised. AE, DI, MC, VI. (X) (310) 438-2881

The Chart House Steak & Seafood $$ ◆◆
At Long Beach Marina. 215 Marina Dr. Features steak, fresh seafood, chicken & prime rib. View of the marina. A/C. Early bird specials; children's menu. Open 5 pm-10 pm; Fri-10:30 pm; Sat-11 pm. Cocktails & lounge. AE, DI, DS, MC, VI. (X) (310) 598-9411

Collage Restaurant Continental $$ ◆◆
762 Pacific Ave at 8th St. Nice selection of French & contemporary cuisine. Open 11:30 am-2:30 & 5:30-10 pm; Sat 5:30 pm-11 pm; closed Sun, Mon for dinner, 1/1, 9/7, 11/25 & 12/25. Cocktails & lounge. AE, MC, VI. (X) (310) 437-3324

El Torito Mexican ◆◆
8 mi se on SR 1. 6605 E Pacific Coast Hwy. Casual atmosphere, varied selection of cuisine. A/C. Children's menu. Open 11 am-11 pm; Fri & Sat-midnight; Sun 9:30 am-11 pm; closed 11/25 & 12/25. Cocktails & lounge. AE, DI, MC, VI. (X) (310) 594-6917

Fish Tale Seafood $$ ◆◆
3/4 mi s of I-405. 2050 Bellflower Blvd. Attractive country atmosphere. A/C. Children's menu. Open 11 am-10 pm; Fri & Sat-11 pm; Sun 10 am-10 pm; closed 11/25 & 12/25. Cocktails & lounge. Reserv advised. AE, CB, DI, MC, VI. (X) (L) (310) 594-8771

555 East Restaurant American $$$ ◆◆◆
Downtown. 555 E Ocean Blvd. Attractively decorated. Nice selection of beef, veal, poultry, pasta & fresh seafood. A/C. Open 11:30 am-3:30 & 5-10 pm; Fri-11 pm; Sat 5 pm-11 pm; Sun 5 pm-10 pm; closed 12/25. Cocktails & lounge. Valet parking. Reserv advised. AE, DI, DS, MC, VI. (X) (310) 437-0626

Gazzella Italian $$ ◆◆
2 blks n of Ocean Blvd, corner of Atlantic & Broadway. 525 E Broadway. Selections of veal, chicken, seafood, lamb, salads & pastas. Semi-formal atmosphere. Live entertainment Wed-Sat, 6 pm-11 pm. A/C. Open 11 am-2:30 & 5-11 pm; Sat & Sun from 5 pm; closed 7/4, 11/25 & 12/25. Cocktails & lounge. Valet parking. AE, DI, MC, VI. (X) (310) 438-2881

L'Opera Ristorante Italian $$ ◆◆◆
1 blk n of Ocean Blvd. 101 Pine Ave. Classic & modern Italian dishes in a restored bank building. Pasta & desserts prepared on premises. A/C. Open 11:30 am-11 pm; Fri-midnight; Sat 5 pm-midnight; Sun 5 pm-10:30 pm. Cocktails. Valet parking. Reserv advised for dinner. AE, DI, DS, MC, VI. (X) (310) 491-0000

Simon & Seafort's Steak, Chop & Oyster House   American $$ ◆◆
2 blks s of Ocean Ave, at Catalina Landing. 340 Golden Shore. Nice selection of fresh seafood; also steaks, poultry & pasta. A/C. Children's menu. Open 11 am-2:15 & 5:30-10 pm; Sat 5 pm-11 pm; Sun 4:30 pm-9 pm; closed 7/4, 11/25 & 12/25. Cocktails & lounge. Reserv advised. AE, DI, MC, VI.   ⊗ (310) 435-2333

Williamsburg Restaurant   American $ ◆◆
Downtown. 355 E First St. Buffet restaurant. Attractive early American decor. A/C. Children's menu. Open 11 am-8 pm; closed 1/1 & 12/25. Beer & wine. MC, VI.   ⊗ (310) 590-0220

LOS ANGELES — 3,485,400   (See map pages A206 & A207)

Establishments in Los Angeles are divided into Downtown, Central & Western Areas and San Fernando Valley.

Airport Accommodations-SEE FOLLOWING LISTINGS IN LOS ANGELES (Central & Western Areas):

- ⊕ **Airport Century Inn, 1 mi e of airport.**
  Best Western Suite Hotel, 1 1/2 mi e of airport
  Courtyard by Marriott, 1 3/4 mi s of airport.
- ⊕ **Crown Sterling Suites-Los Angeles Airport, 1/2 mi s of airport.**
- ⊕ **Days Inn-Airport, 1 1/2 mi e of airport.**
- ⊕ **Embassy Suites Hotel-LAX/Century, 1/2 mi s of airport.**
- ⊕ **Hacienda Hotel-L. A. Airport, 1 1/2 mi s of airport.**
  Hampton Inn-Los Angeles International Airport, 1 1/2 mi e of airport
- ⊕ **Holiday Inn-Crowne Plaza, 1/4 mi e of airport.**
- ⊕ **Holiday Inn Express, Los Angeles Int'l Airport, 1 1/2 mi e of airport.**
  Holiday Inn-International Airport, 1 1/4 mi e of airport.
  Hyatt at Los Angeles Airport, across from entrance.
- ⊕ **LAX Hotel, 1 1/4 mi s of airport.**
- ⊕ **Los Angeles Airport Hilton & Towers, 3/4 mi e of airport.**
  Los Angeles Airport Marriott Hotel, 1/2 mi e of airport.
- ⊕ **Quality Hotel-Los Angeles Airport, 1 1/4 mi e of airport.**
- ⊕ **Sheraton Los Angeles Airport Hotel, 1/4 mi e of airport.**
- ⊕ **Stouffer Concourse Hotel, 1 1/4 mi e of airport.**
- ⊕ **Tsa-Kwa-Luten Lodge, 1/2 mi e of airport.**
- ⊕ **Viscount Hotel-Los Angeles, 1/2 mi e of airport.**

LOS ANGELES (Downtown) (See LOS ANGELES (Downtown) AREA spotting map page A208; see index below)

Index of Establishments on the LOS ANGELES (Downtown) AREA Spotting Map

---

Best Western Dragon Gate Inn **18**   **Rates Subject to Change**   *Motor Inn*   ◆◆
⊕ All year   1P .... 49.00   2P/1B .... 52.00   2P/2B .... 57.00   XP 5
50 units. 2 blks n of US 101 in Chinatown. 818 N Hill St. (90012) Refrigerators; A/C; C/TV; radios; phones; comb or shower baths. Pay garage. Reserv deposit required. AE, DI, DS, MC, VI. ● Restaurant; 8 am-7 pm; $4.50-$6.50. *(See ad below)*   ⊗ Ⓓ Ⓛ (213) 617-3077

Best Western The Mayfair **8**   Rates Guaranteed   *Hotel*   ◆◆
All year   1P 75.00- 115.00   2P/1B 85.00- 130.00   2P/2B 85.00- 130.00   XP 15   F
Senior discount. 295 units. 5 blks w of Figueroa St. 1256 W 7th St. (90017) A/C; C/TV; pay movies; VCPs. Radios; phones; comb or shower baths. Exercise rm. Fee for: airport transp. Garage & parking ramp. Pets, $30 deposit required. AE, DI, DS, MC, VI. ● Dining rm; 6 am-11 am, 11:30-2:30 & 6-10:30 pm; Sat & Sun from 7 am; $11-$16; cocktails. FAX (213) 484-2769 *(See ad p A205)*   ⊗ Ⓢ Ⓓ Ⓛ (213) 484-9789

The Biltmore Los Angeles **13**   Rates Guaranteed   *Hotel*   ◆◆◆◆
⊕ All year   1P 180.00- 265.00   2P/1B 190.00- 265.00   2P/2B 190.00- 265.00   XP 20   F
704 units. 506 S Grand Ave at 5th St. (90071) A long established hotel. Beautifully decorated lobby & public facilities. Check-in 3 pm. A/C; C/TV; pay movies; radios; phones. Sauna; whirlpool; heated indoor pool. Pay valet garage. No pets. AE, CB, DI, MC, VI. ● 2 restaurants & coffeeshop; 6:30 am-11 pm; a la carte entrees about $10-$17; cocktails; entertainment. Also, Bernard's, see separate listing. FAX (213) 612-1628   ⊗ Ⓢ Ⓓ Ⓛ (213) 624-1011

Checkers Hotel 11   AAA Special Value Rates   Hotel ◆◆◆◆
All year   1P 180.00- 190.00   2P/1B   180.00- 190.00   2P/2B   180.00- 190.00   XP 35
188 units. 535 S Grand Ave. (90071) A/C; C/CATV; movies; radios; phones. Saunas; rooftop lap pool & whirlpool; steam-room; exercise rm. Pay valet garage & parking lot. Pets, AE, DI, DS, MC, VI. ● Dining rm; 7-11 am, 11:30-2:30 & 5:30-10 pm; closed for lunch Sat; Sun brunch 11 am-2:30 pm; a la carte entrees about $16-$32; 24 hr rm service; cocktails. A Preferred Hotel. FAX (213) 626-9906   ⊗ Ⓢ Ⓓ (213) 624-0000

Holiday Inn Convention Center 6   AAA Special Value Rates   Hotel ◆◆◆
All year   1P 89.00- 129.00   2P/1B   104.00- 129.00   2P/2B   104.00- 129.00   XP 15   F
195 units. 1020 S Figueroa St at Olympic Blvd. (90015) A/C; C/CATV; movies; radios; phones. Coin laundry. Small pool; sauna; exercise rm. Garage. Pets, in travel kennel. AE, DI, DS, MC, VI. ● Dining rm; 6 am-2 & 5-10 pm; $9-$18; cocktails. FAX (213) 748-6028   ⊗ Ⓢ Ⓓ (213) 748-1291

Holiday Inn-Downtown 10   Rates Subject to Change   Hotel ◆◆
All year   ....   2P/1B   ....   89.00   2P/2B   ....   99.00   XP 9   F
Senior discount. 205 units. 1 blk w of SR 110. 750 Garland Ave at 8th St. (90017) A/C; C/CATV; pay movies; radios; phones. Coin laundry. Pool. Parking ramp. Pets. Monthly rates avail. Reserv deposit required. AE, DI, DS, MC, VI. ● Dining rm; 6 am-2 & 5-10:30 pm; $7.50-$15; cocktails. FAX (213) 628-1201   ⊗ Ⓓ (213) 628-5242

Hyatt Regency Los Angeles 9   Rates Subject to Change   Hotel ◆◆◆
Sun-Thurs   1P 139.00- 214.00   ....   2P/2B   164.00- 239.00   XP 25   F
Fri & Sat   1P 95.00- 144.00   ....   2P/2B   95.00- 144.00   XP 25   F
Senior discount. 485 units. 3 blks e of SR 110; at Broadway Plaza. 711 S Hope St at 7th St. (90017) Lobby adjoins shopping plaza. Check-in 3 pm. A/C; C/CATV; free & pay movies; radios; phones. Rental refrigerators. Whirlpool; exercise rm. Pay valet garage. No pets. Wkly & monthly rates avail. AE, DI, DS, MC, VI. ● 2 restaurants; 6 am-11 pm; $10-$14.50; cocktails. FAX (213) 629-3230   ⊗ Ⓢ Ⓓ 🅰 (213) 683-1234

Los Angeles Hilton Hotel and Towers 12   Rates Subject to Change   Hotel ◆◆◆
🚲 All year   1P 160.00- 201.00   2P/1B   180.00- 221.00   2P/2B   180.00- 221.00   XP 20   F
900 units. Adjacent to SR 110. 930 Wilshire Blvd at Figueroa St. (90017) Extensive public facilities & shopping areas. Check-in 3 pm. A/C; C/CATV; free & pay movies; radios; phones. Htd pool; exercise rm. Pay valet garage. No pets. Monthly rates avail. AE, DI, DS, MC, VI. ● 3 dining rms & coffeeshop; 24 hours; $7-$23; cocktails; entertainment. Also, Cardini, see separate listing. FAX (213) 488-9869 *(See ad p 22)* ⊗ Ⓢ Ⓓ 🅰 (213) 629-4321

Metro Plaza Hotel 19   AAA Special Value Rates   Hotel ◆◆◆
🚲 All year   1P   ....   59.00   2P/1B   ....   69.00   2P/2B   ....   75.00   XP 6   F
82 units. Corner of Main & Macy sts. 711 N Main St. (90012) Across from Olvera St; 1/2 blk from Amtrak. Refrigerators; A/C; C/CATV; radios; phones. Coin laundry. Sauna; whirlpool. Garage. No pets. 2 rooms with spa & sauna, $99. Reserv deposit required. AE, DI, DS, MC, VI. ● Restaurant & coffeeshop; 6 am-10 pm; $7.95-$16.95. FAX (213) 620-0200 *(See ad p A209)*   ⊗ Ⓢ Ⓓ (213) 680-0200

Miyako Inn 16   Rates Subject to Change   Hotel ◆◆
All year   1P 85.00- 95.00   2P/1B   95.00- 105.00   2P/2B   95.00- 105.00   XP 15   F
Senior discount. 174 units. In Little Tokyo area. 328 E First St. (90012) Refrigerators; A/C; C/CATV; free & pay movies; radios; phones. Fee for: sauna, massage. Pay valet parking ramp. Airport transp. No pets. Monthly rates avail. AE, DI, MC, VI. ● Restaurant & coffeeshop; 7 am-10 pm; $6-$14; cocktails.   ⊗ Ⓢ Ⓓ (213) 617-2000

The New Otani Hotel 17   Rates Subject to Change   Hotel ◆◆◆
All year   1P 135.00- 170.00   2P/1B   160.00- 180.00   2P/2B   160.00- 180.00   XP 15   F
Senior discount. 440 units. In Civic Center-Little Tokyo area. 120 S Los Angeles St. (90012) Extensive public facilities & shopping areas. Second floor Japanese garden. Refrigerators; A/C; C/CATV; pay movies; radios; phones. Fee for: sauna, whirlpool, massage. Pay garage. No pets. AE, CB, DI, MC, VI. ● 2 dining rms & coffeeshop; 5:30 am-midnight; $7-$30; 24 hour room service; cocktails; entertainment. Also, A Thousand Cranes Restaurant, see separate listing. FAX (213) 622-0980   ⊗ Ⓢ Ⓓ (213) 629-1200

Sheraton Grande Hotel 15   Rates Subject to Change   Hotel ◆◆◆
All year   1P 175.00- 250.00   2P/1B   200.00- 275.00   2P/2B   200.00- 275.00   XP 25   F
Senior discount. 469 units. Adjacent to SR 110. 333 S Figueroa St. (90071) Check-in 3 pm. A/C; C/CATV; free & pay movies; radios; phones. Htd pool. Fee for: airport transp. Pay valet garage. No pets. Reserv deposit required. AE, DI, DS, MC, VI. ● 3 dining rms; 6:30 am-midnight; $10-$30; 24 hour room service; cocktails; entertainment. Also, Scarlatti, see separate listing. FAX (213) 613-0291   ⊗ Ⓢ Ⓓ 🅰 (213) 617-1133

Terrace Manor Bed & Breakfast 3   Rates Subject to Change   Historic Bed & Breakfast ◆◆◆
All year [BP]   ....   2P/1B   70.00- 100.00   XP
5 units. 2 blks e of Alvarado St; between Hoover & Pico blvds. 1353 Alvarado Terr. (90006) 1902 registered historic landmark located in residential area. Smoke free premises. Comb or shower baths. 1 2-bedrm unit. No pets. Reserv deposit required, 5 days refund notice. AE, DS, MC, VI.   ⊗ Ⓓ (213) 381 1478

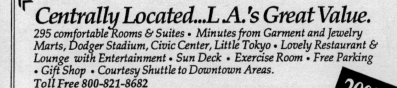

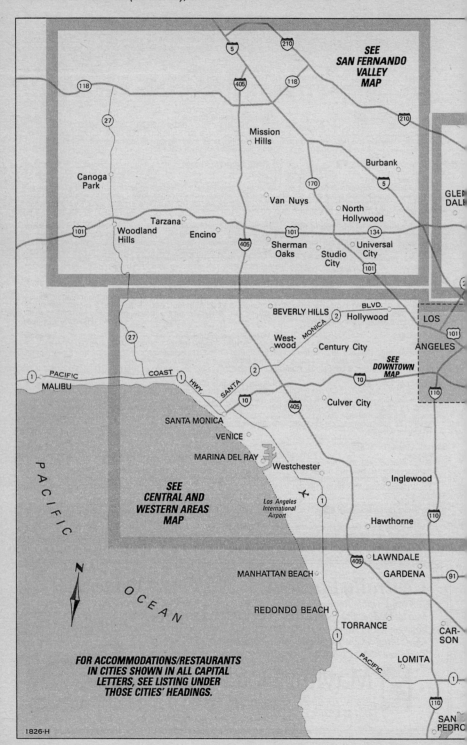

SEE
SAN FERNANDO
VALLEY
MAP

Mission
Hills

Burbank

Canoga
Park

GLEN
DALE

Van Nuys

North
Hollywood

Tarzana
Woodland
Hills

Encino

Universal
City

Sherman
Oaks

Studio
City

BEVERLY HILLS   BLVD.
Hollywood   LOS

West-
wood

Century City

ANGELES

SEE
DOWNTOWN
MAP

PACIFIC   COAST
MALIBU   HWY   SANTA

SANTA MONICA

VENICE

MARINA DEL RAY   Westchester

SEE
CENTRAL AND
WESTERN AREAS
MAP

Culver City

Inglewood

Los Angeles
International
Airport

Hawthorne

PACIFIC   OCEAN

LAWNDALE
GARDENA

MANHATTAN BEACH

CAR-
SON

REDONDO BEACH

TORRANCE

LOMITA

PACIFIC

FOR ACCOMMODATIONS/RESTAURANTS
IN CITIES SHOWN IN ALL CAPITAL
LETTERS, SEE LISTING UNDER
THOSE CITIES' HEADINGS.

SAN
PEDRO

1826-H

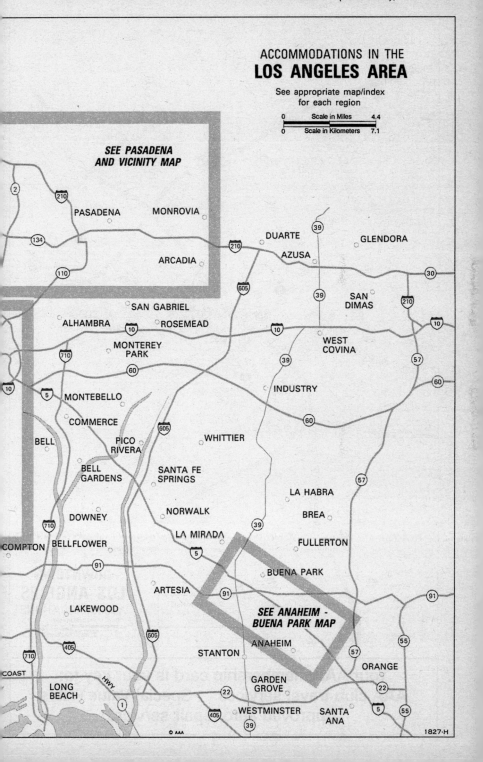

ACCOMMODATIONS IN THE
LOS ANGELES AREA

See appropriate map/index
for each region

0   Scale in Miles   4.4
0   Scale in Kilometers   7.1

**SEE PASADENA
AND VICINITY MAP**

2
210
PASADENA   MONROVIA
134   DUARTE   39   GLENDORA
110   AZUSA
                  ARCADIA   210
605   39   SAN
                                                  DIMAS   30
         SAN GABRIEL   210
ALHAMBRA   ROSEMEAD   10   10
710   MONTEREY   WEST
         PARK   COVINA   57
         60   39   60
10
5   MONTEBELLO   INDUSTRY
                                            60
         COMMERCE
605
BELL   PICO   WHITTIER
           RIVERA
         BELL   57
         GARDENS   SANTA FE
                     SPRINGS   LA HABRA
         DOWNEY   NORWALK   BREA
710   LA MIRADA   39
                     5   FULLERTON
COMPTON BELLFLOWER
         91   BUENA PARK
           ARTESIA   91   91
LAKEWOOD   **SEE ANAHEIM -
                              BUENA PARK MAP**
         605   ANAHEIM
710 405   STANTON   57   ORANGE
COAST   GARDEN   22   55
         LONG   22   GROVE
         BEACH   WESTMINSTER   SANTA   5   55
         1   405   39   ANA

© AAA   1827-H

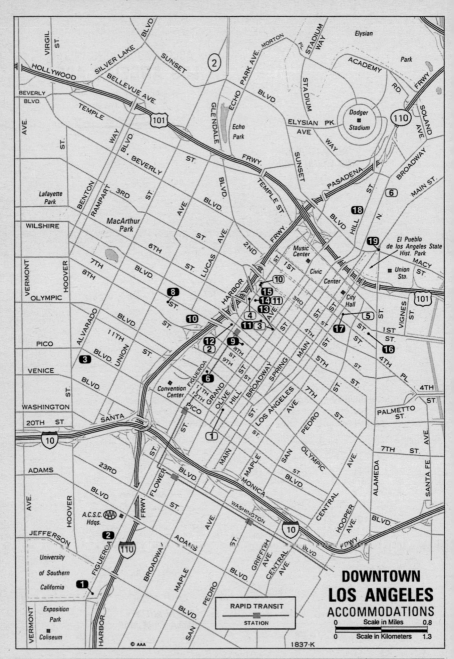

DOWNTOWN
LOS ANGELES
ACCOMMODATIONS

Scale in Miles   0.8
Scale in Kilometers   1.3

1837-K

RAPID TRANSIT

STATION

University Hilton-Los Angeles ❶   AAA Special Value Rates   *Hotel*   ◆◆◆
ⓐ All year   1P 95.00-135.00   2P/1B 110.00-150.00   2P/2B 110.00-150.00   XP 15   F
241 units. 1 blk w of SR 110, Harbor Frwy, exit Exposition Blvd. 3540 S Figueroa St. (90007) 200 refrigerators; A/C; C/CATV; movies; radios; phones. Htd pool; whirlpool. Pay parking lot. No pets. Monthly rates avail. AE, DI, DS, MC, VI. ● Dining rm & coffeeshop; 6:30 am-10:30 pm; $7-$15; cocktails. FAX (213) 746-3255 *(See ad p 22)*
Ⓧ Ⓢ Ⓓ (213) 748-4141

Vagabond Inn Figueroa ❷   Rates Subject to Change   *Motor Inn*   ◆◆
ⓐ All year [CP]   1P 55.00-65.00   2P/1B 65.00-70.00   2P/2B 65.00-75.00   XP 5   F
72 units. 1/2 mi sw of SR 110, Adams Blvd exit. 3101 S Figueroa St. (90007) A/C; C/CATV; movies; radios; phones. 6 2-bedrm units. Htd pool. Pets, $5 extra charge. AE, DI, DS, MC, VI. ● Coffeeshop; 6 am-10 pm; $4.50-$7.50.
FAX (213) 746-9106   Ⓧ Ⓓ (213) 746-1531

The Westin Bonaventure ⓮   Rates Guaranteed   *Hotel*   ◆◆◆◆
ⓐ All year   1P 89.00-150.00   2P/1B 89.00-150.00   2P/2B 89.00-150.00   XP 25   F
1474 units. 404 S Figueroa St. (90071) Dramatically designed lobby area. Extensive public facilities & shopping areas. Check-in 3 pm. A/C; C/CATV; pay movies; radios; phones. Htd pool. Pay valet garage. Small pets only. AE, DI, DS, MC, VI. ● Dining rm & coffeeshop; 6 am-1 am; $7-$30; 24 hour room service; cocktails; entertainment. Also, Top of Five, see separate listing. FAX (213) 612-4800   Ⓧ Ⓢ Ⓓ Ⓛ (213) 624-1000

A Thousand Cranes Restaurant ⑤   Ethnic $$ ◆◆
In The New Otani Hotel. Japanese restaurant with 3-6 persons & 1-25 person tatami rooms. Tempura & sushi bar. Garden view from most areas. Sun brunch. A/C. Open 11:30 am-2 & 6-10 pm. Cocktails & lounge. Entertainment. Reserv advised. AE, DI, MC, VI.   Ⓧ (213) 629-1200

Bernard's ③   Continental $$$$ ◆◆◆◆
In The Biltmore Los Angeles. An elegant dining room featuring expertly prepared cuisine. A/C. Dress code. Open 11:30 am-2 & 6-10 pm; Fri-10:30 pm; Sat 6 pm-10:30 pm; closed Sun & major holidays. Cocktails. Valet parking. Reserv advised. AE, CB, DI, MC, VI.   Ⓧ (213) 612-1580

Cardini ② Italian $$$ ◆◆◆
In the Los Angeles Hilton Hotel and Towers. Selections of seafood, lamb, veal, chicken & pastas. A/C. Open 11:30 am-2 & 5:30-10 pm; Sat 6 pm-10:30 pm; closed Sun. Cocktails & lounge. Entertainment. Pay valet parking. AE, DI, DS, MC, VI.   Ⓧ (213) 629-3236

Little Joe's ⑥ Italian $$ ◆
1 1/4 mi n of US 101, in Chinatown area. 900 N Broadway. Extensive selection of entrees. Informal atmosphere. A/C. Children's menu. Open 11:30 am-9 pm; closed Sun & major holidays. Cocktails & lounge. Valet parking. AE, DI, DS, MC, VI.   (213) 489-4900

Scarlatti ⑩ Italian $$$$ ◆
In Sheraton Grande Hotel. Formerly Ravel. Formal decor & service. Beautifully decorated. A/C. Open 5:30 pm-10 pm; closed Sun & Mon. Cocktails. Valet parking. Reserv advised. AE, DI, DS, MC, VI.   Ⓧ (213) 617-1133

Sonora Cafe ④   Southwest American $$$ ◆◆
445 S Figueroa St. An attractive restaurant serving a nice selection of Southwestern cuisine. A/C. Open 11 am-2:30 & 5:30-10 pm; Sat from 5:30 pm; Sun 5 pm-9 pm; closed 1/1, 7/4 & 12/25. Cocktails & lounge. Pay garage. Reserv advised. AE, CB, DI, MC, VI.   Ⓧ (213) 624-1800

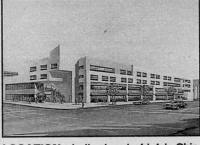

Top of Five (11) Continental $$$ ◆◆◆
On the 35th floor of the Westin Bonaventure. Panoramic view. Mesquite broiled seafood, black angus steaks, lamb, chicken, veal & pasta. Hot rock cooking by guest at tableside. A/C. Open 11:30 am-2:30 & 6-10:30 pm; Fri-Sun 6 pm-11 pm. Cocktails & lounge. Entertainment & dancing. Pay valet parking. Reserv advised. AE, DI, DS, MC, VI.
⊗ (213) 612-4743

The Tower (1) French $$$$ ◆◆◆
1150 S Olive St. On 32nd floor of Transamerica Center Building with panoramic view of city. Formal atmosphere. A/C. Open 11:30 am-2 & 5:30-9:30 pm; Sat from 5:30 pm; closed Sun & major holidays. Cocktails & lounge. Valet parking. Reserv advised. AE, CB, DI, MC, VI.
⊗ (213) 746-1554

LOS ANGELES (Central & Western Areas) — (See LOS ANGELES (Central & Western Areas) spotting map pages A212 & A213; see index starting below) See also BEVERLY HILLS, MARINA DEL REY/VENICE & SANTA MONICA

Index of Establishments on the LOS ANGELES (Central & Western Areas) AREA Spotting Map

(See LOS ANGELES (Central & Western Areas) spotting map pages A212 & A213)

SANTA MONICA

⊕ Comfort Inn	171
⊕ Oceana Hotel................................	172
⊕ Best Western Santa Monica Gateway Hotel ...	173
⊕ Radisson Huntley Hotel......................	174
⊕ Miramar Sheraton Hotel.....................	175
⊕ Pacific Shore Hotel	176
Holiday Inn-Bayview Plaza.....................	177
⊕ Shangri-La Hotel	178
⊕ Loews Santa Monica Beach Hotel	179
Channel Road Inn Bed & Breakfast.............	180
Guest Quarters Suite Hotel	181
⊕ Hotel Santa Monica........................	182

RESTAURANTS

Chinois on Main	75
Cafe Casino	76
Valentino Restaurant	77
Knoll's Black Forest Inn	78
Madame Wu's Garden	79
Bob Burns Restaurant.........................	80
Michael's	82

BEVERLY HILLS

The Peninsula Beverly Hills....................	188
Regent Beverly Wilshire.......................	189
⊕ Beverly Hilton.............................	190

RESTAURANTS

Lawry's The Prime Rib	88
La Scala Boutique	89
L'Escoffier	90
Trader Vic's..................................	91
Ruth's Chris Steak House	92
El Torito Grill	93
Prego..	94
Matsuhisa	95
La Veranda	96

MARINA DEL REY/VENICE

⊕ Foghorn Hotel..............................	195
⊕ Marina Pacific Hotel & Suites...............	196
⊕ Doubletree Hotel Marina Beach..............	197
⊕ Best Western-Jamaica Bay Inn	198
Marina International Hotel	199
⊕ Marina Motel	200
Marina del Rey Marriott	201
⊕ The Mansion Inn............................	202
⊕ Jolly Roger Hotel	203
⊕ The Ritz-Carlton, Marina del Rey	204

RESTAURANTS

Cafe Del Rey	100
Rueben's	100
The Dining Room	101
Stones	102

Airport Century Inn 92   Rates Guaranteed   *Motor Inn* ◆◆◆
⊕ Mon-Thurs   1P 59.00- 64.00   2P/1B   64.00- 69.00   2P/2B   64.00- 69.00   XP 8   F
Fri-Sun   1P 54.00- 59.00   2P/1B   58.00- 63.00   2P/2B   58.00- 63.00   XP 8   F
Senior discount. 147 units. 1 mi e of airport at Aviation Blvd. 5547 W Century Blvd. (90045) A/C; C/CATV; movies; rental VCPs. Radios; phones; shower or comb baths. Coin laundry. Htd pool. Airport transp. Reserv deposit required. AE, DI, DS, MC, VI. ● Coffeeshop; 24 hours; $5-$9; cocktails. FAX (310) 649-0311 *(See ad p A214)*
     D (310) 649-4000

Airport Marina Hotel 123   Rates Guaranteed   *Motor Inn* ◆◆
⊕ All year   1P .... 89.00   2P/1B   .... 89.00   2P/2B   .... 89.00   XP 10   F
Senior discount. 756 units. On SR 1, 2 mi nw of airport. 8601 Lincoln Blvd at Manchester Blvd. (90045) Check-in 3 pm. A/C; C/TV; pay movies; 500 radios; phones; comb or shower baths. Htd pool. Airport transp. No pets. AE, DI, DS, MC, VI. ● Coffeeshop; 6:30 am-10:30 pm; $6.75-$17.50; cocktails. FAX (310) 337-1883   (310) 670-8111

Bel Age Hotel 156   Rates Subject to Change   *Suites Hotel* ◆◆◆◆
All year   1P 195.00- 550.00   2P/1B   195.00- 550.00   2P/2B   195.00- 550.00   XP 25
189 units. 1/2 blk s of Sunset Blvd. 1020 N San Vicente Blvd. (West Hollywood, 90069) European elegance. 1-bedroom suites with living room. Refrigerators; A/C; C/CATV; movies; radios; phones. Whirlpool; heated rooftop pool. Pay valet garage. No pets. AE, CB, DI, MC, VI. ● Dining rm & restaurant; 7 am-11 pm; a la carte entrees about $12-$35; 24 hour room service; cocktails. Also, Diaghlev, see separate listing. FAX (310) 854-0926   S D (310) 854-1111

Best Western Airpark Hotel 125   Rates Guaranteed   *Motel* ◆◆◆
⊕ 6/1-8/31 [CP]   1P 56.00- 66.00   2P/1B   62.00- 74.00   2P/2B   64.00- 76.00   XP 6   F
9/1-5/31 [CP]   1P 52.00- 60.00   2P/1B   56.00- 65.00   2P/2B   59.00- 70.00   XP 6   F
70 units. Adjacent to I-405, Manchester Blvd E exit. 640 W Manchester Blvd. (Inglewood, 90301) Refrigerators; A/C; C/CATV; radios; phones. Coin laundry. Pool; sauna; whirlpool; 1 indoor whirlpool. Airport transp. No pets. 5 rooms with whirlpool tub, $80-$120. Reserv deposit required; 7 days refund notice. AE, DI, DS, MC, VI. Restaurant opposite. FAX (310) 674-1137 *(See ad p A215)*   S D & (310) 677-7378

Best Western Airport Plaza Inn 133   Rates Guaranteed   *Motel* ◆◆◆
⊕ 6/1-8/31 [CP]   1P 54.00- 69.00   2P/1B   60.00- 69.00   2P/2B   61.00- 71.00   XP 6   F
9/1-5/31 [CP]   1P 49.00- 59.00   2P/1B   54.00- 66.00   2P/2B   56.00- 68.00   XP 6   F
54 units. 3/4 mi ne of I-405, exit La Tijera Blvd to Centinela, 1/2 blk e of La Cienega. 1730 Centinela Ave. (Inglewood, 90302) Refrigerators; A/C; C/CATV; movies; radios; phones. Coin laundry. Sauna; whirlpool; 6 rooms with whirlpool tub. Airport transp. No pets. Reserv deposit required. AE, DI, DS, MC, VI. FAX (310) 337-1919 *(See ad p A216)*   D (310) 568-0071

Best Western Executive Motor Inn
Mid-Wilshire 72   AAA Special Value Rates   *Motel* ◆◆
⊕ All year [CP]   1P 55.00- 65.00   2P/1B   55.00- 65.00   2P/2B   60.00- 69.00   XP 3- 8   F
90 units. 1 blk n of Wilshire Blvd. 603 S New Hampshire Ave. (90005) Refrigerators; A/C; C/CATV; phones. Coin laundry. Htd indoor pool; sauna; indoor whirlpool; exercise rm. Garage. No pets. AE, CB, DI, MC, VI. FAX (213) 380-5413 *(See ad below)*   ⊗ D (213) 385-4444

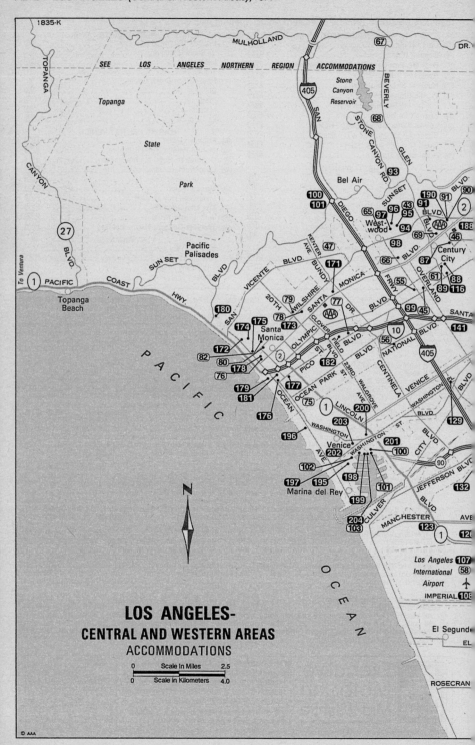

LOS ANGELES-
CENTRAL AND WESTERN AREAS
ACCOMMODATIONS

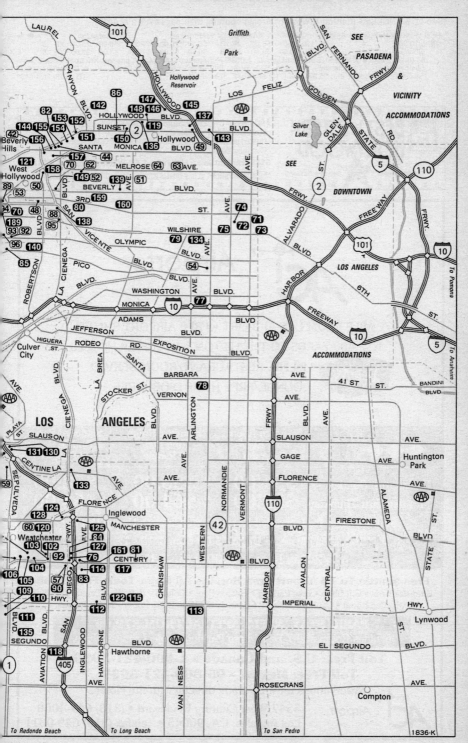

(See LOS ANGELES (Central & Western Areas) spotting map pages A212 & A213)

Best Western Hollywood 145

			AAA Special Value Rates				Motor Inn			◆◆
ⓐⓐ 6/10-9/7	1P 60.00-	65.00	2P/1B	65.00- 70.00	2P/2B	70.00- 75.00	XP 5		
9/8-6/9	1P 54.00-	59.00	2P/1B	59.00- 63.00	2P/2B	63.00- 68.00	XP 5	F

85 units. 2 blks e of Vine St. 6141 Franklin Ave. (90028) Refrigerators; A/C; C/TV; phones. Htd pool. Pets, $25 deposit required. 45 efficiencies, $10 extra. Wkly & monthly rates avail. AE, CB, DI, MC, VI. ● Coffeeshop; 6:30 am-9 pm; Sun from 7 am; $5-$7. FAX (213) 962-0536 *(See ad below)*   Ⓓ (213) 464-5181

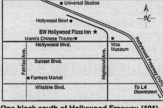

(See LOS ANGELES (Central & Western Areas) spotting map pages A212 & A213)

Best Western Hollywood Plaza Inn 🔲147🔲   Rates Guaranteed   *Motor Inn*   ◆◆◆
🅰🅰 6/1-9/30   1P 69.00- 79.00   2P/1B   75.00- 85.00   2P/2B   75.00- 85.00   XP 6   F
10/1-10/31 & 3/1-5/31   1P 62.00- 72.00   2P/1B   68.00- 78.00   2P/2B   68.00- 78.00   XP 6   F
11/1-2/28   1P 58.00- 68.00   2P/1B   63.00- 73.00   2P/2B   63.00- 73.00   XP 6   F
82 units. 1/2 mi n of Hollywood Blvd. 2011 N Highland Ave. (90068) Refrigerators; A/C; C/CATV; movies; radios;
phones. Coin laundry. Htd pool. No pets. 2 rooms with whirlpool tub, $95-$120. Reserv deposit required; 7 days
refund notice. AE, CB, DI, MC, VI. ● Coffeeshop; 7 am-1:30 & 5:30-9 pm; $5-$8. FAX (213) 851-1836 *(See ad
p A215)*   ⊗ Ⓓ 🅂 (213) 851-1800

Best Western Royal Palace Hotel 🔲99🔲   Rates Guaranteed   *Apartment Motel*   ◆◆
🅰🅰 6/15-9/15 [CP]   1P 60.00- 75.00   2P/1B   65.00- 81.00   2P/2B   75.00- 81.00   XP 6   F
Senior discount. 55 units. 1/4 mi s of Pico Blvd. 2528 S Sepulveda Blvd. (90064) OPEN ALL YEAR. Refrigerators;
A/C; C/CATV; movies; phones; shower baths. 42 kitchens. Coin laundry. Small htd pool; sauna; whirlpool; exercise rm. No pets. Reserv deposit required. AE, DI, DS, MC, VI. FAX (310) 478-4133   Ⓓ (310) 477-9066

See WHAT THE 🅰🅰 MEANS.

(See LOS ANGELES (Central & Western Areas) spotting map pages A212 & A213)

Best Western Suite Hotel **161**　　　　　　Rates Subject to Change　　　　　　*Motel*
6/1-8/31 [CP]　　　　　1P 79.00- 95.00 2P/1B 89.00- 99.00 2P/2B 89.00- 99.00 XP 10　　F
9/1-5/31 [CP]　　　　　1P 69.00- 85.00 2P/1B 79.00- 95.00 2P/2B 79.00- 95.00 XP 10　　F
Senior discount. 80 units. Adjacent to I-405, Century Blvd e exit, 1 1/2 mi e of airport. 5005 W Century Blvd. (90304) Rating withheld pending completion of construction. Scheduled to open August, 1992. Refrigerators; A/C; C/CATV; movies; radios; phones. Htd pool; whirlpool. Parking ramp. No pets. Reserv deposit required. AE, DI, DS, MC, VI. FAX (310) 674-1137 *(See ad below)*　　　　　　⊗ Ⓢ Ⓓ (310) 677-7733

Best Western Sunset Plaza Hotel **151**　　　　　Rates Guaranteed　　　　　　*Motel*　◆◆◆
🅰🅱 5/16-9/30 [CP]　　　　1P 79.00- 92.00 2P/1B 79.00- 92.00 2P/2B 82.00- 92.00 XP 8　　F
10/1-5/15 [CP]　　　　　1P 69.00- 85.00 2P/1B 79.00- 95.00 2P/2B 75.00- 85.00 XP 8　　F
Senior discount. 86 units. 2 blks e of La Cienega Blvd. 8400 Sunset Blvd. (West Hollywood, 90069) Refrigerators; A/C; C/CATV; VCPs; radios; phones. 22 kitchens. Coin laundry. Htd pool. Garage. No pets. 6 1-bedroom apartments, $140-$165 for 2 persons. Reserv deposit required. AE, CB, DI, MC, VI. FAX (213) 656-4158 *(See ad p A218)*　　　⊗ Ⓓ (213) 654-0750

The Beverly Grand Hotel **139**　　　　　　Rates Subject to Change　　　　　*Motor Inn*　◆◆
Fri & Sat [BP]　　　　　1P .... 65.00 2P/1B .... 75.00 2P/2B 75.00- 85.00 XP 15
Sun-Thurs [BP]　　　　　1P .... 59.00 2P/1B .... 65.00 2P/2B 65.00- 75.00 XP 15
41 units. 3 blks w of La Brea Ave. 7257 Beverly Blvd. (90036) A/C; C/CATV; phones. Garage. No pets. Refrigerators, $5 daily. Wkly rates avail. AE, DI, MC, VI. Coffeeshop; 7:30 am-10 pm; $18. FAX (213) 930-0716 Ⓢ Ⓓ (213) 939-1653

Beverly Hills Comstock Hotel **91**　　　　　Rates Subject to Change　　　　*Apartment Hotel*　◆◆◆
All year　　　　　　　1P 95.00- 195.00 2P/1B 95.00- 195.00 2P/2B 150.00- 290.00 XP　　　F
Senior discount. 116 units. 1 blk e of Beverly Glen Dr. 10300 Wilshire Blvd. (90024) A/C; C/CATV; pay movies; radios; phones; comb or shower baths. 73 kitchens. Htd pool; whirlpool. Pay valet garage. Pets, $500 deposit required. 12 2-bedroom apartments, $190-$295. Monthly rates avail. AE, DI, DS, MC, VI. ● Dining rm; 6:30 am-10:30 pm; $12-$20; cocktails. FAX (310) 278-3325　　　　　　　　　　　　　　　　　　　　　Ⓓ (310) 275-5575

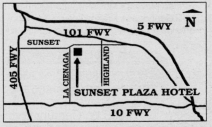

(See LOS ANGELES (Central & Western Areas) spotting map pages A212 & A213)

Beverly Laurel Motor Hotel 159   Rates Subject to Change   *Motel* ◆◆
ⓐ All year   1P .... 51.00 2P/1B .... 57.00 2P/2B .... 57.00 XP 5
52 units. 3 blks w of Fairfax Ave. 8018 Beverly Blvd. (90048) Refrigerators; A/C; C/CATV; phones; shower or comb baths. Htd pool. 10 kitchen units, $10 extra. Wkly rates avail. AE, DI, MC, VI. Coffeeshop adjacent. *(See ad p A217)*   Ⓓ (213) 651-2441

Beverly Plaza Hotel 80   Rates Subject to Change   *Hotel* ◆◆◆
ⓐ All year   1P .... 92.00 2P/1B .... 100.00 2P/2B .... 100.00 XP 10   F
Senior discount. 98 units. 2 blks e of La Cienega Blvd. 8384 W 3rd St. (90048) A/C; C/CATV; radios; phones. Small htd pool; saunas; exercise rm. Pay valet garage. No pets. Reserv deposit required. AE, DI, DS, MC, VI. ● Dining rm; 7 am-10:30 pm; $8-$15; 24 hour room service; cocktails. FAX (213) 653-3464
                                                     ⊗ Ⓢ Ⓓ Ⓚ (213) 658-6600

Brentwood Suites Hotel 100   Rates Guaranteed   *Motel* ◆◆◆
ⓐ All year [CP]   1P 85.00- 105.00 2P/1B 85.00- 105.00 2P/2B 85.00- 105.00 XP 8
60 units. Adjacent to I-405, Sunset Blvd exit, 1/2 mi n. 199 N Church Ln. (90049) Check-in 3 pm. A/C; C/TV; phones. Efficiencies. Coin laundry. Small htd pool; sauna; indoor whirlpool. Pets, $30 deposit required. Wkly & monthly rates avail. AE, CB, DI, MC, VI. FAX (310) 471-4285 *(See ad below)*   Ⓓ Ⓚ (310) 476-6255

Carlyle Inn 140   Rates Subject to Change   *Motor Inn* ◆◆◆
All year [BP]   1P .... 120.00 2P/1B .... 140.00 2P/2B .... 140.00 XP 25   F
Senior discount. 32 units. 1 blk s of Olympic Blvd. 1119 S Robertson Blvd. (90035) Charming rooms & suites overlooking courtyard area. Afternoon tea served 4-6 pm. Refrigerators; A/C; C/CATV; VCPs; radios; phones. Whirlpool; sun deck. No pets. Executive suites, $145 for up to 2 persons. Reserv deposit required. Complimentary beverages each evening. AE, CB, DI, MC, VI. Dining rm; 7 am-10:30 & 4-6 pm; $5.95; cocktails. FAX (310) 859-0496
                                                ⊗ Ⓢ Ⓓ Ⓚ (310) 275-4445

Century City Inn 89   Rates Subject to Change   *Motel* ◆◆◆
ⓐ All year [CP]   1P .... 104.00 2P/1B .... 114.00 2P/2B .... 114.00 XP 10   F
Senior discount. 46 units. 2 blks e of Beverly Glen. 10330 W Olympic Blvd. (90064) Refrigerators; A/C; C/CATV; pay movies; VCPs. Radios; phones; comb or shower baths. All rooms with whirlpool tub. Pay valet garage. No pets. Microwaves. Reserv deposit required. AE, DI, DS, MC, VI. FAX (310) 277-1633   ⊗ Ⓓ Ⓚ (310) 553-1000

(See LOS ANGELES (Central & Western Areas) spotting map pages A212 & A213)

Century Plaza Hotel & Tower 87   Rates Subject to Change   *Hotel*   ◆◆◆◆
All year   1P 175.00- 275.00   2P/1B 200.00- 300.00   2P/2B 200.00- 300.00   XP 25   F
Senior discount. 1072 units. Century City. 2025 Avenue of the Stars. (90067) An impressive hotel with many public facilities & shops. Across from ABC Entertainment Center. A/C; C/CATV; free & pay movies; radios; phones; comb or shower baths. 2 htd pools; saunas; whirlpools; exercise rm. Pay valet garage & parking lot. Small pets only. AE, DI, DS, MC, VI. ● Dining rm, 4 restaurants & coffeeshop; 6 am-1 am; $11-$26; cocktails; entertainment. Also, La Chaumiere, see separate listing. FAX (310) 551-3355   ⊗ ⓢ ⓓ ⓚ (310) 277-2000

Chesterfield Hotel Beverly Hills/Century City 88   Rates Subject to Change   *Motor Inn*   ◆◆◆
4/16-7/5 & 9/8-1/31   1P 99.00- 129.00   ....   2P/2B 109.00- 139.00   XP 10
2/1-4/15   1P 109.00- 129.00   2P/1B 119.00- 139.00   2P/2B 119.00- 139.00   XP 10
7/6-9/7   1P .... 125.00   2P/1B .... 135.00   2P/2B .... 135.00   XP 10
136 units. 2 blks e of Beverly Glen. 10320 W Olympic Blvd. (90064) Check-in 3 pm. A/C; C/CATV; free & pay movies; rental VCPs. Radios; phones. Whirlpool; exercise rm. Garage. AE, DI, DS, MC, VI. ● Coffeeshop; 6:30 am-11 & 6-10 pm; $9-$17; cocktails. FAX (310) 203-0563   ⊗ ⓢ ⓓ ⓚ (310) 556-2777

Comfort Inn 78   AAA Special Value Rates   *Motel*   ◆◆
All year   1P 52.00- 57.00   2P/1B 48.00- 67.00   2P/2B 62.00- 72.00   XP 10   F
41 units. 2 blks s of Martin Luther King Blvd. 4122 S Western Ave. (90062) 38 refrigerators; A/C; C/TV; movies; radios; phones; shower or tub baths. 1 2-bedrm unit. Indoor whirlpool. No pets. AE, DI, DS, MC, VI. *(See ad below)*   ⊗ ⓓ ⓚ (213) 294-5200

Comfort Inn Mid-Wilshire 71   AAA Special Value Rates   *Motel*   ◆
All year   1P 44.00- 49.00   2P/1B 48.00- 54.00   2P/2B 48.00- 54.00   XP 5   F
120 units. 1 blk e of Vermont Ave. 3400 W 3rd St. (90020) 19 refrigerators; A/C; C/CATV; movies; 110 radios; phones; shower or comb baths. Htd pool. No pets. 4 kitchens, $5 extra. Wkly rates avail. Reserv deposit required. AE, CB, DI, MC, VI. Coffeeshop adjacent. FAX (213) 385-8517 *(See ad p A219)*   ⊗ ⓓ (213) 385-0061

Courtyard by Marriott 111   Rates Subject to Change   *Motor Inn*   ◆◆◆
Sun-Thurs   1P .... 92.00   2P/1B .... 92.00   2P/2B .... 92.00   XP
Fri & Sat   1P .... 72.00   2P/1B .... 72.00   2P/2B .... 72.00   XP
Senior discount. 146 units. 2 blks s of SR 1, Sepulveda Blvd; 1 3/4 mi s of airport. 2000 E Mariposa Ave. (El Segundo, 90245) Many rooms with balcony overlooking courtyard. Check-in 3 pm. 12 refrigerators; A/C; C/CATV; free & pay movies; radios; phones. Coin laundry. Htd pool; indoor whirlpool; exercise rm. Airport transp. No pets. Suites $110 Sun-Thurs; $72 Fri & Sat. AE, DI, DS, MC, VI. ● Dining rm; 6:30 am-2 & 5-10 pm; Sat & Sun from 7 am; $7.95-$12.95; cocktails. FAX (310) 322-4401 *(See ad p A221)*   ⊗ ⓢ ⓓ ⓚ (310) 322-0700

(See LOS ANGELES (Central & Western Areas) spotting map pages A212 & A213)

Crown Sterling Suites-Los Angeles Airport 108

All year [BP] — Rates Guaranteed — Suites Motor Inn ◆◆◆
2P/1B .... 99.00   2P/2B .... 99.00   XP   F

Senior discount. 350 units. 1 blk w of Sepulveda Blvd; 1/2 mi s of Los Angeles Airport. 1440 E Imperial Ave. (El Segundo, 90245) Beautifully decorated & landscaped interior courtyard. A/C; C/CATV; free & pay movies; radios; phones. Htd indoor pool; sauna; indoor whirlpool; steamroom. Garage. Airport transp. Pets, $10 extra charge. Microwaves & refrigerators. Maximum rate for up to 4 persons. Wkly & monthly rates avail. Complimentary beverages each evening. AE, DI, DS, MC, VI. ● Restaurant; 11 am-10 pm; $9.50-$20; cocktails. FAX (310) 322-0954 *(See ad below)*   (310) 640-3600

Culver City Travelodge 129

All year — Rates Subject to Change — Motel ◆◆◆
1P 57.00- 65.00   2P/1B 62.00- 70.00   2P/2B 62.00- 70.00   XP 5   F

36 units. 1/4 blk e of Sepulveda Blvd. 11180 Washington Pl. (Culver City, 90232) Large rooms. Refrigerators; A/C; C/CATV; movies; radios; phones; comb or shower baths. No pets. Wkly rates avail 2/1-3/31. Reserv deposit required. AE, DI, DS, MC, VI. Coffeeshop adjacent. FAX (310) 839-4628 *(See ad p A222)*   (310) 839-1111

(See LOS ANGELES (Central & Western Areas) spotting map pages A212 & A213)

Days Inn-Airport [84] ◆◆
Rates Subject to Change | Motor Inn
⊕ 6/1-8/31 1P .... 69.00 2P/1B .... 69.00 2P/2B .... 69.00 XP 10 F
9/1-5/31 1P .... 59.00 2P/1B .... 59.00 2P/2B .... 59.00 XP 10 F
252 units. Adjacent to I-405, Century Blvd E exit; 1 1/2 mi e of airport. 5101 W Century Blvd. (Inglewood, 90304) A/C; C/CATV; free & pay movies; radios; phones. Pool. Airport transp. No pets. Wkly & monthly rates avail. AE, DI, DS, MC, VI. ● Restaurant; 6 am-11 pm; $5-$13; cocktails. FAX (310) 677-7871 *(See ad p A223)*
⊗ Ⓢ Ⓓ 🅶 (310) 419-1234

Days Inn Airport Center [124] ◆◆
Rates Guaranteed | Motor Inn
⊕ All year 1P 49.00- 59.00 2P/1B 54.00- 64.00 2P/2B 54.00- 64.00 XP 5 F
Senior discount. 47 units. 1 blk w of I-405, Manchester Blvd exit. 901 W Manchester Blvd. (Inglewood, 90301) Formerly Airport Courtesy Inn. 21 refrigerators; A/C; C/CATV; movies; radios; phones. 11 2-bedrm units. Coin laundry. Pool. Airport transp. No pets. 11 2-bedroom units. $60-$72. AE, DI, DS, MC, VI. ● Coffeeshop; 6 am-8 pm; Sun-3 pm; $4-$6; beer & wine. FAX (310) 649-3837 *(See ad p A224)*
⊗ Ⓓ (310) 649-0800

Days Inn-Wilshire [134] ◆◆
AAA Special Value Rates | Motor Inn
All year 1P 55.00- 65.00 2P/1B 65.00- 75.00 2P/2B 65.00- 75.00 XP 6 F
86 units. 3900 Wilshire Blvd. (90010) A/C; C/CATV; movies; radios; phones. Parking ramp. No pets. Reserv deposit required. AE, DI, DS, MC, VI. ● Dining rm; 7 am-10:30 pm; $8-$11. FAX (213) 736-5038 ⊗ Ⓢ Ⓓ (213) 736-5222

Diamond Inn [122] ◆
Rates Subject to Change | Motel
⊕ All year 1P .... 40.00 2P/1B .... 40.00 2P/2B .... 50.00 XP
41 units. 2 1/2 mi e of I-405. 3735 W Imperial Hwy. (Inglewood, 90303) A/C; C/CATV; movies; radios; phones. No pets. 3 rooms with whirlpool, $70-$80. AE, MC, VI.
Ⓓ (310) 674-1278

Doubletree Club Hotel Los Angeles [135] ◆◆◆
Rates Subject to Change | Motor Inn
Sun-Thurs [BP] 1P .... 92.00 2P/1B .... 102.00 2P/2B .... 102.00 XP 10 F
Fri & Sat [BP] 1P .... 69.00 2P/1B .... 79.00 2P/2B .... 79.00 XP 10 F
Senior discount. 215 units. 1 blk e of SR 1, Sepulveda Blvd. 1985 E Grand Ave. (El Segundo, 90245) A/C; C/CATV; free & pay movies; radios; phones. Htd pool; whirlpool; exercise rm. Parking ramp & parking lot. Airport transp. No pets. Complimentary beverages each evening. AE, DI, DS, MC, VI. FAX (310) 322-4758 ⊗ Ⓢ Ⓓ 🅶 (310) 322-0999

(See LOS ANGELES (Central & Western Areas) spotting map pages A212 & A213)

Dunes Motel-Sunset **143**   Rates Subject to Change   *Motor Inn* ◆◆
│ All year   1P .... 54.00 2P/1B .... 54.00 2P/2B .... 62.20 XP 5   F
57 units. 1 blk e of US 101, exit Sunset Blvd. 5625 Sunset Blvd. (90028) A/C; C/TV; movies; radios; phones. No pets. Reserv deposit required. AE, CB, DI, MC, VI. ● Restaurant; 7 am-9 pm; closed Sun; $5-$10; cocktails. *(See ad below)*   Ⓓ (213) 467-5171

Dunes Motor Hotel-Wilshire **79**   Rates Subject to Change   *Motel* ◆◆
│ All year   1P .... 54.00 2P/1B .... 54.00 2P/2B .... 62.20 XP 5   F
58 units. 2 blks w of Crenshaw Blvd. 4300 Wilshire Blvd. (90010) A/C; C/TV; movies; radios; phones. Coin laundry. Htd pool. No pets. 6 efficiencies, $10 extra. Reserv deposit required. AE, DI, MC, VI. Coffeeshop; 7:30 am-3 pm. *(See ad below)*   Ⓓ (213) 938-3616

Econo Lodge **74**   Rates Subject to Change   *Motel* ◆◆
│ All year   1P .... 45.00 2P/1B .... 49.00 2P/2B .... 49.00 XP 5
Senior discount. 50 units. 2 blks n of Wilshire Blvd. 457 S Mariposa Ave. (90020) Refrigerators; A/C; C/CATV; movies; phones. Pool; sauna; whirlpool; exercise rm. Garage. No pets. 3 rooms with whirlpool tub, $65. AE, CB, DI, MC, VI. FAX (213) 382-3888 *(See ad below)*   ⊗ Ⓓ (213) 380-6910

(See LOS ANGELES (Central & Western Areas) spotting map pages A212 & A213)

Econo Lodge-Hollywood `142`   Rates Subject to Change   *Motel*   ◆
⊕ All year   1P .... 39.00   2P/1B .... 45.00   2P/2B .... 48.00   XP 6   F
Senior discount. 43 units. 1 1/2 blks n of Melrose Ave. 777 N Vine St. (90038) 15 refrigerators; A/C; C/CATV; movies; radios; phones. Coin laundry. Pool. No pets. AE, DS, MC, VI. Restaurant opposite. *(See ad below)*
            ⊗ Ⓓ (213) 463-5671

Econo Lodge LAX `81`   AAA Special Value Rates   *Motel*   ◆ ◆
⊕ All year   1P .... 35.00   2P/1B .... 42.00   2P/2B .... 50.00   XP 5
Senior discount. 41 units. 1 3/4 mi e I-405. 4123 W Century Blvd. (Inglewood, 90304) A/C; C/CATV; movies; radios; phones. Pets. AE, DS, MC, VI. FAX (310) 672-7295
            ⊗ Ⓢ Ⓓ (310) 672-7285

Embassy Suites Hotel-LAX/Century `126`   Rates Guaranteed   *Suites Motor Inn*   ◆ ◆ ◆
⊕ All year [BP]   1P .... 99.00   2P/1B .... 99.00   2P/2B .... 99.00   XP
215 units. 1 blk n of Century Blvd; 1/2 mi e of airport. 9801 Airport Blvd. (90045) A/C; C/CATV; free & pay movies; radios; phones. Coin laundry. Htd indoor pool; sauna; whirlpool; exercise rm. Pay garage. Airport transp. Pets, $15 extra charge. Microwaves & refrigerators. Monthly rates avail. Reserv deposit required. Complimentary beverages each evening. AE, DI, DS, MC, VI. ● Restaurant; 11 am-11 pm; $11.95-$16.95; cocktail lounge.
FAX (310) 215-1952   ⊗ Ⓢ Ⓓ Ⓑ (310) 215-1000

Farmer's Daughter Motel `160`   Rates Subject to Change   *Motel*   ◆ ◆
⊕ 6/20-8/31   1P .... 65.00   2P/1B .... 65.00   2P/2B .... 65.00   XP 3
9/1-6/19   1P .... 58.00   2P/1B .... 58.00   2P/2B .... 58.00   XP 3
66 units. Opposite Farmers Market. 115 S Fairfax Ave. (90036) Check-in 3 pm. Refrigerators; A/C; C/CATV; movies; radios; phones. Small htd pool. No pets. Reserv deposit required. AE, MC, VI.
            Ⓓ (213) 937-3930

Four Seasons Hotel `70`   Rates Subject to Change   *Hotel*   ◆ ◆ ◆ ◆
⊕ All year   1P 250.00- 355.00   2P/1B 275.00- 355.00   2P/2B 275.00- 355.00   XP 25
285 units. Corner of Burton Way. 300 S Doheny Dr. (90048) Check-in 3 pm. A/C; C/CATV; free & pay movies; VCPs. Radios; phones. Htd pool; whirlpool; exercise rm. Fee for: massage. Pay valet parking lot. Reserv deposit required. AE, CB, DI, MC, VI. ● Dining rm & restaurant; 6 am-11 pm; $25-$33; cocktails; entertainment.
FAX (310) 859-3824   ⊗ Ⓢ Ⓓ Ⓑ (310) 273-2222

Hacienda Hotel-L. A. Airport `110`   Rates Subject to Change   *Hotel*   ◆ ◆
⊕ Mon-Thurs   1P 52.00- 60.00   2P/1B 60.00- 68.00   2P/2B 60.00- 68.00   XP 8   F
Fri-Sun   1P .... 49.00   2P/1B .... 49.00   2P/2B .... 49.00   XP 8   F
Senior discount. 630 units. On SR 1; 1 1/2 mi s of airport. 525 Sepulveda Blvd. (El Segundo, 90245) A/C; C/CATV; free & pay movies; radios; phones; comb or shower baths. Coin laundry. Htd pool; whirlpool. Parking lot. Airport transp. No pets. Reserv deposit required. AE, DI, DS, MC, VI. ● Dining rm & coffeeshop; 24 hours; $7-$16.95; cocktails; entertainment. FAX (310) 615-0217 *(See ad below)*   ⊗ Ⓢ Ⓓ Ⓑ (310) 615-0015

(See LOS ANGELES (Central & Western Areas) spotting map pages A212 & A213)

Hallmark Hotel 150   **AAA Special Value Rates**   *Motel*   ◆◆
All year [CP]   1P 56.00- 60.00   2P/1B   60.00- 66.00   2P/2B   65.00- 75.00   XP 10   F
74 units. 1 blk e of La Brea Ave. 7023 Sunset Blvd. (90028) A/C; C/CATV; movies; radios; phones; shower or
comb baths. 8 efficiencies, no utensils. Htd pool. Garage. Small pets only. 6 rooms with whirlpool tub, $100.
Wkly rates avail. AE, DI, DS, MC, VI. FAX (213) 962-9748   (D) (213) 464-8344

Hampton Inn-Los Angeles International
Airport 83   Rates Subject to Change   *Motel*   ◆◆◆
All year [CP]   1P 69.00- 85.00   2P/1B   79.00- 95.00   2P/2B   89.00- 95.00   XP 10
150 units. From I-405, exit Century Blvd, 1 blk w & 2 blks s; 1 1/2 mi e of airport. 10300 La Cienega Blvd. (Inglewood, 90304) A/C; C/CATV; free & pay movies; radios; phones. Sauna; exercise rm. Limited garage & parking lot. Airport transp. No pets. Complimentary beverages each evening. AE, DI, DS, MC, VI. FAX (310) 645-6925
         ⊗ Ⓢ Ⓓ 🅐 (310) 337-1000

Hilgard House Hotel 96   Rates Subject to Change   *Motel*   ◆◆◆
All year [CP]   1P 99.00- 109.00   2P/1B   99.00- 109.00   2P/2B   99.00- 109.00   XP 10   F
Senior discount. 47 units. 3 blks n of Wilshire Blvd. 927 Hilgard Ave. (90024) Refrigerators; A/C; C/CATV; movies;
radios; phones. 15 rooms with whirlpool tub. Garage. No pets. Reserv deposit required. AE, CB, DI, MC, VI.
FAX (310) 208-1972   (D) (310) 208-3945

(See LOS ANGELES (Central & Western Areas) spotting map pages A212 & A213)

Holiday Inn-Crowne Plaza 🔲105   **AAA Special Value Rates**   *Hotel* ◆◆◆
🅰 **All year**   1P 126.00- 141.00   2P/1B 141.00- 156.00 2P/2B 141.00- 156.00 XP 15   F
615 units. 1/4 mi e of airport. 5985 W Century Blvd. (90045) Check-in 3 pm. A/C; C/CATV; free & pay movies; radios; phones. Coin laundry. Small htd pool; sauna; whirlpool; exercise rm. Pay valet parking ramp. Airport
transp. No pets. AE, DI, DS, MC, VI. ● Dining rm & coffeeshop; 6 am-11 pm; $7.50-$27; 24 hour room service;
cocktails; entertainment. FAX (310) 417-3608   ⊗ Ⓢ Ⓓ 🅖 (310) 642-7500

Holiday Inn Express, Los Angeles Int'l
  Airport 🔲114   **AAA Special Value Rates**   *Motel* ◆◆
🅰 **5/29-9/15 [CP]**   1P 64.00- 79.00 2P/1B   64.00- 84.00 2P/2B 74.00- 84.00 XP 5   F
  9/16-5/28 [CP]   1P 59.00- 74.00 2P/1B   64.00- 79.00 2P/2B 69.00- 79.00 XP 5
105 units. 1 blk e of I-405; 1 1/2 mi e of airport. 4922 W Century Blvd. (Inglewood, 90304) Formerly Rodeway
Inn-Los Angeles Airport. 55 refrigerators; A/C; C/CATV; movies; radios; phones. Pool; 33 rooms with whirlpool
tub. No pets. AE, DI, DS, MC, VI. FAX (310) 671-1804 *(See ad p A225)*   ⊗ Ⓢ Ⓓ 🅖 (310) 671-7213

Holiday Inn-Hollywood 🔲146   **Rates Subject to Change**   *Hotel* ◆◆◆
All year   1P 85.00- 120.00 2P/1B 100.00- 135.00 2P/2B 100.00- 135.00 XP 15
Senior discount. 470 units. 1 blk n of Hollywood Blvd. 1755 N Highland Ave. (90028) A/C; C/CATV; free & pay movies;
radios; phones. Coin laundry. Htd pool. Pay parking ramp. Pets. AE, DI, DS, MC, VI. ● Restaurant; revolving rooftop
dining room; 6 am-11 pm; $8-$22; cocktails; entertainment. FAX (213) 466-9072   ⊗ Ⓓ 🅖 (213) 462-7181

(See LOS ANGELES (Central & Western Areas) spotting map pages A212 & A213)

Holiday Inn-International Airport **127**   Rates Subject to Change   *Motor Inn*   ◆◆
All year   1P 82.00- 89.00   2P/1B   92.00- 99.00   2P/2B   92.00- 96.00   XP 10   F
Senior discount. 402 units. 1 1/4 mi e of airport; 1/2 blk n of Century Blvd. 9901 S La Cienega Blvd. (90045) A/C;
C/CATV; free & pay movies; radios; phones. Coin laundry. Htd pool; exercise rm. Airport transp. Pets. AE, DI, MC,
VI. ● Dining rm; 6 am-midnight; $7-$13; cocktails. FAX (310) 670-3619   ⊗ Ⓓ ⅃ (310) 649-5151

Hollywood Celebrity Hotel **148**   Rates Subject to Change   *Motel*   ◆◆
⊕ 5/1-9/30 [CP]   1P   .... 68.00   2P/1B   .... 78.00   2P/2B   .... 83.00   XP 5   F
   10/1-4/30 [CP]   1P   .... 65.00   2P/1B   .... 73.00   2P/2B   .... 73.00   XP 5   F
Senior discount. 39 units. 1 blk n of Hollywood Blvd. 1775 Orchid Ave. (90028) Art deco motif. A/C; C/TV; radios;
phones. Rental refrigerators. Pets, $25 deposit required. AE, CB, DI, MC, VI.   Ⓓ (213) 850-6464

Hollywood Metropolitan Hotel **137**   AAA Special Value Rates   *Hotel*   ◆◆
⊕ All year [CP]   1P 85.00- 115.00   2P/1B 85.00- 115.00   2P/2B   .... 95.00   XP 10   F
90 units. 1 blk w of US 101, exit Sunset Blvd. 5825 Sunset Blvd. (90028) 12-story hi-rise. A/C; C/CATV; phones.
Garage. No pets. AE, DI, DS, MC, VI. Restaurant; 7 am-10 pm; $7.50-$17; cocktails. FAX (213) 465-1380
                                                                              ⊗ Ⓢ Ⓓ (213) 962-5800

Hollywood Roosevelt Hotel **136**   Rates Subject to Change   *Hotel*   ◆◆
All year   1P 105.00- 160.00 2P/1B 125.00- 180.00 2P/2B 125.00- 180.00 XP 20   F
Senior discount. 330 units. 7000 Hollywood Blvd. (90028) Long established hotel. Interesting Hollywood memorablia on
mezzanine level. A/C; C/CATV; radios; phones. Htd pool; whirlpool. Pay valet garage & parking lot. No pets. AE, CB, DI,
MC, VI. ● Dining rm; 6:30 am-midnight; a la carte entrees about $12-$18; cocktails; entertainment. FAX (213) 462-8056
                                                                              ⊗ Ⓓ (213) 466-7000

Hotel Bel-Air **93**   Rates Subject to Change   *Hotel*   ◆◆◆◆
                          1P 225.00- 395.00 2P/1B 245.00- 435.00 2P/2B 245.00- 435.00 XP 20
92 units. 1/2 mi n of Sunset Blvd. 701 Stone Canyon Rd. (90077) Quiet, secluded location on extensive, beautifully landscaped grounds. Check-in 3 pm. Refrigerators; A/C; C/CATV; movies; radios; phones. 5 2-bedrm units. Htd pool. Valet
parking lot. No pets. Luxury level rooms avail. Suites & apartments, $480-$2,000. Reserv deposit required. AE, CB, DI,
MC, VI. ● Dining rm; 7 am-10:30, noon-2:30 & 6:30-10 pm; a la carte entrees about $35-$55; cocktails; entertainment.
A Preferred Hotel. FAX (310) 476-5890   Ⓓ (310) 472-1211

Hotel Del Capri **94**   AAA Special Value Rates   *Suites Motel*   ◆◆◆
⊕ All year [CP]   1P 85.00- 110.00   2P/1B   95.00- 120.00   2P/2B 105.00- 120.00 XP 10   F
81 units. 5 blks e of Westwood Blvd. 10587 Wilshire Blvd. (90024) Attractively landscaped. 65 refrigerators; A/C;
C/CATV; radios; phones; comb or shower baths. 45 efficiencies. Coin laundry. Htd pool; whirlpool tubs. 2-deluxe
suites, $140 for up to 2 persons. Wkly rates avail. AE, CB, DI, MC, VI. FAX (310) 470-9999   Ⓓ (310) 474-3511

Hotel Nikko at Beverly Hills **138**   Rates Subject to Change   *Hotel*   ◆◆◆◆
⊕ All year   1P 220.00- 325.00 2P/1B 245.00- 350.00 2P/2B 245.00- 350.00 XP
304 units. 465 S La Cienega Blvd at San Vicente. (90048) Spacious rooms decorated in a contemporary oriental
motif. A/C; C/CATV; movies; radios; phones. Htd pool; saunas; exercise rm. Fee for: massage. Pay valet garage.
AE, DI, DS, MC, VI. ● Dining rm & restaurant; 6:30 am-2:30 & 5:30-11 pm; a la carte entrees about $10-$20; 24
hour room service; cocktails. FAX (310) 247-0315   ⊗ Ⓢ Ⓓ ⅃ (310) 247-0400

Hotel Sofitel Ma Maison **149**   Rates Subject to Change   *Hotel*   ◆◆◆◆
All year   1P 190.00- 210.00 2P/1B 210.00- 230.00 2P/2B 210.00- 230.00 XP 20
Senior discount. 311 units. 2 1/2 mi n of I-10, exit La Cienega Blvd; Beverly Blvd at La Cienega Blvd, across from Beverly Center. 8555 Beverly Blvd. (90048) Check-in 3 pm. A/C; C/CATV; free & pay movies; radios; phones. Htd pool;
sauna; exercise rm. Fee for: massage. Pay valet garage. Pets, $20 extra charge. Reserv deposit required. AE, MC,
VI. ● Dining rm & restaurant; 6 am-midnight; a la carte entrees about $7.95-$45; cocktails. Also, Ma Maison, see separate listing. FAX (310) 657-2816   ⊗ Ⓢ Ⓓ (310) 278-5444

Howard Johnson-Lax **128**   Rates Subject to Change   *Motor Inn*   ◆◆
⊕ All year   1P   .... 53.00   2P/1B   .... 59.00   2P/2B   .... 59.00   XP 6   F
Senior discount. 160 units. 1/2 blk S Manchester Ave. 8620 Airport Blvd. (90045) Check-in 3 pm. Refrigerators;
A/C; C/CATV; radios; phones. Htd pool; whirlpool. Airport transp. No pets. AE, DI, DS, MC, VI. ● Restaurant;
6:30 am-10 pm; $6.95-$12.95. FAX (310) 645-2958   ⊗ Ⓢ Ⓓ (310) 645-7700

Howard Johnson Plaza Hotel **130**   AAA Special Value Rates   *Motor Inn*   ◆◆
⊕ All year   1P 63.00- 75.00   2P/1B   69.00- 88.00   2P/2B   69.00- 88.00   XP 10   F
200 units. Adjacent to I-405, Sepulveda Blvd exit. 5990 Green Valley Cir. (Culver City, 90230) 7 refrigerators; A/C;
C/CATV; free & pay movies; radios; phones. Htd pool. Airport transp. No pets. Microwaves. AE, DI, DS, MC,
VI. ● Dining rm; 6 am-10 pm; $9-$14; cocktails. FAX (310) 645-7045   ⊗ Ⓓ (310) 641-7740

Hyatt at Los Angeles Airport **107**   Rates Guaranteed   *Hotel*   ◆◆◆
Sun-Thurs   1P 155.00- 165.00 2P/1B 170.00- 180.00 2P/2B 170.00- 180.00 XP 15   F
Fri & Sat   1P 99.00- 125.00   2P/1B   99.00- 125.00   2P/2B   99.00- 100.00 XP   F
596 units. On SR 1, across from airport entrance. 6225 W Century Blvd at Sepulveda Blvd. (90045) Check-in 3 pm. 80
refrigerators; A/C; C/CATV; free & pay movies; radios; phones. Htd pool; sauna; exercise rm. Pay valet parking lot &
ramp. Airport transp. No pets. AE, DI, DS, MC, VI. ● Dining rm & restaurant; 6 am-midnight; $6.25-$30; cocktails; entertainment. FAX (310) 641-6924   ⊗ Ⓓ (310) 670-9000

Hyatt on Sunset **152**   Rates Subject to Change   *Hotel*   ◆◆◆
262 units. 2 blks e of La Cienega Blvd. 8401 Sunset Blvd. (West Hollywood, 90069) A/C; C/CATV; free & pay movies;
radios; phones. Rooftop pool. Pay valet parking lot. No pets. AE, DI, DS, MC, VI. ● Dining rm; 6:30 am-11 pm; $10-
$20; cocktails. FAX (213) 650-7024   ⊗ Ⓢ Ⓓ (213) 656-1234
                          1P 135.00- 165.00 2P/1B 155.00- 185.00 2P/2B   .... 155.00 XP 20   F

J W Marriott at Century City **116**   Rates Subject to Change   *Hotel*   ◆◆◆◆
⊕ Mon-Fri   1P 259.00- 279.00 2P/1B 289.00- 309.00 2P/2B 289.00- 309.00 XP 30   F
   Sat & Sun   1P   .... 199.00 2P/1B   .... 199.00 2P/2B   .... 199.00 XP 30   F
Senior discount. 375 units. 1/2 mi s of Santa Monica Blvd. 2151 Avenue of the Stars. (90067) Nicely decorated
rooms, many with balcony or patio. Check-in 3 pm. A/C; C/CATV; movies; radios; phones. 2 htd pools, 1 indoor;
saunas; indoor whirlpool; steamroom; health club. Fee for: tanning bed; massage. Pay garage. No pets. AE, DI,
DS, MC, VI. ● Dining rm; 6:30 am-10:30 pm; Sat & Sun from 7 am; $17.95-$30; afternoon tea served 3:30 pm-5
pm; cocktail lounge. FAX (310) 785-9240   ⊗ Ⓢ Ⓓ ⅃ (310) 277-2777

La Mirage Inn **113**   Rates Subject to Change   *Motel*   ◆
⊕ All year   1P   .... 45.00   2P/1B   .... 45.00   2P/2B   .... 60.00   XP
Senior discount. 34 units. 2 blks s of Imperial Hwy. 11711 S Western Ave. (90047) Refrigerators; A/C; C/CATV;
movies; radios; phones. No pets. 4 rooms with whirlpool tub, $80. AE, MC, VI.   Ⓓ (213) 418-0888

(See LOS ANGELES (Central & Western Areas) spotting map pages A212 & A213)

La Mirage Inn 112
All year   Rates Subject to Change   Motel   ◆◆
1P .... 46.00   2P/1B .... 46.00   2P/2B .... 55.00   XP 5
Senior discount. 47 units. 3/4 mi e of I-405, exit Imperial Hwy. 4501 W Imperial Hwy. (Inglewood, 90304) Refrigerators; A/C; C/CATV; movies; 43 radios; phones. No pets. 4 rooms with whirlpool, $80. AE, MC, VI.
ⓈⒹ⊜ (310) 671-6017

LAX Hotel 109
All year [CP]   AAA Special Value Rates   Motel   ◆◆
1P 45.00- 50.00   2P/1B 51.00- 56.00   2P/2B 57.00- 62.00   XP 5
94 units. On SR 1, 1 1/4 mi s of airport. 1804 E Sycamore at Sepulveda Blvd. (El Segundo, 90245) A variety of nicely furnished units. Refrigerators; A/C; C/CATV; movies; rental VCPs. Radios; phones; comb or shower baths. 37 kitchens, 5 efficiencies. Coin laundry. Htd pool. Airport transp. Pets, $200 deposit required. Wkly rates avail. AE, DI, DS, MC, VI. FAX (310) 322-4475 (See ad p A230)
⊗ Ⓓ (310) 615-1073

Le Dufy Hotel 157
All year   AAA Special Value Rates   Motor Inn   ◆◆◆
1P 145.00- 215.00   2P/1B 145.00- 215.00   XP
103 units. 3 blks s of Sunset Blvd, 1 blk n of Santa Monica Blvd. 1000 Westmount Dr. (West Hollywood, 90069) 1-bedroom suites with living room & gas fireplace. Refrigerators; A/C; C/CATV; movies; radios; phones; comb or shower baths. 64 kitchens. Coin laundry. Htd pool; sauna; whirlpool. Pay garage. No pets. Monthly rates avail. AE, CB, DI, MC, VI. ● Dining rm; 7 am-11 pm; $10-$20. FAX (310) 854-6744
⊗ Ⓓ (310) 657-7400

Le Montrose Suite Hotel De Gran Luxe 121
All year   AAA Special Value Rates   Motor Inn   ◆◆◆
1P 135.00- 185.00   2P/1B 135.00- 185.00   XP   F
109 units. 2 blks s of Sunset Blvd, 1 blk e of Doheny. 900 Hammond St at Cynthia. (West Hollywood, 90069) Formerly Valadon Hotel. Spacious, attractively furnished rooms & suites. Check-in 3 pm. Refrigerators; A/C; C/CATV; movies; VCPs. Radios; phones. 73 efficiencies. Coin laundry. Whirlpool; heated rooftop pool; lighted tennis-1 court; bicycles. Pay garage. Wkly & monthly rates avail. AE, CB, DI, MC, VI. ● Dining rm; guests only, 7 am-10:45 pm; $10-$20; cocktails. FAX (310) 657-9192 (See ad below)
Ⓓ (310) 855-1115

Le Parc Hotel 158
All year   Rates Subject to Change   Motor Inn   ◆◆◆
1P 110.00- 255.00   2P/1B 110.00- 255.00   2P/2B 110.00- 255.00   XP 25   F
Senior discount. 154 units. 1 blk n of Melrose Ave & 1 blk w of La Cienega Blvd. 733 N West Knoll Dr. (West Hollywood, 90069) Spacious, nicely decorated rooms. Refrigerators; A/C; C/CATV; movies; VCPs. Radios; phones. 98 efficiencies. Sauna; whirlpool; rooftop heated pool; lighted tennis-1 court; exercise rm. Pay valet garage. Monthly rates avail. AE, CB, DI, MC, VI. ● Dining rm; guests only 7 am-10:30 pm; 24 hour room service; cocktails. FAX (310) 659-7812
Ⓓ (310) 855-8888

Le Reve Hotel 144
All year   Rates Subject to Change   Motel   ◆◆◆
1P 100.00- 160.00   2P/1B 100.00- 160.00   .... XP 25
77 units. 1 blk n of Santa Monica Blvd; 2 blks s of Sunset Blvd. 8822 Cynthia St at Larrabe. (West Hollywood, 90069) Rooms & 1-bedroom units with living room; most with gas fireplace. Refrigerators; A/C; C/CATV; movies; radios; phones. 16 efficiencies. Coin laundry. Whirlpool; rooftop pool. Pay garage. No pets. Monthly rates avail. AE, CB, DI, MC, VI. Room service avail. FAX (310) 657-2623
Ⓓ (310) 854-1114

Los Angeles Airport Hilton & Towers 102
All year   AAA Special Value Rates   Hotel   ◆◆◆
1P 135.00- 165.00   2P/1B 150.00- 180.00   2P/2B 150.00- 180.00   XP 15   F
1279 units. 3/4 mi e of airport. 5711 W Century Blvd. (90045) Check-in 3 pm. A/C; C/CATV; free & pay movies; radios; phones. Coin laundry. Htd pool; saunas; whirlpools. Fee for: racquetball-2 courts; health club. Pay valet garage & parking ramp. Airport transp. Pets. AE, DI, DS, MC, VI. ● Dining rm & restaurant; 24 hours; $7-$25; cocktails; entertainment. Also, Alexander's, see separate listing. FAX (310) 410-6250 (See ad p 22)
⊗ ⓈⒹ⊜ (310) 410-4000

Los Angeles Airport Marriott Hotel 104
Sun-Thurs   Rates Subject to Change   Hotel   ◆◆◆
1P 144.00- 154.00   2P/1B 154.00- 165.00   2P/2B 154.00- 165.00   XP 10   F
Fri & Sat   1P .... 119.00   2P/1B .... 119.00   2P/2B .... 119.00   XP 10   F
1012 units. 1/2 mi e of airport. 5855 W Century Blvd. (90045) Check-in 3 pm. 15 refrigerators; A/C; C/CATV; free & pay movies; radios; phones. Coin laundry. Htd pool; saunas; whirlpool; exercise rm. Valet garage & parking lot. Airport transp. Pets. AE, DI, DS, MC, VI. ● 2 dining rms, restaurant & coffeeshop; 6 am-midnight; $7-$25; 24 hour room service; cocktails; entertainment. FAX (310) 337-5358
⊗ ⓈⒹ⊜ (310) 641-5700

Mondrian Hotel 153
All year   Rates Subject to Change   Hotel   ◆◆◆
1P 160.00- 325.00   2P/1B 160.00- 325.00   2P/2B 160.00- 325.00   XP 25
219 units. 2 blks e of La Cienega Blvd. 8440 Sunset Blvd. (West Hollywood, 90069) Rooms nicely decorated in a contemporary decor. Refrigerators; A/C; C/CATV; movies; radios; phones. Htd pool; whirlpool; health club & massage. Pay valet garage. Monthly rates avail. AE, DI, DS, MC, VI. ● Dining rm; 7 am-10:30 pm; a la carte entrees about $14.50-$25; cocktails; entertainment. FAX (213) 650-5215
ⓈⒹ⊜ (213) 650-8999

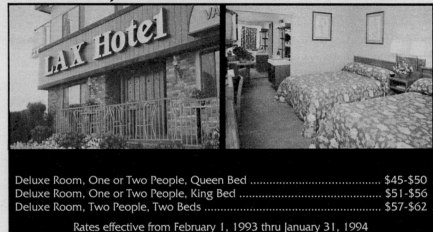
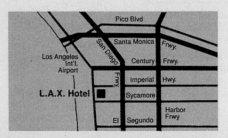

(See LOS ANGELES (Central & Western Areas) spotting map pages A212 & A213)

Orchid Suites Hotel 119   Rates Guaranteed   *Apartment Motel*   ◆◆
6/1-9/1	1P 60.00-	70.00	2P/1B	65.00-	70.00	2P/2B	60.00-	70.00	XP	5
2/1-5/30 & 9/2-10/31	1P 55.00-	65.00	2P/1B	55.00-	65.00	2P/2B	55.00-	65.00	XP	5
11/1-1/31	1P 50.00-	60.00	2P/1B	50.00-	60.00	2P/2B	50.00-	60.00	XP	5

Senior discount. 40 units. 1 blk n of Hollywood Blvd. 1753 N Orchid Ave. (90028) A/C; C/TV; phones. Coin laundry. Htd pool. Garage. No pets. Studio & 1-bedroom suites with efficiency or kitchen. Wkly rates avail. AE, DI, DS, MC, VI. Restaurant opposite. FAX (213) 874-9931   Ⓓ (213) 874-9678

Pacifica Hotel 132   Rates Guaranteed   *Hotel*   ◆◆◆
Mon-Thurs	1P	....	75.00	2P/1B	....	75.00	2P/2B	....	75.00	XP 10	F
Fri-Sun	1P	....	69.00	2P/1B	....	69.00	2P/2B	....	69.00	XP 10	F

Senior discount. 360 units. Adjacent to I-405, Jefferson Blvd exit. 6161 Centinela Ave. (Culver City, 90230) Check-in 3 pm. Refrigerators; 368 A/C; pay movies; 368 radios; 368 phones; 368 comb baths. Htd pool; whirlpool. Fee for: health club. Parking lot. Airport transp. No pets. AE, DI, DS, MC, VI. ● Dining rm; 6 am-10 pm; $11-$19; cocktails; entertainment. FAX (310) 649-4411   ⊗ Ⓢ Ⓓ ⓛ (310) 649-1776

Park Sunset Hotel 154   Rates Guaranteed   *Motor Inn*   ◆◆
All year	1P	....	69.00	2P/1B	....	69.00	2P/2B	....	69.00	XP 10	F

Senior discount. 84 units. 2 blks e of La Cienega Blvd. 8462 Sunset Blvd. (West Hollywood, 90069) A/C; C/CATV; pay movies; VCPs. Radios; phones; comb or shower baths. 16 kitchens. Coin laundry. Htd pool. No pets. 16 1-bedroom suites with microwave, $139. Wkly rates avail. AE, DI, DS, MC, VI. ● Restaurant; 7 am-11 pm; $6-$12; beer & wine.   ⊗ Ⓓ (213) 654-6470

Quality Hotel-Los Angeles Airport 76   AAA Special Value Rates   *Hotel*   ◆◆
All year	1P 55.00-	75.00	2P/1B	60.00-	80.00	2P/2B	60.00-	80.00	XP 10	F

278 units. 1 1/4 mi e of airport. 5249 W Century Blvd. (90045) Check-in 3 pm. A/C; C/TV; pay movies; radios; phones. Coin laundry. Htd pool; exercise rm. Pay parking ramp. Airport transp. No pets. Wkly & monthly rates avail. AE, DI, DS, MC, VI. ● Dining rm & coffeeshop; 6 am-10 pm; $10-$16; cocktails. FAX (310) 641-8214 *(See ad below)*   ⊗ Ⓢ Ⓓ (310) 645-2200

Radisson Bel Air Summit Hotel 101   Rates Subject to Change   *Motor Inn*   ◆◆◆
All year	1P 109.00-	139.00	2P/1B	119.00-	149.00	2P/2B	119.00-	149.00	XP 10	F

Senior discount. 162 units. In Brentwood area; 1 blk w of I-405. 11461 Sunset Blvd. (90049) Attractive grounds. Spacious, nicely decorated rooms, many with balcony or patio. Check-in 3 pm. Refrigerators; A/C; C/CATV; pay movies; radios; phones. Htd pool; tennis-1 court. No pets. AE, DI, DS, MC, VI. ● Dining rm; 7 am-10:30 pm; $11-$21; cocktails; entertainment. FAX (310) 471-6310   Ⓓ ⓛ (310) 476-6571

Ramada Hotel 131   Rates Guaranteed   *Motor Inn*   ◆◆◆
All year	1P 85.00-	95.00	2P/1B	95.00-	105.00	2P/2B	95.00-	105.00	XP 10	

Senior discount. 259 units. Adjacent to I-405, Sepulveda Blvd exit, 1/4 blk n Centinela. 6333 Bristol Pkwy. (Culver City, 90230) 13 refrigerators; A/C; C/CATV; pay movies; radios; phones. Htd pool; whirlpool; exercise rm. Airport transp. Pets. AE, CB, DI, MC, VI. ● Dining rm; 6 am-11 pm; $10-$18; cocktails. FAX (310) 670-9026 *(See ad p A232)*   Ⓓ (310) 670-3200

Ramada Hotel 85   Rates Guaranteed   *Hotel*   ◆◆◆
All year	1P	....	85.00	2P/1B	....	85.00	2P/2B	....	95.00	XP 10	F

260 units. 1/2 blk n of Pico Blvd. 1150 S Beverly Dr. (90035) A/C; C/CATV; pay movies; radios; phones. Htd pool. Valet parking ramp. No pets. Wkly & monthly rates avail. Reserv deposit required; 3 days refund notice. AE, DI, DS, MC, VI. ● Dining rm; 6 am-10 pm; $9.95-$16.95; cocktails; entertainment. FAX (310) 277-4469   Ⓓ (310) 553-6561

(See LOS ANGELES (Central & Western Areas) spotting map pages A212 & A213)

Ramada Hotel-Airport South 118   AAA Special Value Rates   *Motor Inn* ◆◆◆
All year   1P .... 79.00   2P/1B .... 79.00   2P/2B .... 79.00   XP 10
169 units. Adjacent to I-405. 5250 El Segundo Blvd. (Hawthorne, 90250) A/C; C/CATV; movies; radios; phones. Coin laundry. Htd pool; indoor whirlpool; 9 rooms with whirlpool tub; exercise rm. Garage. Airport transp. No pets. Wkly rates avail. AE, DI, MC, VI. ● Restaurant; 6 am-10 pm; $7.50-$12.95; cocktail lounge. FAX (310) 536-9535   ⊗ Ⓢ Ⓓ Ⓛ (310) 536-9800

Ramada-West Hollywood 82   Rates Subject to Change   *Hotel* ◆◆◆
All year [CP]   1P 109.00- 119.00   2P/1B 119.00- 129.00   2P/2B 119.00- 129.00   XP 15   F
177 units. 1 blk w of La Cienega Blvd. 8585 Santa Monica Blvd. (West Hollywood, 90069) Contemporary decor. A/C; C/CATV; pay movies; radios; phones. Coin laundry. Htd pool. Pay garage. No pets. 22 loft suites, $189-$269. Wkly & monthly rates avail. AE, DI, DS, MC, VI. ● Restaurant; 11:30 am-11 pm; a la carte entrees about $9-$17; cocktails. FAX (310) 652-2135   ⊗ Ⓢ Ⓓ Ⓛ (310) 652-6400

Renaissance-Lax 120   Rates Subject to Change   *Hotel* ◆◆◆◆
All year   1P 130.00- 195.00   2P/1B 145.00- 210.00   2P/2B 145.00- 210.00   XP 15   F
505 units. 1 blk n of Century Blvd; 1/2 mi e of airport. 9620 Airport Blvd. (90045) Check-in 3 pm. A/C; C/CATV; pay movies; radios; phones. Htd pool; sauna; whirlpool; exercise rm. Pay valet garage. Airport transp. No pets. AE, DI, DS, MC, VI. ● 2 restaurants; 6 am-11 pm; $12.75-$22.75; 24 hour room service; cocktails. FAX (310) 337-4826   ⊗ Ⓢ Ⓓ Ⓛ (310) 337-2800

Royal Palace Westwood 97   Rates Subject to Change   *Apartment Motel* ◆◆
6/15-9/15 [CP]   1P 60.00- 82.00   2P/1B 66.00- 96.00   2P/2B 76.00- 96.00   XP 6   F
Senior discount. 36 units. Westwood; 1 1/2 blks n of Wilshire Blvd. 1052 Tiverton Ave. (90024) OPEN ALL YEAR. Studio & 1-bedroom apartments; 6 small units. A/C; C/CATV; movies; radios; phones; comb or shower baths. 30 kitchens. Exercise rm. No pets. Wkly & monthly rates avail. AE, CB, DI, MC, VI. FAX (310) 824-3732   Ⓓ (310) 208-6677

Salisbury House 77   Rates Guaranteed   *Bed & Breakfast* ◆◆
All year [BP]   1P 65.00- 90.00   2P/1B 70.00- 85.00   2P/2B 70.00- 95.00   XP 10
5 units. 2 blks n of I-10 & 2 blks w of Western Ave; from I-10, Western Ave exit. 2273 W 20th St. (90018) 1909 California Craftsman home in residential area. Nicely decorated rooms. Check-in 3 pm. 4 refrigerators; 2 TV; 3 shower or tub baths. 1 2-bedrm unit. No pets. Wkly rates avail. Reserv deposit required; 3 days refund notice. AE, MC, VI.   ⊗ Ⓓ (213) 737-7817

Sheraton Los Angeles Airport Hotel 106   Rates Subject to Change   *Hotel* ◆◆◆
All year   1P 115.00- 155.00   2P/1B 135.00- 175.00   2P/2B 135.00- 175.00   XP 20   F
807 units. 1/4 mi e of airport. 6101 W Century Blvd. (90045) Formerly Sheraton Plaza La Reina Hotel. Check-in 3 pm. A/C; C/CATV; free & pay movies; radios; phones. Coin laundry. Htd pool; whirlpool; exercise rm. Pay valet parking ramp. Airport transp. Reserv deposit required. AE, DI, DS, MC, VI. ● Dining rm & restaurant; 6 am-10 pm; $7.25-$14.25; cocktails; entertainment. FAX (310) 410-1267   ⊗ Ⓢ Ⓓ Ⓛ (310) 642-1111

Sheraton Town House 73   Rates Subject to Change   *Hotel* ◆◆
All year   1P 95.00- 125.00   2P/1B 95.00- 125.00   2P/2B 95.00- 125.00   XP 15   F
272 units. 4 blks e of Vermont Ave. 2961 Wilshire Blvd. (90010) Check-in 3 pm. 35 refrigerators; A/C; C/TV; free & pay movies; radios; phones. Coin laundry. Htd pool; sauna; lighted tennis-4 courts. Pay valet garage. Small pets only. Reserv deposit required. AE, DI, DS, MC, VI. ● Dining rm & coffeeshop; 6:30 am-10:30 pm; $7.50-$20; cocktails; entertainment. FAX (213) 487-7148   Ⓢ Ⓓ (213) 382-7171

Westin Hotel-Los Angeles Airport 90   Rates Subject to Change   *Hotel* ◆◆◆◆
All year   1P 159.00- 199.00   2P/1B 169.00- 209.00   2P/2B 169.00- 209.00   XP 10   F
Senior discount. 750 units. 1 1/4 mi e of airport. 5400 W Century Blvd. (90045) Check-in 3 pm. A/C; C/CATV; free & pay movies; radios; phones. Htd pool; sauna; whirlpool; exercise rm. Pay valet parking ramp. Airport transp. No pets. AE, DI, DS, MC, VI. ● Dining rm & restaurant; 24 hrs; $8-$20; cocktails; entertainment. Also, Trattoria Grande, see separate listing. FAX (310) 670-1948   ⊗ Ⓢ Ⓓ Ⓛ (310) 216-5858

(See LOS ANGELES (Central & Western Areas) spotting map pages A212 & A213)

Sunset Marquis Hotel & Villas 155   Rates Subject to Change   *Suites Motor Inn* ◆◆◆◆
All year   1P 215.00- 500.00   2P/1B   215.00- 500.00   2P/2B   215.00- 500.00   XP 30
118 units. 1/2 blk s of Sunset Blvd. 1200 N Alta Loma Rd. (West Hollywood, 90069) 1-bedroom units with living room.
Attractive grounds. Refrigerators; A/C; C/CATV; movies; VCPs. Radios; phones. 18 kitchens. Coin laundry. 2 htd pools;
sauna; whirlpool; exercise rm. No pets. Private villas, $650-$1,000. Reserv deposit required. AE, DI, MC, VI. ● Dining
rm; 6:30 am-12:30 am; a la carte entrees about $14.50-$28; cocktails. FAX (310) 652-5300   (D) (310) 657-1333

Travelodge Inglewood 117   Rates Subject to Change   *Motel* ◆◆
⊕ All year [CP]   1P ....   48.00   2P/1B ....   53.00   2P/2B ....   58.00   XP 5   F
Senior discount. 46 units. 1 1/4 mi e of I-405. 4300 W Century Blvd. (Inglewood, 90304) Refrigerators; A/C;
C/CATV; movies; rental VCPs. Radios; phones. Coin laundry. Whirlpool. Airport transp. No pets. 4 rooms with
whirlpool tub, $80. AE, DI, DS, MC, VI. FAX (310) 412-1294   ⊗ (D) (ᴸ) (310) 419-1011

Travelodge-Inglewood South 115   Rates Subject to Change   *Motel* ◆
⊕ All year   ....   2P/1B ....   38.00   2P/2B ....   47.00   XP
Senior discount. 40 units. 1 mi e of Hawthorne Blvd. 3649 W Imperial Hwy. (Inglewood, 90303) A/C; C/CATV;
movies; radios; phones. Whirlpool. No pets. 5 rooms with whirlpool tub, $50. AE, DI, DS, MC, VI.
FAX (310) 771-0486   ⊗ (D) (310) 677-0112

Travelodge-Los Angeles West 141   Rates Subject to Change   *Motel* ◆◆
⊕ All year   1P ....   56.00   2P/1B ....   61.00   2P/2B ....   75.00   XP 5   F
55 units. 2 mi e from I-405, Santa Monica Blvd exit. 10740 Santa Monica Blvd. (90025) Refrigerators; A/C; C/CATV;
movies; radios; phones; shower or comb baths. Htd pool. No pets. Wkly rates avail. Reserv deposit required.
AE, DI, DS, MC, VI. FAX (310) 470-3117   ⊗ (D) (310) 474-4576

Travelodge-Sunset/La Brea 86   Rates Subject to Change   *Motel* ◆
⊕ Fri & Sat   1P 52.00- 62.00   2P/1B   57.00- 67.00   2P/2B   60.00- 70.00   XP 5   F
Sun-Thurs   1P 45.00- 55.00   2P/1B   50.00- 60.00   2P/2B   55.00- 65.00   XP 5   F
Senior discount. 43 units. In Hollywood area. 7051 Sunset Blvd. (90028) A/C; C/TV; phones; shower or comb
baths. Htd pool. AE, CB, DI, MC, VI. FAX (213) 465-6088   (D) (213) 462-0905

Viscount Hotel-Los Angeles 103   Rates Subject to Change   *Hotel* ◆
⊕ All year   1P ....   75.00   2P/1B ....   85.00   2P/2B ....   85.00   XP 10   F
Senior discount. 570 units. 1/2 mi e of airport; 1 blk n of Century Blvd. 9750 Airport Blvd. (90045) Check-in 3 pm.
A/C; C/CATV; pay movies; radios; phones. Htd pool; exercise rm. Pay parking lot. Airport transp. Small pets only,
$20 deposit. AE, DI, DS, MC, VI. ● Restaurant; 6 am-10:30 pm; $8-$20; cocktails; entertainment.
FAX (310) 216-7029   ⊗ (310) 645-4600

Westwood Marquis Hotel and Gardens 95   Rates Guaranteed   *Suites Hotel* ◆◆◆◆
⊕ All year   1P 220.00- 325.00   2P/1B   220.00- 325.00   2P/2B ....   250.00   XP 20
Senior discount. 258 units. Westwood Village, 3 blks n of Wilshire Blvd. 930 Hilgard Ave. (90024) Elegant hotel;
1 to 3-bedroom suites with living room. Afternoon tea, 3 pm-5 pm. A/C; C/CATV; movies; radios; phones. Coin
laundry. 2 htd pools; saunas; whirlpools; exercise room; health club. Fee for: massage. Pay valet garage. No
pets. Monthly rates avail. Reserv deposit required. AE, CB, DI, MC. ● 2 dining rms; 6:30 am-11 pm; a la carte
entrees about $17-$23; cocktails; entertainment. Also, Dynasty Room, see separate listing. A Preferred Hotel.
FAX (310) 824-0355   ⊗ (D) (310) 208-8765

Westwood Plaza Hotel 98   Rates Subject to Change   *Hotel* ◆◆
All year   1P 120.00- 130.00   2P/1B   130.00- 140.00   2P/2B ....   130.00   XP 10   F
Senior discount. 295 units. 10740 Wilshire Blvd. (90024) A/C; C/CATV; movies; radios; phones. Htd pool; sauna; whirl-
pool; exercise rm. Parking ramp. No pets. AE, DI, DS, MC, VI. ● Dining rm; 7 am-10 pm; $7.50-$16.50; cocktails.
FAX (310) 475-5220   ⊗ (D) (310) 475-8711

Wilshire Plaza Hotel 75   Rates Guaranteed   *Hotel* ◆◆◆
All year   1P 120.00- 135.00   2P/1B   140.00- 155.00   2P/2B   140.00- 155.00   XP
Senior discount. 396 units. 3515 Wilshire Blvd at Normandie Ave. (90010) Formerly Hyatt Wilshire. A/C; C/CATV; free &
pay movies; radios; phones. Htd pool. Pay valet garage. Wkly & monthly rates avail. AE, CB, DI, MC, VI. ● Dining rm;
6 am-midnight; $23; cocktails; entertainment. FAX (213) 386-7379   ⊗ (D) (213) 381-7411

RESTAURANTS

Adriano's 67   Italian $$$ ◆◆◆
2 1/2 mi e of I-405; Mulholland Dr exit. 2930 Beverly Glen Cr. In Glen Centre, atop Beverly Glen Canyon. Northern Italian
cuisine. Patio dining. Open 6 pm-10:30 pm; Fri & Sat-11 pm; also 11:30 am-3 pm Tues-Thurs; closed Mon.
   (310) 475-9807

Alexander's 60   Continental $$$ ◆◆◆
In Los Angeles Airport Hilton & Towers. An elegant dining room. Sun brunch, 10:30 am-2:30 pm, $17.95. A/C. Open 6
pm-10 pm. Cocktails & lounge. Pay valet parking. Reserv advised. AE, DI, DS, MC, VI. (See ad p 22)
   ⊗ (213) 410-4000

Brentwood Bar & Grill 47   American $$$ ◆◆◆
In Brentwood; 1/4 mi nw of I-405, exit Wilshire Blvd; 1 blk e of Barrington. 11647 San Vicente Blvd. A/C. Open 11:30
am-2:30 & 6-10:30 pm; Fri & Sat-11 pm; closed major holidays. Cocktails & lounge. Valet parking. Reserv advised. AE,
CB, DI, MC, VI.   ⊗ (310) 820-2121

California Place 58   American $$ ◆◆
L. A. International Airport. Located in Theme Building with panoramic view of airport. Sun brunch, 10 am-2:30 pm. A/C.
Open 11 am-4:30 & 5-9:30 pm; Sun from 10 am. Cocktails & lounge. AE, CB, MC, VI.   ⊗ (310) 646-5471

The Chart House 65   American $$ ◆◆
In Westwood, 2 blks n of Wilshire Blvd. 1097 Glendon Ave. Casual atmosphere. Nice selection of steaks, prime rib &
seafood. A/C. Open 11:30 am-2 & 5-10 pm; Fri-11 pm; Sat 5 pm-11 pm; Sun 5 pm-10 pm. Cocktails & lounge. AE, DI,
DS, MC, VI.   ⊗ (310) 208-8034

Chaya Brasserie 53   Ethnic $$$ ◆◆◆
8741 Alden Dr. Dine in a twenty-first century Quonset hut. French, Japanese & Italian entrees. A/C. Open 11:30 am-2:30
& 6-10:30 pm; Fri-11 pm; Sat 6 pm-11 pm; Sun 6 pm-10 pm. Cocktails & lounge. Valet parking. Reserv required. AE, DI,
MC, VI.   ⊗ (310) 859-8833

Citrus 64   French $$$$ ◆◆◆
1 blk w of Highland Ave. 6703 Melrose Ave. Contemporary decor. Interesting selection of French & California cuisine.
A/C. Open noon-2:30 & 6:30-10 pm; Sat 6 pm-11 pm; closed Sun & holidays. Cocktails. Pay valet parking. Reserv advised. AE, DI, MC, VI.   ⊗ (213) 857-0034

(See LOS ANGELES (Central & Western Areas) spotting map pages A212 & A213)

Diaghilev ㊷ Ethnic $$$$ ◆◆◆◆
West Hollywood, in Bel Age Hotel. An elegant dining room serving superbly prepared Russian cuisine. A/C. Open 6:30 pm-10 pm; closed Sun & Mon. Cocktails & lounge. Valet parking. Reserv advised. AE, CB, DI, MC, VI.
⊗ (310) 854-1111

Dynasty Room ㊸ Continental $$$$ ◆◆◆◆
At Westwood Marquis Hotel & Gardens. Elegant dining room with attentive service & creative dishes artfully presented. A/C. Dress code. Open 6 pm-10:30 pm; Fri & Sat-11 pm. Cocktails. Valet parking. Reserv advised. AE, DI, MC, VI.
(310) 208-8765

El Cholo (54) Mexican $ ◆◆
2 blks s of Olympic Blvd. 1121 S Western Ave. A charming, long established, family owned & operated restaurant. A/C. Children's menu. Open 11 am-10 pm; Fri & Sat-11 pm; Sun-9 pm; closed 7/4, 11/25 & 12/25. Cocktails & lounge. Valet parking. Reserv advised. AE, MC, VI. ⊗ (213) 734-2773

Emilio's Ristorante (51) Italian $$$ ◆◆◆
6602 Melrose Ave at Highland Ave. Very attractive restaurant with several small dining areas. A/C. Open 5 pm-midnight; also Thurs & Fri 11:30 am-2:30 pm; closed 11/25 & 12/25. Cocktails. Valet parking. Reserv advised. AE, CB, DI, MC, VI.
⊗ (213) 935-4922

Four Oaks (68) Ethnic $$$ ◆◆◆
In Bel Air, 1/2 mi n of Sunset Blvd. 2181 N Beverly Glen. Charming century-old house. California-French cuisine. Sun brunch. A/C. Open 11:30 am-2 & 6-10 pm; Mon 6 pm-10 pm; Sun 10:30 am-2:30 & 6-10 pm. Cocktails & lounge. Valet parking. Reserv advised. MC, VI. ⊗ (310) 470-2265

Junior's Restaurant (55) Ethnic $ ◆
AAA In Rancho Park area, 1/4 blk n of Pico Blvd. 2379 Westwood Blvd. Very popular Jewish restaurant & delicatessen. Large selection of salads, sandwiches, entrees, kosher style foods & bakery. A/C. Children's menu. Open 6 am-11 pm; Fri-midnight; Sat 7 am-midnight; closed 11/25, 12/24 & Jewish holidays. Beer & wine. AE, MC, VI.
⊗ (310) 475-5771

La Bruschetta (66) Italian $$$ ◆◆
1/2 mi ne of I-405; Santa Monica Blvd. 1621 Westwood Blvd. A/C. Open noon-2 & 6-10:30 pm; Sat 6 pm-10:30 pm; closed Sun. Beer & wine. Valet parking. Reserv required. AE, CB, DI, MC, VI. ⊗ (310) 477-1052

La Chaumiere ㊻ French $$$ ◆◆◆
At Century Plaza Hotel and Tower. Dine in a relaxed, but refined setting; beautiful view. A/C. Dress code. Open 5:30 pm-10:30 pm. Cocktails & lounge. Valet parking. Reserv required. AE, DI, DS, MC, VI. ⊗ (310) 551-3360

Le Chardonnay (62) French $$$$ ◆◆◆◆
5 blks e of La Cienega Blvd. 8284 Melrose Ave. Elegant French bistro decor. A/C. Open noon-2 & 6-10 pm; Fri-11 pm; Sat 6 pm-11 pm; closed Sun & major holidays. Cocktails. Pay valet parking. Reserv advised. AE, DI, MC, VI.
⊗ (213) 655-8880

L'Orangerie (70) French $$$$ ◆◆◆◆◆
903 N La Cienega Blvd. Formal dining in a classic French atmosphere. A/C. Dress code. Open 6:30 am-11 pm; closed 1/1 & 12/25. Cocktails & lounge. Pay valet parking. Reserv advised. AE, CB, DI, MC, VI. ⊗ (310) 652-9770

Lunaria (69) French $$$ ◆◆◆
2 1/4 mi e of I-405; Santa Monica Blvd exit. 10351 Santa Monica Blvd. A/C. Open 11:30 am-2:30 & 6-10 pm; Sat 6 pm-10 pm; Sun 5:40 pm-9:30 pm; closed major holidays. Cocktails & lounge. Entertainment. Valet parking. Reserv required. AE, CB, DI, MC, VI. ⊗ (310) 282-8870

MaBe' ㊽ French $$$ ◆◆
1 blk e of Robertson Blvd. 8722 W 3rd St. European villa-like setting. A/C. Open 11 am-2 am; closed major holidays. Cocktails & lounge. Reserv advised. AE, MC, VI. ⊗ (310) 276-6223

Ma Maison (52) Continental $$$$ ◆◆◆
In Hotel Sofitel Ma Maison. Popular restaurant with casual atmosphere. A/C. Open 11:30 am-2:30 & 5:30-10:30 pm; Sat-11 pm; closed Sun & major holidays. Cocktails. Pay valet parking. Reserv advised. AE, CB, DI, MC, VI.
(310) 278-5444

The Old Spaghetti Factory ㊾ Italian $ ◆
In Hollywood; 2 blks e of Gower. 5939 Sunset Blvd. A popular, uniquely decorated, informal restaurant serving spaghetti with a large choice of sauces. A/C. Children's menu. Open 11:30 am-2 & 5-10 pm; Fri-11 pm; Sat 5 pm-11 pm; Sun 4 pm-10 pm; closed 11/25, 12/24 & 12/25. Cocktails & lounge. MC, VI. ⊗ (213) 469-7149

Orleans Restaurant (56) Ethnic $$ ◆◆◆
At Barrington. 11705 National Blvd. Nicely appointed restaurant serving expertly prepared Cajun-Creole cuisine. A/C. Open 11:30 am-2 & 6-9:30 pm; Fri-10:00 pm; Sat 5:00 pm-10:00 pm. Cocktails & lounge. Valet parking. Reserv advised. AE, DI, MC, VI. ⊗ (310) 479-4187

Patina (63) French $$$$ ◆◆◆◆
1 blk w of Cahuenga Blvd. 5955 Melrose Ave. Superbly prepared French & California cuisine. A/C. Open 11:30 am-2 & 6-9:30 pm; Mon 6 pm-9:30 pm; Sat 5:30 pm-10 pm; Sun 6 pm-9:30 pm. Cocktails & lounge. Pay valet parking. Reserv advised. AE, MC, VI. ⊗ (213) 467-1108

Primi (61) Italian $$$ ◆◆◆
2 1/4 mi ne of I-10, Overland Ave exit. 10543 W Pico Blvd. A/C. Open 11:30 am-2:30 & 5-11 pm; Sun 5:30 pm-10 pm; closed major holidays. Cocktails. Valet parking. Reserv advised. AE, CB, DI, MC, VI. ⊗ (310) 475-9235

Red Car Grill ㊹ American $$$ ◆◆◆
In Ramada West Hollywood. Nice selection of American cuisine served in comfortable surroundings. A/C. Open noon-2:30 & 5:30-10 pm; Sat 5:30 pm-11 pm; Sun 5:30 pm-10 pm; closed major holidays. Cocktails & lounge. Valet parking. AE, CB, DI, MC, VI. ⊗ (310) 652-9263

Reuben's (59) American $$ ◆
In Westchester area. 6531 S Sepulveda Blvd. Nice selection of prime rib, steaks & seafood. A/C. Early bird specials; children's menu. Open 11:30 am-10:30 pm; Fri & Sat-11:30 pm; Sun 10:30 am-2:30 & 4-10:30 pm. Cocktails & lounge. Entertainment. AE, DI, DS, MC, VI. ⊗ (213) 776-1300

Sisley Italian Kitchen ㊺ Italian $$ ◆◆
2 1/4 mi nw of I-10, Overland Ave exit, in Westside Pavilion Shopping Center. 10800 W Pico Blvd. A nice selection of Northern & Southern Italian cuisine. A/C. Open 11 am-10 pm; Fri & Sat-10:30 pm. Cocktails. Reserv advised. AE, MC, VI. ⊗ (310) 446-3030

(See LOS ANGELES (Central & Western Areas) spotting map pages A212 & A213)

Trattoria Grande **57**   Northern Italian $$$ ◆◆◆
In Westin Hotel-Los Angeles Airport. Attractive dining room. Italian oriented menu featuring homemade pasta & fresh seafood. A/C. Open 11:30 am-2:30 & 6-11 pm; Sat & Sun from 6 pm; closed 11/25 & 12/25. Cocktails. AE, DI, DS, MC, VI.
                                                                    ⊗ (310) 216-5858

Trumps **50**   American $$$ ◆◆◆
In West Hollywood. 8764 Melrose Ave at Robertson. Popular restaurant featuring California cuisine. Afternoon tea, 3:30 pm-5:30 pm Mon-Sat. A/C. Open 11:45 am-3 & 6-11:30 pm; Fri & Sat-1 am; closed Sun, 1/1, 7/4 & 12/25. Cocktails & lounge. Valet parking. Reserv advised. AE, DI, MC, VI.
                                                                    ⊗ (310) 855-1480

LOS ANGELES (San Fernando Valley) (See LOS ANGELES (San Fernando Valley) AREA spotting map page A236; see index starting below)

Index of Establishments on the LOS ANGELES (San Fernando Valley) AREA Spotting Map

---

Airtel Plaza Hotel 34   Rates Guaranteed   *Motor Inn* ◆◆◆
All year .... 2P/1B .... 69.00 2P/2B .... 69.00 XP 10
268 units. 3/4 mi w of I-405; exit Sherman Way. 7277 Valjean Ave at Sherman Way. (Van Nuys, 91406) Adjacent to Van Nuys Airport. Spacious rooms. A/C; C/CATV; free & pay movies; radios; phones. Htd pool; whirlpools; 14 rooms with whirlpool tub; parking spaces for private planes; exercise rm. No pets. AE, DI, DS, MC, VI. ● Dining rm & coffeeshop; 6:30 am-10 pm; $10-$18; cocktails. FAX (818) 785-8864 *(See ad p A237)*
                                                    ⊗ Ⓢ Ⓓ Ⓚ (818) 997-7676

Best Western Canoga Park Motor Inn 42   AAA Special Value Rates   *Motor Inn* ◆◆
All year 1P 49.00- 59.00 2P/1B 54.00- 64.00 2P/2B 54.00- 64.00 XP 5 F
Senior discount. 46 units. 1 1/2 mi n of US 101. 20122 Vanowen St at Winnetka Ave. (Canoga Park, 91306) A/C; C/CATV; movies; radios; phones; comb or shower baths. Htd pool; sauna; whirlpool. Small pets only. 8 efficiencies with microwave, $10 extra. Wkly & monthly rates avail. AE, DI, DS, MC, VI. ● Coffeeshop; 7 am-11 am; $5-$7; cocktails. FAX (818) 883-1202 *(See ad below)*
                                                              Ⓓ (818) 883-1200

Best Western Mission Hills Inn 49   Rates Subject to Change   *Motel* ◆◆
6/21-9/15 [CP] 1P .... 63.00 2P/1B .... 68.00 2P/2B .... 72.00 XP 5
9/16-6/20 [CP] 1P .... 59.00 2P/1B .... 64.00 2P/2B .... 68.00 XP 5
Senior discount. 119 units. 1 blk s of SR 118, 1/4 mi e of I-405. 10621 Sepulveda Blvd. (Mission Hills, 91345) Patios or balconies. Refrigerators; A/C; C/CATV; movies; rental VCPs. Radios; phones. Coin laundry. Pool. No pets. AE, CB, DI, MC, VI. Coffeeshop adjacent. FAX (818) 895-1446
                                                    ⊗ Ⓓ (818) 891-1771

Carriage Inn 31   Rates Guaranteed   *Motor Inn* ◆◆◆
All year .... 2P/1B .... 59.00 2P/2B .... 59.00 XP F
183 units. Adjacent to I-405, Burbank Blvd exit. 5525 Sepulveda Blvd. (Sherman Oaks, 91411) A/C; C/TV; pay movies; radios; phones. Htd pool; whirlpool. No pets. 13 rooms with microwave & refrigerator, $5 extra. AE, DI, DS, MC, VI. ● Dining rm & coffeeshop; 6 am-10 pm; $9-$16; live piano music Fri & Sat night; cocktails. FAX (818) 782-9373 *(See ad p A238)*
                                                    ⊗ Ⓓ (818) 787-2300

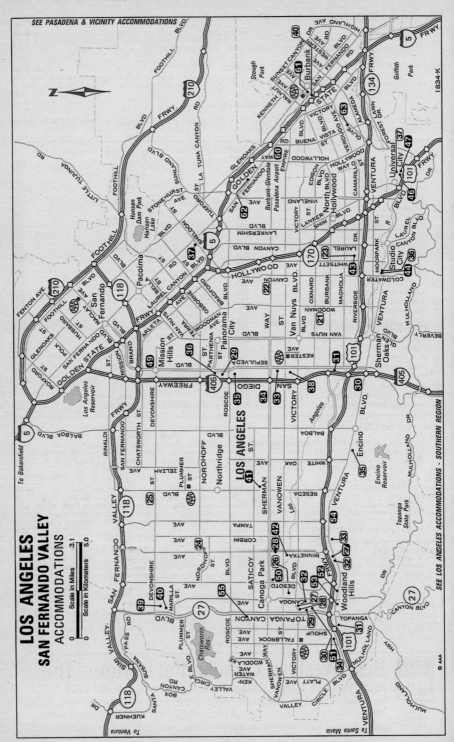

LOS ANGELES
SAN FERNANDO VALLEY
ACCOMMODATIONS

Scale in Miles
Scale in Kilometers

(See LOS ANGELES (San Fernando Valley) spotting map page A236)

The Chatsworth Hotel 55   Rates Subject to Change   Motor Inn   ◆◆◆
All year   1P .... 79.00 2P/1B .... 79.00 2P/2B .... 79.00 XP 10   F
Senior discount. 150 units. 2 mi s of US 118, exit Topanga Canyon Rd. 9777 Topanga Canyon Rd. (91311) A/C; C/TV;
movies; radios; phones. Coin laundry. Htd pool; whirlpool; exercise rm. 6 suites, $130-$165. Wkly & monthly rates avail.
AE, DI, MC, VI. ● Restaurant; 6:30 am-10 pm; $11.95-$16.95. FAX (818) 998-3573   ⊗ Ⓢ Ⓓ Ⓚ (818) 709-7054

Clarion Suites Warner Palms 28   Rates Guaranteed   Suites Motel   ◆◆◆
All year [BP]   1P 69.00- 99.00 2P/1B 69.00- 99.00 2P/2B 69.00- 109.00 XP 10   F
100 units. 1/2 blk w of Winnetka Ave. 20200 Sherman Way. (Canoga Park, 91306) 1-bedroom suites with living
room. Some patios or balconies. Refrigerators; A/C; C/CATV; movies; VCPs. Radios; phones. Coin laundry. Pool;
lighted tennis-1 court. No pets. Microwaves. Complimentary beverages each evening. AE, DI, DS, MC, VI.
FAX (818) 228-8268 (See ad p A240)   ⊗ Ⓓ (818) 883-8250

Comfort Inn North Hills/Van Nuys 36   AAA Special Value Rates   Motel   ◆◆
All year   1P 43.00- 60.00 2P/1B 50.00- 65.00 2P/2B .... 65.00 XP 5   F
59 units. 3/4 mi ne of I-405; exit Roscoe Blvd. 8647 Sepulveda Blvd. (North Hills, 91343) 43 refrigerators; A/C;
C/CATV; movies; radios; phones; comb or shower baths. Small pool. No pets. AE, DI, DS, MC, VI.
FAX (818) 893-1536   ⊗ Ⓓ Ⓚ (818) 893-3776

(See LOS ANGELES (San Fernando Valley) spotting map page A236)

Choose an establishment with the ⊛ next to its listing!

(See LOS ANGELES (San Fernando Valley) spotting map page A236)

Emerson Inn 37   Rates Subject to Change   *Motel*   ◆◆
🌀 All year   1P 42.00- 54.00 2P/1B 42.00- 54.00 2P/2B 50.00- 54.00 XP 4
30 units. 3/4 mi n of I-5, then just w of Sheldon; exit Sheldon. 9417 San Fernando Rd. (Sun Valley, 91352) 3-story, no elevator. Refrigerators; A/C; C/CATV; movies; radios; phones. No pets. 4 rooms with whirlpool tub, $54 for up to 2 persons. AE, DS, MC, VI.   ⊗ Ⓓ ⬢ (818) 768-6600

Holiday Inn-Van Nuys 35   AAA Special Value Rates   *Motor Inn*   ◆◆
🌀 All year   1P 64.00-100.00 2P/1B 76.00- 112.00 2P/2B 76.00- 112.00 XP 12   F
130 units. 1/2 blk e of I-405, Roscoe Blvd exit. 8244 Orion St. (Van Nuys, 91406) A/C; C/CATV; free & pay movies; radios; phones. Rental refrigerators. Coin laundry. Htd pool; exercise rm. No pets. AE, DI, DS, MC, VI. ● Dining rm; 6 am-2 & 5:30-10 pm; $8-$15; cocktails.   ⊗ Ⓓ ⬢ (818) 989-5010

Holiday Inn-Woodland Hills 53   AAA Special Value Rates   *Motor Inn*   ◆◆◆
All year   1P 88.00-102.00 2P/1B 88.00-102.00 2P/2B 98.00-112.00 XP 10   F
127 units. Adjacent to US 101, DeSoto St exit. 21101 Ventura Blvd. (Woodland Hills, 91364) A/C; C/TV; free & pay movies; radios; phones. Coin laundry. Pool. No pets. Wkly & monthly rates avail. AE, DI, DS, MC, VI. ● Dining rm; 6:30 am-2 & 5-10 pm; $8-$16; cocktails. FAX (818) 340-6550   ⊗ Ⓓ ⬢ (818) 883-6110

Howard Johnson Lodge 41   Rates Subject to Change   *Motel*   ◆◆
🌀 All year [CP]   1P .... 50.00 2P/1B .... 55.00 2P/2B .... 55.00 XP 5   F
Senior discount. 74 units. 2 blks w of Sherman Way. 7432 Reseda Blvd. (Reseda, 91335) Refrigerators; A/C; C/TV; movies; radios; phones. Small pool; whirlpool; 6 rooms with whirlpool; 1 with sauna. No pets. 17 suites with microwave & refrigerator. Wkly rates avail. AE, DI, DS, MC, VI. *(See ad p A238)* ⊗ Ⓓ ⬢ (818) 344-0324

Mikado Best Western Motor Hotel 43   Rates Guaranteed   *Motor Inn*   ◆◆◆
🌀 6/1-9/15 & 12/16-1/31 [BP]   1P .... 85.00 2P/1B .... 95.00 2P/2B .... 95.00 XP 10   F
2/1-5/31 & 9/16-12/15 [BP]   1P .... 80.00 2P/1B .... 90.00 2P/2B .... 90.00 XP 10
Senior discount. 58 units. Adjacent to US 101, between Coldwater Canyon & Laurel Canyon Ave exits. 12600 Riverside Dr. (North Hollywood, 91607) 9 refrigerators; A/C; C/TV; radios; phones. Pool; whirlpool. No pets. 2 1-bedroom efficiencies & 1 1-bedroom apartment, $100-$150. AE, DI, DS, MC, VI. ● Restaurant; 11:30 am-2:30 & 5:30-10:30 pm; Sat & Sun 5:30 pm-9:30 pm; $16-$20; cocktails. Also restaurant, see separate listing. *(See ad below)*   Ⓓ (818) 763-9141

Radisson Valley Center Los Angeles 30   Rates Subject to Change   *Hotel*   ◆◆◆
🌀 All year   1P 84.00-130.00 2P/1B 94.00-140.00 2P/2B 114.00-120.00 XP 10   F
215 units. At jct of I-405 & US 101, 2 blks w of Sepulveda Blvd. 15433 Ventura Blvd. (Sherman Oaks, 91403) Formerly Valley Hilton. A/C; C/CATV; free & pay movies; radios; phones. Rental refrigerators. Htd pool; whirlpool; exercise rm. Pay parking ramp. No pets. Monthly rates avail. AE, DI, DS, MC, VI. ● Dining rm; 6:30 am-10 pm; Fri & Sat-midnight; $11-$18; cocktails; entertainment. FAX (818) 981-3175 *(See ad p A240)*   ⊗ Ⓢ Ⓓ (818) 981-5400

(See LOS ANGELES (San Fernando Valley) spotting map page A236)

Ramada Limited 54 ◆◆
All year [CP]   Rates Subject to Change   *Motel*
1P 59.00- 65.00   2P/1B   59.00- 65.00   2P/2B   65.00- 75.00 XP 8
Senior discount. 47 units. 1/4 mi s of US 101; exit Tampa. 19170 Ventura Blvd. (91356) Formerly Chalet Lodge.
Refrigerators; A/C; C/CATV; movies; radios; phones; shower or comb baths. Htd pool; whirlpool. No pets. AE,
DI, DS, MC, VI. Coffeeshop adjacent. FAX (818) 344-3112   (D) (818) 345-9410

7-Star Suites Hotel 39 ◆◆
All year [CP]   AAA Special Value Rates   *Motel* F
1P 59.00- 159.00   2P/1B   59.00- 159.00   2P/2B   59.00- 159.00 XP 7   F
75 units. 3/4 mi w of De Soto Ave. 21603 Devonshire St. (Chatsworth, 91311) Refrigerators; A/C; C/CATV;
movies; radios; phones. Small htd pool; whirlpool; 36 rooms with whirlpool. No pets. Wkly & monthly rates avail.
AE, DI, MC, VI. FAX (818) 718-6666   ⊗ Ⓢ Ⓓ 🅶 (818) 998-8888

Sheraton Universal Hotel 46 ◆◆◆
All year   Rates Subject to Change   *Hotel*
1P 140.00- 200.00   2P/1B   160.00- 220.00   ....   XP 20   F
446 units. Adjacent to US 101, exit Lankershim Blvd. 333 Universal Terrace Pkwy. (Universal City, 91608) At Universal Studios. Check-in 3 pm. A/C; C/CATV; free & pay movies; radios; phones. Htd pool; whirlpool; exercise
rm. Pay valet garage. No pets. Reserv deposit required. AE, DI, DS, MC, VI. ● Restaurant; 6 am-11 pm; $11-$20;
cocktails. FAX (818) 985-4980   ⊗ Ⓢ Ⓓ 🅶 (818) 980-1212

Sportsmen's Lodge Hotel 44 ◆◆◆
All year   Rates Guaranteed   *Motor Inn*
1P 98.00- 108.00   2P/1B   108.00- 118.00   2P/2B   108.00- 118.00 XP 10   F
Senior discount. 193 units. 1 mi s of US 101, Coldwater Canyon Ave exit. 12825 Ventura Blvd. (Studio
City, 91604) Many balconies. A/C; C/CATV; movies; radios; phones. Htd pool; whirlpool; exercise rm. No pets.
Monthly rates avail. AE, DI, DS, MC, VI. ● Restaurant & coffeeshop; 6:30 am-10 pm; $10-$18; cocktails; enter-
tainment. FAX (213) 877-3898 *(See ad p A243)*   ⊗ (D) (818) 769-4700

Summerfield Suites Hotel 40 ◆◆◆
Sun-Thurs [BP]   1P .... 128.00   2P/1B   .... 128.00   2P/2B   .... 158.00 XP
Fri & Sat [BP]   1P .... 80.00   2P/1B   .... 80.00   2P/2B   .... 130.00 XP
114 units. 1/4 blk e of Topanga Canyon Blvd. 21902 Lassen St. (Chatsworth, 91311) 1- & 2-bedroom suites with living
room & kitchen. Many fireplaces. 3-story building, no elevator. Check-in 3 pm. A/C; C/CATV; movies; VCPs. Radios;
phones. 27 2-bedrm units. Coin laundry. Htd pool; whirlpool; exercise rm. Microwaves. Pets, $6 extra charge; $250 deposit required, $50-$75 non-refundable. Complimentary beverages each evening. AE, DI, DS, MC, VI.
FAX (818) 773-0351   ⊗ Ⓢ Ⓓ 🅶 (818) 773-0707

Travelodge Van Nuys-Sepulveda 33 ◆◆
All year [CP]   1P .... 45.00   2P/1B   .... 45.00   2P/2B   .... 45.00 XP 6
Senior discount. 75 units. 3/4 mi se of I-405, Sherman Way exit. 6909 Sepulveda Blvd. (Van Nuys, 91405) Refrig-
erators; A/C; C/CATV; movies; radios; phones. Small htd pool. Reserv deposit required. AE, DI, DS, MC, VI.
FAX (818) 782-0239 *(See ad p A241)*   (D) 🅶 (818) 787-5400

(See LOS ANGELES (San Fernando Valley) spotting map page A236)

Universal City Hilton & Towers **47**   Rates Subject to Change   *Hotel*   ◆◆◆
🏨 Sun-Thurs   1P 129.00- 180.00   2P/1B   129.00- 180.00   2P/2B 129.00- 180.00   XP 20   F
Fri & Sat   1P 105.00- 145.00   2P/1B   105.00- 145.00   2P/2B 105.00- 145.00   XP 20   F
450 units. Adjacent to US 101, exit Lankershim Blvd. 555 Universal Terrace Pkwy. (Universal City, 91608)
Check-in 3 pm. 20 refrigerators; A/C; C/CATV; free & pay movies; radios; phones. Htd pool; whirlpool; exercise
rm. Pay valet garage. No pets. AE, DI, DS, MC, VI. ● 2 dining rms; 6:30 am-11 pm; $20-$30; cocktails.
FAX (818) 509-2031   ⊗ Ⓢ Ⓓ Ⓚ   (818) 506-2500

Vagabond Inn **27**   Rates Subject to Change   *Motor Inn*   ◆◆
🏨 All year [CP]   1P 45.00- 60.00   2P/1B   50.00- 65.00   2P/2B   55.00- 70.00   XP 5   F
100 units. Adjacent to US 101, Winnetka Ave exit. 20157 Ventura Blvd. (Woodland Hills, 91364) A/C; C/CATV;
movies; VCPs. Radios; phones; comb or shower baths. Rental refrigerators. Htd pool; whirlpool. Small pets
only, $5 extra charge. AE, DI, DS, MC, VI. ● Coffeeshop; 24 hours; $5-$8; beer & wine. FAX (818) 716-5333 *(See
ad p A243)*   ⊗ Ⓓ Ⓚ   (818) 347-8080

Voyager Motor Inn **38**   AAA Special Value Rates   *Motel*   ◆◆
🏨 All year [CP]   1P 39.00- 48.00   2P/1B   44.00- 50.00   2P/2B   46.00- 65.00   XP 5   F
122 units. 3/4 mi ne of I-405; exit Victory Blvd. 6500 Sepulveda Blvd. (Van Nuys, 91411) A/C; C/CATV; movies;
phones. 39 efficiencies. Coin laundry. Htd pool; whirlpool. No pets. Wkly rates avail. AE, DI, DS, MC, VI.
FAX (818) 782-3718   ⊗ Ⓓ   (818) 997-6007

Warner Center Hilton & Towers **32**   Rates Subject to Change   *Hotel*   ◆◆◆
All year   1P 99.00- 149.00   2P/1B   119.00- 169.00   2P/2B 119.00- 169.00   XP 15
327 units. 1/2 blk s of Victory Blvd. 6360 Canoga Ave. (Woodland Hills, 91367) Check-in 3 pm. 30 refrigerators; A/C;
C/CATV; pay movies; radios; phones. Fee for: health club. Pay valet garage. No pets. AE, DI, DS, MC,
VI. ● Restaurant; 6 am-11 pm; $12-$14; cocktails; entertainment. FAX (818) 595-1090   ⊗ Ⓢ Ⓓ Ⓚ   (818) 595-1000

Warner Center Marriott Hotel **51**   Rates Subject to Change   *Hotel*   ◆◆◆◆
All year   1P 150.00- 170.00   2P/1B   170.00- 190.00   2P/2B -170.00- 190.00   XP 15
463 units. 3/4 mi n of US 101, exit Topanga Canyon Blvd. 21850 Oxnard St. (Woodland Hills, 91367) Check-in 3 pm. 30
refrigerators; A/C; C/CATV; movies; radios; phones. Coin laundry. Htd indoor/outdoor pool; saunas; whirlpool; exercise
rm. Fee for: massage. Pay valet garage. Monthly rates avail. AE, DI, DS, MC, VI. ● 2 dining rms; 6:30 am-11 pm; $6-
$20; cocktails. Also, Pearls, see separate listing. FAX (818) 347-0007   ⊗ Ⓢ Ⓓ Ⓚ   (818) 887-4800

Warner Center Motor Inn **50**   AAA Special Value Rates   *Motor Inn*   ◆◆
🏨 All year [CP]   1P 40.00- 65.00   2P/1B   45.00- 70.00   2P/2B   45.00- 70.00   XP 5
90 units. 1/4 blk s of Sherman Way. 7132 DeSoto Ave. (Canoga Park, 91303) Refrigerators; A/C; C/CATV; movies;
VCPs. 65 radios; phones; shower or comb baths. 4 efficiencies. Coin laundry. Htd pool. Pets, $8 extra charge. 4
1-bedroom apartments, $55-$75 for 2-4 persons. Microwave rental, $5. 5 rooms with whirlpool, $60-$80. Wkly
rates avail. Reserv deposit required. AE, CB, DI, MC, VI. ● Restaurant; 11:30 am-10 pm; closed Mon; $7-$15;
cocktails. FAX (818) 992-8885 *(See ad p A243)*   ⊗ Ⓓ Ⓚ   (818) 346-5400

Warner Gardens Motel **52**   Rates Guaranteed   *Motel*   ◆
🏨 All year   1P .... 46.00   2P/1B   46.00- 51.00   2P/2B   50.00- 58.00   XP   F
Senior discount. 39 units. 2 blks e of Topanga Canyon Blvd. 21706 Ventura Blvd. (Woodland Hills, 91364) A/C;
C/CATV; movies; phones. Small pool; whirlpool. No pets. Wkly & monthly rates avail. AE, CB, DI, MC, VI.
FAX (818) 704-1062   ⊗ Ⓓ Ⓚ   (818) 992-4426

RESTAURANTS

Adagio Ristorante **34**   Northern Italian $$$ ◆◆
1/2 mi w of Shoup. 22841 Ventura Blvd. Selection of pastas, veal, chicken, seafood, beef & lamb. A/C. Children's menu.
Open 11:30 am-2:30 & 5:30-10 pm; Sat & Sun from 5:30 pm; closed Mon, 1/1, 7/4, 11/25 & 12/25. Cocktails. Reserv
advised weekends. AE, DI, MC, VI.   (818) 346-5279

Adam's Restaurant **35**   American $$ ◆
In Encino; 2 blks e of White Oak Ave. 17500 Ventura Blvd. Casual, informal atmosphere. Features barbecue ribs,
chicken, seafood, mesquite broiled steaks, pasta & salad bar. A/C. Children's menu. Open 11:30 am-2:30 & 5-10 pm; Fri
& Sat-11 pm; Sun 10 am-2 & 4-10 pm; closed 11/25 & 12/25. Cocktails & lounge. AE, DI, DS, MC, VI.
    ⊗ (818) 990-7427

Black Angus **27**   American $$ ◆◆
In Woodland Hills; 1 blk e of Topanga Canyon Blvd. 21720 Victory Blvd. Formerly Velvet Turtle Restaurant. Attractive
restaurant featuring lamb, beef, seafood & chicken. A/C. Early bird specials; children's menu. Open 11:30 am-10 pm; Fri
& Sat-11 pm; Sun 11 am-10 pm; closed 12/25. Cocktails & lounge. Reserv advised Fri & Sat. AE, DI, DS, MC, VI.
    ⊗ Ⓚ (818) 703-6160

(See LOS ANGELES (San Fernando Valley) spotting map page A236)

Bob Burns Restaurant ㉙   American $$ ◆◆
Woodland Hills; 1 blk e of Topanga Canyon Blvd. 21821 Oxnard St. Attractive Scottish decor. Nice selection of seafood, steaks, prime rib, chicken, lamb & pasta. Sandwich Bar $5.25-$7.45. A/C. Open 11:30 am-10 pm, Fri & Sat-11 pm; Sun 10:30 am-3 & 4-10 pm; closed 1/1, 5/31, 7/4 & 9/6. Cocktails & lounge. Entertainment. AE, DI, DS, MC, VI.
⊗ ⓵ (818) 883-2145

Brunello Ristorante ㉝   Continental $$ ◆◆
Tarzana; 1/2 mi w of Tampa Ave, in the Capri Plaza. 19598 Ventura Blvd. Small, charming restaurant with a nice selection of Italian Continental cuisine. Sun brunch. A/C. Open 11 am-3 & 5-10 pm; Fri-11 pm; Sat 5 pm-11 pm; Sun noon-9 pm. Cocktails & lounge. Reserv advised. AE, DI, DS, MC, VI.
⊗ (818) 708-9922

Charley Brown's Restaurant ㉜   American $$ ◆◆
Woodland Hills, 1 mi w of Winnetka Ave. 20401 Ventura Blvd. Nice selection of steaks, seafood & chicken. Informal atmosphere. A/C. Early bird specials; children's menu. Open 11:30 am-2:30 & 5-10 pm; Fri & Sat-11 pm; Sun 10 am-2 & 4-9 pm. Cocktails & lounge. AE, DI, DS, MC, VI.
⊗ (818) 348-1812

Ellie's Old Heidelberg ㉑   German $$ ◆◆
Van Nuys; 1/2 blk w of Woodman Ave. 13726 Oxnard St. Old World atmosphere. A/C. Children's menu. Open 11 am-10 pm; Fri & Sat-11 pm; Sun 4 pm-10 pm; closed Mon, 1/1 & 12/25. Cocktails & lounge. Valet parking. AE, MC, VI.
⊗ (818) 997-9396

Furr's Cafeteria ㉒   American $ ◆
North Hollywood; 3/4 mi w of SR 170, Hollywood Frwy. 13055 Sherman Way. Nice selection of salads, entrees & desserts. Buffet, $5.49. A/C. Open 11 am-8 pm; Fri & Sat-8:30 pm; closed 12/25. MC, VI.
⊗ ⓵ (818) 982-8366

The Garden Room ㊱   American $$ ◆◆
At the Sportsmen's Lodge Hotel. 12833 Ventura Blvd. Steak, seafood, chicken, duck, trout, fetuccini, veal & salads. Bread & pastries baked on premises. Mon night Glatt Kosher dinners. Sun brunch, 10:30 am-2 pm. A/C. Early bird specials; children's menu. Open 5:30 pm-9:30 pm; Sat-10 pm; Sun 10:30 am-2 & 4:30-9 pm; closed 1/1 & 12/25. Cocktails & lounge. Entertainment & dancing. Minimum, $5. Reserv advised. AE, MC, VI.
⊗ (818) 984-0202

Lautrec ㉛   French $$ ◆◆
In Woodland Hills; 2 blks w of Topanga Canyon Blvd. 22160 Ventura Blvd. Very attractive, semiformal restaurant. Outdoor patio dining weather permitting. A/C. Open 11 am-3 & 5-10 pm; Sat-11 pm; Sun from 10 am; closed 1/1, 7/4, & 12/25. Cocktails & lounge. Pay valet parking. Reserv advised. AE, DI, MC, VI.
⊗ (818) 704-1185

Mikado Restaurant ㉓   **Ethnic**   **$$**   ◆◆
⓮ At Mikado Best Western Motor Hotel. Features Japanese food & sushi bar. Casual atmosphere. A/C. Open 11:30 am-2:30 & 5:30-10:30 pm; Sat from 5:30 pm; Sun 5:30 pm-9:30 pm; closed 11/26. Cocktails & lounge. Reserv advised Fri evenings. AE, DI, DS, MC, VI. *(See ad p A239)*
⊗ (818) 763-9141

The Olive Garden ㉔   Italian $$ ◆◆
On sw corner of Nordhoff Pl & Corbin St. 19724 Nordhoff Pl. Selection of pasta, chicken, veal, lasagna & spaghetti. Casual atmosphere. A/C. Children's menu. Open 11 am-10 pm; Fri & Sat-11 pm. Cocktails & lounge. AE, DI, DS, MC, VI.
⊗ (818) 772-6090

Pearls ㉚   Seafood $$ ◆◆◆
In Warner Center Marriott Hotel. Nicely decorated dining room specializing in fresh seafood. Semiformal atmosphere. A/C. Cocktails & lounge. Dancing. Reserv advised; accepted up to 10 pm. AE, DI, DS, MC, VI.
⊗ (818) 887-4800

Reubens ㉖   American $$ ◆◆
1/4 mi sw of US 101; exit Desoto St. 21055 Ventura Blvd. Steaks & fresh seafood, informal atmosphere. A/C. Early bird specials; children's menu. Open 11:30 am-2:30 & 5-10 pm; Fri & Sat 5 pm-10:30 pm; Sun 5 pm-9:30 pm. Cocktails & lounge. Entertainment & dancing. Reserv advised Fri & Sat. AE, DI, DS, MC, VI.
⊗ (818) 347-1083

Reuben's ㉕   American $$ ◆◆
Northridge; 1/4 mi w of Reseda Blvd. 18711 Devonshire St. Sun buffet brunch. Selection of steaks & fresh seafood. A/C. Early bird specials; children's menu. Open 11:30 am-2:30 & 5-10 pm; Fri-11 pm; Sat 5 pm-11 pm; Sun 10 am-2 & 5-10 pm. Cocktails & lounge. Entertainment & dancing. Reserv advised. AE, DI, DS, MC, VI.
⊗ ⓵ (818) 363-3115

Reuben's Summer House ㉘   American $$ ◆◆
In Woodland Hills; 1/2 blk e of Topanga Canyon Blvd. 21870 Victory Blvd. Beautifully decorated. Features prime rib, steak & seafood. A/C. Early bird specials; children's menu. Open 11:30 am-3 & 5-10 pm; Fri & Sat-11 pm; Sun 10 am-2 & 5-10 pm. Cocktails & lounge. Entertainment. AE, DI, DS, MC, VI.
⊗ (818) 883-3030

Victoria Station ㊲   American $$ ◆◆
At entrance to Universal Studios Hollywood, from US 101, exit Lankershim Blvd. 100 Universal Terrace Pkwy. Authentic replica of the Victoria Station in London. Fresh seafood, steaks, chicken, pastas, salad, sandwiches & prime rib. Patio dining in summer months. A/C. Open 11:30 am-4 & 5-10 pm; Fri & Sat-11 pm; closed 11/25 & 12/25. Cocktails & lounge. Entertainment. Valet parking. Reserv advised. AE, MO, VI.
⊗ (818) 622-9190

LOS BANOS — 14,500

Bonanza Motel   **Rates Subject to Change**   *Motor Inn*   ◆◆
⓮ All year   1P 30.50- 33.50   2P/1B   36.50- 39.50   2P/2B   39.50- 42.50 XP 4
Senior discount. 38 units. On SR 152. 349 W Pacheco Blvd. (93635) A/C; C/CATV; radios; phones; comb or shower baths. Small pool. 1 2-bedroom unit, $60 for up tp 4 persons. Pets, $3 extra charge also $20 deposit. Reserv deposit required. AE, CB, MC, VI. Coffeeshop adjacent.
⊗ Ⓓ (209) 826-3871

RESTAURANT

Carlo's   Continental $$$ ◆◆◆
⓮ On SR 152. 400 Pacheco Blvd. Varied menu. Few Italian entrees. A/C. Children's menu. Open 11:30 am-10 pm; Sun-9:30 pm; closed 1/1, 4/11, 11/25 & 12/25. Cocktails & lounge. Minimum $6. Reserv advised. AE, MC, VI.
⊗ ⓵ (209) 826-2331

LOS GATOS — 27,400

La Hacienda Inn   **Rates Subject to Change**   *Motor Inn*   ◆◆◆
⓮ All year [CP]   1P 78.00- 105.00   2P/1B   83.00- 110.00   2P/2B   .... 89.00 XP 10
Senior discount. 20 units. 1 mi w on SR 9. 18840 Saratoga-Los Gatos Rd. (95030) Attractively landscaped. Some large units, patios, few studios; 6 fireplace units. Refrigerators; A/C; C/TV; radios; phones; shower or comb baths. 3 kitchens. Pool; whirlpool. No pets. Wkly & monthly rates avail. Reserv deposit required. AE, CB, DI, MC, VI. Restaurant adjacent. FAX (408) 354-7590
Ⓢ Ⓓ (408) 354-9230

Lodge at Villa Felice   AAA Special Value Rates   *Motor Inn*   ◆◆◆◆
⊛ All year [CP]   1P 98.00- 119.00   2P/1B   98.00- 119.00   2P/2B   98.00- 119.00   XP 10
33 units. 1 mi n between Blossom Hill Rd & Lark Ave. 15350 S Winchester Blvd. (95030) Many rooms with view
of Lake Vasona. Few rooms with whirlpool, fireplace, steam-shower. Check-in 3 pm. Refrigerators; A/C; C/CATV;
movies; radios; phones; comb or shower baths. 1 2-bedrm unit, 1 kitchen. Small pool; whirlpool. No pets. 1
2-bedroom apartment, $200 for 2 person. Reserv deposit required. AE, CB, DI, MC, VI. ● Restaurant, see sepa-
rate listing. FAX (408) 354-1826   ⊗ Ⓢ Ⓓ ⓐ (408) 395-6710

Los Gatos Lodge   AAA Special Value Rates   *Motor Inn*   ◆◆
All year [CP]   1P .... 79.00   2P/1B .... 89.00   2P/2B .... 89.00   XP 10   F
125 units. 11 mi sw of US 101; off SR 17 via E Los Gatos exit. 50 Saratoga Ave. (95032) Extensive landscaped grounds. Balconies & patios. A/C; C/CATV; radios; phones; comb or shower baths. 1 2-bedrm unit, 8 efficiencies. Coin laundry. Pool; putting green. Pets. 8 efficiency units, $119 for up to 2 persons. [MAP] avail. AE, DI, DS, MC, VI. ● Restaurant; 6:30 am-9:30 pm; Fri & Sat-10 pm; $10-$25; cocktails; entertainment. FAX (408) 354-5451   ⊗ Ⓓ (408) 354-3300

Los Gatos Motor Inn   Rates Subject to Change   *Motel*   ◆◆
All year [CP]   1P 62.00- 69.00   2P/1B 65.00- 74.00   2P/2B .... 75.00   XP 5   F
Senior discount. 60 units. 11 mi sw of US 101; off SR 17, via E Los Gatos exit. 55 Saratoga Ave. (95032) 6 refrigerators; A/C; C/TV; movies; phones; shower or comb baths. Pool. Reserv deposit required. AE, CB, DI, MC, VI. Restaurant opposite. FAX (408) 356-7502   ⊗ Ⓓ (408) 356-9191

Toll House Hotel   Rates Guaranteed   *Hotel*   ◆◆◆
All year   1P 89.00- 93.00   2P/1B 89.00- 93.00   2P/2B 89.00- 93.00   XP
Senior discount. 98 units. 1/4 mi w of jct I-880 & SR 9; exit SR 9, Santa Cruz Ave, 1 blk n. 140 S Santa Cruz Ave. (95030) Many rooms with balcony. Check-in 3 pm. 10 refrigerators; A/C; C/CATV; radios; phones. 6 rooms with whirlpool bath. Garage. No pets. AE, DI, MC, VI. ● Dining rm; 6 am-9 pm; Fri & Sat-10 pm; $13-$28; cocktails. FAX (408) 395-3730   ⊗ Ⓢ Ⓓ Ⓖ (408) 395-7070

Village Inn Motel   Rates Guaranteed   *Motel*   ◆◆
All year   1P 50.00- 52.00   2P/1B 55.00- 57.00   2P/2B .... 57.00   XP 5
23 units. 2 blks w; exit SR 17 via Saratoga-Los Gatos Rd. 235 W Main St. (95030) Refrigerators; A/C; C/TV; phones; shower or comb baths. 1 2-bedrm unit. Pool. No pets. Monthly rates avail. Reserv deposit required. AE, CB, DI, MC, VI. *(See ad below)*   ⊗ Ⓓ (408) 354-8120

RESTAURANTS

California Cafe   American $$$ ◆◆
In Old Town. 50 University Ave. Contemporary California cuisine in a casual, upscale atmosphere. A/C. Open 11:30 am-10 pm; Fri & Sat-10:30 pm; Sun 10 am-2:30 & 4:30-9 pm; closed 12/25. Cocktails & lounge. Reserv advised. AE, CB, DI, MC, VI.   ⊗ (408) 354-8118

La Hacienda Restaurant   Continental $$$ ◆◆
In La Hacienda Inn. Italian specialties. A/C. Children's menu. Open 11 am-11 pm; Sun 10 am-10 pm; closed 12/25. Cocktails & lounge. Entertainment. Minimum $8. Reserv advised. AE, DI, DS, MC, VI.   ⊗ (408) 354-6669

Villa Felice   Continental $$ ◆◆
Adjacent to Lodge at Villa Felice. Picturesque location overlooking Lake Vasona. Italian specialties & pastas. A/C. Dress code. Open 11:30 am-2 & 5-10 pm; Sun 10 am-2:30 & 3-9:30 pm; closed major holidays. Cocktails & lounge. Dancing. Minimum $5. Reserv advised. AE, DI, MC, VI.   ⊗ (408) 395-6711

LOS OLIVOS — 300

Los Olivos Grand Hotel   Rates Subject to Change   *Country Inn*   ◆◆◆◆
Fri & Sat   1P 210.00- 325.00   2P/1B 210.00- 325.00   2P/2B .... 230.00   XP
Sun-Thurs   1P 160.00- 300.00   2P/1B 160.00- 300.00   2P/2B .... 180.00   XP
21 units. 1/2 mi s of SR 154. 2860 Grand Ave. (PO Box 526, 93441) Charming country inn atmosphere. Spacious, beautifully decorated rooms with gas fireplaces. Check-in 3 pm. Refrigerators; A/C; C/CATV; radios; phones. Htd pool; whirlpool. No pets. Reserv deposit required; 3 days refund notice. AE, DS, MC, VI. Remington's Restaurant, see separate listing. FAX (805) 688-1942   ⊗ Ⓢ Ⓓ (805) 688-7788

RESTAURANTS

Mattei's Tavern   American $$ ◆
On SR 154. Dining in a historic stagecoach stop. Nice selection of steaks, prime rib, seafood & other entrees. A/C. Open 5:30 pm-9 pm; Sat & Sun noon-3 & 4:30-10 pm; closed 12/24 & 12/25. Cocktails & lounge. Reserv advised. MC, VI.   (805) 688-4820

Remington's Restaurant   Continental $$ ◆◆◆
In Los Olivos Grand Hotel. A/C. Open 7 am-3 & 5:30-9 pm; Sat & Sun 8 am-3 & 5:30-10 pm. Cocktails. AE, DI, MC, VI.   ⊗ (805) 688-7788

LOS OSOS

Best Western Sea Pines Golf Resort   Rates Subject to Change   *Motor Inn*   ◆◆◆
6/1-9/15   1P 89.00- 119.00   2P/1B 89.00- 119.00   2P/2B 89.00- 119.00   XP 10   F
9/16-5/31   1P 69.00-109.00   2P/1B 69.00-109.00   2P/2B 69.00-109.00   XP 10   F
Senior discount. 48 units. On Sea Pines Golf Course. 1945 S Solano St. (93402) 13 rooms with bay view & 14 with fairway views. A/C; C/CATV; radios; phones. Putting green. Fee for: 9 hole executive golf course. No pets. 15 rooms with fireplace. 6 1-bedroom suites with fireplace, $139-$149. AE, DI, DS, MC, VI. ● Restaurant; 9 am-3 & 5-9 pm; Sat & Sun from 8 am; closed Mon & Tues for dinner; $10.95-$19.95; beer & wine. *(See ad p A285)*   ⊗ Ⓓ (805) 528-5252

RESTAURANT

Rodney's   Continental $$ ◆◆
1/4 mi s of Santa Ysabel St. 1315 2nd St. Small charming restaurant. Selections of steaks, veal, quail, ribs, chicken, lamb, fettuccine & fresh seafood. Early bird specials; children's menu. Open 4:30 pm-9 pm, Fri & Sat-10 pm; closed Tues & 1/10-1/22. Beer & wine. MC, VI.   ⊗ (805) 528-0459

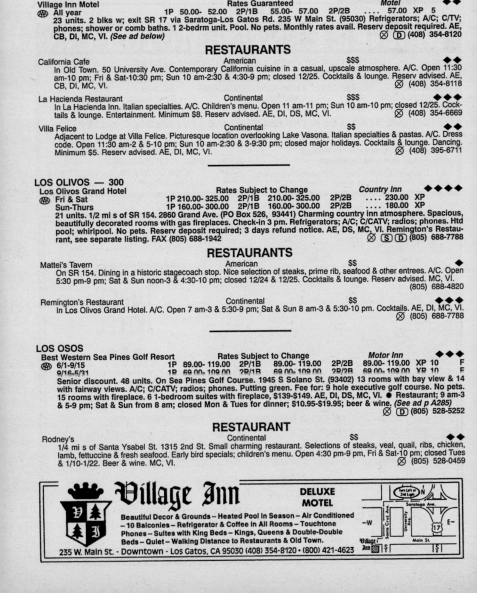

Village Inn
DELUXE MOTEL
Beautiful Decor & Grounds – Heated Pool In Season – Air Conditioned – 10 Balconies – Refrigerator & Coffee In All Rooms – Touchtone Phones – Suites with King Beds – Kings, Queens & Double-Double Beds – Quiet – Walking Distance to Restaurants & Old Town.
235 W. Main St. - Downtown - Los Gatos, CA 95030 (408) 354-8120 • (800) 421-4623

LYNWOOD — 61,900
Century Frwy Travelodge   AAA Special Value Rates   *Motel* ◆◆ F
All year   1P .... 44.00   2P/1B .... 44.00   2P/2B .... 55.00   XP 5
Senior discount. 49 units. Adjacent n side of I-105 (Century Frwy), exit Long Beach Blvd 2 blks s of Imperial Hwy. 11401 Long Beach Blvd. (90262) A/C; C/CATV; movies; radios; phones. Htd pool; whirlpool. No pets. 8 rooms with whirlpool, $65-$75. AE, MC, VI. FAX (310) 763-0548   ⊗ Ⓢ Ⓓ (310) 763-4029

MADERA — 29,300
Best Western Madera Valley Inn   Rates Subject to Change   *Motor Inn* ◆◆◆
⊛ All year   1P 52.00-58.00   2P/1B 58.00-61.00   2P/2B 60.00-66.00   XP 4
Senior discount. 93 units. 3 blks n; e off Frwy 99 via Central Madera. 317 North G St. (93637) A/C; C/TV; movies; radios; phones. Pool. Pets. 2 1-bedroom suites, $107 for up to 2 persons. Monthly rates avail. Reserv deposit required; 3 days refund notice. AE, CB, DI, MC, VI. ● Coffeeshop; 6 am-9 pm; $7-$13; cocktails.
   ⊗ Ⓓ (209) 673-5164

RESTAURANT
Lucca's   Italian $$$ ◆◆
3 blks n on SR 99 business rt. 325 N Gateway Dr. Homemade pastas. Also, American dishes. A/C. Children's menu. Open 11:30 am-9:30 pm; Sun from 10 am; closed Mon & major holidays. Cocktails & lounge. MC, VI.
   ⊗ (209) 674-6744

MALIBU — 11,700
Malibu Beach Inn   Rates Subject to Change   *Motel* ◆◆◆
All year [CP]   1P 150.00-210.00   2P/1B 150.00-210.00   ....   XP 10
47 units. Adjacent to Malibu Pier. 22878 Pacific Coast Hwy. (90265) Balconies with ocean view, 42 fireplaces. Check-in 3 pm. Refrigerators; A/C; C/CATV; pay movies; VCPs. Radios; phones. Beach; swimming; fishing; exercise rm. No pets. 2 night minimum stay weekends. Reserv deposit required; 3 days refund notice. AE, CB, DI, MC, VI. FAX (310) 456-1499 *(See ad below)*   Ⓢ Ⓓ ♿ (310) 456-6444

Malibu Country Inn   Rates Subject to Change   *Motel* ◆◆
⊛ 5/22-9/15 [BP]   ....   2P/1B 115.00-255.00   2P/2B 135.00-285.00   XP 10
9/16-5/21 [BP]   ....   2P/1B 95.00-195.00   2P/2B 115.00-225.00   XP 10
14 units. 7 mi n, corner of Westward Beach Rd & US 1 (Pacific Coast Hwy). 6506 Westward Beach Rd. (90265) Check-in 3 pm. Refrigerators; C/TV; radios; phones; comb or shower baths. 1 2-bedrm unit. Small htd pool. No pets. AE, DS, MC, VI. FAX (310) 457-1349   Ⓓ (310) 457-9622

RESTAURANTS
Beau Rivage   Ethnic $$$ ◆◆
2 mi n of Malibu Canyon Rd. 26025 Pacific Coast Hwy. Mediteranean cuisine with emphasis on French & Italian entrees. Sun brunch, 11 am-4 pm. A/C. Open 5 pm-11 pm; Sun-10 pm; closed major holidays. Cocktails. Reserv required. AE, CB, DI, MC, VI.   ⊗ (310) 456-5733

Granita   Ethnic $$$ ◆◆◆
5 1/2 mi n, in Malibu Colony Plaza. 23725 W Malibu Rd. Featuring Mediterranean cuisine. Outdoor dining weather permitting. A/C. Open 5:30 pm-10:30 pm; Wed-Fri 11:30 am-2:30 pm. Cocktails & lounge. Reserv advised. AE, DI, MC, VI.   ⊗ (310) 456-0488

MAMMOTH LAKES — 4,800

Alpenhof Lodge — Rates Subject to Change — *Motor Inn* ◆◆
Fri-Sun 11/1-5/15   1P 78.00- 115.00   2P/1B 78.00- 115.00   2P/2B 86.00- 95.00   XP 10
Mon-Thurs 11/1-5/15   1P 68.00- 115.00   2P/1B 68.00- 115.00   2P/2B 75.00- 85.00   XP 10
5/16-10/31   1P 51.00- 59.00   2P/1B 51.00- 75.00   2P/2B 59.00- 65.00   XP 10
48 units. 1 mi w on SR 203. (PO Box 1157, 93546) Some fireplaces. Check-out 10 am. C/CATV; movies; phones; comb or shower baths. Coin laundry. Sauna; whirlpools; pool open in summer. No pets. Wkly rates avail. Reserv deposit required; 7 days refund notice. AE, DS, MC, VI. ● The Matterhorn Restaurant, see separate listing.
FAX (619) 934-7614   (D) (619) 934-6330

Alpine Lodge — Rates Subject to Change — *Motel* ◆
Fri-Sun 11/1-5/15   1P 75.00- 95.00   2P/1B 75.00- 95.00   2P/2B 84.00- 95.00   XP 10
Mon-Thurs   1P 65.00- 90.00   2P/1B 65.00- 90.00   2P/2B 74.00- 95.00   XP 10
5/16-10/31   1P 54.00- 80.00   2P/1B 54.00- 80.00   2P/2B 62.00- 68.00   XP 10
Senior discount. 66 units. 1 1/4 mi w on SR 203. 6209 Minaret RD. (PO Box 389, 93546) Check-in 3 pm. Check-out 10 am. C/CATV; radios; phones; comb or shower baths. Sauna; indoor whirlpool. Parking lot. No pets. 4 2-bedroom housekeeping cottages with full kitchen & utensils $100-$150; 2 night minimum stay. MC, VI. *(See ad p A245)*   (D) (619) 934-8526

Econolodge Wildwood Inn — Rates Subject to Change — *Motel* ◆◆
Fri & Sat 11/1-4/30 [CP]   1P 54.00- 69.00   2P/1B 59.00- 79.00   2P/2B .... 89.00   XP 5   F
5/1-10/31 [CP]   1P 44.00- 49.00   2P/1B 49.00- 59.00   2P/2B 69.00- 79.00   XP 5   F
Sun-Thurs 11/1-4/30 [CP]   1P 49.00- 59.00   2P/1B 54.00- 69.00   2P/2B .... 69.00   XP 5   F
Senior discount. 31 units. 1/4 mi w on SR 203. (PO Box 568, 93546) Formerly Wildwood Inn. Check-out 10 am. 6 refrigerators; C/CATV; movies; radios; phones. Whirlpool; heated pool open in summer; fish cleaning & freezing facilities. Pets. 2 night minimum stay Fri & Sat 11/20-4/30. Wkly rates avail. Reserv deposit required; 7 days refund notice; 30 days in ski season. AE, DI, DS, MC, VI. FAX (619) 934-6156   (D) (619) 934-6855

North Village Inn — Rates Guaranteed — *Motel* ◆
Fri & Sat 11/1-4/30 [CP]   1P 59.00- 69.00   2P/1B 59.00- 69.00   2P/2B 59.00- 69.00   XP
Sun-Thurs 11/1-4/30 [CP]   1P 49.00- 59.00   2P/1B 49.00- 59.00   2P/2B 49.00- 59.00   XP
5/1-10/31 [CP]   1P 42.00- 54.00   2P/1B 42.00- 54.00   2P/2B 42.00- 54.00   XP
Senior discount. 12 units. On Lake Mary Rd, 100 yards n of SR 203. 103 Lake Mary Rd. (PO Box 1984, 93546) Various accommodations on tree shaded grounds. 4 smaller units with common lounge area. Check-out 10 am. Refrigerators; C/CATV; phones; shower or comb baths. Whirlpool. Pets, $100 deposit required. 3 kitchen units with fireplace, $59-$107. Wkly rates avail. Reserv deposit required; 7 days refund notice. AE, DS, MC, VI. FAX (619) 934-6144   (D) (619) 934-2525

Quality Inn — Rates Subject to Change — *Motel* ◆◆◆
Fri & Sat 11/1-4/30 [CP]   1P 94.00- 99.00   2P/1B .... 99.00   2P/2B .... 94.00   XP 5   F
Sun-Thurs 11/1-4/30 [CP]   1P 69.00- 79.00   2P/1B .... 84.00   2P/2B .... 79.00   XP 5   F
5/1-10/31 [CP]   1P .... 69.00   2P/1B .... 84.00   2P/2B .... 79.00   XP 5   F
Senior discount. 61 units. 1/4 mi w on SR 203. (PO Box 3507, 93546) Check-out 10 am. 3 refrigerators; C/CATV; movies; phones. 1 efficiency. Indoor whirlpool. Garage. No pets. 2 night minimum stay Fri & Sat 11/20-4/30. Wkly rates avail. Reserv deposit required; 7 days refund notice; 30 days in ski season. AE, DI, DS, MC, VI. FAX (619) 934-5165   ⊗ (S)(D) (619) 934-5114

Royal Pines Resort — Rates Subject to Change — *Apartment Motel* ◆◆
11/1-4/30   1P 55.00- 60.00   2P/1B 60.00- 65.00   2P/2B 60.00- 74.00   XP 7
5/1-10/31   1P .... 44.00   2P/1B .... 44.00   2P/2B 48.00- 53.00   XP 7
26 units. 1/2 mi w on SR 203, on Viewpoint Rd. (PO Box 348, 93546) Check-out 10 am. C/CATV; movies; radios; phones; comb or shower baths. 7 kitchens, 14 efficiencies. Whirlpool. Pets, $5 in housekeeping units. Wkly rates avail. Reserv deposit required; 7 days refund notice. MC, VI.   (D) (619) 934-2306

Shilo Inn — Rates Subject to Change — *Motel* ◆◆◆
Fri & Sat 11/15-4/16 [CP]   1P 128.00- 150.00   2P/1B 128.00- 150.00   2P/2B 128.00- 150.00   XP 12   F
1/1-4/15 & 11/16-12/31 [CP]   1P 93.00- 120.00   2P/1B 93.00- 120.00   2P/2B 93.00- 120.00   XP 12   F
Sun-Thurs 4/16-11/15 [CP]   1P 74.00- 120.00   2P/1B 74.00- 120.00   2P/2B 74.00- 120.00   XP 12   F
71 units. On SR 203, 1/2 blk e of Old Mammoth Rd. (PO Box 2179, 93546) Well-equipped rooms with microwave & refrigerator. A/C; C/CATV; movies; rental VCPs. Radios; phones. Coin laundry. Htd indoor pool; sauna; indoor whirlpool; steamroom; exercise rm. Garage. Pets, $6 extra charge. Wkly & monthly rates avail. Reserv deposit required; 7 days refund notice; 30 days in ski season. AE, DI, DS, MC, VI. FAX (619) 934-7594 *(See ad below)*   ⊗ (S)(D)(&) (619) 934-4500

Sierra Lodge — Rates Subject to Change — *Motel* ◆◆◆
Fri & Sat 11/1-4/30 [CP]   ....   2P/1B 110.00- 130.00   2P/2B 110.00- 130.00   XP 10   F
Sun-Thurs 11/1-4/30 [CP]   ....   2P/1B 85.00- 95.00   2P/2B 85.00- 95.00   XP 10   F
5/1-10/31 [CP]   ....   2P/1B 60.00- 75.00   2P/2B 60.00- 75.00   XP 10   F
Senior discount. 35 units. 1/4 mi w on SR 203. 3540 Main St. (PO Box 9228, 93546) All rooms have microwave & refrigerator. Attractive guest lounge with fireplace. Designated smoking areas. Check-in 4 pm. O/OATV; movies; radios; phones. Whirlpool. Garage. No pets. Wkly rates avail in summer. Reserv deposit required; 3 days refund notice in winter. MC, VI. FAX (619) 934-7231   ⊗ (S)(D) (619) 934-8881

Snow Goose Bed & Breakfast Inn — AAA Special Value Rates — *Bed & Breakfast* ◆◆
Fri & Sat 11/15-5/31 [BP]   ....   2P/1B .... 98.00   2P/2B .... 98.00   XP 10
Sun-Thurs 11/15-5/31 [BP]   ....   2P/1B .... 78.00   2P/2B .... 78.00   XP 10   F
6/1-11/14 [BP]   ....   2P/1B .... 58.00   2P/2B .... 58.00   XP 6   F
18 units. 1 blk w on SR 203, 1 blk n on Forest Tr. (PO Box 946, 93546) Check-out 10 am. C/CATV; phones; comb or shower baths. Whirlpool. No pets. 2 efficiencies, $10 extra. 4 2-bedroom apartments. Wkly rates avail. Reserv deposit required; 30 days refund notice 11/15-5/31. Complimentary beverages each evening. AE, DI, DS, MC, VI.   (D) (619) 934-2660

Swiss Chalet Motel   Rates Subject to Change   *Motel* ◆◆
- Fri & Sat 11/15-5/14   1P .... 60.00   2P/1B .... 60.00   2P/2B .... 64.00   XP 6
- Sun-Thurs 11/15-5/14   1P .... 53.00   2P/1B .... 53.00   2P/2B .... 57.00   XP 6
- 5/15-11/14   1P .... 42.00   2P/1B .... 42.00   2P/2B .... 46.00   XP 6

Senior discount. 21 units. 1/2 mi w on SR 203. Viewpoint Rd. (PO Box 16, 93546) Check-out 10 am. 18 refrigerators; C/CATV; movies; phones; shower baths. Sauna; indoor whirlpool. No pets. 2 efficiencies, $3 extra. Reserv deposit required; 7 days refund notice. AE, DS, MC, VI.   Ⓓ (619) 934-2403

Travelodge Mammoth Mountain   Rates Subject to Change   *Motel* ◆◆
- Fri & Sat 11/1-5/1   1P .... 88.00   2P/1B .... 88.00   2P/2B .... 98.00   XP
- Sun-Thurs 11/1-5/1   1P .... 68.00   2P/1B .... 68.00   2P/2B .... 78.00   XP
- 5/2-10/31   1P .... 58.00   2P/1B .... 58.00   2P/2B .... 68.00   XP

Senior discount. 61 units. 1 1/4 mi w on SR 203, on Minaret Rd. (PO Box 390, 93546) Refrigerators; C/CATV; 50 radios; phones. Htd indoor pool; sauna; whirlpool. Garage. No pets. 2-night minimum stay weekends 11/1-5/1. Reserv deposit required. AE, DI, DS, MC, VI. FAX (619) 934-8007   ⊗ Ⓓ (619) 934-8576

Viking Inn   Rates Subject to Change   *Motel* ◆◆
- Fri & Sat 11/15-4/30 [CP]   1P 49.00- 59.00   2P/1B 49.00- 59.00   2P/2B 55.00- 65.00   XP 5   F
- Sun-Thurs 11/15-4/30 [CP]   1P 44.00- 54.00   2P/1B 44.00- 54.00   2P/2B 50.00- 60.00   XP 5   F
- 5/1-11/14 [CP]   1P 39.00- 49.00   2P/1B 39.00- 49.00   2P/2B 39.00- 49.00   XP 5   F

10 units. 1 blk s of SR 203. 113 Center St. (PO Box 3338, 93546) Check-in 3 pm. Check-out 10 am. C/CATV; movies; phones; comb or shower baths. 1 2-bedrm unit. Whirlpool. No pets. 2 2-room units, $49-$69. Reserv deposit required; 21 days refund notice. AE, MC, VI. FAX (619) 924-2950   ⊗ Ⓓ (619) 934-2873

White Stag Inn   Rates Subject to Change   *Motel* ◆◆
- Fri & Sat 11/15-4/30   1P 54.00- 59.00   2P/1B 54.00- 59.00   2P/2B .... 68.00   XP 10
- Sun-Thurs 11/15-4/30   1P 44.00- 49.00   2P/1B 44.00- 49.00   2P/2B .... 58.00   XP 10
- 5/1-11/14   1P .... 42.00   2P/1B .... 42.00   2P/2B .... 47.00   XP 6

Senior discount. 21 units. 3/4 mi w on SR 203. (PO Box 45, 93546) 7 refrigerators; C/CATV; movies; phones; shower or comb baths. Sauna; fish cleaning & freezing facilities. No pets. 5 efficiencies, $5 extra. Wkly rates avail. Reserv deposit required; 7 days refund notice. AE, DS, MC, VI.   Ⓓ (619) 934-7507

RESTAURANTS

The Matterhorn Restaurant   Continental $$ ◆◆
At Alpenhof Lodge. Attractive, cozy restaurant. Open 7 am-10 & 5:30-9 pm; Sat-10 pm. Beer & wine. AE, MC, VI.   ⊗ (619) 934-3369

Nevados   American $$ ◆◆
3/4 mi w on SR 203. Minaret Rd at Main St. Formerly Roget's. Dining in casual atmosphere. Designated smoking areas. Open 5:30 pm-10 pm; in summer from 6 pm; closed June & Oct. Cocktails & lounge. Reserv advised. AE, DI, DS, MC, VI.   ⊗ (619) 934-4466

Ocean Harvest Restaurant   Seafood $$ ◆◆
3 blks s of SR 203, on Old Mammoth Rd. Beef, poultry & a large selection of mesquite broiled seafood. Open 5 pm-10 pm; in summer 6 pm-9:30 pm. Cocktails & lounge. Reserv advised. AE, DS, MC, VI.   ⊗ (619) 934-8539

O'Kelly & Dunn Co   American $$ ◆◆
In Minaret Village shopping center. 437 Old Mammoth Rd, #1. A charming restaurant with country decor. Smoke free premises. A/C. Open 6:30 am-9 pm; closed Tues, 11/25 & 12/25. Beer & wine. AE, DS, MC, VI.   ⊗ (619) 934-9316

Petrello's Ristorante   Italian $$ ◆◆
1/2 mi w on SR 203, on Viewpoint Rd. Casual dining with an attractive view. Nice selection of pasta, veal, chicken & seafood. Designated smoking areas. Children's menu. Open 6 pm-10 pm; in winter from 5:30 pm; closed 4/11, 7/4, 11/25, 12/25, Mon & Tues May & June. Beer & wine. Reserv advised. MC, VI.   ⊗ (619) 934-6767

The Restaurant at Convict Lake   American $$$ ◆◆
4 mi s of SR 203, 1 1/2 mi e of US 395 at Convict Lake turnoff. Attractive restaurant with picturesque view. Designated smoking areas. Open 5:30 pm-9 pm; closed 11/1-11/12. Cocktails. Reserv advised. AE, DS, MC, VI. ⊗ (619) 934-3803

Slocum's Italian & American Grill   Italian $$ ◆◆
On SR 203, 2 blks w of Old Mammoth Rd. Pasta, chicken, beef & seafood entrees. Limted menu in lounge from 4 pm; $6.85-$12.85. Designated smoking areas. Open 5:30 pm-10 pm. Cocktails. Reserv advised. DS, MC, VI.   (619) 934-7647

Whiskey Creek Restaurant   American $$ ◆◆
3/4 mi w on SR 203. Specializing in barbecued ribs, prime rib, steaks & seafood entrees. Designated smoking areas. A/C. Children's menu. Open 5:30 pm-10 pm. Cocktails & lounge. Reserv advised. AE, MC, VI.   ⊗ (619) 934-2555

MANHATTAN BEACH — 32,100

Barnabey's Hotel   AAA Special Value Rates   *Motor Inn* ◆◆◆
- All year [BP]   1P 129.00- 144.00   2P/1B 144.00- 159.00   2P/2B 144.00- 159.00   XP 15   F

128 units. On SR 1; 1/2 blk s of Rosecrans Ave. 3501 N Sepulveda Blvd. (90266) Charming Old English atmosphere. Check-in 3 pm. 20 refrigerators; A/C; C/CATV; free & pay movies; radios; phones; comb or shower baths. Htd indoor pool; whirlpool; jogging track. Valet parking lot. Airport transp. No pets. Some rooms with VCP's. Reserv deposit required. AE, CB, DI, MC, VI. ● Dining rm; 6:30 am-10 & 11-11 pm; $16-$25; cocktails; entertainment. FAX (310) 545-8621   ⊗ Ⓓ (310) 545-8466

Comfort Inn   Rates Subject to Change   *Motel* ◆◆◆
- All year   1P 60.00- 70.00   2P/1B 65.00- 75.00   2P/2B 75.00- 85.00   XP 6   F

Senior discount. 45 units. On SR 1. 850 N Sepulveda Blvd. (90266) 8 refrigerators; A/C; C/CATV; movies; rental VCPs. Radios; phones. Coin laundry. Htd pool; sauna; whirlpool. Garage. Airport transp. No pets. 8 rooms with whirlpool tub & 2-room units $105-$135. Reserv deposit required; 3 days refund notice. AE, DI, DS, MC, VI. FAX (310) 376-3545 *(See ad p A248)*   ⊗ Ⓢ Ⓓ (310) 318-1020

Radisson Plaza Hotel   Rates Guaranteed   *Hotel* ◆◆◆
- Mon-Thurs   1P 120.00- 160.00   2P/1B 120.00- 160.00   2P/2B 120.00- 160.00   XP 20
- Fri-Sun   1P .... 79.00   2P/1B .... 79.00   2P/2B .... 79.00   XP

Senior discount. 380 units. 1/2 mi e of SR 1; 1 blk s of Rosecrans Ave. 1400 Parkview Ave. (90266) Check-in 3 pm. A/C; C/CATV; free & pay movies; radios; phones. Htd pool; saunas; whirlpool; exercise rm. Fee for: par-3 golf. Pay garage. Airport transp. No pets. AE, CB, DI, DS. ● Dining rm & restaurant; 6 am-11 pm; $7-$30; cocktails. FAX (310) 546-7520   ⊗ Ⓢ Ⓓ Ⓖ (310) 546-7511

Residence Inn by Marriott   Rates Subject to Change   *Apartment Motel* ◆◆◆
All year [CP]   1P 89.00- 145.00   2P/1B   89.00- 145.00   2P/2B   104.00- 189.00   XP 10   F
Senior discount. 176 units. On SR 1, 1 mi s of Rosecrans Ave. 1700 N Sepulveda Blvd. (90266) 1-bedroom studios &
split level, 2-bedroom units with living room & kitchen. Many fireplaces. Check-in 3 pm. A/C; C/CATV; movies; VCPs.
Radios; phones. Coin laundry. Htd pool; whirlpools. Airport transp. Pets, $250 deposit required; also $6 extra charge.
Wkly & monthly rates avail. Reserv deposit required. AE, DI, DS, MC, VI. FAX (213) 545-1327
     ⊗ Ⓓ 🅰   (310) 546-7627

Sea View Inn at the Beach   Rates Guaranteed   *Motel* ◆
⊛ 5/1-10/1   1P .... 75.00   2P/1B   .... 75.00   2P/2B   .... 75.00   XP
10/2-4/30   1P .... 65.00   2P/1B   .... 65.00   2P/2B   .... 65.00   XP
8 units. 3 blks s of Rosecrans Ave. 3400 Highland Ave. (90266) Refrigerators; C/CATV; movies; radios; phones;
shower baths. Htd pool. Garage. No pets. Wkly rates avail. Reserv deposit required. AE, MC, VI.
FAX (310) 545-4052   Ⓓ (310) 545-1504

RESTAURANT

Sausalito South   Continental $$ ◆◆
On SR 1, 1 blk s of Rosecrans Ave; in Manhattan Village Shopping Center. 3280 Sepulveda Blvd. Casual San Francisco
atmosphere. Nice selection of seafood, beef, poultry & pasta. A/C. Open 11 am-10 pm; Fri-11 pm; Sat 5 pm-11 pm;
closed Sun, 1/1 & 12/25. Cocktails & lounge. Reserv advised. AE, MC, VI.   ⊗ 🅰 (310) 546-4507

MANTECA — 40,800
Best Western Inn of Manteca   Rates Guaranteed   *Motel* ◆◆◆
⊛ All year   1P 50.00- 60.00   2P/1B   60.00- 70.00   2P/2B   .... 74.00   XP 8
Senior discount. 101 units. At jct of SR 99 & 120, exit Yosemite Ave. 1415 E Yosemite Ave. (95336) Some rooms
with balcony. Refrigerators; A/C; C/CATV; movies; radios; phones. Pool; sauna; whirlpool. No pets. 12 rooms
with kitchen, $10 extra. 30 rooms with whirlpool tub, $75-$125. Wkly rates avail. Reserv deposit required. AE, DI,
DS, MC, VI. Coffeeshop adjacent. FAX (209) 825-4251   ⊗ Ⓢ Ⓓ (209) 825-1415

MARICOPA — 1,200
Best Western Maricopa Inn | Rates Guaranteed | Motel ◆◆
㉟ All year [CP]   1P 45.00- 48.00 2P/1B 45.00- 48.00 2P/2B .... 48.00 XP 6   F
Senior discount. 41 units. 1/2 blk e of jct Hwy 33 & 166. 600 Poso St. (PO Box 608, 93252) 21 refrigerators; A/C;
C/CATV; radios; phones. 11 efficiencies. Small pool; whirlpool. No pets. Wkly rates avail. Reserv deposit required. AE, DI, DS, MC, VI. Coffeeshop opposite.   ⊗ Ⓓ 🅓 (805) 769-8291

MARINA DEL REY/VENICE — 45,735   (See LOS ANGELES (Central & Western Areas) spotting
map pages A212 & A213; see index starting on page A210)
Best Western-Jamaica Bay Inn 🄓🄗🄗 | Rates Guaranteed | Motor Inn ◆◆
㉟ 6/1-9/30   1P .... 115.00 2P/1B .... 115.00 2P/2B .... 115.00 XP 10   F
   10/1-5/31   1P .... 95.00   2P/1B .... 95.00   2P/2B .... 95.00 XP 10   F
42 units. 3/4 mi w of SR 1 (Lincoln Blvd). 4175 Admiralty Way. (Marina del Rey, 90292) At Marina del Rey Beach.
Spacious rooms, some with marina view. A/C; C/CATV; phones. Htd pool; whirlpool; rental bicycles. No pets. 10
rooms with microwave & refrigerator, $100-$145; no utensils. Reserv deposit required. AE, DI, DS, MC,
VI. ● Restaurant & coffeeshop; 6 am-10 pm; $5.50-$10; cocktails. FAX (310) 823-1325 *(See ad below)*
                                                                       Ⓓ (310) 823-5333

Doubletree Hotel Marina Beach 🄓🄗🄗 | Rates Subject to Change | Hotel ◆◆◆◆
㉟ All year   1P 175.00- 215.00 2P/1B 195.00- 235.00 2P/2B 195.00- 235.00 XP 20   F
300 units. 3/4 mi w of SR 1 (Lincoln Blvd). 4100 Admiralty Way. (Marina del Rey, 90292) Check-in 3 pm. A/C;
C/CATV; free & pay movies; radios; phones. Htd pool. Pay valet parking ramp. Airport transp. No pets. AE, DI,
DS, MC, VI. ● Dining rm & restaurant; 6 am-10 pm; $15-$35; cocktails; entertainment. Also, Stones, see separate listing. FAX (310) 301-6890 *(See ad below)*   ⊗ Ⓢ Ⓓ 🅓 (310) 301-3000

Foghorn Hotel 🄓🄗🄗 | Rates Subject to Change | Motel ◆◆
㉟ 4/1-9/30   1P 70.00- 100.00 2P/1B 80.00- 110.00 2P/2B 80.00- 110.00 XP 10
24 units. 2 blks s of Washington St. 4140 Via Marina. (Marina Del Rey, 90292) OPEN ALL YEAR. At Marina Del
Rey Beach. Refrigerators; A/C; C/CATV; movies; VCPs. Phones; comb or shower baths. Beach. Reserv deposit
required. AE, CB, DI, MC, VI. Restaurant adjacent. FAX (310) 578-1964   Ⓓ (310) 823-4626

(See LOS ANGELES (Central & Western Areas) spotting map pages A212 & A213)

Jolly Roger Hotel 203   Rates Subject to Change   *Motel* ◆
Ⓟ All year [CP]   1P 47.00- 61.00   2P/1B   47.00- 61.00   2P/2B   57.00- 71.00   XP 10
84 units. 2 blks w of SR 1 (Lincoln Blvd). 2904 Washington Blvd. (Marina del Rey, 90291) A/C; C/TV; VCPs; radios; phones. Small htd pool; whirlpools. No pets. Reserv deposit required. AE, MC, VI. FAX (310) 301-9461 *(See ad below)*   D (310) 822-2904

The Mansion Inn 202   AAA Special Value Rates   *Motel* ◆◆◆
Ⓟ All year [CP]   1P 79.00- 125.00   2P/1B   79.00- 125.00   2P/2B   89.00- 125.00   XP 10   F
43 units. 327 Washington Blvd. (Marina del Rey, 90291) 2 1/2 blks to beach. Attractive decor. Check-in 3 pm. A/C; C/CATV; movies; radios; phones. No pets. Wkly & monthly rates avail. AE, DI, DS, MC, VI. FAX (310) 827-0289   ⊗ D (310) 821-2557

Marina del Rey Marriott 201   Rates Subject to Change   *Motor Inn* ◆◆◆
All year   1P .... 139.00   2P/1B   .... 159.00   2P/2B   .... 159.00   XP 10   F
Senior discount. 283 units. 1/2 blk e of SR 1 (Lincoln Blvd); 1 blk n of jct SR 90. 13480 Maxella Ave. (Marina del Rey, 90291) Check-in 4 pm. 10 refrigerators; A/C; C/CATV; free & pay movies; radios; phones. Htd pool; whirlpool; rental bicycles; exercise rm. Parking lot. Pets. Airport transportation from 6 am-10:30 am. Wkly rates avail. AE, DI, DS, MC, VI. ● Dining rm; 6:30 am-10 pm; $8-$16; cocktails. FAX (310) 823-2996   ⊗ D Ⓜ (310) 822-8555

Marina International Hotel 199   AAA Special Value Rates   *Motel* ◆◆◆
Mon-Thurs   1P 110.00- 288.00   2P/1B   125.00- 288.00   2P/2B   125.00- 288.00   XP 20-60   F
Fri-Sun   1P 85.00- 115.00   2P/1B   85.00- 115.00   2P/2B   85.00- 115.00   XP 20-60   F
135 units. 3/4 mi w of SR 1 (Lincoln Blvd). 4200 Admiralty Way. (Marina del Rey, 90292) A/C; C/CATV; free & pay movies; radios; phones; comb or shower baths. Htd pool; whirlpool. Garage. Airport transp. No pets. Monthly rates avail. AE, CB, DI, MC, VI. Coffeeshop; 6:30 am-10 & 11-1:30 pm; $10.50-$16; cocktails. FAX (310) 301-6687   Ⓞ D (310) 301-2000

Marina Motel 200   Rates Subject to Change   *Motel* ◆◆
Ⓟ All year [CP]   1P 54.00- 64.00   2P/1B   55.00- 69.00   2P/2B   60.00- 70.00   XP 5   F
31 units. 1 blk w of SR 1 (Lincoln Blvd). 3130 Washington Blvd. (Venice, 90291) Nicely furnished rooms. A/C; C/TV; phones. No pets. 1 kitchen unit, $75-$80. 2 rooms with refrigerator & microwave $65-$70. AE, CB, DI, MC, VI. Restaurant opposite. FAX (310) 821-6167   ⊗ D (310) 821-5086

Marina Pacific Hotel & Suites 196   Rates Subject to Change   *Motor Inn* ◆
Ⓟ 6/10-9/15   1P 95.00- 120.00   2P/1B   95.00- 120.00   2P/2B   95.00- 120.00   XP 10
9/16-6/9   1P 85.00- 105.00   2P/1B   85.00- 105.00   2P/2B   85.00- 105.00   XP 10
92 units. 1697 Pacific Ave. (Venice, 90291) Adjacent to beach. Some rooms with ocean view. Refrigerators; A/C; C/CATV; movies; radios; phones; comb or shower baths. Coin laundry. Garage. No pets. 35 suites with kitchen & gas fireplace, $125-$250. Monthly rates avail. AE, CB, DI, MC, VI. Coffeeshop; 7 am-5 pm. FAX (310) 452-5479   Ⓞ D (310) 452-1111

The Ritz-Carlton, Marina del Rey 204   Rates Subject to Change   *Hotel* ◆◆◆◆◆
Ⓟ All year   1P 225.00- 325.00   2P/1B   225.00- 325.00   2P/2B   225.00- 325.00   XP 25
306 units. 4375 Admiralty Way. (Marina del Rey, 90292) A/C; C/CATV; free & pay movies; radios; phones. Htd pool; saunas; whirlpool; charter yachts; rental bicycles; exercise rm. Fee for: lighted tennis-3 courts; massage. Pay valet garage. Airport transp. No pets. AE, CB, DI, MC, VI. ● Restaurant; 6:30 am-11 pm; $15-$29; 24 hour room service. Also, The Dining Room, see separate listing. FAX (310) 823-2403   ⊗ Ⓞ D Ⓜ (310) 823-1700

RESTAURANTS

Cafe Del Rey 103   American $$$ ◆◆◆
4451 Admiralty Way. Lively atmosphere, overlooks yacht harbor. A/C. Open 11:30 am-2:30 & 5:30-10:30 pm; Fri & Sat-11 pm; Sun 10:30 am-3 & 5-10:30 pm; closed 12/25. Cocktails & lounge. Valet parking. Reserv advised. AE, DI, DS, MC, VI.   ⊗ (310) 823-6395

The Dining Room 101   Continental $$$ ◆◆◆
In The Ritz-Carlton, Marina del Rey. Well-appointed restaurant with formal & friendly service. A/C. Children's menu. Open 6:30 am-10:30 pm; closed Sun & Mon. Cocktails & lounge. Valet parking. Reserv advised. AE, CB, DI, MC, VI.   ⊗ (310) 823-1700

Rueben's 100   American $$ ◆◆
In Marina del Rey; 3/4 mi w of Lincoln Blvd (SR1). 4211 Admiralty Way. Casual dining with marina view. A/C. Early bird specials; children's menu. Open 11:30 am-4 & 5-10 pm; Fri-11 pm; Sat 11:30 am-11 pm; Sun 10 am-3 & 4-10 pm. Cocktails & lounge. Pay valet parking. AE, DI, DS, MC, VI.   ⊗ Ⓜ (310) 823-5341

Stones 102   Continental $$$ ◆◆◆
In Doubletree Hotel Marina Beach. Nicely appointed dining room with view of hotel grounds. A/C. Open 6 am-10 pm. Cocktails & lounge. Valet parking. Reserv advised. AE, DI, DS, MC, VI. *(See ad p A249)*   ⊗ (310) 301-3000

MARIPOSA — 1,200

Best Western Yosemite Way Station — Rates Subject to Change — *Motel* ◆◆
4/1-10/31 [CP] 1P .... 76.00 2P/1B .... 76.00 2P/2B .... 76.00 XP 4
11/1-3/31 [CP] 1P .... 56.00 2P/1B .... 56.00 2P/2B .... 56.00 XP 4
78 units. On SR 140 at SR 49S. 4999 Hwy 140. (PO Box 1989, 95338) Check-in 3 pm. A/C; C/CATV; pay movies; phones. Pool; whirlpool. No pets. Reserv deposit required. AE, CB, DI, MC, VI. Restaurant opposite. FAX (209) 966-6353 *(See ad p A551)* ⊗ Ⓢ Ⓓ Ⓛ (209) 966-7545

E. C. Yosemite Motel — Rates Subject to Change — *Motel* ◆◆
4/1-10/31 1P .... 55.00 2P/1B .... 55.00 2P/2B .... 55.00 XP 5
Senior discount. 28 units. At jct SR 49 & 140N. 5180 Jones St. (PO Box 1989, 95338) OPEN ALL YEAR. Check-in 3 pm. A/C; C/CATV; movies; phones. Small pool; whirlpool. No pets. Reserv deposit required; 3 days refund notice. AE, MC, VI. Coffeeshop opposite. Ⓢ Ⓓ (209) 742-6800

Mariposa Hotel-Inn — Rates Subject to Change — *Bed & Breakfast* ◆◆
2/1-12/31 [CP] 1P 68.00- 80.00 2P/1B 68.00- 80.00 2P/2B 68.00- 80.00 XP 10
5 units. Center. 5029 Hwy 140. (PO Box 745, 95338) OPEN 2/1-12/31. On second floor of converted historic building circa 1901. Cozy individually decorated units. Check-in 3 pm. A/C; C/CATV; radios; comb or shower baths. No pets. Reserv deposit required. AE, MC, VI. Coffeeshop opposite. ⊗ Ⓓ (209) 966-4676

Mariposa Lodge — Rates Subject to Change — *Motel* ◆◆
Fri & Sat 4/1-9/30 1P .... 55.00 2P/1B .... 70.00 2P/2B .... 70.00 XP 6
Sun-Thurs 4/1-9/30 1P .... 55.00 2P/1B .... 65.00 2P/2B .... 65.00 XP 6
10/1-3/31 1P .... 35.00 2P/1B .... 50.00 2P/2B .... 50.00 XP 5
44 units. On SR 140. (PO Box 733, 95338) 13 refrigerators; A/C; C/CATV; pay movies; phones; shower or comb baths. Small pool; whirlpool. Few VCP's. Reserv deposit required; 7 days refund notice. AE, DI, DS, MC, VI. *Independant Motels of America.* FAX (209) 742-7038 *(See ad below and p A551)* ⊗ Ⓓ (209) 966-3607

Miners Inn — Rates Subject to Change — *Motel* ◆◆
4/1-9/30 1P .... 49.95 2P/1B .... 59.95 2P/2B .... 69.95 XP 6
10/1-3/31 1P .... 34.95 2P/1B .... 44.95 2P/2B .... 54.95 XP 5
Senior discount. 64 units. On SR 140 at SR 49N. (PO Box 246, 95338) Check-in 3 pm. A/C; C/CATV; phones; comb or shower baths. Pool; whirlpool. No pets. 4 individually decorated units with whirlpool bath, $125 for 2 persons. Wkly & monthly rates avail. AE, DI, DS, MC, VI. Cocktail lounge; coffeeshop adjacent. FAX (209) 966-2343 *(See ad below and p A551)* ⊗ Ⓓ Ⓛ (209) 742-7777

Yosemite Gold Rush Inn — Rates Subject to Change — *Motel* ◆◆
4/1-10/31 [CP] 1P 49.00- 72.00 2P/1B 59.00- 72.00 2P/2B .... 70.00 XP 6
11/1-3/31 [CP] 1P .... 35.00 2P/1B .... 45.00 2P/2B .... 55.00 XP 6
61 units. 1 blk e of jct SR 140 & 49S. 4994 Bullion St. (PO Box 1989, 95338) Check-in 3 pm. A/C; C/CATV; pay movies; phones; comb or shower baths. 2 2-bedrm units, 2 kitchens. Small pool; whirlpool. No pets. Reserv deposit required; 14 days refund notice. AE, MC, VI. FAX (209) 966-4655 *(See ad p A252 and p A549)* ⊗ Ⓢ Ⓓ (209) 966-4344

MARTINEZ — 31,800
John Muir Inn — Rates Subject to Change — *Motel* ◆◆
All year [CP]   1P 49.50- 64.00   2P/1B   54.00- 69.00   2P/2B   54.00- 69.00   XP 10   F
117 units. 2 1/4 mi w of jct I-680 & SR 4, exit SR 4 at Pine/Center. 445 Muir Station Rd. (94553) A/C; C/CATV; movies; 57 radios; phones; comb or shower baths. 8 kitchens, 8 efficiencies. Small pool; whirlpool. No pets. AE, DI, DS, MC, VI. Restaurant opposite. FAX (510) 228-4810   ⊗ Ⓢ Ⓓ ⌷ (510) 229-1010

MARYSVILLE — 12,300
Oxbow Motel — Rates Subject to Change — *Motel* ◆
All year   1P .... 32.00   2P/1B   .... 34.00   2P/2B   .... 38.00   XP 4
Senior discount. 40 units. 1/2 mi s on SR 70; exit e off N Beale Rd-Yuba College; northbound SR 70 exit Feather River Blvd. 1078 N Beale Rd. (95901) Refrigerators; A/C; C/CATV; movies; radios; phones. Small pool. No pets. AE, CB, DI, MC, VI. Coffeeshop opposite. FAX (916) 472-7989   ⊗ Ⓓ ⌷ (916) 742-8238

RESTAURANT

The Cannery Restaurant — American — $$ ◆◆
In an old cannery; approach via 6th St. 606 J St. Steak & seafood. A/C. Children's menu. Open 11:30 am-2:30 & 5:30-9:30 pm; Fri & Sat-10 pm; closed Sun & major holidays. Cocktails & lounge. Minimum, $4. AE, MC, VI.
    ⊗ (916) 743-3005

MENDOCINO — 1,000   See also ALBION & LITTLE RIVER
Big River Lodge-Stanford Inn by the Sea   Rates Subject to Change   *Complex*   ◆◆◆◆
◉ All year [BP]   1P 135.00- 250.00   2P/1B 135.00- 250.00   2P/2B 135.00- 250.00   XP 20
25 units. 1/2 mi s; 1/2 mi e on Comptche-Ukiah Rd. (PO Box 487, 95460) Spacious grounds. Rustic setting. Most
rooms with ocean view. Fireplaces. Check-in 4 pm. Refrigerators; C/CATV; movies; radios; phones; comb or
shower baths. Htd indoor pool; sauna; whirlpool; rental canoes; bicycles. Pets. Wkly rates avail. Reserv deposit
required; 7 days refund notice. AE, DI, DS, MC, VI. FAX (707) 937-0305 *(See ad p A252)* ⊗ Ⓓ (707) 937-5615

Blackberry Inn   Rates Subject to Change   *Motel*   ◆◆
All year [CP]   1P 65.00- 100.00 2P/1B   70.00- 120.00 2P/2B   75.00- 120.00 XP 5
13 units. 1 blk e of SR 1. 44951 Larkin Rd. (95460) Western town facades. Attractively appointed rooms, some fireplaces; ocean view. C/CATV. 2 efficiencies. No pets. Wkly rates avail. Reserv deposit required. MC, VI.
                      (D) (707) 937-5281

Hill House Inn   Rates Subject to Change   *Motor Inn*   ◆◆◆
All year   1P 80.00- 195.00 2P/1B   80.00- 195.00 2P/2B   80.00- 195.00 XP 15
44 units. W of & adjacent to SR 1, via Little Lake St to stop sign, right to entrance on Pallette Dr. 10701 Pallette Dr. (PO Box 625, 95460) Victorian decor. View of ocean from a few units. C/CATV; 22 radios; phones. No pets. 2-night mimimum stay with Sat reserve. Reserv deposit required; 5 days refund notice. AE, MC, VI. ● Restaurant; 7-10 am, 11:30-2 & 6-9 pm; $11-$20; cocktails. FAX (707) 937-1123 *(See ad p A253)*
                    (D) (S) 937-0554

Mendocino Hotel & Garden Suites   Rates Guaranteed   *Historic Hotel*   ◆◆◆
Fri & Sat   1P 65.00- 275.00 2P/1B   65.00- 275.00 2P/2B   65.00- 275.00 XP 20
Sun-Thurs   1P 50.00- 200.00 2P/1B   50.00- 200.00 2P/2B   50.00- 200.00 XP 20
51 units. Center. 45080 Main St. (PO Box 587, 95460) Restored 1878 Victorian hotel. 2- & 3-story, no elevator. Few small rooms. Check-in 3 pm. 25 C/CATV; phones; 40 comb or shower baths. Limited parking lot. No pets. Reserv deposit required. AE, MC, VI. ● Dining rm, see separate listing. FAX (707) 937-0513 *(See ad p A253)*
                    (D) (707) 937-0511

Reed Manor   Rates Subject to Change   *Bed & Breakfast*   ◆◆◆◆
All year [CP]   1P 175.00- 350.00 2P/1B   175.00- 350.00 2P/2B   175.00- 350.00 XP 50
5 units. W of SR 1 via Little Lake St, right on Lansing St, right on Palette Dr. (PO Box 127, 95460) Individually decorated, spacious units; gas fireplaces, private decks. Village or ocean views. Designated smoking areas. Refrigerators; C/CATV; VCPs; radios; phones. No pets. All units with whirlpool bath. 2-night minimum stay weekends. Reserv deposit required; 4 days refund notice. MC, VI. Restaurant opposite.   ⊗ (D) (707) 937-5446

RESTAURANT

Mendocino Hotel Dining Room   American $$ ◆◆
In Mendocino Hotel & Garden Suites. Victorian decor. Glass-enclosed courtyard. California cuisine. Open 8 am-2:30 & 6-9:30 pm. Cocktails & lounge. Reserv advised. AE, MC, VI. *(See ad p A253)*   ⊗ (707) 937-0511

MENLO PARK — 28,000   (See SAN FRANCISCO (Southern Region) AREA spotting map page A444 ; see index starting on page A443) See also PALO ALTO
Menlo Park Inn 175   Rates Subject to Change   *Motel*   ◆◆◆
All year [CP]   1P 60.00- 70.00 2P/1B   65.00- 75.00 2P/2B   65.00- 75.00 XP 5   F
Senior discount. 30 units. Center; on SR 82. 1315 El Camino Real. (94025) Modern attractive rooms. Refrigerators; A/C; C/CATV; phones. No pets. All rooms with microwave & refrigerator. 4 units with whirlpool tub. AE, DI, DS, MC, VI. FAX (415) 328-7539 *(See ad p A255)*   ⊗ (S) (D) (S) (415) 326-7530

Stanford Park Hotel Best Western 176   Rates Subject to Change   *Hotel*   ◆◆◆◆
All year   1P 160.00- 250.00 2P/1B   170.00- 260.00 2P/2B   170.00- 260.00 XP 10
Senior discount. 163 units. On SR 82, 1/2 mi ne of Stanford University. 100 El Camino Real. (94025) 28 fireplaces, attractively appointed & spacious rooms. 9 refrigerators; A/C; C/CATV; pay movies; radios; phones. Pool; sauna; whirlpool; exercise rm. Parking lot. No pets. AE, DI, DS, MC, VI. ● Restaurant; 6 am-11:30 pm; $8-$18; cocktails. FAX (415) 322-0975 *(See ad inside back cover)*   ⊗ (S) (D) (S) (415) 322-1234

RESTAURANT

The Velvet Turtle 80   American $$ ◆◆
2 mi w of SR 82 via Sand Hill Rd; in Sharon Heights Shopping Center. 325 Sharon Park Dr. Nice selection of varied entrees. Comfortable seating. A/C. Early bird specials; children's menu. Open 11:30 am-2:30 & 5-9:30 pm; Fri-10:30 pm; Sat 5 pm-10:30 pm; Sun 5 pm-9 pm. Cocktails & lounge. Reserv advised. AE, CB, DI, MC, VI.   ⊗ (415) 854-3813

MERCED — 56,200

Best Western Inn — Rates Guaranteed — *Motel* ◆◆
◈ All year — 1P 38.00- 52.00 2P/1B 38.00- 52.00 2P/2B 40.00- 56.00 XP 5
Senior discount. 42 units. 1 1/2 mi s; e of & adjacent to SR 99, exit Childs Ave northbound, SR 140 southbound.
1033 Motel Dr. (95340) Refrigerators; A/C; C/CATV; radios; phones; shower or comb baths. 3 2-bedrm units.
Small pool. No pets. 2 units with whirlpool bath, $10 extra. Reserv deposit required. AE, CB, DI, MC, VI. Restaurant adjacent. FAX (209) 384-7272 — ⊗ Ⓓ (209) 723-2163

Best Western Pine Cone Inn — AAA Special Value Rates — *Motor Inn* ◆◆◆
◈ All year — 1P .... 57.00 2P/1B .... 62.00 2P/2B .... 62.00 XP 5 — F
97 units. 1/2 mi n off SR 99, Gustine-Sonora exit. 1213 V St. (95340) A/C; C/CATV; phones; comb or shower baths.
Pool. No pets. AE, DI, DS, MC, VI. Restaurant adjacent. FAX (209) 722-8551 *(See ad below)* ⊗ Ⓓ (209) 723-3711

Merced Travelodge — AAA Special Value Rates — *Motor Inn* ◆◆◆
◈ 5/16-9/15 — 1P 51.00- 58.00 2P/1B 53.00- 65.00 2P/2B 55.00- 61.00 XP 5 — F
9/16-5/15 — 1P 45.00- 53.00 2P/1B 47.00- 55.00 2P/2B 50.00- 55.00 XP 5 — F
119 units. Childs Ave exit off SR 99. 2000 E Childs Ave. (95340) 90 refrigerators; A/C; C/CATV; movies; 90 radios;
phones. Pool. No pets. Monthly rates avail. Reserv deposit required. AE, DI, DS, MC, VI. ● Eagles Nest, see
separate listing. FAX (209) 723-0127 — ⊗ Ⓓ (209) 723-3121

RESTAURANTS

The Branding Iron — Steak & Seafood — $$ ◆◆
E of SR 99. 640 W 16th St. Casual, western decor; also patio dining. A/C. Children's menu. Open 11:30 am-2 & 5:30-
9:30 pm; Sat from 5:30 pm; Sun 5 pm-9 pm. Cocktails & lounge. Reserv advised. AE, MC, VI. — ⊗ (209) 722-1822

Eagles Nest — American — $$ ◆
At Merced Travelodge. Upscale family restaurant with background music. California cuisine using fresh ingredients. A/C.
Early bird specials; children's menu. Open 6 am-10 pm. Cocktails & lounge. AE, DI, DS, MC, VI. — ⊗ (209) 723-1041

Sir James — Steak & Seafood — $$ ◆
1 1/2 mi s off SR 99, near Yosemite Hwy. 1111 Motel Dr. Seafood & poultry. A/C. Early bird specials. Open 5:30 pm-10
pm; Sun-9:30 pm; closed 1/1, 4/11, 11/25 & 12/25. Cocktails. Dancing. Reserv advised. AE, CB, DI, MC, VI.
⊗ (209) 723-5552

MILLBRAE — 20,400   See SAN FRANCISCO (Southern Region)

MILL VALLEY — 13,000

Howard Johnson Motor Lodge		AAA Special Value Rates				Motor Inn			◆
6/1-10/31	1P 81.00	2P/1B 86.00	2P/2B 86.00	XP 5	F
11/1-5/31	1P 75.00	2P/1B 78.00	2P/2B 78.00	XP 5	F

100 units. 4 mi n of Golden Gate Bridge; w off US 101 at the Richardson Bay Bridge on the Stinson Beach turn-off. 160 Shoreline Hwy. (94941) A/C; C/CATV; 25 radios; phones. Pool; wading pool. Pets, $10 extra charge. Reserv deposit required. AE, DI, DS, MC, VI. ● Coffeeshop; 7 am-3 & 6-10 pm; closed Mon & Tues; $9-$16; cocktails. FAX (415) 331-1859   ⊗ (D) (415) 332-5700

Mill Valley/Sausalito Travelodge		Rates Subject to Change				Motel			◆
6/25-9/5	1P 59.00- 67.00	2P/1B 64.00- 67.00	2P/2B 69.00	XP 5	F
5/1-6/24 & 9/6-10/31	1P 53.00- 61.00	2P/1B 58.00- 61.00	2P/2B 63.00	XP 5	F
11/1-4/30	1P 49.00- 57.00	2P/1B 54.00- 57.00	2P/2B 59.00	XP 5	F

Senior discount. 45 units. US 101 exit Seminary Dr. 707 Redwood Hwy. (94941) A/C; C/CATV; radios; phones; shower or comb baths. 2 family units $109, 6/25-9/5; $99, 9/6-10/31 & 5/1-6/24; $95, 11/1-4/30 for up to 4 persons. 8 rooms with whirlpool bath, $9 extra. AE, DI, DS, MC, VI. Restaurant adjacent. FAX (415) 383-0312
⊗ (D) (415) 383-0340

MILPITAS — 50,700   See also SAN JOSE

Beverly Heritage Hotel		Rates Subject to Change				Hotel			◆◆◆
All year [CP]	1P 79.00	2P/1B 79.00	2P/2B 79.00	XP 10	

Senior discount. 196 units. 2 mi n of San Jose Airport, nw quad of I-880 & Montague Expwy. 1820 Barber Ln. (95035) Large rooms, 21 with skylights. Check-in 3 pm. 30 refrigerators; A/C; C/CATV; movies; VCPs. Radios; phones. Pool; wading pool; whirlpool; bicycles; exercise rm. Airport transp. No pets. 2 suites with whirlpool tub, $150-$250 for 2 persons. [BP] Sat & Sun. Monthly rates avail. Complimentary beverages each evening. AE, DI, DS, MC, VI. ● Brandon's, see separate listing. FAX (408) 432-8617 *(See ad p A456)*   ⊗ (S)(D) (408) 943-9080

Brookside Inn		Rates Subject to Change				Motor Inn			◆
ⓐⓐ Sun-Thurs [CP]	1P 49.00	2P/1B 44.00	2P/2B 44.00	XP 5	F
Fri & Sat [CP]	1P 39.00	2P/1B 39.00	2P/2B 39.00	XP	

70 units. 4 mi n San Jose Airport; exit I880 Calaveras Blvd N at Abbott Ave. 400 Valley Way. (95035) Formerly Best Western Brookside Inn. 9 refrigerators; A/C; C/CATV; movies; phones. Pool. Pets, $10 extra charge. Microwave & refrigerator, $5 daily. Wkly & monthly rates avail. Reserv deposit required. AE, DI, DS, MC, VI. ● Restaurant; 11:30 am-2 & 5-10 pm; $6-$12. FAX (408) 262-6866   ⊗ (S)(D) (408) 263-5566

Crown Sterling Suites Milpitas		Rates Subject to Change				Suites Hotel			◆◆◆
ⓐⓐ Sun-Thurs [BP]	1P 115.00- 125.00	2P/1B 140.00	2P/2B 135.00	XP 15	
Fri & Sat [BP]	1P 89.00	2P/1B 89.00	2P/2B 89.00	XP	

267 units. Exit I-680 Calaveras Blvd E SR 237. 901 Calaveras Blvd. (95035) Formerly Embassy Suites. Exotic atrium lobby with glass elevators, waterfall & lagoon. Check-in 3 pm. A/C; C/CATV; movies; radios; phones. Coin laundry. Indoor pool; sauna; whirlpool; steambaths. Parking ramp. Airport transp. Complimentary beverages each evening. AE, CB, DI, MC, VI. ● Restaurant; 11 am-midnight; $10-$20; cocktails; entertainment. FAX (408) 262-8604 *(See ad below)*   ⊗ (S)(D)(&) (408) 942-0400

Economy Inns of America		AAA Special Value Rates				Motel			◆◆
ⓐⓐ All year [CP]	1P 39.90	2P/1B 49.90	2P/2B 49.90	XP 7	

124 units. 4 mi n of San Jose Airport, exit I880 Calaveras Blvd; adjacent to Serra Shopping Center. 270 S Abbott Ave. (95035) Check-in 3 pm. A/C; C/CATV; movies; phones. Pool. Pets. 1 2-bedroom unit, $69 for up to 4 persons. AE, MC, VI.   ⊗ (S)(D)(&) (408) 946-8889

Holiday Inn San Jose North   Rates Guaranteed   *Hotel*   ◆◆◆
◍ Mon-Thurs   1P .... 84.00   2P/1B   .... 84.00   2P/2B .... 84.00 XP 10   F
  Fri-Sun   1P .... 59.00   2P/1B   .... 59.00   2P/2B .... 59.00 XP   F
  Senior discount. 305 units. Sw quadrant of I-880 & SR 237. 777 Bellew Dr. (95035) A/C; C/CATV; free & pay
  movies; radios; phones. Coin laundry. Pool; sauna; whirlpool; exercise rm. Parking lot. Airport transp. No pets.
  Luxury level rooms avail. AE, DI, DS, MC, VI. ● Restaurant; 6 am-2 & 5-10 pm; $7-$13; cocktails.
  FAX (408) 321-9599   ⊗ Ⓢ Ⓓ ⒧ (408) 321-9500

Milpitas Travelodge   Rates Subject to Change   *Motel*   ◆◆
◍ All year [CP]   1P 45.00- 50.00 2P/1B   50.00- 55.00 2P/2B   .... 56.00 XP 5
  Senior discount. 39 units. 4 mi n of San Jose Airport, exit I-880 at Calaveras Blvd. 378 W Calaveras Blvd. (95035)
  Refrigerators; A/C; C/CATV; movies; phones; shower or comb baths. 2 2-bedrm units. Pool. No pets. Reserv de-
  posit required. AE, CB, DI, MC, VI. Restaurant adjacent. FAX (408) 263-0416   ⊗ Ⓓ (408) 263-0500

Sheraton San Jose At Silicon Valley   Rates Subject to Change   *Hotel*   ◆◆◆◆
◍ Sun-Thurs   1P 110.00- 130.00 2P/1B   120.00- 140.00 2P/2B 120.00- 140.00 XP 10   F
  Fri & Sat   1P 69.00- 85.00   2P/1B   69.00- 85.00   2P/2B   69.00- 85.00 XP V
  Senior discount. 229 units. 4 mi n of San Jose Airport; 1/4 mi nw of I-880 & Montague Expwy. 1801 Barber Ln.
  (95035) Attractively landscaped pool courtyard. Check-in 3 pm. A/C; C/CATV; radios; phones. Pool;
  whirlpool; exercise rm. Airport transp. No pets. 24 suites with balcony, $140 for up to 2 persons. Monthly rates
  avail. AE, DI, DS, MC, VI. ● Restaurant; 6:30 am-10:30 pm; $8-$18; cocktails. FAX (408) 943-0484 *(See ad
  p A256)*   ⊗ Ⓢ Ⓓ ⒧ (408) 943-0600

Super 8 Motel   AAA Special Value Rates   *Motel*   ◆◆
◍ All year [CP]   1P 45.00- 60.00 2P/1B   50.00- 60.00 2P/2B   55.00- 65.00 XP 5
  80 units. 6 mi n of San Jose Airport, exit I-880 at Montague E, n on Main St. 485 S Main St. (95035) A/C; C/CATV;
  movies; 59 radios; phones. Coin laundry. No pets. 2 2-bedroom units with microwave, refrigerator & whirlpool
  tub, $85 for up to 2 persons. Wkly rates avail. Reserv deposit required. AE, DI, DS, MC, VI. FAX (408) 262-6128
                                                                     ⊗ Ⓢ Ⓓ ⒧ (408) 946-1615

RESTAURANTS

Brandon's   American $$ ◆◆◆
◍ At Beverly Heritage Hotel. Varied menu, attractive comfortable setting, fresh seafood specialties. Sun
  brunch 10 am-2:30 pm. A/C. Open 6-10:30 am, 11-2:30 & 5:30-10:30 pm; Sat 7:30 am-2:30 & 5:30-11 pm; Sun 7:30
  am-10 & 5-10 pm. Cocktails & lounge. AE, DI, MC, VI.   ⊗ (408) 432-6311

Marie Callender's Restaurant   American $$ ◆◆
◍ Exit I-880 Calaveras Rd, s on Abbott. 333 S Abbott Ave. Homestyle cooking & speciality pies. A/C. Children's
  menu. Open 11 am-10 pm; closed 1/1 & 12/25. Beer & wine. AE, MC, VI.   ⊗ (408) 263-7437

MIRAMAR — See SAN DIEGO

MIRANDA — 400
Miranda Gardens Resort   Rates Subject to Change   *Cottages*   ◆◆
◍ 5/1-10/31   1P 45.00- 145.00 2P/1B   45.00- 145.00 2P/2B   60.00- 145.00 XP 10
  16 units. In the village. 6766 Avenue of the Giants. (PO Box 186, 95553) OPEN ALL YEAR. Spacious, shaded
  grounds; quiet location in the redwoods. Cozy single or duplex cottages. Refrigerators; C/TV; shower or comb
  baths. 8 2-bedrm units, 9 efficiencies. Pool 5/15-10/15; nature trails. Pets, $5 extra charge. 4 cabins with fireplace
  & 2 with whirlpool tub, $165. Pets not permitted in these cabins. Reserv deposit required; 7 days refund notice.
  AE, DI, DS, MC, VI. *(See ad p A148)*   Ⓓ (707) 943-3011

MISSION BAY PARK — See SAN DIEGO

MISSION HILLS — 32,000   See LOS ANGELES (San Fernando Valley)

MISSION VALLEY — See SAN DIEGO

MISSION VIEJO — 72,800   See also LAGUNA HILLS & LAKE FOREST
Hampton Inn   Rates Guaranteed   *Motel*   ◆◆
◍ All year [CP]   1P .... 57.00   2P/1B   .... 64.00   2P/2B   .... 64.00 XP
  Senior discount. 147 units. Just e of I-5; Oso Pkwy exit. 26328 Oso Pkwy. (92691) Check-in 3 pm. A/C; C/CATV;
  free & pay movies; phones. Htd pool; whirlpool. Pets. Rental microwaves & refrigerator units, $5 daily. Wkly
  rates avail. AE, DI, DS, MC, VI. FAX (714) 582-3287   ⊗ Ⓢ Ⓓ ⒧ (714) 582-7100

MI-WUK VILLAGE — 1,000

Christmas Tree Inn   Rates Subject to Change   *Motel* ◆◆
Fri & Sat   1P .... 49.95 2P/1B .... 55.00 2P/2B .... 55.00 XP 5
Sun-Thurs   1P .... 45.00 2P/1B .... 49.95 2P/2B .... 49.95 XP 5
16 units. 15 mi e of Sonora; on SR 108. 24685 SR 108. (PO Box 700, 95346) A/C; C/CATV; phones. Pool; whirl-pool. No pets. Rental microwaves & refrigerators. Wkly & monthly rates avail. Reserv deposit required; 3 days refund notice. AE, DI, DS, MC, VI. FAX (209) 586-2247   ⊗ Ⓓ (209) 586-1005

Mi-Wuk Motor Lodge   Rates Subject to Change   *Motel*
6/15-9/1 & weekends   1P 41.00- 46.00 2P/1B 41.00- 57.00 2P/2B 45.00- 60.00 XP 5
17 units. 15 mi e of Sonora on SR 108. (PO Box 70, 95346) OPEN ALL YEAR. Rating withheld pending comple-tion of renovation. Wooded area. C/CATV; VCPs; radios; phones; shower or comb baths. Coin laundry. Pool. Pets, $3 extra charge. 2-night minimum stay weekends. 1 housekeeping apartment, $67-$79 for 2-6 persons. Wkly rates avail. Reserv deposit required; 7 days refund notice. CB, DI, DS, MC, VI. FAX (209) 586-3031 *(See ad p A257)*   ⊗ Ⓓ (209) 586-3031

MODESTO — 164,700

Best Western Mallards Inn   AAA Special Value Rates   *Motel* ◆◆◆◆
All year   1P 67.00- 87.00 2P/1B 72.00- 92.00 2P/2B 72.00- 92.00 XP 6   F
126 units. Exit SR 99 at Briggsmore Blvd, 1/4 mi n on Sisk Rd. (95350) Check-in 3 pm. A/C; C/CATV; movies; VCPs. Radios; phones. Pool; whirlpool. AE, DI, DS, MC, VI. Cafeteria; 6:30 am-9:30 & 6-10 pm; beer & wine. FAX (209) 577-1717 *(See ad below)*   ⊗ Ⓢ Ⓓ Ⓖ (209) 577-3825

Best Western Town House Lodge   AAA Special Value Rates   *Motel* ◆◆
All year [CP]   1P 45.00- 50.00 2P/1B 53.00- 58.00 2P/2B 55.00- 60.00 XP 8
59 units. 1 mi e off Frwy 99; exit via Central Modesto at I St. 909 16th St. (95354) 42 refrigerators; A/C; C/CATV; movies; radios; phones; shower or comb baths. Pool. No pets. Wkly rates avail. AE, DI, DS, MC, VI. FAX (209) 579-9546 *(See ad p A257)*   ⊗ Ⓓ (209) 524-7261

Chalet Motel   AAA Special Value Rates   *Motel* ◆
All year   1P 36.00- 42.00 2P/1B 42.00- 48.00 2P/2B 42.00- 48.00 XP 6
40 units. 1/2 mi ne on SR 108. 115 Downey Ave. (95354) A/C; C/CATV; movies; 20 radios; phones; shower or comb baths. Small pool. No pets. 8 rooms with whirlpool tub, extra charge. Wkly rates avail. AE, DI, DS, MC, VI. Coffeeshop adjacent. *(See ad below)*   Ⓓ (209) 529-4370

Holiday Inn of Modesto   Rates Subject to Change   *Motor Inn* ◆◆
All year   1P .... 75.00 2P/1B .... 85.00 2P/2B .... 85.00 XP   F
Senior discount. 186 units. SR 99 exit Briggsmore Ave. 1612 Sisk Rd. (95350) A/C; C/CATV; VCPs; radios; phones. 2 pools, 1 indoor; wading pool; sauna; whirlpool; putting green; lighted tennis-2 courts; playground; exercise rm. No pets. AE, CB, DI, MC, VI. ● Restaurant; 6:30 am-2 & 5-10 pm; $9-$15; cocktails. FAX (209) 527-5074   ⊗ Ⓓ (209) 521-1612

Motel Orleans   Rates Subject to Change   *Motel*
All year   1P .... 32.00 2P/1B .... 37.00 2P/2B .... 39.00 XP 5
Senior discount. 70 units. SR 99 exit Kansas Ave. 500 Kansas Ave. (95351) 3-story, no elevator. A/C; C/CATV; phones; comb or shower baths. Coin laundry. Pool. No pets. Reserv deposit required; 3 days refund notice. AE, DI, DS, MC, VI. ● Coffeeshop; 5:30 am-9 pm; Sun 6 am-3 pm; $6-$12; beer & wine. ⊗ Ⓓ Ⓖ (209) 578-5400

Ramada Inn   AAA Special Value Rates   *Motel* ◆◆◆
All year [CP]   1P 62.00- 92.00 2P/1B 70.00- 100.00 2P/2B .... 75.00 XP 8   F
115 units. SR 99 exit Briggsmore Ave, 1 blk s. 2001 W Orangeburg Ave. (95350) Few rooms with microwave & wet bar. Check-in 3 pm. Refrigerators; A/C; C/CATV; movies; VCPs. Radios; phones. Pool; whirlpool. No pets. AE, DI, DS, MC, VI. FAX (209) 521-6034   ⊗ Ⓢ Ⓓ Ⓖ (209) 521-9000

Red Lion Hotel · Rates Subject to Change · *Hotel* ◆◆◆
Sun-Thurs 1P 96.00- 116.00   2P/1B 106.00- 127.00   2P/2B 106.00- 127.00   XP 10   F
Fri & Sat 1P .... 85.00   2P/1B .... 85.00   2P/2B .... 85.00   XP 10   F
265 units. SR 99 northbound exit central Modesto; southbound exit Maze Blvd; at Convention Center Plaza. 1150 9th St. (95354) Tastefully appointed rooms & public areas. Check-in 3 pm. A/C; C/CATV; pay movies; radios; phones. Htd pool; whirlpool; exercise rm. Pay valet garage. Airport transp. Pets. Suites, $225-$395. AE, DI, DS, MC, VI. ● Dining rm & coffeeshop; 6 am-11 pm; $8-$20; cocktails; entertainment. FAX (209) 526-6096 *(See ad p A3)*
⊗ Ⓢ Ⓓ ⓐ (209) 526-6000

Sundial Lodge · Rates Subject to Change · *Motor Inn* ◆◆
🅐 All year 1P .... 48.00   2P/1B .... 52.00   2P/2B .... 56.00   XP 4
48 units. On SR 108; southbound Frwy 99 exit e via Briggsmore Ave, s on McHenry Ave; northbound exit Central Modesto. 808 McHenry Ave. (95350) Few rooms with balcony. A/C; C/CATV; movies; phones; shower or comb baths. Small pool. No pets. 1 efficiency, $10 extra. AE, MC, VI. ● Dining rm, see separate listing. FAX (209) 521-2692
⊗ Ⓓ (209) 523-5642

Super 8 Motel · Rates Guaranteed · *Motel* ◆
🅐 All year 1P .... 44.00   2P/1B .... 48.00   2P/2B .... 51.00   XP 4   F
Senior discount. 80 units. SR 99 exit Briggsmore Ave. 2025 W Orangeburg Ave. (95350) A/C; C/CATV; movies; phones. Pool. No pets. Wkly rates avail. AE, DI, DS, MC, VI. Coffeeshop opposite. FAX (209) 575-4118
⊗ Ⓓ (209) 577-8008

Vagabond Inn · Rates Subject to Change · *Motel* ◆◆
🅐 All year [CP] 1P 38.00- 48.00   2P/1B 42.00- 52.00   2P/2B .... 57.00   XP 5   F
99 units. 2 mi n on SR 108; from SR 99, exit Briggsmore Ave; 2 1/4 mi e to McHenry Ave, then 2 blks s. 1525 McHenry Ave. (95350) A/C; C/CATV; movies; radios; phones. Pool. Pets, $3 daily extra charge. AE, DI, DS, MC, VI. Coffeeshop adjacent. FAX (209) 575-2015 *(See ad below)*
⊗ Ⓓ (209) 521-6340

Western Host Motor Hotel · Rates Guaranteed · *Motel* ◆◆◆
🅐 All year 1P .... 39.00   2P/1B .... 45.00   2P/2B .... 45.00   XP 5   F
104 units. 1 3/4 mi n on SR 108; exit Briggsmore Ave; from SR 99, 2 1/4 mi e, then 1/2 mi s on McHenry Ave. 1312 McHenry Ave. (95350) A/C; C/CATV; movies; radios; phones; comb or shower baths. Coin laundry. Pool; whirlpool. No pets. Reserv deposit required. AE, CB, DI, MC, VI. Restaurant adjacent. FAX (209) 527-2033 *(See ad below)*
⊗ Ⓓ (209) 527-1010

RESTAURANT

Sundial Lodge Dining Room · American · $$ · ◆◆
In Sundial Lodge. Varied menu. Attractive decor. A/C. Early bird specials. Open 5 am-10 pm; Fri & Sat-11 pm; closed 12/25. Cocktails & lounge. AE, MC, VI.
⊗ (209) 524-4375

MOJAVE — 2,900

Scottish Inns · Rates Subject to Change · *Motel* ◆◆
🅐 All year 1P 35.00- 45.00   2P/1B 42.00- 50.00   2P/2B 40.00- 55.00   XP 5
25 units. On SR 14 (Sierra Hwy). 16352 Sierra Hwy. (93501) A/C; C/CATV; movies; phones. Small pool; whirlpool. Small pets only, $5. Microwave & refrigerator. AE, DI, DS, MC, VI.
⊗ Ⓓ ⓐ (805) 824-9317

Western Inn · Rates Subject to Change · *Motor Inn* ◆◆
🅐 All year 1P .... 33.00   2P/1B .... 35.00   2P/2B .... 35.00   XP 2
Senior discount. 23 units. On SR 14 (Sierra Hwy). 16200 Sierra Hwy. (93501) A/C; C/CATV; movies; radios; phones. Pool; whirlpool. Wkly rates avail. MC, VI. Coffeeshop; 7 am-10 pm; $3.25-$9; beer. FAX (805) 824-3605
⊗ Ⓢ Ⓓ (805) 824-3601

MONROVIA — 35,800   (See PASADENA & VICINITY AREA spotting map page A327; see index starting on page A326)

Holiday Inn **7**   AAA Special Value Rates   *Motor Inn* ◆◆◆
🏧 All year   1P .... 75.00   2P/1B .... 79.00   2P/2B .... 75.00   XP 10   F
174 units. Adjacent to I-210, exit Huntington Dr. 924 W Huntington Dr. (91016) Check-in 3 pm. A/C; C/CATV; movies; radios; phones. Coin laundry. Htd pool; whirlpool. Fee for: airport transp. Pets. Monthly rates avail. AE, CB, DI, MC, VI. ● Restaurant; 6 am-10 pm; $9.95-$15.95; cocktails. FAX (818) 357-1900
⊗ Ⓢ Ⓓ Ⓛ (818) 357-1900

Howard Johnson Plaza Hotel **8**   AAA Special Value Rates   *Motor Inn* ◆◆◆
🏧 All year   1P 59.00- 125.00   2P/1B   69.00- 135.00   2P/2B   69.00- 140.00   XP 10   F
151 units. Adjacent to I-210, Huntington Dr exit. 700 W Huntington Dr. (91016) A/C; C/CATV; movies; phones. Htd pool; whirlpools; exercise rm. No pets. Wkly rates avail. AE, CB, DI, MC, VI. ● Dining rm; 6 am-2 & 5-10 pm; $7.50-$13; cocktails; entertainment. FAX (818) 357-2786 *(See ad below)*   ⊗ Ⓢ Ⓓ Ⓛ (818) 357-5211

Oak Tree Inn **9**   Rates Subject to Change   *Motel* ◆◆◆
🏧 All year [CP]   1P 45.00- 60.00   2P/1B   45.00- 60.00   2P/2B   45.00- 60.00   XP 5
Senior discount. 56 units. Adjacent to I-210, Huntington Dr exit. 788 W Huntington Dr. (91016) Refrigerators; A/C; C/CATV; movies; radios; phones. Htd pool; whirlpool. No pets. Wkly & monthly rates avail. AE, DI, DS, MC, VI. FAX (818) 301-0657 *(See ad p A259)*   ⊗ Ⓢ Ⓓ Ⓛ (818) 358-8981

MONTEBELLO — 59,600

Holiday Inn   Rates Subject to Change   *Motor Inn* ◆◆◆
All year   1P .... 49.00   2P/1B .... 49.00   2P/2B .... 49.00   XP
Senior discount. 156 units. N side adjacent to I-5, exit Slauson Ave. 7709 Telegraph Rd. (90640) A/C; C/CATV; movies; radios; phones. Coin laundry. Pool. AE, DI, DS, MC, VI. ● Restaurant; 6 am-10 pm; $8.95-$15.95; cocktails. FAX (213) 721-4410   ⊗ Ⓢ Ⓓ (213) 724-1400

MONTEREY — 32,000   (See MONTEREY PENINSULA spotting map pages A262 & A263; see index starting below) See also CARMEL, MARINA, PACIFIC GROVE, PEBBLE BEACH & SEASIDE

Index of Establishments on the MONTEREY PENINSULA AREA Spotting Map

---

(See MONTEREY PENINSULA spotting map pages A262 & A263)

Delfino's on The Bay	7	
⊕ Abalonetti	8	
Mark Thomas' Outrigger	9	
⊕ Whaling Station Inn	10	
⊕ Sardine Factory	11	

PACIFIC GROVE
⊕ Olympia Motor Lodge	55
⊕ Rosedale Inn	56
⊕ Pacific Gardens Inn	57
⊕ Executive Lodge	58
⊕ Larchwood Inn Motel	59
⊕ Pacific Grove Inn	60
⊕ Borg's Ocean Front Motel	61
⊕ Best Western Butterfly Trees Lodge	62
⊕ Lighthouse Lodge	63
⊕ The Wilkies Motel	64
⊕ Butterfly Grove Inn	65
⊕ Pacific Grove Motel	66
⊕ Quality Inn	67

RESTAURANTS
Old Bath House Restaurant	15
⊕ Fandango	16
El Cocodrilo	17

PEBBLE BEACH
⊕ The Inn at Spanish Bay	72
⊕ The Lodge at Pebble Beach	73

CARMEL
⊕ Best Western Carmel's Town House Lodge	77
⊕ Carmel Studio Lodge	78
⊕ Best Western Bay View Inn	79
⊕ Carmel Village Inn	81
⊕ Pine Inn	82
⊕ Carmel Normandy Inn	83
⊕ Lobos Lodge	84

⊕ Cypress Inn	85
⊕ Coachman's Inn	86
⊕ Wayside Inn	87
⊕ Carriage House Inn	88
Cobblestone Inn	89
⊕ Adobe Inn-Carmel	90
⊕ Colonial Terrace Inn	91
⊕ Carmel Mission Inn-Best Western	92
⊕ Carmel River Inn	93
⊕ Highlands Inn	94
⊕ Tickle Pink Inn	95
⊕ Carmel Oaks Inn	96
La Playa Hotel	97
⊕ Carmel Sands Lodge	98
⊕ Ocean View Lodge	99
⊕ Horizon Inn	100
⊕ Carmel Tradewinds Inn	101
⊕ Hofsas House	102
⊕ Dolores Lodge	103
⊕ Carmel Fireplace Inn	104
⊕ Dolphin Inn	105
⊕ Svendsgaard's	106
⊕ Carmel Wayfarer Inn	107
⊕ Carmel Garden Court	108
⊕ Candle Light Inn	109

RESTAURANTS
Casanova	21
Clam Box	22
Rio Grill	23
⊕ Anton & Michel	24
Adobe Inn Bully III	25
⊕ Sans Souci	26
From Scratch	27
Silver Jones	28

Arbor Inn 30

		Rates Subject to Change						*Motel*		◆
⊕ Fri & Sat 6/15-10/31 [CP]	1P	69.00- 109.00	2P/1B	69.00- 109.00	2P/2B	79.00- 119.00	XP 10		F
Sun-Thurs 6/15-10/31 &									
Fri-Sat 11/1-6/14 [CP]	1P	59.00- 99.00	2P/1B	59.00- 99.00	2P/2B	69.00- 109.00	XP 10		F
Sun-Thurs 11/1-6/14 [CP]	1P	49.00- 89.00	2P/1B	49.00- 89.00	2P/2B	59.00- 99.00	XP 5		F

Senior discount. 56 units. 1/2 mi s; SR 1 exit Munras Ave. 1058 Munras Ave. (93940) 12 rooms with fireplace.
C/CATV; 34 radios; phones. Whirlpool. No pets. Wkly rates avail. Reserv deposit required. AE, DI, DS, MC, VI.
FAX (408) 372-4687   ⊗ Ⓓ (408) 372-3381

Bay Park Hotel 41

		Rates Subject to Change						*Motor Inn*		◆◆◆
⊕ 6/15-9/30	1P	79.00- 129.00	2P/1B	79.00- 129.00	2P/2B	79.00- 129.00	XP 7		F
10/1-6/14	1P	69.00- 109.00	2P/1B	69.00- 109.00	2P/2B	69.00- 109.00	XP 7		F

80 units. 1 mi s; SR 1 exit Munras Ave. 1425 Munras Ave. (93940) 20 refrigerators; A/C; C/CATV; radios; phones.
Pool; whirlpool. Pets. AE, DI, DS, MC, VI. ● Restaurant; 7 am-2 & 5:30-9 pm; $9-$14; cocktails.
FAX (408) 373-4258 *(See ad p A109 and below)*   ⊗ Ⓓ (408) 649-1020

With your AAA membership card and exclusive Hertz discount card,
you are recognized all over the world as a special customer.

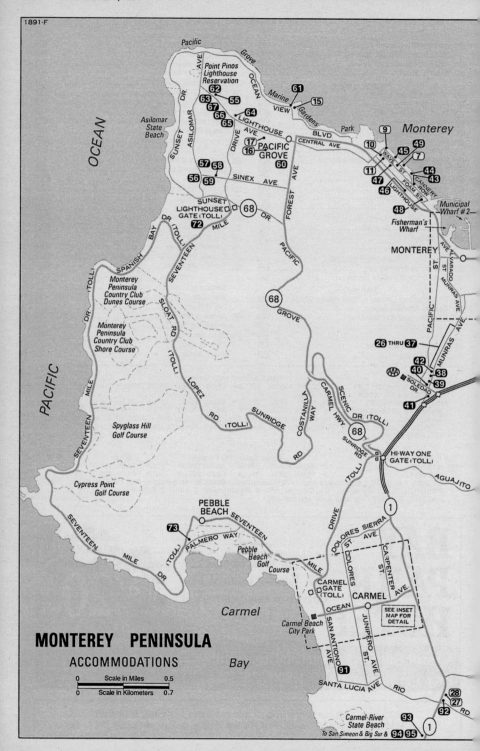

1891-F

MONTEREY PENINSULA

ACCOMMODATIONS

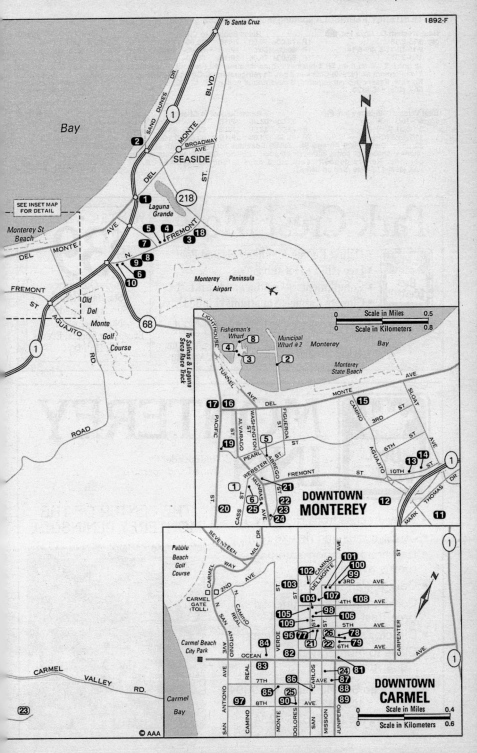

(See MONTEREY PENINSULA spotting map pages A262 & A263)

Best Western De Anza Inn **5** ◆◆◆

								Motel			
6/15-9/15	1P	70.00-	99.00	2P/1B	80.00-	110.00	2P/2B	85.00-	115.00	XP	8
9/16-10/31 & 4/1-6/14	1P	60.00-	80.00	2P/1B	65.00-	89.00	2P/2B	75.00-	95.00	XP	8
11/1-3/31	1P	60.00-	75.00	2P/1B	65.00-	89.00	2P/2B	70.00-	90.00	XP	8

Rates Subject to Change

42 units. 1 3/4 mi n on SR 1 business rt; northbound exit Fremont St, southbound exit Del Rey Oaks, SR 218. 2141 Fremont St. (93940) Check-in 3 pm. 14 refrigerators; C/CATV; pay movies; radios; phones. Pool; whirlpool. No pets. Reserv deposit required; 3 days refund notice. AE, DI, DS, MC, VI. Restaurant & coffeeshop adjacent. FAX (408) 646-8130   ⊗ ⑤ Ⓓ Ⓚ (408) 646-8300

Best Western Monterey Inn **23** ◆◆◆

								Motel			
6/1-10/31 [CP]	1P	83.00-	103.00	2P/1B	83.00-	103.00	2P/2B	88.00-	108.00	XP	8
3/1-5/31 [CP]	1P	73.00-	83.00	2P/1B	73.00-	83.00	2P/2B	78.00-	98.00	XP	8
11/1-2/28 [CP]	1P	63.00-	73.00	2P/1B	63.00-	73.00	2P/2B	68.00-	88.00	XP	8

Rates Subject to Change

80 units. Center. 825 Abrego St. (93940) Spacious rooms, few with view. 30 refrigerators; C/CATV; radios; phones; shower or comb baths. Small pool; whirlpool. Garage. No pets. 9 rooms with fireplace, $98-$118 for 2 persons. Reserv deposit required; 3 days refund notice. AE, CB, DI, DS. Coffeeshop adjacent. FAX (408) 373-3246 *(See ad below)*   ⊗ ⑤ Ⓓ Ⓚ (408) 373-5345

(See MONTEREY PENINSULA spotting map pages A262 & A263)

Best Western Park Crest Motel 31   Rates Subject to Change   *Motel*   ◆◆◆
🐸 Fri & Sat 6/15-9/30 [CP]   1P   69.00- 159.00   2P/1B   75.00- 159.00   2P/2B   79.00- 159.00   XP 10
53 units. 1/2 mi s; SR 1 exit Munras Ave. 1100 Munras Ave. (93940) OPEN ALL YEAR. Few units with view of bay.
2 units with private lanai. C/CATV; movies; radios; phones; comb or shower baths. 2 2-bedrm units. Swimming
pool open 4/15-10/31. No pets. Reserv deposit required. AE, CB, DI, MC, VI. FAX (408) 372-2317 *(See ad p A264)*
                                               ⊗ Ⓓ (408) 372-4576

Best Western Ramona Inn 3   Rates Subject to Change   *Motel*   ◆◆

🐸 7/1-8/31 [CP]	1P	....	75.00	2P/1B	....	80.00	2P/2B	....	85.00 XP 10 F
9/1-10/31 [CP]	1P	....	60.00	2P/1B	....	65.00	2P/2B	....	76.00 XP 10 F
11/1-6/30 [CP]	1P	....	55.00	2P/1B	....	60.00	2P/2B	....	65.00 XP 10 F

Senior discount. 34 units. 1 3/4 mi n on SR 1 business rt; northbound exit Fremont St, southbound exit Del Rey
Oaks, SR 218. 2332 Fremont St. (93940) C/CATV; movies; radios; phones. Small pool; whirlpool. No pets. 4 units
with refrigerator & microwave, $8 extra. Wkly rates avail. Reserv deposit required. AE, DI, DS, MC, VI. Restau-
rant adjacent.   ⊗ Ⓓ (408) 373-2445

(See MONTEREY PENINSULA spotting map pages A262 & A263)

Best Western Steinbeck Lodge **38**   Rates Subject to Change   *Motel*   ◆◆
🏵 Fri & Sat 6/15-9/30 [CP]   1P 69.00- 159.00   2P/1B   75.00- 159.00   2P/2B   79.00- 159.00 XP 10
32 units. 3/4 mi s; SR 1 exit Munras Ave. 1300 Munras Ave. (93940) OPEN ALL YEAR. 8 refrigerators; C/CATV; 22
radios; phones. Pool. No pets. Reserv deposit required. AE, DI, DS, MC, VI. *(See ad p A265)*
⊗ Ⓓ (408) 373-3203

Best Western Victorian Inn **46**   Rates Subject to Change   *Motel*   ◆◆◆
🏵 Fri & Sat 6/1-10/31 [CP]   1P 149.00- 189.00   2P/1B 149.00- 189.00   2P/2B 149.00- 189.00 XP 10   F
Sun-Thurs 6/1-10/31 & Fri-Sat
11/1-5/31 [CP]   1P 139.00- 169.00   2P/1B 139.00- 169.00   2P/2B 139.00- 169.00 XP 10   F
Sun-Thurs 11/1-5/31 [CP]   1P 119.00- 149.00   2P/1B 119.00- 149.00   2P/2B 119.00- 149.00 XP 10   F
Senior discount. 68 units. 2 blks w of Cannery Row. 487 Foam St. (93940) All units with gas burning fireplace.
Check-in 3 pm. Refrigerators; C/CATV; pay movies; radios; phones. Whirlpool. Garage. Pets, $25 extra charge.
Reserv deposit required. AE, DI, DS, MC, VI. Restaurant adjacent. FAX (408) 373-4815 Ⓢ Ⓓ 🅰 (408) 373-8000

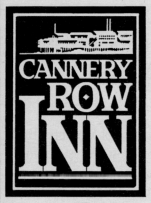

PATRONIZE AAA/CAA ESTABLISHMEMTS

(See MONTEREY PENINSULA spotting map pages A262 & A263)

Californian Motel 6 — Motel ◆
Rates Subject to Change
Fri & Sat — 1P 49.00- 61.00 2P/1B 59.00- 85.00 2P/2B 69.00- 99.00 XP 6 F
Sun-Thurs 6/1-9/30 — 1P 34.00- 49.00 2P/1B 39.00- 65.00 2P/2B 42.00- 74.00 XP 6 F
Sun-Thurs 10/1-5/31 — 1P .... 29.00 2P/1B 34.00- 38.00 2P/2B 38.00- 45.00 XP 6 F
Senior discount. 47 units. 1 3/4 mi n; northbound exit Fremont St, southbound exit Casa Verde. 2042 Fremont St. (93940) C/CATV; movies; radios; phones; comb or shower baths. 12 kitchens. Pool; whirlpool. Pets. Wkly rates avail in winter. Reserv deposit required. AE, DI, DS, MC, VI. (See ad p A266) ⊗ Ⓓ (408) 372-5851

Cannery Row Inn 48 — Motel ◆◆
Rates Subject to Change
6/1-10/31 [CP] — 1P 85.00- 150.00 2P/1B 85.00- 150.00 2P/2B 90.00- 150.00 XP 10
11/1-5/31 [CP] — 1P 65.00- 130.00 2P/1B 65.00- 130.00 2P/2B 85.00- 130.00 XP 10
Senior discount. 32 units. 200 Foam St. (93940) Some rooms with view. Many with gas fireplace. Check-in 3 pm. Refrigerators; C/CATV; radios; phones. Whirlpool. Garage. No pets. 2-night minimum stay weekends. Reserv deposit required; 3 days refund notice. AE, MC, VI. FAX (408) 649-2566 (See ad p A266) Ⓢ Ⓓ 🅱 (408) 649-8580

Carmel Hill Motor Lodge 39 — Motel ◆
Rates Subject to Change
Fri & Sat — 1P 60.00- 65.00 2P/1B 65.00- 85.00 2P/2B 85.00- 110.00 XP 10
Sun-Thurs 5/15-10/31 — 1P 50.00- 85.00 2P/1B 60.00- 90.00 2P/2B 80.00- 100.00 XP 10
Sun-Thurs 11/1-5/14 — 1P 40.00- 50.00 2P/1B 45.00- 55.00 2P/2B 50.00- 65.00 XP 10
38 units. 1 mi s; SR 1 exit via Munras Ave. 1374 Munras Ave. (93940) C/CATV; phones; shower baths. Small pool. No pets. Reserv deposit required. AE, MC, VI. ⊗ Ⓓ (408) 373-3252

Casa Munras Garden Hotel 25 — Motor Inn ◆◆◆
Rates Guaranteed
All year — 1P 71.00- 126.00 2P/1B 71.00- 126.00 2P/2B 81.00- 126.00 XP 12
150 units. 700 Munras Ave. (PO Box 1351, 93940) Spacious landscaped grounds. Colorful garden. Few fireplaces. Check-in 3 pm. C/CATV; radios; phones; comb or shower baths. 1 kitchen. Htd pool. No pets. 4 suites with fireplace, $149-$350 for up to 2 persons. Reserv deposit required. AE, CB, DI, MC, VI. ● Dining rm & coffeeshop; 7 am-2 & 5-9 pm; $9-$16; cocktails; entertainment. FAX (408) 375-1365 (See ad p A110 and below) Ⓓ (408) 375-2411

Colton Inn 20 — Motel ◆◆◆
Rates Subject to Change
4/1-10/31 — 1P 89.00- 96.00 2P/1B 89.00- 96.00 2P/2B 96.00- 104.00 XP
11/1-3/31 — 1P 78.00- 84.00 2P/1B 78.00- 84.00 2P/2B 78.00- 92.00 XP
Senior discount. 50 units. In Old Monterey. 707 Pacific St. (93940) Some fireplaces. C/CATV; radios; phones. 7 efficiencies, no utensils. Sauna. No pets. Reserv deposit required. AE, CB, DI, MC, VI. Sun deck. FAX (408) 373-6987 (See ad p A268) ⊗ Ⓓ 🅱 (408) 649-6500

(See MONTEREY PENINSULA spotting map pages A262 & A263)

Comfort Inn-Carmel Hill 34   Rates Subject to Change   *Motel*   ◆◆

Fri & Sat	1P	....	75.00	2P/1B	....	80.00	2P/2B	....	85.00	XP 5	F
Sun-Thurs 6/16-10/31	1P	50.00-	65.00	2P/1B	60.00-	75.00	2P/2B	70.00-	80.00	XP 5	F
Sun-Thurs 4/1-6/15	1P	48.00-	65.00	2P/1B	50.00-	70.00	2P/2B	50.00-	70.00	XP 5	F
Sun-Thurs 11/1-3/31	1P	40.00-	55.00	2P/1B	45.00-	55.00	2P/2B	50.00-	60.00	XP 5	F

Senior discount. 29 units. 3/4 mi s; SR 1 exit Munras Ave. 1252 Munras Ave. (93940) C/CATV; VCPs; phones; shower or comb baths. Small pool. No pets. 1 2-bedroom unit, $120 5/1-10/1 for up to 6 persons. Reserv deposit required; 3 days refund notice. AE, DI, DS, MC, VI.   ⊗ Ⓓ (408) 372-2908

Comfort Inn-Del Monte Beach 1   Rates Subject to Change   *Motel*   ◆◆◆

6/29-9/30	1P	64.00-	119.00	2P/1B	64.00-	119.00	2P/2B	69.00-	129.00	XP 6	F
5/1-6/28	1P	59.00-	109.00	2P/1B	59.00-	109.00	2P/2B	69.00-	109.00	XP 6	F
10/1-4/30	1P	45.00-	109.00	2P/1B	45.00-	109.00	2P/2B	50.00-	109.00	XP 6	F

Senior discount. 47 units. E of SR 1; exit SR 218 Seaside-Del Rey Oaks. 2401 Del Monte Ave. (93940) Few units overlooking small lake. C/CATV; radios; phones. No pets. Reserv deposit required; 3 days refund notice. AE, CB, DI, MC, VI. FAX (408) 373-4813 *(See ad below)*   ⊗ Ⓢ Ⓓ Ⓚ (408) 373-7100

Comfort Inn-Munras Ave 37   Rates Subject to Change   *Motel*   ◆◆

Fri & Sat 6/2-9/30	1P	....	80.00	2P/1B	....	90.00	2P/2B	....	95.00	XP 5	F
Sun-Thurs 6/2-9/30	1P	55.00-	65.00	2P/1B	65.00-	75.00	2P/2B	75.00-	85.00	XP 5	F
Fri & Sat 10/1-6/1	1P	50.00-	70.00	2P/1B	55.00-	75.00	2P/2B	55.00-	75.00	XP 5	F
Sun-Thurs 10/1-6/1	1P	50.00-	60.00	2P/1B	50.00-	60.00	2P/2B	50.00-	60.00	XP 5	F

Senior discount. 36 units. 3/4 mi s; SR 1 exit Munras Ave. 1262 Munras Ave. (93940) 5 refrigerators; C/CATV; pay movies; VCPs. Phones; shower or comb baths. 3 2-bedrm units. Pool. No pets. [CP] avail. AE, DI, DS, MC, VI. FAX (408) 646-1950   ⊗ Ⓓ (408) 372-8088

Cypress Gardens Motel 32   Rates Subject to Change   *Motel*   ◆◆

5/28-10/31 & Fri-Sat [CP]	1P	....	84.00	2P/1B	....	84.00	2P/2B	....	104.00	XP 10	F
Sun-Thurs 11/1-5/27 [CP]	1P	59.00-	79.00	2P/1B	59.00-	79.00	2P/2B	69.00-	89.00	XP 10	F

Senior discount. 46 units. 1/2 mi s; SR 1 exit Munras Ave. 1150 Munras Ave. (93940) Nicely landscaped grounds. Check-in 3 pm. 12 refrigerators; C/CATV; 28 radios; phones. 1 2-bedrm unit. Pool; whirlpool. Pets. 1- & 2-bedroom suites with kitchen & fireplace, $150-$225. Reserv deposit required; 3 days refund notice. AE, CB, DI, MC, VI. FAX (408) 649-1329 *(See ad p A102)*   ⊗ Ⓓ (408) 373-2761

Cypress Tree Inn 4   Rates Subject to Change   *Motel*   ◆◆

5/1-10/31 & weekends	1P	52.00-	92.00	2P/1B	62.00-	94.00	2P/2B	66.00-	110.00	XP 6
11/1-4/30	1P	46.00-	62.00	2P/1B	48.00-	64.00	2P/2B	58.00-	68.00	XP 6

55 units. 1 3/4 mi n on SR 1 business rt; northbound exit N Fremont St, southbound exit Del Rey Oaks, SR 218. 2227 N Fremont St. (93940) Few rooms with patio. Check-in 4 pm. Refrigerators; C/CATV; radios; phones. 6 kitchens. Coin laundry. Sauna; whirlpool. No pets. 10 rooms with hot tub, $95-$195 for 2 persons. Reserv deposit required; 3 days refund notice. MC, VI. FAX (408) 372-2940 *(See ad p A269)*   Ⓓ (408) 372-7586

(See MONTEREY PENINSULA spotting map pages A262 & A263)

Days Inn-Monterey 36   Rates Subject to Change   *Motel*   ◆◆
5/15-9/30   1P 65.00- 85.00   2P/1B   75.00- 95.00   2P/2B   85.00-125.00   XP 10
10/1-5/14   1P 45.00- 65.00   2P/1B   50.00- 75.00   2P/2B   55.00- 80.00   XP 10
Senior discount. 34 units. 3/4 mi s; SR 1 exit Munras Ave. 1288 Munras Ave. (93940) Formerly The Monterey Pines. Refrigerators; C/CATV; pay movies; VCPs. Radios; phones; shower or comb baths. No pets. 6 units with whirlpool & fireplace, $125-$150 for up to 2 persons. Microwaves. [CP] avail. Reserv deposit required; 3 days refund notice. AE, DI, DS, MC, VI.   ⊗ Ⓓ (408) 375-2168

Del Monte Pines Motel 42   Rates Subject to Change   *Motel*   ◆◆
Fri & Sat 5/15-10/31 [CP]   1P 64.00-104.00   2P/1B   69.00-104.00   2P/2B   74.00- 119.00   XP 10
Sun-Thurs 5/15-10/31 [CP]   1P 59.00- 89.00   2P/1B   64.00- 94.00   2P/2B   69.00- 99.00   XP 10
Fri & Sat 11/1-5/14 [CP]   1P 54.00- 84.00   2P/1B   59.00- 84.00   2P/2B   64.00- 99.00   XP 10
Sun-Thurs 11/1-5/14 [CP]   1P 49.00- 79.00   2P/1B   54.00- 84.00   2P/2B   59.00- 94.00   XP 5
Senior discount. 19 units. 1/4 mi s; SR 1 exit Munras Ave. 1298 Munras Ave. (93940) C/CATV; movies; 15 radios; phones; shower or comb baths. Small pool. No pets. Reserv deposit required. AE, DI, DS, MC, VI.   ⊗ Ⓓ (408) 375-2323

Doubletree Hotel 16   Rates Subject to Change   *Motor Inn*   ◆◆◆
2/1-11/21   1P 125.00- 185.00   2P/1B   140.00- 200.00   2P/2B   140.00- 200.00   XP 15
11/22-1/31   1P 115.00- 175.00   2P/1B   130.00- 190.00   2P/2B   130.00- 190.00   XP 15
374 units. Corner of Pacific & Del Monte aves, adjacent to Monterey Conference Center; entrance at Alvarado St. 2 Portola Plaza. (93940) Few rooms overlooking bay & harbor. Check-in 3 pm. C/CATV; pay movies; radios; phones. Pool; whirlpool. Fee for: tennis-3 courts. Pay valet garage. No pets. Monthly rates avail. Reserv deposit required. AE, CB, DI, MC, VI. ● 2 restaurants; 6 am-10 pm; $10-$20; cocktails; entertainment. FAX (408) 372-0620 *(See ad p A270)*   ⊗ Ⓓ (408) 649-4511

(See MONTEREY PENINSULA spotting map pages A262 & A263)

Driftwood Motel 18

		Rates Subject to Change							Motel			◆
Fri & Sat 6/1-10/31	1P	55.00-	75.00	2P/1B	60.00-	80.00	2P/2B	60.00-	80.00	XP	5	F
Sun-Thurs 6/1-10/31	1P	45.00-	60.00	2P/1B	50.00-	70.00	2P/2B	50.00-	70.00	XP	5	F
Fri & Sat 11/1-5/31	1P	40.00-	60.00	2P/1B	45.00-	65.00	2P/2B	45.00-	65.00	XP	5	F
Sun-Thurs 11/1-5/31	1P	32.00-	40.00	2P/1B	36.00-	45.00	2P/2B	36.00-	45.00	XP	5	F

Senior discount. 14 units. 1 3/4 mi n on SR 1 business rt; northbound exit Fremont St, southbound exit Del Rey Oaks, SR 218. 2362 N Fremont St. (93940) C/CATV; phones; shower baths. No pets. Wkly & monthly rates avail. Reserv deposit required; 3 days refund notice. AE, DI, DS, MC, VI. FAX (408) 655-1621   ⊗ Ⓓ (408) 372-5059

El Adobe Inn 27

		Rates Subject to Change							Motel			◆◆
5/26-10/31 & Fri-Sat [CP]	1P	74.00-	89.00	2P/1B	74.00-	89.00	2P/2B	74.00-	89.00	XP	10	F
11/1-5/25 & Sun-Thurs [CP]	1P	54.00-	79.00	2P/1B	54.00-	79.00	2P/2B	54.00-	79.00	XP	10	F

Senior discount. 26 units. 1/4 mi s; SR 1 traffic exit via Munras Ave. 936 Munras Ave. (93940) 8 refrigerators; C/CATV; movies; phones; shower or comb baths. Hot tub. Pets. Reserv deposit required; 3 days refund notice. AE, DI, DS, MC, VI. *(See ad p A102)*   ⊗ Ⓓ (408) 372-5409

El Dorado Inn 26

		Rates Subject to Change							Motel			◆
Fri & Sat 5/15-10/31 [CP]	1P	59.00-	99.00	2P/1B	59.00-	99.00	2P/2B	79.00-	120.00	XP	10	F
Sun-Thurs 5/15-10/31 [CP]	1P	49.00-	79.00	2P/1B	49.00-	79.00	2P/2B	69.00-	109.00	XP	10	F
Fri & Sat 11/1-5/14 [CP]	1P	49.00-	69.00	2P/1B	49.00-	69.00	2P/2B	59.00-	79.00	XP	10	F
Sun-Thurs 11/1-5/14 [CP]	1P	39.00-	59.00	2P/1B	39.00-	59.00	2P/2B	49.00-	69.00	XP	10	F

15 units. 2 blks s; corner El Dorado St & Munras Ave. 900 Munras Ave. (93940) Few fireplaces. C/CATV; movies; phones; shower or comb baths. No pets. Reserv deposit required. AE, DI, DS, MC, VI.   ⊗ Ⓓ (408) 373-2921

(See MONTEREY PENINSULA spotting map pages A262 & A263)

Fairgrounds Travelodge **10**   Rates Subject to Change   *Motor Inn* ◆◆
♿ 4/1-10/31   1P .... 55.00 2P/1B .... 60.00 2P/2B .... 65.00 XP 10   F
   11/1-3/31   1P .... 45.00 2P/1B .... 50.00 2P/2B .... 55.00 XP 6   F
Senior discount. 103 units. At jct SR 1 & Fremont St. 2030 Fremont St. (93940) Large rooms. Check-in 3 pm. 20
refrigerators; C/CATV; pay movies; VCPs. Radios; phones; shower or comb baths. 1 2-bedrm unit. Coin laundry.
Pool. No pets. Reserv deposit required. AE, CB, DI, MC, VI. Restaurant adjacent. Cocktails. FAX (408) 649-8741
                                                 ⊗ ⒟ (408) 373-3381

Holiday Inn Express **47**   Rates Subject to Change   *Motel* ◆◆◆
♿ Fri & Sat [CP]   1P 105.00- 155.00 2P/1B 105.00- 155.00 2P/2B 105.00- 155.00 XP 10
   Sun-Thurs [CP]   1P 95.00- 125.00 2P/1B   95.00- 125.00 2P/2B 95.00- 125.00 XP 10
43 units. 1 blk from bay. 443 Wave St. (93940) Formerly Steinbeck Gardens Inn. Check-in 3 pm. 6 refrigerators;
C/CATV; radios; phones. Whirlpool. Garage. No pets. Reserv deposit required. Complimentary beverages each
evening. AE, DI, MC, VI. FAX (408) 372-1969 *(See ad p A269)*   ⊗ Ⓢ ⒟ Ⓓ 🔧 (408) 372-1800

(See MONTEREY PENINSULA spotting map pages A262 & A263)

Holiday Inn Resort 🟦 12   Rates Subject to Change   *Motor Inn*   ◆◆◆
⊕ 4/1-10/31   1P 112.00- 172.00   2P/1B   112.00- 172.00   2P/2B 112.00- 159.00   XP 15   F
Senior discount. 204 units. E off SR 1 via Aguajito Rd; southbound exit Fisherman's Wharf. 1000 Aguajito Rd.
(93940) OPEN ALL YEAR. All rooms with balcony. Check-in 4 pm. 30 refrigerators; A/C; C/CATV; pay movies;
VCPs. Radios; phones. Pool; sauna; whirlpool; putting green; tennis-2 courts. Garage & parking lot. Pets. Reserv deposit required. AE, DI, DS, MC, VI. ● Restaurant; 6:30 am-10 pm; $9-$22; cocktails. FAX (408) 655-8608
(See ad p A271)   ⊗ Ⓢ Ⓓ ⓰ (408) 373-6141

Hotel Pacific 🟦 17   Rates Subject to Change   *Motel*   ◆◆◆◆
⊕ All year [CP]   1P 144.00- 214.00   2P/1B   144.00- 214.00   2P/2B 144.00- 214.00   XP 20
Senior discount. 104 units. 2 blks s of Fisherman's Wharf. 300 Pacific St. (93940) Adobe style; all rooms have
deck, wet bar & fireplace; few with view. Check-in 4 pm. Refrigerators; C/CATV; movies; radios; phones. 1
2-bedrm unit. Whirlpools. Garage. No pets. Reserv deposit required. Complimentary beverages each evening.
AE, MC, VI. FAX (408) 373-6921   Ⓢ Ⓓ ⓰ (408) 373-5700

Howard Johnson Lodge 🟦 24   Rates Subject to Change   *Motel*   ◆◆
⊕ 5/15-10/15 [CP]   1P 60.00- 75.00   2P/1B   75.00- 99.00   2P/2B   85.00- 120.00   XP 10   F
    10/16-5/14 [CP]   1P 45.00- 55.00   2P/1B   49.00- 85.00   2P/2B   65.00- 85.00   XP 10   F
55 units. Exit SR 1 at Fremont St; 3/4 mi w & 1/4 mi s on Abrego St. 850 Abrego St. (93940) Formerly San Carlos
Inn. Few large rooms with ocean view. C/CATV; 24 radios; phones; comb or shower baths. Whirlpool. No pets.
2-night minimum stay weekends 5/15-10/15. Wkly rates avail. Reserv deposit required; 3 days refund notice. AE,
CB, DI, MC, VI. FAX (408) 649-6353 *(See ad p A271)*   ⊗ Ⓓ (408) 649-6332

**Hyatt Regency-Monterey Resort & Conference
Center** 🟦 11   Rates Subject to Change   *Resort Complex*   ◆◆◆◆
⊕ All year   1P 135.00- 215.00   2P/1B   160.00- 240.00   2P/2B 160.00- 240.00   XP 25   F
Senior discount. 575 units. 1 mi n off SR 1; northbound exit Aguajito Rd, southbound exit Monterey. 1 Old Golf
Course Rd. (93940) Landscaped grounds. Some suites with fireplace. Check-in 3 pm. C/CATV; pay movies; radios; phones; comb or shower baths. 2 pools, 1 htd; whirlpools; rental bicycles; health & fitness center. Fee for:
golf-18 holes, tennis-6 courts, 2 lighted. Parking lot. No pets. [MAP] avail. Monthly rates avail. Reserv deposit
required. AE, CB, DS, MC, VI. ● Dining rm; 6:30 am-11 pm; a la carte entrees about $14-$25; cocktails; entertainment. FAX (408) 375-3960   ⊗ Ⓓ ⓰ (408) 372-1234

(See MONTEREY PENINSULA spotting map pages A262 & A263)

The Mariposa Inn 🆊   AAA Special Value Rates   *Motel*   ◆◆
🛆 All year [CP]   1P 68.00- 98.00   2P/1B   68.00- 120.00   2P/2B   80.00- 120.00   XP   8
51 units. 3/4 mi s; SR 1 exit Munras Ave. 1386 Munras Ave. (93940) Few fireplaces. Balconies. Check-in 3 pm. 15 refrigerators; C/CATV; pay movies; radios; phones. Small pool; whirlpool. No pets. 10 townhouses, $100-$160 for up to 4 persons; 4 with whirlpool bath $165. Wkly rates avail. Reserv deposit required. AE, DI, DS, MC, VI.
(See ad p A272)   Ⓢ Ⓓ (408) 649-1414

Monterey Bay Inn 🆉   Rates Subject to Change   *Motel*   ◆◆◆
🛆 Fri & Sat 6/1-10/31 [CP]   1P 149.00- 269.00   2P/1B   149.00- 269.00   ....   XP 10   F
Sun-Thurs 6/1-10/31 & Fri-Sat
11/1-5/31 [CP]   1P 129.00- 249.00   2P/1B   129.00- 249.00   ....   XP 10   F
Sun-Thurs 11/1-5/31 [CP]   1P 119.00- 229.00   2P/1B   119.00- 229.00   ....   XP 10   F
Senior discount. 47 units. 242 Cannery Row. (93940) Many bay views; balconies. Check-in 4 pm. Refrigerators; C/CATV; pay movies; radios; phones. Sauna; whirlpools; exercise equipment. Garage. No pets. Reserv deposit required. AE, DI, DS, MC, VI. FAX (408) 373-7603   ⊗ Ⓢ Ⓓ Ⓖ (408) 373-6242

Monterey Beach Hotel-Best Western 🄯   Rates Subject to Change   *Motor Inn*   ◆◆◆
🛆 7/1-10/31   1P 89.00- 169.00   2P/1B   89.00- 169.00   2P/2B   89.00- 159.00   XP 10
Senior discount. 196 units. 2 1/2 mi n off SR 1; exit Del Rey Oaks. 2600 Sand Dunes Dr. (93940) OPEN ALL YEAR. Most units have ocean view. Check-in 4 pm. 15 refrigerators; A/C; C/CATV; movies; radios; phones. Pool; beach; whirlpool; jogging track. Pets. Reserv deposit required; 3 days refund notice. AE, DI, DS, MC, VI. ● Restaurant; 6:30 am-2:30 & 5-10 pm; $12-$25; cocktail lounge. FAX (408) 393-1912   ⊗ Ⓓ Ⓖ (408) 394-3321

Monterey Downtown Travelodge 🄌   Rates Guaranteed   *Motel*   ◆◆
🛆 2/1-10/31   1P   60.00- 95.00   2P/1B   65.00- 95.00   2P/2B   65.00- 95.00   XP 10   F
11/1-1/31   1P   45.00- 65.00   2P/1B   45.00- 65.00   2P/2B   49.00- 77.00   XP 10   F
Senior discount. 49 units. Center; corner Fremont St. 675 Munras Ave. (93940) 6 refrigerators; C/CATV; pay movies; radios; phones; shower or comb baths. Pool. No pets. Covered & lot parking. Reserv deposit required. AE, DI, DS, MC, VI. Coffeeshop opposite. FAX (408) 373-8693 *(See ad below)*   ⊗ Ⓓ (408) 373-1876

Monterey Fireside Lodge 🄬   Rates Guaranteed   *Motel*   ◆
🛆 Sun-Thurs 5/1-10/31 & Fri-Sat
[CP]   1P 66.00- 90.00   2P/1B   66.00- 90.00   2P/2B   ....   99.00   XP 10
Sun-Thurs 11/1-4/30 [CP]   1P 55.00- 79.00   2P/1B   66.00- 79.00   2P/2B   ....   80.00   XP 10
Senior discount. 23 units. Off SR 1, on Frontage Rd; exit Camino Aguajito Rd. 1131 10th St. (93940) Gas-log fireplaces. Check-in 3 pm. Refrigerators; C/CATV; movies; phones. 1 kitchen, 6 efficiencies. Whirlpool. Pets, $10 extra charge. AE, DI, DS, MC, VI.   Ⓓ (408) 373-4172

Monterey Marriott 🄐   AAA Special Value Rates   *Hotel*   ◆◆◆
🛆 All year   1P 150.00- 170.00   2P/1B   150.00- 170.00   2P/2B   150.00- 170.00   XP 15   F
341 units. Adjacent to Monterey Conference Center. 350 Calle Principal. (93940) Formerly Monterey Sheraton. Many rooms with view of bay. Check-in 3 pm. Refrigerators; A/C; C/CATV; pay movies; radios; phones. Htd pool; sauna; whirlpool; health club. Fee for: massage. Pay valet garage. Pets. AE, CB, DS, MC, VI. ● Dining rm & restaurant; 6:30 am-11 pm; $16-$26; cocktails; entertainment. FAX (408) 372-2968   ⊗ Ⓢ Ⓓ Ⓖ (408) 649-4234

Monterey Motor Lodge 🄐   AAA Special Value Rates   *Motel*   ◆◆
🛆 6/1-10/31 [CP]   1P 85.00- 95.00   2P/1B   85.00- 95.00   2P/2B   90.00- 110.00   XP   4-10
2/1-5/31 [CP]   1P 69.00- 75.00   2P/1B   69.00- 75.00   2P/2B   79.00- 85.00   XP   4-10
11/1-1/31 [CP]   1P 49.00- 69.00   2P/1B   49.00- 69.00   2P/2B   59.00- 79.00   XP 10
45 units. 2 blks from State Beach. 55 Camino Aguajito. (93940) C/CATV; radios; phones; shower baths. 2 2-bedrm units. Pool. Pets, $10 extra charge. Reserv deposit required. AE, DI, DS, MC, VI. Restaurant adjacent. FAX (408) 655-2933   ⊗ Ⓓ (408) 372-8057

(See MONTEREY PENINSULA spotting map pages A262 & A263)

Monterey Plaza **44**　　　　　　AAA Special Value Rates　　　　　*Hotel*　◆◆◆◆
　All year　　　　　　1P 150.00- 280.00　2P/1B　150.00- 280.00　2P/2B 150.00- 280.00 XP 20　　F
290 units. 400 Cannery Row. (93940) Large rooms; views of bay from many balconies. Check-in 4 pm. 12 refrigerators; C/CATV; pay movies; radios; phones; comb or shower baths. Exercise rm. Pay valet garage. No pets. 15 1- & 2-bedroom suites, $300-$675 for up to 6 persons. Reserv deposit required. AE, CB, DI, MC, VI. ● Restaurant; 7 am-10 pm; a la carte entrees about $12-$20; cocktails. Also, Delfino's On The Bay, see separate listing. FAX (408) 646-0285
　　　　　　　　　　　　　　　　　　　　　　　⊗ Ⓢ Ⓓ Ⓐ (408) 646-1700

Munras Lodge **28**　　　　　　　Rates Subject to Change　　　　　*Motel*　◆◆◆
⓪ Fri & Sat 6/15-9/30 [CP]　1P 69.00- 179.00　2P/1B　75.00- 179.00　2P/2B　79.00- 179.00 XP 10
　Sun-Thurs 6/15-9/30 & Fri &
　Sat 10/1-6/14 [CP]　　　1P 55.00- 179.00　2P/1B　59.00- 179.00　2P/2B　59.00- 179.00 XP 10
　Sun-Thurs 10/1-6/14 [CP]　1P 45.00- 179.00　2P/1B　49.00- 179.00　2P/2B　55.00- 99.00 XP 10
29 units. 1/2 mi s; SR 1 exit via Munras Ave. 1010 Munras Ave. (93940) Many gas burning fireplaces. Few rooms with whirlpool bath. Check-in 3 pm. 4 refrigerators; C/CATV; movies; radios; phones. Sauna; whirlpool. No pets. Reserv deposit required. AE, DI, DS, MC, VI. FAX (408) 372-3505 *(See ad below)*　　⊗ Ⓓ (408) 646-9696

Otter Inn **49**　　　　　　　　Rates Subject to Change　　　　　*Motel*　◆◆◆
⓪ All year　　　　　　　1P 75.00- 160.00　2P/1B　75.00- 160.00　2P/2B　75.00- 160.00 XP 10
31 units. 1 blk w of Cannery Row. 571 Wave St. (93940) Many rooms with ocean view. Check-in 3 pm. 13 refrigerators; C/CATV; radios; phones; 28 comb baths. Whirlpool. Garage. No pets. 3 2-bedrm units for up to 6 persons; 4 units with whirlpool bath & fireplace $110-$190. Monthly rates avail. Reserv deposit required; 3 days refund notice. AE, MC, VI. *(See ad p A274)*　　　　　⊗ Ⓢ Ⓓ Ⓐ (408) 375-2299

Padre Oaks **35**　　　　　　　Rates Subject to Change　　　　　*Motel*　◆◆
⓪ Fri-Sat & 6/16-8/31　　1P　....　80.00　2P/1B　....　85.00　2P/2B　....　90.00 XP　5
　Sun-Thurs 6/16-8/31 & Fri-Sat
　5/1-6/15 & 9/1-10/15　　1P　....　60.00　2P/1B　....　65.00　2P/2B　....　70.00 XP　5
　Fri-Sat 10/16-4/30　　　1P　....　50.00　2P/1B　....　55.00　2P/2B　....　60.00 XP　5
　Sun-Thurs 9/1-6/15　　　1P　....　40.00　2P/1B　....　45.00　2P/2B　....　50.00 XP　5
Senior discount. 20 units. 1/4 mi s; SR 1 exit Munras Ave. 1278 Munras Ave. (93940) C/CATV; movies; radios; phones; shower baths. 1 2-bedrm unit. Pool. No pets. Reserv deposit required; 5 days refund notice. AE, DS, MC, VI. *(See ad below)*　　　　　　　　　　　⊗ Ⓓ (408) 373-3741

Ramada Limited **8**　　　　　　Rates Subject to Change　　　　　*Motel*　◆
⓪ Fri-Sat 5/2-10/31 [CP]　1P 80.00- 90.00　2P/1B　85.00- 95.00　2P/2B　95.00- 110.00 XP 10　F
　Sun-Thurs 5/2-10/31 [CP] 1P 55.00- 70.00　2P/1B　65.00- 85.00　2P/2B　75.00- 95.00 XP 10　F
　Fri & Sat 11/1-5/1 [CP]　1P 50.00- 70.00　2P/1B　55.00- 75.00　2P/2B　60.00- 75.00 XP 10　F
　Sun-Thurs 11/1-5/1 [CP]　1P 45.00- 50.00　2P/1B　48.00- 52.00　2P/2B　50.00- 55.00 XP 10　F
Senior discount. 48 units. 1 3/4 mi n; SR 1 northbound exit Fremont St, southbound Casa Verde. 2058 N Fremont St. (93940) Formerly Franciscan Inn. Some small rooms. Check-in 3 pm. 8 refrigerators; C/CATV; 5 radios; phones; comb or shower baths. 1 2-bedrm unit. Small pool; sauna; whirlpool. No pets. Few VCP's & microwaves, $10 extra charge. Reserv deposit required; 3 days refund notice. AE, CB, DI, MC, VI. FAX (408) 375-9701
　　　　　　　　　　　　　　　　　　　　　　　　⊗ Ⓓ (408) 375-9511

(See MONTEREY PENINSULA spotting map pages A262 & A263)

Rancho Monterey Motel 33				Rates Subject to Change				Motel			◆
⑭ Fri & Sat 6/16-9/30 [CP]	1P	65.00-	85.00	2P/1B	65.00-	85.00	2P/2B	75.00-	90.00	XP 10	
Sun-Thurs 6/16-9/30 [CP]	1P	50.00-	65.00	2P/1B	50.00-	65.00	2P/2B	60.00-	75.00	XP 10	
Fri & Sat 10/1-6/15 [CP]	1P	40.00-	55.00	2P/1B	45.00-	65.00	2P/2B	50.00-	70.00	XP 5	
Sun-Thurs 10/1-6/15 [CP]	1P	34.00-	45.00	2P/1B	36.00-	55.00	2P/2B	40.00-	65.00	XP 5	

27 units. 1/2 mi s; SR 1 exit via Munras Ave. 1200 Munras Ave. (93940) 4 refrigerators; C/CATV; phones; shower or comb baths. 1 2-bedrm unit. Pool. No pets. Wkly & monthly rates avail. Reserv deposit required; 3 days refund notice. AE, MC, VI. *(See ad below)*   ⊗ Ⓓ (408) 372-5821

Sand Dollar Inn 22				Rates Subject to Change				Motel			◆◆
⑭ 5/1-10/31 [CP]	1P	69.00-	99.00	2P/1B	74.00-	109.00	2P/2B	84.00-	109.00	XP 5	F
11/1-4/30 [CP]	1P	59.00-	99.00	2P/1B	64.00-	104.00	2P/2B	74.00-	99.00	XP 5	F

Senior discount. 63 units. Center. 755 Abrego St at Fremont St. (93940) Some units with small deck or patio; many fireplaces, gas or woodburning. Check-in 3 pm. 20 refrigerators; C/CATV; phones; comb or shower baths. 2 2-bedrm units. Coin laundry. Pool; whirlpool. Pets, $25 deposit required. Reserv deposit required. DI, DS, MC, VI. Cocktail lounge; coffeeshop adjacent. FAX (408) 372-0916 *(See ad p A277)*   Ⓓ (408) 372-7551

(See MONTEREY PENINSULA spotting map pages A262 & A263)

Scottish Fairway Motel 7 — Rates Subject to Change — *Motel* ◆

Fri & Sat	1P	48.00-	60.00	2P/1B	58.00-	84.00	2P/2B	69.00-	98.00	XP	5	
Sun-Thurs 5/1-9/30	1P	36.00-	48.00	2P/1B	42.00-	68.00	2P/2B	46.00-	72.00	XP	5	
Sun-Thurs 10/1-4/30	1P	33.00-	39.00	2P/1B	35.00-	52.00	2P/2B	42.00-	56.00	XP	5	

Senior discount. 42 units. 1 3/4 mi n on SR 1 business rt; northbound exit Fremont St, southbound exit Casa Verde Way, 1/2 blk s on Fremont St. 2075 Fremont St. (93940) C/CATV; movies; phones; comb or shower baths. 12 2-bedrm units, 6 kitchens, 7 efficiencies, no utensils. Small pool. No pets. Wkly rates avail. Reserv deposit required; 3 days refund notice. AE, DI, DS, MC, VI. *(See ad p A276)* ⊗ (D) (&) (408) 373-5551

Spindrift Inn 45 — Rates Subject to Change — *Motel* ◆◆◆

Fri & Sat 6/1-10/31 [CP]	1P	179.00-	319.00	2P/1B	179.00-	319.00	2P/2B	....	319.00	XP	10	F
Fri & Sat 11/1-5/31 & Sun-Thurs 6/1-10/31 [CP]	1P	169.00-	289.00	2P/1B	169.00-	289.00	2P/2B	....	289.00	XP	10	F
Sun-Thurs 11/1-5/31 [CP]	1P	149.00-	269.00	2P/1B	149.00-	269.00	2P/2B	....	269.00	XP	10	F

Senior discount. 41 units. 652 Cannery Row. (93940) On the bay. All units with fireplace & elegant furnishings. Check-in 4 pm. Refrigerators; C/CATV; pay movies; radios; phones. Pay valet parking lot. No pets. Reserv deposit required. AE, DI, DS, MC, VI. Restaurant adjacent. FAX (408) 646-5342 (S) (D) (&) (408) 646-8900

Stage Coach Lodge 14 — Rates Subject to Change — *Motel* ◆

5/31-10/25 & Fri-Sat	1P	49.00-	140.00	2P/1B	49.00-	140.00	2P/2B	49.00-	140.00	XP	5
Sun-Thurs 10/26-5/30	1P	35.00-	59.00	2P/1B	35.00-	59.00	2P/2B	48.00-	70.00	XP	5

Senior discount. 25 units. Off SR 1, on frontage road; exit Camino Aquajito Rd. 1111 10th St. (93940) Few rooms with view of Carmel Hills. Check-in 3 pm. C/CATV; phones. Small pool; sauna. No pets. Few refrigerators & microwaves. Wkly & monthly rates avail. AE, DI, DS, MC, VI. *(See ad below)* ⊗ (D) (408) 373-3632

Respect Property—Public and Private.

(See MONTEREY PENINSULA spotting map pages A262 & A263)

Super 8 Motel ⑨				Rates Subject to Change						Motel			◆◆
🏾 Fri & Sat 4/1-10/31	1P	58.00-	62.00	2P/1B	65.00-	80.00	2P/2B	75.00-	80.00	XP	5	F
Sun-Thurs 6/16-10/31	1P	....	58.00	2P/1B	58.00-	62.00	2P/2B	62.00-	66.00	XP	5	F
Sun-Thurs 4/1-6/15	1P	48.00-	52.00	2P/1B	52.00-	56.00	2P/2B	58.00-	62.00	XP	5	F
11/1-3/31	1P	32.00-	39.00	2P/1B	39.00-	48.00	2P/2B	44.00-	48.00	XP	5	F

Senior discount. 46 units. 1 3/4 mi n; northbound exit Fremont St, southbound exit Casa Verde. 2050 Fremont St. (93940) C/CATV; movies; VCPs. Phones; comb or shower baths. Sauna; whirlpool. No pets. Reserv deposit required. AE, CB, DI, MC, VI.   Ⓧ Ⓓ (408) 373-3081

RESTAURANTS

Abalonetti ⑧   Steak & Seafood $$ ◆◆
🏾 On Fisherman's Wharf. 57 Fisherman's Wharf. View of Monterey Bay. Specializing in calamari. Outdoor dining weather permitting. Children's menu. Open 10 am-9 pm; closed 11/25 & 12/25. Lounge. Pay parking lot. AE, CB, DI, MC, VI. *(See ad below)*   Ⓧ (408) 373-1851

Bindel's ①   American $$ ◆◆◆
In Old Monterey. 500 Hartnell St. California cuisine & fresh seafood; in restored 1834 Stokes adobe. A/C. Open 11 am-10 pm; Sat 4 pm 10:30 pm; Sun 11 am-3 & 5-10 pm. Cocktails & lounge. Reserv advised. AE, DS, MC, VI.
Ⓧ (408) 373-3737

The Clock Garden ⑤   American $$ ◆◆
🏾 In Old Monterey. 565 Abrego St. Charming casual atmosphere. Open 10 am-10 pm; closed 1/1, 11/25, 12/24 & 12/25. Cocktails & lounge. Minimum $5. Reserv advised. AE, DI, MC, VI.   (408) 375-6100

Delfino's on The Bay ⑦   Northern Italian $$$$
In Monterey Plaza. 400 Cannery Row. Tastefully appointed. European specialties. A/C. Children's menu. Open 7 am-11, 11:30-2 & 6-10 pm; Fri & Sat-10:30 pm; Sun 7 am-2:30 & 6-10 pm. Cocktails & lounge. Entertainment. Parking avail. Reserv advised. AE, DI, DS, MC, VI.   Ⓧ Ⓑ (408) 646-1706

Domenico's ③   Seafood $$$ ◆◆
🏾 On historic Old Fisherman's Wharf. 50 Fisherman's Wharf. Overlooking marina. Mesquite grilled seafood; pastas. Open 11:30 am-2:30 & 5-9:30 pm; Fri-10 pm; Sat 11:30 am-3 & 4-10 pm; Sun 11 am-3 & 4-9:30 pm; closed 11/25 & 12/25. Cocktails & lounge. Minimum $10. Pay parking lot. Reserv advised. AE, CB, DI, MC, VI. *(See ad p A279)*   Ⓧ (408) 372-3655

Mark Thomas' Outrigger ⑨   Steak & Seafood $$$ ◆◆
700 Cannery Row. Over the water at Monterey Bay. Early bird specials; children's menu. Open 11:30 am-10 pm; Sun from 11 am; closed 11/25 & 12/25. Cocktails & lounge. Pay parking lot. MC, VI.   Ⓧ (408) 372-8543

Mike's Seafood Restaurant ④   Seafood $$ ◆
🏾 On historic Old Fisherman's Wharf. 25 Fisherman's Wharf. View of Monterey Bay. Family restaurant. Early bird specials; children's menu. Open 9:30 am-9:30 pm; Sat & Sun-10 pm; closed 12/25. Cocktails & lounge. Minimum $4. AE, MC, VI.   Ⓧ (408) 372-6153

Sandbar & Grill ②   Seafood $$ ◆◆
🏾 #9 Wharf 2. Overlooking marina. Also pastas, steaks & ribs. Children's menu. Open 11:30 am-11 pm; Fri-midnight; Sat 10:30 am-midnight; closed 11/25 & 12/25. Cocktails. Entertainment. Minimum, $5. Pay parking lot. AE, MC, VI.   (408) 373-2818

Sardine Factory ⑪   Seafood $$$ ◆◆◆
🏾 In Cannery Row area. 701 Wave St. Attractive decor. California regional & Italian specialties. A/C. Dress code. Children's menu. Open 5 pm-10:30 pm; Fri & Sat-11 pm; Sun 2 pm-10 pm; closed 12/17-12/25. Cocktails & lounge. Minimum $8. Valet parking. Reserv advised. AE, CB, DI, MC, VI.   Ⓧ (408) 373-3775

The Whaler ⑥   Steak & Seafood $$ ◆◆
635 Cass St. A/C. Early bird specials; children's menu. Open 11:30 am-3 & 5-10 pm; Fri & Sat-11 pm; closed 11/26, 12/24 & 12/25. Cocktails & lounge. AE, CB, DI, MC, VI.   (408) 373-1933

Whaling Station Inn ⑩   Steak & Seafood $$$ ◆◆◆
🏾 In Cannery Row area. 763 Wave St. Victorian decor. Mesquite wood broiler. House appetizer, soup & salad included with full dinner. A/C. Children's menu. Open 5 pm-10 pm; Sat-10:30 pm; closed 1/1, 11/25, 12/25 & 4/11. Cocktails & lounge. Minimum $10. Parking avail. Reserv advised. AE, DI, DS, MC, VI. *(See ad p A279)*   Ⓧ (408) 373-3778

MONTEREY PARK — 60,700

Best Western Monterey Park Inn   Rates Subject to Change   *Motel*   ◆◆
⑭ All year   1P 44.00- 54.00   2P/1B   48.00- 56.00   2P/2B   52.00- 65.00   XP   5
Senior discount. 55 units. 2 blks s of I-10. 420 N Atlantic Blvd. (91754) 50 refrigerators; A/C; C/CATV; movies; radios; phones. Coin laundry. Small pool; whirlpool. No pets. Wkly & monthly rates avail. Reserv deposit required. AE, DI, DS, MC, VI. FAX (818) 281-6499   ⓓ (818) 289-5090

Best Western Park Hotel   Rates Guaranteed   *Motel*   ◆◆
⑭ All year   1P   ....   44.00   2P/1B   ....   46.00   2P/2B   ....   50.00   XP   4
Senior discount. 90 units. Adjacent to SR 60 n side, exit Garfield & Wilcox; 1 blk ne of westbound exit, 3/4 mi e of eastbound exit. 434 Potrero Grande Dr. (91754) A/C; C/TV; movies; phones. Sauna; indoor whirlpool. Garage. No pets. Wkly & monthly rates avail. Reserv deposit required. AE, CB, DI, MC, VI. FAX (213) 722-0710
     ⊗ Ⓢ ⓓ Ⓚ (213) 728-8444

Garvey Inn   Rates Subject to Change   *Motel*   ◆
⑭ All year   1P   ....   36.00   2P/1B   ....   38.00   2P/2B   ....   45.00   XP
Senior discount. 48 units. 1/2 mi s of I-10; exit New Ave. 1040 E Garvey Ave. (91754) A/C; C/TV; movies; radios; phones. 8 2-bedrm units. Coin laundry. Whirlpool. No pets. Wkly rates avail. Reserv deposit required; 3 days refund notice. AE, MC, VI. FAX (818) 280-8988   Ⓢ ⓓ Ⓚ (818) 280-8989

Grand Inn   Rates Subject to Change   *Motel*   ◆
🏨 All year   1P .... 44.00   2P/1B   .... 47.00   2P/2B   .... 51.00   XP   3
33 units. 1 blk se of I-10; exit Garfield. 118 E Hellman Ave. (91754) Refrigerators; A/C; C/CATV; movies; radios; phones; comb or shower baths. Coin laundry. No pets. Wkly & monthly rates avail. AE, MC, VI.
FAX (818) 280-0949   Ⓓ Ⓑ (818) 307-1071

Lincoln Plaza Hotel   Rates Subject to Change   *Motor Inn*   ◆ ◆
🏨 All year   1P 68.00- 72.00   2P/1B   78.00- 82.00   2P/2B   .... 78.00   XP 10
145 units. 3/4 mi s of I-10, 1 blk e on Garvey Ave; exit Garfield Ave. 123 S Lincoln Ave. (91754) A/C; C/CATV; radios; phones. Pool; whirlpool. Airport transp. No pets. AE, MC, VI. ● Restaurant & coffeeshop; 6:30 am-3 am; a la carte entrees about $6-$10; cocktail lounge. FAX (818) 571-4005   ⊗ Ⓢ Ⓓ Ⓑ (818) 571-8818

MONTEREY PENINSULA — See CARMEL, MARINA, MONTEREY, PACIFIC GROVE, PEBBLE BEACH & SEASIDE

MORENO VALLEY — 118,800

Best Western Image Suites   Rates Subject to Change   *Motor Inn*   ◆ ◆ ◆
🏨 All year [BP]   1P 50.00- 60.00   2P/1B   55.00- 65.00   2P/2B   55.00- 65.00   XP   5   F
125 units. N side of SR 60, exit Perris Blvd. 24840 Elder Ave. (92387) A/C; C/CATV; pay movies; radios; phones. Coin laundry. No pets. 43 1-bedroom suites, with refrigerator & microwave. Reserv deposit required. AE, CB, DI, MC, VI. ● Coffeeshop; 6 am-9 pm; Sun 7 am-2 pm; $3.75-$8.50. FAX (909) 247-9337
                                           ⊗ Ⓢ Ⓓ (909) 924-4546

Econo Lodge   Rates Subject to Change   *Motel*   ◆ ◆
🏨 All year   1P .... 32.95   2P/1B   .... 36.00   2P/2B   39.00- 42.00   XP   3   F
35 units. Adjacent to SR 60, 1/4 mi w of Perris Blvd. 24810 Sunnymead Blvd. (92388) A/C; C/CATV; movies; radios; phones. Whirlpool. No pets. Reserv deposit required. AE, MC, VI.   ⊗ Ⓓ Ⓑ (909) 247-8582

Holiday Inn Express   AAA Special Value Rates   *Motel*   ◆ ◆ ◆
🏨 All year   1P .... 40.00   2P/1B   .... 45.00   2P/2B   .... 45.00   XP   5   F
86 units. Adjacent to SR 60, exit Pigeon Pass Rd, then 1/2 mi e. 23330 Sunnymead Blvd. (92388) Formerly Rodeway Inn. A/C; C/CATV; movies; rental VCPs. Phones. 12 efficiencies. Coin laundry. Htd pool; whirlpool. No pets. 3 rooms with whirlpool tub, $70. Wkly rates avail. AE, DI, DS, MC, VI. FAX (909) 243-8635
                                          ⊗ Ⓢ Ⓓ (909) 242-0699

RESTAURANTS

Frangipanis Restaurant   Italian $$ ◆ ◆
1/2 mi w of Heacock Rd. 23580 Sunnymead Blvd. Nice selection of pasta, veal, chicken & seafood. A/C. Open 11:30 am-2:30 & 5-11 pm. Cocktails & lounge. AE, CB, DI, MC, VI.   ⊗ (909) 242-8023

Mrs. Knott's Restaurant & Bakery   American $ ◆ ◆
Adjacent to SR 60, exit Pigeon Pass Rd; in Town Gate Center. 12625-T Frederick St. Variety of salads, sandwiches & entrees including their well-known complete chicken dinner. A/C. Children's menu. Open 7 am-9 pm; Fri & Sat-10 pm; closed 12/25. Cocktails. AE, DS, MC, VI.   ⊗ (909) 697-4483

MORGAN HILL — 23,900

Best Western Country Inn   AAA Special Value Rates   *Motel*   ◆ ◆ ◆
🏨 All year [CP]   1P 54.00- 66.00   2P/1B   59.00- 71.00   2P/2B   66.00- 76.00   XP   5
84 units. E of & adjacent to US 101; northbound exit Tennant Ave, southbound exit E Dunne Ave. 16525 Condit Rd. (95037) Refrigerators; A/C; C/CATV; movies; radios; phones. Coin laundry. Small pool; whirlpool. Pets. Reserv deposit required. AE, CB, DI, MC, VI. Restaurant adjacent.   ⊗ Ⓢ Ⓓ Ⓑ (408) 779-0447

Executive Inn   Rates Subject to Change   *Motel*   ◆ ◆
🏨 All year [CP]   1P 65.00- 85.00   2P/1B   65.00- 85.00   2P/2B   65.00- 85.00   XP 10   F
Senior discount. 30 units. E of US 101; Dunne Ave exit, s 1 1/2 blk. 16505 Condit Rd. (95037) All units with parlor area. Refrigerators; A/C; C/CATV; pay movies; VCPs. Radios; phones. Pool. No pets. Microwaves. Most units with whirlpool bath. Reserv deposit required. AE, DI, DS, MC, VI. FAX (408) 778-2090 *(See ad below)*
                                          Ⓓ Ⓑ (408) 778-0404

Morgan Hill Inn   AAA Special Value Rates   *Motel*   ◆
🏨 5/15-9/30   1P 40.00- 46.00   2P/1B   44.00- 50.00   2P/2B   50.00- 60.00   XP   5
    10/1-5/14   1P 36.00- 42.00   2P/1B   40.00- 46.00   2P/2B   42.00- 50.00   XP   5
23 units. 1 mi n on US 101 business rt. 16250 Monterey Hwy. (95037) 10 refrigerators; A/C; C/CATV; movies; phones. 1 2-bedrm unit. No pets. Microwaves. Reserv deposit required; 3 days refund notice. AE, CB, DI, MC, VI.
                                          Ⓢ Ⓓ (408) 779-1900

RESTAURANT

Cooperage   American $$ ◆ ◆ ◆
E of & adjacent to US 101; northbound exit Tennant Ave, southbound exit E Dunne Ave. 16695 Condit Rd. Formerly Golden Oak. Spacious, converted old winery. Also pasta & California selections. A/C. Children's menu. Open 11 am-9 pm; Sat from 5 pm; Sun 10 am-2 & 5-9 pm; closed 11/25 & 12/25. Cocktails & lounge. Reserv advised. AE, CB, DI, MO, VI.   ⊗ Ⓑ (408) 779-8085

MORRO BAY — 9,700   See also CAYUCOS & LOS OSOS

Bay View Lodge   Rates Subject to Change   *Motel*   ◆ ◆ ◆
🏨 6/1-10/1 & Fri-Sat   ....   2P/1B   56.00- 68.00   2P/2B   68.00- 74.00   XP   8
    10/2-5/31   ....   2P/1B   46.00- 57.00   2P/2B   57.00- 68.00   XP   8
22 units. 225 Harbor St at Market Ave. (93442) Some ocean view rooms. 16 rooms with gas fireplace. Refrigerators; C/CATV; movies; VCPs. Radios; phones; shower or comb baths. Coin laundry. Whirlpool. No pets. Reserv deposit required. AE, MC, VI. *(See ad p A281)*   ⊗ Ⓓ (805) 772-2771

Best Value Inn

				Rates Subject to Change			Motel			◆◆
6/15-9/15 & Weekends	1P	52.00- 67.00	2P/1B	52.00- 67.00	2P/2B	57.00- 72.00	XP	5		F
9/16-10/31 & 4/1-6/14	1P	45.00- 55.00	2P/1B	45.00- 55.00	2P/2B	50.00- 60.00	XP	5		F
11/1-3/31	1P	30.00- 45.00	2P/1B	35.00- 45.00	2P/2B	40.00- 50.00	XP	5		F

Senior discount. 32 units. 220 Beach St at Market Ave. (93442) 12 refrigerators; C/CATV; movies; radios; phones; shower or comb baths. Small pets only. Wkly & monthly rates avail. Reserv deposit required. AE, DS, MC, VI.

⊗ Ⓓ (805) 772-3333

Best Western El Rancho   Rates Guaranteed   *Motor Inn*   ◆◆
6/11-9/6   ....   2P/1B   69.00- 87.00   2P/2B   69.00- 89.00 XP 7
4/2-6/10 & 9/7-1/31   ....   2P/1B   51.00- 69.00   2P/2B   55.00- 74.00 XP 5
2/1-4/1   ....   2P/1B   49.00- 59.00   2P/2B   53.00- 69.00 XP 5
27 units. 2 mi n; from SR 1 northbound exit Main St; southbound exit San Jacinto St. 2460 Main St. (93442) Refrigerators; C/CATV; movies; radios; phones; shower or comb baths. Coin laundry. Htd pool. Pets, $4 extra
charge. 7 microwaves. AE, DI, DS, MC, VI. ● Coffeeshop; 7 am-10 pm; a la carte entrees about $4-$10; beer &
wine. *(See ad p A281)*   ⊗ Ⓓ (805) 772-2212

Best Western San Marcos Motor Inn   Rates Subject to Change   *Motel*   ◆◆◆
5/25-9/12 [CP]   1P 62.00- 94.00   2P/1B   62.00- 94.00   2P/2B   67.00- 99.00 XP 5
5/1-5/24 & 9/13-10/31 [CP] 1P 54.00- 74.00   2P/1B   54.00- 74.00   2P/2B   58.00- 78.00 XP 5
11/1-4/30 [CP]   1P 41.00- 72.00   2P/1B   46.00- 72.00   2P/2B   50.00- 77.00 XP 5
Senior discount. 32 units. 250 Pacific Ave at Morro Ave. (93442) Many rooms with ocean view. Check-in 3 pm.
Refrigerators; C/CATV; movies; radios; phones; shower baths. Whirlpool. No pets. Wkly & monthly rates avail.
Reserv deposit required. AE, DI, DS, MC, VI. FAX (805) 772-6844 *(See ad p A283)*   ⊗ Ⓓ (805) 772-2248

Best Western Tradewinds Motel   Rates Subject to Change   *Motel*   ◆◆
Sun-Thurs 6/16-9/15 & Fri-Sat 1P 60.00- 70.00   2P/1B   60.00- 70.00   2P/2B   65.00- 75.00 XP 5
Sun-Thurs 4/1-6/15 &
9/16-10/31   1P 40.00- 50.00   2P/1B   46.00- 56.00   2P/2B   49.00- 59.00 XP 5
Sun-Thurs 11/1-3/31   1P 35.00- 45.00   2P/1B   39.00- 49.00   2P/2B   44.00- 54.00 XP 5
Senior discount. 24 units. 225 Beach St & Market Ave. (93442) Refrigerators; C/CATV; movies; radios; phones.
Whirlpool. Reserv deposit required. AE, DI, DS, MC, VI. Coffeeshop adjacent.   Ⓓ (805) 772-7376

Blue Sail Inn   Rates Subject to Change   *Motel*   ◆◆◆
All year   ....   2P/1B   60.00- 95.00   2P/2B   60.00- 95.00 XP
48 units. Corner Market Ave & Harbor St. 851 Market Ave. (93442) Most with balcony & harbor view. 7 gas fireplaces. Refrigerators; C/CATV; movies; radios; phones. Whirlpool. Garage. No pets. Reserv deposit required.
AE, DI, DS, MC, VI. *(See ad below)*   ⊗ ⓈⒹⒷ (805) 772-7132

Breakers Motel   Rates Subject to Change   *Motel*   ◆◆◆
◉ 5/1-10/15   ....   2P/1B 70.00- 96.00   2P/2B 70.00- 86.00 XP 10
   10/16-4/30   ....   2P/1B 60.00- 88.00   2P/2B 60.00- 78.00 XP 10
25 units. Morro Bay Blvd at Market Ave. (PO Box 1447, 93443) Nicely decorated rooms, most with ocean view. Some with woodburning fireplaces. Refrigerators; 15 A/C; C/CATV; movies; radios; phones; shower or comb baths. Htd pool; whirlpool. Reserv deposit required. AE, DI, DS, MC, VI. Restaurant opposite. *(See ad p A282)*
⊗ Ⓓ (805) 772-7317

Econo Lodge   Rates Subject to Change   *Motel*   ◆◆
◉ Fri & Sat 6/11-9/30   1P 65.00- 85.00   2P/1B 70.00- 90.00   2P/2B 75.00- 95.00 XP 5
   Fri & Sat 10/1-6/10   1P 44.00- 65.00   2P/1B 48.00- 70.00   2P/2B 55.00- 75.00 XP 5
   Sun-Thurs 6/11-9/30   1P 40.00- 55.00   2P/1B 45.00- 60.00   2P/2B 50.00- 65.00 XP 5
   Sun-Thurs 10/1-6/10   1P 38.00- 50.00   2P/1B 40.00- 55.00   2P/2B 45.00- 60.00 XP 5
18 units. Corner of Beach St. 1100 Main St. (93442) Formerly Morro Bay Motel. A/C; C/CATV; movies; phones. 1 2-bedrm unit, 4 efficiencies, no utensils. No pets. Wkly rates avail 10/1-6/14. Reserv deposit required. AE, DI, DS, MC, VI. Coffeeshop adjacent.
⊗ Ⓓ 🄶 (805) 772-5609

El Morro Lodge   Rates Guaranteed   *Motel*   ◆◆◆
◉ All year [CP]   1P 45.00- 90.00   2P/1B 50.00- 90.00   2P/2B 50.00- 90.00 XP 8
27 units. 2 blks sw of SR 1; exit Main St. 1206 Main St. (93442) Most rooms with balcony. 12 gas fireplaces. 8 refrigerators; C/CATV; movies; radios; phones. Coin laundry. Whirlpool. No pets. 1 suite with whirlpool, fireplace & private balcony, $160-$175. Reserv deposit required. AE, DI, MC, VI. *(See ad below)*
Ⓓ 🄶 (805) 772-5633

Embarcadero Inn   Rates Subject to Change   *Motel*   ◆◆◆
◉ 4/1-10/15 [CP]   ....   2P/1B 70.00- 115.00   2P/2B 95.00- 115.00 XP 10
   10/16-3/31 [CP]   ....   2P/1B 55.00- 95.00   2P/2B 75.00- 95.00 XP 10
32 units. S of Marina St on The Embarcadero. 456 Embarcadero. (93442) Harbor views; most units with balcony; 19 units with gas fireplace. Check-in 3 pm. Refrigerators; C/CATV; VCPs; radios; phones. 2 indoor whirlpools. Garage. No pets. 4 units with microwave. 3 suites, $120-$160. Reserv deposit required. AE, DI, DS, MC, VI. *(See ad p A284)*
⊗ Ⓢ Ⓓ (805) 772-2700

Gold Coast   Rates Subject to Change   *Motel*   ◆◆
◉ Fri & Sat   1P 45.00- 75.00   2P/1B 50.00- 75.00   2P/2B 55.00- 85.00 XP 5
   Sun-Thurs   1P 30.00- 45.00   2P/1B 35.00- 50.00   2P/2B 45.00- 55.00 XP 5
17 units. 1 blk s of Morro Bay Blvd. 670 Main St. (93442) C/CATV; movies; radios; phones. Small pets only, $5 extra. Reserv deposit required. AE, DI, DS, MC, VI.
⊗ Ⓓ (805) 772-7740

Harbor House Inn   Rates Subject to Change   *Motel*   ◆◆◆
◉ 6/1-9/30 & Fri-Sat   1P .... 60.00   2P/1B 60.00- 70.00   2P/2B 65.00- 75.00 XP
   Sun-Thurs 10/1-5/31 1P .... 45.00   2P/1B 50.00- 60.00   2P/2B 56.00- 75.00 XP
46 units. On Main St between Beach & Dune sts. 1095 Main St. (93442) 15 refrigerators; C/CATV; movies; VCPs. Radios; phones; comb or shower baths. Whirlpool. No pets. Reserv deposit required. AE, DI, DS, MC, VI. Restaurant opposite.
⊗ Ⓢ Ⓓ 🄶 (805) 772-2711

AAA — we've got it all — travel agency services, maps, TourBooks, insurance and even emergency towing service.

The Inn at Morro Bay   **AAA Special Value Rates**   *Motor Inn*   ◆◆◆
All year   ....   2P/1B   85.00- 200.00   2P/2B   85.00- 200.00   XP
96 units. 1 mi s on Main St; at entrance to state park & golf course. 19 Country Club Rd. (93442) Bayfront. On spacious grounds. Some rooms with gas fireplace. Many patios or balconies. Check-in 3 pm. 60 refrigerators; C/CATV; rental VCPs; radios; phones; comb or shower baths. Htd pool; fishing; bicycles. No pets. Reserv deposit required; 3 days refund notice. AE, DI, DS, MC, VI. ● Dining rm; 7-11 am, 11:30-2 & 5-9 pm; $15.25-$19.50; entertainment. Also restaurant, see separate listing. FAX (805) 772-4779 *(See ad below)* ⊗ Ⓓ (805) 772-5651

Keystone Motel   **Rates Guaranteed**   *Motel*   ◆◆
5/15-9/31   ....   2P/1B   40.00- 65.00   2P/2B   60.00- 78.00   XP   2- 4
10/1-5/14   ....   2P/1B   40.00- 56.00   2P/2B   56.00- 65.00   XP   2- 4
21 units. 540 Main St. (93442) 15 refrigerators; C/CATV; movies; phones. No pets. Reserv deposit required. AE, DI, DS, MC, VI.   ⊗ Ⓓ (805) 772-7503

La Serena Inn   **Rates Subject to Change**   *Motel*   ◆◆◆
4/1-10/1 [CP]   ....   2P/1B   68.50- 145.00   2P/2B   68.50- 145.00   XP   5
10/2-3/31 [CP]   ....   2P/1B   58.50- 135.00   2P/2B   58.50- 135.00   XP   5
Senior discount. 37 units. Corner Morro Ave & Dunes St. 990 Morro Ave. (PO Box 1711, 93443) 15 rooms with ocean view, 4 with gas fireplace. 2 refrigerators; A/C; C/CATV; movies; radios; phones. 1 2-bedrm unit. Sauna. Garage. No pets. Reserv deposit required. AE, MC, VI. FAX (805) 772-5665 *(See ad p A285)*   ⊗ Ⓢ Ⓓ Ⓛ (805) 772-5665

Sea Air Inn | | Rates Subject to Change | | | | | | *Motel* | | | ◆◆
5/1-9/30 & Fri-Sat | 1P | 38.00- | 60.00 | 2P/1B | 40.00- | 65.00 | 2P/2B | 45.00- | 75.00 | XP | 5 | F
Sun-Thurs 10/1-4/30 | 1P | 30.00- | 50.00 | 2P/1B | 35.00- | 55.00 | 2P/2B | 40.00- | 65.00 | XP | 5 | F

25 units. 845 Morro Ave & Morro Bay Blvd. (93442) Some ocean view rooms. 3 refrigerators; C/CATV; movies; phones; comb or shower baths. 1 2-bedrm unit. No pets. Reserv deposit required. AE, MC, VI. Restaurant adjacent. *(See ad below)*   Ⓓ (805) 772-4437

Sundown Motel	Rates Subject to Change			Motel	◆◆

◉ 5/15-9/30   1P 32.00- 60.00   2P/1B 32.00- 70.00   2P/2B 36.00- 75.00 XP 4
    10/1-5/14   1P 30.00- 55.00   2P/1B 32.00- 60.00   2P/2B 32.00- 65.00 XP 4
Senior discount. 17 units. 1/4 mi s. 640 Main St. (93442) C/CATV; movies; phones; shower baths. Wkly & monthly rates avail. Reserv deposit required. AE, DS, MC, VI. *(See ad p A285)*   ⊗ Ⓓ (805) 772-7381

The Twin Dolphin	Rates Subject to Change			Motel	◆◆◆

◉ 5/1-10/31 [CP]   1P 55.00- 80.00   2P/1B 55.00- 80.00   2P/2B 55.00- 80.00 XP 5
    11/1-4/30 [CP]   1P 45.00- 65.00   2P/1B 45.00- 65.00   2P/2B 45.00- 65.00 XP 5
31 units. Corner Marina St & Morro Ave. 590 Morro Ave. (93442) Some units with ocean view. 4 refrigerators; A/C; C/CATV; movies; radios; phones; shower baths. Whirlpool. Garage. No pets. Wkly & monthly rates avail. Reserv deposit required. DS, MC, VI.   ⊗ Ⓢ Ⓓ ⬛ (805) 772-4483

Villager Motel	Rates Subject to Change			Motel	◆◆

◉ Fri & Sat 6/11-9/10   1P 60.00- 85.00   2P/1B 65.00- 90.00   2P/2B 70.00- 95.00 XP 6
    Fri & Sat 9/11-6/10   1P 40.00- 60.00   2P/1B 45.00- 65.00   2P/2B 50.00- 70.00 XP 6
    Sun-Thurs   1P 35.00- 50.00   2P/1B 40.00- 55.00   2P/2B 45.00- 60.00 XP 6
22 units. 1098 Main St at Beach St. (93442) C/CATV; movies; 18 radios; phones; shower baths. Indoor whirlpool. No pets. Reserv deposit required; 3 days refund notice. AE, DI, DS, MC, VI. Coffeeshop opposite. *(See ad below)*   ⊗ Ⓓ (805) 772-1235

RESTAURANTS

Brannigan's Reef   Steak & Seafood $$ ◆◆
Market Ave & Morro Bay Blvd. 781 Market Ave. Steaks, seafood, chicken, salads & prime rib. Sun brunch 10 am-2 pm. View of bay. Children's menu. Open 11:30 am-3 & 4-9 pm; Fri & Sat-10 pm; Sun 10 am-2 & 4-9 pm; closed for lunch 6/7-5/30. Cocktails & lounge. Entertainment. AE, MC, VI.   ⊗ (805) 772-7321

Galley Restaurant   Seafood $$ ◆◆
◉ 899 Embarcadero. On waterfront overlooking bay. Seafood, beef & chicken. Casual atmosphere. Children's menu. Open 11 am-9 pm; Sat, Sun & 6/1-9/15 to 9:30 pm; closed 12/1-12/25. Beer & wine. Reserv advised. MC, VI.   ⊗ (805) 772-2806

Great American Fish Company   Seafood $$ ◆◆
◉ 1185 Embarcadero. On waterfront, overlooking bay. Nice selection of mesquite broiled seafood & steaks. Children's menu. Open 11 am-10 pm; 4/1-11/1 to 9 pm. Cocktails & lounge. MC, VI.   ⊗ (805) 772-4407

Harbor Hut Restaurant   Seafood $$ ◆◆
◉ 1205 Embarcadero. On waterfront, overlooking bay. Casual, informal atmosphere. Nice selection of pasta, mesquite broiled steaks & seafood. Open 11 am-10 pm; 4/1-11/1 to 9 pm. Cocktails & lounge. Reserv advised. AE, DS, MC, VI.   (805) 772-2255

Hoppe's at 901   Continental $$$ ◆◆
◉ 901 Embaacadero. Specializing in fresh seafood, steaks, venison, chicken & vegetarian selections. View of bay. Brunch served 11 am-2 pm. Children's menu. Open 5 pm-9 pm; Fri 11 am-2 & 5-9 pm; Sat & Sun 11 am-2 & 5-10 pm; closed Tues. Beer & wine. Reserv advised. AE, MC, VI.   ⊗ (805) 772-9012

The Inn at Morro Bay Dining Room | American | $$$ | ◆◆◆
At Inn at Morro Bay. Attractive dining room serving regional cuisine. All seating features a view of bay. Sun brunch 11 am-2 pm. Early bird specials. Open 7-11 am, 11:30-2 & 5-9 pm; Sun 7 am-2 & 5:30-9 pm. Cocktails & lounge. Entertainment. Reserv advised weekends. AE, DI, DS, MC, VI. *(See ad p A284)*   ⊗ (805) 772-5651

Rose's Landing Restaurant | Seafood | $$ | ◆◆
🏵 725 Embarcadero. On waterfront, overlooking bay. Casual atmosphere. Seafood, beef, chicken & salads. A/C. Early bird specials & senior discount; children's menu. Open 11:30 am-3 & 5-10 pm; Sat 11:30 am-3 & 4-10 pm; Sun from 4 pm. Cocktails & lounge. Entertainment. Reserv advised. AE, MC, VI.   ⊗ (805) 772-4441

MOUNTAIN VIEW — 67,500

Best Western Inn — AAA Special Value Rates — Motel — ◆◆◆
🏵 All year [CP] 1P 62.00- 72.00 2P/1B 62.00- 72.00 2P/2B 67.00- 77.00 XP 6   F
58 units. 3/4 mi se, on SR 82. 93 El Camino Real W. (94040) Large rooms, attractively decorated. Refrigerators; A/C; C/CATV; movies; VCPs. Radios; phones; shower or comb baths. 6 kitchens, 22 efficiencies. Coin laundry. Small pool; whirlpool; exercise rm. No pets. All rooms with microwave. Wkly rates avail. Reserv deposit required. AE, DI, DS, MC, VI. Restaurant adjacent. FAX (415) 967-4834 *(See ad p A286)*   ⊗ Ⓓ (415) 967-6957

Best Western Mountain View Inn — AAA Special Value Rates — Motel — ◆◆◆
🏵 Sun-Thurs [CP] 1P 64.00- 72.00 2P/1B 64.00- 72.00 2P/2B 65.00- 75.00 XP 5
Fri & Sat [CP] 1P 49.00- 59.00 2P/1B 55.00- 65.00 2P/2B 58.00- 67.00 XP 5
72 units. 1 1/4 mi s of US 101, exit Rengstorff Rd; 2 blks w on El Camino Real (SR 82). 2300 El Camino Real W. (94040) Refrigerators; A/C; C/CATV; movies; radios; phones; comb or shower baths. 1 kitchen, no utensils. Coin laundry. Small pool; sauna; whirlpool; exercise rm. No pets. 6 rooms with whirlpool, $85. All rooms with microwave. AE, DI, DS, MC, VI. Restaurant adjacent. FAX (415) 962-9011   ⊗ Ⓢ Ⓓ Ⓛ (415) 962-9912

Best Western Tropicana Lodge — AAA Special Value Rates — Motel — ◆◆
🏵 All year [CP] 1P 55.00- 75.00 2P/1B 60.00- 80.00 2P/2B 65.00- 80.00 XP 4
60 units. Exit US 101 Shoreline S, 2 mi to SR 82, then 1/4 mi w. 1720 El Camino Real W. (94040) 35 refrigerators; A/C; C/CATV; movies; 30 radios; phones; shower or comb baths. Pool; sauna. Pets. AE, DI, DS, MC, VI. Restaurant adjacent. FAX (415) 961-1471 *(See ad p A286)*   ⊗ Ⓓ (415) 961-0220

County Inn — AAA Special Value Rates — Motel — ◆◆◆
🏵 Sun-Thurs [CP] 1P .... 89.00 2P/1B .... 99.00 2P/2B .... 109.00 XP 10 F
Fri & Sat [CP] 1P .... 65.00 2P/1B .... 65.00 2P/2B .... 65.00 XP 10 F
52 units. 1 blk s off US 101; exit via Moffett Blvd. 850 Leong Dr. (94043) Attractive & comfortable rooms. Refrigerators; A/C; C/CATV; movies; VCPs. Radios; phones. Coin laundry. Pool; bicycles. No pets. AE, DI, DS, MC, VI. Restaurant adjacent. FAX (415) 965-9099   ⊗ Ⓓ (415) 961-1131

Crestview Motel — Rates Subject to Change — Motel — ◆◆
🏵 Mon-Thurs [BP] 1P .... 69.00 2P/1B .... 74.00 2P/2B .... 84.00 XP 5   F
Fri-Sun [BP] 1P .... 51.75 2P/1B .... 55.00 2P/2B .... 63.00 XP 5   F
Senior discount. 66 units. On SR 82, 1/2 mi e of SR 85. 901 E El Camino Real. (94040) A/C; C/CATV; movies; VCPs. Radios; phones. Efficiencies, no utensils. Coin laundry. No pets. Most rooms with large whirlpool tub, stereo & cassette player. AE, DI, DS, MC, VI.   ⊗ Ⓢ Ⓓ (415) 966-8848

Residence Inn By Marriott — Rates Subject to Change — Suites Motel — ◆◆
All year [BP] 1P .... 134.00 2P/1B .... 134.00 2P/2B .... 159.00 XP
Senior discount. 112 units. US 101, exit S Rengstorff; e on El Camino Real. 1854 El Camino Real. (94040) 1 & 2 bedroom units with fireplace. Check-in 3 pm. A/C; C/CATV; movies; radios; phones. Kitchens. Coin laundry. Pool; whirlpool; sports court. Pets, $50-$75 non-refundable fee, also $6 daily extra charge. [CP]. Wkly & monthly rates avail. Reserv deposit required. AE, DI, DS, MC, VI. FAX (415) 969-4997   ⊗ Ⓓ (415) 940-1300

Rodeway Inn — AAA Special Value Rates — Motel — ◆◆
🏵 All year [CP] 1P 56.00- 65.00 2P/1B 62.00- 70.00 2P/2B 62.00- 70.00 XP 5   F
50 units. West of US 101, exit Moffett Blvd West. 55 Fairchild Dr. (94043) Refrigerators; A/C; C/CATV; movies; radios; phones. Coin laundry. Pool; whirlpool. No pets. 6 rooms with whirlpool tub, $70. Microwaves. Reserv deposit required. AE, DI, DS, MC, VI. FAX (415) 964-4542 *(See ad below)*   ⊗ Ⓓ (415) 967-6856

San Antonio Inn — Rates Subject to Change — Motel — ◆
🏵 5/1-11/1 [CP] 1P .... 40.00 2P/1B .... 42.00 2P/2B .... 44.00 XP
11/2-4/30 [CP] 1P .... 38.00 2P/1B .... 40.00 2P/2B .... 42.00 XP
Senior discount. 54 units. On SR 82, 1/4 mi w of San Antonio Rd. 2650 El Camino Real. (94040) A/C; C/TV; movies; radios; phones. Pool. No pets. Many rooms with microwave & refrigerator. Wkly rates avail. Reserv deposit required. AE, CB, DI, MC, VI. Restaurant adjacent. FAX (415) 948-7214   ⊗ Ⓓ (415) 948-1036

MOUNT SHASTA — 3,500

Mountain Air Lodge   *Motel* ◆◆
ⓐ All year   Rates Subject to Change
1P 32.00- 38.00 2P/1B 36.00- 44.00 2P/2B 46.00- 56.00 XP 5
38 units. Exit I-5 central, 1 mi s. 1121 S Mount Shasta Blvd. (96067) Shaded grounds. A/C; C/CATV; movies; phones; comb or shower baths. 12 2-bedrm units. Whirlpools; recreation room. Pets, $5 extra charge. 4 kitchens, $7 extra; 2 family units $130 for up to 10 persons. Reserv deposit required. AE, DI, DS, MC, VI.
ⓓ (916) 926-3411

Strawberry Valley Inn   *Motel*
ⓐ All year [CP]   Rates Subject to Change
1P .... 42.50 2P/1B .... 46.50 2P/2B 52.50- 62.50 XP 6   F
15 units. Exit I-5 Central exit, 1/2 mi e, then 1/2 mi s. 1142 S Mt Shasta Blvd. (96067) C/CATV; radios; phones; shower or comb baths. 4 2-bedrm units. Complimentary beverages each evening. AE, DS, MC, VI.
⊗ ⓓ (916) 926-2052

Swiss Holiday Lodge   *Motel* ◆◆
ⓐ All year   Rates Guaranteed
1P 32.95- 38.95 2P/1B 36.95- 42.95 2P/2B 38.95- 56.95 XP 4
21 units. E of I-5 at McCloud/SR 89 exit. 2400 S Mt. Shasta Blvd. (PO Box 335, 96067) Most rooms with view of Mt. Shasta. A/C; C/CATV; radios; phones; shower baths. Rental refrigerators. 1 kitchen. Small pool; whirlpool. Pets. 1-bedroom apartments, $90 for up to 6 persons. Wkly rates avail. Reserv deposit required; 3 days refund notice. AE, DI, DS, MC, VI. *(See ad below)*   ⊗ ⓓ (916) 926-3446

The Tree House Best Western   *Motor Inn* ◆◆◆
ⓐ All year   AAA Special Value Rates
1P 56.00- 72.00 2P/1B 64.00- 72.00 2P/2B 72.00-130.00 XP 8
95 units. E off & adjacent to I-5; exit Central Mt Shasta, 2nd exit. (PO Box 236, 96067) Nicely landscaped grounds. 40 refrigerators; A/C; C/CATV; phones. 7 2-bedrm units. Indoor pool. Pets. Reserv deposit required. AE, DI, DS, MC, VI. ● Dining rm, see separate listing. FAX (916) 926-3542 *(See ad p A287)* ⊗ ⓓ ⓛ (916) 926-3101

RESTAURANTS

Bellissimo Restaurant & Gallery   American $$ ◆◆
ⓐ Exit I-5 Central, 1/4 mi e. 204A W Lake St. California cuisine featuring fresh, seasonal produce & seafood. Creative homemade desserts. Large selection of espresso coffee. A/C. Open 3/15-10/15 & 11/15-1/15 from 11 am-9 pm; Fri & Sat-10 pm; closed Tues, Wed, 11/26 & 12/25. Beer & wine. MC, VI.   ⊗ (916) 926-4461

Michael's Restaurant   Italian $$ ◆◆
Exit I-5 at Central, 1/4 mi e. 313 N Mt Shasta Blvd. Casual atmosphere, varied menu. A/C. Children's menu. Open 11 am-9 pm; closed Sun, Mon & major holidays. Beer & wine. Reserv advised. AE, MC, VI.   (916) 926-5288

Tree House Restaurant   American $$ ◆◆
In The Tree House Best Western. Varied menu. View of Mt Shasta. A/C. Children's menu. Open 6:30 am-2 & 5-9:30 pm; Sun 6:30 am-1:30 & 4-9 pm. Cocktails & lounge. Reserv advised. AE, CB, DI, MC, VI. *(See ad p A287)*   ⊗ (916) 926-3101

MURRIETA

RESTAURANT

The Fish Exchange   Seafood $$ ◆◆
From I-15, take Murrieta Hot Springs Rd 1/2 mi w; 1/2 mi n on Jefferson, then 1/2 mi w on Ivy. 24910 Washington. Casual dining. Nice selection of fresh seafood. A/C. Open 11:30 am-9 pm; Fri-9:30 pm; Sat noon-9:30 pm; Sun 10 am-3 & 4-9 pm; closed 7/4, 11/25 & 12/25. Beer & wine. AE, MC, VI.   ⊗ (714) 677-9449

MYERS FLAT

Myers Country Inn   *Bed & Breakfast* ◆◆
ⓐ 6/1-10/30 [CP]   Rates Subject to Change
1P .... 55.00 2P/1B .... 60.00 2P/2B .... 60.00 XP 10
11/1-5/31 [CP]   1P .... 45.00 2P/1B .... 45.00 2P/2B .... 45.00 XP 10
Senior discount. 10 units. W of & adjacent to US 101 exit Myers Flat. 12913 Ave of the Giants. (95554) Check-in 4 pm. No pets. MC, VI. Restaurant opposite.   ⊗ ⓓ (707) 943-3259

RESTAURANT

Knight's Restaurant   American $$ ◆◆
W of US 101 on Ave of the Giants. 12866 Ave of the Giants. Casual atmosphere, booth & counter seating. Fresh ingredients, creative preparation. A/C. Open 3/1-12/1 from 11:30 am-9 pm; Sun from 8 am; closed Mon 9/30-6/30. Beer & wine. MC, VI.   ⊗ (707) 943-3411

NAPA — 61,800

Best Western Inn   Rates Guaranteed   Motel   ◆◆◆

5/1-10/31	1P	70.00- 80.00	2P/1B	89.00- 99.00	2P/2B	89.00- 99.00	XP 10	F
11/1-4/30	1P	59.00- 69.00	2P/1B	69.00- 89.00	2P/2B	69.00- 89.00	XP 10	F

68 units. At jct SR 121 & Soscal Ave. (94559) Check-in 3 pm. A/C; C/CATV; movies; radios; phones. Pool; whirlpool. Few deluxe rooms, $119-$159 for up to 2 persons. Reserv deposit required. AE, DI, DS, MC, VI. Coffeeshop adjacent. FAX (707) 255-0709   ⊗ Ⓢ Ⓓ 🅰 (707) 257-1930

The Chablis Lodge   Rates Subject to Change   Motel   ◆◆

Fri & Sat 5/1-10/31	1P	74.00- 79.00	2P/1B	79.00- 84.00	2P/2B	.... 84.00	XP 5
Sun-Thurs 5/1-10/31	1P	54.00- 59.00	2P/1B	64.00- 69.00	2P/2B	.... 69.00	XP 5
Fri & Sat 11/1-4/30	1P	59.00- 69.00	2P/1B	64.00- 79.00	2P/2B	.... 69.00	XP 5
Sun-Thurs 11/1-4/30	1P	49.00- 59.00	2P/1B	54.00- 64.00	2P/2B	.... 59.00	XP 5

34 units. 1 blk w off SR 29 via Redwood Rd, 1 1/2 blks s. 3360 Solano Ave. (94558) Refrigerators; A/C; C/CATV; movies; radios; phones. 7 efficiencies. Small pool; whirlpool. No pets. Few rooms with whirlpool, $10-$20 extra charge. Wkly & monthly rates avail. Reserv deposit required. AE, CB, DI, MC, VI. FAX (707) 226-6862 *(See ad p A288)*   ⊗ Ⓓ (707) 257-1944

The Chateau   Rates Subject to Change   Motel   ◆◆◆

Fri & Sat 4/1-10/31 [CP]	1P	.... 75.00	2P/1B	.... 85.00	2P/2B	.... 85.00	XP 10	F
Sun-Thurs 4/1-10/31 [CP]	1P	.... 65.00	2P/1B	.... 75.00	2P/2B	.... 75.00	XP 10	F
11/1-3/31 [CP]	1P	.... 60.00	2P/1B	.... 70.00	2P/2B	.... 70.00	XP 10	F

115 units. W of & adjacent to SR 29 at W Salvador Ave. 4195 Solano Ave. (94558) Check-in 3 pm. A/C; C/CATV; movies; phones. 4 2-bedrm units. Pool; whirlpool. No pets. Reserv deposit required. AE, DI, DS, MC, VI. Coffeeshop adjacent. FAX (707) 253-0906 *(See ad below)*   ⊗ Ⓓ 🅰 (707) 253-9300

Clarion Inn Napa Valley   Rates Subject to Change   Motor Inn   ◆◆◆

Fri & Sat 5/27-11/26	1P	.... 109.00	2P/1B	.... 119.00	2P/2B	.... 119.00	XP 10	F
Fri-Sat 4/1-5/26	1P	.... 89.00	2P/1B	.... 99.00	2P/2B	.... 99.00	XP 10	F
Sun-Thurs 4/1-11/26 & Fri-Sat								
11/27-3/31	1P	.... 79.00	2P/1B	.... 89.00	2P/2B	.... 89.00	XP 10	F
Sun-Thurs 11/27-3/31	1P	.... 59.00	2P/1B	.... 69.00	2P/2B	.... 69.00	XP 10	F

Senior discount. 191 units. 1 blk w off SR 29 via Redwood Rd, 1/2 blk n. 3425 Solano Ave. (94558) Check-in 3 pm. A/C; C/CATV; pay movies; radios; phones. Pool; whirlpool; lighted tennis-2 courts. Pets, $200 deposit required. Reserv deposit required. AE, DI, DS, MC, VI. ● Restaurant; 7 am-2 & 5-10 pm; $9-$14; cocktails. FAX (707) 253-7433 *(See ad p A290)*   ⊗ Ⓓ 🅰 (707) 253-7433

The Elm House   Rates Guaranteed   Motel   ◆◆

Fri & Sat 4/1-11/31 [CP]	1P	.... 130.00	2P/1B	.... 130.00	2P/2B	.... 130.00	XP 10
Sun-Thurs 4/1-11/31 & Fri-Sat							
12/1-3/31 [CP]	1P	.... 90.00	2P/1B	.... 90.00	2P/2B	.... 90.00	XP 10
Sun-Thurs 12/1-3/31 [CP]	1P	.... 60.00	2P/1B	.... 65.00	2P/2B	.... 65.00	XP 5

Senior discount. 16 units. Exit SR 29 at 1st St; 1 1/2 blks s on California Blvd. 800 California Blvd. (94559) Residential location. Check-in 3 pm. Refrigerators; A/C; C/CATV; radios; phones; comb or shower baths. Whirlpool. No pets. Few rooms with woodburning fireplace, $10-$15 extra. Reserv deposit required; 3 days refund notice. AE, MC, VI. FAX (707) 255-8609 *(See ad p A290)*   ⊗ Ⓢ Ⓓ (707) 255-1831

Inn at Napa Valley, A Crown Sterling Suites   Rates Guaranteed   *Hotel*   ◆◆
⑳ All year [BP]   1P .... 102.00   2P/1B .... 102.00   2P/2B .... 102.00 XP 15
205 units. Adjacent to SR 29; exit e 1st St. 1075 California Blvd. (94559) 1-bedroom suites with living room.
Check-in 4 pm. Refrigerators; A/C; C/CATV; free & pay movies; radios; phones. 2 pools, 1 indoor; sauna; whirlpool; rental bicycles. Parking lot. No pets. Wkly & monthly rates avail. Reserv deposit required. AE, CB, DS, MC,
VI. ● Restaurant; 11 am-2 & 5-10 pm; a la carte entrees about $9-$15; cocktails. FAX (707) 253-9202 *(See ad
below)*   ⊗ Ⓢ Ⓓ 🅢 (707) 253-9540

John Muir Inn ◆◆◆
All year [CP]   Rates Subject to Change   *Motel*
1P 75.00- 95.00 2P/1B 75.00- 95.00 2P/2B 75.00- 95.00 XP 10   F
59 units. E of & adjacent to SR 29; exit e Trower Ave. 1998 Trower Ave. (94558) Check-in 3 pm. 55 refrigerators; A/C; C/CATV; movies; VCPs. Radios; phones. 15 efficiencies. Pool; whirlpool. No pets. 3 rooms with whirlpool tub, $15 extra. AE, DI, DS, MC, VI. Coffeeshop adjacent. FAX (707) 258-0943 *(See ad below)*
Ⓧ Ⓢ Ⓓ (707) 257-7220

Napa Valley Travelodge ◆
Fri & Sat 5/1-10/31   Rates Subject to Change   *Motel*
Fri & Sat 5/1-10/31   1P 70.00- 85.00 2P/1B 75.00- 90.00 2P/2B .... 90.00 XP 10 F
Sun-Thurs 5/1-10/31   1P 55.00- 65.00 2P/1B 60.00- 70.00 2P/2B .... 75.00 XP 10 F
11/1-4/30   1P 50.00- 65.00 2P/1B 55.00- 70.00 2P/2B .... 75.00 XP 10 F
44 units. At 2nd & Coombs sts, across from courthouse. 853 Coombs St. (94559) A/C; C/TV; 25 radios; phones. Small pool. Limited parking lot. No pets. Reserv deposit required; 3 days refund notice. AE, DI, DS, MC, VI. *(See ad below)*
Ⓧ Ⓓ (707) 226-1871

Silverado Country Club Resort   AAA Special Value Rates   *Resort Complex* ◆◆◆◆
3/16-11/25   1P 130.00- 600.00 2P/1B 130.00- 600.00 2P/2B 130.00- 600.00 XP 15 F
11/25-3/15   1P 120.00- 175.00 2P/1B 120.00- 175.00 2P/2B 120.00- 175.00 XP 15 F
260 units. 5 3/4 mi e of Napa via SR 121. 1600 Atlas Peak Rd. (94558) Outstanding recreational facilities. Cottages; 1-to 3-bedroom efficiency or kitchen apartments; many fireplaces. Check-in 5 pm. A/C; C/CATV; VCPs; radios; phones; shower or comb baths. 8 pools; rental bicycles. Fee for: golf-36 holes, tennis-23 courts, 3 lighted. No pets. Maximum rates for up to 6 persons. Reserv deposit required; 3 days refund notice. AE, DI, DS, MC, VI. ● 2 dining rms & restaurant; 6-11 am, 11:30-2:30 & 6:30-11 pm; a la carte entrees about $17-$28; reservations required; dress code; cocktails. FAX (707) 257-5407
Ⓓ (707) 257-0200

RESTAURANTS

Jonesy's Famous Steak House   Steakhouse $$ ◆
At Napa County Airport. 2044 Airport Rd. Also, chicken & fresh fish. A/C. Children's menu. Open 11:30 am-9 pm, Fri & Sat-9 pm; 4/4-10/31 to 8 pm; closed Mon, 1/1, 11/25 & 12/23-12/25. Cocktails. Minimum $4. AE, DI, DS, MC, VI.
Ⓧ (707) 255-2003

Napa Valley Wine Train   Continental $$$$ ◆◆◆
⊕ Exit SR 29 at 1st St, e on 1st St 3/4 mi then 4 blks n on Soscal Ave. 1275 McKinstry St. Restored turn-of-the-century pullman cars; 36 mi round trip excursion through scenic wine country. 3 hour fine dining experience. Prix fixe, 3 entree choices. A/C. Open seatings at 11:30 am & 6:30 pm; Sat & Sun seatings at 12:20 pm & 6 pm; closed first 2 weeks in Jan & for dinner Mon. Cocktails. Reserv advised. AE, CB, DI, MC, VI. *(See ad p 114)*
                                                                      ⊗ (707) 253-2111

Ruffino's   Northern Italian $$ ◆◆
645 First St. Also, steak & seafood. A/C. Children's menu. Open 11:30 am-2 & 5-10 pm; Sun 11:30 am-2 & 4:30-9:30 pm; closed Sat, 1/1, 11/26, 12/24-12/26 & 3 weeks in June. Cocktails & lounge. Minimum $6. Reserv advised. MC, VI.
                                                                      ⊗ (707) 255-4455

NAPA VALLEY — See CALISTOGA, NAPA, ST. HELENA & YOUNTVILLE

NATIONAL CITY — 54,200   (See SAN DIEGO spotting map pages A376 & A377; see index starting on page A374)

Econo Lodge 🄻🄻🄻   *Motel*   ◆
⊕ Sun-Thurs 5/21-9/11   1P .... 39.95 2P/1B .... 42.95 2P/2B .... 49.95 XP 5   F
  Fri & Sat 5/21-9/11   1P .... 42.95 2P/1B .... 45.95 2P/2B .... 49.95 XP 5   F
  9/12-5/20   1P .... 34.95 2P/1B .... 35.95 2P/2B .... 39.95 XP 5
  Sun-Thurs 9/12-5/20   1P .... 35.95 2P/1B .... 35.95 2P/2B .... 39.95 XP 5
70 units. 1 blk w of I-805, exit Plaza Blvd. 1640 E Plaza Blvd. (91950) 52 refrigerators; A/C; C/CATV; movies; rental VCPs. Radios; phones. Pool. No pets. Wkly rates avail. AE, DS, MC, VI. *(See ad below)*
                                                         ⊗ Ⓢ Ⓓ 🄰 (619) 474-9202

Radisson Inn National City 🄻🄻🄻   *Hotel*   ◆◆◆
⊕ All year   1P .... 49.00 2P/1B .... 49.00 2P/2B .... 49.00 XP 5   F
180 units. Adjacent to I-5, 8th St. Exit. 700 National City Blvd. (91950) Many rooms with harbor view. Check-in 3 pm. A/C; C/CATV; pay movies; radios; phones. Coin laundry. Htd pool; whirlpool; exercise rm. Parking lot. Wkly & monthly rates avail. AE, DI, DS, MC, VI. ● Coffeeshop; 6 am-10 pm; $5.95-$11.50; cocktails; cocktail lounge. FAX (619) 336-1628 *(See ad p A405)*
                                                         ⊗ Ⓢ Ⓓ 🄰 (619) 336-1100

Radisson Suites National City 🄻🄻🄻   *Suites Hotel*   ◆
⊕ All year [CP]   1P .... 59.00 2P/1B .... 64.00 2P/2B .... 64.00 XP 5
Senior discount. 170 units. Adjacent to I-5, 8th St exit. 810 National City Blvd. (91950) Rating withheld pending completion of construction. 1 to 2-bedroom suites with living room, bedroom, refrigerator & microwave. Many with bay view. Check-in 3 pm. A/C; C/CATV; pay movies; phones. Whirlpool. Garage. No pets. 12 2-bedroom suites $99, $5 extra for up to 6 persons. Complimentary beverages each evening. AE, DI, DS, MC, VI. FAX (619) 336-1628 *(See ad p A405)*
                                                         ⊗ Ⓢ Ⓓ 🄰 (619) 336-1100

Sweetwater Inn 🄻🄻🄻   *Motel*   ◆
⊕ 6/1-9/18   1P .... 47.00 2P/1B .... 47.00 2P/2B .... 51.00 XP 5   F
  9/19-5/31   1P .... 42.00 2P/1B .... 42.00 2P/2B .... 46.00 XP 5
38 units. 2 blks e of I-805, exit Sweetwater Rd. 2435 Sweetwater Rd. (91950) A/C; C/CATV; movies; radios; phones. Htd pool. No pets. 9 rooms with microwave & refrigerator. Wkly & monthly rates avail. Reserv deposit required. AE, MC, VI.
                                                           Ⓢ Ⓓ 🄰 (619) 470-8877

NEEDLES — 5,200

Best Motel   *Motel*   ◆
⊕ All year   1P .... 25.00 2P/1B .... 28.00 2P/2B .... 30.00 XP 6
Senior discount. 29 units. 1 mi nw on I-40 business loop; from I-40 westbound exit J St, eastbound exit W Broadway. 1900 W Broadway. (92363) 4 refrigerators; A/C; C/CATV; 6 radios; phones; shower baths. Pool. Pets. Wkly & monthly rates avail. Reserv deposit required; 3 days refund notice. AE, DI, DS, MC, VI. Restaurant adjacent. *(See ad below)*
                                                              ⊗ Ⓓ (619) 326-3824

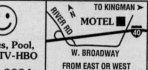

Best Western Colorado River Inn

			Rates Subject to Change			*Motel*		
6/1-9/31	1P	.... 55.00	2P/1B	.... 60.00	2P/2B	.... 60.00	XP	5
4/2-5/31 & 10/1-10/31	1P	.... 50.00	2P/1B	.... 55.00	2P/2B	.... 55.00	XP	5
11/1-4/1	1P	.... 40.00	2P/1B	.... 45.00	2P/2B	.... 45.00	XP	5

Senior discount. 62 units. From I-40, E Broadway/River Rd exit. 2271 W Broadway. (92363) Scheduled to open August, 1992. A/C; C/CATV; movies; phones. Indoor pool; sauna; whirlpool. Pets. 9 mini suites, $65-$85. AE, DI, DS, MC, VI. Restaurant adjacent. FAX (619) 326-4562   (S) (D) (619) 326-4552

Best Western Overland Motel ◆◆

			Rates Subject to Change			*Motor Inn*		
4/16-9/30	1P	36.00- 50.00	2P/1B	48.00- 60.00	2P/2B	48.00- 60.00	XP	5
10/1-4/15	1P	34.00- 44.00	2P/1B	44.00- 56.00	2P/2B	44.00- 56.00	XP	5

Senior discount. 41 units. Downtown; on Business Loop I-40; eastbound exit J St, westbound exit E Broadway. 712 Broadway. (92363) 4 refrigerators; A/C; C/CATV; movies; phones; comb or shower baths. 4 2-bedrm units. Pool. Small pets only, $5. Reserv deposit required. AE, DI, DS, MC, VI. ● Coffeeshop; 5:30 am-9 pm; $4.50-$7.95; cocktails. FAX (619) 326-3274   (D) (619) 326-3821

Days Inn ◆◆◆

			Rates Subject to Change			*Motel*		
4/1-10/30	1P	40.00- 50.00	2P/1B	50.00- 65.00	2P/2B	50.00- 65.00	XP	5

60 units. From I-40, W Broadway/River Rd exit. 1111 Pashard St. (92363) OPEN ALL YEAR. A/C; C/CATV; movies; phones; Pool; indoor whirlpool & sauna. Pets. Microwave avail. AE, DI, DS, MC, VI. FAX (619) 326-4002
⊗ (S) (D) (619) 326-5660

Imperial 400 Motel ◆

			Rates Subject to Change			*Motel*		
4/1-9/30	1P	.... 28.00	2P/1B	.... 36.00	2P/2B	.... 38.00	XP	8
10/1-3/31	1P	.... 22.00	2P/1B	.... 22.00	2P/2B	.... 22.00	XP	5

31 units. Downtown, on Business Loop I-40, eastbound exit J St, westbound exit E Broadway. 644 Broadway. (92363) Refrigerators; A/C; C/CATV; movies; phones. Pool. Small pets only. Wkly rates avail. Reserv deposit required. AE, MC, VI.   (D) (619) 326-2145

River Valley Motor Lodge F

			Rates Subject to Change			*Motel*		
5/1-10/15	1P	21.00- 26.00	2P/1B	22.00- 30.00	2P/2B	26.00- 34.00	XP	3

Senior discount. 27 units. 1 mi nw on I-40 business loop; from I-40 westbound exit J St, eastbound exit W Broadway. 1707 W Broadway. (92363) OPEN ALL YEAR. Refrigerators; A/C; C/CATV; movies; phones; comb or shower baths. Pool. Small pets only. Wkly rates avail. Reserv deposit required in summer. AE, CB, DI, MC, VI.
(See ad below)   ⊗ (D) (619) 326-3839

Travelers Inn F

			Rates Subject to Change			*Motel*		
All year	1P	.... 29.95	2P/1B	.... 35.95	2P/2B	.... 35.95	XP	4

121 units. Adjacent to I-40, exit J St downtown. 1195 3rd Street Hill. (92363) 5 refrigerators; A/C; C/CATV; movies; phones. Coin laundry. Htd pool; whirlpool. No pets. 5 suites, $36.95-$57.95 for 2 persons. Reserv deposit required. AE, DI, MC, VI. FAX (619) 326-4980   ⊗ (S) (D) (&) (619) 326-4900

NEVADA CITY — 2,900   See also GRASS VALLEY

Northern Queen Inn ◆◆

			Rates Subject to Change			*Motel*		
All year	1P	50.00- 53.00	2P/1B	50.00- 53.00	2P/2B	53.00- 62.00	XP	3- 5

Senior discount. 85 units. 1/2 mi w, adjacent & s of SR 20 & 49, exit Sacramento St. 400 Railroad Ave. (95959) Some cottages with woodburning stoves, overlooking creek. Check-in 3 pm. Refrigerators; A/C; C/CATV; radios; phones; comb or shower baths. Htd pool; whirlpool. No pets. 8 1-story cottage units, $75-$90; 8 2-story cottage units $85-$100, for up to 2 persons. Reserv deposit required. AE, CB, DI, MC, VI. Restaurant; 7 am-9 pm; Fri & Sat-9:30 pm; a la carte entrees about $7-$17; cocktails. *(See ad below)*   ⊗ (D) (916) 265-5824

RESTAURANT

Peter Selaya's   American $$ ◆◆
Opposite City Hall. 320 Broad St. California cuisine in a victorian atmosphere. Smoke free premises. A/C. Children's menu. Open 6 pm-9 pm; Sat 5:30 pm-9:30 pm; Sun 5 pm-9 pm; closed Mon & major holidays. Beer & wine. Reserv advised. AE, MC, VI.   ⊗ (916) 265-5697

NEWARK — 37,900

Newark-Fremont Hilton ◆◆◆

			Rates Guaranteed			*Hotel*		
Mon-Thurs	1P	.... 78.00	2P/1B	.... 93.00	2P/2B	.... 93.00	XP 15	F
Fri-Sun	1P	.... 69.00	2P/1B	.... 69.00	2P/2B	.... 69.00	XP	

Senior discount. 311 units. Exit I-880, Stevenson Blvd W. 39900 Balentine Dr. (94560) Courtyard & tower units. Check-in 3 pm. A/C; C/CATV; movies; radios; phones. Pool; sauna; whirlpool; exercise rm. Parking lot. Airport transp. No pets. Wkly & monthly rates avail. AE, DI, DS, MC, VI. ● Dining rm & restaurant; 6 am-10 pm; $10-$20; cocktails. FAX (510) 651-7829 *(See ad p 22)*   ⊗ (S) (D) (&) (510) 490-8390

Woodfin Suites		AAA Special Value Rates				*Suites Motel*			◆◆◆
Mon-Thurs [BP]	1P	.... 84.00	2P/1B	.... 84.00	2P/2B	.... 84.00	XP 10		F
Fri & Sat [BP]	1P	.... 79.00	2P/1B	.... 79.00	2P/2B	.... 79.00	XP 10		F

148 units. Exit I-880 at Mowry Ave W; 1/4 mi s on Cedar Blvd. 39150 Cedar Blvd. (94560) 1- & 2-bedroom suites with living room & kitchen, most with fireplace. Check-in 4 pm. A/C; C/CATV; movies; VCPs. Radios; phones. 16 2-bedrm units. Coin laundry. Pool; whirlpool. Airport transp. Pets, credit cardt deposit, $5 daily extra charge. Wkly & monthly rates avail. Reserv deposit required. AE, DI, DS, MC, VI. FAX (510) 795-8874   ⊗ Ⓓ ⓢ (510) 795-1200

NEWPORT BEACH — 66,600

Best Western Bay Shores Inn		Rates Subject to Change				*Motel*			◆◆◆
ⓐ 6/16-9/10 [CP]	1P	.... 92.00	2P/1B	.... 99.00	2P/2B	.... 99.00	XP 7		
3/3-6/15 [CP]	1P	.... 85.00	2P/1B	.... 92.00	2P/2B	.... 92.00	XP 7		
9/11-3/2 [CP]	1P	.... 75.00	2P/1B	.... 82.00	2P/2B	.... 82.00	XP 7		

20 units. 1 mi sw of SR 1, on Balboa Peninsula. 1800 W Balboa Blvd. (92663) Sun deck with partial view of ocean & bay. A/C; C/TV; VCPs; radios; phones. Coin laundry. No pets. 1 2-bedroom unit with full kitchen, $169-$209. 1 unit with whirlpool bathtub. Reserv deposit required. AE, DI, DS, MC, VI. FAX (714) 675-4977 *(See ad below)*   ⊗ Ⓓ (714) 675-3463

Four Seasons Hotel		Rates Guaranteed				*Hotel*			◆◆◆◆◆
ⓐ All year		1P 195.00- 265.00	2P/1B	225.00- 295.00	2P/2B	225.00- 295.00	XP 30		F

Senior discount. 285 units. In Newport Center; 3/4 mi e of SR 1. 690 Newport Center Dr. (92660) An elegant hotel in a contemporary setting. Check-in 3 pm. A/C; C/CATV; free & pay movies; radios; phones. Htd pool; saunas; whirlpool; bicycles; exercise rm. Fee for: lighted tennis-2 courts; massage. Pay valet garage. Airport transp. Pets. Monthly rates avail. AE, CB, DI, MC, VI. ● 2 dining rms & restaurant; 6:30 am-10:30 pm; a la carte entrees about $11-$40; 24 hour room service; cocktails; entertainment. Also, The Pavilion, see separate listing. FAX (714) 759-0568   ⊗ ⓢ Ⓓ ⓢ (714) 759-0808

Hyatt Newporter		Rates Subject to Change				*Resort Hotel*			◆◆◆
All year		1P 119.00- 179.00	2P/1B	144.00- 204.00	2P/2B	119.00- 179.00	XP 25		F

Senior discount. 410 units. 1/2 mi n of SR 1. 1107 Jamboree Rd. (92660) Spacious, beautifully landscaped grounds. 4 3-bedroom villas with private pools. Check-in 4 pm. A/C; C/CATV; free & pay movies; radios; phones. 3 htd pools; wading pool; putting green; rental bicycles; exercise rm. Fee for: par-3 golf, lighted tennis-16 courts; massage. Valet parking lot. Airport transp. Pets. Wkly & monthly rates avail. Reserv deposit required. AE, DI, DS, MC, VI. ● Coffeeshop; 6 am-10 pm; $14.50-$25; cocktails; entertainment. FAX (714) 759-3253   ⊗ Ⓓ ⓢ (714) 729-1234

Le Meridien-Newport Beach		AAA Special Value Rates				*Hotel*			◆◆◆◆
ⓐ All year		1P 140.00- 190.00	2P/1B	160.00- 210.00	2P/2B	160.00- 210.00	XP 20		F

435 units. 1 mi s of I-405. 4500 MacArthur Blvd. (92660) Very attractive rooms. Contemporary decor. Check-in 3 pm. A/C; C/CATV; free & pay movies; radios; phones. Htd pool; saunas; whirlpool; lighted tennis-2 courts; rental bicycles; exercise rm. Fee for: massage. Pay valet garage & parking lot. Airport transp. Some VCP's. Wkly & monthly rates avail. AE, DI, DS, MC, VI. ● 2 dining rms; 6:30 am-11 pm; a la carte entrees about $9-$26; cocktails; entertainment. Also, Antoine, see separate listing. FAX (714) 476-0153   ⊗ ⓢ Ⓓ ⓢ (714) 476-2001

Newport Beach Marriott Hotel		Rates Subject to Change				*Hotel*			◆◆◆
ⓐ All year		1P 144.00- 149.00	2P/1B	164.00- 169.00	2P/2B	164.00- 169.00	XP 15		

586 units. 1/2 mi e of SR 1. 900 Newport Center Dr. (92660) Some rooms with view of bay & ocean. Check-in 4 pm. 30 refrigerators; A/C; C/CATV; free & pay movies; radios; phones. Coin laundry. 2 htd pools; saunas; whirlpools; rental bicycles; exercise rm. Fee for: lighted tennis-8 courts; massage. Parking lot. Airport transp. Pets. AE, DI, DS, MC, VI. ● Restaurant; 6:30 am-2 & 5-11 pm; $7.95-$16.95; cocktails; entertainment. FAX (714) 640-5055   ⊗ ⓢ Ⓓ ⓢ (714) 640-4000

Newport Beach Marriott Suites   Rates Subject to Change   *Suites Hotel* ◆◆◆◆

Sun-Thurs	1P	....	139.00	2P/1B	....	139.00	2P/2B	.... 139.00 XP 10	
Fri & Sat	1P	....	99.00	2P/1B	....	99.00	2P/2B	.... 99.00 XP 10	F
Fri & Sat 9/4-6/21	1P	....	99.00	2P/1B	....	99.00	2P/2B	.... 99.00 XP 10	

Senior discount. 250 units. At intersection of Jamboree Rd & Bayview Way. 500 Bayview Circle. (92660) Check-in 3 pm. Refrigerators; A/C; C/CATV; movies; radios; phones. Coin laundry. Htd pool; saunas; whirlpool; rental bicycles; exercise rm. Valet parking lot. Airport transp. AE, DI, DS, MC, VI. ● Dining rm; 6 am-9:30 & 11:30-10 pm; $4.95-$17.95; cocktails. FAX (714) 854-3937   ⊗ Ⓢ Ⓓ 🅑 (714) 854-4500

Newport Channel Inn   **AAA Special Value Rates**   *Motel* ◆◆
(AAA)

6/11-9/11	1P	57.00-	65.00	2P/1B	57.00-	65.00	2P/2B	.... 65.00 XP 5	F
3/26-6/10 & 9/12-10/31	1P	43.00-	49.00	2P/1B	43.00-	49.00	2P/2B	.... 48.00 XP 5	F
11/1-3/25	1P	39.00-	44.00	2P/1B	39.00-	44.00	2P/2B	.... 43.00 XP 5	F

30 units. On SR 1, 1 mi nw of jct SR 55. 6030 W Pacific Coast Hwy. (92663) Across from beach. C/TV; radios; phones; shower baths. No pets. Reserv deposit required in season. AE, DI, DS, MC, VI. Restaurant adjacent. *(See ad p A294)*   ⊗ Ⓓ (714) 642-3030

Newport Classic Inn   **AAA Special Value Rates**   *Motor Inn* ◆◆◆
(AAA)

6/1-8/31 [CP]	1P	....	86.00	2P/1B	....	96.00	2P/2B	.... 96.00 XP	F
9/1-5/31 [CP]	1P	....	76.00	2P/1B	....	86.00	2P/2B	.... 86.00 XP	F

50 units. 1 mi w of Jamboree. 2300 W Coast Hwy. (92663) Check-in 3 pm. A/C; C/TV; radios; phones. Htd pool; sauna; whirlpool; rental bicycles; exercise rm. Airport transp. No pets. Rooms with whirlpool bathtub, $10 extra. AE, DI, DS, MC, VI. Restaurant; 11:30 am-2 & 5-10 pm; Fri & Sat-11 pm; $11.50-$25; cocktails. FAX (714) 631-5659 *(See ad below)*   Ⓢ Ⓓ 🅑 (714) 722-2999

Portofino Beach Hotel   **Rates Guaranteed**   *Bed & Breakfast* ◆◆◆
(AAA) All year [CP]   1P 100.00- 235.00   2P/1B   100.00- 235.00   2P/2B 110.00- 125.00 XP 15
15 units. Located at Newport Pier. 2306 W Oceanfront. (92663) Oceanfront hotel with European decor. Some rooms with full or partial ocean view. Many rooms with whirlpool tub. Check-in 3 pm. A/C; C/TV; radios; phones; comb or shower baths. Coin laundry. Valet parking lot. No pets. Reserv deposit required; 3 days refund notice. AE, CB, DI, MC, VI. Restaurant; 5:30 pm-10 pm; cocktails. FAX (714) 723-4370 *(See ad p A296)* Ⓓ (714) 673-7030

Sheraton Newport Beach   **Rates Guaranteed**   *Hotel* ◆◆◆
All year [BP]   1P 110.00- 155.00   2P/1B   135.00- 165.00   2P/2B   .... 135.00 XP 10   F
Senior discount. 338 units. 1 mi s of I-405; 1/2 mi s of John Wayne/Orange County Airport. 4545 MacArthur Blvd. (92660) Check-in 3 pm. A/C; C/CATV; free & pay movies; radios; phones. Htd pool; whirlpool; lighted tennis-2 courts; exercise rm. Parking lot. Airport transp. No pets. Monthly rates avail. Reserv deposit required. Complimentary beverages each evening. AE, CB, DI, MC, VI. ● Dining rm & 2 coffeeshops; 6:30 am-10 pm; $7-$25; cocktails. FAX (714) 833-3927   ⊗ Ⓢ Ⓓ 🅑 (714) 833-0570

RESTAURANTS

Antoine   French $$$$ ◆◆◆◆
In Hotel Le Meridien-Newport Beach. An elegant, formal dining room featuring excellently prepared & served entrees. A/C. Dress code. Open 6 pm-11 pm; closed Sun & Mon. Cocktails & lounge. Valet parking. Reserv advised. AE, DI, DS, MC, VI.   ⊗ (714) 476-2001

Bob Burns   American $$ ◆◆◆
In Newport Center; next to Broadway. 37 Fashion Island. Olde English decor. A/C. Early bird specials; children's menu.
Open 11 am-10 pm; Fri & Sat-11 pm; closed 1/1 & 12/25. Cocktails & lounge. Entertainment. Reserv advised. AE, DI,
DS, MC, VI.   ⊗ (714) 644-2030

The Cannery Restaurant   Steak & Seafood $$ ◆◆
⊕ 1 mi s of SR 1; on Balboa Peninsula. 3010 Lafayette Ave at 31st St. An interesting waterfront restaurant in the
former Western Canners Co packing plant. Brunch cruises Sat & Sun, $25 by reservation only. A/C. Children's
menu. Open 11:30 am-3 & 5-10 pm; Sun 10 am-2:30 & 5-10 pm; closed 11/25 & 12/25. Cocktails & lounge. Entertainment. Valet parking. Reserv advised. AE, CB, DI, MC, VI.   ⊗ (714) 675-5777

Five Crowns   American $$ ◆◆◆
In Corona Del Mar on SR 1. 3801 E Coast Hwy. Old English inn atmosphere. Specializing in prime rib. A/C. Children's
menu. Open 5 pm-10 pm; Fri & Sat-11 pm; Sun 10:30 am-3 & 4-10 pm; closed 7/4 & 12/25. Cocktails & lounge. Pay
valet parking. Reserv advised. AE, DI, DS, MC, VI.   ⊗ (714) 760-0331

Josh Slocum's Restaurant   Steak & Seafood $$ ◆◆
1/4 mi se on SR 1 (Pacific Coast Hwy). 2601 W Coast Hwy. Nautical decor, overlooking Newport Bay. Early bird spe-
cials. Open 5 pm-9:30 pm; Fri-10:30 pm; Sat 4:30 pm-10:30 pm; Sun 4:30 pm-9:30 pm; closed 11/25 & 12/25. Cocktails
& lounge. Valet parking. Reserv advised. AE, MC, VI.   ⊗ (714) 642-5935

The Old Spaghetti Factory   Italian $ ◆
1 mi s of SR 1, Pacific Coast Hwy. 2110 Newport Blvd. A popular, uniquely decorated, family-type restaurant serving
spaghetti with a large choice of sauces. A/C. Children's menu. Open 5 pm-10 pm; Fri & Sat-midnight; Sat from noon;
Sun noon-10 pm; closed 11/25, 12/24 & 12/25. Cocktails & lounge. MC, VI.   ⊗ (714) 675-8654

The Pavilion   Continental $$$$ ◆◆◆
At Four Seasons Hotel. Sun brunch 10 am-2:30 pm, $34-$39; children from 5-12, $22. Excellent food & service. A/C.
Open 6:30-10:30 am, 11:30-2:30 & 6-10:30 pm; Sat from 6 pm; Sun 10 am-2:30 & 6-10:30 pm. Cocktails. Parking avail.
Reserv advised. AE, CB, DI, MC, VI.   ⊗ (714) 759-0808

Trees Restaurant   American $$ ◆◆
4 blks s of Mac Arthur; 1 blk w of Pacific Coast Hwy. 440 Heliotrope. Friendly & inviting atmosphere. Diverse menu. Open
6 pm-10:30 pm; Fri & Sat-11 pm. Cocktails. Reserv advised. MC, VI.   ⊗ (714) 673-0910

21 Ocean Front   Seafood $$$ ◆◆◆
2100 W Ocean Front. At the beach; across from Newport Pier. Expertly prepared selections. A/C. Dress code. Open 5:30
pm-11 pm; closed 11/25 & 12/25. Cocktails & lounge. Valet parking. Reserv advised. AE, CB, DI, MC, VI.
     ⊗ (714) 675-2566

NIPOMO

The Kaleidoscope Inn Bed & Breakfast — Rates Guaranteed — *Historic Bed & Breakfast* ◆◆
All year [BP] 1P .... 75.00 2P/1B .... 80.00 .... XP 10
3 units. 1/2 mi e on US 101; exit Tefft/Napomo, then 1 blk s on Thompson Rd & 1 blk e on Dana St. 130 E Dana St. (PO Box 1297, 93444) Historical Victorian house built in 1886. Smoke free premises. Check-in 3 pm. Shower or comb baths. No pets. 1 whirlpool tub. Wkly rates avail. Reserv deposit required. AE, MC, VI. ⊗ Ⓓ (805) 929-5444

NORCO

Howard Johnson Lodge — Motel — Under Construction
55 units. 1/4 mi sw from I-15, exit Second St. 1695 Hammer Ave. (91760) Scheduled to open July, 1992. A/C; C/TV; phones. Pool; whirlpool. No pets. 3 deluxe suites. (714) 278-8886

NORTH HOLLYWOOD — 82,600   See LOS ANGELES (San Fernando Valley)

NORWALK — 94,300

Best Western Norwalk Inn — AAA Special Value Rates — *Motel* ◆◆◆
⊛ All year [CP] 1P 45.00- 52.00 2P/1B 45.00- 52.00 2P/2B 49.00- 52.00 XP 4 F
88 units. 1/4 blk e of I-605; exit Firestone Blvd. 10902 Firestone Blvd. (90650) Refrigerators; A/C; C/CATV; movies; radios; phones. Coin laundry. Pool; sauna; whirlpool. No pets. Wkly & monthly rates avail. AE, DI, DS, MC, VI. FAX (310) 929-4027 (See ad p A296) ⊗ Ⓢ Ⓓ 🅖 (310) 929-8831

Econo Lodge — Rates Guaranteed — *Motel* ◆◆
⊛ All year [CP] 1P 39.00- 55.00 2P/1B 44.00- 65.00 2P/2B 49.00- 59.00 XP 5 F
Senior discount. 43 units. 1/4 mi w of I-5; southbound exit San Antonio Dr/Norwalk; northbound exit Firestone Blvd. 12225 E Firestone Blvd. (90650) Refrigerators; A/C; C/CATV; movies; radios; phones. Coin laundry. Pool; whirlpool; 4 rooms with whirlpool spa. No pets. Microwaves. Wkly rates avail. Reserv deposit required. AE, DI, DS, MC, VI. FAX (310) 864-7373 ⊗ Ⓓ 🅖 (310) 868-0791

Sheraton Norwalk Hotel — Rates Subject to Change — *Motor Inn* ◆◆◆
⊛ All year 1P .... 94.00 2P/1B .... 104.00 2P/2B .... 104.00 XP 10 F
175 units. Adjacent to I-5, exit Norwalk Blvd. 13111 Sycamore Dr. (90650) Check-in 3 pm. A/C; C/CATV; movies; radios; phones. Htd pool; whirlpool. Airport transp. No pets. Reserv deposit required. AE, DI, DS, MC, VI. ● Restaurant; 6 am-10:30 pm; $8.25-$14.95; cocktails; entertainment. FAX (310) 868-4486 ⊗ Ⓢ Ⓓ (310) 863-6666

NOVATO — 47,600

Rush Creek Novato Travelodge — Rates Subject to Change — *Motel* ◆
⊛ All year 1P .... 55.00 2P/1B .... 62.00 2P/2B .... 65.00 XP 5
Senior discount. 50 units. 1 mi n, exit US 101 Atherton Ave San Martin Dr; 1 blk w. 7600 Redwood Blvd. (94945) A/C; C/CATV; movies; radios; phones; comb or shower baths. Coin laundry. Small pool; whirlpool; exercise rm. Pets, $5 extra charge. AE, DI, DS, MC, VI. FAX (415) 898-0828 ⊗ Ⓢ Ⓓ 🅖 (415) 892-7500

OAKDALE — 12,000

Holiday Motel — Rates Subject to Change — *Motel* ◆
⊛ All year [CP] 1P 39.00- 51.00 2P/1B 44.00- 56.00 2P/2B 51.00- 63.00 XP 6 F
32 units. 1 mi e on SR 108 & 120. 950 East F St. (95361) A/C; C/CATV; phones; comb or shower baths. 1 2-bedrm unit. Small pool. No pets. Monthly rates avail. Reserv deposit required. AE, MC, VI. ⊗ Ⓓ 🅖 (209) 847-7023

Ramada Inn — AAA Special Value Rates — *Motel* ◆◆◆
⊛ 5/1-9/30 1P .... 71.00 2P/1B .... 77.00 2P/2B .... 77.00 XP 6 F
10/1-4/30 1P .... 65.00 2P/1B .... 71.00 2P/2B .... 71.00 XP 6 F
70 units. 3/4 mi e on SR 108 & 120. 825 East F St. (95361) Check-in 3 pm. A/C; C/CATV; movies; rental VCPs. Radios; phones; comb or shower baths. Htd pool; whirlpool. No pets. Reserv deposit required. AE, DI, DS, MC, VI. Coffeeshop adjacent. FAX (209) 847-9546 ⊗ Ⓓ 🅖 (209) 847-8181

OAKHURST — 2,000

Best Western Yosemite Gateway Inn — Rates Subject to Change — *Motel* ◆◆◆
⊛ 5/16-9/25 1P 68.00- 78.00 2P/1B 68.00- 78.00 2P/2B 74.00- 80.00 XP 6
9/26-10/31, 4/1-5/15 &
12/25-12/31 1P 50.00- 58.00 2P/1B 50.00- 58.00 2P/2B 54.00- 58.00 XP 4
11/1-12/24 & 1/1-3/31 1P 44.00- 50.00 2P/1B 44.00- 52.00 2P/2B 50.00- 54.00 XP 4
118 units. On SR 41; 3/4 mi n of jct SR 49. 40530 Hwy 41. (93644) In nicely landscaped hillside oakgrove. 71 refrigerators; A/C; C/CATV; movies; 108 radios; phones. 7 kitchens, 4 efficiencies. Coin laundry. 2 pools, 1 htd, 1 indoor; sauna; whirlpools; exercise rm. 2 1-bedroom suites & 15 2-bedroom units with microwave & wet bar, $100 for up to 6 persons. AE, DI, DS, MC, VI. Cocktail lounge; restaurant adjacent. FAX (209) 683-3813 (See ad p A549) ⊗ Ⓓ 🅖 (209) 683-2378

Chateau du Sureau — Rates Subject to Change — *Country Inn* ◆◆◆◆
⊛ All year [BP] 1P 250.00- 350.00 2P/1B 250.00- 350.00 .... XP
9 units. W of SR 41 at Victoria Ln. 48688 Victoria Ln. (PO Box 577, 93644) Individually, richly appointed; antiques, oils, objects D'art. Provencal ambiance. Closed 1/2-1/24. A/C; 2 C/CATV; phones. Small pool. Parking lot. Reserv deposit required; 7 days refund notice. MC, VI. ● Dining rm & restaurant. Also, Erna's Elderberry House, see separate listing. FAX (209) 683-0800 ⊗ Ⓓ 🅖 (209) 683-6860

Days Inn — Rates Subject to Change — *Motel* ◆◆
⊛ 5/1-10/31 [CP] 1P .... 75.00 2P/1B .... 85.00 2P/2B .... 85.00 XP 5 F
11/1-4/30 [CP] 1P .... 45.00 2P/1B .... 55.00 2P/2B .... 55.00 XP 5 F
Senior discount. 42 units. On SR 41; 3/4 mi n of jct SR 49. 40662 Hwy 41. (93644) Check-in 3 pm. Refrigerators; A/C; C/CATV; pay movies; radios; phones. Small pool. No pets. 1 unit with whirlpool bath, $59-$99 for up to 2 persons. Reserv deposit required; 3 days refund notice. AE, DI, MC, VI. Coffeeshop adjacent. FAX (209) 658-8481 (See ad p A549) ⊗ Ⓢ Ⓓ (209) 642-2525

Shilo Inn — Rates Subject to Change — *Motel* ◆◆◆
4/16-9/15 [CP] 1P 90.00- 105.00 2P/1B 90.00- 105.00 2P/2B 90.00- 105.00 XP 10 F
9/16-4/15 [CP] 1P 75.00- 92.00 2P/1B 75.00- 92.00 2P/2B 75.00- 92.00 XP 10 F
Senior discount. 80 units. On SR 41; 3/4 mi n of jct SR 49. 40644 Hwy 41. (93644) Large rooms. All with microwave. Check-in 4 pm. Refrigerators; A/C; C/CATV; pay movies; radios; phones. Coin laundry. Small pool; whirlpool; steamroom; exercise rm. No pets. Wkly & monthly rates avail. Reserv deposit required. AE, DI, DS, MC, VI. Coffeeshop adjacent. FAX (209) 683-3386 (See ad p A550) ⊗ Ⓢ Ⓓ 🅖 (209) 683-3555

RESTAURANTS

Erna's Elderberry House   French $$$$ ◆◆◆◆
W of SR 41 at Victoria Ln. 48688 Victoria Ln. California cuisine with European influence; prix fixe, 7-course dinner changed daily. Country French ambiance. Smoke free premises. A/C. Open 11:30 am-1 & 5:30-8:30 pm; Mon & Sat from 5:30 pm; closed Tues, 7/4, 1/2-1/31 & Mon in winter. Cocktails & lounge. Reserv advised. MC, VI. ⊗ (209) 683-6800

Viewpoint   American $$ ◆◆
🏢 On SR 41; 3/4 mi n of jct SR 49. 40530 Hwy 41. Family restaurant. A/C. Open 7 am-9:30 pm. Cocktails & lounge. Reserv advised. AE, CB, DI, MC, VI.   ⊗ 🅱 (209) 683-5200

OAKLAND — 372,200   (See OAKLAND/BERKELEY spotting map pages A300 & A301; see index starting below)   See also BERKELEY, EMERYVILLE & SAN LEANDRO

Airport Accommodations-See listings for:

🏢 Best Western Park Plaza Hotel, 1 1/2 mi e of airport.
🏢 Days Inn-Oakland Airport, 2 1/4 mi e of airport.
🏢 Hampton Inn-Oakland Airport, 2 1/2 mi e of airport.
🏢 Holiday Inn-Oakland Airport, 2 1/4 mi e of airport
🏢 Oakland Airport Hilton, 1 1/4 mi e of airport.

Index of Establishments on the OAKLAND/BERKELEY AREA Spotting Map

---

Best Western Park Plaza Hotel 18   Rates Guaranteed   *Motor Inn*   ◆◆◆
🏢 Sun-Thurs   1P 78.00- 94.00   2P/1B   88.00- 104.00   2P/2B   88.00- 104.00   XP 10   F
  Fri & Sat   1P 64.00- 84.00   2P/1B   69.00- 89.00   2P/2B   69.00- 89.00   XP 5
Senior discount. 185 units. 1 1/2 mi e of Oakland Airport, w of I-880, exit Hegenberger Rd, 3/4 mi. 150 Hegenberger Rd. (94621) Check-in 3 pm. A/C; C/CATV; free & pay movies; radios; phones. Pool; sauna; indoor whirlpool; exercise rm. Limited parking lot. Airport transp. No pets. AE, DI, DS, MC, VI. ● Restaurant; 6 am-10 pm, Sat & Sun from 7 am; $6-$11; cocktails. FAX (510) 635-9661   ⊗ Ⓓ (510) 635-5300

Best Western Thunderbird Inn 17   Rates Guaranteed   *Motel*   ◆◆
🏢 Mon-Thurs   1P 55.00- 70.00   2P/1B   65.00- 80.00   2P/2B   65.00- 80.00   XP 10   F
Senior discount. 101 units. Exit I-880 Broadway, 1/4 mi w, at entrance to Jack London Sq. 233 Broadway. (94607) OPEN ALL YEAR. A/C; C/CATV; movies; phones; comb or shower baths. Pool; saunas. Limited garage. No pets. 2 1-bedroom suites $125-$150 for 2 persons. Reserv deposit required. AE, DI, DS, MC, VI. Coffeeshop adjacent. FAX (510) 452-4634   ⊗ Ⓓ (510) 452-4565

The Claremont Resort, Spa & Tennis Club 16   Rates Guaranteed   *Resort Hotel*   ◆◆◆◆
🏢 All year   1P 159.00- 250.00   2P/1B   179.00- 270.00   2P/2B   179.00- 270.00   XP 20
239 units. In Berkeley Hills; on SR 13, 1 mi n of jct SR 24, exit I-80 via Ashby Ave. Ashby & Domingo aves. (94623) Renovated 1915 chateau resort, with European style spa. Beautifully landscaped grounds; many rooms with view of San Francisco bay. Check-in 3 pm. A/C; C/CATV; free & pay movies; radios; phones; comb or shower baths. 40 2-bedrm units. 2 htd pools; saunas; whirlpool; 2 indoor whirlpools; tennis-10 courts, 6 lighted. Fee for: steamroom; health club & massage. Pay parking lot. Airport transp. No pets. Luxury level rooms avail. Monthly rates avail. Reserv deposit required. AE, DI, DS, MC, VI. ● Restaurant & 2 coffeeshops; 6:30 am-10 pm; $25-$40; cocktails. A *Preferred Hotel*. FAX (510) 843-6239   ⊗ Ⓢ Ⓓ 🅱 (510) 843-3000

Days Inn-Oakland Airport 15   Rates Subject to Change   *Motor Inn*   ◆
🏢 All year   1P 59.00- 75.00   2P/1B   65.00- 84.00   2P/2B   65.00- 84.00   XP 1-10   F
Senior discount. 142 units. 2 1/4 mi e of Oakland Airport; e of I-880, exit Hegenberger Rd. 8350 Edes Ave. (94621) Some small rooms. A/C; C/TV; free & pay movies; radios; phones. Small pool. Airport transp. Small pets only, $10 daily. [MAP] avail. Monthly rates avail. Reserv deposit required; 3 days refund notice. AE, DI, DS, MC, VI. ● Coffeeshop; 24 hours; $5-$10; beer & wine. FAX (510) 569-4652   ⊗ Ⓢ Ⓓ 🅱 (510) 568-1880

(See OAKLAND/BERKELEY spotting map pages A300 & A301)

Executive Inn Embarcadero Cove 🆖 Rates Subject to Change *Motel* ◆◆◆
⊕ All year [CP] 1P 68.00- 90.00 2P/1B 72.00- 94.00 2P/2B 72.00- 88.00 XP 4 F
146 units. W of I-880, southbound exit 16th/Embarcadero, northbound exit 5th Ave/Embarcadero. 1755 Embarcadero Dr. (94606) Most rooms have view of Estuary, some spacious rooms. Check-in 4 pm. 23 refrigerators; A/C; C/CATV; movies; radios; phones; comb or shower baths. Coin laundry. Pool; whirlpool; exercise rm. Airport transp. No pets. 1 king suite with fireplace, microwave, refrigerator & whirlpool tub, overlooking the Estuary, $150 for 2 persons. Reserv deposit required. AE, DI, DS, MC, VI. FAX (510) 536-6006 *(See ad below)*
⊗ Ⓢ Ⓓ Ⓚ (510) 536-6633

Hampton Inn-Oakland Airport 🆓 Rates Guaranteed *Motel* ◆◆
⊕ All year [CP] 1P 57.00- 61.00 2P/1B 64.00- 68.00 2P/2B .... 66.00 XP F
149 units. 2 1/2 mi e of Oakland Airport; e of I-880, exit Hegenberger Rd. 8465 Enterprise Way. (94621) A/C; C/TV; free & pay movies; phones. Htd pool; whirlpool. Airport transp. No pets. Microwave/refrigerators avail. Monthly rates avail. AE, DI, DS, MC, VI. FAX (510) 632-4713 ⊗ Ⓢ Ⓓ Ⓚ (510) 632-8900

Holiday Inn-Oakland Airport 🆓 Rates Subject to Change *Motor Inn* ◆◆◆
All year 1P 79.00- 95.00 2P/1B 85.00- 105.00 2P/2B 85.00- 105.00 XP 10 F
Senior discount. 290 units. 2 1/4 mi e of Oakland Airport; e of I-880, exit Hegenberger Rd. 500 Hegenberger Rd. (94621) Check-in 3 pm. 60 refrigerators; A/C; C/CATV; free & pay movies; radios; phones. Coin laundry. Pool; exercise rm. Airport transp. Pets. Luxury level rooms avail. Monthly rates avail. Reserv deposit required; 3 days refund notice. AE, DI, DS, MC, VI. ● Restaurant; 6:30 am-2 & 5-10 pm; $7-$12; cocktails. FAX (510) 636-1539 ⊗ Ⓓ (510) 562-5311

Lake Merritt Hotel 🆙 AAA Special Value Rates *Hotel* ◆◆◆
⊕ All year [CP] 1P 79.00- 149.00 2P/1B 79.00- 149.00 2P/2B 79.00- 149.00 XP 10 F
Senior discount. 51 units. Exit I-880 at Broadway, 3/4 mi e to 17th St, 6 blks s. 1800 Madison St. (94612) Refurbished 1927 art deco style hotel, most rooms overlook Lake Merritt. Refrigerators; C/CATV; movies; radios; phones; comb or shower baths. 42 efficiencies. Limited garage. Airport transp. Reserv deposit required. AE, CB, DI, MC, VI. ● Coffeeshop; 6:30-10 am, 11:30-2:30 & 5-10 pm; $12-$25; cocktail lounge. FAX (415) 832-7150
⊗ Ⓓ (510) 832-2300

Oakland Airport Hilton 🆑 AAA Special Value Rates *Motor Inn* ◆◆◆◆
⊕ All year 1P 120.00- 140.00 2P/1B 140.00- 160.00 2P/2B 140.00- 160.00 XP 20 F
362 units. 1 1/4 mi e of Oakland Airport; w of I-880, exit Hegenberger Rd 1 mi. 1 Hegenberger Rd. (PO Box 2549, 94614) Spacious rooms. Some studio & patio units. Attractive landscaping. A/C; C/CATV; free & pay movies; radios; phones. 7 2-bedrm units. Pool; whirlpool; exercise rm. Airport transp. 1 & 2-bedroom suites, $300-$500 for 2 persons. Pets, $25 extra per stay. AE, DI, DS, MC, VI. ● Restaurant & coffeeshop; 6 am-11 pm; $7.50-$24; cocktails. FAX (510) 635-0244 *(See ad p 22)* ⊗ Ⓢ Ⓓ Ⓚ (510) 635-5000

Waterfront Plaza Hotel 🔟 Rates Subject to Change *Hotel* ◆◆◆
⊕ All year 1P 145.00- 165.00 2P/1B 160.00- 180.00 2P/2B 160.00- 180.00 XP 15
144 units. 1/2 mi w off I-880 exit Broadway; 1 blk n of Jack London Sq. Ten Washington St. (94607) On Inner Harbor; many rooms with harbor view. Some balconies & fireplaces. Check-in 3 pm. A/C; C/CATV; movies; VCPs. Radios; phones; comb or shower baths. Pool; sauna; whirlpool; dock; exercise rm. Pay valet garage. Airport transp. No pets. Luxury level rooms avail. All rooms with mini bars & safe. Reserv deposit required. AE, DI, DS, MC, VI. ● Restaurant; 6:30 am-10 pm; $15-$30; cocktails. FAX (510) 832-5695 ⊗ Ⓢ Ⓓ Ⓚ (510) 836-3800

RESTAURANTS

Bay Wolf Restaurant ⑩ American $$$ ◆◆◆
⊕ Exit I-580 at Oakland Ave, n on Mac Arthur Blvd 1/4 mi, 2 blks e on Piedmont Ave. 3853 Piedmont Ave. Attractive converted house, street parking. California cuisine with strong Mediterranean influence. Smoking not permitted. Open 11:30 am-2 & 6-9:30 pm; Fri-9:30 pm; Sat 5:30 pm-9:30 pm; Sun 5:30 pm-9 pm; closed major holidays. Beer & wine. Reserv advised. MC, VI. ⊗ (510) 655-6004

Gingerbread House ⑫ Regional American $$$ ◆◆
⊕ W of & adjacent to I-880, northbound exit Broadway, w at Brush, exit 980 11th/12th, w to 5th St. 741 5th St. Hand-painted Victorian house with gazebo seating. Cajun specialties. Homey atmosphere. Diners seated at 6 pm & 8:30 pm. Open 11:30 am-1:30 & 6-8:30 pm; Sat 11:30 am-1:30 & 4-8:30 pm; closed Sun & Mon. Wine. Reserv required. AE, CB, DI, MC, VI. ⊗ (510) 444-7373

La Brasserie Restaurant ⑪ Provincial French $$ ◆◆
1/4 mi s of I-580, exit Grand Ave. 542 Grand Ave. Casual atmosphere. A/C. Dress code. Children's menu. Open 5:30 pm-9:30 pm; Sun 5 pm-9 pm; closed Mon, Tues, 7/4 & 12/25. Beer & wine. Minimum, $6.60. Reserv advised. AE, CB, DI, MC, VI. ⊗ (510) 893-6206

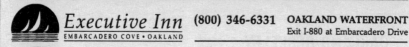

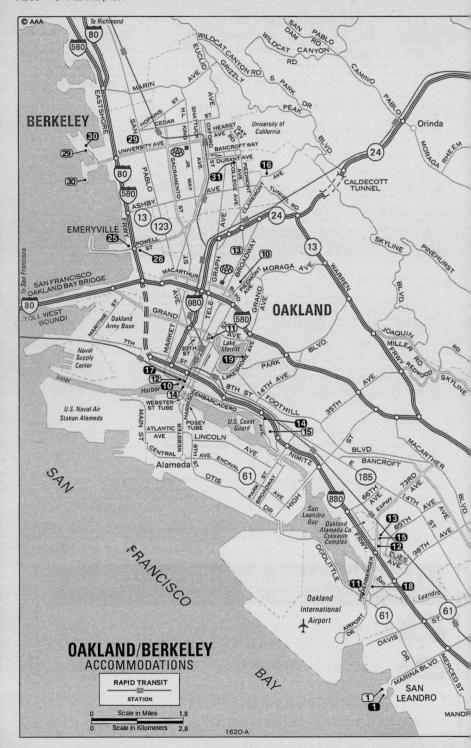

OAKLAND/BERKELEY
ACCOMMODATIONS

RAPID TRANSIT
STATION

Scale in Miles 0 — 1.8
Scale in Kilometers 0 — 2.8

1620-A

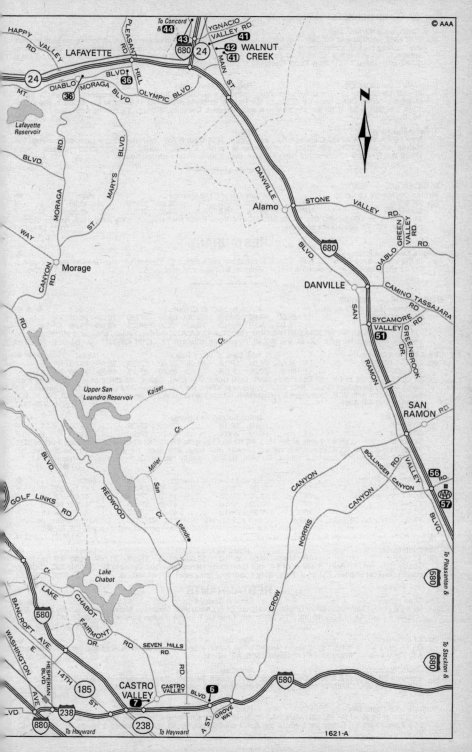

© AAA

1621-A

(See OAKLAND/BERKELEY spotting map pages A300 & A301)

L. J. Quinn's Lighthouse ⑮   Seafood $$ ◆◆
  ⊕ W of I-880, southbound exit 16th Ave, northbound exit 5th Ave. 51 Embarcadero Cove. A lighthouse built in 1903, overlooking marina; varied menu featuring contemporary American cooking. Pasta specialities. Casual atmosphere. Children's menu. Open 11:30 am-2:30 & 5:30-9 pm; Sat 11:30-4 pm & 5:30-10 pm; Sun 11:30 am-3 pm & 4:30-9 pm; closed 1/1, 11/26 & 12/25. Cocktails & lounge. Minimum, $10. Reserv advised. MC, VI.
        ⊗ (510) 536-2050

Ristorante Il Pescatore ⑭   Regional Italian $$ ◆◆
  At Jack London Sq. 57 Jack London Sq. Varied menu, tuscan cuisine, fresh seafood specialities, homemade pasta. Overlooks marina. Opera singers entertain on last Thurs of month at dinner. A/C. Open 11:30 am-10:30 pm; Sat 11 am-10:30 pm; Sun 11 am-10:30 pm; closed Mon & major holidays. Cocktails. Minimum $9. Parking avail. Reserv advised. AE, DI, MC, VI.
        ⊗ (510) 465-2188

Ti Bacio Ristorante ⑬   Italian $$ ◆
  Near Broadway; SR 24 exit Claremont Ave, e on Clifton. 5301 College Ave. Innovative, health-conscious cooking. Traditional veal dishes made with turkey. Nice selection of seafood & pasta. Smoking not permitted on premises. Open 4 pm-10 pm; Sun from 10 am; closed major holidays. Beer & wine. Reserv advised. MC, VI.
        ⊗ (510) 428-1703

OCCIDENTAL — 800

Negri's Occidental Lodge

		Rates Subject to Change				Motel			◆
⊕ Fri & Sat	1P	.... 48.00	2P/1B	.... 48.00	2P/2B	.... 48.00	XP 5		F
Sun-Thurs	1P	.... 38.00	2P/1B	.... 42.00	2P/2B	.... 42.00	XP 5		F

24 units. In the village. (PO Box 84, 95465) C/CATV. Pool. Small pets only, $3. Wkly rates avail. Reserv deposit required. MC, VI. Restaurant opposite.   Ⓓ (707) 874-3623

RESTAURANT

Negri's Italian Restaurant   Italian $ ◆
  In the village. 3700 Bohemian Hwy. Modest decor-family restaurant. A/C. Children's menu. Open 11 am-9 pm; Fri & Sat-10 pm; closed 12/24. Cocktails & lounge. Minimum $4. Reserv advised. AE, DI, MC, VI.
        (707) 823-5301

OCEANSIDE — 128,400

Best Western Marty's Valley Inn

		Rates Subject to Change				Motel			◆◆◆
⊕ 6/25-9/11 [CP]	1P	63.00- 66.00	2P/1B	63.00- 69.00	2P/2B	70.00- 74.00	XP 5		F
9/12-6/24 [CP]	1P	55.00- 59.00	2P/1B	59.00- 65.00	2P/2B	63.00- 65.00	XP 4		F

111 units. 2 mi e on SR 76. 3240 E Mission Ave. (92054) A/C; C/CATV; movies; radios; phones. 2 efficiencies, no utensils. Htd pool. No pets. AE, DI, DS, MC, VI. Restaurant adjacent. FAX (619) 439-3311 ⊗ Ⓓ (619) 757-7700

Best Western Oceanside Inn

		AAA Special Value Rates				Motel			◆◆◆
⊕ 7/1-9/15 [CP]	1P	64.00- 85.00	2P/1B	64.00- 85.00	2P/2B	70.00- 80.00	XP 6		
9/16-6/30 [CP]	1P	59.00- 80.00	2P/1B	59.00- 80.00	2P/2B	65.00- 75.00	XP 6		

80 units. Adjacent to I-5, exit Oceanside Blvd. 1680 Oceanside Blvd. (92054) Attractive pool & courtyard area. Large, nicely furnished rooms. A/C; C/CATV; movies; VCPs. Radios; phones. Htd pool; saunas; whirlpool. No pets. 21 rooms with VCP, microwave & refrigerator; also some rental VCP's. Monthly rates avail. AE, CB, DI, MC, VI. FAX (619) 967-8969   ⊗ Ⓓ (619) 722-1821

El Camino Inn

		Rates Subject to Change				Motel			◆◆
⊕ 6/15-9/15	1P	.... 75.00	2P/1B	.... 75.00	2P/2B	.... 75.00	XP 5		F
9/16-6/14	1P	.... 64.00	2P/1B	.... 69.00	2P/2B	.... 69.00	XP 5		F

Senior discount. 43 units. N side of SR 78, 1 1/2 mi e of I-5; from SR 78 exit El Camino Real, then 1 blk e. 3170 Vista Way. (92056) C/CATV; movies; radios; phones. Htd pool; whirlpool; playground; exercise rm. Fee for: golf-18 holes, tennis-7 courts, 4 lighted. No pets. Wkly & monthly rates avail. Reserv deposit required. AE, DI, DS, MC, VI.   ⊗ Ⓓ (619) 757-2200

Oceanside Travelodge

		Rates Subject to Change				Motel			◆
⊕ Fri & Sat 6/15-9/15	1P	.... 47.00	2P/1B	.... 49.00	2P/2B	.... 52.00	XP 5		F
Sun-Thurs 6/15-9/15	1P	.... 44.00	2P/1B	.... 46.00	2P/2B	.... 47.00	XP 5		F
2/16-6/14	1P	.... 40.00	2P/1B	.... 42.00	2P/2B	.... 45.00	XP 5		F
9/16-2/15	1P	.... 38.00	2P/1B	.... 40.00	2P/2B	.... 42.00	XP 5		F

Senior discount. 28 units. Adjacent to I-5, exit Hill St. 1401 N Hill St. (92054) A/C; C/CATV; movies; phones; shower or comb baths. 2 2-bedrm units. Coin laundry. No pets. Reserv deposit required. AE, CB, DI, MC, VI.
        ⊗ Ⓓ (619) 722-1244

Sandman Motel

		Rates Guaranteed				Motel			◆
⊕ All year	1P	36.00- 43.00	2P/1B	37.00- 45.00	2P/2B	41.00- 49.00	XP 4		

Senior discount. 81 units. 1 blk w of I-5, exit Oceanside Harbor Dr. 1501 Carmelo Dr. (92054) A/C; C/CATV; movies; radios; phones. Htd pool. Pets. Wkly & monthly rates avail. AE, DI, MC, VI.   Ⓓ (619) 722-7661

RESTAURANTS

The Chart House   Steak & Seafood $$ ◆◆
  1/2 mi w of I-5, Oceanside Harbor Dr exit. 314 Harbor Dr S. Overlooking Oceanside Marina. Contemporary decor. A/C. Children's menu. Open 5 pm-10 pm; Fri & Sat-11 pm. Cocktails & lounge. Reserv advised. AE, CB, DI, MC, VI.
        ⊗ 🄻 (619) 722-1345

Furr's Family Dining   American $ ◆
  On SR 76; 2 blks e of I-5. 1531 Mission Ave. Attractive cafeteria serving large selection of salads, entrees & desserts. A/C. Open 11 am-8:30 pm; Sun-8 pm; closed 12/25. AE, MC, VI.   ⊗ 🄻 (619) 433-5553

The Grove Restaurant   American $ ◆◆
  2 mi e on SR 76. 3232 E Mission Dr. Very attractive restaurant. Selection of salads, sandwiches & entrees. Sun brunch, 9:30 am-3 pm. A/C. Children's menu. Open 11:30 am-9 pm; Fri & Sat-10 pm; Sun 9:30 am-9:30 pm. Cocktails & lounge. MC, VI.   ⊗ 🄻 (619) 757-7711

Hungry Hunter Restaurant   Steak & Seafood $$ ◆◆
  1/4 blk w of I-5 at Jct SR 78. 1221 Vista Way. Attractive country atmosphere. A/C. Early bird specials. Open 11:30 am-2:30 & 5-9:30 pm; Fri-10 pm; Sat 5 pm-10 pm; Sun 4 pm-9:30 pm; closed 12/25. Cocktails & lounge. AE, CB, DI, MC, VI.   ⊗ (619) 433-2633

OJAI — 7,600

Best Western Casa Ojai AAA Special Value Rates *Motel* ◆◆
Fri & Sat [CP] 1P 80.00- 90.00 2P/1B 90.00- 100.00 2P/2B 95.00- 105.00 XP 5 F
Sun-Thurs [CP] 1P 55.00- 65.00 2P/1B 65.00- 75.00 2P/2B 70.00- 80.00 XP 6 F
45 units. 3/4 mi e on SR 150. 1302 E Ojai Ave. (93023) 6 refrigerators; A/C; C/CATV; phones. Htd pool; whirlpool. Reserv deposit required weekends. AE, DI, DS, MC, VI. FAX (805) 640-8247 ⊗ Ⓓ (805) 646-8175

Ojai Valley Inn & Country Club Rates Subject to Change *Resort Complex* ◆◆◆
All year [BP] 1P 190.00- 250.00 2P/1B 190.00- 250.00 2P/2B 190.00- 250.00 XP 25 F
212 units. 1 mi w on SR 150, 1/4 mi s. Country Club Rd. (PO Box L, 93023) Charming resort on several acres of nicely landscaped grounds. 16 suites with fireplaces. Check-in 3 pm. A/C; C/CATV; pay movies; radios; phones. 2 htd pools; saunas; whirlpool; putting green; recreational program; bicycles; playground; exercise rm. Fee for: golf-18 holes, tennis-8 courts, 4 lighted. Small pets only. Reserv deposit required; 3 days refund notice. AE, DI, DS, MC, VI. ● Dining rm & restaurant; 6:30 am-11 pm; $18-$35; 24 hour room service; cocktails. FAX (805) 646-7969 ⊗ Ⓢ Ⓓ Ⓖ (805) 646-5511

RESTAURANT

Ranch House Restaurant Continental $$$ ◆◆◆
From jct SR 150 & 33; 3/4 mi nw on Maricopa Rd, 1/3 mi w on El Roblar, then 1/2 mi s. Corner of S Lomita & Besant Rd. Colorful lush garden foliage, patio dining, homemade breads & desserts. Beef, lamb, chicken & fresh seafood. Menu changes weekly. Informal atmosphere. Open 11:30 am-1:30; seatings for dinner at 6 pm & 8:30 pm; Sun 1 pm-3:30 pm; seatings for dinner at 7:30 pm; closed Mon, Tues & for lunch 10/2-4/14. Beer & wine. Reserv required for dinner. AE, DI, MC, VI. ⊗ (805) 646-2360

ONTARIO — 133,200

Airport Accommodations-See listings for:

- ⓐ Best Western Ontario Airport Motel, 1/2 mi n of airport
- ⓐ Country Side Suites, (, 1/2 mi n of airport.
- ⓐ Country Suites By Carlson, 3/4 mi n of airport
- ⓐ Doubletree Club Hotel, 1 mi n of airport.
- ⓐ Marriott Hotel-Ontario, 1 mi ne of airport.
- Red Lion Hotel, 3/4 mi n of airport.
- Residence Inn by Marriott, 1 1/4 mi n of airport.
- Super 8 Lodge, 1 mi n of airport.

Best Ontario Inn Rates Subject to Change *Motel* ◆
All year 1P .... 35.00 2P/1B .... 45.00 2P/2B .... 45.00 XP 5
Senior discount. 42 units. 1 mi w of Euclid Ave, at Mountain. 1045 W Mission Blvd. (91762) A/C; C/CATV; movies; radios; phones. Coin laundry. Small htd pool; whirlpool. No pets. Wkly rates avail. AE, CB, DI, MC, VI. Ⓢ Ⓓ (909) 391-6668

Best Western Ontario Airport Motel AAA Special Value Rates *Motel* ◆◆
All year [CP] 1P 44.00- 50.00 2P/1B 54.00- 60.00 2P/2B .... 54.00 XP 5 F
150 units. 1/2 mi s of I-10, Vineyard Ave exit, 1/2 mi nof Ontario Airport. 209 N Vineyard Ave. (91764) 38 refrigerators; A/C; C/CATV; movies; phones. Coin laundry. Htd pool; whirlpool. Airport transp. AE, CB, DI, MC, VI. Restaurant adjacent. Ⓓ (909) 983-9600

Comfort Inn Airport South AAA Special Value Rates *Motel* ◆◆
All year 1P 36.00- 40.00 2P/1B 40.00- 45.00 2P/2B .... 45.00 XP 3 F
45 units. 1/2 blk n of SR 60, Pomona Frwy, exit Euclid Ave. 2301 S Euclid Ave. (91762) A/C; C/CATV; movies; radios; phones. Pool; whirlpool. No pets. 5 rooms with whirlpool tub, $70. Wkly rates avail. AE, CB, DI, MC, VI. ⊗ Ⓢ Ⓓ (909) 986-3556

Country Inn AAA Special Value Rates *Motel* ◆◆
All year [CP] 1P 39.00- 45.00 2P/1B 43.00- 49.00 2P/2B 43.00- 49.00 XP 4- 5 F
71 units. Adjacent to SR 60, exit Grove Ave. 2359 S Grove Ave. (91761) Formerly Rodeway Inn. Some rooms with VCP's. A/C; C/CATV; movies; 50 radios; phones. Htd pool; whirlpool. Pets, $50 deposit required. 8 rooms with whirlpool tub, $70. Wkly rates avail. AE, DI, DS, MC, VI. FAX (909) 923-4504 ⊗ Ⓢ Ⓓ (909) 923-1887

Country Side Suites Rates Guaranteed *Motel* ◆◆◆◆
All year [BP] 1P .... 65.00 2P/1B .... 65.00 2P/2B .... 65.00 XP 10 F
Senior discount. 105 units. 1/2 mi s of I-10, Vineyard Ave exit, 1/2 mi n of Ontario Airport. 204 N Vineyard Ave. (91764) Attractively decorated in a country French theme. Refrigerators; A/C; C/CATV; movies; radios; phones. Htd pool; whirlpool. Airport transp. No pets. 6 rooms with whirlpool tub, $75. Wkly rates avail. Complimentary beverages each evening. AE, DI, MC, VI. FAX (909) 986-4227 *(See ad p A205)* ⊗ Ⓢ Ⓓ Ⓖ (909) 986-8550

Country Suites By Carlson   Rates Guaranteed   *Apartment Motel*   ◆◆
All year [CP]   1P 62.00- 72.00   2P/1B   62.00- 72.00   2P/2B   .... 72.00   XP 10   F
120 units. 2 1/2 blks s of I-10; 3/4 mi n of airport. 231 N Vineyard Ave. (91764) Studio & 1-to 2-bedroom suites with kitchen. A/C; C/TV; free & pay movies; radios; phones. 12 2-bedrm units, efficiencies. Coin laundry. Htd pool; whirlpool. Pets, $100 deposit required. Wkly rates avail. AE, CB, DI, MC, VI. FAX (909) 983-0858 *(See ad p A303)*   ⊗ Ⓓ (909) 983-8484

Days Inn   Rates Subject to Change   *Motel*   ◆
All year   1P 45.00- 55.00   2P/1B   49.00- 59.00   2P/2B   49.00- 59.00   XP 5
Senior discount. 50 units. Adjacent to I-10, exit 4th St, then 1 blk w. 1405 E 4th St. (91764) A/C; C/TV; movies; radios; phones. Small pool. No pets. 3 rooms with whirlpool tub, $80. AE, DI, DS, MC, VI. Restaurant adjacent. FAX (909) 391-1216   ⊗ Ⓢ Ⓓ (909) 983-7411

Doubletree Club Hotel   Rates Subject to Change   *Motor Inn*   ◆◆◆
Sun-Thurs [BP]   1P .... 64.00   2P/1B   .... 64.00   2P/2B   .... 64.00   XP 10
Fri & Sat [BP]   1P .... 59.00   2P/1B   .... 59.00   2P/2B   .... 59.00   XP
Senior discount. 171 units. 1/4 mi s of I-10, Vineyard Ave exit; 1 mi n of Ontario Airport. 429 N Vineyard Ave. (91764) Check-in 3 pm. A/C; C/TV; free & pay movies; radios; phones. Htd pool; whirlpool; exercise rm. Airport transp. No pets. Complimentary beverages each evening. AE, DI, DS, MC, VI. Light meals avail 5 pm-10 pm. FAX (909) 391-2369 *(See ad below)*   ⊗ Ⓢ Ⓓ Ⓚ (909) 391-6411

Fairfield Inn by Marriott   Rates Subject to Change   *Motel*   ◆◆
All year   1P .... 43.95   2P/1B   .... 43.95   2P/2B   .... 45.95   XP
Senior discount. 117 units. S side of I-10, exit Haven Ave; then 1/2 mi w. 3201 Centrelake Dr. (91761) A/C; C/CATV; phones. Htd pool. Airport transp. No pets. AE, DI, DS, MC, VI. *(See ad p A221)*   ⊗ Ⓢ Ⓓ Ⓚ (909) 395-9300

Holiday Inn   Rates Guaranteed   *Motor Inn*   ◆◆◆
All year   1P 67.00- 80.00   2P/1B   67.00- 80.00   2P/2B   67.00- 80.00   XP   F
Senior discount. 186 units. Adjacent to I-10, exit Vineyard Ave, 1 blk s then 1 blk w. 1801 East G St. (91764) A/C; C/CATV; free & pay movies; radios; phones. Coin laundry. Pool. Airport transp. Pets. AE, CB, DI, MC, VI. ● Dining rm; 6 am-1:30 & 5:30-10 pm; Sat & Sun from 7 am; $7-$12; cocktails. FAX (909) 986-4724   Ⓓ (909) 983-3604

Howard Johnson Lodge-Ontario Airport South   AAA Special Value Rates   *Motel*   ◆◆
All year [CP]   1P 40.00- 72.00   2P/1B   44.00- 72.00   2P/2B   44.00- 72.00   XP 8   F
62 units. Adjacent to SR 60, exit Archibald Ave. 2425 S Archibald Ave. (91761) A/C; C/CATV; movies; radios; phones. 4 2-bedrm units. Small pool; 8 rooms with whirlpool tub. Pets, $5 extra charge. AE, CB, DI, MC, VI. Restaurant adjacent.   ⊗ Ⓢ Ⓚ (909) 923-2728

Inn Suites Ontario Airport Hotel   Rates Guaranteed   *Motor Inn*   ◆◆◆
All year [CP]   1P .... 62.00   2P/1B   .... 68.00   2P/2B   68.00- 76.00   XP   F
Senior discount. 150 units. Adjacent to I-10, exit Haven Ave, 1/2 blk n, then 1/2 blk w. 3400 Shelby St. (91764) Refrigerators; A/C; C/CATV; movies; radios; phones. Htd pool; whirlpool; exercise rm. Airport transp. Pets, $50 deposit required. Microwaves. 42 1-bedroom suites. Wkly & monthly rates avail. Complimentary beverages each evening. AE, CB, DI, MC, VI. ● Dining rm; 6:30-10 am, 11-2 & 5-9 pm; $7-$16; cocktails. FAX (909) 941-1445   ⊗ Ⓢ Ⓓ (909) 466-9600

DOUBLETREE
CLUB HOTEL · ONTARIO AIRPORT

For AAA members, we're taking a little off the top.

$59 *weekends* / $64 *weekdays* Stay in a beautiful room at a trimmed rate not far from Mt. Baldy and Lake Arrowhead. Call your travel professional or 909-391-6411. 429 N. Vineyard Ave. 1-800-528-0444.

Rates are based on single or double occupancy and subject to availability.

Marriott Hotel-Ontario   Rates Subject to Change   *Motor Inn* ◆◆◆

Sun-Thurs   1P .... 79.00   2P/1B .... 79.00   2P/2B .... 79.00   XP 15   F
Fri & Sat   1P .... 59.00   2P/1B .... 59.00   2P/2B .... 59.00   XP 15   F
299 units. 1 mi ne of Ontario Airport; 1/2 mi e of Vineyard Ave. 2200 E Holt Blvd. (91764) A/C; C/CATV; pay movies; radios; phones; comb or shower baths. Htd pool; sauna; whirlpool. Fee for: lighted tennis-1 court; racquetball-3 courts; steamroom; health club & massage. Airport transp. No pets. AE, CB, DI, MC, VI. ● 2 dining rms; 6 am-midnight; deli 24 hours; $5-$16; cocktails. FAX (909) 391-6151 *(See ad p A304)*
⊗ Ⓢ Ⓓ Ⓛ (909) 986-8811

Mountain Inn   Rates Guaranteed   *Motel* ◆

All year   1P .... 35.00   2P/1B .... 38.00   2P/2B .... 46.00   XP 3   F
Senior discount. 42 units. 1 blk n of SR 60, exit Mountain Ave. 2289 S Mountain Ave. (91761) A/C; movies; phones. Pool. No pets. 8 rooms with whirlpool tub, $48 for 2 persons. AE, DS, MC, VI. Coffeeshop opposite. FAX (909) 391-6601
⊗ Ⓢ Ⓓ Ⓛ (909) 391-1708

Ontario Airport Hilton   Rates Subject to Change   *Hotel* ◆◆◆

All year   1P 110.00- 140.00   2P/1B 120.00- 150.00   2P/2B 120.00- 150.00   XP 15   F
Senior discount. 308 units. Adjacent to I-10, Haven Ave exit. 700 N Haven Ave. (91764) Check-in 3 pm. A/C; C/CATV; free & pay movies; radios; phones. Htd pool; whirlpool; exercise rm. Parking lot. Airport transp. No pets. AE, CB, DI, MC, VI. ● Dining rm & restaurant; 5 am-midnight; $8-$22; cocktails. FAX (909) 948-9309 *(See ad p 22)*
⊗ Ⓢ Ⓓ Ⓛ (909) 980-0400

Quality Inn Airport   Rates Subject to Change   *Motel* ◆◆◆

All year [CP]   1P 49.00- 76.00   2P/1B 57.00- 76.00   2P/2B 57.00- 76.00   XP 8   F
Senior discount. 106 units. 1 blk w of Vineyard Ave; 3/4 mi w of Ontario Airport. 1818 E Holt Blvd. (91761) A/C; C/CATV; movies; radios; phones. Coin laundry. Htd pool; sauna; whirlpool. Airport transp. No pets. Complimentary beverages each evening. AE, DI, DS, MC, VI. FAX (909) 391-3449 *(See ad below)*
⊗ Ⓢ Ⓓ Ⓛ (909) 988-8466

Red Lion Hotel   Rates Subject to Change   *Motor Inn* ◆◆◆

Sun-Thurs   1P .... 79.00   2P/1B .... 79.00   2P/2B .... 79.00   XP 15   F
Fri & Sat   1P .... 59.00   2P/1B .... 59.00   2P/2B .... 59.00   XP 15   F
340 units. 1/4 mi s of I-10 Vineyard Ave exit; 3/4 mi n of Ontario Airport. 222 N Vineyard Ave. (91764) A/C; C/CATV; pay movies; radios; phones. 11 2-bedrm units. Htd pool; whirlpool; exercise rm. Airport transp. Pets. AE, DI, DS, MC, VI. ● Dining rm & coffeeshop; 6 am-11 pm; $7-$23; cocktails; entertainment. FAX (909) 983-8851 *(See ad p A3)*
⊗ Ⓓ Ⓛ (909) 983-0909

Residence Inn by Marriott   AAA Special Value Rates   *Apartment Motel* ◆◆◆

All year   1P 99.00- 129.00   2P/1B .... 99.00   2P/2B 99.00- 129.00   XP 10   F
200 units. From I-10 exit Vineyard Ave, 2 blks s then 1 blk e; 1 1/4 mi n of Ontario Airport. 2025 East D St. (91764) Studio & 2-story, 2-bedroom units with living room & kitchen. Many fireplaces. A/C; C/CATV; movies; VCPs. Radios; phones. Coin laundry. Htd pool; whirlpool; sports court. Airport transp. Pets, $35 non-refundable fee; also $6 daily extra charge. Wkly & monthly rates avail. AE, DI, DS, MC, VI. FAX (909) 983-3843
⊗ Ⓢ Ⓓ Ⓛ (909) 983-6788

Super 8 Lodge   Rates Guaranteed   *Motel* ◆◆

All year   1P 41.00- 51.00   2P/1B 48.00- 58.00   2P/2B 52.00- 62.00   XP 4   F
Senior discount. 135 units. Adjacent to I-10, Vineyard exit; 1 mi n of Ontario Airport. 514 N Vineyard Ave. (91764) A/C; C/TV; movies; phones. Pool; whirlpool. Airport transp. No pets. AE, DI, DS, MC, VI. Coffeeshop adjacent. FAX (909) 988-2115
⊗ Ⓢ Ⓓ Ⓛ (909) 983-2886

Travelodge-Central   AAA Special Value Rates   *Motel* ◆

All year   1P 41.00- 43.00   2P/1B 45.00- 47.00   2P/2B 46.00- 48.00   XP 5   F
33 units. 1 mi s of I-10, Euclid Ave exit. 755 N Euclid Ave. (91762) A/C; C/CATV; movies; phones; shower or comb baths. Rental refrigerators. 1 2-bedrm unit. Htd pool; whirlpool. Pets. 4 microwaves. Wkly rates avail. AE, CB, DI, MC, VI. Restaurant adjacent.
Ⓓ (909) 984-1775

RESTAURANTS

El Torito Restautant   Mexican $ ◆◆

Adjacent to I-10, exit Haven Ave, 1 blk n, then 2 blks e. 3680 Inland Empire St. Popular, colorfully decorated restaurant. Sunday brunch 9 am-2 pm. A/C. Children's menu. Open 11 am-11 pm; Fri-midnight; Sun 9 am-10 pm; closed 11/25 & 12/25. Cocktails & lounge. AE, CB, DI, MC, VI.
⊗ (909) 944-9102

La Cheminee   French $$$ ◆

2 blks sw of I-10, 1 blk w of Mountain Ave. 1133 W 6th St. Formal decor & service. Nice selection of entrees. A/C. Open 11:30 am-2:30 & 5:30-9:30 pm; Sat 6 pm-10 pm; closed Sun, 11/25 & 12/25. Cocktails & lounge. Entertainment & dancing. AE, CB, DI, MC, VI.
⊗ (909) 983-7900

Panda Inn   Chinese $$ ◆

Adjacent to I-10; exit Haven Ave, 1 blk s then 1/2 mi w. 3223 E Centrelake Dr. Large, attractive restaurant serving a nice selection of Mandarin cuisine. A/C. Open 11:30 am-10:30 pm. Cocktails & lounge. Reserv advised. AE, CB, DI, MC, VI.
⊗ (909) 983-2888

Rosa's   Italian $$$ ◆

1 1/2 blks s of I-10. 425 N Vineyard Ave. Attractively decorated dining room. Formal service. A/C. Open 11:30 am-10 pm; Sat 5 pm-11 pm; Sun 4 pm-9 pm; closed major holidays. Cocktails & lounge. Reserv advised. AE, CB, DI, MC, VI.
⊗ (909) 391-1971

ORANGE — 110,700

Airport Accommodations
Orange County-John Wayne Airport
See Costa Mesa, Irvine, Newport Beach

Best Western El Camino Inn — Rates Subject to Change — *Motel* ◆◆
All year [CP] — 1P 42.00- 51.00 2P/1B 45.00- 54.00 2P/2B 47.00- 56.00 XP 3 F
Senior discount. 56 units. At jct SR 55 & 91; from SR 55, exit Lincoln Ave, 3/4 mi n on Tustin Ave; from SR 91, exit Tustin Ave, 3/4 mi s. 3191 N Tustin Ave. (92665) Refrigerators; A/C; C/CATV; movies; 50 radios; phones; comb or shower baths. 7 efficiencies. Htd pool. No pets. Reserv deposit required. AE, DI, DS, MC, VI.
⊗ Ⓓ (714) 998-0360

Big A Motel — Rates Subject to Change — *Motel* ◆◆
All year — 1P 35.00- 45.00 2P/1B .... 35.00 2P/2B 37.00- 45.00 XP 4 F
Senior discount. 40 units. 1/2 blk s of Katella Ave. 1250 N Glassell St. (92667) A/C; C/CATV; movies; radios; phones. 2 kitchens, 11 efficiencies, no utensils. Coin laundry. Small htd pool; whirlpool. No pets. 2 units with kitchen, $45-$75. Wkly & monthly rates avail. AE, CB, MC, VI.
⊗ Ⓓ (714) 633-4478

Doubletree Hotel At The City — Rates Subject to Change — *Hotel* ◆◆◆
All year — 1P 125.00- 145.00 2P/1B 135.00- 155.00 2P/2B 135.00- 155.00 XP 10 F
Senior discount. 451 units. 1 blk w of I-5; southbound exit The City Dr, northbound exit Chapman Ave. 100 The City Dr at Chapman Ave. (92668) Check-in 3 pm. A/C; C/CATV; pay movies; radios; phones. Htd pool; whirlpool; lighted tennis-2 courts. Parking lot. Airport transp. Pets, $75 deposit. AE, DI, DS, MC, VI. ● Dining rm & coffeeshop; 6 am-11 pm; $9-$25; cocktails. FAX (714) 978-3839 *(See ad p A45)* ⊗ Ⓢ Ⓓ (714) 634-4500

Hilton Suites-Orange — Rates Subject to Change — *Suites Hotel* ◆◆◆
All year — 1P 130.00- 165.00 2P/1B 145.00- 180.00 2P/2B 145.00- 180.00 XP 15 F
230 units. 1 blk e of I-5; southbound State College Blvd, northbound Chapman Ave. 400 North State College Blvd. (92668) 1 bedroom suites with living room, refrigerator & microwave. Check-in 3 pm. A/C; C/CATV; movies; VCPs. Radios; phones. Small htd indoor pool; sauna; exercise rm. Parking lot. Complimentary beverages each evening. AE, DI, DS, MC, VI. ● Dining rm; 11:30 am-1:30 & 5:30-10 pm; $5.75-$14.95; cocktails. FAX (714) 938-0930 *(See ad p 22)* ⊗ Ⓢ Ⓓ Ⓖ (714) 938-1111

Orange Travelodge — AAA Special Value Rates — *Motel* ◆◆◆
5/1-9/15 — 1P .... 45.00 2P/1B .... 50.00 2P/2B .... 60.00 XP 4 F
9/16-4/30 — 1P .... 40.00 2P/1B .... 45.00 2P/2B .... 55.00 XP 4 F
32 units. 1 mi e of I-5. 1302 W Chapman Ave. (92668) 16 refrigerators; A/C; C/CATV; movies; radios; phones; shower or comb baths. 8 2-bedrm units. Pool. No pets. AE, DI, DS, MC, VI. FAX (714) 633-9469
⊗ Ⓓ (714) 633-7720

Orange Tustin Inn — Rates Subject to Change — *Motel* ◆◆
All year — 1P .... 40.00 2P/1B .... 44.00 2P/2B .... 44.00 XP 4 F
Senior discount. 41 units. 1 blk n of SR 22, Garden Grove Frwy. 639 S Tustin Ave. (92666) A/C; C/CATV; movies; phones. No pets. 4 2-bedroom units with efficiencies, $88; no utensils. Reserv deposit required. AE, DI, DS, MC, VI. FAX (714) 771-2815
Ⓓ (714) 771-7460

Ramada Inn-South Anaheim — Rates Subject to Change — *Motor Inn* ◆◆
All year [CP] — 1P 39.00- 59.00 2P/1B 39.00- 59.00 2P/2B 39.00- 59.00 XP 6 F
Senior discount. 143 units. Adjacent to I-5; 1 blk n of Chapman Ave. 101 N State College Blvd. (92668) Check-in 3 pm. A/C; C/CATV; movies; radios; phones. Rental refrigerators. Coin laundry. Htd pool; whirlpool; lighted tennis-2 courts. No pets. Wkly & monthly rates avail. Reserv deposit required. AE, DI, DS, MC, VI. ● Restaurant; 11 am-10 pm; $6.95-$13.95; cocktails. FAX (714) 634-4751 ⊗ Ⓓ (714) 634-9500

The Residence Inn by Marriott — Rates Guaranteed — *Apartment Motel* ◆◆◆
All year [BP] — 1P 89.00- 115.00 2P/1B 89.00- 115.00 2P/2B 99.00- 145.00 XP
105 units. Adjacent to I-5; 1 blk n of Chapman Ave. 201 N State College Blvd. (92668) 1-bedroom studios & 26 split level 2-bedroom suites with living room; many with fireplace. Check-in 3 pm. A/C; C/CATV; movies; VCPs. Radios; phones. Coin laundry. Htd pool; whirlpool. Pets $250 deposit, $50 non-refundable; also $6 daily extra charge. Complimentary beverages each evening. AE, CB, DI, MC, VI. Complimentary dinner buffet, Mon-Fri. FAX (714) 978-6257
⊗ Ⓓ Ⓖ (714) 978-7700

RESTAURANT

Reubens — Steak & Seafood — $$ ◆◆
From SR 55, exit Lincoln Ave, 1 1/2 blks s on Tustin Ave; from SR 91, exit Tustin Ave, 1/2 mi s. 2585 N Tustin Ave. Nice selection. A/C. Early bird specials; children's menu. Open 11:30 am-3 & 5-10 pm; Fri-11 pm; Sat 5 pm-11 pm; Sun 5 pm-10 pm. Cocktails & lounge. Entertainment. Reserv advised. AE, DI, DS, MC, VI. ⊗ (714) 998-1542

ORLAND — 5,100

Amber Light Inn Motel — Rates Subject to Change — *Motel* ◆◆
All year — 1P 26.00- 28.00 2P/1B 28.00- 34.00 2P/2B 32.00- 36.00 XP 2- 3
Senior discount. 40 units. Exit I-5 via Chico, SR 32 off-ramp, then 1/4 mi e on Newville Rd. 828 Newville Rd. (95963) A/C; C/CATV; radios; phones; shower or comb baths. Pool; whirlpool. Reserv deposit required. AE, MC, VI. Coffeeshop opposite. ⊗ Ⓓ Ⓖ (916) 865-7655

Orland Inn — Rates Subject to Change — *Motel* ◆◆
All year — 1P 28.00- 32.00 2P/1B 32.00- 36.00 2P/2B .... 40.00 XP 4 F
Senior discount. 40 units. 1/2 mi s; northbound exit I-5E via Orland-Fairgrounds, southbound exit I-5E via CR 16; adjacent to I-5 in Stony Creek Shopping Center. 1052 South St. (95963) A/C; C/CATV; radios; phones. Pool. Small pets only. Wkly & monthly rates avail. Reserv deposit required. AE, DI, DS, MC, VI. ⊗ Ⓓ (916) 865-7632

OROVILLE — 12,000

Best Western Grand Manor Inn — Rates Subject to Change — *Motel* ◆◆◆
⊛ All year [CP]   1P 53.00- 85.00 2P/1B   64.00- 91.00 2P/2B   64.00- 75.00 XP 6
Senior discount. 53 units. SR 70 exit E Montgomery. 1470 Feather River Blvd. (95965) Refrigerators; A/C; C/CATV; radios; phones. Coin laundry. Pool; sauna; whirlpool; exercise rm. Parking lot. Pets. Reserv deposit required; 3 days refund notice. AE, DI, DS, MC, VI. FAX (916) 533-5862   ⊗ Ⓢ Ⓓ Ⓖ (916) 533-9673

The Villa Motel — Rates Subject to Change — *Motel* ◆◆
⊛ All year   1P .... 48.00 2P/1B   .... 50.00 2P/2B   .... 54.00 XP 4
Senior discount. 20 units. 1/4 mi e off SR 70 exit E Montgomery; 1/2 mi n off SR 162 (Oroville Dam Blvd). 1527 Feather River Blvd. (95965) A/C; C/CATV; movies; 18 radios; phones; shower baths. Pool. No pets. Reserv deposit required; 3 days refund notice. AE, CB, DI, MC, VI.   Ⓓ (916) 533-3930

RESTAURANT

The Depot — Steak & Seafood — $$ ◆◆
4 blks ne of courthouse. 2191 High St. Varied menu. A/C. Early bird specials; children's menu. Open 11 am-2:30 & 4-9:30 pm; Fri-10 pm; Sat 4 pm-10 pm; Sun 9:30 am-2 & 3:30-9:30 pm; closed 12/25. Cocktails & lounge. AE, DS, MC, VI.   ⊗ (916) 534-9101

OXNARD — 142,200

Casa Sirena Marina Resort — Rates Guaranteed — *Motor Inn* ◆◆◆
⊛ All year   1P .... 65.00 2P/1B   .... 65.00 2P/2B   .... 65.00 XP 10   F
Senior discount. 275 units. 1/2 mi w of Victoria Blvd via Channel Islands Blvd at Channel Islands Harbor. 3605 Peninsula Rd. (93035) Many rooms overlooking marina. Check-in 3 pm. Refrigerators; C/CATV; pay movies; radios; phones. 24 2-bedrm units, 24 efficiencies. Htd pool; saunas; whirlpools; putting green; lighted tennis-1 court; rental bicycles; exercise rm. No pets. Wkly & monthly rates avail. AE, MC, VI. ● Coffeeshop; 6:30 am-10 pm. Also, Lobster Trap Restaurant, see separate listing. FAX (805) 985-4329 *(See ad p A306)*   ⊗ Ⓓ (805) 985-6311

Casa Via Mar Inn & Tennis Club — Rates Subject to Change — *Motel* ◆◆◆
⊛ All year [BP]   1P 59.00- 69.00 2P/1B   69.00- 79.00 2P/2B   69.00- 77.00 XP 10   F
74 units. 5 blks w of Ventura Rd. 377 W Channel Islands Blvd. (Port Hueneme, 93041) Some rooms with patio or balcony. Refrigerators; C/TV; VCPs; radios; phones; comb or shower baths. 31 efficiencies. Htd pool; whirlpool; tennis-6 courts. No pets. Reserv deposit required. AE, CB, DI, MC, VI. FAX (805) 948-6222 Ⓓ Ⓖ (805) 984-6222

Country Inn at Port Hueneme — Rates Guaranteed — *Motel* ◆◆◆
⊛ Sun-Thurs [BP]   1P .... 76.00 2P/1B   .... 76.00 2P/2B   .... 76.00 XP 10   F
  Fri & Sat [BP]   1P .... 69.00 2P/1B   .... 69.00 2P/2B   .... 69.00 XP 10   F
Senior discount. 135 units. Port Hueneme & Ventura rds. 350 E Hueneme Rd. (Port Hueneme, 93041) Check-in 3 pm. Refrigerators; A/C; C/CATV; VCPs; radios; phones. 8 kitchens. Coin laundry. Htd pool; whirlpool; 12 rooms with whirlpool bathtub. No pets. Microwaves & wet bars. Complimentary beverages each evening. AE, DI, DS, MC, VI. FAX (805) 986-4399 *(See ad below)*   ⊗ Ⓢ Ⓓ Ⓖ (805) 986-5353

Financial Plaza Hilton   Rates Guaranteed   *Motor Inn*   ◆◆◆
ⓐⓑ All year   1P .... 63.00 2P/1B .... 63.00 2P/2B .... 63.00 XP 10   F
Senior discount. 160 units. 2 blks s of US 101 exit Vineyard Ave. 600 Esplanade Dr. (93030) Check-in 3 pm. Refrigerators; A/C; C/CATV; VCPs; radios; phones. Htd pool; whirlpool; lighted tennis-1 court; jogging track. No pets. AE, DI, DS, MC, VI. ● Restaurant; 6:30 am-10 pm; $9-$17.50; cocktails; entertainment. FAX (805) 485-2061
(See ads p 22 and p A307)   ⊗ Ⓢ Ⓓ Ⓐ (805) 485-9666

Radisson Suite Hotel At River Ridge   Rates Subject to Change   *Apartment Motor Inn*   ◆◆◆
ⓐⓑ All year [BP]   1P .... 69.00 2P/1B .... 69.00 2P/2B .... 69.00 XP 10   F
Senior discount. 250 units. 1 3/4 mi sw of US 101, exit Vineyard Ave. 2101 W Vineyard Ave. (93030) Check-in 3 pm. Refrigerators; A/C; C/CATV; movies; VCPs. Radios; phones. 60 2-bedrm units, kitchens. Coin laundry. 2 htd pools; whirlpools; exercise rm. Fee for: golf-18 holes, lighted tennis-5 courts. Airport transp. No pets. 60 loft suites with fireplace & kitchen, $99. 120 fireplace units. Monthly rates avail. AE, DI, DS, MC, VI. ● Restaurant; 6:30 am-10 pm; $9-$17; cocktails. *(See ad below)*   ⊗ Ⓓ Ⓐ (805) 988-0130

RESTAURANTS

Furr's Cafeteria   American $ ◆◆
1 blk e of Ventura Rd. 1301 W Channel Island. A/C. Open 11 am-8 pm; closed 12/25. AE, MC, VI. ⊗ (805) 483-0187

The Greek   Greek $$ ◆◆
3 blks s of US 101 on the nw corner of Oxnard Blvd & Vineyard Ave; exit Vineyard Ave. 2343 N Oxnard Blvd. Steaks, seafood, lamb, chicken, vegetarian plate, pasta & casseroles. A/C. Children's menu. Open 11 am-10 pm; Fri-11 pm; Sat & Sun 5 pm-11 pm. Beer & wine. Entertainment & dancing. Reserv advised Fri & Sat. AE, DI, DS, MC, VI.
                                                                                  ⊗ (805) 981-1891

Lobster Trap Restaurant   Steak & Seafood $$ ◆◆
In Casa Sirena Marina Resort. Overlooking marina. Salads, seafood, chicken, steak & prime rib. Sun brunch 10 am-2 pm. A/C. Early bird specials. Open 11:30 am-10 pm. Cocktails & lounge. Entertainment & dancing. AE, CB, DI, MC, VI.
                                                                                  ⊗ (805) 985-6361

The Whales Tail   Seafood $$ ◆◆
3/4 mi se of Channel Island Blvd, via Harbor Blvd (Channel Island Harbor). 3950 Bluefin Cir. Fresh seafood, steaks, salads, chicken, pasta & rack of lamb. View of harbor. A/C. Open 11:15 am-3 & 5-10:30 pm, Fri & Sat to 11 pm; Sun 10:30 pm-2:30 & 4-10:30 pm; closed 12/25. Cocktails & lounge. Entertainment & dancing. Reserv advised Fri & Sat. AE, DS, MC, VI.   ⊗ (805) 985-2511

PACIFIC BEACH — 34,300   See SAN DIEGO

PACIFIC GROVE — 16,100   (See MONTEREY PENINSULA spotting map pages A262 & A263; see index starting on page A260)

Best Western Butterfly Trees Lodge 62   AAA Special Value Rates   *Motel*   ◆◆
ⓐⓑ 3/1-10/31 [CP]   1P 69.00- 109.00 2P/1B 69.00- 109.00 2P/2B .... 109.00 XP 8   F
    11/1-2/28 [CP]   1P 59.00- 99.00   2P/1B 59.00- 99.00   2P/2B .... 99.00 XP 8   F
66 units. 1 mi w. 1150 Lighthouse Ave. (93950) Some fireplaces. 7 refrigerators; C/CATV; radios; phones; comb or shower baths. Pool; sauna; whirlpool. Pets, $10 extra charge. Reserv deposit required; 3 days refund notice. Complimentary beverages each evening. AE, DI, DS, MC, VI. FAX (408) 372-4385   ⊗ Ⓓ (408) 372-0503

Borg's Ocean Front Motel 61   Rates Subject to Change   *Motel*   ◆
ⓐⓑ All year   1P 48.00- 80.00 2P/1B 48.00- 90.00 2P/2B 62.00- 95.00 XP
60 units. 1/2 mi n on the bay. 635 Ocean View Blvd. (93950) Some units with ocean view. C/CATV; phones; shower or comb baths. 6 2-bedrm units. No pets. 3-night minimum stay in 6 kitchen units, 10 extra. Reserv deposit required. AE, MC, VI. Restaurant adjacent.   Ⓓ (408) 375-2406

(See MONTEREY PENINSULA spotting map pages A262 & A263)

Butterfly Grove Inn 🆖   Rates Subject to Change   *Motel*   ◆
♿ 6/1-9/20 & Fri-Sat   1P 50.00- 65.00   2P/1B   65.00- 75.00   2P/2B   65.00- 90.00   XP 8
    9/21-5/31 & Sun-Thurs   1P 45.00- 55.00   2P/1B   55.00- 65.00   2P/2B   65.00- 75.00   XP 8
Senior discount. 28 units. 3/4 mi w. 1073 Lighthouse Ave. (93950) 9 refrigerators; C/CATV; radios; phones; comb or shower baths. 9 2-bedrm units. Pool; whirlpool. Reserv deposit required; 3 days refund notice. AE, CB, DI, MC, VI.   Ⓓ (408) 373-4921

Executive Lodge 🆖   Rates Guaranteed   *Motel*   ◆◆◆
♿ 6/15-9/30 & Fri-Sat [CP]   1P 120.00- 150.00   2P/1B   120.00- 150.00   2P/2B   120.00- 150.00   XP 10   F
    Sun-Thurs 10/1-6/14 [CP]   1P 95.00- 125.00   2P/1B   95.00- 125.00   2P/2B   95.00- 125.00   XP 10   F
30 units. Off SR 68 at Asilomar Ave; e on Sinex Ave corner Dennett & Sinex aves. 660 Dennett Ave. (93950) Quiet forest setting. Some spacious rooms with balcony; some with gas burning fireplace. Check-in 3 pm. Refrigerators; C/CATV; radios; phones. 10 2-bedrm units, 8 kitchens, 9 efficiencies, no utensils. No pets. Wkly & monthly rates avail. Reserv deposit required; 3 days refund notice. MC, VI. FAX (408) 373-2698 ⊗ Ⓓ 🦽 (408) 373-8777

Larchwood Inn Motel 🆖   Rates Subject to Change   *Motel*   ◆
♿ All year   1P .... 63.00   2P/1B   .... 70.00   2P/2B   .... 80.00   XP 5
24 units. 1 mi w; 1 blk n off SR 68 & entrance to Asilomar conference grounds. 740 Crocker Ave. (93950) All units have pressed-log fireplaces. C/CATV; phones. No pets. 2-night minimum stay weekends. Reserv deposit required. MC, VI. *(See ad p A308)*   Ⓓ (408) 373-1114

Lighthouse Lodge 🆖   AAA Special Value Rates   *Motel*   ◆◆◆
♿ All year [BP]   1P 159.00- 209.00   2P/1B   159.00- 209.00   2P/2B   179.00- 209.00   XP 10
29 units. 1 mi w. 1249 Lighthouse Dr. (93950) Landscaped, natural setting. Few ocean view; many balconies or patios. Gas fireplaces. Check-in 4 pm. Refrigerators; C/CATV; radios; phones; comb or shower baths. All rooms with whirlpool tub. Garage & parking lot. All units have wet bar & microwave. Wkly & monthly rates avail. Reserv deposit required; 3 days refund notice. AE, MC, VI. FAX (408) 655-4922 *(See ad below)*
                                    ⊗ Ⓢ Ⓓ 🦽   (408) 655-2111

Olympia Motor Lodge 🆖   Rates Guaranteed   *Motel*   ◆◆
♿ All year   1P 40.00- 80.00   2P/1B   44.00- 90.00   2P/2B   48.00- 94.00   XP 5
Senior discount. 38 units. 1 mi w. 1140 Lighthouse Ave. (93950) Japanese motif; some rooms with ocean view & balcony. C/CATV; phones. Coin laundry. Pool. 8 efficiencies, $5 extra. Reserv deposit required. AE, DI, MC, VI. Coffeeshop adjacent.   Ⓓ (408) 373-2777

Pacific Gardens Inn 🆖   Rates Guaranteed   *Motel*   ◆◆◆
♿ 3/1-10/31 & weekends [CP]   1P 88.00- 93.00   2P/1B   88.00- 93.00   2P/2B   88.00- 98.00   XP 10
    11/1-2/28 [CP]   1P 70.00- 75.00   2P/1B   70.00- 75.00   2P/2B   78.00- 88.00   XP 10
Senior discount. 27 units. Off SR 68 at Asilomar Blvd, 1/2 blk from Asilomar Conference Center. 701 Asilomar Blvd. (93950) 25 rooms with woodburning fireplace. Refrigerators; C/CATV; radios; phones. 2 2-bedrm units, 6 kitchens. Whirlpools. No pets. 3 1- & 2-bedroom units with parlor, $115-$145 for up to 4 persons. Reserv deposit required. AE, MC, VI.   Ⓓ (408) 646-9414

(See MONTEREY PENINSULA spotting map pages A262 & A263)

Pacific Grove Inn 60   AAA Special Value Rates   *Historic Bed & Breakfast* ◆◆◆
- Fri & Sat 7/1-10/31 [BP]   1P 67.50- 87.50   2P/1B   77.50- 97.50   2P/2B   87.50-107.50   XP 16
- Sun-Thurs 3/1-6/30 [BP]   1P 57.50- 77.50   2P/1B   67.50- 87.50   2P/2B   77.50- 97.50   XP 13
- Sun-Thurs 11/1-2/28 [BP]   1P 47.50- 67.50   2P/1B   57.50- 77.50   2P/2B   67.50- 87.50   XP 11
16 units. 1/4 mi s; 3 1/2 mi w of SR 1 via SR 68 & Forest Ave. 581 Pine Ave. (93950) Charming 1904 Queen Anne Victorian. Most rooms with fireplace, some with ocean view. Smoke free premises. 3-story, no elevator. Refrigerators; C/CATV; radios; phones; comb or shower baths. 2 2-bedrm units. Limited parking lot. No pets. 2 bedroom units $87.50-$147.50 for up to 4 persons. Reserv deposit required; 3 days refund notice. AE, DI, DS, MC, VI. *(See ad p A309)* ⊗ Ⓢ Ⓓ (408) 375-2825

Pacific Grove Motel 66   Rates Subject to Change   *Motel* ◆
- Sun-Thurs 5/28-9/6 & Fri-Sat   1P 54.00- 74.00   2P/1B   59.00- 94.00   2P/2B   59.00- 94.00   XP 5
- Sun-Thurs 9/7-5/27   1P 44.00- 59.00   2P/1B   49.00- 69.00   2P/2B   49.00- 69.00   XP 5
30 units. 1 mi w; 3 blks w off Seventeen Mile Dr. Lighthouse Ave & Grove Acre. (93950) Refrigerators; C/CATV; 6 radios; phones; shower or comb baths. Pool; whirlpool; playground. No pets. 6 2-bedroom units $79-$121, for up to 6 persons. 2-night minimum stay on weekends. Reserv deposit required; 3 days refund notice. AE, DS, MC, VI. *(See ad below)* Ⓓ (408) 372-3218

Quality Inn 67   Rates Subject to Change   *Motel* ◆◆◆
- 5/1-10/31 [CP]   1P 80.00- 140.00   2P/1B   90.00- 150.00   2P/2B   100.00- 140.00   XP 10   F
- 11/1-4/30 [CP]   1P 70.00- 130.00   2P/1B   80.00- 140.00   2P/2B   90.00- 120.00   XP 10   F
49 units. 3/4 mi w, 1 blk w off Seventeen Mile Dr. 1111 Lighthouse Ave. (93950) Landscaped & skylight interior corridors. 11 A/C; C/CATV; movies; radios; phones. 6 2-bedrm units, 6 efficiencies. Htd pool; sauna; whirlpool. No pets. Rooms with fireplace, $10 extra. 4 suite $280-$350 for up to 6 persons. Wkly & monthly rates avail. Reserv deposit required; 3 days refund notice. Complimentary beverages each evening. AE, DS, DI, MC, VI. FAX (408) 646-5976 *(See ad p A272)* ⊗ Ⓢ Ⓓ Ⓖ (408) 646-8885

Rosedale Inn 56   Rates Subject to Change   *Motel* ◆◆◆
- 6/1-9/30 [CP]   1P 115.00- 185.00   2P/1B   115.00- 185.00   2P/2B   115.00- 185.00   XP 10   F
Senior discount. 18 units. Corner of Asilomar & Sinex aves; across from Asilomar Conference Center. 775 Asilomar Ave. (93950) OPEN ALL YEAR. Attractive decor, fireplaces & microwaves. Refrigerators; A/C; C/CATV; pay movies; VCPs. Radios; phones. 3 kitchens. Whirlpool baths. No pets. Reserv deposit required; 3 days refund notice. AE, DI, DS, MC, VI. FAX (408) 655-0691 *(See ad p A276)* ⊗ Ⓓ Ⓖ (408) 655-1000

The Wilkies Motel 64   AAA Special Value Rates   *Motel* ◆◆
- 6/1-9/30   1P 70.00- 85.00   2P/1B   70.00- 85.00   2P/2B   70.00- 85.00   XP 6   F
- 10/1-5/31   1P 50.00- 75.00   2P/1B   50.00- 75.00   2P/2B   50.00- 75.00   XP 6   F
24 units. 3/4 mi w; 1 blk w off Seventeen Mile Dr. 1038 Lighthouse Ave. (93950) Few rooms with partial ocean view. C/CATV; phones; shower baths. No pets. 2 kitchens, $10 extra. 2 night minimum stay weekends. Wkly & monthly rates avail in winter. Reserv deposit required; 3 days refund notice. AE, DS, MC, VI. *(See ad below)* ⊗ Ⓓ (408) 372-5960

RESTAURANTS

El Cocodrilo 17   Ethnic $ ◆◆
Center. 701 Lighthouse Ave. Caribbean & Latin-American specialties. Designated smoking areas. A/C. Children's menu. Open 5 pm-10 pm; Sat-11 pm; closed Tues, 11/25 & 12/25. Beer & wine. Reserv advised. MC, VI. ⊗ (408) 655-3311

Fandango 16   Continental $$ ◆◆
- 223 17th St. Mesquite-grilled seafood & meats. European specialties served in informal Mediterranean atmosphere. Open 11 am-2 & 5:30-10 pm; Sun 10 am-2:30 & 5:30-10 pm. Cocktails. Reserv advised. AE, CB, DI, MC, VI. ⊗ (408) 372-3456

(See MONTEREY PENINSULA spotting map pages A262 & A263)

Old Bath House Restaurant ⑮   Continental $$$ ◆◆◆
1/2 mi n. 620 Ocean View Blvd. View of bay. Fresh seafood. Mesquite grilled meats. Designated smoking areas. Open
5 pm-10:30 pm; Sat 4 pm-11 pm; Sun 3 pm-10:30 pm. Cocktails & lounge. Minimum $8. Reserv advised. AE, CB, DI,
MC, VI.   ⊗ (408) 375-5195

PALMDALE — 68,800

Holiday Inn Palmdale-Lancaster   Rates Subject to Change   *Motor Inn*   ◆◆
All year   1P 50.00- 60.00 2P/1B   60.00- 70.00 2P/2B   60.00- 70.00 XP 10   F
Senior discount. 153 units. Palmdale Hwy & SR 14. 38630 5th St W. (93551) Formerly Days Inn. Check-in 3 pm. 8 re-
frigerators; A/C; C/CATV; pay movies; radios; phones. Htd pool; whirlpool. AE, DI, DS, MC, VI. ● Coffeeshop; 6 am-10
pm; $7-$12; cocktails. FAX (805) 947-9957   ⊗ Ⓢ Ⓓ Ⓛ (805) 947-8055

Ramada Inn   Rates Guaranteed   *Motor Inn*   ◆◆
⊕ All year [BP]   1P 48.00- 58.00 2P/1B   53.00- 63.00 2P/2B   53.00- 63.00 XP 5   F
Senior discount. 135 units. Adjacent to SR 14; exit Palmdale Blvd. 300 W Palmdale Blvd. (93551) Check-in 3 pm.
A/C; C/CATV; movies; VCPs. Radios; phones. Rental refrigerators. Coin laundry. Htd pool; whirlpool; exercise
rm. No pets. Wkly & monthly rates avail. AE, DI, DS, MC, VI. ● Restaurant; 6 am-10 pm; $8-$14; cocktails; en-
tertainment. FAX (805) 947-9593   ⊗ Ⓓ Ⓛ (805) 273-1200

Super 8 Motel   AAA Special Value Rates   *Motel*   ◆◆
All year   1P   .... 32.00 2P/1B   .... 35.00 2P/2B   .... 40.00 XP 3   F
94 units. Adjacent to jct SR 14 & 138; exit Palmdale Blvd. 200 W Palmdale Blvd. (93550) 65 refrigerators; A/C; C/CATV;
movies; radios; phones. Htd pool; whirlpool. No pets. Wkly & monthly rates avail. AE, DI, DS, MC, VI. Restaurant adja-
cent. FAX (805) 266-4521 *(See ad below)*   ⊗ Ⓓ Ⓛ (805) 273-8000

RESTAURANTS

JE's Old Firehouse   American $$ ◆◆
1 3/4 mi e on SR 138 (Palmdale) from SR 14, exit Palmdale Blvd. 1643 E Palmdale Blvd. Replica of an 1890 firehouse,
uniquely decorated & furnished. Prime rib, pork ribs, chicken, seafood & steaks cooked over mesquite broiler. A/C. Children's menu. Open 11 am-10 pm; Fri & Sat-11 pm; Sun 10 am-2:30 & 4-10 pm. Cocktails & lounge. Entertainment &
dancing. MC, VI.   ⊗ Ⓛ (805) 273-0833

Mr. B's Restaurant   American $$ ◆◆◆
19 1/2 mi e via Palmdale Blvd, 1 1/4 mi n via 170th St E; in the Lake Los Angeles area. Wide selection of wines. Selec-
tion of steak, lamb, seafood & chicken. A/C. Children's menu. Open 5 pm-9 pm; Fri & Sat-10 pm; Sun 4 pm-9 pm; closed
Mon, 12/24 & 12/25. Cocktails & lounge. Reserv advised Weekends. AE, DI, DS, MC, VI. ⊗ (805) 264-2169

PALM DESERT — 23,300   (See map page A315)

Casa Larrea Motel   AAA Special Value Rates   *Motel*   ◆◆
⊕ 2/1-5/30 [CP]   ....   2P/1B .... 54.00 2P/2B   .... 54.00 XP 11
   12/23-1/31 [CP]   ....   2P/1B .... 52.00 2P/2B   .... 52.00 XP 11
   10/29-12/22 [CP]   ....   2P/1B .... 47.00 2P/2B   .... 47.00 XP 11
   5/31-10/28 [CP]   ....   2P/1B .... 36.00 2P/2B   .... 36.00 XP 11
20 units. 2 blks s of SR 111, between San Luis Rey & Portola Ave. 73-771 Larrea St. (92260) Patios. Refrigera-
tors; A/C; C/CATV; phones; shower or comb baths. 5 efficiencies. 2 htd pools; whirlpool; bicycles. No pets. 1
2-bedroom housekeeping unit; 6 kitchen units, $10-$14 extra. Reserv deposit required; 7 days refund notice. AE,
MC, VI.   Ⓓ (619) 568-0311

Deep Canyon Inn   Rates Subject to Change   *Motel*   ◆◆
⊕ 12/1-5/31 [CP]   1P 80.00- 95.00 2P/1B   85.00-105.00 2P/2B   85.00-185.00 XP 10
   9/15-11/30 [CP]   1P .... 65.00 2P/1B   65.00- 75.00 2P/2B   75.00-140.00 XP 10
   6/1-9/14 [CP]   1P 45.00- 65.00 2P/1B   55.00- 75.00 2P/2B   55.00- 85.00 XP 10
30 units. 1 blk s of SR 111 via Deep Canyon Rd. 74-470 Abronia Tr. (92260) Nicely landscaped. Check-in 3 pm.
Refrigerators; A/C; C/CATV; movies; phones; comb or shower baths. 3 2-bedrm units, 16 efficiencies. Htd pool;
whirlpool; bicycles. Monthly rates avail. Reserv deposit required. AE, CB, DI, MC, VI. FAX (619) 341-9120
                                                                     Ⓓ (619) 346-8061

(See map page A315)

Embassy Suites Hotel

		Rates Subject to Change			Suites Motor Inn	◆◆◆
2/1-4/24 [BP]	1P 149.00- 209.00	2P/1B 149.00- 209.00	2P/2B 149.00- 209.00	XP 15		F
4/25-6/19 & 9/17-1/31 [BP]	1P 99.00- 159.00	2P/1B 99.00- 159.00	2P/2B 99.00- 159.00	XP 15		F
6/20-9/16 [BP]	1P 69.00- 125.00	2P/1B 69.00- 125.00	2P/2B 69.00- 125.00	XP 15		F

199 units. 1 1/2 mi e on SR 111. 74-700 Hwy 111. (92260) Nicely landscaped courtyard & pool area. Check-in 4 pm. Refrigerators; A/C; C/CATV; movies; radios; phones. Htd pool; whirlpool; putting green; lighted tennis-6 courts; exercise rm; jogging track. No pets. Reserv deposit required. Complimentary beverages each evening. AE, DI, DS, MC, VI. ● Restaurant; 11:30 am-3 & 5-10 pm; $12-$20; cocktails. FAX (619) 340-9519   ⊗ Ⓢ Ⓓ (619) 340-6600

Howard Johnson Hotel

ⓐ		AAA Special Value Rates			Motel	◆◆
1/1-3/31 [CP]	1P 85.00- 105.00	2P/1B 90.00- 105.00	2P/2B 90.00- 105.00	XP 5		F
12/1-12/31 & 4/1-4/30 [CP]	1P 70.00- 90.00	2P/1B 75.00- 90.00	2P/2B 75.00- 90.00	XP 5		F
5/1-5/31 & 10/1-11/30 [CP]	1P 60.00- 80.00	2P/1B 65.00- 80.00	2P/2B 65.00- 80.00	XP 5		F
6/1-9/30 [CP]	1P 50.00- 65.00	2P/1B 55.00- 70.00	2P/2B 55.00- 70.00	XP 5		F

131 units. 1 1/2 mi e on SR 111. (92260) Check-in 3 pm. 12 refrigerators; A/C; C/CATV; movies; phones. Htd pool; saunas; whirlpool; tennis-1 court. No pets. Wkly & monthly rates avail. Reserv deposit required. AE, CB, DI, MC, VI. Restaurant adjacent. FAX (619) 340-4303   ⊗ Ⓢ Ⓓ ⓛ (619) 340-4303

International Lodge

ⓐ		Rates Subject to Change			Apartment Motel	◆◆◆
1/1-4/30	1P 85.00	2P/1B 85.00	2P/2B 85.00	XP 10		
5/1-6/30 & 9/1-12/31	1P 60.00	2P/1B 60.00	2P/2B 60.00	XP 10		
7/1-8/31	1P 45.00	2P/1B 45.00	2P/2B 45.00	XP 10		

51 units. 1/2 blk s of SR 111 via Panorama Dr. 74-380 El Camino. (92260) Spacious, individually decorated rooms. A/C; C/CATV; radios; phones; shower baths. Efficiencies. Coin laundry. 2 htd pools; whirlpool. No pets. Wkly & monthly rates avail. Reserv deposit required. AE, MC, VI. *(See ad p A311)*   Ⓓ (619) 346-6161

Marriott's Desert Springs Resort & Spa

		Rates Subject to Change			Resort Hotel	◆◆◆◆
12/23-5/30	....	2P/1B 260.00- 330.00	2P/2B 260.00- 330.00	XP 10		
9/13-12/22	....	2P/1B 200.00- 250.00	2P/2B 200.00- 250.00	XP 10		
5/31-7/4 & 8/30-9/12	....	2P/1B 145.00- 195.00	2P/2B 145.00- 195.00	XP 10		
7/5-8/29	....	2P/1B 125.00- 165.00	2P/2B 125.00- 165.00	XP 10		

891 units. 1 1/2 mi n of SR 111 via Cook St. 74-855 Country Club Dr. (92260) Beautifully landscaped grounds. Impressive lobby. Check-in 4 pm. A/C; C/CATV; movies; radios; phones. 3 htd pools; whirlpools. Fee for: sauna, golf-36 holes, tennis-16 courts, 8 lighted; health club & massage. Garage. No pets. AE, CB, DI, MC, VI. ● 4 dining rms, 3 restaurants & coffeeshop; 6 am-11 pm; $8.95-$30; cocktails; entertainment. FAX (619) 341-1872   Ⓢ Ⓓ ⓛ (619) 341-2211

Shadow Mountain Resort & Racquet Club

ⓐ		AAA Special Value Rates			Resort Motor Inn	◆◆◆
2/1-4/29	....	2P/1B 135.00- 165.00	2P/2B 135.00- 165.00	XP 15		
4/30-5/20 & 9/24-2/10	....	2P/1B 115.00- 130.00	2P/2B 115.00- 130.00	XP 15		
5/21-9/23	....	2P/1B 85.00- 100.00	2P/2B 85.00- 100.00	XP 15		

120 units. 1/2 mi s of SR 111. 45-750 San Luis Rey. (92260) Tennis resort. Rooms, studios, 1 to 3-bedroom apartments & villas. Check-in 3 pm. A/C; C/CATV; radios; phones. 53 kitchens, 67 efficiencies. Coin laundry. 4 htd pools; saunas; whirlpools; tennis-16 courts, 4 lighted; paddle tennis-2 courts; rental bicycles. No pets. Wkly & monthly rates avail. Reserv deposit required; 3 days refund notice. AE, MC, VI. ● Restaurant; 7:30 am-5 pm; Fri & Sat-10 pm; closed 6/1-9/30; $8-$14; cocktails. FAX (619) 346-6518   (619) 346-6123

Travelers Inn

ⓐ		AAA Special Value Rates			Motel	◆◆◆
1/15-5/27 [CP]	1P 67.00- 82.00	2P/1B 78.00- 93.00	2P/2B 78.00- 93.00	XP 7		
10/15-1/14 [CP]	1P 64.00- 78.00	2P/1B 75.00- 89.00	2P/2B 75.00- 89.00	XP 7		
5/28-10/14 [CP]	1P 42.00	2P/1B 49.00	2P/2B 49.00	XP 7		

115 units. On SR 111, 1 blk e of Fred Waring Dr. 72-322 Hwy 111. (92260) A/C; C/CATV; movies; radios; phones. Htd pool; whirlpool; putting green. No pets. AE, CB, DI, MC, VI. FAX (619) 773-3575   ⊗ Ⓢ Ⓓ ⓛ (619) 341-9100

Vacation Inn

		AAA Special Value Rates			Motel	◆◆◆
12/25-5/31 [CP]	1P 82.00- 108.00	2P/1B 85.00- 108.00	2P/2B 85.00- 108.00	XP 10		F
6/1-6/30 & 9/15-12/24 [CP]	1P 61.00- 87.00	2P/1B 64.00- 87.00	2P/2B 61.00- 87.00	XP 10		F
7/1-9/14 [CP]	1P 39.00- 62.00	2P/1B 39.00- 62.00	2P/2B 43.00- 62.00	XP 10		F

130 units. 1 1/2 mi e on SR 111. 74-715 Hwy 111. (92260) Balconies or patios. Check-in 3 pm. Refrigerators; A/C; C/CATV; pay movies; radios; phones. 10 efficiencies. Htd pool; whirlpool; putting green; tennis-2 courts; exercise rm. No pets. Reserv deposit required. AE, CB, DI, MC, VI. FAX (619) 773-9413 *(See ad below)* ⊗ Ⓢ Ⓓ Ⓔ (619) 340-4441

RESTAURANTS

Casuelas Cafe
Mexican $ ◆◆
Between San Luis Rey & Larkspur. 73-703 Highway 111. A/C. Open 11 am-10 pm; Fri & Sat-11 pm. Cocktails & lounge. CB, DI, DS, MC, VI.   ⊗ (619) 568-0011

Cedar Creek Inn
American $$ ◆◆
1 blk s of SR 111, corner San Pablo & El Paseo. 73-445 El Paseo. Attractive restaurant featuring a nice selection of salads, sandwiches, entrees & a large selection of homemade desserts. A/C. Open 11 am-9 pm; closed Sun. Cocktails & lounge. Reserv advised. MC, VI.   ⊗ (619) 340-1236

Club 74
French $$$ ◆◆
1 blk s of Hwy 111. 73-061 El Paseo. Sweeping view of mountains and city lights. Nice selection of varied entrees. A/C. Open 11:30 am-2:30 & 5:30-10 pm. Cocktails. Reserv advised. AE, MC, VI.   (619) 568-2782

Cuistot
French $$$ ◆◆
1 blk s of Hwy 111. 73-111 El Paseo. A/C. Open 11:30 am-2:30 & 6-10 pm; Sun 6 pm-10 pm; closed Mon. Cocktails. Reserv advised. MC, VI.   ⊗ (619) 340-1000

(See map page A315)

LG's Steak House   Steakhouse $$$ ◆◆◆
At jct SR 111 & El Paseo. 74-225 Hwy 111. Southwestern decor. Dining in pueblo-style landmark building. Entrees include steak, chicken & seafood. A/C. Open 5 pm-11 pm. Cocktails & lounge. Entertainment. Valet parking. Reserv advised. AE, DI, MC, VI.   ⊗ (619) 779-9799

Mancuso's   Italian $$ ◆◆◆
On SR 111, at Fred Waring Dr. 72-281 Hwy 111. Elegant decor. Italian & continental cuisine. A/C. Open 5 pm-10:30 pm; closed 11/25 & 12/25. Cocktails & lounge. Valet parking. Reserv advised. AE, CB, DI, MC, VI.   ⊗ (619) 340-6610

Reuben's   Steak & Seafood $$ ◆◆
On SR 111, at Fred Waring Dr. 72-291 Hwy 111. Attractive country decor. A/C. Early bird specials. Open noon-2 & 4-9 pm; Fri & Sat-10 pm; Sun 10 am-2:30 & 4:30-9 pm; closed 12/25. Cocktails & lounge. Valet parking. AE, CB, DI, MC, VI.   ⊗ (619) 568-9388

Ristorante Mamma Gina   Italian $$$ ◆◆◆
1 blk s of SR 111. 73-705 El Paseo. Northern Italian cuisine featuring homemade pasta, chicken & veal specialties. A/C. Open 5:15 pm-10 pm; closed 12/25 & 7/5-9/13. Cocktails. Reserv advised. AE, MC, VI.   ⊗ (619) 568-9898

Robert Cunard's   Continental $$$ ◆◆◆
At jct SR 74 & Hwy 111 in Stanley B's Plaza. 73-101 Hwy 111. California-Continental cuisine in an elegant atmosphere. A/C. Open 9/14-7/1 from 4:30 pm-10 pm; Fri & Sat-10:30 pm; closed 12/25. Cocktails & lounge. Entertainment. Valet parking. Reserv advised. AE, MC, VI.   ⊗ (619) 773-3337

Rusty Pelican   Seafood $$ ◆◆
1 mi w on SR 111. 72-191 Hwy 111. A/C. Open 5 pm-10 pm; Fri-11 pm; Sat 4:30 pm-11 pm; Sun 4:30 pm-10 pm; closed 11/25 & 12/25. Cocktails & lounge. Valet parking. Reserv advised. AE, CB, DI, MC, VI.   ⊗ (619) 346-8065

Ruth's Chris Steak House   Steakhouse $$$$ ◆◆◆
At jct Hwy 111 & Portola. 74-040 Hwy 111. Casual atmosphere. A/C. Open 5 pm-10 pm; Fri & Sat-10:30 pm. Cocktails & lounge. Reserv advised. AE, MC, VI.   ⊗ (619) 779-1998

Senor Salsa   Mexican $ ◆◆
1 blk s of SR 111, corner of San Luis Rey & El Paseo. 73-725 El Paseo. Very festive atmosphere. Specialties include carnitas & fajitas. A/C. Open 11 am-10 pm; closed Mon. Cocktails & lounge. AE, MC, VI.   ⊗ (619) 346-0245

Tai Ping   Chinese $$ ◆◆◆
⊛ 1 blk s of SR 111; corner El Paseo & Lupine Ln. 45-299 Lupine Ln. Nicely appointed restaurant serving expertly prepared Cantonese & Mandarin cuisine. A/C. Open 11/29-5/31 from 5:30 pm-10 pm; closed 12/25. Cocktails & lounge. Reserv advised. AE, MC, VI.   ♿ (619) 340-1836

PALM SPRINGS — 40,200   (See PALM SPRINGS AREA spotting map page A314; see index below)   See also DESERT HOT SPRINGS, INDIAN WELLS, INDIO, LA QUINTA, PALM DESERT & RANCHO MIRAGE

Index of Establishments on the PALM SPRINGS AREA Spotting Map

---

Adriatic Villa **2**   Rates Subject to Change   *Motel*   ◆◆

		2P/1B	77.00- 145.00	2P/2B	77.00- 145.00	XP 10
12/1-7/6	....	2P/1B	77.00- 145.00	2P/2B	77.00- 145.00	XP 10
7/7-11/30	....	2P/1B	57.00- 125.00	2P/2B	57.00- 125.00	XP 10

20 units. 2 mi n. 2300 N Palm Canyon Dr. (92262) A/C; C/CATV; phones. 2 kitchens, 18 efficiencies. Coin laundry. Htd pool; sauna; whirlpool. No pets. Wkly & monthly rates avail. Reserv deposit required; 3 days refund notice. AE, MC, VI.   Ⓓ (619) 325-5024

(See PALM SPRINGS spotting map below)

American Hotel 30   Rates Guaranteed   *Motel*   ◆

10/1-7/7	....		2P/1B	38.00- 48.00	2P/2B	44.00- 54.00	XP	6
7/8-9/30	1P	.... 30.00	2P/1B	30.00- 38.00	2P/2B	38.00- 46.00	XP	5

Senior discount. 15 units. 1 mi s. 1200 S Palm Canyon Dr. (92264) A/C; C/CATV; phones; shower baths. Htd pool. Airport transp. No pets. 7 kitchens, $10 extra. Wkly rates avail. Reserv deposit required. AE, MC, VI.

Ⓓ (619) 320-4399

Arenas Inn 29   Rates Subject to Change   *Apartment Motel*   ◆◆

9/1-5/30	1P	95.00- 120.00	2P/1B	95.00- 120.00	2P/2B	120.00- 165.00	XP
5/31-8/31	1P	57.00- 72.00	2P/1B	57.00- 72.00	2P/2B	72.00- 99.00	XP

Senior discount. 11 units. 1/2 mi w of Palm Canyon Dr. 680 W Arenas Rd. (92262) Spacious 1 & 2-bedroom suites with kitchen. A/C; C/CATV; radios; phones; shower or comb baths. 2 2-bedrm units. Coin laundry. Pool; whirlpool. No pets. Wkly & monthly rates avail. Reserv deposit required; 3 days refund notice. MC, VI. FAX (619) 322-7572   ⊗ Ⓓ (619) 325-0551

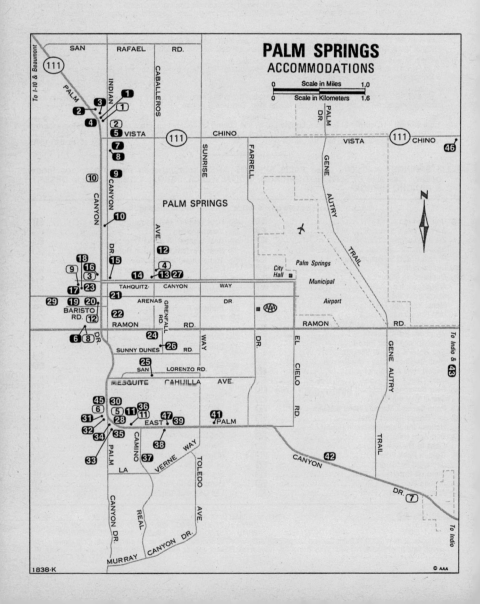

(See PALM SPRINGS spotting map page A314)

A Sunbeam Inn **8**   Rates Subject to Change   *Apartment Motel* ◆

10/15-6/10 [CP]	....	2P/1B	49.00- 75.00	2P/2B	49.00- 75.00	XP 10	
6/11-10/14 [EP]	....	2P/1B	35.00- 49.00	2P/2B	35.00- 49.00	XP 10	

15 units. 1 1/4 mi n; 1 1/4 blks e of Palm Canyon. 291 Camino Monte Vista. (92262) Refrigerators; A/C; C/CATV; radios; phones; shower or comb baths. Htd pool. No pets. 2 2-bedroom kitchen apartments $110; 7 1-bedroom kitchen apartments. Microwaves. Wkly & monthly rates avail. Reserv deposit required; 3 days refund notice in summer; 7 days in winter. AE, MC, VI.   ⒹD (619) 323-3812

The Autry Resort Hotel **42**   AAA Special Value Rates   *Resort Hotel* ◆◆◆◆

1/1-5/31 & 10/1-12/31	1P 135.00- 225.00	2P/1B	135.00- 225.00	2P/2B	135.00- 225.00	XP 20	F
6/1-9/30	1P 85.00- 110.00	2P/1B	85.00- 110.00	2P/2B	85.00- 110.00	XP 20	F

184 units. 4 1/2 mi se on Palm Canyon Dr. 4200 E Palm Canyon Dr. (92264) Beautifully landscaped grounds. Many rooms with patio or balcony. Check-in 3 pm. 66 refrigerators; A/C; C/CATV; movies; radios; phones; comb or shower baths. 3 htd pools; whirlpools; exercise rm. Fee for: tennis-10 courts, 2 lighted; massage. Airport transp. No pets. 11 bungalow suites, $250-$400 in season. Reserv deposit required; 3 days refund notice. AE, DI, DS, MC, VI. ● Dining rm; 7 am-11 pm; $10-$30; cocktails; entertainment. FAX (619) 324-6104 ⊗ ⒹD (619) 328-1171

Best Western A Aloha Tropics **33**   Rates Subject to Change   *Motel* ◆◆

Weekends 12/24-4/30	1P 76.00- 110.00	2P/1B	76.00- 110.00	2P/2B	82.00- 130.00	XP 8
Weekends 5/1-6/4	1P 54.00- 100.00	2P/1B	54.00- 100.00	2P/2B	60.00- 130.00	XP 8
Weekends 9/30-12/23	1P 49.00- 90.00	2P/1B	49.00- 90.00	2P/2B	55.00- 110.00	XP 8
Weekends 6/5-9/29	1P 34.00- 69.00	2P/1B	34.00- 69.00	2P/2B	42.00- 69.00	XP 8

Senior discount. 142 units. 1 1/2 mi s. 411 E Palm Canyon Dr. (92264) A/C; C/CATV; phones; comb or shower baths. 24 2-bedrm units, 50 kitchens. Coin laundry. 2 htd pools; whirlpools. No pets. Reserv deposit required. AE, DI, DS, MC, VI. ● Coffeeshop; 24 hours; $4-$7; cocktail lounge. FAX (619) 323-3493 ⊗ ⒹD (619) 327-1391

Best Western Host Motor Hotel **31**   Rates Subject to Change   *Motel* ◆◆◆

12/25-7/5 [CP]	....	2P/1B	69.00- 98.00	2P/2B	78.00- 98.00	XP 6	F
10/1-12/24 [CP]	....	2P/1B	49.00- 78.00	2P/2B	58.00- 78.00	XP 6	F
7/6-9/30 [CP]	....	2P/1B	39.00- 68.00	2P/2B	48.00- 68.00	XP 6	F

Senior discount. 72 units. 1 1/2 mi s at jct E Palm Canyon Dr. 1633 S Palm Canyon Dr. (92264) A/C; C/CATV; movies; radios; phones. Rental refrigerators. Htd pool; whirlpool. No pets. Wkly & monthly rates avail. Reserv deposit required. AE, DI, DS, MC, VI. FAX (619) 325-9177   ⊗ ⒹD (619) 325-9177

Best Western Royal Sun Hotel **34**   Rates Subject to Change   *Motel* ◆◆

12/25-5/25 [CP]	....	2P/1B	59.00- 89.00	2P/2B	64.00- 94.00	XP 8
10/1-12/24 [CP]	....	2P/1B	49.00- 69.00	2P/2B	55.00- 75.00	XP 8
5/26-9/30 [CP]	....	2P/1B	39.00- 59.00	2P/2B	45.00- 65.00	XP 8

Senior discount. 66 units. 1 1/2 mi se on Palm Canyon Dr, 1 blk s. 1700 S Palm Canyon Dr. (92264) Balconies or patios. Refrigerators; A/C; C/CATV; free & pay movies; radios; phones. Coin laundry. Htd pool; sauna; whirlpool. No pets. Luxury level rooms avail. 2 1-bedroom efficiency apartments, $100-$140 in season. 2 suites with whirlpool, $125-$150 in season. Wkly & monthly rates avail. Reserv deposit required. AE, DI, DS, MC, VI. Restaurant opposite. FAX (619) 322-1796 *(See ad p A316)* ⊗ ⒹD (619) 327-1564

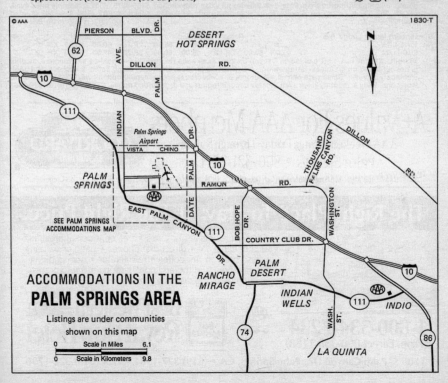

ACCOMMODATIONS IN THE
PALM SPRINGS AREA

Listings are under communities shown on this map

(See PALM SPRINGS spotting map page A314)

Cambridge Inn 🕙   Rates Subject to Change   *Motel* ◆
ᴬᴬᴬ 12/25-4/30   1P .... 38.00   2P/1B .... 38.00   2P/2B .... 42.00   XP 4
     5/1-12/24   1P .... 30.00   2P/1B .... 30.00   2P/2B .... 32.50   XP 4
61 units. 1 mi s. 1277 S Palm Canyon Dr. (92264) 13 refrigerators; A/C; C/CATV; phones; shower or comb baths. Htd pool. Pets, $10 extra charge. Wkly & monthly rates avail. Reserv deposit required. AE, DI, DS, MC, VI.
Ⓓ (619) 325-5574

Casa Cody Country Inn 🕙   Rates Guaranteed   *Historic Motel* ◆◆
12/18-4/30 [CP]   1P 65.00- 105.00   2P/1B 65.00- 105.00   2P/2B 65.00- 160.00   XP 10
5/1-7/5 & 10/1-12/17 [CP]   1P 60.00- 95.00   2P/1B 60.00- 95.00   2P/2B 60.00- 150.00   XP 10
7/6-9/30 [CP]   1P 40.00- 60.00   2P/1B 40.00- 60.00   2P/2B 40.00- 105.00   XP 10
Senior discount. 17 units. 2 blks w of SR 111, 1 blk s of Tahquitz Canyon Way. 175 S Cahuilla Rd. (92262) Restored historic inn on attractive grounds. Quiet location with studios. 1 & 2-bedroom villas, many with woodburning fireplace; also 2 smaller units. 10 A/C; C/CATV; phones; comb or shower baths. 2 2-bedrm units, 15 efficiencies. 2 htd pools; whirlpool. Pets. Wkly & monthly rates avail. Reserv deposit required; 3 days refund notice. AE, MC, VI. FAX (619) 325-8610
Ⓓ (619) 320-9346

Courtyard by Marriott 🕗   Rates Subject to Change   *Motor Inn* ◆◆◆
1/1-5/31   1P .... 66.00   2P/1B .... 66.00   2P/2B .... 66.00   XP 10
6/1-12/31   1P .... 34.00   2P/1B .... 34.00   2P/2B .... 34.00   XP 10
Senior discount. 149 units. 1 mi e of Indian Canyon Dr. 1300 Tahquitz Canyon Way. (92262) Check-in 4 pm. A/C; C/CATV; free & pay movies; radios; phones. Coin laundry. Htd pool; whirlpool; exercise rm. Airport transp. No pets. Wkly rates avail. Reserv deposit required. AE, CB, DI, MC, VI. ● Dining rm; 6:30 am-2 & 5-10 pm; Sat & Sun 7 am-10 pm; $6.95-$12.95; cocktails. FAX (619) 322-6091 *(See ad below)* ⊗ Ⓢ Ⓓ 🅖 (619) 322-6100

Desert Hills Apt. Hotel 🕗   Rates Subject to Change   *Apartment Motel* ◆◆◆
ᴬᴬᴬ 12/20-4/20   ....   2P/1B 60.00- 115.00   2P/2B 60.00- 115.00   XP 10
4/21-6/10 & 9/16-12/19   ....   2P/1B 55.00- 105.00   2P/2B 55.00- 105.00   XP 10
6/11-9/15   ....   2P/1B 50.00- 80.00   2P/2B 50.00- 80.00   XP 10
14 units. 1/2 mi w of Palm Canyon Dr. 601 W Arenas Rd. (92262) Spacious, attractively furnished rooms. Refrigerators; A/C; C/CATV; radios; phones; comb or shower baths. 11 kitchens. Htd pool; whirlpool; bicycles. No pets. 1 2-bedroom apartment $150, 12/20-4/20. Microwave. Monthly rates avail. Reserv deposit required; 7 days refund notice. DS, MC, VI. FAX (619) 325-6423 ⊗ Ⓓ (619) 325-2777

Doubletree Resort at Desert Princess Country Club 🕙   Rates Subject to Change   *Resort Complex* ◆◆◆
ᴬᴬᴬ 1/8-4/24   1P .... 110.00   2P/1B .... 110.00   2P/2B .... 110.00   XP 15   F
10/1-1/6   1P .... 83.00   2P/1B .... 83.00   2P/2B .... 83.00   XP 15   F
4/25-6/12   1P .... 80.00   2P/1B .... 80.00   2P/2B .... 80.00   XP 15   F
6/13-9/30   1P .... 50.00   2P/1B .... 50.00   2P/2B .... 50.00   XP 15   F
289 units. 3 mi e of SR 111 on Vista Chino at Landau. 67-967 Vista Chino. (PO Box 1644, 92263) Spacious grounds. Nicely furnished rooms with patio or balcony. Check-in 3 pm. Refrigerators; A/C; C/CATV; free & pay movies; radios; phones. Htd pool; whirlpools; racquetball-2 courts; exercise rm. Fee for: golf-27 holes, tennis-10 courts, 5 lighted. Airport transp. Pets. 1- & 2-bedroom villas with kitchen, $155-$375. Wkly & monthly rates avail. AE, DI, MC, VI. ● Dining rm & coffeeshop; 6:30 am-10 pm; $7.50-$19; cocktails. FAX (619) 322-6853 *(See ad p A317)* ⊗ Ⓢ Ⓓ 🅖 (619) 322-7000

Duesenberg Motor Lodge 🕖   Rates Guaranteed   *Motel* ◆
ᴬᴬᴬ 11/15-6/15   ....   2P/1B 50.00- 65.00   2P/2B 50.00- 65.00   XP 10
6/16-11/14   1P 45.00- 60.00   2P/1B 45.00- 60.00   2P/2B 45.00- 60.00   XP 10
13 units. 1 1/2 mi n. 1/4 blk e of Indian Canyon Dr. 269 Chuckwalla Rd. (92262) Alcohol free environment, alcohol is not permitted on premises. Refrigerators; A/C; C/CATV; phones; shower or comb baths. 6 kitchens. Htd pool; whirlpool; bicycles. Small pets only. 4 1-bedroom & 1 2-bedroom housekeeping bungalows, $85-$105 for up to 2 persons. Wkly & monthly rates avail. Reserv deposit required; 3 days refund notice. MC, VI. Ⓓ (619) 325-2567

(See PALM SPRINGS spotting map page A314)

El Rancho Lodge 47

			Rates Subject to Change				Motel	◆◆◆
10/1-5/31 [CP]		....	2P/1B	61.00- 80.00	2P/2B	61.00- 80.00	XP 20	
6/1-9/30 [CP]		....	2P/1B	40.00- 55.00	2P/2B	40.00- 55.00	XP 20	

19 units. 2 mi se on Palm Canyon Dr. 1330 E Palm Canyon Dr. (92264) Check-in 3 pm. Refrigerators; A/C; C/CATV; radios; phones; shower or comb baths. 9 kitchens, 6 efficiencies. Coin laundry. Htd pool; whirlpool. No pets. 2-night minimum stay weekends. Monthly rates avail. Reserv deposit required; 7 days refund notice. AE, DS, MC, VI.   (D) (619) 327-1339

Emerald Court Resort Hotel 43

			Rates Guaranteed				Motel	◆◆
1/1-6/1 [CP]	1P	60.00- 70.00	2P/1B	70.00- 80.00	2P/2B	70.00- 80.00	XP 10	
10/15-12/31 [CP]	1P	50.00- 65.00	2P/1B	60.00- 75.00	2P/2B	60.00- 75.00	XP 10	

23 units. 5 mi e; 1/4 mi e of Date Palm Dr. 69-375 Ramon Rd. (Cathedral City, 92234) OPEN 10/15-6/1. A/C; C/CATV; radios; phones. Htd pool; whirlpool; lighted tennis-5 courts. No pets. Wkly rates avail. Reserv deposit required. MC, VI.   (D) (619) 324-4521

Four Seasons Apartment Hotel 19

			Rates Subject to Change				Apartment Motel	◆◆◆◆
2/1-3/31	1P	100.00- 130.00		....	2P/2B	100.00- 130.00	XP 15	
4/1-5/31 & 12/16-1/31	1P	90.00- 115.00		....	2P/2B	90.00- 115.00	XP 15	
10/1-12/15	1P	75.00- 100.00		....	2P/2B	75.00- 100.00	XP 15	
6/1-9/30	1P	55.00- 75.00		....	2P/2B	55.00- 75.00	XP 15	

11 units. 5 blks w of Palm Canyon Dr. 290 San Jacinto Dr at Baristo Dr. (92262) Spacious, beautifully decorated 1-bedroom suites with kitchen, also 1 2-bedroom unit & 1 hotel room. Refrigerators; A/C; C/CATV; radios; phones. Htd pool; whirlpool; bicycles. No pets. Microwaves. Monthly rates avail. Reserv deposit required; 14 days refund notice. MC, VI.   (D) (619) 325-6427

Golden Palm Villa 26

			Rates Subject to Change				Motel	◆◆
9/1-6/1		....	2P/1B	55.00- 85.00	2P/2B	55.00- 85.00	XP	

21 units. 3/4 mi e of Palm Canyon Dr, via Ramon Rd, then 1 blk s. 601 Grenfall Rd. (92264) OPEN 9/1-6/1. Quiet area; nicely landscaped grounds. Refrigerators; A/C; C/CATV; phones; shower or comb baths. Coin laundry. 2 htd pools; whirlpools. Airport transp. No pets. 9 studio efficiencies & 6 1-bedroom apartments, $6-$10 extra. Monthly rates avail. Reserv deposit required; 7 days refund notice. AE, DS, MC, VI. FAX (619) 327-7273   (D) (619) 327-1408

Hampton Inn 1

			Rates Subject to Change				Motel	◆◆◆
Fri & Sat 1/19-5/26 [CP]	1P	64.00- 74.00	2P/1B	79.00- 84.00	2P/2B	.... 74.00	XP	F
Fri & Sat 9/14-1/18 [CP]	1P	49.00- 59.00	2P/1B	54.00- 64.00	2P/2B	.... 54.00	XP	F
5/27-9/13 [CP]	1P	39.00- 49.00	2P/1B	44.00- 54.00	2P/2B	.... 44.00	XP	F

96 units. 1 1/2 mi n. 2000 N Palm Canyon Dr. (92262) Check-in 3 pm. 28 refrigerators; A/C; C/CATV; movies; radios; phones. Htd pool; whirlpool. No pets. Wkly & monthly rates avail. AE, CB, DI, MC, VI. FAX (619) 320-2261   ⊗ Ⓢ (D) (Ⓛ) (619) 320-0555

(See PALM SPRINGS spotting map page A314)

Holiday Inn Palm Mountain Resort 23   Rates Subject to Change   *Motor Inn* ◆◆◆
12/25-5/24	1P	89.00- 139.00	2P/1B	89.00- 139.00	2P/2B	99.00- 139.00	XP 10
9/4-12/24	1P	59.00- 89.00	2P/1B	59.00- 89.00	2P/2B	69.00- 99.00	XP 10
5/25-9/3	1P	49.00- 79.00	2P/1B	49.00- 79.00	2P/2B	49.00- 79.00	XP 10

Senior discount. 121 units. 1 blk w of Palm Canyon Dr. 155 S Belardo. (92262) Many rooms with patio or balcony. Check-in 3 pm. Refrigerators; A/C; C/CATV; radios; phones; comb or shower baths. Htd pool; whirlpool; putting green; 3 rooms with whirlpool tub; exercise rm. No pets. Microwaves. AE, DI, DS, MC, VI. ● Restaurant; 7 am-10:30, 11:30-2 & 5-10 pm; $10.25-$19.50. FAX (619) 323-8937 *(See ad below)*   Ⓓ 🅛 (619) 325-1301

Hyatt Regency Suites Palm Springs 16   Rates Subject to Change   *Suites Hotel* ◆◆◆◆
1/1-5/2		....	2P/1B	199.00- 229.00	2P/2B	199.00- 229.00	XP 25 F

Senior discount. 194 units. 285 N Palm Canyon Dr. (92262) Check-in 3 pm. A/C; C/CATV; movies; radios; phones. 5 2-bedrm units. Htd pool; sauna; whirlpool; exercise rm. Fee for: health club. Pay valet garage. Airport transp. Pets, $50 deposit required. Monthly rates avail. Reserv deposit required. AE, CB, DI, MC, VI. ● 2 dining rms & restaurant; 7 am-11 pm; Fri & Sat-midnight; $10-$21; cocktails; entertainment. FAX (619) 322-6009   ⊗ Ⓢ Ⓓ 🅛 (619) 322-9000

Ingleside Inn 6   Rates Subject to Change   *Hotel* ◆◆◆
10/1-5/31 [CP]	1P	95.00- 375.00	2P/1B	95.00- 375.00	2P/2B	95.00- 375.00	XP 20
Fri & Sat 6/1-9/30 [CP]	1P	86.00- 338.00	2P/1B	86.00- 338.00	2P/2B	86.00- 338.00	XP 20
Sun-Thurs 6/1-9/30 [CP]	1P	76.00- 310.00	2P/1B	76.00- 310.00		....	XP

29 units. 1 blk w of Palm Canyon Dr. 200 W Ramon Rd. (92264) Each room or villa contains beautifully restored antiques. Many rooms with woodburning fireplaces; some private patios. Refrigerators; A/C; C/CATV; movies; VCPs. Radios; phones; comb or shower baths. Htd pool; whirlpool; croquet lawn. Parking lot. Airport transp. 2 bedroom suites, $450-$550 for 1 or 2 persons. Wkly & monthly rates avail. Reserv deposit required. AE, MC, VI. ● Melvyn's, see separate listing. FAX (619) 325-0710   Ⓓ (619) 325-0046

La Mancha Private Villas & Court Club 12   AAA Special Value Rates   *Resort Complex* ◆◆◆◆
12/16-5/4		....	2P/1B	140.00- 750.00	2P/2B	305.00- 850.00	XP 25
5/5-7/13 & 9/30-12/15		....	2P/1B	135.00- 695.00	2P/2B	255.00- 790.00	XP 25
7/14-9/29		....	2P/1B	95.00- 470.00	2P/2B	155.00- 585.00	XP 25

69 units. 3/4 mi e of Palm Canyon Dr, via Alejo Rd. 444 Avenida Caballeros. (PO Box 340, 92262) Spacious, beautifully furnished 1 to 3-bedroom villas, some with private whirlpool; others with private pool & whirlpool. Refrigerators; A/C; C/CATV; rental VCPs; radios; phones. 10 2-bedrm units, 14 3-bedrm units, 54 kitchens. Htd pool; saunas; whirlpool; putting green; rental bicycles; exercise rm. Fee for: tennis-7 courts, 4 lighted; 2 lighted paddle courts; croquet court. Airport transp. No pets. Wkly & monthly rates avail. Reserv deposit required; 3 days refund notice. AE, CB, DI, MC, VI. ● Dining rm; open to public by reservation only; 7 am-2 & 5-9 pm; a la carte entrees about $14.50-$22.50; cocktails. FAX (619) 323-5928 *(See ad p A319)*   Ⓓ 🅛 (619) 323-1773

Las Brisas Resort Hotel 22   Rates Subject to Change   *Motel* ◆◆◆
1/12-4/18 [CP]	1P	85.00- 95.00	2P/1B	95.00- 105.00	2P/2B	95.00- 105.00	XP 10 F/
5/25-9/12 [CP]	1P	39.00- 49.00	2P/1B	44.00- 54.00	2P/2B	44.00- 54.00	XP 10 F
4/19-5/24 & 9/13-1/11 [CP]	1P	55.00- 65.00	2P/1B	60.00- 70.00		....	XP 5 F

90 units. 1/4 mi s. 222 S Indian Canyon Dr. (92262) Check-in 3 pm. Refrigerators; A/C; C/CATV; movies; radios; phones. Coin laundry. Htd pool; whirlpool; 8 rooms with whirlpool. Airport transp. No pets. Reserv deposit required. AE, DI, DS, MC, VI. FAX (619) 320-1371   ⊗ Ⓢ Ⓓ (619) 325-4372

Monte Vista Apt. Hotel 10   Rates Subject to Change   *Apartment Motel* ◆
10/1-6/1	1P	.... 50.00	2P/1B	.... 55.00	2P/2B	.... 77.00	XP 8

32 units. Downtown, on SR 111. 414 N Palm Canyon Dr. (92262) OPEN ALL YEAR. Rooms & 1-bedroom apartments; some studios. A/C; C/CATV; radios; shower or comb baths. Coin laundry. Htd pool; whirlpool. No pets. Wkly & monthly rates avail. Reserv deposit required. AE, MC, VI.   Ⓓ (619) 325-5641

(See PALM SPRINGS spotting map page A314)

Morningside Inn **9**		AAA Special Value Rates			Motel		◆◆
10/1-5/31 [CP]	....	2P/1B	55.00- 95.00	2P/2B	55.00- 95.00	XP 10	
6/1-9/30 [CP]	....	2P/1B	40.00- 75.00	2P/2B	40.00- 75.00	XP 10	

11 units. 1 mi n. 888 N Indian Canyon Dr. (92262) Refrigerators; A/C; C/CATV; 4 radios; phones; comb or shower baths. 7 kitchens. Htd pool; whirlpool. No pets. Wkly & monthly rates avail. Reserv deposit required; 3 days refund notice. AE, MC, VI. (D) (619) 325-2668

Orchid Tree Inn **20**			Rates Guaranteed			Apartment Motel		◆◆
11/1-5/31	1P	60.00- 250.00	2P/1B	60.00- 250.00	2P/2B	60.00- 250.00	XP 15	
6/1-7/5 & 9/1-10/31	1P	55.00- 200.00	2P/1B	55.00- 200.00	2P/2B	55.00- 200.00	XP 15	
7/6-8/31	1P	45.00- 150.00	2P/1B	45.00- 150.00	2P/2B	45.00- 150.00	XP 10	

Senior discount. 36 units. 1 blk w of SR 111, S Palm Canyon Dr. 261 S Belardo Rd. (92262) Nicely landscaped grounds & garden areas. A/C; C/CATV; radios; phones; comb or shower baths. 2 htd pools; whirlpool. No pets. 30 kitchen units $9-$10 extra charge; 2-night minimum stay. Wkly & monthly rates avail. Reserv deposit required; 7 days refund notice. AE, MC, VI. FAX (619) 325-3855 *(See ad below)* (D) (619) 325-2791

(See PALM SPRINGS spotting map page A314)

Palm Springs Hilton Resort **14**   AAA Special Value Rates   *Hotel*   ◆◆◆
		2P/1B	195.00- 295.00	2P/2B	195.00- 295.00	XP 20	F
12/28-5/31	....						
6/1-7/5 & 9/3-12/27	....	2P/1B	145.00- 235.00	2P/2B	145.00- 235.00	XP 20	F
7/6-9/2	....	2P/1B	80.00- 130.00	2P/2B	80.00- 130.00	XP 20	F

259 units. 1 blk e of Indian Canyon Dr. 400 E Tahquitz Canyon Way. (92262) Attractively landscaped courtyard & pool area. Balconies or patios. Check-in 3 pm. A/C; C/CATV; movies; radios; phones. Htd pool; sauna; whirlpools. Fee for: lighted tennis-6 courts; health spa. Pay valet parking lot. Airport transp. Pets, $300 deposit required. Reserv deposit required; 3 days refund notice. AE, CB, DI, MC, VI. ● 2 dining rms; 6:30 am-10 pm; $8.50-$30; cocktails; entertainment. FAX (619) 320-2126 *(See ad p 22)*   Ⓢ Ⓓ Ⓛ (619) 320-6868

Palm Springs Marquis Hotel & Villas **21**   Rates Guaranteed   *Hotel*   ◆◆◆
ⓐⓐ 2/1-4/10	1P 149.00- 299.00	2P/1B	149.00- 299.00	2P/2B	149.00- 299.00	XP 20	F
4/1-6/12 & 9/18-1/31	1P 119.00- 230.00	2P/1B	119.00- 230.00	2P/2B	119.00- 230.00	XP 20	F
6/13-9/17	1P 65.00- 155.00	2P/1B	65.00- 155.00	2P/2B	65.00- 155.00	XP 15	F

Senior discount. 264 units. 1/2 blk s of Tahquitz Canyon Way. 150 S Indian Canyon Dr. (92262) Spacious rooms; 1- & 2-bedroom suites. Patios or balconies. Check-in 4 pm. Refrigerators; A/C; C/CATV; pay movies; radios; phones. 101 kitchens. 2 htd pools; whirlpools; exercise rm. Fee for: lighted tennis-2 courts. Pay valet garage. Airport transp. No pets. Wkly & monthly rates avail. Reserv deposit required; 3 days refund notice. AE, CB, DI, MC, VI. ● Dining rm & restaurant; 6 am-midnight; $7-$25; cocktails. FAX (619) 322-2380
                                                         ⊗ Ⓢ Ⓓ Ⓛ (619) 322-2121

Palm Tee Hotel **39**   Rates Subject to Change   *Apartment Motel*   ◆◆
| 10/1-5/31 [CP] | .... | 2P/1B | 56.00- 125.00 | 2P/2B | 56.00- 125.00 | XP 10 |
| 6/1-9/30 [CP] | .... | 2P/1B | 39.00- 75.00 | 2P/2B | 39.00- 75.00 | XP 10 |

15 units. 2 1/2 mi se. 1590 E Palm Canyon Dr. (92264) Most rooms with patio or balcony. Refrigerators; A/C; C/CATV; radios; phones; comb or shower baths. Htd pool; whirlpool. Airport transp. No pets. 7 efficiency apartments & 2 studio efficiencies. Wkly rates avail. Reserv deposit required; 7 days refund notice. AE, DS, MC, VI. Ⓓ (619) 327-1293

Place In The Sun **25**   AAA Special Value Rates   *Apartment Motel*   ◆◆◆
| 11/1-4/30 | 1P 65.00- 105.00 | 2P/1B | 65.00- 105.00 | 2P/2B | 65.00- 105.00 | XP 12 |
| 5/1-6/30 & 9/1-10/31 | 1P 60.00- 90.00 | 2P/1B | 60.00- 90.00 | 2P/2B | 60.00- 90.00 | XP 12 |

16 units. 3 1/2 blks e of Palm Canyon Dr, via Mesquite Ave & Random Rd. 754 San Lorenzo Rd. (92264) OPEN 9/1-6/30. Attractive grounds. Studio & 1-bedroom apartments. Patios. A/C; C/CATV; phones. 14 kitchens, 2 efficiencies. Htd pool; whirlpool. No pets. Wkly & monthly rates avail. Reserv deposit required; 7 days refund notice. MC, VI.
                                                                      Ⓓ (619) 325-0254

(See PALM SPRINGS spotting map page A314)

Quality Inn 38   AAA Special Value Rates   *Motel* ◆◆◆

12/26-7/6	1P	49.00- 99.00	2P/1B	59.00- 99.00	2P/2B	59.00- 119.00	XP 10		F
7/7-12/25	1P	35.00- 69.00	2P/1B	49.00- 69.00	2P/2B	49.00- 69.00	XP 5		F

124 units. 2 1/4 mi se on Palm Canyon Dr. 1269 E Palm Canyon Dr. (92264) Spacious grounds. 28 1-bedroom units with living room. Check-in 3 pm. 80 refrigerators; A/C; C/CATV; free & pay movies; phones. Coin laundry. Htd pool; wading pool; whirlpool. Pets, $10 extra charge. 1 bedroom suites, $119-$169 12/26-7/6; $79-$89 7/7-12/25. Wkly & monthly rates avail. Reserv deposit required. AE, DI, DS, MC, VI. Restaurant adjacent. FAX (619) 323-4234 *(See ad p A320)*   ⊗ Ⓓ (619) 323-2775

Ramada Hotel Resort 41   AAA Special Value Rates   *Motor Inn* ◆◆

2/1-5/31	1P	69.00- 129.00	2P/1B	69.00- 129.00	2P/2B	69.00- 129.00	XP 15		F
10/1-1/31	1P	49.00- 109.00	2P/1B	49.00- 109.00	2P/2B	49.00- 109.00	XP 15		F
6/1-9/30	1P	39.00- 99.00	2P/1B	39.00- 99.00	2P/2B	39.00- 99.00	XP 15		F

255 units. 2 1/2 mi se on Palm Canyon Dr. 1800 E Palm Canyon Dr. (92264) Check-in 3 pm. 195 refrigerators; A/C; C/CATV; pay movies; phones. 2 2-bedrm units. Coin laundry. Htd pool; saunas; whirlpools; exercise rm. No pets. Wkly & monthly rates avail. Reserv deposit required. AE, DI, DS, MC, VI. ● Coffeeshop; 7 am-2 & 5-9 pm; $6.95-$13.95; cocktail lounge. FAX (619) 322-1075 *(See ad p A320)*   ⊗ Ⓓ (619) 323-1711

Riviera Resort & Racquet Club 5   Rates Subject to Change   *Hotel* ◆◆◆

1/14-4/13	1P	135.00- 195.00	2P/1B	135.00- 195.00	2P/2B	135.00- 195.00	XP 20		F
4/14-6/8 & 9/15-1/13	1P	115.00- 175.00	2P/1B	115.00- 175.00	2P/2B	115.00- 175.00	XP 20		F
6/9-9/14	1P	70.00- 105.00	2P/1B	70.00- 105.00	2P/2B	70.00- 105.00	XP 20		F

Senior discount. 480 units. 1 1/2 mi n. 1600 N Indian Canyon Dr. (92262) Formerly Radisson Palm Springs Resort. Check-in 3 pm. A/C; C/CATV; movies; radios; phones. 2 htd pools; wading pool; whirlpools; tennis-3 courts, 2 lighted; exercise rm. Parking lot. Airport transp. Reserv deposit required. AE, MC, VI. ● Dining rm; 6:30 am-11 pm; $13.50-$25.50; cocktails. FAX (619) 327-4323 *(See ad below)*   ⊗ Ⓢ Ⓓ (619) 327-8311

(See PALM SPRINGS spotting map page A314)

Shilo Inn 🔳4   Rates Subject to Change   *Motel*   ◆◆◆
Weekends 12/16-6/15 [CP]   1P 105.00- 115.00   2P/1B 105.00- 115.00   2P/2B 105.00- 115.00   XP 10   F
Weekends 9/16-12/15 [CP]   1P 95.00- 105.00   2P/1B 95.00- 105.00   2P/2B 95.00- 105.00   XP 10   F
Weekends 6/16-9/15 [CP]   1P 69.00- 79.00   2P/1B 69.00- 79.00   2P/2B 69.00- 79.00   XP 10   F
124 units. 1 1/2 mi n. 1875 N Palm Canyon Dr. (92262) Nicely landscaped grounds. Patios or balconies. Check-in 3 pm. Refrigerators; A/C; C/CATV; movies; radios; phones. 4 kitchens. Coin laundry. 2 htd pools; sauna; whirlpools; exercise rm. Airport transp. Wkly rates avail. Reserv deposit required. AE, DI, DS, MC, VI. Restaurant opposite. FAX (619) 320-9543 *(See ad p A320)*   ⊗ Ⓢ Ⓓ 🅹 (619) 320-7676

Spa Hotel & Mineral Springs 🔳15   Rates Subject to Change   *Hotel*   ◆◆
⊛ 12/27-6/1   1P 85.00- 135.00   2P/1B 85.00- 135.00   2P/2B 85.00- 135.00   XP 20   F
10/1-12/26   1P 65.00- 105.00   2P/1B 65.00- 105.00   2P/2B 65.00- 105.00   XP 20   F
6/2-9/30   1P 45.00- 95.00   2P/1B 45.00- 95.00   2P/2B 45.00- 95.00   XP 10   F
Senior discount. 230 units. 100 N Indian Canyon Dr, at Tahquitz Canyon Dr. (PO Box 1787, 92263) Check-in 4 pm. A/C; C/CATV; phones. 26 efficiencies. Htd pool; outdoor hot mineral pool, hot mineral whirlpool; health spa; steamroom. Fee for: lighted tennis-3 courts. Parking lot. Airport transp. No pets. Wkly rates avail. Reserv deposit required; 3 days refund notice. AE, CB, DI, MC, VI. Restaurant; cocktails. FAX (619) 325-3344   ⊗ Ⓓ 🅹 (619) 325-1461

Stardust Hotel 🔳28   Rates Subject to Change   *Motel*   ◆
⊛ 10/1-5/31 [CP]   1P 65.00- 75.00   2P/1B 65.00- 75.00   2P/2B 65.00- 85.00   XP 15
6/1-9/30 [EP]   1P 59.00- 65.00   2P/1B 59.00- 65.00   2P/2B 65.00- 75.00   XP 15
Senior discount. 9 units. 1 1/2 mi s on Palm Canyon Dr, 1 blk w. 1610 Via Entrada. (92264) Refrigerators; A/C; C/CATV; shower or comb baths. 2 kitchens, 3 efficiencies. Htd pool; whirlpool; bicycles. Airport transp. No pets. Wkly & monthly rates avail. Reserv deposit required; 3 days refund notice. MC, VI.   Ⓓ (619) 325-5152

Sun Spot Hotel 🔳24   Rates Subject to Change   *Motel*   ◆◆
⊛ 11/1-5/31   1P 50.00- 65.00   2P/1B 50.00- 65.00   2P/2B 50.00- 65.00   XP
6/1-7/6 & 9/1-10/31   1P 45.00- 55.00   2P/1B 45.00- 55.00   2P/2B 45.00- 55.00   XP
7/7-8/31   1P 40.00- 50.00   2P/1B 40.00- 50.00   2P/2B 40.00- 50.00   XP
20 units. 1/2 mi e of Palm Canyon Dr. 1035 E Ramon Rd. (92262) 12 rooms with private patio. Refrigerators; A/C; C/CATV; phones; shower or comb baths. Coin laundry. Htd pool; whirlpool; putting green. Airport transp. No pets. 10 kitchens, $5-$10 extra. 4 deluxe units, $55-$70. 3 2-room units. Microwaves. Reserv deposit required; 7 days refund notice. AE, DS, MC, VI. *(See ad p A321)*   Ⓓ (619) 327-1288

Super 8 Lodge 🔳3   Rates Subject to Change   *Motel*   ◆◆
10/1-6/30   1P .... 55.00   2P/1B .... 65.00   2P/2B .... 69.00   XP 5   F
7/1-9/30   1P .... 49.00   2P/1B .... 55.88   2P/2B .... 59.88   XP 5   F
Senior discount. 63 units. 1 1/2 mi n. 1900 N Palm Canyon Dr. (92262) Refrigerators; A/C; C/CATV; movies; radios; phones. Htd pool; whirlpool. No pets. Reserv deposit required; 3 days refund notice. AE, DI, DS, MC, VI. Restaurant adjacent.   Ⓢ Ⓓ 🅹 (619) 322-3757

Tiki Spa Hotel & Suites 🔳37   Rates Subject to Change   *Apartment Motel*   ◆◆
⊛ 12/16-5/15   ....   2P/1B 77.00- 115.00   2P/2B 77.00- 115.00   XP 7   F
5/16-7/5 & 10/1-12/15   ....   2P/1B 57.00- 95.00   2P/2B 57.00- 95.00   XP 7   F
7/6-9/30   ....   2P/1B 48.00- 89.00   2P/2B 48.00- 89.00   XP 7   F
28 units. 2 mi se on Palm Canyon Dr, 1/4 mi s. 1910 S Camino Real. (92264) Spacious rooms, many with private patio. Refrigerators; A/C; C/CATV; phones; comb or shower baths. 21 efficiencies. Htd pool; saunas; whirlpools; bicycles. Airport transp. No pets. 3 2-bedroom apartments. Wkly & monthly rates avail. Reserv deposit required. AE, MC, VI. Cafeteria; 9 am-3 pm. *(See ad below)*   Ⓓ (619) 327-1349

Travelodge-Palm Springs 🔳35   Rates Subject to Change   *Motel*   ◆◆
⊛ 12/24-6/12   ....   2P/1B 55.00- 75.00   2P/2B 65.00- 79.00   XP 10   F
9/2-12/23   ....   2P/1B 45.00- 59.00   2P/2B 55.00- 69.00   XP 10   F
6/13-9/1   ....   2P/1B 35.00- 45.00   2P/2B 39.00- 55.00   XP 10   F
Senior discount. 158 units. 1 1/2 mi s. 333 E Palm Canyon Dr. (92264) Many balconies or patios. A/C; C/CATV; movies; rental VCPs. Phones; shower or comb baths. Coin laundry. 2 htd pools; whirlpool; volleyball court. No pets. Wkly rates avail. Reserv deposit required. AE, CB, DI, MC, VI. Restaurant adjacent. FAX (619) 320-4672   ⊗ Ⓓ (619) 327-1211

(See PALM SPRINGS spotting map page A314)

Vagabond Inn 32   **AAA Special Value Rates**   *Motel*   ◆◆◆

12/25-5/2	1P 66.00- 76.00	2P/1B	66.00- 76.00	2P/2B	72.00- 79.00	XP	6
5/3-6/12	1P 54.00- 75.00	2P/1B	54.00- 75.00	2P/2B	58.00- 79.00	XP	6
9/24-12/24	1P 46.00- 59.00	2P/1B	46.00- 59.00	2P/2B	52.00- 62.00	XP	6
6/13-9/23	1P 36.00- 46.00	2P/1B	36.00- 46.00	2P/2B	40.00- 50.00	XP	3

120 units. 1 1/2 mi s at jct E Palm Canyon Dr. 1699 S Palm Canyon Dr. (92264) A/C; C/CATV; radios; phones. Rental refrigerators. 1 2-bedrm unit. Htd pool; saunas; whirlpool. No pets. Reserv deposit required; 3 days refund notice in season. AE, DI, DS, MC, VI. Coffeeshop; 7 am-3 pm. FAX (619) 322-9269 *(See ad p A322)*
                                                          ⊗ (D) (619) 325-7211

Villa Rosa Inn 11   **Rates Guaranteed**   *Motel*   ◆◆

10/1-7/4 [CP]	....	2P/1B	65.00- 85.00	....	XP	
7/5-9/30 [CP]	....	2P/1B	45.00- 65.00	....	XP	

6 units. 2 mi se on Palm Canyon Dr, 1 1/2 blks n. 1577 S Indian Tr. (92264) Smoke free premises. A/C; C/CATV; radios; shower or comb baths. Htd pool. No pets. A/C. 1-bedroom suites with kitchen, $85-$110 for 2 persons. 2-night minimum stay weekends. 4 kitchen units. Microwaves. Wkly & monthly rates avail. Reserv deposit required; 3 days refund notice. AE, MC, VI. Restaurant opposite.
                                                          ⊗ (D) (619) 327-5915

Villa Royale Bed & Breakfast Inn 36   **Rates Subject to Change**   *Country Inn*   ◆◆◆

10/1-7/6 [CP]	1P 75.00- 250.00	2P/1B	75.00- 250.00	2P/2B	75.00- 250.00	XP	25
7/7-9/30 [CP]	1P 60.00- 150.00	2P/1B	60.00- 150.00	2P/2B	60.00- 150.00	XP	25

31 units. 2 mi se on Palm Canyon Dr, 1 blk n. 1620 S Indian Tr. (92264) Charming inn with beautifully landscaped courtyards & individually decorated rooms & suites. Many with fireplaces. A/C; C/CATV; pay movies; rental VCPs. Radios; phones; shower or comb baths. 4 2-bedrm units, 20 efficiencies. 2 htd pools; whirlpool. No pets. 2-night minimum stay weekends. Wkly & monthly rates avail. Reserv deposit required; 10 days refund notice. AE, MC, VI. ● Europa Restaurant, see separate listing. FAX (619) 322-4151
                                                          (D) (619) 327-2314

Wyndham Palm Springs 13   **Rates Subject to Change**   *Hotel*   ◆◆◆

1/1-5/31	....	2P/1B	185.00- 240.00	2P/2B	185.00- 240.00	XP 25	F
10/1-12/31	....	2P/1B	155.00- 200.00	2P/2B	155.00- 200.00	XP 25	F
6/1-7/4 & 9/1-9/30	....	2P/1B	135.00- 159.00	2P/2B	135.00- 159.00	XP 25	F
7/5-8/31	....	2P/1B	79.00- 109.00	2P/2B	79.00- 109.00	XP 25	F

410 units. 3 blks e of Indian Canyon Dr. 888 E Tahquitz Canyon Way. (92262) A/C; C/CATV; pay movies; radios; phones. Htd pool; sauna; whirlpools; health club. Parking lot. Airport transp. No pets. Reserv deposit required. AE, CB, DI, MC, VI. ● 2 dining rms; 6:30 am-11 pm; $8-$27; cocktails; entertainment. FAX (619) 322-5351 *(See ad p A324)*
                                                ⊗ (S) (D) (க) (619) 322-6000

RESTAURANTS

Banducci's Bit of Italy 5   **Italian**   **$$**   ◆
1 mi s. 1260 S Palm Canyon Dr. Popular, long established restaurant. Informal decor & service. Indoor & outdoor patio dining. A/C. Children's menu. Open 5 pm-11 pm. Cocktails & lounge. Valet parking. Reserv advised in season. AE, MC, VI.
                                                          ⊗ (619) 325-2537

Billy Reed's Restaurant 1   **American**   **$$**   ◆
1 1/2 mi n. 1800 N Palm Canyon Dr. Popular restaurant featuring a large selection of salads, sandwiches & entrees. Victorian decor. A/C. Early bird specials. Open 7 am-11 pm; closed 12/25. Cocktails & lounge. Entertainment. AE, DI, DS, MC, VI.
                                                          ⊗ (619) 325-1946

Bono 2   **Italian**   **$$$**   ◆◆
1 1/2 mi n. 1700 N Indian Canyon Dr. Attractive restaurant featuring nice selection of Southern Italian cuisine. A/C. Open 11:30 am-3 & 5:30-10 pm; Fri & Sat-11 pm; closed 1/1 & 12/25. Cocktails & lounge. Entertainment. MC, VI.
                                                          ⊗ (619) 322-6200

Cedar Creek Inn 6   **American**   **$$**   ◆◆◆
1 mi s. 1555 S Palm Canyon Dr. Very attractive restaurant featuring a large selection of salads, sandwiches, entrees & homemade desserts. A/C. Open 11 am-9 pm; closed major holidays. Cocktails & lounge. Entertainment. Reserv advised. MC, VI.
                                                          ⊗ (619) 325-7300

Europa Restaurant 11   **Continental**   **$$**   ◆◆
At Villa Royale Bed & Breakfast Inn. A nice selection of pasta, veal & lamb. Dining in the pool courtyard, weather permitting. A/C. Open 11:30 am-2 & 5:30-10 pm; Fri & Sat-11 pm; closed Mon. Lounge. Reserv advised. AE, MC, VI.
                                                        ⊗ (619) 327-2314

Eveleen's 10   **French**   **$$$**   ◆◆◆
664 N Palm Canyon Dr. Small, quaint restaurant situated in a charming adobe building. A/C. Dress code. Open 8/1-7/1 from 0 pm-10 pm; closed Tues. Cocktails & lounge. Reserv advised. MC, VI.
                                                        ⊗ (619) 325-4766

(See PALM SPRINGS spotting map page A314)

Las Casuelas Terraza ⑫   Mexican $ ◆◆
Downtown. 222 S Palm Canyon Dr. Popular restaurant. Indoor & patio dining. A/C. Open 11 am-10 pm; Sun from 10 am. Cocktails & lounge. Entertainment. AE, DI, MC, VI.   ⊗ (619) 325-2794

Le Vallavris ⑨   French $$$ ◆◆◆
3 blks w of Palm Canyon Dr. 385 W Tahquitz Canyon Way. Fine dining in a beautifully decorated restaurant & tree-shaded patio. Sun brunch, 11:30 am-3 pm. A/C. Open 11:30 am-3 & 6-11 pm. Cocktails & lounge. Valet parking. Reserv advised. AE, CB, DI, MC, VI.   (619) 325-5059

Marie Callender's ③   American $ ◆
1/2 blk n of Tahquitz Canyon Way. 123 N Palm Canyon Dr. Very attractive restaurant with a nice selection of salads, sandwiches & entrees. Also, Heritage Theater on upper level, extra charge. A/C. Children's menu. Open 8 am-11 pm; Sun-10 pm. Cocktails & lounge. AE, MC, VI.   ⊗ (619) 323-7437

Melvyn's ⑧   Continental $$$ ◆◆◆
At Ingleside Inn. Garden setting; enclosed patio dining. Sat & Sun brunch 9 am-3 pm. A/C. Open noon-3 & 6-11 pm. Cocktails & lounge. Entertainment. Valet parking. Reserv advised. AE, MC, VI.   ⊗ (619) 325-2323

Otani-A Garden Restaurant ④   Ethnic $$$ ◆◆◆
3 blks e of Indian Canyon Dr; across from convention center. 266 Avenida Caballeros. Japanese cuisine. Tempura & sushi bar. Sun brunch. A/C. Open 11 am-2 & 5-10 pm; Sat 5 pm-10 pm; Sun 11 am-2:30 & 5-10 pm. Cocktails & lounge. Reserv advised. AE, DI, MC, VI.   ⊗ (619) 327-6700

Siamese Gourmet Restaurant ⑦   Ethnic $$ ◆◆
5 mi se on Palm Canyon Dr, at Gene Autry Tr. 4711 E Palm Canyon Dr. Small restaurant serving nice selection of Thai cuisine. A/C. Open 11:30 am-2:30 & 4:30-10 pm; Sun from 4:30 pm. Beer & wine. Reserv advised. AE, DI, MC, VI.   (619) 328-0057

PALO ALTO — 55,900   See also MENLO PARK

Best Western Creekside Inn   Rates Subject to Change   *Motor Inn*   ◆◆◆
🅰 All year   1P 69.00- 85.00   2P/1B   71.00- 87.00   2P/2B   .... 77.00 XP 3
136 units. On SR 82; 1/4 s of Oregon Expwy/Page Mill Rd. 3400 El Camino Real. (94306) Landscaped grounds. Many spacious rooms, some studios. 79 refrigerators; A/C; C/TV; movies; radios; phones; comb or shower baths. 9 2-bedrm units, 6 kitchens, 8 efficiencies. 2 pools. No pets. Reserv deposit required. AE, CB, DI, MC, VI. ● Fresco, see separate listing. FAX (415) 493-6787   ⊗ Ⓓ (415) 493-2411

Country Inn Motel   Rates Subject to Change   *Motel*   ◆◆
🅰 All year   1P 41.00- 45.00   2P/1B   41.00- 45.00   2P/2B   .... 47.00 XP 6
27 units. On SR 82 (El Camino Real). 4345 El Camino Real. (94306) Attractive, well-maintained rooms. 12 A/C; C/CATV; 13 radios; phones; shower or comb baths. 12 kitchens. Pool. No pets. AE, CB, DI, MC, VI. FAX (415) 949-4190   Ⓓ (415) 948-9154

Days Inn ◆◆
⊕ All year [CP]   Rates Subject to Change   *Motel*   F
1P 49.00- 90.00   2P/1B   55.00- 95.00   2P/2B   60.00- 100.00   XP 6
23 units. 2 1/2 mi s of Stanford University Campus, on El Camino Real. 4238 El Camino Real. (94306) Attractive modern decor. A/C; C/CATV; movies; radios; phones; comb or shower baths. Pets, $10 extra charge. All rooms with microwave & refrigerator. Wkly rates avail. Reserv deposit required; 3 days refund notice. AE, DI, DS, MC, VI. FAX (415) 494-6112   ⊗ Ⓓ (415) 493-4222

Holiday Inn-Palo Alto ◆◆◆
4/1-9/25   Rates Guaranteed   *Motor Inn*   F
1P 124.00- 142.00   2P/1B   134.00- 152.00   2P/2B   134.00- 152.00   XP 10
342 units. Exit US 101 Embarcadero W; 2 mi to SR 82; 1/2 mi n; opposite Stanford University. 625 El Camino Real. (94301) OPEN ALL YEAR. Landscaped, tree-shaded grounds. Some balconies. A/C; C/CATV; movies; radios; phones. 12 kitchens. Pool; exercise rm. No pets. Some rooms with whirlpool tub. Monthly rates avail. Reserv deposit required. AE, DI, DS, MC, VI. ● Restaurant; 6:30 am-10:30 pm; $8-$18; cocktails. FAX (415) 327-7362   ⊗ Ⓢ Ⓓ (415) 328-2800

Hyatt Palo Alto ◆◆
Sun-Thurs   Rates Guaranteed   *Motor Inn*   F
1P 115.00- 175.00   2P/1B   145.00- 175.00   2P/2B   145.00- 175.00   XP 15
Fri & Sat   1P 75.00- 175.00   2P/1B   75.00- 175.00   2P/2B   75.00- 175.00   XP 15   F
Senior discount. 200 units. 3 1/2 mi s on SR 82. 4290 El Camino Real. (94306) Attractively landscaped grounds. Check-in 3 pm. A/C; C/CATV; movies; radios; phones. Pool; wading pool; sauna; lighted tennis-2 courts; health club. Pets, $50 deposit required. AE, DI, DS, MC, VI. ● Restaurant; 6:30 am-10:30 pm; $10-$20; cocktails. FAX (415) 493-5879   ⊗ Ⓓ (415) 493-0800

Hyatt Rickeys ◆◆◆
Sun-Thurs   Rates Guaranteed   *Motor Inn*   F
1P 115.00- 145.00   2P/1B   145.00- 170.00   2P/2B   145.00- 170.00   XP 25
Fri & Sat   1P 75.00- 110.00   2P/1B   75.00- 110.00   2P/2B   75.00- 110.00   XP 25   F
Senior discount. 347 units. 3 1/4 mi s on SR 82. 4219 El Camino Real. (94306) Attractively landscaped grounds. Few fireplaces, balconies or patios; few studios. Check-in 3 pm. 20 refrigerators; A/C; C/CATV; movies; radios; phones; comb or shower baths. Pool; putting green. Pets, $50 deposit required. AE, DI, DS, MC, VI. ● Restaurant; 6:30 am-10:30 pm; $10-$21; cocktails. FAX (415) 424-0836   ⊗ Ⓓ Ⓑ (415) 493-8000

Oak Motel ◆
⊕ All year   AAA Special Value Rates   *Motel*
1P .... 35.85   2P/1B .... 41.65   2P/2B .... 47.15   XP 5
39 units. On SR 82. 4279 EL Camino Real. (94306) A/C; C/CATV; movies; radios; phones. 2 efficiencies, no utensils. Coin laundry. Pool. No pets. All rooms have microwave & refrigerator. Wkly & monthly rates avail. Reserv deposit required. AE, DI, DS, MC, VI. FAX (415) 493-3593   Ⓓ (415) 493-6644

Sky Ranch Motel ◆
⊕ All year   Rates Guaranteed   *Motel*
1P 40.00- 48.00   2P/1B   46.00- 52.00   2P/2B   46.00- 52.00   XP 4
Senior discount. 27 units. 2 1/2 mi s of Stanford University Campus, on El Camino Real. 4234 El Camino Real. (94306) Refrigerators; A/C; C/CATV; movies; VCPs. Radios; phones; shower or comb baths. No pets. Microwaves. Reserv deposit required. AE, DI, DS, MC, VI. FAX (415) 493-0858 (See ad below)   ⊗ Ⓓ (415) 493-7221

Stanford Terrace Inn ◆◆◆
⊕ All year [CP]   Rates Subject to Change   *Motel*   F
1P 95.00- 100.00   2P/1B   100.00- 105.00   2P/2B   105.00- 180.00   XP 10
Senior discount. 79 units. W off SR 82; s edge of Stanford University Campus. 531 Stanford Ave. (94306) Service oriented. A/C; C/CATV; movies; VCPs. Radios; phones; 80 comb or shower baths. 13 kitchens. Coin laundry. Small pool. Garage. No pets. All rooms with microwave & refrigerator. Reserv deposit required. AE, DI, MC, VI. FAX (415) 857-0343   ⊗ Ⓓ (415) 857-0333

Townhouse Motel ◆◆
⊕ All year [CP]   Rates Guaranteed   *Motel*
1P 39.00- 44.00   2P/1B   43.00- 47.00   2P/2B   47.00- 50.00   XP 4
23 units. Exit US 101 Oregon Expwy; 3 mi w to SR 82 se. 4164 El Camino Real. (94306) A/C; C/CATV; movies; phones; shower or comb baths. No pets. All rooms with microwave & refrigerator. Wkly rates avail. Reserv deposit required. AE, CB, DI, MC, VI. Restaurant adjacent. FAX (415) 493-3418 (See ad below)   Ⓓ (415) 493-4492

RESTAURANTS

Fresco Restaurant   American $$ ◆◆
⊕ On SR 82; s of Page Mill Rd/Oregon Expwy at B W Creekside Inn. 3398 El Camino Real. Creative California cuisine, casual atmosphere. A/C. Open 6 am-11 pm; Fri-11:30 pm; Sat 7 am-11:30 pm; Sun 7 am-11 pm; closed 11/25 & 12/25. Cocktails. Reserv advised. AE, DI, MC, VI.   ⊗ (415) 493-3470

Ming's Villa   Regional Chinese $$ ◆◆
Exit US 101 Embarcadero Rd e. 1700 Embarcadero Rd. Specialities include dim sum on carts, fresh seafood, chinese barbecue, Cantonese style. Comfortable seating. A/C. Open 11:30 am-3 & 5-10 pm. Cocktails & lounge. Reserv advised. AE, DI, MC, VI.   (415) 856-7700

Nataraja Restaurant   Ethnic $$ ◆◆
2 mi w of US 101, exit University Ave. 117 University Ave. Indian Tandoori, Moghlai & North Indian specialties. A/C. Open 11 am-2 & 6-10 pm; Sun 11 am-3 & 6-10 pm; closed Mon, 7/4, 11/26 & 12/25. Cocktails & lounge. Valet parking. Reserv advised. AE, CB, DI, MC, VI.   ⊗ (415) 321-6161

Scott's Seafood Grill   Seafood $$$ ◆
Exit US 101 at Embarcadero Rd E. 2300 E Bayshore Rd. New England atmosphere; casual dining, pasta & chicken dishes. A/C. Open 11:30 am-9:30 pm; Mon-9 pm; Sat 5 pm-10 pm; closed Sun & major holidays. Cocktails & lounge. Reserv advised. AE, CB, DI, MC, VI.   ⊗ (415) 856-1046

PALOS VERDES ESTATES

RESTAURANT

La Rive Gauche   French $$$ ◆◆
1 blk w of Malaga Cove Plaza. 320 Tejon Pl. A/C. Open 5:30 pm-10 pm; also, 11:30 am-3 pm Tues-Fri. Cocktails & lounge. Entertainment. Reserv advised. AE, CB, DI, MC, VI.   ⊗ (310) 378-0267

PARADISE — 25,400

Lantern Motel   Rates Guaranteed   Motel   ◆◆
⊕ All year   1P .... 36.00 2P/1B .... 38.00 2P/2B 41.00- 45.00 XP 4
16 units. 1 blk w off Skyway. 5799 Wildwood Ln. (95969) Quiet location among pine trees. A/C; C/TV; radios; phones; shower baths. Pool. No pets. Reserv deposit required. AE, DI, DS, MC, VI. Coffeeshop opposite.
                    ⊗ Ⓓ (916) 877-5553

Palos Verdes Motel   Rates Subject to Change   Motel   ◆
⊕ All year   1P .... 35.00 2P/1B .... 37.00 2P/2B .... 39.00 XP 3
17 units. 1 1/2 mi w. 5423 Skyway. (PO Box 458, 95967) A/C; C/CATV; radios; phones; shower or comb baths. Small pool. Pets. 6 kitchens, $10 extra. Wkly rates avail. Reserv deposit required. AE, DI, DS, MC, VI. FAX (916) 872-2615   ⊗ Ⓓ (916) 877-2127

Ponderosa Gardens Motel   Rates Subject to Change   Motel   ◆◆◆
⊕ All year   1P 47.00- 65.00 2P/1B 48.00- 65.00 2P/2B .... 55.00 XP 5
36 units. Center; 2 blks e. 7010 Skyway. (95969) Secluded setting among pine trees. A/C; C/CATV; radios; phones. Coin laundry. Pool; whirlpool. Pets, $5 extra charge. 1 kitchen, $10 extra. Reserv deposit required. AE, CB, DI, MC, VI. FAX (916) 872-2993   ⊗ Ⓓ (916) 872-9094

PASADENA — 131,600   (See PASADENA & VICINITY AREA spotting map page A327; see index starting below)

Index of Establishments on the PASADENA & VICINITY AREA Spotting Map

---

Best Western Colorado Inn ⓯   Rates Subject to Change   Motel   ◆◆
⊕ All year [CP]   1P .... 56.00 2P/1B .... 62.00 2P/2B .... 66.00 XP 6
Senior discount. 77 units. 3/4 mi s of I-210, exit Sierra Madre Blvd. 2156 E Colorado Blvd. (91107) Refrigerators; A/C; C/CATV; movies; radios; phones. Coin laundry. Small htd pool; whirlpool. No pets. AE, DI, DS, MC, VI.
                    Ⓢ Ⓓ Ⓛ (818) 793-9339

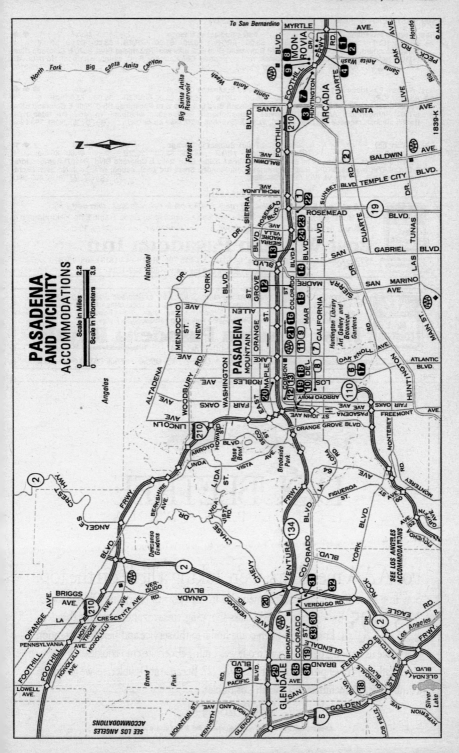

(See PASADENA & VICINITY spotting map page A327)

Best Western Pasadena Inn 23
(AAA) All year [CP]   Rates Subject to Change   *Motel*   ◆◆
                                  1P 48.00- 58.00   2P/1B   53.00- 63.00   2P/2B   53.00- 63.00   XP 5   F
Senior discount. 63 units. From I-210, exit Rosemead Blvd S; 2 blks w of Rosemead Blvd. 3570 E Colorado Blvd.
(91107) Refrigerators; A/C; C/CATV; movies; radios; phones. Coin laundry. Pool; sauna; whirlpool. No pets. AE,
CB, DI, MC, VI. FAX (818) 405-9948 *(See ad below)*   (D) (818) 796-9100

Best Western Pasadena Royale 22
(AAA) All year [CP]   Rates Subject to Change   *Motel*   ◆◆◆
                                  1P 50.00- 68.00   2P/1B   55.00- 73.00   2P/2B   55.00- 73.00   XP 5   F
Senior discount. 61 units. From I-210, exit Rosemead Blvd S; 2 blks w of Rosemead Blvd. 3600 E Colorado Blvd.
(91107) Refrigerators; A/C; C/CATV; movies; radios; phones. Pool; sauna; whirlpool. No pets. Wkly rates avail.
Reserv deposit required. AE, CB, DI, MC, VI. FAX (818) 568-2827 *(See ad below)*   (S) (D) (&) (818) 793-0950

Comfort Inn 14
(AAA) All year [CP]   Rates Subject to Change   *Motel*   ◆◆◆
                                  1P 49.00- 50.00   2P/1B   54.00- 55.00   2P/2B   .... 57.00   XP 5   F
Senior discount. 50 units. 1/2 mi s of I-210; exit Sierra Madre Blvd. 2462 E Colorado Blvd. (91107) Refrigerators;
A/C; C/CATV; movies; VCPs. Radios; phones. Coin laundry. Small htd pool; sauna; whirlpool. No pets. Micro-
waves. AE, CB, DI, MC, VI. FAX (818) 796-0966   (⊗) (S) (D) (&) (818) 405-0811

(See PASADENA & VICINITY spotting map page A327)

Doubletree Hotel-Pasadena 20   Rates Guaranteed   *Hotel*   ◆◆◆◆
🌐 All year   1P 90.00- 145.00   2P/1B 100.00- 155.00   2P/2B 100.00-155.00   XP 10   F
Senior discount. 355 units. 2 blks n of Colorado Blvd. 191 N Los Robles Ave at Walnut Ave. (91101) A/C; C/CATV; free & pay movies; radios; phones. Htd pool; sauna; whirlpool; steamroom; health club. Fee for: airport transp. Pay valet garage. No pets. AE, CB, DI, MC, VI. ● Dining rm; 6 am-11 pm; a la carte entrees about $10-$18; cocktails. FAX (818) 795-7669 *(See ad p A328)*   ⊗ Ⓢ Ⓓ ✆ (818) 792-2727

Holiday Inn 19   Rates Guaranteed   *Motor Inn*   ◆◆◆
All year   1P 88.00- 115.00   2P/1B 100.00- 125.00   2P/2B 100.00-125.00   XP 12   F
Senior discount. 318 units. 2 blks s of Colorado Blvd. 303 E Cordova St. (91101) A/C; C/CATV; free & pay movies; radios; phones. Pool; lighted tennis-2 courts. Pay garage. Pets. Monthly rates avail. AE, CB, DI, MC, VI. ● Dining rm; 6 am-10 pm; $9-$17; cocktails. FAX (818) 584-1390   ⊗ Ⓓ (818) 449-4000

Pasadena Hilton 18   AAA Special Value Rates   *Hotel*   ◆◆◆
All year   1P 119.00- 150.00   2P/1B 134.00- 175.00   2P/2B 134.00- 175.00   XP 15   F
291 units. 2 blks s of Colorado Blvd. 150 S Los Robles Ave. (91101) Check-in 3 pm. A/C; C/CATV; free & pay movies; radios; phones. Coin laundry. Htd pool; exercise rm. Pay valet garage. Small pets only, $25 extra charge. AE, CB, DI, MC, VI. ● Dining rm; 6:30 am-11 pm; $10-$18; cocktails. FAX (818) 584-3148 *(See ad p 22)*   Ⓢ Ⓓ (818) 577-1000

The Ritz Carlton, Huntington Hotel 17   Rates Subject to Change   *Hotel*   ◆◆◆◆
All year   1P 145.00- 240.00   2P/1B 145.00- 240.00   2P/2B 145.00- 240.00   XP 25
Senior discount. 383 units. 1 1/2 mi s of Colorado Blvd. 1401 S Oak Knoll Ave. (91106) Elegant decor in quiet residential area. Main building, garden units & cottages on several acres of nicely landscaped grounds. Check-in 3 pm. A/C; C/CATV; movies; radios; phones. Htd pool; whirlpool; exercise rm. Fee for: tennis-3 courts. Pay valet garage. No pets. AE, CB, DI, MC, VI. ● 3 dining rms; 6:30 am-11 pm; a la carte entrees about $12-$40; 24 hour room service; cocktails. FAX (818) 568-3159   ⊗ Ⓢ Ⓓ (818) 568-3900

Rodeway Inn 24   AAA Special Value Rates   *Motel*   ◆◆◆
🌐 All year   1P 43.00- 48.00   2P/1B 48.00- 53.00   2P/2B 52.00- 57.00   XP 5   F
70 units. From I-210, exit Madre Ave, 1 blk s, then 1 blk w. 3321 E Colorado Blvd. (91107) 62 refrigerators; A/C; C/TV; movies; radios; phones. Coin laundry. Small pool; sauna; whirlpool. No pets. 2 suites with whirlpool. Reserv deposit required. AE, CB, DS, MC, VI. FAX (818) 796-9780   ⊗ Ⓢ Ⓓ 🔧 (818) 796-9291

Saga Motor Hotel 16   Rates Guaranteed   *Motel*   ◆
🌐 All year   1P 49.00- 53.00   2P/1B 49.00- 56.00   2P/2B 49.00- 56.00   XP 5   F
Senior discount. 69 units. 3/4 mi s of I-210; westbound Allen Ave exit, eastbound Hill Ave exit, across from Pasadena City College. 1633 E Colorado Blvd. (91106) 12 refrigerators; A/C; C/CATV; movies; phones. Htd pool. No pets. AE, CB, DI, MC, VI. *(See ad below)*   Ⓓ (818) 795-0431

Travelodge-Pasadena Central 12   Rates Subject to Change   *Motel*   ◆
🌐 All year   1P ....   2P/1B .... 39.00   2P/2B .... 45.00   XP 5
53 units. 3 blks w of Sierra Madre Blvd. 2131 E Colorado Blvd. (91107) A/C; C/CATV; movies; radios; phones. Coin laundry. Pool; whirlpool. No pets. DI, DS, MC, VI.   Ⓓ (818) 796-6001

(See PASADENA & VICINITY spotting map page A327)

Vagabond Inn **13**   Rates Subject to Change   *Motel*   ◆
🏵 All year [CP]   1P 42.00- 52.00 2P/1B   47.00- 57.00 2P/2B   52.00- 62.00 XP 5   F
70 units. 3/4 mi sw of I-210, Madre Ave exit. 2863 E Colorado Blvd. (91107) A/C; C/CATV; movies; radios; phones.
Htd pool. Pets, $5 extra charge. AE, CB, DI, MC, VI. FAX (818) 578-9791 *(See ad p A329)* ⊗ Ⓓ (818) 449-3020

Westway Inn **21**   AAA Special Value Rates   *Motel*   ◆◆◆
🏵 All year   1P 44.00- 49.00 2P/1B   48.00- 53.00 2P/2B   52.00- 56.00 XP 4   F
61 units. 3/4 mi s of I-210, westbound Allen Ave exit, eastbound Hill Ave exit, across from Pasadena City College. 1599 E Colorado Blvd. (91106) Refrigerators; A/C; C/CATV; movies; radios; phones. Coin laundry. Small
pool; sauna; whirlpool. No pets. 4 rooms with whirlpool, $74. Reserv deposit required. AE, CB, DS, MC, VI.
FAX (818) 449-3493   ⊗ Ⓢ Ⓓ (818) 304-9678

RESTAURANTS

Bistro 45 **11**   French $$$ ◆◆◆
1 blk s of Colorado Blvd. 45 S Mentor Ave. Nice selection of French & California cuisine. A/C. Open 11:30 am-2:30 &
6-10 pm; Sat 5:30 pm-midnight; Sun 5 pm-midnight; closed Mon, 1/1, 11/25 & 12/25. Cocktails & lounge. Valet parking.
Reserv advised. AE, CB, DI, MC, VI.   ⊗ (818) 795-2478

The Chronicle **7**   Continental $$ ◆◆◆
5 blks s of Colorado Blvd; via Lake Ave. 897 Granite Dr. Nice selection of beef, seafood & house specialties. A/C. Open
11:30 am-2:30 & 5-10 pm; Fri-11 pm; Sat 11:30 am-2:30 & 5-11 pm; Sun 5 pm-10 pm; closed major holidays. Cocktails
& lounge. Valet parking. Reserv advised. AE, CB, DI, MC, VI.   ⊗ Ⓛ (818) 792-1179

The Georgian Room **6**   French $$$$ ◆◆◆
In The Ritz Carlton, Huntington Hotel. Elegant dining in restored Old World atmosphere. A/C. Dress code. Open 6 pm-10
pm; closed Mon & Tues. Cocktails. Entertainment. Valet parking. Reserv required. AE, CB, DI, MC, VI. (818) 568-3900

Maldonado's **9**   Continental $$$$ ◆◆◆
1202 E Green St. A small, charming restaurant. Light opera or musical comedies nightly. A/C. Open 11:30 am-2:30 pm,
dinner seatings at 6 pm & 9 pm; Sat 6 pm-9 pm; Sun dinner seatings at 5 pm & 8 pm; closed Mon & major holidays.
Cocktails. Pay valet parking. Reserv advised. AE, MC, VI.   ⊗ Ⓛ (818) 796-1126

Pappagallo Ristorante **12**   Italian $$ ◆◆◆
1/2 blk s of Colorado Blvd, in Old Town area. 42 S Pasadena Ave. Colorfully decorated dining room & tree shaded patio.
Nice selection of pasta, seafood & veal. A/C. Open 11:30 am-2:30 & 5-10:30 pm; Fri-11:30 pm; Sat 11:30 am-3 & 5-11:30
pm; Sun 5 pm-9:30 pm; closed Mon & major holidays. Cocktails & lounge. Valet parking. Reserv advised. AE, MC, VI.
                                                                        ⊗ (818) 578-0224

Parkway Grill **8**   American $$$ ◆◆◆
510 S Arroyo Pkwy. Popular restaurant serving an interesting selection of pasta, pizza, grills & main courses. Sun brunch
10:30 am-2:30 pm. A/C. Open 11:30 am-2:30 & 5:30-11 pm; Fri-midnight; Sat 5 pm-midnight; Sun 5 pm-10 pm; closed
7/4, 11/25 & 12/25. Cocktails & lounge. Valet parking. Reserv advised. AE, CB, DI, MC, VI.   ⊗ (818) 795-1001

Ritz Grill **10**   American $$ ◆◆◆
In Old Town area. 168 W Colorado Blvd. Nice variety of entrees. Attractive dining room & outdoor patio. A/C. Open 11
am-2:30 & 5-10 pm; Fri-11 pm; Sat 5 pm-11 pm; Sun 10:30 am-3 & 5-9 pm; closed major holidays. Cocktails & lounge.
Valet parking. Reserv advised. AE, MC, VI.   ⊗ (818) 405-0806

Yujean Kang's **13**   Chinese $$$ ◆◆◆
In Old Town area, 1 1/2 blks n of Colorado Blvd. 67 N Raymond Ave. Features gourmet Chinese cuisine. A/C. Open
11:30 am-2:30 & 5-9:30 pm; Fri & Sat-10 pm; closed 11/25. Beer & wine. Reserv advised. AE, CB, DI, MC, VI.
                                                                        ⊗ (818) 585-0855

PASO ROBLES — 12,100

Adelaide Motor Inn   Rates Subject to Change   *Motel*   ◆◆◆
🏵 4/30-10/10   1P 40.00- 48.00 2P/1B   40.00- 48.00 2P/2B   .... 50.00 XP 5
  10/11-4/29   1P 36.00- 45.00 2P/1B   36.00- 45.00 2P/2B   47.00- 48.00 XP 5
Senior discount. 67 units. 1 blk w of US 101, exit SR 46, Fresno. 1215 Ysabel Ave. (93446) Refrigerators; A/C;
C/CATV; movies; rental VCPs. Radios; phones; comb or shower baths. Coin laundry. Htd pool; 2 rooms with
whirlpool tub. No pets. 1 2-bedroom unit with microwave, $74-$81. Reserv deposit required. AE, DI, DS, MC, VI.
Restaurant adjacent. FAX (805) 238-3497 *(See ad below)*   ⊗ Ⓓ Ⓛ (805) 238-2770

Best Western Black Oak Motor Lodge   Rates Subject to Change   *Motor Inn*   ◆◆◆
🏵 5/2-10/14   1P 51.50- 68.00 2P/1B   51.50- 68.00 2P/2B   57.00- 66.00 XP 6
  10/15-5/1   1P 47.50- 64.00 2P/1B   47.50- 64.00 2P/2B   53.00- 62.00 XP 6
Senior discount. 110 units. 1 mi n; adjacent to US 101, exit SR 46 Fresno, 1 blk w. 1135 24th St. (93446) Refrigerators; A/C; C/CATV; radios; phones; comb or shower baths. 2 2-bedrm units. Coin laundry. Htd pool; wading
pool; sauna; whirlpool; 2 rooms with whirlpool tub. No pets. 18 microwaves. Reserv deposit required. AE, DI,
DS, MC, VI. ● Coffeeshop; 6 am-8:30 pm; $5.50-$10.95; beer & wine. Also restaurant, see separate listing.
FAX (805) 238-0726   ⊗ Ⓓ Ⓛ (805) 238-4740

Melody Ranch Motel   Rates Guaranteed   *Motel*   ◆
🏵 5/20-9/16   1P 34.00- 40.00 2P/1B   40.00- 44.00 2P/2B   42.00- 46.00 XP 3
19 units. 1/4 mi s on US 101 business rt. 939 Spring St. (93446) OPEN ALL YEAR. A/C; C/CATV; radios; phones;
shower baths. Pool. No pets. Reserv deposit required. AE, CB, DI, MC, VI.   Ⓓ (805) 238-3911

Travelodge Paso Robles   Rates Subject to Change   *Motel* ◆◆
⊕ 5/1-10/1   1P 38.00- 48.00   2P/1B   42.00- 58.00   2P/2B 48.00- 75.00 XP 5   F
   10/2-4/30   1P 34.00- 45.00   2P/1B   38.00- 48.00   2P/2B 45.00- 65.00 XP 5   F
Senior discount. 31 units. 1 mi n on US 101 business rt. 2701 Spring St. (93446) Spacious landscaped grounds.
Refrigerators; A/C; C/CATV; movies; radios; phones; shower or comb baths. Htd pool. Small pets only, $4. 6 mi-
crowaves. Wkly rates avail. AE, DI, DS, MC, VI.   ⊗ ⑩ (805) 238-0078

RESTAURANTS

Black Oak Restaurant   American $$ ◆
⊕ 1 mi n; adjacent to US 101, exit SR 46E, Fresno, 1 blk w. 1535 24th St. Selections of steak, pork, chicken, bar-
becue spare ribs & seafood. A/C. Early bird specials. Open 7 am-10:30 pm. Cocktails & lounge. AE, DS, MC, VI.
                                                                                       ⊗ (805) 238-6330

Lolo's Mexican Food   Mexican $
⊕ 1/2 mi s on US 101 business rt. 305 Spring St. Casual atmosphere. Selections of early California Mexican cui-
sine. A/C. Children's menu. Open 11 am-9 pm; Fri & Sat-10 pm; closed 11/25 & 12/25. Beer & wine. MC, VI.
                                                                                       ⊗ (805) 239-5777

PEBBLE BEACH — 4,300   (See MONTEREY PENINSULA spotting map pages A262 & A263; see index starting on page A260)

The Inn at Spanish Bay 🔢   Rates Subject to Change   *Resort Complex* ◆◆◆◆
⊕ All year   1P 230.00- 335.00   2P/1B 230.00- 335.00   2P/2B 230.00- 335.00 XP 25
270 units. W of SR 1 on 17 Mile Dr. 2700 17 Mile Dr. (93953) All rooms have bay or forest view, gas-burning fire-
place; many with balcony or patio. Surrounded by Scottish-Links golf course. Check-in 4 pm. C/CATV; pay
movies; radios; phones. Pool; beach; saunas; whirlpools; putting green; tennis-8 courts, 2 lighted; rental bicy-
cles; health club. Fee for: golf-18 holes, riding, exercise rm. Valet parking lot. Airport transp. No pets. [AP] avail.
Service charge: $15. Reserv deposit required; 3 days refund notice. AE, CB, DI, MC, VI. ● Dining rm, restaurant
& coffeeshop; 6:30 am-10 pm; a la carte entrees about $18-$40; cocktails; entertainment. FAX (408) 647-7443
                                                                           Ⓢ Ⓓ Ⓛ (408) 647-7500

The Lodge at Pebble Beach 🔢   Rates Subject to Change   *Resort Complex* ◆◆◆◆
⊕ All year   1P 280.00- 425.00   2P/1B 280.00- 425.00   2P/2B 280.00- 425.00 XP 25
161 units. Off SR 1, on 17 Mile Dr. (PO Box 1128, 93953) Beautiful, oceanfront location. Panoramic view. Many
with woodburning fireplace. Check-in 4 pm. C/CATV; pay movies; radios; phones. Pool; wading pool; beach;
sauna; whirlpool; nature trails; rental bicycles; 10 units with whirlpool tub. Fee for: golf-18 holes, par-3 golf,
tennis-14 courts; riding, exercise rm. Airport transp. Pets. Service charge: $15. Reserv deposit required; 3 days
refund notice. AE, CB, DI, MC, VI. ● Dining rm, 2 restaurants & coffeeshop; 6:30 am-10:30 pm; a la carte en-
trees about $18-$40; cocktails. FAX (408) 624-6357   ⑩ (408) 624-3811

PERRIS

Best Western Lake Perris Inn   Rates Subject to Change   *Motel*
⊕ All year   1P .... 45.00   2P/1B   ....   45.00   2P/2B   ....   55.00 XP 5
105 units. 1 blk w of I-215, exit SR 74W, 4th St. 480 S Redlands Ave. (92376) Rating withheld pending completion
of construction. Scheduled to open September, 1992. Refrigerators; A/C; C/CATV; movies; radios; phones. Htd
pool; whirlpool. 12 rooms with whirlpool tub, $65; 2 & 3 bedroom suites, $75-$95. AE, DI, DS, MC, VI.
                                                                                       ⊗ (909) 943-5577

PETALUMA — 43,200

Best Western Petaluma Inn   Rates Subject to Change   *Motel* ◆◆
⊕ All year   1P 50.00- 56.00   2P/1B   56.00- 60.00   2P/2B 61.00- 68.00 XP 6
Senior discount. 75 units. 1 blk e off US 101, Washington St exit. 200 S McDowell Blvd. (94954) Few small rooms.
A/C; C/CATV; movies; radios; phones; shower or comb baths. Pool. No pets. Reserv deposit required. AE, DI,
DS, MC, VI. Coffeeshop adjacent. FAX (707) 778-3111   ⊗ ⑩ (707) 763-0994

Quality Inn-Petaluma   Rates Subject to Change   *Motel* ◆◆◆
⊕ 5/1-10/31 [CP]   1P 59.00- 89.00   2P/1B   64.00- 99.00   2P/2B 66.00-102.00 XP 5   F
   11/1-4/30 [CP]   1P 54.00- 84.00   2P/1B   59.00- 94.00   2P/2B 61.00- 94.00 XP 5   F
Senior discount. 110 units. US 101 northbound exit Old Redwood Hwy-Penngrove, southbound exit Petaluma
Blvd N-Penngrove, e side adjacent to US 101. 5100 Montero Way. (94954) Refrigerators; A/C; C/CATV; movies;
radios; phones; comb or shower baths. Coin laundry. Pool; sauna; whirlpool. Pets, $20 deposit required. Few
rooms with wet bar & hot plate, $5 extra, some with whirlpool bath & hot plate. Reserv deposit required. AE, DI,
DS, MC, VI. Restaurant adjacent. FAX (707) 664-8566 *(See ad p A332)*   ⑭ ⑪ Ⓛ (707) 664-1166

RESTAURANTS

Fino Cucina Italiana   Italian $$ ◆◆
US 101, exit E Washington/Central Petaluma; corner E Washington & Petaluma Blvd N. 208 Petaluma Blvd N. Art deco
decor. A/C. Open 11 am-2 & 5-9:30 pm; Sat & Sun 5 pm-10 pm; closed Mon, 1/1, 11/26 & 12/25. Beer & wine. Minimum,
$7. Reserv advised. AE, MC, VI.   ⊗ (707) 762-5966

Sonoma Joe's   Steak & Seafood $$ ◆◆
3 mi n, e off US 101; northbound exit Old Redwood Hwy-Penngrove; southbound exit Petaluma Blvd N-Penngrove. 5151
Montero Way. Steaks, ribs & seafood. Lunch features salad & pasta bar. A/C. Children's menu. Open 11 am-9 pm; Sat
5 pm-10 pm; Sun 10 am-9 pm; closed Mon, 7/4, 11/25, 12/24 & 12/25. Cocktails & lounge. Minimum $4. Reserv advised.
AE, MC, VI.   ⊗ (707) 795-5800

Steamer Gold Landing   Steak & Seafood $$ ◆◆
1 mi w off US 101, E Washington St exit; 2 blks s on Water St; 1 Water St. On Petaluma River; in historical building. A/C. Children's menu. Open 11:30 am-2:30 & 5-9 pm; Fri & Sat-10 pm; Sun 10:30 am-2:30 & 5-9 pm; closed 7/4, 11/25 & 12/25. Cocktails & lounge. Entertainment & dancing. Minimum $5. Reserv advised. AE, MC, VI.   ⊗ (707) 763-6876

PHELAN — 100

Economy Inn   Rates Subject to Change   *Motel*   ◆
All year   1P .... 48.00   2P/1B   .... 54.00   2P/2B   .... 57.00   XP 6
47 units. On SR 138 at jct I-15, exit Palmdale/Silverwood Lake. 8317 Hwy 138. (Cajon Pass, 92371) A/C; C/CATV; 20 radios; phones. 9 efficiencies. Coin laundry. Htd pool. Pets. Rooms with 3 beds, $70. AE, DI, DS, MC, VI.
    Ⓢ Ⓓ (619) 249-6777

PICO RIVERA — 59,200

Pico Rivera Travelodge   Rates Guaranteed   *Motel*   ◆◆◆
All year   1P 42.00- 45.00   2P/1B   48.00- 52.00   2P/2B   .... 55.00   XP 4   F
Senior discount. 47 units. On SR 19; 1 mi n of I-5. 7222 Rosemead Blvd. (90660) Refrigerators; A/C; C/CATV; movies; radios; phones; shower baths. Htd pool; 5 rooms with whirlpool. No pets. AE, DI, DS, MC, VI.
    Ⓓ (310) 949-6648

PINE VALLEY — 600

Pine Valley Lodge   Rates Subject to Change   *Motel*   ◆
Fri & Sat 4/1-12/31   1P .... 59.95   2P/1B   .... 59.95   2P/2B   .... 69.95   XP
Sun-Thurs 4/1-12/31 & Fri-Sat
1/1-3/31   1P .... 49.95   2P/1B   .... 49.95   2P/2B   .... 59.95   XP 5
Sun-Thurs 1/1-3/31   1P .... 39.95   2P/1B   .... 39.95   2P/2B   .... 49.95   XP
26 units. 1/2 mi n of I-8. 28857 Old Hwy 80. (PO Box 178, 92082) Tree-shaded grounds. A/C; C/CATV; radios; phones; comb or shower baths. Efficiencies. Coin laundry. Htd pool; lighted tennis-2 courts. No pets. Wkly rates avail. Reserv deposit required. AE, DS, MC, VI. Restaurant adjacent.
    ⊗ Ⓓ (619) 473-8711

Sunrise Motel   Rates Subject to Change   *Motel*   ◆
All year   1P .... 39.95   2P/1B   .... 45.95   2P/2B   .... 49.95   XP 4   F
Senior discount. 22 units. 3/4 mi n of I-8. 28940 Old Hwy 80. (PO Box 370, 91962) Refrigerators; A/C; C/CATV; phones. Pets, $20 deposit required. All units with microwave. Some rooms with VCP. Wkly & monthly rates avail. Reserv deposit required. AE, DI, DS, MC, VI. Coffeeshop adjacent.
    ⊗ Ⓢ Ⓓ Ⓛ (619) 473-8777

PIONEER — 200

Pioneer Resorts II Lodge   Rates Subject to Change   *Motel*   ◆◆
All year   ....   2P/1B   49.00- 73.00   2P/2B   56.00- 71.00   XP 8
25 units. 1/2 mi w on SR 88. 24144 Hwy 88. (PO Box 2019, 95666) Check-in 3 pm. A/C; C/CATV; radios; phones. Pool; whirlpool. No pets. 1 kitchen, $64-$79 for up to 4 persons. Reserv deposit required. AE, MC, VI. Restaurant adjacent.
    ⊗ Ⓓ Ⓛ (209) 295-3490

PISMO BEACH — 7,700   See also GROVER CITY

Best Western Shelter Cove Lodge   Rates Subject to Change   *Motel*   ◆◆◆
6/1-10/5 [CP]   1P 108.00- 118.00   2P/1B   108.00- 118.00   2P/2B   108.00- 118.00   XP 10   F
10/6-5/31 [CP]   1P 88.00- 98.00   2P/1B   88.00- 98.00   2P/2B   88.00- 98.00   XP 10   F
Senior discount. 52 units. 1 1/2 mi n; adjacent to US 101 & SR 1. 2651 Price St. (93449) 4 rooms with wood-burning fireplace. Ocean view & balcony. Check-in 3 pm. Refrigerators; A/C; C/CATV; rental VCPs; radios; phones. Htd pool; whirlpool. No pets. AE, DI, DS, MC, VI. *(See ad p A333)*   Ⓢ Ⓓ (805) 773-3511

Best Western Shore Cliff Lodge   Rates Guaranteed   *Motor Inn*   ◆◆◆
All year   1P 83.00- 95.00   2P/1B   83.00- 95.00   2P/2B   89.00- 100.00   XP 10   F
Senior discount. 99 units. 1 mi n; adjacent to US 101 & SR 1. 2555 Price St. (93449) Spacious ocean view rooms. Balcony or patio. Stairway to ocean. Check-in 3 pm. A/C; C/CATV; pay movies; radios; phones. Htd pool; sauna; whirlpool; lighted tennis-2 courts. No pets. 9 efficiencies, $10 extra. 6 2-bedroom housekeeping apartments, $185-210 for up to 4 persons. Reserv deposit required. AE, DI, DS, MC, VI. ● Restaurant, see separate listing. FAX (805) 773-2341 *(See ad p A333)*   ⊗ Ⓢ Ⓓ (805) 773-4671

The Cliffs at Shell Beach   AAA Special Value Rates   *Motor Inn*   ◆◆◆
All year   1P 110.00- 160.00   2P/1B   110.00- 160.00   2P/2B   110.00- 160.00   XP 15   F
166 units. 3 mi n; adjacent to US 101 & SR 1, northbound exit Spyglass Dr; southbound Shell Beach Rd. 2757 Shell Beach Rd. (93449) Many balconies. Check-in 3 pm. 110 refrigerators; A/C; C/CATV; pay movies; radios; phones. Coin laundry. Htd pool; sauna; whirlpool; indoor whirlpool; exercise rm. Fee for: massage. No pets. 27 suites with whirlpool tub, $170-$290. AE, DI, DS, MC, VI. ● Sea Cliffs Restaurant, see separate listing. FAX (805) 770-0764 *(See ad p A334)*   ⊗ Ⓢ Ⓓ Ⓛ (805) 773-5000

Edgewater Motel AAA Special Value Rates *Motel* ◆◆
5/1-9/30 [CP] .... 2P/1B 55.00- 85.00 2P/2B 65.00- 85.00 XP F
10/1-4/30 [CP] .... 2P/1B 55.00- 70.00 2P/2B 65.00- 75.00 XP F
92 units. 1/4 mi n on SR 1; 2 blks w of US 101. 280 Wadsworth Ave. (93449) At beach. Some ocean view rooms.
1 2-bedroom apartment. Refrigerators; C/CATV; radios; phones. Coin laundry. Htd pool; whirlpool; 9 units with
whirlpool tub. No pets. 2 efficiencies & 19 1-bedroom apartments, $85-$135 for up to 4 persons. Wkly & monthly
rates avail. Reserv deposit required. AE, DI, DS, MC, VI. FAX (805) 773-5121 *(See ad p A335)* Ⓓ (805) 773-4811

Kon Tiki Inn   **Rates Guaranteed**   *Motor Inn* ◆◆◆
⊛ 3/19-10/3   1P   72.00- 88.00   2P/1B   72.00- 88.00   2P/2B   72.00- 88.00   XP 14
86 units. 1/2 mi n on SR 1, at jct US 101. 1621 Price St. (93449) OPEN ALL YEAR. Ocean view rooms. Private
stairway to beach. 4 rooms with woodburning fireplace. Check-in 3 pm. Refrigerators; 46 A/C; C/CATV; movies;
radios; phones. Coin laundry. Htd pool; whirlpools; lighted tennis-2 courts; racquetball-4 courts. Fee for: health
club. No pets. Reserv deposit required. AE, MC, VI. ● Restaurant; 7 am-9 pm; $14.50-$26.95; cocktails; entertainment. FAX (805) 773-6541   ⊗ Ⓓ Ⓛ (805) 773-4833

Ocean Palms   **Rates Subject to Change**   *Motel*   ◆◆
⊛ Fri & Sat 4/1-9/14   1P .... 55.00 2P/1B .... 65.00 2P/2B .... 75.00 XP 5
  Fri & Sat 9/15-3/31   1P .... 45.00 2P/1B .... 45.00 2P/2B .... 55.00 XP 5
  Sun-Thurs 4/1-9/14   1P .... 32.00 2P/1B .... 42.00 2P/2B .... 46.00 XP 5
  Sun-Thurs 9/15-3/31   1P .... 28.00 2P/1B .... 38.00 2P/2B .... 42.00 XP 5
20 units. Northbound adjacent w side of US 101 exit Price St, southbound 1 blk sw of US 101 exit Hinds St. 390
Ocean View Ave. (93449) 18 refrigerators; C/CATV; movies; radios; phones; shower or comb baths. 6 efficien-
cies. Htd pool. No pets. AE, DS, MC, VI. Restaurant opposite.   ⊗ Ⓓ (805) 773-4669

Quality Suites　　　　　　　　　　Rates Guaranteed　　　　　　　　*Suites Motel*　◆◆◆
　5/15-9/7 [BP]　　1P 89.00- 119.00　2P/1B 98.00- 128.00　2P/2B 98.00- 128.00　XP 9　F
　9/8-5/14 [BP]　　1P 79.00- 109.00　2P/1B 88.00- 118.00　2P/2B 88.00- 118.00　XP 9　F
Senior discount. 133 units. 2 mi s adjacent to US 101 exit 4th St. 651 Five Cities Dr. (93449) Refrigerators; A/C; C/CATV; VCPs; radios; phones. Coin laundry. Htd pool; wading pool; whirlpool; putting green. Small pets only, $6. 1-bedroom suites with living room & microwave. Complimentary beverages each evening. AE, DI, DS, MC, VI. FAX (805) 773-5177
　⊗ Ⓢ Ⓓ Ⓛ (805) 773-3773

Sandcastle Inn　　　　　　　AAA Special Value Rates　　　　　　*Motel*　◆◆◆
　♿ Fri-Sat [CP]　　1P 95.00- 145.00　2P/1B 95.00- 145.00　2P/2B 95.00- 145.00　XP 10　F
　Sun-Thurs [CP]　　1P 75.00- 130.00　2P/1B 75.00- 130.00　2P/2B 75.00- 130.00　XP　　F
59 units. 1/4 mi s on SR 1; 3 blks w of US 101. 100 Stimson Ave. (93449) On beach. Many rooms with ocean view, patio or balcony. Check-in 4 pm. Refrigerators; C/CATV; VCPs; radios; phones. Whirlpool. Suites, $155-$255. Wkly & monthly rates avail. AE, DI, DS, MC, VI. FAX (805) 773-0771 *(See ad p A334)*
　⊗ Ⓢ Ⓓ Ⓛ (805) 773-2422

Sea Crest Resort Motel　　　　Rates Subject to Change　　　　　*Motel*　◆◆◆
　♿ 4/1-10/31　　　　.......　　2P/1B 65.00- 135.00　2P/2B 65.00- 135.00　XP 5
Senior discount. 160 units. 3/4 mi n; adjacent to US 101 & SR 1. 2241 Price St. (93449) OPEN ALL YEAR. Ocean view rooms. Private stairway to beach. Rooms with patio or balcony. Check-in 3 pm. Refrigerators; C/TV; movies; 110 radios; phones; comb or shower baths. 5 2-bedrm units. Htd pool; whirlpools; 4 rooms with whirlpool. No pets. Reserv deposit required. AE, DI, DS, MC, VI. Restaurant adjacent. *(See ad p A336)*
　Ⓓ (805) 773-4608

Sea Gypsy Motel　　　　　　Rates Subject to Change　　　*Apartment Motel*　◆◆
　♿ All year　　　1P 40.00- 55.00　2P/1B 45.00- 55.00　2P/2B 65.00- 100.00　XP 10
77 units. 1 blk w of SR 1. 1020 Cypress. (93449) At beach. Most rooms with ocean view. Check-in 3:30 pm. Refrigerators; C/CATV; phones; comb or shower baths. 3 2-bedrm units. Coin laundry. Small htd pool; whirlpool. No pets. 47 kitchen units with microwave. Wkly & monthly rates avail. Reserv deposit required. AE, DS, MC, VI. FAX (805) 773-9286 *(See ad p A336)*
　Ⓓ (805) 773-1801

SeaVenture Hotel

		Rates Subject to Change				Motor Inn		◆◆
⊕ 6/1-9/16 [CP]	1P 89.00- 159.00	2P/1B	89.00- 159.00	2P/2B	89.00- 159.00	XP 12		F
9/17-5/31 [CP]	1P 79.00- 148.00	2P/1B	79.00- 148.00	2P/2B	79.00- 148.00	XP 10		F

Senior discount. 52 units. 1/4 mi s on SR 1; 3 blks w of US 101. 100 Oceanview Ave. (93449) At beach. Many rooms with ocean view. Refrigerators; C/CATV; movies; radios; phones; shower or comb baths. 20 rooms with whirlpool on balcony. No pets. Monthly rates avail. DS, DI, MC, VI. ● Restaurant; 5 pm-10 pm; $14-$23.95; cocktails. FAX (805) 773-4693 *(See ad p A337)*   ⊗ Ⓓ 🛗 (805) 773-4994

Shell Beach Motel

		Rates Subject to Change				Motel		◆◆
⊕ Fri & Sat 5/15-10/31	....	2P/1B	65.00- 100.00	2P/2B	65.00- 120.00	XP 5		F
Sun-Thurs 5/15-10/31	....	2P/1B	60.00- 95.00	2P/2B	60.00- 105.00	XP 5		F
Fri & Sat 11/1-5/14	....	2P/1B	60.00- 90.00	2P/2B	60.00- 90.00	XP 5		F
Sun-Thurs 11/1-5/14	....	2P/1B	55.00- 80.00	2P/2B	55.00- 80.00	XP 5		F

9 units. 2 mi n; adj to US 101 & SR 1. 653 Shell Beach Rd. (93449) 2 blocks from beach. Attractively decorated & furnished in country English decor. Refrigerators; C/CATV; movies; radios; phones; comb or shower baths. Small htd pool. No pets. Reserv deposit required; 3 days refund notice. AE, DS, MC, VI. ⊗ Ⓓ (805) 773-4373

Spyglass Inn
AAA Special Value Rates | *Motor Inn* ◆◆◆

Fri & Sat	1P	84.00- 125.00	2P/1B	84.00- 125.00	2P/2B	84.00- 125.00	XP 10		F
Sun-Thurs	1P	74.00- 105.00	2P/1B	74.00- 105.00	2P/2B	74.00- 105.00	XP 10		F

82 units. 3 mi n; adjacent to US 101 & SR 1, Spyglass Dr exit. 2705 Spyglass Dr. (93449) Spacious rooms; many with ocean view. Check-in 3 pm. C/CATV; VCPs; radios; phones; comb or shower baths. Htd pool; whirlpool; miniature golf. Pets, $10 extra charge. 2 1-bedroom housekeeping units, $104-$139 for 2 persons. Wkly & monthly rates avail. AE, DI, DS, MC, VI. ● Restaurant, see separate listing. *(See ad p A338)*

⊗ Ⓓ Ⓖ (805) 773-4855

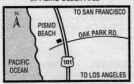

RESTAURANTS

F McLintock's Saloon & Dining House   Steakhouse $$ ◆◆
Adjacent to US 101 & SR 1 between Spyglass Dr & Price St exits. 750 Mattie Rd. Very popular restaurant with ocean view. Informal western atmosphere. Nice selection of steaks & seafood. Sun ranch breakfast 9 am-1:30 pm. A/C. Early bird specials; children's menu. Open 11:30 am-10:30 pm; Sun 9 am-1:30 & 2-9:30 pm; closed 1/1, 11/25, 12/24 & 12/25. Cocktails & lounge. Entertainment. DS, MC, VI. *(See ad p A337)*   ⊗ (805) 773-1892

Marie Callender's   American $ ◆
3/4 mi n; adjacent to US 101 & SR 1. 2131 Price St. Sun brunch 8 am-1:30 pm. Casual atmosphere. Pies are a specialty. Children's menu. Open 7 am-10 pm; Fri & Sat-11 pm; Sun 8 am-10 pm; closed 12/25. Beer & wine. AE, DS, MC, VI.   ⊗ (805) 773-0606

Rosa's Italian Restaurant   Italian $ ◆◆
Northbound 1 blk nw of US 101, exit Price St, southbound 1 blk sw of US 101; exit Hinds St. 491 Price St. Steak, veal, chicken & seafood. Pizza & nice selection of Italian cusine. Children's menu. Open 11:30 am-2 & 4-10 pm; Sat-Mon 4 pm-10 pm; closed 11/25 & 12/25. Beer & wine. AE, DS, MC, VI.   ⊗ (805) 773-0551

Sea Cliffs Restaurant   Seafood $$ ◆◆
In The Cliffs at Shell Beach. Selections of fresh fish, steaks, chicken, pasta, lamb & prime rib. Ocean view. A/C. Early bird specials. Open 7 am-9:30 pm; Fri & Sat-11 pm. Cocktails & lounge. Entertainment & dancing. Valet parking. Reserv advised. AE, DI, DS, MC, VI.   ⊗ (805) 773-3555

Shore Cliff Restaurant   Seafood $$ ◆◆
At Best Western Shore Cliff Lodge. Casual atmosphere. Ocean view. Selections of salads, chicken & steak. Sun brunch 10 am-2 pm. A/C. Early bird specials; children's menu. Open 7 am-9 pm; Fri & Sat-10 pm. Cocktails & lounge. Entertainment & dancing. Reserv advised. AE, DI, DS, MC, VI.   ⊗ (805) 773-4671

Spyglass Inn Restaurant   Seafood $$ ◆
In Spyglass Inn. Nautical decor, located on a cliff overlooking the ocean. Fresh seafood, chicken & steaks. Heated patio dining. A/C. Early bird specials; children's menu. Open 7-11 am, 11:30-2 & 4:30-9:30 pm; Fri & Sat-10:30 pm; Sun 7 am-2 & 4-9:30 pm. Cocktails & lounge. Dancing. Reserv advised. AE, MC, VI. *(See ad below)*   ⊗ (805) 773-1222

PLACENTIA — 41,300

Fairfield Inn By Marriott   Rates Subject to Change   Motel   ◆◆
All year   1P .... 39.95   2P/1B .... 42.95   2P/2B .... 46.95   XP 3
Senior discount. 135 units. 1/4 mi w of SR 57, exit Orangethorpe Ave. 710 W Kimberly Ave. (92670) Check-in 3 pm. A/C; C/CATV; movies; radios; phones. Htd pool. No pets. AE, DI, DS, MC, VI. FAX (714) 996-4410 *(See ad p A33)*
⊗ Ⓢ Ⓓ 🄵 (714) 996-4410

Quality Hotel at Placentia   Rates Subject to Change   Motor Inn   ◆◆◆
All year   1P 49.00- 58.00   2P/1B 54.00- 63.00   2P/2B 54.00- 63.00   XP 5
Senior discount. 102 units. 1 1/2 blks e of SR 57; exit Orangethorpe Ave. 118 E Orangethorpe Ave. (92670) Large, well-appointed rooms. 32 refrigerators; A/C; C/CATV; movies; radios; phones. Htd pool; sauna; whirlpool; 10 rooms with whirlpool; exercise rm. No pets. Reserv deposit required. AE, DI, DS, MC, VI. ● Coffeeshop; 24 hours; $7-$10. FAX (714) 528-4837   ⊗ Ⓢ Ⓓ 🄵 (714) 528-7778

Residence Inn By Marriott   Rates Subject to Change   Apartment Motel   ◆◆◆
Mon-Fri [CP]   1P 79.00- 105.00   2P/1B 79.00- 105.00   2P/2B 79.00- 105.00   XP 10   F
Sat & Sun [CP]   1P 65.00- 89.00   2P/1B 65.00- 89.00   2P/2B 65.00- 89.00   XP 10   F
112 units. 1/4 mi w of SR 57, exit Orangethorpe Ave. 700 W Kimberly Ave. (92670) Most units with woodburning fireplace. Check-in 3 pm. A/C; C/CATV; movies; radios; phones. 28 2-bedrm units, kitchens. Coin laundry. Htd pool; whirlpool. Pets, $35-$45 non-refundable deposit. Wkly & monthly rates avail. AE, DI, DS, MC, VI. FAX (714) 993-1043
⊗ Ⓢ Ⓓ (714) 996-0555

PLACERVILLE — 7,400 See also CAMERON PARK & POLLOCK PINES

Best Western Placerville Inn   AAA Special Value Rates   Motel   ◆◆◆
All year   1P 58.00- 68.00   2P/1B 64.00- 74.00   2P/2B 64.00- 74.00   XP 6   F
105 units. 2 mi w; exit US 50 at Missouri Flat Rd s. 6850 Green Leaf Dr. (95667) A/C; C/CATV; movies; radios; phones. Pool; whirlpool. Reserv deposit required. AE, DI, DS, MC, VI. Restaurant adjacent. FAX (916) 622-9376 *(See ad p A339)*   ⊗ Ⓢ Ⓓ 🄵 (916) 622-9100

Days Inn   AAA Special Value Rates   Motel   ◆◆
5/1-9/1 [CP]   1P 47.00- 53.00   2P/1B 53.00- 63.00   2P/2B .... 65.00   XP 4   F
45 units. US 50 exit s Schnell School Rd. 1332 Broadway. (95667) OPEN ALL YEAR. A/C; C/CATV; movies; phones; comb or shower baths. No pets. AE, DI, DS, MC, VI. Coffeeshop adjacent. FAX (916) 622-2080 *(See p A339)*   ⊗ Ⓓ 🄵 (916) 622-3124

Gold Trail Motor Lodge ⊛

			Rates Subject to Change					*Motel*			◆
5/1-9/30	1P	....	41.00	2P/1B	....	46.00	2P/2B	46.00-	51.00	XP	5
10/1-4/30	1P	....	36.00	2P/1B	....	41.00	2P/2B	41.00-	46.00	XP	5

Senior discount. 32 units. 2 mi e; exit Point View Dr off US 50. 1970 Broadway. (95667) Nicely landscaped shaded grounds. A/C; C/CATV; movies; 28 radios; phones; shower or comb baths. 1 2-bedrm unit. Pool. Pets, $5 extra charge. Wkly rates avail. Reserv deposit required; 3 days refund notice. AE, CB, DI, MC, VI.
⊗ Ⓓ (916) 622-2906

Mother Lode Motel ⊛

			Rates Subject to Change					*Motel*			◆
4/1-9/30	1P	39.00-	48.00	2P/1B	39.00-	48.00	2P/2B	46.00-	51.00	XP	5
10/1-3/31	1P	34.00-	43.00	2P/1B	34.00-	43.00	2P/2B	41.00-	46.00	XP	5

Senior discount. 21 units. 2 mi e; adjacent to US 50; exit Point View Dr. 1940 Broadway. (95667) Some small modest rooms. A/C; C/CATV; movies; phones; shower baths. Pool. Pets, $5 extra charge. Reserv deposit required; 3 days refund notice. AE, CB, DI, MC, VI.
⊗ Ⓓ (916) 622-0895

PLEASANT HILL — 30,700

Residence Inn By Marriott-Pleasant Hill

			Rates Subject to Change				*Suites Motel*		◆◆◆
All year [CP]	1P	....	89.00	2P/1B	....	89.00	2P/2B	....	119.00 XP

126 units. Exit I-680 Willow Pass Rd, to Taylor W; s Contra Costa Blvd, e on Ellinwood Dr, n on Ellinwood Way. 700 Ellinwood Way. (94523) Check-in 3 pm. A/C; C/CATV; movies; VCPs. Radios; phones. 28 2-bedrm units, kitchens. Coin laundry. Pool; whirlpool; sports court; exercise rm. Pets, $100 deposit required; also, $6 daily. AE, DI, DS, MC, VI. Restaurant adjacent. FAX (510) 689-1098
⊗ Ⓢ Ⓓ (510) 689-1010

PLEASANTON — 50,600   See also LIVERMORE & SAN RAMON

Courtyard by Marriott

			Rates Subject to Change					*Motor Inn*			◆◆◆
Sun-Thurs	1P	85.00-	105.00	2P/1B	95.00-	115.00	2P/2B	95.00-	115.00	XP	10
Fri & Sat	1P	....	65.00	2P/1B	....	65.00	2P/2B	....	65.00	XP	

Senior discount. 145 units. I-580 off Hopyard Rd exit, 1/2 mi s. 5059 Hopyard Rd. (94588) Attractive, landscaped courtyard. Check-in 3 pm. A/C; C/CATV; movies; radios; phones. Coin laundry. Pool; indoor whirlpool; exercise rm. No pets. Wkly & monthly rates avail. AE, DI, DS, MC, VI. ● Restaurant; 6:30 am-2 & 5-10 pm; $7-$13; cocktails. FAX (510) 463-0113 *(See ad below)*
⊗ Ⓢ Ⓓ Ⓛ (510) 463-1414

Doubletree Club   Rates Guaranteed   *Hotel* ◆◆

Sun-Thurs [BP]	1P	....	89.00	2P/1B	....	89.00	2P/2B	....	99.00 XP 10 F
Fri & Sat [BP]	1P	....	59.00	2P/1B	....	59.00	2P/2B	....	59.00 XP

171 units. 1/2 mi sw of jct I-580 & I-680; exit I-580 at Foothill Rd, 1/4 mi s, then 1/4 mi e on Canyon Way. 5990 Stoneridge Mall Rd. (94588) Check-in 3 pm. A/C; C/CATV; movies; radios; phones. Pool; sauna; whirlpool; exercise rm. Parking lot. Pets, $15 deposit required. Complimentary beverages each evening. AE, DI, DS, MC, VI. ● Cafeteria; 6-11 am, 11:30-1:30 & 5-10 pm; cocktail lounge. FAX (510) 463-3330 *(See ad below)*
⊗ Ⓢ Ⓓ (510) 463-3330

Holiday Inn   AAA Special Value Rates   *Hotel* ◆◆◆

Mon-Thurs	1P	80.00-	89.00	2P/1B	90.00-	99.00	2P/2B	....	90.00 XP 15 F
Fri-Sun	1P	....	61.00	2P/1B	....	66.00	2P/2B	....	66.00 XP 15 F

248 units. Exit I-580 at Foothill Rd, 1/4 mi s. 11950 Dublin Canyon Rd. (94588) Attractive lobby & public areas. Check-in 3 pm. 22 refrigerators; A/C; C/CATV; movies; radios; phones. Coin laundry. Pool; whirlpool; exercise rm. Parking lot. Pets, $10 extra charge. Wkly rates avail. AE, CB, DI, MC, VI. ● Restaurant; 6 am-10 pm; Sat & Sun from 7 am; $6-$15; cocktails. FAX (510) 463-2585
⊗ Ⓢ Ⓓ (510) 847-6000

Pleasanton Hilton   Rates Guaranteed   *Hotel* ◆◆◆

Sun-Thurs	1P	79.00-129.00	2P/1B	79.00-129.00	2P/2B	79.00-129.00 XP 10 F
Fri & Sat	1P	59.00- 79.00	2P/1B	59.00- 79.00	2P/2B	59.00- 79.00 XP 10 F

296 units. In se quadrant at jct I-580 & I-680. 7050 Johnson Dr. (94588) A/C; C/CATV; movies; radios; phones. 2 pools; whirlpool; health club. Fee for: tennis-18 courts, 4 lighted, 14 indoor; racquetball-4 courts. Parking lot. Pets. Monthly rates avail. AE, DI, DS, MC, VI. ● Restaurant; 6 am-11 pm; Sat & Sun 7 am-10 pm; $6-$17; cocktails. FAX (510) 463-3801 *(See ad p 22)*
⊗ Ⓢ Ⓓ Ⓚ (510) 463-8000

Sheraton Pleasanton   Rates Subject to Change   *Motor Inn* ◆◆◆◆

Mon-Thurs	1P	77.00- 97.00	2P/1B	87.00-107.00	2P/2B	87.00-107.00 XP 10 F
Fri & Sat	1P	57.00- 77.00	2P/1B	57.00- 77.00	2P/2B	57.00- 77.00 XP 10

214 units. 1/2 mi e of jct I-680 & I-580, exit I-580 at Hopyard Rd, then 1/2 mi s. 5115 Hopyard Rd. (94588) Attractive, landscaped garden area. Check-in 3 pm. 10 refrigerators; A/C; C/CATV; movies; radios; phones. Pool; whirlpool; exercise rm. No pets. AE, DI, DS, MC, VI. ● Velvet Turtle, see separate listing. FAX (510) 847-9455 *(See ad below)*
⊗ Ⓢ Ⓓ Ⓚ (510) 460-8800

Super 8 Lodge   Rates Guaranteed   *Motel* ◆◆

All year	1P	....	52.00	2P/1B	....	55.00	2P/2B	....	58.00 XP 4 F

Senior discount. 101 units. Exit I-580 at Hopyard Rd, 2 blks s. 5375 Owens Ct. (94566) Check-in 3 pm. A/C; C/TV; movies; radios; phones. Pool; whirlpool. Pets, $10 extra charge. 25 rooms with microwave & refrigerator. Wkly rates avail. AE, DI, DS, MC, VI. Coffeeshop adjacent. FAX (510) 734-8843
⊗ Ⓢ Ⓓ (510) 463-1300

RESTAURANTS

Maestro's Caffe Italiano   Italian $$ ◆◆

Exit I-580 Hopyard Rd, 1/4 mi s. 5100 Hopyard Rd. Comfortable attractive surroundings, casual atmosphere; seafood specialties. A/C. Children's menu. Open 11:30 am-3 & 4:30-10 pm; Sat 4 pm-11 pm; Sun 4 pm-10 pm; closed 11/26 & 12/25. Cocktails & lounge. Reserv advised. AE, MC, VI.
⊗ (510) 463-8773

Pleasanton Hotel Restaurant   Continental $$ ◆◆

Downtown, 2 mi e of I-680, Bernal Ave ext. 855 Main St. Varied menu. In historic 1851 building. A/C. Open 11:30 am-2 & 5-9 pm; Fri & Sat-10 pm; Sun 10 am-2 & 4:30-9 pm; closed 9/6 & 12/25. Cocktails & lounge. Entertainment & dancing. Reserv advised. AE, DI, DS, MC, VI.
⊗ (510) 846-8106

Velvet Turtle   American $$ ◆◆

In Sheraton Pleasanton. Varied menu, very attractive, comfortable atmosphere. A/C. Early bird specials. Open 6:30 am-3 & 5-10:30 pm; Fri-11 pm; Sat 7:30 am-3 & 5-11 pm; Sun 7:30 am-3 & 4-9 pm. Cocktails & lounge. Dancing. Reserv advised. AE, DI, MC, VI. *(See ad below)*
⊗ (510) 460-0444

PLYMOUTH — 800

Shenandoah Inn — Motel ◆◆◆

			Rates Subject to Change				
Fri & Sat [CP]	1P	.... 58.00	2P/1B	.... 65.00	2P/2B	.... 65.00	XP 7
Sun-Thurs [CP]	1P	.... 52.00	2P/1B	.... 60.00	2P/2B	.... 60.00	XP 7

47 units. 1 mi s on SR 49. 17674 Village Dr. (95669) Check-in 3 pm. A/C; C/CATV; movies; 40 radios; phones. Pool; whirlpool. Pets, $25 & $6 daily deposit required. 1 mini suite Fri & Sat, $110; Sun-Thurs, $99 for up to 4 persons. Reserv deposit required. AE, DI, DS, MC, VI. FAX (209) 245-4498   ⊗ Ⓢ Ⓓ Ⓛ (209) 245-4491

POINT ARENA

Wharfmaster's Inn — Motel

			Rates Subject to Change		
3/15-10/31 [CP]	1P	95.00- 175.00	2P/1B	95.00- 175.00	.... XP 10

Senior discount. 25 units. 1 mi w of SR 1 via Iversen or Port Rd. 785 Port Rd. (PO Box 674, 95468) OPEN ALL YEAR. Rating withheld pending completion of construction. Scheduled to open summer, 1992. Overlooking wharf; most units with view, fireplace & whirlpool bath. Check-in 3 pm. C/CATV; VCPs; radios; phones. 1 2-bedrm unit. Dock; fishing. No pets. 2-bedroom apartment with fireplace, $285 for up to 6 persons. Designated smoking areas. Wkly rates avail. Reserv deposit required; 5 days refund notice. AE, DS, MC, VI. Restaurant adjacent. FAX (707) 882-4114   ⊗ Ⓓ (707) 882-3171

POINT LOMA — See SAN DIEGO

POINT REYES NATIONAL SEASHORE — See BODEGA BAY

POLLOCK PINES — 1,900

RESTAURANT

Haven Restaurant — American — $$ ◆

Off US 50 at Sly Park, 1/2 mi w. 6396 Pony Express Tr. Variety of sandwiches, omelettes & a few hot entrees. Open 11 am-9 pm; Sat 8 am-9 pm; Sun 8 am-9 pm; closed 11/26 & 12/25. Beer & wine. Minimum $4.   (916) 644-3448

POMONA — 131,700

Sheraton Suites Fairplex — Hotel — Under Construction

247 units. 2 mi n of I-10, exit Fairplex Dr. 600 W McKinley Ave. (91768) Scheduled to open fall 1992. Adjacent to Fairplex Exhibition Center. Refrigerators; A/C; C/CATV; phones. 1 2-bedrm unit. Htd pool; sauna; whirlpool; exercise rm. Parking lot. Airport transp. Pets, $75 non-refundable deposit required. 1 2-bedroom unit; also deluxe lanai units. Microwave & wetbar in all rooms. Monthly rates avail. Reserv deposit required. AE, DI, DS, MC, VI. Restaurant; cocktails; entertainment. FAX (909) 622-3577   ⊗ Ⓢ Ⓓ (909) 622-2220

Shilo Inn Hilltop Suites Hotel — Suites Motor Inn ◆◆◆

			Rates Subject to Change				
All year [CP]	1P	114.00- 134.00	2P/1B	114.00- 134.00	2P/2B	114.00- 134.00	XP 12 F

Senior discount. 130 units. Adjacent to SR 57 Temple Ave exit. 3101 Temple Ave. (91768) 1-bedroom suites with refrigerator, microwave & wet bar. A/C; C/CATV; movies; VCPs. Radios; phones. Coin laundry. Small htd pool; sauna; whirlpool; steamroom; exercise rm. Garage. Airport transp. No pets. Wkly & monthly rates avail. AE, DI, DS, MC, VI. ● Restaurant; 6 am-11 pm; $6.95-$17.95; cocktails. FAX (909) 598-5654   ⊗ Ⓢ Ⓓ Ⓛ (909) 598-7666

Shilo Inn Hotel-Diamond Bar/Pomona   Rates Subject to Change   *Motor Inn*   ◆◆◆
All year [CP]   1P 84.00-104.00   2P/1B 84.00-104.00   2P/2B 84.00-104.00   XP 10   F
Senior discount. 160 units. Adjacent to I-10, exit Temple Ave exit. 3200 Temple Ave. (91768) Refrigerators; A/C; C/CATV; movies; rental VCPs. Radios; phones. Coin laundry. Htd pool; sauna; whirlpool; steamroom; exercise rm. Airport transp. Pets, $6 extra charge. Microwaves. Wkly & monthly rates avail. AE, CB, DI, MC, VI. ● Restaurant; 6 am-10 pm; $10-$15; cocktails. FAX (909) 594-5862 *(See ad p A341)*   ⊗ Ⓢ Ⓓ 🅱 (909) 598-0073

RESTAURANTS

Pomona Valley Mining Co   Steak & Seafood $$
Adjacent to I-10, exit Dudley St. 1777 Gillette Rd. Replica of an old mine. On hillside overlooking Pomona Valley. A/C. Children's menu. Open 11:30 am-3 & 5-10 pm; Fri-11 pm; Sat 5 pm-11 pm; Sun 10 am-3 & 5-10 pm; closed 12/25. Cocktails & lounge. Entertainment. AE, MC, VI.   🅱 (909) 623-3515

Rillo's Restaurant   Italian $$
1/4 mi w of Towne Ave. 510 E Foothill Blvd. Large selection of pasta, veal, chicken & seafood. A/C. Early bird specials. Open 11:30 am-2:30 & 4:30-10 pm; Sat & Sun from 4:30 pm; closed 11/25, 12/25 & 7/1-7/15. Cocktails & lounge. AE, MC, VI.   ⊗ (909) 621-4954

PORTERVILLE — 23,200

Best Western Porterville Inn   Rates Subject to Change   *Motel*   ◆◆◆
All year [CP]   1P 45.00-55.00   2P/1B 50.00-60.00   2P/2B 55.00-65.00   XP 5
Senior discount. 120 units. 3/4 mi e of SR 65 on SR 190, then 1 blk s on Jaye St & 1/2 blk e. 350 W Montgomery Ave. (93257) Check-in 3 pm. Refrigerators; A/C; C/TV; movies; rental VCPs. Phones. Coin laundry. Htd pool; whirlpool; exercise rm. No pets. AE, DI, DS, MC, VI. FAX (209) 781-8910   ⊗ Ⓢ Ⓓ 🅱 (209) 781-7411

RESTAURANT

Palace Dining Room   American $$ ◆◆
On 2nd floor, at the ne corner of Oak Ave & Main St. 22 E Oak Ave. Selections of seafood, chicken, rack of lamb, steak & lobster. Bread baked on premises. A/C. Open 11:30 am-2 & 5-9 pm; Sat 5 pm-9 pm; closed Sun & Mon. Cocktails & lounge. Entertainment. Reserv advised weekends. DS, MC, VI.   (209) 784-7086

PORT HUENEME — 20,300 See OXNARD

POWAY — 43,500 See also RANCHO BERNARDO

Poway Country Inn   Rates Guaranteed   *Motel*   ◆◆
All year   ....   2P/1B 38.00-42.00   2P/2B .... 44.00   XP 4   F
Senior discount. 44 units. 4 3/4 mi e of I-15, on CR S-4. 13845 Poway Rd. (92064) 13 refrigerators; A/C; C/CATV; movies; radios; phones. Coin laundry. Pool; whirlpool. No pets. 4 efficiencies, 1 unit with kitchen, $65 for up to 4 persons. Wkly rates avail. AE, DI, DS, MC, VI.   ⊗ Ⓓ (619) 748-6320

Poway Travelodge   Rates Guaranteed   *Motel*   ◆◆
All year   1P .... 35.00   2P/1B .... 38.00   2P/2B .... 40.00   XP 4
Senior discount. 47 units. 2 1/2 mi e of I-15, on CR S-4. 12448 Poway Rd. (92064) A/C; C/CATV; movies; radios; phones. Htd pool; whirlpool; 5 rooms with whirlpool tubs. No pets. AE, DI, MC, VI. ⊗ Ⓢ Ⓓ (619) 748-7311

PROJECT CITY — 1,700 See REDDING

RAMONA — 8,200

Ramona Valley Inn   Rates Subject to Change   *Motel*   ◆◆
All year [CP]   ....   2P/1B 42.00-50.00   2P/2B 47.00-55.00   XP   F
Senior discount. 39 units. 1/4 mi n on SR 78. 416 Main St. (92065) A/C; C/CATV; phones. Rental refrigerators. 1 2-bedrm unit. Coin laundry. Pool. No pets. 4 efficiencies, $5 extra. Wkly rates avail. Reserv deposit required. AE, DI, ER, MC, VI. Restaurant opposite.   ⊗ (619) 789-6433

RANCHO BERNARDO — See also POWAY

Carmel Highland Doubletree Golf & Tennis
Resort   Rates Guaranteed   *Resort Complex*   ◆◆◆
All year   1P 99.00-129.00   2P/1B 109.00-129.00   2P/2B 109.00-129.00   XP   F
Senior discount. 174 units. 2 1/2 mi s on I-15, exit Carmel Mountain Rd, then 1 blk w. 14455 Penasquitos Dr. (San Diego, 92129) Check-in 3 pm. A/C; C/CATV; pay movies; phones. Coin laundry. 2 htd pools; sauna; whirlpools; putting green; steamroom. Fee for: golf-18 holes, lighted tennis-6 courts; exercise rm & massage. Parking lot. Airport transp. Small pets only. Reserv deposit required. AE, DI, DS, MC, VI. ● Restaurant & coffeeshop; 6:30 am-11 pm; cocktails; entertainment. FAX (619) 672-9166 *(See ad p A343)*   ⊗ Ⓓ (619) 672-9100

Doubletree Club Hotel — Rates Guaranteed — *Motor Inn* ◆◆◆

Mon-Thurs [BP]	1P	....	65.00	2P/1B	....	65.00	2P/2B	....	65.00	XP 10 F
Fri-Sun [BP]	1P	....	55.00	2P/1B	....	55.00	2P/2B	....	55.00	XP 10 F

210 units. From I-15, exit Rancho Bernardo Rd, 1 blk e, then 1 blk s to Bernardo Plaza Ct. 11611 Bernardo Plaza Ct. (San Diego, 92128) A/C; C/CATV; pay movies; radios; phones. Htd pool; whirlpool; exercise rm. No pets. Monthly rates avail. Complimentary beverages each evening. AE, CB, DI, MC, VI. Light meals avail, 5 pm-10:30 pm; cocktails. FAX (619) 451-7948 *(See ad p A342)*   ⊗ Ⓢ Ⓓ (619) 485-9250

Holiday Inn Rancho Bernardo — Rates Guaranteed — *Motel* ◆◆◆

All year [BP]	1P	62.00- 68.00	2P/1B	62.00- 68.00	2P/2B	62.00- 68.00	XP 10 F

Senior discount. 179 units. 1 blk w of I-15, exit Rancho Bernardo Rd. 17065 W Bernardo Dr. (San Diego, 92127) Formerly Best Western Rancho Bernardo. Some balconies or patios. A/C; C/CATV; movies; radios; phones. Coin laundry. Htd pool; sauna; whirlpools; 8 suites with whirlpool tub; exercise rm. Pets, $10 extra charge. 13 efficiencies, $10 extra. Wkly & monthly rates avail. Complimentary beverages each evening. AE, CB, DI, MC, VI. Restaurant adjacent. FAX (619) 485-6530 *(See ad p A400)*   ⊗ Ⓓ (619) 485-6530

La Quinta Inn — Rates Subject to Change — *Motel* ◆◆◆

All year	1P	45.00- 52.00	2P/1B	51.00- 58.00	2P/2B	.... 51.00	XP 3 F

120 units. 3 mi s on I-15; exit Rancho Penasquitos Blvd. 10185 Paseo Montril. (San Diego, 92129) A/C; C/CATV; free & pay movies; radios; phones. Rental refrigerators. Htd pool. Small pets only. AE, DI, DS, MC, VI. Coffeeshop adjacent. FAX (619) 538-0476   ⊗ Ⓢ Ⓓ Ⓛ (619) 484-8800

Radisson Suite Hotel — Rates Subject to Change — *Motor Inn* ◆◆◆

All year [BP]	1P	79.00- 109.00	2P/1B	89.00- 119.00	2P/2B	89.00- 119.00	XP 10 F

177 units. From I-15, exit Rancho Bernardo Rd, 1 blk w, 3 blks s on W Bernardo Rd, then 1/2 blk w. 11520 W Bernardo Ct. (San Diego, 92127) Check-in 3 pm. Refrigerators; A/C; C/CATV; VCPs; radios; phones. Coin laundry. Htd pool; whirlpool; exercise rm. Small pets only. Microwaves. Complimentary beverages each evening. AE, CB, DI, MC, VI. Dining rm; 6 am-9:30 & 5-10 pm; Sat & Sun 7 am-11 & 5-10 pm; limited menu with light meals for dinner; $3-$5; cocktails. FAX (619) 451-5629 *(See ad p A407)*   ⊗ Ⓓ Ⓛ (619) 451-6600

Ramada Limited Suites — AAA Special Value Rates — *Motel* ◆◆

6/16-9/5 [CP]	1P	59.00- 64.00	2P/1B	64.00- 69.00	....		XP
9/6-6/15 [CP]	1P	54.00- 59.00	2P/1B	59.00- 64.00	....		XP

105 units. 3 mi s on I-15; exit Rancho Penasquitos Blvd, then 2 blk w. 12979 Rancho Penasquitos Blvd. (San Diego, 92129) Formerly Comfort Suites North. Refrigerators; A/C; C/CATV; movies; radios; phones. Htd pool; whirlpool. No pets. Microwaves. Wkly rates avail. AE, DI, DS, MC, VI. FAX (619) 484-7945   ⊗ Ⓓ Ⓛ (619) 484-3300

Rancho Bernardo Inn — Rates Subject to Change — Resort Complex ◆◆◆◆

		1P		2P/1B		2P/2B			
1/1-3/31		190.00- 235.00		190.00- 235.00		190.00- 235.00	XP 15		F
4/1-6/30 & 10/1-12/31		160.00- 205.00		160.00- 205.00		160.00- 205.00	XP 15		F
7/1-9/30		125.00- 180.00		125.00- 180.00		125.00- 180.00	XP 15		F

287 units. 2 mi ne of I-15, exit Rancho Bernardo Rd. 17550 Bernardo Oaks Dr. (San Diego, 92128) On several acres of beautifully landscaped grounds. Patios & balconies. Check-in 4 pm. A/C; C/CATV; rental VCPs; radios; phones. 2 htd pools; whirlpools; rental bicycles. Fee for: golf-45 holes, tennis-12 courts, 4 lighted; health club & massage; airport transp. No pets. Package plans avail. Reserv deposit required; 3 days refund notice. AE, DI, MC, VI. ● 2 dining rms; 6:30 am-10 pm; $9-$21; afternoon tea served 4 pm-5 pm; cocktails; entertainment. Also, El Bizcocho Restaurant, see separate listing. FAX (619) 673-0311 *(See ad p 144)* ⊗ Ⓓ Ⓛ (619) 487-1611

Rancho Bernardo Travelodge — Rates Subject to Change — Motel ◆◆

		1P		2P/1B		2P/2B			
All year [CP]		.... 55.00		.... 62.00		.... 70.00	XP 8		F

Senior discount. 49 units. From I-15, exit Rancho Bernardo Rd, 1 blk w, then 2 blks s. 16929 W Bernardo Dr. (San Diego, 92127) A/C; C/CATV; movies; 25 radios; phones. 2 2-bedrm units. Htd pool. Pets, $5 extra charge. AE, DI, DS, MC, VI. Restaurant adjacent. *(See ad p A410)* ⊗ Ⓓ Ⓛ (619) 487-0445

Residence Inn by Marriott — AAA Special Value Rates — Suites Motel

		1P		2P/1B		2P/2B			
All year [CP]		109.00- 139.00		.... 109.00		.... 139.00	XP 10		F

123 units. 2 1/2 mi s on I-15, exit Carmel Mountain Rd, then 1 blk e. 11002 Rancho Carmel Dr. (San Diego, 92128) Attractively decorated 1- & 2-bedroom suites. A/C; C/CATV; movies; VCPs. Radios; phones. 22 2-bedrm units, kitchens. Coin laundry. Htd pool; whirlpool; exercise rm. Pets, $100 deposit $50 non-refundable, plus $6 daily extra charge. Wkly & monthly rates avail. AE, CB, DI, MC, VI. FAX (619) 673-1913 ⊗ Ⓢ Ⓓ (619) 673-1900

RESTAURANTS

Anthony's Fish Grotto — Seafood — $$ ◆◆
1 blk w of Bernardo Center Dr. 11666 Avena Pl. Popular family dining. Large selection of seafood. A/C. Children's menu. Open 11:30 am-8:30 pm; closed major holidays. Cocktails & lounge. AE, DI, DS, MC, VI. ⊗ Ⓛ (619) 451-2070

El Bizcocho Restaurant — French — $$$$ ◆◆◆
In Rancho Bernardo Inn. An elegant, beautifully decorated dining room with formal decor & service. Sun brunch 10 am-2:30 pm. A/C. Dress code. Open 6 pm-10 pm; Fri & Sat-10:30 pm. Cocktails & lounge. Reserv advised. AE, CB, DI, MC, VI. *(See ad p 144)* Ⓛ (619) 487-1611

Hungry Hunter — Steak & Seafood — $$ ◆◆
In Town Center Shopping Plaza; 1/2 mi e of I-15, Rancho Bernardo Rd exit; via Bernardo Center Dr. 11940 Bernardo Plaza Dr. Popular, attractive restaurant with a nice selection of steaks, prime rib & seafood. A/C. Children's menu. Open 11:30 am-2 & 5-10 pm; Fri-10:30 pm; Sat 5 pm-10:30 pm; Sun 4 pm-9 pm; closed 12/25. Cocktails & lounge. Entertainment. Reserv advised. AE, DI, DS, MC, VI. ⊗ Ⓛ (619) 485-1263

Japanese Restaurant Yae — Ethnic — $$ ◆◆
1 blk w of Bernardo Center Dr. 11616 Iberia Pl. Traditional Japanese menu in main dining room or tableside preparation in the Teppanyaki room. Sushi bar. A/C. Open 11:30 am-2 & 5-10 pm; Sat from 5 pm-10 pm; Sun 4:30 pm-9 pm; closed 1/1 & 11/25. Cocktails & lounge. AE, CB, DI, MC, VI. ⊗ Ⓛ (619) 485-0390

Valentino's — Italian — $$ ◆◆
1 blk e of I-15; In the Mercado Center. 11828 Rancho Bernardo Rd. Small, charming restaurant serving a nice selection of Northern Italian cuisine. A/C. Open 11 am-2 & 5-10 pm; Sat from 5 pm; closed Sun, 1/1, 11/25 & 12/25. Cocktails. AE, CB, DI, MC, VI. ⊗ (619) 451-3200

RANCHO CORDOVA — 42,900 (See SACRAMENTO AREA spotting map page A360; see index starting on page A359)

Best Western Heritage Inn ㊺ — Rates Subject to Change — Motor Inn ◆◆◆

		1P		2P/1B		2P/2B		
All year		56.00- 62.00		58.00- 64.00		56.00- 62.00	XP 5	

Senior discount. 126 units. 9 mi e of Sacramento; exit US 50 s Sunrise Blvd. 11269 Pointe East Dr. (95742) A/C; C/CATV; movies; 45 radios; phones. Pool; sauna; whirlpool. No pets. Some units with whirlpool tub. Reserv deposit required. AE, DI, DS, MC, VI. ● Restaurant; 6 am-2 & 6-10 pm; $7-$15; cocktail lounge. FAX (916) 635-7198 *(See ad p A364)* ⊗ Ⓢ Ⓓ (916) 635-4040

Comfort Inn ㊽ — AAA Special Value Rates — Motel

		1P		2P/1B		2P/2B			
All year [BP]		49.00- 74.00		49.00- 74.00		.... 54.00	XP 10		F

112 units. 7 mi e of Sacramento, exit US 50 eastbound Mather Field Rd; westbound Mather Field AFB. 3240 Mather Field Rd. (95670) Check-in 3 pm. A/C; C/CATV; radios; phones. 8 efficiencies, no utensils. Coin laundry. Pool; whirlpool. Airport transp. Pets, $100 deposit required. AE, DI, DS, MC, VI. Coffeeshop adjacent. FAX (916) 362-0903 *(See ad below)* ⊗ Ⓢ Ⓓ Ⓛ (916) 363-3344

Courtyard by Marriott ㊼ — Rates Subject to Change — Motor Inn ◆◆◆

		1P		2P/1B		2P/2B		
Sun-Thurs		.... 75.00		.... 85.00		.... 85.00	XP	
Fri & Sat		.... 58.00		.... 58.00		.... 58.00	XP	

Senior discount. 145 units. 8 mi e of Sacramento; s of & adjacent to US 50, Zinfandel Dr exit. 10683 White Rock Rd. (95670) Check-in 3 pm. A/C; C/CATV; free & pay movies; radios; phones. Coin laundry. Pool; whirlpool; exercise rm. No pets. 14 suites, $72-$99 for up to 4 persons. Wkly rates avail. AE, DI, DS, MC, VI. ● Restaurant; 6:30-10 am, 11-2 & 5-10 pm; $9.50-$13.50; cocktails. FAX (916) 638-6776 *(See ad p A363)* ⊗ Ⓢ Ⓓ Ⓛ (916) 638-3800

Days Inn ㊷ — AAA Special Value Rates — Motor Inn ◆◆

		1P		2P/1B		2P/2B			
All year		49.00- 75.00		55.00- 75.00		.... 75.00	XP 10		F

130 units. 9 mi e of Sacramento; exit US 50 via Sunrise Blvd S. 11131 Folsom Blvd. (95670) A/C; C/CATV; pay movies; radios; phones. Pool; whirlpool. No pets. AE, DI, DS, MC, VI. ● Coffeeshop; 6 am-2 & 5-10 pm; $8-$12; cocktails. FAX (916) 635-3297 ⊗ Ⓢ Ⓓ Ⓛ (916) 635-0666

(See SACRAMENTO spotting map page A360)

Economy Inn's of America [51]   Rates Subject to Change   *Motel*   ◆◆
⊕ All year [CP]   1P .... 34.90   2P/1B .... 42.90   2P/2B .... 42.90 XP 7
Senior discount. 123 units. Exit Hwy 50 at Hazel Ave, 2 blks s. 12249 Folsom Blvd. (95670) A/C; C/CATV; movies;
radios; phones. Pool. Pets. Wkly rates avail. AE, MC, VI. Coffeeshop adjacent. FAX (916) 985-3622
                                                                                      ⊗ Ⓢ Ⓓ (916) 351-1213

Fairfield Inn by Marriott [50]   Rates Subject to Change   *Motor Inn*   ◆◆
All year   1P 40.95- 43.95   2P/1B 46.95- 49.95   2P/2B 49.95- 52.95 XP 3   F
117 units. 8 mi e of Sacramento, s of & adjacent to US 50, Zenfandel Dr exit. 10713 White Rock Rd. (95670) A/C; C/TV;
movies; radios; phones. Pool. No pets. AE, DI, DS, MC, VI. Coffeeshop adjacent. *(See ad p A363)*
                                                                                      ⊗ Ⓓ (916) 631-7500

Quality Suites [49]   AAA Special Value Rates   *Hotel*   ◆◆◆
All year [BP]   1P 77.00- 95.00   2P/1B 77.00- 95.00   2P/2B 77.00- 95.00 XP 7   F
127 units. 9 mi e of Sacramento; exit US 50 S Sunrise Blvd. 11260 Point East Dr. (95742) Few rooms with whirlpool tub;
few poolside with patio. Check-in 3 pm. A/C; C/CATV; VCPs; radios; phones. Coin laundry. Htd pool; whirlpool; exercise
rm. Parking lot. Airport transp. No pets. Microwaves. AE, DS, MC, VI. Restaurant adjacent. FAX (916) 638-4287
                                                                                      ⊗ Ⓢ Ⓓ (916) 638-4141

Sheraton Rancho Cordova
Hotel-Sacramento [53]   AAA Special Value Rates   *Hotel*   ◆◆◆◆
All year   1P 89.00- 110.00   2P/1B 99.00- 125.00   2P/2B 99.00- 125.00 XP 15   F
265 units. 9 mi e of Sacramento, s of & adjacent to US 50; Sunrise Blvd exit. 11211 Point East Dr. (95742) Check-in 3
pm. A/C; C/CATV; pay movies; radios; phones. Small htd pool; whirlpool; exercise rm. Parking lot. No pets. AE, DI, DS,
MC, VI. ● Restaurant; 6 am-10:30 pm; a la carte entrees about $7-$16; cocktail lounge. FAX (916) 638-5803
                                                                                      ⊗ Ⓢ Ⓓ Ⓑ (916) 638-1100

RANCHO CUCAMONGA — 101,400

Best Western Heritage Inn   Rates Subject to Change   *Motel*
All year [CP]   1P 49.00- 68.00   2P/1B 52.00- 76.00   2P/2B 57.00- 76.00 XP 5
Senior discount. 117 units. 1/2 mi e of Haven Ave, 1/4 blk s of Foothill Blvd. 8179 Spruce Ave. (91730) Scheduled to
open September, 1992. A/C; C/CATV; movies; phones. Pool; whirlpool. No pets. AE, CB, DI, MC, VI.   (909) 466-1111

RESTAURANTS

Cask'N Cleaver   American $$ ◆
1/2 mi w of Vineyard Ave. 8689 Ninth St. Informal dining. Nice selection of steaks, seafood & chicken. A/C. Children's
menu. Open 11:30 am-2 & 5-9:30 pm; Fri & Sat-10:30 pm; Sun 4:30 pm-9:30 pm; closed major holidays. Cocktails &
lounge. AE, DS, MC, VI.   ⊗ (909) 982-7108

Magic Lamp Inn   American $$$ ◆◆
On SR 66, 1 1/4 mi e of Euclid Ave. 8189 Foothill Blvd. Attractive early American decor. Nice selection of prime rib,
steaks, seafood & house specialties. A/C. Open 11:30 am-2:30 & 5-10 pm; Sat & Sun 5 pm-10 pm; closed 12/25. Cocktails & lounge. Entertainment. Reserv advised. AE, CB, DI, MC, VI.   ⊗ (909) 981-8659

Sycamore Inn   American $$ ◆◆◆
On SR 66, 1 1/2 mi e of Euclid Ave. 8318 Foothill Blvd. Fine dining in historic, popular, long-established restaurant. Ex-
tensive wine list. A/C. Children's menu. Open 11:30 am-2:30 & 5-10 pm; Fri-11 pm; Sat 5 pm-11 pm; Sun 10:30 am-2:30
& 3-10 pm; closed 12/25. Cocktails & lounge. AE, CB, DI, MC, VI.   Ⓑ (909) 982-1104

RANCHO MIRAGE — 9,800   (See map page A315)

Marriott's Rancho Las Palmas Resort   Rates Subject to Change   *Resort Hotel* ◆◆◆◆
⊕ 1/1-5/15   1P .... 175.00   2P/1B .... 175.00   2P/2B .... 175.00 XP 10
5/16-6/5 & 9/12-12/31 1P .... 145.00   2P/1B .... 145.00   2P/2B .... 145.00 XP 10
6/6-9/11   1P .... 75.00   2P/1B .... 75.00   2P/2B .... 75.00   XP 10
456 units. 1/4 mi n of SR 111. 41-000 Bob Hope Dr. (92270) On several acres of beautifully landscaped grounds.
Balconies or patios. Check-in 4 pm. A/C; C/CATV; pay movies; radios; phones. Coin laundry. 2 htd pools; whirl-
pools; rental bicycles; exercise rm. Fee for: golf-27 holes, tennis-26 courts, 8 lighted; airport transp. Parking lot.
Pets. Reserv deposit required; 10 days refund notice. AE, DI, DS, MC, VI. ● Dining rm, restaurant & coffeeshop;
6:30 am-11 pm; $7.95-$30; cocktails; entertainment. FAX (619) 568-5845 *(See ad p A346)*
                                                                                      Ⓓ Ⓑ (619) 568-2727

The Ritz-Carlton, Rancho Mirage   Rates Guaranteed   *Resort Hotel* ◆◆◆◆
⊕ 12/27-5/31   1P 275.00- 395.00   2P/1B 275.00- 395.00   2P/2B 275.00- 395.00 XP 25   F
9/12-12/26   1P 200.00- 350.00   2P/1B 200.00- 350.00   2P/2B 200.00- 350.00 XP 25   F
6/1-9/11   1P 119.00- 179.00   2P/1B 119.00- 179.00   2P/2B 119.00- 179.00 XP 25   F
238 units. 1/2 mi s of SR 111. 68-900 Frank Sinatra Dr. (92270) Hilltop location. Elegantly decorated public facil-
itites & guest rooms. Check-in 3 pm. A/C; C/CATV; movies; rental VCPs. Radios; phones. Htd pool; whirlpool;
putting green; steamroom; exercise rm. Fee for: lighted tennis-10 courts; massage. Pay valet garage. No pets.
Reserv deposit required; 7 days refund notice. AE, DI, DS, MC, VI. ● Dining rm & restaurant; 6:30 am-10 pm; a
la carte entrees about $12-$30; dress code for dinner; 24 hour room service; cocktails. Also, The Dining Room,
see separate listing. FAX (619) 321-6928   ⊗ Ⓢ Ⓓ (619) 321-8282

The Westin Mission Hills Resort   AAA Special Value Rates   *Resort Hotel* ◆◆◆◆
1/3-5/22   1P 250.00- 385.00   2P/1B 250.00- 385.00   2P/2B 250.00- 385.00 XP 25   F
9/12-1/2   1P 175.00- 295.00   2P/1B 175.00- 295.00   2P/2B 175.00- 295.00 XP 25   F
5/23-7/10   1P 135.00- 250.00   2P/1B 135.00- 250.00   2P/2B 135.00- 250.00 XP 25   F
7/11-9/11   1P 115.00- 225.00   2P/1B 115.00- 225.00   2P/2B 115.00- 225.00 XP 25   F
512 units. 2 mi sw from I-10, exit Bob Hope Dr. 71-333 Dinah Shore Dr. (92270) On several acres of grounds. Attractive
Moroccan architecture, spacious rooms with patio or balcony. Check-in 4 pm. A/C; C/CATV; pay movies; radios; phones.
3 htd pools; whirlpools; volleyball & croquet; steamroom. Fee for: golf-36 holes, tennis-17 courts, 7 lighted; exercise rm
& massage. Parking lot. Airport transp. Pets. $100 deposit required. Deluxe suites $245-$425 for 1 to 2 persons. Reserv
deposit required; 5 days refund notice. AE, CB, DI, MC, VI. ● Dining rm, restaurant & cafeteria; 6 am-11 pm; a la carte
entrees about $11-$24; 24 hour room service; cocktails. FAX (619) 321-2955   ⊗ Ⓢ Ⓓ Ⓑ (619) 328-5955

RESTAURANTS

Charley Brown's   Steak & Seafood $$ ◆◆
2 mi w on SR 111. 70-190 Hwy 111. Informal dining. Nice selection of steaks, prime rib & seafood. A/C. Early bird spe-
cials. Open 5 pm-10 pm; Fri & Sat-11 pm; closed 12/25. Cocktails & lounge. Valet parking. Reserv advised. AE, CB, DI,
MC, VI.   ⊗ (619) 328-3131

(See map page A315)

The Chart House   American $$ ◆◆
2 1/4 mi w on SR 111. 69-934 Hwy 111. Casual atmosphere. Nice selection of steaks, prime rib & seafood. A/C. Children's menu. Open 5:30 pm-9:30 pm; Fri-10 pm; Sat 5 pm-10 pm; Sun 5 pm-9:30 pm. Cocktails & lounge. Valet parking. AE, DI, DS, MC, VI.   ⊗ (619) 324-5613

The Dining Room   French $$$$ ◆◆◆◆
At The Ritz-Carlton, Rancho Mirage. Dining in formal elegance. A/C. Dress code. Open 9/7-5/31 from 6 pm-10 pm; Fri & Sat-10:30 pm. Cocktails. Pay valet parking. Reserv advised. AE, DI, DS, MC, VI.   ⊗ (619) 321-8282

Kobe Japanese Steak House   Ethnic $$ ◆
On SR 111, 1 blk e of Frank Sinatra Dr. 69-838 Hwy 111. Tableside preparation by Japanese chefs. Group seating. A/C. Children's menu. Open 5:30 pm-10 pm; Fri & Sat-11 pm; closed 11/25. Cocktails & lounge. Valet parking. Reserv advised. AE, CB, DI, MC, VI.   ⊗ (619) 324-1717

Las Casuelas Nuevas   Mexican $$ ◆
On SR 111. 70-050 Hwy 111. Colorfully decorated dining room & outdoor patio. Sun brunch 10 am-2 pm. A/C. Children's menu. Open 11 am-10 pm; Fri & Sat-11 pm; Sun 10 am-10 pm; closed 11/25 & 12/25. Cocktails & lounge. Entertainment. Valet parking. AE, CB, DI, MC, VI.   ⊗ 🅱 (619) 328-8844

Lord Fletcher Inn   American $$ ◆◆
1 mi w on SR 111. 70-385 Hwy 111. Fine English fare served in atmosphere of Old England. A/C. Open 9/1-6/30 from 5 pm-10 pm; Fri & Sat-11 pm; closed 12/25 & Sun-Mon 6/1-6/30. Cocktails. Valet parking. Reserv advised. MC, VI.   ⊗ 🅱 (619) 328-1161

Marie Callender's   American $
On SR 111, 1/2 blk e of Frank Sinatra Dr. 69-830 Hwy 111. A casual, attractive family type restaurant with a nice selection of salads, sandwiches, pasta & chicken. Large selection of pies. A/C. Open 11 am-11 pm; Sat from 8 am; Sun 8 am-10 pm; closed 11/25 & 12/25. Cocktails & lounge. AE, MC, VI.   ⊗ (619) 328-0844

Scoma's of San Francisco   Seafood $$$ ◆◆◆
On SR 111; 1 blk w of Frank Sinatra Dr. 69-620 Hwy 111. Formal decor & service. A/C. Open 9/1-7/5 from 5 pm-11 pm; closed 11/25. Cocktails & lounge. Valet parking. Reserv advised. AE, CB, DI, MC, VI.   ⊗ (619) 328-9000

Wally's Desert Turtle   Continental $$$ ◆◆◆
71-775 Hwy 111. A/C. Open 9/28-5/31 from 6:30 pm-10 pm; Fri & Sat-10:30 pm. Cocktails & lounge. Reserv advised. MC, VI.   ⊗ (619) 568-9321

RANCHO PALOS VERDES — 46,300

RESTAURANT

Admiral Risty Restaurant Steak & Seafood $$ ◆◆
🚲 Just s of Hawthorne Blvd. 31250 Palos Verdes Dr W. Seafood, steak, chicken, salad & pasta. 4 styles of seafood preparation. Ocean view. A/C. Children's menu. Open 5 pm-10 pm; Fri & Sat-11 pm; Sun 10 am-3 & 4-9:30 pm; closed 11/25 & 12/25. Cocktails & lounge. Entertainment. Reserv advised Fri & Sat. AE, DI, DS, MC, VI.
Ⓢ (310) 377-0050

RANCHO SANTA FE — 4,000

The Inn at Rancho Santa Fe Rates Subject to Change *Resort Complex* ◆◆◆
🚲 All year 1P 80.00- 185.00 2P/1B 80.00- 185.00 2P/2B 80.00- 185.00 XP
83 units. In downtown area; on CR S8. Linea del Cielo at Paseo Delicias. (PO Box 869, 92067) Long established inn; atmosphere of gracious charm. Rooms in cottages & main building on several acres of beautifully landscaped, tree-shaded grounds. Check-in 3 pm. 70 refrigerators; A/C; C/TV; radios; phones; comb or shower baths. 6 2-bedrm units, 1 3-bedrm unit, 19 efficiencies. Htd pool; tennis-3 courts; exercise rm. Fee for: airport transp. 1- & 2-bedroom cottages, $250-$485. Many with patio & some with fireplace. Wkly & monthly rates avail. Reserv deposit required; 3 days refund notice. AE, CB, DI, MC, VI. ● Dining rm; 7:30 am-10, noon-2:30 & 6:30-9 pm; $18-$25; cocktails. FAX (619) 759-1604 *(See ad below)* Ⓓ (619) 756-1131

Rancho Valencia Resort Rates Subject to Change *Resort* ◆◆◆◆
🚲 All year 1P 275.00- 410.00 2P/1B 275.00- 410.00 2P/2B 275.00- 410.00 XP 35 F
43 units. From I-5, take Via De La Valle 1 1/4 mi e, then 1/2 mi s on El Camino Real, 2 1/2 mi e on San Dieguito, then 1 mi n on Rancho Dieguito & Rancho Valencia. 5921 Valencia Cir. (PO Box 9126, 92067) Nestled among the rolling hills. Reminiscent of early California haciendas. Spacious units, all with fireplace & patio. Check-in 4 pm. A/C; C/CATV; movies; radios; phones. Htd pool; saunas; whirlpools; tennis-18 courts; exercise rm. Fee for: massage. No pets. 3-bedroom hacienda with pool. [AP] avail. Reserv deposit required; 7 days refund notice. AE, MC, VI. ● Dining rm; 7 am-10 pm; a la carte entrees about $16-$25; cocktails. 24 hour room service. A *Preferred Hotel.* FAX (619) 756-0165 ⊗ Ⓓ 🅱 (619) 756-1123

RESTAURANTS

Delicias American $$$ ◆◆◆
Downtown area. 6106 Paseo Delicias. An attractive dining room & outdoor patio serving a nice selection of California/French cuisine. A/C. Open 11 am-2:30 & 6-9:30 pm; Fri-10:30 pm; Sat 6 pm-10:30 pm; Sun 10:30 am-2:30 & 6-9:30 pm; closed 12/25. Cocktails & lounge. Reserv advised. AE, CB, DI, MC, VI. Ⓢ (619) 756-8000

Mille Fleurs French $$$$ ◆◆◆
Downtown. 6009 Paseo Delicias. Elegant country French decor. Menu changes daily. A/C. Open 11:30 am-2:30 & 6-10 pm; Sat & Sun from 6 pm; closed 12/25. Cocktails & lounge. Reserv advised. AE, MC, VI. Ⓢ (619) 756-3085

RED BLUFF — 12,400

Cinderella Riverview Motel AAA Special Value Rates *Motel* ◆
🚲 All year 1P 32.00- 44.00 2P/1B 36.00- 46.00 2P/2B 38.00- 48.00 XP 4 F
40 units. 1 blk w off I-5; exit via SR 36W. 600 Rio St. (96080) Some units face river. Some with balcony. 4 refrigerators; A/C; C/CATV; movies; phones; shower or comb baths. 1 2-bedrm unit. Coin laundry. Pool; fishing. Small pets only, $50 deposit. Reserv deposit required. AE, DI, DS, MC, VI. FAX (916) 527-7051 Ⓢ Ⓓ (916) 527-5490

Lamplighter Lodge Rates Subject to Change *Motel* ◆◆
🚲 All year [CP] 1P 32.00- 36.00 2P/1B 38.00- 44.00 2P/2B 40.00- 44.00 XP 4
Senior discount. 51 units. I-5 exit via business loop. 210 S Main St. (96080) Few large rooms. 10 refrigerators; A/C; C/CATV; movies; phones; shower or comb baths. Pool. No pets. AE, DI, DS, MC, VI. Restaurant adjacent. FAX (916) 527-5878 Ⓢ Ⓓ (916) 527-1150

Value Lodge Rates Subject to Change *Motel* ◆◆
🚲 All year 1P 40.00- 46.00 2P/1B 45.00- 50.00 2P/2B .... 50.00 XP 4
60 units. Exit I-5, SR 36W-Central District; 1/2 blk s on Gilmore Rd. 30 Gilmore Rd. (96080) Formerly Nendels Valu Inn. 9 refrigerators; A/C; C/CATV; movies; phones. Coin laundry. Small pool. Some rooms with microwave. AE, DI, DS, MC, VI. FAX (916) 527-1702 Ⓢ Ⓓ 🅱 (916) 529-2028

RESTAURANT

J & C Green Barn Restaurant American $ ◆◆
🚲 Exit I-5. 5 Chestnut Ave. Long established, family atmosphere, varied menu. A/C. Open 11 am-9 pm; closed 11/25 & 12/25. Cocktails & lounge. AE, MC, VI. Ⓢ (916) 527-7390

REDDING — 66,500

Best Western Hilltop Inn   AAA Special Value Rates   *Motor Inn*   ◆◆◆
All year [CP]   1P 69.00- 84.00   2P/1B   85.00- 94.00   2P/2B   79.00- 94.00   XP 12   F
112 units. Exit I-5 Cypress Ave E; 1/4 mi n on Hilltop Dr. 2300 Hilltop Dr. (96002) A/C; C/CATV; movies; rental VCPs. Radios; phones. Coin laundry. Pool; wading pool; whirlpool. No pets. Reserv deposit required. AE, DI, DS, MC, VI. ● Dining rm & coffeeshop; 11 am-11 pm; $9-$16; cocktails. Also, C. R. Gibbs Restaurant, see separate listing. FAX (916) 221-2867 *(See ad below)*   ⊗ ⒟ Ⓛ (916) 221-6100

Best Western Hospitality House   Rates Subject to Change   *Motel*   ◆◆
5/16-10/15   1P 42.00- 52.00   2P/1B   46.00- 52.00   2P/2B   .... 49.00   XP 6   F
63 units. 1 mi n on SR 273; exit I-5 299E, 1/4 mi w, 1/2 mi s on Market St. 532 N Market St. (96003) OPEN ALL YEAR. A/C; C/CATV; phones; comb or shower baths. Pool. Pets. Reserv deposit required. AE, CB, DS, MC, VI. Restaurant adjacent. *(See ad below)*   ⊗ ⒟ (916) 241-6464

Best Western Ponderosa Inn   Rates Subject to Change   *Motor Inn*   ◆◆
5/15-10/31   1P .... 45.00   2P/1B   .... 51.00   2P/2B .... 53.00   XP 6
11/1-5/14   1P .... 39.00   2P/1B   .... 45.00   2P/2B .... 47.00   XP 6
Senior discount. 70 units. 1 1/2 mi w of I-5, exit Cypress Ave. 2220 Pine St. (96001) A/C; C/CATV; phones. 1 2-bedrm unit. Pool; wading pool. Small pets only. Reserv deposit required; 3 days refund notice. AE, DI, DS, MC, VI. ● Restaurant; 6 am-10 pm; $5-$11; cocktails. FAX (916) 241-5949   ⊗ ⒟ (916) 241-6300

Colony Inn ◆
🌐 All year 75 units. Exit I-5 at Cypress Ave W; 1/2 mi s on Bechelli. 2731 Bechelli Ln. (96002) Attractive modern rooms. A/C; C/CATV; movies; phones. Pool. No pets. Wkly rates avail. Reserv deposit required. AE, CB, DI, MC, VI. *(See ad p A348)*

	Rates Guaranteed			*Motel*
1P 34.00	2P/1B 38.00	2P/2B 42.00	XP 5	

⊗ Ⓓ (916) 223-1935

Days Hotel-Redding ◆◆
🌐 6/1-9/6
9/7-5/31
Senior discount. 144 units. Exit I-5 Cypress Ave E, 1/2 mi n. 2180 Hilltop Dr. (96002) A/C; C/CATV; movies; radios; phones. Pool; whirlpool. Airport transp. Pets, $25 deposit required. Wkly & monthly rates avail. AE, DS, DI, MC, VI. ● Restaurant; 6:30 am-10 pm; Sun-9 pm; $6-$19; cocktails. FAX (916) 223-4727

				Motor Inn	
1P 65.00- 79.00	2P/1B 75.00- 89.00	2P/2B 75.00- 89.00	XP 10		F
1P 54.00- 69.00	2P/1B 64.00- 79.00	2P/2B 64.00- 79.00	XP 10		F

⊗ Ⓓ 🔊 (916) 221-8200

Grand Manor Inn ◆◆◆
🌐 All year [CP]
Senior discount. 71 units. Exit I-5 Cypress Ave E; 3/4 mi n on Hilltop Dr. 850 Mistletoe Ln. (96002) Refrigerators; A/C; C/CATV; movies; phones; comb or shower baths. Pool; sauna; whirlpool; exercise rm. No pets. Reserv deposit required. AE, DI, DS, MC, VI. Restaurant adjacent. FAX (916) 222-8106 *(See ad below)*

	Rates Subject to Change			*Motel*
1P 58.00- 78.00	2P/1B 63.00- 83.00	2P/2B 63.00- 88.00	XP 5	

⊗ Ⓢ Ⓓ 🔊 (916) 221-4472

Holiday Inn of Redding ◆◆◆
🌐 All year
163 units. Exit I-5 via SR 44 & 299/Hilltop, 1/4 mi s. 1900 Hilltop Dr. (96002) Check-in 3 pm. A/C; C/CATV; movies; 80 radios; phones. Coin laundry. Htd indoor pool; wading pool; sauna; whirlpool; exercise rm. Airport transp. Pets. Monthly rates avail. AE, DI, DS, MC, VI. ● Restaurant; 6 am-10 pm; $6-$15; cocktails. FAX (916) 222-3008

	Rates Guaranteed			*Motor Inn*	
1P 66.00- 72.00	2P/1B 72.00- 82.00	2P/2B 72.00- 82.00	XP 7		F

Ⓓ (916) 221-7500

Motel Orleans-East ◆◆
🌐 All year
Senior discount. 89 units. Exit I-5 Cypress Ave E; 1/4 mi n. 2059 Hilltop Dr. (96002) A/C; C/CATV; phones. Small pool. No pets. Reserv deposit required; 3 days refund notice. AE, DI, DS, MC, VI.

	Rates Subject to Change			*Motel*
1P 34.00	2P/1B 39.00	2P/2B 41.00	XP 4	

⊗ Ⓓ (916) 221-6530

Red Lion Inn ◆◆◆
🌐 All year
194 units. Exit I-5 via SR 44 & 299 Hilltop Dr. 1830 Hilltop Dr. (96002) Nicely landscaped pool area. Many large units. Balconies & patios. Check-in 3 pm. A/C; C/CATV; movies; radios; phones; comb or shower baths. Htd pool; wading pool; whirlpool; putting green. Airport transp. Pets. AE, DI, DS, MC, VI. ● Dining rm & coffeeshop; 6 am-11 pm; $6-$15; cocktails; entertainment. FAX (916) 221-0324 *(See ad p A3)*

	Rates Subject to Change			*Motor Inn*	
1P 81.00- 101.00	2P/1B 90.00- 118.00	2P/2B 93.00- 113.00	XP 15		F

⊗ Ⓓ (916) 221-8700

Shasta Dam El Rancho Motel ◆
🌐 All year
14 units. 7 mi n; w of I-5, at Shasta Dam-Central Valley exit; n at Union School Rd, Cascade Blvd. 1529 Cascade Blvd. (PO Box 1033, Project City, 96079) Tree-shaded location. A/C; C/TV; phones; shower baths. 1 2-bedrm unit. Pool. Pets. 6 efficiencies, $6 extra. Reserv deposit required. AE, CB, DS, MC, VI.

	Rates Guaranteed			*Motel*
1P 26.00- 30.00	2P/1B 28.00- 34.00	2P/2B 30.00- 36.00	XP 4	

⊗ Ⓓ (916) 275-1065

Super 8 Motel ◆
🌐 All year
Senior discount. 80 units. Exit I-5; Churn Creek Rd E. 5175 Churn Creek Rd. (96002) Some small rooms. A/C; C/CATV; movies; 50 radios; phones. Pool; sauna; indoor whirlpool. No pets. AE, DI, DS, MC, VI. FAX (916) 221-8881

	Rates Guaranteed			*Motel*
1P 41.88	2P/1B 45.88	2P/2B 48.88	XP 4	

⊗ Ⓢ Ⓓ 🔊 (916) 221-8881

Vagabond Inn ◆◆
🌐 All year [CP]
71 units. W off I-5 via Cypress Ave. 536 E Cypress Ave. (96002) A/C; C/CATV; movies; radios; phones. Pool. Pets, $5 extra charge. AE, DI, DS, MC, VI. Coffeeshop adjacent. FAX (916) 221-4247 *(See ad below)*

	Rates Subject to Change			*Motel*	
1P 47.00- 65.00	2P/1B 52.00- 70.00	2P/2B 57.00- 75.00	XP 5		F

⊗ Ⓓ (916) 223-1600

RESTAURANTS

C. R. Gibbs Restaurant   American $$ ◆◆
In Best Western Hilltop Inn. Varied menu; featuring peeled shrimp appetizers. A/C. Children's menu. Open 5:30 pm-10 pm; Sun-9 pm; closed 11/25 & 12/25. Cocktails & lounge. AE, CB, DI, MC, VI.

⊗ (916) 221-2335

Hatch Cover   Seafood $$ ◆◆
Exit I-5 Cypress Ave W; 1/2 mi n on Hemsted Dr. 202 Hemsted Dr. Casual atmosphere, beef & chicken specialties, excellent view of Sacramento River. A/C. Open 11:30 am-2 & 5:30-9:30 pm; Fri-10 pm; Sat 5:30 pm-10 pm; Sun 5 pm-9:30 pm, 6/1-9/1 to 10 pm; closed 1/1, 11/26, 12/24 & 12/25. Cocktails & lounge. Minimum, $4. AE, MC, VI.

⊗ (916) 223-5606

Marie Callender's   American $ ◆◆
    Exit I-5 Hilltop Dr, 1/2 mi s. 1987 Hilltop Dr. Casual atmosphere, home baked pies. A/C. Children's menu. Open 7 am-11 pm; Fri-Sun to 11:30 pm; closed 11/25 & 12/25. Beer & wine. Reserv advised. AE, DI, MC, VI.
                                                        ⊗ (916) 223-4310

Nello's Place   Italian $$ ◆◆
    W off I-5, northbound exit Bechelli Ln, n 2 mi, southbound exit Cypress Ave, 1/4 mi w, s on Bechelli 1 mi. 3055 Bechelli Ln. A/C. Early bird specials; children's menu. Open 5 pm-10 pm; closed Mon, 1/1, 11/25 & 12/25. Cocktails & lounge. Reserv advised. AE, MC, VI.
                                                        ⊗ (916) 223-1636

REDLANDS — 60,400

Best Western Sandman Motel   Rates Subject to Change   *Motel*   ◆◆
    All year [CP]   1P 38.00- 48.00   2P/1B   43.00- 53.00   2P/2B   48.00- 58.00 XP 6   F
Senior discount. 66 units. Adjacent to I-10, exit Tennessee St. 1120 W Colton Ave. (92374) A/C; C/CATV; movies; phones. 7 efficiencies. Htd pool; whirlpool. No pets. Wkly rates avail. AE, DI, DS, MC, VI. Coffeeshop adjacent. FAX (909) 792-7612 *(See ad p A371)*   ⊗ Ⓓ (909) 793-2001

Redlands Inn   Rates Subject to Change   *Motel*   ◆◆
    All year   1P .... 28.00   2P/1B   .... 28.00   2P/2B   .... 32.00 XP 4   F
55 units. 1/2 blk sw of I-10, exit Tennessee St. 1235 W Colton Ave. (92373) 20 refrigerators; A/C; C/CATV; movies; phones. Pool. No pets. Wkly rates avail. AE, DI, DS, MC, VI. FAX (909) 798-0880   ⊗ Ⓓ (909) 793-6648

Redlands Motor Lodge   Rates Subject to Change   *Motel*   ◆◆
    All year   1P .... 32.95   2P/1B   .... 36.95   2P/2B   .... 39.95 XP 4
30 units. 1/2 blk n of I-10, exit Alabama St. 1151 Arizona St. (92374) A/C; C/CATV; movies; radios; phones; comb or shower baths. No pets. 5 rooms with whirlpool tub, $65. AE, DS, MC, VI. Restaurant adjacent.
                                           ⊗ Ⓢ Ⓓ (909) 798-2432

Stardust Motel   Rates Subject to Change   *Motel*   ◆
    All year   1P .... 28.95   2P/1B   .... 32.95   2P/2B   .... 38.95 XP 2
Senior discount. 20 units. N of I-10; westbound exit 6th St, eastbound exit Orange St; 1 blk to Colton Ave. 200 The Terrace. (92374) A/C; C/CATV; movies; radios; phones; shower or comb baths. 2 2-bedrm units. Pool. No pets. Reserv deposit required. AE, CB, DI, MC, VI.   ⊗ Ⓓ (909) 793-2571

RESTAURANTS

Furr's Family Dining   American $ ◆
    Adjacent to I-10, exit Tennessee Ave. 1330 Industrial Park. Large selection of salads, entrees & desserts. A/C. Open 11 am-8 pm; closed 12/25. MC, VI.   ⊗ (909) 792-3024

Griswold's Smorgasbord   American $ ◆
    2 mi e, adjacent to I-10, exit Ford St. 1025 Parkford Dr. Attractive Scandinavian decor. Sun brunch 7 am-1 pm. A/C. Children's menu. Open 7-11 am, 11:30-4 & 5-8 pm; Fri-8:30 pm; Sat 7 am-8:30 pm; Sun 7 am-8 pm. Beer & wine. AE, DI, MC, VI.   ⊗ (909) 793-2158

Joe Greensleeves   American $$$ ◆◆◆
    Downtown, 1/2 blk n of Redlands Blvd. 222 N Orange. Interesting selection of well-prepared contemporary cuisine. A/C. Open 5:30 pm-9:30 pm; closed Sun, Mon, 1/1, 11/25 & 12/25. Beer & wine. Reserv advised. AE, MC, VI. (909) 792-6969

Reuben's   Steak & Seafood $$ ◆
    2 mi e, adjacent to I-10, exit Ford St. 1045 Parkford Dr. Attractive restaurant. Nice selection of steaks, prime rib & seafood. A/C. Early bird specials. Open 11:30 am-2:30 & 5-9 pm; Fri-10 pm; Sat 5 pm-10 pm; Sun 10 am-2 & 5-9 pm; closed 12/25. Cocktails & lounge. AE, DI, DS, MC, VI.   ⊗ (909) 793-2221

Vesuvio   Italian $$ ◆◆
    Downtown, in Centennial Plaza. 101 E Redlands Blvd. Very attractive restaurant featuring pasta, veal, seafood & poultry. A/C. Open 11 am-3 & 5-10 pm; Sat from 5 pm; Sun 10 am-2 & 5-10 pm; closed major holidays. Cocktails & lounge. Entertainment & dancing. Reserv advised. AE, CB, DS, MC, VI.   ⊗ (909) 792-9399

REDONDO BEACH — 60,200

Best Western Galleria Inn   AAA Special Value Rates   *Motel*   ◆◆◆
    All year [CP]   1P 56.00- 66.00   2P/1B   59.00- 69.00   2P/2B   59.00- 69.00 XP 6
38 units. 1 mi w of I-405. 2740 Artesia Blvd. (90278) Refrigerators; A/C; C/CATV; movies; radios; phones. Coin laundry. Sauna; whirlpool. No pets. 6 rooms with whirlpool tub, $90-$120. Reserv deposit required; 7 days refund notice. AE, DI, DC, MC, VI. FAX (310) 793 7136 *(See ad p A316)*   ⊗ Ⓓ ① (310) 370-4353

Best Western Redondo Beach Inn — AAA Special Value Rates — *Motor Inn* ◆◆◆

6/1-8/31	1P	74.00-	90.00	2P/1B	74.00-	90.00	2P/2B	74.00- 90.00	XP 5	F
9/1-5/31	1P	70.00-	86.00	2P/1B	70.00-	86.00	2P/2B	70.00- 86.00	XP 5	F

101 units. 1 3/4 mi se on SR 1. 1850 S Pacific Coast Hwy. (90277) 42 refrigerators; A/C; C/TV; movies; radios; phones. Small htd pool; sauna; indoor whirlpool; exercise rm. No pets. 1 suite with whirlpool, $160. Reserv deposit required. AE, DI, DS, MC, VI. ● Coffeeshop; 6 am-1 pm; $5.95-$8.95. FAX (310) 540-3675 *(See ad p A533)*
Ⓓ 🔁 (310) 540-3700

Best Western Sunrise-Redondo Beach — AAA Special Value Rates — *Motor Inn* ◆◆◆

6/1-8/31	1P	75.00-	85.00	2P/1B	80.00-	90.00	2P/2B	85.00- 90.00	XP 10	F
9/1-5/31	1P	65.00-	75.00	2P/1B	70.00-	80.00	2P/2B	75.00- 85.00	XP 5	F

111 units. 1/2 mi w of SR 1 (Pacific Coast Hwy). 400 N Harbor Dr. (90277) Some rooms with ocean view. Check-in 3 pm. Refrigerators; A/C; C/CATV; pay movies; radios; phones. Htd pool; whirlpool. Airport transp. No pets. Wkly & monthly rates avail. AE, DI, DS, MC, VI. ● Dining rm; 6 am-10 pm; $7-$12; cocktails. FAX (310) 376-7384 *(See ad p A350)*
⊗ Ⓓ 🔁 (310) 376-0746

Holiday Inn Crowne Plaza — Rates Subject to Change — *Hotel* ◆◆◆◆

All year	1P	....	95.00	2P/1B	.... 95.00	2P/2B	.... 95.00	XP 20	F

339 units. 1/2 mi w of SR 1 (Pacific Coast Hwy) at King Harbor. 300 N Harbor Dr. (90277) Many rooms with harbor view. Balconies. Check-in 3 pm. A/C; C/CATV; pay movies; radios; phones. Coin laundry. Htd pool; saunas; whirlpool; lighted tennis-1 court; rental bicycles; exercise rm. Fee for: massage. Parking ramp & pay garage. No pets. AE, DI, DS, MC, VI. ● Restaurant; 6 am-10 pm; $9-$13; cocktails; entertainment. FAX (310) 376-1930
⊗ Ⓢ Ⓓ 🔁 (310) 318-8888

Palos Verdes Inn — AAA Special Value Rates — *Hotel* ◆◆◆

All year	1P	90.00-	110.00	2P/1B	100.00-120.00	2P/2B	100.00-120.00	XP 10	F

110 units. 1 1/2 mi se on SR 1. 1700 S Pacific Coast Hwy. (90277) Many rooms with balconies. Check-in 3 pm. 13 refrigerators; A/C; C/TV; pay movies; radios; phones. Htd pool; whirlpool. Parking lot. No pets. Wkly & monthly rates avail. Reserv deposit required. AE, CB, DI, MC, VI. ● Dining rm & restaurant; 7 am-midnight; $9-$18.50; cocktails; entertainment. Also, Chez Melange, see separate listing. FAX (310) 316-4863 *(See ad p A350)*
⊗ Ⓓ (310) 316-4211

Portofino Hotel & Yacht Club — Rates Subject to Change — *Motor Inn* ◆◆◆

All year	1P	129.00-	159.00	2P/1B	129.00-159.00	2P/2B	129.00-159.00	XP 10	F

165 units. At the marina at King Harbor, 3/4 mi w of SR 1 (Pacific Coast Hwy); 1/4 mi w of Harbor Dr. 260 Portofino Way. (90277) Patio or balconies. Most rooms have a harbor or ocean view. A/C; C/CATV; pay movies; radios; phones. Coin laundry. Small htd pool; whirlpool; bicycles; exercise rm. Pets. 8 rooms with oversize whirlpool tub, $159-$245. Monthly rates avail. AE, DI, DS, MC, VI. ● Dining rm, restaurant & coffeeshop; 6 am-10 pm; $15-$25; cocktails; entertainment. FAX (310) 372-7329 *(See ad below)*
⊗ Ⓢ Ⓓ 🔁 (310) 379-8481

Travelodge-Redondo Beach Pier — AAA Special Value Rates — *Motel* ◆◆

6/1-9/15 [CP]	1P	....	61.00	2P/1B	.... 67.00	2P/2B	.... 71.00	XP 6	F
9/16-5/31 [CP]	1P	....	56.00	2P/1B	.... 62.00	2P/2B	.... 66.00	XP 6	F

37 units. 1/2 blk n of Torrance Blvd. 206 S Pacific Coast Hwy. (90277) Refrigerators; A/C; C/TV; movies; radios; phones. Small htd pool; whirlpool. No pets. Wkly rates avail. AE, DI, DS, MC, VI. FAX (310) 379-0190 *(See ad below)*
⊗ Ⓢ Ⓓ 🔁 (310) 318-1811

RESTAURANTS

The Blue Moon Saloon — Seafood — $$$ ◆◆
On the waterfront in Redondo Beach Marina. 207 N Harbor Dr. Casual atmosphere & harbor view. Seafood, steaks, chicken, pasta & salads. Live band & dancing Fri 9 pm-1:30 am. Early bird specials. Open 11 am-2 & 5-10 pm; Sat 10 am-11 pm; Sun 10 am-10 pm; closed 11/25 & 12/24. Cocktails & lounge. Entertainment. Reserv advised weekends. AE, MC, VI.
⊗ (310) 374-3411

Catalina Grill — American — $$ ◆◆
1814 S Catalina Ave. Sandwiches, chicken, steaks & fish grilled over open fire of mesquite & apple wood. Also salads, pastas & some Mexican cuisine. Casual atmosphere. A/C. Open 11:30 am-4:30 & 5-10 pm; Sun 9:30 am-2:30 & 5-10 pm. Cocktails. AE, DI, DS, MC, VI.
⊗ (310) 316-7716

Chez Melange — Continental — $$ ◆◆◆
In Palos Verdes Inn. Selection of chicken, steak, duck, lamb, salads & pastas prepared in the southwestern, Italian, or oriental flair. Oyster, caviar & champagne bar. A/C. Open 7 am-midnight. Cocktails & lounge. Reserv advised. AE, MC, VI.
⊗ (310) 540-1222

Le Beaujolais — French — $$$ ◆
1/4 blk n of Francica Ave. 522 S Pacific Coast Hwy. Fresh seafood, chicken, duck, quiche, pasta & salads. Sat & Sun brunch, 10 am-3 pm. Open 11:30 am-3 & 5:30-10 pm. Cocktails. Reserv advised. AE, DI, MC, VI. ⊗ (310) 543-5100

Marie Callender's — American — $ ◆
1/2 mi w of I-405. 2979 Artesia Blvd. Casual atmosphere. Selection of entrees, salads, sandwiches & homemade pies. A/C. Children's menu. Open 8 am-10 pm; Fri & Sat 11 pm. Beer & wine. AE, DS, MC, VI. ⊗ (310) 371-5500

Millie Riera's Seafood Grotto   Seafood $$ ◆◆
   1700 Esplanade at Ave I. Overlooks ocean. Nice selection of seafood. A/C. Open 11:30 am-9:30 pm; Fri-11 pm; Sat 4 pm-11 pm; Sun 3 pm-10 pm; closed major holidays & 12/24. Cocktails & lounge. Pay valet parking. Reserv advised. AE, MC, VI.   (310) 375-0531

Reuben's   Steak & Seafood $$$ ◆◆
   At the marina at King Harbor, 1/2 mi w of SR 1 (Pacific Coast Hwy). 230 Portofino Way. Harbor view with casual atmosphere. Features fresh seafood, chicken & steaks. Sun brunch 10 am-2 pm. A/C. Early bird specials; children's menu. Open 11:30 am-10 pm; Fri & Sat-11 pm; Sun 10 am-2 & 4-10 pm. Cocktails & lounge. Entertainment & dancing. Reserv advised. AE, DI, DS, MC, VI.   ⊗ (310) 379-8363

REDWOOD CITY — 66,100   (See SAN FRANCISCO (Southern Region) AREA spotting map page A444 ; see index starting on page A443)

Best Western Executive Suites 160   Rates Subject to Change   *Motel*   ◆◆◆
⊕ All year [CP]   1P 65.00- 95.00 2P/1B 75.00- 105.00 2P/2B 85.00- 105.00 XP 10
   Senior discount. 28 units. Exit US 101 at SR 84W 1/2 mi, 1 mi s on SR 82, then 1/4 blk e on 5th Ave. 25 5th Ave. (94063) Attractive comfortable rooms. A/C; C/CATV; movies; VCPs. Radios; phones. 1 efficiency. Coin laundry. Sauna; whirlpool; rooms with whirlpool tub; steamroom; exercise rm. No pets. All rooms with microwave & refrigerator. Reserv deposit required; 7 days refund notice. AE, DI, DS, MC, VI. FAX (415) 365-1429   ⊗ Ⓢ Ⓓ (415) 366-5794

Best Western Sundial Motel 162   Rates Subject to Change   *Motel*   ◆◆
⊕ 6/1-8/31   1P 52.00- 60.00 2P/1B 56.00- 64.00 2P/2B 58.00- 66.00 XP 5   F
   Senior discount. 26 units. 3/4 mi s on SR 82. 316 El Camino Real. (94062) OPEN ALL YEAR. A/C; C/CATV; movies; radios; phones; shower or comb baths. Small pool. No pets. Some rooms with microwave & refrigerator. Reserv deposit required. AE, DI, DS, MC, VI. Coffeeshop adjacent. FAX (415) 364-9380   ⊗ Ⓓ (415) 366-3808

Comfort Inn 165   Rates Subject to Change   *Motel*   ◆◆
⊕ All year   1P 55.00- 65.00 2P/1B 55.00- 65.00 2P/2B 70.00- 85.00 XP 5
   Senior discount. 52 units. Exit US 101 Whipple Ave, 1/2 mi w, the 1 mi s on El Camino Real. 1818 El Camino Real. (94063) Refrigerators; A/C; C/CATV; movies; VCPs. Phones. 10 kitchens. Pool; sauna; whirlpool. No pets. 11 suites with whirlpool, $90 for 2 persons. All rooms with microwave & VCP. Reserv deposit required; 3 days refund notice. AE, CB, DI, MC, VI. FAX (415) 369-6481 *(See ad below)*   ⊗ Ⓓ (415) 599-9636

Continental Garden Motel 164   Rates Guaranteed   *Motel*   ◆
⊕ All year [CP]   1P 42.00- 48.00 2P/1B 44.00- 50.00 2P/2B 46.00- 58.00 XP 4   F
   Senior discount. 70 units. 1 mi s on SR 82; 1/4 mi s of jct SR 84. 2650 El Camino Real. (94061) Well back from highway on attractively landscaped grounds. Some balconies. 35 refrigerators; A/C; C/CATV; movies; 62 radios; phones; shower or comb baths. Coin laundry. Pool; whirlpool. No pets. 5 kitchen apartments, $48-$60 for 2 persons. Wkly rates avail. Reserv deposit required. AE, DI, DS, MC, VI. *(See ad below)*   ⊗ Ⓓ (415) 369-0321

(See SAN FRANCISCO (Southern Region) spotting map page A444)

Hotel Sofitel San Francisco Bay 163   Rates Subject to Change   Hotel   ◆◆◆◆
Sun-Thurs	1P 135.00- 250.00	2P/1B	150.00- 250.00	2P/2B	150.00- 250.00	XP 20
Fri & Sat	1P 95.00	2P/1B	.... 95.00	2P/2B	.... 95.00	XP 20

319 units. Exit US 101 at Marine World Pkwy E, 1/2 mi s on Twin Dolphin Dr. 223 Twin Dolphin Dr. (94065) Some rooms overlooking tidal waters & San Francisco Bay. Check-in 3 pm. Refrigerators; A/C; C/CATV; movies; radios; phones. Pool; sauna; exercise rm; jogging track. Fee for: massage. Parking ramp. Airport transp. No pets. Reserv deposit required. AE, CB, DI, MC, VI. ● Dining rm & restaurant; 6 am-10 pm; $9-$23; cocktails. FAX (415) 598-0459
Ⓧ Ⓢ Ⓓ ⓢ (415) 598-9000

Howard Johnson Motor Lodge 161   Rates Subject to Change   Motel   ◆◆
⊕ 7/16-9/4	1P 74.00- 84.00	2P/1B	84.00- 94.00	2P/2B	84.00- 94.00	XP 10	F
2/1-7/15 & 9/5-11/18	1P 69.00- 79.00	2P/1B	79.00- 89.00	2P/2B	79.00- 89.00	XP 10	F
11/19-1/31	1P 59.00- 79.00	2P/1B	59.00- 89.00	2P/2B	59.00- 89.00	XP 10	F

Senior discount. 125 units. W off & adjacent to US 101; exit Whipple Ave. 485 Veterans Blvd. (94063) Balconies & patios. 16 refrigerators; A/C; C/CATV; movies; phones. Coin laundry. Pool; wading pool. Airport transp. Pets. AE, CB, DI, MC, VI. Restaurant adjacent. FAX (415) 365-1119 *(See ad below)*
Ⓧ Ⓓ (415) 365-5500

RESTAURANT

Farmhouse 75   American $ ◆
W of US 101, exit Whipple Rd, s on Convention Way. 386 Convention Way. Casual atmosphere, family oriented. A/C. Children's menu. Open 11:30 am-9 pm; Fri & Sat 10 pm; Sat-11 pm; Sun 12 pm-9 pm; closed 12/25. Cocktails & lounge. Dancing. Reserv advised. AE, CB, DI, MC, VI.
Ⓧ (415) 369-3337

REEDLEY — 14,200

Edgewater Inn   AAA Special Value Rates   Motel   ◆◆◆
⊕ All year [CP]	1P 46.00	2P/1B	.... 52.00	2P/2B	.... 52.00	XP 6	F

47 units. 12 mi e of SR 99 via Manning Hwy. 17777 E Manning Ave. (93654) 1/4 block to Kings River. 5 refrigerators; A/C; C/TV; pay movies; phones. Pool; whirlpool; playground. No pets. [MAP]. Reserv deposit required. AE, DS, MC, VI. FAX (209) 637-7777
Ⓧ Ⓓ ⓢ (209) 637-7777

RESEDA — 79,800   See LOS ANGELES (San Fernando Valley)

RIALTO — 72,400

Best Western Empire Inn   Rates Subject to Change   Motor Inn   ◆◆◆
⊕ 5/1-10/31	1P 50.00- 65.00	2P/1B	57.00- 70.00	2P/2B	57.00- 70.00	XP 7	
11/1-4/30	1P 45.00- 60.00	2P/1B	52.00- 65.00	2P/2B	52.00- 65.00	XP 7	

100 units. 1/2 mi nw of I-10, exit Riverside Ave. 475 W Valley Blvd. (92376) Rating withheld pending completion of construction. Scheduled to open September, 1992. A/C; C/CATV; movies; radios; phones. Coin laundry. Htd pool; sauna; whirlpool; 10 rooms with whirlpool tub; exercise rm. No pets. AE, DI, DS, MC, VI. Restaurant; 6 am-10 pm. FAX (909) 877-0841
Ⓧ Ⓢ Ⓓ (909) 877-0690

Rialto Travelodge   Rates Subject to Change   Motel   ◆◆◆
⊕ All year	1P 38.00	2P/1B	.... 42.00	2P/2B	.... 45.00	XP 4	

Senior discount. 50 units. 3 mi n of I-10; exit Riverside Ave. 425 Foothill Blvd. (92376) Refrigerators; A/C; C/CATV; radios; phones; comb or shower baths. Pool. No pets. Microwaves. 4 rooms with whirlpool spa, $75. Wkly rates avail. AE, MC, VI.
Ⓧ Ⓢ Ⓓ ⓢ (909) 820-0705

RICHMOND — 87,400

Days Hotel-Richmond/Hilltop   Rates Guaranteed   Hotel   ◆◆◆
⊕ All year	1P 60.00- 90.00	2P/1B	70.00- 100.00	2P/2B	70.00- 100.00	XP 10	F

Senior discount. 150 units. Exit I-80 Hilltop Dr N. 3150 Garrity Way. (94806) A/C; C/CATV; movies; radios; phones. Pool; whirlpool; exercise rm. Parking lot. No pets. Wkly & monthly rates avail. AE, CB, DI, MC, VI. ● Restaurant; 6 am-10 pm; $8-$18; cocktails. FAX (510) 262-0927
Ⓧ Ⓢ Ⓓ ⓢ (510) 262-0700

RESTAURANT

Hotel Mac Restaurant   Continental $$ ◆◆
1 blk s of Cutting Blvd; 1 mi w of Richmond-San Rafael Bridge toll booth, in Pt. Richmond. 50 Washington Ave. Nicely restored building. Varied menu. A/C. Open 11:30 am-2:30 & 5:30-10 pm; Sat from 5:30 pm; Sun 4:30 pm-9 pm; closed major holidays & for dinner Mon. Cocktails & lounge. Reserv advised. AE, DI, MC, VI.
Ⓧ (510) 233-0576

RIDGECREST — 27,700

Carriage Inn
⟨AAA⟩ All year
163 units. Corner China Lake Blvd & Drummond Ave. 901 N China Lake Blvd. (93555) Check-in 3 pm. A/C; C/CATV; free & pay movies; radios; phones. Htd pool; sauna; whirlpool; exercise rm. No pets. 80 rooms with microwave & refrigerator, $5 extra. AE, DI, DS, MC, VI. ● Dining rm & coffeeshop; 6 am-10 pm; $3.95-$19.25; cocktails. FAX (619) 446-6408 *(See ad below)*

	AAA Special Value Rates			*Motor Inn*	◆◆◆
1P 54.00- 59.00	2P/1B	54.00- 59.00	2P/2B	54.00- 59.00 XP 10	F

⊗ Ⓓ ⓑ (619) 446-7910

Econo Lodge
⟨AAA⟩ Sun-Thurs
Fri & Sat
54 units. On Inyokern Rd (SR 178) 1 blk w of China Lake Blvd. 201 Inyokern Rd. (93555) Refrigerators; A/C; C/CATV; movies; phones. No pets. Microwaves, $2 extra charge. AE, CB, DI, MC, VI. FAX (619) 446-5740

	Rates Subject to Change			*Motel*	◆◆
1P 44.00	2P/1B	.... 46.00	2P/2B	.... 50.00 XP 2	
1P 35.00	2P/1B	.... 35.00	2P/2B	.... 39.00 XP 2	

⊗ Ⓓ (619) 446-2551

Heritage Inn
⟨AAA⟩ All year [CP]
125 units. 1050 N Norma. (PO Box 640, 93556) 73 refrigerators; A/C; C/CATV; movies; rental VCPs. Radios; phones. 43 efficiencies, utensils, deposit required. Coin laundry. Htd pool; whirlpool; exercise rm. Pets. Wkly rates avail. AE, CB, DI, MC, VI. ● Restaurant; 5 pm-10 pm; closed Sun; $10-$16; beer & wine. FAX (619) 446-2884

	AAA Special Value Rates			*Motor Inn*	◆◆◆
1P 69.00- 87.00	2P/1B	75.00- 93.00	2P/2B	75.00- 93.00 XP 6	F

⊗ Ⓓ (619) 446-6543

Heritage Suites
⟨AAA⟩ All year [CP]
46 units. 1/2 blk e of Norma. 919 N Heritage Dr. (PO Box 640, 93556) Formerly Heritage House. A/C; C/CATV; movies; rental VCPs. Radios; phones. 42 kitchens. Coin laundry. Htd pool; whirlpool; exercise rm. Pets. Rental microwaves. Wkly & monthly rates avail. Reserv deposit required. AE, DI, DS, MC, VI. FAX (619) 446-2884

	AAA Special Value Rates			*Suites Motor Inn*	◆◆◆
1P 89.00-105.00	2P/1B	95.00-111.00	2P/2B	.... 111.00 XP 6	

⊗ Ⓓ (619) 446-7951

RIO VISTA — 3,300

RESTAURANT

The Point Restaurant   American $$ ◆◆
⟨AAA⟩ 1/2 mi s of SR 12, via Main or Front sts; then s on Second St. 120 Marina Dr. On the river. Docking facilities. Glassed in garden room on deck for brunch & lunch. Casual atmosphere, varied menu. A/C. Children's menu. Open 11:30 am-9 pm; Sun from 10 am; closed Mon, 12/25-12/30. Cocktails & lounge. Reserv advised. MC, VI.

⊗ (707) 374-5400

RIVERSIDE — 226,500
Best Western of Riverside   Rates Subject to Change   *Motel*   ◆◆
Ⓐ All year   1P .... 45.00 2P/1B .... 50.00 2P/2B .... 52.00 XP 6   F
Senior discount. 62 units. 7 mi sw on SR 91, exit Tyler Rd, then 2 blks w on Magnolia Ave. 10518 Magnolia Ave.
(92505) Refrigerators; A/C; C/TV; movies; radios; phones. 1 2-bedrm unit, 4 efficiencies, no utensils. Htd pool;
whirlpool. No pets. Reserv deposit required; 7 days refund notice. AE, CB, DS, MC, VI. FAX (909) 359-6749
Ⓧ Ⓓ Ⓢ (909) 359-0770

Days Inn   Rates Subject to Change   *Motel*
All year   1P 45.00- 55.00   2P/1B   45.00- 55.00   ....   XP   F
Senior discount. 66 units. 7 mi sw on SR 91 exit Tyler Rd, then 1 blk s on Magnolia Ave. 10545 Magnolia Ave. (92505) Scheduled to open October, 1992. 33 refrigerators; A/C; C/CATV; movies; radios; phones. Pool. No pets. Microwave avail. Deluxe suites & 6 rooms with whirlpool tub, $60-$70 for 1 or 2 persons. Wkly rates avail. Reserv deposit required. AE, DI, DS, MC, VI. *(See ad p A355)*   Ⓢ Ⓓ 🅑 (909) 358-2808

Days Inn Hotel   Rates Guaranteed   *Motor Inn* ◆◆◆
All year   1P 55.00- 65.00   2P/1B   65.00- 75.00   2P/2B   65.00- 75.00   XP 10   F
Senior discount. 163 units. 1/2 mi w of I-215 & SR 60, exit University Ave. 1510 University Ave. (92507) A/C; C/CATV; movies; radios; phones. Htd pool; whirlpool. No pets. AE, DI, DS, MC, VI. ● Coffeeshop; 6 am-10 pm; $6-$9; cocktails. FAX (909) 787-6783   ⊗ Ⓢ Ⓓ 🅑 (909) 788-8989

Dynasty Suites   Rates Subject to Change   *Motel* ◆◆◆
All year   ....   2P/1B   39.95- 44.95   2P/2B   44.95- 49.95   XP   5   F
Senior discount. 33 units. From SR 60, exit University Ave; 1/2 blk n. 3735 Iowa Ave. (92507) Refrigerators; A/C; C/CATV; movies; VCPs. Radios; phones. Small htd pool. Pets, $10 extra charge. 2 suites with whirlpool spa, $79. Microwaves avail. AE, DI, DS, MC, VI. Restaurant opposite. FAX (909) 369-2807 *(See ad p A354)*   ⊗ Ⓓ 🅑 (909) 369-8200

Econo Lodge   Rates Subject to Change   *Motel* ◆◆
All year [CP]   1P .... 39.90   2P/1B .... 42.90   2P/2B .... 44.90   XP   5   F
Senior discount. 32 units. 6 mi sw on SR 91, exit Van Buren, then 1 mi N. 9878 Magnolia Ave. (92503) Refrigerators; A/C; C/CATV; movies; radios; phones. No pets. AE, DI, DS, MC, VI. FAX (909) 688-6606   ⊗ Ⓓ (909) 687-3090

Garden Inn   Rates Subject to Change   *Motel* ◆◆
All year   1P 35.00- 45.00   2P/1B   35.00- 45.00   2P/2B .... 45.00   XP   5
Senior discount. 30 units. 6 mi sw on SR 91, exit Van Buren, then 3/4 mi n. 9328 Magnolia Ave. (92503) Refrigerators; A/C; C/CATV; movies; radios; phones. 13 rooms with whirlpool tub. No pets. 1 deluxe spa room, $50-$55 for 2 persons. Wkly rates avail. Reserv deposit required. AE, MC, VI.   Ⓓ (909) 689-1300

Hampton Inn   Rates Guaranteed   *Motel* ◆◆◆
All year [CP]   1P .... 49.00   2P/1B .... 54.00   2P/2B .... 54.00   XP   5   F
123 units. 1/2 mi w of I-215 & SR 60, exit University Ave. 1590 University Ave. (92507) Check-in 3 pm. A/C; C/CATV; movies; radios; phones. Htd pool. No pets. Wkly rates avail. AE, DI, DS, MC, VI. FAX (909) 782-8052   ⊗ Ⓗ (909) 683-6000

Holiday Inn   Rates Guaranteed   *Motor Inn* ◆◆◆
All year   1P 64.00- 69.00   2P/1B   68.00- 75.00   2P/2B   68.00- 75.00   XP   4   F
Senior discount. 207 units. 1/2 blk w of I-215 & SR 60; exit University Ave. 1200 University Ave. (92507) A/C; C/CATV; movies; radios; phones. Coin laundry. Htd pool; saunas; whirlpool; exercise rm. Parking ramp. Pets. Monthly rates avail. Reserv deposit required; 3 days refund notice. AE, CB, DI, MC, VI. ● Dining rm; 6:30 am-2 & 5-10 pm; $4.95-$8.75; cocktails; entertainment. FAX (909) 682-7095   Ⓓ (909) 682-8000

Sheraton Riverside   Rates Subject to Change   *Hotel* ◆◆◆
All year   1P   84.00   2P/1B .... 94.00   2P/2B .... 89.00   XP 10   F
Senior discount. 296 units. 1 mi w of SR 91, exit 7th St; 1 mi s of SR 60 exit Market St. 3400 Market St. (92501) A/C; C/CATV; movies; radios; phones. Htd pool; whirlpool. Parking ramp. Airport transp. No pets. Monthly rates avail. AE, CB, DI, MC, VI. ● Dining rm & coffeeshop; 6:30 am-10 pm; $7.25-$19.75; cocktails. FAX (909) 369-7127   ⊗ Ⓢ Ⓓ (909) 784-8000

Super 8 Motel   Rates Subject to Change   *Motor Inn* ◆◆
All year   1P .... 32.88   2P/1B .... 32.88   2P/2B .... 39.88   XP   5   F
Senior discount. 103 units. Adjacent to I-215 & SR 60; exit University Ave. 1199 University Ave. (92507) Formerly Howard Johnson Lodge. A/C; C/CATV; movies; phones. Coin laundry. Htd pool; wading pool. Pets. Wkly & monthly rates avail. AE, DS, MC, VI. ● Restaurant; 6 am-midnight; Fri & Sat 24 hours; $4-$6; cocktails. FAX (909) 369-6645   ⊗ Ⓓ (909) 682-9011

Travelodge-La Sierra   Rates Subject to Change   *Motel* ◆◆◆
All year [CP]   1P .... 39.00   2P/1B   39.00- 69.00   2P/2B   39.00- 69.00   XP   6   F
Senior discount. 42 units. 8 mi sw on SR 91, exit La Sierra, then 1/2 mi n. 11043 Magnolia Ave. (92505) A/C; C/CATV; movies; VCPs. Radios; phones. Coin laundry. Small htd pool; 26 rooms with whirlpool tub. No pets. Wkly rates avail. AE, DI, DS, MC, VI. Restaurant opposite. FAX (909) 785-5655   ⊗ Ⓢ Ⓓ 🅑 (909) 688-5000

RESTAURANTS

Pitruzzelo's Restaurant   Italian $$ ◆◆
Adjacent to I-215; 1 3/4 mi n of jct SR 60 exit Center St Highgrove. 287 W La Cadena Dr. Nice selection of Italian cuisine, mesquite broiled steaks & seafood. Extensive wine list. A/C. Early bird specials. Open 11 am-2 pm; Thurs & Fri 11 am-3 & 5-10 pm; Sat from 5 pm; closed Sun, 11/25 & 12/25. Cocktails & lounge. AE, CB, DI, MC, VI.   ⊗ 🅑 (909) 686-6787

Reuben's   American $$ ◆
2 1/2 mi s; 1/2 mi w of SR 91, Central Ave exit. 3640 Central Ave. Selection of steaks, seafood & chicken. A/C. Early bird specials; children's menu. Open 11:30 am-2:30 & 5-10 pm; Sat from 5 pm; Sun 9:30 am-2 & 4:30-9:30 pm; closed 12/25. Cocktails & lounge. AE, CB, DI, MC, VI.   ⊗ (909) 683-3842

ROCKLIN — 19,000

First Choice Inn   Rates Subject to Change   *Suites Motel* ◆◆
All year [CP]   1P 60.00- 85.00   2P/1B   65.00- 90.00   2P/2B   65.00- 90.00   XP   5   F
Senior discount. 90 units. US 80 e exit Rocklin Rd; westbound exit Rocklin. 4420 Rocklin Rd. (95677) Check-in 3 pm. Refrigerators; A/C; C/TV; movies; radios; phones. Coin laundry. Pool; whirlpool. Pets, $50 deposit required. Microwaves. Wkly & monthly rates avail. AE, DI, DS, MC, VI. Coffeeshop adjacent. FAX (916) 624-5982   ⊗ Ⓢ Ⓓ 🅑 (916) 624-4500

Ramada Inn   Rates Subject to Change   *Motel* ◆◆
All year   1P 50.00- 60.00   2P/1B   55.00- 65.00   2P/2B   55.00- 65.00   XP   5   F
Senior discount. 65 units. Exit I-80 Rocklin Rd, 1/4 mi to Granite Dr then 1/2 mi e. 4515 Granite Dr. (95677) Adjacent to freeway. Refrigerators; A/C; C/CATV; movies; radios; phones. 1 kitchen. Coin laundry. Pool; sauna. No pets. Rooms with whirlpool, $80 for 2 persons. Reserv deposit required; 3 days refund notice. AE, CB, DI, MC, VI. FAX (916) 632-0335 *(See ad p A357)*   ⊗ Ⓓ 🅑 (916) 632-0101

ROHNERT PARK — 36,300
Best Western Inn   AAA Special Value Rates   *Motel*   ◆◆◆
🏨 5/1-9/31   1P 36.00- 48.00 2P/1B   44.00- 54.00 2P/2B   44.00- 54.00 XP   4   F
145 units. W side of US 101; exit w via Rohnert Park Expwy. 6500 Redwood Dr. (94928) OPEN ALL YEAR. A/C;
C/CATV; movies; radios; phones. Pool; whirlpool. No pets. Reserv deposit required; 3 days refund notice. AE,
DI, DS, MC, VI. Coffeeshop adjacent. FAX (707) 584-3848 *(See ad below)*   ⊗ Ⓓ 🔲 (707) 584-7435

Red Lion Hotel   Rates Subject to Change   *Motor Inn*   ◆◆◆◆
All year   1P 101.00- 128.00 2P/1B 110.00- 140.00 2P/2B 110.00- 140.00 XP 15   F
245 units. 3 mi s of Santa Rosa; exit US 101, Golf Course Dr. 1 Red Lion Dr. (94928) California Spanish architecture.
Check-in 3 pm. A/C; C/CATV; pay movies; radios; phones. Htd pool; whirlpool; tennis-2 courts; exercise rm. Pets, $50
deposit required. AE, DI, DS, MC, VI. ● Dining rm & coffeeshop; 6 am-11 pm; a la carte entrees about $6-$21; cocktail lounge; entertainment. FAX (707) 586-9726 *(See ad p A3)*   ⊗ Ⓢ Ⓓ 🔲 (707) 584-5466

ROSAMOND — 2,900
Devonshire Inn Motel   Rates Guaranteed   *Motel*   ◆◆
🏨 All year [CP]   1P .... 49.00 2P/1B   .... 49.00 2P/2B   .... 59.00 XP
Senior discount. 30 units. 1/2 blk e of SR 14, exit Edwards/Rosamond. 2076 Rosamond Blvd. (PO Box
2080, 93560) Refrigerators; A/C; C/CATV; movies; radios; phones. Coin laundry. Small htd pool; whirlpool. Pets.
Reserv deposit required. AE, DI, DS, MC, VI.   ⊗ Ⓓ 🔲 (805) 256-3454

ROSEMEAD — 51,600

Flamingo Inn   **AAA Special Value Rates**   *Motel*   ◆
🏧 All year   1P .... 35.00 2P/1B .... 40.00 2P/2B .... 45.00 XP 5
40 units. 3/4 mi se of I-10; exit Walnut Grove. 8621 E Garvey Ave. (91770) Refrigerators; A/C; C/CATV; movies; radios; phones. Coin laundry. Small pool; 6 rooms with whirlpool tub. No pets. Wkly rates avail. Reserv deposit required. AE, DS, MC, VI.   (D) (&) (818) 571-0171

Holiday Inn Express   **Rates Subject to Change**   *Motel*   ◆◆◆
All year [CP]   1P 59.00- 69.00 2P/1B 59.00- 69.00 2P/2B .... 59.00 XP 5   F
Senior discount. 70 units. Adjacent to SR 60, exit San Gabriel Blvd. 705 N San Gabriel Blvd. (91770) A/C; C/CATV; movies; rental VCPs. Radios; phones. Coin laundry. Htd pool; whirlpool. Airport transp. No pets. 2 deluxe suites, $129 for up to 4 persons. Microwave & refrigerators. Wkly & monthly rates avail. Reserv deposit required. AE, DI, DS, MC, VI. FAX (213) 887-9236   ⊗ (D) (213) 726-2227

Motel VIP   **Rates Subject to Change**   *Motel*   ◆
🏧 All year   1P .... 34.00 2P/1B .... 37.00 2P/2B .... 37.00 XP
32 units. 1 mi s of I-10, exit San Gabriel Blvd. 2619 S San Gabriel Blvd. (91770) Refrigerators; A/C; C/CATV; movies; radios; phones. No pets. MC, VI.   (D) (818) 571-6626

Sheraton Rosemead Hotel   **Rates Subject to Change**   *Hotel*   ◆◆◆
🏧 All year   1P 85.00- 135.00 2P/1B 95.00- 145.00 2P/2B 95.00- 145.00 XP 10
148 units. Adjacent to SR 60, exit San Gabriel Blvd. 888 Montebello Blvd. (91770) Across from Montebello Towne Center. A/C; C/CATV; movies; radios; phones. Htd pool; sauna; whirlpool; exercise rm. Parking lot. No pets. 6 rooms with whirlpool, $215 for 2 persons. AE, CB, DI, MC, VI. ● Dining rm; 6:30 am-10:30 pm; Sun brunch 10 am-2 pm; $7.95-$16.95; cocktails. FAX (213) 721-8028   ⊗ (S)(D)(&) (213) 722-8800

Travelodge-Rosemead East   **AAA Special Value Rates**   *Motel*   ◆◆
🏧 All year   1P .... 42.00 2P/1B .... 46.00 2P/2B .... 48.00 XP 6   F
56 units. 3/4 mi sw of I-10, exit Walnut Grove. 8463 E Garvey Ave. (91770) 35 refrigerators; A/C; C/CATV; movies; radios; phones. Small htd pool; whirlpool. No pets. 3 rooms with whirlpool tub, $60. AE, DI, DS, MC, VI. FAX (818) 572-7416   ⊗ (D) (818) 571-5555

Vagabond Inn   **Rates Subject to Change**   *Motor Inn* ◆◆
🏧 All year [CP]   1P 44.00- 54.00 2P/1B 49.00- 59.00 2P/2B 54.00- 64.00 XP 5   F
99 units. On SR 19, 1 blk n of I-10. 3633 N Rosemead Blvd. (91770) A/C; C/TV; rental VCPs; radios; phones. Pool; whirlpool. Pets, $5 daily extra charge. AE, DI, DS, MC, VI. Coffeeshop; 24 hours; $5.50-$9.50; cocktails. *(See ad below)*   ⊗ (D) (818) 288-6661

ROSEVILLE — 44,700   (See SACRAMENTO AREA spotting map page A360; see index starting on page A359)

Best Western Roseville Inn 🅞   **Rates Subject to Change**   *Motel*   ◆◆
🏧 4/1-9/30 [CP]   1P 48.00- 55.00 2P/1B 52.00- 55.00 2P/2B .... 54.00 XP 4
Senior discount. 130 units. Exit w off I-80 via Douglas, 1 blk n. 220 Harding Blvd. (95678) OPEN ALL YEAR. 28 refrigerators; A/C; C/CATV; movies; 70 radios; phones; comb or shower baths. Pool; saunas; whirlpool; 20 rooms with whirlpool tub. Pets, $5 extra charge. 4 kitchens, $12 extra. AE, DI, DS, MC, VI. Restaurant adjacent. FAX (916) 782-8335 *(See ad p A364)*   ⊗ (D) (916) 782-4434

Heritage Inn 🅐   **Rates Subject to Change**   *Motel*   ◆◆
🏧 All year   1P 49.00- 59.00 2P/1B 52.00- 62.00 2P/2B 52.00- 62.00 XP 5   F
Senior discount. 101 units. Exit w off I-80 via Douglas, 1/2 blk n. 204 Harding Blvd. (95678) Large rooms. 80 refrigerators; A/C; C/CATV; movies; radios; phones. Pool; whirlpool. No pets. 12 rooms with whirlpool bath. Reserv deposit required. AE, DI, DS, MC, VI. Coffeeshop adjacent. *(See ad p A364)*   ⊗ (D) (916) 782-4466

ROWLAND HEIGHTS — 28,300   See also INDUSTRY

Best Western Executive Inn   **AAA Special Value Rates**   *Motel* ◆◆◆
🏧 All year [CP]   1P 62.00- 78.00 2P/1B 64.00- 79.00 2P/2B .... 68.00 XP 4   F
135 units. North side of SR 60, exit Nogales St, then 1/4 mi w. 18880 E Gale Ave. (91748) 22 refrigerators; A/C; C/CATV; movies; radios; phones. Coin laundry. Htd pool; whirlpool. No pets. Wkly rates avail. AE, DI, DS, MC, VI. Restaurant adjacent. FAX (818) 810-3222   ⊗ (S)(D)(&) (818) 810-1818

RUNNING SPRINGS — 500

Cloud 9 Lodge   **Rates Subject to Change**   *Cottages* ◆
🏧 All year   ....   2P/1B 45.00- 70.00 2P/2B   80.00 XP
8 units. 1/4 mi e of jct SR 18 & 330; 1 blk n of SR 18. 2642 Dade Dr. (PO Box 54, 92382) Nicely landscaped, tree-shaded grounds, 7 kitchen cottages with 1-to 2-bedrooms & living room. Fireplaces. Also 1 motel room. C/CATV; phones. Sauna. No pets. Wkly rates avail. Reserv deposit required; 5 days refund notice. AE, DI, DS, MC, VI.   (D) (909) 867-2400

RESTAURANT

The Lodge   American $$ ◆◆
6 mi ne off SR 18 at Green Valley Lake. 33655 Green Valley Lake Rd. Open 5 pm-8:30 pm; Fri 5:30 pm-9 pm; Sat 7 am-10; noon-2 & 5:30-9 pm; Sun 9 am-2 & 5:30-8 pm; closed Mon, Tues, 1/1 & 12/25. Cocktails. Reserv required Fri & Sat nights. MC, VI.   ⊗ (909) 867-4281

RUTHERFORD

Auberge Du Soleil   Rates Subject to Change   *Country Inn* ◆◆◆
All year   1P 295.00- 740.00   2P/1B 295.00- 740.00   2P/2B 295.00- 740.00 XP
48 units. 1/4 mi n of jct 128 & Silverado Tr. 180 Rutherford Hill Rd. (94573) 33 acres overlooking Napa Valley. Peaceful
setting. All rooms with woodburning fireplaces. Refrigerators; A/C; C/TV; movies; VCPs. Radios; phones. Sauna; indoor
olympic size lap pool; tennis-3 courts; steambaths. Fee for: steamroom; massage. No pets. 12 rooms with whirlpool bath.
AE, CB, DI, MC, VI. ● Dining rm & coffeeshop; 7 am-10:30, 11-2:30 & 6-9:30 pm; $22-$47; Reservations required;
cocktails; cocktail lounge. FAX (707) 963-8764   Ⓓ (707) 963-1211

SACRAMENTO — 369,400   (See SACRAMENTO AREA spotting map page A360; see index starting below)   See also RANCHO CORDOVA

Airport Accommodations-See listing for:

🏨 Host International Hotel, at airport entrance

Index of Establishments on the SACRAMENTO AREA Spotting Map

Best Western Harbor Inn & Suites ❶   **AAA Special Value Rates**   *Motel*   ◆◆◆
🏨 Mon-Thurs 5/1-1/31   1P 58.00- 78.00 2P/1B 63.00- 83.00 2P/2B 63.00- 83.00 XP 5   F
   Mon-Thurs 2/1-4/30   1P 55.00- 75.00 2P/1B 60.00- 80.00 2P/2B 60.00- 80.00 XP 5   F
   Fri-Sun   1P 51.00- 71.00 2P/1B 56.00- 76.00 2P/2B 56.00- 76.00 XP 5   F
138 units. 4 mi w; exit Business Loop 80 via Harbor Blvd. 1250 Halyard Dr. (West Sacramento, 95691) A/C;
C/CATV; movies; radios; phones. Pool; whirlpools; 12 steambaths. Airport transp. 15 suites $72, $77 for 2 per-
sons; $65, $70 for 2 persons weekends. AE, DI, DS, MC, VI. Coffeeshop opposite. FAX (916) 373-1507 *(See ad
below)*   ⊗ Ⓓ (916) 371-2100

Best Western Ponderosa Motor Inn ❸   Rates Subject to Change   *Motel*   ◆◆◆
🏨 All year [CP]   1P 64.00- 82.00 2P/1B 69.00- 87.00 2P/2B 77.00- 92.00 XP 8   F
Senior discount. 98 units. Downtown, 3 blks from capitol, between 11th & 12th sts. 1100 H St. (95814) A/C; C/TV;
movies; radios; phones. Pool. Limited garage. No pets. Reserv deposit required. AE, CB, DI, MC, VI. Restaurant
adjacent. FAX (916) 441-5961 *(See ad p A361)*   ⊗ Ⓢ Ⓓ Ⓑ (916) 441-1314

 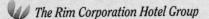

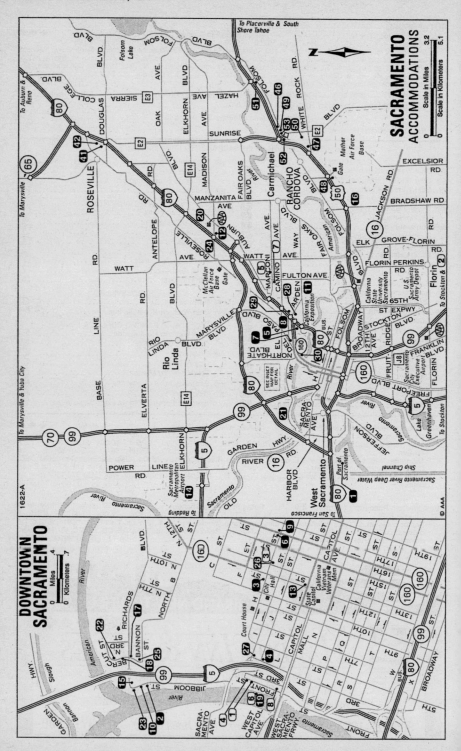

(See SACRAMENTO spotting map page A360)

Best Western Sandman Motel ❷   AAA Special Value Rates   *Motel* ◆◆◆

			1P		2P/1B			2P/2B			XP		
5/1-9/31			1P	44.00- 54.00	2P/1B	48.00- 60.00		2P/2B	52.00- 62.00		XP	4	F
10/1-4/31			1P	41.00- 50.00	2P/1B	45.00- 56.00		2P/2B	48.00- 58.00		XP	4	F

115 units. 2 1/4 mi nw of Business Loop 80, off I-5 exit Richards Blvd. 236 Jibboom St. (95814) A/C; C/TV; movies; radios; phones. Coin laundry. Pool; whirlpool. Airport transp. No pets. Reserv deposit required; 3 days refund notice. AE, DI, DS, MC, VI. Coffeeshop adjacent. FAX (916) 443-8346 *(See ad below)* ⊗ ⒟ (916) 443-6515

Beverly Garland Hotel ❺   Rates Subject to Change   *Motor Inn* ◆◆◆

		1P		2P/1B		2P/2B		XP		
Mon-Thurs 2/1-11/19 & 12/31-1/31		1P	80.00- 85.00	2P/1B	90.00- 95.00	2P/2B	.... 95.00	XP	10	F
Fri-Sun 2/1-11/19 & 12/31-1/31		1P	.... 55.00	2P/1B	.... 55.00	2P/2B	.... 65.00	XP	10	F
12/18-12/30		1P	.... 55.00	2P/1B	.... 55.00	2P/2B	.... 65.00	XP	10	F
11/20-12/17		1P	.... 60.00	2P/1B	.... 60.00	2P/2B	.... 60.00	XP	10	F

206 units. W off Business Loop 80 via Exposition Blvd. 1780 Tribute Rd. (95815) Check-in 3 pm. A/C; C/CATV; pay movies; radios; phones. Coin laundry. Pool; whirlpool. Airport transp. Pets, $25 deposit required. AE, DI, DS, MC, VI. ● Restaurant & coffeeshop; 6 am-9 pm; Sat & Sun 6 am-1 & 5-9 pm; a la carte entrees about $8-$14; cocktails. FAX (916) 921-9147 ⊗ ⒟ ⬓ (916) 929-7900

Canterbury Inn ❼   Rates Guaranteed   *Motor Inn* ◆◆

		1P		2P/1B		2P/2B		XP		
All year [CP]		1P	.... 55.00	2P/1B	.... 65.00	2P/2B	.... 65.00	XP	10	F

Senior discount. 151 units. 3 mi e of Capitol via SR 160, 16th St extension. 1900 Canterbury Rd. (95815) Check-in 4 pm. A/C; C/CATV; movies; radios; phones. Pool; whirlpool. Airport transp. Pets, $100 deposit required. Reserv deposit required. AE, DI, DS, MC, VI. ● Restaurant; 11 am-2 & 4-10 pm, Fri & Sat-11 pm; closed Sun; $10-$16; cocktails. FAX (916) 641-8594 *(See ad p A362)* ⊗ ⒟ (916) 927-3492

Clarion Hotel ❻   Rates Guaranteed   *Hotel* ◆◆◆

		1P		2P/1B		2P/2B		XP		
All year		1P	89.00- 99.00	2P/1B	99.00- 109.00	2P/2B	99.00- 109.00	XP	15	F

Senior discount. 239 units. On SR 160; 1 1/4 mi n of Business Loop 80, 16th St exit. 700 16th St. (95814) A/C; C/TV; pay movies; VCPs. Radios; phones; comb or shower baths. Pool. Parking lot. No pets. Luxury level rooms avail. Reserv deposit required. AE, DI, DS, MC, VI. ● Restaurant; 6:30 am-2:30 & 5-10 pm; $11-$19; cocktails. FAX (916) 442-8129 *(See ad p A362)* ⊗ ⒟ (916) 444-8000

Courtyard by Marriott-Natomas ㉑   Rates Subject to Change   *Motor Inn* ◆◆◆

		1P		2P/1B		2P/2B		XP		
Sun-Thurs		1P	.... 78.00	2P/1B	.... 88.00	2P/2B	.... 88.00	XP	10	F
Fri & Sat		1P	.... 62.00	2P/1B	.... 62.00	2P/2B	.... 62.00	XP		

Senior discount. 151 units. I-5 exit W Garden Hwy; 1st stop light, Gateway Oak Dr, 1 blk n. 2101 River Plaza Dr. (95833) Check-in 3 pm. A/C; C/CATV; free & pay movies; radios; phones. Coin laundry. Pool; whirlpool; exercise rm. Airport transp. No pets. Wkly rates avail. AE, DI, DS, MC, VI. ● Restaurant; 6:30 am-2 & 5-10 pm; $9-$15; cocktails. FAX (916) 922-1872 *(See ad p A363)* ⊗ ⒮ ⒟ ⬓ (916) 922-1120

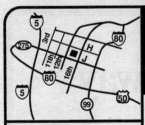

(See SACRAMENTO spotting map page A360)

Crossroads Inn 🔟   Rates Subject to Change   *Motel*   ◆
🏶 All year   1P 38.00- 60.00   2P/1B   41.00- 60.00   2P/2B   47.00- 55.00   XP   3
28 units. 2 1/4 mi nw of business loop 80; I-5 exit Richards Blvd. 221 Jibboom St. (95814) Refrigerators; A/C;
C/CATV; movies; radios; phones. Small pets, $20 deposit. Reserv deposit required. AE, DI, DS, MC, VI.
                                                                        ⊗ ⑪ (916) 442-7777

(See SACRAMENTO spotting map page A360)

Days Inn 23   Rates Guaranteed   *Motor Inn*   ◆
⊛ All year   1P 52.00- 58.00 2P/1B 55.00- 68.00 2P/2B 55.00- 68.00 XP 10   F
Senior discount. 173 units. 2 1/4 mi nw of Business Loop 80; off I-5 exit Richards Blvd W. 200 Jibboom St.
(95814) A/C; C/CATV; free & pay movies; phones. Pool. Airport transp. Pets, $10 daily extra charge. Wkly &
monthly rates avail. Reserv deposit required. AE, DI, DS, MC, VI. ● Coffeeshop; 5 am-11 pm; $6-$10.
FAX (916) 447-3621 *(See ad below)*   ⊗ Ⓓ Ⓢ (916) 448-8100

(See SACRAMENTO spotting map page A360)

Delta King River Boat Hotel 🔟   AAA Special Value Rates   *Historical*   ◆◆
Fri & Sat [CP]   1P .... 125.00   2P/1B .... 135.00 ....   XP 10
Sun-Thurs [CP]   1P .... 85.00   2P/1B .... 95.00 ....   XP 10
44 units. I-5 exit J St (Old Sacramento). 1000 Front St. (95814) A 1927 restored sternwheeler riverboat permanently docked on Sacramento River waterfront. On national register of historic places. Check-in 3 pm. A/C; C/CATV; movies; radios; phones; shower or comb baths. Pay parking ramp. Airport transp. No pets. Reserv deposit required. AE, DI, MC, VI. ● entertainment. Pilothouse Restaurant, see separate listing. FAX (916) 444-5314   (S)(D) (916) 444-5464

Discovery Inn 🔞   AAA Special Value Rates   *Motel*   ◆◆◆
Ⓐ All year [CP]   1P 60.00- 70.00   2P/1B   65.00- 75.00   2P/2B   65.00- 75.00 XP 5   F
100 units. 2 1/4 mi nw of Business Loop 80; off I-5 exit, E Richards Blvd. 350 Bercut Dr. (95814) Check-in 3 pm. 14 refrigerators; A/C; C/TV; movies; radios; phones. Pool; whirlpool. Airport transp. AE, DI, MC, VI. Restaurant & coffeeshop adjacent. FAX (916) 444-2809 *(See ad below)*   ⊗ (S)(D) (916) 442-6971

Fountain Suites Hotel 🔢   Rates Subject to Change   *Motor Inn*   ◆◆◆
Ⓐ All year [CP]   1P 86.00- 106.00   2P/1B   101.00- 121.00   2P/2B .... 101.00 XP 15   F
Senior discount. 305 units. 2 1/4 mi nw of Business Loop 80; off I-5, exit Richards Blvd. 321 Bercut Dr. (95814) Attractive landscaped grounds. Check-in 3 pm. A/C; C/TV; pay movies; radios; phones. Coin laundry. Pool; whirlpool. Airport transp. No pets. AE, DI, DS, MC, VI. Coffeeshop adjacent. Cocktails. FAX (916) 441-6530 *(See ad p A365)*   ⊗ (S)(D) (916) 441-1444

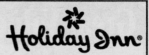

(See SACRAMENTO spotting map page A360)

Governors Inn 🏛 **17**
Rates Subject to Change   *Motel* ◆◆◆
🏩 All year [CP]   1P .... 60.00 2P/1B .... 60.00 2P/2B .... 65.00 XP
133 units. 2 1/4 mi nw of Business Loop 80; I-5 exit E Richards Blvd. 210 Richards Blvd. (95814) A/C; C/CATV;
free & pay movies; phones; shower or comb baths. Pool; whirlpool; exercise rm. Airport transp. No pets. Refrigerator avail, extra charge. AE, DI, DS, MC, VI. Coffeeshop opposite. FAX (916) 448-7382 *(See ad below)*
⊗ Ⓢ Ⓓ (916) 448-7224

Holiday Inn Capitol Plaza **4**
AAA Special Value Rates   *Hotel* ◆◆◆
All year   1P 72.00- 84.00 2P/1B 76.00- 90.00 2P/2B 76.00- 90.00 XP 8   F
368 units. I-5 exit J st. 300 J St. (95814) Check-in 3 pm. A/C; C/CATV; movies; radios; phones. Pool; saunas. Garage.
Pets. AE, DI, DS, MC, VI. ● Dining rm & coffeeshop; 6 am-11 pm; Sun-10 pm; $9-$28; cocktails. FAX (916) 446-0100
⊗ Ⓢ Ⓓ Ⓑ (916) 446-0100

Holiday Inn North East **20**
Rates Subject to Change   *Motor Inn* ◆◆◆
All year   1P .... 66.00 2P/1B .... 66.00 2P/2B .... 66.00 XP 6   F
230 units. 9 mi e; exit I-80 at Madison Ave, 1/4 mi e. 5321 Date Ave. (95841) A/C; C/CATV; free & pay movies; radios;
phones. Indoor/outdoor pool; sauna; whirlpool; exercise rm. Airport transp. Pets. Monthly rates avail. Reserv deposit required; 3 days refund notice. AE, DI, DS, MC, VI. ● Dining rm & coffeeshop; 6 am-10 pm; $9-$19; cocktails.
FAX (916) 334-2868   ⊗ Ⓢ Ⓓ (916) 338-5800

(See SACRAMENTO spotting map page A360)

Host International Hotel 🏨 **14**   **AAA Special Value Rates**   *Motel*   ◆
🏢 All year   1P .... 85.00   2P/1B .... 90.00   2P/2B .... 90.00   XP 10
89 units. 11 mi nw from capitol; 6 mi nw of I-80, off I-5 at the Sacramento Metropolitan Airport. 6945 Airport Blvd. (95837) Underground concourse connection direct with airport terminal. Check-in 3 pm. A/C; C/CATV; movies; radios; phones. Pool; whirlpool. Garage. No pets. AE, DI, DS, MC, VI. Restaurant opposite. FAX (916) 929-8636
    ⊗ Ⓓ (916) 922-8071

Howard Johnson Hotel 🏨 **16**   **Rates Subject to Change**   *Motor Inn*   ◆
🏢 All year   1P .... 61.00   2P/1B .... 66.00   2P/2B .... 66.00   XP 5
126 units. 5 1/2 mi e of jct I-80 & SR 50; exit 50 at Bradshaw Rd, 2 blks s. 3343 Bradshaw Rd. (95827) 18 refrigerators; A/C; C/TV; movies; radios; phones. Indoor/outdoor pool; sauna; whirlpool. Pets, $20 deposit required. 4 suites, $100 for up to 4 persons. AE, DI, DS, MC, VI. ● Restaurant; 6:30 am-2 & 5-10 pm; $9-$14; cocktails. FAX (916) 366-1266
    ⊗ Ⓓ (916) 366-1266

Hyatt Regency 🏨 **13**   Rates Subject to Change   *Hotel*   ◆◆◆◆
Sun-Thurs   1P 130.00- 165.00   2P/1B 150.00- 185.00   2P/2B 150.00- 185.00   XP 20   F
Fri & Sat   1P 89.00- 125.00   2P/1B 89.00- 125.00   2P/2B 89.00- 125.00   XP 20   F
Senior discount. 500 units. 1/2 blk from Capitol at 12th & L sts. 1209 L St. (95814) Mediterranean style architecture. Check-in 3 pm. A/C; C/CATV; free & pay movies; radios; phones. Small htd pool; whirlpool; exercise rm. Pay valet parking ramp. No pets. Luxury level rooms avail. Some microwaves & refrigerators, extra charge. 30 suites, $350-$795 for up to 2 persons. Reserv deposit required. AE, DI, DS, MC, VI. ● Dining rm & restaurant; 6 am-11 pm; a la carte entrees about $15-$28; cocktails; entertainment; nightclub. FAX (916) 321-6699
    ⊗ Ⓢ Ⓓ 🅱 (916) 443-1234

La Quinta Inn 🏨 **12**   Rates Subject to Change   *Motel*   ◆◆
🏢 All year   1P 52.00- 59.00   2P/1B 58.00- 65.00   2P/2B .... 58.00   XP 5   F
129 units. 9 mi e; exit I-80 at Madison Ave. 4604 Madison Ave. (95841) Check-in 3 pm. A/C; C/CATV; free & pay movies; radios; phones. Small pool. Small pets only. 1 suite, $79 for up to 2 persons. AE, DI, DS, MC, VI. Coffeeshop adjacent. FAX (916) 331-7160
    ⊗ Ⓢ Ⓓ 🅱 (916) 348-0900

Mansion View Lodge 🏨 **9**   Rates Subject to Change   *Motel*   ◆
🏢 All year   1P .... 36.00   2P/1B .... 40.00   2P/2B .... 42.00   XP 4
Senior discount. 41 units. On SR 160, 1 mi n of Business Loop 80, I-80 business loop eastbound exit 15th St, westbound 16th St, I-5 exit J St. 711 16th St. (95814) 25 refrigerators; A/C; C/TV; movies; 14 radios; phones; shower or comb baths. 2 2-bedrm units. Pets, $6 extra charge. Wkly rates avail. Reserv deposit required. AE, DI, DS, MC, VI. Restaurant opposite. FAX (916) 441-3194 *(See ad below)*
    Ⓓ (916) 443-6631

Marriott Residence Inn 🏨 **11**   **AAA Special Value Rates**   *Motel*   ◆◆◆
All year [CP]   1P 98.00- 118.00   2P/1B 98.00- 118.00   2P/2B 98.00- 118.00   XP
176 units. 2 1/2 mi n of jct SR 16 & US 50, exit Howe Ave. 1530 Howe Ave. (95825) 1-bedroom suites with living room & kitchen. Many with fireplace. Check-in 3 pm. Refrigerators; A/C; C/CATV; free & pay movies; radios; phones. Coin laundry. Pool; whirlpools. Airport transp. No pets. Reserv deposit required. AE, DI, DS, MC, VI. FAX (916) 921-5664
    ⊗ Ⓢ Ⓓ (916) 920-9111

Motel Orleans 🏨 **10**   Rates Subject to Change   *Motel*   ◆
🏢 All year   1P .... 35.00   2P/1B .... 40.00   2P/2B .... 44.00   XP 5
Senior discount. 69 units. 2 1/4 mi nw of Business Loop 80 off I-5; exit I-5 via Richards Blvd. 228 Jibboom St. (95814) A/C; C/TV; phones; comb or shower baths. Coin laundry. Pool. No pets. Reserv deposit required; 3 days refund notice. AE, DI, DS, MC, VI. Coffeeshop adjacent.
    ⊗ Ⓓ (916) 443-4811

Radisson Hotel 🏨 **30**   Rates Subject to Change   *Motor Inn*   ◆◆◆
🏢 All year   1P .... 72.00   2P/1B .... 82.00   2P/2B .... 82.00   XP 10
Senior discount. 309 units. 3 1/2 mi e via 16th St, SR 160; exit via Cantebury Rd. 500 Leisure Ln. (95815) Early California architecture. Some rooms with patios or decks; some rooms overlook small lake. Check-in 4 pm. A/C; C/CATV; pay movies; radios; phones. Pool; whirlpool; rental bicycles; exercise rm & massage. Fee for: paddleboats. Airport transp. Pets, $50 deposit required. Monthly rates avail. Reserv deposit required. AE, DI, DS, MC, VI. ● Restaurant; 6 am-11 pm; a la carte entrees about $7-$18; cocktails. FAX (916) 649-9463 *(See ad p A367)*
    ⊗ Ⓓ 🅱 (916) 922-2020

Red Lion Hotel 🏨 **28**   Rates Subject to Change   *Motor Inn*   ◆◆◆
Sun-Thurs   1P 100.00- 137.00   2P/1B 117.00- 143.00   2P/2B 117.00- 143.00   XP 15   F
Fri & Sat   1P .... 82.00   2P/1B .... 82.00   2P/2B .... 82.00   XP 15   F
448 units. 3 1/2 mi e; 1 blk off Business Loop 80; exit via Arden Way. 2001 Point West Way. (95815) Spacious grounds. Check-in 3 pm. 11 refrigerators; A/C; C/CATV; pay movies; radios; phones. 6 2-bedrm units. 2 pools; exercise rm. Airport transp. Pets. AE, DI, DS, MC, VI. ● Dining rm & coffeeshop; 6 am-11 pm; Fri & Sat-midnight; $9-$22; cocktails; entertainment. FAX (916) 924-4913 *(See ad p A3)*
    ⊗ Ⓓ 🅱 (916) 929-8855

(See SACRAMENTO spotting map page A360)

Red Lion's Sacramento Inn **29** Rates Subject to Change *Motor Inn* ◆◆◆
Sun-Thurs 1P 85.00- 105.00 2P/1B 97.00- 117.00 2P/2B 97.00- 117.00 XP 15 F
Fri & Sat 1P .... 65.00 2P/1B .... 65.00 2P/2B .... 65.00 XP 15 F
378 units. Exit Business Loop 80 via Arden Way in Arden Fair Shopping Plaza lot. 1401 Arden Way. (95815) Spacious grounds. Some patios. Many balconies. Check-in 3 pm. 9 refrigerators; A/C; C/CATV; pay movies; radios; phones; shower or comb baths. 5 2-bedrm units. 3 pools; wading pool; putting green; exercise rm. Airport transp. Pets. AE, DI, DS, MC, VI. ● 2 restaurants; 6 am-10 pm; Fri & Sat-midnight; $9-$15; cocktails; entertainment. FAX (916) 922-0386
(See ad p A3) ⊗ ⒟ Ⓛ (916) 922-8041

Sacramento Hilton Inn **8** Rates Subject to Change *Hotel* ◆◆◆
All year 1P .... 99.00 2P/1B .... 109.00 2P/2B .... 109.00 XP 12 F
325 units. At jct Business Loop 80 & Arden Way; exit W Arden Way. 2200 Harvard St. (95815) Check-in 3 pm. A/C; C/CATV; movies; radios; phones. Htd pool; sauna; whirlpool; fitness center; 15 rms with whirlpool bath. Parking lot. Airport transp. Pets, $50 deposit required. 5 suites, $125-$250 for up to 4 persons. Reserv deposit required. AE, DI, DS, MC, VI. ● Dining rm & coffeeshop; 6 am-11 pm; $7-$18.50; cocktails. FAX (916) 922-8418 *(See ads p 22 and below)*
⊗ Ⓢ ⒟ Ⓛ (916) 922-4700

(See SACRAMENTO spotting map page A360)

Sterling Hotel 🅰️26   Rates Subject to Change   *Hotel*   ◆◆◆
All year   1P 95.00- 225.00   2P/1B   95.00- 225.00   2P/2B   95.00- 225.00 XP
12 units. I-5 exit J St. 1300 H St. (95814) Beautifully restored 1894 mansion. Smoke free premises. 3 story, no elevator.
Check-in 3 pm. A/C; C/CATV; radios; phones. All rooms with whirlpool tub. Limited parking lot. No pets. Reserv deposit
required. AE, DI, MC, VI. ● Chanterelle, see separate listing. FAX (916) 448-8066   ⊗ Ⓓ (916) 448-1300

Super 8 Executive Suites 🅰️25   Rates Subject to Change   *Motel*   ◆◆
🏨 All year [CP]   1P 52.00- 65.00   2P/1B   54.00- 75.00   2P/2B   58.00- 85.00 XP 5
40 units. 2 1/4 mi nw of Business Loop 80; I-5 exit E Richards Blvd. 216 Bannon St. (95814) Check-in 3 pm. Refrigerators; A/C; C/CATV; movies; VCPs. Radios; phones. Coin laundry. Sauna; whirlpool. No pets. Few rooms
with whirlpool. Microwaves. Reserv deposit required. AE, DI, DS, MC, VI. FAX (916) 447-5153
                                                                              ⊗ Ⓢ Ⓓ (916) 447-5400

Super 8 Lodge 🅰️24   Rates Guaranteed   *Motel*   ◆◆
All year   1P .... 44.00   2P/1B   .... 48.00   2P/2B   .... 52.00 XP 5   F
Senior discount. 128 units. N of & adjacent to I-80; exit Madison Ave. 4317 Madison Ave. (95842) 3-story, no elevator.
A/C; C/CATV; phones. Pool. No pets. Wkly & monthly rates avail. AE, DI, DS, MC, VI. Coffeeshop adjacent.
FAX (916) 331-8916   ⊗ Ⓢ Ⓓ Ⓚ (916) 334-7430

Vagabond Inn 🅰️27   Rates Subject to Change   *Motel*   ◆◆
🏨 All year [CP]   1P 50.00- 64.00   2P/1B   55.00- 69.00   2P/2B   .... 74.00 XP 5   F
107 units. 8 blks w of Capitol; adjacent to Chinese Cultural Center & Old Sacramento Historic Quarter; exit J St.
909 3rd St. (95814) A/C; C/CATV; movies; radios; phones. 1 2-bedrm unit. Pool. Airport transp. Pets, $5 daily
extra charge. Reserv deposit required. AE, DI, DS, MC, VI. Coffeeshop adjacent. FAX (916) 448-0364 *(See ad*
below)   ⊗ Ⓓ Ⓚ (916) 446-1481

RESTAURANTS

Aldo's 🄻5️⃣   Northern Italian $$$ ◆◆◆
In Town & Country Village at Fulton Ave & Marconi St. 2914 Pasatiempo Ln. Varied selection of classic French & Cali-
fornia specialties. A/C. Open 11:30 am-2:30 & 6-10:30 pm; Sun-2:30 pm; closed major holidays. Cocktails & lounge.
Minimum, $10. Reserv advised. AE, CB, DI, MC, VI.   ⊗ (916) 483-5031

California Fats 🄻4️⃣   Chinese $$$ ◆◆
In Old Sacramento historic area. 1015 Front St. California-Pacific cuisine, eastern seasonings; bold rustic-modern de-
sign on 3 levels. Wok & grill cooking. A/C. Children's menu. Open 11:30 am-2 & 5:30-10 pm; Sat-11 pm; Sun 10:30 am-2
& 5:30-10 pm; closed 1/1, 11/26 & 12/25. Cocktails & lounge. Pay parking lot. Reserv advised. AE, MC, VI.
                                                                              ⊗ (916) 441-7966

Chanterelle 🄻3️⃣   Continental $$ ◆◆◆
In Sterling Hotel. California French. Varied menu. Smoke free premises. A/C. Open 7-9 am, 11:30-2 & 5:30-10 pm; Sat
& Sun 8:30 am-2 & 5:30-10 pm; closed major holidays. Cocktails. Reserv advised. AE, MC, VI.   ⊗ (916) 442-0451

Coral Reef 🄻7️⃣   American $$ ◆◆
6 blks s off Business Loop 80; frwy exit via Fulton Ave. 2795 Fulton Ave. Polynesian decor. Also, Cantonese cuisine fea-
tured. A/C. Open 11:30 am-2 & 5-10 pm; Sat 5 pm-11 pm; Sun 4 pm-10 pm; closed Mon for lunch, 11/26 & 12/25. Cocktails & lounge. Reserv advised. AE, CB, DI, MC, VI.   ⊗ (916) 483-5551

Fat City Bar & Grill 🄻1️⃣   American $$ ◆◆
In Old Sacramento historic area. 1001 Front St. Turn-of-the-century cafe. A/C. Open 11:30 am-2:30 & 5:30-10 pm; Fri-11
pm; Sat 10:30 am-2:30 & 5:30-11 pm; Sun 10:30 am-2:30 & 5:30-10 pm; closed 1/1 for lunch, 11/26 & 12/25. Cocktails
& lounge. Minimum, $7. Pay parking lot. AE, MC, VI.   ⊗ (916) 446-6768

The Firehouse 🄻8️⃣   Continental $$$$ ◆◆
In Old Sacramento historic area. 1112 2nd St. Former quarters of Sacramento Fire Company. Period decor. A/C. Open
11:30 am-2 & 5:30-10 pm; Sat from 5:30 pm; closed Sun & major holidays. Cocktails & lounge. Reserv advised. AE, MC,
VI.   ⊗ (916) 442-4772

Kallie's Restaurant 🄻2️⃣   American $$ ◆
🏨 7 mi s of Business Loop 80; on SR 99 exit Mack Rd E. 7770 Stockton Blvd. Family restaurant, varied menu. A/C.
Early bird specials; children's menu. Open 11 am-10 pm; Sat 8 am-11 pm; Sun 8 am-9 pm; closed 7/4. Cocktails
& lounge. Entertainment. Reserv advised. AE, MC, VI.   ⊗ (916) 423-2128

Pilothouse Restaurant 🄻6️⃣   Continental $$$ ◆◆
On Delta King, Old Scramento Waterfront. 1000 Front St. Turn-of-the-century decor. Smoke free premises. A/C. Open
11:30 am-2 & 5-10 pm; Sun 10 am-2 & 5-10 pm. Cocktails. Pay parking ramp. Reserv advised. AE, DI, DS, MC, VI.
                                                                              ⊗ (916) 441-4440

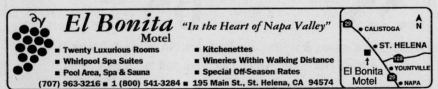

ST. HELENA — 5,000

El Bonita Motel

		Rates Subject to Change			Motel		◆◆
5/23-10/31	1P 65.00- 89.00	2P/1B	65.00- 95.00	2P/2B	69.00- 99.00	XP 9	
11/1-5/22	1P 46.00- 75.00	2P/1B	49.00- 79.00	2P/2B	49.00- 85.00	XP 9	

42 units. 3/4 mi s on SR 29. 195 Main St. (94574) Few small rooms with art deco motif. A/C; C/TV; movies; radios; phones; comb or shower baths. 2 2-bedrm units, 6 efficiencies. Pool; sauna; whirlpool. Pets, $10 extra charge. Wkly & monthly rates avail. Reserv deposit required; 3 days refund notice. AE, DI, DS, MC, VI. FAX (707) 963-8838 *(See ad p A291 and p A368)*   ⊗ Ⓓ (707) 963-3216

Harvest Inn

		Rates Subject to Change		Motel	◆◆◆◆
Fri & Sat [CP]	....	2P/1B	110.00- 325.00	....	XP 10
Sun-Thurs 4/1-11/30 [CP]	....	2P/1B	100.00- 290.00	....	XP 10
Sun-Thurs 12/1-3/31 [CP]	....	2P/1B	90.00- 260.00	....	XP 10

54 units. 1 1/2 mi s on SR 29. One Main St. (94574) English Tudor design. Many fireplaces. Antique furnishings. Check-in 4 pm. A/C; C/CATV; radios; phones. 2 pools; whirlpools; rental bicycles. Pets. 2-night minimum stay weekends. Reserv deposit required. AE, DS, MC, VI. FAX (707) 963-4402   Ⓓ (707) 963-9463

Meadowood Resort

		Rates Subject to Change			Resort Motor Inn		◆◆◆◆
All year	1P 225.00- 365.00	2P/1B	225.00- 365.00	2P/2B	225.00- 365.00	XP 25	F

82 units. Exit SR 29 & 128 at Pope St; 3/4 mi e to Silverado Tr, 100 ft n then 1 blk e on Howell Mountain Rd to Meadowood Ln. 900 Meadowood Ln. (94574) Many rooms with woodburning fireplace. Charming country lodges on 250 acres wooded private reserve, nicely landscaped. Check-in 4 pm. Refrigerators; A/C; C/CATV; movies; phones; comb or shower baths. 24 2-bedrm units, 12 3-bedrm units. 2 pools; nature program & trails. Fee for: par-3 golf, tennis-7 courts; professional croquet course; health club & massage. No pets. 2-night minimum stay weekends. Reserv deposit required; 7 days refund notice. AE, DI, MC, VI. ● Dining rm & restaurant; 7:30 am-9:30 pm; a la carte entrees about $25-$35. A *Preferred Hotel*. FAX (707) 963-3532   Ⓓ Ⓛ (707) 963-3646

Rancho Caymus Inn

		AAA Special Value Rates			Motel		◆◆◆
Fri & Sat [CP]	1P 115.00- 150.00	2P/1B	115.00- 150.00	....		XP 15	
Sun-Thurs [CP]	1P 100.00- 135.00	2P/1B	100.00- 135.00	....		XP 15	

26 units. 4 mi s in Rutherford, 1 blk e of SR 29 & SR 129. 1140 Rutherford Rd. (PO Box 78, Rutherford, 94573) Early California, Spanish hacienda architecture. Many rooms with woodburning fireplace. Check-in 3 pm. Refrigerators; A/C; C/TV; radios; phones. 1 2-bedrm unit, 5 kitchens. No pets. 5 suites with whirlpool bath, $200-$295 for 2 persons. 2 night minimum stay weekends 4/1-11/30. Wkly & monthly rates avail. Reserv deposit required; 3 days refund notice. AE, MC, VI. Restaurant adjacent. FAX (707) 963-5387   Ⓓ (707) 963-1777

Vineyard Inn

		Rates Subject to Change			Suites Motel		
4/1-11/14 [CP]	1P 145.00	2P/1B	.... 155.00	2P/2B	.... 155.00	XP 10	
11/15-3/31 [CP]	1P 115.00	2P/1B	.... 125.00	2P/2B	.... 125.00	XP 10	

21 units. 3/4 mi s on SR 29. 201 Main St. (94574) Scheduled to open fall, 1992. Rating withheld pending inspection. Check-in 3 pm. Refrigerators; A/C; C/CATV; radios; phones. Pool; whirlpool. No pets. Reserv deposit required. AE, CB, DI, MC, VI. *(See ad below)*   ⊗ (707) 963-1000

Wine Country Inn

		Rates Subject to Change			Lodge		◆◆◆
All year [CP]	1P 75.00- 135.00	2P/1B	95.00- 155.00	2P/2B	130.00- 150.00	XP 20	

24 units. 2 mi n & e off SR 29, in the Napa Valley Wine Country. 1152 Lodi Ln. (94574) Balconies or patios, many fireplaces. 10 refrigerators; A/C; phones; comb or shower baths. Pool; whirlpool. No pets. Reserv deposit required; 3 days refund notice. AE, MC, VI. FAX (707) 963-9018   Ⓓ (707) 963-7077

SALINAS — 108,800

Appling Inn

		Rates Subject to Change			Motel		◆◆
All year	1P 35.00- 59.00	2P/1B	45.00- 69.00	2P/2B	50.00- 79.00	XP 5	

Senior discount. 44 units. E of & adjacent to US 101; exit Sanborn Rd southbound, Fairview Ave northbound. 1030 Fairview Ave. (93905) 6 refrigerators; C/CATV; movies; radios; phones. No pets. Reserv deposit required; 3 days refund notice. AE, MC, VI. FAX (408) 757-0567   ⊗ Ⓓ (408) 422-6486

Best 5 Motel

		Rates Subject to Change			Motel		◆
All year	1P 35.00- 59.00	2P/1B	45.00- 69.00	2P/2B	50.00- 79.00	XP 5	

Senior discount. 59 units. E of US 101; Monterey Peninsula exit. 180 S Sanborn Rd. (93905) 3-story, no elevator. 5 refrigerators; A/C; C/CATV; radios; phones; comb or shower baths. No pets. Reserv deposit required; 3 days refund notice. AE, MC, VI.   ⊗ Ⓓ (408) 422-5111

Best Western Airport Motor Inn

		Rates Subject to Change			Motel		◆◆
7/1-10/15 [CP]	1P 75.00- 85.00	2P/1B	80.00- 90.00	2P/2B	85.00- 95.00	XP 6	F
4/1-6/30 [CP]	1P 55.00- 60.00	2P/1B	60.00- 65.00	2P/2B	65.00- 75.00	XP 6	F
10/16-3/31 [CP]	1P 38.00- 44.00	2P/1B	40.00- 46.00	2P/2B	44.00- 50.00	XP 6	F

Senior discount. 96 units. Adjacent to US 101, exit Airport Blvd. 555 Airport Blvd. (93905) 34 refrigerators; A/C; C/CATV; pay movies; 31 radios; phones. Coin laundry. Pool. Pets, $6 extra charge. 4 units with whirlpool bath $125 for up to 2 persons. Wkly rates avail. Reserv deposit required; 7 days refund notice. AE, DI, DS, MC, VI. Coffeeshop 24 hrs adjacent. FAX (408) 424-1741   ⊗ Ⓓ (408) 424-1741

Comfort Inn
All year [CP]   Rates Subject to Change   *Motel*   ◆◆
1P 49.00- 98.00   2P/1B   54.00- 98.00   2P/2B   65.00- 110.00   XP 8   F
Senior discount. 32 units. 1 blk e of US 101; Market St exit. 144 Kern St. (93905) A/C; C/CATV; radios; phones. No pets. Wkly rates avail. Reserv deposit required; 4 days refund notice. AE, DI, DS, MC, VI. Coffeeshop opposite. FAX (408) 758-3611   ⊗ Ⓢ Ⓓ Ⓚ   (408) 758-8850

Days Inn
4/1-10/15   Rates Subject to Change   *Motel*   ◆◆
1P 60.00- 70.00   2P/1B   70.00- 80.00   2P/2B   ....   90.00   XP 6   F
10/16-3/31   1P 35.00- 45.00   2P/1B   45.00- 55.00   2P/2B   ....   58.00   XP 6   F
Senior discount. 32 units. Adjacent to US 101, Airport Blvd exit. 1226 de la Torre St. (93905) Formerly Steinbeck Inn. A/C; C/CATV; pay movies; phones. Pets, $5 extra charge. Wkly & monthly rates avail. Reserv deposit required; 3 days refund notice. AE, DI, DS, MC, VI. Coffeeshop opposite. FAX (408) 424-1741   ⊗ Ⓢ Ⓓ Ⓚ   (408) 759-9900

El Dorado Motel
All year   Rates Subject to Change   *Motel*   ◆◆
1P 28.00- 38.00   2P/1B   38.00- 56.00   2P/2B   44.00- 60.00   XP 8
Senior discount. 44 units. 1 mi n on US 101 business rt; southbound US 101 exit Boronda Rd, northbound via N Main St. 1351 N Main St. (93906) Few small units. 4 refrigerators; C/CATV; 10 radios; phones; shower or comb baths. Whirlpool. Pets, $6 extra charge. Wkly & monthly rates avail. DS, MC, VI.   ⊗ Ⓓ (408) 449-2442

Laurel Inn Motel
All year   Rates Subject to Change   *Motel*   ◆◆
1P 48.00- 58.00   2P/1B   56.00- 85.00   2P/2B   60.00- 90.00   XP 6- 8
145 units. Adjacent to US 101, exit Laurel Dr. 801 W Laurel Dr. (93906) Spanish design. Some units with gas fireplace. 10 refrigerators; C/CATV; movies; radios; phones; comb or shower baths. 3 2-bedrm units. Pool; sauna; whirlpool. No pets. Reserv deposit required; 3 days refund notice. AE, DI, DS, MC, VI. Coffeeshop adjacent. FAX (408) 449-2476   ⊗ Ⓓ (408) 449-2474

Ramada Inn
7/1-9/30   1P   ....   69.00   2P/1B   ....   79.00   2P/2B   ....   89.00   XP 10
Rates Subject to Change   *Motel*   ◆◆
4/1-6/30   1P   ....   59.00   2P/1B   ....   69.00   2P/2B   ....   79.00   XP 10
10/1-3/31   1P   ....   49.00   2P/1B   ....   59.00   2P/2B   ....   69.00   XP 10
Senior discount. 162 units. Adjacent to e side of US 101, exit N Main St. 808 N Main St. (93906) A/C; C/CATV; 50 radios; phones. Pool; wading pool; whirlpool. Reserv deposit required; 3 days refund notice. AE, CB, DI, MC, VI. ● Dining rm & coffeeshop; 6 am-2 & 5-10 pm; $9-$15; cocktails. FAX (408) 424-5628 *(See ad below)*
       ⊗ Ⓓ (408) 424-8661

Vagabond Inn
All year [CP]   Rates Subject to Change   *Motel*   ◆◆
1P 35.00- 50.00   2P/1B   40.00- 55.00   2P/2B   45.00- 60.00   XP 5   F
70 units. E off & adjacent to US 101 bypass; exit Market St. 131 Kern St. (93905) A/C; C/CATV; radios; phones. Pool. Pets, $5 extra charge. AE, CB, DI, MC, VI. Coffeeshop adjacent. FAX (408) 758-9835 *(See ad below)*
       ⊗ Ⓓ Ⓚ   (408) 758-4693

RESTAURANT

Italian Villa   Italian $$ ◆
2 mi sw on SR 68. 64 Monterey Rd. Specializing in oakwood barbecued steaks. A/C. Early bird specials; children's menu. Open 11 am-10 pm; Sun 3 pm-9 pm; closed major holidays. Cocktails & lounge. Reserv advised. AE, MC, VI.   ⊗ (408) 424-6266

SAN BERNARDINO — 164,200

Best Western Sands Motel
All year   AAA Special Value Rates   *Motor Inn*   ◆◆
1P   ....   52.00   2P/1B   ....   55.00   2P/2B   ....   60.00   XP 3- 6   F
54 units. Adjacent to I-215, exit 5th St. 606 North H St. (92410) A/C; C/CATV; movies; rental VCPs. Radios; phones. Pool; whirlpool. Pets. Reserv deposit required; 3 days refund notice. AE, DI, DS, MC, VI. ● Coffeeshop; 6 am-7:30 pm; $4.95-$7.95; beer & wine. FAX (909) 889-8394 *(See ad below)*   ⊗ Ⓓ (909) 889-8391

Comfort Inn   Rates Subject to Change   *Motel*   ◆◆◆
All year   1P .... 46.00   2P/1B .... 51.00   2P/2B .... 51.00   XP 5   F
Senior discount. 50 units. Adjacent to I-10, exit Waterman Ave; 1 blk n. 1909 S Business Center Dr. (92408) Refrigerators; A/C; C/CATV; movies; VCPs. Phones. Pool. No pets. Microwaves. Reserv deposit required. AE, DI, DS, MC, VI. Restaurant opposite. FAX (909) 889-0090   ⊗ D ⅃ (909) 889-0090

La Quinta Motor Inn   Rates Subject to Change   *Motel*   ◆◆◆
All year   1P 51.00- 58.00   2P/1B 59.00- 66.00   2P/2B .... 59.00   XP 5   F
153 units. 1/4 mi nw of I-10, Waterman Ave exit. 205 E Hospitality Ln. (92408) Check-in 3 pm. A/C; C/CATV; free & pay movies; radios; phones. Htd pool. AE, DI, DS, MC, VI. Restaurant adjacent. FAX (909) 884-3864
   ⊗ D (909) 888-7571

Maruko Hotel & Convention Center   AAA Special Value Rates   *Hotel*   ◆◆◆
All year   1P .... 65.00   2P/1B .... 75.00   2P/2B .... 75.00   XP 10
237 units. 1/2 mi e of I-215, exit 2nd St. 295 North E St. (92401) A/C; C/CATV; pay movies; radios; phones. Whirlpool; airport transportation to Ontario International Airport. Parking ramp. No pets. AE, DI, DS, MC, VI. ● Dining rm & coffeeshop; 6:30 am-11 pm; $9-$15; cocktails; entertainment. FAX (909) 381-5288   ⊗ Ⓢ D (909) 381-6181

Ramada Inn   AAA Special Value Rates   *Hotel*   ◆◆◆
All year   1P .... 59.00   2P/1B .... 69.00   2P/2B .... 69.00   XP 10   F
116 units. Adjacent to I-215, University Pkwy exit. 2000 Ostrems Way. (92407) 3/4 mi w of California State University. A/C; C/CATV; movies; radios; phones. Small htd pool; whirlpool. Garage. AE, DI, DS, MC, VI. ● Restaurant; 6:30 am-10 pm; Fri & Sat-11 pm; $10.95-$14.95; cocktails. FAX (909) 880-3792   ⊗ Ⓢ D ⅃ (909) 887-3001

San Bernardino Hilton   AAA Special Value Rates   *Hotel*   ◆◆◆
All year   1P .... 85.00   2P/1B .... 95.00   2P/2B .... 95.00   XP 10   F
247 units. Adjacent to I-10, exit Waterman Ave. 285 E Hospitality Ln. (92408) Refrigerators; A/C; C/CATV; movies; radios; phones. Htd pool; whirlpool; airport transportation to Ontario International Airport. Parking lot. No pets. AE, DI, DS, MC, VI. ● Dining rm; 6:30 am-11 pm; Sun from 7 am; $10-$18; cocktails. FAX (909) 381-4299 *(See ad p 22)*
   ⊗ Ⓢ D ⅃ (909) 889-0133

San Bernardino Travelodge   Rates Subject to Change   *Motel*   ◆◆
All year [CP]   1P .... 40.00   2P/1B .... 45.00   2P/2B .... 50.00   XP 5
90 units. 1/4 mi nw of I-10, exit Waterman Ave. 225 E Hospitality Ln. (92408) A/C; C/CATV; movies; rental VCPs. Phones. 7 2-bedrm units. Htd pool. No pets. Rental microwaves & refrigerators. AE, DI, DS, MC, VI. Restaurant adjacent. FAX (909) 885-6925   ⊗ D (909) 888-6777

Super 8 Motel   Rates Guaranteed   *Motel*   ◆◆
All year   1P .... 43.00   2P/1B .... 47.00   2P/2B .... 49.00   XP 5   F
Senior discount. 81 units. 1 blk n of I-10, exit Waterman Ave. 294 E Hospitality Ln. (92408) 5 refrigerators; A/C; C/TV; phones. Pool; whirlpool. No pets. Wkly & monthly rates avail. AE, DI, DS, MC, VI. Restaurant adjacent. FAX (909) 888-5120   ⊗ Ⓢ D ⅃ (909) 381-1681

Super 8 San Bernardino-215 Frwy   AAA Special Value Rates   *Motel*   ◆◆
All year [CP]   1P 38.00- 48.00   2P/1B 40.00- 50.00   2P/2B 41.00- 51.00   XP 5   F
58 units. 1/2 blk e of I-215, exit 5th St. 777 W 6th St. (92410) Formerly Oak Creek Inn. Refrigerators; A/C; C/CATV; movies; radios; phones; shower or comb baths. Htd pool; sauna; whirlpool. No pets. AE, DI, DS, MC, VI. Coffeeshop opposite. FAX (909) 884-7127 *(See ad below)*   ⊗ D (909) 889-3561

RESTAURANTS

Bobby McGee's Conglomeration   American $$ ◆
2 blks nw of I-10, Waterman Ave exit. 1905 S Commerce Ctr E & Hospitality Ln. Unusual decor. Informal service by costumed waiters & waitresses. Selection of steaks & seafood. A/C. Children's menu. Open 5 pm-10 pm; Fri-11 pm; Sat 4 pm-11 pm; Sun 4 pm-10 pm; closed 12/25. Cocktails & lounge. Dancing. Reserv advised. AE, CB, DI, MC, VI.
   ⊗ (909) 884-7233

Bon Appetito   Italian $$ ◆◆
1 blk w of Waterman Ave. 246 E Baseline. A small, charming Italian restaurant. Large selection of pasta, veal, seafood & steaks. A/C. Open 11:30 am-2 & 4:30-9 pm; Fri-10 pm; Sat 4:30 pm-10 pm; closed Sun, Mon & major holidays. Cocktails & lounge. MC, VI.   (909) 884-5054

El Torito   Mexican $ ◆◆
2 blks nw of I-10, Waterman Ave exit. 118 E Hospitality Ln. Popular, colorfully decorated restaurant. A/C. Children's menu. Open 11 am-11 pm; Fri & Sat-midnight; Sun 9 am-10 pm; closed 11/25 & 12/25. Cocktails & lounge. Reserv advised. AE, CB, DI, MC, VI.   ⊗ (909) 381-2316

Lotus Garden Restuarant   Chinese $$ ◆◆
3 blks nw of I-10, Waterman Ave exit. 111 E Hospitality Ln. Large, nicely decorated restaurant. A/C. Children's menu. Open 11:30 am-9:30 pm; Fri & Sat-10:30 pm. Cocktails & lounge. AE, CB, DI, MC, VI.   ⊗ (909) 381-6171

SAN CARLOS — 26,200   (See SAN FRANCISCO (Southern Region) AREA spotting map page A444 ; see index starting on page A443)

Days Inn-San Carlos 🔲156   Rates Subject to Change   *Motel*   ◆◆
Ⓐ All year [CP]   1P .... 46.00 2P/1B .... 49.00 2P/2B .... 54.00 XP 5
Senior discount. 29 units. US 101 northbound exit Holly St w to El Camino n 1/4 mi southbound US 101 exit Ralston w to El Camino, s 1/4 mi. 26 El Camino Real. (94070) A/C; C/CATV; movies; phones. Htd pool. No pets. Reserv deposit required. AE, DI, DS, MC, VI. FAX (415) 508-1476 *(See ad p A447)*   ⊗ Ⓓ (415) 591-5771

San Carlos Inn 🔲155   Rates Subject to Change   *Motel*   ◆◆
Ⓐ All year [CP]   1P .... 44.00 2P/1B .... 42.00 2P/2B .... 50.00 XP 5
32 units. Exit US 101, Holly St, 1/2 mi s on El Camino Real (SR 82). 1562 El Camino Real. (94070) Refrigerators; A/C; C/CATV; movies; VCPs. Radios; phones. No utensils. Sauna; whirlpool; 7 rooms with whirlpool. No pets. 4 efficiencies, $55-$60. All rooms with microwave. Wkly rates avail. Reserv deposit required. AE, CB, DI, MC, VI. FAX (415) 591-6655 *(See ad p A467)*   Ⓓ 🔳 (415) 591-6655

SAN CLEMENTE — 41,100

Best Western Casablanca Inn   AAA Special Value Rates   *Motel*   ◆◆◆
Ⓐ All year [CP]   1P .... 64.00 2P/1B 69.00-109.00 2P/2B 69.00-109.00 XP 5
42 units. 3/4 mi sw of I-5, exit Avenida Pico. 1601 N El Camino Real. (92672) Check-in 3 pm. Refrigerators; A/C; C/CATV; movies. Radios; phones. 13 rooms with whirlpool bathtub. No pets. Monthly rates avail. Reserv deposit required. AE, DI, DS, MC, VI. FAX (714) 361-3825   ⊗ ⓈⒹⒷ (714) 361-1644

Casa Clemente Resort & Convention Center   Rates Subject to Change   *Motor Inn*   ◆◆
All year [BP]   1P 73.00- 79.00 2P/1B 83.00- 89.00 2P/2B .... 83.00 XP 10   F
Senior discount. 110 units. Adjacent to I-5, exit Ave Pico, then 1/2 mi s on frontage road. 35 Calle de Industrias. (92672) Formerly Ramada Inn. 25 refrigerators; A/C; C/CATV; movies; rental VCPs. Radios; phones. Htd pool. No pets. Wkly & monthly rates avail. Reserv deposit required. AE, DI, DS, MC, VI. ● Dining rm; 7 am-1:30 & 5-10 pm; $9-$16; cocktails. FAX (714) 498-8800   ⊗ ⓄⒹⒷ (714) 498-8800

Econo Lodge   Rates Subject to Change   *Motel*   ◆◆
All year   1P 45.00- 50.00 2P/1B 50.00- 55.00 2P/2B 60.00- 65.00 XP 5   F
Senior discount. 31 units. 2002 S El Camino Real. (92672) Refrigerators; A/C; C/CATV; movies; rental VCPs. Radios; phones. 1 2-bedrm unit. Garage. No pets. Rooms with whirlpool, $75-$90. Wkly rates avail. Reserv deposit required. AE, DI, DS, MC, VI. Coffeeshop adjacent.   ⊗ Ⓓ (714) 361-2110

Holiday Inn-San Clemente Resort   Rates Subject to Change   *Motor Inn*   ◆◆◆
Ⓐ All year   1P .... 70.00- 95.00 2P/2B 70.00- 95.00 XP 10   F
Senior discount. 72 units. Off I-5, southbound exit El Camino Real, northbound exit Ave Presidio. 111 S Avenida de Estrella. (92672) Many rooms with ocean view & balcony. Check-in 3 pm. Refrigerators; A/C; C/CATV; movies; radios; phones. Htd pool; whirlpool. Pets. 11 rooms with whirlpool spa, $145 for 2 persons. Wkly & monthly rates avail. AE, DI, DS, MC, VI. ● Dining rm; 6:30 am-2 & 5-10 pm; $9-$16; cocktails. FAX (714) 361-2472   ⊗ ⓈⒹⒷ (714) 361-3000

Motel San Clemente   Rates Subject to Change   *Motel*   ◆◆
Ⓐ 5/1-9/30   1P 40.00- 55.00 2P/1B 50.00- 60.00 2P/2B 55.00- 75.00 XP 5
10/1-4/30   1P 40.00- 45.00 2P/1B 45.00- 50.00 2P/2B 50.00- 60.00 XP 5
18 units. 1/2 mi s. 1819 S Camino Real. (92672) A/C; C/CATV; radios; phones; comb or shower baths. No pets. Reserv deposit required. AE, CB, DI, MC, VI. *(See ad below)*   ⊗ ⓈⒹⒷ (714) 492-1960

Oceanview Inn & Suites   Rates Guaranteed   *Motel*   ◆◆
Ⓐ All year   1P .... 53.00 2P/1B .... 58.00 2P/2B .... 63.00 XP 5   F
43 units. 1301 N El Camino Real. (92672) Formerly San Clemente North Travelodge. Refrigerators; A/C; C/CATV; movies; phones; comb or shower baths. No pets. 8 rooms with whirlpool, $59-$119. Reserv deposit required. AE, DI, DS, MC, VI. FAX (714) 492-1140 *(See ad p A373)*   ⊗ ⓈⒹⒷ (714) 361-0636

AAA restaurant expertise
saves you time and costly explorations.

San Clemente Beach Travelodge   Rates Subject to Change   *Motel* ◆◆
All year [CP]   1P 39.00- 49.00 2P/1B 45.00- 55.00 2P/2B 49.00- 69.00 XP 5 F
Senior discount. 19 units. Adjacent to I-5; southbound exit Calafia; northbound exit Magdalena. 2441 S El Camino Real. (92672) Some rooms with balcony. 3 small units. 16 refrigerators; A/C; C/CATV; free & pay movies; VCPs. Radios; phones; comb or shower baths. 1 2-bedrm unit. 5 spa rooms. Garage. No pets. AE, DI, DS, MC, VI. FAX (714) 498-5954 *(See ad p A374)*   ⊗ Ⓢ Ⓓ (714) 498-5954

RESTAURANTS

The Pasta House   Italian $$ ◆◆◆
1/2 mi s. 1925 S El Camino Real. Formerly Andreinos. Small charming restaurant. A/C. Open 4:30 pm-9 pm; closed Sun & major holidays. Beer & wine. Reserv advised. AE, MC, VI.   ⊗ 🅐 (714) 492-9955

Swiss Chalet   German $$ ◆◆◆
Downtown. 216 N El Camino Real. Charming decor, also specializing in Swiss entrees. A/C. Children's menu. Open 5 pm-9 pm; closed Sun & Mon. Beer & wine. Reserv advised. MC, VI. ⊗ 🅐 (714) 492-7931

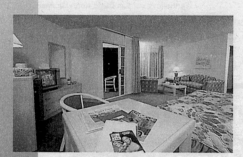

SAN DIEGO — 1,110,500 (See SAN DIEGO spotting map pages A376 & A377; see index starting below) See also DEL MAR, EL CAJON & RANCHO BERNARDO

Airport Accommodations-See listings for:

- Sheraton Grand on Harbor Island, 1/4 mi s of airport.
- Sheraton Harbor Island Hotel, 1/4 mi s of airport.
- Travelodge Hotel-Harbor Island, 1/2 mi s of airport.

Index of Establishments on the SAN DIEGO AREA Spotting Map

(See SAN DIEGO spotting map pages A376 & A377)

🏨 Handlery Hotel & Country Club	51
🏨 Town and Country Hotel	52
Hyatt Regency San Diego	53
🏨 Comfort Inn-La Mesa	54
🏨 La Mesa Lodge	55
Wyndham Garden Hotel	56
🏨 Super 8 Mission Bay	57
🏨 La Mesa Country Inn	58
🏨 National Budget Inn	59
San Diego Marriott Mission Valley	60
🏨 Pacific Terrace Inn	61
🏨 Radisson Hotel-San Diego	62
🏨 San Diego Mission Valley Hilton	63
🏨 Comfort Suites Hotel Circle	64
🏨 Holiday Inn-Hotel Circle	65
🏨 Days Inn-Hotel Circle	66
🏨 Vagabond Inn-Misson Valley	67
Holiday Inn Montgomery Field	68
🏨 Kings Inn	69
🏨 Regency Plaza Hotel	70
🏨 Howard Johnson Hotel Circle	71
🏨 Ramada Inn-Hotel Circle	72
🏨 Hotel Circle Inn & Suites	73
🏨 Beach Haven Inn	74
🏨 Best Western Hacienda Hotel-Old Town	75
🏨 Sheraton Harbor Island Hotel	76
🏨 Sheraton Grand on Harbor Island	77
🏨 Travelodge Hotel-Harbor Island	78
🏨 Seapoint Hotel	79
🏨 Best Western Posada Inn	80
Best Western Hotel-San Diego Central	81
🏨 Econo Lodge	82
🏨 Humphrey's Half Moon Inn	83
🏨 The Bay Club Hotel & Marina	84
🏨 Best Western Shelter Island Marina Inn	85
🏨 Old Town Travelodge	86
🏨 Days Inn Suites	87
Holiday Inn-Harbor View	88
🏨 Holiday Inn On The Bay	89
🏨 Best Western Bayside Inn	90
🏨 Howard Johnson Hotel Harbor View	91
🏨 Rodeway Inn-Balboa Park/Downtown	92
🏨 Comfort Inn-Downtown	93
🏨 The Westgate	94
🏨 The Bristol Court Hotel	95
🏨 U. S. Grant Hotel	96
🏨 Loews Coronado Bay Resort	97
🏨 Doubletree Hotel at Horton Plaza	98
🏨 Super 8 Harborside	99
🏨 Marriott San Diego Marina	100
🏨 Best Western Suites-Coronado Island	101
🏨 Glorietta Bay Inn-Coronado	103
Hampton Inn-Kearny Mesa	104
🏨 Le Meridien San Diego At Coronado	105
🏨 Lamplighter Inn & Suites	106
Vacation Inn-Old Town	107
🏨 Embassy Suites-San Diego Bay	108
🏨 Radisson Hotel Harbor View	109
🏨 Holiday Inn Express-Sea World Area	110
🏨 Comfort Inn-Airport at Old Town	111
🏨 Ramada Hotel Bay View	112
San Diego Marriott Suites-Downtown	113
🏨 The Pan Pacific Hotel	114
Crown City Inn	115
🏨 Pacific Shores Inn	116
Executive Hotel & Suites	117

🏨 Best Western Blue Sea Lodge	119
🏨 Crown Point View Suite-Hotel	120

RESTAURANTS

Salmon House	14
🏨 Shanghai	15
Garcia's of Scottsdale	16
Casa de Bandini	17
Cafe Pacifica	18
Islands Restaurant	19
Baci's	20
Tradewinds Restaurant	21
Madeo Ristorante	22
Anthony's Fish Grotto	23
Bobby McGee's Conglomeration	24
California Cafe Bar & Grill	25
Furr's Fine Family Dining	26
Monterey Whaling Company	27
El Torito	28
Dockside Broiler	29
Kings Grille	30
The Tickled Trout	31
Acapulco	32
Tio Leo's	33
🏨 Hob Nob Hill	34
Reuben's	35
Spencer's	36
🏨 Tom Ham's Lighthouse	37
🏨 Shelter Island's Bali Hai Restaurant	38
Humphrey's	39
Anthony's Star of the Sea Room	41
Anthony's Fish Grotto	42
Grant Grill	45
Harbor House Restaurant	46
The Old Spaghetti Factory	47
The Brigantine	48
The Chart House 1887	49
Peohe's	50
First Avenue Bar & Grill	51

NATIONAL CITY

🏨 Radisson Suites National City	130
🏨 Sweetwater Inn	131
🏨 Radisson Inn National City	132
🏨 Econo Lodge	133

CHULA VISTA

🏨 Best Western Cavalier Motor Hotel	137
🏨 Vagabond Inn	138
🏨 All Seasons Inns	139
Ramada Inn-San Diego South	140
🏨 La Quinta Inn	141
🏨 Rodeway Inn	142
🏨 Palomar Inn	143
🏨 Otay Valley Inn	144
🏨 Chula Vista Travelodge	145

RESTAURANTS

Anthony's Fish Grotto	55
La Fonda Roberto's	56
Furr's Family Dining	58

IMPERIAL BEACH

🏨 Hawaiian Gardens Suite-Hotel	150

RESTAURANT

Hungry Hunter Restaurant	62

SAN YSIDRO

🏨 Americana Inn & Suites	155
🏨 International Motor Inn	157

The Bay Club Hotel & Marina 84   **AAA Special Value Rates**   *Motor Inn* ◆◆◆
🏨 **All year [BP]**   1P 110.00- 140.00   2P/1B 110.00- 150.00   2P/2B 110.00-150.00 XP 10   F
105 units. On Shelter Island. 2131 Shelter Island Dr. (92106) Spacious rooms, most with view of bay or marina. Check-in 4 pm. Refrigerators; A/C; C/CATV; radios; phones. Coin laundry. Htd pool; whirlpool; exercise rm. Airport transp. No pets. Reserv deposit required. AE, DI, DS, MC, VI. ● Dining rm; 6:30 am-10 pm; Sat & Sun from 7 am; $14-$19; cocktails. FAX (619) 225-1604 *(See ad p A378)*   ⊗ Ⓢ Ⓓ (619) 224-8888

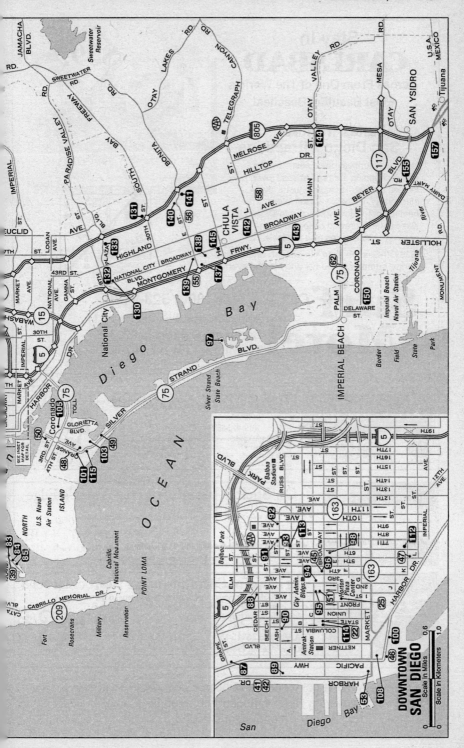

DOWNTOWN
SAN DIEGO

AAA has it covered. We publish 23 TourBooks annually,
covering North America from Florida to Alaska
and all of Canada.

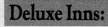
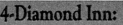

Treat Yourself to a *Suite*.

MINI-SUITE

2 & 3 ROOM FAMILY SUITE (LIVING ROOM)

MINI-SUITE

1 OR 2 PERSONS
- 1 Bed • 1 Bath
- Full Kitchen
*September to May $55
June to August $65

2 ROOM FAMILY SUITE

UP TO 6 PERSONS
Bedroom with 2 Beds • 1 Bath
- Large Living Room w/Sofa Bed
- 2 TVs • Full Kitchen
with Dining Table
*September to May $69 to $79
June to August $99 to $109

3 ROOM FAMILY SUITE

UP TO 10 PERSONS
Large Living Room w/ Sofa Bed
- 2 Bedrooms/ 2 Full Baths
1 with choice of King or 2 Beds
- 1 with 2 beds • 3 TVs
Full Kitchen with Dining Table
*Sept. to May $109 to $119
June to August $159 to $169

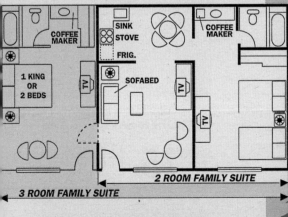

COFFEE MAKER

SINK
STOVE

FRIG.

COFFEE MAKER

1 KING OR 2 BEDS

TV

SOFABED

TV

TV

2 ROOM FAMILY SUITE

3 ROOM FAMILY SUITE

24 HR. TOLL FREE RESERVATIONS:
(800) 772-7711
CANADA: (800) 621-4222

*Higher Rates for some weekends, holiday periods & special events. Offers subject to limited availability.

Radisson

H O T E L   S A N   D I E G O

Located in the heart of San Diego, this magnificent 14-story hotel is one of the city's finest with lavish accommodations, superb service, complete comfort and luxury featuring . . .

- *260 exquisitely decorated rooms*
- *Plaza Club — full concierge service*
- *Large heated outdoor pool and spa*
- *Sweetwater's, one of San Diego's finer restaurants*
- *Intermezzo Lounge for Happy Hour, hors d'oeuvres and live entertainment*
- *Full Health Club facilities*
- *Complimentary airport shuttle*
- *Non-smoking rooms*
- *Room Service*
- *Outstanding meeting facilities*

Located in San Diego's famous Mission Valley and CLOSE TO EVERYTHING . . . 8 minutes to Downtown, Airport, Zoo, Beaches, Seaworld and directly opposite the beautiful Mission Valley Mall, Fashion Valley Malls and 1 mile to Jack Murphy Stadium.

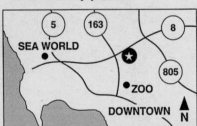

Radisson Hotel
THE TWO NATION VACATION

MEXICO ADVENTURE PACKAGES

**ENSENADA PACKAGE
3 DAYS/2 NIGHTS**
- 2 Nights Deluxe Radisson accommodations
- 1 Day-long Tour to – Ensenada, Mexico Round Trip, per person Lunch included
- 1 Full Breakfast Buffet per person
- Includes taxes, (Plaza Club extra)

**2 People
$295**

**TIJUANA PACKAGE
3 DAYS/2 NIGHTS**
- 2 Nights Deluxe Radisson accommodations
- 1 Day-long Tour to – Tijuana, Mexico Round Trip, per person
- 1 Full Breakfast Buffet per person
- Includes taxes, (Plaza Club extra)

**2 People
$254**

Proof of citizenship required for travel into Mexico

SAN DIEGO ADVENTURE PACKAGES

MOONLIGHT ON THE BAY–DINNER CRUISE
3 DAYS/2 NIGHTS — AVAILABLE WED. THRU SUN.
- 2-Hour Bay Cruise with Dinner, Hosted Beverage Service, Live Band and Dancing
- 2 Nights Deluxe Radisson accommodations
- Airport/Amtrak Transfers• 2 Full Breakfast Buffets per person
- 2 Old Town Trolley City Tours• Includes taxes (Plaza Club extra)

**ADVENTURE #1
3 DAYS/2 NIGHTS**
- 2 Nights Deluxe Radisson accommodations
- 1 Welcome drink in the Intermezzo Lounge
- 2 Full Breakfast Buffets per person
- CHOICE of San Diego Zoo Admission, including Guided Bus Tour & Aerial Tram Ride - OR - 2 Day Sea World Pass for Admissions, Shows & Attractions
- Includes taxes (Plaza Club extra)

**ADVENTURE #2
4 DAYS/2 NIGHTS**
- 3 Nights Deluxe Radisson accommodations
- 1 Welcome drink in the Intermezzo Lounge
- 3 Full Breakfast Buffets per person
- San Diego Zoo Admission, including Guided Bus Tour & Aerial Tram Ride
- 2 Day Sea World Pass including Admissions, Shows & Attractions
- Includes taxes (Plaza Club extra)

ROOM OCCUPANCY	MOONLIGHT CRUISE	ADVENTURE PKG #1	ADVENTURE PKG #2	EXTRA NIGHTS
2 PEOPLE	$295.00	$225.00	$350.00	ROOM
3 PEOPLE	$350.00	$255.00	$405.00	ONLY
4 PEOPLE	$412.00	$285.00	$460.00	$75.00

• PRICE IS PER PACKAGE, NOT PER PERSON •
All packages subject to change

(See SAN DIEGO spotting map pages A376 & A377)

Beach Haven Inn 74 ◆◆
AAA Special Value Rates *Motel*

6/15-9/14		1P	75.00- 95.00	2P/1B	75.00- 95.00	2P/2B	85.00-105.00	XP 10	F
9/15-6/14		1P	60.00- 90.00	2P/1B	60.00- 90.00	2P/2B	70.00- 90.00	XP 5	F

23 units. In Pacific Beach area. 4740 Mission Blvd. (92109) 1 block to beach. Nicely decorated rooms 1-bedroom apartments. Refrigerators; A/C; C/CATV; movies; rental VCPs. Phones. Coin laundry. Htd pool; whirlpool. 19 kitchens, $85-$100. Pets, $50 deposit required; small pets under 20 pounds. Wkly & monthly rates avail except summer. Reserv deposit required; 3 days refund notice. AE, DI, DS, MC, VI. FAX (619) 544-1257 *(See ad below)*
⊗ Ⓓ Ⓖ (619) 272-3812

Best Western Airport Inn 40 ◆◆◆
AAA Special Value Rates *Motor Inn*

7/1-9/7		1P	69.00- 75.00	2P/1B	75.00- 81.00	2P/2B	.... 75.00	XP 7	F
9/8-6/30		1P	60.00- 65.00	2P/1B	60.00- 90.00	2P/2B	.... 65.00	XP 6	F

105 units. 1/2 blk e of Rosecrans St. 2901 Nimitz Blvd. (92106) A/C; C/CATV; movies; phones. Rental refrigerators. Htd pool. Garage & parking lot. No pets. Wkly & monthly rates avail. Reserv deposit required. AE, DI, DS, MC, VI. ● Coffeeshop; 6 am-10 pm; $4.50-$8; cocktails. FAX (619) 224-4025 *(See ad below)*
⊗ Ⓓ (619) 224-3655

Best Western Bayside Inn 90 ◆◆◆
AAA Special Value Rates *Hotel*

7/1-9/4 [CP]		1P	80.00- 92.00	2P/1B	80.00- 92.00	2P/2B	86.00- 98.00	XP 6	
9/5-6/30 [CP]		1P	70.00- 82.00	2P/1B	70.00- 82.00	2P/2B	76.00- 88.00	XP 6	

122 units. 555 W Ash St at Columbia. (92101) Many rooms with view of harbor. 3 refrigerators; A/C; C/CATV; free & pay movies; radios; phones. Htd pool; whirlpool. Parking ramp. Airport transp. No pets. Monthly rates avail. AE, DI, DS, MC, VI. ● Restaurant; 6:30 am-2 & 5-10 pm; $8-$12; cocktails. FAX (619) 239-8060
⊗ Ⓢ Ⓓ (619) 233-7500

Ⓖ = The lodging establishment or restaurant can accommodate wheelchair travelers.

(See SAN DIEGO spotting map pages A376 & A377)

Best Western Blue Sea Lodge 119   Rates Subject to Change   *Motel* ◆◆◆
6/15-9/15 [CP]   1P 110.00- 125.00 2P/1B 120.00- 135.00 2P/2B 130.00- 150.00 XP 15   F
9/16-6/14 [CP]   1P 95.00- 115.00 2P/1B 110.00- 125.00 2P/2B 120.00- 140.00 XP 15   F
Senior discount. 100 units. Pacific Beach area, 1/2 blk w of Mission Blvd. 707 Pacific Beach Dr. (92109) At the beach. Many balconies & ocean views. Check-in 3 pm. A/C; C/CATV; movies; phones; shower or comb baths. 48 efficiencies. Coin laundry. Htd pool; whirlpool. No pets. Reserv deposit required. AE, DI, DS, MC, VI. Restaurant adjacent. FAX (619) 488-7276 *(See ad p A384)*   Ⓢ Ⓓ Ⓖ (619) 488-4700

Best Western Hacienda Hotel-Old Town 75   Rates Guaranteed   *Motor Inn* ◆◆◆
All year   1P 99.00- 109.00 2P/1B 109.00- 119.00 2P/2B 107.00- 117.00 XP 10   F
Senior discount. 149 units. Juan & Harney sts. 4041 Harney St. (92110) Beautifully landscaped, terraced hillside location. Check-in 3 pm. Refrigerators; A/C; C/CATV; pay movies; VCPs. Radios; phones. Htd pool; whirlpool; exercise rm. Garage & parking lot. Airport transp. No pets. Microwave in all units. Reserv deposit required. AE, CB, DI, MC, VI. ● Restaurant; 6:30 am-10 pm; $6-$13; cocktails. Also, Acapulco, see separate listing. FAX (619) 298-4707 *(See ad below)*   ⊗ Ⓓ Ⓖ (619) 298-4707

Best Western Hotel-San Diego Central 81   AAA Special Value Rates   *Hotel* ◆◆◆
5/15-9/15 [CP]   1P .... 74.00 2P/1B .... 79.00 2P/2B .... 74.00 XP 6   F
9/16-5/14 [CP]   1P .... 69.00 2P/1B .... 74.00 2P/2B .... 69.00 XP 6   F
174 units. Adjacent to I-15, 2 mi n of I-8. 3805 Murphy Canyon Rd. (92123) Formerly Best Western Hotel Kearney Mesa. Check-in 3 pm. A/C; C/CATV; free & pay movies; radios; phones. Coin laundry. Htd pool; whirlpool; exercise rm. Garage & parking lot. No pets. 2 room suites with wet bar, microwave & refrigerator $89-$99. Reserv deposit required. AE, DI, DS, MC, VI. ● Dining rm; 6:30 am-9:30 pm; $7.95-$14.50; cocktails. FAX (619) 277-3442 ⊗ Ⓢ Ⓓ (619) 277-1199

Best Western Inn-Miramar/San Diego 31   AAA Special Value Rates   *Motel* ◆◆◆
6/18-9/5 [CP]   1P .... 53.00 2P/1B .... 59.00 2P/2B .... 59.00 XP 6   F
9/6-6/17 [CP]   1P .... 50.00 2P/1B .... 56.00 2P/2B .... 56.00 XP 6   F
101 units. 1/2 blk w of I-15, exit Miramar Rd. 9310 Kearny Mesa Rd. (92126) A/C; C/CATV; movies; VCPs. Radios; phones. Coin laundry. Htd pool; whirlpool; exercise rm. No pets. Some rooms with refrigerator & microwave. AE, DI, DS, MC, VI. Restaurant adjacent. FAX (619) 536-1368   ⊗ Ⓓ Ⓖ (619) 578-6600

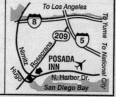

(See SAN DIEGO spotting map pages A376 & A377)

Best Western Posada Inn ⑧⓪		AAA Special Value Rates					Motel			◆◆◆
ⓐ 7/1-9/6	1P	.... 79.00	2P/1B	.... 85.00	2P/2B	91.00- 97.00	XP 6			F
9/7-6/30	1P	.... 69.00	2P/1B	.... 75.00	2P/2B	81.00- 87.00	XP 6			F

112 units. Point Loma area, 2 blks s of Rosecrans St. 5005 N Harbor Dr. (92106) Many rooms with harbor view. A/C; C/CATV; movies; radios; phones. Small htd pool; whirlpool; exercise rm. Airport transp. No pets. AE, DI, DS, MC, VI. Restaurant opposite. FAX (619) 224-2186 *(See ad p A385)*   ⊗ ⒟ ⓺ (619) 224-3254

Best Western Seven Seas ㉘		Rates Guaranteed					Hotel		◆◆
ⓐ 7/1-9/5	1P	.... 61.00	2P/1B	.... 61.00	2P/2B	.... 61.00	XP		F
9/6-6/30	1P	.... 51.00	2P/1B	.... 51.00	2P/2B	.... 51.00	XP		F

Senior discount. 309 units. 411 S Hotel Cir. (92108) 51 refrigerators; A/C; C/CATV; movies; radios; phones. 9 efficiencies. Coin laundry. Htd pool; whirlpools. Parking lot. Airport transp. AE, DI, DS, MC, VI. ● Restaurant & coffeeshop; 6 am-midnight; $6-$16. FAX (619) 291-6933 *(See ad below)*   ⊗ ⒟ (619) 291-1300

Best Western Shelter Island Marina Inn ⑧⑤		AAA Special Value Rates					Motor Inn		◆◆
ⓐ 6/1-8/31	1P	.... 80.00	2P/1B	.... 90.00	2P/2B	.... 90.00	XP 10		F
9/1-5/31	1P	.... 70.00	2P/1B	.... 80.00	2P/2B	.... 80.00	XP 10		F

97 units. On Shelter Island. 2051 Shelter Island Dr. (92106) Most rooms with view of marina or harbor. Check-in 3 pm. A/C; phones; shower or comb baths. Htd pool; whirlpool. Fee for: dock. Airport transp. No pets. 29 suites with kitchen, $115-$155. Reserv deposit required. AE, DI, DS, MC, VI. ● Dining rm; 6:30 am-10 pm; $9-$17; cocktails; entertainment. FAX (619) 222-9760   ⊗ ⒟ (619) 222-0561

Best Western Suites-Coronado Island ⑩①		Rates Subject to Change					Motel		◆◆◆
ⓐ 6/1-9/18 [CP]	1P	85.00- 125.00	2P/1B	93.00- 129.00	2P/2B	95.00- 129.00	XP 8		F
9/19-5/31 [CP]	1P	75.00- 115.00	2P/1B	83.00- 115.00	2P/2B	85.00- 115.00	XP 8		F

Senior discount. 63 units. Corner of SR 75 & Orange Ave. 275 Orange Ave. (Coronado, 92118) A/C; C/CATV; movies; VCPs. Radios; phones. 3 2-bedrm units, efficiencies. Coin laundry. Small htd pool; whirlpool. Garage. No pets. All rooms with microwave & refrigerator. Reserv deposit required. AE, DI, DS, MC, VI. FAX (619) 437-0188 *(See ad below)*   ⊗ ⓢ ⒟ ⓺ (619) 437-1666

(See SAN DIEGO spotting map pages A376 & A377)

The Bristol Court Hotel 95
⊛ All year [CP]   1P 104.00- 124.00   2P/1B   114.00- 134.00   2P/2B   114.00- 134.00   XP 15   Hotel ◆◆◆
Senior discount. 99 units. 1055 1st Ave at C St. (92101) Check-in 3 pm. A/C; C/CATV; VCPs; phones.
Racquetball-2 courts; health club. Pay valet garage. Airport transp. No pets. AE, DI, DS, MC, VI. ● Dining rm; 11
am-2:30 pm & 5-10 pm; Sat & Sun from 5 pm; $10-$15; cocktails. Also, First Avenue Bar & Grill, see separate
listing. FAX (619) 232-0118   ⊗ ⒟ ⑤   (619) 232-6141

California Lodge Suites 33
⊛ All year [CP]   1P .... 45.00   2P/1B   .... 50.00   2P/2B   .... 55.00   XP 20   Motel ◆
Senior discount. 165 units. 1 blk w of I-805, exit Clairmont Mesa Blvd. 5415 Clairmont Mesa Blvd. (92117) Refrig-
erators; A/C; C/CATV; radios; phones. 110 efficiencies. Coin laundry. No pets. AE, DI, DS, MC, VI.
FAX (619) 569-4957   ⊗ ⒟ (619) 560-0545

Catamaran Resort Hotel 32
⊛ All year   ......   2P/1B   130.00- 190.00   2P/2B   130.00- 190.00   XP   Resort Hotel ◆◆◆
Senior discount. 312 units. 3 blks s of Grand Ave; on Mission Bay. 3999 Mission Blvd. (92109) Many rooms over-
looking bay; balconies or patios. Check-in 4 pm. Refrigerators; A/C; C/CATV; pay movies; radios; phones. 68 ef-
ficiencies. Htd pool; beach; rental boats; rental bicycles; exercise rm. Fee for: windsurfing & sailing instructions.
Pay valet garage & parking lot. No pets. Bay view rooms, $250. Reserv deposit required. AE, DI, DS, MC,
VI. ● Restaurant; 6:30 am-10 pm; Fri & Sat-11 pm; $6.95-$21.50; cocktails; entertainment. FAX (619) 488-1081
                                                                 ⊗ ⒟ (619) 488-1081

Comfort Inn-Airport at Old Town 111
⊛ All year   1P 39.95- 49.95   2P/1B   46.95- 56.95   2P/2B   .... 56.95   XP 7   Motel ◆◆◆
121 units. E side of I-5, exit Old Town Ave, 1/2 mi s on San Diego Ave. 1955 San Diego Ave. (92110) Located in
Old Town area. A/C; C/CATV; movies; radios; phones. Coin laundry. Whirlpool. Garage & parking lot. No pets.
AE, DI, DS, MC, VI. FAX (619) 543-1182   ⊗ ⑤ ⒟ (619) 543-1130

Comfort Inn-Downtown 93
⊛ 5/25-9/9 [CP]   1P 49.00- 67.00   2P/1B   .... 55.00   2P/2B   .... 78.00   XP 5   Motel ◆◆
  9/10-5/24 [CP]   1P 46.00- 65.00   2P/1B   .... 51.00   2P/2B   .... 74.00   XP 5   F
Senior discount. 67 units. 719 Ash St at 7th Ave. (92101) A/C; C/CATV; radios; phones; shower baths. Whirlpool.
Garage & parking lot. Airport transp. No pets. 3 rooms with microwave & refrigerator. Wkly & monthly rates avail.
Reserv deposit required. AE, DI, DS, MC, VI. FAX (619) 239-0138 *(See ad below)*   (619) 232-2525

Comfort Inn-La Mesa 54
⊛ 5/24-9/4 [CP]   1P .... 49.50   2P/1B   .... 54.50   2P/2B   .... 58.50   XP 5   Motel ◆◆
128 units. Fletcher Pkwy, 1/4 blk e of Baltimore Dr. 8000 Parkway Dr. (La Mesa, 92042) OPEN ALL YEAR. 30 refrigerators; A/C; C/CATV; movies; rental VCPs. Radios; phones. Coin laundry. Small pool; whirlpool. No pets. AE,
DI, DS, MC, VI. FAX (619) 698-6347 *(See ad below)*   ⊗ ⑤ ⒟ ⑤ (619) 698-7747

Comfort Inn-Mission Bay 35
⊛ 7/1-9/15   1P .... 44.95   2P/1B   .... 51.95   2P/2B   .... 61.95   XP 7   Motel ◆◆
  9/16-6/30   1P .... 39.95   2P/1B   .... 46.95   2P/2B   .... 56.95   XP 7   F
Senior discount. 63 units. 3/4 mi nw, SR 209 Rosecrans St. 3747 Midway Dr. (92110) A/C; C/CATV; movies; rental
VCPs. Radios; phones; comb or shower baths. Coin laundry. Parking lot. No pets. 2 2-room suites with whirlpool tub, refrigerator & microwave, $89.95. Few units with microwave & refrigerator, $15 extra. Wkly & monthly
rates avail. AE, DI, DS, MC, VI. Restaurant opposite. FAX (619) 222-2123 *(See ad below)* ⊗ ⒟ (619) 225-1295

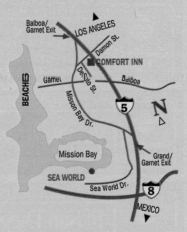

(See SAN DIEGO spotting map pages A376 & A377)

Comfort Inn-Sea World Area 27
ⓐ Fri & Sat 6/1-8/31 [CP] .... Rates Subject to Change
Sun-Thurs 6/1-8/31 [CP] ....
9/1-5/31 [CP] ....

									Motel	◆◆
		2P/1B	59.00- 79.00	2P/2B	59.00- 89.00	XP	5			F
		2P/1B	59.00- 69.00	2P/2B	59.00- 79.00	XP	5			F
		2P/1B	46.00- 59.00	2P/2B	46.00- 69.00	XP	5			F

Senior discount. 85 units. From I-5, northbound exit Grand/Garnet, southbound exit Balboa/Garnet; 1 blk e of Mission Bay Dr. 4610 DeSoto St. (92109) Formerly Mission Bay Travelodge. A/C; C/CATV; movies; VCPs. Radios; phones. Coin laundry. Htd pool; whirlpool. Garage. No pets. Wkly & monthly rates avail. Reserv deposit required; 3 days refund notice. AE, DI, DS, MC, VI. Restaurant adjacent. FAX (619) 483-4010 *(See ad p A388)*
⊗ Ⓢ Ⓓ Ⓛ (619) 483-9800

Comfort Suites Hotel Circle 64
ⓐ 5/21-9/15 [CP]   AAA Special Value Rates   *Motel*   ◆◆◆

1P	61.00- 72.00	2P/1B	66.00- 82.00	2P/2B	66.00- 82.00	XP	8		F

122 units. S side of I-8, exit Mission Center Rd. 631 Camino Del Rio S. (92108) OPEN ALL YEAR. Refrigerators; A/C; C/CATV; movies; radios; phones. Coin laundry. Htd pool; whirlpool; exercise rm. Airport transp. No pets. Reserv deposit required. AE, DI, DS, MC, VI. FAX (619) 294-3444 *(See ad starting on p A394)*
⊗ Ⓢ Ⓓ Ⓛ (619) 294-3444

Courtyard by Marriott 30
Fri & Sat 7/1-9/30 Rates Subject to Change
Sun-Thurs
Fri & Sat 10/1-6/30

							Motor Inn	◆◆◆
1P	....	89.00	2P/1B	....	89.00	2P/2B	.... 89.00 XP	
1P	....	79.00	2P/1B	....	79.00	2P/2B	.... 79.00 XP 10	
1P	....	68.00	2P/1B	....	68.00	2P/2B	.... 68.00 XP 10	

149 units. 1/2 mi e I-805; exit Mira Mesa. 9650 Scranton. (92121) Check-in 3 pm. 18 refrigerators; A/C; C/CATV; free & pay movies; radios; phones. Coin laundry. Htd pool; indoor whirlpool; exercise rm. No pets. AE, DI, DS, MC, VI. ● Restaurant; 6:30 am-2 & 5-10 pm; Sat & Sun from 7 am; $5.95-$14.95; cocktails. FAX (619) 558-4539 *(See ad below)*
⊗ Ⓢ Ⓓ Ⓛ (619) 558-9600

Crown City Inn 115
5/1-9/15 Rates Subject to Change
9/16-4/30

							Motor Inn	◆◆
1P	59.50- 65.00	2P/1B	59.50- 65.00	2P/2B	65.00- 75.00 XP			
1P	49.50- 59.50	2P/1B	49.50- 59.50	2P/2B	62.50- 72.50 XP			

33 units. 520 Orange Ave. (Coronado, 92118) Attractively decorated rooms. Check-in 3 pm. A/C; C/CATV; movies; radios; phones; shower or comb baths. Coin laundry. Small pool. Limited parking lot. No pets. Some rooms with microwave & refrigerator. Wkly & monthly rates avail. Reserv deposit required. AE, DI, DS, MC, VI. ● Restaurant; 8 am-2 & 5-9 pm; $6.50-$11.95. FAX (619) 435-6750 *(See ad below)*
⊗ Ⓓ (619) 435-3116

Crown Point View Suite-Hotel 120
ⓐ 6/15-9/14 & 12/15-4/14 [CP]   AAA Special Value Rates   *Apartment Motel*   ◆◆◆
9/15-12/14 & 4/15-6/14 [CP]

1P	80.00- 95.00	2P/1B	80.00- 125.00	2P/2B	95.00- 150.00	XP	5-10	F
1P	70.00- 85.00	2P/1B	75.00- 95.00	2P/2B	85.00- 125.00	XP	5-10	F

19 units. 1/4 blk s of Pacific Beach Dr. 4088 Crown Point Dr. (92109) Well-equipped studios, 1- & 2-bedroom apartments. Check-in 3 pm. C/CATV; movies; phones. Coin laundry. Pets. 7-night minimum stay. Wkly & monthly rates avail. Reserv deposit required; 14 days refund notice. AE, DI, DS, MC, VI. *(See ad p A390)*
Ⓓ (619) 272-0676

Dana Inn & Marina 39
ⓐ All year   Rates Guaranteed   *Motor Inn*   ◆◆

1P	69.50- 129.50	2P/1B	79.50- 139.50	2P/2B	79.50- 139.50	XP	10	F

Senior discount. 196 units. In Mission Bay Park. 1710 W Mission Bay Dr. (92109) Check-in 4 pm. 8 refrigerators; A/C; C/TV; radios; phones; shower or comb baths. Coin laundry. Htd pool; whirlpool; rental boats; tennis-2 courts; rental bicycles. Fee for: dock. Airport transp. No pets. Reserv deposit required. AE, DI, DS, MC, VI. ● Restaurant; 7 am-10 pm; $6-$10; beer & wine. FAX (619) 222-5916 *(See ad p A391)* ⊗ Ⓓ (619) 222-6440

Days Inn-Hotel Circle 66
ⓐ All year   Rates Guaranteed   *Motor Inn*   ◆◆

1P	55.50- 69.50	2P/1B	59.50- 69.50	2P/2B	59.50- 79.50	XP	10	F

Senior discount. 282 units. S side of I-8. 543 Hotel Circle S. (92108) Check-in 4 pm. Refrigerators; A/C; C/CATV; movies; radios; phones. 49 efficiencies. Coin laundry. Htd pool; whirlpool. No pets. Reserv deposit required. AE, DI, DS, MC, VI. ● Coffeeshop; 6:30 am-9 pm; Sun from 7 am; $3-$7. FAX (619) 298-6029
⊗ Ⓓ Ⓛ (619) 297-8800

(See SAN DIEGO spotting map pages A376 & A377)

Days Inn Suites ⟨87⟩   Rates Subject to Change   *Motel*   ◆◆

	1P	49.00- 55.00	2P/1B	49.00- 55.00	2P/2B	58.00- 75.00	XP 5
6/26-9/7							
9/8-6/25	1P	43.00- 46.00	2P/1B	45.00- 49.00	2P/2B	50.00- 55.00	XP 5

Senior discount. 66 units. 1/2 blk s of Grape St; from I-5 southbound exit Front St, northbound exit Hawthorn St. 1919 Pacific Hwy. (92101) Formerly 7 + 1 Mototel. 1 block to Embarcadero. Refrigerators; A/C; C/CATV; movies; radios; phones. 2 2-bedrm units. Coin laundry. Htd pool. No pets. Reserv deposit required. AE, DI, DS, MC, VI. FAX (619) 233-6977 *(See ad below)*   ⊗ Ⓓ (619) 232-1077

(See SAN DIEGO spotting map pages A376 & A377)

Days Suites-Point Loma **46**   AAA Special Value Rates   *Motel*   ◆◆
  All year [BP]   1P 55.00- 84.00   2P/1B   59.00- 89.00   2P/2B   59.00- 89.00 XP 7   F
  159 units. 3/4 mi w of jct I-5 & I-8. 3350 Rosecrans St. (92110) 78 1-bedroom suites with living room. Check-in 3 pm.
  Refrigerators; A/C; C/CATV; movies; rental VCPs. Phones. Coin laundry. Htd pool; whirlpool. Airport transp. No pets. AE,
  DI, DS, MC, VI. FAX (619) 224-9800   ⊗ Ⓓ 🛇 (619) 224-9800

Doubletree Hotel at Horton Plaza **98**   Rates Guaranteed   *Hotel*   ◆◆◆◆
  ⓐ All year   1P .... 99.00   2P/1B   .... 109.00   2P/2B   .... 109.00 XP 15   F
  450 units. 1 blk s of Broadway, adjacent to Horton Plaza. 910 Broadway Cir. (92101) Formerly Omni San Diego
  Hotel. Check-in 3 pm. 10 refrigerators; A/C; C/CATV; free & pay movies; radios; phones. Htd pool; saunas; indoor whirlpool. Fee for: lighted tennis-2 courts; health club & massage; airport transp. Pay valet garage. No
  pets. AE, DI, DS, MC, VI. ● 2 restaurants; 6:30 am-11 pm; $7.95-$21; cocktails. FAX (619) 239-0509 *(See ad*
  below)   ⊗ Ⓢ Ⓓ 🛇 (619) 239-2200

Econo Lodge **82**   Rates Subject to Change   *Motel*   ◆◆
  ⓐ 6/17-9/3 [CP]   1P 41.00- 49.00   2P/1B   46.00- 58.00   2P/2B   46.00- 58.00 XP 5
  9/4-6/16 [CP]   1P 36.00- 40.00   2P/1B   45.00- 50.00   2P/2B   45.00- 50.00 XP 3
  Senior discount. 45 units. 2 blks n of SR 94 Frwy; exit Spring St. 4210 Spring St. (La Mesa, 91941) A/C; C/CATV;
  movies; radios; phones. Coin laundry. No pets. Microwaves & refrigerators. Wkly rates avail. AE, MC, VI.
  FAX (619) 469-0654 *(See ad p A393)*   ⊗ Ⓓ (619) 589-7288

Econolodge Sports Arena **41**   AAA Special Value Rates   *Motel*   ◆◆
  ⓐ All year   1P 42.00- 53.00   2P/1B   42.00- 53.00   2P/2B   48.00- 55.00 XP 5
  150 units. Adjacent to I-5 & I-8; Sports Arena area. 3880 Greenwood St. (92110) Formerly Budget Motels of
  America. 38 refrigerators; A/C; C/CATV; movies; radios; phones. Coin laundry. No pets. Wkly & monthly rates
  avail. AE, DI, DS, MC, VI. FAX (619) 574-1437   ⊗ Ⓢ Ⓓ 🛇 (619) 543-9944

(See SAN DIEGO spotting map pages A376 & A377)

Embassy Suites-San Diego Bay 108   Rates Subject to Change   *Suites Hotel* ◆◆◆
All year [BP]   1P 119.00- 189.00   2P/1B   129.00- 199.00   2P/2B   129.00- 199.00   XP 15   F
Senior discount. 337 units. Corner Pacific Hwy & Market St. 601 Pacific Hwy. (92101) Suites with living room & efficiency. Check-in 4 pm. Refrigerators; A/C; C/CATV; free & pay movies; radios; phones. Coin laundry. Htd indoor pool; sauna; whirlpool; exercise rm. Pay valet garage. Airport transp. Reserv deposit required; 3 days refund notice. Complimentary beverages each evening. AE, DI, DS, MC, VI. ● Restaurant; 9:30 am-midnight; $9-$15; cocktails; entertainment. FAX (619) 239-1520   ⊗ Ⓢ Ⓓ Ⓛ (619) 239-2400

Executive Hotel & Suites 117   Rates Guaranteed   *Motel* ◆◆◆
All year [CP]   1P   59.00- 78.00   2P/1B   59.00- 78.00   2P/2B   59.00- 78.00   XP   4   F
Senior discount. 198 units. Adjacent to I-5 & I-8; Sports Arena area. 3888 Greenwood St. (92110) 100 refrigerators; A/C; C/CATV; movies; radios; phones; comb or shower baths. Coin laundry. Htd pool; whirlpool. Airport transp. No pets. Reserv deposit required; 3 days refund notice. AE, DI, DS, MC, VI. FAX (619) 291-8333   ⊗ Ⓢ Ⓓ Ⓛ (619) 299-6633

Fabulous Inn-San Diego 49   Rates Guaranteed   *Motel* ◆◆
6/15-9/7 [CP]   1P   56.00- 66.00   2P/1B   60.00- 70.00   2P/2B   65.00- 75.00   XP   5
3/1-6/14 & 9/8-11/30 [CP]   1P   49.00- 56.00   2P/1B   52.00- 60.00   2P/2B   57.00- 65.00   XP   5
12/1-2/29 [CP]   1P   46.00- 51.00   2P/1B   49.00- 54.00   2P/2B   52.00- 60.00   XP   5
176 units. Adjacent to I-8, exit Taylor St. 2485 Hotel Circle Pl. (92108) Check-in 4 pm. 74 refrigerators; A/C; C/CATV; movies; radios; phones. Coin laundry. Htd pool; whirlpool; 70 rooms with whirlpool tub. No pets. Wkly & monthly rates avail. Reserv deposit required. AE, DI, DS, MC, VI. Restaurant adjacent. FAX (619) 297-6179 *(See ad p A392)*   ⊗ Ⓓ (619) 291-7700

Glorietta Bay Inn-Coronado 103   Rates Subject to Change   *Motel* ◆◆
6/15-9/7   1P   79.00- 179.00   2P/1B   99.00- 179.00   2P/2B   99.00- 179.00   XP 10
9/8-6/14   1P   79.00- 129.00   2P/1B   89.00- 129.00   2P/2B   89.00- 129.00   XP 10
Senior discount. 98 units. On SR 75. 1630 Glorietta Blvd at Orange Ave. (Coronado, 92118) In 2-story buildings around the historic Spreckel's mansion. Some rooms with bay view. Nicely landscaped. Check-in 4 pm. Refrigerators; A/C; C/CATV; radios; phones; comb or shower baths. 20 kitchens, 12 efficiencies. Coin laundry. Htd pool; rental bicycles. No pets. Reserv deposit required; 3 days refund notice. AE, CB, DI, MC, VI. FAX (619) 435-6182   ⊗ Ⓓ (619) 435-3101

Grosvenor Inn 45   Rates Guaranteed   *Motor Inn* ◆◆◆
5/21-9/15   1P   ....   62.00   2P/1B   ....   62.00   2P/2B   ....   62.00   XP
9/16-5/20   1P   ....   55.00   2P/1B   ....   55.00   2P/2B   ....   55.00   XP
206 units. 1/4 mi sw of jct I-5 & I-8, exit Rosecrans St. 3145 Sports Arena Blvd at Rosecrans St. (92110) Check-in 3 pm. Refrigerators; A/C; C/CATV; free & pay movies; radios; phones. Coin laundry. Htd pool; whirlpool. Airport transp. No pets. Wkly & monthly rates avail. Reserv deposit required. AE, DI, DS, MC, VI. ● Restaurant & coffeeshop; 7 am-10 pm; $5-$9; cocktails. FAX (619) 225-0958 *(See ad starting on p A394)*   ⊗ Ⓓ (619) 225-9999

Hampton Inn-Kearny Mesa 104   Rates Subject to Change   *Motel* ◆◆◆
All year [CP]   1P 68.00- 74.00   2P/1B   80.00- 74.00   2P/2B   78.00- 84.00   XP   F
151 units. Adjacent to SR 163; exit Clairmont Mesa. 5434 Kearny Mesa Rd. (92111) 10 refrigerators; A/C; C/CATV; free & pay movies; radios; phones. Coin laundry. Htd pool. No pets. Rooms with refrigerator & microwave, $54-$66, for 7 to 30 day stay. Some rooms with VCP. AE, DI, DS, MC, VI. FAX (619) 292-4410   ⊗ Ⓢ Ⓓ Ⓛ (619) 292-1482

Hanalei Hotel 50   Rates Subject to Change   *Hotel* ◆◆
All year   1P 80.00- 110.00   2P/1B   90.00- 120.00   2P/2B   90.00- 120.00   XP 10
424 units. N side of I-8. 2270 Hotel Cir. (92108) Beautifully landscaped grounds. Polynesian atmosphere. Check-in 3 pm. 158 refrigerators; A/C; C/CATV; pay movies; radios; phones. Htd pool; whirlpool. No pets. Reserv deposit required. AE, DI, DS, MC, VI. ● Coffeeshop; 6:30 am-9:30 pm; in summer-10 pm; $7-$10.75; cocktails; entertainment. Also, Islands Restaurant, see separate listing. FAX (619) 297-6049 *(See ad p A397)*   ⊗ Ⓓ Ⓛ (619) 297-1101

Four San Diego Lo
Convenience

GROSVENOR INN, Sports Arena
- 206 guest rooms with refrigerators.
- Complimentary in-room coffee, FREE HBO & remote.
- Large heated pool & spa • restaurant.
- FREE airport shuttle • FREE parking.
- Walk to Old Town & shopping.
- 3 blocks off (I-5 & I-8) exit Rosecrans.
  3145 Sports Arena Blvd.
  (619) 225-9999

$55 9/15/ to 5/20
$62 5/21 to 9/14

COMFORT SUITES, Hotel Circle
- Deluxe mini suites with refrigerators
- Remote control TV, FREE HBO • Exercise room.
- FREE continental breakfast.
- 10 minutes to Sea World, Zoo, Stadium shopping centers.
- In the heart of Mission Valley • I-8 exit.
  631 Camino del Rio South
  (619) 294-3444

$62 9/15/ to 5/20
$72 5/21 to 9/14

SUPER 8, Mission Bay
- 117 deluxe rooms.
- FREE coffee • HBO.
- Swimming pool.
- Next to Mission Bay Golf & Mission Bay Parks
- Walk to restaurants.
- Directly off I-5 next to Mission Bay.
  4540 Mission Bay Drive
  (619) 274-7888

$44 9/15/ to 5/20
$54 5/21 to 9/14

GROSVENOR HO
Toll FREE
Nationwide

**Rates valid for 1 to 4 persons in room.
Must ask for AAA rate**

cations offering . . .
& Comfort

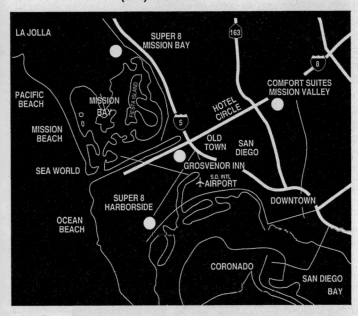

America Is Turning In At Howard Johnson.

More And More, When Travelers Are Looking For Super Rates And Great Value, They're Turning To Howard Johnson.

For business and pleasure, today's travelers are choosing Howard Johnson wherever they go. Howard Johnson's super rates offer the best lodging value available, with all the comfort and convenience you've come to expect.

Howard Johnson offers you many ways to save you money. Our Family Packages, where kids stay free, make savings on travel a breeze for the whole family. And if you're a senior, our Road Rally discounts offer even more savings.

When traveling on business, look to the Executive Section at Howard Johnson properties for special amenities. Your complimentary wake-up and coffee service, a morning newspaper and a welcome snack on arrival all serve to make your stay more relaxing and enjoyable.

Whatever your reason for traveling, look for Howard Johnson's over 575 locations throughout the United States, Mexico and Canada to welcome you.

FOR RESERVATIONS CALL
1·800·I·GO·HOJO
OR YOUR LOCAL TRAVEL PROFESSIONAL
1-800-446-4656

When The Sun Goes Down, America Turns To Orange.

®1993 Hospitality Franchise Systems, Inc.

(See SAN DIEGO spotting map pages A376 & A377)

Handlery Hotel & Country Club 🖬   AAA Special Value Rates   *Motor Inn* ◆◆
🚲 5/16-10/16   1P 65.00- 85.00   2P/1B 75.00- 95.00   2P/2B 75.00- 95.00 XP 10   F
216 units. N side of I-8. 950 Hotel Cir N. (92108) OPEN ALL YEAR. Check-in 3 pm. A/C; C/CATV; movies; radios;
phones. 2 htd pools; wading pool; paddle tennis court; exercise rm. Fee for: golf-27 holes, tennis-8 courts, 6
lighted; racquetball-2 courts; massage. No pets. AE, DI, MC, VI. ● Dining rm & 2 coffeeshops; 24 hours; $5-$15;
cocktails; entertainment. FAX (619) 298-9793 *(See ad p A398)*   ⊗ Ⓓ (619) 298-0511

Heritage Park Bed & Breakfast Inn 🖬   AAA Special Value Rates   *Bed & Breakfast* ◆◆
🚲 All year [BP]   1P 80.00- 120.00   2P/1B 80.00- 120.00   2P/2B 80.00- 120.00 XP 15
8 units. Off Juan St, in Old Town area. 2470 Heritage Park Row. (92110) Delightful victorian style home in Heri-
tage Park. Some rooms with shared bath. Smoking in restricted areas. Check-in 3 pm. 4 comb or shower baths.
Airport transp. No pets. 2-night minimum stay Fri & Sat 7/1-8/31. Reserv deposit required; 7 days refund notice.
MC, VI. FAX (619) 299-6832   ⊗ Ⓢ Ⓓ (619) 299-6832

Holiday Inn Express-Sea World Area 🖬   Rates Subject to Change   *Motel* ◆◆◆
🚲 All year [CP]   1P 58.00- 68.00   2P/1B 66.00- 76.00   2P/2B 66.00- 76.00 XP 10   F
Senior discount. 70 units. 1 3/4 mi sw of jct I-5 & I-8; from I-5 southbound exit Rosecrans St, northbound exit I-8
& Sports Arena Blvd. 3950 Jupiter St. (92110) A/C; C/CATV; movies; radios; phones. Coin laundry. Small htd
pool; whirlpool. Garage. No pets. AE, DI, DS, MC, VI. FAX (619) 226-1409 *(See ad p A400)*
⊗ Ⓢ Ⓓ ▣ (619) 226-8000

spotting map pages A376 & A377)

View 88   Rates Guaranteed   *Motor Inn* ◆◆◆
1P 80.00- 118.00   2P/1B   90.00- 128.00   2P/2B   90.00- 128.00   XP 10
. 203 units. Adjacent to I-5; southbound exit Front St, northbound exit 6th Ave. 1617 1st Ave. (92101) A/C;
pay movies; radios; phones. Rental refrigerators. Coin laundry. Pool. Garage & parking ramp. Airport
. Monthly rates avail. Reserv deposit required. AE, DI, DS, MC, VI. ● Dining rm; 6 am-10 pm; $6.95-
$14.95; ...ails. FAX (619) 233-6228   ⊗ Ⓓ (619) 239-6171

Holiday Inn-Hotel Circle 65   Rates Subject to Change   *Hotel* ◆◆◆
🅐🅐 All year   ....   2P/1B   69.00- 89.00   2P/2B   79.00- 99.00   XP 10   F
Senior discount. 316 units. S side of I-8. 595 Hotel Circle S. (92108) Check-in 3 pm. 5 refrigerators; A/C; C/CATV;
movies; radios; phones. Coin laundry. Htd pool; whirlpool; exercise rm. Parking lot. No pets. Reserv deposit re-
quired; 3 days refund notice. AE, DI, DS, MC, VI. ● Dining rm; 6:30 am-10 pm; $6-$18; cocktails; entertainment.
FAX (619) 297-7362 *(See ad p A399)*   ⊗ Ⓢ Ⓓ ⓔ (619) 291-5720

Holiday Inn Montgomery Field 68   Rates Guaranteed   *Motor Inn* ◆◆◆
All year   1P 76.00- 104.00   2P/1B   84.00- 112.00   2P/2B   84.00- 112.00   XP 8   F
Senior discount. 225 units. From SR 163, southbound exit Balboa Ave, 1 mi se via Kearny Villa Rd, northbound exit
Kearny Villa Rd, 3/4 mi ne. 8110 Aero Dr. (92123) 7 refrigerators; A/C; C/CATV; free & pay movies; radios; phones. Coin
laundry. Htd pool; sauna; whirlpool; exercise rm. Airport transp. Pets. Monthly rates avail. Reserv deposit required; 3
days refund notice. AE, DI, DS, MC, VI. ● Restaurant; 6 am-10 pm; $6-$12; cocktails; entertainment.
FAX (619) 277-8888   ⊗ Ⓢ Ⓓ ⓔ (619) 277-8888

Holiday Inn On The Bay 89   Rates Subject to Change   *Hotel* ◆◆◆
🅐🅐 All year   1P 68.00- 98.00   2P/1B   68.00- 98.00   2P/2B   68.00- 98.00   XP 15   F
Senior discount. 600 units. 1355 N Harbor Dr at Ash St. (92101) Many rooms with view of harbor or city skyline.
Check-in 3 pm. 30 refrigerators; A/C; C/CATV; free & pay movies; radios; phones. Coin laundry. Htd pool; whirl-
pool. Pay parking lot & garage. Airport transp. Small pets only. Reserv deposit required. AE, DI, DS, MC,
VI. ● Restaurant; 6 am-10 pm; $6-$17; cocktails; entertainment. FAX (619) 232-4924 *(See ad below)*
     ⊗ Ⓓ ⓔ (619) 232-3861

STOP! YOU'VE FOUND A PERFECT NEW HOTEL AT A PERFECT LOCATION.

Holiday Inn
AT HOTEL CIRCLE • SEA WORLD / ZOO AREA

Spacious New Rooms at an Introductory AAA Rate...

FEATURES: 320 completely renovated rooms with King or 2 Queens ■ Rainbow Cafe offers a delightfully casual setting featuring California cuisine at its best ■ Piano Bar offers a festive Happy Hour ■ Gift Shop ■ Video Game Room ■ Fitness Center ■ Room Service ■ Sparkling Heated Pool & Spa ■ FREE fresh brewed coffee In Room ■ FREE In-Room Movie Channel (Showtime) ■ FREE Parking ■ Refrigerator available

$59*
AAA MEMBER SPECIAL
UP TO 4 PERSONS
PER ROOM, PER NIGHT

* July - August & holidays $69 to $79.
Subject to limited availability.

LOCATION: on famous Hotel Circle within seven minutes to Sea World, San Diego Zoo, Mission Bay, Airport, Historic Old Town, J.M.Stadium, Downtown and Miles of Sandy Beaches, Opposite San Diego's Largest Shopping Malls.

AAA THREE DIAMOND AWARD

1-800-433-2131

595 Hotel Circle South, San Diego California 92108 (619) 291-5720 FAX (619) 297-7362

In San Diego...Three Great Locations

All three locations are minutes away from San Diego Main Attractions!

RANCHO BERNARDO
17065 W. Bernardo Dr.
San Diego, CA 92127
(off I-15 at Rancho
Bernardo Rd.)

(619) 485-6530

$59.00*

- **Closest Hotel to the Wild Animal Park**
- Comp. Con'tl Breakfast
- Pool & Spa
- In-room Movies

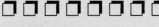

SAN DIEGO NORTH MIRAMAR
9335 Kearny Mesa Rd.
San Diego, CA 92126
(off I-15 at Miramar Rd.)

(619) 695-2300

$64.00*

- **Minutes from Zoo, Sea World, Mission Bay & Beaches**
- Comp. Con'tl Breakfast & Happy Hour
- Pool, Spa & Sauna
- In-room movies
- Marie Callenders Restaurant

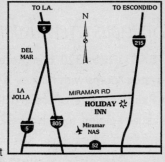

EXPRESS

SEA WORLD AREA
3950 Jupiter Street
San Diego, CA 92110
(I-8 at Sports Arena Blvd.)

(619) 226-8000

$59.00*

- **Only 1/2 mile from Sea World, Mission Bay & Beaches**
- Comp. Con'tl Breakfast
- Pool & Spa

* Up to 4 people based on availability. 6/26/93 - 9/6/93 and Holidays add $5.00 more.

Call Toll Free: (800) 356-3307

(See SAN DIEGO spotting map pages A376 & A377)

Holiday Inn San Diego North-Miramar 🄸🄸   Rates Subject to Change   *Motor Inn* ◆◆◆
🄰🄰 All year [CP]   1P 75.00- 95.00 2P/1B 85.00- 105.00 2P/2B 85.00- 105.00 XP 10
Senior discount. 155 units. Adjacent to I-15; exit Miramar Rd. 9335 Kearny Mesa Rd. (92126) Refrigerators; A/C; C/CATV; free & pay movies; radios; phones. 15 2-bedrm units. Coin laundry. Htd pool; sauna; whirlpool; exercise rm. No pets. Some units with microwave & refrigerator, $85-$115. Wkly & monthly rates avail. Complimentary beverages each evening. AE, DI, DS, MC, VI. ● Restaurant; 6 am-10 pm; $5.50-$10.50; cocktails. FAX (619) 578-7925 *(See ad p A400)*   ⊗ Ⓢ Ⓓ ♿ (619) 695-2300

Hotel Circle Inn & Suites 🄸🄸   Rates Subject to Change   *Motor Inn* ◆◆
🄰🄰 6/1-8/31   ....   2P/1B 59.00- 89.00 2P/2B 59.00- 99.00 XP 5
9/1-5/31   ....   2P/1B 49.00- 69.00 2P/2B 49.00- 79.00 XP 5
Senior discount. 196 units. S side of I-8. 2201 Hotel Circle S. (92108) A/C; C/CATV; movies; radios; phones; comb or shower baths. Coin laundry. Htd pool; whirlpool. Pets. 24 2-room suites with kitchen, $69-$119. Wkly rates avail. Reserv deposit required; 3 days refund notice. AE, DI, DS, MC, VI. ● Coffeeshop; 6:30 am-11:30 pm; $6-$8.50; cocktails. FAX (619) 542-1227 *(See ad starting on p A380)*   ⊗ Ⓓ (619) 291-2711

Howard Johnson Hotel Circle 🄸🄸   Rates Subject to Change   *Motel* ◆◆
🄰🄰 6/1-9/15 [CP]   1P .... 64.00 2P/1B .... 69.00 2P/2B .... 74.00 XP 6 F
9/16-5/31 [CP]   1P .... 45.00 2P/1B .... 49.00 2P/2B .... 55.00 XP 6 F
Senior discount. 81 units. S side of I-8. 1631 Hotel Circle S. (92108) A/C; C/CATV; pay movies; radios; phones. Htd pool; whirlpool. No pets. Reserv deposit required. AE, DI, DS, MC, VI. FAX (619) 298-5321   ⊗ Ⓢ Ⓓ (619) 293-7792

Howard Johnson Hotel Harbor View 🄸🄸   AAA Special Value Rates   *Motor Inn* ◆◆
🄰🄰 All year   1P 59.00- 89.00 2P/1B 69.00- 89.00 2P/2B 69.00- 89.00 XP 10 F
135 units. 1430 7th Ave at Ash St. (92101) Many rooms with balcony. 13 refrigerators; A/C; C/CATV; free & pay movies; rental VCPs. Radios; phones. Coin laundry. Small htd pool; exercise rm. Airport transp. No pets. Wkly & monthly rates avail. Reserv deposit required; 3 days refund notice. AE, DI, DS, MC, VI. ● Coffeeshop; 6 am-10 pm; Sat & Sun from 7 am; $3.95-$6.95. FAX (619) 239-0138   ⊗ Ⓓ (619) 696-0911

Humphrey's Half Moon Inn 🄸🄸   Rates Guaranteed   *Motor Inn* ◆◆◆
🄰🄰 All year   1P 79.00- 159.00 2P/1B 89.00- 169.00 2P/2B 89.00- 169.00 XP 10 F
Senior discount. 182 units. On Shelter Island. 2303 Shelter Island Dr. (92106) Tropically landscaped grounds. Most rooms with bay or yacht harbor view. Check-in 4 pm. 80 refrigerators; A/C; C/CATV; movies; radios; phones; comb or shower baths. Coin laundry. Htd pool; whirlpool; bicycles. Fee for: boat slips. Airport transp. No pets. 30 suites with kitchen, $125-$250. Reserv deposit required. AE, DI, DS, MC, VI. ● Restaurant, see separate listing. FAX (619) 224-3478 *(See ad p A391)*   ⊗ Ⓓ ♿ (619) 224-3411

(See SAN DIEGO spotting map pages A376 & A377)

Hyatt Islandia 42   Rates Subject to Change   *Motor Inn* ◆◆◆
All year   1P 109.00- 185.00   2P/1B   124.00- 205.00   2P/2B   124.00- 184.00   XP 15   F
Senior discount. 423 units. In Mission Bay Park; off W Mission Bay Dr. 1441 Quivira Rd. (92109) Variety of accommodations. Low rise units in garden setting, tower units with bay view & marina suites on yacht harbor. Check-in 4 pm. 34 refrigerators; A/C; C/CATV; free & pay movies; VCPs. Radios; phones; comb or shower baths. Htd pool; whirlpool. Fee for: dock, fishing, airport transp. No pets. Luxury level rooms avail. Reserv deposit required. AE, DI, DS, MC, VI. ● Dining rm & restaurant; 6 am-11 pm; $7-$20; cocktails; entertainment.
FAX (619) 224-0348 *(See ad p A401)*   ⊗ Ⓓ (619) 224-1234

Hyatt Regency San Diego 53   Rates Subject to Change   *Hotel*
All year   1P 189.00- 209.00   2P/1B   189.00- 209.00   2P/2B   189.00- 209.00   XP 20
875 units. Harbor Dr & Market Pl. One Market Pl. (92101) Rating withheld pending completion of construction. Scheduled to open December, 1992. Check-in 3 pm. A/C; C/CATV; pay movies; radios; phones. Htd pool; sauna; whirlpool; tennis-4 courts; exercise rm. Pay valet garage. No pets. AE, DI, DS, MC, VI. ● 2 restaurants; 6 am-10 pm; $12-$30.
FAX (619) 239-5678   Ⓢ Ⓓ (619) 232-1234

Kings Inn 69   Rates Guaranteed   *Motor Inn* ◆◆
All year   1P   ....   57.00   2P/1B   ....   57.00   2P/2B   ....   57.00   XP 10
140 units. S side of I-8. 1333 Hotel Circle S. (92108) Check-in 3 pm. A/C; C/CATV; pay movies; phones. Htd pool; whirlpool. Fee for: airport transp. No pets. Reserv deposit required; 14 days refund notice. AE, DI, DS, MC, VI. ● Coffeeshop; 6:30 am-9:30 pm; $5-$8.50; cocktails. Also, Kings Grille, see separate listing.
FAX (619) 296-5255 *(See ad below)*   ⊗ Ⓓ (619) 297-2231

La Mesa Country Inn 58   Rates Subject to Change   *Motel* ◆◆
6/1-9/15   1P   ....   36.00   2P/1B   ....   41.00   2P/2B   ....   46.00   XP 5
9/16-5/31   1P   ....   29.00   2P/1B   ....   33.00   2P/2B   ....   38.00   XP 5
61 units. 1/2 blk w of La Mesa Blvd. 7911 University Ave. (La Mesa, 91941) A/C; C/CATV; 30 radios; phones. Coin laundry. Pool; exercise rm. No pets. Some rooms with microwave & refrigerator. AE, MC, VI.
                                                           Ⓢ Ⓓ (619) 466-5988

La Mesa Lodge 55   Rates Subject to Change   *Motel* ◆◆
All year   1P 31.00- 35.00   2P/1B   35.00- 38.00   2P/2B   38.00- 42.00   XP 5
39 units. 1/2 mi s of I-8; eastbound Fletcher Pkwy exit, westbound El Cajon Blvd exit. 7961 El Cajon Blvd at Baltimore Dr. (La Mesa, 91941) A/C; C/CATV; movies; radios; phones. Efficiencies. Coin laundry. Small pool. No pets. Wkly rates avail. Reserv deposit required. AE, MC, VI. Restaurant opposite. *(See ad p A403)*
                                                                Ⓓ (619) 697-3444

Lamplighter Inn & Suites 106   AAA Special Value Rates   *Motel* ◆◆
6/1-9/5   1P 40.86- 60.86   2P/1B   43.86- 63.86   2P/2B   45.86- 59.86   XP 5   F
63 units. 1 mi sw of I-8; exit 70th St. 6474 El Cajon Blvd. (92115) OPEN ALL YEAR. A/C; C/CATV; movies; radios; phones; comb or shower baths. Rental refrigerators. 32 kitchens. Coin laundry. Htd pool. Microwave rental. 2 2-room family units with kitchen $72-$85. Wkly & monthly rates avail. AE, DI, DS, MC, VI. Restaurant adjacent.
(See ad p A403)   ⊗ Ⓓ Ⓢ (619) 582-3088

(See SAN DIEGO spotting map pages A376 & A377)

Le Meridien San Diego At Coronado 105   Rates Subject to Change   *Hotel* ◆◆◆◆
(AAA) All year   1P 165.00- 250.00   2P/1B   165.00- 250.00   2P/2B   165.00- 250.00   XP 15   F
300 units. 1 1/2 blks e of 4th St at Glorietta Blvd & 2nd St. 2000 2nd St. (Coronado, 92118) Balconies with view
of bay or lagoon. Check-in 3 pm. A/C; C/CATV; free & pay movies; radios; phones. 3 htd pools; sauna; whirlpools; dock; water skiing; children's program; rental bicycles; jogging trail; health club. Fee for: lighted tennis-6
courts; massage. Pay valet garage. No pets. 1 & 2-bedroom villas, $180-$650. Reserv deposit required; 3 days
refund notice. AE, DI, DS, MC, VI. ● Dining rm & restaurant; 6:30 am-10 pm; $14-$23; 24 hour room service;
cocktails; entertainment. FAX (619) 435-3032   ⊗ Ⓢ Ⓓ Ⓛ (619) 435-3000

Loews Coronado Bay Resort 97   Rates Subject to Change   *Hotel* ◆◆◆◆
(AAA) All year   1P 180.00- 220.00   2P/1B   200.00- 240.00   2P/2B   200.00- 240.00   XP 20   F
Senior discount. 442 units. 5 3/4 mi s of Coronado Bridge, via Silver Strand Blvd. 4000 Coronado Bay Rd. (Coro-
nado, 92118) Check-in 3 pm. A/C; C/CATV; free & pay movies; radios; phones. 3 htd pools; saunas; whirlpools;
rental boats; marina; water skiing; children's program; rental bicycles; exercise rm. Fee for: lighted tennis-5
courts; massage. Pay valet parking ramp. Small pets only. Bayside suites, $280-$475. AE, DI, DS, MC,
VI. ● Dining rm & restaurant; 6 am-10:30 pm; $9.25-$26; 24 hour room service; cocktails; entertainment.
FAX (619) 424-4400   ⊗ Ⓢ Ⓓ (619) 424-4000

Marriott San Diego Marina 100   Rates Subject to Change   *Hotel* ◆◆◆◆
(AAA) All year   1P 149.00- 179.00   2P/1B   159.00- 179.00   2P/2B   159.00- 179.00   XP 20   F
Senior discount. 1355 units. Adjacent to Seaport Village. 333 W Harbor Dr. (92101) An impressive bayfront hotel.
Most rooms with harbor view. Check-in 4 pm. A/C; C/CATV; free & pay movies; radios; phones. Coin laundry. 2
htd pools; sauna; whirlpools; marina; small electric power boats; scuba instruction 5/1-10/31; children's pro-
gram; exercise rm. Fee for: lighted tennis-6 courts; massage. Pay valet garage & parking lot. Airport transp.
Pets. Reserv deposit required. AE, DI, DS, MC, VI. ● 2 dining rms & 2 restaurants; 6:30 am-11:30 pm; Fri & Sat-1
am; $6-$30; 24 hour room service; cocktails; entertainment. FAX (619) 234-8678 ⊗ Ⓢ Ⓓ Ⓛ (619) 234-1500

National Budget Inn 59   Rates Subject to Change   *Apartment Motel* ◆◆
(AAA) All year   1P 31.00- 35.00   2P/1B   35.00- 38.00   2P/2B   38.00- 42.00   XP 5   F
Senior discount. 41 units. From I-8; eastbound 70th St exit to El Cajon Blvd, 3/4 mi e; westbound El Cajon Blvd
exit, 1 mi w. 7475 El Cajon Blvd. (La Mesa, 91941) A/C; C/CATV; movies; radios; phones. Efficiencies. Coin
laundry. Small htd pool; whirlpool. No pets. Wkly & monthly rates avail. Reserv deposit required. AE, MC, VI.
Coffeeshop opposite. *(See ad p A404)*   ⊗ Ⓓ (619) 697-9005

Old Town Travelodge 86   Rates Guaranteed   *Motel* ◆◆◆
(AAA) All year [CP]   1P 39.00- 44.00   2P/1B   44.00- 59.00   2P/2B   49.00- 54.00   XP 5   F
Senior discount. 79 units. Adjacent to I-5, exit Old Town Ave, 1 blk n via Frontage Rd. 2380 Moore St. (92110)
Check-in 3 pm. 8 refrigerators; A/C; C/CATV; rental VCPs; phones. Coin laundry. Htd pool; whirlpool; 8 whirlpool
tubs. No pets. Microwaves. AE, DI, DS, MC, VI. FAX (619) 291-4717 *(See ad p A404)* ⊗ Ⓓ Ⓛ (619) 291-9100

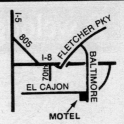

(See SAN DIEGO spotting map pages A376 & A377)

Pacific Shores Inn 116

		Rates Subject to Change				*Motel*		◆
6/14-9/15	1P 73.00- 90.00	2P/1B 73.00- 90.00	2P/2B 78.00- 95.00	XP 10	F
9/16-6/13	1P 58.00- 85.00	2P/1B 58.00- 85.00	2P/2B 63.00- 90.00	XP 5	F

56 units. In Pacific Beach area. 4802 Mission Blvd. (92109) 1/2 block from public beach. A/C; C/CATV; movies; radios; phones; comb or shower baths. Coin laundry. Htd pool; whirlpool. 6 kitchen units, $71-$115. 22 efficiency units, $5 extra; no utensils. Wkly & monthly rates avail. Reserv deposit required; 3 days refund notice. AE, DI, DS, MC, VI. FAX (619) 483-9276   Ⓓ (619) 483-6300

Pacific Terrace Inn 61

		AAA Special Value Rates				*Motel*		◆◆◆◆
6/15-9/14 [CP]	1P 150.00- 190.00	2P/1B 150.00- 190.00	2P/2B 150.00- 200.00	XP 10	F
9/15-6/14 [CP]	1P 110.00- 175.00	2P/1B 110.00- 175.00	2P/2B 125.00- 185.00	XP 5	F

73 units. Pacific Beach Area; 1 blk w of Mission Blvd. 610 Diamond St. (92109) Beachfront. Large rooms with balcony or patio, most with ocean view. Check-in 4 pm. Refrigerators; A/C; C/CATV; movies; radios; phones. 40 efficiencies. Coin laundry. Htd pool; whirlpool; 8 rooms with whirlpool tub. Garage. Airport transp. No pets. Wkly & monthly rates avail. Reserv deposit required; 3 days refund notice. AE, DI, DS, MC, VI. FAX (619) 274-3341 *(See ad p A379 and below)*   ⊗ Ⓢ Ⓓ 🅰 (619) 581-3500

(See SAN DIEGO spotting map pages A376 & A377)

The Pan Pacific Hotel 114 ♦♦♦♦
All year

		Rates Subject to Change		Hotel	
	1P 130.00- 150.00	2P/1B 150.00- 170.00	2P/2B 150.00- 170.00	XP 15	F

Senior discount. 436 units. At Emerald-Shapery Center between Columbia & State. 400 W Broadway. (92101) Check-in 4 pm. A/C; C/CATV; pay movies; radios; phones. 3 2-bedrm units. Htd pool; whirlpool. Fee for: health club & massage. Pay valet garage. Airport transp. No pets. Reserv deposit required. AE, DI, DS, MC, VI. ● Dining rm; 6 am-10 pm; $12-$25; 24 hour room service; cocktails. FAX (619) 239-3274

⊗ Ⓢ Ⓓ ⓬ (619) 239-4500

Quality Suites 34 ♦♦♦
7/1-9/2 [CP]
9/3-6/30 [CP]

			AAA Special Value Rates		Suites Motel	
1P	....	89.00	2P/1B	....	99.00	2P/2B	....	99.00	XP 10
1P	....	79.00	2P/1B	....	89.00	2P/2B	....	89.00	XP

130 units. Just e of I-15; exit Mira Mesa Blvd. 9880 Mira Mesa Blvd. (92131) 1-bedroom suites with living room & microwave. Check-in 3 pm. Refrigerators; A/C; C/CATV; movies; VCPs. Radios; phones. 5 2-bedrm units. Htd pool; whirlpool; exercise rm. No pets. Reserv deposit required. Complimentary beverages each evening. AE, DI, DS, MC, VI. Restaurant adjacent. FAX (619) 530-2000

⊗ Ⓢ Ⓓ ⓬ (619) 530-2000

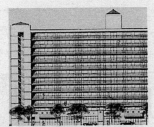

(See SAN DIEGO spotting map pages A376 & A377)

Radisson Hotel Harbor View 109   Rates Guaranteed   *Hotel* ◆◆◆
All year   1P 109.00- 129.00   2P/1B   109.00- 129.00   2P/2B   109.00- 129.00   XP 10   F
Senior discount. 333 units. 1646 Front St. (92101) Check-in 3 pm. A/C; C/CATV; free & pay movies; radios; phones. Rental refrigerators. Htd pool; sauna; whirlpool; exercise rm. Pay garage. Airport transp. Small pets only. Suites with whirlpool tub, $159-$189. AE, DI, DS, MC, VI. ● Restaurant; 6:30 am-11 pm; $9-$22; cocktails.
FAX (619) 238-9461 *(See ad below)*   ⊗ Ⓢ Ⓓ Ⓛ (619) 239-6800

Radisson Hotel-San Diego 62   Rates Guaranteed   *Hotel* ◆◆◆
All year   1P   79.00- 125.00   2P/1B   89.00- 135.00   2P/2B   89.00- 135.00   XP 10
Senior discount. 260 units. S side of I-8, exit Mission Center Rd. 1433 Camino Del Rio S. (92108) Many balconies. Check-in 3 pm. A/C; C/CATV; pay movies; radios; phones. Htd pool; whirlpool; exercise rm. Parking lot. Airport transp. Small pets only. AE, DI, DS, MC, VI. ● Dining rm; 6:30-10:30 am, 11:30-2 & 5:30-11 pm; Sun brunch 10 am-2 pm; $8-$12; cocktails. FAX (619) 497-0854 *(See ad starting on p A382)*
     ⊗ Ⓢ Ⓓ Ⓛ (619) 260-0111

Ramada Hotel Bay View 112   Rates Guaranteed   *Hotel* ◆◆◆
5/24-9/7   1P   ....   99.00   2P/1B   ....   109.00   2P/2B   ....   109.00   XP 15   F
9/8-5/23   1P   ....   89.00   2P/1B   ....   99.00   2P/2B   ....   99.00   XP 15   F
Senior discount. 312 units. 660 K St at 6th Ave. (92101) Check-in 3 pm. A/C; C/CATV; free & pay movies; radios; phones. Coin laundry. Sauna; whirlpool; exercise rm. Pay garage. Airport transp. No pets. 2 room suites, $129-$139. Reserv deposit required. AE, DI, DS, MC, VI. ● Restaurant; 6 am-11 pm; $5.95-$17.75; cocktails. FAX (619) 231-8199 *(See ad p A407)*   ⊗ Ⓢ Ⓓ Ⓛ (619) 696-0234

Ramada Hotel-Old Town 47   Rates Subject to Change   *Motor Inn* ◆◆◆
All year [BP]   1P 99.00- 109.00   2P/1B   109.00- 119.00   2P/2B   109.00- 129.00   XP 10   F
Senior discount. 152 units. Adjacent to I-5, exit Old Town Ave. 2435 Jefferson St. (92110) Check-in 3 pm. 25 refrigerators; A/C; C/CATV; radios; phones. Htd pool; whirlpool. Airport transp. No pets. Wkly & monthly rates avail. Reserv deposit required. Complimentary beverages each evening. AE, DI, DS, MC, VI. ● Restaurant; 6 am-2 & 5-10 pm; $8-$14; cocktails. FAX (619) 297-2078 *(See ad p A408)*   ⊗ Ⓢ Ⓓ Ⓛ (619) 260-8500

Ramada Inn-Hotel Circle 72   Rates Guaranteed   *Motor Inn* ◆◆◆
All year   1P 65.00- 75.00   2P/1B   70.00- 89.00   2P/2B   70.00- 89.00   XP 10   F
Senior discount. 183 units. S side of I-8. 2151 Hotel Circle S. (92108) Check-in 3 pm. A/C; C/CATV; movies; radios; phones. Rental refrigerators. Htd pool; whirlpool. No pets. Reserv deposit required. AE, DI, DS, MC, VI. ● The Tickled Trout, see separate listing. FAX (619) 294-7531   ⊗ Ⓢ Ⓓ Ⓛ (619) 291-6500

Red Lion Hotel/San Diego 48   Rates Subject to Change   *Hotel* ◆◆◆
All year   1P 133.00- 153.00   2P/1B   143.00- 163.00   2P/2B   143.00- 163.00   XP 10   F
300 units. Adjacent to SR 163, exit Friars Rd. 7450 Hazard Center Dr. (92108) Check-in 3 pm. A/C; C/CATV; pay movies; radios; phones. 2 htd pools, 1 indoor; sauna; whirlpool; lighted tennis-2 courts; exercise rm. Valet parking lot. Airport transp. AE, DI, DS, MC, VI. ● Dining rm & coffeeshop; 6 am-11 pm; $9-$18; cocktails; entertainment. FAX (619) 297-5499 *(See ad p A3)*   ⊗ Ⓢ Ⓓ Ⓛ (619) 297-5466

(See SAN DIEGO spotting map pages A376 & A377)

Regency Plaza Hotel 🔟 ♿
All year | Rates Guaranteed | Motor Inn ◆◆◆
1P .... 69.00   2P/1B .... 79.00   2P/2B .... 79.00   XP 15   F
Senior discount. 217 units. S side of I-8. 1515 Hotel Circle S. (92108) Check-in 3 pm. A/C; C/CATV; pay movies; radios; phones. Coin laundry. Htd pool; sauna; whirlpool; exercise rm. Valet parking ramp. Airport transp. No pets. 29 large rooms with wet bar & refrigerator. Reserv deposit required. AE, DI, DS, MC, VI. ● Dining rm; 6 am-12 pm; $12-$30; cocktails; entertainment. FAX (619) 260-0147   ⊗ Ⓓ Ⓑ (619) 291-8790

Residence Inn by Marriott Kearny Mesa 26 ♿
All year [CP] | Rates Subject to Change | Apartment Motel ◆◆◆
.... 2P/1B .... 75.00   2P/2B .... 129.00   XP 10
Senior discount. 144 units. Adjacent to SR 163, exit Clairemont Mesa. 5400 Kearny Mesa Rd. (92111) 1-bedroom studios & 2-bedroom suites with living room & kitchen. Check-in 4 pm. A/C; C/CATV; movies; rental VCPs. Radios; phones. Coin laundry. Small htd pool; whirlpools. Pets, $6 daily extra charge & $50 cleaning fee. Wkly & monthly rates avail. AE, DI, DS, MC, VI. FAX (619) 278-2100   ⊗ Ⓓ (619) 278-2100

Rodeway Inn-Balboa Park/Downtown 92 ♿ | AAA Special Value Rates | Motel ◆◆
5/28-9/5 [CP]   1P 59.00- 64.00   2P/1B   64.00- 74.00   2P/2B .... 74.00   XP 5   F
9/6-10/31 & 1/1-5/27 [CP]   1P 49.00- 54.00   2P/1B   54.00- 64.00   2P/2B .... 64.00   XP 5   F
11/1-12/31 [CP]   1P 44.00- 49.00   2P/1B   49.00- 54.00   2P/2B   54.00- 59.00   XP 5   F
45 units. Ash St at 9th Ave. 833 Ash St. (92101) 6 refrigerators; A/C; C/CATV; movies; radios; phones. Saunas; indoor whirlpool. No pets. AE, DI, DS, MC, VI. Coffeeshop opposite. FAX (619) 235-6951   ⊗ Ⓓ (619) 239-2285

San Diego Hilton Beach & Tennis Resort 37 ♿ | AAA Special Value Rates | Resort Complex ◆◆◆◆
All year   1P 130.00- 235.00   2P/1B   150.00- 235.00   2P/2B   150.00- 235.00   XP 20   F
354 units. Adjacent to I-5; 1/2 mi n of Sea World Dr exit. 1775 E Mission Bay Dr. (92109) In Mission Bay Park. Attractive tropical setting. Spacious rooms with patio or balcony. Check-in 3 pm. Refrigerators; A/C; C/CATV; free & pay movies; radios; phones. Coin laundry. Htd pool; wading pool; beach; sauna; whirlpools; dock; putting green; social program; children's program; rental bicycles; playground; exercise rm. Fee for: sailboats, windsurfing, scuba lessons during summer; water skiing, lighted tennis-5 courts; massage. Airport transp. Pets, $10 extra charge. Monthly rates avail. Reserv deposit required in season; 3 days refund notice. AE, DI, DS, MC, VI. ● Dining rm; 6:30 am-11 pm; $7-$12; cocktails; entertainment. Also, Tradewinds Restaurant, see separate listing. FAX (619) 275-7991 (See ad p 22)   ⊗ Ⓢ Ⓓ Ⓑ (619) 276-4010

(See SAN DIEGO spotting map pages A376 & A377)

San Diego Marriott Mission Valley **60**   AAA Special Value Rates   *Hotel*   ◆◆◆
All year [BP]   1P .... 149.00   2P/1B .... 159.00   2P/2B .... 159.00   XP   F
350 units. 1/4 mi n of I-8; exit Stadium Way. 8757 Rio San Diego Dr. (92108) Many balconies. Check-in 3 pm. A/C;
C/CATV; free & pay movies; radios; phones. Rental refrigerators. Coin laundry. Htd pool; sauna; whirlpool; lighted
tennis-2 courts; exercise rm. Fee for: airport transp. Valet parking lot. Pets. AE, DI, MC, VI. ● Restaurant; 6:30 am-11
pm; $9-$18; cocktails; entertainment. FAX (619) 692-0769   ⊗ Ⓢ Ⓓ Ⓛ (619) 692-3800

San Diego Marriott Suites-Downtown **113**   Rates Subject to Change   *Suites Hotel*   ◆◆◆
All year   1P .... 170.00   2P/1B .... 180.00   2P/2B .... 180.00   XP 5   F
264 units. Adjacent to Symphony Hall. 701 A St corner 7th Ave. (92101) Check-in 4 pm. Refrigerators; A/C; C/CATV; free
& pay movies; radios; phones. Htd indoor pool; sauna; whirlpool; exercise rm. Pay valet garage. Airport transp. Pets, $50
deposit required. Reserv deposit required. AE, DI, DS, MC, VI. ● Restaurant; 6:30 am-11 pm; Sat & Sun from 7 am;
$12-$20; cocktails. FAX (619) 696-1555   ⊗ Ⓢ Ⓓ (619) 696-9800

San Diego Mission Valley Hilton **63**   Rates Subject to Change   *Hotel*   ◆◆◆◆
⊕ 2/1-9/6   1P 89.00- 119.00   2P/1B 99.00- 129.00   2P/2B 99.00- 129.00   XP 10   F
9/7-1/31   1P 79.00- 109.00   2P/1B 89.00- 119.00   2P/2B 89.00- 119.00   XP 10
350 units. Adjacent to I-8, exit Mission Center Rd. 901 Camino del Rio S. (92108) Formerly Doubletree Hotel.
Check-in 3 pm. 150 refrigerators; A/C; C/CATV; pay movies; radios; phones. Htd pool; sauna; whirlpool; exercise rm. Valet garage & parking ramp. Pets, $200 deposit, also $50 extra charge. AE, DI, DS, MC,
VI. ● Restaurant; 6:30 am-10 pm; Fri & Sat-11 pm; $8.95-$21.95; cocktails; entertainment. Also, Monterey
Whaling Company, see separate listing. FAX (619) 296-9561   ⊗ Ⓢ Ⓓ Ⓛ (619) 543-9000

San Diego Princess Resort **38**   Rates Subject to Change   *Resort Complex*   ◆◆◆
⊕ 4/2-9/18   1P 150.00- 195.00   2P/1B 150.00- 195.00   2P/2B 150.00- 195.00 XP 15   F
9/19-4/1   1P 120.00- 160.00   2P/1B 135.00- 175.00   2P/2B 135.00- 175.00 XP 15   F
Senior discount. 462 units. In Mission Bay Park at W Vacation Rd & Ingraham St. 1404 W Vacation Rd. (92109)
Bungalows & motel units on several acres of beautifully landscaped grounds on Mission Bay. Check-in 4 pm.
Refrigerators; A/C; C/CATV; pay movies; radios; phones. 145 efficiencies. Coin laundry. 5 pools, 2 htd; beach;
whirlpool; rental boats; marina; water skiing; putting green; recreational program; rental bicycles; jogging track.
Fee for: lighted tennis-6 courts; massage. Parking lot. Pets. Studio & 2 room efficiencies, $215-$345. Reserv deposit required; 3 days refund notice. AE, CB, DI, MC, VI. ● Restaurant & coffeeshop; 7 am-10 pm; in summer-11
pm; $6-$23.50. Also, Dockside Broiler, see separate listing. FAX (619) 581-5929 *(See ad below)*
                                                                          ⊗ Ⓓ (619) 274-4630

Seapoint Hotel **79**   Rates Guaranteed   *Motor Inn*   ◆◆
⊕ All year   1P 65.00- 109.00   2P/1B 75.00- 119.00   2P/2B 75.00- 119.00   XP 10   F
Senior discount. 242 units. Point Loma Area; 2 blks s of Rosecrans St. 4875 N Harbor Dr. (92106) Check-in 4 pm.
24 refrigerators; A/C; C/CATV; movies; radios; phones; comb or shower baths. Coin laundry. Htd pool; whirlpool;
exercise rm. Airport transp. No pets. Reserv deposit required. AE, DI, DS, MC, VI. ● Coffeeshop; 6 am-10 pm;
$5-$7; cocktails. FAX (619) 224-3629 *(See ad p A391)*   ⊗ Ⓓ Ⓛ (619) 224-3621

(See SAN DIEGO spotting map pages A376 & A377)

Sheraton Grand on Harbor Island 77   Rates Subject to Change   *Hotel* ◆◆◆◆
All year   1P 150.00- 170.00   2P/1B   150.00- 170.00   2P/2B 150.00- 170.00   XP 20   F
350 units. 1/4 mi s of airport. 1590 Harbor Island Dr. (92101) Spacious rooms overlooking bay or yacht harbor. 30 refrigerators; A/C; C/CATV; free & pay movies; radios; phones. Htd pool; whirlpool; rental bicycles. Pay parking lot. Airport transp. No pets. AE, DI, DS, MC, VI. ● Dining rm; 6 am-11 pm; $14-$22.50; 24 hour room service; cocktails. Also, Spencer's, see separate listing. FAX (619) 291-4877   ⊗ Ⓢ Ⓓ 🔳 (619) 291-6400

Sheraton Harbor Island Hotel 76   Rates Subject to Change   *Motor Inn* ◆◆◆◆
All year   1P 150.00- 170.00   2P/1B   150.00- 170.00   2P/2B 150.00- 160.00   XP 20   F
Senior discount. 700 units. 1/4 mi s of airport. 1380 Harbor Island Dr. (92101) Most rooms overlooking bay or yacht harbor. Check-in 3 pm. 50 refrigerators; A/C; C/CATV; free & pay movies; radios; phones. Coin laundry. 2 htd pools; 2 wading pools; sauna; whirlpool; rental boats; rental bicycles; playground. Fee for: dock, lighted tennis-4 courts; health club & massage. Pay parking lot. Airport transp. Pets. Reserv deposit required. AE, CB, DI, MC, VI. ● Dining rm, restaurant & coffeeshop; 6 am-11 pm; $9-$23; cocktails; entertainment. FAX (619) 546-0643   ⊗ Ⓢ Ⓓ 🔳 (619) 291-2900

Super 8 Harborside 99   AAA Special Value Rates   *Motor Inn* ◆◆
6/1-9/30   1P .... 60.00   2P/1B   .... 70.00   2P/2B .... 80.00   XP 10   F
10/1-5/31   1P .... 50.00   2P/1B   .... 60.00   2P/2B .... 70.00   XP 10   F
86 units. Corner of Fenelon. 1403 Rosecrans St. (92106) Check-in 3 pm. 20 refrigerators; A/C; C/CATV; movies; phones. Htd pool. Airport transp. No pets. Wkly & monthly rates avail. Reserv deposit required; 3 days refund notice. AE, DI, DS, MC, VI. ● Restaurant; 7:30 am-9 pm; $6.95-$15; cocktails. FAX (619) 225-9461
(See ad starting on p A394)   ⊗ Ⓓ 🔳 (619) 225-9461

Super 8 Mission Bay 57   AAA Special Value Rates   *Motel* ◆◆
5/21-9/15   1P .... 52.00   2P/1B   .... 60.00   2P/2B .... 60.00   XP 10   F
9/16-5/20   1P .... 50.00   2P/1B   .... 58.00   2P/2B .... 58.00   XP 10   F
117 units. Northbound, 1/2 mi nw of I-5, exit Grand Ave/Garnet Ave; southbound, 1/4 mi sw, exit Balboa Ave. 4540 Mission Bay Dr. (92109) 16 refrigerators; A/C; C/CATV; movies; radios; phones. Small htd pool. No pets. Monthly rates avail. Reserv deposit required. AE, DI, DS, MC, VI. FAX (619) 274-7888 *(See ad starting on p A394)*
   ⊗ Ⓢ Ⓓ 🔳 (619) 274-7888

Town and Country Hotel 52   Rates Subject to Change   *Complex* ◆◆
All year   1P 72.00- 110.00   2P/1B   87.00- 125.00   2P/2B 87.00- 125.00   XP 10   F
955 units. N side of I-8. 500 Hotel Circle N. (92108) On several acres of nicely landscaped grounds. Check-in 3 pm. A/C; C/CATV; pay movies; radios; phones. 4 pools, 1 htd; whirlpool. No pets. Reserv deposit required. AE, DI, DS, MC, VI. ● Restaurant & 2 coffeeshops; 6:30 am-midnight; $5-$15; cocktails; entertainment. FAX (619) 291-3584 *(See ad p A411)*   ⊗ Ⓓ (619) 291-7131

Travelodge Clairemont Mesa 29   Rates Guaranteed   *Motel* ◆◆
6/1-9/12 [CP]   1P .... 39.00   2P/1B   .... 43.00   2P/2B .... 49.00   XP 8   F
9/13-5/31 [CP]   1P .... 35.00   2P/1B   .... 39.00   2P/2B .... 44.00   XP 8   F
Senior discount. 88 units. 1/2 blk w of I-805. 5550 Clairemont Mesa Blvd. (92117) 20 refrigerators; A/C; C/CATV; movies; radios; phones. Coin laundry. No pets. Wkly rates avail. AE, DI, DS, MC, VI. Restaurant adjacent. FAX (619) 268-4353   ⊗ Ⓓ (619) 560-4551

Travelodge Hotel-Harbor Island 78   Rates Guaranteed   *Motor Inn* ◆◆◆
4/1-10/31   1P .... 79.00   2P/1B   .... 79.00   2P/2B .... 79.00   XP 10   F
11/1-3/31   1P .... 69.00   2P/1B   .... 69.00   2P/2B .... 69.00   XP 10   F
208 units. On Harbor Island; 1/2 mi s of airport. 1960 Harbor Island Dr. (92101) Overlooking bay or yacht harbor. A/C; C/CATV; movies; rental VCPs. Radios; phones. Htd pool; sauna; whirlpool; exercise rm. Airport transp. No pets. AE, DI, DS, MC, VI. ● Dining rm; 6:30 am-2:30 & 5:30-10 pm; Sat & Sun-10:30 pm; $13-$20; cocktails; entertainment. FAX (619) 293-0689   ⊗ Ⓢ Ⓓ 🔳 (619) 291-6700

Travelodge Sports Arena 43   Rates Subject to Change   *Motor Inn* ◆◆
5/14-9/15 [CP]   1P .... 62.00   2P/1B   .... 68.00   2P/2B .... 70.00   XP 10   F
9/16-5/13 [CP]   1P .... 52.00   2P/1B   .... 58.00   2P/2B .... 60.00   XP 10   F
Senior discount. 307 units. 3/4 mi sw of jct I-5 & I-8; from I-5, southbound exit Rosecrans St, northbound exit I-8W, then exit Sports Arena Blvd. 3737 Sports Arena Blvd. (92110) Check-in 3 pm. A/C; C/CATV; pay movies; radios; phones. Coin laundry. Htd pool; whirlpool. Airport transp. No pets. AE, DI, DS, MC, VI. ● Coffeeshop; 6 am-11 pm; $5-$9; cocktails. FAX (619) 224-9248 *(See ad below)*   ⊗ Ⓢ 🔳 (619) 226-3711

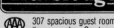

(See SAN DIEGO spotting map pages A376 & A377)

U. S. Grant Hotel 96
AAA Special Value Rates   Hotel ◆◆◆◆
All year   1P 135.00- 155.00   2P/1B   155.00- 175.00   2P/2B   155.00- 175.00   XP 20
280 units. 326 Broadway. (92101) Completely rebuilt & refurbished, historic hotel. Elegant decor. Check-in 3 pm. A/C; C/CATV; pay movies; rental VCPs. Radios; phones. Rental refrigerators. Exercise rm. Fee for: massage. Pay valet garage. Airport transp. No pets. AE, DI, DS, MC, VI. ● Dining rm; 6 am-11 pm; a la carte entrees about $15.50-$19.50; 24 hour room service; cocktails; entertainment. Also, Grant Grill, see separate listing. A *Preferred Hotel*. FAX (619) 232-3626 *(See ad p A412)*   ⊗ Ⓢ Ⓓ Ⓚ (619) 232-3121

Vacation Inn-Old Town 107
Rates Guaranteed   Motel ◆◆◆
5/16-9/15 [CP]   1P 85.50- 104.50   2P/1B   85.50- 104.50   2P/2B   95.50- 114.50   XP 10   F
9/16-5/15 [CP]   1P 69.50- 89.50   2P/1B   69.50- 89.50   2P/2B   79.50- 99.50   XP 10   F
Senior discount. 125 units. 2 blks e of I-5; Old Town area; exit Old Town Ave. 3900 Old Town Ave. (92110) Microwaves. Check-in 3 pm. Refrigerators; A/C; C/CATV; free & pay movies; radios; phones. Coin laundry. Htd pool; whirlpool. Garage. Airport transp. No pets. AE, DI, DS, MC, VI. *(See ad p A412)*   ⊗ Ⓢ Ⓓ Ⓚ (619) 299-7400

Vagabond Inn-Misson Valley 67
Rates Subject to Change   Motel ◆
All year [CP]   1P 41.00- 57.00   2P/1B   46.00- 62.00   2P/2B   51.00- 67.00   XP 5   F
88 units. S side of I-8. 625 Hotel Circle South. (92108) 6 refrigerators; A/C; C/CATV; movies; radios; phones. 2 2-bedrm units. 2 pools, 1 htd; whirlpool. Pets, $5 extra charge. AE, DI, DS, MC, VI. Restaurant adjacent. FAX (619) 692-9009 *(See ad p A412)*   ⊗ Ⓓ (619) 297-1691

(See SAN DIEGO spotting map pages A376 & A377)

The Westgate 94   Rates Subject to Change   *Hotel* ◆◆◆◆
♨ All year   1P 134.00- 154.00   2P/1B   144.00- 164.00   2P/2B   144.00- 164.00   XP 10
223 units. 1055 2nd Ave at C St. (92101) An elegant hotel; exquisite furnishings & decor. 120 refrigerators; A/C; C/CATV; movies; radios; phones. Exercise rm. Fee for: massage. Pay garage. Airport transp. No pets. Reserv deposit required. AE, CB, DI, MC, VI. ● Dining rm & restaurant; 6 am-11 pm; a la carte entrees about $10-$30; 24 hour room service; cocktails; entertainment. FAX (619) 232-4526   ⊗ Ⓓ (619) 238-1818

Wyndham Garden Hotel 56   Rates Subject to Change   *Motor Inn* ◆◆◆
Mon-Thurs   1P 89.00- 99.00   2P/1B   99.00- 109.00   2P/2B   99.00- 109.00   XP 10   F
Fri-Sun   1P .... 54.00   2P/1B   .... 54.00   2P/2B   .... 54.00   XP 10   F
180 units. 1 mi e of I-805; exit Mira Mesa Blvd. 5975 Lusk Blvd. (92121) Check-in 3 pm. A/C; C/CATV; pay movies; radios; phones. Rental refrigerators. Coin laundry. Htd pool; whirlpool; exercise rm. No pets. Reserv deposit required. AE, DI, DS, MC, VI. ● Restaurant; 6:30 am-2 pm & 5-10 pm; Sat & Sun-7 am; $10.25-$16.25; cocktails. FAX (619) 558-0421 *(See ad p A413)*   ⊗ Ⓢ Ⓓ Ⓑ (619) 558-1818

RESTAURANTS

Acapulco 32   Mexican $ ◆◆
At Best Western Hacienda Hotel-Old Town. Patio dining overlooking Old Town. Sun brunch, $7.95. A/C. Children's menu. Open 6:30 am-10 pm; Fri & Sat-11 pm. Cocktails & lounge. Reserv advised. AE, DI, MC, VI.   ⊗ (619) 260-8124

(See SAN DIEGO spotting map pages A376 & A377)

Anthony's Fish Grotto ㊷   Seafood $ ◆
On the Embarcadero. 1360 Harbor Dr. Large selection of seafood served in very popular restaurant overlooking bay. A/C. Early bird specials; children's menu. Open 11:30 am-8:30 pm; closed major holidays & Easter. Cocktails & lounge. AE, DI, DS, MC, VI.   ⊗ 🄻 (619) 232-5103

Anthony's Fish Grotto ㉓   Seafood $ ◆◆
In La Mesa; just n of I-8 exit Severin Dr. 9530 Murray Dr. Very popular restaurant offering wide variety of fresh seafood & chicken. Fresh fish market on premises. A/C. Early bird specials; children's menu. Open 11:30 am-8:30 pm; closed major holidays. Cocktails & lounge. AE, DI, DS, MC, VI.   ⊗ 🄻 (619) 463-0368

Anthony's Star of the Sea Room ㊶   Seafood $$$ ◆◆◆
On the Embarcadero. 1360 Harbor Dr. Elegant decor; continental service. A/C. Dress code. Open 5:30 pm-10:30 pm; closed major holidays & 4/11. Cocktails & lounge. Reserv required. AE, DI, DS, MC, VI.   ⊗ 🄻 (619) 232-7408

Baci's ⑳   Italian $$ ◆◆◆
From I-5, northbound exit Tecolote Rd, southbound exit Clairemont Dr; 1/2 mi s of Clairemont Dr. 1955 Morena Blvd. Small intimate Italian restaurant featuring homemade pasta, seafood & veal specialties. A/C. Open 11:30 am-2:30 & 5:30-10:30 pm; Sat from 5:30 pm; closed Sun & major holidays. Cocktails & lounge. Reserv advised wkends. AE, CB, DI, MC, VI.   ⊗ (619) 275-2094

Bobby McGee's Conglomeration ㉔   American $$ ◆◆
In La Mesa; adjacent to I-8, in Grossmont Center. 5500 Grossmont Center Dr. Uniquely decorated restaurant. Informal, casual service by costumed waiters & waitresses. Prime rib & seafood. A/C. Early bird specials; children's menu. Open 5 pm-9:30 pm; Fri-10 pm; Sat 5 pm-10 pm; Sun 4:30 pm-9:30 pm; closed 12/25. Cocktails & lounge. Dancing. Reserv advised. AE, CB, DI, MC, VI.   ⊗ (619) 589-0444

The Brigantine ㊽   Seafood $$ ◆◆
In Coronado; on SR 75. 1333 Orange Ave. Also features steaks. Limited menu in lounge 3 pm-6 pm Mon-Fri. A/C. Early bird specials; children's menu. Open 11:30 am-2:30 & 5-10:30 pm; Fri-11:30 pm; Sat 5 pm-11:30 pm; Sun 5 pm-10:30 pm; closed 11/25 & 12/25. Cocktails & lounge. Reserv advised. AE, DI, MC, VI.   ⊗ (619) 435-4166

Cafe Pacifica ⑱   Seafood $$ ◆◆
In Old Town area. 2414 San Diego Ave. Small, charming restaurant. A/C. Open 11:30 am-2 & 6-10 pm; Sat from 6 pm; Sun 5:30 pm-9:30 pm; closed 11/25 & 12/25. Cocktails. Valet parking. Reserv advised. AE, CB, DI, MC, VI.   ⊗ (619) 291-6666

California Cafe Bar & Grill ㉕   American $$ ◆◆◆
In Horton Plaza-upper level. Patio seating avail. Varied menu; some pasta & pizza selections. A/C. Open 11:30 am-9:30 pm; Fri & Sat-10 pm; Sun 11 am-9:30 pm; closed 12/25. Cocktails & lounge. Reserv advised. AE, DI, DS, MC, VI.   ⊗ (619) 238-5440

Casa de Bandini ⑰   Mexican $ ◆◆◆
In Old Town San Diego State Park, 1 blk s of Bazaar del Mundo. 2754 Calhoun St. Delightful dining in historical landmark & colorful outdoor patio area. Seafood entrees. A/C. Open 11 am-9:30 pm; Fri & Sat-10 pm; Sun 10 am-9:30 pm; closed 1/1, 11/25 & 12/25. Cocktails & lounge. Entertainment. AE, DI, DS, MC, VI.   ⊗ (619) 297-8211

(See SAN DIEGO spotting map pages A376 & A377)

The Chart House 1887 ⑭9️⃣   Steak & Seafood $$$ ◆◆◆
  On SR 75; in Coronado. 1701 Strand Way. Casual, informal dining in the former Del Coronado Hotel boathouse. Early
  bird specials; children's menu. Open 5 pm-10:30 pm. Cocktails & lounge. Reserv advised. AE, CB, DI, MC, VI.
                                                                                   ⊗ (619) 435-0155

Dockside Broiler ㉉9️⃣   Seafood $$ ◆◆◆
  At San Diego Princess Resort. Beautifully appointed restaurant overlooking Mission Bay. Nice selection of steaks & con-
  tinental entrees. A/C. Open 5 pm-10 pm. Cocktails & lounge. Reserv advised. AE, CB, DI, MC, VI. *(See ad p A409)*
                                                                               ⊗ 🅱️ (619) 274-4630

El Torito ㉘8️⃣   Mexican $ ◆◆
  S side of I-8, exit Mission Center Rd. 445 Camino Del Rio South. Sun brunch 9 am-2 pm. A/C. Children's menu. Open
  11 am-10 pm; Fri & Sat-11 pm; Sun 9 am-10 pm; closed 11/25 & 12/25. Cocktails & lounge. AE, DI, DS, MC, VI.
                                                                                   ⊗ (619) 296-6154

First Avenue Bar & Grill ㉑5️⃣1️⃣   American $$ ◆◆◆
  In the Bristol Court Hotel. A/C. Open 11 am-2:30 & 5-10 pm; Sat & Sun from 5 pm. Cocktails & lounge. Entertainment.
  AE, DI, DS, MC, VI.   ⊗ (619) 232-6141

Furr's Fine Family Dining ㉖6️⃣   American $ ◆
  3893 54th St at University Ave. Formerly Furrs Cafeteria. Large selection of salads, entrees & desserts. A/C. Open 11
  am-8 pm; Fri & Sat-8:30 pm. AE, MC, VI.   ⊗ (619) 287-6791

Garcia's of Scottsdale ㉖1️⃣6️⃣   Mexican $ ◆◆
  1/4 mi sw of jct I-5 & I-8. 3106 Sports Arena Blvd at Rosecrans St. Colorfully decorated. A/C. Children's menu. Open 11
  am-10 pm; Fri & Sat-11 pm; closed 11/25 & 12/25. Cocktails & lounge. AE, MC, VI.   ⊗ 🅱️ (619) 223-5441

Grant Grill ㉖4️⃣5️⃣   American $$$ ◆◆◆
  In US Grant Hotel. A/C. Open 7 am-2:30 & 5:30-11 pm. Cocktails & lounge. Reserv advised. AE, DI, DS, MC, VI.
                                                                               ⊗ 🅱️ (619) 232-3121

Harbor House Restaurant ㉖4️⃣6️⃣   Seafood $$ ◆◆◆
  In Seaport Village. 831 W Harbor Dr. Fine harbor view dining. Sun brunch $15.95. A/C. Children's menu. Open 11:30
  am-10 pm; Fri & Sat-11 pm; Sun 10 am-10 pm. Cocktails & lounge. Reserv advised. AE, DS, MC, VI.
                                                                                   ⊗ (619) 232-1141

Hob Nob Hill ㉚3️⃣4️⃣   American $$ ◆
  🅰️🅱️ **1/2 blk n of Ivy St. 2271 First Ave. Popular family type restaurant featuring a large selection of entrees & daily
  specials. Pies & pastries baked on premises. A/C. Children's menu. Open 7 am-9 pm; closed Sat, major holidays
  & 12/23-1/6. Beer & wine. Reserv advised. AE, MC, VI.   ⊗ 🅱️ (619) 239-8176**

Humphrey's ㉚3️⃣9️⃣   Seafood $$$ ◆
  At Humphrey's Half Moon Inn. Sun brunch 10 am-2 pm, $16.95. A/C. Open 7 am-10 pm; Sat-11 pm; Sun-9 pm. Cock-
  tails & lounge. Entertainment. Reserv advised Fri & Sat evening. AE, DI, DS, MC, VI.   ⊗ (619) 224-3577

Islands Restaurant ㉑1️⃣9️⃣   Ethnic $$ ◆◆
  In Hanalei Hotel. Polynesian, also American dishes, served in an attractive South Seas atmosphere. Sat & Sun brunch.
  A/C. Early bird specials; children's menu. Open 11 am-2 & 5-10 pm; Fri-11 pm; Sat & Sun 9:30 am-2:30 & 5-10 pm.
  Cocktails & lounge. Entertainment. AE, DI, DS, MC, VI.   ⊗ (619) 297-1101

Kings Grille ㉚3️⃣0️⃣   American $$ ◆◆
  In Kings Inn. A/C. Children's menu. Open 11:30 am-9 pm; Fri-10 pm; Sat 5 pm-10 pm; Sun 9:30 am-2 & 5-9 pm. Cock-
  tails & lounge. AE, DI, DS, MC, VI. *(See ad p A402)*   ⊗ 🅱️ (619) 297-2231

Madeo Ristorante ㉒2️⃣   Italian $$$ ◆◆
  Located in Emerald Shapery Center. 402 W Broadway. Excellent food & service. A/C. Open 11:30 am-3 & 5:30-11 pm.
  Cocktails & lounge. Pay valet garage. Reserv advised weekends. AE, DI, MC, VI.   ⊗ (619) 239-5888

Monterey Whaling Company ㉒7️⃣   Seafood $$ ◆◆
  In San Diego Mission Valley Hilton. 901 Camino del Rio S. A/C. Children's menu. Open 6:30 am-3 & 5-10 pm; Fri &
  Sat-11 pm. Cocktails & lounge. Entertainment & dancing. Valet parking. AE, DI, DS, MC, VI.   ⊗ 🅱️ (619) 543-9000

The Old Spaghetti Factory ㉔4️⃣7️⃣   Italian $ ◆
  In the Gaslamp Quarter, 1 blk n of Harbor Dr. 275 Fifth Ave, corner of K St. Very popular uniquely decorated, family type
  restaurant featuring spaghetti with a large choice of sauces. A/C. Children's menu. Open 5 pm-10 pm; Fri-11 pm; Sat
  4:30 pm-11 pm; Sun 4 pm-10 pm; closed 11/25, 12/24 & 12/25. Cocktails & lounge.   ⊗ (619) 233-4323

Peohe's ㉚5️⃣0️⃣   Seafood $$$ ◆◆
  2 blks s of Orange Ave; The Old Ferry Landing Plaza. 1201 First St. Bay view & patio dining. Sun brunch 10:30 am-2
  pm. A/C. Children's menu. Open 11:30 am-2:30 & 5-10 pm; Fri & Sat-11 pm; Sun 10:30 am-10 pm. Cocktails & lounge.
  Reserv advised. AE, DI, DS, MC, VI.   ⊗ (619) 437-4474

Heuben's ㉚3️⃣5️⃣   American $$ ◆◆
  On Harbor Island. 880 E Harbor Island Dr. Fine view of harbor & city skyline. Selection of steaks & seafood. Sun brunch
  9:30 am-2:30 pm, $14.95. A/C. Early bird specials; children's menu. Open 9:30 am-10 pm; Fri & Sat-11 pm; Sun 9:30
  am-2:30 & 4-10 pm; closed 12/25. Cocktails & lounge. Reserv advised Sat. AE, DI, DS, MC, VI. ⊗ 🅱️ (619) 291-5030

Salmon House ㉑1️⃣4️⃣   Seafood $$ ◆◆
  In Mission Bay Park, at Marina Village. 1970 Quivira Way. Informal restaurant overlooking Quivira Basin. Features Al-
  derwood broiled salmon & other seafood entrees. Sun brunch 10 am-3 pm, $15.95. A/C. Early bird specials; children's
  menu. Open 11:30 am-3 & 4:30-10 pm; Fri & Sat 11 pm; Sun 10 am-3 & 4:30-10 pm. Cocktails & lounge. Reserv advised. AE, DI, MC, VI.   ⊗ 🅱️ (619) 223-2234

Shanghai ㉑1️⃣5️⃣   Chinese $ ◆
  🅰️🅱️ **In Mission Bay Park, at Marina Village. 1930 Quivira Way. Features Mandarin cuisine & Mongolian barbequed
  beef, lamb & pork. Overlooking Quivira Basin. Sun brunch $8.95. A/C. Open 11:30 am-9:30 pm; Fri-10:30 pm; Sat
  noon-10:30 pm; Sun 11 am-9:30 pm. Reserv advised. AE, CB, DI, MC, VI.   ⊗ (619) 226-6200**

Shelter Island's Bali Hai Restaurant ㉚3️⃣8️⃣   Ethnic $$ ◆◆
  🅰️🅱️ **2230 Shelter Island Dr. South Seas motif; beautiful location overlooking bay. Patio dining in summer, Polynesian
  cuisine, also beef, poultry & seafood. Sun brunch 10 am-2 pm $9.95. A/C. Open 11:30 am-3:30 & 5-10 pm; Fri-
  11:30 pm; Sat 5 pm-11:30 pm; Sun 10 am-2 & 4-10 pm; closed 12/25. Cocktails & lounge. Reserv advised. AE, DI,
  DS, MC, VI.   ⊗ (619) 222-1181**

Spencer's ㉚3️⃣6️⃣   American $$$ ◆◆◆
  In Sheraton Grand on Harbor Island. Sun brunch 11 am-3 pm, $15.95. A/C. Children's menu. Open 6 am-10:30 pm; Fri
  & Sat-11 pm. Cocktails & lounge. Pay valet parking. Reserv advised. AE, DI, DS, MC, VI.   ⊗ (619) 692-2777

(See SAN DIEGO spotting map pages A376 & A377)

The Tickled Trout ③① Seafood $$ ◆◆
In Ramada Inn-Hotel Circle. English pub decor. A/C. Open 6:30 am-2 & 5-10 pm; Sat & Sun 6:30 am-noon & 5-10 pm; closed 1/1, 11/25 & 12/25. Cocktails & lounge. AE, DI, DS, MC, VI. ⊗ ⓑ (619) 291-6505

Tio Leo's ③③ Mexican $
1/2 mi n of Taylor via Morena Blvd. 5302 Napa St. Family owned. Good food; prepared using traditional Mexican recipes. A/C. Children's menu. Open 7 am-10 pm; Fri & Sat-11 pm; closed 1/1, 11/25 & 12/25. Cocktails & lounge. Reserv advised. AE, DI, DS, MC, VI. ⊗ (619) 542-1462

Tom Ham's Lighthouse ③⑦ American $$ ◆
⊕ On Harbor Island. 2150 Harbor Island Dr. Early California decor; overlooks bay & city skyline. A/C. Early bird specials; children's menu. Open 11:15 am-3:30 & 5-10 pm; Fri-11 pm; Sat 5 pm-11 pm; Sun 10 am-2:30 & 4-10 pm; closed 12/25. Cocktails & lounge. Entertainment. Reserv advised. AE, DI, DS, MC, VI. ⊗ (619) 291-9110

Tradewinds Restaurant ②① Seafood $$ ◆◆◆
In San Diego Hilton Beach & Tennis Resort. Nautical decor. California cuisine. Sun Brunch 10:30 am-2:30 pm, $14.50. A/C. Open 6 pm-11 pm; closed Sun for dinner & Mon 9/1-6/30. Cocktails & lounge. Entertainment. AE, DI, DS, MC, VI.
(See ad p 22) ⊗ ⓑ (619) 276-4010

SAN DIMAS — 32,400

Best Western San Dimas Inn	AAA Special Value Rates				Motel		◆◆◆
⊕ All year [CP]	1P 55.00- 65.00	2P/1B	60.00- 75.00	2P/2B	65.00	XP 5-10	F

134 units. Adjacent to I-210, exit Arrow Hwy. 204 N Village Ct. (91773) Refrigerators; A/C; C/CATV; movies; phones; comb or shower baths. Htd pool; whirlpool. No pets. AE, CB, DI, MC, VI. FAX (909) 592-7903 ⊗ Ⓓ ⓑ (909) 599-2362

Comfort Suites	AAA Special Value Rates				Motel		◆◆◆
All year [BP]	1P 74.00- 84.00	2P/1B	84.00- 94.00	2P/2B 84.00- 94.00	XP 8		F

60 units. 1/4 mi e of I-210, exit Arrow Hwy. 501 W Bonita. (91773) Check-in 4 pm. A/C; C/CATV; pay movies; radios; phones. Efficiencies. Coin laundry. Htd pool; whirlpool. No pets. Reserv deposit required; 3 days refund notice. Complimentary beverages each evening. AE, CB, DI, MC, VI. FAX (909) 599-1546 ⊗ Ⓓ (909) 592-0500

RESTAURANT

Cask N Cleaver American $$ ◆
Adjacent to I-210, exit Arrow Hwy. 125 N Village Ct. Casual dining. Nice selection of steaks, seafood & chicken. A/C. Open 11:30 am-2:30 & 5-9 pm; Fri-11 pm; Sat 5 pm-11 pm; Sun 4:30 pm-9:30 pm; closed major holidays. Cocktails & lounge. AE, MC, VI. ⊗ (909) 592-1646

SAN FRANCISCO — 724,000

Establishments in San Francisco are divided into Downtown, Northern Region and Southern Region.

Airport Accommodations-SEE FOLLOWING LISTINGS IN SAN FRANCISCO (Southern Region):

⊕ Best Western El Rancho Inn, 3 1/2 mi w of airport.
⊕ Best Western Grosvenor Hotel, 1 3/4 mi n of airport.
Clarion Hotel, 1/2 mi s of airport.
Courtyard by Marriott, 2 mi nw of airport.
⊕ Crown Sterling Suites-Burlingame, 1 1/2 mi s of airport.
⊕ Crown Sterling Suites-South San Francisco, 1 1/2 mi s of airport
⊕ Days Inn-Airport, 1 1/2 mi s of airport
⊕ Doubletree Hotel-San Francisco Airport, 1 1/4 mi s of airport
Holiday Inn Crowne Plaza, 1 1/2 mi s of airport.
Hyatt Regency-San Francisco Airport, 3 mi s of airport.
⊕ La Quinta Motor Inn, 2 1/2 mi n of airport
Millwood Inn, 3 1/2 mi w of airport
⊕ Radisson Inn, 3 1/2 mi n of airport
⊕ Ramada San Francisco Airport, 2 1/2 mi s of airport.
⊕ Ritz Motel, 2 1/2 mi nw of airport
⊕ San Francisco Airport Hilton, at airport entrance.
San Francisco Airport Marriott, 2 mi s of airport.
Sheraton-San Francisco Airport, 2 1/2 mi s of airport.
⊕ Vagabond Inn-Airport, 1 mi s of airport
⊕ The Westin Hotel-San Francisco Airport, 1/2 mi s of airport

SAN FRANCISCO (Downtown) (See SAN FRANCISCO (Downtown) AREA spotting map page A416; see index below)

(See also SAN MATEO)

Index of Establishments on the SAN FRANCISCO (Downtown) AREA Spotting Map

(See SAN FRANCISCO (Downtown) spotting map below)

⊕ Bedford Hotel	㉕
⊕ Four Seasons Clift Hotel	㉖
⊕ The Raphael.	㉗
⊕ The Westin St. Francis.	㉘
⊕ Villa Florence	㉙
⊕ The Handlery Union Square Hotel	㉚
⊕ Hotel Nikko	㉛
San Francisco Hilton	㉜
⊕ Parc Fifty Five Hotel	㉝
⊕ Hotel Britton	㉞
⊕ Best Western Flamingo Motor Inn	㉟
⊕ Best Western Carriage Inn	㊱
⊕ Best Western Americana	㊲
⊕ Monticello Inn	㊳
⊕ Shannon Court Hotel	㊴
⊕ San Francisco Marriott.	㊵
⊕ The Prescott Hotel.	㊷
⊕ Warwick Regis Hotel.	㊸
⊕ King George Hotel	㊹
⊕ Hotel Juliana	㊺

RESTAURANTS

The Waterfront Restaurant	①
Ernie's	②
⊕ John's Grill	③
Blue Fox.	④
Empress of China	⑤
Kan's.	⑥
Mason's.	⑦
Yamato Restaurant	⑧
Carnelian Room	⑨
⊕ Schroeder's Restaurant	⑩
Scott's Seafood Grill	⑪
Lehr's Greenhouse	⑫
Trader Vic's	⑬
Cityscape	⑮
⊕ New Joe's.	⑯
The Iron Horse	⑰
Victor's	⑱
Palio D'Asti	⑲

ANA Hotel San Francisco ⑭   **AAA Special Value Rates**   *Hotel* ◆◆◆◆
All year   1P 155.00- 195.00   2P/1B 180.00- 220.00   2P/2B 180.00- 220.00   XP 25   F
675 units. 1 1/2 blks n of Moscone Convention Center. 50 3rd St. (94103) Some units with bay view. Check-in 3 pm.
A/C; C/TV; pay movies; radios; phones. Pay valet garage. No pets. Suites, $350-$1400 for up to 2 persons. Reserv deposit required; 3 days refund notice. AE, CB, DI, MC, VI. ● Restaurant; 6:30 am-10:30 pm; a la carte entrees about
$12.50-$24; cocktails. FAX (415) 543-8268   ⊗ Ⓢ Ⓓ Ⓓ Ⓐ (415) 974-6400

DOWNTOWN
SAN FRANCISCO
ACCOMMODATIONS

(See SAN FRANCISCO (Downtown) spotting map page A416)

Bedford Hotel 🅂25   Rates Guaranteed   *Hotel* ◆◆
🏨 All year   1P   .... 79.00   2P/1B   .... 79.00   2P/2B   .... 79.00   XP 10   F
Senior discount. 144 units. 3 1/2 blks w of Union Square. 761 Post St. (94109) Check-in 3 pm. Refrigerators; C/CATV; pay movies; VCPs. Radios; phones. 3 2-bedrm units. Pay valet garage. Airport transp. No pets. Wkly & monthly rates avail. Reserv deposit required. AE, DI, DS, MC, VI. ● Restaurant; 7 am-10 & 6-9 pm; a la carte entrees about $7-$15; cocktails. FAX (415) 563-6739   ⊗ Ⓢ Ⓓ (415) 673-6040

Best Western Americana 🅂37   Rates Guaranteed   *Motor Inn* ◆◆◆
🏨 All year   1P 68.00- 93.00   2P/1B 74.00- 99.00   2P/2B 79.00-104.00   XP 10   F
Senior discount. 142 units. 1 1/2 blks s of Market St. 121 7th St. (94103) C/CATV; movies; radios; phones; comb or shower baths. 14 2-bedrm units. Coin laundry. Htd pool; saunas. Garage & parking lot. No pets. 18 family units, $90-$150 for 4-6 persons. Reserv deposit required. AE, DI, DS, MC, VI. ● Dining rm & coffeeshop; 6:30 am-10:30 pm; a la carte entrees about $7-$14; cocktails. FAX (415) 626-3974 *(See ad below)*   Ⓓ (415) 626-0200

Best Western Canterbury Whitehall Hotel 🅂22   AAA Special Value Rates   *Hotel* ◆◆
🏨 All year   1P 85.00- 109.00   2P/1B 95.00- 115.00   2P/2B 99.00- 129.00   XP 10   F
250 units. Between Taylor & Jones sts. 750 Sutter St. (94109) 234 refrigerators; A/C; C/TV; free & pay movies; 240 radios; phones. Exercise rm. Limited pay garage. No pets. AE, DI, DS, MC, VI. ● Restaurant; 6:30 am-10 pm; Fri & Sat-11 pm; $8-$22.50; cocktails. Lehr's Greenhouse. FAX (415) 474-5856   ⊗ Ⓓ (415) 474-6464

(See SAN FRANCISCO (Downtown) spotting map page A416)

Best Western Carriage Inn 🆖   Rates Guaranteed   *Motel*   ◆◆◆
🏨 All year [CP]   1P 74.00- 94.00   2P/1B   84.00- 109.00   2P/2B   84.00- 109.00   XP 10   F
Senior discount. 48 units. 1 1/2 blks s of Market St. 140 7th St. (94103) Large rooms. Victorian decor. A/C;
C/CATV; movies; radios; phones. Whirlpool. Garage. Pets. 5 rooms with fireplace, $15 extra. Reserv deposit re-
quired. AE, DI, DS, MC, VI. Restaurant opposite. FAX (415) 626-3974 *(See ad p A417)* ⊗ Ⓓ 🅛 (415) 552-8600

Best Western Flamingo Motor Inn 🆖   Rates Guaranteed   *Motel*   ◆◆
🏨 All year   1P 55.00- 75.00   2P/1B   59.00- 79.00   2P/2B   63.00- 83.00   XP   5   F
Senior discount. 36 units. 1 blk s of Market St; 3 blks from Civic Center. 114 7th St. (94103) Some small rooms.
C/CATV; movies; radios; phones; shower or comb baths. No pets. Reserv deposit required. AE, DI, DS, MC, VI.
Restaurant opposite. FAX (415) 626-3974 *(See ad below)*   Ⓓ (415) 621-0701

Campton Place Hotel, Kempinski San
Francisco 🆖   Rates Subject to Change   *Hotel*   ◆◆◆◆
All year   1P 185.00- 320.00   2P/1B   185.00- 320.00   2P/2B   210.00- 270.00   XP
120 units. 1/2 blk n of Union Square. 340 Stockton St. (94108) Refined atmosphere; residential character. A/C; C/CATV;
movies; radios; phones. 10 2-bedrm units. Pay valet garage. Pets, $25 non-refundable deposit required. Suites, $395-
$800 for 2 persons. AE, DI, DS, MC, VI. ● Dining rm; 7-10:30 am, 11:30-2:30 & 5:30-10:30 pm; Sat & Sun from 8 am;
a la carte entrees about $18-$28; cocktails. FAX (415) 955-8536   ⊗ Ⓢ Ⓓ (415) 781-5555

Chancellor Hotel 🆖   AAA Special Value Rates   *Hotel*   ◆◆◆
🏨 Wed-Sat   1P .... 97.00   2P/1B   .... 114.00   2P/2B   .... 114.00   XP 15
Sun-Tues   1P .... 90.00   2P/1B   .... 104.00   2P/2B   .... 104.00   XP 15
140 units. 1/2 blk n off Union Square. 433 Powell St. (94102) Few small rooms. Check-in 3 pm. C/TV; pay movies;
radios; phones. Pay garage. No pets. Reserv deposit required. AE, DI, DS, MC, VI. ● Dining rm; 7 am-3 & 5-9:30
pm; Sun-3 pm; $10-$18; cocktails. FAX (415) 362-1403 *(See ad below)*   ⊗ Ⓓ (415) 362-2004

The Donatello 🆖   Rates Guaranteed   *Hotel*   ◆◆◆◆
All year   1P 155.00- 215.00   2P/1B   170.00- 215.00   2P/2B   170.00- 215.00   XP 25   F
Senior discount. 95 units. 1 blk w of Union Square, at Mason St. 501 Post St. (94102) Few studios. A/C; C/TV; radios;
phones. Pay valet garage. Airport transp. No pets. Reserv deposit required. AE, DI, DS, MC, VI. ● Restaurant; 7 am-
10:30 & 6-10:30 pm; a la carte entrees about $18-$28; cocktails. FAX (415) 885-8842   Ⓓ (415) 441-7100

Fairmont Hotel & Tower 🆖   Rates Guaranteed   *Hotel*   ◆◆◆◆◆
🏨 All year   1P 135.00- 225.00   2P/1B   135.00- 225.00   2P/2B   135.00- 225.00   XP 30
Senior discount. 596 units. Atop Nob Hill, at California St. 950 Mason St. (94108) Good to excellent varied sized
rooms. A/C; C/CATV; free & pay movies; radios; phones. Fee for: health club. Pay valet garage. No pets. 60
suites, $450-$1200 for up to 2 persons. Reserv deposit required. AE, DI, DS, MC, VI. ● 5 restaurants & coffeeshop; 6 am-3 & 5-midnight; a la carte entrees about $14-$30; cocktails; name entertainment. Also, Mason's Restaurant, see separate listing. FAX (415) 772-5013   ⊗ Ⓓ (415) 772-5000

(See SAN FRANCISCO (Downtown) spotting map page A416)

Four Seasons Clift Hotel 26 ◆◆◆◆◆
All year   Rates Subject to Change   *Hotel*
1P 205.00- 320.00   2P/1B   205.00- 350.00   2P/2B   205.00- 350.00   XP 20   F
329 units. 2 blks w of Union Square, at Taylor St. 495 Geary St. (94102) Service oriented hotel. Check-in 3 pm. Refrigerators; A/C; C/CATV; movies; radios; phones. Exercise rm. Fee for: airport transp. Pay valet garage. Reserv deposit required. AE, CB, DI, MC, VI. ● Dining rm; 6:30 am-2 & 5:30-10 pm; a la carte entrees about $25-$35; cocktails. FAX (415) 441-4621   ⊗ Ⓢ Ⓛ (415) 775-4700

Galleria Park Hotel 12 ◆◆
Mon-Thurs   AAA Special Value Rates   *Hotel*
1P   .... 140.00   2P/1B   .... 140.00   2P/2B   .... 140.00   XP
Fri-Sun   1P   .... 99.00   2P/1B   .... 99.00   2P/2B   .... 99.00   XP
177 units. 2 blks ne of Union Square. 191 Sutter St. (94104) Check-in 3 pm. Refrigerators; A/C; C/CATV; pay movies; radios; phones; comb & shower baths. Jogging track. Pay garage. No pets. Suites, $145-$325 for up to 2 persons. Reserv deposit required. AE, DI, DS, MC, VI. ● 2 restaurants; 7 am-10 pm; a la carte entrees about $9-$16; cocktail lounge. FAX (415) 433-4409   ⊗ Ⓓ (415) 781-3060

Grand Hyatt San Francisco 16 ◆◆◆◆
All year   Rates Subject to Change   *Hotel*
1P   .... 205.00   2P/1B   .... 235.00   2P/2B   .... 235.00   XP 25
Senior discount. 693 units. On Union Square at Post St. 345 Stockton St. (94108) Check-in 3 pm. A/C; C/CATV; free & pay movies; radios; phones. Exercise rm. Pay valet garage. No pets. Reserv deposit required. AE, DI, DS, MC, VI. ● Restaurant & cafeteria; 6:30 am-10:30 pm; $13-$35; cocktails; entertainment. FAX (415) 392-2536   ⊗ Ⓓ (415) 398-1234

The Handlery Union Square Hotel 30 ◆◆◆
All year   AAA Special Value Rates   *Hotel*
1P 110.00- 145.00   2P/1B   120.00- 160.00   2P/2B   120.00- 160.00   XP 10   F
377 units. 1 1/2 blks sw of Union Square. 351 Geary St. (94102) Some large rooms; few studios. Check-in 3 pm. 93 A/C; C/CATV; pay movies; radios; phones; comb or shower baths. 8 2-bedrm units. Htd pool; sauna. Pay valet garage. No pets. Reserv deposit required. AE, DI, DS, MC, VI. Restaurant adjacent. FAX (415) 781-0269 *(See ad below)*   ⊗ Ⓓ (415) 781-7800

Holiday Inn-Financial District 2 ◆◆◆
6/1-10/31   Rates Subject to Change   *Hotel*
1P 125.00- 155.00   2P/1B   140.00- 170.00   2P/2B   116.00- 175.00   XP 15
566 units. 1 blk from Chinatown. 750 Kearny St. (94108) OPEN ALL YEAR. A/C; C/CATV; pay movies; radios; phones. Coin laundry. Pool. Pay garage. No pets. AE, DI, DS, MC, VI. ● Restaurant & coffeeshop; 6 am-10 pm; $9.50-$21.50; cocktails. FAX (415) 765-7891   ⊗ Ⓓ (415) 433-6600

Holiday Inn-Union Square 17 ◆◆◆
All year   AAA Special Value Rates   *Hotel*
1P 140.00- 175.00   2P/1B   165.00- 195.00   2P/2B   165.00- 195.00   XP 20   F
401 units. 1 blk n off Union Square, corner Powell St. 480 Sutter St. (94108) Check-in 3 pm. A/C; C/TV; pay movies; radios; phones. Pay garage. No pets. Reserv deposit required. AE, DI, DS, MC, VI. ● Restaurant; 6:30-10:30 am, 11:30-2:30 & 6-10 pm; $11.50-$20.50; cocktails. FAX (415) 989-8823   ⊗ Ⓓ (415) 398-8900

(See SAN FRANCISCO (Downtown) spotting map page A416)

Hotel Britton 🆖   Rates Guaranteed   *Hotel*   ◆◆
🅰 All year   1P 45.00- 65.00   2P/1B   52.00- 72.00   2P/2B   59.00- 79.00 XP 7   F
Senior discount. 79 units. 1 blk s of Market St; 3 blks s of Civic Center. 112 7th St. (94103) C/CATV; movies; radios; phones; comb or shower baths. 8 2-bedrm units. Coin laundry. Limited pay parking lot. No pets. Reserv deposit required. AE, DI, DS, MC, VI. ● Coffeeshop; 7 am-2 & 5-10 pm; Thurs-Sat from 4 am; $6-$9.
FAX (415) 626-3974 *(See ad below)*   ⊗ Ⓓ (415) 621-7001

Hotel Nikko 🆖   AAA Special Value Rates   *Hotel*   ◆◆◆◆
🅰 All year   1P 205.00- 265.00   2P/1B   225.00- 285.00   2P/2B   245.00- 285.00   XP 25
522 units. 3 blks w of Union Square. 222 Mason St. (94102) Contemporary Japanese styling. Check-in 3 pm. A/C; C/CATV; pay movies; radios; phones. Htd indoor pool; whirlpool. Fee for: health club. Pay valet garage. No pets. Suites, $375-$1300 for up to 2 persons. Reserv deposit required. AE, CB, DI, MC, VI. ● 2 restaurants; 6:30 am-10 pm; a la carte entrees about $15-$40; cocktails. FAX (415) 394-1106   ⊗ Ⓢ Ⓓ (415) 394-1111

The Huntington Hotel 🆖   Rates Subject to Change   *Hotel*   ◆◆◆
All year   1P 165.00- 215.00   2P/1B   185.00- 235.00   2P/2B   185.00- 235.00   XP 30
140 units. Atop Nob Hill at Taylor St. 1075 California St. (94108) Some large, richly appointed rooms. Check-in 3 pm. 87 refrigerators; C/CATV; radios; phones. Pay valet garage. No pets. 40 units with seperate parlor. AE, DI, DS, MC, VI. ● Restaurant; 7-11 am, 11:30-2:30 & 5:30-11 pm; $20-$45; cocktails; cocktail lounge; entertainment. A *Preferred Hotel.* FAX (415) 474-6227   Ⓓ (415) 474-5400

Hyatt Regency-San Francisco 🆖   Rates Subject to Change   *Hotel*
Sun-Thurs   1P 195.00- 230.00   2P/1B   225.00- 260.00   2P/2B   225.00- 260.00   XP 30   F
Fri & Sat   1P 129.00- 189.00   2P/1B   129.00- 189.00   2P/2B   129.00- 189.00 XP 30   F
Senior discount. 803 units. Foot of California St. 5 Embarcadero Center. (94111) Outstanding public rooms. Rating withheld pending completion of renovation. Closed April, May & June, 1993. Check-in 3 pm. A/C; C/CATV; free & pay movies; radios; phones. Pay valet garage. No pets. Reserv deposit required. AE, DI, DS, MC, VI. ● 2 restaurants & coffeeshop; rooftop dining rm; 6:30 am-midnight; a la carte entrees about $8-$24; cocktails; entertainment. FAX (415) 398-2567
     ⊗ Ⓢ Ⓓ (415) 788-1234

(See SAN FRANCISCO (Downtown) spotting map page A416)

Hotel Juliana 45   Rates Subject to Change   *Hotel* ◆◆◆
All year   1P .... 114.00   2P/1B .... 114.00   2P/2B 114.00-130.00   XP 12
Senior discount. 107 units. Downtown. 590 Bush St. (94108) Cozy homelike atmosphere. Attractive rooms. Refrigerators; A/C; C/CATV; movies; radios; phones. Pay valet garage. 22 suites, $140-$150 for 2 persons. Reserv deposit required; 3 days refund notice. AE, CB, DI, MC, VI. Restaurant adjacent. FAX (415) 391-8447
   ⊗ Ⓓ (415) 392-2540

King George Hotel 44   AAA Special Value Rates   *Hotel* ◆◆
All year   1P .... 97.00   2P/1B .... 107.00   2P/2B .... 107.00   XP 10
137 units. 1 1/2 blks w of Union Square. 334 Mason St. (94102) Some small rooms. Service oriented staff. C/TV; pay movies; phones. Pay parking ramp. No pets. Reserv deposit required. AE, DI, DS, MC, VI. FAX (415) 391-6976
(See ad below)   Ⓢ Ⓓ (415) 781-5050

Mandarin Oriental 11   Rates Subject to Change   *Hotel* ◆◆◆◆
All year   1P 245.00-355.00   2P/1B 280.00-390.00   2P/2B 280.00-390.00   XP 45   F
160 units. In Financial District. 222 Sansome St. (94104) Top 11 floors of 48 story First Interstate Center Bldg. View of bay. A/C; C/CATV; free & pay movies; VCPs. Radios; phones. Pay valet garage. No pets. AE, DI, DS, MC, VI. ● Dining rm & restaurant; 7 am-10 pm; a la carte entrees about $19-$25. FAX (415) 433-0289   ⊗ Ⓓ (415) 885-0999

Mark Hopkins Inter-Continental 6   Rates Subject to Change   *Hotel* ◆◆◆◆
Sun-Thurs   1P 180.00-275.00   2P/1B 200.00-305.00   2P/2B 200.00-305.00   XP 30   F
Fri-Sat & holidays   1P 169.00-189.00   2P/1B 169.00-189.00   2P/2B 169.00-189.00   XP 30   F
391 units. Corner California & Mason sts. 1 Nob Hill. (94108) Panoramic view from many rooms. Quiet refined atmosphere. Check-in 3 pm. A/C; C/CATV; pay movies; radios; phones. Exercise rm. Pay valet garage. No pets. Reserv deposit required. AE, CB, DI, MC, VI. ● Restaurant; 6:30 am-10:30 pm; $25-$50; cocktails; entertainment. FAX (415) 421-3302   ⊗ Ⓓ Ⓖ (415) 392-3434

Monticello Inn 38   Rates Guaranteed   *Hotel* ◆◆
All year [CP]   1P .... 99.00   2P/1B .... 99.00   2P/2B .... 99.00   XP 15
91 units. 2 1/2 blks w of Union Square. 127 Ellis St. (94102) Colonial theme. Check-in 3 pm. A/C; C/CATV; radios; phones; shower or comb baths. Pay valet garage & parking lot. No pets. Wkly & monthly rates avail. Reserv deposit required. Complimentary beverages each evening. AE, DI, DS, MC, VI. ● Restaurant; 11:30 am-11:30 pm; a la carte entrees about $7-$14; cocktails. FAX (415) 398-2650   ⊗ Ⓢ Ⓓ (415) 392-8800

The Pan Pacific Hotel 20   AAA Special Value Rates   *Hotel* ◆◆◆◆
All year   1P 185.00-325.00   2P/1B 185.00-350.00   2P/2B .... 230.00   XP 25
330 units. 1 blk w of Union Square at Mason St. 500 Post St. (94102) Refrigerators; A/C; C/CATV; free & pay movies; radios; phones. Pay valet garage. Airport transp. Pets. 19 suites, $550-$1500 for up to 2 persons. Reserv deposit required. AE, CB, DI, DS, MC, VI. ● Restaurant; 6:30 am-11, noon-2:30 & 5:30-10 pm; a la carte entrees about $14-$28; cocktails. FAX (415) 398-0267   ⊗ Ⓢ Ⓓ Ⓖ (415) 771-8600

Parc Fifty Five Hotel 33   Rates Subject to Change   *Hotel* ◆◆◆◆
All year   1P 155.00-175.00   2P/1B 170.00-190.00   2P/2B 170.00-190.00   XP 15   F
1005 units. 3 blks w of Union Square. 55 Cyril Magnin St. (94102) Tiered exterior affording maximum views. Check-in 3 pm. A/C; C/CATV; free & pay movies; radios; phones; comb or shower baths. Fee for: fitness center. Pay valet garage. No pets. AE, DI, DS, MC, VI. ● 3 restaurants; 6:30 am-11 pm; a la carte entrees about $12-$21; cocktails. FAX (415) 296-8054   ⊗ Ⓢ Ⓓ Ⓖ (415) 392-8000

Park Hyatt Hotel 13   Rates Subject to Change   *Hotel* ◆◆◆◆
Sun-Thurs   1P .... 230.00   2P/1B .... 255.00   2P/2B .... 255.00   XP 25   F
Fri & Sat   1P .... 169.00   2P/1B .... 169.00   2P/2B .... 169.00   XP 30   F
360 units. In Financial District; At Clay St. 333 Battery St. (94111) Understated elegance. Few rooms with view of bay, some with balconies. Check-in 4 pm. Refrigerators; A/C; C/CATV; free & pay movies; radios; phones. Pay valet garage. No pets. Luxury level rooms avail. Reserv deposit required. AE, DI, DS, MC, VI. ● Restaurant; 6 am-10 pm; a la carte entrees about $12-$25; cocktails; entertainment. FAX (415) 421-2433
   ⊗ Ⓢ Ⓓ Ⓖ (415) 392-1234

Petite Auberge 8   Rates Subject to Change   *Hotel* ◆◆◆
All year [BP]   1P 110.00-160.00   2P/1B 110.00-160.00   ....   XP 15
26 units. Exit US 101 (Van Ness Ave) at Bush St, 6 1/2 blks e. 863 Bush St. (94108) French country inn atmosphere. Some units with fireplace. C/CATV; radios; phones; comb or shower baths. Pay valet parking ramp. No pets. 1 mini-suite with whirlpool bath, $210 for 2 persons. Reserv deposit required. AE, MC, VI. FAX (415) 775-5717
   Ⓢ Ⓓ (415) 928-6000

(See SAN FRANCISCO (Downtown) spotting map page A416)

The Prescott Hotel ㊷   Rates Subject to Change   Hotel   ◆◆◆
🏵 All year   1P .... 165.00   2P/1B .... 165.00   2P/2B .... 165.00   XP 10   F
Senior discount. 167 units. 1 1/2 blk w of Union Square. 545 Post St. (94102) Check-in 3 pm. A/C; C/CATV; pay movies; radios; phones; comb or shower baths. Pay valet garage. No pets. 48 1-bedroom suites, $215 for up to 2 persons. Reserv deposit required. Complimentary beverages each evening. AE, DI, DS, MC, VI. ● Restaurant; 7 am-midnight; a la carte entrees about $17-$24; cocktail lounge. FAX (415) 563-6831
⊗ Ⓢ Ⓓ ⤵ (415) 563-0303

The Raphael ㉗   Rates Guaranteed   Hotel   ◆◆
🏵 All year   1P 94.00- 115.00   2P/1B 104.00- 125.00   2P/2B 104.00- 125.00   XP 10   F
152 units. 1 blk w off Union Square. 386 Geary St. (94102) A/C; C/CATV; free & pay movies; radios; phones; comb or shower baths. Pay garage. No pets. Reserv deposit required. AE, DI, DS, MC, VI. ● Restaurant; 7 am-midnight; Fri & Sat-1 am; a la carte entrees about $12-$20; cocktails. FAX (415) 397-2447 ⊗ Ⓓ (415) 986-2000

The Ritz-Carlton ㉓   Rates Subject to Change   Hotel   ◆◆◆◆
All year   1P 185.00- 345.00   2P/1B 185.00- 345.00   2P/2B 185.00- 345.00   XP
336 units. 4 blks n of Union Square at California St. 600 Stockton St. (94108) Neo-classical structure. Check-in 3 pm. A/C; C/CATV; free & pay movies; radios; phones. Indoor pool; saunas; whirlpool; health club. Pay valet garage. No pets. 44 suites, $500-$3,000. Reserv deposit required. AE, DI, DS, MC, VI. ● Dining rm & restaurant; 6:30 am-11 pm; $25-$60; cocktail lounge; entertainment. FAX (415) 296-8559
⊗ Ⓢ Ⓓ ⤵ (415) 296-7465

(See SAN FRANCISCO (Downtown) spotting map page A416)

Royal Pacific Motor Inn ❶   Rates Subject to Change   *Motel*   ◆◆◆
🛆 All year   1P .... 72.00   2P/1B .... 74.00   2P/2B .... 76.00   XP 5
74 units. Between Grant Ave & Stockton St, adjacent to Chinatown. 661 Broadway. (94133) Some balconies. Check-in 3 pm. 12 A/C; C/TV; phones; comb or shower baths. Coin laundry. Sauna; exercise rm. No pets. Limited parking lot & adjacent garage, RV's not permitted. Reserv deposit required. AE, CB, DI, MC, VI. Restaurant adjacent. FAX (415) 781-6688 *(See ad p A422)*   ⊗ Ⓓ (415) 781-6661

San Francisco Hilton ㉜   Rates Subject to Change   *Hotel*   ◆◆◆◆
All year   1P 170.00- 225.00   2P/1B 195.00- 250.00   2P/2B 195.00- 250.00   XP 25   F
1891 units. 3 blks w of Union Square. 333 O'Farrell St. (94102) Few small rooms. A/C; C/CATV; pay movies; radios; phones. Pool; exercise rm. Pay valet garage & parking ramp. No pets. AE, DI, DS, MC, VI. ● 5 restaurants; 6 am-2 am; $13-$34; cocktails; entertainment. Also, Cityscape Restaurant, see separate listing. FAX (415) 771-6807 *(See ad p 22)*   ⊗ Ⓢ Ⓓ ⓐ (415) 771-1400

San Francisco Marriott ㊵   Rates Subject to Change   *Hotel*   ◆◆◆◆
🛆 Sun-Thurs   1P .... 205.00   2P/1B .... 235.00   2P/2B .... 235.00   XP 20   F
    Fri & Sat   1P .... 149.00   2P/1B .... 149.00   2P/2B .... 169.00   XP 20   F
Senior discount. 1500 units. 2 blks s of Union Square; 1 blk n of Moscone Center. 55 Fourth St. (94103) Check-in 4 pm. A/C; C/CATV; free & pay movies; radios; phones. Htd indoor pool; health club. Pay valet garage. Suites, $325-$2000 for up to 2 persons. AE, DI, DS, MC, VI. ● Restaurant & coffeeshop; 6:30 am-11 pm; $8-$18; cocktails. FAX (415) 896-6175   ⊗ Ⓢ Ⓓ ⓐ (415) 896-1600

Shannon Court Hotel ㊴   Rates Guaranteed   *Hotel*   ◆◆◆
🛆 All year [CP]   1P .... 85.00   2P/1B .... 85.00   2P/2B .... 85.00   XP 10   F
173 units. 3 blks w of Union Square, between Jones & Taylor sts. 550 Geary St. (94102) Refrigerators; C/TV; movies; radios; phones. Pay valet parking lot. No pets. Reserv deposit required. AE, DI, DS, MC, VI. ● Restaurant; 6 am-11 pm; a la carte entrees about $7-$11. FAX (415) 928-6813   ⊗ Ⓢ Ⓓ ⓐ (415) 775-5000

Sheraton Palace Hotel ❿   Rates Subject to Change   *Historic Hotel*   ◆◆◆
All year   1P 195.00- 295.00   2P/1B 215.00- 315.00   2P/2B 215.00- 315.00   XP 20   F
Senior discount. 550 units. 4 blks e of Union Square; 8 blks w of Ferry Bldg & Embarcadero. 2 New Montgomery St. (94105) A 1909 San Francisco landmark restored to its original elegance. Check-in 3 pm. Refrigerators; A/C; C/CATV; pay movies; radios; phones; comb or shower baths. Htd indoor pool; sauna; whirlpool; exercise rm. Pay valet garage. No pets. 32 suites, $400-$1800 for up t 2 persons. Reserv deposit required. AE, CB, DI, MC, VI. ● Dining rm & 2 restaurants; 6:30 am-midnight; a la carte entrees about $9-$18; cocktail lounge. FAX (415) 543-0671   ⊗ Ⓢ Ⓓ ⓐ (415) 392-8600

Sir Francis Drake Hotel ⓲   Rates Subject to Change   *Hotel*   ◆
All year   1P 110.00- 170.00   2P/1B 120.00- 180.00   2P/2B 120.00- 180.00   XP 20   F
Senior discount. 417 units. 1/2 blk off Union Square at Sutter St. 450 Powell St. (94102) Few small rooms. Check-in 3 pm. 100 A/C; C/TV; pay movies; radios; phones; comb or shower baths. Exercise rm. Pay valet garage. Small pets only, $75 deposit. Reserv deposit required. AE, CB, DI, MC, VI. ● Restaurant; 6:30 am-10 pm; $10-$17; cocktails. FAX (415) 391-8719   Ⓓ (415) 392-7755

(See SAN FRANCISCO (Downtown) spotting map page A416)

Stouffer Stanford Court 7   Rates Subject to Change   Hotel   ◆◆◆◆
🐫 Sun-Thurs   1P 195.00- 295.00   2P/1B 225.00- 325.00   2P/2B 225.00- 325.00 XP 30   F
    Fri-Sat   1P 169.00- 265.00   2P/1B 169.00- 265.00   2P/2B 169.00- 265.00 XP 30   F
    Senior discount. 402 units. Atop Nob Hill, at Powell St. 905 California St. (94108) Check-in 3 pm. A/C; C/CATV;
    free & pay movies; VCPs. Radios; phones. Pay valet garage. 36 suites, $450-$925 for up to 2 persons. Reserv
    deposit required. AE, CB, DI, MC, VI. ● Restaurant; 6:30 am-2:30 & 5:30-11 pm; a la carte entrees about $17-$28;
    cocktails. FAX (415) 391-0513   ⊗ Ⓢ Ⓓ (415) 989-3500

Villa Florence 29   Rates Subject to Change   Hotel   ◆◆◆
🐫 All year   1P .... 109.00   2P/1B   .... 109.00   2P/2B   .... 109.00 XP 15   F
    Senior discount. 177 units. 1/2 blk off Union Square. 225 Powell St. (94102) Check-in 3 pm. Refrigerators; 140
    A/C; C/CATV; pay movies; radios; phones; comb or shower baths. Pay garage. No pets. Reserv deposit required.
    AE, DI, DS, MC, VI. ● Restaurant; 7 am-11 pm; a la carte entrees about $7-$16; cocktails. FAX (415) 397-1006
                                                                          ⊗ Ⓢ Ⓓ (415) 397-7700

Warwick Regis Hotel 43   AAA Special Value Rates   Hotel   ◆◆◆
🐫 All year [CP]   1P 95.00- 130.00   2P/1B 105.00- 205.00   2P/2B 105.00- 205.00 XP 15
    86 units. 2 blks w of Union Sq. 490 Geary St. (94102) English & French antiques. Check-in 3 pm. Refrigerators;
    C/CATV; pay movies; radios; phones; comb or shower baths. Pay garage. No pets. AE, DI, DS, MC, VI. Restau-
    rant adjacent. FAX (415) 441-8788   ⊗ Ⓓ (415) 928-7900

(See SAN FRANCISCO (Downtown) spotting map page A416)

The Westin St. Francis [28]   **Rates Subject to Change**   *Hotel* ◆◆◆◆
⊕ All year   1P 160.00- 280.00   2P/1B 195.00- 315.00   2P/2B 195.00- 315.00   XP 35   F
1200 units. On Union Square. 335 Powell St. (94102) Nationally famous hotel. Tower units. Outstanding facilities. Imposing public rooms. Few small guestrooms. Check-in 3 pm. A/C; C/TV; pay movies; radios; phones. Exercise rm. Pay valet garage. Pets. AE, CB, DI, MC, VI. ● 2 dining rms & coffeeshop; 6 am-11 pm; $15-$33; cocktails; entertainment. FAX (415) 774-0124 *(See ad p A423)*   ⊗ Ⓓ (415) 397-7000

White Swan Inn [9]   **Rates Guaranteed**   *Hotel* ◆◆◆
All year [BP]   ....   2P/1B 145.00- 165.00   ....   XP 15
26 units. Exit US 101 (Van Ness Ave) at Bush St. 845 Bush St. (94108) English country-inn atmosphere. Fireplaces. Refrigerators; C/CATV; radios; phones; comb or shower baths. Pay valet garage. No pets. Reserv deposit required. AE, MC, VI. FAX (415) 775-5717   Ⓢ Ⓓ (415) 775-1755

York Hotel [24]   **AAA Special Value Rates**   *Hotel* ◆◆
⊕ All year [CP]   1P 95.00- 110.00   2P/1B   95.00- 110.00   2P/2B   95.00- 110.00   XP 10   F
96 units. 5 blks w of Union Square. 940 Sutter St. (94109) Art deco style. Few small rooms. Check-in 3 pm. 45 refrigerators; C/TV; pay movies; radios; phones. Exercise rm. Pay garage. No pets. Reserv deposit required. Complimentary beverages each evening. AE, DI, DS, MC, VI. Cocktail lounge; entertainment; nightclub. FAX (415) 885-2115   ⊗ Ⓓ (415) 885-6800

(See SAN FRANCISCO (Downtown) spotting map page A416)

RESTAURANTS

Blue Fox ④ Northern Italian $$$$ ◆◆◆
In the financial district. 659 Merchant St. Distinctive Italian restaurant. Menu changes daily; also prix fixe, $55. A/C. Dress code. Open 5:30 pm-11 pm; closed Sun, major holidays & 1st week January & July. Cocktails & lounge. Pay valet parking. Reserv required. AE, CB, DI, MC, VI. ⊗ (415) 981-1177

Carnelian Room ⑨ American $$$$ ◆◆◆
Atop Bank of America Center on 52 floor. 555 California St. Spectacular panoramic view. Seasonal California cuisine. A/C. Dress code. Open 6 pm-10 pm; Sun from 10 am; closed 1/1, 11/25 & 12/25. Cocktails & lounge. Pay garage. Reserv advised. AE, CB, DI, MC, VI. ⊗ (415) 433-7500

Cityscape ⑮ American $$$ ◆◆◆
In San Francisco Hilton. 333 O'Farrell St. Panoramic view. A/C. Open 5:30 pm-10 pm; Fri & Sat-11 pm. Cocktails. Entertainment. Parking avail. Reserv advised. AE, CB, DI, MC, VI. *(See ad p 22)* ⊗ (415) 771-1400

Empress of China ⑤ Chinese $$$ ◆◆
In Chinatown, on top floor of China Trade Center Building. 838 Grant Ave. Oriental decor; regional specialties. A/C. Dress code. Open 11:30 am-3 & 5 pm-11 pm; Sun 12:30 pm-11 pm. Cocktails & lounge. Minimum $13. Reserv advised. AE, DI, MC, VI. ⊗ (415) 434-1345

Ernie's ② French $$$$ ◆◆◆◆
847 Montgomery St. Excellent cuisine; elegant atmosphere. Prix fixe menu Sun-Thurs, $38. A/C. Dress code. Open 11:30 am-2:30 & 5:30-10:30 pm; Sat & Sun from 5:30 pm; closed major holidays. Cocktails & lounge. Pay valet parking. Reserv advised. AE, DI, MC, VI. ⊗ (415) 397-5971

The Iron Horse ⑰ Italian $$ ◆◆
1 1/2 blks e of Union Square. 19 Maiden Ln. Contemporary Northern Italian cusine. Street parking. A/C. Children's menu. Open 11:30 am-10:30 pm; Sun from 5 pm; closed 11/25 & 12/25. Cocktails & lounge. Minimum, $8. Reserv advised. AE, DI, DS, MC, VI. ⊗ (415) 362-8133

John's Grill ③ Steak & Seafood $$$ ◆◆
🍸 2 1/2 blks s of Union Square. 63 Ellis St. Continental cuisine. A/C. Open 11 am-10 pm; closed Sun, 1/1, 7/4 & 12/25. Cocktails. AE, MC, VI. ⊗ (415) 986-0069

Kan's ⑥ Chinese $$ ◆◆
In Chinatown. Upstairs at 708 Grant Ave. Long-established Chinese restaurant featuring Cantonese dishes. A/C. Open 11:30 am-2 & 4:30-10 pm; Sun from 4 pm; closed 11/26 & 12/25. Cocktails & lounge. Minimum $8. Reserv advised. AE, DI, DS, VI. ⊗ (415) 982-2388

Lehr's Greenhouse ⑫ American $$ ◆◆
Between Taylor & Jones sts, in Best Western Canterbury Whitehall Hotel. 740 Sutter St. Indoor garden dining. California cuisine. A/C. Open 6:30 am-10 pm; Fri & Sat-11 pm; Sun 6:30 am-10 pm. Cocktails & lounge. Minimum $7. Pay parking lot. Reserv advised. AE, CB, DI, MC, VI. ⊗ (415) 474-6478

Mason's ⑦ American $$$ ◆◆◆◆
On the Arcade floor of the Fairmont Hotel & Tower. A/C. Dress code. Open 5 pm-10 pm; Sat 5 pm-11 pm; closed Sun, 5/25, 7/4 & 9/7. Cocktails & lounge. Entertainment. Parking avail. Reserv advised. AE, DI, MC, VI. ⊗ (415) 392-0113

New Joe's ⑯ Italian $$ ◆◆
🍸 1/2 blk sw of Union Square. 347 Geary St. Family restaurant; also American cuisine. A/C. Children's menu. Open 7 am-11 pm; closed 12/25. Cocktails & lounge. Minimum, $5. Pay garage. Reserv advised. AE, CB, DI, MC, VI. ⊗ (415) 989-6733

Palio D'Asti ⑲ Italian $$ ◆◆◆
In financial district. 640 Sacramento St. Piedmonteses & other regional specialties. Relaxed high-tech atmosphere. A/C. Open 11:30 am-11 pm; Sat 5 pm-11 pm; closed Sun & major holidays. Cocktails. Pay valet parking. Reserv required. AE, DI, DS, MC, VI. ⊗ (415) 395-9800

Schroeder's Restaurant ⑩ German $$ ◆◆
🍸 In the Financial District, between California & Sacramento sts. 240 Front St. Bavarian specialties; Old World charm. Children's menu. Open 11 am-9 pm; Sat from 5 pm; closed Sun & major holidays. Cocktails. Minimum, $5. Reserv advised. AE, DI, MC, VI. ⊗ (415) 421-4778

Scott's Seafood Grill ⑪ Seafood $$$ ◆◆
On Podium level. 3 Embarcadero Center. In the heart of the Financial District. A/C. Open 11 am-10 pm; Fri & Sat-11 pm; Sun 4:30 pm-9:30 pm; closed 1/1, 7/4, 11/26, 12/25. Cocktails & lounge. Minimum $5. Reserv advised. AC, DI, MC, VI. ⊗ (415) 981-0622

(See SAN FRANCISCO (Downtown) spotting map page A416)

Trader Vic's ⑬ — Ethnic — $$$ ◆◆
Off Taylor St, between Post & Sutter sts. 20 Cosmo Pl. Polynesian cuisine & decor. A/C. Dress code. Open 5 pm-11 pm; Fri & Sat to midnight; Sun 5 pm-10 pm; closed major holidays. Cocktails & lounge. Pay valet parking. Reserv advised. AE, MC, VI. ⊗ (415) 776-2232

Victor's ⑱ — American — $$$$ ◆◆◆◆
Atop The Westin St. Francis, on Union Square. Seasonal California specialties using freshest ingredients. A/C. Dress code. Open 6 pm-10:30 pm. Cocktails. Pay valet parking. Reserv required. AE, CB, DI, MC, VI. ⊗ (415) 956-7777

The Waterfront Restaurant ① — Seafood — $$$ ◆◆
1 1/2 mi s of Fisherman's Wharf on The Embarcadero. Pier 7. View of harbor. Open 11:30 am-10:30 pm; Sun from 10 am; closed 7/4, 12/24 & 12/25. Cocktails. Pay valet parking. Reserv advised. AE, CB, DI, MC, VI. ⊗ (415) 391-2696

Yamato Restaurant ⑧ — Ethnic — $$$ ◆◆◆
Off Grant Ave. 717 California St. Japanese cuisine & traditional decor; sushi bar, tatami rooms. A/C. Children's menu. Open noon-2 & 5-10 pm; Sat & Sun from 5 pm; closed Mon & 1/1, 11/26 & 12/25. Cocktails & lounge. Reserv advised. AE, CB, DI, MC, VI. (415) 397-3456

SAN FRANCISCO (Northern Region) (See SAN FRANCISCO (Northern Region) spotting map pages A428 & A429; see index below)

Index of Establishments on the SAN FRANCISCO (Northern Region) AREA Spotting Map

---

Alamo Square Inn 🏨102 — Rates Subject to Change — *Bed & Breakfast* ◆◆
All year [BP] — 1P 85.00- 175.00 — 2P/1B 85.00- 175.00 — 2P/2B .... 100.00 XP 25
14 units. Exit 101, Fell St; 5 blks w, 2 blks n opposite Alamo Square. 719 Scott St. (94117). Smoke free premises. 5 C/TV; radios; phones; shower or comb baths. 2 kitchens. Coin laundry. Limited parking lot. No pets. Reserv deposit required; 7 days refund notice. AE, MC, VI. ⊗ Ⓓ (415) 922-2055

The Archbishops Mansion 🏨88 — Rates Subject to Change — *Historic Bed & Breakfast* ◆◆◆
🏨 All year [CP] — .... 2P/1B 100.00- 295.00 — 2P/2B 100.00- 295.00 XP 20
15 units. Exit US 101, Fell St; 4 blks w, 2 blks n on Steiner opposite Alamo Square. 1000 Fulton St. (94117). Elegant. European antiques. Many rooms with fireplace. Check-in 3 pm. C/CATV; radios; phones; comb or shower baths. 1 2-bedrm unit. 2 rooms with whirlpool. Limited parking lot. No pets. 2-night minimum stay weekends. Wkly rates avail. Reserv deposit required; 7 days refund notice. Complimentary beverages each evening. AE, MC, VI. FAX (415) 885-3193 ⓈⒹ (415) 563-7872

Beck's Motor Lodge 🏨84 — AAA Special Value Rates — *Motel* ◆◆
5/1-10/31 — 1P 71.00- 86.00 — 2P/1B 75.00- 90.00 — 2P/2B 84.00- 99.00 XP 7
11/1-4/30 — 1P 62.00- 77.00 — 2P/1B 66.00- 81.00 — 2P/2B 74.00- 89.00 XP 7
57 units. 2222 Market St. (94114) 2 gas fireplaces. Few studios. Refrigerators; 10 A/C; C/TV; movies; radios; phones; shower or comb baths. Coin laundry. Reserv deposit required. AE, DI, DS, MC, VI. Restaurant opposite. *(See ad p A430)* Ⓓ (415) 621-8212

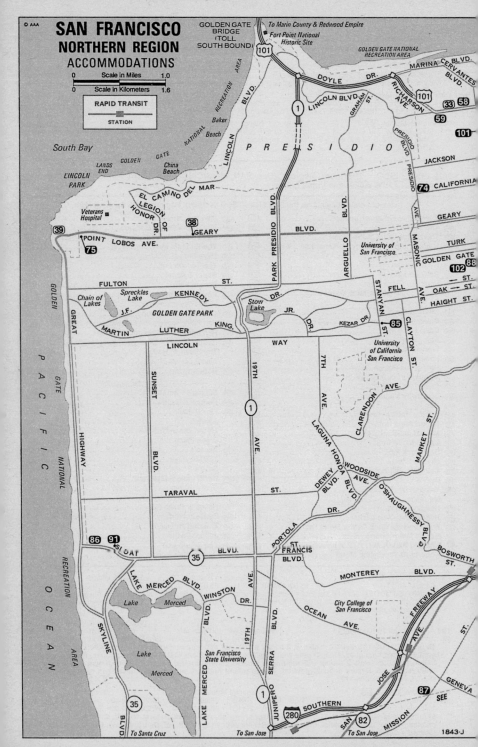

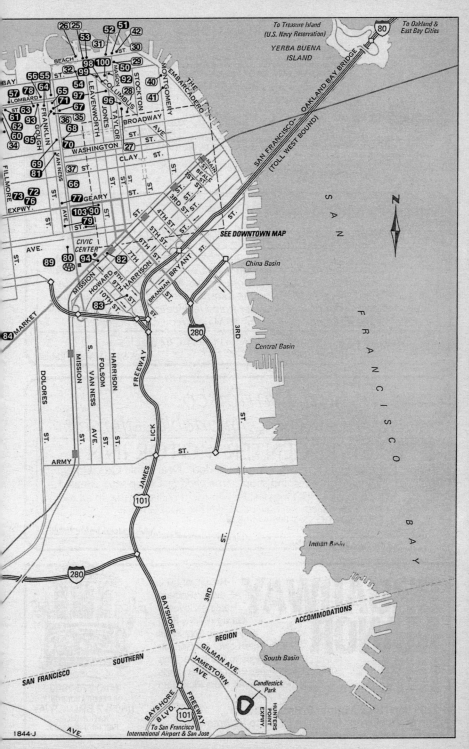

1844-J

(See SAN FRANCISCO (Northern Region) spotting map pages A428 & A429)

Best Western Civic Center Motor Inn 83   AAA Special Value Rates   *Motel*   ◆◆
 5/1-10/31   1P 65.00- 83.00 2P/1B 75.00- 90.00 2P/2B 80.00- 95.00 XP 7
 11/1-4/30   1P 60.00- 75.00 2P/1B 67.00- 80.00 2P/2B 75.00- 85.00 XP 7
 57 units. 1 1/2 blks n off frwy; Civic Center exit, at Harrison St. 364 9th St. (94103) Some studio units. Refrigerators; C/TV; movies; radios; phones; shower or comb baths. Coin laundry. Small pool. Reserv deposit required. AE, DI, DS, MC, VI. Coffeeshop; 7 am-2 pm; Sat & Sun-noon. FAX (415) 621-0833 *(See ad below)*
                                                                                                    Ⓓ (415) 621-2826

Broadway Manor Inn 69   Rates Guaranteed   *Motor Inn*   ◆
 6/16-9/14   1P .... 73.00 2P/1B .... 73.00 2P/2B .... 78.00 XP 8   F
 9/15-6/15   1P .... 49.00 2P/1B .... 59.00 2P/2B .... 62.00 XP 8   F
 Senior discount. 56 units. On US 101, at Broadway. 2201 Van Ness Ave. (94109) C/TV; movies; phones. Limited garage & parking lot. No pets. Reserv deposit required. AE, DI, DS, MC, VI. ● Coffeeshop; 7 am-2 pm; $7-$10; beer & wine. FAX (415) 928-0460 *(See ad below)*   ⊗ Ⓓ (415) 776-7900

Buena Vista Motor Inn
1599 Lombard Street
San Francisco, Ca 94123
1-800-835-4980
(415) 923-9600

Lombard Motor Inn
1475 Lombard Street
San Francisco, Ca 94123
1-800-835-3639
(415) 441-6000

Star Motel
1727 Lombard Street
San Francisco, Ca 94133
1-800-835-8143 Additional Discounts Available
(415) 346-8250

Three Great Choices at One Great Price

$78.

AAA Members
Single or Double Occupancy
Winter Rates

We are minutes from <u>San Francisco's</u> favorite attractions

(See SAN FRANCISCO (Northern Region) spotting map pages A428 & A429)

Buena Vista Motor Inn 78   Rates Subject to Change   *Motel*   ◆◆◆
All year   1P .... 73.00 2P/1B .... 78.00 2P/2B .... 78.00 XP 6   F
50 units. On US 101, Lombard St, at Gaugh St. 1599 Lombard St. (94123) Check-in 3 pm. A/C; C/TV; radios; phones; comb or shower baths. Limited garage. No pets. Reserv deposit required. AE, DI, DS, MC, VI. FAX (415) 441-4775 *(See ad p A431)*   ⊗ Ⓢ Ⓓ 🛇 🛗 (415) 923-9600

Capri Motel 62   Rates Guaranteed   *Motel*   ◆
All year   1P .... 54.00 2P/1B .... 68.00 2P/2B .... 72.00 XP 8
46 units. Off US 101, 1 blk s of Lombard St at Buchanan St. 2015 Greenwich St. (94123) C/CATV; phones; shower or comb baths. No pets. 1 1-bedroom unit with kitchen, $78, 1 with efficiency $90. 2-bedroom units with efficiency, $146 for up to 6 persons. Reserv deposit required. AE, DI, DS, MC, VI. FAX (415) 346-3256   Ⓓ (415) 346-4667

Castle Inn Motel 68   Rates Guaranteed   *Motel*   ◆◆
6/1-9/15   1P 65.00- 70.00 2P/1B 65.00- 78.00 2P/2B 75.00- 85.00 XP 10
9/16-5/31   1P 48.00- 52.00 2P/1B 50.00- 58.00 2P/2B 58.00- 65.00 XP 8
25 units. 1/2 blk e of US 101 (Van Ness Ave.). 1565 Broadway. (94109) Refrigerators; 23 A/C; C/TV; radios; phones. Garage. No pets. Reserv deposit required; 3 days refund notice. AE, DI, DS, MC, VI. *(See ad below)*   ⊗ Ⓓ (415) 441-1155

Cathedral Hill Hotel 77   Rates Guaranteed   *Hotel*   ◆◆◆
All year   1P 105.00- 170.00 2P/1B 125.00- 190.00 2P/2B 140.00- 240.00 XP 20
Senior discount. 400 units. On US 101 between Geary & Post sts. 1101 Van Ness Ave. (94109) Small & large units. Check-in 3 pm. A/C; C/TV; pay movies; radios; phones. Pool & garden patio on 4th floor. Garage. No pets. AE, DI, DS, MC, VI. ● Dining rm & coffeeshop; 6:30 am-11 pm; $7-$30; cocktails. FAX (415) 441-2841   ⊗ Ⓢ Ⓓ (415) 776-8200

Chelsea Motor Inn 60   Rates Guaranteed   *Motel*   ◆◆◆
All year   1P .... 73.00 2P/1B .... 78.00 2P/2B .... 78.00 XP 7
60 units. On US 101 at Fillmore St. 2095 Lombard St. (94123) Check-in 3 pm. A/C; C/CATV; radios; phones. Garage. No pets. Reserv deposit required. AE, CB, DI, MC, VI. FAX (415) 567-6475 *(See ad p A433)*   Ⓓ (415) 563-5600

Columbus Motor Inn 97   Rates Guaranteed   *Motel*   ◆◆◆
5/15-10/15   1P .... 92.00 2P/1B .... 97.00 2P/2B .... 97.00 XP 10
10/16-5/14   1P .... 73.00 2P/1B .... 78.00 2P/2B .... 78.00 XP 7
45 units. 4 blks from Fisherman's Wharf; between Francisco & Chestnut sts. 1075 Columbus Ave. (94133) Check-in 3 pm. A/C; C/CATV; radios; phones. Garage. No pets. 6 2-room units, $137 5/15-10/15, $108 10/16-5/14 for up to 4 persons. Reserv deposit required. AE, CB, DI, MC, VI. FAX (415) 928-2174 *(See ad p A433)*   ⊗ Ⓓ (415) 885-1492

Coventry Motor Inn 61   Rates Guaranteed   *Motel*   ◆◆◆
All year   1P .... 73.00 2P/1B .... 78.00 2P/2B .... 78.00 XP 7
69 units. On US 101; at Buchanan St. 1901 Lombard St. (94123) Check-in 3 pm. A/C; C/CATV; radios; phones. Garage. No pets. Reserv deposit required. AE, CB, DI, MC, VI. FAX (415) 921-8745 *(See ad p A433)*   Ⓓ (415) 567-1200

Cow Hollow Motor Inn & Suites 58   Rates Guaranteed   *Motel*   ◆◆◆
All year   1P .... 73.00 2P/1B .... 78.00 2P/2B .... 78.00 XP 7
129 units. On US 101 at Steiner St. 2190 Lombard St. (94123) Very good rooms. Check-in 3 pm. A/C; C/CATV; radios; phones. Garage. No pets. 12 1- & 2-bedroom suites with wood burning fireplace & antiques, $175-$225, for up to 4 persons. Reserv deposit required. AE, CB, DI, MC, VI. Coffeeshop; 6:30 am-2:30 pm; $4.95-$8. FAX (415) 922-8515 *(See ad p A433 and p A434)*   ⊗ Ⓓ (415) 921-5800

DeVille Motor Inn   **$48 SPECIAL* 10/16 – 6/15**
2599 Lombard Street   ✓ *Spacious Rooms*   ✓ *Great Location*
San Francisco, CA 94123   ✓ *In-Room Coffee*   ✓ *Elevator*
(415) 346-4664   **Sun.–Thurs. for 2 people/1 bed with mention of this ad. Includes AAA discount. Weekends & Holidays excluded. Extra bed additional charge.*

CASTLE INN
For Reservations Call Toll Free
1-800-822-7853
U.S. & Canada
(415) 441-1155

Conveniently located near Fisherman's Wharf, Ghirardelli Square, Chinatown and Cable Cars

- Color Cable TV AM/FM Radio
- King & Queen Beds
- Covered Parking
- Refrigerators
- Free Tour Pick-Up

1565 Broadway • at Van Ness Ave., SF • CA 94109

(See SAN FRANCISCO (Northern Region) spotting map pages A428 & A429)

Days Inn [91]
		Rates Subject to Change							Motel		◆
7/1-9/15 [CP]	1P	80.00-	95.00	2P/1B	85.00-	95.00	2P/2B	....	95.00	XP 10	F
5/15-6/30 [CP]	1P	70.00-	85.00	2P/1B	75.00-	85.00	2P/2B	....	85.00	XP 10	F
9/16-5/14 [CP]	1P	60.00-	70.00	2P/1B	60.00-	65.00	2P/2B	....	75.00	XP 10	F

Senior discount. 33 units. 3 blks from beach. 2600 Sloat Blvd. (94116) Refrigerators; C/CATV; radios; phones; comb or shower baths. Garage. No pets. 3 family units, $105-$130 for up to 4 persons. Microwaves. Reserv deposit required; 3 days refund notice. AE, DI, DS, MC, VI. FAX (415) 665-5440 ⊗ Ⓢ Ⓓ ⓛ (415) 665-9000

Days Inn-Civic Center [89]
		Rates Guaranteed							Motel		◆◆
All year [CP]	1P	60.00-	70.00	2P/1B	65.00-	75.00	2P/2B	....	80.00	XP 10	

Senior discount. 40 units. 2 1/2 blks w of US 101, Van Ness Ave. 465 Grove St. (94102) Refrigerators; C/CATV; VCPs; phones. Limited parking lot. No pets. Microwave; few wet bars. 6 units with whirlpool bath, $70-$90 for up to 2 persons. AE, DI, DS, MC, VI. FAX (415) 864-4040 ⊗ Ⓓ (415) 864-4040

De Ville Motor Inn [59]
	Rates Guaranteed							Motel		◆◆
6/15-10/15	....		2P/1B	60.00-	80.00	2P/2B	64.00-	84.00	XP 4
10/16-6/14	....		2P/1B	48.00-	68.00	2P/2B	52.00-	72.00	XP 4

40 units. On US 101; 1 1/2 blks from Presidio. 2599 Lombard St. (94123) C/CATV; radios; phones; shower or comb baths. No pets. 2 family units with parlor $90-$100 for up to 6 persons. Reserv deposit required; 3 days refund notice. AE, DS, MC, VI. FAX (415) 929-8128 *(See ad p A432)* Ⓓ (415) 346-4664

(See SAN FRANCISCO (Northern Region) spotting map pages A428 & A429)

Francisco Bay Motel 64   Rates Guaranteed   *Motel* ◆◆
🏵 All year   1P 48.50- 72.50   2P/1B   52.50- 82.50   2P/2B   56.50- 82.50 XP 8
34 units. On US 101. 1501 Lombard St. (94123) Few small rooms. 6 refrigerators; A/C; C/TV; radios; phones; shower or comb baths. 1 kitchen. No pets. Reserv deposit required; 3 days refund notice. AE, CB, DI, MC, VI.
FAX (415) 567-7082 *(See ad p A434)*   ⊗ Ⓓ (415) 474-3030

Holiday Inn-Civic Center 82   AAA Special Value Rates   *Motor Inn* ◆◆◆
🏵 All year   1P 88.00- 140.00   2P/1B   98.00- 160.00   2P/2B   98.00- 160.00 XP 15   F
Senior discount. 389 units. 2 blks from Civic Auditorium; 1/2 blk s off Market St & BART Station. 50 8th St. (94103) A/C; C/CATV; movies; radios; phones. Coin laundry. Htd pool. Garage. No pets. AE, DI, DS, MC, VI. ● Restaurant; 6 am-10 pm; $8-$15; cocktails. FAX (415) 552-1084   ⊗ Ⓓ Ⓛ (415) 626-6103

Holiday Inn-Fisherman's Wharf 100   AAA Special Value Rates   *Motor Inn* ◆◆◆
🏵 All year   1P 105.00- 155.00   2P/1B   110.00- 160.00   2P/2B   110.00- 160.00 XP 15   F
580 units. 3 blks from the bay & Fisherman's Wharf; 2 blks from Ghiradelli Square. 1300 Columbus Ave. (94133) Check-in 3 pm. A/C; C/CATV; movies; radios; phones. Coin laundry. Small pool. No pets. Limited pay garage & parking lot. AE, DI, DS, MC, VI. ● 2 restaurants; 6 am-10 pm; $9-$18; cocktails. FAX (415) 771-7006
     ⊗ Ⓓ (415) 771-9000

Holiday Inn-Golden Gateway 66   Rates Subject to Change   *Hotel* ◆◆◆
All year   1P 99.00- 123.00   2P/1B   114.00- 136.00   2P/2B   123.00- 142.00 XP 15   F
494 units. On US 101 at Pine St. 1500 Van Ness Ave. (94109) Some small rooms. A/C; C/CATV; free & pay movies; radios; phones. Pool. Pay garage. No pets. AE, DS, DI, MC, VI. ● Coffeeshop; 6:30 am-10:30 pm; $10-$16; cocktails.
FAX (415) 776-7155   ⊗ Ⓓ (415) 441-4000

Holiday Lodge 81   Rates Subject to Change   *Motel* ◆◆
🏵 6/1-10/31   1P .... 84.00   2P/1B   .... 88.00   2P/2B   .... 88.00 XP 10   F
11/1-5/31   1P .... 64.00   2P/1B   .... 69.00   2P/2B   .... 69.00 XP 10   F
Senior discount. 65 units. On US 101 at Jackson. 1901 Van Ness Ave. (94109) Some units overlook pool, garden patio. C/TV; movies; radios; phones; comb or shower baths. Small pool. No pets. Wkly rates avail 11/1-4/30. Reserv deposit required. AE, DI, MC, VI. Restaurant opposite. FAX (415) 474-7046   Ⓓ (415) 776-4469

Howard Johnson Lodge at Fisherman's
Wharf 53   Rates Subject to Change   *Motel* ◆◆◆
🏵 7/1-10/31   1P .... 113.00   2P/1B   .... 123.00   2P/2B   .... 123.00 XP 10   F
3/1-6/30   1P .... 93.00   2P/1B   .... 103.00   2P/2B   .... 103.00 XP 10   F
11/1-2/28   1P .... 83.00   2P/1B   .... 93.00   2P/2B   .... 93.00 XP 10   F
Senior discount. 128 units. In the Fisherman's Wharf area, adjacent to the Cannery, between Jones & Leavenworth sts. 580 Beach St. (94133) Check-in 3 pm. A/C; C/CATV; free & pay movies; radios; phones; comb or shower baths. Coin laundry. Garage. No pets. Reserv deposit required. AE, DI, DS, MC, VI. Restaurant adjacent.
FAX (415) 441-7307   ⊗ Ⓢ Ⓛ (415) 775-3800

Hyatt Fisherman's Wharf 96   Rates Subject to Change   *Hotel* ◆◆◆
4/1-10/31   1P 129.00- 175.00   2P/1B   154.00- 200.00   2P/2B   154.00- 200.00 XP 25   F
11/1-3/31   1P 115.00- 155.00   2P/1B   140.00- 180.00   2P/2B   140.00- 180.00 XP 25   F
Senior discount. 313 units. 2 blks from wharf; at Taylor St. 555 North Point St. (94133) Check-in 3 pm. A/C; C/CATV; pay movies; radios; phones. Coin laundry. Htd pool; sauna; whirlpool; recreational program; exercise rm. Pay valet garage. No pets. Reserv deposit required; 3 days refund notice. AE, DI, DS, MC, VI. ● Restaurant; 6:30 am-10 pm; Fri & Sat-11 pm; $15-$22. FAX (415) 563-2218   ⊗ Ⓢ Ⓓ Ⓛ (415) 563-1234

Hyde Park Suites 54   AAA Special Value Rates   *Suites Motel* ◆◆
🏵 All year   1P 165.00- 190.00   2P/1B   165.00- 190.00   2P/2B   .... 220.00 XP 10   F
24 units. 6 blks from Fisherman's Wharf, at North Point St. 2655 Hyde St. (94109) On cable car line. Some units with view of bay. Check-in 3 pm. C/CATV; radios; phones. Kitchens. Coin laundry. Limited valet garage. No pets. Reserv deposit required. Complimentary beverages each evening. AE, DI, DS, MC, VI. FAX (415) 346-8058
     Ⓓ (415) 771-0200

Inn at the Opera 80   Rates Guaranteed   *Hotel* ◆◆◆
All year [CP]   1P 110.00- 205.00   2P/1B   120.00- 215.00   2P/2B   195.00- 215.00 XP 10   F
47 units. 1 blk w of City Hall. 333 Fulton St. (94102) English furnishings. Check-in 3 pm. C/CATV; movies; VCPs. Radios; phones. Pay garage. No pets. Reserv deposit required. AE, MC, VI. ● Dining rm; 7 am-10:30 pm; a la carte entrees about $8-$25; cocktails. FAX (415) 861-0821   ⊗ Ⓢ Ⓓ (415) 863-8400

Laurel Motor Inn 74   AAA Special Value Rates   *Motel* ◆◆
🏵 All year [CP]   1P 70.00- 90.00   2P/1B   78.00- 98.00   2P/2B   78.00- 98.00 XP 8   F
Senior discount. 49 units. 1 mi w of US 101 (Van Ness Ave); 1 mi e of Park Presido Blvd (SR 1) at California St. 444 Presidio Ave. (94115) Check-in 3 pm. C/CATV; movies; radios; phones; shower or comb baths. Coin laundry. Garage. Pets. 18 kitchens, $10 extra. Reserv deposit required. AE, DI, DS, MC, VI. Cocktail lounge; restaurant opposite. FAX (415) 928-1866 *(See ad below)*   ⊗ Ⓓ (415) 567-8467

(See SAN FRANCISCO (Northern Region) spotting map pages A428 & A429)

Lombard Motor Inn 🔢 65   Rates Subject to Change   *Motel* ◆◆◆
🏨 All year   1P .... 73.00   2P/1B   78.00   2P/2B   78.00   XP   6
48 units. 1 blk off Van Ness Ave on US 101. 1475 Lombard St. (94123) Check-in 3 pm. A/C; C/TV; radios; phones; comb or shower baths. Garage. No pets. Reserv deposit required. AE, DI, DS, MC, VI. FAX (415) 441-4291 *(See ad p A431)*   ⊗ Ⓓ (415) 441-6000

Lombard Plaza Motel 🔢 57   Rates Subject to Change   *Motel* ◆
🏨 5/24-10/31   ....   2P/1B   59.00- 69.00   2P/2B   69.00- 79.00   XP 12
     11/1-5/23   ....   2P/1B   45.00- 69.00   2P/2B   49.00- 69.00   XP 12
31 units. On US 101. 2026 Lombard St. (94123) 8 A/C; C/TV; movies; radios; phones; shower or comb baths. Limited parking lot. No pets. Wkly rates avail. AE, DS, MC, VI. FAX (415) 921-5275   Ⓓ (415) 921-2444

Mission Serra Motel 🔢 87   Rates Guaranteed   *Motel* ◆◆
🏨 All year   1P 40.00- 49.00   2P/1B   45.00- 55.00   2P/2B   51.00- 60.00   XP   5   F
Senior discount. 52 units. 5 mi s; exit I-280 via Geneva Ave, 1/2 mi e to Mission St, then 1/2 mi s. 5630 Mission St. (94112) C/CATV; 40 radios; phones; shower or comb baths. 8 2-bedrm units. Coin laundry. No pets. 7 efficiencies & 9 kitchens, $6-$10 extra. Wkly rates avail. Reserv deposit required. AE, DI, DS, MC, VI. *(See ad below)*   ⊗ Ⓢ Ⓓ (415) 584-5020

Miyako Hotel 🔢 76   AAA Special Value Rates   *Hotel* ◆◆◆
🏨 All year   1P 92.00- 149.00   2P/1B   92.00- 169.00   2P/2B   92.00- 169.00   XP 20   F
218 units. 1 mi w of Union Square, at Laguna St in Japan Center. 1625 Post St. (94115) Japanese garden courtyard. Check-in 3 pm. Refrigerators; A/C; C/TV; pay movies; radios; phones. Pay valet garage. No pets. Authentic Japanese suites, $250 & a few western-style suites with sauna, $180-$250. 4 Japanese rooms $180. AE, DI, DS, MC, VI. ● Restaurant; 6:30 am-10:30 pm; a la carte entrees about $15-$22; cocktails; entertainment. FAX (415) 921-0417 *(See ad p A426)*   ⊗ Ⓢ Ⓓ (415) 922-3200

(See SAN FRANCISCO (Northern Region) spotting map pages A428 & A429)

Miyako Inn-Best Western 🔢   Rates Guaranteed   *Motor Inn* ◆◆
🏵 All year   1P .... 81.00 2P/1B .... 91.00 2P/2B .... 89.00 XP 10   F
Senior discount. 125 units. 1 mi w of Union Square; 5 blks w of US 101 at Sutter & Buchanan sts; 1 blk from the Japan Center. 1800 Sutter St. (94115) A/C; C/TV; phones. 60 steambaths. No pets. Rooms with steambath, $6 extra. Limited pay garage & parking lot. AE, DI, DS, MC, VI. ● Dining rm; 7 am-10 pm; $8-$17; beer & wine.
FAX (415) 923-1064 *(See ad p A420)*   ⊗ Ⓢ Ⓓ Ⓛ (415) 921-4000

Nob Hill Motel 🔢   Rates Guaranteed   *Motel* ◆◆
🏵 6/1-9/15   1P 65.00- 70.00 2P/1B 65.00- 78.00 2P/2B 75.00- 85.00 XP 10
9/16-5/31   1P 48.00- 52.00 2P/1B 50.00- 58.00 2P/2B 58.00- 65.00 XP 8
29 units. 1/2 blk e of US 101, Van Ness Ave. 1630 Pacific Ave. (94109) Large rooms. Refrigerators; C/TV; radios; phones; shower or comb baths. No pets. Covered parking. Reserv deposit required; 3 days refund notice. AE, DI, DS, MC, VI. *(See ad p A436)*   ⊗ Ⓓ (415) 775-8160

Pacific Heights Inn 🔢   Rates Subject to Change   *Motel* ◆◆
🏵 All year [CP]   1P 59.00- 89.00 2P/1B 59.00- 89.00 2P/2B 75.00- 98.00 XP
Senior discount. 40 units. 1/2 blk w of US 101 (Van Ness Ave). 1555 Union St. (94123) Few small rooms. Refrigerators; C/CATV; radios; phones; shower or comb baths. 5 2-bedrm units, 17 kitchens. 8 rms with whirlpool bath. 1 apartment, $95-$150 for up to 4 persons. Wkly rates avail. Reserv deposit required. AE, DI, DS, MC, VI.
FAX (415) 776-8176 *(See ad below)*   ⊗ Ⓓ (415) 776-3310

The Phoenix Inn 🔢   Rates Subject to Change   *Motel* ◆◆
🏵 All year [CP]   1P .... 84.00 2P/1B .... 89.00 2P/2B .... 89.00 XP 10   F
44 units. 2 blks e of US 101 (Van Ness Ave). 601 Eddy St. (94109) C/CATV; movies; radios; phones. Pool. Limited parking lot. No pets. 2 suites, $125-$135 for up to 2 persons. Reserv deposit required. AE, DI, MC, VI. ● Restaurant; 11:30 am-2:30 & 6-10 pm; closed Mon; a la carte entrees about $9-$15; cocktails.
FAX (415) 885-3109   Ⓓ (415) 776-1380

Quality Hotel by the Bay 🔢   Rates Subject to Change   *Motor Inn* ◆◆
🏵 7/1-9/6 [CP]   1P 63.00- 85.00 2P/1B 75.00- 81.00 2P/2B 87.00- 97.00 XP 12   F
9/7-10/31 [CP]   1P 59.00- 75.00 2P/1B 71.00- 77.00 2P/2B 81.00- 87.00 XP 12   F
11/1-6/30 [CP]   1P 56.00- 69.00 2P/1B 68.00- 74.00 2P/2B 75.00- 81.00 XP 12   F
Senior discount. 136 units. On US 101 at Lombard St. 2775 Van Ness Ave. (94109) Many units with view of Bay, 6 blocks away from Golden Gate Bridge. A/C; C/TV; pay movies; radios; phones. Exercise rm. Limited pay garage. No pets. Reserv deposit required. AE, DI, DS, MC, VI. ● Restaurant; 6:30 am-9 & 6:30-9:30 pm; $9-$14; beer & wine. FAX (415) 441-3990   ⊗ Ⓓ (415) 928-5000

Queen Anne Hotel 🔢   AAA Special Value Rates   *Hotel* ◆◆◆
🏵 All year [CP]   1P 99.00- 150.00 2P/1B 99.00- 150.00 2P/2B 99.00- 150.00 XP 20
49 units. 1 3/4 mi w of Union Square, exit US 101 (Van Ness Ave) at Sutter St; 4 blks w. 1590 Sutter St. (94109) Individually appointed rooms in a restored Victorian building. Few fireplaces. Check-in 3 pm. 4 refrigerators; C/TV; radios; phones; comb or shower baths. Limited pay parking lot. No pets. Limited parking opposite. 4 units with parlor, $175-$275 for 2 persons. Monthly rates avail. Reserv deposit required. AE, CB, DI, MC, VI.
FAX (415) 775-5212   ⊗ Ⓢ Ⓓ (415) 441-2828

Ramada Hotel-Fisherman's Wharf 🔢   AAA Special Value Rates   *Motor Inn* ◆◆◆
🏵 6/17-10/16   1P 112.00- 225.00 2P/1B 127.00- 240.00 2P/2B 127.00- 240.00 XP 15   F
10/17-6/16   1P 95.00- 150.00 2P/1B 110.00- 175.00 2P/2B 110.00- 175.00 XP 15   F
231 units. 2 blks from the wharf, between Jones & Taylor sts at Columbus Ave. 590 Bay St. (94133) A/C; C/CATV; pay movies; radios; phones. Limited pay garage. No pets. [BP] avail. Wkly & monthly rates avail. Reserv deposit required. AE, DI, DS, MC, VI. ● Restaurant; 6 am-1:30 & 5-10 pm; $11-$18; cocktails. FAX (415) 771-8945
                             ⊗ Ⓓ Ⓛ (415) 885-4700

Ramada Inn 🔢   Rates Subject to Change   *Hotel* ◆◆◆
🏵 All year   1P 105.00- 145.00 2P/1B 115.00- 155.00 2P/2B 115.00- 155.00 XP 12   F
Senior discount. 460 units. 1 blk from Civic Auditorium. 1231 Market St. (94103) San Francisco landmark. Check-in 3 pm. A/C; C/CATV; movies; phones; comb or shower baths. Limited pay garage. No pets. 13 suites, $220-$300 for up to 2 persons. Reserv deposit required; 3 days refund notice. AE, DI, DS, MC, VI. ● Restaurant; 6:30 am-2:30 & 5-10 pm; $10-$19; cocktails. FAX (415) 861-1460 *(See ad p A438)* ⊗ Ⓢ Ⓓ Ⓛ (415) 626-8000

Redwood Inn 🔢   Rates Subject to Change   *Motel* ◆◆
🏵 4/1-11/30   1P .... 70.00 2P/1B .... 75.00 2P/2B .... 80.00 XP 6
12/1-3/31   1P .... 60.00 2P/1B .... 65.00 2P/2B .... 70.00 XP 6
33 units. On US 101. 1530 Lombard St. (94123) 31 refrigerators; A/C; C/CATV; radios; phones. No pets. 4 kitchens, $5 extra. Reserv deposit required. AE, CB, DI, MC, VI. *(See ad p A439)*   Ⓓ (415) 776-3800

(See SAN FRANCISCO (Northern Region) spotting map pages A428 & A429)

Roberts-At-The-Beach Motel 86		Rates Subject to Change					Motel		◆
6/15-8/31	1P	.... 53.00	2P/1B	.... 53.00	2P/2B	.... 58.00	XP	5	
9/1-11/30 & 4/1-6/14	1P	.... 49.00	2P/1B	.... 49.00	2P/2B	.... 54.00	XP	5	
12/1-3/31	1P	.... 40.00	2P/1B	.... 45.00	2P/2B	.... 51.00	XP	5	

30 units. 1 blk from beach, opposite zoo, at 46th Ave. 2828 Sloat Blvd. (94116) C/CATV; radios; phones; shower or comb baths. Coin laundry. No pets. 7-night minimum stay in 2 housekeeping units, $67-$72 for 3-4 persons. AE, MC, VI.   (D) (415) 564-2610

Rodeway Inn 103		Rates Guaranteed					Motel		◆
All year	1P	.... 59.00	2P/1B	.... 59.00	2P/2B	.... 59.00	XP	6	F

Senior discount. 73 units. 2 blks e of US 101 (Van Ness Ave) corner of Larkin St. 895 Geary St. (94109) A/C; C/CATV; radios; phones. Garage. No pets. AE, CB, DI, MC, VI. FAX (415) 771-5667   ⊗ (D) (415) 441-8220

Rodeway Inn 55		AAA Special Value Rates					Motel		◆◆
6/1-8/31	1P	75.00- 125.00	2P/1B	85.00- 125.00	2P/2B	95.00- 135.00	XP	10	F
4/1-5/31 & 9/1-10/31	1P	65.00- 115.00	2P/1B	75.00- 115.00	2P/2B	85.00- 125.00	XP	10	F
11/1-3/31	1P	55.00- 105.00	2P/1B	65.00- 105.00	2P/2B	75.00- 115.00	XP	10	F

73 units. On US 101 between Van Ness Ave & Franklin St; 1 1/2 mi e of Golden Gate Bridge. 1450 Lombard St. (94123) Check-in 3 pm. 38 A/C; C/TV; radios; phones; comb or shower baths. 2 2-bedrm units, 2 kitchens, 4 efficiencies, no utensils. Pets. AE, CB, DI, MC, VI. Restaurant adjacent. FAX (415) 673-3232 *(See ad below)*
⊗ (D) (415) 673-0691

San Francisco Marriott Fisherman's Wharf 98		Rates Subject to Change					Hotel		◆◆◆
All year	1P	.... 148.00	2P/1B	.... 148.00	2P/2B	.... 148.00	XP	20	

256 units. 3 blks from the wharf; at Columbus Ave & Bay St. 1250 Columbus Ave. (94133) Check-in 3 pm. A/C; C/CATV; pay movies; radios; phones. Sauna; exercise rm. Limited pay valet parking lot. AE, CB, DI, MC, VI. ● Dining rm; 6:30 am-10 pm; $12-$30; cocktails. FAX (415) 474-2099   ⊗ (S) (D) (ℬ) (415) 775-7555

(See SAN FRANCISCO (Northern Region) spotting map pages A428 & A429)

Seal Rock Inn 🟤**75**
ⓐ	5/16-9/14					Rates Subject to Change			*Motel*	◆◆

ⓐ 5/16-9/14	1P	79.00- 100.00	2P/1B	83.00- 104.00	2P/2B	83.00- 104.00	XP 4- 8
9/15-5/15	1P	66.00- 90.00	2P/1B	70.00- 95.00	2P/2B	70.00- 95.00	XP 4- 8

27 units. 5 mi w of Civic Center; 1 blk from beach; end of Geary St. 545 Point Lobos Ave. (94121) Some fireplaces. Refrigerators; C/CATV; radios; phones; shower or comb baths. Small pool. Parking ramp. No pets. 11 efficiencies, $4 extra. 2-night minimum stay weekends. Reserv deposit required. AE, CB, DI, MC, VI. Coffeeshop; 7 am-4 pm; Wed-Sun to 10 pm. *(See ad below)*   ⓓ (415) 752-8000

Sheraton at Fisherman's Wharf 🟤**50**   AAA Special Value Rates   *Hotel*   ◆◆◆

4/10-10/31	1P	145.00- 230.00	2P/1B	145.00- 230.00	2P/2B	145.00- 230.00	XP 20	F
11/1-1/31	1P	110.00- 190.00	2P/1B	110.00- 190.00	2P/2B	110.00- 170.00	XP 20	F
2/1-4/9	1P	100.00- 180.00	2P/1B	100.00- 180.00	2P/2B	100.00- 160.00	XP 20	F

525 units. 1 1/2 blks from the wharf, between Beach & North Point sts. 2500 Mason St. (94133) Check-in 3 pm. 15 refrigerators; A/C; C/CATV; pay movies; radios; phones. Pool. Pay valet garage. Pets. Reserv deposit required. AE, DI, DS, MC, VI. ● Restaurant; 6:30 am-10 pm; Fri & Sat-11 pm; $12-$30; cocktails. Also, Mason Beach Grill, see separate listing. FAX (415) 956-5275 *(See ad below)*   ⊗ Ⓢ Ⓓ 🅰 (415) 362-5500

The Sherman House 🟤**101**   Rates Subject to Change   *Historic Hotel*   ◆◆◆
All year	1P	235.00- 750.00	2P/1B	235.00- 750.00	2P/2B	.... 175.00	XP

14 units. US 101 (Lombard St) exit Fillmore St; 4 blks s. 2160 Green St. (94123) French-Italianate Victorian built in 1876. 4-story, no elevator. Wood burning fireplaces. 12 refrigerators; C/CATV; radios; phones. Pay valet garage. No pets. 2 units with whirlpool bath. Reserv deposit required; 4 days refund notice. AE, CB, DI, MC, VI. ● Dining rm; 7 am-11, 11:30-2 & 5:30-10 pm; a la carte entrees about $20-$28. FAX (415) 563-1882   Ⓢ Ⓓ (415) 563-3600

Stanyan Park Hotel 🟤**85**   Rates Subject to Change   *Historic Bed &*
ⓐ All year [CP]	1P	78.00- 96.00	2P/1B	78.00- 96.00	2P/2B	88.00- 96.00	XP

Breakfast

36 units. 2 1/2 mi w. 750 Stanyan St. (94117) Victorian; some rooms with view of Golden Gate Park; period decor with modern conveniences. C/TV; radios; phones. 4 2-bedrm units, 6 kitchens. Limited pay parking lot. No pets. 4 2-bedroom suites with kitchen, $120-$170 for up to 4 persons. Reserv deposit required. AE, DI, DS, MC, VI. FAX (415) 668-5454   ⓓ (415) 751-1000

Star Motel 🟤**63**   Rates Subject to Change   *Motel*   ◆◆
ⓐ All year	1P	.... 64.00	2P/1B	.... 70.00	2P/2B	.... 74.00	XP 6

52 units. On US 101. 1727 Lombard St. (94123) Few small rooms. Check-in 3 pm. A/C; C/TV; phones; shower or comb baths. No pets. Reserv deposit required. AE, DI, DS, MC, VI. FAX (415) 441-4469 *(See ad p A431)*   ⊗ ⓓ (415) 346-8250

Super 8 Motel 🟤**93**   Rates Subject to Change   *Motel*   ◆◆
ⓐ All year	1P	55.00- 75.00	2P/1B	69.00- 79.00	2P/2B	.... 84.00	XP 8

Senior discount. 32 units. On US 101, between Scott & Divisadero sts. 2440 Lombard St. (94123) 3-story, no elevator. Refrigerators; 16 A/C; C/TV; pay movies; VCPs. Phones. Sauna. Limited garage. No pets. Rooms with whirlpool bath, $15 extra. Micrwaves. Reserv deposit required. AE, CB, DI, MC, VI. Restaurant adjacent.   ⊗ Ⓢ Ⓓ (415) 922-0244

(See SAN FRANCISCO (Northern Region) spotting map pages A428 & A429)

Travelodge Hotel at the Wharf 🔲**52**   AAA Special Value Rates   *Motor Inn*   ◆◆
🏚 5/1-10/31   1P 105.00- 125.00 2P/1B   115.00- 135.00 2P/2B 120.00- 155.00 XP 10   F
11/1-4/30   1P 75.00- 105.00 2P/1B   75.00- 115.00 2P/2B   85.00- 135.00 XP 10   F
250 units. At Fishermans Wharf. 250 Beach St. (94133) Some rooms with view of bay. Check-in 3 pm. 90 A/C; C/TV; pay movies; phones; shower or comb baths. Pool. Parking ramp. No pets. Reserv deposit required. AE, DI, DS, MC, VI. ● Coffeeshop; 7 am-2 pm; $7-$13; cocktail lounge. FAX (415) 392-6700 ⊗ Ⓓ (415) 392-6700

The Tuscan Inn 🔲**92**   Rates Subject to Change   *Hotel*   ◆◆◆
🏚 All year   1P .... 123.00 2P/1B   .... 123.00 2P/2B .... 123.00 XP 20   F
220 units. 2 blks w of Pier 39 at Mason St. 425 Northpoint St. (94133) Some rooms with view of bay. Check-in 3 pm. Refrigerators; A/C; C/CATV; pay movies; radios; phones. Limited pay valet garage. No pets. 12 units with VCP, CD player & parlor $195 for up to 2 persons. Reserv deposit required. AE, DI, DS, MC, VI. ● Restaurant; 6:30 am-10:30 pm; a la carte entrees about $10-$18; cocktails. FAX (415) 561-1199 ⊗ Ⓢ Ⓓ (415) 561-1100

Vagabond Inn-Midtown 🔲**67**   Rates Subject to Change   *Motel*   ◆◆
🏚 All year [CP]   1P 65.00- 97.00 2P/1B   70.00- 102.00 2P/2B   75.00- 107.00 XP 5   F
132 units. On US 101, at Filbert St. 2550 Van Ness Ave. (94109) Some small rooms. C/CATV; movies; radios; phones; comb or shower baths. 7 2-bedrm units. Small pool. Limited parking ramp. No pets. Reserv deposit required. AE, DI, DS, MC, VI. Cocktail lounge; coffeeshop adjacent. FAX (415) 776-5689 *(See ad below)* Ⓢ (415) 776-7500

Valu Inn by Nendel's 🔲**79**   AAA Special Value Rates   *Motel*   ◆◆
🏚 All year   1P 62.00- 66.00 2P/1B   72.00- 76.00 2P/2B   74.00- 78.00 XP 5
59 units. 1 blk w of US 101, at Eddy St. 900 Franklin St. (94109) C/CATV; movies; radios; phones. 1 2-bedrm unit. Whirlpool; exercise rm. Garage. No pets. Reserv deposit required; 3 days refund notice. AE, CB, MC, VI. FAX (415) 474-1652 *(See ad below)* Ⓓ (415) 885-6865

The Wharf Inn 🔲**51**   Rates Subject to Change   *Motel*   ◆◆
🏚 6/1-10/31   1P 98.00- 118.00 2P/1B   98.00- 118.00 2P/2B 103.00- 118.00 XP
3/1-5/31   1P 83.00- 103.00 2P/1B   83.00- 103.00 2P/2B   88.00- 103.00 XP
11/1-2/29   1P 68.00- 98.00 2P/1B   73.00- 98.00 2P/2B   83.00- 98.00 XP
51 units. Fisherman's Wharf area, at Beach St. 2601 Mason St. (94133) Check-in 3 pm. C/TV; movies; 12 radios; phones; shower or comb baths. Garage. No pets. 1 2-bedroom efficiency apartments, $190-$250 for 4 persons. Reserv deposit required. AE, DI, DS, MC, VI. Restaurant adjacent. FAX (415) 776-2181 *(See ad p A442)* ⊗ Ⓓ (415) 673-7411

RESTAURANTS

Alioto's 🔲**31**   Italian $$$ ◆◆
🏚 8 Fisherman's Wharf. Overlooking fishing fleet. Established since 1928. Regional Sicilian, also seafood specialties. A/C. Open 11 am-11 pm; closed 12/25. Cocktails & lounge. Minimum $10. Reserv advised. AE, CB, DI, MC, VI. *(See ad p 165)* ⊗ (415) 673-0183

(See SAN FRANCISCO (Northern Region) spotting map pages A428 & A429)

Amelios ㉘ French $$$$ ◆◆◆◆
In the North Beach area, at Union St. 1630 Powell St. Prixe fixe; choice of entree from seasonal menu; cozy contemporary atmosphere. Dress code. Open 5:30 pm-9:30 pm; closed Sun, Mon, 1/1 & 12/25. Cocktails. Minimum $17. Pay valet parking. Reserv advised. AE, DI, MC. ⊗ (415) 397-4339

Castagnola's Restaurant ㊷ Seafood $$$ ◆◆
1 blk w Fishermans Wharf; at Jones St. 286 Jefferson St. Since 1952. Casual atmosphere. A/C. Children's menu. Open 9 am-10 pm. Cocktails. Minimum $5. Reserv advised. AE, CB, DI, MC, VI. ⊗ (415) 776-5015

Chic's Place ㉚ Seafood $$$ ◆
On the Embarcadero, se of Fisherman's Wharf. 202-A Pier 39. Early San Francisco decor. View of marina & bay. A/C. Children's menu. Open 9 am-11 pm. Cocktails. Pay garage. Reserv advised. AE, CB, DI, MC, VI. ⊗ (415) 421-2442

The Cliff House ㊴ American $$$ ◆◆
⊕ At Ocean Beach, 6 mi w of downtown area. 1090 Point Lobos. Seafood & Beverage Co downstairs. Popular landmark overlooking Seal Rocks & ocean. Varied menu, casual attractive atmosphere, specialties include omelettes. Open 9 am-10:30 pm; Fri-11 pm; Sat & Sun 8:30 am-11 pm. Cocktails & lounge. Minimum, $7. AE, DI, MC, VI. ⊗ (415) 386-3330

Dynasty Fantasy ㊳ Chinese $$ ◆◆
⊕ 4 mi w of Civic Center. 6139 Geary Blvd. Traditional & innovative cuisine. Open 11:30 am-2:30 & 5-10 pm; closed Mon, 11/26 & 12/25. Beer & wine. AE, MC, VI. ⊗ (415) 386-3311

Fior D' Italia ㉗ Italian $$ ◆◆
⊕ 601 Union St. An older north beach institution. Dress code. Open 11:30 am-10:30 pm; Sat 10:30 am-11:30 pm; Sun 10:30 am-10:30 pm. Cocktails & lounge. Pay valet parking. Reserv advised. AE, CB, DI, MC, VI.
(415) 986-1886

Golden Turtle ㉟ Ethnic $$ ◆◆
On US 101. 2211 Van Ness Ave. Vietnamese custom decor cuisine. A/C. Open 11:30 am-3 & 5-11 pm; closed Mon & 12/24-12/31. Beer & wine. Minimum $5. Reserv advised. AE, MC, VI. ⊗ (415) 441-4419

Harris' ㊱ Steakhouse $$$ ◆◆◆
On US 101, at Pacific Ave. 2100 Van Ness Ave. Old San Francisco atmosphere, featuring dry-aged, mid-western beef & fresh seafood. A/C. Open 5 pm-11 pm; also Wed 11:30 am-2 pm; closed 1/1 & 12/25. Cocktails & lounge. Entertainment. Minimum, $8. Parking avail. Reserv advised. AE, DI, MC, VI. ⊗ (415) 673-1888

House of Prime Rib ㊲ American $$$ ◆◆◆
On US 101. 1906 Van Ness Ave. Cart brought to guest's table for individual cuts. Also fresh fish, & specialty items. A/C. Children's menu. Open 5:30 pm-10 pm; Sat 5 pm-10 pm; Sun 4 pm-10 pm. Cocktails & lounge. Pay valet parking. Reserv advised. AE, MC, VI. ⊗ (415) 885-4605

Julius' Castle ㊵ Ethnic $$$ ◆◆◆
⊕ On east slope of Telegraph Hill, off Union St. 1541 Montgomery St. Excellent views, romantic setting. Continental, Northern Italian & French cuisine. A/C. Dress code. Open 5-10 pm; closed 12/25. Cocktails & lounge. Pay valet parking. Reserv advised. AE, DS, DI, MC, VI. ⊗ (415) 362-3042

The Mandarin ㉜ Northern Chinese $$$$ ◆◆
Nw corner of Ghirardelli Square; on top floor of Woolen Mill Bldg. 900 N Point St. Excellently prepared cuisine. Szechwan cuisine also offered. A/C. Open noon-11 pm; closed 11/26 & 12/25. Cocktails & lounge. Minimum $10. Pay garage. Reserv advised. AE, CB, DI, MC, VI. ⊗ (415) 673-8812

Mason Beach Grill ㉙ American $$ ◆◆
In Sheraton at Fisherman's Wharf. A/C. Children's menu. Open 6:30 am-10 pm; Fri & Sat-11 pm. Cocktails & lounge. Pay garage. Reserv advised. AE, DI, DS, MC, VI. *(See ad p A440)* ⊗ (415) 362-5500

North India Restaurant ㉞ Ethnic $$ ◆◆◆
⊕ 1 blk s of US 101, Lombard St. 3131 Webster St. North Indian & Pakistani Tandoori cooking. Early bird specials; children's menu. Open 11:30 am-2 & 5-10:30 pm; Sat & Sun from 5 pm; closed 11/25 & 12/25. Wine. Pay parking lot. Reserv advised. AE, DI, MC, VI. ⊗ (415) 931-1556

Pompei's Grotto ㉖ Seafood $$ ◆◆
⊕ At Fisherman's Wharf. 340 Jefferson St. Casual dining, pasta specialties with emphasis on Northern Italian preparation. Long established, family owned. Children's menu. Open 8 am-11 pm; closed 11/25 & 12/25. Cocktails & lounge. Minimum $4. Pay parking lot. Reserv advised. AE, CB, DI, MC, VI. ⊗ (415) 776-9265

Scoma's Restaurant ㉕ Seafood $$$ ◆◆
⊕ Fisherman's Wharf, Pier 47. Casual atmosphere, popular landmark restaurant. A/C. Open 11:30 am-11 pm; closed 11/26, 12/24 & 12/25. Cocktails & lounge. Minimum, $8. Pay valet parking. AE, DI, DS, MC, VI. ⊗ (415) 771-4383

(See SAN FRANCISCO (Northern Region) spotting map pages A428 & A429)

Scott's Seafood Grill (33) Seafood $$$ ◆
On US 101 at Scott St. 2400 Lombard St. Casual atmosphere. Open 11:30 am-10:30 pm; Fri & Sat-11 pm; Sun 9:30 am-10:30 pm; closed 11/26 & 12/25. Cocktails. Minimum, $6. Reserv advised. AE, DS, MC, VI. ⊗ (415) 563-8988

The Shadows (41) French $$$ ◆◆◆
1 blk se of Telegraph Hill. 1349 Montgomery St. Contemporary European specialties. A/C. Children's menu. Open 5 pm-10 pm; closed 11/26 & 12/25. Cocktails & lounge. Pay valet parking. Reserv advised. AE, CB, DI, MC, VI. ⊗ **(415) 982-5536**

SAN FRANCISCO (Southern Region) (See SAN FRANCISCO (Southern Region) AREA spotting map page A444; see index starting below)

Index of Establishments on the SAN FRANCISCO (Southern Region) AREA Spotting Map

---

Americana Inn Motel 130 Rates Guaranteed *Motel* ◆
All year 1P 45.00- 60.00 2P/1B 45.00- 60.00 2P/2B .... 55.00 XP 5
17 units. 3 mi n of airport, on SR 82; exit US 101 via I-380 northbound or Grand Ave southbound. 760 El Camino Real. (94080) Refrigerators; A/C; C/TV; pay movies; VCPs. Phones. Sauna; 3 rooms with whirlpool bath. No pets. Reserv deposit required. AE, DI, DS, MC, VI. Restaurant adjacent. (D) **(415) 589-0404**

Best Western El Rancho Inn 110 Rates Guaranteed *Motor Inn* ◆◆◆
All year 1P 74.00- 84.00 2P/1B 84.00- 94.00 2P/2B 89.00- 99.00 XP 5
Senior discount. 295 units. 2 1/2 mi w of airport; 14 mi s of San Francisco, US 101 exit w on Millbrae Ave, then 3/4 mi n on SR 82. 1100 El Camino Real. (Millbrae, 94030) Spacious grounds. 215 A/C; C/CATV; free & pay movies; radios; phones; comb or shower baths. Coin laundry. 2 pools; whirlpools; exercise rm. Airport transp. No pets. 1-to 3-bedroom apartments, $112-$152 for up to 8 persons. 1 unit wiht whirlpool tub, $129 for 2 persons. Wkly & monthly rates avail. AE, DI, DS, MC, VI. ● Restaurant; 6 am-2 pm; outside dining weather permitting 5 pm-10 pm; $11-$18; cocktails. FAX (415) 871-7150 *(See ad p A445 and p A450)* ⊗ (D) **(415) 588-8500**

SAN FRANCISCO SOUTHERN REGION ACCOMMODATIONS

SEE SAN FRANCISCO NORTHERN REGION ACCOMMODATIONS MAP

Scale in Miles   0 — 3.2
Scale in Kilometers   0 — 5.1

OCEAN

PACIFIC

San Francisco Bay

John Daly Blvd
Southern Frwy
Daly City
Guadalupe Canyon Pkwy
Candlestick Park
Sharp Park Beach
Sharp Park Rd
Skyline Blvd
W Borough Blvd
Hickey Blvd
Chestnut Ave
El Camino Real
Hillside Blvd
Bayshore Blvd
PACIFICA
SOUTH SAN FRANCISCO
San Bruno Ave
Montara
San Andreas Lake
Millbrae
Millbrae Ave
Trousdale Rd
Junipero
San Francisco International Airport
Coyote Point Park
Broadway
Burlingame
Moss Beach
Pilarcitos Lake
San Mateo Creek
Hayne Rd
El Cerrito Ave
Peninsula Ave
San Mateo Bridge
To Hayward
(Toll)
Princeton
El Granada
Miramar
SAN MATEO
FOSTER CITY
Hillsdale Blvd
3rd Ave
Half Moon Bay State Beach
Lower Crystal Springs Reservoir
Crystal Springs Rd
Polhemus Rd
Hillsdale Blvd
Alameda De Las Pulgas
Half Moon Bay
HALF MOON BAY
Higgins
Pilarcitos
Half Moon Bay Rd
Crystal Springs Creek
Upper Crystal Springs Reservoir
Ralston Ave
BELMONT
San Carlos Ave
SAN CARLOS
Holly St
REDWOOD CITY
Whipple Ave
El Camino Real
Purisima Creek Rd
Purisima
Canada Rd
Edgewood Rd
Alameda De Las Pulgas
Woodside Rd
MENLO PARK
Coast Rd
Huddart Park
Kings Mtn Rd
Skyline Blvd
WOODSIDE
Lobitos Cr Cutoff
Tunitas
To Santa Cruz
To San José
To San José

1829-D

© AAA

(See SAN FRANCISCO (Southern Region) spotting map page A444)

Best Western Grosvenor Hotel **133**   AAA Special Value Rates   *Hotel* ◆◆◆
⊕ All year   1P 74.00- 89.00 2P/1B   74.00- 89.00 2P/2B   80.00- 85.00 XP 5
203 units. 11 1/4 mi s; 1 3/4 mi n of airport, e off US 101 Frwy via S Airport Blvd. 380 S Airport Blvd. (South San
Francisco, 94080) A/C; C/CATV; pay movies; radios; phones. Small pool. Airport transp. No pets. 20 units with
steambath, 9 with whirlpool bath, $5 extra. AE, DI, DS, MC, VI. ● Restaurant; 6 am-10 pm; Fri & Sat-11 pm; $10-
$18; cocktails. FAX (415) 589-3495   ⊗ Ⓓ Ⓑ (415) 873-3200

Clarion Hotel **111**   Rates Subject to Change   *Motor Inn* ◆◆◆
All year   1P 109.00- 119.00 2P/1B   109.00- 119.00 2P/2B 109.00- 129.00 XP 10 F
435 units. 1/2 mi s of airport; e off US 101 Frwy at Millbrae exit. 401 E Millbrae Ave. (Millbrae, 94030) Nicely landscaped
grounds. A/C; C/CATV; pay movies; radios; phones. Pool; whirlpool; exercise rm. Airport transp. No pets.
Reserv deposit required. AE, DI, DS, MC, VI. ● Coffeeshop; 6 am-11 pm; $16-$21; cocktails. FAX (415) 697-8735 *(See
ad below and p A450)*   Ⓢ Ⓓ Ⓑ (415) 692-6363

Comfort Inn-Airport West **122**   Rates Subject to Change   *Motel* ◆◆
⊕ All year [CP]   1P 68.00- 75.00 2P/1B   75.00- 78.00 2P/2B   75.00- 78.00 XP 5 F
Senior discount. 99 units. 14 mi s; 3 1/2 mi w of airport; US 101 exit exit w on Millbrae Ave, 1 mi n on SR 82.
1390 El Camino Real. (Millbrae, 94030) 54 refrigerators; A/C; C/CATV; phones; comb or shower baths. 39
kitchens, utensils, extra charge. Coin laundry. Pool; sauna; whirlpool. Garage. Airport transp. No pets.
1-bedroom apartment $130; 3 kitchens with fireplace $90; 10 rooms with whirlpoolbath, $90 for up to 2 persons.
Wkly rates avail. Reserv deposit required. AE, DI, DS, MC, VI. Restaurant adjacent. FAX (415) 952-0474 *(See ad
p A450)*   ⊗ Ⓢ Ⓓ Ⓑ (415) 952-3200

Comfort Suites **129**   AAA Special Value Rates   *Motel* ◆◆
⊕ 5/21-5/30 [CP]   1P .... 85.00 2P/1B   .... 95.00 2P/2B   .... 95.00 XP 10 F
5/31-5/20 [EP]   1P .... 79.00 2P/1B   .... 88.00 2P/2B   .... 88.00 XP 10 F
165 units. 3 mi n of airport; e of & adjacent to US 101, Grand Ave exit. 121 E Grand Ave. (S San Francisco, 94003)
A/C; C/CATV; pay movies; VCPs. Radios; phones. Coin laundry. Whirlpool. Airport transp. No pets. Wkly &
monthly rates avail. AE, DI, DS, MC, VI. FAX (415) 588-2231 *(See ad below)*   ⊗ Ⓢ Ⓓ Ⓑ (415) 589-7766

Courtyard by Marriott **135**   Rates Subject to Change   *Motor Inn* ◆◆◆
Sun-Thurs   1P .... 88.00 2P/1B   .... 98.00 2P/2B   .... 98.00 XP 10
Fri & Sat   1P .... 69.00 2P/1B   .... 79.00 2P/2B   .... 79.00 XP 10
Senior discount. 147 units. 2 mi nw of Airport; US 101N to I-380, exit El Camino Real S & right on Bayhill Dr. 1050 Bay-
hill Dr. (San Bruno, 94066) Check-in 3 pm. A/C; C/CATV; pay movies; radios; phones. Coin laundry. Small indoor pool;
whirlpool; exercise rm. Airport transp. No pets. Maximum rates for up to 4 persons. Wkly rates avail. AE, DI, DS, MC,
VI. ● Restaurant; 6:30 am-2 & 5-10 pm; $7-$12; cocktails. FAX (415) 952-4707 *(See ad p A447)*
    ⊗ Ⓢ Ⓓ Ⓑ (415) 952-3333

(See SAN FRANCISCO (Southern Region) spotting map page A444)

Crown Sterling Suites-Burlingame 🆔 ◆◆◆◆
Rates Guaranteed — Suites Hotel
🏾 All year [BP] 1P .... 102.00 2P/1B .... 102.00 2P/2B .... 102.00 XP 10
340 units. 1 1/2 mi s of the airport; southbound US 101, Broadway-Burlingame exit; northbound, Anza Blvd. 150 Anza Blvd. (Burlingame, 94010) On the bay. Many view rooms. Complimentary beverages 5:30-7:30 pm. Check-in 3 pm. Refrigerators; A/C; C/CATV; pay movies; radios; phones. Coin laundry. Htd indoor pool; sauna; whirlpools; putting green. Airport transp. No pets. Microwaves. Wkly & monthly rates avail. Reserv deposit required. AE, DI, DS, MC, VI. ● Dining rm; 11 am-2:30 & 5-10 pm; $10-$17; cocktails. FAX (415) 343-8137 *(See ad below)*
⊗ Ⓢ Ⓓ (415) 342-4600

Crown Sterling Suites-South San Francisco 🆔 ◆◆◆
Rates Guaranteed — Suites Hotel
🏾 All year [BP] 1P .... 86.00 2P/1B .... 86.00 2P/2B .... 86.00 XP 10 F
Senior discount. 313 units. 2 mi n of airport; exit US 101 via Grand Ave, e 2 blks. 250 Gateway Blvd. (94080) Some rooms with bay view. Check-in 3 pm. Refrigerators; A/C; C/CATV; pay movies; VCPs. Radios; phones. Htd indoor pool; sauna; whirlpool; recreational program; exercise rm. Parking lot. Airport transp. No pets. Microwaves. Monthly rates avail. Complimentary beverages each evening. AE, DI, DS, MC, VI. ● Restaurant; 11 am-3 & 5-10 pm; $13-$18; cocktails. FAX (415) 876-0305 *(See ad below)*
⊗ Ⓢ Ⓓ (415) 589-3400

(See SAN FRANCISCO (Southern Region) spotting map page A444)

Days Inn-Airport 120   Rates Guaranteed   *Motor Inn*   ◆◆
Fri & Sat 7/1-9/6	1P 80.00- 90.00	2P/1B	90.00-100.00	2P/2B	90.00-100.00	XP 10	F
Sun-Thurs 7/1-9/6	1P 75.00- 80.00	2P/1B	85.00- 90.00	2P/2B	85.00- 90.00	XP 10	F
9/7-6/30	1P 70.00- 75.00	2P/1B	80.00- 85.00	2P/2B	80.00- 85.00	XP 10	F

Senior discount. 200 units. 1 1/2 mi s of airport; southbound US 101, exit Broadway-Burlingame, northbound exit e Anza Blvd. 777 Airport Blvd. (Burlingame, 94010) Check-in 3 pm. A/C; C/CATV; pay movies; 60 radios; phones. Pool. Airport transp. Pets, $10 extra charge. AE, DI, DS, MC, VI. ● Coffeeshop; 24 hours; $6-$14. FAX (415) 342-2635 *(See ad p A448)*   ⊗ Ⓢ Ⓓ Ⓖ (415) 342-7772

Days Inn-South San Francisco 127   AAA Special Value Rates   *Motel*   ◆◆
5/1-9/30	1P 54.00- 60.00	2P/1B	60.00- 70.00	2P/2B	70.00- 80.00	XP 6	F
10/1-4/30	1P 50.00- 55.00	2P/1B	55.00- 64.00	2P/2B	64.00- 72.00	XP 6	

49 units. On SR 82, 3/4 mi s of Hickey Blvd; I-280 exit, Hickey Blvd; adjacent to Kaiser Hospital. 1330 El Camino Real. (94080) C/CATV; radios; phones; shower or comb baths. 5 2-bedrm units. Swimming pool open 5/1-9/30. No pets. Reserv deposit required. AE, DI, DS, MC, VI. FAX (415) 589-6756   ⊗ Ⓓ (415) 589-8875

Doubletree Hotel-San Francisco Airport 118   Rates Subject to Change   *Hotel*   ◆◆◆
Mon-Thurs	1P 79.00	2P/1B	.... 79.00	2P/2B	.... 79.00	XP 10	F
Fri-Sun	1P 69.00	2P/1B	.... 69.00	2P/2B	.... 69.00	XP 10	F

Senior discount. 291 units. 1 1/2 mi s of airport; southbound US 101, Broadway-Burlingame exit, northbound Anza Blvd. 835 Airport Blvd. (Burlingame, 94010) Many rooms with bay view. Check-in 3 pm. A/C; C/CATV; pay movies; radios; phones. Exercise rm. Parking lot. Airport transp. Special bay view rooms $124; 6 suites $150; for up to 2 persons. Pets, $20 charge non-refundable. Wkly rates avail. Reserv deposit required. AE, CB, DI, MC, VI. ● Restaurant; 6:30-11 am, 11:30-2 & 5-10 pm; $10-$22; cocktails. FAX (415) 340-8851 *(See ad below)*   ⊗ Ⓢ Ⓓ Ⓖ (415) 344-5500

HoJo Inn 128   Rates Subject to Change   *Motel*   ◆
4/1-9/30	1P 55.00	2P/1B	.... 60.00	2P/2B	.... 60.00	XP 5	

Senior discount. 21 units. Exit US 101 at Grand Ave, 1/4 mi n on Airport Blvd. 701 Airport Blvd. (South San Francisco, 94080) OPEN ALL YEAR. Formerly Sierra Inn Motel. A/C; C/TV; radios; phones. No pets. 4 rooms with whirlpool tub, $55 for up tp 2 persons. Reserv deposit required. AE, DI, DS, MC, VI. FAX (415) 952-8311   ⊗ Ⓓ Ⓖ (415) 952-2505

Holiday Inn Crowne Plaza 121   AAA Special Value Rates   *Hotel*   ◆◆◆◆
All year	1P 104.00- 125.00	2P/1B	114.00- 135.00	2P/2B	114.00- 135.00	XP 10	F

405 units. 16 mi s; 1 1/2 mi s of airport, southbound US 101, exit Broadway-Burlingame; northbound exit e Anza Blvd, 4 blks. 600 Airport Blvd. (Burlingame, 94010) Many units overlooking bay. Check-in 3 pm. A/C; C/CATV; pay movies; radios; phones. Htd indoor pool; saunas; whirlpool; exercise rm. Garage. Airport transp. No pets. AE, DI, DS, MC, VI. ● Dining rm & restaurant; 6 am-11 pm; $12-$20; cocktails. FAX (415) 343-1546 ⊗ Ⓢ Ⓓ Ⓖ (415) 340-8500

(See SAN FRANCISCO (Southern Region) spotting map page A444)

Hyatt Regency-San Francisco Airport **115**   Rates Subject to Change   *Hotel*   ◆◆◆◆
  Sun-Thurs   1P .... 165.00   2P/1B .... 190.00   2P/2B .... 190.00   XP 25
  Fri & Sat   1P ....   89.00   2P/1B ....   89.00   2P/2B ....   89.00   XP 25
  791 units. 3 mi s of airport, exit US 101 at Old Bayshore Hwy-Broadway or Broadway-Burlingame. 1333 Bayshore Hwy.
  (Burlingame, 94010) Some rooms with view of bay or hills. Eight-story atrium with translucent-fabric roof. Check-in 3 pm.
  A/C; C/CATV; pay movies; radios; phones. Small pool; saunas; whirlpool; health club; exercise rm. Fee for: massage.
  Parking ramp. Airport transp. No pets. Reserv deposit required. AE, DI, DS, MC, VI. ● Dining rm & restaurant; 6:30
  am-11 pm; also deli 24 hours; a la carte entrees about $15-$35; cocktails; entertainment; nightclub. FAX (415) 347-5948
                                                                          ⊗ Ⓢ Ⓓ (415) 347-1234

La Quinta Motor Inn **134**   Rates Subject to Change   *Motel*   ◆◆◆
  ⓐ All year   1P 66.00- 73.00   2P/1B 74.00- 81.00   2P/2B ....   74.00   XP 5   F
  174 units. 2 1/2 mi n of airport, exit US 101 at S Airport Blvd. 20 Airport Blvd. (South San Francisco, 94080)
  Check-in 3 pm. A/C; C/CATV; free & pay movies; radios; phones. Coin laundry. Small pool; whirlpool; exercise
  rm. Airport transp. AE, DI, DS, MC, VI. Coffeeshop adjacent. FAX (415) 589-6770 ⊗ Ⓢ Ⓓ Ⓖ (415) 583-2223

(See SAN FRANCISCO (Southern Region) spotting map page A444)

Millwood Inn 137   Rates Subject to Change   *Motel*   ◆◆
⊕ All year [CP]   1P 52.00- 56.00 2P/1B   52.00- 56.00 2P/2B 58.00- 62.00 XP 4
Senior discount. 34 units. 14 mi s in Millbrae; 3 1/2 mi w of airport; US 101 exit w on Millbrae Ave, 1 mi n on SR
82. 1375 El Camino Real. (Millbrae, 94030) Check-in 3 pm. Refrigerators; A/C; C/CATV; movies; radios; phones;
shower baths. Coin laundry. No pets. 5 kitchens, $15 extra. All rooms have VCR & microwave. Wkly rates avail
9/16-4/30. Reserv deposit required. AE, DI, DS, MC, VI. FAX (415) 875-4354 *(See ads p A450)*
                                                                              Ⓓ (415) 583-3935

Oyster Point Marina Inn 138   Rates Guaranteed   *Motor Inn*   ◆◆◆
⊕ All year [CP]   1P 99.00-109.00 2P/1B   109.00-119.00 2P/2B 109.00-119.00 XP 12   F
Senior discount. 30 units. 4 mi n of airport; e of US 101; exit Oyster Point Blvd northbound, South San Francisco southbound & 1/4 mi e on Oyster Point Blvd. 425 Marina Blvd. (South San Francisco, 94080) All units with
bay view & gas fireplace. Check-in 3 pm. 10 refrigerators; A/C; C/CATV; movies; radios; phones. Beach; jogging
trail. Airport transp. No pets. 1 unit with sauna. Reserv deposit required. AE, DI, DS, MC, VI. ● Restaurant; 11:30
am-2:30 & 5:30-9:30 pm; $15-$30; beer & wine. FAX (415) 737-0795   ⊗ Ⓢ Ⓓ (415) 737-7633

Radisson Inn 132   AAA Special Value Rates   *Hotel*   ◆◆◆
⊕ All year [CP]   1P 80.00-110.00 2P/1B   80.00-110.00 2P/2B 80.00-110.00 XP 10   F
224 units. 3 1/2 mi n of airport; exit US 101 at S Airport Blvd. 275 S Airport Blvd. (94080) Check-in 3 pm. 12 refrigerators; A/C; C/CATV; pay movies; radios; phones. Saunas; whirlpool; exercise rm. Parking lot. Airport
transp. Monthly rates avail. AE, DI, DS, MC, VI. ● Restaurant & coffeeshop; 6-10 am, 11:30-2 & 5:30-10 pm; a la
carte entrees about $10-$18; cocktail lounge; entertainment. FAX (415) 873-4524 *(See ad below)*
                                                                          ⊗ Ⓓ Ⓑ (415) 873-3550

Ramada San Francisco Airport 116   AAA Special Value Rates   *Hotel*   ◆◆◆
⊕ All year   1P 82.00-106.00 2P/1B   88.00-112.00 2P/2B 88.00-112.00 XP 10   F
144 units. 15 mi se; 2 1/2 mi s of airport; off US 101 via Old Bayshore Hwy northbound, Broadway-Burlingame
southbound. 1250 Old Bayshore Hwy. (Burlingame, 94010) Many rooms facing the bay. A/C; C/CATV; pay
movies; radios; phones. Pool. Parking lot. Airport transp. No pets. AE, DI, DS, MC, VI. ● Restaurant; 6:30 am-11
pm; $11-$17; cocktails. FAX (415) 348-8838 *(See ad below)*   ⊗ Ⓓ (415) 347-2381

Ritz Motel 124   Rates Subject to Change   *Motel*   ◆
⊕ All year   1P .... 40.00 2P/1B   .... 40.00 2P/2B .... 48.00 XP 4
23 units. 2 1/2 mi nw of airport; US 101 to I-380, exit El Camino Real S, SR 82. 151 El Camino Real. (San
Bruno, 94066) 15 refrigerators; C/TV; movies; VCPs. Radios; phones; shower or comb baths. No pets. AE, DS,
MC, VI. Restaurant opposite.   Ⓓ (415) 589-3553

Royal Inn 126   Rates Subject to Change   *Motel*   ◆
⊕ Fri & Sat   1P .... 45.00 2P/1B   .... 50.00 2P/2B .... 55.00 XP 5
17 units. 1/2 mi e of I-280, Hickey Blvd exit. 120 Hickey Blvd. (South San Francisco, 94080) OPEN ALL YEAR.
3-story, no elevator. A/C; C/CATV; pay movies; VCPs. Radios; phones; comb or shower baths. No pets. 5 rooms
with whirlpool bath, $5 extra. Reserv deposit required. AE, DI, DS, MC, VI.   Ⓢ Ⓓ Ⓑ (415) 755-0724

(See SAN FRANCISCO (Southern Region) spotting map page A444)

San Bruno Inn 131   Rates Subject to Change   *Motel*
ⓐ All year   1P .... 45.00   2P/1B .... 45.00   2P/2B .... 55.00   XP 5
28 units. 11 mi s; 4 1/2 mi nw of San Francisco International Airport, exit US 101 at San Bruno Ave, then 3 blks
s on El Camino Real. 500 El Camino Real. (94066) Rating withheld pending completion of construction. Refrigerators; A/C; C/CATV; movies; VCPs. Radios; phones. Sauna; whirlpool. Reserv deposit required. AE, CB, DI,
MC, VI. Coffeeshop opposite. *(See ad below)*   ⊗ Ⓓ (415) 871-4000

San Francisco Airport Hilton 136   Rates Subject to Change   *Hotel* ◆◆◆◆
ⓐ All year   1P 139.00- 159.00   2P/1B 155.00- 175.00   2P/2B 155.00- 175.00   XP 16   F
530 units. 13 mi s; off US 101, at airport entrance. Check-in 3 pm.
A/C; C/CATV; pay movies; radios; phones. Pool; whirlpool; exercise rm. Parking lot. Airport transp. Pets. 76
units with lanai or patio. AE, CB, DI, MC, VI. ● Dining rm & coffeeshop; 6 am-11 pm; $16-$35; cocktails; entertainment. Also, Barronshire, see separate listing. FAX (415) 589-4696 *(See ad p 22)*
                                                     ⊗ Ⓢ Ⓓ Ⓛ (415) 589-0770

San Francisco Airport Marriott 113   *Hotel* ◆◆◆◆
Sun-Thurs   1P .... 159.00   2P/1B .... 159.00   2P/2B .... 159.00   XP
Fri & Sat   1P .... 133.00   2P/1B .... 133.00   2P/2B .... 133.00   XP
684 units. 13 1/2 mi s; 2 mi s of airport, exit US 101 at Millbrae Ave E. 1800 Old Bayshore Hwy. (Burlingame, 94010)
On the Bay, many rooms with view. Check-in 3 pm. A/C; C/CATV; pay movies; radios; phones. Coin laundry. Indoor pool;
saunas; whirlpool; health club. Valet parking lot & pay garage. Airport transp. Pets. Wkly rates avail. AE, CB, DI, MC,
VI. ● Restaurant & coffeeshop; 6 am-11 pm; $11-$25; cocktails; entertainment. FAX (415) 692-8016
                                                     ⊗ Ⓢ Ⓓ Ⓛ (415) 692-9100

Sheraton-San Francisco Airport 119   Rates Subject to Change   *Hotel* ◆◆◆
All year   1P .... 109.00   2P/1B .... 119.00   2P/2B .... 119.00   XP 15
302 units. 15 mi s; southbound US 101, Broadway-Burlingame exit, northbound Old Bayshore Hwy. 1177 Airport Blvd.
(Burlingame, 94010) Some rooms with bay view. A/C; C/CATV; movies; radios; phones. Htd indoor/outdoor pool; whirlpool; exercise rm. Parking lot. Airport transp. Reserv deposit required. AE, CB, DI, MC, VI. ● Restaurant; 6 am-11 pm;
$10-$20; cocktails; entertainment. FAX (415) 342-9200   ⊗ Ⓢ Ⓓ (415) 342-9200

Super 8 Lodge 125   Rates Guaranteed   *Motel* ◆◆
ⓐ All year   1P .... 55.00   2P/1B .... 60.00   2P/2B .... 60.00   XP 4   F
Senior discount. 117 units. 4 mi n of the airport; exit US 101 at S Airport Blvd. 111 Mitchell Ave. (94080) A/C;
C/CATV; phones. Airport transp. No pets. Wkly rates avail. Reserv deposit required. AE, DI, DS, MC, VI.
FAX (415) 871-8377   ⊗ Ⓓ Ⓛ (415) 877-0770

Vagabond Inn-Airport 114   Rates Subject to Change   *Motel* ◆◆
ⓐ All year [CP]   1P 60.00- 75.00   2P/1B 65.00- 80.00   2P/2B 70.00- 90.00   XP 5   F
91 units. 14 mi s; exit US 101E via Millbrae Ave. 1640 Bayshore Hwy. (Burlingame, 94010) Some rooms overlook
the bay. A/C; C/CATV; pay movies; radios; phones. 1 2-bedrm unit. Coin laundry. Sauna. Airport transp. Pets, $5
extra charge. AE, DI, DS, MC, VI. Restaurant adjacent. FAX (415) 692-5314 *(See ad p A441)*
                                                     ⊗ Ⓓ Ⓛ (415) 692-4040

The Westin Hotel-San Francisco Airport 112   Rates Subject to Change   *Hotel* ◆◆◆◆
ⓐ Mon-Thurs   1P 119.00- 155.00   2P/1B 119.00- 155.00   2P/2B 115.00- 155.00   XP 20   F
388 units. 1/2 mi s of airport; e of US 101, Millbrae exit. 1 Old Bayshore Hwy. (Millbrae, 94030) OPEN ALL YEAR.
Tropical landscaped grounds. Check-in 3 pm. A/C; C/CATV; pay movies; radios; phones. Htd indoor pool; sauna;
whirlpool; exercise rm. Parking lot. Airport transp. AE, CB, DI, MC, VI. ● Restaurant & coffeeshop; 6 am-11 pm;
a la carte entrees about $15-$50; cocktail lounge. FAX (415) 872-8111 *(See ad p A450)*
                                                    ⊗ Ⓢ Ⓓ Ⓛ (415) 692-3500

RESTAURANTS

Barronshire 53   American $$$ ◆◆
In San Francisco Airport Hilton. A/C. Children's menu. Open 6 pm-10:30 pm; Sun 10:30 am-2:30 pm; closed 5/30, 7/4
& 9/6. Cocktails & lounge. Minimum $11. Reserv advised. AE, CB, DI, MC, VI. *(See ad p 22)*   ⊗ (415) 875-3035

Gulliver's 50   American $$ ◆◆
3/4 mi s of airport; exit US 101E via Millbrae Ave or e via Broadway-Burlingame. 1699 Old Bayshore Hwy. English pub
atmosphere. Prime rib. A/C. Open 11:30 am-2:30 pm, 5:30-9:30 pm; Fri & Sat 10:30 pm; Sun 5 pm-9:30 pm. Cocktails
& lounge. Reserv advised. AE, DI, MC, VI.   ⊗ (415) 692-6060

Jin Jiang 51   Chinese $$$ ◆◆◆
16 1/2 mi s; 4 mi s of airport; exit US 101 at Old Bayshore Hwy-Broadway-Burlingame. 433 Airport Blvd. 5th-floor pent-
house overlooking bay. Oriental art & furnishings. A/C. Open 11:30 am-2 & 5:30-10 pm; Fri-10:30 pm; Sat 5:30 pm-10:30
pm; Sun 5 pm-10 pm; closed 1/1 & 12/25. Cocktails & lounge. Minimum $10. Reserv advised. AE, MC, VI.
                                                             ⊗ (415) 348-1133

(See SAN FRANCISCO (Southern Region) spotting map page A444)

Vanessi's ⑤②   American $$$ ◆◆
   In Burlingame; 2 mi s of airport on w side of US 101; exit frwy via Broadway to Carolan 1 blk, then w on Cadillac Way.
   1095 Rollins Rd. Varied menu. A/C. Open 11 am-10 pm; Fri & Sat-11:30 pm; closed Major holidays. Cocktails & lounge.
   Reserv advised. AE, DI, MC, VI.   ⊗ (415) 342-4922

SAN GABRIEL — 37,100

Garden Inn Motel   Rates Subject to Change   *Motel*   ◆
🅰 All year   1P .... 35.00   2P/1B .... 35.00   2P/2B .... 40.00 XP
   41 units. On SR 19, 1 1/2 mi n of jct I-10. 5318 Rosemead Blvd. (91776) 23 refrigerators; A/C; C/TV; radios;
   phones. No pets. 7 rooms with whirlpool tub, $50-$60. AE, DS, MC, VI. FAX (818) 286-3791 Ⓓ (818) 285-8866

Quality Inn   AAA Special Value Rates   *Motel*   ◆◆
🅰 All year [CP]   1P .... 50.00   2P/1B .... 58.00   2P/2B .... 60.00 XP 8   F
   42 units. From I-10, take San Gabriel Blvd 2 mi n, then 1/2 mi e on Las Tunas. 1114 E Las Tunas Dr. (91776) Re-
   frigerators; A/C; movies; phones. Coin laundry. Small pool; whirlpool. No pets. Wkly rates avail. Reserv
   deposit required. AE, CB, DI, MC, VI. FAX (818) 285-8391 *(See ad p A452)*   ⊗ Ⓓ (818) 285-0921

RESTAURANT

Panchito's   Mexican $$ ◆
   2 blks w of San Gabriel Mission. 261 S Mission Dr. Colorfully decorated restaurant, also featuring marinated steaks &
   shrimp. A/C. Children's menu. Open 11:30 am-9:30 pm; Fri-10:30 pm; Sat 5 pm-10:30 pm; Sun 4 pm-9:30 pm; closed
   Mon & major holidays. Cocktails & lounge. AE, CB, DI, MC, VI.   ⊗ (818) 284-8830

SAN JACINTO

Crown Motel   Rates Guaranteed   *Motel*   ◆◆
🅰 All year   1P 36.00- 42.00 2P/1B 42.00- 48.00   2P/2B 48.00- 54.00 XP 4   F
   Senior discount. 21 units. 2 blks n on SR 79. 138 S Ramona Blvd. (92583) Refrigerators; A/C; C/CATV; movies;
   radios; phones; comb or shower baths. Pool; whirlpool. Pets. 9 rooms with microwave. 2 rooms with whirlpool
   tub, $75. Wkly rates avail. Reserv deposit required. AE, DI, DS, MC, VI. FAX (909) 654-6184
                                                                       ⊗ Ⓓ (909) 654-7133

SAN JOSE — 782,200   See also CAMPBELL, CUPERTINO & MILPITAS

Airport Plaza Inn   Rates Subject to Change   *Motel*   ◆◆◆
🅰 All year [CP]   1P .... 60.00   2P/1B .... 60.00   2P/2B .... 70.00 XP 5
   40 units. US 101 exit I-880; 1 1/4 mi sw of San Jose International Airport. 2118 The Alameda. (95126) Some large
   rooms. Refrigerators; A/C; C/CATV; movies; VCPs. Radios; phones. 2 efficiencies, no utensils. Small pool;
   sauna; whirlpool; exercise rm. No pets. 5 units with whirlpool, $75. Some rooms with microwave. Reserv deposit
   required. AE, CB, DI, MC, VI. FAX (408) 243-5478   ⊗ Ⓢ Ⓓ Ⓛ (408) 243-2400

Best Western Gateway Inn — AAA Special Value Rates — *Motor Inn* ◆◆◆

Sun-Thurs [CP]	1P	65.00- 72.00	2P/1B	70.00- 77.00	2P/2B	70.00- 77.00	XP	5	
Fri & Sat [CP]	1P	55.00- 60.00	2P/1B	60.00- 65.00	2P/2B	60.00- 65.00	XP	5	

147 units. Exit US 101 Trimble Rd E; 1 mi N E of San Jose International Airport. 2585 Seaboard Ave. (95131) Attractive Modern rooms. Refrigerators; A/C; C/TV; movies; radios; phones. Pool; indoor whirlpool; steamroom. Airport transp. No pets. AE, DI, DS, MC, VI. Restaurant adjacent. FAX (408) 435-8879 *(See ad p A453)*
⊗ Ⓓ (408) 435-8800

Best Western Inn — Rates Subject to Change — *Motel* ◆◆

All year [CP]	1P	48.00- 58.00	2P/1B	50.00- 60.00	2P/2B	52.00- 68.00	XP	5	

Senior discount. 72 units. 1 blk e off SR 82. 455 S 2nd St. (95113) Refrigerators; A/C; C/CATV; movies; radios; phones; shower or comb baths. 2 kitchens. Pool; sauna; indoor whirlpool; steamroom; exercise rm. No pets. Some rooms with microwave. Wkly rates avail. Reserv deposit required. AE, DI, DS, MC, VI. Cocktail lounge; restaurant adjacent. FAX (408) 298-2477 *(See ad below)*
⊗ Ⓓ (408) 298-3500

Best Western San Jose Lodge — Rates Guaranteed — *Motel* ◆◆

All year	1P	56.00- 62.00	2P/1B	59.00- 65.00	2P/2B	62.00- 68.00	XP	5	F

Senior discount. 75 units. 1 mi e of San Jose International Airport; s off US 101; exit via N 1st St. 1440 N 1st St. (95112) A/C; C/CATV; movies; phones; shower or comb baths. Pool. Small pets only. AE, DI, DS, MC, VI. Coffeeshop adjacent. FAX (408) 437-9519
⊗ Ⓓ (408) 453-7750

Comfort Inn — Rates Subject to Change — *Motel* ◆◆

6/1-9/30	1P	55.00- 70.00	2P/1B	60.00- 75.00	2P/2B	60.00- 70.00	XP	10	F
2/1-5/31 & 10/1-1/31	1P	52.00- 65.00	2P/1B	57.00- 70.00	2P/2B	57.00- 70.00	XP	7	F

Senior discount. 58 units. 3/4 mi s of jct I-280 & SR 82, S 1st St. 1215 S 1st St. (95110) 47 refrigerators; A/C; C/CATV; movies; VCPs. Radios; phones. 22 efficiencies, no utensils. Some rooms with whirlpool tub. No pets. AE, DI, DS, MC, VI. FAX (408) 280-0569 *(See ad p A453)*
Ⓓ (408) 280-5300

Comfort Inn-Airport — Rates Subject to Change — *Motel* ◆◆

All year	1P	56.00- 70.00	2P/1B	62.00- 78.00	2P/2B	62.00- 78.00	XP	7	F

Senior discount. 56 units. 1 mi e of San Jose Airport; at E Rosemary St. 1310 N 1st St. (95112) A/C; C/CATV; movies; VCPs. 30 radios; phones; shower or comb baths. Pool; whirlpool. Airport transp. No pets. Some rooms with microwave & refrigerator. AE, DI, DS, MC, VI. FAX (408) 453-1890 *(See ad p A453)* ⊗ Ⓓ (408) 453-1100

Courtyard by Marriott — Rates Subject to Change — *Motor Inn* ◆◆◆

Sun-Thurs	1P	.... 94.00	2P/1B	.... 104.00	2P/2B	.... 104.00	XP	
Fri & Sat	1P	.... 68.00	2P/1B	.... 68.00	2P/2B	.... 68.00	XP	

151 units. 1/2 mi e of San Jose International Airport, via Airport Parkway, 1/4 mi s US 101 exit n 1st St, 1/4 mi w to Skyport Dr. 1727 Technology Dr. (95110) Check-in 3 pm. A/C; C/CATV; movies; radios; phones. Coin laundry. Pool; indoor whirlpool; exercise rm. Airport transp. No pets. Reserv deposit required. AE, DI, DS, MC, VI. ● Restaurant; 6 am-2 & 5-10 pm; $8-$14; cocktail lounge. FAX (408) 441-8039 *(See ad below)*
⊗ Ⓢ Ⓓ (408) 441-6111

Days Inn — Rates Subject to Change — *Motel* ◆◆◆

All year [CP]	1P	50.00- 60.00	2P/1B	55.00- 65.00	2P/2B	65.00- 75.00	XP	5	

Senior discount. 33 units. 1 blk s of jct G21 (Capitol Expwy) & SR 82 (Monterey Rd). 4170 Monterey Rd. (95111) Refrigerators; A/C; C/CATV; movies; radios; phones. 4 kitchens, 9 efficiencies. Pool; whirlpool. Small pets only. 3 rooms with whirlpool, extra charge. Reserv deposit required; 3 days refund notice. AE, DI, DS, MC, VI.
⊗ Ⓓ (408) 224-4122

Fairmont Hotel — Rates Guaranteed — *Hotel* ◆◆◆◆

Sun-Thurs	1P	135.00- 175.00	2P/1B	155.00- 195.00	2P/2B	155.00- 195.00	XP	25	F
Fri & Sat	1P	.... 89.00	2P/1B	.... 89.00	2P/2B	.... 89.00	XP	25	F

541 units. At Fairmont Plaza. 170 S Market St. (95113) 16 poolside units with lanais; elegant decor. Check-in 3 pm. Refrigerators; A/C; C/CATV; movies; radios; phones. Pool; saunas; steamroom; health club. Fee for: massage. Pay valet garage. Airport transp. No pets. 1 bedroom suites, $400-$500 for 2 persons; 2 bedroom suites, $1300-$1800. Reserv deposit required. AE, DI, DS, MC, VI. ● 4 restaurants; 6 am-midnight; $14-$28; afternoon tea; cocktails. Also, Les Saisons, see separate listing. FAX (408) 287-1648 ⊗ Ⓢ Ⓓ Ⓛ (408) 998-1900

Holiday Inn-Airport
All year   Rates Subject to Change   *Motor Inn*   ◆◆
                 1P 71.00- 78.00   2P/1B   78.00- 88.00   2P/2B   73.00- 83.00   XP 10   F
Senior discount. 192 units. 1/2 mi e of San Jose Airport; US 101 exit N 1st St, s 1/2 mi to Rosemary St E. 1355 N 4th St. (95112) A/C; C/CATV; pay movies; phones. Coin laundry. Pool. Airport transp. Pets. AE, DI, DS, MC, VI. ● Restaurant; 6 am-10 pm; $7-$14; cocktails. FAX (408) 453-5340 *(See ad below)* ⊗ Ⓓ 🅶 (408) 453-5340

Holiday Inn-Park Center Plaza
All year   Rates Subject to Change   *Hotel*   ◆◆◆
                 1P   72.00   2P/2B   89.00   XP 10   F
Senior discount. 232 units. Opposite Convention Center; 6 blks n off I-280, exit via Almaden-Vine. 282 Almaden Blvd. (95113) A/C; C/CATV; movies; radios; phones. Pool; exercise rm. Parking ramp. Airport transp. No pets. Reserv deposit required; 3 days refund notice. AE, DI, DS, MC, VI. ● Restaurant; 6 am-10 pm; $7-$20; cocktails; entertainment. FAX (408) 289-9081 ⊗ Ⓢ Ⓓ 🅶 (408) 998-0400

Holiday Inn South San Jose
Sun-Thurs [EP]   Rates Subject to Change   *Motor Inn*   ◆◆◆
Sun-Thurs [EP]   1P   79.00   2P/1B   79.00   2P/2B   79.00   XP 10
Fri & Sat [BP]   1P   59.00   2P/1B   59.00   2P/2B   59.00   XP 10
Senior discount. 150 units. Exit US 101; Bernal Rd E. 399 Silicon Valley Blvd. (95138) Attractive modern decor. Check-in 3 pm. A/C; C/CATV; movies; radios; phones. Pool; whirlpool; exercise rm. Airport transp. No pets. 24 luxury suites, $109 for 2 persons. Monthly rates avail. Complimentary beverages each evening. AE, DI, DS, MC, VI. ● Restaurant; 6 am-10 & 5-10 pm; Fri & Sat-11 pm; $12-$30; cocktails. FAX (408) 972-0157 *(See ad below)* ⊗ Ⓢ Ⓓ 🅶 (408) 972-7800

Homewood Suites
Sun-Thurs [CP]   AAA Special Value Rates   *Suites Motel*   ◆◆◆
Sun-Thurs [CP]   1P 129.00- 139.00   2P/1B   129.00- 139.00   2P/2B   159.00   XP
Fri & Sat [CP]   1P 89.00- 99.00   2P/1B   89.00- 99.00   2P/2B   119.00   XP
142 units. Exit US 101 Trimble Rd, 1 1/4 mi e, 2 mi ne San Jose Int'l Airport. 10 W Trimble Rd. (95131) 1- & 2-bedroom suites, comfortable attractive decor. Check-in 3 pm. A/C; C/CATV; VCPs; radios; phones. 14 2-bedrm units, kitchens. Coin laundry. Pool; sports court; exercise rm. Airport transp. Pets $200 deposit, plus $75 extra charge. Wkly & monthly rates avail. AE, DI, DS, MC, VI. Restaurant adjacent. FAX (408) 428-0222 ⊗ Ⓢ Ⓓ 🅶 (408) 428-9900

Hyatt San Jose
Ⓐ Sun-Thurs   Rates Subject to Change   *Motor Inn*   ◆◆◆
Sun-Thurs   1P 89.00- 139.00   2P/1B   114.00- 154.00   2P/2B   114.00- 154.00   XP 25   F
Fri & Sat   1P   69.00   2P/1B   69.00   2P/2B   69.00   XP 25   F
Senior discount. 474 units. 1/2 mi e of San Jose International Airport via Aiport Pkwy; w of US 101, exit N 1st St. 1740 N 1st St. (95112) Spacious grounds. Some compact rooms. A/C; C/CATV; movies; radios; phones; comb or shower baths. 3 2-bedrm units. Pool; whirlpool; exercise rm. Airport transp. Small pets only, $50. Wkly & monthly rates avail. AE, DI, DS, MC, VI. ● Dining rm & coffeeshop; 5:30 am-midnight; $7-$21; cocktails. FAX (408) 453-0259 ⊗ Ⓓ (408) 993-1234

Le Baron Hotel   Rates Subject to Change   *Hotel*   ◆◆◆
  Sun-Thurs   1P 75.00- 105.00   2P/1B   75.00- 105.00   2P/2B 79.00- 105.00 XP 10   F
  Fri & Sat   1P .... 65.00   2P/1B   .... 65.00   2P/2B   .... 65.00 XP 10   F
Senior discount. 329 units. 1/4 mi s off US 101, exit N 1st St, 1 mi e of San Jose International Airport Pkwy, s on N 1st St. 1350 N 1st St. (95112) Attractive rooms. Check-in 3 pm. 55 refrigerators; A/C; C/CATV; movies; radios; phones; comb or shower baths. Small pool; exercise rm. Parking lot. Airport transp. No pets. Monthly rates avail. Reserv deposit required; 14 days refund notice. AE, CB, DI, MC, VI. ● Restaurant & coffeeshop; 6 am-11 pm; $7-$25; cocktails. FAX (408) 437-9693   ⊗ Ⓓ (408) 453-6200

The President Inn   Rates Subject to Change   *Motel*   ◆◆◆
🆎 All year [CP]   1P 65.00- 80.00   2P/1B   70.00- 85.00   2P/2B   .... 75.00 XP 10   F
Senior discount. 45 units. Exit US 101 Tully, s on Monterey Rd. 3200 Monterey Rd. (95111) Attractive modern decor. Refrigerators; A/C; C/CATV; movies; phones. Coin laundry. Pool; whirlpool; exercise rm. No pets. 5 units with wet bar & whirlpool tub, $220-$280. All rooms have microwave & refrigerator. Reserv deposit required. AE, DI, DS, MC, VI. Restaurant adjacent. FAX (408) 972-2632 *(See ad p A455)*   ⊗ Ⓓ (408) 972-2200

Choose an establishment with the 🆎 next to its listing!

Radisson Plaza Hotel, San Jose Airport   AAA Special Value Rates   *Hotel*   ◆◆◆◆
Sun-Thurs   1P .... 109.00   2P/1B .... 109.00   2P/2B .... 119.00   XP 12
Fri & Sat   1P 69.00- 84.00   2P/1B 69.00- 84.00   2P/2B .... 84.00   XP 12
187 units. 1/2 mi n San Jose airport; US 101 exit n 1st St. 1471 N 4th St. (95112) French Provincial appointments; attractive public areas. A/C; C/CATV; pay movies; radios; phones. Htd pool; indoor whirlpool; exercise rm; jogging track. Parking ramp & parking lot. Airport transp. No pets. AE, CB, DI, MC, VI. ● Restaurant; 6 am-10 pm; $9-$20; cocktails. FAX (408) 437-8819   ⊗ Ⓢ Ⓓ 🄴 (408) 452-0200

Red Lion Hotel   Rates Subject to Change   *Motor Inn*   ◆◆◆◆
All year   1P 138.00- 169.00   2P/1B 147.00- 178.00   2P/2B 147.00- 178.00   XP 15   F
506 units. 1/4 mi e of San Jose International Airport Way, s of & adjacent to US 101 exit N 1st St. 2050 Gateway Pl. (95110) Large rooms. Check-in 3 pm. A/C; C/CATV; movies; radios; phones. Pool; sauna; whirlpool; exercise rm; jogging track. Airport transp. AE, DI, DS, MC, VI. ● Dining rm & coffeeshop; 6 am-11 pm; Fri & Sat-midnight; $8-$30; cocktails; entertainment. FAX (408) 437-9507 (See ad p A3)   ⊗ Ⓢ Ⓓ 🄴 (408) 453-4000

Rodeway Inn   Rates Subject to Change   *Motel*   ◆◆
All year   1P 45.00- 70.00   2P/1B 48.00- 78.00   2P/2B 52.00- 78.00   XP 5   F
95 units. Exit US 101W via Tully Rd; 1/4 mi n of fairgrounds on SR 82. 2112 Monterey Hwy. (95112) Some small units. Attractive landscaping. 87 refrigerators; A/C; C/CATV; movies; radios; phones; comb or shower baths. 2 2-bedrm units. Coin laundry. Pool. No pets. 5-night minimum stay in 14 efficiencies & 4 kitchens, $10 extra; utensils, deposit required. AE, CB, DI, MC, VI. ● Restaurant & coffeeshop; 24 hours; $10-$15; beer & wine. (See ad below)   ⊗ Ⓓ (408) 294-1480

Hotel Sainte Claire   Rates Subject to Change   *Historic Hotel*   ◆◆
All year   1P 79.00- 150.00   2P/1B 94.00- 150.00   2P/2B 94.00- 150.00   XP 15
Senior discount. 170 units. Opposite conventio center. 302 S Market St. (95113-2889) Restored historic 1926 hotel, rating withheld pending completion of restoration. Check-in 3 pm. A/C; C/CATV; free & pay movies; radios; phones. Steamroom; exercise rm. Fee for: massage. Valet garage. Airport transp. No pets. 17 suites with wet bar, whirlpool tub & steam room, $135-$795 for 2 persons. Reserv deposit required. AE, DI, DS, MC, VI. ● 3 restaurants; $15-$40; cocktails. FAX (408) 279-5803   ⊗ Ⓢ Ⓓ (408) 295-2000

San Jose Hilton & Towers   Rates Subject to Change   *Hotel*
All year   1P 125.00- 135.00   2P/1B .... 150.00   2P/2B .... 140.00   XP 15   F
355 units. 300 Almaden Blvd. (95113) Rating withheld pending completion of construction. Check-in 4 pm. A/C; C/CATV; pay movies; radios; phones. Pool; whirlpool. Valet garage. Airport transp. No pets. Reserv deposit required. AE, DI, DS, MC, VI. ● Restaurant; 6 am-midnight; $10-$25; cocktails.   ⊗ Ⓢ Ⓓ (408) 287-2100

Travelodge-San Jose Convention Center   AAA Special Value Rates   *Motel*   ◆
All year   1P .... 50.00   2P/1B .... 55.00   2P/2B .... 60.00   XP 5   F
26 units. 1 mi s of I-280 & SR 82, via N 1st St. 1415 Monterey Rd. (95110) A/C; C/CATV; movies; radios; phones. 1 2-bedrm unit. No pets. 4 units with whirlpool tub, $10 extra for up to 2 persons. Reserv deposit required. AE, DI, DS, MC, VI. Coffeeshop opposite. FAX (408) 993-8744   Ⓓ 🄴 (408) 993-1711

Valley Inn [CP]   Rates Guaranteed   *Motel*   ◆◆
All year   1P 49.00- 54.00   2P/1B 54.00- 59.00   2P/2B 59.00- 64.00   XP 5
Senior discount. 26 units. 1/2 mi w of I-880, 1 1/2 mi SW of San Jose Int'l Airport. 2155 The Alameda. (95126) Refrigerators; A/C; C/CATV; movies; VCPs. Radios; phones; comb or shower baths. No pets. 7 rooms with whirlpool, $64-$109 for 2 persons. All rooms have microwave & refrigerator. Wkly rates avail. Reserv deposit required. AE, DI, DS, MC, VI.   Ⓓ 🄴 (408) 241-8500

Valley Park Hotel   Rates Subject to Change   *Motel*   ◆◆
All year [BP]   1P .... 89.00   2P/1B .... 95.00   2P/2B 105.00- 115.00   XP 6
Senior discount. 55 units. Exit I-880, Stevens Creek/San Carlos; 1/4 mi e. 2404 Stevens Creek Blvd. (95128) All units with extra large whirlpool tub. A/C; C/CATV; movies; VCPs. Radios; phones. Efficiencies. Coin laundry. Parking lot. No pets. Wkly rates avail. AE, DI, DS, MC, VI.   ⊗ Ⓢ Ⓓ 🄴 (408) 293-5000

RESTAURANTS

Emiles Restaurant   French $$$ ◆◆◆
Center. 545 S 2nd St. Swiss specialties, emphasis on lite healthy preparation. Warm inviting atmosphere. A/C. Open 11:30 am-2 & 5:30-9:30 pm; Sat 5:30 pm-10 pm; closed Sun, Mon, 11/25, 12/25, 1/1-1/10 & 7/1-7/10. Cocktails. Minimum $7.50. Reserv advised. AE, CB, DI, MC, VI.   ⊗ (408) 289-1960

Eulipia Restaurant & Bar   American $$ ◆◆
374 S 1st St. Creative contemporary cooking, attractive decor. A/C. Open 11:30 am-2 & 5:30-9:30 pm; Sat 5:30 pm-11 pm; Sun 4:30 pm-9 pm; closed major holidays. Cocktails & lounge. Pay parking lot. Reserv advised. AE, MC, VI.   ⊗ (408) 280-6161

Les Saisons   Continental $$$$ ◆◆◆◆
In The Fairmont Hotel. Features California influenced cuisine in a warm & elegant atmosphere. A/C. Dress code. Open 11:30 am-2:30 & 6-10:30 pm; Sat & Sun from 6 pm. Cocktails & lounge. Entertainment. Reserv advised. AE, CB, DI, MC, VI.   ⊗ (408) 998-3950

Lou's Village   Seafood $$$ ◆◆
3 1/2 mi s on SR 17 from jct US 101; 1 1/4 mi e on W San Carlos St. 1465 W San Carlos St. Cheerful surrounding, casual atmosphere. Varied menu. A/C. Children's menu. Open 11:30 am-10 pm; Fri-11 pm; Sat & Sun 4:30 pm-11 pm; closed major holidays. Cocktails & lounge. Minimum, $5. Reserv advised. AE, DI, MC, VI.   (408) 293-4570

The Old Spaghetti Factory   Italian $ ◆
1 blk n of W Santa Clara St. 51 N San Pedro St. Family restaurant. Victorian decor casual atmosphere. A/C. Children's menu. Open 11:30 am-2 & 5-10 pm; Fri-11 pm; Sat 5 pm-11 pm; Sun 4 pm-10 pm; closed 11/25, 12/24 & 12/25. Cocktails & lounge. MC, VI.   ⊗ (408) 288-7488

Pasquale's Italian Garden Restaurant   Italian $$ ◆◆◆
E of SR 82 at E Williams St. 476 S 1st St. Cuisine prepared with Italian influence. Garden dining 4/1-9/30. A/C. Dress code. Open 11:30 am-2:30 & 5-11 pm; Sat from 5 pm; Sun 10:30 am-2:30 & 4:30-9:30 pm. Cocktails & lounge. Valet parking. Reserv advised. AE, CB, DI, MC, VI.   ⊗ (408) 286-1770

SAN JUAN BAUTISTA — 1,600

San Juan Inn		Rates Subject to Change				Motel		◆◆
⊕ 3/1-11/30	1P	.... 42.00	2P/1B	.... 60.00	2P/2B	.... 60.00	XP	6
12/1-2/28	1P	.... 42.00	2P/1B	.... 50.00	2P/2B	.... 50.00	XP	6

42 units. At jct SR 156 & Alameda St. (PO Box 1080, 95045) Quiet location, attractively landscaped grounds. 19 refrigerators; A/C; C/CATV; phones. Pool; whirlpool. Pets, $5 extra charge. Wkly rates avail. Reserv deposit required; 3 days refund notice. AE, DI, MC, VI.   ⊗ Ⓓ (408) 623-4380

RESTAURANTS

Cademartori's   Italian $$ ◆
3 blks w at 1st & San Jose sts, adjacent to historic mission grounds. Steaks; homemade ravioli. Children's menu. Open 11:30 am-2 & 5-9 pm; Fri & Sat-10 pm; Sun 1 pm-9 pm; closed Mon, 12/25 & 1/1-1/10. Cocktails & lounge. Reserv advised. AE, CB, DI, MC, VI.   (408) 623-4511

The Faultline   Continental $$$ ◆◆
2 mi e off US 101 on SR 156. 11 Franklin St. View of San Juan Valley. Limited menu changes daily, all fresh ingredients. Smoke free premises. A/C. Dress code. Open 11:30 am-3 & 5-6:30 pm; Sat 11:30 am-3 & 4:30-6:30 pm; Sun 11:30 am-3 & 3:30-6:30 pm; closed Tues & major holidays. Beer & wine. Reserv required. MC, VI.   ⊗ (408) 623-2117

SAN JUAN CAPISTRANO — 26,200

Best Western Capistrano Inn		AAA Special Value Rates				Motel		◆◆◆
⊕ All year	1P 59.00- 75.00	2P/1B	59.00- 75.00	2P/2B	62.00- 72.00	XP	6	F

108 units. On SR 74, 1/2 blk e of I-5. 27174 Ortega Hwy. (92675) A/C; C/CATV; movies; radios; phones. 8 efficiencies. Htd pool; whirlpool. Pets. Complimentary breakfast & evening beverages on weekdays. Wkly & monthly rates avail. Reserv deposit required; 3 days refund notice. AE, DI, DS, MC, VI. Coffeeshop adjacent. FAX (714) 661-8293 *(See ad below)*   ⊗ Ⓓ Ⓛ (714) 493-5661

San Juan Capistrano Travelodge		Rates Subject to Change				Motel		◆◆
⊕ All year	1P	.... 49.00	2P/1B	.... 49.00	2P/2B	.... 59.00	XP	4

Senior discount. 33 units. Adjacent to I-5, exit Avary Pkwy. 28742 Camino Capistrano. (92675) A/C; C/CATV; movies; rental VCPs. Radios; phones. Coin laundry. Whirlpool; all rooms with whirlpool tub. Garage. No pets. 11 efficiencies, $10 extra; no utensils. Wkly rates avail. Reserv deposit required; 3 days refund notice. AE, DI, DS, MC, VI. Restaurant adjacent. *(See ad p A125)*   ⊗ Ⓢ Ⓓ (714) 364-0342

RESTAURANTS

Cafe Mozart   Continental $$ ◆◆◆
In Mercado Village, 1 1/2 blks from Mission San Juan Capistrano. 31952 Camino Capistrano. Delightful dining in casual atmosphere. Several German entrees. Wild game a speciality. A/C. Children's menu. Open 11:30 am-3 & 5:30-10 pm; closed Sun, Mon, 1/1-1/8 & 11/22-11/30. Beer & wine. Entertainment. Reserv advised weekends. AE, CB, DI, MC, VI.   ⊗ Ⓛ (714) 496-0212

El Adobe de Capistrano   Mexican $$ ◆◆
Center 1 1/2 blks from Misson San Juan Capistrano. 31899 Camino Capistrano. Delightful dining in historic landmark. Also Features American cuisine. Sun brunch 10:30 am-3 pm. A/C. Children's menu. Open 11:30 am-10 pm; Fri & Sat-11 pm; Sun 10:30 am-10 pm. Cocktails & lounge. AE, MC, VI.   ⊗ Ⓛ (714) 493-1163

SAN LEANDRO — 68,200   (See OAKLAND/BERKELEY AREA spotting map pages A300 & A301; see index starting on page A298)

Airport Accommodations-See listing for:

⊕ San Leandro Marina Inn, 3 mi s of airport.

San Leandro Marina Inn ❶		AAA Special Value Rates				Motel		◆◆◆
⊕ All year [CP]	1P 83.00- 98.00	2P/1B	89.00- 102.00	2P/2B	87.00- 102.00	XP	4	F

130 units. 3 mi s of Oakland Airport; w of I-880 exit Marina Blvd, 1 1/4 mi w at San Leandro Marina. 60 Can Leandro Marina. (94577) Attractive rooms overlooking marina. 18 refrigerators; A/C; C/CATV; pay movies; radios; phones; comb or shower baths. Htd pool; whirlpool; bicycles. Airport transp. No pets. Reserv deposit required. AE, CB, DI, MC, VI. Restaurant adjacent. FAX (510) 483-4078 *(See ad p A459)*   Ⓢ Ⓓ Ⓛ (510) 895-1311

RESTAURANT

Horatio's ❶   Seafood $$ ◆◆
⊕ At San Leandro Marina; exit I-880 Marina Blvd W; 1 1/4 mi. 60 San Leandro Marina. Attractive surroundings overlooking marina. Casual atmosphere, varied menu. A/C. Children's menu. Open 11:15 am-5 & 5:30 pm-9:30 pm; Fri-10 pm; Sat 5 pm-10 pm; Sun 10 am-2 & 5-9 pm; closed major holidays. Cocktails & lounge. Reserv advised. AE, MC, VI.   ⊗ (510) 351-5556

SAN LUIS OBISPO — 42,000

Apple Farm Inn
Ⓐ All year
Rates Subject to Change — *Motor Inn* ◆◆◆◆
1P 105.00- 185.00   2P/1B   105.00- 185.00   2P/2B   125.00- 150.00   XP 15   F
68 units. 1 1/2 mi n; 2 blks s of jct US 101, Monterey St exit, behind Apple Farm Restaurant. 2015 Monterey St. (93401) Charming country decor & atmosphere. Exquisite early period furnishings. All rooms with gas fireplace. Check-in 4 pm. A/C; C/CATV; radios; phones. Htd pool; whirlpool. Airport transp. No pets. Reserv deposit required. AE, MC, VI. ● Restaurant, see separate listing. FAX (805) 543-3064 *(See ad p A460)*
⊗ Ⓢ Ⓓ ⬛ (805) 544-2040

Apple Farm Trellis Court
Ⓐ All year [CP]
Rates Subject to Change — *Motel* ◆◆◆
1P 60.00- 99.00   2P/1B   60.00- 99.00   2P/2B   75.00- 95.00   XP 15   F
34 units. 1 1/4 mi n, adjacent to US 101, Monterey St exit. 2121 Monterey St. (93401) Charming country decor. All rooms with gas fireplace. Check-in 4 pm. A/C; C/CATV; radios; phones; shower or comb baths. 2 2-bedrm units. Htd pool; whirlpool. No pets. Reserv deposit required. AE, MC, VI. Restaurant adjacent. FAX (805) 543-3064 *(See ad p A460)*
⊗ Ⓓ (805) 544-2040

Best Western Olive Tree Inn
Ⓐ
Rates Subject to Change — *Motor Inn* ◆◆
6/11-9/18	1P	....	53.00	2P/1B	....	65.00	2P/2B	.... 65.00 XP 4
3/2-6/10 & 12/24-1/31	1P	....	45.00	2P/1B	....	49.00	2P/2B	.... 49.00 XP 4
2/1-3/1 & 9/19-12/23	1P	....	42.00	2P/1B	....	46.00	2P/2B	.... 46.00 XP 4

38 units. 3/4 blk w of US 101 at jct SR 1; US 101 northbound Morro Bay exit, southbound Santa Rosa exit. 1000 Olive St. (93405) C/CATV; VCPs; phones. Coin laundry. Htd pool; sauna. No pets. 8 efficiencies, $6 extra. AE, DI, DS, MC, VI. Coffeeshop; 6:30 am-2 pm.
Ⓓ (805) 544-2800

Best Western Royal Oak Motor Hotel
Ⓐ
Rates Subject to Change — *Motor Inn* ◆◆◆
5/1-9/5 [CP]	1P	63.00-	89.00	2P/1B	69.00-	89.00	2P/2B	74.00- 83.00 XP 7
9/6-11/13 [CP]	1P	63.00-	80.00	2P/1B	69.00-	80.00	2P/2B	74.00- 77.00 XP 7
11/14-4/30 [CP]	1P	61.00-	79.00	2P/1B	68.00-	79.00	2P/2B	71.00- 76.00 XP 7

Senior discount. 99 units. 1 1/2 mi s; 1 blk s of jct US 101, Madonna Rd exit. 214 Madonna Rd. (93405) Balconies. 30 refrigerators; C/CATV; rental VCPs; 25 radios; phones. Coin laundry. Htd pool; indoor whirlpool. Pets. AE, DI, DS, MC, VI. ● Restaurant; 7 am-9 pm; Sat & Sun from 7:30 am; $6-$9; cocktails. FAX (805) 544-3026
⊗ Ⓓ ⬛ (805) 544-4410

Look for the 🅐 in our listings!

Best Western Somerset Manor   Rates Subject to Change   *Motor Inn* ◆◆
8/1-8/31   1P 57.00- 67.00   2P/1B   60.00- 70.00   2P/2B   63.00- 67.00 XP 3
5/18-7/31 & 9/1-10/13   1P 47.00- 57.00   2P/1B   50.00- 60.00   2P/2B   53.00- 57.00 XP 3
10/14-5/17   1P 36.00- 46.00   2P/1B   39.00- 49.00   2P/2B   42.00- 46.00 XP 3
40 units. 1 1/4 mi n; 2 blks s of jct US 101, Monterey St exit. 1895 Monterey St. (93401) Check-in 3 pm. A/C; C/CATV; phones; comb or shower baths. Htd pool; whirlpool. No pets. Microwaves & refrigerators. Reserv deposit required. AE, DI, DS, MC, VI. ● Coffeeshop; 6 am-10 pm; $6-$16. FAX (805) 541-2805 *(See ad p A459)*
(D) (805) 544-0973

Budget Motel   Rates Guaranteed   *Motel* ◆
All year [CP]   1P 34.00- 50.00   2P/1B   38.00- 55.00   2P/2B   48.00- 59.00 XP 2- 6
Senior discount. 51 units. 3/4 mi s; 1 blk e of US 101, Marsh St exit. 345 Marsh St. (93401) 13 A/C; C/CATV; movies; phones; shower or comb baths. 2 2-bedrm units. No pets. Reserv deposit required. AE, DI, DS, MC, VI.
⊗ (D) (医) (805) 543-6443

Campus Motel   Rates Subject to Change   *Motel* ◆◆
6/11-9/6   ....   2P/1B   54.00- 69.00   2P/2B   59.00- 79.00 XP 5 F
4/2-6/10   2P/1B   54.00- 64.00   2P/2B   54.00- 69.00 XP 5 F
9/7-4/1   ....   2P/1B   44.00- 49.00   2P/2B   49.00- 59.00 XP 5 F
Senior discount. 35 units. On SR 1, at jct US 101. 404 Santa Rosa St. (93405) Refrigerators; 8 A/C; C/CATV; rental VCPs; radios; phones. Coin laundry. Htd pool; 6 rooms with whirlpool tub; 2 steambaths. Small pets only, $4 extra. 2 microwaves. AE, DI, DS, MC, VI. *(See ad below)* ⊗ (D) (医) (805) 544-0881

Cuesta Canyon Lodge   Rates Subject to Change   *Motor Inn* ◆◆
All year [CP]   1P .... 58.00   2P/1B   .... 68.00   2P/2B   .... 68.00 XP 10
Senior discount. 100 units. 1 1/4 mi n, 2 blks s of jct US 101; northbound Grand Ave exit, southbound Monterey St exit. 1800 Monterey St. (93401) A/C; C/CATV; movies; radios; phones. Htd pool; whirlpool. No pets. AE, DS, MC, VI. ● Restaurant; 11:30 am-midnight; $7.50-$12; cocktails. FAX (805) 541-4698 ⊗ (D) (医) (805) 544-8600

Embassy Suites Hotel   Rates Subject to Change   *Suites Motor Inn* ◆◆◆
All year [BP]   1P 109.00- 119.00   2P/1B   119.00- 129.00   2P/2B   119.00- 129.00 XP 10
Senior discount. 196 units. 1 3/4 mi s; 1/2 mi s of jct Hwy 101; Madonna Rd exit. 333 Madonna Rd. (93405) Check-in 3 pm. A/C; C/CATV; free & pay movies; radios; phones. Coin laundry. Htd indoor pool; whirlpools. Airport transp. No pets. 1-bedroom suites with living room; most with microwave. Monthly rates avail. Complimentary beverages each evening. AE, DI, DS, MC, VI. ● Restaurant; 6:30 am-10 pm; $6-$16. FAX (805) 543-5273 *(See ad p A462)* ⊗ (S) (D) (医) (805) 549-0800

Garden Street Inn Bed & Breakfast   Rates Subject to Change   *Historic Bed & Breakfast* ◆◆◆
All year [BP]   ....   2P/1B   90.00- 120.00   .... XP
13 units. 1/2 mi e of US 101; Marsh St exit. 1212 Garden St. (93401) 1887 restored Italianate Queen Anne style house. Designated smoking areas. Check-in 3 pm. A/C; radios. No pets. 4 suites, $140-$160. 6 rooms with whirlpool, some with gas fireplace. Wkly rates avail. Reserv deposit required; 7 days refund notice. AE, MC, VI. ⊗ (S) (D) (805) 545-9802

Howard Johnson Motor Lodge

			Rates Subject to Change				Motel				◆◆
6/1-9/10	1P	64.00- 89.00	2P/1B	69.00- 94.00	2P/2B	69.00- 94.00	XP	8			F
9/11-9/25 & 4/1-5/31	1P	44.00- 69.00	2P/1B	49.00- 74.00	2P/2B	49.00- 74.00	XP	8			F
9/26-3/31	1P	44.00- 54.00	2P/1B	49.00- 59.00	2P/2B	49.00- 59.00	XP	8			F

Senior discount. 64 units. 2 1/4 mi s; adjacent to US 101, Los Osos Rd exit. 1585 Calle Joaquin. (93405) 27 refrigerators; A/C; C/CATV; movies; rental VCPs. Phones. Coin laundry. Htd pool; wading pool. Wkly & monthly rates avail. AE, DI, DS, MC, VI. Restaurant adjacent. FAX (805) 541-2823 *(See ad p A463)*   ⊗ Ⓓ ⓑ (805) 544-5300

La Cuesta Motor Inn   **AAA Special Value Rates**   *Motel*   ◆◆◆
5/15-9/30 [CP]   1P 65.00- 85.00 2P/1B   70.00- 90.00   2P/2B 71.00- 95.00 XP 10   F
10/1-5/14 [CP]   1P 59.00- 79.00 2P/1B   64.00- 84.00   2P/2B 64.00- 84.00 XP 10   F
72 units. 1 1/4 mi n; 2 blks s of jct US 101, Monterey St exit. 2074 Monterey St. (93401) Balconies. Afternoon tea 3 pm-6 pm. 15 refrigerators; A/C; C/CATV; movies; radios; phones. Htd pool; whirlpool. No pets. AE, DI, DS, MC, VI. Restaurant opposite. FAX (805) 544-0656 *(See ad p A462)*   ⊗ Ⓢ Ⓓ 🅱 (805) 543-2777

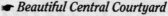

Lamplighter Inn   Rates Subject to Change   *Motel* ◆◆
⊕ 7/20-9/5 [CP]   1P 49.00- 75.00   2P/1B   49.00- 75.00   2P/2B   59.00- 75.00   XP   6
    6/10-7/19 [CP]   1P 42.00- 64.00   2P/1B   45.00- 64.00   2P/2B   54.00- 64.00   XP   6
    4/1-6/9 & 9/6-10/15 [CP]   1P 37.00- 59.00   2P/1B   42.00- 59.00   2P/2B   49.00- 59.00   XP   5
    10/16-3/31 [CP]   1P 35.00- 54.00   2P/1B   39.00- 54.00   2P/2B   45.00- 54.00   XP   5
Senior discount. 40 units. 3/4 mi n; 5 blks s of jct US 101, Monterey St exit. 1604 Monterey St. (93401) Few small units. Refrigerators; A/C; C/CATV; movies; phones; shower or comb baths. 1 2-bedrm unit. Coin laundry. Htd pool; whirlpool. No pets. 11 1-bedroom units with living room & kitchen. Wkly rates avail. AE, MC, VI. FAX (805) 547-7787 *(See ad below)*   ⊗ Ⓓ (805) 547-7777

Madonna Inn   Rates Subject to Change   *Motor Inn* ◆◆◆
    All year   1P .... 72.00   2P/1B   82.00- 180.00   2P/2B   82.00- 180.00   XP   15
109 units. 1 1/2 mi s; adjacent to US 101, Madonna Rd exit. 100 Madonna Rd. (93405) Each room unusually designed & decorated. Check-in 4 pm. 29 A/C; C/CATV; 50 radios; phones; shower or comb baths. 2 2-bedrm units, 2 3-bedrm units. No pets. Reserv deposit required. ● Coffeeshop; 7 am-10:30 pm; $6.95-$13; cocktails. Also dining room, see separate listing. FAX (805) 543-1800 *(See ad below)*   Ⓓ (805) 543-3000

Mid-Town Motel
Fri & Sat 5/1-9/30   1P 75.00- 85.00   2P/1B   75.00- 85.00   2P/2B   95.00- 110.00 XP 10
Sun-Thurs 5/1-9/30   1P 38.00- 46.00   2P/1B   40.00- 50.00   2P/2B   46.00- 55.00 XP 5
10/1-4/30   1P 34.00- 42.00   2P/1B   38.00- 42.00   2P/2B   38.00- 46.00 XP 5

Rates Subject to Change   *Motel*   ◆

32 units. 1/2 mi s; 1/4 mi e of US 101; Marsh St exit. 475 Marsh St. (93401) C/CATV; movies; 25 radios; phones; shower or comb baths. 3 2-bedrm units. Pool. No pets. 10 units with microwave & refrigerator. Reserv deposit required. AE, CB, DI, MC, VI.   ⊗ Ⓓ (805) 543-4533

Peach Tree Inn   Rates Guaranteed   *Motel*   ◆◆
All year [CP]   1P 35.00- 49.00   2P/1B   42.00- 59.00   2P/2B   45.00- 69.00 XP 3- 5
39 units. 1 1/4 mi n; 1 blk s of jct US 101, Monterey St exit. 2001 Monterey St. (93401) A/C; C/CATV; movies; phones; shower or comb baths. No pets. Reserv deposit required; 3 days refund notice. AE, DS, MC, VI.
FAX (805) 543-7673 *(See ad p A463)*   ⊗ Ⓓ (805) 543-3170

Quality Suites   AAA Special Value Rates   *Suites Motel*   ◆◆◆
5/22-9/7 [BP]   1P 99.00- 119.00   2P/1B 109.00- 129.00   2P/2B 109.00- 129.00 XP 10   F
9/8-5/21 [BP]   1P 89.00- 109.00   2P/1B · 99.00- 119.00   2P/2B   99.00- 119.00 XP 10   F
138 units. 3/4 mi n; 5 blks s of jct US 101, Monterey St exit. 1631 Monterey St. (93401) 1-bedroom suites with living room & microwave. Refrigerators; A/C; C/CATV; movies; VCPs. Radios; phones. Coin laundry. Htd pool; wading pool; whirlpool. No pets. Complimentary beverages each evening. AE, DI, DS, MC, VI. FAX (805) 546-9475
(See ad below)   ⊗ Ⓢ Ⓓ Ⓛ (805) 541-5001

Sands Motel & Suites
							Motel		◆◆
5/15-9/15	....	2P/1B	52.00-	89.00	2P/2B	69.00-	99.00	XP	7
3/15-5/15	....	2P/1B	52.00-	69.00	2P/2B	59.00-	74.00	XP	7
2/1-3/15 & 9/16-1/31	....	2P/1B	49.00-	59.00	2P/2B	54.00-	69.00	XP	7

70 units. 1 1/4 mi n; 2 blks s of jct US 101, Monterey St exit. 1930 Monterey St. (93401) Refrigerators; A/C; C/CATV; VCPs; 35 radios; phones; comb or shower baths. Coin laundry. Htd pool. Small pets only, $5 extra. 14 1-bedroom suites with microwave. AE, DI, DS, MC, VI. Restaurant opposite. FAX (805) 544-3529 *(See ad p A465)*
⊗ Ⓢ Ⓓ Ⓛ (805) 544-0500

San Luis Obispo Travelodge
								Motel		◆◆
7/4-9/15	1P	49.00-	59.00	2P/1B	49.00-	69.00	2P/2B	54.00-	78.00	XP 3	F
9/16-7/3	1P	36.00-	49.00	2P/1B	39.00-	49.00	2P/2B	44.00-	59.00	XP 3	F

Senior discount. 38 units. 1 1/4 mi n, 2 blks s of jct US 101; northbound exit Grand Ave, southbound exit Monterey St. 1825 Monterey St. (93401) A/C; C/CATV; phones; shower or comb baths. Htd pool. No pets. Reserv deposit required. AE, DI, DS, MC, VI. *(See ad below)*
⊗ Ⓓ (805) 543-5110

Super 8 Motel
								Motel		◆◆
8/1-8/31 [CP]	1P	49.00-	59.00	2P/1B	54.00-	65.00	2P/2B	54.00-	65.00	XP 5
5/15-7/31 & 9/1-11/15 [CP]	1P	39.00-	49.00	2P/1B	42.00-	59.00	2P/2B	45.00-	59.00	XP 5
11/16-5/14 [CP]	1P	37.00-	49.00	2P/1B	39.00-	49.00	2P/2B	44.00-	55.00	XP 5

Senior discount. 49 units. 1 1/4 mi s of jct US 101, Monterey St exit. 1951 Monterey St. (93401) A/C; C/CATV; movies; phones. Small htd pool. No pets. 5 rooms with microwave & refrigerator. Wkly rates avail. AE, DI, DS, MC, VI. Coffeeshop adjacent.
⊗ Ⓢ Ⓓ Ⓛ (805) 544-7895

Travelodge South
							Motel		◆◆
Fri & Sat 6/16-9/9	....	2P/1B	60.00-	80.00	2P/2B	75.00-	95.00	XP	5
Fri & Sat 9/10-6/15	....	2P/1B	40.00-	70.00	2P/2B	44.00-	80.00	XP	5
Sun-Thurs 6/16-9/9	....	2P/1B	46.00-	60.00	2P/2B	50.00-	75.00	XP	5
Sun-Thurs 9/10-6/15	....	2P/1B	38.00-	60.00	2P/2B	46.00-	66.00	XP	5

Senior discount. 32 units. 1 blk w of US 101 at jct SR 1; US 101 northbound Morro Bay exit, southbound Santa Rosa exit. 950 Olive St. (93405) A/C; C/CATV; movies; phones. 2 efficiencies, no utensils. Whirlpool. No pets. AE, DI, DS, MC, VI. *(See ad below)*
⊗ Ⓢ Ⓓ Ⓛ (805) 544-8886

Vagabond Inn — Rates Subject to Change — *Motel* ◆◆
🏵 All year [CP]   1P 44.00- 63.00   2P/1B   49.00- 68.00   2P/2B   54.00- 73.00   XP 5   F
61 units. 1 1/2 mi s; 1/2 blk s of jct US 101, Madonna Rd exit. 210 Madonna Rd. (93401) A/C; C/CATV; movies; radios; phones. 1 2-bedrm unit. Htd pool. Pets, $5 extra charge. AE, DI, DS, MC, VI. Coffeeshop adjacent. FAX (805) 541-1949 *(See ad p A466)*   ⊗ ⒟ (805) 544-4710

Villa Motel — Rates Subject to Change — *Motel* ◆◆
🏵 6/1-9/30   ....   2P/1B   .... 43.00   2P/2B   .... 53.00   XP 3- 4
    4/1-5/31   ....   2P/1B   .... 39.00   2P/2B   .... 42.00   XP 3- 4
    10/1-3/31   ....   2P/1B   .... 36.00   2P/2B   .... 39.00   XP 3- 4
14 units. 1 mi n; 4 blks s of jct US 101, Monterey St exit. 1670 Monterey St. (93405) A/C; C/CATV; movies; VCPs. Phones; shower or comb baths. Heated pool open 4/1-10/31. No pets. Reserv deposit required. AE, DI, DS, MC, VI. *(See ad below)*   ⊗ ⒟ (805) 543-8071

RESTAURANTS

Apple Farm — American — $ ◆◆
🏵 At Apple Farm Inn. Country charm. Serving homemade soups, desserts & varied entrees. Smoke free premises. A/C. Children's menu. Open 7 am-10 pm. Beer & wine. AE, MC, VI. *(See ad p A460)*   ⊗ (805) 544-6100

Benvenuti Ristorante — Italian — $$ ◆◆
1/2 mi s; 1/4 mi e of US 101; Marsh St exit. 450 Marsh St. Formerly Carmel Beach Restaurant. Charming Victorian house. Nice selection of Italian cuisine. Smoke free premises. A/C. Children's menu. Open 11:30 am-2 & 5:30-10 pm; Sat & Sun from 5:30 pm; closed 1/1, 11/25 & 12/25. Cocktails. Reserv advised. AE, MC, VI.   ⊗ (805) 541-5393

Madonna Inn Dining Room — American — $$ ◆◆◆
In Madonna Inn. Uniquely decorated dining room. Nice selection of complete dinners. Smoke free premises. A/C. Children's menu. Open 5:30 pm-11 pm. Cocktails & lounge. Entertainment & dancing. Reserv advised. ⊗ (805) 543-3000

This Old House — American — $$ ◆◆◆
3 mi nw of US 101; Santa Rosa (SR 1) & Foothill Blvd. 740 W Foothill Rd. Selections of oakwood barbecue, steaks, pork, chicken, ribs & seafood served in a country western atmosphere. Children's menu. Open 5 pm-9:30 pm; Fri-1 pm; Sat 4 pm-10 pm; Sun 4 pm-9:30 pm; closed 11/25 & 12/25. Cocktails & lounge. Reserv advised. AE, DI, MC, VI.   ⊗ (805) 543-2690

SAN MARCOS — 39,000

Quails Inn at Lake San Marcos Resort — AAA Special Value Rates — *Motor Inn* ◆◆◆
🏵 All year   1P 90.00- 125.00   2P/1B   90.00- 125.00   2P/2B   90.00- 115.00   XP 10   F
142 units. 2 mi s of SR 78, Rancho Santa Fe Rd exit, then 1/2 mi e via Lake San Marcos Dr & San Marino Dr; at Lake San Marcos. 1025 La Bonita Dr. (92069) Attractive grounds, lakefront location. Check-in 3 pm. A/C; C/CATV; 62 radios; phones; comb or shower baths. 4 kitchens. 2 htd pools; whirlpool; rental boats & canoes; tennis-4 courts; paddleball-3 courts. Fee for: paddleboats; golf-36 holes. Pets, $10 extra charge. 2 1-bedroom & 2 2-bedroom apartments, $165-$220. Reserv deposit required. AE, DI, DS, MC, VI. ● Restaurant; 7 am-10 pm; $12-$18; cocktails. FAX (619) 744-0748   ⊗ ⒟ (619) 744-0120

San Marcos Travelodge — Rates Subject to Change — *Motor Inn* ◆◆
🏵 All year   1P .... 36.00   2P/1B   .... 38.00   2P/2B   .... 42.00   XP 5   F
Senior discount. 86 units. 1 blk e of SR 78, exit San Marcos Blvd. 517 San Marcos Blvd. (92069) A/C; C/CATV; movies; phones. 11 efficiencies. Coin laundry. Htd pool. No pets. AE, DI, DS, MC, VI. ● Restaurant; 24 hours; $5-$11; beer & wine.   ⊗ ⒟ (619) 471-2800

SAN MATEO — 85,500   (See SAN FRANCISCO (Southern Region) AREA spotting map page A444; see index starting on page A443)

Airport Accommodations-See SAN FRANCISCO:

Best Western San Mateo Inn 145 — Rates Guaranteed — *Motel* ◆◆
🏵 All year   1P 57.00- 67.00   2P/1B   61.00- 71.00   2P/2B   61.00- 71.00   XP 7
Senior discount. 113 units. Adjacent to US 101 Frwy; exit e via E Hillsdale Blvd. 2940 S Norfolk St. (94403) A/C; C/CATV; pay movies; 50 radios; phones; comb or shower baths. 3 2-bedrm units. Indoor whirlpool; exercise rm. Airport transp. No pets. Wkly & monthly rates avail. Reserv deposit required. AE, DI, DS, MC, VI. Coffeeshop adjacent. FAX (415) 341-9999   ⊗ (415) 341-3300

Dunfey San Mateo Hotel 141 — Rates Guaranteed — *Motel* ◆◆◆
All year   1P .... 69.00   2P/1B   .... 69.00   2P/2B   .... 69.00   XP 15   F
Senior discount. 270 units. Nw of jct US 101 & SR 92; exit SR 92 Delaware St, E on Concar Dr. 1770 S Amphlett Blvd. (94402) Some rooms with courtyard view. Check-in 3 pm. A/C; C/CATV; free & pay movies; radios; phones. Coin laundry. Pool. Airport transp. Pets, $50 deposit required. Reserv deposit required. AE, DI, DS, MC, VI. ● Dining rm & coffeeshop; 6 am-10:30 pm; $14-$17; cocktails. FAX (415) 570-0500   ⊗ ⒟ (415) 570-7001

(See SAN FRANCISCO (Southern Region) spotting map page A444)

Holiday Inn Express ⚂ 142   Rates Subject to Change   *Motel* ◆◆◆
All year [CP]   1P 54.00- 59.00   2P/1B   60.00- 65.00   2P/2B   62.00- 67.00   XP 6
Senior discount. 111 units. Northbound exit US 101 Dore Ave; 5B exit US 101 3rd Ave E, reenter US 101 N exit Dore Ave; 5 mi s of San Francisco Airport. 350 N Bayshore Blvd. (94401) Attractive, comfortable rooms. Check-in 3 pm. A/C; C/CATV; movies; radios; phones. 3 2-bedrm units, 6 efficiencies. Coin laundry. Airport transp. No pets. 6 efficiencies, $76-$89. Reserv deposit required; 3 days refund notice. AE, DI, DS, MC, VI.
FAX (415) 343-7108   ⊗ Ⓢ Ⓓ (415) 344-6376

Holiday Inn-San Mateo ⚂ 144   Rates Subject to Change   *Motor Inn* ◆◆◆
All year   1P 79.00- 125.00   2P/1B   85.00- 135.00   2P/2B   89.00- 175.00   XP 6   F
111 units. Adjacent to US 101, exit 3rd Ave E; 1/4 mi n on Bayshore Blvd. 330 N Bayshore Blvd. (94401) Formerly Grand Manor Inn. Few rooms with fireplace. Very comfortable & attractive rooms. Refrigerators; A/C; C/CATV; movies; radios; phones; comb or shower baths. 3 2-bedrm units. Coin laundry. Sauna; indoor whirlpool; exercise rm. Airport transp. No pets. AE, DI, DS, MC, VI. ● Restaurant; 6 am-11 pm; $10-$20; cocktail lounge.
FAX (415) 344-9012   ⊗ Ⓢ Ⓓ (415) 344-3219

Quality Hotel Airport South ⚂ 143   Rates Subject to Change   *Motor Inn* ◆◆◆
All year   1P 65.00- 76.00   2P/1B   73.00- 84.00   2P/2B   73.00- 84.00   XP 8   F
Senior discount. 286 units. 8 mi s of San Francisco International Airport, exit US 101 W Hillside Blvd, 1/2 mi s on SR 82. 4000 S El Camino Real. (94403) Formerly Villa Hotel. Check-in 3 pm. A/C; C/CATV; movies; radios; phones; comb or shower baths. Pool. Airport transp. Pets, $50 deposit required. AE, DI, DS, MC, VI. ● Restaurant & coffeeshop; 24 hours; $6-$16; cocktails; entertainment. FAX (415) 573-0164 *(See ad below)*
          ⊗ Ⓓ (415) 341-0966

Residence Inn by Marriott ⚂ 140   Rates Subject to Change   *Suites Motel* ◆◆◆
All year [CP]   1P .... 124.00   2P/1B   .... 124.00   2P/2B   .... 149.00   XP
159 units. 3/4 mi se from jct US 101 & SR 92; exit SR 92 via Edgewater Blvd. 2000 Winward Way. (94404) 1-bedroom & 2-story 2-bedroom suites with living room & kitchen; patio or balcony; many fireplaces. Check-in 3 pm. A/C; C/CATV; movies; radios; phones. Coin laundry. Pool; whirlpools. Airport transp. Pets, $50 also $6 daily extra charge. Wkly rates avail. Reserv deposit required. Complimentary beverages each evening. AE, DI, DS, MC, VI. FAX (415) 572-9084
          ⊗ Ⓓ ⚿ (415) 574-4700

RESTAURANTS

Borel's Restaurant 71   American $$ ◆◆
Off SR 92, exit s via W Hillsdale Blvd. 2951 Campus Dr. Modern decor. View of San Francisco Bay. Prime rib & seafood. A/C. Open 11:30 am-2 & 6-9:30 pm; Sat 5:30 pm-10:30 pm; Sun 10:30 am-2:30 & 5:30-9:30 pm; closed 12/25. Cocktails & lounge. Minimum $3. Reserv advised. AE, CB, DI, MC, VI.   ⊗ (415) 341-7464

Tino's European Restaurant 70   Italian $$ ◆◆
On SR 82; 1/2 mi n of jct SR 92. 1206 S El Camino Real. Continental cuisine also. A/C. Open 5 pm-11 pm; closed Sun, Mon, 11/25, 12/25 & 7/1-7/19. Cocktails & lounge. Reserv advised. MC, VI.   (415) 573-7555

SAN MIGUEL

San Miguel Mission Inn   Rates Subject to Change   *Motel* ◆◆
5/16-9/15   1P .... 38.00   2P/1B   .... 41.00   2P/2B   .... 45.00   XP 3   F
9/16-5/15   1P .... 30.00   2P/1B   .... 33.00   2P/2B   .... 40.00   XP 3   F
Senior discount. 16 units. Adjacent e side of US 101, 1/4 mi ne of 10th St exit. 1099 K St. (PO Box 58, 93451) A/C; C/CATV; movies; radios; phones. Pets, $10 extra charge. 4 rooms with microwave & refrigerator. Wkly rates avail. MC, VI.   ⊗ Ⓓ (805) 467-3674

SAN PEDRO — 70,900

Best Western San Pedro Grand Hotel   **AAA Special Value Rates**   *Hotel*   ◆◆◆
All year [BP]   1P 85.00- 105.00   2P/1B   95.00- 110.00   2P/2B   95.00- 110.00 XP 10
60 units. 2 blks s of SR 110. 111 S Gaffey. (90731) Beautifully decorated in an Old World, European ambiance.
Check-in 3 pm. Refrigerators; A/C; C/CATV; movies; radios; phones. Small htd pool; whirlpool. Garage. No pets.
4 efficiencies, $10 extra. 4 suites with fireplace, $199-$219. AE, DI, DS, MC, VI. ● Dining rm; 11:30 am-2 &
5:30-10 pm; Sun 10 am-2 pm; $11-$18; cocktails. FAX (310) 831-8262 *(See ad p A468)* ⊗ Ⓓ ⓓ (310) 514-1414

Doubletree Hotel-Los Angeles World Port   **Rates Guaranteed**   *Motor Inn*   ◆◆◆
All year [BP]   1P 79.00- 89.00   2P/1B   89.00- 99.00   2P/2B   89.00- 109.00 XP 10   F
Senior discount. 226 units. 1/4 mi w of 22nd St, at Cabrillo Marina. 2800 Via Cabrillo Marina. (90731) Many rooms
overlooking marina. Check-in 3 pm. A/C; C/CATV; free & pay movies; radios; phones. Htd pool; sauna; whirlpool;
lighted tennis-2 courts; rental bicycles; exercise rm. No pets. Monthly rates avail. Complimentary beverages
each evening. AE, DI, DS, MC, VI. ● 2 restaurants; 6:30 am-10 pm; $10-$20; cocktails. Also, Madeo, see separate listing. FAX (310) 514-8945 *(See ad below)* ⊗ Ⓢ Ⓓ ⓓ (310) 514-3344

Pacific Inn   **Rates Guaranteed**   *Motel*   ◆◆
All year   1P 45.00- 50.00   2P/1B   45.00- 50.00   2P/2B .... 55.00 XP 5   F
Senior discount. 24 units. Corner Pacific & 38th sts. 516 W 38th St. (90731) 2 1/2 blocks from Cabrillo Beach.
C/TV; radios; phones. 2 2-bedrm units. Coin laundry. No pets. 18 1-bedroom units with living room & efficiency,
$5 extra charge; utensils deposit required. Wkly rates avail. Reserv deposit required; 7 days refund notice. AE,
MC, VI.   Ⓓ (310) 514-1247

Sheraton-Los Angeles Harbor Hotel   **Rates Subject to Change**   *Hotel*   ◆◆◆◆
All year   1P .... 79.00   2P/1B .... 89.00   2P/2B .... 89.00 XP 10
244 units. 601 S Palos Verdes St at 6th St. (90731) Check-in 3 pm. A/C; C/CATV; movies; radios; phones. Htd
pool; sauna; whirlpool; exercise rm. Valet parking lot. No pets. AE, DI, DS, MC, VI. ● Moonraker, see separate
listing. FAX (310) 519-8421   ⊗ Ⓢ Ⓓ ⓓ (310) 519-8200

Sunrise Best Western Hotel   Rates Guaranteed   *Motel* ◆◆
Ⓐ Mon-Thurs [CP]   1P 68.00- 125.00   2P/1B 68.00- 125.00   2P/2B 74.00- 125.00 XP 8   F
    Fri-Sun [CP]   1P 61.00- 99.00   2P/1B 61.00- 99.00   2P/2B 66.00- 125.00 XP 8   F
    112 units. 1/2 mi s of I-110, Harbor Blvd exit. 525 S Harbor Blvd. (90731) Across from Los Angeles Maritime Museum. 49 refrigerators; A/C; C/TV; movies; radios; phones. Htd pool; whirlpool. No pets. AE, DI, DS, MC, VI. Coffeeshop adjacent. FAX (310) 519-0380 *(See ad below)*   Ⓧ Ⓓ Ⓖ (310) 548-1080

Vagabond Inn   Rates Subject to Change   *Motel* ◆◆
Ⓐ All year [CP]   1P 44.00- 58.00   2P/1B 49.00- 62.00   2P/2B 54.00- 67.00 XP 5   F
    74 units. 2 blks s of SR 110. 215 S Gaffey. (90731) A/C; C/CATV; movies; radios; phones. Htd pool. Pets, $5 extra charge. AE, DI, DS, MC, VI. Coffeeshop adjacent. FAX (310) 831-2649 *(See ad p A469)*   Ⓧ Ⓓ (310) 831-8911

RESTAURANTS

Madeo Ristorante   Regional Italian $$ ◆◆◆
At the Doubletree Hotel-Los Angeles World Port. Varied selection of salad, pasta, seafood & steak. Buffet 11:30 am-2:30 pm. A/C. Open 11:30 am-2:30 & 5:30-10:30 pm; Fri & Sat-11:30 pm. Cocktails & lounge. AE, DI, DS, MC, VI.   Ⓧ (310) 831-1199

Moonraker   Seafood $$ ◆◆◆
In the Sheraton Los Angeles Harbor Hotel. Selections of fresh seafood, veal, lamb, steak, chicken, prime rib & pasta. Breakfast & lunch buffet Mon-Fri. A/C. Children's menu. Open 6 am-10 pm. Cocktails & lounge. Entertainment & dancing. Pay valet parking. Reserv advised. AE, DI, DS, MC, VI.   Ⓧ (310) 519-8200

Nizetich's Restaurant   Continental $$ ◆◆◆
At Ports O'Call Village. 1050 Nagoya St. Beautiful restaurant with view of Los Angeles Harbor. A/C. Open 11:30 am-2 & 5:30-10 pm; Fri-11 pm; Sat 5:30 pm-11 pm; Sun 5 pm-9 pm; closed Tues, 1/1, 12/24 for dinner & 12/25. Cocktails & lounge. Entertainment. Reserv advised. AE, MC, VI.   Ⓧ (310) 514-3878

SAN RAFAEL — 48,400   See also CORTE MADERA

Embassy Suites Hotel   AAA Special Value Rates   *Suites Hotel* ◆◆◆◆
    All year [BP]   1P 99.00- 150.00   2P/1B 99.00- 165.00   2P/2B 99.00- 165.00 XP 15   F
    235 units. US 101 northbound exit e San Pedro Dr, southbound exit Freitas Pkwy; adjacent to Marin Conty Civic Center. 101 McInnis Pkwy. (94903) Garden atrium. Check-in 3 pm. A/C; C/CATV; free & pay movies; radios; phones. Coin laundry. Htd indoor pool; whirlpool; exercise rm. Parking lot. Pets, $50 deposit required. Complimentary beverages each evening. AE, DI, DS, MC, VI. ● Restaurant; 11 am-10 pm; Fri & Sat-11 pm; a la carte entrees about $8-$20; cocktails. FAX (415) 499-9268   Ⓧ Ⓢ Ⓓ Ⓖ (415) 499-9222

Holiday Inn   Rates Subject to Change   *Hotel* ◆◆◆
    All year   1P 89.00- 110.00   2P/1B 99.00- 122.00   2P/2B 99.00- 122.00 XP 12
    224 units. 3 mi n in Terra Linda, off US 101; exit Terra Linda off-ramp. 1010 Northgate Dr. (94903) On knoll overlooking valley & hills. A/C; C/CATV; free & pay movies; radios; phones. Pool; whirlpool; exercise rm. Parking lot. Pets, $50 deposit required. 5 suites, $200-$250 for up to 4 persons. Reserv deposit required. AE, DI, DS, MC, VI. ● Restaurant; 6:30 am-2:30 & 5:30-10 pm; $9-$15; cocktails. FAX (415) 479-6739 *(See ad p A471)*   Ⓧ Ⓓ Ⓖ (415) 479-8800

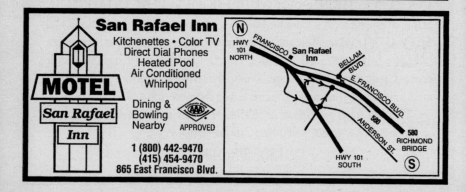

San Rafael Inn ♿
6/15-9/30   **Rates Subject to Change**   *Motel*   ◆
6/15-9/30   1P 48.00- 54.00   2P/1B   50.00- 60.00   2P/2B   56.00- 65.00   XP   5
10/1-6/14   1P 40.00- 46.00   2P/1B   46.00- 54.00   2P/2B   50.00- 56.00   XP   5
Senior discount. 32 units. Off US 101; exit E Francisco Blvd, 1 blk n. 865 Francisco Blvd E. (94901) A/C; C/TV; movies; radios; phones; comb or shower baths. 2 2-bedrm units, 4 efficiencies, no utensils. Small pool; whirlpool. No pets. 2 rooms with whirlpool bath, extra charge. Reserv deposit required. AE, CB, DI, MC, VI. *(See ad p A470)*   ⊗ Ⓓ (415) 454-9470

Villa Inn ♿
All year   **Rates Subject to Change**   *Motel*   ◆◆
All year   1P 58.50- 68.00   2P/1B   63.50- 75.00   2P/2B   66.50- 80.00   XP   5   F
Senior discount. 60 units. Off US 101; southbound Lincoln Ave off-ramp, northbound Central San Rafael exit, 3 blks n then 3 blks w on Fourth St. 1600 Lincoln Ave. (94901) Refrigerators; A/C; C/CATV; radios; phones; shower or comb baths. 3 2-bedrm units. Coin laundry. Htd pool; whirlpool. Pets, $20; no cats extra charge. 3-night minimum stay in 9 kitchens, $8 extra. Reserv deposit required. AE, DI, DS, MC, VI. Cocktail lounge; restaurant adjacent. *(See ad below)*   ⊗ Ⓓ (415) 456-4975

RESTAURANT

Le Chalet Basque   French $$ ◆
1 mi e of Marin Civic Center. 405 N San Pedro Rd. Family dinners. Patio dining, weather permitting. A/C. Children's menu. Open 11:30 am-2 & 5-10 pm; Sat from 5 pm; Sun 10:30 am-2 & 4-9 pm; closed Mon, 11/26, 12/25, last 2 weeks of Aug & 1st week of Sept. Cocktails & lounge. Minimum $4. Reserv advised. MC, VI.   ⊗ (415) 479-1070

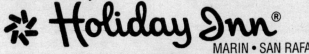

SAN RAMON — 35,300   (See OAKLAND/BERKELEY AREA spotting map pages A300 & A301; see index starting on page A298)   See also LIVERMORE & PLEASANTON

Residence Inn by Marriott 57

		Rates Subject to Change				Suites Motel	◆◆◆
Sun-Thurs [CP]	1P	.... 109.00	2P/1B	.... 109.00	2P/2B	.... 139.00	XP
Fri & Sat [CP]	1P	.... 79.00	2P/1B	.... 79.00	2P/2B	.... 109.00	XP

106 units. E of I-680, exit Bollinger Canyon Rd. 1071 Market Pl. (94583) Some units with 2-bedrooms & 2-baths, some fireplaces. A/C; C/CATV; movies; radios; phones. 24 2-bedrm units, kitchens. Coin laundry. Pool; whirlpool; sports court; exercise rm. Pets, $75, also $5 daily extra charge. Wkly & monthly rates avail. Reserv deposit required. Complimentary beverages each evening. AE, DI, DS, MC, VI. FAX (510) 277-0687   ⊗ Ⓢ Ⓓ 🅱 (510) 277-9292

San Ramon Marriott At Bishop Ranch 56

		Rates Guaranteed				Hotel	◆◆◆
ⓐ Sun-Thurs	1P	.... 135.00	2P/1B	.... 145.00	2P/2B	.... 145.00	XP 10
Fri & Sat	1P	85.00- 100.00	2P/1B	85.00- 100.00	2P/2B	85.00- 100.00	XP

Senior discount. 368 units. Exit I-680 Bollinger Canyon Rd E; N Sunset; w on Bishop Dr. 2600 Bishop Dr. (94583) Very attractive rooms & public areas. Check-in 3 pm. A/C; C/CATV; movies; radios; phones. Coin laundry. Htd indoor/outdoor pool; saunas; indoor whirlpool; exercise rm. Valet parking lot. Pets. AE, DI, DS, MC, VI. ● Restaurant; 6 am-11 pm; $10-$16; cocktail lounge; nightclub. FAX (510) 275-9443
   ⊗ Ⓢ Ⓓ 🅱 (510) 867-9200

SAN SIMEON — See also CAMBRIA

Best Western Green Tree Inn

		Rates Subject to Change				Motel	◆◆◆
ⓐ 6/16-9/30	1P	.... 68.00	2P/1B	.... 68.00	2P/2B	.... 72.25	XP 10
10/1-6/15	1P	.... 55.25	2P/1B	.... 55.25	2P/2B	.... 59.50	XP 10

Senior discount. 115 units. 3 1/2 mi s on SR 1. 9250 Castillo Dr. (93452) Check-in 3 pm. A/C; C/CATV; movies; phones. 25 efficiencies. Coin laundry. Htd indoor pool; whirlpool; lighted tennis-2 courts. No pets. AE, DI, DS, MC, VI. Restaurant adjacent. FAX (805) 927-1473 *(See ad p A473)*   ⊗ Ⓓ 🅱 (805) 927-4691

California Seacoast Lodge   Rates Subject to Change   *Motel*   ◆◆◆
6/1-9/30 [CP]   ....   2P/1B   65.00- 100.00   2P/2B   65.00- 100.00   XP   5
10/1-5/31 [CP]   ....   2P/1B   55.00- 95.00   2P/2B   55.00- 95.00   XP   5
57 units. 3 1/2 mi s on SR 1. 9215 Hearst Dr. (93452) Many rooms with ocean view, 36 gas-log fireplaces. Check-in 3 pm. 37 refrigerators; C/CATV; VCPs; phones. Small htd pool. No pets. 14 rooms with whirlpool tub, $80-$125. Reserv deposit required; 3 days refund notice. AE, DI, MC, VI. *(See ad p A475)*   ⊗ Ⓓ 🅖 (805) 927-3878

Carriage Inn   Rates Guaranteed   *Motor Inn*   ◆◆◆
6/1-9/30   ....   2P/1B   65.00- 115.00   2P/2B   73.00- 120.00   XP   5
10/1-5/31   ....   2P/1B   50.00- 95.00   2P/2B   55.00- 100.00   XP   5
Senior discount. 48 units. 3 1/2 mi s on SR 1. 9280 Castillo Dr. (93452) Spacious rooms. 6 refrigerators; C/CATV; phones. Whirlpool; indoor whirlpool. No pets. Reserv deposit required. AE, DS, MC, VI. ● Restaurant; 6:30 am-8 pm; $7.70-$11.70; beer & wine. FAX (805) 927-4800   ⊗ Ⓓ (805) 927-9659

El Rey Inn   Rates Subject to Change   *Motor Inn*   ◆◆◆
6/7-9/5, Fri & Sat 4/2-6/6 &
9/6-10/31 [CP]   ....   2P/1B   74.00- 94.00   2P/2B   ....   74.00   XP   5
Sun-Thurs 11/1-4/1, 9/6-6/6 &
Fri-Sat 11/1-4/1 [CP]   ....   2P/1B   64.00- 84.00   2P/2B   ....   64.00   XP   5
Senior discount. 56 units. 3 1/2 mi s on SR 1. 9260 Castillo Dr. (PO Box 200, 93452) Spacious rooms, some with ocean view. Some gas fireplaces, many balconies. 12 refrigerators; C/CATV; movies; phones. 2 2-bedrm units. Coin laundry. Small htd pool; whirlpools; 10 rooms with whirlpool tub. No pets. 2 2-room suites with whirlpool $139-$159. Reserv deposit required. AE, DS, MC, VI. Restaurant; 5:30 pm-9 pm; $12.95-$16.95; beer & wine. FAX (805) 927-8268 *(See ad p A476)*   Ⓓ (805) 927-3998

San Simeon Lodge   Rates Subject to Change   *Motor Inn*   ◆
6/1-9/30   ....   2P/1B   50.00- 70.00   2P/2B   50.00- 75.00   XP   5
10/1-5/31   ....   2P/1B   35.00- 50.00   2P/2B   40.00- 100.00   XP   5
63 units. 3 1/2 mi s on SR 1. 9520 Castillo Dr. (93452) Check-in 3 pm. C/CATV; phones; shower or comb baths. Htd pool. No pets. 2 4-bedroom units. Reserv deposit required; 3 days refund notice. AE, DI, MC, VI. ● Restaurant; 7 am-2 & 5-9 pm; $10-$15; cocktails. *(See ad p A478)*   ⊗ Ⓓ (805) 927-4601

Silver Surf Motel

		Rates Guaranteed					*Motel*	◆◆
7/2-9/5	....	2P/1B	55.00-	65.00	2P/2B	55.00-	80.00	XP	5
9/6-7/1	....	2P/1B	35.00-	45.00	2P/2B	35.00-	65.00	XP	5

Senior discount. 72 units. 3 1/2 mi s on SR 1. 9390 Castillo Dr. (93452) Some rooms with ocean view. Some balconies. Check-in 3 pm. C/CATV; phones; shower or comb baths. 1 2-bedrm unit. Small htd indoor pool; whirlpool. 4 rooms with gas fireplace, $49-$85. Reserv deposit required. AE, DI, DS, MC, VI. Restaurant adjacent. FAX (805) 927-3225 *(See ad p A473)*   ⊗ Ⓓ (805) 927-4661

RESTAURANT

Europa Restaurant — Continental — $$ — ◆◆
3 1/2 mi s on SR 1. 9240 Castillo Dr. American & European food with homemade touch. Specialties include fresh seafood, pasta & desserts made on premises. Smoke free premises. A/C. Children's menu. Open 5:30 pm-9 pm; closed 12/1-12/25. Beer & wine. Minimum, $8. MC, VI.   ⊗ (805) 927-3087

SANTA ANA — 293,700

Best Western Santa Anna Inn

| | | Rates Subject to Change | | | | | | *Motel* | ◆◆ |
| All year | | 1P 50.00- | 54.00 | 2P/1B | 54.00- | 64.00 | 2P/2B | 54.00- | 64.00 | XP | 6 |

Senior discount. 122 units. 1/4 mi n of I-5, exit Main St. 2600 N Main St. (92701) 40 refrigerators; A/C; C/CATV; movies; radios; phones. Htd pool; whirlpool. No pets. AE, DI, DS, MC, VI. Restaurant adjacent. FAX (714) 543-0841   ⊗ Ⓓ Ⓖ (714) 836-5141

See the Sample Listing in the front of this book.

Comfort Suites — AAA Special Value Rates — *Motel* ◆◆◆
All year [CP]   1P 55.00- 59.00   2P/1B   65.00- 69.00   2P/2B   71.00- 75.00   XP 10   F
130 units. 1 blk w of SR 55, exit Dyer Rd. 2620 Hotel Terrace Dr. (92701) A/C; C/CATV; movies; VCPs. Radios; phones.
Coin laundry. Htd pool; whirlpool. Airport transp. No pets. Microwaves. Wkly & monthly rates avail. AE, DI, DS, MC, VI.
Restaurant opposite. FAX (714) 979-9650   ⊗ ⑤Ⓓ🖢 (714) 966-5200

Courtyard by Marriott — Rates Subject to Change — *Motor Inn* ◆◆◆
⚅ All year   1P .... 59.00   2P/1B .... 59.00   2P/2B .... 59.00   XP 10
145 units. 1 1/2 mi n of I-405, Harbor Blvd exit. 3002 S Harbor Blvd. (92704) Check-in 3 pm. 5 refrigerators; A/C;
C/CATV; movies; radios; phones. Coin laundry. Htd pool; indoor whirlpool; exercise rm. No pets. Wkly rates
avail. AE, DI, DS, MC, VI. ● Dining rm; 6:30 am-2 & 5-10 pm; Sat & Sun from 7 am; $8.25-$13.25; cocktails.
FAX (714) 545-8439   ⊗ ⑤Ⓓ🖢 (714) 545-1001

GOING UP?
Expect elevators in establishments of four or more stories.
We tell you in the listings if there are none.

Crown Sterling Suites Orange County Airport   Rates Subject to Change   *Suites Motor Inn*   ◆◆◆

Sun-Thurs [BP]	1P	....	99.00	2P/1B	.... 109.00	2P/2B	.... 109.00	XP 10	F
Fri & Sat 6/1-9/15 [BP]	1P	....	89.00	2P/1B	60.00- 89.00	2P/2B	.... 89.00	XP 10	F
Fri & Sat 9/16-5/31 [BP]	1P	....	79.00	2P/1B	.... 79.00	2P/2B	.... 79.00	XP 10	F

306 units. Adjacent to SR 55; exit Dyer Rd. 1325 E Dyer Rd. (92705) Beautifully landscaped atruim area. 1-bedroom suites with living room, refrigerator & microwave. A/C; C/CATV; free & pay movies; radios; phones. Htd indoor pool; sauna; whirlpool; steamroom. Airport transp. No pets. Monthly rates avail. Complimentary beverages each evening. AE, DI, DS, MC, VI. ● Dining rm; 11 am-11 pm; $9.75-$23.50; cocktails; entertainment. FAX (714) 662-1651 *(See ad below)*   ⊗ Ⓢ Ⓓ Ⓛ (714) 241-3800

Days Inn   AAA Special Value Rates   *Motor Inn*   ◆

All year	1P	55.00- 75.00	2P/1B	60.00- 75.00	2P/2B	60.00- 75.00	XP 10	F

146 units. 3 blks w of I-5, First St exit. 1600 E First St. (92701) Check-in 3 pm. 15 refrigerators; A/C; C/CATV; movies; 75 radios; phones. Htd pool; saunas; indoor whirlpool; exercise rm. Airport transp. Pets, $35 deposit required. Reserv deposit required. AE, DI, DS, MC, VI. ● Restaurant; 6 am-2 & 5-9 pm; $5.95-$10.95; cocktails. FAX (714) 543-0856   ⊗ Ⓢ Ⓓ (714) 835-3051

Doubletree Club Hotel — Rates Guaranteed — *Motel* ◆◆◆
Sun-Thurs [BP] ... 1P .... 73.00 2P/1B .... 83.00 2P/2B .... 83.00 XP 10 ... F
Fri & Sat [BP] ... 1P .... 53.00 2P/1B .... 53.00 2P/2B .... 53.00 XP ... F
Senior discount. 170 units. 1 blk w of SR 55, exit MacArthur Blvd. 7 Hutton Centre Dr. (92707) Check-in 3 pm. A/C; C/CATV; free & pay movies; radios; phones; comb or shower baths. Htd pool; whirlpool; exercise rm. Airport transp. No pets. Wkly & monthly rates avail. Reserv deposit required. Complimentary beverages each evening. AE, DI, DS, MC, VI. Cocktail lounge. FAX (714) 662-7935 *(See ad p A478)* ⊗ Ⓢ Ⓓ Ⓛ (714) 751-2400

Howard Johnson Lodge — Rates Guaranteed — *Motel* ◆◆◆
All year [CP] ... 1P 49.00- 59.00 2P/1B 49.00- 59.00 2P/2B 54.00- 64.00 XP 5 ... F
Senior discount. 144 units. 1 blk w of SR 55, exit Dyer Rd W. 2700 Hotel Terrace Dr. (92705) A/C; C/CATV; movies; radios; phones. Rental refrigerators. Htd pool; whirlpool; exercise rm. No pets. Some rooms with refrigerator & microwave, $5 extra. Wkly rates avail. AE, DI, DS, MC, VI. FAX (714) 434-6228 *(See ad p A17 and p A162)* ⊗ Ⓢ Ⓓ Ⓛ (714) 432-8888

Howard Johnson Motor Lodge — AAA Special Value Rates — *Motor Inn* ◆◆
All year ... 1P 46.00- 56.00 2P/1B 56.00- 66.00 2P/2B 61.00- 71.00 XP 5 ... F
155 units. 1/4 mi e of I-5, exit 17th St. 939 E 17th St. (92701) 62 refrigerators; A/C; C/CATV; movies; radios; phones. 2 efficiencies. Coin laundry. Htd pool; sauna; whirlpool. Small pets only. Wkly rates avail. AE, DI, DS, MC, VI. Coffeeshop; 6 am-2 pm; Sat & Sun 7 am-12 pm. FAX (714) 568-1641 *(See ad below)* ⊗ Ⓓ (714) 558-3700

Irvine Host Hotel-Best Western — Rates Guaranteed — *Motor Inn* ◆◆◆
All year [CP] ... 1P 52.20- 55.80 2P/1B 52.20- 55.80 2P/2B 52.20- 55.80 XP 8
Senior discount. 150 units. 1/2 blk e of SR 55, exit Dyer Rd. 1717 E Dyer Rd. (92705) A/C; C/CATV; movies; VCPs. Phones. Coin laundry. Htd pool; sauna; whirlpool. Airport transp. No pets. Microwaves & refrigerators. Wkly & monthly rates avail. AE, DI, DS, MC, VI. ● Restaurant; 6 am-10:30 pm; Sat & Sun from 7 am; $7.50-$12; cocktails. FAX (714) 261-1265 *(See ad p A162)* ⊗ (714) 261-1515

Nendels Inn-Santa Ana — Rates Guaranteed — *Motor Inn* ◆
All year [CP] ... 1P .... 38.00 2P/1B .... 41.00 2P/2B .... 48.00 XP 5 ... ●
Senior discount. 52 units. 1/2 mi w of I-5; First St exit. 1519 E First St. (92701) Formerly Vagabond Inn. A/C; C/CATV; movies; radios; phones. Rental refrigerators. 2 2-bedrm units. Htd pool; playground. Pets, $3 extra charge. Wkly rates avail. AE, DI, DS, MC, VI. ● Coffeeshop; 6 am-10 pm; $4.95-$9.95; beer & wine. FAX (714) 547-4327 ⊗ Ⓓ (714) 547-9426

Orange Tree Motel — Rates Guaranteed — *Motel* ◆
All year ... 1P 30.00- 34.00 2P/1B 34.00- 40.00 2P/2B 36.00- 42.00 XP 4
48 units. 1/2 blk s of SR 22, Glassell St exit. 2720 N Grand Ave. (92701) 32 refrigerators; A/C; C/CATV; movies; phones. Small pool. No pets. Reserv deposit required. AE, DI, DS, MC, VI. Ⓓ (714) 997-2330

Quality Suites — AAA Special Value Rates — *Suites Motel* ◆◆◆
All year [BP] ... 1P 85.00- 95.00 2P/1B 85.00- 95.00 2P/2B 85.00- 95.00 XP 10 ... F
177 units. 1 blk w of SR 55, exit Dyer Rd. 2701 Hotel Terrace Dr. (92705) 1-bedroom suites with living room & microwave. A/C; C/CATV; movies; VCPs. Radios; phones. Coin laundry. Htd pool; whirlpool. Airport transp. No pets. Wkly & monthly rates avail. Complimentary beverages each evening. AE, DI, DS, MC, VI. FAX (714) 641-8936 *(See ad below)* ⊗ Ⓢ Ⓓ (714) 957-9200

Radisson Suite Hotel-Santa Ana — Rates Guaranteed — *Suites Motel* ◆◆◆
All year [BP] ... 1P 89.00- 105.00 2P/1B 89.00- 105.00 2P/2B 95.00- 115.00 XP
Senior discount. 122 units. 1 blk w of SR 55, exit Dyer Rd. 2710 Hotel Terrace Dr. (92705) Check-in 3 pm. Refrigerators; A/C; C/CATV; free & pay movies; radios; phones. Htd pool; whirlpool; exercise rm. Parking lot. Airport transp. No pets. Reserv deposit required; 3 days refund notice. AE, DI, DS, MC, VI. FAX (714) 241-1008 *(See ads p A162 and starting on p A10)* ⊗ Ⓢ Ⓓ (714) 556-3838

Ramada Hotel   AAA Special Value Rates   *Motor Inn*   ◆◆◆
⊕ All year   1P 69.00- 99.00   2P/1B   69.00- 99.00   2P/2B   69.00- 99.00 XP   F
183 units. Adjacent to SR 55, exit Dyer Rd. 2726 S Grand Ave. (92705) A/C; C/CATV; pay movies; radios; phones. Coin laundry. Htd pool; whirlpool; exercise rm. Airport transp. No pets. 115 rooms with microwave & refrigerator. Wkly & monthly rates avail. Reserv deposit required. AE, DI, DS, MC, VI. ● Dining rm & coffeeshop; 6 am-2 & 4-11 pm; $6-$13.95; cocktails. FAX (714) 966-1889 *(See ad below)*   ⊗ Ⓢ Ⓓ ⊠   (714) 966-1955

Rodeway Inn Harbor Park   Rates Subject to Change   *Motel*   ◆◆◆
⊕ All year   1P 35.00- 45.00   2P/1B   40.00- 50.00   2P/2B   45.00- 60.00 XP   5   F
Senior discount. 88 units. 1 mi s of SR 22; Harbor Blvd exit. 1104 N Harbor Blvd. (92703) A/C; C/CATV; movies; VCPs. Radios; phones. 34 efficiencies, no utensils. Coin laundry. Htd pool; saunas; whirlpool; 8 rooms with whirlpool. No pets. Wkly rates avail. Reserv deposit required. AE, DI, DS, MC, VI. FAX (714) 554-7538   Ⓢ Ⓓ ⊠ (714) 554-1177

RESTAURANTS

Antonello Ristorante   Northern Italian $$$ ◆◆◆◆
In South Coast Plaza Village; 1/2 blk n of Sunflower; 1 blk w of Bristol. 3800 S Plaza Dr. An elegant restaurant. A/C. Open 11:30 am-2 & 5:45-10 pm; Fri-11 pm; Sat 5:45 pm-11 pm; closed Sun & major holidays. Cocktails & lounge. Valet parking. Reserv advised. AE, CB, DI, MC, VI.   ⊗ (714) 751-7153

Gandhi Indian Cuisine   Ethnic $$ ◆◆
In South Coast Plaza Village; 1 blk w of Bristol. 1621-D Sunflower. Attractively decorated restaurant specializing in curry & tandoori dishes. Open 11:30 am-2:30 & 5:30-10 pm; Fri-11 pm; closed 1/1, 11/25 & 12/25. Cocktails. AE, DI, MC, VI.   ⊗ (714) 556-7273

SANTA BARBARA — 85,600   (See SANTA BARBARA AREA spotting map page A482; see index below)

Index of Establishments on the SANTA BARBARA AREA Spotting Map

(See SANTA BARBARA spotting map page A482)

El Encanto Hotel & Garden Villas	㊸
ⓐ Villa Rosa	㊹
ⓐ Blue Quail Inn	㊺
ⓐ The Upham	㊻
ⓐ Hacienda Motel	㊼

RESTAURANTS

Michael's Waterside	①
Wine Cask Restaurant	②
Maxis	③
Downey's	④

Andria's Harborside Restaurant	⑤
Original Enterprise Fish Company	⑥
Cattlemen's Restaurant	⑦
Citronelle Restaurant	⑧
The Palace Cafe	⑨
The Chart House	⑩
Cafe del Sol	⑪
Ristorante Piatti	⑫
Chad's	⑬

Ambassador By The Sea Motel ⑪   Rates Subject to Change   *Motel*   ◆◆
ⓐ 5/1-10/1   ....   2P/1B   88.00- 158.00   2P/2B   88.00- 128.00   XP 10
10/2-4/30   ....   2P/1B   58.00- 128.00   2P/2B   58.00- 98.00   XP 10
32 units. 3 blks s of US 101, between Bath St & Chapala. 202 W Cabrillo Blvd. (93101) Across from beach with spacious grounds. C/TV; radios; phones; shower or comb baths. 4 2-bedrm units. Small htd pool. No pets. 2 efficiencies, $10 extra. Reserv deposit required. AE, DI, DS, MC, VI. FAX (805) 965-9937   Ⓓ (805) 965-4577

Bath Street Inn ㉙   Rates Subject to Change   *Bed & Breakfast*   ◆◆
7/1-9/30 & Fri-Sat [BP]   1P   90.00- 120.00   2P/1B   95.00- 125.00   ....   XP 15
Sun-Thurs 10/1-6/30 [BP]   1P   70.00- 100.00   2P/1B   75.00- 105.00   ....   XP 15
8 units. 2 1/2 blks s of Mission St. 1720 Bath St. (93101) 1873 Queen Anne Victorian house in residential area. Smoke free premises. 3 radios; shower or comb baths. Bicycles. No pets. 2-night minimum stay weekends. Reserv deposit required; 3 days refund notice. AE, MC, VI. *(See ad below)*   ⊗ Ⓓ (805) 682-9680

Bayberry Inn ㉗   Rates Subject to Change   *Bed & Breakfast*   ◆◆
All year   1P   85.00- 135.00   2P/1B   85.00- 135.00   ....   XP
8 units. 111 W Valerio St at Chapala. (93101) 1886 Federal style house located in residential area. 4 units with wood-burning fireplace. Smoke free premises. Check-in 3 pm. Comb or tub baths. 2 night minimum stay weekends. Reserv deposit required; 7 days refund notice. AE, DS, MC, VI.   ⊗ Ⓓ (805) 682-3199

Best Western-El Patio Beachside Inn ⑬   AAA Special Value Rates   *Motor Inn*   ◆◆
ⓐ 5/28-9/6   1P   94.00- 140.00   2P/1B   100.00- 140.00   2P/2B   104.00- 140.00   XP 8   F
9/7-5/27   1P   85.00- 132.00   2P/1B   91.00- 132.00   2P/2B   95.00- 132.00   XP 8   F
60 units. 4 blks s of US 101. 336 W Cabrillo Blvd & Castillo St. (93101) Across from beach & yacht harbor. Check-in 3 pm. A/C; C/CATV; movies; phones; comb or shower baths. 3 2-bedrm units. Htd pool. Small pets only, $20. Complimentary breakfast Mon-Fri. Wkly & monthly rates avail. AE, DI, DS, MC, VI. ● Andria's Harborside, see separate listing. FAX (805) 966-6626 *(See ad below)*   ⊗ Ⓓ (805) 965-6556

Best Western Encina Lodge ㉛   AAA Special Value Rates   *Motor Inn*   ◆◆◆
ⓐ All year   1P   98.00- 130.00   2P/1B   104.00- 134.00   2P/2B   104.00- 134.00   XP 6
122 units. 1/2 mi n of US 101; exit Mission St, 1 blk s of Santa Barbara Cottage Hospital. 2220 Bath St. (93105) Spacious grounds. Some patios & balconies. Check-in 3 pm. Refrigerators; 100 A/C; C/CATV; movies; radios; phones; comb or shower baths. Coin laundry. Htd pool; sauna; whirlpool. Airport transp. No pets. 33 1 & 2-bedroom kitchen apartments, 3 bi-level. Wkly & monthly rates avail. Reserv deposit required. AE, CB, DI, MC, VI. ● Restaurant; 7:30 am-9:30 pm; $11-$19; cocktails. FAX (805) 563-9319 *(See ad p A483)* Ⓓ (805) 682-7277

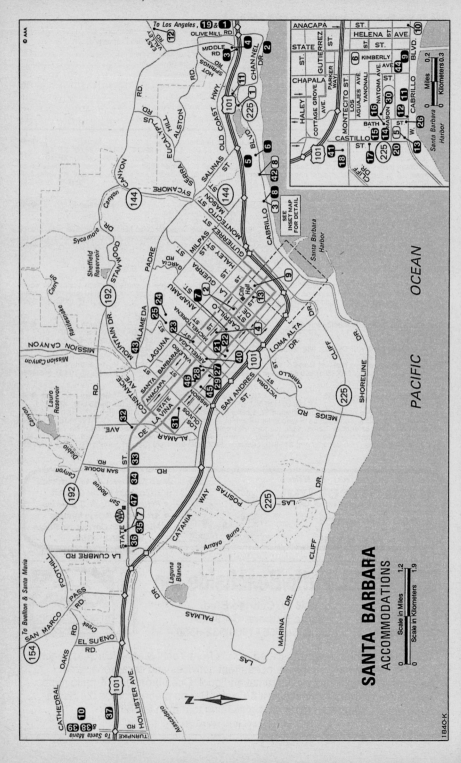

SANTA BARBARA
ACCOMMODATIONS

(See SANTA BARBARA spotting map page A482)

Best Western Pepper Tree Inn 36 ⊕
Rates Subject to Change — *Motor Inn* ◆◆◆

5/28-9/5 [CP]	1P	92.00- 116.00	2P/1B	98.00- 122.00	2P/2B	98.00- 122.00	XP 6
9/6-1/31 [CP]	1P	90.00- 114.00	2P/1B	96.00- 120.00	2P/2B	96.00- 120.00	XP 6
2/1-5/27 [CP]	1P	86.00- 110.00	2P/1B	92.00- 116.00	2P/2B	92.00- 116.00	XP 6

150 units. 3 1/2 mi nw; 1/2 mi e of jct US 101. 3850 State St. (93105) Attractively decorated rooms with patio or balcony. Check-in 3 pm. Refrigerators; A/C; C/CATV; movies; radios; phones. Coin laundry. 2 htd pools; sauna; whirlpools; exercise rm. Fee for: massage. Airport transp. No pets. Reserv deposit required. AE, DI, DS, MC, VI. ● Restaurant; 6 am-9:30 pm; Fri & Sat-11 pm; $8.50-$16; cocktails. FAX (805) 682-2410 *(See ad below)*
⊗ Ⓓ (805) 687-5511

Best Western South Coast Inn 39 ⊕
Rates Subject to Change — *Motel* ◆◆◆

All year [CP]	1P	89.00- 140.00	2P/1B	99.00- 140.00	2P/2B	99.00- 140.00	XP 10 F

121 units. 7 mi nw, adjacent to US 101; between Patterson & Fairview Ave exits. 5620 Calle Real. (Goleta, 93117) Check-in 3 pm. A/C; C/CATV; free & pay movies; phones. Htd pool; whirlpool. No pets. AE, DI, DS, MC, VI. FAX (805) 683-4466 *(See ad p A484)*
⊗ Ⓢ Ⓓ Ⓖ (805) 967-3200

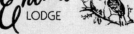

(See SANTA BARBARA spotting map page A482)

Blue Quail Inn 45   **Rates Subject to Change**   *Bed & Breakfast*   ◆◆
🅐🅑 5/16-10/31 & Fri-Sun 11/1-5/15
[BP]   ....   2P/1B   82.00- 165.00   ....   XP 20
Mon-Thurs 11/1-5/15 [BP]   ....   2P/1B   74.00- 149.00   ....   XP 20
9 units. From US 101, northbound exit Arrellaga St, southbound exit Mission. 1908 Bath St. (93101) Attractively furnished rooms in main house & cottages on nicely landscaped grounds. Designated smoking areas. Check-in 3 pm. 7 comb baths. No pets. 2-night minimum stay weekends. Reserv deposit required; 3 days refund notice. AE, MC, VI.   ⊗ Ⓓ (805) 687-2300

Cathedral Oaks Lodge 37   **Rates Subject to Change**   *Motel*   ◆◆◆
🅐🅑 All year [CP]   1P 74.00- 78.00   2P/1B   84.00- 88.00   2P/2B   84.00- 88.00 XP 10
126 units. 5 mi nw on US 101; exit Turnpike Rd, 1 blk n. 4770 Calle Real. (93110) Attractive, landscaped grounds. Many Balconies or patios. Check-in 3 pm. A/C; C/CATV; movies; phones. Rental refrigerators. 1 2-bedrm unit. Coin laundry. Htd pool; whirlpool. No pets. Reserv deposit required weekends. AE, CB, DI, MC, VI. Restaurant opposite. FAX (805) 964-0075 *(See ad p A485)*   ⊗ Ⓓ 🅖 (805) 964-3511

The Cheshire Cat 28   **Rates Subject to Change**   *Bed & Breakfast*   ◆◆◆
Fri-Sun [BP]   1P 119.00- 195.00   2P/1B   119.00- 249.00   ....   XP
Mon-Thurs [BP]   1P 75.00- 179.00   2P/1B   79.00- 190.00   ....   XP
14 units. 36 W Valerio St at Chapala. (93101) 1880 Queen Anne & Victorian homes located in residential area. 3 fireplaces. Smoking in designated areas. Check-in 3 pm. 3 refrigerators; 1 C/CATV; phones; shower or comb baths. Whirlpool; 3 rooms with whirlpool tub. No pets. 2-night minimum stay weekends. Reserv deposit required; 7 days refund notice. MC, VI.   ⊗ Ⓓ (805) 569-1610

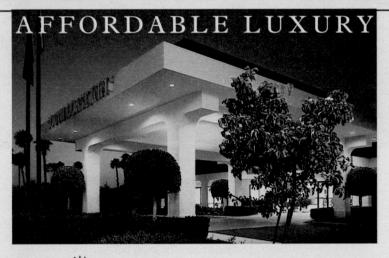

Choose an establishment with the 🅐🅑🅐 next to its listing!

One of the most beautiful lodges in the West....

126 beautiful rooms and suites with individual heat and air conditioning, each with private patio or balcony • Central Hall • Heated pool and jacuzzi • Remote control color cable TV with HBO movies • In-room brewed coffee • Bedside lighting controls. • Direct dial phones with free local calls • Children under 12 free • Complimentary full continental breakfast • Lush gardens • Lagoons with waterfall and fountain, friendly ducks and Koi fish • Five minutes to downtown, UCSB, shopping & entertainment.

**10%
SPECIAL
DISCOUNT
to
AAAMembers**

(off posted rates)

800-654-1965

Cathedral Oaks Lodge

(Formerly Turnpike Lodge)

4770 Calle Real, Santa Barbara 93110
(805) 964-3511 • Highway 101 at Turnpike Road Exit

(See SANTA BARBARA spotting map page A482)

Coast Village Inn ❹   Rates Subject to Change   *Motel*   ◆◆
ⓐ Fri-Sat 5/15-9/14 [CP]   1P   80.00- 95.00   2P/1B   80.00- 95.00   2P/2B   85.00- 95.00   XP   5   F
Fri-Sat 9/15-5/14 & Sun-Thurs
5/15-9/14 [CP]   1P   70.00- 85.00   2P/1B   70.00- 85.00   2P/2B   75.00- 85.00   XP   5   F
Sun-Thurs 9/15-5/14 [CP]   1P   60.00- 75.00   2P/1B   60.00- 75.00   2P/2B   65.00- 75.00   XP   5   F
Senior discount. 25 units. In Montecito, from US 101 exit Olive Mill Rd, then 1/4 mi N. 1188 Coast Village Rd.
(93108) Designated smoking areas. C/CATV; radios; phones; shower or comb baths. 2 kitchens. Htd pool. No
pets. Wkly & monthly rates avail. Reserv deposit required. AE, MC, VI. Restaurant adjacent. *(See ad p A484)*
                                                ⊗ Ⓓ (805) 969-3266

Eagle Inn ㉚   Rates Subject to Change   *Apartment Motel*   ◆◆
ⓐ Fri & Sat 6/11-9/30 [CP]   1P   85.00- 110.00   2P/1B   85.00- 110.00   2P/2B   90.00- 120.00   XP   5   F
Fri & Sat 10/1-6/10 [CP]   1P   75.00- 85.00   2P/1B   75.00- 85.00   2P/2B   85.00- 110.00   XP   5   F
Sun-Thurs 6/11-9/30 [CP]   1P   65.00- 70.00   2P/1B   65.00- 70.00   2P/2B   70.00- 95.00   XP   5   F
Sun-Thurs 10/1-6/10 [CP]   1P   50.00- 60.00   2P/1B   50.00- 60.00   2P/2B   60.00- 75.00   XP   5   F
Senior discount. 17 units. 3 blks s of US 101. 232 Natoma Ave at Bath St. (93101) 1 1/2 blocks to beach. C/CATV;
phones; comb or shower baths. 13 kitchens. Coin laundry. No pets. Wkly rates avail. AE, DI, DS, MC, VI.
                                                     Ⓓ (805) 965-3586

El Encanto Hotel & Garden Villas ㊸   Rates Subject to Change   *Cottages*   ◆◆◆
All year   1P   120.00- 350.00   2P/1B   120.00- 350.00   2P/2B   120.00- 350.00   XP   F
84 units. 1 1/2 mi n of US 101, exit Mission St; 1/2 mi e of Mission Santa Barbara. 1900 Lasuen Rd. (93103) Cottages
& bungalows on several acres of beautifully landscaped grounds. Check-in 3 pm. C/CATV; movies; radios; phones. 6
2-bedrm units. Htd pool; tennis-1 court. No pets. Monthly rates avail. Reserv deposit required; 3 days refund notice. AE,
DI, MC, VI. ● Dining rm; 7 am-9:30 pm; Fri & Sat-10 pm; a la carte entrees about $11-$18; cocktails.
FAX (805) 687-3903 *(See ad below)*   ⊗ (805) 687-5000

El Prado Motor Inn ㊵   Rates Subject to Change   *Motel*   ◆
ⓐ 6/1-9/15 [CP]   1P   55.00- 90.00   2P/1B   60.00- 90.00   2P/2B   60.00- 100.00   XP   5   F
9/16-5/31 [CP]   1P   50.00- 80.00   2P/1B   55.00- 80.00   2P/2B   55.00- 90.00   XP   5   F
66 units. 1601 State St. (93101) 22 refrigerators; A/C; C/CATV; movies; phones; comb or shower baths. Htd pool. 6 2-bedrm
units, 2 efficiencies. Htd pool. Garage & parking lot. No pets. Wkly & monthly rates avail. AE, DI, DS, MC, VI.
FAX (805) 966-6502   ⊗ Ⓓ (805) 966-0807

Fess Parker's Red Lion Resort ❽   Rates Subject to Change   *Motor Inn*   ◆◆◆◆
ⓐ All year   1P   190.00- 290.00   2P/1B   190.00- 290.00   2P/2B   190.00- 290.00   XP   15   F
360 units. 3 blks s of US 101 via Milpas St. 633 E Cabrillo Blvd. (93103) Across from beach on spacious landscaped
grounds. Balcony or patio. Check-in 4 pm. A/C; C/CATV; free & pay movies; radios; phones. Coin laundry. Htd pool;
sauna; whirlpool; putting green; rental bicycles; exercise rm. Fee for: lighted tennis-3 courts. Airport transp. Pets, $50
deposit required. Reserv deposit required; 3 days refund notice. AE, DI, DS, MC, VI. ● Coffeeshop; 6:30 am-11 pm;
$7-$12; cocktails. Also, Maxi's, see separate listing. FAX (805) 564-4964 *(See ad p A3)* ⊗ Ⓢ Ⓓ 🅿 (805) 564-4333

Four Seasons Biltmore ❷   Rates Subject to Change   *Resort Complex*   ◆◆◆
ⓐ All year   1P   290.00- 360.00   2P/1B   290.00- 360.00   2P/2B   290.00- 360.00   XP   30   F
234 units. 1/4 mi s of US 101, in Montecito area, exit Olive Mill Rd. 1260 Channel Dr. (93108) An elegant oceanfront resort on spacious, beautifully landscaped grounds. Spanish architecture. Large rooms in lodge & cottages. Garden or ocean views. Check-in 3 pm. Refrigerators; C/CATV; movies; VCPs. Radios; phones. 2 htd
pools; beach; saunas; whirlpools; putting green; social program; recreational program; children's program; bicycles. Fee for: lighted tennis-3 courts; massage. Pets, in cottages only. Reserv deposit required. AE, MC,
VI. ● 2 dining rms & restaurant; 6:30 am-10 pm; Fri & Sat 11:30 pm; $14-$40; afternoon tea 3 pm-5 pm; 24 hour
room service; cocktails; entertainment. FAX (805) 969-4212   ⊗ Ⓓ 🅿 (805) 969-2261

Franciscan Inn ⓰   Rates Subject to Change   *Motel*   ◆◆◆
ⓐ 5/15-9/15 & Fri-Sat 9/16-5/14
[CP]   1P   65.00- 85.00   2P/1B   75.00- 115.00   2P/2B   90.00- 145.00   XP   8
Sun-Thurs 9/16-5/14 [CP]   1P   55.00- 85.00   2P/1B   60.00- 89.00   2P/2B   70.00- 145.00   XP   8
53 units. 2 1/2 blks s of US 101. 109 Bath St. (93101) 1 block to beach. Check-in 3 pm. 30 refrigerators; 13 A/C;
C/CATV; movies; radios; phones; comb or shower baths. 4 2-bedrm units, 24 efficiencies. Coin laundry. Htd
pool; whirlpool. No pets. AE, CB, DI, MC, VI. FAX (805) 564-3295 *(See ad p A487)* ⊗ Ⓓ 🅿 (805) 963-8845

The Glenborough Inn ㉑   Rates Subject to Change   *Bed & Breakfast*   ◆◆
ⓐ 5/21-9/5 & Fri-Sat 9/6-5/20
[BP]   1P   65.00- 155.00   2P/1B   65.00- 155.00   ....   XP   10
Sun-Thurs 9/6-5/20 [BP]   1P   60.00- 120.00   2P/1B   60.00- 125.00   ....   XP   10
12 units. 1327 Bath St. (93101) 3 homes built in 1880's & early 1900's. Located in residential area. Smoke free
premises. Check-in 3 pm. 5 comb baths. Whirlpool. Parking lot. No pets. 3 suites with fireplace. 2 night-minimum
stay weekends. Monthly rates avail. Reserv deposit required; 7 days refund notice. AE, CB, DI, MC, VI.
                                                     ⊗ Ⓓ (805) 966-0589

(See SANTA BARBARA spotting map page A482)

Hacienda Motel ④			Rates Subject to Change					Motel			◆
⑩ 6/16-9/14		1P	54.00-	69.00	2P/1B	54.00-	74.00	2P/2B	64.00-	79.00	XP 5
9/15-6/15		1P	44.00-	54.00	2P/1B	44.00-	64.00	2P/2B	49.00-	69.00	XP 5

Senior discount. 31 units. 3643 State St. (93105) 26 refrigerators; C/CATV; movies; phones; shower or comb baths. 5 kitchens. No pets. Wkly rates avail. Reserv deposit required. AE, DI, MC, VI.   Ⓓ (805) 687-6461

(See SANTA BARBARA spotting map page A482)

Harbor View Inn ⑨   Rates Subject to Change   *Motel*   ◆◆◆
⊛ All year [CP]   1P 85.00-215.00 2P/1B 85.00-215.00 2P/2B 100.00-165.00 XP 15
64 units. 3 blks s of US 101; 1/2 blk w of State St. 28 W Cabrillo Blvd. (93101) Across from beach & Stearn's
Wharf. Comfortable original rooms to spacious, beautifully furnished rooms in newer wing. Check-in 3 pm. 34
refrigerators; 28 A/C; C/CATV; radios; phones; comb or shower baths. 2 2-bedrm units. Htd pool; whirlpool. No
pets. Reserv deposit required. Complimentary beverages each evening. AE, CB, DI, MC, VI. Restaurant adjacent.
FAX (805) 963-7967 *(See ad p A487)*   Ⓢ Ⓓ Ⓛ (805) 963-0780

Harbour Carriage House ㊶   AAA Special Value Rates   *Bed & Breakfast*   ◆◆
All year   ....   2P/1B   85.00-185.00 2P/2B .... 145.00 XP 10
9 units. 1/2 blk w of Castillo St. 420 W Montecito St. (93101) Rooms in 1895 French country style home & new carriage
house. Smoke free premises. Check-in 3 pm. Comb or shower baths. No pets. 2-night minimum stay weekends. Reserv
deposit required; 5 days refund notice. AE, MC, VI.   ⊗ Ⓓ (805) 962-8447

Holiday Inn-Santa Barbara/Goleta ㊳   AAA Special Value Rates   *Motor Inn*   ◆◆
All year   1P 86.00-125.00 2P/1B 96.00-135.00 2P/2B 96.00-135.00 XP 10
Senior discount. 154 units. 7 mi nw adjacent to US 101; between Patterson & Fairview Ave exits. 5650 Calle Real. (Goleta, 93117) A/C; C/CATV; pay movies; phones. Htd pool. Airport transp. Pets. AE, DI, DS, MC, VI. ● Dining rm; 6 am-2
& 5-10 pm; $11-$17; cocktails. *(See ad below)*   ⊗ Ⓓ Ⓛ (805) 964-6241

Inn On Summer Hill ⑲   Rates Subject to Change   *Bed & Breakfast*   ◆◆◆◆
⊛ Fri-Sun 5/1-9/30 [BP]   ....   2P/1B 175.00-250.00 2P/2B .... 185.00 XP 20
Mon-Thurs 5/1-9/30 [BP]   ....   2P/1B 155.00-210.00 2P/2B .... 175.00 XP 20
Mon-Thurs 10/1-4/30 [BP]   ....   2P/1B 135.00-200.00 2P/2B .... 145.00 XP 20
16 units. N side of US 101; northbound exit Evans St, southbound exit Summerland then 1/2 mi e. 2520 Lillie
Ave. (Summerland, 93067) Beautifully decorated rooms in an Early American motif. Ocean view. Gas fireplaces.
Smoke free premises. Check-in 3 pm. Refrigerators; A/C; C/CATV; VCPs; radios; phones. Whirlpool. No pets. 2
night minimum stay weekends. Reserv deposit required; 5 days refund notice. AE, MC, VI. FAX (805) 969-9998
(See ad below)   ⊗ Ⓓ (805) 969-9998

Kings Inn of Santa Barbara ⑮   Rates Subject to Change   *Motel*   ◆◆
⊛ 5/15-9/30   1P 74.00- 88.00 2P/1B 74.00- 88.00 2P/2B 74.00- 88.00 XP 6
10/1-5/14   1P 50.00- 70.00 2P/1B 50.00- 70.00 2P/2B 50.00- 70.00 XP 6
45 units. 1 1/2 blks s of US 101. 128 Castillo St. (93101) 2 blocks from beach. Many rooms with patio or balcony.
Check-in 3 pm. 39 refrigerators; A/C; C/CATV; radios; phones. Small htd pool; saunas; whirlpool. No pets. Wkly
& monthly rates avail. AE, CB, DI, MC, VI. FAX (805) 687-2271   ⊗ Ⓓ (805) 963-4471

(See SANTA BARBARA spotting map page A482)

Marina Beach Motel 26		Rates Subject to Change				Motel			◆◆
⊕ Fri & Sat 5/15-9/15 [CP]	1P 75.00- 135.00	2P/1B	75.00- 140.00	2P/2B	80.00- 200.00	XP	7		F
Fri & Sat 9/16-5/14 [CP]	1P 55.00- 125.00	2P/1B	55.00- 125.00	2P/2B	55.00- 185.00	XP	7		F
Sun-Thurs 5/15-9/15 [CP]	1P 55.00- 95.00	2P/1B	55.00- 100.00	2P/2B	60.00- 145.00	XP	7		F
Sun-Thurs 9/16-5/14 [CP]	1P 40.00- 85.00	2P/1B	42.00- 95.00	2P/2B	45.00- 130.00	XP	7		F

31 units. 21 Bath St. (93101) 1/2 blk to beach. C/CATV; movies; phones; shower or comb baths. 17 efficiencies. No pets. 2 night minimum stay weekends. Reserv deposit required. AE, DI, DS, MC, VI. FAX (805) 564-4102 *(See ad below)*
⊗ Ⓓ (805) 963-9311

Mason Beach Inn 14		Rates Subject to Change				Motel			◆◆
⊕ 5/15-9/4	....	2P/1B	68.00- 115.00	2P/2B	68.00- 115.00	XP	6		
2/1-5/14 & 9/5-10/31	....	2P/1B	58.00- 105.00	2P/2B	58.00- 105.00	XP	6		
11/1-1/31	....	2P/1B	55.00- 95.00	2P/2B	55.00- 95.00	XP	6		

44 units. 2 blks s of US 101, southbound exit Castillo St. Northbound exit Cabrillo Blvd, then n to Castillo. 324 W Mason St. (93101) 1 block from beach. A/C; C/CATV; radios; phones. Htd pool; whirlpool. No pets. 3 suites with microwave & refrigerator, $95-$145. Wkly rates avail. Reserv deposit required. AE, DI, DS, MC, VI. *(See ad below)*
⊗ Ⓢ Ⓓ (805) 962-3203

Montecito Inn 3		AAA Special Value Rates				Historic Hotel		◆◆◆
⊕ 5/16-9/30 [CP]	1P 130.00- 145.00	2P/1B	130.00- 145.00	2P/2B	.... 175.00	XP		
10/1-5/15 [CP]	1P 105.00- 120.00	2P/1B	105.00- 120.00	2P/2B	.... 150.00	XP		

52 units. In Montecito, adjacent to US 101, exit Olive Mill Rd. 1295 Coast Village Rd. (93108) Charming, Historic Inn built in 1928. 2 blocks from beach. Check-in 3 pm. 17 refrigerators; C/CATV; movies; radios; phones; shower or comb baths. Htd pool; sauna; whirlpool; bicycles; exercise rm. Valet garage. No pets. Wkly & monthly rates avail. Reserv deposit required. AE, DI, DS, MC, VI. ● Restaurant; 11:30 am-2:30 & 5:30-10 pm; $7-$14; cocktails. FAX (805) 969-0623
⊗ Ⓢ Ⓓ (805) 969-7854

(See SANTA BARBARA spotting map page A482)

Mountain View Inn 33 — Rates Subject to Change — *Motel* ◆◆
Fri & Sat 6/15-9/15 [CP]   1P   .... 83.00   2P/1B   .... 85.00   2P/2B   .... 87.00   XP   5
Sun-Thurs 6/15-9/15 [CP]   1P   .... 68.00   2P/1B   .... 70.00   2P/2B   .... 72.00   XP   5
Fri & Sat 9/16-6/14 [CP]   1P   .... 61.00   2P/1B   .... 67.00   2P/2B   .... 69.00   XP   5
Sun-Thurs 9/16-6/14 [CP]   1P   .... 46.00   2P/1B   .... 52.00   2P/2B   .... 54.00   XP   5
Senior discount. 34 units. 1 mi e of US 101, exit Los Positas, corner of State & De La Vina sts. 3055 De La Vina St. (93105) Adjacent to city park. Refrigerators; C/CATV; movies; phones. Small htd pool. No pets. Reserv deposit required. AE, DS, MC, VI. *(See ad p A488)*   (D) (805) 687-6636

Old Yacht Club Inn 5 — Rates Subject to Change — *Bed & Breakfast* ◆◆
6/1-9/30 & Fri-Sun [BP]   1P 80.00- 135.00   2P/1B   80.00- 140.00   ....   XP 30
Mon-Thurs 10/1-5/31 [BP]   1P   55.00- 115.00   2P/1B   65.00- 115.00   ....   XP 30
Senior discount. 9 units. 1/2 blk n of Cabrillo Blvd. 431 Corona Del Mar. (93103) 1912 California Craftsman & 1920 Early California homes in residential area. 2 blks to beach. Smoke free premises. Phones; shower or comb baths. Bicycles; 1 room with whirlpool tub. No pets. 2-night minimum stay weekends. Reserv deposit required; 7 days refund notice. AE, DS, MC, VI. FAX (805) 962-3989 *(See ad below)*   ⊗ (D) (805) 962-1277

The Olive House 25 — Rates Subject to Change — *Bed & Breakfast* ◆◆
All year [CP]   1P 80.00- 125.00   2P/1B   85.00- 125.00   ....   XP
6 units. 1 mi e of US 101; northbound exit Arrellaga St; southbound exit Mission St. 1604 Olive St, 1/4 blk n of Arrellaga. (93101) 1904 California Craftsman house located in a residential area. Smoke free premises. Check-in 3 pm. Radios; comb, shower, or tub baths. Parking lot. No pets. 2-night minimum stay weekends. Reserv deposit required; 7 days refund notice. MC, VI. *(See ad below)*   ⊗ (D) (805) 962-4902

The Parsonage 24 — Rates Subject to Change — *Bed & Breakfast* ◆◆
5/1-10/30 & Fri-Sun 11/1-4/30
[BP]   1P 85.00- 160.00   2P/1B   85.00- 160.00   ....   XP
Mon-Thurs 11/1-4/30 [BP]   1P 76.50- 144.00   2P/1B   76.50- 144.00   ....   XP
6 units. 1 mi e of US 101; northbound exit Arrellaga St; southbound exit Mission St. 1600 Olive St, at Arrellaga St. (93101) 1892 Victorian house in a residential area. Smoke free premises. Comb or shower baths. No pets. 2-night minimum stay weekends. Wkly rates avail. Reserv deposit required; 7 days refund notice. MC, VI.   ⊗ (D) (805) 962-9336

Polynesian Inn 18 — Rates Subject to Change — *Motel* ◆
Fri & Sat 6/1-8/31   1P 75.00- 79.00   2P/1B   75.00- 79.00   2P/2B   79.00- 90.00   XP   5
Sun-Thurs 6/1-8/31 & Fri-Sat
9/1-5/31   1P 65.00- 79.00   2P/1B   65.00- 79.00   2P/2B   69.00- 79.00   XP   5
Sun-Thurs 9/1-5/31   1P 52.00- 67.00   2P/1B   55.00- 67.00   2P/2B   60.00- 70.00   XP   5
41 units. 2 blks sw of US 101; 1 blk w of Castillo St. 433 W Montecito St. (93101) 3 blocks from beach. C/CATV; phones. Coin laundry. Htd pool; whirlpool. No pets. 22 kitchens, $10 extra. Wkly & monthly rates avail. Reserv deposit required. AE, DI, DS, MC, VI. FAX (805) 962-9428   ⊗ (D) (805) 963-7851

Quality Suites 10 — AAA Special Value Rates — *Suites Motel* ◆◆◆
5/22-9/6 [BP]   1P 120.00- 140.00   2P/1B   120.00- 140.00   2P/2B   120.00- 140.00   XP 10   F
75 units. From US 101, exit Patterson Ave, 1/2 mi s; then 1/2 mi w on Hollister Ave. 5490 Hollister Ave. (93111) OPEN ALL YEAR. Spacious grounds. Check-in 3 pm. Refrigerators; A/C; C/CATV; movies; VCPs. Radios; phones. Htd pool; whirlpool. No pets. Microwave in all suites. Monthly rates avail. Reserv deposit required. Complimentary beverages each evening. AE, CB, DS, MC, VI. *(See ad below)*   ⊗ (805) 683-6722

The Sandman Inn 35 — AAA Special Value Rates — *Motor Inn* ◆◆
All year [CP]   1P 84.00- 94.00   2P/1B   84.00- 94.00   2P/2B   94.00- 104.00   XP 10   F
110 units. 3 mi nw; 3/4 mi e of jct US 101. 3714 State St. (93105) Check-in 3 pm. 67 refrigerators; 100 A/C; C/CATV; phones; comb or shower baths. 7 2-bedrm units. Coin laundry. Htd pool; whirlpool. Airport transp. No pets. 6 kitchens & 11 efficiencies, $10 extra. Monthly rates avail. Reserv deposit required. AE, CB, DI, MC, VI. ● The Cattlemen's Restaurant, see separate listing. FAX (805) 687-6581 *(See ad p A491)*   ⊗ (D) (805) 687-2468

(See SANTA BARBARA spotting map page A482)

Sandpiper Lodge 34		Rates Subject to Change					*Motel*			◆
⊕ 5/15-9/30	1P 58.00-68.00	2P/1B	58.00-68.00	2P/2B	58.00-68.00	XP 5				
10/1-5/14	1P 48.00-58.00	2P/1B	48.00-58.00	2P/2B	48.00-58.00	XP 5				

73 units. 3 mi nw; 3/4 mi e of US 101. 3525 State St. (93105) 33 refrigerators; C/CATV; radios; phones. 16 2-bedrm units. Small pool. No pets. 7-night minimum stay in 3 1-bedroom apartments. Wkly & monthly rates avail. AE, CB, DI, MC, VI. Coffeeshop opposite. FAX (805) 687-2271   ⊗ Ⓓ (805) 687-5326

(See SANTA BARBARA spotting map page A482)

Santa Barbara Inn 42   Rates Subject to Change   *Motor Inn* ◆◆◆

4/2-10/30	1P 149.00- 189.00	2P/1B	149.00- 189.00	2P/2B	149.00- 189.00	XP	
10/31-4/1	1P 99.00- 139.00	2P/1B	99.00- 139.00	2P/2B	99.00- 139.00	XP	

71 units. 3 blks s of US 101, exit Milpas St. 901 Cabrillo Blvd. (93103) Across from beach. Spacious rooms with ocean or mountain views. Refrigerators; C/CATV; radios; phones. Htd pool; whirlpool. Valet parking lot. No pets. Reserv deposit required. AE, DI, DS, MC, VI. ● Citronelle Restaurant, see separate listing. FAX (805) 966-6584
(See ad p A491)   ⊗ Ⓢ Ⓓ (805) 966-2285

Sheraton Santa Barbara Hotel 6   Rates Subject to Change   *Motor Inn* ◆◆◆

5/22-10/10	1P 139.00- 205.00	2P/1B	139.00- 205.00	2P/2B	139.00- 205.00	XP 15		F
10/11-11/28	1P 119.00- 195.00	2P/1B	119.00- 195.00	2P/2B	119.00- 195.00	XP 15		F
11/29-5/21	1P 115.00- 179.00	2P/1B	115.00- 179.00	2P/2B	115.00- 179.00	XP 15		F

174 units. 2 blks e of Milpas St, southbound US 101 exit Milpas St; northbound exit Cabrillo Blvd. 1111 E Cabrillo Blvd. (93103) Across from beach. Many ocean or mountain view rooms. Check-in 4 pm. A/C; C/CATV; pay movies; radios; phones; comb or shower baths. Htd pool. Fee for: health club & massage. Garage. No pets. Reserv deposit required; 3 days refund notice. AE, CB, DI, MC, VI. ● Restaurant; 6:30 am-10:30 pm; $11-$20; cocktails. FAX (805) 962-0985   ⊗ Ⓢ Ⓓ Ⓚ (805) 963-0744

Simpson House Inn 23   Rates Subject to Change   *Bed & Breakfast* ◆◆◆

5/1-9/30 & Fri-Sun [BP]	1P 95.00- 200.00	2P/1B	95.00- 200.00	....	XP
Mon-Thurs 10/1-4/30 [BP]	1P 76.00- 160.00	2P/1B	76.00- 160.00	....	XP

10 units. 1 1/2 blks e of State St. 121 E Arrellaga St. (93101) 1874 Victorian house on spacious grounds. Smoke free premises. Phones; 9 comb or shower baths. Bicycles. No pets. Wkly rates avail. AE, DS, MC, VI.
      ⊗ Ⓓ (805) 963-7067

Summerland Inn 1   Rates Subject to Change   *Motel* ◆◆◆

Fri & Sat [CP]	1P 75.00- 120.00	2P/1B	75.00- 120.00	2P/2B	90.00- 120.00	XP 15	
Sun-Thurs [CP]	1P 55.00- 90.00	2P/1B	65.00- 90.00	2P/2B	80.00- 90.00	XP 15	

Senior discount. 10 units. Adjacent to US 101, northbound exit Evans St, southbound Summerland exit. 2161 Ortega Hill Rd. (PO Box 1209, Summerland, 93067) Charming country inn decor. 2 units with gas fireplace. Smoke free premises. Check-in 3 pm. 2 A/C; C/CATV; phones; shower or comb baths. No pets. 2-night minimum stay weekends. Wkly & monthly rates avail. Reserv deposit required; 3 days refund notice. AE, DI, DS, MC, VI.
      ⊗ Ⓓ (805) 969-5225

Tiffany Inn 22   Rates Subject to Change   *Bed & Breakfast* ◆◆◆

6/1-9/30 & Fri-Sun [BP]	....	2P/1B	75.00- 175.00	....	XP
Mon-Thurs 10/1-5/31 [BP]	....	2P/1B	60.00- 130.00	....	XP

7 units. 1323 De La Vina St. (93101) 1898 Colonial Revival style house located in residential area. 5 units with woodburning fireplace. Smoke free premises. Check-in 3 pm. 5 comb or shower baths. 2 rooms with whirlpool bath. No pets. 2 night minimum stay weekends. Reserv deposit required; 7 days refund notice. AE, MC, VI.
      ⊗ Ⓓ (805) 963-2283

Travelodge Santa Barbara Beach 20   Rates Subject to Change   *Motel* ◆◆

5/1-9/15	1P 70.00- 105.00	2P/1B	80.00- 105.00	2P/2B	95.00- 110.00	XP 6		F
9/16-4/30	1P 60.00- 85.00	2P/1B	65.00- 85.00	2P/2B	75.00- 85.00	XP 6		F

Senior discount. 19 units. 3 blks s of US 101. 22 Castillo St. (93101) 1/2 block from beach. 4 rooms with patios. A/C; C/CATV; movies; radios; phones. No pets. AE, DI, DS, MC, VI. Restaurant adjacent. FAX (805) 965-6125
      Ⓓ (805) 965-8527

Tropicana Inn 17   Rates Subject to Change   *Motel* ◆◆◆

5/21-9/5 [CP]	1P 90.00- 139.00	2P/1B	90.00- 139.00	2P/2B	99.00- 170.00	XP 5	
9/6-5/20 [CP]	1P 75.00- 120.00	2P/1B	75.00- 120.00	2P/2B	80.00- 150.00	XP 5	

31 units. Northbound US 101 exit Cabrillo Blvd, 3 mi w to Castillo St, then 2 1/2 blks n; southbound exit Castillo St. 223 Castillo St. (93101) 2 blocks to beach & harbor. Designated smoking areas. Check-in 3 pm. Refrigerators; C/CATV; rental VCPs; radios; phones; comb or shower baths. Htd pool; whirlpool. 3 studio kitchens & 13 1-bedroom apartments, 2 day minimum stay weekends. Wkly & monthly rates avail. Reserv deposit required. AE, DI, DS, MC, VI. FAX (805) 962-9428   ⊗ Ⓓ (805) 966-2219

The Upham 46   AAA Special Value Rates   *Historic Hotel* ◆◆

All year [CP]	1P 95.00- 165.00	2P/1B	95.00- 165.00	2P/2B	.... 150.00	XP 10	F

49 units. From US 101 exit Mission St, 3 blks n, turn 6 blks e. 1404 De la Vina St at Sola St. (93101) A historic Victorian hotel & garden cottages established in 1871. Check-in 3 pm. C/CATV; phones. Parking lot. No pets. Reserv deposit required; 3 days refund notice. AE, CB, DI, MC, VI. ● Restaurant; 11:30 am-2 & 6-9 pm; a la carte entrees about $9-$19; beer & wine. FAX (805) 962-0058   Ⓓ (805) 962-0058

Vagabond Inn-Midtown 7   Rates Subject to Change   *Motel* ◆

All year [CP]	1P 50.00- 58.00	2P/1B	55.00- 63.00	2P/2B	60.00- 68.00	XP 5		F

46 units. 1/2 mi e of US 101, exit Mission St. 1920 State St. (93101) A/C; C/CATV; movies; radios; phones; comb or shower baths. 2 2-bedrm units. Pool. Pets, $5 extra charge. AE, DI, DS, MC, VI. FAX (805) 682-6854
      Ⓓ (805) 569-1521

Vagabond Inn-State St 32   Rates Subject to Change   *Motel* ◆◆

All year [CP]	1P 46.00- 68.00	2P/1B	51.00- 73.00	2P/2B	56.00- 78.00	XP 5		F

55 units. 1 1/2 miles nw. 2819 State St. (93105) Many patios or balconies. 53 A/C; C/CATV; movies; radios; phones; comb or shower baths. Pool. Pets, $5 extra charge. AE, DI, DS, MC, VI. FAX (805) 687-4432 *(See ad below)*
      ⊗ Ⓓ (805) 687-6444

(See SANTA BARBARA spotting map page A482)

| Villa Rosa **44** | | | Rates Subject to Change | | *Bed & Breakfast* | ◆◆ |

Villa Rosa **44** Rates Subject to Change *Bed & Breakfast* ◆◆
🏨 Fri-Sat & 7/1-9/30 [CP]   1P 90.00- 190.00 2P/1B 90.00- 190.00 .... XP
Sun-Thurs 10/1-6/30 [CP]   1P 80.00- 160.00 2P/1B 80.00- 160.00 .... XP
18 units. 1 blk from beach. 15 Chapala St. (93101) A classic 1930's Spanish style building. Rooms decorated in an attractive southwest theme. Check-in 3 pm. 3 C/CATV. Small pool; whirlpool. Limited parking lot. No pets. 2-night minimum stay weekends. Reserv deposit required; 5 days refund notice. AE, MC, VI. FAX (805) 962-7159
ⓓ (805) 966-0851

West Beach Inn **12** Rates Subject to Change *Motel* ◆◆◆
🏨 6/11-9/7 & Fri-Sat 9/8-6/10
[CP]   1P 105.00- 155.00 2P/1B 105.00- 155.00 2P/2B 120.00- 155.00 XP 15
Sun-Thurs 9/8-6/10 [CP]   1P 77.00- 120.00 2P/1B 77.00- 120.00 2P/2B 97.00- 120.00 XP 15
44 units. 4 blks s of US 101. 306 W Cabrillo Blvd & Bath St. (93101) Across from yacht harbor & beach. Some patios or balconies. Check-in 4 pm. Refrigerators; A/C; C/CATV; movies; radios; phones. Coin laundry. Htd pool; saunas; whirlpool. No pets. 2 deluxe 1-bedroom apartments, $160-$230. Reserv deposit required; 3 days refund notice. AE, CB, DI, MC, VI. FAX (805) 564-4210 *(See ad below)*
⊗ ⓓ (805) 963-4277

RESTAURANTS

Andria's Harborside Restaurant **5** Seafood $$ ◆◆
At Best Western-El Patio Beachside Inn. Across from beach & yacht harbor. Nice selection of seafood & limited selection of steaks, chicken & pasta. Oyster bar. A/C. Children's menu. Open 6 am-midnight; Fri & Sat-1 am. Cocktails & lounge. AE, DS, MC, VI. *(See ad p A481)*
⊗ (805) 966-3000

Cafe del Sol **11** American $$ ◆◆
1/2 blk s of US 101, exit Cabrillo Blvd. 30 Los Patos Way. Casual dining. Nice selection of seafood, chicken, steaks & Mexican specialties. Sun brunch. A/C. Open 11:30 am-3 & 5:30-10 pm; Sun 10 am-2:30 & 5:30-10 pm; closed 1/1, 11/25 & 12/25. Cocktails & lounge. MC, VI.
⊗ (805) 969-0448

Cattlemen's Restaurant **7** American $$ ◆
At The Sandman Inn. Western decor. Casual dining with a selection of beef, seafood & barbeque specialties. Sun brunch. A/C. Open 5 pm-10 pm; Sun 10 am-2:30 & 6-9 pm; closed 1/1 & 12/25. Cocktails & lounge. Entertainment. Reserv advised. AE, MC, VI.
⊗ (805) 687-2828

Chad's **13** American $$ ◆
1 blk w of State St, 1/2 blk n of Cota. 625 Chapala St. Regional American cuisine served in a charming home built in 1876. Smoke free premises. Open 11:30 am-10 pm; closed Sun & major holidays. Cocktails. MC, VI.
⊗ (805) 568-1876

The Chart House **10** Steak & Seafood $$$ ◆◆
1 blk s of State St, across from beach. 101 E Cabrillo Blvd. Casual dining. Nice selection of steaks, prime rib, rack of lamb & fresh seafood. A/C. Open 5:30 pm-10 pm; Fri & Sat 5 pm-11 pm; Sun 5 pm-10 pm. Cocktails & lounge. AE, CB, DI, MC, VI.
⊗ (805) 966-2112

Santa Barbara at its best

Across the street from the beach and harbor • Walking distance to downtown • 44 immaculate rooms with ocean and garden views • Complimentary continental breakfast and afternoon wine and cheese

- Heated pool and whirlpool
- Cable television

West Beach Inn
At the Harbor

Nationwide	800-423-5991
California	800-233-5743
FAX	805-564-4210

805-963-4277

306 West Cabrillo Boulevard, Santa Barbara, California 93101

(See SANTA BARBARA spotting map page A482)

Citronelle Restaurant ⑧   French $$$$ ◆◆◆
   In Santa Barbara Inn. 901 Cabrillo Blvd. Fine dining with a panoramic ocean view. Interesting selection of French & California cuisine. Sun brunch. A/C. Open 7-10 am, noon-2:30 & 6-9:30 pm; Sun 7-10 am, 11:30-2:30 & 6-9:30 pm. Cocktails & lounge. Pay valet parking. Reserv advised. AE, CB, DI, MC, VI.   ⊗ (805) 963-0111

Downey's ④   American $$$ ◆◆◆
   Downtown. 1305 State St. Small restaurant serving excellently prepared & presented cuisine. Menu changes daily. A/C.
   Open 11:30 am-1:45 & 5:30-9 pm; Fri-9:30 pm; Sat 5:30 pm-9:30 pm; Sun 5:30 pm-9 pm; closed Mon, 1/1 & 12/25. Beer
   & wine. Reserv advised. AE, MC, VI.   (805) 966-5006

Maxis ③   Continental $$$ ◆◆◆
   In Fess Parker's Red Lion Resort. Elegant decor. Sun brunch 10 am-2 pm. A/C. Open 6 pm-10 pm; closed Mon & Tues.
   Cocktails & lounge. Valet parking. Reserv advised. AE, DI, DS, MC, VI.   ⊗ (805) 564-4333

Michael's Waterside ①   French $$$$ ◆◆◆
   adjacent to US 101, exit Cabrillo Blvd, 1 blk s, then 1 blk w, across from Andree Clark Bird Refuge. 50 Los Patos Way.
   Elegant dining room featuring French cuisine. Also, the more casual Bistro Room. A/C. Dress code. Open 6 pm-9 pm;
   Fri & Sat-9:30 pm; closed Sun. Cocktails & lounge. Reserv advised. AE, CB, DI, MC, VI.   ⊗ (805) 969-0307

Original Enterprise Fish Company ⑥   Seafood $$ ◆◆◆
   1 blk s of US 101. 225 State St. Casual dining. Nautical decor. Large selection of mesquite broiled seafood. Children's
   menu. Open 11:30 am-10 pm; Fri & Sat-11 pm; Sun 3 pm-10 pm; closed 11/25 & 12/25. Beer & wine. Reserv advised.
   AE, MC, VI.   ⊗ (805) 962-3313

The Palace Cafe ⑨   American $$$ ◆◆◆
   Downtown area; 3 blks nw of US 101, 1/2 blk e of State St. 8 E Cota St. Casual dining. Interesting selection of Cajun,
   Creole & Caribbean cuisine. A/C. Open 5:30 pm-11 pm; Fri & Sat-midnight. Beer & wine. MC, VI. ⊗ (805) 966-3133

Ristorante Piatti ⑫   Italian $$ ◆◆
   1 mi n of US 101, exit San Ysidro Rd; In Montecito. 516 San Ysidro Rd at E Valley Rd. Selection of pasta, pizza, sea-
   food & veal. Indoor or outdoor patio dining. A/C. Open 11:30 am-2:30 & 5-10 pm; Fri-11 pm; Sat noon-11 pm; Sun 10
   am-10 pm; closed 1/1, 11/25 & 12/25. Cocktails & lounge. Reserv advised. MC, VI.   ⊗ (805) 969-7520

Wine Cask Restaurant ②   American $$$ ◆◆◆
   Downtown. 813 Anacapa St. California cuisine served in an attractive dining room or an outdoor courtyard. Extensive
   wine list. Smoking in designated areas. A/C. Open 11:30 am-2:30 & 5:30-9 pm; Fri-10 pm; Sat 5:30 pm-10 pm; Sun 5:30
   pm-9 pm; closed 4/11 & 12/25. Beer & wine. Reserv advised. AE, MC, VI.   ⊗ (805) 966-9463

SANTA CLARA — 93,600

Best Western Santa Clara Holiday Lodge   Rates Subject to Change   Motel   ◆◆
   ㊹ All year [CP]   2P/1B   51.00- 59.00   2P/2B   60.00- 66.00 XP 5   F
   Senior discount. 52 units. 2 blks w of Lawrence Expwy; on SR 82. 4341 El Camino Real. (95051) Very attractive
   & comfortable rooms. Refrigerators; A/C; C/CATV; movies; VCPs. Radios; phones. Pool. No pets. All rooms with
   microwave. Wkly rates avail. Reserv deposit required. AE, CB, DI, MC, VI. Restaurant opposite.
   FAX (408) 244-3366   ⊗ Ⓓ (408) 244-3366

Biltmore Hotel & Suites/Silicon Valley   Rates Subject to Change   Motor Inn   ◆◆◆
   ㊹ Sun-Thurs   1P 85.00- 140.00   2P/1B 105.00- 150.00   2P/2B 115.00- 210.00 XP 10
        Fri & Sat   1P 59.00- 79.00   2P/1B   59.00- 79.00   2P/2B   59.00- 79.00 XP 10
   262 units. E of & adjacent to US 101; exit Montague Expwy; 1 mi s of Great America. 2151 Laurelwood Rd.
   (95054) 2-story building & tower. Check-in 3 pm. A/C; C/TV; movies; radios; phones. 6 2-bedrm units. Pool; whirlpool; exercise rm. Parking lot. Airport transp. No pets. AE, CB, DI, MC, VI. ● Restaurant; 6 am-11 pm; $10-$20;
   cocktail lounge. FAX (408) 988-0225 *(See ad below)*   ⊗ Ⓓ Ⓖ (408) 988-8411

Budget Inn
All year   Rates Subject to Change   *Motel* ◆
All year   1P .... 44.00   2P/1B .... 46.00   2P/2B .... 52.00 XP 4
31 units. Exit US 101 at San Tomas Expwy; 2 mi s, then 1/4 mi w on El Camino Real (SR 82). 2499 El Camino Real.
(95051) Formerly EL Camino Inn. 15 refrigerators; A/C; C/CATV; movies; phones. Pets. Reserv. deposit required. AE, DI,
DS, MC, VI. Restaurant opposite. FAX (408) 244-9541   ⊗ Ⓓ (408) 244-9610

Days Inn ⍟
All year   Rates Guaranteed   *Motor Inn* ◆◆
All year   1P 59.00- 79.00   2P/1B   69.00- 89.00   2P/2B 59.00- 89.00 XP 10   F
Senior discount. 168 units. 1/2 mi e off US 101; exit Great American Pkwy; 3/4 mi s of Great America Theme Park.
4200 Great America Pkwy. (95054) Check-in 3 pm. A/C; C/CATV; pay movies; radios; phones. Htd pool; whirlpool.
Airport transp. Pets, $50 deposit required. Wkly & monthly rates avail. AE, DI, DS, MC, VI. ● Restaurant; 6 am-2
& 5-9 pm; $6-$14. FAX (408) 988-0976 *(See ad below)*   ⊗ Ⓢ Ⓓ Ⓚ (408) 980-1525

Econo Lodge ⍟
All year [CP]   AAA Special Value Rates   *Motel* ◆◆
All year [CP]   1P 50.00- 100.00   2P/1B   55.00- 95.00   2P/2B 61.00- 95.00 XP 5   F
70 units. On SR 82; 1/2 mi w of San Tomas Expwy; US 100 exit s Bowers Ave. 2930 El Camino Real. (PO Box
2841, 95051) Refrigerators; A/C; C/CATV; movies; VCPs. Radios; phones. 18 2-bedrm units, 1 3-bedrm unit, 17
kitchens. Small pool. Pets, $5 extra charge. Wkly & monthly rates avail. Reserv deposit required. AE, DI, DS, MC,
VI. Coffeeshop adjacent. FAX (408) 247-0623 *(See ad below)*   ⊗ Ⓓ (408) 241-3010

Embassy Suites Hotel — AAA Special Value Rates — *Suites Hotel* ◆◆◆
Mon-Thurs [BP]   1P .... 119.00   2P/1B .... 119.00   ....   XP 15   F
Fri-Sun [BP]   1P .... 99.00   2P/1B .... 99.00   ....   XP 15   F
257 units. W of US 101; Great America Pkwy exit. 2885 Lakeside Dr. (95054) Some small units. 1- & 2-bedroom suites with living room. Check-in 3 pm. 241 refrigerators; A/C; C/CATV; movies; radios; phones. 1 2-bedrm unit. Coin laundry. Small indoor pool; sauna; whirlpool; exercise rm. Parking lot. Airport transp. No pets. Wkly & monthly rates avail. Complimentary beverages each evening. AE, CB, DI, MC, VI. ● Restaurant; 11 am-2:30 & 5-10 pm; Fri & Sat-11 pm; $8-$20; cocktail lounge. FAX (408) 988-7529   ⊗ Ⓢ Ⓓ Ⓛ (408) 496-6400

Granada Inn-Silicon Valley — Rates Guaranteed — *Motel* ◆
⑱ All year [CP]   1P .... 39.00   2P/1B .... 39.00   2P/2B .... 47.00 XP 4
Senior discount. 67 units. Exit US 101, San Tomas Expwy; 3 mi s, w on El Camino Real. 2515 El Camino Real. (95051) A/C; C/CATV; movies; VCPs. Radios; phones; shower or comb baths. Efficiencies. Coin laundry. No pets. Wkly rates avail. AE, DI, DS, MC, VI. Restaurant adjacent. FAX (408) 241-8559 *(See ad p A494)*
   ⊗ Ⓓ (408) 241-2841

Howard Johnson Lodge — AAA Special Value Rates — *Motel* ◆
All year   1P 75.00- 80.00   2P/1B 80.00- 90.00   2P/2B 80.00- 90.00 XP 10   F
95 units. W of jct I-280 & Lawrence Expwy; exit Stevens Creek Blvd. 5405 Stevens Creek Blvd. (95051) A/C; C/CATV; movies; phones. Coin laundry. Pool; wading pool. Pets, $10 extra charge. AE, DI, DS, MC, VI. Beer & wine; restaurant adjacent. FAX (408) 446-2936 *(See ad below)*   ⊗ Ⓓ (408) 257-8600

Mariani's Inn — Rates Subject to Change — *Motor Inn* ◆◆◆
⑱ All year [CP]   1P .... 60.00   2P/1B .... 68.00   2P/2B .... 68.00 XP 8
Senior discount. 126 units. 1 mi w on SR 82, between Kiely Blvd & San Tomas Expwy; 3 mi from Great America Theme Park. 2500 El Camino Real. (95051) Refrigerators; A/C; C/TV; movies; radios; phones; shower or comb baths. 4 2-bedrm units, 47 kitchens. Coin laundry. Pool. No pets. 2 2-bedroom cottages, $125. AE, CB, DI, MC, VI. ● $11-$24. Restaurant, see separate listing. FAX (408) 243-5745 *(See ad below)*   ⊗ Ⓓ (408) 243-1431

Quality Suites   Rates Subject to Change   *Suites Motel* ◆◆◆

Sun-Thurs [BP]	1P 139.00- 154.00	2P/1B	139.00- 154.00	2P/2B	139.00- 154.00	XP 10	F
Fri & Sat [BP]	1P 79.00- 94.00	2P/1B	79.00- 94.00	2P/2B	79.00- 94.00	XP 10	F

Senior discount. 221 units. W of US 101, exit Lawrence Expwy, s on Oakmead, at Peterson Way. 3100 Lakeside Dr. (95054) Check-in 4 pm. A/C; C/CATV; movies; VCPs. Radios; phones. Coin laundry. Pool; whirlpool; exercise rm. Parking ramp. Airport transp. No pets. All units with microwave, wet bar & mini bar. Reserv deposit required; 3 days refund notice. Complimentary beverages each evening. AE, DI, DS, MC, VI. FAX (407) 748-1496 *(See ad p A496)*   ⊗ Ⓢ Ⓓ Ⓛ (408) 748-9800

Santa Clara Marriott Hotel   Rates Subject to Change   *Hotel* ◆◆◆

Sun-Thurs	1P 165.00	2P/1B	.... 180.00	2P/2B	.... 180.00	XP 15	F
Fri & Sat	1P 119.00	2P/1B	.... 119.00	2P/2B	.... 119.00	XP 15	F

758 units. 1/2 mi e off US 101; exit Great America Pkwy; 3/4 mi s of Great America Theme Park. 2700 Mission College. (95054) Spanish design. Many balconies; some patios. Check-in 3 pm. A/C; C/CATV; movies; radios; phones. Coin laundry. Indoor/outdoor pool; whirlpool; lighted tennis-4 courts; exercise rm. Parking ramp. Airport transp. AE, DI, DS, MC, VI. ● 2 restaurants; 6 am-1:30 am; Sat & Sun from 7 am; $6-$30; cocktails. FAX (408) 727-4353   ⊗ Ⓢ Ⓓ Ⓛ (408) 988-1500

Santa Clara Travelodge   Rates Guaranteed   *Motel* ◆

4/1-10/30	1P 50.00	2P/1B	.... 52.00	2P/2B	.... 56.00	XP 5	F
11/1-3/30	1P 42.00	2P/1B	.... 45.00	2P/2B	.... 48.00	XP 5	F

Senior discount. 43 units. 2 1/4 mi s on US 101 exit Lawrence Expwy, 2 blks e on El Camino Real (SR 82). 3477 El Camino Real. (95051) A/C; C/CATV; movies; phones. Whirlpool. Some rooms with microwave & refrigerator. Wkly rates avail. AE, CB, DI, MC, VI.   ⊗ Ⓓ (408) 984-3364

The Vagabond Inn   Rates Subject to Change   *Motel* ◆◆

All year	1P 40.00- 50.00	2P/1B	45.00- 55.00	2P/2B	50.00- 60.00	XP 5	F

70 units. On SR 82; se corner of Lawrence Expwy cloverleaf. 3580 El Camino Real. (95051) A/C; C/CATV; movies; radios; phones. Pool. Pets, $5 extra charge. AE, DI, DS, MC, VI. Coffeeshop adjacent. FAX (408) 247-3386 *(See ad below)*   ⊗ Ⓓ (408) 241-0771

The Westin Hotel-Santa Clara   Rates Guaranteed   *Hotel*

Sun-Thurs	1P 165.00	2P/1B	.... 185.00	2P/2B	.... 185.00	XP 15	
Fri & Sat	1P 89.00	2P/1B	.... 89.00	2P/2B	.... 89.00	XP 15	

500 units. 3/4 mi e off US 101, exit Great America Pkwy; at Santa Clara Convention Center. 5101 Great America Pkwy. (95054) Formerly Doubletree Hotel. Rating witheld pending completion of renovations. Check-in 3 pm. A/C; C/CATV; movies; radios; phones. Pool; saunas; whirlpool; steamroom; exercise rm. Fee for: golf-18 holes, lighted tennis-5 courts. Parking ramp & parking lot. Airport transp. Pets. AE, CB, DI, MC, VI. ● Dining rm & restaurant; 6:30 am-11 pm; $10-$30; cocktails. FAX (408) 986-1838   ⊗ Ⓢ Ⓓ Ⓛ (408) 986-0700

Woodcrest Hotel   Rates Subject to Change   *Hotel* ◆◆◆

Sun-Thurs [BP]	1P 114.00- 124.00	2P/1B	129.00- 139.00	2P/2B	129.00- 139.00	XP 15	F
Fri & Sat [BP]	1P 69.00- 99.00	2P/1B	69.00- 99.00	2P/2B	69.00- 99.00	XP 15	F

Senior discount. 60 units. W of jct I-280 & Lawrence Expwy, exit Stevens Creek Blvd. 5415 Stevens Creek Blvd. (95051) Formerly Woodmark Hotel of Santa Clara. Very attractive rooms. Check-in 3 pm. 12 refrigerators; A/C; C/CATV; movies; VCPs. Radios; phones; comb or shower baths. Parking ramp. No pets. Luxury level rooms avail. 1 Suite with whirlpool tub & fireplace. Wkly rates avail. Reserv deposit required. AE, DI, MC, VI. Complimentary evening deli buffet. FAX (408) 446-9739   ⊗ Ⓢ Ⓓ (408) 446-9636

RESTAURANTS

Arthur's   American $$$ ◆◆

Exit US 101 Great America Pkwy W. 2875 Lakeside Dr. Elegant decor, very popular; varied menu with continental flair. A/C. Open 11 am-3 & 5-10 pm; Sat from 5 pm; closed Sun & major holidays. Cocktails & lounge. Reserv advised. AE, CB, DI, MC, VI.   ⊗ (408) 980-1666

Mariani's   Continental $$ ◆◆◆

On SR 82, 1/4 mi w of San Tomas, at Mariani's Inn. 2500 El Camino Real. Modern comfortable decor, varied menu featuring pasta, seafood, chops & poultry. A/C. Children's menu. Open 6:30 am-11 pm; Mon-10 pm; Sun 11 am-2 & 4-10 pm; closed 12/25. Cocktails & lounge. Entertainment. Reserv advised. AE, CB, DI, MC, VI.   ⊗ (408) 243-1431

SANTA CLARITA — 110,600

Hampton Inn   Rates Subject to Change   *Motel* ◆◆◆

5/25-9/7 [CP]	1P 69.00- 76.00	2P/1B	76.00- 86.00	2P/2B	79.00- 86.00	XP	
9/8-5/24 [CP]	1P 59.00- 65.00	2P/1B	66.00- 72.00	2P/2B	69.00- 72.00	XP	

130 units. Adjacent to I-5 w side; exit Lyons Ave. 25259 The Old Rd. (91381) A/C; C/CATV; movies; radios; phones. Coin laundry. Htd pool; whirlpool. Small pets only. Monthly rates avail. AE, DS, MC, VI. FAX (805) 253-1683 *(See ad below)*   ⊗ Ⓢ Ⓣ Ⓛ (805) 253-2400

Hilton Garden Inn   Rates Subject to Change   *Motor Inn* ◆◆◆
⊕ All year   1P 79.00-109.00   2P/1B   89.00-119.00   2P/2B   89.00-119.00 XP 10   F
Senior discount. 152 units. Adjacent to I-5, 1/4 mi nw, exit Magic Mountain Pkwy. 27710 The Old Rd. (91355)
Some rooms with balcony. 5 refrigerators; A/C; C/CATV; free & pay movies; radios; phones. Coin laundry. Htd
pool; whirlpool; exercise rm. Small pets only. Monthly rates avail. AE, DI, DS, MC, VI. ● Restaurant; 6:30-10 am,
11:30-2 & 5-10 pm; $7.95-$12.95; cocktails. FAX (805) 254-9399   ⊗ Ⓢ Ⓓ (805) 254-8800

Santa Clarita Travelodge   Rates Subject to Change   *Motel* ◆◆
⊕ All year [CP]   1P .... 55.00   2P/1B   .... 55.00   2P/2B   .... 60.00 XP 5
54 units. 2 1/2 mi nw of SR 14; northbound exit Sierra Hwy, southbound exit Sierra Hwy via Princessa. 17843
Sierra Hwy. (91351) Check-in 3 pm. 52 refrigerators; A/C; C/CATV; movies; radios; phones. Small htd pool; whirlpool. No pets. AE, DI, DS, MC, VI. Restaurant opposite. FAX (805) 252-5286 *(See ad below)*
     ⊗ Ⓓ Ⓛ (805) 252-1716

RESTAURANTS

El Torito   Mexican $ ◆◆
Adjacent to I-5, w side exit Magic Mountain Pkwy. 27510 The Old Rd. Sun brunch 9 am-2 pm. A/C. Children's menu.
Open 11 am-10 pm; Fri & Sat-11 pm; closed 11/25 & 12/25. Cocktails & lounge. AE, DI, DS, MC, VI. ⊗ (805) 254-2994

Inagika   Ethnic $$$ ◆◆
1/2 mi e of I-5; exit Magic Mountain Pkwy at the Valencia Country Club. 27330 N Tourney Rd. Large variety of Japanese
cuisine, steaks, chicken, seafood, sushi, teppen grill & traditional Kaiseki dinner. Light jazz Fri & Sat, 7 pm-11 pm. A/C.
Open 11:30 am-2 & 5:30-10 pm; Fri-10:30 pm; Sat noon-10:30 pm; Sun noon-9 pm. Cocktails & lounge. Valet parking.
Reserv advised. AE, DI, DS, MC, VI.   ⊗ (805) 259-2942

SANTA CRUZ — 49,000   See also APTOS, CAPITOLA & SCOTTS VALLEY

Babbling Brook Bed & Breakfast Inn   Rates Subject to Change   *Bed & Breakfast* ◆◆◆
⊕ All year [BP]   1P 85.00-135.00   2P/1B   85.00-135.00   2P/2B   85.00-135.00 XP 15
12 units. 1 1/2 blks sw of SR 1. 1025 Laurel St. (95060) 3 2-story duplexes in cozy shaded setting along brook.
Many units with fireplace. Smoke free premises. Check-in 3 pm. C/CATV; radios; phones; comb or shower baths.
No pets. 2 rooms with whirlpool bath. 2-night minimum stay with Sat reservations. Reserv deposit required; 3
days refund notice. AE, DI, DS, MC, VI. FAX (408) 427-2457   ⊗ Ⓓ (408) 427-2437

Best Western All Suites Inn   Rates Guaranteed   *Suites Motel* ◆◆◆
⊕ 5/1-9/30 [CP]   1P 105.00-160.00   2P/1B   105.00-165.00   2P/2B   115.00-165.00 XP 10
10/1-4/30 [CP]   1P 85.00-150.00   2P/1B   85.00-160.00   2P/2B   95.00-145.00 XP 10
41 units. Exit SR 1 & 17 via Central District. 500 Ocean St. (95060) All units with whirlpool bath, microwave &
some fireplaces. Check-in 3 pm. Refrigerators; A/C; C/CATV; radios; phones. Small htd indoor pool; sauna. No
pets. Reserv deposit required; 3 days refund notice. AE, CB, DI, MC, VI. Restaurant opposite. FAX (408) 429-1903
     ⊗ Ⓢ Ⓓ Ⓛ (408) 458-9898

Best Western Inn   Rates Subject to Change   *Motel* ◆◆
⊕ 6/1-9/30   1P 65.00- 80.00   2P/1B   75.00- 90.00   2P/2B   80.00- 95.00 XP 10
4/1-5/31   1P 50.00- 65.00   2P/1B   60.00- 75.00   2P/2B   70.00- 85.00 XP 10
10/1-3/31   1P 45.00- 60.00   2P/1B   55.00- 70.00   2P/2B   65.00- 80.00 XP 10
26 units. Off jct SR 1 & 17; e side of Ocean St. 126 Plymouth St. (95060) Refrigerators; A/C; C/CATV; movies;
radios; phones. 1 2-bedrm unit. Sauna; whirlpool; 2 rooms with whirlpool. No pets. [CP] avail. Reserv deposit
required; 3 days refund notice. AE, DI, DS, MC, VI. Coffeeshop opposite.   ⊗ Ⓢ Ⓓ (408) 425-4717

Best Western Torch-Lite Inn   Rates Subject to Change   *Motel* ◆◆
⊕ 6/1-9/15   1P .... 74.00   2P/1B   .... 79.00   2P/2B   .... 87.00 XP 8
4/15-5/31   1P .... 55.00   2P/1B   .... 59.00   2P/2B   .... 67.00 XP 8
9/16-4/14   1P .... 49.00   2P/1B   .... 49.00   2P/2B   .... 57.00 XP 8
38 units. 3 blks from beach. 500 Riverside Ave. (95060) C/CATV; phones; comb or shower baths. Pool; putting
green. No pets. 4 kitchens, $8 extra. Reserv deposit required. AE, CB, DI, MC, VI. *(See ad p A499)*
     ⊗ Ⓓ (408) 426-7575

Candlelite Inn   Rates Subject to Change   *Motel* ◆◆
⊕ Fri & Sat 5/1-10/31   1P 70.00- 90.00   2P/1B   70.00-100.00   2P/2B   75.00-120.00 XP 5
Sun-Thurs 5/1-10/31   1P 40.00- 70.00   2P/1B   40.00- 70.00   2P/2B   65.00- 80.00 XP 5
42 units. 3 blks w off SR 1 & 17, exit Central District. 1101 Ocean St. (95060) 16 refrigerators; C/CATV; free & pay
movies; phones. Pool. No pets. Reserv deposit required. AE, DI, MC, VI. Coffeeshop adjacent.
     ⊗ Ⓓ (408) 427-1616

Carousel Motel

		AAA Special Value Rates					*Motel*			◆◆
Fri & Sat 4/1-10/31	1P	80.00- 125.00	2P/1B	80.00- 125.00	2P/2B	....	99.00	XP 10		F
Sun-Thurs 6/1-9/6	1P	72.00- 125.00	2P/1B	72.00- 125.00	2P/2B	....	96.00	XP 10		F
Fri & Sat 11/1-3/31	1P	65.00- 90.00	2P/1B	65.00- 90.00	2P/2B	....	76.00	XP 10		F
Sun-Thurs 9/7-5/31	1P	49.00- 65.00	2P/1B	49.00- 65.00	2P/2B	....	62.00	XP 10		

34 units. 1/2 blk from the boardwalk & beach. 110 Riverside Ave. (95060) Some rooms with view of amusement park. Balconies or patios. Check-in 3 pm. C/CATV; radios; phones; comb or shower baths. No pets. 2-night minimum stay weekends 4/1-10/31. Wkly rates avail 11/1-3/31. Reserv deposit required. AE, MC, VI. *(See ad below)*
⊗ (D) 🔲 (408) 425-7090

Chaminade

	Rates Subject to Change			*Resort Complex*	◆◆◆
All year	1P 125.00- 135.00	2P/1B	125.00- 145.00	2P/2B 125.00- 145.00	XP 25

Senior discount. 152 units. 1 1/2 mi e of SR 17 & 1; exit SR 1 at Soquel Ave, 1/2 blk w to Paul Sweet Rd then 1/2 mi n. 1 Chaminade Ln. (95065) Quiet, hillside location. Public areas overlook Santa Cruz & the Pacific. Check-in 4 pm. 10 refrigerators; A/C; C/CATV; movies; radios; phones. Htd pool; saunas; whirlpools; men's & women's therapy pools; lighted tennis-4 courts; health club; jogging track. Fee for: massage. Valet parking lot. No pets. Reserv deposit required. AE, DI, DS, MC, VI. ● Dining rm, restaurant & coffeeshop; 7 am-9:30 pm; $20-$35; cocktails. FAX (408) 476-4798
⊗ (S)(D) 🔲 (408) 475-5600

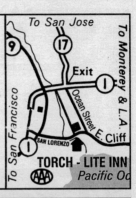

Comfort Inn-Santa Cruz   Rates Subject to Change   *Motel*   ◆◆◆
⊛ 5/1-9/30 [CP]   1P 79.00- 109.00   2P/1B   79.00- 109.00   2P/2B   89.00- 119.00   XP 10   F
   10/1-4/30 [CP]   1P 69.00- 99.00   2P/1B   69.00- 99.00   2P/2B   79.00- 109.00   XP 10   F
Senior discount. 63 units. Off jct SR 1 & 17; e side of Ocean St. 110 Plymouth St. (95060) Nicely landscaped
grounds. 22 refrigerators; A/C; C/CATV; radios; phones. 4 efficiencies, no utensils. Small pool; sauna; whirlpool;
16 rooms with whirlpool bath. No pets. Luxury level rooms avail. 4 rooms with gas fireplace. Some VCP's. Wkly
& monthly rates avail. Reserv deposit required. AE, DI, DS, MC, VI. Coffeeshop opposite. FAX (408) 426-0923 *(See
ad below)*   ⊗ Ⓢ Ⓓ 🅚 (408) 426-2664

Dream Inn   Rates Subject to Change   *Motor Inn* ◆◆◆
⊛ 6/12-9/12   1P 159.00- 255.00   2P/1B 165.00- 255.00   2P/2B 159.00- 255.00   XP 10
Senior discount. 164 units. 175 W Cliff Dr. (95060) OPEN ALL YEAR. Overlooking beach. Balconies & patios.
Check-in 4 pm. Refrigerators; A/C; C/TV; pay movies; radios; phones. Pool; sauna; whirlpool. No pets. Reserv
deposit required. AE, DI, DS, MC, VI. ● Dining rm & coffeeshop; 6:30 am-10 pm; $12-$22; cocktails; entertainment. FAX (408) 427-2025 *(See ad below)*   ⊗ Ⓓ (408) 426-4330

ONLY **BEACHFRONT HOTEL** IN
SANTA CRUZ

Dream Inn
On The Beach

175 West Cliff Dr.
Santa Cruz, CA 95060
(408) 426-4330

HSI Reservations
(800) 421-6662
In 310 area - 452-5448

- Ocean Front Rooms
- On The Beach
- Free Parking
- Sauna
- Pool • Spa
- Room Service
- Restaurant
- Surf Diner
- Lounge

In AAA Listings, "Weekends" means Friday and Saturday nights.

Holiday Inn-Santa Cruz
📷 4/1-9/30

		AAA Special Value Rates		Motor Inn	◆◆◆

| 4/1-9/30 | 1P 89.00- 125.00 | 2P/1B 89.00- 125.00 | 2P/2B .... 112.00 | XP 10 | F |
| 10/1-3/31 | 1P 79.00- 96.00 | 2P/1B 79.00- 96.00 | 2P/2B .... 89.00 | XP 10 | F |

169 units. Exit SR 1 & 17 via Central District. 611 Ocean St. (95060) Some small rooms. Check-in 4 pm. A/C; C/CATV; radios; phones. Pool; whirlpool. No pets. AE, DI, DS, MC, VI. ● Restaurant; 6:30 am-10 pm; $7-$16; cocktails. FAX (408) 429-1044 *(See ad p A499)*   ⊗ Ⓓ (408) 426-7100

The Inn at Pasatiempo
📷

		Rates Subject to Change		Motor Inn	◆◆◆
Fri & Sat 5/1-10/15 [BP]	1P 80.00- 90.00	2P/1B 90.00- 100.00	2P/2B 90.00- 100.00	XP 10	
Sun-Thurs & Fri-Sat					
10/16-4/30 [BP]	1P 70.00- 80.00	2P/1B 80.00- 90.00	2P/2B 80.00- 90.00	XP 10	

Senior discount. 54 units. 3/4 mi n of jct SR 1 & 17; exit SR 17 via Pasatiempo Dr. (95060) Attractive landscaped garden, adjacent to Pasatiempo Golf Course. Check-in 3 pm. C/CATV; pay movies; radios; phones; shower or comb baths. Pool. No pets. Reserv deposit required. AE, CB, DI, MC, VI. ● Dining rm; 7-10 am, 11:30-2:30 & 5-10 pm; $12-$20; cocktails. FAX (408) 426-1737   ⊗ Ⓓ (408) 423-5000

Mission Inn
📷 5/1-9/30

		Rates Subject to Change		Motel	◆◆
5/1-9/30	1P 65.00- 85.00	2P/1B 75.00- 95.00	2P/2B 110.00	XP 5	
10/1-4/30	1P 53.00- 65.00	2P/1B 58.00- 70.00	2P/2B 75.00	XP 5	

42 units. 2 1/2 mi sw of jct SR 1 & SR 17, on SR 1 northbound. 2250 Mission St. (95060) A/C; C/CATV; phones. Sauna; whirlpool. No pets. Large unit with whirlpool bath, $145 for 2 persons. Reserv deposit required; 3 days refund notice. AE, MC, VI. Restaurant adjacent.   ⊗ Ⓢ Ⓓ (408) 425-5455

Motel Continental
📷

		Rates Subject to Change		Motel	◆
Fri & Sat 5/12-9/16	....	2P/1B 68.50- 88.50	2P/2B 78.50- 98.50	XP 10	
Fri & Sat 9/17-5/11	....	2P/1B 58.50- 78.50	2P/2B 68.50- 88.50	XP 10	
Sun-Thurs 5/12-9/16	....	2P/1B 48.50- 68.50	2P/2B 68.50- 88.50	XP 10	
Sun-Thurs 9/17-5/11	....	2P/1B 38.50- 58.50	2P/2B 48.50- 68.50	XP 10	

31 units. 5 blks from beach between Broadway & Soquel Ave. 414 Ocean St. (95060) Some small rooms. Refrigerators; A/C; C/CATV; phones. Whirlpool. Pets. Reserv deposit required; 3 days refund notice. AE, CB, DI, MC, VI.   Ⓓ (408) 429-1221

National 9 Motel
📷

		Rates Guaranteed		Motel	◆◆
5/16-10/31 & Fri-Sat	1P 65.00	2P/1B 75.00	2P/2B 85.00	XP 4	
Sun-Thurs 11/1-5/15	1P 40.00	2P/1B 45.00	2P/2B 55.00	XP 4	

21 units. Off jct SR 1 & 17; e side of Ocean St. 130 Plymouth St. (95060) C/CATV; phones. Small pool. No pets. Reserv deposit required. AE, MC, VI. Coffeeshop opposite.   ⊗ Ⓓ (408) 426-4515

Ocean Pacific Inn
📷 All year [CP]

		Rates Subject to Change		Motel	
All year [CP]	1P 60.00- 125.00	2P/1B 70.00- 125.00	2P/2B 70.00- 125.00	XP	

Senior discount. 57 units. 6 blks se of SR 1. 120 Washington. (85060) Rating withheld pending completion of construction. 28 refrigerators; A/C; C/CATV; movies; VCPs. Radios; phones. Coin laundry. Htd pool. Pets, $50 deposit required. MC, VI. FAX (408) 848-5269   ⊗ Ⓓ (408) 457-1234

Pacific Inn
📷

		Rates Subject to Change		Motel	◆◆
Fri & Sat 5/12-9/16	....	2P/1B 68.50- 88.50	2P/2B 78.50- 98.50	XP 10	
Fri & Sat 9/17-5/11	....	2P/1B 58.50- 78.50	2P/2B 68.50- 88.50	XP 10	
Sun-Thurs 5/12-9/16	....	2P/1B 48.50- 68.50	2P/2B 68.50- 88.50	XP 10	
Sun-Thurs 9/17-5/11	....	2P/1B 38.50- 58.50	2P/2B 48.50- 68.50	XP 10	

36 units. 1 mi from jct SR 1 & 17. 330 Ocean St. (95060) Refrigerators; A/C; C/CATV; movies; phones. Indoor/outdoor pool; 4 rms with whirlpool bath. Pets. Reserv deposit required; 3 days refund notice. AE, DS, MC, VI.   ⊗ Ⓢ Ⓓ (408) 425-3722

Riverside Garden Inn
(AAA) Fri & Sat 6/15-9/30 [CP]   Rates Subject to Change   *Motel*   ◆◆
    Fri & Sat 10/1-6/14 & Sun-   1P 58.00- 98.00   2P/1B   58.00- 98.00   2P/2B   58.00- 98.00 XP 10   F
    Thurs 6/15-9/30 [CP]   1P 48.00- 88.00   2P/1B   48.00- 88.00   2P/2B   48.00- 88.00 XP 10   F
    Sun-Thurs 10/1-6/14 [CP]   1P 45.00- 78.00   2P/1B   45.00- 78.00   2P/2B   45.00- 78.00 XP 10   F
    80 units. 4 blks from beach. 600 Riverside Ave. (95060) Nicely landscaped. Check-in 3 pm. C/CATV; radios;
    phones. Small htd pool; whirlpools; few units with whirlpool bath. No pets. Wkly rates avail. Reserv deposit re-
    quired. AE, DI, DS, MC, VI. *(See ad below)*   ⊗ Ⓢ Ⓓ Ⓛ (408) 458-9660

Sandpiper Lodge
(AAA) All year   Rates Subject to Change   *Motel*   ◆◆
                                   1P 59.00- 69.00   2P/1B   69.00- 89.00   2P/2B   79.00- 99.00 XP 10
    25 units. E Cliff Dr, 4 1/2 blks from beach. 111 Ocean St. (95060) Many balconies. Check-in 3 pm. C/CATV;
    phones; comb or shower baths. 4 indoor whirlpools. Limited garage. No pets. Reserv deposit required. AE, DI,
    DS, MC, VI.   ⊗ Ⓓ (408) 429-8244

Sea & Sand Inn
(AAA) Fri & Sat [CP]   Rates Guaranteed   *Motel*   ◆◆
    Sun-Thurs 6/1-9/6 [CP]   1P 115.00- 190.00   2P/1B 115.00- 190.00   2P/2B   .... 145.00 XP 10   F
    Sun-Thurs 4/1-5/31 [EP]   1P 105.00- 175.00   2P/1B 105.00- 175.00   2P/2B   .... 130.00 XP 10   F
    Sun-Thurs 9/7-3/31 [EP]   1P 90.00- 155.00   2P/1B   90.00- 155.00   2P/2B   .... 110.00 XP 10   F
                                   1P 75.00- 155.00   2P/1B   75.00- 155.00   2P/2B   .... 90.00 XP 10   F
    Senior discount. 20 units. Overlooking the wharf. 201 W Cliff Dr. (95060) On a cliff with panoramic ocean view.
    Country inn decor. Check-in 3 pm. C/CATV; pay movies; VCPs. Radios; phones; shower baths. Beach; 3 rooms
    with whirlpool bath. No pets. 2 housekeeping apartments, $175-$190 for up to 2 persons. 2-night minimum stay
    on weekends. Reserv deposit required. AE, MC, VI. Restaurant adjacent. FAX (408) 427-3400 *(See ad p A499)*
                                                                              ⊗ Ⓓ (408) 427-3400

Sunset Inn
(AAA) 5/1-9/30   Rates Subject to Change   *Motel*   ◆
    10/1-4/30   1P   .... 60.00   2P/1B   .... 65.00   2P/2B   .... 75.00 XP 10
                                   1P   .... 45.00   2P/1B   .... 60.00   2P/2B   .... 60.00 XP 10
    Senior discount. 28 units. Exit SR 1 at Mission St, 2 1/2 mi w. 2424 Mission St. (95060) C/CATV; phones. No pets.
    4 kitchens, $10 extra. Reserv deposit required; 3 days refund notice. AE, DS, MC, VI.   Ⓓ (408) 423-3471

Travelodge Riviera Motel
(AAA) 5/15-9/15   Rates Subject to Change   *Motel*   ◆◆
    9/16-10/31 & 3/1-5/14   1P 55.00- 80.00   2P/1B   60.00- 85.00   2P/2B   70.00- 95.00 XP 10
    11/1-2/29   1P 55.00- 65.00   2P/1B   55.00- 70.00   2P/2B   60.00- 75.00 XP 10
                                   1P 45.00- 55.00   2P/1B   50.00- 60.00   2P/2B   55.00- 65.00 XP 10
    63 units. 3 blks from beach. 619 Riverside Ave. (95060) Check-in 3 pm. C/CATV; pay movies; 50 radios; phones.
    33 2-bedrm units, 7 kitchens, no utensils. Indoor pool; whirlpool. No pets. 5 rooms with whirlpool bath, $85-$110
    for up to 2 persons. Wkly & monthly rates avail. Reserv deposit required. AE, DI, DS, MC, VI.
                                                                              ⊗ Ⓓ (408) 423-9515

RESTAURANTS

Crow's Nest   Steak & Seafood $$ ◆◆
(AAA) 1 1/4 mi e, at s shore Santa Cruz Small Crafts Harbor via Murray St bridge. 2218 E Cliff Dr. Fresh seafood. View
    of bay. Lively atmosphere, popular with locals. A/C. Children's menu. Open 11:30 am-2:30 & 5:30-10 pm; Sat &
    Sun 11:30 am-3 & 5-10 pm; closed 12/25. Cocktails & lounge. Entertainment & dancing. Pay parking lot. Reserv
    advised. AE, DI, MC, VI.   ⊗ (408) 476-4560

Hollins House   Continental $$ ◆◆
(AAA) 1/2 mi n of jct SR 1 & 17; w of SR 17, Pasatiempo Dr exit; at golf course. 20 Club House Rd. Overlooking city &
    bay. Open 11:30 am-2:30 & 5:30-9:30 pm; Sat from 5:30 pm; Sun 10 am-2 pm; closed Mon, 1/1-1/14 & for dinner
    Tues & Sun. Cocktails & lounge. Reserv advised. AE, MC, VI.   ⊗ (408) 459-9177

Sea Cloud   American $$ ◆◆
    On 2nd floor. Municipal Wharf 49B. California cuisine & fresh seafood. Panoramic bay & shoreline views. Elevator. Ca-
    sual. Children's menu. Open 11:30 am-2:30 & 5-9:30 pm; Sat-10 pm; closed 12/24 & 12/25. Lounge. Pay parking lot.
    Reserv advised. AE, MC, VI.   ⊗ (408) 458-9393

SANTA FE SPRINGS — 15,500

Best Western Sandman Motel

			Rates Subject to Change				*Motel*	◆◆
7/1-8/31 [CP]	1P	.... 47.00	2P/1B	.... 50.00	2P/2B	.... 52.00	XP	3
9/1-6/30 [CP]	1P	.... 39.00	2P/1B	.... 42.00	2P/2B	.... 45.00	XP	3

56 units. Adjacent to I-5, exit Carmenita Rd. 13530 E Firestone Blvd. (90670) Refrigerators; A/C; C/CATV; movies; 20 radios; phones. Coin laundry. Pool. Pets, $5 extra charge. Reserv deposit required in summer. AE, DS, MC, VI. Coffeeshop adjacent. FAX (310) 921-2451   ⊗ Ⓢ Ⓓ (310) 921-8571

SANTA MARIA — 61,300

Best Western Big America

			AAA Special Value Rates				*Motor Inn*	◆◆◆
All year [CP]	1P	55.00- 85.00	2P/1B	55.00- 85.00	2P/2B	60.00- 90.00	XP	7

104 units. On SR 135, 1/2 mi sw of jct US 101, exit Broadway. 1725 N Broadway. (93454) Refrigerators; A/C; C/CATV; movies; phones. Htd pool; whirlpool. Reserv deposit required. AE, DI, DS, MC, VI. ● Restaurant; 6 am-9 pm; $6-$13. FAX (805) 922-9865 *(See ad below)*   ⊗ Ⓓ Ⓖ (805) 922-5200

Howard Johnson Lodge

			Rates Subject to Change				*Motel*	◆◆
6/16-9/4	1P	49.00- 59.00	2P/1B	54.00- 64.00	2P/2B	54.00- 59.00	XP	8	F
9/5-12/31 & 4/11-6/15	1P	44.00- 54.00	2P/1B	49.00- 59.00	2P/2B	49.00- 54.00	XP	8	F
1/1-4/10	1P	39.00- 49.00	2P/1B	44.00- 54.00	2P/2B	44.00- 49.00	XP	8	F

Senior discount. 64 units. Adjacent to US 101, Main St exit. 210 S Nicholson Ave. (93454) A/C; C/CATV; movies; phones. Coin laundry. Htd pool; wading pool; whirlpool. Pets. AE, DI, DS, MC, VI. Restaurant adjacent. FAX (805) 928-9222 *(See ad p A504)*   ⊗ Ⓓ Ⓖ (805) 922-5891

Hunter's Inn

			Rates Guaranteed				*Motel*	◆◆
All year	1P	49.00- 59.00	2P/1B	55.00- 69.00	2P/2B	58.00- 75.00	XP	6

Senior discount. 70 units. 1 1/2 mi s on US 101 business rt & SR 135. 1514 S Broadway. (93454) 12 rooms with patio or balcony. 30 refrigerators; C/CATV; movies; phones. 5 2-bedrm units. Htd pool; whirlpool. Pets, $5 extra charge. Microwaves avail. Wkly & monthly rates avail. Reserv deposit required. AE, DI, DS, MC, VI. Coffeeshop opposite. FAX (805) 925-1523 *(See ad p A502)*   ⊗ Ⓓ (805) 922-2123

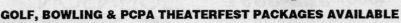

Ramada Suites   Rates Subject to Change   *Suites Motor Inn* ◆◆◆
 Fri & Sat   1P 65.00- 150.00 2P/1B 65.00- 150.00 2P/2B 65.00- 150.00 XP 10 F
 Sun-Thurs   1P 55.00- 96.00 2P/1B 55.00- 96.00 2P/2B 55.00- 96.00 XP 10 F
Senior discount. 210 units. 2 mi n, adjacent to US 101; Broadway exit. 2050 N Preisker Ln. (93454) Check-in 4 pm. Refrigerators; A/C; C/CATV; movies; radios; phones. 4 2-bedrm units. Coin laundry. Htd pool; whirlpool. Pets, $30 extra charge. 1-bedroom suites with living room & efficiency. Monthly rates avail. AE, DI, DS, MC, VI. ● Restaurant; 6 am-2 & 5-10 pm; $6.95-$17.95; cocktails. FAX (805) 928-0356 *(See ad p A503)*
⊗ Ⓢ Ⓓ 🅰 (805) 928-6000

Santa Maria Airport Hilton   Rates Subject to Change   *Hotel* ◆◆◆
 All year   1P .... 59.00   .... 59.00 2P/2B .... 59.00 XP 10
190 units. From US 101, exit Betteravia Rd, 2 1/4 mi w, then 1 3/4 mi s on Skyway Dr; adjacent to airport. 3455 Skyway Dr. (93455) Some balconies. Check-in 3 pm. A/C; C/CATV; movies; rental VCPs. Radios; phones. Htd pool; whirlpool. Parking lot. Airport transp. No pets. Monthly rates avail. AE, DI, DS, MC, VI. ● Dining rm & coffeeshop; 6 am-10 pm; $10-$26; cocktails; entertainment. FAX (805) 928-5251 *(See ad below & p 22)*
⊗ Ⓢ Ⓓ 🅰 (805) 928-8000

Our **bold type** listings have a special interest in serving you!

Santa Maria Inn
AAA All year — Rates Guaranteed — *Historic Hotel* ◆◆◆
1P 69.00- 83.00 2P/1B 69.00- 83.00 2P/2B 69.00- 83.00 XP 10 F
Senior discount. 166 units. 1/2 mi s on SR 135 & US 101 business rt. 801 S Broadway. (93454) Old English Country motif. Attractively decorated rooms in the original restored building. Very spacious rooms in the new tower section. Check-in 3 pm. Refrigerators; 142 A/C; C/CATV; VCPs; radios; phones. 12 2-bedrm units. Htd pool; sauna; whirlpool; 40 rooms with whirlpool tub; exercise rm. Garage & parking lot. Airport transp. No pets. AE, DI, MC, VI. ● Dining rm; 6 am-10 pm; $11-$21; cocktails. Also, Santa Maria Inn Restaurant, see separate listing. FAX (805) 928-5690 *(See ad below)* ⊗ Ⓢ Ⓓ ⓑ (805) 928-7777

Western Host Motor Hotel
AAA — Rates Guaranteed — *Motel* ◆◆
Fri-Sun 5/1-9/30   1P 39.00- 59.00 2P/1B 47.00- 59.00 2P/2B 49.00- 69.00 XP 5 F
10/1-4/30   1P 35.00- 45.00 2P/1B 40.00- 50.00 2P/2B 45.00- 55.00 XP 5 F
Mon-Thurs 5/1-9/30 1P 35.00- 39.00 2P/1B 40.00- 45.00 2P/2B 45.00- 50.00 XP 5 F
81 units. On SR 166; 1 blk w of jct US 101. 1007 E Main St. (93454) 57 refrigerators; A/C; C/CATV; pay movies; rental VCPs. Radios; phones; shower or comb baths. Htd pool; whirlpool; tennis-2 courts. Small pets only, $3 extra. AE, DI, MC, VI. Coffeeshop adjacent. *(See ad below)* ⊗ Ⓓ (805) 922-4505

RESTAURANTS

Central City Broiler — American — $$ ◆◆
1 mi n on US 101 business rt & SR 135. 1520 N Broadway. Early American decor. Selection of barbecue, steaks, chicken, seafood & prime rib. A/C. Early bird specials; children's menu. Open 11:30 am-2 & 5-9 pm; Fri-10 pm; Sat 5 pm-10 pm; Sun 5 pm-9 pm; closed 1/1, 12/24 & 12/25. Cocktails & lounge. AE, MC, VI. ⊗ (805) 922-3700

Santa Maria Inn Restaurant — American — $$
AAA In Santa Maria Inn. Very attractive dining room, selection of prime rib, steaks, seafood, chicken & continental entrees. Sun brunch 10 am-2 pm. A/C. Early bird specials. Open 11 am-10 pm. Cocktails & lounge. Entertainment. Reserv advised. AE, DI, MC, VI. (805) 928-7777

SANTA MONICA — 86,900   (See LOS ANGELES (Central & Western Areas) spotting map pages A212 & A213; see index starting on page A210) See also LOS ANGELES (Central & Western Areas)

Best Western Santa Monica Gateway
Hotel 🔲173 — Rates Guaranteed — *Motel* ◆◆◆
AAA All year   1P 69.00- 99.00 2P/1B 69.00- 99.00 2P/2B 69.00- 99.00 XP 5
Senior discount. 125 units. 1 1/4 mi e of SR 1 (Lincoln Blvd). 1920 Santa Monica Blvd. (90404) A/C; C/CATV; radios; phones. Exercise rm. Garage. No pets. Refrigerators & microwaves, $10 extra charge. Reserv deposit required; 7 days refund notice. AE, DI, DS, MC, VI. FAX (310) 829-9211 ⊗ Ⓢ Ⓓ ⓑ (310) 829-9100

Channel Road Inn Bed & Breakfast 🔲180 — Rates Subject to Change — *Historic Bed & Breakfast* ◆◆◆
All year [BP] 2P/1B 95.00- 180.00 2P/2B 95.00- 225.00 XP 15
14 units. 1 blk e of Pacific Coast Hwy. 219 W Channel Rd. (90402) 1910 Colonial Revival house furnished with period antiques. 1 block from beach, some rooms with ocean view. Smoke free premises. Check-in 3 pm. C/TV; radios; phones; comb or shower baths. Whirlpool; bicycles. No pets. Reserv deposit required; 3 days refund notice. MC, VI. FAX (310) 454-9920 ⊗ Ⓢ Ⓓ ⓑ (310) 459-1920

Comfort Inn 🔲171 — Rates Subject to Change — *Motel* ◆◆
5/28-10/2   1P 75.00- 75.00 2P/1B 75.00- 85.00 2P/2B .... 85.00 XP 10 F
10/3-5/27   1P 55.00- 65.00 2P/1B 65.00- 75.00 2P/2B .... 75.00 XP 10 F
Senior discount. 101 units. 1 1/2 mi e of SR 1 (Lincoln Blvd). 2815 Santa Monica Blvd. (90404) 10 refrigerators; A/C; C/CATV; movies; radios; phones; comb or shower baths. Htd pool. No pets. AE, DI, DS, MC, VI. *(See ad p A506)* ⊗ Ⓓ (310) 828-5517

(See LOS ANGELES (Central & Western Areas) spotting map pages A212 & A213)

Guest Quarters Suite Hotel **181**   AAA Special Value Rates   *Suites Hotel* ◆◆◆
    All year   1P 165.00- 185.00 2P/1B 185.00- 205.00 2P/2B 185.00- 205.00 XP 20
    253 units. Adjacent to I-10, exit 4th St; 1 blk s. 1707 Fourth St. (90401) 1-bedroom suites with living room & balcony overlooking atrium. Check-in 3 pm. A/C; C/CATV; movies; radios; phones. Pool; sauna; whirlpool; exercise rm. Pay valet garage. No pets. Wkly & monthly rates avail. AE, DI, DS, MC, VI. ● Restaurant; 6 am-10 pm; $7.95-$21.95; cocktails.
    FAX (310) 452-7399   ⊗ Ⓢ Ⓓ Ⓛ (310) 395-3332

Holiday Inn-Bayview Plaza **177**   AAA Special Value Rates   *Hotel* ◆◆◆
    All year   1P 99.00-129.00 2P/1B 99.00-139.00 2P/2B 99.00-139.00 XP 10   F
    309 units. 1 blk w of Lincoln Ave. 530 Pico Blvd. (90405) Check-in 4 pm. A/C; C/CATV; movies; radios; phones. Coin laundry. Htd pool; whirlpool; exercise rm. Garage. No pets. AE, DI, DS, MC, VI. ● Dining rm; 6:30 am-11 pm; 1/1-4/30 6 am-2 & 5-11 pm; $5.50-$18; cocktails; entertainment. FAX (310) 399-2504   ⊗ Ⓢ Ⓓ Ⓛ (310) 399-9344

Hotel Santa Monica **182**   Rates Subject to Change   *Motel* ◆◆
🏛️ 6/1-11/14 [CP]   1P .... 69.00 2P/1B .... 69.00 2P/2B .... 79.00 XP 10   F
    11/15-5/31 [CP]   1P .... 59.00 2P/1B .... 59.00 2P/2B .... 69.00 XP 10   F
    Senior discount. 99 units. From I-10, exit Centinela Ave; 3 blks w. 3102 W Pico Blvd. (90405) Check-in 3 pm. 49 refrigerators; A/C; C/CATV; phones. 37 kitchens. Coin laundry. No pets. Microwaves. Wkly rates avail. Reserv deposit required. AE, DI, DS, MC, VI. Restaurant opposite. FAX (310) 450-8843 *(See ad below)*
                                                        ⊗ Ⓓ (310) 450-5766

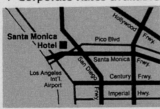

(See LOS ANGELES (Central & Western Areas) spotting map pages A212 & A213)

Loews Santa Monica Beach Hotel 179   Rates Subject to Change   *Hotel*   ◆◆◆◆
♿ All year   1P 195.00- 450.00   2P/1B   195.00- 450.00   2P/2B 195.00- 450.00 XP 20   F
350 units. 1700 Ocean Ave. (90401) Many ocean view rooms. Check-in 3 pm. A/C; C/CATV; movies; radios; phones. Htd indoor/outdoor pool; whirlpool; rental bicycles; steamroom; health club. Fee for: massage. Pay valet garage. Pets, $100 deposit required. AE, CB, DI, MC, VI. ● Restaurant & coffeeshop; 6:30 am-11 pm; Sun brunch 10:30 am-2:30 pm; $14.95-$27; 24 hour room service; cocktails; entertainment. FAX (310) 458-0020
⊗ Ⓢ Ⓓ ♿ (310) 458-6700

Miramar Sheraton Hotel 175   Rates Subject to Change   *Hotel*   ◆◆◆
♿ All year   1P 125.00- 350.00   2P/1B   145.00- 370.00   2P/2B 145.00- 370.00 XP 20   F
Senior discount. 305 units. 101 Wilshire Blvd at Ocean Ave. (90401) Many rooms with balcony overlooking ocean. Check-in 3 pm. A/C; C/CATV; movies; radios; phones; comb or shower baths. Htd pool; health club. Limited pay parking lot. No pets. AE, DI, DS, MC, VI. ● Dining rm & coffeeshop; 6 am-11:30 pm; $6.95-$22.50; 24 hour room service; cocktails; entertainment. FAX (310) 458-7912
⊗ Ⓓ ♿ (310) 576-7777

Oceana Hotel 172   AAA Special Value Rates   *Suites Motel*   ◆
♿ All year [CP]   1P 99.00- 109.00   2P/1B   119.00- 149.00   2P/2B 119.00- 149.00 XP 10   F
60 units. 3 blks n of Wilshire Blvd. 849 Ocean Ave. (90403) 48 1-bedroom & 9 2-bedroom kitchen suites; also 4 studio units. Some balconies, some with ocean view. C/CATV; movies; rental VCPs. Phones. Coin laundry. Htd pool. Garage. No pets. 2-bedroom apartments, $159-$189 for up to 4 persons. Wkly & monthly rates avail. AE, CB, DI. FAX (310) 458-1182
Ⓓ (310) 393-0486

Pacific Shore Hotel 176   Rates Subject to Change   *Motor Inn*   ◆◆◆
♿ All year   1P 115.00- 145.00   2P/1B   125.00- 155.00   2P/2B 125.00- 155.00 XP 15   F
Senior discount. 168 units. 1819 Ocean Blvd. (90401) Some rooms with ocean view. Check-in 3 pm. 11 refrigerators; A/C; C/CATV; pay movies; radios; phones. Coin laundry. Pool; saunas; whirlpool. No pets. AE, DI, MC, VI. Restaurant adjacent. FAX (310) 394-6657 *(See ad below)*
⊗ Ⓢ Ⓓ ♿ (310) 451-8711

Radisson Huntley Hotel 174   Rates Guaranteed   *Hotel*   ◆◆◆
♿ All year   1P 95.00- 145.00   ....   2P/2B 105.00- 155.00 XP 10   F
213 units. 1 blk n of Wilshire Blvd. 1111 Second St. (90403) Check-in 3 pm. A/C; C/TV; radios; phones. Pay valet garage. No pets. Wkly & monthly rates avail. AE, CB, DI, MC, VI. ● Restaurant & coffeeshop; 6 am-midnight; $5.75-$19.95; cocktails; entertainment. FAX (310) 458-9776 *(See ad p A231)*
⊗ Ⓢ Ⓓ ♿ (310) 394-5454

Shangri-La Hotel 178   Rates Subject to Change   *Motel*   ◆◆◆
♿ All year [CP]   1P 110.00- 205.00   2P/1B   110.00- 205.00   2P/2B   .... 230.00 XP 15
55 units. 1 blk s of Wilshire Blvd. 1301 Ocean Ave. (90401) Built in 1939. Designed in art deco style. Located across from Palisades Park. Check-in 3 pm. Refrigerators; C/TV; 20 radios; phones. 7 2-bedrm units, 47 kitchens. Coin laundry. No pets. AE, DI, DS, MC, VI. Afternoon tea served 2:30 pm-4 pm. FAX (310) 451-3351 *(See ad p A508)*
Ⓓ (310) 394-2791

(See LOS ANGELES (Central & Western Areas) spotting map pages A212 & A213)

RESTAURANTS

Bob Burns Restaurant (80)   American $$ ◆◆
202 Wilshire Blvd. Nice selection of seafood and other entrees. A/C. Open 11:30 am-11 pm; Fri & Sat-midnight; Sun 10:30 am-10:30 pm; closed 1/1, 7/4 & 12/25. Cocktails & lounge. Valet parking. AE, CB, DI, MC, VI. ⊗ (310) 393-6777

Cafe Casino (76)   American $ ◆◆
1299 Ocean Ave at Arizona Ave. Cafeteria. Charming atmosphere of a French sidewalk cafe. A/C. Open 7 am-10 pm; Fri & Sat-11 pm; closed 12/25. Beer & wine. MC, VI.   ⊗ (310) 394-3717

Chinois on Main (75)   Chinese $$$ ◆◆◆
1/2 mi w of SR 1 (Lincoln Blvd). 2709 Main St. Casual atmosphere. California-Chinese cuisine. A/C. Open 11:30 am-2 & 6-10:30 pm; Sat from 6 pm; Sun 5:30 pm-10 pm; closed for lunch Mon & Tues. Cocktails & lounge. Reserv required. AE, CB, DI, MC, VI.   ⊗ (310) 392-9025

Knoll's Black Forest Inn (78)   German $$ ◆◆◆
2454 Wilshire Blvd. Charming restaurant. A/C. Open 11:30 am-3 & 5:30-10:30 pm; Sat & Sun from 5 pm; closed Mon & 12/25. Cocktails & lounge. Valet parking. Reserv advised. AE, CB, DI, MC, VI.   ⊗ (310) 395-2212

Madame Wu's Garden (79)   Chinese $$ ◆◆
2201 Wilshire Blvd. Nice selection of Cantonese, Mandarin & Szechwan dishes. A/C. Open 11:30 am-10 pm; Fri-11 pm; Sat 5 pm-11:30 pm; Sun noon-10 pm; closed 11/25. Cocktails & lounge. Pay valet parking. Reserv advised. AE, CB, DI, MC, VI.   ⊗ (310) 828-5656

Michael's (82)   American $$$$ ◆◆◆
1/2 blk n of Wilshire Blvd. 1147 3rd St. Patio dining in attractive garden weather permitting. Sat & Sun brunch. Sat & Sun 10:30 am-2 pm. A/C. Dress code. Open noon-2 & 6:30-10 pm; Sat & Sun 10:30 am-2 & 6:30-10 pm; closed major holidays. Cocktails. Reserv advised. AE, DI, MC, VI.   ⊗ (310) 451-0843

Valentino Restaurant (77)   Italian $$$ ◆◆◆
1/4 mi w of Centinela Ave. 3115 Pico Blvd. Also Continental cuisine. A/C. Open 5:30 pm-10:30 pm; Fri & Sat-11:30 pm; closed Sun & major holidays. Cocktails. Pay valet parking. Reserv required. AE, CB, DI, MC, VI.   (310) 829-4313

SANTA NELLA — 100

Best Western Andersen's Inn — Rates Subject to Change — Motel ◆
All year — 1P 50.00- 56.00 2P/1B 52.00- 58.00 2P/2B 56.00- 62.00 XP 6 F
Senior discount. 94 units. E off & adjacent to I-5; 4 mi n of SR 152, Pacheco Pass Rd; exit I-5 via Santa Nella-Gustine SR 33. 12367 Hwy 33S. (95322) Danish architecture. A/C; C/CATV; phones. Coin laundry. Pool. 8 rooms with whirlpool bath, $5 extra. AE, DI, DS, MC, VI. Restaurant adjacent. FAX (209) 827-1449 *(See ad p A508)*
⊗ Ⓓ 🛆 (209) 826-5534

Holiday Inn Mission de Oro — AAA Special Value Rates — Motor Inn ◆◆◆
5/30-9/19 — 1P 39.95- 59.95 2P/1B 49.95- 69.95 2P/2B 59.95- 64.95 XP 10 F
9/20-5/29 — 1P 39.95- 49.95 2P/1B 49.95- 59.95 2P/2B 49.95- 54.95 XP 10 F
159 units. 3 1/2 mi n of jct SR 152; w off & adjacent to I-5; southbound exit Gilroy-SR 33, northbound exit SR 33-Gustine-Santa Nella. 13070 Hwy 33S. (95322) Spacious. Surrounding an attractive early California-style plaza. 15 refrigerators; A/C; C/CATV; pay movies; radios; phones. Pool; whirlpools; playground; 9 rooms with whirlpool bath. Pets. AE, DI, DS, MC, VI. ● Restaurant; 6:30 am-10 pm; $6-$15; cocktails. FAX (209) 826-8071 *(See ad below)*
⊗ Ⓢ Ⓓ (209) 826-4444

La Fontaine Inn — AAA Special Value Rates — Motel ◆◆
All year [CP] — 1P .... 59.00 2P/1B .... 66.00 2P/2B .... 66.00 XP 7 F
100 units. 2 blk e of I-5; SR 33 exit. 28976 W Plaza Dr. (95322) Formerly LaFontaine Travelodge. Refrigerators; A/C; C/CATV; radios; phones. Coin laundry. Htd pool; whirlpool; exercise rm. Wkly & monthly rates avail. AE, DI, DS, MC, VI. Coffeeshop opposite. FAX (209) 826-9039 *(See ad below)*
⊗ Ⓢ Ⓓ 🛆 (209) 826-8282

SANTA PAULA — 25,100

Santa Paula Travelodge — Rates Subject to Change — Motel ◆◆
All year [CP] — 1P .... 43.00 2P/1B .... 49.00 2P/2B .... 59.00 XP 10
Senior discount. 52 units. 1/4 blk n of SR 126; exit Peck Rd. 350 S Peck Rd. (93060) 8 refrigerators; A/C; C/CATV; movies; rental VCPs. Radios; phones. 3 efficiencies, no utensils. Small htd pool; whirlpool; 10 rooms with whirlpool tub. No pets. Wkly rates avail. AE, DI, DS, MC, VI. Restaurant adjacent. FAX (805) 525-4230
⊗ Ⓢ Ⓓ (805) 525-1561

The White Gables Inn — Rates Subject to Change — Historic Bed & Breakfast ◆◆◆
4/1-10/31 [BP] — 2P/1B 85.00- 115.00 — XP 20
11/1-3/31 [BP] — 2P/1B 70.00- 100.00 — XP 20
3 units. From SR 126 exit 10th St (SR 150), 1/2 mi n then 4 blks w. 715 E Santa Paula St. (93060) Historical 1894 Victorian Queen Anne house located in a designated historical district. 3-story, no elevator. 1 room with balcony. Designated smoking areas. Check-in 3 pm. Radios; comb or shower baths. Parking lot. No pets. Spacious 3rd floor suite with sitting room, bedroom, kitchen & bath. Reserv deposit required.
⊗ Ⓓ (805) 933-3041

RESTAURANT

Familia Diaz — Mexican — $ — ◆
Adjacent northside of SR 126; exit 10th St (SR 150). 245 S 10th St. Casual atmosphere. A/C. Children's menu. Open 11 am-2 & 4:30-9 pm; Sat & Sun 11 am-9 pm; closed major holidays & 8/2-8/13. Cocktails & lounge. DS, MC, VI.
(805) 525-2813

SANTA ROSA — 113,300

Best Western Garden Inn — Rates Guaranteed — Motel ◆◆◆
4/1-10/31 — 1P 45.00- 60.00 2P/1B 55.00- 70.00 2P/2B .... 70.00 XP 5
Senior discount. 78 units. 1 mi s on US 101 business rt; northbound exit Baker Ave; southbound exit Corby Ave. 1500 Santa Rosa Ave. (95404) OPEN ALL YEAR. 41 refrigerators; A/C; C/CATV; movies; radios; phones; comb or shower baths. 5 2-bedrm units. Coin laundry. 2 pools. Pets, $10 extra charge. Reserv deposit required. AE, DI, DS, MC, VI. Coffeeshop; 6:30 am-11 am. FAX (707) 526-4903 *(See ad below)*
⊗ Ⓓ 🛆 (707) 546-4031

Best Western Hillside Inn   Rates Guaranteed   *Motel* ◆◆◆
ⓐ 4/1-10/31   1P .... 46.00   2P/1B .... 50.00   2P/2B .... 54.00   XP 4   F
     11/1-3/31   1P .... 44.00   2P/1B .... 46.00   2P/2B .... 49.00   XP 4   F
36 units. 2 1/2 mi e off US 101 on SR 12, at Farmers Ln & 4th St. 2901 4th St. (95409) Some balconies & patios. A/C; C/CATV; radios; phones. 7 2-bedrm units. Coin laundry. Pool; sauna. 17 efficiencies & 19 kitchens, $4 extra. Reserv deposit required. AE, DI, DS, MC, VI. Coffeeshop; 6:30 am-3 pm; beer & wine. *(See ad below)*
     Ⓓ (707) 546-9353

Days Inn   Rates Guaranteed   *Motor Inn* ◆◆◆
ⓐ Fri & Sat 5/1-9/30   1P 75.00- 95.00   2P/1B 85.00- 105.00   2P/2B 85.00- 105.00   XP 10   F
    Sun-Thurs 5/1-9/30   1P 65.00- 85.00   2P/1B 75.00- 95.00   2P/2B 75.00- 95.00   XP 10   F
    2/1-4/30 & 10/1-1/31   1P 55.00- 75.00   2P/1B 65.00- 85.00   2P/2B 65.00- 85.00   XP 10   F
Senior discount. 135 units. US 101, exit downtown w; adjacent to Railroad Square, Old Town. 3rd & Railroad St. (95401) Check-in 3 pm. A/C; C/CATV; free & pay movies; radios; phones. Pool; whirlpool. No pets. Reserv deposit required. AE, DI, DS, MC, VI. ● Coffeeshop; 6 am-2 & 5-10 pm; a la carte entrees about $8-$14; cocktail lounge. FAX (707) 573-0272 *(See ad p A510)*
     ⊗ Ⓢ Ⓓ ⓓ (707) 573-9000

Doubletree Hotel-Santa Rosa   Rates Guaranteed   *Motor Inn* ◆◆◆◆
ⓐ 5/22-11/1   1P 89.00- 119.00   2P/1B 89.00- 119.00   2P/2B 89.00- 119.00   XP 10   F
   2/1-5/21 & 11/2-1/31   1P 79.00- 109.00   2P/1B 79.00- 109.00   2P/2B 79.00- 109.00   XP 10   F
Senior discount. 247 units. US 101; exit e via Mendocino-Old Redwood Hwy; 3 blks n top of the hill. 3555 Round Barn Blvd. (95403) Check-in 3 pm. 26 refrigerators; A/C; C/CATV; pay movies; radios; phones. Pool; whirlpool; jogging track. No pets. AE, DI, DS, MC, VI. ● Dining rm; 6:30 am-10:30 pm; a la carte entrees about $11-$20; cocktails. FAX (707) 545-2807 *(See ad below)*
     ⊗ Ⓢ Ⓓ ⓓ (707) 523-7555

AAA CampBooks — valuable additions for members
who enjoy outdoor vacations.

El Rancho Tropicana   Rates Subject to Change   Motor Inn   ◆◆

4/16-10/16	1P	60.00-	75.00	2P/1B	70.00-	85.00	2P/2B	80.00-	85.00	XP	5
10/17-1/31	1P	55.00-	70.00	2P/1B	65.00-	80.00	2P/2B	65.00-	80.00	XP	5
2/1-4/15	1P	50.00-	65.00	2P/1B	60.00-	75.00	2P/2B	60.00-	75.00	XP	5

Senior discount. 270 units. 1 1/2 mi s on US 101 business rt; northbound exit Hearn, southbound exit Santa Rosa Ave. 2200 Santa Rosa Ave. (95407) Spacious grounds. Many large rooms. Few studio units & housekeeping apartments. Check-in 3 pm. A/C; C/CATV; movies; 168 radios; phones; shower or comb baths. 10 2-bedrm units. 3 pools; wading pool; whirlpool; tennis-4 courts; playground. No pets. Reserv deposit required; 4 days refund notice. AE, DI, DS, MC, VI. ● Dining rm & coffeeshop; 24 hours; $9-$20; cocktails; entertainment. FAX (707) 576-1033 *(See ad below)*
(D) (707) 542-3655

Flamingo Resort Hotel   Rates Subject to Change   Motor Inn   ◆◆◆
(AAA) 4/1-10/31   1P 66.00- 94.00   2P/1B   76.00- 94.00   2P/2B   76.00- 94.00 XP 11   F
137 units. Off SR 12, at Farmers Ln. 2777 Fourth St. (95405) OPEN ALL YEAR. Attractively landscaped grounds. Check-in 3 pm. A/C; C/CATV; pay movies; phones. Htd pool; wading pool; whirlpool; tennis-5 courts; jogging track. Fee for: health club. Airport transp. No pets. AE, DI, MC, VI. ● Dining rm; 6:30 am-11 pm; a la carte entrees about $8-$15; cocktails. FAX (707) 528-1404 *(See ad below)*   ⊗ (S) (D) (707) 545-8530

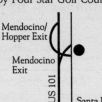

FountainGrove Inn ⓐ ⑭
All year [CP] Rates Guaranteed Motor Inn ◆◆◆◆
1P .... 75.00 2P/1B .... 85.00 2P/2B .... 85.00 XP 10 F
Senior discount. 85 units. 2 mi n off US 101; exit Mendocino Ave/Old Redwood Hwy; 1/4 mi s to Fountain Grove Pkwy. 101 Fountain Grove Pkwy. (95403) Atrium lobby of natural wood & stone. Water cascades over stone lobby wall. Check-in 4 pm. Refrigerators; A/C; C/CATV; free & pay movies; radios; phones. Small pool; whirlpool. No pets. 4 suites $125-$175 for up to 2 persons. Wkly & monthly rates avail. Reserv deposit required. AE, DI, DS, MC, VI. ● Equus Restaurant, see separate listing. FAX (707) 544-3126 *(See ad p A512)*
⊗ Ⓓⅉ (707) 578-6101

Heritage Inn ⓐ
All year Rates Subject to Change Motor Inn ◆
1P .... 47.00 2P/1B .... 62.00 2P/2B .... 85.00 XP 6 F
Senior discount. 96 units. 1 1/2 mi n on US 101, northbound exit W Old Redwood Hwy/Mendocino Ave, southbound exit Hopper Ave. 870 Hopper Ave. (95403) Refrigerators; A/C; C/CATV; movies; radios; phones. Pool. 5 suites with whirlpool bath, $115. Pets, $20 deposit, small dogs only. Wkly rates avail. Reserv deposit required. AE, CB, DI, MC, VI. Restaurant adjacent. FAX (707) 571-0145 *(See ad p A364)* ⊗ ⑤Ⅾⅉ (707) 545-9000

Hotel La Rose ⓐ
All year AAA Special Value Rates Historical ◆◆◆
.... 2P/1B 60.00- 85.00 2P/2B .... 75.00 XP 15 F
49 units. 2 blk w off US 101, exit downtown Santa Rosa Ave; on Railroad Square. 308 Wilson St. (95401) Cobblestone hotel built in 1907. English country atmosphere. Check-in 3 pm. A/C; C/CATV; radios; phones; comb or shower baths. No pets. Wkly & monthly rates avail. Reserv deposit required; 3 days refund notice. AE, MC, VI. Dining rm; 11:30 am-2 & 5:30-9 pm Tues-Fri, Sat 5:30 pm-9 pm; closed Sun-Mon; a la carte entrees about $10-$16; cocktails. FAX (707) 579-3247 ⊗ ⑤Ⅾ (707) 579-3200

Los Robles Lodge ⓐ
All year AAA Special Value Rates Motor Inn ◆◆◆
1P 65.00- 85.00 2P/1B 70.00- 90.00 2P/2B 70.00- 90.00 XP 5 F
105 units. 1 mi n off US 101; exit via Steele Ln. 925 Edwards Ave. (95401) Check-in 4 pm. Refrigerators; A/C; C/CATV; movies; rental VCPs. Radios; phones; comb or shower baths. Coin laundry. Pool; wading pool; whirlpool; outdoor fitness center. Airport transp. Pets. Wkly & monthly rates avail. Reserv deposit required. AE, DI, DS, MC, VI. ● Restaurant & coffeeshop; 6 am-10 pm; $8-$29; cocktails. Also dining room, see separate listing. FAX (707) 575-5826 ⊗ Ⅾ (707) 545-6330

Sandman Motel ⓐ
All year AAA Special Value Rates Motel ◆◆◆
1P 38.00- 47.00 2P/1B 42.00- 52.00 2P/2B 44.00- 54.00 XP 4 F
112 units. 2 3/4 mi n off US 101; exit Mendocino Ave. 3421 Cleveland Ave. (95403) Check-in 4 pm. A/C; C/CATV; movies; radios; phones. Pool; whirlpool. No pets. Reserv deposit required; 3 days refund notice. AE, DI, DS, MC, VI. Coffeeshop adjacent. FAX (707) 544-8710 *(See ad below)* ⊗ Ⅾ (707) 544-8570

Santa Rosa Downtown Travelodge ⓐ
All year Rates Subject to Change Motel ◆
1P .... 45.00 2P/1B .... 58.00 2P/2B .... 70.00 XP 5 F
44 units. Exit e 3 blks off US 101 via College Ave, at Mendocino Ave. 635 Healdsburg Ave. (95401) A/C; C/CATV; movies; 26 radios; phones; shower or comb baths. Pool; sauna. Pets. Wkly rates avail. Reserv deposit required. AE, DI, DS, MC, VI. ⊗ Ⅾⅉ (707) 544-4141

Santa Rosa Travelodge ⓐ
7/1-10/31 AAA Special Value Rates Motel ◆◆
1P .... 50.00 2P/1B .... 63.00 2P/2B .... 65.00 XP 5 F
11/1-6/30 1P .... 48.00 2P/1B .... 55.00 2P/2B .... 55.00 XP 5 F
31 units. 1 1/2 mi s on US 101 business rt; northbound exit US 101 via Baker Ave, southbound Santa Rosa Ave-Corby. 1815 Santa Rosa Ave. (95407) A/C; C/CATV; movies; phones; shower or comb baths. 4 2-bedrm units. Pool. Reserv deposit required. AE, DI, DS, MC, VI. ⊗ Ⅾ (707) 542-3472

Super 8 Lodge ⓐ
All year Rates Guaranteed Motel ◆◆
1P .... 42.00 2P/1B .... 46.00 2P/2B .... 50.00 XP 5 F
Senior discount. 100 units. 1 mi n off US 101; exit via Steele Ln. 2632 Cleveland Ave. (95403) A/C; C/CATV; phones. Pool. No pets. AE, DI, DS, MC, VI. Coffeeshop opposite. FAX (707) 542-9738 ⊗ ⑤Ⅾ (707) 542-5544

Vintners Inn ⓐ
All year [CP] Rates Subject to Change Lodge ◆◆◆◆
1P 118.00- 195.00 2P/1B 118.00- 195.00 2P/2B 118.00- 195.00 XP 10
44 units. 2 mi n on US 101; exit w off US 101 via River Rd-Mark West Springs Rd. 4350 Barnes Rd. (95403) Surrounded by vineyards & country charm; Country French decor. Some fireplaces. Check-in 3 pm. Refrigerators; A/C; C/CATV; rental VCPs; radios; phones. Whirlpool. No pets. Reserv deposit required; 3 days refund notice. AE, CB, DI, MC, VI. ● John Ash & Company, see separate listing. ⑤Ⅾ (707) 575-7350

RESTAURANTS

Equus Restaurant Continental $$$ ◆◆◆
In FountainGrove Inn. A/C. Open 11:30 am-2:30 & 5:30-9:30 pm; Fri & Sat-10 pm; Sun 10 am-2:30 & 5-9 pm. Cocktails. Minimum, $8. Reserv advised. AE, DI, DS, MC, VI. ⊗ (707) 578-6101

John Ash & Company   French $$$ ◆◆◆
At Vintners Inn. Emphasis on local foods. Smoking not permitted. A/C. Open 11:30 am-2 & 5:30-9:30 pm; Sat 5 pm-10 pm; Sun 10:30 am-2 & 5:30-9 pm; closed Mon, 1/1 & 12/25. Cocktails. Reserv advised. AE, DI, MC, VI.
     ⊗ (707) 527-7687

La Gare French Restaurant   French $$$ ◆◆
US 101, exit downtown; 2 blks w; 1/2 blk s of Railroad Square. 208 Wilson St. Smoke free premises. A/C. Children's menu. Open 5:30 pm-10 pm; Fri & Sat from 5 pm; Sun 5 pm-9 pm; closed Mon, 1/1, 11/25 & 12/25. Beer & wine. Minimum, $8. Reserv advised. AE, DI, MC, VI.
     ⊗ (707) 528-4355

Lisa Hemenway's   American $$ ◆◆
On SR 12 in Montgomery Village; in Village Court Mall area. 714 Village Ct. California cuisine, emphasis on fresh Sonoma County products. A/C. Open 11:30 am-2:30 & 5:30-9:30 pm; closed Sun-Mon for dinner & major holidays. Beer & wine. Reserv advised. DI, MC, VI.
     ⊗ (707) 526-5111

Los Robles Lodge Dining Room   American $$ ◆◆
In Los Robles Lodge. Also continental dishes featured. A/C. Children's menu. Open 11 am-2 & 5-10 pm; Sun 10 am-2 & 4:30-9 pm; closed 2/17, 7/4 & 9/7. Cocktails & lounge. Dancing. Parking avail. Reserv advised. AE, DI, DS, MC, VI.
     ⊗ (707) 545-6330

SANTEE — 52,900
Best Western Santee   Rates Subject to Change   *Motel*   ◆◆◆
🏮 All year [CP]   1P .... 45.00   2P/1B .... 50.00   2P/2B .... 59.00   XP 5   F
Senior discount. 47 units. 1/2 blk e of Magnolia Ave. 10726 Woodside Ave. (92071) 5 refrigerators; A/C; C/CATV; radios; phones; comb or shower baths. Small pool; whirlpool. No pets. Wkly rates avail. Reserv deposit required. AE, DI, DS, MC, VI. Restaurant opposite. *(See ad p A386)*   ⊗ Ⓢ Ⓓ (619) 449-2626

SAN YSIDRO   (See SAN DIEGO spotting map pages A376 & A377; see index starting on page A374 A374)
Americana Inn & Suites 155   AAA Special Value Rates   *Motel*   ◆◆
🏮 All year   1P 35.00- 38.00   2P/1B 39.00- 42.00   2P/2B 39.00- 42.00   XP 5   F
126 units. Adjacent to I-5, exit Dairy Mart Rd. 815 San Ysidro Blvd. (92173) Formerly Rodeway Inn San Diego South. Refrigerators; A/C; C/CATV; movies; phones. Coin laundry. Htd pool; whirlpool. No pets. Monthly rates avail. AE, CB, DI, MC, VI. Coffeeshop adjacent. FAX (619) 428-0693   ⊗ Ⓓ (619) 428-5521

International Motor Inn 157   Rates Guaranteed   *Motel*   ◆
🏮 All year   1P 38.00- 41.00   2P/1B 38.00- 41.00   2P/2B 38.00- 41.00   XP 2   F
Senior discount. 100 units. Adjacent to I-5, exit Via de San Ysidro, then 1 blk se. 190 E Calle Primera. (92173) 42 refrigerators; A/C; C/CATV; movies; radios; phones. 34 efficiencies. Coin laundry. Htd pool; whirlpool. AE, CB, DI, MC, VI. Coffeeshop adjacent. FAX (619) 428-3618   ⊗ Ⓓ Ⓖ (619) 428-4486

SARATOGA — 28,100   See also LOS GATOS
The Inn at Saratoga   Rates Subject to Change   *Motor Inn*   ◆◆◆
🏮 All year [CP]   1P 145.00- 245.00   2P/1B 145.00- 245.00   2P/2B .... 145.00   XP 15
46 units. Center; 1/2 blk n of SR 9. (95070) Tastefully appointed. Patios or balconies overlooking adjacent park or creek. Check-in 3 pm. Refrigerators; A/C; C/CATV; radios; phones. 1 2-bedrm unit. 7 rooms with whirlpool bath. No pets. 15 units with VCP. Reserv deposit required. AE, DI, MC, VI. Restaurant opposite. FAX (408) 741-0981 *(See ad below)*   ⊗ Ⓢ Ⓓ Ⓖ (408) 867-5020

RESTAURANTS

La Mere Michelle   French $$$ ◆◆◆
On SR 9. 14467 Big Basin Way. Quiet, refined ambiance. A/C. Open 11:30 am-2 & 6-10 pm; closed Mon & major holidays. Cocktails & lounge. Reserv advised. AE, CB, DI, MC, VI.   ⊗ (408) 867-5272

The Plumed Horse   French $$$ ◆◆◆◆
1/4 mi sw on SR 9. 14555 Big Basin Way. Relaxing old-world charm. Frequent menu changes & fresh seasonal products. Outstanding wine cellar. Designated smoking areas. A/C. Open 6 pm-10 pm; closed Sun & major holidays. Cocktails & lounge. Entertainment & dancing. Pay valet parking. Reserv advised. AE, CB, DI, MC, VI. ⊗ Ⓖ (408) 867-4711

SAUSALITO — 7,200   See also CORTE MADERA, MILL VALLEY & TIBURON
RESTAURANTS

Hotel Alta Mira Dining Room   American $$$ ◆
Center; w on Princess St from Bridgeway; n on Bulkley Ave. 125 Bulkley Ave. Hillside location with excellent view of San Francisco Bay area. Varied menu; popular for lunch & Sun brunch. Terrace dining. Dress code. Children's menu. Open 7:30 am-11 pm. Cocktails & lounge. Pay valet parking. Reserv advised. AE, CB, MC, VI.   (415) 332-1350

The Spinnaker   Seafood $$ ◆◆
100 Spinnaker Dr. Dining room over water. Varied menu. A/C. Children's menu. Open 11 am-11 pm; Fri & Sat-midnight; closed 11/26 & 12/25. Cocktails & lounge. Minimum $3. Valet parking. Reserv advised. AE, DI, MC, VI. (415) 332-1500

SCOTTS VALLEY — 8,600

Best Western Inn-Scotts Valley   Rates Guaranteed   *Motel*   ◆◆◆

5/1-9/15	1P	....	60.00	2P/1B	....	65.00	2P/2B	.... 70.00 XP 6
9/16-4/30	1P	....	55.00	2P/1B	....	60.00	2P/2B	.... 65.00 XP 6

Senior discount. 58 units. Adjacent to SR 17; southbound exit Scotts Valley Dr, northbound exit Granite Creek/Glenwood Dr, 1/4 mi w to Scotts Valley Dr. 6020 Scotts Valley Dr. (95066) Refrigerators; A/C; C/CATV; radios; phones. Coin laundry. Small pool; sauna; whirlpool. Reserv deposit required. AE, DI, DS, MC, VI. Coffeeshop adjacent. FAX (408) 439-8752   ⊗ Ⓢ Ⓓ 🄴 (408) 438-6666

SEAL BEACH — 25,100

Radisson Inn of Seal Beach   Rates Subject to Change   *Motel*   ◆◆◆

All year [CP]	1P	86.00- 106.00	2P/1B	96.00- 116.00	2P/2B	96.00- 116.00	XP 10

71 units. 1 blk s of SR 1, Pacific Coast Hwy. 600 Marina Dr. (90740) A/C; C/CATV; movies; radios; phones. Small htd pool; whirlpool; exercise rm. Garage. No pets. AE, DI, DS, MC, VI. Restaurant opposite. FAX (310) 493-7501
(See ad below)   ⊗ Ⓢ Ⓓ 🄴 (310) 493-7501

The Seal Beach Inn and Gardens   Rates Guaranteed   *Bed & Breakfast*   ◆◆

All year [BP]	1P	98.00- 155.00	2P/1B	98.00- 165.00	2P/2B	98.00- 165.00	XP 10

Senior discount. 23 units. 3 blks s of SR 1, Pacific Coast Hwy. 212 5th St. (90740) Beautifully restored 60 year-old inn furnished with many antiques & historical pieces. Garden settings throughout. Smoke free premises. Check-in 4 pm. 19 refrigerators; 1 A/C; C/CATV; radios; phones; comb or shower baths. 2 2-bedrm units, 11 kitchens, 5 efficiencies. Small pool. Limited parking lot. No pets. Wkly rates avail. Reserv deposit required; 3 days refund notice. Complimentary beverages each evening. AE, DI, MC, VI. FAX (310) 799-0483
   ⊗ Ⓓ (310) 493-2416

RESTAURANT

Spaghettini   Italian $$ ◆◆
1/2 blk n of I-405, exit Seal Beach Blvd. 3005 Old Ranch Pkwy. Very attractive restaurant featuring a nice selection of pasta, gourmet pizza, seafood, steaks & chicken. A/C. Early bird specials; children's menu. Open 11 am-3:30 & 4:30-10 pm; Sat 4:30 pm-10:30 pm; Sun 4 pm-9:30 pm; closed 11/25 & 12/25. Cocktails & lounge. Reserv advised. AE, DI, DS, MC, VI.   ⊗ (310) 596-2199

SEASIDE — 38,900

Bay Breeze Inn   Rates Subject to Change   *Motel*   ◆◆

Fri & Sat [CP]	1P	46.00- 68.00	2P/1B	56.00- 88.00	2P/2B	66.00- 102.00	XP 5
Sun-Thurs 5/1-9/30 [CP]	1P	36.00- 58.00	2P/1B	39.00- 68.00	2P/2B	46.00- 82.00	XP 5
Sun-Thurs 10/1-4/30 [CP]	1P	33.00- 39.00	2P/1B	35.00- 52.00	2P/2B	42.00- 56.00	XP 5

Senior discount. 50 units. 1/4 mi e off SR 1; exit Seaside-Sand City. 2049 Fremont Blvd. (93955) A/C; C/CATV; phones. 9 efficiencies, no utensils. 1 unit with fireplace, $10 extra. Wkly rates avail. AE, DI, DS, MC, VI. *(See ad p A276)*
   ⊗ Ⓓ (408) 899-7111

Best Western Magic Carpet Lodge   Rates Subject to Change   *Motel*   ◆◆

5/24-9/22	1P	60.00- 70.00	2P/1B	70.00- 90.00	2P/2B	75.00- 95.00	XP 5	F
9/23-5/23	1P	40.00- 60.00	2P/1B	45.00- 70.00	2P/2B	50.00- 80.00	XP 5	F

40 units. 1 mi se of jct SR 1 & 218; 1 1/2 mi n on Fremont Blvd. 1875 Fremont Blvd. (93955) C/CATV; 24 radios; phones. 3 efficiencies, no utensils. Small pool. No pets. 2 night minimum stay weekends. Wkly & monthly rates avail. Reserv deposit required. AE, CB, DI, MC, VI. *(See ad p A278)*   ⊗ Ⓓ (408) 899-4221

Days Inn   Rates Guaranteed   *Motor Inn*   ◆◆

Fri & Sat	1P	70.00- 95.00	2P/1B	80.00- 115.00	2P/2B	80.00- 115.00	XP 10	F
Sun-Thurs 6/15-9/15	1P	65.00- 87.00	2P/1B	76.00- 105.00	2P/2B	76.00- 105.00	XP 10	F
Sun-Thurs 9/14-6/14	1P	53.00- 75.00	2P/1B	59.00- 81.00	2P/2B	59.00- 81.00	XP 10	F

Senior discount. 143 units. E of SR 1; exit SR 218, Seaside/Del Rey Oaks. 1400 Del Monte Blvd. (93955) A/C; C/TV; pay movies; radios; phones. Small pool; whirlpool; jogging track. Pets, $5 extra charge. Wkly & monthly rates avail. AE, DI, DS, MC, VI. ● Coffeeshop; 6 am-10 pm; $6-$12. FAX (408) 394-7125 *(See ad p A273)*
   ⊗ Ⓢ Ⓓ 🄴 (408) 394-5335

Pacific Best Inn   Rates Subject to Change   *Motel*   ◆◆
⊕ Fri & Sat 5/1-9/30   1P .... 89.00   2P/1B .... 89.00   2P/2B .... 99.00   XP 5
   Sun-Thurs 5/1-9/30 & Fri-Sat
   10/1-4/30   1P .... 69.00   2P/1B .... 69.00   2P/2B .... 79.00   XP 5
   Sun-Thurs 10/1-4/30   1P .... 45.00   2P/1B .... 50.00   2P/2B .... 60.00   XP 5
20 units. E of SR 1; Fremont Blvd exit. 1141 Fremont Blvd. (93955) A/C; C/CATV; phones. No pets. 2 2-bedroom units, $89-$155 for up to 4 persons. Reserv deposit required; 3 days refund notice. AE, DS, MC, VI. Coffeeshop opposite.   ⊗ (D) 🅖 (408) 899-1881

Seaside Motel 8   Rates Subject to Change   *Motel*   ◆
⊕ Fri-Sat & 5/1-9/30   1P .... 85.00   2P/1B .... 85.00   2P/2B .... 95.00   XP
   Sun-Thurs 10/1-4/30   1P .... 50.00   2P/1B .... 50.00   2P/2B .... 60.00   XP
Senior discount. 17 units. E of SR 1; Fremont Blvd exit. 1131 Fremont Blvd. (93955) 6 refrigerators; C/CATV; radios; phones; shower baths. Pets, $25 deposit required. Rates for up to 4 persons. Reserv deposit required. AE, DS, MC, VI. Coffeeshop opposite.   (D) (408) 394-8881

Thunderbird Motel   Rates Subject to Change   *Motel*   ◆
⊕ 6/18-9/16   1P 35.00- 60.00   2P/1B 38.00- 70.00   2P/2B 45.00- 90.00   XP 5
   9/17-6/17   1P 28.00- 45.00   2P/1B 30.00- 50.00   2P/2B 38.00- 70.00   XP 5
33 units. 1/4 mi n on SR 1 business rt. 1933 Fremont Blvd. (93955) C/CATV; phones; shower or comb baths. 7 efficiencies. Small pool. No pets. Wkly rates avail. Reserv deposit required; 3 days refund notice. DI, MC, VI. *(See ad p A277)*   ⊗ (D) (408) 394-6797

SEPULVEDA — 56,200 See LOS ANGELES (San Fernando Valley)

SEQUOIA AND KINGS CANYON NATIONAL PARKS — See also THREE RIVERS

The establishments below do not meet all AAA standards but are listed as a service to members who may wish to stay in the parks. All housekeeping accommodations are without bath.

Cedar Grove Lodge   Rates Subject to Change   *Lodge*
   5/1-10/11   1P .... 80.00   ....   2P/2B .... 80.00   XP 6   F
18 units. 31 mi ne of Grant Grove, at end of SR 180; reached by paved 2-lane winding mountain road. (Sequoia National Park, 93633) OPEN 5/1-10/11. On the banks of the Kings River. Check-in 4 pm. A/C; shower or comb bath. Coin laundry. Fishing; hiking trails. No pets. For reservations specify Cedar Grove Lodge; Guest Services, PO Box 789, Three Rivers, CA 93271. Reserv deposit required; 3 days refund notice. MC, VI. ● Coffeeshop; 7 am-7 pm; $6.75-$11.95.
FAX (209) 335-2364   ⊗ (D) 🅖 (209) 561-3314

Giant Forest Lodge   Rates Subject to Change   *Complex*
   All year   1P 40.00- 115.00   ....   2P/2B 40.00- 115.00   XP 6   F
244 units. In Giant Forest Village. (Sequoia National Park, 93262) Accommodations include modern motel units, 1- & 2-room cottages with bath, very modest canvas top cabins without bath. Check-in 4 pm. 149 radios; 149 comb baths. Cabins without bath have woodburning stoves; many have outdoor patio woodburning cooking stoves; central restroom & shower facilities; skiing; tobogganing; hiking trails. No pets. For reservations specify Giant Forest Lodge; Guest Services, PO Box 789, Three Rivers CA 93271. MC, VI. Restaurant & lounge in summer; cafeteria open all year.
FAX (209) 565-3249   ⊗ 🅖 (209) 561-3314

Grant Grove Lodge   Rates Subject to Change   *Cottages*
   All year   1P 40.00- 70.00   ....   2P/2B 40.00- 70.00   XP 6   F
52 units. On SR 180, in Grant Grove Village. (Kings Canyon National Park, 93633) Very modest roofed or canvas top cabins without baths; most have wood heating stoves & oil lamps. In pine-shaded forest. Check-in 4 pm. 9 comb baths. Many cabins with outdoor patio, 9 with tub baths, electric lights & heat. Central restroom & shower facilities; ski trails; hiking trails. For reservations specify Grant Grove Lodge; Guest Services, PO Box 789, Three Rivers CA 93271. Reserv deposit required; 3 days refund notice. MC, VI. ● Coffeeshop; 7 am-7 pm; 5/6-9/10 to 9 pm; $5-$9.95; cocktails.
FAX (209) 335-2364   (209) 561-3314

Montecito-Sequoia Lodge   Rates Subject to Change   *Lodge*
⊕ All year   1P .... 75.00   2P/1B .... 75.00   ....   XP 48
37 units. 10 mi s of Grant Grove off General's Hwy. (PO Box 858, Grant Grove, 93633) Accommodations include lodge rooms & 8 cabins with central bath. Check-in 4 pm. Comb baths. Htd pool; whirlpool; rental canoes; lighted tennis-2 courts; ski trails; recreational program. Fee for: water skiing, sailing, paddleboats. No pets. Reservations: 472 Deodara Dr, Los Altos, CA 94024; (800) 227-9900 or (415) 967-8612. [AP], [BP] & [MAP] avail. Reserv deposit required; 10 days refund notice. AE, DI, DS, MC, VI. Dining rm; 7:30-9 am, 12:30-1:30 & 6-7:30 pm; buffet about $16; cocktail lounge. FAX (415) 967-1365 *(See ad below)*   (209) 565-3388

Stony Creek Lodge   Rates Subject to Change   *Lodge*
   5/22-9/11   1P .... 80.00   2P/1B .... 80.00   2P/2B .... 80.00   XP 7   F
11 units. Midway between Grant Grove Village & Giant Forest Village. (Sequoia National Park, 93262) OPEN 5/22-9/11. All units on second floor of main lodge. Check-in 4 pm. Radios; shower or comb baths. Coin laundry. Hiking trails. No pets. For reservations specify Stony Creek Lodge Guest Services, PO Box 789, Three Rivers CA 93271. Reserv deposit required; 3 days refund notice. MC, VI. ● Restaurant; 7 am-9 pm; $4.95-$11.95; beer & wine. ⊗ (D) (209) 561-3314

SHASTA LAKE — 800

Bridge Bay Resort Rates Subject to Change *Resort Motor Inn* ◆
5/1-9/30   1P .... 69.00 2P/1B .... 69.00 2P/2B .... 69.00 XP 8
10/1-4/30   1P .... 55.00 2P/1B .... 55.00 2P/2B .... 55.00 XP 8
40 units. 12 mi n of Redding, off I-5; 1 mi s of Bridge Bay Rd turnoff. 10300 Bridge Bay Rd. (Redding, 96003) Overlooking Lake Shasta. A/C; C/CATV; movies; radios; phones; shower baths. 3 2-bedrm units. Htd pool; beach; rental boats & motors; boat ramp; fishing; water skiing. Fee for: houseboats. Pets. 8 kitchens, $90-$150 for up to 4 persons. Reserv deposit required; 7 days refund notice. AE, MC, VI. ● Restaurant; 7 am-2 & 5-10 pm; $9-$18; cocktails. *(See ad below)*
ⓓ (916) 275-3021

SHELTER ISLAND — See SAN DIEGO

SHERMAN OAKS — 136,900   See LOS ANGELES (San Fernando Valley)

SIERRA CITY — 100

Herrington's Sierra Pines AAA Special Value Rates *Motor Inn* ◆◆
Ⓐ 4/1-11/30   1P 55.00- 70.00 2P/1B 55.00- 70.00 2P/2B 60.00- 75.00 XP 5
20 units. 1/2 mi w on SR 49. (PO Box 235, 96125) OPEN 4/1-11/30. Spacious grounds on north fork of Yuba River. View of Sierra Buttes & river. Balconies. C/CATV; movies; shower baths. Fishing. Fee for: trout pond fishing. Pets. 1 cottage with kitchen & fireplace for up to 4 persons, $80-$90. Wkly rates avail. Reserv deposit required; 7 days refund notice. MC, VI. ● Dining rm; 8 am-11 & 5-9 pm; $9-$25; cocktails. ⓓ (916) 862-1151

SIERRA MADRE

RESTAURANT

Restaurant Lozano American $$ ◆◆
1 mi n of I-210. 44 N Baldwin Ave. Interesting selection of southwestern, Italian & Caribbean cuisine. A/C. Open 11 am-3 & 5-9 pm; Fri & Sat-10 pm; Sun 11 am-9 pm; closed major holidays. Beer & wine. Reserv advised. AE, CB, DI, MC, VI.
⊗ (818) 355-5945

SILVER LAKE (Amador County) — See KIT CARSON

SIMI VALLEY — 100,200

Clarion Hotel Rates Subject to Change *Motor Inn* ◆◆◆
All year [BP]   1P 70.00- 90.00 2P/1B 80.00- 100.00 2P/2B 80.00- 100.00 XP 10 F
Senior discount. 120 units. 1 mi s of SR 118; exit Madera Rd. 1775 Madera Rd. (93065) Many balconies. 2 mi n of The Ronald Reagan Presidential Library. Check-in 3 pm. C/CATV; free & pay movies; radios; phones. 16 2-bedrm units, 1 3-bedrm unit. Coin laundry. Htd pool; whirlpool; exercise rm. Pets. AE, DI, DS, MC, VI. ● Restaurant; 6:30 am-1 am; $7-$12. FAX (805) 527-9969 *(See ad below)* ⊗ Ⓢ ⓓ ⓑ (805) 584-6300

Radisson-Simi Valley Rates Guaranteed *Motor Inn* ◆◆◆
Ⓐ All year   1P 69.00- 89.00 2P/1B 72.00- 92.00 2P/2B 72.00- 92.00 XP 10 F
Senior discount. 195 units. Adjacent to SR 118; exit 1st St. 999 Enchanted Way. (93065) A/C; C/CATV; free & pay movies; radios; phones. Htd pool; whirlpool; exercise rm. Pets, $500 fee non-refundable. AE, DI, DS, MC, VI. ● Restaurant; 6 am-11 pm; $9-$15; cocktails; entertainment. FAX (805) 583-2779 *(See ad p A518)* ⊗ Ⓢ ⓓ ⓑ (805) 583-2000

Travelodge Rates Guaranteed *Motel* ◆◆◆
Ⓐ All year [CP]   1P .... 62.00 2P/1B .... 72.00 2P/2B .... 76.00 XP 6 F
Senior discount. 96 units. Adjacent s side SR 118, exit Erringer Rd. 2550 Erringer Rd. (93065) Check-in 3 pm. 50 refrigerators; A/C; C/TV; free & pay movies; phones. Coin laundry. Htd pool; sauna; whirlpool; 36 rooms with whirlpool; exercise rm. No pets. 6 1-bedroom suites with microwave & refrigerator, $120-$145. Reserv deposit required; 14 days refund notice. AE, DI, DS, MC, VI. Restaurant adjacent. FAX (805) 527-5629
⊗ Ⓢ ⓓ ⓑ (805) 584-6006

RESTAURANT

Reuben's American $$ ◆◆
1 blk s of SR 118, exit Sycamore Dr. 2410 N Sycamore Dr. Casual atmosphere. Featuring steaks & seafood. A/C. Open 11:30 am-3 & 5-10 pm; Sat & Sun 5 pm-11 pm. Cocktails & lounge. Entertainment & dancing. AE, DI, DS, MC, VI.
Ⓧ (805) 527-6601

SMITH RIVER — 2,000

Best Western Ship Ashore Motel Rates Subject to Change *Motor Inn* ◆◆
⑬ 6/16-10/31	1P	.... 54.00	2P/1B	.... 60.00	2P/2B	.... 64.00	XP 6	
11/1-6/15	1P	.... 46.00	2P/1B	.... 52.00	2P/2B	.... 54.00	XP 6	

50 units. 2 3/4 mi n on US 101; 3 mi s of OR-CA stateline. (PO Box 75, 95567) View of Smith River. Entrance through trailer park. 1 2-bedroom apartment with fireplace. 42 refrigerators; C/CATV; movies; radios; phones. Coin laundry. Indoor hot tub; rental boats & motors; fishing. Fee for: boat dock & ramp. No pets. 3 kitchen suites. 8 efficiencies, $4-$10 extra. 15 rooms with whirlpool tub, $20-$25 extra. Reserv deposit required. AE, DI, DS, MC, VI. ● Restaurant; 6 am-10 pm; $8-$22; cocktails. FAX (707) 487-7070 Ⓓ (707) 487-3141

SOLEDAD — 7,100

Best Western Valley Harvest Inn Rates Subject to Change *Motor Inn* ◆◆◆
⑬ 5/1-9/30	1P	57.00- 79.00	2P/1B	65.00- 85.00	2P/2B	.... 75.00	XP 9		F
4/30	1P	51.50- 71.50	2P/1B	58.50- 76.50	2P/2B	.... 67.50	XP 9		F

Senior discount. 60 units. 1/2 mi s on US 101. 1155 Front St. (93960) Check-in 3 pm. A/C; C/CATV; pay movies; 30 radios; phones. 4 efficiencies, no utensils. Coin laundry. Pool; whirlpool. No pets. Wkly rates avail. AE, DI, DS, MC, VI. ● Restaurant & coffeeshop; 6 am-10 pm; $9-$20; cocktails. FAX (408) 678-3011
Ⓧ Ⓓ Ⓖ (408) 678-3833

SOLVANG — 4,700 See also BALLARD & BUELLTON

Best Western King Frederik Motel Rates Subject to Change *Motel* ◆◆◆
⑬ All year	1P	53.00- 68.00	2P/1B	57.00- 68.00	2P/2B	.... 68.00	XP 6	F

45 units. On SR 246. 1617 Copenhagen Dr. (93463) A/C; C/CATV; phones; comb or shower baths. Htd pool; whirlpool. No pets. Reserv deposit required. AE, DI, DS, MC, VI. Ⓓ (805) 688-5515

Chimney Sweep Inn Rates Guaranteed *Motel* ◆◆◆
⑬ All year [CP]	1P	65.00- 80.00	2P/1B	65.00- 80.00	2P/2B	75.00- 85.00	XP 10	F

28 units. 1 blk s of SR 246. 1554 Copenhagen Dr. (93463) A/C; C/CATV; radios; phones; comb or shower baths. Whirlpool. No pets. 8 split-level loft rooms, $90-$125; 6 cottage units with fireplace, $165-$225. Wkly rates avail. Reserv deposit required. AE, DS, MC, VI. *(See ad p A519)* Ⓧ Ⓓ (805) 688-2111

Danish Country Inn Rates Guaranteed *Motel* ◆◆◆
⑬ Fri & Sat [BP]	1P	.... 73.00	2P/1B	.... 73.00	2P/2B	.... 73.00	XP 10	F
Sun-Thurs [BP]	1P	.... 62.00	2P/1B	.... 62.00	2P/2B	.... 62.00	XP 9	

Senior discount. 82 units. 3 blks w on SR 246. 1455 Mission Dr. (93463) Spacious rooms. Check-in 3 pm. Refrigerators; A/C; C/CATV; rental VCPs; radios; phones. Small htd pool; whirlpool. Garage. No pets. 6 split-level loft rooms, $109-$190 for 2 persons. Reserv deposit required. Complimentary beverages each evening. AE, DI, MC, VI. FAX (805) 688-1156 *(See ad p A519)* Ⓧ Ⓢ Ⓓ (805) 688-2018

Dannebrog Inn Rates Guaranteed *Motel* ◆◆◆
⑬ Fri & Sat 6/1-9/30 [CP]	....	2P/1B	.... 85.00	2P/2B	.... 85.00	XP 5	
Sun-Thurs 6/1-9/30 & Fri & Sat 10/1-5/31 [CP]	....	2P/1B	.... 65.00	2P/2B	.... 65.00	XP 5	
Sun-Thurs 10/1-5/31 [CP]	....	2P/1B	.... 50.00	2P/2B	.... 55.00	XP 5	

Senior discount. 75 units. 3 blks w on SR 246. 1450 Mission Dr. (93463) 25 refrigerators; A/C; C/CATV; phones; comb or shower baths. Htd indoor pool; recreational program. No pets. 2 rooms with whirlpool spa, $95-$185. Reserv deposit required. AE, DI, MC, VI. FAX (805) 688-0026 Ⓓ (805) 688-3210

Hamlet Motel — Rates Subject to Change — *Motel* ◆

Fri & Sat			....	2P/1B	60.00- 80.00	2P/2B	65.00- 95.00	XP 10
Sun-Thurs	1P	35.00- 45.00	2P/1B	45.00- 60.00	2P/2B	65.00- 95.00	XP 5

14 units. 1 blk w on SR 246. 1532 Mission Dr. (93463) 6 refrigerators; C/CATV; movies; phones; shower or comb baths. 1 2-bedrm unit. No pets. Reserv deposit required. AE, DI, DS, MC, VI. Restaurant opposite. FAX (805) 686-1301 *(See ad p A518)* ⊗ Ⓓ (805) 688-4413

Kronborg Inn — Rates Subject to Change — *Motel* ◆◆

6/16-9/15 & Fri-Sat 9/16-6/15 [CP]	1P	65.00- 75.00	2P/1B	65.00- 75.00	2P/2B	70.00- 80.00	XP 10
Sun-Thurs 4/1-6/15 & 9/16-10/31 [CP]	1P	50.00- 60.00	2P/1B	50.00- 60.00	2P/2B	55.00- 65.00	XP 10
Sun-Thurs 11/1-3/31 [CP]	1P	40.00- 50.00	2P/1B	40.00- 50.00	2P/2B	45.00- 55.00	XP 10

Senior discount. 39 units. 5 blks w on SR 246. 1440 Mission Dr. (93463) Check-in 3 pm. Refrigerators; A/C; C/CATV; movies; phones. Htd pool; whirlpool. Wkly rates avail. AE, CB, DI, MC, VI. FAX (805) 688-1821 ⊗ Ⓓ Ⓖ (805) 688-2383

Petersen Village Inn — Rates Subject to Change — *Motor Inn* ◆◆◆◆

All year [CP]	1P	95.00- 155.00	2P/1B	95.00- 155.00	....	XP 10

40 units. On SR 246. 1576 Mission Dr. (93463) Charming, elegant Old World ambiance with spacious, beautifully decorated rooms. 1 smaller unit. Check-in 3 pm. A/C; C/CATV; phones; comb or shower baths. No pets. Reserv deposit required. Complimentary beverages each evening. AE, MC, VI. Restaurant adjacent. FAX (805) 688-5732 *(See ad p A520)* ⊗ Ⓢ Ⓓ (805) 688-3121

The Royal Copenhagen Motel — Rates Subject to Change — *Motel* ◆◆◆

All year	1P	60.00- 75.00	2P/1B	65.00- 75.00	2P/2B	60.00- 75.00	XP 6

48 units. On SR 246. 1579 Mission Dr. (93463) Very attractive Scandinavian decor. A/C; C/CATV; radios; phones; shower baths. Htd pool. No pets. 4 split-level loft rooms, $85. Reserv deposit required. AE, MC, VI. *(See ad p A521)* ⊗ Ⓓ (805) 688-5561

Svendsgaard's Danish Lodge Rates Subject to Change *Motel* ◆◆◆
All year [CP] 1P 44.00- 86.00 2P/1B 44.00- 86.00 2P/2B 49.00- 86.00 XP 6
48 units. On SR 246 at Alisal Rd. 1711 Mission Dr. (93463) Many rooms with fireplace. Refrigerators; A/C; C/CATV; 40 radios; phones; comb or shower baths. 3 2-bedrm units. Pool; whirlpool. No pets. 4 kitchens, $5 extra. Wkly rates avail. Reserv deposit required. AE, DI, DS, MC, VI. *Independant Motels of America. (See ad p A520)*
⊗ Ⓓ (805) 688-3277

Three Crowns Inn Rates Subject to Change *Motel* ◆◆
Fri & Sat 1P 50.00- 75.00 2P/1B 50.00- 75.00 2P/2B 60.00- 80.00 XP 5
Sun-Thurs 1P .... 40.00 2P/1B 40.00- 45.00 2P/2B .... 50.00 XP 5
27 units. 1 1/2 blks w on SR 246. 1518 Mission Dr. (93463) A/C; C/CATV; radios; phones. 2 2-bedrm units. No pets. Reserv deposit required. AE, MC, VI. Restaurant opposite. *(See ad below)*
⊗ Ⓓ (805) 688-4702

Tivoli Inn AAA Special Value Rates *Motel* ◆◆◆
All year [CP] 1P 85.00- 195.00 2P/1B 85.00- 195.00 2P/2B 85.00- 195.00 XP
29 units. 1 blk s of SR 246. 1564 Copenhagen Dr. (93463) Charming, Old World decor. Nicely decorated rooms with fireplace. Check-in 3 pm. A/C; C/TV; radios; phones. 6 2-bedrm units, 1 3-bedrm unit. No pets. Reserv deposit required. AE, CB, DI, MC, VI. FAX (805) 686-0032
Ⓢ Ⓓ (805) 688-0559

Viking Motel	Rates Subject to Change			Motel		◆
ⒶⒶⒶ Sat	1P 52.00- 78.00	2P/1B 52.00- 78.00	2P/2B 58.00- 85.00	XP 6		
Sun-Fri	1P 32.00- 54.00	2P/1B 32.00- 54.00	2P/2B 36.00- 60.00	XP 6		

Senior discount. 12 units. 2 blks w on SR 246. 1506 Mission Dr. (93463) A/C; C/CATV; movies; phones; shower or comb baths. Pets, $8 extra charge. Reserv deposit required. AE, DI, DS, MC, VI. *(See ad below)*

Ⓓ (805) 688-1337

RESTAURANTS

Alexander's Copenhagen Inn Restaurant   Ethnic $$ ◆
1/2 blk s of SR 246. 467 Alisal Rd. Danish cuisine with Danish country decor. Outdoor courtyard patio. Also American cuisine. A/C. Open 11 am-9 pm; Sun from-9 am. Beer & wine. Reserv advised. MC, VI.   ⊗ (805) 688-6622

Bit 'O Denmark Restaurant   American $$ ◆
ⒶⒶⒶ 1/2 blk s of SR 246. 473 Alisal Rd. Nice selection of American & Danish entrees. Smorgasbord lunch & dinner. A/C. Children's menu. Open 8 am-9 pm; Fri & Sat-9:30 pm; closed 12/25. Beer & wine. AE, CB, DI, MC, VI.
(805) 688-5426

The Danish Inn Restaurant   Ethnic $$ ◆◆
1 blk w on SR 246. 1547 Mission Dr. Attractive restaurant featuring Scandinavian & Continental cuisine. Lunch & dinner smorgasbord. A/C. Open 7 am-11 & 11:30-10 pm. Cocktails & lounge. Reserv advised. AE, DI, DS, MC, VI.
⊗ (805) 688-4813

Massimi Ristorante   Italian $$ ◆◆◆
On SR 246; in Petersen Village Sq. 1588 Mission Dr. A small, charming restaurant with indoor & outdoor patio dining. Open 5:30 pm-9:30 pm; also 11:30 am-2:30 pm Wed-Fri; closed Mon & major holidays. Beer & wine. Reserv advised. AE, MC, VI.   (805) 688-0027

SONOMA (95476) — 8,100

Best Western Sonoma Valley Inn	Rates Subject to Change			Motel		◆◆◆
ⒶⒶⒶ Fri & Sat 4/1-10/30 [CP]	1P 125.00- 135.00	2P/1B 125.00- 135.00	2P/2B 125.00- 135.00	XP 10	F	
Fri & Sat 11/1-3/31 [CP]	1P 90.00- 100.00	2P/1B 90.00- 100.00	2P/2B 90.00- 100.00	XP 10	F	
Sun-Thurs 4/1-10/30 [CP]	1P 95.00	2P/1B 95.00	2P/2B 95.00	XP 10	F	
Sun-Thurs 11/1-3/31 [CP]	1P 75.00	2P/1B 75.00	2P/2B 75.00	XP 10	F	

72 units. 1 blk w of Town Plaza. 550 2nd St W. Many rooms with fireplace. Check-in 3 pm. Refrigerators; A/C; C/CATV; free & pay movies; radios; phones. Coin laundry. Pool; whirlpool. Pets, $10 deposit required. Reserv deposit required. AE, DI, DS, MC, VI. Coffeeshop opposite. FAX (707) 938-0935 *(See ad below)*

⊗ Ⓢ Ⓓ Ⓛ (707) 938-9200

Sonoma Mission Inn
🄰🄰 5/1-10/31
11/1-4/30

	Rates Subject to Change		Resort Motor Inn	◆◆◆◆
1P 165.00- 295.00	2P/1B	165.00- 295.00	2P/2B 165.00- 295.00 XP 30	
1P 135.00- 270.00	2P/1B	135.00- 270.00	2P/2B 135.00- 270.00 XP 30	

Senior discount. 170 units. 2 1/2 mi n on SR 12. 18140 Sonoma Hwy. (PO Box 1447) A mixture of Mediterranean & Spanish-Californian architecture. Spacious, landscaped grounds. Extensive spa facilities; some fireplaces. Check-in 4 pm. A/C; C/CATV; VCPs; radios; phones; comb or shower baths. 1 2-bedrm unit. 2 pools; sauna; whirlpools; lighted tennis-2 courts. Fee for: health club. No pets. Reserv deposit required. AE, DI, MC, VI. ● 2 restaurants; 7 am-10 pm; a la carte entrees about $10.50-$33; cocktails. A *Preferred Hotel.* FAX (707) 938-4250
⊗ Ⓢ Ⓓ (707) 938-9000

RESTAURANT

La Casa   Mexican $ ◆◆
Opposite San Francisco Solano Mission. 121 E Spain St. Traditional specialties. A/C. Children's menu. Open 11:30 am-9:30 pm; Fri & Sat-10 pm; closed 11/26, 12/24, 12/25 & Easter. Cocktails. Reserv advised. AE, CB, DI, MC, VI.
⊗ (707) 996-3406

SONORA — 4,200   See also COLUMBIA, MI-WUK VILLAGE & TWAIN HARTE

Aladdin Motor Inn
🄰🄰 5/1-9/30
10/1-4/30

	Rates Subject to Change		Motel	◆◆
1P 50.00	2P/1B	.... 60.00	2P/2B .... 65.00 XP 5	
1P 47.00	2P/1B	.... 53.00	2P/2B .... 58.00 XP 5	

60 units. 3 1/2 mi e on SR 108. 14260 Mono Way. (95370) Refrigerators; A/C; C/CATV; movies; rental VCPs. Phones. Coin laundry. Pool; whirlpool. Pets, $40 small dogs deposit required. Reserv deposit required. AE, DI, DS, MC, VI. Coffeeshop adjacent. FAX (209) 532-1522
⊗ Ⓢ Ⓓ 🅑 (209) 533-4971

Best Western Sonora Oaks Motor Hotel
🄰🄰 5/1-9/30
10/1-12/31
1/1-4/30

	AAA Special Value Rates		Motel	◆◆◆
1P 60.00- 70.00	2P/1B	65.00- 75.00	2P/2B 70.00- 80.00 XP 5	F
1P 58.00- 68.00	2P/1B	63.00- 73.00	2P/2B 68.00- 78.00 XP 5	F
1P 56.00- 66.00	2P/1B	61.00- 71.00	2P/2B 66.00- 72.00 XP 5	F

70 units. 3 1/2 mi e on SR 108; corner of Hess Ave. 19551 Hess Ave. (95370) Quiet, country setting. A/C; C/CATV; movies; rental VCPs. Phones; comb or shower baths. Htd pool; whirlpool. Pets. Reserv deposit required. AE, DI, DS, MC, VI. Coffeeshop adjacent. FAX (209) 532-1964 *(See ad below)*
⊗ Ⓓ (209) 533-4400

Sonora Gold Lodge
🄰🄰 All year

	Rates Subject to Change		Motel	◆
1P 48.00- 50.00	2P/1B	52.00- 64.00	2P/2B 52.00- 64.00 XP 5	

42 units. 1/2 mi sw on SR 108 business rt & 49. 480 Stockton St. (95370) Tree-shaded grounds. Some small rooms. A/C; C/CATV; 10 radios; 24 phones; shower or comb baths. No pets. AE, DS, MC, VI. *(See ad p A522)*
⊗ Ⓓ (209) 532-3952

Sonora Towne House Motel
🄰🄰 5/1-10/31

	AAA Special Value Rates		Motel	◆
1P 55.00- 60.00	2P/1B	60.00- 65.00	2P/2B 60.00- 65.00 XP 5	

112 units. 3 blks e on SR 108 business rt. 350 S Washington St. (95370) OPEN ALL YEAR. A/C; C/CATV; movies; 75 radios; phones; shower or comb baths. 2 pools; hot tub. No pets. Reserv deposit required. AE, DI, DS, MC, VI. FAX (209) 532-9000
Ⓓ (209) 532-3633

SONORA PASS AREA — See MI-WUK VILLAGE, SONORA & TWAIN HARTE

SOUTH SAN FRANCISCO — 54,300   See SAN FRANCISCO (Southern Region)

SOUTH GATE — 86,300

Value Inn by Nendels
All year

	Rates Subject to Change		Motel	◆◆
1P 37.00	2P/1B	.... 37.00	2P/2B .... 47.00 XP 10	

30 units. 3/4 mi nw of I-710, 3 blk n of Imperial Hwy; exit Imperial Hwy. 10352 Atlantic Ave. (90280) A/C; C/CATV; movies; radios; phones. No pets. 3 rooms with whirlpool, $51. AE, MC, VI.
⊗ Ⓢ Ⓓ 🅑 (213) 567-9218

SOUTH LAKE TAHOE — 21,600   See LAKE TAHOE (Southern Region)

STANTON — 30,500

Best Western Cypress Inn
🄰🄰 5/26-9/8 [CP]

	Rates Subject to Change		Motel	◆◆◆
1P 45.00- 59.00	2P/1B	51.00- 65.00	2P/2B .... 59.00 XP 6	

68 units. 1/2 blk e of Knott Ave. 7161 W Katella Ave. (90680) OPEN ALL YEAR. Refrigerators; A/C; C/CATV; movies; radios; phones. Coin laundry. Htd pool; sauna; whirlpool; exercise rm. No pets. 10 suites, $71. 12 rooms with whirlpool tub, $81-$91. AE, DI, DS, MC, VI. FAX (714) 527-7737 *(See ad p A54)* ⊗ Ⓢ Ⓓ 🅑 (714) 527-6680

Daystop of Anaheim/Buena Park
🄰🄰 All year [CP]

	AAA Special Value Rates		Motel	◆◆
1P 42.00- 58.00	2P/1B	46.00- 62.00	2P/2B 46.00- 62.00 XP 5	F

28 units. On SR 39; 2 blks s of Ball Rd. 10301 Beach Blvd. (90680) A/C; C/CATV; movies; radios; phones; comb or shower baths. No pets. 9 rooms with microwave & refrigerator. 10 rooms with VCP. Reserv deposit required. AE, DI, DS, MC, VI.
⊗ Ⓓ 🅑 (714) 826-6060

STOCKTON — 210,900

Best Western Charter Way Inn   AAA Special Value Rates   *Motel* ◆◆
All year   1P 45.00- 52.00   2P/1B   50.00- 57.00   2P/2B   52.00- 62.00 XP 5   F
80 units. 1 3/4 mi s at jct I-5 & SR 4; 3 mi w of SR 99. 550 W Charter Way. (95206) A/C; C/CATV; movies; radios; phones. Pool. Pets. Wkly rates avail. Reserv deposit required; 5 days refund notice. AE, DI, DS, MC, VI. Coffeeshop adjacent. FAX (209) 463-1638   (D) (209) 948-0321

Econo Lodge of Stockton   Rates Subject to Change   *Motel* ◆◆
All year   1P .... 33.00   2P/1B   .... 38.00   2P/2B   .... 42.00 XP 5   F
Senior discount. 69 units. Exit I-5 w 8th St off ramp; 1/4 mi s of jct SR 4. 2210 S Manthey Rd. (95206) 3-story building, no elevator. A/C; C/CATV; movies; radios; phones; comb or shower baths. 2 2-bedrm units. Coin laundry. Pool. No pets. 2-large units, $60-$70 for up to 6 persons. Reserv deposit required; 3 days refund notice. AE, DS, ER, MC, VI.   ⊗ (D) 🖫 (209) 466-5741

Holiday Inn Plum Tree Plaza   AAA Special Value Rates   *Motor Inn* ◆◆◆
All year   1P .... 85.00   2P/1B   85.00- 93.00   2P/2B   85.00- 93.00 XP 8   F
209 units. Exit I-5 March Ln 2 mi e, corner El Dorado St. 111 E March Ln. (95207) Check-in 3 pm. A/C; C/CATV; movies; radios; phones. Pool; whirlpool. Airport transp. Small pets only, $50 deposit. Monthly rates avail. AE, DI, DS, MC, VI. ● Coffeeshop; 6 am-10 pm; $7-$17; cocktails. FAX (209) 474-7612   ⊗ Ⓢ (D) 🖫 (209) 474-3301

La Quinta Inn   Rates Subject to Change   *Motel* ◆◆
All year   1P 51.00- 59.00   2P/1B   59.00- 66.00   2P/2B   .... 59.00 XP 5   F
153 units. Exit w off I-5, March Ln. 2710 W March Ln. (95219) Check-in 3 pm. A/C; C/CATV; free & pay movies; radios; phones. Pool. Small pets only. AE, DI, DS, MC, VI. Coffeeshop adjacent. FAX (209) 472-0732
    ⊗ (D) 🖫 (209) 952-7800

Motel Orleans   Rates Subject to Change   *Motel* ◆◆
All year   1P .... 33.00   2P/1B   .... 38.00   2P/2B   .... 40.00 XP 5
Senior discount. 70 units. E off SR 99 at jct SR 88. 3951 Budweiser Ct. (95215) 3-story, no elevator. A/C; C/TV; movies; phones; comb or shower baths. Coin laundry. Pool. No pets. Reserv deposit required; 3 days refund notice. AE, DI, DS, MC, VI. Coffeeshop adjacent.   ⊗ Ⓢ (D) 🖫 (209) 931-9341

Stockton Hilton   Rates Subject to Change   *Hotel* ◆◆
All year   1P 85.00- 125.00   2P/1B   97.00- 137.00   2P/2B   97.00- 137.00 XP 12   F
Senior discount. 198 units. Exit e off I-5 via March Ln. 2323 Grand Canal Blvd. (95207) Some balconies. Check-in 3 pm. A/C; C/CATV; pay movies; radios; phones. Pool; whirlpool. Parking lot. No pets. AE, CB, DI, MC, VI. ● Coffeeshop; 6:30 am-2 & 5-11 pm; a la carte entrees about $7-$17; cocktails. FAX (209) 473-8908   ⊗ (D) 🖫 (209) 957-9090

Stockton Inn Best Western   Rates Guaranteed   *Motor Inn* ◆◆◆
All year   1P .... 51.00   2P/1B   .... 51.00   2P/2B   .... 58.00 XP 10   F
141 units. E off SR 99 at jct SR 88. 4219 Waterloo Rd. (95215) Spacious grounds. Many large rooms. Check-in 3 pm. A/C; C/CATV; movies; 74 radios; phones. Pool; wading pool; whirlpool. No pets. Reserv deposit required. AE, DI, DS, MC, VI. ● Restaurant; 6 am-3 & 5-10 pm; Sat & Sun from 7 am; $8-$16.50; cocktails. FAX (209) 931-0423 *(See ad below)*   ⊗ (D) (209) 931-3131

Vagabond Inn   AAA Special Value Rates   *Motel* ◆
All year [CP]   1P 36.00- 40.00   2P/1B   38.00- 43.00   2P/2B   .... 45.00 XP 5
100 units. 1 blk n; w off El Dorado St via Weber; southbound SR 99 traffic exit Wilson Way, northbound w via Mariposa Rd to Charter Way; I-5 exit Downtown. 33 N Center St. (95202) A/C; C/TV; VCPs; radios; phones. Pool. Pets, $3 extra charge. Reserv deposit required; 7 days refund notice. AE, DI, DS, MC, VI. Coffeeshop adjacent. FAX (209) 948-1220   ⊗ (D) 🖫 (209) 948-6151

RESTAURANTS

Alberts   Continental $$$ ◆◆
6 mi n; adjacent to SR 99; exit via Hammer Ln. 8103 Hwy 99N. Refined atmosphere. Varied menu. Featuring Portugeese dishes. A/C. Dress code. Children's menu. Open 5 pm-10 pm; Sun 4 pm-9 pm; closed 7/4, 11/26 & 12/25. Cocktails & lounge. Minimum $5. Reserv advised. MC, VI.   ⊗ (209) 476-1763

LeBistro   Continental $$$$ ◆◆◆
Adjacent to I-5, exit Benjamin Holt Dr, in Village Square Center behind Lyons. 3121 W Benjamin Holt Dr. Specializing in seafood. A/C. Open 11:30 am-2 & 5:30-10 pm; Sat from 5:30 pm; Sun 5 pm-9 pm. Cocktails & lounge. Reserv advised. AE, DI, DS, MC, VI.   ⊗ (209) 951-0885

On Lock Sam   Chinese $
3 blks s, I-5 exit downtown. 333 S Sutter St. Cantonese cuisine since 1898. A/C. Open 11:30 am-10 pm; Sat-11 pm; closed 11/25 & 12/25. Cocktails & lounge. Reserv advised. AE, MC, VI.   ⊗ (209) 466-4561

Shannon's Restaurant   Seafood $$$ ◆◆
Exit e off I-5 via March Ln; opposite Quail Lakes Shopping Center. 4722 Quail Lakes Dr. Also steak & chicken. A/C. Children's menu. Open 11 am-2:30 & 5:30-10 pm; Fri-11 pm; Sat 5 pm-11 pm; Sun 9:30 am-2:30 & 4:30-9 pm; closed 12/25. Cocktails & lounge. Entertainment. Reserv advised. AE, DS, MC, VI.   ⊗ (209) 952-1637

Ye Olde Hoosier Inn   American $ ◆
1 mi ne on SR 99 business rt. 1537 N Wilson Way. Family restaurant. Furnished in antiques. A/C. Children's menu. Open 6:30 am-9 pm; Sat & Sun from 7 am-9 pm; closed 5/31, 7/4 & 12/25.   ⊗ (209) 463-0271

STUDIO CITY — 45,100   See LOS ANGELES (San Fernando Valley)

SUGAR PINE — 300   See SONORA

SUNNYVALE — 117,200

Best Western Sunnyvale Inn   AAA Special Value Rates   *Motel*   ◆◆
All year   1P 54.00- 64.00   2P/1B   58.00- 72.00   2P/2B   64.00- 72.00   XP 4   F
88 units. N off & adjacent to US 101; exit via Mathilda Ave, 1 blk e on Ross Dr. 940 Weddell Dr. (94089) Few small rooms. 6 refrigerators; A/C; C/CATV; movies; phones; comb or shower baths. Small pool. No pets. AE, CB, DI, MC, VI. ● Coffeeshop; 6 am-2 pm; $4.25-$8.25; cocktails. FAX (408) 734-1462   ⊗ Ⓢ Ⓓ (408) 734-3742

Captain's Cove Motel   Rates Subject to Change   *Motel*   ◆
All year [CP]   1P .... 59.00   2P/1B   .... 61.00   2P/2B   .... 61.00   XP 5
Senior discount. 102 units. Exit US 101 at Mathilda Ave, 1/4 mi s. 600 N Mathilda Ave. (94086) Refrigerators; A/C; C/CATV; movies; VCPs. Radios; phones; shower or comb baths. 91 efficiencies. Coin laundry. Pets, $25 deposit required. Wkly rates avail. AE, DI, DS, MC, VI. FAX (408) 739-5439   ⊗ Ⓓ (408) 735-7800

Comfort Inn   Rates Subject to Change   *Motel*   ◆◆◆
All year [CP]   1P 67.00- 82.00   2P/1B   72.00- 87.00   2P/2B   .... 75.00   XP 5   F
Senior discount. 52 units. Exit US 101 at Mathilda Ave 1/4 mi s. 595 N Mathilda Ave. (94086) Refrigerators; A/C; C/CATV; movies; VCPs. Radios; phones. Coin laundry. Sauna; whirlpool; 12 rooms with whirlpool tub. No pets. All rooms with microwave. AE, CB, DI, MC, VI. FAX (408) 749-0367   ⊗ Ⓢ Ⓓ ⓛ (408) 749-8000

Days Inn   Rates Subject to Change   *Motel*   ◆◆◆
All year [CP]   1P 60.00- 70.00   2P/1B   65.00- 75.00   2P/2B   70.00- 75.00   XP
Senior discount. 36 units. Exit US 101 at Mathilda Ave; 1/4 mi s. 590 N Mathilda Ave. (94086) Formerly Mathilda Lodge. A/C; C/CATV; movies; radios; phones. Coin laundry. No pets. 2 rooms with large whirlpool, $80 for 2 persons. All rooms with microwave & refrigerator. Some units with whirlpool bath. Reserv deposit required. AE, DI, DS, MC, VI. FAX (408) 737-1177   ⊗ Ⓢ Ⓓ ⓛ (408) 737-1177

Friendship Inn-Sunnyvale   Rates Subject to Change   *Motel*   ◆◆
All year [CP]   1P .... 45.00   2P/1B   45.00- 55.00   2P/2B   .... 60.00   XP 5
40 units. On SR 82, 1/2 mi e of Wolfe Rd. 958 E El Camino Real. (94087) Refrigerators; A/C; C/CATV; movies; VCPs. Phones. 20 efficiencies, no utensils. Coin laundry. Sauna. No pets. Wkly rates avail. AE, DI, MC, VI. FAX (408) 245-7372   ⊗ Ⓢ Ⓓ (408) 733-8800

Holiday Inn-Sunnyvale   AAA Special Value Rates   *Motor Inn*   ◆◆◆
All year [BP]   1P 99.00- 109.00   2P/1B   109.00- 119.00   2P/2B   109.00- 119.00   XP 10
176 units. N off & adjacent to US 101; exit via Lawrence Expwy N. 1217 Wildwood Ave. (94089) A/C; C/CATV; movies; radios; phones; 179 comb baths. Coin laundry. Pool; whirlpool. No pets. AE, DI, DS, MC, VI. ● Dining rm & restaurant; 6 am-2 & 5-10 pm; $6-$25; cocktails. FAX (408) 732-2628   ⊗ Ⓓ ⓛ (408) 245-5330

Maple Tree Inn   AAA Special Value Rates   *Motel*   ◆◆◆
All year [CP]   1P 70.00- 75.00   2P/1B   75.00- 79.00   2P/2B   75.00- 79.00   XP 6   F
180 units. Exit US 101 at Fair Oaks Ave, 2 1/2 mi s to SR 82 (El Camino Real), then 1/4 mi e. 711 E El Camino Real. (94087) Some small rooms. A/C; C/CATV; movies; radios; phones. 1 2-bedrm unit. Coin laundry. Pool. No pets. 1 apartment with kitchen for up tp 8 persons, $110-$135. AE, CB, DI, MC, VI. *(See ad below)*   ⊗ Ⓢ Ⓓ (408) 720-9700

Quality Inn-Sunnyvale   AAA Special Value Rates   *Motel*   ◆◆
Sun-Thurs [CP]   1P .... 68.00   2P/1B   .... 68.00   2P/2B   .... 68.00   XP 5   F
Fri & Sat [CP]   1P .... 50.00   2P/1B   .... 50.00   2P/2B   .... 50.00   XP 5   F
72 units. Exit US 101 at Lawrence Expwy, 1 mi n to Persian Dr, then 1/4 mi w. 1280 Persian Dr. (94089) Refrigerators; A/C; C/CATV; movies; radios; phones. Small pool. No pets. Some rooms with microwave. AE, DI, DS, MC, VI. FAX (408) 744-0660   ⊗ Ⓢ Ⓓ (408) 744-0660

Radisson Haus Inn-Sunnyvale   AAA Special Value Rates   *Hotel*   ◆◆◆
Sun-Thurs   1P .... 105.00   2P/1B   .... 115.00   2P/2B   .... 115.00   XP 10   F
Fri & Sat   1P .... 59.00   2P/1B   .... 59.00   2P/2B   .... 59.00   XP 10   F
136 units. 1/4 mi w of Lawrence Expwy; on SR 82. 1085 E El Camino Real. (94087) Attractive rooms & public areas. A/C; C/CATV; movies; radios; phones. Pool; whirlpool; exercise rm. Garage. No pets. 12 suites with refrigerator & whirlpool; $135 for 2 persons. Reserv deposit required. Complimentary beverages each evening. AE, CB, DI, MC, VI. ● Restaurant; 6:30 am-2 & 5-10 pm; Sun from 10:30 am; $10-$18; cocktails. FAX (408) 984-7120   ⊗ Ⓡ Ⓓ ⓛ (408) 247-0000

Residence Inn by Marriott ◆◆◆
		Rates Subject to Change			*Apartment Motel*
Sun-Thurs [CP]	1P 124.00- 149.00	2P/1B	124.00- 149.00	2P/2B	124.00- 149.00 XP
Fri & Sat [EP]	1P 69.00- 89.00	2P/1B	69.00- 89.00	2P/2B	69.00- 89.00 XP

231 units. Exit US 101 Lawrence Expwy S; then e on Oakmead. 750 Lakeway Dr. (94086) 1-bedroom suites with living room & kitchen. Check-in 3 pm. A/C; C/CATV; movies; VCPs. Radios; phones. 58 2-bedrm units. Coin laundry. Small pool; whirlpools; sports court. Airport transp. Pets, $50-$100 extra charge; also $6 daily. Reserv deposit required. Complimentary beverages each evening. AE, DI, DS, MC, VI. FAX (408) 737-9722   ⊗ ⓓ ⓑ (408) 720-1000

Residence Inn by Marriott ◆◆◆
		Rates Subject to Change			*Apartment Motel*
All year [CP]	1P 128.00- 148.00	2P/1B	128.00- 148.00	2P/2B	128.00- 148.00 XP

Senior discount. 247 units. US 101 exit Lawrence Expwy S, Duane Ave W, Stewart Dr S. 1080 Stewart Dr. (94086) 1 & 2-bedroom suites with kitchen. Check-in 3 pm. A/C; C/CATV; movies; VCPs. Radios; phones. Efficiencies. Coin laundry. Pool; whirlpools; sports court. Airport transp. Pets, $50-$100 extra charge; also $6 daily. Wkly rates avail. AE, DI, DS, MC, VI. FAX (408) 720-8749   ⊗ ⓢ ⓓ ⓑ (408) 720-8893

Sheraton Sunnyvale Inn ⓐⓐ ◆◆◆
		Rates Subject to Change			*Motor Inn*	
Mon-Wed	1P 95.00- 120.00	2P/1B	105.00- 130.00	2P/2B	105.00- 130.00 XP 10	F
Thurs-Sun	1P 60.00	2P/1B	.... 60.00	2P/2B	.... 60.00 XP 10	F

Senior discount. 174 units. E off US 101, exit Mathilda Ave, Sunnyvale exit. 1100 N Mathilda Ave. (94089) A/C; C/CATV; movies; radios; phones. Pool; whirlpool; exercise rm. Airport transp. No pets. Wkly & monthly rates avail. AE, DI, DS, MC, VI. ● Restaurant; 6:30 am-10 pm; $7-$20; cocktail lounge. FAX (408) 734-8276 *(See ad p A527)*   ⊗ ⓢ ⓓ ⓑ (408) 745-6000

Sundowner Inn ◆◆◆
		AAA Special Value Rates			*Motel*	
Sun-Thurs [CP]	1P 101.00	2P/1B	.... 111.00	2P/2B	.... 111.00 XP 10	F
Fri & Sat [CP]	1P 65.00	2P/1B	.... 65.00	2P/2B	.... 65.00 XP 10	F

105 units. Sw corner of SR 237 & Mathilda Ave; e off US 101. 504 Ross Dr. (94089) Attractive comfortable rooms. Check-in 3 pm. Refrigerators; A/C; C/CATV; movies; VCPs. Radios; phones. Coin laundry. Htd pool; sauna; bicycles; exercise rm. No pets. 7 suites with wet bar, refrigerator & microwave, $150-$175 for 2 persons. Reserv deposit required. AE, DI, DS, MC, VI. Restaurant adjacent. FAX (408) 747-0580   ⊗ ⓓ (408) 734-9900

Sunnyvale Hilton ◆◆◆◆
		Rates Subject to Change			*Motor Inn*	
Sun-Thurs [EP]	1P 105.00- 150.00	2P/1B	120.00- 165.00	2P/2B	120.00- 165.00 XP 15	F
Fri & Sat [BP]	1P 65.00- 110.00	2P/1B	80.00- 125.00	2P/2B	80.00- 125.00 XP 15	F

Senior discount. 372 units. S off & adjacent to US 101, exit Lawrence Expwy. 1250 Lakeside Dr. (94086) Lagoon & colorfully landscaped grounds. Spacious modern rooms. A/C; C/CATV; movies; radios; phones. Pool; sauna; whirlpool; exercise rm; jogging track. Airport transp. No pets. Wkly rates avail. AE, DI, DS, MC, VI. ● Restaurant & coffeeshop; 6:30 am-11 pm; $10-$20; cocktails. FAX (408) 737-7147 *(See ad below)*   ⊗ ⓓ ⓑ (408) 738-4888

Super 8 Sunnyvale ⓐⓐ ◆◆
		Rates Subject to Change			*Motel*
All year [CP]	1P 42.00- 48.00	2P/1B	44.00- 54.00	2P/2B	46.00- 64.00 XP 6

Senior discount. 64 units. 2 1/2 blks w of Lawrence Expwy; on SR 82. 1071 E El Camino Real. (94087) Formerly Motel Orleans. Very well maintained, comfortable rooms. Refrigerators; A/C; C/CATV; movies; radios; phones. Pool. No pets. Wkly rates avail. Reserv deposit required; 3 days refund notice. AE, DI, DS, MC, VI. Restaurant opposite.   ⊗ ⓢ ⓓ (408) 244-9000

The Vagabond Inn ⓐⓐ ◆◆
		Rates Subject to Change			*Motel*	
All year [CP]	1P 40.00- 52.00	2P/1B	45.00- 55.00	2P/2B	50.00- 60.00 XP 5	F

60 units. S off US 101; exit via Mathilda Ave S. 816 Ahwanee Ave. (94086) A/C; C/CATV; movies; radios; phones. 1 2-bedrm unit. Pool. No pets. AE, DI, DS, MC, VI. Coffeeshop adjacent. FAX (408) 734-1675 *(See ad below)*   ⓓ (408) 734-4607

Valu-Inn by Nendels ⓐⓐ ◆
		Rates Subject to Change			*Motel*	
All year	1P 54.00	2P/1B	.... 54.00	2P/2B	59.00 XP 5	F

59 units. Exit US 101 at Mathilda Ave, 2 mi s, then 1/4 mi w on El Camino Real (SR 82). 852 W El Camino Real. (94087) 21 refrigerators; A/C; C/CATV; movies; rental VCPs. Radios; phones. Indoor whirlpool. No pets. 8 rooms with whirlpool, $5 extra. Wkly & monthly rates avail. Reserv deposit required. AE, DI, MC, VI. FAX (408) 773-0420   ⊗ ⓢ ⓓ ⓑ (408) 773-1234

Woodfin Suites   Rates Subject to Change   Suites Motel   ◆◆◆
  Sun-Thurs [BP]   1P 115.00- 132.00 2P/1B 125.00- 142.00 2P/2B 125.00- 142.00 XP 10   F
  Fri & Sat [BP]   1P .... 79.00   2P/1B .... 79.00   2P/2B .... 79.00   XP 10   F
  Senior discount. 88 units. Exit US 101 at Fair Oaks; 2 1/2 mi w to SR 82E. 635 E El Camino Real. (94087) 1- &
  2-bedroom suites, most with fireplace. Check-in 4 pm. A/C; C/CATV; movies; VCPs. Radios; phones. Coin laundry. Small
  pool; whirlpool. Airport transp. No pets. Monthly rates avail. Reserv deposit required. Complimentary beverages each
  evening. AE, DI, DS, MC, VI. FAX (408) 738-0840   Ⓓ (408) 738-1700

Wyndham Garden Hotel   Rates Subject to Change   Hotel   ◆◆◆
  Mon-Thurs   1P .... 105.00   2P/1B .... 115.00   2P/2B .... 115.00   XP 10   F
  Fri-Sun   1P .... 44.00   2P/1B .... 44.00   2P/2B .... 44.00   XP 10   F
  180 units. Exit US 101 Lawrence Expwy N; at nw quadrant of SR 237 & Lawrence Expwy. 1300 Chesapeake Terr.
  (94089) Check-in 3 pm. A/C; C/CATV; movies; radios; phones. Coin laundry. Pool; indoor whirlpool; exercise rm. Parking
  lot. Airport transp. No pets. Reserv deposit required. AE, CB, DI, MC, VI. ● Restaurant; 6:30 am-2:30 & 5-10 pm; $9-
  $15; cocktails. FAX (408) 745-0759 (See ad p A456)   ⊗ Ⓢ Ⓓ Ⓑ (408) 747-0999

RESTAURANTS

California Cafe Bar & Grill   American $$ ◆◆
  At Wolfe Rd. 855 E Homestead Rd. Creative California cuisine, varied menu, emphasis on unique preparation. Outside
  dining, special desserts. Casual atmosphere. A/C. Children's menu. Open 11:30 am-2:30 & 5:30-9:30 pm; Fri-10 pm; Sat
  5 pm-10 pm; Sun 10 am-2:30 & 5-9 pm; closed 11/26, 12/25; Easter & Super Bowl Sun. Cocktails & lounge. Reserv ad-
  vised. AE, CB, DI, MC, VI.   ⊗ (408) 739-7670

Pezzella's Villa Napoli   Italian $$ ◆◆◆
  Ⓦ W of Mary Ave. 1025 W El Camino Real. Comfortable attractive dining room; seafood, steak, veal & pasta spe-
  cialties. Family owned for 3 generations. A/C. Children's menu. Open 11:30 am-3 & 5-10:30 pm; Sat from 5 pm;
  closed Sun, Mon, mid-August to Labor day & major holidays. Cocktails & lounge. Reserv advised. AE, DI, MC,
  VI.   ⊗ (408) 738-2400

The Velvet Turtle   Continental $$ ◆◆
  1/2 mi e of SR 85, exit Fremont Ave, in DeAnza Square. 1306 S Mary Ave. Varied menu; casual atmosphere. A/C. Chil-
  dren's menu. Open 11:30 am-2:30 & 5-10 pm; Sat 5 pm-10 pm; Sun 10 am-2:30 & 4-9 pm. Cocktails & lounge. Reserv
  advised. AE, CB, DI, MC, VI.   ⊗ (408) 738-4070

SUNSET BEACH — 1,800
Best Western Sunset Beach Inn   Rates Subject to Change   Motel   ◆◆◆
  ⊛ All year [CP]   1P 79.00- 150.00 2P/1B   79.00- 150.00 2P/2B   79.00- 150.00 XP 10   F
  Senior discount. 50 units. On SR 1; adjacent to Bolsa Chica State Beach. 17205 Pacific Coast Hwy at Warner
  Ave. (PO Box 1188, 90742) Most rooms with patio or balcony. Refrigerators; A/C; C/CATV; movies; radios;
  phones. Whirlpool. Garage. No pets. AE, DI, DS, MC, VI. FAX (310) 592-4093   Ⓓ Ⓑ (714) 840-2431

Harbour Inn   AAA Special Value Rates   Motel   ◆◆◆
  ⊛ All year [CP]   1P 59.00- 89.00   2P/1B   69.00- 99.00   2P/2B   69.00- 99.00   XP 10   F
  23 units. On SR 1. 16912 Pacific Coast Hwy. (PO Box 1439, 90742) Spacious rooms. A/C; C/CATV; movies; ra-
  dios; phones. No pets. Some refrigerators & microwaves. Wkly & monthly rates avail. Reserv deposit required.
  AE, DI, DS, MC, VI. FAX (310) 592-3547   Ⓓ (310) 592-4770

Ramada Inn Sunset Beach   Rates Subject to Change   Motel   ◆◆
  ⊛ 6/15-9/14 [CP]   1P .... 89.00   2P/1B .... 89.00   2P/2B .... 69.00   XP 5   F
  9/15-6/14 [CP]   1P .... 69.00   2P/1B .... 69.00   2P/2B .... 69.00   XP 5   F
  Senior discount. 25 units. 16555 Pacific Coast Hwy. (90742) Microwaves in most rooms. Refrigerators; A/C;
  C/CATV; radios; phones. 2 2-bedrm units, 2 kitchens, 23 efficiencies. Coin laundry. Whirlpool; 1 room with whirl-
  pool. Garage. No pets. Wkly rates avail. Reserv deposit required. AE, DI, DS, MC, VI. FAX (310) 592-5617
                                                                                 Ⓓ (310) 592-1993

SUSANVILLE — 7,300
Best Western Trailside Inn   Rates Guaranteed   Motel   ◆◆◆
  ⊛ 4/1-10/31   1P 46.00- 68.00   2P/1B   48.00- 68.00   2P/2B   48.00- 68.00   XP 4
  Senior discount. 90 units. 1 1/2 mi e on SR 36. 2785 Main St. (96130) OPEN ALL YEAR. A/C; C/CATV; movies;
  phones. Pool. 4 units with seating area & whirlpool bath, $74 for up to 2 persons. AE, DI, DS, MC, VI. Coffeeshop
  adjacent. (See ad below)   ⊗ Ⓓ (916) 257-4123

River Inn Motel   Rates Subject to Change   Motel   ◆◆
  ⊛ 5/1-10/31   1P 32.00- 36.00   2P/1B   36.00- 42.00   2P/2B   38.00- 45.00   XP 4
  Senior discount. 49 units. 3/4 mi e on SR 36. 1710 Main St. (96130) OPEN ALL YEAR. A/C; C/CATV; movies;
  phones. Small pool. Pets. Reserv deposit required; 10 days refund notice. AE, DS, DI, MC, VI. Coffeeshop adja-
  cent. FAX (916) 257-4950   ⊘ Ⓓ (916) 257-6051

Super Budget Motel   Rates Subject to Change   *Motel*   ◆◆
🆎 5/1-10/31   1P   34.00-   40.00   2P/1B   37.00-   44.00   2P/2B   ....   46.00   XP   5
69 units. 1 3/4 mi e on SR 36 & 1/2 blk n. 2975 Johnstonville Rd. (96130) OPEN ALL YEAR. Large rooms. A/C; C/CATV; movies; radios; phones. Pool; Small pool open 5/1-9/30. Wkly & monthly rates avail. AE, DI, DS, MC, VI.
     ⊗ Ⓓ 🅿 (916) 257-2782

TAHOE CITY — 1,800 See LAKE TAHOE (NORTHERN REGION)

TAHOE VISTA — See LAKE TAHOE (NORTHERN REGION)

TARZANA — See LOS ANGELES (San Fernando Valley)

TEHACHAPI — 5,800
Best Western Mountain Inn   Rates Subject to Change   *Motor Inn*   ◆
🆎 All year   1P   ....   45.56   2P/1B   ....   48.89   2P/2B   ....   51.11   XP   3   F
Senior discount. 75 units. 3 blks w on SR 58 business rt. 416 W Tehachapi Blvd. (93561) 50 refrigerators; A/C; C/CATV; movies; radios; phones. Small pool & whirlpool; closed in winter. Pets. Wkly rates avail. AE, DI, DS, MC, VI. ● Coffeeshop; 24 hours; $7-$9.25; cocktails. FAX (805) 822-6197   ⊗ Ⓓ 🅿 (805) 822-5591

Tehachapi Summit Travelodge   Rates Subject to Change   *Motor Inn*   ◆◆◆
🆎 All year   1P   46.00-   53.00   2P/1B   53.00-   60.00   2P/2B   53.00-   60.00   XP   10   F
Senior discount. 80 units. 2 mi e on SR 58 business rt adjacent to SR 58 eastbound exit Monolith; westbound exit 1st Tehachapi exit. 500 Steuber Rd. (PO Box 140, 93581) Balconies. Check-in 3 pm. A/C; C/CATV; phones. Htd pool; whirlpool. 5 suites with microwave & refrigerator, $58-$61. AE, CB, DI, MC, VI. ● Restaurant; 6 am-10 pm; $7-$16.95; cocktails; entertainment. Also, The Summit Dining Hall & Saloon, see separate listing. FAX (805) 822-1337 *(See ad below)*   ⊗ Ⓓ 🅿 (805) 823-8000

RESTAURANT

The Summit Dining Hall & Saloon   Steakhouse $$ ◆◆
At The Tehachapi Summit Travelodge. Informal western atmosphere. Sandwiches, salad, chicken, pork, seafood & steaks. Prime rib Fri & Sat 5 pm-9 pm; ages 5-12, $2.50, under 5 free. A/C. Early bird specials; children's menu. Open 5:30 am-10 pm. Cocktails & lounge. Entertainment & dancing. AE, DI, MC, VI. *(See ad below)*   ⊗ (805) 823-1000

TEMECULA — 27,100
Best Western Country Inn   Rates Subject to Change   *Motel*   ◆◆◆
🆎 Fri & Sat   1P   ....   42.75   2P/1B   ....   45.09   2P/2B   ....   51.30   XP   4
Sun-Thurs   1P   ....   39.00   2P/1B   ....   42.00   2P/2B   ....   48.00   XP   4
Senior discount. 74 units. Adjacent to I-15, exit Winchester Rd, 1 blk w then 1/2 mi s. 27706 Jefferson Ave. (92590) 60 refrigerators; A/C; C/CATV; movies; radios; phones. Coin laundry. Htd pool; sauna; whirlpool. No pets. 6 rooms with whirlpool tub, 2 with fireplace, $85-$115. AE, DI, DS, MC, VI. FAX (909) 699-7995
     ⊗ Ⓓ 🅿 (909) 676-7378

Best Western Guest House Inn   Rates Subject to Change   *Motel* ◆◆
🏢 All year   1P 43.00- 46.00   2P/1B   49.00- 55.00   2P/2B   54.00- 64.00 XP 5
Senior discount. 24 units. From I-15, Rancho California Rd exit, 1 blk w to Front St, 1 blk s to Moreno, then 1 blk e. 41873 Moreno Rd. (92590) A/C; C/CATV; movies; radios; phones. Small pool; whirlpool. No pets. Reserv deposit required. AE, DI, DS, MC, VI. Restaurant adjacent. FAX (909) 694-8520   ⊗ Ⓓ (909) 676-5700

Butterfield Inn   Rates Subject to Change   *Motel* ◆◆
🏢 Fri & Sat   1P   ....   38.00   2P/1B   ....   43.00   2P/2B   ....   45.00 XP 5
Sun-Thurs   1P   ....   33.00   2P/1B   ....   38.00   2P/2B   ....   40.00 XP 5
Senior discount. 39 units. Adjacent to I-15, exit SR 79S, then 1 mi n. 28718 Front St. (92590) 5 refrigerators; A/C; C/CATV; movies; radios; phones. Coin laundry. Small pool; whirlpool. No pets. Reserv deposit required. AE, DS, MC, VI.   ⊗ Ⓓ (909) 676-4833

Doubletree Suites Hotel   Rates Subject to Change   *Suites Hotel* ◆◆◆
🏢 Fri & Sat   1P   ....   85.00   2P/1B   ....   85.00   2P/2B   ....   85.00 XP 10
Sun-Thurs   1P   ....   69.00   2P/1B   ....   69.00   2P/2B   ....   69.00 XP 10
136 units. 1 blk e of I-15, exit Rancho California Rd. 29345 Rancho California Rd. (92591) On spacious grounds. Refrigerators; A/C; C/CATV; free & pay movies; VCPs. Radios; phones. Htd pool; whirlpool; exercise rm. Parking lot. No pets. Microwaves. AE, CB, DI, MC, VI. ● Restaurant; 6:30 am-9:30 pm; $8-$15; cocktails. FAX (909) 699-3928 *(See ad below)*   ⊗ Ⓢ Ⓓ Ⓛ (909) 676-5656

Loma Vista Bed & Breakfast   Rates Subject to Change   *Bed & Breakfast* ◆◆◆
🏢 All year [BP]   1P 95.00- 125.00   2P/1B   95.00- 125.00   ....   XP 25
6 units. 4 mi e of I-15, on Rancho California Rd. 33350 La Serena Way. (92591) Hillside location, nicely decorated & furnished rooms. Smoke free premises. Check-in 3 pm. A/C. No pets. Reserv deposit required; 7 days refund notice. DS, MC, VI.   ⊗ Ⓓ (909) 676-7047

Ramada Inn   Rates Subject to Change   *Motel* ◆◆
All year [CP]   1P   ....   49.00   2P/1B   ....   59.00   2P/2B   ....   59.00 XP 5   F
Senior discount. 70 units. 1/4 mi nw of I-15; exit SR 79-Indio. 28980 Front St. (92592) Refrigerators; A/C; C/CATV; movies; phones. Htd pool; whirlpool. Pets, $35 deposit required. 34 rooms with microwave. Wkly rates avail. AE, DS, MC, VI. Restaurant adjacent. FAX (909) 699-3400   ⊗ Ⓢ Ⓓ (909) 676-8770

Temecula Creek Inn   Rates Subject to Change   *Resort Motor Inn* ◆◆◆
🏢 All year   1P 115.00- 145.00   2P/1B   115.00- 145.00   2P/2B   115.00- 145.00 XP 20
80 units. From I-15, use SR 79 south exit, 3/4 mi e to Pala Rd, then 1/4 mi se. 44501 Rainbow Canyon Rd. (92592) On nicely landscaped grounds overlooking golf course. Patios or balconies. Check-in 3 pm. Refrigerators; A/C; C/CATV; radios; phones; comb or shower baths. Htd pool; whirlpool; tennis-2 courts. Fee for: golf-27 holes. Reserv deposit required. AE, DI, DS, MC, VI. ● Temet Grill, see separate listing. FAX (909) 676-3422 *(See ad p 185)*   ⊗ Ⓓ (909) 676-5631

RESTAURANTS

Cafe Champagne   American $$$ ◆◆◆
4 mi e of I-15; exit Rancho California Rd. 32575 Rancho California Rd. At Culbertson Winery. Nicely prepared California cuisine served in an attractive dining room or outdoor terrace. A/C. Open 11 am-9 pm; closed 1/1, 11/25 & 12/25. Wine. Reserv advised weekends. MC, VI.   ⊗ (909) 699-0088

Delaney's   Seafood $$ ◆◆
1 1/2 blks ne of I-15; exit Rancho California Rd; in The Tower Plaza. 27511 Ynez Rd. Attractive nautical decor. Sun brunch 10 am-2 pm. A/C. Children's menu. Open 11:30 am-9 pm; Fri & Sat-10 pm; closed 11/25 & 12/25. Cocktails & lounge. AE, DI, MC, VI.   ⊗ 🔊 (909) 676-1113

Dos Gringos   Mexican $ ◆◆
In the Old Abode Plaza Shopping Center; 1/2 mi s of Winchester Rd. 27645 Jefferson Ave. Casual atmosphere. Wide variety of Mexican cuisine including steaks, chicken & shrimp dishes. Sun brunch 11 am-2 pm. A/C. Children's menu. Open 11:30 am-9 pm; Sat 11:30 am-10 pm; Sun 11 am-9 pm; closed 11/25 & 12/25. Beer & wine. AE, DS, MC, VI.
                                                                                                                  ⊗ (909) 699-4722

Mexico Chiquito   Mexican $ ◆
From I-15, exit Rancho California Rd, 1 blk w to Front St, 1 blk s to Moreno, then 1 blk e. 41841 Moreno Rd. Sun brunch 10 am-2 pm; buffet Mon-Thurs 11 am-2 pm. A/C. Children's menu. Open 11 am-9 pm; Sat & Sun from 8 am; closed 1/1, 11/25 & 12/25. Cocktails & lounge. MC, VI.   ⊗ 🔊 (909) 676-2933

Temet Grill   American $$ ◆
At the Temecula Creek Inn. Overlooking golf course. Sun brunch 10 am-2:30 pm. A/C. Open 6:30 am-10 pm; Sat & Sun from 6 am. Cocktails & lounge. Entertainment. Reserv advised. AE, MC, VI. *(See ad p 185)*   ⊗ (909) 676-5631

TEMPLE CITY — See SAN GABRIEL

TEMPLETON — 800

RESTAURANT

A J Spurs   American $$ ◆
⊛ 1 1/4 mi se of 101; exit Main St. 508 Main St. Barbecue chicken, quail, steaks, ribs & seafood. Western casual atmosphere. A/C. Early bird specials; children's menu. Open 4 pm-9:30 pm; Sat & Sun 2 pm-9:30 pm; closed 1/1, 11/25, 12/24 & 12/25. Cocktails & lounge. Reserv advised No reserv accepted Sat. AE, MC, VI.   (805) 434-2700

TERRA LINDA — See SAN RAFAEL

THOUSAND OAKS — 104,400
Best Western Oaks Lodge   AAA Special Value Rates   *Motel*   ◆◆
⊛ All year [CP]   1P 46.00- 56.00 2P/1B 51.00- 61.00 2P/2B 46.00- 56.00 XP 5   F
76 units. From US 101, 1 blk n, then 1 blk nw on Thousand Oaks Blvd; exit Moorpark Rd. 12 Conejo Blvd. (91360) 20 refrigerators; A/C; C/TV; movies; radios; phones; comb or shower baths. Coin laundry. Pool; whirlpool. No pets. 7-night minimum stay in 6 efficiencies, $5 extra. AE, DI, DS, MC, VI.   ⊗ Ⓓ (805) 495-7011
FAX (805) 495-0647

Days Inn ◆◆◆
🌐 All year   **AAA Special Value Rates**   *Motor Inn*   F
1P 55.00- 60.00 2P/1B 55.00- 70.00 2P/2B 55.00- 70.00 XP 10
124 units. 1 blk se of US 101, exit Ventu Park Rd. 1320 Newbury Rd. (91320) 20 refrigerators; A/C; C/TV; free & pay movies; radios; phones. Coin laundry. Htd pool; whirlpool. No pets. Wkly & monthly rates avail. AE, DI, DS, MC, VI. ● Restaurant; 6 am-1 & 5-9:30 pm; $7-$12; cocktails. FAX (805) 498-5783 *(See ad p A530)*
⊗ Ⓢ Ⓓ Ⓛ (805) 499-5910

Econo Lodge ◆◆
🌐 5/26-9/1 [CP]   **Rates Subject to Change**   *Motel*
1P 38.00- 44.00 2P/1B 42.00- 48.00 2P/2B 44.00- 54.00 XP 5 F
9/2-5/25 [CP]   1P 36.00- 40.00 2P/1B 38.00- 44.00 2P/2B 40.00- 50.00 XP 5 F
Senior discount. 60 units. 3 blks ne of US 101, exit Rancho Rd. 1425 Thousand Oaks Blvd. (91362) A/C; C/CATV; radios; phones. Small pool. No pets. Wkly rates avail. AE, DI, DS, MC, VI. FAX (805) 494-1295
⊗ Ⓓ (805) 496-0102

Howard Johnson Hotel ◆◆
🌐 All year   **Rates Subject to Change**   *Motor Inn*
1P 47.00- 60.00 2P/1B 52.00- 70.00 2P/2B 52.00- 70.00 XP 5 F
Senior discount. 107 units. Adjacent to US 101, exit Moorpark Rd, then 1/4 mi w. 75 W Thousand Oaks Blvd. (91360) 7 refrigerators; A/C; C/TV; free & pay movies; radios; phones. Coin laundry. Small htd pool; whirlpool. Pets. 4 suites with microwave & refrigerator. Wkly & monthly rates avail. AE, DI, DS, MC, VI. ● Restaurant; 6 am-10 pm; $5-$9; cocktails. FAX (805) 497-1875
⊗ Ⓓ Ⓛ (805) 497-3701

RESTAURANTS

Black Angus   American $$ ◆◆
Adjacent to US 101, exit Moorpark Rd, 1/2 mi w. 139 W Thousand Oaks Blvd. Beef, seafood, chicken, pastas, salads & prime rib. A/C. Children's menu. Open 11 am-10 pm; Fri & Sat-11 pm; closed 12/25. Cocktails & lounge. Reserv advised Fri & Sat. AE, DI, DS, MC, VI. ⊗ (805) 497-0757

Hunan Chinese Restaurant   Chinese $ ◆
🌐 Corner of Moorpark Rd & Janss St, s end of shopping plaza. 1352 N Moorpark Rd. Authentic Hunan style cooking. A/C. Open 11:30 am-9:30 pm; Fri & Sat-10 pm. Beer & wine. Minimum, $4-$6. AE, MC, VI.
⊗ (805) 371-0075

THOUSAND PALMS — 1,700
Travelers Inn ◆◆
🌐 11/1-5/31   **AAA Special Value Rates**   *Motel*
1P .... 35.95 2P/1B .... 41.95 2P/2B .... 41.95 XP 4
6/1-10/31   1P .... 31.95 2P/1B .... 37.95 2P/2B .... 37.95 XP 4
116 units. Adjacent to I-10, exit Ramon Rd. 72-215 Varner Rd. (92276) A/C; C/CATV; movies; phones. Htd pool; whirlpool. No pets. AE, DI, MC, VI. FAX (619) 343-3082
⊗ Ⓢ Ⓓ Ⓛ (619) 343-1381

THREE RIVERS — 1,400
Best Western Holiday Lodge ◆◆
🌐 All year [CP]   **Rates Subject to Change**   *Motel*
1P 46.00- 72.00 2P/1B 48.00- 72.00 2P/2B 53.00- 76.00 XP 4
44 units. 2 mi sw on SR 198. (PO Box 129, 93271) 10 deluxe units. Refrigerators; A/C; C/CATV; radios; phones; comb or shower baths. 1 2-bedrm unit. Pool; whirlpool; playground. Pets. Reserv deposit required. AE, DI, DS, MC, VI.
⊗ Ⓓ Ⓛ (209) 561-4119

Buckeye Tree Lodge ◆◆
🌐 All year   **Rates Subject to Change**   *Motel*
1P 39.00- 52.00 2P/1B 46.00- 55.00 2P/2B 46.00- 61.00 XP 4
12 units. 6 mi ne on SR 198, 1/2 mi sw from entrance to Sequoia National Park. 46000 Sierra Dr. (93271) In canyon setting. All rooms with patio or deck overlooking the Kaweah River. 7 refrigerators; A/C; C/CATV; shower or comb baths. Pool; fishing. Pets, $4 extra charge. 1 efficiency, $6 extra. 1 2-room cottage with fireplace & kitchen, $97 for up to 4 persons. Wkly rates avail. Reserv deposit required; 3 days refund notice. AE, DI, DS, MC, VI.
Ⓓ (209) 561-5900

Lazy J Ranch Motel ◆◆
🌐 All year   **Rates Subject to Change**   *Motel*
1P 40.00- 54.00 2P/1B 44.00- 54.00 2P/2B 56.00- 80.00 XP 5
18 units. 2 1/2 mi sw on SR 198. 39625 Sierra Dr. (93271) Tree shaded spacious grounds. Refrigerators; A/C; C/CATV; radios; shower or comb baths. 3 2-bedrm units, 7 kitchens. Coin laundry. Pool; fishing; playground. Pets. 5 cottages with kitchen, $70 for 2 persons. Wkly rates avail. Reserv deposit required; 3 days refund notice. AE, DI, MC, VI. *Independant Motels of America.*
Ⓓ (209) 561-4449

The River Inn ◆
🌐 4/1-10/31   **Rates Subject to Change**   *Motel*
1P .... 48.00 2P/1B 51.00- 55.00 2P/2B 55.00- 59.00 XP 3
11/1-3/31   1P .... 35.00 2P/1B .... 38.00 2P/2B .... 40.00 XP 3
12 units. 5 mi ne on SR 198, 1 1/2 mi sw from entrance to Sequoia National Park. 45176 Sierra Dr. (93271) Scenic mountain view. Refrigerators; A/C; C/CATV; shower or comb baths. Pets, $3 extra charge. Wkly rates avail. Reserv deposit required; 3 days refund notice. DI, DS, MC, VI.
Ⓓ (209) 561-4367

Sierra Lodge ◆◆
🌐 4/1-10/31   **Rates Subject to Change**   *Motel*
1P 45.00- 50.00 2P/1B 48.00- 55.00 2P/2B .... 48.00 XP 3
11/1-3/31   1P 35.00- 45.00 2P/1B 39.00- 55.00 2P/2B .... 46.00 XP 3
22 units. 2 mi ne on SR 198, 3 mi sw from entrance to Sequoia National Park. 43175 Sierra Dr. (93271) 7 units with fireplace. Refrigerators; A/C; C/CATV; radios; phones; comb or shower baths. Pool. 1 1-bedroom suite with efficiency, $65-$70. 4 2-bedroom suites with efficiency, $70-$135. Wkly rates avail. Reserv deposit required. AE, DI, MC, VI. FAX (209) 561-3264
⊗ Ⓓ (209) 561-3681

TIBURON — 7,500 See also CORTE MADERA, MILL VALLEY & SAN RAFAEL

Tiburon Lodge   AAA Special Value Rates   Motel   ◆◆◆
🅰 All year   1P 85.00- 105.00 2P/1B 110.00- 120.00 2P/2B 100.00- 110.00 XP 15   F
97 units. In village; 1 blk from bay; 4 mi e of US 101; exit Tiburon-Belvedere. 1651 Tiburon Blvd. (94920) Few
studios. Check-in 3 pm. 64 A/C; C/CATV; movies; radios; phones; shower or comb baths. Pool. Pets, $15 daily
extra charge. 3 apartments $125-$175 for 2-4 persons. 21 rooms with whirlpool tub $140-$250 for up to 2 persons. Reserv deposit required; 3 days refund notice. AE, DI, DS, MC, VI. Restaurant; 7-11 am; Sat & Sun-1 pm.
FAX (415) 435-2451 *(See ad p A425)*   ⊗ Ⓓ (415) 435-3133

TORRANCE — 133,100

City Inn   Rates Subject to Change   Motel   ◆◆◆
🅰 Sun-Thurs [CP]   1P .... 65.00 2P/1B   .... 70.00 2P/2B   .... 70.00 XP 5   F
Fri & Sat [CP]   1P .... 58.50 2P/1B   .... 58.50 2P/2B   .... 58.50 XP 5   F
Senior discount. 51 units. 1/2 blk e of Hawthorne Blvd. 3673 Torrance Blvd. (90503) Refrigerators; A/C; C/TV;
movies; radios; phones. Whirlpool. Garage. No pets. 1 kitchen unit, $125 for up to 4 persons. Wkly & monthly
rates avail. AE, MC, VI. FAX (310) 316-9349 *(See ad p A531)*   ⊗ Ⓢ Ⓓ Ⓚ (310) 316-5570

Courtyard by Marriott   Rates Subject to Change   Motor Inn   ◆◆◆
Sun-Thurs   1P 75.00- 85.00 2P/1B   75.00- 85.00 2P/2B   75.00- 85.00 XP 10
Fri & Sat   1P .... 65.00 2P/1B   .... 65.00 2P/2B   .... 65.00 XP 10
Senior discount. 149 units. 1 blk w of Crenshaw Blvd. 2633 W Sepulveda Blvd. (90505) Check-in 3 pm. 4 refrigerators;
A/C; C/CATV; free & pay movies; radios; phones. Coin laundry. Htd pool; whirlpool; exercise rm. No pets. Wkly rates
avail. AE, DI, DS, MC, VI. ● Restaurant; 6:30 am-2 & 5-10 pm; $7-$14; cocktails. FAX (310) 533-0564 *(See ad
p A221)*   ⊗ Ⓢ Ⓓ Ⓚ (310) 533-8000

Days Inn   AAA Special Value Rates   Motel   ◆◆
🅰 All year   1P 55.00- 65.00 2P/1B   .... 70.00 2P/2B   60.00- 70.00 XP 5   F
92 units. 1/4 mi w of Hawthorne Blvd. 4111 Pacific Coast Hwy. (90505) Formerly Quality Inn. 29 refrigerators; A/C;
C/CATV; movies; radios; phones. 4 kitchens, no utensils. Pool. Pets, $40 deposit required. 4 units with whirlpool,
$145. Wkly rates avail. AE, DI, DS, MC, VI. Cocktail lounge; entertainment. FAX (310) 378-8171 *(See ad below)*
                                                                                       ⊗ Ⓓ (310) 378-8511

Del Amo Inn   Rates Subject to Change   Motel   ◆
🅰 All year   1P .... 46.00 2P/1B   .... 48.00 2P/2B   .... 55.00 XP 5   F
Senior discount. 31 units. 1/2 mi n of Torrance Blvd. 20534 Hawthorne Blvd. (90503) 14 refrigerators; A/C; C/TV;
movies; radios; phones. No pets. 5-night minimum stay in 4 efficiencies. Wkly rates avail. AE, DI, DS, MC, VI.
                                                                                       Ⓓ Ⓚ (310) 542-9417

Holiday Inn Torrance Harbor Gateway   Rates Subject to Change   Hotel   ◆◆◆
🅰 All year   1P 95.00- 105.00 2P/1B 105.00- 115.00 2P/2B 105.00- 115.00 XP 10   F
Senior discount. 338 units. S of jct I-110 & I-405, 1/2 mi s of 190th St. 19800 S Vermont Ave. (90502) 20 refriger-
ators; A/C; C/CATV; free & pay movies; radios; phones. Small htd pool; sauna; whirlpool; exercise rm. Garage.
No pets. Monthly rates avail. AE, DI, DS, MC, VI. ● Dining rm; 6 am-2 & 5:30-10 pm; $12-$19; cocktails; cocktail
lounge; entertainment. Also, Pasta's Ristorante, see separate listing. FAX (310) 327-8296
                                                                                       ⊗ Ⓢ Ⓓ Ⓚ (310) 781-9100

Howard Johnson Lodge   Rates Subject to Change   Motor Inn   ◆◆
🅰 All year   1P 52.00- 58.00 2P/1B   58.00- 64.00 2P/2B   58.00- 64.00 XP 6
Senior discount. 88 units. 1 mi e of Hawthorne Blvd. 2880 Pacific Coast Hwy. (90505) Refrigerators; A/C; C/TV;
movies; radios; phones. Coin laundry. Htd pool; whirlpool. No pets. 12 rooms with microwave. Wkly rates avail.
AE, DI, DS, MC, VI. ● Coffeeshop; 6 am-9 pm; Sun-2 pm; $5-$7. FAX (310) 775-6661   Ⓓ (310) 325-0660

Residence Inn by Marriott   Rates Guaranteed   Suites Motel ◆◆◆
All year [CP]   1P 124.00- 162.00 2P/1B 124.00- 162.00 2P/2B 124.00- 162.00 XP 10
Senior discount. 247 units. 1/2 blk e of Hawthorne Blvd. 3701 Torrance Blvd. (90503) 1 & 2-bedroom suites with living
room. 123 fireplaces. Check-in 4 pm. A/C; C/CATV; pay movies; rental VCPs. Radios; phones. 61 2-bedrm units. Coin
laundry. Htd pool; whirlpools. Pets, $100 deposit, $50 non-refundable; $6 extra charge. Fully equipped kitchen in every
unit. Wkly & monthly rates avail. AE, DI, DS, MC, VI. FAX (310) 543-3026   ⊗ Ⓓ Ⓚ (310) 543-4566

Summerfield Suites Hotel   Rates Subject to Change   Suites Motel ◆
Sun-Thurs [CP]   ....   2P/1B   .... 129.00 2P/2B   .... 159.00 XP 10
Fri & Sat [CP]   ....   2P/1B   .... 89.00 2P/2B   .... 104.00 XP 10
144 units. Between 190th St & Del Amo Blvd. 19901 Prairie Ave. (90503) 1- & 2-bedroom suites with living room. 22 fireplaces. Check-in 3 pm. Refrigerators; A/C; C/CATV; free & pay movies; VCPs. Radios; phones. 49 2-bedrm units,
kitchens. Coin laundry. Htd pool; whirlpool; sports court; putting green; exercise rm. Pets, $250 non-refundable fee. Com-
plimentary beverages each evening. AE, DI, DS, MC, VI. FAX (310) 542-9628   ⊗ Ⓢ Ⓓ Ⓚ (310) 371-8525

Torrance Business Center Courtyard by Marriott   Rates Subject to Change   Motor Inn   ◆◆◆
Sun-Thurs   1P .... 64.00 2P/1B   .... 64.00 2P/2B   .... 64.00 XP 10   F
Fri & Sat   1P .... 44.00 2P/1B   .... 44.00 2P/2B   .... 44.00 XP
Senior discount. 149 units. Adjacent to I-405; exit Western Ave. 1925 W 190th St. (90504) Check-in 3 pm. 8 refriger-
ators; A/C; C/CATV; free & pay movies; radios; phones. Coin laundry. Htd pool; whirlpool; exercise rm. No pets. Wkly rates
avail. AE, DI, DS, MC, VI. ● Restaurant; 6:30 am-2 & 5-10 pm; Sat & Sun from 7 am; $7.25-$12.25; cocktails.
FAX (310) 532-9161   ⊗ Ⓢ Ⓓ Ⓚ (310) 532-1722

Torrance Holiday Inn   AAA Special Value Rates   Hotel   ◆◆◆
All year   1P 89.00- 109.00 2P/1B   99.00- 119.00 2P/2B   96.00- 116.00 XP 10
386 units. 1 blk s of Torrance Blvd. 21333 Hawthorne Blvd. (90503) Refrigerators; A/C; C/CATV; movies; radios; phones.
Htd pool; sauna; whirlpool; rental bicycles; exercise rm. Parking lot. Pets. Wkly & monthly rates avail. AE, DI, DS, MC,
VI. ● Restaurant; 6 am-2 & 5-10 pm; $7.95-$13.95; cocktails; entertainment. FAX (310) 540-2065
                                                                                       ⊗ Ⓢ Ⓓ Ⓚ (310) 540-0500

Torrance Marriott Rates Subject to Change *Hotel* ◆◆◆◆
Sun-Thurs 1P .... 145.00 2P/1B .... 165.00 2P/2B .... 165.00 XP
Fri & Sat 1P .... 89.00 2P/1B .... 89.00 2P/2B .... 89.00 XP
487 units. 1 blk s of Torrance Blvd; off Hawthorne Blvd. 3635 Fashion Way. (90503) Most rooms with balcony. Check-in 3 pm. 40 refrigerators; A/C; C/CATV; free & pay movies; radios; phones. Coin laundry. Htd indoor/outdoor pool; saunas; whirlpool; exercise rm. Valet garage & parking lot. No pets. AE, DI, DS, MC, VI. ● Dining rm & 2 restaurants; 6 am-11 pm; $8.50-$20.95; cocktails; cocktail lounge; entertainment. Also, Jasmines, see separate listing. FAX (310) 543-6076
⊗ Ⓢ Ⓓ ⑤ (310) 316-3636

Travelodge AAA Special Value Rates *Motel* ◆◆
⊛ All year 1P .... 53.00 2P/1B .... 58.00 2P/2B .... 61.00 XP 6 F
53 units. 1/4 blk e of Crenshaw Blvd. 2448 Sepulveda Blvd. (90501) 15 refrigerators; A/C; C/CATV; movies; radios; phones. 1 2-bedrm unit. Small pool. No pets. Wkly rates avail. AE, DI, DS, MC, VI. FAX (310) 539-6420
⊗ Ⓓ ⑤ (310) 539-9888

RESTAURANTS

Jasmines Continental $$$ ◆◆◆
In Torrance Marriott. 3635 Fashion Way. Informal atmosphere. Featuring seafood, steaks, duck & pasta. Japanese breakfast, 6 am-11 am. A/C. Open 6 pm-10 pm; Fri & Sat-11 pm; closed Sun & Mon. Cocktails. Valet parking. AE, DI, DS, MC, VI. ⑤ (310) 316-3636

Miyako Restaurant Ethnic $$ ◆◆
On SR 107, Hawthorne Blvd. 24 Del Amo Fashion Square. Japanese specialties served in quiet, refined atmosphere. A/C. Children's menu. Open 11:30 am-2 & 5:30-10 pm; Sat from 5:30 pm; Sun 4 pm-9 pm; closed 7/4, 11/25 & 12/25. Cocktails. Reserv advised. AE, MC, VI. ⊗ Ⓓ (310) 542-8677

Pasta's Ristorante Continental $$ ◆◆
⊛ In the Holiday Inn Torrance Harbor Gateway. Selections of steaks, seafood, chicken, veal chops, salads, pizzas, calzones & pastas. Traditional & Japanese breakfast. A/C. Early bird specials. Open 6 am-10 pm. Cocktails & lounge. AE, DI, DS, MC, VI. ⊗ Ⓓ (310) 515-0600

Reuben's American $$ ◆◆
On SR 107, 1 blk s of Carson St. 21815 Hawthorne Blvd. Featuring steaks, seafood, chicken & fettuccine. A/C. Children's menu. Open 11:30 am-3 & 5-10 pm; Sat 5 pm-11 pm; Sun 4 pm-10 pm. Cocktails & lounge. AE, DI, DS, MC, VI. ⊗ ⑤ (310) 542-4100

Velvet Turtle American $$ ◆◆
1/2 mi e of Hawthorne Blvd. 3210 W Sepulveda Blvd. Featuring beef, lamb, chicken & fresh seafood. Semi-formal atmosphere. Sun brunch 10 am-3 pm. A/C. Open 11:30 am-3 & 5-10 pm; Sat 5 pm-10:30 pm; Sun 10 am-3 & 4:30-9:30 pm. Cocktails & lounge. Valet parking. Reserv advised. AE, DI, DS, MC, VI. ⊗ (310) 534-1701

TRABUCO CANYON — See LAGUNA HILLS

TRACY — 33,600

Phoenix Lodge Rates Subject to Change *Motel* ◆◆
⊛ All year 1P .... 40.00 2P/1B .... 42.00 2P/2B .... 44.00 XP 4
60 units. Off I-205, exit at Central Tracy. 3511 N Tracy Blvd. (95376) 3-story building, no elevator. Check-in 3 pm. A/C; C/CATV; movies; phones; comb or shower baths. Coin laundry. Pool. No pets. Reserv deposit required. AE, MC, VI. Coffeeshop opposite. FAX (209) 835-8041 ⊗ Ⓓ (209) 835-1335

TRINIDAD — 400
Bishop Pine Lodge ◆◆
			Rates Subject to Change				*Cottages*			
4/1-10/15	1P	60.00- 65.00	2P/1B	60.00- 65.00	2P/2B	70.00- 75.00	XP	5
10/16-3/31	1P	50.00- 55.00	2P/1B	50.00- 55.00	2P/2B	60.00- 65.00	XP	5

13 units. W of US 101; northbound exit Trinidad, then 2 mi n of Patricks Point Dr; southbound exit Seawall, then 1 mi s on Patrick Point Dr. 1481 Patricks Point Dr. (95570) Garden setting among pines & redwoods. C/CATV; movies; radios; phones; shower or comb baths. 6 efficiencies. Forest & coast hiking trails; exercise rm. Pets, $5 extra charge. 2 2-bedroom units, $85-$95 for 2-4 persons. 1-duplex cottage with hot tub, $90 for 2 persons. 6 efficiencies & 4 kitchens, $5 extra. 2 night minimum stay. Reserv deposit required; 14 days refund notice. AE, DS, MC, VI.　Ⓓ (707) 677-3314

RESTAURANT
Seascape Restaurant　Seafood　$$　◆
At the pier, 1/4 mi w of US 101. On harbor; rustic decor. Variety of omelets, beef, chicken & pasta. Early bird specials; children's menu. Open 7 am-9 pm; closed 11/25 & 12/25. Beer & wine. MC, VI.　⊗ (707) 677-3762

TRUCKEE — 2,400   (See LAKE TAHOE (Northern Region) AREA spotting map page A177; see index starting on page A176)
Best Western Truckee Tahoe Inn 25 ◆◆◆
			Rates Subject to Change				*Motel*			
Fri & Sat 1/3-4/10 & 6/15-9/20 [CP]	1P	68.00- 85.00	2P/1B	79.00- 90.00	2P/2B	75.00- 95.00	XP	7	F
Sun-Thurs 1/3-4/10 & 6/15-9/20 [CP]	1P	52.00- 85.00	2P/1B	56.00- 90.00	2P/2B	56.00- 95.00	XP	7	F
Fri & Sat 4/11-6/14 & 9/21-1/2 [CP]	1P	58.00- 76.00	2P/1B	67.00- 83.00	2P/2B	64.00- 70.00	XP	7	F
Sun-Thurs 4/11-6/14 & 9/21-1/2 [CP]	1P	50.00- 68.00	2P/1B	58.00- 75.00	2P/2B	56.00- 62.00	XP	7	F

100 units. 1 1/2 mi se of I-80, via SR 267 exit. 11331 SR 267. (96161) Attractive courtyard garden, pool & spa area. A/C; C/CATV; movies; radios; phones. Coin laundry. Pool; sauna; whirlpool; exercise rm. Fee for: golf-9 holes. No pets. AE, DI, DS, MC, VI. FAX (916) 587-8173　⊗ Ⓢ Ⓓ (916) 587-4525

Donner Lake Village 26 ◆◆
			Rates Subject to Change				*Apartment Motel*			
7/1-9/7 & 12/18-1/2	1P	90.00- 205.00	2P/1B	90.00- 205.00	2P/2B	90.00- 205.00	XP	5	F
1/3-3/31	1P	70.00- 165.00	2P/1B	70.00- 165.00	2P/2B	70.00- 165.00	XP	5	F
4/1-6/30 & 9/8-12/17	1P	60.00- 130.00	2P/1B	60.00- 130.00	2P/2B	60.00- 130.00	XP	5	F

64 units. 6 mi w; I-80 exit Donner Lake, on Old Hwy 40 at w end of lake. 15695 Donner Pass Rd, suite 101. (96161) Studio, 1- & 2-bedroom units. Some lakefront units. Check-in 3 pm. C/CATV; 30 radios; phones. Coin laundry. Beach; swimming; saunas; rental boats & canoes; marina; fishing; water skiing. No pets. Reserv deposit required; 5 days refund notice. AE, CB, DI, MC, VI. FAX (916) 587-8782 *(See ad p A182)*　⊗ Ⓓ (916) 587-6081

RESTAURANT
The Left Bank 11　Provincial French　$$$　◆◆
Center. 10098 Commercial Row. Intimate rustic decor. Varied menu Country French with California-Oriental flair. A/C. Early bird specials. Open 11 am-4 & 5-10 pm. Beer & wine. Reserv advised. AE, MC, VI.　(916) 587-4694

TULARE — 33,200
Best Western Town & Country Lodge ◆◆◆
			Rates Subject to Change				*Motor Inn*		
All year [CP]	1P	.... 47.00	2P/1B	.... 52.50	2P/2B	.... 52.50	XP	6

Senior discount. 93 units. Adjacent W side SR 99, Blackstone/Prosperity exit. 1051 N Blackstone. (93274) Refrigerators; A/C; C/CATV; radios; phones; comb or shower baths. Pool; whirlpool. Reserv deposit required. AE, DI, DS, MC, VI. Restaurant adjacent. Cocktails. FAX (209) 688-2163 *(See ad below)*　⊗ Ⓓ Ⓢ (209) 688-7537

RESTAURANT
El Dorado Mexican Restaurant　Mexican　$　◆◆
1/4 mi e of SR 99, SR 137 & Central Tulare off ramp. 1776 E Tulare Ave. Long established restaurant with good selection of American dishes including fresh seafood. Tamales, chips & salsa made on premises. A/C. Children's menu. Open 11 am-9 pm; Fri & Sat-10 pm; Sun-8 pm; closed Mon & major holidays. Cocktails & lounge. AE, MC, VI.　⊗ (209) 686-0061

TURLOCK — 42,200

Almond Tree Inn — Rates Subject to Change — *Motel* ◆◆
ⓐ All year 1P .... 36.00 2P/1B .... 40.00 2P/2B .... 40.00 XP 4
Senior discount. 92 units. Exit Hwy 99, Lander exit. 200 W Glenwood Ave. (95380) A/C; C/CATV; movies; VCPs. Phones; comb or shower baths. Small pool. No pets. Reserv deposit required. AE, CB, DI, MC, VI. Coffeeshop adjacent. FAX (209) 668-0144
ⒹⓈ (209) 668-3400

Best Western Orchard Inn — Rates Guaranteed — *Motel* ◆◆
ⓐ All year 1P 47.00- 53.00 2P/1B 53.00- 59.00 2P/2B 57.00- 63.00 XP 6
Senior discount. 72 units. 5 mi n; exit SR 99 at Taylor Rd. 5025 N Golden State Blvd. (95380) 39 refrigerators; A/C; C/CATV; movies; VCPs. 50 radios; phones; comb or shower baths. Pool; whirlpool. Pets. 15 efficiencies, $10 extra. Few rooms with whirlpool tub, extra charge. Wkly rates avail. AE, DI, DS, MC, VI. Coffeeshop adjacent. FAX (209) 634-6588 *(See ad p A534)*
ⓍⒹⓈ (209) 667-2827

The Gardens Best Western Motor Inn — AAA Special Value Rates — *Motor Inn* ◆◆◆
ⓐ All year 1P 48.00- 58.00 2P/1B 54.00- 64.00 2P/2B 56.00- 66.00 XP 6 F
95 units. Exit SR 99 at Fulkerth Rd, then 1 mi e. 1119 Pedras Rd. (95380) A/C; C/CATV; VCPs; phones; shower or comb baths. Pool. Fee for: bowling. No pets. Suites, $90-$100 up to 2 persons. AE, DS, DI, MC, VI. Coffeeshop adjacent. FAX (209) 632-0231
ⓍⒹ (209) 634-9351

TUSTIN — 50,700

RESTAURANTS

The Barn Restaurant & Saloon — American — $$ ◆◆
1/2 mi e of SR 55, exit Edinger Ave. 14982 Red Hill Ave. Large restaurant with several dining areas. Western atmosphere. A/C. Early bird specials; children's menu. Open 11 am-2 & 5-9 pm; Fri & Sat-10 pm; Sat 5 pm-10 pm; Sun 5 pm-9 pm; closed major holidays. Cocktails & lounge. Entertainment. Reserv advised weekends. AE, DI, DS, MC, VI.
Ⓧ (714) 259-0115

Mimi's Cafe — American — $ ◆◆
Adjacent to SR 55. 17231 17th St. Attractive family restaurant with French cafe decor. Nice selection of salads, sandwiches & entrees. A/C. Children's menu. Open 6 am-11 pm; closed 11/25 & 12/25. Beer & wine. AE, DI, MC, VI.
Ⓧ (714) 544-5522

Nieuport 17 Restaurant — American — $$ ◆◆◆
Corner of Irvine; in Plaza Lafayette. 13051 Newport Blvd. Decorated with authentic aviation memorabilia. Nice selection of varied entrees. A/C. Dress code. Children's menu. Open 11 am-10 pm; Fri-11 pm; Sat 5 pm-11 pm; Sun 5 pm-10 pm; closed major holidays. Cocktails & lounge. Entertainment. Valet parking. Reserv advised. AE, DI, MC, VI.
Ⓧ (714) 731-5130

Revere House Restaurant — American — $$ ◆◆
Adjacent to SR 55, 4th St exit; 1/2 mi e of I-5, First St exit. 900 W First St & Tustin Ave. Charming Early-American atmosphere. Sun brunch 10 am-3 pm, $10.95. A/C. Early bird specials; children's menu. Open 11 am-10 pm; Fri-11 pm; Sat 5 pm-11 pm; Sun 10 am-3 & 5:30-9 pm; closed major holidays. Cocktails & lounge. Entertainment. Reserv advised. AE, MC, VI.
Ⓧ (714) 543-9319

TWAIN HARTE — 1,400

Eldorado Motel — Rates Subject to Change — *Motel* ◆
ⓐ All year 1P .... 45.00 2P/1B .... 49.00 2P/2B .... 65.00 XP 5
Senior discount. 11 units. Exit SR 108 via Twain Harte; corner Twain Harte Dr & Blackhawk Dr, opposite golf course. (PO Box 368, 95383) C/CATV; shower baths. Pets, $5 extra charge. 2 rooms with kitchens, $10 extra. Wkly rates avail. Reserv deposit required. AE, DS, MC, VI.
Ⓓ (209) 586-4479

Wildwood Inn Motor Lodge — Rates Subject to Change — *Motel* ◆
ⓐ All year 1P .... 52.00 2P/1B .... 57.00 2P/2B .... 57.00 XP 5
Senior discount. 21 units. Center. 22960 Meadow Dr. (PO Box 457, 95383) A/C; C/CATV; radios; phones; shower baths. No pets. Reserv deposit required. MC, VI.
Ⓓ (209) 586-2900

RESTAURANT

Kelly's Kitchen — American — $$ ◆
ⓐ 3 mi e on SR 108, at Sugar Pine; 14 mi e of Sonora. 24181 SR 108. Family restaurant with mountain view. Varied menu; specializing in homemade pies. A/C. Children's menu. Open 4 pm-10 pm; Sat & Sun 7 am-10 pm; closed 12/25. Cocktails & lounge. Reserv advised. MC, VI.
(209) 586-3283

TWENTYNINE PALMS — 11,800

Best Western Gardens Motel — Rates Subject to Change — *Motel* ◆◆◆
ⓐ All year 1P .... 54.00 2P/1B .... 58.00 2P/2B .... 62.00 XP 8
Senior discount. 71 units. 1 3/4 mi w on SR 62. 71487 Twentynine Palms Hwy. (92277) A/C; C/CATV; rental VCPs; radios; phones. Htd pool; whirlpool. 8 1-bedroom units with kitchen, $84-$90. AE, DI, DS, MC, VI. FAX (619) 367-2584
Ⓧ Ⓓ (619) 367-9141

Circle 'C' — Rates Subject to Change — *Motel* ◆
All year [CP] 1P .... 70.00 2P/1B .... 85.00 2P/2B .... 85.00 XP 20
11 units. 1 1/2 mi w on SR 62, 1 blk n. 6340 El Rey Ave. (92277) Nicely landscaped pool area. Spacious, exceptionally well maintained rooms. Check-in 3 pm. Refrigerators; A/C; C/CATV; VCPs; radios; phones. 10 kitchens. Coin laundry. Htd pool; whirlpool. No pets. Reserv deposit required. AE, CB, DI, MC, VI.
Ⓓ (619) 367-7615

UKIAH — 14,600

Best Western Inn — *Motel* ◆◆◆
ⓐ 5/1-10/15 [CP] 1P 44.00- 52.00 2P/1B 46.00- 58.00 2P/2B 52.00- 65.00 XP 5
10/16-4/30 [EP] 1P 42.00- 48.00 2P/1B 46.00- 52.00 2P/2B 48.00- 55.00 XP 5
40 units. E off US 101 bypass; exit Talmage off-ramp. 601 Talmage Rd. (95482) 22 refrigerators; A/C; C/CATV; 10 radios; phones. Small pool; putting green. Airport transp. No pets. Reserv deposit required; 3 days refund notice. AE, DI, DS, MC, VI.
Ⓧ Ⓓ (707) 462-8868

Discovery Inn
◉ 5/1-9/30   AAA Special Value Rates   Motel ◆◆◆
5/1-9/30   1P 42.00- 52.00   2P/1B   44.00- 56.00   2P/2B   48.00- 62.00   XP   5   F
154 units. 1 1/2 mi n on US 101 business rt; exit US 101 via N State St. 1340 N State St. (95482) OPEN ALL YEAR. Some rooms with private balcony. Few small rooms. 117 refrigerators; A/C; C/CATV; movies; radios; phones; comb or shower baths. 1 2-bedrm unit, 7 kitchens. Coin laundry. Pool; sauna; whirlpool; lighted tennis-1 court. No pets. Reserv deposit required; 3 days refund notice. AE, DI, DS, MC, VI. Coffeeshop adjacent. FAX (707) 462-1249 *(See ad below)*   ⊗ Ⓓ (707) 462-8873

Ukiah Travelodge   Rates Subject to Change   Motel ◆◆
◉ 5/1-10/15 [CP]   1P 42.00- 50.00   2P/1B   44.00- 52.00   2P/2B   46.00- 56.00   XP   5
10/16-4/30 [EP]   1P 36.00- 42.00   2P/1B   40.00- 46.00   2P/2B   42.00- 50.00   XP   5
Senior discount. 40 units. 2 blks s on US 101 business rt; northbound exit US 101W via Perkins off-ramp, southbound exit Central off-ramp. 406 S State St. (95482) Formerly Best Western Willow Tree Inn. A/C; C/CATV; movies; radios; phones; shower baths. 1 2-bedrm unit. Pool. No pets. Reserv deposit required; 3 days refund notice. AE, DI, DS, MC, VI. Restaurant opposite.   ⊗ Ⓓ (707) 462-8611

Vichy Springs Resort   Rates Subject to Change   Historical ◆◆
All year [BP]   1P 80.00- 135.00   2P/1B   105.00- 135.00   2P/2B   105.00- 150.00   XP   25
14 units. 3 mi e; exit US 101 via e Perkins St/Vichy Springs Rd. 2605 Vichy Springs Rd. (95482) Restored buildings circa 1864. Motel rooms & 2 cottages. Smoke free premises. Check-in 3 pm. A/C; radios; phones; shower or comb baths. 1 2-bedrm unit, 2 kitchens. Whirlpool; 4 outdoor & 6 indoor mineral baths, outdoor olympic pool, heated 5/1-10/31; mountain bike trails; nature program. Fee for: massage. Parking lot. No pets. Wkly & monthly rates avail. Reserv deposit required; 4 days refund notice. AE, DI, DS, MC, VI. FAX (707) 462-9516   ⊗ Ⓓ (707) 462-9515

Western Traveler Motel   Rates Subject to Change   Motel ◆◆
◉ 6/15-9/15   1P 36.00- 44.00   2P/1B   44.00- 52.00   2P/2B   44.00- 56.00   XP   5
9/16-6/14   1P 32.00- 38.00   2P/1B   38.00- 45.00   2P/2B   42.00- 49.00   XP   5
Senior discount. 56 units. Exit US 101 via Gobbi St W. 693 S Orchard Ave. (95482) 20 refrigerators; A/C; C/CATV; pay movies; VCPs. Phones. 2 2-bedrm units. Small pool; whirlpool. Pets, $5 extra charge. 2 family units $75; 9/16-6/14 $60 for up to 5 persons. Reserv deposit required. AE, DI, DS, MC, VI. Coffeeshop adjacent. FAX (707) 468-8268 *(See ad below)*   ⊗ Ⓓ (707) 468-9167

UNION CITY — 53,800

Best Western Wellex Inn   AAA Special Value Rates   *Motel* ◆◆
All year [CP]   1P   54.00-   69.00   2P/1B   59.00-   74.00   2P/2B   ....   64.00   XP   5
75 units. Exit I-880 Alvarado-Niles Rd W. 31140 Alvarado-Niles Rd. (94587) Central pool & spa area. A/C; C/CATV; movies; radios; phones. Pool; whirlpool. No pets. Wkly & monthly rates avail. Reserv deposit required. AE, DI, DS, MC, VI. FAX (510) 475-0910   ⊗ Ⓢ Ⓓ (510) 475-0600

Holiday Inn   Rates Guaranteed   *Motor Inn* ◆◆
Sun-Thurs   1P   ....   68.00   2P/1B   ....   68.00   2P/2B   ....   74.00   XP   5
Fri & Sat   1P   ....   59.00   2P/1B   ....   64.00   2P/2B   ....   64.00   XP   5
266 units. Exit I-880 at Alvarado-Niles Rd, 1/4 mi e. 32083 Alvarado-Niles Rd. (94587) Check-in 3 pm. A/C; C/CATV; movies; phones. Coin laundry. Pool; sauna; whirlpool; lighted tennis-1 court; racquetball-1 court; exercise rm. Airport transp. No pets. Wkly & monthly rates avail. AE, DI, DS, MC, VI. ● Restaurant; 6 am-10 pm; Fri & Sat 6:30 am-10 pm; $5-$25; cocktails. FAX (510) 489-7642   ⊗ Ⓢ Ⓓ Ⓛ (510) 489-2200

UNIVERSAL CITY — See LOS ANGELES (San Fernando Valley)

UPLAND — 63,400

Comfort Inn   Rates Subject to Change   *Motel* ◆◆
All year   1P   ....   39.00   2P/1B   ....   40.00   2P/2B   ....   45.00   XP   2   F
Senior discount. 62 units. Adjacent to I-10, exit Mountain Ave, 1 blk w. 1282 W 7th St. (91786) 20 refrigerators; A/C; C/TV; movies; radios; phones. Pool. No pets. AE, DI, DS, MC, VI. FAX (909) 985-9136 *(See ad below)*   ⊗ Ⓓ (909) 985-8115

RESTAURANTS

Charley's Grill & Pub   American $$ ◆◆
1 blk w of Central Ave. 2035 W Foothill Blvd. Old English decor. Features prime rib, steaks & seafood. A/C. Children's menu. Open 5 pm-9:30 pm; Fri & Sat-10 pm; Sun 4:30 pm-9:30 pm; closed 1/1, 7/4 & 12/25. Cocktails & lounge. AE, MC, VI.   ⊗ (909) 982-4513

El Gato Gordo   Mexican $
1 blk w of Mountain Ave. 1241 Foothill Blvd. Colorfully decorated. Casual atmosphere. A/C. Children's menu. Open 11:30 am-10 pm; Sun 10 am-10 pm; closed major holidays. Cocktails & lounge. AE, DS, MC, VI.   ⊗ (909) 981-8380

Mimi's Cafe   American $ ◆◆
1 mi n of I-10, exit Mountain Ave. 370 N Mountain Ave. Colorful French cafe atmosphere. Nice selection of sandwiches, salads & entrees. A/C. Children's menu. Open 7 am-11 pm; closed 11/25 & 12/25. Beer & wine. AE, MC, VI.   ⊗ (909) 982-3038

VACAVILLE — 71,500

Best Western Heritage Inn   Rates Subject to Change   *Motel* ◆◆
6/1-9/30 [CP]   1P   ....   42.00   2P/1B   ....   46.00   2P/2B   ....   48.00   XP   5   F
Senior discount. 41 units. 1 1/8 mi e; n side of I-80, Monte Vista exit. 1420 E Monte Vista Ave. (95688) OPEN ALL YEAR. A/C; C/CATV; phones. Pool. Some rooms with microwave & refrigerator. Wkly & monthly rates avail. Reserv deposit required; 3 days refund notice. AE, DI, DS, MC, VI. Coffeeshop adjacent. FAX (707) 447-8649 *(See ad p A364)*   ⊗ Ⓓ (707) 448-8453

Quality Inn-Vacaville   Rates Subject to Change   *Motor Inn* ◆◆
All year   1P   47.00-   49.00   2P/1B   ....   54.00   2P/2B   ....   52.00   XP   5   F
Senior discount. 120 units. S side of I-80; exit Leisure Town Rd 1/4 mi e of I-505 interchange. 950 Leisure Town Rd. (95687) Check-in 3 pm. A/C; C/CATV; radios; phones; comb or shower baths. Pool; whirlpool. No pets. AE, DI, DS, MC, VI. ● Restaurant; 6:30 am-10 pm; $7-$15. Also, Vaca Joe's Restaurant, see separate listing. FAX (707) 449-0109   ⊗ Ⓓ Ⓛ (707) 446-8888

Vacaville Super 8   Rates Subject to Change   *Motel* ◆◆
All year   1P   ....   39.88   2P/1B   ....   43.88   2P/2B   ....   46.88   XP   3
53 units. N of & adjacent to I-80, exit Monte Vista Ave. 101 Allison Ct. (95688) A/C; C/TV; movies; radios; phones. Small pool. Pets. AE, CB, DI, MC, VI.   ⊗ Ⓢ Ⓓ Ⓛ (707) 449-8884

RESTAURANTS

Black Oak Restaurant   American $$ ◆
S side of I-80, at jct I-505. 320 Orange Dr. Booth seating, casual atmosphere, basic varied menu. A/C. Children's menu. Open 6 am-11 pm. Beer & wine. AE, MC, VI.   ⊗ (707) 448-1311

Coffee Tree   American $
S side of I-80 at jct I-505. Varied but limited menu. Casual atmosphere, counter & booth seating. A/C. Children's menu. Open 5:30 am-midnight; closed 12/25. Beer & wine. AE, MC, VI.   ⊗ (707) 448-8435

The Nut Tree   Western American $$ ◆◆
1 1/2 mi e on n side of I-80. Known for western-style food & use of fresh fruit & vegetables. Popular for breakfast & lunch. A/C. Children's menu. Open 7 am-9 pm; closed 12/25. Cocktails. Reserv advised. AE, MC, VI.   ⊗ (707) 448-1818

Vaca Joe's Restaurant   Italian $$ ◆◆
At Quality Inn-Vacaville. 980 Leisure Town Rd. Varied menu, seafood specialties. A/C. Children's menu. Open 6:30 am-10 pm; Fri & Sat-11 pm; closed 11/25 & 12/25. Cocktails. AE, DI, DS, MC, VI.   ⊗ (707) 447-4633

VALENCIA — See SANTA CLARITA

VALLEJO — 109,200

Comfort Inn   Rates Subject to Change   *Motor Inn* ◆◆
⑳ 3/31-10/31 [CP]   1P 48.00- 72.00 2P/1B   52.00- 75.00   2P/2B   .... 72.00 XP 7   F
    11/1-3/30 [CP]   1P 48.00- 52.00 2P/1B   52.00- 66.00   2P/2B   62.00- 72.00 XP 7   F
Senior discount. 80 units. Exit I-80 Columbus Pkwy 1/2 mi e; 1/4 mi s on Admiral Callaghan Ln. 1185 Admiral Callaghan Ln. (94591) Check-in 3 pm. A/C; C/CATV; movies; radios; phones. Coin laundry. Pool; sauna; whirlpool; steamroom; exercise rm. No pets. Luxury level rooms avail. Reserv deposit required. AE, DI, DS, MC, VI. FAX (707) 552-8623   ⊗ Ⓢ Ⓓ Ⓐ (707) 648-1400

Ramada Inn   AAA Special Value Rates   *Motel* ◆◆
All year [CP]   1P 55.00- 62.00 2P/1B   59.00- 66.00   2P/2B   66.00- 89.00 XP 7   F
131 units. 1/4 mi e exit I-80 at Columbus Pkwy; 1/2 mi s on Admiral Callaghan Ln. 1000 Admiral Callaghan Ln. (94591) Attractive lobby. Refrigerators; A/C; C/CATV; movies; phones. 1 kitchen, 19 efficiencies. Coin laundry. Htd pool; whirlpool. No pets. Reserv deposit required. AE, DI, DS, MC, VI. Coffeeshop adjacent. FAX (707) 642-1148   ⊗ Ⓢ Ⓓ Ⓐ (707) 643-2700

Royal Bay Inn
⊕

		Rates Subject to Change						Motel		◆◆
5/1-9/14 [CP]	1P	39.00-	50.00	2P/1B	43.00-	60.00	2P/2B	48.00- 68.00	XP 5	F
9/15-4/30 [CP]	1P	35.00-	45.00	2P/1B	39.00-	55.00	2P/2B	42.00- 62.00	XP 5	F

Senior discount. 78 units. E off & adjacent to I-80; exit via Tennessee St-Mare Island. 44 Admiral Callaghan Ln. (94590) A/C; C/CATV; movies; radios; phones. Coin laundry. Pool. Pets, $5 extra charge. Wkly rates avail. Reserv deposit required. AE, DI, DS, MC, VI. Coffeeshop adjacent. FAX (707) 643-4719 *(See ad p A538)*
⊗ Ⓓ ⓚ (707) 643-1061

VAN NUYS — See LOS ANGELES (San Fernando Valley)

VENTURA — 83,400

Bella Maggiore Inn
⊕

		AAA Special Value Rates						Hotel		◆◆◆
All year [BP]	1P	75.00- 150.00		2P/1B	75.00- 150.00			......	XP 10	

24 units. 1/4 mi n of US 101, exit California St (Downtown). 67 S California St. (93001) Renovated historical landmark built in 1926. Attractive southern European ambiance. Check-in 3 pm. 4 refrigerators; 10 A/C; C/TV; radios; phones; comb or shower baths. 2 rooms with whirlpool tub. Parking lot. No pets. Wkly rates avail. Reserv deposit required. AE, DI, DS, MC, VI. Restaurant adjacent.
⊗ Ⓓ (805) 652-0277

Best Western Inn of Ventura
⊕

		Rates Subject to Change						Motel		◆◆
4/1-9/30	1P	52.00-	62.00	2P/1B	58.00-	68.00	2P/2B	60.00- 70.00	XP 5	
10/1-3/31	1P	48.00-	58.00	2P/1B	54.00-	64.00	2P/2B	56.00- 66.00	XP 5	

75 units. 2 blks e of California St; from US 101, northbound exit California St, southbound exit Ventura Ave. 708 E Thompson Blvd. (93001) A/C; C/CATV; movies; phones; shower or comb baths. Htd pool; whirlpool. No pets. Reserv deposit required in summer. AE, DI, DS, MC, VI. Coffeeshop adjacent.
⊗ Ⓓ (805) 648-3101

Clocktower Inn-A Clarion Carriage House

		AAA Special Value Rates						Motor Inn		◆◆
All year [CP]	1P	70.00-	90.00	2P/1B	80.00- 100.00		2P/2B	.... 90.00	XP 10	F

49 units. 1/2 mi nw of US 101; northbound exit California St, southbound exit Ventura Ave. 181 E Santa Clara. (93001) Attractive southwest decor. Adjacent to Mission San Buenaventura & Mission Park. 5 rooms with fireplace & 8 with balcony. Check-in 3 pm. A/C; C/CATV; radios; phones. No pets. Wkly & monthly rates avail. Reserv deposit required. AE, DI, DS, MC, VI. ● Restaurant; 11 am-2:30 & 5-9 pm; closed Mon; $11-$20; cocktails. FAX (805) 643-1432
⊗ Ⓢ Ⓓ Ⓚ (805) 652-0141

Country Inn at Ventura
⊕

		Rates Guaranteed						Motel		◆◆◆
All year [BP]	1P	....	66.00	2P/1B	....	66.00	2P/2B	.... 66.00	XP 10	F

Senior discount. 120 units. 1 blk e of California St & 1 blk s of Thompson Blvd; from US 101; northbound exit California St, southbound exit Ventura Ave. 298 Chestnut St. (93001) Some balconies, ocean & mountain views. Check-in 3 pm. Refrigerators; A/C; C/CATV; pay movies; VCPs. Radios; phones. Coin laundry. Htd pool; whirlpool. Garage & parking lot. No pets. Microwaves. Reserv deposit required. Complimentary beverages each evening. AE, DI, MC, VI. FAX (805) 648-7126 *(See ad p A538)*
⊗ Ⓢ Ⓓ Ⓚ (805) 653-1434

Doubletree Hotel at Ventura
⊕

		Rates Guaranteed						Motor Inn		◆◆◆
All year	1P	89.00- 119.00		2P/1B	99.00- 129.00		2P/2B	99.00- 129.00	XP 10	

Senior discount. 285 units. Adjacent to w side of US 101, exit Seaward Ave. 2055 Harbor Blvd. (93001) 1 blk to San Buenaventura State Beach. Attractively landscaped courtyard & pool area. Check-in 3 pm. A/C; C/CATV; free & pay movies; phones. Rental refrigerators. Htd pool; saunas; whirlpool; exercise rm. Pets, $50 deposit required. Reserv deposit required. AE, DI, DS, MC, VI. ● Restaurant; 6:30 am-10 pm; Sat & Sun from 7 am; $9-$16; cocktails. FAX (805) 643-7137 *(See ad below)*
⊗ Ⓢ Ⓓ Ⓚ (805) 643-6000

Harbortown Marina Resort
⊕

		AAA Special Value Rates						Motor Inn		◆◆◆
2/1-11/14 [BP]	1P	79.00-	99.00	2P/1B	79.00-	99.00	2P/2B	79.00- 99.00	XP 10	F
11/15-1/31 [BP]	1P	....	69.00	2P/1B	....	69.00	2P/2B	.... 69.00	XP 10	F

150 units. From US 101, exit Seaward Ave, then 1 1/2 mi s on Harbor Blvd, at Ventura Harbor. 1050 Schooner Dr. (93001) Many rooms with marina view & balcony or patio. Check-in 4 pm. C/CATV; movies; radios; phones. 4 2-bedrm units. Htd pool; whirlpool; lighted tennis-3 courts. No pets. Monthly rates avail. Reserv deposit required. Complimentary beverages each evening. AE, CB, DI, MC, VI. ● Restaurant; 6:30 am-10 pm; $12-$22; cocktails; entertainment. FAX (805) 658-6347 *(See ad p A540)*
⊗ Ⓢ Ⓓ Ⓚ (805) 658-1212

DOUBLETREE
H O T E L · V E N T U R A

For AAA members, we're taking a little off the top.

Stay in a beautiful room at a trimmed rate just 2 blocks from the beach and minutes $65 from beautiful Santa Barbara and exciting Los Angeles. Call your travel professional or 805-643-6000. 2055 Harbor Blvd. (Seaward Ave. exit on Hwy. 101.)

1-800-528-0444

Rate is based on single or double occupancy and subject to availability. Includes breakfast.

INN on the BEACH
Oceanfront Cape Cod Hotel

ALL 24 ROOMS HAVE BEACHFRONT BALCONIES

Complimentary Continental Breakfast
Intimate Setting • Beachfront Balconies

for reservations call (805) 652-2000
1175 SEAWARD AVE., VENTURA, CA 93001

Holiday Inn Beach Resort
Hotel ◆◆◆
All year   1P 80.00- 90.00 2P/1B 90.00- 100.00 2P/2B 90.00- 100.00 XP 10   F
Rates Subject to Change
Senior discount. 260 units. Adjacent to US 101; northbound exit California St, southbound exit Main St. 450 E Harbor Blvd. (93001) A multi-story, beachfront hotel. Check-in 4 pm. 25 refrigerators; A/C; C/CATV; free & pay movies; radios; phones. Htd pool; wading pool; playground; exercise rm. Garage & parking lot. No pets. Monthly rates avail. Reserv deposit required. AE, DI, DS, MC, VI. ● Dining rm; 6 am-10 pm, Fri & Sat 11 pm; $13-$17; cocktails; entertainment. FAX (805) 653-6202   ⊗ Ⓓ Ⓢ Ⓔ (805) 648-7731

Inn on the Beach
Motel ◆◆
All year   1P 80.00- 130.00 2P/1B 80.00- 130.00 2P/2B 80.00- 130.00 XP 5   F
Rates Subject to Change
24 units. 1/2 mi w of US 101; exit Seaward Ave. 1175 S Seaward Ave. (93001) At the Beach. Patio or balcony. Ocean View. Check-in 3 pm. 4 refrigerators; A/C; C/CATV; movies; radios; phones. No pets. Reserv deposit required. AE, DI, DS, MC, VI. *(See ad p A539)*   ⊗ Ⓢ Ⓓ Ⓔ (805) 652-2000

La Mer European Bed & Breakfast
Historic Bed & Breakfast ◆◆
All year [BP]   1P 100.00- 150.00 2P/1B 105.00- 155.00 .... XP
Rates Subject to Change
5 units. 1/2 mi n of US 101; northbound exit California St, southbound exit Ventura Ave, 1 blk W of California st. 411 Poli St. (93001) All rooms individually furnished in a different European motif. House built in 1890. Check-in 4 pm. Radios; tub or shower baths. Parking lot. No pets. 2-night minimum stay weekends. Reserv deposit required; 7 days refund notice. MC, VI.   ⊗ Ⓓ (805) 643-3600

La Quinta Inn
Motel ◆◆◆
All year [CP]   1P 51.00- 58.00 2P/1B 56.00- 63.00 2P/2B .... 56.00 XP 5   F
Rates Subject to Change
142 units. 1/2 blk s of US 101; exit Victoria Ave. 5818 Valentine Rd. (93003) Check-in 3 pm. A/C; C/CATV; free & pay movies; radios; phones. Rental refrigerators. Htd pool; whirlpool. Pets. AE, DI, DS, MC, VI. Restaurant adjacent. FAX (805) 642-2840   ⊗ Ⓢ Ⓓ Ⓔ (805) 658-6200

Pierpont Inn
Motor Inn ◆◆
All year   1P 64.00- 66.00 2P/1B 72.00- 77.00 2P/2B 72.00- 77.00 XP 8   F
Rates Subject to Change
Senior discount. 70 units. Adjacent to US 101; northbound Sanjon Rd exit, southbound Seaward Ave exit. 550 Sanjon Rd. (93001) Across freeway from beach. Attractive grounds. Many rooms with ocean view. Many rooms with balcony. Check-in 3 pm. C/CATV; movies; radios; phones; shower or comb baths. Htd pool; rental bicycles. No pets. 8 suites with balcony, $118. 2 cottages, $115-$200. AE, DI, DS, MC, VI. ● Dining rm, see separate listing. FAX (805) 641-1501 *(See ad below)*   ⊗ Ⓓ (805) 653-6144

Vagabond Inn
Motor Inn ◆◆
4/16-9/14 [CP]   1P .... 46.00 2P/1B .... 63.00 2P/2B .... 65.00 XP 5   F
9/15-4/15 [CP]   1P .... 46.00 2P/1B .... 48.00 2P/2B .... 50.00 XP 5   F
Rates Guaranteed
Senior discount. 82 units. 1/4 mi e on US 101 business rt; from US 101 northbound exit California St, southbound exit Ventura Ave. 756 E Thompson Blvd. (93001) A/C; C/CATV; movies; radios; phones. 2 2-bedrm units. Htd pool; whirlpool; playground. No pets. AE, DI, DS, MC, VI. ● Coffeeshop; 24 hours; $5-$10. FAX (805) 648-5613 *(See ad p A538)*   ⊗ Ⓓ (805) 648-5371

RESTAURANTS

The Chart House
Steak & Seafood $$ ◆◆
Adjacent to US 101; northbound Sanjon Rd exit, southbound Seaward Ave exit. 567 Sanjon Rd. Contemporary-style restaurant overlooking the ocean. Features steak, fresh seafood, chicken & prime rib. A/C. Children's menu. Open 5:30 pm-10 pm; Fri-10:30 pm; Sat 5 pm-11 pm; Sun 5 pm-10 pm. Cocktails & lounge. AE, DI, MC, VI.   ⊗ (805) 643-3725

Old Vienna Restaurant
German $$ ◆◆
1/4 mi e of Mills Rd. 3845 Telegraph Rd. Large selection, including venison, roast goose in season. A/C. Children's menu. Open 11:30 am-2 & 5-9:30 pm; Fri-10 pm; Sat 5 pm-10 pm; Sun 11 am-2 & 4:30-9 pm; closed Mon & 12/25. Cocktails. Reserv advised weekends. AE, DI, DS, MC, VI.   ⊗ (805) 654-1214

Pierpont Inn
American $$ ◆◆
In Pierpont Inn. Fine ocean view dining at inn established 1928. Entrees include beef, chicken & seafood. Desserts made on premises. Children's menu. Open 7-10:30 am, 11:30-2 & 4:30-8:30 pm; Sat 7-10:30 am, 11:30-3 & 5:30-10 pm; Sun 8 am-3 & 5-8:30 pm. Cocktails & lounge. Entertainment. Reserv advised. AE, DI, DS, MC, VI. *(See ad below)*   ⊗ (805) 653-6144

Seafood & Beverage Co
Seafood $$ ◆◆
1/2 mi nw of US 101; northbound exit California St, southbound exit Ventura Ave, 3 blks w of California St. 211 E Santa Clara St. Several dining areas in a historical landmark; 1912 Victorian home. A/C. Children's menu. Open 11:30 am-9 pm; closed 11/25 & 12/25. Cocktails & lounge. Reserv advised weekends. AE, MC, VI.   ⊗ (805) 643-3264

Yolanda's Mexican Cafe
Mexican $ ◆◆
1/2 mi e of Seaward Ave. 2753 E Main. Colorfully decorated restaurant. Southwestern cuisine. A/C. Children's menu. Open 11 am-10 pm; Fri & Sat-11 pm; Sun 10 am-9 pm; closed 11/25 & 12/25. Cocktails & lounge. Reserv advised. AE, MC, VI.   ⊗ (805) 643-2700

VICTORVILLE — 40,700 See also HESPERIA

Best Western-Green Tree Inn Rates Guaranteed   *Motor Inn* ◆◆◆
All year   1P 46.00- 70.00 2P/1B 50.00- 76.00 2P/2B 50.00- 76.00 XP 6   F
Senior discount. 168 units. Adjacent to I-15, SR 18W, Palmdale Rd exit. 14173 Green Tree Blvd. (92392) 72 refrigerators; A/C; C/CATV; phones. Htd pool; wading pool; indoor whirlpool; 6 rooms with whirlpool tub. No pets. 72 1-bedroom suites with living room. AE, CB, DI, MC, VI. ● Dining rm & coffeeshop; 24 hours; $6-$17; cocktails; entertainment. FAX (619) 245-7745   ⊗ Ⓓ 🅛 (619) 245-3461

Budget Inn   Rates Subject to Change   *Motel* ◆
All year   1P 30.00- 32.00 2P/1B 32.00- 36.00 2P/2B 36.00- 42.00 XP 5
Senior discount. 40 units. Adjacent to I-15, exit SR 18W, Palmdale Rd. 14153 Kentwood Blvd. (92392) Refrigerators; A/C; C/CATV; movies; phones. Small pets only. AE, DI, DS, MC, VI. Restaurant opposite.
⊗ Ⓢ Ⓓ (619) 241-8010

Economy Inn   Rates Subject to Change   *Motel* ◆
All year   1P 28.88- 32.88 2P/1B 36.88- 38.88 2P/2B .... 40.88 XP 3
16 units. 1 blk w of I-15, exit Mojave Dr. 15822 Mojave Dr. (92392) Refrigerators; A/C; C/CATV; movies; phones; comb baths. 2 rooms with whirlpool, $40.88. AE, DI, DS, MC, VI.   Ⓓ (619) 241-0075

Hi Desert Travelers Motel   Rates Guaranteed   *Motel* ◆◆◆
All year [CP]   1P .... 45.00 2P/1B .... 51.00 2P/2B .... 49.00 XP 6   F
Senior discount. 94 units. Adjacent to I-15, between Bear Valley Rd & Palmdale Rd exits. 13409 Mariposa Rd. (92392) 14 1-bedroom suites with living room & microwave. Refrigerators; A/C; C/CATV; movies; rental VCPs. Radios; phones. Pool; whirlpools. Pets, $20 deposit required. AE, CB, DI, MC, VI. FAX (619) 241-3627   ⊗ Ⓢ Ⓓ (619) 241-1577

Holiday Inn   AAA Special Value Rates   *Hotel* ◆◆◆
All year   1P .... 51.00 2P/1B 57.00- 60.00 2P/2B 55.00- 61.00 XP 6   F
162 units. Adjacent to I-15, exit SR 18W, Palmdale Rd. 15494 Palmdale Rd. (92392) A/C; C/CATV; VCPs; radios; phones. Coin laundry. Htd pool. No pets. AE, CB, DI, MC, VI. ● Dining rm & coffeeshop; 6 am-10 pm; $5.95-$15.95; cocktails; entertainment. FAX (619) 245-6649   ⊗ Ⓓ (619) 245-6565

Scottish Inns   Rates Subject to Change   *Motel* ◆
All year   1P 22.00- 26.00 2P/1B 28.00- 32.00 2P/2B 32.00- 36.00 XP 3
Senior discount. 21 units. Adjacent to I-15, exit Mojave Dr; 2 blks w. 15499 Village Dr. (92392) A/C; C/CATV; movies; rental VCPs. Phones. Pool. Pets, $50 deposit required. AE, DS, MC, VI.   Ⓓ (619) 243-5858

Victorville-Apple Valley Travelodge   Rates Subject to Change   *Motel* ◆◆
All year   1P .... 2P/1B .... 32.00 2P/2B .... 37.00 XP   F
Senior discount. 98 units. 2 mi n on I-15, exit Stoddard Wells Rd, 1/2 blk w. 16868 Stoddard Wells Rd. (92392) A/C; C/CATV; movies; rental VCPs. Phones. Coin laundry. Pool. Pets. 10 rooms with whirlpool, $57.99 for up to 2 persons. Wkly rates avail. AE, DI, DS, MC, VI. FAX (619) 243-4432   ⊗ Ⓢ Ⓓ (619) 243-7700

RESTAURANTS

Cask 'N' Cleaver   American $$ ◆
From I-15, exit SR 18, Palmdale Rd, 1 blk w, then 3 blks s. 13885 Park Ave. Casual dining. Features a selection of steaks, seafood & chicken. A/C. Early bird specials. Open 11:30 am-2 & 5-9:30 pm; Fri-10:30 pm; Sat 5 pm-10:30 pm; Sun 5 pm-9:30 pm; closed 1/1, 11/25 & 12/25. Cocktails & lounge. AE, MC, VI.   ⊗ (619) 241-7318

Marie Callender's   American $
Adjacent to I-15, exit Bear Valley Rd, then 2 blks ne. 12180 Mariposa Rd. Attractively decorated. Nice selection of sandwiches, salads, pasta, seafood & chicken. A/C. Open 6:30 am-10 pm; Fri & Sat-11 pm; Sun 8 am-10 pm; closed 11/25 & 12/25. Cocktails & lounge. AE, MC, VI.   ⊗ (619) 241-6973

VISALIA — 75,600

Best Western Visalia Inn Motel   Rates Guaranteed   *Motel* ◆◆
All year [CP]   1P .... 53.00 2P/1B .... 57.00 2P/2B .... 62.00 XP 6
40 units. 2 blks n of SR 198. 623 W Main St. (93291) Refrigerators; A/C; C/CATV; movies; radios; phones. Small pool. Small pets only. AE, DI, DS, MC, VI. Restaurant opposite.   Ⓓ (209) 732-4561

Econo Lodge   Rates Guaranteed   *Motor Inn* ◆
All year   1P .... 39.00 2P/1B .... 42.00 2P/2B .... 44.00 XP 5   F
Senior discount. 49 units. 1/2 mi s of SR 198; exit Mooney Blvd. 1400 S Mooney Blvd. (93277) 10 refrigerators; A/C; C/CATV; movies; radios; phones; shower or comb baths. Pool. No pets. AE, DI, DS, MC, VI. Coffeeshop; 6 am-2 pm. FAX (209) 739-7520   ⊗ Ⓓ (209) 732-6641

El Rancho Motel   Rates Subject to Change   *Motel* ◆
All year   1P 28.00- 30.00 2P/1B 32.00- 36.00 2P/2B 38.00- 40.00 XP 5   F
Senior discount. 16 units. On SR 198; 1 1/2 mi w of jct SR 63. 4506 W Mineral King Ave. (93291) A/C; C/CATV; radios; phones; shower baths. No pets. Reserv deposit required. AE, DI, DS, MC, VI. Restaurant opposite.
⊗ Ⓓ (209) 734-9271

Holiday Inn Plaza Park   Rates Subject to Change   *Motor Inn* ◆◆◆
All year   1P 66.00- 75.60 2P/1B 72.00- 81.00 2P/2B 72.00- 81.00 XP 6   F
Senior discount. 260 units. On SR 198; 1/2 mi e of jct SR 99, adjacent to Visalia Airport. 9000 W Airport Dr. (93277) Check-in 3 pm. 5 refrigerators; A/C; C/CATV; free & pay movies; radios; phones. Coin laundry. 2 htd pools, 1 indoor; saunas; whirlpool; indoor whirlpool; indoor putting green; exercise rm. Pets. Reserv deposit required; 3 days refund notice. AE, DI, DS, MC, VI. ● Dining rm; 6 am-10 pm; $9.95-$24.95; cocktails. FAX (209) 651-5000   ⊗ Ⓓ 🅛 (209) 651-5000

Lamp Liter Inn   Rates Subject to Change   *Motor Inn* ◆◆
2/1-11/30   1P 59.00- 65.00 2P/1B 65.00- 75.00 2P/2B 69.00- 75.00 XP 6   F
12/1-1/31   1P 45.00- 50.00 2P/1B 49.00- 55.00 2P/2B 49.00- 60.00 XP 6   F
Senior discount. 100 units. On SR 198; 1/2 mi w of jct SR 63. 3300 W Mineral King Ave. (93291) Spacious landscaped grounds. 9 refrigerators; A/C; C/CATV; movies; radios; phones; shower or comb baths. Pool. No pets. Monthly rates avail. Reserv deposit required. AE, DI, DS, MC, VI. ● Dining rm & coffeeshop; 6 am-10 pm; $8.50-$18; cocktails; entertainment. FAX (209) 732-1840   Ⓓ (209) 732-4511

Parkway Inn   *Rates Subject to Change*   *Motel* ◆◆
4/1-11/30   1P .... 38.00 2P/1B   42.00- 45.00 2P/2B 48.00- 52.00 XP 5
12/1-3/31   1P .... 35.00 2P/1B   40.00- 42.00 2P/2B 42.00- 46.00 XP 5
38 units. On SR 198; 1 3/4 mi w of SR 63. 4801 W Mineral King Ave. (93277) 23 refrigerators; A/C; C/CATV; phones. Small pool. No pets. Reserv deposit required. AE, CB, DI, MC, VI.   ⊗ ⒟ (209) 627-2885

Visalia Radisson Hotel   *Rates Subject to Change*   *Hotel* ◆◆◆
All year   1P .... 78.00 2P/1B   .... 78.00 2P/2B   .... 78.00 XP 10
Senior discount. 201 units. 1 blk e of SR 198, corner Mineral King Ave & Court St; exit Central-Visalia. 300 S Court St. (93291) A/C; C/CATV; pay movies; radios; phones. Htd pool; whirlpool; exercise rm. Parking lot. No pets. Monthly rates avail. Reserv deposit required. AE, DI, DS, MC, VI. Restaurant; 6 am-11 pm; $7-$24; cocktails; entertainment. FAX (209) 636-8224 *(See ad p A543)*   ⊗ Ⓢ ⒟ (209) 636-1111

RESTAURANTS

The Chinowth House   American $ ◆◆
1/2 blk s of Mineral King Ave. 505 S Chinowth Rd. Restored home specializing in home cooked food. A/C. Children's menu. Open 7 am-2 & 5-8:30 pm; 5/9, 6/20 & 4/11 7 am-2 pm; Sun 7 am-7:30 pm; closed Mon & 12/25. MC, VI.   ⊗ (209) 734-6301

The Depot Restaurant   American $$ ◆◆
Downtown; 2 blks n of Main St. 207 E Oak St at Church St. Attractive restaurant in former railroad depot. Selections of steaks, chicken & seafood. A/C. Children's menu. Open 11:30 am-2:30 & 5-10 pm; Fri & Sat-11 pm; closed Sun & major holidays. Cocktails & lounge. Reserv advised wkends. AE, DS, MC, VI.   ⊗ (209) 732-8611

The Vintage Press   American $$$ ◆◆◆
Downtown; 1 blk n of Main St. 216 N Willis St. Varied selection of fresh seafood, steaks & chicken served in attractive dining rooms or garden patio area. California cuisine. A/C. Children's menu. Open 11:30 am-2 & 6-10:30 pm; Fri & Sat-11 pm; closed Sun, 12/25 & for lunch major holidays. Cocktails & lounge. Reserv advised. AE, CB, DI, MC, VI.   ⊗ (209) 733-3033

VISTA — 71,900
La Quinta Inn   *Rates Subject to Change*   *Motel* ◆◆◆
All year   1P 46.00- 53.00 2P/1B   54.00- 61.00 2P/2B   .... 54.00 XP 5   F
106 units. Adjacent to SR 78, exit Sycamore Ave. 630 Sycamore Ave at Thibodo Rd. (92083) A/C; C/CATV; free & pay movies; radios; phones. Htd pool. Pets. AE, DI, DS, MC, VI. Restaurant adjacent. FAX (619) 598-1732   ⊗ ⒟ 🅶 (619) 727-8180

WALNUT — See WALNUT

WALNUT CREEK — 60,600   (See OAKLAND/BERKELEY AREA spotting map pages A300 & A301; see index starting on page A298)

Doubletree Hotel Walnut Creek 41   **Rates Guaranteed**   *Hotel* ◆◆◆◆
♿ All year   1P 109.00- 129.00   2P/1B   124.00- 144.00   2P/2B   124.00- 144.00   XP 15   F
Senior discount. 337 units. E of I-680; exit N Main St; 1/4 mi s at Parkside Dr. 2355 N Main. (94596) Attractive public areas. Check-in 3 pm. A/C; C/CATV; pay movies; radios; phones. Pool; whirlpool; exercise rm. Valet garage & parking lot. No pets. Monthly rates avail. AE, DS, DI, MC, VI. ● Restaurant; 6:30 am-11 pm; $8-$25; cocktails. FAX (510) 934-6374 *(See ad p A542)*   ⊗ Ⓢ Ⓓ ♿ (510) 934-2000

Embassy Suites Hotel 44   **AAA Special Value Rates**   *Suites Hotel* ◆◆◆◆
♿ All year [BP]   1P .... 145.00   2P/1B .... 169.00   2P/2B .... 169.00   XP 15   F
249 units. E of & adjacent to I-680, northbound exit Treat Blvd, southbound exit Oak Park Blvd at Bart Station. 1345 Treat Blvd. (94596) Attractive atrium landscaping. Check-in 3 pm. A/C; C/CATV; movies; radios; phones. Efficiencies. Coin laundry. Indoor pool; sauna; whirlpool; exercise rm. Garage. No pets. Reserv deposit required; 3 days refund notice. Complimentary beverages each evening. AE, DI, DS, MC, VI. ● Restaurant; 11 am-11 pm; $10-$25; cocktail lounge. FAX (510) 256-7233   ⊗ Ⓢ Ⓓ ♿ (510) 934-2500

Holiday Inn of Walnut Creek 43   **Rates Subject to Change**   *Motor Inn* ◆◆◆
All year   1P .... 68.00   2P/1B .... 68.00   2P/2B .... 68.00   XP 8   F
151 units. I-680 northbound exit Geary/Treat, w to N Main St, 1/4 mi s; southbound exit OakPark, w to N Main St. 2730 N Main St. (94596) Attractive courtyard setting. A/C; C/CATV; movies; radios; phones. Pool; whirlpool; jogging track. Garage. No pets. AE, DS, DI, MC, VI. ● Restaurant; 6:30 am-10 pm; $7-$15; cocktails. FAX (510) 256-7672   ⊗ Ⓢ Ⓓ ♿ (510) 932-3332

Walnut Creek Motor Lodge 42   **Rates Subject to Change**   *Motel* ◆◆
♿ All year   1P 50.00- 55.00   2P/1B   55.00- 65.00   2P/2B   60.00- 70.00   XP 5
Senior discount. 72 units. 2 blks e off I-680 & SR 24; northbound exit e via Ygnacio Valley Rd, southbound exit e via N Main St. 1960 N Main St. (94596) A/C; C/CATV; movies; radios; phones. Pool; whirlpool. No pets. 8 efficiencies, $10 extra. Monthly rates avail. AE, CB, DI, MC, VI. Restaurant adjacent. FAX (510) 932-5989   ⊗ Ⓓ (510) 932-2811

RESTAURANT

Maximillian's Restaurant & Cafe 41   French $$$ ◆◆◆
I-680 & SR at Ygnacio Valley Rd; s on California Blvd, e on La Cassie. 1604 Locust St. Formal French dining room upstairs, cafe with light Mediterranean style cuisine downstairs. Attractive contemporary decor. A/C. Dress code. Open 11:30 am-3 & 5-11 pm; Sat 5 pm-11 pm; closed Sun & major holidays. Cocktails & lounge. Reserv advised. AE, CB, DI, MC, VI.   ⊗ (510) 932-1474

WATSONVILLE — 31,100

Best Western Inn ◆◆
⊛ 7/1-8/31

			Rates Subject to Change				Motel	
	1P	62.50- 72.50	2P/1B	74.50- 84.50	2P/2B	76.50- 86.50	XP 10	
9/1-10/31 & 4/1-6/30	1P	52.50- 62.50	2P/1B	54.50- 64.50	2P/2B	56.50- 66.50	XP 10	
11/1-3/31	1P	48.50- 58.50	2P/1B	52.50- 62.50	2P/2B	54.50- 64.50	XP 10	

42 units. Jct SR 152 & Freedom Blvd. 740 Freedom Blvd. (95076) Refrigerators; A/C; C/CATV; pay movies; phones; comb or shower baths. Coin laundry. Small pool; whirlpool. Reserv deposit required; 3 days refund notice. AE, DI, DS, MC, VI. Coffeeshop opposite. FAX (408) 761-1785 ⊗ Ⓢ Ⓓ (408) 724-3367

El Rancho Motel ◆
⊛ 5/15-10/15

			Rates Subject to Change				Motel	
	1P	32.50- 42.50	2P/1B	39.50- 59.50	2P/2B	42.50- 52.50	XP	3- 5
10/16-5/14	1P	30.00- 32.00	2P/1B	30.00- 45.00	2P/2B	36.50- 45.50	XP	3- 5

Senior discount. 12 units. 3 mi s, across Pajaro Golf Course; 1 mi from SR 1 & Salinas Rd turnoff. 976 Salinas Rd. (95076) Quiet location. C/CATV; 7 radios; phones; shower baths. 2 2-bedrm units. Pets, $5 extra charge. 4 efficiencies, $180 weekly; 10/16-5/14. Reserv deposit required. AE, CB, DI, MC, VI. Ⓓ (408) 722-2766

National 9 Motel ◆◆
⊛ 5/15-10/14 & Fri-Sat

			Rates Subject to Change				Motel	
	1P	.... 55.00	2P/1B	.... 65.00	2P/2B	.... 75.00	XP 10	
Sun-Thurs 10/15-5/14	1P	.... 35.00	2P/1B	.... 40.00	2P/2B	.... 45.00	XP 10	

Senior discount. 1/2 mi n off Main St; southbound exit SR 1 at Watsonville-Gilroy, northbound exit at Riverside Dr. 1 Western Dr. (95076) C/CATV; movies; phones; shower baths. 1 2-bedrm unit. Small pool. Reserv deposit required. AE, DI, DS, MC, VI. Coffeeshop opposite. ⊗ Ⓓ (408) 724-1116

RESTAURANT

Mt Madonna Inn Restaurant .... Continental .... $$ ◆◆
7 mi e on the summit of Hecker Pass, SR 152. 1285 Hecker Pass Rd. Panoramic View of valley & cities below; also fresh seafood. A/C. Children's menu. Open 5 pm-10 pm; Sat noon-4 & 5-10 pm; Sun noon-9 pm; closed Mon-Wed & 12/25. Cocktails & lounge. Entertainment & dancing. Minimum $5. Reserv advised. AE, CB, DI, MC, VI.
⊗ (408) 724-2275

WEAVERVILLE — 2,800

49er Motel ◆◆
⊛ 5/1-9/30

			Rates Guaranteed				Motel	
	1P	32.00- 34.00	2P/1B	36.00- 38.00	2P/2B	38.00- 40.00	XP 3	
10/1-4/30	1P	30.00- 32.00	2P/1B	34.00- 36.00	2P/2B	34.00- 36.00	XP 3	

13 units. On SR 299. 718 Main St. (PO Box 1608, 96093) A/C; C/CATV; movies; radios; phones; shower baths. 1 kitchen. Pool. Pets. Reserv deposit required. AE, DI, DS, MC, VI. Restaurant opposite. Ⓓ (916) 623-4937

Motel Trinity ◆
⊛ All year

			Rates Subject to Change				Motel	
	1P	30.00- 55.00	2P/1B	33.00- 55.00	2P/2B	36.00- 58.00	XP 4	F

Senior discount. 25 units. 1/2 mi e on SR 299. 1112 Main St. (PO Box 1179, 96093) Attractive mountain setting. Refrigerators; A/C; C/CATV; movies; phones; comb or shower baths. 4 2-bedrm units, 3 kitchens. Pool; enclosed whirlpool. No pets. 3 rooms with whirlpool bath, $10 extra. Reserv deposit required. AE, DI, DS, MC, VI. Ⓓ (916) 623-2129

Weaverville Victorian Inn ◆◆◆
⊛ All year

			AAA Special Value Rates					
	1P	.... 49.00	2P/1B	.... 58.00	2P/2B	.... 59.00	XP 8	

61 units. On SR 299. 1709 Main St. (PO Box 2400, 96093) 28 refrigerators; A/C; C/CATV; movies; VCPs. Radios; phones. Pool enclosed in winter. 7 suites with whirlpool tub, $80 for 2 persons. Package plans avail. Wkly rates avail. Reserv deposit required. AE, DI, DS, MC, VI. FAX (916) 623-4264 ⊗ Ⓢ Ⓓ Ⓛ (916) 623-4432

WEED — 3,100

Sis-Q-Inn Motel ◆◆
⊛ All year

			Rates Guaranteed				Motel	
	1P	29.50- 35.00	2P/1B	35.55- 42.00	2P/2B	39.50- 46.00	XP 5	F

22 units. Exit I-5, s Weed. 1825 Shastina Dr. (96094) View of Mt. Shasta from most units. A/C; C/CATV; movies; phones. 5 2-bedrm units. Indoor whirlpool. Pets, $3 extra charge. Reserv deposit required. AE, MC, VI. Restaurant opposite. ⊗ Ⓓ (916) 938-4194

WESTCHESTER — See LOS ANGELES (Southern Region)

WEST COVINA — 96,100

Best Western West Covina Inn ◆◆◆
⊛ All year [CP]

			AAA Special Value Rates				Motel	
	1P	48.00- 57.00	2P/1B	53.00- 62.00	2P/2B	53.00- 62.00	XP 5	F

126 units. Adjacent to I-10, exit Grand Ave. 3275 E Garvey Ave. (91791) A/C; C/CATV; free & pay movies; radios; phones. 10 efficiencies. Coin laundry. Pool; whirlpool; exercise rm. No pets. 8 rooms with whirlpool tub, $90. Wkly & monthly rates avail. AE, CB, DI, MC, VI. FAX (818) 332-6977 (See ad below) ⊗ Ⓢ Ⓓ Ⓛ (818) 915-1611

Comfort Inn ◆◆◆
⊛ All year [CP]

			AAA Special Value Rates				Motel	
	1P	42.00- 49.00	2P/1B	47.00- 52.00	2P/2B	49.00- 59.00	XP 5	F

58 units. S side of I-10 between Barranca & Citrus Ave exits. 2804 E Garvey Ave S. (91791) Refrigerators; A/C; C/CATV; movies; rental VCPs. Radios; phones. Small pool; whirlpool. No pets. AE, DI, DS, MC, VI. FAX (818) 915-6077 ⊗ Ⓓ (818) 915-6077

Embassy Suites Hotel ◆◆◆
⊛ Mon-Thurs [BP]

			Rates Guaranteed				Suites Motor Inn	
	1P	.... 89.00	2P/1B	.... 89.00	2P/2B	.... 89.00	XP 10	F
Fri-Sun [BP]	1P	.... 79.00	2P/1B	.... 79.00	2P/2B	.... 79.00	XP 10	F

264 units. Adjacent to I-10, Holt Ave exit. 1211 E Garvey St. (Covina, 91724) Very attractively landscaped. 1-bedroom suites, with living room & efficiency. A/C; C/CATV; movies; radios; phones. Coin laundry. Htd pool; whirlpool. No pets. Monthly rates avail. Reserv deposit required. Complimentary beverages each evening. AE, DI, DS, MC, VI. ● Velvet Turtle Restaurant, see separate listing. FAX (818) 331-0773 ⊗ Ⓢ Ⓓ (818) 915-3441

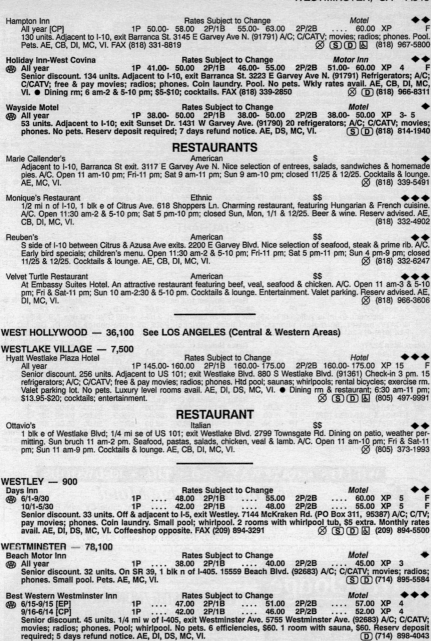

Hampton Inn   Rates Subject to Change   *Motel*   ◆◆
🏵 All year [CP]   1P 50.00- 58.00   2P/1B   55.00- 63.00   2P/2B   .... 60.00 XP   F
130 units. Adjacent to I-10, exit Barranca St. 3145 E Garvey Ave N. (91791) A/C; C/CATV; movies; radios; phones. Pool.
Pets. AE, CB, DI, MC, VI. FAX (818) 331-8819   ⊗ ⓈⒹ🅔 (818) 967-5800

Holiday Inn-West Covina   Rates Subject to Change   *Motor Inn*   ◆◆
🏵 All year   1P 41.00- 50.00   2P/1B   46.00- 55.00   2P/2B   51.00- 60.00 XP 4   F
Senior discount. 134 units. Adjacent to I-10, exit Barranca St. 3223 E Garvey Ave N. (91791) Refrigerators; A/C;
C/CATV; free & pay movies; radios; phones. Coin laundry. Pool. No pets. Wkly rates avail. AE, CB, DI, MC,
VI. ● Dining rm; 6 am-2 & 5-10 pm; $5-$10; cocktails. FAX (818) 339-2850   ⊗ Ⓓ (818) 966-8311

Wayside Motel   Rates Subject to Change   *Motel*   ◆
🏵 All year   1P 38.00- 50.00   2P/1B   38.00- 50.00   2P/2B   38.00- 50.00 XP 3- 5
53 units. Adjacent to I-10; exit Sunset Dr. 1431 W Garvey Ave. (91790) 20 refrigerators; A/C; C/CATV; movies;
phones. No pets. Reserv deposit required; 7 days refund notice. AE, DS, MC, VI.   ⓈⒹ (818) 814-1940

RESTAURANTS

Marie Callender's   American $ ◆
Adjacent to I-10, Barranca St exit. 3117 E Garvey Ave N. Nice selection of entrees, salads, sandwiches & homemade
pies. A/C. Open 11 am-10 pm; Fri-11 pm; Sat 9 am-11 pm; Sun 9 am-10 pm; closed 11/25 & 12/25. Cocktails & lounge.
AE, MC, VI.   ⊗ (818) 339-5491

Monique's Restaurant   Ethnic $$ ◆◆◆
1/2 mi n of I-10, 1 blk e of Citrus Ave. 618 Shoppers Ln. Charming restaurant, featuring Hungarian & French cuisine.
A/C. Open 11:30 am-2 & 5-10 pm; Sat 5 pm-10 pm; closed Sun, Mon, 1/1 & 12/25. Beer & wine. Reserv advised. AE,
CB, DI, MC, VI.   (818) 332-4902

Reuben's   American $$ ◆
S side of I-10 between Citrus & Azusa Ave exits. 2200 E Garvey Blvd. Nice selection of seafood, steak & prime rib. A/C.
Early bird specials; children's menu. Open 11:30 am-2 & 5-10 pm; Fri-11 pm; Sat 5 pm-11 pm; Sun 4 pm-9 pm; closed
11/25 & 12/25. Cocktails & lounge. AE, CB, DI, MC, VI.   ⊗ (818) 332-6247

Velvet Turtle Restaurant   American $$ ◆◆
At Embassy Suites Hotel. An attractive restaurant featuring beef, veal, seafood & chicken. A/C. Open 11 am-3 & 5-10
pm; Fri & Sat-11 pm; Sun 10 am-2:30 & 5-10 pm. Cocktails & lounge. Entertainment. Valet parking. Reserv advised. AE,
DI, MC, VI.   ⊗ (818) 966-3606

WEST HOLLYWOOD — 36,100   See LOS ANGELES (Central & Western Areas)

WESTLAKE VILLAGE — 7,500

Hyatt Westlake Plaza Hotel   Rates Subject to Change   *Hotel*   ◆◆◆
All year   1P 145.00- 160.00   2P/1B   160.00- 175.00   2P/2B 160.00- 175.00 XP 15   F
Senior discount. 256 units. Adjacent to US 101; exit Westlake Blvd. 880 S Westlake Blvd. (91361) Check-in 3 pm. 15
refrigerators; A/C; C/CATV; free & pay movies; radios; phones. Htd pool; saunas; whirlpools; rental bicycles; exercise rm.
Valet parking lot. No pets. Luxury level rooms avail. AE, DI, DS, MC, VI. ● Dining rm & restaurant; 6:30 am-11 pm;
$13.95-$20; cocktails; entertainment.   ⊗ ⓈⒹ🅔 (805) 497-9991

RESTAURANT

Ottavio's   Italian $$ ◆◆
1 blk e of Westlake Blvd; 1/4 mi se of US 101; exit Westlake Blvd. 2799 Townsgate Rd. Dining on patio, weather per-
mitting. Sun bruch 11 am-2 pm. Seafood, pastas, salads, chicken, veal & lamb. A/C. Open 11 am-10 pm; Fri & Sat-11
pm; Sun 11 am-9 pm. Cocktails & lounge. AE, CB, DI, MC, VI.   ⊗ (805) 373-1993

WESTLEY — 900

Days Inn   Rates Subject to Change   *Motel*   ◆◆
🏵 6/1-9/30   1P   .... 48.00   2P/1B   .... 55.00   2P/2B   .... 60.00 XP 5   F
   10/1-5/30   1P   .... 42.00   2P/1B   .... 48.00   2P/2B   .... 55.00 XP 5   F
Senior discount. 33 units. Off & adjacent to I-5, exit Westley. 7144 McKraken Rd. (PO Box 311, 95387) A/C; C/TV;
pay movies; phones. Coin laundry. Small pool; whirlpool. 2 rooms with whirlpool tub, $5 extra. Monthly rates
avail. AE, DI, DS, MC, VI. Coffeeshop opposite. FAX (209) 894-3291   ⊗ ⓈⒹ🅔 (209) 894-5500

WESTMINSTER — 78,100

Beach Motor Inn   Rates Subject to Change   *Motel*   ◆
🏵 All year   1P   .... 38.00   2P/1B   .... 40.00   2P/2B   .... 45.00 XP 3
Senior discount. 32 units. On SR 39, 1 blk n of I-405. 15559 Beach Blvd. (92683) A/C; C/CATV; movies; radios;
phones. Small pool. Pets. AE, MC, VI.   ⓈⒹ (714) 895-5584

Best Western Westminster Inn   Rates Subject to Change   *Motel*   ◆◆◆
🏵 6/15-9/15 [EP]   1P   .... 47.00   2P/1B   .... 51.00   2P/2B   .... 57.00 XP 4
   9/16-6/14 [CP]   1P   .... 42.00   2P/1B   .... 46.00   2P/2B   .... 52.00 XP 4
Senior discount. 45 units. 1/4 mi w of I-405, exit Westminster Ave. 5755 Westminster Ave. (92683) A/C; C/CATV;
movies; radios; phones. Pool; whirlpool. No pets. 6 efficiencies, $60. 1 room with sauna, $60. Reserv deposit
required; 5 days refund notice. AE, DI, DS, MC, VI.   Ⓓ (714) 898-4043

Travelodge of Westminster　　　　　Rates Subject to Change　　　　　*Motel*　◆◆◆

		1P		2P/1B		2P/2B		XP	
4/1-10/1		39.00	....	45.00	....	47.00	....	5	F
10/2-3/31		37.00	....	42.00	....	45.00	....	5	F

Senior discount. 46 units. On SR 39, 1/2 mi s of jct SR 22. 13659 Beach Blvd. (92683) Refrigerators; A/C; C/CATV; movies; radios; phones. Coin laundry. Htd pool; whirlpool. No pets. 4 rooms with whirlpool tub, $85. Wkly rates avail. AE, CB, DI, MC, VI. *(See ad below)*　　　⊗ Ⓢ Ⓓ (714) 373-3200

Westminster Gateway Travelodge　　　　　Rates Guaranteed　　　　　*Motel*　◆◆

		1P		2P/1B		2P/2B		XP	
6/1-9/30		39.00	....	42.00	....	50.00	....	5	F
10/1-5/31		36.00	....	39.00	....	45.00	....	5	F

60 units. 1/2 mi e of I-405; exit Westminster Ave. 6601 Westminster Ave. (92683) A/C; C/CATV; radios; phones; comb baths. Small pool. No pets. 5 rooms with whirlpool tub, $65. Wkly rates avail. AE, DI, MC, VI.
FAX (714) 895-2140　　　⊗ Ⓢ Ⓓ (714) 898-5598

WESTWOOD — 2,100　See LOS ANGELES (Central & Western Areas)

WHITTIER — 77,700

Vagabond Inn　　　　　Rates Subject to Change　　　　　*Motel*　◆◆

		1P		2P/1B		2P/2B		XP	
All year [CP]		35.00- 49.00		40.00- 54.00		45.00- 59.00		5	F

50 units. 1 1/4 mi e. 14125 E Whittier Blvd. (90605) A/C; C/TV; VCPs; radios; phones. Rental refrigerators. Pool. Pets, $5 extra charge. AE, DI, DS, MC, VI. FAX (310) 698-8716 *(See ad p A545)*　　　⊗ Ⓓ (310) 698-9701

Whittier Hilton　　　　　Rates Guaranteed　　　　　*Hotel*　◆◆◆

		1P		2P/1B		2P/2B		XP	
All year		85.00- 125.00		100.00- 140.00		100.00- 140.00		15	F

Senior discount. 206 units. 7320 Greenleaf Ave. (90602) Check-in 3 pm. 10 refrigerators; A/C; C/CATV; movies; radios; phones. Htd pool; whirlpool; exercise rm. Parking lot. No pets. Wkly & monthly rates avail. AE, CB, DI, MC, VI. ● Dining rm; 6:30 am-10:30 pm; $7.95-$18.95; cocktails; entertainment. FAX (310) 945-8511　⊗ Ⓢ Ⓓ ⑤ (310) 945-8511

RESTAURANT

Reuben's　　　　　Steak & Seafood　　　　　$$　◆◆

2 1/2 mi e on SR 72. 15360 E Whittier Blvd. Attractive restaurant. A/C. Children's menu. Open 11:30 am-2:30 & 5-10 pm; Fri-11 pm; Sat 5 pm-11 pm; Sun 10 am-2 & 4-10 pm; closed 12/25. Cocktails & lounge. Entertainment & dancing. AE, DI, DS, MC, VI.　　　⊗ ⑤ (310) 947-9511

WILLIAMS — 2,300

Comfort Inn　　　　　Rates Subject to Change　　　　　*Motel*　◆◆

		1P		2P/1B		2P/2B		XP	
All year [CP]		43.00	....	48.00	....	48.00	....	5	F

Senior discount. 61 units. Adjacent to I-5, exit W SR 20 business rt; 2 blks n. 400 C St. (PO Box 729, 95987) A/C; C/CATV; movies; 60 radios; phones. Small pool; whirlpool. Pets, $5 extra charge. AE, DI, DS, MC, VI. FAX (916) 473-2418　　　⊗ Ⓢ Ⓓ (916) 473-2381

Stage Stop Motel　　　　　Rates Subject to Change　　　　　*Motel*　◆

		1P		2P/1B		2P/2B		XP	
4/1-11/15		38.00- 40.00		38.00- 45.00		50.00	....	5	F

Senior discount. 25 units. Exit I-5 via SR 20 business rt, 3 blks w. 330 7th St. (95987) OPEN ALL YEAR. Refrigerators; A/C; C/CATV; movies; phones; shower or comb baths. 2 2-bedrm units. Small pool; whirlpool. Pets, $5 extra charge. Reserv deposit required; 3 days refund notice. AE, DS, MC, VI.　　　⊗ Ⓓ (916) 473-2281

WILLITS — 5,000

Baechtel Creek Inn　　　　　Rates Subject to Change　　　　　*Motel*　◆◆

		1P		2P/1B		2P/2B		XP	
6/1-9/30 [CP]		56.00- 65.00		59.00- 65.00		65.00- 68.00		3	
4/1-5/31 & 10/1-10/31 [CP]		49.00- 56.00		52.00- 56.00		59.00- 62.00		3	
11/1-3/31 [CP]		45.00- 52.00		49.00- 52.00		52.00- 55.00		3	

46 units. 1/2 mi s of jct SR 20, 1 blk w of US 101. 101 Gregory Ln. (95490) A/C; C/CATV; radios; phones. Pool; whirlpool. No pets. Reserv deposit required; 3 days refund notice. AE, DI, DS, MC, VI. Restaurant opposite.
FAX (707) 459-0226　　　⊗ Ⓓ ⑤ (707) 459-9063

Holiday Lodge Motel · **AAA Special Value Rates** · · · · · · · *Motel* ◆
5/15-9/30 · · · · · · 1P · · · · 42.00 · 2P/1B · 48.00- 52.00 · 2P/2B · 52.00- 57.00 · XP · 5
10/1-5/14 · · · · · · 1P · · · · 38.00 · 2P/1B · 42.00- 45.00 · 2P/2B · 45.00- 50.00 · XP · 5
16 units. 1 1/4 mi s on US 101. 1540 S Main St. (95490) A/C; C/CATV; movies; phones; comb or shower baths. 1 efficiency. Small pool. No pets. Reserv deposit required. AE, MC, VI. *(See ad p A546)* ⊗ Ⓓ (707) 459-5361

Old West Inn · **Rates Subject to Change** · · · · · · · *Motel* ◆
5/15-10/31 · · · · · 1P · 48.00- 58.00 · 2P/1B · 55.00- 65.00 · 2P/2B · 60.00- 65.00 · XP · 10
11/1-5/14 · · · · · · 1P · 40.00- 45.00 · 2P/1B · 45.00- 55.00 · 2P/2B · 50.00- 55.00 · XP · 6
Senior discount. 19 units. 1 mi s on US 101. 1221 S Main St. (95490) Early western theme rooms & facades. 10 refrigerators; C/CATV; phones. Small pool open 5/15-9/30. No pets. AE, DI, DS, MC, VI. FAX (707) 459-3009
⊗ Ⓓ (707) 459-4201

RESTAURANT

South Main Restaurant · · · · · · · · · · · · · · · · **American** · · · · · · · · · · · · · · · · · $ ◆
Center; on US 101. 708 S Main St. Popular with local families. A/C. Open 7 am-9 pm; Sun 8 am-3 pm; closed 11/25 & 12/25. Beer & wine. MC, VI. ⊗ (707) 459-9335

WILLOW CREEK — 1,000

RESTAURANT

Cinnabar Sam's · **American** · · · · · · · · · · · · · · · · · $$ ◆
1/4 mi e on SR 299. 19 Willow Way. Casual American food, steak, fajitas, seafood & homemade desserts. Outdoor dining. A/C. Children's menu. Open 11:30 am-2:30 & 5-9 pm; 4/19-11/25 7:30 am-10 pm; Sat 11:30 am-9 pm; 4/19-11/25 7:30 am-10 pm; Sun 10 am-9 pm; 4/19-11/25 7:30 am-10 pm; closed 11/25 & 12/25. Beer & wine. MC, VI.
(916) 629-3437

WILLOWS — 6,000

Best Western Golden Pheasant Inn · · · · · · · **AAA Special Value Rates** · · · · *Motor Inn* ◆◆◆
All year · · · · · · 1P · 45.00- 55.00 · 2P/1B · 51.00- 61.00 · 2P/2B · 54.00- 64.00 · XP · 5
104 units. E side of I-5; exit frwy via Willow-Elk Creek-Glenn Rd. 249 N Humboldt Ave. (95988) Nicely landscaped lawn area. Spanish design. A/C; C/CATV; VCPs; 74 radios; phones. Coin laundry. 2 pools. Reserv deposit required. AE, DI, DS, MC, VI. ● WillowBrooke, see separate listing. FAX (916) 934-4275 *(See ad below)*
⊗ Ⓓ Ⓖ (916) 934-4603

Blue Gum Inn · **Rates Guaranteed** · · · · · · · · · · · *Motel* ◆
5/1-10/31 · · · · · · 1P · · · · 28.00 · 2P/1B · · · · 38.00 · 2P/2B · · · · 42.00 · XP · 5
11/1-4/30 · · · · · · 1P · · · · 26.00 · 2P/1B · · · · 29.00 · 2P/2B · · · · 36.00 · XP · 5
30 units. 5 mi n; exit I-5 via Bayliss-Blue Gum Rd, 1 3/4 mi n on business Rt. (Rt 2, Box 171A, 95988) Landscaped lawn; eucalyptus grove. A/C; C/CATV; radios; phones; shower baths. 1 kitchen. Pool. Pets, $6 extra charge. Some microwaves & refrigerators. Wkly rates avail. Reserv deposit required. AE, MC, VI. Restaurant adjacent.
FAX (916) 934-7737 Ⓓ (916) 934-5401

Cross Roads West Inn · · · · · · · · · · · · · · · · **Rates Subject to Change** · · · · · · · *Motel* ◆
All year · · · · · · 1P · · · · 26.00 · 2P/1B · · · · 33.00 · 2P/2B · · · · 36.00 · XP · 6
41 units. E side of I-5; exit via Willow-Elk Creek-Glenn Rd. 452 N Humboldt Ave. (95988) A/C; C/CATV; 30 phones. Small pool. Pets. Reserv deposit required. MC, VI. Coffeeshop adjacent. ⊗ Ⓓ (916) 934-7026

RESTAURANTS

Franco's · **Continental** · · · · · · · · · · · · · · · · · $$ ◆
1/2 mi s on Old Hwy 99. 610 S Tehama St. American cuisine & steaks. A/C. Early bird specials; children's menu. Open 11 am-2 & 4:30-10 pm; Sat 4:30 pm-11 pm; Sun 4:30 pm-9:30 pm; closed 7/4, 11/26 & 12/25. Cocktails & lounge. Minimum $3.00. Reserv advised. MC, VI. ⊗ (916) 934-4273

WillowBrooke   Continental $$ ◆◆
At Best Western Golden Pheasant Inn. American cuisine. A/C. Children's menu. Open 6 am-10 pm; dining rm only 11 am-2 & 5:30-9:30 pm, Sat 5:30 pm-10 pm, Sun brunch 10 am-2 pm. Cocktails & lounge. Minimum $8. Reserv advised. AE, DI, DS, MC, VI. *(See ad p A547)*   ⊗ (916) 934-2878

WILMINGTON — 40,000

Crescent Inn   Rates Guaranteed   *Motel*   ◆◆
⊕ All year   1P   ....   40.00   2P/1B   ....   45.00   2P/2B   ....   55.00   XP 5
Senior discount. 22 units. 1/4 mi e of I-110, exit Pacific Coast Hwy. 1104 W Pacific Coast Hwy. (90744) A/C; C/TV; movies; radios; phones. No pets. 4 rooms with efficiencies, extra charge; no utensils. Wkly rates avail. Reserv deposit required. AE, MC, VI.   ⊗ Ⓢ Ⓓ (310) 830-9898

Quality Inn South Bay   Rates Guaranteed   *Motel*   ◆◆◆
⊕ All year [CP]   1P 49.00- 59.00 2P/1B 55.00- 60.00 2P/2B 59.00- 64.00 XP 6   F
Senior discount. 72 units. Just w of I-110; exit Pacific Coast Hwy. 1402 W Pacific Coast Hwy. (90744) Refrigerators; A/C; C/CATV. Radios; phones. Coin laundry. Htd pool; whirlpool. Garage. No pets. Wkly rates avail. AE, DI, DS, MC, VI. Coffeeshop adjacent. FAX (310) 835-2225   ⊗ Ⓓ Ⓑ (310) 834-3400

WOODLAND — 39,800

Cinderella Motel   Rates Subject to Change   *Motel*   ◆
⊕ All year   1P   ....   35.00   2P/1B   ....   38.00   2P/2B   ....   42.00   XP 3
Senior discount. 30 units. 3/4 mi w on I-5 business loop; northbound I-5 exit first Woodland exit, southbound exit Main St. 99 W Main St. (95695) Refrigerators; A/C; C/CATV; movies; radios; phones; shower or comb baths. Pool; whirlpool. Pets, dogs only. Reserv deposit required; 3 days refund notice. AE, DI, DS, MC, VI. FAX (916) 668-0332 *(See ad p A547)*   ⊗ Ⓓ (916) 662-1091

Comfort Inn   Rates Subject to Change   *Motel*   ◆◆
⊕ All year   1P 45.00- 55.00 2P/1B 48.00- 58.00 2P/2B 52.00- 65.00 XP 6
51 units. I-5 northbound exit SR 113 Woodland; southbound exit Main St. 1562 E Main St. (95695) 48 refrigerators; A/C; C/CATV; radios; phones. 24 kitchens, no utensils. Whirlpool. Pets, $6 deposit required. AE, DS, MC, VI. *(See ad below)*   Ⓑ (916) 666-3050

Phoenix Inn   Rates Subject to Change   *Motel*   ◆
⊕ All year   1P   ....   34.00   2P/1B   ....   36.00   2P/2B   ....   40.00   XP 3
53 units. I-5 northbound exit Woodland; southbound exit Main St; SR 113 exit Main St. 1524 E Main St. (95695) 3 story, no elevator. A/C; C/CATV; movies; phones; comb or shower baths. Coin laundry. Pool. No pets. Wkly rates avail. Reserv deposit required. AE, MC, VI. Coffeeshop adjacent.   ⊗ Ⓢ Ⓓ Ⓑ (916) 666-3800

Woodland Shadow Motel   Rates Subject to Change   *Motel*   ◆◆
⊕ All year   1P 40.00- 55.00 2P/1B 44.00- 60.00 2P/2B 48.00- 65.00 XP 5
123 units. I-5 exit Yuba City/Davis SR 113N, 1/4 mi w. 584 N East St. (95695) 28 refrigerators; A/C; C/CATV; movies; radios; phones. Pool; whirlpools. No pets. AE, DI, MC, VI. Coffeeshop adjacent. FAX (916) 662-2804   ⊗ Ⓓ (916) 666-1251

WOODLAND HILLS — See LOS ANGELES (San Fernando Valley)

WOODSIDE — 5,000   (See SAN FRANCISCO (Southern Region) AREA spotting map page A444; see index starting on page A443)

RESTAURANT

Bella Vista Restaurant ㊺   Continental $$$ ◆◆
On SR 35, between SR 92 & 84; n of SR 84. 13451 Skyline Blvd. In the redwoods. Some tables with a view. A/C. Open 5:30 pm-10:30 pm; Sat-11 pm; Sun 4:30 pm-10 pm; closed Mon, 1/1, 11/26, 12/24 & 12/25. Cocktails & lounge. Minimum $10. Reserv advised. AE, DI, MC, VI.   ⊗ (415) 851-1229

YORBA LINDA — 34,300
Country Side Suites   Rates Guaranteed   *Motel*   ◆◆◆
🏨 All year [BP]   1P .... 60.00 2P/1B .... 70.00 2P/2B .... 70.00 XP 10
   Senior discount. 112 units. Adjacent to SR 91, exit Weir Canyon Rd. 22677 Oak Crest Cir. (92687) Attractive
   French country decor. Refrigerators; A/C; C/CATV; movies; radios; phones; comb or shower baths. Htd pool;
   whirlpool. No pets. All rooms with whirlpool tub. Wkly rates avail. Complimentary beverages each evening. AE,
   DI, DS, MC, VI. Restaurant adjacent. FAX (714) 283-3927 *(See ad p A295)*   ⊗ Ⓢ Ⓓ Ⓚ (714) 921-8688

RESTAURANT

El Torito Restaurant   Mexican $$ ◆◆
   Adjacent to SR 91, exit Weir Canyon. 22699 Oakhurst Cir. Colorfully decorated; southwest motif. A/C. Children's menu.
   Open 11 am-10 pm; Fri & Sat-11 pm; Sun 9 am-10 pm; closed 11/25 & 12/25. Cocktails & lounge. AE, CB, DI, MC, VI.
                                                                          ⊗ (714) 921-2335

IF THE ROOM YOU GET
ISN'T THE ROOM YOU RESERVED . . .
Do you have written confirmation?
Has the management offered you a choice of
another room there or elsewhere?
Know what to do. Read the Making Reservations section
in Tips for the TourBook Traveler.

YOSEMITE NATIONAL PARK — See also BASS LAKE, COULTERVILLE, EL PORTAL, FISH CAMP, MARIPOSA & OAKHURST

Reservations should be made well in advance for all types of accommodations; write Yosemite Park & Curry Company, Yosemite National Park, CA 95389, or phone (209) 252-4848. Rates may be revised or adjusted in fall & spring with NPS approval. Park visitors may contact the Reservation Office near the park headquarters in Yosemite Valley.

The Ahwahnee   Rates Subject to Change   *Historic Hotel*   ◆◆◆◆
2/9-11/25 & Fri-Sat   1P .... 201.25 2P/1B .... 208.00 2P/2B .... 208.00 XP 20   F
Sun-Thurs 11/26-2/8   1P .... 181.12 2P/1B .... 187.20 2P/2B .... 187.20 XP 20   F
123 units. In Yosemite Valley; 3/4 mi e beyond Park Headquarters. (95389) Spacious shaded setting; spectacular views. Check-in 5 pm. 20 refrigerators; 100 A/C; C/TV; radios; phones. Pool; tennis-2 courts. Valet parking lot. No pets. 24 duplex cottages. [AP]. Reserv deposit required; 3 days refund notice. DI, DS, MC, VI. ● Dining rm; 7-11 am, 11:30-4 & 5:30-10 pm; a la carte entrees about $18-$30; afternoon tea at 5 pm; dress code for dinner; cocktails. FAX (209) 456-0542   ⊗ Ⓓ ▣ (209) 252-4848

The Redwoods   Rates Subject to Change   *Resort Cottages*   ◆◆
🆎 5/1-9/30   1P 78.00- 279.00 2P/1B   78.00- 280.00 2P/2B   78.00- 280.00 XP 10-20
10/1-4/30   1P 71.00- 255.00 2P/1B   68.00- 243.00 2P/2B   68.00- 243.00 XP 10-20
Senior discount. 81 units. 6 mi inside the southern entrance via SR 41 & Chilhualna Falls Rd. (PO Box 2085, Wawona Station, 95389) Wooded setting. 1 to 5-bedroom homes, fully equipped, many with deluxe furnishings. Most with woodburning fireplace. Few small studio cabins. Check-in 3 pm. 10 TV, 67 C/TV; 40 radios; 19 phones; comb or shower baths. 41 2-bedrm units, 17 3-bedrm units, kitchens. Pets. Wkly rates avail in winter. Reserv deposit required; 10 days refund notice. MC, VI. FAX (209) 375-6400 *(See ad p A552)*   Ⓓ (209) 375-6666

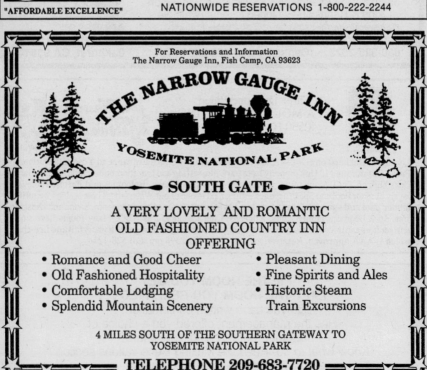

The establishments below do not meet all AAA standards but are listed as a service to members who may wish to stay in the park.

Curry Village

			Rates Subject to Change				Cottages			
3/25-10/28	1P	43.75- 72.25	2P/1B	43.75- 72.25	2P/2B	43.75- 72.25	XP	3- 8
Fri & Sat 10/29-3/24	1P	25.75- 63.00	2P/1B	25.75- 63.00	2P/2B	25.75- 63.00	XP	3- 8
Sun-Thurs 10/29-3/24	1P	24.50- 49.30	2P/1B	24.50- 56.75	2P/2B	24.50- 56.75	XP	3- 8

621 units. In Yosemite Valley; 2 mi e & across the Merced River from Park Headquarters. (95389) Modest, rustic accommodations. No food or cooking allowed in tent-cabin area. Check-in 5 pm. 19 phones; 115 shower, tub, or comb baths. Pool; rental bicycles. Fee for: rafting in summer; ice skating, riding. No pets. Tent cabins, $30 for up to 2 persons, extra person $4. Cabins without bath $43.75 for up to 2 persons, extra person $5. [AP] avail. Reserv deposit required; 3 days refund notice. CB, DI, DS, MC, VI. Cafeteria; grill 4/11-11/30; 7-10 am & 5-8 pm. FAX (209) 456-0542
(D) (209) 252-4848

Wawona Hotel

		Rates Subject to Change				Historic Hotel	
4/1-11/30	1P	63.25- 85.25	2P/1B	63.25- 85.25	2P/2B	63.25- 85.25	XP

105 units. On SR 41; 27 mi s from Yosemite Valley; 8 mi from the Mariposa Grove of Big Trees. (95389) OPEN 4/1-11/30. Charming setting on spacious grounds. Modest older units. Check-in 5 pm. 50 tub or comb baths. Pool; tennis-1 court. Fee for: golf-9 holes, riding. No pets. Maximum rates for up to 2 persons. Reserv deposit required; 3 days refund notice. AE, DI, DS, MC, VI. ● Dining rm; 7:30 am-11, noon-1:30 & 6-8 pm; buffet only noon-1:30 pm; $12-$24; cocktails. FAX (209) 456-0542
⊗ (S)(D) (209) 252-4848

In Yosemite National Park-six miles inside the south entrance-Hwy 41

AAA APPROVED

R The **EDWOODS**

Badger Pass Ski Resort: 17 miles
Mariposa Grove: 7 miles
Yosemite Valley Floor: 25 miles
Glacier Point: 25 miles
Wawona Golf Course: 1 mile
Historic Train Ride: 8 miles

One to five bedrooms, privately owned, fully furnished homes, most with fireplace, nestled within forest and wildlife. Close to 3 fishing streams, waterfall, swimming holes, hiking trails and stables. From rustic redwood log cabins to spacious modern homes. 7th night free: off-season

P.O. Box 2085, Wawona, CA 95389 - Call: 209-375-6666 or Fax 209-375-6400

The Pines RESORT

At Beautiful Bass Lake - Just 14 Miles from Southern Entrance to Yosemite

Condo-type Chalets with Kitchens
Pool • Sauna
Whirlpool • Tennis
Ducey's on the Lake Suites

1(800) 350-7463

AAA APPROVED ®

P.O. Box 109, Bass Lake, CA 93604

CEDAR LODGE

a "Beary" Nice Place to Stay!

Just 8 Miles from Yosemite Park Entrance

206 modern rooms, from moderate to elegant.
We have something to suit every taste, including...

- Deluxe Kings with in-room spa-tubs
- Family Units with mini or full kitchens
- Elegant Suites with 4-poster beds and private spas
- Fine Restaurant, Lounge and new "50's" Diner
- Swimming pools and access to the Merced River

800-321-5261 or (209) 379-2612
P.O. Box C, El Portal, CA 95318

Yosemite Lodge

			Rates Subject to Change					*Motor Inn*			
3/24-10/27	1P	48.25-	89.25	2P/1B	48.25-	89.25	2P/2B	48.25-	89.25	XP	6-12
Fri & Sat 10/28-3/23	1P	48.25-	72.75	2P/1B	48.25-	72.75	2P/2B	48.25-	72.75	XP	6-12
Sun-Thurs 10/28-3/23	1P	48.25-	68.75	2P/1B	48.25-	68.75	2P/2B	48.25-	68.75	XP	6-12

495 units. In Yosemite Valley; 3/4 mi w of Park Headquarters; near the foot of Yosemite Falls. (95389) Varied accommodations from cabins without bath to motel rooms. Check-in 5 pm. 286 phones; 395 shower or comb baths. Pool; rental bicycles. No pets. Reserv deposit required; 3 days refund notice. CB, DI, DS, MC, VI. ● Restaurant, coffeeshop & cafeteria; 7 am-9 pm; $14-$25; cocktail lounge. FAX (209) 456-0542   ⊗ (209) 252-4848

YOUNTVILLE — 3,300

Napa Valley Lodge Best Western   *Motel* ◆◆◆◆
⊛ All year [CP]

			Rates Subject to Change					*Motel*	◆◆◆◆
All year [CP]	1P 122.00- 165.00	2P/1B	132.00- 165.00	2P/2B	132.00- 165.00	XP 10			

Senior discount. 55 units. 1/2 mi n, off SR 29; exit Madison St. (PO Box L, 94599) Some rooms overlooking vineyards & hills. Balconies or patios. Refrigerators; A/C; C/CATV; radios; phones. 3 2-bedrm units. Htd pool; sauna; whirlpool; exercise rm. No pets. 11 rooms with fireplace, $10 extra. Reserv deposit required. AE, DI, DS, MC, VI. Restaurant opposite. FAX (707) 944-9362 *(See ads inside back cover and p A291)*   ⊗ Ⓓ & (707) 944-2468

Vintage Inn   *Motel* ◆◆◆◆
⊛ Fri & Sat [CP]

			Rates Subject to Change					*Motel*	◆◆◆◆
Fri & Sat [CP]	1P 144.00- 164.00	2P/1B	154.00- 174.00	2P/2B	154.00- 174.00	XP 25			
Sun-Thurs [CP]	1P 124.00- 144.00	2P/1B	134.00- 154.00	2P/2B	134.00- 154.00	XP 25			

80 units. Center; SR 29 exit Yountville. 6541 Washington St. (94599) Vineyard, mountain & town views. Balconies or patios, all with fireplace & whirlpool tub. Check-in 3 pm. Refrigerators; A/C; C/CATV; free & pay movies; VCPs. Radios; phones. Htd pool; whirlpool; tennis-2 courts; rental bicycles. Airport transp. Pets, $25 daily extra charge. 2-night minimum stay weekends 4/1-11/15. Reserv deposit required. AE, CB, DI, MC, VI. Restaurant adjacent. Cocktails. FAX (707) 944-1617   ⊗ Ⓓ & (707) 944-1112

RESTAURANTS

California Cafe Bar & Grill   American $$$ ◆◆
SR 29 exit Madison St; in Washington Square. 6795 Washington St. Contemporary California cuisine, featuring fresh grilled meats & fish. Smoke free premises. A/C. Open 11:30 am-9 pm; Sat-10 pm; Sun 10 am-9:30 pm. Cocktails. Reserv advised required weekends. AE, DI, DS, MC, VI.   ⊗ (707) 944-2330

Domaine Chandon   French $$$$ ◆◆◆◆
⊛ W off SR 29; adjacent to Veteran's Home. 1 California Dr. California cuisine for lunch & French for dinner. A/C. Dress code. Open 11:30 am-2:30 & 6-9 pm; closed Mon & Tues for dinner, 12/25 & January. Wine. Reserv required (14-day advance notice). AE, DI, MC, VI.   ⊗ (707) 944-2892

Mama Nina's   Northern Italian $$
1/4 mi n; SR 29 exit Madison St. 6772 Washington St. Varied menu from several parts of Italy. A/C. Children's menu. Open 5-10 pm, 9 pm 11/1-3/31; Fri-Sun 11:30 am-3 & 5-10 pm; closed 11/26 & 12/25. Cocktails & lounge. Minimum $9. Reserv advised. MC, VI.   ⊗ (707) 944-2112

Piatti Ristorante   Italian $$$
SR 29 exit E Yountville-Veterans Home, 1 blk n. 6480 Washington St. Few tables with view of vineyard. A/C. Open 11:30 am-2:30 & 5-10 pm; Fri & Sat-11 pm; Sat noon-11 pm; Sun noon-10 pm; closed 1/1, 11/26 & 12/25. Cocktails. Reserv advised. MC, VI.   ⊗ (707) 944-2070

YREKA — 6,600

Best Western Miner's Inn   *Motel* ◆◆◆
⊛ All year

			Rates Subject to Change					*Motel*	◆◆◆
All year	1P 44.00	2P/1B	.... 49.00	2P/2B	.... 55.00	XP 5			

Senior discount. 135 units. 1 blk w off I-5 via Central Yreka. 122 E Miner St. (96097) Large rooms. A/C; C/CATV; phones; comb or shower baths. 15 2-bedrm units. 2 pools. Small pets only. 15 2-bedroom units with kitchen, $85 for 2 persons. AE, DI, DS, MC, VI. Coffeeshop adjacent. FAX (916) 842-4480   ⊗ Ⓓ & (916) 842-4355

Klamath Motor Lodge   *Motel* ◆◆
⊛ All year

			Rates Subject to Change					*Motel*	◆◆
All year	1P 36.00	2P/1B	.... 40.00	2P/2B	.... 42.00	XP 3			

28 units. Northbound exit I-5 Ft Jones N 1 1/4 mi; southbound exit Central Yreka s 3/4 mi. 1111 S Main St. (96097) Attractively landscaped grounds. 10 refrigerators; A/C; C/CATV; movies; radios; phones; shower or comb baths. 2 2-bedrm units. Pool. No pets. Reserv deposit required. AE, CB, DI, MC, VI.   ⊗ Ⓓ (916) 842-2751

Motel Orleans   *Motel* ◆
⊛ All year

			Rates Subject to Change					*Motel*	◆
All year	1P 32.00	2P/1B	.... 37.00	2P/2B	.... 39.00	XP 4			

Senior discount. 53 units. Exit I-5 at jct SR 3. 1804B Fort Jones Rd. (PO Box 778, 96097) 3-story, no elevator. A/C; C/CATV; phones; comb or shower baths. Pool. No pets. Reserv deposit required; 3 days refund notice. AE, DI, DS, MC, VI. Restaurant opposite.   ⊗ Ⓓ & (916) 842-1612

Thunderbird Lodge   *Motel* ◆
⊛ All year

			Rates Guaranteed					*Motel*	◆
All year	1P 32.00	2P/1B	.... 35.00	2P/2B	.... 40.00	XP 3			

Senior discount. 44 units. 1/4 mi s; I-5 via Central Yreka exit. 526 S Main St. (96097) A/C; C/CATV; movies; phones; shower baths. Pool. Pets. Wkly rates avail. AE, DI, DS, MC, VI.   ⊗ Ⓓ (916) 842-4404

Wayside Inn   *Motel* ◆
⊛ 6/1-8/31

			Rates Subject to Change					*Motel*	◆
6/1-8/31	1P 34.00	2P/1B	.... 40.00	2P/2B	.... 44.00	XP 4			
9/1-5/31	1P 32.00	2P/1B	.... 40.00	2P/2B	.... 42.00	XP 4			

Senior discount. 44 units. Northbound exit I-5 Ft Jones, 1 mi n; southbound exit Central Yreka, 1 mi s. 1235 S Main St. (96097) Attractively decorated rooms, some covered parking. Refrigerators; A/C; C/CATV; movies; phones; comb or shower baths. Coin laundry. Pool; whirlpool. Pets, $3 extra charge. 3 kitchens, $32-$48 for 2 persons. 1 unit with whirlpool tub, fireplace, microwave, refrigerator & VCP, $135-$150. Wkly & monthly rates avail. AE, DI, DS, MC, VI. Restaurant adjacent. *(See ad below)*   ⊗ Ⓓ (916) 842-4412

RESTAURANT

Old Boston Shaft Restaurant   Continental $$ ◆◆
⑭ Exit I-5 at jct SR 3. 1801 Fort Jones Rd. Varied menu, American/European featuring beef, seafood, veal & European desserts. A/C. Open 11 am-2:30 & 5-9:30 pm; Fri-10 pm; Sat 5 pm-10 pm; closed Sun & 12/25. Cocktails & lounge. Reserv advised. MC, VI.   ⊗ (916) 842-5768

YUBA CITY — 27,400

The Bonanza Inn Best Western   Rates Subject to Change   Motor Inn   ◆◆
⑭ All year [CP]   1P 70.00- 74.00 2P/1B   74.00- 78.00   2P/2B 78.00- 82.00 XP 4
Senior discount. 125 units. 2 mi w of Marysville; 1 blk n off SR 20. 1001 Clark Ave. (95991) A/C; C/CATV; free & pay movies; radios; phones. Pool; whirlpool. No pets. Reserv deposit required. AE, DI, DS, MC, VI. ● Dining rm & coffeeshop; 6 am-10 pm; $10-$24; cocktails. FAX (916) 674-0563   ⊗ Ⓓ (916) 674-8824

Motel Orleans   Rates Subject to Change   Motel   ◆◆
⑭ All year   1P .... 32.00 2P/1B   .... 37.00   2P/2B .... 40.00 XP 5
Senior discount. 53 units. E of & adjacent to SR 99, 1/8 mi s of jct SR 20, exit SR 99 at Bridge St. 730 Palora Ave. (95991) 3 story, no elevator. A/C; C/CATV; phones; comb or shower baths. Coin laundry. Small pool. No pets. Reserv deposit required; 3 days refund notice. AE, DI, DS, MC, VI.   ⊗ Ⓓ (916) 674-1592

Yuba City Motor Inn   Rates Subject to Change   Motel   ◆◆◆
⑭ All year [CP]   1P 53.00- 63.00 2P/1B   57.00- 67.00   2P/2B 57.00- 67.00 XP 6   F
88 units. On SR 99, 1 blk s of jct SR 20. 894 W Onstott Rd. (95991) A/C; C/CATV; radios; phones. Coin laundry. Pool; sauna; whirlpool; exercise rm. No pets. AE, DI, DS, MC, VI. Restaurant adjacent. FAX (916) 674-1266
⊗ Ⓓ Ⓖ (916) 674-4000

RESTAURANT

The Refuge Restaurant & Lounge   American $$ ◆◆
SR 99 exit; w SR 20 1 blk, 3 blks n, then 1 blk w. 1501 Butte House Rd. Prime rib, steak & fresh seafood. A/C. Children's menu. Open 11:30 am-2 & 5:30-9 pm; Sat 5:30 pm-10 pm; Sun 10 am-2 & 5-9 pm; closed 7/4 & 12/25. Cocktails. Minimum $5. Reserv advised. AE, MC, VI.   ⊗ (916) 673-7620

YUCCA VALLEY — 8,300

Desert View Motel   Rates Subject to Change   Motel   ◆◆
⑭ All year   1P 36.50- 39.50 2P/1B   39.50- 45.50   2P/2B 42.50- 48.50 XP 5
Senior discount. 14 units. 2 mi e on SR 62, 1 blk s on Airway Ave. 57471 Primrose Dr. (92284) A/C; C/CATV; movies; radios; phones; shower or comb baths. Pool. No pets. Reserv deposit required. AE, DS, MC, VI.
⊗ Ⓓ (619) 365-9706

Oasis of Eden Inn & Suites   Rates Subject to Change   Motel   ◆◆◆
⑭ All year [CP]   1P 38.75- 64.75 2P/1B   39.75- 79.75   2P/2B 39.75- 79.75 XP 5
39 units. 1/2 mi e on SR 62. 56377 Twentynine Palms Hwy. (92284) Attractive grounds. A/C; C/CATV; phones. 2 efficiencies. Htd pool; whirlpool. No pets. Wkly & monthly rates avail. Reserv deposit required. AE, CB, DI, MC, VI.   ⊗ Ⓓ Ⓖ (619) 365-6321

Yucca Inn   Rates Subject to Change   Motor Inn   ◆
⑭ All year   ....   2P/1B   39.00- 47.00   2P/2B 39.00- 47.00 XP 5
72 units. 1 mi w on SR 62; 1 blk n. 7500 Camino Del Cielo. (92284) A/C; C/CATV; phones; comb or shower baths. Htd pool; sauna; whirlpools; bicycles; exercise rm. No pets. 17 1-bedroom kitchen apartments, $55-$58. Reserv deposit required. AE, DI, DS, MC, VI. ● Restaurant; 7 am-2 pm; Fri-Sun to 9 pm; $9.50-$14; cocktails.
⊗ Ⓓ Ⓖ (619) 365-3311

NEVADA

BATTLE MOUNTAIN — 2,800

Best Western Big Chief Motel   Rates Subject to Change   Motel   ◆◆
⑭ All year [CP]   1P .... 45.00 2P/1B   .... 51.00   2P/2B .... 55.00 XP 6   F
Senior discount. 58 units. N of I-80; exit 229 eastbound, 233 westbound. 434 W Front St. (PO Box 471, 89820) Some small units. 26 refrigerators; A/C; C/CATV; phones; comb or shower baths. 8 efficiencies, no utensils. Coin laundry. Whirlpool; pool open 5/15-9/15. Pets, $10 deposit required. 18 units with microwave, $3 extra. AE, DI, DS, MC, VI. FAX (702) 635-2418   ⊗ Ⓓ (702) 635-2416

Holiday Inn Express
AAA Special Value Rates — *Motel* ◆◆
All year [CP]　1P .... 44.00　2P/1B .... 49.00　2P/2B .... 49.00　XP 5　F
72 units. N of I-80, exit 229 eastbound; 233 westbound. 521 E Front St. (89820) Formerly VIP's Motor Inn. Refrigerators; A/C; C/CATV; radios; phones. Coin laundry. Pets, $10 deposit required. Microwaves. Wkly rates avail. AE, DI, DS, MC, VI. FAX (702) 635-5788 　⊗ Ⓢ Ⓓ 🅺 (702) 635-5880

BEATTY

Burro Inn
Rates Subject to Change — *Motor Inn* ◆
All year　1P .... 29.00　2P/1B .... 34.00　2P/2B .... 36.00　XP 2
62 units. 4 blks s on SR 95. Third St & Hwy 95. (PO Box 7, 89003) A/C; C/CATV; 24 radios; phones. Coin laundry. Pets, $4 extra charge. AE, MC, VI. ● Restaurant; 24 hours; $6-$15; cocktail lounge. Casino. FAX (702) 553-2892　Ⓓ (702) 553-2225

Exchange Club Motel
Rates Guaranteed — *Motel* ◆
All year　1P 35.00- 38.00　2P/1B 38.00- 42.00　2P/2B .... 42.00　XP 5
44 units. On US 95. (PO Box 97, 89003) Refrigerators; A/C; C/CATV; radios; phones. Coin laundry. No pets. 1 unit with whirlpool bath, $65 for 2 persons. Reserv deposit required. AE, MC, VI. ● Coffeeshop; 24 hours; $6-$13; cocktails. Casino.　Ⓓ (702) 553-2333

BOULDER CITY — 13,200

Best Western Lighthouse Inn
Rates Guaranteed — *Motel* ◆◆◆
All year　1P 52.00- 58.00　2P/1B .... 62.00　2P/2B .... 62.00　XP 10
70 units. 1 mi e via SR 93. 110 Ville Dr. (89005) Some rooms with view of Lake Mead. A/C; C/CATV; movies; phones. Coin laundry. Pool; whirlpool. No pets. Reserv deposit required. AE, DI, DS, MC, VI. FAX (702) 293-6547　⊗ Ⓢ Ⓓ 🅺 (702) 293-6444

El Rancho Boulder Motel
Rates Subject to Change — *Motel* ◆◆◆
All year　1P 42.00- 60.00　2P/1B 46.00- 60.00　2P/2B 60.00- 80.00　XP 10
39 units. On US 93. 725 Nevada Hwy. (89005) Spanish style. Refrigerators; A/C; C/CATV; movies; radios; phones. 9 2-bedrm units. Pool. No pets. 16 kitchens, $10 extra. Monthly rates avail. Reserv deposit required; 7 days refund notice. AE, DI, DS, MC, VI. Coffeeshop adjacent. FAX (702) 293-6685　⊗ Ⓓ (702) 293-1085

Sands Motel
Rates Subject to Change — *Motel* ◆
All year　1P 32.00- 38.00　2P/1B 38.00- 44.00　2P/2B 40.00- 48.00　XP 6
25 units. On US 93. 809 Nevada Hwy. (89005) Some small units. Refrigerators; A/C; C/CATV; movies; phones; comb or shower baths. 2 2-bedrm units. No pets. 5 kitchens, $6 extra. Wkly rates avail. Reserv deposit required; 3 days refund notice. AE, DI, DS, MC, VI.　⊗ Ⓓ (702) 293-2589

CARSON CITY — 40,300

Best Western Trailside Inn — *Motel* ◆◆
Rates Subject to Change
6/1-10/31　1P 46.00- 56.00　2P/1B 51.00- 61.00　2P/2B 54.00- 64.00　XP 5
4/1-5/31　1P 38.00- 42.00　2P/1B 43.00- 48.00　2P/2B 45.00- 50.00　XP 5
11/1-1/31　1P 36.00- 42.00　2P/1B 41.00- 45.00　2P/2B 43.00- 47.00　XP 5
2/1-3/31　1P 34.00- 38.00　2P/1B 39.00- 43.00　2P/2B 41.00- 45.00　XP 5
Senior discount. 67 units. 1/2 mi n on US 395. 1300 N Carson St. (89701) 36 refrigerators; A/C; C/CATV; movies; phones. Small pool. No pets. Reserv deposit required; 3 days refund notice. AE, DI, DS, MC, VI.　⊗ Ⓓ (702) 883-7300

Hardman House Motor Inn — *Motel* ◆◆
AAA Special Value Rates
4/15-10/15　1P 45.00- 55.00　2P/1B 50.00- 60.00　2P/2B 55.00- 65.00　XP 6
10/16-4/14　1P 35.00- 45.00　2P/1B 40.00- 50.00　2P/2B 45.00- 55.00　XP 6
62 units. On US 395. 917 N Carson St. (89701) A/C; C/CATV; radios; phones. Limited garage. No pets. Wkly & monthly rates avail. Reserv deposit required. AE, DI, DS, MC, VI. Coffeeshop opposite. FAX (702) 887-0321　⊗ Ⓢ Ⓓ (702) 882-7744

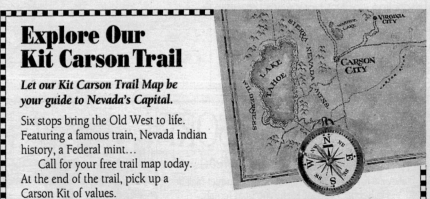

Motel Orleans	Rates Subject to Change					Motel		◆◆
Fri & Sat	1P	....	38.00	2P/1B	....	43.00	2P/2B	....	48.00	XP	5
Sun-Thurs	1P	....	32.00	2P/1B	....	37.00	2P/2B	....	42.00	XP	5

Senior discount. 58 units. 1 1/4 mi s on US 50 & 395. 2731 S Carson St. (89701) A/C; C/CATV; phones. Coin laundry. Small pool; whirlpool. No pets. Reserv deposit required; 3 days refund notice. AE, DI, DS, MC, VI.
⊗ ⑤ (702) 882-2007

The Ormsby House	Rates Subject to Change					Hotel		◆
6/1-9/30	1P	....	55.00	2P/1B	....	60.00	2P/2B	....	60.00	XP	10
10/1-5/31	1P	....	44.00	2P/1B	....	54.00	2P/2B	....	54.00	XP	10

200 units. On US 395, opposite state building. 600 S Carson St. (PO Box 1890, 89702) Check-in 3 pm. A/C; C/TV; radios; phones. Pool open 6/1-9/30. Garage & parking lot. No pets. AE, CB, DI, MC, VI. ● Restaurant & coffeeshop; 24 hours; $7-$21; buffet about $7-$10; cocktails; entertainment. Casino.
Ⓢ Ⓓ (702) 882-1890

RESTAURANT

Heidi's Family Restaurant — American — $ — ◆
🏵 At jct US 395 & 50E. 1020 North Carson St. Family restaurant, noted for breakfast. A/C. Children's menu. Open 6 am-9 pm; Tues & Wed to 2 pm; closed 12/25. MC, VI.
⊗ (702) 882-0486

COTTONWOOD COVE

Cottonwood Cove Motel	Rates Subject to Change					Motel		◆
All year	1P	....	85.00	2P/1B	....	85.00	2P/2B	....	80.00	XP	6

24 units. Between Las Vegas & Needles; 14 mi e of Searchlight, off US 95. (PO Box 1000, 89046) Overlooking Lake Mojave. Check-in 3 pm. A/C; C/CATV; rental VCPs; phones; shower or comb baths. Beach; swimming; marina & ramp; fishing. Fee for: houseboats, powerboats, water skiing & equipment. No pets. Reserv deposit required; 3 days refund notice. AE, MC, VI. ● Coffeeshop; 7 am-8 pm; 9/6-5/27 to 7 pm; $4-$8. FAX (702) 297-1464 *(See ad below)*
Ⓓ (702) 297-1464

DAYTON

RESTAURANT

Mia's Swiss Restaurant — Ethnic — $$ — ◆
🏵 US 50 exit e Main St. 65 Pike St. In State Historical Building built in 1863. Swiss Cuisine. A/C. Open 11:30 am-2 & 5-10 pm; closed Sun & major holidays; except 11/25. Cocktails. Reserv advised. AE, MC, VI. ⊗ (702) 246-3993

ECHO BAY

Echo Bay Resort   Rates Subject to Change   *Motor Inn* ◆
All year   1P .... 69.00   2P/1B .... 74.00   2P/2B 69.00- 84.00 XP 6
52 units. On Lake Mead; 4 mi e of SR 169. Lake Mead. (Overton, 89040) A/C; C/CATV; radios; phones. Coin laundry. Rental boats; marina; fishing; water skiing. Fee for: houseboats. Pets, $50 deposit required. 4 family rooms, $84 for up to 4 persons. Reserv deposit required. MC, VI. ● Restaurant; 7 am-8:30 pm; 5/1-9/30 6 am-9:30 pm; $6-$15; cocktails. FAX (702) 394-4182 *(See ad p A556)*   (D) (702) 394-4000

ELKO — 18,400

Best Western Gold Rush Inn   Rates Guaranteed   *Motel* ◆◆◆
5/15-9/15   1P 49.00- 59.00   2P/1B   54.00- 64.00   2P/2B 59.00- 69.00 XP 8
Senior discount. 109 units. S of I-80 exit 303, 1 mi w. 1930 Idaho St. (89801) OPEN ALL YEAR. Spacious attractive rooms. Refrigerators; A/C; C/CATV; movies; radios; phones. 3 2-bedrm units. Coin laundry. Indoor pool; whirlpool; exercise rm. 34 units with microwave & wet bar. AE, DI, DS, MC, VI. FAX (702) 753-7910   (S) (D) (702) 738-8787

Best Western Red Lion Motor Inn   Rates Subject to Change   *Motor Inn* ◆◆◆
All year   1P 55.00- 63.00   2P/1B   63.00- 73.00   2P/2B 63.00- 73.00 XP 10   F
151 units. I-80 exit 303. 2050 Idaho St. (89801) Large rooms. 12 refrigerators; A/C; C/CATV; movies; radios; phones; comb or shower baths. 17 2-bedrm units. Coin laundry. Pool open 6/1-9/15. Pets. AE, DI, DS, MC, VI. ● Coffeeshop; 24 hours in summer; $5-$10; cocktails. Casino. FAX (702) 738-1798 *(See ad p A3)*   (D) (702) 738-8421

Best Western The Marquis Motor Inn   Rates Subject to Change   *Motel* ◆◆◆
5/16-9/30   1P .... 49.00   2P/1B .... 54.00   2P/2B .... 59.00 XP 5
10/1-5/15   1P .... 44.00   2P/1B .... 49.00   2P/2B .... 54.00 XP 5
Senior discount. 49 units. 4 blks e on I-80 business rt. 837 Idaho St. (89801) Large rooms. 15 refrigerators; A/C; C/CATV; movies; phones. 3 2-bedrm units. Small pool open 6/1-9/15. AE, DI, DS, MC, VI. FAX (702) 738-0118   (D) (702) 738-7261

Econo Lodge   Rates Subject to Change   *Motel* ◆
All year   1P .... 35.00   2P/1B .... 40.00   2P/2B .... 45.00 XP 6   F
Senior discount. 61 units. S of I-80; exit 303, 1 mi w. 1785 Idaho St. (89801) 3-story no elevator. 21 refrigerators; A/C; C/CATV; radios; phones. Indoor whirlpool; small exercise room. No pets. Some microwaves avail. AE, DI, DS, MC, VI. FAX (702) 753-7347   ⊗ (S) (D) (702) 753-7747

Holiday Inn   AAA Special Value Rates   *Motor Inn* ◆◆◆
All year   1P 53.00- 63.00   2P/1B   61.00- 69.00   2P/2B 63.00- 75.00 XP 8   F
170 units. I-80 exit 303. 3015 Idaho St. (PO Box 1830, 89801) 7 refrigerators; A/C; C/CATV; movies; radios; phones. Coin laundry. Indoor pool; whirlpool; exercise rm. Pets. AE, DI, DS, MC, VI. ● Restaurant; 6 am-10 pm; $7-$16; cocktails. FAX (702) 753-7906 *(See ad p A3)*   ⊗ (D) (702) 738-8425

National 9 El Neva Motel   Rates Subject to Change   *Motel* ◆◆
5/16-9/10   1P 38.00- 44.00   2P/1B   38.00- 48.00   2P/2B 44.00- 54.00 XP 4   F
9/11-5/15   1P 29.00- 38.00   2P/1B   32.00- 42.00   2P/2B 36.00- 44.00 XP 4   F
Senior discount. 28 units. Eastbound I-80 exit 301; 1 1/2 mi s to Idaho St. 736 Idaho St. (89801) Refrigerators; A/C; C/CATV; movies; phones. Microwaves. Wkly rates avail in winter. AE, DI, DS, MC, VI. Restaurant opposite. FAX (702) 738-3447 *(See ad below)*   ⊗ (D) (702) 738-7152

National 9 Topper's Motel   Rates Subject to Change   *Motel* ◆◆
5/16-9/10   1P 38.00- 44.00   2P/1B   38.00- 48.00   2P/2B 44.00- 54.00 XP 4   F
9/11-5/15   1P 29.00- 38.00   2P/1B   32.00- 42.00   2P/2B 36.00- 44.00 XP 4   F
Senior discount. 33 units. S of I-80; exit 303, 3/4 mi w. 1500 Idaho St. (89801) Refrigerators; A/C; C/CATV; phones. Microwaves. AE, DI, DS, MC, VI. Coffeeshop adjacent. FAX (702) 753-9881 *(See ad below)* ⊗ (D) (702) 738-7245

Red Lion Inn & Casino   Rates Subject to Change   *Motor Inn* ◆
All year   1P 65.00- 73.00   2P/1B   75.00- 83.00   2P/2B 75.00- 83.00 XP 8   F
223 units. I-80 exit 303. 2065 Idaho St. (89801) Large rooms; A/C; C/CATV; movies; radios; phones. 2 2-bedrm units. Pool open 6/1-9/30. Airport transp. Pets. AE, DI, DS, MC, VI. ● Dining rm & coffeeshop; 24 hours; $9-$15; cocktails; entertainment. Casino. FAX (702) 753-9859 *(See ad p A3)*   ⊗ (S) (D) (702) 738-2111

Rodeway Inn   Rates Subject to Change   *Motel* ◆
5/15-9/4   1P 42.00- 46.00   2P/1B   46.00- 50.00   2P/2B 48.00- 54.00 XP 5   F
9/5-5/14   1P 35.00- 38.00   2P/1B   38.00- 42.00   2P/2B 44.00- 46.00 XP 5   F
Senior discount. 65 units. 1 mi e on I-80 business route. 1300 Idaho St. (89801) 13 refrigerators; A/C; C/CATV; phones. Pool open 5/25-9/15. Pets. Wkly rates avail. AE, DI, DS, MC, VI. Coffeeshop adjacent. FAX (702) 753-5076   ⊗ (D) (702) 738-7000

Shilo Inn   Rates Subject to Change   *Motel* ◆◆◆
5/16-9/6 [CP]   1P 72.00- 83.00   2P/1B   72.00- 83.00   2P/2B 72.00- 83.00 XP 10   F
9/7-5/15 [CP]   1P 62.00- 73.00   2P/1B   62.00- 73.00   2P/2B 62.00- 73.00 XP 10   F
Senior discount. 70 units. N of I-80, exit 301. 2401 Mountain City Hwy. (89801) Check-in 3 pm. Refrigerators; A/C; C/CATV; pay movies; radios; phones. 16 kitchens. Coin laundry. Indoor pool; sauna; whirlpool; steambaths & steamroom; exercise rm. Airport transp. Pets, $6 extra charge. Microwaves & wet bars. Kitchen units, $70-$110 for up to 2 persons. Wkly & monthly rates avail. AE, CB, DI, DS, VI. Coffeeshop opposite. FAX (702) 738-6247   ⊗ (S) (D) (702) 738-5522

Thunderbird Motel   Rates Subject to Change   *Motel* ◆◆◆
All year   1P 39.00- 43.00   2P/1B   43.00- 49.00   2P/2B 49.00- 57.00 XP 10   F
Senior discount. 70 units. On I-80 business rt. 345 Idaho St. (89801) A/C; C/CATV; movies; radios; phones. Pool open 6/1-9/30. Pets. AE, DI, DS, MC, VI. Restaurant opposite. *(See ad p A3)*   ⊗ (D) (702) 738-7115

RESTAURANT

Nevada Dinner House   Ethnic $$ ◆◆
2 blks s of I-80 business rt. 351 Silver St. Family-style meals; several choices of entree; also American cuisine comfortable seating. Basque cuisine. A/C. Children's menu. Open 5 pm-10 pm; Sun-9 pm; closed Mon, 11/25 & 12/25. Cocktails & lounge. AE, MC, VI.   **(702) 738-8485**

ELY — 5,300

Fireside Inn   Rates Subject to Change   *Motel*   ◆◆
All year   1P .... 34.00 .... 2P/2B .... 41.00 XP 4
Senior discount. 15 units. 3 mi n on US 93. McGill Hwy. (HC 33 Box 33400, 89301) A/C; C/TV; phones. 1 2-bedrm unit. Pets, $4 extra charge. Reserv deposit required. AE, DS, MC, VI. ● Restaurant, see separate listing.
     ⊗ Ⓓ **(702) 289-3765**

Steptoe Valley Inn   Rates Subject to Change   *Bed & Breakfast*   ◆◆
6/1-9/30 [BP]   1P .... 62.00 2P/1B .... 73.00 2P/2B 73.00- 80.00 XP 6
5 units. 3 blks n of US 93. 220 E 11th St. (PO Box 151110, 89315) OPEN 6/1-9/30. Reconstructed 1907 grocery store. Private balconies, landscaped yard with gazebo & lawn. Smoke free premises. Check-in 3 pm. A/C; C/CATV; shower or comb baths. No pets. Reserv deposit required. AE, MC, VI.   ⊗ Ⓓ **(702) 289-8687**

RESTAURANT

Fireside Inn Restaurant   American $$ ◆
In Fireside Inn. Varied menu, casual atmosphere, Italian specialties. Breakfast 6/1-10/31 only. A/C. Children's menu. Open 6 am-10 & 5-10 pm; Sun 6 am-11 & 5-10 pm; closed 11/25 & 12/25. Cocktails & lounge. Reserv advised. AE, DS, MC, VI.   **(702) 289-3765**

FALLON — 6,400

Comfort Inn   Rates Subject to Change   *Motel*   ◆◆
4/1-9/30 [CP]   1P 46.00- 51.00 2P/1B 51.00- 56.00 2P/2B .... 60.00 XP 5   F
49 units. On US 50; 5 blks w of jct US 95. 1830 W Williams Ave. (89406) OPEN ALL YEAR. Check-in 3 pm. 12 refrigerators; A/C; C/CATV; pay movies; radios; phones. Small pool; whirlpool. No pets. 6 rooms with whirlpool bath, $56-$75 for 2 persons. Reserv deposit required. AE, DI, DS, MC, VI. Coffeeshop opposite. FAX (702) 423-0663
     ⊗ Ⓢ Ⓓ Ⓛ **(702) 423-5554**

Lariat Motel   Rates Guaranteed   *Motel*   ◆◆
All year   .... 2P/1B 34.00- 36.00 2P/2B 38.00- 40.00 XP 4
18 units. 8 blks w on US 50 & 95. 850 W Williams Ave. (PO Box 649, 89406) Some large rooms. A/C; C/CATV; radios; phones; shower baths. Pool. No pets. 1 unit with 3-beds, $50 for up to 6 persons. Reserv deposit required. MC, VI. Restaurant opposite.   ⊗ Ⓓ **(702) 423-3181**

Western Motel   Rates Guaranteed   *Motel*   ◆◆
All year   1P .... 32.00 2P/1B .... 36.00 2P/2B .... 38.00 XP 5
Senior discount. 22 units. 1 blk off US 50 & 95. 125 S Carson St. (PO Box 290, 89406) 16 refrigerators; A/C; C/CATV; movies; phones; comb or shower baths. Small pool. Wkly rates avail. Reserv deposit required. AE, CB, DI, MC, VI. Restaurant opposite.   Ⓓ **(702) 423-5118**

FERNLEY

Super 8 Motel   Rates Subject to Change   *Motel*   ◆
All year   1P .... 37.88 2P/1B .... 40.88 2P/2B .... 43.88 XP 3
Senior discount. 36 units. Adjacent & s of I-80, exit 48. 1350 Newlands Dr. (89408) A/C; C/CATV; phones. No pets. AE, DI, DS, MC, VI. Coffeeshop adjacent.   ⊗ Ⓓ Ⓛ **(702) 575-5555**

GARDNERVILLE — 2,600

Topaz Lodge   Rates Subject to Change   *Motel*   ◆◆
All year   1P 39.00- 48.00 2P/1B 39.00- 48.00 2P/2B 39.00- 48.00 XP 2
59 units. 22 mi s on US 395S, at Topaz Lake. 1979 US 395S. (PO Box 187, 89410) All rooms with view of Topaz Lake. A/C; C/CATV; movies; phones; comb or shower baths. Small pool; playground. Pets, $5 deposit required. AE, DS, MC, VI. ● Coffeeshop; 24 hours; $6-$9; casino; cocktails. FAX (702) 266-3338   Ⓓ Ⓛ **(702) 266-3338**

Westerner Motel   Rates Subject to Change   *Motel*   ◆◆
4/1-10/31   1P .... 35.00 2P/1B .... 40.00 2P/2B .... 43.00 XP 3- 5
11/1-03/31   1P .... 30.00 2P/1B .... 32.00 2P/2B .... 34.00 XP 3- 5
25 units. 3/4 mi s on US 395. 1353 US 395S. (PO Box 335, 89410) A/C; C/CATV; phones. Pool. Reserv deposit required. AE, DS, MC, VI.   ⊗ Ⓓ **(702) 782-3602**

HAWTHORNE — 3,700

El Capitan Motor Lodge   Rates Subject to Change   *Motor Inn*   ◆◆
All year   1P 28.00- 32.00 2P/1B 35.00- 38.00 2P/2B 38.00- 42.00 XP 5   F
103 units. 1 blk off US 95. 540 F St. (PO Box 1000, 89415) Refrigerators; A/C; C/CATV; phones. 4 2-bedrm units. Pool. Pets, $10 deposit required. Reserv deposit required. AE, DI, DS, MC, VI. ● Restaurant; 24 hours; $6-$15; cocktails. Casino. FAX (702) 324-6229   Ⓓ **(702) 945-3321**

HENDERSON — 80,400

Best Western Lake Mead Motel   Rates Subject to Change   *Motel*   ◆◆
All year   1P 37.00- 51.00 2P/1B 42.00- 56.00 2P/2B 42.00- 56.00 XP 5   F
Senior discount. 58 units. On SR 146; 1/2 mi w off Boulder Hwy, US 93 & 95. 85 W Lake Mead Dr. (89015) 42 refrigerators; A/C; C/CATV; movies; phones. Coin laundry. Small pool. No pets. Wkly & monthly rates avail. Reserv deposit required. AE, DI, DS, MC, VI. FAX (702) 564-7642   ⊗ Ⓓ **(702) 564-1712**

INDIAN SPRINGS

Indian Springs Motor Hotel   Rates Subject to Change   *Motel*   ◆
All year   1P .... 35.00 2P/1B .... 35.00 2P/2B .... 37.00 XP
45 units. On US 95, 45 mi n of Las Vegas. (PO Box 270, 89018) A/C; C/TV; phones. Coin laundry. Pets, $6 extra charge. AE, DI, DS, MC, VI. ● Coffeeshop; 6 am-10 pm; $7-$10; cocktail lounge. 24 hour casino.
     Ⓓ Ⓛ **(702) 879-3700**

JACKPOT

Cactus Pete's Resort Casino
Rates Subject to Change — Hotel ◆◆◆◆

		1P		2P/1B		2P/2B		XP
5/21-11/28	1P	45.00-	90.00	2P/1B	45.00- 90.00	2P/2B	45.00- 90.00	XP 10
2/14-5/20	1P	40.00-	80.00	2P/1B	40.00- 80.00	2P/2B	40.00- 80.00	XP 10
11/29-2/13	1P	35.00-	65.00	2P/1B	35.00- 65.00	2P/2B	35.00- 65.00	XP 10

290 units. On SR 93. (PO Box 508, 89825) Check-in 4 pm. A/C; C/CATV; movies; radios; phones; comb or shower baths. Pool; whirlpool; lighted tennis-4 courts. Fee for: golf-18 holes. Parking lot. No pets. 4 units with whirlpool bath & wet bar, $100-$125 for 2 persons. Reserv deposit required. AE, DI, DS, MC, VI. ● Dining rm, 2 restaurants & coffeeshop; 24 hours; $11-$20; buffet 5 pm-10 pm, $6-$8; casino; cocktails; entertainment. FAX (702) 755-2737 ⊗ Ⓢ Ⓓ Ⓚ (702) 755-2321

Horseshu Hotel & Casino
Rates Subject to Change — Motel ◆◆◆

		1P		2P/1B		2P/2B		XP
5/21-11/28	1P	35.00-	60.00	2P/1B	35.00- 60.00	2P/2B	35.00- 60.00	XP 10
2/14-5/20	1P	30.00-	55.00	2P/1B	30.00- 55.00	2P/2B	30.00- 55.00	XP 10
11/29-2/13	1P	25.00-	50.00	2P/1B	25.00- 50.00	2P/2B	25.00- 50.00	XP 10

120 units. On Hwy 93. Dice Rd. (PO Box 508, 89825) A/C; C/CATV; radios; phones. Pool. Fee for: golf-18 holes. Pets. Reserv deposit required. AE, DI, DS, MC, VI. ● Restaurant; 24 hours; $4-$10; casino; cocktails. ⊗ Ⓓ (702) 755-7777

JEAN

Primadonna Resort & Casino
Rates Subject to Change — Motor Inn ◆◆

	1P		2P/1B		2P/2B		XP	
Fri & Sat	1P	.... 31.00	2P/1B	.... 31.00	2P/2B	.... 31.00	XP 5	F
Sun-Thurs	1P	.... 18.00	2P/1B	.... 18.00	2P/2B	.... 18.00	XP 5	F

661 units. E of & adjacent to I-15, State Line exit, 45 mi s of Las Vegas. (PO Box 95997, Las Vegas, 89193) Ferris wheel, carousel & monorail. Check-in 3 pm. A/C; C/CATV; pay movies; radios; phones. Pool; whirlpool; putting green. No pets. 2-night minimum stay Fri & Sat; for up to 4 persons. AE, DI, DS, MC, VI. ● Restaurant & coffeeshop; 24 hours; $5-$13.50; buffet, $3-$4; casino; cocktails; entertainment. FAX (702) 874-1749 ⊗ Ⓢ Ⓓ (702) 382-1212

Whiskey Pete's Hotel & Casino
Rates Subject to Change — Motor Inn ◆◆

	1P		2P/1B		2P/2B		XP
Fri & Sat	1P	.... 31.00	2P/1B	.... 31.00	2P/2B	.... 31.00	XP 5
Sun-Thurs	1P	.... 18.00	2P/1B	.... 18.00	2P/2B	.... 18.00	XP 5

258 units. W of & adjacent to I-15, State line exit, 45 mi s of Las Vegas. (PO Box 93718, 89193) Check-in 3 pm. A/C; C/CATV; pay movies; phones. Pool; wading pool; whirlpool. No pets. Maximum 4 persons per room. 2-day minimum stay Fri-Sat. AE, DI, DS, MC, VI. ● Restaurant & coffeeshop; 24 hours; $5-$13.50; buffet, $3.80; Casino; cocktails; entertainment. FAX (702) 874-1554 ⊗ Ⓢ Ⓓ Ⓚ (702) 382-4388

LAKE MEAD NATIONAL RECREATION AREA — See BOULDER CITY, COTTONWOOD COVE, ECHO BAY & LAUGHLIN

LAKE TAHOE — See CALIFORNIA

LAS VEGAS — 258,300   (See LAS VEGAS AREA spotting map page A560; see index below)

Most establishments in Las Vegas do not confirm advance reservations at a definite rate. Advance reservations for Saturday only are extremely difficult.

Index of Establishments on the LAS VEGAS AREA Spotting Map

AAA Plus provides you extended services like up to 100 miles of towing free.

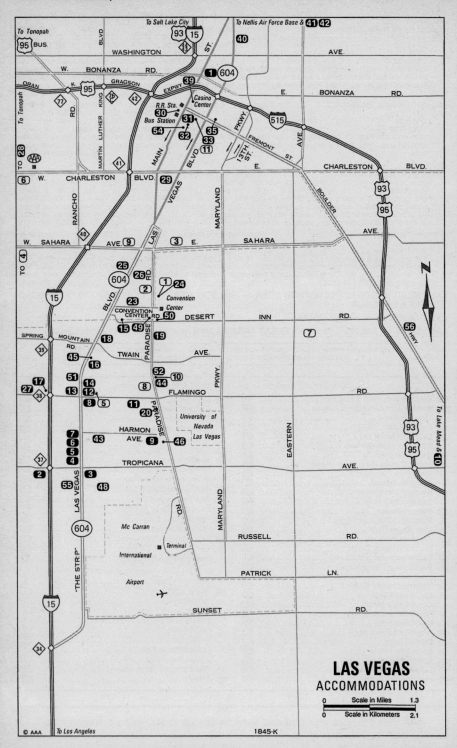

LAS VEGAS
ACCOMMODATIONS

Scale in Miles

Scale in Kilometers

© AAA   To Los Angeles   1845-K

(See LAS VEGAS spotting map page A560)

Alexis Park Resort Hotel **9**   Rates Subject to Change   *Resort Hotel*   ◆◆◆
All year   1P 95.00- 585.00   2P/1B   95.00- 585.00   2P/2B   95.00- 585.00 XP 15
Senior discount. 500 units. I-15 exit e Tropicana Ave; 2 blks w UNLV, 2 mi s of Convention Center. 375 E Harmon Ave. (89109) Spacious landscaped grounds. All units with wet bar. 1- & 2-bedroom suites many with gas fireplace. Check-in 4 pm. Refrigerators; A/C; C/CATV; free & pay movies; radios; phones. 3 pools; saunas; whirlpools; putting green; lighted tennis-2 courts; 250 rooms with whirlpool. Fee for: health club & massage. Parking lot. 12 2-bedroom, 2-story suites; $335-$1150 for up to 4 persons. Reserv deposit required. AE, DI, DS, MC, VI. ● Restaurant & coffeeshop; 6 am-midnight; $12-$80; 24 hours room service; cocktails; entertainment. FAX (702) 796-4334 ⊗ Ⓢ Ⓓ (702) 796-3300

Arizona Charlie's Hotel **28**   Rates Subject to Change   *Motor Inn*   ◆◆
⊕ Fri-Sat   1P .... 40.00   2P/1B   .... 40.00   2P/2B   .... 40.00 XP 4
  Sun-Thurs   1P .... 28.00   2P/1B   .... 28.00   2P/2B   .... 28.00 XP 4
100 units. 1 mi nw of I-15; Charleston Blvd exit. 740 S Decatur Blvd, at Evergreen Ave. (89107) Old West atmosphere. A/C; C/TV; phones. Small pool. No pets. AE, DI, DS, MC, VI. ● Coffeeshop; 24 hour; $7-$11; buffet, $4; Casino; cocktail lounge. FAX (702) 258-5196   ⊗ Ⓢ Ⓓ (702) 258-5111

Bally's Casino Resort-Las Vegas **8**   Rates Subject to Change   *Hotel*   ◆◆◆
● All year   1P 84.00- 175.00   2P/1B   84.00- 175.00   2P/2B   84.00- 175.00 XP 15   F
2827 units. 4 1/2 mi s on the Strip. 3645 Las Vegas Blvd S. (PO Box 96505, 89109) Check-in 3 pm. A/C; C/CATV; pay movies; radios; phones. 2827 3-bedrm units. Pool; sauna; whirlpool; tennis-10 courts, 4 lighted. Fee for: health club. Valet parking lot. No pets. Reserv deposit required. AE, DI, DS, MC, VI. ● 4 restaurants & 3 coffeeshops; 24 hrs; $8-$34; casino; cocktails; name entertainment. FAX (702) 739-4405 ⊗ Ⓢ Ⓓ Ⓛ (702) 739-4111

Barbary Coast Hotel **12**   Rates Subject to Change   *Hotel*   ◆◆◆
  Fri & Sat   1P .... 75.00   2P/1B   .... 75.00   2P/2B   .... 75.00 XP 5
  Sun-Thurs   1P .... 50.00   2P/1B   .... 50.00   2P/2B   .... 50.00 XP 5
200 units. 1 3/4 mi s on the Strip. 3595 Las Vegas Blvd S. (PO Box 19030, 89132) Gay 90's decor. A/C; C/CATV; free & pay movies; radios; phones. Parking ramp. No pets. 12 suites $150-$350 for up to 2 persons. Reserv deposit required. AE, DI, DS. ● Restaurant & coffeeshop; 24 hours; $7-$20; cocktails. Casino. FAX (702) 737-6304
                                                                ⊗ Ⓢ Ⓓ Ⓛ (702) 737-7111

Barcelona Motel **42**   Rates Subject to Change   *Motor Inn*   ◆
⊕ Fri & Sat   1P .... 45.00   2P/1B   .... 49.50   2P/2B   .... 50.00 XP 5
  Sun-Thurs   1P .... 35.00   2P/1B   .... 42.50   2P/2B   .... 42.50 XP 5
Senior discount. 179 units. 7 mi ne; 1/2 mi from Nellis AFB; I-15 exit 48 via Craig Rd. 5011 E Craig Rd. (89115) 112 refrigerators; A/C; C/TV; pay movies; phones; comb or shower baths. 83 kitchens, no utensils. Coin laundry. Small pool; whirlpool. Pets, $20 extra charge. Wkly & monthly rates avail. Reserv deposit required. AE, DI, DS, MC, VI. ● Coffeeshop; 24 hours; $6-$10; cocktails. Small casino. FAX (702) 644-6510   ⊗ Ⓓ (702) 644-6300

Best Western Main Street Inn **1**   Rates Subject to Change   *Motor Inn*   ◆◆
⊕ Fri & Sat   1P 50.00- 58.00   ....   2P/2B   55.00- 60.00 XP 7
  Sun-Thurs 5/27-8/29   1P 40.00- 48.00   ....   2P/2B   45.00- 50.00 XP 7
  Sun-Thurs 8/30-5/26   1P 39.00- 44.00   ....   2P/2B   44.00- 46.00 XP 7
Senior discount. 91 units. I-15N, exit 43E; I-15S, exit 44E. 1000 N Main St. (89101) Formerly Best Western Downtown Convention Center Inn. 13 refrigerators; A/C; C/TV; radios; phones. Coin laundry. Small pool. Pets, $7. Reserv deposit required. AE, DI, DS, MC, VI. ● Restaurant; 24 hours; $8-$12; cocktail lounge. Ⓓ (702) 382-3455

Best Western Mardi Gras Inn **19**   AAA Special Value Rates   *Motor Inn*   ◆◆
⊕ 12/28-12/31   1P 78.00- 88.00   2P/1B   88.00- 98.00   ....   XP 6   F
  1/1-5/31 & 9/1-11/30   1P 51.00- 61.00   2P/1B   57.00- 67.00   ....   XP 6   F
  6/1-8/31   1P 50.00- 60.00   2P/1B   50.00- 60.00   ....   XP 6   F
  12/1-12/27   1P 40.00- 48.00   2P/1B   40.00- 48.00   ....   XP 6
314 units. 1/2 mi s of Convention Center. 3500 Paradise Rd. (89109) Refrigerators; A/C; C/CATV; free & pay movies; radios; phones. Coin laundry. Pool; whirlpool. Airport transp. No pets. AE, DI, DS, MC, VI. ● Restaurant; 6:30 am-11 pm; $9-$14; cocktails. Slot casino. FAX (702) 733-6994 *(See ad below)*
                                                                   Ⓓ (702) 731-2020

(See LAS VEGAS spotting map page A560)

Best Western Nellis Motor Inn 41 | Rates Subject to Change | *Motel* ◆◆
Fri & Sat 5/25-9/3	1P 49.50	2P/1B 54.00	2P/2B 54.00	XP 6	F
Fri & Sat 9/4-5/24	1P 47.00	2P/1B 51.00	2P/2B 51.00	XP 6	F
Sun-Thurs 5/25-9/3	1P 43.00	2P/1B 49.50	2P/2B 49.50	XP 6	F
Sun-Thurs 9/4-5/24	1P 38.50	2P/1B 44.00	2P/2B 44.00	XP 6	F

Senior discount. 52 units. 7 mi ne; 1/4 mi from Nellis AFB; exit I-15, exit 48 e. 5330 E Craig Rd. (89115) A/C; C/CATV; free & pay movies; phones. Coin laundry. Pool; playground. Pets, $50 also $6 daily deposit required. Reserv deposit required. AE, DI, DS, MC, VI. Coffeeshop opposite. *(See ad p A561)*   ⊗ Ⓓ (702) 643-6111

Best Western Parkview Inn 40 | Rates Subject to Change | *Motel* ◆◆
Fri & Sat	1P 48.00	2P/1B 52.00	2P/2B 58.00	XP 6	
Sun-Thurs 5/27-8/29	1P 40.00	2P/1B 42.00	2P/2B 50.00	XP 6	
Sun-Thurs 8/30-5/26	1P 38.00	2P/1B 40.00	2P/2B 44.00	XP 6	

Senior discount. 56 units. 8 blks n on US 91 & 93. 905 Las Vegas Blvd N. (89101) A/C; C/TV; radios; phones. Coin laundry. Small pool. Pets, $6 daily extra charge. Reserv deposit required; 14 days refund notice. AE, DI, DS, MC, VI.   ⊗ Ⓓ (702) 385-1213

Blair House Hotel 15 | Rates Subject to Change | *Apartment Motel* ◆◆
Fri & Sat [CP]	1P 75.00	2P/1B 75.00	2P/2B 75.00	XP 10	F
Sun-Thurs [CP]	1P 55.00	2P/1B 55.00	2P/2B 55.00	XP 10	F

Senior discount. 224 units. Exit I-15 at Sahara to Strip, 1/4 mi e. 344 E Desert Inn Rd. (89109) Check-in 3 pm. A/C; C/CATV; free & pay movies; phones. Kitchens. Coin laundry. Pool; whirlpool. No pets. Reserv deposit required. AE, DI, DS, MC, VI. FAX (702) 792-9042   ⊗ Ⓢ Ⓓ (702) 792-2222

Boardwalk Hotel-Casino 6 | AAA Special Value Rates | *Motor Inn* ◆◆
Sat	1P 48.00- 90.00	2P/1B 48.00- 90.00	2P/2B 48.00- 90.00	XP 6	F
Sun-Fri	1P 34.00	2P/1B 34.00	2P/2B 34.00	XP 6	F

201 units. 4 3/4 mi s on the Strip. 3750 Las Vegas Blvd S. (89109) A/C; C/CATV; pay movies; 120 radios; phones. Coin laundry. 2 pools. Pets, $50 deposit, also $10 daily extra charge. AE, DI, DS, MC, VI. ● 2 coffeeshops; 24 hours; a la carte entrees about $5-$11; cocktails. Casino. FAX (702) 739-8152   ⊗ Ⓓ ⅃ (702) 735-1167

Caesars Palace 13 | Rates Subject to Change | *Hotel* ◆◆◆◆
All year	1P 95.00-160.00	2P/1B 110.00-175.00	2P/2B 120.00-175.00	XP 20	F

1515 units. 4 1/2 mi s on the Strip, I-15 exit E Flamingo Rd. 3570 Las Vegas Blvd S. (89109) Attractively landscaped grounds & marble statuary. Large rooms. The forum shops common areas that resemble Roman streetscape, elegant shopping mall. Check-in 3 pm. A/C; C/CATV; movies; radios; phones. 2 pools, 1 htd; sauna; whirlpool; tennis-4 courts, 2 lighted. Fee for: health club. Valet ramp & parking lot. No pets. Reserv deposit required. AE, DS, MC, VI. ● 7 restaurants & coffeeshop; 24 hours; $10-$60; buffet, $12; casino; cocktail lounge; name entertainment. 24 hour room service. FAX (702) 731-6636   Ⓢ Ⓓ ⅃ (702) 731-7110

California Hotel 39 | Rates Subject to Change | *Hotel* ◆◆
Fri & Sat	1P 50.00	2P/1B 50.00	2P/2B 50.00	XP 5	
Sun-Thurs	1P 40.00	2P/1B 40.00	2P/2B 40.00	XP 5	

650 units. In downtown Casino Center Area. 1st & Ogden. (PO Box 630, 89125) A/C; C/TV; phones. Swimming pool open 4/1-10/31. Valet garage & parking lot. No pets. Reserv deposit required. AE, DI, DS, MC, VI. ● 2 restaurants & coffeeshop; 24 hours; $8-$25; cocktails. Casino. FAX (702) 388-2610   Ⓢ Ⓓ ⅃ (702) 385-1222

Carriage House 43 | AAA Special Value Rates | *Apartment* ◆◆
All year	1P 85.00-190.00	2P/1B 85.00-190.00	2P/2B 85.00-190.00	XP	

143 units. 1 blk e off the strip. 105 E Harmon Ave. (89109) Check-in 3 pm. A/C; C/CATV; free & pay movies; radios; phones; comb or shower baths. 15 2-bedrm units, 91 kitchens, 15 efficiencies. Coin laundry. Pool; whirlpool; lighted tennis-1 court. Airport transp. No pets. 15, 2-bedroom units, $190-$245 for 2-8 persons. Reserv deposit required. AE, DI, DS, MC, VI. ● Restaurant; 7 am-10 & 5:30-11 pm; $9-$16; cocktails. FAX (702) 798-1020 *(See ad below)*   ⊗ Ⓢ Ⓓ (702) 798-1020

Center Strip Inn 7 | Rates Subject to Change | *Motel* ◆◆
Fri & Sat [CP]	1P 49.95- 69.95	2P/1B 59.95- 69.95	2P/2B 69.95- 89.95	XP 10	
Sun-Thurs [CP]	1P 29.95- 39.95	2P/1B 39.95- 49.95	2P/2B 39.95- 59.95	XP 10	

92 units. 4 1/2 mi s on the Strip. 3688 Las Vegas Blvd S. (89109) Refrigerators; A/C; C/TV; movies; VCPs. Radios; phones. 4 2-bedrm units. Coin laundry. Pool. No pets. Wkly rates avail. Reserv deposit required. AE, DI, MC, VI. Coffeeshop adjacent. FAX (702) 736-2521 *(See ad p A563)*   Ⓓ (702) 739-6066

Center Strip Travelodge 45 | Rates Subject to Change | *Motel* ◆◆◆
8/15-5/31	1P 49.00	2P/1B 49.00	2P/2B 59.00	XP 7	F
6/1-8/14	1P 39.00	2P/1B 39.00	2P/2B 49.00	XP 7	F

Senior discount. 160 units. 4 mi s on the Strip. 3419 Las Vegas Blvd S. (89109) A/C; C/TV; pay movies; radios; phones. Pool. No pets. Reserv deposit required. AE, DI, DS, MC, VI. Restaurant adjacent. FAX (702) 737-9165   ⊗ Ⓓ (702) 734-6801

(See LAS VEGAS spotting map page A560)

Circus Circus Hotel **25**   Rates Subject to Change   *Hotel*   ◆◆
  All year   1P 30.00- 50.00 2P/1B 30.00- 50.00 2P/2B 30.00- 50.00 XP 6   F
2793 units. 2 3/4 mi s on the Strip. 2880 Las Vegas Blvd S. (PO Box 14967, 89114) Credit cards are not accepted to
guarantee reservations. A/C; C/TV; phones; comb or shower baths. 3 pools; whirlpool; circus entertainment 11 am-
midnight. Valet ramp & parking lot. No pets. Reserv deposit required. ● 3 restaurants & 2 coffeeshops; 24 hours; $5-
$18; buffet, $4; cocktails. Casino. FAX (702) 734-5897   ⊗ Ⓢ Ⓓ 🅰 🄳 (702) 734-0410

Comfort Inn South **48**   Rates Subject to Change   *Motel*   ◆◆
🅰🅰 Fri & Sat [CP]   1P .... 55.00 2P/1B .... 60.00 2P/2B .... 60.00 XP 5   F
  Sun-Thurs [CP]   1P .... 38.00 2P/1B .... 42.00 2P/2B .... 42.00 XP 5   F
Senior discount. 106 units. 1/2 mi e of I-15; Tropicana Ave exit. 5075 S Koval Ln. (89109) A/C; C/CATV; movies;
phones. Small pool. No pets. Monthly rates avail. Reserv deposit required. AE, DI, DS, MC, VI. FAX (702) 736-0726
                                                                      ⊗ 🄳 (702) 736-3600

The **Resorts Index** specializes in lodgings with extensive on-premises recreational facilities.

(See LAS VEGAS spotting map page A560)

Courtyard By Marriott 🆔   Rates Subject to Change   *Motor Inn* ◆◆◆
All year   1P .... 82.00 2P/1B .... 92.00 2P/2B .... 92.00 XP   F
149 units. 3 blks e off strip; 1 blk to convention center. 3275 Paradise Rd. (89109) Attractively decorated rooms. Check-in 3 pm. A/C; C/TV; free & pay movies; radios; phones. Coin laundry. Pool; whirlpool; exercise rm. Airport transp. No pets. AE, DI, DS, MC, VI. ● Restaurant; 6:30 am-2 & 5-10 pm; $8-$16; cocktails. FAX (702) 796-7981 *(See ad p A563)*
⊗ Ⓢ Ⓓ 🅙 (702) 791-3600

Days Inn Downtown 🆔   Rates Subject to Change   *Motel* ◆
🆔 Fri & Sat   1P .... 50.00 2P/1B .... 60.00 2P/2B .... 60.00 XP 10
Sun-Thurs   1P .... 36.00 2P/1B .... 46.00 2P/2B .... 46.00 XP 10
Senior discount. 147 units. On US 93 & 95 business rt. 707 E Fremont St. (89101) Few small rooms. A/C; C/CATV; phones. Pool. No pets. 7 1-bedroom suites, $60-$110. Reserv deposit required. AE, DI, DS, MC, VI. Coffeeshop; 24 hours; $3-$5; cocktails. Slot casino. FAX (702) 388-9622
⊗ Ⓓ (702) 388-1400

Desert Inn Hotel and Casino 🆔   Rates Guaranteed   *Resort Complex* ◆◆◆
🆔 9/1-5/31   1P 90.00- 175.00 2P/1B 90.00- 175.00 2P/2B 90.00- 175.00 XP 15   F
6/1-8/31   1P 75.00- 150.00 2P/1B 75.00- 150.00 2P/2B 75.00- 150.00 XP 15   F
821 units. On the Strip; I-15 northbound exit e Flamingo Ave, southbound exit e Sahara Ave. 3145 Las Vegas Blvd S. (89109) Attractive landscaped grounds. Check-in 3 pm. Refrigerators; A/C; C/CATV; pay movies; radios; phones. 95 2-bedrm units. Htd pool; sauna; whirlpool; lighted tennis-10 courts; jogging track. Fee for: golf-18 holes, spa; health club. Valet parking lot. No pets. Reserv deposit required. AE, DI, DS, MC, VI. ● Dining rm, 2 restaurants & coffeeshop; 24 hours; $8-$34; casino; 24 hour room service; cocktails; name entertainment. A *Preferred Hotel.* FAX (702) 733-4774
Ⓓ 🅙 (702) 733-4444

Econo Lodge 🆔   AAA Special Value Rates   *Motel* ◆
🆔 Fri & Sat   1P 45.00- 50.00 2P/1B 50.00- 55.00 2P/2B .... 55.00 XP 10
Sun-Thurs   1P 35.00- 40.00 2P/1B 40.00- 45.00 2P/2B .... 45.00 XP 10
128 units. 1/2 blk s of Charleston Blvd; halfway between the strip & the downtown Casino Center. 1150 Las Vegas Blvd S. (89104) A/C; C/TV; VCPs; phones. 3 kitchens, no utensils. Small pool. Limited parking lot. No pets. AE, DI, DS, MC, VI. FAX (702) 382-9180
⊗ Ⓓ (702) 382-6001

Econo Lodge-Downtown 🆔   Rates Subject to Change   *Motel* ◆
🆔 Fri & Sat   1P .... 38.00 2P/1B .... 38.00 2P/2B .... 48.00 XP 5   F
Sun-Thurs   1P .... 32.00 2P/1B .... 32.00 2P/2B .... 38.00 XP 5   F
Senior discount. 48 units. Exit I-15 downtown Casino Center. 520 S Casino Center Blvd. (89101) Refrigerators; A/C; C/TV; phones. 4 kitchens, no utensils. Coin laundry. No pets. 4 1-bedroom apartments, $69-$95 for up to 4 persons. Reserv deposit required; 3 days refund notice. AE, DI, DS, MC, VI. FAX (702) 384-8580
⊗ Ⓓ (702) 384-8211

Emerald Springs Inn 🆔   Rates Subject to Change   *Motor Inn* ◆◆◆
🆔 All year [CP]   1P 49.00- 165.00 2P/1B 49.00- 165.00 2P/2B 49.00- 165.00 XP 15   F
150 units. I-15 exit E Flamingo Rd. 325 E Flamingo Rd. (89109) Refrigerators; A/C; C/CATV; free & pay movies; radios; phones. Pool; whirlpool; exercise rm. Airport transp. No pets. AE, DI, DS, MC, VI. ● Restaurant; 6:30 am-2 pm; $10-$20; cocktails. FAX (702) 731-9784 *(See ad below)*
⊗ Ⓢ Ⓓ 🅙 (702) 732-9100

Excalibur Hotel & Casino 🆔   Rates Subject to Change   *Hotel* ◆◆◆
🆔 Fri & Sat   1P 60.00- 70.00 2P/1B 60.00- 70.00 2P/2B 60.00- 70.00 XP 7   F
Sun-Thurs   1P 39.00- 47.00 2P/1B 39.00- 47.00 2P/2B 39.00- 47.00 XP 7   F
4032 units. 5 1/2 mi s on the strip; I-15 exit E Tropicana Ave. 3850 Las Vegas Blvd S. (PO Box 96778, 89193) Medieval castle theme. A/C; C/TV; pay movies; phones; shower baths. 2 htd pools. Valet parking lot. Pets. Rooms with whirlpool bath, $110 for up to 2 persons. Reserv deposit required. AE, DI, DS, MC, VI. ● Dining rm, 5 restaurants & coffeeshop; 24 hours; $5-$30; buffet, $5; casino; cocktails; entertainment. 24 hour room service. FAX (702) 597-7009
⊗ Ⓢ Ⓓ (702) 597-7777

Fairfield Inn by Marriott 🆔   Rates Subject to Change   *Motel* ◆◆
9/1-2/1   1P .... 50.95 2P/1B .... 56.95 2P/2B .... 56.95 XP 3   F
2/2-6/1   1P .... 47.95 2P/1B .... 53.95 2P/2B .... 53.95 XP 3   F
6/2-8/31   1P .... 43.95 2P/1B .... 49.95 2P/2B .... 49.95 XP 3   F
Senior discount. 129 units. I-15 exit E Flamingo Rd; 3 blks n of convention center. 3850 Paradise Rd. (89109) Check-in 3 pm. A/C; C/CATV; movies; radios; phones. Pool; whirlpool. Airport transp. No pets. AE, DI, DS, MC, VI. Restaurant adjacent. FAX (702) 791-0899 *(See ad p A563)*
⊗ Ⓢ Ⓓ (702) 791-0899

(See LAS VEGAS spotting map page A560)

Flamingo Hilton-Las Vegas 🔢14 ◆◆◆
All year Rates Subject to Change *Hotel*
1P 72.00- 122.00 2P/1B 72.00- 122.00 2P/2B 72.00- 122.00 XP 16 F
3529 units. 4 mi s on the Strip. 3555 Las Vegas Blvd S. (89109) Many tower, few garden rooms. 180 refrigerators; A/C; C/CATV; pay movies; radios; phones. 2 pools; whirlpool. Fee for: lighted tennis-4 courts; steamroom; health club & massage. Valet ramp & parking lot. No pets. Reserv deposit required; 3 days refund notice. AE, DI, DS. ● 5 restaurants & cafeteria; 24 hours; $7-$20; buffet, $5-$8; cocktails; entertainment. Casino.
FAX (702) 733-3528 Ⓢ Ⓓ (702) 733-3111

Four Queens Hotel 🔢33 ◆◆◆
9/29-5/28 & Fri-Sat Rates Subject to Change *Hotel*
1P 47.00- 57.00 2P/1B 47.00- 57.00 2P/2B 47.00- 57.00 XP 8 F
Sun-Thurs 5/29-9/28 1P .... 47.00 2P/1B .... 47.00 2P/2B .... 47.00 XP 8 F
Senior discount. 709 units. In downtown Casino Center area. 202 E Fremont St. (89101) Check-in 4 pm. A/C; C/TV; pay movies; phones; comb or shower baths. Valet garage. No pets. 38 suites, $85-$95 for up to 2 persons. Reserv deposit required. AE, DI, DS, MC, VI. ● Restaurant & coffeeshop; 24 hours; $7-$29; casino; cocktails; entertainment. FAX (702) 383-0631 Ⓢ Ⓓ ♿ (702) 385-4011

Gold Coast Hotel 🔢27 ◆◆◆
 Rates Guaranteed *Hotel*
Fri & Sat 1P .... 50.00 2P/1B .... 50.00 2P/2B .... 50.00 XP
Sun-Thurs 1P .... 35.00 2P/1B .... 35.00 2P/2B .... 35.00 XP
722 units. 1 blk w of I-15, exit Flamingo Rd W. 4000 W Flamingo Rd. (PO Box 80750, 89180) Colonial-Spanish architecture. A/C; C/CATV; free & pay movies; radios; phones. Pool; whirlpool. Fee for: bowling, movie theaters. Valet ramp & parking lot. No pets. 18 suites with wet bar & refrigerator, $100-$150 for 2 persons. Reserv deposit required. AE, DI, DS, MC, VI. ● Dining rm, restaurant & coffeeshop; 24 hours; $5-$17; buffet, $6; cocktails; entertainment. Casino.
FAX (702) 367-8575 ⊗ Ⓢ Ⓓ (702) 367-7111

Golden Nugget Hotel 🔢31 ◆◆◆◆
All year AAA Special Value Rates *Hotel*
1P 58.00- 130.00 2P/1B 58.00- 130.00 2P/2B 58.00- 130.00 XP 12 F
1907 units. In downtown Casino Center area. 129 E Fremont St. (PO Box 2016, 89125) Large rooms, attractive contemporary decor. A/C; C/CATV; radios; phones. Pool; whirlpool; video arcade. Fee for: steamroom; health club & massage. Valet parking ramp. No pets. 1 & 2-bedroom suites, $210-$300 for 2 persons. Reserv deposit required. AE, DI, DS, MC, VI. ● 2 dining rms, restaurant & coffeeshop; 24 hours; $10-$35; buffet $10;24 hour room service; cocktails; name entertainment. Casino. FAX (702) 386-8362 Ⓢ Ⓓ (702) 385-7111

Harrah's-Las Vegas 🔢16 ◆◆◆
Fri & Sat 2/12-5/30 & 9/3-11/4 Rates Subject to Change *Hotel*
1P 95.00- 120.00 2P/1B 95.00- 120.00 2P/2B 95.00- 120.00 XP 10
Fri & Sat 2/1-2/11, 5/31-9/12 &
11/5-1/31 1P 92.00- 118.00 2P/1B 92.00- 118.00 2P/2B 92.00- 118.00 XP 10
Sun-Thurs 2/12-5/30 & 9/3-11/4 1P 75.00- 100.00 2P/1B 75.00- 100.00 2P/2B 75.00- 100.00 XP 10
Sun-Thurs 2/1-2/11, 5/31-9/2 &
11/15-1/31 1P 62.00- 88.00 2P/1B 62.00- 88.00 2P/2B 62.00- 88.00 XP 10
Senior discount. 1725 units. 4 mi s on the Strip. 3475 Las Vegas Blvd S. (89109) Formerly Holiday Casino/Holiday Inn. Check-in 3 pm. A/C; C/CATV; free & pay movies; radios; phones. Coin laundry. Pool; whirlpool. Fee for: health club. Valet ramp & parking lot. No pets. 48 suites $175-$350 for up to 2 persons. Reserv deposit required; 3 days refund notice. AE, DI, DS, MC, VI. ● 4 restaurants & coffeeshop; 24 hours; $9-$29; buffet, $6; cocktails; entertainment.
FAX (702) 369-6014 ⊗ Ⓢ Ⓓ (702) 369-5000

Howard Johnson Hotel & Casino 🔢2 ◆◆
Fri & Sat Rates Subject to Change *Hotel*
1P .... 79.00 2P/1B .... 79.00 2P/2B .... 79.00 XP 10
Sun-Thurs 1P .... 49.00 2P/1B .... 49.00 2P/2B .... 49.00 XP 10
150 units. Adjacent to I-15; Tropicana W exit. 3111 W Tropicana Ave. (89103) Convenient to airport & strip. Check-in 3 pm. A/C; C/CATV; pay movies; radios; phones. Pool; whirlpool. Parking lot. Airport transp. No pets. 1 bedroom apartment with kitchen, $250-$350, for up to 4 persons. Reserv deposit required. AE, DI, DS, MC, VI. ● Coffeeshop; 6 am-10 pm; $5-$12; cocktail lounge. Slot casino. FAX (702) 798-7138 ⊗ Ⓓ (702) 798-1111

Lady Luck Casino & Hotel 🔢32 ◆◆
All year Rates Subject to Change *Hotel*
1P 39.00- 75.00 2P/1B 39.00- 75.00 2P/2B 39.00- 75.00 XP 8
791 units. 3rd & Ogden. 206 N 3rd St. (PO Box 1060, 89125) Few poolside units. Refrigerators; A/C; C/CATV; pay movies; radios; phones. Pool. Valet parking ramp. Airport transp. No pets. 165 suites with whirlpool bath $50-$90 for 2 persons. Reserv deposit required. AE, DI, DS, MC, VI. ● 3 dining rms, restaurant & coffeeshop; 24 hrs; $7-$22; buffet, $5; cocktails. FAX (702) 384-2832 ⊗ Ⓢ Ⓓ ♿ (702) 477-3000

La Quinta Motor Inn 🔢5 ◆◆
Fri & Sat Rates Subject to Change *Motel*
1P 50.00, 66.00 2P/1B 67.00- 74.00 2P/2B .... 67.00 XP 8 F
Sun-Thurs 1P 49.00- 56.00 2P/1B 57.00- 64.00 2P/2B .... 57.00 XP 8 F
114 units. 5 1/2 mi s on the Strip. 3782 Las Vegas Blvd S. (89109) Spanish exterior design. A/C; C/CATV; free & pay movies; radios; phones. Pool. Airport transp. Small pets only. AE, DI, DS, MC, VI. Coffeeshop adjacent.
FAX (702) 736-1129 ⊗ Ⓓ (702) 739-7457

Las Vegas Hilton 🔢24 ◆◆◆◆
All year Rates Guaranteed *Hotel*
1P 85.00- 180.00 2P/1B 85.00- 180.00 2P/2B 85.00- 180.00 XP 25 F
3174 units. 2 3/4 mi s; 4 blks e off the Strip; adjacent to Convention Center. 3000 Paradise Rd. (PO Box 93147, 89193) A/C; C/CATV; pay movies; radios; phones. Pool; putting green; lighted tennis-6 courts; playground. Fee for: health club & massage. Valet ramp & parking lot. No pets. 300 suites, $290-$950 for up to 2 persons. Reserv deposit required; 3 days refund notice. AE, DI, DS, MC, VI. ● Coffeeshop; 12 restaurants; 24 hours; $8-$35; buffet, $7-$10; cocktails; name entertainment. Also, Benihana Village, see separate listing.
FAX (702) 732-5249 ⊗ Ⓢ Ⓓ ♿ (702) 732-5111

The Mirage 🔢51 ◆◆◆◆
Fri & Sat Rates Guaranteed *Hotel*
1P 109.00- 159.00 2P/1B 109.00- 159.00 2P/2B 109.00- 159.00 XP 15 F
Sun-Thurs 1P 79.00- 109.00 2P/1B 79.00- 109.00 2P/2B 79.00- 109.00 XP 15 F
3044 units. 3 1/2 mi s on strip. 3400 Las Vegas Blvd S. (PO Box 9193, 89109) Lavish grounds & unique public areas. Check-in 3 pm. A/C; C/CATV; movies; radios; phones. 2 htd pools; wading pool; whirlpools; health club. Fee for: massage. Valet parking lot. No pets. 1 & 2-bedroom suites, $400-$750 for 2 persons. Reserv deposit required. AE, CB, MC, VI. ● Dining rm, 7 restaurants & coffeeshop; 24 hours; $6-$50; buffet, $6.50-$9.50; Sun $12.50; cocktails. Casino. FAX (702) 791-7446 ⊗ Ⓢ Ⓓ ♿ (702) 791-7111

Ramada Makes Short Vacations An Overnight Success.

Wherever you travel this year, Ramada has a variety of packages that offer fun and excitement at rates that are sure to please your budget.

Family Fun

One to two nights' accommodations for families with features like free tickets and transportation to area attractions. It's great fun for the whole family.

Bed & Breakfast

These packages offer one or more relaxing nights at very special rates. Included is a big, comfortable room, all the amenities Ramada is known for, plus a terrific breakfast served daily.

Steal-A-Weekend

Friday and Saturday night accommodations at special low rates that will keep you coming back time and again. These weekend rates often include tickets and transportation to exciting local attractions at no additional cost.

Ramada offers many additional packages, with features as varied as the areas in which the properties are located. Offering city night life or country relaxation, beaches and boating, golf and tennis, sporting events and sightseeing. You make the choice.

Call Ramada's Package Hotline at 1-800-544-9772, and make your plans now.

RAMADA®

INNS, HOTELS, SUITES AND RESORTS.

FOR RESERVATIONS CALL

1-800-2-RAMADA

(1-800-272-6232)

OR YOUR LOCAL TRAVEL PROFESSIONAL

©1993 Ramada Franchise Systems, Inc.

(See LAS VEGAS spotting map page A560)

Plaza Suite Hotel by Howard Johnson 🔲20   Rates Subject to Change   *Motor Inn* ◆◆◆
9/1-11/15	1P	95.00- 125.00	2P/1B	95.00- 125.00	2P/2B	....	125.00	XP 15	F
12/28-6/14	1P	75.00- 85.00	2P/1B	75.00- 85.00	2P/2B	....	85.00	XP 15	F
6/15-8/31	1P	65.00- 75.00	2P/1B	65.00- 75.00	2P/2B	....	75.00	XP 15	F
11/16-12/27	1P	55.00- 65.00	2P/1B	55.00- 65.00	2P/2B	....	65.00	XP 15	F

202 units. Exit I-15 Flamingo, e 1/2 mi to Paradise, s 1/4 mi. 4255 S Paradise Rd. (89109) 197 refrigerators; A/C; C/CATV; free & pay movies; radios; phones. Pool; sauna; whirlpool; exercise rm. Pets. Reserv deposit required. AE, DI, DS, MC, VI. ● Restaurant; 6 am-midnight; $8-$20; cocktails. FAX (702) 369-3770   ⊗ Ⓢ Ⓓ 🅈 (702) 369-4400

Quality Inn Sunrise Suites 🔲56   Rates Subject to Change   *Apartment Motel* ◆◆
Fri & Sat	1P	48.00- 78.00	2P/1B	48.00- 78.00	2P/2B	48.00- 78.00	XP 10		
Sun-Thurs	1P	36.00- 66.00	2P/1B	36.00- 66.00	2P/2B	36.00- 66.00	XP 10		F

Senior discount. 305 units. Off SR 93/95, 1 mi s of Desert Inn Rd. 4575 Boulder Hwy. (89121) Formerly Fountain Suites. Full suites & few motel rooms with seating area. Check-in 3 pm. A/C; C/CATV; free & pay movies; 143 radios; phones. Efficiencies, no utensils. Coin laundry. Pool; whirlpool. No pets. Wkly & monthly rates avail. Reserv deposit required. AE, DI, DS, MC, VI. Deli 6 am-10 pm. FAX (702) 434-2619   ⊗ Ⓢ Ⓓ 🅈 (702) 434-0848

Residence Inn by Marriott 🔲50   Rates Subject to Change   *Apartment Motel* ◆◆◆
All year [CP]	1P	90.00- 120.00	2P/1B	90.00- 120.00	2P/2B	129.00- 165.00	XP

192 units. 3 blks e off the Strip; opposite convention center. 3225 Paradise Rd. (89109) Complimentary snakcs & beverages 5 pm-6:30 pm weekdays. Check-in 4 pm. A/C; C/CATV; free & pay movies; 48 2-bedrm units, kitchens. Coin laundry. Htd pool; whirlpools; sports court. Parking lot. Airport transp. Pets, $7 extra charge. Maximum rates for up to 4 persons. Wkly & monthly rates avail. Reserv deposit required. AE, DI, DS, MC, VI. FAX (702) 796-9300   ⊗ Ⓢ Ⓓ (702) 796-9300

Rio Suite Hotel & Casino 🔲17   Rates Subject to Change   *Hotel* ◆◆◆
Fri & Sat	1P	....	99.00	2P/1B	....	99.00	2P/2B	....	99.00	XP 10	F
Sun-Thurs	1P	....	81.00	2P/1B	....	81.00	2P/2B	....	81.00	XP 10	F

430 units. Exit I-15 at Flamingo Rd, 1/4 mi w. 3700 W Flamingo Rd. (PO Box 14160, 89103) Large rooms, attractive decor. Sand beach at pool. Refrigerators; A/C; C/CATV; movies; phones. Htd pool; whirlpool; exercise rm. Valet parking lot. No pets. AE, CB, DI, MC, VI. ● Dining rm, 3 restaurants & coffeeshop; 24 hours; $8-$30; buffet, $7; casino; 24 hour room service; cocktails. FAX (702) 252-0080   ⊗ Ⓢ Ⓓ (702) 252-7777

Riviera Hotel 🔲26   Rates Subject to Change   *Hotel* ◆◆◆
All year	1P	59.00- 95.00	2P/1B	59.00- 95.00	2P/2B	59.00- 95.00	XP 12	F

2200 units. 2 3/4 mi s on the Strip. 2901 Las Vegas Blvd S. (89109) Check-in 3 pm. 300 refrigerators; A/C; C/CATV; pay movies; phones. Pool; whirlpool; lighted tennis-2 courts. Fee for: health club. Valet ramp & parking lot. No pets. Reserv deposit required. AE. ● 3 restaurants & coffeeshop; 24 hours; $7-$35; buffet, $7; casino; cocktails; entertainment. FAX (702) 794-9451   Ⓢ Ⓓ (702) 734-5110

Rodeway Inn 🔲4   AAA Special Value Rates   *Motel* ◆
🅰 Fri & Sat	1P	....	65.00	2P/1B	....	65.00	2P/2B	....	65.00	XP 5	F
Sun-Thurs	1P	....	45.00	2P/1B	....	45.00	2P/2B	....	45.00	XP 5	F

97 units. 5 1/2 mi s on the Strip. 3786 Las Vegas Blvd S. (89109) A/C; C/CATV; movies; phones. 5 2-bedrm units. Pool. Pets, $5 extra charge. AE, DI, DS, MC, VI. Coffeeshop opposite. FAX (702) 736-6058 *(See ad below)*   ⊗ Ⓓ (702) 736-1434

Sam's Town Hotel 🔲10   Rates Subject to Change   *Hotel* ◆◆
All year	1P	....	45.00	2P/1B	....	45.00	2P/2B	....	45.00	XP 5	

197 units. On US 93 & 95 at Nellis Blvd. 5111 Boulder Hwy. (89122) A/C; C/TV; phones. Pool. Fee for: bowling. Valet ramp & parking lot. No pets. Reserv deposit required. AE, DI, DS, MC, VI. ● 3 restaurants & coffeeshop; 24 hours; $6-$18; buffet, $7; cocktails. Casino. FAX (702) 454-8060   ⊗ Ⓓ 🅈 (702) 456-7777

(See LAS VEGAS spotting map page A560)

Sheffield Inn 44   **AAA Special Value Rates**   *Apartment Motel*   ◆◆
All year [CP]   1P 85.00- 98.00   2P/1B   85.00- 98.00   2P/2B   85.00- 98.00   XP
228 units. 3/4 mi s of convention center, exit I-15 Flamingo Ave E; 1/2 mi e of strip. 3970 Paradise Rd. (89109)
Some units with balconies, few with patios. Check-in 4 pm. A/C; C/CATV; movies; VCPs. Radios; phones. 9
2-bedrm units, 51 kitchens, 120 efficiencies. Coin laundry. Small pool; whirlpool; units with whirlpool tub. Air-
port transp. No pets. Maximum rates for up to 6 persons. 42 1-bedroom units $125, 9 2-bedroom units, $200.
Wkly & monthly rates avail. Reserv deposit required. AE, DI, DS, MC, VI. Restaurant adjacent. FAX (702) 796-9000
(See ad p A569)   ⊗ Ⓓ ⑤ (702) 796-9000

Somerset House Motel 23   **Rates Subject to Change**   *Motel*   ◆◆
Fri & Sat   1P ....   33.00   2P/1B   ....   45.00   2P/2B   ....   45.00   XP 3   F
Sun-Thurs   1P ....   28.00   2P/1B   ....   36.00   2P/2B   ....   36.00   XP 3   F
Senior discount. 104 units. 3 mi s; e off the Strip. 294 Convention Center Dr. (89109) Check-in 3 pm. Refrigera-
tors; A/C; C/CATV; movies; phones. 63 kitchens, 17 efficiencies. Coin laundry. Pool. No pets. Wkly rates avail.
Reserv deposit required. AE, CB, DI, MC, VI. FAX (702) 369-2388 *(See ad below)*   ⊗ Ⓓ (702) 735-4411

St Tropez All Suites Hotel 46   **Rates Subject to Change**   *Apartment*   ◆◆◆
All year   1P 90.00- 125.00   2P/1B   90.00- 125.00   2P/2B   115.00- 135.00   XP 12
Senior discount. 149 units. 2 mi s of convention center at Paradise Rd. 455 E Harmon Ave. (89109) Surrounding attrac-
tive landscaped grounds. Courtyard units with patio or deck. Check-in 3 pm. A/C; C/CATV; radios; phones. Pool;
whirlpool; exercise rm. Airport transp. No pets. Reserv deposit required. Complimentary beverages each evening. AE,
DI, DS, MC, VI. Cocktail lounge; restaurant adjacent. FAX (702) 369-1150   ⊗ Ⓓ (702) 369-5400

Tropicana Hotel 3   **Rates Subject to Change**   *Hotel*   ◆◆◆
Fri & Sat   1P 79.00- 129.00   2P/1B   79.00- 129.00   2P/2B   79.00- 129.00   XP 10
Sun-Thurs   1P 55.00- 99.00   2P/1B   55.00- 99.00   2P/2B   55.00- 99.00   XP 10
1910 units. 5 1/2 mi s on the Strip. 3801 Las Vegas Blvd S. (PO Box 97777, 89193) Tropical landscaping, pools, ponds
& waterfalls. Tower & garden rooms. Check-in 3 pm. A/C; C/CATV; pay movies; 1600 radios; phones. Indoor/outdoor
pool; whirlpools. Fee for: sauna, exercise room; health club & massage. Valet parking lot. No pets. 120 suites, $225 for
up to 2 persons. Reserv deposit required. AE. ● 5 restaurants & 2 coffeeshops; 24 hours; $6-$32; Fri & Sat buffet,
$6;24 hour room service; cocktails; entertainment. Casino. FAX (702) 739-2469   Ⓢ Ⓓ ⑤ (702) 739-2222

Union Plaza Hotel 30   **Rates Guaranteed**   *Hotel*   ◆◆
All year   1P ....   50.00   2P/1B   ....   50.00   2P/2B   ....   50.00   XP 8
1037 units. Adjacent to Casino Center. 1 Main St. (PO Box 760, 89125, 89101) 100 refrigerators; A/C; C/TV;
phones. Coin laundry. Pool; lighted tennis-4 courts; jogging track. Valet parking ramp. No pets. Reserv deposit
required. AE, DI, DS, MC, VI. ● 2 restaurants & coffeeshop; 24 hours; $6-$15; casino; cocktails; entertainment.
FAX (702) 382-8281   Ⓢ Ⓓ ⑤ (702) 386-2110

RESTAURANTS

Alpine Village Inn ②   German $$ ◆◆◆
Opposite Las Vegas Hilton. 3003 Paradise Rd. European atmosphere. Excellent Swiss & American dishes. Raths-
keller serves a la carte items. Imported & domestic beer & wine. A/C. Children's menu. Open 5 pm-11 pm. Cock-
tails & lounge. Minimum $4. Valet parking. Reserv advised. AE, DI, DS, MC, VI.   ⊗ (702) 734-6888

Andre's ⑪   French $$$$ ◆◆◆
At Lewis St. 401 S 6th St. Country-French decor; several dining rooms. A/C. Open 6 pm-11 pm. Cocktails &
lounge. Valet parking. Reserv advised. AE, MC, VI.   ⊗ (702) 385-5016

Battista's Hole In The Wall ⑤   Italian $$ ◆◆
1/4 mi e of strip; off Flamingo. 4041 Audrie. Unique decor; casual atmosphere. Dinners include wine & cappuccino. A/C.
Open 5 pm-11 pm; closed 11/28, 5/27 & three weeks at Christmas. Cocktails & lounge. Minimum $6. Reserv advised.
AE, CB, DI, MC, VI.   (702) 732-1424

Benihana Village ①   Ethnic $$$ ◆◆◆
In Las Vegas Hilton. Hibachi & Robata Yaki style cooking. Japanese village atmosphere including running streams & rain
storms. A/C. Children's menu. Open 6 pm-11 pm. Cocktails & lounge. Entertainment. Reserv advised. AE, CB, DI, MC,
VI.   (702) 732-5801

Country Inn ⑥   American $$ ◆◆◆
Exit I-15 Charleston, 4 mi w; s Rainbow, 1/4 mi. 1401 S Rainbow. Attractive country decor; traditional dishes. Friendly
atmosphere. A/C. Open 7 am-10 pm; Fri & Sat-11 pm; closed 12/25. Beer & wine. AE, CB, DI, MC, VI.
                                                          ⊗ (702) 254-0520

Country Inn ⑦   American $$ ◆◆
2 mi e of the strip. 2425 E Desert Inn Rd. Attractive country decor; casual atmosphere. A/C. Open 7 am-10 pm; Fri &
Sat-11 pm; closed 12/25. Beer & wine. AE, CB, DI, MC, VI.   ⊗ (702) 731-5035

(See LAS VEGAS spotting map page A560)

Famous Pacific Fish Co ⑧   Seafood $$ ◆◆
Exit I-15, Flamingo E 1 mi; 1/2 mi n. 3925 S Paradise Rd. Attractive fish house decor; casual atmosphere. A/C. Children's menu. Open 11 am-10 pm; Fri & Sat-11 pm; closed 11/25 & 12/25. Cocktails & lounge. Reserv advised. AE, CB, DI, MC, VI.   ⊗ (702) 796-9676

Golden Steer ⑨   Steakhouse $$$ ◆◆
Exit I-15 Sahara, 1/4 mi e; 1 blk w of strip. 308 W Sahara Ave. Varied menu; chicken, veal & seafood. Quiet atmosphere. A/C. Open 5 pm-11:45 pm; closed 11/25 & 12/25. Cocktails & lounge. Valet parking. Reserv required. AE, CB, DI, MC, VI.   (702) 384-4470

Philips Supper House ④   Steak & Seafood $$$ ◆◆◆
2 3/4 mi w of the Strip, between Arville St & Decatur Blvd. 4545 W Sahara Ave. Prime eastern beef, seafood & Italian specialties. A/C. Open 5 pm-11 pm. Cocktails & lounge. Reserv advised. AE, DI, DS, MC, VI.   ⊗ (702) 873-5222

Tony Roma's ③   Southwest American $
2 mi s on the Strip; 1 mi e on E Sahara Ave. 620 E Sahara Ave. A place for ribs. A/C. Children's menu. Open 11 am-10 pm; Fri & Sat midnight; closed 12/25. Cocktails & lounge. AE, DI, DS, MC, VI.   ⊗ (702) 733-9914

Yolie's Brazilian Steak House ⑩   Ethnic $$ ◆◆
On upper level, Citybank Park Plaza. 3900 Paradise Rd, Suite Z. Informal atmosphere, variety of meats served from a skewer. Also lamb, chicken & fish specialties. A/C. Children's menu. Open 11:30 am-11 pm; Sat & Sun from 5 pm. Cocktails & lounge. Entertainment. Reserv advised. AE, CB, DI, MC, VI.   (702) 794-0700

LAUGHLIN

Bayshore Inn   Rates Subject to Change   *Motel*   ◆◆

Fri & Sat	1P	....	55.00	2P/1B	....	65.00	2P/2B	....	65.00	XP 7	F
Sun-Thurs	1P	....	22.00	2P/1B	....	30.00	2P/2B	....	30.00	XP 7	F

Senior discount. 105 units. 7 mi s of Davis Dam. 1955 W Casino Dr. (PO Box 31377, 89029) A/C; C/CATV; phones. Pool; whirlpool; boat ramp; fishing. Reserv deposit required. AE, DI, DS, MC, VI. FAX (702) 299-9194
     Ⓢ Ⓓ (702) 299-9010

Best Western Riverside Resort   Rates Guaranteed   *Motor Inn*   ◆◆◆
⊛

Fri & Sat	1P	....	62.00	2P/1B	....	62.00	2P/2B	....	62.00	XP 8
Sun-Thurs	1P	....	42.00	2P/1B	....	42.00	2P/2B	....	42.00	XP 8

659 units. 2 mi s of Davis Dam; across river from Bullhead City, AZ. 1650 S Casino Way. (PO Box 500, 89029) On the Colorado River. A/C; C/CATV; pay movies; phones; comb or shower baths. 2 pools; fishing. Valet parking lot. No pets. AE, DI, DS, MC, VI. ● Dining rm & restaurant; 24 hours; $7-$30; also buffet, $4; cocktails; name entertainment. Casino. FAX (702) 298-2614   Ⓢ Ⓓ Ⓛ (702) 298-2535

Colorado Belle Hotel & Casino   Rates Subject to Change   *Hotel*   ◆◆◆
⊛

Fri & Sat	1P	49.00-	59.00	2P/1B	49.00- 59.00	2P/2B	49.00- 59.00	XP		F
Sun-Thurs	1P	....	32.00	2P/1B	.... 32.00	2P/2B	.... 32.00	XP		F

1238 units. Center; 3 mi s of Davis Dam. 2100 S Casino Dr. (PO Box 2304, 89029) On the Colorado River. A/C; C/TV; phones; shower baths. 2 pools; whirlpool; fishing; water skiing. Valet parking lot. No pets. Suites, 6 with whirlpool bath, $85-$120 for up to 4 persons. Reserv deposit required. AE, DI, DS, MC, VI. ● 3 restaurants & coffeeshop; 24 hours; $7-$25; also buffet, $5; casino; cocktails. FAX (702) 298-2285
     ⊗ Ⓢ Ⓓ Ⓛ (702) 298-4000

Edgewater Hotel   Rates Subject to Change   *Hotel*   ◆◆◆
⊛

Fri & Sat	1P	49.00- 59.00	2P/1B	49.00- 59.00	2P/2B	49.00- 59.00	XP
Sun-Thurs	1P	22.00- 27.00	2P/1B	22.00- 27.00	2P/2B	22.00- 27.00	XP

1450 units. Center; 3 mi s of Davis Dam. 2020 S Casino Dr. (PO Box 30707, 89029) On the Colorado River, some rooms with river view. A/C; C/CATV; phones; shower or comb baths. Pool; whirlpool; fishing; water skiing. Fee for: 10 river cruise. Valet ramp & parking lot. No pets. Maximum rates for up to 4 persons. Reserv deposit required. AE, DI, DS, MC, VI. ● Dining rm & coffeeshop; 24 hours; $5-$20; also buffet $4; cocktails; entertainment. Casino. FAX (702) 298-8165   ⊗ Ⓢ Ⓓ (702) 298-2453

Flamingo Hilton Laughlin   AAA Special Value Rates   *Hotel*   ◆◆◆
⊛

Fri & Sat	1P	....	65.00	2P/1B	....	65.00	2P/2B	....	65.00	XP 7
Sun-Thurs	1P	....	35.00	2P/1B	....	35.00	2P/2B	....	35.00	XP 7

2000 units. 2 mi s of Davis Dam. 1900 S Casino Dr. (PO Box 30630, 89029) Check-in 3 pm. A/C; C/CATV; pay movies; phones. Pool; lighted tennis-3 courts. Parking lot. No pets. Reserv deposit required. AE, DI, DS, MC, VI. ● 2 restaurants & coffeeshop; 24 hours; $9-$21; buffet, $5; casino; cocktails; entertainment. FAX (702) 298-5177   ⊗ Ⓢ Ⓓ Ⓛ (702) 298-5111

Harrah's Casino Hotel

								Rates Subject to Change							Hotel ◆◆◆
Fri & Sat	1P	55.00-	90.00	2P/1B	55.00-	90.00	2P/2B	55.00-	90.00	XP	7

1658 units. 5 mi s of Davis Dam; on the river. 2900 S Casino Dr. (PO Box 33000, 89029) OPEN ALL YEAR. Southwest architecture. On the Colorado River. Check-in 3 pm. A/C; C/CATV; pay movies; phones; comb or shower baths. 2 pools; beach; whirlpool. Valet ramp & parking lot. No pets. Reserv deposit required. AE, DI, DS, MC, VI. ● Dining rm, 2 restaurants & coffeeshop; 24 hours; also buffet $8; Fri $13; $10-$25; casino; cocktails; entertainment; nightclub. Also, William Fisk's steakhouse, see separate listing. FAX (702) 298-6896   ⊗ Ⓢ Ⓓ Ⓛ (702) 298-4600

Ramada Express Hotel & Casino

								Rates Subject to Change							Hotel ◆◆◆
Fri & Sat	1P	54.00-	59.00	2P/1B	54.00-	59.00	2P/2B	54.00-	59.00	XP	7
Sun-Thurs	1P	....	34.00	2P/1B	....	34.00	2P/2B	....	34.00	XP	7

406 units. 3 mi s of Davis Dam. 2121 S Casino Dr. (PO Box 658, 89029) A/C; C/TV; pay movies; phones; shower baths. Pool; recreational program; train ride. Valet parking lot. No pets. Reserv deposit required. AE, DI, DS, MC, VI. ● Restaurant & coffeeshop; 24 hours; $10-$20; buffet, $7; casino; cocktail lounge. FAX (702) 298-4619 *(See ad below)*   ⊗ Ⓢ Ⓓ Ⓛ (702) 298-4200

RESTAURANT

William Fisk's Steakhouse   Steak & Seafood $$$ ◆◆
In Harrah's Del Rio. 2900 S Casino Dr. Varied menu; intimate dining atmosphere overlooking Colorado River. A/C. Dress code. Open 6 pm-10 pm; Fri & Sat-11 pm. Cocktails. Valet parking. Reserv advised. AE, DI, DS, MC, VI. (702) 298-6832

LOVELOCK — 2,300

Best Western Sturgeon's Motel

								Rates Subject to Change			Motor Inn ◆◆◆	
⑱ 5/1-8/31	1P	....	49.50	2P/1B	....	52.80	2P/2B	....	52.80	XP	7	F
9/1-12/31	1P	....	41.80	2P/1B	....	47.30	2P/2B	....	47.30	XP	7	F
1/1-4/30	1P	....	38.50	2P/1B	....	44.00	2P/2B	....	44.00	XP	7	F

Senior discount. 74 units. Eastbound exit I-80 exit 105; westbound exit 107. 1420 Cornell Ave. (PO Box 56, 89419) Some large rooms. A/C; C/CATV; 24 radios; phones. Coin laundry. Indoor pool. No pets. 2 units with whirlpool bath, $63 for up to 2 persons. Reserv deposit required. AE, CB, DI, MC, VI. ● Restaurant & coffeeshop; 24 hours; $8-$20; casino; cocktails; entertainment. FAX (702) 273-2278   ⊗ Ⓓ Ⓛ (702) 273-2971

MESQUITE — 1,900

Virgin River Hotel & Casino

								Rates Subject to Change			Motor Inn ◆◆	
Fri & Sat	1P	....	45.00	....			2P/2B	....	45.00	XP	4
Sun-Thurs	1P	19.95-	24.95	....			2P/2B	19.95-	24.95	XP	4

379 units. W of & adjacent to I-15, exit 122. PO Box 1620. (89024) Check-in 3 pm. A/C; C/CATV; radios; phones. Pool; whirlpool; video arcade. Pets, $25 deposit required. 2 suites, Fri & Sat $125; Sun-Thurs $100 for up to 2 persons. AE, DS, MC, VI. ● Restaurant; 24 hours; $9-$15; casino; cocktails. FAX (702) 346-7780   ⊗ Ⓢ Ⓓ (702) 346-7777

MINDEN

Carson Valley Inn

					AAA Special Value Rates					Motor Inn ◆◆◆	
⑱ Fri & Sat 4/1-10/31	1P	....	69.00	2P/1B	....	69.00	2P/2B	....	69.00	XP	6
Fri & Sat 11/1-3/31	1P	....	59.00	2P/1B	....	59.00	2P/2B	....	59.00	XP	6
Sun-Thurs 4/1-10/31	1P	....	59.00	2P/1B	....	59.00	2P/2B	....	59.00	XP	6
Sun-Thurs 11/1-3/31	1P	....	49.00	2P/1B	....	49.00	2P/2B	....	49.00	XP	6

158 units. Center; on US 395N. 1627 US 395N. (89423) View of mountains or ranch land. Check-in 3 pm. A/C; C/CATV; phones. Whirlpools. No pets. 7 suites, $89-$149 for up to 2 persons. Reserv deposit required. AE, DI, DS, MC, VI. ● 2 restaurants; 24 hours; $6-$17; casino; cocktails; entertainment. FAX (702) 782-7472   ⊗ Ⓢ Ⓓ (702) 782-9711

RESTAURANT

Heidi's Family Restaurant   American $ ◆
⑱ E side of US 395, 1/4 mi n of Minden-Gardnerville city limit. 1595 Hwy 395. Family restaurant noted for breakfast. A/C. Children's menu. Open 6:30 am-2 pm; closed 12/25. MC, VI.   ⊗ (702) 782-2930

RENO — 133,900

Airport Accommodations-See listing for:

Best Western Airport Plaza Hotel, 2 blks n of airport entrance.

Best Western Airport Plaza Hotel — Rates Subject to Change — *Hotel* ◆◆◆
All year   1P 58.00- 190.00   2P/1B   66.00- 220.00   2P/2B   68.00- 220.00   XP 10   F
Senior discount. 270 units. US 395 & 580, exit E Plume-Villa Nova. 1981 Terminal Way. (89502) Opposite Cannon International Airport. A/C; C/CATV; movies; radios; phones. 15 2-bedrm units. Pool; sauna; whirlpool; exercise rm. Airport transp. 16 units with fireplace, $125-$300 for up to 2 persons. Reserv deposit required. AE, DI, DS, MC, VI. ● Restaurant; 5:30 am-11 pm; a la carte entrees about $9-$20; cocktail lounge. Slot casino.
FAX (702) 348-9722   ⊗ Ⓢ Ⓓ (702) 348-6370

Best Western Continental Lodge — Rates Subject to Change — *Motor Inn* ◆◆◆
5/1-10/31 & wkends   1P .... 57.00   2P/1B   .... 63.00   2P/2B   .... 63.00   XP 6
11/1-4/30   1P .... 45.00   2P/1B   .... 51.00   2P/2B   .... 51.00   XP 6
Senior discount. 103 units. 1 mi s on US 395. 1885 S Virginia St. (89502) Rooms with balcony or patio. Land-scaped gardens. A/C; C/CATV; movies; radios; phones. No pets. Pool; whirlpool. Airport transp. No pets. Reserv deposit required; 3 days refund notice. AE, DI, DS, MC, VI. ● Restaurant; 6 am-10 pm; $15-$19; cocktails; entertainment. FAX (702) 324-5402   ⊗ Ⓓ (702) 329-1001

Best Western Daniel's Motor Lodge — AAA Special Value Rates — *Motel* ◆◆
4/1-10/31   1P 40.00- 60.00   2P/1B   54.00- 65.00   2P/2B   60.00- 80.00   XP 7
11/1-3/31   1P 40.00- 50.00   2P/1B   45.00- 55.00   2P/2B   51.00- 61.00   XP 7
82 units. In casino area, on US 395; jct I-80 business rt. 375 N Sierra St. (89501) Many large rooms. A/C; C/CATV; movies; phones. No pets. Reserv deposit required. AE, DI, DS, MC, VI.   ⊗ Ⓓ (702) 329-1351

Circus Circus — Rates Subject to Change — *Hotel* ◆◆
Fri & Sat   1P .... 48.00   2P/1B   .... 48.00   2P/2B   .... 48.00   XP 6   F
Sun-Thurs 2/1-11/24 1P .... 39.00   2P/1B   .... 39.00   2P/2B   .... 39.00   XP 6   F
Sun-Thurs 11/25-1/31 1P .... 23.00   2P/1B   .... 23.00   2P/2B   .... 23.00   XP 6   F
1625 units. Corner N Virginia & Fifth sts; 1 blk n off I-80 business rt. 500 N Sierra St. (PO Box 5880, 89513) Check-in 3 pm. A/C; C/TV; radios; phones. Valet garage. No pets. 2-night minimum stay weekends. Reserv deposit required. AE, DI, DS. ● Restaurant & coffeeshop; 24 hours; $5-$13; buffet about $4-$6; cocktails; entertainment. Casino.
FAX (702) 329-0599   ⊗ Ⓢ Ⓓ Ⓛ (702) 329-0711

Clarion Hotel Casino — Rates Subject to Change — *Motor Inn* ◆◆◆
6/19-11/14   1P 45.00- 149.00   2P/1B   45.00- 149.00   2P/2B   49.00- 154.00   XP 6   F
2/1-6/18 & 11/15-11/31 1P 35.00- 139.00   2P/1B   39.00- 139.00   2P/2B   39.00- 139.00   XP 6   F
Senior discount. 303 units. 3 mi s on US 395. 3800 S Virginia St. (89502) Some motel rooms. A/C; C/CATV; pay movies; radios; phones. Pool; sauna; whirlpool; exercise rm. Valet parking lot. Airport transp. No pets. 11 suites, $125-$295 for up to 2 persons. Wkly & monthly rates avail. Reserv deposit required. AE, DI, DS, MC, VI. ● Coffeeshop & cafeteria; 24 hours; $7-$14; casino; cocktails; entertainment. FAX (702) 826-7860 *(See ad below)*   ⊗ Ⓓ Ⓛ (702) 825-4700

Colonial Inn Hotel & Casino ··· AAA Special Value Rates ··· *Motor Inn* ◆◆◆
◉ Sat	1P	67.00-	71.00	2P/1B	67.00-	71.00	2P/2B	69.00-	73.00	XP 10
2/28-11/27	1P	47.00-	51.00	2P/1B	47.00-	51.00	2P/2B	49.00-	53.00	XP 10
Sun-Fri 11/28-2/27	1P	45.00-	49.00	2P/1B	45.00-	49.00	2P/2B	47.00-	51.00	XP 10

168 units. Off 2nd St. 250 N Arlington. (89501) A/C; C/TV; radios; phones. Pool; sauna. Limited garage & parking lot. No pets. Reserv deposit required. AE, CB, DI, MC, VI. ● Restaurant; 6 am-midnight; $6-$10.50; cocktail lounge. Slot casino. FAX (702) 323-4588
Ⓢ Ⓓ (702) 322-3838

Colonial Motor Inn-West ··· AAA Special Value Rates ··· *Motel* ◆◆◆
◉ Sat	1P	66.00-	71.00	2P/1B	67.00-	71.00	2P/2B	69.00-	73.00	XP 10
Sun-Fri 2/28-11/27	1P	47.00-	51.00	2P/1B	47.00-	51.00	2P/2B	49.00-	53.00	XP 10
Sun-Fri 11/28-2/27	1P	45.00-	49.00	2P/1B	45.00-	49.00	2P/2B	47.00-	51.00	XP 10

100 units. 1 blk off I-80 business rt; 1 blk from casinos. 232 West St. (89501) A/C; C/TV; radios; phones. Pool; sauna. Limited garage & parking lot. No pets. Reserv deposit required. AE, CB, DI, MC, VI. FAX (702) 323-4588
Ⓓ (702) 786-5038

Days Inn ··· Rates Subject to Change ··· *Motor Inn* ◆
◉ Fri & Sat	1P	35.00-	70.00	2P/1B	45.00-	75.00	2P/2B	45.00-	75.00	XP 10
Sun-Thurs	1P	35.00-	60.00	2P/1B	35.00-	60.00	2P/2B	35.00-	59.00	XP 10

Senior discount. 137 units. S of & adjacent to I-80; exit Wells Ave. 701 E 7th St. (89512) A/C; C/CATV; pay movies; radios; phones. Pool. Pets, $6 extra charge. Reserv deposit required. AE, DI, DS, MC, VI. ● Coffeeshop; 6 am-10 pm; $5-$8. FAX (702) 329-4338
⊗ Ⓓ (702) 786-4070

Eldorado Hotel ··· Rates Subject to Change ··· *Hotel* ◆◆◆
◉ Fri & Sat 4/1-10/31	1P	88.00-	98.00	2P/1B	88.00-	98.00	2P/2B	88.00-	98.00	XP 8
Sun-Thurs 4/1-10/31 & Fri-Sat										
11/1-3/31	1P	68.00-	78.00	2P/1B	68.00-	78.00	2P/2B	68.00-	78.00	XP 8
Sun-Thurs 11/1-3/31	1P	55.00-	65.00	2P/1B	55.00-	65.00	2P/2B	55.00-	65.00	XP 8

785 units. In the casino area, 4th & Virginia sts. (PO Box 3399, 89505) Check-in 3 pm. A/C; C/CATV; pay movies; radios; phones. Pool; whirlpool. Valet garage & parking lot. Airport transp. No pets. Reserv deposit required. AE, DI, DS, MC, VI. ● 2 dining rms, 4 restaurants & coffeeshop; 24 hrs; a la carte entrees about $5.50-$28; also buffet about $7-$12.50; cocktails; entertainment. Casino. FAX (702) 322-7124
⊗ Ⓢ Ⓓ Ⓑ (702) 786-5700

Fitzgeralds Hotel ··· Rates Subject to Change ··· *Hotel* ◆◆◆
Fri & Sat	1P	60.00-	92.00	2P/1B	60.00-	92.00	2P/2B	60.00-	92.00	XP 8
Sun-Thurs	1P	38.00-	75.00	2P/1B	38.00-	75.00	2P/2B	38.00-	75.00	XP 8

350 units. In casino area. 255 N Virginia St. (89501) Check-in 3 pm. A/C; C/CATV; pay movies; radios; phones. Valet parking lot. No pets. Reserv deposit required. AE, DI, DS, MC, VI. ● Restaurant; 24 hours; $4-$9.50; buffet about $5; cocktails. Casino. FAX (702) 786-7180 *(See ad below)*
Ⓢ Ⓓ Ⓑ (702) 786-3663

Flamingo Hilton-Reno ··· Rates Subject to Change ··· *Hotel* ◆◆◆
Fri & Sat	1P	99.00-	159.00	2P/1B	99.00-	159.00	2P/2B	99.00-	159.00	XP 15	F
Sun-Thurs	1P	59.00-	69.00	2P/1B	59.00-	69.00	2P/2B	59.00-	69.00	XP 15	F

604 units. 1 blk s off I-80 business rt; 1 blk w off S Virginia St; between W 2nd & Commercial sts. 255 N Sierra St. (PO Box 1291, 89504) Check-in 3 pm. A/C; C/TV; pay movies; radios; phones. Valet garage & parking ramp. Airport transp. No pets. Reserv deposit required. AE, DI, DS, MC, VI. ● Dining rm, 2 restaurants & coffeeshop; 24 hours; $6-$30; cocktails; entertainment. Casino. FAX (702) 785-7057
Ⓢ Ⓓ Ⓑ (702) 322-1111

GateKeeper Inn ··· Rates Subject to Change ··· *Motel* ◆
◉ 4/1-11/15 & weekends	1P	....	50.00	2P/1B	....	55.00	2P/2B	....	60.00	XP 6
11/16-3/31	1P	....	34.00	2P/1B	....	38.00	2P/2B	....	40.00	XP 6

28 units. 2 blks w of casinos, corner West & 5th sts. 221 W 5th St. (89503) Check-in 4 pm. A/C; C/CATV; phones. No pets. Reserv deposit required. AE, DS, MC, VI.
⊗ Ⓓ (702) 786-3500

HOJO INNS.

TODAY'S ANSWER FOR THE ECONOMY MINDED TRAVELER.

In these times, finding a good value is more important than ever. And that's why Howard Johnson® is proud to offer its economical lodging facilities… Hojo Inns.

Hojo Inns offer a perfect combination of comfortable, attractive rooms, friendly, courteous service and the quality and value you've come to expect from Howard Johnson.

That's what Hojo Inns are about, no expensive frills…just a lot of comfort and convenience for today's budget conscious travelers.

So, the next time you're on the road, check into a HoJo Inn, and find out why economical lodging has never been better.

HoJo Inn
By Howard Johnson

FOR RESERVATIONS CALL
1·800·I·GO·HOJO
OR YOUR LOCAL TRAVEL PROFESSIONAL

®1993 Hospitality Franchise Systems, Inc.

Holiday Inn-Convention Center ◆◆

Rates Subject to Change — *Motor Inn*

Fri & Sat 4/1-10/31	1P	50.00- 60.00	2P/1B	50.00- 60.00	2P/2B	50.00- 60.00	XP	5		F
Sun-Thurs 4/1-10/31 & Fri-Sat 11/1-3/31	1P	40.00- 50.00	2P/1B	40.00- 50.00	2P/2B	40.00- 50.00	XP	5		F
Sun-Thurs 11/1-3/31	1P	30.00- 40.00	2P/1B	30.00- 40.00	2P/2B	30.00- 40.00	XP	5		F

Senior discount. 153 units. 4 mi s on US 395. 5851 S Virginia St. (89502) A/C; C/CATV; free & pay movies; radios; phones. Coin laundry. Pool; whirlpool. Airport transp. Pets. Reserv deposit required. AE, DI, DS, MC, VI. ● Restaurant; 6:30 am-10 pm; $8-$15; cocktails. FAX (702) 826-3835   ⊗ Ⓓ (702) 825-2940

Holiday Inn-Downtown ◆◆◆

AAA Special Value Rates — *Motor Inn*

All year	1P	65.00- 88.00	2P/1B	65.00- 88.00	2P/2B	65.00- 88.00	XP	5	F

286 units. 12 blks e; I-80 via Wells. 1000 E 6th St. (89512) Few small rooms. A/C; C/CATV; free & pay movies; radios; phones. Pool. Airport transp. Pets. 6 suites, $125-$195 for up to 2 persons. AE, DI, DS, MC, VI. ● Restaurant; 6:30 am-2 & 5-10 pm; Fri & Sat-11 pm; a la carte entrees about $6-$19; cocktails. Casino. FAX (702) 786-2447 *(See ad p A572)*   ⊗ Ⓢ Ⓓ (702) 786-5151

La Quinta Inn ◆◆

Rates Subject to Change — *Motel*

Fri & Sat	1P	51.00- 58.00	2P/1B	59.00- 66.00	2P/2B	.... 59.00	XP	5	F
Sun & Thurs	1P	46.00- 53.00	2P/1B	54.00- 61.00	2P/2B	.... 54.00	XP	5	F

130 units. US 395 northbound exit airport, southbound exit Villanova Dr. 4001 Market St. (89502-3110) Check-in 3 pm. A/C; C/CATV; free & pay movies; radios; phones. Pool. Airport transp. Pets. AE, DI, DS, MC, VI. Coffeeshop adjacent. FAX (702) 348-8794   ⊗ Ⓓ Ⓢ (702) 348-6100

Miner's Inn ◆

Rates Subject to Change — *Motel*

Fri & Sat 4/1-11/1	1P	.... 48.00	2P/1B	.... 48.00	2P/2B	.... 50.00	XP	4	
Fri & Sat 11/2-3/31	1P	.... 35.00	2P/1B	.... 35.00	2P/2B	.... 40.00	XP	4	
Sun-Thurs 4/1-11/1	1P	.... 34.00	2P/1B	.... 30.00	2P/2B	.... 38.00	XP	4	
Sun-Thurs 11/2-3/31	1P	.... 28.00	2P/1B	.... 25.00	2P/2B	.... 32.00	XP	4	

71 units. Opposite University of Nevada. 1651 N Virginia St. (89503) A/C; C/CATV; phones. Rental refrigerators. Pool. No pets. Rental microwaves. Reserv deposit required; 3 days refund notice. AE, DI, DS, MC, VI.   ⊗ Ⓓ (702) 329-3464

RIVER HOUSE MOTOR HOTEL

Right on the Truckee River. River Balcony. One Block from Casinos. Pets Accepted

2 People/2 Beds Rate : Sunday - Thursday	$46 - $50
Friday - Saturday	$50 - $60
Friday - Saturday - Holidays & Special Events	$65 - $110

2 Lake Street, Reno, Nevada 89505 • (702) 329 - 0036

ON THE ROAD AGAIN.

When the driving's done for the day, shift gears and treat yourself to the full-throttle fun of the Reno Hilton.
- 2,001 Spacious Rooms • Superb Dining • Dazzling Entertainment
- Health & Tennis

Club • Olympic-Size Pool • Indoor Golf • Shopping Mall • 50-Lane Bowling Center.

So join us, you're always in the driver's seat for a good time at the Reno Hilton!

THE NEW RENO HILTON.

Reservations: 800-648-5080

Reno Hilton
🏩 All year

	Rates Subject to Change			*Hotel* ◆◆◆
1P 69.00- 119.00	2P/1B	69.00- 119.00	2P/2B	69.00- 119.00 XP 10 F

2001 units. 1/2 mi s of jct I-80 & US 395; US 395 exit Mill St. 2500 E 2nd St. (89595) Formerly Bally's-Reno. Spacious. A/C; C/CATV; pay movies; radios; phones. Pool. Fee for: tennis-8 courts, 3 lighted, 5 indoor; bowling; health club. Valet parking lot. Airport transp. No pets. Suites, $150-$544 up to 2 persons. Reserv deposit required. AE, DI, DS, MC, VI. ● 5 restaurants & coffeeshop; 24 hrs; $7-$36; buffet about $5; cocktails; name entertainment. Casino. FAX (702) 789-2418 *(See ad p A574)*   ⊗ Ⓢ Ⓓ Ⓢ (702) 789-2000

River House Motor Hotel
🏩 Fri & Sat 3/1-11/1
   Sun-Thurs 3/1-11/1
   11/2-2/28

	Rates Subject to Change			*Motel* ◆
1P 50.00- 60.00	2P/1B	50.00- 60.00	2P/2B	50.00- 60.00 XP 2
1P 46.00- 50.00	2P/1B	46.00- 50.00	2P/2B	46.00- 50.00 XP 2
1P 30.00	2P/1B	.... 35.00	2P/2B	.... 35.00 XP

33 units. Corner of 1st St. 2 Lake St. (PO Box 2425, 89505) Few rooms with river view balcony. A/C; C/TV; phones; shower or comb baths. Pets, $8 daily extra charge. Wkly rates avail 1/5-3/5. Reserv deposit required. AE, DI, MC, VI. *(See ad p A574)*   Ⓓ (702) 329-0036

Rodeway Inn
🏩 4/1-10/31
   11/1-3/31

	AAA Special Value Rates			*Motel* ◆◆
1P 47.00- 77.00	2P/1B	57.00- 77.00	2P/2B	57.00- 77.00 XP 9 F
1P 37.00- 67.00	2P/1B	47.00- 67.00	2P/2B	47.00- 67.00 XP 6 F

210 units. US 395 exit W Mill St. 2050 Market St. (89502) A/C; C/CATV; pay movies; radios. Pool; sauna; whirlpool. Airport transp. Pets, $5 daily extra charge. 70 efficiencies, units, $57-$77 for up to 4 persons; no utensils. Wkly rates avail. Reserv deposit required. AE, DI, DS, MC, VI. FAX (702) 786-3884 *(See ad below)*   ⊗ Ⓢ Ⓓ (702) 786-2500

Seasons Inn
🏩 Fri & Sat
   Sun-Thurs 4/1-10/31
   Sun-Thurs 11/1-3/31

	Rates Subject to Change			*Motel* ◆◆
1P 60.00	2P/1B	.... 65.00	2P/2B	.... 75.00 XP 6
1P 42.00	2P/1B	.... 45.00	2P/2B	.... 48.00 XP 6
1P 34.00	2P/1B	.... 38.00	2P/2B	.... 40.00 XP 6

Senior discount. 56 units. 2 blks w of casinos; corner West & 5th sts. 495 West St. (89503) A/C; C/CATV; movies; phones. Pets, $25 deposit required. Reserv deposit required. AE, DI, DS, MC, VI.   ⊗ Ⓢ Ⓓ (702) 322-6000

Thunderbird Motel
🏩 All year

	Rates Subject to Change			*Motel* ◆
1P	2P/1B	.... 75.00	2P/2B	80.00- 90.00 XP 10

27 units. On US 395, 2 blks from casinos. 420 N Virginia St. (89501) A/C; C/TV; phones. 1 2-bedrm unit. No pets. Reserv deposit required. AE, CB, DI, MC, VI.   Ⓓ (702) 329-3578

Town House Motor Lodge
🏩 Fri & Sat 5/1-10/31
   Sun-Thurs 5/1-10/31
   Fri & Sat 11/1-4/30
   Sun-Thurs 11/1-4/30

	AAA Special Value Rates			*Motel* ◆
1P 68.00	2P/1B	.... 70.00	2P/2B	.... 85.00 XP 5
1P 48.00	2P/1B	.... 48.00	2P/2B	.... 60.00 XP 5
1P 48.00	2P/1B	.... 50.00	2P/2B	.... 60.00 XP 5
1P 38.00	2P/1B	.... 42.00	2P/2B	.... 48.00 XP 5

79 units. 2 blks s off I-80 business rt; 3 blks w of casinos. 303 W 2nd St. (89503) A/C; C/CATV; 40 radios; phones. Pool. No pets. Reserv deposit required. AE, CB, DI, MC, VI. FAX (702) 323-1791   Ⓓ (702) 323-1821

Vagabond Inn
🏩 All year [CP]

	Rates Subject to Change			*Motel* ◆◆
1P 36.00- 59.00	2P/1B	41.00- 64.00	2P/2B	.... 64.00 XP 5 F

130 units. 2 1/2 mi s on US 395. 3131 S Virginia St. (89502) Few bunk beds. Check-in 3 pm. A/C; C/CATV; VCPs; radios; phones. 7 2-bedrm units. Pool. Pets, $5 daily extra charge. Reserv deposit required. AE, DI, DS, MC, VI. Restaurant adjacent. FAX (702) 825-3096 *(See ad below)*   ⊗ Ⓓ (702) 825-7134

Wonder Lodge
🏩 Fri & Sat 7/1-10/31
   Fri & Sat 11/1-6/30
   Sun-Thurs 7/1-10/31
   Sun-Thurs 11/1-6/30

	Rates Guaranteed			*Motel* ◆
1P 42.00	2P/1B	.... 42.00	2P/2B	.... 54.00 XP
1P 39.00	2P/1B	.... 39.00	2P/2B	.... 52.00 XP
1P 37.00	2P/1B	.... 37.00	2P/2B	.... 50.00 XP
1P 32.00	2P/1B	.... 32.00	2P/2B	.... 46.00 XP

63 units. 1 blk off I-80 business rt; 2 blks from casinos. 430 Lake St. (89501) Large rooms. Check-in 3 pm. A/C; C/TV; phones. Pool. No pets. Reserv deposit required. AE, CB, DI, MC, VI.   Ⓓ (702) 786-6840

RESTAURANTS

Heidi's Family Restaurant American $ ◆
⊕ On US 395 2 mi s, adjacent to Park Lane Mall. 2450 S Virginia St. Noted for breakfast. A/C. Children's menu. Open 6:30 am-2 pm; closed 12/25. MC, VI. ⊗ (702) 826-3336

La Table Francaise French $$$$ ◆◆◆
1 mi w of Keystone. 3065 W 4th St. Excellently prepared cuisine. A/C. Open 6 pm-10 pm; closed Sun, 1/1, 7/4 & 12/25. Cocktails. Reserv advised. AE, MC, VI. ⊗ (702) 323-3200

Rapscallion Seafood $$ ◆◆
1555 S Wells. Fresh seafood flown in daily. A/C. Children's menu. Open 11:30 am-5 & 5:30-10:30 pm; Fri-11 pm; Sat 5:30 pm-11 pm; Sun 10 am-3 & 5:30-10:30 pm; closed 11/25, 12/25 & for lunch 7/4. Cocktails & lounge. Reserv advised. AE, MC, VI. ⊗ (702) 323-1211

SPARKS — 55,600

John Ascuaga's Nugget Courtyard AAA Special Value Rates *Motel* ◆◆◆
⊕ All year 1P 65.00- 79.00 2P/1B 65.00- 79.00 2P/2B 65.00- 79.00 XP 10 F
157 units. On I-80 business loop; exit I-80 via Rock Blvd. 1225 B St. (PO Box 797, 89431) Some rooms with balcony. Check-in 3 pm. A/C; C/CATV; radios; phones; comb or shower baths. Pool; exercise rm. No pets. Reserv deposit required. AE, DI, DS, MC, VI. Restaurant adjacent. FAX (702) 356-3434 ⊗ ⒟ (702) 356-3300

John Ascuaga's Nugget Hotel AAA Special Value Rates *Hotel* ◆◆◆
⊕ All year 1P 89.00- 115.00 2P/1B 89.00- 115.00 2P/2B 89.00- 115.00 XP 10 F
610 units. I-80 eastbound exit Nugget Ave westbound exit Rock Blvd. 1100 Nugget Ave. (89431) Check-in 3 pm. A/C; C/CATV; radios; phones. Htd indoor pool; whirlpool; exercise rm. Valet parking lot. Airport transp. No pets. Reserv deposit required. AE, DI, DS, MC, VI. Dining rm, 2 restaurants & 2 coffeeshops; 24 hours; $6-$29; buffet about $9-$16; Sun brunch $10; casino; cocktails; entertainment. FAX (702) 356-4198 ⊗ Ⓢ ⒟ (702) 356-3300

McCarren House Inn AAA Special Value Rates *Motor Inn* ◆
Fri & Sat 7/1-10/15 1P .... 55.00 2P/1B .... 55.00 2P/2B .... 55.00 XP 10 F
Fri & Sat 2/1-6/30 & 10/16-1/31 1P .... 47.00 2P/1B .... 47.00 2P/2B .... 47.00 XP 10 F
Sun-Thurs 7/1-10/15 1P .... 47.00 2P/1B .... 47.00 2P/2B .... 47.00 XP 10 F
Sun-Thurs 2/1-6/30 &
10/16-1/31 1P .... 39.00 2P/1B .... 39.00 2P/2B .... 39.00 XP 10 F
220 units. 1 1/4 mi e; s off & adjacent to I-80; exit McCarran Blvd. 55 E Nugget Ave. (89431) Check-in 3 pm. A/C; C/CATV; movies; radios; phones. Pool. Airport transp. No pets. Reserv deposit required; 3 days refund notice. AE, DI, DS, MC, VI. ● Restaurant; 6 am-10 pm, Sun-9 pm; $6-$13; cocktails. FAX (702) 359-6065 ⊗ Ⓢ ⒟ (702) 358-6900

Nendels Inn of Reno/Sparks Rates Subject to Change *Motel* ◆◆
⊕ All year 1P .... 40.00 2P/1B .... 40.00 2P/2B .... 50.00 XP 5
90 units. Exit I-80 at McCarran Blvd, 1 blk n to B St. 60 East B St. (89431) Check-in 3 pm. A/C; C/CATV; phones. Coin laundry. No pets. Reserv deposit required. AE, DI, DS, MC, VI. Ⓢ ⒟ (702) 356-7770

Victorian Inn Rates Subject to Change *Motel* ◆◆
⊕ Fri & Sat 1P 48.00- 54.00 2P/1B 48.00- 54.00 2P/2B 60.00- 64.00 XP 4
Sun-Thurs 4/1-10/31 1P 36.00- 40.00 2P/1B 36.00- 42.00 2P/2B 42.00- 48.00 XP 6
Sun-Thurs 11/1-3/31 1P 30.00- 34.00 2P/1B 32.00- 38.00 2P/2B 40.00- 44.00 XP 6
21 units. On I-80 business loop; exit I-80 via Rock Blvd. 1555 B St. (89431) Formerly Coach Lite Motel. A/C; C/CATV; phones. No pets. Reserv deposit required. AE, DS, MC, VI. ⊗ ⒟ (702) 331-3203

TONOPAH — 2,000

Best Western Hi Desert Inn Rates Subject to Change *Motel* ◆◆◆
All year 1P .... 42.00 2P/1B .... 48.00 2P/2B .... 52.00 XP 6
62 units. On US 6 & 95. (PO Box 351, 89049) A/C; C/CATV; movies; phones. 1 2-bedrm unit. Pool & whirlpool 5/15-10/15. Reserv deposit required. AE, DI, DS, MC, VI. Coffeeshop opposite. FAX (702) 482-3300 ⊗ ⒟ (702) 482-3511

Jim Butler Motel Rates Guaranteed *Motel* ◆◆
⊕ All year 1P .... 29.00 2P/1B .... 35.00 2P/2B .... 35.00 XP 4
Senior discount. 25 units. On US 6 & 95. (PO Box 1352, 89049) Very good rooms. A/C; C/CATV; movies; phones. AE, DI, DS, MC, VI. Restaurant opposite. FAX (702) 482-5240 *(See ad below)* ⊗ ⒟ (702) 482-3577

WELLS — 1,400

Best Western Sage Motel — Rates Subject to Change — Motel ◆◆

5/15-9/15	1P	40.00-	50.00	2P/1B	45.00-	55.00	2P/2B	45.00-	55.00 XP 5
9/16-5/14	1P	30.00-	40.00	2P/1B	35.00-	45.00	2P/2B	35.00-	45.00 XP 5

Senior discount. 24 units. I-80 exit 352, 1/2 mi w. 576 6th St. (PO Box 343, 89835) A/C; C/CATV; movies; phones; shower or comb baths. 1 2-bedrm unit. Pool open 6/15-9/15. Reserv deposit required. AE, DI, DS, MC, VI.
⊗ Ⓓ (702) 752-3353

Ranch House Inn — Rates Subject to Change — Motel

5/15-9/15	1P	....	38.00	2P/1B	....	42.00	2P/2B	....	44.00 XP 5	F
9/16-5/14	1P	....	32.00	2P/1B	....	36.00	2P/2B	....	38.00 XP 5	F

58 units. E of I-80; at jct US 40 & US 93; exit 352A. 930 6th St. (PO Box 302, 89835) Rating withheld pending completion of renovation. Scheduled to open Spring, 1993. A/C; C/CATV; phones; comb or shower baths. AE, DI, DS, MC, VI.
Ⓓ (702) 752-3384

RestInn Suites Motel — Rates Subject to Change — Motel ◆

4/17-11/15	1P 36.95-	52.95	2P/1B	38.95-	52.95	2P/2B	38.95-	52.95 XP 4	F
11/16-4/16	1P 34.95-	38.95	2P/1B	34.95-	38.95	2P/2B	34.95-	42.95 XP 4	F

Senior discount. 57 units. 1 blk n jct US 93; I-80 exit 352A. 1250 E 6th St. (PO Box 237, 89835) Check-in 3 pm. Refrigerators; A/C; C/CATV; phones. Coin laundry. 22 units with microwave & love seat. AE, DS, MC, VI. Coffeeshop opposite.
⊗ Ⓢ Ⓓ (702) 752-2277

WENDOVER

Nevada Crossing Hotel — Rates Subject to Change — Hotel ◆◆

Fri & Sat	1P	....	50.00	2P/1B	....	50.00	2P/2B	....	50.00 XP 5
Sun-Thurs	1P	....	40.00	2P/1B	....	40.00	2P/2B	....	40.00 XP 5

137 units. I-80 exit W Wendover; 1/4 mi e. 1035 Wendover Blvd. (PO Box 2457, 89883) A/C; C/CATV; phones. Htd indoor pool; indoor whirlpool. No pets. 4 1-bedroom efficiencies, $60; Fri & Sat for up to 2 persons, $50 Sun-Thurs. AE, DI, DS, MC, VI. Restaurant adjacent. Casino connected; cocktails. *(See ad p A576)*
Ⓢ Ⓓ ⓖ (702) 664-2900

WENDOVER, UTAH — 1,400

Best Western Salt Flat Inn — AAA Special Value Rates — Motel ◆◆◆

Sat [CP]	1P	45.00-	70.00	2P/1B	45.00-	70.00	2P/2B	50.00-	75.00 XP 5
Fri [CP]	1P	35.00-	60.00	2P/1B	35.00-	60.00	2P/2B	35.00-	60.00 XP 5
Sun-Thurs 5/16-9/15 [CP]	1P	35.00-	48.00	2P/1B	35.00-	50.00	2P/2B	40.00-	55.00 XP 5
Sun-Thurs 9/16-5/15 [CP]	1P	30.00-	40.00	2P/1B	30.00-	40.00	2P/2B	30.00-	40.00 XP 5

24 units. In town, off I-80, exit Utah 2. (PO Box 400, 84083) Check-in 3 pm. A/C; C/CATV; movies; phones. Htd pool; sauna; whirlpool; steamroom; exercise rm. Airport transp. No pets. Reserv deposit required; 30 days refund notice. AE, DI, DS, MC, VI.
⊗ Ⓓ (801) 665-7811

State Line Inn — Rates Subject to Change — Motel ◆◆◆

Fri & Sat	1P	43.00-	48.00	2P/1B	43.00-	48.00	2P/2B	43.00-	48.00 XP 5	F
Sun-Thurs	1P	29.00-	34.00	2P/1B	29.00-	34.00	2P/2B	29.00-	34.00 XP 5	F

101 units. 295 E Wendover Blvd. (PO Box 789, Wendover, UT, 84083) Check-in 3 pm. A/C; C/CATV; phones. Htd pool; whirlpool. No pets. AE, DI, DS, MC, VI.
Ⓢ Ⓓ (801) 665-2226

Western Ridge Motel — Rates Subject to Change — Motel ◆◆

Sat	1P	45.00-	55.00	2P/1B	48.00-	58.00	2P/2B	58.00-	68.00 XP 5	F
Fri	1P	35.00-	45.00	2P/1B	35.00-	45.00	2P/2B	35.00-	45.00 XP 5	F
Sun-Thurs	1P	26.00-	34.00	2P/1B	30.00-	36.00	2P/2B	30.00-	36.00 XP 5	F

55 units. In town, exit I-80, Utah 2. (PO Box 400, 84083) Check-in 3 pm. A/C; C/CATV; movies. 10 2-bedrm units. Htd pool. Pets. Reserv deposit required. AE, DI, DS, MC, VI.
⊗ Ⓓ (801) 665-2211

WINNEMUCCA — 6,300

Best Western Holiday Motel — Rates Subject to Change — Motel ◆◆◆

All year	1P	65.00-	75.00	2P/1B	75.00-	85.00	2P/2B	75.00-	85.00 XP 10

40 units. S of I-80; eastbound exit 176; westbound exit 178. 670 W Winnemucca Blvd. (89445) A/C; C/CATV; movies; radios; phones. Pool open 6/1-9/15. Pets. AE, DI, DS, MC, VI. FAX (702) 623-4221 *(See ad p A3)*
⊗ Ⓓ (702) 623-3684

Best Western Red Lion Inn & Casino — Rates Subject to Change — Motor Inn ◆◆◆

4/1-10/14	1P	70.00-	80.00	2P/1B	80.00-	90.00	2P/2B	80.00-	90.00 XP 10	F
10/15-3/31	1P	....	55.00	2P/1B	....	65.00	2P/2B	....	65.00 XP 10	F

107 units. S of I-80; eastbound exit 176, westbound exit 178. 741 W Winnemucca Blvd. (89445) Some large rooms. A/C; C/CATV; movies; radios; phones. 6 2-bedrm units. Swimming pool open 6/15-9/15. AE, DI, DS, MC, VI. ● Restaurant; 24 hours; $7-$16; cocktails. Casino. FAX (702) 623-5702 *(See ad p A3)*
⊗ Ⓓ ⓖ (702) 623-2565

Gold Country Inn — Rates Subject to Change — Motor Inn ◆◆◆

6/15-9/30	1P	65.00-	75.00	2P/1B	75.00-	85.00	2P/2B	75.00-	85.00 XP 10	F
10/1-6/14	1P	49.00-	59.00	2P/1B	59.00-	69.00	2P/2B	59.00-	69.00 XP 10	F

Senior discount. 71 units. S of I-80; eastbound exit 176, westbound exit 178. 921 W Winnemucca Blvd. (89445) A/C; C/CATV; movies; radios; phones. 1 2-bedrm unit, 15 kitchens. AE, DI, DS, MC, VI. Restaurant adjacent. FAX (702) 623-9190
⊗ Ⓢ Ⓓ (702) 623-6999

Pyrenees Motel — Rates Guaranteed — Motel ◆◆

5/1-10/31	1P	....	40.00	2P/1B	....	45.00	2P/2B	....	48.00 XP 4
11/1-4/30	1P	....	35.00	2P/1B	....	38.00	2P/2B	....	42.00 XP 4

Senior discount. 46 units. S of I-80; eastbound exit 176, westbound exit 178. 714 W Winnemucca Blvd. (89445) 17 refrigerators; A/C; C/CATV; phones; comb or shower baths. Pets. 6 units with microwave. AE, DI, DS, MC, VI. Coffeeshop opposite. FAX (702) 623-4892
⊗ Ⓓ ⓖ (702) 623-1116

Thunderbird Motel Rates Subject to Change *Motel* ◆◆◆
(辿) All year 1P 60.00- 63.00 2P/1B 65.00- 75.00 2P/2B 65.00- 75.00 XP 10 F
50 units. S of I-80; eastbound exit 176, westbound exit 178. 511 W Winnemucca Blvd. (89445) Many large rooms.
A/C; C/CATV; movies; radios; phones. Small pool open 6/1-9/15. Pets. 2 units with small conference area,
$75-$80 for up to 2 persons. AE, DI, DS, MC, VI. FAX (702) 623-4234 *(See ad p A3)* ⊗ Ⓓ (702) 623-3661

Town House Motel Rates Guaranteed *Motel* ◆◆◆
(辿) 6/1-9/30 .... 2P/1B .... 44.00 2P/2B .... 49.00 XP 5
4/1-5/31 & 10/1-10/31 .... 2P/1B .... 37.00 2P/2B .... 42.00 XP 5
11/1-3/31 .... 2P/1B .... 30.00 2P/2B .... 35.00 XP 5
19 units. S of I-80; eastbound exit 176, westbound exit 178; at 4 St. 375 Monroe St. (89445) A/C; C/CATV; movies;
radios; phones; comb or shower baths. Pool open 6/1-9/5. No pets. AE, DI, DS, MC, VI. *(See ad p A577)*
⊗ Ⓓ (702) 623-3620

Val-U Inn AAA Special Value Rates *Motel* ◆◆
(辿) 5/1-9/30 1P .... 45.00 2P/1B .... 50.00 2P/2B .... 55.00 XP 4
10/1-4/30 1P .... 39.00 2P/1B .... 41.00 2P/2B .... 45.00 XP 4
80 units. S of I-80; eastbound exit 176, westbound exit 178. 125 E Winnemucca Blvd. (89445) Few small rooms.
A/C; C/CATV; phones. Sauna; pool open 5/1-9/30; steamroom. Pets, $5 extra charge. AE, DI, DS, MC, VI.
FAX (702) 623-4722 ⊗ Ⓓ (702) 623-5248

RESTAURANTS

Martin Hotel Dining Room Ethnic $$ ◆
4 blks s off I-80 business rt. Railroad & Melarkey sts. Family-style full dinners include choice of steak, lamb & other en-
trees, house wine & dessert. Basque cuisine. A/C. Children's menu. Open 11 am-2 & 5-9:30 pm; Sat & Sun 5 pm-9:30
pm; closed 11/25 & 12/25. Cocktails & lounge. MC, VI. (702) 623-3197

Ormachea's Dinner House Ethnic $$ ◆◆
On US 95N at 2nd & Melarkey St. Family-style dinners. Choice of entree. Complimentary house wine, ice cream in-
cluded. Smoking permitted in lounge only. Basque cuisine. A/C. Children's menu. Open 6 pm-10 pm; closed Sun, Mon,
major holidays & Feb. Cocktails & lounge. Parking avail. MC, VI. ⊗ (702) 623-3455

BAJA CALIFORNIA

All rates are quoted in approximate U. S. Dollars. Mexican lodging establishments are required by law to quote and
charge in pesos according to rates set by the Ministry of Tourism.

CABO SAN LUCAS, B. C. S. — 11,000

Hotel Calinda Quality Beach Cabo San Lucas *Motor Inn* ◆◆◆
12/21-5/31 1P 100.00- 125.00 2P/1B 100.00- 125.00 2P/2B 100.00- 125.00 XP 15 F
6/1-12/20 1P 60.00- 80.00 2P/1B 60.00- 80.00 2P/2B 60.00- 80.00 XP 15 F
125 units. 5.7 km e on Mex 1. (PO Box 12) On bluff overlooking ocean. Attractive landscaping. Check-in 3 pm. A/C; 30
C/CATV; phones. 3 pools, 2 small; beach; whirlpools; charter fishing; tennis-3 courts. Fee for: snorkeling. Limited parking
lot. No pets. For reservations: (800) 228-5151. Service charge: 10%. Reserv deposit required. AE, DI, MC, VI. ● Dining
rm; 7 am-11 pm; $11-$22; cocktails. FAX (684) 3-0077 (684) 3-0044

Hotel Finisterra *Motor Inn* ◆◆◆
All year 1P 90.00- 130.00 2P/1B 99.00- 130.00 2P/2B 99.00- 130.00 XP 10-15 F
197 units. 1 km s. (APDO Postal NO. 1) Spectacular location on bluff overlooking ocean. 87 new units under contruction.
Scheduled to open fall, 1992. A/C; C/CATV; movies; radios; comb or shower baths. 2 2-bedrm units, 42 efficiencies. 2
pools; sauna; charter fishing; tennis-2 courts, 2 lighted extra charge; exercise rm. Fee for: skin diving, snorkeling; massage. No pets. For reservations: (213) 583-3393; (800) 347-2252 & (714) 827-3933. Service charge: 15%. Reserv deposit required; 7 days refund notice. MC, VI. ● Dining rm; 6:30 am-9:30 pm; $9-$20; cocktails; entertainment.
FAX (684) 3-0590 (684) 3-0000

Hotel Twin Dolphin [AP] *Resort Motor Inn* ◆◆◆◆
10/1-8/31 [AP] 1P .... 220.00 .... 2P/2B .... 300.00 XP 150
56 units. 11.9 km e on Mex 1. (PO Box 52) OPEN 10/1-8/31. On hillside overlooking ocean. Desert landscaping. Spacious rooms with patio. Refrigerators; A/C; shower baths. 6 2-bedrm units. Htd pool; beach; charter fishing, surf fishing;
putting green; lighted tennis-2 courts; nature trails; exercise rm; jogging track. Fee for: skin diving, snorkeling; massage.
No pets. For reservations: 1625 W Olympic Blvd, Suite 1, Los Angeles 90015; (800) 421-8925) (213) 386-3940. Service
charge: 15%. Reserv deposit required; 14 days refund notice. MC, VI. ● Dining rm; 7-9:30 am, 12:30-2 & 7-9 pm, public
by reserv only; $24; cocktails; entertainment. FAX (684) 3-0077 (684) 3-0259

Melia San Lucas *Resort Hotel* ◆◆◆
12/20-4/19 1P 144.00- 174.00 2P/1B 154.00- 174.00 2P/2B 164.00- 174.00 XP 35
4/20-12/19 1P 128.00- 158.00 2P/1B 138.00- 158.00 2P/2B 138.00- 158.00 XP 35
187 units. 2 blks e of Mex 1; at El Medano Beach. El Medano. Attractive pueblo style architecture around central landscaped grounds & pool overlooking bay & Land's End. Refrigerators; A/C; C/CATV; movies; phones. 2 pools; beach;
rental boats; charter fishing. Fee for: water skiing, windsurfing. Parking lot. No pets. For reservations: (800) 336-3542.
Monthly rates avail. Service charge: 10%. Reserv deposit required; 15 days refund notice. AE, MC, VI. ● Dining rm &
2 restaurants; 5 am-11 pm; $6-$30; 24 hour room service; cocktails; entertainment. FAX (684) 3-0420 (684) 3-1000

Pueblo Bonito Resort Rates Subject to Change *Resort Motor Inn* ◆◆◆
12/21-4/30 1P 135.00- 160.00 .... 2P/2B 135.00- 160.00 XP 35 F
5/1-12/20 1P 110.00- 135.00 .... 2P/2B 110.00- 135.00 XP 35 F
141 units. 3 blks s of Mex 1, El Medano Beach S/N. (PO Box 460) Beachfront location. Spacious, nicely furnished rooms
& suites. Balconies. A/C; C/CATV; phones. Efficiencies. Htd pool; beach; charter fishing; exercise rm. No pets. For reservations: (800) 262-4500. Service charge: 10%. Reserv deposit required; 7 days refund notice. AE, MC, VI. ● 2 restaurants; 7 am-10 pm; $6-$15; cocktails. FAX (684) 3-1995 (684) 3-1976

Villa Alfonso's *Bed & Breakfast* ◆◆
11/1-4/18 [BP] 1P 100.00- 135.00 2P/1B 100.00- 135.00 2P/2B .... 100.00 XP 15
4/19-10/31 [BP] 1P 75.00- 100.00 2P/1B 75.00- 100.00 2P/2B .... 75.00 XP 5
12 units. 0.6 km s of Mex 1. 16 de Septiembre at El Medano. (PO Box 3) Attractively furnished rooms in restored colonial home, 1 block to beach. A/C; shower or comb baths. Rooftop sun deck with whirlpool; heated
lap pool; 2 rooms with whirlpool tub. No pets. For reservations: (800) 347-2252; (714) 827-3933. Service charge: 15%.
Reserv deposit required; 14 days refund notice. MC, VI. ● Restaurant, see separate listing. (684) 3-0739

RESTAURANTS

Carlos & Charlie'e   Mexican $$ ◆◆
Blvd Marina #20. Popular restaurant serving a wide variety of entrees. A/C. Open noon-midnight. Cocktails. AE, CB, DI, MC, VI.   (684) 3-1280

Da Giorgio Restaurant   Italian $$ ◆◆◆
5 km e on Mex 1, then 1 km s; adjacent to Misiones Del Cabo. An impressive, open-air, palapa covered restaurant with view of ocean & Land's End. Features pasta, seafood & pizza. Open 8 am-11 pm. Cocktails & lounge. Valet parking. AE, MC, VI.

Peacocks (Pavo Real) Restaurant   Continental $$$ ◆◆
2 blks s of Mex 1, on Paseo de Pescador. Nice selection of European cuisine. Open 6 pm-11 pm; closed Mon in summer. Cocktails & lounge.   (684) 3-1858

Ristorante Galeon Italiano   Italian $$ ◆◆
1 km s. Blvd Marina S/N. Dining room & balcony seating overlooking town & bay. Nice selection of seafood, pasta, veal & pizza. A/C. Open 4 pm-11 pm. Cocktails & lounge. MC, VI.   (684) 3-0443

Romeo Y Julieta Ristorante   Italian $$ ◆◆
1/2 km s; Blvd Marina at Pedregal. Pasta, seafood & pizza served in a quaint hacienda. Open 4 pm-11 pm. Cocktails & lounge. MC, VI.   (684) 3-0225

Villa Alfonso's Restaurant   Nouvelle Mexican $$$$ ◆◆
1 km s of Mex 1 (in Villa Alfonso's). 16 de Septiembre at El Medano. Dining room & patio service in Mexican-colonial home, featuring international nouvelle cuisine. Prix fixe 6-course dinners, choice of 5 entrees. Open 6 pm-10:30 pm. Cocktails. Reserv advised. MC, VI.   (684) 3-0739

CATAVINA, B. C.

Hotel La Pinta   *Motor Inn*
All year   1P   .... 55.00   ....   2P/2B   .... 60.00 XP 10
28 units. On Mex 1. (APDO Postal 179, San Quintin, B. C.) Best avail. Isolated, attractive desert setting. Check-in 3 pm. 4 refrigerators; A/C; C/TV; shower baths. Small pool; wading pool. No pets. For reservations: Mexico Resorts International, PO Box 120637, Chula Vista, CA 92012; (800) 336-5454. MC, VI. ● Restaurant; 7 am-10 pm; $7-$15; cocktails. Phone Radiophone to Hotel La Pinta in Ensenada.

ENSENADA, B. C. — 260,900

Casa del Sol Motel   Rates Subject to Change   *Motel*   ◆
All year   1P   .... 53.00 1P/1B   .... 53.00 2P/2B   .... 68.00 XP 8
Senior discount. 48 units. 1 km s. 1001 Ave Adolfo Lopez Mateos & Blancarte. (PO Box 557) A/C; C/CATV; radios; phones; shower baths. 1 kitchen. Pool. Limited parking lot. No pets. For reservations: (800) 528-1234. Reserv deposit required. MC, VI. Cocktail lounge; restaurant adjacent. FAX (66) 78-1570   Phone (66) 78-1570

Ensenada Travelodge   *Motor Inn*   ◆◆
All year   1P 42.00- 45.00 2P/1B 55.00- 60.00 2P/2B 65.00- 70.00 XP 12   F
Senior discount. 52 units. 1 km s. 130 Ave Blancarte & Adolfo Lopez Mateos. A/C; C/CATV; movies; rental VCPs. Radios; phones; shower baths. Htd pool; whirlpool. No pets. 1 whirlpool suite, $125-$150. For reservations: (800)255-3050. Reserv deposit required; 3 days refund notice. AE, MC, VI. ● Restaurant; 7:30 am-11 pm; $6.50-$10; cocktail lounge. FAX (66) 78-4005   ⊗ Phone (66) 78-1601

Estero Beach Resort Hotel   *Resort Complex*   ◆◆
4/1-9/30   ....   2P/1B 64.00- 78.00 2P/2B 66.00- 88.00 XP 8
Fri-Sun 10/1-3/31   ....   2P/1B 54.00- 68.00 2P/2B 56.00- 78.00 XP 8
Mon-Thurs 10/1-3/31   ....   2P/1B 44.00- 62.00 2P/2B 46.00- 68.00 XP 8
107 units. 10.5 km s on Mex 1, 1.5 km w. (PO Box 86) Beachfront. Attractive grounds. Many rooms with balcony or patio. 17 refrigerators; C/CATV; movies; comb or shower baths. 10 kitchens, no utensils. Swimming; rental canoes; boat ramp; water skiing; rental boats, jet skis, wave runners, 4/1-10/1; rental bicycles; playground. Fee for: fishing, tennis-3 courts; riding. No pets. Reserv deposit required; 3 days refund notice. MC, VI. ● Restaurant; 7 am-10 pm; $8-$10; cocktails. FAX (66) 76-6925   ⊗ Phone (66) 76-6225

Punta Morro Hotel Suites   *Apartment Motor Inn*   ◆◆
6/1-9/30 & Sat & Sun 10/1-5/31 1P 68.00- 86.00 2P/1B 68.00- 86.00 2P/2B 68.00- 86.00 XP
Mon-Fri 10/1-5/31   1P 58.00- 69.00 2P/1B 58.00- 69.00 2P/2B 58.00- 69.00 XP
24 units. 5 km n on Mex 1. (Apartado Postal 2891) All units with terrace & ocean view. Refrigerators; C/CATV; phones; shower baths. 21 kitchens. Pool; whirlpool. No pets. 9 2-bedroom apartments, $95-$116 for up to 4 persons; 3 3-bedroom apartments, $130-$156 for up to 6 persons. Reservations: PO Box 434263 San Diego CA, 92143. Reserv deposit required; 7 days refund notice. AE, MC, VI. ● Restaurant; 1 pm-10 pm; $9.90-$20.45; cocktails. FAX (66) 74-4490   Phone (66) 78-3507

San Nicholas Resort Hotel   *Motor Inn*   ◆◆
Fri & Sat   1P 00.00- 78.00 2P/1B 78.00 00.00 2P/2B 78.00- 88.00 XP 8
Sun-Thurs   1P 58.00- 68.00 2P/1B 68.00- 78.00 2P/2B 68.00- 78.00 XP 8
Senior discount. 140 units. 1.5 km se on Ave Adolfo Lopez Mateos, at Ave Guadalupe. (PO Box 19) 35 refrigerators; A/C; C/CATV; radios; phones; shower baths. Htd pool; whirlpool. Parking lot. No pets. For reservations: PO Box 437060, San Ysidro, Ca 92143. 4 small suites & 3 whirlpool suites, $130-$260. Reserv deposit required; 3 days refund notice. AE, MC, VI. ● Restaurant & coffeeshop; 7 am-11 pm; $5-$17; cocktails; entertainment. FAX (66) 76-4930   Phone (66) 76-1901

RESTAURANTS

El Rey Sol Restaurant   French $$ ◆◆◆
1 km s at Ave Adolfo Lopez Mateos & Ave Blancarte. Attractive restaurant. Also offers a large selection of Mexican cuisine. A/C. Open 7:30 am-11 pm. Cocktails. AE, MC, VI.   PHONE (66) 78-1733

Enrique's Restaurant   Mexican $
2.3 km n on Mex 1D. Small restaurant serving a selection of steaks & seafood. Children's menu. Open 8 am-11:30 pm; closed 1/1, 5/1, 9/16 & 12/25. Cocktails. MC, VI.   PHONE (66) 78-2461

Haliotis   Seafood $
2 blks s of Calle Gral Augustin Sangines. Calle Delante O Sangines 179. Small informal restaurant. Specializing in fresh seafood; also serving chicken & beef. A/C. Open 1 pm-11 pm; closed Tues. Beer & wine. MC, VI. PHONE (66) 76-3720

La Cueva de los Tigres   Seafood $$ ◆◆
4 km se on Mex 1, 0.8 km w on gravel road. Attractive beachfront restaurant also serving a nice selection of steaks & Mexican specialties. Children's menu. Open 11 am-midnight; closed 1/1, 3/20, 5/1, 9/16 & 12/25. Cocktails & lounge. MC, VI.   PHONE (66) 78-2653

GUERRERO NEGRO, B. C. S. — 16,000

Hotel La Pinta   *Motor Inn*

All year	1P	....	55.00	....	2P/2B	.... 60.00 XP 10	F

27 units. 7.5 km ne on Mex 1 at 28th parallel. Best avail. C/TV; shower baths. No pets. For reservations: Mexico Resorts International, PO Box 120637, Chula Vista CA 92012; (800) 336-5454. MC, VI. ● Restaurant; 7 am-10 pm; $6-$15; cocktails.   (685) 7-1300

RESTAURANT

Malarrimo Restaurant   Seafood $ ◆
1 km w of Mex 1, at east edge of town. Open 7:30 am-10:30 pm; closed 12/25. Cocktails.

LA PAZ, B. C. S. — 166,000

Cabanas de Los Arcos   *Motel* ◆◆

All year	1P	....	58.00	....	2P/2B	.... 60.00 XP 5	F

Senior discount. 52 units. Center; 1/2 blk off Paseo Alvaro Obregon opposite the Malecon; adjacent to Hotel Los Arcos. (PO Box 112) 1/2 block from beach. Tropical garden setting. Some bungalows. A/C; C/CATV; movies; radios; phones; shower baths. Htd pool; charter fishing. No pets. Street parking only. For reservations 4422 Cerritos Ave, Los Alamitos CA 90720; or (800) 347-2252. Reserv deposit required; 7 days refund notice. AE, MC, VI. Restaurant adjacent.   (682) 2-2744

Hotel Gran Baja   *Resort Hotel*   F

All year	1P	....	60.00	....	2P/2B	.... 65.00 XP 5	F

112 units. 3.3 km w on Mex 1, 1 km n via Jalisco St toward bay. (PO Box 223) Multi-story beachfront hotel. All rooms with view of La Paz Bay. A/C; C/CATV; radios; phones. Pool; wading pool; beach; water skiing; charter fishing, surf fishing. Fee for: lighted tennis-2 courts. Parking lot. No pets. For reservations (800) 346-3942. Reserv deposit required. AE, DI, MC, VI. ● Restaurant; 6 am-midnight; $8-$20; cocktails. FAX (682) 2-0755   (682) 2-3900

Hotel Los Arcos   *Hotel* ◆◆

All year	1P 58.00- 60.00	....	2P/2B	60.00- 62.00 XP 5	F

Senior discount. 130 units. Center. Alvaro Obregon 498. (PO Box 112) Across from beach, overlooking La Paz Bay. A/C; C/CATV; movies; radios; phones; shower baths. Pool; charter fishing. Fee for: sauna. Limited parking lot. No pets. For reservations: 4422 Cerritos Ave, LosAlamitos CA 90720; or (800) 347-2252. Reserv deposit required; 7 days refund notice. AE, MC, VI. ● Cafeteria; 6 am-11 pm; $4-$8; cocktails. Also, Restaurant Bermejo, see separate listing. FAX (682) 5-4313   (682) 2-2744

Hotel Palmira   *Motor Inn*

12/16-4/30	1P	....	55.00	....	2P/2B	.... 60.00 XP 7	F
5/1-12/15	1P	....	45.00	....	2P/2B	.... 50.00 XP 7	F

Senior discount. 120 units. 2.5 km n on Carretera a Pichilingue, Mex 11, the road to ferry terminal. (PO Box 442) Across from bay. Attractive tropical landscaping. A/C; C/CATV; radios; phones; shower baths. Pool; wading pool; charter fishing; playground. Fee for: lighted tennis-1 court. No pets. Wkly rates avail. Reserv deposit required. AE, CB, DI, MC, VI. ● Restaurant; 7 am-10:30 pm; $5-$12; cocktails. Disco. FAX (682) 2-3727   (682) 2-4000

La Concha Beach Resort   *Resort Hotel* ◆◆◆

10/1-7/31	....	2P/1B	.... 85.00	2P/2B	.... 85.00 XP 15	
8/1-9/30	....	2P/1B	.... 70.00	2P/2B	.... 70.00 XP 15	

Senior discount. 107 units. 5 km ne; on Carretera a Pichilingue, Mex 11. (Apartado Postal 607) On attractively landscaped tree-shaded, oceanfront grounds. Rooms with bay view & balcony. Refrigerators; 66 C/CATV; phones; shower baths. Htd pool; beach; rental boats; fishing; charter fishing. Fee for: water skiing, scuba diving, snorkeling, windsurfing, parasailing; sightseeing tours. No pets. For reservations: (800) 999-2252; (310) 943-1369. Reserv deposit required; 3 days refund notice. AE, MC, VI. ● Restaurant; 7 am-10:30 pm; $6-$12; cocktails; entertainment. FAX (682) 2-6218   (682) 2-6544

RESTAURANTS

El Molina Steak House   Steak & Seafood $$ ◆
Across from Marina de La Paz. Topete Y Legaspy. Palapa setting with a selection of steaks, seafood & poultry. Open noon-midnight. Cocktails & lounge. MC, VI.   (682) 2-6191

El Taste   Mexican $$ ◆
Paseo Alvaro Obregon. Overlooking the Malecon & Bay. Featuring seafood & beef dishes. Open 8 am-midnight. Cocktails. MC, VI.   (682) 2-8121

La Paz-Lapa de Carlos 'n Charlies   Mexican $$ ◆
1 km sw; on Paseo Alvaro Obregon. Informal beachfront dining. Large selection of steaks, seafood & Mexican specialties. Children's menu. Open noon-11 pm; closed Tues. Cocktails & lounge. MC, VI.   (682) 2-6025

Restaurant Bermejo   Mexican $$ ◆◆
In Hotel Los Arcos. Attractive dining room with view of bay. Nice selection of seafood, pasta, steaks & Mexican specialties. A/C. Open noon-11 pm. Cocktails & lounge. AE, MC, VI.   (682) 2-2744

LORETO, B. C. S. — 9,000

Stouffer Presidente-Loreto   *Resort Motor Inn* ◆◆

ⓐ 4/1-8/31	1P 80.00- 105.00	2P/1B	80.00- 105.00	2P/2B	80.00- 105.00 XP 20	F
9/1-3/31	1P 70.00- 95.00	2P/1B	70.00- 95.00	2P/2B	70.00- 95.00 XP 20	F

230 units. 8 km s on Mex 1, then 1 km e in Nopolo. Blvd Mision de Loreto. On spacious, attractively landscaped oceanfront grounds; most rooms have ocean view & patio or balcony. A/C; C/CATV; movies; phones; shower baths. 2 htd pools; beach; fishing; charter fishing, scuba diving, snorkeling, sailing & windsurfing. Fee for: riding. No pets. For reserv: (800) 468-3571. AE, DI, MC, VI. ● Restaurant; 7 am-11 pm; $12-$25; cocktails. FAX (683) 3-0377   (683) 3-0700

RESTAURANT

El Nido Restaurant   Steak & Seafood $$ ◆◆
1 km e off Mex 1; at town entrance. Salvatierra 154. Ranch atmosphere featuring mesquite broiled steaks & seafood. A/C. Open noon-11 pm; closed 12/25. MC, VI.   (683) 3-0284

LOS BARRILES, B. C. S.

Hotel Punta Pescadero — *Resort Motor Inn* ◆◆
All year   1P .... 85.00   .... 2P/2B .... 85.00 XP 25
21 units. 12 km n of Mex 1, via narrow unpaved road with steep grades & sharp turns. (APDO Postal 362, La Paz, BCS) Secluded resort on picturesque sandy beach. All rooms have patio & ocean view. Also 2 4-bedroom villas. Phone 682-3636, ext 186. Refrigerators; A/C; C/CATV; shower baths. Pool; beach; rental boats; charter fishing, ski boats; tennis-2 courts, 1 lighted; 3500 ft paved landing strip, unicom 122.8; air taxi avail from La Paz or Los Cabos. Fee for: fishing, scuba diving equipment. For reservations: PO Box 1044, Los Altos, CA 94023 or (800)426-2252. Service charge: 10%. Reserv deposit required; 15 days refund notice. MC, VI. ● Dining rm; 6:30-9:30 am, lunch seating-1 pm, dinner seating-7pm;$16;cocktails.

MEXICALI, B. C. — 602,400

Holiday Inn — *Motor Inn* ◆◆◆
All year   .... 2P/1B .... 67.00 2P/2B .... 67.00 XP 12   F
171 units. 7.1 km se of border. 2220 Blvd Benito Juarez. (PO Box 5497, Calexico, CA, 92231) A/C; C/CATV; movies; radios; phones. Pool; wading pool. Fee for: lighted tennis-1 court. No pets. 47 1-bedroom suites, $87 for 2 persons. For reservations: (800) 465-4329. AE, CB, DI, MC, VI. ● Dining rm & restaurant; 7 am-1 am; $6-$14; cocktails; entertainment. FAX (65) 66-4901   ⊗ Phone (65) 66-1300

Holiday Inn Crown Plaza — *Hotel* ◆◆◆
All year   1P .... 98.00 2P/1B .... 98.00 2P/2B .... 98.00 XP 20   F
158 units. 7.2 km s of border Civic Center area. Blvd Lopez Mateos y Av de Los Heroes 201. (21000) A/C; C/CATV; movies; radios; phones. Pool. Garage & parking lot. No pets. AE, MC, VI. ● 2 restaurants; 6:30 am-midnight; $7-$22; cocktails. FAX (65) 57-0555   ⊗ Ⓓ Phone (65) 57-3600

Hotel Calafia — *Motor Inn* ◆
All year   .... 2P/1B .... 54.00 2P/2B .... 54.00 XP 8   F
173 units. 3 km se of border. Calzada Justo Sierra 1495. (21230) A/C; C/CATV; movies; phones; shower baths. Pool. No pets. AE, CB, DI, MC, VI. ● Restaurant & coffeeshop; 6 am-midnight; $5-$12; cocktails.   Phone (65) 68-3311

Hotel Lucerna — *Motor Inn* ◆◆
All year   1P .... 57.00 2P/1B .... 62.00 2P/2B .... 62.00 XP 12
190 units. 7.2 km se of border. 2151 Blvd Benito Juarez. (PO Box 2300, Calexico, CA, 92231) Attractive, nicely landscaped grounds. Refrigerators; A/C; C/CATV; movies; radios; phones; comb or shower baths. 2 pools, 1 htd. No pets. Reserv deposit required. AE, DI, MC, VI. ● 2 dining rms & coffeeshop; 7 am-11:30 pm; $9-$15; cocktails; entertainment. Also, Rivoli, see separate listing. FAX (65) 66-1000   Phone (65) 66-1000

RESTAURANT

Rivoli   French $$$ ◆◆◆
In Hotel Lucerna. Open 7 pm-1 am; closed Sun. Cocktails. AE, DI, MC, VI.   PHONE (65) 66-1000

MULEGE, B. C. S. — 38,600

RESTAURANTS

El Nido Steakhouse   Steak & Seafood $$ ◆
E edge of town center, on Calle Romero Rubio. Ranch atmosphere. Featuring mesquite broiled steaks, shrimp & seafood. A/C. Open 1 pm-10 pm; closed 12/25. Cocktails & lounge. MC, VI.   (685) 3-0221

Las Casitas Restaurant   Mexican $$ ◆
In Town Center Callejon de los Estudiantes & Ave Independencia. Attractive patio setting. Specializing in beef & seafood dishes. Open 7 am-10 pm; closed 12/25. Cocktails & lounge.   (685) 3-0019

ROSARITO, B. C.

Las Rocas Hotel & Suites — *Motor Inn* ◆◆◆
6/1-9/30 & Fri & Sat [CP]   .... 2P/1B   70.00- 150.00 2P/2B   130.00- 150.00 XP 10   F
Sun-Thurs 10/1-5/31 [EP]   .... 2P/1B   49.00- 99.00 2P/2B   93.00- 99.00 XP 10   F
Senior discount. 74 units. 10 km s on Mex Hwy 1. (PO Box 8851, Chula Vista, CA 91912) On a bluff overlooking ocean. All rooms with ocean view. C/CATV; movies. Pool; whirlpools; tennis-1 court. No pets. 1- & 2-bedroom penthouses with outdoor whirlpool, $119-$230. Deluxe rooms with microwave, refrigerator & fireplace $74-$150. For reservations (800) 733-6394. Reserv deposit required; 3 days refund notice. AE, MC, VI. ● Dining rm & coffeeshop; 7:30 am-10:30 pm; $9-$16; cocktails. FAX (66) 12-2140   Phone (66) 12-2140

RESTAURANTS

El Nido Steakhouse   Steak & Seafood $ ◆◆
In town. Benito Juarez 67. Ranch atmosphere featuring mesquite broiled steaks, shrimp & seafood. A/C. Open 8 am-midnight; closed 9/16 & 12/25. Cocktails.   PHONE (66) 12-1431

Los Pelicanos   Steak & Seafood $ ◆◆
On the beach. Calle Ebano 113. Nice selection of mesquite broiled steaks, shrimp & seafood. A/C. Open 8 am-midnight; closed 9/16 & 12/25. Cocktails. MC, VI.   PHONE (66) 12-1757

SAN FELIPE, B. C. — 11,000

Hotel Las Misiones San Felipe — *Motor Inn* ◆◆
All year   1P .... 72.00 2P/1B .... 72.00 2P/2B .... 72.00 XP 15
Senior discount. 241 units. On road to airport, 3.2 km s of jct Mex 5. 138 Avenida Mision de Loreto. (PO Box 7544, Calexico, CA 92231) Many rooms with balconies overlooking Gulf of California. 20 refrigerators; A/C; C/CATV; movies; phones; comb or shower baths. 7 efficiencies, utensils, extra charge. 3 pools, 1 htd; 2 wading pools; beach; volleyball court. Fee for: lighted tennis-2 courts. No pets. For reservations: Mexico Resorts International 740 Bay Blvd, Suite 105, Chula Vista, CA 92910 (619) 422-6900, CA (800) 336-5454. Reserv deposit required; 3 days refund notice. AE, MC, VI. ● Coffeeshop; 7 am-11 pm; $10-$14; cocktails. FAX (65) 77-1283   Phone (65) 77-1281

RESTAURANT

El Nido Steakhouse   Steakhouse $ ◆◆
On Mar de Cortez; 1/2 km s of town center. Nicely decorated ranch atmosphere. Featuring mesquite broiled steaks, shrimp & seafood. A/C. Open 2 pm-11 pm; closed Wed. Cocktails.

SAN IGNACIO, B. C. S. — 2,000

Hotel La Pinta   *Motor Inn*
All year   1P .... 58.00   ....   2P/2B .... 60.00 XP 10
Senior discount. 28 units. 2.5 km w of jct Mex 1, towards town plaza. Apartado Postal 37. (23930) Best avail. Attractive tropical landscaping. A/C; C/TV; shower baths. Small pool; wading pool. No pets. For reservations: Mexico Resorts International PO Box 120637, Chula Vista CA 92012; (800) 336-5454. Reserv deposit required; 3 days refund notice. MC, VI. ● Restaurant; 7 am-10:30 pm; $6-$15; cocktails.   (685) 4-0300

SAN JOSE DEL CABO, B. C. S. — 15,000

Casa Del Mar Hotel   *Motor Inn*   Under Construction
31 units. 11 1/2 km w on Mex 1, in Cabo Real. Scheduled to open September, 1992. A/C; C/CATV; phones. Pool; beach. Fee for: golf-9 holes. No pets. Restaurant; cocktail lounge.

Hotel Conrad Los Cabos   *Resort Hotel*   Under Construction
239 units. 10 km w on Mex 1. Beachfront resort. Scheduled to open January, 1993. A/C; C/TV; phones. 2 pools; exercise rm. No pets. 2 restaurants; cocktails. *A Hilton Hotel.*

Fiesta Inn   *Motor Inn*   ◆◆
12/21-4/9   1P .... 90.00   2P/1B .... 90.00   2P/2B .... 90.00 XP 20   F
4/20-12/20   1P .... 65.00   2P/1B .... 65.00   2P/2B .... 65.00 XP 15   F
Senior discount. 151 units. 1/2 km e off Mex 1. Blvd Malecon San Jose. (APDO Postal 124) Attractively landscaped grounds on the beach. Rooms with patio or balcony & ocean or garden views. A/C; C/CATV; movies; phones. Htd pool; beach; charter fishing. No pets. For reservations: (800) 343-7821. AE, MC, VI. ● Restaurant; 7 am-10:30, noon-5 & 6:30-10:30 pm; $4-$12; cocktails. FAX (684) 2-0480   (684) 2-0793

Hotel Posada Real Los Cabos   *Motor Inn*   ◆◆
12/20-4/19   1P .... 95.00   2P/1B .... 95.00   2P/2B .... 95.00 XP 10
4/20-12/19   1P .... 65.00   2P/1B .... 65.00   2P/2B .... 65.00 XP 10
Senior discount. 150 units. 1/2 km e, off Mex 1. Malecon San Jose. (PO Box 51) On the beach; most rooms with ocean view. A/C; C/CATV; phones; shower baths. Pool; wading pool; whirlpools; charter boats. Fee for: lighted tennis-1 court. No pets. For reservations: (800) 528-1234. Reserv deposit required; 3 days refund notice. AE, MC, VI. ● Restaurant; 7 am-10:30 pm; $4-$14; cocktails.   (684) 2-0155

Howard Johnson Plaza Suite Hotel & Resort   *Apartment Hotel*   ◆◆◆
12/16-4/15   1P 95.00- 140.00   ....   2P/2B 95.00- 140.00 XP
4/16-12/15   1P 90.00- 129.00   ....   2P/2B 90.00- 129.00 XP
172 units. 0.5 km e of Mex 1. Paseo Finisterra 1. (PO Box 152) Attractive Mexican colonial & Moorish-style buildings surrounding courtyard & pool. Hotel rooms & 1-3 bedroom apartments. A/C; C/CATV; movies; phones. Htd pool; charter fishing, sailing, scuba diving. Fee for: golf-9 holes, tennis-2 courts. Valet parking lot. No pets. For reservations (800) 654-2000. Reserv deposit required; 7 days refund notice. AE, MC, VI. ● Restaurant; 7 am-11 pm; $6-$14; cocktails. FAX (684) 2-0806   (684) 2-0999

Melia Cabo Real   *Resort Motor Inn*   ◆◆◆
12/20-4/19   1P .... 128.00   2P/1B .... 138.00   2P/2B .... 138.00 XP 35
4/20-12/19   1P .... 100.00   2P/1B .... 110.00   2P/2B .... 110.00 XP 35
Senior discount. 309 units. 11 km w on Mex 1. Carretera Cabo San Lucas km 19.5. Spacious oceanfront grounds. Desert landscaping. A/C; C/CATV; phones. Pool; beach; sauna; charter fishing. Fee for: golf-9 holes, lighted tennis-1 court. Pets. For reservations: (800) 336-3542. Monthly rates avail. Service charge: 15%. Reserv deposit required; 15 days refund notice. AE, MC, VI. ● 4 restaurants; 24 hours; $6-$20; cocktails; entertainment. FAX (684) 3-1003 (Ⓓ) (684) 3-0967

Stouffer Presidente Los Cabos   *Resort Motor Inn*   ◆◆◆
(AAA) 12/21-4/26   1P 110.00- 170.00   2P/1B 110.00- 170.00   2P/2B 110.00- 170.00 XP 20   F
4/27-12/20   1P 70.00- 110.00   2P/1B 70.00- 110.00   2P/2B 70.00- 110.00 XP 15   F
Senior discount. 240 units. 2 1/2 km e of Mex 1. Paseo San Malecon at Blvd Mijares. (APDO Postal 2) Attractive location with beautifully landscaped spacious grounds; on the beach. Check-in 3 pm. A/C; C/CATV; movies; phones; shower baths. Htd pool; wading pool; charter fishing; tennis-2 courts, 2 lighted extra charge. No pets. For reservations: (800) 468-3571. Service charge: 10%. Reserv deposit required; 3 days refund notice. AE, CB, DI, MC, VI. ● Dining rm & 2 restaurants; 7 am-10:30 pm; $10-$18; 24 hour room service; cocktails. Disco. FAX (684) 2-0232   (684) 2-0211

RESTAURANTS

Da Giorgio Restaurant   Italian $$ ◆◆
9 km w on Mex 1; near Palmilla. Dining in a hilltop villa overlooking Bay of San Jose. A/C. Open 3 pm-11 pm. Cocktails & lounge. AE, MC, VI.

Damiana   Mexican   ◐◐   ◆
Downtown; at Town Plaza. Blvd Mijares 8. Patio & inside dining in quaint atmosphere. Specializing in Mexican seafood & regional dishes. Open 11 am-11 pm; closed 12/25. Cocktails & lounge.   (684) 2-0499

Ivan's European Restaurant   Continental $$ ◆
Downtown. Blvd Mijares No. 16. On second floor overlooking town plaza & city hall. Nice selection of European cuisine. A/C. Open 6 pm-11 pm. Cocktails.

SAN QUINTIN, B. C.

Hotel La Pinta   *Motor Inn*
All year   1P .... 55.00   ....   2P/2B .... 58.00 XP 10   F
58 units. 16 km s on Mex 1, 4 1/2 km to outer San Quintin Bay. (Apartado Postal 168) Best avail. On beach, most rooms with ocean view. Check-in 3 pm. 20 refrigerators; C/TV; movies; shower baths. Fishing. No pets. For reservations: Mexico Resorts International, PO Box 120637, Chula Vista, CA 92012; (800) 336-5454. Reserv deposit required; 3 days refund notice. MC, VI. ● Restaurant; 7:30 am-10:30 pm; $6-$15; cocktails.   Phone (66) 65-2878

Check out our **bold** listings!

TIJUANA, B. C. — 742,700

Hotel Fiesta Americana Tijuana | Rates Subject to Change | *Hotel* ◆ ◆ ◆
All year   1P 111.00- 145.00   2P/1B   111.00- 145.00   2P/2B   111.00- 145.00   XP 15   F
422 units. 0.6 km e of Ave Rodriquez. Blvd Agua Caliente No. 4500. (PO Box BC, Chula Vista, CA, 92012) Check-in 3 pm. A/C; C/CATV; movies; radios; phones. Htd pool; saunas; whirlpool; tennis-2 courts. Fee for: exercise rm. Garage. No pets. For reservations: (800)343-7811 or 343-7815. Reserv deposit required; 3 days refund notice. AE, CB, DI, MC, VI. ● 2 dining rms & coffeeshop; 24 hours; $4.50-$15; 24 hour room service; disco; cocktails; entertainment; nightclub. Also, Place De La Concorde, see separate listing. FAX (66) 81-7016   Ⓢ Ⓓ Phone (66) 81-7014

Hotel Paraiso-Radisson | Rates Subject to Change | *Hotel* ◆ ◆
All year   1P 72.00- 80.00   2P/1B   82.00- 90.00   2P/2B   82.00- 90.00   XP 10   F
Senior discount. 200 units. Adjacent to Tijuana Country Club golf course. Blvd Agua Caliente No. 1. (PO Box 1588, San Ysidro, CA, 92073) 40 refrigerators; A/C; C/CATV; movies; radios; phones. Htd pool; whirlpool; exercise rm. Parking lot. No pets. For Reservations: (800)333-3333. Wkly rates avail. Reserv deposit required; 3 days refund notice. AE, MC, VI. ● Dining rm; 7 am-midnight; $11-$18; cocktails. FAX (66) 81-7200   ⊗ Ⓓ Phone (66) 86-3637

Hotel Lucerna | Rates Subject to Change | *Hotel* ◆ ◆
All year   1P ....   65.00   2P/1B   70.00- 75.00   2P/2B   70.00- 75.00   XP 12   F
168 units. E side in Rio Tijuana area. Paseo de los Heroes at Ave Rodriquez. A/C; C/CATV; movies; radios; phones. Pool. Parking lot. No pets. For reservations: PO Box 437910 San Ysidro CA 92143; or (800) 582-3762. 10 apartments with microwave & refrigerator, $105. Reserv deposit required; 3 days refund notice. AE, DI, MC, VI. ● Restaurant & coffeeshop; 7 am-11 pm; $3-$8; cocktails; entertainment. Also, Rivoli, see separate listing. FAX (66) 34-2400   Ⓚ Phone (66) 84-2000

RESTAURANTS

Alcazar del Rio | Continental | $$$ ◆ ◆ ◆
Zona del Rio; opposite Sears Shopping Center. Paseo de los Heroes 56-A. International dishes served in formal dining room with refined service. A/C. Open noon-midnight; closed major holidays. Cocktails. MC, VI.   PHONE (66) 84-2672

Boccaccio's | Italian | $$
3.5 km se. Blvd Agua Caliente 2500. Refined atmosphere. Nice variety of seafood; steaks & Mexican dishes served also. A/C. Open 1 pm-midnight; closed major holidays. Cocktails. Reserv advised. MC, VI.   PHONE (66) 86-2266

Place De La Concorde | French | $$$ ◆ ◆ ◆ ◆
At Hotel Fiesta Americana Tijuana. Blvd Aqua Caliente No 4500. A beautiful, elegant dining room. A/C. Open 6 pm-midnight; closed Sun & major holidays. Cocktails. AE, CB, DI, MC, VI.   PHONE (66) 81-7014

Rivoli | French | $$
In Hotel Lucerna. Attractive dining room. A/C. Open 7 am-midnight; Sun 7 am-2 pm; closed major holidays. Cocktails & lounge. AE, MC, VI.   PHONE (66) 84-2000

BAJA CALIFORNIA, MEXICO

RATES—All rates are quoted in approximate U.S. dollars. Much of the information in this book is necessarily compiled some time in advance of publication. **Rates are subject to change and are for information only.**

Mexican lodging establishments catering to the tourist trade are required to quote and charge in pesos according to the maximum prices that the Ministry of Tourism sets periodically. The government-approved rate must be posted by the front desk and in each room. The establishment must abide by these posted rates. An establishment may apply for a rate change, but cannot charge different rates until it has received and posted new rate forms. Ceiling prices in pesos have been established for restaurants as well. These rates do not include any room, food or beverage tax.

Any violations of posted rates should be reported with documentation—either the bill itself or a photocopy—to the Ministry of Tourism and AAA. This enables both agencies to make a full investigation on your behalf. Rate complaints should be directed to the Ministry of Tourism through the following representative: Director, Mexican Government Tourist Office, 405 Park Ave., Suite 1002, New York, NY 10022.

RESERVATIONS—Confirmed reservations should be obtained for accommodations in the states of Baja California and Baja California Sur. Most establishments require a 1-day deposit with reservations. If you find it impossible to use your reservation, notify the establishment. If notification is by mail, allow sufficient time for postal transit and delivery. Most establishments require 3 to 10 days' cancellation notice for deposit refund; a minimum of 10 days is suggested. Establishments in Ensenada do not refund deposits on cancellation of holiday reservations.

FOR YOUR INFORMATION

Three handy sections to help make your vacation planning easier.

AAA Clubs and Branch Offices

Need a sheet map or Triptik map? Run out of travelers checks? Want the latest update on local road conditions? All this information and more awaits you at more than 1,000 AAA and CAA clubs and offices across the United States and Canada—a boon for travelers in an unfamiliar state, province or city. Each listing provides the office address, phone number and hours of service.

Temperature Chart

Knowing what clothes to pack for a trip can make the difference between pleasant vacationing and unpleasant surprises. Use the temperature chart to help determine your on-the-road wardrobe. The chart, found in each TourBook, lists average monthly maximum and minimum temperatures for representative cities.

Driving Distances Map

For safety's sake, it makes sense to take regular breaks while driving on the open road. The driving distances map is a quick and useful reference for trip planning—from a 1-day excursion to a cross-country jaunt. It provides both the mileage and the average driving time (excluding stops) between towns and cities located throughout a state or province.

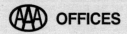 OFFICES

Names of main offices are listed in dark type; names of branch offices, in light type. All are closed Saturdays, Sundays and holidays unless otherwise indicated.

The type of service provided is designated after the phone number of each office:

✚ = Auto travel services, including books/maps, marked maps and on-demand Triptik maps

● = Auto travel services, including books/maps, marked maps, but no on-demand Triptik maps

■ = Provides books/maps only. No marked maps or on-demand Triptik maps available

▲ = Travel agency service

CALIFORNIA

ALHAMBRA—(See San Gabriel).

ANAHEIM—Auto. Club of So. Calif., 150 W. Vermont Ave., 92805. M-F 9-5. (714) 774-2392.✚▲

ANAHEIM—Auto. Club of So. Calif., 5500 E. Santa Ana Canyon Rd., 92807. M-F 9-5. (714) 921-2850.✚▲

ANGELS CAMP—Calif. State Auto. Assn., 451 S. Main, Hwy. 49; *Mailing Address: PO Box 594, 95221.* M-F 8:30-5. (209) 736-4517.✚

ANTIOCH—Calif. State Auto. Assn., 2615 Somersville Rd.; *Mailing Address: PO Box 2239, 94531.* M-F 8:30-5. (510) 754-2210.✚

ARCADIA—Auto. Club of So. Calif., 420 E. Huntington Dr.; *Mailing Address: PO Box K, 91066.* M-F 9-5. (818) 445-5441.✚▲

ARTESIA—Auto. Club of So. Calif., 18642 S. Gridley Rd.; *Mailing Address: PO Box 6087, 90701.* M-F 9-5. (310) 924-6636.✚▲

AUBURN—Calif. State Auto. Assn., 2495 Bell Rd., 95603. M-F 8:30-5. (916) 885-6561.✚

AZUSA—Auto. Club of So. Calif., 1167 E. Alosta Ave., 91702. M-F 9-5. (818) 963-8531.✚▲

BAKERSFIELD—Auto. Club of So. Calif., 1500 Commercial Way; *Mailing Address: PO Box 12003, 93389.* M-F 9-5. (805) 327-4661.✚▲

BEACH CITIES—(See Manhattan Beach).

BERKELEY—Calif. State Auto. Assn., 1775 University Ave.; *Mailing Address: PO Box 310, 94701.* M-F 8:30-5. (510) 845-8890.✚

BEVERLY HILLS—(See Century City).

BISHOP—Auto. Club of So. Calif., 187 W. Pine St.; *Mailing Address: PO Box 1028, 93514.* M-F 9-5. (619) 872-8241.✚

BLYTHE—Auto. Club of So. Calif., 221 E. Hobsonway, 92225. M-F 9-5. (619) 922-3194.✚

BURBANK—Auto. Club of So. Calif., 550 N. 3rd St.; *Mailing Address: PO Box 4069, 91503.* M-F 9-5. (818) 843-2833.✚

CAPITOLA—Calif. State Auto. Assn., 4400 Capitola Rd.; *Mailing Address: PO Box 250, 95010.* M-F 8:30-5. (408) 479-9830.✚▲

CENTURY CITY—Auto. Club of So. Calif., 1950 Century Park E., 90067. M-F 9-5. (310) 277-0900.✚▲

CHICO—Calif. State Auto. Assn., 1160 E. 1st Ave.; *Mailing Address: PO Box 1120, 95927.* M-F 8:30-5. (916) 891-8601.✚

CHINO—Auto. Club of So. Calif., 11911 Central Ave.; *Mailing Address: PO Box 1846, 91708.* M-F 9-5. (714) 591-9451.✚▲

CHULA VISTA—Auto. Club of So. Calif., 569 Telegraph Canyon Rd.; *Mailing Address: PO Box 1267, 92012.* M-F 9-5. (619) 421-0410.✚

CLOVIS—Calif. State Auto. Assn., 1595 W. Shaw Ave., 93612. M-F 8:30-5. (209) 298-9121.✚▲

CONCORD—Calif. State Auto. Assn., 2055 Meridian Park Blvd.; *Mailing Address: PO Box 4019, 94524.* M-F 8:30-5. (510) 671-2708.✚▲

COSTA MESA—Auto. Club of So. Calif., 659 W. 19th St.; *Mailing Address: PO Box 10865, 92627.* M-F 9-5. (714) 645-3300.✚

COVINA—Auto. Club of So. Calif., 325 E. Rowland St., 91723. M-F 9-5. (818) 967-9321.✚

CULVER CITY—Auto. Club of So. Calif., 4512 Sepulveda Blvd.; *Mailing Address: PO Box 2100, 90231.* M-F 9-5. (310) 390-9866.✚

CUPERTINO—Calif. State Auto. Assn., 1601 Saratoga-Sunnyvale Rd.; *Mailing Address: PO Box 161685, 95016.* M-F 8:30-5. (408)996-3553.✚▲

DALY CITY—Calif. State Auto. Assn., 1617 Southgate Ave., 94015. M-F 8:30-5. (415) 994-8400.✚▲

DEL MAR—Auto. Club of So. Calif., 12835 Point Del Mar Way, 92014. M-F 9-5. (619) 481-7181✚▲

DOWNEY—Auto. Club of So. Calif., 8500 E. Florence Ave., 90240. M-F 9-5. (310) 861-2231.✚

DUBLIN—Calif. State Auto. Assn., 7035 Dublin Blvd.; *Mailing Address: PO Box 2489, 94568.* M-F 8:30-5. (510) 829-2021.✚

EL CENTRO—Auto. Club of So. Calif., 300 S. Imperial Ave., Suite 12; *Mailing Address: PO Box 3007, 92244.* M-F 9-5. (619) 352-6731.✚

ESCONDIDO—Auto. Club of So. Calif., 800 La Terraza Boulevard, 92025. M-F 9-5. (619) 745-2124.✚▲

EUREKA—Calif. State Auto. Assn., 707 L St.; *Mailing Address: PO Box 1308, 95502.* M-F 8:30-5. (707) 443-5087.✚

FAIRFIELD—Calif. State Auto. Assn., 222 Acacia St.; *Mailing Address: PO Box 90, 94533.* M-F 8:30-5. (707) 422-1820.✚

FRESNO—Calif. State Auto. Assn., 5040 N. Forkner Ave.; *Mailing Address: PO Box 9300, 93791.* M-F 8:30-5. (209) 435-8450.✚▲

FULLERTON—Auto. Club of So. Calif., 2101 N. Harbor Blvd., 92635. M-F 9-5. (714) 871-2333.✚

GARDENA—Auto. Club of So. Calif., 2416 W. El Segundo Blvd.; *Mailing Address: PO Box 1398, 90249.* M-F 9-5. (310) 323-4000.✚

GARDEN GROVE—Auto. Club of So. Calif., 10402 Westminster Ave.; *Mailing Address: PO Box 1018, 92642.* M-F 9-5. (714) 638-1330.✚

GILROY—Calif. State Auto. Assn., 1395 Hecker Pass Hwy.; *Mailing Address: PO Box 1765, 95021.* M-F 8:30-5. (408) 847-2300.✚

GLENDALE—Auto. Club of So. Calif., 1233 E. Broadway; *Mailing Address: PO Box 9280, 91206.* M-F 9-5. (818) 240-2200.✚▲

GLENDORA—(See Azusa).

GRASS VALLEY—Calif. State Auto. Assn., 113-B Dorsey Dr., 95945. M-F 8:30-5. (916) 272-9011.✚

GREENBRAE—Calif. State Auto. Assn., 100 Drake's Landing Rd., 94904. M-F 8:30-5. (415) 925-1200.✚▲

HACIENDA HEIGHTS—Auto. Club of So. Calif., 2245 S. Hacienda Blvd.; *Mailing Address: PO Box 5400, 91745.* M-F 9-5. (818) 961-9331.✚

HANFORD—Calif. State Auto. Assn., 780 N. Irwin St.; *Mailing Address: PO Box G-988, 93232.* M-F 8:30-5. (209) 582-9071.✚

HAYWARD—Calif. State Auto. Assn., 1580 Chabot Ct.; *Mailing Address: PO Box 3368, 94540.* M-F 8:30-5. (510) 784-0900.✚▲

HEMET—Auto. Club of So. Calif., 450 W. Stetson Ave., 92343. M-F 9-5. (714) 652-6202.✚▲

HOLLISTER—Calif. State Auto. Assn., 191 San Felipe Rd., Suite M; *Mailing Address: PO Box 780, 95024.* M-F 8:30-5. (408) 637-7457.✚

HOLLYWOOD—Auto. Club of So. Calif., 4773 Hollywood Blvd., 90027. M-F 9-5. (213) 666-2420.✚

HUNTINGTON BEACH—Auto. Club of So. Calif., 7891 Talbert Ave.; *Mailing Address: PO Box 1370, 92647.* M-F 9-5. (714) 848-2227.✚

HUNTINGTON PARK—Auto. Club of So. Calif., 7301 State St.; *Mailing Address: PO Box 3127, 90255.* M-F 9-5. (213) 582-6481.✚

INDIO—Auto. Club of So. Calif., 45-915 Oasis St.; *Mailing Address: PO Box AAA, 92202.* M-F 9-5. (619) 347-0961.✚

INGLEWOOD—Auto. Club of So. Calif., 1234 Centinela Ave., 90302. M-F 9-5. (310) 673-5170.✚

JACKSON—Calif. State Auto. Assn., 2092 W. Hwy. 88; *Mailing Address: PO Box 668, 95642.* M-F 8:30-5. (209) 223-2761.✚

KINGS BEACH—Calif. State Auto. Assn., 7717 N. Lake Blvd.; *Mailing Address: PO Box 19, 96148.* M-F 8:30-5. (916) 546-4245.✚

LAFAYETTE—Calif. State Auto. Assn., 3390 Mt. Diablo Blvd.; *Mailing Address: PO Box 1699, 94549.* M-F 8:30-5. (510) 283-9450.✚

LAGUNA—(See South Laguna).

LAGUNA HILLS—Auto. Club of So. Calif., 25181 Paseo De Alicia; *Mailing Address: PO Box 2249, 92654.* M-F 9-5. (714) 951-1400.✚▲

LA HABRA—Auto. Club of So. Calif., 1700 W. La Habra Blvd.; *Mailing Address: PO Box 815, 90633.* M-F 9-5. (310) 694-3711.✚▲

LAKEPORT—Calif. State Auto. Assn., 1464 Parallel Dr., 95453. M-F 8:30-5. (707) 263-4807.✚

LAKE TAHOE—(See South Lake Tahoe).

LA MESA—Auto. Club of So. Calif., 8765 Fletcher Pkwy.; *Mailing Address: PO Box 8900, 91944.* M-F 9-5. (619) 464-7001.✚▲

LANCASTER—Auto. Club of So. Calif., 1055 W. Ave. J; *Mailing Address: PO Box 1899, 93539.* M-F 9-5. (805) 948-7661.✚

LIVERMORE—(See Dublin).

LODI—Calif. State Auto. Assn., 1335 S. Fairmont Ave.; *Mailing Address: PO Box 610, 95241.* M-F 8:30-5. (209) 334-9671.✚

LOMPOC—Auto. Club of So. Calif., 816 E. Ocean Ave.; *Mailing Address: PO Box 340, 93438.* M-F 9-5. (805) 735-2731.✚

LONG BEACH—Auto. Club of So. Calif., 4800 Los Coyotes Diagonal, 90815. M-F 9-5. (310) 597-2421.✚▲

LOS ANGELES—Auto. Club of So. Calif., 2601 S. Figueroa St.; *Mailing Address Terminal Annex Box 30432, 90030.* M-F 9-5. (213) 741-3111.✚▲

LOS ANGELES—(Also see Century City, Hollywood and South Los Angeles).

LOS CERRITOS—(See Artesia).

LOS GATOS—Calif. State Auto. Assn., 101 Blossom Hill Rd., 95030. M-F 8:30-5. (408) 395-6411.✚

MADERA—Calif. State Auto. Assn., 221 North G St.; *Mailing Address: PO Box 1200, 93639.* M-F 8:30-5. (209) 673-3586.✚

MANHATTAN BEACH—Auto. Club of So. Calif., 700 S. Aviation Blvd., 90266. M-F 9-5. (310) 376-0521.✚▲

MANTECA—Calif. State Auto. Assn., 145 Trevino Ave., *Mailing Address: PO Box 2215, 95336.* M-F 8:30-5. (209) 239-1252.✚

MARYSVILLE—Calif. State Auto. Assn., 1205 D St.; *Mailing Address: PO Box 430, 95901.* M-F 8:30-5. (916) 742-5531.✚

MERCED—Calif. State Auto. Assn., 3065 M St.; *Mailing Address: PO Box 2227, 95344.* M-F 8:30-5. (209) 723-9143.✚

MODESTO—Calif. State Auto. Assn., 3525 Coffee Rd.; *Mailing Address: PO Box 579570, 95357.* M-F 8:30-5. (209) 523-9171.✚▲

MONTEBELLO—Auto. Club of So. Calif., 2444 W. Beverly Blvd., 90640. M-F 9-5. (213) 725-6545.✚

MONTEREY—Calif. State Auto. Assn., 53 Soledad Dr.; *Mailing Address: PO BIN 711, 93942.* M-F 8:30-5. (408) 373-3021.✚

MONTROSE—Auto. Club of So. Calif., 2112 Montrose Ave.; *Mailing Address: P. O. Box 508, 91020.* M-F 9-5. (818) 249-3971.✚

MORENO VALLEY—Auto. Club of So. Calif., 12240-B Perris Blvd.; *Mailing Address: PO Box 8200, 92303.* M-F 9-5. (714) 243-6344.✚

MOUNTAIN VIEW—Calif. State Auto. Assn., 900 Miramonte Ave.; *Mailing Address: PO Box 391840, 94039.* M-F 8:30-5. (415) 965-7000.✚▲

NAPA—Calif. State Auto. Assn., 800 Trancas St.; *Mailing Address: PO Box 3630, 94558.* M-F 8:30-5. (707) 226-9961.✚▲

NEWARK—Calif. State Auto. Assn., 39600 Balentine Dr.; *Mailing Address: PO Box 324, 94560.* M-F 8:30-5. (510) 770-9280.✚▲

NEWPORT BEACH—Auto. Club of So. Calif., 3880 Birch St., 92660. M-F 9-5. (714) 476-8880.✚▲

NORTH LONG BEACH—Auto. Club of So. Calif., 4565 California Ave., 90807. M-F 9-5. (310) 428-6461.✚

NORTHRIDGE—Auto. Club of So. Calif., 9440 Reseda Blvd.; *Mailing Address: PO Box 646, 91328.* M-F 9-5. (818) 993-1616.✚▲

NORWALK—Auto. Club of So. Calif., 12901 Norwalk Blvd.; *Mailing Address: PO Box 59298, 90652.* M-F 9-5. (310) 868-0541.✚

OAKLAND—Calif. State Auto. Assn., 380 W. MacArthur Blvd., 94609. M-F 8:30-5. (510) 652-1812.✚▲

OCEANSIDE—Auto. Club of So. Calif., 3330 Vista Way; *Mailing Address: PO Box 1128, 92054.* M-F 9-5. (619) 433-6261.✚

ONTARIO—(See Upland).

OROVILLE—Calif. State Auto. Assn., 1430 Feather River Blvd.; *Mailing Address: PO Box 152, 95965.* M-F 8:30-5. (916) 533-3931.✚

PALM SPRINGS—Auto. Club of So. Calif., 300 S. Farrell Dr.; *Mailing Address: PO Box 1587, 92263.* M-F 9-5. (619) 320-1121.✚▲

PALO ALTO—Calif. State Auto. Assn., 430 Forest Ave.; *Mailing Address: PO Box 1673, 94302.* M-F 8:30-5. (415) 321-0470.✚▲

PARADISE—Calif. State Auto. Assn., 6332 Clark Rd., 95969. M-F 8:30-5. (916) 872-2236.✚

PASADENA—Auto. Club of So. Calif., 801 E. Union St., 91101. M-F 9-5. (818) 795-0601.✚▲

PETALUMA—Calif. State Auto. Assn., 111 Lynch Creek Way; *Mailing Address: PO Box 750249, 94975.* M-F 8:30-5. (707) 763-0973.✚

PLACERVILLE—Calif. State Auto. Assn., 1323 Broadway; *Mailing Address: PO Box 969, 95667.* M-F 8:30-5. (916) 622-4084.✚

PORTERVILLE—Auto. Club of So. Calif., 24 W. Morton Ave.; *Mailing Address: PO Box 31, 93258.* M-F 9-5. (209) 784-6500.✚

QUINCY—Calif. State Auto. Assn., 20 Crescent St.; *Mailing Address: PO Box 3920, 95971.* M-F 8:30-5. (916) 283-1014.✚

RED BLUFF—Calif. State Auto. Assn., 151 Sale Ln.; *Mailing Address: PO Box 219, 96080.* M-F 8:30-5. (916) 527-4304.✚

REDDING—Calif. State Auto. Assn., 943 Mission De Oro Dr., 96003. M-F 8:30-5. (916) 222-2722.✚

REDLANDS—Auto. Club of So. Calif., 413 E. Palm Ave.; *Mailing Address: PO Box 1047, 92373.* M-F 9-5. (714) 793-3357.✚

REDWOOD CITY—Calif. State Auto. Assn., 20 El Camino Real, 94062. M-F 8:30-5. (415) 364-0620.✚

RESEDA—(See Van Nuys).

RIDGECREST—Auto. Club of So. Calif., 114 S. Gemstone, Suite A, 93555. M-F 9-5. (619) 375-8426.✚

RIVERSIDE—Auto. Club of So. Calif., 6927 Magnolia Ave.; *Mailing Address: PO Box 2217, Magnolia Ctr., 92516.* M-F 9-5. (714) 684-4250.✚▲

ROSEVILLE—Calif. State Auto. Assn., 2100 Professional Dr., 95661. M-F 8:30-5. (916) 784-3232.✚▲

SACRAMENTO—Calif. State Auto. Assn., 4333 Florin Rd.; *Mailing Address: PO Box 9834, 95823.* M-F 8:30-5. (916) 422-6511.✚

SACRAMENTO—Calif. State Auto. Assn., 15 Bicentennial Cir.; *Mailing Address: PO Box 260810, 95826.* M-F 8:30-5. (916) 381-3355.✚▲

SACRAMENTO—Calif. State Auto. Assn., 4745 Chippendale Dr., 95841. M-F 8:30-5. (916) 331-7610.✚▲

SALINAS—Calif. State Auto. Assn., 1045 Post Drive, *Mailing Address: PO Box 3010, 93912.* M-F 8:30-5. (408) 424-2521.✛

SAN BERNARDINO—Auto. Club of So. Calif., 808 W. 2nd St.; *Mailing Address: PO Box 2128, 92406.* M-F 9-5. (714) 381-2211.✛

SAN DIEGO—Auto. Club of So. Calif., 815 Date St.; *Mailing Address: PO Box 1031, 92112.* M-F 9-5. (619) 233-1000.✛▲

SAN DIEGO—Auto. Club of So. Calif., 4973 Clairemont Dr., Suite C; *Mailing Address: PO Box 17527, 92117.* M-F 9-5. (619) 483-4960.✛▲

SAN DIEGO—Auto. Club of So. Calif., 12630 Sabre Sprgs. Pkwy. 301, 92128. M-F 9-5. (619) 486-0786.✛

SAN FERNANDO—Auto. Club of So. Calif., 1075 N. Maclay Ave., 91340. M-F 9-5. (818) 365-0611.✛

SAN FRANCISCO—Calif. State Auto. Assn., 150 Van Ness Ave.; *Mailing Address: PO Box 1860, 94101.* M-F 8:30-5. (415) 565-2012.✛▲

SAN GABRIEL—Auto. Club of So. Calif., 215 S. Mission Dr.; *Mailing Address: PO Box C, 91778.* M-F 9-5. (818) 289-4491.✛

SAN JOSE—Calif. State Auto. Assn., 5340 Thornwood Dr.; *Mailing Address: PO Box 23910, 95153.* M-F 8:30-5. (408) 629-1911.✛▲

SAN LUIS OBISPO—Auto. Club of So. Calif., 1445 Calle Joaquin; *Mailing Address: PO Box 4040, 93403.* M-F 9-5. (805) 543-6454.✛

SAN MATEO—Calif. State Auto. Assn., 1650 S. Delaware Ave.; *Mailing Address: PO Box 5925, 94402.* M-F 8:30-5. (415) 572-1160.✛▲

SAN PABLO—Calif. State Auto. Assn., 14560 San Pablo Ave.; *Mailing Address: PO Box 7, 94806.* M-F 8:30-5. (510) 233-8800.✛

SAN PEDRO—Auto. Club of So. Calif., 852 N. Western Ave.; *Mailing Address: PO Box 669, 90733.* M-F 9-5. (310) 547-2412.✛

SAN RAFAEL—Calif. State Auto. Assn., 99 Smith Ranch Rd.; *Mailing Address: PO Box B, 94913.* M-F 8:30-5. (415) 472-6700.✛▲

SAN RAMON—Calif. State Auto. Assn., 1081 Market Place, *Mailing Address: PO Box 888, 94583.* M-F 8:30-5. (510) 830-9797.✛▲

SANTA ANA—Auto. Club of So. Calif., 1901 N. Tustin Ave.; *Mailing Address: PO Box 11763, 92711.* M-F 9-5. (714) 973-1211.✛▲

SANTA BARBARA—Auto. Club of So. Calif., 3712 State St.; *Mailing Address: P. O. Drawer 3860, 93130.* M-F 9-5. (805) 682-5811.✛▲

SANTA CLARA—Calif. State Auto. Assn., 80 Saratoga Ave.; *Mailing Address: PO Box 70, 95103.* M-F 8:30-5. (408) 985-9300.✛▲

SANTA CLARITA—Auto. Club of So. Calif., 23770 Valencia Blvd., 91355. M-F 9-5. (805)259-6222.✛

SANTA CRUZ—(See Capitola).

SANTA MARIA—Auto. Club of So. Calif., 2033 B So. Broadway; *Mailing Address: PO Box 1308, 93456.* M-F 9-5. (805) 922-6731.✛

SANTA MONICA—Auto. Club of So. Calif., 2730 Santa Monica Blvd., 90404. M-F 9-5. (310) 829-9731.✛▲

SANTA ROSA—Calif. State Auto. Assn., 1500 Farmers Ln.; *Mailing Address: PO Box 2906, 95405.* M-F 8:30-5. (707) 544-1010.✛▲

SERRAMONTE—(See Daly City).

SIMI VALLEY—Auto. Club of So. Calif., 2837 Cochran St., 93065. M-F 9-5. (805) 522-7330.✛

SONOMA—Calif. State Auto. Assn., 650 Second St.; *Mailing Address: PO Box 1909, 94576.* M-F 8:30-5. (707) 996-1083.✛

SONORA—Calif. State Auto. Assn., 301 S. Shepherd St.; *Mailing Address: PO Box 877, 95370.* M-F 8:30-5. (209) 532-3134.✛

SOUTH LAGUNA—Auto. Club of So. Calif., 32355 Coast Hwy, 92677. M-F 9-5. (714) 499-1381.✛

SOUTH LAKE TAHOE—Calif. State Auto. Assn., 961 Emerald Bay Rd. (Hwy. 89), 96150. M-F 8:30-5. (916) 541-4434.✛

SOUTH LOS ANGELES—Auto. Club of So. Calif., 9621 S. Vermont Ave., 90044. M-F 9-5. (213) 754-2831.✛

STOCKTON—Calif. State Auto. Assn., 49 W. Yokuts Ave.; *Mailing Address: PO Box 7608, 95207.* M-F 8:30-5. (209) 952-4100.✛▲

SUNNYVALE—Calif. State Auto. Assn., 755 S. Bernardo Ave.; *Mailing Address: PO Box 61448, 94088.* M-F 8:30-5. (408) 739-4422.✛

SUSANVILLE—Calif. State Auto. Assn., 550 Ash St.; *Mailing Address: PO Box 1360, 96130.* M-F 8:30-5. (916) 257-6144.✛

TEMECULA—Auto. Club of So. Calif., 27727 Jefferson Ave., Suite 103, 92390. M-F 9-5. (714) 694-9403.✛

THOUSAND OAKS—Auto. Club of So. Calif., 100 E. Wilbur Rd.; *Mailing Address: PO Box 1046, 91360.* M-F 9-5. (805) 497-0911.✛▲

TORRANCE—Auto. Club of So. Calif., 2606 Sepulveda Blvd.; *Mailing Address: PO Box 4298, 90510.* M-F 9-5. (310) 325-3111.✛▲

TURLOCK—Calif. State Auto. Assn., 2160 Geer Rd.; *Mailing Address: PO Box 736, 95381.* M-F 8:30-5. (209) 668-2722.✛

UKIAH—Calif. State Auto. Assn., 601 Kings Ct.; *Mailing Address: PO Box 600, 95482.* M-F 8:30-5. (707) 462-3861.✛

UPLAND—Auto. Club of So. Calif., 1021 E. Foothill Blvd.; *Mailing Address: PO Box 1449, 91786.* M-F 9-5. (714) 981-2961.✛▲

VALENCIA—(See Santa Clarita).

VALLEJO—Calif. State Auto. Assn., 1183 Admiral Callaghan Ln.; *Mailing Address: PO Box 4483, 94590.* M-F 8:30-5. (707) 552-0592.✛▲

VAN NUYS—Auto. Club of So. Calif., 6725 Kester Ave.; *Mailing Address: PO Box 2096, 91404.* M-F 9-5. (818) 997-6230.✛▲

VENTURA—Auto. Club of So. Calif., 1501 S. Victoria Ave.; *Mailing Address: PO Box 3618, Ventura St. 93006.* M-F 9-5. (805) 644-7171.✛▲

VICTORVILLE—Auto. Club of So. Calif., 12490 Amargosa Rd.; *Mailing Address: PO Box 1478, 92392.* M-F 9-5. (619) 245-6666.✛

VISALIA—Auto. Club of So. Calif., 300 S. Mooney Blvd.; *Mailing Address: PO Box 1150, 93279.* M-F 9-5. (209) 732-8045.✛

WATSONVILLE—Calif. State Auto. Assn., 617 E. Lake Ave., 95076. M-F 8:30-5. (408) 722-8151.✛

WEST VALLEY—(See Woodland Hills).

WHITTIER—Auto. Club of So. Calif., 8522 S. Painter Ave.; *Mailing Address: PO Box 4766, 90607.* M-F 9-5. (310) 698-3721.✛

WILLOWS—Calif. State Auto. Assn., 855 W. Wood St.; *Mailing Address: PO Box 1007, 95988.* M-F 8:30-5. (916) 934-4648.✛

WOODLAND—Calif. State Auto. Assn., 95 W. Lincoln Ave.; *Mailing Address: PO Box 789, 95695.* M-F 8:30-5. (916) 662-9344.✛

WOODLAND HILLS—Auto. Club of So. Calif., 22708 Victory Blvd.; *Mailing Address: PO Box 2500, 91365.* M-F 9-5. (818) 883-2660.✛▲

YREKA—Calif. State Auto. Assn., 500 N. Main St.; *Mailing Address: PO Box 410, 96097.* M-F 8:30-5. (916) 842-4416.✛

NEVADA

CARSON CITY—Calif. State Auto. Assn., 2901 S. Carson St., 89701. M-F 8:30-5. (702) 883-2470.✛

LAKE TAHOE—(See South Lake Tahoe, California).

LAS VEGAS—Calif. State Auto. Assn., 3312 W. Charleston Blvd.; *Mailing Address: PO Box 26719, 89126.* M-F 8:30-5. (702) 870-9171.✛▲

RENO—Calif. State Auto. Assn., 199 E. Moana Ln.; *Mailing Address: PO Box 7020, 89510.* M-F 8:30-5. (702) 826-8800.✛

Temperature Averages - Maximum/Minimum
From the records of the National Weather Service

	JAN.	FEB.	MAR.	APR.	MAY	JUNE	JULY	AUG.	SEPT.	OCT.	NOV.	DEC.
CALIFORNIA												
Bakersfield	57 / 37	63 / 41	69 / 45	76 / 50	85 / 56	92 / 62	100 / 68	98 / 66	92 / 61	81 / 53	69 / 43	59 / 39
Barstow	59 / 31	63 / 34	70 / 40	77 / 45	84 / 51	96 / 60	101 / 67	100 / 65	92 / 57	80 / 47	70 / 37	60 / 30
Bishop	53 / 21	56 / 25	64 / 30	73 / 38	81 / 44	90 / 50	97 / 55	95 / 52	89 / 47	77 / 37	64 / 28	55 / 23
Bridgeport	38 / 9	41 / 12	48 / 19	59 / 27	66 / 33	74 / 38	84 / 45	83 / 44	77 / 37	65 / 29	53 / 21	44 / 15
Chico	54 / 36	60 / 39	67 / 41	73 / 44	82 / 49	91 / 55	98 / 59	96 / 58	88 / 53	79 / 47	66 / 40	55 / 36
Eureka	54 / 41	54 / 42	55 / 43	56 / 45	58 / 48	60 / 51	61 / 52	61 / 53	62 / 51	60 / 59	58 / 45	55 / 43
Fresno	55 / 36	61 / 39	67 / 42	75 / 47	83 / 52	90 / 57	99 / 63	97 / 60	91 / 56	80 / 48	67 / 39	56 / 37
Indio	70 / 39	75 / 45	80 / 50	86 / 57	93 / 63	102 / 72	107 / 78	106 / 76	101 / 69	91 / 58	80 / 46	71 / 39
Los Angeles	65 / 47	66 / 48	69 / 50	71 / 53	74 / 56	77 / 59	83 / 63	83 / 63	82 / 61	77 / 57	73 / 52	68 / 49
Merced	55 / 36	62 / 39	66 / 41	73 / 45	81 / 50	91 / 56	97 / 61	95 / 59	88 / 54	79 / 47	67 / 39	56 / 35
Mount Shasta	41 / 25	47 / 28	52 / 30	60 / 35	68 / 40	75 / 46	85 / 51	85 / 49	78 / 45	66 / 38	53 / 31	45 / 27
Needles	64 / 39	70 / 45	77 / 49	86 / 55	94 / 63	104 / 71	108 / 80	105 / 78	98 / 67	85 / 55	72 / 46	63 / 40
Redding	54 / 37	59 / 40	64 / 43	71 / 48	80 / 54	88 / 61	97 / 67	95 / 65	87 / 59	77 / 52	64 / 44	56 / 38
Sacramento	53 / 39	59 / 42	65 / 44	72 / 47	80 / 52	89 / 56	95 / 59	94 / 58	90 / 57	79 / 51	65 / 44	55 / 40
San Diego	65 / 46	65 / 48	67 / 50	68 / 54	70 / 57	72 / 60	76 / 63	77 / 65	77 / 62	73 / 58	71 / 51	67 / 48
San Francisco	55 / 42	58 / 43	62 / 45	64 / 47	67 / 50	70 / 52	72 / 54	72 / 54	74 / 54	71 / 51	64 / 46	57 / 43
Santa Barbara	64 / 43	65 / 44	66 / 46	68 / 48	69 / 50	72 / 53	76 / 56	77 / 57	76 / 55	74 / 51	72 / 46	67 / 43
Truckee	38 / 16	38 / 16	46 / 21	53 / 29	60 / 36	73 / 41	81 / 43	81 / 41	73 / 37	63 / 30	52 / 24	40 / 15
Willits	49 / 31	53 / 34	56 / 35	64 / 39	70 / 43	77 / 47	86 / 52	86 / 50	83 / 49	71 / 44	57 / 38	50 / 34
NEVADA												
Beatty	55 / 25	59 / 30	66 / 33	73 / 39	81 / 46	92 / 55	99 / 61	97 / 59	89 / 52	76 / 43	65 / 33	55 / 26
Elko	35 / 10	40 / 16	49 / 22	60 / 29	69 / 35	79 / 41	91 / 48	89 / 45	80 / 36	66 / 28	49 / 19	39 / 14
Ely	37 / 9	40 / 13	47 / 20	58 / 28	67 / 34	77 / 40	87 / 48	85 / 47	77 / 38	63 / 29	49 / 18	41 / 13
Hawthorne	45 / 23	49 / 26	57 / 31	64 / 36	72 / 44	82 / 52	90 / 59	89 / 59	79 / 51	67 / 40	57 / 31	46 / 24
Las Vegas	55 / 32	60 / 36	69 / 42	79 / 51	88 / 60	98 / 69	105 / 76	102 / 73	95 / 66	81 / 53	66 / 40	57 / 33
Reno	47 / 17	51 / 21	57 / 25	65 / 30	73 / 34	81 / 39	91 / 45	90 / 43	83 / 37	71 / 29	58 / 21	49 / 17

CALIFORNIA-NEVADA
DRIVING DISTANCES

MILES: *210* AVERAGE TIME (EXCLUDING STOPS): 4:10

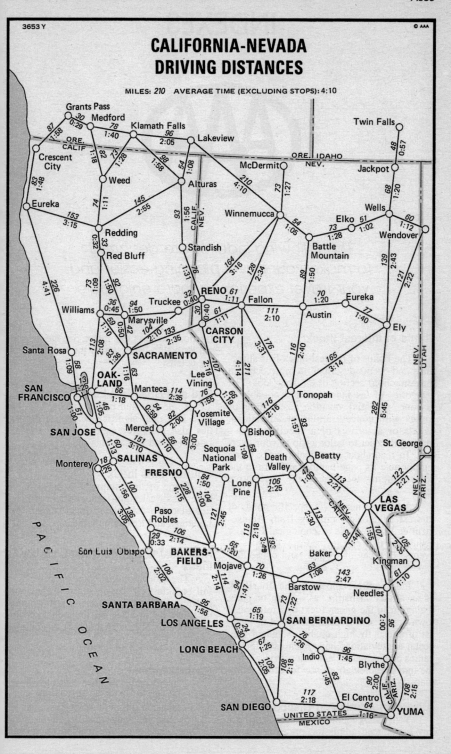

INDEXES

*The following indexes are designed
to make your travel planning easier and
your travel experience more enjoyable.*

Points of Interest Index

The Points of Interest Index lists attractions and events described in more detail in the Attractions section of the TourBook. The categories of the index make it possible to discover potential vacation destinations or routes with concentrations of attractions, events or activities of a specific type—making it easier to tailor a trip to your interests. To read about a particular index entry, simply note its page number and turn to the corresponding location in the descriptive text.

AAA uses nearly 200 specific points of interest categories, ranging from Amusement & Theme Parks to Zoological Parks & Exhibits. Also categorized are 15 types of events, 13 types of exhibits and collections and 10 types of sports events.

Index entries appear in the TourBook as an attraction listing, as a town or place listing, or in the general text of a referenced town or place. A ★ denotes a point of interest of unusually high quality. Standard U.S. postal abbreviations have been used for the names of states and Canadian provinces. See the Index Abbreviations box for other abbreviations used.

Attraction Admission Discount Index

Your AAA membership card can be a key to reduced admission prices at the attractions listed in this index. See the individual attraction listing under the town heading for details.

Bed and Breakfast Lodging Index

Some bed and breakfasts listed might have historical significance. Those properties also are referenced in the Historical Lodgings and Restaurants Index.

Country Inns Index

Some of the country inns listed might have historical significance. Those properties also are referenced in the Historical Lodgings and Restaurants Index.

Historical Lodgings & Restaurants Index

The indication that Continental [CP] or full breakfast [BP] is included in the room rate reflects whether a property is a bed-and-breakfast facility. See the individual accommodation listing under the town heading for details.

Resorts Index

Many establishments are located in resort areas; however, the resorts in this index have extensive on-premises recreational facilities. See the individual accommodation listings under the town heading for details.

POINTS OF INTEREST INDEX

INDEX ABBREVIATIONS

NB....................... national battlefield		NRA.................. national recreation area	
NBP.................national battlefield park		NS........................ national seashore	
NC................... national cemetery		NWR.................national wildlife refuge	
NF.......................national forest		PHS........... provincial historic(al) site	
NHM......... national historic(al) monument		PP.............................. provincial park	
NHP.................national historic(al) park		SF...................................... state forest	
NHS...................national historic(al) site		SHM.............. state historic(al) monument	
NL.................... national lakeshore		SHP.....................state historic(al) park	
NME................ national memorial		SHS......................... state historic(al) site	
NMO....................national monument		SME.........................state memorial	
NMP.................... national military park		SP.. state park	
NP................................ national park		SRA...................... state recreation area	

EXHIBITS & COLLECTIONS-ANIMALS & BIRDS

EXHIBITS & COLLECTIONS-AVIATION

EXHIBITS & COLLECTIONS-CLOCKS

EXHIBITS & COLLECTIONS-COINS

EXHIBITS & COLLECTIONS-DOLLS & TOYS

EXHIBITS & COLLECTIONS-HISTORICAL

EXHIBITS & COLLECTIONS-INDIAN

EXHIBITS & COLLECTIONS-MUSIC

EXHIBITS & COLLECTIONS-SCIENCE

HISTORIC DOCUMENTS, MANUSCRIPTS & RARE BOOKS

HISTORIC SITES

HORSE FARMS

INDIAN BURIAL GROUNDS

INDIAN MOUNDS, REMAINS, RUINS

INDIAN PICTOGRAPHS & PETROGLYPHS

INDIAN RESERVATIONS & VILLAGES

INDUSTRIAL TOURS

MUSIC EVENTS

MUSIC HALLS & OPERA HOUSES

MUSIC SCHOOLS

NATIONALITIES & ETHNIC AREAS

NATURAL PHENOMENA

NATURE CENTERS

NATURE TRAILS

NAUTICAL TOURS

OBSERVATORIES

PAINTINGS

PARKS, CITY; STATE; PROVINCIAL

Attraction Admission Discount Index
See individual attraction listings for details.

California

ATTRACTION ADMISSIONS DISCOUNT (cont'd)

BED & BREAKFAST LODGING INDEX

Some bed and breakfasts listed below might have historical significance. Those properties are also referenced in the Historical index. The indication that continental [CP] or full breakfast [BP] is included in the room rate reflects whether a property is a Bed-and-Breakfast facility.

BAJA CALIFORNIA

Accommodation

CALIFORNIA

Accommodations

BED & BREAKFAST (cont'd)

Wainwright Inn Bed
 & Breakfast........................Big Bear Lake
Wine and Roses Country
 Inn...Lodi

NEVADA

Accommodation
Steptoe Valley Inn.................................Ely

COUNTRY INNS INDEX

Some of the following country inns can also be considered as bed-and-breakfast operations. The indication that continental [CP] or full breakfast [BP] is included in the room rate reflects whether a property is a Bed-and-Breakfast facility.

CALIFORNIA

Accommodations
Auberge Du Soleil ....Rutherford
Benbow Inn...............................Garberville
Captain's
 Alpenhaus.........Lake Tahoe (Northern Region)
Chateau du Sureau ....Oakhurst
Lighthouse Lodge ....Pacific Grove
Los Olivos Grand Hotel ....Los Olivos

Madrona Manor ....Healdsburg
Saddleback Inn-
 Arrowhead ....Lake Arrowhead
Thatcher Inn ....Hopland
Villa Royale Bed &
 Breakfast Inn ....Palm Springs

Restaurant
Little River Inn Restaurant ....Little River

HISTORICAL LODGINGS & RESTAURANTS INDEX

Some of the following historical lodgings can also be considered as bed-and-breakfast operations. The indication that continental [CP] or full breakfast [BP] is included in the room rate reflects whether a property is a Bed-and-Breakfast facility.

CALIFORNIA

Accommodations
An Elegant Victorian Mansion ....Eureka
Benbow Inn ....Garberville
Casa Cody Country Inn ....Palm Springs
Casa Laguna Inn ....Laguna Beach
Channel Road Inn Bed &
 Breakfast ....Santa Monica
Cypress Inn ....Carmel
Eureka Inn ....Eureka
Garden Street Inn Bed &
 Breakfast ....San Luis Obispo
Hotel Arcata ....Arcata
Hotel Jeffery ....Coulterville
Hotel Sainte
 Claire ....San Jose
La Mer European Bed &
 Breakfast ....Ventura
Mendocino Hotel & Garden
 Suites ....Mendocino
Montecito Inn ....Santa Barbara
Olallieberry Inn ....Cambria
Pacific Grove Inn ....Pacific Grove
Santa Maria Inn ....Santa Maria
Sheraton Palace
 Hotel ....San Francisco (Downtown)
Stanyan Park
 Hotel ....San Francisco (Northern Region)

Terrace Manor Bed &
 Breakfast ....Los Angeles (Downtown)
The Ahwahnee ....Yosemite National Park
The Archbishops
 Mansion ....San Francisco (Northern Region)
The Cain House ....Bridgeport
The Kaleidoscope Inn Bed
 & Breakfast ....Nipomo
The Sherman
 House ....San Francisco (Northern Region)
The Upham ....Santa Barbara
The White Gables Inn ....Santa Paula
Union Hotel ....Benicia
Wawona Hotel ....Yosemite National Park

Restaurants
Benbow Inn Dining
 Room ....Garberville
Casa de Bandini ....San Diego
City Hotel Dining Room ....Columbia
El Adobe de
 Capistrano ....San Juan Capistrano
Joshua's Restaurant ....Paso Robles
Lark Creek Inn ....Larkspur
Mattei's Tavern ....Los Olivos
Pleasanton Hotel Restaurant ....Pleasanton
Sycamore Inn ....Rancho Cucamonga
The Cannery Restaurant ....Newport Beach
The Chart House 1887 ....San Diego

RESORTS INDEX

Many establishments are located in resort areas; however, the following places have extensive on-premises recreational facilities:

BAJA CALIFORNIA

Accommodations

Estero Beach
  Resort Hotel ....Ensenada, B.C.
Hotel Conrad
  Los Cabos ....San Jose del Cabo, B.C.S.
Hotel Gran Baja ....La Paz, B.C.S.
Hotel Punta Pescadero ....Los Barriles, B.C.S.
Hotel Twin Dolphin ....Cabo San Lucas, B.C.S.
La Concha Beach Resort ....La Paz, B.C.S.
Melia Cabo Real ....San Jose del Cabo, B.C.S.
Melia San Lucas ....Cabo San Lucas, B.C.S.
Pueblo Bonito Resort .....Cabo San Lucas, B.C.S.
Stouffer Presidente
  Los Cabos ....San Jose del Cabo, B.C.S.
Stouffer Presidente-Loreta ....Loreto, B.C.S.

CALIFORNIA

Accommodations

Bridge Bay Resort ....Shasta Lake
Carmel Highland Doubletree
  Golf & Tennis Resort ....Rancho Bernardo
Catamaran Resort Hotel ....San Diego
Chaminade ....Santa Cruz
Disneyland Hotel ....Anaheim
Doubletree Resort at Desert Princess
  Country Club ....Palm Springs
Drakesbad Guest
  Ranch ....Lassen Volcanic National Park
Ducey's on the Lake ....Bass Lake
Four Seasons Biltmore ....Santa Barbara
Furnace Creek
  Inn ....Death Valley National Monument
Furnace Creek
  Ranch ....Death Valley National Monument
Highland Springs Resort ....Beaumont
Hyatt Grand Champions
  Resort ....Indian Wells
Hyatt Newporter ....Newport Beach
Hyatt Regency Lake Tahoe Resort &
  Casino ....Lake Tahoe (Northern Region)
Hyatt Regency-Monterey Resort &
  Conference Center ....Monterey
Industry Hills &
  Sheraton Resort ....Industry
Kirkwood Resort ....Kirkwood
Konocti Harbor Resort & Spa ....Kelseyville
La Casa Del Zorro
  Resort Hotel ....Borrego Springs
La Costa Resort and Spa ....La Costa
La Mancha Private Villas &
  Court Club ....Palm Springs
Lake Arrowhead Hilton
  Resort ....Lake Arrowhead
Lawrence Welk Resort ....Escondido
Marriott's Desert Springs Resort
  & Spa ....Palm Desert
Marriott's Rancho Las Palmas
  Resort ....Rancho Mirage
Marriott's Tenaya Lodge ....Fish Camp
Meadowood Resort ....St. Helena
Ojai Valley Inn & Country
  Club ....Ojai
Pala Mesa Resort ....Fallbrook
Quail Lodge ....Carmel Valley
Rancho Bernardo Inn ....Rancho Bernardo
Resort at Squaw
  Creek ....Lake Tahoe (Northern Region)
San Diego Hilton Beach &
  Tennis Resort ....San Diego
San Diego Princess Resort ....San Diego
Shadow Mountain Resort &
  Racquet Club ....Palm Desert
Silverado Country Club
  Resort ....Napa
Singing Hills Lodge ....El Cajon
Sonoma Mission Inn ....Sonoma
Stouffer Esmeralda Resort ....Indian Wells
Temecula Creek Inn ....Temecula
The Autry Resort Hotel ....Palm Springs
The Claremont Resort, Spa &
  Tennis Club ....Oakland
The Inn at Rancho
  Santa Fe ....Rancho Santa Fe
The Inn at Spanish Bay ....Pebble Beach
The Lodge at Pebble Beach ....Pebble Beach
The Redwoods ....Yosemite National Park
The Ridge
  Tahoe ....Lake Tahoe (Southern Region)
The Ritz-Carlton,
  Laguna Niguel ....Laguna Niguel
The Ritz-Carlton, Rancho
  Mirage ....Rancho Mirage
The Westin Mission Hills
  Resort ....Rancho Mirage

NEVADA

Accommodations

Alexis Park Resort Hotel ....Las Vegas
Desert Inn Hotel and Casino ....Las Vegas

SHOW YOUR MEMBERSHIP CARD
WHEN YOU REGISTER
AT AAA APPROVED ESTABLISHMENTS.

BOOK PRODUCTION STAFF

D. JAMES McDOWELL: *Senior Vice President of Association Services*
Tracy Brueggeman: Manager, Association Services

NATIONAL TRAVEL

TOM CROSBY: *Managing Director*
Gayle Anderson: Administrative Secretary; Jane Bloodworth: Manager, Special Projects; Pat Budowick: Project Analyst; Gail Acebes: Product Manager.

APPROVED ACCOMMODATIONS INSPECTIONS

KRISTINA KRAUSE: *Director*
Liz Allatt, Jim Babich, Dale Banks, Jeremy Barrett, Diane Bazelides, Dawn Belden, Rosalyn Betts, Guy Bianco, George Boomer, John Campbell, Dan Chandler, Kim Clausen, Carol Clifton, Carol Damato, Don Elder, Kathy Gibson, Kelly Giewont, John Grady, Lynn Green, Bill Greene, Bill Grunwald, Larry Hamilton, Gene Hamrick, Nancy Hansen, Ed Herold, Jo Ann Higgins, David House, Ray Kaczmarek, Eileen Kitchen, Linda Lilley, Alan Lima, Bruce Martin, Sue McCormick, Steven McGrandle, Irene McLarty, Pat McMahon, Walter Merkler, Dan Morris, Michel Mousseau, Stacey Mower, Vincent Munoz, Virginia Price, Mike Radigan, Pamela Ragar, Peter Robotham, Marcia Rowland, Jan Roza, Linda Russ, Patrick Schardin, Virginia Schley, Lynn Schneider, Marcia Schneider, Bruce Scott, Robert Sheron, Bernie Tamayo, Diane Thomas, Margarite Toro, Bruce Turgen, Bill Vieregg, Nick Vilardell, Rod Volk, Charles Walker Jr., Fred Weber, Bob Wedge.

APPROVED ACCOMMODATIONS MARKETING & SALES

HAROLD YANKELEVITZ: *Staff Director*
Judy Erickson: Administrative Secretary; Glenn Cooper: Sales Manager; Patty Griffiths: Sales Coordinator; Deborah Canton and McLean Jones: Sales Assistants; Shirley Cortese: Industry Relations Supervisor; Kim Hardenbergh: Industry Relations Coordinator; Erin Higgins: Industry Relations Assistant; Patricia Sanderson: Word Processor; Deborah Berry, Mary Carrico, Millie Constantino and Debbie Gish: Correspondents; Don Balyeat, Joel Brown, Dann Chappelear, Paul Dodson, Jay Donahue, Tom Foley, Emilie Heitman, Carol Johnson, Bill King, Joe Perko, Harry Reeves, Ian Sutherland, Ken Tabacca, Harris Vincent and Bob Wildmann: Regional Sales Managers.

MEMBER RELATIONS AND TRAVELMATCH MARKETING & SUPPORT

DEBORAH F. RANSON: *Director*
Nancy Leem: Assistant. **Club Auto Travel Services**—Bill Hughes: Supervisor; Cindy Pitt: Assistant; Earlene Cavender: Communications Specialist; Pat Sindlinger: Coordinator.**Member Relations**—Gwen White: Supervisor; Harry Bumba, Martha Norton, Darlene Ortiz, Frances Piper and Patricia Tichonoff: Coordinators; Jennifer Burney and Karen Dunn: Assistants. **Travel Trend Analysis**—Karen Hardzewicz: Supervisor.

PUBLISHING

W.C. HOLLIBAUGH JR.: *Director*
Eugenia Stefan: Administrative Secretary
CARTOGRAPHIC SERVICES—Elke Owen: Chief Cartographer; Linda Orman: Administrative Secretary. **Automated Cartography**—Ross Morres: System Manager; Kevin McGraw and Scott Peterson: Supervisors; Kim Trench: Clerk; Christopher Anderson, Beth Anthony, Curtis Burner, Joseph Esteban, Gerrad Finan, Carl Hagerty, Gail Horan, Michael Imlay, Timothy Kidwell, David McAllister, Julie Rediker and Glenn Sottardi: System Operators. **Cartography**—Randy Schwaband and Tom Urbanowicz: Unit Supervisors; Mark Dodich, Peter Everett, Mike Gibson, Mike Hirschmann, Don Melhorn, Laura Myers and Scott Wade: Cartographic Techs. **Data Research**—Mike Camarano: Manager; Mike Mouser: Highway Information Supervisor; Goffrey Baldwin and Mike Gilbride: Compilation Techs; Bob Hawkinson, Harry Jones, Cindi Kalb and John Swartchick: Road Reporters; Nancy Grobmyer: D & C Research Tech; Mela-

nie Fuller: Editorial Assistant; Betty White: Highway Information Specialist; Amy Rew: Research Supervisor; Grace Kenyon, Doyle Kirkland, Linda McDuffie, Mary Mills, Bob Modrzejewski, Linda Nowinski, Sandy Stansbury and Ismael Villafane: Research Techs; Meg Duda and Linda Indolfi: Data Research Clerks. **Production Standards**—David Anderson: Manager; Barbara Clark: Cartographic Coordinator; Cynthia Etchison, Jerry Heflin and Terry Strefling: Map Editors; Christine Freshwater: Cartographic Production Assistant.

EDITORIAL SERVICES—Bill Wood: Editor-in-Chief; Peggy Cole: Administrative Secretary.
Advertising Processing—Nantambu Ahota: Supervisor; Sharon Kurir: Clerk; Mary Saah: Ad Coordination Manager; Jeff Acker, Tamara DeGayner and Teri Sliman: Ad Quality Assurance Analysts; Ann DeVane, Patty Maggi, Michelle Noble and Gerzell Sanders: Senior Ad Coordinators; Janet Foss: Ad Coordinator. **DataBase**—Laurie Myers: Supervisor; Cindy Hood: Clerk; Joyce Bishop: DataBase Coordinators; Maureen Schoen: Senior DataBase Proofing Specialist; Mary Cednick, Nancy Downer, Roberta Hughes, JoAnn Proulx, Judy Turner and Lynn Valdes: DataBase Proofing Specialists. **Editorial**—Greg Weekes: Managing Editor; Stephanie Simpson: Clerk; Margene Bonachea, Curtis Hewston and Suzanne Lemon: Senior Associate Editors; Michelle Brady, Debbie Burton, Penny Cload, Valerie Hood, Bobbi McLean, Lisa Peterson and Cynthia Psaraklis: Associate Editors; Julie Metzinger: Senior Editorial Assistant; Charlotte Simmons and Lynda Wiland: Editorial Assistants.

PRODUCTION SERVICES—N.A. Daniels: Operations Manager; Olga Brooks: Administrative Secretary; Lisa Oelschlager: Supervisor, Production & Schedules; Diane Norden and Tracy Schramm: Clerks. **Graphics**—Jan Coyne: Supervisor; Ruth Del Manzano: Operations Associate; Kelly Atterbury: Customer Service Representative; Elizabeth McCall: Photo Researcher; Marilyn Hatchett, Chuck Henderson, Frank Goldsmith and Joanne McNamara: Artists. **Photo Lab**—Jim Shillabeer: Supervisor; Orrin Love and Jeff Schmidt: Unit Supervisors; Lorne Corbett: Coordinator; Scott Boetel, Daniel Donahoe, Lisa Hales, Christine Lomas, Hai Son Nguyen, Mike Shimko, Shawn Smith, Susan Stofko and James Thompson: Techs; Walt Hamler and Mike Siedzinski: Photographers. **Typography**—Beverly Donovan: Supervisor; Christine Carter and Marina Kopko: Senior Typographers; Carolyn Frost, Phyllis Hodges, Warren Ironmonger, Mario Ruta and Janice Simmons: Typographers; Paula Jobin: Coordinator; Cassandra Young: Quality/Verification Specialist.

QUALITY ASSURANCE—Jim Hutton: Manager; Terry Lane and Susan Sears: Senior QA Analysts; Andrea Payne: QA Analyst; Larry Rew: Database Analyst.
TECHNICAL SUPPORT—W. Kristian Berger, Daniel W. Macaluso: Technical Analysts.

CLUB CONTACTS FOR ATTRACTION UPDATES

California—Automobile Club of Southern California: Norma E. Palmer; California State Automobile Association: Josephina Beaumont, Patricia Dent, Leslie G. Kelley. **Nevada/Baja California**—Automobile Club of Southern California: R. Clark Hunter; California State Automobile Association: Josephina Beaumont, Patricia Dent, Leslie G. Kelley.

WESTERN CLUB INSPECTIONS

Automobile Club of Southern California: Ronald Alexander, Karen Clyne, Alice Coen, Virginia Cunanan, Clarence Garlough, Alisa Moncrief, Ginger Nichols, Danielle Roberts, Penny Rodgers, Charles Smith, Graham Wood. **California State Automobile Association:** Oralia Alvarez, Jose Carrion, Leora Crosetti, Jack Kahle, David Mendricks, Roger Tennyson, Judith Trainor.

A company that doesn't know what its customers think won't be in business very long. A company that knows but doesn't act has an equally poor survival chance. AAA has thrived for more than 90 years. We want to perform even better. **CAN YOU HELP US?** Please complete this questionnaire and mail to: TourBook Survey, Box 59, 1000 AAA Drive, Heathrow, FL 32746-5063.

1. How many years have you been a member of AAA/CAA?_____

2. Do you have a BASIC or PLUS membership? ☐ BASIC ☐ PLUS

3. In which state(s)/province(s) did you stop to eat or stay overnight? (Check all that apply and write in spaces provided any additional states/provinces where you stayed or ate):

State	Eat	Stay
California	_____	_____
Neveda	_____	_____
_____	_____	_____
_____	_____	_____

4. To what extent do you supplement the AAA TourBook with non-AAA travel information materials? ☐ Never ☐ Sometimes ☐ Always

5. What type of non-AAA/CAA travel information materials do you use?
   ☐ Travel Guide   ☐ City Map
   ☐ Travel Brochure   ☐ State Map
   ☐ Magazine   ☐ Travel Video
   ☐ Newspaper   ☐ Other_____

6. Specifically describe the kind/content of information you obtained from non-AAA/CAA travel materials:

_____
_____

7. Why did you use the materials? (Check all that apply):
   ☐ Materials were free
   ☐ I already had materials
   ☐ Information was more concise
   ☐ Information was easier to use
   ☐ Materials provided information that AAA/CAA materials could not provide. Specify:

_____
_____

8. In your opinion, what is the most important travel information AAA/CAA does not provide?

_____
_____

9. If AAA/CAA were to provide a 24 hour, toll-free number through which you could request Triptik routings that would be mailed to you, how likely would you be to use this service?
   ☐ Very likely   ☐ Somewhat unlikely
   ☐ Somewhat likely   ☐ Very unlikely

10. If AAA/CAA were to provide a 24 hour, toll-free number through which you could make airline reservations, how likely would you be to use this service?
   ☐ Very likely   ☐ Somewhat unlikely
   ☐ Somewhat likely   ☐ Very unlikely

11. If AAA/CAA were to provide a 24 hour, toll-free number through which you could make car rental and hotel reservations, how likely would you be to use this service?
   ☐ Very likely   ☐ Somewhat unlikely
   ☐ Somewhat likely   ☐ Very unlikely

12. Currently, TourBooks are free to members and not available to non-members. On a scale of 1 to 10, where 1 is "not very likely" and 10 is "very likely," how likely would you be to renew your AAA/CAA membership if TourBooks remain free to members, but were also sold in retail outlets such as bookstores at a competitive price?

Not Very Likely   *Very Likely*

1   2   3   4   5   6   7   8   9   10

13. AAA/CAA is considering offering AAA/CAA TourBook information through an on-line home computer service such as Prodigy or CompuServe which charges subscribers approximately $20 a month. Again, using the same scale as in Question 12, how likely would you be to renew your AAA/CAA membership if members and non-members could access TourBook information through a home computer?

Not Very Likely   *Very Likely*

1   2   3   4   5   6   7   8   9   10

14. On a scale of 1 to 5, with 1 being "not very clear" and 5 being "very clear," please rate the clarity of:

TourBook Lodging Listing Rate Options:	*Not Very Clear*				*Very Clear*
Guaranteed rates	1	2	3	4	5
Special value rates	1	2	3	4	5
Rates subject to change	1	2	3	4	5
Discounts Displayed in TourBook advertisements	1	2	3	4	5
Passport Discounts	1	2	3	4	5

15. How much influence does a TourBook advertisement have on your selection of:

Attractions	❏ Great deal	❏ Some	❏ None
Lodgings	❏ Great deal	❏ Some	❏ None
Restaurants	❏ Great deal	❏ Some	❏ None

16. If you have ever patronized an establishment as a result of seeing an advertisement in the TourBook, what feature of the ad most influenced your selection? (Check all that apply):

❏ Pictures/Graphics   ❏ Toll-free reservation/information number
❏ Color advertisements   ❏ Other_____
❏ Rates/discounts

17. How much influence does the AAA/CAA logo next to a TourBook listing have on your selection of:

Lodgings	❏ Great deal	❏ Some	❏ None
Restaurants	❏ Great deal	❏ Some	❏ None

18. What one recommendation would you make to improve the usefulness of the TourBook?

_____

_____

19. Which of the following information found in the FAST FACTS or THE INFORMED TRAVELER box in the Attractions section of the TourBook did you use? (Check all that apply):

❏ Camping   ❏ Seat Belt/Child Restraint Laws   ❏ Firearms Laws
❏ State Population   ❏ Helmets for Motorcyclists   ❏ Fire Phone #
❏ Area   ❏ Police (non emergency) #   ❏ Holidays
❏ Capital   ❏ Time and Temperature #   ❏ Newspaper
❏ Highest Point   ❏ Taxes   Listing
❏ Visitor Information #   ❏ State Welcome Centers   ❏ Time zones
❏ Listing of Radio & TV Stations   ❏ City Population/Altitude   ❏ Lowest Point
❏ Minimum Age for Drivers   ❏ Emergency Phone #   ❏ What to Wear

20. In the city and place listings of the TourBook, would you like to see more shopping information?   ❏ Yes   ❏ No

If yes, what types of shopping information? (Check all that apply):
❏ Factory Outlet Malls   ❏ Farmers Markets   ❏ Theme Stores
❏ Regional Malls   ❏ Specialty Stores   ❏ Flea Markets
❏ Strip Shopping Centers

TELL US WHAT YOU THINK

Dear Loyal Member:

How are we doing? The lodging and restaurant establishments in this TourBook are inspected and rated every year by an experienced AAA field inspector to help you select establishments that will be suitable for you.

On the reverse side is a survey form that allows you to provide us with your impressions of the accuracy and consistency of our work. Please feel free to reproduce this form and return to us at the address below as often as you like. We value your contribution. Although it isn't possible to acknowledge each response individually, we sincerely thank you for your input!

Sincerely,

Neil Docken
American Automobile Association
Approved Accommodations – Inspections
Box 51
1000 AAA Drive
Heathrow, Florida 32746-5063

622

TELL US WHAT YOU THINK

Property Name _____

City _____ State _____ Phone _____

Check one:

____ Lodging	____ Restaurant
Arr. Date _____ Dep. Date _____	Date of Visit _____
Room # _____	Meal: __ B __ L __ D
Current Rating _____	Current Rating _____

Based on my overall experience the establishment:

____ Exceeded expectations at the rating.

____ Met expectations at the rating.

____ Did not meet expectations at the rating.

Comments:

_____

_____

_____

_____

_____

_____

_____

_____

Member _____ Membership # _____

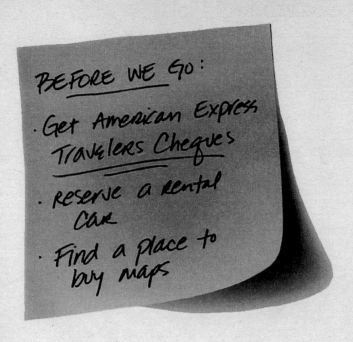

Or just go to AAA

You don't have to drive to one place for maps, to another for reservations and to still another for American Express® Travelers Cheques. AAA has all of this and much more in one place.

What's more, if you're a AAA member, the American Express Travelers Cheques are *fee-free*. They're available at over 1,000 participating AAA offices in the U.S. and Canada. And if they're lost or stolen, American Express can hand-deliver a

Travelers Cheque refund to you just about anywhere you are.

All of which means that, instead of driving all over town to get things for your trip, you can be very single-minded.

Looks like someone found a way to beat our low AAA rates.

But we think you'll find our beds more comfortable than this rollaway. Of course, if you're a AAA member, chances are you already know about us.

In fact, your suggestions have helped us discover what we could do to make your stay more enjoyable. And now we're busy improving to give you even more of the kind of things you want.

So if you'd like to see what we're up to, come spend a little quality time with us. The number here is: **800-367-2250**.

Travelodge.

The Sign of Value.